CONGRESSIONAL QUARTERLY

Almanac

97th CONGRESS

1st SESSION 1981

VOLUME XXXVII

Congressional Quarterly Inc.

Washington, D.C.

CQ 1981 Almanac

Editor and President
Eugene Patterson

Publisher
Wayne P. Kelley

Executive Editor
Peter A. Harkness

General Manager
Robert C. Hur

Director, Research and Development
Robert E. Cuthriell

EDITORIAL DEPARTMENT
Charles W. Hucker (*Managing Editor*)
Kathryn Waters Gest (*Asst. Managing Editor*)
Alan Ehrenhalt (*Political Editor*)

News Editors: Martha Angle, Marsha Canfield, Mary Cohn, John Felton, Peg O'Hara

Reporters: Irwin B. Arieff, Nadine Cohodas, Christopher Colford, Rhodes Cook, Harrison Donnelly, Phil Duncan, Ross Evans, Pamela Fessler, Bill Keller, Kathy Koch, Larry Light, Ann Pelham, Andy Plattner, Judy Sarasohn, Dale Tate, Pat Towell, Elizabeth Wehr, Laura B. Weiss, Richard Whittle, Elder Witt

Production Editor: David Long

Editorial Coordinator: Colleen McGuiness

Editorial Assistants: Renee Amrine, Kathryn Creel, Eugene J. Gabler, Rob Gurwitt, Susan C. Hodge, Chris Russell, Evelyn Russell, Amy Stern

RESEARCH DEPARTMENT: Michael L. Koempel (*Director*), Wayne Walker (*Asst. Director*), Edna Frazier-Cromwell (*Librarian*), Diane Huffman (*Indexer*), Ricka P. Wolf (*Seminars*), Sharon Clayton, Rapheal Clemencia, Reid Dulberger, Beth Easterly, Walter E. Eling, Jennifer Greene, James M. McCarthy, Julia C. McCue, Barbara L. Miracle, Florence A. Mosebach, Mary Anne Rothwell, Debra F. Sessoms, T. Siafa Sherman Jr.

ART DEPARTMENT: Richard A. Pottern (*Director*), Robert O. Redding, Cheryl B. Rowe

PRODUCTION: I.D. Fuller (*Manager*), Maceo Mayo (*Asst. Manager*), Sydney E. Garriss (*Computer Services*)

SALES AND PROMOTION: James V. Bullard (*Manager*)

CONTROLLER: Jonathan C. Angier

BOOK DEPARTMENT: David R. Tarr (*Director*)

NEWSLETTERS: Kenneth B. Dalecki (*Editor*)

CONGRESSIONAL MONITOR: Michaela Buhler (*Editor*), Robert Healy (*Managing Editor*)

EDITORIAL RESEARCH REPORTS: Hoyt Gimlin (*Editor*), Sandra Stencel (*Managing Editor*)

Chairman of the Board: Nelson Poynter (1903-1978)

Library of Congress No. 47-41081
International Standard Book No. 0-87187-231-5

Copyright 1982 by Congressional Quarterly Inc.
1414 22nd Street, N.W., Washington, D.C. 20037

Congressional Quarterly Inc.

Congressional Quarterly Inc. is an editorial research service and publishing company serving clients in the fields of news, education, business and government. Congressional Quarterly, in its basic publication, the CQ Weekly Report, covers Congress, government and politics. Congressional Quarterly also publishes hardbound reference books and paperback books on public affairs. The service was founded in 1945 by Henrietta and Nelson Poynter.

An affiliated service, Editorial Research Reports, publishes reports each week on a wide range of subjects. Editorial Research Reports also publishes hardbound and paperback books.

Almanac Editor: Mary Cohn
Editorial Coordinator: Renee Amrine
Assistant Editors: Martha Angle, Marsha Canfield, John Felton, Kathryn Waters Gest, Peg O'Hara, Elder Witt
Editorial Assistants: Eugene J. Gabler, Sumie Kinoshita, David Long, Colleen McGuiness, Evelyn Russell
Other Contributors: Irwin B. Arieff, Nadine Cohodas, Harrison Donnelly, Reid Dulberger, Phil Duncan, Dan Elmer, Ross Evans, Pamela Fessler, Gail Gregg, Bill Keller, Kathy Koch, Larry Light, Julia McCue, Florence A. Mosebach, Ann Pelham, Andy Plattner, Judy Sarasohn, Dale Tate, Pat Towell, Elizabeth Wehr, Laura B. Weiss, Richard Whittle
Roll-Call Charts: Barbara L. Miracle, Colleen McGuiness; **Vote Studies:** Wayne Walker, Jennifer Greene
Indexers: Janet Hoffman, Kathryn Creel, Diane Huffman, Debra Sessoms
Production: I.D. Fuller (manager), Maceo Mayo (assistant manager)

SUMMARY TABLE OF CONTENTS

TABLE OF CONTENTS

Chapter 1 — 97th Congress, First Session

Chapter 2 — Economic Policy

Chapter 3 — Foreign Policy

Chapter 4 — Defense

Chapter 5 — Budget and Appropriations

Chapter 6 — Congress and Government

Chapter 7 — Law Enforcement/Judiciary

Chapter 8 — Energy

Chapter 9 — Health/Education/Welfare

Chapter 10 — Environment

Chapter 11 — Agriculture

Chapter 12 — Transportation/Commerce/Consumers

APPENDICES

Special Reports

Political Report

Voting Studies

Lobby Registrations

Presidential Messages

Public Laws

Roll-Call Charts

Index

ERRATA

1980 Almanac: P. 125, col. 1, reconciliation: Conferees dropped Senate provisions permitting reallocation of money between the Old Age and Survivors (OASI) and Disability Insurance (DI) trust funds. Identical reallocation provisions already had been enacted in separate legislation (HR 7670 — PL 96-403) cleared Sept. 25. **P. 380**, Jordan box, and **P. 398**, col. 1, Weicker amendment to Justice Department authorization: The 1978 ethics act was PL 95-521, not 96-521.

1979 Almanac: P. 24-S, vote 130, Endangered Species Act: The corrected breakdown is: Passed 91-5: R 41-4; D 50-1 (ND 34-0, SD 16-1).

GLOSSARY OF CONGRESSIONAL TERMS

Act—The term for legislation which has passed both houses of Congress and has been signed by the president or passed over his veto, thus becoming law.

Also used technically for a bill that has been passed by one house and engrossed. *(See Engrossed.)*

Adjournment Sine Die—Adjournment without definitely fixing a day for reconvening; literally "adjournment without a day." Usually used to connote the final adjournment of a session of Congress. A session can continue until noon, Jan. 3, of the following year, when by law it automatically terminates.

Adjournment to a Day Certain—Adjournment under a motion or resolution which fixes the next time of meeting. Neither house can adjourn for more than three days without the concurrence of the other. A session of Congress is not ended by adjournment to a day certain.

Amendment—Proposal of a member of Congress to alter the language or stipulations in a bill or act. It is usually printed, debated, and voted upon in the same manner as a bill.

Appeal—A senator's challenge of a ruling or decision made by the presiding officer of the Senate. The senator appeals to members of the chamber to override the decision. If carried by a majority vote, the appeal nullifies the chair's ruling. In the House the decision of the Speaker traditionally has been final, with no appeal to the members to reverse his stand. To appeal a ruling would be considered an attack on the Speaker.

Appropriation Bill—Grants the actual monies approved by authorization bills, but not necessarily to the total permissible under the authorization bill. An appropriation bill originates in the House, and normally is not acted on until its authorization measure is enacted. General appropriations bills are supposed to be enacted by the seventh day after Labor Day before the start of the fiscal year to which they apply, but in recent years this has rarely happened. *(See Continuing Appropriations.)* In addition to general appropriations bills, there are two specialized types. *(See Deficiency and Supplemental.)*

Authorization Bill—Authorizes a program, specifies its general aim and conduct, and unless "open-ended," puts a ceiling on monies that can be used to finance it. Usually enacted before the related appropriation bill is passed. *(See Contract Authorization.)*

Bills—Most legislative proposals before Congress are in the form of bills, and are designated as HR (House of Representatives) or S (Senate) according to the house in which they originate and by a number assigned in the order in which they were introduced, from the beginning of each two-year congressional term. "Public bills" deal with general questions, and become Public Laws if approved by Congress and signed by the president. "Private bills" deal with individual matters such as claims against the government, immigration and naturalization cases, land titles, etc., and become Private Laws if approved and signed.

The introduction of a bill, and its referral to an appropriate committee for action, follows the process given in "How A Bill Becomes Law." *(See also Concurrent Resolution, Joint Resolution, Resolution, in this Glossary.)*

Bills Introduced—In the Senate, any number of senators may join in introducing a single bill. In the House, until 1967 only one member's name could appear on a single bill. Between 1967 and 1978 there was a limit of 25 cosponsors on any one bill. A resolution adopted in 1978 eliminated the ceiling on the number of cosponsors, beginning at the start of the 96th Congress.

Many bills in reality are committee bills and are introduced under the name of the chairman of the committee or subcommittee as a formality. All appropriation bills fall into this category, as do many other bills, particularly those dealing with complicated, technical subjects. A committee frequently holds hearings on a number of related bills, and may agree on one of them or on an entirely new bill. *(See Clean Bill and By Request.)*

Bills Referred—When introduced a bill is referred to the committee which has jurisdiction over the subject with which the bill is concerned. The appropriate reference for bills is spelled out in Senate and House rules. Committee jurisdictions in the House were reorganized in 1974. Bills are referred by the Speaker in the House and the presiding officer in the Senate. Appeals may be made from their decisions.

Budget—The document sent to Congress by the president in January of each year estimating government revenue and expenditures for the ensuing fiscal year and recommending appropriations in detail. The president's budget message forms the basis for congressional hearings and legislation on the year's appropriations.

By Request—A phrase used when a senator or representative introduces a bill at the request of an executive agency or private organization but does not necessarily endorse the legislation.

Calendar—An agenda or list of pending business before committees of either chamber. The House uses five legislative calendars. *(See Consent, Discharge, House, Private and Union Calendar.)*

In the Senate, all legislative matters reported from committee go on a single calendar. They are listed there in order, but may be called up irregularly by the majority leader either by a motion to do so, or by obtaining the unanimous consent of the Senate. Frequently the minority leader is consulted to assure unanimous consent. Only cloture can limit debate on bills thus called up. *(See Call of the Calendar.)*

The Senate also uses one non-legislative calendar, for treaties, etc. *(See Executive Calendar.)*

Calendar Wednesday—In the House on Wednesdays, committees may be called in the order in which they appear in Rule X of the House Manual, for the purpose of bringing up any of their bills from the House or the Union Calendars, except bills which are privileged. General debate is limited to two hours. Bills called up from the Union Calendar are considered in Committee of the Whole. Calendar Wednesday is not observed during the last two weeks of a session, and may be dispensed with at other times — by a two-thirds vote. It usually is dispensed with.

Call of the Calendar—Senate bills which are not brought up for debate by a motion or a unanimous consent

agreement are brought before the Senate for action when the calendar listing them in order is "called." Bills considered in this fashion are usually non-controversial, and debate is limited to five minutes for each senator on a bill or on amendments to it.

Chamber—Meeting place for the total membership of either the House or the Senate, as distinguished from the respective committee rooms.

Clean Bill—Frequently after a committee has finished a major revision of a bill, one of the committee members, usually the chairman, will assemble the changes plus what is left of the original bill into a new measure and introduce it as a "clean bill." The new measure, which carries a new number, is then sent to the floor for consideration. This often is a timesaver, as committee-recommended changes do not have to be considered one at a time by the chamber.

Clerk of the House—Chief administrative officer of the House of Representatives with duties corresponding to those of the secretary of the Senate. *(See Secretary of the Senate.)*

Cloture—The process by which a filibuster can be ended in the Senate, other than by unanimous consent. A motion for cloture can apply to any measure before the Senate, including a proposal to change the chamber's rules. It requires 16 senators' signatures for introduction and the votes of three-fifths of the entire Senate membership (60 if there are no vacancies), except that to end a filibuster against a proposal to amend the Standing Rules of the Senate a two-thirds vote of senators present and voting is required. It is put to a roll-call vote one hour after the Senate meets on the second day following introduction of the motion. If voted, cloture limits each senator to one hour of debate. A proposal must come to a final vote after 100 hours of debate.

Committee—A subdivision of the House or Senate which prepares legislation for action by the parent chamber, or makes investigations as directed by the parent chamber. There are several types of committees. *(See Standing, Select or Special.)* Most standing committees are divided into subcommittees, which study legislation, hold hearings, and report their recommendations to the full committee. Only the full committee can report legislation for action by the House or Senate.

Committee of the Whole—The working title of what is formally "The Committee of the Whole House [of Representatives] on the State of the Union." Unlike other committees, it has no fixed membership. It is comprised of any 100 or more House members who participate — on the floor of the chamber — in debating or altering legislation before the body. Such measures, however, must first have passed through the regular committees and be on the calendar.

Technically, the Committee of the Whole considers only bills directly or indirectly appropriating money, authorizing appropriations, or involving taxes or charges on the public. Actually, the Committee of the Whole often considers other types of legislation. Because the Committee of the Whole need number only 100 representatives, a quorum is more readily attained, and business is expedited. Before 1971, members' positions were not individually recorded on votes taken in Committee of the Whole except for automatic roll calls in the absence of a quorum.

When the full House resolves itself into the Committee of the Whole, it supplants the Speaker with a "chairman."

The measure is debated or amended, with votes on amendments as needed. When the committee completes its action on the measure, it dissolves itself by "rising." The Speaker returns, and the full House hears the erstwhile chairman of the committee report that group's recommendations.

At this time members may demand a roll-call vote on any amendment *adopted* in the Committee of the Whole. The last vote is on passage of the legislation in question.

Concurrent Resolution—A concurrent resolution, designated H Con Res or S Con Res, must be adopted by both houses but does not require the signature of the president and does not have the force of law. Concurrent resolutions generally are used to make or amend rules applicable to both houses or to express the sentiment of the two houses. A concurrent resolution, for example, is used to fix the time for adjournment of a Congress. It might also be used to convey the congratulations of Congress to another country on the anniversary of its independence.

Conference—A meeting between the representatives of the House and Senate to reconcile differences between the two houses over provisions of a bill. Members of the conference committee are appointed by the Speaker and the president of the Senate and are called "managers" for their respective chambers. A majority of the managers for each house must reach agreement on the provisions of the bill (often a compromise between the versions of the two chambers) before it can be sent up for floor action in the form of a "conference report." There it cannot be amended, and if not approved by both chambers, the bill may go back to conference under certain situations, or a new conference may be convened. Elaborate rules govern the conduct of the conferences. All bills which are passed by the House and Senate in slightly different form need not be sent to conference; either chamber may "concur" in the other's amendments. *(See Custody of the Papers.)*

Congressional Record — The daily, printed account of proceedings in both House and Senate chambers, with debate, statements and the like incorporated in it. Committee activities are not covered, except that their reports to the parent body are noted. Highlights of legislative and committee action are embodied in a Digest section of the *Record,* and members are entitled to have their extraneous remarks printed in an appendix known as "Extension of Remarks." They may edit and revise remarks made on the floor, and frequently do, so that quotations reported by the press are not always found in the *Record.*

Beginning on March 1, 1978, the *Record* incorporated a procedure to distinguish remarks spoken on the floor of the House and Senate from undelivered speeches. At the direction of Congress, all speeches, articles and other materials members inserted in the *Record* without actually reading them on the floor were set off by large black dots. However, a loophole allows a member to avoid the dots if he delivers any portion of the speech in person.

Congressional Terms of Office—Begin on Jan. 3 of the year following a general election and are for two years for representatives and six years for senators.

Consent Calendar—Members of the House may place on this calendar any bill on the Union or House Calendar which is considered to be non-controversial. Bills on the Consent Calendar are normally called on the first and third Mondays of each month. On the first occasion when a bill is called in this manner, consideration may be blocked by the

objection of any member. On the second time, if there are three objections, the bill is stricken from the Consent Calendar. If less than three members object, the bill is given immediate consideration.

A bill on the Consent Calendar may be postponed in another way. A member may ask that the measure be passed over "without prejudice." In that case, no objection is recorded against the bill, and its status on the Consent Calendar remains unchanged.

A bill stricken from the Consent Calendar remains on the Union or House Calendar.

Continuing Appropriations—When a fiscal year begins and Congress has not yet enacted all the regular appropriation bills for that year, it passes a joint resolution "continuing appropriations" for government agencies at rates generally based on their previous year's appropriations.

Contract Authorizations—Found in both authorization and appropriation bills, these authorizations are stop-gap provisions which permit the federal government to let contracts or obligate itself for future payments from funds not yet appropriated. The assumption is that funds will be available for payment when contracted debts come due.

Correcting Recorded Votes—Rules prohibit members from changing their votes after the result has been announced. But frequently, hours, days, or months after a vote has been taken, a member announces that he was "incorrectly recorded." In the Senate, a request to change one's vote almost always receives unanimous consent. In the House, members are prohibited from changing their votes if tallied by the electronic voting system installed in 1973. If taken by roll call, it is permissible if consent is granted. Errors in the text of the *Record* may be corrected by unanimous consent.

Custody of the Papers—To reconcile differences between the House and Senate versions of a bill, a conference may be arranged. The chamber with "custody of the papers" — the engrossed bill, engrossed amendments, messages of transmittal — is the only body empowered to request the conference. That body then has the advantage of acting last on the conference report when it is submitted.

Deficiency Appropriations—An appropriation to cover the difference between an agency's regular appropriation and the amount deemed necessary for it to operate for the full fiscal year. In recent years deficiency bills have usually been called supplemental appropriations.

Dilatory Motion—A motion, usually made upon a technical point, for the purpose of killing time and preventing action on a bill. The rules outlaw dilatory motions, but enforcement is largely within the discretion of the presiding officer.

Discharge a Committee—Occasionally, attempts are made to relieve a committee from jurisdiction over a measure before it. This is rarely a successful procedure, attempted more often in the House than in the Senate.

In the House, if a committee does not report a bill within 30 days after the bill was referred to it, any member may file a discharge motion. This motion, treated as a petition, needs the signatures of 218 members (a majority of the House). After the required signatures have been obtained, there is a delay of seven days. Then, on the second and fourth Mondays of each month, except during the last

six days of a session, any member who has signed the petition may be recognized to move that the committee be discharged. Debate on the motion to discharge is limited to 20 minutes, and if the motion is carried, consideration of the bill becomes a matter of high privilege.

If a resolution to consider a bill *(see Rule)* is held up in the Rules Committee for more than seven legislative days, any member may enter a motion to discharge the committee. The motion is handled like any other discharge petition in the House.

Occasionally, to expedite non-controversial legislative business, a committee is discharged upon unanimous consent of the House, and a petition is not required. *(For Senate procedure, see Discharge Resolution.)*

Discharge Calendar—The House calendar to which motions to discharge committees are referred when they have the necessary 218 signatures and are awaiting action.

Discharge Petition—In the House, a motion to discharge a committee from considering a bill. The motion, or petition, requires signatures of 218 House members.

Discharge Resolution—In the Senate, a special motion that any senator may introduce to relieve a committee from consideration of a bill before it. The resolution can be called up on a motion for approval or disapproval, in the same manner as other matters of Senate business. *(For House procedure, see Discharge a Committee.)*

Division Vote—Same as Standing Vote. *(See below.)*

Enacting Clause—Key phrase in bills beginning, "Be it enacted by the Senate and House of Representatives...." A successful motion to strike it from legislation kills the measure.

Engrossed Bill—The final copy of a bill as passed by one chamber, with the text as amended by floor action and certified to by the clerk of the House or the secretary of the Senate.

Enrolled Bill—The final copy of a bill which has been passed in identical form by both chambers. It is certified to by an officer of the house of origin (House clerk or Senate secretary) and then sent on for signatures of the House Speaker, the Senate president, and the U.S. president. An enrolled bill is printed on parchment.

Entitlement Program—A federal program that guarantees a certain level of benefits to persons who meet the requirements set by law. It thus leaves no discretion to Congress as to how much money to appropriate.

Executive Calendar—This is an additional, non-legislative calendar, in the Senate, on which presidential documents such as treaties and nominations are listed.

Executive Document—A document, usually a treaty, sent to the Senate by the president for consideration or approval. These are identified for each session of Congress as Executive A, 95th Congress, 1st Session; Executive B, etc. They are referred to committee in the same manner as other measures. Unlike legislative documents, however, treaties do not die at the end of a Congress, but remain "live" proposals until acted on by the Senate or withdrawn by the president.

Executive Session—Meeting of a Senate or a House committee (or, occasionally, of the entire chamber) which only the group's members are privileged to attend. Fre-

quently witnesses appear at committee meetings in executive session, and other members of Congress may be invited, but the public and press are not allowed to attend.

Expenditures—The actual spending of money as distinguished from the appropriation of it. Expenditures are made by the disbursing officers of the administration; appropriations are made only by Congress. The two are rarely identical in any fiscal year; expenditures may represent money appropriated one, two or more years previously.

Filibuster—A time-delaying tactic used by a minority in an effort to prevent a vote on a bill which probably would pass if brought to a vote. The most common method is to take advantage of the Senate's rules permitting unlimited debate, but other forms of parliamentary maneuvering may be used. The stricter rules in the House make filibusters more difficult, but they are attempted from time to time through various delaying tactics arising from loopholes in House rules.

Fiscal Year—Financial operations of the government are carried out in a 12-month fiscal year, beginning on Oct. 1 and ending on Sept. 30. The fiscal year carries the date of the calendar year in which it ends.

Floor Manager—A member, usually representing sponsors of a bill, who attempts to steer it through debate and amendment to a final vote in the chamber. Floor managers are frequently chairmen or ranking members of the committee that reported the bill. Managers are responsible for apportioning the time granted supporters of the bill for debating it. The minority leader or the ranking minority member of the committee often apportions time for the minority party's participation in the debate.

Frank—A member's facsimile signature on envelopes, used in lieu of stamps, for his official outgoing mail, thus postage-free. Also the privilege of sending mail postage-free.

Germane—Pertaining to the subject matter of the measure at hand. All House amendments must be germane to the bill. The Senate requires that amendments be germane only when they are proposed to general appropriation bills, bills being considered under cloture, or, often, when proceeding under an agreement to limit debate.

Grandfather Clause — A provision exempting persons already engaged in an activity from rules or legislation restricting or prohibiting that activity.

Grandfather clauses are sometimes added to legislation in order to avoid antagonizing groups with established interests in the activities being restricted.

Grants-in-Aid—Payments by the federal government which aid the recipient state, local government or individual in administering specified programs, services or activities.

Hearings—Committee sessions for hearing witnesses. At hearings on legislation, witnesses usually include specialists, government officials and spokesmen for persons affected by the bills under study. Hearings related to special investigations bring forth a variety of witnesses. Committees sometimes use their subpoena power to summon reluctant witnesses. The public and press may attend "open" hearings, but are barred from "closed" or "executive" hearings.

Hold-Harmless Clause—A provision added to legislation to ensure that recipients of federal funds do not receive less in a future year than they did the previous year, if a new formula for allocating such funds would result in a reduction in the amount. To hold a state or city government "harmless" means that neither would be responsible for providing the additional funds or services to make up the difference between the level of benefits previously received and that which would be allowed under the new formula. The federal government would be obliged to provide the additional funds or benefits. This clause has been used most frequently to soften the impact of sudden reductions in federal aid.

Hopper—Box on House clerk's desk where bills are deposited on introduction.

House—The House of Representatives, as distinct from the Senate, although each body is a "house" of Congress.

House Calendar—Listing for action by the House of Representatives of public bills which do not directly or indirectly appropriate money or raise revenue.

Immunity—Constitutional privilege of members of Congress to make verbal statements on the floor and in committee for which they cannot be sued or arrested for slander or libel. Also, freedom from arrest while traveling to or from sessions of Congress or on official business. Members in this status may be arrested only for treason, felonies or a breach of the peace, as defined by congressional manuals.

Joint Committee—A committee composed of a specified number of members of both the House and Senate. Usually a joint committee is investigative in nature, such as the Joint Economic Committee. Others have housekeeping duties such as the joint committees on Printing and on the Library of Congress.

Joint Resolution—A joint resolution, designated H J Res or S J Res, requires the approval of both houses and the signature of the president, just as a bill does, and has the force of law if approved. There is no real difference between a bill and a joint resolution. The latter is generally used in dealing with limited matters, such as a single appropriation for a specific purpose.

Joint resolutions also are used to propose amendments to the Constitution. They do not require a presidential signature, but become a part of the Constitution when three-fourths of the states have ratified them.

Journal—The official record of the proceedings of the House and Senate. The Journal records the actions taken in each chamber, but, unlike the *Congressional Record*, it does not include the verbatim report of speeches, debates, etc.

Law—An act of Congress which has been signed by the president, or passed over his veto by Congress; for example, the Civil Rights Act of 1964 (HR 7152) became Public Law 88-352 during the 88th Congress.

Legislative Day—The "day" extending from the time either house meets after an adjournment until the time it next adjourns. Because the House normally adjourns from day to day, legislative days and calendar days usually coincide. But in the Senate, a legislative day may, and

frequently does, extend over several calendar days. *(See Recess.)*

Legislative Veto—A procedure permitting either the House or Senate, or both chambers, to review proposed executive branch regulations or actions and block or modify those with which they disagree. The specifics of the procedure may vary, but Congress generally provides for a legislative veto by including in a specific piece of legislation a provision that administrative rules or actions taken to implement the legislation are to go into effect at the end of a designated period of time unless blocked by either or both houses.

Lobby—A group seeking to influence the passage or defeat of legislation. Originally the term referred to persons frequenting the lobbies or corridors of legislative chambers in order to speak to lawmakers.

The definition of a lobby and the activity of lobbying is a matter of differing interpretation. By some definitions, lobbying is limited to attempts at direct influence by personal interview and persuasion. Under other definitions, lobbying includes attempts at indirect influence, such as persuading members of a group to write or visit their representative or senators, or attempting to create a climate of opinion favorable to a desired legislative action.

The right to attempt to influence legislation is based on the First Amendment to the Constitution, which says Congress shall make no law abridging the right of the people "to petition the government for a redress of grievances."

Majority Leader—Chief strategist and floor spokesman for the party in nominal control in either chamber. He is elected by his party colleagues and is virtually program director for his chamber, since he usually speaks for its majority.

Majority Whip—In effect, the assistant majority leader, in House or Senate. His job is to help marshal majority forces in support of party strategy and legislation.

Manual—The official handbook in each house prescribing its organization, procedures and operations in detail. The Senate manual contains standing rules, orders, laws and resolutions affecting Senate business; the House manual is for operations affecting that chamber. Both volumes contain previous codes under which Congress functioned and from which it continues to derive precedents. Committee powers are outlined. The rules set forth in the manuals may be changed by chamber actions also specified by the manuals.

Marking Up a Bill—Going through a measure, in committee or subcommittee, taking it section by section, revising language, penciling in new phrases, etc. If the bill is extensively revised, the new version may be introduced as a separate bill, with a new number. *(See Clean Bill.)*

Minority Leader—Floor leader for the minority party. *(See Majority Leader.)*

Minority Whip—Performs duties of whip for the minority party. *(See Majority Whip.)*

Morning Hour—The time set aside at the beginning of each legislative day for the consideration of regular routine business. The "hour" is of indefinite duration in the House, where it is rarely used. In the Senate it is the first two hours of a session following an adjournment, as distinguished from a recess. The morning hour can be terminated earlier if the morning business has been completed. The business includes such matters as messages from the president, communications from the heads of departments, messages from the House, the presentation of petitions, reports of standing and select committees, and the introduction of bills and resolutions.

During the first hour of the morning hour in the Senate, no motion to proceed to the consideration of any bill on the calendar is in order except by unanimous consent. During the second hour, motions can be made but must be decided without debate. Senate committees may meet while the Senate is in the morning hour.

Motion—Request by a member for any one of a wide array of parliamentary actions. He "moves" for a certain procedure, or the consideration of a measure or a vote, etc. The precedence of motions, and whether they are debatable, is set forth in the House and Senate manuals.

Nominations—Appointments to office by the executive branch of the government, subject to Senate confirmation. Although most nominations win quick Senate approval, some are controversial and become the topic of hearings and debate. Sometimes senators object to appointees for patronage reasons — for example, when a nomination to a local federal job is made without consulting the senators of the state concerned. Then a senator may use the stock objection that the nominee is "personally obnoxious" to him. Usually other senators join in blocking such an appointment out of courtesy to their colleague.

One Minute Speeches—Addresses by House members at the beginning of a legislative day. The speeches may cover any subject, but are limited strictly to one minute's duration. By unanimous consent, members may also be recognized to address the House for longer periods after completion of all legislative business for the day. Senators, by unanimous consent, are permitted to make speeches of a predetermined length during the Morning Hour.

Override a Veto—If the president disapproves a bill and sends it back to Congress with his objections, Congress may override his veto by a two-thirds vote in each chamber. The Constitution requires a recorded vote. The question put to each house is: "Shall the bill pass, the objections of the president to the contrary notwithstanding?" *(See also Pocket Veto and Veto.)*

Pair—A "gentlemen's agreement" between two lawmakers on opposite sides to withhold their votes on roll calls so their absence from Congress will not affect the outcome of a recorded vote. If passage of the measure requires a two-thirds majority, a pair would require two members favoring the action to one opposed to it.

Two kinds of pairs — special and general — are used; neither is counted in vote totals. The names of lawmakers pairing on a given vote and their stands, if known, are printed in the *Congressional Record*.

The special pair applies to one or a series of roll-call votes on the same subject. On special pairs, lawmakers usually specify how they would have voted.

A general pair in the Senate, now rarely used in the chamber, applies to all votes on which the members pairing are on opposite sides, and it lasts for the length of time pairing senators agree on. It usually does not specify a senator's stand on a given vote.

The general pair in the House differs from the other pairs. No agreement is involved and the pair does not tie up votes. A representative expecting to be absent may notify the House clerk he wishes to make a "general" pair. His name then is paired arbitrarily with that of another member desiring a general pair, and the list is printed in the *Congressional Record.* He may or may not be paired with a member taking the opposite position. General pairs in the House give no indication of how a member would have voted. *(See Record Vote.)*

Petition—A request or plea sent to one or both chambers from an organization or private citizens' group asking support of particular legislation or favorable consideration of a matter not yet receiving congressional attention. They are referred to appropriate committees and are considered or not, according to committee decisions.

Pocket Veto—The act of the president in withholding his approval of a bill after Congress has adjourned — either for the year or for a specified period. However, the U.S. Court of Appeals for the District of Columbia Circuit on Aug. 14, 1974, upheld a congressional challenge to a pocket veto used by former President Nixon during a six-day congressional recess in 1970. The court declared that it was an improper use of the pocket veto power. When Congress is in session, a bill becomes law without the president's signature if he does not act upon it within 10 days, excluding Sundays, from the time he gets it. But if Congress adjourns within that 10-day period, the bill is killed without the president's formal veto.

Point of Order—An objection raised by a member that the chamber is departing from rules governing its conduct of business. The objector cites the rule violated, the chair sustaining his objection if correctly made. Order is restored by the chair's suspending proceedings of the chamber until it conforms to the prescribed "order of business." Members sometimes raise a "point of no order" — when there is noise and disorderly conduct in the chamber.

President of the Senate—Presiding officer of the upper chamber, normally the vice president of the United States. In his absence, a president pro tempore (president for the time being) presides.

President pro tempore—The chief officer of the Senate in the absence of the vice president. He is elected by his fellow senators. The recent practice has been to elect to the office the senator of the majority party with longest continuous service.

Previous Question—In this sense, a "question" is an "issue" before the House for a vote and the issue is "previous" when some other topic has superseded it in the attention of the chamber. A motion for the previous question, when carried, has the effect of cutting off all debate and forcing a vote on the subject originally at hand. If, however, the previous question is moved and carried before there has been any debate on the subject at hand and the subject is debatable, then 40 minutes of debate is allowed before the vote. The previous question is sometimes moved in order to prevent amendments from being introduced and voted on. The motion for the previous question is a debate-limiting device and is not in order in the Senate.

Private Calendar—Private House bills dealing with individual matters such as claims against the government, immigration, land titles, etc., are put on this calendar.

When it is before the chamber, two members may block a private bill, which then is recommitted to committee.

Backers of a private bill thus recommitted have another recourse. The measure can be put into an "omnibus claims bill" — several private bills rolled into one. As with any bill, no part of an omnibus claims bill may be deleted without a vote. When a private bill goes back to the floor in this form, it can be defeated only by a majority of those present. The private calendar can be called on the first and third Tuesdays of each month.

Privilege—Privilege relates to the rights of members of Congress and to the relative priority of the motions and actions they may make in their respective chambers. The two are distinct. "Privileged questions" concern legislative business. "Questions of privilege" concern legislators themselves. *(See below.)*

Privileged Questions—The order in which bills, motions and other legislative measures are considered by Congress is governed by strict priorities. A motion to table, for instance, is more privileged than a motion to recommit. Thus, a motion to recommit can be superseded by a motion to table, and a vote would be forced on the latter motion only. A motion to adjourn, however, would take precedence over this one, and is thus considered of the "highest privilege."

Pro Forma Amendment—*(See Strike Out the Last Word.)*

Questions of Privilege—These are matters affecting members of Congress individually or collectively.

Questions affecting the rights, safety, dignity and integrity of proceedings of the House or Senate as a whole are questions of privilege of the House or Senate, as the case may be.

Questions involving individual members are called questions of "personal privilege." A member's rising to a question of personal privilege is given precedence over almost all other proceedings. An annotation in the House rules points out that the privilege of the member rests primarily on the Constitution, which gives him a conditional immunity from arrest and an unconditional freedom to speak in the House.

Quorum—The number of members whose presence is necessary for the transaction of business. In the Senate and House, it is a majority of the membership (when there are no vacancies, this is 51 in the Senate and 218 in the House). A quorum is 100 in the Committee of the Whole House. If a point of order is made that a quorum is not present, the only business in order is either a motion to adjourn or a motion to direct the sergeant-at-arms to request the attendance of absentees.

Readings of Bills—Traditional parliamentary law required bills to be read three times before they were passed. This custom is of little modern significance except in rare instances. Normally the bill is considered to have its first reading when it is introduced and printed, by title, in the *Congressional Record.* Its second reading comes when floor consideration begins. (This is the most likely point at which there is an actual reading of the bill, if there is any.) The third reading (usually by title) takes place when action has been completed on amendments.

Recess—Distinguished from adjournment in that a recess does not end a legislative day and, therefore, does not

interfere with unfinished business. The rules in each house set forth certain matters to be taken up and disposed of at the beginning of each legislative day. The House, which operates under much stricter rules than the Senate, usually adjourns from day to day. The Senate often recesses.

Recommit to Committee—A simple motion, made on the floor after a bill has been debated, to return it to the committee which reported it. If approved, recommittal usually is considered a death blow to the bill. In the House a motion to recommit can be made only by a member opposed to the bill, and in recognizing a member to make the motion, the Speaker gives the minority position preference over the majority.

A motion to recommit may include instructions to the committee to report the bill again with specific amendments or by a certain date. Or the instructions may be to make a particular study, with no definite deadline for final action. If the recommittal motion includes instructions, and it is adopted, floor action on the bill continues and the committee does not formally reconsider the legislation.

Reconsider a Vote—A motion to reconsider the vote by which an action was taken has, until it is disposed of, the effect of suspending the action. In the Senate the motion can be made only by a member who voted on the prevailing side of the original question, or by a member who did not vote at all. In the House it can be made only by a member on the prevailing side.

A common practice after close votes in the Senate is a motion to reconsider, followed by a motion to table the motion to reconsider. On this motion to table, senators vote as they voted on the original question, to enable the motion to table to prevail. The matter is then finally closed and further motions to reconsider are not entertained. In the House, as a routine precaution, a motion to reconsider usually is made every time a measure is passed. Such a motion almost always is tabled immediately, thus shutting off the possibility of future reconsideration except by unanimous consent.

Motions to reconsider must be entered in the Senate within the next two days of actual session after the original vote has been taken. In the House they must be entered either on the same day or on the next succeeding day the House is in session.

Recorded Vote—A vote upon which each member's stand is individually made known. In the Senate, this is accomplished through a roll call of the entire membership, to which each senator on the floor must answer "yea," "nay" or, if he does not wish to vote, "present." Since January 1973, the House has used an electronic voting system both for yeas and nays and other recorded votes in the Committee of the Whole. *(See Teller Vote.)*

The Constitution requires yea-and-nay votes on the question of overriding a veto. In other cases, a recorded vote can be obtained by the demand of one-fifth of the members present.

Report—Both a verb and a noun, as a congressional term. A committee which has been examining a bill referred to it by the parent chamber "reports" its findings and recommendations to the chamber when the committee returns the measure. The process is called "reporting" a bill.

A "report" is the document setting forth the committee's explanation of its action. House and Senate reports are numbered separately and are designated S Rept or H Rept. Conference reports are numbered and designated in the same way as regular committee reports.

Most reports favor a bill's passage. Adverse reports are occasionally submitted, but more often, when a committee disapproves a bill, it simply fails to report it at all. Some laws require that committee reports (favorable or adverse) be made. When a committee report is not unanimous, the dissenting committeemen may file a statement of their views, called minority views and referred to as a minority report. Sometimes a bill is reported without recommendation.

Rescission—An item in an appropriation bill rescinding, or canceling, funds previously appropriated but not spent. Also, the repeal of a previous appropriation by the president to cut spending, if approved by Congress under procedures in the Budget and Impoundment Control Act of 1974.

Resolution—A simple resolution, designated H Res or S Res, deals with matters entirely within the prerogatives of one house or the other. It requires neither passage by the other chamber nor approval by the president, and does not have the force of law. Most resolutions deal with the rules of one house. They also are used to express the sentiments of a single house, as condolences to the family of a deceased member or to give "advice" on foreign policy or other executive business. *(Also see Concurrent and Joint Resolutions.)*

Rider—An amendment, usually not germane, which its sponsor hopes to get through more easily by including it in other legislation. Riders become law if the bills embodying them do. Riders providing legislative directives in appropriations bills are outstanding examples, though technically they are banned. The House, unlike the Senate, has a strict germaneness rule; thus riders are usually Senate devices to get legislation enacted quickly or to bypass lengthy House consideration, and, possibly, opposition.

Rule—The term has two specific congressional meanings. A rule may be a standing order governing the conduct of House or Senate business and listed in the chamber's book of rules. The rules deal with duties of officers, order of business, admission to the floor, voting procedures, etc.

In the House, a rule also may be a decision made by its Rules Committee about the handling of a particular bill on the floor. The committee may determine under which standing rule a bill shall be considered, or it may provide a "special rule" in the form of a resolution. If the resolution is adopted by the House, the temporary rule becomes as valid as any standing rule, and lapses only after action has been completed on the measure to which it pertains.

A special rule sets the time limit on general debate. It may also waive points of order against provisions of the bill in question, such as non-germane language, or against specified amendments intended to be proposed to the bill. It may even forbid all amendments or all amendments except, in some cases, those proposed by the legislative committee that handled the bill. In this instance it is known as a "closed" or "gag" rule as opposed to an "open" rule, which puts no limitation on floor action, thus leaving the bill completely open to alteration. *(See Suspend the Rules.)*

Secretary of the Senate—Chief administrative officer of the Senate, responsible for direction of duties of Senate employees, education of pages, administration of oaths,

receipt of registration of lobbyists and other activities necessary for the continuing operation of the Senate.

Select or Special Committee—A committee set up for a special purpose and, generally, for a limited time by resolution of either House or Senate. Most special committees are investigative in nature.

Senatorial Courtesy—Sometimes referred to as "the courtesy of the Senate," it is a general practice — with no written rule — applied to consideration of executive nominations. Generally, it means that nominations from a state are not to be confirmed unless they have been approved by the senators of the president's party of that state, with other senators following their lead in the attitude they take toward such nominations. *(See Nominations.)*

Sine Die—See Adjournment *sine die.*

Slip Laws—The first official publication of a bill that has been enacted into law. Each is published separately in unbound single-sheet or pamphlet form. It usually takes two to three days from the date of presidential approval to the time when slip laws become available.

Speaker—The presiding officer of the House of Representatives, elected by its members.

Special Session—A session of Congress after it has adjourned *sine die,* completing its regular session. Special sessions are convened by the president of the United States under his constitutional powers.

Standing Committees—Committees permanently authorized by House and Senate rules. The standing committees of the House were last reorganized by the committee reorganization act of 1974. The last major reorganization of Senate committees was in the Legislative Reorganization Act of 1946.

Standing Vote—A non-recorded vote used in both the House and Senate. A standing vote, also called a division vote, is taken as follows: Members in favor of a proposal stand and are counted by the presiding officer. Then members opposed stand and are counted. There is no record of how individual members voted. In the House, the presiding officer announces the number for and against. In the Senate, usually only the result is announced.

Statutes-at-Large—A chronological arrangement of the laws enacted in each session of Congress. Though indexed, the laws are not arranged by subject matter nor is there an indication of how they affect previous law. *(See U.S. Code.)*

Strike from the Record—Remarks made on the House floor may offend some member, who moves that the offending words be "taken down" for the Speaker's cognizance, and then expunged from the debate as published in the *Congressional Record.*

Strike Out the Last Word—A move whereby House members are entitled to speak for a fixed time on a measure then being debated by the chamber. A member gains recognition from the chair by moving to strike out the last word of the amendment or section of the bill then under consideration. The motion is pro forma, and customarily requires no vote.

Substitute—A motion, an amendment, or an entire bill introduced in place of pending business. Passage of a

substitute measure kills the original measure by supplanting it. A substitute may be amended.

Supplemental Appropriations—Normally, these are passed after the regular (annual) appropriations bills, but before the end of the fiscal year to which they apply. Also referred to as "deficiencies."

Suspend the Rules—Often a time-saving procedure for passing bills in the House. The wording of the motion, which may be made by any member recognized by the Speaker, is: "I move to suspend the rules and pass the bill. . . ." A favorable vote by two-thirds of those present is required for passage. Debate is limited to 40 minutes and no amendments from the floor are permitted. If a two-thirds favorable vote is not attained, the bill may be considered later under regular procedures. The suspension procedure is in order on the first and third Mondays and Tuesdays of each month and usually is reserved for non-controversial bills.

Table a Bill—The motion to "lay on the table" is not debatable in either house, and is usually a method of making a final, adverse disposition of a matter. In the Senate, however, different language is sometimes used. The motion is worded to let a bill "lie on the table," perhaps for subsequent "picking up." This motion is more flexible, merely keeping the bill pending for later action, if desired.

Teller Vote—In the House, members file past tellers and are counted as for or against a measure, but they are not recorded individually. The teller vote is not used in the Senate. In the House, tellers are ordered upon demand of one-fifth of a quorum. This is 44 in the House, 20 in the Committee of the Whole.

The House also has a recorded teller vote procedure, now largely supplanted by the electronic voting procedure, under which the individual votes of members are made public just as they would be on a yea-and-nay vote. This procedure, introduced in 1971, forced members to take a public position on amendments to bills considered in the Committee of the Whole. *(See Recorded Vote.)*

Treaties—Executive proposals — in the form of resolutions of ratification — which must be submitted to the Senate for approval by two-thirds of the senators present. Before they act on such foreign policy matters, senators usually send them to committee for scrutiny. Treaties are read three times and debated in the chamber much as are legislative proposals. After approval by the Senate, they are ratified by the president.

Unanimous Consent—Synonymous with Without Objection. *(See below.)*

Union Calendar—Bills which directly or indirectly appropriate money or raise revenue are placed on this House calendar according to the date reported from committee.

U.S. Code—A consolidation and codification of the general and permanent laws of the United States arranged by subject under 50 titles, the first six dealing with general or political subjects, and the other 44 alphabetically arranged from agriculture to war and national defense. The code is now revised every six years and a supplement is published after each session of Congress.

Veto—Disapproval by the president of a bill or joint resolution, other than one proposing an amendment to the

Constitution. When Congress is in session, the president must veto a bill within 10 days, excluding Sundays, after he has received it; otherwise it becomes law with or without his signature.

When the president vetoes a bill, he returns it to the house of its origin with a message stating his objections. The veto then becomes a question of high privilege. *(See Override a Veto.)*

When Congress has adjourned, the president may pocket veto a bill by failing to sign it. *(See Pocket Veto.)*

Voice Vote—In either the House or Senate, members answer "aye" or "no" in chorus, and the presiding officer decides the result. The term also is used loosely to indicate action by unanimous consent or without objection.

Whip—See Majority Whip.

Without Objection—Used in lieu of a vote on non-controversial motions, amendments or bills, which may be passed in either the House or the Senate if no member voices an objection.

HOW A BILL BECOMES LAW

Note: Parliamentary terms used below are defined in the Glossary.

INTRODUCTION OF BILLS

A House member (including the resident commissioner of Puerto Rico and non-voting delegates of the District of Columbia, Guam, the Virgin Islands, and American Samoa) may introduce any one of several types of bills and resolutions by handing it to the clerk of the House or placing it in a box called the hopper. A senator first gains recognition of the presiding officer to announce the introduction of a bill. If objection is offered by any senator the introduction of the bill is postponed until the following day.

As the next step in either the House or Senate, the bill is numbered, referred to the appropriate committee, labeled with the sponsor's name, and sent to the Government Printing Office so that copies can be made for subsequent study and action. Senate bills may be jointly sponsored and carry several senators' names. Until 1978, the House limited the number of members who could co-sponsor any one bill; the ceiling was eliminated at the beginning of the 96th Congress. A bill written in the Executive Branch and proposed as an administration measure usually is introduced by the chairman of the congressional committee which has jurisdiction.

Bills—Prefixed with "HR" in the House, "S" in the Senate, followed by a number. Used as the form for most legislation, whether general or special, public or private.

Joint Resolutions—Designated H J Res or S J Res. Subject to the same procedure as bills, with the exception of a joint resolution proposing an amendment to the Constitution. The latter must be approved by two-thirds of both houses and is thereupon sent directly to the administrator of general services for submission to the states for ratification rather than being presented to the president for his approval.

Concurrent Resolutions—Designated H Con Res or S Con Res. Used for matters affecting the operations of both houses. These resolutions do not become law.

Resolutions—Designated H Res or S Res. Used for a matter concerning the operation of either house alone and adopted only by the chamber in which it originates.

COMMITTEE ACTION

A bill is referred to the appropriate committee by a House parliamentarian on the Speaker's order, or by the Senate president. Sponsors may indicate their preferences for referral, although custom and chamber rule generally govern. An exception is the referral of private bills, which are sent to whatever group is designated by their sponsors. Bills are technically considered "read for the first time" when referred to House committees.

When a bill reaches a committee it is placed upon the group's calendar. At that time it comes under the sharpest congressional focus. Its chances for passage are quickly determined — and the great majority of bills fall by the legislative roadside. Failure of a committee to act on a bill is equivalent to killing it; the measure can be withdrawn from the group's purview only by a discharge petition signed by a majority of the House membership on House bills, or by adoption of a special resolution in the Senate. Discharge attempts rarely succeed.

The first committee action taken on a bill usually is a request for comment on it by interested agencies of the government. The committee chairman may assign the bill to a subcommittee for study and hearings, or it may be considered by the full committee. Hearings may be public, closed (executive session), or both. A subcommittee, after considering a bill, reports to the full committee its recommendations for action and any proposed amendments.

The full committee then votes on its recommendation to the House or Senate. This procedure is called "ordering a bill reported." Occasionally a committee may order a bill reported unfavorably; most of the time a report, submitted by the chairman of the committee to the House or Senate, calls for favorable action on the measure since the committee can effectively "kill" a bill by simply failing to take any action.

When a committee sends a bill to the chamber floor, it explains its reasons in a written statement, called a report, which accompanies the bill. Often committee members opposing a measure issue dissenting minority statements which are included in the report.

Usually, the committee "marks up" or proposes amendments to the bill. If they are substantial and the measure is complicated, the committee may order a "clean bill" introduced, which will embody the proposed amendments. The original bill then is put aside and the "clean bill," with a new number, is reported to the floor.

The chamber must approve, alter, or reject the committee amendments before the bill itself can be put to a vote.

FLOOR ACTION

After a bill is reported back to the house where it originated, it is placed on the calendar.

Bills and Resolutions

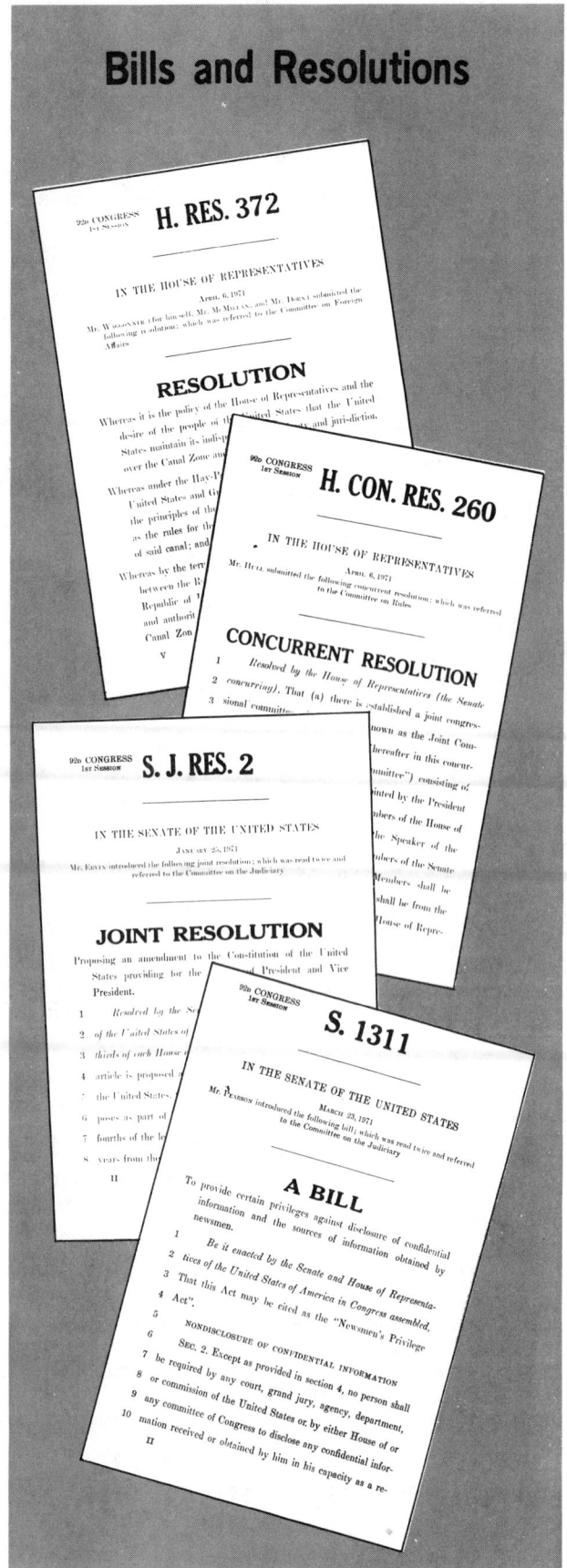

There are five legislative calendars in the House, issued in one cumulative calendar titled *Calendars of the United States House of Representatives and History of Legislation.* The House calendars are:

The Union Calendar to which are referred bills raising revenues, general appropriation bills and any measures directly or indirectly appropriating money or property. It is the Calendar of the Committee of the Whole House on the State of the Union.

The House Calendar to which are referred bills of a public character not raising revenue or appropriating money or property.

The Consent Calendar to which are referred bills of a non-controversial nature that are passed without debate when the Consent Calendar is called on the first and third Mondays of each month.

The Private Calendar to which are referred bills for relief in the nature of claims against the United States or private immigration bills that are passed without debate when the Private Calendar is called the first and third Tuesdays of each month.

The Discharge Calendar to which are referred motions to discharge committees when the necessary signatures are signed to a discharge petition.

There is only one legislative calendar in the Senate and one "executive calendar" for treaties and nominations submitted to the Senate. When the Senate Calendar is called, each senator is limited to five minutes' debate on each bill.

DEBATE. A bill is brought to debate by varying procedures. If a routine measure, it may await the call of the calendar. If it is urgent or important, it can be taken up in the Senate either by unanimous consent or by a majority vote. The policy committee of the majority party in the Senate schedules the bills that it wants taken up for debate.

In the House, precedence is granted if a special rule is obtained from the Rules Committee. A request for a special rule is usually made by the chairman of the committee that favorably reported the bill, supported by the bill's sponsor and other committee members. The request, considered by the Rules Committee in the same fashion that other committees consider legislative measures, is in the form of a resolution providing for immediate consideration of the bill. The Rules Committee reports the resolution to the House where it is debated and voted upon in the same fashion as regular bills. If the Rules Committee should fail to report a rule requested by a committee, there are several ways to bring the bill to the House floor — under suspension of the rules, on Calendar Wednesday or by a discharge motion.

The resolutions providing special rules are important because they specify how long the bill may be debated and whether it may be amended from the floor. If floor amendments are banned, the bill is considered under a "closed rule," which permits only members of the committee that first reported the measure to the House to alter its language, subject to chamber acceptance.

When a bill is debated under an "open rule," amendments may be offered from the floor. Committee amendments are always taken up first, but may be changed, as may all amendments up to the second degree, i.e., an amendment to an amendment to an amendment is not in order.

Duration of debate in the House depends on whether the bill is under discussion by the House proper or before

the House when it is sitting as the Committee of the Whole House on the State of the Union. In the former, the amount of time for debate is determined either by special rule or is allocated with an hour for each member if the measure is under consideration without a rule. In the Committee of the Whole the amount of time agreed on for general debate is equally divided between proponents and opponents. At the end of general discussion, the bill is read section by section for amendment. Debate on an amendment is limited to five minutes for each side.

Senate debate is usually unlimited. It can be halted only by unanimous consent by "cloture," which requires a three-fifths majority of the entire Senate except for proposed changes in the Senate rules. The latter requires a two-thirds vote.

The House sits as the Committee of the Whole when it considers any tax measure or bill dealing with public appropriations. It can also resolve itself into the Committee of the Whole if a member moves to do so and the motion is carried. The Speaker appoints a member to serve as the chairman. The rules of the House permit the Committee of the Whole to meet with any 100 members on the floor, and to amend and act on bills with a quorum of the 100, within the time limitations mentioned previously. When the Committee of the Whole has acted, it "rises," the Speaker returns as the presiding officer of the House and the member appointed chairman of the Committee of the Whole reports the action of the committee and its recommendations (amendments adopted).

VOTES. Voting on bills may occur repeatedly before they are finally approved or rejected. The House votes on the rule for the bill and on various amendments to the bill. Voting on amendments often is a more illuminating test of a bill's support than is the final tally. Sometimes members approve final passage of bills after vigorously supporting amendments which, if adopted, would have scuttled the legislation.

The Senate has three different methods of voting: an untabulated voice vote, a standing vote (called a division) and a recorded roll call to which members answer "yea" or "nay" when their names are called. The House also employs voice and standing votes, but since January 1973 yeas and nays have been recorded by an electronic voting device, eliminating the need for time-consuming roll calls.

Another method of voting, used in the House only, is the teller vote. Traditionally, members filed up the center aisle past counters; only vote totals were announced. Since 1971, one-fifth of a quorum can demand that the votes of individual members be recorded, thereby forcing them to take a public position on amendments to key bills. Electronic voting now is commonly used for this purpose.

After amendments to a bill have been voted upon, a vote may be taken on a motion to recommit the bill to committee. If carried, this vote removes the bill from the chamber's calendar. If the motion is unsuccessful, the bill then is "read for the third time." An actual reading usually is dispensed with. Until 1965, an opponent of a bill could delay this move by objecting and asking for a full reading of an engrossed (certified in final form) copy of the bill. After the "third reading," the vote on final passage is taken.

The final vote may be followed by a motion to reconsider, and this motion itself may be followed by a move to lay the motion on the table. Usually, those voting for the bill's passage vote for the tabling motion, thus safeguarding the final passage action. With that, the bill has been

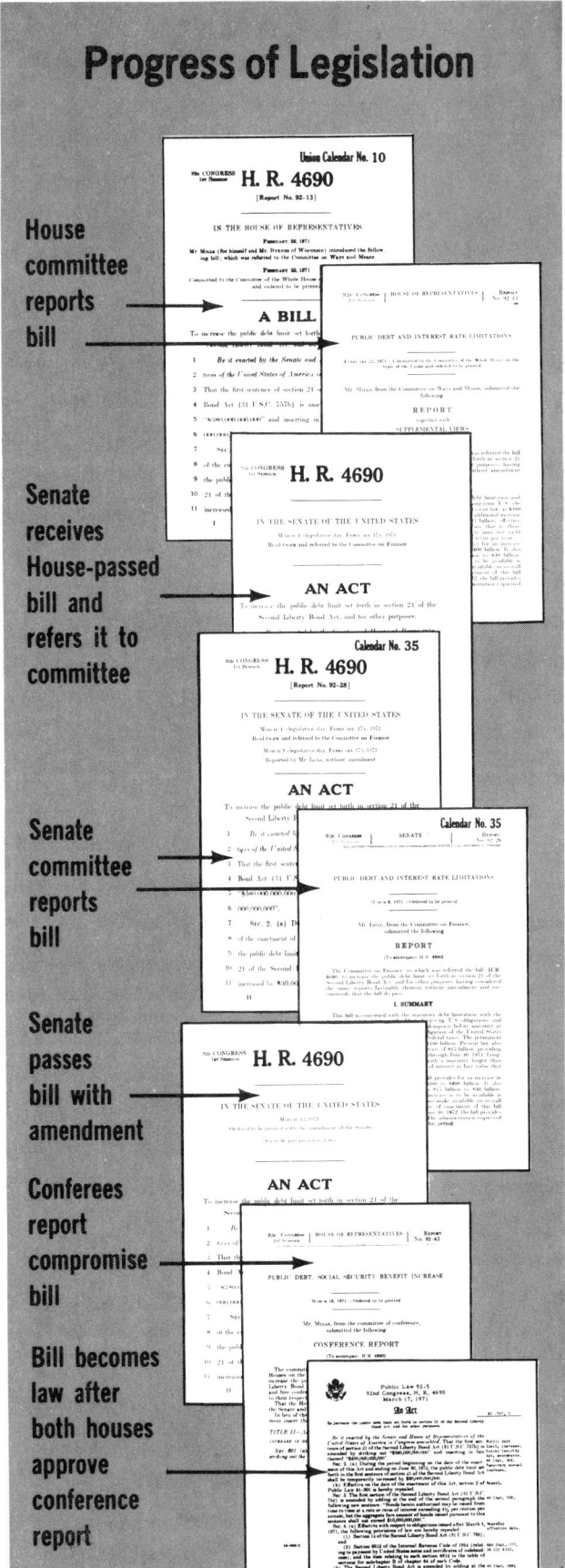

Progress of Legislation

House committee reports bill

Senate receives House-passed bill and refers it to committee

Senate committee reports bill

Senate passes bill with amendment

Conferees report compromise bill

Bill becomes law after both houses approve conference report

formally passed by the chamber. While a motion to reconsider a Senate vote is pending on a bill, the measure cannot be sent to the House.

ACTION IN SECOND HOUSE

After a bill is passed it is sent to the other chamber. This body may then take one of several steps. It may pass the bill as is — accepting the other chamber's language. It may send the bill to committee for scrutiny or alteration, or reject the entire bill, advising the other house of its actions. Or it may simply ignore the bill submitted while it continues work on its own version of the proposed legislation. Frequently, one chamber may approve a version of a bill that is greatly at variance with the version already passed by the other house, and then substitute its amendments for the language of the other, retaining only the latter's bill designation.

A provision of the Legislative Reorganization Act of 1970 permits a separate House vote on any non-germane amendment added by the Senate to a House-passed bill and requires a majority vote to retain the amendment. Previously the House was forced to act on the bill as a whole; the only way to defeat the non-germane amendment was to reject the entire bill.

Often the second chamber makes only minor changes. If these are readily agreed to by the other house, the bill then is routed to the White House for signing. However, if the opposite chamber basically alters the bill submitted to it, the measure usually is "sent to conference." The chamber that has possession of the "papers" (engrossed bill, engrossed amendments, messages of transmittal) requests a conference and the other chamber must agree to it. If the second house does not agree, the bill dies.

CONFERENCE. A conference undertakes to harmonize conflicting House and Senate versions of a legislative bill. The conference is usually staffed by senior members (conferees), appointed by the presiding officers of the two houses, from the committees that managed the bills. Under this arrangement the conferees of one house have the duty of trying to maintain their chamber's position in the face of amending actions by the conferees (also referred to as "managers") of the other house.

The number of conferees from each chamber may vary, the range usually being from three to nine members in each group, depending upon the length or complexity of the bill involved. There may be five representatives and three senators on the conference committee, or the reverse. But a majority vote controls the action of each group so that a larger representation does not give one chamber a voting advantage over the other chamber's conferees.

Theoretically, conferees are not allowed to write new legislation in reconciling the two versions before them, but this curb sometimes is bypassed. Many bills have been put into acceptable compromise form only after new language was provided by the conferees. The 1970 Reorganization Act attempted to tighten restrictions on conferees by forbidding them to introduce any language on a topic that neither chamber sent to conference or to modify any topic beyond the scope of the different House and Senate versions.

Frequently the ironing out of difficulties takes days or even weeks. Conferences on involved appropriation bills sometimes are particularly drawn out.

As a conference proceeds, conferees reconcile differences between the versions, but generally they grant concessions only insofar as they remain sure that the chamber they represent will accept the compromises. Occasionally, uncertainty over how either house will react, or the positive refusal of a chamber to back down on a disputed amendment, results in an impasse, and the bills die in conference even though each was approved by its sponsoring chamber.

Conferees sometimes go back to their respective chambers for further instructions, when they report certain portions in disagreement. Then the chamber concerned can either "recede and concur" in the amendment of the other house, or "insist on its amendment."

When the conferees have reached agreement, they prepare a conference report embodying their recommendations (compromises). The reports, in document form, must be submitted to each house.

The conference report must be approved by each house. Consequently, approval of the report is approval of the compromise bill. In the order of voting on conference reports, the chamber which asked for a conference yields to the other chamber the opportunity to vote first.

FINAL STEPS. After a bill has been passed by both the House and Senate in identical form, all of the original papers are sent to the enrolling clerk of the chamber in which the bill originated. He then prepares an enrolled bill which is printed on parchment paper. When this bill has been certified as correct by the secretary of the Senate or the clerk of the House, depending on which chamber originated the bill, it is signed first (no matter whether it originated in the Senate or House) by the Speaker of the House and then by the president of the Senate. It is next sent to the White House to await action.

If the president approves the bill he signs it, dates it and usually writes the word "approved" on the document. If he does not sign it within 10 days (Sundays excepted) and Congress is in session, the bill becomes law without his signature.

However, should Congress adjourn before the 10 days expire, and the president has failed to sign the measure, it does not become law. This procedure is called the pocket veto.

A president vetoes a bill by refusing to sign it and before the 10-day period expires, returning it to Congress with a message stating his reasons. The message is sent to the chamber which originated the bill. If no action is taken there on the message, the bill dies. Congress, however, can attempt to override the president's veto and enact the bill, "the objections of the president to the contrary notwithstanding." Overriding of a veto requires a two-thirds vote of those present, who must number a quorum and vote by roll call.

Debate can precede this vote, with motions permitted to lay the message on the table, postpone action on it, or refer it to committee. If the president's veto is overridden by a two-thirds vote in both houses, the bill becomes law. Otherwise it is dead.

When bills are passed finally and signed, or passed over a veto, they are given law numbers in numerical order as they become law. There are two series of numbers, one for public and one for private laws, starting at the number "1" for each two-year term of Congress. They are then identified by law number and by Congress — i.e., Private Law 21, 90th Congress; Public Law 250, 90th Congress (or PL 90-250).

HOW A BILL BECOMES LAW

This graphic shows the most typical way in which proposed legislation is enacted into law. There are more complicated, as well as simpler, routes, and most bills fall by the wayside and never become law. The process is illustrated with two hypothetical bills, House bill No. 1 (HR 1) and Senate bill No. 2 (S 2).

Each bill must be passed by both houses of Congress in identical form before it can become law. The path of HR 1 is traced by a solid line, that of S 2 by a broken line. However, in practice most legislation begins as similar proposals in both houses.

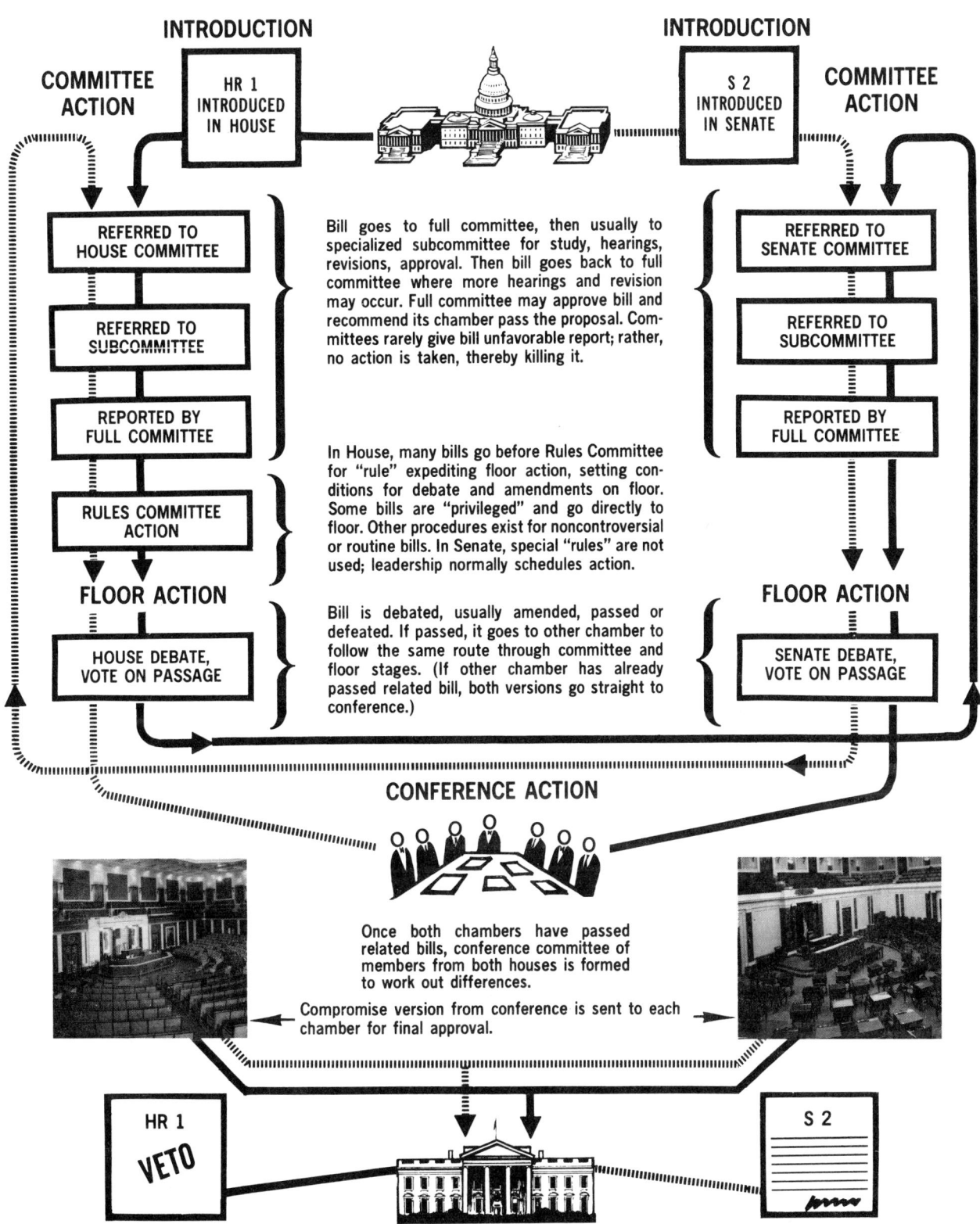

INTRODUCTION

COMMITTEE ACTION

HR 1 INTRODUCED IN HOUSE

REFERRED TO HOUSE COMMITTEE

REFERRED TO SUBCOMMITTEE

REPORTED BY FULL COMMITTEE

RULES COMMITTEE ACTION

FLOOR ACTION

HOUSE DEBATE, VOTE ON PASSAGE

INTRODUCTION

COMMITTEE ACTION

S 2 INTRODUCED IN SENATE

REFERRED TO SENATE COMMITTEE

REFERRED TO SUBCOMMITTEE

REPORTED BY FULL COMMITTEE

FLOOR ACTION

SENATE DEBATE, VOTE ON PASSAGE

Bill goes to full committee, then usually to specialized subcommittee for study, hearings, revisions, approval. Then bill goes back to full committee where more hearings and revision may occur. Full committee may approve bill and recommend its chamber pass the proposal. Committees rarely give bill unfavorable report; rather, no action is taken, thereby killing it.

In House, many bills go before Rules Committee for "rule" expediting floor action, setting conditions for debate and amendments on floor. Some bills are "privileged" and go directly to floor. Other procedures exist for noncontroversial or routine bills. In Senate, special "rules" are not used; leadership normally schedules action.

Bill is debated, usually amended, passed or defeated. If passed, it goes to other chamber to follow the same route through committee and floor stages. (If other chamber has already passed related bill, both versions go straight to conference.)

CONFERENCE ACTION

Once both chambers have passed related bills, conference committee of members from both houses is formed to work out differences.

Compromise version from conference is sent to each chamber for final approval.

HR 1 **VETO**

S 2

Compromise version approved by both houses is sent to President who can either sign it into law or veto it and return it to Congress. Congress may override veto by a two-thirds majority vote in both houses; bill then becomes law without President's signature.

97TH CONGRESS, FIRST SESSION

GOP Seeks Fruits of Victory as 97th Convenes

The 97th Congress, which convened Jan. 5, was distinctly different from its immediate predecessor. For the first time since January 1955, Republicans controlled the Senate. In the House, the Democrats were still in the majority, though by a slimmer margin than they enjoyed during the 96th Congress. And the conservative leanings of many of their numbers threatened to make the Democratic leadership's grasp on House proceedings a sometimes thing.

As Congress opened, Senate Republicans reveled in their unwonted majority status. The new Senate majority leader, Howard H. Baker Jr., R-Tenn., plowed through the routine opening exercises with obvious relish and to the accompaniment of much applause and backslapping from his GOP colleagues. On the other hand, if House Republicans returned to the Capitol feeling peppy over their 33-seat gain in membership, their continuing second-class status in that chamber was soon driven home in a series of opening-day GOP defeats. On party-line votes, House Democrats beat back several Republican efforts to dramatize the two parties' differences on economic and procedural questions.

The House Republicans accepted their losses philosophically, however, immediately vowing future confrontations with the Democrats over the same issues.

The change in control in the Senate meant that the entire committee leadership shifted to the Republicans and that the Democrats were relegated to minority status. Democrats retained control of the committee structure in the House, but election defeats and the increased number of Republicans forced several changes in party and committee leadership. House Democrats refused, however, to revamp party ratios on four key committees to reflect the GOP membership gains in the House.

The Senate

The Senate spent its opening day on largely ceremonial matters. New members were sworn in, some routine housekeeping measures were adopted and committee assignments were formally ratified. The Republican leadership proposed no changes in the Senate rules.

Most of the key organizational decisions had been made at party caucuses held in early December 1980. Republicans elected their new leaders Dec. 2, while Democrats chose theirs Dec. 4.

THE MAJORITY LEADERSHIP

Baker was unopposed as the new Senate majority leader. Elected majority whip — also unopposed — was Ted Stevens, Alaska. Baker and Stevens, both considered GOP moderates, served during the 96th Congress as the Senate's minority leader and minority whip.

In the sole contested GOP race, James A. McClure, Idaho, a conservative, defeated moderate John Heinz, Pa., 33-20 for chairmanship of the Senate Republican Confer-

ence, a GOP policy-making body. Heinz had chaired the Republican Senatorial Campaign Committee during the highly successful 1980 campaign and was an early favorite. However, conservatives fought hard to elect McClure, explaining he would balance the party leadership. Other senators mentioned Heinz' wealth and aloof personality as factors in the race.

Bob Packwood, Ore., was uncontested to succeed Heinz as chairman of the campaign committee. Robert Dole, Kan., also had campaigned for the post but dropped out of the race at the last minute.

GOP senators also re-elected John Tower, Texas, chairman of the the Republican Policy Committee, and Jake Garn, Utah, was re-elected secretary of the Republican Conference. Republican Strom Thurmond, S.C., became Senate president pro tempore even though Democrat John C. Stennis, Miss., had more seniority. The president pro tempore is third in the line of presidential succession.

THE MINORITY LEADERSHIP

On the other side of the aisle, Democrats routinely elected previous majority leader Robert C. Byrd, W.Va., as

---

97th Congress Leadership

SENATE

President Pro Tempore — Strom Thurmond, R-S.C

Majority Leader — Howard H. Baker Jr., R-Tenn..

Majority Whip — Ted Stevens, R-Alaska

Republican Conference Chairman — James A. McClure, R-Idaho

Republican Conference Secretary — Jake Garn, R-Utah

Minority Leader — Robert C. Byrd, D-W.Va.

Minority Whip — Alan Cranston, D-Calif.

Democratic Conference Secretary — Daniel K. Inouye, D-Hawaii

HOUSE

Speaker — Thomas P. O'Neill Jr., D-Mass.

Majority Leader — Jim Wright, D-Texas

Majority Whip — Thomas S. Foley, D-Wash.

Minority Leader — Robert H. Michel, R-Ill.

Minority Whip — Trent Lott, R-Miss.

Chairman of the Conference — Jack F. Kemp, R-N.Y.

Republican Policy Committee Chairman — Dick Cheney, R- Wyo.

Public Laws

A total of 145 bills cleared by Congress in 1981 became public laws. Following is a list of the number of public laws enacted since 1966:

Year	Public Laws	Year	Public Laws
1981	145	1973	247
1980	426	1972	483
1979	187	1971	224
1978	410	1970	505
1977	223	1969	190
1976	383	1968	391
1975	205	1967	249
1974	402	1966	461

minority leader and chairman of the Democratic Conference for the 97th Congress. Californian Alan Cranston, majority whip in the 96th Congress, was unopposed for minority whip, and Daniel K. Inouye, Hawaii, retained his post as secretary of the conference.

In a Dec. 1, 1980, meeting, Senate Democrats eliminated a party rule giving new senators a leg up in obtaining choice committee assignments if their predecessors retired early, permitting them to gain a few days' seniority by being appointed to fill the vacancy just before the end of a Congress. Senate Republicans had eliminated a similar rule in August 1980. Seniority still counted in obtaining such Senate perquisites as choice of office and parking space assignments.

COMMITTEE ASSIGNMENTS

The new Senate committee assignments — handed down in the closing days of the 96th Congress — reinforced the assumption that the 97th Congress would take a sharp turn to the right. With new GOP chairmen and Republican majorities, the Senate's committees were more anti-government and significantly more conservative on fiscal matters than committees of the 96th Congress had been.

The composition of the new panels, especially Energy and Environment, also meant the Senate was likely to worry more over Western U.S. concerns than Eastern ones and to favor the smaller, less developed states over the nation's industrial areas.

Committee Ratios

Republicans moved to increase by one the size of the Appropriations, Judiciary and Special Aging committees. Increased by two were the Budget, Energy, Environment, Foreign Relations, Rules, Select Intelligence and Veterans' Affairs committees. Republicans reduced by one the size of the Senate Agriculture Committee. Republicans assigned themselves a two-seat margin of control over the Democrats on the Budget, Energy, Environment, Finance, Judiciary, Rules, Joint Economic and Veterans' Affairs committees. They outnumbered Democrats by only one on Agriculture, Appropriations, Armed Services, Banking, Commerce, Foreign Relations, Governmental Affairs, Labor, Select Intelligence, Special Aging and Select Small Business.

Meanwhile the Democrats' heavy losses in November dictated substantial shuffling of minority leadership positions on the Senate committees. Only one surviving Democrat — Dennis DeConcini, Ariz. — actually lost a committee assignment as a result of the Republican Senate majority. He was forced off the Rules Committee when that panel's Democratic membership was reduced from seven to four. DeConcini, however, picked up a seat on the Veterans' Affairs Committee.

Chairmen, Ranking Democrats. Following are the chairmen and ranking minority members of Senate committees approved when Congress convened Jan. 5:

● Agriculture — Chairman: Jesse Helms, R-N.C., replacing Herman E. Talmadge, D-Ga., who lost re-election. Ranking Democrat: Walter D. Huddleston, Ky.

● Appropriations — Chairman: Mark O. Hatfield, R-Ore., replacing Warren G. Magnuson, D-Wash., who lost re-election. Ranking Democrat: William Proxmire, Wis.

● Armed Services — Chairman: John Tower, R-Texas, replacing John C. Stennis, D-Miss. Ranking Democrat: Stennis.

● Banking, Housing and Urban Affairs — Jake Garn, R-Utah, replacing William Proxmire, D-Wis. Ranking Democrat: Harrison A. Williams Jr., N.J.

● Budget — Pete V. Domenici, R-N.M., replacing Ernest F. Hollings, D-S.C. Ranking Democrat: Hollings.

Membership Changes, 97th Congress

HOUSE

Party	Member	Died	Resigned	Successor	Party	Elected	Sworn In
R	Dave Stockman - Mich.		1/27/81	Mark Siljander	R	4/21/81	4/28/81
D	Gladys Noon Spellman - Md.		2/24/81*	Steny Hoyer	D	5/19/81	6/3/81
R	Tennyson Guyer - Ohio	4/12/81		Michael G. Oxley	R	6/25/81	7/21/81
R	Jon Hinson - Miss.		4/13/81	Wayne Dowdy	D	7/7/81	7/9/81
D	Raymond F. Lederer - Pa.		5/5/81	Joseph F. Smith	D	7/21/81	7/28/81
D	William R. Cotter - Conn.	9/8/81					
D	Eugene V. Atkinson - Pa.		Atkinson switched to the Republican Party on Oct. 14, 1981.				

* Rep. Spellman suffered cardiac arrest four days before the November general election and remained in a trance-like state of consciousness from that time. Although she was elected to the 97th Congress, she was never sworn in as a member. On Feb. 24, 1981, the House voted to declare her seat vacant.

● Commerce, Science and Transportation — Bob Packwood, R-Ore., replacing Howard W. Cannon, D-Nev. Ranking Democrat: Cannon.

● Energy and Natural Resources — James A. McClure, R-Idaho, replacing Henry M. Jackson, D-Wash. Ranking Democrat: Jackson.

● Environment and Public Works — Robert T. Stafford, R-Vt., replacing Jennings Randolph, D-W. Va. Ranking Democrat: Randolph.

● Finance — Robert Dole, R-Kan., replacing Russell B. Long, D-La. Ranking Democrat: Long.

● Foreign Relations — Charles H. Percy, R-Ill., replacing Frank Church, Idaho, who lost re-election. Ranking Democrat Claiborne Pell, R.I.

● Governmental Affairs — William V. Roth Jr., R-Del., replacing Abraham Ribicoff, D-Conn., who retired. Ranking Democrat: Thomas F. Eagleton, Mo.

● Judiciary — Strom Thurmond, R-S.C., replacing Edward M. Kennedy, D-Mass. Ranking Democrat: Joseph R. Biden, Del.

● Labor and Human Resources — Orrin G. Hatch, R-Utah, replacing Harrison A. Williams Jr. Ranking Democrat: Edward M. Kennedy, Mass.

● Rules and Administration — Charles McC. Mathias Jr., R-Md., replacing Claiborne Pell, R.I. Ranking Democrat: Wendell H. Ford, Ky.

● Select Ethics — Chairman: Malcolm Wallop, R-Wyo., replacing Howell Heflin, Ala. Ranking Democrat: Heflin.

● Select Indian Affairs — William S. Cohen, R-Maine, replacing John Melcher, D-Mont. Ranking Democrat: Melcher.

● Select Intelligence — Chairman: Barry Goldwater, R-Ariz., replacing Birch Bayh, D-Ind. who lost re-election. Ranking Democrat: Daniel Patrick Moynihan, N.Y.

● Select Small Business — Chairman: Lowell P. Weicker Jr., R-Conn., replacing Gaylord Nelson, D-Wis., who lost re-election. Ranking Democrat: Sam Nunn, Ga.

● Special Aging — John Heinz, R-Pa., replacing Lawton Chiles, D-Fla. Ranking Democrat: Chiles.

● Veterans' Affairs — Alan K. Simpson, R-Wyo., replacing Alan Cranston, D-Calif. Ranking Democrat: Cranston.

The House

The House began its opening day formalities with the election of a Speaker. It then proceeded to swear in new members and to adopt its rules for the next two years.

For Speaker, the House re-elected Thomas P. O'Neill Jr., D-Mass., over the Republican candidate, Robert H. Michel, Ill., by a 234-182 vote. No other candidates were nominated, and the vote was strictly along party lines. *(Vote 1, p. 2-H)*

Following the vote, O'Neill told his House colleagues he would try to "seek the common ground" with the Republican Senate and the Republican president. "When differences occur, as they no doubt will, we will air them in an atmosphere of constructive dialogue rather than partisan recrimination." Rep. Michel, the new Republican leader, also pledged to cooperate with the Democrats "in the best interest of the American people."

His GOP colleagues then went on to launch a vigorous offensive against the rules package the Democrats were proposing for the 97th Congress.

The Democrats were seeking only minor changes in the House rules, having decided in December 1980 to defer

---

Spellman Vacancy

For the first time in its history, the House in 1981 approved a resolution declaring a vacancy because of a member's disability.

The resolution (H Res 80) declared vacant Maryland's 5th Congressional District. The seat had been held by Democrat Gladys Noon Spellman, who had remained hospitalized in a semiconscious state since suffering a heart attack Oct. 31, 1980. Spellman first entered the House in 1975. A week after suffering her heart attack, she was re-elected with more than 80 percent of the vote. However, her disability prevented her from being sworn in as a member of the 97th Congress.

Two days after the House acted, Maryland Gov. Harry R. Hughes, D, called for a May 19 general election to fill the seat.

The election was won by Democrat Steny Hoyer. *(Details, p. 4-B)*

In the only similar action, the House in late 1972 and early 1973 voted to declare two seats vacant after a court declared that the members elected to those seats were legally dead. The members — Reps. Hale Boggs, D-La. (1941-43; 1947-73), and Nicholas J. Begich, D-Alaska (1971-72) — had been passengers in a plane that disappeared without a trace in October 1972.

The Constitution gives the House the power to "be the Judge of the . . . Qualifications of its own members."

---

action on more controversial proposals intended to help fend off Republican riders on appropriations bills. The rules changes the Democrats sought proposed to give the Speaker flexibility in avoiding quorum calls requested during routine legislative business, in clustering votes on bills taken under a suspension of the rules and in taking up a continuing resolution after Dec. 15 of any fiscal year.

Republicans countered with two rules changes that dealt with the congressional budget process. One would have required the House to tie federal spending to a gradually declining percentage of the gross national product. The second would have transferred jurisdiction over the 1974 Congressional Budget Act from the Rules Committee to the Budget Committee.

House consideration of the two GOP amendments was blocked 216-179. *(Vote 2, p. 2-H)*

Claiming that the Democrats had stacked the membership on several key committees, Republicans then offered an amendment that made the ratio between the number of Democrats and the number of Republicans on those committees more to the GOP's liking. That amendment was turned back, largely along party-line votes. The House then approved its rules by voice vote. *(Details, committee ratio fight, p. 9)*

THE MAJORITY LEADERSHIP

Like the Senate, House Democrats and Republicans had elected their leadership in December. House Democrats had few leadership contests. House Speaker O'Neill and House Majority Leader Jim Wright, Texas, were unopposed for re-election at the Democrats' Dec. 8, 1980, party caucus.

Reagan Is Eighth Sitting U.S. President . . .

President Reagan was wounded in the chest March 30 in an assassination attempt. The attack came at about 2:30 p.m. as he walked toward his limousine after addressing the AFL-CIO Building and Construction Trades Department at the Washington Hilton Hotel.

A man standing with reporters, who were waiting for the president outside the hotel, fired six shots from a .22-caliber pistol. One of the bullets hit Reagan in the chest. Three others also were wounded — press secretary James S. Brady, who was the most seriously hurt with a bullet wound in his brain; Secret Service agent Timothy J. McCarthy, and D.C. policeman Thomas K. Delahanty.

The alleged assailant later was identified as John Warnock Hinckley Jr., 25.

Secret Service agents quickly hustled Reagan into the limousine, which sped first toward the White House but then went to the George Washington University Medical Center, about six blocks from the White House, when agents learned that Reagan had been hit.

Initial news reports of the attack said the president had not been hurt. And when the injury was first announced, reports also gave the clear impression that it was relatively minor.

However, later accounts reported that the president could have died from his injuries if they had not been promptly treated. Witnesses and doctors reported that Reagan collapsed after walking into the hospital emergency room, that he was coughing blood, having trouble breathing and required blood transfusions to stabilize his condition. He then was wheeled into surgery to remove the bullet from his left lung. The operation lasted more than two hours.

Meanwhile, law enforcement officers at the Washington Hilton Hotel had seized Hinckley immediately after the shots were fired. The son of a wealthy Colorado oil executive had neither job nor fixed address, and his parents said he had undergone psychiatric treatment.

Letters found in his Washington hotel room indicated that Hinckley was in love with teen-age movie actress Jodie Foster, and that he had planned the assassination attempt as a "historical act" to win her "respect and love."

Hinckley was charged the night of the shooting with attempting to kill the president and with assaulting a Secret Service agent with a deadly weapon. A psychiatric examination was ordered and he was found competent to stand trial, although further tests were ordered after he attempted suicide in November. At year's end his trial date had not been set.

Who Was in Charge?

One question raised by the shooting was who, really, was running the country in the hours immediately after the assassination attempt.

The decision by Secretary of State Alexander M. Haig Jr. to make a nationally televised statement that he was "in control" at the White House contributed to the muddle and reportedly prompted a behind-the-scenes squabble in the administration.

Meanwhile, however, Vice President George Bush stepped into the delicate role of substituting for the president without appearing to supplant him. Bush and members of the Cabinet decided not to invoke the 25th Amendment, the constitutional procedure for declaring the president disabled and transferring authority to the vice president. *(1967 Almanac p. 300)*

Some of the confusion may have been attributable to the fact that the president's top spokesman, press secretary Brady, had been critically wounded himself.

The word from James A. Baker III, White House chief of staff, and other sources was that high-ranking staff members had gathered quickly at the hospital while a number of Cabinet members collected in the White House "situation room," a communications center where National Security Council meetings take place.

A triangular chain of communication was established between the hospital, the situation room and the airplane carrying Bush back to Washington from Texas, where he had canceled a speaking engagement.

This chain, Baker said, was meant to keep the government functioning and to ensure that the constitutional procedure for delegating presidential authority to Bush could be activated, if needed.

The administration had, at all times, been ready "for any contingency that might arise," he said.

Legal opinions on the constitutional line of succession and provisions governing presidential disability were sought and delivered the same day by the Justice Department. *(Line of succession, Congress and the Nation Vol. I, p. 1435)*

Defense Secretary Caspar W. Weinberger "took charge of the national defense moves that were made, and we contacted leaders around the world," according to Sen. Alan Cranston, D-Calif., Senate minority whip, who was briefed with other congressional leaders on March 31 by White House Counsel Edwin Meese III.

The next day, Reagan and his three top aides — Meese, Baker and Deputy Chief of Staff Michael K. Deaver — had their customary morning meeting, held in Reagan's hospital room instead of in the Oval Office.

Contributing to the image of normalcy, Reagan signed a dairy bill (S 509) on his breakfast tray. And Reagan's schedule — a meeting with congressional leaders, a luncheon discussion with Dutch Prime Minister Andreas van Agt — went unchanged, although Bush filled in for the president. *(Dairy bill, p. 550)*

The assassination attempt also raised questions about Secret Service protection, and additional funds for agents were included in the Treasury-Post Office appropriation bil. *(Story, p. 355)*

Past Assassination Attempts

President Reagan was the eighth sitting American president to be the victim of an assassination attempt.

Of the five who were actually wounded, he was the only one to live. The four killed by assassins' bullets were Abraham Lincoln, James A. Garfield, William McKinley

... To Be Target of Assassination Attempt

and John F. Kennedy. The three who escaped injury were Andrew Jackson, Harry S Truman and Gerald R. Ford.

Following is a summary of the assassination attempts on the eight sitting presidents:

Andrew Jackson was in the rotunda of the U.S. Capitol when he was shot at on Jan. 30, 1835, by Richard Lawrence. The assailant's two pistols misfired and Jackson was unhurt. Lawrence was tried and found insane. He spent the rest of his life in prisons and mental hospitals.

Abraham Lincoln was shot April 14, 1865, as he watched a play at Ford's Theater in Washington, D.C. He died April 15. The assassin, John Wilkes Booth, fled. On April 26 he was cornered in a barn in nearby Maryland and shot to death by law officers. Four co-conspirators were hanged on July 7.

James A. Garfield was shot in the back July 2, 1881, at the train station in Washington, D.C. He died Sept. 19. His murderer, Charles J. Guiteau, who had been refused an ambassadorial position by Garfield, was hanged June 30, 1882.

William McKinley was about to shake hands with Leon Czologosz when Czologosz shot him on Sept. 6, 1901, in Buffalo, N.Y. McKinley died eight days later. Czologosz was electrocuted Oct. 29 for the crime.

Harry S Truman escaped death Nov. 1, 1950, when two Puerto Rican nationalists shot their way into Blair House in Washington, D.C., where Truman was living while the White House was being renovated. One of the assailants, Griselio Torresola, and a White House guard were killed during the shoot-out. The other gunman, Oscar Collazo, was sentenced to death, but Truman reduced the sentence to life imprisonment. In 1979 President Carter commuted the sentence and Collazo, 64, returned to Puerto Rico.

John F. Kennedy was shot with a high-powered rifle while riding in a motorcade in Dallas, Texas, on Nov. 22, 1963. He died almost immediately. Lee Harvey Oswald, arrested for the murder, was shot and killed two days later in the Dallas police station by a bystander, nightclub owner Jack Ruby. Ruby was convicted of murder and later died in prison.

Gerald R. Ford in 1975 escaped would-be assassins' bullets twice in one month. Both incidents occurred in California. On Sept. 5 in Sacramento, Lynette "Squeaky" Fromme, a 26-year-old follower of convicted murderer and cult leader Charles Manson, aimed a pistol at Ford as he reached out to shake her hand. A Secret Service agent grabbed the gun and it did not fire. On Sept. 22, Sara Jane Moore, 45, shot at Ford as he left a San Francisco hotel. A bystander grabbed her arm and the shot was deflected. Moore had been questioned by police and Secret Service agents the day before the shooting; she was charged with carrying a concealed weapon and then released. *(1975 Almanac pp. 519, 907)*

The two women were the first persons tried under the 1965 law (PL 89-141) making it a federal crime to attempt to kill the president, vice president or the next person in line of succession, a law passed after President Kennedy's assassination. Both women were sentenced to life imprisonment. *(1965 law, 1965 Almanac p. 582)*

Ronald Reagan was wounded by gunfire March 30, 1981, as he emerged from the Washington Hilton Hotel after making a speech. His press secretary, a Secret Service agent and a Washington, D.C., policeman also were shot. Seized and charged with the assaults was John W. Hinckley Jr.

Other Shootings

Former President Theodore Roosevelt was shot and seriously wounded on Oct. 14, 1912, in Milwaukee, Wis., while campaigning again for the presidency on the Bull Moose ticket. His assailant, John Schrank, was committed to a Wisconsin state hospital for the insane. He died in 1943.

President-elect Franklin D. Roosevelt was riding in an open car in Miami, Fla., when Giuseppe Zangara fired at him on Feb. 15, 1933. A woman in the crowd grabbed Zangara's arm and the bullet missed Roosevelt, hitting Chicago Mayor Anton J. Cermak, who was riding with him. Cermak died March 6, and Zangara was electrocuted March 20.

Sen. Robert F. Kennedy, D-N.Y. (1965-68), was a candidate for president in 1968 when he was shot and killed in a Los Angeles hotel the night of the 1968 California primary. He was shot just after midnight on June 5, and died the next day. Kennedy's assailant, Sirhan Sirhan, was sentenced to death, but the sentence was commuted to life imprisonment in 1972 when the Supreme Court declared capital punishment unconstitutional. He would be eligible for parole on Sept. 1, 1984.

George C. Wallace was campaigning for the Democratic presidential nomination when he was shot at a Laurel, Md., shopping center on May 15, 1972. The injury left him paralyzed from the waist down. Three bystanders also were injured. Wallace's attacker, Arthur Bremer, was sentenced to 63 years in prison, but an appeals court later reduced the sentence to 53 years. Bremer was sent to the Maryland Correctional Institute in Hagerstown.

Assaults on Congressmen

At least eight members of Congress had been assaulted by robbers on the streets of Washington, D.C., in 10 years preceding the Reagan assassination attempt.

Sen. John C. Stennis, D-Miss., was the most seriously injured. He was shot twice on Jan. 30, 1973, during an armed robbery in front of his home. He underwent emergency surgery and almost died.

In addition, three members of Congress had been assassinated, but not in the capital. Sen. Huey Long, D-La. (1932-35), was shot while in the rotunda of the Louisiana State Capitol in Baton Rouge on Sept. 8, 1935. On June 6, 1968, Sen. Robert F. Kennedy, D-N.Y. (1965-68), was assassinated in a Los Angeles hotel the night of the California primary. Rep. Leo J. Ryan, D-Calif. (1973-78), was gunned down on Nov. 18, 1978, on an airstrip in Guyana. *(Violent deaths among members of Congress, 1978 Almanac p. 7)*

At that caucus Wright announced he had named Rep. Thomas S. Foley, Wash., majority whip for the 97th Congress. Foley, a moderate, replaced Rep. John Brademas, Ind., who lost his bid for re-election.

Rep. Dan Rostenkowski, Ill., was Wright's first choice for the whip job. But Rostenkowski announced Dec. 5 that he instead would seek the chairmanship of the Ways and Means Committee, succeeding Rep. Al Ullman, Ore., who also was defeated in the 1980 elections.

Reflecting conservative Democrats' increasing numbers in the House, a number of lesser posts were filled by moderates and conservatives, many of them Southerners.

Rep. Gillis W. Long, La., a moderate, was elected chairman of the Democratic Caucus, succeeding Foley. Long won with 146 votes to 53 for Rep. Charlie Rose, N.C., and 41 for Matthew F. McHugh, N.Y.

Appointed by Wright to be chief deputy majority whip — the leadership position formerly held by Rostenkowski — was Rep. Bill Alexander, Ark., a moderate. Rep. Richard A. Gephardt, D-Mo., another moderate, was named chief of task forces, a new post in the Democratic leadership. Gephardt's role was to supplement the existing whip system by seeking to form coalitions to help shepherd key bills through the House.

Wright and O'Neill named three Southern conservatives to the Democratic Steering and Policy Committee: Reps. Tom Bevill, Ala., Bo Ginn, Ga., and Wes Watkins, Okla. The Steering and Policy panel made Democratic committee assignments, nominated committee chairmen and played a role in party policy making. Following the November election, an informal group of 34 conservative Democrats met with Democratic leaders to ask for a greater voice in party affairs. Among their suggestions was to put more conservatives on the Steering and Policy Committee as well as on other key panels.

THE MINORITY LEADERSHIP

In choosing their leaders Dec. 8, House Republicans selected candidates known for their flexibility and willingness to negotiate with the Democrats over those known more as strong partisans or rigid ideologues. For the post of minority leader, the Republicans chose Rep. Michel, a skilled legislative technician with a good working relationship with the Democratic leadership. Michel succeeded John J. Rhodes, Ariz, who voluntarily stepped down from the House GOP leadership. Republicans subsequently dubbed Rhodes their "leader emeritus."

Michel told his colleagues after his election that he would need their help in staging "commando raids for votes" on the Democratic side of the aisle. "We've got to be on the offensive" in order to overcome the Democrats' superior numbers, he said. "The bottom line is enactment of the Reagan program [and] the battle will be in the House."

Michel had been minority whip since 1974. His opponent in the race for minority leader, Guy Vander Jagt, Mich., was known more for his oratory than for his parliamentary ability. As chairman of the National Republican Congressional Committee he had spent most of 1979 and 1980 traveling across the country touting GOP House candidates and raising money for their campaigns.

In the election Michel won 103 votes to Vander Jagt's 87. Prior to the balloting both candidates had claimed victory. Vander Jagt had even sent thank-you notes to the 102 Republicans he thought had promised to support his candidacy. The difference in the final tally was blamed on members who had promised their vote to both candidates.

In other House GOP races:

● Jack F. Kemp, N.Y., was elected chairman of the Republican Conference, the policy making group composed of all House Republicans. He defeated John H. Rousselot, Calif., by a vote of 107-77. Three other candidates — Reps. Bill Goodling, Pa., Henry J. Hyde, Ill., and Thomas N. Kindness, Ohio — dropped out of the race and were not nominated. Kemp succeeded Samuel L. Devine, Ohio, who was defeated for re-election.

● Trent Lott, Miss., was elected minority whip, the position held by Michel in the 96th Congress. Lott defeated Bud Shuster, Pa., by a vote of 96-90.

● Dick Cheney, Wyo., defeated Rep. Marjorie S. Holt, Md., 99-68 for the chairmanship of the Republican Policy Committee, the post previously held by Shuster. A third candidate in the race, Rep. Eldon Rudd, Ariz., was eliminated on an earlier ballot.

● Rep. Edward R. Madigan, Ill., defeated Robert S. Walker, Pa., for chairmanship of the Republican Research Committee.

● Reps. Jack Edwards, Ala., and Clair W. Burgener, Calif., were unopposed for re-election as conference vice chairman and secretary, respectively.

COMMITTEE CHANGES

In the 96th Congress House Democrats did not get around to electing committee chairmen until late January 1979. For the 97th Congress, they had completed the task by Dec. 11, 1980, nearly a month before the new Congress convened.

It's Official: Reagan Won

President-elect Reagan's landslide victory became official Jan. 6 when a joint session of Congress counted the votes of the Electoral College.

Only about 200 members were present for the brief ceremony. As expected, Reagan and his running mate, George Bush, received 489 electoral votes, while President Jimmy Carter and Vice President Walter F. Mondale tallied 49.

The congressional vote-counting ritual was the final step in the presidential election, a process defined by the Constitution. The electoral votes were cast in each state capital and the District of Columbia Dec. 15 by the 538 electors who were chosen Nov. 4 by more than 83 million voters.

Mondale presided over the counting of the electoral votes in his role as president of the Senate. Members gave him a standing ovation when the votes for him were announced. Carter and Mondale carried only six states and the District of Columbia.

This was the first election in the last four where all the electors were faithful to their state's choice for president.

In 1977, a Republican elector from the state of Washington, who was pledged to Gerald R. Ford, voted instead for Reagan. In 1973, a Republican elector from Virginia cast his ballot for the Libertarian Party ticket. In 1969, a North Carolina Republican elector defected to George C. Wallace, the American Independent Party candidate.

In the only significant contest for a committee chairmanship, House Democrats elected James R. Jones, Okla., to chair the Budget Committee in the 97th Congress. Jones defeated David R. Obey, Wis., a liberal who was more senior than Jones. Jones replaced Rep. Robert N. Giaimo, Conn., who retired. Jones and Obey tied on the first ballot with 100 votes each to 39 votes for Rep. Paul Simon, Ill. On the second ballot Jones and Obey tied once more with 118 votes each. The third ballot gave Jones 121 votes and Obey 116.

For every other House panel on which the top job was vacant for the new Congress, the Democratic Caucus selected the highest-ranking eligible Democrat on the committee. All incumbent chairmen were re-elected.

Elected to fill vacant chairmanships were:

- Fernand J. St Germain, R.I., Banking, replacing Henry S. Reuss, Wis., who gave up his Banking chairmanship to head the Joint Economic Committee.
- John D. Dingell, Mich., Commerce, succeeding Harley O. Staggers, W. Va., who retired.
- E. "Kika" de la Garza, Texas, Agriculture, succeeding Thomas S. Foley, Wash., who stepped down to become minority whip.
- Augustus F. Hawkins, Calif., House Administration, replacing Frank Thompson Jr., N.J. who was defeated for re-election.
- Walter B. Jones, N.C., Merchant Marine, replacing John M. Murphy, N.Y., who was defeated for re-election.
- William D. Ford, Mich., Post Office and Civil Service, succeeding James M. Hanley, N.Y., who retired.
- James J. Howard, N.J., Public Works and Transportation, succeeding Harold T. Johnson, Calif., who lost re-election.
- Parren J. Mitchell, Md., Small Business, succeeding Neal Smith, Iowa, who preferred to take an Appropriations subcommittee chairmanship.
- Louis Stokes, Ohio, Standards of Official Conduct, succeeding Charles E. Bennett, Fla., who was required to step down under a caucus rule limiting service on the ethics panel to two consecutive terms.
- G. V. "Sonny" Montgomery, Miss., Veterans, Agriculture, succeeding Ray Roberts, Texas, who retired.
- Dan Rostenkowski, Ill., Ways and Means, succeeding Al Ullman, Ore., who was defeated for re-election.

In the only close vote, de la Garza was approved as Agriculture chairman by a 110-92 tally. An expected challenge to Walter Jones failed to materialize after he agreed to appoint next-ranking Mario Biaggi, N.Y., Merchant Marine vice chairman for the 97th Congress.

Re-elected as chairmen were: Jamie L. Whitten, Miss., Appropriations; Melvin D. Price, Ill., Armed Forces; Ronald V. Dellums, Calif., District of Columbia; Carl D. Perkins, Ky., Education and Labor; Clement J. Zablocki, Wis. Foreign Relations; Jack Brooks, Texas, Government Operations; Morris K. Udall, Ariz., Interior; Peter W. Rodino Jr., N.J., Judiciary; Richard Bolling, Mo., Rules; and Don Fuqua, Fla., Science and Technology.

Ratio Dispute. Despite the Democrats' early start, formal approval of these and other House committee assignments was delayed until Jan. 28 by a dispute over the party ratios on several key committees. *(House committee roster, p. 60)*

While the ratio of House Democrats to Republicans was about 5-to-4 in the 97th Congress, Speaker O'Neill and the House Democratic Caucus insisted on retaining a 3-2 ratio on the Appropriations and Budget committees, a

---

Reagan Vetoes

President Reagan vetoed only two bills in his first year in office.

Congress made no attempt to override the formal veto of a continuing appropriations resolution (H J Res 357) for fiscal 1982. Reagan vetoed, the measure Nov. 23. *(Story, p. 294)*

The second veto was a pocket veto, accomplished by Reagan's rejection, after Congress adjourned, of a bill (HR 4353) that would have reduced bankruptcy fees for a single company. In a Dec. 29 memorandum of disapproval, Reagan said the bill amounted to "special relief in the guise of general legislation." *(Story, p. 436)*

When Congress is in session, a bill becomes law without the president's signature if he does not act upon it within 10 days, excluding Sundays, from the time he receives it. But if Congress adjourns within that 10-day period, the bill is killed, or pocket vetoed, without the president's formal veto.

Reagan's two vetoes matched the total number of vetoes cast by George Washington in his two terms as president. Seven presidents vetoed no bills during their tenures. The greatest number of vetoes, 635, was cast by Franklin D. Roosevelt. More recently, Jimmy Carter vetoed two bills in his first year in office, 1977; Gerald R. Ford vetoed 27 in 1974; Richard M. Nixon, none in 1969; Lyndon B. Johnson, 6 in 1964; and John F. Kennedy, 8 in 1961.

1981
1. H J Res 357 (Continuing Appropriations).
   Vetoed: Nov. 23.
   No Override Attempt.
2. HR 4353 (Bankruptcy Fees on Lifetime Communities Inc.).
   Pocket vetoed: Dec. 29.

---

more than 2-1 ratio on the Rules Committee and a ratio of slightly less than 2-to-1 on the Ways and Means Committee.

Democratic leaders argued that these larger margins were necessary to retain procedural control of the House, but Republicans charged the Democrats with attempting to alter the results of the Republican landslide in the November elections.

Barber B. Conable Jr., R-N.Y., irked over the Ways and Means ratio in particular, had attempted to press the issue in private, and talks between him and Ways and Means Chairman Rostenkowski continued until Jan. 2, just three days before the 97th Congress was to begin.

Throughout the negotiations, however, Speaker O'Neill refused to budge. It was the Speaker's intransigence that convinced Conable the Republicans should go public with the dispute on the session's opening day.

Committee ratios traditionally have been laid out by the majority party and have not been included in House rules. But to dramatize the issue, as Conable had suggested, Michel Jan. 5 offered a privileged motion to make the ratios more to the GOP's liking and to write those new ratios into the rules.

As expected, the GOP proposal on committee ratios also was turned back, largely along party lines. But the debate gave the Republicans a prominent forum in which

Senate Cloture Votes, 1977-81

Following is a list of all cloture votes taken by the Senate from 1977 through 1981. Cloture motions required a majority of three-fifths of the total Senate (60 members) for adoption, under a rule adopted in 1975; previously cloture could be invoked by a two-thirds majority vote of those senators present and voting.

Since 1979, Senate rules had required a final vote on a measure on which cloture had been invoked after no more than 100 hours of post-cloture debate.

The seven cloture votes in 1981 brought to 168 the total number of cloture votes taken since the adoption of Rule 22 first allowed them in 1917. *(Cloture votes 1919-76, 1977 Almanac p. 813)*

Issue	Date	Vote	Yeas Needed
Draft Resisters Pardons	Jan. 24, 1977	53-43	60
Campaign Financing	July 29, 1977	49-45	60
Campaign Financing	Aug. 1, 1977	47-46	60
Campaign Financing	Aug. 2, 1977	52-46	60
Natural Gas Pricing	Sept. 26, 1977	77-17	60
Labor Law Revision	June 7, 1978	42-47	60
Labor Law Revision	June 8, 1978	49-41	60
Labor Law Revision	June 13, 1978	54-43	60
Labor Law Revision	June 14, 1978	58-41	60
Labor Law Revision	June 15, 1978	58-39	60
Labor Law Revision	June 22, 1978	53-45	60
Revenue Act of 1978	Oct. 9, 1978	62-28	60
Energy Taxes	Oct. 14, 1978	71-13	60
Windfall Profits Tax	Dec. 12, 1979	53-46	60
Windfall Profits Tax	Dec. 13, 1979	56-40	60
Windfall Profits Tax	Dec. 14, 1979	56-39	60
Windfall Profits Tax	Dec. 17, 1979	84-14	60
Lubbers Nomination	April 21, 1980	46-60	60
Lubbers Nomination	April 22, 1980	62-34	60
Rights of Institutionalized	April 28, 1980	44-39	60
Rights of Institutionalized	April 29, 1980	56-34	60
Rights of Institutionalized	April 30, 1980	53-35	60
Rights of Institutionalized	May 1, 1980	60-34	60
Bottlers' Antitrust Immunity	May 15, 1980	86-6	60
Draft Registration Funding	June 10, 1980	62-32	60
Zimmerman Nomination	Aug. 1, 1980	51-35	60
Zimmerman Nomination	Aug. 4, 1980	45-31	60
Zimmerman Nomination	Aug. 5, 1980	63-31	60
Alaska Lands	Aug. 18, 1980	63-25	60
Vessel Tonnage/ Strip Mining	Aug. 21, 1980	61-32	60
Fair Housing Amendments	Dec. 3, 1980	51-39	60
Fair Housing Amendments	Dec. 4, 1980	62-32	60
Fair Housing Amendments	Dec. 9, 1980	54-43	60
Breyer Nomination	Dec. 9, 1980	68-28	60
Justice Department Authorization	July 10, 1981	38-48	60
Justice Department Authorization	July 13, 1981	54-32	60
Justice Department Authorization	July 29, 1981	59-37	60
Justice Department Authorization	Sept. 10, 1981	57-33	60
Justice Department Authorization	Sept. 16, 1981	61-36	60
Justice Department Authorization	Dec. 10, 1981	64-35	60
State, Justice, Commerce, Judiciary Appropriations	Dec. 11, 1981	59-35	60

to air their grievances. On the 180-220 vote, only one Democrat, Rep. Larry P. McDonald, Ga., voted along with the Republicans. *(Vote 3, p. 2-H)*

That was not the end of the matter, however. On Jan. 22, Republicans caught the Democratic leadership off guard with their proposal to amend the usually routine resolution approving committee assignments by adding three more Republicans to Ways and Means and one more member to the Rules Committee. When a quorum call showed only 10 more Democrats on the floor than Republicans, Speaker O'Neill delayed a vote on the resolution and quickly adjourned the chamber.

A week later, Democrats Jan. 28 voted as a bloc to defeat a Republican proposal to add two GOP members to the Ways and Means Committee. The Republican plan was rejected 172-221. The House by voice vote then formally re-established its committees and approved committee assignments for the new Congress. *(Vote 4, p. 2-H)*

Still piqued, 14 House Republicans in July filed a suit in District of Columbia federal court challenging the constitutionality of the Democrats' decision to stack the Appropriations, Budget, Rules and Ways and Means committees. It asked the court to order that committee ratios reflect the ratio of Democrats to Republicans in the House as a whole. The U.S. District Court for the District of Columbia dismissed the suit Oct. 8.

Committee Rules Changes. The House Democratic Caucus approved several changes in the rules governing committee membership. On Jan. 21 it voted to limit the number of subcommittees and similar committee sub-units that could be established by the House's standing committees in the 97th Congress. Under the new rule, Rules and Ways and Means could have up to six subcommittees and Appropriations could retain all 13 of its subcommittees. All other standing committees would be limited to no more than eight subcommittees or the number of subcommittees they had as of Jan. 1, whichever was fewer. A committee with more than 35 members and fewer than six subcommittees could increase to six if it so desired.

The rule affected the Education and Labor, Agriculture, Budget and Banking committees, all of which had more than eight subcommittees in the 96th Congress.

On Jan. 28, the caucus waived a party rule limiting members of the Judiciary and District of Columbia committees to only one other legislative committee assignment.

PARTY DISCIPLINE

House Democratic leaders, promising "amnesty" for party members who defected to President Reagan earlier in 1981 on tax and budget votes, threatened to withhold prestigious committee assignments from those who strayed from the fold in the future.

The leadership position was proclaimed Sept. 16 by Majority Leader Wright at a special meeting of the party caucus. Speaker O'Neill did not publicly endorse the plan, but an O'Neill aide said the Speaker had no serious objection to it.

Wright said there would be "amnesty for what's happened in the past," but that the Democratic Steering and Policy Committee would take members' future behavior into account in awarding committee assignments.

The idea in dealing with an errant Democrat, Wright said, was "not to punish that person, but just to refrain from rewarding them. Nobody is going to be asked to leave the party."

The caucus did not vote on his plan, Wright said after the meeting, but "I think it's a position that most members of the caucus embrace."

The closed-door meeting, billed as a "harmony session," was convened by caucus Chairman Gillis W. Long of Louisiana in response to calls from some Democrats for disciplinary action against party colleagues who had voted to support Reagan's economic program. But sentiment for punishment dissipated over the August recess.

No disciplinary resolution was put before the caucus, participants said, and the only specific measure discussed to foster party loyalty was the position set forth by Wright.

Party Switches. A month later House Democrats deferred altogether a decision over the committee assignments of two-term Pennsylvania Rep. Eugene V. Atkinson. Atkinson stunned Democrats with his Oct. 14 announcement that he was switching to the Republican side of the aisle.

Party leaders promptly threatened to seek House approval to oust Atkinson from his committee seats and to nominate Democratic replacements at the party's Oct. 21 caucus meeting. But when the time came, the caucus instead referred the matter to its Steering and Policy Committee for further consideration. Atkinson was on the Public Works, Government Operations and Select Aging committees.

The controversy centered on who in the House controlled committee assignments after they were made. Democratic leaders maintained Atkinson was obliged to give his seats back to the Democratic Caucus and to seek new assignments from the Republicans. But GOP leaders said he was entitled to keep the seats he had.

Recent House tradition supported the Democrats' position. But to win on the House floor, the Democratic leadership needed the support of Southern conservatives, who had abandoned their party in droves on other important issues in 1981.

One other Democrat — Bob Stump of Arizona — announced Sept. 24 that he would become a Republican but not until the 98th Congress. Thus his committee assignments were not an issue. ∎

Members of the 97th Congress, First Session . . .

As of Dec. 31, 1981
Representatives

D 242; R 192
1 Vacancy [1]

A

Addabbo, Joseph P., D-N.Y. (7)
Akaka, Daniel K., D-Hawaii (2)
Albosta, Don, D-Mich. (10)
Alexander, Bill, D-Ark. (1)
Anderson, Glenn M., D-Calif. (32)
Andrews, Ike, D-N.C. (4)
Annunzio, Frank, D-Ill. (11)
Anthony, Beryl Jr., D-Ark. (4)
Applegate, Douglas, D-Ohio (18)
Archer, Bill, R-Texas (7)
Ashbrook, John M., R-Ohio (17)
Aspin, Les, D-Wis. (1)
Atkinson, Eugene V., R-Pa. (25)
AuCoin, Les, D-Ore. (1)

B

Badham, Robert E., R-Calif. (40)
Bafalis, L. A. "Skip", R-Fla. (10)
Bailey, Don, D-Pa. (21)
Bailey, Wendell, R-Mo. (8)
Barnard, Doug Jr., D-Ga. (10)
Barnes, Michael D., D-Md. (8)
Beard, Robin L., R-Tenn. (6)
Bedell, Berkley, D-Iowa (6)
Beilenson, Anthony C., D-Calif. (23)
Benedict, Cleve, R-W. Va. (2)
Benjamin, Adam Jr., D-Ind. (1)
Bennett, Charles E., D-Fla. (3)
Bereuter, Douglas K., R-Neb. (1)
Bethune, Ed, R-Ark. (2)
Bevill, Tom, D-Ala. (4)
Biaggi, Mario, D-N.Y. (10)
Bingham, Jonathan B., D-N.Y. (22)
Blanchard, James J., D-Mich. (18)
Bliley, Thomas J. Jr., R-Va. (3)
Boggs, Lindy (Mrs. Hale), D-La. (2)
Boland, Edward P., D-Mass. (2)
Bolling, Richard, D-Mo. (5)
Boner, Bill, D-Tenn. (5)
Bonior, David E., D-Mich. (12)
Bonker, Don, D-Wash. (3)
Bouquard, Marilyn Lloyd, D-Tenn. (3)
Bowen, David R., D-Miss. (2)
Breaux, John B., D-La. (7)
Brinkley, Jack, D-Ga. (3)
Brodhead, William M., D-Mich. (17)
Brooks, Jack, D-Texas (9)
Broomfield, William S., R-Mich. (19)
Brown, Clarence J., R-Ohio (7)
Brown, George E. Jr., D-Calif. (36)
Brown, Hank, R-Colo. (4)
Broyhill, James T., R-N.C. (10)
Burgener, Clair W., R-Calif. (43)
Burton, John L., D-Calif. (5)
Burton, Phillip, D-Calif. (6)
Butler, M. Caldwell, R-Va. (6)
Byron, Beverly B., D-Md. (6)

C

Campbell, Carroll A. Jr., R-S.C. (4)
Carman, Gregory W., R-N.Y. (3)
Carney, William, R-N.Y. (1)
Chappell, Bill Jr., D-Fla. (4)
Chappie, Gene, R-Calif. (1)
Cheney, Dick, R-Wyo. (AL)
Chisholm, Shirley, D-N.Y. (12)
Clausen, Don H., R-Calif. (2)
Clay, William, D-Mo. (1)
Clinger, William F. Jr., R-Pa. (23)
Coats, Dan, R-Ind. (4)
Coelho, Tony, D-Calif. (15)
Coleman, E. Thomas, R-Mo. (6)
Collins, Cardiss, D-Ill. (7)
Collins, James M., R-Texas (3)
Conable, Barber B. Jr., R-N.Y. (35)
Conte, Silvio O., R-Mass. (1)
Conyers, John Jr., D-Mich. (1)

D

Corcoran, Tom, R-Ill. (15)
Coughlin, Lawrence, R-Pa. (13)
Courter, Jim, R-N.J. (13)
Coyne, Jim, R-Pa. (8)
Coyne, William J., D-Pa. (14)
Craig, Larry E., R-Idaho (1)
Crane, Daniel B., R-Ill. (22)
Crane, Philip M., R-Ill. (12)
Crockett, George W. Jr., D-Mich. (13)

D'Amours, Norman E., D-N.H. (1)
Daniel, Dan, D-Va. (5)
Daniel, Robert W. Jr., R-Va. (4)
Danielson, George E., D-Calif. (30)
Dannemeyer, William E., R-Calif. (39)
Daschle, Thomas A., D-S.D. (1)
Daub, Hal, R-Neb. -2)
Davis, Robert W., R-Mich. (11)
Deckard, Joel, R-Ind. (8)
de la Garza, E. "Kika", D-Texas (15)
Dellums, Ronald V., D-Calif. (8)
DeNardis, Lawrence J., R-Conn. (3)
Derrick, Butler, D-S.C. (3)
Derwinski, Edward J., R-Ill. (4)
Dickinson, William L., R-Ala. (2)
Dicks, Norman D., D-Wash. (6)
Dingell, John D., D-Mich. (16)
Dixon, Julian C., D-Calif. (28)
Donnelly, Brian J., D-Mass. (11)
Dorgan, Byron L., D-N.D. (AL)
Dornan, Robert K., R-Calif. (27)
Dougherty, Charles F., R-Pa. (4)
Dowdy, Wayne, D-Miss. (4)
Downey, Thomas J., D-N.Y. (2)
Dreier, David, R-Calif. (35)
Duncan, John J., R-Tenn. (2)
Dunn, Jim, R-Mich. (6)
Dwyer, Bernard J., D-N.J. (15)
Dymally, Mervyn M., D-Calif. (31)
Dyson, Roy, D-Md. (1)

E

Early, Joseph D., D-Mass. (3)
Eckart, Dennis E., D-Ohio (22)
Edgar, Robert W., D-Pa. (7)
Edwards, Don, D-Calif. (10)
Edwards, Jack, R-Ala. (1)
Edwards, Mickey, R-Okla. (5)
Emerson, Bill, R-Mo. (10)
Emery, David F., R-Maine (1)
English, Glenn, D-Okla. (6)
Erdahl, Arlen, R-Minn. (1)
Erlenborn, John N., R-Ill. (14)
Ertel, Allen E., D-Pa. (17)
Evans, Billy Lee, D-Ga. (8)
Evans, Cooper, R-Iowa (3)
Evans, David W., D-Ind. (6)
Evans, Thomas B. Jr., R-Del. (AL)

F

Fary, John G., D-Ill. (5)
Fascell, Dante B., D-Fla. (15)
Fazio, Vic, D-Calif. (4)
Fenwick, Millicent, R-N.J. (5)
Ferraro, Geraldine A., D-N.Y. (9)
Fiedler, Bobbi, R-Calif. (21)
Fields, Jack, R-Texas (8)
Findley, Paul, R-Ill. (20)
Fish, Hamilton Jr., R-N.Y. (25)
Fithian, Floyd, D-Ind. (2)
Flippo, Ronnie G., D-Ala. (5)
Florio, James J., D-N.J. (1)
Foglietta, Thomas M., D-Pa. (1)
Foley, Thomas S., D-Wash. (5)
Ford, Harold E., D-Tenn. (8)
Ford, William D., D-Mich. (15)
Forsythe, Edwin B., R-N.J. (6)
Fountain, L. H., D-N.C. (2)
Fowler, Wyche Jr., D-Ga. (5)
Frank, Barney, D-Mass. (4)
Frenzel, Bill, R-Minn. (3)
Frost, Martin, D-Texas (24)
Fuqua, Don, D-Fla. (2)

G

Garcia, Robert, D-N.Y. (21)

Gaydos, Joseph M., D-Pa. (20)
Gejdenson, Sam, D-Conn. (2)
Gephardt, Richard A., D-Mo. (3)
Gibbons, Sam, D-Fla. (7)
Gilman, Benjamin A., R-N.Y. (26)
Gingrich, Newt, R-Ga. (6)
Ginn, Bo, D-Ga. (1)
Glickman, Dan, D-Kan. (4)
Goldwater, Barry M. Jr., R-Calif. (20)
Gonzalez, Henry B., D-Texas (20)
Goodling, Bill, R-Pa. (19)
Gore, Albert Jr., D-Tenn. (4)
Gradison, Bill, R-Ohio (1)
Gramm, Phil, D-Texas (6)
Gray, William H. III, D-Pa. (2)
Green, Bill, R-N.Y. (18)
Gregg, Judd, R-N.H. (2)
Grisham, Wayne, R-Calif. (33)
Guarini, Frank J., D-N.J. (14)
Gunderson, Steve, R-Wis. (3)

H

Hagedorn, Tom, R-Minn. (2)
Hall, Ralph M., D-Texas (4)
Hall, Sam B. Jr., D-Texas (1)
Hall, Tony P., D-Ohio (3)
Hamilton, Lee H., D-Ind. (9)
Hammerschmidt, John Paul, R-Ark. (3)
Hance, Kent, D-Texas (19)
Hansen, George, R-Idaho (2)
Hansen, James V., R-Utah (1)
Harkin, Tom, D-Iowa (5)
Hartnett, Thomas F., R-S.C. (1)
Hatcher, Charles, D-Ga. (2)
Hawkins, Augustus F., D-Calif. (29)
Heckler, Margaret M., R-Mass. (10)
Hefner, W. G. "Bill", D-N.C. (8)
Heftel, Cecil, D-Hawaii (1)
Hendon, Bill, R-N.C. (11)
Hertel, Dennis M., D-Mich. (14)
Hightower, Jack, D-Texas (13)
Hiler, John, R-Ind. (3)
Hillis, Elwood, R-Ind. (5)
Holland, Ken, D-S.C. (5)
Hollenbeck, Harold C., R-N.J. (9)
Holt, Marjorie S., R-Md. (4)
Hopkins, Larry J., R-Ky. (6)
Horton, Frank, R-N.Y. (34)
Howard, James J., D-N.J. (3)
Hoyer, Steny, D-Md. (5)
Hubbard, Carroll Jr., D-Ky. (1)
Huckaby, Jerry, D-La. (5)
Hughes, William J., D-N.J. (2)
Hunter, Duncan L., R-Calif. (42)
Hutto, Earl, D-Fla. (1)
Hyde, Henry J., R-Ill. (6)

I, J

Ireland, Andy, D-Fla. (8)
Jacobs, Andrew Jr., D-Ind. (11)
Jeffords, James M., R-Vt. (AL)
Jeffries, Jim, R-Kan. (2)
Jenkins, Ed, D-Ga. (9)
Johnston, Eugene, R-N.C. (6)
Jones, Ed, D-Tenn. (7)
Jones, James R., D-Okla. (1)
Jones, Walter B., D-N.C. (1)

K

Kastenmeier, Robert W., D-Wis. (2)
Kazen, Abraham Jr., D-Texas (23)
Kemp, Jack F., R-N.Y. (38)
Kildee, Dale E., D-Mich. (7)
Kindness, Thomas N., R-Ohio (8)
Kogovsek, Ray, D-Colo. (3)
Kramer, Ken, R-Colo. (5)

L

LaFalce, John J., D-N.Y. (36)
Lagomarsino, Robert J., R-Calif. (19)
Lantos, Tom, D-Calif. (11)
Latta, Delbert L., R-Ohio (5)
Leach, Jim, R-Iowa (1)
Leath, Marvin, D-Texas (11)
LeBoutillier, John, R-N.Y. (6)
Lee, Gary A., R-N.Y. (33)
Lehman, William, D-Fla. (13)

Leland, Mickey, D-Texas (18)
Lent, Norman F., R-N.Y. (4)
Levitas, Elliott H., D-Ga. (4)
Lewis, Jerry, R-Calif. (37)
Livingston, Bob, R-La. (1)
Loeffler, Tom, R-Texas (21)
Long, Clarence D., D-Md. (2)
Long, Gillis W., D-La. (8)
Lott, Trent, R-Miss. (5)
Lowery, Bill, R-Calif. (41)
Lowry, Mike, D-Wash. (7)
Lujan, Manuel Jr., R-N.M. (1)
Luken, Thomas A., D-Ohio (2)
Lundine, Stanley N., D-N.Y. (39)
Lungren, Dan, R-Calif. (34)

M

Madigan, Edward R., R-Ill. (21)
Markey, Edward J., D-Mass. (7)
Marks, Marc L., R-Pa. (24)
Marlenee, Ron, R-Mont. (2)
Marriott, Dan, R-Utah (2)
Martin, David O'B., R-N.Y. (30)
Martin, James G., R-N.C. (9)
Martin, Lynn, R-Ill. (16)
Matsui, Robert T., D-Calif. (3)
Mattox, Jim, D-Texas (5)
Mavroules, Nicholas, D-Mass. (6)
Mazzoli, Romano L., D-Ky. (3)
McClory, Robert, R-Ill. (13)
McCloskey, Paul N. Jr., R-Calif. (12)
McCollum, Bill, R-Fla. (5)
McCurdy, Dave, D-Okla. (4)
McDade, Joseph M., R-Pa. (10)
McDonald, Larry P., D-Ga. (7)
McEwen, Bob, R-Ohio (6)
McGrath, Raymond J., R-N.Y. (5)
McHugh, Matthew F., D-N.Y. (27)
McKinney, Stewart B., R-Conn. (4)
Mica, Daniel A., D-Fla. (11)
Michel, Robert H., R-Ill. (18)
Mikulski, Barbara A., D-Md. (3)
Miller, Clarence E., R-Ohio (10)
Miller, George, D-Calif. (7)
Mineta, Norman Y., D-Calif. (13)
Minish, Joseph G., D-N.J. (11)
Mitchell, Donald J., R-N.Y. (31)
Mitchell, Parren J., D-Md. (7)
Moakley, Joe, D-Mass. (9)
Moffett, Toby, D-Conn. (6)
Molinari, Guy V., R-N.Y. (17)
Mollohan, Robert H., D-W. Va. (1)
Montgomery, G. V. "Sonny", D-Miss. (3)
Moore, Henson, R-La. (6)
Moorhead, Carlos J., R-Calif. (22)
Morrison, Sid, R-Wash. (4)
Mottl, Ronald M., D-Ohio (23)
Murphy, Austin J., D-Pa. (22)
Murtha, John P., D-Pa. (12)
Myers, John T., R-Ind. (7)

N

Napier, John L., R-S.C. (6)
Natcher, William H., D-Ky. (2)
Neal, Stephen L., D-N.C. (5)
Nelligan, James L., R-Pa. (11)
Nelson, Bill, D-Fla. (9)
Nichols, Bill, D-Ala. (3)
Nowak, Henry J., D-N.Y. (37)

O

Oakar, Mary Rose, D-Ohio (20)
Oberstar, James L., D-Minn. (8)
Obey, David R., D-Wis. (7)
O'Brien, George M., R-Ill. (17)
O'Neill, Thomas P. Jr., D-Mass. (8)
Ottinger, Richard L., D-N.Y. (24)
Oxley, Michael G., R-Ohio (4)

P

Panetta, Leon E., D-Calif. (16)
Parris, Stan, R-Va. (8)
Pashayan, Charles Jr., R-Calif. (17)
Patman, Bill, D-Texas (14)
Patterson, Jerry M., D-Calif. (38)
Paul, Ron, R-Texas (22)
Pease, Don J., D-Ohio (13)

...Governors, Supreme Court, Cabinet Rank Officers

Pepper, Claude, D-Fla. (14)
Perkins, Carl D., D-Ky. (7)
Petri, Thomas E., R-Wis. (6)
Peyser, Peter A., D-N.Y. (23)
Pickle, J. J., D-Texas (10)
Porter, John Edward, R-Ill. (10)
Price, Melvin, D-Ill. (23)
Pritchard, Joel, R-Wash. (1)
Pursell, Carl D., R-Mich. (2)

Q

Quillen, James H., R-Tenn. (1)

R

Rahall, Nick J. II, D-W. Va. (4)
Railsback, Tom, R-Ill. (19)
Rangel, Charles B., D-N.Y. (19)
Ratchford, William R., D-Conn. (5)
Regula, Ralph, R-Ohio (16)
Reuss, Henry S., D-Wis. (5)
Rhodes, John J., R-Ariz. (1)
Richmond, Fred, D-N.Y. (14)
Rinaldo, Matthew J., R-N.J. (12)
Ritter, Don, R-Pa. (15)
Roberts, Clint, R-S.D. (2)
Roberts, Pat, R-Kan. (1)
Robinson, J. Kenneth, R-Va. (7)
Rodino, Peter W. Jr., D-N.J. (10)
Roe, Robert A., D-N.J. (8)
Roemer, Buddy, D-La. (4)
Rogers, Harold, R-Ky. (5)
Rose, Charlie, D-N.C. (7)
Rosenthal, Benjamin S., D-N.Y. (8)
Rostenkowski, Dan, D-Ill. (8)
Roth, Toby, R-Wis. (8)
Roukema, Marge, R-N.J. (7)
Rousselot, John H., R-Calif. (26)
Roybal, Edward R., D-Calif. (25)
Rudd, Eldon, R-Ariz. (4)
Russo, Marty, D-Ill. (3)

S

Sabo, Martin Olav, D-Minn. (5)
St Germain, Fernand J., D-R.I. (1)
Santini, James D., D-Nev. (AL)
Savage, Gus, D-Ill. (2)
Sawyer, Harold S., R-Mich. (5)
Scheuer, James H., D-N.Y. (11)
Schneider, Claudine, R-R.I. (2)
Schroeder, Patricia, D-Colo. (1)
Schulze, Richard T., R-Pa. (5)
Schumer, Charles E., D-N.Y. (16)
Seiberling, John F., D-Ohio (14)
Sensenbrenner, F. James Jr., R-Wis. (9)
Shamansky, Bob, D-Ohio (12)
Shannon, James M., D-Mass. (5)
Sharp, Philip R., D-Ind. (10)
Shaw, E. Clay Jr., R-Fla. (12)
Shelby, Richard C., D-Ala. (7)
Shumway, Norman D., R-Calif. (14)
Shuster, Bud, R-Pa. (9)
Siljander, Mark, R-Mich. (4)
Simon, Paul, D-Ill. (24)
Skeen, Joe, R-N.M. (2)
Skelton, Ike, D-Mo. (4)
Smith, Albert Lee Jr., R-Ala. (6)
Smith, Christopher H., R-N.J. (4)
Smith, Denny, R-Ore. (2)
Smith, Joseph F., D-Pa. (3)
Smith, Neal, D-Iowa (4)
Smith, Virginia, R-Neb. (3)
Snowe, Olympia J., R-Maine (2)
Snyder, Gene, R-Ky. (4)
Solarz, Stephen J., D-N.Y. (13)
Solomon, Gerald B. H., R-N.Y. (29)
Spence, Floyd, R-S.C. (2)
Stangeland, Arlan, R-Minn. (7)
Stanton, J. William, R-Ohio (11)
Stark, Fortney H. "Pete", D-Calif. (9)
Staton, David Michael, R-W.Va. (3)
Stenholm, Charles W., D-Texas (17)
Stokes, Louis, D-Ohio (21)
Stratton, Samuel S., D-N.Y. (28)
Studds, Gerry E., D-Mass. (12)
Stump, Bob, D-Ariz. (3)
Swift, Al, D-Wash. (2)
Synar, Mike, D-Okla. (2)

T

Tauke, Tom, R-Iowa (2)
Tauzin, W. J. "Billy", D-La. (3)
Taylor, Gene, R-Mo. (7)
Thomas, William M., R-Calif. (18)
Traxler, Bob, D-Mich. (8)
Trible, Paul S. Jr., R-Va. (1)

U, V

Udall, Morris K., D-Ariz. (2)
Vander Jagt, Guy, R-Mich. (9)
Vento, Bruce F., D-Minn. (4)
Volkmer, Harold L., D-Mo. (9)

W

Walgren, Doug, D-Pa. (18)
Walker, Robert S., R-Pa. (16)
Wampler, William C., R-Va. (9)
Washington, Harold, D-Ill. (1)
Watkins, Wes, D-Okla. (3)
Waxman, Henry A., D-Calif. (24)
Weaver, James, D-Ore. (4)
Weber, Ed, R-Ohio (9)
Weber, Vin, R-Minn. (6)
Weiss, Ted, D-N.Y. (20)
White, Richard C., D-Texas (16)
Whitehurst, G. William, R-Va. (2)
Whitley, Charles, D-N.C. (3)
Whittaker, Bob, R-Kan. (5)
Whitten, Jamie L., D-Miss. (1)
Williams, Lyle, R-Ohio (19)
Williams, Pat, D-Mont. (1)
Wilson, Charles, D-Texas (2)
Winn, Larry Jr., R-Kan. (3)
Wirth, Timothy E., D-Colo. (2)
Wolf, Frank R., R-Va. (10)
Wolpe, Howard, D-Mich. (3)
Wortley, George C., R-N.Y. (32)
Wright, Jim, D-Texas (12)
Wyden, Ron, D-Ore. (3)
Wylie, Chalmers P., R-Ohio (15)

X, Y, Z

Yates, Sidney R., D-Ill. (9)
Yatron, Gus, D-Pa. (6)
Young, C. W. Bill, R-Fla. (6)
Young, Don, R-Alaska (AL)
Young, Robert A., D-Mo. (2)
Zablocki, Clement J., D-Wis. (4)
Zeferetti, Leo C., D-N.Y. (15)

Delegates

de Lugo, Ron, R-V.I.
Fauntroy, Walter E., D-D.C.
Sunia, Fofo I. F., D-American Samoa
Won Pat, Antonio Borja, D-Guam

Resident Commissioner

Corrada, Baltasar, New Prog.-Puerto Rico

Senators

R 53; D 47 [2]

Abdnor, James, R-S.D.
Andrews, Mark, R-N.D.
Armstrong, William L., R-Colo.
Baker, Howard H. Jr., R-Tenn.
Baucus, Max, D-Mont.
Bentsen, Lloyd, D-Texas
Biden, Joseph R. Jr., D-Del.
Boren, David L., D-Okla.
Boschwitz, Rudy, R-Minn.
Bradley, Bill, D-N.J.
Bumpers, Dale, D-Ark.
Burdick, Quentin N., D-N.D.
Byrd, Harry F. Jr., Ind.-Va.
Byrd, Robert C., D-W. Va.
Cannon, Howard W., D. Nev.
Chafee, John H., R-R.I.
Chiles, Lawton, D-Fla.
Cochran, Thad, R-Miss.
Cohen, William S., R-Maine
Cranston, Alan, D-Calif.
D'Amato, Alfonse, R-N.Y.

Danforth, John C., R-Mo.
DeConcini, Dennis, D-Ariz.
Denton, Jeremiah, R-Ala.
Dixon, Alan J., D-Ill.
Dodd, Christopher J., D-Conn.
Dole, Robert, R-Kan.
Domenici, Pete V., R-N.M.
Durenberger, David, R-Minn.
Eagleton, Thomas F., D-Mo
East, John P., R-N.C.
Exon, J. James, D-Neb.
Ford, Wendell H., D-Ky.
Garn, Jake, R-Utah
Glenn, John, D-Ohio
Goldwater, Barry, R-Ariz.
Gorton, Slade, R-Wash.
Grassley, Charles E., R-Iowa
Hart, Gary, D-Colo.
Hatch, Orrin G., R-Utah
Hatfield, Mark O., R-Ore.
Hawkins, Paula, R-Fla.
Hayakawa, S. I. "Sam", R-Calif.
Heflin, Howell, D-Ala.
Heinz, John, R-Pa.
Helms, Jesse, R-N.C.
Hollings, Ernest F., D-S.C.
Huddleston, Walter D., D-Ky.
Humphrey, Gordon J., R-N.H.
Inouye, Daniel K., D-Hawaii
Jackson, Henry M., D-Wash.
Jepsen, Roger W., R-Iowa
Johnston, J. Bennett, D-La.
Kassebaum, Nancy Landon, R-Kan.
Kasten, Robert W. Jr., R-Wis.
Kennedy, Edward M., D-Mass.
Laxalt, Paul, R-Nev.
Leahy, Patrick J., D-Vt.
Levin, Carl, D-Mich.
Long, Russell B., D-La.
Lugar, Richard G., R-Ind.
Mathias, Charles McC. Jr., R-Md.
Matsunaga, Spark M., D-Hawaii
Mattingly, Mack, R-Ga.
McClure, James A., R-Idaho
Melcher, John, D-Mont.
Metzenbaum, Howard M., D-Ohio
Mitchell, George J., D-Maine
Moynihan, Daniel Patrick, D-N.Y.
Murkowski, Frank H., R-Alaska
Nickles, Don, R-Okla.
Nunn, Sam, D-Ga.
Packwood, Bob, R-Ore.
Pell, Claiborne, D-R.I.
Percy, Charles H., R-Ill.
Pressler, Larry, R-S.D.
Proxmire, William, D-Wis.
Pryor, David, D-Ark.
Quayle, Dan, R-Ind.
Randolph, Jennings, D-W. Va.
Riegle, Donald W. Jr., D-Mich.
Roth, William V. Jr., R-Del.
Rudman, Warren B., R-N.H.
Sarbanes, Paul S., D-Md.
Sasser, Jim, D-Tenn.
Schmitt, Harrison "Jack", R-N.M.
Simpson, Alan K., R-Wyo.
Specter, Arlen, R-Pa.
Stafford, Robert T., R-Vt.
Stennis, John C., D-Miss.
Stevens, Ted, R-Alaska
Symms, Steven D., R-Idaho
Thurmond, Strom, R-S.C.
Tower, John, R-Texas
Tsongas, Paul E., D-Mass.
Wallop, Malcolm, R-Wyo.
Warner, John W., R-Va.
Weicker, Lowell P. Jr., R-Conn.
Williams, Harrison A. Jr., D-N.J.
Zorinsky, Edward, D-Neb.

Governors

D 27; R 23

Ala.—Fob James, D
Alaska—Jay S. Hammond, R
Ariz.—Bruce Babbitt, D
Ark.—Frank D. White, R
Calif.—Edmund G. Brown Jr., D
Colo.—Richard D. Lamm, D
Conn.—William A. O'Neill, D
Del.—Pierre S. "Pete" du Pont IV, R
Fla.—Robert Graham, D
Ga.—George Busbee, D
Hawaii—George Ariyoshi, D
Idaho—John V. Evans, D
Ill.—James R. Thompson, R
Ind.—Robert D. Orr, R
Iowa—Robert Ray, R
Kan.—John Carlin, D
Ky.—John Y. Brown, D
La.—David C. Treen, R
Maine—Joseph E. Brennan, D
Md.—Harry R. Hughes, D
Mass.—Edward J. King, D
Mich.—William G. Milliken, R
Minn.—Albert H. Quie, R
Miss.—William Winter, D
Mo.—Christopher S. "Kit" Bond, R
Mont.—Ted Schwinden, D
Neb.—Charles Thone, R
Nev.—Robert F. List, R
N.H.—Hugh Gallen, D
N.J.—Thomas Kean, R
N.M.—Bruce King, D
N.Y.—Hugh L. Carey, D
N.C.—James B. Hunt Jr., D
N.D.—Allen I. Olsen, R
Ohio—James A. Rhodes, R
Okla.—George Nigh, D
Ore.—Victor L. Atiyeh, R
Pa.—Richard L. Thornburgh, R
R.I.—J. Joseph Garrahy, D
S.C.—Richard Riley, D
S.D.—William J. Janklow, R
Tenn.—Lamar Alexander, R
Texas—William Clements, R
Utah—Scott M. Matheson, D
Vt.—Richard A. Snelling, R
Va.—Charles Robb, D
Wash.—John Spellman, R
W. Va.—John D. "Jay" Rockefeller IV, D
Wis.—Lee Sherman Dreyfus, R
Wyo.—Ed Herschler, D

Supreme Court

Burger, Warren E.—Minn., Chief Justice
Blackmun, Harry A.—Minn.
Brennan, William J. Jr.—N.J.
Marshall, Thurgood—N.Y.
O'Connor, Sandra Day—Ariz.
Powell, Lewis F. Jr.—Va.
Rehnquist, William H.—Ariz.
Stevens, John Paul—Ill.
White, Byron R.—Colo.

Cabinet

Baldrige, Malcolm—Commerce
Bell, T. H.—Education
Block, John R.—Agriculture
Donovan, Raymond J.—Labor
Edwards, James B.—Energy
Haig, Alexander M. Jr.—State
Lewis, Drew—Transportation
Pierce, Samuel R. Jr.—HUD
Regan, Donald T.—Treasury
Schweiker, Richard S.—HHS
Smith, William French—Attorney General
Watt, James G.—Interior
Weinberger, Caspar W.—Defense

Other Officers with Cabinet Rank

Brock, William E. III—U.S. Trade Representative
Bush, George—Vice President
Casey, William J.—CIA Director
Kirkpatrick, Jeane J.—U.N. Representative
Meese, Edwin III—Counselor to the President
Stockman, David A.—OMB Director

[1] Conn. 1st Dist.
[2] Includes Harry F. Byrd Jr. (Va.) elected as an independent.

97th Took Bold Steps to Reduce Federal Role

Dominated by Republicans for the first time in 2½ decades and guided by a forceful and popular president, Congress took bold steps in 1981 toward reducing the federal government's scope.

Following the wishes of President Reagan, the 97th Congress slashed government spending, cut taxes for individuals and businesses, slimmed down federal regulatory activities and generally sought to dispel the notion that people and institutions should look to Washington to solve their problems.

In giving Reagan most of what he asked for, Congress was acting under the belief that it was responding to the mandate of the 1980 elections. That political tide not only swept a conservative Republican into the White House, but also floated the GOP into its first Senate majority since January 1955 and eroded Democratic control of the House.

But by agreeing so wholeheartedly to the president's program, legislators risked laying a trap for themselves in 1982.

If the president's program was clearly succeeding by the fall, their gamble would have paid off and they could claim their winnings at the polls.

But if the economy remained in disarray, then the result could be a massive rejection of the president's supporters in the 1982 election.

Reagan's Personal Triumph

In all, the first session of the 97th Congress was a great personal triumph for Reagan. Congressional approval of his plan was due largely to his own efforts and strength. But if the president's program were to founder, he would have only himself to blame.

When Reagan entered office in January, he laid out what appeared to some to be contradictory goals for his presidency. In order to revitalize the economy and strengthen the nation, he said, he would cut federal spending yet increase spending for defense, reduce taxes yet balance the budget.

Many traditional Republicans in Congress were uneasy with this "supply-side" economic approach. But the GOP leaders in both houses proved to be effective and loyal lieutenants for their president.

Reagan himself was the administration's best lobbyist. He promised that his plan, if approved, would have immediate results. The mere expectation of the changes to be wrought by his recovery program would spur the economy upward, he said.

As the first session drew to a close in December, the returns on the Reagan program were not all in, but the results were at best mixed.

Congress had enacted $35.2 billion in fiscal 1982 program cuts and cut nearly $4 billion more from appropriations, had approved a cut in individual and business taxes totaling $749 billion over a five-year period, and had added about $18 billion to the fiscal 1982 defense budget drafted by President Carter the year before.

But the federal deficit for the year appeared to be

First Session Summary

Working late into the night on several major pieces of legislation, the first session of the 97th Congress completed its legislative business on Dec. 16, 1981. The Senate adjourned *sine die* at 10:28 p.m. and the House, after rejecting an earlier motion to adjourn, followed suit at 11:22 p.m.

The session, which convened at noon on Jan. 5, 1981, lasted 346 days and tied with the first session of the 95th Congress and the second session of the 76th Congress as the 14th longest in history. The third session of the 76th Congress, from Jan. 3, 1940 to Jan. 3, 1941, is the longest on record. *(CQ Guide to Congress 2nd Edition, p. 339)*

The Senate met for 165 days during the year, the House for 163 days. There were 8,719 bills and resolution (2,478 Senate and 6,241 House) introduced during the session, an increase of 4,296 from 1980 but fewer than the 10,171 bills and resolutions introduced during the first session of the 96th Congress.

President Reagan signed into law 145 public bills that were cleared during the session. In 1980, President Carter signed 426 public bills into law. Reagan vetoed two bills. Neither veto was overridden. *(Vetoes, p. 9)*

During 1981, the House took 353 recorded votes, substantially below the record-setting 834 votes taken in 1978, and the fewest since 1972. The Senate's 483 recorded votes fell 205 below the record 688 taken in 1976 and were the fewest since 1971.

Following are the recorded congressional vote totals between 1971 and 1981:

Year	House	Senate	Total
1981	353	483	836
1980	604	531	1,135
1979	672	497	1,169
1978	834	516	1,350
1977	706	635	1,341
1976	661	688	1,349
1975	612	602	1,214
1974	537	544	1,081
1973	541	594	1,135
1972	329	532	861
1971	320	423	743

heading over the $100 billion mark, and the economy was in a period not of unprecedented growth but of decline.

And in the process of getting his program enacted, Reagan exhausted his winning coalition, stretched congressional procedures out of shape and bruised sensitive legislators' egos.

Almost all the sweeping budget cuts Congress approved were made in one package, the budget "reconciliation" bill. The use of the reconciliation method in such a massive way — more ambitious than Congress had contemplated in 1974 when it invented the legislative device — was criticized by some members as an abuse of the budget process.

The one budget bill touched on virtually every federal activity except defense. Included in it were a multitude of changes in existing law, including provisions to tighten eligibility for food stamps and public assistance, to cut funds for subsidized housing programs, to reduce school lunch subsidies, to impose a needs test for guaranteed student loans and to cut Medicaid payments to the states.

Party Loyalties Distorted

In a sense, Congress did work its will on Reagan's economic proposals — by passing even more generous tax cuts for business and high-income investors than he initially had asked for. Ironically, Democrats abetted this turn of events by engaging in a fruitless bidding war for interest groups' support.

Traditional party interests and loyalties were distorted in other ways as well. Republicans were able to win their twin economic victories only with the help of Democratic defectors in the House, mostly a group of Southern conservatives calling themselves "Boll Weevils." Such defections led House Democratic leaders to threaten discipline of such errant colleagues in the future.

In September, when Reagan proposed a second package of $13 billion in further spending cuts and $3 billion in unspecified revenue increases for 1982, the president's coalition began to crumble.

Even members who had worked hard for Reagan's first round of cuts had no stomach for a second in a single year.

Moderate House Republicans threatened to desert him unless he shielded their pet programs. Conservative Democrats threatened to bail out over the growing deficit, and the Reagan team was split over tax increases.

The president maintained symbolic pressure on Congress to make additional spending cuts — even bringing the government to a halt for a day in late November by vetoing a temporary funding resolution.

But Congress was unwilling to make the cuts he demanded. The appropriations process ground to a halt, and the government limped through the end of the year on a series of temporary resolutions.

The appropriations logjam ended just five days before the session's end, when the president announced he would sign any individual appropriations bills that came in under the ceilings set in the stopgap funding measure that cleared Congress on Dec. 11.

Defense, Foreign Affairs

On defense, Congress granted Reagan's request for significant spending increases and approved his call for an interim MX missile basing plan and production of the B-1 bomber that had been canceled by President Carter four years before. The $200 billion fiscal 1982 Defense appropriation was the largest peacetime appropriations bill ever approved.

Following a dramatic lobbying effort by the president, the Senate narrowly voted to permit the sale to Saudi Arabia of sophisticated radar planes and other arms, a victory Reagan said was essential to his conduct of foreign policy.

In another example of Reagan's persuasive powers, Congress cleared its first foreign aid appropriations bill since 1978. Earlier bills had fallen victim to partisan differences in Congress over the proper ratio of military-to-economic aid. The same issue had kept the fiscal 1982 bill in limbo all year.

But at the last minute, Reagan rallied to his side a sufficient number of Republicans to push the measure through a reluctant Congress.

In the fields of health, education and the social services, Congress approved the transformation of many domestic aid programs into block grants that transferred power from the federal government to the states and localities — although Reagan did not get all he asked for in that area.

Congress approved a new four-year farm bill that came close to Reagan's requested spending cuts in subsidy programs. The measure continued most existing price support and other farm programs with moderate increases except for the dairy program, whose support rates were reduced sharply. It included a one-year extension of food stamps with new enforcement authority to discourage fraud and abuse.

Despite the sweeping changes Congress made, several important controversies remained unresolved.

In an embarrassment for the president, Congress refused to even consider his proposal to overhaul the Social Security system, and Reagan subsequently withdrew it. Legislators then abandoned their own efforts to achieve a comprehensive reform of the retirement system, opting instead to seek a temporary solution.

A scheduled reauthorization of the Clean Air Act also became mired in controversy and was put off.

The House approved by a wide margin legislation to extend the 1965 Voting Rights Act, but the bill got nowhere in the Senate during 1981.

Legislation to deregulate the telecommunications industry and to restructure the American Telephone & Telegraph Co. cleared the Senate but was still pending in the House.

Social Issues Debated

Congress debated proposals to permit school prayer, curb busing and ban abortions. But at year's end, these volatile social issues remained to be resolved.

A constitutional amendment giving the states and Congress joint authority to restrict abortion was approved by a Senate Judiciary subcommittee and was pending before the full committee at session's end. Also pending before the Senate panel was a bill declaring that human life begins at conception and allowing states to pass anti-abortion laws.

The Senate adopted a far-reaching curb on the use of court-ordered busing for racial balance as an amendment to a Justice Department reauthorization bill, but the measure subsequently became enmeshed in a filibuster.

A filibuster also stymied efforts to enact legislation allowing voluntary school prayer.

Congress never acted on Reagan campaign promises to deregulate natural gas and abolish the Education and Energy departments because the administration never formally proposed them.

Muted Boasts

At session's end, Republican legislators hailed the year's accomplishments in glowing terms.

"We helped define a new direction for national government and national politics in this country," said House Minority Leader Robert H. Michel, R-Ill., following adjournment.

But the leaders conceded that considerable challenges still faced the GOP in 1982. "This situation wasn't created in a year. We can't clean it up in a year," said Senate Majority Whip Ted Stevens, R-Alaska.

For the Democrats, House Chief Deputy Majority Whip Bill Alexander, D-Ark., said, "it was necessary to fight each round, but it was fortunate that we did not win. Had we won and changed Ronald Reagan's economic plan, the president could have pointed to us and accused us of being responsible for the mess we find ourselves in today."

Agriculture

Dairy Price Supports. President Reagan won a strategically important victory over the well-financed dairy lobby in March when Congress canceled a scheduled increase in dairy price supports (S 509).

Reagan painted the victory as an important first step on the road to a balanced budget. The fight divided the dairy lobby internally and also helped set up stresses among commodity groups that later aided the administration drive for a low-cost omnibus farm bill.

Grain Embargo. Less than a year after approving certain interest-free loans for farmers to compensate for the embargo of grain sales to Russia, Congress reinstated the interest charges. President Reagan signed the legislation (S 1395) July 23.

The bill ended a mandatory interest waiver established in December 1980 on loans for 1980 and 1981 grain crops stored in the farmer-held reserve.

The 1980 legislation was intended to aid farmers adversely affected by President Carter's Jan. 4, 1980, announcement establishing the embargo. Reagan ended the embargo April 24, honoring a campaign pledge to farmers and eliminating a major irritant for Agriculture Committee members who had begun drafting four-year farm legislation.

Farm Bill. Stringent budget constraints pressured commodity groups into competing directly for shares of a smaller federal pie and shattered their customary vote-trading relationships. Consequently, the process of writing a four-year farm bill (S 884) was prolonged and painful.

The Senate reluctantly complied with Reagan's demands for less-generous price support increases than commodity groups wanted. But House farm interests shepherded a far more costly bill all the way to conference before bowing to administration pressures.

The final version continued major crop price supports with moderate increases, and pruned existing support rates for dairy products. It also kept sugar and peanut programs, despite earlier House votes to eliminate them.

Farm groups were split, with corn, cotton, sugar and soybean producers supporting S 884 and dairymen and others calling the bill inadequate. That division, along with opposition from consumer and urban critics of the sugar and peanut programs, made enactment doubtful until the last day of the session, Dec. 16, when the House finally cleared S 884.

Reconciliation. Federal financing for farms, water and waste disposal projects and telephone and electrical systems tightened up with the passage of the budget reconciliation bill (HR 3982).

The measure capped federal or federally backed lending for these purposes, while raising interest rates. It also shifted from the federal budget to the private sector certain commodity inspection fees and included a short-lived price support increase for dairymen.

Commerce

Communications Rewrite. Legislation to deregulate much of the telecommunications industry and restructure the American Telephone & Telegraph Co. (AT&T) was passed by the Senate. The House Energy and Commerce Committee planned to consider related legislation (HR 5158) in 1982.

The Senate measure (S 898) was the first such bill to reach the floor of either chamber in the five years Congress had been considering revisions of the 1934 Communications Act.

It would allow AT&T to enter new unregulated and computer-oriented markets, such as data processing, currently forbidden to it under a 1956 consent decree. However, the monopoly would have to set up a separate subsidiary to handle the new services.

The sale of telephone and other customer-premises equipment would be deregulated, but regulation of basic telephone service would continue.

Public Broadcasting. The Corporation for Public Broadcasting (CPB) received authorizations in the budget reconciliation bill (HR 3982) of $130 million annually for fiscal 1984-86, a total of $80 million more than President Reagan requested. Congress also allowed several public station licensees to experiment with advertisements, now generally barred by law.

Late-year budget cuts in the continuing appropriations resolution (H J Res 370) reduced the fiscal 1984 funding for public broadcasting to a level of $105.6 million. Public stations feared that the cut would cripple their programming of nationally acclaimed shows, such as the "MacNeil-Lehrer Report" and "Sesame Street."

Reagan argued that taxpayers should not be required to subsidize the entertainment of others. However, critics responded that the government should aid public broadcasting because it provides a cultural service.

Congress also included a provision from a separately passed House bill (HR 3238) that directed the CPB to allocate funds for direct station aid, national programming and other costs, according to a formula. The formula was designed to end the fighting between CPB and stations over who would control federal funds.

Public broadcasting received advance appropriations. Congress had approved appropriations of $172 million for fiscal 1982 and $137 million for 1983.

Broadcasting Revisions. Changes in radio and television regulation approved by Congress drew criticism that citizens would be seriously limited in challenging licenses.

The reconciliation legislation established seven-year licenses for radio stations and five-year licenses for televi-

sion stations, lengthening both from three years under previous law. Some consumer, religious and labor groups claimed the extension would make it difficult for citizens to protest inadequate broadcasting. The bill also provided for a lottery to allocate new licenses.

However, the final compromise dropped Senate proposals that would have eliminated the current license renewal procedure of comparing the license holder with other applicants and would have freed radio stations from most federal news and public affairs requirements.

Shortly before adjournment, the Senate Commerce Committee approved new legislation (S 1629) including the radio provisions that had been dropped in reconciliation.

Tourism. Legislation (S 304) to beef up the federal role in promoting foreign tourism to the United States was enacted after key members of Congress scaled back their original plans to win administration approval.

The measure replaced the U.S. Travel Service (USTS) with an upgraded agency to be known as the U.S. Travel and Tourism Administration. The new agency was placed under the Commerce Department. Many members had contended that the USTS had not done an adequate job of funneling tourist dollars into the U.S. economy. But others objected that the government should not be involved in promoting a private industry.

The administration had objected strongly to creating an independent agency outside the Commerce Department, as proposed by the Senate and by a House subcommittee.

Product Liability. Congress enacted legislation (HR 2120) to help businesses insure themselves against damage claims involving their products.

Businesses had complained that product liability insurance was either prohibitively expensive or simply not available. The new law generally pre-empted state laws that restricted the formation of business "risk retention groups" for self-insurance or "purchasing groups" to buy product liability insurance jointly at favorable rates.

The insurance industry had fought similar legislation in 1980, partly because the proposals required Commerce Department approval of risk retention groups, which the industry argued would be an unwarranted federal intrusion into a state-regulated area. The 1981 measure did not provide for federal regulation.

Daylight-Saving Time. Although the House approved a bill (HR 4437) extending daylight-saving time (DST) for an additional two months each year, opponents continued to block action in the Senate Commerce Committee.

Critics argued that the longer morning darkness would cause problems for farmers and schoolchildren in rural areas in the Western time zones.

Supporters said the change would result in more daylight hours for work and recreation, as well as a significant energy savings because of the reduced need for electricity.

As passed by the House, the bill would extend the current six-month DST to eight months by starting DST on the first Sunday of March.

It would continue to allow a state to exempt from DST all its area or a portion in a different time zone from the rest of the state.

Consumer Product Safety Commission (CPSC). House supporters of the CPSC successfully protected the

agency from dismantlement by slipping supporting language into the reconciliation bill.

CPSC emerged from the budget battles bruised but retained its status as an independent regulatory agency.

Business critics had complained that CPSC did not understand manufacturing and that it overregulated in its efforts to protect consumers.

The Reagan administration originally wanted to abolish the agency, and there was strong support in the House and Senate to put CPSC under the Commerce Department. Consumer advocates said that would bury the agency within a department with strong connections to business.

HR 3982 authorized $33 million in fiscal 1982 and $35 million in 1983, cuts that would require heavy staff reductions. The bill also allowed one chamber of Congress to veto CPSC rules if the other chamber did not object and directed the agency to rely on voluntary safety standards developed by industry groups when possible.

National Consumer Cooperative Bank. The Co-op Bank, also targeted by the Reagan administration for extinction, found an unlikely source of support in the House for its survival. Eighteen Republicans saved it by threatening to vote against a GOP alternative plan for the entire federal budget if the plan did not include funds for the bank.

The final reconciliation compromise scheduled the bank to become a private financial institution by Dec. 31, 1981, or 10 days after enactment of fiscal 1982 appropriations legislation for the bank, whichever was later. This would be several years sooner than originally planned.

The measure also included a fiscal 1982 authorization of $47 million for the bank's market-rate loans to co-ops and $14 million for low-interest loans. The continuing appropriations resolution (H J Res 370) reduced those amounts to $41 million and $4.8 million.

Congress

Abscam. A two-year House investigation growing out of the FBI's "Abscam" corruption probe came abruptly to a close in August when the House Committee on Standards of Official Conduct dismissed a recommendation by its attorney that charges of wrongdoing be voted against Rep. John P. Murtha, D-Pa.

The committee's attorney, E. Barrett Prettyman Jr., subsequently resigned in protest, but the panel nevertheless closed its books on Abscam.

The Senate put off until 1982 final consideration of its sole Abscam disciplinary case. Senate leaders announced Dec. 1 that they would wait until the second session before scheduling a debate on a Senate Ethics Committee recommendation (S Res 204) that Harrison A. Williams Jr., D-N.J., be expelled for his involvement in Abscam.

In all, the Abscam probe resulted in the criminal conviction of seven members of Congress, only one of whom — Sen. Williams — remained a member as of the end of 1981. Of the other six only one — Rep. Michael "Ozzie" Myers, D-Pa. (1976-80) — was expelled, though two others — Reps. John W. Jenrette Jr., D-S.C. (1975-80), and Raymond F. Lederer, D-Pa. (1977-81) — resigned from the House in order to stop expulsion proceedings against them.

Three other convicted members — Reps. Richard Kelly, R-Fla. (1975-81), John M. Murphy, D-N.Y. (1963-

81), and Frank Thompson Jr., D-N.J. (1955-81) — were defeated for re-election before the House could act against them.

Ethics Code. In another matter related to congressional ethics, the Senate Select Ethics Committee put off indefinitely a plan to revise the Senate's 1977 ethics code. The committee began the revision project in early 1981 but dropped it in order to pursue its investigation of Williams.

A separate effort to revise House disciplinary procedures was bottled up in the Rules Committee at the end of the first session.

Congressional Pay, Benefits. Shying from a pay increase during a time of budget restraint, Congress instead gave its members several less direct methods of increasing their take-home pay. Two fiscal 1982 continuing resolutions (H J Res 325, H J Res 370), a black lung benefits bill (HR 5159) and a House rules change (H Res 305) gave members three new ways to take home more money.

Members were given an automatic annual cost-of-living raise equal to the raise given most white-collar federal workers, beginning in 1983. Beginning in 1981, senators and representatives were permitted to deduct from their income taxes the expenses they incur while in Washington. Also as of 1981, senators were no longer limited in the amount of outside income they could earn in addition to their official salaries, while the ceiling on House members' outside earnings was increased from 15 percent of their official salary to 30 percent.

Franking Law Revisions. Legislation revising the congressional franking privilege (S 1224) cleared Congress Oct. 13.

The measure's supporters said its principal purpose was to write into statute many of the restrictions imposed on the use of the frank by the House and Senate since passage of the original franking statute in 1973. But the law also altered several of the restrictions, easing some and strengthening others.

The most significant change made by the new law authorized senators to frank statewide mass mailings, a privilege previously granted only to House members.

New Caucus Rules. New regulations adopted in October by the House Administration Committee required special-interest caucuses and similar legislative service organizations in the House to relinquish all outside funding or sever their official ties with Congress by 1983.

Under the new rules, caucuses would be allowed to continue to accept outside funds after 1982 only if they set up separate non-profit foundations with private offices, staffs and facilities. The crackdown on legislative service organizations was prompted by a Sept. 18 report by the Chicago-based Better Government Association charging that outside contributions to such groups violated the spirit of House ethics rules.

Election Law, FEC. The Senate Rules Committee began work in late fall on revising the federal election code, amid attacks on the Federal Election Commission (FEC) by its opponents. Proposals for revamping the law ranged from minor streamlining changes to abolishing the commission.

By threatening to cut off funding for the FEC, Roger W. Jepsen, R-Iowa, led a group of GOP senators trying to speed up the timetable for action on revising the election law. They failed Nov. 20 in a bid to grant money to the agency only until March 15, 1982.

Rules Chairman Charles McC. Mathias Jr., R-Md., resisted the Jepsen maneuver. He introduced a bill (S 1851) that would increase the legal limits on campaign donations, which some felt were set too low because of inflation. Jepsen wanted to close the FEC and transfer its financial disclosure function to the General Accounting Office and its enforcement role to the Justice Department.

Despite complaints by the Jepsen faction that Mathias was delaying, no legislation moved during the first session.

Senate Television. Debate on a proposal (S Res 20) to permit live broadcast coverage of the Senate was put off until 1982 by Senate Majority Leader Howard H. Baker Jr., R-Tenn. Baker had been optimistic about the Senate's approval of the plan before the end of the first session. But on Nov. 30 he announced he was postponing the Senate's consideration of the matter because the year was rapidly coming to a close.

Defense

Defense Spending. True to his campaign pledge to beef up U.S. defenses, President Reagan began the year with a large boost in President Carter's fiscal 1982 defense budget — an increase from $196 billion to $222 billion. But by October, facing skyrocketing projections of the fiscal 1982 deficit, Reagan cut his earlier request by some $8 billion. The cuts came from a wide range of procurement programs and operating accounts.

At the end of the session, Congress appeared headed for approval of essentially the level of funding included in the October request. But during Senate debate on the defense appropriations bill (HR 4995) in early December, the Reagan position came under fire from both flanks.

On the one hand, Democrats mounted a concerted attack on the October reductions which, they said, sacrificed the combat-readiness of conventional combat forces. On eight amendments, voting along nearly straight party lines, Republicans blocked Democrats' efforts to increase appropriations by amounts totaling more than $1 billion for various "readiness-related" programs cut by Reagan.

On the other hand, several Republicans — including such senior members as Finance Committee Chairman Robert Dole, R-Kan. — warned the administration during the debate that they would demand a tighter budgetary rein on the Pentagon in future fiscal years.

Congress cleared defense authorization and appropriations bills (S 815 and HR 4995, respectively) that approved the Reagan spending program on most major points.

MX Missile. After eight months of deliberation, the administration killed the mobile version of the MX missile long-favored by the Air Force and proposed in 1979 by the Carter administration.

Reagan essentially deferred until 1984 a decision on how to base the new intercontinental missile in a way that would not be vulnerable to Soviet missile attack. To prevent any delay in deploying the new missiles while a new basing technique was developed, Reagan announced Oct. 2, the first few dozen of a planned 100 MXs would be deployed in existing missile silos that would be

"superhardened" with additional concrete.

Administration officials conceded that the improved silos would become vulnerable to increasingly accurate Soviet missiles within a few years, but they said that would be time enough to select and develop an improved MX basing system.

The decision — especially the superhardened interim bases — enraged members of the Senate Armed Services Committee, who had supported the Air Force-Carter version.

But efforts to block the $2 billion included in the budget to continue MX development were rejected in both houses.

In a series of hearings in November, Senate Armed Services lambasted the administration's superhardening proposal and pressed the administration to speed selection of a long-term MX basing that would include many of the mobility features of the Carter version Reagan rejected in October.

The maneuvering was capped by a complex amendment to the defense appropriations bill — adopted by a 90-4 vote — designed to signal acute congressional skepticism toward the superhardening proposal. The amendment was retained in the final defense appropriations bill (HR 4995).

B-1 Bomber. Like his overall increase in the defense budget, Reagan's decision to begin production of the B-1 bomber — canceled by Carter in 1977 — redeemed a campaign pledge.

And like the defense budget increase, the B-1 program lost some of its longtime supporters, who warned that the bomber program — which would cost nearly $40 billion counting inflation — might siphon money away from more critically needed weapons programs.

In particular, some congressional defense specialists worried that the B-1 program might slow down development of the new "stealth" bomber, designed to evade radar and thus penetrate Soviet territory long after the B-1 became vulnerable to Russian air defenses.

For a brief period in November, the B-1 appeared to face a serious threat on Capitol Hill because of doubts that it could cope with Soviet defenses any better than existing B-52 bombers.

But by late November, administration officials were presenting a solid front of opinion that the B-1 could penetrate defenses through the mid-1990s. And to circumvent widespread unease over the B-1's cost, the administration circulated estimates that it would cost nearly as much to modify and continue operating B-52s through the rest of the century ($93 billion) as it would to follow the president's program of building B-1s and then stealths ($114 billion).

Efforts to block the B-1 outright were handily defeated in both the House and the Senate during late November and early December consideration of the defense appropriations bill (HR 4995).

Senate Democratic critics of the program were no more successful in their effort to shift funds from the B-1 to stealth and a range of conventional combat-readiness measures. Senate Republicans closed ranks behind the B-1 almost unanimously.

Rapid Deployment Force, Indian Ocean Bases. Congress continued to support the general idea of beefing up the Rapid Deployment Force (RDF). RDF was the umbrella concept under which the Pentagon was improving its ability to move large combat forces into distant trouble spots where there were no permanent U.S. military bases — notably the oil-producing Persian Gulf region.

But in its October budget retrenchment, the administration slowed its own plans to deploy a fleet of cargo ships that would store the tanks and other heavy equipment of a Marine division near potential trouble spots.

And, as had been the case in 1980, Congress was strongly skeptical about a proposal to develop from scratch a new, long-range transport plane called the C-17 (formerly called the CX). The final version of the defense authorization bill (S 815) allowed only $15 million of the $169.7 million requested for the C-17.

Both the House and Senate versions of the defense appropriations bill (HR 4995) disallowed continuation of the C-17, directing the Pentagon to concentrate on purchasing existing, wide-body transport planes.

Repeating the pattern of earlier years, the House proposed a deep reduction — nearly 40 percent — in the $541 million appropriations request for construction projects designed to facilitate RDF deployment to the Middle East. The cut was recommended by the House Appropriations Committee, which maintained that much more of the cost of U.S. efforts to defend Persian Gulf oil supplies should be borne by U.S. allies in Europe and Japan who were far more dependent on those supplies than the United States was.

The Senate version of the military construction appropriations bill (HR 4241) restored the House cuts, and conferees provided funding for all projects except for the upgrading of facilities at Ras Banas in Egypt.

Military Pay Raise. Reagan's proposed $4.8 billion pay raise for military personnel drew no significant congressional objection. But the Senate Armed Services Committee fought the administration and the House Armed Services panel to a draw over the distribution of the pay hike.

Reagan and the House committee favored an across-the-board hike of 14.3 percent for all enlisted personnel and officers. It was argued that this would restore military purchasing power to the levels established by the large military pay hikes accompanying the start of the all-volunteer policy in 1973.

But the Senate panel insisted that money should be diverted from the proposed raises for low-ranking enlisted personnel to give higher raises to mid-level and senior enlisted persons. According to the Senate committee, shortages in experienced enlisted personnel were the most serious manpower problem facing the services.

The Senate proposed a pay raise costing about as much as the House bill, but ranging from a 7 percent increase for recruits to raises of more than 20 percent for some very senior sergeants.

As House and Senate conferees squared off over the pay raise bill, the administration offered a counterproposal, under which raises would have ranged from 10.7 percent for recruits to 16.5 percent for top sergeants. The House conferees were adamant that recruit raises not drop below 10 percent. Eventually the Senate conferees agreed to a package (S 1181) that basically followed the Pentagon proposal, with raises ranging from 10 percent for privates to 17 percent for top sergeants.

Battleships, Aircraft Carrier. Congress deep-sixed a proposal to re-activate the mothballed aircraft car-

rier *Oriskany*, for which Reagan's March budget included more than $400 million. Of the four congressional defense panels, only the House Armed Services approved the idea. The Senate Armed Services Committee was particularly harsh in its opposition, insisting that the rehabilitation would take too long and cost too much, considering the limited combat power of the ship.

But a proposal to reactivate mothballed battleships and equip them with long-range cruise missiles won a firm congressional endorsement. Three times during the year, amendments to cancel funding for one of the first two ships — the *New Jersey* or the *Iowa* — were turned back by comfortable margins in the Senate, where opposition to the move was centered.

The supplemental appropriations bill for fiscal 1981 (HR 3512) and the fiscal 1982 defense appropriations bill (HR 4995) included a total of $328 million for the *New Jersey*. The 1982 bills also included $90 million to begin work on the *Iowa*.

Economic Affairs

Banking. Major banking reform legislation was put on hold in 1981 because various segments of the financial industry could not reach a consensus on what should be in the bill.

Congress wanted to help the savings and loan industry, which had been suffering severe losses because of inflation and competition from new investment sources. But the House and Senate chose different routes to try to provide that relief.

The House Oct. 28 passed emergency legislation (HR 4603) that would expand financial aid to all thrift institutions and allow commercial banks and savings and loans to acquire troubled savings institutions across state lines.

In the Senate, Banking Committee Chairman Jake Garn, R-Utah, proposed sweeping banking deregulation legislation (S 1720) that would eliminate most existing distinctions between S&Ls and commercial banks, as well as providing the emergency aid proposed by the House. Garn's bill also would allow banks and savings institutions to get into investment businesses by permitting them to operate, manage and sell interest in mutual funds.

Although his committee held extensive hearings on the bill, Garn refused to move to markup until banks and S&Ls reached agreement on the legislation.

Budget/Reconciliation. Although the fiscal 1982 budget provided President Reagan with heady victories, economic realities later scuttled his budget goals.

Congress July 31 gave final approval to omnibus "reconciliation" legislation (HR 3982) that dramatically curtailed the shape and scope of many government programs. The bill cut nearly $35.2 billion from the $740 billion spending level projected by the Congressional Budget Office for fiscal 1982.

Drafted under reconciliation instructions contained in the first fiscal 1982 budget resolution (H Con Res 115), the bill consolidated in a single package cuts sought by Reagan in his March budget proposals.

The idea of using reconciliation to carry through Reagan's pledge to trim federal spending was advanced by Office of Management and Budget Director David A. Stockman. The reconciliation process was created by the 1974 Congressional Budget Act as a means of forcing committees to comply with congressionally approved spending levels. It had been used only once previously — in 1980.

That Reagan was able to succeed in his early efforts to slash the budget in the Republican-controlled Senate was no surprise. In the House, however, victory was attributable to two factors:

● Republicans to a man stood behind the administration's alternative, known as Gramm-Latta, to the Budget Committee's version of the first budget resolution.

● A sizable group of conservative Democrats, dubbed "Boll Weevils," voted with the GOP.

That same coalition prevailed in the House when the reconciliation bill itself came to the floor. With the help of conservative Democrats, the Republicans turned aside the $37.7 billion package of cuts recommended by the House authorizing committees. In its place they won approval of a substitute package known as Gramm-Latta II, which had been hastily developed with administration help and which closely followed the Senate bill.

In signing his reconciliation and tax cut bills Aug. 13, Reagan boasted that they marked "an end to the excessive growth in government bureaucracy and government spending and government taxing."

Within weeks after enactment of the reconciliation package, however, the administration was forced to acknowledge that its economic program was not achieving the desired effects.

Faced with soaring deficit projections spawned by stubbornly high interest rates and inflation, Reagan Sept. 24 announced a second budget-slashing initiative. This time he asked Congress to save $13 billion by paring appropriations measures and making changes in non-discretionary entitlement programs such as Medicaid and food stamps. He also called for $3 billion in new revenues.

Congressional response was negative, however, especially among Republicans. GOP members of the Senate Appropriations Committee said they could not cut more than $5 billion from fiscal 1982 appropriations. And House Republicans said they would not attempt to raise taxes — not in an election year and not in a recession. Reagan himself ultimately agreed to settle for $4 billion in cuts and to postpone his entitlement and tax proposals.

One result of the Republican stalemate was that the appropriations process ground to a standstill, and most of the government was funded under a series of short-term continuing appropriations resolutions.

The GOP stalemate over the Sept. 24 initiative also delayed action on the second, and supposedly binding, budget resolution for fiscal 1982.

Senate Budget Committee Chairman Pete V. Domenici, R-N.M., insisted that Congress had to acknowledge that future budget deficits would be enormous unless substantial cuts were made and that it was necessary in 1981 to at least lay out a blueprint for how to achieve these savings. Domenici, however, could not get his committee to agree on what direction to take.

In the House Budget Committee, many Republicans were unwilling to draft a resolution that showed just how bad the deficit outlook was, and Democrats were disinclined to move ahead without knowing what the administration wanted. In the end the committee reported a pro forma second resolution that was simply a carbon copy of the resolution Congress had approved in May. That measure had contemplated a deficit of $37.65 billion for fiscal 1982 — far below current projections.

The Senate Budget Committee reluctantly followed

suit but added language noting the prospect of deficits ranging from $95 billion to $165 billion in fiscal 1982-84 if no further cuts were made.

The Senate approved its version of the resolution (S Con Res 50) Dec. 9 by a slim 49-48 margin after adding "sense of the Senate" language calling for a revised resolution by March 1982 that would achieve a balanced budget by fiscal 1984. The House accepted the Senate language and approved the resolution Dec. 10, 206-200.

Debt Limit. Congress in 1981 was forced to boost the federal debt limit above the trillion dollar mark — a level often cited by Reagan as evidence of the need to curtail government spending.

The bill (H J Res 265), cleared Sept. 29, lifted the debt ceiling to $1,079,800,000,000 through Sept. 30, 1982.

Earlier in the year, debt limit legislation provided Reagan with his first legislative victory when Congress approved a measure (HR 1553) increasing the debt limit to $985 billion through Sept. 30, 1981. Many Republicans who never in their careers had voted to boost the ceiling — calling such votes "fiscally irresponsible" — acceded to their president's request for a $50 billion increase.

Tax Cuts. One of the Reagan administration's major legislative achievements for the year was enactment of the Economic Recovery Tax Act of 1981 (HR 4242).

Fashioned during a fierce "bidding war" between the administration and congressional Democrats, the measure called for $749 billion in business and individual tax cuts for fiscal 1982-86. The main components were a 23 percent across-the-board cut in individual income tax rates; accelerated depreciation of capital investments; savings incentives; and tax relief for oil producers, married couples and estates. The bill was the linchpin of the administration's supply-side economic theory, which stated that reduced taxes would encourage savings and spur productivity and economic growth.

However, it also proved an important political victory for the Reagan administration and confirmed what had already been shown during earlier budget votes — the Democratic majority had lost control of the House to a coalition of Republicans and conservative Democrats.

A House Ways and Means Committee bill, which targeted more of the tax relief to lower- and middle-income groups, was defeated on the House floor July 29 by a vote of 238-195 after an intense lobbying effort by the administration. A White House-backed substitute subsequently passed.

The Senate measure, passed July 31, also was generally in line with the administration's proposals.

When conferees completed their negotiations Aug. 1, Treasury Secretary Donald T. Regan boasted that the administration had received "95 percent" of what it wanted.

In September, Reagan took a new tack on taxes. He called for $22 billion in tax hikes — euphemistically labeled "revenue enhancements" — over the next three years to reduce the budget deficit. However, faced with a recession and numerous political hurdles, the administration postponed submitting specifics of these proposals until 1982.

Education

Elementary and Secondary Education. The Reagan administration's efforts to consolidate programs of aid to elementary and secondary education met with mixed success.

The president proposed lumping 44 education programs into two block grants. In place of existing categorical programs, states would get funds to use as they wished to help children with special educational needs and to improve school programs.

The proposal ran into heavy opposition, however, largely because of fears that it would undermine the two core federal programs: aid for the education of disadvantaged and handicapped children. A lengthy deadlock in the Senate Labor and Human Resources Committee finally produced a compromise plan that maintained the separate status of those programs, while establishing one block grant out of a variety of small programs.

The changes were part of the budget reconciliation bill (HR 3982). The bill also revised the education program for the disadvantaged, in an effort to simplify its administration, and reduced funding levels.

Impact Aid. Congress took a step toward the goal, sought for decades by half a dozen presidents, of eliminating the impact aid program of assistance to school districts educating the children of federally connected parents.

The reconciliation bill provided for a phase-out, over three years, of "B" payments, which went to school districts with children whose parents either lived or worked on federal property. Assistance for children whose parents both lived and worked on federal property would continue, however. HR 3982 cut impact aid funding to $475 million in fiscal 1982, from about $725 million in 1981.

College Student Aid. Congress cut the rapidly growing guaranteed student loan (GSL) program, but not as much as President Reagan wanted.

To hold down costs, the administration proposed two major changes: use of a "needs test" to limit eligibility for GSL loans; and an end to the federal subsidy of interest costs for students who were still in school.

The termination of in-school interest subsidies was opposed by banks as well as higher education interests and did not receive serious congressional attention.

However, the reconciliation bill established a modified version of the needs test. Under the bill, students from families with annual incomes over $30,000 could get loans only in the amounts needed to cover their educational costs, after other forms of aid and parental contributions were taken into account. Those from families with incomes under $30,000 could continue to borrow the existing annual maximum of $2,500.

The reconciliation bill also limited funding for "Pell grants" for college students to amounts well below the estimated cost of full operation of the program. That was expected to mean smaller grants for several million low- and middle-income students.

Energy

Nuclear Breeder Reactor. Over the objections of environmental and taxpayer groups, Congress supported continued funding of the Clinch River (Tenn.) nuclear breeder reactor. But opponents in both chambers, basing their arguments mainly on economic grounds, came closer than they ever had to killing it.

President Carter unsuccessfully tried for four years to

scrap the project, which would generate electricity and produce more plutonium fuel than it consumed. It currently was estimated to cost at least $3.2 billion; $1 billion had been spent but construction had not yet started.

President Reagan left Clinch River funding out of his initial energy budget but later added $254 million for it at the urging of Senate Majority Leader Howard H. Baker Jr., R-Tenn.

In May, the House Science Committee voted 22-18 to kill the reactor, but that decision was overturned in the budget reconciliation bill (HR 3982). During consideration of the energy and water appropriations bill (HR 4144), both the House and Senate rejected amendments to delete Clinch River funding. The House vote was 186-206, the Senate vote, 46-48.

The House bill provided $228 million for Clinch River, the Senate bill $180 million. Conferees agreed to provide $195 million.

Nuclear Waste. After nearly 40 years without a national program to dispose of radioactive waste, Congress was preparing again to try to enact such a policy. An effort to do so failed at the end of the 96th Congress.

Two Senate committees (Energy and Environment) in late autumn approved different versions of a bill (S 1662) setting a timetable for locating and approving construction of a permanent nuclear waste repository by the year 2000. Sponsors hoped for floor action soon after Congress returned in January 1982.

Floor fights were expected over how to treat nuclear waste from the military weapons program and what kind of waste storage to have. Senators from Louisiana and Mississippi, who feared nuclear wastes would be stored permanently in underground salt formations in their region, favored long-term, monitored waste storage vaults instead. The Energy Committee supported such monitored storage; Environment did not.

In the House, three committees have jurisdiction over the waste issue. The Science and Technology Committee Nov. 20 approved a bill (HR 5016) that would establish a national waste repository by the mid-1990s. An Interior subcommittee had finished work on a similar bill (HR 3809). The Energy and Commerce Committee had not yet acted, but just before Congress adjourned its leaders wrote a compromise bill that might be agreeable to the Interior Committee.

Energy Deregulation. Congress made only a feeble attempt to overturn Reagan's Jan. 28 lifting of price controls on domestic crude oil. The Senate voted 24-68 against an amendment to reimpose oil price controls that would have expired anyway on Sept. 30, 1981. There was no House vote.

Reagan was expected to have a much more difficult time decontrolling natural gas prices. Unlike oil decontrol, gas decontrol would require legislation. Reagan's advisers recommended that he seek a bill to remove all gas price controls over three years, but he deferred the issue until 1982.

While the administration philosophically supported elimination of controls on natural gas, it feared the inflationary effect: Residential gas bills could double. Also, to secure votes for his tax cut, Reagan promised not to tax the windfall profits the gas companies would get as a result of decontrol. Such a sweetener was believed necessary to win congressional approval of gradual oil decontrol in 1979.

Strategic Oil Reserve. In what members admitted was a budget gimmick, Congress declared the Strategic Petroleum Reserve (SPR) "off budget." It thus managed to provide the $3.9 billion the president had requested for fiscal 1982 to fill the nation's emergency oil tank, while reducing the budget by that amount.

The push to knock SPR out of the budget began in the Senate Budget Committee in March. Some members thought the reserve could be financed privately through the sale of "oil bonds," but the financial community and the administration opposed that idea. By then, SPR funding was out of the budget, and members had no stomach for putting it back. To the dismay of the congressional energy committees, the "off-budget" idea snowballed and became part of the budget reconciliation bill (HR 3982).

The bill set up a separate SPR account for which Congress would have to authorize and appropriate money annually. It also ordered the reserve to be filled at a rate of at least 300,000 barrels a day. The SPR held a little more than 200 million barrels of oil at the end of 1981.

Alaska Gas Pipeline. Congress Dec. 10 cleared a package of waivers submitted by Reagan in hopes of facilitating private financing for a $40 billion pipeline to bring natural gas from Alaska to the continental United States. But there was still no guarantee that the consortium trying to build the 4,800-mile line could secure the necessary financing.

The waivers altered the 1977 decision to build the pipeline, shifting to gas consumers part of the risk of delay or non-completion of the project.

Although consumer groups fought the waivers, pipeline sponsors brought in dozens of top-flight lobbyists to work for them. The Senate approved the waiver package by a vote of 75-19 on Nov. 19 (S J Res 115). The House voted twice on the issue. It passed a resolution (H J Res 341) that was identical to the Senate version by a vote of 233-173 Dec. 9. For parliamentary reasons it then approved the Senate resolution Dec. 10, 230-188, clearing the waivers.

Emergency Oil Allocation. Although Reagan said he did not need or want authority to allocate oil supplies and set prices in a petroleum shortage, Congress was insisting on giving him those powers.

The previous presidential authority expired Sept. 30 with the end of the 1973 Emergency Petroleum Allocation Act. The administration declared that in a future crisis the energy marketplace would allocate and price oil, not the government.

But the Senate Oct. 29, by a vote of 85-7, passed a bill (S 1503) to give the president the authority to act in an undefined "severe shortage." The House passed a similar bill (HR 4700) by a vote of 244-136 Dec. 14. A conference committee met briefly Dec. 15, but did not come up with a compromise version and was to meet again after Congress reconvened in 1982.

Nuclear Licensing. As part of a two-year authorization for the Nuclear Regulatory Commission (HR 2330), the House gave the agency authority to allow nuclear power plants to operate before public hearings were complete. The Senate Environment Committee reported a similar bill (S 1207) in May, but fear of controversial amendments blocked floor action.

Proponents of the change argued that it would save electric consumers over $1 billion in replacement power

costs at 11 plants that would be ready to operate while hearings were still going on. The administration and the nuclear industry strongly supported the provision.

The House soundly rejected — 90-304 — opponents' arguments that public safety would be jeopardized by the speeded-up licensing procedure. Opponents also argued that delays caused by public hearings were not as serious as proponents claimed.

Environment

Clean Air. A rewrite of the Clean Air Act, touted early in the year as the major environmental battle of 1981, turned into a war nobody wanted to fight. The Sept. 30 expiration date for the program's authorization came and went. The Reagan administration failed to recommend a comprehensive rewrite, and money to continue the program was included in various appropriations measures — providing some breathing space while House and Senate committees worked on the reauthorization.

Numerous public opinion polls throughout the year showed exceptionally strong support for the act. Convinced they could use the clean air law as a campaign rallying point in 1982, House Democrats kept the bill in the Energy and Commerce Subcommittee on Health and the Environment through 1981, holding lengthy and detailed hearings.

In the Senate, the Environment and Public Works Committee began markup Nov. 17 and displayed no appetite for a major overhaul of the act. In their first test votes, panel members indicated they wanted to keep the law largely intact and to prevent the administration from relaxing its provision through regulation changes.

Clean Water. Congress incorporated many of the reforms sought by President Reagan in its reauthorization (HR 4503) of the federal sewer grant program, after House and Senate conferees Dec. 10 overcame a temporary impasse in their efforts to reconcile two widely differing versions of the bill.

The president wanted to halt federal funds for future population growth, which would have meant less federal money for dozens of expanding Sun Belt sewer systems and more money for sewage treatment plants in urban Frost Belt cities.

The House wanted to "grandfather in" most Sun Belt construction projects already under way, but the Senate had wanted more of the cutbacks proposed by the administration.

In the conference agreement, which cleared both houses Dec. 16, the president got much of what he had asked for, but the changes would be phased in more slowly. All plants and equipment now eligible for 75 percent federal funding would remain so until fiscal 1985. After that, only sewage treatment plants, large sewer lines and repairs of leaky pipes could be paid for with federal funds, but at a 55 percent federal share. Governors could use up to 20 percent of a state's money for items Reagan did not want funded.

The president signed the $2.4 billion measure Dec. 29, and was expected to send a supplemental fiscal 1982 request to Congress to provide money for the grants.

Wilderness Leasing. The House Interior and Insular Affairs Committee twice signaled its strong opposition to the administration's plan to open up wilderness areas to oil and gas leasing.

Although the Wilderness Act of 1964 allowed such leasing in the nation's 80 million acres of designated wilderness until Dec. 31, 1983, very few leases had been granted. Soon after Interior Secretary James G. Watt took office, he announced that he planned to allow more leases in those areas, some of which lie along the oil-rich Overthrust Belt.

The first objection to that policy by the Interior Committee came in May, when the panel invoked an obscure provision of the Federal Land Policy and Management Act of 1976 (FLPMA) to prevent any leasing in Montana's Bob Marshall Wilderness Area just outside of Glacier National Park.

That action was quickly challenged in court and remained in litigation at year's end.

In the fall, word leaked out that the Interior Department had leased 700 acres of New Mexico's Capitan Wilderness Area without conducting environmental impact studies and without notifying Congress. Congress learned that the department was reviewing hundreds of similar applications for leases in wilderness areas, including California's Los Padres National Forest on the Big Sur coast.

That prompted a 41-1 committee vote Nov. 20 to ask the administration not to issue any oil and gas leases in wilderness areas until June 1, 1982, while Congress considered changing the law to prevent leasing in wilderness areas except for national security reasons. Watt agreed to go along with the moratorium, effectively delaying for six months further confrontations with the committee.

Parks Policy. Congress rejected Watt's proposal to use the popular Land and Water Conservation Fund, statutorily earmarked for parkland purchases, to upgrade existing national parks and wildlife refuges.

As part of the Reagan budget, Watt proposed to clamp a moratorium on federal and state park purchase grants while using acquisition money for maintenance. Congress provided extra money for upgrading deteriorating park facilities but refused to allow acquisition funds to be used for that purpose.

In addition, Congress provided money for park acquisition in both its budget reconciliation (HR 3982) and Interior Department appropriations (HR 4035) measures.

Water Policy Board. Congress did not complete action on a measure (S 1095, HR 3432) to create a new national water policy board, a bipartisan effort to prevent Watt from dominating national water policy.

The bills would establish a board to set guidelines for deciding which water projects to build and to coordinate often-conflicting water supply and water pollution programs. Watt opposed creation of a policy board, preferring to coordinate federal water programs in the president's Cabinet Council on Natural Resources and the Environment, which he headed.

An attempt to insert the board authorization into the budget reconciliation measure (HR 3982) was derailed. But fiscal 1982 funding was provided in HR 3982 for a water policy board, provided an authorization cleared Congress.

HR 3432 was reported by three House committees, and S 1095 was reported by the Senate Environment and Public Works Committee. Both bills were awaiting floor action in their respective chambers.

'Tenn-Tom' Waterway. By narrow margins in both

houses, Congress decided to continue funding for the Tennessee-Tombigbee Waterway, the largest water project in the nation's history. The 232-mile-long canal, linking the Tennessee and Tombigbee rivers to provide barges a route through Mississippi and Alabama to the Gulf Coast, had been estimated to cost up to $3 billion.

Both the House and Senate rejected attempts to delete funding for the project from the fiscal 1982 energy and water development appropriations bill (HR 4144 — PL 97-88), but opponents came closer to killing the project than they ever had in the past. The final version of the bill included $189 million for Tenn-Tom.

Supporters of the project argued that it would be foolish to kill it when more than $1 billion already had been spent on it. They put the total cost at $1.8 billion, not $3 billion, and claimed the canal would generate several million dollars a year in user fees. They also said it was needed to transport Appalachian coal to the sea for export. Opponents called it an economic and environmental disaster.

Foreign Policy

Saudi AWACS. President Reagan narrowly won his first major foreign policy test in Congress when the Senate failed Oct. 28, in a dramatic 48-52 vote, to disapprove his plan to sell Saudi Arabia five sophisticated Airborne Warning and Control System (AWACS) radar planes and other air defense equipment.

The vote came on a concurrent resolution to disapprove the sale (H Con Res 194). The House had approved H Con Res 194 on Oct. 14 by an overwhelming vote of 301-111.

The AWACS vote was a stunning victory for Reagan because 50 senators — one less than the majority needed to block the sale — had cosponsored the resolution of disapproval. In the end, Reagan won by persuading seven first-term GOP senators among those cosponsors to switch their positions.

The $8.5 billion arms package also included tanker planes, plus fuel tanks and highly sophisticated AIM-9L air-to-air missiles for 60 F-15 fighter planes that Congress agreed to sell the Saudis in 1978 after a similar fight with the Carter administration.

Israel strongly opposed the AWACS sale, viewing it as a threat to Israeli air superiority. The American Jewish community campaigned against it, and many members of Congress opposed it as a threat to Israel.

Saudi Arabia cast the deal as a test of U.S.-Saudi relations. Reagan won the issue after he put his personal prestige on the line by arguing that a congressional veto would impair his ability to conduct foreign policy.

El Salvador. Both houses of Congress voted to impose conditions on U.S. arms aid to the ruling centrist junta in El Salvador after the Reagan administration, in a "white paper" on the conflict in the tiny Central American nation, declared a leftist insurgency there to be a "textbook case of indirect armed aggression by communist powers through Cuba."

Soon after taking office, the administration declared it would support the junta with military aid to help repulse the leftists and with economic assistance to help relieve social unrest. Strong opposition to that policy arose in Congress when the administration announced in March that it would send El Salvador extra fiscal 1981 military aid and military advisers.

Critics warned that increasing U.S. involvement in the Salvadoran conflict threatened "another Vietnam," though the administration pledged to keep U.S. personnel out of the fighting.

Congress agreed to a compromise of sorts by approving the aid requests but attaching conditions designed to help win a negotiated settlement and to protect human rights. The conditions were included in the fiscal 1982 foreign aid authorization bill (S 1196).

Foreign Aid. Always an unpopular program, foreign aid was the source of especially rancorous partisan and philosophical disputes within Congress in a year when domestic spending was cut beyond all previous proportions.

Congress was hamstrung in trying to fashion a foreign aid program by a fundamental disagreement between conservative Republicans and liberal Democrats over the ratio of military to development aid. The Reagan administration asked Congress to substantially increase U.S. military aid while stringing out contributions to some international development banks to reduce federal spending.

No foreign aid appropriations bill had passed Congress for two years, and for months 1981 seemed certain to be the third year in a row that this would be true.

The House Appropriations Committee reported its aid appropriations bill (HR 4559) on Sept. 22. But the dispute over military vs. development aid made Democrats reluctant to bring the measure to the floor.

Meanwhile, Senate Republican leaders wanted to get Reagan his foreign aid program. They tried to do so by passing the Senate version of the aid appropriations bill (S 1802) on Nov. 17 — violating the tradition that the House must pass appropriations bills first.

The House finally took up the bill Dec. 11 and passed it with support from key Republicans who stressed the "national security" role of foreign aid. The conference report cleared Dec. 16.

At the same time, Congress also completed the companion foreign aid authorization, which contained authorities the Reagan administration wanted to implement its own foreign aid program.

The Senate passed its version of the 1982 aid authorization bill (S 1196) first — with no violation of tradition involved — by a close vote of 40-33 on Oct. 22.

As with the aid appropriations bill, House Democrats were reluctant to act on their version of the authorization bill (HR 3566) without assurances of Republican votes. But the House passed the bill Dec. 9, again with greater than usual Republican backing. A compromise version was settled Dec. 14, and Congress cleared the measure Dec. 16.

Among its major provisions, the authorization bill gave the president leeway to provide aid and arms sales to Argentina, Chile and Pakistan, but retained a controversial limit on U.S. aid to warring factions in Angola.

State Department Authorization. The House rejected the annual State Department authorization bill (HR 3518) Sept. 17 in a move widely regarded as an indicator of how reluctant members were to vote for any foreign spending in light of reduced domestic outlays.

In addition, some House members apparently voted against the bill because it was brought to the floor when Reagan was revising his budget requests, and the bill did not reflect the latest administration requests for State Department spending.

The House passed another version (HR 4814) of the bill Oct. 29 after it was amended to the lower spending levels sought by Reagan in September.

The Senate had passed its version (S 1193) on June 18. But the reluctance to deal with foreign spending measures apparently extended to the conference on the State Department bill. A House-Senate conference had not completed work on the bill in time for adjournment.

Peace Corps. Congress made the Peace Corps independent again after 10 years of its operating under the aegis of the ACTION agency. It was placed under ACTION in 1971 by President Nixon.

Some congressional backers of the Peace Corps had long advocated returning its independence. The ties were officially broken when Congress cleared the fiscal 1982-83 foreign aid authorization bill (S 1196) on Dec. 16.

The move to untie the two agencies picked up steam after Reagan nominated Thomas W. Pauken, a former Army intelligence officer who served in Vietnam in the late 1960s, as director of ACTION.

Proponents of separating the agencies feared Pauken's background would taint the Peace Corps' reputation for being free of involvement in intelligence activities.

Opponents said the separation was a slap at Pauken and would be too costly.

Intelligence Identities. For the second year running, legislation that would make it a crime to disclose the name of a U.S. intelligence agent had wide support in Congress but fell victim to the crush of business before the Christmas recess.

Liberal foes of the so-called names-of-agents bill were able to prevent the measure (S 391) from coming to the Senate floor when it finally was scheduled on both Dec. 15 and 16, the last two days of the first session of the 97th Congress.

The House (HR 4) and Senate bills were almost identical, establishing in their most controversial provision a crime punishable by up to three years in prison and a fine of up to $15,000 for anyone who deliberately reveals the identity of a U.S. agent.

The House passed HR 4 on Sept. 23 after amending it to permit a conviction if a prosecutor proved a defendant had "reason to believe" it would disrupt U.S. intelligence operations for him to disclose an agent's name.

The House Intelligence Committee had proposed a standard of proof under which a prosecutor would have to prove that a defendant exposed an agent "with the intent to impair or impede" U.S. intelligence.

In acting on its version (S 391) on Oct. 6, the Senate Judiciary Committee voted 9-8 in favor of the "intent" standard preferred by a majority of the House Intelligence Committee.

Sens. John H. Chafee, R-R.I., and Henry M. Jackson, D-Wash., were planning to offer an amendment on the Senate floor to reverse the Judiciary Committee action and restoring the "reason to believe" standard passed by the House.

World Bank. After two years of struggle, Congress authorized a politically unpopular $3.24 billion U.S. donation to the International Development Association (IDA), an arm of the World Bank that made no-interest loans to the world's poorest nations.

The authorization, which ratified a pledge made by President Carter in 1979, got past its critics in Congress when supporters hit upon the tactic of including it in the budget reconciliation bill (HR 3982).

But conservative Republican critics of IDA continued to buck the Reagan administration's qualified support for IDA, with significant success.

First, they were able to demand that the reconciliation bill contain limits on appropriations, forcing U.S. payments to be spread over at least four years. Carter had proposed that the payments be made in equal installments of $1.08 billion in fiscal 1980, 1981 and 1982.

Senate critics also managed to cut IDA's fiscal 1981 payment to $500 million during action on the supplemental 1981 appropriations bill (HR 3512), and the 1982 installment was cut to $700 million in the foreign aid appropriations bill (HR 4559), which Congress cleared Dec. 16.

The Reagan administration originally had proposed to make the IDA donation in payments of $540 million in fiscal 1981, $850 million in 1982 and $1.8 billion in 1983.

In the bills containing IDA funding, Congress also approved with little debate an $8.8 billion contribution to another World Bank agency, the International Bank for Reconstruction and Development. Only $658 million of that amount must be paid to the bank; the remainder was a loan guarantee.

Pakistan Aid, Arms. Reagan sought much warmer relations with Pakistan in hopes of countering the influence of the Soviet occupation of Afghanistan. Despite concerns about Pakistan's dictatorship and its efforts to acquire a nuclear weapons capability, Congress went along without much complaint.

The administration proposed to give Pakistan $3.2 billion in economic and military aid over six years and to sell Pakistan 40 F-16 fighter planes, with at least part of the sale to be financed by Saudi Arabia.

But aid to Pakistan had been barred since 1979 under a law that banned aid to nations suspected of trying to develop nuclear weapons. The administration asked Congress to modify the law to permit the aid.

The Republican Senate obliged in S 1196, its version of the fiscal 1982 foreign aid authorization bill, by waiving the law for six years and approving an initial $100 million.

But when it marked up its version of the aid bill (HR 3566) in the spring, the Democratic-controlled House Foreign Affairs Committee deferred the request because details of the Pakistan aid package were unsettled.

In mid-November, the House committee demonstrated its favorable attitude toward aiding Pakistan when it joined with the Senate Foreign Relations Committee in failing to veto the F-16 sale, which was controversial for a variety of reasons.

On Dec. 14, a House-Senate conference on the fiscal 1982-83 foreign aid authorization bill (S 1196) gave the president authority to provide the aid to Pakistan — but with a provision giving Congress the right to veto the president's action. That action became final when Congress cleared the conference report on S 1196 on Dec. 16.

Government

Small Business Administration. Congress raised interest rates substantially on most SBA business loans and cut the amount of loss covered by disaster loans.

The provisions were included in the budget reconcili-

ation legislation (HR 3982).

The rate for direct business loans was increased to match the cost of money to the government plus up to 1 percent. At the time of enactment, the change produced a rate of 15.3 percent. Previously, borrowers had paid between 3 and about 12 percent.

Lawmakers also raised the rate on SBA disaster loans and reduced the amount of the loss covered from 100 percent to 85 percent. Businesses unable to obtain credit elsewhere would pay an 8 percent rate; the rate had been 5 percent. Credit-worthy businesses would pay the prevailing market rate; under previous law their rate had equaled the government's cost of money plus up to 1 percent.

Arts Funding. Congress balked at the 50 percent budget cut the Reagan administration proposed for the arts and humanities endowments and instead authorized a funding cut of 25 percent.

The reconciliation legislation authorized $119.3 million for the National Endowment for the Arts (NEA) and $113.7 million for the National Endowment for the Humanities (NEH) annually for fiscal 1982-1984.

Reagan originally asked for only $88 million in fiscal 1982 budget authority for NEA and $85 million for the NEH.

In September, he requested further reductions to $77.4 million for NEA and $74.8 million for NEH.

The fiscal 1982 Interior Appropriations bill (HR 4035) contained $143.4 million for NEA and $130.5 million for the NEH, both amounts exceeding the reconciliation bill. The bill passed when no point of order was raised against the conflict, committee aides said.

Postal Service. Two U.S. Postal Service subsidies were cut by Congress in a move that could mean higher rates for non-profit organizations and other subsidized mail users.

The reconciliation bill cut the fiscal 1982 authorization for the public service subsidy that supports delivery to unprofitable areas by $394 million to $250 million for fiscal 1982.

The House included in the fiscal 1982 appropriations bill (HR 4121) for the Treasury, Postal Service and other general government operations $300 million for the public service subsidy. The Senate approved $250 million. The administration's revised September budget request called for eliminating the public service subsidy.

The "revenue foregone" subsidy, which makes up for income lost to the Postal Service through subsidies primarily to charities and other non-profit mailers, was reduced to $696 million, a cut of $416 million.

The House included in HR 4121 $500 million for revenue foregone; the Senate $619.2 million, nearly identical to the administration's September request.

Reconciliation also deflated the nine-digit ZIP code that the Postal Service said it needed to increase efficiency and cut costs.

The bill postponed the start of the new code until Oct. 1, 1983, but did allow the agency to buy new machinery required to process the code and to advertise, train personnel and take other preliminary steps.

Federal Pay Raise. White-collar federal employees got a 4.8 percent pay raise on Oct. 1, the amount recommended by Reagan and included by Congress in the reconciliation legislation.

The raise was considerably less than the recommendation of a pay comparability committee, which would have amounted to about 15 percent.

The reconciliation package also cut the frequency of federal retirees' cost-of-living adjustments from twice yearly to annually.

A stopgap funding measure (H J Res 370) approved by Congress Dec. 11 raised the pay level for federal executives just below Cabinet officials and members of Congress, to $59,500 a year. Other executives also got increases.

Regulatory Reform. House and Senate committees continued to work toward regulatory reform legislation (S 1080, HR 746) that would change the way agencies make regulations.

The House Judiciary Committee and the Senate Governmental Affairs and Judiciary committees appeared to have agreed that regulatory agencies should be required to assess the costs and benefits of any proposed rule that would cost business at least $100 million a year to comply with.

But a compromise worked out by the staffs of the two Senate panels and the bill approved by the House Judiciary Committee differed on several points.

The House committee struck key portions of the so-called "Bumpers amendment." Named after its sponsor, Sen. Dale Bumpers, D-Ark., the amendment would make it easier to challenge agency rules in court by erasing the benefit of doubt currently given by law to agencies. The Senate consensus bill retained the provision.

The two Senate committees gave the Office of Management and Budget largely unrestricted authority to oversee independent and executive agencies' cost-benefit tests. Under the House committee bill, independent agencies would still have to do the cost-benefit tests, but OMB could not monitor their performance.

Freedom of Information Act. Efforts to revise the Freedom of Information Act (FOIA) drew strong criticism from the press as hearings were held in the House and a subcommittee markup was held in the Senate in 1981.

Enacted in 1966 and amended in 1974, FOIA opened previously secret government files to the public. The Reagan administration and Sen. Orrin G. Hatch, R-Utah, chairman of the Judiciary Constitution Subcommittee, maintained that the law must be reconstructed to protect vital government documents, national security and law enforcement efforts.

The administration bill (S 1751, HR 4805) would further restrict the release of law enforcement and business information and would allow agencies to charge higher fees to cover the estimated $57 million annual cost of meeting requests for information.

Hatch's measure (S 1730), as introduced, would give law enforcement agencies fewer exemptions from disclosure requirements than the administration plan. But it would add more protection for businesses that complained about confidential information given to regulatory agencies being made public.

The Constitution Subcommittee Dec. 14 by a 3-2 vote approved a version of S 1730 that borrowed heavily from the administration bill. For example, it gave broad new powers to the attorney general to exempt all information relating to terrorism, organized crime and foreign counterintelligence investigations.

The measure also made it easier for the Central Intelli-

gence Agency (CIA) to stop disclosure of sensitive information.

Press critics had complained that the Hatch bill would subvert the law, making it difficult for Americans to keep tabs on government operations. Rep. Glenn English, D-Okla., also introduced a bill (HR 2021) that would provide more rights for businesses. He said he would wait for Senate action before marking up a bill.

Veterans' Disability Pay. Congress cleared Oct. 2 and sent to the president a bill (S 917) to provide an 11.2 percent average annual cost-of-living increase in payments for veterans with service-connected disabilities.

The measure also provided an across-the-board 11.2 percent increase for families of severely disabled veterans and families of veterans who died from service-connected causes.

The bill, the result of a compromise worked out by the House and Senate Veterans' committees, also made available to veterans graduated-payment loans that required smaller monthly payments during the first several years of a mortgage and larger payments in later years.

Health

Medicaid. In an effort to hold down soaring federal health care costs, Congress agreed after a bitter battle to cut Medicaid payments to the states in fiscal 1982-84.

Medicaid, the health care program for the poor and disabled, cost the federal government about $16.5 billion in 1981. The federal government paid about 55 percent of Medicaid costs, the states the rest.

Congress refused to put a rigid "cap" on federal payments, as President Reagan requested. But as part of the reconciliation bill (HR 3982), it reduced payments to the states by 3 percent in fiscal 1982, 4 percent in 1983 and 4.5 percent in 1984.

The states, already hurting from high Medicaid bills, bitterly fought Reagan's proposal to limit the annual increase in federal payments to 5 percent. Health care costs were rising three times that fast, they protested.

The Senate agreed to a cap but raised it to 9 percent. The states' position prevailed in the House, however. Some members who otherwise supported an administration-backed reconciliation substitute refused to go along with the Medicaid cap, so sponsors never brought it to a vote. Instead, the House bill called for spending cuts of 3 percent in 1982, 2 percent in 1983 and 1 percent in 1984.

Conferees raised the cuts to 3, 4 and 4.5 percent, respectively. The Congressional Budget Office estimated the cuts would reduce federal Medicaid spending by about $1 billion a year. Because of rising health care costs, however, the federal share was still expected to be $600 million higher in 1982 than in 1981, and $2.3 billion higher in 1983.

Medicare. The reconciliation bill also made changes in Medicare designed to save more than $1 billion a year. Although the bulk of the savings were achieved through bookkeeping changes and repealing new benefits that had not yet gone into effect, the bill also required elderly Medicare beneficiaries to pay a greater share of the cost of their care.

Federal Medicare costs totaled about $42.5 billion in 1981.

The president originally said Medicare would be exempt from cuts as part of his "social safety net." But he later asked for about $1 billion in savings, and Congress cut even deeper than that.

Block Grants. Another bitter battle on the reconciliation bill came over Reagan's proposal to end 25 categorical health programs and channel their funds into two block grants to the states — with a 25 percent cut.

Congress went along with the reduction in funding, for savings estimated at about $1 billion a year in fiscal 1982-84. But it balked at the block grant proposal. The Senate Labor and Human Resources Committee deadlocked on the issue for weeks, until a compromise finally was worked out. And House Republicans failed to get enough votes to include their health provisions in the reconciliation bill, so the watered-down block grants approved by the Education and Labor Committee were adopted.

The final bill lumped 19 programs into four block grants but imposed a number of conditions on how the money was to be spent, rather than giving the states total control as Reagan wanted. It also reauthorized as separate programs several of the programs Reagan wanted to put into block grants. These included family planning and migrant health centers, which supporters feared some states might not choose to fund.

Health Manpower. With the doctor shortages of the 1960s and early 1970s gone and a surplus forecast, Congress ended "capitation" grants to medical schools and substantially reduced spending for other programs of aid to health professionals. The changes were part of the budget reconciliation bill.

Under the capitation grant program, the government had paid medical schools up to $2,100 per student in an effort to encourage schools to expand their enrollments. President Reagan, like President Carter before him, called for an end to the program.

Congress continued loan programs and other aid for health-profession students but cut their authorization levels to less than half the fiscal 1980 levels. It refused to go along with Reagan's request to eliminate the National Health Service Corps, which provided scholarships to doctors and other health professionals who in return served in a medically underserved area.

Health Planning, PSROs. Congress declined to go along with Reagan administration requests to kill the health planning system and the Professional Standards Review Organization (PSRO) program. It did make substantial cuts in both, however, as part of the reconciliation bill.

The health planning program was intended to curb unneeded hospital construction or expansions and prevent duplication of services, which added to health care costs. PSROs are groups of physicians that monitor federal health care programs to determine whether services are necessary and of high quality. The administration said both programs represented excessive federal regulation and had not proved effective.

Congress extended the planning program for one year but authorized only $102 million for it, compared to spending of $117 million in 1981 and $158 million in 1980. It allowed the secretary of health and human services to terminate PSROs that he found to be ineffective; no more than 30 percent of the nation's 185 PSROs could be terminated in 1982, however.

PHS Hospitals. Congress finally did what economy-minded presidents since Dwight D. Eisenhower had wanted to do: It ended federal funding of the eight hospitals and 27 clinics operated by the Public Health Service (PHS) and repealed the right of merchant seamen to free medical care, an entitlement that dated to 1798. The actions were taken as part of the budget reconciliation bill.

The bill authorized funding in fiscal 1982 to continue care for seamen already under treatment and to assist in the transfer of the PHS hospitals to state, local or private control.

Congress provided the funding for hospitals in an emergency supplemental appropriation in July (H J Res 308) and in the continuing resolutions (H J Res 368, H J Res 370) approved in November and December.

Food Safety. Once again Congress put off action on a promised revision of the nation's food safety laws. The chairmen of three of the four committees with jurisdiction over food safety introduced legislation (S 1442, HR 4014) in June to overhaul existing laws, but no action was taken on it. The administration still had not sent Congress its food safety proposals, and hearings — postponed several times — finally were set for January 1982.

Consumer groups attacked the legislation introduced by Sens. Orrin G. Hatch, R-Utah, and Jesse Helms, R-N.C., and Rep. E. "Kika" de la Garza, D-Texas. Although sponsors said the bill was simply intended to give the food industry more flexibility, critics said it would increase the possibility that consumers would be exposed to chemicals that could cause cancer or other diseases. Under the bill, a food additive would be considered safe unless it could be shown that its use posed a "significant risk" to health. The existing law, known as the Delaney clause, flatly prohibited the use of any additive found to induce cancer in animals or humans.

Pending a full-scale revision of the food safety laws, Congress passed legislation (S 1278) extending for two more years the 1977 law prohibiting the Food and Drug Administration from banning the use of the artificial sweetener saccharin in diet foods and soft drinks.

Koop Nomination. After months of controversy, Dr. C. Everett Koop was confirmed by the Senate Nov. 16 as surgeon general and director of the U.S. Public Health Service (PHS). Opposed by PHS professionals and feminist groups, the prominent Philadelphia pediatric surgeon nonetheless won easy approval, 68-24.

Although Senate critics focused primarily on Koop's alleged lack of credentials to head the PHS — they argued that his experience was largely in clinical medicine rather than in public health — it was his outspoken anti-abortion views that underlay much of the opposition. Koop had written and spoken against abortion, Planned Parenthood and some forms of birth control.

Earlier, in the budget reconciliation bill, Congress removed age limits on the surgeon general and other members of the PHS, which initially had held up the 65-year-old Koop's appointment, and required that the surgeon general have "specialized training or significant experience in public health programs."

Veterans' Health Care. Vietnam veterans finally won their long fight to get medical treatment for veterans suffering from ailments attributed to Agent Orange, the herbicide used to defoliate jungles in Vietnam. Legislation

(HR 3499) directing the Veterans Administration (VA) to provide the care cleared Congress Oct. 16.

Veterans' groups for years had sought to get treatment and compensation for veterans exposed to Agent Orange in Vietnam. They claimed exposure had resulted in a wide array of health problems. The VA had rejected their claims.

The bill also extended for three years another program strongly backed by Vietnam veterans' organizations — the "storefront" readjustment counseling centers that the Reagan administration wanted to abolish as an economy move. HR 3499 also required the VA to maintain a minimum number of hospital and nursing home beds — more than the administration wanted, extended the period in which veterans could use certain educational benefits, and established a new small-business loan program for veterans.

Reagan expressed concern about the cost of some of the provisions in the bill, but signed it into law Nov. 3.

Housing/Development

Enterprise Zones. House and Senate proposals to provide tax breaks to encourage urban redevelopment in specified areas of cities (S 1310, HR 3824) remained at the hearing stage in 1981.

To the distress of the proposal's chief sponsors, Reps. Jack F. Kemp, R-N.Y., and Robert Garcia, D-N.Y., and Sens. Rudy Boschwitz, R-Minn., and John H. Chafee, R-R.I., the administration had not taken a position on the legislation.

The bills called for establishing 10 to 25 "enterprise zones" in decaying urban areas. Tax incentives would include eliminating the capital gains tax on investment within a zone and excluding from taxation half of all income earned by zone enterprises.

HUD Authorization. Congress made substantial cuts in housing programs in fiscal 1982 authorizations for the Department of Housing and Urban Development (HUD) that were included in the budget reconciliation bill (HR 3982).

The authorization for additional subsidized housing units in 1982 was cut from 260,000 proposed by the outgoing Carter administration to 153,000.

In the community development area, Congress went along with the administration's request to ease federal controls over Community Development Block Grants, which cities and counties used for a variety of urban aid projects.

Although the administration wanted to end the popular Urban Development Action Grants program (UDAG), Congress refused to comply and authorized $500 million for the program.

On Dec. 10 Congress completed final action on a $60.38 billion fiscal 1982 appropriations bill for HUD and several independent agencies that provided funding for about 142,321 additional housing units.

Labor/Retirement

CETA Jobs. Congress finished off the remnants of the public service jobs program authorized by the Comprehensive Employment and Training Act (CETA).

In their heyday, the CETA jobs programs had em-

ployed more than 700,000 people. But the programs fell from their 1978 peak to about 300,000 at the beginning of 1981, in part because of heavy congressional criticism of the programs' alleged waste.

The budget reconciliation bill (HR 3982) eliminated funding for the jobs programs in fiscal 1982. It provided continued funding for CETA job training programs but at reduced levels.

Railroad Retirement. Faced with impending bankruptcy, the railroad retirement system was kept afloat with a compromise funding plan approved by Congress as part of budget reconciliation (HR 3982) and the Economic Recovery Tax Act (HR 4242).

The package, put together after lengthy negotiations between rail labor and management, called for both benefit cuts and increased railroad retirement taxes to keep the system from going broke as early as April 1982. The measure ended several years of dispute between the rail industry and the federal government over the financial problems of the system, which is subsidized by the Treasury.

The new provisions were expected to keep the retirement program, which pays benefits to 1 million retirees, their dependents and survivors, solvent for the next 10 years. Net budget savings from the legislation were estimated at $620 million for fiscal 1982-84.

Social Security. As it had done in the past, Congress put off the politically sensitive task of overhauling the financially troubled Social Security system.

This time, a highly charged partisan atmosphere hampered all substantive action. Democrats, burned by Republicans on tax and budget cuts, seized on the issue to illustrate their claims that the administration was attempting to balance the budget on the backs of the needy. Congressional Republicans, unnerved by the public furor that greeted Social Security cuts proposed by President Reagan on May 12, were reluctant to go out on a limb alone.

Instead, Congress agreed to a stopgap measure (HR 4331) that would keep the system's largest trust fund, the Old-Age and Survivors' Insurance (OASI), from going broke in the fall of 1982. HR 4331 allowed OASI to borrow money from the healthier Hospital Insurance and Disability Insurance trust funds — but only through the end of 1982, forcing Congress to take another look at the troubled system sometime in 1982.

Meanwhile, President Reagan withdrew his spring proposals Sept. 24 when he called for the formation of a bipartisan commission to come up with recommendations for solving Social Security's funding problems. He proposed that the panel not report until 1983, effectively putting off any further debate until after the 1982 elections. However, House and Senate conferees expressed hope that the one-year interfund borrowing provision in HR 4331 would force an earlier reporting date for the panel.

HR 4331 also included provisions to restore the $122 minimum monthly Social Security benefit for all current recipients. Congress had eliminated the benefit earlier in the year as part of budget reconciliation (HR 3982), but retreated after adverse public reaction.

Trade Adjustment Assistance. The trade adjustment assistance program — often criticized as a social program gone awry — was substantially cut back by Congress as part of the budget reconciliation bill (HR 3982).

The measure pared $2.6 billion from the program for fiscal 1982-84 by tightening eligibility requirements and by requiring claimants to exhaust all unemployment compensation benefits before collecting trade adjustment assistance. The program was designed to help those who lose their jobs as a result of competition from imports.

Cited as proof of the program's inefficiency was a 1980 General Accounting Office (GAO) study that found the payments were sometimes a disincentive for claimants to look for work and, in other cases, were often received in a lump sum after the claimant had found another job.

Unemployment Compensation. Congress rejected a controversial Reagan administration proposal that those currently receiving unemployment compensation be required to accept minimum-wage jobs after 13 weeks of benefits.

But it did include in the budget reconciliation bill (HR 3982) provisions to cut the federal-state program more than $3.1 billion for fiscal 1982-84. Congress eliminated the nationwide extended benefit program and benefits for those who voluntarily quit military service. It also tightened requirements governing federal loans to states that did not have sufficient unemployment tax revenues to cover benefit payments.

Law Enforcement/Judiciary

Voting Rights. By an overwhelming 389-24 margin, the House passed a bill (HR 3112) Oct. 5 extending key enforcement sections of the 1965 Voting Rights Act. The Senate did not consider the measure in 1981, but the Judiciary Committee's Constitution Subcommittee was expected to begin hearings on the current law in January 1982.

Final House action on HR 3112 came after 9½ hours of debate during which supporters of the bill fended off several weakening amendments.

As approved by the House, HR 3112 would make permanent in 1984 a provision requiring states covered by the act to get Justice Department approval for any election law changes. The bill also included a new "bail-out" section to allow covered states to get out from under the act if they meet certain conditions.

Busing. After breaking a three-month filibuster, the Senate Sept. 16 adopted an amendment to a Justice Department authorization bill (S 951) sharply restricting the authority of federal courts to order school busing for racial balance. The bill returned to the floor in December, but remained stalled at adjournment, with Sen. Lowell P. Weicker Jr., R-Conn., threatening to employ additional delaying tactics to block its passage.

Under the amendment sponsored by J. Bennett Johnston, D-La., federal judges could order students bused only to the nearest school. The attorney general could file a lawsuit on behalf of students who believed they had been bused in violation of this standard, thus opening the way for overturning existing busing orders.

Two other anti-busing bills were pending in the Senate Judiciary Committee. One (S 1760) would prohibit the courts from ordering busing and would allow existing busing orders to be vacated unless a judge made specified findings to support the order. The second bill (S 1647) would prevent federal courts from ordering busing, trans-

ferring teachers or closing schools to achieve racial balance. Any existing busing order would be vacated upon the request of any state or local educational agency affected by the order.

No busing legislation moved in the House. However, a Judiciary Committee subcommittee held extensive hearings on the school desegregation issue, largely in an effort to derail a petition by Ronald M. Mottl, D-Ohio, to discharge the committee from considering a proposed anti-busing amendment to the Constitution.

O'Connor Nomination. By a 99-0 vote, the Senate Sept. 15 confirmed President Reagan's nomination of Sandra Day O'Connor as the first woman justice of the Supreme Court. The 51-year-old Arizona appeals court judge, who became the 102nd justice, replaced Potter Stewart. Stewart retired July 3, 1981.

Legal Services Corporation. The Legal Services Corporation (LSC), slated for extinction by the Reagan administration, survived at least until March 31, 1982 through the stopgap continuing appropriations resolution (H J Res 370). The measure included $241 million for the corporation.

The money was appropriated even though legislation authorizing the LSC had not been cleared.

Despite the threat of a presidential veto, the House voted 245-137 on June 18 to reauthorize the corporation for two years at $241 million annually — the same amount that was put in H J Res 370.

The authorization (HR 3480) passed only after the adoption of several amendments restricting the activities of LSC lawyers. Among them was an amendment barring legal aid lawyers from bringing any "class action" lawsuits against state, local and federal governments.

A Senate bill (S 1533) reauthorizing the LSC for three years at $100 million annually was pending on the Senate calendar.

President Reagan wanted to abolish the seven-year-old LSC and let states provide legal aid to the poor through social services block grants.

Criminal Code. For the third time since 1977, the Senate Judiciary Committee approved a bill (S 1630) to revise and update federal criminal laws. Like its predecessors, S 1630 was a controversial measure, drawing sharp criticism from groups ranging from the conservative Moral Majority — which contended the bill was too lenient on many crimes — to the American Civil Liberties Union — which argued that the bill threatened civil liberties by including new offenses.

Two criminal code bills (HR 4711, HR 1647) were pending in a House Judiciary Committee subcommittee at the end of 1981. Under a committee agreement, one of the bills was expected to be sent to the full committee by Jan. 31, 1982.

Abortion. A Senate Judiciary Committee subcommittee approved a bill July 9 (S 158) that would allow states to ban abortion and would prohibit federal courts from striking down any new state abortion law. It was the first anti-abortion measure to come out of a subcommittee since the 1973 Supreme Court decision that legalized abortion.

S 158 was not considered by the full committee, however. The panel was expected to consider the measure early in 1982 along with a proposed constitutional amendment

that would give Congress and the states joint authority to regulate abortion (S J Res 110). The amendment proposal was approved by the Constitution Subcommittee on Dec. 16.

Immigration Reform. Immigration subcommittees of the Senate and House Judiciary committees held extensive hearings in the fall on the decades-old immigration laws. Both chambers passed a non-controversial bill (HR 4327) to streamline naturalization proceedings and to make operations of the Immigration and Naturalization Service more efficient.

No major reform legislation moved in either chamber, however.

In October, the Reagan administration began circulating its wide-ranging proposal to revise immigration laws. The most dramatic provisions in the proposal were those giving the president authority to declare an emergency that could last for up to a year, with broad powers to seal any harbor, port, airport or road, and to restrict Americans' travel to named countries. The administration's bill was introduced Oct. 22 in both the House and the Senate (HR 4832, S 1765).

Overseas Bribery. The Senate Nov. 23 passed a bill (S 708) to ease the law prohibiting U.S. companies from bribing foreign officials.

Passed by voice vote, S 708 would limit prosecutions to companies or corporate officials who "knowingly" falsify records or directly order that a bribe offer be made. Entitled the Business Accounting and Foreign Trade Simplification Act, the bill also would allow companies to keep less strict records than mandated by current law.

Under the Foreign Corrupt Practices Act of 1977, corporate officers could be liable if they merely have "reason to believe" that bribes are being made. The proponents of S 708 argued that existing law discouraged exports.

The measure still had to get through the House, where it faced considerable skepticism. The House Commerce Subcommittee on Finance held hearings on the measure, but no markups were contemplated.

Transportation

Amtrak, Conrail. The federally subsidized passenger and freight railroads evaded administration proposals that some critics predicted would have destroyed Amtrak and Conrail.

The Reagan administration sought to limit Amtrak's fiscal 1982 authorization to $613 million. The railroad said that would allow trains to run only in the Northeast Corridor between Washington and Boston.

Amtrak found support among members from outside the Northeast who were concerned that their states would lose service and from Northeastern members who feared Amtrak would lose congressional support if it served only their area.

Congress included $735 million for Amtrak in the reconciliation legislation (HR 3982), which Amtrak officials said would allow most national service to continue.

But lawmakers also required Amtrak to recover at least 50 percent of its operating costs from the fare box or other non-federal sources in fiscal 1982.

To prevent Conrail from continuing to be a drain on the federal budget, the administration wanted Congress to

give the transportation secretary flexibility to dispose of unprofitable Conrail lines.

But House members, particularly from the Northeast and Midwest, feared that breaking up Conrail for sale would mean the loss of vital service. A compromise was crafted to assure them that the secretary would make a good-faith effort to sell the railroad as one system.

The reconciliation legislation barred the secretary from selling Conrail except as a single system until June 1, 1984, if Conrail were determined to be profitable. If Conrail were deemed unprofitable, it could be sold piecemeal after Oct. 31, 1983.

Highways. The House and Senate approved a late-session compromise to resolve a dispute over the scope of highway legislation that had pitted the House against the administration and the Senate and forced some states to delay Interstate highway projects.

President Reagan and the Senate wanted major cost-cutting changes in the highway program, with multiyear authorizations to allow states to plan.

House members wanted to wait until 1982, when more would be known about available revenue. Also, some members wanted to tie the politically popular highway program to mass transit legislation in an effort to fight expected budget cuts in transit aid.

The differing points of view were incorporated into versions of HR 3210 passed by each chamber.

States were affected because even though Interstate construction funds had been authorized through fiscal 1990 by previous law, new legislation was needed to direct the transportation secretary to apportion fiscal 1983 funds. States normally obligate funds a year in advance.

HR 3210, as passed by the House, would reduce the Interstate construction authorization for fiscal 1983 to $3.1 billion, from the existing level of $3.2 billion.

The Senate version would authorize a total of about $28 billion for fiscal 1982-1990, a reduction of $800 million from existing authorizations. Both bills would tighten eligibility requirements for funds and would expand the Interstate repair program.

The compromise would provide limited legislation redefining eligibility for Interstate construction funds, expanding the Interstate repair program and directing the secretary to apportion funds only for fiscal 1983. Congress was expected to enact a comprehensive measure in 1982.

Bus Deregulation. A bill passed by the House (HR 3663) would significantly reduce 46 years' worth of government regulation of the intercity bus industry.

The bill, if enacted, would be the fourth measure passed by Congress in recent years to increase transportation competition and to give industries more flexibility. Trucking and railroad deregulation laws were passed in 1980 and an airline deregulation measure was approved in 1978.

The bus legislation, supported by the industry, would allow companies to establish new routes and drop unprofitable ones more easily. The Interstate Commerce Commission would be allowed to pre-empt state restrictions on bus firms under some conditions.

The bill would give companies some flexibility to raise and lower rates without government review. But it would limit their ability to set rates collectively by narrowing their exemption from antitrust laws.

Industry officials contended that regulations were un-

necessarily restrictive and inhibited operations and competition. The administration was expected to seek further deregulatory provisions in the Senate in 1982.

Airport Development. Congress granted a temporary funding reprieve to the federally supported airport development program that expired in 1980, but a stalemate continued over the scope and direction of the program.

The reconciliation bill authorized $450 million in fiscal 1981 for airport development, including new and expanded runways. The fiscal 1981 supplemental appropriations bill (HR 3512) provided for $450 million, but no money could be spent because the authorization had expired Sept. 30, 1980.

Separate legislation involved the direction of the program. A House committee bill (HR 2643) would maintain the existing structure of the program, contrary to a Senate committee plan (S 508) to "defederalize," or drop, the largest airports from the development funding program. S 508 was designed to remove the government as middleman and to allow the airports to negotiate with the airlines for development funds.

A similar dispute resulted in the lapse in the program the previous year.

Maritime Subsidies. Major changes in maritime policies were included in the reconciliation bill.

The legislation included Reagan's plan to eliminate new construction subsidies for fiscal 1982. The subsidies were designed to help make U.S. ships competitive with foreign vessels.

Another change allowed owners of U.S.-flag ships under limited circumstances to buy or to build foreign vessels in fiscal 1982 and 1983 and still be eligible for federal operating subsidies. Previously, ships had to be built in American yards to qualify for the subsidies, and an American operator accepting subsidies could own only U.S.-built ships.

Maritime Administration. Congress transferred the Maritime Administration from the Commerce Department to the Transportation Department, for the first time giving one department responsibility for all transportation programs.

President Johnson first proposed the transfer in 1966 along with the creation of the Transportation Department, but industry opposition scuttled the plan. Industry officials accepted the new proposal (HR 4074) when it was renewed by President Reagan because they believed maritime issues would receive strong support from Transportation Secretary Drew Lewis.

User Fees. Congress strongly resisted Reagan's plan for new and increased user fees to shift the burden of paying for special services from general taxpayers to those who benefit from the services.

None of his plans for aviation (HR 2930), inland waterways (S 810), port development (S 809) and Coast Guard user fees were enacted in 1981. However, congressional panels worked to modify some of them.

Many members of Congress generally agreed with the concept of user fees. But they and some special interests contended that Reagan's plans called for excessive charges and did not give enough weight to the benefits the general public received from the services, such as the economic boost an area received from a busy airport.

Welfare

AFDC. Congress made major cuts in Aid to Families with Dependent Children (AFDC) benefits to working parents.

Reflecting the Reagan administration's philosophy that welfare payments should go only to people who had no other sources of income, the reconciliation bill (HR 3982) sharply curtailed the "work incentives" in existing law, which allowed families with substantial earned income to receive AFDC benefits.

In most cases, AFDC mothers with no other income would not be severely hurt by HR 3982. However, some would be required to do community service work in exchange for their benefits. The bill allowed states to set up "workfare" programs, under which able-bodied adult recipients would have to work a certain number of hours each month.

Anti-Poverty Programs. Two of the last major bastions of the 1960s' War on Poverty, the Community Services Administration (CSA) and Head Start, met sharply different fates in the 97th Congress.

Long a target of conservatives for its funding of local anti-poverty groups, the CSA was abolished by the budget reconciliation bill (HR 3982). In its place the bill established a community services block grant, which would fund local anti-poverty agencies through the states.

The Head Start program for low-income preschool children did much better; in fact, it was one of the few anti-poverty programs to win an increase in funding. Although there was a brief mix-up, in which the program's authorization was inadvertently dropped from the House version of the reconciliation bill, Head Start received a fiscal 1982 authorization of $950 million, compared with $820 million in 1981.

Child Nutrition. Child nutrition programs suffered major cuts as Congress reduced subsidies for school meals and tightened eligibility for free and reduced-price meals.

The reconciliation bill limited federal payments to schools for all breakfasts and lunches served to students. The subsidy cuts led to cost increases in "full-price" meals served to middle-income students and a doubling of the cost of "reduced-price" meals (from 20 cents to 40 cents) to children from families with incomes between $11,000 and $15,600 a year. The bill also lowered the amount of family income students could have and still receive free or reduced-price meals.

Critics of the cuts warned that many school lunch programs might be forced to shut down altogether, as paying students quit buying the meals because of the higher prices.

Food Stamps. The food stamp program was scaled back substantially but not as much as the Reagan administration and congressional conservatives had sought.

The budget reconciliation bill tightened eligibility for food stamps, held down inflation-based adjustments in benefit levels and cut benefits to people during their first month on the program, among other changes. All told, the bill cut fiscal 1982 food stamp costs by $1.7 billion, in part by throwing an estimated 1.1 million people off the program.

However, the legislation did not include an administration-backed proposal to reduce benefits to families whose children got federally subsidized free lunches at school.

The conference agreement on the omnibus farm bill (S 884) authorized the program for fiscal 1982, at an $11.3 billion level. Conferees on the farm bill had to settle for a one-year extension of the food stamp provisions instead of the expected four-year measure because they were unable to resolve a dispute over the timing of cost-of-living increases in benefits.

Senate—Birth Dates, Occupations, Religions, Seniority

(Seniority rank is within the member's party.)

ALABAMA
Heflin (D)—June 19, 1921. Occupation: lawyer, judge. Religion: Methodist. Seniority: 37.

Denton (R)—July 15, 1924. Occupation: naval officer, educator, broadcasting executive. Religion: Roman Catholic. Seniority: 34.

ALASKA
Murkowski (R)—March 28, 1933. Occupation: banker. Religion: Roman Catholic. Seniority: 34.

Stevens (R)—Nov. 18, 1923. Occupation: lawyer. Religion: Episcopalian. Seniority: 5.

ARIZONA
DeConcini (D)—May 8, 1937. Occupation: lawyer. Religion: Roman Catholic. Seniority: 32.

Goldwater (R)—Jan. 1, 1909. Occupation: author, department store executive. Religion: Episcopalian. Seniority: 6.

ARKANSAS
Bumpers (D)—Aug. 12, 1925. Occupation: farmer, hardware company executive, lawyer, governor. Religion: Methodist. Seniority: 24.

Pryor (D)—Aug. 29, 1934. Occupation: newspaper publisher, lawyer, governor. Religion: Presbyterian. Seniority: 34.

CALIFORNIA
Cranston (D)—June 19, 1914. Occupation: author, journalist, real estate executive. Religion: Protestant. Seniority: 16.

Hayakawa (R)—July 18, 1906. Occupation: author, educator, psychologist. Religion: Methodist. Seniority: 18.

COLORADO
Hart (D)—Nov. 28, 1937. Occupation: author, educator, lawyer. Religion: Protestant. Seniority: 25.

Armstrong (R)—March 16, 1937. Occupation: broadcasting executive. Religion: Lutheran. Seniority: 27.

CONNECTICUT
Dodd (D)—May 27, 1944. Occupation: lawyer. Religion: Roman Catholic. Seniority: 39.

Weicker (R)—May 16, 1931. Occupation: lawyer. Religion: Episcopalian. Seniority: 10.

DELAWARE
Biden (D)—Nov. 20, 1942. Occupation: lawyer. Religion: Roman Catholic. Seniority: 21.

Roth (R)—July 22, 1921. Occupation: lawyer. Religion: Episcopalian. Seniority: 9.

FLORIDA
Chiles (D)—April 3, 1930. Occupation: lawyer. Religion: Presbyterian. Seniority: 18.

Hawkins (R)—June 24, 1927. Occupation: vitamin retailer, public official. Religion: Mormon. Seniority: 34.

GEORGIA
Nunn (D)—Sept. 8, 1938. Occupation: farmer, lawyer. Religion: Methodist. Seniority: 19.

Mattingly (R)—Jan. 7, 1931. Occupation: corporate executive. Religion: Methodist. Seniority: 34.

HAWAII
Inouye (D)—Sept. 7, 1924. Occupation: lawyer. Religion: Methodist. Seniority: 12.

Matsunaga (D)—Oct. 8, 1916. Occupation: lawyer. Religion: Episcopalian. Seniority: 29.

IDAHO
Symms (R)—April 23, 1938. Occupation: fruitgrower, fitness club owner. Religion: Methodist. Seniority: 31.

McClure (R)—Dec. 27, 1924. Occupation: lawyer. Religion: Methodist. Seniority: 12.

ILLINOIS
Dixon (D)—July 7, 1927. Occupation: lawyer. Religion: Presbyterian. Seniority: 40.

Percy (R)—Sept. 27, 1919. Occupation: banker, corporate executive. Religion: Christian Scientist. Seniority: 3.

INDIANA
Quayle (R)—Feb. 4, 1947. Occupation: newspaper publisher, lawyer. Religion: Presbyterian. Seniority: 33.

Lugar (R)—April 4, 1932. Occupation: farmer, educator, tool company executive. Religion: Methodist. Seniority: 20.

IOWA
Grassley (R)—Sept. 17, 1933. Occupation: farmer, educator. Religion: Baptist. Seniority: 32.

Jepsen (R)—Dec. 23, 1928. Occupation: insurance salesman, marketing executive. Religion: Lutheran. Seniority: 29.

KANSAS
Dole (R)—July 22, 1923. Occupation: lawyer. Religion: Methodist. Seniority: 7.

Kassebaum (R)—July 29, 1932. Occupation: broadcasting executive. Religion: Episcopalian. Seniority: 22.

KENTUCKY
Ford (D)—Sept. 8, 1924. Occupation: insurance executive, governor. Religion: Baptist. Seniority: 23.

Huddleston (D)—April 15, 1926. Occupation: broadcasting executive. Religion: Methodist. Seniority: 21.

LOUISIANA
Johnston (D)—June 10, 1932. Occupation: lawyer. Religion: Baptist. Seniority: 20.

Long (D)—Nov. 3, 1918. Occupation: lawyer. Religion: Methodist. Seniority: 2.

MAINE
Mitchell (D)—Aug. 20, 1933. Occupation: lawyer, judge. Religion: Roman Catholic. Seniority: 38.

Cohen (R)—Aug. 28, 1940. Occupation: author, educator, lawyer. Religion: Unitarian. Seniority: 27.

MARYLAND
Sarbanes (D)—Feb. 3, 1933. Occupation: lawyer. Religion: Greek Orthodox. Seniority: 31.

Mathias (R)—July 24, 1922. Occupation: lawyer. Religion: Episcopalian. Seniority: 7.

MASSACHUSETTS
Kennedy (D)—Feb. 22, 1932. Occupation: author, lawyer. Religion: Roman Catholic. Seniority: 11.

Tsongas (D)—Feb. 14, 1941. Occupation: author, lawyer. Religion: Greek Orthodox. Seniority: 35.

MICHIGAN
Levin (D)—June 28, 1934. Occupation: educator, lawyer. Religion: Jewish. Seniority: 37.

Riegle (D)—Feb. 4, 1938. Occupation: educator, pricing analyst. Methodist. Seniority: 28.

MINNESOTA
Boschwitz (R)—Nov. 7, 1930. Occupation: plywood company owner, lawyer. Religion: Jewish. Seniority: 24.

Durenberger (R)—Aug. 19, 1934. Occupation: adhesive manufacturing company executive, lawyer. Religion: Roman Catholic. Seniority: 21.

MISSISSIPPI

Stennis (D)—Aug. 3, 1901. Occupation: lawyer, judge. Religion: Presbyterian. Seniority: 1.

Cochran (R)—Dec. 7, 1937. Occupation: lawyer. Religion: Baptist. Seniority: 23.

MISSOURI

Eagleton (D)—Sept. 4, 1929. Occupation: lawyer. Religion: Roman Catholic. Seniority: 15.

Danforth (R)—Sept. 5, 1936. Occupation: clergyman, lawyer. Religion: Episcopalian. Seniority: 16.

MONTANA

Baucus (D)—Dec. 11, 1941. Occupation: lawyer. Religion: United Church of Christ. Seniority: 33.

Melcher (D)—Sept. 6, 1924. Occupation: veterinarian, cattle feedlot operator. Religion: Roman Catholic. Seniority: 30.

NEBRASKA

Exon (D)—Aug. 9, 1921. Occupation: office equipment retailer, governor. Religion: Episcopalian. Seniority: 36.

Zorinsky (D)—Nov. 11, 1928. Occupation: tobacco and candy wholesaler. Religion: Jewish. Seniority: 26.

NEVADA

Cannon (D)—Jan. 26, 1912. Occupation: lawyer. Religion: Mormon. Seniority: 8.

Laxalt (R)—Aug. 2, 1922. Occupation: hotel-casino owner, lawyer, governor. Religion: Roman Catholic. Seniority: 14.

NEW HAMPSHIRE

Rudman (R)—May 13, 1930. Occupation: lawyer. Religion: Jewish. Seniority: 34.

Humphrey (R)—Oct. 9, 1940. Occupation: airline pilot. Religion: Baptist. Seniority: 29.

NEW JERSEY

Bradley (D)—July 28, 1943. Occupation: author, professional basketball player. Religion: Protestant. Seniority: 37.

Williams (D)—Dec. 10, 1919. Occupation: lawyer. Religion: Presbyterian. Seniority: 7.

NEW MEXICO

Domenici (R)—May 7, 1932. Occupation: lawyer. Religion: Roman Catholic. Seniority: 13.

Schmitt (R)—July 3, 1935. Occupation: author, educator, astronaut, geologist. Religion: Methodist. Seniority: 20.

NEW YORK

Moynihan (D)—March 16, 1927. Occupation: author, educator. Religion: Roman Catholic. Seniority: 32.

D'Amato (R)—Aug. 1, 1937. Occupation: lawyer. Religion: Roman Catholic. Seniority: 34.

NORTH CAROLINA

East (R)—May 5, 1931. Occupation: author, educator, lawyer. Religion: Christian. Seniority: 34.

Helms (R)—Oct. 18, 1921. Occupation: journalist, association director, broadcasting executive. Religion: Baptist. Seniority: 13.

NORTH DAKOTA

Burdick (D)—June 19, 1908. Occupation: lawyer. Religion: United Church of Christ. Seniority: 9.

Andrews (R)—May 9, 1926. Occupation: farmer. Religion: Episcopalian. Seniority: 30.

OHIO

Glenn (D)—July 18, 1921. Occupation: astronaut, soft drink company executive. Religion: Presbyterian. Seniority: 22.

Metzenbaum (D)—June 4, 1917. Occupation: newspaper publisher, parking lot executive, lawyer. Religion: Jewish. Seniority: 27.

OKLAHOMA

Boren (D)—April 21, 1941. Occupation: educator, lawyer, governor. Religion: Methodist. Seniority: 36.

Nickles (R)—Dec. 6, 1948. Occupation: machine company executive. Religion: Roman Catholic. Seniority: 34.

OREGON

Hatfield (R)—July 12, 1922. Occupation: author, educator, governor. Religion: Baptist. Seniority: 4.

Packwood (R)—Sept. 11, 1932. Occupation: lawyer. Religion: Unitarian. Seniority: 8.

PENNSYLVANIA

Heinz (R)—Oct. 23, 1938. Occupation: educator, management consultant. Religion: Episcopalian. Seniority: 19.

Specter (R)—Feb. 12, 1930. Occupation: educator, lawyer. Religion: Jewish. Seniority: 34.

RHODE ISLAND

Pell (D)—Nov. 22, 1918. Occupation: investment executive. Religion: Episcopalian. Seniority: 10.

Chafee (R)—Oct. 22, 1922. Occupation: lawyer, governor. Religion: Episcopalian. Seniority: 17.

SOUTH CAROLINA

Hollings (D)—Jan. 1, 1922. Occupation: lawyer, governor. Religion: Lutheran. Seniority: 14.

Thurmond (R)—Dec. 5, 1902. Occupation: lawyer, judge, governor. Religion: Baptist. Seniority: 1.

SOUTH DAKOTA

Abdnor (R)—Feb. 23, 1923. Occupation: rancher. Religion: Methodist. Seniority: 31.

Pressler (R)—March 29, 1942. Occupation: lawyer. Religion: Roman Catholic. Seniority: 28.

TENNESSEE

Sasser (D)—Sept. 30, 1936. Occupation: lawyer. Religion: Methodist. Seniority: 32.

Baker (R)—Nov. 15, 1925. Occupation: lawyer. Religion: Presbyterian. Seniority: 3.

TEXAS

Bentsen (D)—Feb. 11, 1921. Occupation: finance holding institution executive, lawyer, judge. Religion: Presbyterian. Seniority: 17.

Tower (R)—Sept. 29, 1925. Occupation: educator. Religion: Methodist. Seniority: 2.

UTAH

Garn (R)—Oct. 12, 1932. Occupation: insurance executive. Religion: Mormon. Seniority: 15.

Hatch (R)—March 22, 1934. Occupation: lawyer. Religion: Mormon. Seniority: 20.

VERMONT

Leahy (D)—March 31, 1940. Occupation: lawyer. Religion: Roman Catholic. Seniority: 25.

Stafford (R)—Aug. 8, 1913. Occupation: lawyer, governor. Religion: Congregationalist. Seniority: 11.

VIRGINIA

Byrd (Ind)—Dec. 20, 1914. Occupation: newspaper editor and publisher, applegrower. Religion: Episcopalian. Seniority: 13.

Warner (R)—Feb. 18, 1927. Occupation: farmer, lawyer. Religion: Episcopalian. Seniority: 26.

WASHINGTON

Jackson (D)—May 31, 1912. Occupation: lawyer. Religion: Presbyterian. Seniority: 3.

Gorton (R)—Jan. 8, 1928. Occupation: lawyer. Religion: Episcopalian. Seniority: 34.

WEST VIRGINIA

Byrd (D)—Nov. 20, 1917. Occupation: lawyer. Religion: Baptist. Seniority: 6.

Randolph (D)—March 8, 1902. Occupation: journalist, educator, airline executive. Religion: Seventh Day Baptist. Seniority: 5.

WISCONSIN

Kasten (R)—June 19, 1942. Occupation: shoe manufacturing company executive. Religion: Episcopalian. Seniority: 33.

Proxmire (D)—Nov. 11, 1915. Occupation: author, journalist, printing company executive. Religion: Episcopalian. Seniority: 4.

WYOMING

Simpson (R)—Sept. 2, 1931. Occupation: lawyer. Religion: Episcopalian. Seniority: 25.

Wallop (R)—Feb. 27, 1933. Occupation: rancher, meatpacking plant executive. Religion: Episcopalian. Seniority: 20.

House—Birth Dates, Occupations, Religions, Seniority

(Seniority rank is within the member's party)

ALABAMA

1 Edwards (R)—Sept. 20, 1928. Occupation: lawyer. Religion: Presbyterian. Seniority: 7.

2 Dickinson (R)—June 5, 1925. Occupation: railroad executive, lawyer, judge. Religion: Methodist. Seniority: 7.

3 Nichols (D)—Oct. 16, 1918. Occupation: cotton gin company president, fertilizer manufacturing company executive. Religion: Methodist. Seniority: 19.

4 Bevill (D)—March 27, 1921. Occupation: lawyer. Religion: Baptist. Seniority: 19.

5 Flippo (D)—Aug. 15, 1937. Occupation: accountant. Religion: Church of Christ. Seniority: 44.

6 Smith (R)—Aug. 31, 1931. Occupation: insurance salesman. Religion: Baptist. Seniority: 37.

7 Shelby (D)—May 6, 1934. Occupation: lawyer. Religion: Presbyterian. Seniority: 48.

ALASKA

AL Young (R)—June 9, 1933. Occupation: educator, riverboat captain. Religion: Episcopalian. Seniority: 22.

ARIZONA

1 Rhodes (R)—Sept. 18, 1916. Occupation: insurance executive, lawyer. Religion: Methodist. Seniority: 1.

2 Udall (D)—June 15, 1922. Occupation: author, professional basketball player, lawyer. Religion: Mormon. Seniority: 10.

3 Stump (D)—April 4, 1927. Occupation: farmer. Religion: Seventh-Day Adventist. Seniority: 44.

4 Rudd (R)—July 15, 1920. Occupation: FBI agent, lawyer. Religion: Roman Catholic. Seniority: 28.

ARKANSAS

1 Alexander (D)—Jan. 16, 1934. Occupation: lawyer. Religion: Episcopalian. Seniority: 22.

2 Bethune (R)—Dec. 19, 1935. Occupation: FBI agent, lawyer. Religion: Methodist. Seniority: 33.

3 Hammerschmidt (R)—May 4, 1922. Occupation: lumber company executive. Religion: Presbyterian. Seniority: 11.

4 Anthony (D)—Feb. 21, 1938. Occupation: lawyer. Religion: Episcopalian. Seniority: 48.

CALIFORNIA

1 Chappie (R)—March 28, 1920. Occupation: rancher, public official. Religion: Roman Catholic. Seniority: 37.

2 Clausen (R)—April 27, 1923. Occupation: banker, air ambulance service president, insurance executive. Religion: Lutheran. Seniority: 6.

3 Matsui (D)—Sept. 17, 1941. Occupation: lawyer. Religion: Methodist. Seniority: 48.

4 Fazio (D)—Oct. 11, 1942. Occupation: journalist, public official. Religion: Episcopalian. Seniority: 48.

5 Burton, John (D)—Dec. 15, 1932. Occupation: lawyer. Religion: Roman Catholic. Seniority: 35.

6 Burton, Phillip (D)—June 1, 1926. Occupation: lawyer. Religion: Unitarian. Seniority: 15.

7 Miller (D)—May 17, 1945. Occupation: lawyer. Religion: Roman Catholic. Seniority: 38.

8 Dellums (D)—Nov. 24, 1935. Occupation: educator, social worker, consultant. Religion: Protestant. Seniority: 26.

9 Stark (D)—Nov. 11, 1931. Occupation: banker. Religion: Unitarian. Seniority: 30.

10 Edwards (D)—Jan. 6, 1915. Occupation: title company executive, lawyer. Religion: Unitarian. Seniority: 13.

11 Lantos (D)—Feb. 1, 1928. Occupation: educator, economist. Religion: Jewish. Seniority: 51.

12 McCloskey (R)—Sept. 29, 1927. Occupation: educator, lawyer. Religion: Presbyterian. Seniority: 12.

13 Mineta (D)—Nov. 12, 1931. Occupation: insurance executive. Religion: Methodist. Seniority: 38.

14 Shumway (R)—July 28, 1934. Occupation: lawyer. Religion: Mormon. Seniority: 33.

15 Coelho (D)—June 15, 1942. Occupation: congressional aide. Religion: Roman Catholic. Seniority: 48.

16 Panetta (D)—June 28, 1938. Occupation: lawyer. Religion: Roman Catholic. Seniority: 44.

17 Pashayan (R)—March 27, 1941. Occupation: tire retailer, lawyer. Religion: Protestant. Seniority: 33.

18 Thomas (R)—Dec. 6, 1941. Occupation: educator, public official. Religion: Baptist. Seniority: 33.

19 Lagomarsino (R)—Sept. 4, 1926. Occupation: lawyer. Religion: Roman Catholic. Seniority: 23.

20 Goldwater (R)—July 15, 1938. Occupation: stockbroker. Religion: Episcopalian. Seniority: 15.

21 Fiedler (R)—April 22, 1937. Occupation: author, interior decorator, drugstore owner. Religion: Jewish. Seniority: 37.

22 Moorhead (R)—May 6, 1922. Occupation: lawyer. Religion: Presbyterian. Seniority: 21.

23 Beilenson (D)—Oct. 26, 1932. Occupation: lawyer. Religion: Jewish. Seniority: 44.

24 Waxman (D)—Sept. 12, 1939. Occupation: lawyer. Religion: Jewish. Seniority: 38.

25 Roybal (D)—Feb. 10, 1916. Occupation: educator, social worker. Religion: Roman Catholic. Seniority: 13.

26 Rousselot (R)—Nov. 1, 1927. Occupation: public relations executive, management consultant. Religion: Christian Scientist. Seniority: 17.

27 Dornan (R)—April 3, 1933. Occupation: journalist, commercial pilot, television producer and moderator. Religion: Roman Catholic. Seniority: 28.

28 Dixon (D)—Aug. 8, 1934. Occupation: public official, lawyer. Religion: Episcopalian. Seniority: 48.

29 Hawkins (D)—Aug. 31, 1907. Occupation: real estate salesman. Religion: Methodist. Seniority: 13.

30 Danielson (D)—Feb. 20, 1915. Occupation: FBI agent, lawyer. Religion: Protestant. Seniority: 26.

31 Dymally (D)—May 12, 1926. Occupation: author, educator, data processing executive. Religion: Episcopalian. Seniority: 51.

32 Anderson (D)—Feb. 21, 1913. Occupation: savings and loan executive. Religion: Episcopalian. Seniority: 22.

33 Grisham (R)—Jan. 10, 1923. Occupation: real estate salesman. Religion: Methodist. Seniority: 33.

34 Lungren (R)—Sept. 22, 1946. Occupation: lawyer. Religion: Roman Catholic. Seniority: 33.

35 Dreier (R)—July 5, 1952. Occupation: public relations executive. Religion: Christian Scientist. Seniority: 37.

36 Brown (D)—March 6, 1920. Occupation: management consultant. Religion: Methodist. Seniority: 28.

37 Lewis (R)—Oct. 21, 1934. Occupation: insurance executive, public official. Religion: Presbyterian. Seniority: 33.

38 Patterson (D)—Oct. 25, 1934. Occupation: lawyer. Religion: Congregationalist. Seniority: 38.

39 Dannemeyer (R)—Sept. 22, 1929. Occupation: lawyer. Religion: Lutheran. Seniority: 33.

40 Badham (R)—June 9, 1929. Occupation: hardware company executive. Religion: Lutheran. Seniority: 28.

41 Lowery (R)—May 2, 1947. Occupation: public relations excecutive. Religion: Roman Catholic. Seniority: 37.

42 Hunter (R)—May 31, 1948. Occupation: lawyer. Religion: Baptist. Seniority: 37.

43 Burgener (R)—Dec. 5, 1921. Occupation: real estate salesman. Religion: Mormon. Seniority: 21.

COLORADO

1 Schroeder (D)—July 30, 1940. Occupation: educator, lawyer. Religion: Congregationalist. Seniority: 30.

2 Wirth (D)—Sept. 22, 1939. Occupation: corporate executive. Religion: Episcopalian. Seniority: 38.

3 Kogovsek (D)—Aug. 19, 1941. Occupation: public official. Religion: Roman Catholic. Seniority: 48.

4 Brown (R)—Feb. 12, 1940. Occupation: meatpacking company executive, lawyer. Religion: United Church of Christ. Seniority: 37.

5 Kramer (R)—Feb. 19, 1942. Occupation: lawyer. Religion: Jewish. Seniority: 33.

CONNECTICUT

1 Vacant.

2 Gejdenson (D)—May 20, 1948. Occupation: dairyfarmer. Religion: Jewish. Seniority: 51.

3 DeNardis (R)—March 18, 1938. Occupation: educator. Religion: Roman Catholic. Seniority: 37.

4 McKinney (R)—Jan. 30, 1931. Occupation: tire retailer. Religion: Episcopalian. Seniority: 19.

5 Ratchford (D)—May 24, 1934. Occupation: lawyer. Religion: Unitarian. Seniority: 48.

6 Moffett (D)—Aug. 18, 1944. Occupation: educator, congressional aide. Religion: Roman Catholic. Seniority: 38.

DELAWARE

AL Evans (R)—Nov. 5, 1931. Occupation: mortgage broker, insurance executive, lawyer. Religion: Episcopalian. Seniority: 28.

FLORIDA

1 Hutto (D)—May 12, 1926. Occupation: educator, advertising executive. Religion: Baptist. Seniority: 48.

2 Fuqua (D)—Aug. 20, 1933. Occupation: farmer. Religion: Presbyterian. Seniority: 13.

3 Bennett (D)—Dec. 2, 1910. Occupation: author, lawyer. Religion: Disciples of Christ. Seniority: 3.

4 Chappell (D)—Feb. 3, 1922. Occupation: lawyer. Religion: Methodist. Seniority: 22.

5 McCollum (R)—July 12, 1944. Occupation: lawyer. Religion: Episcopalian. Seniority: 37.

6 Young (R)—Dec. 16, 1930. Occupation: insurance executive. Religion: Methodist. Seniority: 19.

7 Gibbons (D)—Jan. 20, 1920. Occupation: lawyer. Religion: Presbyterian. Seniority: 13.

8 Ireland (D)—Aug. 23, 1930. Occupation: banker. Religion: Episcopalian. Seniority: 44.

9 Nelson (D)—Sept. 29, 1942. Occupation: lawyer. Religion: Episcopalian. Seniority: 48.

10 Bafalis (R)—Sept. 28, 1929. Occupation: banker. Religion: First Christian Church. Seniority: 21.

11 Mica (D)—Feb. 4, 1944. Occupation: educator, congressional aide. Religion: Roman Catholic. Seniority: 48.

12 Shaw (R)—April 19, 1939. Occupation: nurseryman, lawyer, judge. Religion: Roman Catholic. Seniority: 37.

13 Lehman (D)—Oct. 5, 1913. Occupation: educator, automobile dealer. Religion: Jewish. Seniority: 30.

14 Pepper (D)—Sept. 8, 1900. Occupation: lawyer. Religion: Baptist. Seniority: 13.

15 Fascell (D)—March 9, 1917. Occupation: lawyer. Religion: Protestant. Seniority: 6.

GEORGIA

1 Ginn (D)—May 31, 1934. Occupation: educator, rural electric co-op executive, congressional aide. Religion: Baptist. Seniority: 30.

2 Hatcher (D)—July 1, 1939. Occupation: lawyer. Religion: Episcopalian. Seniority: 51.

3 Brinkley (D)—Dec. 22, 1930. Occupation: lawyer. Religion: Baptist. Seniority: 19.

4 Levitas (D)—Dec. 26, 1930. Occupation: lawyer. Religion: Jewish. Seniority: 38.

5 Fowler (D)—Oct. 6, 1940. Occupation: lawyer. Religion: Presbyterian. Seniority: 45.

6 Gingrich (R)—June 17, 1943. Occupation: educator. Religion: Baptist. Seniority: 33.

7 McDonald (D)—April 1, 1935. Occupation: physician. Religion: Independent Methodist. Seniority: 38.

8 Evans (D)—Nov. 10, 1941. Occupation: lawyer. Religion: Christian. Seniority: 44.

9 Jenkins (D)—Jan. 4, 1933. Occupation: lawyer. Religion: Baptist. Seniority: 44.

10 Barnard (D)—March 20, 1922. Occupation: banker. Religion: Baptist. Seniority: 44.

HAWAII

1 Heftel (D)—Sept. 30, 1924. Occupation: broadcasting executive. Religion: Mormon. Seniority: 44.

2 Akaka (D)—Sept. 11, 1924. Occupation: educator, public official. Religion: Congregationalist. Seniority: 44.

IDAHO

1 Craig (R)—July 20, 1945. Occupation: real estate salesman, cattle and grain farmer. Religion: Methodist. Seniority: 37.

2 Hansen (R)—Sept. 14, 1930. Occupation: educator, printer, insurance salesman. Religion: Mormon. Seniority: 24.

ILLINOIS

1 Washington (D)—April 15, 1922. Occupation: lawyer. Religion: African Methodist Episcopal Zion. Seniority: 51.

2 Savage (D)—Oct. 30, 1925. Occupation: journalist, newspaper publisher. Religion: Protestant. Seniority: 51.

3 Russo (D)—Jan. 23, 1944. Occupation: lawyer. Religion: Roman Catholic. Seniority: 38.

4 Derwinski (R)—Sept. 15, 1926. Occupation: savings and loan executive. Religion: Roman Catholic. Seniority: 3.

5 Fary (D)—April 11, 1911. Occupation: real estate salesman, tavern owner. Religion: Roman Catholic. Seniority: 39.

6 Hyde (R)—April 18, 1924. Occupation: lawyer. Religion: Roman Catholic. Seniority: 25.

7 Collins (D)—Sept. 24, 1931. Occupation: auditor, accountant. Religion: Baptist. Seniority: 32.

8 Rostenkowski (D)—Jan. 2, 1928. Occupation: insurance executive. Religion: Roman Catholic. Seniority: 8.

9 Yates (D)—Aug. 27, 1909. Occupation: lawyer. Religion: Jewish. Seniority: 16.

10 Porter (R)—June 1, 1935. Occupation: lawyer, public official. Religion: Presbyterian. Seniority: 35.

11 Annunzio (D)—Jan. 12, 1915. Occupation: educator, labor union executive. Religion: Roman Catholic. Seniority: 17.

12 Crane, Philip M. (R)—Nov. 3, 1930. Occupation: author, educator. Religion: Methodist. Seniority: 16.

13 McClory (R)—Jan. 31, 1908. Occupation: lawyer. Religion: Christian Scientist. Seniority: 5.

14 Erlenborn (R)—Feb. 8, 1927. Occupation: lawyer. Religion: Roman Catholic. Seniority: 7.

15 Corcoran (R)—May 23, 1939. Occupation: railroad executive, public official. Religion: Roman Catholic. Seniority: 28.

16 Martin (R)—Dec. 26, 1939. Occupation: educator, public official. Religion: Roman Catholic. Seniority: 37.

17 O'Brien (R)—June 17, 1917. Occupation: lawyer. Religion: Roman Catholic. Seniority: 21.

18 Michel (R)—March 2, 1923. Occupation: congressional aide. Religion: Apostolic Christian. Seniority: 2.

19 Railsback (R)—Jan. 22, 1932. Occupation: lawyer. Religion: United Church of Christ. Seniority: 11.

20 Findley (R)—June 23, 1921. Occupation: author, publisher. Religion: United Church of Christ. Seniority: 4.

21 Madigan (R)—Jan. 13, 1936. Occupation: automobile taxi and leasing company executive. Religion: Roman Catholic. Seniority: 21.

22 Crane, Daniel B. (R)—Jan. 10, 1936. Occupation: dentist. Religion: Methodist. Seniority: 33.

23 Price (D)—Jan. 1, 1905. Occupation: journalist. Religion: Roman Catholic. Seniority: 2.

24 Simon (D)—Nov. 29, 1928. Occupation: author, educator, newspaper editor and publisher. Religion: Lutheran. Seniority: 38.

INDIANA

1 Benjamin (D)—Aug. 6, 1935. Occupation: lawyer. Religion: Eastern Catholic. Seniority: 44.

2 Fithian (D)—Nov. 3, 1928. Occupation: farmer, educator. Religion: Methodist. Seniority: 38.

3 Hiler (R)—April 24, 1953. Occupation: foundry executive. Religion: Roman Catholic. Seniority: 37.

4 Coats (R)—May 16, 1943. Occupation: lawyer. Religion: Protestant. Seniority: 37.

5 Hillis (R)—March 6, 1926. Occupation: lawyer. Religion: Presbyterian. Seniority: 19.

6 Evans (D)—Aug. 17, 1946. Occupation: educator. Religion: Roman Catholic. Seniority: 38.

7 Myers (R)—Feb. 8, 1927. Occupation: farmer, banker. Religion: Episcopalian. Seniority: 11.

8 Deckard (R)—March 7, 1942. Occupation: radio newsman, broadcasting executive. Religion: Protestant. Seniority: 33.

9 Hamilton (D)—April 20, 1931. Occupation: lawyer. Religion: Methodist. Seniority: 17.

10 Sharp (D)—July 15, 1942. Occupation: educator, congressional aide. Religion: Methodist. Seniority: 38.

11 Jacobs (D)—Feb. 24, 1932. Occupation: lawyer. Religion: Roman Catholic. Seniority: 36.

IOWA

1 Leach (R)—Oct. 15, 1942. Occupation: propane gas marketer. Religion: Episcopalian. Seniority: 28.

2 Tauke (R)—Oct. 11, 1950. Occupation: lawyer. Religion: Roman Catholic. Seniority: 33.

3 Evans (R)—May 26, 1924. Occupation: farmer, engineer. Religion: Methodist. Seniority: 37.

4 Smith (D)—March 23, 1920. Occupation: farmer, lawyer. Religion: Methodist. Seniority: 8.

5 Harkin (D)—Nov. 19, 1939. Occupation: lawyer. Religion: Roman Catholic. Seniority: 38.

6 Bedell (D)—March 5, 1921. Occupation: fishing tackle manufacturer. Religion: Methodist. Seniority: 38.

KANSAS

1 Roberts (R)—April 20, 1936. Occupation: congressional aide. Religion: Methodist. Seniority: 37.

2 Jeffries (R)—June 1, 1925. Occupation: investment consultant. Religion: Presbyterian. Seniority: 33.

3 Winn (R)—Aug. 22, 1919. Occupation: homebuilder, real estate developer. Religion: Christian Church. Seniority: 11.

4 Glickman (D)—Nov. 24, 1944. Occupation: lawyer. Religion: Jewish. Seniority: 44.

5 Whittaker (R)—Sept. 18, 1939. Occupation: optometrist. Religion: Christian Church. Seniority: 33.

KENTUCKY

1 Hubbard (D)—July 7, 1937. Occupation: lawyer. Religion: Baptist. Seniority: 38.

2 Natcher (D)—Sept. 11, 1909. Occupation: lawyer. Religion: Baptist. Seniority: 5.

3 Mazzoli (D)—Nov. 2, 1932. Occupation: educator, lawyer. Religion: Roman Catholic. Seniority: 26.

4 Snyder (R)—Jan. 26, 1928. Occupation: farmer, real estate salesman, lawyer. Religion: Lutheran. Seniority: 10.

5 Rogers (R)—Dec. 31, 1937. Occupation: lawyer. Religion: Baptist. Seniority: 37.

6 Hopkins (R)—Oct. 25, 1933. Occupation: stockbroker. Religion: Methodist. Seniority: 33.

7 Perkins (D)—Oct. 15, 1912. Occupation: lawyer. Religion: Baptist. Seniority: 3.

LOUISIANA

1 Livingston (R)—April 30, 1943. Occupation: lawyer. Religion: Episcopalian. Seniority: 30.

2 Boggs (D)—March 13, 1916. Occupation: educator. Religion: Roman Catholic. Seniority: 31.

3 Tauzin (D)—June 14, 1943. Occupation: lawyer. Religion: Roman Catholic. Seniority: 49

4 Roemer (D)—Oct. 4, 1943. Occupation: farmer, banker, data processing executive. Religion: Methodist. Seniority: 51.

5 Huckaby (D)—July 19, 1941. Occupation: farmer, engineer, corporate executive. Religion: Methodist. Seniority: 44.

6 Moore (R)—Oct. 4, 1939. Occupation: lawyer. Religion: Episcopalian. Seniority: 26.

7 Breaux (D)—March 1, 1944. Occupation: lawyer. Religion: Roman Catholic. Seniority: 27.

8 Long (D)—May 4, 1923. Occupation: farmer, investment broker, lawyer. Religion: Baptist. Seniority: 29.

MAINE

1 Emery (R)—Sept. 1, 1948. Occupation: engineer, public official. Religion: Congregationalist. Seniority: 25.

2 Snowe (R)—Feb. 21, 1947. Occupation: concrete company executive, public official. Religion: Greek Orthodox. Seniority: 33.

MARYLAND

1 Dyson (D)—Nov. 15, 1948. Occupation: lumber company executive. Religion: Roman Catholic. Seniority: 51.

2 Long (D)—Dec. 11, 1908. Occupation: author, educator. Religion: Presbyterian. Seniority: 13.

3 Mikulski (D)—July 20, 1936. Occupation: educator, socialworker, public official. Religion: Roman Catholic. Seniority: 44.

4 Holt (R)—Sept. 17, 1920. Occupation: lawyer. Religion: Presbyterian. Seniority: 21.

5 Hoyer (D)—June 14, 1939. Occupation: lawyer. Religion: Baptist. Seniority: 52.

6 Byron (D)—July 27, 1932. Occupation: civic activist. Religion: Episcopalian. Seniority: 48.

7 Mitchell (D)—April 29, 1922. Occupation: educator. Religion: Episcopalian. Seniority: 26.

8 Barnes (D)—Sept. 3, 1943. Occupation: lawyer. Religion: Protestant. Seniority: 48.

MASSACHUSETTS

1 Conte (R)—Nov. 9, 1921. Occupation: lawyer. Religion: Roman Catholic. Seniority: 3.

2 Boland (D)—Oct. 1, 1911. Occupation: public official. Religion: Roman Catholic. Seniority: 4.

3 Early (D)—Jan. 31, 1933. Occupation: educator. Religion: Roman Catholic. Seniority: 38.

4 Frank (D)—March 31, 1940. Occupation: public official. Religion: Jewish. Seniority: 51.

5 Shannon (D)—April 4, 1952. Occupation: lawyer. Religion: Roman Catholic. Seniority: 48.

6 Mavroules (D)—Nov. 1, 1929. Occupation: personnel supervisor. Religion: Greek Orthodox. Seniority: 48.

7 Markey (D)—July 11, 1946. Occupation: lawyer. Religion: Roman Catholic. Seniority: 42.

8 O'Neill (D)—Dec. 9, 1912. Occupation: insurance salesman. Religion: Roman Catholic. Seniority: 4.

9 Moakley (D)—April 27, 1927. Occupation: lawyer. Religion: Roman Catholic. Seniority: 30.

10 Heckler (R)—June 21, 1931. Occupation: lawyer. Religion: Roman Catholic. Seniority: 11.

11 Donnelly (D)—March 2, 1947. Occupation: educator. Religion: Roman Catholic. Seniority: 48.

12 Studds (D)—May 12, 1937. Occupation: teacher. Religion: Episcopalian. Seniority: 30.

MICHIGAN

1 Conyers (D)—May 16, 1929. Occupation: lawyer. Religion: Baptist. Seniority: 17.

2 Pursell (R)—Dec. 19, 1932. Occupation: publisher, educator, real estate salesman, office equipment retailer. Religion: Baptist. Seniority: 28.

3 Wolpe (D)—Nov. 2, 1939. Occupation: author, educator. Religion: Jewish. Seniority: 48.

4 Siljander (R)—June 11, 1951. Occupation: restaurant executive. Religion: Nondenominational Christian. Seniority: 38.

5 Sawyer (R)—March 21, 1920. Occupation: lawyer. Religion: Episcopalian. Seniority: 28.

6 Dunn (R)—July 21, 1943. Occupation: homebuilder. Religion: Episcopalian. Seniority: 37.

7 Kildee (D)—Sept. 16, 1929. Occupation: educator. Religion: Roman Catholic. Seniority: 44.

8 Traxler (D)—July 21, 1931. Occupation: lawyer. Religion: Episcopalian. Seniority: 34.

9 Vander Jagt (R)—Aug. 26, 1931. Occupation: lawyer. Religion: Presbyterian. Seniority: 9.

10 Albosta (D)—Dec. 5, 1925. Occupation: farmer. Religion: Roman Catholic. Seniority: 48.

11 Davis (R)—July 31, 1932. Occupation: funeral director. Religion: Episcopalian. Seniority: 33.

12 Bonior (D)—June 6, 1945. Occupation: probation officer, public official. Religion: Roman Catholic. Seniority: 44.

13 Crockett (D)—Aug. 10, 1909. Occupation: lawyer, judge. Religion: Baptist. Seniority: 50.

14 Hertel (D)—Dec. 7, 1948. Occupation: lawyer. Religion: Roman Catholic. Seniority: 51.

15 Ford (D)—Aug. 6, 1927. Occupation: lawyer. Religion: United Church of Christ. Seniority: 17.

16 Dingell (D)—July 8, 1926. Occupation: lawyer. Religion: Roman Catholic. Seniority: 7.

17 Brodhead (D)—Sept. 12, 1941. Occupation: lawyer. Religion: Roman Catholic. Seniority: 38.

18 Blanchard (D)—Aug. 8, 1942. Occupation: lawyer. Religion: Unitarian. Seniority: 38.

19 Broomfield (R)—April 28, 1922. Occupation: insurance salesman, public official. Religion: Presbyterian. Seniority: 2.

MINNESOTA

1 Erdahl (R)—Feb. 27, 1931. Occupation: farmer. Religion: Lutheran. Seniority: 33.

2 Hagedorn (R)—Nov. 27, 1943. Occupation: farmer. Religion: Lutheran. Seniority: 25.

3 Frenzel (R)—July 31, 1928. Occupation: warehouse company executive. Religion: unspecified. Seniority: 19.

4 Vento (D)—Oct. 7, 1940. Occupation: teacher. Religion: Roman Catholic. Seniority: 44.

5 Sabo (D)—Feb. 28, 1938. Occupation: public official. Religion: Lutheran. Seniority: 48.

6 Weber (R)—July 24, 1952. Occupation: publisher. Religion: Roman Catholic. Seniority: 37.

7 Stangeland (R)—Feb. 8, 1930. Occupation: farmer. Religion: Lutheran. Seniority: 29.

8 Oberstar (D)—Sept. 10, 1934. Occupation: congressional aide. Religion: Roman Catholic. Seniority: 38.

MISSISSIPPI

1 Whitten (D)—April 18, 1910. Occupation: author, educator, lawyer. Religion: Presbyterian. Seniority: 1.

2 Bowen (D)—Oct. 21, 1932. Occupation: educator. Religion: Baptist. Seniority: 30.

3 Montgomery (D)—Aug. 5, 1920. Occupation: insurance executive. Religion: Episcopalian. Seniority: 19.

4 Dowdy (D)—July 27, 1943. Occupation: broadcasting executive, lawyer. Religion: Methodist. Seniority: 53.

5 Lott (R)—Oct. 9, 1941. Occupation: lawyer. Religion: Baptist. Seniority: 21.

MISSOURI

1 Clay (D)—April 30, 1931. Occupation: real estate salesman, insurance company executive. Religion: Roman Catholic. Seniority: 22.

2 Young (D)—Nov. 27, 1923. Occupation: pipefitter. Religion: Roman Catholic. Seniority: 44.

3 Gephardt (D)—Jan. 31, 1941. Occupation: lawyer. Religion: Baptist. Seniority: 44.

4 Skelton (D)—Dec. 20, 1931. Occupation: lawyer. Religion: Christian. Seniority: 44.

5 Bolling (D)—May 17, 1916. Occupation: author, educator. Religion: Episcopalian. Seniority: 3.

6 Coleman (R)—May 29, 1943. Occupation: lawyer. Religion: Protestant. Seniority: 27.

7 Taylor (R)—Feb. 10, 1928. Occupation: automobile dealer. Religion: Methodist. Seniority: 21.

8 Bailey (R)—July 31, 1940. Occupation: automobile dealer. Religion: Baptist. Seniority: 37.

9 Volkmer (D)—April 4, 1931. Occupation: lawyer. Religion: Roman Catholic. Seniority: 44.

10 Emerson (R)—Jan. 1, 1938. Occupation: corporate executive. Religion: Presbyterian. Seniority: 37.

MONTANA

1 Williams (D)—Oct. 30, 1937. Occupation: educator. Religion: Roman Catholic. Seniority: 48.

2 Marlenee (R)—Aug. 8, 1935. Occupation: rancher. Religion: Lutheran. Seniority: 28.

NEBRASKA

1 Bereuter (R)—Oct. 6, 1939. Occupation: educator. Religion: Lutheran. Seniority: 33.

2 Daub (R)—April 23, 1941. Occupation: feed company executive. Religion: Presbyterian. Seniority: 37.

3 Smith (R)—June 30, 1911. Occupation: farmer. Religion: Methodist. Seniority: 25.

NEVADA

AL Santini (D)—Aug. 13, 1937. Occupation: educator, lawyer, judge. Religion: Roman Catholic. Seniority: 38.

NEW HAMPSHIRE

1 D'Amours (D)—Oct. 14, 1937. Occupation: educator, lawyer. Religion: Roman Catholic. Seniority: 38.

2 Gregg (R)—Feb. 14, 1947. Occupation: lawyer. Religion: Protestant. Seniority: 37.

NEW JERSEY

1 Florio (D)—Aug. 29, 1937. Occupation: lawyer. Religion: Roman Catholic. Seniority: 38.

2 Hughes (D)—Oct. 17, 1932. Occupation: lawyer. Religion: Episcopalian. Seniority: 38.

3 Howard (D)—July 24, 1927. Occupation: educator. Religion: Roman Catholic. Seniority: 17.

4 Smith (R)—March 4, 1953. Occupation: sporting goods wholesaler. Religion: Roman Catholic. Seniority: 37.

5 Fenwick (R)—Feb. 25, 1910. Occupation: editor, public official. Religion: Protestant. Seniority: 25.

6 Forsythe (R)—Jan. 17, 1916. Occupation: dairyfarm manager, association executive. Religion: Society of Friends. Seniority: 18.

7 Roukema (R)—Sept. 19, 1929. Occupation: educator. Religion: Protestant. Seniority: 37.

8 Roe (D)—Feb. 28, 1924. Occupation: public official. Religion: Roman Catholic. Seniority: 25.

9 Hollenbeck (R)—Dec. 29, 1938. Occupation: lawyer. Religion: Roman Catholic. Seniority: 28.

10 Rodino (D)—June 7, 1909. Occupation: lawyer. Religion: Roman Catholic. Seniority: 3.

11 Minish (D)—Sept. 1, 1916. Occupation: labor union executive. Religion: Roman Catholic. Seniority: 13.

12 Rinaldo (R)—Sept. 1, 1931. Occupation: industrial relations consultant. Religion: Roman Catholic. Seniority: 21.

13 Courter (R)—Oct. 14, 1941. Occupation: lawyer. Religion: Methodist. Seniority: 33.

14 Guarini (D)—Aug. 20, 1924. Occupation: lawyer. Religion: Roman Catholic. Seniority: 48.

15 Dwyer (D)—Jan. 24, 1921. Occupation: insurance salesman. Religion: Roman Catholic. Seniority: 51.

NEW MEXICO

1 Lujan (R)—May 12, 1928. Occupation: insurance salesman. Religion: Roman Catholic. Seniority: 14.

2 Skeen. (R)—June 30, 1927. Occupation: rancher. Religion: Roman Catholic. Seniority: 37.

NEW YORK

1 Carney (R)—July 1, 1942. Occupation: air conditioning salesman, public official. Religion: Roman Catholic. Seniority: 33.

2 Downey (D)—Jan. 28, 1949. Occupation: personnel manager, public official. Religion: Methodist. Seniority: 38.

3 Carman (R)—Jan. 31, 1937. Occupation: lawyer. Religion: Episcopalian. Seniority: 37.

4 Lent (R)—March 23, 1931. Occupation: lawyer. Religion: Methodist. Seniority: 19.

5 McGrath (R)—March 27, 1942. Occupation: educator, public official. Religion: Roman Catholic. Seniority: 37.

6 LeBoutillier (R)—May 26, 1953. Occupation: author, lecturer. Religion: Episcopalian. Seniority: 37.

7 Addabbo (D)—March 17, 1925. Occupation: lawyer. Religion: Roman Catholic. Seniority: 9.

8 Rosenthal (D)—June 8, 1923. Occupation: lawyer. Religion: Jewish. Seniority: 12.

9 Ferraro (D)—Aug. 26, 1935. Occupation: lawyer. Religion: Roman Catholic. Seniority: 48.

10 Biaggi (D)—Oct. 26, 1917. Occupation: police detective, lawyer. Religion: Roman Catholic. Seniority: 22.

11 Scheuer (D)—Feb. 6, 1920. Occupation: lawyer. Religion: Jewish. Seniority: 36.

12 Chisholm (D)—Nov. 30, 1924. Occupation: author, educator, consultant. Religion: Methodist. Seniority: 22.

13 Solarz (D)—Sept. 12, 1940. Occupation: educator. Religion: Jewish. Seniority: 38.

14 Richmond (D)—Nov. 15, 1923. Occupation: manufacturing company executive. Religion: Jewish. Seniority: 38.

15 Zeferetti (D)—July 15, 1927. Occupation: corrections officer. Religion: Roman Catholic. Seniority: 38.

16 Schumer (D)—Nov. 23, 1950. Occupation: lawyer. Religion: Jewish. Seniority: 51.

17 Molinari (R)—Nov. 23, 1928. Occupation: lawyer. Religion: Roman Catholic. Seniority: 37.

18 Green (R)—Oct. 16, 1929. Occupation: lawyer. Religion: Jewish. Seniority: 31.

19 Rangel (D)—June 11, 1930. Occupation: lawyer. Religion: Roman Catholic. Seniority: 26.

20 Weiss (D)—Sept. 17, 1927. Occupation: lawyer. Religion: Jewish. Seniority: 44.

21 Garcia (D)—Jan. 9, 1933. Occupation: computer engineer. Religion: Protestant. Seniority: 46.

22 Bingham (D)—April 24, 1914. Occupation: journalist, lawyer. Religion: United Church of Christ. Seniority: 17.

23 Peyser (D)—Sept. 7, 1921. Occupation: insurance executive. Religion: Episcopalian. Seniority: 47.

24 Ottinger (D)—Jan. 27, 1929. Occupation: lawyer. Religion: Jewish. Seniority: 37.

25 Fish (R)—June 3, 1926. Occupation: lawyer. Religion: Episcopalian. Seniority: 14.

26 Gilman (R)—Dec. 6, 1922. Occupation: lawyer. Religion: Jewish. Seniority: 21.

27 McHugh (D)—Dec. 6, 1938. Occupation: lawyer. Religion: Roman Catholic. Seniority: 38.

28 Stratton (D)—Sept. 27, 1916. Occupation: broadcast journalist, educator, public official. Religion: Presbyterian. Seniority: 8.

29 Solomon (R)—Aug. 14, 1930. Occupation: insurance salesman. Religion: Presbyterian. Seniority: 33.

30 Martin (R) April 26, 1944. Occupation: lawyer. Religion: Roman Catholic. Seniority: 37.

31 Mitchell (R)—May 8, 1923. Occupation: optometrist. Religion: Methodist. Seniority: 21.

32 Wortley (R)—Dec. 8, 1926. Occupation: newspaper publisher. Religion: Roman Catholic. Seniority: 37.

33 Lee (R)—Aug. 18, 1933. Occupation: educator, public official. Religion: Protestant. Seniority: 33.

34 Horton (R)—Dec. 12, 1919. Occupation: lawyer. Religion: Presbyterian. Seniority: 5.

35 Conable (R)—Nov. 2, 1922. Occupation: lawyer. Religion: Methodist. Seniority: 7.

36 LaFalce (D)—Oct. 6, 1939. Occupation: lawyer. Religion: Roman Catholic. Seniority: 38.

37 Nowak (D)—Feb. 21, 1935. Occupation: lawyer. Religion: Roman Catholic. Seniority: 38.

38 Kemp (R)—July 13, 1935. Occupation: professional football player, broadcast journalist, association executive, public relations officer. Religion: Presbyterian. Seniority: 19.

39 Lundine (D)—Feb. 4, 1939. Occupation: lawyer. Religion: Protestant. Seniority: 40.

NORTH CAROLINA

1 Jones (D)—Aug. 19, 1913. Occupation: office supply company executive. Religion: Baptist. Seniority: 18.

2 Fountain (D)—April 23, 1913. Occupation: lawyer. Religion: Presbyterian. Seniority: 4.

3 Whitley (D)—Jan. 3, 1927. Occupation: congressional aide, lawyer. Religion: Baptist. Seniority: 44.

4 Andrews (D)—Sept. 2, 1925. Occupation: lawyer. Religion: Baptist. Seniority: 30.

5 Neal (D)—Nov. 7, 1934. Occupation: newspaper publisher, mortgage banker. Religion: Episcopalian. Seniority: 38.

6 Johnston (R)—March 3, 1936. Occupation: real estate holding company president, printing company executive, lawyer. Religion: Methodist. Seniority: 37.

7 Rose (D)—Aug. 10, 1939. Occupation: lawyer. Religion: Presbyterian. Seniority: 30.

8 Hefner (D)—April 11, 1930. Occupation: broadcasting executive. Religion: Baptist. Seniority: 38.

9 Martin (R)—Dec. 11, 1935. Occupation: educator. Religion: Presbyterian. Seniority: 21.

10 Broyhill (R)—Aug. 19, 1927. Occupation: furniture factory executive. Religion: Baptist. Seniority: 5.

11 Hendon (R)—Nov. 9, 1944. Occupation: funeral director, sugarbeet processing equipment supplier. Religion: Episcopalian. Seniority: 37.

NORTH DAKOTA

AL Dorgan (D)—May 14, 1942. Occupation: author, public official. Religion: Lutheran. Seniority: 51.

OHIO

1 Gradison (R)—Dec. 28, 1928. Occupation: investment broker. Religion: Jewish. Seniority: 25.

2 Luken (D)—July 9, 1925. Occupation: lawyer. Religion: Roman Catholic. Seniority: 43.

3 Hall (D)—Jan. 16, 1942. Occupation: real estate salesman. Religion: Presbyterian. Seniority: 48.

4 Oxley (R)—Feb. 11, 1944. Occupation: FBI agent, lawyer. Religion: Lutheran. Seniority: 39.

5 Latta (R)—March 5, 1920. Occupation: lawyer. Religion: Church of Christ. Seniority: 3.

6 McEwen (R)—Jan. 12, 1950. Occupation: real estate developer. Religion: Protestant. Seniority: 37.

7 Brown (R)—June 18, 1927. Occupation: newspaper editor and publisher, farm owner, broadcasting executive. Religion: Presbyterian. Seniority: 8.

8 Kindness (R)—Aug. 26, 1929. Occupation: lawyer. Religion: Presbyterian. Seniority: 25.

9 Weber (R)—July 26, 1931. Occupation: lawyer. Religion: Baptist. Seniority: 37.

10 Miller (R)—Nov. 1, 1917. Occupation: electrical engineer. Religion: Methodist. Seniority: 11.

11 Stanton (R)—Feb. 20, 1924. Occupation: automobile dealer, public official. Religion: Roman Catholic. Seniority: 7.

12 Shamansky (D)—April 18, 1927. Occupation: lawyer. Religion: Jewish. Seniority: 51.

13 Pease (D)—Sept. 26, 1931. Occupation: newspaper editor. Religion: Protestant. Seniority: 44.

14 Seiberling (D)—Sept. 8, 1918. Occupation: lawyer. Religion: Presbyterian. Seniority: 26.

15 Wylie (R)—Nov. 23, 1920. Occupation: lawyer. Religion: Methodist. Seniority: 11.

16 Regula (R)—Dec. 3, 1924. Occupation: lawyer. Religion: Episcopalian. Seniority: 21.

17 Ashbrook (R)—Sept. 21, 1928. Occupation: newspaper publisher, lawyer. Religion: Baptist. Seniority: 4.

18 Applegate (D)—March 27, 1928. Occupation: real estate salesman. Religion: Presbyterian. Seniority: 44.

19 Williams (R)—Aug. 23, 1942. Occupation: barber. Religion: Church of Christ. Seniority: 33.

20 Oakar (D)—March 5, 1940. Occupation: educator. Religion: Roman Catholic. Seniority: 44.

21 Stokes (D)—Feb. 23, 1925. Occupation: lawyer. Religion: African Methodist Episcopal Zion. Seniority: 22.

22 Eckart (D)—April 6, 1950. Occupation: lawyer. Religion: Roman Catholic. Seniority: 51.

23 Mottl (D)—Feb. 6, 1934. Occupation: lawyer. Religion: Roman Catholic. Seniority: 38.

OKLAHOMA

1 Jones (D)—May 5, 1939. Occupation: lawyer. Religion: Roman Catholic. Seniority: 30.

2 Synar (D)—Oct. 17, 1950. Occupation: rancher, real estate salesman, lawyer. Religion: Episcopalian. Seniority: 48.

3 Watkins (D)—Dec. 15, 1938. Occupation: real estate salesman, homebuilder. Religion: Presbyterian. Seniority: 44.

4 McCurdy (D)—March 30, 1950. Occupation: lawyer. Religion: Lutheran. Seniority: 51.

5 Edwards (R)—July 12, 1937. Occupation: author, journalist, lawyer. Religion: Episcopalian. Seniority: 28.

6 English (D)—Nov. 30, 1940. Occupation: petroleum landman. Religion: Methodist. Seniority: 38.

OREGON

1 AuCoin (D)—Oct. 21, 1942. Occupation: journalist, public relations executive, engineering firm administrator. Religion: Protestant. Seniority 38.

2 Smith (R)—Jan. 19, 1938. Occupation: newspaper publisher, pilot. Religion: Protestant. Seniority: 37.

3 Wyden (D)—May 3, 1949. Occupation: lawyer. Religion: Jewish. Seniority: 51.

4 Weaver (D)—Aug. 8, 1927. Occupation: homebuilder. Religion: Protestant. Seniority: 38.

PENNSYLVANIA

1 Foglietta (D)—Dec. 3, 1928. Occupation: lawyer. Religion: Roman Catholic. Seniority: 51.

2 Gray (D)—Aug. 20, 1941. Occupation: clergyman. Religion: Baptist. Seniority: 48.

3 Smith (D)—Jan. 24, 1920. Occupation: accountant. Religion: Roman Catholic. Seniority: 54.

4 Dougherty (R)—June 26, 1937. Occupation: educator. Religion: Roman Catholic. Seniority: 33.

5 Schulze (R)—Aug. 7, 1929. Occupation: household appliance retailer, public official. Religion: Presbyterian. Seniority: 25.

6 Yatron (D)—Oct. 16, 1927. Occupation: professional boxer, ice cream manufacturer. Religion: Greek Orthodox. Seniority: 22.

7 Edgar (D)—May 29, 1943. Occupation: clergyman. Religion: Methodist. Seniority: 38.

8 Coyne (R)—Nov. 17, 1946. Occupation: author, chemical company executive, consultant. Religion: Presbyterian. Seniority: 37.

9 Shuster (R)—Jan. 23, 1932. Occupation: farmer, corporate executive. Religion: United Church of Christ. Seniority: 21.

10 McDade (R)—Sept. 29, 1931. Occupation: lawyer. Religion: Roman Catholic. Seniority: 5.

11 Nelligan (R)—Feb. 14, 1929. Occupation: accountant. Religion: Roman Catholic. Seniority: 37.

12 Murtha (D)—June 17, 1932. Occupation: carwash operator. Religion: Roman Catholic. Seniority: 33.

13 Coughlin (R)—April 11, 1929. Occupation: lawyer. Religion: Episcopalian. Seniority: 14.

14 Coyne (D)—Aug. 24, 1936. Occupation: accountant. Religion: Roman Catholic. Seniority: 51.

15 Ritter (R)—Oct. 21, 1940. Occupation: educator, metallurgist, engineer. Religion: Unitarian. Seniority: 33.

16 Walker (R)—Dec. 23, 1942. Occupation: educator. Religion: Presbyterian. Seniority: 28.

17 Ertel (D)—Nov. 7, 1936. Occupation: lawyer. Religion: Lutheran. Seniority: 44.

18 Walgren (D)—Dec. 28, 1940. Occupation: lawyer. Religion: Roman Catholic. Seniority: 44.

19 Goodling (R)—Dec. 5, 1927. Occupation: educator. Religion: Methodist. Seniority: 25.

20 Gaydos (D)—July 3, 1926. Occupation: lawyer. Religion: Roman Catholic. Seniority: 20.

21 Bailey (D)—July 21, 1945. Occupation: lawyer. Religion: Presbyterian. Seniority: 48.

22 Murphy (D)—June 17, 1927. Occupation: lawyer. Religion: Roman Catholic. Seniority: 44.

23 Clinger (R)—April 4, 1929. Occupation: lawyer. Religion: Presbyterian. Seniority: 33.

24 Marks (R)—Feb. 12, 1927. Occupation: lawyer. Religion: Jewish. Seniority: 28.

25 Atkinson (R)—April 5, 1927. Occupation: insurance executive. Religion: Roman Catholic. Seniority: 40.

RHODE ISLAND

1 St Germain (D)—Jan. 9, 1928. Occupation: lawyer. Religion: Roman Catholic. Seniority: 9.

2 Schneider (R)—March 25, 1947. Occupation: environmental activist, television producer and moderator. Religion: Roman Catholic. Seniority: 37.

SOUTH CAROLINA

1 Hartnett (R)—Aug. 7, 1941. Occupation: real estate salesman. Religion: Roman Catholic. Seniority: 37.

2 Spence (R)—April 9, 1928. Occupation: lawyer. Religion: Lutheran. Seniority: 19.

3 Derrick (D)—Sept. 30, 1936. Occupation: lawyer. Religion: Episcopalian. Seniority: 38.

4 Campbell (R)—July 24, 1940. Occupation: farmer, real estate salesman, parking lot president, restaurant executive. Religion: Episcopalian. Seniority: 33.

5 Holland (D)—Nov. 24, 1934. Occupation: lawyer. Religion: Methodist. Seniority: 38.

6 Napier (R)—May 16, 1947. Occupation: lawyer. Religion: Presbyterian. Seniority: 37.

SOUTH DAKOTA

1 Daschle (D)—Dec. 9, 1947. Occupation: congressional aide, public official. Religion: Roman Catholic. Seniority: 48.

2 Roberts (R)—Jan. 30, 1935. Occupation: rancher. Religion: Methodist. Seniority: 37.

TENNESSEE

1 Quillen (R)—Jan. 11, 1916. Occupation: publisher, banker, real estate and insurance salesman. Religion: Methodist. Seniority: 5.

2 Duncan (R)—March 24, 1919. Occupation: lawyer. Religion: Presbyterian. Seniority: 7.

3 Bouquard (D)—Jan. 3, 1929. Occupation: broadcasting executive. Religion: Church of Christ. Seniority: 38.

4 Gore (D)—March 31, 1948. Occupation: journalist, homebuilder. Religion: Baptist. Seniority: 44.

5 Boner (D)—Feb. 14, 1945. Occupation: educator, banker, lawyer. Religion: Methodist. Seniority: 48.

6 Beard (R)—Aug. 21, 1939. Occupation: educator. Religion: Methodist. Seniority: 21.

7 Jones (D)—April 20, 1912. Occupation: agricultural agent and inspector. Religion: Presbyterian. Seniority: 23.

8 Ford (D)—May 20, 1945. Occupation: mortician. Religion: Baptist. Seniority: 38.

TEXAS

1 Hall (D)—Jan. 11, 1924. Occupation: lawyer. Religion: Church of Christ. Seniority: 41.

2 Wilson (D)—June 1, 1933. Occupation: lumberyard executive. Religion: Methodist. Seniority: 30

3 Collins (R)—April 29, 1916. Occupation: corporate executive. Religion: Baptist. Seniority: 13.

4 Hall (D)—May 3, 1923. Occupation: feed company executive, banker, lawyer, judge. Religion: Methodist. Seniority: 51.

5 Mattox (D)—Aug. 29, 1943. Occupation: lawyer. Religion: Baptist. Seniority: 44.

6 Gramm (D)—July 8, 1942. Occupation: author, educator, economist, consultant. Religion: Episcopalian. Seniority: 48.

7 Archer (R)—March 22, 1928. Occupation: feed company executive, lawyer. Religion: Roman Catholic. Seniority: 19.

8 Fields (R)—Feb. 3, 1952. Occupation: cemetery executive, lawyer. Religion: Baptist. Seniority: 37.

9 Brooks (D)—Dec. 18, 1922. Occupation: lawyer. Religion: Methodist. Seniority: 4.

10 Pickle (D)—Oct. 11, 1913. Occupation: public relations and advertising executive. Religion: Methodist. Seniority: 14.

11 Leath (D)—May 6, 1931. Occupation: banker. Religion: Presbyterian. Seniority: 48.

12 Wright (D)—Dec. 22, 1922. Occupation: advertising executive. Religion: Presbyterian. Seniority: 6.

13 Hightower (D)—Sept. 6, 1926. Occupation: lawyer. Religion: Baptist. Seniority: 38.

14 Patman (D)—March 26, 1927. Occupation: rancher, lawyer. Religion: Methodist. Seniority: 51.

15 de la Garza (D)—Sept. 22, 1927. Occupation: lawyer. Religion: Roman Catholic. Seniority: 17.

16 White (D)—April 29, 1923. Occupation: lawyer. Religion: Episcopalian. Seniority: 17.

17 Stenholm (D)—Oct. 26, 1938. Occupation: cottongrower. Religion: Lutheran. Seniority: 48.

18 Leland (D)—Nov. 27, 1944. Occupation: pharmacist. Religion: Roman Catholic. Seniority: 48.

19 Hance (D)—Nov. 14, 1942. Occupation: lawyer. Religion: Baptist. Seniority: 48.

20 Gonzalez (D)—May 3, 1916. Occupation: lawyer, public official. Religion: Roman Catholic. Seniority: 11.

21 Loeffler (R)—Aug. 1, 1946. Occupation: rancher, lawyer. Religion: Lutheran. Seniority: 33.

22 Paul (R)—Aug. 20, 1935. Occupation: physician. Religion: Episcopalian. Seniority: 32.

23 Kazen (D)—Jan. 17, 1919. Occupation: lawyer. Religion: Roman Catholic. Seniority: 19.

24 Frost (D)—Jan. 1, 1942. Occupation: lawyer. Religion: Jewish. Seniority: 48.

UTAH

1 Hansen (R)—Aug. 14, 1932. Occupation: insurance executive, land developer. Religion: Mormon. Seniority: 37.

2 Marriott (R)—Nov. 2, 1939. Occupation: pension consultant, insurance underwriter. Religion: Mormon. Seniority: 28.

VERMONT

AL Jeffords (R)—May 11, 1934. Occupation: lawyer. Religion: Congregationalist. Seniority: 25.

VIRGINIA

1 Trible (R)—Dec. 29, 1946. Occupation: lawyer. Religion: Episcopalian. Seniority: 28.

2 Whitehurst (R)—March 12, 1925. Occupation: educator, broadcast journalist. Religion: Methodist. Seniority: 14.

3 Bliley (R)—Jan. 28, 1932. Occupation: funeral director. Religion: Roman Catholic. Seniority: 37.

4 Daniel, Robert W. Jr. (R)—March 17, 1936. Occupation: farmer, educator, financial analyst. Religion: Episcopalian. Seniority: 21.

5 Daniel, Dan (D)—May 12, 1914. Occupation: textile company executive. Religion: Baptist. Seniority: 22.

6 Butler (R)—June 2, 1925. Occupation: lawyer. Religion: Episcopalian. Seniority: 20.

7 Robinson (R)—May 14, 1916. Occupation: applegrower, applepacking company executive. Religion: Quaker. Seniority: 19.

8 Parris (R)—Sept. 9, 1929. Occupation: automobile dealer, commercial pilot, banker, lawyer. Episcopalian. Seniority: 36.

9 Wampler (R)—April 21, 1926. Occupation: journalist, carpet retailer. Religion: Presbyterian. Seniority: 10.

10 Wolf (R)—Jan. 30, 1939. Occupation: lawyer. Religion: Presbyterian. Seniority: 37.

WASHINGTON

1 Pritchard (R)—May 5, 1925. Occupation: envelope manufacturer. Religion: Presbyterian. Seniority: 21.

2 Swift (D)—Sept. 12, 1935. Occupation: broadcasting executive. Religion: Unitarian. Seniority: 48.

3 Bonker (D)—March 7, 1937. Occupation: auditor. Religion: Presbyterian. Seniority: 38.

4 Morrison (R)—May 13, 1933. Occupation: fruitgrower, nurseryman. Religion: Methodist. Seniority: 37.

5 Foley (D)—March 6, 1929. Occupation: educator, lawyer. Religion: Roman Catholic. Seniority: 17.

6 Dicks (D)—Dec. 14, 1940. Occupation: congressional aide, lawyer. Religion: Lutheran. Seniority: 44.

7 Lowry (D)—March 8, 1939. Occupation: public official. Religion: Baptist. Seniority: 48.

WEST VIRGINIA

1 Mollohan (D)—Sept. 18, 1909. Occupation: insurance salesman, public official. Religion: Baptist. Seniority: 21.

2 Benedict (R)—March 21, 1935. Occupation: dairy farmer. Religion: Episcopalian. Seniority: 37.

3 Staton (R)—Feb. 11, 1940. Occupation: data processing executive. Religion: Methodist. Seniority: 37.

4 Rahall (D)—May 20, 1949. Occupation: broadcasting executive, travel agent. Religion: Presbyterian. Seniority: 44.

WISCONSIN

1 Aspin (D)—July 21, 1938. Occupation: educator. Religion: Episcopalian. Seniority: 26.

2 Kastenmeier (D)—Jan. 24, 1924. Occupation: lawyer. Religion: Unspecified. Seniority: 8.

3 Gunderson (R)—May 10, 1951. Occupation: public official. Religion: Lutheran. Seniority: 37.

4 Zablocki (D)—Nov. 18, 1912. Occupation: educator, musician. Religion: Roman Catholic. Seniority: 3.

5 Reuss (D)—Feb. 22, 1912. Occupation: author, nurseryman, banker, lawyer. Religion: Episcopalian. Seniority: 6.

6 Petri (R)—May 28, 1940. Occupation: lawyer, public official. Religion: Lutheran. Seniority: 34.

7 Obey (D)—Oct. 3, 1938. Occupation: real estate salesman. Religion: Roman Catholic. Seniority: 24.

8 Roth (R)—Oct. 10, 1938. Occupation: real estate salesman. Religion: Roman Catholic. Seniority. 33.

9 Sensenbrenner (R)—June 14, 1943. Occupation: lawyer. Religion: Episcopalian. Seniority: 33.

WYOMING

AL Cheney (R)—Jan. 30, 1941. Occupation: financial consultant. Religion: Methodist. Seniority: 33.

Seniority in the 97th Congress

Senate Seniority

Senate rank generally is determined according to the official date of the beginning of a member's service, which is Jan. 3 except in the case of new members sworn in after Congress is in session. For those appointed or elected to fill unexpired terms, the date of the appointment, certification or swearing-in determines the senator's rank.

When members are sworn in on the same day, custom decrees that those with prior political experience take precedence. Counted as political experience, in order of importance, is senatorial, House and gubernatorial service. Information on prior experience is given where applicable. The dates following senator's names refer to the beginning of their present service.

REPUBLICANS

1. Thurmond—Nov. 7, 1956[1]
2. Tower—June 15, 1961
3. Baker—Jan. 3, 1967
    Percy—Jan. 3, 1967
4. Hatfield—Jan. 10, 1967
5. Stevens—Dec. 24, 1968
6. Goldwater (ex-senator)—Jan. 3, 1969
7. Dole (ex-representative, four House terms—Jan. 3, 1969
    Mathias (ex-representative, four House terms)—Jan. 3, 1969
8. Packwood—Jan. 3, 1969
9. Roth—Jan. 1, 1971
10. Weicker—Jan. 3, 1971
11. Stafford—Sept. 16, 1971
12. McClure (ex-representative)—Jan. 3, 1973
13. Helms—Jan. 3, 1973
    Domenici—Jan. 3, 1973
14. Laxalt—Dec. 18, 1974
15. Garn—Dec. 21, 1974
16. Danforth—Dec. 27, 1976
17. Chafee—Dec. 29, 1976
18. Hayakawa—Jan. 2, 1977
19. Heinz (ex-representative)—Jan. 3, 1977
20. Hatch—Jan. 3, 1977
    Lugar—Jan. 3, 1977
    Schmitt—Jan. 3, 1977
    Wallop—Jan. 3, 1977
21. Durenberger—Nov. 8, 1978
22. Kassebaum—Dec. 23, 1978
23. Cochran—Dec. 27, 1978
24. Boschwitz—Dec. 30, 1978
25. Simpson—Jan. 1, 1979
26. Warner—Jan. 2, 1979
27. Armstrong (ex-representative, three House terms)—Jan. 3, 1979
    Cohen (ex-representative, three House terms)—Jan. 3, 1979
28. Pressler (ex-representative, two House terms)—Jan. 3, 1979
29. Jepsen—Jan. 3, 1979
    Humphrey—Jan. 3, 1979
30. Andrews (ex-representative, eight and one-half House terms)—Jan. 3, 1981
31. Abdnor (ex-representative, four House terms)—Jan. 3, 1981
    Symms (ex-representative, four House terms)—Jan. 3, 1981
32. Grassley (ex-representative, three House terms)—Jan. 3, 1981
33. Kasten (ex-representative, two House terms)—Jan. 3, 1981
    Quayle (ex-representative, two House terms)—Jan., 3, 1981
34. D'Amato—Jan. 3, 1981
    Denton—Jan. 3, 1981
    East—Jan. 3, 1981
    Gorton—Jan. 3, 1981

Hawkins—Jan. 3, 1981
Mattingly—Jan. 3, 1981
Murkowski—Jan. 3, 1981
Nickles—Jan. 3, 1981
Rudman—Jan. 3, 1981
Specter—Jan. 3, 1981

DEMOCRATS

1. Stennis—Nov. 5, 1947
2. Long—Dec. 31, 1948
3. Jackson—Jan. 3, 1953
4. Proxmire—Aug. 28, 1957
5. Randolph—Nov. 5, 1958
6. Byrd (W.Va.) (ex-representative, three House terms)—Jan. 3, 1959
7. Williams (ex-representative, one and one-half House terms)—Jan. 3, 1959
8. Cannon—Jan. 3, 1959
9. Burdick—Aug. 8, 1960
10. Pell—Jan. 3, 1961
11. Kennedy—Nov. 7, 1962
12. Inouye—Jan. 3, 1963
13. Byrd (Va.)—Nov. 12, 1965²
14. Hollings—Nov. 9, 1966
15. Eagleton—Dec. 28, 1968
16. Cranston—Jan. 3, 1969
17. Bentsen (ex-representative)—Jan. 3, 1971
18. Chiles—Jan. 3, 1971
19. Nunn—Nov. 8, 1972
20. Johnston—Nov. 14, 1972
21. Biden—Jan. 3, 1973
    Huddleston—Jan. 3, 1973
22. Glenn—Dec. 24, 1974
23. Ford—Dec. 28, 1974
24. Bumpers (ex governor)—Jan. 3, 1975
25. Hart—Jan. 3, 1975
    Leahy—Jan. 3, 1975
26. Zorinsky—Dec. 28, 1976
27. Metzenbaum—Dec. 29, 1976
28. Riegle—Dec. 30, 1976
29. Matsunaga (ex-representative, seven House terms)—Jan. 3, 1977
30. Melcher (ex-representative, three and one-half House terms)—Jan. 3, 1977
31. Sarbanes (ex-representative, three House terms)—Jan. 3, 1977
32. DeConcini—Jan. 3, 1977
    Moynihan—Jan. 3, 1977
    Sasser—Jan. 3, 1977
33. Baucus—Dec. 15, 1978
34. Pryor (ex-representative, three and one-half House terms; ex-governor)—Jan. 3, 1979
35. Tsongas (ex-representative, two House terms)—Jan. 3, 1979
36. Boren (ex-governor)—Jan. 3, 1979
    Exon (ex-governor)—Jan. 3, 1979
37. Bradley—Jan. 3, 1979
    Heflin—Jan. 3, 1979
    Levin—Jan. 3, 1979
38. Mitchell—May 8, 1980

39. Dodd (ex-representative)—Jan. 3, 1981
40. Dixon—Jan. 3, 1981

---

1 Thurmond began his Senate service Nov. 7, 1956, as a Democrat. He became a Republican Sept. 16, 1964. The Republican Conference allowed his seniority to count from his 1956 election to the Senate.

2 Although elected as an independent, Byrd caucuses with the Democrats and receives committee assignments from them.

House Seniority

House rank generally is determined according to the official date of the beginning of a member's service, which is Jan. 3 except in the case of members elected to fill vacancies, when the date of election determines rank.

When members enter the House on the same day, those with prior House experience take precedence, starting with those with the longest consecutive service. Experience as a senator or governor is disregarded. Information on prior experience is given where applicable. The dates following members' names refer to the beginning of their present service.

DEMOCRATS

1. Whitten (Miss.)—Nov. 4, 1941
2. Price (Ill.)—Jan. 3, 1945
3. Bennett (Fla.)—Jan. 3, 1949
   Bolling (Mo.)—Jan. 3, 1949
   Perkins (Ky.)—Jan. 3, 1949
   Rodino (N.J.)—Jan. 3, 1949
   Zablocki (Wis.)—Jan. 3, 1949
4. Boland (Mass.)—Jan. 3, 1953
   Brooks (Texas)—Jan. 3, 1953
   Fountain (N.C.)—Jan. 3, 1953
   O'Neill (Mass.)—Jan. 3, 1953
5. Natcher (Ky.)—Aug. 1, 1953
6. Fascell (Fla.)—Jan. 3, 1955
   Reuss (Wis.)—Jan. 3, 1955
   Wright (Texas)—Jan. 3, 1955
7. Dingell (Mich.)—Dec. 13, 1955u
8. Kastenmeier (Wis.)—Dec. 13, 1959
   Rostenkowski (Ill.)—Jan. 3, 1959
   Smith (Iowa)—Jan. 3, 1959
   Stratton (N.Y.)—Jan. 3, 1959
9. Addabbo (N.Y.)—Jan 3, 1961
   St Germain (R.I.)—Jan. 3, 1961
10. Udall (Ariz.)—May 2, 1961
11. Gonzalez (Texas)—Nov. 4, 1961
12. Rosenthal (N.Y.)—Feb. 20, 1962
13. Edwards (Calif.)—Jan. 3, 1963
    Fuqua (Fla.)—Jar 3, 1963
    Gibbons (Fla.)—Jan. 3, 1963
    Hawkins (Calif.—Jan. 3, 1963
    Long (Md.)—Jan. 3, 1963
    Minish (N.J.)—Jan. 3, 1963
    Pepper (Fla.)—Jan. 3, 1963

   Roybal (Calif.)—Jan. 3, 1963
14. Pickle (Texas)—Dec. 21, 1963
15. Burton, Phillip (Calif.)—Feb. 18, 1964
16. Yates (Ill.) (seven terms previously)—Jan. 3, 1965
17. Annunzio (Ill.)—Jan. 3, 1965
    Bingham (N.Y.)—Jan. 3, 1965
    Conyers (Mich.)—Jan. 3, 1965
    de la Garza (Texas)—Jan. 3, 1965
    Foley (Wash.)—Jan. 3, 1965
    Ford (Mich.)—Jan. 3, 1965
    Hamilton (Ind.)—Jan. 3, 1965
    Howard (N.J.)—Jan. 3, 1965
    White (Texas)—Jan. 3, 1965
18. Jones (N.C.)—Feb. 5, 1966
19. Bevill (Ala.)—Jan. 3, 1967
    Brinkley (Ga.)—Jan. 3, 1967
    Kazen (Texas)—Jan. 3, 1967
    Montgomery (Miss.)—Jan 3, 1967
    Nichols (Ala.)—Jan. 3, 1967
20. Gaydos (Pa.)—Nov. 5, 1968
21. Mollohan (W.Va.) (two terms previously)—Jan. 3, 1969
22. Alexander (Ark.)—Jan. 3, 1969
    Anderson (Calif.)—Jan. 3, 1969
    Biaggi (N.Y.)—Jan 3, 1969
    Chappell (Fla.)—Jan. 3, 1969
    Chisholm (N.Y.)—Jan. 3, 1969
    Clay (Mo.)—Jan. 3, 1969
    Daniel (Va.)—Jan. 3, 1969
    Stokes (Ohio)—Jan. 3, 1969
    Yatron (Pa.)—Jan. 3, 1969
23. Jones (Tenn.)—March 25, 1969
24. Obey (Wis.)—April 1, 1969
25. Roe (N.J.)—Nov. 4, 1969
26. Aspin (Wis.)—Jan. 3, 1971
    Danielson (Calif.)—Jan. 3, 1971
    Dellums (Calif.)—Jan. 3, 1971
    Mazzoli (Ky.)—Jan. 3, 1971
    Mitchell (Md.)—Jan. 3, 1971
    Rangel (N.Y.)—Jan. 3, 1971
    Seiberling (Ohio)—Jan. 3, 1971
27. Breaux (La.)—Sept. 30, 1972
28. Brown (Calif.) (four terms previously)—Jan. 3, 1973
29. Long (La.) (one term previously)—Jan. 3, 1973
30. Andrews (N.C.)—Jan. 3, 1973
    Bowen (Miss.)—Jan. 3, 1973
    Ginn (Ga.)—Jan. 3, 1973
    Jones (Okla.)—Jan. 3, 1973
    Lehman (Fla.)—Jan. 3, 1973
    Moakley (Mass.)—Jan. 3, 1973
    Rose (N.C.)—Jan. 3, 1973
    Schroeder (Colo.)—Jan. 3, 1973
    Stark (Calif.)—Jan. 3, 1973
    Studds (Mass.)—Jan. 3, 1973
    Wilson (Texas)—Jan. 3, 1973
31. Boggs (La.)—March 20, 1973
32. Collins (Ill.)—June 5, 1973
33. Murtha (Pa.)—Feb. 5, 1974
34. Traxler (Mich.)—April 16, 1974
35. Burton, John L. (Calif.)—June 4, 1974
36. Jacobs (Ind.) (four terms previously)—Jan. 3, 1975

Scheuer (N.Y.) (four terms previously)—Jan. 3, 1975
37. Ottinger (N.Y.) (three terms previously)—Jan. 3, 1975
38. AuCoin (Ore.)—Jan. 3, 1975
Bedell (Iowa)—Jan. 3, 1975
Blanchard (Mich.)—Jan. 3, 1975
Bonker (Wash.)—Jan. 3, 1975
Bouquard (Tenn.)—Jan. 3, 1975
Brodhead (Mich.)—Jan. 3, 1975
D'Amours (N.H.)—Jan. 3, 1975
Derrick (S.C.)—Jan. 3, 1975
Downey (N.Y.)—Jan. 3, 1975
Early (Mass.)—Jan. 3, 1975
Edgar (Pa.)—Jan. 3, 1975
English (Okla.)—Jan. 3, 1975
Evans (Ind.)—Jan. 3, 1975
Fithian (Ind.)—Jan. 3, 1975
Florio (N.J.)—Jan. 3, 1975
Ford (Tenn.)—Jan. 3, 1975
Harkin (Iowa)—Jan. 3, 1975
Hefner (N.C.)—Jan. 3, 1975
Hightower (Texas)—Jan. 3, 1975
Holland (S.C.)—Jan. 3, 1975
Hubbard (Ky.)—Jan. 3, 1975
Hughes (N.J.)—Jan. 3, 1975
LaFalce (N.Y.)—Jan. 3, 1975
Levitas (Ga.)—Jan. 3, 1975
McDonald (Ga.)—Jan. 3, 1975
McHugh (N.Y.)—Jan. 3, 1975
Miller (Calif.)—Jan. 3, 1975
Mineta (Calif.)—Jan. 3, 1975
Moffett (Conn.)—Jan. 3, 1975
Mottl (Ohio)—Jan. 3, 1975
Neal (N.C.)—Jan. 3, 1975
Nowak (N.Y.)—Jan. 3, 1975
Oberstar (Minn.)—Jan. 3, 1975
Patterson (Calif.)—Jan. 3, 1975
Richmond (N.Y.)—Jan. 3, 1975
Russo (Ill.)—Jan. 3, 1975
Santini (Nev.)—Jan. 3, 1975
Sharp (Ind.)—Jan. 3, 1975
Simon (Ill.)—Jan. 3, 1975
Solarz (N.Y.)—Jan. 3, 1975
Waxman (Calif.)—Jan. 3, 1975
Weaver (Ore.)—Jan. 3, 1975
Wirth (Colo.)—Jan. 3, 1975
Zeferetti (N.Y.)—Jan. 3, 1975
39. Fary (Ill.)—July 15, 1975
40. Lundine (N.Y.)—March 8, 1976
41. Hall, Sam B. Jr. (Texas)—June 19, 1976
42. Markey (Mass.)—Nov. 2, 1976
43. Luken (Ohio) (one term previously)—Jan. 3, 1977
44. Akaka (Hawaii)—Jan. 3, 1977
Applegate (Ohio)—Jan. 3, 1977
Barnard (Ga.)—Jan. 3, 1977
Beilenson (Calif.)—Jan. 3, 1977
Benjamin (Ind.)—Jan. 3, 1977
Bonior (Mich.)—Jan. 3, 1977
Dicks (Wash.)—Jan. 3, 1977
Ertel (Pa.)—Jan. 3, 1977
Evans (Ga.)—Jan. 3, 1977
Flippo (Ala.)—Jan. 3, 1977
Gephardt (Mo.)—Jan. 3, 1977
Glickman (Kan.)—Jan. 3, 1977

Gore (Tenn.)—Jan. 3, 1977
Heftel (Hawaii)—Jan. 3, 1977
Huckaby (La.)—Jan. 3, 1977
Ireland (Fla.)—Jan. 3, 1977
Jenkins (Ga.)—Jan. 3, 1977
Kildee (Mich.)—Jan. 3, 1977
Mattox (Texas)—Jan. 3, 1977
Mikulski (Md.)—Jan. 3, 1977
Murphy (Pa.)—Jan. 3, 1977
Oakar (Ohio)—Jan. 3, 1977
Panetta (Calif.)—Jan. 3, 1977
Pease (Ohio)—Jan. 3, 1977
Rahall (W.Va.)—Jan. 3, 1977
Skelton (Mo.)—Jan. 3, 1977
Stump (Ariz.)—Jan. 3, 1977
Vento (Minn.)—Jan. 3, 1977
Volkmer (Mo.)—Jan. 3, 1977
Walgren (Pa.)—Jan. 3, 1977
Watkins (Okla.)—Jan. 3, 1977
Weiss (N.Y.)—Jan. 3, 1977
Whitley (N.C.)—Jan. 3, 1977
Young (Mo.)—Jan. 3, 1977
45. Fowler (Ga.)—April 5, 1977
46. Garcia (N.Y.)—Feb. 14, 1978
47. Peyser (N.Y.) (three terms previously as a Republican)—Jan. 3, 1979
48. Albosta (Mich.)—Jan. 3, 1979
Anthony (Ark.)—Jan. 3, 1979
Bailey (Pa.)—Jan. 3, 1979
Barnes (Md.)—Jan. 3, 1979
Boner (Tenn.)—Jan. 3, 1979
Byron (Md.)—Jan. 3, 1979
Coelho (Calif.)—Jan. 3, 1979
Daschle (S.D.)—Jan. 3, 1979
Dixon (Calif.)—Jan. 3, 1979
Donnelley (Mass.)—Jan. 3, 1979
Fazio (Calif.)—Jan. 3, 1979
Ferraro (N.Y.)—Jan. 3, 1979
Frost (Texas)—Jan. 3, 1979
Gramm (Texas)—Jan. 3, 1979
Gray (Pa.)—Jan. 3, 1979
Guarini (N.J.)—Jan. 3, 1979
Hall (Ohio)—Jan. 3, 1979
Hance (Texas)—Jan. 3, 1979
Hutto (Fla.)—Jan. 3, 1979
Kogovsek (Colo.)—Jan. 3, 1979
Leath (Texas)—Jan. 3, 1979
Leland (Texas)—Jan. 3, 1979
Lowry (Wash.)—Jan. 3, 1979
Matsui (Calif.)—Jan. 3, 1979
Mavroules (Mass.)—Jan. 3, 1979
Mica (Fla.)—Jan. 3, 1979
Nelson (Fla.)—Jan. 3, 1979
Ratchford (Conn.)—Jan. 3, 1979
Sabo (Minn.)—Jan. 3, 1979
Shannon (Mass.)—Jan. 3, 1979
Shelby (Ala.)—Jan. 3, 1979
Stenholm (Texas)—Jan. 3, 1979
Swift (Wash.)—Jan. 3, 1979
Synar (Okla.)—Jan. 3, 1979
Williams (Mont.)—Jan. 3, 1979
Wolpe (Mich.)—Jan. 3, 1979
49. Tauzin (La.)—May 17, 1980
50. Crockett (Mich.)—Nov. 4, 1980
51. Coyne (Pa.)—Jan. 3, 1981
Dorgan (N.D.)—Jan. 3, 1981
Dwyer (N.J.)—Jan. 3, 1981

Dymally (Calif.)—Jan. 3, 1981
Dyson (Md.)—Jan. 3, 1981
Eckart (Ohio)—Jan. 3, 1981
Foglietta (Pa.)—Jan. 3, 1981
Frank (Mass.)—Jan. 3, 1981
Gejdenson (Conn.)—Jan. 3, 1981
Hall, Ralph M. (Texas)—Jan. 3, 1981
Hatcher (Ga.)—Jan. 3, 1981
Hertel (Mich.)—Jan. 3, 1981
Lantos (Calif.)—Jan. 3, 1981
McCurdy (Okla.)—Jan. 3, 1981
Patman (Texas)—Jan. 3, 1981
Roemer (La.)—Jan. 3, 1981
Savage (Ill.)—Jan. 3, 1981
Schumer (N.Y.)—Jan. 3, 1981
Shamansky (Ohio)—Jan. 3, 1981
Washington (Ill.)—Jan. 3, 1981
Wyden (Ore.)—Jan. 3, 1981
52. Hoyer (Md.)—May 19, 1981
53. Dowdy (Miss.)—July 7, 1981
54. Smith (Pa.)—July 21, 1981

REPUBLICANS

1. Rhodes (Ariz.)—Jan. 3, 1953
2. Broomfield (Mich.)—Jan. 3, 1957
Michel (Ill.)—Jan. 3, 1957
3. Conte (Mass.)—Jan. 3, 1959
Derwinski (Ill.)—Jan. 3, 1959
Latta (Ohio)—Jan. 3, 1959
4. Ashbrook (Ohio)—Jan. 3, 1961
Findley (Ill.)—Jan. 3, 1961
5. Broyhill (N.C.)—Jan. 3, 1963
Horton (N.Y.)—Jan. 3, 1963
McClory (Ill.)—Jan. 3, 1963
McDade (Pa.)—Jan. 3, 1963
Quillen (Tenn.)—Jan. 3, 1963
6. Clausen (Calif.)—Jan. 22, 1963
7. Conable (N.Y.)—Jan. 3, 1965
Dickinson (Ala.)—Jan. 3, 1965
Duncan (Tenn.)—Jan. 3, 1965
Edwards (Ala.)—Jan. 3, 1965
Erlenborn (Ill.)—Jan. 3, 1965
Stanton (Ohio)—Jan. 3, 1965
8. Brown (Ohio)—Nov. 2, 1965
9. Vander Jagt (Mich.)—Nov. 8, 1966
10. Snyder (Ky.) (one term previously)—Jan. 3, 1967
Wampler (Va.) (one term previously)—Jan. 3, 1967
11. Hammerschmidt (Ark.)—Jan. 3, 1967
Heckler (Mass.)—Jan. 3, 1967
Miller (Ohio)—Jan. 3, 1967
Myers (Ind.)—Jan. 3, 1967
Railsback (Ill.)—Jan. 3, 1967
Winn (Kan.)—Jan. 3, 1967
Wylie (Ohio)—Jan. 3, 1967
12. McCloskey (Calif.)—Dec. 12, 1967
13. Collins (Texas)—Aug. 24, 1968
14. Coughlin (Pa.)—Jan. 3, 1969
Fish (N.Y.)—Jan. 3, 1969
Lujan (N.M.)—Jan. 3, 1969
Whitehurst (Va.)—Jan. 3, 1969

15. Goldwater (Calif.)—April 29, 1969
16. Crane, Philip M. (Ill.)—Nov. 25, 1969
17. Rousselot (Calif.)—June 20, 1970
18. Forsythe (N.J.)—Nov. 3, 1970
19. Archer (Texas)—Jan. 3, 1971
   Frenzel (Minn.)—Jan. 3, 1971
   Hillis (Ind.)—Jan. 3, 1971
   Kemp (N.Y.)—Jan. 3, 1971
   Lent (N.Y.)—Jan. 3, 1971
   McKinney (Conn.)—Jan. 3, 1971
   Robinson (Va.)—Jan. 3, 1971
   Spence (S.C.)—Jan. 3, 1971
   Young (Fla.)—Jan. 3, 1971
20. Butler (Va.)—Nov. 7, 1972
21. Bafalis (Fla.)—Jan. 3, 1973
   Beard (Tenn.)—Jan. 3, 1973
   Burgener (Calif.)—Jan. 3, 1973
   Daniel (Va.)—Jan. 3, 1973
   Gilman (N.Y.)—Jan. 3, 1973
   Holt (Md.)—Jan. 3, 1973
   Lott (Miss.)—Jan. 3, 1973
   Madigan (Ill.)—Jan. 3, 1973
   Martin (N.C.)—Jan. 3, 1973
   Mitchell (N.Y.)—Jan. 3, 1973
   Moorhead (Calif.)—Jan. 3, 1973
   O'Brien (Ill.)—Jan. 3, 1973
   Pritchard (Wash.)—Jan. 3, 1973
   Regula (Ohio)—Jan. 3, 1973
   Rinaldo (N.J.)—Jan. 3, 1973
   Shuster (Pa.)—Jan. 3, 1973
   Taylor (Mo.)—Jan. 3, 1973
22. Young (Alaska)—March 20, 1973
23. Lagomarsino (Calif.)—March 5, 1974
24. Hansen (Idaho) (two terms previously)—Jan. 3, 1975
25. Emery (Maine)—Jan. 3, 1975
   Fenwick (N.J.)—Jan. 3, 1975
   Goodling (Pa.)—Jan. 3, 1975
   Gradison (Ohio)—Jan. 3, 1975
   Hagedorn (Minn.)—Jan. 3, 1975
   Hyde (Ill.)—Jan. 3, 1975
   Jeffords (Vt.)—Jan. 3, 1975
   Kindness (Ohio)—Jan. 3, 1975
   Schulze (Pa.)—Jan. 3, 1975
   Smith (Neb.)—Jan. 3, 1975
26. Moore (La.)—Jan. 7, 1975
27. Coleman (Mo.)—Nov. 2, 1976
28. Badham (Calif.)—Jan. 3, 1977
   Corcoran (Ill.)—Jan. 3, 1977
   Dornan (Calif.)—Jan. 3, 1977
   Edwards (Okla.)—Jan. 3, 1977
   Evans (Del.)—Jan. 3, 1977
   Hollenbeck (N.J.)—Jan. 3, 1977

Leach (Iowa)—Jan. 3, 1977
Marlenee (Mont.)—Jan. 3, 1977
Marks (Pa.)—Jan. 3, 1977
Marriott (Utah)—Jan. 3, 1977
Pursell (Mich.)—Jan. 3, 1977
Rudd (Ariz.)—Jan. 3, 1977
Sawyer (Mich.)—Jan. 3, 1977
Trible (Va.)—Jan. 3, 1977
Walker (Pa.)—Jan. 3, 1977
29. Stangeland (Minn.)—Feb. 22, 1977
30. Livingston (La.)—Aug. 27, 1977
31. Green (N.Y.)—Feb. 14, 1978
32. Paul (Texas) (one-half of one term previously)—Jan. 3, 1979
33. Bereuter (Neb.)—Jan. 3, 1979
   Bethune (Ark.)—Jan. 3, 1979
   Campbell (S.C.)—Jan. 3, 1979
   Carney (N.Y.)—Jan. 3, 1979
   Cheney (Wyo.)—Jan. 3, 1979
   Clinger (Pa.)—Jan. 3, 1979
   Courter (N.J.)—Jan. 3, 1979
   Crane, Daniel B. (Ill.)—Jan. 3, 1979
   Dannemeyer (Calif.)—Jan. 3, 1979
   Davis (Mich.)—Jan. 3, 1979
   Deckard (Ind.)—Jan. 3, 1979
   Dougherty (Pa.)—Jan. 3, 1979
   Erdahl (Minn.)—Jan. 3, 1979
   Gingrich (Ga.)—Jan. 3, 1979
   Grisham (Calif.)—Jan. 3, 1979
   Hopkins (Ky.)—Jan. 3, 1979
   Jeffries (Kan.)—Jan. 3, 1979
   Kramer (Colo.)—Jan. 3, 1979
   Lee (N.Y.)—Jan. 3, 1979
   Lewis (Calif.)—Jan. 3, 1979
   Loeffler (Texas)—Jan. 3, 1979
   Lungren (Calif.)—Jan. 3, 1979
   Pashayan (Calif.)—Jan. 3, 1979
   Ritter (Pa.)—Jan. 3, 1979
   Roth (Wis.)—Jan. 3, 1979
   Sensenbrenner (Wis.)—Jan. 3, 1979
   Shumway (Calif.)—Jan. 3, 1979
   Snowe (Maine)—Jan. 3, 1979
   Solomon (N.Y.)—Jan. 3, 1979
   Tauke (Iowa)—Jan. 3, 1979
   Thomas (Calif.)—Jan. 3, 1979
   Whittaker (Kan.)—Jan. 3, 1979
   Williams (Ohio)—Jan. 3, 1979
34. Petri (Wis.)—April 3, 1979
35. Porter (Ill.)—Jan. 22, 1980
36. Parris (Va.) (one term previously)—Jan. 3, 1981
37. Bailey (Mo.)—Jan. 3, 1981
   Benedict (W.Va.)—Jan. 3, 1981

Bliley (Va.)—Jan. 3, 1981
Brown (Colo.)—Jan. 3, 1981
Carman (N.Y.)—Jan. 3, 1981
Chappie (Calif.)—Jan. 3, 1981
Coats (Ind.)—Jan. 3, 1981
Coyne (Pa.)—Jan. 3, 1981
Craig (Idaho)—Jan. 3, 1981
Daub (Neb.)—Jan. 3, 1981
DeNardis (Conn.)—Jan. 3, 1981
Dreier (Calif.)—Jan. 3, 1981
Dunn (Mich.)—Jan. 3, 1981
Emerson (Mo.)—Jan. 3, 1981
Evans (Iowa)—Jan. 3, 1981
Fiedler (Calif.)—Jan. 3, 1981
Fields (Texas)—Jan. 3, 1981
Gregg (N.H.)—Jan. 3, 1981
Gunderson (Wis.)—Jan. 3, 1981
Hansen (Utah)—Jan. 3, 1981
Hartnett (S.C.)—Jan. 3, 1981
Hendon (N.C.)—Jan. 3, 1981
Hiler (Ind.)—Jan. 3, 1981
Hunter (Calif.)—Jan. 3, 1981
Johnston (N.C.)—Jan. 3, 1981
LeBoutillier (N.Y.)—Jan. 3, 1981
Lowery (Calif.)—Jan. 3, 1981
Martin (N.Y.)—Jan. 3, 1981
Martin (Ill.)—Jan. 3, 1981
McCollum (Fla.)—Jan. 3, 1981
McEwen (Ohio)—Jan. 3, 1981
McGrath (N.Y.)—Jan. 3, 1981
Molinari (N.Y.)—Jan. 3, 1981
Morrison (Wash.)—Jan. 3, 1981
Napier (S.C.)—Jan. 3, 1981
Nelligan (Pa.)—Jan. 3, 1981
Roberts (S.D.)—Jan. 3, 1981
Roberts (Kan.)—Jan. 3, 1981
Rogers (Ky.)—Jan. 3, 1981
Roukema (N.J.)—Jan. 3, 1981
Schneider (R.I.)—Jan. 3, 1981
Shaw (Fla.)—Jan. 3, 1981
Skeen (N.M.)—Jan. 3, 1981
Smith (Ala.)—Jan. 3, 1981
Smith (N.J.)—Jan. 3, 1981
Smith (Ore.)—Jan. 3, 1981
Staton (W.Va.)—Jan. 3, 1981
Weber (Ohio)—Jan. 3, 1981
Weber (Minn.)—Jan. 3, 1981
Wolf (Va.)—Jan. 3, 1981
Wortley (N.Y.)—Jan. 3, 1981
38. Siljander (Mich.)—April 21, 1981
39. Oxley (Ohio)—June 25, 1981
40. Atkinson (Pa.)—Oct. 14, 1981[1]

---

1 Atkinson began his House service Jan. 3, 1979 as a Democrat. He became a Republican on Oct. 14, 1981. ■

Senate Committees, 97th Congress, First Session

(As of Sept. 28, 1981)

Agriculture, Nutrition, and Forestry

Agriculture in general, including farm credit and security, crop insurance, soil conservation and rural electrification; forestry in general; human nutrition, school nutrition programs, food stamp program, and matters relating to food, nutrition and hunger.

Phone: 224-2035

R 9 - D 8

Jesse Helms, R-N.C., chairman*

Robert Dole, Kan.	*Walter D. Huddleston, Ky.**
S. I. "Sam" Hayakawa, Calif.	*Patrick J. Leahy, Vt.*
	Edward Zorinsky, Neb.
Richard G. Lugar, Ind.	*John Melcher, Mont.*
Thad Cochran, Miss.	*David Pryor, Ark.*
Rudy Boschwitz, Minn.	*David L. Boren, Okla.*
Roger W. Jepsen, Iowa	*Alan J. Dixon, Ill.*
Paula Hawkins, Fla.	*Howell Heflin, Ala.*
Mark Andrews, N.D.	

Agricultural Credit and Rural Electrification

Hawkins - chairman

Jepsen	*Zorinksy*
Andrews	*Heflin*
	Boren

Agricultural Production, Marketing, and Stabilization of Prices

Cochran - chairman

Helms	*Huddleston*
Andrews	*Zorinsky*
Boschwitz	*Melcher*
Hawkins	*Dixon*
	Leahy

Agricultural Research and General Legislation

Lugar - chairman

Dole	*Boren*
Hayakawa	*Huddleston*
Boschwitz	*Pryor*
Andrews	*Heflin*

Foreign Agricultural Policy

Boschwitz - chairman

Lugar	*Dixon*
Cochran	*Pryor*
Dole	*Boren*
Jepsen	*Zorinsky*
Hawkins	

Forestry, Water Resources, and Environment

Hayakawa - chairman

Jepsen	*Melcher*

Nutrition

Dole - chairman

Hayakawa	*Leahy*
Lugar	*Melcher*
Hawkins	*Dixon*

Rural Development, Oversight, and Investigations

Andrews - chairman

Lugar	*Pryor*
Boschwitz	*Leahy*

Soil and Water Conservation

Jepsen - chairman

Cochran	*Heflin*
Hayakawa	*Huddleston*

* Chairman and ranking minority member are members ex officio *of all subcommittees of which they are not regular members.*

Appropriations

Appropriations of government revenues.

Phone: 224-3471

R 15 - D 14

Mark O. Hatfield, R-Ore., chairman*

Ted Stevens, Alaska	*William Proxmire, Wis.**
Lowell P. Weicker Jr., Conn.	*John C. Stennis, Miss.*
James A. McClure, Idaho	*Robert C. Byrd, W.Va.*

Paul Laxalt, Nev.
Jake Garn, Utah
Harrison "Jack" Schmitt, N.M.
Thad Cochran, Miss.
Mark Andrews, N.D.
James Abdnor, S.D.
Robert W. Kasten Jr., Wis.
Alfonse, D'Amato, N.Y.
Mack Mattingly, Ga.
Warren B. Rudman, N.H.
Arlen Specter, Pa.

Daniel K. Inouye, Hawaii
Ernest F. Hollings, S.C.
Thomas F. Eagleton, Mo.
Lawton Chiles, Fla.
J. Bennett Johnston, La.
Walter D. Huddleston, Ky.
Quentin N. Burdick, N.D.
Patrick J. Leahy, Vt.
Jim Sasser, Tenn.
Dennis DeConcini, Ariz.
Dale Bumpers, Ark.

Agriculture, Rural Development, and Related Agencies

Phone: 224-7240

Cochran - chairman

McClure	*Eagleton*
Andrews	*Stennis*
Abdnor	*Byrd*
Kasten	*Chiles*
Mattingly	*Burdick*
Specter	*Sasser*

Defense

Phone: 224-7255

Stevens - chairman

Weicker	*Stennis*
Garn	*Proxmire*
McClure	*Inouye*
Schmitt	*Hollings*
Andrews	*Eagleton*
Kasten	*Chiles*
D'Amato	*Johnston*
Rudman	*Huddleston*

District of Columbia

Phone: 224-7220

D'Amato - chairman

Weicker	*Leahy*
Specter	*Bumpers*

Energy and Water Development

Phone: 224-7260

Hatfield - chairman

McClure	*Johnston*
Garn	*Stennis*
Schmitt	*Byrd*

Cochran	*Hollings*
Abdnor	*Huddleston*
Kasten	*Burdick*
Mattingly	*Sasser*

Foreign Operations

Phone: 224-7274

Kasten - chairman

Hatfield	*Inouye*
D'Amato	*Johnston*
Rudman	*Leahy*
Specter	*DeConcini*

HUD—Independent Agencies

Phone: 224-7253

Garn - chairman

Weicker	*Huddleston*
Laxalt	*Stennis*
Schmitt	*Proxmire*
D'Amato	*Leahy*
Specter	*Sasser*

Interior, and Related Agencies

Phone: 224-7262

McClure - chairman

Stevens	*Byrd*
Laxalt	*Johnston*
Garn	*Huddleston*
Schmitt	*Leahy*
Cochran	*DeConcini*
Andrews	*Burdick*
Rudman	*Bumpers*

Labor, Health and Human Services, Education, and Related Agencies

Phone: 224-7283

Schmitt - chairman

Hatfield	*Proxmire*
Weicker	*Byrd*
Stevens	*Hollings*
Andrews	*Eagleton*
Abdnor	*Chiles*
Rudman	*Burdick*
Specter	*Inouye*

Legislative Branch

Phone: 224-7295

Mattingly - chairman

Stevens	*Bumpers*
Hatfield	*Hollings*

Military Construction

Phone: 224-7271

Laxalt - chairman

Garn	*Sasser*
Mattingly	*Inouye*

State, Justice, Commerce, the Judiciary, and Related Agencies

Phone: 224-7244

Weicker - chairman

Stevens	*Hollings*
Laxalt	*Inouye*
Cochran	*DeConcini*
Rudman	*Bumpers*

Transportation and Related Agencies

Phone: 224-0330

Andrews - chairman

Cochran	*Chiles*
Abdnor	*Stennis*
Kasten	*Byrd*
D'Amato	*Eagleton*

Treasury, Postal Service, and General Government

Phone: 224-2726

Abdnor - chairman

Laxalt	*DeConcini*
Mattingly	*Proxmire*

* Chairman and ranking minority member are members ex officio of all subcommittees of which they are not regular members.

Armed Services

Military affairs, Panama Canal and Canal Zone, strategic and critical materials; aeronautical and space activities peculiar to or primarily associated with development of weapons systems or military operations, Selective Service System, national security aspects of nuclear energy.

Phone: 224-3871

R 9 - D 8

John Tower, R-Texas, chairman*

Strom Thurmond, S.C.	*John C. Stennis, Miss.**
Barry Goldwater, Ariz.	*Henry M. Jackson, Wash.*
John W. Warner, Va.	*Howard W. Cannon, Nev.*
Gordon J. Humphrey, N.H.	*Harry F. Byrd Jr., Va.*
William S. Cohen, Maine	*Sam Nunn, Ga.*
Roger W. Jepsen, Iowa	*Gary Hart, Colo.*
Dan Quayle, Ind.	*J. James Exon, Neb.*
Jeremiah Denton, Ala.	*Carl Levin, Mich.*

Manpower and Personnel

Jepsen - chairman

Cohen	*Exon*
Quayle	*Byrd*
Denton	*Nunn*

Military Construction

Thurmond - chairman

Warner	*Hart*
Humphrey	*Jackson*
Denton	*Cannon*
	Exon

Preparedness

Humphrey - chairman

Goldwater	*Levin*
Jepsen	*Jackson*

Sea Power and Force Projection

Phone: 224-2127

Cohen - chairman

Humphrey	*Byrd*
Quayle	*Nunn*
Denton	*Hart*

Strategic and Theater Nuclear Forces

Warner - chairman

Thurmond	*Jackson*
Goldwater	*Cannon*
Cohen	*Nunn*
Quayle	*Hart*
	Exon

Tactical Warfare

Goldwater - chairman

Thurmond	*Cannon*
Warner	*Byrd*
Jepsen	*Levin*

* *Chairman and ranking minority member are members* ex officio *of all subcommittees.*

Banking, Housing, and Urban Affairs

Banking and currency generally; financial matters other than taxes and appropriations; public and private housing; economic controls; urban affairs; export and foreign trade promotion and export controls.

Phone: 224-7391

R 8 - D 7

Jake Garn, R-Utah, chairman*

John Tower, Texas	*Harrison A. Williams Jr., N.J.*
John Heinz, Pa.	*William Proxmire, Wis.*
William L. Armstrong, Colo.	*Alan Cranston, Calif.*
Richard G. Lugar, Ind.	*Donald W. Riegle Jr., Mich.*
Alfonse D'Amato, N.Y.	*Paul S. Sarbanes, Md.*
John H. Chafee, R.I.	*Christopher J. Dodd, Conn.*
Harrison "Jack" Schmitt, N.M.	*Alan J. Dixon, Ill.*

Consumer Affairs

Chafee - chairman

D'Amato	*Dodd*
Schmitt	*Dixon*

Economic Policy

Armstrong - chairman

Heinz	*Riegle*
Lugar	*Cranston*
Chafee	*Sarbanes*

Financial Institutions

Tower - chairman

Garn	*Cranston*
Lugar	*Williams*
D'Amato	*Proxmire*
Schmitt	*Dixon*

Housing and Urban Affairs

Phone: 224-5404

Lugar - chairman

Garn	*Williams*
Tower	*Proxmire*
Heinz	*Cranston*
Armstrong	*Sarbanes*
D'Amato	*Riegle*

International Finance and Monetary Policy

Phone: 224-0891

Heinz - chairman

Garn	*Proxmire*
Armstrong	*Williams*
Chafee	*Dodd*

Rural Housing and Development

Phone: 224-5404

Schmitt - chairman

Heinz	*Dixon*
Lugar	*Dodd*

Securities

D'Amato - chairman

Tower	*Sarbanes*
Schmitt	*Riegle*

* *Chairman is a member* ex officio *of all subcommittees of which he is not a regular member.*

Budget

Federal budget generally; Congressional Budget Office.

Phone: 224-0642

R 12 - D 10

Pete V. Domenici, R-N.M., chairman

William L. Armstrong, Colo.	*Ernest F. Hollings, S.C.*
Nancy Landon Kassebaum, Kan.	*Lawton Chiles, Fla.*
Rudy Boschwitz, Minn.	*Joseph R. Biden Jr., Del.*
Orrin G. Hatch, Utah	*J. Bennett Johnston, La.*
John Tower, Texas	*Jim Sasser, Tenn.*
Mark Andrews, N.D.	*Gary Hart, Colo.*
Steven D. Symms, Idaho	*Howard M. Metzenbaum, Ohio*

Charles E. Grassley, Iowa
Robert W. Kasten Jr., Wis.
Dan Quayle, Ind.
Slade Gorton, Wash.

Donald W. Riegle Jr., Mich.
Daniel Patrick Moynihan,
N.Y.
J. James Exon, Neb.

No standing subcommittees.

Commerce, Science and Transportation

Interstate commerce in general, transportation, merchant marine and navigation, safety and transportation, Coast Guard, inland waterways except construction; communications, regulation of consumer products and services, standards and measurement, highway safety; science, engineering, and technology research and development and policy; non-military aeronautical and space sciences, marine fisheries, coastal zone management; oceans, weather and atmospheric activities.

Phone: 224-5115

R 9 - D 8

Bob Packwood, R-Ore., chairman*

Barry Goldwater, Ariz.
Harrison "Jack" Schmitt,
N.M.
John C. Danforth, Mo.
Nancy Landon Kassebaum,
Kan.
Larry Pressler, S.D.
Slade Gorton, Wash.
Ted Stevens, Alaska
Robert W. Kasten Jr., Wis.

*Howard W. Cannon, Nev.**
Russell B. Long, La.
Ernest F. Hollings, S.C.
Daniel K. Inouye, Hawaii
Wendell H. Ford, Ky.
Donald W. Riegle Jr., Mich.
J. James Exon, Neb.
Howell Heflin, Ala.

Aviation

Phone: 224-4852

Kassebaum - chairman

Goldwater	*Cannon*
Danforth	*Inouye*
Stevens	*Exon*

Business, Trade, and Tourism

Phone: 224-2670

Pressler - chairman

Packwood	*Exon*

Communications

Phone: 224-8144

Goldwater - chairman

Schmitt	*Hollings*
Pressler	*Inouye*
Stevens	*Ford*

Consumer

Phone: 224-4768

Kasten - chairman

Danforth	*Ford*

Merchant Marine

Phone: 224-4766

Gorton - chairman

Stevens	*Inouye*
Kasten	*Long*

National Ocean Policy Study

Phone: 224-8170

Packwood - chairman
Stevens - vice chairman

Schmitt	*Cannon*
Pressler	*Long*
Gorton	*Hollings*
	Inouye

Science, Technology, and Space

Phone: 224-8172

Schmitt - chairman

Goldwater	*Riegle*
Kassebaum	*Ford*
Gorton	*Hollings*
Kasten	*Heflin*

Surface Transportation

Phone: 224-4852

Danforth - chairman

Pressler	*Long*
Schmitt	*Hollings*
Kassebaum	*Riegle*
Gorton	*Heflin*

* *Chairman and ranking minority member are members* ex officio *of all subcommittees of which they are not regular members.*

Energy and Natural Resources

Energy policy generally; energy regulation and conservation, research and development; solar energy systems; nuclear energy; naval petroleum; oil and gas; hydro-electric power; coal; mining; public parks and recreation areas; territorial possessions of the United States.

Phone: 224-4971

R 11 - D 9

James A. McClure, R-Idaho, chairman*

Mark O. Hatfield, Ore.	Henry M. Jackson, Wash.*
Lowell P. Weicker Jr., Conn.	J. Bennett Johnston, La.
Pete V. Domenici, N.M.	Dale Bumpers, Ark.
Malcolm Wallop, Wyo.	Wendell H. Ford, Ky.
John W. Warner, Va.	Howard M. Metzenbaum, Ohio
Gordon J. Humphrey, N.H.	
Frank H. Murkowski, Alaska	Spark M. Matsunaga, Hawaii
Don Nickles, Okla.	
John P. East, N.C.	John Melcher, Mont.
John Heinz, Pa.	Paul E. Tsongas, Mass.
	Bill Bradley, N.J.

Energy and Mineral Resources

Phone: 224-4236

Warner - chairman

Heinz	Matsunaga
Humphrey	Johnston
Wallop	Bumpers
Murkowski	Bradley

Energy Conservation and Supply

Phone: 224-4136

Weicker - chairman

Hatfield	Metzenbaum
Humphrey	Matsunaga
East	Tsongas
Heinz	Bradley

Energy Regulation

Phone: 224-5356

Humphrey - chairman

Nickles	Johnston
Domenici	Ford
East	Metzenbaum
Heinz	Melcher

Energy Research and Development

Phone: 224-4431

Domenici - chairman

East	Ford
Nickles	Johnston
Weicker	Bumpers
Warner	Tsongas

Public Lands and Reserved Water

Phone: 224-5161

Wallop - chairman

Hatfield	Bumpers
Warner	Metzenbaum
Murkowski	Matsunaga
Domenici	Melcher

Water and Power

Phone: 224-5726

Murkowski - chairman

Hatfield	Melcher
Weicker	Ford
Wallop	Tsongas
Nickles	Bradley

* Chairman and ranking minority member are members ex officio of all subcommittees.

Environment and Public Works

Environmental policy, research and development; ocean dumping, fisheries and wildlife, Outer Continental Shelf, solid waste disposal and recycling, toxic substances and other pesticides; public works, bridges and dams; water, air and noise pollution; federal buildings and grounds; flood control; construction and maintenance of highways.

Phone: 224-6176

R 9 - D 7

Robert T. Stafford, R-Vt., chairman*

Howard H. Baker Jr., Tenn.	Jennings Randolph, W.Va.*
Pete V. Domenici, N.M.	Lloyd Bentsen, Texas
John H. Chafee, R.I.	Quentin N. Burdick, N.D.
Alan K. Simpson, Wyo.	Gary Hart, Colo.

James Abdnor, S.D.
Steven D. Symms, Idaho
Slade Gorton, Wash.
Frank H. Murkowski, Alaska

Daniel Patrick Moynihan,
N.Y.
George J. Mitchell, Maine
Max Baucus, Mont.

Environmental Pollution

Chafee - chairman

Simpson	*Mitchell*
Symms	*Hart*
Gorton	*Moynihan*

Nuclear Regulation

Simpson - chairman

Baker	*Hart*
Domenici	*Mitchell*
Symms	*Baucus*

Regional and Community Development

Murkowski - chairman

Baker	*Burdick*
Domenici	*Bentsen*
Chafee	*Mitchell*

Toxic Substances and Environmental Oversight

Gorton - chairman

Simpson	*Baucus*
Abdnor	*Burdick*
Murkowski	*Hart*

Transportation

Symms - chairman

Stafford	*Bentsen*
Baker	*Randolph*
Chafee	*Burdick*
Abdnor	*Moynihan*

Water Resources

Abdnor - chairman

Domenici	*Moynihan*
Gorton	*Bentsen*
Murkowski	*Baucus*

* Chairman and ranking minority member are members ex officio of all subcommittees of which they are not regular members.

Finance

Taxes, tariffs, foreign trade, import quotas, Social Security, revenue sharing.

Phone: 224-4515

R 11 - D 9

Robert Dole, R-Kan., chairman

Bob Packwood, Ore.	*Russell B. Long, La.*
William V. Roth Jr., Del.	*Harry F. Byrd Jr., Va.*
John C. Danforth, Mo.	*Lloyd Bentsen, Texas*
John H. Chafee, R.I.	*Spark M. Matsunaga,*
John Heinz, Pa.	*Hawaii*
Malcolm Wallop, Wyo.	*Daniel Patrick Moynihan,*
David Durenberger, Minn.	*N.Y.*
William L. Armstrong, Colo.	*Max Baucus, Mont.*
Steven D. Symms, Idaho	*David L. Boren, Okla.*
Charles E. Grassley, Iowa	*Bill Bradley, N.J.*
	George J. Mitchell, Maine

Economic Growth, Employment, and Revenue Sharing

Heinz - chairman

Roth	*Mitchell*
	Moynihan

Energy and Agricultural Taxation

Wallop - chairman

Symms	*Bradley*
Durenberger	*Mitchell*
	Bentsen

Estate and Gift Taxation

Symms - chairman

Grassley	*Boren*
	Byrd

Health

Phone: 224-5470

Durenberger - chairman

Dole	*Baucus*
Packwood	*Bradley*
Heinz	*Long*

International Trade

Danforth - chairman

Roth	*Bentsen*
Chafee	*Matsunaga*
Heinz	*Moynihan*
Wallop	*Boren*
Armstrong	*Bradley*
Grassley	*Byrd*
Symms	*Baucus*

Oversight of the Internal Revenue Service

Grassley - chairman

Dole   *Baucus*

Savings, Pensions, and Investment Policy

Chafee - chairman

Packwood   *Matsunaga*
Roth   *Mitchell*

Social Security and Income Maintenance Programs

Phone: 224-5470

Armstrong - chairman

Durenberger   *Moynihan*
Danforth   *Boren*
Dole   *Long*

Taxation and Debt Management

Phone: 224-5487

Packwood - chairman

Danforth   *Byrd*
Chafee   *Bentsen*
Wallop   *Matsunaga*
Armstrong   *Long*

Foreign Relations

Relations of the United States with foreign nations generally; treaties; International Red Cross; diplomatic service; United Nations; foreign loans; foreign interventions and declarations of war; protection of U.S. citizens abroad; matters relating to food, hunger and nutrition in foreign countries.

Phone: 224-4651

R 9 - D 8

Charles H. Percy, R-Ill., chairman*

Howard H. Baker Jr., Tenn.   *Claiborne Pell, R.I.**
Jesse Helms, N.C.   *Joseph R. Biden Jr., Del.*
S. I. "Sam" Hayakawa,   *John Glenn, Ohio*
   Calif.   *Paul S. Sarbanes, Md.*
Richard G. Lugar, Ind.   *Edward Zorinsky, Neb.*
Charles McC. Mathias Jr.,   *Paul E. Tsongas, Mass.*
   Md.   *Alan Cranston, Calif.*
Nancy Landon Kassebaum,   *Christopher J. Dodd, Conn.*
   Kan.
Rudy Boschwitz, Minn.
Larry Pressler, S.D.

African Affairs

Phone: 224-5481

Kassebaum - chairman

Helms   *Tsongas*
Hayakawa   *Glenn*
Mathias   *Dodd*

Arms Control, Oceans, International Operations, and Environment

Phone: 224-4651

Pressler - chairman

Percy   *Cranston*
Baker   *Zorinsky*

East Asian and Pacific Affairs

Phone: 224-5481

Hayakawa - chairman

Baker   *Glenn*
Helms   *Tsongas*
Boschwitz   *Cranston*

European Affairs

Phone 224-5481

Lugar - chairman

Mathias   *Biden*
Boschwitz   *Sarbanes*
Pressler   *Zorinsky*

International Economic Policy

Phone 224-4192

Mathias - chairman

Percy   *Dodd*
Lugar   *Biden*
Kassebaum   *Sarbanes*

Near Eastern and South Asian Affairs

Phone 224-5481

Boschwitz - chairman

Baker   *Sarbanes*
Helms   *Glenn*
Pressler   *Cranston*

Western Hemisphere Affairs

Phone 224-3866

Helms - chairman

Hayakawa	*Zorinsky*
Lugar	*Tsongas*
Kassebaum	*Dodd*

* Chairman and ranking minority member are members ex officio *of all subcommittees of which they are not regular members.*

Governmental Affairs

Budget and accounting measures; reorganization of the executive branch; general governmental and administrative problems; intergovernmental relationships between the federal government and the states and municipalities, and between the United States and international organizations of which the United States is a member; postal service; federal civil service.

Phone: 224-4751

R 9 - D 8

William V. Roth Jr., R-Del., chairman*

Charles H. Percy, Ill.	*Thomas F. Eagleton, Mo.**
Ted Stevens, Alaska	*Henry M. Jackson, Wash.*
Charles McC. Mathias Jr., Md.	*Lawton Chiles, Fla.*
John C. Danforth, Mo.	*Sam Nunn, Ga.*
William S. Cohen, Maine	*John Glenn, Ohio*
David Durenberger, Minn.	*Jim Sasser, Tenn.*
Mack Mattingly, Ga.	*David Pryor, Ark.*
Warren B. Rudman, N.H.	*Carl Levin, Mich.*

Civil Service, Post Office, and General Services

Phone: 224-2254

Stevens - chairman

Mathias	*Pryor*

Congressional Operations and Oversight

Phone: 224-3643

Mattingly - chairman

Stevens	*Pryor*

Energy, Nuclear Proliferation, and Government Processes

Phone: 224-9515

Percy - chairman

Durenberger	*Glenn*
Cohen	*Jackson*
Mattingly	*Levin*

Federal Expenditures, Research and Rules

Phone: 224-0241

Danforth - chairman

Percy	*Chiles*
Durenberger	*Jackson*

Governmental Efficiency and the District of Columbia

Phone: 224-4161

Mathias - chairman

Rudman	*Eagleton*

Intergovernmental Relations

Phone: 224-4718

Durenberger - chairman

Danforth	*Sasser*
Mattingly	*Nunn*

Oversight of Government Management

Phone: 224-5538

Cohen - chairman

Stevens	*Levin*
Rudman	*Pryor*

Permanent Subcommittee on Investigations

Phone: 224-3721

Roth - chairman
Rudman - vice chairman

Percy	*Nunn*
Mathias	*Jackson*
Danforth	*Chiles*
Cohen	*Glenn*
	Sasser

* Chairman and ranking minority member are members ex officio *of all subcommittees of which they are not regular members.*

Judiciary

Federal courts and judges, penitentiaries, civil rights, civil liberties, constitutional amendments, monopolies and unlawful restraints of trade, interstate compacts, immigration and naturalization, apportionment of representatives, meetings of Congress and attendance of members, claims against the United States, patents generally, bankruptcy, mutiny, espionage, counterfeiting, and holidays and celebrations.

Phone: 224-5225

R 10 - D 8

Strom Thurmond, R-S.C., chairman*

Charles McC. Mathias Jr., Md.	*Joseph R. Biden Jr., Del.**
Paul Laxalt, Nev.	*Edward M. Kennedy, Mass.*
Orrin G. Hatch, Utah	*Robert C. Byrd, W.Va.*
Robert Dole, Kan.	*Howard M. Metzenbaum, Ohio*
Alan K. Simpson, Wyo.	*Dennis DeConcini, Ariz.*
John P. East, N.C.	*Patrick J. Leahy, Vt.*
Charles E. Grassley, Iowa	*Max Baucus, Mont.*
Jeremiah Denton, Ala.	*Howell Heflin, Ala.*
Arlen Specter, Pa.	

Agency Administration

Phone: 224-3282

Grassley - chairman

Laxalt	*Metzenbaum*
Specter	*Baucus*

The Constitution

Phone: 224-8191

Hatch - chairman

Thurmond	*DeConcini*
Grassley	*Leahy*

Courts

Phone: 224-1674

Dole - chairman

Thurmond	*Heflin*
Simpson	*Baucus*
East	

Criminal Law

Phone: 224-5617

Mathias - chairman

Laxalt	*Biden*
Specter	*Metzenbaum*
Dole	

Immigration and Refugee Policy

Phone: 224-4031

Simpson - chairman

Thurmond	*Kennedy*
Grassley	*DeConcini*

Juvenile Justice

Phone: 224-7801

Specter - chairman

Denton	*Metzenbaum*
Mathias	*Kennedy*

Regulatory Reform

Phone: 224-3980

Laxalt - chairman

Dole	*Leahy*
Mathias	*Byrd*
Simpson	

Security and Terrorism

Phone: 224-6136

Denton - chairman

Hatch	*Biden*
East	*Leahy*

Separation of Powers

Phone: 224-6791

East - chairman

Hatch	*Baucus*
Denton	*Heflin*

* Chairman and ranking minority member are members ex officio of all subcommittees of which they are not regular members.

Labor and Human Resources

Education, labor, health and public welfare generally.

Phone: 224-5375

R 9 - D 7

Orrin G. Hatch, R-Utah, chairman*

Robert T. Stafford, Vt.	*Edward M. Kennedy, Mass.**
Dan Quayle, Ind.	*Jennings Randolph, W.Va.*
Paula Hawkins, Fla.	*Harrison A. Williams Jr., N.J.*

Don Nickles, Okla.
Lowell P. Weicker Jr.,
  Conn.
Gordon J. Humphrey, N.H.
Jeremiah Denton, Ala.
John P. East, N.C.

Claiborne Pell, R.I.
Thomas F. Eagleton, Mo.
Donald W. Riegle Jr., Mich.
Howard M. Metzenbaum,
  Ohio

Aging, Family, and Human Services

Phone: 224-3491

Denton - chairman

Weicker
Humphrey

Eagleton
Metzenbaum

Alcoholism and Drug Abuse

Phone: 224-5630

Humphrey - chairman

Denton
Hatch

Riegle
Williams

Education, Art and Humanities

Phone: 224-2962

Stafford - chairman

East
Quayle
Weicker
Denton

Pell
Kennedy
Randolph
Eagleton

Employment and Productivity

Phone: 224-6306

Quayle - chairman

Hawkins
Nickles
Hatch

Metzenbaum
Riegle
Pell

Handicapped

Phone: 224-6265

Weicker - chairman

Stafford
East
Nickles

Randolph
Williams
Eagleton

Investigations and General Oversight

Phone: 224-8789

Hawkins - chairman

Humphrey

Kennedy

Labor

Phone: 224-5546

Nickles - chairman

Hatch
East
Stafford
Quayle
Hawkins

Williams
Kennedy
Randolph
Riegle

* Chairman and ranking minority member are members ex officio of all subcommittees of which they are not regular members.

Rules and Administration

Senate administration generally, contested elections, presidential succession, and management of the Library of Congress, the Smithsonian Institution, Government Printing Office, etc.

Phone: 224-6352

R 7 - D 5

Charles McC. Mathias Jr., R-Md., chairman

Mark O. Hatfield, Ore.
Howard H. Baker Jr., Tenn.
James A. McClure, Idaho
Jesse Helms, N.C.
John W. Warner, Va.
Robert Dole, Kan.

Wendell H. Ford, Ky.
Howard W. Cannon, Nev.
Claiborne Pell, R.I.
Robert C. Byrd, W.Va.
Harrison A. Williams Jr., N.J.

No standing subcommittees.

Select Ethics

Studies and investigates standards and conduct of Senate members and employees and may recommend remedial action.

Phone: 224-2981

R 3 - D 3

Malcolm Wallop, R-Wyo., chairman
Howell Heflin, D-Ala., vice chairman

Jesse Helms, N.C.
Mack Mattingly, Ga.

David Pryor, Ark.
Thomas F. Eagleton, Mo.

No standing subcommittees.

Select Indian Affairs

Legislation dealing with Indian affairs; studies all problems relating to Indians including, but not limited to, Indian land management and trust responsibilities, Indian education, health, special services and loan programs and Indian claims against the United States.

Phone: 224-2251

R 4 - D 3

William S. Cohen, R-Maine, chairman

Barry Goldwater, Ariz.	*John Melcher, Mont.*
Mark Andrews, N.D.	*Daniel K. Inouye, Hawaii*
Slade Gorton, Wash.	*Dennis DeConcini, Ariz.*

No standing subcommittees.

Select Intelligence

Legislative and budgetary authority over the Central Intelligence Agency, the Federal Bureau of Investigation and other components of the federal intelligence community.

Phone: 224-1700

R 8 - D 7

Barry Goldwater, R-Ariz., chairman*
*Daniel Patrick Moynihan, D-N.Y. - vice chairman**

Jake Garn, Utah	*Walter D. Huddleston, Ky.*
John H. Chafee, R.I.	*Joseph R. Biden Jr., Del.*
Richard G. Lugar, Ind.	*Daniel K. Inouye, Hawaii*
Malcolm Wallop, Wyo.	*Henry M. Jackson, Wash.*
David Durenberger, Minn.	*Patrick J. Leahy, Vt.*
William V. Roth Jr., Del.	*Lloyd Bentsen, Texas*
Harrison "Jack" Schmitt, N.M.	

Analysis and Production

Lugar - chairman
Jackson - vice chairman

Garn	*Bentsen*
Wallop	
Durenberger	

Budget

Wallop - chairman
Inouye - vice chairman

Garn	*Jackson*
Durenberger	*Leahy*
Roth	*Bentsen*

Collection and Foreign Operations

Chafee - chairman
Huddleston - vice chairman

Garn	*Biden*
Lugar	*Inouye*
Durenberger	*Jackson*
Schmitt	

Legislation and the Rights of Americans

Schmitt - chairman
Leahy - vice chairman

Garn	*Huddleston*
Chafee	

* Chairman and ranking minority member are members ex officio of all subcommittees.

Select Small Business

Problems of small business; oversight of Small Business Administration.

Phone: 224-5175

R 9 - D 8

Lowell P. Weicker Jr., R-Conn., chairman*

Bob Packwood, Ore.	*Sam Nunn, Ga.**
Orrin G. Hatch, Utah	*Walter D. Huddleston, Ky.*
S. I. "Sam" Hayakawa, Calif.	*Dale Bumpers, Ark.*
Rudy Boschwitz, Minn.	*Jim Sasser, Tenn.*
Slade Gorton, Wash.	*Max Baucus, Mont.*
Don Nickles, Okla.	*Carl Levin, Mich.*
Warren B. Rudman, N.H.	*Paul E. Tsongas, Mass.*
Alfonse D'Amato, N.Y.	*Alan J. Dixon, Ill.*

Advocacy and the Future of Small Business

Hayakawa - chairman

Rudman	*Tsongas*

Capital Formation and Retention

Packwood - chairman

Hatch	*Nunn*
Boschwitz	*Sasser*

Export Promotion and Market Development

Boschwitz - chairman

Hayakawa	*Huddleston*

Government Procurement

Nickles - chairman

Weicker   *Sasser*

Government Regulation and Paperwork

Hatch - chairman

D'Amato   *Bumpers*
Gorton   *Huddleston*

Innovation and Technology

Rudman - chairman

Packwood   *Levin*

Productivity and Competition

Gorton - chairman

Nickles   *Baucus*

Urban and Rural Economic Development

D'Amato - chairman

Weicker   *Dixon*

* Chairman and ranking minority member are members ex officio *of all subcommittees of which they are not regular members.*

Special Aging

Studies and investigates problems of the aging and reports findings and makes recommendations to the Senate, but cannot report legislation.

Phone: 224-5364

R 8 - D 7

John Heinz, R-Pa., chairman

Pete V. Domenici, N.M.   *Lawton Chiles, Fla.*
Charles H. Percy, Ill.   *John Glenn, Ohio*
Nancy Landon Kassebaum,   *John Melcher, Mont.*
  Kan.   *David Pryor, Ark.*
William S. Cohen, Maine   *Bill Bradley, N.J.*
Larry Pressler, S.D.   *Quentin N. Burdick, N.D.*
Charles E. Grassley, Iowa   *Christopher J. Dodd, Conn.*
David Durenberger, Minn.

No standing subcommittees.

Veterans' Affairs

Veterans' measures generally; pensions, armed forces life insurance, rehabilitation, education, medical care and treatment of veterans, veterans' hospitals, national cemeteries.

Phone: 224-9126

R 7 - D 5

Alan K. Simpson, R.-Wyo., chairman

Strom Thurmond, S.C.   *Alan Cranston, Calif.*
Robert T. Stafford, Vt.   *Jennings Randolph, W.Va.*
Robert W. Kasten Jr., Wis.   *Spark M. Matsunaga,*
Jeremiah Denton, Ala.   *Hawaii*
Frank H. Murkowski, Alaska   *Dennis DeConcini, Ariz.*
Arlen Specter, Pa.   *George J. Mitchell, Maine*

No standing subcommittees.

Senate Republican Leaders

Chairman of the Conference - James A. McClure, Idaho
Secretary of the Conference - Jake Garn, Utah
President Pro Tempore - Strom Thurmond, S.C.
Floor Leader - Howard H. Baker Jr., Tenn.
Whip - Ted Stevens, Alaska

Policy Committee

Phone: 224-2946

John Tower, Texas, Chairman

Mark Andrews, N.D.   Mack Mattingly, Ga.
William L. Armstrong, Colo.   Charles H. Percy, Ill.
Jeremiah Denton, Ala.   William V. Roth Jr., Del.
Robert Dole, Kan.   Harrison "Jack" Schmitt,
Pete V. Domenici, N.M.   N.M.
Orrin G. Hatch, Utah   Robert T. Stafford, Vt.
Mark O. Hatfield, Ore.   Strom Thurmond, S.C.
John Heinz, Pa.   Malcolm Wallop, Wyo.
Jesse Helms, N.C.
Nancy Landon Kassebaum,
  Kan.

Committee on Committees

Makes Republican committee assignments.

Phone: 224-4814

Richard G. Lugar, Ind., chairman

James Abdnor, S.D.	Charles E. Grassley, Iowa
Rudy Boschwitz, Minn.	S. I. "Sam" Hayakawa,
John H. Chafee, R. I.	Calif.
Alfonse D'Amato, N. Y.	Frank H. Murkowski, Alaska
John C. Danforth, Mo.	Dan Quayle, Ind.
David Durenberger, Minn.	Alan K. Simpson, Wyo.
Barry Goldwater, Ariz.	Arlen Specter, Pa.
Slade Gorton, Wash.	Lowell P. Weicker Jr., Conn.

National Republican Senatorial Committee

Phone: 224-2351

Bob Packwood, Ore., chairman

Thad Cochran, Miss.	Frank H. Murkowski, Alaska
William S. Cohen, Maine	Don Nickles, Okla.
John P. East, N.C.	Larry Pressler, S. D.
Slade Gorton, Wash.	Dan Quayle, Ind.
Paula Hawkins, Fla.	Warren B. Rudman, N. H.
Gordon J. Humphrey, N.H.	Alan K. Simpson, Wyo.
Roger W. Jepsen, Iowa	Steven D. Symms, Idaho
Robert W. Katsen Jr., Wis.	John W. Warner, Va.
Paul Laxalt, Nev.	
Charles McC. Mathias Jr., Md.	

Senate Democratic Leaders

Chairman of the Conference - *Robert C. Byrd, W.Va.*
Secretary of the Conference - *Daniel K. Inouye, Hawaii*
Floor Leader - *Byrd*
Whip - *Alan Cranston, Calif.*
Chief Deputy Whip - *Spark M. Matsunaga, Hawaii*
Deputy Whips - *Max Baucus, Mont.; Alan J. Dixon, Ill.; Christopher J. Dodd, Conn.; J. James Exon, Neb.; Wendell H. Ford, Ky.; John Glenn, Ohio; Walter D. Huddleston, Ky.; Patrick J. Leahy, Vt.; David Pryor, Ark.; Donald W. Riegle Jr., Mich.; Paul S. Sarbanes, Md.*

Policy Committee

Phone: 224-5551

Robert C. Byrd, W.Va., chairman

Lloyd Bentsen, Texas	Walter D. Huddleston, Ky.
Dale Bumpers, Ark.	Daniel K. Inouye, Hawaii†
Quentin N. Burdick, N.D.	Henry M. Jackson, Wash.
Alan Cranston, Calif.†	John Melcher, Mont.
J. James Exon, Neb.	Daniel Patrick Moynihan,
John Glenn, Ohio	N.Y.

Gary Hart, Colo.	Claiborne Pell, R.I.
Ernest F. Hollings, S.C.	William Proxmire, Wis.
	Paul S. Sarbanes, Md.

† Members ex officio from the leadership.

Legislative Review

Phone: 224-5551

Dale Bumpers, Ark., chairman

Lloyd Bentsen, Texas	Daniel Patrick Moynihan,
J. James Exon, Neb.	N.Y.
Gary Hart, Colo.	William Proxmire, Wis.
John Melcher, Mont.	Paul S. Sarbanes, Md.

Steering Committee

Phone: 224-5551

Robert C. Byrd, W.Va., chairman

Joseph R. Biden Jr., Del.	Russell B. Long, La.
David L. Boren, Okla.	Howard M. Metzenbaum,
Howard W. Cannon, Nev.	Ohio
Lawton Chiles, Fla.	George J. Mitchell, Maine
Alan Cranston, Calif.	Sam Nunn, Ga.
Dennis DeConcini, Ariz.	David Pryor, Ark.
Thomas F. Eagleton, Mo.	Donald W. Riegle Jr., Mich.
Wendell H. Ford, Ky.	Jim Sasser, Tenn.
Daniel K. Inouye, Hawaii†	John C. Stennis, Miss.
Edward M. Kennedy, Mass.	Harrison A. Williams Jr., N.J.
Patrick J. Leahy, Vt.	Edward Zorinsky, Neb.

† Member ex officio from the leadership.

Senatorial Campaign Committee

Phone: 224-2447

Wendell H. Ford, Ky., chairman
Bill Bradley, N.J., vice chairman

Max Baucus, Mont.	Thomas F. Eagleton, Mo.
Joseph R. Biden Jr., Del.	John Glenn, Ohio
Dale Bumpers, Ark.	Gary Hart, Colo.
Robert C. Byrd, W.Va.†	Daniel K. Inouye, Hawaii†
Lawton Chiles, Fla.	Henry M. Jackson, Wash.
Alan Cranston, Calif.†	Carl Levin, Mich.
Alan J. Dixon, Ill.	Russell B. Long, La.
Christopher J. Dodd, Conn.	Paul E. Tsongas, Mass.

† Members ex officio from the leadership.

House Committees, 97th Congress, First Session

(As of Sept. 28, 1981)

Agriculture

Agriculture and forestry in general; farm credit and security, crop insurance, soil conservation, rural electrification and development.

Phone: 225-2171

D 24 - R 19

E. "Kika" de la Garza, D-Texas, chairman*

Thomas S. Foley, Wash.	William C. Wampler, Va.*
Walter B. Jones, N.C.	Paul Findley, Ill.
Ed Jones, Tenn.	James M. Jeffords, Vt.
George E. Brown Jr., Calif.	Tom Hagedorn, Minn.
David R. Bowen, Miss.	E. Thomas Coleman, Mo.
Charlie Rose, N.C.	Ron Marlenee, Mont.
Fred Richmond, N.Y.	Larry J. Hopkins, Ky.
James Weaver, Ore.	William M. Thomas, Calif.
Tom Harkin, Iowa	George Hansen, Idaho
Berkley Bedell, Iowa	Arlan Stangeland, Minn.
Glenn English, Okla.	Pat Roberts, Kan.
Floyd Fithian, Ind.	Bill Emerson, Mo.
Leon E. Panetta, Calif.	John L. Napier, S.C.
Jerry Huckaby, La.	Joe Skeen, N.M.
Dan Glickman, Kan.	Sid Morrison, Wash.
Charles Whitley, N.C.	Clint Roberts, S.D.
Tony Coelho, Calif.	Steve Gunderson, Wis.
Thomas A. Daschle, S.D.	Cooper Evans, Iowa
Beryl Anthony Jr., Ark.	Gene Chappie, Calif.
Charles W. Stenholm, Texas	
Harold L. Volkmer, Mo.	
Charles Hatcher, Ga.	
Byron L. Dorgan, N.D.	

Conservation, Credit, and Rural Development

Phone: 225-1867

Jones, Tenn. - chairman

Bedell	Jeffords
Glickman	Coleman
Daschle	Roberts, Kan.
Dorgan	Napier
Bowen	Skeen
Harkin	Morrison
English	Roberts, S.D.
Fithian	Gunderson
Panetta	Evans
Anthony	
Richmond	

Cotton, Rice, and Sugar

Phone: 225-1867

Bowen - chairman

Huckaby	Thomas
Coelho	Stangeland
Anthony	Emerson
Stenholm	Napier
Hatcher	Morrison
Jones, Tenn.	Gunderson
Whitley	Chappie
Foley	
English	

Department Operations, Research, and Foreign Agriculture

Phone: 225-8405

Brown - chairman

Richmond	Wampler
Foley	Thomas
Bowen	Roberts, Kan.
Fithian	Emerson
Volkmer	Evans

Domestic Marketing, Consumer Relations, and Nutrition

Phone: 225-1867

Richmond - chairman

Panetta	Coleman
Glickman	Findley
Coelho	Hansen
Harkin	Chappie
Foley	

Forests, Family Farms, and Energy

Phone: 225-8406

Weaver - chairman

Foley	Marlenee
Brown	Hansen
Bedell	Stangeland
Huckaby	Skeen
Panetta	Morrison
Daschle	Chappie
Anthony	
Dorgan	

Livestock, Dairy, and Poultry

Phone: 225-8405

Harkin - chairman

Volkmer	*Hagedorn*
Jones, Tenn.	*Jeffords*
Rose	*Hopkins*
Whitley	*Hansen*
Coelho	*Skeen*
Stenholm	*Gunderson*
Hatcher	

Tobacco and Peanuts

Phone: 225-1867

Rose - chairman

Jones, N.C.	*Hopkins*
Whitley	*Wampler*
Hatcher	*Napier*
English	*Roberts, S.D.*
Stenholm	

Wheat, Soybeans, and Feed Grains

Phone: 225-2171

Foley - chairman

English	*Findley*
Fithian	*Hagedorn*
Weaver	*Marlenee*
Glickman	*Stangeland*
Daschle	*Roberts, Kan.*
Stenholm	*Emerson*
Volkmer	*Roberts, S.D.*
Dorgan	*Evans*
Bedell	
Huckaby	

* Chairman and ranking minority member are members ex officio of all subcommittees.

Appropriations

Appropriations of government revenues.

Phone: 225-2771

D 33 - R 22

Jamie L. Whitten, D-Miss., chairman*

Edward P. Boland, Mass.	*Silvio O. Conte, Mass.**
William H. Natcher, Ky.	*Joseph M. McDade, Pa.*
Neal Smith, Iowa	*Jack Edwards, Ala.*
Joseph P. Addabbo, N.Y.	*John T. Myers, Ind.*
Clarence D. Long, Md.	*J. Kenneth Robinson, Va.*

Sidney R. Yates, Ill.	*Clarence E. Miller, Ohio*
David R. Obey, Wis.	*Lawrence Coughlin, Pa.*
Edward R. Roybal, Calif.	*C. W. Bill Young, Fla.*
Louis Stokes, Ohio	*Jack F. Kemp, N.Y.*
Tom Bevill, Ala.	*Ralph Regula, Ohio*
Bill Chappell Jr., Fla.	*Clair W. Burgener, Calif.*
Bill Alexander, Ark.	*George M. O'Brien, Ill.*
John P. Murtha, Pa.	*Virginia Smith, Neb.*
Bob Traxler, Mich.	*Eldon Rudd, Ariz.*
Joseph D. Early, Mass.	*Carl D. Pursell, Mich.*
Charles Wilson, Texas	*Mickey Edwards, Okla.*
Lindy (Mrs. Hale) Boggs, La.	*Bob Livingston, La.*
Adam Benjamin Jr., Ind.	*Bill Green, N.Y.*
Norman D. Dicks, Wash.	*Tom Loeffler, Texas*
Matthew F. McHugh, N.Y.	*Jerry Lewis, Calif.*
Bo Ginn, Ga.	*Carroll A. Campbell Jr., S.C.*
William Lehman, Fla.	*John Edward Porter, Ill.*
Jack Hightower, Texas	
Martin Olav Sabo, Minn.	
Julian C. Dixon, Calif.	
Vic Fazio, Calif.	
W.G. "Bill" Hefner, N.C.	
Les AuCoin, Ore.	
Daniel K. Akaka, Hawaii	
Wes Watkins, Okla.	
William H. Gray III, Pa.	
Bernard J. Dwyer, N.J.	

Agriculture, Rural Development and Related Agencies

Phone: 225-2638

Whitten - chairman

Traxler	*Smith*
Alexander	*Robinson*
McHugh	*Myers*
Natcher	*Lewis*
Hightower	
Akaka	
Watkins	

Commerce, Justice, State, and Judiciary

Phone: 225-3351

Smith, Iowa - chairman

Alexander	*O'Brien*
Early	*Miller*
Hightower	*Campbell*
Dwyer	

Defense

Phone: 225-2847

Addabbo - chairman

Chappell	*Edwards, Ala.*
Murtha	*Robinson*
Dicks	*McDade*

Wilson	*Young*
Hefner	
Ginn	

District of Columbia

Phone: 225-5338

Dixon - chairman

Natcher	*Coughlin*
Stokes	*Green*
Wilson	*Porter*
Lehman	

Energy and Water Development

Phone: 225-3421

Bevill - chairman

Boland	*Myers*
Boggs	*Burgener*
Chappell	*Smith*
Fazio	*Rudd*
Watkins	
Benjamin	

Foreign Operations

Phone: 225-2041

Long - chairman

Obey	*Kemp*
Yates	*Edwards, Okla.*
McHugh	*Livingston*
Lehman	*Lewis*
Wilson	*Porter*
Dixon	
Gray	

HUD - Independent Agencies

Phone: 225-3241

Boland - chairman

Traxler	*Green*
Stokes	*Coughlin*
Boggs	*Young*
Sabo	

Interior

Phone: 225-3081

Yates - chairman

Long	*McDade*
Murtha	*Regula*
Dicks	*Loeffler*
AuCoin	

Labor - HHS - Education

Phone: 225-3508

Natcher - chairman

Smith	*Conte*
Obey	*O'Brien*
Roybal	*Pursell*
Stokes	*Livingston*
Early	*Porter*
Dwyer	

Legislative

Phone: 225-5338

Fazio - chairman

Murtha	*Burgener*
Traxler	*Conte*
Benjamin	*Lewis*
Dicks	*Campbell*

Military Construction

Phone: 225-3047

Ginn - chairman

Bevill	*Regula*
Hefner	*Burgener*
Addabbo	*Edwards, Okla.*
Long	*Loeffler*
Chappell	
Alexander	

Transportation

Phone: 225-2141

Benjamin - chairman

Lehman	*Coughlin*
Sabo	*Conte*
AuCoin	*Edwards, Ala.*
Gray	*Pursell*

Treasury - Postal Service - General Government

Phone: 225-5834

Roybal - chairman

Addabbo	*Miller*
Akaka	*Rudd*
Yates	*Campbell*
Obey	

* Chairman and ranking minority member are members ex officio *of all subcommittees of which they are not regular members.*

Armed Services

All matters related to the national military establishment; conservation, development and use of naval petroleum and oil shale reserves; strategic and critical materials; scientific research and development in support of the armed services; Selective Service System.

Phone: 225-4151

D 25 - R 19

Melvin Price, D-Ill., chairman

Charles E. Bennett, Fla.	William L. Dickinson, Ala.
Samuel S. Stratton, N.Y.	G. William Whitehurst, Va.
Richard C. White, Texas	Floyd Spence, S.C.
Bill Nichols, Ala.	Robin L. Beard, Tenn.
Jack Brinkley, Ga.	Donald J. Mitchell, N.Y.
Robert H. Mollohan, W.Va.	Marjorie S. Holt, Md.
Dan Daniel, Va.	Robert W. Daniel Jr., Va.
G.V. "Sonny" Montgomery, Miss.	Elwood Hillis, Ind.
Les Aspin, Wis.	David F. Emery, Maine
Ronald V. Dellums, Calif.	Paul S. Trible Jr., Va.
Patricia Schroeder, Colo.	Robert E. Badham, Calif.
Abraham Kazen Jr., Texas	Charles F. Dougherty, Pa.
Antonio Borja Won Pat, Guam[1]	Jim Courter, N.J.
Larry P. McDonald, Ga.	Larry J. Hopkins, Ky.
Bob Stump, Ariz.	Robert W. Davis, Mich.
Beverly B. Byron, Md.	Kenneth B. Kramer, Colo.
Nicholas Mavroules, Mass.	Duncan L. Hunter, Calif.
Earl Hutto, Fla.	James L. Nelligan, Pa.
Ike Skelton, Mo.	Thomas F. Hartnett, S.C.
Marvin Leath, Texas	
Dave McCurdy, Okla.	
Thomas M. Foglietta, Pa.	
Roy Dyson, Md.	
Dennis M. Hertel, Mich.	
Vacancy	

Investigations

Phone: 225-4221

White - chairman

Mollohan	Beard
Aspin	Daniel
Kazen	Mitchell
Mavroules	Hopkins
Stratton	Davis
Brinkley	Nelligan
Daniel	

Military Installations and Facilities

Phone: 225-1240

Brinkley - chairman

Montgomery	Trible
Kazen	Whitehurst
Won Pat	Mitchell
Hutto	Dickinson
Foglietta	Dougherty
Dyson	Kramer
Bennett	

Military Personnel and Compensation

Phone: 225-7560

Nichols - chairman

Montgomery	Mitchell
Aspin	Holt
Won Pat	Hillis
Byron	Hopkins
Skelton	Hunter
Bennett	Hartnett
White	

Procurement and Military Nuclear Systems

Phone: 225-7160

Stratton - chairman

Byron	Holt
Mavroules	Hillis
Leath	Badham
McCurdy	Courter
Hertel	Kramer
Price	Hunter
Vacancy	

Readiness

Phone: 225-7991

Dan Daniel - chairman

Schroeder	Whitehurst
Stump	Dickinson
Skelton	Spence
Leath	Hillis
McCurdy	Nelligan

Research and Development

Phone: 225-3168

Price - chairman

Mollohan	Dickinson
Dellums	Courter
Schroeder	Beard
McDonald	Daniel
Stump	Emery
Hutto	Badham
White	Davis
Nichols	

Seapower and Strategic and Critical Materials

Phone: 225-6704

Bennett - chairman

Mollohan	*Spence*
McDonald	*Emery*
Hutto	*Trible*
Foglietta	*Dougherty*
Dyson	*Hartnett*
Hertel	

[1] *Delegate from Guam not counted in party ratios.*

Banking, Finance and Urban Affairs

Banks and banking, including deposit insurance and federal monetary policy; money and credit, including currency; gold and silver, including coinage; valuation and revaluation of the dollar; urban development; housing generally; economic stabilization; control of prices; international finance; financial aid to commerce and industry.

Phone: 225-4247

D 25 - R 19

Fernand J. St Germain, D-R.I., chairman

Henry S. Reuss, Wis.	*J. William Stanton, Ohio*
Henry B. Gonzalez, Texas	*Chalmers P. Wylie, Ohio*
Joseph G. Minish, N.J.	*Stewart B. McKinney, Conn.*
Frank Annunzio, Ill.	*George Hansen, Idaho*
Parren J. Mitchell, Md.	*Jim Leach, Iowa*
Walter E. Fauntroy, D.C.[1]	*Thomas B. Evans Jr., Del.*
Stephen L. Neal, N.C.	*Ron Paul, Texas*
Jerry M. Patterson, Calif.	*Ed Bethune, Ark.*
James J. Blanchard, Mich.	*Norman D. Shumway, Calif.*
Carroll Hubbard Jr., Ky.	*Stan Parris, Va.*
John J. LaFalce, N.Y.	*Ed Weber, Ohio*
David W. Evans, Ind.	*Bill McCollum, Fla.*
Norman E. D'Amours, N.H.	*Gregory W. Carman, N.Y.*
Stanley N. Lundine, N.Y.	*George C. Wortley, N.Y.*
Mary Rose Oakar, Ohio	*Marge Roukema, N.J.*
Jim Mattox, Texas	*Bill Lowery, Calif.*
Bruce F. Vento, Minn.	*Jim Coyne, Pa.*
Doug Barnard Jr., Ga.	*Douglas K. Bereuter, Neb.*
Robert Garcia, N.Y.	*David Dreier, Calif.*
Mike Lowry, Wash.	
Charles E. Schumer, N.Y.	
Barney Frank, Mass.	
Bill Patman, Texas	
William J. Coyne, Pa.	
Steny Hoyer, Md.	

Consumer Affairs and Coinage

Phone: 225-9181

Annunzio - chairman

St Germain	*Paul*
Gonzalez	*Evans*
Minish	*Wylie*
Patman	*Carman*
Hoyer	

Domestic Monetary Policy

Phone: 225-7315

Fauntroy - chairman

Mitchell	*Hansen*
Neal	*Paul*
Barnard	*McCollum*
Reuss	*Lowery*
Blanchard	*Weber*
Hubbard	*Coyne*
Patman	

Economic Stabilization

Phone: 225-7145

Blanchard - chairman

Lundine	*McKinney*
Vento	*Shumway*
Evans	*Paul*
D'Amours	*Bethune*
Oakar	*Parris*
Garcia	*Wortley*
St Germain	*Roukema*
Minish	*Coyne*
Annunzio	*Bereuter*
Fauntroy	
Schumer	
Coyne	

Financial Institutions Supervision, Regulation and Insurance

Phone: 225-3851

St Germain - chairman

Annunzio	*Wylie*
Hubbard	*Hansen*
D'Amours	*Leach*
Mattox	*Bethune*
Minish	*McKinney*
Barnard	*Shumway*
LaFalce	*Weber*
Evans	*McCollum*

Oakar
Vento
Garcia
Schumer
Patman

Lowery
Wortley

General Oversight and Renegotiation

Phone: 225-2828

Minish - chairman

Gonzalez
Annunzio
Mitchell
Barnard
Fauntroy
Oakar
Mattox
Frank

Parris
McCollum
Weber
Roukema
Carman
Wortley
Bereuter

Housing and Community Development

Phone: 225-7054

Gonzalez - chairman

St Germain
Fauntroy
Patterson
LaFalce
Blanchard
Evans
Lundine
Oakar
Vento
Garcia
Lowry
Mitchell
Hubbbard
D'Amours
Schumer
Frank
Coyne
Hoyer

Stanton
Wylie
McKinney
Evans
Leach
Bethune
Roukema
Coyne
Wortley
Carman
McCollum
Lowery
Bereuter
Dreier

International Development Institutions and Finance

Phone: 225-7054

Patterson - chairman

LaFalce
Oakar
Neal
Reuss
Lowry

Evans
Stanton
Coyne
Dreier

International Trade, Investment and Monetary Policy

Phone: 225-1271

Neal - chairman

Lundine
Barnard
Patterson
LaFalce
Mattox
Lowry
Frank
Coyne
St Germain

Leach
Hansen
Shumway
Stanton
Parris
Carman
Dreier

¹ *Delegate from District of Columbia not counted in party ratios.*

Budget

Federal budget generally; Congressional Budget Office.

Phone: 225-7200

D 18 - R 12

James R. Jones, D-Okla., chairman

Jim Wright, Texas
David R. Obey, Wis.
Paul Simon, Ill.
Norman Y. Mineta, Calif.
Jim Mattox, Texas
Stephen J. Solarz, N.Y.
Timothy E. Wirth, Colo.
Leon E. Panetta, Calif.
Richard A. Gephardt, Mo.
Bill Nelson, Fla.
Les Aspin, Wis.
W.G. "Bill" Hefner, N.C.
Thomas J. Downey, N.Y.
Adam Benjamin Jr., Ind.
Brian J. Donnelly, Mass.
Beryl Anthony Jr., Ark.
Phil Gramm, Texas

Delbert L. Latta, Ohio*
Ralph Regula, Ohio
Bud Shuster, Pa.
Bill Frenzel, Minn.
Jack F. Kemp, N.Y.
James G. Martin, N.C.
Paul S. Trible Jr., Va.
Ed Bethune, Ark.
Lynn Martin, Ill.
Albert Lee Smith Jr., Ala.
Eugene Johnston, N.C.
Bobbi Fiedler, Calif.

No standing subcommittees.

District of Columbia

All measures relating to municipal affairs of the District of Columbia except its appropriations.

Phone: 225-4457

D 7 - R 4

Ronald V. Dellums, D-Calif., chairman

Walter E. Fauntroy, D.C.[1]
Romano L. Mazzoli, Ky.
Fortney H. "Pete" Stark, Calif.
Mickey Leland, Texas
William H. Gray III, Pa.
Michael D. Barnes, Md.
Mervyn M. Dymally, Calif.

Stewart B. McKinney, Conn.
Stan Parris, Va.
Thomas J. Bliley Jr., Va.
Marjorie S. Holt, Md.

Mario Biaggi, N.Y.
Ike F. Andrews, N.C.
Paul Simon, Ill.
George Miller, Calif.
Austin J. Murphy, Pa.
Ted Weiss, N.Y.
Baltasar Corrada, P.R.[1]
Dale E. Kildee, Mich.
Peter A. Peyser, N.Y.
Pat Williams, Mont.
William R. Ratchford, Conn.
Ray Kogovsek, Colo.
Harold Washington, Ill.
Dennis E. Eckart, Ohio

Ken Kramer, Colo.
Arlen Erdahl, Minn.
Thomas E. Petri, Wis.
Millicent Fenwick, N.J.
Marge Roukema, N.J.
Eugene Johnston, N.C.
Lawrence J. DeNardis, Conn.
Larry E. Craig, Idaho
Wendell Bailey, Mo.

Fiscal Affairs and Health

Phone: 225-2661

Dellums - chairman

Fauntroy	*McKinney*
Stark	*Bliley*
Leland	*Parris*
Gray	

Government Operations and Metropolitan Affairs

Phone: 225-4001

Gray - chairman

Stark	*Parris*
Barnes	*McKinney*
Fauntroy	*Holt*
Vacancy	

Judiciary and Education

Phone: 225-1612

Dymally - chairman

Mazzoli	*Bliley*
Barnes	*Holt*
Vacancy	*Vacancy*
Vacancy	

[1] *Delegate from District of Columbia not counted in party ratios.*

Education and Labor

Education, labor and welfare matters.

Phone: 225-4527

D 19 - R 14

Carl D. Perkins, D-Ky., chairman*

Augustus F. Hawkins, Calif.
William D. Ford, Mich.
Phillip Burton, Calif.
Joseph M. Gaydos, Pa.
William Clay, Mo.

*John M. Ashbrook, Ohio**
John N. Erlenborn, Ill.
James M. Jeffords, Vt.
Bill Goodling, Pa.
E. Thomas Coleman, Mo.

Elementary, Secondary, and Vocational Education

Phone: 225-4368

Perkins - chairman

Ford	*Goodling*
Andrews	*Jeffords*
Miller	*Coleman*
Corrada	*Erdahl*
Kildee	*Petri‡*
Williams	*Roukema*
Hawkins	*DeNardis*
Biaggi	*Craig*
Ratchford	
Washington	

Employment Opportunities

Phone: 225-1927

Hawkins - chairman

Clay	*Jeffords*
Weiss	*Petri*
Corrada	*Fenwick*
Simon	*DeNardis‡*
Washington	

Health and Safety

Phone: 225-6876

Gaydos - chairman

Murphy	*Kramer*
Kogovsek	*Johnston*
Washington	*Craig‡*

Human Resources

Phone: 225-1850

Andrews - chairman

Corrada	*Petri*
Williams	*Coleman‡*

Labor-Management Relations

Phone: 225-5768

Burton - chairman

Clay	*Ashbrook*
Ford	*Erlenborn*
Biaggi	*Kramer*
Kildee	*Fenwick*
Weiss	*Johnston*
Peyser	

Labor Standards

Phone: 225-5331

Miller - chairman

Burton	*Erlenborn*
Williams	*Fenwick*
Ratchford	*Roukema‡*
Murphy	*Johnston*
Kildee	*Bailey*

Postsecondary Education

Phone: 225-8881

Simon - chairman

Ford	*Coleman*
Peyser	*Erlenborn*
Gaydos	*Erdahl‡*
Weiss	*DeNardis*
Andrews	*Bailey*
Eckart	

Select Education

Phone: 225-5954

Murphy - chairman

Miller	*Erdahl*
Biaggi	*Jeffords*
Simon	*Bailey‡*

* Chairman and ranking minority member are members ex officio of all subcommittees of which they are not regular members. However, Rep. Ashbrook received Committee consent to have other minority members serve ex officio in his place. These members are indicated by double daggers (‡).

‡ See footnote designated (*), above.

¹ Resident commissioner from Puerto Rico not counted in party ratios.

Energy and Commerce

National energy policy generally; interstate and foreign commerce.

Phone: 225-2927

D 24 - R 18

John D. Dingell, D-Mich., chairman*

James H. Scheuer, N.Y.	*James T. Broyhill, N.C.**
Richard L. Ottinger, N.Y.	*Clarence J. Brown, Ohio*
Henry A. Waxman, Calif.	*James M. Collins, Texas*
Timothy E. Wirth, Colo.	*Norman F. Lent, N.Y.*
Philip R. Sharp, Ind.	*Edward R. Madigan, Ill.*
James J. Florio, N.J.	*Carlos J. Moorhead, Calif.*
Toby Moffett, Conn.	*Matthew J. Rinaldo, N.J.*
Jim Santini, Nev.	*Marc L. Marks, Pa.*
Edward J. Markey, Mass.	*Tom Corcoran, Ill.*
Thomas A. Luken, Ohio	*Gary A. Lee, N.Y.*
Doug Walgren, Pa.	*William E. Dannemeyer,*
Albert Gore Jr., Tenn.	*Calif.*
Barbara A. Mikulski, Md.	*Bob Whittaker, Kan.*
Ronald M. Mottl, Ohio	*Tom Tauke, Iowa*
Phil Gramm, Texas	*Don Ritter, Pa.*
Al Swift, Wash.	*Harold Rogers, Ky.*
Mickey Leland, Texas	*Cleve Benedict, W.Va.*
Richard C. Shelby, Ala.	*Daniel R. Coats, Ind.*
Cardiss Collins, Ill.	*Thomas J. Bliley Jr., Va.*
Mike Synar, Okla.	
W.J. "Billy" Tauzin, La.	
Ron Wyden, Ore.	
Ralph M. Hall, Texas	

Commerce, Transportation, and Tourism

Phone: 225-1467

Florio - chairman

Santini	*Lent*
Mikulski	*Madigan*
Scheuer	*Lee*
Moffett	

Energy Conservation and Power

Phone: 226-2424

Ottinger - chairman

Moffett	*Moorhead*
Markey	*Rinaldo*
Gore	*Collins*
Gramm	*Corcoran*
Swift	*Whittaker*
Leland	*Tauke*
Shelby	*Ritter*
Synar	*Rogers*
Wyden	*Benedict*
Hall	
Walgren	
Collins	

Fossil and Synthetic Fuels

Phone: 226-2500

Sharp - chairman

Moffett	Brown
Markey	Collins
Gore	Corcoran
Gramm	Lee
Swift	Dannemeyer
Leland	Tauke
Shelby	Rogers
Collins	Benedict
Synar	Coats
Tauzin	
Hall	
Wirth	

Health and the Environment

Phone: 225-4952

Waxman - chairman

Scheuer	Madigan
Luken	Brown
Walgren	Dannemeyer
Mikuski	Whittaker
Wyden	Ritter
Florio	Benedict
Moffett	Bliley
Shelby	
Gramm	
Leland	

Oversight and Investigations

Phone: 225-4441

Dingell - chairman

Santini	Marks
Walgren	Lent
Gore	Whittaker
Mottl	Ritter
Luken	Rogers
Shelby	Coats
Synar	Broyhill
Tauzin	
Wyden	

Telecommunications, Consumer Protection, and Finance

Phone: 225-9304

Wirth - chairman

Mottl	Collins

Scheuer	Rinaldo
Markey	Moorhead
Luken	Marks
Swift	Tauke
Waxman	Bliley
Collins	
Tauzin	

* Chairman and ranking minority member are members ex officio *of all subcommittees of which they are not regular members.*

Foreign Affairs

Relations of the United States with other nations and international organizations and movements.

Phone: 225-5021

D 21 - R 16

Clement J. Zablocki, D-Wis., chairman*

L.H. Fountain, N.C.	William S. Broomfield, Mich.*
Dante B. Fascell, Fla.	
Benjamin S. Rosenthal, N.Y.	Edward J. Derwinski, Ill.
Lee H. Hamilton, Ind.	Paul Findley, Ill.
Jonathan B. Bingham, N.Y.	Larry Winn Jr., Kan.
Gus Yatron, Pa.	Benjamin A. Gilman, N.Y.
Stephen J. Solarz, N.Y.	Robert J. Lagomarsino, Calif.
Don Bonker, Wash.	Bill Goodling, Pa.
Gerry E. Studds, Mass.	Joel Pritchard, Wash.
Andy Ireland, Fla.	Millicent Fenwick, N.J.
Dan Mica, Fla.	Robert K. Dornan, Calif.
Michael D. Barnes, Md.	Jim Leach, Iowa
Howard Wolpe, Mich.	Arlen Erdahl, Minn.
George W. Crockett Jr., Mich.	Toby Roth, Wis.
	Olympia J. Snowe, Maine
Bob Shamansky, Ohio	John LeBoutillier, N.Y.
Sam Gejdenson, Conn.	Henry J. Hyde, Ill.
Mervyn M. Dymally, Calif.	
Dennis E. Eckart, Ohio	
Tom Lantos, Calif.	
David R. Bowen, Miss.	

Africa

Phone: 225-3157

Wolpe - chairman

Crockett	Goodling
Solarz	Erdahl
Studds	Snowe
Eckart	Dornan

Asian and Pacific Affairs

Phone: 225-3044

Solarz - chairman

Dymally	*Pritchard*
Ireland	*Dornan*
Lantos	*Leach*
Bowen	*Hyde*

Europe and the Middle East

Phone: 225-3345

Hamilton - chairman

Fountain	*Findley*
Rosenthal	*Fenwick*
Shamansky	*Roth*
Lantos	*Snowe*

Human Rights and International Organizations

Phone: 225-5318

Bonker - chairman

Rosenthal	*Leach*
Barnes	*LeBoutillier*
Gejdenson	*Pritchard*
Dymally	*Hyde*

Inter-American Affairs

Phone: 225-9404

Barnes - chairman

Yatron	*Gilman*
Studds	*Lagomarsino*
Mica	*Goodling*
Gejdenson	*Dornan*

International Economic Policy and Trade

Phone: 225-3246

Bingham - chairman

Eckart	*Lagomarsino*
Bonker	*Erdahl*
Wolpe	*Gilman*
Shamansky	*Fenwick*

International Operations

Phone: 225-3424

Fascell - chairman

Ireland	*Derwinski*
Yatron	*Winn*
Mica	*Pritchard*
Crockett	*Roth*

International Security and Scientific Affairs

Phone: 225-8926

Zablocki - chairman

Fountain	*Broomfield*
Fascell	*Winn*
Hamilton	*LeBoutillier*
Bingham	*Derwinski*

* Chairman and ranking minority member are members ex officio of all subcommittees of which they are not regular members.

Government Operations

Budget and accounting measures; overall economy and efficiency of government, including federal procurement; reorganization in the executive branch; inter-governmental relations; general revenue sharing; National Archives.

Phone: 225-5051

D 23 - R 17

Jack Brooks, D-Texas, chairman*

L.H. Fountain, N.C.	*Frank Horton, N.Y.**
Dante B. Fascell, Fla.	*John N. Erlenborn, Ill.*
Benjamin S. Rosenthal, N.Y.	*Clarence J. Brown, Ohio*
Don Fuqua, Fla.	*Paul N. McCloskey Jr., Calif.*
John Conyers Jr., Mich.	*Thomas N. Kindness, Ohio*
Cardiss Collins, Ill.	*Robert S. Walker, Pa.*
John L. Burton, Calif.	*M. Caldwell Butler, Va.*
Glenn English, Okla.	*Lyle Williams, Ohio*
Elliott H. Levitas, Ga.	*Joel Deckard, Ind.*
David W. Evans, Ind.	*William F. Clinger Jr., Pa.*
Toby Moffett, Conn.	*Raymond J. McGrath, N.Y.*
Henry A. Waxman, Calif.	*Hal Daub, Neb.*
Floyd Fithian, Ind.	*John Hiler, Ind.*
Ted Weiss, N.Y.	*Wendell Bailey, Mo.*
Mike Synar, Okla.	*Lawrence J. DeNardis, Conn.*
Eugene V. Atkinson, Pa.	*Judd Gregg, N.H.*
Stephen L. Neal, N.C.	*Michael G. Oxley, Ohio*
Doug Barnard Jr., Ga.	
Peter A. Peyser, N.Y.	
Barney Frank, Mass.	
Harold Washington, Ill.	
Tom Lantos, Calif.	

Commerce, Consumer, and Monetary Affairs

Phone: 225-4407

Rosenthal - chairman

Conyers	*Williams*
Atkinson	*Daub*
Neal	*Clinger*
Barnard	*Hiler*
Peyser	

Environment, Energy and Natural Resources

Phone: 225-6427

Moffett - chairman

Fithian	*Deckard*
Synar	*Hiler*
Lantos	*Gregg*
Atkinson	*Vacancy*
Frank	

Government Activities and Transportation

Phone: 225-7920

Burton - chairman

Evans	*Walker*
Weiss	*Bailey*
Peyser	*McGrath*
Lantos	*Daub*
Waxman	

Government Information and Individual Rights

Phone: 225-3741

English - chairman

Weiss	*Kindness*
Waxman	*Erlenborn*
Burton	*Bailey*
Conyers	

Intergovernmental Relations and Human Resources

Phone: 225-2548

Fountain - chairman

Frank	*Brown*
Levitas	*McGrath*
Fithian	*DeNardis*
Neal	

Legislation and National Security

Phone: 225-5147

Brooks - chairman

Fascell	*Horton*
Fuqua	*Erlenborn*
Levitas	*Butler*
Evans	*Clinger*
Waxman	

Manpower and Housing

Phone: 225-6751

Collins - chairman

Washington	*McCloskey*
Conyers	*Butler*
Atkinson	*Vacancy*
Rosenthal	

* Chairman and ranking minority member are members ex officio of all subcommittees of which they are not regular members.

House Administration

House administration generally; printing and correction of the Congressional Record; federal elections generally; management of the Library of Congress, supervision of the Smithsonian Institution, etc.

Phone: 225-2061

D 11 - R 8

Augustus F. Hawkins, D-Calif., chairman*

Frank Annunzio, Ill.	*Bill Frenzel, Minn.**
Joseph M. Gaydos, Pa.	*William L. Dickinson, Ala.*
Ed Jones, Tenn.	*Robert E. Badham, Calif.*
Robert H. Mollohan, W.Va.	*Newt Gingrich, Ga.*
Joseph G. Minish, N.J.	*William M. Thomas, Calif.*
Charlie Rose, N.C.	*Gary A. Lee, N.Y.*
John L. Burton, Calif.	*Jim Coyne, Pa.*
William R. Ratchford, Conn.	*Lynn Martin, Ill.*
Al Swift, Wash.	
William J. Coyne, Pa.	

Accounts

Phone: 225-7884

Annunzio - chairman

Rose	*Badham*
Burton	*Thomas*
Ratchford	*Lee*
Swift	*Martin*
Coyne	*Frenzel*
Gaydos	

Contracts and Printing

Phone: 225-2444

Gaydos - chairman

Jones	*Gingrich*
Minish	*Martin*

Office Systems

Phone: 225-1608

Mollohan - chairman

Burton	*Thomas*
Swift	*Lee*

Personnel and Police

Phone: 225-7552

Minish - chairman

Annunzio	*Lee*
Ratchford	*Coyne*

Services

Phone: 225-4568

Jones - chairman

Mollohan	*Dickinson*
Rose	*Coyne*

Policy Group on Information and Computers

Phone: 225-5428

Rose - chairman

Burton	*Coyne*
Coyne	*Thomas*

* Chairman and ranking minority member are members ex officio of all subcommittees of which they are not regular members.

Interior and Insular Affairs

Public lands, parks, natural resources, territorial possessions of the United States, Indian affairs, regulation of domestic nuclear energy industry.

Phone: 225-2761

D 23 - R 17

Morris K. Udall, D-Ariz., chairman*

Phillip Burton, Calif.	*Manuel Lujan Jr., N.M.**
Robert W. Kastenmeier, Wis.	*Don H. Clausen, Calif.*
Abraham Kazen Jr., Texas	*Don Young, Alaska*
Jonathan B. Bingham, N.Y.	*Robert J. Lagomarsino, Calif.*
John F. Seiberling, Ohio	*Dan Marriott, Utah*
Antonio Borja Won Pat, Guam[1]	*Ron Marlenee, Mont.*
James D. Santini, Nev.	*Dick Cheney, Wyo.*
James Weaver, Ore.	*Charles Pashayan Jr., Calif.*
	Douglas K. Bereuter, Neb.

George Miller, Calif.	*David O'B. Martin, N.Y.*
James J. Florio, N.J.	*Larry E. Craig, Idaho*
Philip R. Sharp, Ind.	*Bill Hendon, N.C.*
Edward J. Markey, Mass.	*Hank Brown, Colo.*
Baltasar Corrada, P.R.[1]	*David Michael Staton, W.Va.*
Austin J. Murphy, Pa.	*Denny Smith, Ore.*
Nick J. Rahall, II, W.Va.	*James V. Hansen, Utah*
Bruce F. Vento, Minn.	*Vacancy*
Jerry Huckaby, La.	
Jerry M. Patterson, Calif.	
Ray Kogovsek, Colo.	
Pat Williams, Mont.	
Dale E. Kildee, Mich.	
Tony Coelho, Calif.	
Beverly B. Byron, Md.	
Ron de Lugo, V.I.[1]	
Sam Gejdenson, Conn.	

Energy and the Environment

Phone: 225-8331

Udall - chairman

Bingham	*Lujan*
Seiberling	*Marriott*
Weaver	*Cheney*
Sharp	*Bereuter*
Markey	*Martin*
Corrada	*Staton*
Murphy	*Smith*
Rahall	*Vacancy*
Vento	
Huckaby	
Williams	
Gejdenson	

Insular Affairs

Phone: 225-9297

Won Pat - chairman

Burton	*Lagomarsino*
Seiberling	*Clausen*
Corrada	*Bereuter*
Kildee	*Smith*
De Lugo	
Udall	

Mines and Mining

Phone: 225-1661

Santini - chairman

Kazen	*Marriott*
Murphy	*Young*
Rahall	*Martin*
Huckaby	*Craig*
Kogovsek	*Staton*
Byron	

Oversight and Investigations

Phone: 225-2196

Markey - chairman

Coelho	*Marlenee*
Patterson	*Hendon*
Florio	*Brown*
Byron	*Vacancy*
Gejdenson	

Public Lands and National Parks

Phone: 225-3681

Seiberling - chairman

Burton	*Young*
Kastenmeier	*Clausen*
Kazen	*Lagomarsino*
Bingham	*Marlenee*
Won Pat	*Cheney*
Santini	*Pashayan*
Weaver	*Craig*
Florio	*Hendon*
Vento	*Brown*
Kogovsek	*Hansen*
Williams	
Kildee	
Byron	
De Lugo	
Gejdenson	

Water and Power Resources

Phone: 225-6042

Kazen - chairman

Udall	*Clausen*
Weaver	*Lujan*
Miller	*Pashayan*
Patterson	*Bereuter*
Kogovsek	*Hansen*
Coelho	

* Chairman and ranking minority member are members ex officio of all subcommittees of which they are not regular members.
1 Delegates from Guam and the Virgin Islands and the Resident Commissioner from Puerto Rico not counted in party ratios.

Judiciary

Courts and judicial proceedings generally; constitutional amendments; civil rights; civil liberties; interstate compacts; immigration and naturalization; apportionment of representatives; meetings of Congress and attendance of members; presidential succession; national penitentiaries; patents; copyrights; trademarks; protection of trade and commerce against unlawful restraints and monopolies; subversive activities affecting the internal security of the United States.

Phone: 225-3951

D 16 - R 12

Peter W. Rodino Jr., D-N.J., chairman

Jack Brooks, Texas	*Robert McClory, Ill.*
Robert W. Kastenmeier, Wis.	*Tom Railsback, Ill.*
Don Edwards, Calif.	*Hamilton Fish Jr., N.Y.*
John Conyers Jr., Mich.	*M. Caldwell Butler, Va.*
John F. Seiberling, Ohio	*Carlos J. Moorhead, Calif.*
George E. Danielson, Calif.	*John M. Ashbrook, Ohio*
Romano L. Mazzoli, Ky.	*Henry J. Hyde, Ill.*
William J. Hughes, N.J.	*Thomas N. Kindness, Ohio*
Sam B. Hall Jr., Texas	*Harold S. Sawyer, Mich.*
Mike Synar, Okla.	*Dan Lungren, Calif.*
Patricia Schroeder, Colo.	*F. James Sensenbrenner Jr.,*
Billy Lee Evans, Ga.	*Wis.*
Dan Glickman, Kan.	*Bill McCollum, Fla.*
Harold Washington, Ill.	
Barney Frank, Mass.	

Administrative Law and Governmental Relations

Phone: 225-5741

Danielson - chairman

Synar	*Moorhead*
Evans	*Kindness*
Glickman	*McClory*

Civil and Constitutional Rights

Phone: 225-1680

Edwards - chairman

Kastenmeier	*Hyde*
Schroeder	*Sensenbrenner*
Washington	*Lungren*

Courts, Civil Liberties, and Administration of Justice

Phone: 225-3926

Kastenmeier - chairman

Brooks	*Railsback*
Danielson	*Sawyer*
Frank	*Butler*

Crime

Phone: 225-1695

Hughes - chairman

		Norman E. D'Amours, N.H.	*Thomas B. Evans Jr., Del.*
Kastenmeier	*Sawyer*	James L. Oberstar, Minn.	*Robert W. Davis, Mich.*
Conyers	*Ashbrook*	William J. Hughes, N.J.	*William Carney, N.Y.*
Hall	*Fish*	Barbara A. Mikulski, Md.	*Charles F. Dougherty, Pa.*

Criminal Justice

Phone: 225-0406

Conyers - chairman

		Mike Lowry, Wash.	*Norman D. Shumway, Calif.*
		Earl Hutto, Fla.	*Jack Fields, Texas*
Edwards	*Sensenbrenner*	Brian J. Donnelly, Mass.	*Claudine Schneider, R.I.*
Seiberling	*Kindness*	W.J. "Billy" Tauzin, La.	*E. Clay Shaw Jr., Fla.*
Hall	*McCollum*	Thomas M. Foglietta, Pa.	

Bill Patman, Texas
Fofo I.F. Sunia,
 American Samoa[1]
Dennis M. Hertel, Mich.
Roy Dyson, Md.

Immigration, Refugees, and International Law

Phone: 225-5727

Mazzoli - chairman

Coast Guard and Navigation

Phone: 225-8204

Studds - chairman

Hall	*Fish*	Hughes	*Young*
Schroeder	*Lungren*	Tauzin	*Lent*
Frank	*McCollum*	Biaggi	*Evans*

Monopolies and Commercial Law

Phone: 225-2825

Rodino - chairman

		Bonker	*Davis*
		Oberstar	*Dougherty*
		Mikulski	*Shumway*
Brooks	*McClory*	Lowry	*Fields*
Edwards	*Butler*	Hutto	*Shaw*
Seiberling	*Railsback*	Foglietta	
Mazzoli	*Moorhead*	Dyson	
Hughes	*Hyde*		
Evans			

Fisheries and Wildlife Conservation and the Environment

Phone: 225-7307

Breaux - chairman

Merchant Marine and Fisheries

Merchant marine generally; Coast Guard; oceanography and marine affairs; maintenance and operation of the Panama Canal and administration of the Canal Zone; fisheries and wildlife.

Phone: 225-4047

D 20 - R 15

Walter B. Jones, D-N.C., chairman*

Bowen	*Forsythe*
Bonker	*McCloskey*
Oberstar	*Pritchard*
Lowry	*Young*
Hutto	*Emery*
Donnelly	*Evans*
Patman	*Davis*
Sunia	*Carney*
Dyson	*Dougherty*
Anderson	*Shumway*
Studds	*Schneider*
D'Amours	
Hughes	
Tauzin	
Hertel	

Mario Biaggi, N.Y.	*Gene Snyder, Ky.**
Glenn M. Anderson, Calif.	*Paul N. McCloskey Jr., Calif.*
John B. Breaux, La.	*Edwin B. Forsythe, N.J.*
Gerry E. Studds, Mass.	*Joel Pritchard, Wash.*
David R. Bowen, Miss.	*Don Young, Alaska*
Carroll Hubbard Jr., Ky.	*Norman F. Lent, N.Y.*
Don Bonker, Wash.	*David F. Emery, Maine*

Merchant Marine

Phone: 225-3426

Biaggi - chairman

Anderson	McCloskey	Mary Rose Oakar, Ohio	Daniel B. Crane, Ill.
Mikulski	Young	Charles E. Schumer, N.Y.	Wayne R. Grisham, Calif.
Foglietta	Davis	Steny Hoyer, Md.	Frank R. Wolf, Va.
Hertel	Dougherty	George E. Danielson, Calif.	Vacancy
Hubbard	Shumway	Ronald V. Dellums, Calif.	
Donnelly	Fields	Ron de Lugo, V.I.[1]	
Patman	Shaw	Gus Savage, Ill.	
Sunia			
Breaux			

Oceanography

Phone: 225-7508

D'Amours - chairman

Dyson	Pritchard
Studds	Emery
Hughes	Carney
Mikulski	Schneider
Hertel	

Panama Canal and Outer Continental Shelf

Phone: 225-8186

Hubbard - chairman

Breaux	Lent
Bowen	Forsythe
Foglietta	Young
Anderson	Emery
Mikulski	Carney
Lowry	Fields
Tauzin	

* Chairman and ranking minority member are members ex officio of all subcommittees.
1 Delegate from American Samoa not counted in party ratios.

Post Office and Civil Service

Postal and federal civil services; census and the collection of statistics generally; Hatch Act; holidays and celebrations.

Phone: 225-4054

D 15 - R 11

William D. Ford, D-Mich., chairman*

Morris K. Udall, Ariz.	Edward J. Derwinski, Ill.*
William Clay, Mo.	Gene Taylor, Mo.
Patricia Schroeder, Colo.	Benjamin A. Gilman, N.Y.
Robert Garcia, N.Y.	Tom Corcoran, Ill.
Mickey Leland, Texas	Jim Courter, N.J.
Geraldine A. Ferraro, N.Y.	Charles Pashayan Jr., Calif.
Don Albosta, Mich.	William E. Dannemeyer,
Gus Yatron, Pa.	Calif.

Census and Population

Phone: 225-6741

Garcia - chairman

Yatron	Courter
Leland	Crane
Oakar	Grisham
Vacancy	

Civil Service

Phone: 225-4025

Schroeder - chairman

Udall	Pashayan
Clay	Taylor
Yatron	Courter
Danielson	Wolf
Vacancy	

Compensation and Employee Benefits

Phone: 225-6831

Oakar - chairman

Albosta	Dannemeyer
Danielson	Crane
Hoyer	
Savage	

Human Resources

Phone: 225-2821

Ferraro - chairman

Dellums	Corcoran
Danielson	Gilman
Schumer	Wolf
Hoyer	

Investigations

Phone: 225-6295

Ford - chairman

Clay	Derwinski
Udall	Pashayan
Garcia	Grisham

Postal Operations and Services

Phone: 225-9124

Clay - chairman

Albosta	*Taylor*
Ferraro	*Corcoran*
Oakar	*Wolf*
de Lugo	*Vacancy*
Dellums	

Postal Personnel and Modernization

Phone: 225-3718

Leland - chairman

Garcia	*Gilman*
Clay	*Dannemeyer*
Dellums	*Grisham*
Schumer	

* Chairman and ranking minority member are members ex officio of all subcommittees of which they are not regular members.

Public Works and Transportation

Public buildings and roads; flood control; improvement of rivers and harbors; water power; pollution of navigable waters; transportation (except railroads).

Phone: 225-4472

D 25 - R 19

James J. Howard, D-N.J., chairman*

Glenn M. Anderson, Calif.	*Don H. Clausen, Calif.**
Robert A. Roe, N.J.	*Gene Snyder, Ky.*
John B. Breaux, La.	*John Paul Hammerschmidt, Ark.*
Norman Y. Mineta, Calif.	
Elliott H. Levitas, Ga.	*Bud Shuster, Pa.*
James L. Oberstar, Minn.	*Barry M. Goldwater Jr., Calif.*
Henry J. Nowak, N.Y.	
Robert W. Edgar, Pa.	*Tom Hagedorn, Minn.*
Marilyn Lloyd Bouquard, Tenn.	*Arlan Stangeland, Minn.*
	Newt Gingrich, Ga.
John G. Fary, Ill.	*William F. Clinger Jr., Pa.*
Robert A. Young, Mo.	*Gerald B. H. Solomon, N.Y.*
Allen E. Ertel, Pa.	*Harold C. Hollenbeck, N.J.*
Billy Lee Evans, Ga.	*Joel Deckard, Ind.*
Ronnie G. Flippo, Ala.	*Wayne Grisham, Calif.*
Nick J. Rahall II, W.Va.	*Jim Jeffries, Kan.*
Douglas Applegate, Ohio	*Jack Fields, Texas*
Geraldine A. Ferraro, N.Y.	*Guy V. Molinari, N.Y.*

Eugene V. Atkinson, Pa.
Don Albosta, Mich.
Bill Boner, Tenn.
Ron de Lugo, V.I.[1]
Gus Savage, Ill.
Fofo I.F. Sunia, American Samoa[1]
Buddy Roemer, La.
Brian J. Donnelly, Mass.
Ray Kogovsek, Colo.

E. Clay Shaw Jr., Fla.
Bob McEwen, Ohio
Frank R. Wolf, Va.

Aviation

Phone: 225-9161

Mineta - chairman

Levitas	*Snyder*
Ferraro	*Hammerschmidt*
Atkinson	*Shuster*
Boner	*Goldwater*
de Lugo	*Hagedorn*
Roemer	*Gingrich*
Anderson	*Hollenbeck*
Oberstar	*Deckard*
Fary	*Grisham*
Young	*Wolf*
Ertel	
Rahall	
Applegate	
Sunia	
Nowak	

Economic Development

Phone: 225-6151

Oberstar - chairman

Bouquard	*Hagedorn*
Roe	*Hammerschmidt*
Flippo	*Shuster*
Applegate	*Clinger*
Albosta	*Hollenbeck*
Savage	*Deckard*
Sunia	*McEwen*
Donnelly	
Nowak	
Edgar	

Investigations and Oversight

Phone: 225-3274

Levitas - chairman

Mineta	*Goldwater*
Roe	*Stangeland*
Ferraro	*Gingrich*
Albosta	*Solomon*
Boner	*Hollenbeck*

Savage
Roemer
Fary
Flippo

Molinari
McEwen

Public Buildings and Grounds

Phone: 225-9161

Fary - chairman

Mineta
Levitas
Donnelly
Bouquard

Stangeland
Solomon
Jeffries

Surface Transportation

Phone: 225-4472

Anderson - chairman

Edgar
Ertel
Rahall
Applegate
Atkinson
Boner
Nowak
Young
Evans
Albosta
de Lugo
Savage
Sunia
Donnelly
Kogovsek
Breaux

Shuster
Snyder
Hagedorn
Stangeland
Gingrich
Clinger
Deckard
Fields
Molinari
Shaw
McEwen

Water Resources

Phone: 225-0060

Roe - chairman

Breaux
Flippo
Ferraro
Roemer
Anderson
Oberstar
Nowak
Edgar
Fary
Young
Ertel
Evans
Rahall

Hammerschmidt
Snyder
Clinger
Solomon
Grisham
Jeffries
Fields
Molinari
Shaw
Wolf

* Chairman and ranking minority member are members ex officio of all subcommittees.

Rules

Rules and order of business of the House.

Phone: 225-9486

D 11 - R 5

Richard Bolling, D-Mo., chairman

Claude Pepper, Fla.
Gillis W. Long, La.
Joe Moakley, Mass.
Shirley Chisholm, N.Y.
Leo C. Zeferetti, N.Y.
Butler Derrick, S.C.
Anthony C. Beilenson, Calif.
Martin Frost, Texas
David E. Bonior, Mich.
Tony P. Hall, Ohio

James H. Quillen, Tenn.
Delbert L. Latta, Ohio
Trent Lott, Miss.
Gene Taylor, Mo.
John J. Rhodes, Ariz.

Legislative Process

Phone: 225-9641

Long - chairman

Chisholm
Zeferetti
Derrick

Lott
Taylor

Rules of the House

Phone: 225-9091

Moakley - chairman

Beilenson
Frost
Pepper
Bonior
Hall

Taylor
Rhodes
Lott

Science and Technology

Scientific and astronautical research and development generally; National Aeronautics and Space Administration; National Aeronautics and Space Council; National Science Foundation; outer space; science scholarships; Bureau of Standards; National Weather Service; civil aviation research and development; environmental research and development; energy research and development (except nuclear research and development).

Phone: 225-6371

D 23 - R 17

Don Fuqua, D-Fla., chairman*

Robert A. Roe, N.J.
George E. Brown Jr., Calif.
James H. Scheuer, N.Y.
Richard L. Ottinger, N.Y.
Tom Harkin, Iowa
Marilyn Lloyd Bouquard,
  Tenn.
James J. Blanchard, Mich.
Doug Walgren, Pa.
Ronnie G. Flippo, Ala.
Dan Glickman, Kan.
Albert Gore Jr., Tenn.
Robert A. Young, Mo.
Richard C. White, Texas
Harold L. Volkmer, Mo.
Howard Wolpe, Mich.
Bill Nelson, Fla.
Stanley N. Lundine, N.Y.
Allen E. Ertel, Pa.
Bob Shamansky, Ohio
Ralph M. Hall, Texas
Dave McCurdy, Okla.
Mervyn M. Dymally, Calif.

Larry Winn Jr., Kan.*
Barry M. Goldwater Jr.,
  Calif.
Hamilton Fish Jr., N.Y.
Manuel Lujan Jr., N.M.
Harold C. Hollenbeck, N.J.
Robert S. Walker, Pa.
Edwin B. Forsythe, N.J.
William Carney, N.Y.
Margaret M. Heckler, Mass.
F. James Sensenbrenner Jr.,
  Wis.
Vin Weber, Minn.
Judd Gregg, N.H.
Raymond J. McGrath, N.Y.
Joe Skeen, N.M.
Claudine Schneider, R.I.
Jim Dunn, Mich.
Bill Lowery, Calif.

Energy Development and Applications

Phone: 225-4494

Fuqua - chairman

Harkin	*Fish*
Blanchard	*Sensenbrenner*
White	*Weber*
Volkmer	*Gregg*
Wolpe	*Skeen*
Nelson	*Schneider*
Ertel	*McGrath*
McCurdy	*Dunn*
Roe	*Walker*
Scheuer	
Ottinger	
Bouquard	
Young	

Energy Research and Production

Phone: 225-8056

Bouquard - chairman

Roe	*Lujan*
Ottinger	*Forsythe*
Young	*Lowery*
Lundine	*Goldwater*
Flippo	*Hollenbeck*
Volkmer	
Wolpe	

Investigations and Oversight

Phone: 225-2121

Gore - chairman

Shamansky	*Walker*
Volkmer	*Lujan*

Natural Resources, Agriculture Research and Environment

Phone: 225-1064

Scheuer - chairman

Brown	*Carney*
Blanchard	*Sensenbrenner*
Walgren	*Schneider*
White	

Science, Research and Technology

Phone: 225-8844

Walgren - chairman

Brown	*Heckler*
Shamansky	*Weber*
Dymally	*Gregg*
Lundine	*Skeen*
Ertel	*Forsythe*
Hall	
McCurdy	

Space Science and Applications

Phone: 225-7858

Flippo - chairman

Nelson	*Hollenbeck*
Brown	*McGrath*
Bouquard	*Lowery*
Hall	

Transportation, Aviation and Materials

Phone: 225-9662

Glickman - chairman

Hall	*Goldwater*
Harkin	*Dunn*
Shamansky	*Hollenbeck*
Dymally	*Carney*
Flippo	

* Chairman and ranking minority member are members ex officio *of all subcommittees of which they are not regular members.*

Select Aging

Studies and investigates problems of aging.

Phone: 225-9375

D 32 - R 23

Claude Pepper, D-Fla., chairman*

Edward R. Roybal, Calif.	Matthew J. Rinaldo, N.J.*
Mario Biaggi, N.Y.	William C. Wampler, Va.
Ike Andrews, N.C.	John Paul Hammerschmidt, Ark.
John L. Burton, Calif.	
Don Bonker, Wash.	Marc L. Marks, Pa.
Thomas J. Downey, N.Y.	Ralph Regula, Ohio
James J. Florio, N.J.	Robert K. Dornan, Calif.
Harold E. Ford, Tenn.	Harold C. Hollenbeck, N.J.
William J. Hughes, N.J.	Norman D. Shumway, Calif.
Marilyn Lloyd Bouquard, Tenn.	Olympia J. Snowe, Maine
	Dan Lungren, Calif.
James D. Santini, Nev.	Millicent Fenwick, N.J.
David W. Evans, Ind.	James M. Jeffords, Vt.
Stanley N. Lundine, N.Y.	Tom Tauke, Iowa
Mary Rose Oakar, Ohio	Thomas E. Petri, Wis.
Thomas A. Luken, Ohio	Judd Gregg, N.H.
Geraldine A. Ferraro, N.Y.	Dan Coats, Ind.
Beverly B. Byron, Md.	George C. Wortley, N.Y.
William R. Ratchford, Conn.	Hal Daub, Neb.
Dan Mica, Fla.	Larry E. Craig, Idaho
Henry A. Waxman, Calif.	Pat Roberts, Kan.
Mike Synar, Okla.	Bill Hendon, N.C.
Eugene V. Atkinson, Pa.	Gregory W. Carman, N.Y.
Butler Derrick, S.C.	Cooper Evans, Iowa
Bruce F. Vento, Minn.	
Barney Frank, Mass.	
Tom Lantos, Calif.	
Bob Shamansky, Ohio	
Ron Wyden, Ore.	
Don Albosta, Mich.	
George W. Crockett Jr., Mich.	
Bill Boner, Tenn.	

Health and Long-Term Care

Phone: 225-2381

Pepper - chairman

Andrews	Marks
Bonker	Regula
Ford	Lungren
Bouquard	Fenwick
Luken	Jeffords
Ratchford	Wortley
Mica	Daub
Atkinson	Craig
Derrick	Roberts
Wyden	
Florio	
Evans	
Oakar	

Housing and Consumer Interests

Phone: 225-4242

Roybal - chairman

Santini	Hammerschmidt
Byron	Dornan
Lantos	Wortley
Shamansky	Hendon
Crockett	Carman
Lundine	Vacancy
Synar	

Human Services

Phone: 225-4348

Biaggi - chairman

Florio	Rinaldo
Hughes	Hammerschmidt
Lundine	Shumway
Vento	Snowe
Albosta	Lungren
Ferraro	Tauke
Ratchford	Petri
Crockett	Craig
Boner	

Retirement Income and Employment

Phone: 225-4045

Burton - chairman

Downey	Wampler
Evans	Hollenbeck
Oakar	Shumway
Ferraro	Jeffords
Waxman	Gregg
Synar	Coats
Frank	Hendon
Vento	Carman
Lantos	
Wyden	

* Chairman and ranking minority member are members ex officio of all subcommittees of which they are not regular members.

Select Intelligence

Legislative and budgetary authority over the Central Intelligence Agency, the Federal Bureau of Investigation and other components of the federal intelligence community.

Phone: 225-4121

D 9 - R 5

Edward P. Boland, D-Mass., chairman*

Clement J. Zablocki, Wis.   J. Kenneth Robinson, Va.

Charlie Rose, N.C.
Romano L. Mazzoli, Ky.
Norman Y. Mineta, Calif.
Wyche Fowler Jr., Ga.
Lee H. Hamilton, Ind.
Albert Gore Jr., Tenn.
Bob Stump, Ariz.

John M. Ashbrook, Ohio
Robert McClory, Ill.
G. William Whitehurst, Va.
C. W. Bill Young, Fla.

Glenn English, Okla.
Billy Lee Evans, Ga.
James H. Scheuer, N.Y.
Cardiss Collins, Ill.
Daniel K. Akaka, Hawaii
Frank J. Guarini, N.J.
Robert T. Matsui, Calif.

Robert K. Dornan, Calif.
Lawrence J. DeNardis, Conn.
E. Clay Shaw Jr., Fla.
Michael G. Oxley, Ohio

Legislation

Phone: 225-7310

Mazzoli - chairman

| Fowler | McClory |
| Hamilton | Ashbrook |

No standing subcommittees.

Oversight and Evaluation

Phone: 225-5657

Rose - chairman

| Fowler | Ashbrook |
| Gore | Young |

Small Business

Assistance to and protection of small business, including financial aid; participation of small business enterprises in federal procurement and government contracts.

Phone: 225-5821

D 23 - R 17

Parren J. Mitchell, D-Md., chairman*

Program and Budget Authorization

Phone: 225-7690

Boland - chairman

Zablocki	Robinson
Mineta	Whitehurst
Stump	Young

* Chairman of full committee is a voting member of all subcommittees. House Majority Leader Jim Wright, D-Texas and Minority Leader Robert H. Michel, R-Ill., are members ex officio *of the full committee.*

Select Narcotics Abuse and Control

Studies and reviews the problems of narcotics abuse and control, including international trafficking, enforcement, prevention, international treaties, organized crime, drug abuse in the U.S. armed forces, treatment and rehabilitation.

Phone: 225-1753

D 11 - R 8

Leo C. Zeferetti, D-N.Y., chairman

Peter W. Rodino Jr., N.J.
Charles B. Rangel, N.Y.
Fortney H. "Pete" Stark, Calif.

Tom Railsback, Ill.
Robin L. Beard, Tenn.
Benjamin A. Gilman, N.Y.
Lawrence Coughlin, Pa.

Neal Smith, Iowa
Joseph P. Addabbo, N.Y.
Henry B. Gonzalez, Texas
John J. LaFalce, N.Y.
Berkley Bedell, Iowa
Fred Richmond, N.Y.
Henry J. Nowak, N.Y.
Thomas A. Luken, Ohio
Andy Ireland, Fla.
Ike Skelton, Mo.
Billy Lee Evans, Ga.
Charles W. Stenholm, Texas
Romano L. Mazzoli, Ky.
Nicholas Mavroules, Mass.
George W. Crockett Jr., Mich.
Charles Hatcher, Ga.
Ron Wyden, Ore.
Dennis E. Eckart, Ohio
Byron L. Dorgan, N.D.
Gus Savage, Ill.
Buddy Roemer, La.
John G. Fary, Ill.

Joseph M. McDade, Pa.*
Silvio O. Conte, Mass.
J. William Stanton, Ohio
William S. Broomfield, Mich.
Dan Marriott, Utah
Lyle Williams, Ohio
Olympia J. Snowe, Maine
Daniel B. Crane, Ill.
John Hiler, Ind.
David Michael Staton, W.Va.
Vin Weber, Minn.
Hal Daub, Neb.
Christopher H. Smith, N.J.
Ed Weber, Ohio
David Dreier, Calif.
Guy V. Molinari, N.Y.
Mark Siljander, Mich.

Antitrust and Restraint of Trade Activities Affecting Small Business

Phone: 225-6026

Luken - chairman

Eckart	Williams
Gonzalez	Daub
Bedell	Siljander

Energy, Environment and Safety Issues Affecting Small Business

Phone: 225-8944

Bedell - chairman

Mavroules	*Conte*
Hatcher	*Hiler*
Eckart	*Molinari*

Export Opportunities and Special Small Business Problems

Phone: 225-9368

Ireland - chairman

Skelton	*Broomfield*
Stenholm	*Staton*
Wyden	*Weber, Ohio*
Crockett	*Dreier*
Smith	

General Oversight

Phone: 225-9321

LaFalce - chairman

Mazzoli	*Stanton*
Addabbo	*Smith*
Richmond	*Weber, Ohio*
Luken	*Dreier*
Roemer	*Snowe*
Crockett	

SBA and SBIC Authority, Minority Enterprise and General Small Business Problems

Phone: 225-5821

Mitchell - chairman

Smith	*McDade*
Addabbo	*Hiler*
Gonzalez	*Staton*
Richmond	*Daub*
Hatcher	*Smith*
Savage	

Tax, Access to Equity Capital and Business Opportunities

Phone: 225-7797

Nowak - chairman

Evans	*Marriott*
Dorgan	*Snowe*

Savage	*Crane*
Roemer	*Weber, Minn.*
Fary	

* Chairman and ranking minority member are members ex officio of all subcommittees of which they are not regular members.

Standards of Official Conduct

Studies and investigates standards of conduct of House members and employees and may recommend action.

Phone: 225-7103

D 6 - R 6

Louis Stokes, D-Ohio, chairman

Nick J. Rahall II, W.Va.	*Floyd Spence, S.C.*
Bill Alexander, Ark.	*Barber B. Conable Jr., N.Y.*
Charles Wilson, Texas	*John T. Myers, Ind.*
Ken Holland, S.C.	*Edwin B. Forsythe, N.J.*
Don Bailey, Pa.	*Hank Brown, Colo.*
	James V. Hansen, Utah

No standing subcommittees.

Veterans' Affairs

Veterans' measures generally; pensions, armed forces insurance, rehabilitation, education, medical care and treatment of veterans, veterans' hospitals and housing.

Phone: 225-3527

D 17 - R 14

G. V. "Sonny" Montgomery, D-Miss., chairman*

Don Edwards, Calif.	*John Paul Hammerschmidt,*
George E. Danielson, Calif.	*Ark.**
Jack Brinkley, Ga.	*Margaret M. Heckler, Mass.*
Ronald M. Mottl, Ohio	*Chalmers P. Wylie, Ohio*
Robert W. Edgar, Pa.	*Elwood Hillis, Ind.*
Sam B. Hall Jr., Texas	*Harold S. Sawyer, Mich.*
Douglas Applegate, Ohio	*Gerald B. H. Solomon, N.Y.*
Marvin Leath, Texas	*Jim Jeffries, Kan.*
Bill Boner, Tenn.	*Bob McEwen, N.Y.*
Richard C. Shelby, Ala.	*Jim Dunn, Mich.*
Dan Mica, Fla.	*Christopher H. Smith, N.J.*
Thomas A. Daschle, S.D.	*Albert Lee Smith Jr., Ala.*
Bob Stump, Ariz.	*Denny Smith, Ore.*
Phil Gramm, Texas	*Mark Siljander, Mich*
Austin J. Murphy, Pa.	*Vacancy*
Byron L. Dorgan, N.D.	
Antonio Borja Won Pat, Guam[1]	

Compensation, Pension and Insurance

Phone: 225-3569

Hall - chairman

Montgomery	*Wylie*
Danielson	*Hammerschmidt*
Brinkley	*Smith, Ala.*
Applegate	*Smith, Ore.*
Murphy	*Siljander*

Education, Training and Employment

Phone: 225-9166

Edgar - chairman

Edwards	*Heckler*
Leath	*Wylie*
Boner	*Jeffries*
Daschle	*Smith, Ore.*
Gramm	*Siljander*

Hospitals and Health Care

Phone: 225-9154

Mottl - chairman

Edwards	*Hammerschmidt*
Applegate	*Heckler*
Boner	*Hillis*
Shelby	*Solomon*
Mica	*McEwen*
Daschle	*Dunn*
Gramm	*Smith, N.J.*
Edgar	*Smith, Ala.*
Dorgan	

Housing and Memorial Affairs

Phone: 225-9164

Leath - chairman

Brinkley	*Sawyer*
Mottl	*McEwen*
Shelby	*Smith, N.J.*
Mica	*Dunn*
Won Pat	

Oversight and Investigations

Phone: 225-3541

Montgomery - chairman

Danielson	*Hillis*
Stump	*Hammerschmidt*
Hall	*Sawyer*

Mica	*Solomon*
Leath	*Jeffries*
Won Pat	

* *Chairman and ranking minority member are members ex officio of all subcommittees of which they are not regular members.*

¹ *Delegate from Guam not counted in party ratios.*

Ways and Means

Revenue measures generally; tariffs and trade agreements; Social Security; tax exempt foundations and charitable trusts.

Phone: 225-3625

D 23 - R 12

Dan Rostenkowski, D-Ill., chairman*

Sam Gibbons, Fla.	*Barber B. Conable Jr., N.Y.**
J. J. Pickle, Texas	*John J. Duncan, Tenn.*
Charles B. Rangel, N.Y.	*Bill Archer, Texas*
Fortney H. "Pete" Stark, Calif.	*Guy Vander Jagt, Mich.*
	Philip M. Crane, Ill.
James R. Jones, Okla.	*Bill Frenzel, Minn.*
Andrew Jacobs Jr., Ind.	*James G. Martin, N.C.*
Harold E. Ford, Tenn.	*L. A. "Skip" Bafalis, Fla.*
Ken Holland, S.C.	*Richard T. Schulze, Pa.*
William M. Brodhead, Mich.	*Bill Gradison, Ohio*
Ed Jenkins, Ga.	*John H. Rousselot, Calif.*
Richard A. Gephardt, Mo.	*Henson Moore, La.*
Thomas J. Downey, N.Y.	
Cecil Heftel, Hawaii	
Wyche Fowler Jr., Ga.	
Frank J. Guarini, N.J.	
James M. Shannon, Mass.	
Marty Russo, Ill.	
Don J. Pease, Ohio	
Kent Hance, Texas	
Robert T. Matsui, Calif.	
Don Bailey, Pa.	
Vacancy	

Health

Phone: 225-7785

Jacobs - chairman

Rangel	*Gradison*
Ford	*Duncan*
Holland	*Crane*
Vacancy	

Oversight

Phone: 225-2743

Rangel - chairman

Gibbons	*Crane*
Pickle	*Moore*
Jenkins	*Duncan*
Guarini	*Martin*
Shannon	
Russo	

Pease	*Schulze*
Hance	
Brodhead	
Bailey	

* Chairman and ranking minority member are members ex officio of all subcommittees of which they are not regular members.

Public Assistance and Unemployment Compensation

Phone: 225-1025

Ford - chairman

Stark	*Bafalis*
Pease	*Rousselot*
Hance	*Gradison*
Matsui	*Moore*
Bailey	
Vacancy	

Select Revenue Measures

Phone: 225-9710

Stark - chairman

Holland	*Duncan*
Fowler	*Schulze*
Russo	*Vander Jagt*
Matsui	*Moore*
Heftel	
Guarini	

Social Security

Phone: 225-9263

Pickle - chairman

Jacobs	*Archer*
Gephardt	*Gradison*
Shannon	*Rousselot*
Brodhead	*Crane*
Heftel	
Fowler	

Trade

Phone: 225-3943

Gibbons - chairman

Rostenkowski	*Vander Jagt*
Jones	*Archer*
Jenkins	*Frenzel*
Downey	*Bafalis*

House Democratic Leaders

Speaker—Thomas P. O'Neill Jr., Mass.
Chairman of the Caucus—Gillis W. Long, La.
Secretary of the Caucus—Geraldine A. Ferraro, N.Y.
Floor Leader—Jim Wright, Texas
Whip—Thomas S. Foley, Wash.

Chief Deputy Whip—Bill Alexander, Ark.

Deputy Whips—George E. Danielson, Calif.; Richard A. Gephardt, Mo.; Joe Moakley, Mass.; Benjamin S. Rosenthal, N.Y.

At-Large Whips—Tom Bevill, Ala.; Tony Coelho, Calif.; Dennis E. Eckart, Ohio; William D. Ford, Mich.; Martin Frost, Texas; Carroll Hubbard Jr., Ky.; Ray Kogovsek, Colo.; Mickey Leland, Texas; Norman Y. Mineta, Calif.; Parren J. Mitchell, Md.; John P. Murtha, Pa.; Mary Rose Oakar, Ohio; Dan Rostenkowski, Ill.; Patricia Schroeder, Colo.; Pat Williams, Mont.

Assistant Whips, by zone numbers:

1. William R. Ratchford, Conn.—Connecticut, Massachusetts, Rhode Island, New Hampshire
2. Charles B. Rangel, N.Y. and Henry J. Nowak, N.Y.—New York
3. Allen E. Ertel, Pa.—Pennsylvania
4. Michael D. Barnes, Md.—Maryland, New Jersey
5. Charles Whitley, N.C.—North Carolina, Virginia
6. Elliott H. Levitas, Ga.—Georgia, South Carolina
7. James J. Blanchard, Mich.—Michigan
8. Martin Olav Sabo, Minn.—Minnesota, Wisconsin
9. Lee H. Hamilton, Ind.—Indiana, Kentucky
10. Don J. Pease, Ohio—Ohio, West Virginia
11. G.V. "Sonny" Montgomery, Miss.—Louisiana, Mississippi, Tennessee
12. Andy Ireland, Fla.—Alabama, Florida
13. Ike Skelton, Mo.—Iowa, Missouri
14. Sidney R. Yates, Ill.—Illinois
15. Richard C. White, Texas and Henry B. Gonzalez, Texas—Texas
16. Mike Synar, Okla.—Arkansas, Kansas, Oklahoma
17. Thomas A. Daschle, S.D. and Byron L. Dorgan, N.D.—Arizona, Colorado, Montana, Nevada, North Dakota, South Dakota
18. Norman D. Dicks, Wash.—Hawaii, Oregon, Washington
19. Anthony C. Beilenson, Calif. and Leon E. Panetta, Calif.—California

The nine states not covered — Alaska, Delaware, Idaho, Maine, Nebraska, New Mexico, Utah, Vermont and Wyoming — have no Democratic representatives.

Steering and Policy Committee

Scheduling of legislation and Democratic committee assignments.

Phone: 225-7187

Thomas P. O'Neill Jr., Mass., chairman
Jim Wright, Texas, vice chairman
Gillis W. Long, La., 2nd vice chairman

Adam Benjamin Jr., Ind.	James R. Jones, Okla.†
Tom Bevill, Ala	Norman Y. Mineta, Calif.
Mario Biaggi, N.Y.	Joe Moakley, Mass.
Richard Bolling, Mo.†	John P. Murtha, Pa.
John B. Breaux, La.	Charles B. Rangel, N.Y.
Phillip Burton, Calif.	Dan Rostenkowski, Ill.†
Geraldine A. Ferraro, N.Y.†	Fernand J. St Germain, R.I.
Thomas S. Foley, Wash.†	Patricia Schroeder, Colo.
William D. Ford, Mich.	W. J. "Billy" Tauzin, La.
Richard A. Gephardt, Mo.	Wes Watkins, Okla.
Bo Ginn, Ga.	Jamie L. Whitten, Miss.†
W. G. "Bill" Hefner, N.C.	Charles Wilson, Texas
William J. Hughes, N.J.	Timothy E. Wirth, Colo.

† Members ex officio *from the leadership.*

Democratic Congressional Campaign Committee

Phone: 789-2920

Tony Coelho, Calif., chairman
Dan Rostenkowski, Ill., vice chairman

Frank Annunzio, Ill.	Kenneth L. Holland, S.C
Beryl Anthony Jr., Ark.	Ed Jones, Tenn.
Les AuCoin, Ore.	James R. Jones, Okla.
Tom Bevill, Ala.	Clarence D. Long, Md.
Lindy (Mrs. Hale) Boggs, La.	Gillis W. Long, La.†
Don Bonker, Wash.	Thomas A. Luken, Ohio
David R. Bowen, Miss.	Robert H. Mollohan, W.Va.
Bill Chappell Jr., Fla.	William H. Natcher, Ky.
William Clay, Mo.	James L. Oberstar, Minn.
Baltasar Corrada, P.R.	Thomas P. O'Neill Jr., Mass.†
Norman E. D'Amours, N.H.	J. J. Pickle, Texas
Dan Daniel, Va.	William R. Ratchford, Conn.
Thomas A. Daschle, S.D.	Fred Richmond, N.Y.
Ron de Lugo, V.I.	Fernand J. St Germain, R.I.
John D. Dingell, Mich.	James D. Santini, Nev.
Byron Dorgan, N.D.	Patricia Schroeder, Colo.
Joseph D. Early, Mass.	Fofo I. F. Sunia,
Walter E. Fauntroy, D.C.	American Samoa
Floyd Fithian, Ind.	Morris K. Udall, Ariz.
James J. Florio, N.J.	Henry A. Waxman, Calif.
L. H. Fountain, N.C.	Pat Williams, Mont.

Thomas S. Foley, Wash.†	Antonio Borja Won Pat,
Wyche Fowler Jr., Ga.	Guam
Dan Glickman, Kan.	Jim Wright, Texas†
Tom Harkin, Iowa	Gus Yatron, Pa.
Cecil Heftel, Hawaii	Clement J. Zablocki, Wis.

† Members ex officio *from the leadership.*

Personnel Committee

Phone: 225-4068

Joe Moakley, Mass., chairman

Joseph P. Addabbo, N.Y.	Augustus F. Hawkins, Calif.
Bo Ginn, Ga.	Thomas P. O'Neill Jr., Mass.

House Republican Leaders

Chairman of the Conference—*Jack F. Kemp, N.Y.*
Vice Chairman of the Conference—*Jack Edwards, Ala.*
Secretary of the Conference—*Clair W. Burgener, Calif.*
Floor Leader—*Robert H. Michel, Ill.*
Whip—*Trent Lott, Miss.*
Chief Deputy Whip—*David F. Emery, Maine*
  Deputy Whips—*Tom Loeffler, Texas and Sid Morrison, Wash.*

The assistant minority whips are divided into four divisions, each with an overall regional whip and assistant whips in charge of specific numbers of members as follows:

New England and Middle Atlantic Division—*Joseph M. McDade, Pa.(10 states, 46 members)*
  James Courter, N.J. (11 members)
  David O'B. Martin, N.Y. (13 members)
  Richard T. Schulze, Pa. (11 members)
  Gerald B. H. Solomon, N.Y. (11 members)
Midwest Division—*Edward J. Derwinski, Ill. (7 states, 50 members)*
  Tom Corcoran, Ill. (16 members)
  Arlan Stangeland, Minn. (14 members)
  J. William Stanton, Ohio (11 members)
  Vin Weber, Minn. (9 members)
Western and Plains Division—*John H. Rousselot, Calif. (15 states, 46 members)*
  Hank Brown, Colo. (14 members)
  Mickey Edwards, Okla. (7 members)
  Robert J. Lagomarsino, Calif. (16 members)
  Manuel Lujan Jr., N.M. (9 members)
Border and Southern Division—*Bob Livingston, La. (15 states, 49 members)*
  Robin L. Beard Jr., Tenn. (13 members)
  William L. Dickinson, Ala. (9 members)
  John L. Napier, S.C. (16 members)
  Paul S. Trible Jr., Va. (11 members)

The three states not listed — Hawaii, Nevada and North Dakota — do not have Republican representatives.

Committee on Committees

Makes Republican committee assignments.

Phone: 225-0600

Robert H. Michel, Ill, chairman

Bill Archer, Texas
L. A. "Skip" Bafalis, Fla.
William S. Broomfield, Mich.
Hank Brown, Colo.
James T. Broyhill, N.C.
Clair W. Burgener, Calif.
Dick Cheney, Wyo.
E. Thomas Coleman, Mo.
Silvio O. Conte, Mass.
Larry Craig, Idaho
Hal Daub, Neb.
William L. Dickinson, Ala.
John J. Duncan, Tenn.
Mickey Edwards, Okla.
Cooper Evans, Iowa
Thomas B. Evans Jr., Del.
Edwin B. Forsythe, N.J.
Bill Frenzel, Minn.
Newt Gingrich, Ga.
Judd Gregg, N.H.
John Paul Hammerschmidt, Ark.
James V. Hansen, Utah
John Hiler, Ind.
Marjorie S. Holt, Md.

Frank Horton, N.Y.
James M. Jeffords, Vt.
Delbert L. Latta, Ohio
Manuel Lujan Jr., N.M.
Ron Marlenee, Mont.
Joseph M. McDade, Pa.
Stewart B. McKinney, Conn.
Henson Moore, La.
Sid Morrison, Wash.
John T. Myers, Ind.
Clint Roberts, S.D
Hal Rogers, Ky.
Toby Roth, Wis.
Eldon Rudd, Ariz.
Claudine Schneider, R.I.
Denny Smith, Ore.
Virginia Smith, Neb.
Olympia J. Snowe, Maine
Gene Snyder, Ky.
Floyd D. Spence, S.C.
David Michael Staton, W.Va.
William C. Wampler, Va.
Larry Winn Jr., Kan.
Don Young, Alaska

Personnel Committee

Phone: 225-0833

John T. Myers, Ind., chairman

Bobbi Fiedler, Calif.
Edwin B. Forsythe, N.J.
Bill Frenzel, Minn.
Gary A. Lee, N.Y.

Dan Lungren, Calif.
Gene Snyder, Ky.
Chalmers P. Wylie, Ohio

Policy Committee

Advises on party action and policy.

Phone: 225-6168

Dick Cheney, Wyo., chairman

Robert E. Badham, Calif.
Douglas K. Bereuter, Neb.
Clair W. Burgener, Calif.
Carroll A. Campbell Jr., S.C.
Dan Coats, Ind.
James M. Collins, Texas
Barber B. Conable Jr., N.Y.
Silvio O. Conte, Mass.
Jack Edwards, Ala.
John N. Erlenborn, Ill.
Thomas B. Evans Jr., Del.
Edwin B. Forsythe, N.J.
Bill Goodling, Pa.
Judd Gregg, N.H.
George Hansen, Idaho
Jack F. Kemp, N.Y.

Delbert L. Latta, Ohio
Jim Leach, Iowa
Trent Lott, Miss.
Edward R. Madigan, Ill.
Robert H. Michel, Ill.
Henson Moore, La.
Carlos J. Moorhead, Calif.
James H. Quillen, Tenn.
John J. Rhodes, Ariz.
Christopher H. Smith, N.J.
Floyd D. Spence, S.C.
Tom Tauke, Iowa
Guy Vander Jagt, Mich.
Vin Weber, Minn.
Chalmers P. Wylie, Ohio

National Republican Congressional Committee

Phone: 479-7070

Guy Vander Jagt, Mich., chairman

Robin L. Beard Jr., Tenn.
Cleve Benedict, W.Va.
Ed Bethune, Ark.
Clarence J. Brown, Ohio
Clair W. Burgener, Calif.†
Carroll A. Campbell Jr., S.C.
Dick Cheney, Wyo.
James A. Collins, Texas
Lawrence Coughlin, Pa.
Hal Daub, Neb.
Robert W. Davis, Mich.
Lawrence J. DeNardis, Conn.
Edward J. Derwinski, Ill.
Charles F. Dougherty, Pa.
Jack Edwards, Ala.†
Mickey Edwards, Okla.
Bill Emerson, Mo.
David F. Emery, Maine
Thomas B. Evans Jr., Del.
Newt Gingrich, Ga.
Judd Gregg, N.H.
Tom Hagedorn, Minn.
George Hansen, Idaho
Margaret M. Heckler, Mass.
Elwood Hillis, Ind.
Marjorie S. Holt, Md.
Larry J. Hopkins, Ky.
James M. Jeffords, Vt.
Eugene Johnston, N.C.

Jack F. Kemp, N.Y.†
Ken Kramer, Colo.
John LeBoutillier, N.Y.
Norman F. Lent, N.Y.
Bob Livingston, La.
Trent Lott, Miss.
Edward R. Madigan, Ill.†
Ron Marlenee, Mont.
Dan Marriott, Utah
Robert H. Michel, Ill.†
Stan Parris, Va.
Thomas E. Petri, Wis.
Joel Pritchard, Wash.
John J. Rhodes, Ariz.
Matthew J. Rinaldo, N.J.
Clint Roberts, S.D.
John H. Rousselot, Calif.
Claudine Schneider, R.I.
Joe Skeen, N.M.
Albert Lee Smith Jr., Ala.
Denny Smith, Ore.
Tom Tauke, Iowa
Gene Taylor, Mo.
Larry Winn Jr., Kan.
Frank R. Wolf, Va.
C. W. Bill Young, Fla.
Don Young, Alaska

† Members ex officio from the leadership.

Research Committee

Phone: 225-0871

Edward R. Madigan, Ill., chairman

Robert E. Badham, Calif.	Jack F. Kemp, N.Y.
Clair W. Burgener, Calif.	Gary A. Lee, N.Y.
Dick Cheney, Wyo.	Jerry Lewis, Calif.

Jim Coyne, Pa.	*Trent Lott, Miss.*
Lawrence J. DeNardis, Conn.	*James G. Martin, N.C.*
Jack Edwards, Ala.	*Bob McEwen, Ohio*
Arlen Erdahl, Minn.	*Robert H. Michel, Ill.†*
Jack Fields, Texas	*Thomas E. Petri, Wis.*
Bill Green, N.Y.	*Guy Vander Jagt, Mich.*
Bill Hendon, N.C.	

† Member ex officio *from the leadership.*

Joint Committees, 97th Congress, First Session

Joint Committees are set up to examine specific questions and are established by public law. Membership is drawn from both chambers and both parties. When a senator serves as chairman, the vice chairman is usually a representative, and vice versa. The chairmanship usually rotates from one chamber to the other at the beginning of each Congress.

Democrats are listed on the left in Roman type; Republicans are on the right in italics.

Economic

Studies and investigates all recommendations included in the president's annual Economic Report to Congress and reports findings and recommendations to the House and Senate.

Phone: 224-5171

Rep. Henry S. Reuss, D-Wis., chairman
Sen. Roger W. Jepsen, R-Iowa, vice chairman

Senate Members

Lloyd Bentsen, Texas	*William V. Roth Jr., Del.*
William Proxmire, Wis.	*James Abdnor, S.D.*
Edward M. Kennedy, Mass.	*Steven D. Symms, Idaho*
Paul S. Sarbanes, Md.	*Paula Hawkins, Fla.*
	Mack Mattingly, Ga.

House Members

Richard Bolling, Mo.	*Clarence J. Brown, Ohio*
Lee H. Hamilton, Ind.	*Margaret M. Heckler, Mass.*
Gillis W. Long, La.	*John H. Rousselot, Calif.*
Parren J. Mitchell, Md.	*Chalmers P. Wylie, Ohio*
Fred Richmond, N.Y.	

Agriculture and Transportation

Sen. Abdnor - chairman
Rep. Heckler - vice chairman

Senate Members

Bentsen   *Hawkins*

House Members

Long
Bolling

Economic Goals and Intergovernmental Policy

Rep. Hamilton - chairman
Sen. Bentsen - vice chairman

Senate Members

Hawkins
Symms
Mattingly

House Members

Bolling

International Trade, Finance and Security Economics

Rep. Long - chairman
Sen. Proxmire - vice chairman

Senate Members

Symms
Jepsen
Mattingly

House Members

Richmond

Investment, Jobs, and Prices

Rep. Reuss - chairman
Sen. Kennedy - vice chairman

Senate Members

Sarbanes   *Roth*

House Members

Mitchell   *Wylie*
                                           Brown
                                           Heckler

Monetary and Fiscal Policy

Sen. Jepsen - chairman
Rep. Rousselot - vice chairman

Senate Members

Sarbanes

House Members

Reuss   *Wylie*
Hamilton

Trade, Productivity, and Economic Growth

Sen. Roth - chairman
Rep. Brown - vice chairman

Senate Members

Kennedy   *Abdnor*
Proxmire

House Members

Mitchell   *Rousselot*
Richmond

Library

Phone: 225-0392

Rep. Augustus F. Hawkins, D-Calif., chairman
Sen. Charles McC. Mathias Jr., R-Md., vice chairman

Senate Members

Claiborne Pell, R.I.   *Mark O. Hatfield, Ore.*
Harrison A. Williams Jr., N.J.   *Howard H. Baker Jr., Tenn.*

House Members

Al Swift, Wash.   *Newt Gingrich, Ga.*
William J. Coyne, Pa.   *Jim Coyne, Pa.*

No standing subcommittees.

Printing

Phone: 224-5241

Sen. Charles McC. Mathias Jr., R-Md., chairman
Rep. Augustus F. Hawkins, D-Calif., vice chairman

Senate Members

Howard W. Cannon, Nev.   *John W. Warner, Va.*
Wendell H. Ford, Ky.   *Mark O. Hatfield, Ore.*

House Members

Joseph M. Gaydos, Pa.   *Newt Gingrich, Ga.*
Ed Jones, Tenn.   *Lynn Martin, Ill.*

No standing subcommittees.

Taxation

Phone: 225-3621

Rep. Dan Rostenkowski, D-Ill., chairman
Sen. Robert Dole, R-Kan., vice chairman

Senate Members

Russell B. Long, La.   *Bob Packwood, Ore.*
Harry F. Byrd Jr., Va.   *William V. Roth Jr., Del.*

House Members

Sam Gibbons, Fla.   *Barber B. Conable Jr., N.Y.*
J.J. Pickle, Texas   *John J. Duncan, Tenn.*

No standing subcommittees.

MAJOR
CONGRESSIONAL
ACTION

CQ

Economic Policy

Despite hopes that President Reagan's strikingly different brand of economics would spur American business to new heights, 1981 ended with the United States buffeted by its second recession in two years.

Reagan's solution to the economic woes of the nation was a largely untested theory called supply-side economics. Simply put, supply-siders held that by returning taxes to businesses and workers and by restricting the growth of government, Americans would have more incentive to work harder and to save more. That would lead to increased investment, higher productivity and a decline in inflation, they said. *(Keynesians vs. supply-siders, box, next page)*

To aim the economy in the supply-side direction, the president March 10 requested that Congress cut more than $40 billion from fiscal 1982 spending and reduce taxes by $53.9 billion.

Using his considerable political acumen, Reagan was able to push through budget and tax bills that very closely mirrored his requests. His victory was short-lived, however. Later in the year, as the economy slipped into recession, the president was unable to generate congressional backing for a second round of massive budget cuts.

The Economy

Reagan inherited a sluggish economy, still beset by high inflation and high interest rates.

When he took office in January, the prime lending rate was hovering between 20 and 20-1/2 percent. Inflation, as measured by the Consumer Price Index (CPI) was rising, approaching 12 percent annually. The unemployment rate stood at 7.4 percent.

By the second quarter of 1981, inflation began abating. Final figures for 1981 showed that consumer prices rose only 8.9 percent during the year — the first time the annual rate had fallen below double digits since 1978.

But that was the only rosy signal. Interest rates, as reflected by the prime lending rate, remained stubbornly high — not dipping below the 20 percent rate until September. These high interest rates infected the whole economy — but especially the rate-sensitive housing and automobile sectors.

Recession

High interest rates, coupled with a continued restrictive monetary policy being followed by the Federal Reserve Board, started the economy on its downward slide, and by August the nation had entered a recession.

By December nine million Americans were unemployed — an 8.8 percent unemployment rate. In the final quarter of the year, the nation's "real" gross national product (GNP) — the total output of goods and services, adjusted for inflation — fell at an annual rate of 4.7 percent.

Toward the end of the year interest rates began to decline. The prime rate at the end of December stood at 15-3/4 percent, but many economists warned that the relief from high interest rates was only temporary.

Budget and Taxes

Before leaving office Jan. 20, Jimmy Carter sent Congress his last budget — a budget that reflected his belief that income tax cuts would increase inflation and that spending on domestic programs for the needy could not be substantially reduced.

The document was merely symbolic, however. For not long after Reagan was sworn in, he sent Congress his own budget blueprint — one that called for the largest tax cut in the history of the United States and for massive, across-the-board cuts in all areas of domestic spending except defense.

Reagan told the American people his program was "evenhanded" and could be accomplished "without harm to government's legitimate purpose or to our responsibilty to all who need our benevolence."

Few would have believed that such a monumental shift in the role and focus of government would be accomplished as quickly as it was. But in little more than six months Congress approved the major elements of Reagan's proposals.

Reagan's success in achieving $35.2 billion in budget cuts for fiscal 1982 — a total of $130.6 billion in reductions in fiscal 1981-84 — stemmed in part from the unique use of a congressional budget-cutting tool known as reconciliation. The reconciliation vehicle allowed the House and Senate Budget committees to package together individual budget cuts proposed by authorizing committees into one bill, which they then sent to the floor for a single, up-or-down vote in each chamber.

The administration billed it as a vote on the Reagan economic program — an economic program that was the mandate of the last presidential election. The strategy worked. With a solid phalanx of Republican votes and enough help from Southern conservative Democrats, the administration was able to vanquish the Democratic-controlled House on key budget votes. In the Senate there was no question that the newly conservative-leaning body would support Reagan overwhelmingly.

On the tax front Reagan displayed the same political finesse that he had shown in the budget battle. Originally the president supported a tax cut that included only two elements: personal rate reductions totaling 30 percent over three years, and accelerated depreciation schedules for businesses to write off the cost of investing in plants and equipment more quickly.

During the give and take of the legislative process that lean tax measure grew fat with provisions considered crucial for victory. Democrats in the House engaged in the bidding war too. But in the end the power and pull of the president made the difference.

The final version of the bill was expected to deprive the Treasury of $749 billion over the next five years. But its

'Supply-Siders' Disputed Keynes

Supply-side theorists challenged the basic assumption of post-World-War-II economic policy, which had focused on controlling the demand for goods and services, rather than the supply.

Following the teachings of the British economist John Maynard Keynes, postwar policy was designed largely to eliminate unemployment. Keynes argued that joblessness results from inadequate "demand," which in turn reflects insufficient income in the hands of consumers. The Keynesian remedy for this problem is to increase demand, either by cutting taxes or increasing spending. Once people start spending their additional income, Keynesians said, the demand for goods and services will rise, production will increase and the unemployed will be offered jobs.

The focus of Keynesian theory on unemployment is not surprising; it was born during the 1930s, when joblessness was a chronic problem. Later, when inflation also came to be recognized as an economic worry, Keynes' successors said demand-oriented policies could correct that too.

They argued that, just as unemployment occurs when demand falls short of the economy's productive capacity, inflation results when demand *exceeds* economic capacity. If everybody is producing as much as they can, increasing incomes merely compel consumers to bid up the prices for the limited quantity of goods and services produced, according to this theory. The Keynesian cure for inflation is thus to restrain purchasing power, either by cutting back government spending or raising taxes, until demand again comes into line with supply.

While Keynesian policies would cure inflation by reducing demand — a course that sounded to many a lot like accepting a lower standard of living — the supply-siders said they could curb inflation by quickly increasing supply. The key, they said, is to reduce taxes and thus increase the incentives to produce.

The supply-siders disputed the Keynesian notion that once the government maintains an adequate level of demand, supply will be assured. The supply-siders said that people produce not merely in response to demand, but to increase their own income.

The fulcrum of economic activity, according to supply-siders, is the marginal rate of taxation, the rate on the last dollar earned. People continually are deciding between work and leisure, and between saving and consumption. The higher the marginal tax rate, the less incentive a person has to work rather than be idle, or to save rather than consume, they contended. By reducing marginal tax rates, supply-siders concluded, the government can encourage more work and saving, in the process increasing income and economic well-being.

proponents claimed that it would provide the investment incentives necessary to stimulate economic growth and speed recovery from the recession.

Within weeks after enactment of the budget and tax

measures, however, the administration was forced to acknowledge that its economic program was not achieving the desired effects. Rather than buoy Wall Street and send the economy on an upward course, approval of the Reagan program seriously shook the financial markets, which feared soaring federal deficits that would perpetuate inflation and high interest rates. Continued massive federal borrowing would "crowd out" the private sector in credit markets, they maintained.

Reagan responded Sept. 24 by proposing a package of $13 billion in additional budget cuts and $3 billion in "revenue enhancements," or increased taxes, but Congress — still smarting from the earlier battles — rebuffed the president's plan.

The White House did go nose to nose with Congress over a temporary appropriations resolution which it said did not cut deeply enough into fiscal 1982 spending. The president's Sept. 24 proposal called for 12 percent reductions in all appropriated funds. After the president vetoed the first funding resolution, Congress squeezed out enough money — $4 billion — to win Reagan's approval of the measure. But that was only one-quarter of the total savings he had requested.

Monetary Policy

As in previous years, it was the Federal Reserve Board that shouldered most of the burden in the fight to lower inflation in 1981.

Despite considerable congressional rhetoric about unacceptably high interest rates — rates that members said were crippling small-business men, farmers, the home building and auto industries, Federal Reserve Chairman Paul A. Volcker and his colleagues stuck to their restrictive monetary policy. Financial markets' fears of big budget deficits were the main cause of high interest rates, Volcker maintained.

The Fed's stated target for the basic money supply was a growth rate of 3.5 to 6 percent. Over the course of the year, however, the money supply grew more slowly than even the bottom end of the target. While Fed officials emphasized that they could not control the money supply with precision, the Fed's failure to meet its target prompted occasional sniping from administration officials, notably Treasury Secretary Donald T. Regan.

The Deficit Issue

President Reagan said in his inaugural address that decades of deficit spending, if continued, would "guarantee tremendous social, cultural, political and economic upheavals."

Through most of 1981 the president stressed the importance of gradually limiting deficits with the prospect of balancing the budget by fiscal 1984, as he had pledged during his 1980 campaign.

But as the recession took hold, pushing deficit forecasts to $100 billion for fiscal 1982 and to even higher levels in fiscal 1983-84, the president began to backpedal. Acknowledging that he probably would not be able to balance the budget by 1984, Reagan said that balancing the budget had been only a "goal."

The important factor, administration officials maintained, was that the deficit as a percentage of GNP was on a downward trend.

—By Dale Tate

Congress Enacts President Reagan's Tax Plan

In a stunning endorsement of President Reagan's economic policies, Congress Aug. 4 completed action on legislation providing a $37.7 billion tax cut in fiscal 1982. The action came only four days after lawmakers gave final approval to a $35.2 billion package of fiscal 1982 "reconciliation" budget savings — the other major item in Reagan's economic program. *(Reconciliation, p. 256)*

The final version of the tax bill (HR 4242 — PL 97-34) reflected a wide range of concessions made to ensure enactment of Reagan's revolutionary tax cut policies. But none of the many changes and add-ons to the legislation did damage to the heart of the Reagan supply-side plan — across-the-board reductions in individual income taxes and faster write-offs for capital investment to spur productivity and economic growth.

The form of the package changed substantially. Reagan originally had wanted a "clean bill," with other popular tax plans saved for a second tax measure later in the year.

But, bowing to the realities of politics, the president reshaped the package several times, giving in on some details while standing firm on the central theme. By doing so, Reagan forced Democrats, intent on passing their own alternative tax plan, to move closer and closer to the administration position.

"This is President Reagan's economic tax recovery plan," Treasury Secretary Donald T. Regan told reporters Aug. 1 after a conference agreement was reached on the two versions of the bill passed by the House and Senate earlier in the week. Regan boasted that the administration received "95 percent" of what it had sought.

Democrats were more than happy to agree and shift all responsibility for the economic consequences to Reagan.

"Make no mistake about it," Rep. Dan Rostenkowski, D-Ill., chairman of the House Ways and Means Committee, told colleagues before the final vote. "This is the president's bill. It outlines a bold — and risky — economic strategy. Only time will tell whether the risks involved ... were worth taking."

The Economic Recovery Tax Act of 1981 was expected to put $749 billion — more money than the federal government was expected to spend in fiscal 1982 — back in the hands of business and individual taxpayers over the next five years. Opponents insisted that the plan would aggravate inflation and lead to uncontrollable budget deficits.

Reagan signed the bill Aug. 13 while vacationing in California. The Senate had given its final approval to the measure Aug. 3 by a vote of 67-8. The House had cleared the package the following day on a 282-95 vote. *(Senate vote 248, p. 42-S; House vote 179, p. 62-H)*

Background

In approving Reagan's tax cut bill, Congress veered sharply away from the tax policies that had guided Democratic-dominated Congresses of the past.

Democratic tax bills tended to be relatively more generous to people at the low end of the income scale. And they generally placed emphasis on closing "loopholes" — limiting the special treatment afforded certain kinds of income. That approach culminated in the Tax Reform Act of 1976 (PL 94-455). *(1976 Almanac p. 41)*

Only two years later, however, Congress signaled a change of course in the Revenue Act of 1978 (PL 95-600). Riding the crest of a middle class "taxpayer's revolt," lawmakers reversed some of the prized liberal "reforms" of the past and approved individual cuts skewed toward the upper end of the income scale. *(1978 Almanac p. 219)*

Evolution of Bill

Reagan's 1981 tax legislation originated with a bill that initially was given little serious chance of passage. The measure, introduced simultaneously in 1977 by Sen. William V. Roth Jr., R-Del., and Rep. Jack F. Kemp, R-N.Y., called for a three-year average income tax cut of approximately 33 percent, future indexing of taxes to offset the effects of inflation and reductions in business taxes.

Interestingly, what became known as the Kemp-Roth plan originally called for rate cuts that targeted more of the relief to those in the lower- and middle-income brackets, not unlike the alternative tax plans Democrats tried so desperately to get Reagan and the majority of Congress to accept in 1981.

It was not until the Republican Party, and its presidential candidate Ronald Reagan, latched onto Kemp-Roth during the 1980 campaign that the proposal was given serious attention.

On the steps of the Capitol June 25, 1980, Senate and House Republicans unanimously pledged their support to a revised version of Kemp-Roth: a one-year, 10 percent, across-the-board tax cut for individuals and a plan to allow business faster write-offs of investment in plant and equipment. The accelerated depreciation plan was one business groups and several members of Congress had been working on since passage of the 1978 tax bill.

Simultaneously, Reagan backed such a tax cut for Jan. 1, 1981, followed by additional 10 percent cuts in individual income taxes in each of the next two years and indexing.

But soon after, Reagan began changing, if not his tune, at least the words of his song:

● Aug. 21, 1980. The Democratic-controlled Senate Finance Committee approved a $39 billion tax cut that combined individual income tax relief to offset increased Social Security taxes and the effects of inflation with incentives for business investment. Candidate Reagan said he backed the bill, but the plan, strongly opposed by President Carter, never reached the Senate floor. *(1980 Almanac p. 295)*

● Feb. 18, 1981. Reagan announced his tax plans to Congress. He called for $53.9 billion in tax cuts in 1982, starting with a 10 percent cut in individual income tax rates July 1, 1981 (six months later than he originally had proposed), and additional 10 percent cuts on July 1 in each of the two succeeding years. Indexing was dropped, but his business depreciation plan remained intact. Reagan promised a second tax bill for such measures as relief from the "marriage penalty" tax. In the months that followed, the administration showed no willingness to compromise.

● June 4, 1981. Bowing to the pressures of a tight budget and a Congress less than enthusiastic about the original tax cut package, Reagan offered an alternative. He proposed $37.4 billion in tax cuts for 1982, reduced the first rate reduction to 5 percent, delayed it until Oct. 1, 1981, and put in some popular "sweeteners," including savings incentives and marriage penalty relief.

● June 9, 1981. Business groups remained cool toward the June 4 plan, so before the package (HR 3849) was introduced in Congress by Reps. Barber B. Conable Jr., R-N.Y., and Kent Hance, D-Texas, the administration added more tax advantages for business.

● July 24, 1981. With a close vote on the House floor only a few days away, the administration proposed its final legislation. The basic concept remained — across-the-board cuts and investment incentives — but the floodgate on "sweeteners" was opened in an attempt to win a handful of swing House votes.

Major Provisions

As signed into law, the Economic Recovery Tax Act of 1981 (HR 4242 — PL 97-34) included the following major provisions (all effective Jan. 1, 1982, unless otherwise noted):

Individual Tax Cuts

● **Rate Cuts.** Reduced all individual income tax rates by 5 percent Oct. 1, 1981, 10 percent July 1, 1982, and an additional 10 percent July 1, 1983. Each cut would be applied to marginal tax rates, or those rates imposed on the last dollar of income. The changes were to be reflected in lower withholding in paychecks beginning Oct. 1.

● **Investment Income.** Reduced the top rate on investment, or "unearned," income from 70 percent to 50 percent, the existing maximum for earned income.

● Reduced the maximum rate on capital gains — which were taxed at 40 percent of the investment income rate — from 28 percent to 20 percent, effective June 10, 1981.

● **Indexing.** Increased individual income tax brackets, the zero bracket amount and the personal exemption to reflect annual increases in the Consumer Price Index (CPI), beginning with the 1985 tax year. For example, if the CPI increased 10 percent during the preceding year, the lowest tax bracket, currently $3,400 to $5,500 would be changed to $3,740 ($3,400 plus 10 percent) to $6,050 ($5,500 plus 10 percent). The tax rates would remain the same.

● **Marital Deductions.** Allowed two-earner married couples filing joint returns in 1982 to deduct 5 percent of up to $30,000 (a maximum deduction of $1,500) of the lesser of their two incomes. The deduction would increase to 10 percent (a maximum of $3,000) in 1983 and after.

● **Child Care.** Increased to 30 percent from 20 percent the tax credit for child and dependent day care expenses in connection with the taxpayer's employment, for those earning $10,000 or less. The credit would be reduced one percentage point for each $2,000 in additional income, up to $28,000. Those earning over $28,000 would be eligible for a 20 percent credit.

● Increased the maximum amount of expenses eligible for the credit from $2,000 to $2,400 for one dependent and from $4,000 to $4,800 for two or more dependents.

● **Charitable Contributions.** Allowed individuals who did not itemize deductions on their tax returns to deduct charitable contributions as follows: up to 25 percent of contributions of $100 or less (a $25 maximum deduction) in 1982 and 1983; 25 percent of up to $300 in 1984 (a $75 maximum); 50 percent with no cap in 1985; and 100 percent in 1986. The provision would expire after 1986.

● **Sale of Residence.** Extended from 18 months to 24 months the period an individual was allowed to defer taxes

on proceeds from the sale of a primary residence if that money was used to buy another home at the same or greater cost. The provision applied to all sales after July 20, 1981, and in cases where the 18-month "rollover" period had not expired by July 20, 1981.

● Increased from $100,000 to $125,000 the one-time exclusion from tax of capital gains from the sale of a home by those aged 55 and over, effective July 21, 1981.

● **Foreign Earned Income.** Allowed an individual working overseas to exclude from tax up to $75,000 of foreign earned income in 1982. The exclusion would increase $5,000 each year over the next four years to $95,000 in 1986 and after. The provision, if elected by the taxpayer, would replace current tax breaks for the excess living costs of those working abroad.

● Provided an allowance for "reasonable" housing costs in excess of a base amount, 16 percent of the salary of a grade GS-14, Step 1, government worker (the current base amount would be $6,059).

Business Tax Cuts

● **Accelerated Depreciation.** Replaced the complex existing system for depreciating assets over their "useful" lives with a simplified approach called the Accelerated Cost Recovery System (ACRS). Under ACRS, investments in plant and equipment would be grouped in four classes, each having a standard schedule of deductions that could be taken over a fixed recovery period. Businesses could write off the value of an asset over three, five, 10 or 15 years at an accelerated rate. The provisions were made retroactive to Jan. 1, 1981.

● Classified assets as follows:

Three years: Automobiles, light trucks, equipment used in research and development, racehorses, and machinery and equipment that under existing law had a depreciation range of up to four years. A one-time, 6 percent investment tax credit would be allowed.

Five years: All other machinery and equipment, public utilities with a current depreciation range of 18 years or less, single-use farm structures (such as hen houses) and some petroleum storage facilities. A 10 percent investment tax credit would be allowed.

Ten years: Public utility property with a current depreciation range from 18.5 years to 25 years, railroad tank cars, some mobile homes and other structures (such as theme parks). A 10 percent investment credit would be allowed.

Fifteen years: Public utility property with a current depreciation range of more than 25 years and all other buildings. A 10 percent investment tax credit would be available for the public utility property only.

● Permitted taxpayers to depreciate an asset over a period of time longer than that designated in one of the four depreciation classes.

● Allowed through 1984 all assets except 15-year real estate to be written off using an accelerated depreciation system that combined the 150 percent declining balance and straight-line methods. The declining balance method allowed a firm to deduct 15 percent of the total value of the investment the first year and 15 percent of the undepreciated value in each subsequent year. Under the straight-line method, assets would depreciated an equal percentage each year — for example, 10 percent for each of 10 years.

● Allowed all assets except 15-year real estate to be depreciated in 1985 at an even faster rate using 175 percent

Tax Bill's Estimated Revenue Impact

(Fiscal years, in millions of dollars)

Provisions	1981	1982	1983	1984	1985	1986
Individual income taxes	$− 39	$−26,929	$−71,098	$−114,684	$−148,237	$−196,143
Business tax cuts	−1,562	−10,657	−18,599	− 28,275	− 39,269	− 54,468
Energy taxes	−−	− 1,320	− 1,742	− 2,242	− 2,837	− 3,619
Savings incentives	−−	− 247	− 1,797	− 4,208	− 5,740	− 8,375
Estate and gift taxes	−−	− 204	− 2,114	− 3,218	− 4,248	− 5,568
Tax straddles[1]	37	623	327	273	249	229
Administrative provisions	−−	1,182	2,048	1,856	718	592
Miscellaneous provisions	− 1	− 104	243	535	53	− 275
Totals	**$−1,565**	**$−37,656**	**$−92,732**	**$−149,963**	**$−199,311**	**$−267,627**

[1] *Figures do not reflect transactions entered into after Dec. 31, 1981.*

SOURCE: Joint Committee on Taxation

declining balance (17.5 percent of the undepreciated value would be written off in the early years) and after 1985, using 200 percent declining balance (20 percent of the undepreciated value written off in the early years).

● Allowed structures other than low-income housing to be depreciated using the 175 percent declining balance method, with straight-line depreciation for the later years; 200 percent declining balance could be used for low-income housing.

● Gave taxpayers the option of substituting straight-line depreciation for all of the above methods.

● **Small Business Depreciation.** Allowed "expensing," or the immediate deduction, by small businesses of the cost of new or used machinery and equipment, of up to $5,000 in 1982 and 1983, $7,500 in 1984 and 1985, and $10,000 after 1985.

● **Used Property.** Increased from $100,000 to $125,000 in 1981 through 1984, and to $150,000 in 1985, the maximum amount of used property eligible for an investment tax credit.

● **Credit Carryover.** Extended from seven to 15 years the period over which businesses could carry forward unused tax credits and offset them against future tax liability.

● **Leasing.** Liberalized leasing laws to make it easier to transfer investment tax credit and accelerated depreciation benefits from businesses that were not profitable enough to use such benefits to businesses that could use them.

● **Rehabilitation of Old Buildings.** Increased the current 10 percent investment tax credit for the rehabilitation of old buildings to 15 percent for buildings 30-39 years old, 20 percent for buildings 40 years and older, and 25 percent for certified historic structures.

● Allowed more rapid depreciation (175 percent declining balance instead of straight-line) for buildings constructed on the site of a demolished historic structure.

● **Research and Development.** Allowed a 25 percent tax credit for new spending on research and development above and beyond the average annual amount spent on such activities over the three preceding years. The provision applied to all expenditures made after June 30, 1981, through Dec. 31, 1985.

● Increased deductions for corporate contributions of new equipment to a university or college for research.

● **Foreign Research.** Allowed firms to offset all of their U.S. research and development expenses against U.S. income, instead of against both foreign and U.S. income. The provision aimed to prevent the moving abroad of U.S. corporate research activities.

● **Accumulated Earnings.** Increased from $150,000 to $250,000 the amount of earnings a business could accumulate without paying an accumulated earnings tax.

● Exempted from the provision service corporations in health, law, engineering, architecture, accounting, actuarial science, performing arts and consulting.

● **Shareholder Size.** Increased from 15 to 25 the maximum number of shareholders a small business could have and still retain the option of having its individual shareholders, not both the corporation and the shareholders, taxed on income.

● **Small Business Accounting.** Simplified the use of "last in, first out" (LIFO) accounting. LIFO is generally an attractive accounting method to use during times of high inflation, but, under current law, had been considered too complex for small businesses to undertake.

● **Corporate Rate Reductions.** Reduced the lowest corporate income tax rates from 17 percent on the first $25,000 of income to 16 percent in 1982 and 15 percent in 1983, and from 20 percent on the next $25,000 to 19 percent in 1982 and 18 percent in 1983.

● **"Incentive" Stock Options.** Created so-called "incentive" stock options for employees to buy their employer's stock and for which the employee would be taxed only when the stock purchased under the option was sold. Under existing law, employees were taxed on ordinary income at the time they were granted such options.

● **Targeted Jobs Tax Credit.** Extended for one year the targeted jobs tax credit program created by the 1978 tax bill (PL 95-600), which was due to expire at the end of 1981, and expanded the group of disadvantaged workers for which employers could receive the credit. *(Background, 1978 Almanac p. 221)*

● **Mutual Savings Banks.** Provided preferential tax treatment for mutual savings banks that converted into stock associations.

● **Trucking Licenses.** Allowed trucking firms a five-year deduction for the loss in value of their operating licenses resulting from the 1980 trucking deregulation bill. *(1980 Almanac p. 242)*

Energy Provisions

● **Royalty Owners.** Increased from $1,000 to $2,500 the tax credit allowed small oil royalty owners to offset the windfall profits tax in 1981. *(Tax, 1980 Almanac p. 473)*

● Provided an exemption from the windfall profits tax on oil production of two barrels a day for 1982-84 and three barrels of oil a day for 1985 and after. (Although the values of the barrel-a-day exemptions varied with the price of oil, they were likely to be substantially higher than the $2,500 credit.)

● **"Stripper" Oil.** Exempted from the windfall profits tax all independently produced oil from "stripper" wells — those that produce an average of 10 barrels of oil a day or less. The provision would begin in 1983.

● **Newly Discovered Oil.** Reduced from 30 percent to 15 percent by 1986 the windfall profits tax on newly discovered oil. The reduction would be phased in: 27.5 percent in 1982; 25 percent in 1983; 22.5 percent in 1984; 20 percent in 1985; and 15 percent in 1986 and after.

● **Charitable Organizations.** Expanded the current exemption from the windfall profits tax for charitable organizations to include homes for disadvantaged children.

Savings Incentives

● **Individual Retirement Accounts (IRAs).** Increased to the lesser of $2,000 or 100 percent of compensation (from $1,500 or 15 percent of compensation) the amount an individual could deduct for annual contributions to an IRA.

● Increased from $1,750 to $2,250 the deduction for contributions to "spousal" IRAs, those set up by a working spouse for both himself, or herself, and a non-working spouse. A requirement that contributions must be equally divided between the two spouses was dropped.

● Allowed deductible IRA contributions both for those not covered and for those covered by an employer-sponsored plan. In cases where an individual was covered by an employer-sponsored plan, voluntary contributions to that plan would be deductible up to $2,000.

● Permitted divorced spouses to contribute at least $1,125 a year to an IRA that had been set up for them by the other spouse. Under existing law, such persons could no longer contribute to such an IRA after divorce.

● **Self-Employed Retirement Plans (Keogh).** Increased from $7,500 to $15,000 the amount a self-employed individual could deduct for contributions to his or her own retirement plan.

● **Dividend and Interest Exclusion.** Repealed as of Jan. 1, 1982, the current $200 exclusion ($400 for couples) allowed for interest and dividend income, and reinstated a previous $100 ($200 for couples) exclusion for dividend income only.

● Allowed taxpayers, beginning in 1985, to exclude 15 percent of up to $3,000 ($6,000 for couples) of interest income.

● **Savings Certificates.** Allowed banks, savings and loans, credit unions and other depository institutions to issue one-year savings certificates that would yield 70 percent of the yield on one-year Treasury bills (currently about 14 percent).

● Permitted individuals to exclude up to $1,000 of the interest on such certificates; couples could exclude up to $2,000.

● Permitted the certificates to be issued only from Oct. 1, 1981, through Dec. 31, 1982, and stipulated that they must be offered in denominations of $500.

● Required institutions, other than credit unions, issuing the certificates to make at least 75 percent of their net new savings available for home or agricultural loans.

● **Employee Stock Ownership Plans (ESOPs).** Replaced the existing additional 1 percent investment tax credit allowed employers for contributions to tax credit ESOPs with a payroll-based tax credit. The new credit would be phased in gradually up to .75 percent of compensation of employees covered by the plan in 1985. The provision would expire Dec. 31, 1987.

● Increased from 15 percent of payroll to 25 percent the tax deductions allowed employers for contributions to an ESOP that borrowed money to buy stock in the company, provided the contribution was used to pay off the loan.

● Repealed a requirement that voting rights be transferred to employees participating in a profit-sharing ESOP.

● **Dividend Reinvestment.** Allowed public utilities shareholders who elected to receive dividends in the form of newly issued common stock rather than cash to exclude from tax up to $750 a year ($1,500 for joint returns). The provision would expire at the end of 1985.

● **Legal Service Plans.** Extended through Dec. 31, 1984, the current exclusion from employee income of employer contributions to, and the value of benefits received from, a prepaid legal service plan for employees. The existing provision would have expired Dec. 31, 1981.

Estate and Gift Taxes

● **Exemption.** Increased from $175,625 to $600,000 by 1987 the total amount of estate and gift transfers that would be exempt from estate and gift taxes. The change would be phased in as follows: $225,000 in 1982; $275,000 in 1983; $325,000 in 1984; $400,000 in 1985; $500,000 in 1986; and $600,000 in 1987 and after. By 1987 less than 1 percent of all estates would be taxed.

● **Estate Value.** Made it easier to base the value of an estate on its current use rather than to use its generally higher fair market value when determining taxes.

● **Rate Reduction.** Reduced the top estate and gift tax rate from the current 70 percent to 50 percent by 1985. The rate was set at 65 percent in 1982, 60 percent in 1983 and 55 percent in 1984. When fully phased in, the top rate would apply to gifts and estates over $2.5 million.

● **Marital Deduction.** Repealed existing limits on tax-free estate and gift transfers between spouses.

● **Gift Tax.** Increased the annual gift tax exclusion from $3,000 to $10,000 per donee, with an unlimited exclusion for tuition and medical expenses; allowed gift taxes to be paid on an annual rather than quarterly basis.

● **Generation-Skipping Tax.** Extended for one year, to Jan. 1, 1983, current transitional exemptions from the tax on generation-skipping transfers. *(1976 Almanac p. 41)*

Commodity Tax Straddles

● **Annual Tax.** Restricted the use of a tax shelter technique called the commodity tax straddle by imposing a maximum 32 percent tax on the net gain of an individual's commodity futures holdings as of the last day of a tax year, even if the gain had yet to be realized. The straddle, which

Individual Cuts Under Tax Bill*

One-earner family of four

Annual Income	1982	1983	1984
$ 10,000	$ 52	$ 78	$ 83
20,000	228	371	464
30,000	405	744	914
50,000	947	1,754	2,158
60,000	1,255	2,370	2,928
100,000	2,137	4,648	5,822

Two-earner family of four

Annual Income	1982	1983	1984
$ 10,000	$ 69	$ 110	$ 113
20,000	275	456	544
30,000	499	916	1,079
50,000	1,191	2,191	2,570
60,000	1,547	2,895	3,423
100,000	2,749	5,748	6,872

* Includes rate cuts, marriage "penalty" tax break and reduction in top rate on investment income. These provisions were identical in the House and Senate versions of the tax bill. Assumptions: All income is earned income, and itemized deductions equal 23 percent of income. In two-earner families, the second wage earner earns 25 percent of the family's income.

SOURCE: Joint Committee on Taxation

involved the purchase of offsetting futures contracts, had been used widely to avoid or defer taxes.

● **Exemption.** Exempted professional hedgers — those who buy or sell futures as a protection against price fluctuations in commodities they use or supply — from the annual tax on straddles.

Administrative Changes

● **Railroad Retirement Taxes.** Increased Railroad Retirement System taxes 2.25 percentage points for rail management and two percentage points for employees to keep the troubled fund from going broke.

● **Corporate Tax Payments.** Increased from 60 percent to 80 percent the amount of estimated tax a large corporation must pay in the current tax year. The percentage increase would be phased in gradually: 65 percent in 1982; 75 percent in 1983; and 80 percent in 1984.

● **Estimated Taxes.** Increased from $100 to $500 by 1985 the minimum amount of income tax liability over the amount withheld that required an individual to declare or pay estimated taxes for the following year.

● **Tax Court Fee.** Increased from $10 to $60 the fee for filing a petition in U.S. Tax Court.

● **Penalties.** Increased miscellaneous penalties, including the penalty for filing a false W-4 form, on which deductions are claimed for tax withholding.

● **Tax return Confidentiality.** Clarified existing law to ensure that the Internal Revenue Service could refuse to disclose information used to develop standards for auditing tax returns if it would impair tax-collecting operations.

Miscellaneous Provisions

● **State Legislators.** Allowed state legislators to deduct per diem expenses during legislative sessions, even if they did not stay overnight in the state capital, provided they lived more than 50 miles away. The provision was made retroactive to Jan. 1, 1976.

● **Fringe Benefits.** Extended the current prohibition on the taxation of fringe benefits until Dec. 31, 1983.

● **Campaign Committees.** Reduced taxes on the income, such as interest income, of a congressional candidate's principal campaign committee. Under existing law, all such income was taxed at 46 percent; under the bill, it would be taxed at the graduated corporate rate, from 15 percent to 46 percent.

● **Mass Transit.** Allowed use of tax-exempt industrial development bonds for any bus, subway car, rail car or similar equipment leased to a public mass transit system.

● **Volunteer Fire Departments.** Allowed volunteer fire departments to issue tax-exempt bonds for the purchase or improvement of a firehouse or fire truck.

● **Telephone Excise Tax.** Extended the telephone excise tax at 1 percent through 1984.

● **Employee Awards.** Allowed employees a deduction of up to $400 per item for awards given by their company for length of service, productivity or safety.

● **Adoption Expenses.** Allowed a deduction of up to $1,500 for expenses incurred in the adoption of a disadvantaged or hard-to-place child.

Reagan Proposals

In a televised speech to a joint session of Congress Feb. 18, President Reagan called for $53.9 billion in individual and business tax cuts in fiscal 1982.

The heart of the two-part bill was a proposal to cut individual income tax rates by 10 percent a year for three years. The individual tax breaks mirrored the Kemp-Roth tax proposal — the centerpiece of Reagan's economic plank during the presidential campaign.

The second feature of the Reagan tax package was a speed-up in the rate at which businesses could deduct the cost of purchasing new plants and equipment.

Reagan pledged to send to Congress at an "early date" a second tax parcel, including proposals to index income tax brackets; do away with the marriage penalty, which discriminated against working married couples; provide tuition tax credits; and revise inheritance taxation.

"Unlike some past tax 'reforms,' this is not merely a shift of wealth between different sets of taxpayers," Reagan said in describing his controversial individual tax cut plan. "This proposal for an equal reduction in everyone's tax rates will expand our national prosperity, enlarge national incomes and increase opportunities for all Americans." *(Text of speech, p. 15-E)*

Individual Cuts

Following through on a campaign pledge, Reagan proposed to cut marginal tax rates by 10 percent a year for three years.

Under existing law, the maximum marginal tax rate was 70 percent. But that rate affected only unearned or investment income, such as interest and dividends, because the tax code imposed a maximum rate of 50 percent on earned income, such as wages, salaries and fees.

As a result of the personal rate cuts, once the top marginal rate dropped to 50 percent the distinction between earned income and unearned income would be eliminated. The administration hoped that this change, along

with the fact that individuals would have more disposable income, would lead to more savings.

In fact, administration officials believed the tax cuts should result in a 2 percent increase in the rate of savings, which would amount to between $44 billion and $60 billion. These savings, they claimed, would help finance the deficit without the need to step up growth of the money supply. "That's what we're betting on, that's what we're counting on," said one official.

Another side effect of the rate reductions was a cut in the capital gains rate. Under existing law, 60 percent of net capital gains were excluded from an individual's income when computing taxes, leaving 40 percent included in income that was taxed at normal rates.

As a result of the president's proposal, however, the maximum tax rate on that 40 percent would be reduced from the current 70 percent to 50 percent as individual tax cuts were phased in. Thus, the top capital gains rate would be reduced gradually from a maximum of 28 percent to 20 percent in 1984 — that is, 40 percent of the 50 percent marginal rate.

If the tax cuts were not enacted, the administration said in documents accompanying the president's speech, "federal taxes would consume a rapidly increasing share of the national income — rising to 23.4 percent of GNP [gross national product] after 1985." Under the president's program, the Treasury Department said, tax receipts would drop to 20.4 percent of GNP in 1982 and 19.3 percent by 1985.

Individual rate reductions would cost the Treasury $44.2 billion in fiscal 1982, rising to $162.4 billion in fiscal 1986.

Business Cuts

In order to do away with the "obsolete, needlessly complex and economically counterproductive" depreciation system for business investments, Reagan proposed a simplified "accelerated cost recovery system."

The president said the change would "provide the new investment which is needed to create millions of new jobs between now and 1986 and to make America competitive once again in world markets."

The effect of the president's faster and simpler depreciation schedule would be to provide businesses with $9.7 billion for investment in fiscal 1982, rising to $44.2 billion in fiscal 1985. Those figures also reflected the loss in revenues to the Treasury.

The plan was a slightly altered version of the "10-5-3" accelerated depreciation plan, which had great bipartisan support in both houses of Congress in 1980.

While the proposed personal income tax reductions would not take effect until July 1, 1981, the business tax breaks would be retroactive to Jan. 1, 1981. However, the program would be phased in "progressively" over a five-year period for machinery and buildings acquired before 1985.

Under existing law, businesses that wanted to write off the cost of capital investments had to use a complicated system that placed plants and machinery in categories according to their "useful lives." Businesses were then allowed to deduct the cost of their investments over the useful life period. But the depreciation schedules were so stretched out that it could take up to 40 years to write off certain buildings and up to 28 years to depreciate some types of machinery.

The Reagan plan attempted to simplify the system

and accelerate the rate at which these investments could be written off. Specifically, the program would replace the complex useful life provisions with "easily identified" classes, each having a standard schedule of deductions that could be taken over a fixed recovery period.

These classes were:

●Three-year property. Outlays for autos and light trucks, and machinery and equipment used in research and development activities. These assets could be written off in three years, as follows: 33 percent in the first year, 45 percent in the second and 22 percent in the third.

●Five-year property. Outlays for machinery and equipment including public utility property. After a phase-in period, property in this class would be written off in five years: 20 percent in the year acquired and 32 percent, 24 percent, 16 percent and 8 percent in succeeding years.

●Ten-year property. Factory buildings, retail stores and warehouses used by owners and public utility property could be written off over 10 years: 10 percent, 18 percent, 16 percent, 14 percent, 12 percent, 10 percent, 8 percent, 6 percent, 4 percent and 2 percent.

Finally, there would be two new depreciation categories — a 15-year and an 18-year category — for other types of real estate. These depreciation periods would be "audit proof" — that is, they would not require subsequent audit. The costs would be written off on a "straight-line basis," so that the same percentage of the original cost could be written off each year.

In addition to the changes in the depreciation schedules, the president's plan would allow increases in the investment tax credit to take effect at once, as opposed to the depreciation reforms, which would be phased in: 6 percent for investments in the three-year write-off category, an increase of 2-2/3 percent, and the full 10 percent investment tax credit for investments in the five-year category, as compared to the 6-1/2 percent credit currently used.

Rostenkowski Counterproposal

The new chairman of the House Ways and Means Committee, Rep. Dan Rostenkowski, D-Ill., April 9 outlined an alternative one-year tax cut proposal that he said "strikes that essential political and economic balance to pass Congress" while preserving the spirit of the president's plan.

Rostenkowski called for a tax cut of $40 billion in fiscal 1982, of which $28 billion would go to individuals and $12 billion to business. The size was close to the $38 billion target set by the House Budget Committee in drafting the first fiscal 1982 budget resolution. *(Resolution, p. 247)*

Under the tax chairman's plan, marginal rates would be reduced for all taxpayers — although not as sharply as the president's 10 percent rate reduction — and tax brackets would be widened so that slight increases in income would not push an individual into a higher bracket.

These cuts, while affecting all taxpayers, would be designed to help especially those in the $20,000-$50,000 income range. The standard deduction and the earned income credit would be liberalized to help those in the lower income brackets.

The Rostenkowski package included two proposals that long had had widespread GOP support: reducing the top marginal rate on unearned income from 70 percent to 50 percent, which would help those at the upper end of the income scale, and easing the marriage penalty, which would benefit two-earner families.

Rostenkowski called for an increase in the amount of money that could be sheltered from taxes through an Individual Retirement Account (IRA) — a proposal sponsored in the Senate by Republican Finance Committee Chairman Robert Dole, Kan., in a move to increase funds available for investment.

The House chairman also proposed a dividend reinvestment plan for public utilities.

Finally, Rostenkowski sought to allow businesses to depreciate their capital investments more easily and quickly. He did not endorse the president's "10-5-3" proposal, however. Although he did not outline a specific depreciation plan of his own, several standards he set down differed from the administration's approach.

Republican reaction to Rostenkowski's overture, which was carefully designed to embrace the basic principles of the Reagan plan, was respectful but negative. Treasury Secretary Regan called the individual cuts "puny."

Rep. Conable, the ranking minority member of the Ways and Means Committee, said the package was not the "consensus" bill Rostenkowski claimed.

In a conference with reporters April 14, Conable held out prospects for an eventual tax bill compromise.

While Reagan had barred any retreat for the time being, Conable said, the president's "implication was that he might be open to compromise later."

Conable said he thought Reagan's "tough position has resulted in Rostenkowski proposing a much more conservative bill than he would have."

Administration Revisions

Despite the unenthusiastic congressional response to his Feb. 18 tax proposals, the president spurned all compromise suggestions for nearly two months. On June 4, however, Reagan finally proposed major changes.

The new plan, backed by congressional Republicans and a group of dissident House Democrats, scaled back individual cuts to provide a 5 percent cut in marginal tax rates effective Oct. 1, 1981, and 10 percent rate cuts on July 1, 1982, and July 1, 1983. It also dropped the top rate on investment income to 50 percent, cut almost 30 percent of the business tax relief in the original plan and added a potpourri of tax bonuses for individuals that were selected to lure support from conservative Democrats.

The bipartisan group that supported the revised plan was pitted against the majority of House Democrats, who had joined in support of a two-year, 15 percent across-the-board tax cut adorned with special relief for the middle class.

After several weeks of negotiations, Ways and Means Democrats, led by Rostenkowski, had tentatively agreed to go about halfway to meet the administration's original tax proposal. Despite this major shift, however, the president decided he would go to the mat for his three-year tax cut.

Both Reagan and his aides acknowledged that the tax cut battle would be much tougher, and the vote closer, than the budget fight he won earlier in the year. Nonetheless, the president told reporters, "If we don't have the votes, we'll get them."

Once again Reagan was counting on the support of many of the members of the Conservative Democratic Forum (CDF). But on the day Reagan announced his new three-year plan, Rep. Charles W. Stenholm, D-Texas, coordinator of the CDF, said the 47-member group was split between those who supported the president and those who would opt for a two-year measure. Another CDF representative, Rep. Phil Gramm, D-Texas, claimed the president had 20 solid votes among the conservative Democrats.

The new administration tax package would reduce Treasury revenues by $37.4 billion in fiscal 1982, almost $17 billion less than the president's original tax plan, according to administration estimates, and would lower the projected fiscal 1982 deficit to less than $30 billion, from $45 billion. The plan would cost $92.1 billion in fiscal 1983 and $144.5 billion in 1984. Over the three years, individuals would receive $224.8 billion in tax relief, businesses $49.2 billion.

The cost of the Democratic alternative would be $41 billion in fiscal 1982 — substantially less than the original Reagan plan but more than the revamped version.

Compromise Abandoned

The gulf between the administration and House Democrats widened as the House Ways and Means Committee prepared to begin drafting a tax bill June 10.

The administration June 9 restored to its tax plan approximately $40 billion in business tax reductions for fiscal 1981-86. The revision was an attempt to woo back business groups, who were angered at the scaled-back depreciation proposal announced by Reagan June 4. His revised proposal (HR 3849) was introduced by Conable and Hance.

House Democrats, meanwhile, hardened their position by backing away from the compromise they had offered earlier that called for a two-year, 15 percent across-the-board cut in individual income tax rates.

Rostenkowski said after a caucus meeting June 9 that committee Democrats had abandoned the idea of across-the-board rate cuts and were leaning toward a cut that would primarily help the $10,000-$50,000 income group. The across-the-board proposal had been made only for negotiating purposes with the administration, he said, "but the negotiations have been concluded."

The administration's June 9 plan called for a $38 billion tax cut in 1982, $16 billion less than its original Feb. 18 proposal and slightly higher than the revised plan announced June 4. The June 4 plan would have restored $50 billion in business taxes for fiscal 1981-86. HR 3849 would reduce the administration's original $172.9 billion depreciation cut by only $10 billion over that same period, and in later years would actually give business a greater tax reduction than the administration originally proposed.

The original business cuts were scaled back so that the administration could add several other tax-cut provisions in an attempt to win broad support for its plan, especially among conservative House Democrats.

Senate Committee Action

Pressuring the Ways and Means Committee to act quickly on tax legislation, the Senate Finance Committee began work on its own bill June 18. After four days of markup, the committee June 25 adopted by a 19-1 vote a package almost identical to that requested by President Reagan.

It attached its tax cut package to a House-passed debt limit measure (H J Res 266), a maneuver that would make it possible to circumvent the constitutional mandate that all revenue-raising measures originate in the House. The committee reported its version of the bill July 6 (S Rept 97-144).

Finance Chairman Robert Dole, R-Kan., denied he was trying to upstage the Ways and Means Committee on its tax-writing privileges but said he learned as a Boy Scout "to be prepared." The administration had pushed for Aug. 1 enactment of the bill so that its across-the-board rate cuts could go into effect Oct. 1.

The sole dissenting vote was cast by Bill Bradley, D-N.J., who made several unsuccessful attempts during the course of the rapid four-day markup to change the president's proposal.

Bradley called the administration plan "inflationary and inequitable" and said most of the tax reductions were geared toward those in the upper-income brackets, instead of toward those in the middle brackets. "They are the primary tax-paying public and they deserve some relief," he said. Other committee Democrats also criticized the plan as a bill for the rich. Their "welfare has been our almost exclusive preoccupation," said George J. Mitchell, D-Maine.

"This is a tax reduction program, not a redistributive one," countered Dole, who managed to keep all but a few special-interest tax provisions from loading down the bill.

The committee approved by a 15-4 vote the core of Reagan's plan: a three-year, 25 percent across-the-board cut in individual income tax rates and an accelerated depreciation plan for business.

The committee also agreed with Reagan to lower the top marginal tax rate individuals pay on investment income to 50 percent. And it accepted administration proposals to lower the marriage penalty, to increase deductions for contributions to retirement plans set up by individuals and the self-employed, and to allow a 25 percent tax credit for wages paid for research and development. It reduced estate and gift taxes, increased tax relief for American workers overseas, and increased tax credits for the rehabilitation of old buildings and for small oil royalty owners subject to the windfall profits tax.

Changes in Reagan Plan

But the panel also made several revisions and additions to the Reagan proposal. The administration, which had wanted a "clean" bill, grudgingly accepted the changes as the inevitable price for Senate passage.

Among the major additions to Reagan's bill was a so-called "all-savers" plan, promoted by savings and loan institutions to counter dwindling deposits. The provision would allow banks, credit unions and savings and loans to issue one-year certificates that would earn 70 percent of the yield on a one-year Treasury bill. Individuals could exclude up to $1,000 of the certificate interest from their incomes; couples could exclude up to $2,000. The certificates would be issued for one year only, from Oct. 1, 1981, through Sept. 30, 1982.

The provision would mean an estimated $4.6 billion in lost government revenues by 1984. To offset the cost, the panel agreed to allow the current $200 ($400 for a joint return) exclusion for dividend and interest income to revert to prior law — a $100 ($200 for a joint return) exclusion for dividend income.

Attempts by Sen. Lloyd Bentsen, D-Texas, to extend the all-savers provision over three years and to target the savings to help the housing industry were defeated, basically along party lines. Bentsen would have required that institutions could issue savings certificates only to the extent that they held home mortgages in their portfolios.

The committee also agreed to an amendment, offered by William L. Armstrong, R-Colo., to adjust individual income, capital gains, and estate and gift taxes to reflect increases in the Consumer Price Index, beginning in 1985. The move, approved by a 9-5 vote, would in effect do away with "bracket creep," through which inflation pushes individuals into higher and higher tax brackets. The indexing provisions were to be offered as a committee amendment to the Finance bill, requiring a separate vote on the Senate floor. This was done, according to committee aides, because of strong administration opposition to including the provision in the bill, although Reagan favored indexation at a later time.

In other changes to the administration plan, the committee voted to:

● Impose an annual 32 percent tax on commodity futures contracts to close a well-publicized tax loophole by which investors converted ordinary income into a long-term capital gain, which was taxed at a lower rate. The move was expected to save the government $1.3 billion in 1982.

● Gradually decrease the windfall profits tax on newly discovered oil from the current 30 percent rate to 15 percent in 1986, at an estimated cost to the government through 1986 of $2.6 billion.

● Allow firms to expense, or write off in the year of purchase, the first $5,000 of the value of machinery and equipment. The write-off amount would gradually increase to $10,000 by 1986.

● Liberalize the tax on stock options given employees as part of their work benefits, and increase tax credits for company contributions to employee stock ownership plans. Both moves were intended to encourage workers to take an interest in their company's growth.

● Remove the current $10,000 cap on the investment tax credit that businesses could claim for investment in used equipment, a move intended to help small business.

● Allow truckers a deduction for the loss in value of their operating licenses that they claimed resulted from the 1980 trucking deregulation bill. *(1980 Almanac p. 242)*

Defeated were an amendment by John Heinz, R-Pa., to allow ailing industries a refund for past unused investment tax credits, and a measure proposed by Daniel Patrick Moynihan, D-N.Y., to provide tax credits to offset tuition paid at private elementary and secondary schools.

House Committee Action

Setting the administration's proposal (HR 3849) aside, the House Ways and Means Committee began in mid-June to fashion a substantially different package. Despite prodding by the Senate and the administration, the House panel did not approve its tax cut bill (HR 4242 — H Rept 97-201) until July 23.

Business Taxes

The panel tentatively agreed June 17 and 18 to cut corporate income tax rates and to substitute expensing for the current system of business depreciation.

Sam Gibbons, D-Fla., head of a Democratic task force on depreciation that drew up the proposal, said the plan would be more "even-handed" in its treatment of different kinds of businesses than the administration's business tax proposal, and that it also would be less complex.

But Democrats on the panel acknowledged that the move was a gamble and that success of their measure would depend in part on how much business backing resulted.

"This is all part of a package," said Thomas J. Downey, D-N.Y. "With this, individual rate cuts, plus some other sweeteners, it's conceivable, just conceivable, that our package will be a lot more attractive."

Treasury Secretary Regan immediately denounced the measure as a "last-minute, scattershot scheme." Assistant Treasury Secretary John E. Chapoton told the committee the expensing proposal — especially in the early years before it was fully phased in — would fall far short of providing business with the investment incentive needed for economic recovery.

The Ways and Means business tax relief measure would help both capital- and labor-intensive industries, according to Gibbons. The Reagan proposal, he said, would not benefit labor-intensive industries, such as research firms, because it targeted tax relief at capital investment.

The committee plan also avoided what some Democrats saw as an administration tax cut so generous as to provide some businesses with a government subsidy.

The plan would gradually lower the top corporate income tax rate paid by companies with annual incomes over $100,000 from the current 46 percent to 34 percent. The rate would drop to 43 percent in 1984, 40 percent in 1985, 37 percent in 1986 and 34 percent after 1986.

Gibbons said his task force also would propose that corporate taxes be lowered for firms earning under $100,000, but details had yet to be worked out.

Under the committee expensing plan, business would be allowed to write off the entire cost of machinery and equipment in the year of its purchase, instead of depreciating its cost over a period of time.

The provision would not be fully effective under the Ways and Means proposal until 1990, however, because an immediate effective date would put too great a strain on the federal budget, Gibbons said. Instead, the panel agreed to phase the provision in. The panel would phase out the current investment tax credit of up to 10 percent.

The committee measure was expected to equal the cost of the administration's business proposal, estimated by the Joint Taxation Committee to be $485 billion through 1990.

The plan also would provide:

● A 10-year depreciation for public utility property currently depreciated over 18-25 years and a 15-year depreciation of public utility property currently depreciated over 25 years. The Reagan plan would depreciate all such property over 10 years.

● Depreciation of all structures over a 15-year period, at a rate lower than that recommended by the administration for all except low-income housing.

● An increased tax credit for the rehabilitation of buildings over 30 years old, also proposed by Reagan.

● A refund of approximately $3.3 billion in unused investment tax credits to certain distressed industries — airlines, automobile manufacturers, mining, paper, railroads and steel — to be used by those industries to invest in new capital.

Savings and Investment

The panel agreed June 24 to several tax relief measures to encourage savings and investment. It accepted the administration proposal to raise the deductions from $7,500 to $15,000 for contributions to a Keogh plan, a retirement plan set up by the self-employed. It agreed to increase deductions for contributions to individual retirement accounts (IRAs) to $2,000 for individuals not covered by an employer-sponsored pension plan and to $1,000 for

individuals who are covered by employer-sponsored plans. It also voted to allow an additional non-deductible contribution equal to the maximum deductible amount.

The committee also:

● Adopted a savings certificate plan similar to that approved by the Finance Committee with the exception that only institutions holding home mortgages could issue the certificates and that certificates would be offered at a minimum denomination of no greater than $500.

● Agreed to let public utilities shareholders exclude up to $1,500 ($3,000 for a married couple) if they decided to receive dividends in the form of more utility stock instead of cash.

Small Business

Resuming markup July 9, following the Independence Day recess, the committee agreed to several provisions designed to help small businesses. The provisions, expected to cost almost $10 billion over the next five years, would:

● Broaden corporate income tax brackets gradually over the next three years so that many firms would fall into a lower tax bracket than under existing law. Also, tax rates in each of the brackets would be lowered by as much as 10 points.

These new provisions would be in addition to a gradual decrease in the top corporate tax rate, from 46 percent to 34 percent, approved earlier by the committee.

● Increase from $150,000 to $250,000 the amount of money a firm could accumulate before it was subject to an accumulated earnings tax.

In other action, the panel approved:

● A restriction, less stringent than one adopted by the Senate Finance Committee, on the use of commodity tax straddles to avoid paying taxes.

● A 25 percent tax credit for new expenditures made by a company for research and development within the company or for research the company has contracted an outside institution, such as a university, to do. There also would be an increased charitable deduction for contributions of new research equipment to a college or university.

Individual Cuts

After rejecting the president's 33-month, 25 percent across-the-board tax cut, the committee July 14 adopted its two-year, 15 percent proposal by a 22-13 vote, basically along party lines. The one exception: Hance, who voted with the Republicans.

The Democratic plan would cut average individual income tax rates by 5 percent Oct. 1, 1981, and by an additional 10 percent July 1, 1982. It would skew the cuts so that those earning under $50,000 would receive more than the average cut; those earning over $50,000 would receive less.

In addition to rate cuts, the committee agreed to:

● Drop the top tax rate on investment income from 70 percent to 60 percent in 1982 and 50 percent in 1983.

● Increase the zero bracket amount (formerly the standard deduction) from $2,300 to $2,500 for individuals and from $2,600 to $3,000 for joint returns.

● Increase the earned income credit for low-income families from 10 percent to 11 percent of the first $5,000 of income. Also, the credit would be phased out at a higher income level — $12,000, instead of the current $10,000.

● Reduce the marriage penalty tax by allowing two-income couples to deduct 10 percent, up to $5,000, of the lesser of the two incomes.

• Increase the credit for child care from 20 percent to 25 percent of up to $2,400 of such expenses for one child ($4,800 for two or more dependents).

The total package would mean a loss in revenues for fiscal 1982-86 of $419 billion, compared with $500 billion for individual cuts approved by the Senate Finance Committee.

The House committee estimated that under the Democratic proposal in 1983 those earning under $50,000 would receive 76.5 percent of the tax relief, while this same group would receive only 67.7 percent of the relief under the Senate and administration plan.

Other Provisions

In addition to cuts in individual taxes, the Ways and Means Committee agreed to:

• Provide a more generous reduction in estate and gift taxes than that approved by the Senate. The committee agreed to gradually increase the current $175,625 exemption to $600,000 by 1987 and to reduce the top tax rate on estates and gifts from the current 70 percent to 50 percent by 1985. The Senate bill would only increase the exemption.

Ways and Means agreed with the Senate to increase the annual gift tax exclusion from $3,000 to $10,000 and to do away with estate and gift taxes for transfers between spouses.

• Increase taxes to keep the troubled Railroad Retirement System from going broke as early as April 1982. Under an agreement reached by railroad labor and management and accepted by the committee, employer taxes to the pension fund would increase from 9.5 percent to 11.75 percent of payroll and employees would pay a new 2 percent tax. Also, the system would be allowed to borrow money from the Treasury on a short-term basis to cover shortfalls if there were a delay in transfer of money to the fund from the Social Security system.

These changes, plus some benefit cuts proposed in the House reconciliation bill, were expected to provide the system with increased funds of $4.1 billion for fiscal 1982-86.

• Exclude from taxes the first $75,000 of income earned abroad, with an additional allowance for housing costs in excess of a base amount.

• Increase from $50 to $1,000 the penalty for filing a false W-4 form, on which deductions are claimed for withholding of taxes.

• Extend the congressional moratorium on the taxation of fringe benefits through May 31, 1983. *(1979 Almanac p. 325)*

• Increase and extend the targeted jobs tax credit, scheduled to expire at the end of 1981, through Jan. 1, 1985. *(1978 Almanac p. 221)*

Political Bidding War

Before reporting the bill, the panel, at 2 a.m. July 22, adopted by an 18-17 vote a provision allowing the exemption of 500 barrels of oil a day from the windfall profits tax, at a cost to the Treasury of approximately $7 billion over the next five years.

The oil "sweetener" emerged from days of negotiation among Democrats anxious to hold the votes of conservative party members — many of whom came from oil-producing states — when the tax bill reached the House floor.

But not to be outbid, the White House and House Republicans hastily revised Reagan's 25 percent, across-the-board tax cut and crafted a new package expected to cost over $730 billion through fiscal 1986.

Added to Reagan's individual rate cuts and accelerated depreciation plans were tax breaks for oil producers, annual indexation of tax rates to offset inflation, relief from estate and gift taxes, increased charitable deductions, and a host of other measures designed, for the most part, to win a handful of swing votes.

Both Republicans and Democrats admitted their bills were more products of a political bidding war than blueprints for sound economic policy. Conable said, "If I were writing this bill, I would write it differently and so would every other member of this Congress." But he said Republicans had little choice if they wanted to enact the heart of Reagan's economic program.

Both sides conceded the outcome in the House was too close to call. Democrats claimed firm commitments from 12 of 29 conservative Democrats who defected to Reagan on a recent budget vote and said they hoped for some GOP help as well. *(Budget, vote 95, p. 40-H)*

But the Republicans rolled out their heavy artillery for the final battle. At a GOP pep rally July 24, President Reagan personally urged House Republicans to stick together in "these last critical days," calling the tax cut "the most crucial item left on our agenda for prosperity."

Senate Floor Action

While the Ways and Means Committee was marking up HR 4242, the Senate took its bill to the floor July 15 and approved its provisions July 29. In deference to House prerogatives on revenue measures, however, the Senate stopped short of final passage pending receipt of the House bill.

The key Senate test came July 29 when the Finance Committee's version as amended on the floor was approved 89-11. Thirty-seven of the Senate's 47 Democrats voted for the bill, while one Republican — Charles McC. Mathias Jr. of Maryland — voted against it. *(Vote 239, p. 41-S)*

On July 31, the Senate formally received HR 4242 from the House, which had passed the measure two days earlier. The Senate then substituted language from its own bill and appointed conferees for negotiations to resolve differences between the two versions.

During 12 days of debate, the Senate considered 118 amendments and adopted 80.

Indexation

The Senate July 16 agreed to index taxes to offset the effects of inflation. It adopted by a 57-40 vote the committee amendment requiring the indexation of individual income taxes to prevent so-called "bracket creep," which results when inflation pushes taxpayers into higher and higher tax brackets. *(Vote 191, p. 35-S)*

Under the provision, all income tax brackets, the zero bracket amount (formerly the standard deduction) and the personal exemption (currently $1,000 per person) would be increased annually by an amount equal to the increase in the Consumer Price Index over the previous fiscal year.

The indexing would begin in 1985, the year after the proposed 25 percent rate cut would be in full effect. According to the Joint Committee on Taxation, indexation could mean $12.6 billion in lost revenues for fiscal 1985 and $37.4 billion in 1986.

Opponents argued that indexation would take away

Tax Vote Defectors

Forty-eight Democrats defected July 29 and voted for the Reagan-backed tax cut substitute in the House. Only one Republican — James M. Jeffords of Vermont — voted against the Reagan tax plan. *(Vote 166, p. 58-H)*

Listed below are the 48 defecting Democrats. An asterisk (*) indicates a member voted with the Reagan administration May 7 on the Gramm-Latta substitute for the first fiscal 1982 budget resolution. *(Vote 30, p. 20-H)*

A dagger (†) indicates a member sided with President Reagan June 25 on the key vote on the rule to consider the omnibus budget reconciliation bill. *(Vote 95, p. 40-H)*

Atkinson, Pa.*†	Hightower, Texas*†
Barnard, Ga.*†	Hubbard, Ky.
Biaggi, N.Y.	Huckaby, La.*†
Boner, Tenn.	Hutto, Fla.*†
Bouquard, Tenn.*	Ireland, Fla.*†
Bowen, Miss.*	Jones, Tenn.*
Brinkley, Ga.*	Leath, Texas*†
Byron, Md.*†	Levitas, Ga.*
Chappell, Fla.*†	Luken, Ohio*
Daniel, D., Va.*†	Lundine, N.Y.
de la Garza, Texas	Mazzoli, Ky.*
Dicks, Wash.	McCurdy, Okla.
Dyson, Md.*	McDonald, Ga.*†
English, Okla.*	Mica, Fla.*
Evans, Ga.*†	Montgomery, Miss.*†
Fountain, N.C.*	Mottl, Ohio*†
Fuqua, Fla.*	Nelson, Fla.*
Ginn, Ga.*	Nichols, Ala.*†
Glickman, Kan.	Roemer, La.*†
Gramm, Texas*†	Santini, Nev.*†
Hall, R., Texas*†	Shelby, Ala.*†
Hall, S., Texas*†	Stenholm, Texas*†
Hance, Texas*†	Stump, Ariz.*†
Hatcher, Ga.*	Yatron, Pa.*

congressional ability to target future tax reductions, result in bloated budget deficits and prove inflationary by giving taxpayers more take-home pay during times of high inflation. "What this measure does is create a whole new class of citizens who can shrug their shoulders at inflation," said John H. Chafee, R-R.I.

But supporters countered that the plan would put a hold on government spending and force Congress to go on record when it needed to increase taxes, instead of allowing inflation to do the job more painlessly.

'All-Savers'

The Senate also agreed to revise the committee's "all-savers" plan to allow savings and loans, credit unions and commercial banks to issue one-year tax-exempt savings certificates. While the measure was intended to help the financially troubled savings and loan industry and to spur individual savings, there were doubts, even among committee members, that it would do the latter.

"Maybe it was an 'all-subsidy' plan, but not an 'all-savers' plan," said Finance Chairman Dole.

With the help of the administration, a new plan was devised that won Senate approval. It provided that the certificates could be issued over a 15-month period, from Oct. 1, 1981, through Dec. 31, 1982. It would continue the committee provision that each certificate earn 70 percent of the yield on the one-year Treasury bill, with up to $1,000 of interest deductible for individuals, $2,000 for couples.

In addition, beginning in 1984, a 15 percent exclusion of interest income would be allowed for up to $3,000 of interest for an individual ($6,000 for a couple). However, first deducted from the interest income would be any consumer debt interest, other than interest on home mortgages and business loans, that had been paid during the year by the taxpayer. This would be done to prevent individuals from borrowing money to buy the certificates and getting two tax breaks — one on the interest income, another on the interest payment.

The measure was attached on a 56-40 vote to an amendment by Lloyd Bentsen, D-Texas, that required institutions issuing the certificates to use 75 percent of the additional savings income for home or farm loans. The Bentsen amendment was approved by a vote of 86-10. *(Votes 192, 196, p. 35-S)*

Banking Committee Chairman Jake Garn, R-Utah, tried unsuccessfully to broaden the Bentsen provision to include school, car and small business loans. *(Votes, 193-195, p. 35-S)*

Social Security

The Senate also tabled, largely along party lines, an amendment by Daniel Patrick Moynihan, D-N.Y., to allow the Old Age and Survivors' Insurance Trust Fund to borrow from other Social Security trust funds. The 51-45 vote came after lengthy debate over the solvency of the financially troubled pension system. Moynihan and other Democrats argued that the administration had overblown the seriousness of Social Security's problems so that it could cut benefits to help balance the budget in 1984. Moynihan claimed that interfund borrowing alone could keep the funds solvent well into the next century.

But Republicans contended the system could go broke as early as 1982 and that a major overhaul of benefits and funding were required for long-term solvency. Dole called Moynihan's plan a "Band-Aid that won't stop the bleeding even for three years."

The action came two days after the Senate unanimously approved a "sense of the Senate" resolution opposing taxation of Social Security benefits. *(Votes 187-188, p. 34-S; Social Security, p. 117)*

Subsequently, the Senate adopted an amendment instructing the Finance Committee to report a bill by Nov. 15 that would allow borrowing among the three Social Security trust funds. The vote was 89-4. *(Vote 218, p. 38-S)*

Windfall Profits Tax

An amendment by Lloyd Bentsen, D-Texas, to exempt from the windfall profits tax 1,000 barrels of oil a day for independent producers and 10 barrels a day for royalty owners was tabled by a vote of 61-38. *(Vote 209, p. 37-S)*

In its place, Finance Chairman Dole offered a four-year phase-out of all windfall profits taxes on newly discovered oil, which, with a second-degree amendment to expand the exemption, would have cost the Treasury about $11 billion through 1986.

Democrats balked and began a filibuster. After moving to table his own amendment to test its support, Dole —

finding unexpectedly strong opposition to his plan — agreed to withdraw the amendment. *(Vote 210, p. 37-S)*

Heating Tax Credit

The Senate reversed itself July 28 on an amendment offered by Sen. Warren B. Rudman, R-N.H., and voted 71-25 to provide a tax credit for the costs of heating a home. *(Vote 234, p. 40-S)*

A day earlier, the Senate voted 47-48 to reject a similar amendment by Sen. Edward M. Kennedy, D-Mass., to allow an annual credit of up to $300 for heating costs for three years. *(Vote 224, p. 39-S)*

Both amendments were designed to help people living in the Northeast and Midwest, although all taxpayers would be eligible.

According to a Rudman aide, after the Kennedy amendment was rejected, Rudman personally lobbied his colleagues and tried to get the administration to endorse the proposal. He also scaled it down to a maximum credit of $200, which would be in effect only for the 1981 tax year.

The administration still opposed the amendment, as did Dole. But Rudman persuaded 25 of his fellow senators to switch their votes and support his scaled-down amendment.

Being a Republican apparently helped: 22 of the 25 senators changing their votes were Republicans.

Under the amendment that was approved, taxpayers could get a maximum $200 tax credit for their heating costs if their income was $15,000 or less. A smaller credit would be available to those earning between $15,000 and $25,000.

Rudman said the amendment would cost the government $400 million (the Kennedy amendment was estimated to cost about $600 million a year).

The Senate amendment subsequently was dropped in conference.

Charitable Contributions

An amendment by Bob Packwood, R-Ore., to allow those who did not itemize deductions on their tax returns to take a deduction for charitable contributions was adopted overwhelmingly.

The provision would phase in the deduction, allowing taxpayers a 25 percent deduction up to $100 in 1982 and 1983, a 25 percent deduction with no limit in 1984, a 50 percent deduction in 1985, and a 100 percent deduction in 1986. The provision would expire at the end of 1986, giving Congress the opportunity to decide whether the deduction actually increased contributions to charity and should be continued.

The measure, approved by a 97-1 vote (S. I. "Sam" Hayakawa, R-Calif., was the only dissenter), was expected to result in a revenue loss of about $4.8 billion over the next five years. *(Vote 203, p. 36-S)*

Other Amendments Adopted

In other action, the Senate accepted amendments to:
● Reduce corporate income tax rates over the next two years. The current 17 percent rate on the first $25,000 of income would be lowered to 16 percent in 1982, and to 15 percent in 1983. The current 20 percent rate for the next $25,000 would be cut to 19 percent in 1982 and 18 percent in 1983. The provision, aimed primarily at helping small businesses, was adopted by a vote of 92-0. *(Vote 199, p. 36-S)*
● Impose a $150,000 cap on the amount of used property eligible for a 10 percent investment tax credit and change

the method used for recapturing the credit if the property was sold. The committee bill had eliminated the current $100,000 cap.
● Allow widowed or divorced spouses to contribute up to $1,125 a year to an individual retirement account (IRA) that had been set up for them by the other spouse. Under current law, such persons could no longer contribute to such an IRA once they had been divorced or their spouse had died.
● Eliminate the requirement that closely held (generally family-owned) companies participating in an employee stock ownership plan pass on voting rights to employees participating in the plan. The measure was adopted by a 94-3 vote. *(Vote 205, p. 37-S)*
● Reduce the rate at which structures other than low-income housing could be depreciated over 15 years and offset allowable depreciation of rehabilitated buildings by the amount of the tax credit received for renovation. The vote was 56-40. *(Vote 206, p. 37-S)*
● Require that the tax-exempt "all-savers" certificate approved earlier be available in denominations of as little as $500 to attract small investors.
● Permit greater access by law enforcement officials to Internal Revenue Service files for use in combating drug traffic and organized crime. The provision was adopted by voice vote after a motion to table the measure was defeated 28-66. *(Vote 225, p. 39-S)*
● Simplify and lessen the penalty for use of what is called "last in, first out" (LIFO) inventory accounting, which is a more advantageous method during periods of high inflation. The measure was approved by a vote of 94-0. *(Vote 226, p. 39-S)*
● Increase from 5 percent to 10 percent the charitable deduction allowed corporations. The vote was 88-5. *(Vote 221, p. 39-S)*
● Allow a one-time, $1,500 maximum credit for the adoption of certain disadvantaged children.
● Allow taxpayers in South Alabama a $10 credit for each pecan tree planted to replace one destroyed by Hurricane Frederick in 1979.
● Increase the current 20 percent child care credit to 30 percent for those earning less than $10,000, reduce it one percentage point for each additional $1,000 in income up to $30,000 and allow a 20 percent credit for those earning $30,000 or more. The ceiling on the amount of day care expenses eligible for the credit would be increased from $2,000 to $2,400 for one dependent and from $4,000 to $4,800 for two or more dependents. The vote was 94-1. *(Vote 227, p. 39-S)*
● Exempt homes for orphaned or handicapped children from paying a windfall profits tax on oil royalties.

Amendments Rejected

Not all amendments proposed on the floor fared so well. The Senate also:
● Rejected 26-71 a substitute tax-cut package offered by Ernest F. Hollings, D-S.C., which included a one-year 10 percent cut in individual taxes in 1983 and targeted the cuts to provide more relief to those earnings under $50,000. *(Vote 211, p. 37-S)*
● Tabled an amendment by Donald W. Riegle Jr., D-Mich., to maintain the $122 minimum monthly Social Security benefit for those currently receiving it and those who would be entitled to receive it at any time in 1981. The vote was 52-46, largely along party lines. *(Vote 207, p. 37-S)*
● Tabled, 54-46, an amendment by Kennedy to increase

by 5 percent the existing energy conservation tax credit for commercial and industrial energy users and to increase the size of the home-owner's tax credit. *(Vote 208, p. 37-S)*

● Tabled, 62-36, an amendment by Bradley that would have lowered the maximum tax on capital gains from 28 percent to 15 percent. *(Vote 189, p. 35-S)*

● Rejected, 24-61, a Bradley amendment to limit the tax cut to one year. *(Vote 201, p. 36-S)*

● Tabled, 56-40, an amendment by Alfonse D'Amato, R-N.Y., that would have made permanent the current $200 exclusion ($400 for joint returns) of interest and dividend income. Under the committee bill, that exclusion would be replaced after 1982 with a $100 ($200 for joint returns) exclusion for dividend income only. *(Vote 190, p. 35-S)*

House Floor Action

Reagan's tax cut triumph was assured July 29 when the Democratic-controlled House bowed to a tidal wave of public pressure generated by the president's July 27 televised appeal for support and adopted his package in place of a Ways and Means Committee version.

Forty-eight Democrats defected to Reagan in the crucial showdown as the House voted 238-195 to adopt provisions of the administration substitute sponsored by Conable and Hance in place of the Ways and Means bill. Only one Republican, James M. Jeffords of Vermont, broke ranks. *(Defectors box, p. 101; vote 166, p. 58-H)*

Reagan's Pressure Felt

The House vote was touted by some as a test, after Reagan's budget victory a month earlier, of who had true control of the House — the Democratic majority or administration-backed Republicans in coalition with conservative Democrats.

Rostenkowski, in his first floor battle as chairman of the Ways and Means Committee, warned, "If we accept the president's substitute, we accept his dominance of our House for the months ahead. We surrender to the political and economic whim of his White House."

A day before the vote, both sides labeled the outcome too close to call. But as debate was about to begin, House Speaker Thomas P. O'Neill Jr., D-Mass., all but conceded the battle was lost — largely as a result of heavy lobbying by the president, his aides and voters mobilized by Reagan's television appeal.

Democrats responded to Reagan with TV commentaries of their own but spent much of their time discussing Social Security, an issue on which they felt the president was more vulnerable.

"We are experiencing a telephone blitz like this nation has never seen. It's had a devastating effect," said O'Neill the morning of the vote.

In floor debate, Republicans called for a "new beginning" and an end to worn-out economic policies of the past. Democrats predicted high inflation and bloated budget deficits and defended their own program for targeting tax relief to low- and middle-income Americans.

Some members condemned both packages for the series of "sweeteners," especially tax breaks for oil producers that were attached to win Southern Democratic support. "I don't mind if the eyes of Texas are upon me," said Barney Frank, D-Mass. "I just don't want the hands of Texas in my pockets."

Members had their first test vote on a liberal tax cut

alternative (HR 4269) sponsored by Morris K. Udall, D-Ariz., that called for a scaled-down version of the committee bill and a balanced budget in 1982. It was defeated 144-288, with one vote of "present." *(Vote 165, p. 58-H)*

The House also adopted a committee amendment to strike from the bill a section dealing with federal loans to states for unemployment compensation, an issue resolved earlier that day during a budget reconciliation conference.

The vote on the Conable-Hance substitute followed, and the bill as amended was then passed 323-107. *(Vote 167, p. 58-H)*

Conference Action

The conference agreement (H Rept 97-215, S Rept 97-176) was the product of an all-night session July 31 during which House and Senate conferees worked out the differences between the two versions of the tax cut bill.

Major disagreements were few, with the exception of oil-related tax breaks, in large part because both bills had been written with strong White House influence.

The Senate accepted House provisions to give oil royalty owners more generous exemptions from the windfall profits tax and to totally exempt "stripper" wells — those that produce 10 barrels or less of oil a day — from the tax after 1982. The two measures were expected to cost $8.4 billion through fiscal 1986.

House plans to freeze the oil depletion allowance at 22 percent and to allow a tax credit for wood-burning stoves were dropped, as was a Senate provision to give tax credits for home heating costs. Both measures reduced the windfall profits tax on newly discovered oil from 30 percent to 15 percent by 1986, a $3.2 billion tax break.

The House accepted Senate-passed child-care credits, stricter curbs on the commodity tax straddle and increased tax benefits for employee stock ownership plans. The Senate accepted House-passed tax breaks for homes sold but rejected a provision to reduce to six months from one year the holding period for capital gains.

A number of miscellaneous special-interest provisions were dropped, including tax breaks for planting pecan trees and what Finance Chairman Dole dubbed the "Gong Show amendment" — a tax credit for investment in TV game shows.

Last-Ditch Opposition

The bill did not complete its congressional journey without some last-ditch Democratic attempts to reduce $11.8 billion in tax breaks for oil producers included in the package.

Sen. Kennedy kept the Senate in session two days after its scheduled Aug. 1 recess to vote on a motion to send the bill back to conference. He called the tax breaks for independent oil producers and royalty owners an "unfair and unnecessary giveaway" at a time "when millions of average families are being asked to sacrifice as part of the administration's economic program."

But his pleas were quickly rebuffed by impatient, and in some cases angry, senators who wanted to head off for their summer vacations before an air traffic controllers' strike put a kink in their getaway plans.

Dole called the debate little more than a "media event" and denied Kennedy's accusations that the tax breaks would go to "big oil." After two hours of debate, Kennedy's motion failed, 20-55. *(Vote 247, p. 42-S)*

The following day in the House, Ways and Means Democrat James M. Shannon, Mass., attempted to prevent a final vote on the bill until oil tax breaks could be trimmed back. But his plan to raise a point of order against the conference report was blocked by Rostenkowski, who won approval of the measure under suspension of the rules, a procedure that requires a two-thirds vote.   ∎

Debt Limit Increases

Congress twice during 1980 enacted legislation increasing the "temporary" limit on the public debt, ultimately boosting the ceiling above the trillion-dollar mark for the first time (H J Res 265 — PL 97-49).

Had Congress failed to act, the debt limit would have fallen to its "permanent" $400 billion level, leaving the government unable to meet its borrowing needs.

In considering the second debt limit bill, Congress used shortcut procedures established in 1979 to depoliticize the debt process. However, the earlier increase (HR 1553 — PL 97-2), which was requested by President Reagan as one of his first official acts, sailed through Congress under regular procedures with unaccustomed Republican support.

Fiscal 1981: $985 Billion

Handing Reagan his first legislative victory, Congress Feb. 6 completed action on legislation (HR 1553 — PL 97-2) increasing the public debt ceiling to $985 billion through Sept. 30, 1981.

Final action came when the Senate approved on a 73-18 vote the measure the House had passed a day earlier by a 305-104 margin. *(House vote 7, p. 4-H; Senate vote 23, p. 6-S)*

Had Congress failed to act, outstanding debt would have hit the existing $935.1 billion ceiling by mid-February. *(Existing ceiling, 1980 Almanac p. 301)*

'Rapid Conversion'

Just before the Senate vote on the bill, Finance Committee Chairman Robert Dole, R-Kan., noted that there had "been a lot of rapid conversion around here on this issue."

In both chambers, Republicans who never in their careers had voted to increase the debt limit — calling such votes "fiscally irresponsible" — were queueing up to accede to their president's request to boost the ceiling by another $50 billion.

"I see for the first time some glimmer of hope that we will bring federal spending under control," reasoned Rep. Marjorie S. Holt, R-Md.

GOP members argued that President Reagan was not responsible for the ballooning deficit that made the increase necessary. It was leftover business from the Carter administration, they maintained.

Although a majority of Democrats in both houses voted for the measure, they made the Republicans squirm before the final votes were taken.

In the House many Democrats stood beside their chairs, arms folded, watching their Republican colleagues vote "aye" before they cast their own votes.

In the Senate, the partisanship was more explicit. Minority Leader Robert C. Byrd, D-W.Va., offered an amend-

ment to set the debt limit at $963 billion, which he said would be sufficient to finance the debt through May 1981.

"We think the Senate ought to have a debt limit figure based on the assumptions of the Reagan administration and the president's economic package," Byrd said, rather than the Carter administration's assumptions upon which the $985 billion was based.

But Byrd's attempt to lower the debt ceiling figure was killed on a tabling motion offered by Majority Leader Howard H. Baker Jr., R-Tenn. The vote was 52-41. *(Vote 22, p. 6-S)*

Sen. Howard M. Metzenbaum, D-Ohio, had planned to offer an amendment to require the president to re-control oil prices, but agreed to withhold his proposal.

Earlier, Senate Republicans seemed to pose as much of a problem for the president's debt limit increase as the Democrats. Sens. Orrin G. Hatch, R-Utah, and William L. Armstrong, R-Colo., wanted to attach several budget reform amendments — including one to give the president impoundment and rescission powers. Armstrong made it clear that the budget reforms would surface again, but he did not press to attach them to the debt limit bill.

Conservative Sen. James A. McClure, R-Idaho, withdrew an amendment to raise the debt limit to $1.04 trillion. McClure argued that it was a "more realistic estimate" of what would be needed through the year. He said it would be wiser to do it now so the Reagan administration would not be blamed for breaking the trillion dollar mark. Reagan opposed the proposal.

Administration Plea

Before reporting the debt limit bill (H Rept 97-1), the House Ways and Means Committee Feb. 2 heard Treasury Secretary Donald T. Regan and Director of the Office of Management and Budget David A. Stockman plead their case for the increase.

Stockman, who voted against raising the debt limit every time it came up during his two terms in the House (1977-81) was asked to explain his sudden turnabout.

"I voted against those debt ceiling bills because I had no confidence anybody was developing a plan to control spending," Stockman answered. "I have confidence such a plan is being developed now because I am writing it."

Regan, calling the need for the debt limit increase "one of the most disheartening things I've faced," said that if the ceiling were not increased "as early as this Friday [Feb. 6] the existing debt limit will introduce an element of uncertainty in the market and will affect Treasury's decisions on borrowings."

Fiscal 1982: Trillion-Dollar Limit

Senate passage Sept. 29 by a 64-34 vote cleared the second bill (H J Res 265 — PL 97-49), increasing the debt ceiling to $1,079,800,000,000 through Sept. 30, 1982. The existing $985 billion limit was scheduled to expire Oct. 1. *(Vote 295, p. 50-S)*

The Finance Committee had approved the measure Sept. 15 without a written report.

Senate Republicans warned that without the debt limit increase, government borrowing would be impaired and government checks, including Social Security payments, might not be honored.

The House had approved the resolution as part of its first fiscal 1982 budget resolution. Under a procedure established in 1979, the $1.0798 trillion debt limit figure

contained in the budget resolution was incorporated in H J Res 265, which the House then sent to the Senate without a separate vote. *(Budget resolution, p. 247; procedure, 1979 Almanac p. 305)*

The procedure was designed to insulate the debt ceiling increases from political pressures that often had caused them to fail in the House. In keeping with history, however, the debt limit bill once again became a political football.

In the past, it was fiscally conservative Republicans who refused to vote for debt limit increases. In action on H J Res 265, however, the Democrats were playing the game. They offered a series of amendments, many of which involved repealing parts of the recently passed tax cut. One Democrat talked the night away in an effort to hold the debt ceiling below a trillion dollars.

Proxmire Talkathon

William Proxmire, D-Wis., spoke from early in the evening of Sept. 28 to mid-morning Sept. 29, urging his colleagues to keep the debt limit to $995 billion as a means to hold down spending.

Proxmire's speech, running 16 hours and 12 minutes, caused the first all-night session of the Senate since debate on draft registration in June 1980. It apparently was the fourth longest speech in Senate history.

The record for the longest speech ever given in the Senate was held by Strom Thurmond, R-S.C., who filibustered the Civil Rights Act of 1957 for 24 hours and 18 minutes. Runners-up were Wayne Morse, D-Ore. (1945-69), who spoke for 22 hours and 26 minutes on tidelands oil legislation in 1953, and Robert M. LaFollette Sr., R-Wis. (1906-25), who spoke for 18 hours and 23 minutes on a currency bill in 1908. *(1980 Almanac pp. 18, 47)*

"I wanted some way I could call attention to this very serious economic blunder," Proxmire told reporters after he finished his talkathon.

Proxmire never threatened to hold up passage of the debt limit increase, which Finance Chairman Dole repeatedly told members was absolutely essential for the orderly operation of government.

If the resolution were not passed before Oct. 1, Dole warned, a financial crisis might be precipitated because the government could no longer borrow money. Dole raised the threat that senior citizens might not be able to cash their Social Security checks by Oct. 5.

Amendments Tabled

Dole's admonitions to approve the bill without amendments so the increase could be sent directly to the president, worked in the end — but not until Democrats and one Republican offered a number of amendments.

Amendments that were tabled and thus killed included proposals offered by:

● William L. Armstrong, R-Colo., to enhance the president's power to rescind appropriated funds by requiring a two-house veto of any rescission, instead of the existing method, which required two-house approval. Tabled 84-15. *(Vote 289, p. 49-S)*

● J. James Exon, D-Neb., and Bill Bradley, D-N.J., to cut the third year of the newly enacted individual income tax cut by the amount needed to get the deficit down to the $42.5 billion figure estimated by the administration. Tabled 56-43. *(Vote 290, p. 49-S; tax cut, p. 91)*

● Proxmire, to hold the debt ceiling increase to $995 billion. Tabled 63-33. *(Vote 292, p. 50-S)*

● Daniel Patrick Moynihan, D-N.Y., to advance the expiration date for the debt limit to March 31, 1982. Tabled 53-44. *(Vote 294, p. 50-S)*

● Gary Hart, D-Colo., to reduce the tax deduction for business meals from 100 percent to 70 percent and earmark the difference in savings to restore funding for the school lunch program to the level it enjoyed before the budget reconciliation cuts. Tabled 58-30. *(Vote 286, p. 49-S)*

One-Day Increase

In addition to approving the fiscal 1982 debt limit increase, the Senate Sept. 29 gave final approval to an increase for the remainder of fiscal 1981 (H J Res 266 — PL 97-48). This resolution raised the debt ceiling through Sept. 30, 1981, to $999.8 billion.

The Treasury Department had estimated it would bump up against the existing $985 billion limit Sept. 30 and thus would be precluded from issuing approximately $13 billion in securities to the civil service retirement trust fund on Oct. 1.

Dole told the Senate that if the issue were delayed, the trust fund would lose about $4.5 million per day — $350,000 for each $1 billion of uninvested funds.

The Senate approved H J Res 266 by voice vote after deleting tax cut provisions that had been attached to the measure earlier in the session.   ∎

Cash Discount Ban Ends

Congress completed action July 14 on legislation that would permit merchants to offer unlimited discounts on cash purchases while prohibiting them from imposing surcharges on credit card sales.

The bill (HR 31 — PL 97-25) repealed the existing 5 percent ceiling on discounts merchants were permitted to offer customers for cash purchases. It also extended until Feb. 27, 1984, a prohibition on surcharges for purchases by credit card. This ban had lapsed Feb. 27 while Congress considered the extension legislation.

The House originally passed HR 31 Feb. 24 by a 372-4 vote. The Senate approved its version (S 414 — S Rept 97-23) March 12 by voice vote after rejecting, 41-56, an amendment to delete the credit card surcharge provisions. *(House vote 8, p. 6-H; Senate vote 28, p. 9-S)*

Deadlock

Subsequently, however, Senate and House conferees deadlocked over an unrelated Senate amendment designed to remove legal obstacles to the nomination of Dr. C. Everett Koop as surgeon general of the United States. The 64-year-old Koop, an outspoken foe of abortion, was over the statutory age limit for the post. *(Koop controversy, p. 492)*

Seeking to end the stalemate, the House May 4 passed by a 296-43 vote a separate bill (HR 3132) that incorporated the basic provisions of HR 31 but deleted the nongermane amendment. The Senate never acted on that measure. *(Vote 22, p. 18-H)*

Conferees on HR 31 finally agreed June 17 to accept the disputed Senate language after discovering that other provisions of law still would bar Koop's appointment. The House adopted the conference report (H Rept 97-159) June 24 by a 398-9 vote and the Senate cleared the measure by a standing vote July 14. *(Vote 90, p. 38-H)*

Provisions

As enacted into law, HR 31:

● Repealed the existing 5 percent ceiling on the discount merchants might offer to customers who paid by cash without being subject to certain truth in lending disclosure requirements and state usury laws.

● Eliminated existing regulatory restrictions that discouraged cash discounts.

● Extended for three years, until Feb. 27, 1984, a prohibition on surcharges for purchases by credit card or under open-end credit plans.

● Required the Federal Reserve Board to study and report to Congress in two years on the effect of charge card transactions on card issuers, merchants and consumers.

● Permitted lenders to comply with new civil liability provisions of 1980 amendments (PL 96-221) to the Truth in Lending Act before the April 1, 1982, effective date. *(Amendments, 1980 Almanac p. 236)*

● Extended until Dec. 31, 1982, the time that a national bank could hold real estate, if it was acquired before Dec. 31, 1979, and was carried at nominal value on that date. *(Previous legislation, 1980 Almanac p. 275)*

● Waived provisions of the Public Health Service Act of 1944 (PL 78-410) that established a mandatory retirement age for the surgeon general of the United States. ∎

Railroad Retirement System

Congress July 31 approved a major overhaul of the Railroad Retirement system in an effort to avert a financial shortfall in the system as early as April 1982.

Changes made in the system by the budget reconciliation bill (HR 3982 — PL 97-35) were part of a package agreed to by rail labor and management, which included increased railroad retirement taxes adopted during the first week of August as part of President Reagan's Economic Recovery Tax Act of 1981 (HR 4242 — PL 97-34).

The final legislation was a compromise of provisions drafted by the House Ways and Means and Senate Finance committees, which were incorporated in the reconciliation savings measures reported by the House Budget Committee (H Rept 97-158) and its Senate counterpart (S 1377 —S Rept 97-139). *(Reconciliation bill legislative history, p. 256; tax bill, p. 91)*

The Reagan administration proposed a far different change from that finally accepted by Congress, in part because rail labor and management had not yet come up with a plan to solve the system's financial difficulties. The administration proposed in its March budget that a 1980 benefit increase be repealed until rail labor and management came up with a plan to put the pension system back on a sound footing. *(Background, 1980 Almanac p. 295, 1974 Almanac p. 254)*

The changes made in the reconciliation bill were expected to save approximately $620 million for fiscal 1982-84. The amount was a net figure; many of the reconciliation changes involved benefit increases offered in exchange for the $1.7 billion increase in rail employee and employer taxes for fiscal 1982-84 adopted as part of HR 4242.

The major changes included a more generous benefit formula, authority for short-term borrowing from the Treasury and restricted "windfall" benefits — extra benefits given retirees as a result of a major revision of the Railroad

Retirement system in 1974. These changes, combined with the tax increases, were expected to keep the system solvent for the next 10 years.

Major Provisions

As cleared by Congress, Title XI of HR 3982 included the following provisions (generally effective Oct. 1, 1981):

● Changed the method used for computing so-called Tier II rail pension benefits — those above and beyond what a retiree would have received under Social Security — to prevent the benefit from eroding with inflation.

● Provided for permanent annual cost-of-living increases of Tier II benefits.

● Ended the use of general retirement funds to pay for windfall benefits. This provision was expected to result in immediate payment reductions for some 400,000 current recipients of windfall benefits.

● Eliminated pre-retirement cost-of-living indexing of windfall benefits.

● Eliminated new windfall benefits for non-dependent spouses who might be eligible for such benefits as a result of a recent court case. New windfall benefits also would be eliminated for all other spouses, widows or widowers of railroad employees. The bill made the provision effective on the day of enactment.

● Adjusted the formula for reducing future benefit increases of early retirees to be consistent with the formula used for such benefits under Social Security.

● Lowered from 50 percent to 45 percent the amount of an employee's Tier II benefit granted a spouse, but removed existing caps on such spousal benefits.

● Revised the survivors' Tier II benefit formula to include a lower cost-of-living increase.

● Allowed for limited authority to borrow from the Treasury funds to cover temporary funding shortfalls.

● Instituted an "early warning system" that required the Railroad Retirement Board to alert Congress to future funding problems. This report would be triggered whenever the board was required to borrow from the Treasury 50 percent or more of the money it needed to pay basic, Social Security-equivalent benefits.

● Required that employees receive credit for actual months of service, rather than having months of service rounded up to the next highest year, for calculating benefits.

● Expanded the category of workers considered "currently connected" with the rail industry who qualified for more generous survivors' and supplemental benefits.

● Allowed divorced wives to collect basic benefits, equivalent to Social Security benefits, if they were married to the employee for at least 10 years, were no longer married and were at least 65 years old.

● Expanded basic benefit coverage to include surviving divorced wives and mothers and remarried widows.

● Eliminated, for workers hired on or after Oct. 1, 1981, supplemental benefits given to those with long-term rail service. ∎

Unemployment Benefits Cut

The federal-state unemployment compensation program was reduced more than $3.1 billion for fiscal 1982-84 by the budget reconciliation bill (HR 3982 — PL 97-35).

Major changes involved the extended benefits program, which provided recipients with benefits for up to 13 weeks — on top of the 26 weeks of regular benefits — during periods of high unemployment, and federal loans to states that did not have sufficient unemployment tax revenues to cover benefit payments. *(Background, 1980 Almanac p. 293; Congress and the Nation Vol. IV, p. 709)*

The final legislation, cleared July 31, was a compromise of provisions drafted by the House Ways and Means and Senate Finance committees, which were incorporated in the reconciliation savings measures reported by the House Budget committee (H Rept 97-158) and its Senate counterpart (S 1377 — S Rept 97-139). *(Reconciliation legislative history, p. 256)*

President Reagan had asked Congress to eliminate the nationwide extended benefits program, to tighten eligibility for state extended benefits and to eliminate benefits for those who voluntarily quit military service, all of which Congress approved. However, it turned down a more controversial Reagan proposal under which claimants could be required to accept minimum-wage jobs after collecting 13 weeks of unemployment benefits. *(Reagan's budget request, p. 278)*

Major Provisions

As cleared by Congress, Title XXIV of HR 3982 made the following changes in unemployment compensation programs:

● Eliminated immediately the requirement that all states provide up to 13 weeks of extended unemployment benefits when the national insured unemployment rate (IUR) exceeded 4.5 percent.

● Excluded persons receiving extended unemployment benefits from the calculation of the IUR used to trigger extended benefits in states.

● Raised the triggers used to determine whether the extended benefits program would be available in a state, as follows:

1) The mandatory trigger, under which states had to provide extended benefits would rise to 5 percent unemployment, from 4 percent under existing law; as under existing law, this trigger would apply only if the state IUR was at least 20 percent higher than the state average over the two previous years.

2) The optional trigger, under which states could choose to provide extended benefits, would rise to 6 percent, from 5 percent under existing law.

● Made the provision effective for weeks beginning after Sept. 25, 1982.

● Required extended benefits claimants who had worked at least 20 weeks or had the "equivalent" in wages (defined as either 40 times the claimant's current weekly insurance payment or 1.5 times the claimant's wages over the quarter with the highest wages during a one-year base period prior to unemployment). The provision was effective for weeks beginning after Sept. 25, 1982.

● Disqualified from any unemployment compensation those who voluntarily left military service at the end of their enlistment term and were eligible to re-enlist; effective for those who left the service on or after July 1, 1981.

● Required states to amend their unemployment compensation laws to allow for the above changes before employers in the state could be eligible for a 2.7 percent federal credit against taxes paid under the Federal Unemployment Tax Act (FUTA).

● Imposed an interest rate of up to 10 percent on loans made to states from the federal unemployment insurance trust fund between April 1, 1982, and Dec. 31, 1987.

● Set limits on the federal penalty imposed on states for failing to repay loans received from the federal unemployment insurance trust fund, if the states took certain steps to improve the solvency of their unemployment compensation programs. The provision was effective from Oct. 1, 1981, through Dec. 31, 1987. ▪

Trade Adjustment Aid Cut

The trade adjustment assistance program, designed to help those who lost their jobs as a result of competition from imports, was trimmed back substantially as part of the budget reconciliation package (HR 3982 — PL 97-35), cleared July 31.

Congress cut $2.6 billion from the program for fiscal 1982-84 by accepting administration requests to tighten eligibility and to require that claimants exhaust all unemployment compensation benefits before collecting trade adjustment assistance. *(Reagan's budget, p. 278)*

The provisions, drafted by the House Ways and Means and Senate Finance committees, were incorporated in the reconciliation savings measures reported by the House Budget committee (H Rept 97-158) and its Senate counterpart (S 1377 — S Rept 97-139). *(Reconciliation legislative history, p. 256)*

The reductions were made in part because of criticisms that the program had not worked as originally intended. The Senate committee report cited a 1980 General Accounting Office study that found the weekly cash payments did little to help displaced workers adjust to their unemployment, were often received in lump sums after the claimant had found a job and might have been a disincentive for some to look for work. *(Background, 1979 Almanac p. 327; 1974 Almanac p. 553; Congress and the Nation Vol. IV, p. 131)*

Major Provisions

As cleared by Congress, Title XXV of HR 3982 included the following provisions (all effective after Sept. 30, 1981, unless otherwise indicated):

● Extended for one year, to Sept. 30, 1983, the trade adjustment assistance program for workers and firms.

● Tightened the standard under which eligibility for trade adjustment assistance benefits were determined. Benefits would be provided to groups of workers only when it was found that foreign import competition was a "substantial cause" for the loss of their jobs. Existing law stipulated that import competition must have "contributed importantly" to the layoffs. The provision was effective 180 days after enactment.

● Required workers to exhaust all unemployment compensation benefits before qualifying for trade adjustment assistance.

● Limited an individual's weekly payment under the adjustment assistance program to the amount received under unemployment insurance.

● Limited an individual's combined unemployment compensation and trade adjustment assistance payments to 52 weeks.

● Disqualified from benefits those workers who refused

to seek or accept "suitable work" if prospects of returning to their line of work were not good.

● Authorized the secretary of labor to require workers to accept training or expand their job search, after the first eight weeks of eligibility.

● Required that job training be made available to workers, if certain other conditions were met.

● Increased job search and relocation allowances from a maximum of $500 for each worker to $600.

● Expanded the secretary of labor's responsiblity to inform all workers about the program, its benefits and how to apply, effective on the day of enactment.

● Eliminated most retroactive lump-sum payments by limiting benefit payments to weeks of unemployment more than 60 days after workers filed a petition to qualify for assistance.

● Liberalized the requirement that workers must be employed for 26 weeks during the year preceding unemployment by allowing certain leave to be counted in the 26-week period.

● Authorized the secretary of commerce to provide each eligible industry with up to $2 million a year in technical assistance, including establishment of industry-wide programs to develop new products, effective on the day of enactment.

CETA Jobs Programs

The omnibus budget reconciliation bill (HR 3982 — PL 97-35) finished off the troubled public service jobs programs authorized by the Comprehensive Employment and Training Act (CETA).

The two programs, which at one time had provided 725,000 jobs, were terminated at the end of fiscal 1981. The reconciliation bill authorized no funds for them in fiscal 1982.

One of the programs, authorized by CETA Title II-D, provided jobs to low-income persons with long-term employment problems. The other, CETA Title VI, was for people thrown out of work by short-term fluctuations in the economy. At the beginning of 1981, they provided about 300,000 jobs.

The Reagan administration had sought termination of the public service employment programs, which over the years had been plagued with reports of fraud, abuse and waste. *(Background, 1978 Almanac p. 287)*

The reconciliation bill, cleared July 31, included provisions drafted by the House Education and Labor and Senate Labor committees, which were incorporated in the savings measures reported by the House Budget committee (H Rept 97-158) and its Senate counterpart (S 1377 — S Rept 97-139). *(Reconciliation legislative history, p. 256)*

The reconciliation legislation also ordered reductions in other CETA job training programs. However, Congress put off until 1982 consideration of a full-scale revision of the program.

Provisions

As cleared by Congress, the employment and training provisions (Title VII) of HR 3982:

● Provided no funds for the public service jobs programs authorized by Titles II-D and VI of CETA.

● Authorized the following amounts for other parts of CETA in fiscal 1982: $1.43 billion for job training pro-

grams; $219 million for national programs, including the National Commission for Employment Policy; $576.2 million for youth employment and training; $628.3 million for the Job Corps; $766.1 million for summer youth jobs; $274.7 million for joint programs with businesses; and $75.5 million for administration of the programs.

● Increased to 85 percent from 75 percent the percentage of youth employment and training funds going to local government prime sponsors; reduced to 6 percent from 16 percent the share of funds for Labor Department discretionary programs.

● Allowed prime sponsors to transfer up to 20 percent of funds between youth employment and training and summer youth employment programs.

● Provided that, if Congress did not complete action on reauthorization or replacement of CETA by Sept. 10, 1982, the 1982 authorization levels would apply in fiscal 1983.

● Prohibited appropriations for the Youth Conservation Corps (YCC) in fiscal years 1982-84.

● Limited spending for administration of the Employment Service to $677.8 million in fiscal 1982.

Economic Development

Congress rejected President Reagan's proposal to shut down the Economic Development Administration (EDA).

Title XVIII of the final version of the budget reconciliation bill (HR 3982 — PL 97-35) authorized $290 million in fiscal 1982 funding for EDA, a Commerce Department agency that was created in 1965 to provide economic and community development aid to depressed areas. *(Background, 1980 Almanac p. 306, 1979 Almanac p. 310)*

The reconciliation bill also authorized $215 million for the Appalachian Regional Commission in fiscal 1982, with $165 million earmarked for highways and $50 million for other projects. Reagan had sought to terminate funding for the non-highway programs.

As Reagan requested, the measure repealed the network of eight regional planning commissions authorized under Title V of the Public Works and Economic Development Act of 1965 (PL 89-136).

The House version of HR 3982 had authorized $360 million for EDA in fiscal 1982, while the Senate had acceded to Reagan's request to provide only $50 million to close down EDA programs. Although conferees agreed to spare the agency, the funding level they approved was sharply below the $1 billion fiscal 1982 authorization voted by Congress in 1980. *(Reconciliation legislative history, p. 256; Reagan budget, p. 278)*

CETA Youth Jobs Programs

Legislation (S 1070 — PL 97-14) to extend through Sept. 30, 1982, the authorization for youth employment programs under the Comprehensive Employment and Training Act (CETA) cleared Congress June 2.

In his fiscal 1982 budget, President Reagan had proposed that the youth programs be joined with other parts of CETA in a single program of job training for the disadvantaged. But that proposal was sidetracked at least until 1982, when Congress was to consider reauthorization of the whole CETA system.

The Senate passed S 1070 by voice vote May 12. The House passed an identical bill (HR 3337) June 2 by a 309-84 vote under suspension of the rules. It then approved S 1070 by voice vote, thus clearing the measure for the president's signature. *(Vote 49, p. 28-H)*

Legislative History

The authorization for the CETA youth programs, established by Congress in 1977, expired at the end of fiscal 1980. The three programs — the Youth Incentive Entitlement Pilot Projects, the Youth Community Conservation and Improvement Projects, and the Youth Employment and Training Program — were intended to test various ways of improving the job prospects of disadvantaged youths aged 16-21. *(1977 Almanac p. 116)*

President Carter in 1980 proposed that the existing youth programs be made part of his combined youth education and employment program. Congressional consideration of that measure, which passed the House but not the Senate, precluded action on a simple extension of the programs. *(1980 Almanac p. 440)*

The existing programs continued to operate under the authority of continuing appropriations resolutions for fiscal 1981. Two of the resolutions (PL 96-369, PL 96-536) were passed in the 96th Congress and extended funding authority through June 5, 1981. A third continuing appropriations measure (HR 3512), extended spending through Sept. 30, 1981. *(1980 legislation, 1980 Almanac pp. 168, 218; 1981 extension, p. 281)*

Unlike other, widely criticized CETA programs, the youth programs enjoyed substantial support in Congress. So Reagan's proposal to combine the youth programs with the job training programs authorized by CETA Title II met heavy opposition.

Arguing that the whole CETA structure would be reexamined during the reauthorization process in 1982, both the House and Senate Labor committees decided to report simple one-year extensions of the programs.

Preoccupied with its budget cutting efforts, the administration did not oppose the simple extension. The Office of Management and Budget said the legislation was "not necessarily inconsistent with the president's program."

The bill authorized "such sums as may be necessary" in fiscal 1982 for the youth programs, which were funded at $875 million in fiscal 1981. The Congressional Budget Office estimated that the cost of the bill would be $947 million in 1982, but Senate committee staff predicted that actual funding would be no more than $600 million.

Committee Action

The House Education and Labor Committee approved HR 3337 by voice vote May 5 (H Rept 97-36).

In the Senate committee, however, five Republicans opposed the bill because it did not include Reagan's consolidation proposal. The five — Don Nickles, Okla., Jeremiah Denton, Ala., Paula Hawkins, Fla., John P. East, N.C., and Gordon J. Humphrey, N.H. — said in the committee report that the main CETA training program was more effective than the existing youth programs in serving young people.

The Senate bill originally was approved by the committee as S 648 (S Rept 97-46). But the bill ran into Congressional Budget Act problems because it contained an authorization for fiscal year 1981 as well as 1982. Under the Budget Act deadlines, the fiscal 1981 authorization had to have been reported by May 15, 1980.

So S 648 was stripped of the fiscal 1981 authorization and brought to the floor as S 1070.

Overseas Investment

Congress Oct. 2 approved legislation (HR 3136 — PL 97-65) expanding the activities of the Overseas Private Investment Corp. (OPIC), which insures American investors in foreign countries against political risks.

Final congressional action on the bill came when the House accepted a Senate amendment that would bring OPIC's direct loan program for small businesses under the appropriations process. OPIC's authority to issue new loans expired Oct. 1.

The bill extended for four years, to Sept. 30, 1985, OPIC's authority to issue new insurance and added civil strife to the risks against which the agency could insure. It also removed restrictions on OPIC activities in 18 countries.

In addition, the legislation required OPIC to reimburse taxpayers for the $106 million appropriated for startup costs in the corporation's early years. Since 1974, OPIC had been operating on a self-sustaining basis without federal appropriations.

The Reagan administration supported OPIC's extension. But the administration opposed a House provision, which was retained in the final bill, that continued the OPIC direct loan program for small businesses.

Both House and Senate versions of the bill included administration-requested language eliminating specific restrictions against OPIC support of projects involving copper, citrus, sugar and palm oil.

Existing law barred OPIC from supporting any project likely to reduce significantly U.S. employment in a particular industry or in the economy as a whole.

Background

OPIC was created in 1969 (PL 91-175) and went into full operation in 1971. It was designed to encourage private U.S. business ventures in developing countries by providing insurance against the risks of war, expropriation and non-convertibility of currency. *(1969 Almanac p. 434)*

According to the House Foreign Affairs Committee, OPIC had insured or helped finance 337 investment projects in 58 countries since 1978, resulting in a total U.S. investment of $4.6 billion. The projects were expected to generate more than $3.4 billion in direct U.S. exports during the first five years of their operation.

OPIC had reserves and capital of almost $700 million, and fiscal 1980 net income was $65 million, the panel said.

Legislative History

The House passed its version of the bill (H Rept 97-195) Sept. 22 by voice vote.

The ease of passage contrasted with the difficulty that OPIC's renewal faced in 1977. House supporters then were forced to withdraw legislation from the floor after active labor opposition developed. Labor contended that OPIC aggravated U.S. economic problems by encouraging firms to invest abroad rather than at home. The House finally approved the extension (PL 95-268) on a second try in 1978. *(1978 Almanac p. 267)*

The Senate originally included OPIC extension in its

broader foreign aid bill (S 1196 — S Rept 97-83). In an attempt to meet the Sept. 30 deadline, when OPIC's authority to issue new insurance expired, the Senate Sept. 25 substituted the OPIC provisions of S 1196 for HR 3136. *(Foreign aid authorization, p. 161)*

There was no formal conference to resolve the differences between the House and Senate versions. Instead, each chamber made amendments to the other's version of the bill over a period of a week.

Provisions

As signed into law, HR 3136:

- Extended for four years, to Sept. 30, 1985, OPIC's authority to issue foreign investment political risk insurance and loan guarantees.
- Increased the per capita income limit for countries eligible for special consideration by OPIC to $680 in 1979 dollars from $520 in 1975 dollars.
- Raised the per capita limit to $2,950 in 1979 dollars from $1,000 in 1975 dollars for countries in which OPIC activity was restricted. The effect would be to remove limitations on support for projects in Cyprus, Taiwan, French Guyana, Malta, Surinam, Yugoslavia, Barbados, Argentina, Portugal, Romania, Costa Rica, Brazil, Fiji, Chile, Korea, Panama, Turkey and Jamaica.
- Required OPIC when deciding whether to finance a project to consider among other factors whether a foreign

nation's performance requirements on the investment would reduce substantially the positive trade benefits likely to accrue to the United States from the investment.
- Expanded the OPIC board of directors to 15 members from 13 and required the appointment of a Labor Department official.
- Added civil strife as a political risk that could be covered by OPIC insurance. OPIC must submit an analysis of planned civil strife insurance to the House Foreign Affairs Committee and the Senate Foreign Relations Committee at least 60 days before issuance.
- Mandated the continued transfer of OPIC revenues to the Direct Investment Fund (DIF) to provide direct loans for small-business projects. Beginning in fiscal 1982, at least 10 percent of OPIC's net income from the preceding fiscal year plus repayments of previous DIF financing were to be transferred to the fund.

DIF loans could be authorized only to the extent provided in appropriations acts.
- Repealed specific restrictions on OPIC support for projects involving copper, palm oil, sugar and citrus.
- Required OPIC to submit to Congress by June 30, 1982, a report on methods for determining whether particular investments or types of investments would be made if OPIC support was not provided.
- Required OPIC to reimburse the Treasury over an indefinite period for the $106 million that the corporation had received in appropriations.   ▮

Reagan Housing Plans Generally Approved

President Reagan got much of what he asked for in Department of Housing and Urban Development (HUD) programs in the budget reconciliation bill (HR 3982 — PL 97-35) passed by Congress July 31.

For subsidized housing, Congress cut even more from the fiscal 1982 budget than the president requested.

In March, Reagan proposed funds for 175,000 additional units of subsidized housing in fiscal 1982, a substantial cut from the 260,000 units proposed by the outgoing Carter administration.

(Subsidized housing includes the Section 8 rental assistance program and public housing, which is owned and operated by public housing authorities.)

The reconciliation bill provided $18.09 billion for assisted housing, which would cover about 153,000 additional units in fiscal 1982. That was down from the House version of 158,000 units but a hike from the Senate proposal of 150,000 units.

Congress also met Reagan's request to ease federal controls over Community Development Block Grants, which cities and counties use for a variety of urban projects.

The amount authorized for the grants for fiscal 1982 was $4.17 billion, with $500 million set aside for the popular Urban Development Action Grant (UDAG) program. UDAG funds are intended to help local governments stimulate private development.

Reagan at one time proposed combining UDAG with the block grants, but Congress did not go along with that suggestion.

In addition, Reagan wanted states, rather than the federal government, to administer the community develop-

ment grants to small cities — those with populations under 50,000. Congress instead gave states the option to administer the small-cities program.

The 1974 Emergency Home Purchase Assistance Act (PL 93-449) failed to be reauthorized when conferees did not include House language extending the law through 1982. The Senate bill had no similar provision.

The act was designed to aid the housing industry by allowing the government to buy conventional mortgages that were not government insured. It was called the "Brooke-Cranston" law after its chief sponsors, Sen. Alan Cranston, D-Calif., and former Sen. Edward W. Brooke, R-Mass. (1967-1979).

Congress also decided to phase out the Section 235 low-income homeownership assistance program.

Provisions

As cleared by Congress, Title III of HR 3982:

Community Development

- **Block Grants.** Required a community or state seeking a Community Development Block Grant (CDBG) to prepare a statement explaining its goals and how the money would be used.
- **Public Participation.** Required that citizens be told the amount of funds available to the grantee and the proposed use of the money.
- Required an opportunity for citizens to comment on the applicant's performance in community development.
- Required a grantee to hold at least one public hearing.

● Required a grantee to certify to HUD that it had complied with requirements concerning publication of its statement of goals and citizen participation.

● **Housing Assistance Plans.** Deleted an existing requirement that small, so-called "non-entitlement" communities competing for discretionary funds prepare housing assistance plans as a part of their community development grant applications.

● Modified the housing assistance plan requirement for a large (over 50,000 population) "entitlement" community — which receives funds by a formula — to include an estimate of housing needs based on low-income persons residing or expected to reside in the community as a result of existing or projected employment opportunities and population.

● **Performance Review.** Required the HUD secretary annually to review communities' performances under their grants to determine if primary objectives were being met. The conference report said conferees wanted "to make clear" that the HUD secretary was not to establish a standard of review more restrictive than under existing law.

● **Planning.** Made community planning activities eligible for CDBG funds to replace the "Section 701" planning program that was eliminated.

● **State Option.** Gave states the option to administer the small-cities' CDBG program. If a state decided not to administer the program, HUD would continue to do so.

● Required any state that decided to administer a small-cities' program to certify to HUD that the state engaged or will engage in community development planning; provided or will provide local governments with technical assistance for community development; will provide state community development funds that are at least 10 percent of the community development funds allocated to the state; and consulted with local elected officials in non-entitlement communities concerning distribution of the federal funds.

● **Urban Development Block Grant (UDAG).** Retained the UDAG program as a separate entity and provided $500 million for each of fiscal 1982 and 1983.

● Provided that if no funds were set aside for UDAG after fiscal 1983, any amount that might later become available would be added to the CDBG account.

● Required grant applicants to provide "satisfactory assurances" to HUD that grants will be handled in accordance with civil rights provisions.

● **Rehabilitation Loans.** Extended Section 312 rehabilitation loans through fiscal 1982 but repealed the authorization of $129 million for fiscal 1982. Loans will be available only from an existing revolving loan fund.

● **Urban Homesteading.** Provided $13.47 million annually for fiscal 1982 and 1983 for urban homesteading.

● **Neighborhood Reinvestment.** Authorized the Neighborhood Reinvestment Corporation at $13.43 million for fiscal 1981 and $14.95 million for fiscal 1982.

Housing Programs

● **Assisted Housing.** Provided $18.09 billion for fiscal 1982 for subsidized housing, for 153,000 additional units.

● Authorized $906.96 million in annual contract authority for the additional units.

● Set aside $75 million from the annual contract authority funds for comprehensive improvement assistance.

● **Housing Mix.** Provided that nationally, the HUD secretary should enter into contracts that result in 55 percent of the subsidies being used for new units; the remaining 45 percent would be used for rehabilitated housing.

● Required the HUD secretary to alter the housing mix in particular communities to accommodate the preferences of local officials. Such alteration would take place after HUD allocated funds to the communities and after HUD consulted with local housing agencies.

● **Set-Asides.** Set aside 17,000 units under the Section 8 rental assistance program for use by state housing finance agencies; not more than 4,000 Section 8 units for the Farmers Home Administration; and 2,500 units under the Indian housing program.

● **Public Housing Subsidies.** Provided $1.5 billion for fiscal 1982 for public housing operating subsidies.

● **Discretionary Funds.** Allowed the HUD secretary to keep up to 15 percent of the available contract authority for all assisted housing for specified purposes, including unforeseeable housing needs and services for the handicapped or for minority enterprises.

In the past, the HUD secretary routinely had kept up to 20 percent of housing money in a discretionary fund, although there was no clear authority for withholding the money nor any limit.

● **Troubled Projects.** Provided $4 million for fiscal 1982 to assist multi-family projects experiencing financial difficulties.

● **Income, Rent.** Set the rent for Section 8 and public housing tenants at the highest of three figures — 30 percent of the family's monthly adjusted income, 10 percent of the family's monthly gross income or that part of a family's welfare payments specifically designated to meet housing costs in states that adjust welfare to cover housing. Existing law set rent at 25 percent of a family's monthly adjusted income or 5 percent of gross monthly income.

● Defined income to mean income from all sources of each member of the household, as determined by criteria established by HUD.

● Left the income eligibility standard for tenants in assisted housing generally at 80 percent of the area median income. However, some of the HUD secretary's discretion was restricted to allow persons who made more than 80 percent of the median income to live in subsidized housing.

In addition, nationally, only 10 percent of the occupants in existing housing as of Oct. 1, 1981, could have incomes between 50 and 80 percent of the median income. The remaining tenants must earn less than 50 percent of the median income.

Finally, as additional units became available, only 5 percent nationally could be occupied by persons whose incomes fell between 50 and 80 percent of the median income.

The conferees said they did not intend that every low-income housing project or individual program meet the specified percentages.

● **Modest Design.** Required the HUD secretary to assure that new Section 8 units be modest in design.

● **Rent Increases.** Limited rent increases in new or substantially rehabilitated Section 8 housing to the amount of operating cost increases incurred by owners of comparable projects in the area suitable for families eligible for the assistance. Where no comparable units exist, the secretary could approve the rent increase using "the best available data" regarding operating cost increases in rental units.

● **Single Rooms.** Allowed the HUD secretary to provide Section 8 funds, in specified circumstances, for single-room dwelling units that did not have individual bathrooms or kitchens.

● **Fraud, Abuse.** Allowed public housing agencies to

retain part of the funds they recovered from money wrongfully paid as a result of fraud and abuse.

● **Income Mix.** Directed the HUD secretary to rescind a regulation that required an owner of assisted housing projects, during the initial renting of units, to rent 30 percent of the units to very low-income families and to try to maintain 30 percent occupancy by such families. After the initial renting, the owner was to use his "best efforts" to keep 30 percent occupancy of such members.

● **Section 235 Home Ownership.** Extended the authorization for the program through fiscal 1982 but set March 31, 1982, as the deadline for making any new HUD financial commitments.

● **Mobile Homes.** Allowed Section 8 subsidies to be used for units in mobile home parks under specified conditions.

● **Tenant Comments.** Allowed subsidized housing tenants in multi-family projects to comment to HUD on an owner's actions only regarding requests for rent increases, conversion of the project to other uses, major physical alterations or partial release of security on the project.

● **FHA Interest.** Extended through Sept. 30, 1982, the HUD secretary's authority to set the Federal Housing Administration interest rate above the statutory maximum of 6 percent to meet the market rate.

● **Emergency Assistance.** Ended the authorization for the 1974 Emergency Home Purchase Assistance Act (PL 93-449).

● **Government National Mortgage Association.** Set the authority of the Government National Mortgage Association to purchase mortgages in fiscal 1982 at $1.97 billion.

● **FHA Insurance.** Set the limit for Federal Housing Administration Insurance authority at $41 billion for fiscal 1982.

● **Elderly, Handicapped.** Set HUD's borrowing limit for elderly and handicapped housing at $6.1 billion in fiscal 1982, some $830 million more than the fiscal 1981 level.

● **Loan Limits.** Increased HUD loan limits for a variety of housing programs, including home improvements for single-family residences, general improvements for apartments, loans for manufactured homes and for lots on which manufactured homes can be placed.

● **Counseling.** Authorized up to $6 million for housing counseling assistance in fiscal 1982 and up to $4 million in fiscal 1983.

● **New Communities.** Authorized up to $33.25 million for new communities in fiscal 1982.

The conferees noted that revenues of $10 million should be available from HUD collections, bringing the actual total for fiscal 1982 to $43.25 million.

● **Congregate Services.** Authorized $40 million for fiscal 1982 for the congregate services programs, which provide aid, including meals and some medical services, to low-income elderly and handicapped persons at home.

Flood, Crime and Riot Insurance

● **Crime, Riot Insurance.** Extended authorizations for crime and riot insurance through Sept. 30, 1982.

● Extended authorization for urban riot reinsurance through Sept. 30 1985.

● Deleted a provision in the urban riot reinsurance program that required state insurance plans for high-risk areas to charge policyholders in those areas the same rate as charged in the private market.

Rural Housing

● Reauthorized for fiscal 1982 the following Farmers Home Administration (FmHA) loan and grant programs for rural housing: $50 million for loans and grants for repairing rural homes of very low-income persons; $25 million for grants for housing for domestic farm workers; $2 million for rural housing technical assistance grants, with half earmarked for counseling buyers and delinquent borrowers; and $2 million for the program that reimburses owners of FmHA-financed housing for construction defects.

● Continued the rental assistance payment contracting authority, which provides rent subsidies for low-income individuals in rural areas.

● Extended through fiscal 1982 the $5 million authorization for the mutual and self-help housing assistance program, under which non-profit groups of low-income persons build their own homes with professional advice.

● Authorized up to $3 million for capital for the land development fund and placed a new ceiling of $5 million on total site and acquisition loans in fiscal 1982.

● Required a report from the secretary of agriculture to Congress by March 1982, covering such subjects as alternatives to the Federal Financing Bank for financing rural housing projects and targeting FmHA housing aid.

Multi-Family Mortgage Foreclosure

● Provided a uniform, non-judicial procedure to cover HUD foreclosures on FHA-insured or HUD-assisted multi-family properties held by HUD and in default. The procedure replaced state laws. Conferees said the new owners — either HUD or another party — must continue the project as a subsidized residence, except in certain circumstances.

Conference

The HUD authorization became entangled in the reconciliation process in June, when House Banking Committee Democrats tried to thwart Senate efforts to cut back drastically on HUD programs. The committee sent its HUD authorization bill (HR 3534) to the Budget Committee for reconciliation purposes.

But in response to the House members' ploy, Senate Republicans, led by Jake Garn, R-Utah, Banking, Housing and Urban Affairs Committee Chairman, added their HUD reauthorization to the Senate reconciliation package (S 1377). The Senate HUD authorization (S 1197 — S Rept 97-87) was passed by a vote of 65-24 June 3. *(Vote 138, p. 26-S)*

The two committees were far apart in their reauthorizations, but all that changed when the House June 26 adopted the so-called "Gramm-Latta II" amendment to the reconciliation bill (HR 3982). The housing and urban aid provisions — which trimmed new housing units and revised the Community Development Block Grant program — brought the House much closer to the Senate.

As a result, there were few controversial issues to be worked out during the three conference meetings which ended July 22.

Agreements reached included:

● **Rent Control.** Conferees agreed to drop a Senate provision that would have prohibited cities with rent control laws from receiving Section 8 money for new units or for substantial rehabilitation.

In exchange, House conferees agreed to drop a provision requiring state insurance plans for high-risk areas to

charge policyholders in those areas the same rate as charged in the private market.

● **Income Eligibility.** The Senate had lowered the income eligibility requirement for new tenants in assisted housing to 50 percent of an area's median income, down from the current 80 percent. The House did not include that provision.

Conferees came up with a three-part compromise that basically left the eligibility standard at 80 percent.

● **Public Housing Operating Subsidies.** Conferees agreed to $1.5 billion for operating subsidies. The House had proposed $1.6 billion; the Senate, $1.2 billion.

● **GNMA.** The Senate agreed to a House provision that set the GNMA's authority to purchase mortgages at $1.97 billion. The Senate figure was $3.2 billion.

● **UDAG.** The House accepted a Senate provision that left UDAG as a separate entity, authorized at $500 million for fiscal 1982 and 1983. The House had made UDAG a separate item in the discretionary fund of the HUD secretary, authorized at $500 million for fiscal 1982.

● **Block Grants**. While both the House and Senate had eased federal controls over the community development block grants, the House accepted Senate provisions that required a more detailed application process. ▌

Export Promotion Plan

The House did not act on Senate-passed legislation aimed at boosting U.S. exports.

The Senate bill (S 734), passed April 8 on a 93-0 vote, would promote the formation of export trading companies to help U.S. firms market their goods abroad. The companies would act as middlemen, providing financial, marketing and transportation services for small and medium-sized firms engaged in foreign trade. *(Vote 83, p. 17-S)*

The legislation would permit banks for the first time to participate as active partners in export trading companies. It also would ease existing antitrust barriers that had inhibited joint exporting activities.

A similar measure passed the Senate in 1980, but a companion bill reported by the House Foreign Affairs Committee became bogged down in other committees and did not reach the House floor before adjournment of the 96th Congress. *(Background, 1980 Almanac p. 291)*

In the House the 1981 legislation was referred jointly to three committees — Banking, Foreign Affairs and Judiciary.

Committee Report

In its March 18 report on S 734 (S Rept 97-27), the Senate Banking Committee said banks — which traditionally had been barred from most commercial activity — "appear to be the best intermediary between the potential U.S. exporter and the foreign buyer because they already have offices (branches) at both ends of the chain and are already communicating with business people on both ends."

The legislation spelled out a number of restrictions on bank participation in export trading companies, however, including provisions that would prohibit a banking organization from:

● Investing more than 5 percent of its capital and surplus in export trading companies.

● Taking a controlling interest or making any invest-

ment of more than $10 million in any export trading company without prior approval of federal bank regulatory agencies.

S 734 also revised the Webb-Pomerene Act of 1918 to clarify antitrust provisions relating to export trade activities. It established a certification procedure permitting the Commerce Department, after consultation with the Justice Department and the Federal Trade Commission, to give export trading companies limited immunity from antitrust laws.

Other provisions of the bill required the secretary of commerce to promote and encourage the formation and operation of export trading companies.

The committee's ranking Democrat, William Proxmire, Wis., charged that the bill would involve the Commerce Department in a "massive conflict of interest situation" by giving it "responsibilities to promote trade and enforce the antitrust laws."

In individual views, Proxmire also blasted the bill's banking provisions. "The sponsors of the bill will not countenance any deviation from their current wisdom," he said. "Thus the Senate will send to the House a bill that mixes banking and commerce unnecessarily. We will have to rely on the House Banking Committee to show greater wisdom than we have done."

In a letter included in the report, Commerce Secretary Malcolm Baldrige indicated the Reagan administration supported the bill.

Floor Amendments

During floor action April 8, the Senate deleted two financing provisions that were opposed by the administration. The provisions would have:

● Authorized $10 million annually for five years for loans and loan guarantees by the Economic Development Administration and Small Business Administration for initial investments and operating expenses of trading companies.

The Senate struck the provision by voice vote after killing a compromise proposal by floor manager John Heinz, R-Pa., that would have cut the authorization to $5 million. The Heinz amendment was tabled 55-38. *(Vote 82, p. 17-S)*

President Reagan wanted to abolish the Economic Development Administration and to cut Small Business Administration credit assistance by 25 percent.

● Authorized $2 million annually for a three-year pilot program of Commerce Department grants to small businesses to help absorb the first-year costs of hiring export managers. The grants were to provide 50 percent of the manager's salary up to a maximum of $40,000. The Senate deleted the pilot program 68-25. *(Vote 81, p. 16-S)*

Senators also tabled, 66-27, a non-germane amendment expressing the sense of the Senate in support of phased decontrol of natural gas. Sponsor J. James Exon, D-Neb., said he wanted to send a message to the administration "that this body does not support immediate decontrol of natural gas prices." *(Vote 80, p. 16-S)* ▌

Export Control Programs

Legislation designed to improve federal enforcement of controls on exports was cleared by Congress Dec. 16. The bill (HR 3567 — PL 97-145) increased the fines for violations of export controls established to protect U.S. national

security interests, and authorized more than $19 million for federal export control programs in fiscal 1982 and 1983.

The Senate agreed to the conference report (H Rept 97-401) on the bill Dec. 15 by a 67-27 vote. The House adopted it by voice vote Dec. 16. *(Senate vote 471, p. 76-S)*

John Heinz, R-Pa., floor manager of the Senate bill, said the higher penalties would improve U.S. defenses against increasing efforts by the Soviet Union to obtain high-technology American goods. The bill raised fines for criminal violation of controls placed on exports for national security purposes to $1 million for corporations and $250,000 for individuals, both up from $100,000. *(Background, 1979 Almanac p. 300)*

Conferees dropped several Senate-passed provisions from the final bill, including one requiring congressional approval for any selective agricultural embargo. A similar provision was in the 1981 farm bill (S 884), conferees noted. *(Farm bill, p. 535)*

The conference compromise did include a House provision barring food embargoes if they would result in malnutrition, except under limited circumstances.

Provisions. As cleared by Congress, HR 3567:

● Authorized $9,659,000 in each of fiscal 1982 and 1983 for federal export control programs.

● Required federal agencies to share among themselves information relevant to the enforcement of export controls.

● Increased fines for willful violations of export controls established for national security purposes to $1 million per violation for corporations and $250,000 for individuals, from $100,000. The maximum civil penalty was increased to $100,000, from $10,000.

● Barred a food embargo if it would result in measurable malnutrition, unless the president determined that the embargo was necessary for U.S. security interests or that the food would not reach needy persons.

● Made clear that existing export control law (PL 96-72) could not be construed to prohibit export embargoes in response to military action by the Soviet Union or its allies against Poland.

Legislative History

The House originally passed HR 3567 June 8 (H Rept 97-57). The Senate passed its version of the measure (S 1112 — S Rept 97-91) Nov. 12.

Embargoes. Before passing the bill, the Senate adopted, 66-20, an amendment that would require the affirmative approval of Congress for any selective embargo on agricultural exports ordered by the president, starting Jan. 21, 1985. If Congress did not adopt a joint resolution approving the president's action within 60 days, the embargo would come to an end. *(Vote 364, p. 61-S)*

Under existing law, Congress could veto agricultural embargoes imposed for reasons of foreign policy or domestic supply problems by adoption of a concurrent resolution within 30 days.

The embargo amendment, sponsored by Charles H. Percy, R-Ill., and Alan J. Dixon, D-Ill., was a response to former President Carter's embargo on grain sales to the Soviet Union following the Soviet invasion of Afghanistan. President Reagan lifted the grain embargo April 24.

"The American farmer is puzzled and confused about a society that restricts trade in their product while allowing business as usual in the trade of other non-agricultural goods...," Percy said.

Heinz argued that the measure would limit the president's flexibility and encourage U.S. allies not to go along

with a proposed embargo if Congress appeared likely to stop it. However, Heinz voted for the amendment after it was revised to take effect following Reagan's first term as president.

The Commerce and State departments opposed the amendment.

Senators also accepted, by a 49-35 vote, an amendment stating the sense of the Senate that there should be an embargo on all U.S. trade to Russia if the Soviet Union, or its allies, engaged in direct military action against Poland. *(Vote 365, p. 61-S)*

The amendment was offered by Heinz as an alternative to stronger language proposed by Minority Leader Robert C. Byrd, D-W.Va. Byrd would have required an embargo unless the president certified to Congress within 30 days of the military action that the embargo would not be in U.S. national security or foreign policy interests.

Interest Rates. The Senate Nov. 10 approved, 50-35, a Heinz amendment directing the administration to emphasize policies that would continue the downward movement of interest rates. *(Vote 359, p. 61-S)*

The amendment was designed to head off a proposal drafted by a 13-member Democratic task force that would have directed the president to ensure an adequate flow of credit to small borrowers at affordable prices. A slightly different version of the Democratic amendment, offered by Lawton Chiles, D-Fla., was rejected 32-52. *(Vote 358, p. 61-S)*

Heinz said the Chiles amendment "attempts to do something we know does not work. Credit allocations have been tried before. They are not the solution."

The Senate also adopted, 77-12, an amendment by Edward M. Kennedy, D-Mass., that directed the president to encourage financial institutions voluntarily to exercise restraint in extending credit for large corporate takeovers. *(Vote 360, p. 61-S)*

Kennedy contended that the flow of credit to "unproductive" merger fights, such as the battles for Conoco and Marathon oil companies, had reduced the availability of credit for housing, the auto industry and small businesses.

Both the Heinz and Kennedy amendments were dropped in conference.

Black Lung Trust Fund

Congress in 1981 agreed to a labor-industry compromise plan to help bail out the financially troubled Black Lung Disability Trust Fund, which pays benefits to coal miners disabled by black lung disease.

The measure (HR 5159 — PL 97-119), cleared Dec. 16, doubled the excise tax on coal paid by coal producers and tightened black lung benefit eligibility requirements in an attempt to wipe out the four-year-old fund's $1.5 billion deficit.

The tax on underground coal was raised to $1 a ton and the tax on surface-mined coal to 50 cents a ton. The higher tax would be in effect until Jan. 1, 1996, or until the trust fund became solvent, whichever came first.

The package, enacted quickly during the last hectic days before Congress adjourned, also was the vehicle for several miscellaneous tax measures, including one that allowed members of Congress to deduct the cost of maintaining a second home in Washington. *(Story, p. 116)*

The House passed HR 5159 by voice vote Dec. 15; the bill contained only the tax increase and other trust fund

provisions. The Senate amended it Dec. 16 to include the unrelated tax provisions and changes in black lung benefit requirements, then passed it, 63-30. Later that day the House agreed, 363-47, to accept the Senate version, clearing it for the president. *(Senate votes 478-480, p. 77-S; House vote 349, p. 114-H)*

Trust Fund Trouble

Senate Finance Committee Chairman Robert Dole, R-Kan., warned Dec. 16 that adoption of the bill was necessary to stop "the hemorrhaging" of the black lung program, which pays benefits to about 200,000 disabled coal miners and their survivors.

Every year since it was established in 1978, the trust fund had distributed more funds than it had taken in. The difference — about $1.5 billion by the end of fiscal 1981 — had come out of general revenues. Dole said the deficit could reach $9 billion by 1995 if no changes were made.

The fund was established in an attempt to shift most of the program's growing burden from the government to mine operators. Financed solely by the coal tax, it generally paid benefits for disabled workers who held mining jobs prior to 1970; in most other cases, the "responsible" operator paid. The trust fund paid when no responsible mine operator could be found, and made temporary payments when operators challenged a claim. *(1978 Almanac p. 266)*

Originally it was predicted that the excise taxes would cover most costs, but liberalized benefits and built-in incentives for operators to challenge claims had strained the fund's resources.

The Joint Committee on Taxation estimated that the new tax would raise $1.5 billion for the trust fund by fiscal 1986, although the increase in total federal revenues would be less because of lower income tax receipts. The Labor Department projected that with the tax increase, the fund would no longer have to borrow funds from the Treasury after 1985 and that its deficit would be wiped out as early as 1994.

While HR 5159 tightened eligibility requirements for benefits, it also transferred the responsibility for about 10,200 unresolved claims to the trust fund, more than offsetting savings from the benefit changes over the next five years. Some members objected to that; they also complained that the increased coal tax would only be passed on to consumers, and said the tightening of eligibility requirements did not go far enough.

"As a result [of previous benefit changes], everyone who has ever seen a coal mine is now entitled to collect the black lung payments," Sen. John H. Chafee, R-R.I., charged. "It seems to me that this is the classic case of a program that has gotten out of control."

Floor Action

Despite the complaints, passage of the bill was accomplished fairly smoothly in what Rep. Barber B. Conable Jr., R-N.Y., called a "rather well-rehearsed scenario."

The measure was based on an agreement worked out in recent months by mine operators, labor groups, insurance companies and the administration. Members of Congress indicated there were strong lobbying efforts by the White House to complete action before adjournment so that the tax increase could go into effect on Jan. 1.

The House took up only the excise tax increase and other trust fund provisions approved by the Ways and Means Committee Dec. 9 (H Rept 97-406). The effect was to bypass the Education and Labor Committee, which has

jurisdiction over black lung benefits. Aides said consideration by that panel could have delayed passage of the benefit cuts, which were considered an essential part of the labor-industry package.

Although the Senate Finance Committee approved its own black lung bill (S 1957) Dec. 14, Dole brought HR 5159 to the floor Dec. 16. The result was to eliminate a Finance Committee provision that would have prevented the trust fund from borrowing from the Treasury after Oct. 1, 1985.

The provision's sponsor, Russell B. Long, D-La., said he had reluctantly agreed to withdraw it after being told it might jeopardize quick passage of the bill. But he vowed to bring up the issue in 1982, saying "it is impossible to have a program of this sort without bankrupting the government, unless someone takes the hard-nosed position."

Dole's substitute also added three tax provisions, including the home maintenance tax break for members of Congress, that had been approved Dec. 15 by the House as part of other bills. *(Story, p. 286)*

Also attached on the Senate floor, by voice vote, was an amendment by Labor and Human Resources Committee Chairman Orrin G. Hatch, R-Utah, that called for the benefit change portion of the package.

Provisions

As cleared by Congress, HR 5159:

● Doubled the manufacturers' excise tax on surface-mined coal to 50 cents a ton and the tax on underground coal to $1 a ton.

● Imposed a cap on the tax equal to 4 percent of the price for which the coal was sold. The existing cap was 2 percent.

● Made the higher tax effective from Jan. 1, 1982, to Jan. 1, 1996, or until the Black Lung Disability Trust Fund became solvent, whichever was earlier.

● Transferred responsibility from coal mine operators to the trust fund for 10,200 black lung claims rejected prior to 1978 changes in benefits, but later approved.

● Eliminated a provision in existing law requiring that the trust fund pay lump sum back benefits when a claim was filed but was contested by the mine operator.

● Increased the interest rate due on trust fund advances to cover claims for which an operator was later found responsible. The rate was increased from 6 percent to the prevailing interest rate; in 1982 it was set at 15 percent.

● Revised the method for determining the interest rate used when the trust fund must repay funds lent by the Treasury so the rate would be closer to the fair market rate.

● Transferred provisions of the Black Lung Disability Trust Fund to the Internal Revenue Code.

Eligibility Standards. Allowed the Labor Department to seek a second physician's opinion in determining whether an applicant's X-rays indicated the presence of black lung disease (pneumoconiosis).

● Ended the provision of existing law that established the presumption, subject to rebuttal, that miners with 10 years' experience in the mines who died as a result of respiratory disease died because of black lung disease.

● Ended the provision that established the presumption that miners with 15 years in the mines who were totally disabled due to respiratory impairment were disabled due to black lung disease, even in the absence of a medical showing of black lung; made both of the above changes applicable to claims filed after enactment of the bill.

● Ended the provision that established a presumption

that survivors of miners who died before March 2, 1978, and who had spent 25 years in the mines before June 30, 1971, were entitled to survivors' benefits. This change would apply to claims filed more than six months after enactment of the bill.

● Ended the provision that allowed a miner's widow, in cases where there was no clear-cut medical evidence, to receive benefits by simply submitting an affidavit that the miner had had black lung before he died. Under the new law, only someone who did not stand to receive benefits in a case would be able to submit an affidavit.

Benefits. Limited payment of survivors' benefits to cases in which the miner died as a result of black lung disease; the change would apply to claims filed after enactment of the bill. Under existing law, survivors' benefits had been awarded in some cases where the miner's death was not due to black lung.

● Reduced black lung benefits for recipients who had earnings above the Social Security excess earnings limit.

● Provided for a study of the relationship between black lung benefits and other workers' compensation benefits.

Miscellaneous Tax Provisions

● Required businesses involved in so-called safe-harbor leasing transactions, in which unprofitable firms could effectively sell unused tax credits to profitable ones, to report such transactions to the Internal Revenue Service within 30 days or by Jan. 31, 1982, for leasing agreements signed in 1981. *(Background, p. 91)*

● Delayed for two years, until Jan. 1, 1984, the effective date of a provision in the 1976 Tax Reform Act that would limit the carry-over of net operating losses for firms with substantial ownership changes.

● Allowed taxpayers to deduct the costs of maintaining a second home for business purposes when it was also used as a residence. While applying to all taxpayers, the primary beneficiaries of this provision would be members of Congress, who under existing law could not deduct such expenses if their families resided with them in Washington.

● Directed the Treasury secretary to determine the "appropriate" amount a member of Congress could deduct for business expenses while Congress was in session without having to substantiate them.

● Allowed certain deductions for a residence that was used as a person's primary place of work for a second job.

● Liberalized rules governing business deductions in cases where a residence was rented to a relative at a fair market rate.   ∎

Miscellaneous Tax Changes

In the final hours before it adjourned Dec. 16, Congress attempted to push through more than two dozen miscellaneous tax changes, but time ran out before a conference could be arranged to work out a final House-Senate agreement.

For the most part, the measures made minor technical changes in tax law, but there also were provisions to award legal fees to individuals unjustly taken to Tax Court, to liberalize the use of mortgage revenue bonds and to repeal several provisions of the budget reconciliation bill (PL 97-35) enacted earlier in the year.

However, three separate tax provisions, attached to a Black Lung Disability Trust Fund bill (HR 5159), cleared both houses. These included provisions allowing members of Congress to deduct the cost of maintaining a home in Washington and requiring firms that sold unused tax credits to report such transactions to the Internal Revenue Service. *(Story, p. 114)*

In the House, there was little debate on the bills (HR 4961, HR 4717) containing the tax provisions, primarily because amendments were not allowed under suspension of the rules. The measures, which had been reported by the Ways and Means Committee Dec. 14 (H Repts 97-404, 405), were adopted by voice vote Dec. 15.

In the Senate, however, floor consideration Dec. 16 of HR 4717 brought numerous amendments and the objections of some members that the bill did too much, too late in the year, with too few available details. The Finance Committee had amended the House bill extensively Dec. 14, including in it a number of the provisions of HR 4961.

"I am troubled about the pattern . . . where we bring up tax bills on the very last day of the session," complained William Proxmire, D-Wis. "The one fundamental safeguard we have is that we know what we are doing."

After several hours of debate and the adoption of half a dozen new provisions, the measure was adopted by voice vote. However, House leaders were reluctant to go to conference, not only because of the numerous Senate amendments but because both houses were preparing to adjourn for the year within a few hours of Senate passage.

House Bills

As approved by the House, HR 4717:

● Deferred for one year the Jan. 1, 1982, effective date of certain regulations governing the taxation of "last-in, first-out" (LIFO) inventories of liquidating companies.

● Extended to 10 years, from three years, the period over which the Federal National Mortgage Association could carry back net operating losses to offset taxes, and shortened the time period over which they could be carried forward.

● Required companies that sell, or "lease," their unused tax credits to other firms to report such transactions. This provision was later passed as part of the black lung bill.

Major provisions of HR 4961:

● Allowed the awarding of up to $50,000 in legal fees to a party against which "unreasonable" tax proceedings were brought by the United States.

● Allowed taxpayers who accrued deductions for taxes paid to other jurisdictions to take the deductions at an earlier date.

● Repealed a provision of the budget reconciliation bill and allowed those who voluntarily left military service after two years to collect unemployment compensation for 13 weeks.

● Repealed a reconciliation provision that required states to charge a 10 percent fee for collecting child support payments for families not in the Aid to Families with Dependent Children program.

According to Ways and Means, the two bills, if enacted, could cost about $1.4 billion in lost revenues and increased outlays over the next five years. Revenue figures were not available for the Senate bill.

Senate Bill

The Senate version of HR 4717 included a hodgepodge of tax provisions ranging from tax breaks for fishermen to increased annuities for the survivors of tax court judges. Included in the more than 20 amendments added by the

Finance Committee were ones that would:
- Ease requirements under which eligibility for Trade Adjustment Assistance benefits were determined.
- Allow the awarding of up to $25,000 in tax court legal fees.
- Extend for one year the existing exemption of the wages of certain fishermen from unemployment taxes.

Amendments were added on the floor to:
- Prohibit the use of "small issue" tax-exempt industrial development bonds (IDBs) for massage parlors, race tracks, golf courses and suntan facilities.
- Cut substantially the excise tax on gambling.
- Liberalize restrictions on the use of tax-exempt mortgage revenue bonds to finance housing costs. ∎

Interim Social Security Changes Approved

Putting off action on a long-range Social Security financing plan, Congress Dec. 16 cleared legislation to restore the $122 minimum monthly Social Security benefit and to patch up the troubled retirement system through the end of 1982.

House-Senate conferees reached agreement on the Social Security bill (HR 4331 — PL 97-123) Dec. 14, only two days before the end of the session. The Senate approved the conference report on the bill (H Rept 97-409) by a 96-0 vote Dec. 15; the House approved it the following day, 412-10. *(Senate vote 472, p. 76-S; House vote 347, p. 112-H)*

The final package restored the minimum payment for all three million current recipients but eliminated the benefit for those who became eligible for Social Security after Dec. 31, 1981.

To pay for much of the $6.1 billion, five-year cost of restoring the benefit, Congress agreed to extend the 6.7 percent payroll tax to the first six months of sick pay, beginning Jan. 1, 1982. Under existing law, sick pay was taxed only in cases where employees were not covered by a specific company sick pay plan or system.

The bill also allowed the financially troubled Old-Age and Survivor's Insurance (OASI) Trust Fund, expected to go broke sometime in the fall of 1982, to borrow from the two other, healthier Social Security trust funds. However, this provision was to expire on Dec. 31, 1982, forcing Congress to address the sticky issue of Social Security's funding problems again in 1982.

The ranking Democrat on the Senate Finance Subcommittee on Social Security, Daniel Patrick Moynihan, D-N.Y., praised the bill for putting "a little cheer in the holiday season" for minimum benefit recipients while giving Congress "some breathing room for devising a longer-term solution to the question of Social Security funding."

But others criticized Congress for not addressing the long-term funding of Social Security, which the Reagan administration said could face a deficit of up to $111 billion over the next five years.

"We have ducked the main issue and handled some really minor housekeeping things which were easy to agree on," said Sen. William L. Armstrong, R-Colo., chairman of the Social Security Subcommittee. "It is a travesty to suggest that we have fulfilled our responsibility."

Reconciliation Retreat

Congress eliminated the minimum benefit in July as part of President Reagan's budget reconciliation package (PL 97-35). However, the public outcry was so great that both houses and the administration beat a hasty retreat.

In passing HR 4331 July 31, the House agreed to restore the minimum payment for all current and future recipients. The Senate passed HR 4331 Oct. 15, but it reinstated the payment only for current recipients who lived in the United States and did not have government pensions in excess of $300 a month.

In a Sept. 24 speech, President Reagan called for Congress to restore the minimum benefit, which only a few months before he had asked it to eliminate. "It was never our intention to take this support away from those who truly need it," he said. *(Text of speech, p. 30-E)*

The benefit set a floor for monthly Social Security payments and was intended to provide some protection for those with low earnings under the system. Without it, retirees received benefits based solely on prior earnings.

The administration argued that many receiving the payment, such as former government workers, had other pensions to rely on. It maintained that those who depended on the minimum could receive assistance from the Supplemental Security Income (SSI) program for the elderly poor.

Democrats countered that no one knew for certain what would happen to many of the current recipients.

As approved by Congress, HR 4331 restored the minimum benefit retroactively for 4,400 beneficiaries who were not given the minimum payment in November and December in compliance with the reconciliation bill, which eliminated the payment for new recipients as of Nov. 1.

The measure also allowed members of religious orders, who became eligible for Social Security in 1972, to continue to start receiving the minimum payment for the next 10 years.

Final Provisions

As cleared by Congress, HR 4331:
- Continued the $122 minimum monthly benefit for all those eligible as of Jan. 1, 1982.
- Allowed members of religious orders to become eligible for the minimum until Dec. 31, 1991.
- Permitted borrowing among the Old Age and Survivor's Insurance (OASI), Disability Insurance (DI) and Hospital Insurance (HI) trust funds until Dec. 31, 1982.
- Extended the payroll tax to the first six months of sick pay, with the exception of payments attributable to an employee's contribution to a third-party sick pay plan.
- Made it a felony to alter or counterfeit a Social Security card.
- Required the Department of Health and Human Services (HHS) to contract by Jan. 1, 1982, to set up Aid to Families with Dependent Children home health aid experiments in at least seven states.
- Waived the Federal Privacy Act for prisoners so government agencies could give prisoners' Social Security numbers to HHS to prevent them from receiving illegal disability benefits.

● Required HHS to report to Congress in 90 days on its efforts to prevent Social Security payments from being sent to deceased individuals.

Financing Crisis

In 1977, Congress approved large payroll tax increases aimed at keeping the system solvent well into the next century. *(1977 Almanac p. 161)*

However, it was soon apparent that continued bad economic conditions were rapidly eroding trust fund reserves. In 1980, Congress temporarily reallocated funds from the Disability Insurance Trust Fund to OASI (PL 96-403). It was understood even then, however, that something more had to be done.

Not only was the system currently confronting a short-term cash-flow problem caused by recent inflation and high unemployment, but it faced a major funding crisis after the turn of the century. By that time, it was projected, there would be too few workers contributing to the system to support the millions of retirees from the so-called baby boom generation.

Because of the imminent bankruptcy of OASI, Social Security's largest trust fund, many members of Congress and other observers thought 1981 might be the year to resolve the vexing, and politically touchy, problem of Social Security financing.

The administration had expressed an interest in overhauling the system, and the chairman of the Ways and Means Subcommittee on Social Security, J. J. Pickle, D-Texas, began markup of major Social Security legislation (HR 3207) shortly after the 97th Congress convened. His bill would gradually raise the retirement age to 68 by the year 2000 and use general revenues to fund part of the HI trust fund.

But what mood for action there may have been at the start of the year rapidly dissolved with the proposal by the administration May 12 of drastic cuts in the Social Security program, including large penalties for early retirement and reductions in disability benefits.

It was, said Armstrong, a "masterpiece in bad timing."

Congress was in the throes of its greatest budget-cutting battle, and Democrats, tasting their first defeats at the hands of the new GOP administration, were in no mood for the spirit of "bipartisanship" called for in the Social Security debate.

The party quickly latched onto the issue, charging that the administration was cutting the program not to save it, but to help balance the budget. With the tone thus set, further efforts at overhauling Social Security proved futile. On Sept. 24, Reagan withdrew his proposals and called for the formation of a 15-member bipartisan commission to study the problem. Members of the panel were appointed Dec. 16, and Reagan gave it a Dec. 31, 1982, reporting deadline.

Administration Proposals

"The crisis is inescapable," said Health and Human Services Secretary Richard S. Schweiker, in announcing the administration proposals May 12. "Today we move to face it head-on and solve it. If we do nothing, the system would go broke as early as fall 1982, breaking faith with the 36 million Americans depending on Social Security."

The administration predicted that its program would not only allow the system to remain solvent, but permit the reduction of payroll taxes below the current 6.65 percent rate by 1990. Most provisions would affect only workers going on the rolls after Jan. 1, 1982.

"This means that the young person entering the labor force next year would pay an average of $33,600 less in Social Security taxes over his/her lifetime, a reduction of over 10 percent," said Schweiker.

The administration estimated that enactment of all of its Social Security proposals, including those sent up as part of its March budget package, could save $81.9 billion by the end of 1986.

Reagan's March budget included proposals to eliminate the minimum benefits program, end benefits for postsecondary students aged 18-22, tighten eligibility for disability benefits and eliminate the lump sum death benefit in cases where there were no surviving spouse or children.

Details of Plan

Highlight of the president's May 12 package was a controversial plan to reduce benefits for those who elected to retire early, starting in January 1982. Under the existing system, those who retired at age 62 received 80 percent of the benefits they would be entitled to if they had retired at age 65. President Reagan wanted those early benefits reduced to 55 percent of full benefits to encourage people to remain in the work force longer.

Another controversial proposal called for a three-month delay of an annual cost-of-living (COLA) increase scheduled for July 1982. The administration estimated the deferral would save at least $6.3 billion over the next five years.

In addition to the delayed COLA and reduced benefits for early retirees, major administration proposals would:

● Eliminate "windfall" benefits for retirees, such as government employees, who worked only a few years under Social Security but could collect relatively high benefits under current formulas. The administration proposed figuring in other pension receipts for these "double dippers" when calculating their Social Security benefits.

● Phase out the retirement earnings limits by 1986. Currently, recipients ages 65 through 71 lost $1 in benefits for every $2 earned each year over $5,500. The administration would permit $10,000 in outside earnings in 1983, $15,000 in 1984, $20,000 in 1985, with no earnings limits thereafter.

● Revise the formula used to determine a recipient's initial benefit by using only 50 percent of a wage index, instead of the full index currently in use. The purpose, the administration said, was to correct past overindexing, and the change would apply only through 1987, when the distortion should be corrected. The change would reduce a recipient's primary benefit by an estimated 7 percent.

● End children's benefits for retirees under age 65.

● Place a cap on benefits for families of retired and deceased workers to prevent such benefits from exceeding what had been the worker's net take-home pay.

● Tax sick pay for the first six months of a worker's illness. Sick pay was not subject to the payroll tax under existing law.

● Raise from 20 to 30 the number of quarters out of the past 40 that a worker must be in the work force to qualify for disability benefits.

● Consider only medical factors — instead of age, education and work experience — in determining if a worker qualified for disability benefits and extend from 12 to 24 months the anticipated period of disability required.

Retreat

The Reagan administration's announcement of its Social Security "reform" plan set off a tempest in Congress.

Following a week of attack on the proposals by members of both parties, the administration began to retreat.

"We are willing to entertain other ideas," Schweiker told the House Select Committee on Aging May 21.

Later in the day, President Reagan sent a letter to congressional leaders trying to smooth over the flap surrounding his proposal.

"This administration is not wedded to any single solution," he said. "We recognize that members have alternative answers. This diversity is healthy so long as it leads to constructive debate and then to an honest legislative response."

Reagan said his administration was committed to only three principles: preserving basic benefits and the integrity of the system's three trust funds, minimizing Social Security taxes and eliminating abuses in the system.

The backpedaling followed attacks on the proposals by members of both houses, many besieged by calls from angry constituents fearing their benefits would be drastically cut. While Republicans were far from quiet about their concern over the proposals, Democrats waged their assault with obvious glee.

The House Democratic Caucus May 20 unanimously adopted a resolution calling the proposed changes an "unconscionable breach of faith" and vowing not to "destroy the program or a generation of retirees."

Senate Democrats said they would use "every rule in the book" to prevent enactment of Reagan's proposals and took the first step toward fulfilling that promise during action on a supplemental appropriations bill (HR 3512). The Senate unanimously adopted an amendment opposing key parts of Reagan's proposed cuts in Social Security benefits after heading off harsher Democratic-sponsored language by a one-vote margin. *(Supplemental bill, p. 281)*

Republicans, while praising Reagan for bringing the sensitive issue of Social Security financing into the open, kept their distance from his specific plans. Senate Finance Committee Chairman Robert Dole, R-Kan., said he had not been consulted on the proposal and predicted there would have to be compromise before a way was found to ensure the solvency of the system.

Reconciliation Changes Approved

In the massive budget reconciliation bill (HR 3982 — PL 97-35), cleared July 31, Congress agreed to eliminate the minimum benefit and approved some other Social Security cutbacks sought by the president. But it rejected Reagan's proposals to reduce benefits for early retirees and to delay the July 1982 COLA increase. *(Reconciliation, p. 256)*

Major Provisions

As signed into law, Title XXII of HR 3982 made the following major cutbacks in Social Security programs:

● Eliminated the $122 minimum monthly payment for all new recipients beginning with the December 1981 payment and for all current recipients for benefits paid after February 1982. Such recipients would instead receive benefits based on prior earnings.

● Changed age limitations on Supplemental Security Income to allow individuals aged 60 to 64 who would be eligible for the minimum benefit before December to qualify for offsetting SSI payments if they met other eligibility requirements.

● Eliminated the $255 lump-sum death payment for deaths occurring after Aug. 31, 1981, in cases where there were no surviving spouses or dependent children.

● Required that those electing to retire at age 62, and their dependents, begin to receive Social Security benefits in the first full month of their entitlement. Under existing law, if a worker retired in the middle of the month, he received benefits for the entire month. The provision was to take effect for September 1981 benefits.

● Extended for one year, until Jan. 1, 1983, current limits on outside earnings for those under age 72. The age cap had been scheduled to drop to 70 in 1982.

● Eliminated payments for a parent caring for a child receiving benefits when the child reached age 16. Under existing law, these benefits ended when the child turned 18. The provision did not apply to parents caring for a disabled child. It was to take effect for current recipients two years after the bill was signed into law; for all new recipients, two months after enactment.

● Eliminated benefits for new postsecondary students aged 18-22 after August 1982. Payments for current recipients and those eligible for such benefits before Sept. 1, 1981, who entered postsecondary school before May 1, 1982, were to be phased out gradually, 25 percent each year for the next four years through July 1985. Cost-of-living adjustments and payments for summer months were eliminated for all recipients.

● Reduced disability benefits by the amount received from other federal, state or local disability programs if combined benefits exceeded 80 percent of the worker's prior earnings. Current law only offset disability benefits with workers' compensation payments.

● Made the offset provision applicable to workers aged 64 and under and their dependents, instead of those under 62 as current law required. The offsets would be made as soon as the non-Social Security payments began. The provision, which affected only new recipients, applied to those who became disabled no more than five months before the bill became law.

● Eliminated reimbursement of state vocational rehabilitation programs, except in cases where it could be shown that the program had resulted in taking a disabled person off the Social Security rolls.

● Required rounding to the next lowest 10 cents at each stage of the benefit calculation except for the final benefit amount, which would be rounded to the next lowest dollar. Under existing law benefits were rounded to the next highest 10 cents.

Minimum Benefit Dispute

Achieving a compromise on the Social Security provisions was one of the most difficult tasks that faced the conferees on the reconciliation bill.

Differences between the two chambers involved disability requirements, vocational rehabilitation, the earnings limitation for retirees and timing for elimination of the Social Security minimum benefit, to which both houses had acceded. The minimum benefit controversy briefly jeopardized the conference report on the reconciliation bill.

On July 21 the House by a 405-13 vote adopted a nonbinding resolution (H Res 181) urging reconciliation conferees to take steps "to ensure that Social Security benefits

are not reduced for those currently receiving them." *(Vote 136, p. 50-H)*

An attempt the same day to attach a minimum benefits amendment to the Senate tax bill failed, however, 52-46. *(Vote 207, p. 37-S)*

Despite such reservations, reconciliation conferees from the House Ways and Means and Senate Finance committees abided by the decisions previously reached in each chamber. On July 23, they decided to halt the minimum benefit at the end of February 1982 for all those currently receiving it.

No one, including the Democratic sponsors of the House Social Security resolution, really expected the conferees to reverse the previously adopted House position on minimum benefits.

But the Democrats, with thousands of senior citizens marching on the Capitol to protest changes in the Social Security system, wanted to force Republicans to be counted on the minimum benefits issue.

House Minority Leader Robert H. Michel, R-Ill., released GOP members to vote for the essentially toothless resolution when it came up July 21 on the House floor. Eager to escape the trap set by the Democrats, Republicans did so in droves.

After the conference report on the reconciliation bill was filed July 29, Democrats staged a last-ditch effort to restore the minimum Social Security benefits which had been eliminated in the conference agreement.

House Rules Committee Chairman Richard Bolling, D-Mo., threatened to refuse to convene his panel to clear the reconciliation bill for floor action unless the conference was reopened to restore the minimum benefits provisions.

But after bipartisan House and Senate leaders met behind closed doors, the issue was resolved by allowing two separate House votes — one on the conference report and one on a bill (HR 4331) to reinstate the minimum benefit. *(Votes 176-79, p. 62-H)*

Minimum Benefit Restored

The House passed HR 4331 July 31, voting to reinstate the minimum benefit by a 404-20 margin. *(Vote 178, p. 62-H)*

The bill then went to the Senate, where an attempt to gain immediate consideration of the measure was rebuffed, 57-30. *(Vote 245, p. 42-S)*

The Senate finally passed its version of HR 4331 by a 95-0 vote Oct. 15. The Senate bill restored the payment for most current beneficiaries and made stopgap arrangements to keep the OASI trust fund from going broke in 1982. *(Vote 312, p. 53-S)*

Finance Committee Chairman Dole called the measure "the cosmetic approach" to Social Security's financial ills. It was proposed by his panel Sept. 24 after efforts to draft a more comprehensive bill failed.

"What we have done is take the easy way out," Dole said, adding that under certain economic conditions, the system could still run out of money sometime during 1984.

Democrats, relying on more optimistic economic assumptions, countered as they had throughout the Social Security debate that the system would be financially sound through the end of the decade with passage of the Senate measure.

Moynihan, ranking Democrat on the Social Security Subcommittee, called the bill "a gracious retreat" by Re-

publicans from the controversial Social Security proposals Reagan made earlier in the year. "It is a responsible change of opinion," he said.

To keep the system from going broke, the Senate measure would permanently reallocate payroll taxes from the healthier Disability trust fund to the OASI fund.

It also would reallocate taxes designated for the Hospital trust fund to OASI through 1984. HI, which financed Medicare, faced its own financial problems by the end of the decade.

The bill would allow OASI to borrow funds from the DI trust fund through 1990, if the payroll tax reallocations proved insufficient to keep the OASI fund afloat.

As passed by the Senate, HR 4331 would continue the full minimum benefit for all three million current recipients except those living overseas and those with government pensions over $300 a month.

It also provided that members of religious orders, who became eligible for Social Security in 1972, could continue to start receiving the minimum payment for the next 10 years.

The Senate measure provided that all those receiving government pensions would have their so-called "windfall" Social Security benefits reduced one dollar for each dollar their government pension exceeded $300 a month. They, and all others no longer eligible for the minimum, would still continue to receive a monthly benefit based on their earnings while covered by Social Security.

To offset the cost of restoring the minimum benefit, the Senate agreed to apply the payroll tax to the first six months of all sick pay and to lower the maximum family retirement and survivor benefit to 150 percent of the worker's primary insurance amount (PIA). Under existing law, such benefits could range from 150 percent to 188 percent.

Restoration of the minimum was expected to cost the Social Security trust fund $4.5 billion for fiscal 1982-86. According to the Congressional Budget Office, the payroll tax change would raise $2.4 billion for fiscal 1982-86, and the benefit cut would save $2.9 billion over the same period.

Senate Floor Amendments

The Senate rejected two Democratic amendments to HR 4331, but not before the minority party took a few jabs at Reagan's economic recovery program.

A proposal by Thomas F. Eagleton, D-Mo., to repeal a provision of the new tax cut law (PL 97-34) reducing taxes on newly discovered oil and to use the funds to build an emergency reserve for Social Security was tabled, 65-30. Eagleton called the tax break a "gratuitous bonanza" for oil companies. *(Vote 309, p. 53-S)*

Also tabled, by a 50-47 vote along straight party lines, was an amendment by Minority Leader Robert C. Byrd, D-W.Va., requiring the administration to specify by Nov. 15 all budget cuts it planned to propose for fiscal 1982-4. *(Vote 310, p. 53-S)*

By voice vote, the Senate agreed to:

● Override provisions of the Federal Privacy Act to allow access to prison records so that disability payments to inmates can be stopped.

● Make it a felony to misuse a Social Security number.

● Extend the Highway Trust Fund though fiscal 1990 and to extend highway taxes, including the gasoline excise tax, through fiscal 1989. This was a procedural maneuver in a separate House-Senate dispute over highway legislation. *(Story, Transportation chapter, p. 553)*

Conference Dispute

The major dispute of the six-week-long conference was whether the cost of restoring the benefit would be offset with other tax increases or benefit cuts. For almost a month, conferees could not agree to meet.

In addition to taxing sick pay, the Senate-passed version of HR 4331 would have lowered maximum family retirement and survivor benefits, raising approximately $2 billion over the next five years. However, House conferees steadfastly refused to accept the benefit cut.

The deadlock was broken as adjournment neared and members faced the prospect of returning home without having resolved the emotional Social Security issue.

Senate and House Republican conferees agreed to accept only the sick pay tax, which was expected to raise $4.4 billion over the next five years, on the condition that interfund borrowing be allowed for just one year. The Senate bill had provided for interfund borrowing over the next 10 years and for reallocation of payroll taxes. Conferees dropped the reallocation plan.

Reps. Barber B. Conable Jr., R-N.Y., and Bill Gradison, R-Ohio, refused to sign the conference agreement unless the Dec. 31, 1982, deadline on interfund borrowing was included. "There are those of us who feel that if this isn't dealt with in 1982, it won't be dealt with until the end of 1984, and that by then the trust funds will be in much more serious trouble," said Conable.

For one conference member, the one-year limit on interfund borrowing was not enough. Rep. Bill Archer, R-Texas, ranking minority member of the Social Security Subcommittee, did not sign the final conference report (H Rept 97-409) because of his dissatisfaction with the bill's temporary patch-up of Social Security's funding problems. ∎

Aid for Savings & Loans

Congress did not complete action in 1981 on legislation to help the ailing savings and loan industry.

The House Oct. 28 passed a short-term emergency measure (HR 4603) authorizing federal bank regulators to provide expanded financial aid to savings and loan associations (S&Ls) and allowing banks and S&Ls to acquire troubled savings and loans across state lines.

In the Senate, however, Banking Committee Chairman Jake Garn, R-Utah, decided not to act on the House bill. Instead, he planned to move forward in 1982 on a broader measure making long-range structural changes in the financial services industry, including provisions that would allow savings and loans to offer many of the services provided by commercial banks.

Many thrift institutions — S&Ls, mutual savings banks and credit unions — were in precarious financial condition because of record high interest rates and competitive pressures from commercial banks and unregulated financial institutions.

Congress showed its willingness to support the distressed thrift industry by including in the 1981 tax cut bill (HR 4242 — PL 97-34) an "all savers" provision authorizing depository institutions to issue one-year, tax-exempt certificates at attractive interest rates. *(Story, p. 91)*

In addition, Congress Dec. 16 cleared a bill (HR 4879 — PL 97-110) that expanded the ability of savings and loans to swap low-yield mortgages for securities or cash. The bill eliminated the existing 20 percent ceiling on the

---

Bank Regulatory Agencies

Under the American dual banking system, banks and savings and loan associations may be chartered and regulated by state or federal authorities. In practice, however, most banking institutions are subject to some degree of federal regulation.

Federal Reserve System. All federally chartered banks and many state chartered banks are members of the Federal Reserve, which serves as the country's central bank. Under the Depository Institutions Deregulation and Monetary Control Act of 1980 (PL 96-221), the Federal Reserve Board may establish reserve requirements for all depository institutions, including those that are not members of the Federal Reserve System. The Fed also has supervisory power over state banks that are members of the system.

Comptroller of the Currency. The comptroller, an official of the Treasury Department, charters and supervises national banks. The comptroller's approval is necessary for the establishment of new national banks and for mergers and consolidations where the surviving institution is a national bank. His office also periodically appraises the financial condition and management of all national banks.

Federal Deposit Insurance Corp. (FDIC). The FDIC insures the desposits in most state and federally chartered commercial banks and supervises the insured state-chartered commercial banks that are not part of the Federal Reserve System. The corporation's income consists of assessments on deposits held by insured banks.

Federal Home Loan Bank Board (FHLBB). The FHLBB charters and supervises federal savings and loan associations and provides loans to institutions engaged in mortgage financing. This includes savings and loans and homestead associations, savings and cooperative banks, and insurance companies. All federal savings and loans and all state chartered S&Ls insured by the FDIC are required to be members of the bank board system.

Federal Savings and Loan Insurance Corp. (FSLIC). The corporation insures savings in all federally chartered savings and loans and in state chartered S&Ls that apply and qualify for such insurance.

Depository Institutions Deregulation Committee (DIDC). This panel was set up by the 1980 banking law to plan the deregulation of the nation's depository institutions. The committee had five members: the chairman of the Federal Reserve Board, Paul A. Volcker; the secretary of the Treasury, Donald T. Regan; the chairman of the Federal Home Loan Bank Board, Richard T. Pratt; the chairman of the Federal Deposit Insurance Corp., Irving Sprague; and the chairman of the National Credit Union Administration, Lawrence Connell.

---

amount of older mortgages that the Federal National Mortgage Association and the Federal Home Loan Mortgage Corp. could include in their portfolios.

Mixed Support

During House debate on HR 4603, William J. Stanton, R-Ohio, the Banking Committee's ranking Republican,

said the administration did not "favor" the House bill, because it did not address the "thrift industry's long-term structural difficulties."

In testimony before the Senate Banking Committee Oct. 19, Treasury Secretary Donald T. Regan said, "The thrift industry has always had problems in high interest rate periods and it will continue to have them in future years if fundamental changes are not made in the way it does business."

Regan did not support all elements of the broad approach taken by Garn in legislation (S 1720) introduced early in October. The administration did, however, fully endorse a proposal known as the "powers" bill (S 1703), which was put together by the Federal Home Loan Bank Board (FHLBB). The FHLBB bill, while far more encompassing than the House-passed emergency legislation, did not go as far as Garn's measure.

While not disagreeing with the need to look at long-range restructuring of financial institutions, Federal Reserve Board Chairman Paul A. Volcker told the Senate panel Oct. 29 that the provisions of the House-passed "regulators" bill should "be enacted immediately." He said it would give regulatory agencies the "flexibility and authority needed to deal with the transitional problems" of the thrift industry caused "by the extraordinarily high level of market rates."

Background

Competitive pressures from commercial banks and unregulated financial institutions had imposed growing strains on S&Ls and other thrift institutions in recent years.

The primary business of savings and loans was providing home loans. And the rates they had to pay on new high-yield savings instruments to obtain funds for lending far exceeded the yields they received on their mortgage loans — a high proportion of which were long-term and had low interest rates.

In 1980, almost two-thirds of the thrift institutions' approximately $500 billion in mortgage investments carried interest rates of less than 10 percent. At the same time short-term rates were well above that level.

S&Ls also had to compete with an array of new and attractive investment instruments for new deposits — money market and mutual funds that paid much higher yields than traditional passbook accounts were permitted to pay.

FHLBB Chairman Richard T. Pratt told the House Banking Committee July 14 that 80 percent of the nation's 4,600 savings and loans were suffering operating losses. One-third of the S&Ls were not "viable under today's conditions," he said.

Pratt said there were 263 S&Ls in what the regulatory agency called the "most troubled" category. The failure of these institutions could lead to losses of up to $60 billion.

The sale of assets and federal insurance would offset the $60 billion figure by $15 billion, Pratt said, leaving a $45 billion net loss.

In 1980 Congress attempted to ease the problems of the banking industry by enacting the Depository Institutions Deregulation and Monetary Control Act (PL 96-221).

Major provisions of the act ordered a six-year phase-out of interest rate ceilings on savings accounts, authorized federally insured financial institutions to offer interest-bearing NOW checking accounts, gave S&Ls new consumer lending powers and required all depository institutions to maintain reserves as directed by the Federal Reserve Board. *(Background, 1980 Almanac p. 275)*

However, the industry's plight intensified following enactment of the law, as interest rates soared to record levels in 1981.

House Action

The House Banking Committee reported HR 4603 Oct. 6 (H Rept 97-272), and the House passed the measure Oct. 28 by a 371-46 vote. *(Vote 268, p. 86-H)*

Banking Committee Chairman Fernand J. St Germain, D-R.I., and other proponents of HR 4603 argued that banking regulators needed more flexibility to provide assistance while thrifts were experiencing financial problems. Provisions of the emergency legislation would expire Sept. 30, 1982.

But opponents of the measure claimed the bill would open the door to takeovers of small banks by large "New York" banks. "You are just giving the large banks of the country the power to gobble up the small banks and savings and loan institutions all over the country," said Carl D. Perkins, D-Ky.

During floor consideration, the House accepted two amendments, by Bill McCollum, R-Fla., that were designed to allay these fears by narrowing the scope of the measure.

One of McCollum's amendments permitted banks and savings and loans to acquire only ailing S&Ls or mutual savings banks. The original legislation also would have allowed them to acquire foundering commercial banks with assets above $2 billion.

The other McCollum amendment required the FHLBB and the Federal Deposit Insurance Corp. (FDIC) to give equal consideration to protection of federal insurance funds and to the order of preference for mergers listed in HR 4603. As written, the bill gave "paramount" consideration to the loss of insurance funds.

The order of merger preference outlined in the measure required regulators first to try to select for a merger an institution of the same type within the same state. Next in priority was an institution of the same type in a different state, then an institution of a different type within the same state and, finally, a different institution in a different state.

House Provisions

As passed by the House, other major provisions of HR 4603, the Depository Insurance Flexibility Act, would:

● Expand the circumstances under which the FDIC and the Federal Savings and Loan Insurance Corp. (FSLIC) could provide financial aid to insured banks and savings and loans.

The bill would allow the FDIC to purchase the securities of an insured bank as well as make contributions to it. It also would authorize the FDIC to provide aid in order to help prevent insolvency, restore a closed bank to normal operation and to reduce losses to the FDIC that resulted when the financial resources of a significant number of insured institutions were threatened.

The FSLIC could provide assistance to insured institutions when severe financial conditions threatened the stability of a significant number of insured institutions or when such aid would reduce the threat to the FSLIC. The aid could take the form of deposits or purchase of an institution's securities, in addition to the current approach

of making contributions or loans, or purchasing the assets of the troubled S&L.

● Authorize the FHLBB to approve the conversion of a mutual savings and loan or a mutual savings bank into either a federal stock savings and loan or a federal stock savings bank if an institution were in receivership; if existing financial conditions threatened the stability of the institution; or if either the FDIC or FSLIC had contracted to assist the institution through loans, contributions or asset purchases.

● Allow the FSLIC to approve a merger or a transfer of assets and liabilities between two FSLIC-insured institutions or between an insured institution and any other company if the FSLIC found that severe financial conditions threatened the stability of a significant number of insured institutions or the stability of an insured institution with significant financial resources. The order of preference for mergers is listed above.

● Relax the prohibition on FSLIC borrowing from sources other than the Treasury Department. The FSLIC could borrow from Federal Home Loan banks at interest rates at least as high as the banks' current marginal cost of funds.

● Allow the National Credit Union Association (NCUA) to arrange emergency mergers for troubled credit unions and authorize the NCUA to borrow, under emergency conditions, from the NCUA Central Liquidity Facility to advance funds to the Share Insurance Fund.

Garn Bill

The Garn bill, called the Financial Institutions Restructuring and Services Act of 1981, contained seven titles covering a broad range of major banking law changes.

"In essence, what this legislation represents is a shifting of gears to facilitate the stability and growth of our financial system," Garn said when he proposed S 1720. He added that there were provisions in the massive bill that he did not fully support, but were advocated by other members of the Banking Committee and deserved to be considered as part of the overall dialogue on banking issues.

The major elements of the Garn bill would:

● **Depository Institutions Restructuring.** Extend to savings and loans powers enjoyed by commercial banks. The bill would permit savings and loans to offer checking accounts, make commercial loans and invest in real estate and in corporate debt instruments.

● Pre-empt or strike down state laws that prohibited banks from enforcing due-on-sale prohibitions that were contained in many mortgage contracts, which denied the new buyer the right to assume the old mortgage. These prohibitions were enacted to protect consumers' rights to assume mortgages at lower interest rates.

The Garn bill would require the holder of the mortgage to pay off the balance of the mortgage when selling the property. Under the Garn bill, the due-on-sale provisions would be enforced for all lenders approved by the Department of Housing and Urban Development.

● Authorize the FSLIC, when severe financial conditions threatened the stability of a significant number of savings and loan institutions, to approve interstate and cross-industry mergers — but only after reasonable efforts were made to find intra-industry and in-state merger partners.

● Authorize the FDIC under the same "severe financial conditions" test to make loans, investments or deposits in distressed insured banks.

● Authorize the FDIC to approve an interstate acquisition for a closed commercial bank with $2 billion in assets, but only after exhausting the possibilities of an in-state or adjacent state merger.

● **National and Member Banks.** Raise the limit on the amount of money a national or member bank could lend to a single borrower from 10 percent to 15 percent of capital and surplus.

● Revise the Federal Reserve Act to permit unlimited transactions, except for "classified" loans, between a member bank and its sister subsidiaries in a multi-bank holding company.

● Exempt from the reserve requirements of the 1980 banking deregulation act those financial institutions with less than $5 million in deposits.

● **Securities Activities.** Authorize banks and thrift institutions to operate, manage and sell interests in mutual funds.

● Authorize national banks to deal in and underwrite municipal revenue bonds.

● **Other Provisions.** Pre-empt state consumer usury ceilings, but give states a three-year period to override the pre-emptions. The House Banking Subcommittee on Consumer Affairs Oct. 21 rejected a bill (HR 2501) containing this provision.

The 1980 banking deregulation law lifted state usury ceilings on most other loans, including agriculture and business loans above $25,000.

● Facilitate emergency mergers or acquisitions of a failing credit union.

● Broaden real estate lending authority for credit unions.

● Generally prohibit insurance activities by bank holding companies.

● Redefine "creditor" in truth-in-lending laws to apply only to professional creditors.

● Increase deposit insurance coverage on individual retirement (IRA) and Keogh retirement accounts from $100,000 to $200,000.

Garn also introduced a separate measure (S 1721), called the Federal Deposit Insurance Consolidation Act of 1981, which would merge the FSLIC and NCUA into the FDIC.

Export-Import Bank Loans

Intensive lobbying saved the Export-Import Bank from sharp budget cuts proposed by the Reagan administration in 1981.

The bank, which loans money to foreign countries for purchase of American products, was to be the administration's symbolic budgetary swipe at big business, proof that the ax was not falling on social programs alone.

Two-thirds of Ex-Im loans benefited seven large companies such as Boeing and Westinghouse that produced aircraft, nuclear plants and other high-technology exports. Reagan proposed in March to whittle the loan levels well below President Carter's figures.

"I've got to take something out of Boeing's hide to make this look right," Office of Management and Budget Director David A. Stockman told a magazine interviewer. "You can measure me on this, because I'll probably lose but I'll give it a helluva fight."

But Stockman evidently spent most of his effort fight-

ing the issue within the administration, where Commerce Secretary Malcolm Baldrige and U.S. Trade Representative William E. Brock III were outspoken Ex-Im supporters. The president went along with Stockman on cutting Ex-Im, but the administration showed little enthusiasm for the fight once it reached Congress.

Meanwhile, companies that profited from Ex-Im launched a busy lobbying campaign, arguing that jobs and the trade balance were at stake. They won successive victories in:

● The fiscal 1981 supplemental appropriations bill (HR 3512). The president proposed a $5.1 billion direct loan limit; Congress approved $5.461 billion. *(Story, p. 281)*

● The fiscal 1982 reconciliation measure (HR 3982).

The bill included a $10.478 billion ceiling on the Ex-Im Bank's direct lending authority in fiscal 1982 and 1983. Conferees accepted Senate language designating $5.065 billion of the total for fiscal 1982 and $5.413 billion for fiscal 1983. The bill permitted the administration to allocate some of the fiscal 1983 lending authority for fiscal 1982 use if necessary to combat foreign predatory financing. *(Story, p. 256)*

The Reagan budget had proposed a fiscal 1982 limit of $4.4 billion, $600 million less than President Carter requested before he left office in January.

● The 1982 foreign aid appropriation (HR 4559).

The final 1982 appropriation bill gave the bank $4.4 billion in direct loan authority (compared to a $3.9 billion revised Reagan request) and $9.2 billion for loan guarantees (Reagan wanted $8.2 billion). *(Story, p. 339)*

On the House floor Dec. 11, Rep. Harold L. Volkmer, D-Mo., offered an amendment to cut $500 million from the loan figure, but conceded that "undoubtedly the individual industries that are affected by this Export-Import Bank have sufficient clout on this floor in order to make sure that they win the day whatever the amount." His amendment failed without a roll call.

The business victory aside, the administration faced continuing resistance from Ex-Im backers, led by members of its own party, over the bank's lending policies. Sen. John Heinz, R-Pa., held up two Reagan appointments to the bank's board out of unhappiness with the bank's rising interest rates and suspicion that the bank might not lend out all the money Congress had given it. ∎

Foreign Policy

In their first year in office, President Reagan and his team delivered what they had implicitly promised — an America unafraid to upset adversaries and allies alike in the name of gaining renewed respect.

The administration assumed power vowing to get tough with the Soviet Union and other of America's Nemeses, notably Cuba and Libya. It did — and U.S. relations with each of those nations became more and more testy as 1981 went by.

But the price for confronting America's foes often proved to be discomfort or protest on the part of U.S. allies, many of whom who did not share the Reagan view that the world's major problems flowed from communist or Libyan mischief.

Even relations with Israel declined as Prime Minister Menachem Begin, uneasy with administration efforts to woo Arab states into a "strategic consensus" against the Soviet Union, pursued increasingly aggressive policies that embarrassed the United States.

In addition, Reagan's past statements expressing sympathy for South Africa and Taiwan, though not translated into dramatic policy changes, threatened the improved relations with black Africa and mainland China that President Carter had counted among his major achievements.

Human Rights. The new administration rejected Carter's dedication to holding anti-communist authoritarian governments publicly accountable for their human rights records by withholding aid to those with unsuitable ones.

Reagan and his aides said they would promote human rights through "quiet diplomacy" instead, relying on the carrot rather than the stick to foster liberty and justice in those nations whose rulers recognized the Soviet threat.

The policy shift was greeted with suspicion and outrage by Reagan's domestic and foreign critics. It also contributed to one of Reagan's few defeats in Congress — the withdrawal under pressure of his nominee for assistant secretary of state for human rights, Ernest W. Lefever.

An underlying issue was Lefever's belief in a controversial theory put forth by Reagan's ambassador to the United Nations, Jeane Kirkpatrick. She postulated a distinction between totalitarian and authoritarian governments on human rights, asserting that the latter held out more hope of reform.

Critics replied that those being tortured under authoritarian states would take little comfort in the distinction, and Kirkpatrick's theory drew scorn from administration opponents.

But in November the administration adopted a new and stronger human rights policy that implied an even-handed approach to totalitarian and authoritarian governments alike. That mollified some opponents, and they were further reassured when Reagan named Elliot Abrams, his assistant secretary of state for international organizations, to take over the job denied Lefever.

Nuclear Non-proliferation. Reagan similarly abandoned Carter's use of the stick to try to stop the spread of nuclear weapons, again preferring the carrot. The State Department under Reagan argued that the way to disabuse nations of the notion that they needed nuclear weapons was to make them feel sufficiently secure to forgo the expense and trouble of developing the bomb.

Critics were less vocal in this realm. Even liberal Democrats who normally opposed Reagan agreed that Carter's policy of invoking sanctions against nations trying to acquire nuclear weapons had not fully succeeded. But it was well into the year when Reagan unveiled his non-proliferation policy; he was criticized in the interim for lacking one.

The administration put its policy into practice in seeking warmer relations with Pakistan to counter the influence of the Soviet occupation of Afghanistan. Despite concerns about Pakistan's military dictatorship and its efforts to acquire a nuclear weapons capability, Congress went along without much complaint.

Reagan proposed to give Pakistan $3.2 billion in economic and military aid over six years and to sell Pakistan 40 high performance F-16 fighter planes, with at least part of the sale to be financed by Saudi Arabia. But U.S. aid to Pakistan had been withheld since 1979 under a law that banned aid to nations suspected of trying to develop nuclear weapons.

The administration asked Congress to modify the law to permit the aid, and after surprisingly little struggle, Congress did — but it also added a provision that gave Congress the right to veto the president's action.

Arms Sales Policy

Likewise, in advocating large increases in military aid and arms sales to friendly nations early in the year, Reagan was charged with failing to develop his own guidelines and goals on arms transfers before dropping Carter's, which had attempted to discourage them.

On July 9 the Reagan administration declared its policy on sales of conventional arms to be one of dealing "with the world as it is, rather than as we would like it to be." Arms transfers would be "considered on a case-by-case basis" and would be an "essential element" of U.S. global strategy, said a policy directive signed by Reagan.

The directive made formal a policy already evident in administration requests that Congress repeal restrictions on arms sales to Argentina and other countries.

Carter had put the "burden of persuasion" on advocates rather than opponents of specific arms sales. He also had emphasized the human rights records of potential arms buyers, and flatly banned sales to some nations.

A Reagan administration official said the new policy would not ignore human rights but would not make them the "sole criteria" for approving or disapproving specific sales. The Reagan policy also allowed U.S. embassy person-

nel to aggressively assist arms dealers — a function forbade them under Carter.

Policy Faulted

The "no policy" charge often was broadened beyond specific issues such as human rights and arms sales. Some Democratic critics contended that the administration in fact had no foreign policy at all — just a vague notion that a hard line against Moscow and more defense spending was needed.

But there was also a more charitable and perhaps more accurate assessment: The administration had tried to put off formulating major foreign policies while it got its economic package through Congress, but foreign events could not be postponed. The administration had to react, with or without detailed policies.

Meanwhile, Reagan's political opponents were galvanized by administration plans to step up military aid to El Salvador and to sell sophisticated Airborne Warning and Control System (AWACS) radar planes to Saudi Arabia.

Congress stopped short of undercutting Reagan's support for the centrist junta in El Salvador, in the end doing nothing more than setting conditions on further U.S. aid.

The opposition was far stronger on the AWACS sale, which led to a bitter battle in Congress that Reagan barely won. A congressional veto of the plan to sell AWACS to the Saudis was avoided only through Reagan's personal lobbying of the Senate.

Once Reagan turned his attention to foreign affairs, he enjoyed two other significant successes.

In a speech billed as his first major foreign policy address, Reagan was able on Nov. 18 to cool passions somewhat in Europe over the issue of arms control, where the strong anti-Soviet line adopted by his administration had raised fears of nuclear war. After a series of massive demonstrations in Europe against NATO plans to deploy nuclear missiles there, Reagan proposed to cancel the deployment if the Soviet Union dismantled similar weapons.

He also won a foreign policy victory on the home front when he invested his prestige in a fight to get two foreign aid bills through Congress. His efforts helped win passage of the first aid appropriations bill in three years.

The Reagan Team

In addition to their hard line against the Soviet Union, the Reagan foreign policy team was characterized by a proclivity for controversy.

Haig. Reagan chose as his secretary of state Alexander M. Haig Jr., the former Army general and NATO commander known for his loyal service as President Nixon's White House chief of staff during the Watergate scandal.

The nomination sparked fierce initial opposition from some senators, and Haig's confirmation hearings before the Senate Foreign Relations Committee consumed five days — the longest on record for a secretary of state.

Haig's strong performance under questioning and his expertise on foreign affairs overwhelmed the opposition, and he was confirmed by a vote of 93-6 on Jan. 21. But he remained controversial, declaring himself Reagan's foreign policy "vicar" and engaging in jealous turf fights over policy formulation with other administration figures.

His disputes with others in the administration made Haig an issue in himself. Reagan implicitly rebuked Haig by naming Vice President George Bush as head of "crisis management" in foreign policy. Haig openly complained

that "someone" in the White House — presumed to be Richard V. Allen, the White House national security adviser — was waging a political "guerrilla campaign" against him. Reagan finally had to call Haig and Allen before him to lecture them about their feuding.

There was also Haig's nervous, agitated appearance before television cameras at the White House on March 30, minutes after an attempted assassination of Reagan, when Haig declared — in a quavering voice that belied his words — "I am in control here at the White House."

Haig and other administration foreign policy-makers also publicly contradicted one another at times on what U.S. policy was, thereby committing a sin for which they had castigated the Carter administration: Failure to speak with one voice.

Moreover, Haig tended toward the bellicose in his statements, hinting at various times, for example, that the United States was contemplating military action against Cuba and Nicaragua for their aid to El Salvador's leftist guerrillas.

Yet in the most conservative American administration in years, Haig also proved himself an internationalist who could take the diplomatic approach, as was demonstrated by his success in smoothing over a dispute between Israel and the allies in Europe over European participation in a new Sinai peace-keeping force.

In addition, despite friction with some members of Congress, Haig proved instrumental in the administration's victory on foreign aid.

Allen, Casey, Clark. Reagan's conduct of foreign policy was hampered all year by questions about the conduct of security adviser Allen and CIA Director William J. Casey. Another issue was the competence of Reagan's choice for deputy secretary of state, his longtime California confidant William P. Clark.

Allen promised that he would stay out of the limelight — unlike previous national security advisers Henry A. Kissinger and Zbigniew Brzezinski — but proved unable to keep the vow. A rivalry with Haig over foreign policy kept Allen in the headlines, and allegations of wrongdoing on his part led to his forced resignation on Jan. 4, 1982, despite Justice Department and White House investigations that cleared him of illegal or unethical conduct.

Casey, a "venture capitalist" whose past wheeling and dealing had involved him in a number of civil suits, got into political hot water in July. Max Hugel, the man Casey picked to head the CIA's clandestine services, resigned on July 14 after being accused of unethical and illegal business practices in the past.

The political waters got hotter for Casey on July 23, when Barry Goldwater, R-Ariz., chairman of the Senate Intelligence Committee, declared that Casey should resign. A committee probe, however, eventually found Casey merely not "unfit to serve."

Clark, a California judge, seemed an embarrassing choice for deputy secretary of state at first, revealing a limited knowledge of foreign affairs in confirmation hearings. But he had been chosen because of Reagan's confidence in him, and he later won a reputation as a quick study able to smooth relations between Haig and the White House. So when Allen was forced to resign in January, Clark replaced him.

Relations with Moscow

Reagan changed the tone of U.S. relations with Moscow as early as his first press conference as president, on

Jan. 31, when he unhesitatingly replied in answer to a reporter's question that he firmly believed that the goal of the Soviets was world domination.

In a comment that was startling for a president to make, Reagan then added that the Soviets "reserve unto themselves the right to commit any crime, to lie, to cheat, in order to attain that, and that is moral [in their view], not immoral, and we operate on a different set of standards."

The remark made it evident that U.S.-Soviet relations would continue on the downhill course that had begun under Carter following the Soviet invasion of Afghanistan in December 1979.

The dialogue between the United States and the Soviet Union in 1981 was rife with charge and countercharge as the administration put into practice the hard line Reagan had promised.

But at first the administration was less strident in its actions. It approved the sale of pipeline technology to the Soviets over conservative objections, and Reagan kept a campaign promise to farmers by lifting a grain embargo against Moscow — the most severe sanction Carter had imposed for the invasion of Afghanistan.

Early in the year, Reagan and Haig declared that future arms negotiations with the Soviets would depend on Soviet behavior around the world — a stipulation that heightened concern about Reagan among domestic and international arms control advocates.

But the administration nevertheless went ahead with scheduled U.S.-Soviet talks on reducing nuclear forces in Europe — even after publicly blaming and imposing economic sanctions on the Soviets for the imposition of martial law in Poland by authorities there on Dec. 13.

El Salvador

The administration set out early in the year to shore up the embattled centrist junta in El Salvador, where leftist guerrillas attempted a "final offensive" in an effort to topple the junta in the days before Reagan took office.

Haig declared that the United States would "draw the line" in El Salvador against communist interference in Central America. Expanding on last-minute actions by Carter, Reagan decided to assist the government of Jose Napoleon Duarte by sending El Salvador more arms aid and U.S. military advisers — a decision that raised cries of "another Vietnam" in the United States.

Haig solicited congressional support for the policy on Feb. 17 by showing key members of Congress evidence that communist nations were funneling arms to leftist guerrillas in El Salvador.

Meanwhile, Reagan's opponents charged that the Salvadoran government had failed to rein in its security forces, which the critics charged with brutal murders and other violence, and consequently should get no U.S. military aid.

The administration sought to establish the validity of its approach by releasing a "white paper" on Feb. 23 detailing what the State Department called a "textbook case of indirect armed aggression by communist powers through Cuba." The accuracy of the white paper later was called into question by the press.

But the policy itself met its first challenge in the House Appropriations Foreign Operations Subcommittee, where Chairman Clarence D. Long, D-Md., and other Democrats were leery of sending more arms and advisers to El Salvador. Reagan barely won a symbolic March 24 vote in the subcommittee on a request to shift $5 million in fiscal 1981 funds from other accounts to El Salvador's.

The 8-7 subcommittee vote proved a solid indicator of how Congress would react to the Reagan policy — with skeptical acquiescence.

Still, the only action Congress took later in the year was to approve conditions on aid to El Salvador under the fiscal 1982-83 foreign aid authorization bill, with the president to certify whether they had been met.

Middle East

The Middle East was chief among the regions of the world whose problems would not await formal policies. Haig asserted that the United States would foster a "strategic consensus" among the nations of the Middle East against the Soviet threat. Critics said "strategic consensus" was mere theory, not a policy.

The critics charged that Haig's theory was misconceived in any event because for some Arab nations the Soviet threat was not a concern that could override their enmity for Israel.

Another central criticism was that the theory was leading Reagan and Haig to pay inadequate attention to the Arab-Israeli dispute. This charge was said to be demonstrated in the administration's failure to push Egypt and Israel to make progress on Palestinian autonomy talks provided for under their 1979 peace treaty.

Meanwhile, the administration scored a success in the Middle East by reacting to events, as opposed to implementing its policy, when Philip C. Habib, a special ambassador named by Reagan, was able with Saudi help to arrange a cease-fire in southern Lebanon between Israel and the Palestine Liberation Organization (PLO).

But Reagan's major Middle East initiative was his decision to go ahead with a suggestion raised in the Carter administration and to sell five sophisticated AWACS (Airborne Warning and Control System) radar planes to Saudi Arabia.

AWACS. Reagan narrowly won this first major foreign policy test in Congress when the Senate failed Oct. 28, by a dramatic 48-52 vote, to disapprove the sale of AWACS and other air defense equipment to Saudi Arabia. The vote came on a concurrent resolution to disapprove the sale (H Con Res 194) which the House had passed Oct. 14 by an overwhelming vote of 301-111.

The Senate vote on AWACS was a stunning victory for Reagan because 50 senators — one less than the majority needed to block the sale — had cosponsored the resolution of disapproval. In the end, Reagan won by persuading seven first-term GOP senators among those cosponsors to switch their positions.

The $8.5 billion arms package also included tanker planes, plus fuel tanks and highly sophisticated AIM-9L air-to-air missiles for 60 F-15 fighter planes that Congress agreed to sell the Saudis in 1978 after a similar fight with the Carter administration.

Israel strongly opposed the AWACS sale, viewing it as a threat to Israeli air superiority in the region. The American Jewish community campaigned against it, and many members of Congress opposed it as a threat to Israel.

Saudi Arabia cast the deal as a test of U.S.-Saudi relations. Reagan won the issue after he put his personal prestige on the line by arguing that a congressional veto would impair his ability to conduct foreign policy.

But the deal left a bitter taste in the mouths of some of Israel's closest supporters in Congress, and it contributed to a decline in relations between the United States and Israel that was manifested in other ways as well.

Israel. U.S. relations with Israel began to sour when the administration confirmed in February that it would sell the AWACS to the Saudis. But a shock wave hit the relationship on June 7, when Israeli Prime Minister Begin dispatched U.S.-supplied F-16 jet fighters to bomb a nuclear reactor in Iraq.

The Iraq raid strained American support for Israel, though many in Congress and elsewhere defended the preemptive strike as, in Begin's phrase, "an act of supreme, legitimate self-defense."

Reagan responded by delaying delivery of four more F-16s already bought by Israel. Though nothing came of it, the administration also said it was examining whether Israel had violated U.S. laws forbidding the use of U.S.-supplied weaponry for other than defensive purposes.

But the Iraq raid seemed to demonstrate nothing so much as Israeli frustration at administration efforts to court the Arabs — a frustration manifested again on July 17 in an even more controversial Israeli raid.

Amid clashes between Israel and the PLO in southern Lebanon, Israeli jets struck again, this time bombing a PLO headquarters in Beirut — and killing more than 200 civilians.

The Beirut raid occurred on the very day the State Department had been prepared to release the F-16s that were withheld after the Iraq raid. Instead, on July 20 Reagan extended the suspension of F-16 deliveries to six more planes in addition to the four being withheld.

Reagan lifted the suspensions on Aug. 17, and the planes were later delivered. But the incident left sour feelings on both sides — as later events demonstrated.

After the AWACS issue was resolved, the administration sought to soothe the Israelis by agreeing to a plan for "strategic cooperation," to include special arrangements with Israel regarding the use of U.S. military aid. But even that deal was threatened when Begin surprised the United States and the world by getting the Knesset to vote — in whirlwind fashion — to extend Israeli law to the Golan Heights, strategic territory captured from Syria in the 1967 Arab-Israeli war.

Egypt. One of the year's most dramatic foreign events was the Oct. 6 assassination of Egyptian President Anwar el-Sadat, who was gunned down by extremists who disguised themselves as soldiers and ambushed him from a military parade. Sadat's death raised the specter of instability in his nation, which remained vital to U.S. hopes for peace and stability in the region.

However, Sadat's successor, Vice President Hosni Mubarak, quickly promised upon taking office that he would continue Sadat's moderate foreign policy, and Mubarak kept that pledge. He pursued a moderate line toward Israel, in part because of an intense interest in seeing Israel carry through on its pledge under the 1979 Egyptian-Israeli peace treaty to withdraw all its forces from the Sinai peninsula on April 25, 1982.

In connection with that, Congress agreed with little debate to permit up to 1,200 U.S. military personnel to be stationed in the Sinai in a multilateral peace-keeping force to be established after the Israeli withdrawal. The administration persuaded Britain, Colombia, Fiji, France, Italy, the Netherlands and Uruguay, to contribute forces as well.

Relations With Libya

The administration's tough talk was never stronger than when directed at Libya and that nation's strongman leader, Muammar Qaddafi. And here the administration supplemented its words with action.

Declaring Qaddafi a major source of arms and money for international terrorists and a military threat to his African neighbors, the administration ordered the Libyan diplomatic mission in Washington closed in May.

Libyan military operations in neighboring Chad led the administration in June to pledge military aid to African nations, such as the Sudan, that wanted to resist Libyan interventionism.

U.S.-Libyan tensions escalated in August when Reagan went ahead with U.S. naval maneuvers in disputed waters of the Mediterranean Sea near the Libyan coast and U.S. Navy jets shot down two Libyan fighter planes that challenged them.

Finally, Reagan himself publicly ascribed truth to reports that Qaddafi had dispatched assassination squads to the United States to try to kill the president or other top U.S. officials.

Despite all of that, the administration successfully opposed moves by liberal Democrats in Congress to enact an embargo on Libyan oil to the United States. But Reagan did advise Americans working for oil companies in Libya to leave that nation for their own safety, implying possible sanctions or other action against Libya in the future.

Cuba, Nicaragua. The administration also sought to be forceful with Cuba and Nicaragua, openly warning both to stop aiding and abetting the leftist guerrillas seeking power in El Salvador.

The war of words with those two nations remained mainly that, though the administration did suspend $15 million of $75 million in economic aid Congress had voted for Nicaragua in 1980 after a bitter battle. The aid never was resumed.

Reagan and Foreign Aid

The AWACS victory was by far Reagan's most prominent foreign policy success in Congress, but another feather in his cap was rapid House action in the final days of the session on two stalled foreign aid bills.

Foreign aid, especially U.S. donations to multilateral development banks, became an unusually contentious issue in a year when Congress was making unprecedented reductions in domestic programs. But after personal appeals from Reagan and Haig, the House quickly passed aid authorization and appropriations bills that had been in limbo because of past Republican opposition to foreign aid.

Among its major provisions, the authorization bill gave the president leeway to provide arms aid or sales to Argentina, Chile and Pakistan, but it left intact a controversial limit on U.S. aid to warring factions in Angola.

On the aid appropriations bill, Congress had been hamstrung by a fundamental disagreement between conservatives (mostly Republicans) and liberals (mostly Democrats) over the proper ratio of military-to-development aid. The issue was never resolved, but compromises were reached to satisfy the president's desire for a bill that would embody a Reagan foreign aid program.

Reagan's support also helped get through Congress an overdue authorization for a $3.24 billion donation to the International Development Association (IDA), a World Bank arm that made no-interest loans to poor nations.

The authorization ratified a pledge made by President Carter in 1979. But conservative critics of IDA continued to buck Reagan's qualified support by stretching out the appropriations needed to make actual payments.

—By Richard Whittle

Senate Supports Reagan on AWACS Sale

President Reagan narrowly won the first major test of his authority in foreign policy Oct. 28 when the Senate, in a dramatic 48-52 vote, rejected a resolution to disapprove the sale to Saudi Arabia of five Airborne Warning and Control System (AWACS) radar planes and other arms. *(Details of items in sale, box, p. 130)*

Fifty senators had cosponsored a version of the resolution. But the president's appeals for loyalty led eight first-term senators among the cosponsors — seven of them Republicans — to switch at the last minute and vote against the resolution. *(Vote 335, p. 56-S)*

A majority of each house would have had to pass the veto resolution (H Con Res 194) for it to take effect under a 1976 law that gave Congress the right to veto major arms sales. Congress had 30 days after receiving formal notice of the $8.5 billion sale on Oct. 1 to do so; the House had voted 301-111 against the sale Oct. 14. *(House vote 243, p. 80-H)*

The Senate vote to allow the sale preserved Congress' record of never having used its arms sale veto power, though the threat of a veto had forced previous administrations to alter the terms of other weapons deals.

It also gave Reagan a momentous victory in a contest that had pitted his presidency against another of Washington's most potent lobbies — the American Jewish community, which fought the deal because of Israel's strong opposition to it.

The debate, which began in earnest in the spring, had centered on fears that Saudi Arabia might use the AWACS (Airborne Warning and Control System) planes against Israel in concert with other Arab nations or might fail to guard the AWACS's secrets from falling into unfriendly hands.

But in the final days before the issue was decided, the White House relentlessly portrayed the question as a matter of presidential power and prestige, arguing that Reagan would lose his credibility in Saudi Arabia and other foreign lands if the Senate scotched the deal.

That aspect was especially important because the AWACS sale had become the most visible symbol of Reagan's policy in the Middle East. The policy rested in large part on the U.S. ability to hold together a "strategic consensus" among nations that opposed Soviet adventurism in the region.

But in order to gain his victory, the president was forced at the 11th hour to spend large amounts of political capital wooing senators whose support might have been gained much earlier.

Administration officials were ecstatic about the vote. Reagan characterized the Senate action as "the upper chamber at its best." *(Statement, p. 26-E)*

The seven Republicans who cosponsored the anti-AWACS resolution but then switched were: Mark Andrews of North Dakota, William S. Cohen of Maine, Slade Gorton of Washington, Orrin G. Hatch of Utah, Roger W. Jepsen of Iowa, Larry Pressler of South Dakota, and Alan K. Simpson of Wyoming. Another cosponsor, Edward Zorinsky, D-Neb., also voted with the president.

Background

The AWACS sale had its origins in a study of Saudi military needs, conducted by the U.S. Defense Department in 1974. Partly as a result of that study — coupled with the U.S. desire to develop closer ties with its largest supplier of imported oil — the United States began selling Saudi Arabia large quantities of weapons and weapons-related services.

From 1974 to mid-1981, Saudi Arabia contracted to buy $32.1 billion worth of weapons and services from the United States. Of that amount, $8.6 billion was for weapons, ammunition, spare parts and equipment; the remaining $23.5 billion was for services, such as design and construction supervision of several new air, naval and army bases.

In 1978, Congress agreed after a bruising political battle to allow the sale to Saudi Arabia of 60 F-15 fighters, costing $2.5 billion; that was the first sale of the advanced warplanes to any country other than a close U.S. ally. The sale was part of a package, which included 50 F-5E planes for Egypt and 15 F-15s and 150 F-16 fighters for Israel. *(1978 Almanac p. 405)*

During debate on that sale, the Carter administration promised Congress that Saudi Arabia would not be sold equipment, such as long-range fuel tanks, multiple-ejection bomb racks or advanced Sidewinder air-to-air missiles, to enhance the offensive capability of the F-15s. The Carter administration also assured Congress that Saudi Arabia would not be sold sophisticated air surveillance aircraft, such as the E-2C "Hawkeye" or the E-3A AWACS.

Saudi Arabia's first experience with AWACS came in April 1979, when President Carter sent two of the planes to Saudi Arabia during a border war between North and South Yemen. In September of that year, Saudi Arabia asked the United States to conduct a study of that country's need for an airborne surveillance system. The following February, before the study was completed, Saudi Arabia put the AWACS plane on a list of equipment it wanted to buy.

Meanwhile, throughout 1980, the Carter administration and Congress publicly debated whether to reverse the 1978 promise not to sell the Saudis advanced equipment for the F-15s. In response to reports that the administration was considering selling Saudi Arabia the fuel tanks, bomb racks and other items, 68 senators wrote Carter on July 8 opposing such a sale. Faced with opposition and the upcoming election, the Carter administration postponed a decision on the matter.

In October 1980, following the outbreak of war between Iran and Iraq, Carter sent four AWACS planes to Saudi Arabia, their mission to detect threats to the Saudi oil fields. Manned by American crews, those planes remained in Saudi Arabia through the rest of 1980 and all of 1981. Congressional reports later said the performance of those planes greatly increased the Saudis' interest in having their own AWACS.

The study of Saudi Arabia's air surveillance needs was completed in December 1980. According to various reports, the study made no recommendations but did list the costs and equipment needed for various methods of air surveillance.

There later was wide dispute about whether the Carter administration had committed the United States to sell AWACS to Saudi Arabia, or merely had led Saudi officials to believe that such a sale might be possible.

Details of Saudi Arms Sale

The $8.5 billion "Royal Saudi Air Force enhancement package" included the following items:

AWACS

Five E-3A AWACS, at a total cost of $5.8 billion, to be delivered beginning in 1985. Four U.S. Air Force AWACS had operated in Saudi Arabia since October 1980. They were to remain until replaced by the Saudi AWACS.

The AWACS — a Boeing 707 airliner with a distinctive "radome" mounted on top — carried complex electronic equipment capable of detecting low-flying aircraft at 175 nautical miles and high-altitude bombers at 360 nautical miles. Its computers could track hundreds of aircraft simultaneously.

A Defense Department document submitted to the House Foreign Affairs and Senate Foreign Relations committees said the Saudi planes would not contain key items used in U.S. AWACS.

The elements to be left out, the document said, were: a Joint Tactical Information Distribution System, which could securely communicate information the AWACS radars pick up to large numbers of fighter planes; Electronic Counter-Counter Measures to prevent an opponent from jamming AWACS communications; a jam-resistant communication system known as HAVE QUICK; and three computer consoles, in addition to the nine now used, that were to be added to future U.S. AWACS.

In describing the sale, one State Department official said the Saudi AWACS would operate under "strictures" that would limit access to the planes to Saudi and U.S. nationals and forbid the transfer of the aircraft or their secrets to any third country.

He said 400 Americans — 30 U.S. Air Force personnel and 370 civilian contract employees — would help operate and maintain the AWACS when they were deployed in 1985. Some Americans always would be needed, he said.

Other Items

101 sets of conformal fuel tanks that could be fitted to the Saudi F-15s to boost their fuel capacity by 9,750 pounds. Delivery of the tanks, valued at $110 million, would begin in late 1983 or early 1984.

Six to eight KC-707 tanker aircraft, worth up to $2.4 billion. The tankers would allow Saudi Arabia to refuel both its F-15s and F-5 aircraft in-flight. Saudi Arabia had requested six KC-707s with an option to buy two more. Delivery of the tanks was to begin in 1984.

1,177 AIM-9L heat-seeking air-to-air missiles, at a cost of $200 million, to replace AIM-9P missiles the Saudis possessed. The AIM-9Ls would allow the Saudi F-15s to score hits on enemy aircraft from head-on rather than having to maneuver behind them, as the AIM-9P required.

The missiles would be taken from U.S. supplies, as the United States replaced its AIM-9Ls with more advanced AIM-9M missiles.

The Reagan Approach

On Feb. 26, 1981, Reagan administration officials told congressional committees that the United States had agreed to sell the advanced AIM-9L Sidewinder air-to-air missiles and long-range fuel tanks for their F-15s. The United States also had agreed "in principle" to sell Saudi Arabia tanker planes for mid-air refueling of the F-15s and a radar surveillance plane, possibly the AWACS. Those decisions were made public on March 6 by the State Department.

Opposition to the sale immediately mounted in Congress. Between March 24 and April 7, 44 senators and 78 House members made floor speeches denouncing the sale. The speeches were organized by Republicans, including Rep. Jack F. Kemp, of New York and Sens. Bob Packwood of Oregon and Roger W. Jepsen of Iowa.

The only congressional leader who immediately moved to support the weapons sale was John Tower, R-Texas, chairman of the Senate Armed Services Committee.

Arguments Against Sale

During their floor speeches, members advanced several broad arguments against the sale:

● Selling advanced weapons to the Saudis would aggravate regional tensions, forcing Israel to buy more arms.

● The Saudis did not need the enhanced F-15s and the AWACS for their own defense. Several members said the Saudis could defend themselves against their most likely opponents: Iraq, Iran and South Yemen. They said the new arms would be of little use against an attack by the Soviet Union.

● The weapons would increase the threat to Israel. Several members noted that the enhanced F-15s could strike anywhere in Israel from bases deep in Saudi Arabia.

● The new weapons could contribute to instability in Saudi Arabia. Several members compared the Saudi regime to Iran under the former shah.

● An increasing number of members were questioning the conventional wisdom that Saudi Arabia was a "moderate" among Arab and oil-producing nations.

Noting that the Saudis have called for a holy war against Israel, Rep. Kemp said: "We thought back in 1978 that agreeing to sell the Saudis the F-15s . . . would result in Saudi commitment to the security interests we hold in common. Instead, we have seen the Saudis time and time again act as antagonists, opposing rather than supporting our interests."

● The United States could not be certain the Saudis could maintain the secrets of the AWACS. Joseph P. Addabbo, D-N.Y., chairman of the House Defense Appropriations Subcommittee, said: "There is no one who can guarantee what type of government, pro-United States, anti-United States or violently opposed to Israel, will be in control of those weapons one year or five years from now. . . ."

● The Saudis had offered nothing to the United States in return for the equipment. Some members noted that the Saudis had refused to allow U.S. troops on Saudi soil.

Israeli Opposition

During a Middle East trip April 3-9, Secretary of State Alexander M. Haig Jr., discussed the sale in Saudi Arabia and Israel. In an attempt to reduce Israeli opposition to the sale of advanced arms to Saudi Arabia, Haig promised Israel an extra $300 million annually in military aid for

fiscal years 1983 and 1984. That was to be in addition to the $1.4 billion in military grants and loans Israel already was receiving each year.

Haig reportedly offered to make the extra $600 million an outright grant, rather than a loan, because Israel had compiled a multibillion-dollar debt in buying arms from the United States.

But Israeli Prime Minister Menachem Begin spurned Haig's arguments that the sale would not jeopardize Israel's security. Begin publicly told Haig April 6 that allowing Saudi Arabia to buy AWACS planes would present "a very serious threat to Israel."

Begin's statement prompted several American Jewish groups to start lobbying against the sale.

Nevertheless, on April 21 the White House announced that the United States would sell Saudi Arabia five AWACS planes in addition to the other equipment. However, the White House said Congress would not receive official notice of the sale until after the June 30 Israeli elections.

Begin again denounced the sale, expressing his "profound regret" at Reagan's decision.

Administration Launches Campaign

The administration began its campaign to sell the AWACS deal. The day after Begin's protest:

● A senior White House official stressed that 30 U.S. Air Force personnel and 410 American civilians would be needed to fly and maintain the AWACS. This argument was aimed at easing fears that the Saudis might use the AWACS against Israel or lose control of their secrets.

● A State Department spokesman said the Saudi AWACS would not threaten Israel because they would "have no radio monitoring, photo reconnaissance or intelligence-gathering capabilities." He said the Saudi AWACS would be unable to detect "militarily significant" ground activity, could not coordinate with aircraft from other nations without joint training and the use of U.S. computers and would need U.S. spare parts and maintenance.

● Haig met April 23 with 30 leaders of American Jewish organizations and urged them to "keep your powder dry until you see the bottom line" of the Saudi deal. His statement reflected the argument that the Saudis might not get the most sophisticated version of AWACS.

Israeli Raids

On June 7, Begin sent U.S.-supplied F-16 jets on a bombing mission that destroyed a nuclear power plant near Baghdad, Iraq. Begin said the raid was justified because Iraq planned to use the plant to produce nuclear bombs against Israel.

But the United States condemned the raid, and temporarily suspended the delivery of new jets to Israel. The raid — coupled with the July 17 Israeli bombing of Palestinian outposts in Beirut, Lebanon, killing more than 100 civilians — shook even Israel's staunchest supporters in the United States.

Several members of Congress suggested that the widespread anger at Israel's actions might help Reagan win approval of the AWACS sale in Congress.

The raid on Iraq, however, clearly helped Begin politically in his own country. Previously, most observers expected that Begin's conservative coalition would be swept out of office by the Labor Party. But in the June 30 elections, Begin managed to hold onto power, with the aid a fundamentalist religious party in the Knesset (parliament).

In spite of the criticisms of Israel, opposition to the AWACS sale continued to harden. At the instigation of the American-Israel Public Affairs Committee, a pro-Israel lobbying group, 54 senators sent Reagan a letter on June 24 asking that he "refrain from sending this proposal to Congress." Among the signers were 34 Democrats and 20 Republicans.

In the House, 224 members signed a resolution asserting that the House "objects to the proposed sale."

In response, Reagan wrote Congress on Aug. 4, asking members to keep open minds on the issue. "I hope that no one will prejudge our proposal before it is presented," the president wrote. "We will make a strong case to the Congress that it is in the interest of our country, the Western alliance and stability in the Middle East."

Official Proposal

Under standard procedures for major arms sales, the administration officially notified Congress of the AWACS package sale in two steps: On August 24, the Defense Department sent Congress an "informal notice" with details of the sale; that was followed Oct. 1 with the formal notice, which kicked off the 30 day period in which Congress could veto the sale. *(Box, p. 132)*

The $8.5 billion package included the five AWACS planes, 101 sets of conformal fuel tanks for the Saudi F-15s, six to eight KC-707 fuel tanker aircraft, and 1,177 AIM-9L Sidewinder air-to-air missiles. *(Details, box, p. 130)*

Defending the sale, administration officials said the AWACS planes were needed to improve Saudi Arabia's ability to defend its oil fields, to preserve Western access to Persian Gulf oil supplies, to guard against Soviet intrusions in the area, to show U.S. resolve to guarantee the region's security and to cement U.S.-Saudi ties.

"This proposed sale is a cornerstone of the president's policy to strengthen the strategic environment in the Middle East," James L. Buckley, under secretary of state for security assistance, said in announcing the sale.

Begin met with Reagan in Washington September 9, and reaffirmed his opposition to the sale. Begin also took his campaign against the sale to Capitol Hill on September 10.

A week later, Senate opponents, led by Packwood, said 50 senators had cosponsored a resolution to reject it. That same day, Haig told the Senate Foreign Relations Committee that the administration was "taking steps to assure that Israeli concerns are met."

Joint Control Issue

In mid-September, the issue of who would control the operation and information produced by the AWACS emerged as the central point of debate.

John Glenn, D-Ohio, potentially a key senator because of his background as an astronaut and Marine Corps pilot, led a movement insisting that the United States retain "joint control" of the AWACS planes through the 1990s.

To reduce concern about the abuse of loss of the AWACS secrets, the administration had said the planes sold to the Saudis would not include some of the most sensitive equipment used on U.S. AWACS. Instead, Glenn proposed selling Saudi Arabia the more advanced plane and, in return, insisting that American crewmen be stationed on board the planes.

Saudi officials, however, reportedly rejected the Glenn proposal, and Glenn became a determined opponent of the sale.

Administration Campaign

On Oct. 1, the day Congress was officially notified of the sale, Reagan and Haig launched campaigns to secure its approval in the Senate. Admitting that the House was certain to vote against the sale, administration officials concentrated their efforts on blocking the veto in the Republican-controlled House.

Reagan raised the AWACS issue in an Oct. 1 White House news conference, indirectly criticizing Israel's adamant opposition by declaring: "It is not the business of other nations to make American foreign policy."

Later Reagan was asked about charges that the Saudi government was unstable and might fall, resulting in a loss of the AWACS planes to forces unfriendly to the United States, as happened with other valued U.S. military equipment when the shah of Iran was overthrown.

The president replied simply that the United States would not allow that to happen.

"I have to say that, Saudi Arabia, we will not permit to be an Iran," Reagan said. "There is no way — as long as Saudi Arabia and the OPEC nations . . . provide the bulk of the energy that is needed to turn the wheels of industry in the Western world — there's no way that we could stand by and see that taken over by anyone that would shut off that oil."

Haig Testimony

Haig appeared Oct. 1 before the Senate Foreign Relations Committee to defend the sale. Haig first briefed committee members in closed session, then testified in a public session.

Chairman Charles H. Percy, R-Ill., a sale supporter, said Haig in the private session had offered "new assurances" that the Saudis would protect the secrets of the AWACS planes and would not use them against Israel.

But others, including Glenn, said they were still dissatisfied.

Haig's appearance came after a week of frantic maneuvering by the administration that apparently was aimed at getting the Saudis to agree to some form of joint U.S.-Saudi control. Haig said he was bringing the committee "arrangements" that should alleviate their concerns. He rejected the phrase "joint control," however.

When Haig also was unable to say that American personnel would be allowed to fly with the Saudi AWACS

AWACS Subject to Congressional Veto Under 1976 Law

A 1976 amendment to the Arms Export Control Act (PL 94-329) gave Congress an opportunity to reject sales of U.S. military equipment, such as the AWACS for Saudi Arabia, that exceed dollar thresholds.

The thresholds — later doubled in the fiscal 1982 foreign aid authorization bill — were $7 million in the case of a single item and $25 million in the case of a package of military equipment. *(1976 Almanac p. 213)*

Under the law, Congress could reject such sales by adopting a concurrent resolution of disapproval within 30 calendar days of receiving formal notice of the proposed sale from the executive branch. The House and Senate resolutions must be identical.

However, a "gentleman's agreement" reached with the Ford administration when the arms export law was reviewed in 1976 entitled Congress to informal notice of a proposed arms sale 20 days before the formal notice. The 20-day informal notice was a compromise agreed to after some members of Congress suggested the 30-calendar-day period for a congressional veto should be made 30 legislative days or should be lengthened.

The Carter and Reagan administrations had abided by that agreement. But the Reagan administration went a step further in the case of the AWACS, giving Congress its informal notice on Aug. 24, yet saying the 20-day informal review period would not begin until Sept. 9, when Congress returned to work from its August recess.

The Reagan administration also modified the normal informal notice by giving details of the AWACS notice in unclassified form. The nuts and bolts of such notices normally are classified.

Veto Waiver

Even if he had lost the Senate vote on selling AWACS planes to Saudi Arabia, President Reagan had two legal powers to proceed with the sale.

One power was granted in the 1976 Arms Export Control Act.

Under section 36(b) of the law, the president must send Congress an unclassified notice describing major sales before he can issue a formal "letter of offer" to the country buying the weapons or services.

The president could waive Congress's right to veto the sale by stating in his notice to Congress that "an emergency exists which requires such sale in the national security interests of the United States."

If the president said there was such an emergency, he must give Congress "a detailed justification for his determination, including a description of the emergency circumstances which necessitate the immediate issuance of the letter of offer and a discussion of the national security interests involved."

Congress added the requirement for the justification in the International Security Assistance Act of 1979 (PL 96-92). *(1979 Almanac p. 124)*

The Reagan administration's Oct. 1 notice of the sale of AWACS radar planes and other weapons to Saudi Arabia did not mention an "emergency."

A second presidential power to prevent a congressional arms sale veto was attached to the fiscal 1981 foreign aid bill (PL 96-533). That law allowed the president to waive most legal restrictions (such as the congressional veto) on foreign aid and arms sales if he notified Congress that doing so "is vital to the national security interests of the United States."

Before using the waiver, the law said, the president "shall consult with, and shall provide a written policy justification to" the congressional foreign policy and Appropriations committtees. *(1980 Almanac p. 313)*

throughout their service life, Glenn declared that without such a stipulation the deal was "doomed."

Alluding to Glenn's support for the military concept behind the sale proposal, Haig declared: "I would hate to have an advocate for the solution become an albatross that drags it down to defeat." But Glenn said he would vote against the bargain unless the Saudis agreed to let Americans fly with their AWACS crews.

Haig said the arrangements governing the use of the Saudi AWACS "respond to the fundamental concerns about the sale that have been raised during the course of our consultations with the Congress."

Implying concessions by the Saudis, he said they had agreed that:

● All information derived from their AWACS planes would be shared with the United States.

● None of the information would be shared "with any other parties without U.S. consent."

● "Only carefully-screened Saudi and U.S. nationals will be permitted to be involved with these aircraft."

● "Given the shortage of Saudi air crews and technicians ... there will be an American presence in the aircraft and on the ground well into the 1990s."

● "There will be no operation of Saudi AWACS outside Saudi airspace" — an implicit pledge the planes would not be used against Israel.

● "There will be extensive and elaborate security measures for safeguarding equipment and technology."

Committee Response

Percy was the only panel member present who voiced sympathy with the administration's position after Haig's briefing. He said the need for AWACS in Saudi Arabia was demonstrated the previous night when a plane from Iran, which was at war with Iraq, flew across the Persian Gulf and bombed an oil facility in Kuwait between Iraq and the Saudi oil fields on the east coast of the Arabian peninsula.

Haig testified that the four U.S. AWACS stationed in Saudi Arabia monitored the Iranian raid from start to finish.

The administration had argued that the Saudis needed the five AWACS to provide 24-hour radar coverage of the Persian Gulf at distances that would give Saudi fighters time to scramble and intercept intruders before they reach the oil fields.

Haig eagerly agreed with Percy on the significance of the Iranian raid, calling it "a dramatic and, I think, God-given warning" of the need for the AWACS in Saudi Arabia.

But others on the committee reiterated their criticisms of the sale and their demands for tighter controls.

"Without effective controls, the sale of AWACS and the F-15 enhancement package constitutes a clear threat to Israel. I do not believe effective controls are possible," said Claiborne Pell, R.I., ranking panel Democrat. "We simply cannot place our reliance on understandings."

Joseph R. Biden Jr., D-Del., said Haig had failed to persuade him as well. Acknowledging the validity of administration warnings that rejecting the sale risked damaging U.S.-Saudi relations, Biden said he believed greater damage could result from going ahead. "I'm afraid we're in a position here where we are limiting damage," he said. Biden also said that while he did not equate Saudi Arabia with Iran before the fall of the shah, there was a similarity in that the royal family could be overthrown easily.

"If the top five princes were bumped off tomorrow

there'd be chaos — isn't that what we're afraid of?" Biden asked. Haig replied that one reason for the AWACS sale was to increase Saudi stability.

Haig emphasized the importance of the sale to U.S. relations with Saudi Arabia and, as a consequence, to U.S. policy in the Middle East. He said the sale would help foster Saudi cooperation in a U.S. effort to forge a "strategic consensus" among nations there to resolve their differences and guard against Soviet encroachment.

But Rudy Boschwitz, R-Minn., another sale opponent, noted that the Saudis had billed the issue as a test of U.S. friendship despite a long history of U.S. military sales and other friendly gestures. "What's going to be the next litmus test?" he asked.

Boschwitz also dismissed administration arguments that the Saudis have been a moderating influence on oil price increases among members of the Organization of Petroleum Exporting Countries (OPEC).

He said Saudi Arabia had opposed U.S. efforts to fill the Strategic Petroleum Reserve, and he noted Saudi opposition to the Camp David peace accords negotiated by Israel and Egypt under Carter's guidance.

Haig responded that the United States had differences with all nations, even its close allies such as Israel — an allusion to disputes with.Israel over its use of U.S. aircraft outside Israel.

He added that the ruling Saudi royal family was obliged to engage in a certain amount of anti-U.S. politics to maintain its standing in the Arab world. "The radical Arab movement is not an inconsequential concern in the region," Haig said.

Haig was followed by Defense Secretary Caspar W. Weinberger and Gen. David C. Jones, chairman of the Joint Chiefs of Staff, who also had testified Sept. 28 before the Senate Armed Services Committee on the military issues involved in the sale.

Sadat Assassination

The House Foreign Affairs Committee — a hotbed of opposition to the AWACS sale — was scheduled to vote on the issue Oct. 6, but postponed the vote that morning when news of the assassination of Egyptian President Anwar Sadat reached Washington.

Sadat's assassination shifted the focus of the debate on the sale, giving Reagan new hope of winning on the issue.

The emphasis in the days before had been on the demands of key senators that the Saudis agree to joint U.S. control of the sophisticated surveillance planes.

But with Sadat's death, the administration quickly began to argue that the loss of America's best Arab friend made it imperative that Congress not jeopardize U.S. ties with Saudi Arabia — or Reagan's stature — by blocking the deal.

Recalling Sadat's support for the sale, Haig asserted at an Oct. 7 news conference that for Congress to reject it would "make a mockery of all President Sadat stood for."

By contrast, critics argued that the assassination demonstrated with chilling clarity how unstable were even the strongest of Middle East regimes. They said it reinforced the argument that to sell AWACS to the ruling royal Saudi family risked losing it to U.S. foes in a *coup d'etat*.

The administration countered that, as presidential counselor Edwin Meese III put it the day Sadat was killed, the assassination did "not indicate instability in the Middle East any more than the shooting of President Reagan indicates instability in the United States."

Reagan Team May Draw Key Lessons . . .

On the way to its intoxicating, uphill victory on the Saudi arms sale, the Reagan administration may have learned some hard lessons about how — and how not — to lobby Congress on a foreign policy issue.

Despite the president's ultimate success, a wide variety of critics said the White House, by maladroit handling of the issue, gave opponents of the sale a large head start, then had to invest precious political capital to catch up.

Specific criticisms ranged from the initial conception of the arms package to allegations (heatedly denied) of small favors bestowed on wavering senators.

But the most common objection was that the administration unnecessarily let the sale become a divisive referendum on Reagan's ability to conduct foreign policy.

"I know of no one on either side who does not think this has been grossly mishandled," said Sen. John Glenn, D-Ohio, who voted against the sale after unsuccessful efforts to negotiate a compromise.

Critics faulted the administration's conduct of the AWACs campaign on a number of points:

Conception

Many senators, including a number who supported the sale, said the administration failed from the outset to recognize the repercussions of the sale or to establish its place in an overall Mideast policy.

Sen. Charles McC. Mathias Jr., R-Md., who voted for the sale, said the administration talked as if Saudi Arabia were "some kind of a sideshow going on down in the [Persian] gulf."

"I would hope one of the lessons they would learn would be the importance of having a coherent strategy into which an issue of this sort can be fitted," Mathias said.

I. M. Destler, director of the Carnegie Endowment's Project on Executive-Congressional Relations in Foreign Policy, added that where the Saudi-U.S. relationship required nuance and delicacy, Reagan's decision to sell AWACS led to a massive public confrontation that "contradicts or cuts into the whole way we ought to be managing our relations with the Saudis."

"Because of the failure to be sensitive to the politics of this issue, [Reagan] dug himself an enormous hole, and was only able to dig out of it with great effort and at a considerable cost," Destler said.

Consultation

Several senators complained that the administration neglected to inform or consult with Congress as the deal was hatched.

"This whole exercise could have been prevented had there been proper consultation with the Congress," said AWACS opponent Sen. Claiborne Pell, D-R.I.

Frederick G. Dutton, a lawyer representing the Saudis, compared Reagan's performance with President Carter's 1978 sale of F-15 aircraft to Saudi Arabia.

"The Carter people, though they were generally thought of as inept, lined up Ribicoff to take much of the heat.... It was organized before it really was sprung publicly." Sen. Abraham Ribicoff, D-Conn. (1963-81), was a prominent supporter of Israel who backed the 1978 sale.

Coordination

The chairmanship of the interdepartmental committee handling the AWACS was assigned first to Defense Under Secretary Fred C. Ikle, then to National Security Adviser Richard V. Allen, and finally, in early October, to White House Chief of Staff James A. Baker III. Senators complained that Allen, known as a "substance man" rather than a salesman, was not adept at responding to their misgivings about the sale.

In addition, bickering among the various departments frequently spilled into the press.

Timing

Rumors that AWACs would be sold to the Saudis circulated in March. The administration confirmed them in April. Months passed — and opposition hardened — before the administration did any lobbying on the package.

By the time the president himself became aggressively involved, in September, opponents of the sale had more than half of the Senate publicly on record as critical of the sale. Moreover, several senators said, the president was not well-versed in particulars of the sale in his first few meetings with senators.

Sen. Slade Gorton, R-Wash., who became a swing vote in the administration's favor, complained: "Just to wander around here and say, 'As soon as you see the whole thing, you'll be satisfied,' which was what we were

---

The day after Sadat was felled, Reagan hosted 43 of the Senate's 53 Republicans at the White House and urged them anew to back him on the sale.

Responding to Reagan's entreaties, Sens. Hatch and Simpson said afterward that they would support Reagan despite having cosponsored the Senate version of the resolution of disapproval (S Con Res 37). That left S Con Res 37 with 48 cosponsors, three less than the majority of 51 required for its adoption.

The joint control issue, which before Sadat's death seemed likely to kill the deal in the Senate, remained a fundamental problem for the president.

But a hopeful note was struck for the administration

on that score when Senate Armed Services Committee members Sam Nunn, D-Ga., and John W. Warner, R-Va., introduced a resolution (S Res 228) addressing that issue. S Res 228 stated the sense of the Senate that before selling AWACS to any nation the president should certify that the recipient had accepted six safeguards on their use.

The safeguards essentially matched arrangements with the Saudis disclosed by Haig Oct. 1 before the Foreign Relations Committee. But the measure seemed to offer a way to satisfy the demands of some senators for written safeguards, for Warner said that Reagan had pledged to "advise the Senate in writing that he will meet each of the requirements" if adopted.

. . . From Difficult Struggle Over AWACS

hearing from Richard Allen for months, is not an appropriate way to handle an issue of this magnitude."

In a speech to the U.S. Chamber of Commerce Oct. 28, presidential aide Baker said that during the spring White House attention was trained on the House fight over budget and taxes, and "one thing we didn't need when we were winning votes on the floor of the House of Representatives by four or five votes was another divisive issue out there."

Charles H. Percy, R-Ill., chairman of the Senate Foreign Relations Committee, added that while the late start was "a strategic mistake," after the president "got deeply, personally involved, they more than made up for it."

But J. Brian Atwood, who handled congressional relations for the State Department under Carter, said Reagan might not yet realize the price of letting his opposition get ahead.

"A lot of those senators who reversed themselves under great pressure have been embarrassed by this whole thing. They're perceived by a lot of people as being weak, and they're going to suffer the political consequences of it," he said.

The next time, Atwood said, those senators would be less willing to take risks for Reagan. He recalled that after a series of controversial foreign policy battles, President Carter "had absolutely run out of political capital" to sell his Strategic Arms Limitation Treaty.

Bargaining

When Israeli Prime Minister Menachem Begin visited Reagan in September, the White House offered to establish a closer military partnership in the Mideast.

Though the proposal was designed to mitigate Israeli objections to the AWACS sale, Reagan neglected to link the two issues. Begin promptly went to the press and renewed his attack on the Saudi sale.

Atwood said the concessions to Israel could have been used as a way of winning over dubious senators to the issue — as Carter did with several concessions in 1978 — especially if the administration had allowed senators to share in the execution.

"Congress wants a piece of the action," Atwood said. "The White House should have allowed members of Congress to claim credit for that kind of security enhancement."

The White House apparently learned this lesson late in the game. A decisive factor in the final victory was a presidential letter that allowed several freshmen senators to claim they had wrested serious concessions from the administration.

Anti-Semitism Issue

Administration officials spoke of Jewish opposition to AWACS in ways that many Jews, and some senators, found offensive.

Glenn, for example, said he was astonished when Reagan told a group of senators that AWACS foe Bob Packwood, R-Ore., was so adamant because he hoped to enhance Republican fund-raising in Jewish communities.

The administration also raised the specter of Israeli meddling in U.S. policy and, more indirectly, the possibility of an anti-Jewish backlash if the sale failed.

Hyman Bookbinder, Washington representative for the American Jewish Committee, called such statements "tragic, poisonous," and said the administration "probably lost half of the new Jewish support they picked up in 1980."

Side Deals

Some critics said the deliberations were demeaned by a last-minute aura of horse-trading. Beginning with a *Wall Street Journal* story Oct. 14, various news accounts reported half a dozen instances where administration favors were bestowed on marginal senators: acceleration of a U.S. attorney appointment for a candidate favored by Sen. Charles E. Grassley, R-Iowa, money for a Public Health Service hospital special to Gorton; a hint that the president might not campaign in 1982 against Sen. Dennis DeConcini, D-Ariz.; and approval of a coal-fired power plant for Sen. John Melcher, D-Mont.

None of these was tied to the president, and the senators involved all strongly denied that their votes were influenced by the alleged favors.

Reagan himself said "there have been no deals made."

Sen. Mark Andrews, R-N.D., who was lobbied heavily, said on PBS's "MacNeil-Lehrer Report" that he never heard any hint of a reward: "You don't buy votes when you're talking about your national security. You might when you're talking about a tax or budget issue."

House Action

The administration sustained its first formal defeat on the issue Oct. 7 when the Foreign Affairs Committee approved, by a 28-8 vote, H Con Res 194 to disapprove the entire AWACS sale package. The committee vote demonstrated the difficulty of trying to gauge how members of Congress would approach the issue. The panel's chairman, Democrat Clement J. Zablocki of Wisconsin, voted against the resolution, while ranking Republican William S. Broomfield of Michigan voted for it.

The committee filed its report (H Rept 97-268) the same day.

The committee vote on the issue was:

Aye:

Democrats (18) — Dante B. Fascell, Fla.; Benjamin S. Rosenthal, N.Y.; Lee H. Hamilton, Ind.; Jonathan B. Bingham, N.Y.; Gus Yatron, Pa.; Stephen J. Solarz, N.Y.; Don Bonker, Wash.; Gerry E. Studds, Mass.; Andy Ireland, Fla.; Daniel A. Mica, Fla.; Michael D. Barnes, Md.; Howard Wolpe, Mich.; George W. Crockett Jr., Mich.; Bob Shamansky, Ohio; Dennis E. Eckart, Ohio; Sam Gejdenson, Conn.; Mervyn M. Dymally, Calif.; Tom Lantos, Calif.

Republicans (10) — William S. Broomfield, Mich.; Edward J. Derwinski, Ill.; Larry Winn Jr., Kan.; Benjamin A. Gilman, N.Y.; Millicent Fenwick, N.J.; Robert K.

Dornan, Calif.; Jim Leach, Iowa; Arlen Erdahl, Minn.; Olympia J. Snowe, Maine; John LeBoutillier, N.Y.

Nay:

Democrats (3) — Chairman Clement J. Zablocki, Wis.; L. H. Fountain, N.C.; David R. Bowen, Miss.

Republicans (5) — Paul Findley, Ill.; Robert J. Lagomarsino, Calif.; Joel Pritchard, Wash.; Toby Roth, Wis.; Henry J. Hyde, Ill.

Present: Bill Goodling, R-Pa.

House Vote

On Oct. 14, following a debate that repeated arguments that had been made for or against the sale for months, the House voted 301-111 to adopt the resolution disapproving the sale. The overwhelming vote had been expected, and the administration had made little efffort to avert a negative vote in the House. *(Vote 243, p. 80-H)*

Senate Committee Action

The stage was set Oct. 15 for a Senate showdown on the issue, as the Senate Foreign Relations Committee approved by a vote of 9-8 and sent to the Senate a resolution (S Con Res 37) disapproving the sale. The committee filed its report on the issue (S Rept 97-249) the same day.

Despite the adverse vote for Reagan, there was evidence that White House lobbying and the president's pleas for support were having the desired effect on some senators.

The committee vote was closer than many observers had expected, with the majority consisting of the panel's eight Democrats plus Rudy Boschwitz, R-Minn. Three Republicans whose positions had been unclear — S. I. "Sam" Hayakawa of California, Charles McC. Mathias Jr. of Maryland and Larry Pressler of South Dakota — voted as Reagan wished.

Most surprising was the vote of Pressler, who had been one of 50 cosponsors of the resolution of disapproval. Pressler revealed just before the vote that Reagan had telephoned him as the committee was debating the measure and persuaded him to switch his position.

Pressler said he specifically was influenced by Reagan's promise to include in a letter to the Senate the substance of a resolution (S Res 227) Pressler introduced Oct. 7 calling for the United States to offer Israel radar jamming equipment to counter the Saudi AWACS.

But U.S. Air Force Maj. Gen. Richard Secord had testified before Pressler at a committee hearing that Israel had no interest in radar jamming equipment. Secord said Israel's ability to jam air communications was "well known."

Mathias seemed to be still uncertain of whether he was right to support the sale, for he left open the possibility that he might vote against it in the full Senate.

He also cautioned his colleagues that more was involved than the sale of airplanes to Saudi Arabia. He said the AWACS would be but a first step in an "extended and intimate political and military association with a country with which we already have substantial economic ties."

Mathias said having Americans in Saudi Arabia to maintain the AWACS would "simultaneously create and symbolize a guarantee by the United States of the security of the Persian Gulf in a way far more significant than President Carter's statement on that subject of Jan. 23, 1980."

Carter at that time declared that the United States would use military force if necessary to protect the Persian Gulf and its oil from outside powers. *(Background, 1980 Almanac p. 310)*

Hayakawa said he was uncomfortable with the sale but had been reassured by Reagan.

By meeting with several senators at the White House, Reagan was able to gain support prior to the committee vote. On Oct. 14, Republicans Ted Stevens of Alaska, Mack Mattingly of Georgia and Dan Quayle of Indiana announced they would support the sale. All three had expressed doubts about it previously.

Committee Debate

The Foreign Relations vote was taken in the afternoon of Oct. 15 before a packed and excited audience, only hours after James Buckley and other State Department officials appeared before the panel one last time to defend the sale.

Chairman Percy urged the committee to reject S Con Res 37. He said it was important that Reagan be trusted in the Arab world so that Saudi Arabia and other moderate Arab states might move toward peace with Israel. "There is a perception that the United States will not deal with Arab nations in full partnership in guaranteeing the security of the area," he said, and failure to approve the AWACS deal would "affirm that perception."

"A defeat of the AWACS sale would also deal a devastating blow to the power and prestige of the presidency," Percy said, warning that the sale's defeat would "place upon the shoulders of those who vote against it responsibility for the consequences."

Majority Leader Howard H. Baker Jr., R-Tenn., who rarely attended Foreign Relations Committee meetings, came to the AWACS vote to display his support for Reagan.

Alluding to arguments that the sale should not go forward because it might endanger the security of Israel, Baker said: "Anyone who believes the security of Israel will be enhanced by reducing our influence in the Arab world is fundamentally wrong."

Baker also praised the administration's handling of the campaign to get Congress to approve the sale. He said the White House had engaged in "extraordinary" consultation with members of Congress in an effort to assuage their doubts so that they could vote for the deal.

But Democrats Claiborne Pell of Rhode Island and Glenn of Ohio criticized the administration on the same point, complaining that they had been asked for their suggestions on the AWACS package only after Reagan had submitted it to Congress.

Glenn said the sale had been "as poorly handled as anything I've seen in my seven years on Capitol Hill."

Sale foes Joseph R. Biden Jr., D-Del., and Paul E. Tsongas, D-Mass., both lamented that there would be "no winners" no matter which way the Senate voted.

Biden said he opposed the deal because it "is not in the interest of the United States" to give the highly-prized AWACS planes to Saudi Arabia and risk their loss or the compromise of their secrets. But he said proponents of the sale were correct when they argued that "failure to sell the weapons will damage our relations with the Saudis."

Tsongas said that, "No matter how the vote comes out, we have three losers." If the sale was approved, he said, Israel would be endangered, the United States would risk losing the AWACS's secrets and the Saudis no longer would be able to resist Arab efforts to involve them militarily in a war against Israel. If it was disapproved, Saudi Arabia would lose face, the United States would lose Saudi

good will and Arab trust, and Israel would suffer a backlash from those who felt the Jewish nation had too much influence on U.S. policy.

On the other side, Richard G. Lugar, R-Ind., and Nancy Landon Kassebaum, R-Kan., argued that the president must be supported and U.S. relations with Saudi Arabia must be preserved and improved.

"We've reached the point when we should reach out to Arab states," Kassebaum said.

Glenn repeated his frustration that the administration had not persuaded the Saudis to agree to joint U.S. control of the AWACS. He also complained that the administration, seeking to comfort those fearful for Israel's security, had pledged to remove some equipment from the Saudi AWACS that was included in the version of the aircraft used by the United States.

"It seems to me we want the highest-rated AWACS," Glenn said. "To do that, we need Americans [on board]."

Boschwitz said he feared that if Congress accepted the AWACS sale there would be further military equipment offered to Saudi Arabia later.

Some opponents of the AWACS sale had noted that when the Carter administration persuaded Congress in 1978 to allow the Saudis to buy 60 F-15s, it promised that items now offered the Saudis would not be offered. "Frankly, I'm afraid that we are going to see quite soon an AWACS enhancement package," Boschwitz said.

Alan Cranston, D-Calif., said he continued to believe it was not in the U.S. national interest to go ahead with the sale, in particular the AWACS and 1,177 AIM-9L Sidewinder missiles included in the package.

Cranston also said the United States should not "submit to another 'litmus test'" of its friendship for Saudi Arabia and should refuse "to continue to pump sophisticated weapons of war to both sides in that volatile region."

Answering the argument of proponents that Congress should not undercut the president's authority to make foreign policy, Cranston harked back to Reagan's fierce opposition to the 1978 treaties giving the Panama Canal to Panama.

Said Cranston: "I would like to paraphrase the words of Ronald Reagan when he opposed President Carter on the Panama Canal issue. 'We built the AWACS. We paid for them. We should keep them.'"

Final Testimony

In the administration's last formal plea for Congress to go along with the sale, Buckley asserted that events in the Middle East demonstrated the need for the Saudi sale.

"The Iranian air attack [of Oct. 1] on Kuwaiti oil facilities underscored the need of our friends to acquire adequate air defense systems, both to protect their petroleum resources and enhance stability by deterring attacks by regional powers," Buckley said.

"The assassination of President Sadat is a reminder to us all that our policies in the area must be built on the firm foundation of a mutuality of interests so that we may develop enduring relationships not only with particular leaders and governments, but with the peoples and nations of the Middle East that are of particular importance to us," he added.

Buckley said that a veto of the sale would raise "the question of whether the United States can be relied upon" to provide for Arab security.

Pell told Buckley that to defeat the AWACS sale would be "no more of a letdown of the president than not

to accept SALT II." Opposition from conservatives such as Reagan helped lead to Carter's withdrawal of the Strategic Arms Limitation Treaty he had signed with the Soviet Union.

Buckley, a former senator from New York (1971-77), said that was not the case. He said the Constitution gave the Senate the power to advise and consent on treaties and they, therefore, "occupy a special niche." The right of Congress to veto arms sales existed only in a statute Congress passed.

Most of the arguments raised for and against the sale during the hearing had been heard before at length.

But Percy raised a new one when he compared the Saudi deal to a 1978 sale of F-5 aircraft to Egypt. Percy said the F-5 sale had helped persuade Sadat to trust the United States and negotiate peace with Israel.

Deals Made?

Glenn took the administration to task for its political handling of the issue. He said he was outraged by tactics described in an Oct. 14 *Wall Street Journal* article that said the administration was trading political favors to win support of senators. *(Lobbying, box, p. 134)*

Glenn said he had heard no denial of the Journal article from the White House, and so he assumed it was true. If so, he said, "It just is political bribery, and I just can't use any other word for it." He said such charges were "very disturbing" when the issues involved affected U.S. national security.

Richard Fairbanks, assistant secretary of state for congressional relations, vowed to Glenn that the "press reports about wheeling and dealing and trading are not true." He said no one in the State Department had engaged in such tactics and he said he did not "know of any" such moves by the White House lobbying team.

The hearing ended on a rancorous note when Biden charged that implicit in the administration's arguments was that the sale should be approved because it would be good for Boeing Aircraft Co., the maker of the AWACS, and other contractors that stood to profit from it.

Buckley and State Department Counselor Robert C. McFarlane heatedly denied the administration ever had made such an argument.

Armed Services Action

The Foreign Relations Committee's vote followed by a few hours the Senate Armed Services Committee's approval, on a 10-5 vote, of a report declaring the AWACS sale to be in the U.S. interest and no threat to Israel.

Armed Services had no official role in considering the sale, but Chairman John Tower wanted his panel to be on record favoring it.

The two committee votes came after former Presidents Carter, Ford and Nixon declared their support for the AWACS sale. The three presidents had attended Sadat's funeral in Cairo on Oct. 10.

Carter said he thought the sale to be unwise but that the president, having made the commitment, should not be reversed by Congress.

Senate Floor Action

As the Senate vote on the issue neared, a turning point seemed to be an Oct. 21 speech against the sale by Minority Leader Robert C. Byrd, D-Va. His opposition came as a blow to the administration, which had hoped to win his

support and consequently gain other Democratic votes as well.

Byrd Speech

In his Senate speech, Byrd reviewed the range of arguments for and against the sale, and he said he thought he could argue the case either way — "to a point."

But Byrd also raised some new points in the debate. He argued, for example, that the sale might destabilize Saudi Arabia, rather than ensure its security. The sale would "vault Saudi Arabia into the position of being America's chief client state in the Middle East," Byrd said. Because of that, radical Arab groups "will perceive the Saudis as having sold out to 'the Great Satan,' America."

The administration had said the AWACS sale would improve U.S.-Saudi relations and could help induce the Saudis to cooperate in moving toward a Middle East peace.

But Byrd said that because the AWACS would be a focus for anti-Americanism among radical Arabs, it might have the opposite effect, making it more difficult politically for Saudi Arabia to act in concert with the United States.

Byrd also castigated the administration for pursuing a Middle East policy aimed at unifying the United States, Israel and Arab states against the threat of the Soviet Union on the premise that this could move the Arabs and Israel toward peace.

He said the administration should first focus on trying to help resolve the Arab-Israeli dispute, which Byrd said "transcends everything" for Arabs.

Byrd also argued that the sale would restrict Israel's ability to take the risks that might lead to peace.

"Their willingness to take such risks will be predicated upon their full confidence that the United States will stick by them," Byrd said. "Approval of the sale will give [Israeli] Prime Minister Begin no maneuvering room whatsoever to make these decisions."

In summary, Byrd said: "I do not believe this sale serves the best interests of the United States. Quite the contrary, I think it places those interests in jeopardy."

Senate Vote

The 48-52 Senate vote rejecting the resolution to veto the AWACS sale came at 5 p.m. on Oct. 28, following eight hours of debate.

As late as about two hours before the roll call, opponents, led by Republican Bob Packwood of Oregon and Democrat Alan Cranston of California, believed they could get the 51 votes needed to win.

But the tale was told, Cranston said after the vote, when Republican William S. Cohen of Maine, took the floor during the eight-hour debate to say he had changed his mind.

"Senator Cohen's decision was a turning point," Cranston said.

Cohen, whose father was Jewish but who was himself a Unitarian, told the Senate he had decided to support the sale after meeting with Reagan the previous day and receiving his assurance "that he will not allow Israel's qualitative and quantitative military edge to be eroded."

But Cohen said at the heart of his decision was the fear that, given Israel's opposition to the sale and the history of anti-Semitism, a rejection of the sale might "allow Israel to become a scapegoat" if another Arab-Israeli war erupted as an ultimate consequence.

"Israel can survive only if it is militarily superior to its enemies and only if the people of the United States remain clear in their understanding of Israel's struggle and unequivocal in their commitment to its existence," Cohen said.

If the sale were rejected and conflict in the Middle East occurred again, he said, "I do not want to hear any voices in the United States say [of the Israelis]: 'If only they had not been so intransigent; if only they had agreed not to interfere; if only they had not brought this mess — this death — upon themselves.'"

Cohen's speech came only hours after freshman Republican Slade Gorton of Washington, a cosponsor of the anti-AWACS resolution, helped turn the momentum in Reagan's direction by confirming that his mind, too, had been changed by presidential persuasion.

Gorton's intentions had become known the previous day, when it was also disclosed that Mark Andrews, R-S.D., probably would do the same, which he did.

Reagan Letter

Gorton said his and Andrews' votes were won by a letter Reagan had promised weeks earlier and sent to the Senate on the day of the vote. In it, Reagan offered assurances that the Saudi AWACS would not be misused or compromised. *(Text, p. 25-E)*

In a press conference after he told the Senate his decision, Gorton said he, Andrews and four other Republicans met Oct. 6 — the day Egyptian President Sadat was assassinated — to work out a draft of assurances they wanted from Reagan.

The draft was given to Vice President George Bush and James A. Baker III, the White House chief of staff, the next day, Gorton said. But the White House kept the text of the letter open until the day of the vote so it could be altered to meet the concerns of as many senators as possible.

The other GOP senators who sought the letter were Robert W. Kasten Jr. of Wisconsin, Mack Mattingly of Georgia, Frank H. Murkowski of Alaska and Dan Quayle of Indiana. All but Kasten voted against the resolution of disapproval.

"The letter was very important," said Percy, chairman of the Foreign Relations Committee. "It was an assurance senators wanted."

But sale foe John Glenn dismissed the Reagan letter as meaningless. Besides the fact that it was not binding, he said, "there wasn't anything new in it."

Reagan's letter said Saudi Arabia had consented to a "detailed plan" to ensure the security of the AWACS and its components, to share all information gathered by the planes with the United States, to desist from sharing the planes or their information with any third country, and to operate the planes only over Saudi territory unless it had U.S. consent to do otherwise.

The president also pledged that the sale would enhance "the stability and security of the area."

Perhaps most importantly, Reagan assured the Senate, the "agreements as they concern organizational command and control structure for the operation of AWACS are of such a nature to guarantee that the commitments above will be honored."

Opponents of the sale noted that each of those commitments already had been made by Haig in testimony before the Foreign Relations Committee on Oct. 1. Most of the commitments were no more specific than the routine requirements of U.S. arms sales contracts with foreign governments.

But a key issue had been the administration's inability to meet demands for joint U.S. control of the Saudi AWACS.

Gorton said Reagan's assurance that the command structure would "guarantee that the commitments. . . .will be honored" satisfied him on that point. In fact, Gorton said he himself had written that paragraph of Reagan's letter.

"It is very difficult for me to see how that commitment can be made without some form of American control or joint crewing," Gorton said.

An equally key part of the letter, Gorton told the Senate, was that Reagan promised to cancel the deal, under which the first AWACS aircraft was to be delivered in 1985, "in the event any of the agreements is breached."

"This does not mean that I . . . am totally happy with this proposal," Gorton said. "But it does swing the balance to a different ultimate conclusion from our conclusions at the time of the submission of this proposed sale."

Nevertheless, some opponents of the sale compared the Reagan letter to one sent to Congress in 1978 by Defense Secretary Harold Brown, in which Brown promised that the F-15s sold to Saudi Arabia that year would not get some of the equipment included in the AWACS package.

Carl Levin, D-Mich., told the Senate that "given the consistency of the [Reagan administration's] commitment to the pledges made in Secretary Brown's letter, I would suggest that we ought to view the promises of the president with at least a healthy degree of skepticism if not cynicism."

Other Switches

Cranston said Edward Zorinsky of Nebraska, the only Democrat to cosponsor the resolution but vote against it, had acknowledged that a visit with Reagan on the day of the vote had changed his mind as well.

"Ed Zorinsky said the president told him, 'How can I meet with a foreign leader and have him believe I'm in charge of the government if I can't sell five airplanes?'" Cranston said, repeating Zorinsky's explanation for switching.

Three other first-term Republicans had cosponsored the resolution of disapproval but announced well before the vote that they had changed their minds: Orrin G. Hatch of Utah, Larry Pressler of South Dakota and Alan K. Simpson of Wyoming.

Jepsen Switch

The first firm indication that Reagan was likely to pull out the victory came the day before the vote, when Roger Jepsen, R-Iowa, surprised Washington by announcing he had changed his mind.

Jepsen was key because in May he had declared: "This sale undermines the security of Israel" and "I pledge my efforts and my vote to block this sale."

In a news conference, Jepsen said he had decided to support the deal "after prayerful and careful deliberation."

Jepsen said three factors had led him to switch. First, he said he had been given "highly classified information" that eased his concerns. Secondly, he said the "national and worldwide attention created by this debate have changed the stakes involved" by making it clear that a defeat for Reagan "would curb his ability to achieve the many foreign and domestic policy objectives necessary for world peace and domestic economic stability."

Finally, Jepsen said that when he ran for the Senate in 1978, he told the people of Iowa "a senator should be the hired man of the people." He said "large numbers of Iowans" had urged him to support Reagan on the AWACS sale. "This senator has heard their voice," Jepsen said.

Jepsen added that he had "spent all weekend discussing this with my wife," who he said was fervently religious and a strong supporter of Israel, and she had agreed with his decision.

Under questioning by reporters, Jepsen said he received his classified information from the administration and from Sen. Jeremiah Denton, R-Ala., a former U.S. Navy admiral and test pilot.

But sale opponents Glenn and Biden derisively demanded during the debate the next day that the Senate go into closed session so Jepsen could share his "highly classified information."

"I suggest that it might be in order for the distinguished senator from Iowa, who has that highly classified information, to perhaps take us into closed session so that we could share that information, which we apparently have not been given," Glenn said.

As the debate drew to a close, Jepsen took the floor to respond. He protested the insinuation that he had been misleading in citing classified information as a reason for his switch.

But when Biden asked if there was "anything that you know of that warrants our being brought into closed session," Jepsen replied: "No."

Senate Debate

Despite the intense interest in the issue, the final day's debate was lackluster for the most part, less resembling a true debate than the religious revival practice of various individuals standing up to "witness" the reasons for their faith.

But the arguments for and against the sale were repeated and dissected at length.

Proponents of the sale said it would warm U.S.-Saudi relations and encourage the Saudis to be constructive in efforts to achieve a Middle East peace. Saudi Arabia had been moderate in its oil pricing policies, they said, and was instrumental in getting a cease-fire in Lebanon earlier in the year between Israel and Palestinian guerrillas.

Opponents of the sale charged that any signs of moderation on the part of the Saudis merely reflected a Saudi conclusion that moderation was temporarily useful and did not reflect the true Saudi character. The Saudis remained sworn to destroy Israel, they said, and had rejected the Camp David peace process despite the hope it offered for a Middle East peace.

Proponents of the sale said that vetoing it would chill U.S.-Saudi relations and confirm the suspicion in Arab nations that the United States will always put Israel first in considering its Middle East policies, creating further opportunities for Soviet influence in the Arab world.

In the wake of the assassination of Egyptian President Sadat, the proponents said, it would be a critical mistake for the United States to risk the loss of its second-best Arab friend, Saudi Arabia.

Opponents of the sale said the Saudis eventually would recover their pride if the planes were withheld and, in any event, had nowhere else to turn. They would have to rely on the United States to prevent any Soviet military moves into the region, they said.

The sale proponents reiterated the administration's argument that the combination of the AWACS and fitting the Saudi F-15s with the AIM-9L missile would be a giant step toward defending Saudi oil fields on the east coast of the Arabian peninsula from air attacks that might be launched across the Persian Gulf by the Soviet Union, Iran or Iraq.

With its ability to detect low-level incoming aircraft at least 15 minutes in advance, the proponents said, the AWACS would give Saudi fighter planes time enough to meet an attacker before the foe could strike the oil fields.

Opponents said those same capabilities would endanger Israel by altering the military balance in the region.

In past Middle East wars, the opponents said, the lack of a significant air capability had left the Saudis unable to add militarily to the Arab war effort. With AWACS and F-15s equipped with AIM-9L missiles, they said, the Saudis might not be able to sit out the next war — thus endangering Israel.

'Joint Control'

The opponents also said the United States should not entrust the AWACS to sole Saudi control. Only joint U.S.-Saudi control would provide confidence that the planes would not be used against Israel and would not be compromised, they said.

Proponents said joint U.S. control was politically impossible, given Saudi sensitivities about possible Arab charges that they had become an American client. They argued that if the United States refused to sell the Saudis the AWACS, the Saudis would acquire a similar plane from Britain or another source, and the result would be a loss of U.S. influence in the region.

Those in favor of the sale also argued that in the event of a Persian Gulf conflict involving the United States, the Saudi AWACS would be a valuable air surveillance system compatible with U.S. forces and already in place.

Moreover, those for the sale argued that to veto it after Reagan had invested so much prestige would undercut his ability to conduct foreign policy, perhaps irrevocably. If the sale were defeated, they said, no foreign government would feel it could rely on Reagan's commitments. ∎

Canada Maritime Treaty

A treaty designed to resolve an East Coast maritime boundary dispute between the United States and Canada was approved by the Senate April 29.

The Senate vote was 91-0. *(Vote 84, p. 18-S)*

In the treaty (Exec U, 96th Cong, 1st Sess), the two countries agreed to submit the dispute to the World Court for binding arbitration. The disagreement involved jurisdiction over fishing and oil leasing in the Georges Bank off Cape Cod, one of the world's richest fishing grounds.

Canada had not ratified the treaty as of the end of 1981.

Background

The treaty was one of two agreements (Exec U, V; 96th Cong, 1st sess) signed March 29, 1979, after nearly two years of active negotiation.

The Maritime Boundary Settlement Treaty provided for World Court binding arbitration of a dispute between the United States and Canada over about 5,000 square miles of the Georges Bank. Overlapping claims resulted in the mid-1970s when both countries claimed control over the seas within 200 miles of their coasts.

In addition to determining fishing grounds, the treaty aimed to resolve conflicting claims over offshore oil fields in the Georges Bank. Both countries already had taken steps to claim the area for oil production. The United States had issued leases for drilling in the area, prompting outcries from fishermen and environmentalists.

Under the boundary treaty, the two countries agreed to ask the International Court of Justice (the World Court) to appoint a special five-member panel to arbitrate the conflicting claims. If the court failed to appoint such a panel within six months after the treaty took effect, the two countries could jointly appoint a five-member panel to arbitrate the dispute.

State Department officials said the arbitration process could take several years. In the meantime, Reagan said the United States would allow Canadians to fish in all areas claimed by Canada.

A companion East Coast Fisheries Agreement would have established conservation guidelines for North Atlantic fishing grounds. Its most controversial provisions would have set shares of various fish species that could be caught by U.S. and Canadian fishermen.

In the disputed Georges Bank area, the fishing treaty allocated 73 percent of the scallops to Canadian fishermen, and 83 percent of the cod, 79 percent of the haddock and 66 percent of the herring to the United States.

A major goal of the treaty was to foster conservation of fish stocks that, in some cases, could be depleted in a few years to dangerously low levels.

U.S. fishermen were especially upset by the share of scallops allocated to Canada because of their high market value. They also complained that the treaty was permanent and would have allowed only minor changes in the fishing allocations.

In 1980, Sens. Claiborne Pell, D-R. I., and Edward M. Kennedy, D-Mass., proposed amending the fishing treaty to terminate it after three years and to give the United States control over scallop fishing in the western portion of the Georges Bank.

Those senators also advocated separating the fishing and maritime boundary treaties. However, Carter administration officials said that Canada had demanded the linking of the two treaties.

In submitting the treaties to the Senate in 1979, Carter said they were fair to both countries and "an important contribution to good relations" between them. Delay in approving them could lead to "serious irritants" in relations, he said.

But the Senate did delay action on the treaties. The Senate Foreign Relations Committee did not hold hearings on them until April, 1980. Following the hearings, administration officials attempted to work out a compromise acceptable to both Canada and the New England fishermen.

While the Senate delayed, Canadian officials fumed. Mark MacGuigan, Canada's secretary of state for external affairs, said the dispute over the treaty "is not only the most serious bilateral issue we have with the United States. It is the most serious bilateral issue we have with any country."

Fishing Treaty Withdrawn

Shortly after taking office, President Reagan assigned a special ambassador, Rozanne Ridgway, to review the two

treaties. As a result of that review, Reagan determined that chances for Senate approval of the fishing treaty were nil.

In a March 6 letter to Charles H. Percy, R-Ill., chairman of the Senate Foreign Relations Committee, Reagan said he was withdrawing the controversial fishing treaty and asked the Senate to quickly approve the maritime boundaries settlement treaty. The two treaties had been legally linked, but Reagan proposed amending the boundaries treaty to permit it to take effect without the fisheries agreement.

"After examining the matter, it is clear to me that the fishery treaty cannot be ratified in a form that would be acceptable to Canada," Reagan said in a reference to the Pell-Kennedy amendments.

Reagan announced withdrawal of the fishing treaty just four days before he visited Ottawa, Canada, where he met with Prime Minister Pierre Trudeau and addressed the Canadian Parliament.

Expressing displeasure with Reagan's action, Trudeau refused to say whether he would accept the separation of the two treaties. "The boundaries are one thing, and the management of the fisheries is another, but they have to go together," he said at press conference March 12.

Senate Response

Percy said that even though both countries were unhappy with the failure to resolve both the fishing and boundary issues, "maybe we'll be equally unhappy" once the fisheries treaty was withdrawn.

At a Foreign Relations Committee hearing March 18, U. S. fishing lobbyists and six New England senators said they were pleased with Reagan's decision to separate the two treaties.

"I would like to commend President Reagan for recognizing the futility of attempting to link" the two treaties, Pell said. The fishing pact was "very much against the interests of our fishermen," he said.

Pell rejected claims that the Georges Bank would be overfished if there were no formal agreement restricting catches. Even if scallops were overfished, he said, "they will regenerate themselves" because it will no longer be economical to fish for them.

"I don't think we should get too worried about letting a little time go by" before seeking another fishing agreement, he said.

In response, Ambassador Ridgway told the committee that the United States would not seek to renegotiate the fishing treaty until after the Georges Bank boundaries were established.

Several senators said they were concerned about Trudeau's statement that Canadians might try to "grab" all the fishing in the Georges Bank.

But William S. Cohen, R-Maine, said: "I don't think there will be an attempt by anybody to grab it all."

In one concession to Canada, Reagan had said the United States would allow Canadians to fish in all of the Georges Bank area claimed by Canada. In the past, the United States prevented Canadians from fishing in part of the area, while Canada kept U.S. fishermen out of another part.

Cohen said he approved of that concession if "it is not intended to set any sort of a precedent."

Mark B. Feldman, acting legal adviser for the State Department, said the concession would not set a precedent or affect the U.S. boundary case before the World Court.

Senate Action

The Foreign Relations Committee reported the boundary treaty April 1 (Exec Rept 97-5), with technical amendments removing references to the fishing treaty.

In supporting Senate approval of the boundary treaty April 29, Kennedy said the boundary dispute "has gone on too long and has affected our relationship too deeply. Now it is time to put aside our differences and move on." ∎

Wallenberg Citizenship

On Oct. 5, in large part because of efforts by the Hungarian-born Rep. Tom Lantos, D-Calif., Raoul Wallenberg became the second person in modern American history to be awarded honorary citizenship. The first was former British Prime Minister Winston Churchill, in 1963.

Wallenberg, a Swedish diplomat operating in Hungary toward the end of World War II, was instrumental in getting Lantos and his wife Annette safely out of Nazi-controlled Hungary. Shortly afterward, Wallenberg was arrested by the invading Russians and has not been seen since. For several years, Mrs. Lantos, founder of the International Free Raoul Wallenberg Committee, worked for his release.

Congress voted to make Wallenberg an honorary citizen and instructed the president to ascertain from the Soviet Union Wallenberg's whereabouts and to secure his freedom. Lantos said he hoped Wallenberg's new status would force the Soviets to cooperate.

The Senate acted on Aug. 3, passing by voice vote a resolution (S J Res 65) making Wallenberg an honorary citizen. The House on Sept. 22 passed a similar resolution (H J Res 220), introduced by Lantos, on a 396-2 vote, then formally replaced it with the Senate resolution. President Reagan signed the Senate resolution into law (PL 97-54) on Oct. 5. *(Vote 200, p. 68-H)*

The two House members who voted against the resolution were John M. Ashbrook, R-Ohio, and Henry J. Hyde, R-Ill. An aide said Ashbrook voted that way simply because "John doesn't think Congress should be granting American citizenship to anyone."

Hyde, who said he was "not entirely comfortable" with his vote, agreed that Wallenberg was "an incredible hero." But he said Wallenberg's actions were "for a religious group with very little connection with America."

In 1980 Congress overwhelmingly passed a more modest resolution (S Con Res 117) expressing concern over Wallenberg's fate.

Protected Hungarian Jews

Wallenberg was a Swedish businessman when World War II broke out. He had studied architecture at the University of Michigan, which now holds an annual lecture in his honor. In 1944 the United States asked Sweden, as a neutral nation, to aid in protecting the lives of Hungarian Jews facing extermination by the Nazis. Wallenberg volunteered to help, and he has been credited by Jewish groups with saving at least 100,000 lives.

To do this he pulled Jews off trains headed for death camps, printed thousands of special passports allowing Jews to escape from the Nazis and established "safe houses" — one of which Lantos used. ∎

Development Banks Put in Reconciliation

Authorizations for U.S. contributions to four international development banks and their affiliates were included in the omnibus reconciliation bill (HR 3982 — PL 97-35) that cut $35.2 billion in federal spending for fiscal 1982. *(Reconciliation, p. 256)*

The House Banking Committee had attached authorizations for the development banks, such as the World Bank, to the reconciliation bill in a political maneuver. Committee members argued that bank funding — always an unpopular item on Capitol Hill — might not pass as separate legislation. Committee members argued, successfully, that the only way to get the bank funding through Congress was to attach it to legislation that was certain to be passed.

The major issue was a $3.24 billion authorization for the International Development Association, an arm of the World Bank that made no-interest loans to the world's poorest nations.

The conference agreement on reconciliation produced victories both for President Reagan, who supported funding for IDA, and for some of his Republican supporters in the House, who opposed the funding. The final reconciliation bill authorized the IDA funds, but placed limits on annual donations that might be unacceptable to the World Bank.

Reagan had proposed to pay the IDA donation in installments of $540 million in fiscal 1981, $850 million in 1982 and $1.85 billion in fiscal 1983 to meet a three-year schedule stipulated in a 1979 understanding with other IDA donors.

But Congress reduced the Reagan request by $40 million for fiscal 1981, and the reconciliation bill placed limits on future appropriations of $850 million in fiscal 1982 and $945 million in fiscal 1983. That meant that, at a minimum, a fourth installment of $945 million would be necessary to complete the $3.24 billion payment.

Congress appropriated the $500 million for IDA in 1981 in the omnibus continuing resolution (HR 3512 — PL 97-12), which cleared June 4. *(Continuing resolution, p. 281)*

The reconciliation bill also authorized $8.8 billion for the U.S. share of a $40 billion general capital increase for the International Bank for Reconstruction and Development (IBRD), the World Bank agency that made loans at near-market interest rates.

As envisioned in the original proposal, the bill limited actual appropriations to be paid-in to the IBRD to 7.5 percent of the U.S. share, or $658 million. The remaining $8.1 billion was "callable capital" that served to guarantee the bank's borrowing. A separate appropriation would be required before any of that sum could be called.

Other Development Banks

Other development bank authorizations included in the reconciliation bill were:

● $360 million, the Reagan request, for a U.S. subscription to the African Development Bank, which had asked some non-African nations to become members. Of that amount, $90 million was to be paid in over five years. The rest was callable capital. The bill limited appropriations of the U.S. subcription to no more than $18 million in each of fiscal years 1982, 1983 and 1984. The fiscal 1981 continuing appropriations bill contained another $18 million. The final payment would be made in fiscal 1985.

● $275 million to restore a 10 percent cut Congress made in 1980 in a $2.7 billion U.S. donation to an $8 billion replenishment of the Inter-American Development Bank (IADB), of which $206 million was to be paid-in capital. Of the $275 million, $20.6 million, or 7.5 percent, was to be paid in. *(1980 Almanac p. 343)*

● $70 million to restore a 10 percent cut Congress made in 1980 in a $700 million U.S. donation to the IADB's concessional lending facility, the Fund for Special Operations (FSO). The U.S. contribution was scheduled to be made in four installments of $175 million each in fiscal years 1980-83, and conferees stipulated that no more than $175 million could be appropriated in fiscal years 1982 and 1983 to complete the U.S. payments.

The bill also authorized $15.7 million for fiscal 1982 to cover part of the $600 million U.S. share of a previous FSO replenishment that was to have been paid in 1977-79 but of which Congress never appropriated $125.3 million. The administration proposed to pay the remaining $109 million in installments of $31 million in fiscal 1983 and $39.3 million in each of fiscal years 1984 and 1985.

● $67 million to make up a 15 percent cut Congress made in 1980 in a $445 million U.S. donation to the second replenishment of the Asian Development Fund, the concessional arm of the Asian Development Bank. Conferees stipulated that no more than $111 million could be appropriated for these payments in each of fiscal 1982 and 1983.

The bill also authorized $14 million as partial payment of an overdue U.S. donation of $56 million to the Asian fund's first replenishment, to which the United States pledged $180 million.

Background

The international development banks posed an ironic political problem for the Reagan administration.

As had happened previously in his young administration, Republican President Reagan found himself asking conservative GOP members of Congress to alter their stance on one of their pet issues.

The World Bank and other multilateral development banks were traditional targets of many Republicans, especially in the House, where conservative opposition killed one bank funding bill and substantially reduced another one in 1980. *(1980 Almanac pp. 343, 347)*

Moreover, conservative GOP members had reviled Democrats for years for supporting U.S. donations to multilateral banks, which they disliked on a variety of counts.

During political campaigns, Democrats who had voted to contribute to the banks, or for other foreign aid, often were charged by Republican opponents with being spendthrift.

IDA VI

Known as the "soft loan window" of the World Bank, IDA was established to make loans at no interest to the poorest nations to help them develop their economies. IDA's donors had replenished its capital five times since it was founded in 1960.

Foreign Aid Cuts Made in Reconciliation Bill

The impact of budget reconciliation on fiscal 1982 U.S. foreign affairs programs was to be borne by relatively small programs, according to reductions effected by the Senate Foreign Relations and House Foreign Affairs committees.

Both panels were instructed to cut $250 million in fiscal 1982 budget authority from the current policy baseline and their reconciliation cuts generally were similar. Foreign Relations made $267 million in cuts.

The committees took their reconciliation cuts from small accounts because in many instances the current policy baselines for them were higher than the Reagan request. In some cases this allowed the committees to authorize amounts higher than Reagan requested but still get credit for reconciliation cuts.

For example, Reagan asked $95 million for Peace Corps operations in fiscal 1982, but the reconciliation baseline was $114 million. Thus, though both committees added $10 million to the Peace Corps request, making it $105 million, each received credit for cutting the Peace Corps by $9 million below the reconciliation baseline.

Conference Agreement

Conferees from the House Foreign Affairs and Senate Foreign Relations committees had little difficulty reaching agreement on the four differences in reconciliation cuts falling within their joint jurisdiction. Conferees resolved their differences by July 29 in a "paper conference" conducted largely by staff.

The reconciliation bill:

● Authorized $256 million, the House figure, for fiscal 1982 voluntary contributions to international organizations, primarily the United Nations. That was $27 million more than the Senate figure and a savings of $29 million from the reconciliation baseline. The fiscal 1981 continuing resolution (H J Res 412 — PL 96-86) appropriated $210 million for that item.

● Authorized $455 million, the Senate figure, for assessed contributions to international organizations, such as the United Nations.

That was stated as a reconciliation savings of $100 million. However, $40 million of that savings was not an actual cut in the amount the United States would spend on assessed contributions but resulted from a Senate amendment accelerating a Reagan plan to defer some U.S. payments until later years. Under the amendment, the deferments would occur over three years instead of four.

The House had authorized $495 million, the amount Reagan requested. The final $455 million figure was up from $397 million in the fiscal 1981 continuing resolution and $376 million in fiscal 1981 authority that remained after a budget rescission.

● Authorized $20 million, the House figure, for the American Schools and Hospitals Abroad program, the amount appropriated in fiscal 1981 and a $2 million reconciliation savings. The Senate bill had authorized the program at $12 million. Reagan requested only $7.5 million.

● Deleted a House authorization of $2 million to establish the African Development Foundation, which Congress authorized in 1980 but did not fund. The deletion voided a reconciliation savings of $176,000. The administration requested no funding for the foundation.

The bill also authorized these items which were not in dispute between the two houses:

● $37.7 million, the Reagan request, for International Narcotics Control. The fiscal 1981 authorization was $38.6 million.

● $12 million, the Reagan request, for the Inter-American Foundation. The 1981 authorization was $16 million.

● $105 million for the Peace Corps, an increase of $10 million above the Reagan request. The 1981 authorization was $118 million.

● $98.3 million, the Reagan request, for the Board for International Broadcasting. The 1981 authorization was $86.8 million.

● $18.3 million for the Arms Control and Disarmament Agency, an increase of $1.5 million above the Reagan request. The 1981 authorization was $20.7 million.

● $27 million, the Reagan request, for International Disaster Assistance. The 1981 authorization was $25 million.

In December 1979, after 18 months of negotiations, the United States agreed with 32 other donor nations to a sixth replenishment of $12 billion, known as IDA VI. The U.S. share of $3.24 billion was to have been made in three installments of $1.08 billion each.

IDA VI was to have gone into effect on July 1, 1980, but Congress failed to authorize the U.S. share. The agreement could not go into effect without the United States.

Rather than let IDA run out of funds, other donors tided the bank over with a $1.6 billion "bridging arrangement," but those advance contributions were exhausted in April, 1981.

The Reagan administration, intent on cutting federal spending, debated internally whether to attempt to renegotiate the IDA VI agreement. An early plan by David A. Stockman, director of the Office of Management and Budget, was to revoke the U.S. pledge to IDA VI and negotiate to cut the donation in half.

Instead, Reagan in March proposed stretching out the U.S. payments, with the following schedule: $540 million in fiscal 1981, $850 million in fiscal 1982 and $1.85 billion in fisal 1983. He asked Congress to appropriate the payments in separate appropriations bills, including a fiscal 1981 supplemental appropriation for the first installment.

The amounts in the annual appropriations could be altered without abrogating the U.S. commitment to IDA. But the $3.24 billion total pledge could not be cut without either breaching or renegotiating IDA VI.

Capital Increase

Also facing Congress was a request to authorize the U.S. share of a General Capital Increase (GCI) for the

World Bank that was agreed to in January 1980. The GCI was to double — from $40 billion to $80 billion — the capital available to the World Bank's "hard loan" window, which made loans to developing countries at near commercial interest rates.

The intention was to allow the bank, formally called the International Bank for Reconstruction and Development (IBRD), to increase its lending by 5 percent in real terms, after inflation, during the 1980s.

The U.S. share was to be 21.95 percent of the GCI, or $8,807,561,350. Only 7.5 percent of that amount, or $658.3 million, had to be appropriated as "paid-in capital." Reagan in March proposed appropriating that amount in six equal installments of $109.7 million each, beginning in fiscal 1982.

The remaining amount was "callable capital," similar to a loan guarantee.

If Congress had failed to authorize the U.S. pledge, the United States would have lost its veto over changes in the World Bank's charter.

Congressional debate on the issue came during a period of transition for the bank. Robert S. McNamara, bank president since 1968, retired in April, and was succeeded by A. W. Clausen, former president of BankAmerica Corp.

Foreign Relations Committee

By voice vote on March 25, the Senate Foreign Relations Committee ordered reported an administration bill (S 786 — S Rept 97-36) authorizing $3.24 billion over three years for IDA.

The bill had been introduced for the administration by committee Chairman Charles H. Percy, R-Ill., only the previous day.

The Foreign Relations Committee was able to move so rapidly on the IDA VI authorization bill because Percy and most other members of the committee strongly supported multilateral development banks.

But their haste derived from pressure being put on the United States by other IDA donors, who were scheduled to meet in Paris the following week to discuss how to proceed in the face of the U.S. delay.

Before voting on the measure, Percy announced that he had spoken to Jesse Helms, R-N.C., the most strident World Bank opponent on the committee. Percy said Helms, who was not present, raised no objection to reporting S 786 without delay.

S 786 also authorized U.S. membership in the African Development Bank (AFDB), with an initial subscription of $360 million in AFDB which would require federal budget outlays of $90 million over five years.

As written by the administration, the bill also would have authorized late contributions to the Inter-American Development Bank (IADB), the IADB's Fund for Special Operations and to the Asian Development Fund.

But to smooth the way, the committee deleted those provisions and later inserted them in another bill, S 1195. The committee reported that bill (S Rept 97-76) on May 15.

In a committee hearing on bank issues, Ernest B. Johnston Jr., a deputy assistant secretary of state, pledged that "the Reagan administration is committed to an all-out maximum effort to pass this legislation...."

R. T. McNamar, deputy secretary of the Treasury, reiterated the argument that multilateral aid made economic sense because pooled contributions allowed far greater aid to poor nations than did bilateral aid.

But in keeping with a pronounced Reagan administration emphasis on military-related aid over development assistance, McNamara and Johnston also noted that nations important to U.S. interests were major IDA aid recipients.

"One has only to list a few of the major IDA borrowers — India, Bangladesh, Egypt, Indonesia, Sudan, Pakistan and Kenya — to see the strategic importance of the political stability these [multilateral] institutions offer," Johnston said.

Senate Floor Action

The Senate passed S 786 April 29 on a vote of 58-32. In a switch from previous years, most Republicans supported the bill. *(Vote 87, p. 18-S)*

In arguing for the bill, Foreign Relations Chairman Percy repeatedly emphasized administration support for it.

Percy inserted in the *Congressional Record* a joint letter from Secretary of State Alexander M. Haig Jr. and Treasury Secretary Donald T. Regan. The letter asked for support for "prompt passage of this legislation, which is vital to U.S. foreign policy and to international economic relations."

On two separate votes, the Senate rejected an amendment by Dennis DeConcini, D-Ariz., to cut IDA funding by $810 million, or 25 percent.

First, by a 30-61 vote, the Senate refused to table a Percy substitute that provided full funding and merely stated how the first two portions of the IDA money would be appropriated: $540 million in fiscal year 1981 and $850 million in fiscal 1982. *(Vote 85, p. 18-S)*

Next, the Senate formally accepted the Percy substitute, on a vote of 58-33. *(Vote 86, p. 18-S)*

DeConcini argued that funding in the IDA bill represented a "hefty" increase over previous years at the same time domestic programs were being reduced.

"If this country cannot afford to continue providing support at existing levels [for] programs that directly benefit Americans, then we cannot afford to continue year after year to augment our contribution to these institutions over which we, as the Congress, have virtually no control," he said.

On June 17, the Senate passed by a 65-27 vote S 1195, authorizing the $8.8 billion U.S. contribution to the International Bank for Reconstruction and Development. S 1195 also authorized payments to the Inter-American Development Bank (IADB), the IADB Fund for Special Operations and the Asian Development Fund. *(Vote 156, p. 29-S)*

House Banking Committee Action

By voice vote and with little debate, the House Banking Committee May 6 approved HR 3439 authorizing the $3.24 billion U.S. contribution to IDA. The committee never formally reported the measure, however.

Despite administration requests for rapid action, resistance to the measure among many hard-line conservatives remained strong. Because of that, House Democratic leaders had said they would not move the IDA VI legislation in 1980 until the Senate passed it and the administration persuaded House Republicans to back it.

Senate passage of S 786 on April 29, with Republican support, apparently led House Banking Committee Chairman Fernand J. St Germain, D-R.I., and other committee Democrats to proceed with HR 3439.

Other contributions in the House bill were:

• The U.S. contribution to the General Capital Increase of the IBRD. In an attempt to reduce the political hurdles facing such a large contribution, the committee dropped the $8.8 billion figure from the bill. As reported, the bill specifically authorized only the $658.3 million in paid-in capital.

Instead of authorizing the $8.15 billion in callable capital, the bill merely instructed the U.S. representative to the bank to subscribe the full U.S. share due the IBRD. The bill also eliminated the requirement that callable capital be included in appropriations bills.

• $360 million for an initial U.S. subscription to the African Development Bank.

• $275 million for the U.S. subscription to the Inter-American Development Bank (IADB) and $70 million for a contribution to the IADB's Fund for Special Operations.

• $66.8 million for the Asian Development Fund (ADF).

Reconciliation Action

Faced with seemingly insurmountable political problems on the development banks issue, Democrats on the House Banking Committee decided to use budget reconciliation to get the bank authorizations — especially the $3.24 billion for IDA — past House critics.

For a time, Senate Budget Committee policy threatened to kill the strategy. That committee maintained for several weeks that "extraneous" matter — items not making reconciliation savings — should not be put in the reconciliation bill.

Banking Committee Strategy

On June 8, the full Banking Committee agreed to a plan by Democrats to put funding for IDA VI and several other development banks into its reconciliation package.

Committee Democrats originally wanted to put the banks in the reconciliation bill to help offset cuts in domestic housing programs. The proposed tradeoff between foreign and domestic funds was thwarted, however, when the House Budget Committee ruled that Banking could claim no credit toward reconciliation by limiting the fiscal 1982 payment to IDA VI.

Some Republicans then said IDA VI should be taken to the floor as a separate bill.

But because of its political sensitivity, the Democrats insisted on putting IDA VI into the reconciliation bill. To comply with the Budget Committee ruling, the Banking Committee limited fiscal 1982 and 1983 authorizations for all development banks by subtracting IDA VI authorizations from the other banks.

The committee authorized the full $3.24 billion for IDA VI but limited appropriations to $298 million in fiscal 1982, $540 million in fiscal 1983 and $540 million in fiscal 1984. The rest of the IDA funds were to be appropriated later.

That payment schedule would have breached the 1979 understanding that the United States would make its contribution within three years. But Banking Committee aides said that was part of the strategy. The hope, they said, was that the schedule would lead the administration to lobby the Senate to include IDA VI in its reconciliation bill.

Banking aides said that if the committee's plan survived House floor action on reconciliation, and the Senate put the development banks into its version, a House-Senate conference could agree to the full IDA VI authorization and delete the limits on the payments.

Banking Committee Republicans accepted the strategy "only because it seemed far easier to get it through this way," said James C. Orr, committee minority counsel.

The strategy essentially worked, but through a different route: the House retained the authorizations for the banks in its reconciliation bill, but the Senate did not include them in its version. The issue was left to the House-Senate conference committee on the reconciliation bill.

Reconciliation Conference

Conferees agreed July 29 to leave the $3.24 billion for IDA in the reconciliation bill (HR 3982).

The agreement on IDA — the final issue in the mammoth reconciliation conference — was reached only after Reagan telephoned IDA's fiercest critics — Rep. C. W. "Bill" Young, R-Fla., and Rep. Jack F. Kemp, R-N.Y. — July 28 to say he wanted IDA in the bill. Kemp and Young acquiesced to let the reconciliation conference conclude. But Young said they did so reluctantly and would not retreat in a fight over the 1982 foreign aid appropriations bill, in which they were holding hostage an $850 million installment on the IDA donation. *(Appropriations bill, p. 339)*

Though the IDA VI authorization's presence in reconciliation promised IDA a victory its supporters had feared unattainable, World Bank officials said terms the conferees attached made it uncertain IDA could accept it. Under a 1979 understanding, the $3.24 billion U.S. share of the $12 billion replenishment was to be paid in three years, with IDA VI taking effect only with the U.S. share.

But to appease Kemp and Young, the conferees put "caps" on IDA VI appropriations of $850 million in fiscal 1982 and $945 million in 1983 — meaning the remaining $945 million could be paid in 1984 at the earliest, stretching out U.S. payments to at least four years.

The conference version was a distinct improvement for IDA over the original reconciliation bill, which contained more stringent caps.

Other Banks. Conferees also kept in the reconciliation bill authorizations for other development banks: the International Bank for Reconstruction and Development, the non-controversial "hard loan" window of the World Bank; the African Development Bank; the Inter-American Development Bank and its Fund for Special Operations; and the Asian Development Fund. ∎

Non-Proliferation

President Reagan on July 16 announced his policy on steps the United States would take to restrict the spread of nuclear weapons.

The next day, both houses of Congress unanimously passed resolutions calling on Reagan to take more sweeping and specific nuclear non-proliferation actions than his policy embraced.

Sen. John Glenn, D-Ohio, and Rep. Dennis E. Eckart, D-Ohio, introduced the resolutions prior to Reagan's announcement, saying they hoped to prod the president into

Canada. The final summit communiqué, issued July 21, mentioned non-proliferation only in passing.

Reagan Policy

Although most of its points were vaguely worded, the Reagan policy added up to a sharp change in emphasis from former President Carter's non-proliferation policy.

Carter had emphasized U.S. restrictions on exports of nuclear material and equipment that could be used to build weapons. In asking other countries to restrict nuclear exports, the United States should set an example by restricting its own exports, Carter said. *(1977 Almanac p. 27-E)*

The Reagan policy emphasized the opposite: By improving its reputation as a reliable supplier of nuclear technology to other countries, the United States could win back some of the nuclear business it lost under Carter and would be in a better position to enforce non-proliferation standards, the president said.

Reagan also put greater reliance than did Carter on international inspections (called "safeguards") of nuclear facilities to detect nuclear weapons-building efforts.

Reagan's "policy framework" included seven points under which the United States would:

● "Seek to prevent the spread of nuclear explosives to additional countries as a fundamental national security and foreign policy objective."

● "Strive to reduce the motivation for acquiring nuclear explosives by working to improve regional and global stability and to promote understanding of the legitimate security concerns of other states."

As an example of what it meant by that point, the administration proposed to restore military aid and advanced weapons sales to Pakistan. Carter had accused Pakistan of developing a nuclear weapons capability, but Reagan aides said Pakistan might be persuaded to drop that effort if it felt militarily secure. On September 16, the administration presented Congress with a plan for $3.18 billion in economic and military aid to Pakistan over six years.

● "Continue to support adherence to the Treaty on the Non-proliferation of Nuclear Weapons and to the Treaty for the Prohibition of Nuclear Weapons in Latin America (Treaty of Tlateloco) by countries that have not accepted those treaties."

Reagan said he would "promptly" ask the Senate to ratify Protocol I to the Treaty of Tlateloco, which would prevent the United States from basing nuclear weapons in its territories in Latin America (such as Puerto Rico). The protocol had been stalled in the Senate since 1978. *(Box, this page.)*

● "View a material violation of these treaties or an international safeguards agreement as having profound consequences for international order and United States bilateral relations, and also view any nuclear explosion by a non-nuclear-weapon state with grave concern."

● "Strongly support and continue to work with other nations to stengthen the International Atomic Energy Agency [IAEA] to provide for an improved international safeguards regime."

● "Seek to work more effectively with other countries to forge agreement on measures for combatting the risks of proliferation."

● "Continue to inhibit the transfer of nuclear materials, equipment and technology, particularly where the danger

---

Latin Nuclear Arms Treaty

The Senate Nov. 13 approved, on a 79-0 vote, Protocol I to the Treaty for the Prohibition of Nuclear Weapons in Latin America, known as the Treaty of Tlatelolco. *(Vote 371, p. 62-S)*

Under the protocol the United States agreed not to base nuclear weapons in Latin America. The full treaty established a nuclear-free zone in Latin America, with nations of the region agreeing not to make, test, use, store, deploy or possess nuclear weapons.

Although not a direct party to the treaty, the United States was invited to participate through Protocol I which applied to nations possessing territories in Latin America. U.S. territories in the region were Puerto Rico, the Virgin Islands and the Guantanamo Naval Base in Cuba.

The United States signed the protocol May 26, 1977, and President Carter sent it to the Senate a year later. The Senate Foreign Relations Committee held hearings in August 1978, but delayed action because of questions about whether the agreement would affect the U.S. right to transport ships and planes armed with nuclear weapons in Latin America.

In urging its approval, the Reagan administration insisted the United States was not prohibited from transporting nuclear weapons in the region.

The Foreign Relations Committee then added several understandings, the most important of which stated the U.S. declaration of its right to transport ships and planes throughout the region regardless of their cargo or armaments. The committee reported the protocol Oct. 19 (Exec Rept 97-21) by a unanimous vote.

Previous Ratifications

Protocol I also had been ratified by Great Britain and the Netherlands. France had signed the protocol but had not ratified it.

The United States in 1971 ratified the treaty's Protocol II, which bound nations possessing nuclear weapons to respect the nuclear-free zone in Latin America and not to use or threaten to use nuclear weapons against any parties to the treaty. Protocol II also was ratified by the Soviet Union, France, China and Great Britain.

Twenty-two Latin American nations had ratified the Treaty of Tlatelolco itself and had agreed to be bound by its terms.

But the treaty could not enter into full legal force until all the following steps had been taken: France and the United States had ratified Protocol I, Argentina and Cuba had ratified the treaty, as did Chile and Brazil. However, at the end of 1981, both Chile and Brazil refused to be bound by its terms until all other eligible nations had ratified the treaty and protocols.

---

stating his long-delayed non-proliferation policy.

Immediately following Reagan's announcement, Glenn and Eckart pushed for passage of the resolutions in order to persuade the president to raise non-proliferation issues at the July 20-21 economic summit meeting in Ottawa,

of proliferation demands, and to seek agreement on requiring IAEA safeguards on all nuclear activities in non-nuclear-weapon states as a condition for any significant new supply commitment."

The Washington Post reported in October that the administration was considering several additional steps to ease restrictions on exports of nuclear technology and supplies.

U.S. As Reliable Supplier

Much of Reagan's statement concerned making the United States a "reliable supplier" of nuclear technology and equipment to nations that were not proliferation threats.

Critics of Carter's policy, especially the nuclear industry, argued that restricting U.S. nuclear exports reduced the U.S. leverage over other countries. Since other nations could no longer rely on the United States for nuclear supplies, they turned to other suppliers, such as France, which did not impose the same restrictions, the critics said.

"We must re-establish this nation as a predictable and reliable supplier of peaceful nuclear cooperation under adequate safeguards," Reagan said in endorsing that view. "If we are not such a partner, other countries will tend to go their own ways, and our influence will diminish."

Reprocessing Technology

Reagan's most direct break with Carter concerned exports of reprocessing and breeder reactor technology, which could be used to create weapons-grade plutonium. Carter had banned exports of those items and halted reprocessing and breeder reactor plants in the United States.

Reagan said the administration would not inhibit reprocessing and breeder reactor development "in nations with advanced nuclear power programs where it does not constitute a proliferation risk." He did not set specific standards for determining what nations would be permitted to buy that technology. However, congressional aides said Reagan's policy was directed at allowing exports of those items to Japan.

Reagan also did not set out a policy covering exports of uranium enrichment technology, which could convert natural uranium into highly enriched fuel capable of making atomic weapons.

Safeguards

Before entering into "any significant new nuclear supply commitment" with another nation, Reagan said, the United States would require that the nation accept international safeguards on all its nuclear facilities (called "full-scope safeguards").

Reagan's statement did not say whether the United States would continue to press for adoption of full-scope safeguards by nations that already had nuclear agreements with the United States but which had refused to accept the safeguards. Those nations included India, South Africa, Argentina, Brazil and Spain.

Neither Reagan's two-page statement nor an accompanying four-page "fact sheet" mentioned the Nuclear Non-proliferation Act (NNPA), the 1978 law (PL 95-242) that established U.S. non-proliferation policy. *(1978 Almanac p. 350)*

The law placed strict controls on all nuclear exports and prohibited exports after March 1980 to countries that refused to accept full-scope safeguards. The president could waive that prohibition, but Congress could override

his approval of an export.

Spokesmen for the nuclear industry had complained that the law was too rigid and placed too many hurdles in the way of nuclear exports.

Reagan said he would direct U.S. agencies to expedite export requests that met conditions of the law.

Congressional Resolutions

The Senate and House July 17 adopted similar resolutions on the non-proliferation issue.

The strongest and most specific resolution was S Res 179, adopted by the Senate 88-0. *(Vote 200, p. 36-S)*

Referring to the Ottawa summit meeting, Glenn said President Reagan had "a unique opportunity to exert nuclear non-proliferation leadership for the whole world," by raising the issue with leaders representing the most important nuclear supplier nations.

Glenn wrote to Reagan early in June suggesting a meeting of all nuclear supplier nations. Glenn's resolution said the president should confer with other supplier nations to tighten controls on nuclear trade and to take several steps beyond Reagan's declared policy, including:

● A temporary worldwide moratorium on transfers of uranium enrichment and reprocessing equipment to "sensitive areas, such as the Middle East and South Asia."

● Limiting the size of research reactors (such as the Iraqi reactor destroyed June 7, 1981, by Israel), eliminating the use of weapons-grade uranium in those reactors and requiring importing nations to return spent nuclear fuel to the nations that supplied the original fuel.

● Making nuclear exports only to nations that accepted safeguards on all their nuclear facilities. Only the United States and Canada required those safeguards.

● Imposing sanctions on nations that violated safeguards.

The resolution also called on the president to work to strengthen international safeguards and to formulate a "clear" U.S. policy on nuclear trade.

Glenn later said Reagan's policy "is God, flag and motherhood. It can be interpreted in any way." And Glenn said he was "very disappointed" that Reagan apparently did not push other leaders at the Ottawa summit to adopt tighter controls on nuclear exports.

"We may be at a watershed time," he said. "Five or six nations now have this [bomb-making] technology. It won't be long before 15 or 20 or 50 nations will have the same capability. It will truly be a mad world."

Support for Reagan's policy came from James A. McClure, R-Idaho, chairman of the Senate Energy Committee and a staunch advocate of the nuclear industry.

Arguing that Carter's policy amounted to "nuclear isolationism," McClure said he was especially pleased by Reagan's decision to drop the ban on exports of reprocessing technology and breeder reactors. The Reagan policy, McClure told the Senate, "more realistically, and certainly more correctly, will distinguish between nations with advanced nuclear programs such as Japan and Germany, and the use of sensitive technologies in other nations where the risk of proliferation is more realistically a consideration."

House Resolution

The House also passed a resolution (H Res 177) calling for non-proliferation steps beyond Reagan's policy. The resolution was passed 365-0, with two members (Larry P.

McDonald, D-Ga., and Ron Paul, R-Texas), voting "present." *(Vote 133, p. 50-H)*

The resolution asked the president to "develop and implement a United States nuclear non-proliferation policy which aggressively and creatively strengthens the political, institutional and technical barriers to the further spread of nuclear weapons," including "concrete methods for achieving restraint on the part of all nuclear suppliers."

It called for "credible" sanctions against nations that misuse nuclear material and said the president should fully implement the Nuclear Non-proliferation Act.

An aide said Eckart, the resolution's sponsor, believed Reagan's policy was "ambiguous" and "didn't go far enough," especially in the area of imposing sanctions against countries that develop nuclear weapons.

Although applauding Reagan's "preliminary steps," House Foreign Affairs Committee Chairman Clement J. Zablocki, D-Wis., expressed concern about the emphasis on making the United States a reliable nuclear supplier. Zablocki said Reagan's actions "will not in themselves solve the problems of proliferation — especially if we permit our desire to be a reliable supplier to lead to the approval of requests for nuclear cooperation which will abet the spread of nuclear capability rather than inhibit its spread." ∎

Intelligence Authorization

The House and Senate Nov. 18 cleared for the president a fiscal 1982 intelligence authorization bill (HR 3454 — PL 97-89) approving secret amounts of spending by the Central Intelligence Agency and other U.S. spy services.

The House approved the conference report on HR 3454 (H Rept 97-332) by a vote of 379-22. *(Vote 294, p. 96-H)*

The Senate approved the report by voice vote with only perfunctory discussion of it.

While spending authorized by HR 3454 was secret, Edward P. Boland, D-Mass., chairman of the House Intelligence Committee, said the conferees had given the Reagan administration "almost everything that it asked for."

The bill also contained a secret, supplemental fiscal 1981 authorization for intelligence agency spending.

Committee member J. Kenneth Robinson, R-Va., said he also wanted to "emphasize that the programs authorized by the bill are very close to the requests of the president."

When the House passed HR 3454 on July 13, Boland had said the House bill contained a "net reduction" from President Reagan's request, compared to a "substantial addition" to Reagan's request by the Senate Intelligence Committee.

Robinson also disclosed that HR 3454 "provides for acquisition of a new classified technical collection capability which I believe will be of great benefit to our country." He, of course, did not describe that item.

Conference Action

Both houses of Congress had passed their versions of the fiscal 1982 intelligence authorization bill in July. Final action by conferees was delayed because amounts for military intelligence had to be considered in conjunction with the fiscal 1982 defense authorization bill, which in turn was delayed for several months while the administration delib-

erated on its strategic weapons policies. *(Defense authorization, p. 212)*

In actions that were made public, conferees:

● Accepted the House authorization of $13.6 million and 220 personnel — $1.8 million and 25 personnel less than Reagan wanted — for the staff of the director of central intelligence. The director supervised all intelligence agencies and also was director of the Central Intelligence Agency (CIA). The Senate originally approved $15.4 million.

● Authorized $11.9 million for a Federal Bureau of Investigation domestic counterintelligence program which the Senate had not included in its version of the bill.

● Agreed to Senate provisions establishing a senior cryptologic executive service within the National Security Agency (NSA) similar to the senior executive service for other federal employees, and a senior executive service for civilian personnel in the Defense Intelligence Agency.

● Agreed to a House provision permitting the director of the NSA to make grants for research into cryptology, which involved writing and breaking coded messages.

● Accepted a Senate provision prohibiting unauthorized persons from using the names, initials or seals of the CIA and NSA for commercial or improper purposes, and gave those agencies authority to seek U.S. district court injunctions to halt such activities.

The unauthorized use would have to be done in a "manner reasonably calculated to convey the impression that such use is approved, endorsed or authorized" by the agency in question.

News stories had said the provision was intended to prevent the sale of novelty T-shirts bearing the CIA seal, but the conference report said such items were specifically exempt from the provision so long as the seller did not represent himself as having the endorsement of the CIA.

A House committee aide said the provision was intended to prevent more serious fraudulent uses of the CIA and NSA emblems.

● Dropped a Senate provision that would have made it a federal crime to kill, attempt to kill, kidnap or extort either CIA personnel acting in the line of duty, intelligence defectors or specified foreign "visitors" to the United States.

House committee member Robert McClory, R-Ill., said the House conferees agreed that the provision "has clear merit" but wanted House committees to have a chance to hold hearings on the issue.

After the provision was dropped from HR 3454, House Committee Chairman Boland introduced a bill (HR 4940) to establish penalties for assaulting intelligence agents and the measure was referred to the House Judiciary Committee.

● Agreed to a modification of a House provision requiring that no funds authorized in the bill could be spent for purposes other than those for which they were proposed unless the House and Senate Intelligence committees were notified at least 15 days in advance.

● Agreed to a modification of a Senate provision authorizing CIA personnel to carry firearms to perform authorized CIA duties.

Conferees stipulated that such authority would be limited within the United States to the protection of classified materials, training CIA personnel to use firearms, maintaining security at CIA installations or other property, and protecting CIA personnel, defectors and their families or foreign visitors in the United States under the auspices of the CIA.

Other Provisions

As cleared for the president, HR 3454 also authorized:
- $84.6 million for the CIA Retirement and Disability System.
- The NSA to establish a cryptologic linguist reserve of persons who could make and break codes in foreign languages.
- Allowances and benefits for CIA employees comparable to those offered members of the Foreign Service, as well as special travel allowances.

Committee Action

Uncle Sam's spy agencies needed better linguists, judging by provisions in fiscal 1982 intelligence authorization bills approved by House and Senate committees.

But under both measures, the NSA, which invented and broke secret codes used by spies and diplomats, was to establish a "cryptologic linguist reserve." A "cryptologic linguist" could make or break codes in a foreign language. The NSA would train current and former NSA employees or others eligible for the linguist reserve and pay the linguists bonuses for honing their skills.

Both measures would let the NSA make grants to persons or institutions providing language training unavailable in government. "NSA is particularly interested in supporting language programs in the more esoteric languages for which other sources of students and instruction do not exist," the Senate committee's report said.

Though the amounts authorized by the bills for CIA and other intelligence agency spending were secret, the House Intelligence Committee's report on HR 3454 said the "administration requested a substantial increase" in fiscal 1982 over the amount of fiscal 1981 intelligence agency spending. Although some portions of the request were unjustified, the committee said, "in general, the committee supports the level of effort requested...."

Senate Committee

The Senate Intelligence Committee reported S 1127 (S Rept 97-57) on May 6. The bill was then jointly referred to the Armed Services, Governmental Affairs and Judiciary committees, which were to jointly report S 1127 by July 10.

Armed Services approved S 1127 on June 3 after amending portions dealing with secret military intelligence spending, a committee aide said.

Governmental Affairs was expected to include the NSA under provisions in S 1127 authorizing a senior executive service within the Defense Intelligence Agency.

Judiciary ordered S 1127 reported on June 24 after deleting provisions the Intelligence Committee put in to streamline and make permanent the FBI's authority to set up fake businesses used in counterintelligence operations.

Authority to set up such "proprietaries" normally was provided in the annual Justice Department authorization bill and applied to criminal investigations as well as counterintelligence operations. A committee aide said Judiciary preferred to retain that system.

Judiciary also approved a provision to make it a federal crime to kill or attempt to kill, to kidnap, assault or attempt to extort U.S. secret agents, intelligence sources or defectors under U.S. protection.

The Senate bill also:
- Authorized $15.4 million for the staff of the director of central intelligence, the amount requested, but $2.9 million

less than fiscal 1981.
- Authorized $84.6 million for the Central Intelligence Agency Retirement and Disability System, up from $55.3 million in fiscal 1981.
- Prohibited unauthorized persons from using the names, initials or seals of the Central Intelligence Agency or National Security Agency for commercial or improper purposes.
- Authorized allowances and benefits for CIA employees comparable to those paid the Foreign Service and authorized special allowances for intelligence assignments.

House Committee

The House Intelligence Committee ordered HR 3454 reported (H Rept 97-101, Pt. 1) on May 7. The bill also was referred to the House Armed Services Committee, which reported it (H Rept 97-101, Pt. 2) on June 12 without amendment.

As reported, HR 3454 authorized secret amounts for fiscal 1982, a secret supplemental for fiscal 1981 and the establishment of a cryptologic linguist reserve. It also:
- Authorized $13.6 million in fiscal 1982 for the staff of the director of central intelligence.
- Authorized $11.9 million in fiscal 1982 for an FBI counterterrorism program.
- Authorized $84.6 million for the CIA retirement fund.
- Authorized the same allowances and benefits as in S 1127.

Floor Action

The House passed its bill (HR 3454) July 13 by voice vote under suspension of the rules. The Senate inserted the text of S 1127 into the House bill before passing it by voice vote July 16.

The only amounts made public were fiscal 1982 authorizations for: the staff of the director of central intelligence ($13.6 million in the House bill, $15.4 million in the Senate bill); $11.9 million in the House bill for an FBI counterterrorism program; and $84.6 million in both bills for the CIA retirement fund. Both bills also made secret supplemental intelligence authorizations for fiscal 1981.

Edward P. Boland, D-Mass., chairman of the House Intelligence Committee, said HR 3454 contained a "net reduction" from President Reagan's spending request, yet allowed growth over fiscal 1981 levels.

Referring to the Senate bill, Boland said the House bill's reduction from the president's request was "in contrast to a substantial addition by the other body."

Both bills permitted the National Security Agency to establish a "cryptologic linguist reserve" of persons who can make and break codes in foreign languages.

There was no debate on the question in either house, but House Intelligence Committee member Romano L. Mazzoli, D-Ky., urged that the House in the future consider making the total amount of the intelligence budget public. Mazzoli said doing so "would not provide particularly useful information to our enemies" and would "certainly be helpful to members."

Final Action

Conferees filed their report Nov. 16 (H Rept 97-332). HR 3454 was cleared for the president's signature Nov. 18 when the House, by a 379-22 vote, and the Senate, by voice vote, approved the conference version. *(Vote 294, p. 96-H)*

Intelligence Agencies Order

President Reagan Dec. 4 loosened restrictions imposed by President Carter on U.S. intelligence agencies, but only after revising a proposed executive order to ease concerns raised by members of Congress over earlier drafts.

Reagan said his order was "designed to provide America's intelligence community with clearer, more positive guidance and to remove the aura of suspicion and mistrust that can hobble our nation's intelligence efforts."

Members of the House and Senate Intelligence committees had criticized three previous drafts of the order for going too far in easing the safeguards Carter erected against spy agency abuses of the rights of Americans.

The Senate committee had unanimously asked Reagan to make 18 changes in the third draft, and a committee aide said the final order was generally acceptable to members of that panel because 15 of the changes were made.

Edward P. Boland, D-Mass., chairman of the House committee, said the final order "retreats from the worst departures from the Carter order" proposed earlier by Reagan aides. But Boland said he was concerned by a section allowing spy agencies to collect "significant foreign intelligence" about even those U.S. citizens not suspected of illegal actions or of being employed by foreign powers.

Carter's Executive Order 12036, issued Jan. 24, 1978, limited physical surveillance of Americans to suspected foreign agents, terrorists, narcotics dealers and current or former intelligence employees thought to endanger secret intelligence methods and sources. *(1978 Almanac p. 360)*

Spying on Americans

While reaction from members of the two Intelligence committees was favorable, *The Washington Post* quoted Rep. Don Edwards, D-Calif., as saying Reagan's order was "really pretty bad." Edwards was chairman of the Judiciary Subcommittee on Civil and Constitutional Rights.

Edwards complained that the order "still puts the CIA smack into secretly operating within the United States" and he said it left Americans overseas "wide open to surveillance, regardless of any connection to foreign governments or criminal activity."

At an Edwards' subcommittee hearing on the executive order Dec. 15, Stansfield Turner, director of the CIA during the Carter administration, said the order risked infringing on the rights of Americans. Turner said the order also raised the possibility of CIA intrusion into domestic matters normally handled by the FBI.

Representatives of the American Civil Liberties Union said the order represented a "grave threat to civil liberties" by allowing CIA intelligence-gathering about Americans.

Carter had barred electronic surveillance, television monitoring, physical searches and mail surveillance of Americans unless the president approved the techniques and the attorney general approved specific applications.

Reagan's order permitted "electronic surveillance, unconsented physical search, mail surveillance, physical surveillance, or monitoring devices" to be used, so long as they were done under procedures established by the head of the agency using the techniques "in cooperation with the attorney general." Those procedures were to "protect constitutional and other legal rights and limit use of [the resulting] information to lawful government purposes."

The Reagan order also permitted intelligence agencies to use physical surveillance against "United States persons" abroad, but only "to obtain significant information that cannot reasonably be acquired by other means."

A "United States person" was defined as a U.S. citizen, a permanent resident alien whose status was known to the intelligence agency concerned, "an unincorporated association substantially composed" of U.S. citizens or permanent resident aliens, or a corporation incorporated in the United States — unless it was "directed and controlled by a foreign government or governments."

A central concern when the earlier drafts of the order were circulated was that Reagan's order would fail to adequately limit Central Intelligence Agency (CIA) operations within the United States, and the Reagan order left some members of Congress dissatisfied on that point.

Daniel Patrick Moynihan, D-N.Y., a member of the Senate committee, said he was satisfied that the order made it clear that the CIA was to operate primarily abroad. But Moynihan said there still were "a very few provisions" that could "pose problems" if they were "misinterpreted or stretched beyond the legitimate intent of their authors."

Authorities

The 17-page Executive Order 12333 permitted the CIA and other agencies besides the Federal Bureau of Investigation to collect "significant foreign intelligence" within the United States provided the effort was not aimed at monitoring domestic activities of "United States persons."

The order also authorized the CIA to conduct domestic or foreign covert operations approved by the president, if they were undertaken to further "national foreign policy objectives abroad" and "not intended to influence United States political processes, public opinion, policies, or media." Carter had prohibited domestic covert operations.

Reagan's order further authorized the CIA to mount counterintelligence activities in the United States in coordination with the FBI but "without assuming or performing any internal security functions."

The order permitted intelligence agencies to infiltrate domestic organizations "in accordance with procedures established by the head of the agency concerned and approved by the attorney general" but "only if it is essential to achieving lawful purposes as determined by the agency head or designee."

Infiltrators could not try to influence the activities of the organization or its members unless working "on behalf of the FBI in the course of a lawful investigation" or the organization "is composed primarily of individuals who are not United States persons and is reasonably believed to be acting on behalf of a foreign power."

Reagan issued another order (Executive Order 12334) to continue the Intelligence Oversight Board begun by Carter and to recommission the 19-member Foreign Intelligence Advisory Board, which Carter had disbanded.

The Intelligence Oversight Board — three private citizens appointed by the president — was to inform him of any "intelligence activities" that any member believes "are in violation of the Constitution or laws of the United States, executive orders or presidential directives."

Reagan said the orders had been "carefully drafted — in consultation with the congressional committees — to maintain the legal protection of all American citizens."

"Contrary to a distorted image that emerged during the last decade, there is no inherent conflict between the intelligence community and the rights of our citizens," he said, alluding to scandals that led to stricter congressional oversight of spy agencies and to Carter's order. ∎

Sinai Peace-Keeping Force

Congress Dec. 16 cleared a resolution (S J Res 100 — PL 97-132) authorizing the president to send up to 1,200 U.S. soldiers and to spend $125 million in fiscal 1982 to support a new 2,500-member peace-keeping force in the Sinai Peninsula.

The force was to be established under the Egyptian-Israeli peace treaty of 1979, which required that Israel completely withdraw from the Sinai by April 25, 1982. Israeli forces had occupied parts of the peninsula since the 1973 Arab-Israeli war.

Final action on S J Res 100 came after the Senate agreed by voice vote, with a minor amendment, to a version the House had passed on Nov. 19. The House cleared S J Res 100 for the president later Dec. 16, also by voice vote.

But even before Congress had approved that key element of the Camp David accords, an angry dispute erupted between Israel and the United States over Israel's annexation of the Golan Heights, shaking the foundations of the Camp David peace process.

At the urging of Prime Minister Menachem Begin, the Israeli Knesset voted Dec. 14 to effectively annex the Golan Heights — captured from Syria by Israel in the six-day war of 1967 — by extending Israeli law to the region.

On Dec. 17, the United Nations Security Council unanimously adopted a resolution calling Israel's action "null and void" and demanding that it be reversed.

Floor Action

The Senate passed its version of the Sinai resolution (S J Res 100) on Oct. 7. That resolution authorized U.S. participation in the peace-keeping force, but placed few restrictions on the U.S. role.

The House adopted a more restrictive resolution (H J Res 349) Nov. 19, on a vote of 368-13. *(Vote 309, p. 100-H)*

The House resolution placed a limit of 1,200 on the number of U.S. military personnel that could be assigned to the force. Administration officials had told Congress the U.S. force would include an 800-man infantry batallion, a 350-man logistics unit and about 50 civilian observers.

The bill also authorized the U.S. share of the costs of the Sinai mission: $125 million in fiscal 1982.

In addition, the United States was to pay an estimated $35 million a year to run the force starting in fiscal 1983.

Of the 13 House members who voted against the resolution, only one — Rep. Hank Brown, R-Colo. — spoke against it on the House floor.

Brown complained that the resolution called for "sending American armed forces to a potential theater of military conflict. It would be tragic for this body to risk American lives where Congress is unwilling to meet our responsibilities to those who wear our country's uniform."

Henry B. Gonzalez, D-Texas, offered an amendment prohibiting the use of drafted soldiers in the Sinai force but withdrew it after Clement J. Zablocki, D-Wis., chairman of the House Foreign Affairs Committee, noted that the United States had no military draft at the moment.

The resolution required the president to send Congress reports by April 30, 1982, and by Jan. 15 of each succeeding year, describing: the activities and composition of the force; all U.S. costs in contributing to the force; and the results of discussions with Egypt and Israel regarding the future of the Sinai force.

Final Provisions

As cleared by Congress, S J Res 100:

● Stated that Congress considered the Sinai force an "essential stage" in the search for a comprehensive Middle East peace and hoped the force would help Israel and Egypt fulfill the Camp David accords and establish a "self-governing authority in order to provide full autonomy in the West Bank and Gaza."

● Authorized the president to assign no more than 1,200 U.S. military personnel to participate in the force.

● Required the president, before assigning any U.S. personnel, to notify Congress of the names of the other countries to participate, the number of personnel they would contribute and the duties those personnel would be assigned.

● Directed that if countries committed to participate withdrew, leaving less than four foreign nations with military personnel assigned to the force, "every possible effort must be made by the United States" to replace them so as to keep at least four foreign countries involved.

● Required that U.S. personnel perform no functions not specified for United Nations Forces and Observers under the Israeli-Egyptian peace treaty.

● Permitted the president to assign as many U.S. civilian observers to the Sinai force as he deemed appropriate.

● Limited U.S. funding for the force to no more than 60 percent of the budget for establishing it in fiscal 1982 and no more than 33.3 percent in each succeeding fiscal year. The United States had agreed to provide $35 million per year to the force beginning in fiscal 1983, with Israel and Egypt to provide equal amounts.

● Authorized the appropriation of $125 million in fiscal 1982 for the U.S. share of the force's budget, to remain available until spent. Congress already had appropriated another $10 million in fiscal 1981 to help establish the force. The $125 million for fiscal 1982 was appropriated in the first continuing resolution (H J Res 325 — PL 97-51), cleared Oct. 1.

● Authorized any U.S. government agency to provide administrative and technical support to the Sinai force without reimbursement, so long as doing so would not mean "significant incremental costs to the United States."

● Authorized the president to provide military training to foreign military personnel participating in the force.

● Required the president to report to the Speaker of the House and the chairman of the Senate Foreign Relations Committee no later than April 30, 1982, and by Jan. 15 of each succeeding year on:

The Sinai force's activities during the preceding year; the composition of the force and the duties of its component military units; all costs to the United States in connection with the force during the preceding year, whether or not the United States was reimbursed for those costs; what it would have cost the United States to maintain the same military personnel if they had been assigned to the United States instead; what amounts the United States had been reimbursed by the Sinai force; the types of property, support or services provided to the force by the United States without reimbursement; the results of any discussions with Egypt and Israel on the possibility of reducing or eliminating the Sinai force.

● Stated that nothing in S J Res 100 was intended "to signify approval by the Congress of any agreement, understanding, or commitment made by the executive branch" other than to participate in the Sinai force. ∎

Agents' Identities Bills

Legislation (HR 4, S 391) to make it a federal crime to expose the names of U.S. secret agents passed the House in 1981, but never made it to the Senate floor.

A threatened filibuster by Sen. Bill Bradley, D-N.J., prevented Senate leaders from taking up the measure in the final days of the congressional rush to adjournment.

Similar legislation also died in 1980, when bills (S 2216, HR 5615) were reported by the Intelligence and Judiciary committees of both houses but failed to reach the floor of either house because of the crush of business. *(1980 Almanac p. 87)*

Background

The agents' identities legislation got an apparent boost June 29 when the Supreme Court denied a former CIA agent's claim of a First Amendment right to uncover his erstwhile colleagues.

Civil libertarians and other opponents of the "names-of-agents" bills had argued that such a law would be unconstitutional under First Amendment guarantees of free speech and free press because it would apply even to disclosures of names gleaned from public sources.

But among the court's findings in its June 29 decision against expatriate former CIA agent Philip Agee was that Agee's practice of disclosing the names of alleged CIA agents was action, not just speech, and "clearly not protected by the Constitution."

The court ruled 7-2 against Agee's contention, based on First Amendment and other grounds, that the president had no right to revoke his passport for national security reasons.

"Assuming *arguendo* that First Amendment protections reach beyond our national boundaries," Chief Justice Warren E. Burger wrote for the 7-2 majority, "Agee's First Amendment claim has no foundation. The revocation of Agee's passport rests in part on the content of his speech: specifically, his repeated disclosures of intelligence operations and names of intelligence personnel. Agee's disclosures, among other things, have the declared purpose of obstructing intelligence operations and the recruiting of intelligence personnel. They are clearly not protected by the Constitution. The mere fact that Agee is also engaged in criticism of the [U.S.] government does not render his conduct beyond the reach of the law."

Whether the court's opinion of Agee's disclosures would apply to disclosures prosecuted under a names-of-agents law was speculative, especially since the bills that were under consideration in Congress also applied to persons who had not had Agee's access to CIA information.

Further, Burger specifically discussed Agee's "declared purpose" of disrupting U.S. intelligence operations. One unresolved issue was whether a names-of-agents law should apply only to defendants who harbor such malintent, as HR 4 would have done, or should bar disclosures made merely with "reason to believe" they would harm U.S. intelligence, part of the standard proposed under S 391.

Aim of Legislation

The so-called "names-of-agents" legislation was aimed at punishing CIA critics such as Agee and sometime associates of his — Louis Wolf, William H. Schaap and Ellen Ray — who published *Covert Action Information Bulletin,* a Washington-based pamphlet that regularly listed alleged CIA agents.

The Covert Action editors angered many members of Congress in 1980 when they accused 15 Americans in Jamaica of being CIA agents. The charge apparently led to violent but unsuccessful attacks against two on the list.

Backers of the legislation said they wanted to punish Agee and the Covert Action editors without affecting "legitimate journalists" who might name an agent incidentally in the course of writing a "legitimate" story about the CIA or another spy agency.

But the American Civil Liberties Union, the Society of Professional Journalists/Sigma Delta Chi and other press groups argued that it was impossible for Congress to pass such a law without putting orthodox journalists in danger of prosecution, and thus chilling public debate over the activities of U.S. intelligence agencies.

House Committee Action

In an eager voice vote, the House Intelligence Committee July 22 approved its version of the names-of-agents legislation (HR 4) after adopting a subcommittee amendment narrowing the bill to make it more palatable to House critics.

The original version of HR 4 made it illegal for a private citizen to disclose an agent's identity "with the intent to impair or impede" U.S. intelligence.

The amended version was more specific, stipulating that the law would apply to private citizens only if they disclosed an agent's identity with the intent to disrupt U.S. intelligence "by the fact of such identification and exposure."

The more specific language was adopted as a compromise to avoid having HR 4 referred to the House Judiciary Committee, where civil liberties specialists in 1980 tried to cripple the names-of-agents bill by amendment.

The committee filed its report (H Rept 97-221) on Sept. 10.

House Floor Action

The House Sept. 23 eagerly passed the bill, but first expanded it — over Intelligence Committee protests — to cover negligent as well as malicious disclosures.

HR 4, passed by a 354-56 vote, imposed jail terms of up to 10 years and fines of up to $50,000 upon active or former intelligence agency personnel who exposed U.S. agents. It imposed a jail term of up to three years and a fine of up to $15,000 upon a private citizen convicted of the same crime. *(Vote 207, p. 70-H)*

Among those voting against HR 4 was Edward P. Boland, D-Mass., the Intelligence Committee chairman, who had pushed for three years for a so-called "names-of-agents" law.

"This bill gives me great troubles in its present form," Boland lamented before the vote.

Scope Broadened

Boland's "troubles" arose from an amendment by John M. Ashbrook, R-Ohio, to enable a prosecutor to convict a private citizen who had exposed an agent by proving the defendant merely had "reason to believe" the exposure might "impair or impede" U.S. intelligence. The amendment was adopted by a 226-181 vote. *(Vote 205, p. 70-H)*

Ashbrook's standard of proof, which the Justice De-

partment had said would cover cases of "negligence," replaced stricter Intelligence Committee language.

As reported by the Intelligence Committee on July 22, HR 4 would have required proof that a defendant had exposed an agent "with the intent to impair or impede" U.S. intelligence "by the fact of" the exposure.

Intelligence Committee leaders warned against relaxing that standard. They said some constitutional scholars believed that without a specific "intent" standard, the courts might rule the law an unconstitutional abridgment of First Amendment rights to free speech and free press.

Ashbrook said that was debatable, and he argued that Congress also had a right to interpret the Constitution.

"The determination of this body carries weight with the Supreme Court, and we should not back down simply because some lawyer or some scholar ... says this might not be constitutional," Ashbrook said. "We have the right on the record to say that we believe our actions are constitutional."

Ashbrook noted that the CIA preferred the "reason to believe" standard, which matched language in S 391.

He also criticized the "intent" standard as an "American Civil Liberties Union [ACLU] compromise," which he said the CIA agreed to in exchange for an ACLU promise "that their supporters would not try to delay this bill."

The ACLU and various press groups had opposed the "reason to believe" standard on the ground that it would have a "chilling effect" on "legitimate" journalists. Such journalists, they argued, might disclose an agent's identity incidentally in the course of exposing agency abuses. While their intent might be to improve intelligence operations, the journalists would have reason to believe that exposing an agent might first impair those operations.

Others said any law forbidding persons who had not had authorized access to government secrets from disclosing an agent's identity must be unconstitutional. "No amount of tinkering can rehabilitate a law which criminalizes constitutionally protected freedoms of speech, press and political expression," said Don Edwards, D-Calif.

Ted Weiss, D-N.Y., protested that, "after witnessing the happenings of this day, one might think with some justification that if an amendment were offered to strike the First Amendment to the Constitution of the United States, that it probably would carry."

Other Amendments

After winning on his first amendment, Ashbrook offered another to make it a crime to falsely identify someone as a U.S. secret agent.

Romano L. Mazzoli, D-Ky., chairman of the Intelligence Subcommittee on Legislation, said the panel had considered but rejected such a provision because, "It essentially makes it a crime to call somebody a bad name."

Ashbrook withdrew his amendment in exchange for promises that the committee would re-examine the issue.

The House then rejected an amendment by Weiss to make disclosure of an agent's identity legal if the identity were determined from "information previously available from public sources or unclassified materials." Agee and others said the identities of covert agents could be extrapolated from old editions of the State Department's *Biographic Register*.

Weiss said his amendment was an attempt to shore up the constitutionality of HR 4. But Intelligence Committee member Robert McClory, R-Ill., argued that the bill was intended to protect agent identities "whether the information comes from public sources or private sources." Weiss' amendment failed on a standing vote of 3-38.

The House next rejected by voice vote an amendment by Charles E. Bennett, D-Fla., to allow the attorney general to seek, and U.S. district courts to grant, court orders to stop "any person [who] is about to engage in conduct that would constitute a violation" of the names-of-agents law.

The committee leaders lost on one other issue when the House adopted by a 313-94 vote an amendment by Gerald B. H. Solomon, R-N.Y., extending HR 4's protection to retired as well as active agents. *(Vote 206, p. 70-H)*

Senate Committee Action

A bare majority of the Senate Judiciary Committee voted Oct. 6 to weaken the Senate version (S 391) of the bill.

The standard of proof required to convict a private citizen under the Senate version as introduced by John H. Chafee, R-R.I., was the same as in the version passed by the House: A prosecutor would have to prove a defendant had exposed U.S. agents "with reason to believe" the disclosure would harm U.S. intelligence.

By a 9-8 vote, Senate Judiciary adopted an amendment by Joseph R. Biden Jr., D-Del., to require instead that a prosecutor prove the defendant had exposed U.S. agents "with the intent to impair or impede" U.S. intelligence "by the fact of such identification" — the standard the House Intelligence Committee had approved.

Republicans Charles McC. Mathias Jr. of Maryland and Arlen Specter of Pennsylvania joined seven of the panel's eight Democrats in voting for Biden's amendment. Howell Heflin, D-Ala., voted "present."

By an 11-7 vote, the committee also adopted an amendment by Max Baucus, D-Mont., exempting the Peace Corps from a provision requiring the president to give U.S. agents better "cover" and requiring government agencies to provide it if the president requested they do so.

In its report (S Rept 97-201), the committee said: "S 391 strikes a proper and constitutional balance between the needs of a free society for information that might contribute to informed debate on public policy issues and the compelling concerns of the men and women who serve our nation's intelligence agencies at great risk and sacrifice." ∎

Lefever and Human Rights

President Reagan's first major congressional defeat on a foreign policy issue came June 5, when the Senate Foreign Relations Committee voted 13-4 to recommend that the Senate reject the nomination of Ernest W. Lefever as assistant secretary of state for human rights and humanitarian affairs.

Hours after the vote, Lefever asked that his nomination be withdrawn.

Nominees had been forced to withdraw before a committee vote in the past, but committee experts said Lefever's case was the first time in recent memory — possibly the first time ever — that Foreign Relations had taken the step of voting against a presidential nominee.

The vote against Lefever came after several weeks of bitter controversy over Lefever's commitment to human rights and his truthfulness with the committee. The vote was a setback for Reagan because the president strongly backed Lefever until the very end.

Secretary of State Alexander M. Haig Jr. in June appointed Lefever as a consultant to the State Department on terrorism, nuclear non-proliferation and other issues.

Following Lefever's withdrawal, there was speculation that the Reagan administration might allow the State Department human rights post to go unfilled. But leading congressional advocates of a strong U.S. human rights policy repeatedly urged Reagan to fill the post.

On Oct. 30, Reagan nominated Elliott Abrams to the position; Abrams was confirmed by the Senate Nov. 20 without controversy. A former assistant to Democratic Sens. Daniel Patrick Moynihan of New York and Henry M. Jackson of Washington, Abrams had been serving as assistant secretary of state for international organizations.

At the time of Abrams' appointment, Haig approved a State Department memorandum stating that "human rights is at the core of our foreign policy because it is central to what America is and stands for."

Background

Lefever's nomination generated controversy on two counts: first, because of the man himself, who proclaimed his devotion to human rights but had his sincerity questioned by his opponents; secondly, because of the rancor of the human rights debate.

Lefever, was a former pacifist and ordained minister who earned Bachelor of Divinity and Ph.D. degrees in Christian ethics from Yale University. He renounced his pacifism, he testified, after seeing Nazi concentration camps following World War II while working as a YMCA relief volunteer.

He spent most of his life as a scholar of ethics and foreign policy, holding teaching or research positions at several universities in the Washington, D.C., area. Since 1976 Lefever had been president of the Ethics and Public Policy Center, a non-profit foundation established under the auspices of Georgetown University but later separated from the school.

Earlier in his career, Lefever was an active and orthodox liberal idealist, according to testimony given the committee. For example, he said he opposed the anti-communist crusade of Sen. Joseph R. McCarthy, R-Wis. (1947-57), and participated in the American civil rights movement.

But his philosophy evolved over the years toward conservatism. His statements and writings on the Carter human rights policy earned him conservative admiration and liberal enmity.

Even before his nomination was announced in February, the rumor that he would be named led some 35 groups, including church and liberal foreign policy interest groups, to form an Ad Hoc Committee of the Human Rights Community to fight the nomination. This group and other opponents charged that Lefever was at best indifferent to human rights concerns and therefore unqualified for the post.

His foes raised various other charges against him, questioning his integrity and that of his Ethics and Public Policy Center, for example, by alleging that the foundation had received financial support from the government of South Africa — a charge Lefever denied during his hearings.

The protest led to a dispute between Lefever and Foreign Relations Chairman Charles H. Percy, R-Ill., over whether Lefever had privately said he believed the opposition was "orchestrated by communist sources." Lefever denied believing that.

Rights Debate

For all the criticism of Lefever personally, the root issue was the Reagan human rights policy in general.

Lefever and other critics of the Carter policy complained that it alienated friendly authoritarian regimes, such as Argentina's, while overlooking greater human rights abuses by totalitarian communist nations such as the Soviet Union.

These critics, including Reagan, said abuses in anti-communist authoritarian regimes could be reduced most readily by offering their leaders the security of U.S. friendship and quietly using the influence thus gained.

Advocates of the Carter policy contended that it saved lives and prevented torture in many cases by focusing world attention on specific rights abuses. They said the "quiet diplomacy" policy advocated by some Reagan aides would mean ignoring human rights abuses by anti-communist U.S. allies while publicly condemning abuses only in Marxist nations.

The Reagan camp argued that the strategic importance of many nations under authoritarian rule outweighed the ability of the United States to influence their internal policies and dictated dealing with them even though their internal policies were distasteful.

Critics of the Reagan approach said it is immoral to remain silent in the face of brutality, no matter how strategically important the nation committing it.

But the other side charged that the Carter administration remained silent about human rights abuses in communist nations and in countries such as Saudi Arabia, sacrificing morals to economics or politics. Rep. Henry J. Hyde, R-Ill., said while testifying on Lefever's behalf: "It has been accurately stated that when America develops a car that runs on bananas and not gasoline, we will crack down hard on human rights in the OPEC countries and be far more tolerant of abuses in Central and South America."

Reagan officials also said authoritarian regimes offered hope for reform because they did not base their ideological legitimacy on unadulterated state control, as did totalitarian states.

Critics of the Reagan line disputed the significance of such distinctions, saying human rights abuses such as torture, murder or detention without trial were unconscionable no matter who committed them.

Hearings

During Senate Foreign Relations Committee hearings on the nomination May 18-19, Chairman Percy and most committee Democrats pelted Lefever with hostile questions.

Republican members Jesse Helms, N.C.; S. I. "Sam" Hayakawa, Calif.; and Richard G. Lugar, Ind., defended Lefever.

In his statement, Lefever outlined the human rights positions that helped generate the opposition to him.

He pledged his commitment to defending human rights, but he said: "We must recognize that there are moral and political limits to what the United States government can and should do to modify the internal behavior of another sovereign state. We wish that all peoples enjoyed the blessings of liberty as we do, but wishing, or preaching, or threatening will not make it so."

He also criticized the Carter approach, saying: "The policies of the last administration have been less than effective and have at times confused both friend and foe."

Lefever said he opposed cutting off assistance to nations whose governments violated human rights, as was done under Carter with Argentina, Guatemala, El Salvador and others. Said Lefever: "In some cases we must provide economic or military aid to a besieged ally whose human rights record is not blameless."

That Lefever faced a rough hearing was evident when Percy began by saying the committee had to determine whether Lefever stood for a mere change of style in U.S. human rights policy or "wants to abandon human rights" as a U.S. policy concern.

Claiborne Pell, D-R.I., ranking minority member, said Lefever's nomination was important for its symbolism. If Lefever were confirmed, he said: "The message to the world could be that the United States has slackened its concern for human rights around the world."

Alan Cranston, D-Calif., was far more blunt. Said Cranston: "I believe the symbolic and substantive duties of the assistant secretary for human rights are too important to allow the position to be warped into becoming simply a bully pulpit for redbaiting."

Helms, on the other hand, predicted that Lefever would be confirmed and counseled him to understand that "both the opposition to your nomination and some of the support is on a partisan basis."

Percy and others registered various complaints about Lefever, but one frequent complaint was about his July 12, 1979, testimony before the House Foreign Affairs Subcommittee on International Organizations, in which he said:

"In my view, the U.S. should remove from the statute books all clauses that establish a human rights standard or condition that must be met by another sovereign government before our government transacts normal business with it unless specifically waived by the president."

At his confirmation hearing, Lefever told the senators: "That is no longer my position. That was too flat a statement." Asked again later whether he still believed the rights standards should be expunged from the law, he characterized his 1979 statement as a "goof."

But Lefever's critics declined to accept that. On the second day of the hearings, Lefever opponent Louis Henkin, a Columbia University international law professor and president of the U.S. Institute for Human Rights, said he doubted Lefever's sincerity. "I do not believe that this law can be faithfully executed by this man, who doesn't believe this law should exist," Henkin said.

Lefever's supporters and Lefever himself described him as a lifelong defender of human rights whose more "realistic" approach could achieve better results than the idealistic approach taken under Carter.

In testimony characteristic of those supporting Lefever, Sen. John Tower, D-Texas, said on the second day: "Absent from Dr. Lefever's approach will be the dual standard which has berated human rights shortcomings of our friends and ignored the brutal oppressions of our enemies."

The previous day, Lefever had told Hayakawa, "I am a confirmed do-gooder." He promised to be "an equal and forceful advocate [of human rights] wherever the wretched of the Earth are crying out for help."

But Democrats Cranston, Paul E. Tsongas, Mass., and Edward Zorinsky, Neb., pressed Lefever to explain why his criticisms of human rights abuses in his writings centered on the Soviet Union. They asked him to name other countries as rights abusers.

Lefever responded that it was not his "style" to name individual countries, nor would he make it his practice as assistant secretary for human rights. "I do not regard myself as a one-man *Good Housekeeping* Seal of Approval going around the world giving my blessing to one country and not another," he said.

Other Charges

Percy and the Democrats raised a variety of peripheral questions that Lefever responded to testily, starting with a dispute over his refusal to turn over the Ethics and Public Policy Center's financial records.

Lefever at first refused, saying he had to protect the privacy of his donors. But Percy said he needed the records to examine the charge that South Africa was helping fund the foundation. That led Lefever to note that the FBI had investigated the charge and found nothing. "Isn't the FBI's word sufficient for you?" he asked Percy at one point.

Lefever ultimately agreed to turn over the records on the understanding that only Percy, Pell and four aides would be allowed access to them.

Another question raised about the foundation was whether it had contracted for a study on the marketing of infant formula in Third World countries in exchange for grants from the Nestlé Co., a maker of infant formula. Lefever denied it, but the intensity of the questioning, in which Tsongas and Christopher J. Dodd, D-Conn., revealed circumstantial evidence to support the charge, led Lefever at one point to request a recess in the hearing.

Nestlé Charges

Lefever's troubles were heightened by a May 22 *Washington Post* article, which disputed Lefever's testimony about whether a group he headed took money from the Nestlé Corp. in exchange for supporting the sale of infant milk formula in poor nations.

Cranston, Tsongas and Dodd then said they wanted more evidence on why the Ethics and Policy Center received $25,000 from Nestlé and later reprinted and distributed an article favoring infant formula exports. They charged that Levefer had given the committee "misleading and evasive testimony" when he denied any connection between the Nestlé donations and his foundation's position on the infant formula issue.

Lefever's involvement in the issue was especially controversial because on May 21 the United States cast the lone dissenting vote against a World Health Organization (WHO) code calling for a worldwide ban on advertising and promotion of baby formula. Infant formulas were powdered-milk substitutes used instead of breast-feeding. They often were mixed with polluted water in poor nations, and some health experts said that had caused as many as a million infant deaths a year.

Lefever acknowledged in his May 18 hearing that he had discussed his opposition to the WHO code with Jeane J. Kirkpatrick, the U.S. ambassador to the United Nations. But he denied that the Ethics and Policy Center's support for infant formula makers was an exchange for Nestlé contributions.

Committee Action

The committee vote to recommend that Lefever be rejected, thought to be unprecedented in committee history, occurred the day after Lefever appeared before the committee in a closed session lasting more than five and a half hours, defending his views on the role of human rights in foreign policy and further explaining his dealings with the Nestlé Corp.

The committee voted against Lefever's nomination June 5 without debate.

Percy, the committee chairman, and four other Republicans voted with the committee's eight Democrats to report the nomination unfavorably. The motion to do so was made by Rudy Boschwitz, R-Minn.

Voting to recommend against Lefever with Percy and Boschwitz were Republicans Nancy Landon Kassebaum, Kan.; Charles McC. Mathias Jr., Md.; and Larry Pressler, S.D.; and Democrats Pell; Cranston; Joseph R. Biden Jr., Del.; John Glenn, Ohio; Paul S. Sarbanes, Md.; Zorinsky; Tsongas and Dodd.

Voting against reporting the nomination unfavorably, and thus in favor of Lefever, were Republicans Howard H. Baker, Tenn.; Helms; Hayakawa; and Lugar.

Percy said he voted against the nomination because Lefever's past opposition to laws imposing sanctions against nations with poor human rights records would undermine the credibility of U.S. human rights policy. He noted that Lefever had retreated from that position in his confirmation hearings, but said he found the recantation unconvincing.

"On the basis of his long-held and firmly expressed views on human rights and foreign policy, Dr. Lefever's confirmation would be an unfortunate symbol and signal to the rest of the world," Percy said.

"His confirmation would be especially unfortunate if his intention, as the State Department's chief advocate of human rights, is to pursue quiet diplomacy as his general strategy," Percy said, for in his view Lefever "fails to display the personal empathy and diplomatic qualities necessary to make such a strategy work."

Hayakawa, defending Lefever, said he found a closed committee session of June 4 distasteful because of the tone of questions about contributions from the Nestlé Corp. to the Ethics and Policy Center.

"The questioning of Dr. Lefever about the contributions had the flavor of accusing him of being some sort of intellectual prostitute," Hayakawa said.

If Lefever's institute was suspect because of corporate contributions, he said, so were ideologically opposite ones such as the Brookings Institution and the Institute for Policy Studies.

Hayakawa also defended Lefever's past statements questioning the role of human rights in foreign policy. Academicians were free to make more "absolute statements" than politicians, Hayakawa said, and it was understandable if Lefever's views had been "corrected" by public life.

Kassebaum took a different tack, saying she was a friend of Lefever's but had voted against him because he had become too controversial.

"He became a lightning rod" for critics of the Reagan administration's change of emphasis in human rights policy, Kassebaum said, "and because of that, I think, [Lefever] lost the ability to function effectively as an assistant secretary of state."

Lefever Withdrawal

Alvin P. Drischler, deputy assistant secretary of state for congressional relations, said Lefever decided to withdraw after consulting with his Senate supporters on the prospects for winning a floor fight over the nomination.

"The decision was made by him," Drischler said. "We [the State Department] were prepared to go ahead and support him on a floor fight, and so was the White House."

It was unclear whether the Republican-controlled Senate would have confirmed Lefever, who proved to be one of the most controversial of Reagan's nominees but had been staunchly defended by Reagan and his deputies.

"Our whip-counts were close," said State Department lobbyist Drischler. "We thought it was a fair shot."

In the days before the committee vote, Baker had warned the White House the nomination was in trouble, but he later predicted Lefever would be confirmed on a close vote.

Drischler said some of Lefever's Senate supporters had argued in meetings after the committee vote that a floor fight might damage the emerging Reagan policy on human rights as well as Lefever personally.

"His friends got together and talked to him about it," Drischler said, "with the view in mind of protecting the policy, and him as well." ∎

Casey, Hugel Controversies

The Senate Intelligence Committee concluded after a four-month investigation - that CIA Director William J. Casey had been lax in complying with ethics laws but that "no basis has been found for concluding that Mr. Casey is unfit to hold office as director of Central Intelligence."

The report (S Rept 97-285), issued Dec. 1, said Casey failed to disclose more than $250,000 in investments and almost $500,000 in personal debts and contingent liabilities. The disclosures should have been made in a financial disclosure statement required of presidential appointees, the committee said.

Casey also failed to list more than 70 legal clients he represented during the four years before he became CIA director, the existence of four civil suits to which he was a party, and his services as a member of the board of directors of several corporations and foundations.

Sen. Joseph R. Biden Jr., D-Del., took exception to the report's central finding, saying he had lost faith in Casey because of Casey's "consistent pattern of omissions, misstatements and contradictions in his dealings with this and other committees of Congress."

But other members of the committee — eight Republicans and six Democrats — approved the report.

An intelligence officer in World War II, Casey was named CIA director after serving as President Reagan's 1980 campaign manager. He was unanimously confirmed by the Senate Jan. 28.

Committee Investigation

The Intelligence Committee in July began its investigation into allegations of financial misconduct on Casey's behalf, after similar charges toppled Max C. Hugel, Casey's deputy for covert operations.

Senate Majority Leader Howard H. Baker Jr., R-Tenn., an *ex-officio* member of the committee, said July 16 the panel had ordered its staff to review "the whole package" of allegations against Casey and Hugel.

Hugel resigned July 14, hours after *The Washington Post* published a lengthy article detailing charges by two stockbrokers that Hugel had engaged in insider trading and manipulation of the stock of Brother International Corp., an export-import firm he headed in the early 1970s.

The charges, which Hugel denied, were brought to *The Washington Post* by former Wall Street stockbrokers Thomas and Samuel McNell, who were brothers. The Post

published excerpts from tape recordings made by the McNells of conversations in which Hugel provided them with advance information on the performance of Brother International.

The McNells also alleged that Hugel improperly financed McNell Securities, their brokerage and the principal firm selling Brother International stock. They further charged that Hugel organized a phased purchase of 15,000 shares of Brother International stock with individual buys of 3,000 shares timed to exaggerate buyer interest in the company.

Casey's choice of Hugel to direct CIA spy operations was controversial from the start because Hugel had no intelligence agency background. Many in the intelligence community considered experience a necessity for that job. Hugel previously had been in business in New Hampshire and worked on the Reagan campaign staff in 1980.

The day after the *Post* story about Hugel, it was revealed that a federal judge in New York had ruled on May 19 that Casey and other directors of a defunct New Orleans firm, Multiponics Inc., knowingly misled investors in an effort to raise $3.5 million in capital for the agribusiness corporation in 1968.

Casey was a director, corporate secretary and legal counsel to the firm, which went bankrupt in 1971. Multiponics investors sued Casey and others, seeking damages on the ground that Multiponics' directors did not tell them the firm had a multimillion-dollar debt.

The judge, Charles E. Stewart, Nov. 10 withdrew his ruling that Casey knowingly misled investors. Stewart cited Casey's sworn affidavit that, as an "outside" director of the firm, he was unaware of a circular that allegedly misled the investors.

In the midst of the Intelligence Committee's probe, chairman Barry Goldwater, R-Ariz., said Casey should resign.

In a news conference July 23, Goldwater raised questions about whether Casey was forthright with the committee during his confirmation hearings. And Goldwater said Casey's choice of Hugel was sufficient cause for Casey to quit.

But Goldwater later signed the committee report approving Casey. ∎

State Department Authority

Congress failed in 1981 to enact an authorization bill for the State Department, in large part because House Republicans helped defeat the bill the first time it reached the House floor.

The key action came Sept. 17, when 131 House Republicans were joined by 95 Democrats in flatly rejecting HR 3518, which authorized $3 billion in fiscal 1982 and $3.1 billion in fiscal 1982 for State Department operations and for payments to the United States and other international organizations.

Later, on Oct. 29, the House passed a revised bill, which met revised administration requests for $2.9 billion in fiscal 1982 and $2.8 billion in fiscal 1983. But House-Senate conferees did not work out a compromise measure in time for action before adjournment.

Senate Committee Action

As reported by the Senate Foreign Relations Committee, S 1193 (S Rept 97-71) authorized $3.124 billion in fiscal 1982 and $2.837 billion in fiscal 1983 for the State Department, the International Communication Agency, the Board for International Broadcasting and the Arms Control and Disarmament Agency. President Reagan did not request a fiscal 1983 spending level for the arms control agency, and the committee set none, authorizing "such sums as may be necessary."

The fiscal 1982 and 1983 authorizations in S 1193 cut Reagan's fiscal 1982 request by $26 million and his fiscal 1983 request by $32 million.

On an amendment by John Glenn, D-Ohio, the Senate committee accelerated an administration proposal to defer paying in each of the next four fiscal years one-quarter of U.S. contributions to 15 international organizations, including the United Nations and its specialized agencies.

The administration proposed to shift U.S. contributions to international organizations to the end of the fiscal year, not cut them, but to do so over four years rather than abruptly. The committee decided under Glenn's amendment to phase in the deferral over three years instead of four.

Among other things, S 1193 also:

● Authorized $4.5 million for the Asia Foundation and $12 million for the Inter-American Foundation.

● Increased the Reagan request for ACDA by $1.5 million in fiscal 1982 to provide funds for possible arms limitation talks with the Soviet Union.

● Earmarked $18.7 million for resettlement of Soviet and Eastern European refugees in Israel.

● Earmarked $2 million to reopen U.S. consulates in Turin, Italy; Salzburg, Austria; Goteborg, Sweden; Bremen, West Germany; Nice, France; Mandalay, Burma; and Brisbane, Australia — posts closed by President Carter in 1980 to save money.

● Earmarked $45.8 million in fiscal 1982 and 1983 for the Organization of American States.

● Authorized the secretary of state to extend the duration of passports from five to 10 years and raise the passport fee from the existing $10, probably to $25.

Senate Floor Action

The Senate passed S 1193 by a vote of 88-4 on June 18 after adopting an amendment by Alan Cranston, D-Calif., on June 17 to separate the Peace Corps from ACTION. *(Vote 158, p. 30-S)* The Peace Corps issue was the meatiest legislative provision contested, and it only briefly. (The Peace Corps was actually separated from ACTION when Congress cleared S 1196, the fiscal 1982-1983 foreign aid authorizations bill.)

On the State Department bill, the issue was decided when the Senate voted 45-52 against a motion by Jesse Helms, R-N.C., to table Cranston's amendment, which Cranston had shielded from crippling amendments by offering a substitute that merely changed one word. Following Helms' defeat, the Senate adopted Cranston's amendment by voice vote. *(Vote 155, p. 29-S)*

The Peace Corps was placed under ACTION in 1971.

Cranston, referring to ACTION Director Thomas Pauken, acknowledged that "much of the impetus for the separation of the Peace Corps from the ACTION agency

State Department Authorizations, Fiscal 1982-83

Following are the amounts for the fiscal 1982 and 1983 State Department authorizations in S 1193 and HR 4814 *(in thousands of dollars):*

Program	Fiscal 1982			Fiscal 1983		
	March Request	Senate-Passed	House-Passed*	March Request	Senate-Passed	House-Passed*
State Department Administration	$1,318,754	$1,318,754	$1,245,637	$1,248,059	$1,248,059	$1,248,059
International Organizations	563,806	523,806	503,462	554,436	514,436	514,436
International Commissions	22,508	22,508	19,808	22,432	22,432	22,432
Science and Technology agreements	3,700	3,700	3,700	3,700	3,700	3,700
Migration and Refugee Assistance	553,100	560,850	504,100	460,000	467,750	460,000
Subtotal	**$2,461,868**	**$2,429,618**	**$2,276,707**	**$2,288,627**	**$2,256,377**	**$2,248,627**
International Communication Agency	561,402	561,402	494,034	482,340	482,340	482,340
Board for International Broadcasting	98,317	98,317	86,519	98,317	98,317	98,317
Inter-American Foundation	12,000	12,000	10,560	†	0	12,800
Arms Control and Disarmament Agency	16,768	18,268	0	†	†	0
Asia Foundation	0	4,500	0	0	0	0
Total	**$3,150,355**	**$3,124,105**	**$2,867,820**	**$2,869,284**	**$2,837,034**	**$2,842,084**

* Revised request.
† Such sums as may be necessary.

arose out of the nomination of an individual with a background in military intelligence work to serve as the director of the ACTION agency."

Pauken served with U.S. military intelligence units in Vietnam.

But Cranston also argued that, aside from dispelling suspicions of Peace Corps connections with U.S. intelligence agencies, separating the Peace Corps from ACTION would remove it from "unnecessary layers of bureaucracy — a bureaucracy that saps its strength and vitality."

Helms objected that the amendment was "in fact, a slap in the face to a distinguished American, Mr. Pauken." But despite the close vote on Helms' motion to table, his was the only voice raised against the proposal.

Non-Immigrant Visas

With Foreign Relations Chairman Charles H. Percy's, R-Ill., acquiescence, the Senate agreed by voice vote to an amendment by Alan K. Simpson, R-Wyo., that deleted a provision authorizing the secretary of state and attorney general to waive a requirement that all foreign visitors to the United States acquire non-immigrant entrance visas.

The administration had requested authority to waive the visa requirement for citizens of 24 countries, mostly European, who want to visit the United States for 90 days or less, either for business or pleasure.

Supporters of the waiver argued that the U.S. visa requirement was inequitable, and the State Department said it created undue paperwork and expense. The Senate passed the non-immigrant visa waiver in 1980 but the measure failed to make it through the House. *(1980 Almanac p. 357)*

But Simpson, chairman of the Judiciary Subcommittee on Immigration and Refugee Policy, said he wanted to examine the issue during his panel's consideration of a "comprehensive overhaul of immigration laws."

UNESCO

The Senate took only two roll-call votes on other amendments to S 1193. The first came June 17 on an amendment by Daniel Patrick Moynihan, D-N.Y., stating the sense of the Congress that the president should withhold the portion of the U.S. contribution to the United Nations Educational, Scientific and Cultural Organization (UNESCO) intended for projects to regulate the world's press. The Moynihan amendment was adopted by a vote of 99-0. *(Vote 154, p. 29-S)*

Developing and communist nations complained that the Western press discriminated against them in its coverage and consequently retarded their progress. UNESCO, dominated by those nations, had identified the Western news media as "a source of moral and cultural pollution" and in 1981 had discussed proposals to license journalists.

Moynihan's proposal was an amendment to an amendment offered by Dan Quayle, R-Ind., that merely would have expressed Congress' opposition to UNESCO's efforts to "regulate news content and formulate rules and regulations for the world press."

The Quayle amendment, as modified by the Moynihan amendment, was adopted by voice vote.

Infant Formula

The other roll-call vote on an amendment came June 18 on a measure by David Durenburger, R-Minn., and

Patrick J. Leahy, D-Vt., stating among other things that Congress "urges the United States government and the breastmilk substitute industry to support the basic aim" of the International Code of Marketing of Breastmilk Substitutes adopted in May by the World Health Organization (WHO) and to "cooperate with the governments of all countries in their efforts to implement the Code."

The amendment was adopted 89-2. *(Vote 157, p. 29-S)*

The amendment was a response to the administration's decision to cast a solitary vote on May 21 against the WHO infant formula code. Robert Dole, R-Kan., and some other Republicans had objected to the amendment because, Dole said, it was intended to "nick the administration a bit."

Other Amendments

The Senate adopted other amendments by voice vote:

● By Moynihan, instructing the president to reduce the U.S. contribution to the United Nations by the amount of the payment used for international organizations or projects that promoted the Palestine Liberation Organization.

● By William V. Roth Jr., R-Del., allowing the Japan-United States Friendship Commission to invest a $2 million gift from the government of Japan.

● By Roth, requiring that each chief of a United States diplomatic mission in a foreign country "shall have as a principal duty the promotion of United States exports to that country."

● By Claiborne Pell, D-R.I., and Percy, merging the Board for International Broadcasting with the board of Radio Free Europe/Radio Liberty.

● By Helms, designating Voice of America radio broadcasts to Cuba as "Radio Free Cuba."

● By Walter D. Huddleston, D-Ky., requiring the president to report to Congress on the total cost of domestic and foreign assistance for refugees and Cuban and Haitian entrants to the United States.

House Committee Action

As reported by the House Foreign Affairs Committee on May 19, HR 3518 (H Rept 97-102, Pt. 1) did not include ACDA and left the fiscal 1982 request for the State Department, ICA and the broadcasting board unchanged at $3.134 billion.

But HR 3518 increased the Reagan request from $2.869 billion to $3.674 billion for fiscal 1983, increasing various items in the bill by 17 percent to compensate for anticipated inflation overseas.

The committee bill authorized:

● $2.5 billion in fiscal 1982 and $2.9 billion in 1983 for the State Department, including $564 million in 1982 and $554 million in 1983 for contributions to international organizations such as the United Nations.

● $561 million in fiscal 1982 and $657 million in fiscal 1983 — the latter an increase of $175 million over the Reagan request — for the International Communication Agency (ICA), which ran the Voice of America.

● For the Board for International Broadcasting, which supervised Radio Free Europe and Radio Liberty, a fiscal 1981 supplemental authorization of $600,000 plus $98.3 million in fiscal 1982 and $115 million in fiscal 1983.

● $12 million in fiscal 1982 and $20 million in fiscal 1983 for the Inter-American Foundation, which made small grants to non-government agencies in Latin America and the Caribbean.

The House passed a separate bill (HR 3467 — H Rept 97-55) on June 8 authorizing fiscal 1982 and 1983 spending by the arms agency and dropping "disarmament" from its name. *(Story, p. 240)*

In HR 3518, the House committee, unlike the Senate panel, accepted the administration's plan to defer U.S. payments to international organizations over the four fiscal years beginning in fiscal 1982.

Foreign Affairs also put into HR 3518 provisions giving the secretary of state authority to retaliate in kind against foreign nations that impose penalties or refuse to grant certain privileges to U.S. missions on their soil.

Because those provisions affected the District of Columbia government's jurisdiction over foreign embassies or other properties in Washington, D.C., HR 3518 was referred sequentially to the House District of Columbia Committee, which reported the bill (H Rept 97-102, Pt. 2) on June 19.

The District Committee opposed a Foreign Affairs Committee move to take away the District of Columbia Zoning Commission's jurisdiction to determine the location of foreign missions. Foreign Affairs had given the jurisdiction to the National Capital Planning Commission, a joint federal-local planning board.

An aide said Ronald V. Dellums, D-Calif., chairman of the District Committee, hoped the State Department and District of Columbia could reach a compromise on the issue that Dellums could offer as a floor amendment to HR 3518.

Senate Foreign Relations Committee Chairman Percy introduced the Senate version of the foreign missions reciprocity measure (S 854) on April 1, but his committee did not act on the bill.

As reported by the committees, HR 3518 and S 1193 were generally identical otherwise.

House Action

The House first cut $496 million out of the fiscal 1983 State Department budget that the Foreign Affairs Committee had proposed. Then 131 House Republicans were joined by 95 Democrats in flatly rejecting the fiscal 1982-83 State Department authorization bill.

Most Foreign Affairs Committee leaders were shocked by the Sept. 17 action on HR 3518.

The bill failed on a vote of 165-226. *(Vote 199, p. 68-H)*

Clement J. Zablocki, D-Wis., chairman of the Foreign Affairs Committee, took the floor the next day to chastise Republicans who helped vote down the budget of a State Department their party controlled.

Said Zablocki: "If the Republican Party cannot, and will not, support its own president and secretary of state, how can we ask others to do so? Under a parliamentary system of government, defeat of such a bill would be tantamount to a vote of 'no confidence.' Maybe that is the problem. Maybe the minority party in the House has no confidence in the ability of the president or the secretary of state to carry out the foreign policy of this country."

Indeed, several Democrats who traditionally supported the State Department funding voted against the bill. One senior House Democrat had a ready explanation: "The liberals on the Democratic side were not about to support a bill that the Republicans, with their own administration, were not going to support."

The defeat of the bill did not force the State Depart-

ment to close its doors when the new fiscal year began Oct. 1, since its appropriations were included in an omnibus continuing resolution (H J Res 325).

Escaping Budget Cuts

But despite Zablocki's assertion that the vote expressed a lack of confidence in the administration, others said the refusal to pass the routine bill reflected how little stomach the House had for spending money abroad in the days of domestic austerity.

"The agencies and programs funded by this bill have apparently and miraculously escaped the budget-cutting knife," complained Minority Whip Trent Lott, R-Miss., in urging his colleagues to defeat the bill even after they had cut $496 million from the fiscal 1983 portion of it.

"I am not going to go back home and try to defend all these other budget cuts if we do not make the necessary cuts in foreign aid and the State Department," Lott said.

For fiscal 1982, the Foreign Affairs Committee had approved the amount Reagan requested, which was $485 million more than the 1981 authorization. But for fiscal 1983, the committee added $805 million to Reagan's request — a 17 percent increase in some accounts to compensate for inflation.

"It is absolutely impossible for this member to justify the expenditure of $6 billion on the programs funded by this bill after the cuts this Congress has voted for in various domestic programs," Lott said.

Lott's stance clearly surprised and rankled Edward J. Derwinski, R-Ill., minority floor leader for HR 3518.

"At the risk of being impolite to my distinguished whip," Derwinski said addressing Lott, "may I point out that even the State Department is part of the administration. . . ?"

After the vote, Derwinski admitted his surprise at the outcome, which he attributed to "confusion and misunderstanding; absence of alertness by the House leadership, by the White House, by the State Department. Nobody saw it coming. A lot of the freshmen thought they were voting on foreign aid."

But, contrary to Derwinski's view, Dante B. Fascell, D-Fla., chairman of the International Operations Subcommittee and majority floor manager of HR 3518, said he had expected the defeat. "It was no surprise to me," Fascell said later. "We all knew from January . . . that any foreign aid, anything that had the name 'foreign' on it, was in trouble."

The House rejected HR 3518 after adopting a variety of amendments, the most significant being one by Hank Brown, R-Colo., to cut the fiscal 1983 authorization for State Department operations by $496 million. His amendment reduced the 1983 figure from $1.744 billion to $1.248 billion, the Reagan request.

"I think in the present climate of 20 percent interest rates, of skyrocketing deficits, of an economy that faces terrible problems, that it would be the height of irresponsibility for us to go ahead with a major increase in expenditures that is beyond what even the executive has requested," Brown said.

Fascell and Derwinski protested. Fascell had said earlier that State Department manpower was being cut by 550 persons in fiscal 1982, leaving it with 16,285 on its payroll.

"This puts the Department of State, which is already the smallest department in government, at a 1959 operating level," Fascell said. "We all know how their responsiblity has increased from the time in 1959, when we

recognized only 77 nations, and now we recognize 146."

Fascell said the committee increased the Reagan request to compensate for expected inflation and avoid cutting 1,000 more persons from State's payroll.

Brown's amendment was adopted by a standing vote of 42-18.

UNESCO Amendment

A roll-call vote came on an amendment by Robin L. Beard, R-Tenn., to prohibit payment of U.S. funds to the United Nations Educational Scientific and Cultural Organization (UNESCO) if it should adopt any programs or policies aimed at regulating the press. The United States provided one-quarter of UNESCO's $45 million annual budget.

Beard's amendment, adopted by a vote of 372-19, required the secretary of state to report by Feb. 1 of each year whether UNESCO had done so. *(Vote 198, p. 68-H)*

"There is, I believe, a number of UNESCO members willing to adopt some sort of system aimed at controlling the world's press, and it is near to a majority," Beard said, referring to debate in UNESCO on a proposed "New World Information Order."

The House also adopted by voice vote the following amendments:

● By Fascell, as a compromise between the Foreign Affairs and District of Columbia committees, to create a District of Columbia Foreign Missions Commission to govern where chanceries of foreign missions can be located in Washington, D.C.

● By William S. Broomfield, R-Mich., to restrict to two the number of persons from each foreign mission in Washington, D.C., entitled to use diplomatic license plates on a motor vehicle and enjoy special traffic privileges.

● By Zablocki, to prohibit the administration from opening any new U.S. consulates unless it also reopened consulates in Salzburg, Austria; Bremen, Germany; Nice, France; Turin, Italy; Goteburg, Sweden; Mandalay, Burma; and Brisbane, Australia.

President Carter ordered those consulates closed to save money. Congress in 1979 ordered them reopened under the fiscal 1980-81 State Department bill (PL 96-60), but the Carter administration did not comply. Zablocki said the Reagan administration also had not complied, yet had plans to open three new consulates in the People's Republic of China, which his amendment would prohibit unless the others were reopened.

● By Larry P. McDonald, D-Ga., to cut U.S. funds for international organizations and conferences, such as the United Nations, from $564 million to $470 million in 1982, and to retain the fiscal 1983 figure at $470 million, rather than the $554 million proposed by Foreign Affairs.

McDonald said his amendment was intended to match the amount approved by the House Sept. 9 in the 1982 State, Justice and Commerce appropriations bill (HR 4169). In HR 4169, the House adopted an amendment by McDonald that cut the international organizations account by $70 million. The amount approved by the House Appropriations Committee for international conferences (a separate account) already was $24 million less than the amount approved by House Foreign Affairs in HR 3518.

● By Derwinski, to redesignate the ICA as the U.S. Information Agency (USIA), which was its name until April 1978.

Later House Action

Five weeks after rejecting HR 3518, the House Oct. 29 passed a revised bill (S 1193) by a vote of 317-58. *(Vote 274, p. 88-H)*

Republican leaders said the revised bill passed for two reasons: its funding levels were lower than the original measure, and the Reagan administration actively lobbied for the revised bill.

The revised bill included the amendments the House had added to HR 3518. But it cut $171.4 million in fiscal 1982 and $251 million in fiscal 1983 from the floor-amended version of HR 3518.

As passed, the new bill matched the administration's revised requests, which were made in September.

The House passed the bill after rejecting a motion by Derwinski to recommit it to Foreign Affairs with instructions to transfer to the International Communication Agency $36 million in fiscal 1982 and $43 million in fiscal 1983 from the accounts for State Department operations for U.S. donations to international organizations. The vote was 63-318. *(Vote 273, 88-H)* ∎

Aid Bill Gives President Broader Authority

President Reagan won broader control over U.S. foreign aid in a fiscal 1982 aid authorization bill signed Dec. 29 (PL 97-113), but Congress refused simply to drop the controls on aid that gave it a say in U.S. foreign policy.

Conferees on the fiscal 1982 and 1983 foreign aid authorization bill (S 1196) met Dec. 11 and Dec. 14 and reached agreement on the bill after the second meeting.

The House adopted the conference report (H Rept 97-413) by voice vote on Dec. 16. The Senate cleared the bill for the president later that day by a 55-42 vote, with 30 Republicans and 25 Democrats supporting it. *(Vote 476, p. 76-S)*

The bill authorized $5.9 billion for fiscal 1982 and — in an unusual step — $5.96 billion for fiscal 1983.

A majority of both parties in the Senate voted in favor of the report, but 22 Democrats — an unusually large number — opposed the measure.

In S 1196, Reagan won a modified victory on one of his most urgent foreign policy initiatives — improving U.S. relations with Pakistan by embarking on a six-year, $3.2-billion economic and military aid program for that nation.

But the administration had to give up on another priority when it was forced to abandon its plea for the repeal of a law banning covert aid to warring factions in Angola. It did so to get Democrats to go along with lifting bans on arms sales or aid to Argentina and Chile.

Provisions

For fiscal years 1982 and 1983, S 1196:

Two-Year Bill

● Authorized funds for both fiscal 1982 and 1983. The fiscal 1982 authorizations were limited to $5,901,070,000. Fiscal 1983 authorizations were limited to $5,960,570,000. *(Chart, p. 166)*

Pakistan

● Allowed the president to waive for Pakistan, until Sept. 30, 1987, the so-called "Symington amendment" in PL 94-329 banning aid to nations dealing in nuclear enrichment technology. For any other country dealing in unsafeguarded enrichment technology, the president could use the authority in PL 94-329 to waive the aid ban only if he certified to Congress that he had "reliable assurances" that the nation was not seeking to develop nuclear weapons.

● Banned economic or military aid to any country that transferred a nuclear device to a non-nuclear weapons state, and to any non-nuclear weapons state that received a nuclear device from another country. Non-nuclear weapons states were defined as nations that were not known to possess nuclear weapons.

● Gave Congress the right to veto, by passing a concurrent resolution of disapproval within 30 days, any presidential waiver of an aid ban imposed under the non-proliferation laws on dealings in enrichment and reprocessing equipment.

● Allowed the president to waive an aid ban imposed against a nation that transferred, received or exploded a nuclear device, but provided that the ban would be automatically re-imposed unless Congress authorized further aid by passing a joint resolution within 30 days.

● Required a secret report to Congress from the president on his reasons if he chose to waive an aid ban for a nation dealing in enrichment or reprocessing equipment.

El Salvador

● Stated that "Congress recognizes that the efforts of the government of El Salvador to achieve [a peaceful settlement of the conflict in that nation] are affected by the activities of forces beyond its control."

● Required that the junta in El Salvador be "achieving substantial control" over its armed forces in order to receive U.S. aid.

● Permitted aid to the government of El Salvador if it had "demonstrated its good faith efforts to begin discussions with all major political factions in El Salvador" who had shown themselves willing to find an "equitable political solution" — the solution to include a renunciation of military or paramilitary operations.

● Required the president, before providing military aid or arms sales to El Salvador, to certify to Congress that the government of that nation was making a concerted and significant effort to comply with internationally recognized human rights. The president would have to make his certification to Congress within 30 days of enactment of the bill and every 180 days thereafter. If he did not make a certification, he would have to suspend all U.S. aid and arms shipments to El Salvador initiated after enactment of the bill and withdraw all U.S. military advisers from the country. The president also was required to certify that the Salvadoran government had made good faith efforts to investigate the murders of six U.S. citizens in El Salvador in December 1980 and January 1981.

● Called on the government of El Salvador to reform its human rights practices, to seek to control its own armed forces, to continue economic and political reforms, to conduct free elections as soon as possible and to end extremist

violence on all sides.

● Stated that economic assistance to El Salvador should emphasize revitalizing the private sector. The bill also urged the president to set aside a portion of El Salvador's economic aid to provide guarantees to private U.S. banks willing to make loans to private Salvadoran businesses.

Argentina, Chile

● Allowed U.S. aid or arms sales to Argentina if the president certified to Congress that the government of Argentina had made significant progress in complying with internationally recognized principles of human rights and that providing aid or sales was in the U.S. national interest.

● Allowed U.S. aid or arms sales to Chile if the president certified to Congress that the government of Chile had made significant progress in complying with internationally recognized principles of human rights; that providing aid or sales was in the U.S. national interest; and that the Chilean government was not aiding or abetting international terrorism and had taken steps to cooperate in the U.S. investigation of the 1976 slaying in Washington, D.C., of former Chilean Ambassador Orlando Letelier.

Military Aid

● Authorized $800 million in Foreign Military Sales (FMS) loans that did not have to be repaid: $550 million for Israel, $200 million for Egypt and $50 million for the Sudan.

● Authorized $3,269,525,000 in regular FMS loans. Of that amount, $280 million was earmarked for Greece.

● Authorized special repayment terms on FMS loans for Egypt, Greece, Turkey, the Sudan and Somalia: 30 years to repay the loans, with an initial 10-year grace period on repayment of principal. Regular FMS loans required repayment within 20 years.

● Authorized $238.5 million in Military Assistance Program (MAP) grants, including $38.5 million to phase out previous MAP grant programs; and the remainder to be divided among countries selected by the administration for concessional aid.

● Authorized $42 million for the International Military Education and Training program, under which foreign officers received U.S. training.

● Authorized $19 million for the U.S. share of United Nations peace-keeping operations.

Limits on Arms Sales

● Required sales of weapons, military equipment or defense services made through U.S. government channels to be reported to Congress if they exceeded $14 million for a single item or $50 million for a package of items.

● Allowed Congress 15 days to review U.S. arms sales to NATO and its member countries, Japan, New Zealand and Australia. The provision also applied to sales of U.S. arms among those countries and transfers of U.S. equipment from those countries to other countries.

Defense Leases

● Placed Defense Department leases of defense equipment to foreign nations under the same congressional controls and scrutiny as U.S. government arms sales. Proposed leases of equipment valued at $14 million or more (or $50 million or more for a package of items) had to be reported to Congress 30 days in advance and could be disapproved by Congress within the 30-day period.

● Allowed the president to override Congress' right to veto a defense lease by certifying that there was an emergency requiring the lease and that U.S. national security interests required it. Congressional review of leases would not apply to NATO or its members, Japan, Australia or New Zealand.

● Required the president in each case of a defense lease to determine that there were "compelling foreign policy and national security reasons" for leasing rather than selling the equipment. In most cases, the president also would have to certify that the United States would recover all its costs in connection with a lease.

Other Arms Provisions

● Set at $75 million the value of Defense Department arms, equipment or services the president could provide to a foreign country in an emergency in any one year.

● Repealed a $100 million limit on individual sales of arms or military equipment abroad that could be made through private channels. Under the previous limit, individual sales over that amount had to be made through the U.S. government.

● Directed the Secretary of Defense to establish a revolving Special Defense Acquisition Fund, to be used for advance purchases of weapons and equipment frequently ordered by U.S. arms loan recipients. The fund was limited to $300 million in fiscal 1982 and to $600 million in fiscal 1983 and afterwards. The fund was to be replenished with a portion of payments made to the United States from the FMS program. The president was required to report to Congress by Dec. 31 of each year on the use of the funds.

● Required the president to make a periodic review of items on the U.S. "munitions list" to determine what items did not need to be on the list, and to report to Congress 30 days before removing any item from the list. Arms and military equipment included on the list were subject to U.S. government export regulations.

● Authorized the Defense Department to add equipment valued at $130 million in fiscal 1982 and $125 million in 1983 to the war reserve stockpile in South Korea.

● Authorized limits on the number of military advisers that could be routinely assigned to nations purchasing arms through the U.S. government. Up to six advisers could be stationed in any one country; a greater number could be provided only if Congress was notified 30 days in advance. Groups of more than six advisers were approved for Egypt, Greece, Indonesia, Jordan, Morocco, the Philippines, Portugal, Saudi Arabia, South Korea, Spain, Thailand and Turkey. The bill stated that the provision of advisory and training assistance "shall be kept to an absolute minimum."

● Required the president to report to Congress within 48 hours of the outbreak of hostilities or terrorist acts that might endanger American lives or property in any country where U.S. military advisers were stationed.

● Prohibited arms sales or military aid to any country if the president determined and reported to Congress that its government was engaged in a consistent pattern of acts of intimidation or harassment directed against individuals in the United States.

Economic Aid

● Authorized up to $75 million in fiscal 1982 for a Special Requirements Fund under the Economic Support Fund (ESF) program. The money could be used to provide

emergency aid to nations. The president was required to notify the House Foreign Affairs, Senate Foreign Relations and House and Senate Appropriations committees 15 days before spending any of the fund. (The related aid appropriations bill, HR 4559, reduced the fund to $25 million in fiscal 1982.)

● Authorized the president to transfer, or "reprogram," up to $75 million each year among accounts to provide emergency aid to foreign countries "when the national interests of the United States urgently require economic support to promote economic or political stability." In using this authority, the president could transfer up to 5 percent from the the funds earmarked for any one country.

● Earmarked the following amounts in ESF for both fiscal 1982 and 1983: Israel, $785 million; Egypt, $750 million; Pakistan, $100 million; Cyprus, $15 million; Tunisia, $5 million; Costa Rica, $15 million; Lebanon, $5 million; Poland, $5 million.

● Of the amount earmarked for Cyprus, $5 million in fiscal 1982 and $10 million in fiscal 1983 was to be used for scholarship programs to bring Cypriots to the United States for education.

● Earmarked $21 million each for Israel and Egypt in fiscal 1982 to replace funds that were transferred in fiscal 1981 from those nations' accounts to Liberia and El Salvador.

● Authorized all ESF money for Israel and Egypt as grants; for Turkey, ESF aid was to be two-thirds grant and one-third loan.

● Authorized up to $50 million of the amount for Egypt in both fiscal 1982 and 1983 to be used for agricultural extension services to aid small farmers.

● Authorized up to $11 million in fiscal 1982 and 1983 for a Middle East special requirements fund. The president was required to report to Congress at the end of each fiscal year on the use of the fund.

● Authorized up to $4 million in fiscal 1982 for scientific and technological projects that would promote regional cooperation among Israel, Egypt and other nations in the Middle East.

● Earmarked $5 million in ESF funds for Poland, with the money to be used to help relieve severe food and medical supply shortages in Poland. The funds were to be distributed through private agencies.

● Prohibited new ESF aid to Syria.

● Stated the sense of Congress that $7 million should be made available in fiscal 1982 and 1983 for relief programs in Lebanon.

● Prohibited the use of ESF money to construct, maintain, operate or supply fuel to any nuclear facility abroad unless the president certified to Congress that such spending was "indispensable to the achievement of non-proliferation objectives which are uniquely significant and of paramount importance to the United States."

● Directed that at least 15 percent of the funds used for commodity import programs be allocated to finance the purchase of agricultural commodities and products of U.S. origin.

Nicaragua

● Earmarked $20 million in ESF aid to Nicaragua in fiscal years 1982 and 1983. In providing the aid, the president was directed to take into account the Nicaraguan government's respect for human rights, its role in international terrorism and its commitment to the Organization of American States. The aid also was to be targeted to the

private sector "to the maximum extent feasible." The president was further directed to report to Congress every six months on the use of the Nicaraguan aid.

Development Aid

● Prohibited the use of U.S. Agency for International Development (AID) funds to perform abortions or to carry out research concerning abortions.

● Authorized up to $5 million in fiscal 1982 under the AID agriculture, rural development and nutrition account to aid developing countries in establishing or improving programs to encourage improved infant feeding practices. The president was required to report to Congress on the implementation of the provision.

● Earmarked $38 million, or 16 percent of the AID population and health account, whichever was less, for the United States Fund for Population Activities.

● Earmarked $4 million in fiscal 1982 and 1983 to finance scholarships for education in the United States of black South African students disadvantaged by virtue of South African legal restrictions.

● Authorized the president to furnish assistance to help developing countries protect and manage their environmental and natural resources. The bill also required the U.S. agencies administering aid programs to prepare environmental impact statements for programs that would significantly affect "the environment of the global commons outside the jurisdiction of any one country, the environment of the United States or other aspects of the environment which the president may specify." The president was permitted to make exceptions to the requirement for an environmental impact statement in an emergency, or in a case where the requirement would be seriously detrimental to the foreign policy interests of the United States.

● Permitted disbursement of Sahel Development Program funds to any nation only if the administrator of AID determined that the government of that nation would maintain a system of accounts for use of the funds that would provide adequate identification of, and control over, receipts and expenditures.

● Prohibited, with limited exceptions, the granting of funds after Dec. 31, 1984, to any U.S. private or voluntary organization that did not receive at least 20 percent of its funds for international activities from non-U.S. government sources.

International Organizations

● Earmarked funds for several programs under the "international organizations" account, but stated that the president could spend either the amount proposed by Congress or a percentage of the total international organizations account, whichever was less. The earmarked programs were: UNICEF, $45 million, or 19.6 percent of the international organizations account; United Nations Development Program, $134.5 million, or 59.5 percent; United Nations Environment Fund, $10 million, or 4.4 percent; United Nations Trust Fund for Southern Africa, $400,000, or .159 percent; United Nations Institute for Training and Research, $500,000, or .196 percent.

● Earmarked $500,000 under a separate account for the United Nations Decade for Women.

● Authorized up to $180 million for the International Fund for Agricultural Development, with no more than $40.5 million authorized to be appropriated in fiscal 1982.

Food for Peace

● Required the president, before entering into agreements to provide Food for Peace aid, to consider whether a recipient country had undertaken programs to reduce illiteracy and improve the health of the rural poor.

● Beginning in fiscal 1983, prohibited any one country from receiving more than 30 percent of the total dollar amount of financing made available under Title I of the Food for Peace program.

● Required that, of the 1.7 million metric tons of agricultural commodities that must be distributed under Title II of the Food for Peace program, 1.2 million tons must be distributed through nonprofit voluntary agencies and the World Food Program.

Peace Corps

● Established the Peace Corps as an independent agency, effective upon enactment of the bill, and provided for the transfer to the control of the Peace Corps of personnel, assets, liability, contracts, personnel records and unexpended balances primarily used by the Peace Corps.

● Provided that the establishment of the Peace Corps as an independent agency shall not cause full-time and permanent part-time personnel in that agency to be separated, reduced in rank or to otherwise suffer loss of employment benefits.

● Required the director of the Peace Corps to continue to exercise all functions in effect on Dec. 14, 1981.

● Authorized the Peace Corps to procure legal services in foreign countries.

Other Policy Provisions

● Repealed a 1978 ban on the use of U.S. foreign aid to spray the herbicide paraquat on marijuana. The bill directed the secretary of state to inform the secretary of health and human services if funds were used for that purpose, and the latter official was to monitor the impact of paraquat spraying on the health of marijuana users. The bill also earmarked $100,000 for research on substances that would leave a mark on marijuana or other illicit crops if sprayed on those crops along with herbicides.

● Expressed support for continued U.S. efforts to resolve Lebanon's problems. Among the principles to guide U.S. policy was "restoration of Lebanon's sovereignty free from outside domination or occupation."

● Condemned the use of toxic or chemical weapons in Laos, Cambodia and Afghanistan and urged the president to seek an explanation from the Soviet Union of its alleged involvement in the use of those weapons.

● Required the president to report to Congress within 30 days of enactment of the bill on whether recipients of U.S. aid represented at a September 1981 meeting of nonaligned nations had dissociated themselves from a communiqué issued following the meeting. The communiqé harshly criticized the United States. The president also was directed to consider whether any proposed recipient of U.S. aid had dissociated itself from the communiqué.

● Extended to Taiwan eligibility for up to 20,000 U.S. immigrant visas per year. The eligibility was inadvertently eliminated in 1979.

● Urged the president to undertake diplomatic initiatives to secure payment by the Soviet Union of its overdue contributions to the United Nations.

● Reaffirmed congressional support for various laws enacted to promote human rights. The bill also stated the sense of Congress that a strong commitment to human rights should continue to be a central feature of U.S. foreign policy.

● Authorized up to $15 million in development aid to Haiti in fiscal 1982, but stated that the aid was to be provided only if the president determined that Haiti was cooperating with the United States to prevent illegal emigration, had assured the United States it would cooperate in implementing aid programs and was not engaging in "a consistent pattern of gross violations of internationally recognized human rights;" required the president to report to Congress every six months on actions by the government of Haiti to restrict illegal emigration; and permitted military aid to Haiti in fiscal years 1982 and 1983 if the aid was used to help halt significant illegal emigration from Haiti to the United States. The latter provision waived a law that prohibited recipient nations from using U.S. aid to train or support their internal police forces.

● Required the president to make a comprehensive report to Congress on his approach to foreign aid. A preliminary report was to be delivered by March 31, 1982, with a final report due June 30, 1982.

● Directed the president to submit a classified report to Congress each year stating, for each country receiving U.S. aid, the extent and effectiveness of International Atomic Energy Agency safeguards at that country's nuclear facilities. The report also was to cover the capabilities, actions and intentions of each recipient country with regard to making or acquiring a nuclear explosive device.

● Authorized the president to furnish an unspecified amount of aid to persons displaced by the civil war in El Salvador. The president also was authorized to provide $5 million per year in aid to Belize to help that nation accept refugees from Haiti.

● Consolidated numerous reports on aid that various agencies were required to give Congress, and repealed provisions in foreign aid laws that were outdated or had been duplicated.

● Placed the AID Inspector General under the Inspector General Act, making that official a presidential appointee.

● Required a report to Congress no later than 120 days after enactment on the external debt burdens of Egypt, Israel and Turkey and on the impact of Arab sanctions on the Egyptian economy.

Senate, House Committee Reports

As reported by the Senate Foreign Relations Committee on May 15 (S Rept 97-83), S 1196 authorized appropriations of $5.778 billion for fiscal 1982 bilateral foreign aid.

The House committee bill, HR 3566, authorized spending $6.027 billion in fiscal 1982 and $6.216 billion in fiscal 1983. It was reported May 19 (H Rept 97-58).

One Year or Two? As in previous years, the panels split on a question of congressional policy — whether to authorize foreign aid programs for two years at a time, rather than annually.

The House committee, at the determined urging of Chairman Clement J. Zablocki, D-Wis., reported a two-year bill, contemplating no substantial changes in aid levels for fiscal 1983 except for inflation. The Senate panel, following the wishes of Chairman Charles H. Percy, R-Ill., rejected that proposal.

Reagan got less money for foreign aid in fiscal 1982

and less flexibility in using it than he requested, under the committee bills.

The bills generally approved the Reagan administration's emphasis on military-related aid at the expense of development assistance.

Both bills would substantially boost the foreign aid authorization over fiscal 1981, which was $4.982 billion (HR 6942 — PL 96-533). *(1980 Almanac p. 313)*

Nevertheless, as reported by the committees, the bills made appreciable cuts in Reagan's $6.7 billion original March request for military, economic and development aid.

The Senate committee bill (S 1196) cut the Reagan request by about $900 million, providing $5.8 billion. Likewise, the House committee bill (HR 3566) provided $6.0 billion, reducing the Reagan request by about $654 million.

The House committee said its reduction was made to conform to the policy of austerity being practiced in almost all phases of the federal budget in 1981. The Senate committee's $900 million cut was necessary to comply with a Senate amendment to the fiscal 1982 budget reconciliation resolution, S Con Res. 9. *(Reconciliation, p. 247)*

Presidential Power

While each measure paid tribute to Reagan requests for greater executive control over the foreign aid dollar, each also reflected a continued congressional determination to keep a hand on the foreign policy tiller.

For example, both committees approved a Reagan request for repeal of a law prohibiting military aid or sales to Argentina. But each panel also said future aid or sales to that nation should be made only if the president could certify that the military government of Argentina had met certain conditions to atone in part for its poor human rights record.

Both panels placed conditions on military aid to El Salvador.

Both committees also reacted coolly to Reagan requests for foreign aid contingency funds unencumbered by congressional spending instructions. Each committee cut those requests; despite its Republican majority, the Senate committee was the more severe, deleting them.

Each committee also approved strict new controls over the president's power to lease defense equipment or services to foreign countries.

However, each also agreed to requests to ease controls on certain arms sales to major U.S. allies.

Clark Amendment

Perhaps the most testy issue facing the committees was a Reagan request for repeal of the Clark amendment, which effectively banned aid to anti-Marxist rebels in Angola. *(1976 Almanac p. 213)*

The Senate committee agreed to repeal the Clark amendment but also established conditions governing any future aid to factions in Angola. The House panel rejected the repeal request.

House Committee

The House committee spent little time on the Reagan request for the Clark amendment repeal, which its Africa Subcommittee had rejected 7-0. Howard Wolpe, D-Mich., subcommittee chairman, said "this would not be the appropriate time" to repeal the aid ban.

Wolpe said repeal would make the Marxist government of Angola fear renewed U.S. aid to the anti-Marxists

who lost the Angolan civil war. Repeal would make the Angolans more reliant on the estimated 20,000 Cuban troops, which the United States wanted out of Angola, Wolpe said.

Another U.S. aim was to end a struggle over Namibia between leftist guerrillas based in Angola and the white-minority government of South Africa. Wolpe said repeal would lead the Angolans to give up efforts to get the guerrillas to negotiate a settlement.

The full committee rejected the repeal request May 12 by a show of hands of 19-5.

Senate Committee

The Senate panel's May 13 consideration of the Clark amendment was marked by the realism of the eight Democrats on the 17-member committee.

Although they might have been able to win a narrow committee rejection of the repeal request, the Democrats settled for a compromise.

Christopher J. Dodd, D-Conn., said he and his party colleagues decided their only hope for winning a concession on the issue from the Republican-controlled Senate was for the committee to present a united stand.

In debating the issue May 11, Paul E. Tsongas, D-Mass., and Nancy Landon Kassebaum, R-Kan., the Africa Subcommittee chairman, revealed opposite analyses of what effect repeal of the Clark amendment would have on chances for a settlement in Namibia.

Tsongas said getting the Cuban troops out of Angola could be achieved by "delicate negotiation," but only if the Angolans felt the security of the ban on U.S. intervention in their nation.

Kassebaum acknowledged the importance black African leaders attached to the Clark amendment. But she said that "a repeal could be an incentive to Angola to move ahead" in seeking a settlement in Namibia.

Percy proposed to repeal the Clark amendment but to state that it was not Congress' intent to endorse any intervention in Angola. His proposal also would require the president, if he should aid any faction in Angola, to submit a secret report to Congress stating why the aid was in the U.S. national interest, the amounts and kinds of aid, and who would receive it. The president also would have to "take into account" how the aid would affect U.S. interests in other African nations.

Tsongas proposed an additional condition: that the president must determine that "substantial progress" (including a cease-fire and preparations for elections) has been made toward a settlement in Namibia and that U.S. aid in Angola will not impair settlement prospects.

Percy accepted that condition, and the entire amendment was adopted 10-2. Kassebaum and S. I. "Sam" Hayakawa, R-Calif., voted no. Voting yes were Percy; Howard H. Baker Jr., R-Tenn.; Rudy Boschwitz, R-Minn.; Claiborne Pell, D-R.I.; Joseph R. Biden Jr., D-Del.; John Glenn, D-Ohio; Paul S. Sarbanes, D-Md.; Tsongas; Alan Cranston, D-Calif.; and Dodd.

Pakistan

The committees displayed their political complexions in their handling of an administration request to loosen a 1976 law that barred aid to Pakistan because of its efforts to develop nuclear weapons.

The Democratic-controlled House committee said it wanted to wait to see what the administration intended to

Foreign Aid Authorizations, 1982-1983

S 1196 made the following authorizations for foreign aid programs in fiscal 1982 (final amounts for fiscal 1983 were identical to the 1982 amounts, except for $2,723,500,000 for the Economic Support Fund and $139.5 million for the International Fund for Agricultural Development):

(in thousands of dollars)

Program	FY 1982 Revised Request	FY1982 Senate Amount	FY1982 House Amount	FY1982 Final Amount
Foreign Military Sales	$ 990,900	$ 990,900	$ 550,000	$ 800,000
FMS guarantees[2]	(3,063,500)	(3,085,500)	(3,269,525)	(3,269,525)
Special Defense Acquisition Fund	——	(350,000)	150,000	——
Military Assistance Program	63,500	31,400	304,375	238,500
Military Training and Education	41,976	47,700	47,700	42,000
Peacekeeping	19,000	19,000	19,000	19,000
Subtotal, Military aid	1,115,376	1,089,000	1,071,075	1,099,500
Economic Support Fund	2,598,500	2,548,500	2,688,000	2,623,500
Agriculture aid	637,500	689,000	747,679	700,000
Population aid	211,300	216,000	273,370	211,000
Health aid	104,600	127,905	133,405	133,405
Education aid	97,700	109,574	109,574	103,600
Energy aid	——	——	39,446	——
Private voluntary organizations; selected aid	155,700	140,889	178,794	147,200
Science and technology	10,000	10,000	——	——
International Fund for Agriculture Development	39,600	45,000	45,000	40,500
Sahel development	94,600	102,000	86,558	86,558
International organization	189,200	229,050	255,650	218,600
Trade and development	6,078	6,907	10,000	6,907
Subtotal, Development aid	1,546,278	1,676,325	1,879,476	1,647,770
American Schools and Hospitals Abroad	6,600	12,000	20,000	20,000
International Narcotics control	36,700	37,700	37,700	37,700
International disaster aid	23,760	27,000	27,000	27,000
Central American Refugees	——	——	5,000	5,000
Subtotal, Other aid	67,060	76,700	89,700	89,700
Peace Corps	83,600	105,000	105,000	105,000
AID operating expenses	317,000	330,972	343,632	335,600
Cut[3]	——	−67,600	−449,029	——
Total	$5,727,854[1]	$5,758,897	$5,727,854	$5,901,070

[1] *Numbers do not add due to a $40,000 error attributed to the administration.*
[2] *Figures represent the limit on loans that can be extended and are not new budget authority.*

[3] *The Senate reduced the overall amount of the bill by $67.6 million; the House set a maximum of $5,727,854,000 for fiscal 1982, which had the effect of reducing the amount by $449,029,000.*

do about nuclear proliferation and how much aid it wanted to give Pakistan.

The Republican-controlled Senate committee took a more trusting approach. It approved both the modification the administration requested and a late request for $100 million in economic aid for Pakistan. But the committee also directed the president to report on his non-prolifera-

tion policy and Pakistan aid package by Oct. 1, 1981. (Reagan submitted a five-year, $3.2 billion economic and military aid package for Pakistan Sept. 16.) *(Box, p. 172)*

The 1976 law, Section 669 of the Foreign Assistance Act (PL 94-329), prohibited U.S. aid to any nation that dealt in nuclear enrichment equipment, materials or technology but refused to submit to international safeguards

against nuclear proliferation. The president could waive
the law if he certified to Congress that he had "reliable
assurances that the country in question will not acquire or
develop nuclear weapons or assist other nations in doing
so." *(1976 Almanac p. 215)*

The law was sponsored by Sen. Stuart Symington, D-
Mo. (1953-76). President Carter invoked it in 1979, when
he cut off aid to Pakistan and accused that nation of trying
to develop a nuclear bomb.

Pakistan's neighbor and historical enemy, India, exploded a nuclear device in 1974.

After the Soviet invasion of Afghanistan in December
1979, President Carter offered to restore aid to Pakistan
with a $400 million, two-year package. But in March 1980
Pakistan President Mohammed Zia ul-Haq rejected the
offer, calling it "peanuts."

The Reagan administration said it also wanted to offer
aid to Pakistan to help it cope with refugees from Soviet-
occupied Afghanistan and counter the Soviet military presence.

Though the House committee declined to act on the
request to amend the Symington amendment, the committee's report on HR 3566 said it did so "without prejudice to
the administration's efforts to work out a new and closer
relationship to Pakistan."

El Salvador

Both committees decided to place restrictions on aid
to the embattled junta of El Salvador. The Reagan administration pumped millons of dollars of military and economic aid into that country early in 1981, in a demonstration of U.S. resolve to battle leftist guerillas in Central
America.

House Committee

The committee April 29 rejected demands for an immediate cutoff of military aid to El Salvador.

The panel did agree to an amendment by liberal New
York Democrats Stephen J. Solarz and Jonathan B.
Bingham to require the president to certify before sending
further military aid that El Salvador had met six conditions aimed at fostering human and civil rights and a
peaceful settlement of the conflict there.

However, that amendment was adopted only after the
committee dropped a provision giving Congress a veto on
aid to El Salvador after the president's certification.

The amendment to ban all military aid was offered by
Gerry E. Studds, D-Mass. A similar proposal was defeated
earlier by the Inter-American Affairs Subcommittee on a 4-
4 vote.

"The time has come in El Salvador to stop the killing
and start the talking," Studds said, arguing that the Reagan policy did nothing to encourage rightists in the Salvadoran junta to seek a settlement with leftist guerrillas.

But Robert J. Lagomarsino, R-Calif., argued that an
end to U.S. military aid would encourage communist nations and the leftist insurgents to intensify their efforts to
win control of the Central American nation.

"I think one person who would be very happy to have
this amendment passed ... is Fidel Castro," Lagomarsino
said. Administration officials had charged that the Cuban
dictator was funneling arms to the Salvadoran leftists.

Daniel A. Mica, D-Fla., argued that the United States
should continue giving military aid to the government of
junta President Jose Napoleon Duarte, under assault by

both the right and left, because it offered the only hope for
a democratic future in El Salvador.

Studds had complained that the amount planned for
El Salvador was far larger than any military aid being
offered other Latin American nations. But Robert K.
Dornan, R-Calif., who met Duarte in El Salvador during
the Easter recess, said Duarte wanted the $25 million and
should get "this pitiful amount of military aid he wants."

The Studds amendment failed by 9-22, with eight
Democrats joining 14 Republicans in defeating it.

Conditional Aid. The committee next considered the
Solarz-Bingham proposal in its original form, which provided for a legislative veto in addition to setting conditions
on U.S. military aid to El Salvador.

Under the amendment, the president would have to
certify that the government of El Salvador itself had not
violated human rights; was achieving "substantial control"
over its security forces, which were said to have committed
torture, murders and other atrocities; had made progress in
redistributing land among its peasants; intended to hold
free elections at an early date; was seeking a political
resolution of the turmoil there; and was honestly trying to
solve the murders of six Americans killed there in 1980.

Solarz said the proposal was a compromise. He sought
to appeal to Republican members by describing the
amendment as "an approach essentially identical to the
approach we took with our aid to Nicaragua."

Congress in 1980 voted $75 million in economic aid for
leftist Nicaragua, but attached various conditions to the
aid. *(1980 Almanac p. 330)*

"The fundamental question is whether we're going to
put a bottom line on our aid to El Salvador," Solarz said.
He said it would "strengthen the hand of President
Duarte" in controlling his government's military and security forces if U.S. aid was contingent on their good behavior.

Lagomarsino protested that there was no legislative
veto included in Nicaragua's aid restrictions, which conservatives demanded and liberals generally opposed.

Chairman Zablocki said the administration had informed him that Reagan "may very well veto" the foreign
aid bill if Congress included new legislative vetoes in it.
Zablocki suggested removing the legislative veto.

Solarz resisted at first but eventually agreed to an
amendment by David R. Bowen, D-Miss., deleting the congressional veto. Solarz also agreed to an amendment by
Lagomarsino to include among the conditions that the
junta demonstrate "support for the private sector."

With the legislative veto removed, moderate members
of the committee joined Solarz on the issue.

The committee then accepted by voice vote an amendment by Millicent Fenwick, R-N.J., to the Solarz-Bingham
amendment, to stipulate that the Salvador junta "is achieving" rather than "has achieved" substantial control over its
security forces.

With that change, the Solarz-Bingham amendment
was adopted by a vote of 26-7, with all 18 of the panel's 21
Democrats attending voting in favor and eight of the 15
Republicans present joining them.

Following that vote, Inter-American Subcommittee
Chairman Michael D. Barnes, D-Md., offered an amendment to require the 56 U.S. military advisers then in El
Salvador to withdraw within 30 days of the foreign aid bill's
enactment. The same proposal had failed by a vote of 4-4
in Barnes's subcommittee.

After further debate, Barnes's amendment failed by a

vote of 11-19.

Senate Committee

The Senate committee's vote May 11 to put conditions on U.S. military aid to El Salvador followed the lead of the House panel.

Although the conditions demonstrated congressional concern with U.S. policy in El Salvador, they did not materially restrict Reagan from continuing to aid the ruling junta.

The Senate amendment, supported by moderate committee Republicans, was a modified version of a bill introduced by Dodd.

He agreed to match the House committee measure by dropping a provision to let Congress veto military aid to El Salvador.

The conditions would require a report from the president 30 days after the foreign aid bill's enactment and every subsequent six months certifying that the Salvadoran junta had met conditions aimed at protecting human and civil rights and reaching a peaceful end to the conflict.

Among other things, the president would have to certify that the junta had made progress on economic and political reforms and had moved to achieve "substantial control over all elements of its own armed forces so as to bring to an end the indiscriminate torture and murder of Salvadoran citizens by these forces."

Dodd said the stipulations were "conditions the administration already has endorsed" and would not place "any undue burdens on the administration."

Kassebaum said she supported Dodd's measure because of the need for bipartisan backing for U.S. policy. She said placing conditions on U.S. aid would strengthen President Duarte over rightists in the junta by raising the threat of an end to the U.S. arms they needed to fight leftists.

But administration officials said the amendment could have the opposite result, tempting leftists and rightists alike to foster violence in hopes of getting Congress to end U.S. support of the junta.

"Once they're given a substantial incentive to achieve a suspension of American aid, we think they will do that," said James R. Cheek of the State Department's Latin American bureau.

Dodd and Biden countered that the conditions were not absolute. Biden said the committee was asking only for the president's "best judgment."

But Cheek said that even if the administration determined a particular instance of violence was not the junta's fault, congressional critics might not believe that. "The [Salvadoran] government is blamed for everything," he said.

Chairman Percy read a letter from Secretary of State Alexander M. Haig Jr. arguing that extremists in El Salvador "will conclude from the legislation that they can force an end to U.S. assistance . . . by stepping up their violence to the point where it blocks further progress on the reforms. . . ."

But Percy said that with the American public fearful of further U.S. involvement, "we are really on the firing line. We need to find some way to reassure them."

Dodd's amendment was approved by a vote of 11-1, with Richard G. Lugar, R-Ind., casting the only no vote. Voting yes were Republicans Percy, Kassebaum and Larry Pressler, S.D., and Democrats Dodd; Tsongas; Biden; Pell; Cranston; Glenn; Sarbanes; and Edward Zorinsky, Neb.

Argentina

The Senate panel took the lead May 11 in linking U.S. military sales or aid to Argentina to its government's accounting for thousands of "disappeared" persons.

Argentina had been barred from receiving U.S. arms since 1978 because of human rights violations there. The Reagan administration wanted the ban lifted unconditionally.

The House committee had rejected a similar measure May 7, but it followed the Senate panel's suit on May 12. Both committees ignored last-minute letters from Haig urging them to reject any such conditions.

The administration had said that rights abuses in Argentina had sharply declined, and the new president, Gen. Roberto Viola, had promised further reforms. (Viola resigned as president in December 1981).

Pell acknowledged that "the situation is getting better," but he said there was "still a need to know what happened" to those who disappeared during the military's crackdown on terrorism in Argentina in recent years. Pell said he feared that Viola's pledge to account for the disappeared persons was not being carried out. Pell proposed that any arms sales or aid to Argentina be withheld unless the president certified to Congress that Argentina had "made significant progress in complying with internationally recognized principles of human rights. . . ."

His amendment stipulated that Argentina must make "every effort" to account for those who disappeared since 1974. To get U.S. arms, Argentina also would have to release or "bring to justice" those held under a law permitting indefinite detention without charges.

After negotiations, Percy proposed an amendment to require that, in making his certification, the president merely pay "particular attention" to whether Pell's conditions had been met, rather than be bound to them.

The committee approved the Pell-Percy amendment by an 11-1 vote, with Kassebaum voting against it. Voting in favor were Republicans Percy, Pressler, Hayakawa, Baker, plus Democrats Pell, Biden, Sarbanes, Zorinsky, Tsongas, Cranston and Dodd.

House Committee

On May 12, House Inter-American Subcommittee Chairman Barnes proposed adopting the Senate panel's amendment, following lengthy negotiations over wording of the Senate measure.

The committee removed a requirement that Argentina list the disappeared persons. But it rejected an amendment by Larry Winn Jr., R-Kan., to delete the requirement that the president consider whether the Argentine government had brought to justice those held in jail without charges.

The modified amendment was approved by voice vote.

In its early action on May 7, the committee, on a key vote of 15-20, rejected an amendment by Studds that would have made any renewed arms sales to Argentina conditioned on its accounting for thousands of "disappeared" persons.

The administration easily won the vote, in part by bringing visible pressure to bear. John A. Bushnell, acting assistant secretary of state for inter-American affairs, put in a special appearance to argue against Studds's amendment.

Studds had failed in an April attempt to get the Inter-American Affairs Subcommittee to retain the ban on military sales.

In offering his modified proposal to place conditions on repeal of the embargo, he said it "reflects the minimum possible conditions that should be attached to a resumption of military sales to Argentina."

Bushnell said that while the Studds amendment might sound non-controversial in the United States, it would "carry a dynamite impact [in Argentina] that I think many of you do not comprehend."

He said that "accounting for the disappeared" was a "code" phrase for Argentinians that implied a desire to find and punish those responsible for the disappearances, in turn implying government culpability.

"We believe very strongly that the correct action is to remove this major thorn in our relations with Argentina," Bushnell said of the arms embargo.

Don Bonker, D-Wash., chairman of the Human Rights and International Organizations Subcommittee, sided with Studds, saying human rights violations in Argentina had not ceased. Bonker said 900 political prisoners still were being held in Argentine jails without charges against them, and there were reports of government-condoned anti-Semitism in Argentina, where German Nazi war criminals were known to live in hiding.

"If we should enact an unconditional repeal, we would send a message to Argentina that their attitudes about human rights don't matter," Bonker said.

Chairman Zablocki quoted Under Secretary of State James L. Buckley as saying the Organization of American States had investigated the allegations of anti-Semitism and had "found the government was not involved."

Bonker and Barnes disputed that. But Dornan noted that Israel had sold some weapons to Argentina during the U.S. arms embargo. Dornan said that indicated the reports of Argentinian government complicity in anti-Semitism were unfounded.

Voting against the Studds amendment were 13 Republicans and Zablocki, L. H. Fountain, D-N.C.; Gus Yatron, D-Pa.; Dante B. Fascell, D-Fla.; Andy Ireland, D-Fla.; Mica; and David R. Bowen, D-Miss.

Israel, Egypt

As had been the case for years, Israel and Egypt were to receive more than half of all U.S. foreign aid in fiscal 1982. Each measure earmarked about $2.2 billion in aid for Israel, including $1.4 billion in military aid. Egypt was to get about $1.7 billion, $900 million of it military aid.

Both bills provided Israel and Egypt the same amounts of arms loans and Economic Support Fund (ESF) aid authorized in fiscal 1981, plus $21 million each in ESF aid that was taken from their fiscal 1981 payments and used for El Salvador and Liberia instead. In fiscal 1982, Israel would receive $806 million in ESF, and Egypt would get $771 million.

For the second year, both bills also provided that all ESF aid given Israel and Egypt would be a grant. Before fiscal 1981, ESF for Israel and Egypt was two-thirds grant.

As in previous years, each bill also provided that $500 million of Israel's Foreign Military Sales (FMS) loans be forgiven, making that amount a grant. Because both committees changed a Reagan request for a new form of low-interest FMS loans called "direct credits," the terms each offered Israel and Egypt on other arms loans differed.

While the House panel did not approve the request for low-interest arms loans for other countries, it specified that $50 million of Israel's $900 million in regular FMS loans be

made low-interest. It also included Israel among nations getting easy repayment terms on their loans.

Military Aid

S 1196 would authorize a total FMS program for fiscal 1982 of $4.076 billion, requiring appropriations of $991 million to pay for the grant portions. The bill authorized $3.1 billion in FMS loans that required no appropriation.

In addition to Israel and Egypt, major FMS recipients under S 1196 were to be Turkey ($400 million, including a $125 million grant), Greece ($280 million, up $20 million from the Reagan request), South Korea ($167.5 million), Spain ($150 million) and the Sudan ($100 million, including a $50 million grant).

HR 3566 would authorize a combination of FMS loans and Military Assistance Program (MAP) grants to fund an arms sales program totaling $4.068 billion. That included the $550 million grant direct loan for Israel, regular FMS loan guarantees of $3.270 billion and MAP grants of $248 million.

Like the Senate committee, the House committee earmarked $280 million in FMS loans for Greece to restore a traditional ratio of 7:10 for aid to Greece and Turkey.

Unlike the Senate panel, the House committee reduced the administration request for FMS loans for Zaire by $6.5 million. Some members of the House committee opposed aid for Zaire's military government because they said it was corrupt. The Senate committee added $2 million to the request for Lebanon, for a total of $17 million.

Arms Transfers

Both panels compromised with the administration on its requests for reduced congressional control of arms sales to allies and transfers of U.S. arms amongst them.

Both agreed to double the thresholds at which sales of U.S. arms or transfers of U.S.-made arms between allies — "third-country transfers" — must be reported to Congress. The thresholds would be increased from $7 million to $14 million for a single item and from $25 million to $50 million for a package of equipment.

Under existing law, any arms sale reported to Congress could be vetoed if, within 30 days, Congress passed a concurrent resolution disapproving the sale.

The House bill would exempt NATO, Japan, Australia and New Zealand from both the legislative veto and the 30-day notice requirement. Reports to Congress on arms transfers above the reporting thresholds involving those allies still would be required, unless the president certified that an emergency required the immediate transfer.

The Senate bill would reduce the 30-day notice requirement to 15 days on arms transfers involving NATO, its members, or Japan, Australia or New Zealand. The legislative veto provision still would apply to those allies under the Senate bill.

In addition, the Senate bill would repeal a $100 million limit on each individual commercial arms sale to countries other than NATO members, Australia, Japan and New Zealand. Currently, individual arms sales over that amount, except to the key allies, had to be made through the U.S. government.

Special FMS Fund

Though differing in details, each panel agreed to the basic thrust of an administration request for a Special Defense Acquisition Fund to be used for advance purchases

of weapons and equipment frequently ordered by U.S. arms loans recipients.

The Senate committee granted an administration request that the fund be established using about $342 million in FMS receipts and operate as a revolving fund with a portion of FMS receipts going into it annually. However, the panel put a $350 million cap on the size of the fund, which it said Congress could review in future years.

The House committee also approved the new account but rejected the request for a revolving fund, stipulating instead that the size of the fund must be set annually by Congress.

The House panel authorized appropriations of $150 million for the fund in both fiscal 1982 and fiscal 1983.

Military Assistance Program

Despite previous congressional plans to phase out the grant Military Assistance Program (MAP) at the end of 1981, both bills authorized MAP in fiscal 1982.

Starting in the mid-1970s, MAP grants were given to countries such as Spain and Portugal where U.S. military bases were located. The grants were used to buy weapons.

The Senate bill, however, did delete a Reagan request for a $100 million MAP contingency fund and would authorize only $31.4 million for MAP operating expenses.

The House bill would authorize $304 million for MAP grants in each of fiscal 1982 and fiscal 1983, but $248 million of that amount was required to fund the House committee's formula for combining MAP grants with FMS loans to the 15 nations the administration wanted to give low-interest "direct credits."

The House committee bill also would include a MAP contingency fund of $25 million, with the rest of the money for administrative and other expenses.

Defense Drawdown

Partially compensating for its rejection of Reagan's requested MAP contingency fund, the Senate bill would increase from $50 million to $100 million the value of military equipment the president could transfer to allies under emergency power known as "defense drawdown authority." The House bill contained no similar provision.

Reagan used the authority in March to send $20 million in aid to El Salvador.

Military Training

S 1196 would cut $6 million from the president's request for the International Military Education and Training (IMET) program, under which foreign military officers received U.S. training in the United States or abroad.

The Senate bill would authorize a fiscal 1982 IMET program of $41.7 million, an increase of $7.7 million over the fiscal 1981 authorization of $34 million. The Senate report said the committee reduced Reagan's request for IMET "solely for budgetary purposes."

The House bill would grant the full Reagan request in fiscal 1982 and would authorize an IMET program of $51.9 million in fiscal 1983.

Reports on Advisers

Adopting an amendment by Glenn, the Senate bill tightened a provision in the Arms Export Control Act of 1968 requiring that the president report to Congress when hostilities broke out in foreign nations where U.S. military personnel were serving.

Glenn had persistently complained that, despite widespread violence in El Salvador, Reagan declined to report to Congress under the arms export act when he sent U.S. military advisers to help train the Salvadoran military.

Section 21(c) of the Arms Export Control Act required a report to Congress within 48 hours of the outbreak of "significant hostilities" in a nation where U.S. personnel were performing defense services.

Glenn argued that Reagan should have reported to Congress under that law. Reagan administration officials said no report was required because "significant hostilities" in El Salvador began during the Carter administration.

Under the Senate bill, the president would be required to report to Congress within 48 hours of "the existence of, or a change in the status of hostilities or terrorist acts" that might endanger American lives or property in a country. However, the report would be required only if the U.S. military personnel themselves were endangered.

Military Advisory Groups

The Senate committee agreed to an administration request to ease controls on how many U.S. military personnel could be stationed abroad to manage U.S. military aid programs. The House committee, wary of the administration's use of advisers in El Salvador, was less receptive to that idea.

Existing law prohibited the Pentagon from assigning more than six military personnel to any nation to manage a U.S. aid program unless Congress specifically authorized a larger group.

The Senate bill would lift that ceiling. It would provide instead that the president must give Congress advance notice of any plans to increase the number of military personnel in a given country above the level originally proposed to Congress each year.

Congress would have no formal method of blocking the president's plans to increase the number of advisers, but the Senate Foreign Relations and House Foreign Affairs committees could object to such plans.

By contrast, the House bill would retain the statutory limit of six military personnel but would allow the president to waive the limit if he informed Congress 30 days in advance of doing so that such a step was necessary to protect U.S. national interests.

The House bill would authorize military management groups larger than six for Indonesia, South Korea, the Philippines, Thailand, Egypt, Jordan, Morocco, Saudi Arabia, Portugal, Spain, Greece and Turkey.

The House bill admonished: "Advisory and training assistance conducted by military personnel assigned under this section shall be kept to an absolute minimum."

Peacekeeping Operations

Both bills would authorize the administration's request for $19 million in fiscal 1982, a reduction of $6 million, for the U.S. share of United Nations peacekeeping forces in the Sinai peninsula ($10 million) and on Cyprus ($9 million).

The House bill also would bar the president from financing or committing U.S. forces to a new Sinai peacekeeping force scheduled to be created in April 1982, when Israel was to complete its withdrawal from the Sinai under the terms of its 1979 peace treaty with Egypt.

The treaty contemplated a United Nations peacekeeping force for the Sinai, but the Soviet Union had threatened to veto such a proposal. The United States, Egypt and Israel later agreed on an independent peacekeeping force,

including foreign troops. *(Sinai force, p. 151)*

The House committee said the prohibition on including U.S. troops was included to ensure that Congress had the chance to fully review and authorize any such mission. The Senate committee report merely noted that a request for funds for a new Sinai force was "expected."

Economic, Development Aid

Economic Support Fund. Both bills cut the administration request for $2.582 billion in ESF aid, the major source of political aid to U.S. allies. ESF was intended to bolster the economies of friendly governments so they could devote more of their own resources to defense.

The House bill cut the Reagan request by reducing the size of an ESF contingency fund the administration wanted from $250 million to $100 million.

The House committee added $106.5 million in ESF for various countries: $21 million each for Israel and Egypt to replace ESF aid withheld from them in fiscal 1981; $10 million for Morocco; $10 million for Kenya, for a total of $20 million; $10 million for Somalia, for a total of $30 million; $25 million for Costa Rica; $7.5 million for Cyprus, for a total of $15 million; $2 million for Lebanon for humanitarian purposes, for a total of $7 million.

The Senate bill would authorize an ESF program of $2.474 billion, a reduction of $208 million from the Reagan request.

The committee deleted $218 million by subtracting that amount plus the $21 million each additional for Israel and Egypt from the $250 million ESF contingency fund request. It then added $10 million: $5 million earmarked for Tunisia: $2.5 million for Cyprus (for a total of $10 million); and $2.5 million for Costa Rica. It also approved a late administration request for $100 million for Pakistan.

Turkey. The Senate bill also earmarked $300 million for Turkey, and both bills provided for the second year in a row that two-thirds of Turkey's ESF aid would be a grant.

Syria. Angered by Syria's animosity toward the United States and the U.S.-sponsored Middle East peace efforts, the Senate committee prohibited any ESF aid for Syria in fiscal 1982.

The House committee ordered that aid appropriated for Syria in previous years but not obligated under contracts be withheld and deposited in the Treasury. The committee report said between $106 million and $130 million would be affected by the provision.

Nicaragua. The Senate bill repealed conditions on aid to Nicaragua established by Congress in 1980 when it approved $75 million in ESF for that country's Sandinista government. Citing the conditions, the Reagan administration in February suspended the final $15 million payment of the $75 million.

Others. Major ESF requests approved by both committees also included: $75 million for Zimbabwe, $50 million for the Sudan, $50 million for the Philippines, $40 million for El Salvador, $40 million for Jamaica and $20 million for Nicaragua.

Development Assistance

The Senate bill cut $106 million from the $1.399 billion Reagan request for bilateral agriculture, population, health, education, energy and scientific development aid programs administered by the Agency for International Development (AID), reducing the total to $1.293 billion. The fiscal 1981 authorization was $1.350 billion.

The House bill increased Reagan's request for AID programs by $83 million in fiscal 1982, to $1.482 billion, and raised them to $1.614 billion in fiscal 1983.

The Senate cut $39 million from the $728 million request for agriculture, rural development and nutrition aid; $37 million from the $253 million request for population aid; and $37 million from the $178 million request for aid to energy projects, private voluntary organizations (PVOs) and related programs. It would add $7.5 million to the $120 million request for health programs.

The House bill added $20 million to agriculture aid, $20 million for population aid and $13 million for health programs. It also established energy programs as a separate aid category with a $39 million authorization.

Under amendments offered by Sen. Tsongas and Rep. Solarz, each bill directed the president to use up to $5.7 million of fiscal 1982 funds in the education account to finance scholarships in the United States for non-white South African students who were prevented by their nation's racial laws from getting "an adequate undergraduate or professional education."

In its authorization for population programs, the Senate committee included an amendment by Biden prohibiting AID from using any of the funds provided for "biomedical research related to abortions as a method of family planning."

Other Aid

IDCA. The committees disagreed on the value of the International Development Cooperation Agency, a State Department umbrella agency erected in 1979 to coordinate U.S. aid programs. The Senate committee disliked IDCA and voted to abolish it. The House panel took the opposite position, saying that "every effort should be undertaken to expand IDCA's coordinating role. The committee would, therefore, disapprove any effort to weaken or lessen the function and responsibilities of IDCA."

Peace Corps. Each measure authorized $105 million for Peace Corps operations in fiscal 1982, up $10 million from the administration request, and separated the Peace Corps from ACTION, its parent agency since June 1971.

Sahel Development. The Senate bill cut the administration request for the multilateral Sahel Development Program in Africa from $107.5 million to $102 million. The House bill cut the fiscal 1982 authorization to $86.6 million.

But the House committee said $20.4 million remained available for the program from previous authorizations, which it said would permit fiscal 1982 spending for the Sahel program of $107.5 million, the amount requested.

ASHA. As they had done for years, both committees added to the administration request for the American Schools and Hospitals Abroad (ASHA) budgets. The Senate bill increased the Reagan request from $7.5 million to $12 million. The House bill boosted it to $20 million.

International Organizations. The Senate bill authorized $229 million, a $14 million increase over the Reagan request, for contributions to international organizations, such as UN agencies. The House authorized $256 million for that purpose in fiscal 1982 and $278 million in fiscal 1983.

African Foundation. The House bill earmarked $2 million, which Reagan did not request, to establish the African Development Foundation, which Congress authorized in the fiscal 1981 aid authorization bill.

Narcotics Control. Both bills authorized $37.7 million for international narcotics control programs in fiscal

Sale of F-16s to Pakistan Approved . . .

Many foreign policy specialists and observers had seen in the administration's proposal to sell 40 F-16 warplanes to Pakistan the potential for a major battle between President Reagan and Congress.

Under the Arms Export Control Act (PL 94-329), Congress could have blocked the F-16 sale by adopting a concurrent resolution of disapproval within 30 days after formal notice of the sale was delivered on Oct. 23.

But the F-16 issue came on the heels of the debate over selling AWACS radar planes to Saudi Arabia, and many observers agreed that Congress had little taste for yet another confrontation with the president on arms sales. *(AWACS, p. 129)*

The F-16 sale won congressional approval when the Senate Foreign Relations and House Foreign Affairs committees rejected veto resolutions (S Con Res 48 and H Con Res 211, respectively).

The Senate panel voted against S Con Res 48 by 7-10 on Nov. 17, with Democrats John Glenn, Ohio, and Edward Zorinsky, Neb., joining eight of the committee's nine Republicans in supporting the sale. Larry Pressler of South Dakota was the only GOP member against the deal.

The same day, two House Foreign Affairs subcommittees disapproved H Con Res 211 but sent it to the full committee anyway. On Nov. 19, the full committee failed by a vote of 13-13 to approve the measure.

Republicans Millicent Fenwick, N.J., and Olympia J. Snowe of Maine joined 11 Democrats in voting for H Con Res 211. Democrats Clement J. Zablocki, Wis., L. H. Fountain of North Carolina and Dante B. Fascell, Florida, and 10 Republicans voted against it.

Aid Package

The F-16s, costing $1.1 billion, were related to a $3.2 billion package of military and economic aid designed to bolster Pakistan in the wake of the Soviet occupation of neighboring Afghanistan.

Six planes, reportedly to be delivered to Pakistan in 1982, were to be diverted from stocks intended for NATO countries.

The other 34 planes were to be delivered by mid-1984.

In addition to the planes, the administration planned to sell Pakistan tanks, missiles, howitzers, helicopters and armored personnel carriers.

The overall $3.2 bilion Pakistan aid package included:

● Economic, development and food aid totaling $150 million in fiscal 1982, $250 million in 1983, $275 million in 1984, $300 million in 1985 and $325 million annually in 1986 and 1987. Those figures included $50 million for each year in food aid. The rest of the money was to be used to shore up Pakistan's economy and for development programs (such as agriculture and health) run by the Agency for International Development (AID).

In requesting the aid, administration officials stressed that no specific decisions had been made about how it was to be used. In background material, Peter M. McPherson, director of AID, said projections for using the economic aid after fiscal 1982 "are at this point notional."

● Arms loans of $275 million in fiscal 1983, $300 million in 1984, and $326 million annually in 1985, 1986 and 1987. Pakistan also was to receive $800,000 annually in 1983 and 1984 and $1 million annually in 1985 through 1987 for military training.

Arguments For the Sale

James L. Buckley, under secretary of state for security assistance, gave Senate and House committees identical reasons why the administration thought it wise to sell Pakistan F-16 high performance warplanes.

Some members of Congress feared that the administration's willingness to sell F-16s to Pakistan and other nations would lead other countries to expect the United States to sell the aircraft to them as well.

Buckley said the administration was wary of that, but he said Pakistan should be an exception to a general policy of encouraging potential customers to buy other aircraft.

He said the threat to Pakistan posed by the Soviet troops in Afghanistan warranted the sale.

"The intention," Buckley told two House Foreign Affairs subcommittees on Nov. 17, "is twofold: to give Pakistan the ability to handle, with its own resources, incursions and limited cross-border threats from Soviet-backed Afghan forces, and to keep the Soviets from thinking they can coerce and subvert Pakistan with impunity."

He said there was no illusion within the administra-

1982, and both repealed a 1978 ban on the use of U.S. foreign aid to spray the herbicide paraquat on marijuana. Members of Congress from Florida, where much drug smuggling from South America occurred, pushed the paraquat ban repeal.

The Senate bill earmarked $100,000 for research on substances that would leave a mark on marijuana or other illicit crops sprayed with herbicides.

Salvadoran Refugees. The House bill also authorized $5 million in fiscal 1982 and $5.5 million in fiscal 1983 to assist those driven from their homes by the political violence in El Salvador.

OPIC. The Senate bill reauthorized operation of the Overseas Private Investment Corp. (OPIC), which insured American firms investing abroad against political risks such as revolution, until Sept. 30, 1985. The House bill did not include OPIC, which was being considered by the panel's International Economic Policy Subcommittee.

Food for Peace. The House measure authorized a four year extension, to Dec. 31, 1985, of the PL 480 Food for Peace program, which financed shipments of surplus food and grain to poor nations. The Senate bill did not address the program.

Because Egypt had been receiving more than 40 percent of PL 480 aid, the House committee included a provision to take effect in fiscal 1983 that would prohibit more than 30 percent of PL 480 aid from going to any one country in a given year.

. . . In Spite of Questions in Congress

tion that the F-16s would enable Pakistan to withstand a "direct and massive Soviet attack."

But the F-16s, he said, would "raise the cost of potential aggression and . . . demonstrate that a strong security relationship exists between the U.S. and Pakistan which the Soviet Union must take into account in its calculations."

Subcommittee members questioned the sale on several counts.

First, some argued that the F-16 was a more sophisticated aircraft than Pakistan required to meet the Soviet threat in Afghanistan. Rep. Stephen J. Solarz, D-N.Y., said Pakistan could get more planes quicker if it bought an older, less capable fighter such as the F-5, which he said would serve Pakistan's purposes.

But Buckley said that Pakistan's "limited financial resources compel it to purchase a proven aircraft which will serve its needs well into the 1990s." Also, he said, Pakistan "faces a clear and present threat against which the F-16 is an appropriate choice."

Balance of Power

Critics of the sale also worried that it would upset the balance of power between Pakistan and India, which had been enemies ever since Pakistan was created by the 1947 partition of India in which India gained its independence from Britain. Pakistan and India were at war as recently as 1971.

Buckley assured the subcommittees that the balance of power would not be affected. He said India already had a "four- or five-to-one advantage in modern aircraft," was acquiring even more sophisticated Soviet aircraft and was negotiating to buy 150 advanced Mirage 2000 fighters from France.

Few senators attended Buckley's Nov. 12 testimony before the Senate Foreign Relations Committee. But a major concern among those who did was Pakistan's effort to acquire the capacity to build a nuclear weapon. The discussion in the Senate panel centered on the wisdom of waiving the Symington amendment, which had barred aid to Pakistan because of its nuclear activities.

The administration had argued that the best way to get Pakistan to drop its efforts to develop nuclear weapons would be to bolster it enough militarily to make Pakistani President Muhammad Zia ul-Haq feel secure from outside threats.

Pakistan's Intentions

Buckley assurd the Senate committee that Pakistan "does not intend to develop nuclear weapons."

Asked by Glenn whether Zia had been told that U.S. aid would be halted if Pakistan exploded a nuclear device, Buckley said: "There is no doubt whatsoever in the mind of any responsible official in Pakistan, including the president, what the consequences would be."

When Glenn pressed Buckley to say what those consequences were, Buckley replied: "It would be very hard to see, in the event of an explosion, how we could continue the assistance."

But Glenn said he was skeptical that Pakistan would give up its nuclear development efforts. He cited a 1966 vow by the late President Zulfikar Ali Bhutto that if India ever were to explode a nuclear device, Pakistanis would "eat grass" if necessary to match the feat.

India exploded a nuclear device in 1974, Glenn noted, and he said Pakistan had yet to demonstrate that it had given up its "bomb plans."

"No one doubts that the Pakistani government has been working as rapidly as possible toward the capability of a nuclear option," Buckley conceded. However, he added, "No one doubts that the Symington amendment has done nothing to stop it."

Members of both committees also questioned whether Pakistan wanted the F-16s to counter the Soviet threat or really wanted them to improve its position vs. India, and so whether it was clear that the planes were to be used for defensive purposes only, as U.S. law required.

Buckley said Pakistan was sincerely concerned by the Soviet threat and that the preponderance of power enjoyed by India would prevent Pakistan from any aggression in any event.

Glenn asked Buckley if the United States would cut off aid to Pakistan if Pakistan used its F-16s for a preemptive strike against India's nuclear capacity like one Israel launched against Iraq on June 7.

Given India's air power, Buckley said, "It would be almost suicidal for Pakistan to make such a strike."

But as for whether the United States would halt aid to Pakistan in such an event, he said, "We would first have to determine whether it [the strike] was defensive."

Senate Floor Action

The Senate broadly endorsed the Reagan administration view that more U.S. foreign aid must be spent to beef up America's allies militarily and less must go to help poor nations develop their economies.

In a $5.8 billion foreign aid authorization bill passed Oct. 22, the Senate also went along in general with administration insistence that the president needed a freer hand to use U.S. aid dollars as a policy tool.

The vote on S 1196 was 40-33. The Senate worked on the bill Sept. 23, 24, and 30, and Oct. 20, 21 and 22. *(Vote 327, p. 55-S)*

While the Senate imposed conditions on U.S. aid to El Salvador, it gave the president broad leeway to decide whether those conditions had been met. Similarly, while providing for continued congressional participation in U.S. policy toward Angola, Argentina, Chile and Pakistan, the Senate agreed to lift bans imposed in the 1970s on U.S. military aid to those countries.

Moreover, the Senate agreed without debate to double the dollar thresholds at which arms sales must be reported to Congress and were subject to congressional veto. The Senate also doubled, from $50 million to $100 million, the value of military equipment the president could take from U.S. stocks and give to a foreign country in an emergency.

Despite sharp disagreements within the Senate over U.S. policy in a number of troubled regions of the world,

the debate on S 1196 was less than contentious on most issues.

Floor manager Percy, chairman of the Senate Foreign Relations Committee, won compromises on many amendments that allowed them to be handled by voice vote.

Funding Cut. One instance involved an amendment offered by Jesse Helms, R-N.C., to cut all authorizations in the bill by 6 percent — about $350 million.

Percy negotiated a compromise, cutting only $67.6 million from the overall authorization in the bill. Helms accepted it, and it was adopted by voice vote.

El Salvador

The Senate demonstrated Sept. 24 that Congress intended to continue playing chaperon to the Reagan administration in its relationship with the ruling junta in El Salvador.

With Salvadoran junta President Jose Napoleon Duarte bringing his nation's turmoil to the fore again by visiting Washington, the Senate voted to suspend U.S. military aid to El Salvador unless the junta protected human rights and pursued economic and political reforms.

By a vote of 47-51, the Senate rejected an amendment by Helms to transform into mere goals restrictions on aid to El Salvador that had been approved by the Foreign Relations Committee. The Helms amendment also would have deleted support for the junta's policy of land redistribution. *(Vote 275, p. 47-S)*

The vote was a defeat for both the Reagan administration, which opposed congressional restrictions on U.S. aid to El Salvador or any other country, and for Duarte, who visited Capitol Hill Sept. 22.

Percy put into the *Congressional Record* a Sept. 23 letter from Duarte that said the sentiment expressed in the conditions "coincides with my own stated objectives."

But Duarte said conditions would be "an unacceptable imposition on a government friendly to the United States and fully committed to fulfill its pledge."

Helms Amendment

The Helms amendment essentially restated an amendment offered Sept. 23 by Lugar that would have made the conditions goals but included among them land reform.

"The fact is that conditions imposed upon American assistance will help only those who hope to see the end to American support for El Salvador," Lugar said. He predicted that leftists or rightists in El Salvador's civil war could force an end to U.S. aid by making it impossible, for example, for the junta to protect human rights.

Dodd, the Foreign Relations member who wrote the conditions adopted by the committee, argued the reverse. Dodd said conditions on U.S. aid would give Duarte a lever with which to gain control of rightists in the junta by tying continued U.S. arms aid to their good behavior.

Percy joined Dodd in arguing that there was nothing onerous about imposing conditions on aid.

"If I walk into a bank and I say to the banker, 'I want to borrow your money, your depositors' money,' the bank has the right to lay down the conditions. If you accept those conditions, then you accept the money.... Otherwise, you are not likely to get the money," Percy said.

In parliamentary maneuvering Sept. 23, Lugar's amendment was modified when the Senate substituted, by a 54-42 vote, an amendment by Pell, that changed Lugar's goals into conditions. *(Vote 274, p. 47-S)*

Helms offered his amendment as a substitute. After it failed Sept. 24, the Senate formally adopted Pell's amendment by voice vote, thus approving conditions similar to those Foreign Relations proposed.

The Pell amendment required the president to cut off U.S. military aid to El Salvador in fiscal 1982 and 1983 unless he could certify to Congress within 30 days after enactment of the foreign aid bill and every 180 days thereafter that the government of El Salvador, "to the extent not precluded by forces outside its control," was:

• Making "a concerted and significant effort" to safeguard human rights.

• "Moving to achieve control" over its armed forces to stop "indiscriminate torture and murder."

• Implementing economic and political reforms "including the land reform program."

• "Committed to the holding of free elections at an early date and to that end has demonstrated its willingness to negotiate an equitable political resolution of the conflict with any group which renounces and refrains from further military or paramilitary opposition activity."

U.S. Aid

In fiscal 1981, according to the State Department, El Salvador received $136 million in U.S. economic, development and food aid, and $35.5 million in military aid, including the use of U.S. military advisers to train its military and maintain U.S. helicopters on loan.

S 1196 contained $40 million in direct economic aid, $26 million in military aid and $35 million in development aid for El Salvador in fiscal 1982.

The restrictions imposed by the Pell amendment mirrored conditions attached by Congress in 1980 to aid to Nicaragua. *(1980 Almanac p. 330)*

The Nicaragua restrictions were aimed at forcing the leftist government there to hold elections and to respect the rights of private business. By contrast, the Salvadoran restrictions were aimed at forcing a government seen by some as dominated by rightist extremists to make reforms to reduce the political appeal of leftists.

Clark Amendment

A week after imposing conditions on overt aid to El Salvador, the Senate Sept. 30 gave President Reagan an easy victory in his quest for repeal of a 1976 ban on covert aid to factions in Angola.

The repeal of the 1976 Clark amendment was formally approved with the voice vote adoption of an amendment by Kassebaum.

The key vote came when the Senate tabled, 66-29, a proposal by Tsongas to retain the aid ban until March 31, 1983, unless there was a cease-fire in the war between South Africa and Soviet-backed guerrillas based in Angola over neighboring Namibia, which was administered by South Africa. *(Vote 296, p. 50-S)*

Tsongas and other Democrats argued that repeal of the aid ban, enacted in 1976 to prevent covert U.S. aid to pro-Western factions in the Angolan civil war, raised the specter of U.S. intervention and could end cooperation by black African nations in efforts to settle the Namibian dispute. Rebels under pro-Western leader Jonas Savimbi were waging guerrilla warfare against the leftist Angolan government.

Kassebaum's amendment included a stipulation that repeal should not be "construed to be an endorsement by

Congress" of covert aid to the rebels in Angola.

Committee Divided

The Kassebaum amendment voided a compromise the Foreign Relations Committee had adopted by a 10-2 vote during a May 13 markup of S 1196.

It also bared tensions between Chairman Percy and Tsongas, who said Percy and other panel Republicans had reneged on a promise to back the May 13 compromise, claiming they had not fully understood it.

The panel had agreed to repeal the Clark amendment but required the president to submit a secret report to Congress before providing aid to factions in Angola. The compromise also required the president to certify that there had been "substantial progress" toward a Namibian settlement — including a cease-fire and preparations for elections.

Tsongas raised the Clark amendment unexpectedly Sept. 30, the second day of floor action. The pending business was an amendment by George J. Mitchell, D-Maine, stating the sense of Congress that Reagan should fill the post of assistant secretary of state for human rights.

Percy had been urging Mitchell to delete a requirement that the post be filled within 60 days of enactment of S 1196. Tsongas rose to speak in favor of Mitchell's amendment — and then offered a "perfecting" amendment.

His amendment, it turned out, dealt with repeal of the Clark amendment. Tsongas apologized for the maneuver but charged that Percy had refused to agree to allow his amendment to come up for a vote otherwise.

After Percy's motion to table the Tsongas amendment was agreed to, the Senate returned to Mitchell's amendment, which he modified to drop the deadline Percy found objectionable. The amendment was adopted by voice vote.

Kassebaum then offered her amendment, with Percy's support. "In repealing the Clark amendment, Congress is not approving covert aid to Jonas Savimbi," Percy said, referring to the anti-Marxist guerilla leader in Angola. Percy added that the White House had assured him "there is no such plan." Percy noted the fiscal 1981 intelligence authorization bill (PL 96-450) required the president to inform the House and Senate Intelligence committees of any plans for covert action anywhere, so he said Congress would be forewarned if plans changed.

Pakistan

The Senate Oct. 21 approved a ban on U.S. aid to Pakistan or India if they should explode a nuclear device but then broadened it to include all but four nations other than the United States known to possess nuclear arms.

The amendment affecting Pakistan and India was offered by Glenn and adopted by a vote of 51-45. *(Vote 314, p. 54-S)*

The broad ban on aid to non-nuclear weapons nations that exploded nuclear devices was proposed by Helms and adopted by voice vote. Helms said his amendment was an effort to "put some teeth" into U.S. nuclear non-proliferation policy.

However, a Senate aide said the Helms amendment in fact was favored by the administration to remove the stigma from India and Pakistan. The administration had opposed the Glenn amendment.

Reagan had proposed a six-year, $3.2 billion aid package for Pakistan and asked for broader power to waive the Symington amendment, which had barred aid to Pakistan

since 1979 because of its efforts to develop nuclear weapons.

On Oct. 20, arguing that the Foreign Relations Committee had gone too far in modifying the law, Glenn offered and the Senate adopted by voice vote an amendment limiting the waiver for Pakistan to six years — the life of the aid package.

"We want to have Pakistani assistance in resisting Soviet or Soviet-backed moves toward the Persian Gulf," Glenn said. However, he added, "an open-ended waiver on the Symington amendment would, in my view, be a radical change — a radical change that should be resisted."

The Senate also adopted by voice vote another Glenn amendment requiring the president to report to Congress annually on Pakistan's nuclear program and any efforts to develop "a nuclear explosive device."

There was little debate on those two Glenn amendments, but the third met opposition from Reagan allies.

The committee had asserted in S 1196 that the president "should not" use his power to waive the Symington amendment if Pakistan or India exploded a nuclear device. Glenn's amendment changed this to "shall not."

Some administration allies argued that Glenn's approach on this point was too rigid.

"I have no doubt that termination of assistance would, and barring unforeseen circumstances should, be the U.S. response," said James A. McClure, R-Idaho. But Glenn's amendment, McClure said, "would tie our hands now, and provide no flexibility for the president to respond based on an evaluation of all pertinent facts."

McClure said the amendment's "confrontational approach" to Pakistan had been tried "and has failed."

Glenn, however, said U.S. efforts to prevent the spread of nuclear weapons should be backed by firm sanctions, especially against nations that tested such weapons. "If we can't draw the line there, then we are incapable of ever drawing the line anywhere, I would submit," he said.

Helms joined Glenn, declaring that in non-proliferation policy it was time "either we put up or shut up."

After the Glenn amendment passed, Helms proposed that the required aid cutoff be extended to all nations — a proposal that came as a surprise to some, given Helms' support for South Africa and Taiwan, each of whom had been rumored to be seeking nuclear capability.

At the suggestion of Pell, Helms changed his amendment to make the ban apply to "any non-nuclear weapons nation" that exploded a nuclear device. U.S. law defined non-nuclear weapons nations as those other than China, Great Britain, France, the Soviet Union and the United States.

In its only direct vote on aid to Pakistan, the Senate rejected, 28-45, an amendment by Mark O. Hatfield, R-Ore., deleting $100 million for Pakistan from the bill. The money was the first installment of the $3.2 billion aid package. *(Vote 326, p. 55-S)*

Chile, Argentina

Capping a five-year debate on the issue, the Senate Oct. 22 voted to lift a 1976 congressional ban on aid and arms sales to the regime of Gen. Augusto Pinochet in Chile. Congress had imposed the ban in response to the regime's generally poor human rights record. *(1976 Almanac p. 213)*

Helms, who had tried for several years to revoke the ban, finally succeeded in defeating a coalition of liberals

and moderates who had viewed it as a symbol of U.S. determination to protect human rights abroad.

The key vote on the issue came when the Senate refused, 30-57, to table a Helms amendment repealing the Chile aid ban. _(Vote 321, p. 55-S)_

But by a unanimous 86-0 vote, the Senate later adopted a Percy substitute amendment stating that the president could not provide aid or allow arms sales to Chile until he certified to Congress, among other things, that Chile had made "significant progress" in improving human rights. _(Vote 322, p. 55-S)_

Helms said the Chile aid ban was a "restrictive, punitive law" that was even more severe than limitations imposed on "those paragons of human rights: Cambodia, Vietnam, Angola and South Africa."

Edward M. Kennedy, D-Mass., who sponsored the original Chile aid cutoff, countered that Chile refused to cooperate in the U.S. investigation of the assassination of former Chilean Ambassador Orlando Letelier. Letelier was assassinated in Washington in September 1976, and a U.S. grand jury had indicted the former head of the Chilean secret service and other Chilean officials as accomplices.

Chile's refusal to cooperate "represents a mockery of U.S. policy in opposition to state-supported terrorism," Kennedy said.

Percy said his compromise amendment would ensure that the United States will exercise "the utmost care and seriousness" before restoring aid to Chile. He noted that the amendment stated the sense of Congress that Chile should take steps to bring the officials indicted in the Letelier case to justice.

In regard to aid to Argentina, the Senate by voice vote dropped a committee provision that would have demanded a full accounting of "disappeared" persons as a condition for resuming aid. The Senate substituted weaker language expressing "the hope" that Argentina would make such an accounting.

Other Issues

In other action, the Senate narrowly rejected an amendment by Gary Hart, D-Colo., to impose a ban within 90 days on U.S. purchases of Libyan oil.

The Hart amendment was defeated when the Senate adopted, by a 47-44 vote, a substitute offered by Percy that instead called on the president to study how to counter Libyan militarism in North Africa and its alleged use of terrorism around the world. _(Vote 316, p. 54-S)_

Armed Services _vs._ Foreign Relations

After lengthy negotiations on and off the Senate floor, a compromise also was arrived at in a jurisdictional dispute between the Foreign Relations and Armed Services committees.

The dispute arose over provisions in S 1196 establishing new controls over Defense Department leases of excess equipment to foreign nations and establishing a new Special Defense Acquisition Fund for advance purchases of items frequently sold to U.S. arms loan recipients.

Foreign Relations had approved a proposal by Zorinsky to put Pentagon leases of excess arms and other equipment to foreign nations under the laws governing arms sales — and under the committee's review.

A major reason for the proposal was a General Accounting Office report concluding that the leasing authority was intended to allow domestic businesses and individuals to lease Pentagon property but had been expanded into a form of foreign aid not subject to normal controls.

Protesting that Foreign Relations was trying to take away a piece of his panel's turf, John Tower, R-Texas, chairman of the Armed Services Committee, offered an amendment on Oct. 22 to retain the existing law on defense leases, leaving jurisdiction over them with his committee.

In an apparent gesture to those concerned over the Pentagon's use of the authority, Tower's amendment also required the Pentagon to report to Congress 30 days in advance of leasing any single piece of equipment valued at $14 million or more and any package of equipment valued at $50 million or more.

Existing arms export law required reports to Congress of sales of individual items worth $7 million or more and arms packages of $25 million or more, but those thresholds would be doubled by both the Senate and House version of the aid authorization bill.

However, while the Foreign Relations proposal would have permitted Congress to veto any defense leases reported to it by adopting a concurrent resolution of disapproval within 30 days, Tower's amendment provided for no veto.

"It is ludicrous to even consider the removal of the Armed Services Committee from review of defense leases," Tower declared to the Senate.

First, Tower noted that defense leases were allowed only on equipment in excess of U.S. needs. "Only the Armed Services Committee can evaluate what is in excess of current U.S. military needs," he asserted.

Tower added that various reports required by law already had created "an excessive burden on Congress, which is overtaxed by its current workload."

Percy responded by citing the GAO study and the Foreign Relations Committee's "national security oversight concerns" under Senate rules adopted in 1977.

"Under successive administrations," Percy added, "the Defense Department has employed a provision of law originally intended for domestic leases of defense stocks to implement controversial arms transfers. For instance, jets were leased to Pakistan in 1979 and helicopters to El Salvador in 1981 outside the reporting and approval restrictions of the Arms Export Control Act."

The use of defense leases in those instances, Percy said, had an obvious impact on U.S. foreign policy, and "are clearly within the jurisdiction of the Foreign Relations Committee."

Percy moved to table the Tower amendment, but the motion was rejected by a vote of 33-43. _(Vote 323, p. 55-S)_

Then Tower suggested they compromise by sharing jurisdiction over defense leases and the Special Defense Acquisition Fund as well.

After extensive bargaining in the two committees, the Senate adopted Tower's amendment by voice vote. Tower then offered, and the Senate passed by voice vote, an amendment placing authorizations for the Special Defense Acquisition Fund under Armed Services jurisdiction.

Tower explained to the Senate that, under an agreement between Percy and himself, "the Foreign Relations Committee will continue to have its present review of transfers to foreign countries of defense equipment and articles procured by the Special Defense Acquisition Fund. The Armed Services Committee would have legislative jurisdiction over the Special Defense Acquisition Fund, including the ceiling of that fund and procurements to be made from the fund."

Earmarking Authorizations

Another congressional policy question was raised when Robert W. Kasten Jr., R-Wis., offered an amendment to delete from S 1196 most earmarkings, which required that a certain sum be spent only for a specific purpose.

Kasten's amendment exempted earmarks setting aside specific sums for Israel and Egypt, which were popular in Congress.

Congress annually earmarked specific amounts of foreign aid for its favorite countries, and Kasten, chairman of the Appropriations Foreign Operations Subcommittee, complained that the practice was "squeezing" accounts not earmarked.

Kasten said his amendment exempted earmarkings for Israel and Egypt because, "I know as well as anyone that one way or another Congress is going to earmark the funding for these two countries. I suspect this is the one case in this legislation where the earmarking will stay the same no matter the size of the pot."

Kasten said that in S 1196, Foreign Relations had earmarked $189.5 million for three of 14 programs included in an original Reagan request for $229.5 million for voluntary contributions to international organizations, such as the United Nations and the Organization of American States.

But the revised Reagan request asked for only $189.2 million for the entire account, he said, so the three earmarkings could result in 11 other programs going unfunded.

Percy said he understood his committee's earmarkings could create problems in the international organizations account, so he offered a substitute amendment making the three earmarkings in that account by percentages instead of dollar amounts. Percy's substitute retained all earmarkings for accounts other than international organizations.

The Percy amendment earmarked at least 19.6 percent, or up to $45 million, of the international organizations account for the United Nations Childrens Emergency Fund (UNICEF); 58.7 percent, or up to $134.5 million, for the U.N. Development Fund; and 4.4 percent, or up to $10 million, for the U.N. Environmental Program.

Though he said he was "not too fond of that method either," Kasten accepted the Percy substitute, which the Senate then adopted by voice vote.

Contingency Fund

With little discussion, the Senate also adopted another amendment by Kasten to provide a $75 million Economic Support Fund contingency fund for the president to use in disbursing aid to friendly nations in emergencies. The amendment increased the total ESF account to $2.549 billion, from the $2.474 billion approved by the committee.

Reagan originally requested a $250 million ESF contingency fund, but Foreign Relations rejected the request.

Kasten's amendment, cosponsored by Daniel K. Inouye, D-Hawaii, ranking minority member of the Foreign Operations Subcommittee, provided that before spending from the contingency fund, the president must give 15 days notice to the Senate Foreign Relations, House Foreign Affairs and Senate and House Appropriations committees.

This provision, Kasten said, was designed to establish a practice similar to the "reprogramming" procedure, under which the Foreign Operations subcommittees received advance notice of plans to shift money from one aid account to another and could informally veto those plans by expressing their disapproval.

Kasten said such a fund was needed because "it is impossible in January of any year [when the president's budget is submitted] to predict all needs that may arise during a fiscal year beginning nine months in the future."

He said the lack of such a fund had meant in the past that aid was taken away from some countries to provide for others, which Kasten said was a "ludicrous" predicament.

Kasten said that "no better example for the need for such a fund exists" than in the case of the Sudan, which the Reagan administration pledged to help resist Libyan aggression in the wake of the assassination of Egyptian President Anwar Sadat, who was a firm ally of Sudan.

The administration had been limited in backing up that pledge because no funds were available for quick aid to the Sudan, where Kasten said the "major threat to stability . . . is that country's precarious economic situation," which ESF aid might help.

Despite only token opposition, the Kasten amendment originally failed on a voice vote. But Majority Leader Baker moved to reconsider the vote, and that motion was agreed to by a vote of 49-24. *(Vote 325, p. 55-S)*

The Kasten amendment subsequently was adopted by voice vote.

Other Amendments

The Senate also adopted amendments by voice vote:

● By Lawton Chiles, D-Fla., prohibiting aid to Haiti unless the president determined that the government of Haiti "is cooperating with the United States in halting illegal emigration from Haiti."

● By Dodd, earmarking $15 million for economic assistance to Costa Rica.

● By Kennedy, earmarking $5 million to provide food and medical aid to Poland, through private, voluntary agencies "where appropriate."

● By Kennedy, earmarking $5 million for relief, administered by private voluntary agencies, to Lebanon, which had been torn by civil war.

● By Kennedy, authorizing up to $5 million to help developing countries establish programs to "encourage improved infant feeding practices" and to require the president to report to Congress in his budget requests for fiscal 1983 and 1984 on actions by the Agency for International Development to promote breast-feeding.

● By Pell, stating that in authorizing $100 million in ESF aid to Pakistan, Congress intended to "promote the expeditious restoration of full civil liberties and representative government in Pakistan."

● By Kasten, to provide that Congress could revoke obligated foreign aid funds only in an appropriations act.

● By Zorinsky, earmarking $33.275 million for aid to the private sector of Nicaragua, so long as the president certified that Nicaragua was making "substantial progress toward free and fair elections," and the president reported to Congress each six months on how the funds had been spent in Nicarauga.

● By Hayakawa, increasing from $100 million to $160 million the value of ammunition that could be stored in South Korea in fiscal 1982 under U.S. control for use by South Korean armed forces in emergencies.

● By Glenn, requiring the president to report to Congress within six months on how the government could stop or prevent U.S. citizens from "acting in the service of terrorism." The amendment was prompted by disclosures that former CIA employees, members of the U.S. Army

Special Forces and others had hired themselves out to Libyan dictator Muammar Qaddafi to assist in procuring bombs and weapons for use by terrorists.

● By Tower, increasing the International Military Education and Training program authorization to $47.7 million, as requested by Reagan, from the $41.7 million approved by the Foreign Relations Committee.

● By Mark O. Hatfield, R-Ore., requiring that, within 90 days of the bill's enactment, the president report to Congress on the conflict in El Salvador and the views of the major parties on how it could be peacefully resolved. The Hatfield amendment further stated the sense of the Senate that the president should send a special envoy to seek the views on that question of the parties in conflict, democratic governments in Latin America, Canada and European allies of the United States.

● By Helms, as modified by a Percy amendment, to retain an existing law prohibiting the use of U.S. aid money in El Salvador "for the purpose of planning for compensation, or for the purpose of compensation" in connection with the expropriation or nationalization of agricultural or banking enterprises. The committee bill did not retain that law.

● By Percy, to permit the spending of $70 million worth of Polish zlotys held by the U.S. government on joint U.S.-Polish development programs. The zloty could be spent only in Poland. The United States accepted the zlotys in question, which were paid for surplus dairy products, rather than hard currency so as not to worsen the Polish balance-of-payments deficit.

The Senate also adopted:

● By a vote of 92-0, an amendment by William Proxmire, D-Wis., expressing the sense of Congress that the president should "undertake a diplomatic initiative" to get the Soviet Union to pay its arrearages to the United Nations, which it owed more than $180 million. *(Vote 297, p. 50-S)*

● By 92-0, an amendment by Gordon J. Humphrey, R-N.H., providing that Congress condemned the use of chemical or biological agents against the peoples of Laos, Kampuchea (Cambodia) and Afghanistan, and stating the sense of Congress that the president should "seek a satisfactory explanation from the government of the Soviet Union regarding the strong circumstantial and presumptive evidence" that the Soviet Union had used such weapons against the peoples of those nations. *(Vote 298, p. 50-S)*

● By 88-0, an amendment by Daniel Patrick Moynihan, D-N.Y., discouraging the president from providing aid to nations that signed and refused to dissociate themselves from a communiqué critical of the United States that was issued Sept. 28 by the foreign ministers of non-aligned nations meeting at the 36th General Assembly of the United Nations. *(Vote 320, p. 54-S)*

Amendments Rejected

The Senate rejected:

● By 39-48, an amendment by Orrin G. Hatch, R-Utah, to retain the Peace Corps as part of the ACTION agency, rather than making it independent. *(Vote 318, p. 54-S)*

● An amendment by Mack Mattingly, R-Ga., to postpone the independence of the Peace Corps until Oct. 1, 1982. By 49-37, the Senate tabled, and thus killed, the Mattingly amendment. *(Vote 319, p. 54-S)*

● By 28-70, an amendment by John C. Danforth, R-Mo., to repeal a law requiring that 50 percent of all food aid sent

abroad under the Food for Peace program (PL 480) be carried on American ships. *(Vote 313, p. 54-S)*

● By 14-61, an amendment by Helms to prohibit aid to Zimbabwe unless the president could certify to Congress that as of Jan. 1, 1982, no North Korean military advisers were in Zimbabwe. *(Vote 324, p. 55-S)*

● By 28-45, an amendment by Hatfield to delete $100 million in economic assistance for Pakistan. *(Vote 326, p. 55-S)*

House Floor Action

House Republicans who had been key foes of foreign aid in the past held their noses and helped pass a two-year foreign aid authorization bill Dec. 9, heeding the pleas of their party's president and secretary of state.

The House passed the $5.7 billion aid bill (HR 3566) by a vote of 222-184, with 97 Republicans joining 125 Democrats to form the majority. *(Vote 327, p. 106-H)*

The vote came after a day of unusually placid debate in which divisive disputes over foreign policy were set aside in the interest of expediting action on the bill.

A discouraging word was seldom heard about controversial amendments that had been anticipated concerning aid to El Salvador, Angola and Pakistan.

Foreign aid authorization bills had been passed by the House in recent years only after bitter and lengthy debate.

But the measure was boosted by Secretary of State Alexander M. Haig Jr., who made an unusual appearance Dec. 8 before the House Republican Conference and urged GOP members to swallow their qualms and vote for foreign aid.

To stress the administration's interest, President Reagan had delivered the same message the previous evening at a White House meeting of 14 House Republican leaders.

Both Reagan and Haig portrayed foreign aid, especially military aid, as part of the U.S. defense buildup.

Roles Reversed

Reagan and Haig were forced to go to great lengths to help House Democratic leaders get the aid bill through because some Republicans in the past had turned a political profit by attacking Democrats for supporting foreign aid. This year, Democrats demanded GOP help.

The irony of the new political circumstances seemed to be lost on no one on either side of the aisle, but only two members — Democrats Patricia Schroeder, Colo., and Peter A. Peyser, N.Y. — tried to make it a prominent issue.

Though he ultimately voted for HR 3566, Peyser took the floor early in the debate to say he intended to oppose the bill to protest domestic budget cuts, which he said amounted to a "crime that is being committed against the people of our country, the young and the old."

Peyser also complained that he had heard a Republican arguing that Congress must "let the president have a program so that he can carry out foreign policy" — an idea he said had no appeal among Republicans when the president was Democrat Jimmy Carter.

Schroeder circulated a letter on Dec. 8 to other House members in which she noted that HR 3566, as reported by the House Foreign Affairs Committee, contained 23 percent more than was authorized in 1981.

"Rumor has it that some members of the House are reborn foreign aid supporters," wrote Schroeder, who voted "no" on the fiscal 1980 aid authorization and appropriations bills but "aye" on the fiscal 1981 authorization bill.

Quoting anti-aid statements made by Republicans in past debates, Schroeder's letter predicted that some of those statements would "contrast sharply with statements to be made this week."

Schroeder and some other Democrats who had prominently backed foreign aid in the past, such as David R. Obey of Wisconsin, voted against HR 3566, carrying through on warnings that they would not help the Republicans give Reagan his foreign aid bill.

On the other hand, leading Republican critics of foreign aid, such as Jack F. Kemp, N.Y., and Lagomarsino of California, voted for HR 3566.

But a number of conservative GOP members refused to budge from their previous opposition to foreign aid. Among them were John M. Ashbrook, R-Ohio, who demanded a recorded vote on the bill, and Minority Whip Trent Lott, R-Miss.

In all, 16 Republicans who had voted "no" on the three foreign aid authorization and appropriations bills considered by the House in 1979 and 1980 voted for HR 3566.

Eighty-six Republicans and 98 Democrats voted against HR 3566. Reagan won only a handful of converts among conservative Democrats, most from the South, who had routinely opposed foreign aid bills.

Cutbacks

Just before the vote on passage of HR 3566, Schroeder offered an amendment to cut 10 percent from the total but exempted nations with democratically elected governments from any cuts in their aid.

Complaining that HR 3566 would authorize $300 million more than Reagan requested in his revised budget request in September, Schroeder said: "Why should we increase funding for overseas projects that are similar to the ones we are stopping domestically? If we cut the budget, the cuts should be equal."

Schroeder's amendment was defeated when the House adopted a substitute by Zablocki cutting the bill to the $5.7 billion requested by Reagan from the $6 billion approved by Zablocki's committee.

The Zablocki amendment, adopted by voice vote, did not specify which countries' aid, or even which aid accounts, would be cut.

The amendment limited total authorizations for fiscal 1982 to $5,727,854,000 — the amount of President Reagan's revised request. For fiscal 1983, the amendment limited the bill to Reagan's request, which was to be made early in calendar year 1982.

As reported by Foreign Affairs, HR 3566 would have authorized $6,026 million for fiscal 1982. While acting on the bill, the House added $150 million under the Economic Support Fund in fiscal 1982, $100 million for Pakistan and $50 million for the Sudan.

The House then adopted the Zablocki amendment, which had the effect of cutting the fiscal 1982 authorization by $449,029,000.

The Zablocki amendment also sharply squeezed those accounts in the bill not earmarked at specific levels. As passed by the House, the bill earmarked $2.17 billion, nearly all of it for Israel and Egypt. As a result, $3.557 billion in the House bill was open to cuts by the administration.

Comity, Not Conflict

Despite the underlying partisan tension, House leaders succeeded early on in their quest to glide over conflicts on the issues raised by the bill, and the spirit of comity seemed to gain momentum as the debate proceeded.

Characteristic of the proceedings was a decision by Edward J. Derwinski, R-Ill., a senior member of House Foreign Affairs, to withhold an amendment to repeal a law that effectively banned covert aid to factions in Angola.

Derwinski had pledged months before that he would try to get the House to vote a repeal of the Clark amendment. But when the opportunity arose, he declined it.

"For a foreign aid bill, to use that improper designation, this has been a quiet debate," Derwinski said, adding that he did not want to disturb the "calm" of the House by raising the Clark amendment issue.

Pakistan Aid

Similarly, despite a dispute over one of its key provisions, there was no fight on a Foreign Affairs Committee amendment to allow the president to lift a ban on aid to Pakistan and proceed with a six-year, $3.2 billion aid package for that country.

The committee's amendment, which the House adopted by voice vote, expanded the list of nuclear activities proscribed to U.S. aid recipients and made it easier for the president to waive an aid cutoff.

But in a provision that sparked debate in the committee, the amendment also permitted Congress to veto any such presidential waiver within 30 days of its being issued by adopting a concurrent resolution of disapproval.

The committee's amendment originally was offered as a separate bill (HR 5015), sponsored primarily by New York Democrats Jonathan B. Bingham and Stephen J. Solarz. The Foreign Affairs Committee modified and approved HR 5015 on Dec. 8.

In a Nov. 20 committee debate on HR 5015, Zablocki and Henry J. Hyde, R-Ill., had disputed the constitutionality of the concurrent resolution veto and said they would try to delete it when the panel voted on the matter.

The administration opposed the veto provision as well, so the opposition of Zablocki and Hyde threatened to provoke a fight within the committee. But under pressure to get the aid authorization bill through the House and to permit aid to Pakistan, that opposition evaporated.

When Foreign Affairs took up HR 5015 on Dec. 8, James L. Buckley, under secretary of state for security assistance, told the panel the administration opposed the congressional veto provision and wanted to see four other technical changes in the bill.

Solarz and Bingham readily agreed to the latter changes but warned that to drop the congressional veto would risk having the House adopt the politically appealing Senate ban on aid to a nation that exploded a nuclear device.

After private discussions, the committee approved HR 5015 by voice vote, without any move to delete the veto provision.

When the text of HR 5015 was offered Dec. 9 as an amendment to HR 3566 on the floor, once again there was no attempt made to delete the congressional veto provision.

Hyde spoke against it as "an aggrandizement of power by this House that I do not think is constitutional." But rather than fight it on the floor, he said simply: "I would hope that this provision . . . would meet a timely demise in conference."

In addition to permitting aid to Pakistan, the amendment specifically authorized $100 million in Economic Sup-

port Fund (ESF) aid to Pakistan in fiscal 1982.

The House also adopted by voice votes two Zablocki amendments adding funds for Pakistan in fiscal 1983. One added $200 million to the bill for ESF aid to Pakistan; the other added $800,000 for military education and training programs and authorized $275 million for arms loans.

Although Zablocki said on the floor that the additional money was for Pakistan, his amendments did not specifically earmark the money for that country.

Libya

The testiest debate came on the issue of U.S. policy toward Libya and its dictator, Muammar Qaddafi, and led to one of only three recorded votes taken on amendments to HR 3566.

After lengthy discussion and parliamentary maneuvering, the House adopted by 356-46 an amendment stating that Congress "condemns" Libya and "believes" the president should "conduct an immediate review of concrete steps the United States could take," including a ban on Libyan oil, to force Libya to abandon its policies. *(Vote 326, p. 106-H)*

The original version of the amendment was offered by Edward J. Markey, D-Mass. Before the House adopted the Markey amendment, it was modified by voice vote on an amendment by Jim Dunn, R-Mich., that deleted a provision banning aid to Libya.

No aid to Libya had been proposed, but Zablocki argued that an aid ban would be unwise because the government of Libya could change. Morever, he said, "By what stretch of the imagination will any president or will any Congress authorize money for Libya under the circumstances which prevail now?"

U.S. relations with Libya had been declining steadily as a result of evidence that Qaddafi was a major source of support for international terrorists, and because of Libya's militantly anti-American foreign policy.

But the issue had gained in emotional force in the days before HR 3566 was debated when news stories said — and Reagan confirmed — that the administration had evidence Qaddafi had organized a squad of assassins to attempt to kill the president or other top U.S. officials.

This development added to previous demands from Democrats that the United States sever economic ties with Libya, which sells about 40 percent of its oil exports to the United States, and seek to isolate Qaddafi internationally.

Reagan Dec. 10 invalidated U.S. passports for travel to Libya and asked the 1,500 Americans living there to leave.

Additions, Earmarks

In addition to earmarking money for Pakistan, the House adopted an amendment by William S. Broomfield, R-Mich., doubling, to $100 million, ESF aid for the Sudan.

The House adopted another amendment by Zablocki authorizing up to $5 million in economic aid to Poland.

Other Amendments

The House adopted the following amendments by voice vote:

● By Solarz, prohibiting military aid or arms sales to any nation unless the president had certified to Congress that the governing authorities of that country "are not engaged in a consistent pattern of acts of intimidation or harassment directed against individuals in the United States."

Solarz said the amendment was intended as a warning to officials in Taiwan, who he said had engaged in a "wide-

spread, systematic effort" to harass and intimidate Taiwanese and Taiwanese-Americans in the United States.

● By Mary Rose Oakar, D-Ohio, stating the sense of Congress that $7 million should be available for relief efforts in Lebanon by international and private voluntary organizations.

● By Tom Harkin, D-Iowa, authorizing $5 million in fiscal 1982 for programs to establish or improve infant feeding practices, especially breast-feeding, in developing countries. The amendment did not add to or earmark funds in the bill.

● By Christopher H. Smith, R-N.J., prohibiting the use of funds in the bill to provide for abortions or to conduct research on medical techniques likely to cause the death of a fetus after conception.

● By Mica, authorizing the president to provide aid for resettling Haitians in the Central American country of Belize (formerly British Honduras).

● By Ted Weiss, D-N.Y., stating the sense of Congress that the estimated 60,000 Salvadoran refugees who had entered the United States since January 1980 should be permitted to remain under "voluntary departure status" until it is safe for them to return to El Salvador.

● By Lagomarsino, placing several conditions on aid to Nicaragua. Among them were: that aid to Nicaragua would be terminated if the president certified to Congress that the Nicaraguan government was cooperating with or harboring international terrorists, or that Soviet, Cuban or other foreign troops were stationed in Nicaragua and threatened the United States or any Latin American ally of the United States; and that any loans made to Nicaragua must be used to aid the private sector "to the maximum extent possible."

● By Lagomarsino, stating the sense of Congress that economic assistance to El Salvador should aim to revitalize the private sector and support the free market system. The amendment also urged the president to use a portion of U.S. aid to make guarantees to U.S. banks willing to extend credit to private businesses in El Salvador.

● By Solarz, to extend to Taiwan eligibility for up to 20,000 U.S. immigrant visas annually. With an immigrant visa, a foreign citizen can enter the United States and eventually apply for U.S. citizenship. Solarz said Taiwan was inadvertently excluded from the immigrant visa law in 1979 when the United States broke relations with Taiwan and established ties with the Peoples Republic of China.

● By Jim Leach, R-Iowa, stating the sense of Congress that the United States should use diplomacy to seek an end to the use of chemical and toxic weapons in Laos, Cambodia and Afghanistan and should seek an explanation from the Soviet Union of its alleged use of such weapons.

● By Ireland, directing the president, in deciding whether to give aid or make arms sales to a nation represented at a meeting of "non-aligned countries" in September 1981 to consider whether that nation had dissociated itself from a communiqué issued after that meeting.

● By Yatron, stating the sense of Congress that, in providing aid to Turkey, Greece or Cyprus, the president should consider whether their governments were helping promote a peaceful settlement of the Cyprus dispute. The amendment stated that a peaceful solution should require foreign troops to withdraw from Cyprus and allow Cypriot refugees to return to their homes.

● By Toby Moffett, D-Conn., directing the president to report to Congress on what steps have been or could be taken to ensure that no United States citizen was acting in

the service of international terrorism.

Amendments Rejected

The House rejected three amendments: to ban aid to Indonesia, to retain the Peace Corps within the ACTION and to prohibit aid under the bill to governments or organizations that aid or abet international terrorism.

Conference Action

Conferees filed their report (H Rept 97-413) Dec. 15, and the House adopted it by voice vote the next day. The Senate cleared the bill on Dec. 15 on a 55-42 vote. *(Vote 476, p. 76-S)*

As reported, the bill authorized $5,901,070,000 for fiscal 1982. Conferees also accepted the House position that the bill should also authorize funds for fiscal 1983. Figures for the latter year were identical to those for fiscal 1982, except for the Economic Support Fund (which was boosted by $100 million) and the International Fund for Agricultural Development (which was allocated the remaining $139.5 million of a $180 million two-year limit).

Pakistan

The Pakistan aid package could not go forward without amendments to U.S. nuclear non-proliferation laws and was a major issue in the conference on S 1196.

Reagan proposed the aid program for Pakistan as a means of countering the Soviet presence in Afghanistan, which the Soviet Union has occupied since December 1979.

But aid to Pakistan had been barred since 1979 under a U.S. law that prohibited aid to nations dealing in nuclear fuel enrichment technology — which could be used to build nuclear weapons — outside international safeguards.

The law permitted the president to waive the aid ban if he could certify that he had "reliable assurances" the nation in question was not trying to develop nuclear weapons, but the administration had said it could not make that certification for Pakistan.

The Senate had voted to allow the president to waive the law for Pakistan alone for the life of the six-year aid program if he declared it to be in the U.S. national interest to do so. The Senate bill also provided for an automatic and flat ban on aid to any non-nuclear nation that exploded a nuclear device in the future.

The House bill contained provisions rewriting nuclear non-proliferation law to make it easier for the president to waive an aid ban imposed on any nation but giving Congress the right to veto such a waiver.

The House bill also contained a provision applying the aid ban to nations that transferred or received a nuclear device.

Conferees agreed to a compromise that:

• Allowed the president to waive the law banning aid to nations dealing in enrichment technology for Pakistan alone and only until Sept. 30, 1987 — the life of the six-year administration aid program.

For any other country dealing in unsafeguarded enrichment technology, the president could use existing authority to waive the aid ban only if he certified to Congress that he had "reliable assurances" that the nation was not seeking to develop nuclear weapons.

• Banned economic or military aid to any country that transferred a nuclear device to a non-nuclear weapons state, and to any non-nuclear weapons state that received a nuclear device from another country. Non-nuclear weapons

states are defined as nations that are not known to possess nuclear weapons.

Existing law banned aid to nations dealing in enrichment or nuclear fuel reprocessing technology outside international safeguards.

• Gave Congress the right to veto, by passing a concurrent resolution of disapproval within 30 days, any presidential waiver of an aid ban imposed under the non-proliferation laws on dealings in enrichment and reprocessing equipment.

• Allowed the president to waive an aid ban imposed against a nation that transferred, received or exploded a nuclear device, but provided that the ban would be automatically re-imposed unless Congress authorized further aid by passing a joint resolution within 30 days.

• Required a secret report to Congress from the president on his reasons if he chose to waive an aid ban for a nation dealing in enrichment or reprocessing equipment.

Angola

The administration had wanted Congress to repeal the ban on covert aid to factions in the African nation of Angola — a law known as the Clark amendment.

The Senate had granted the request, but Democrats on the House Foreign Affairs Committee had refused to go along, arguing that it would raise the specter of U.S. intervention in Angola and torpedo sensitive negotiations for a peaceful settlement of the conflict in neighboring Namibia.

House Republicans, anxious to get the aid authorization bill through the House, had declined to raise the issue on the floor but pledged to seek the Clark amendment's repeal in conference. However, facing the deadline of impending adjournment, the Republican conferees decided to drop the matter so as to expedite a conference agreement.

El Salvador

Another major issue in the conference on S 1196 was the final wording of conditions to be met by the ruling junta of El Salvador and certified by the president before the junta could receive further U.S. military aid.

For fiscal 1982, the administration requested $26 million in military aid and $40 million in economic aid for El Salvador. Both houses approved those amounts, but they differed slightly on the wording of the restrictions on that aid.

The conditions in both bills were designed to force the Salvadoran junta — under attack by both left-wing guerillas and right-wing terrorists who included members of its own security forces — to safeguard human rights and work for a peaceful settlement of the conflict.

The major differences between the House and Senate conditions on U.S. aid were:

• A Senate stipulation that the junta was to meet the conditions "to the extent not precluded by forces outside its control."

• House language requiring that the president certify that the junta was "achieving control" over its armed forces, in contrast to a less stringent Senate requirement that the junta be "moving to achieve" control over those forces.

• Senate language requiring that the Salvadoran government show a willingness to negotiate a settlement with "groups that renounce and refrain from further military or paramilitary opposition activity." The House bill required the junta to be willing to negotiate with "opposition groups" even if they had not renounced violence.

In the Dec. 14 conference, Rep. Solarz contended that the House language was preferable in the first two cases. "There are no forces outside the control of El Salvador that could justify" a failure by the junta to bring its armed forces under control, Solarz asserted.

Furthermore, Solarz said he feared the Senate language would be satisfied if the junta merely made "cosmetic changes" in the hierarchy of its armed forces, thereby "moving to achieve" control over them.

On the third issue, Sen. Dodd and Solarz argued that it was unreasonable to expect the leftists to renounce violence before sitting down to negotiate, though they should be required to renounce violence in connection with any settlement reached.

After lengthy negotiations, conferees agreed to:

● State that "Congress recognizes that the efforts of the government of El Salvador to achieve these goals are affected by the activities of forces beyond its control."

● Accept the House provision requiring that the junta be "achieving substantial control" over its armed forces.

● Rewrite the provision urging a negotiated settlement of the conflict so that the junta could continue to get U.S. arms aid if it had "demonstrated its good faith efforts to begin discussions with all major political factions in El Salvador" who had shown themselves willing to find an "equitable political solution" — the solution to include a renunciation of military or paramilitary operations.

In providing military aid or arms sales, the president also would have to certify to Congress that El Salvador was making a concerted and significant effort to comply with internationally recognized human rights.

The president would have to make his certification to Congress within 30 days of enactment of the bill and every 180 days thereafter. If he did not make a certification, he would have to suspend all U.S. aid and arms shipments to El Salvador initiated after enactment of the bill and withdraw all U.S. military advisers from the country.

The president also was required to certify that the Salvadoran government had made good faith efforts to investigate the murders of six U.S. citizens in El Salvador in December 1980 and January 1981.

The bill also included lengthy "sense of the Congress" resolutions about El Salvador. The resolutions called on the government to reform its human rights practices, to seek to control its own armed forces, to continue economic and political reforms, to conduct free elections as soon as possible and to end extremist violence on all sides.

The bill stated that economic assistance to El Salvador should emphasize revitalizing the private sector. It also urged the president to set aside a portion of El Salvador's economic aid to provide guarantees to private U.S. banks willing to make loans to private Salvadoran businesses.

Two-Year Bill

In a major policy shift, Senate conferees on S 1196 agreed to a perennial proposal by Zablocki, chairman of the House Foreign Affairs Committee, to make the aid authorizations good for two years rather than one.

Earlier in the year, Zablocki had persuaded the House committee to accept a two-year bill, with fiscal 1983 amounts subject to amendments pending administration requests for that year.

Zablocki argued that it made sense to have a two-year bill for politically unpopular foreign aid programs to avoid having to debate them and vote on the bill in an election year — especially given the anticipated struggle for House

seats in election-year 1982.

Members of the Senate Foreign Relations Committee had opposed the idea in the past, saying the uncertainties of foreign affairs made it unwise to try to set economic and military aid levels so far in advance.

The hectic nature of the administration's struggle to get the aid authorization and appropriations bills through Congress this year apparently persuaded members of the Senate committee that there was merit to Zablocki's stance.

Military Aid

The administration's ambitious requests early in the year for large increases in military aid were whittled down substantially in the final version of S 1196.

As had been the case for several years, Israel and Egypt were to get the bulk of U.S. arms aid — $550 million for Israel in Foreign Military Sales (FMS) arms loans that did not have to be repaid; $200 million for Egypt on the same terms. (In addition, the bill authorized loans that must be repaid of $850 million to Israel and $700 million to Egypt.)

Reagan had asked for $1.482 billion to finance arms loans that would not have to be repaid for Israel, Egypt and 14 other countries under the FMS program. The request later was revised to $991 million.

The administration also had requested a $100 million, unallocated Special Requirements Fund under the grant Military Assistance Program (MAP) to permit the president to give friendly nations quick grants of arms aid.

The Senate had approved $991 million in FMS loans that would not have to be repaid, $500 million of that amount for Israel, $200 million for Egypt and the rest to be divided among the 14 other nations on Reagan's list. The Senate bill also contained $31.4 million for MAP grants and $3,085.5 million in FMS loans to be repaid on regular terms.

The House bill contained: $550 million in FMS loans for Israel that would be forgiven and $304.4 million in MAP grants — $248.4 million of that amount to be divided among Egypt and the 14 other concessional aid recipients. The House also approved $25 million for a Special Requirements Fund and $3,269.5 million in regular FMS loans.

Conferees agreed to compromise figures totaling $1.099 billion in direct spending and $4.369 billion in total military aid:

● $800 million in FMS loans that did not have to be repaid: $550 million for Israel, $200 million for Egypt and $50 million for the Sudan.

● $238.5 million in MAP grants, including $38.5 million to phase out previous MAP grant programs; and the remainder to be divided among the countries the administration wanted to give concessional aid. Technically, that would leave about $25 million for a requested Special Requirements Fund, but that money was not available under the related 1982 appropriations bill.

● $3,269,500,000 in regular FMS loans.

● $42 million for the International Military Education and Training program, under which foreign officers receive U.S. training.

● $19 million for the U.S. share of United Nations peacekeeping operations

Arms Loans

In addition to the FMS loans they would not have to

repay, Israel, Egypt and the Sudan also were to receive, along with other nations, regular FMS loans.

The administration requests and the earmarked amount of loans for the three favored countries were: Israel, $1.4 billion total FMS loans earmarked in the bill, with $550 million to be forgiven; Egypt, $900 million total with $200 million to be forgiven; the Sudan, $100 million with $50 million to be forgiven.

Conferees also earmarked $280 million, the House figure, in FMS loans for Greece and recommended $6 million in FMS loans for Zaire. The House had limited Zaire to $4 million in FMS loans.

Egypt, Greece, Turkey, the Sudan and Somalia also were given favorable terms for repayment of their FMS loans: 30 years to repay the loans, with an initial 10-year grace period on repayment of principal. Regular FMS loans required repayment within 20 years.

Chile, Argentina

Conferees moved to lift bans imposed in the mid-1970s on arms aid and sales to Chile and Argentina, but agreed to impose conditions on future military dealings with those nations.

In 1977, Congress flatly prohibited aid or arms sales to the military government of Argentina because of charges by human rights groups that the Argentine government was responsible for the "disappearances" of thousands of persons. *(1977 Almanac p. 287)*

The Reagan administration asked Congress to repeal that ban, saying the Argentine government was relaxing its dictatorial powers and would respond more quickly to "quiet diplomacy" on human rights. Both houses agreed to repeal the ban, but they replaced it with slightly differing conditions on arms sales or aid to Argentina.

Conferees accepted most of the House provision, which allowed aid or arms sales only if the president certified to Congress that Argentina had made significant progress in complying with internationally recognized principles of human rights and that providing aid or sales was in the U.S. national interest.

Conferees adopted the same two restrictions on aid or arms sales to Chile as were applied to Argentina. A third condition was added: that the Chilean government was not aiding or abetting international terrorism and had taken steps to cooperate in the U.S. investigation of the 1976 slaying in Washington, D.C., of former Chilean Ambassador Orlando Letelier.

Aid and arms sales to Chile were prohibited in 1976. *(1976 Almanac p. 215)*

Special FMS Fund

Both houses had approved the thrust of an administration fund, called the Special Defense Acquisition Fund (SDAF), to be used for advance purchases of weapons and equipment frequently ordered by U.S. arms loan recipients.

Conferees basically accepted the Senate version of the SDAF by establishing a revolving fund limited to $300 million in fiscal 1982 and to $600 million in fiscal 1983 and afterwards. The fund would be replenished with a portion of payments made to the United States from the FMS program. The Pentagon would have to report to Congress on the use of the funds.

However, conferees on the related fiscal 1982 foreign aid appropriations bill (HR 4559) provided no funding for the SDAF, thus killing it.

Development Aid

Bending to the House Foreign Affairs Committee, conferees dropped a Senate provision abolishing the International Development and Cooperation Agency (IDCA), established in 1979 to coordinate foreign aid programs. IDCA has been opposed by leading senators, and Reagan has not nominated a director for IDCA. *(1979 Almanac p. 117)*

While stating opposition to "unnecessary bureaucratic layering," conferees said IDCA should continue to coordinate aid programs and policies "in order to achieve maximum effectiveness." Conferees said Reagan should nominate an IDCA director "as soon as possible."

Peace Corps

Ten years after President Nixon placed the Peace Corps under the ACTION agency, Congress undid the deed by making the corps an independent agency. *(1971 Almanac p. 769)*

The independence move, which got under way in 1979, came in spite of opposition from some conservatives, who saw it as a slap at the current ACTION director, Thomas W. Pauken. Pauken was a former Army intelligence officer who served in Vietnam in the late 1960s.

Proponents of separating the agencies feared Pauken's background would taint the Peace Corps' reputation for being free of involvement in intelligence activities.

The aid authorization bill made the Peace Corps' independence effective upon enactment.

In an effort to prevent the Reagan administration from reducing the independence of the Peace Corps, conferees adopted a modified House provision stating that its director must continue to exercise all functions in effect on Dec. 14, 1981 — the date of the conference agreement.

Other Policy Provisions

Congress traditionally asserted its greatest control over U.S. foreign policy through foreign aid authorization bills, and S 1196 was no exception.

In many cases, as had been the practice for years, the policy statements or changes in the bill were made because one or two members of Congress, or in some cases an entire state delegation, had made pet projects of them.

For example, in 1981, members of the Florida delegation were campaigning to ameliorate the problems posed for their state by drug smuggling from Latin America.

Consequently, Florida members such as Democratic Reps. Ireland and Mica pushed through a provision allowing aid recipients to use U.S. funds to pay for spraying the herbicide paraquat on marijuana fields.

The bill repealed a 1978 ban on the use of U.S. foreign aid to spray the herbicide paraquat on marijuana. The ban was enacted because of the reported harmful effects of paraquat on users of sprayed marijuana. *(1978 Almanac p. 417)*

The bill directed the secretary of state to inform the secretary of health and human services if funds were used for that purpose, and the latter official was to monitor the impact of paraquat spraying on the health of marijuana users.

The bill also earmarked $100,000 for research on substances that would leave a mark on marijuana or other illicit crops if sprayed on those crops along with herbicides.

Similarly, Reps. Leach and Solarz became concerned about allegations that agents of Taiwan had engaged in systematic harassment of Taiwanese and Taiwanese-Americans in the United States.

So S 1196 included a modified version of their House amendment prohibiting arms sales or arms aid to any country if the president determined that its government was engaged in a consistent pattern of acts of intimidation or harassment directed against individuals in the United States. The amendment did not directly mention Taiwan.

Other policy issues involved:

Cyprus. Conferees dropped a House amendment stating the sense of Congress that, in providing aid to Greece, Turkey and Cyprus, the president should take into account whether the governments of those countries were helping promote a peaceful settlement to the Cyprus dispute.

Human Rights. Both houses had included provisions reaffirming the U.S. commitment to improving international respect for human rights. The final version reaffirmed congressional support for various laws that had been enacted to promote human rights. It also stated the sense of Congress that a strong commitment to human rights should continue to be a central feature of U.S. foreign policy.

Haiti. The conference combined House and Senate provisions regarding aid to Haiti. The final bill authorized up to $15 million in development aid to Haiti in fiscal 1982; stated that the aid was to be provided only if the president determined that Haiti was cooperating with the United States to prevent illegal emigration, that Haiti had assured the United States it would cooperate in implementing aid programs and that Haiti was not engaging in "a consistent pattern of gross violations of internationally recognized human rights;" required the president to report to Congress every six months on actions by the government of Haiti to restrict illegal emigration; and permitted military aid to Haiti in fiscal years 1982 and 1983 if the aid was used to help halt significant illegal emigration from Haiti to the United States. The latter provision waived a law that prohibits recipient nations from using U.S. aid to train or support their internal police forces.

Consolidations, Repeals. Conferees accepted the goals of a Senate provision consolidating numerous reports on aid that various agencies are required to give Congress and repealing provisions in foreign aid laws that were outdated or duplicated. However, conferees retained requirements for nine reports, the most widely circulated of them being the annual report on human rights in all foreign nations. ∎

Aid to El Salvador

President Reagan's El Salvador policy passed its first congressional test March 24 — by a slim margin.

On an 8-7 vote, the House Appropriations Subcommittee on Foreign Operations approved a Reagan request to "reprogram" $5 million in fiscal 1981 military loans to El Salvador from funds earmarked for other countries.

The action overrode the wishes of subcommittee Chairman Clarence D. Long, D-Md., who argued strongly against the reprogramming. Long heightened the drama of the vote by visiting El Salvador at his own expense the week before.

Long was joined in opposing the aid by six of the subcommittee's seven other Democrats.

But while the House subcommittee gave Reagan what he wanted, it also made clear that the victory was far less than an unqualified endorsement of the administration's method of backing the Salvadoran government.

In fact, the member who cast the deciding vote, Silvio O. Conte, R-Mass., said he would oppose further military aid until a Salvadoran investigation into the Dec. 2, 1980, murders of four American Catholic women missionaries showed results.

Conte said he had supported the administration in part because "this is the first foreign policy issue this administration had out of the box." He also disclosed that Secretary of State Alexander M. Haig Jr. had lobbied him before the vote, calling to say "why he felt this $5 million reprogramming was important."

The administration apparently sought to smooth the way for the reprogramming in other ways as well. Only three days before the subcommittee vote, the State Department announced that 18 of 54 U.S. military advisers in El Salvador would be withdrawn by July and the rest by September. Much of the criticism of Reagan's El Salvador policy had centered around the use of military advisers.

The subcommittee vote cleared the way for the administration to shift $5 million in Foreign Military Sales (FMS) loans to El Salvador. The Senate Appropriations Foreign Operations Subcommittee had approved the request by a 6-2 vote on March 16.

Congress had no statutory authority to block such reprogrammings, but the Appropriations subcommittees had power over other budget requests, so presidents traditionally did not reprogram funds over their opposition.

It took the votes of Conte, ranking minority member of the full Appropriations Committee, and Jamie L. Whitten, D-Miss., chairman of the Appropriations Committee, to carry the issue for Reagan. Whitten said he, too, had been urged by Haig to vote for the reprogramming.

Whitten and Conte were *ex officio* members of all Appropriations subcommittees, but their presence for the El Salvador vote was considered unusual. Whitten rarely attended individual subcommittee meetings, but Conte told reporters that he had never missed a Foreign Operations Subcommittee markup.

The issue was decided on a motion by Long, who moved that the reprogramming be approved but asked the subcommittee to defeat his motion.

Voting with Long against the reprogramming were Democrats David R. Obey, Wis., Sidney R. Yates, Ill., Matthew F. McHugh, N.Y., William Lehman, Fla., Julian C. Dixon, Calif., and William H. Gray III, Pa.

Voting in favor of the Reagan request, in addition to Conte and Whitten, were Charles Wilson, D-Texas, and Republicans Jack F. Kemp, N.Y., Mickey Edwards, Okla., Bob Livingston, La., Jerry Lewis, Calif., and John Edward Porter, Ill.

In passing a foreign aid authorization bill for fiscal 1982 (S 1196), Congress later passed restrictions in additional aid to El Salvador. *(p. 161)*

Symbolism Debated

Subcommittee members on both sides of the issue agreed that the vote was as much symbol as substance. Reagan already had sent $20 million in military aid to El Salvador on March 2, using emergency power not subject to congressional approval.

Foreign Aid to El Salvador

Following are the amounts of direct U.S. aid to El Salvador provided in fiscal 1981 and scheduled for fiscal 1982, as of January 1982:

Fiscal Year 1981

● $5 million in regular Foreign Military Sales (FMS) loans for "non-lethal" military aid (such as communications equipment), approved by Congress during action on the 1981 foreign aid authorization bill (HR 6942 — PL 96-533).

● $500,000 for training Salvadoran military officers under the International Military Education and Training (IMET) program, also approved by Congress in the 1981 foreign aid bill.

● $5 million in emergency "lethal" military aid given El Salvador by the Carter administration on Jan. 17 under special "defense drawdown" authority. The aid included equipment and the services of military advisers. Congressional approval was not required.

● $20 million in emergency military aid (equipment and advisers) provided by the Reagan administration March 2 under the defense drawdown authority.

● $5 million in additional FMS loans reprogrammed by the Reagan administration with the approval of the Senate and House Appropriations Foreign Operations subcommittees.

● $136.015 million in non-military aid. That included $50.645 million in food aid; $44.9 million under the Economic Support Fund (ESF); $32.792 million in Agency for International Development programs; $5.5 million in housing guarantees; and $2.178 million in disaster aid. Of the total, $63.5 million was transferred from other accounts in April 1981.

Fiscal Year 1982

● $35 million in development assistance.
● $25 million in FMS loans.
● $40 million in ESF assistance.
● $1 million in IMET assistance.

But they disagreed sharply on what approving the additional military aid would symbolize. The administration asked for the aid to help the civilian-military junta governing El Salvador put down a communist insurgency.

"I have concluded that the $5 million really doesn't make that much difference from a military point of view," said Long, who had opposed military aid to El Salvador on the ground that it could lead to "another Vietnam."

Kemp, Lewis and the other advocates of the aid argued that the subcommittee failure to approve it would signal a lack of resolve in Congress to protect U.S. interests against Soviet-bloc intrusions.

The Reagan administration charged Feb. 23 that Cuba and other communist countries had shipped tons of weapons to the leftist insurgents in El Salvador.

Proponents of the aid said to reject it also would indicate to U.S. allies that they could not depend on the United States for help in resisting outside aggression.

"To turn our back on a neighbor — to paraphrase a former president — while that neighbor's house is on fire, would be a terrible mistake," Kemp said, alluding to the analogy used by President Franklin D. Roosevelt to support the lend-lease program of military aid to Britain during the early days of World War II.

But opponents of the aid argued that El Salvador's civil strife was the product of longstanding economic and political inequities in its society, rather than outside interference. They also blamed the civilian-military junta's inability to halt terrorism perpetrated by members of its own security forces as well as by the left.

"When we talk about a friend's house on fire we must ask, 'Who set the friend's house on fire?' " said Democrat Gray. "If the friend sets the house on fire himself, I do not intend to keep helping him put the fire out."

Obey said economic and military aid should be linked to show that the United States was not merely engaged in military intervention.

"If I were the Cubans [or] the Soviets, I would very much want this committee today to approve this military aid separate from the economic assistance," Obey said. "It allows the Cubans and Soviets to make us the issue in Latin America."

Subcommittee Action

Obey moved that the subcommittee delay its vote on the military aid reprogramming until an administration's economic aid reprogramming request could be considered along with it.

The subcommittee defeated that motion by voice vote.

Next, the subcommittee approved the military aid reprogramming. But then Long proposed an amendment to prohibit any of the $5 million from being used to pay for U.S. military advisers to train the Salvadoran military.

The chairman's motion found no sympathy among the subcommittee, however, for other members said the administration had no plans to use the military loans for advisers anyway. "I'm going to vote against this amendment because it don't do nothing to nobody," Obey quipped.

While the $5 million was part of a $25 million emergency aid package that included the services of 20 U.S. military advisers, the administration had said the advisers were being paid for out of the $20 million in aid Reagan sent to El Salvador on his own authority.

Although Long said any of the money could be used for advisers, the subcommittee defeated his motion.

Haig Testimony

Appearing on March 18 and 19 before the House Foreign Affairs and Senate Foreign Relations committees, respectively, Secretary of State Alexander M. Haig Jr. disputed the complaint that the United States was emphasizing military aid to El Salvador. "I emphasize that we're giving three-to-one economic aid to military aid," Haig told the Senate panel.

Reagan's fiscal 1982 foreign aid budget requested an additional $25 million in military loans and $40 million in economic aid for El Salvador.

Haig said El Salvador's junta was addressing the economic and political problems in that country. He listed three positive steps: agrarian reform to give land to peasants and peasant cooperatives; the nationalization of banks; and the appointment of a commission to prepare for free election of a national Assembly in 1982.

He also said the Salvadoran government, with extensive advice from the FBI, had made progress in tracking

down those who killed the American missionaries, though it had yet to identify them.

Opponents of Reagan's policy said that neither President José Napolean Duarte nor the United States had worked hard enough for a peaceful political settlement of the conflict.

But Haig reiterated the administration's view that military aid was necessary because the communist insurgents had been organized by Cuba and supplied with arms by it and other Soviet-bloc nations named in a Feb. 23 State Department "white paper."

Before the House Foreign Affairs Committee, Haig added a more provocative charge. He said the communist assault on El Salvador was part of a "four-phased operation" aimed at "the ultimate takeover of Central America."

First on the list was Nicaragua, he said, where rightist dictator Anastasio Somoza was overthrown in July 1979 by the leftist Sandinistas. On the list after El Salvador, he said, were neighboring Honduras and Guatemala. ■

Richard Allen Resignation

President Reagan Jan. 4, 1982, accepted the resignation of national security adviser Richard V. Allen and replaced him with Deputy Secretary of State William P. Clark — a foreign policy novice but a longtime Reagan confidant.

Allen was forced to resign even though the White House counsel's office cleared him the same day of allegations of misconduct that had led him on Nov. 29, 1981, to take a leave of absence.

Meanwhile, the White House national security apparatus was reorganized to provide the national security adviser frequent and assured access to the president, implying greater power and prestige for Clark than Allen had enjoyed.

The Senate confirmed Clark as deputy secretary of state on Feb. 24, 1981, despite his having confessed to scant knowledge of foreign policy. But Clark later became known as a quick study who reportedly worked well with Secretary of State Alexander M. Haig Jr.

The national security adviser was not subject to Senate confirmation, but some members of Congress had advocated legislation to make it so because holders of the office historically have clashed with secretaries of state.

The Senate passed such a provision in 1979, but the requirement was not enacted into law. *(1979 Almanac p. 134)*

Reagan had said such clashes would not arise in his administration, and Allen had promised to stay out of the limelight. He told reporters when his appointment was announced: "You're seeing a disappearing act right now."

But Allen and Haig nevertheless developed a rivalry that led Reagan to call them into his office in the fall of 1981 and order them to stop competing with and sniping at one another over influence in administration foreign policy.

Because of the rivalry, Allen's departure was deemed evidence that Reagan and his top advisers had become disenchanted with Allen not only for the actions that led to the probes of him but also for his uneasy relations with Haig.

Allen himself told reporters "politics was involved" in his ouster. He said he found it "unusual" that someone could "find himself in a position where his resignation would be submitted and accepted" after being cleared by "a rigorous and meticulous examination."

The Allegations

The Justice Department and White House investigations of Allen were not his first such experience.

Allen was forced to resign from Reagan's presidential campaign just before Election Day 1980 after *The Wall Street Journal* published an article alleging that Allen had enriched his consulting business as a National Security Council aide in the Nixon White House.

The new allegations against Allen were raised in November 1981, when the Japanese newspaper *Mainichi* reported that a U.S. official was being investigated for bribery.

American reporters focused on Allen, who denied accepting a bribe but acknowledged receiving a $1,000 "honorarium" from the Japanese magazine *Shufu-no-Tomo*, or "Friend of the Housewife," when one of its reporters interviewed Mrs. Reagan on Jan. 21, 1981, in the White House.

The interpreter for the interview was Chizuko Takase, the wife of a Japanese friend of Allen's, who gave Allen an envelope at the time of the interview.

Allen later said that he did not realize until returning to quarters in the Executive Office Building that the envelope contained cash. When he did, he said he gave the envelope to his secretary and told her to turn the money over to the proper authorities.

According to various accounts, the secretary forgot to do so, and the envelope was not found until September. When it was, Edwin Meese III, counselor to the president, reported the matter to the Justice Department.

The Justice Department said Dec. 1 that Allen had violated no laws in improperly handling the $1,000.

Meanwhile, the press had raised other questions concerning Allen's sale of his Potomac International Corp. consulting firm to former Reagan speech writer Peter D. Hannaford and Allen's continued contacts with Potomac International clients.

Allen sold Potomac International to the Hannaford Company Inc. public relations firm on Jan. 19, 1981, with payment to be made in installments, and he had received monthly payments from Hannaford since February, it was disclosed.

Allen also kept in contact with Hannaford and some of his clients, an apparent conflict of interest.

It also emerged that Allen had accepted three watches from the Takases, possibly taking one after taking his White House job, and had made errors of omission on his financial disclosure report.

On Dec. 23, the Justice Department cleared Allen of any illegality in any of those actions.

The White House counsel's office likewise said Jan. 4 that those acts did not violate White House standards of conduct. ■

Czech Claims Agreement

Congress approved an agreement between the United States and Czechoslovakia settling claims dating from the end of World War II.

The two governments reached an accord on Nov. 6 to return Czech gold held by the United States since the

communist coup in 1948. The agreement, signed in Prague, would pay $81.5 million for U.S. claims and interest resulting from the takeover in Czechoslovakia.

In S 1946 (PL 97-127), cleared Dec. 16, Congress approved the agreement and set priorities for distribution of the $81.5 million.

Background

When the communists took power in Czechoslovakia in 1948, they seized all foreign-owned property. In retaliation, President Harry S Truman impounded all Czech-owned gold captured by the United States after the war, and succeeded in having the British do the same. The U.S.-held gold totaled about 8.5 metric tons.

In 1958, the Foreign Claims Settlement Commission determined the value of American citizens' lost property at $64 million with 10 years in accrued interest, bringing the total to $113.64 million.

Unable to reach a settlement with Czechoslovakia, the U.S. government confiscated a Czech-owned steel mill and sold it, disbursing the $8.5 million to some of the certified claimants. This action still left more than 2,600 Americans unpaid for about $105 million in claims and interest.

A 1974 Czechoslovakian offer of $20.5 million was accepted by the Nixon administration but rejected by Congress because it fell far short of the amount decided upon by the settlement commission. A renegotiation was ordered under the Trade Act of 1974, which gave Congress final approval of any settlement. *(1974 Almanac p. 555)*

No action was taken between 1974 and 1980, when legislation was introduced in the Senate (S 754) by Daniel Patrick Moynihan, D-N.Y., and in the House (HR 2631) by Jonathan B. Bingham, D-N.Y. Those bills would have authorized liquidation of the U.S.-held gold. The proceeds then would have been used to pay off the remaining certified claimants. As of Dec. 10, 1981, with gold selling at about $400 an ounce, the U.S.-held gold was worth nearly $120 million.

When the negotiations resumed in the summer of 1981, Czechoslovakia made an offer of $64.1 million. Under pressure from Congress, however, the United States demanded more. The increasing value of the gold spurred the Czech government to act quickly.

Under the Nov. 6 agreement, the United States was to return the gold to Czechoslovakia, and that country in turn was to pay $81.5 million to the United States for claims of U.S. citizens, plus interest. In addition, Czechoslovakia agreed to pay the United States $8 million for surplus Army equipment that Czechoslovakia bought in 1946 but never paid for, and to return $1 million in U.S. bank accounts in Czechoslovakia that had been frozen.

Unlike the 1974 agreement, the 1981 settlement did not include a U.S. agreement to provide most-favored-nation status to Czechoslovakia.

'Benes' Group Claims

House and Senate bills to approve the settlement agreement differed on one major point: whether to set aside a portion of the settlement for persons who were not U.S. citizens when their property was confiscated.

Those claimants had been referred to as the "Benes group," because their property was nationalized by the post-war Czech government of Eduard Benes, with a promise of subsequent compensation. That promise was repudiated by the communist government after it took over in February 1948.

Some of those persons became U.S. citizens before the communist takeover, and they pressed their claims with the U.S. Foreign Claims Settlement Commission. But the commission rejected their claims on the grounds that they were not U.S. citizens at the time their property originally was confiscated and therefore were not eligible to file claims under U.S. law.

The Senate bill (S 1946), passed Dec. 11 by voice vote, did not include any payments to members of the Benes group. The bill allocated $79.5 million for claims certified by the commission in 1958, $1.5 million for U.S. citizens whose property was seized after 1958, and $500,000 for U.S. government expenses.

The House bill (HR 5125), passed Dec. 15 by voice vote, set aside $7 million to pay part of their claims. That bill also reserved $72.5 million for certified claimants, $1.5 million for post-1958 claimants and $500,000 for the government.

Bingham said members of the Benes group were "Americans who have long been denied economic justice."

Bill Frenzel, R-Minn., opposed payment of claims to the Benes group as a "bad precedent" for future claims settlements and as "inequitable treatment" of the claimants who were U.S. citizens when their property was confiscated.

The next day, the Senate amended S 1946 to allow a $5.4 million *ex gratia* payment to members of the Benes group. The amended bill stated that the payment was made because of the "extraordinary circumstances" involving those claimants, and did not establish a precedent for payment of similar claims in the future. The amended bill also provided $74.55 million for the certified claimants, $1.5 million for the post-1958 claimants and $50,000 for the U.S. government to cover its expenses.

Ted Stevens, R-Alaska, the bill's manager, told the Senate that the amended bill provided $4.95 million for members of the Benes group, with $925,000 of that amount coming from the fund for post-1958 claimants. However, the text of the bill allowed $5.4 million for the Benes group and the full $1.5 million for post-1958 claimants.

The bill stated the sense of Congress that the U.S. government was entitled to 5 percent ($4.075 million) of the $81.5 million. But the bill gave the government only $50,000, with the remainder diverted to the Benes group.

The House passed the amended bill by voice vote later on Dec. 16, over the protests of Frenzel, who said it was "a miscarriage of justice, a waste of the public funds."

As cleared, the bill required the State Department to carry out the agreement with Czechoslovakia within 60 days of the bill's enactment, with a possible 30-day extension. ∎

U.S.-Iran Agreement

A July 2 Supreme Court decision upholding the hostage release agreement with Iran allowed the United States to follow through on steps already taken to implement the accords. *(Statement on accords, p. 10-E)*

The court's decision also relieved Congress of any necessity to approve the agreement.

President Reagan agreed Feb. 18 to honor the agreement.

In addition to releasing the hostages Jan. 20, Iran agreed to arbitration before a joint Iran-United States Claims Tribunal of any claims by U.S. nationals against

Iran and by Iranian nationals against the United States.

The 52 Americans released by Iran on Inauguration Day were among the 66 Americans — most of them State Department employees — taken hostage in the U.S. Embassy in Tehran on Nov. 4, 1979. Thirteen hostages were released later in November 1979, and another, Richard I. Queen, was released in July 1980. *(1980 Almanac p. 352)*

The United States agreed to return portions of $12 billion in Iranian assets President Carter had frozen on Nov. 14, 1979 in retaliation.

At a Jan. 27 "welcome home" ceremony at the White House for the hostages, Reagan promised that "swift and effective retribution" would be the U.S. response to future acts of terrorism.

"We hear it said that we live in an era of limits to our power," Reagan told the former hostages and an audience of 6,000 gathered on the South Lawn of the White House after a joyous Pennsylvania Avenue parade. "Well, let it also be understood, there are limits to our patience."

Despite his promise of future retribution for others, Reagan said later at his first presidential press conference that he was planning no punitive acts against Iran.

"I'm certainly not thinking of revenge," he said, adding later, "I don't think revenge is worthy of us."

Secretary of State Alexander M. Haig Jr. acknowledged that Reagan's retribution warning was "consciously ambiguous," apparently to avoid limiting potential U.S. responses to terrorism.

U.S.-Iran Negotiations

The agreement with Iran was concluded over months of negotiations. But it was made possible largely by two Algerian diplomats and the head of the Central Bank of Algeria, shuttling between Tehran, Algiers and Washington as intermediaries between the United States and Iran.

Carter's Secretary of State Edmund S. Muskie said that, for all the complexity of the resulting agreement, in the end it was based on four points laid down Sept. 12, 1980, by Iranian leader Ayatollah Khomeini. The same points were endorsed Nov. 2, 1980, by the Iranian Parliament.

Those points were: a U.S. pledge of non-interference in Iranian affairs; the release of Iranian assets frozen by Carter; the dropping of all U.S. government and private claims against Iran; the return to Iran of the wealth of the former shah and his relatives.

But the eventual agreement fell far short of meeting Iran's demands to the letter. It perhaps came closer to what Muskie called the "guiding principle" for the U.S. negotiators — "to return matters, insofar as possible, to where they were before the hostages were seized."

Terms of Settlement

The foundations of the agreement were contained in two formal declarations issued Jan. 19 by the government of Algeria in which the United States and Iran agreed to four points of settlement and mechanisms for implementing them.

The United States pledged not to interfere in Iranian affairs — the simplest point, and one that already had been accepted.

It also pledged to freeze "property and assets in the United States within the control of the estate of the former shah or of any close relative" to facilitate Iranian efforts to recover the assets in the U.S. courts. The United States agreed that, within 30 days of the hostages' release, it would require anyone within its jurisdiction to give the U.S. Treasury any information they had concerning the shah's wealth.

This marked a concession on the part of Iran, for a major Iranian aim had been to recover the late shah of Iran's wealth, which Iran claimed was more than $10 billion. Iran previously had demanded that the United States put up $24 billion as security for the release of the hostages, including $10 billion representing the shah's wealth.

The United States and Iran also agreed to establish an Iran-United States Claims Tribunal, empowered to impose binding arbitration to settle private U.S. claims against Iran and private Iranian claims against the United States — including those before U.S. courts.

Some legal experts argued that Carter's order shifting claims against Iran to the international tribunal violated the constitutional rights of the claimants to due process of law.

The day after the hostages were released, however, a U.S. district court judge in Washington denied a request by a group of claimants for an order blocking the government from unfreezing $50 million in Iran's assets. Judge Gerhard A. Gesell ruled that Carter's power to enter into the agreement with Iran was "beyond question."

But the heart of the bargain — triggering the release of the hostages — governed the handling of Iran's frozen assets.

It was a complex set of transactions that required transcontinental shuffling of billions of dollars in bank deposits, securities and gold. Carter's Treasury Secretary, G. William Miller, called it "perhaps the largest transfer of private interests ever accomplished."

Financial Arrangements

As Muskie told reporters, "The problem was to put in Iran's hands enough assets to make this attractive."

Iran was given back $2.9 billion of its estimated $12 billion in frozen assets. Those assets were returned when Algeria certified — as Reagan finished his inaugural address at 12:25 p.m. (EST) Jan. 20 — that an *Air Algerie* Boeing 727 jet carrying the hostages had left Iran.

But before the Americans flew to freedom, the United States had to place a security deposit of $8 billion — two-thirds of Iran's frozen assets — in a Bank of England escrow account controlled by the Central Bank of Algeria.

The $12 billion in frozen Iranian assets consisted of:

● Almost $2.5 billion held by the U.S. government's Federal Reserve Bank of New York. This included 1.6 million ounces of gold, valued at $940 million, and more than $1.4 billion in securities owned by Iran.

● About $5.5 billion in Iranian bank deposits and interest on them held by European branches of U.S. banks. This amount included $4.7 billion in deposits and $800 million in interest. After Carter's freeze of Iranian assets, the U.S. banks used many of those Iranian deposits to "offset" delinquent loans the banks had made to the government of Iran and other Iranian institutions.

● About $4 billion in Iranian assets in the United States, much of it tied up in lawsuits filed by American businesses with claims against Iran for unpaid bills or expropriated property. This included about $2.2 billion in Iranian deposits in domestic branches of U.S. banks.

Carrying Out the Accords

Iran received $2.9 billion soon after the hostages were released. Of the remaining $9.1 billion, about $5.1 billion

was reserved to pay off loans to Iran that were made or shared in by American banks.

Of that $5.1 billion, $3.7 billion immediately was paid to groups of U.S. and European banks that together had made syndicated loans to Iran. The other $1.4 billion was put into an escrow account in the Bank of England to guarantee that Iran would repay loans made by U.S. banks alone.

That $1.4 billion was to stay in escrow until the banks and Iran could settle on specific amounts of principal and interest owed.

Another $1 billion was placed in escrow to ensure that Iran would pay claims awarded U.S. nationals by the joint claims tribunal. The Supreme Court's decision cleared the way for the transfer abroad of the funds designated for this claims tribunal escrow account.

The claims tribunal escrow account was established in the Bank of England by Feb. 19 after Reagan announced he would honor the hostage accords.

The $1 billion designated for the account was to come from the $4 billion in Iranian assets left in the United States after the release of the hostages.

The Supreme Court decision upheld Carter's right to nullify court actions attaching those funds, and thus permitted the transfer of $1 billion to the claims tribunal escrow account and the other $1 billion to Iran, as specified under the accords.

The agreements called for the Iranian assets in the United States to be transferred abroad by July 19. Half of each dollar transferred abroad went into the claims tribunal escrow account until that account reached $1 billion. The rest went to Iran.

Treasury Regulations

The Treasury Department issued regulations June 4 requiring domestic banks to transfer the Iranian assets to the Federal Reserve Bank of New York.

While the court challenges proceeded, the Claims Tribunal was established, and the State Department, American companies and individuals with claims against Iran prepared to register them with the tribunal.

The claims tribunal — composed of three Americans, three Iranians and three neutrals — was established in stages beginning April 19, with Swedish jurist Gunnar Lagergren chosen by the members as its president. The tribunal held its first organizational meeting July 1 at The Hague, the Netherlands, its seat.

Deadline Extended

The accords originally required that any claims not settled by July 19 would be submitted to arbitration, but Iran later requested, and the United States agreed, to extend that deadline to Oct. 19 to allow further negotiations. The new agreement provided that claims had to be submitted to the claims tribunal no later than Jan. 19, 1982.

The agreements called for American nationals claiming more than $250,000 from Iran to attempt to negotiate a settlement with Iran on their own. If no settlement could be reached, the claimants or Iran could submit such disputes to the claims tribunal.

The U.S. government would represent claimants seeking less than $250,000. David Stewart, administrator of Iranian claims at the State Department, said the United States would try to negotiate a lump sum settlement of all such claims.

If that was achieved, individual claims then would be settled by the U.S. Foreign Claims Settlement Commission, Stewart said. If no lump sum settlement could be reached, either the United States or Iran could take those claims to the claims tribunal. ∎

Defense

Almost without exception, President Reagan got the defense programs that he wanted in 1981. But it turned out that he did not want many of the radical changes espoused by some of his most ideologically committed supporters.

With the $26 billion he initially added to President Carter's proposed defense budget for fiscal 1982, Reagan embarked on a program that slightly accelerated the rate at which existing forces would be modernized with new tanks and warplanes.

The Reagan plan did incorporate two substantial additions to the Carter program: the B-1 bomber, and a bigger Navy with more aircraft carriers.

And it had one very important change: After months of internal wrangling, the administration rejected the basing system for the new MX intercontinental ballistic missile (ICBM) long espoused by the Air Force as the only way to protect U.S. ICBMs from increasingly accurate Soviet missiles.

The only dramatic congressional impact on Reagan's program resulted from the Senate Armed Services Committee's outrage at the MX decision. By year's end, the adminstration appeared headed for deployment at some future date of an MX system that would resemble a much smaller version of the one Reagan originally vetoed.

Otherwise, Congress approved the defense request with no more than the usual quibbles over specific programs. Through mid-summer, there was not even any politically serious challenge to the overall size of Reagan's defense plan, or the general allocation of funds within that budget.

Battles to Come

But two developments in the last third of 1981 raised the possibility that Reagan might encounter more serious challenges to his later defense requests:

Budget Restraint. Prominent members of the Republican congressional leadership began to insist that any further cuts in domestic programs be accompanied by restraint in Pentagon spending. Most of these critics had accepted the president's March budget, which boosted Carter's defense proposal by 14.6 percent while cutting virtually all controllable domestic programs.

Complaints about the Pentagon budget emerged within the Reagan coalition in August and September, when the prospect of a huge deficit drove the administration to reassess the fiscal 1982 budget. Reagan cut his original request by only about half the amount proposed by Budget Director David A. Stockman and some other GOP stalwarts, and Congress approved slightly less than that revised request.

But particularly in the Senate, influential GOP committee chairmen warned that another round of domestic cuts could not be accompanied by continued, rapid growth in the Pentagon budget.

Democrats and 'Readiness.' In November and December, Democratic senators from across the political spectrum charged that Reagan was misallocating his defense budget by underfunding the 'combat-readiness' of forces already in the field. They said, for example, that Reagan was buying too little ammunition and training time in order to pay for complex new weapons.

A series of Democratic amendments that would have added money to the annual defense appropriations bill for ammunition and other readiness-related programs were handily rejected on the Senate floor in December, with nearly solid GOP opposition. But Democratic defense specialists were jubilant that the party had evolved an approach that let nearly all Senate Democrats oppose the administration from "pro-defense" positions.

Though keenly aware of the critical issues they would have to skirt to preserve party unity, Democrats promised to renew their attack on Reagan's fiscal 1983 request.

Roads Not Taken

During the 1980 presidential campaign and the early weeks after Reagan's victory, conservative defense analysts who had been long committed to Reagan predicted that the new administration would break radically with the defense programs of the Nixon, Ford and Carter administrations.

But when Reagan's defense budget appeared in March, its most striking aspect was the administration's apparent disregard of the defense recommendations put forward by some of the president's most conservative allies.

Quick Fixes. The first clear indication came nearly a month before the administration took office, when Defense Secretary-designate Caspar W. Weinberger abruptly dismissed the Reagan Pentagon transition team. The team was headed by William R. Van Cleave, who had been Reagan's campaign adviser on defense.

Personal clashes between Weinberger and Van Cleave reportedly contributed to the break. But at its core, the issue was Van Cleave's three-year-long campaign for a program of "quick fixes" intended to rapidly beef up the U.S. nuclear arsenal. One such proposal was to modify existing ICBMs to permit firing them from movable launchers.

In particular, the package was intended to close the "window of vulnerability:" the period during which Soviet missiles theoretically would be able to destroy all but a handful of U.S. ICBMs in a surprise attack.

Even among Republican defense experts, only a minority of strategic arms specialists shared Van Cleave's view of the transcendent importance of the technical details of the strategic balance. And many questioned the technical effectiveness of Van Cleave's proposals.

But the decisive blow to the quick-fix package was its cost. Early on, it became evident that Reagan's budget increases, while substantial, nevertheless would force the Pentagon to make painful choices among alternatives. Most senior military officers and hard-line defense analysts

placed a much higher priority on improving U.S. conventional forces than on new strategic programs (except for the symbolically potent B-1 bomber).

Defense Over Deterrence. Another course popular among some conservatives but rejected by the new administration was a renewed emphasis on anti-missile defense as a cornerstone of U.S. nuclear policy.

In 1980 and 1981, a group of senators dominated by conservative Western Republicans began to argue that a nuclear attack could be deterred by U.S. defenses able to shoot down Soviet missiles and bombers — rather than by threatening a retaliatory attack.

Their basic premise was that technical developments held out the possibility of virtually leak-proof defense of U.S. territory. New anti-missile missiles would be much more effective than the system briefly deployed and then mothballed in 1976, they maintained. And within a decade, they argued, laser-armed space satellites could destroy Soviet missiles soon after they were launched.

Most senior Pentagon scientists and military brass were skeptical, warning that new defensive arms would require years of development and were a long way from deployment.

Despite some favorable references to new defense techniques, the administration did not request a radical increase in strategic defense funds.

Force Increases. The administration also eschewed calls for a crash program to speed the production of weapons. Nor did it call for any substantial increase in the number of combat units on active duty, except in the Navy.

In February 1980, a group of staff aides to congressional conservatives offered one such proposal, called "A Program for Military Independence." It would have more than doubled the production rate of several kinds of combat planes, armored vehicles and warships, while expanding U.S. forces by five ground divisions, four carrier task forces and nine tactical airwings.

The plan also included Van Cleave's "quick fixes" and an energetic program of strategic defenses.

Using cost estimates that were widely regarded as optimistic, the group maintained that their plan would require $226.6 billion more than the $1 trillion Carter planned to spend on defense in the fiscal years 1981-85. For fiscal 1981 alone, the projected cost of the "Independence" program was $198.7 billion compared to Carter's initial request of $161.8 billion.

Just over a year later, in March 1981, Reagan added $184.4 billion to Carter's last five year defense plan: projecting defense budgets totaling $1.46 trillion in fiscal 1982-86 compared with Carter's planned $1.276 trillion. For fiscal 1982 alone, Reagan's increase was $26 billion.

But those substantial increases could buy only a modest increase in tank and plane production rates. And in September, Reagan's original request was pared back to help cope with ballooning estimates of the federal deficit.

Policy and Ideology. Reagan's supporters in the conservative movement also were disappointed in the president's appointments to senior Pentagon positions.

Some conservative defense specialists faulted Reagan's selection of Weinberger, a longtime Reagan associate, as secretary of defense, because of Weinberger's lack of experience with defense issues.

The criticism became louder when Weinberger insisted — over vigorous conservative opposition — on naming Frank C. Carlucci as deputy secretary. Weinberger had served as Secretary of Health, Education and Welfare in

the Nixon and Ford administrations with Carlucci as his deputy. But conservative critics charged that during Carlucci's tenure as deputy director of the CIA in the Carter administration, he had too willingly cooperated with liberal critics of the agency.

Under strong pressure from congressional defense experts to include some defense specialists in the Pentagon hierarchy, Reagan named as Navy Secretary John F. Lehman Jr., a young but experienced defense analyst who had been a leading GOP critic of Carter's defense policies. Widely regarded as the most bureaucratically aggressive of Weinberger's subordinates, Lehman won for his service the administration's first clear departure from Carter policy: the commitment to a 600-ship navy.

Conservatives also counted as victories the appointments of two other experts to top Pentagon posts: Fred C. Ikle as under secretary for policy, and Richard Perle as assistant secretary in charge of policies involving U.S. relations with the Soviet Union and Europe.

The Reagan Package

Reagan's original defense budget plan, announced March 4, incorporated a substantial, if less than revolutionary, increase over Carter's plan. After an initial surge in fiscal 1981 and 1982, Reagan's plan through fiscal 1986 would have increased the Pentagon budget by about 7 percent annually (above the cost of inflation). Carter's last defense budget projected annual real increases of about 5 percent, but Carter's real growth estimates were based on higher inflation assumptions than Reagan used.

Following are the requests for new obligational authority for the Pentagon in fiscal 1982 and the projected requests for fiscal 1982-86 made by Carter in January and by Reagan in March. The amounts are in billions of dollars:

	1982	1983	1984	1985	1986
Carter	$196.4	$224.0	$253.1	$284.3	$318.3
Reagan	222.2	254.8	289.2	326.5	367.5

Reagan also called for a $6.8 billion increase over the $6.3 billion fiscal 1981 supplemental appropriation requested by Carter.

Legislative Agenda. The only force increase to receive immediate congressional action was for the Navy. Senior admirals and Carter critics long had wanted to increase the Navy from about 450 ships to about 600 ships. Of the $25.8 billion Reagan added to Carter's fiscal 1982 request, $4.2 billion was earmarked for new ships — and for the refurbishment of some older ones then in mothballs. That was to be a first step toward expanding the Navy to 15 carrier task forces instead of the 12 then in the fleet.

In the fiscal 1981 supplemental and the fiscal 1982 requests, $2.5 billion was added for items related to the Rapid Deployment Force (RDF) and other programs designed to ease U.S. intervention in the Persian Gulf area. This nearly doubled Carter's request for such programs.

Another $2.5 billion went to continue development of a new strategic bomber. Reagan's choice of the B-1 for this role was not announced until October. But the 1977 decision to cancel the B-1 long had been featured in the hardliners' indictment of Carter, and it was widely anticipated that Reagan would resurrect that program.

Reflecting the president's often-expressed commitment to an all-volunteer military, he proposed an extraor-

dinary 5.3 percent military pay hike in mid-1981 (costing $2.3 billion) in addition to the regular cost-of-living increase — estimated at 9.1 percent — due Oct. 1.

Reagan also asked for $2 billion in the fiscal 1981 supplemental and $13.7 billion in fiscal 1982 to buy more warplanes, missiles, tanks and communications equipment than Carter had requested in January. In nearly every case, the Reagan plan accelerated purchases to which Carter theoretically was committed. These added funds would buy almost 150 more airplanes, 55 more helicopters, 151 tanks and 136 armored troop carriers than had been included in the Carter budget.

The Skirmishes

For five months after the March budget announcement there was no effective objection in Congress either to the overall size of Reagan's defense budget or to his muscular rhetorical stance toward the Soviet Union.

Several narrower — but still important — defense issues took shape on Capitol Hill during that period.

Rapid Deployment Force

The congressional defense committees maintained their pressure on the Pentagon to simplify the organization of the Rapid Deployment Force.

Some critics had viewed Carter's 1979 creation of the Florida-based RDF headquarters — which would have to draw its combat units from among existing forces — as a weak substitute for a stepped-up U.S. military presence near the oil-rich Persian Gulf.

More fundamentally, they were troubled by the bureaucratic complexity of the RDF setup.

Some of the critics also charged that the RDF was planning for the wrong kind of military operation: the transport, at the request of local governments, of large U.S. units into Middle East countries.

A solution promoted by many of these critics was simply to assign the Persian Gulf mission to the Marine Corps. Bureaucratic complexity would be reduced, they argued, and the Corps had experience in the kind of military operation the critics deemed most likely to be needed in the area: the speedy landing from amphibious ships of small but powerful units that would not depend on a friendly reception ashore.

In April, the Reagan administration averted an immediate showdown with the congressional defense committees over the RDF issue by announcing that the RDF would evolve over three years into an independent command, equal in status to the Atlantic and Pacific commands, thus simplifying some of its organizational arrangements. But the RDF was to remain a multi-service coalition.

As they had done in 1980, the defense committees were far more supportive of proposed new transport ships for the RDF than they were of a new transport plane, called the C-17 (formerly the CX).

Military Pay

After a long battle, Congress essentially split the difference between two approaches to allocating a $4.5 billion military pay raise.

The key issue was a disagreement over the relative gravity of two personnel problems facing the services.

The final compromise sought to satisfy both sides: the **Senate Armed Services** committee and the **House Defense Appropriations Subcommittee**, which wanted large raises

to retain senior enlisted personnel; and the Reagan administration and the House Armed Services Committee, both of which favored an across-the-board raise of 14.3 percent in order to help attract recruits to the services.

Procurement Reform

Congressional committees also differed on the conditions under which they would allow the Pentagon to sign a type of weapons contract called "multi-year procurement."

Under that type of contract, the Defense Department would contract at one time for the total number of weapons of a given type it expected to purchase over a period of several years. Congress still would appropriate funds for each year's slice of the contract on an annual basis.

Proponents argued that the multi-year approach should reduce weapons costs by allowing contractors to plan stable, more efficient production runs and by enabling them to buy raw materials and components in large lots at correspondingly lower prices.

The two Armed Services Committees' strong support for increased use of multi-year contracts encountered opposition from two other congressional panels, the House Government Operations Committee and the House Defense Appropriations Subcommittee.

The only direct battle over the multi-year policy came during House debate on the defense authorization bill, when House Armed Services easily bested its opponents.

Alliance Burden-sharing

Until late summer, when the administration's original budget and deficit estimates came under fire, the most ominous threat to Reagan's plan to increase defense spending was the long-festering congressional resentment over allied defense efforts.

Bipartisan coalitions on the defense committees had become increasingly insistent that Japan and U.S. allies in Europe pay more of the cost of defending their interests.

More than considerations of abstract equity were involved. Many members argued that the much larger portion of the U.S. economy that was diverted to defense production accounted in part for the ability of European and Japanese products to undersell U.S. competitors in world markets.

The most widely discussed aspect of the burden-sharing question involved the rate at which NATO members were increasing their defense budgets in real terms.

In 1978, the alliance agreed to an annual real growth rate of 3 percent, but most members had fallen short of that goal. The largest European NATO members also typically spent a smaller portion of their gross national products (GNP) on defense than did the United States.

As in previous years, the cutting edge of congressional resentment fell on the military construction budgets, with the congressional defense committees insisting that the NATO alliance pay for certain facilities that would beef up the U.S. defense of Western Europe. The committees had become increasingly impatient with allied countries since Washington began bearing the whole cost of the RDF and related facilities in the Persian Gulf region. Those facilities were intended to protect oil supplies that were far more essential to U.S. allies than they were to the United States.

The Big Fights

Reagan's domination of the defense debate was disrupted by two events in the second half of the year: the

budget re-estimates in late summer and his decision on strategic arms policy announced Oct. 2.

New Numbers

By late August, it was evident that "Reaganomics" was not having the predicted psychological impact on the economy. Interest rates soared and stock prices dropped in response to projections that the fiscal 1982 deficit would far outstrip Reagan's estimate of $42.5 billion.

OMB director David A. Stockman and other senior White House aides called for cuts of as much as $30 billion in the projected Pentagon outlays over the period fiscal 1982-84. Because funds for weapons procurement were spent over a period of several years, much larger cuts in actual appropriations requests would have been necessary to reduce outlays by that amount.

Reagan announced Sept. 11 that the planned increase in defense outlays over fiscal 1982-84 would be pared by only $13 billion — $2 billion of which would come out of the fiscal 1982 budget. To achieve that $2 billion outlay cut, Reagan in October proposed an $8 billion cut in his $222 billion defense appropriations request.

Several senior GOP members of Congress called publicly for defense to take a larger share of the cuts needed to control future deficits. In the Senate, Majority Leader Howard H. Baker Jr. of Tennessee, Budget Chairman Pete V. Domenici of New Mexico and Defense Appropriations Subcommittee Chairman Ted Stevens of Alaska, took this position. House Minority Leader Robert H. Michel of Illinois joined them.

Echoing the demand for greater restraint of defense increases were several prominent "Boll Weevils:" Southern Democrats who had backed Reagan's economic plan.

But Reagan insisted he wanted no further cuts in his defense plan and, in the end, most of his complaining allies acceded. The only sizable group of defectors from among his original supporters were a dozen or two "Gypsy Moths:" liberal and moderate Republicans from the Northeast and Midwest who had been unhappy from the outset over Reagan's cuts in domestic programs important to their regions.

In acting on the two major Pentagon appropriations bills in late December, Congress cut less than $1.5 billion from Reagan's total request of $208.2 billion.

Nuclear Arms Program

The year's other major row pitted Reagan against a small group of the Senate's most prominent defense specialists over the future shape of the U.S. nuclear arsenal.

After months of delay, Reagan announced a broad-gauged plan for modernization of U.S. nuclear weaponry Oct. 2. The most controversial elements of the program were his decisions to begin production of the B-1 bomber and to scrap the mobile version of the MX missile long espoused by the Air Force and endorsed by Carter in 1979 with evident reluctance.

Reagan proposed instead to deploy the first few dozen missiles in existing missile silos that would be "superhardened" with additional concrete armor. Future MX deployments would use one of several novel techniques from among which Reagan would choose by 1984.

Several Senate Democrats — joined for a time by some senior Republicans — questioned the prudence of spending between $200 million and $400 million for each B-1, since the administration agreed that a so-called "stealth" bomber, designed to evade enemy detection gear, would replace the B-1 in the 1990s.

Eventually the administration won over the Republican skeptics and the challenge to the B-1 was overcome.

Only a handful of congressional specialists supported the MX version killed by Reagan — which involved shuttling each missile among a few dozen hidden launch sites in order to forestall a Soviet missile attack. The plan had seemed dubious to most members and had been hotly opposed by members from Utah and Nevada, where the launch sites would have been spread over a large area.

The critics of Reagan's October plan, centered in the Senate Armed Services Committee, complained that the initial deployment of a few dozen missiles in existing silos made no sense because they would be vulnerable to a Soviet attack, despite the proposed superhardening.

The Senate seconded this judgment by overwhelmingly approving an amendment to the defense appropriations bill that strongly discouraged — but did not flatly prohibit — the superhardening plan. The provision was incorporated into the final version of the bill.

Arms Control

In the early months of 1981, the administration was belabored by friends and foes of strategic arms control.

On the one hand, some conservatives warned that arms control agreements would induce public misconceptions about Soviet intentions that would undermine support for the U.S. defense buildup.

On the other hand, allied governments in western Europe demanded that Reagan's tough line toward Moscow be paralleled by serious efforts to defuse the East-West military confrontation through arms control.

Initially, conservative skeptics of arms control talks appeared destined for key positions in the Arms Control and Disarmament Agency (ACDA). But by midyear, most of the key arms control posts were in the hands of long-time defense analysts who had opposed Carter's SALT treaty, but who were viewed by conservatives as suspiciously "soft" on the the basic notion of arms control.

In November, the administration embarked on a broad approach to arms control negotiations with Moscow.

The U.S. position, announced by Reagan in a widely heralded speech Nov. 18, proposed a "zero-option:" If Moscow would decommission its 250 SS-20 missiles (and some older, shorter-range weapons), the United States would suspend plans to deploy 108 Pershing II ballistic missiles and 464 ground-launched cruise missiles in Europe.

For years, the Soviet Union had insisted that any limitation of nuclear weapons in Europe take account of all arms capable or reaching Soviet territory, including British and French missile-launching submarines and many warplanes of the NATO countries. By ignoring planes and submarines, Reagan's proposal did not meet that demand.

On Nov. 30, U.S. and Soviet negotiators met in Geneva to seek limitations on the deployment of intermediate-range nuclear weapons based in Europe.

Reagan also proposed Nov. 18 that the two superpowers resume negotiations in 1982 on long-range strategic weapons. The goal, Reagan insisted, should be substantial reductions in the existing strategic arsenals. That would be in contrast to the unratified strategic arms limitation (SALT II) treaty that, Reagan said, would have allowed both countries to continue expanding their nuclear forces.

To symbolize this change, Reagan called the new negotiations START: Strategic Arms Reduction Talks.

—By Pat Towell

Reagan Overcame Critics of His Arms Plan

In spite of widespread skepticism and even outright opposition in Congress, President Reagan's strategic weapons program survived congressional tests virtually unscathed in 1981.

Reagan announced his arms plan Oct. 2, after months of highly publicized indecision.

The president decided to produce the B-1 long-range bomber as a replacement for the aging fleet of B-52s. Reagan for years had criticized President Carter's decision in 1977 to cancel the B-1. *(B-1, 1977 Almanac p. 264)*

Reagan also decided to temporarily base about three dozen new MX intercontinental missiles in existing silos in the United States, pending a decision in 1984 on how to base those missiles permanently. Reagan rejected Carter's controversial plan to shuttle the MX missiles among thousands of shelters scattered across the Utah and Nevada deserts. *(MX background, 1979 Almanac p. 450)*

Both decisions were widely criticized in Congress.

The critics ranged from Senate Armed Services Committee leaders who favored the shuttle version of the MX missile, to liberals and arms control advocates who had opposed both the B-1 bomber and any version of MX.

But a successful challenge to the decisions was a long shot, given the disparate motives of members of Congress who were unhappy with various parts of the plan.

Reagan's program had no shortage of critics, but it did not have to confront a single, coherent counter-position.

Politically, the key critics were Republican leaders of the Senate defense establishment. However, they faced no attractive options:

● Most of them were committed to the shuttle version of MX, but saw no practical chance to resurrect it, given Reagan's adamant opposition.

● Most Armed Services Republicans appeared to support construction of both a B-1 bomber and a "stealth" radar-evading bomber. But some were worried that Reagan might shortchange stealth in order to fund the B-1.

● The Republicans' frustration was deepened — and their criticism somewhat restrained — because the program was put forward by a Republican president. That situation was relished by Democrats, who hammered at several aspects of Reagan's plan.

Outright opposition to the Reagan program diminished substantially following the president's Nov. 18 speech offering to cancel deployment of intermediate-range missiles in Western Europe if the Soviet Union would dismantle its comparable missiles.

In the House, which acted on the defense appropriations bill hours after Reagan's speech, there were calls to back the MX and B-1 decisions in order to give the president bargaining muscle for negotiations with the Soviets.

The Reagan Decision

Reagan announced his five-part, $180 billion strategic arms plan Oct. 2. The announcement followed an eight-month review, during which administration officials openly struggled to come to grips with the complex issues involved. *(Announcement text, p. 23-E)*

Reagan and other administration officials repeatedly stressed that their proposal included five parts of a long-term program to modernize U.S. strategic armaments. However, one key element — the interim basing of the MX missile — amounted to the postponement of a decision.

MX Missile. Defense Secretary Caspar W. Weinberger insisted that the administration's long review would not delay deployment of the first MX missile in 1986.

The first 20-40 missiles were to be based temporarily in existing underground silos. The silos were to be "superhardened:" covered with enough steel and cement to delay for a few years the date when Soviet missiles would have enough power and accuracy to destroy them.

(The Pentagon on Dec. 31 said the first 40 MX missiles would be located in existing Minuteman silos, at a cost of $5.6 billion. But the Minuteman silos would not be superhardened because Congress in late 1981 barred superhardening as part of an interim basing method.)

Reagan planned to rush development of three techniques to protect the full fleet of 100 MXs, and to select at least one for a permanent basing system:

● Airplanes that could patrol aloft for several days, ready to launch MXs in mid-air;

● Underground launchers hidden deep inside mountains, where they could not be destroyed by even the most accurate Soviet missiles;

● Anti-ICBM defenses to protect conventional launch silos. But Weinberger emphasized that existing anti-missile designs could not protect such silos.

Of the three alternatives, the airplane system faced the most opposition in Congress. *(Box, p. 199)*

Bombers. Reagan planned to build 100 modified B-1 bombers to enter service by 1987, while continuing development of a new stealth bomber designed to elude Soviet detection. Carter's plan to rely on existing B-52s until the stealth planes were ready was too risky, Weinberger said, because of untested technical features of the new planes.

Depending on how extensively it was modified from its mid-1970s design, similar uncertainties could delay the B-1. Some proposed revisions would incorporate some stealth features into the plane's design and would alter its center of gravity by giving it a larger bomb load.

Submarine Missiles. Reagan planned to continue building Trident missile-launching submarines at a rate of one per year and to develop by 1989 a new, larger missile called Trident II or D-5. The new missile would have a longer range than the current Trident and enough accuracy to destroy armored Soviet missile silos.

As a near-term boost to U.S. nuclear firepower, the plan would equip anti-ship submarines with nuclear-armed cruise missiles able to strike Soviet territory.

U.S. Defense. The plan would build new ground-based radars, Airborne Warning and Control System radar planes and F-15 interceptors to defend U.S. territory.

Communications. The plan included new communications systems and mobile command posts to ensure that U.S. commanders would continue to control U.S. nuclear forces during a prolonged nuclear war.

The Reaction

In the immediate weeks after Reagan's decision, most debate focused on the MX proposal, specifically in whether it closed the so-called "window of vulnerability" alleged to be confronting U.S. nuclear forces.

This was a reference to the period in the 1980s during which a large part of the U.S. land-based missile force

Funding for MX Missile, B-1 Bomber . . .

Following is a summary of major legislative actions dealing with the MX missile and the B-1 bomber in 1981.

MX Missile

Fiscal 1981 Defense Supplemental Authorization (S 694 — PL 97-39)

On April 7, the Senate voted 79-15 to table an amendment to the bill that would have made a symbolic reduction of $7 million in research funds for the MX basing system. The amendment was offered by Larry Pressler, R-S.D. *(Vote 78, p. 16-S)*

Reagan later withdrew the $7 million request, and the bill, cleared Aug. 4, did not include any MX funds.

Fiscal 1981 Defense Supplemental Appropriation (HR 3512 — PL 97-12)

The bill, cleared June 4, denied $38.4 million in requests associated with the MX because Reagan's decision on basing the missile was then pending.

Conferees on the bill also froze $92 million for MX construction projects that had been appropriated in the regular fiscal 1981 bill.

Fiscal 1982 Defense Department Authorization (S 815 — PL 97-86)

During floor action, the House July 9 rejected an amendment by Ronald V. Dellums, D-Calif., to kill the MX. The vote was 96-316. *(Vote 110, p. 44-H)*

But the House did adopt, by voice vote, an amendment giving Congress 60 days to block the president's decision on basing the MX, once it was announced. That amendment was sponsored by James V. Hansen, R-Utah.

The closest House vote on the MX came when the House rejected, 201-207, an amendment by Paul Simon, D-Ill., that would have required concurrence by both houses in the president's decision. *(Vote 108, p. 44-H)*

The final bill authorized $1,875,200,000 for development of the MX missile basing system. That was a cut of $75 million from Reagan's revised request.

Conferees on the bill earmarked $25 million in a separate ballistic missile account for research on a shuttle-type basing system. In their report (H Report 97-311) — but not in the bill itself — conferees barred any research on a scheme of launching the MX from airplanes.

The bill also established a procedure enabling Congress to veto Reagan's decisions on MX and the B-1 bomber by Nov. 18. But the bill was not cleared until Nov. 17, effectively killing that veto provision.

Fiscal 1982 Defense Department Appropriation (HR 4995 — PL 97-114)

By a one-vote margin, the House Defense Appropriations Subcommittee Oct. 28 deleted $1.9 billion in MX money from the bill. On Nov. 16, the full Appropriations Committee voted 25-23 to restore the money.

Two days later, the House rejected an amendment by Joseph P. Addabbo, D-N.Y., to again delete the MX money. The vote was 139-264. *(Vote 300, p. 98-H)*

The Senate took two actions on the MX. On Dec. 3 it rejected an amendment by David Pryor, D-Ark., to delete the $354 million in the bill for work on interim MX basing. The vote was 35-60. *(Vote 431, p. 70-S)*

And the Senate, by a 90-4 vote, Dec. 2 adopted an amendment by William S. Cohen, R-Maine, and Sam Nunn, D-Ga., discouraging research on the interim basing method Reagan had selected. *(Vote 430, p. 70-S)*

The final bill, cleared Dec. 15, provided $1,913,200,000 for research and development on the MX missile and basing system.

The bill included the Cohen-Nunn amendment, which stipulated that $334 million of the $354 million requested for development of an MX interim basing plan would be used only for existing silos that were not "superhardened." The provision also stipulated that a "deceptive" basing system — one in which each missile was shuttled among several possible launch sites — be among the options under study.

The Cohen-Nunn provision also ordered the administration to make a final MX basing decision by July 1, 1983. Reagan had planned to make his decision by 1984.

Fiscal 1982 Military Construction Authorization (HR 3455 — PL 97-99)

On June 4, by voice vote the House adopted an amendment giving Congress 60 days to block by concurrent resolution the president's plan for basing the MX. The House bill barred use of funds for an MX basing system other than the Carter-approved multiple protected shelter (MPS) plan, unless Reagan recommended it and Congress concurred.

As approved by the House, the bill included $356.5 million for MX construction.

The Senate Nov. 5 eliminated the MX money.

---

theoretically could be destroyed by a fraction of the Soviet ICBM fleet. Reagan said his program would narrow the vulnerability window.

But Reagan's MX plan was derided as possibly less capable than Carter's nuclear arms program by John Tower, R-Texas, chairman of the Senate Armed Services Committee. Tower, a staunch supporter of the shuttle version of MX, said Reagan's MX proposal "only places more lucrative targets in already vulnerable fixed silos."

Tower was among the small but powerful group of defense experts who had long accepted the window theory and who remained committed to the shuttle basing for MX, called "multiple protected shelters" (MPS).

For nearly a year, Tower had downplayed Reagan's campaign attacks on Carter's MPS shuttle plan. Tower had said Reagan would see the merit of the system once he had been fully informed on the issue.

In early August, Tower and William L. Dickinson, R-Ala., senior Republican on the House Armed Services panel, personally lobbied Reagan in behalf of MPS.

The proposed interim deployment of some MXs in superhardened silos would not close the vulnerability window, MPS backers warned. But, confronted with Reagan's adamant refusal to even consider MPS, congressional supporters of that system held out little hope that they could induce Congress to override the president on the basis of complex speculations about the course of a nuclear war.

Tower and other Republicans also were handicapped

... Survived Several Hurdles in Congress

After Reagan's rejection of the MPS system, conferees eliminated the $366 million request relating to the MPS system for MX. The final bill, cleared Dec. 8, did include $11 million for acquisition of MX-related office space near Norton Air Force Base, Calif.

Fiscal 1982 Military Construction Appropriation (HR 4241 — PL 97-106)

The bill, cleared Dec. 15, included $11 million for the MX-related office space near Norton Air Force Base, Calif., but no money for other MX projects.

Conferees on the bill said $92 million in MX funds appropriated in fiscal 1981 but frozen pending Reagan's MX decision could be spent. But the conferees insisted that before any funds could be spent, the Appropriations committees had to be given the following: a detailed plan identifying silos to be used for the MX missiles and the relevant cost estimates; a study of the cost and survivability of superhardened silos; a notice that all environmental requirements had been met; and an audit of previously appropriated MX funds.

Fiscal 1982 Department of Energy Nuclear Weapons Authorization (HR 3413 — PL 97-90)

The bill, cleared Nov. 19, included only $30 million of the $60 million requested for manufacturing facilities for MX warheads. The request had been cut by the House Armed Services Committee.

Fiscal 1981 Energy and Water Appropriation, including Energy Department weapons programs (HR 4144 — PL 97-88)

The House Appropriations Committee approved only $9.1 million of the $60 million request for MX warhead manufacturing facilities. The committee restricted use of the money to engineering and design studies. The Senate Appropriations Committee approved $22.5 million.

The final bill, cleared Nov. 21, provided $9.1 million.

B-1 Bomber

Fiscal 1982 Defense Department Authorization (S 815 — PL 97-86)

During House floor action on the bill, the House July 9 rejected an amendment by Wyche Fowler, D-Ga., to remove an Armed Services Committee provision that tilted use of bomber development money in favor of the B-1. The vote was 153-254. *(Vote 111, p. 44-H)*

The final bill authorized a total of $2.1 billion for the

B-1 program, including $1.801 billion for procurement and $302 million for research and development.

Conferees on the bill cut $100 million from the request for B-1 procurement and all of the $51 million request for spare parts.

Amounts in the bill for development of the "stealth" radar-evading bomber were secret.

The bill also established a procedure enabling Congress to veto Reagan's decisions on MX and the B-1 bomber by Nov. 18. But the bill was not cleared until Nov. 17, effectively killing that veto provision.

Fiscal 1982 Defense Department Appropriation (HR 4995 — PL 97-114)

The Senate Appropriations Committee, on Nov. 17, rejected an amendment by Ernest F. Hollings, D-S.C., to delete the B-1 money from the bill. The committee vote was 7-21.

The full Senate rejected several attempts to change funding levels for the B-1 and stealth bombers.

On the key vote, the Senate Dec. 3 rejected an amendment by Hollings to delete all of the $2.4 billion in the bill for the B-1 and to redistribute $1.8 billion of that amount to conventional weapons and "readiness" programs. The vote was 28-66. *(Vote 434, p. 71-S)*

The Senate also rejected two amendments by Robert C. Byrd, D-W.Va., to add money for stealth.

Key House floor action came Nov. 18 when the House rejected an amendment by Addabbo that would have cut B-1 procurement money from the bill. The vote was 142-263. *(Vote 299, p. 98-H)*

The final bill included $2,092,900,000 for the B-1. Of that amount, $1.801 billion was for procurement and $291.9 million was for research and development.

The procurement money was to be spent only after the president certified to Congress that it was feasible to buy a fleet of 100 B-1s for $20.5 billion (in constant 1981 dollars) or for whatever amount the president justified to Congress. The president also was required to state the current cost estimate of the B-1 fleet in each quarterly report to Congress of major weapon program costs.

The amount in the bill for research on the stealth plane was secret. However, conferees on the bill prohibited a reduction in that amount during fiscal 1982.

Both the B-1 cost-certification and the stealth funding floor began as Senate amendments.

by the problem of attacking one of the most important decisions made by a president of their own party.

"If President Carter had recommended this [MX plan], Sen. Tower would have called for his impeachment," Thomas F. Eagleton, D-Mo., told the Senate Oct. 6.

But on NBC's "Meet the Press" Oct. 4, Tower loyally blamed the decision on Reagan's advisers.

Tower protested that the MX decision was made "within a small circle, without the coordination of the best military expertise."

Top Air Force officials were not consulted about the specifics of the decision before it was announced. Air Force Secretary Verne Orr was told of the decision only after reporters were informed.

The Skeptics

Though they were overshadowed by the technically intricate debates over U.S. missile vulnerability and over various versions of MPS, some influential congressional defense experts never had accepted the iron-bound logic of the window theory and the MPS solution.

As Weinberger made the rounds of the defense committees, Reagan's MX plan drew support from Barry Goldwater, R-Ariz., the second-ranking Republican on Senate Armed Services; Jack Edwards, R-Ala., senior Republican on House Defense Appropriations; and several House Armed Services members.

Defense hard-liners who had opposed MPS followed

no one line of argument. But apart from technical issues and the reluctance of some members to challenge a president, these broad themes emerged from those which backed Reagan's rejection of MPS:

• In common-sense terms, there was an inherent implausibility to playing hide-and-seek with hundreds of giant missiles, as the MPS plan would have done.

• More fundamentally, the technical notion of a window of vulnerability rested on complex scenarios of limited nuclear attacks during a prolonged U.S.-Soviet war, which many persons dismissed as fantastic.

• Many members apparently viewed nuclear arms less in technical terms than in the broader political framework of U.S.-Soviet relations. From that perspective, they saw Reagan's MX decision in the context of his broader plan to increase U.S. military power — including other nuclear arms — and his combative anti-Soviet rhetoric.

From the last point of view, MPS was tainted by its association with Carter, even though the plan earlier had been proposed by the Air Force and the Ford administration and was accepted only reluctantly by Carter.

Outright opposition to the MX missile was confined to a small group of arms control advocates concerned about the missile's great accuracy. In an acute crisis in the future, they warned, Soviet leaders would be under great pressure to fire their long-range missiles for fear that otherwise they would be destroyed by an MX attack.

The Joint Chiefs

Gen. David C. Jones, Joint Chiefs of Staff chairman, was firm in his continued support for MPS in joint appearances with Weinberger before congressional committees.

But, as had been the case when Carter decided not to buy the B-1 in 1977, Jones flatly refused on his own initiative to crusade against a presidential decision.

Under questioning by MPS backers, he readily expressed his skepticism of Reagan's MX plan. But Jones emphasized that, on the whole, he supported Reagan's strategic arms package "with enthusiasm."

Though he and Weinberger flatly disagreed with each other over the survivability of MPS, none of the defense committees drew the two into a point-by-point debate over those technical judgments.

The depth of Jones' skepticism toward Reagan's MX plan was evident only by inference. Asked to rank the B-1, the stealth bomber and MX in order of their importance, Jones ranked MX last because he doubted the chances of long-run success for any of the basing plans Reagan hoped would replace MPS.

Weinberger's Case

In addition to sparring with congressional skeptics over the technical merits of Reagan's decisions, Weinberger pressed a broader political case for the plan.

The MX decision should be viewed as "only one small part" of the overall nuclear arms package, he insisted. The fact that more powerful and more accurate weapons would be added to the U.S. arsenal would itself enhance U.S. ability to deter a Soviet attack, apart from the question of U.S. missile vulnerability, he said.

Weinberger also brushed aside complaints that the MX decision overruled the recommendations of senior military officers. The military had been given a full hearing, he insisted. Gen. Jones concurred in that judgment,

but noted that the Joint Chiefs had not been able to review in detail the final MX decision before it was announced.

In any event, Weinberger insisted repeatedly, the decision had been made by the president, who was elected to make such decisions.

"If we had followed precisely the Air Force recommendations," he said on CBS's "Face the Nation" Oct. 4, "I would have to tell you why I wasn't under the total subservience of the generals and admirals."

Weinberger challenged critics who charged that Reagan's MX decision was politically motivated.

The most prevalent accusation was that Reagan killed off MPS at the insistence of his longtime political ally Sen. Paul Laxalt, R-Nev., who had opposed placing the MPS system in his state and in Utah.

Weinberger and Reagan indignantly denied the charge that Laxalt's influence was the reason for the decision.

Weinberger also denied that Reagan had scrapped MPS in favor of a more distant solution to the missile problem in order to save money.

However, Weinberger acknowledged that Reagan's new arms package would cost less than had been projected for strategic forces through fiscal 1984, the year in which Reagan had pledged to balance the federal budget.

In the first few years, Reagan's plan would avoid the expense of building the vast network of MPS shelters. Any of Reagan's three future MX basing systems likely would cost much more than MPS over the long run; but for the early 1980s, they would be only under development.

Making the MX Work

The administration's technical argument against MPS was that an untrammeled expansion of the Soviet missile force could simply overwhelm the system. With enough warheads, Moscow could fire at all 4,600 planned launch sites, thus ensuring the destruction of all 200 MXs.

"There is no way the United States can build [launch] shelters faster than the Soviet Union can build missiles," Weinberger told Senate Armed Services Oct. 5.

A blue-ribbon panel of defense specialists chaired by Nobel Laureate Charles Townes had attested to the vulnerability of MPS, Weinberger maintained. The Townes panel's analysis of MX alternatives, which Weinberger received in July, never was published.

Jones indirectly rebutted a premise of Weinberger's attack on MPS, saying the MPS plan did include options for dealing with increases in Soviet missiles.

The 4,600 shelters planned for MPS were to be spaced far enough apart that another 4,600 could be distributed among the first batch of shelters. If Moscow deployed enough missile warheads to blanket 9,200 shelters, the addition of an anti-missile defense would have the same effect as scattering the MXs among 18,400 shelters.

Sen. Tower also maintained that Weinberger underestimated the obstacles to an enormous expansion of the Soviet missile force. "That assumes that the Soviets have unlimited technological, industrial and economic resources," Tower said on "Meet the Press." "They have to give up something for it ... [which] is the thing that's going to bring them to the bargaining table most quickly."

'Superhardening'

Reagan's interim MX plan encountered considerable skepticism from the congressional panels that had been

told so often that fixed silos could not be protected against increasingly accurate Soviet warheads.

Weinberger emphasized that the missiles would be put in existing silos only for a few years. He said this would buy the Pentagon enough time to develop a new MX version that could survive in the long run.

Gen. Jones agreed that the superhardened silos could work for a few years. But he told the panels he could not endorse the plan until he saw firm estimates of how strong the silos could be made, how much it would cost, how long it would take and how soon Moscow could give its missiles sufficient accuracy to destroy the newly hardened silos.

One Bomber or Two?

In the first several weeks after Reagan's decision was announced, the proposal to begin production of the B-1 bomber appeared to draw a broader and potentially more powerful range of opposition in Congress than the MX decision, though the plane long had enjoyed broad political support on Capitol Hill.

On several grounds, some members appeared dubious about Reagan's plan for the B-1.

There was widespread criticism that the plane might be too expensive for the relatively few years during which it could penetrate the Soviet defenses.

Several members of the House Defense Appropriations panel had concluded from a secret intelligence briefing July 8 that the existing B-52 could penetrate Soviet air defenses for nearly as long as the B-1.

Pentagon officials appearing before the panel later that same day disagreed but emphasized that the B-1 also would be less vulnerable than the older plane to a Soviet attack on U.S. airfields. The B-1 could take off more quickly and fly out of the area faster; its electronic equipment also would be protected against the destructive electrical effects of a nuclear blast.

The administration also argued that if the stealth plane supplanted the B-1 for missions inside Soviet borders, the B-1 could be used through the 1990s to launch cruise missiles from beyond the reach of Soviet defenses and to carry conventional weapons long distances against other targets.

But House Defense Subcommittee Chairman Joseph P. Addabbo, D-N.Y., told Weinberger Oct. 5: "You do not need that sophisticated a weapon to stand off and fire cruise missiles at the enemy."

A longtime foe of the B-1, Addabbo charged that Reagan had opted for the B-1 simply because of his campaign attacks on Carter's decision not to build the plane.

The administration's central argument for buying an interim bomber was that there was too big a technical gamble in counting on having a large stealth plane ready to replace B-52s by the end of the 1980s. The only stealth planes that had been flown were relatively small.

That argument was conclusive for Rep. Jack Edwards. He said he believed stealth could be accelerated, but added: "I can't guarantee that, and so I am not going to second guess the president."

Counting Costs

The Pentagon insisted that buying the B-1 as an insurance policy against the failure of stealth would not cost much. On July 8, witnesses told the House Appropriations panel that buying both bomber types instead of buying just

'Air Mobile' Opposition

Leading defense experts in Congress placed themselves firmly on record in 1981 against the so-called "air mobile" system for basing the MX missile. That system was one of the three alternatives basing systems the Reagan administration planned to study as a permanent home for the MX.

Late in July, news reports said Defense Secretary Caspar W. Weinberger was leaning toward putting MX missiles aboard 100 C-5A transport planes that would be ready for takeoff within minutes of a warning that Soviet missiles had been launched. Later in the 1980s, the C-5As were to be replaced by a new plane that could cruise for several days at a time.

Those reports brought immediate protests from the leaders of both Armed Services committees.

On Aug. 1, John Tower, R-Texas, chairman of the Senate committee, derided an air mobile system as "too unreliable, too costly and of questionable survivability." He warned that Congress would not approve such a system.

On Aug. 6, House committee Chairman Melvin Price, D-Ill., and ranking Republican William L. Dickinson of Alabama wrote Weinberger predicting that "it would be virtually impossible to gain congressional support for an air-mobile basing mode for MX ... that will do less and cost more than the MPS" system. MPS (multiple protected shelters) was the Carter-approved MX system that would have shuttled each missile at random among a large number of hidden launch sites.

Citing Pentagon data, Price and Dickinson argued that only 13 or 14 U.S. missiles likely would survive a Soviet attack on an airborne MX system. All of the U.S. missiles might be destroyed if there were a delay of only few minutes in warning the planes carrying the missiles of an impending attack, they said.

Tower, Price and Dickinson all reminded Weinberger that Congress opposed a slightly different air mobile plan in 1979. *(1979 Almanac p. 437)*

Conferees on the fiscal 1982 defense authorization bill (S 815 — PL 97-86) said the administration could not spend money under the bill for research on the air mobile system. However, that language was not put in the bill itself, and therefore did not have the force of law.

The fiscal 1982 defense appropriations bill (HR 4995 — PL 97-114), did not restrict spending for research on an air mobile MX system.

the stealth plane would cost only about $2 billion extra through the end of the century.

Buying a fleet of 100 B-1s would cost about $20 billion, the Air Force estimated in July.

But on Oct. 5, Addabbo protested that, by the Air Force's own estimate, that would amount to nearly $30 billion after allowing for inflation. And committee member John Murtha, D-Pa., complained that the estimate did not include the cost of some equipment the planes would need, including the equipment to carry cruise missiles.

Whether or not the B-1 would cost much more in the

long run, several members warned that it inevitably would threaten adequate funding for stealth.

"There simply is not enough money to build both," Addabbo said Oct. 8. "Resurrecting [the B-1] will deprive the United States of the timely introduction" of stealth.

Tower cautiously endorsed the B-1 decision, but said on "Meet the Press" he would choose stealth over the B-1, if forced to choose. "I have some question in my mind about how many B-1s we should build," he said.

Before Reagan announced his plan, there had been speculation that he would commit to buy 50 B-1s with more to be bought only if stealth development were moving slowly.

Senate Committee Hearings

Key hearings on the Reagan arms decisions were held the first week of November by the Senate Armed Services Committee and its subcommittee on strategic warfare.

Opening the full committee hearing Nov. 5, Tower warned Weinberger: "The impression has been left that many important aspects of the president's strategic modernization agenda are as yet undefined, are undergoing continuing review or are subject to considerable debate and confusion within the executive branch."

Among the unanswered questions, Tower said, were the military effectiveness of both Reagan's near-term and long-term proposals for basing MX. In addition, he complained, the administration had not explained the assumptions underlying its claim that its program significantly improved U.S. strategic posture vis-á-vis the Soviet Union.

Unencumbered by political ties to the president, committee Democrats were more harsh in their attacks.

Carl Levin, D-Mich., led the charge. The Reagan strategic arms program was "a shambles," he declared, with current forces being shelved to pay for some short-lived "interim" forces. The proposed interim MX deployment "simply makes bigger missiles more tempting targets," in existing missile silos, he said.

"As to the B-1 bomber, the [Pentagon] will apparently say just about anything to sell it," said Levin, reviewing conflicting claims about its cost and effectiveness.

"You have created an impression that we are weak," he told Weinberger, "and now, by your actions, you are making it a reality."

Weinberger came back swinging. Levin's charges reflected "a substantial ignorance . . . that I think can only be designed to mislead," he said. Allegations that Reagan's plan was weaker than Carter's were "dangerous," because they could feed the impression that the United States was "still the kind of weak and vacillating country that it was during the previous administration."

But none of the committee Republicans weighed in to support Weinberger. Tower later noted, rather mildly, that he did not agree with every one of Levin's charges.

B-1 Questions

Weinberger told the committee he had a firm grip on the estimated cost of the B-1 program. Two tactics would be used to keep costs at the estimated level of $20.5 billion (in fiscal 1982 dollars), he said.

First, the contracts for the program would entail stiff penalties for delays and cost-overruns by the contractor. The program would be closely monitored by the highest officials in the Pentagon, he promised.

To control the incessant stream of design changes that increased production costs for many weapons, Weinberger said, the design of the plane would be "frozen." Changes would have to be approved by top Pentagon officials.

Weinberger flatly denied an assertion by Levin that a Pentagon cost-analysis team had put the B-1's cost at upwards of $27 billion (in fiscal 1982 dollars). Higher estimates included items that were unnecessary or that already were paid for, he said.

Effectiveness. Weinberger's defense of the B-1's cost was overshadowed by his partial corroboration of another, more politically damaging criticism: that the bomber could penetrate Soviet air defenses for only a few years.

The penetration argument surfaced late in October, when a CIA analyst told the Senate Defense Appropriations Subcommittee that the B-1 and the B-52 had about the same ability to penetrate Soviet air defenses.

Subcommittee Chairman Ted Stevens, R-Alaska, among others, began asking why Congress should spend more than $20 billion for a plane that would be useful for only a few years. (Stevens later supported the B-1).

But Air Force and Pentagon officials insisted that B-1s could survive Soviet air defense improvements for many years longer than B-52s.

The CIA witness, the officials said, had erroneously based his estimate on the original B-1 design, which Carter had decided not to build in 1977. The Reagan plan would produce an improved plane that would be 10 times harder than the orginal B-1 (and 100 times harder than the B-52) for Soviet radar to detect.

The improved B-1 — the B-1B — could be relied on to hit Soviet targets well into the 1990s, they insisted.

But during the Nov. 5 hearing, Weinberger said repeatedly that the B-1 — which would not enter service until 1986 — could not be relied on for penetration missions past 1988-90. He nevertheless insisted that the plane was needed to carry out penetration missions between the time the B-52 no longer could penetrate and the time stealth could be deployed.

"What I really worry about is giving up for any period of time the ability to penetrate Soviet airspace," he said.

In a Nov. 10 letter co-signed by CIA Director William Casey, Weinberger appeared to retract his testimony, by saying the B-1 could master "anticipated Soviet air defenses well into the 1990s."

SAC Commander

On Nov. 4, Gen. Bennie L. Davis, commander of the Strategic Air Command (SAC), testified that, taken as a whole, the Reagan strategic package was "a significant beginning" to the process of slowing the decline of U.S. nuclear ability relative to Moscow's.

Although saying he would have preferred the MX shuttle system, Davis supported Reagan's alternative, emphasizing the need to begin production of the MX missile while long-term basing decisions were under consideration.

The B-1 should not be considered simply an "interim" bomber, he insisted. Davis said the B-1 could penetrate Soviet defenses "well into the 1990s. A significant number of stealth planes could not be in the field before the early 1990s, "even under the most optimistic schedule," he said.

Though insisting that he supported the Reagan plan on its technical merits, Davis emphasized that the plan was important as a symbol of American resolve to offset any Soviet nuclear threat.

"... [W]e are sending a crucial message to friends and foes alike: America stands ready to take whatever steps are necessary to protect its vital interests," he said.

Reagan Reductions

Under close questioning by Levin and Nunn, Davis reluctantly conceded that the immediate effect of the Reagan plan would be to reduce the number of U.S. nuclear weapons over the next several years.

Compared to the plans of the Carter administration, Nunn and Levin maintained, the Reagan reduction was even more dramatic. Two factors accounted for the reduction:

● For budgetary reasons, Reagan decided to retire early the 75 oldest B-52s and the 52 Titan missiles. (In the 1982 defense appropriations bill (HR 4995), Congress rejected the B-52 retirement plan.)

● Only about two-thirds of the remaining B-52s would be equipped to carry long-range, nuclear-armed cruise missiles, which could be launched from beyond the reach of Soviet air defenses. This would give SAC about 3,700 cruise missiles instead of the 5,000 or so that were possible in theory if the remaining B-52s were equipped.

"We're really going down in capability over the next four to five years, aren't we?" Nunn asked Davis.

"In absolute numbers, certainly you lose capability," Davis conceded. But he insisted that the decline would not be militarily significant, and over the long run the Reagan program was stronger than the Carter plan.

Although Davis did not make the point, the administration had proposed a short-range expedient to increase the numbers of warheads. That plan involved putting long-range cruise missiles aboard attack submarines — the ships designed to hunt Soviet ships.

SALT Violations

Nunn extracted from Davis the first concession from an executive branch witness that Reagan's plan to put the first few dozen MXs in existing Minuteman missile silos might run afoul of SALT II treaty limitations.

The problem could arise from efforts to superharden the launch sites. The unratified SALT II prohibited enlarging the volume of any existing missile silo by more than 32 percent. *(SALT treaty, 1979 Almanac p. 411)*

Davis conceded that Minuteman silos would have to be enlarged by more than that if they were to be superhardened and still be able to accommodate MX missiles, which were much bigger than Minuteman missiles.

Davis insisted that there was "enough maneuvering room," to avoid "a clear-cut violation" of the prohibition. But under questioning from Nunn, he agreed that, if the Soviet Union did not agree to the silo alterations, they would "technically, probably" constitute a violation.

The next day, Weinberger disputed Davis' concession about SALT violations, insisting that the Minuteman silos could be hardened without violating SALT II.

Opposition Swamped

Congressional critics of the B-1 bomber and the MX missile were easily bested during action on the fiscal 1982 defense appropriations bill (HR 4995). *(p. 311)*

Any immediate chance critics might have had to stop Reagan's nuclear arms proposals disappeared without a trace after the president's Nov. 18 speech proposing the elimination of middle-range U.S. and Soviet nuclear missiles from Europe.

The speech came only a few hours before the House took up the defense spending bill.

House members stampeded to support Regan's B-1 and MX decisions as a symbol of backing for the arms cut initiative and to ensure that the president would enter U.S.-Soviet arms talks Nov. 30 with "bargaining chips."

"Their whole theme was 'bargaining chips,'" complained Addabbo, who led unsuccessful efforts to cut funds for the MX and B-1.

Jack Edwards, R-Ala., who led supporters of Reagan's decisions, agreed that the president's speech had affected House debate. "Unwittingly, the president came along at the right time," Edwards said. "You were either for the president and his effort or you weren't."

Senate Critics

In the Senate, critics of Reagan's decisions took two approaches: Democrats attempted to shift money from the B-1 into improvements in conventional forces, and a bipartisan coalition tied strings on the Pentagon's use of money for basing the MX missiles in silos.

Democratic critics of the B-1 decision included some of the Senate's most respected defense experts — Ernest F. Hollings, D-S.C.; Nunn; and Levin.

They slammed the administration for its alleged inconsistencies in defense policy and charged that Reagan's fall budget cuts shortchanged conventional armed forces in order to fund the B-1.

But their attempts to add money for conventional forces and to delete the B-1 funding all failed, in part because Republicans believed the Democrats really were seeking to embarrass the Reagan administration.

The Overall Package

The overall shape of the Reagan nuclear arms package forced other B-1 skeptics to support the plane.

If the MX missile were being deployed in a fashion certain to survive Soviet attacks, J. James Exon, D-Neb., told the Senate, he might have voted against the B-1. But he saw Reagan's version of MX as vulnerable and reluctantly supported the B-1 as the only militarily significant step to modernize U.S. nuclear forces.

The administration also tried to pacify Republicans on the Senate Armed Services Committee who strongly supported the shuttle version of MX.

A key administration concession, according to Senate aides, was the Pentagon's assurance that, among long-term MX base options, it would consider "deceptive basing." That option would shuttle each missile among several launch sites on the same basic principle as the Carter proposal Reagan had rejected.

However, skeptics were determined to nail down that apparent concession. On Dec. 2, 90 senators voted to amend the defense appropriations bill to discourage the Pentagon from spending several hundred million dollars for research on Reagan's interim MX basing plan. The amendment required the administration to include deceptive basing among its options for the MX.

Democrats proclaimed the Senate action as a direct slap at Reagan; Republicans sought to downplay their differences with the president. Either way, the Senate amendment demonstrated that Congress was not yet totally satisfied about Reagan's strategic arms policies. ∎

1981 Defense Supplemental Authorization

Congress Aug. 4 cleared a $2.7 billion defense supplemental authorization (S 694 — PL 97-39) for fiscal 1981. The Senate adopted the conference report on the measure July 30 by voice vote. The House adopted it Aug. 4.

The bill supplemented the $58.3 billion authorized by the regular fiscal 1981 defense authorization and military construction bills. The final amount was some $300 million lower than President Reagan had requested, but that figure obscured the complicated relationship between the bill and the request.

Conferees on the bill challenged as overly optimistic the administration's claim that a rapid drop in inflation would allow some $219 million to be shaved from the 1981 defense budget.

On the one hand, the final bill cut $435.7 million of the $655 million Reagan wanted to slice from 1981 defense programs. Reagan had said the total 1981 budget could be reduced by that amount because his estimate of inflation was lower than President Carter's — an average of 10 percent for the fiscal year compared to Carter's 10.4 percent estimate. Members of both Armed Services committees had questioned that assumption, but Senate Armed Services approved the Reagan cut. House Armed Services approved all but $219.3 million of it, and the conferees accepted the House version.

On the other hand, the conferees maintained that new authorization was not needed for some of the programs Reagan asked for and the conferees backed. Funds for those programs could be appropriated within existing authorization ceilings, they said.

For example, the conferees endorsed renovation of the battleship *New Jersey* ($89 million in fiscal 1981), but pointed out that the regular fiscal 1981 authorization (PL 96-342) already had provided the needed authorization.

Funding technicalities aside, the final version of S 694 made no major change in Reagan's program.

Provisions

S 694 authorized the following additional amounts for fiscal 1981 *(in thousands of dollars)*:

	Reagan Request	Final Authorization
Procurement		
Aircraft	$ 988,225	$ 988,225
Missiles	247,069	243,569
Navy shipbuilding	317,700	149,900
Armored vehicles	807,300	807,300
Research		
and development	598,300	480,928
Military construction	83,322	71,680
Total	**$3,041,916**	**$2,741,602**

Senate Committee Action

In approving the 1981 supplemental bill (S 694 — S Rept 97-35) on April 1, the Senate Armed Services Committee authorized $2.8 billion for additional weapons procurement and military research, $238.2 million less than the administration request.

The total supplemental defense appropriations request was some $6.5 billion, including pay increases and operations and maintenance costs that did not require specific legislative authorization.

One of the Reagan administration's most publicized moves to quickly boost the size of the Navy was rejected April 1 by the committee. The panel deleted from the $3 billion fiscal 1981 supplemental defense authorization bill $139 million earmarked to reactivate the mothballed aircraft carrier *Oriskany. (See box, p. 204)*

Only two days earlier, Navy Secretary John Lehman had encountered a buzz saw of skeptical questions when he defended the reactivation proposal before the committee's Sea Power Subcommittee. Committee Chairman John Tower, R-Texas, had announced then that he was not sold on the *Oriskany* request.

At the same hearing March 30, Tower warned Lehman that the administration plan to update two battleships might be endangered by continuing uncertainty over how the ships would be used and what their modernization would cost. But the committee version of the supplemental bill included the requested $92 million to begin modernization of the *New Jersey* ($89 million) and to start planning the refurbishment of the *Iowa* ($3 million).

In addition to denying funds for the *Oriskany*, the committee denied $96 million for seven F-18 Navy fighters. Tower told *The Washington Post* that the committee's action was intended as a warning to the Pentagon about cost overruns on the F-18, built by McDonnell Douglas Corp. The regular fiscal 1981 defense authorization and appropriations bills had provided $1.8 billion to buy 60 of the planes, but because of increasing costs only 53 planes could be bought with that amount. The administration request would have restored the fiscal 1981 F-18 purchase to 60 planes.

M-1 Tanks

The committee approved funds requested for production of Army tanks. To continue production of the M-60 tank, the bill provided $148 million for 120 tanks. To buy 209 additional M-1 tanks, designed to replace the M-60, the bill authorized $583 million.

As in the case of the F-18, the supplemental for the M-1 was intended to make whole a fiscal 1981 appropriation that had been outrun by spiraling costs. The regular fiscal 1981 defense bills provided $946 million to buy 569 M-1s, but that amount would have paid for only 360 tanks.

In recognition of development problems that plagued the M-1, the committee bill made the additional procurement money available only after the secretary of defense certified that the tank met certain performance criteria.

Senate Floor Action

The Senate approved S 694 April 7 by voice vote after an afternoon of debate, featuring two former secretaries of the Navy exchanging broadsides over the *New Jersey* issue.

By a vote of 69-23, the Senate tabled an amendment that would have barred use of any money in the bill to reactivate the New Jersey battleship. *(Vote 79, p. 16-S)*

The amendment, by Dale Bumpers, D-Ark., would not have reduced the bill by the $89 million earmarked for the *New Jersey* project.

Bumpers and former Navy Secretary John H. Chafee, R-R.I., charged that the estimate of the project's total cost and timetable — $326 million and 21 months — was far too uncertain to justify the reactivation. Technically, the Navy regarded this as a Class F estimate, which, Bumpers quipped, "is something not too far from flying over the ship in a helicopter and saying, 'I believe it will cost about $270 million to reactivate that ship.' "

The money and the 1,500 men who would man the battleship would be better used on new, modern ships, the two members insisted.

Although the Navy planned to equip the ship with long-range cruise missiles, an underlying current of skepticism ran through the opponents' arguments. "Let us not play around with sounding glorious trumpets for past memories," Chafee declared.

William Proxmire, D-Wisc., was more blunt in referring to the battleship: "They've got to be kidding."

Armed Services Committee Chairman John Tower, R-Texas, Sea Power Subcommittee Chairman William S. Cohen, R-Maine, and former Navy Secretary John W. Warner, R-Va., backed the Navy's contention that the *New Jersey* would add firepower to the fleet relatively quickly and inexpensively. The only new ship that could be bought for the same price was an anti-submarine frigate with only a single missile launcher, they argued.

Contrary to earlier Navy testimony, the plan was to leave on the ship all nine guns, which could fire 2,000 pound shells more than 20 miles. Launchers for 48 cruise missiles would be mounted on the deck.

At first glance, the vote to table Bumpers' amendment was more favorable to the battleship project than the 41-50 vote by which a similar amendment was killed in 1980. Only two senators who had supported the modernization in 1980 switched to opposition in 1981; 12 senators switched from opposition to support. Liberal Democrats predominated among supporters of the amendment. *(1980 action, 1980 Almanac p. 62)*

But the project was in more trouble than the April 7 vote made it appear. Among those voting to table the Bumpers amendment were Ted Stevens, R-Alaska, and Jake Garn, R-Utah, whose announced skepticism portended rough water ahead in the appropriations process.

MX Missile

In its first vote on the issue since late 1979, the Senate voted 79-15 to table an amendment that would have made a symbolic reduction in funds for the MX mobile intercontinental missile. *(Vote 78, p. 16-S)*

The administration was re-examining alternative approaches to keeping the new missile hidden from Soviet observation.

The amendment by Larry Pressler, R-S.D., would have deleted from the supplemental $7 million for research related to MX. The amendment "would be a clear signal to the Pentagon that many people are concerned about the validity of the MX," Pressler said, "and that we would like to know where it is going to be located before moving ahead with more expenditures." The regular fiscal 1981 defense bill appropriated $1.6 billion for MX development.

Tower charged that Pressler's amendment would send a different signal: "He is sending a message to the Soviet Union that we are not serious about maintaining an adequate strategic capability in this country to deter them from a first strike."

Warner said that $5 million of the amount Pressler

targeted was needed to study how effectively the MX missiles could be hidden — information essential to the eventual selection of a plan for deploying MX. The other $2 million at issue was to study the effect of a nuclear blast on the missile itself — information needed regardless of how the missile eventually was deployed, Warner said.

Provisions

As passed by the Senate April 7, S 694 authorized the following amounts for Defense Department programs in fiscal 1981:

	Reagan request	Senate-passed
Procurement		
Aircraft	$ 988,225,000	$ 892,225,000
Missiles	247,069,000	265,969,000
Navy shipbuilding	317,700,000	172,100,000
Tanks and other vehicles	807,300,000	807,300,000
Research and Development	598,300,000	599,600,000
Military Construction	83,322,000	66,440,000
Total	$3,041,916,000	$2,803,634,000

House Committee Action

The House Armed Services Committee reported HR 2614 April 9 (H Rept 97-20). The committee ordered the bill reported April 7 by a 36-1 vote. Dennis M. Hertel, D-Mich., cast the only "nay" vote.

The committee bill authorized $2,640,840,000 for weapons procurement, research and military construction — $401.1 million less than the administration request. The difference did not represent a reduction in programs because the panel said new authorization was not needed for some of the projects dropped from the bill.

Carrier Reactivation

One such project was Reagan's request for funds to begin reactivating the mothballed aircraft carrier *Oriskany* and the battleship *New Jersey*. The committee endorsed both projects, but at first said both had been approved already in the regular fiscal 1981 authorization.

The panel's Sea Power Subcommittee had planned to recommend against approving any of the $317.7 million in new budget authority requested for Navy shipbuilding. The supplemental appropriations bill could provide the funds within the scope of the regular fiscal 1981 defense authorization bill, it concluded.

But when the full committee met to mark up the bill, Chief of Naval Operations Adm. Thomas B. Hayward appealed to subcommittee Chairman Charles E. Bennett, D-Fla., to reverse that position. Hayward asked for a signal of positive support for the *Oriskany's* reactivation to offset the Senate's rejection of the plan.

Senior Republican William L. Dickinson (Ala.) led a handful of members questioning the wisdom of reactivating the ship. The current estimate of the project's total cost — some $500 million — was uncertain, Dickinson said. He noted that the Navy's Atlantic Fleet commander said he would not want the ship if the total cost rose as high as $800 million.

But Bennett and his allies insisted that the reactivation was the only way to expand the carrier force relatively

Battleship Plan Under Way, But *Oriskany* Listing Heavily

The Navy's plan to quickly enlarge its fleet by returning three ships to service met only partial success:

● The supplemental appropriations bill (HR 3512 — PL 97-12) killed the request for $139 million to begin renovating the mothballed aircraft carrier *Oriskany*.

Of the four committees that pass on defense funding requests, only House Armed Services demonstrated any support for the *Oriskany*. Other defense committees cited the ship's age and its inability to carry many of the Navy's more powerful types of combat planes. The Navy and House Armed Services said the ship could supplement a larger carrier in the front lines or could operate on its own where there were no strong enemy air forces.

Bending to political realities, President Reagan finally dropped plans to reactivate the *Oriskany* in September, when he proposed cuts to his 1982 budget.

● Congress in 1981 approved $328 million to reactivate the battleship *New Jersey* and $91 million to begin work on its sister ship, the *Iowa*.

The first $91 million for the *New Jersey* was included in the fiscal 1981 supplemental appropriations bill (HR 3512 — PL 97-12). That bill also included $1 million for early work on the *Iowa*. *(p. 352)*

Another $237 million to complete work on the *New Jersey* was included in the 1982 defense authorization bill (S 815 — PL 97-86) and in the 1982 defense appropriations bill (HR 4995 — PL 97-114). *(Authorization, p. 212; appropriation, p. 311)*

An additional $90 million to buy materials for the *Iowa* was included in the 1982 authorization and appropriations bills. The administration planned to ask for funds to complete the *Iowa* project in its fiscal 1983 budget. Requests to modernize the two other *Iowa*-class battleships were to be made in later years.

Renovation Plans

The basic premise of the Navy's proposal to recommission and modernize the three old warships was the Reagan administration's decision to expand the fleet. The Navy was built around 12 "battle groups," each with an aircraft carrier and its escort ships. The administration was committed to expanding the fleet to at least 15 such squadrons.

The first of the three new carriers needed for this plan was to be included in the fiscal 1983 budget, but the total force of 15 carriers could not be in service until the mid-1990s, when the third additional carrier would be completed. In the meantime, the Navy argued, the three recommissioned veterans could fill in to form battle groups of respectable power — for certain situations. Their merit lay in the relatively low cost and short time needed to put them in service, it was argued.

On March 30, Navy Secretary John Lehman told the Senate Sea Power Subcommittee that the *Oriskany* could be put back into service for about $500 million. Among needed modifications was replacement of the wooden flight deck with one of less hazardous material.

The ship was too small to carry the Navy's most modern warplanes, but it could carry several squadrons of the A-4 fighter-bombers used by the Marine Corps.

The *Oriskany* could operate on its own against an opponent lacking first-line jet fighters, Lehman argued, since the very maneuverable A-4s could double as dogfighters. Against a more powerful opponent, he said, *Oriskany*'s planes could act as bombers under the cover of a big carrier equipped with more sophisticated fighters.

Plans for the battleships were more uncertain. The basic argument for their recall was that, although commissioned during World War II, they were relatively "low-mileage" ships, having spent only about a decade in service. Their armor plate was designed to fend off Japanese battleship shells that were heavier and more powerful than the Soviet anti-ship missiles that were the U.S. Navy's current nemesis. And their sheer size was important — the Navy saw them as "platforms" on which to mount a large number of long-range cruise missiles equipped to strike ships or land targets with either nuclear or conventional warheads.

Each ship carried three turrets, each with three cannons that can fire a 2,000-pound shell more than 20 miles. Lehman told the Senate panel that each ship's rear turret would be removed and replaced by long-range cruise missile launchers. Reportedly, 36 missiles would be fitted at first.

After the ships had been in service for several years, he said, a decision could be made to equip them with a much larger number of missile launchers — up to 320 were mentioned. Alternatively, a flight deck could be mounted on the ships' sterns to operate helicopters or vertical takeoff jets.

Lehman estimated that it would cost $325 million for the initial phase of work on the *New Jersey*, which had been in service briefly during the Vietnam War. For the *Iowa*, which had been in mothballs since the late 1950s, it would cost about $500 million, he estimated, though stressing that the figures were only estimates.

Committee Objections

The comments of several Senate Armed Services Committee members to Lehman had a common theme: Plans for the old ships had become so expensive and so time-consuming that it was unclear whether they met the initial goal of providing an interim increase in naval power relatively quickly and at relatively low cost.

Moreover, Committee Chairman John Tower, R-Texas, and William S. Cohen, R-Maine, warned Lehman that the cost estimates were too uncertain for the committee to make its own judgment about whether the projects were worth the price. And they said the figures were not firm enough for the panel to defend on the Senate floor.

Cohen said the estimated cost of the *Oriskany* project had risen more than 60 percent since late 1980. And Harry F. Byrd Jr., Ind.-Va., asked Lehman why the cost of the *New Jersey* project jumped from $247 million, on March 16, to about $325 million less than two weeks later. After a confused exchange of apparently inconsistent figures, Lehman told Byrd he was "not prepared to back up any figure right now." Later, the Navy said the extra money was for additional weapons.

quickly. "We might get a better ship without very much more money eight or 10 years from now." Bennett said.

By a voice vote, with few "nays," the committee adopted Bennett's amendment to include the $139 million for the reactivation.

Spare Parts. The committee cut by 10 percent the $605 million request for spare parts for Air Force aircraft. The procurement subcommittee said the large parts request could not be managed efficiently.

M-1 Tanks. The committee approved $327.5 million of the $337.5 million requested to offset inflation in the cost of M-1 tanks. Without the additional funds, the Army could have bought only 360 of the 569 tanks planned in fiscal 1981.

House Floor Action

The House passed HR 2614 June 23 by a vote of 360-50. *(Vote 86, p. 38-H)*

The House June 23 declined to take a symbolic slap at U.S. allies in Europe for shirking their share of the cost of defending NATO. It rejected by voice vote an amendment by Don J. Pease, D-Ohio, to the fiscal 1981 supplemental defense authorization bill that would have deleted $1.8 million for construction of an ammunition storage dump for Army troops in West Germany.

Pease cited press reports that West Germany's defense budget would increase by only 1.3 percent in real terms in 1981, less than half the 3 percent annual real growth rate to which the NATO countries had agreed in 1978.

Several members of the House Armed Services Committee agreed that European allies should be encouraged to carry more of the burden of alliance defense. But they said the amendment would complicate diplomatic efforts to that end and would deprive U.S. troops of a needed facility.

The House adopted two amendments by voice vote June 23:

• By Melvin Price, D-Ill., to add $24 million to replace an Air Force reconnaissance plane lost in a crash.

• By Bill Nichols, D-Ala., to enlarge the Army by 4,700 members (to a total of 780,000).

HR 2414 made the following fiscal 1981 supplemental authorizations:

	Senate-passed Amount	House-passed Amount
Procurement		
Aircraft	$ 892,225,000	$ 974,425,000
Missiles	265,969,000	284,769,000
Navy shipbuilding	172,100,000	139,000,000
Tanks and other vehicles	807,300,000	792,300,000
Research and Development	599,600,000	408,528,000
Military Construction	66,440,000	66,440,000
Total	**$2,803,634,000**	**$2,665,462,000**

Conference Report

As reported July 27, the conference report (H Rept 97-204) authorized $2,741,602,000 for weapons procurement, military research and construction in fiscal 1981. This was $76 million above the House-passed amount and $62 million below the Senate version of the bill.

On June 4, Congress enacted the supplemental appro-

priations bill (HR 3512 — PL 97-12), which included $9.3 billion for defense programs, most of which did not require authorization. *(See story, p. 352)*

Following are highlights of the conference action:

Conferees approved the $20 million requested to begin "hardening" the equipment on B-52s so it would not be damaged by the electronic effects of a nuclear explosion. But they insisted that before spending the money, the president adopt a comprehensive program for modernizing the bomber fleet. At the time of conference action, Defense Secretary Caspar W. Weinberger was continuing to puzzle over whether to begin building B-1s or "stealth" bombers.

The House bill had denied the B-52 funds because Reagan had not yet reported his overall bomber plan.

The conferees also approved $41.4 million requested to meet unexpected cost increases in development of the ground-launched cruise missile, designed to hit Soviet targets with nuclear warheads from bases in Europe. The House had proposed shifting $41.2 million of that amount to speed production of a ship-launched version of the cruise missile.

Conferees essentially accepted the House position to speed up production of two fighter planes.

First, they approved a request for $95.9 million to meet unexpected cost increases in the F-18 program. Without the additional funds, only 53 of the planes could have been built instead of the 60 budgeted.

Conferees also approved a House initiative to buy enough components to build 180 F-16s in fiscal 1982 instead of the 120 planes for which components were budgeted. Compared to $65.7 million added to the bill for this purpose in the House, the conference report added $51.1 million and told the Pentagon to make up the difference with already enacted budget authority.

The House had cut by 10 percent the $605.2 million requested for Air Force spare parts. Conferees approved $573.1 million and told the Air Force to use existing authority for the other $32.1 million.

The conferees approved the amounts requested to meet cost overruns for the M-1 tank ($337.5 million) and for the M-2 armored troop carrier ($158.5 million). The House had made small reductions in the two programs.

But the conference report blocked expenditure of $278.1 million of the M-1 funds until the Pentagon certified that the tank's transmission demonstrated adequate durability.

Of $317.7 million requested for warships, only $149.9 million was approved in the conference report. This would pay for components of an Aegis anti-missile system to be put on a cruiser that would be requested in fiscal 1983.

Conferees said existing authority was available to offset all the warship reductions, including $89 million for reactivation of the *New Jersey* and $139 million for reactivation of the *Oriskany*. ∎

Production Act Extended

The House Sept. 24 cleared for the president HR 2903 (PL 97-47), extending the provisions of the Defense Production Act by one year, through Sept. 30, 1982. The Senate had passed the bill Sept. 22.

The administration had asked for a five-year extension of the act, which gave the president the powers to assign

industrial priorities and allocations in order to assure defense production in an emergency and to guarantee loans to defense and aerospace-related contractors.

Sen. William Proxmire, D-Wis., said the extension should be limited to one year in order to give Congress an opportunity to review possible administration proposals to use the act to subsidize and set floor prices for strategic minerals.

The Senate adopted an amendment by Harrison "Jack" Schmitt, R-N.M., extending until March 31, 1982, the deadline for a report to Congress by the Gold Commission. The commission was studying the possibility of a return to the gold standard. Its original deadline was Oct. 7, 1981.

The 17-member commission was established by Congress in 1980 but did not begin its work until the fall of 1981.

The House Sept. 24 accepted the Senate amendment and passed the amended bill by voice vote.   ∎

Stockpiles Put in Budget Bill

The Senate and House Armed Services committees used the reconciliation process to make one more move in their long campaign to force the executive branch to rejuvenate the national stockpile of strategic and critical materials.

The Office of Management and Budget (OMB) and the Budget committees had suggested the sale of surplus silver from the stockpile to collect $572 million of the $966 million by which the Armed Services panels were directed to cut direct spending in fiscal 1982.

But Senate conferees basically accepted a House decision to substitute other surplus commodities for some of the silver and to reduce the amount of the sale to $535 million. The conferees also incorporated into the reconciliation bill "management reforms" for the stockpile that would force the Reagan administration to carry out its announced plans to buy additional commodities that were intended to keep the U.S. economy going during a three-year-long war.

The Armed Services committees had long complained that presidents routinely manipulated the stockpile to improve their budgets cosmetically.

To make up for the $37 million reduction in the stockpile sale proceeds, the conferees accepted a House initiative to create a one-year open-enrollment period for the benefits program for survivors of military retirees.

The Senate and House bills had agreed on the source of the remaining $394 million cut: giving cost-of-living adjustments to military retirees annually instead of every six months. Both houses had made the change contingent on a similar change in benefits for retired civilian workers. The change for civilians also was made in the reconciliation bill (HR 3982 — PL 97-35).

Stockpile Sales

On its face, the principal problem with the stockpile was that it had far too much of some commodities and far too little of others.

But overlaying that technical issue was the stockpile's principal political problem. For at least a decade, presidents had tried to use the stockpiled commodities — worth about $9 billion in 1981 — as a pool of potentially liquid assets to be converted by sale whenever the budget could use a few hundred million dollars.

President Nixon reduced from three years to one year the period for which stockpiled commodities were supposed to suffice. President Ford restored the three-year goal in 1976, and President Carter endorsed it in 1977. But in 1975 and 1976 Ford's defense budget request was reduced by several hundred million dollars by anticipating revenues from stockpile sales which, it was generally assumed, Congress would not — and did not — authorize.

In 1976, the House Armed Services Committee concluded that legislation was needed to insulate the stockpile from budgetary politics. The committee reported a bill to deposit the proceeds of stockpile sales in a revolving fund that could be used only to purchase additional stockpile commodities. Similar legislation finally was enacted in 1979. *(1979 Almanac p. 460)*

Meanwhile, the stockpile was embroiled in a controversy over silver. For years, the stockpile agency had declared surplus all 139.5 million troy ounces of silver in the inventory. The agency said the country would have reliable access to silver from domestic sources, plus Canada and Mexico in case of war.

Congressional opposition to that position was especially strong among members from silver producing states, who were worried about the effect of stockpile sales on silver markets. Rep. Larry P. McDonald, D-Ga., also battled to retain a silver stockpile, arguing that in wartime precious metals could be a uniquely acceptable currency for international commodity barter.

Reconciliation Round

The Reagan administration accepted the position that the silver stockpile was superfluous, and recommended a sell-off from which it projected fiscal 1982 receipts of $572 million.

The House Armed Services Committee explored several alternatives to putting any stockpile sales in the reconciliation package, but the committee ultimately proposed to sell equal proportions of all surpluses currently in inventory to gross an estimated $535 million.

Conferees agreed to this provision and also accepted with modifications a Senate provision requiring that before silver could be sold, the president would have to determine that the silver actually was surplus to defense needs.

Conferees also set a ceiling on the total amount that could be held in the revolving fund into which all stockpile sales receipts were placed.

The effect of the ceiling would be to force the Reagan administration to use the sales proceeds to buy additional amounts of stockpiled commodities now in short supply, rather than simply allowing the funds to accumulate. Such stockpile purchases already were a declared administration policy; the fund ceiling would prevent any second thoughts.

Survivors' Benefits

The retired survivors' benefits change declared an open enrollment period for one year in the Survivor Benefit Plan, under which a military careerist could contribute to a fund from which his or her survivors would be paid an annuity after the military member's death.

The maximum annuity was 55 percent of the military member's retired pay, and smaller annuities — with proportionately smaller contributions — could be chosen.

During the open enrollment period, military members who passed the period when they were eligible to join the benefit plan could join, and personnel already contributing could increase the size of their annuity.

For at least the first five years after the open enrollment, the new contributions to the benefit plan would give the Treasury a net income. At some point, as the newly eligible annuitants began drawing money from the plan, the change would begin to cost the Treasury money. However, precise figures on the ultimate cost were not available.

The House-passed provision had provided that if a military member died within one year of taking advantage of the open enrollment period, his or her survivors would receive only the amount contributed to the plan. In conference, the Senate insisted that the moratorium be extended to two years.

Consultant, Travel Cuts

The Armed Services committees warned that combat effectiveness could be harmed by the reconciliation bill's cuts in two perennial targets of congressional budgeteers: travel and consulting contracts.

The bill would cut consultant fees by $500 million and travel costs by $100 million. If those reductions were allocated by OMB on the basis of proportionally equal reductions in each department, the Pentagon would have to absorb 80 percent of the cuts.

According to the Armed Services conferees, administrative travel — the real bogeyman of travel-cutting crusades — accounted for only about 6 percent of all Pentagon travel. The bulk of the Pentagon's expenditures in this category were to move fuel and supplies to forward-deployed units, to move personnel being transferred among assignments, and to move units to and from training exercises.

Most of the contracts affected by the reduction, according to the conferees, would not be the kind of paper analyses at which the cuts were aimed, but essential services such as recruiting advertising, certain kinds of training and some weapons maintenance that were performed by civilian contractors.

The conferees called the potential erosion of military effectiveness "totally unacceptable." The Senate bill — about which Armed Services conferees complained — had reduced travel by $550 million, but the final bill cut it by only $100 million in fiscal 1982. ∎

Military Pay Increased

Deadlocked over principle, Senate-House conferees on a $4.5 billion military pay raise bill (S 1181 — PL 97-60) used the old tactic of splitting the difference to craft a compromise.

The House approved the compromise Oct. 7 on a 417-1 vote; the Senate approved it the same day by voice vote, clearing the bill for the president. *(House vote 238, p. 78-H)*

Bowing to Senate insistence that senior enlisted personnel receive larger raises than new recruits, the compro-

mise pay table was "targeted," ranging from a 10 percent increase in recruit pay to a 17 percent raise for senior sergeants. The raises were retroactive to Oct. 1.

The differential between ranks covered only about half the range of the original Senate bill, which went from 7 percent for privates to 22 percent for some sergeants major.

The increase in the raise for lower ranks reflected a partial victory for the House, which had backed an administration proposal for a 14.3 percent across-the-board pay hike.

The House across-the-board position prevailed on officer pay. The Senate bill had authorized raises of 9-11 percent for new officers, 12 percent for senior officers and 14-16.5 percent for most mid-career officers.

Also in line with House conferees' concern for attracting high quality enlistees, the bill authorized enlistment bonuses of up to $8,000. The Senate bill had increased the bonus ceiling from the current $5,000 to $7,500, and many Senate conferees were unhappy even with that increase.

The basis for the pay compromise was a proposal of Defense Secretary Caspar W. Weinberger which essentially split the difference between the administration's proposal of a 14.3 percent raise and the percentage increase in the Senate bill for each enlisted rank.

Provisions

As signed into law, S 1181 authorized:

● Pay raises, retroactive to Oct, 1, 1981, ranging from 10 percent for recruits, 14.3 percent for officers and up to 17 percent for the three senior sergeant grades;

● A 14.3 percent increase in the food and housing allowance for personnel who did not live in barracks.

● Enlistment bonuses of up to $8,000.

● Addition of three jobs to the list of hazardous duties for which personnel received extra pay. Eligibility was extended to persons working on aircraft carrier flight decks, in laboratories handling viruses or bacteria or handling toxic fuels.

● Extra pay for weapons control officers on AWACS radar-warning and command planes and increased the extra pay for some aviators.

● Payment of the sea-duty bonus to both crews of a ballistic missile-launching submarine. To increase the amount of time the missile subs were at sea and within range of Soviet targets, they had two crews which made alternate patrols. The provision would give both crews sea-duty pay for the whole time they were assigned to the ship, whether they were on patrol or ashore.

● Payment of a $3,000 bonus to naval officers who volunteered for service in nuclear-powered surface ships, an amount already paid to volunteers for nuclear-powered submarines.

● A re-enlistment bonus of up to $3,000 a year for officers trained as engineers or scientists.

● 5,000 new Navy and Air Force ROTC scholarships.

● Payment of up to $110 per day for up to four days of temporary lodging for a service member and his or her family during a transfer from anywhere in the world to a duty station in the United States;

● Payment for transportation of a service member and dependents returning to the United States on emergency leave;

● Elimination of the ban on draft board membership by persons over 65 years-of-age.

Background

The disagreement between the House and Senate approaches to the military pay bill centered around the basic question of what problem needed the greatest attention: recruitment, especially for the all-volunteer Army, or retention of senior enlisted personnel.

There were at least five specific issues that affected that basic question:

Cost of Living. Under normal circumstances, all military pay would have been increased Oct. 1, 1981 (the start of the 1982 fiscal year) to offset increases in the cost of living. Since 1967, the military pay raise had been linked to the pay hike for federal civil service employees. The civilian pay hike, in turn, was linked to an annual survey of private sector pay raises for professional, administrative, technical and clerical workers (called PATC).

In 1980, President Carter proposed a higher raise for the military than for civilian workers, and Congress enacted a larger military raise than Carter sought.

The Reagan administration's initial plan was for the Oct. 1 military pay raise to equal the rate called for by the civilian PATC survey — projected to reach 9.1 percent.

Comparability Catch Up. Senior military officers and advocates of the all-volunteer Army had long argued for restoring military pay to the level of purchasing power relative to private sector pay that prevailed in 1972. In that year the all-volunteer system was inaugurated with a large pay raise for low-ranking personnel.

Under existing law, the president was allowed to "cap" annual federal pay raises by holding them below the level called for by the PATC survey.

The president also could transfer part of the military pay raise out of members' basic pay and into the allowance for quarters — an amount paid to personnel whose living quarters were not provided by the government. Such reallocation was generally unpopular with military personnel because it would depress various benefits — most notably retired pay — that were computed on the basis of basic pay.

In 1975, 1978 and 1979, Presidents Ford and Carter capped all federal pay raises at levels below those called for by the PATC. Portions of the 1976 and 1977 pay raises also were reallocated to the quarters allowance.

As a gesture of support for military personnel, Reagan proposed a special 5.3 percent pay raise to take effect July 1. This would have restored military basic pay to the level it would have reached had it simply risen at the PATC rate since 1972.

Pay Compression. Military careerists complained that the ratio of pay for senior personnel to junior personnel had steadily declined since the big 1972 boost in recruit pay. The resulting "compression" of the pay table reduced the incentive for enlisted personnel to seek promotions and remain in the service for a full career, it was argued.

According to Senate Armed Services Committee member Sam Nunn, D-Ga., between 1972 and 1981 the average annual compensation of a typical recruit increased by 225 percent (from $5,116 to $16,620). Over the same period, the average compensation of a typical sergeant major — the Army's highest enlisted rank — increased by 92 percent (from $15,121 to $29,026), 19 percent less than the increase in the cost of living.

Pentagon critics blamed this compression, in part, for the services' shortage of senior enlisted personnel — more than 20,000 short in the Navy, about 5,000 in the Army.

But critics of the Senate pay targeting plan insisted that these shortages reflected relatively low re-enlistment rates during the Vietnam War. Since the war and under the all-volunteer era, re-enlistment rates had risen. The Pentagon projected that each service would have enough careerists for larger forces within a few years, even without pay targeting to senior ranks.

Skill Shortages. The shortages of senior enlisted personnel were concentrated in two kinds of job specialties. One kind — such as ground combat — involved unpleasant working conditions and had no civilian counterparts. The other — such as radar maintenance — had direct counterparts in the private sector at wages substantially above military salaries.

The Pentagon used two techniques to offset the disadvantages of these specialties:

● Special pay was awarded for duty at sea, in aircraft or in various hazardous situations such as work on the flight deck of an aircraft carrier.

● Bonuses of up to several thousand dollars were paid for enlistment or re-enlistment in job specialties with serious shortages.

Recruiting. In the early months of fiscal 1981, the services were able to enlist nearly the planned number of recruits while complying with congressionally imposed limits on their educational and test score qualifications.

The proportion of new male enlistees with a high school degree rose from 54 percent in the first half of fiscal 1980 to 73 percent in the first half of fiscal 1981. For the Army alone, the percentage rose from 37 percent to 68 percent.

Over the same period, the proportion of recruits scoring in the upper and middle levels of the enlistment exam rose from 70 percent to 82 percent. For the Army, the proportion rose from 50 percent to 70 percent.

But on May 7, Lawrence J. Korb, assistant secretary of defense for manpower, warned a Senate Armed Services subcommittee against assuming that all was well on the recruiting front.

"Youth unemployment has been extremely high," he said. "In the next few years, things will turn around and prospects in the civilian sector will begin to outweigh the economic advantages of a military career."

The Pentagon projected that the Army might miss its fiscal 1983 recruiting goal by 28,000, Korb warned the panel. That shortage could be reduced by 10,000 or 15,000 if Congress enacted the special 5.3 percent catch-up pay raise, he said.

Irritants. In addition to the big pay issues, the military services hoped to relieve the financial burdens of moving from post to post under orders, a problem that had been a focus of service members' gripes.

In 1980, the travel allowance for military personnel moving between assignments was increased to the level paid civilian federal employees. The services also wanted an expense allowance for temporary lodgings during the move and an authorization for service members to draw their travel allowances in advance.

The Reagan Position

The Reagan administration came to Washington promising to support an adequate level of military compensation to give the all-volunteer system a chance to work — a chance it maintained had been stifled by Carter's tight military budgets.

There was a general consensus among Reagan advisers that a catch-up raise needed to be enacted to restore military pay to its 1972 level of purchasing power and that future pay hikes should not be capped. There also was support for an early signal of the Reagan administration's commitment to more generous compensation policies than Carter had supported.

The administration settled on a two-step approach: a 5.3 percent increase July 1 (to restore the 1972 purchasing power) and a regular cost-of-living hike on Oct. 1, 1981, tentatively set at 9.1 percent.

Combined with the previous 11.7 percent hike, that would have meant three pay raises totaling more than 25 percent in less than a year. That prospect provoked a call from some influential members of Congress for more narrowly focused pay increases.

Administration officials insisted that the special July hike should be across-the-board, as a symbol of national support for military personnel. The October increase might be targeted toward sergeants, they said, but the president should decide that, using his discretion under existing law.

The discussion was outrun by events when it became evident that there would be only one military pay raise in 1981, to take effect Oct. 1.

One reason was that it was unclear whether there was enough money remaining in the fiscal 1981 defense budget ceiling to pay for the July raise. Moreover, neither Armed Services Committee was enthusiastic about the July raise.

House Armed Services

The House Armed Services pay bill (HR 3380), reported May 19 (H Rept 97-109, Pt. 1), set a 14.3 percent pay hike across-the-board.

The panel stated its reason for not targeting the raise:

"If the all-volunteer force is to be afforded a realistic chance of succeeding, a reasonably adequate level of entry pay must be provided. To short-change the pay for those initially entering military service runs counter to our efforts to recruit volunteers."

Even with the full increase for recruit pay and the higher enlistment bonuses authorized in the bill, the panel warned, the Army stood only a 50-50 chance of meeting congressionally mandated limits on recruit quality in fiscal 1982 and probably would fall short in fiscal 1983.

The committee also attacked the assumption that pay between higher and lower enlisted ranks had become "compressed." As enlisted personnel gained seniority, their pay increased at a rate greater than the average pay increases of civilians in comparable jobs, the panel said.

HR 3380 also:

● Authorized the president to reallocate up to 25 percent of the total pay raise among ranks.

● Increased to $10,000 the maximum enlistment bonus and authorized smaller bonuses for persons enlisting for three years. Previously, enlistment bonuses were available only to four-year enlistees.

● Authorized the secretary of each armed service to designate job specialties in which members would receive hazardous duty pay ($110 monthly for officers, $55 for enlisted personnel). Previously, hazardous duty pay was authorized for flying, parachuting, bomb disposal and carrier flight deck crews, among others. The committee dismissed as too cumbersome the arrangements under which each eligible specialty was authorized by law.

● Approved a $15,000 bonus for engineers and scientists who signed up as officers for four years.

● Authorized allowances for temporary lodging during a change-of-assignment move and authorized payment in advance of travel allowances.

House Appropriations

HR 3380 was referred sequentially to the Appropriations Committee because, according to some estimates, it would exceed the defense target set by the first concurrent budget resolution for fiscal 1982.

In its report (H Rept 97-109, Pt. 2) on June 11, the committee said that on the House floor, it would offer the pay table of the Senate Armed Services Committee as an amendment. (For parliamentary reasons, the committee was allowed only to amend the bill by proposing an across-the-board pay raise of 9.1 percent instead of Armed Services' 14.3 percent hike.)

The committee objected to the portion of the pay raise intended to restore military pay to the level of comparability with civilian pay in 1972. That base line was purely arbitrary, the committee said.

According to Appropriations, a Congressional Budget Office study "indicated that military pay is currently closely comparable with civilian pay when you include such newly authorized payments as the variable housing allowance."

The Pentagon had no trouble recruiting and retaining manpower overall, the panel said, and an across-the-board increase was too blunt an instrument to solve shortages in specific skills.

The only rationale for the special raise was as a gesture of support for military personnel, the committee concluded. The panel said it "questions whether a special pay raise costing approximately $2.5 billion a year, including the impact in retired pay, ... is the only way to give this clear indication."

House Floor Action

The House passed 3380, incorporating the administration's request for a 14.3 perent across-the-board hike in the basic pay of all military ranks, Sept. 15 on a 396-1 vote. *(Vote 193, p. 66-H)*

The showdown came when Defense Appropriations Subcommittee Chairman Joseph P. Addabbo, D-N.Y., offered an amendment to HR 3380 that would have substituted the Senate's targeted pay table for House Armed Services' across-the-board hike.

Addabbo's pay proposal differed from the Senate version only in a provision that would have allowed the President to reduce the raise for any pay grade by up to 2 percent — such as from 12 percent to 10 percent — and reallocate the saved money to give some other pay grade a higher raise.

"If we are to retain those men and women from those critical ranks where we are now losing experience in droves," Addabbo argued, "we must provide extra incentive to these people to stay."

He cited a RAND Corp. estimate that it would take two inexperienced enlisted personnel to replace each senior sergeant who decided to leave the service. "It is cheaper to retain one skilled individual than it is to recruit and train the three replacements necessary," Addabbo said. "More-

over, who do you think can better maintain and operate sophisticated, multibillion-dollar weapons systems — a skilled sergeant or a new private first class?" he asked.

Defense Appropriations panel member Norman D. Dicks, D-Wash., insisted that the amendment's lower raises for enlistees would not harm recruiting. "Most surveys show it is not the early salary levels that attracts somebody into the service," he said. "It is a question of his desire for a career and a career responsibility, educational training, things of that nature that really draw him into the military service."

Les Aspin, D-Wis., one of the few Armed Services members to back Addabbo's amendment, warned that to the extent higher pay did attract recruits, they might be the wrong ones. To recruit more ambitious, better educated persons, Aspin suggested, the services likely would have to offer educational benefits in return for time spent in the military.

Bill Nichols, D-Ala., chairman of the Armed Services manpower subcommittee, led the charge against Addabbo's proposal. He warned against discounting the importance of recruit pay because of a mistaken complacency over the currently rosy recruiting picture.

"The recruiting market will become tighter in the future as fewer young people reach military age," he said. "At the same time, the military force is expected to grow. As the civilian job market for young people improves, the competition for high quality recruits will become increasingly tough."

Donald J. Mitchell, R-N.Y., the subcommittee's senior Republican, argued that the Pentagon already targeted about $2 billion annually to attract personnel into specific, hard-to-fill job specialties including sea duty, flight crew duty and nuclear power training. "This is the preferred method," he insisted, "to target to skills, not target to grades [or ranks]."

Addabbo's amendment lost, 170-232, because Republicans and Southern Democrats opposed it by ratios of more than 2-to-1, while Northern Democrats supported it by a slightly smaller ratio. *(Vote 192, p. 66-H)*

Other Amendments

The House adopted by voice vote the following amendments to HR 3380:

● By Ike Skelton, D-Mo., to increase the flight pay for battle controllers who served on AWACS radar warning and command planes.

● By Skelton, to increase the number of ROTC scholarships for the Navy and Air Force.

● By Nichols, a technical amendment to clarify that officers and enlisted personnel on temporary assignments would receive per diem expense allowances under the same rules.

Senate Armed Services

The Senate Armed Services bill (S 1181), introduced May 14 by Manpower Subcommittee Chairman Roger W. Jepsen, R-Iowa, was aimed at pay compression. The bill initially provided raises ranging from 4.8 percent for some privates first class to 21.5 percent for sergeant majors with more than 24 years of service.

A basic goal of Jepsen's pay table was to establish a minimum difference of 10 percent between the basic pay of any two ranks and a minimum difference of 3 percent

between any two longevity steps within a given rank.

Following negotiations, Jepsen's pay table was slightly modified. The raises for sergeants were increased by 1-2 percent and the 4.8 percent raise for overage corporals was boosted to 8 percent (a change affecting only a small number of individuals).

As reported by the committee July 8 (S Rept 97-146), S 1181 included pay raises for enlisted personnel ranging from 7 percent for recruits to 22 percent for some senior sergeant majors. Most persons in the top four sergeant grades would receive raises of 19-20 percent.

Some leading all-volunteer supporters discounted the recruiting impact of the 7 percent pay hike for recruits, since enlistees remained in the lowest pay grades for a relatively brief period. Moreover, according to one Senate staffer, "when you're in basic training, the last thing you're thinking about is how much you make a month. You're thinking about survival."

The raises were tailored to give junior members incentives to seek promotion and more senior members an incentive to stay in the service. For instance:

● The pay of corporals with less than four years seniority was increased 14 percent; for corporals with more than four years in service, the raise was only 13 percent.

● For the lowest-ranking group of sergeants, the largest increases were given to members with 6-8 years seniority, with much smaller raises going to members with more than 12 years of service.

● For the first time, longevity increases were provided at two-year intervals for senior enlisted members with 20-30 years of service. Existing law provided no raises between the 22nd and 26th years of service or between the 26th and 30th years.

Most officers would receive raises of 12-14 percent, with higher raises (15-16.5 percent) for majors and lieutenant colonels to induce more mid-level officers to remain in service. The two most junior officer ranks would receive raises of 9-11 percent.

Enlistment Bonus. The Senate committee increased the maximum enlistment bonus to $7,500, of which no more than $4,000 could be paid in a lump sum at the start of the enlistment. Committee members had been visibly distressed by the proposal to pay enlistment bonuses of $10,000, even after Pentagon witnesses insisted that the maximum level would be paid only infrequently. The panel also authorized a one-year test of bonuses of up to 43,000 for three-year enlistments and added 5,000 Navy and Air Force Reserve Officer Training corps scholarships.

Hazardous Duty Pay. The committee increased enlisted hazardous duty pay from $55 to $83 monthly. It added three skills for which the pay was authorized, including servicing Titan intercontinental missiles, which used a dangerous liquid fuel.

Travel Allowances. The committee liberalized travel allowances along the same general lines as House Armed Services. But it also imposed restrictions on the travel and moving allowances currently paid to members leaving the military. The limits would save $113 million in fiscal 1982, the committee estimated.

Senate Floor Action

There was no formal test in the Senate of support for the administration's across-the-board proposal as an alternative to the Armed Services Committee's targeted in-

crease. The Senate debated — but did not vote on — an amendment that would have slightly increased recruit pay at the expense of officers.

The amendment by Spark M. Matsunaga, D-Hawaii, and Mark O. Hatfield, R-Ore., would have increased the basic pay of the three most junior enlisted grades and the two most junior officer grades so each would receive an increase of 9.1 percent. That had been the administration's January estimate of a "comparability" increase: one that would match the average pay raises given private professional, administrative, technical and clerical workers.

To avoid boosting the cost of the bill, Matsunaga and Hatfield would have paid for those increases by reducing the bill's increases for other officers: cuts of 1 percent for generals and colonels; and .5 percent for captains and majors.

'Backdoor Draft'

Noting that many Armed Services Committee members had called for a return to conscription, Hatfield charged that the panel's low pay raise for recruits was an effort to sabotage the all-volunteer policy.

"If we fail to adopt this amendment, we are opening the backdoor for a return to the draft," he insisted.

He and Matsunaga cited warnings by Defense Secretary Weinberger and Pentagon manpower chief Korb that a reduction in the administration's proposed 14.3 percent hike for recruits would seriously hamper recruiting efforts.

"There is a price to be paid for taking the money away from the entry-level grades," Matsunaga warned. "The price will be paid in terms of the recruitment of less high school graduates — the very people whom the Senate Armed Services Committee has stated time and time again are so necessary."

However Matsunaga and Hatfield emphasized that their amendment did not challenge the Armed Services panel's basic thrust to increase the interval between the basic pay of lower- and higher-ranking enlisted personnel.

They hoped only to avoid the symbolic blow to recruits of providing less than a comparability raise, they said. In fact, the battle was even more purely symbolic than that: according to preliminary estimates by the Labor Department, the "comparability" level will be 9.7 percent, not the 9.1 percent in the Matsunaga-Hatfield amendment.

'Demagogic Appeal'

Unsupported on the Senate floor, Hatfield and Matsunaga faced a solid phalanx of Armed Services Committee members led by Manpower Subcommittee Chairman Jepsen and J. James Exon, Neb., the panel's senior Democrat.

The Army's own view, they insisted, was that the Pentagon's most pressing manpower problem was retention of experienced personnel, not enlistment of new ones.

Committee Chairman John Tower, R-Texas, denounced the "demagogic appeal" of the amendment's claim that it was "taking money out of the officers' pockets and giving it to the enlisted men."

On a technical basis, the proposed money shuffle would not provide enough money to pay for the recruit increases, the committee members maintained, because the bill's raises for generals and admirals were purely theoretical. Because of a government-wide cap on executive branch pay, those officers could not receive the basic pay hikes authorized by the bill. Since the $4.5 billion estimated cost

of the committee's pay hike included no funds for those theoretical raises, additional money would be needed to make up that part of the amendment's diversion of funds to recruit pay.

But the committee's heavier ammunition was the strong endorsement of its approach by Gen. Edward C. Meyer, Army chief of staff, and his manpower deputy, Lt. Gen. Max R. Thurman. Both officers had assured the committee that a relatively small hike in recruit pay would make no substantial difference in the Army's recruiting prospects. Both had agreed with the committee's decision that the more pressing need was to improve retention prospects by reducing pay compression.

The committee position drew further support from three senators who had energetically supported the all-volunteer policy: William S. Cohen, R-Maine, and Carl Levin, D-Mich., of the Armed Services Committee; and William L. Armstrong, R-Colo.

However, Armstrong insisted that once senior enlisted personnel were given higher pay to boost retention, Congress would have to make initial enlistment more attractive by enacting GI Bill-type education benefits. Gen. Meyer had suggested the same double-barreled approach to his service's personnel problems.

Other Amendments

The Senate adopted by voice vote five amendments:

● By Exon, to delete a provision that would allow the Selective Service System to use Social Security records to enforce draft registration. The provision was superfluous, since it was to be included in the conference report on the fiscal 1982 defense authorization bill (S 815) Exon said.

● By Jepsen, a technical amendment to clarify the committee's intent regarding the eligibility of some officers for flight pay.

● By Tower, to provide sea-pay for both of the crews assigned to missile-launching submarines, although one crew always was ashore.

● By Tower, to provide a $3,000 bonus for naval officers volunteering for surface-ship nuclear power training.

● By Rudy Boschwitz, R-Minn., to permit persons over 65 years of age to serve on draft boards.

Conference Report

The conference on S 1181 (H Rept 97-265) underscored the disagreement between personnel specialists of the Senate and House Armed Services committees on the pay issue.

Given the irreconcilable disagreement over the recruiting *vs.* retention issue, House conferees seized on Defense Secretary Weinberger's "targeting" proposal as a reasonable compromise and flatly rejected proposals by Senate members that would have tilted the pay raise more toward senior enlisted personnel.

That proposal essentially split the difference between the administration's proposed 14.3 percent raise and the percentage increase in the Senate bill for each enlisted rank.

The final compromise differed from Weinberger's plan only by reducing the raise for recruits from 10.7 percent to 10 percent and increasing the raise of the three senior sergeant grades from 16.5 percent to 17 percent.

The conference committee accepted the House across-the-board position on pay for officers. Regardless of rank, officers were given 14.3 percent pay raises. ∎

Defense Bill Makes Most of Reagan's Cuts

The fiscal 1982 defense authorization bill (S 815 — PL 97-86) acquiesced in large part to President Reagan's decision to pare some $8 billion from his original defense budget request, of which $6.2 billion came from programs covered by the authorization measure.

As cleared by Congress Nov. 17, the bill authorized $130.7 billion for defense programs, $419.4 million above Reagan's revised October request. The bill was $5.4 billion less than the amount approved by the House and nearly $6 billion less than the Senate-passed authorization.

Though Reagan announced the budget decision on Sept. 11, it was not until Oct. 2 that Congress received his detailed recommendations on where the cuts should be made in his March defense request.

In their November 3 report (H Rept 97-311), conferees on the bill warned that the amounts initially approved by the Senate and House "more nearly reflect the long-term requirements for achieving the marked improvement in national defense posture that is needed."

Any deeper cuts, they insisted, "would seriously compromise the absolute necessity to revitalize our military forces."

The Senate adopted the conference report by voice vote Nov. 5. The House adopted the report Nov. 17 by voice vote, thus clearing the bill for the president.

The bill included a provision allowing Congress to veto Reagan's decisions to build the B-1 bomber and to temporarily base MX intercontinental missiles in fixed silos. But the House Armed Services Committee was able to thwart use of the vetoes by holding up adoption of the conference report on the bill until just before the Nov. 18 deadline for Congress to exercise the power.

In contrast to their far-reaching disagreements with President Carter's defense budgets, the Senate and House Armed Services committees, which wrote the bill, strongly endorsed the Reagan administration's general approach to defense. In their respective, original versions of the bill, the panels' differences with the administration request were relatively modest.

The fiscal 1982 authorization bill was the first one to encompass the budget request for operations and maintenance (O&M) expenses. The Armed Services panels in 1981 decided to extend their authority over O&M so they could review training, maintenance and fuel budgets that affect the combat readiness of units in the field.

The bill also covered manpower levels — though appropriations for military pay did not have to be authorized.

Senate Committee Action

As reported May 6 by the Senate Armed Services Committee (S Rept 97-58), S 815 authorized $136.52 billion for weapons procurement, military research, operations and maintenance, and civil defense. This was $29.86 million more than the Reagan administration request submitted in March.

The committee recommended reductions in the administration's manpower request that would reduce personnel appropriations by $47 million. So the net budgetary impact of the committee bill would be a $17.1 million reduction in the administration's total defense request.

Budget Politics

The panel warmly applauded Reagan's pledge of a sustained buildup in U.S. weaponry that was to be substantially more rapid than the one planned by President Carter. But it warned that the buildup might come under heavy political pressure as the administration continued its drive to restrain other federal spending.

The committee emphasized that it expected the administration to stick to its defense program — that is, to buy the planned number of weapons and training exercises, etc. — even if it meant asking for more money later on.

Unlike the other congressional defense panels, the committee found no reason to reject administration inflation estimates as unrealistically low. But the committee said it would hold Defense Secretary Caspar W. Weinberger and budget director David A. Stockman to their assurances that the administration would seek additional funds if needed to offset higher than projected inflation. Using higher estimates of inflation, the Congressional Budget Office (CBO) had estimated that in fiscal 1982 alone, Reagan's defense budget was understated by $6.4 billion.

Apart from the issue of inflation estimates, the committee warned the Pentagon of the political risk posed by continual increases in weapons costs due to changes in design or production schedule. "Significant cost growth discredits the defense establishment and jeopardizes the future of vital programs," the panel said.

In extreme cases, according to the committee, the services should reconsider the need for a weapon and the acceptability of a cheaper (and less capable) alternative.

However the panel imposed a range of much less draconian measures on four major weapons programs that had experienced very large price increases:

● Despite concern over the durability of the transmission of the new M-1 tank, the committee approved the request for $1.9 billion to buy 720 M-1s. But the committee stipulated that $577.2 million of that figure (the amount added by Reagan to the Carter budget) could not be spent until the secretary of defense certified to the committee that he was satisfied with further tests of the tank's transmission. The committee also approved a $1 billion increase in the projected cost of 1,289 M-1 tanks scheduled for purchase in fiscal 1981-82.

The panel suggested that there was a lesson to be drawn from the delays and cost increases that bedeviled the Army's 18-year-long effort to develop a new tank. The Army had emphasized the potential of revolutionary new types of tank equipment in contrast to Soviet efforts that stressed less sweeping, evolutionary improvements in existing tanks, according to the committee. It ordered the Army to plan an evolutionary approach to any further improvements in the M-1.

● To dramatize its unhappiness with continued inflation in the Army's Blackhawk troop-carrying helicopter, the committee cut $25.1 million from the authorization for 96 Blackhawks (approving $483.6 million), an amount that could be saved by greater contractor efficiency, according to an Army study. The committee complained that costs should have stabilized now that the plane was in its fifth year of production.

● No such cut was made in funds for the Navy's LAMPS

III sub-hunting system, which used computers built into a version of the Blackhawk helicopter, and which also had experienced price increases. The committee approved the request for $585.6 million to buy 18 of the helicopters.

The panel justified its approval by noting that the Navy had been trying hard to control the cost increases, the system had been meeting its performance specifications, and it filled a critical niche in the Navy's anti-submarine war plans.

● The committee denied $147.1 million the Reagan administration added to Carter's defense budget to buy five additional F-18 Navy fighters. It approved only the Carter request for $1.74 billion to buy 58 planes. Continuing price increases and technical problems with the plane's computer dictated a cautious buildup in the production rate, the committee said.

Strategic Warfare

In general, the committee endorsed the strategic war moves embodied in the Reagan budget, ignoring various crash programs proposed by some conservative defense experts to build more nuclear missiles or a more extensive defense against Soviet attack.

Missiles

In addition to approving continued MX development, the committee added $53.7 million to continue production of the Mark 12A ICBM warhead. Three Mark 12As were being put on each of 300 Minuteman III missiles (to replace smaller Mark 12s) and each MX would carry 10 of the warheads. The added funds would buy warheads to convert an additional 150 Minuteman IIIs and would keep the production line running until it was time to begin producing Mark 12As for the MX.

The committee approved the Reagan administration's slight increase in funds to further modernize the existing Minuteman missiles ($185.7 million) and to continue testing new concepts for ICBMs and warheads.

Continued production of Trident I submarine-launched missiles was approved as requested: $783.2 million for 72 missiles. But the committee refused the request for $1.1 billion to build a 10th Trident-launching submarine, citing continued delays in delivery of the first of those ships. (Meantime, Trident missiles were being carried in older missile subs.) The committee added to the bill $110 million to procure components for the next two Trident subs. The $75 million of that amount earmarked for the 10th ship would just about pay for the work that would have been done in fiscal 1982 even if the ship had been fully authorized.

Some conservative critics of the MX mobile ICBM had called for a crash program to accelerate development of a larger Trident II missile, which would be as accurate as the MX. The panel opposed this, approving the $242.9 million for Trident II requested by both Carter and Reagan.

Bombers

The administration request for $2.4 billion to develop a new long-range bomber was approved, but with the proviso that Congress could block the president's choice of the plane to do the job, a decision that was expected in June or July.

Having approved development of a new bomber, the committee cut $16.6 million from the $26.6 million requested for research intended to extend the useful life of B-52s the new planes could replace.

Anti-Missile Defense

The committee approved Reagan's request for nearly half a billion dollars for research on anti-ballistic missile defense. But it expressly refused to increase the administration request for research on powerful laser-armed space satellites that some scientists argued could destroy attacking ICBMs.

Funds also were approved that would allow the administration to buy more F-15 fighter planes in fiscal 1982 than the Carter administration had planned. The additional planes would be used to defend North America against Soviet bombers. By the same token, the committee cut $25.2 million from the request for modification of the 20-year-old F-106, which the additional F-15s would replace.

For civil defense related to a military attack, the committee approved $126.8 million, $6 million less than the administration request.

Warning and Communications

In its most far-reaching change to the administration's strategic war budget, the committee recommended an additional $341.6 million for various improvements in the electronic systems that would warn of an impending attack and on which policy-makers would rely for control of U.S. forces during a nuclear war.

Of this amount, $108.6 million was for programs covered by the authorization bill. The panel recommended the addition of the remaining $233 million to the upcoming defense appropriations bill for types of equipment not currently requiring legislative authorization.

The largest single addition was $109 million for a radar station (called Pave Paws) designed to detect submarine-launched ballistic missile attacks on the Southeastern states. One such radar was in service on both the East and West coasts.

Ground Combat

The committee basically supported the administration plan to modernize heavily armored units that would defend Europe against Soviet attack. But it allocated some additional funds to equip the Rapid Deployment Force (RDF).

Heavy Equipment

Besides approving the request for the M-1 tank and the new troop carrier, the committee approved the $429.4 million requested to build the first 14 copies of a new tank-hunting helicopter (called AAH).

The panel also approved the requested amounts for several development programs aimed at producing long-range anti-tank missiles. The missiles would scatter several non-nuclear warheads to home in on enemy tanks located far behind the battlefront. But the committee warned the Pentagon to coordinate the separate projects.

A $20 million request was approved to equip a factory to make a new type of artillery shell (called a binary munition) that would dispense a lethal nerve gas. Money for this purpose was deleted from the 1981 defense appropriations bill when Sen. Mark O. Hatfield, R-Ore., threatened a filibuster on the issue of chemical weapons.

The committee approved the amounts requested for production of several kinds of anti-aircraft missiles and for

an anti-aircraft tank (called Divad). But it cut $373.4 million from the $900.5 million requested for production of the long-range Patriot anti-aircraft missile. According to the committee, the missile needed more testing to make it more reliable.

Lightweight Tanks

As it had done in previous years, the committee prodded the services to quickly buy a force of armored combat vehicles that would be much lighter than current tanks and thus could more easily be transported to distant trouble spots — near the Persian Gulf, for instance — where there were no U.S. bases.

In response to the committee's urging, the Marine Corps had been testing foreign-designed armored cars that were light enough to be carried by helicopter. The Marines also began developing a new light tank for production in the late 1980s that could be equipped with a very powerful — but still experimental — 75mm cannon. For both the immediate version and the improved version of the weapon, the Army insisted that it needed a more heavily armored vehicle carrying a larger cannon.

The committee endorsed the Marines' approach and denied an Army request for $19 million to develop its own larger version of the future vehicle.

Airlift

The Air Force still had not justified development of a new intercontinental transport plane (called CX), the committee complained. It approved only $1 million of the requested $245.7 million for the project. The panel dismissed as "not militarily valid" the Air Force insistence that the new plane should be designed to carry tanks and other very large items to small airstrips close to trouble spots. Each CX could carry one tank.

Other airlift improvements were fully approved by the committee, including $384.5 million to modify existing Air Force transports and $50.8 million to modify civilian airliners so they could be quickly converted to haul military cargo.

Sealift

Funds were authorized as requested ($722.4 million) to buy nine fast commercial cargo ships that could carry U.S. troops to distant spots. Also approved was a request for $392 million to build two ships and convert one commercial ship that would store arms and equipment for U.S. troops near potential trouble spots. Those vessels all were intended to land U.S. troops in areas already controlled by friendly governments. The committee also pressed the administration to more quickly modernize the amphibious fleet designed to carry Marine units that could shoot their way ashore. It added $374.3 million to build a large landing ship (called an LSD) and to buy components for two more LSDs to be funded in fiscal 1983.

The panel denied $10 million to plan for conversion of the passenger liner *United States* into a hospital ship for use in a Rapid Deployment Force action. The committee said the estimated cost of the conversion — some $380 million in the next year — was too uncertain and alternative approaches to medical care had not been investigated.

Naval Forces

Reagan's pledge to build a larger Navy with at least 15 large carriers (instead of the 12 then in service) won strong committee support. But the panel rejected an administration plan to hasten that buildup by recommissioning a mothballed carrier. And — as it had done previously — it tried to force the Navy to consider some fairly radical approaches to future ship design.

Except for reactivation of the carrier *Oriskany* ($364 million), the committee approved all funds requested for combat ships, including $1 billion for two sub-hunting submarines and $2.9 billion for three Aegis cruisers designed to protect carriers from Soviet missile attack.

The committee also approved the request for $158 million to modernize and reactivate the battleship *New Jersey* and for $88 million to begin modernization of the battleship *Iowa*. The panel also added $79 million to increase the number of cruise missiles and other modern weapons that would be added to the *New Jersey*.

Also approved was the $658-million request for components that would be used in a nuclear-powered aircraft carrier to be funded next year. The committee also added $700 million for three escort frigates to the three requested, for a total frigate authorization of $1.67 billion.

The committee approved several ships designed to resupply combat vessels at sea, including a new refueling tanker ($200 million) and two 15-year-old supply ships that would be bought from the British navy ($37 million).

New Approaches

The committee added to the bill funds for several projects that had long been espoused by Gary Hart, D-Colo., with growing support from Armed Services colleagues, including William S. Cohen, R-Maine, chairman of the Sea Power Subcommittee.

A central theme of the "Hart Navy" was dispersal of the fleet's fighting power over a larger number of ships, any one of which would be less expensive than current first-line combatants. The kingpin of Hart's scheme was a relatively small aircraft carrier — costing about one-third as much as current nuclear carriers — that could carry vertical takeoff jets. Hart stressed that he intended these "light carriers" to supplement, not replace, the Navy's larger nuclear carriers.

Armed Services accused the Navy of dragging its anchor in carrying out previous congressional mandates to at least design such a ship. It added $23 million to design such a ship and barred the use of funds to design any other new ship until the Navy showed the panel a light carrier design that could be funded next year.

The committee also added $10 million to develop a fighter version of the Harrier B vertical takeoff jet.

The committee added small sums to the bill to study other "new Navy" options, including:

● A new amphibious landing ship designed to carry vertical takeoff jets as well as troop helicopters ($4 million);

● Diesel-powered submarines as cheaper supplements to a fleet of about 100 nuclear-powered subs ($5 million). The panel emphasized that this represented no commitment to building the cheaper, non-nuclear ships, but it insisted that it wanted to consider the option.

● A containerized kit to equip large cargo ships with anti-submarine helicopters ($3 million).

Combat Readiness

The panel concluded that Reagan's large increase in the fiscal 1982 defense budget had allowed the services to balance their budget between the costs of buying new equipment and boosting the combat readiness of units

already in the field (through increased training and maintenance spending).

It exhorted the Joint Chiefs of Staff to be sure readiness had a uniformly high priority in the budget planning of all the services. For example, the committee warned, it would matter little that Army units had full ammunition dumps if supporting Air Force squadrons ran out of bombs.

The Pentagon's operations and maintenance (O&M) account, which paid for training, equipment maintenance, fuel and other consumables used up in exercises, covered many facets of "readiness."

The committee recommended $63.58 billion for O&M, $293.2 million more than the budget request. Major changes were the addition of $143 million for Army maintenance and supply programs and $100 million for Army building maintenance.

The committee recommended that in future budgets authorization be required for procurement of ammunition and various other small items that the panel said had a direct impact on readiness.

Manpower

A reduction of 5,300 was recommended in Reagan's proposal to increase the number of uniformed personnel by 44,500. The largest part of the cut (3,400) was to make the Air Force hire more civilians to fill non-combat jobs. The total uniformed manpower ceiling approved by the committee was 2.115 million.

The committee renewed the provision in the fiscal 1981 authorization bill that limited the number of Army recruits who were non-high school graduates or who had low scores on the service's intelligence test.

As had been the case for several years, the committee added several hundred million dollars for aircraft for the National Guard and reserve forces, including 20 anti-tank helicopters ($64.4 million), 12 trainer versions of the A-7 light bomber ($151.6 million) and 12 Hercules transports ($163.4 million).

Repeating the action it took on the 1981 bill, the committee recommended a provision that could increase military pensions once annually to pay cost-of-living increases (instead of the current six-month increases). The change would take effect only if Congress approved a similar change for civilian federal retirees.

Senate Floor Action

In the confusion that continued to surround administration strategic arms policy, conservatives and liberals alike used the fiscal 1982 defense authorization bill to try to nudge Reagan toward their respective theories of how to handle nuclear weapons.

The more aggressive tack was taken by a group dominated by Western conservatives who tried to push the Pentagon toward a radical new strategic policy: They would deter nuclear attack by being able to shoot down attacking Soviet missiles and bombers — rather than by threatening a retaliatory strike.

But liberals who supported the SALT II arms control treaty found enough ambiguity in administration policy pronouncements to extract a vaguely worded endorsement of continued negotiations over nuclear arms control.

The bill (S 815) authorizing $136.5 billion for defense programs was passed May 14 by a 92-1 vote, with Mark O. Hatfield, R-Ore., casting the "no" vote. *(Vote 119, p. 23-S)*

Final Authorization

S 815 authorized the following amounts for military programs in fiscal 1982 *(in thousands of dollars):*

	Reagan October Request	Final Authorization
Procurement		
Aircraft		
Army	$ 1,897,300	$ 1,910,200
Navy, Marine Corps	9,244,500	9,302,500
Air Force	13,843,898	13,773,698
Missiles		
Army	2,210,200	2,146,900
Navy	2,567,000	2,567,000
Marine Corps	223,024	223,024
Air Force	4,204,646	4,186,846
Naval Vessels	8,475,300	8,795,900
Tracked Combat Vehicles		
Army	3,201,300	3,251,200
Marine Corps	281,600	281,739
Torpedoes	516,600	516,600
Other Weapons		
Army	655,400	655,400
Navy	200,200	200,200
Marine Corps	136,483	136,344
Air Force	3,047	3,047
Army National Guard	0	50,000
Total, procurement	47,660,498	48,000,598
Research and development		
Army	3,768,500	3,746,299
Navy	5,888,571	6,072,167
Air Force	8,823,400	8,686,800
Defense Agencies	1,842,000	1,899,847
Total, research and development	20,322,471	20,405,113
Operations and maintenance		
Army	16,864,044	17,024,044
Navy	20,189,810	20,130,410
Marine Corps	1,217,239	1,249,939
Air Force	19,056,552	18,898,140
Department-wide	4,833,607	4,859,207
Total, operations and maintenance	62,161,252	62,161,740
Civil defense	132,842	129,000
GRAND TOTAL	$130,277,063	$130,696,451

Strategic Issues

There were no showdown votes on the conservative effort to push a strategic policy of defense rather than deterrence, so the debate demonstrated their commitment rather than their clout.

The movement's leadership was a small but energetic band of senators, most of whom had not come up through the ranks of the congressional defense establishment. Malcolm Wallop, R-Wyo., Harrison "Jack" Schmitt, R-N.M., Pete V. Domenici, R-N.M., and Howell Heflin, D-Ala., were among the most active members.

Their basic premise was that technical breakthroughs held out the promise of virtually leak-proof defenses of U.S. territory against ballistic missiles and long-range bombers. New anti-missile missiles would be much more effective than the U.S. system briefly deployed and then scrapped in 1976, they maintained, and within a decade this country could orbit laser-armed space satellites able to destroy Soviet missiles soon after they were launched. Moscow was pursuing such defenses energetically, according to the "defense dominance" theorists.

Such an emphasis on defense would radically change U.S. strategic policy, which rested for decades on the assumption that the only sure way to fend off a Soviet nuclear attack was by the threat of retaliation.

The Senate Armed Services Committee had reflected the skepticism of senior Pentagon scientists and military brass toward the defense dominance arguments. The radical new weaponry would require years of basic research, they insisted, and was a long way from deployment.

And there was a political dimension to their opposition: Committee sources feared that the widespread but diffuse unhappiness over the cost and complexity of the MX mobile missile might be catalyzed by the prospect of a defense system that would make a mobile MX seem unnecessary.

A missile defense policy also might have the political advantage of costing less than MX for the next few years.

Advocates of the defense dominance theory dismissed the Pentagon view as typical bureaucratic inertia. They said many senior defense scientists who had spent their whole careers working on nuclear weapons could not imagine that new types of weapons could suddenly end the era of the nuclear balance of terror. And the anti-missile advocates insisted that the defense establishment simply had gotten into the habit of thinking up ways to blow up Russians instead of defending U.S. territory.

Amendments

The defense dominance school won only limited victories during debate on S 815:

● $50 million was added to the bill to accelerate research on lasers that might be used for a satellite-based anti-missile defense. This was only one-fifth of the amount Wallop wanted to add to the bill, but he agreed to accept the lower figure in return for committee support of his amendment. Adopted 91-3. *(Vote 115, p. 22-S)*

The amendment also ordered the Air Force to set up an office to plan a space-laser program.

Wallop might have done well in a showdown: In 1980 the Senate rejected his effort to add $136 million for laser research by a 52-39 vote. A dozen of the 52 no longer were in the Senate; most of them were replaced by conservatives who might have been receptive to Wallop's argument.

● $31.2 million was added for development of a rocket-launched reconnaissance probe designed to observe the size of a Soviet missile attack. The committee accepted the amendment, which was adopted by voice vote.

● Schmitt and William V. Roth Jr., R-Del., decided not to offer an amendment — which Armed Services Chairman John Tower, R-Texas, promised to oppose — that would

have expressed the sense of the Senate that MX should be based in fixed missile silos and protected against a Soviet attack with anti-missile defenses.

● $13 million was added by a Schmitt amendment to substitute 50 multiple-warhead Minuteman III ICBMs for single-warhead Minuteman IIs. The committee accepted the amendment, which was adopted by voice vote.

An amendment by Carl Levin, D-Mich., to require congressional approval of the MX version selected by Reagan, before any money could be spent, was tabled (killed) 59-39. Levin, an MX opponent, insisted that he intended only to ensure congressional review of the decision because of its far-reaching impact. The majority of his supporters were pro-arms control liberals, many of whom were unhappy with MX. *(Vote 113, p. 22-S)*

The only solace for traditional arms control supporters was an amendment by Gary Hart, D-Colo., expressing the Senate's support of various rationales that administration spokesmen had expressed for eventual resumption of arms control talks. The amendment was adopted by voice vote.

Cost-consciousness. Despite the Senate's support of a defense buildup, the need for frugality was a theme of floor debate. This took form in two amendments:

● By Tower, to cut $82 million in various projects to offset additions made by the Senate. Adopted by voice vote.

● By Sam Nunn, D-Ga., to require a series of reports by the Pentagon on major weapons programs with substantial cost increases. Adopted 96-0. *(Vote 116, p. 23-S)*

But cost-reduction arguments did not always prevail. The Senate, 66-29, tabled a Levin amendment that would have cut $200 million from the operations and maintenance account to force organizational consolidations proposed by the General Accounting Office. *(Vote 117, p. 23-S)*

By voice vote, the Senate adopted an amendment by John W. Warner, R-Va., modified by Daniel Patrick Moynihan, D-N.Y., to continue a limited suspension of the Maybank amendment. The Maybank amendment was a provision added to each defense appropriations bill since the early 1950s barring the targeting of defense contracts to areas of high unemployment. The Warner-Moynihan amendment would let the Pentagon target up to $3.4 billion in contracts to high unemployment areas.

Draft Registration. In the face of a threatened filibuster by Hatfield, a staunch foe of draft registration, the Armed Services Committee backed down from an effort to toughen enforcement of the law requiring registration by 18-year-old men.

In order to nullify a federal court ruling, the committee had added to the bill a provision allowing the Selective Service System to have access to any federal record for purposes of ensuring compliance with the law. The committee's intent was to allow the draft agency to identify non-registrants by scanning Social Security records and obtaining their current addresses from the Internal Revenue Service.

Hatfield refused to agree to a time limit for voting on the bill unless the committee would drop the provision, and after hurried negotiations the committee finally agreed.

Earlier Amendments. On May 13 the Senate adopted the following amendments by voice vote:

● By William Proxmire, D-Wis., increasing from $20,000 to $35,000 the maximum amount of serviceman's and veteran's group life insurance;

● By Alan K. Simpson, R-Wyo., to prevent any person who served less than two years of a military enlistment

from receiving any federal benefit for which the person became eligible because of military service;

• By William S. Cohen, R-Maine, prohibiting the Defense Department from entering into any contract with a contractor who has been barred from doing business with any other federal agency;

• By David Pryor, D-Ark., to further limit the Pentagon's ability to award sole-source contracts to consultants;

• By Tower to add $2.8 million for intelligence projects.

House Committee Action

The Armed Services Committee bill, HR 3519, reported May 19 (H Rept 97-71, Pt. 1), authorized $136,046,036,000 for weapons procurement, military research, operations and maintenance and civil defense. This was $445.2 million less than Reagan's request.

House subcommittee chairmen had agreed to keep their respective portions of the bill within the amounts budgeted by the administration. For any funds added to the request, they would find offsetting reductions. The two subcommittees dealing with weapons procurement exceeded the administration procurement request by a total of about half a billion dollars.

It was particularly significant that the House committee accepted the overall funding level. In previous years, critics, including former committee member Richard Ichord, D-Mo. (1961-81), charged the panel with being politically unrealistic in adding more money to the authorization bill than Congress eventually would appropriate.

On the other hand, the House committee showed no disposition to accept the budget figure as an absolute ceiling. By a large margin, the panel rejected amendments by senior Republican William L. Dickinson, Ala., that would have reduced additions to the budget in order to keep the overall recommendation within the budget set by the administration.

The House committee added $518 million for a third submarine-hunting submarine in addition to two requested by Reagan. It also added funds to buy components for two ships that would be funded in next year's budget: $100 million for an Aegis cruiser designed to protect carriers against Soviet missiles and $130 million for a large helicopter carrier designed to carry a Marine landing force.

In addition, the House panel added $437 million for 40 more F-16 fighters than the 120 requested by the Air Force, with the stipulation that the additional planes be given to guard and reserve units.

The panel gave its version of the bill a pronounced tilt toward selection of a version of the B-1 for the bomber role. It required that the funds be spent only on a B-1 version, unless the president recommended a more advanced plane and Congress agreed by concurrent resolution within 60 days.

The committee bill redistributed the budget slightly to spend more money on aircraft procurement, especially for Navy fighters and for several types of Air Force planes to be used by National Guard and reserve units.

Research and development funds were cut by an amount that more than offset the procurement increase, reflecting the committee's concern that too many research programs were being undertaken. The panel reiterated its frequent complaint that the Pentagon was pursuing projects that would be "nice to have," but that were not absolutely essential and were too expensive.

Major development programs the committee voted to kill included a long-range Air Force transport plane called CX ($225.7 million), a navigation satellite system ($311.9 million) and a new Navy destroyer called DDG-X ($121.0 million).

Strategic Warfare

Apart from considering production of the B-1 bomber, Reagan's strategic arms production plans were similar to Carter's. Both professed a commitment to the so-called "triad" of forces, each of which could attack Soviet targets with nuclear warheads: land-based Intercontinental Ballistic Missiles (ICBMs), submarine-launched missiles and a bomber fleet.

The House committee recommended only modest changes in Reagan's request for triad modernization.

ICBMs

The committee approved the $2.4 billion requested to continue development of the MX mobile missile. The committee added a provision requiring congressional endorsement by concurrent resolution if Reagan decided to change the MX basing technique recommended by Carter.

To improve the accuracy of Minuteman III missiles, the panel added $5.5 million; it also added $44.6 million to continue production of the Mark 12A nuclear warhead that was carried by Minuteman and could be used on MX. The committee also added $51 million to a project developing new ICBM warheads.

Bombers

Long a hotbed of support for the B-1 bomber, the committee championed the plane as "the best possible choice" for a new bomber. At the same time, the panel recommended a vigorous program to develop the "stealth" bomber designed to be difficult to detect by enemy radars.

The committee recommended $2.24 billion of the $2.42 billion requested to continue development and begin production of the new bomber. It required congressional consent (by concurrent resolution) if the president decided on some course other than a B-1 version.

To save time and money, the committee recommended that only minimal changes be made in the existing B-1 design, to equip it to carry cruise missiles and to add radar-jamming equipment that was immediately available. However it did not flatly bar use of the money for a modified version of the B-1. The Pentagon had been considering modifications of the B-1 incorporating some stealth technology.

The committee approved the amount requested for production of cruise missiles to be launched by bombers at distant targets ($589.9 million for 440 missiles). Funds requested to modify existing B-52 bombers to carry cruise missiles were approved, but the panel denied $50.1 million requested for modifications that would extend the useful life of the B-52. What was needed, the committee said, was a new bomber.

Submarine Missiles

The committee agreed with its Senate counterpart not to approve the $1 billion requested for construction of a 10th large submarine to launch Trident missiles, citing production delays in the program. But the House panel added $100 million to buy components for the ship. This would pay for work in fiscal 1982 that would have been

done even if the ship had been fully authorized. (The Senate had approved $75 million for the same purpose.)

Approved as requested was $909.9 million to buy 72 Trident I missiles. But the committee approved only $141 million of the $239.5 million requested for a larger, more accurate version, called Trident II. The panel said that the $8 billion estimated cost of the Trident II would make it hard to fund other Navy programs. It told the Navy to increase the accuracy of Trident I.

Pending that decision, the committee approved only $5 million of the $29.87 million requested for the Extremely Low Frequency (ELF) antenna, that could signal submerged submarines, pending Reagan's decision on locating the controversial antenna in Michigan. It also added $10 million to test the use of a laser as an alternative way to communicate with submarines.

Nuclear Defense

As it had done with preceding authorization bills, the committee recommended a large increase in the request for civil defense — $41.2 million in addition to the $132.8 million request.

The increase would be the first installment of a seven-year, $2 billion program to plan ways to temporarily evacuate U.S. cities in a U.S.-Soviet crisis. Armed Services Committee member Donald J. Mitchell, R-N.Y., had led House support for the plan, but each year the Senate had opposed the increase, and most of the House addition had been dropped in conference.

Funds were approved as requested for development of anti-ballistic missile defenses, including a system called LoADs to defend U.S. ICBM launchers. But the committee added no funds to accelerate development of laser-armed space satellites, for which the Senate added $50 million.

Medium-range Missiles

Several missiles with a range of about 1,000 miles were approved at the amounts requested. The medium-range missiles, equipped with nuclear warheads, could strike Soviet targets from launchers in Europe or aboard ships.

In a move that had evoked considerable political dissent within several West European nations belonging to NATO, the alliance agreed in December 1979 to deploy 108 Pershing IIs and 464 GLCMs in Europe beginning in 1983.

To procure the first 39 Pershing II ballistic missiles, the bill included $191.8 million. For 54 ground-launched cruise missiles (GLCM), $329.2 million was authorized. (The first 11 GLCMs were funded in fiscal 1981.)

Ground Combat

The committee made few major changes in the request for programs to nullify the large Soviet tank force and to protect U.S. ground units against Soviet air attack.

For 720 M-1 tanks (and components to be used in M-1s funded next year), the committee recommended $1.82 billion, cutting the budget request by $20 million on the basis of the panel's own cost estimate.

Approved as requested was $429.4 million to procure the first 14 of a new model helicopter (called AAH) equipped with anti-tank guided missiles. But the committee ordered the Pentagon to continue production of the current tank-hunting helicopter (called the Cobra) to equip reserve units. It added $67.2 million to buy 16 new Cobras and $36 million to modernize 87 older model Cobras.

The committee also opposed the Pentagon plan to phase out production of the A-10, a small, armored bomber designed to attack tanks. It approved the $509.4 million requested to buy 60 A-10s, but denied $33 million to close down the production line and instead added $63.1 million for enough A-10 components to buy 40 more planes next year.

Light Tanks

Both Armed Services committees urged the Pentagon to buy lightweight armored vehicles (LAVs) that could be flown to distant trouble spots more easily than M-1 tanks. The new M-1 weighed about 60 tons and the existing M-60 tanks about 54 tons. Either could be flown only one-tank-at-a-time in C-5 transports, of which the Air Force had only 77.

Strictly speaking, LAVs were not tanks since their armor was relatively thin. Those in production for other countries were more like armored cars.

The Army and Marine Corps had been under strong congressional pressure to buy a single type of LAV as an interim measure and to develop another uniform type for future production. The two services disagreed about armament for the vehicle. The Marines wanted a 75mm cannon light enough to be carried by helicopters and the Army wanted a 90mm cannon, clearly too heavy for the Marines.

Like its Senate counterpart, the House panel approved a Marine Corps request for $36.2 million to buy 72 LAVs to be based on types currently produced for other countries. But the House bill approved the administration plan to put the Army in charge of the program. The Senate committee ordered that program control be vested in the Marines.

Anti-aircraft Weapons

The committee approved as requested about $2.1 billion for ground-based anti-aircraft weapons. This included $795.8 million for 364 long-range Patriot missiles and 12 units to launch them; $203.9 million for more than 2,500 Stinger missiles carried by infantrymen and launched from tubes like a bazooka; and $335.5 million for production of the first 50 Divad anti-aircraft tanks.

The committee added $75 million to develop a lightweight, short-range anti-aircraft weapon that could be used by U.S. troops flown to distant spots. The Divad tank would be too heavy for that mission, the committee said.

Also approved as requested was $133 million to begin buying British-built Rapier short-range anti-aircraft missiles to defend U.S. air bases in Britain. The Rapier was to be bought by the United States and operated by British forces.

The committee cut by $116.7 million the request for purchase of the French and German designed Roland, a short-range missile launched from a tank. The panel directed the Pentagon to study the possibility of improving some existing Chaparral missiles to replace some of the planned Rolands. For Roland, the panel recommended $360.3 million.

Air Combat

The committee approved only 30 of the 42 F-15 fighters requested (a reduction of $416.2 million).

It recommended procurement of 160 smaller F-16 fighters instead of the 120 requested (an increase of $329.3 million) and ordered that the 40 additional planes be delivered to National Guard units.

Approved as requested was $721 million for various

kinds of missiles used by fighters to attack other planes.

The committee denied $32.2 million requested for two programs to develop future fighter planes to replace the F-15 and F-16. Modifications of those planes would ensure their continued superiority over Soviet aircraft, the committee maintained.

The panel approved a request for $35 million to develop a jet engine that might be used to replace the engines in current fighter planes. But like its Senate counterpart, the committee insisted that such an engine be selected on a competitive basis. Both committees had been suspicious that the Pentagon would select a single contractor to develop a new engine.

Naval Warfare

Carriers. The committee approved the $658 million requested for components to be used in a sixth nuclear powered aircraft carrier. Nearly $3 billion would have to be appropriated in fiscal 1983 for the carrier itself. The panel also approved $364 million requested to reactivate the mothballed carrier *Oriskany*, though that project appeared doomed because of opposition from Senate Armed Services and both Appropriations committees.

The committee approved administration plans to continue production of several kinds of carrier-borne combat planes whose production the Carter administration had planned to terminate. In the case of the F-14 fighter, the panel added $42.9 million to the request so that a production rate of 30 planes a year could be sustained in fiscal 1983 as well as in fiscal 1982.

In the case of the F-18, which was designed both as a smaller fighter to supplement the F-14 and as a small bomber for the Navy and Marines, the panel concluded that the administration had not gone far enough in increasing the Carter budget. Carter had requested 58 planes ($2.28 billion) and Reagan had increased that to 63 planes ($2.48 billion). The committee recommended procurement of 84 planes ($2.95 billion).

The F-18 had been bedeviled by cost increases and technical problems. In the last quarter of 1980, the Pentagon's cost estimate for 1,300 planes rose nearly 30 percent to almost $38 billion.

The committee maintained its longstanding opposition to development of small carriers designed to carry vertical take-off (V/STOL) jets. It denied funds requested to develop both the ships ($17.5 million) and the V/STOLs ($14.96 million).

However the panel enthusiastically approved the $887.7 million requested to continue development and buy the first 12 copies of the Harrier B, an improved version of a small, British-built, V/STOL bomber used by the Marine Corps. The Senate approved the requests for small carrier and V/STOL research, and added $10 million to develop a fighter version of the Harrier B that could be launched from existing ships and could enter service more quickly than a newly designed plane.

Sub Hunting

The committee added to the bill $518.1 million for a third nuclear submarine designed to hunt enemy subs (in addition to two such ships requested by the administration).

Also approved as requested were three escort frigates ($971.9 million).

To buy the first 18 LAMPS III anti-submarine helicopters and to continue development of the plane, the committee approved the $846 million requested. The helicopter would be carried by frigates and all other recently designed surface combat ships. LAMPS III had experienced large cost increases, but the committee rejected a proposal to kill the program.

The committee approved a Pentagon plan to resume production of the smaller LAMPS I helicopter currently in use. It would continue to equip smaller ships unable to carry the LAMPS III. But the panel ordered a slower pace for LAMPS I, approving procurement of 12 helicopters ($189.3 million) instead of 18 ($238 million).

Surface Combat

Funds to begin equipping the battleships *New Jersey* and *Iowa* with cruise missiles and returning them to service were approved as requested ($246 million). The Navy estimated that it could modernize the *New Jersey* for $329 million, since that ship was in service as recently as 1968-69. The *Iowa* project would cost more.

Also approved was the $2.95 billion requested for three cruisers equipped with the Aegis defense system and designed to protect carriers from Soviet missile attack. The committee added to the bill $100 million to purchase components for another Aegis cruiser to be funded next year.

The committee also added $22 million to produce new 8-inch caliber guns for the newest class of Navy destroyers. The gun was tested in 1978, but procurement plans were killed off by budgetary limits. The largest guns in the fleet were 5-inch caliber.

Future Ships

One reason the House committee opposed V/STOL carriers was members' belief that proponents were willing to buy inferior weapons just to save money. The committee's insistence that capability rather than cost should determine weapons design also was evident in its rejection of Navy plans to design two other new ships: a future anti-aircraft destroyer (called DDG-X) and a small anti-submarine frigate (called FFX). The panel condemned both programs for sacrificing combat power to artificial cost limits.

On the other hand, the committee added $46 million to resume development of a seagoing-sized surface effects ship (SES), designed to move over the water on a trapped air bubble at up to 90 mph. The committee had supported the SES idea in the late 1970s as a future submarine hunter, but it was killed by the Carter administration for budget reasons. More recently, SES had been proposed as a cargo ship.

Rapid Deployment Transports

The committee continued its support for Carter and Reagan administration plans to improve the U.S. capability to rapidly intervene in distant trouble spots. A keystone was the Rapid Deployment Force (RDF).

Airlift

The committee approved only $20 million of the $245.7 million requested to begin developing a long-range cargo plane called CX, designed to carry tanks and other heavy cargo into small landing fields. But the panel added to the bill $150 million to buy a cargo version of existing wide-body commercial jets.

In 1980 the Armed Services panels ordered the Pentagon to report on how a CX fleet would mesh with other air

and sea transports in each of several hypothetical situations. The House committee refused to approve the full fiscal 1982 CX request because that report had not been submitted. It acknowledged the overall shortage of long-range cargo planes, hence the addition of funds to buy existing types.

If a new CX were justified by the Pentagon report, the committee said, the Pentagon could seek congressional approval to use the $150 million for that purpose.

The committee also approved a Pentagon proposal to entice more airlines to modify some of their wide-body transport planes so they could quickly be converted to carry large vehicles in case of mobilization. The Pentagon had offered to pay fo the so-called Civil Reserve Air Fleet (CRAF) modification and for the higher operating cost of the plane — since the modifications added weight to the plane, it used more fuel — but only one plane had been committed.

RDF Ships

The committee approved various supply ships to support the Rapid Deployment Force.

The committee approved as requested the construction of one new pre-positioning ship ($195 million), conversion of two commercial ships to perform the job ($197 million) and purchase of a large commercial barge carrier ($54 million).

The Navy also was buying a fleet of very fast commercial transports that could carry an armored division from the United States to the Persian Gulf in half the time of current transports. The committee approved $465 million to buy eight ships, insisting that $203.3 million could be saved from the budget estimate.

Amphibious Landings

The committee pushed the administration to enlarge the amphibious landing fleet from which Marines would try to shoot their way ashore in the face of enemy troops.

The committee added $427.3 million to build a ship (called an LSD-41) designed to launch landing barges carrying tanks and other large pieces of equipment.

The panel also added $130 million to buy components for a helicopter carrier (called an LHA) that could carry about 1,900 Marines, 30 helicopters to land the troops and several large landing barges to carry their equipment.

Combat Readiness

The Armed Services panels in 1981 decided to extend their authority over operations and maintenance so they could review training, maintenance and fuel budgets that affected the combat readiness of units in the field.

Following the logic, the House committee added a provision bringing ammunition and various kinds of communications and supply equipment within the scope of the annual authorization bill beginning in fiscal 1983.

The committee recommended authorization of $63.28 billion for O&M costs, only $6.9 million less than the amount requested. But according to the panel, it shifted funds within the overall figure to add about $350 million to projects that would directly improve combat-readiness. Among the increases cited by the committee were: $149 million to improve equipment overhaul and supply systems; $70.5 million to reduce the backlog of overdue maintenance in military facilities; and $30.4 million to increase flying hours and flight instruction programs.

Among the committee actions to offset these increases was denial of $94 million requested for a large-scale RDF exercise outside of the United States.

The panel approved funds for one exercise, but said two would put too much of a burden on the Air Force transport fleet.

Civilian Employees

The administration had requested an addition of 30,000 civilians to the Pentagon's civilian work force of nearly one million members. The civilians would perform maintenance, supply and routine administrative chores.

The House committee endorsed this argument, adding 7,000 civilian slots to the administration request. The committee said the administration had assumed that too many federal employees' jobs could be turned over to contractors.

The panel added one provision to prevent the Pentagon from contracting out the operation of any military hospital. It also added a provision to bar contracting of any task unless the senior military commander with jurisdiction over the task certified that the use of contract employees would not impede military operations in case of mobilization.

The committee also ordered the Pentagon to study the effect on combat operations of the large number of contractor-employed civilian technicians who performed essential maintenance on complicated weapons even in combat areas. Any aircraft carrier had about 40 such civilians aboard when it was stationed overseas.

"What happens with these vital civilians in time of crisis or war?" the panel asked. "They certainly cannot shut down the computer and go home at 5 p.m. as has happened during recent mobilization training exercises."

The Government Operations Committee dropped all of the Armed Services-recommended restrictions on civilian contracting.

Manpower

The committee approved a manpower ceiling of 2.12 million for active duty forces — 300 more than the Reagan request.

It added a provision canceling a ceiling of 425,000 on the number of military dependents overseas, which had been enacted at the insistence of the Senate Armed Services Committee in 1980.

The ceiling undermined military morale, the House panel maintained.

Enlistment Quality

The committee proposed changing a provision of the fiscal 1981 authorization bill that was intended to make the services recruit a higher proportion of high school graduates and individuals who score in the upper and middle range of the standard Armed Forces Qualifying Test. The provision was aimed at the Army, which was recruiting an increasing number of non-high school graduates and persons scoring well below the median score on the test. *(1980 Almanac p. 60)*

The new House committee provision would allow the Army to recruit more than 25 percent non-graduates in fiscal 1982 (the current limit) if it increased the proportion of non-graduates who scored in the top half of the test. The panel said some evidence suggested that the test scores were more reliable than graduate status as a predictor of job performance in the military.

Reserves

As both Armed Services committees had done for years, the House panel added several hundred million for aircraft to be used by National Guard and reserve units. The panels complained that the Pentagon routinely short-changed the reserve forces when slicing up the budget pie. In 1981, in addition to $437 million for 40 F-16 fighters, the committee added $515.2 million to buy various new training and transport planes and to modernize other reserve aircraft.

Draft Sign-up

Like its Senate counterpart, the House committee moved to overturn a 1980 federal court ruling and simplify enforcement of the legal requirement for draft registration by 18-year-old males.

To enforce registration, the Selective Service System had planned to use Social Security files to identify non-registrants and Internal Revenue Service (IRS) files to find their current addresses. But the U.S. District Court for the District of Columbia ruled in November 1980 that, under the Privacy Act (PL 93-579), registrants could not be required to list their Social Security number unless the requirement was authorized by law.

The House authorized the president to require registrants to list their Social Security numbers and to direct the Social Security Administration and the IRS to cooperate with the registration enforcement plan.

A similar Senate committee provision had been dropped on the Senate floor in the face of a threatened filibuster.

House Floor Action

The House passed the record defense bill July 16 on a 354-63 vote. Liberal Democrats accounted for most of the "nay" votes. The margin was about the same as that on the fiscal 1981 authorization in 1980. *(Vote 131, p. 50-H)*

The House debated the bill for seven days: June 24, July 8-10 and July 14-16.

The House approved a total authorization of $136,111,036,000 for weapons procurement, military research, and operations and maintenance (including the salaries of civilian Pentagon employees). This was $380.2 million less than the president's request and $410 million less than the Senate version of the bill (S 815).

The bill provided an increase of about 31 percent over the fiscal 1981 bill for Pentagon hardware.

The House Armed Services Committee — which enthusiastically supported Reagan's proposed defense buildup — swept from the board nearly all its ideological and institutional opponents during the seven-day-long House debate on the $136.1 billion fiscal 1982 defense authorization bill (HR 3519).

The only change in the authorization amounts originally proposed by the committee was a $65 million increase recommended by the panel at the Pentagon's request. The House rejected by large margins two attempts to second-guess the committee on the merits of various fighter planes.

Liberals, still smarting from the budget reconciliation bill's deep cuts in social programs, tried to apply to the Pentagon budget the congressional ardor for hunting down "waste, fraud and abuse," but the tactic failed by a margin of nearly 2-1.

Opponents of a provision allowing use of government computer banks to enforce draft registration — including some conservative-libertarians — fared even worse.

What may have been the sweetest victories to the Armed Services Committee involved a series of esoteric changes in defense procurement procedures. In a duel over whether the Pentagon should be subject to a government-wide procurement system, Armed Services repeatedly trounced the Government Operations Committee. Government Operations Chairman Jack Brooks, D-Texas, was widely regarded as one of the most formidable legislative operators in the House.

Only one amendment involving a major defense issue was adopted over Armed Services' objection. It would defer obligation of funds for MX missile bases for 60 days after the president announced his choice of a basing method for that mobile, intercontinental missile.

MX Debate

The only safe conclusion to be drawn from two days of House debate on the MX mobile missile (July 8-9) was that the missile was opposed outright only by a small minority of House members, nearly all of them liberals who advocated a continuation of the last decade's efforts to control nuclear arms.

The House adopted, by voice vote, an amendment by James V. Hansen, R-Utah, that would give Congress a chance to block Reagan's final choice of a basing technique for the missile. But it rejected, by a margin of only six votes (201-207), an amendment by Paul Simon, D-Ill., that would have required congressional concurrence in the president's decision. *(Vote 108, p. 44-H)*

Anti-MX amendments were strongly opposed by the Armed Services Committee, which slanted the defense bill in favor of the Multiple Protective Shelter (MPS) shuttle basing system proposed by Carter and supported by the armed services.

The House battle over the Hansen and Simon procedural amendments took on the aspect of a debate over the merits of MPS since opponents of that system — many of whom opposed any MX version — dominated the debate.

But many supporters of the amendments denied that they were acting on the merits of MX or MPS. They insisted that the issue was purely procedural and that they intended merely to protect Congress' right to review the final decision on a weapons system that would cost more than $50 billion in the next decade.

Simon appeared to concede that supporters of his amendment did not necessarily share his antipathy for MPS. Even if his amendment were adopted, he predicted, Congress would easily endorse MPS if Reagan recommended it.

Hansen, Simon Amendments. Hansen's amendment would drop the committee's preferential treatment of MPS, leaving the MX money available for whatever system the president chose. Within 60 days of his decision, Congress could veto the decision by passing a concurrent resolution. The same provision had been added to the military construction bill, and a similar one was contained in the Senate version of the defense authorization bill.

Simon's amendment — which Hansen opposed — would have amended Hansen's amendment to require congressional approval of Reagan's plan within 60 days.

Simon and his supporters recited a litany of political conservatives — such as columnist James J. Kilpatrick — and retired military officers — such as Adm. Thomas Moorer — who rejected MPS as militarily ineffective.

Absent the limits imposed by the SALT II arms control treaty, which Reagan had shelved, the Russians could easily overwhelm MPS by aiming at all 4,600 potential launching sites, Simon argued.

Citing one cost-estimate for the MPS version, Simon warned, "If you put $56 billion into this fancy system that will not be completed ... until 1989, and then may be useless, ... you are taking it away from ships for the Navy, you are taking it away from aircraft we need, you are taking it away from other things that are real defense needs."

Hansen denounced Simon's amendment as "dilatory" and maintained that his own amendment simply would avoid premature expenditures on MPS pending a presidential decision and a reasonable period for congressional review.

Armed Services members opposed both amendments, warning that they might interrupt current contracts that would take months to renegotiate. Given the accuracy of Soviet ICBMs, MPS was essential to overcome the vulnerability of current U.S. missiles based in fixed underground silos, they maintained.

Moreover, Samuel S. Stratton, D-N.Y., warned that abandonment of MPS would undermine the willingness of allied governments in Europe to accept new nuclear weapons on their own territory. "I can understand the people of Utah and Nevada saying, 'Do not put it in my state,'" he said. "But unfortunately when the security of the nation as a whole is involved, sombody has got to give."

Simon's amendment gained many more votes than any of the amendments he had offered in earlier years that were aimed at slowing MPS. Those earlier efforts all had tried to flatly cut funds for the basing mode.

A number of Republicans who typically did not agree with Simon's efforts to restrain defense spending accounted for much of the additional support received by his amendment to HR 3519.

After Simon's amendment was rejected, Hansen's amendment was adopted by voice vote. However a roll-call vote on the Hansen amendment would be likely before the House passed the bill.

Dellums Amendment. The House on July 9 rejected by a 3-1 margin (96-316) an amendment by Ronald V. Dellums, D-Calif., to kill the MX missile. *(Vote 110, p. 44-H)*

Dellums' amendment was passionately supported by arms control advocates who called the new missile unnecessary and dangerous. It was unnecessary, they said, because the scenario of a Soviet attack on existing U.S. missiles was inherently implausible, since the attack surely would trigger World War III.

MX was dangerous, they maintained, because its power and accuracy made it a potential threat to Soviet ICBMs. "If the Soviet Union perceives our ability to strike them a devastating first strike," warned Thomas J. Downey, D-N.Y., "they will want to use that arsenal in a crisis as opposed to losing it."

MX supporters basically ignored the amendment. The margin by which it was rejected reflected about the same level of support the House had given amendments opposing various strategic weapons in recent years.

Bomber Amendments

An amendment by Wyche Fowler Jr., D-Ga., to remove a committee limitation on bomber development money was rejected 153-254. *(Vote 111, p. 44-H)*

In the same way that it had slanted the bill in favor of

MPS, the committee had built in a presumption in favor of the B-1 bomber.

The committee bill provided that $1.9 billion would be available only to begin production of the B-1, unless Reagan certified that the stealth plane was needed instead, and Congress agreed by concurrent resolution within 60 days. Fowler's amendment would have made the money available for stealth plane research without congressional approval.

The House rejected by voice vote an amendment by Tom Harkin, D-Iowa, that would have allowed the president to kill the B-1 if Congress did not disapprove his decision by concurrent resolution within 60 days.

Contracting Out

The House rejected two efforts by the Government Operations Committee to overturn Armed Services Committee provisions to limit the Pentagon's ability to replace federal employees with civilian contract employees.

Armed Services long had maintained that in several administrations, the Office of Management and Budget (OMB) had pressured the Pentagon to replace federal workers with contract employees so that the administration could claim political credit for reducing the size of the federal work force. Many of the contracts involved housekeeping jobs: food preparation, building security, laundry, and janitorial service.

Though such moves had been justified on the grounds of lower cost for contractor performance, Armed Services complained that the savings frequently were illusory over the long term. Once the staff of federal employees was disbanded, isolated installations — like some military bases — might be at a contractor's mercy, leading to large increases in the contract costs, the panel argued.

Moreover, the panel had complained that many defense jobs were so critical to mobilization requirements that they should not be vulnerable to the vicissitudes of private sector labor relations.

Armed Services added to HR 3519 provisions that would:

● Bar the contracting out of operations of any entire military hospital. Over the objections of the armed services' surgeons general, the Pentagon planned to carry out a 1979 congressional order to contract out the operation of three hospitals as a pilot project.

● Require a senior military commander to certify that the transfer of a task within his command to contract employees would not interfere with his wartime mission.

The Government Operations Committee objected to both provisions, pointing out that the OMB rules governing contracting decisions provided exemptions for jobs that were militarily critical.

The Armed Services provisions would unnecessarily carve out a special Pentagon exemption from government-wide policy, and would allow commanders to protect bureaucratic empires at the cost of unneeded government expense, Government Operations complained.

But Government Operations-backed amendments to delete the Armed Services provisions were defeated by voice votes.

The House also rejected, on a 190-194 vote July 10, a Government Operations effort to kill a provision authorizing the Pentagon to fund research by grants as well as contracts. *(Vote 115, p. 46-H)*

Armed Services had incorporated the provision at the Pentagon's request. The Government Operations panel objected that this exempted the Defense Department from

government-wide policy establishing the circumstances under which grants were a proper means of federal funding.

Procurement System

Armed Services beat its rival on three more issues July 14-15. Rejected were Government Operations amendments that would have:

● Required congressional approval on a case-by-case basis of multi-year contracts for major weapons purchases. The Armed Services bill authorized such contracts. Rejected 133-283. *(Vote 122, p. 48-H)*

● Required all Pentagon computer purchases to be channeled through the General Services Administration, which was the purchasing agent for all federal computers. The Armed Services bill made no change in that system, but the Senate authorization bill would exempt from GSA oversight the purchase of computers for combat-related or intelligence uses. Rejected 118-299. *(Vote 123, p. 48-H)*

● Deleted an Armed Services provision that would raise various dollar thresholds below which defense contracts were administered by simplified procedures. Rejected 109-311. *(Vote 119, p. 46-H)*

Waste, Fraud and Abuse

By a vote of 142-276, the House rejected an amendment by Armed Services member Patricia Schroeder, D-Colo., that would have required the president to recommend to Congress by Jan. 15, 1982, rescissions in the Pentagon budget totaling $8 billion due to waste, fraud, abuse and mismanagement. *(Vote 126, p. 48-H)*

But lest constituents doubt the fervor with which the House watched over the federal purse, it then took 15 minutes for a roll-call vote on an alternative amendment that merely directed the president to recommend any changes he deemed necessary to eliminate waste, fraud, abuse or mismanagement by the Pentagon. That amendment was adopted 416-0. *(Vote 127, p. 48-H)*

Schroeder cited a number of studies alleging that the Pentagon was wasting various amounts annually because of improper or unnecessary spending: $16 billion according to the Republican Study Group; $25 billion according to the National Conservative Foundation; billions and billions, according to numerous reports of the General Accounting Office (GAO), some of which Schroeder stacked on a table in the well of the House.

"We are talking about an over-$220-billion defense budget," Schroeder said. "That [$8 billion target] hardly registers on the scale.... It is just a teeny little bit."

Opponents insisted that Reagan and Defense Secretary Caspar W. Weinberger had already implemented some of the savings called for by the studies. But their basic argument was that Schroeder's amendment was simply a disguised effort to reduce the defense budget. "They do not want to admit that that is what they are really doing, ... so they have put the trappings of waste, fraud and abuse around their proposal," charged Robert S. Walker, R-Pa.

All but a handful of Schroeder's supporters were liberal Democrats.

Military Women

By voice vote, the House rejected an amendment by Schroeder that would have blocked Army plans to slow the rate at which it was adding women members. Army officials announced the slowdown during the spring of 1981, saying they wanted time to study the effect of the last decade's increase in the number of Army women.

Schroeder argued that the slowdown was demoralizing to women already in the Army who feared it portended future limitations on their career prospects. She did not oppose the new study, but pointed out that several earlier studies had shown that women could handle their expanded Army role.

Armed Services Military Personnel Subcommittee Chairman Bill Nichols, D-Ala., opposed the amendment, insisting that the slowdown was modest and only temporary.

Under the slowdown plan, in fiscal 1981 the number of Army women would expand to 65,000 rather than to 69,000. Planned increases to 75,000 in fiscal 1982 and to 87,500 in fiscal 1983 had not been changed, Nichols said.

Senior Civilian Cuts

Another Schroeder amendment, which would have forced the Pentagon to cut its staff of high-ranking civilians by 6 percent by the end of fiscal 1982, was rejected by a vote of 142-249. *(Vote 112, p. 44-H)*

The fiscal 1978 defense authorization act (PL 95-79) had mandated a reduction over three years of about 3,000 in the total of 55,000 Pentagon civilians holding civil service grades GS-13 and above. In 1979 and 1980 Congress deferred the deadline for the reduction. At the Pentagon's request, the Armed Services Committee included in HR 3519 a provision repealing the reduction requirement.

Schroeder protested that removal of the cut order would encourage Pentagon "grade creep": promotions to higher rank for people whose jobs did not change.

But Nichols insisted that the cutbacks would cause a shortage of supervisory personnel to oversee Reagan's defense buildup. Already, he said, the shortage of promotion opportunities might have contributed to the resignation of many Pentagon scientists and engineers.

Communication Satellites

Delays in the space shuttle were responsible for the only changes made by the House in Pentagon hardware programs.

At the recommendation of the Armed Services Committee, the House approved by voice vote an amendment by Chairman Melvin Price, D-Ill., adding $65 million for components of three FLTSATCOM communications satellites that would be purchased in later budgets. Also adopted by voice vote was a companion amendment by Dan Daniel, D-Va., transferring $67 million within the Navy's operations and maintenance account to pay for changes in the contract for a new type of communications satellite called LEASAT.

LEASAT had been designed for launch from the space shuttle; delays in that vehicle forced the slowdown in the LEASAT production contract. Moreover, the committee said, additional FLTSATCOM satellites should be bought as an insurance policy in case existing satellites had to be replaced before the LEASATs could be launched with the shuttle.

Registration Enforcement

The House rejected, 125-290, an amendment by Ted Weiss, D-N.Y., to delete a provision intended to permit the Selective Service System to screen Social Security files to identify 19-year-old males who did not register, as required by law. *(Vote 125, p. 48-H)*

Earlier, the House had adopted by voice vote an amendment offered by Bill Nichols, D-Ala., on behalf of

the Armed Services Committee, deleting a provision that would have authorized Selective Service to obtain from the Internal Revenue Service the addresses of non-registrants.

Fighter Planes

By a vote of 101-316, the House rejected an amendment by Bruce F. Vento, D-Minn., that would have canceled the F/A-18 fighter being purchased for the Navy and Marine Corps. The $3.1 billion in the bill for that project would have been left to the Navy to spread around to other aircraft programs. *(Vote 128, p. 48-H)*

By a slightly smaller margin (148-268) the House rejected an amendment by Toby Moffett, D-Conn., that would have dropped from the bill 12 A-7Ks, a two-seat version of a small bomber used by the Air National Guard, and authorized instead 13 additional F-16 fighters for the Guard. *(Vote 129, p. 50-H)*

Anti-Drug Missions

An amendment by E. Clay Shaw Jr., R-Fla., allowing military personnel to seize illegal drugs and arrest drug smugglers (except on the U.S. mainland) was adopted 248-168. Shaw's proposal amended a Judiciary Committee amendment, as amended by Richard C. White, D-Texas, that would have authorized the military to provide drug-law enforcement information and equipment — including operators for the equipment — but not to arrest. *(Vote 120, p. 46-H)*

The Judiciary amendment had been offered to strike from the Armed Services bill a provision that would have authorized military participation in drug smuggling arrests.

The House also adopted by voice vote an amendment by Ed Bethune, R-Ark., to require a Pentagon study of the effect of military cooperation in drug arrests.

Foreign Vehicles

By a 231-187 vote, the House adopted an amendment by Elwood Hillis, R-Ind., to bar the armed services from purchasing cars and trucks not made in the United States or Canada, without express legislative authorization. *(Vote 130, p. 50-H)*. A substitute by Larry J. Hopkins, R-Ky., that would have barred such purchases unless the secretary of defense reported to Congress that no "suitable" vehicles were available in the United States or Canada, was rejected 38-371. *(Vote 124, p. 48-H)*

Other Amendments

Foreign Languages. Paul Simon, D-Ill., a crusader for the study of foreign languages in the United States, offered an amendment directing the Pentagon to study the feasibility of requiring the study of foreign languages at the national military academies. It was adopted by voice vote after Simon accepted an amendment by Nichols broadening the study to cover the feasibility of paying a bonus to armed service personnel stationed abroad who were proficient in the language of the country (other than English).

Yorktown Bicentennial. Authorized Pentagon expenditures for the celebration of the 200th anniversary of the battle of Yorktown (Va.) were reduced from $1 million to $750,000 — the amount in the Senate bill. The reduction, proposed by Peter A. Peyser, D-N.Y., was adopted by voice vote. The House then rejected by a standing vote (33-60) an amendment by Harold L. Volkmer, D-Mo., that would have removed the authorization entirely.

Yorktown was the climactic battle of the Revolutionary War.

The House also adopted the following amendments by voice vote:

● By Ike Skelton, D-Mo., changing the title of the Navy rank corresponding to brigadier general to "commodore" instead of "commodore admiral." No officers held the rank, which was created in 1980. *(1980 Almanac p. 90)*

Stratton said the Navy originally had insisted on the longer title so that officers holding the rank could be addressed as "admiral." But Stratton praised the simpler form: "If it was good enough for Commodore Perry when he opened Japan, it ought to be good enough for the commodores of today."

● By Thomas E. Petri, R-Wis., to extend for two years a program of forgiving partial repayment of federal student loans for persons who join the armed services.

● By Gerald B. H. Solomon, R-N.Y., to extend for one year a reduction in the minimum number of participants required to justify a junior (high school) ROTC program.

● By Paul S. Trible Jr., R-Va., banning the construction or conversion of any Navy ships in foreign shipyards. Newport News Shipbuilding and Dry Dock, a major Navy shipbuilder, was a major employer in Trible's district.

During the spring of 1981, the Navy was locked in a public dispute with General Dynamics Corp., the only builder of Trident missile submarines and one of two builders — along with Newport News — of anti-ship submarines. Navy Secretary John Lehman said that he would consider ordering ships abroad, if necessary, to get them built on time and cheaply. Lehman's remark had been widely seen as a bargaining ploy.

● By Joseph P. Addabbo, D-N.Y., dropping a committee provision that would have repealed a requirement for an annual Pentagon report to Congress on the independent research and development programs of defense contractors.

● By Harold C. Hollenbeck, R-N.J., expressing the sense of Congress that the Army should improve its ability to independently verify the claims submitted by West German citizens for damage caused by U.S. forces on maneuvers.

● By Jack Brinkley, D-Ga., authorizing the Pentagon to provide planning assistance to communities affected by base closings or weapons contract terminations involving more than 2,500 jobs or 10 percent of the area labor force (whichever was the smaller figure).

● By Henry J. Hyde, R-Ill., barring the military services for one year from accepting men but not women recruits who held a high school equivalency certificate. The amendment had been modified by Schroeder to allow the secretary of defense to waive the prohibition if the gender-based distinction were found to be necessary to military readiness.

● By Thomas S. Foley, D-Wash., requiring the president to make certain findings before selling any silver from the national strategic material stockpile after Sept. 30, 1982.

● By Thomas J. Downey, D-N.Y., requiring the secretary of defense to include in his annual report to Congress the total projected cost of any weapon system costing more than $1 billion.

By voice vote, the House rejected an amendment by Joseph G. Minish, D-N.J., to require the General Accounting Office to study the need for a legislative limit on excess profits in defense contracts. The existing limit — the so-called Vinson-Trammell Act — had been suspended from operation for decades, and the House Armed Services Committee was considering replacing that act with one that would impose excess profit limits only in time of war.

1982 Defense Authorizations

Compared with the president's original (March 1981) request, following are the fiscal 1982 authorizations for the Department of Defense passed by the Senate (S 815) and House (HR 3519) *(in thousands of dollars)*:

	Reagan Request	Senate-passed Authorization	House-passed Authorization
Procurement			
Aircraft			
Army	$ 1,797,400	$ 1,836,700	$ 1,880,300
Navy and Marine Corps	9,352,500	9,331,700	9,902,600
Air Force	14,751,898	15,070,798	15,023,698
Missiles			
Army	2,842,500	2,469,100	2,745,800
Navy	2,555,000	2,555,000	2,484,800
Marine Corps	223,024	223,024	223,024
Air Force	4,658,246	4,718,746	4,593,246
Naval Vessels	10,290,100	10,118,600	10,290,100
Tracked Combat Vehicles			
Army	3,487,300	3,537,300	3,469,500
Marine Corps	281,739	281,739	281,739
Torpedoes	516,600	516,600	516,600
Other Weapons			
Army	655,400	655,400	655,400
Navy	200,200	200,200	200,200
Marine Corps	136,344	136,344	136,344
Air Force	3,047	3,047	3,047
National Guard	—	50,000	—
Subtotal	51,751,298	51,704,298	52,406,398
Research and Development			
Army	3,905,200	3,893,100	3,741,470
Navy	6,086,371	6,155,001	5,699,531
Air Force	9,398,100	9,130,100	8,833,700
Defense Agencies	1,881,400	1,882,550	1,914,797
Director, Test and Evaluation	53,000	53,000	—
Subtotal	21,324,071	21,113,751	20,189,498
Operations and Maintenance			
Army	17,214,300	17,490,300	17,214,044
Navy	21,918,049	21,929,949	21,930,149
Air Force	19,249,340	19,274,420	19,230,740
Defense Agencies	4,901,351	4,881,551	4,901,207
Subtotal	63,283,040	63,576,220	63,276,140
Civil Defense	132,842	126,842	174,000
Grand Total	$136,491,251	$136,521,111	$136,046,036

Conference Action

Strategic Warfare

The conferees' most dramatic action dealing with nuclear war forces was their inclusion of provisions that would allow Congress to block by concurrent resolution Reagan's decision to build the B-1 bomber or his decision to base MX missiles in "superhardened" launch silos. But the provisions were to have no effect, since the pro-B-1 House Armed Services Committee bottled up the conference report until after the Nov. 18 deadline for adoption of blocking resolutions. Sen. Carl Levin, D-Mich., and other Democrats introduced resolutions (S Res 240, 241) to block both programs.

Showdown votes on both programs occurred on the defense appropriations bills in both houses. *(Story, p. 311)*

Bombers

The conferees allowed $2.1 billion for the B-1 bomber program, cutting $100 million from the procurement request and $51 million earmarked for repair parts and spares. The request and authorization figures for the "stealth" bomber, designed to evade detection by enemy radar, were closely held secrets. But during Senate debate of the conference report Nov. 5, Sam Nunn, D-Ga., charged that the administration was deliberately slowing the pace of stealth development.

Reagan's October recommendation to begin retiring the oldest B-52s — the 75 planes of the D model — was approved, for a savings of $18.9 million. But the conferees noted that the timing of the retirements would allow the Pentagon to reverse the decision in the course of deliberations on the fiscal 1983 budget. On Nov. 4, the chief of the Strategic Air Command told a Senate panel he was lobbying to keep some of the planes in service.

ICBMs

Of the $1.95 billion requested in October for development of the MX intercontinental missile, conferees approved $1.875 billion. The conference report did not account for the $75 million difference, but it appeared to reflect most conferees' intense disagreement with Reagan's decision to cancel plans to shuttle each MX missile among several hidden launch sites in order to forestall a Soviet missile attack. *(MX background, p. 196)*

Conferees added $76 million to an ICBM research program, earmarking $25 million of that amount for continued research on shuttle-type basing techniques. In their report — but not in the text of the bill — the conferees also barred any research on launching MX from an airplane. That was one approach Reagan wanted to examine for possible future use with MX. The administration had budgeted $50 million for the air-launched system, which had been harshly criticized by key members of both Armed Services committees. *(Air mobile background, box, p. 199)*

The bill included $34.3 million to complete previously planned production of the Mark-12A nuclear warhead, which was used on some Minuteman ICBMs and which could be used on the MX. But efforts by both houses to fund production of additional Mark-12A warheads were dropped, for a savings of some $44.6 million. The conferees urged the Pentagon to seek congressional approval to divert money to the Mark-12A warhead from other programs, if it decided later to keep that production line going.

The conferees rejected an October request to drop two programs designed to help the Minuteman missile force survive a relatively prolonged nuclear war. For a system that would let airborne command posts re-target and fire the missiles, the conferees dropped $12.3 million for procurement but retained $38.5 million to continue development. For another program that would equip Minuteman silos with long-life batteries to provide electrical power in case commercial power failed, the conferees left in the bill $35 million of $45 million added by the Senate. They also refused Reagan's request to rescind $22.5 million appropriated for the program in fiscal 1981.

Anti-Missile Defense

To accelerate work on the kind of anti-ballistic missile defense system the Army had under development, the con-

ferees authorized $336.7 million. That amount included $35 million of the $52 million Reagan wanted to add in his October budget revision.

But the more exotic kind of anti-missile defenses favored by some conservative senators fared poorly. The conferees approved only $5 million of the $50 million added by the Senate to accelerate development of laser-armed anti-missile satellites. Senate laser proponents led by Malcolm Wallop, R-Wyo., had hoped earlier to add $250 million to the program.

The $5 million brought the total for the program to $64.2 million. Conferees also dropped $31.2 million added by the Senate for a very long-range infrared missile detector intended for use with an anti-missile defense.

Air Combat

In general, the conferees compromised between the amounts approved by the Senate and House for fighter plane production. Approved were 63 Navy F/A-18s ($2.13 billion, plus $343 million for spare parts), 36 Air Force F-15s ($1.08 billion, plus $71 million for spare parts) and 120 Air Force F-16s ($1.82 billion, plus $394 million for spare parts).

The Pentagon's October decision to buy only 20 A-10 tank-hunting planes instead of the 60 requested in March also was approved (with an authorization of $229.7 million).

Future Fighters

For the balance of the 1980s, the Air Force should build on the basic design of its F-15 and F-16 fighters rather than starting from scratch to design new fighters, according to the conferees. They canceled two programs (with a total authorization of $32.2 million) to explore new aircraft designs. But they approved a $42.2 million request for improvements in the F-16 and added $15.3 million to test a new version of that plane (called the F-16E).

Conferees denied a request for $27.3 million to develop a ground attack version of the F-15, though they stressed that the action was not intended to foreclose that plan. The Air Force had not explained to Congress its long-term plans for buying new attack planes, according to the conference report.

To keep an eye on new threats that might face future fighter designs, the conferees added to the bill $5 million.

Warships

In October, the administration abandoned its plan to refurbish the mothballed aircraft carrier *Oriskany*, thus reducing its authorization request by $430 million. The Senate had opposed the reactivation, and the House conferees conceded the issue. The conference report approved $8.8 million of $22 million requested by the Navy to further study ways in which mothballed carriers might be used in the future. *(Oriskany background, box, p. 204)*

Not at issue in the conference was $658 million requested and approved by both houses to buy the nuclear power plant and other components for a large aircraft carrier to be included in the fiscal 1983 budget.

The planned modernization and reactivation of the battleship *New Jersey*, which was to be armed with cruise missiles, had been approved by both houses, though they disagreed over the amount to be authorized. The conference agreed on the higher, Senate figure of $237 million.

Frigates

An October request to slow the production of missile-armed frigates (from three ships to two) was rejected by the conferees, who also turned down a Senate proposal to authorize six of the ships. The three ships authorized ($971.9 million) would provide one new ship for each of the three shipyards able to build these vessels (in Maine, California and Washington state).

In October the administration abandoned a request for $15 million to design a smaller frigate that would be manned by naval reservists, a plan both houses already had rejected. A simplified version of the current missile frigate was to be built for reserve use.

Submarines

Conferees approved the request for two nuclear-powered submarines designed to hunt enemy ships and submarines ($1.1 billion). The House had authorized three of the ships. But the conferees approved $397.9 million to buy components that would be used in three submarines that would be funded in fiscal 1983 and another three in fiscal 1984. The administration had requested such "long lead-time" components for only two subs in fiscal 1983 and one in fiscal 1984. However, the administration was committed in principle to building three subs a year.

Future Fleet

To begin designing a missile-armed destroyer (called DDGX) to replace ships due for retirement in the late 1980s, the conferees approved $101 million. The House had blocked funds for the ship, charging that the design was too small and slow, and lacked sufficient armor and armament because of cost limits imposed by Pentagon budgeters. According to the conference report, the House conferees were satisfied by Navy assurances that the alleged limitations had been removed.

The conference was more restrained in its support of programs to design smaller, less expensive aircraft carriers and submarines powered by fuel oil rather than nuclear power. Senate Armed Services Committee member Gary Hart, D-Colo., long had championed such ships as the only affordable way to substantially increase the size of the U.S. fleet. The Senate panel typically had supported Hart while the Navy and the House Armed Services Committee had been opposed.

The conference report approved about half the amount authorized by the Senate for each program: $10 million to design a light carrier, $2.5 million to design a conventionally powered submarine.

Ground Combat

Tanks. Reagan's October recommendation to buy 660 M-1 tanks instead of the 720 originally requested was rejected. But the conference report authorized $1.42 billion for the purchase — $200 million less than had been budgeted earlier in the year. Savings uncovered during negotiation of the fiscal 1981 tank contract made the reduction possible, according to the report.

Anti-Aircraft Missiles

Proposals in October to slow the modernization of anti-aircraft defenses for U.S. forces in Europe received a mixed reception from the conference. The report rejected a proposal to slow purchase of British-built Rapier missiles to defend U.S. air bases in Britain, authorizing the amount originally requested ($133 million).

The proposal to stop buying French-German-designed Roland missiles was rejected because of the billions already invested in the program and because of its importance as a political symbol of the Pentagon's willingness to buy European weaponry, a sore point in the NATO alliance. The conference report approved $50 million; in March, the administration had requested $529.3 million for the program (including spare parts).

The conference recommendation for the Patriot long-range anti-aircraft missile was slightly below the October request — $670 million instead of $720.8 million. But the conference amount was $183 million above the Senate-passed authorization; Senate Armed Services had complained that the missile was being rushed into production without adequate testing.

Helicopters

The amount requested to buy 96 UH-60 troop-carrying helicopters was approved ($545.2 million). But the conferees denied an additional $126 million requested to fund a multi-year contract, which would cover several years' worth of planned UH-60 purchases.

Both houses had approved the administration request for $365 million to build the first 14 AH-64 tank-hunting helicopters. But conferees learned that an additional $73.4 million would be needed to buy the helicopters, so they increased the authorization to $438.4 million.

Because of steadily increasing costs, the conferees killed a program (called SOTAS) intended to develop a helicopter-borne radar that could detect tanks and other moving targets on the ground behind enemy lines. The conferees conceded the program's potential value, but pointed out that its estimated total cost had risen from $969 million to $2.45 billion, despite a reduction in the number of units planned.

To begin developing a less expensive system for this purpose, the conferees added $5 million to the bill.

National Guard, Reserve Equipment

To buy 20 aircraft and some ground combat equipment for reserve and National Guard forces, the conferees added $214.5 million not requested by the administration. But that was only about half the amount included in the bills passed by the two houses.

The two Armed Services committees for years had accused Democratic and Republican administrations of starving the reserve forces of funds needed for modernization, even while claiming they were relying on those units in U.S. war plans.

Among the reserve items that had been approved by both houses but were dropped in conference was approximately $150 million to continue production of the A-7K, a trainer version of the A-7 light bomber, for use by the Air National Guard.

The Reagan administration, following the lead of its predecessors, argued that the plane was an outmoded, Vietnam-era aircraft, and that buying planes for the National Guard was a lower priority than keeping the regular Air Force well-equipped. But until 1981, the National Guard and its allies in Congress always were able to convince Congress to add money for the planes.

Reserve items authorized by the conference report were $109.5 million for eight C-130 transport planes and $55 million for 12 AH-1S helicopters, an older tank-hunt-

Defense Authorization Bill Slows. . . .

Responding to the budgetary stringency adopted by the administration with its October reductions, conferees on the Defense authorization bill slowed most of the aircraft and ship programs most closely associated with plans for a Rapid Deployment Force (RDF).

Tankers

One exception to that rule was the KC-10, a version of the DC-10 airliner designed to refuel other planes in midair. One mission the Air Force envisioned for these planes was to escort fighter combat planes from the United States to distant trouble spots non-stop.

The administration originally had requested — and both houses had approved — $500 million for eight KC-10 planes. In October, the administration recommended killing the program, but conferees approved $237.4 million for four KC-10s.

Cargo Planes

The conferees remained unconvinced of the Air Force's case for a new wide-body transport plane, called the C-17 (formerly CX). The plane had been designed to carry tanks and other heavy pieces of Army equipment across intercontinental distances to small, relatively primitive airstrips.

Instead of the $169.7 million the administration requested in its October budget revision for the C-17, the conferees approved $15 million for that program and $50 million to procure existing wide-body jets to haul Air Force cargo. As a practical matter, the total of $65 million could be used — with the Armed Services committees'

approval — to fund whatever program for new cargo planes the Pentagon justified to the Armed Services committees, whether that involved the new plane, existing planes or a mix of both types. None of the money could be spent until Congress had been given 30 days' prior notice.

Pre-Positioning Ships

Ships designed to speed the arrival of ground combat troops in distant trouble spots met heavy weather in the conference. Staff members emphasized that this did not reflect any reservations about those programs, but simply the fact that, given the organization of the defense budget and the authorization bill, conferees were forced to choose between combat ships and cargo ships to achieve about $1.5 billion worth of cuts in the shipbuilding budget.

In October, the administration abandoned its plan to build new ships (called T-AKXs) to store the tanks, ammunition and other combat equipment of a Marine division. The ships were to be anchored near potential trouble spots to which Marines could be flown from the United States — at the invitation of a local government — in case of a crisis. In addition to six new ships, six cargo ships currently in commercial service would have been bought and converted for this role under the original plan.

Under the plan announced in October, the Pentagon would contract with civilian firms to provide the "pre-positioning ships" on a long-term charter basis. The October budget dropped a request for $392 million to begin buying the ships and added $60 million to begin chartering them, instead.

ing helicopter than the AH-64s now entering production for the Army.

Personnel

Conferees accepted an October recommendation setting the Army manpower ceiling at 780,300, just 300 more than the fiscal 1981 limit but 6,000 fewer than had been requested in March (for an estimated savings of $62.3 million). Much of the slowdown would be absorbed by temporarily disbanding a brigade based in the United States.

The Pentagon won two and lost one of its battles over personnel policy with the Senate Armed Services Committee. Conferees dropped provisions that limited the number of military dependents overseas and required a 6 percent reduction by fiscal 1983 in the number of senior civilian Pentagon employees. Both changes had been requested by the Defense Department.

But the conferees retained relatively tough Senate-sponsored limits on the number of men who were not high school graduates the Army would be allowed to enlist: no more than 35 percent of its fiscal 1982 inductees.

Conferees also agreed to an earlier deadline set by Senate Armed Services as the date by which the Pentagon should make up a shortage of 249,000 in the pool of reservists who would be called up as casualty replacements in

case of war. The House bill had ordered a Pentagon plan that would correct the problem by 1987. The Senate report on S 815 ordered a plan that would fix the shortage by 1984, the date agreed to by the conferees.

Draft Registration Enforcement

To help the Selective Service System identify 18-year-old men who had not registered for the draft as required by law, conferees included a House-passed provision requiring the secretary of health and human services to make available to the draft agency the names and addresses of Social Security registrants who met the requirements for registration.

Twice in the previous year, the Senate had dropped similar riders from defense bills under filibuster threats from anti-draft crusader Mark O. Hatfield, R-Ore.

Maintenance, Readiness

Conferees included the administration's October proposal to keep only one aircraft carrier in the Indian Ocean full-time instead of two (with one additional carrier in the region about half the time), for a savings of $74.6 million. Carter had ordered two carrier task forces into the region following the December 1979 Soviet invasion of Afghanistan, and Reagan continued that deployment until his October 1981 budget reductions.

. . . .Most RDF Aircraft and Ship Programs

But according to the conference report, the Navy had not adequately worked out the details of the charter arrangement. The conferees denied the $60 million requested for charters, but approved $139 million in new funds (and approved the transfer of $58 million appropriated but not spent on the pre-positioning plan in fiscal 1981) to purchase and begin modifying up to four ships.

The conference action left open the possibility that the Navy could use those funds for the charter plan if it could secure the Armed Services committees' assent to a detailed plan.

The conferees also approved an October request to drop from the bill $54 million to buy an existing cargo ship of the "Seabee-type" designed to carry 38 large barges filled with cargo that also could be used to unload the pre-positioning ships.

Fast Transports

The tight budget also slowed conversion of eight very fast commercial ships to carry an Army division's equipment. Six of the ships (called SL-7s) had been bought in fiscal 1981, and the administration requested $668.4 million in fiscal 1982 to buy the other two and to modify all eight so that tanks and other vehicles could drive on and off the ships under their own power, thus speeding the loading and unloading.

The administration did not change its recommendation in October, but the conferees approved only $184 million in new authorization (and the transfer of $44.4 million appropriated but not spent for the project in fiscal 1981). These funds were earmarked to buy the remaining two SL-7s and to convert two of the eight, leaving the six others to be modified in the future.

To begin designing an experimental cargo ship that would move at high speed on a cushion of trapped air, the conferees added $5 million to the bill. Neither the administration nor the Senate had funded this so-called "surface-effects ship," but the House had authorized $46 million.

Amphibious Assault

The conferees stood by the previous decision of both houses to authorize procurement of an amphibious landing ship (called an LSD-41) that could land Marine Corps units in the face of opposing military forces, unlike the pre-positioned ships. They added $301 million to the bill but dropped an additional $107.3 million that both houses had added to buy components for two more ships to be bought in fiscal 1983. The administration had requested no funds for an LSD in fiscal 1982 and $34 million for components of one ship to be budgeted in fiscal 1983.

Conferees also added to the bill $15 million to begin designing a new amphibious landing ship (called an LHDX) that would resemble a medium-sized aircraft carrier. The ship could launch troop-landing helicopters or vertical takeoff jet bombers as well as landing craft able to carry tanks and other heavy equipment to a beach.

Also added to the bill was $45 million to begin buying components for use in either an LHDX or a similar ship (called an LHA). Five of the LHA ships already were in service.

The conferees turned down most other administration recommendations to pare back operating tempos or maintenance plans.

A proposal to save $81.8 million by cutting two days per quarter from the amount of time the naval fleets based on the U.S. East and West coasts would be under way, was cut in half.

Warning that any cutbacks in flight training time would erode U.S. combat readiness, the conferees rejected a proposed 2 percent cut in Navy flying hours (to save $27.8 million). They added $17.1 million to the Air Force's $3.6 billion budget for flight operating costs.

On the other hand, although the conference report added $78.8 million to the Navy's aircraft spare parts budget (for a total authorization of $1.6 billion), it cut $80 million from the corresponding Air Force budget (leaving a $3.89 billion authorization). The 2 percent Air Force cut was intended to force an administrative consolidation of several spare parts accounts that should reduce parts prices, according to the conference report.

Maintenance

The conferees authorized more than the president's request for major overhauls of Army vehicles (increased by $89 million) and Navy aircraft (increased by $3.2 million).

They also added $41.4 million to the request for Navy aircraft modifications, for a total authorization of $264 million. But they accepted an October recommendation to authorize $897.1 million for major ship alterations — $80 million less than had been budgeted in March.

For maintenance and repair of real property, the conferees approved $2.9 billion, $223.2 million more than the administration's October request.

Other Provisions

The conference report also:

● Required that, in case the cost-per-copy of a major weapon grew by more than 15 percent, the secretary of the service buying the weapon give Congress a written report explaining: the reason for the increase; the names of the responsible civilian and military officials; and the actions taken (and planned) to control future cost growth. If the cost increased by more than 25 percent, the secretary of defense would be required to report to Congress certifying the necessity of the weapon and identifying alternative weapons. If either report was not submitted within a certain time, funds for the weapon would be cut off.

● Authorized $200 million to continue development of the Navstar satellite, which would allow vehicles or individuals to locate their position anywhere on Earth to within an accuracy of 10 yards in any direction. No funds were authorized to begin procurement of the satellites.

The conferees complained that the Pentagon was be-

ing forced to pay for Navstar although many civilian users would benefit from it. They directed the Defense Department to suggest ways other federal agencies could be made to bear some of the cost.

● Authorized military personnel to cooperate with civilian law enforcement officials to assist in drug law enforcement under certain circumstances. The provision expressly barred the participation of military personnel in searches, seizures or arrests, actions which the House bill would have allowed outside the continental United States.

● Accepted a Senate provision to partly suspend the so-called Maybank amendment by allowing the allocation of some non-critical Pentagon contracts to areas of high unemployment. The Maybank amendment, routinely added to defense appropriations bills, barred the Pentagon from paying a premium price for any purchase in order to direct its business to areas of high unemployment.

● Dropped a House provision barring the purchase of foreign-made cars and light trucks, a move the Army had been planning for its forces in Europe.

● Changed the title of the Navy's most junior grade of admirals from "commodore admiral" to "commodore." ∎

Nuclear Weapons Authority

Congress Nov. 19 cleared a bill (HR 3413 — PL 97-90) authorizing $5.12 billion in fiscal 1982 for nuclear weapons programs of the Department of Energy (DOE). That was $123.8 million more than President Reagan had requested.

The bill represented a substantial boost in funding for Energy Department nuclear weapons programs. The amount in the bill was 29 percent greater than the $3.97 billion approved for fiscal 1981. *(1980 Almanac p. 83)*

The House adopted the conference report on the bill Nov. 19 by a vote of 335-55. The Senate adopted it by voice vote the same day. *(Vote 305, 100-H)*

The Energy Department conducted all nuclear research and nuclear weapons production for the Pentagon. The annual authorization bill covered development of nuclear weapons and naval power plants, and manufacture and testing of nuclear weapons.

For the first time in several years, the so-called neutron bomb was not a major issue in congressional consideration of the nuclear weapons bill. The neutron warhead was intended to allow nuclear attacks against any Soviet tank columns that might invade densely populated parts of Western Europe, without causing widespread property damage.

The only time the issue was raised was on June 11, when the House overwhelmingly rejected an amendment to bar use of funds in the bill for development of the high-radiation weapons. *(Background, 1978 Almanac p. 370)*

President Reagan Aug. 6 announced his decision to begin manufacturing the neutron warheads, but to base them in the United States, rather than in Europe. The decision to keep the warheads in the United States was made to avoid disputes in Europe, where the weapon was highly controversial.

The weapons could be transferred to Europe in a matter of hours in the event of a Soviet attack, Defense Secretary Caspar W. Weinberger said.

The warheads would be placed on army cannons and short-range missiles.

Conference Action

Conferees came close to splitting the difference between the House and Senate amounts for the bill by recommending $5,120,200,000. That figure was $123.8 million above the administration request and $55.65 million above the House amount, but $44.9 million below the Senate-approved amount.

The administration did not recommend cuts for DOE nuclear programs in its September budget reductions. All defense-related cuts were made in programs directly under the Pentagon's budget. *(Defense cuts story, p. 240)*

The conference report on the bill (H Rept 97-342) was filed Nov. 18.

Fusion Research

Conferees provided $142.3 million, the Senate amount, for research on the inertial confinement fusion process. Inertial confinement fusion was a process intended to simulate in the laboratory the kinds of explosions produced by a hydrogen bomb; it could be used to test nuclear weapons designs. More than $1 billion has been spent since 1977 on the process.

Both Armed Services committees had complained that the Reagan administration requested too little for the program. The $106 million request was $34.6 million less than the 1981 authorization and $78.2 million less than the Energy Department requested when it submitted its budget to the Office of Management and Budget (OMB).

"No reasons have been offered to the Congress for this precipitous decision to curtail" the program, the conferees said in their report.

Nuclear Material Production

Conferees said a shortage of fuel for nuclear weapons (called "special nuclear materials") "may occur between 1985 and 1990 unless additional measures are taken to remedy the problem of declining production of the aging reactors" in Richland, Wash., and Savannah River, S.C.

Conferees added $10 million — not requested by the administration — for studies of a new reactor to produce weapons-grade nuclear materials.

But in their report, the conferees prohibited the Energy Department from spending any of the money until 30 days after it had told the two Armed Services committees how the money would be used.

Conferees also approved $30 million — $8.2 million more than the administration request — for research on a technique to separate weapons-grade plutonium from spent nuclear fuel. The technique was called laser isotope separation. The process also could be used to clean up nuclear wastes and to produce special isotopes for other purposes.

Nuclear Cleanup

In their report, the conferees said they were cutting the administration request for funds to decontaminate some 500 sites formerly used for mining or processing nuclear materials because the Energy Department and other agencies had not adequately explained the costs and benefits of a massive cleanup. "It is not clear whether the many hundreds of millions of dollars planned to be expended for cleanup of those sites [will] provide any actual health benefits to the public and whether the expense involved in cleanup is justified," conferees said.

Authorizations, DOE Nuclear Weapons Programs

HR 3413 made the following authorizations for Energy Department defense programs in fiscal year 1982:

	Reagan Request	House Amount	Senate Amount	Final Authorization
Naval Reactors	$ 326,500,000	$ 314,500,000	$ 326,500,000	$ 326,500,000
Inertial Confinement Fusion	106,000,000	167,600,000	142,300,000	142,300,000
Weapons Activities	2,964,200,000	2,945,250,000	2,976,400,000	2,958,200,000
Verification Technology	50,000,000	50,000,000	51,500,000	51,500,000
Nuclear Materials Production	1,108,400,000	1,137,800,000	1,185,800,000	1,157,800,000
By-products Management	369,700,000	384,800,000	411,000,000	414,800,000
Security and Safeguards	71,600,000	64,600,000	71,600,000	69,100,000
Total	**$4,996,400,000**	**$5,064,550,000**	**$5,165,100,000**	**$5,120,200,000**

The administration requested $10.2 million for decontamination and decommissioning; conferees approved only $4 million.

Waste Isolation Pilot Plant

Conferees approved $38.6 million, the House amount, to continue the Waste Isolation Pilot Plant in New Mexico. The Reagan administration had requested $6.8 million. Conferees said the larger amount was needed "to assure that construction will proceed at a more satisfactory rate."

The plant, called WIPP, was designed as a demonstration project to dispose of nuclear wastes produced by defense facilities. *(Background, 1979 Almanac p. 436)*

Other Provisions

HR 3413 also:

● Directed the secretary of energy to prepare regulations prohibiting the public dissemination of certain unclassified information concerning nuclear facilities, if the release of the information "could reasonably be expected to result in significant adverse effects" on the public health, safety or national defense by increasing the likelihood of theft, diversion or sabotage of nuclear material or facilities. Types of information to be withheld were: design of production facilities, security measures (including security plans, procedures and equipment), and the design of atomic weapons.

● Prohibited the use of funds authorized in the bill for preparation of environmental impact statements that were not required by law and that were not already under way, for any Energy Department defense facility.

● Required the secretary of energy to notify the House and Senate Armed Services committees before proceeding with any environmental impact statement concerning defense facilities of the Energy Department, if the statement would cost more than $250,000 to prepare. The secretary could not proceed with preparing the statement until 30 days after the notification to the committees, unless during that period he received written permission to do so from both committees.

● Required the president to submit to the Armed Services committees by June 30, 1983, a report setting forth his plans for the permanent disposal of nuclear wastes generated by defense facilities.

● Permitted persons who were authorized to carry firearms under the Atomic Energy Act of 1954 to make arrests while carrying out their official duties.

House Committee Action

Reagan's budget for military nuclear programs was the first one in years to meet with the overall approval of the House Armed Services Committee.

During President Carter's administration, the panel regularly charged that the military nuclear budget was too low. It warned the Energy Department's weapons development and production complex was deteriorating to a point where it would be unable to produce new weapons planned for deployment in the mid-1980s. *(1980 Almanac p. 85)*

But in its report on the fiscal 1982 defense nuclear authorization bill the committee called Reagan's request "more in line with committee expectations."

As reported May 15 by the House Armed Services Committee (H Rept 97-45), HR 3413 authorized $5.06 billion for Energy Department military nuclear programs. This was $68.15 million more than the request.

Fusion Research

For fiscal 1982, the Reagan administration requested $106 million to operate the various intertial confinement fusion projects, $34.6 million less than was provided in fiscal 1981 and $78.2 million less than the Energy Department requested from the Office of Management and Budget. Complaining that the administration had provided no rationale for the cut, the committee increased the fusion research accounts to $156.6 million: the amount appropriated in fiscal 1981 plus 11.5 percent to offset inflation.

Weapons Programs

The committee added only $4 million to the $2.348 billion requested to operate the weapons research and production complex. The funds were added to the $586.1 million requested for research and development which, in turn, was 17 percent more than the 1981 appropriation. Much of the increase was earmarked to enlarge the staffs of the nuclear weapons laboratories at Los Alamos and Albuquerque, N.M., and Livermore, Calif.

The committee approved the $369 million request for weapons testing, saying it would provide a "reasonable number" of tests in addition to those funded in fiscal 1981. The 1982 amount was an increase of 22 percent.

Only $30 million — half the request — was approved to begin building a manufacturing plant for MX missile warheads. The panel said it would be years before any warheads were produced and restraint in funding the plant would ease the problem of paying for other projects.

Reagan requested $418.6 million for construction of plants to produce nuclear material for warheads. Among other projects, this would prepare four reactors for reactivation or modification to produce weapons-grade material. The panel added $21.2 million to the request.

No weapons-grade material had been produced since 1964. (The material in obsolete warheads had been salvaged and recycled into newer weapons). But the committee insisted that additional production would be needed by the mid-1980s to equip planned new weapons.

The committee added a provision barring the use of authorized funds to prepare an environmental impact statement (EIS) for any Energy Department weapons facility unless required by law. The panel said the department had spent millions of dollars — and opened its program to court-imposed delays — by preparing EISs for existing facilities even though they were not required by the 1969 National Environmental Policy Act (NEPA).

Though it did not so recommend in its report, the committee argued that "a very good case" existed for exempting defense facilities from NEPA requirements and protecting environmental concerns by other procedures. Full-blown EISs for defense facilities would risk classified information and would provide saboteurs with a handbook for disruption, the committee warned.

Waste, Byproducts Management

The committee insisted that some byproducts of defense nuclear materials plants could be salvaged in economically usable amounts. It added $5 million for a program to test ways to extract those byproducts.

The panel also added $5 million to the $12.3 million requested for operation and construction of the Waste Isolation Pilot Plant (WIPP) intended to demonstrate safe disposal techniques using waste products from the defense nuclear materials complex.

Charging that current safety standards were unnecessarily strict, the committee approved $4 million of the $10.2 million requested for decontamination and de-commissioning of defense nuclear sites.

"Even the resources of the federal government are not sufficient to correct every insult to the environment created in the past by mining, milling, lumbering, farming and the full range of human economic activities," the committee said. Proposed federal remedial action should be assessed in terms of the risk of the status quo compared with the cost, benefit and risk of the proposed remedy, the committee continued. But the assessment frequently had been based on "emotionalism," it said.

House Floor Action

As it had done several times in the previous four years, the House June 11 voted overwhelmingly for production of the so-called "neutron bomb."

But during debate on the issue, Rep. Samuel S. Stratton, D-N.Y., suggested that deployment of the radiation warheads in Western Europe was stymied for the time being by political opposition in potential host countries. Stratton was a leading proponent of the new weapon.

The radiation warheads were considered during House debate on HR 3413, the fiscal 1982 authorization for military programs of the Energy Department. The bill, which was passed by voice vote, authorized $5.06 billion for nuclear weapons research and production and for the development of naval power reactors.

Radiation Weapons

By a vote of 88-293, the House rejected an amendment by Ted Weiss, D-N.Y., to bar use of any authorized funds for the development or production of high radiation weapons. *(Vote 66, p. 32-H)*

In April 1978, President Carter deferred indefinitely a decision to deploy the new radiation warheads for short-range Lance missiles and 8-inch artillery pieces in Europe. He ordered the design of new nuclear warheads for the weapons, which could quickly be converted to radiation weapons after they had been deployed.

But in 1980, the Senate Armed Services Committee complained that it would take months or years to carry out the conversion unless the high-radiation components were manufactured and stockpiled. The fiscal 1981 authorization bill for Energy Department military programs ordered that production of the components begin immediately. *(1980 Almanac p. 83)*

The fiscal 1982 Energy Department weapons bill contained a secret amount of money to manufacture the high-radiation components.

Presenting his amendment June 11, Weiss argued that the new weapons would increase the risk of nuclear war by fostering the assumption that nuclear weapons could be used in limited scenarios. "The likelihood is," Weiss warned, "that if we were to use the neutron bomb, the Russians would retaliate with full-scale tactical nuclear weapons of larger size . . . [leading to] escalation to the full use of large-scale nuclear weapons on both sides."

Supporting Weiss, John F. Seiberling, D-Ohio, warned that deployment of the radiation weapons could inflame opponents of nuclear weapons in Western Europe, thus endangering the already shaky support of some countries for a plan to deploy nuclear missiles that could hit Soviet targets from European launch sites.

Stratton warned that if the radiation weapons were not deployed, Soviet tank attacks could be met only by the more destructive U.S. nuclear arms now deployed in Europe.

But Stratton also agreed with Seiberling's warning: "The Soviet propaganda campaign has done its job. . . . It is perfectly clear that if the nuclear weapons issue is raised in Europe, we will never even get the modernized [long-range] nuclear force implanted in our NATO position. . . . So for good or evil, the enhanced radiation weapon is a long way from any kind of deployment."

Other Amendments

By a vote of 233-122, the House adopted an amendment by Jack Hightower, D-Texas, barring the use of authorized funds to prepare any environmental impact statement (EIS) not required by law except for EISs already in preparation. *(Vote 67, p. 32-H)*

The Armed Services Committee had included a provision aimed at stopping an EIS for a proposed expansion of the Pantex nuclear weapons plant in Hightower's district. The Energy Department had agreed to prepare the statement as part of an out-of-court settlement to prevent a

lawsuit against the project. The committee said preparation of the statement could delay expansion of the plant.

But Hightower said the EIS should be completed, because breaching the out-of-court settlement could result in an even longer delay.

The House also adopted by voice vote an amendment by Patricia Schroeder, D-Colo., to prevent the Energy Department from replacing federal security guards with a commercial security service at the Los Alamos, N.M., national weapons laboratory.

Senate Committee Action

Reagan's 25 percent increase in the budget for nuclear weapons won applause from the Senate Armed Services Committee, which often had warned that Carter's weapons budgets would not buy enough warheads to equip new Pentagon missiles.

"For the first time in several years, the committee feels comfortable that the requested amount for these defense programs is more nearly at the level that it should be," the panel said in its report (S Rept 97-173) on S 1549, the fiscal 1982 nuclear weapons authorization bill.

Reagan's $5 billion request was more than $1 billion above the amount authorized in fiscal 1981 for defense nuclear programs. The Senate panel recommended a further increase of $168.7 million, for a total authorization of $5.165 billion in S 1549.

Senate Armed Services reported its bill July 30.

The Senate committee's applause for Reagan's fiscal 1982 request was coupled with a warning that "significant real increases" would be needed in future budgets to pay for planned new weapons and for modernization of weapons already in the U.S. stockpile.

Some of the modernizations were designed to render the warheads harmless in case they were seized by terrorists; others were intended to reduce the risk that a fire or other disaster would set off their high explosive "triggers," thus scattering radioactive material. Both features were designed into newer U.S. warheads.

Radiation Weapons. The funds authorized by the bill included an undisclosed amount to continue production of the so-called "neutron bomb" — a high-radiation warhead for Lance missiles and 155mm artillery shells. The administration decided Aug. 6 to begin manufacturing the weapons and stockpiling them in the United States. In case war threatened, they would be flown to Europe to be used against massed Soviet tank forces.

Nuclear Material Production. The Senate panel reiterated its long-held concern that the 1990s might bring a shortage in the Energy Department's production of so-called "special nuclear material." This was the enriched uranium and plutonium used to build nuclear explosives.

The administration was proceeding with plans backed by the two Armed Services committees to resume production of the material at one reactor and to convert two others for production of weapons-grade material.

But the Senate committee warned that at least one new production reactor would be needed by 1990, because of the age of the existing production reactors. The panel added to the bill $40 million for design of a new reactor and told the Energy Department to decide its design and location in fiscal 1982.

The committee also urged accelerated research on the use of lasers to extract weapons-grade material from used

fuel from nuclear power reactors. It added $21.2 million to complete a laboratory to test the laser technique.

Waste Disposal. The panel added $30 million to the $8.6 million requested to continue construction of the Waste Isolation Pilot Plant (WIPP) in New Mexico. In accordance with provisions Congress added to the fiscal 1981 nuclear weapons bill, the plant was be used to demonstrate the long-term storage only of nuclear waste resulting from defense programs and would not require an Energy Department license.

Environmental Impact. "The department is spending too much money in writing unnecessary Environmental Impact Statements (EIS)," the committee said. As an example, it cited an EIS under preparation for a project to modernize the Pantex weapons manufacturing plant.

The committee added to the bill a section expressing the sense of Congress that such statements should be prepared only for "exceptional federal actions ... that represent a significant departure from current operations and can be clearly shown, through the environmental assessment process, to have the potential to affect significantly the quality of the human environment."

The provision also would require 30 days' prior notification to the congressional Armed Services committees of the Energy Department's intent in the future to prepare any EIS costing more than $500,000.

The House Armed Services Committee had added to its bill a provision barring the preparation of an EIS for the Pantex project, but it was dropped by the House.

Senate Floor Action

The Senate passed its version of the bill (S 1549) Nov. 3 by voice vote, after adding three amendments. The Senate did not change the $5.165 billion authorization approved by its Armed Services Committee.

Military Waste

The Senate adopted an amendment by Henry M. Jackson, D-Wash., that sought to head off a dispute concerning jurisdiction over nuclear waste generated by military production plants.

Congress was considering legislation to deal with the growing inventory of nuclear waste. Jackson and others insisted that such legislation not apply to the military. Jackson's amendment required the president to come up with a plan for dealing with military waste by Jan. 31, 1983.

The report was to include a state-by-state breakdown of plans to store the waste and how much that would cost for the next five years.

Secret Information

By voice vote, the Senate adopted an amendment by John W. Warner, R-Va., and Robert T. Stafford, R-Vt., to allow the Energy Department to withhold unclassified information about nuclear weapons programs.

The types of unclassified information that could be withheld from public scrutiny under the amendment included: the design of nuclear weapons production facilities, plans for protection of those facilities, and the design of atomic weapons.

In the past, the Energy Department had released substantial amounts of information about the nuclear weapons program through environmental impact statements and other reports.

Environmental Statements

In order to head off the preparation of an environmental impact statement on the modernization of the Pantex nuclear weapons plant in Amarillo, Texas, the committee had included a provision expressing the sense of Congress that such a statement was not required by the National Environmental Policy Act (NEPA) of 1969.

Stafford offered, and the Senate adopted by voice vote, an amendment directly prohibiting the Energy Department from using authorized funds to prepare environmental impact statements for defense facilities unless the report was already under way or was required by law.

Stafford, chairman of the Senate Environment Committee, said his amendment was aimed at eliminating any possibility that the defense bill would set a new standard under NEPA for environmental impact statements.

Stafford's amendment also gave the congressional Armed Services committees the right to delay new environmental impact statements for defense plants if preparing the statement would cost more than $500,000. Under the amendment, the energy secretary could not proceed with such a statement until 30 days after notifying the committees of his intention to prepare the statement, unless in the interim he received written concurrence from both the House and Senate committees.   ■

Military Construction

Conferees on the $6.55 billion military construction authorization bill (HR 3455 — PL 97-99) renewed their annual demands that other NATO allies and Japan pay for a larger share of U.S. efforts to defend their interests in Western Europe and in the oil-rich Persian Gulf.

Both houses adopted the conference report on the bill by voice vote Dec. 8, clearing the bill for the president.

The conferees issued an unusually blunt warning on the politics of "burden-sharing," as the issue has come to be known. Since Washington was paying the total cost of the so-called Rapid Deployment Force (RDF), designed to intervene in the Persian Gulf, the conferees argued it was imperative that other NATO members paid some of the costs of certain U.S. facilities in Europe.

"Otherwise," the conferees said, "the American people may force the Congress to consider reductions in U.S. defense commitments and such reductions could begin with a reduction in the number of U.S. military personnel deployed in Europe."

House Committee Action

Nearly all of President Reagan's $7 billion military construction budget was approved by the House Armed Services Committee in its version of the fiscal 1982 military construction authorization bill.

The committee insisted on congressional approval of any change President Reagan made in the MX mobile missile system recommended by President Carter. It approved without major change projects to make it easier to deploy U.S. troops to trouble spots in the Persian Gulf.

The committee cut $50.3 million from the $7.028 billion request, approving $6.978 billion. The report (H Rept 97-44) was filed May 15.

MX Construction

The committee approved all but $9.5 million of the $366 million request for construction related to the MX intercontinental missile. But the panel restricted use of the funds until the president decided which specific method to use for protecting the missiles against Soviet attack. The committee took similar action on the 1982 Defense Department authorization bill (HR 3519).

The Carter administration had recommended, and senior military officers still preferred, a design called Multiple Protective Structures (MPS) in which 200 MX missiles would be shuttled among 4,600 covered launch sites in Nevada and Utah. The plan had drawn intense opposition, especially in those two states, and was under review by a blue-ribbon panel appointed by Defense Secretary Caspar W. Weinberger. Reagan later scrapped the MPS plan, and decided instead to temporarily base MX missiles in existing silos pending studies on a permanent basing system.

The House committee decided to bar use of any MX funds for a basing system other than MPS unless the president recommended it and Congress approved his recommendation within 60 days.

The funds approved would be used for: maintenance and overhaul facilities for any of several MX versions ($332.6 million); two test launchers to be built at Vandenberg Air Force Base, Calif. ($12.9 million); and a headquarters building for the project ($11 million).

Denied was a request for $9.5 million to begin buying land for the MX project. Most of the land to be used in the MPS version was federally owned.

RDF, Indian Ocean

The committee did not approve $106.57 million of the administration's request ($531.19 million) for construction related to the Rapid Deployment Force (RDF). But the cuts reflected relatively minor technical disagreements in the timing of the projects rather than any challenge to the RDF plan.

RDF was the umbrella concept under which the Pentagon was trying to increase its capacity to send U.S. forces to distant areas where there were no existing U.S. bases or units. Initial planning for the RDF emphasized deployments to the Persian Gulf or nearby territory on the rim of the Indian Ocean.

Approved as requested were funds to enlarge the U.S. base on the island of Diego Garcia in the Indian Ocean ($237.74 million), and to build facilities in Oman ($78.48 million) and Somalia ($24 million), where supplies and equipment could be stored for U.S. forces. The Oman and Somalia facilities would remain under local sovereignty but would be available to U.S. units under agreements negotiated with those countries.

A similar agreement had been negotiated for naval facilities in Kenya, but the committee approved only $4 million of the $26 million requested for the project, saying that other funds were available to the Pentagon to make up the difference.

The committee cut to $80.4 million the $106.4 million requested for a similar storage facility at Ras Banas, Egypt, on the Red Sea coast. The cut was made because plans for the Air Force part of the facility were not final.

Noting that negotiations with Portugal for access rights still were in progress, the committee denied the $49.57 million requested for RDF facilities at the huge Lajes airfield in the Azores Islands. And the panel refused

Military Construction Authorizations, Fiscal 1982

HR 3455 made the following authorizations for military construction programs in fiscal 1982 (*in thousands of dollars*):

	March Reagan Request	Revised Reagan Request	House- Passed Authorization	Senate- Passed Authorization	Final Authorization
Army	$ 849,616	$ 809,446	$ 878,606	$ 753,556	$ 804,720
Navy	1,175,283	1,175,283	1,217,363	1,240,033	1,240,033
Air Force	1,680,955	1,301,955	1,512,893	1,258,371	1,258,506
Defense Agencies	326,100	326,100	282,100	311,815	282,815
NATO Infrastructure	425,000	425,000	425,000	345,000	345,000
Reserve and National Guard	203,000	203,000	291,702	280,000	280,000
Family Housing	2,368,888	2,368,888	2,379,833	2,300,628	2,335,736
Total	**$7,028,842**	**$6,609,672**	**$6,987,497**	**$6,489,403**	**$6,546,810**

$9 million requested for an RDF headquarters near Tampa, Fla., where the RDF staff was located. The committee cited the administration's plan to eventually locate the RDF staff somewhere near the Indian Ocean.

European Defense

The committee approved more than $1 billion requested for construction projects in Europe and another $425 million for the U.S. share of NATO's common pool for defense construction (called the Infrastructure).

The long-simmering congressional suspicion that other NATO members were shirking their fair share of the defense burden was reflected in two parts of the Armed Services Committee report. The panel approved only $13.1 million of an Air Force request for $37.1 million to equip airfields owned by other NATO members which would house reinforcement airplanes flown to Europe from the United States in case of a crisis. According to the committee, the denied funds were for projects that should have been paid for by the alliance-wide Infrastructure.

The panel approved $18 million requested for the first step in a $400 million Master Restationing Plan to shift Army units in West Germany closer to the East German border. The committee said that the West German government, whose territory would be better protected after the move, should pay some of the cost. But it added that, pending agreement with the German government, U.S. funding was needed to provide basic amenities for U.S. troops.

Guard, Reserves

The committee increased by 43.7 percent the administration request for facilities used by the National Guard and the reserve components of the armed services. Congressional defense panels frequently charged the Pentagon with underfunding those units.

The committee recommendation was for $291.7 million, with the added funds to be used for 64 projects.

Family Housing

The committee added $8.8 million for 200 prefabricated family houses at Fort Irwin, Calif. Alarmed at building costs averaging $78,000 for site-built houses, the com-

mittee urged the Pentagon to experiment with prefabricated housing as a cheaper alternative.

House Floor Action

The House June 4 reiterated its 1980 approval of a factory to build a new type of lethal chemical nerve gas weapon, called binary munitions.

By a vote of 135-220 it rejected an amendment to the bill that would have rescinded a fiscal 1981 appropriation of $3.15 million to build the binary plant. David E. Bonior, D-Mich., offered the amendment. *(Vote 56, p. 30-H)*

There had been no roll-call vote in the House last year on the fiscal 1981 appropriation, but in September 1980 the House supported a related appropriation for binary manufacturing equipment by a slightly larger margin (125-276). *(Background, 1980 Almanac pp. 191, 80)*

Later the same day, the House passed the military construction bill, authorizing $6.98 billion for military construction projects. The vote was 311-36. *(Vote 57, p. 30-H)*

Nerve Gas

Binary munitions were artillery shells containing two chemicals that produced a lethal nerve gas when mixed. The Army argued that the binary shells would be safer for U.S. troops to handle than current nerve gas weapons, since the chemicals would mix only when the shells were fired.

Bonior and his allies argued that the weapons would kill only civilians, since combat troops were equipped with protective clothing. A more militarily effective course would be to spend the money on chemical protective equipment for U.S. troops, they said.

Several members also argued that moving toward binary production would derail U.S.-Soviet chemical arms control negotiations and would be perceived as a commitment to building an especially barbarous type of weapon.

Binary supporters, including G. William Whitehurst, R-Va., countered that Soviet use of its large chemical arsenal would be deterred only by a U.S. ability to retaliate in kind. Troops wearing bulky, chemical protective clothing would be handicapped on the battlefield, they said. They said only the prospect of U.S. binary production would induce Moscow to seek a chemical weapons treaty.

MX Basing

By voice vote, the House adopted an amendment by Paul Simon, D-Ill., giving Congress 60 days to block by concurrent resolution President Reagan's choice of a basing technique for the MX mobile intercontinental missile. A blue-ribbon committee was reviewing alternatives to the Multiple Protective Structure (MPS) basing selected by Carter.

HR 3455 authorized $356.5 million for MX-related construction.

In its version of the bill, the Armed Services Committee had barred use of any funds for an MX basing method other than MPS, unless Reagan recommended it and Congress approved by concurrent resolution.

Colorado Training Land. After nearly 90 minutes of heated debate, the House rejected, 175-209, an amendment by Ray Kogovsek, D-Colo., that would have deleted $30 million to begin buying 244,000 acres of grazing land in southeast Colorado. *(Vote 55, p. 30-H)*

The Army wanted the land to run large-scale combat maneuvers for the 4th Division which was stationed at Fort Carson, about 150 miles northwest of the proposed training area. Land closer to Fort Carson was deemed too expensive.

Kogovsek and his allies argued that the Army's training needs could be met at an existing base, suggesting Fort Bliss, Texas, or Fort Irwin, Calif. Opponents, led by Ken Kramer, R-Colo., in whose district Fort Carson was located, countered that it would cost too much to move troops to those more distant sites for routine training.

Other Amendments. The House also approved by voice vote the following amendments:

● By C.W. Bill Young, R-Fla., restoring $9 million to construct a headquarters for the Rapid Deployment Force at MacDill Air Force Base in Tampa, Fla., near Young's district. The amount had been requested by the administration but was dropped in committee because the Pentagon planned to locate the headquarters near the Persian Gulf.

● By Thomas F. Hartnett, R-S.C., to prevent the Army from closing any Corps of Engineers district office near a harbor with major military installations. The amendment was intended to protect the corps' office in Charleston, S.C., in Hartnett's district.

● By Glenn M. Anderson, D-Calif., authorizing an exchange of land between the Army and the city of Long Beach, Calif.

Family Housing. As passed by the House, the bill included $8.8 million added in committee to place 200 units of manufactured housing at Fort Irwin, Calif. In contrast to prefabricated houses, which were assembled at the house site, manufactured houses consisted of whole houses (or parts of houses) that were trucked to the house site like very large mobile homes.

Senate Committee Action

Insisting that U.S. European allies pay more of the cost of NATO's defense, the Senate Armed Services Committee cut the Pentagon's European construction budget for the fourth consecutive year.

In the $7 billion bill (S 1408), the panel deleted $42 million for Army and Air Force projects intended to improve the combat readiness of U.S. units. The panel endorsed the projects on their merits, but insisted that the allies should pay at least a substantial part of the cost.

The size of the reduction was relatively small only because the Pentagon had not asked for many projects of the type that NATO had funded in the past. Since 1978, the congressional defense committees had driven home the message that they would not shrink from slashing much larger amounts.

The committee did approve more than $1.1 billion for European construction, of which $425 million was the annual U.S. contribution to the NATO Infrastructure fund — the alliance's kitty for construction with common benefits.

As reported by the Senate Armed Services Committee June 22 (S Rept 97-141), the bill authorized $7.028 billion for military construction projects, $910 million less than the administration request.

European Construction

The panel denied $24 million of the $37 million requested for building supply dumps and aircraft parking ramps at European-owned air bases that would be used by U.S. fighters flown to Europe as reinforcements in time of war. Construction costs would average $5 million at each of these so-called "co-located operating bases."

The Air Force conceded that the $24 million was earmarked for facilities eligible for NATO Infrastructure funding. But it maintained that the projects could not await alliance funding, which likely would not be available until 1985. U.S. funds spent on the project could be recouped from the infrastructure later. That argument was not good enough for the committee, which had insisted that it would support such U.S. "pre-financing" only in rare instances.

Also denied was $18 million for the first step in a massive plan to move Army units in West Germany to new bases closer to the East German border. Many U.S. bases were far behind the units' assigned defensive positions. Moreover, many of the barracks and maintenance buildings were antiquated — some dating from the 19th century.

In November 1980, Washington formally asked West Germany to pay for several specific costs of U.S. forces stationed in Germany, including the first phase of the Army's so-called "master re-stationing plan (MRP)," which was estimated to cost $400 million over several years.

The Senate committee said it would provide no U.S. funds for any MRP projects, at least until the Bonn government formally rejected the U.S. request.

The panel approved the $69 million requested for facilities in Italy and the United Kingdom to base ground-launched cruise missiles that could reach Soviet targets. But it complained that the plan to build a new $300 million base in Italy just for the new missiles seemed extravagant, given the number of existing military facilities in Italy. While approving the $57 million request for the Italian base, the committee ordered the Pentagon to look for a cheaper solution before proceeding with the new base.

MX, Trident Bases

The committee approved the request for $366 million to begin construction of the MX missile shuttle system recommended by President Carter and favored by the Air Force.

The committee bill provided that no MX construction funds would be available for base construction until 60 days after the president chose a basing system for MX.

Also authorized was $65 million requested for the first installment of an estimated $1.25 billion to build a base at

King's Bay, Ga., for Trident missile-launching submarines.

The bill authorized the secretary of defense to request appropriations to ease the impact on isolated and rural economies of the MX and Trident bases. Such impact aid had been provided to areas affected by construction of the Safeguard anti-ballistic missile system in North Dakota and the Trident submarine base at Bangor, Wash.

Rapid Deployment

The committee approved $500.2 million of the $531.2 million request to support the Rapid Deployment Force. The largest single slice of the request, $237.7 million, was for air and naval facilities on the British-owned island of Diego Garcia in the Indian Ocean.

Funds also were approved to continue construction of military facilities in Oman, Kenya, Somalia and the Azores Islands. The committee's only change was a reduction to $4 million, from the $26 million request, for naval facilities in Kenya; the committee said the rest was covered by existing authorization.

The committee approved the request for $106.4 million to begin work on facilities at Ras Banas, Egypt, on the coast of the Red Sea, that could house an Army brigade and Air Force units.

Davis-Bacon

S 1408 included a provision exempting military construction projects from the so-called Davis-Bacon Act. The 1931 act required contractors to pay locally prevailing wages on federally funded construction. Business allies in Congress condemned the act as inflationary, arguing that it artificially inflated construction wages, partly by imposing union-scale wages in areas that are not heavily unionized. But organized labor rejected those arguments and fiercely defended Davis-Bacon.

The committee cited estimated savings of 10 percent from such a move.

But in additional views appended to the report, Democrats Henry M. Jackson, Wash., Howard W. Cannon, Nev., Gary Hart, Colo., and Carl Levin, Mich., challenged the savings estimate as unproven. An underpaid work force would be less skilled, thus increasing the risk of shoddy construction and delays in military projects, they warned.

Senate Floor Action

Organized labor won the most recent round of a long-running dispute with congressional conservatives Nov. 5 when the Senate voted against exempting military construction projects from requirements of the Davis-Bacon Act.

The Pentagon exemption was included in the Senate Armed Services Committee's version of the $6.5 billion military construction authorization bill for fiscal 1982 (S 1408). But the Reagan administration did not support the move, and on Nov. 5, the Senate voted 55-42 to adopt an amendment by Henry M. Jackson, D-Wash., deleting the waiver from the bill. *(Vote 354, p. 60-S)*

Before passing the bill, the Senate adopted by voice vote an Armed Services Committee amendment reducing the authorization by $546.6 million below the amount reported by the panel on June 22.

Basically, the amendment incorporated budget reductions announced in September by President Reagan. The largest single change was elimination of all $366 million that had been earmarked for construction associated with the multiple launch-site version of the MX intercontinental missile, favored by the Air Force and recommended by the Carter administration. On Oct. 2, Reagan rejected that basing method.

Two other large reductions were a $155.8 million cut in overseas construction costs due to a strengthening of the dollar in international money markets and a $30.7 million cut for projects related to the Roland anti-aircraft missile, which Reagan had canceled in September.

Passage. After completing work on amendments to S 1408, the Senate substituted the text of that bill for the text of the House-passed version (HR 3455) and passed the latter bill by a vote of 95-2. *(Vote 355, p. 60-S)*

Davis-Bacon Debate

The fight over the Davis-Bacon waiver essentially was a reprise of the battle in 1979, when Senate Armed Services added a similar provision to the fiscal 1980 military construction bill (S 1319). The bill subsequently was referred to the Labor and Human Resources Committee, which recommended deletion of the waiver, and the Senate did so in a series of roll-call votes. *(1979 Almanac, p. 307)*

During the debate on S 1408, supporters maintained that the waiver would save more than $200 million in the annual military construction budget. Application of Davis-Bacon directly inflated construction costs by driving wages up to union levels, they argued. This also increased costs indirectly by making it impossible for small businesses, which could not pay union wages, to vie for federal contracts, thus reducing the competitive pressure on other contractors to hold down costs.

Jackson and his allies retorted that the original purpose of Davis-Bacon remained valid: to keep construction wages in a region relatively stable when they might otherwise be disrupted by a federal project's sudden creation of many new jobs. Administrative changes in the law's application, which were under review by the administration, would relieve the cause of some objections to Davis-Bacon, they said. Among the changes were a reduction in contractors' payroll reporting requirements and a prohibition on using wage rates from a metropolitan area to determine the "prevailing wage" in a rural area.

Northern Democrats supported the Jackson amendment 30-1, while Southern Democrats split 9-6 in favor of the amendment.

Sixteen Republicans, most of them from the party's moderate-to-liberal wing, supported Jackson. Majority Leader Howard H. Baker Jr., R-Tenn., said his vote for Jackson's amendment was based on the administration's opposition to the committee move to exempt defense from Davis-Bacon.

One Davis-Bacon opponent who voted with Jackson was James A. McClure, R-Idaho, chairman of the Energy and Natural Resources Committee. An aide said McClure believed that partial repeal of Davis-Bacon would not succeed in 1981 and would only drive organized labor to greater efforts to maintain it.

Other Amendments

The Senate adopted the following amendments by voice vote:

● By Jackson, permitting certain military personnel, military dependents and military retirees to continue using certain Public Health Service hospitals for at least three years after the facilities were transferred to the control of other public agencies or private, non-profit groups;

● By Strom Thurmond, R-S.C., to delete $14,910,000 for military family housing at a naval air base in Willow Grove, Pa., and to add $14,000,000 for construction at the Philadelphia Navy Yard;

● By Lawton Chiles, D-Fla., to add $9 million for construction of a Rapid Deployment Force headquarters at MacDill Air Force Base in Tampa, Fla.;

● By Sam Nunn, D-Ga., to entitle each state containing a military base from which timber was sold to 25 percent of the net proceeds of the sale, after the base had deducted the cost of managing its timber resources. The state share would be earmarked for roads and schools in the county or counties containing the base.

Conference Report

As reported Dec. 7 (H Rept 97-362), HR 3455 authorized $6,546,810,000 for military construction programs in fiscal 1982. This was $62.9 million less than the Reagan budget as revised in October.

The total authorization contained in the conference report was much closer to the Senate-passed total of $6.49 billion than to the $6.99 billion mark passed by the House in June, but that comparison was misleading. At the time the House acted on HR 3455, Reagan's defense construction budget request was $7.03 billion.

Construction in Europe

The conferees approved $14.5 million of an $18 million request to build maintenance facilities and utilities at Vilseck in West Germany as the first step in the Army's so-called Master Restationing Plan (MRP). The reduction was due solely to an upward re-valuation of the dollar since the budget was formulated.

Under the MRP, Army units in Germany were to be moved over the next several years from antiquated facilities distant from the country's eastern frontier to new posts much closer to the units' planned defensive positions.

The Senate version of the bill denied any U.S. funds for MRP, arguing that West Germany should pay for it since it would receive not only a better defense but also the valuable property being vacated by U.S. units.

The conferees made expenditure of the $14.5 million at Vilseck contingent on agreement by West Germany "to designate a responsible negotiator and start negotiations in good faith toward [West German] funding participation."

The project was approved in HR 3455 only because it was compatible with U.S. plans to deliver new weapons to its forces in Europe, the conferees emphasized. "If Vilseck were suitable only for MRP, the request would not have been approved in the absence of any agreement with the [West Germans] that they would fund the MRP."

The conferees also denied $6.37 million that was requested and approved by the House for supply facilities at air bases in Europe that would be "hardened" against aerial attack. If the program were carried out at all U.S. air bases in Europe, the conferees said, it would be extremely costly. It should be funded instead through the NATO Infrastructure — the alliance's kitty for construction of commonly used or mutually beneficial defense projects.

Both houses previously had cut $24 million from a $37 million request for ammunition and fuel dumps and aircraft parking ramps at European-owned air bases that would be used by U.S. fighters flown to Europe as reinforcements in time of war.

The $24 million was earmarked for facilities eligible for Infrastructure funding, but the Air Force wanted to build them faster than NATO funds would be available.

For the annual U.S. contribution to the Infrastructure, the conferees approved $345 million. The budget requested $425 million for the U.S. contribution, but the conferees said that an upward re-valuation of the dollar in the meantime meant that U.S. commitments could be met with the lower amount.

Rapid Deployment Force

The conferees approved all but $34 million of the $531.2 million requested for projects related to the RDF or other U.S. deployments in the Persian Gulf region.

The House had denied $49.57 million requested for projects at Lajes Air Force Base in the Portuguese-owned Azores Islands because negotiations with Portugal had not yet settled U.S. rights to the field as a staging point for planes flying from the United States to the Middle East.

The conferees approved all but $3 million of the Lajes request, on condition that a formal agreement establishing U.S. rights to use the base be signed with Portugal. The president could waive that condition if he certified to Congress that so doing was in the U.S. security interest.

The House also had approved only $44.4 million of a $70.4 million Air Force request for construction at Ras Banas on Egypt's Red Sea coast, arguing that Air Force plans for the base were not yet firm. Concluding that Air Force plans for Ras Banas were settled, the conferees approved the full $70.4 million request.

Other Provisions

Since Reagan's decision on the MX intercontinental missile killed the planned mobile basing technique, the conferees dropped the $366 million budgeted for that purpose. Left in the bill was $11 million to purchase a county office complex near Norton Air Force Base in California as an MX project headquarters.

The conferees also approved $80 million requested to cover a cost-overrun at a huge wind tunnel to test jet engines being built at Tullahoma, Tenn. The project had been funded in 1976. *(1976 Almanac p. 311)*

The final bill retained a provision, sponsored in the House by Thomas F. Hartnett, R-S.C., aimed at preventing the Army from closing the Corps of Engineers district office in Charleston, S.C., in Hartnett's district. ∎

Theater Nuclear Forces

President Reagan sought Nov. 18 to shift the burden of world public opinion to the Soviet Union on the issues of U.S. and Soviet deployments of intermediate-range nuclear weapons in Europe and on arms control generally.

In a speech to the National Press Club, Reagan offered to cancel controversial plans to deploy U.S. intermediate-range cruise and Pershing II nuclear missiles in Western Europe if the Soviets would dismantle medium- and intermediate-range missiles they already had aimed at Europe.

The Soviet missiles were armed with an estimated 1,100 nuclear warheads. The United States, under a plan endorsed in December 1979 by the North Atlantic Treaty Organization, would deploy 572 single-warhead cruise and Pershing II missiles in Western Europe beginning in 1983.

Whether to proceed with deploying the U.S. missiles

was a burning issue in Europe, where an anti-nuclear movement had flared up in reaction to U.S. failure to ratify the SALT II arms control treaty and continuing uncertainty about U.S. nuclear policy.

Reagan said he had sent a letter to Soviet President Leonid Brezhnev making the so-called "zero option" proposal on theater nuclear forces (TNF) along with other arms control offers he discussed in his speech.

In his speech, Reagan said American negotiators at U.S.-Soviet TNF talks to begin Nov. 30 in Geneva would propose the zero option, which envisioned the Soviets removing new, multiple-warhead SS-20 and older, single-warhead SS-4 and SS-5 missiles from Soviet Europe.

"This would be an historic step," Reagan said. "With Soviet agreement, we could together substantially reduce the dread threat of nuclear war which hangs over the people of Europe. This, like the first step on the moon, would be a giant step for mankind." *(Speech text, p. 27-E)*

Reagan also proposed that the two nations open strategic arms talks "as soon as possible next year." He said the goal should be "truly substantial reductions in our strategic arsenals," as opposed to limits of the sort negotiated in the 1970s under the two SALT (Strategic Arms Limitation Talks) treaties.

"To symbolize this fundamental change in direction," Reagan said, "we will call these negotiations START — Strategic Arms Reduction Talks."

The president said the United States also was willing to "achieve equality at lower levels of conventional forces in Europe." Further, Reagan said he was renewing a U.S. proposal for a conference to discuss disarmament and ways to verify compliance with any agreements so as to "reduce the risk of surprise attack and the chance of war arising out of uncertainty or miscalculation."

Tass, the official Soviet news agency, immediately rejected Reagan's zero option offer.

"The U.S. proposal is a mere propaganda ploy designed to stalemate the Geneva talks and present the American course of escalating the arms race and ensuring military superiority as a peace initiative...," Tass said.

Timing of Speech

Reagan's address was billed as his "first major foreign policy speech," and the timing and circumstances highlighted its role in an administration campaign to calm European fears of U.S. nuclear policy.

The speech was broadcast live on national television. The administration also took pains to get Reagan's message to its primary audience by having the U.S. International Communications Agency help pay for a live broadcast of the speech to Europe via the European Broadcasting Union.

The timing was significant in various ways. Reagan's address not only came just before the Nov. 30 U.S.-Soviet TNF talks in Geneva, but also after a series of large anti-nuclear demonstrations in Western Europe which had placed the administration on the defensive.

It also came just before a Nov. 22-23 visit by Brezhnev to West Germany.

Reagan's speech followed statements by himself and Haig that created a furor over U.S. policy and further fanned the fires of anti-nuclear protest in Europe.

First came Reagan's response when he was asked at an Oct. 17 meeting with newspaper editors if there could be a limited exchange of nuclear weapons between the United States and the Soviet Union.

"I don't honestly know," Reagan replied — but then went on to say: "I could see where you could have the exchange of tactical weapons against troops in the field without it bringing either one of the major powers to pushing the button."

The remark provoked a storm in Europe, where there was fear that the United States and the Soviet Union could use Europe as a nuclear battleground.

Haig, a former NATO commander, evoked further protest when he told the Senate Foreign Relations Committee on Nov. 4 that, in the event of a Soviet attack in Europe, NATO had a contingency plan to fire a nuclear weapon in an unpopulated area "for demonstrative purposes."

Defense Secretary Caspar W. Weinberger and others later contradicted Haig, saying such a plan had been discussed but was not part of NATO doctrine. Still, the incident added to uncertainty about Western nuclear policy.

In his speech, Reagan alluded to the anti-nuclear movement, saying that because Europe's "new generation" was not present at the founding of the Atlantic Alliance, "many of them do not fully understand its roots in defending freedom and rebuilding a war-torn continent."

Reagan said that "some young people question why we need weapons — particularly nuclear weapons — to deter war and assure peaceful development." He added: "I understand their concerns. Their questions deserve to be answered."

The speech came amid increasing congressional pressure for the administration to spell out its arms control policies. For example, Senate Minority Leader Robert C. Byrd, D-W.Va., complained as late as the day before the speech that the administration was contributing to unease in Europe on nuclear arms issues by not developing its own "concrete arms reduction proposals around which the alliance could rally."

Reaction

Congressional leaders said they were pleased with Reagan's speech. House Majority Leader Jim Wright, D-Texas, told the House that Reagan's proposal was "a useful and bold initiative which I think all of us in the House, Democrats and Republicans, do and should support."

Reagan's zero option proposal had been publicized before the speech and reaction in Europe was available even before Reagan spoke.

Chancellor Helmut Schmidt of West Germany took credit for persuading Reagan to offer the proposal. According to foreign dispatches, Schmidt said in a television interview Nov. 17 that Reagan's offer "is the negotiating position the Americans have adopted after long talks with us."

In other quarters the offer was denigrated as an effort to mollify European public opinion at little cost by offering a proposal the Soviets would reject.

President Carter also proposed in the first year of his administration that the United States and the Soviet Union negotiate dramatic nuclear arms reductions. The Soviets flatly rejected that proposal.

The British liberal *Guardian* newspaper headlined an article the day of Reagan's speech: "Reagan Zero Option Ploy to Calm Europe."

But a senior administration official who briefed reporters denied that Reagan's proposal was insincere. "Nothing could be further from the truth," the official said. "There's nothing new or tricky or complex about what's being put forward today."

The official added: "We consider it is now up to the

Soviets to respond to these proposals. If the Soviets have counter proposals that are meaningful and serious, they will be considered." However, he said, "We plan to hold to the schedule [for deploying the cruise and Pershing II missiles] unless there's a breakthrough and an agreement." ∎

Arms Agency Authority

Congress in 1981 failed to enact the biennial authorization for the Arms Control and Disarmament Agency (ACDA).

The House passed an ACDA bill (HR 3467) June 8 by voice vote, but the measure died in the Senate.

Under the House bill, the word "disarmament" would be striken from the agency's title. The House Foreign Affairs Committee had recommended the change to correct the "inaccurate and unfounded perception that the Agency was in some way involved in unilateral disarmament at the expense of our national security."

Committee Action

As reported by the House Foreign Affairs Committee May 15 (H Rept 97-55) the bill authorized $1.5 million more for ACDA operations in fiscal 1982 than President Reagan's request of $16,768 000.

The committee said the agency might need more money to begin negotiations on controlling strategic arms or European-based nuclear weapons. The panel also complained that the original request would reduce the agency's 175-member staff by six and would cut the amount spent for strategic arms-related research by $1.645 million.

HR 3467 also authorized the appropriation of any additional amount needed to pay for such costs as governmentwide pay raises and fluctuations in the value of the dollar against foreign currencies.

For operations of the arms control agency in fiscal 1983, the committee recommended authorization of $19,893,852 — the recommended fiscal 1982 level plus the estimated cost of 8.9 percent inflation.

The Reagan administration had requested an open-ended fiscal 1983 authorization for the agency, setting no ceiling on appropriations. ∎

Reagan Increases, Then Trims, Defense

Carrying out his campaign pledge to boost military spending, President Reagan in March added $32.6 billion to President Carter's proposed Defense Department budget for fiscal years 1981 and 1982.

Reagan's additions included $6.8 billion in new budget authority for a supplemental fiscal 1981 appropriation. On top of the $6.3 billion supplemental requested in January by Carter, that brought Reagan's total planned defense spending for fiscal 1981 to $178 billion.

For fiscal 1982, Reagan asked for $25.8 billion more in budget authority than Carter's $195.7 billion request.

Overall, Reagan proposed $1.638 trillion in defense budget authority for fiscal years 1981 through 1986, compared to Carter's proposed $1.447 trillion.

But six months later, bowing to the fiscal reality of ballooning budget deficits, Reagan agreed to trim his plans for increased defense spending.

On Sept. 11, Reagan announced that defense outlays would be cut by $13 billion over fiscal years 1982-84. Total budget authority — as reflected in defense appropriations bills — would have to be pared by upwards of $28 billion in order to achieve the outlay reductions.

Congress accepted most of Reagan's program: first, the increases proposed in March, then the trims proposed in September.

March Increases

Most of Reagan's $32.6 billion addition to the Defense Department budget for fiscal years 1981 and 1982 was earmarked for projects that the Carter Pentagon would have bought if it had been given enough money.

Some of Reagan's conservative advisers had called for much larger defense budgets to pay for a crash program of new nuclear weapons and expanded conventional forces. But, except for advocating a larger Navy and a new manned bomber, Reagan concentrated on modernizing the equipment and improving the combat-readiness of forces

the Pentagon already had.

Defense Secretary Caspar W. Weinberger told a Senate committee March 4: "The principal shortcoming of the defense budget we inherited is not so much that it omitted critical programs entirely, . . . but rather that [the Carter administration] failed to provide full funding for many programs it conceded were necessary but felt unable to afford."

Navy, Rapid Deployment

The only definite force enlargement budgeted by Reagan was for the Navy, which Reagan had pledged to increase from 450 to 600 ships. The new funds added $4.2 billion to Carter's shipbuilding budget, including the down payment on a $3.7 billion nuclear aircraft carrier and funds to refurbish a smaller carrier and two battleships in mothballs. This was a first step toward expanding the Navy to 15 big combat flotillas instead of the 12 planned by Carter.

Also added to Carter's request were:

● A cruiser carrying the Aegis anti-cruise-missile system to escort aircraft carriers ($840 million); Carter had requested two of these ships.

● A nuclear-powered submarine designed to hunt other submarines ($672 million); Carter had requested one submarine.

● Two frigates designed to escort convoys ($491 million); Carter had requested one ship.

About $2.5 billion was earmarked for the Rapid Deployment Force or for other programs to ease U.S. intervention in the Persian Gulf area. This nearly doubled the amounts requested by Carter in the 1981 supplemental and the 1982 budget for that purpose.

Reagan planned to accelerate the conversion of high-speed cargo ships to carry heavily armed U.S. troops from the United States to distant trouble spots. He also planned to begin work on an amphibious landing ship to let Marines shoot their way into an area against opposition.

Strategic Forces

Reagan asked for $2.5 billion to continue development of a new strategic bomber.

Absent from Reagan's budget were "quick fixes," such as a mobile version of the Minuteman missile, intended to improve the U.S. nuclear arsenal.

To further accelerate development of the LoADs anti-missile system that could defend the MX missile against Soviet attack, Reagan added $129 million.

But there was no dramatic acceleration of efforts to develop exotic anti-missile systems using satellites armed with lasers or charged-particle beam weapons. Both the mobile Minuteman missile and exotic missile defenses had been championed by conservative Reagan advisers.

Broad Increases

The rest of Reagan's increase would go to improve — but not enlarge — the arsenal he inherited from Carter:

● $2.3 billion in fiscal 1981 to cover "fact-of-life" increases in Pentagon operating costs due to inflation, pay raises and the unforeseen deployment of a large fleet to the Indian Ocean ($139 million); estimated fuel price increases accounted for $485 million of this amount.

● $700 million in fiscal 1981 and $2.8 billion in fiscal 1982 to improve military pay, benefits and living conditions; included was $2.3 billion for a 5.3 percent military pay raise to begin in July, 1981. That raise was in addition to the 11.4 percent pay hike enacted by Congress in 1980 and the 9.1 percent raise budgeted for fiscal 1982.

● $2.8 billion in fiscal 1981 and $8.7 billion in fiscal 1982 to improve the combat readiness of U.S. forces. The funds would pay for a higher tempo of training and equipment maintenance and for larger stocks of supplies, spare parts and ammunition. Included was $1.6 billion for spare parts and $543 million for major equipment overhauls. For an additional 2,500 air-to-air missiles, the program added $200 million.

● $2 billion in fiscal 1981 and $13.7 billion in fiscal 1982 to buy more warplanes, missiles, tanks and communications gear than Carter had requested in January; in nearly every case, the Reagan plan would accelerate purchases to which Carter theoretically was committed.

Equipment covered by the added funds included 108 more Air Force planes, 41 combat planes and 31 helicopters for the Navy and 24 more helicopters for the Army.

The Reagan plan also would increase production of Army combat vehicles, adding 151 M-1 tanks and 136 armored troop carriers.

Inflation, Outlay Questions

Within weeks of Reagan's budget request, leading defense specialists in Congress warned that future installments of the promised defense buildup could run into a political minefield of the administration's own making.

The critics warned that the cost of Reagan's defense program would substantially outstrip administration projections for fiscal years 1982-86. If the Reagan team followed past practice, it would force the Pentagon to absorb much of this unbudgeted cost by buying fewer weapons and by cutting back on scheduled maintenance and training.

Even if the administration tried to pay for the higher costs with higher than projected future budgets and with supplemental appropriations, political support for defense spending could be seriously eroded by a succession of "cost overruns," at a time when nearly all other federal programs faced stringent budget limits.

Two questions were at issue:

● How quickly would inflation boost the cost of defense items?

● How quickly would the amounts appropriated each year actually be spent as outlays?

Compared to the Congressional Budget Office (CBO), the administration made much more optimistic predictions on both questions: lower inflation, which was assumed to result from the psychological impact of Reagan's economic policy; and slower spending of defense appropriations, thus making it easier for the administration to project a balanced budget by fiscal 1984.

Weinberger and administration budget chief David A. Stockman insisted that CBO's inflation figures reflected traditional economic thought, ignoring the administration's radical changes in tax and budget policy. The outlay dispute merely reflected several technical disagreements, according to the Pentagon.

But aspects of the economic assumptions in Reagan's defense budget projections encountered strong opposition on four congressional committees, not all of it from Democratic members.

The House Armed Services Committee's report on the fiscal 1981 supplemental defense authorizations bill (HR 2614) included a strong attack on the administration's estimate of defense inflation. *(Supplemental, p. 202)*

The Senate Armed Services Committee accepted the administration's prediction that it would reduce inflation fast enough to cut $655 million from the cost of previously authorized programs this year. But Sam Nunn, D-Ga., and some other committee members deemed unrealistic the administration's projected $2.7 billion reduction in the cost of its fiscal 1982 defense program due to a lower rate of inflation.

In House Government Operations subcommittee hearings April 2 and April 7, Chairman Jack Brooks, D-Texas, and senior Republican Frank Horton, N.Y., were strongly critical of the administration's refusal to allow a higher inflation estimate for the defense budget.

The Budget committees were the arena for most discussion of the outlay issue. Nunn attacked the administration on this issue as well as the inflation question, but neither the Armed Services nor Appropriations committees dealt directly with outlays in their legislation.

The Republican-controlled Senate Budget Committee basically accepted the CBO's higher estimate of the defense spending rate. The House Budget Committee accepted the Reagan defense outlay figures, but under circumstances suggesting that most members of that committee, too, agreed with CBO.

September Cutbacks

As the nation's economic problems worsened — and as projections for the fiscal 1982 deficit soared — the Reagan administration came under increasing pressure to pare back the defense budget.

Defense spending was the subject of a fierce debate within the administration; in late August and early September Stockman argued for substantial defense cuts, ranging as high as $30 billion to $50 billion over the 1982-86 period. Weinberger fought all proposals for big cuts.

On Sept. 11, Reagan announced an agreement for $13 billion cuts in defense outlays over three years: $2 billion in fiscal 1982, $5 billion in 1983 and $6 billion in 1984.

The specific cuts were submitted to Congress Oct. 9.

Not even strategic nuclear weapons or the defense of the Persian Gulf were exempt from Reagan's search defense cuts.

The several hundred adjustments proposed by Reagan included some changes that appeared anomalous in the context of the president's overall defense policy stance. Among them:

● His new strategic program placed great stress on ensuring that nuclear weapons and their command systems could survive the opening hours of a war, but the administration cut several programs with a total cost of less than $100 million that would improve the survivability of existing Minuteman intercontinental missiles. *(Strategic arms, p. 195)*

● Reagan reduced the U.S. fleet in the Indian Ocean to one aircraft carrier task force, with a second carrier due to visit the region from time to time. Two task forces had been in the region since January 1980, immediately after the Soviet invasion of Afghanistan.

There was no simple pattern to the hundreds of changes incorporated in Reagan's budget revisions. The 14 largest changes accounted for two-thirds of the $8 billion reduction. But the Oct. 9 Pentagon booklet summarizing the changes was 162 pages long and included changes in dozens of small research programs, each funded for a few tens of millions of dollars.

Reagan also proposed a small number of new increases: the largest — $381 million — to begin multi-year procurement of the F-16 fighter and two other airplanes in fiscal 1982.

As revised, Reagan's budget provided $214.1 billion for Pentagon programs in fiscal 1982, compared with his March request of $222.1 billion and President Carter's January request of $195.7 billion.

In order to make $2 billion in outlay cuts for 1982, Reagan had to propose $8 billion worth of cuts in budget authority.

Nuclear Forces

Two items accounted for the bulk of Reagan's proposed $2 billion cut in strategic arms programs. A cut of $965 million reflected Reagan's cancellation of the multiple launch-site version of the MX intercontinental missile.

An additional $960.8 million reflected cancellation of the request for a 10th Trident missile-launching submarine. On its face, this marked administration acceptance of a congressional *fait accompli*: Both Armed Services committees had opposed the funding, citing production bottlenecks in the General Dynamics Corp. shipyard where the Trident ships were built.

But in mid-October, Navy Secretary John F. Lehman Jr. announced that the shipyard had solved its internal problems, and he awarded it a contract to build a ship-hunting submarine.

Minuteman. The administration proposed cutting $98.6 million (including some fiscal 1981 money) from two programs aimed at improving the existing force of Minuteman intercontinental missiles.

To save $67.6 million, the administration proposed cancelling the program to equip Minuteman silos with long-lasting batteries that could keep the silos operating for days after commercial power was cut off by a nuclear attack.

Also cut was $31.1 million for a system to let Air Force commanders in airborne command posts re-target and fire Minuteman missiles that survived a Soviet attack.

Both Minuteman cuts appeared to run contrary to the administration's emphasis on "endurance" in its strategic arms program.

Anti-Missile Defense. A proposed $52 million increase in missile defense research apparently was to be funneled into an improved version of the so-called LoAD missile system, which had been tested since the late 1970s. LoAD was designed to protect MX missiles based in the multiple launch-site system, which Reagan rejected.

The huge preponderance of public testimony by Pentagon officials in previous years had been that LoAD would be ineffective against a large wave of Soviet missiles, unless the attacking warheads had to be scattered across a large number of decoy MX sites, as well as the sites containing the real missiles.

But the Pentagon budget summary book — which had several security deletions in its discussion of anti-missile defense — suggested that the new missile defense program would use a LoAD-type system "to defend fixed, non-deceptive ICBM sites." A controversial element of Reagan's strategic policy was the basing — at least temporarily — of MX missiles in fixed silos.

RDF/Indian Ocean

Proposed cuts of more than $1.3 billion were suggested for programs related to the Rapid Deployment Force or to U.S. military power near the Persian Gulf.

About a quarter of that reduction reflected a decision to charter, rather than buy, a fleet of ships (called T-AKXs) on which combat equipment for Marine brigades could be stored near potential trouble spots. In case of a crisis, Marines would be flown to the scene to retrieve the combat gear from the ships.

Reagan dropped a request for $392 million to buy two existing commercial ships and build one new one for this role. He asked instead for $60 million to charter ships designed by private contractors to fit Navy specifications.

Other RDF-related cuts included:

Tanker Planes. Reagan proposed saving $500 million by ending procurement of KC-10s, a version of the DC-10 jetliner able to refuel other planes in midair. Because the plane could carry a large cargo load, in addition to fuel, six KC-10s could escort a fighter squadron and all its maintenance equipment non-stop from the United States to the Middle East in one day. The Air Force already had purchased 12 planes, had budgeted eight more for fiscal 1982 and — according to the House Armed Services Committee — hoped to buy a total of 60.

Indian Ocean Fleet. Reagan also ended the policy dating from January 1980 of keeping two aircraft carrier task forces in the Indian Ocean full time. A proposed reduction of $200.8 million in Navy ship and airplane operating funds would keep one carrier in the Indian Ocean at all times, with a second carrier there about half the time.

The new policy began in mid-October, 1981, when the carrier *America* moved through the Suez Canal, leaving the *Coral Sea* as the only carrier in the Indian Ocean.

CX Plane. The administration's original request for $245.7 million to develop a new, long-range cargo plane (called CX) would be cut to $169.7 million. Even that new amount was much higher than the amounts approved by the Senate Armed Services Committee ($20 million) and the House Armed Services Committee ($1 million).

The panels were alarmed at the $10 billion price tag of a new CX fleet and were barraged with competing propos-

als by Lockheed Corp., offering to sell more C-5 transports, and by the Boeing Corp., offering some 747 freight planes. But the Air Force insisted that the C-5 took up too much room to use it on small landing strips in primitive areas, in contrast to the proposed CX. The 747, the Air Force argued, could carry heavy equipment only to major air terminals equipped with special unloading equipment, unlike the C-5 and the CX.

Heavy Bombers. The president dropped a $20.4 million program to develop modifications to increase the bomb load of 30-odd B-52s assigned to the RDF command to carry high-explosive bombs to intercontinental targets.

The modification would have enabled the planes in this so-called Strategic Projection Force to carry 108 large bombs, four times their existing load.

An Air Force spokesman said the service decided that the planes could do the job with already planned changes that would enable them to carry 54 bombs, because improved navigation gear would make their attacks more accurate.

NATO, Ground Combat

Despite Pentagon warnings of a radical improvement in the quality of Soviet attack planes in Europe in the 1970s, the administration proposed cutting $707 million from various anti-aircraft missile programs.

Production would be slowed for the long-range Patriot missile and the British-made Rapier, a short-range missile that would be used to protect U.S. air bases in Britain. But the bulk of that reduction ($564 million) would come from canceling production of the French-German designed Roland, a short-range missile being bought by the Army to defend airbases and supply depots in Europe.

Tanks. To save $276 million, a planned increase in production of the M-1 tank would be slowed. Instead of the originally requested $1.84 billion for 720 tanks in fiscal 1982, Reagan's new request was for $1.56 billion which, according to the Pentagon, could buy at least 665 tanks.

Heavy Bombers. Retirement of the 75 oldest B-52s — the D model — would save $81 million in fiscal 1982, under the Reagan proposal. These planes lacked some of the modifications given later B-52s that would attack Soviet targets; but the older planes were modified to carry 108 large, high-explosive bombs and had operated in exercises over Central Europe.

NATO Bases. The administration was coming to terms with political reality by cutting $24 million from a $37.1 million request to build fuel and ammunition storage facilities at European-owned airfields. These so-called "colocated operating bases" would be used by U.S.-based fighter squadrons flown to Europe in a crisis.

The two Armed Services committees had insisted that the NATO alliance pay for part of this project, on the grounds that all NATO members would benefit from the strengthened alliance defense.

Warships

A net total of $416 million was cut from the budget by the administration's abandonment of plans to reactivate the mothballed aircraft carrier *Oriskany*. Of the congressional defense panels, only the House Armed Services Committee had shown enthusiasm for the plan to equip the ship with small Marine Corps bombers. The ship would have been used either against relatively weak adversaries or in company with a larger, more modern carrier.

However, the administration asked for $22 million to continue inspecting its mothballed carriers and planning how they might be used in an emergency.

To accelerate the planned reactivation of the battleship *New Jersey* — which was to be equipped with cruise missiles — the administration asked for an increase from $158 million to $237 million, an increase incorporated in the Senate version of the defense authorization bill (S 815).

To save $224 million, the administration canceled its request for one of three missile-armed frigates designed to escort troop and supply convoys. A two-ship order would keep in the frigate business only two of the three shipyards that had been building these ships since the mid-1970s.

The new budget also dropped a request for $19.6 million to design a much smaller frigate to be used by Naval Reserve units. Simplified versions of these larger missile frigates would be built for the reserves.

Tactical Aircraft

The administration proposed reducing procurement of the A-10 anti-tank airplane — $267.4 million for 20 planes instead of $542.4 million for 60 planes.

The administration reduced by $35 million its request for components that would be used in F-15 fighters bought in the fiscal 1983 budget. This was in line with its plan to buy only 30 of the planes the following year, instead of 42 as planned earlier. ∎

Status of Appropriations
97th Congress, First Session
Budget Authority for Fiscal Year 1982

(In millions of dollars)

As of Dec. 16, 1981

	September Administration Request	House	Senate	Final Action	Page
Agriculture and related agencies (HR 4119 — PL 97-103)	$ 22,324[1]	$ 22,731[1]	$ 22,853[1]	$ 22,605[1]	375
Defense Department (HR 4995 — PL 97-114)	200,878	197,443	203,676	199,899	311
District of Columbia (HR 4522 — PL 97-91)	570	521	557	557	290
Energy and Water Development (HR 4144 — PL 97-88)	12,097	13,190	12,764	12,472	301
Foreign Aid (HR 4559 — PL 97-121)	7,775	7,440	7,328	7,495	339
Housing and Urban Development, Veterans, NASA (HR 4034 — PL 97-101)	58,686	62,600	60,506	60,376	334
Interior and related agencies (HR 4035 — PL 97-100)	6,406	11,140	7,359	7,227	369
Labor-Health and Human Services-Education (HR 4560)[2]	82,475	85,188	84,791[3]		331
Legislative Branch (H J Res 325 — PL 97-51)	1,434	1,101[4]	935[4]	1,299[4]	286
Military Construction (HR 4241 — PL 97-106)	7,301	6,888	7,316	7,059	306
State, Justice, Commerce, Judiciary (HR 4169)	8,181	8,684	8,630[3]		364
Transportation and related agencies (HR 4209 — PL 97-102)	9,777	11,090	10,414	10,120	358
Treasury, Postal Service, General Government (HR 4121)	9,142	9,745	9,397[3]		355
1981 Supplemental Appropriations (HR 3512 — PL 97-12)	8,374[5]	5,927	6,694	6,649	281
Public Health Service 1981 Supplemental Appropriations (H J Res 308 — PL 97-26)	16.8	16.8	16.8	16.8	502
1982 Continuing Appropriations (H J Res 370 — PL 97-92)	[6]	[6]	[6]	[6]	329

1 *Includes Section 32 transfer amounts.*
2 *Amounts do not include advance funding for fiscal years 1983 and 1984.*
3 *Committee-approved amount.*
4 *The full-year fiscal 1982 legislative branch appropriation is included in the fiscal 1982 continuing appropriations resolution (H J Res 325 — PL 97-51). The House amount excludes funds for Senate operations, and the Senate amount excludes funds for House operations.*

5 *Includes a net of $776,325,000 in budget estimates not considered by the House. Of this amount, $536,124,000 for the food stamp program was not formally transmitted to Congress.*
6 *The joint resolution, signed by the president Dec. 15, 1981, appropriates interim funding through March 31, 1982, for certain departments for which regular appropriations bills have not been cleared. There is no dollar amount for the resolution.*

Budget and Appropriations

Although the fiscal 1982 budget provided President Reagan with heady victories, economic realities later scuttled his budget goals.

Shortly after taking office in January, Reagan asked Congress to cut $41.4 billion from President Carter's final budget proposals. With former Rep. David A. Stockman, R-Mich. (1977-81), Reagan's Office of Management and Budget (OMB) director, masterminding the campaign, Republican leaders who had just taken control of the Senate agreed to consolidate the budget reductions in one "reconciliation" measure early in the 1981 session. By packaging the budget cuts together, then forcing the House and Senate to vote on a single measure, Republicans hoped to prevent congressional committees and interest groups from chipping away at the president's budget plan.

The strategy worked, far better than many dismayed Democrats could have imagined. By Aug. 13, Reagan had signed into law the deepest and farthest-reaching package of budget cuts that Congress had ever approved.

In September, however, when Reagan proposed a further $16 billion package of spending cuts and revenue increases, Congress made it clear that it had no stomach for the undertaking. In the end, Reagan settled for $4 billion in appropriations cuts and agreed to postpone additional initiatives until 1982.

Reconciliation Victory

The omnibus reconciliation bill Congress cleared July 31 (HR 3982) cut nearly $35.2 billion from the $740 billion spending level projected by the Congressional Budget Office for fiscal 1982. In all, the package trimmed expected outlays in fiscal years 1981-84 by $130.6 billion.

Drafted under reconciliation instructions contained in the first fiscal 1982 budget resolution (H Con Res 115), the bill consolidated in a single package the cuts sought by Reagan in his March budget proposals.

The reconciliation process was created by the 1974 Congressional Budget Act as a means of forcing committees to comply with congressionally approved spending levels. It had been used only once previously, in 1980, on a much smaller scale.

That Reagan was able to succeed in his early efforts to slash the budget in the Republican-controlled Senate was no surprise. In the House, however, victory was attributable to two factors:

● Republicans to a man stood behind the administration's alternative — known as Gramm-Latta for its sponsors, Reps. Phil Gramm, D-Texas, and Delbert L. Latta, R-Ohio — to the Budget Committee's version of the first budget resolution.

● A sizable group of conservative Democrats, dubbed "Boll Weevils," voted with the GOP.

That same coalition prevailed in the House when the reconciliation bill itself came to the floor. With the help of conservative Democrats, the Republicans turned aside the $37.7 billion package of cuts recommended by the House authorizing committees. In its place they won approval of a substitute package known as Gramm-Latta II, which had been hastily developed with administration help and which closely followed the Senate bill.

The sweeping use of reconciliation to enact the president's economic program reflected a fundamental shift in power from the authorizing and Appropriations committees to the Budget committees. Once the reconciliation bill was enacted, the Appropriations committees had little leeway in the levels of funding they could provide, since reconciliation had already set the spending ceilings.

It also represented a shift in power, perhaps only temporary, from the legislative branch to the executive. The reconciliation package the House turned down was a package put together by its own authorizing committees through the normal, though truncated, legislative process. The package the House did accept was designed by the White House, Stockman and the House GOP leadership. The administration claimed that using reconciliation in this way was required because of the urgent need to put the president's economic recovery program in place.

Second Round Cuts

In signing his reconciliation and tax cut bills Aug. 13, Reagan boasted that they marked "an end to the excessive growth in government bureaucracy and government spending and government taxing."

Within weeks after enactment of the reconciliation package, however, the administration was forced to acknowledge that its economic program was not achieving the desired effects.

Faced with soaring deficit projections spawned by stubbornly high interest rates and inflation, Reagan Sept. 24 announced a second budget-slashing initiative. This time he asked Congress to save $13 billion by paring appropriations measures and making changes in non-discretionary entitlement programs such as Medicaid and food stamps. He also called for $3 billion in new revenues.

Congressional response was negative, however, especially among Republicans. GOP members of the Senate Appropriations Committee said they could not cut more than $5 billion from fiscal 1982 appropriations. And House Republicans said they would not attempt to raise taxes — not in an election year and not in a recession.

One result of the Republican stalemate was that the appropriations process ground to a standstill, and most of the government was funded under a series of short-term continuing appropriations resolutions.

The first continuing resolution (H J Res 325) funded government agencies until Nov. 20. When it became apparent that most of the regular appropriations measures would not be enacted by that date, the House and Senate Appropriations committees began drafting a new temporary spending bill.

However, the figures contained in the second measure (H J Res 357), haggled over during an entire weekend by Senate and House conferees, did not reflect sufficient savings to satisfy the president. Reagan cast his first veto when he refused to sign the resolution, closing down the government for a day.

Congress quickly passed an interim measure (H J Res 368) extending funding until Dec. 15, giving it time to piece together yet another continuing resolution that would satisfy both itself and the president.

In the end, Reagan agreed to settle for $4 billion in appropriations cuts and to postpone his entitlement and tax proposals until 1982. The final continuing resolution (H J Res 370) extended funding through March 30, 1982, for programs covered under the three appropriations bills that failed to clear before adjournment. *(Status of appropriations, p. 244)*

Budget Resolution Impasse

The GOP stalemate over the president's Sept. 24 budget-cutting initiative also delayed action on the second, and supposedly binding, budget resolution for fiscal 1982.

Senate Budget Committee Chairman Pete V. Domenici, R-N.M., insisted that Congress had to acknowledge that future budget deficits would be enormous unless substantial cuts were made and that it was necessary in 1981 to at least lay out a blueprint for how to achieve these savings. Domenici, however, could not get his committee to agree on what direction to take.

In the House Budget Committee, many Republicans were unwilling to draft a resolution that showed just how bad the deficit outlook was, and Democrats were disinclined to move ahead without knowing what the administration wanted. In the end the committee reported a pro forma second resolution that was simply a carbon copy of the resolution Congress had approved in May.

That measure had contemplated budget authority of $770.9 billion, outlays of $695.45 billion and revenues of $657.8 billion for fiscal 1982. The resulting deficit of $37.65 billion was far below levels projected by the time Congress took up the second resolution.

The Senate Budget Committee reluctantly followed suit but added language noting the prospect of deficits ranging from $95 billion to $165 billion in fiscal 1982-84 if no further cuts were made.

The Senate approved its version of the resolution (S Con Res 50) Dec. 9 by a slim 49-48 margin after adding "sense of the Senate" language calling for a revised resolution by March 1982 that would achieve a balanced budget by fiscal 1984. The House accepted the Senate language and approved the resolution Dec. 10, 206-200.

—By Dale Tate

First Budget Resolution Follows Reagan Plan

Congress May 21 approved a fiscal 1982 target budget drawn to President Reagan's blueprint — a plan that called for deep cuts in social programs, increased defense outlays and a three-year individual tax cut.

With little debate the House approved the conference report on the first concurrent budget resolution (H Con Res 115 — H Rept 97-46) May 20 by a vote of 244-155. The Senate completed the first round of budget action the next day when it approved the measure by a vote of 76-20. *(House vote 44, p. 24-H; Senate vote 126, p. 24-S)*

The resolution set non-binding fiscal 1982 budget targets, calling for $770.9 billion in budget authority, $695.45 billion in outlays, $657.8 billion in revenues and a $37.65 billion deficit. Looking further into the future, the blueprint forecast a budget surplus of $1.5 billion in fiscal 1984. Binding budget levels were set in a second resolution, cleared Dec. 10. *(Second resolution, p. 267)*

In calling for a $51.3 billion reduction in revenues, H Con Res 115 assumed enactment of the full $53.9 billion tax cut sought by Reagan, partially offset by $2.6 billion in additional user fees. *(Tax cut, p. 91)*

In order to meet the budget targets, the measure also included instructions requiring 14 Senate and 15 House committees to alter existing programs to achieve about $36 billion in fiscal 1982 spending cuts. *(Reconciliation, p. 256)*

After final congressional action on H Con Res 115, which did not require Reagan's signature, White House Deputy Press Secretary Larry Speakes said the president was "extremely pleased that the Congress has acted in record time."

Although the resolution called for the most sweeping redirection of federal programs in a generation, Congress completed action on the measure only six days after the statutory May 15 deadline. The final version closely paralleled the budget Reagan sent to Congress March 10. *(Reagan budget, p. 278)*

In the House, where a coalition of Republicans and conservative Democrats had frustrated efforts to modify the Reagan budget priorities, many Democrats seemed resigned to their defeat. During debate on the conference report, Budget Committee Chairman James R. Jones, D-Okla., said he was voting for the resolution "with very major reservations. The prudence of this economic policy is very suspect at best."

In the Republican-controlled Senate, Budget Chairman Pete V. Domenici, R-N.M., told members, "The blueprint contained in this resolution is clear. It is unequivocal. It responds directly to the mandate of the American people and the requests of our president. And, despite all of the rhetoric about unrealistic numbers of optimistic assumptions, these targets are achievable."

The ranking minority member of the Senate Budget Committee, Ernest F. Hollings, D-S.C., faulted the economic assumptions upon which the budget was predicated, however. The "conference report fails to keep faith with the American people who believe the Congress is committed to balancing the budget by fiscal year 1984," he maintained.

In addition to setting budget targets for fiscal 1982, the resolution revised binding fiscal 1981 budget levels and for the first time set spending, revenue and deficit targets for subsequent fiscal years 1983 and 1984.

The revised fiscal 1981 budget totals accommodated $661.35 billion in outlays, $717.5 billion in budget authority, $603.3 billion in revenues and foresaw a $58.05 billion deficit.

Total outlays for fiscal 1983 would be $732.25 billion; budget authority, $813.75 billion; revenues, $713.2 billion; and the deficit, $19.05 billion. For fiscal 1984 the resolution projected outlays of $773.75 billion, budget authority of $866.45 billion, revenues of $774.8 billion and a $1.05 billion surplus. These "outyear" numbers assumed unspecified spending cuts totaling billions of dollars.

The resolution recommended that the public debt limit be set at $999.8 billion for fiscal 1981 and $1,079,800,000,000 for fiscal 1982. On May 21, under procedures established in 1979, the House incorporated the debt limit figures in H J Res 265 and 266, which it then sent to the Senate. *(Procedures, 1979 Almanac p. 305)*

The conference agreement also included a credit budget that recommended a level of $51.93 billion in direct loan obligations, $85.09 billion in primary guarantee commitments and $70.07 billion in secondary guarantee commitments for fiscal 1982.

House Committee Action

Putting their philosophical differences behind them, conservative and liberal Democrats on the House Budget Committee April 9 endorsed an alternative budget that scaled back the tax cut President Reagan recommended

---

1981-82 Budget Totals Compared

(in billions of dollars)

Fiscal 1982 Targets

	Reagan Budget	House-Passed	Senate-Passed	Final Version
Budget Authority	$772.4	$764.55	$775.90	$770.90
Outlays	695.3	688.80	700.80	695.45
Revenues	650.3	657.80	650.30	657.80
Deficit	−45.0	−31.00	−50.50	−37.65

Fiscal 1981 Revisions[1]

	Second Resolution	House-Passed	Senate-Passed	Final Version
Budget Authority	$694.6	$719.05	$716.00	$717.50
Outlays	632.4	660.00	662.70	661.35
Revenues	605.0	603.30	599.90	603.30
Deficit	−27.4	−56.70	−62.80	−58.05

[1] *Revisions of binding budget levels established by Congress in 1980 (H Con Res 448). (1980 Almanac p. 119)*

and spared many social programs from his budget knife.

The House panel's 17-13 vote in favor of the $714.6 billion spending resolution came as Democrats and conservative Republicans joined forces in the Senate Budget Committee to defeat Reagan's budget. *(Senate action, below)*

Conservative Shift. Although Republicans characterized the Budget Committee action as "business as usual" by Democrats, approval of the stringent 1982 budget represented a major rightward shift by the majority party in the House.

The Democrats did alter many of Reagan's spending proposals. They disagreed with him on the size of his tax reduction. But they acceded to his request for an overall cutback in government spending and accepted to the letter a majority of the budget cuts drafted by the Office of Management and Budget (OMB) under the leadership of Reagan's budget director, ex-Rep. David A. Stockman, R-Mich. (1977-81).

Consistently voting against committee Democrats was Phil Gramm, D-Texas. The conservative Gramm, with administration approval, offered a substitute to Jones' budget that would have cut deeper into spending in order to produce a lower deficit.

That substitute, which was cosponsored by Delbert L. Latta, R-Ohio, ranking minority member on the panel, failed 13-17. Latta's bid to replace the Democratic budget with Reagan's numbers was defeated on a similar vote.

Partisan Entrenchment. During the hectic week of budget action, Budget Chairman Jones made several pleas to the White House for help in devising a spending resolution that would be acceptable to both parties.

Upon assuming the chairmanship at the beginning of the 97th Congress, Jones had hoped to win bipartisan support for the budget. And Republicans on his panel had indicated they could compromise with the conservative Democrat on many issues. But the administration instructed Republicans not to compromise, and the House GOP was under "heavy pressure to march in lockstep and to agree to no changes whatsoever to the Stockman budget," according to House Majority Leader Jim Wright, D-Texas.

At one point during his panel's deliberations, Jones lashed out against the White House stand. He accused the OMB chief of having a "bunker mentality stemming from a gargantuan sense of egotism."

"The administration says it can accept no amendments; that its budget is untouchable. No administration has ever made such demands; and no Congress has ever accepted such demands," a tight-lipped Jones told his committee. "It is not the job of Congress not to think."

The Democratic attack on Reagan's economic program did not go unanswered. Almost before the ink was dry on Jones' proposed budget, Stockman decried the plan as "unacceptable" to the White House.

Treasury Secretary Donald T. Regan charged that the Democrats still were "attempting to balance the budget through higher taxes."

Reagan himself joined the fray. In a letter to House Minority Leader Robert H. Michel, R-Ill., penned from his hospital bed, where he was recovering from a March 30 assassination attempt, the president warned that "too many of our colleagues in the House prefer that we return to business as usual."

He urged Michel to "redouble" efforts to secure passage of "all" the key elements of his program.

Resolution Details

As reported by the House Budget Committee April 16, the first budget resolution (H Con Res 115 — H Rept 97-23) set fiscal 1982 budget authority at $787.65 billion, outlays at $714.55 billion, revenues at $688.95 billion and the deficit at $25.6 billion.

That deficit was $19.4 billion less than the deficit Reagan proposed in his March 10 budget. But because the committee used different economic assumptions to write its spending plan, it claimed that its deficit was half the size of the president's.

Those forecasting differences were hotly debated during initial committee action on the budget. Democrats claimed their figures were based on the latest information, which was two months more current than data the OMB used to prepare its program.

But Republicans charged that the new predictions would result in higher spending. Bobbi Fiedler, R-Calif., said the Democratic figures were derived by "sleight of hand," and Jack F. Kemp, R-N.Y., complained that they were "too pessimistic for the [Republican] majority."

Staff economists for the committee concurred with Reagan that new tax and spending policies would help slow inflation and encourage economic growth. But they cautioned that the changes would not occur as quickly as he predicted.

The House staff forecast an annual inflation rate of 10.4 percent in 1982, unemployment of 7.3 percent, gross national product (GNP) growth of 2.3 percent and interest rates, as reflected by the rate for 91-day Treasury bills, of 12 percent.

Reagan had used an inflation rate of 8.3 percent, unemployment of 7.2 percent, a GNP increase of 4.2 percent and an interest rate of 8.9 percent to calculate his budget.

Using the new inflation and growth figures, the House committee recalculated Reagan's spending and tax requests and came up with a budget authority number of $784.8 billion, outlays of $717.8 billion, revenues of $667.4 billion and a deficit of $50.5 billion.

Comparing its recommendations to those numbers, the committee was able to claim that it had cut an additional $3.2 billion from Reagan's own proposal.

It left room for a one-year, $38 billion tax cut effective Jan. 1, 1982 — almost $16 billion under Reagan's request.

Spending Highlights. Reductions in spending for the Strategic Petroleum Reserve (SPR), a crackdown on "waste, fraud and abuse" and interest payment savings due to a lower deficit helped Jones net extra dollars to restore to domestic programs.

He put funds back into energy conservation, the Consumer Cooperative Bank, mass transit, economic development programs, Medicaid, student loans, training, food stamps, school lunches, legal aid and veterans' health programs.

The spending increases, crafted by Jones during weeks of private consultations with committee members, were designed to win the support of moderate and liberal Democrats who opposed many of the spending cuts proposed by Reagan.

Though pleased with the chairman's final product, they pressed for amendments to restore funds to such programs as rural housing, training and higher education grants. But most of their proposals were rebuffed by a solid block of Republicans and conservative Democrats opposed to add-ons.

Only at the end of the four-day markup session were

some members able to win approval of spending increases.

Timothy E. Wirth, D-Colo., pushed through an amendment permitting states that charged severance taxes on oil pumped within their borders to receive revenue sharing funds. A second successful amendment by the Coloradan restored $150 million in outlays for energy projects.

Norman Y. Mineta, D-Calif., won adoption of a proposal adding back $64 million in outlays and $376 million in budget authority for airport construction grants.

The increases prompted Bill Frenzel, R-Minn., to complain that "this committee is getting to be like the Senate Finance Committee. We're all trying to take care of each other."

Frenzel, other Republicans and two conservative Democrats were able to stop yet another budget increase. Proposed by Beryl Anthony Jr., D-Ark., it would have restored funds for farm home loans.

Defense Battle. As the committee wound up its budget deliberations, conservative Democrats threatened to break ranks with Jones and the party leadership unless funds were added back for the Pentagon.

After hours of huddles with Speaker Thomas P. O'Neill Jr., D-Mass., and majority conservatives, Jones announced he was withdrawing his recommendation that certain Pentagon programs be cut and would support the administration's military outlay request.

That number, $188.9 billion, was $900 million lower than the amount contained in Jones' proposed budget. That was because he estimated the Defense Department would spend out its authorized funds faster than predicted.

The new Budget chairman also said he would talk with the administration to determine whether the budget authority figure for the military should be increased.

His decision to go along with the White House on the outlay number was a way of buying time to negotiate with conservative and liberal Democrats.

Committee member Thomas J. Downey, D-N.Y., said party leaders had been concerned that conservatives would return to their districts during the Easter recess disgruntled with the Democratic budget.

Only a few days earlier at a news conference to announce his budget, Jones had told reporters that military spending should be cut along with social programs.

"We should demand of the Pentagon the same respect for efficiency that we do of other agencies," he said.

Fiscal 1981 Budget. The 1982 budget resolution approved by the committee also increased the spending ceiling for the current fiscal year.

It set a new fiscal 1981 outlay limit of $662.4 billion, budget authority of $723 billion, revenues of $610.9 billion and a deficit of $51.5 billion.

A year earlier, in its first 1981 resolution, Congress had approved a balanced budget for fiscal 1981. But in November, when it recalculated spending during action on the second budget resolution, it increased the deficit to $27.4 billion. *(1981 resolution, 1980 Almanac pp. 108, 119)*

Reagan requested a 1981 spending level that was $7.2 billion lower than the Budget Committee number. But because he proposed a tax reduction for the current fiscal year, his deficit would be higher — $54.9 billion.

The Budget panel's 1981 budget would require $500 million in rescissions of funding already on the books. Reagan had asked that $1.5 billion be rescinded.

Reconciliation. H Con Res 115 also included instructions to 13 authorizing committees to change programs under their jurisdiction to save a total $18 billion.

The Senate committee included such "reconciliation" requirements in a separate resolution passed by the full chamber April 2. The savings it approved totaled $36.9 billion. *(Senate resolution, box, next page)*

The House reconciliation figure was lower than the Senate's because it used a different method to calculate budget reductions, according to Leon E. Panetta, D-Calif., chairman of the committee's reconciliation task force.

By establishing a tighter enforcement mechanism for appropriations bills and requiring $4.2 billion in administrative savings, the House bill contained total savings of about $41 billion, Panetta said.

Under the new enforcement procedure, all appropriations conference reports were to be held at the Speaker's desk until Sept. 25. That would give Congress time to revise the spending measures if it decided to cut spending in the second budget resolution.

The committee budget also provided that the first budget resolution automatically become binding on Sept. 15 if a second resolution had not been adopted by that time.

Senate Committee Action

Initial Defeat

With the help of three Republican defectors, Democrats on the Senate Budget Committee April 9 scuttled the initial version of the first budget resolution for fiscal 1982 — a blueprint that contained all of the elements of President Reagan's economic recovery program.

The stunning 8-12 defeat was the first for Reagan's economic package. And it was the first time the panel's Democrats voted as a bloc.

Conservative GOP Sens. William L. Armstrong, Colo., Charles E. Grassley, Iowa, and Steven D. Symms, Idaho, abandoned their colleagues because they believed the resolution's deficits for fiscal 1981-84 broke faith with Republican pledges to balance the budget. The measure projected deficits of $62.8 billion in fiscal 1981, $53.8 billion in fiscal 1982, $52.2 billion in fiscal 1983 and $44.7 billion in fiscal 1984.

The defeated resolution recommended $775.0 billion in budget authority, $704.1 billion in outlays and $650.3 billion in revenues for fiscal 1982.

Democrats, who voted unanimously against the resolution, twitted the Republicans for no longer "worshipping at the shrine of the balanced budget." They argued that if the committee had adopted different economic assumptions and accepted a smaller tax cut, the resolution would have shown a balanced budget in fiscal 1984.

Daniel Patrick Moynihan, D-N.Y., referring to GOP campaign pledges to balance the budget, increase defense spending and radically cut taxes said: "You promised miracles and you are now encountering reality."

Budget Committee Chairman Domenici tried in vain to persuade his fellow Republicans not to break ranks. "We have taken every single recommendation for cutting the budget the president recommended, plus over $2 billion," Domenici argued.

"The only way we could salve our consciences and vote for the '82 budget was to show credibly that we were on the path of a balanced budget," Armstrong said after the vote. "We're not on a path that puts us in balance, and we have to get on the path that does."

Senate Orders $36.9 Billion in Savings...

In a resounding 88-10 vote, the Republican-controlled Senate April 2 endorsed almost to the letter the wide-ranging roster of budget cuts President Reagan proposed as the "leading edge" of his economic recovery plan. *(Vote 77, p. 16-S)*

The first major step toward enactment of his budget and tax proposals came as the president recovered from a gunshot wound suffered during an attempted assassination March 30.

The Senate's reconciliation savings resolution (S Con Res 9) directed Senate committees to report legislation reducing spending by $36.9 billion in fiscal 1982 and $2.4 billion in fiscal 1981. The instructions subsequently were coordinated with the House instructions in the first fiscal 1982 budget resolution (H Con Res 115). Those instructions guided committees in drafting the huge reconciliation savings bill (HR 3982), which cleared July 31. *(Budget resolution, p. 247; reconciliation bill, p. 256)*

With the backing of Majority Leader Howard H. Baker Jr., R-Tenn., Budget Committee Chairman Pete V. Domenici, R-N.M., was able to keep most Republicans united behind the spending reductions his panel recommended. Only one GOP senator — Lowell P. Weicker Jr., R-Conn., voted against final passage.

Senate Democrats, however, were widely split. Because many of the more conservative members of the party frequently voted with the GOP, liberal Democrats did not come close to winning adoption of the more than 20 amendments they introduced.

One after another, proposals to restore funds for energy programs, school lunches, health care for veterans, community health centers, pensions and urban development projects were defeated.

In the end, all but nine Democrats voted for the savings measure. The final Democratic votes for the resolution did not mean the minority senators approved of how the cuts were allocated, however.

"Republican leaders, whipping their troops into lock-step conformity, refused any accommodation, any compromise that might have brought about truly bipartisan support for much of the president's budget," complained Minority Whip Alan Cranston, D-Calif.

Committee Action

The Budget Committee approved S Con Res 9 March 19 by a 20-0 vote. As reported (S Rept 97-28), the resolution instructed 14 authorizing and appropriations committees to cut $36.4 billion from the fiscal 1982 budget.

With committee Republicans solidly behind him, Budget Chairman Domenici downed nearly every proposed spending add-on and even won approval of $2.3 billion in extra cuts on top of Reagan's requests.

Many of the reductions had been opposed by Democrats. But, arguing that Reagan's economic policies should be given a chance, they joined their GOP colleagues in voting to report the resolution to the Senate floor.

The Democrats' support for the package on the final vote also was an admission of Reagan's popularity and a recognition of their new minority status. "When all is said and done," said Howard M. Metzenbaum, D-Ohio, "the president will get pretty much what he wants."

However, Democrats protested the speeded-up budget-writing timetable enforced by Domenici. Under normal practice, reconciliation instructions would be drafted as part of the first or second budget resolution — not before. "The forced-march nature has harmed the quality of work undertaken this week," complained Gary Hart, D-Colo.

Domenici defended the accelerated schedule on grounds that "extraordinary times demand extraordinary efforts."

Reconciliation Details. In preparing its package of far-reaching cuts, the Budget panel virtually rubber-stamped Reagan's savings proposals. Only a few of the 100-plus recommended reductions were altered. While the resolution required legislative committees to achieve specific savings objectives, they did not have to follow the Budget Committee recommendations on individual program cuts.

Extra funds were added for the Export-Import Bank ($110 million in fiscal 1982 outlays); educational and youth training programs ($653 million); a special nutrition program for pregnant women and infants ($224 million); counseling for Vietnam veterans ($25 million); the social services block grant ($100 million); and unidentified increases in appropriations ($264 million).

But those add-ons were more than offset by deeper cuts, totaling $582 million, in small business loans, subsidized housing, community development programs and Medicare funds.

The overall reduction also was increased by a recommended change in the way the government operated the Strategic Petroleum Reserve (SPR) and by increased fees for boat owners to offset Coast Guard costs. Those changes added $3.05 billion.

Missing from the resolution was another $8.8 billion in cuts recommended by Reagan that the committee decided could not be made through the reconciliation process.

As a concession to the Finance Committee, the reconciliation measure also did not contain Reagan's proposals for increasing taxes for the users of certain government services.

Democratic Squabbles. For most Democrats, the budget-writing session marked the first time they had drafted major legislation as members of the minority — a transformation that appeared to leave them in disarray.

The party's more liberal members and its conservative ranking minority member, Ernest F. Hollings, D-S.C., squabbled openly around the conference table.

At one point, in a long speech defending a proposal to change the cost-of-living index for government programs, Hollings suggested that several of his colleagues — whom he named — had not learned that Americans wanted Congress to cut fat from the budget.

"I don't see how we can become a real majority party if we don't represent the majority," Hollings said.

...Endorses Reagan Reconciliation Cuts

By contrast, committee Republicans exhibited unprecedented solidarity. The party's most conservative members — Charles E. Grassley, R-Iowa; Steven D. Symms, R-Idaho; and Robert W. Kasten Jr., R-Wis. — on occasion left the fold to support a proposal that would cut more deeply into the budget than Reagan recommended. But most votes saw the 12 GOP members tightly aligned.

Cost-of-Living Adjustments. In a surprise switch from his previous position, Domenici bowed to pressure from the White House and opposed a proposal to change the index used to figure cost-of-living adjustments for government retirement programs.

Domenici long had argued that inflation could not be brought under control unless the index was altered. But Reagan, who promised during his campaign that he would not cut basic Social Security benefits, did not recommend such a change.

Hollings, author of the proposal, said changing the index to reflect wage increases rather than rises in the Consumer Price Index (CPI) would "restore equity to the working man."

He said the current CPI index "has overcompensated retirees relative to workers by 8.6 percent over the last three years." The change would save the government $6 billion.

But Domenici protested, "I don't think it's critical that we take everything we can right now. If inflation begins to drop quickly, it will make the disparity smaller."

Every one of Hollings' fellow Democrats opposed the measure, arguing that such benefits not be cut at the same time as other social programs.

"The safety net we have heard so much about is obviously constructed of the cheapest of cheesecloth," J. James Exon, D-Neb., said. Hollings' proposal failed, 5-13.

Economic Assumptions. Democrats also faulted the economic assumptions Reagan's advisers used to calculate his budget.

They charged that his forecast of 8.3 percent inflation in calendar 1982 and real economic growth of 4.2 percent was overly optimistic. As a result, they said, he had underestimated spending and would not be able to meet his goal of balancing the budget in fiscal 1984.

In a letter to Hollings and Domenici, the non-partisan Congressional Budget Office (CBO) agreed that Reagan's forecast was too optimistic. Assuming enactment of his budget and tax cuts, the CBO predicted inflation would be 9.7 percent in 1982 with real economic growth of 2.2 percent.

Using those figures, the CBO calculated that Reagan's 1982 spending proposals would total $715 billion to $720 billion rather than $695 billion. The CBO said his recommended spending cuts would total $42.9 billion rather than the $48.6 billion he claimed.

Senate Floor Action

The Senate approved S Con Res 9 April 2 by an 88-10 vote. The resolution was amended only twice during six days of emotional debate over the recommended cuts.

(Votes 42-77, pp. 12-S—16-S)

Amendments. One of the changes approved by the Senate was a bookkeeping proposal, by Finance Chairman Robert Dole, R-Kan. It deepened the cuts recommended by the Budget Committee by $500 million in fiscal 1982.

The second amendment, by conservative Jesse Helms, R-N.C., trimmed 1982 foreign aid spending by an extra $200 million and switched the funds to the school lunch program.

A longtime foe of foreign aid, Helms chaired the Agriculture Committee, which had jurisdiction over the popular nutrition program for schoolchildren. *(Votes 45-46, p. 12-S)*

The biggest threat to the administration's savings package came in the form of an amendment by Republican John H. Chafee, R.I., to restore $973 million to a variety of urban-oriented programs.

That proposal so worried the White House and the Senate leadership that Vice President George Bush traveled to the Capitol to be on hand to cast a possible tie-breaking vote. Bush used his visit to lobby against the Chafee measure.

Once solid Republican opposition to Chafee's amendment was assured, Southern and Western Democrats joined the GOP to defeat it, 40-59. *(Vote 56, p. 13-S)*

Although Chafee had argued that his proposed add-ons would not benefit one region over another, senators voted along regional lines.

Also rejected by wide margins were two other Republican amendments to restore funds to the Energy Committee for the Strategic Petroleum Reserve. *(Votes 51, 63, p. 13-S)*

The Senate also defeated, 17-81, a similar proposal by Democrat Bill Bradley, N.J., to put the $3 billion for SPR back in the budget without making other offsetting cuts. *(Vote 52, p. 13-S)*

Democratic Split. The long debate on reconciliation appeared to be humbling for Senate Democrats. Time after time, they saw their proposals to restore dollars to social programs soundly defeated.

The Democratic amendment that came closest to succeeding was one by David L. Boren, D-Okla. It would have cut the foreign aid budget by $104 million and added that sum back to the budget for veterans' hospitals. It failed on a nearly straight party-line vote, 44-48. *(Vote 47, 12-S)*

More common were the margins on such amendments as a proposal by Daniel Patrick Moynihan, D-N.Y., to restore $435 million in 1982 outlays for elementary and secondary education and a measure by Edward M. Kennedy, D-Mass., to put back $125 million in fiscal 1982 for health programs. Moynihan lost 33-65; Kennedy, 36-62. *(Votes 55 and 60, pp. 13-S, 14-S)*

Conservative Democrats frequently voted against the add-ons. Former Budget Chairman Hollings opposed most of the amendments by his fellow party members, as did Lawton Chiles, D-Fla., J. Bennett Johnston, D-La., William Proxmire, D-Wis., Lloyd Bentsen, D-Texas, and Sam Nunn, D-Ga.

Economic Assumptions. When the committee began consideration of the budget resolution April 7, Democrats tried unsuccessfully to get the committee to use the Congressional Budget Office's (CBO) economic assumptions, which were considerably less optimistic than the president's.

Ranking minority member Hollings argued that the committee always had used CBO's estimates. "We should have some sense of history, of perspective," he said. And Moynihan maintained the panel should not "politicize its economic assumptions."

But the Republicans voted together and the committee approved the president's assumptions, with one exception: It boosted the interest rate projection from the president's 8.9 percent figure to 12 percent for calendar 1981.

Tax Cuts. The other big item of contention was the size of the president's tax cut and other revenue proposals, which would reduce revenues by a net $51.3 billion in fiscal 1982, jumping to a $144.8 billion reduction by fiscal 1984.

A number of Democratic tax proposals were offered — including the bill approved by the Senate Finance Committee in August 1980 and one by Hollings that nearly halved the revenue loss the president's tax package would cause. *(Finance bill, 1980 Almanac p. 295)*

Hollings told members it was "time to lower our sights, to get back into the land of realism. There is no way to inflate the economy with tax cuts the size of the president's and move to balancing the budget by 1984."

But Domenici countered, "The issue is not do we want more deficits, but do we want something dramatically different" to change the tax structure.

The Republicans voted together against the Democratic proposals. The committee went on to approve, 12-9, revenue estimates that reflected Reagan's personal and business tax cuts.

Domenici denied that the vote to reject the resolution signaled the end of the president's Kemp-Roth tax proposal, which would provide a 30 percent individual rate reduction over three years. But a Budget Committee majority staffer quipped, "There goes the tax cut."

Retirement Benefits. Reversing a position it took in March in action on reconciliation spending cut instructions, the committee approved a Hollings proposal to change the index used to calculate the cost-of-living (COLA) increases for federal retirement programs.

The Hollings proposal would limit the calculation of retirees' COLAs to the lesser of the Consumer Price Index (CPI) or the wage index. It also would delay, starting in fiscal 1982, the COLA payment date from July to October.

Recent wage increases had lagged behind inflation as measured by the CPI. Thus more than 44 million government retirees would receive slightly smaller increases under the Hollings plan.

The administration staunchly opposed the change in figuring the COLA increase. Domenici went along with the president during consideration of reconciliation, although he previously had argued that the budget could not be brought under control until the indexing of major entitlement programs was changed.

This time Domenici voted for Hollings' plan, and the proposal was approved 9-8 — with seven Republicans and two Democrats voting for the index change. One plus for the proposal was that it would save $500 million in fiscal 1981 and $7.8 billion in fiscal 1982.

In one other area of controversy the committee accepted figures in budget authority for defense that gener-

ally reflected the president's request. Although the committee added money for several government functions and cut funds for others, most of the budget generally followed Reagan's original request.

Committee Approval

Relying on economic fine-tuning, the Budget Committee April 28 reversed the earlier defeat and approved a Reagan-backed fiscal 1982 budget resolution (S Con Res 19 — S Rept 97-49) that showed a balanced budget in 1984.

By making mostly cosmetic changes and assuming deeper, unspecified spending cuts, the Republican majority wooed back the three GOP conservative defectors who had voted against the earlier version because of its continuing high deficits. The Republicans also won three Southern Democrats, sealing their 15-6 victory.

Reagan heralded the committee vote as an "important and constructive step." But Democrats on the committee derided the accounting changes as "economic sleight of hand."

"The deficit is still there, it's merely papered over," charged Moynihan.

Domenici insisted, however, that "the changes are reasonable and valid assumptions that do no violence to the [budget] process."

Domenici achieved the savings necessary to win approval of the budget resolution by:

● Accepting the administration figures for defense outlays, thus reducing outlays $5.1 billion in fiscal 1982, $2.1 billion in fiscal 1983 and $7.4 billion in fiscal 1984.

● Requiring the Defense Department to absorb 40 percent of defense pay raise costs by finding economies in other defense areas. This change would reduce budget authority and outlays by $1.9 billion in both fiscal 1983 and 1984.

● Saving 1 percent across-the-board in all areas by increased efforts to reduce waste, fraud and abuse. This would cut outlays by $7.2 billion in fiscal 1983 and $7.7 billion in 1984.

● Increasing rescissions, or cancellations, of previously appropriated funds. This change would save $5 billion in outlays in both fiscal 1983 and 1984.

● Assuming additional unspecified outlay savings of $15.3 billion in fiscal 1983 and $22.7 billion in 1984.

The committee-approved changes trimmed the fiscal 1982 deficit from the committee's original $53.8 billion to $48.8 billion. In fiscal 1983, the deficit would drop to $21.4 billion from the earlier version's $52.3 billion. In fiscal 1984, the budget would be balanced instead of showing a $44.7 billion deficit.

Total fiscal 1982 spending under the Senate resolution, which generally reflected administration requests, would be $699.1 billion.

Before accepting Domenici's package, the committee defeated 7-14 an effort by Donald W. Riegle Jr., D-Mich., to reverse the panel's earlier vote to hold down cost-of-living adjustments (COLAs) in federal retirement benefits. That decision preserved $7.8 billion in fiscal 1982 outlay savings.

House Floor Action

The House May 7 approved the fiscal 1982 budget blueprint backed by President Reagan. Sixty-three Democrats joined all of the House Republicans to overwhelmingly endorse the Reagan budget plan, sponsored by Latta

and Gramm. The vote was 253-176. *(Vote 30, p. 20-H)*

The action was viewed as a vote of confidence in President Reagan's economic recovery program. "Let history show that we provided the margin of difference that changed the course of American government," said House Minority Leader Robert H. Michel, R-Ill., as members prepared to vote.

As passed, the Gramm-Latta measured called for $764.55 billion in budget authority, $688.8 billion in outlays, $657.8 billion in revenues and a $31 billion deficit in fiscal 1982.

Enforcing Reconciliation

In adopting the Gramm-Latta plan, the House turned down a Democratic plan endorsed by the Budget Committee and sponsored by Budget Chairman Jones.

The Budget Committee's plan called for spending totaling $713.7 billion and a $24.7 billion deficit. It accommodated a tax cut of $30.5 billion in fiscal 1982.

Throughout the debate, which began April 30, Democrats stressed the differences between the reconciliation provisions of the two plans and the consequences of these differences.

Instead of the $36.6 billion in fiscal 1982 cuts called for in Gramm-Latta, the Jones plan called upon the authorizing committees to make only $15.8 billion in authorization cuts and asked for $23.6 billion in cuts for programs funded by appropriations, which could be changed in the future.

A "Dear Colleague" letter from the chairmen of all the authorizing committees said that the Reagan proposal "wipes out traditional flexibility afforded under the Budget Act [PL 93-344] for legislative committees to act cooperatively with the Appropriations Committee to comply with the overall spending ceiling established in the Budget Resolution...."

Democrats' Continuing Disarray

In the days preceding the final vote, as the Reagan team lobbied hard for its plan, the Democrats tried a last-ditch effort to entice their own conservative members to support the Budget Committee resolution. They put together an amendment, sponsored by W. G. "Bill" Hefner, D-N.C., to increase the defense outlay numbers in the Budget Committee's resolution by $6.7 billion to $188.8 billion. Those figures were identical to the ones included in Gramm-Latta and requested by the president.

Democratic liberals, such as Californian George Miller, argued that "this country can't afford to pay the price for these 20 or 30 votes" that would be picked up by approval of the amendment. But House leaders, such as Majority Whip Thomas S. Foley, D-Wash., and Majority Leader Jim Wright, D-Texas, contended that the vote on the Hefner amendment gave the House the opportunity to "stand together" on defense policy.

On May 5, the amendment was adopted by voice vote.

However, two Democratic alternatives to the Gramm-Latta budget were defeated by wide margins.

One of them — proposed by the 18-member Congressional Black Caucus and sponsored by Del. Walter E. Fauntroy, D-D.C. — would have balanced the budget in fiscal 1982, restored money for social programs, cut military spending in fiscal 1982 by about $2 billion and provided $56.4 billion in tax relief. The plan was rejected May 6, 69-356. *(Vote 27, p. 18-H)*

The second plan, sponsored by David R. Obey, D-Wis., would have provided more money for social programs and

delayed the tax cut until January 1983. It was defeated May 6, 119-303. *(Vote 28, p. 18-H)*

The next day came the vote on Gramm-Latta. And then the House gave final approval to the resolution, 270-154. *(Vote 31, p. 20-H)*

Senate Floor Action

Before sending the resolution to conference May 12, Senate Democrats tried in vain to restore money to the budget for education, job training and veterans' programs, and to trim the size of the anticipated tax cut. Republicans and conservative Democrats, however, held firm, and the Senate approved a $700.8 billion budget, 78-20. *(Vote 112, p. 22-S)*

Only two Senate Republicans — Lowell P. Weicker Jr., Conn., and Gordon J. Humphrey, N.H. — bolted from their party and voted against approving the Reagan-backed budget.

After four days of debate, the Senate agreed to only one amendment, which boosted outlays and the deficit by $1.7 billion. The amendment, adopted 97-1, advanced to March from October the date on which federal civilian and military retirees receive annual cost-of-living increases. If the Senate rejected the change, argued the amendment's sponsor, Ted Stevens, R-Alaska, these retirees would have to wait 18 months for their benefits increase. *(Vote 110, p. 22-S)*

The Senate, however, twice refused — on May 8 and May 12 — to remove provisions from its resolution changing the formula calculation for COLA benefits, which would have limited the annual hikes for all federal pension beneficiaries — including Social Security recipients and railroad retirees. Budget conferees later struck the COLA change. *(Vote 94, p. 20-S; vote 109, p. 22-S)*

The Senate also defeated several attempts to cut the size of the tax cut included in the resolution. The first amendment, by ranking Budget Committee Democrat Hollings, would have limited the tax cut in fiscal 1982 to $25.5 billion. The Hollings amendment was defeated 14-74. *(Vote 102, p. 21-S)*

The Senate rejected by a 34-63 vote an amendment by Daniel Patrick Moynihan, D-N.Y., to reduce the tax cut to $51.2 billion, about the size envisioned in the bill approved by the Senate Finance Committee in 1980. *(Vote 107, p. 21-S)*

Democrats Bill Bradley, N.J., and Riegle offered amendments that would have added money for social programs such as job training, education and mass transit. Bradley's amendment, defeated 22-76, would have paid for these additions by wiping out two so-called tax "loopholes." Riegle, whose amendment lost 17-81, would have taken money from defense outlays to pay for the social program increases. *(Votes 105, 108, p. 21-S)*

During debate May 7 and 8, senators defeated attempts to increase funding for veterans' programs and make other changes in the resolution. Defeated amendments included those by:

● Thurmond, R-S.C., to add $300 million in budget authority and $150 million in outlays to the Veterans Administration by taking like amounts out of the health function; 36-55. *(Vote 95, p. 20-S)*

● DeConcini, D-Ariz., substitute for the Thurmond amendment to add $400 million in budget authority and $250 million in outlays for the Veterans Administration; 39-52. *(Vote 92, p. 19-S)*

● DeConcini, D-Ariz., to save $3.9 billion in budget authority by cutting funds for consultants, audio-visual programs and public relations; 42-49. *(Vote 96, p. 20-S)*

● Hatch, R-Utah, to delete $100 million for the Legal Services Corporation; 24-72. *(Vote 91, p. 19-S)*

● Kennedy, D-Mass., to restore $400 million in budget authority and outlays for school lunch and other child nutrition programs; 29-58. *(Vote 97, p. 20-S)*

Conference Action

House and Senate budget conferees agreed May 14 on a fiscal 1982 target budget (H Rept 97-46) that envisioned $695.45 billion in outlays in fiscal 1982 — $150 million more than Reagan requested. It anticipated $657.8 billion in revenues, resulting in a $37.65 billion deficit that was $7.35 billion under Reagan's estimate. By fiscal 1984, the resolution predicted a $1.5 billion surplus.

The measure called for a $51.3 billion net reduction in fiscal 1982 revenues — to be achieved by enactment of a $53.9 billion tax cut, partially offset by $2.6 billion in additional user fees.

The resolution also contained "reconciliation" instructions requiring House and Senate committees to cut approximately $36 billion in existing programs.

Pending final action on the second fiscal 1982 budget resolution, the conference agreement barred enrollment of any appropriations or direct spending bill that acceded the amount allocated to it under H Con Res 115. Congress thus would have an opportunity to revise the spending measures if it decided to cut spending in the second resolution.

By the time the conferees met to work out the minor differences between the House and Senate versions of the fiscal 1982 spending plan, many Democrats seemed resigned to their defeat.

"I don't think it is any secret," said Rep. Panetta, head of the House reconciliation task force, "that what we're embarking upon is a gamble. We're testing a theory on the American people. I don't think it's going to work — but it's a theory Congress wants to test."

In contrast to past budget resolutions, the disagreements between the House and Senate versions were fairly narrow. Close to $8 billion of the difference between the Senate's $700.8 billion spending figure and the House's $688.8 billion resulted from differences in economic assumptions — chiefly the difference in assumptions about interest rates.

The House had agreed to use the president's optimistic 8.9 percent interest rate for fiscal 1982, while the Senate used a 12 percent rate. The compromise interest rate went right down the middle — 10.5 percent.

Many Democrats scoffed at the prospect of interest rates, as reflected in 91-day Treasury bill rates, dropping to 10.5 percent in 1982. "There isn't a member on this committee who honestly believes the interest rate is going to be 10.5 percent," Sen. Howard M. Metzenbaum, D-Ohio, charged.

"I do," insisted Latta, the ranking minority member of the House Budget Committee. But he added, "We're going to have high interest rates unless we get spending down."

House Budget Chairman Jones quietly voiced his disagreement with the interest estimates. The interest rates in the compromise, he said, "I believe to be totally unrealistic. . . . I hate to see us play games, or charades or mirrors with the budget."

In addition to splitting the difference on the interest

assumptions, the Senate accepted the House measure's more optimistic growth rates for the remainder of fiscal 1981 and fiscal 1982, as well as the House's higher revenue figures. Both helped lower the anticipated deficit.

Spending Targets

In actual spending areas, the most touchy issue involved Social Security cuts. The Senate had agreed to cut Social Security spending by nearly $6 billion by changing the formula for calculating the cost-of-living adjustment (COLA) and delaying the benefit increase three months in fiscal 1982. Several attempts to delete the provision failed.

On May 12, however, the administration proposed sweeping changes in the Social Security system. It claimed the changes would save $9.1 billion in fiscal 1982 in combination with savings from proposals included in Reagan's March 10 budget. The earlier changes already had been approved by House and Senate committees.

The uproar from constituents and members that followed announcement of the administration plan helped convince conferees to drop the savings assumed by the Senate's COLA changes. That still left Senate outlays for income security programs, including Social Security, $3 billion below the House figure. Domenici proposed, and the conferees agreed, to split the difference.

Confusion remained, however, about how much of the president's suggested cuts would be accommodated by the first resolution compromise. According to Senate staffers, there was room in the resolution for $4.5 billion of the administration's cuts; House staffers thought the resolution would accommodate less — perhaps about $3 billion in cuts.

In the only other area of dispute, fiscal conservative Sen. Orrin G. Hatch, R-Utah, chairman of the Senate Labor and Human Resources Committee, fought successfully to add $500 million in budget authority for education and training.

"I chair a committee that I don't think has ever made a cut in its existence," Hatch said. But he explained that if the additional funds were not agreed to, essential programs for the handicapped would face elimination.

Responding to Hatch's plea, Rep. Stephen J. Solarz, D-N.Y., quipped, "If I didn't know better, I would have thought I heard the distinct accents of a born-again liberal."

The Senate conferees agreed to the fiscal 1982 spending targets 9-2, with J. James Exon, D-Neb., and Metzenbaum voting no. House members agreed to accept the compromise by voice vote.

Reconciliation

The House and Senate were very close on their reconciliation figures: The Senate called for $36.9 billion in cuts, and the House resolution required $36.6 billion. But there were technical differences arising from different assumptions and discrepancies in committee jurisdiction.

The conferees left it up to their respective staffs to work out final details of the reconciliation instructions. But they did agree to require savings amounting to at least $36 billion. *(Final reconciliation instructions, p. 256)*

Conferees agreed to resolve differences in four disputed program areas in reconciliation by: providing more money for child nutrition and the supplemental feeding program for women, infants and children (WIC); cutting out funds for the Small Business Administration's direct loan program; and adding $300 million for Medicare. ∎

Budget Totals Compared, Fiscal 1977-82

(In billions of dollars)

	Budget Authority	Outlays*	Revenues*	Deficit*
Fiscal Year 1977				
Ford Budget	$433.4	$394.2	$351.3	$—43.0
First Resolution	454.2	413.3	362.5	—50.8
Second Resolution	451.55	413.1	362.5	—50.6
Third Resolution	472.9	417.45	347.7	—69.75
Third Resolution amended	470.2	409.2	356.6	—52.6
Actual	464.4	402.7	357.8	—44.9
Fiscal Year 1978				
Ford Budget	480.4	440.0	393.0	—47.0
Carter Revisions	507.3	459.4	401.6	—57.7
First Resolution	503.45	460.95	396.3	—64.65
Second Resolution	500.1	458.25	397.0	—61.25
Actual	500.4	450.8	402.0	—48.8
Fiscal Year 1979				
Carter Budget	568.2	500.2	439.6	—60.6
First Resolution	568.85	498.8	447.9	—50.9
Second Resolution	555.65	487.5	448.7	—38.8
Revised Second Resolution	559.2	494.45	461.0	—33.45
Actual	556.7	493.6	465.9	—27.7
Fiscal Year 1980				
Carter Budget	615.5	531.6	502.6	—29.0
First Resolution	604.4	532.0	509.0	—23.0
Second Resolution	638.0	547.6	517.8	—29.8
Revised Second Resolution	658.9	572.65	525.7	—46.95
Actual	658.8	579.6	520.0	—59.6
Fiscal Year 1981				
Carter Budget	696.1	615.8	600.0	—15.8
Carter Revisions	691.3	611.5	628.0	+16.5
First Resolution	697.2	613.6	613.8	+ 0.2
Second Resolution	694.6	632.4	605.0	—27.4
Revised Second Resolution	717.5	661.35	603.3	—58.05
Actual	718.4	657.2	599.3	—57.9
Fiscal Year 1982				
Carter Budget	809.8	739.3	711.8	—27.5
Reagan Revision	772.4	695.3	650.3	—45.0
First Resolution †	770.9	695.45	657.8	—37.65

Actual figures for fiscal 1977-79 are taken from Carter budget for fiscal 1982; fiscal 1980-81 actual figures are from the Reagan administration.

† Second resolution merely reaffirmed figures in first resolution.

Fiscal 1982 Reconciliation Cuts: $35.2 Billion

Congress completed action July 31 on an omnibus package of "reconciliation" budget cuts (HR 3982 — PL 97-35) that dramatically altered the scope and shape of many government programs.

Final action on what House Budget Committee Chairman James R. Jones, D-Okla., called "clearly the most monumental and historic turnaround in fiscal policy that has ever occurred" came just two days after both the House and Senate approved the other major element of President Reagan's economic recovery program, a three-year tax relief package. *(Tax cuts, p. 91)*

As signed into law Aug. 13, the reconciliation measure (PL 97-35) revised federal programs to slash nearly $35.2 billion from a projected fiscal 1982 spending level of approximately $740 billion, according to Congressional Budget Office (CBO) estimates. *(Final savings, box, p. 259)*

Included in the bill's 27 titles were provisions to tighten income eligibility for food stamps and public assistance, eliminate minimum Social Security benefits, cut funds requested for subsidized housing programs, reduce school lunch subsidies, institute a needs test for guaranteed student loans, cut federal Medicaid payments to the states and consolidate various health and education programs into block grants.

Other provisions of the bill established a framework for ending Conrail subsidies, provided longer terms for radio and TV licenses, reauthorized the Consumer Product Safety Commission, terminated public service employment programs, limited pay raises for federal workers, increased interest rates in lending programs for farmers and small businesses, and made a multitude of other changes in existing law.

Specifics of the legislation are detailed in separate stories elsewhere in this volume. *(Index of stories, box, this page)*

Enactment of HR 3982 ended a remarkably swift journey that began in late February, when Reagan and the Republicans announced they wanted to use reconciliation as the tool to cut expected spending by $48.6 billion in fiscal 1982 and close to $200 billion through the end of fiscal 1984. *(How cuts were fashioned, box, next page)*

The idea of using reconciliation to carry through Reagan's pledge to trim federal spending had been advanced by David A. Stockman, director of the Office of Management and Budget (OMB). Stockman, a former House member (R-Mich., 1977-81), also was responsible for the highly publicized "black book" that formed the basis for the administration's sweeping budget cut proposals. *(Reagan budget, p. 278)*

Reconciliation had been used only once before — in 1980, when Congress believed it could balance the budget in 1981. That exercise reduced the deficit by $8.2 billion by slashing some funds and raising new revenues, although the fiscal 1981 budget remained unbalanced despite the effort. *(1980 Almanac p. 124)*

The 1980 reconciliation bill was, however, far more modest in scale and limited in purpose than Reagan's assault on federal spending, which included widespread and permanent changes in numerous program authorizations.

In 1981, as in 1980, reconciliation became a part of the budget process in conjunction with the first budget resolution, instead of the second resolution as envisioned in the

Reconciliation Stories

For a detailed accounting of the provisions of the Omnibus Reconciliation Act of 1981 (PL 97-35), see stories listed below.

1974 Congressional Budget Act (PL 93-344). *(1974 Almanac p. 145)*

The final version of the bill provided $130.6 billion in reconciliation savings for fiscal 1982-84, a total that fell somewhat short of the instructions given House and Senate committees by the first budget resolution in May. *(Resolution, p. 247)*

House Democrats maintained the $3.5 billion in fiscal 1982 spending restored by reconciliation conferees was justified by the importance of the programs involved.

Jones told House members the conference agreement was "vastly superior to the hastily thrown together and little-understood Gramm-Latta II," the Reagan substitute adopted on the House floor June 26 by a vote of 217-211. *(Vote 102, p. 42-H)*

He said it had been "cleansed of many of the misguided proposals" in both the Senate and House bills.

Senate Budget Chairman Pete V. Domenici, R-N.M., agreed. "The conference has produced a bill that is better than the bill the House passed and is, in many respects, better than the bill the Senate passed," he said.

Reagan lost more than he gained in conference. Deeper cuts than he sought were made in the food stamp program and several other areas. But conferees refused to place a "cap" on federal contributions to the states for Medicaid and declined to create some of the block grants Reagan wanted. In addition, funding was continued for several programs — such as the Economic Development Administration and the non-highway programs of the Appalachian Regional Commission — that Reagan wanted to eliminate.

However, such disappointments were insignificant compared to the overall accomplishment represented by the reconciliation measure — a major change in the direction of government and an abrupt slowdown in the growth of federal spending.

Institutional Fallout

Looking back on the 1981 experience, Domenici concluded that reconciliation "is obviously now a tool — a process for budget restraint, inordinate budget restraint — that you use when you want to do something very different."

The Senate Budget chairman saw the evolution of reconciliation as a major enhancement of the budget process. Others, however, expressed concern that Congress was abandoning its responsibilities and abdicating its powers to the executive branch.

"This is the most excessive use of presidential power and license," said House Rules Committee Chairman Richard Bolling, D-Mo. "And reconciliation is the most brutal and blunt instrument used by a president in an attempt to control the congressional process since [President Richard M.] Nixon used impoundment."

For members deeply involved in the budget process, the swift enactment of massive budget cuts was such a noteworthy accomplishment that they downplayed the importance of the severely truncated legislative process used to consider the bill.

They maintained that the sweep of the legislation included in the measure, involving hundreds of federal programs, did not preclude a well-drafted bill. These members pointed to the marathon meetings of 58 sub-conferences, where more than 250 members worked out final legislative agreements, as proof that the ultimate product was carefully considered.

How Cuts Were Fashioned

Feb. 18. President Reagan announces his first series of budget cuts, asking Congress to slash $41.4 billion from the fiscal 1982 spending request submitted by President Carter. With Reagan budget director David A. Stockman masterminding the effort, Senate GOP leaders agree to use reconciliation as the vehicle for consolidating the budget cuts in one package.

March 10. Reagan sends Congress his completed $48.6 billion package of fiscal 1982 budget cuts.

March 23. The Senate Budget Committee reports reconciliation instructions (S Con Res 9) requiring 14 Senate committees to alter programs to cut $36.4 billion in fiscal 1982 spending. The Republican-controlled panel virtually rubber-stamps Reagan's savings proposals.

April 2. The Senate passes, 88-10, S Con Res 9, ordering committees to cut $36.9 billion from the fiscal 1982 budget.

April 16. The Democratic-controlled House Budget Committee reports the first 1982 budget resolution (H Con Res 115). It includes reconciliation instructions calling for savings of $15.8 billion in fiscal 1982.

May 7. Sixty-three Democrats join all House Republicans to substitute the administration-backed budget and reconciliation instructions known as "Gramm-Latta" by a vote of 253-176. The House then approves H Con Res 115.

May 12. The Senate approves its version of the first fiscal 1982 budget resolution (S Con Res 19), incorporating its reconciliation instructions, 78-20.

May 14. House and Senate conferees on the budget resolution agree on fiscal 1982 spending goals, including reconciliation instructions to the authorizing committees requiring them to craft approximately $36 billion in fiscal 1982 spending cuts by June 12.

June 17. The House and Senate Budget committees assemble cuts made by their chambers' authorizing committees and report their reconciliation packages. Fiscal 1982 cuts total $37.7 billion for the House bill (HR 3982), $39.6 billion for the Senate (S 1377).

June 25. The Senate passes S 1377, 80-15. As passed, it provides $38.1 billion in fiscal 1982 savings.

June 26. By a vote of 217-211, the House substitutes "Gramm-Latta II" — a GOP-designed alternative that closely follows the Senate package — for the cuts agreed to by the House authorizing committees. Gramm-Latta II cuts $37.3 billion in fiscal 1982.

July 15. More than 250 Senate conferees, meeting in 58 sub-conferences, begin to work out the differences between the Senate and House bills.

July 29. Conferees reach final agreement on details of the deepest and most widespread package of budget cuts in the history of Congress.

July 31. The House, by voice vote, and the Senate, by an 80-14 vote, adopt the conference report on the reconciliation bill, clearing it for Reagan's signature. The final package is expected to reduce fiscal 1982 spending by nearly $35.2 billion and make reductions totaling $130.6 billion in fiscal 1982-84.

Aug. 13. Reagan signs the bill (PL 97-35).

"There may be those who will question the impact of reconciliation on the economy and on the budget process; but there is no one who can question that this document represents the ability of this institution to do its job, and to that extent I think our democracy has been well served," said Rep. Leon E. Panetta, D-Calif., chairman of the House Budget Committee's reconciliation task force.

Domenici told his colleagues during Senate floor debate on the conference report that "...the entire reconciliation process has done two crucial things: It has strengthened the legislative process, and it has restored confidence in Congress among the American people."

Sen. William Proxmire, D-Wis., however, contended that "congressional procedures were greatly abused, in spite of the innovative nature of the original reconciliation idea."

Proxmire noted that the normal Senate procedures — hearings, open markups, time for study and reports and the unlimited right to amendments on the floor — were abrogated under reconciliation.

The bill fell under the special rules that applied to budget matters, which made it impossible to filibuster and imposed a 20-hour limit on debate that applied even to the non-budget, substantive and sometimes controversial legislative matters included. Those issues ranged from licensing of radio and television stations to development of product safety standards.

The novelty of the reconciliation process, as well as its magnitude, led to substantial confusion among members of Congress about what they were doing and the ground rules under which they were operating. Meanwhile, the public and special interest groups were denied their usual participation in the congressional decision-making process because of the scope and constrained time frame.

In the House, Rep. Ted Weiss, D-N.Y., lamented during floor debate July 31, "...[W]e are voting today not only on a conference report, but on a process that is out of control."

One outgrowth of the reconciliation process in 1981 was the greatly enhanced power enjoyed by the Budget committees.

Even in the House, where the Budget Committee had much of its work overturned on the floor, the panel still played a large role in shaping the reconciliation package and shepherding it through Congress.

In the Senate, the power of the Republican-controlled Budget Committee was substantial. Not only did Domenici spearhead the idea of tailoring reconciliation to Reagan's budget-cutting needs, but he, with Senate Majority Leader Howard H. Baker Jr., R-Tenn., saw to it that reconciliation was put on a "fast-track" schedule — ensuring that the GOP could take advantage quickly of the overwhelming popularity of Reagan and public enthusiasm for trimming the federal budget.

With some hefty assistance from Stockman and OMB, the Senate Budget Committee drafted instructions that gave authorizing committees a detailed scenario of what and how they could cut. In the end, many Senate committees accepted in large measure the Budget Committee's blueprint.

Committee Action

The 1981 reconciliation instructions required 14 Senate committees and 15 House panels to cut or alter existing programs to save about $36 billion in fiscal 1982. The instructions applied to both authorizations and direct spending — that is, spending to which the government is committed whether or not the appropriations are provided in advance. Direct spending embraced entitlement payments, such as Social Security benefits, veterans' compensation and interest on the public debt, as well as contract authority and authority to incur indebtedness. *(Committee instructions, box, p. 260)*

The Republican-controlled Senate originally approved its reconciliation instructions as separate legislation (S Con Res 9). The action was designed to pressure the Democratic House to act swiftly on the Reagan cuts. The Senate instructions ultimately were coordinated with the House instructions as part of the budget resolution. *(Senate resolution, box, p. 250)*

Although the reconciliation instructions required legislative committees to achieve specific savings objectives, the program reductions on which the savings were based were not binding — legislative committees retained the right to make the cuts in other programs if they chose. In fact, however, some committees had little discretion, given the magnitude of their spending reductions.

The panels were required to report their savings measures to the Budget committees by June 12. The Budget committees then were to assemble the various measures into an omnibus package for House and Senate floor consideration.

Most committees put off as long as possible the painful exercise of transforming budget-cutting rhetoric into actual cuts in spending for federal programs. But when the June 12 deadline arrived, all but one of the panels appeared to have done their jobs, at least on paper. Senate committees exceeded their fiscal 1982 outlay cut instructions by $4.5 billion.

Cuts were made from a baseline figure established by the Congressional Budget Office that reflected anticipated fiscal 1982 spending adjusted for inflation.

Senate Budget Chairman Domenici called the reconciliation effort "the most dramatic reduction in ongoing programs in the history of this country."

"It's almost unbelievable to me that we are at this point today," he marveled.

The one committee that did not comply with reconciliation was the House Energy and Commerce Committee, which was unable to get a majority of votes for a package put together by Chairman John D. Dingell, D-Mich.

Three Energy and Commerce Democrats, who were also members of the Conservative Democratic Forum (CDF), which had provided crucial support for Reagan on the first budget resolution — Phil Gramm, Texas; Richard C. Shelby, Ala.; and James D. Santini, Nev. — refused to go along with their chairman. They cast their lot with the GOP alternative sponsored by James T. Broyhill, R-N.C. By siding with the Republicans, the CDF members made the tally 21-21.

Dingell never held a formal vote. Instead, he decided to write a letter to the Budget Committee outlining his proposal and noting that a majority of the panel's Democrats supported the package.

Another crisis was averted when House Education and Labor Committee Democrats pushed through a proposal that basically met their $12.1 billion reconciliation goal. "We are meeting with a gun pointed at our heads," said Chairman Carl D. Perkins, D-Ky. "The majority of this committee does not want to make these drastic cutbacks."

Final Reconciliation Savings

The final version of the reconciliation package (HR 3982) altered existing programs to achieve the following budget savings *(by House committee jurisdiction, in millions of dollars)*:

	Fiscal 1982		Fiscal 1983		Fiscal 1984	
	Budget Authority Cuts	Outlay Cuts	Budget Authority Cuts	Outlay Cuts	Budget Authority Cuts	Outlay Cuts
Committee						
Agriculture	$ 2,449	$ 3,264	$ 3,042	$ 3,878	$ 3,930	$ 4,661
Armed Services	846	882	767	731	374	374
Banking, Finance and Urban Affairs	13,566	481	15,954	1,154	18,402	2,115
District of Columbia	39	40	56	58	72	69
Education and Labor	10,088	7,297	12,414	10,749	14,261	13,881
Energy and Commerce	7,955	7,115	7,457	7,710	6,686	6,961
Foreign Affairs	376	286	524	463	538	515
Interior and Insular Affairs	820	736	+236[1]	111	68	5
Judiciary	72	30	70	71	59	66
Merchant Marine and Fisheries	242	106	242	212	265	253
Post Office and Civil Service	4,706	5,163	6,253	6,690	7,214	7,555
Public Works and Transportation	6,606	1,411	5,070	3,136	6,371	5,418
Science and Technology	1,395	828	961	1,016	1,209	1,065
Small Business	504	823	540	517	527	506
Veterans' Affairs	110	116	122	127	124	128
Ways and Means	4,140	8,981	4,455	9,822	4,763	10,803
Total Cuts[2]	**$51,900**	**$35,190**	**$55,734**	**$44,033**	**$61,721**	**$51,353**

[1] *Increase in budget authority attributable to an increase in the cap on Interior Department funding; conferees' elimination of a provision to increase the price of government uranium enrichment services; and increased funding for the Naval Petroleum Reserve, requested by the administration.*

[2] *Adjusted for jurisdictional overlap.*

SOURCE: House Budget Committee

Perkins said the committee Democrats agreed to make the cuts in part because they obtained an agreement from the House leadership to allow floor votes on four or five of the more controversial reductions.

House Budget Committee

By law the Budget committees had no authority to touch the reconciliation cuts made by the authorizing committees. They were merely to carry out their "ministerial" function of pulling the various committee actions together into one bill.

But the House Budget Committee, confronted with several technical problems and one substantive one, agreed on a straight party-line vote to report a substitute bill that included three amendments. That measure (HR 3982 — H Rept 97-158), reported June 19, called for fiscal 1982 spending cuts totaling $37.76 billion.

The one truly substantive amendment dealt with the Energy and Commerce Committee, which had deadlocked

over reconciliation. The Budget Committee's substitute included the recommendations of the Energy panel's Democratic majority. However, the Budget Committee agreed to ask the Rules Committee to allow a separate vote on the Energy panel's minority proposal, to be offered by ranking member James T. Broyhill, R-N.C.

Another Budget Committee amendment removed controversial language included in the Post Office and Civil Service provisions that directed the closing of 10,000 small post offices. Although the $100 million cut agreed to by the Post Office Committee remained in the reconciliation package, there were no instructions to the Postal Service about where to make the spending reductions.

Finally, the Budget Committee resolved some jurisdictional problems involving revenues. Several committees reported revenue provisions over which the Ways and Means Committee claimed jurisdiction. The Budget Committee agreed to credit Ways and Means with the savings. These jurisdictional changes, which did not affect savings totals,

Reconciliation Instructions Under H Con Res 115. . .

(In millions of dollars)

SENATE COMMITTEES	Fiscal 1981		Fiscal 1982		Fiscal 1983		Fiscal 1984	
	Budget Authority	Outlays	Budget Authority	Outlays	Budget Authority	Outlays	Budget Authority	Outlays
Agriculture, Nutrition and Forestry:								
Reductions in direct spending		$ −163	$ −474	$ −928	$ −659	$ −618	$ −854	$ −795
Reductions in authorizations	$ −140		−3,193	−3,096	−3,961	−3,825	−4,551	−4,451
Armed Services:								
Reductions in direct spending	−233	−233	−966	−966	−899	−899	−511	−511
Banking, Housing, and Urban Affairs:								
Reductions in authorizations	−5,846	−133	−14,498	−840	−17,450	−2,133	−20,341	−3,779
Commerce, Science and Transportation:								
Reductions in direct spending			−100	−100	−200	−200	−300	−300
Reductions in authorizations			−1,558	−884	−1,598	−1,328	−1,465	−1,337
Energy and Natural Resources:								
Reductions in authorizations	−1,331	−94	−3,714	−3,398	−3,660	−3,627	−3,604	−3,711
Environment and Public Works:								
Reductions in direct spending				−185		−900		−1,365
Reductions in authorizations	−2,350	−68	−4,835	−793	−3,035	−1,840	−3,500	−2,800
Finance:								
Reductions in direct spending	−212	−286	−4,394	−9,218	−4,563	−10,744	−4,675	−11,589
Reductions in authorizations			−96	−112	−114	−132	−149	−177
Foreign Relations:								
Reductions in authorizations			−250	−130	−275	−200	−300	−300
Governmental Affairs:								
Reductions in direct spending				−513		−414		−357
Reductions in authorizations			−4,776	−4,690	−6,360	−6,388	−7,462	−7,440
Judiciary:								
Reductions in authorizations			−116	−13	−133	−81	−144	−124
Labor and Human Resources:								
Reductions in direct spending	−39	−49	−596	−575	−1,481	−1,395	−2,452	−2,311
Reductions in authorizations	−2,388	−414	−10,492	−8,225	−12,539	−11,069	−15,048	−13,746
Small Business:								
Reductions in authorizations	−97	−67	−526	−390	−564	−541	−554	−533
Veterans' Affairs:								
Reductions in direct spending	−14	−14	−110	−110	−108	−108	−106	−106
Total reductions in direct spending	−498	−745	−6,640	−12,595	−7,910	−15,278	−8,898	−17,334
Total reductions in authorizations	−12,152	−776	−44,054	−22,571	−49,689	−31,164	−57,118	−38,398
Appropriations Committee:	−13,300	−1,500		−3,200		−1,800		−1,100
Senate total	−25,950	−3,021	−50,694	−38,366	−57,599	−48,242	−66,016	−56,832
Eliminate double counting between appropriations and authorizing committees	+11,283	+677		+1,865		+1,263		+1,034
Total net savings	$ −14,667	$ − 2,344	$ −50,694	$ −36,501	$ −57,599	$ −46,979	$ −66,016	$ −55,798

included railroad retirement changes by Energy and Commerce, black lung benefit changes by Education and Labor and capital construction grants by Public Works. The Budget Committee also agreed to drop provisions for an oil spill "superfund" user fee which the Merchant Marine Committee included in its actions.

Senate Budget Committee

The Republican-controlled Senate Budget Committee met June 16 and routinely packaged the Senate committees' cuts. Its bill was reported the next day (S 1377 — S

Rept 97-139).

Senate committees had been directed in the instructions to provide $36.5 billion in savings, but this total included rescissions and deferrals that were included in the supplemental fiscal 1981 appropriations bill. Once that bill was approved, the Senate's goal dropped to the House level of $35.1 billion in fiscal 1982 savings. The Senate committees overshot that goal, trimming $39.6 billion. *(Supplemental bill, p. 281)*

The chief area of concern over the Senate bill was the inclusion of "extraneous" legislation that had no budgetary

... Require Committees to Make Deep Program Cuts

(In millions of dollars)

HOUSE COMMITTEES	Fiscal 1982		Fiscal 1983		Fiscal 1984	
	Budget Authority	Outlays	Budget Authority	Outlays	Budget Authority	Outlays
Agriculture:						
Reductions in direct spending	$ −232	$ −693	$ −400	$ −362	$ −580	$ −525
Reductions in authorizations	−1,976	−1,828	−2,606	−2,480	−3,091	−3,000
Armed Srvices:						
Reductions in direct spending	−966	−966	−899	−899	−511	−511
Banking, Finance and Urban Affairs:						
Reductions in authorizations	−13,177	−640	−15,572	−1,398	−17,827	−2,369
District of Columbia:						
Reductions in authorizations	−39	−40	−56	−64	−72	−69
Education and Labor:						
Reductions in direct spending	−1,963	−1,946	−2,916	−2,777	−3,995	−3,801
Reductions in authorizations	−10,136	−8,138	−11,991	−10,745	−14,349	−13,219
Energy and Commerce:						
Reductions in direct spending	−787	−1,103	−1,082	−1,716	−1,355	−2,247
Reductions in authorizations	−4,598	−4,081	−4,898	−4,599	−4,930	−4,789
Foreign Affairs:						
Reductions in authorizations	−250	−130	−275	−200	−300	−300
Interior and Insular Affairs:						
Reductions in authorizations	−755	−309	−736	−504	−714	−594
Merchant Marine and Fisheries:						
Reductions in direct spending	−192	−192	−379	−379	−491	−491
Reductions in authorizations	−147	−15	−60	−32	−71	−60
Post Office and Civil Service:						
Reductions in direct spending		−513		−414		−357
Reductions in authorizations	−4,737	−4,650	−6,304	−6,324	−7,390	−7,371
Public Works and Transportation:						
Reductions in direct spending		−185		−900		−1,365
Reductions in authorizations	−6,346	−1,033	−5,122	−2,665	−6,241	−4,355
Science and Technology:						
Reductions in authorizations	−78	−39	−90	−59	−102	−83
Small Business:						
Reductions in authorizations	−526	−390	−564	−541	−554	−533
Veterans Affairs:						
Reductions in direct spending	−110	−110	−108	−108	−106	−106
Ways and Means:						
Reductions in direct spending	−3,699	−8,247	−3,660	−9,247	−3,511	−9,573
Reductions in authorizations	−978	−994	−1,294	−1,312	−1,647	−1,675
House total	−51,692	−36,242	−59,012	−47,725	−67,837	−57,393
Eliminate double counting resulting from shared jurisdiction	+882	+882	+1,180	+1,180	+1,498	+1,498
	+92	+92	+179	+179	+191	+191
	+24	+152	+54	+54	+132	+132
Total net savings	$ −50,694	$ −35,116	$ −57,599	$ −46,312	$ −66,016	$ −55,572

impact.

Committees had included in their reconciliation recommendations legislation ranging from a reauthorization of federal housing programs to permitting wide trucks to operate on federal-aid highways.

The Budget panel agreed to include in its report language expressing its concern about the failure of certain committees to meet their future-year spending reduction goals and urge that something be done on the floor to bring them into compliance.

GOP House Challenge

After a week of forays and retreats by both parties, the administration and House GOP leaders decided that the reconciliation package drafted by 15 House committees did not make deep enough cuts in entitlement programs, under which the government is obligated to make payments to persons who qualify for them.

"Either we come to grips with the question of entitlement programs now," House Minority Leader Robert H. Michel, R-Ill., said June 19, "or we will have broken our

compact with the American people." Michel said eight of the House committees had done their job well, but "seven left us rather short."

Republicans and some conservative Democrats therefore decided to push an alternative package on the House floor. Their package proposed spending cuts in 10 major areas, which they claimed would save about $20 billion by fiscal 1984.

The Republican/conservative Democratic alternative — known as "Gramm-Latta II" for the sponsors of the House-passed fiscal 1982 budget resolution — would save an additional $5.1 billion in major programs in fiscal 1982. But it also would restore money for some programs, such as educational impact aid.

Even before committees completed their work on reconciliation, a group of dissatisfied House Republicans and conservative Democrats had complained that a number of the spending cuts made by the House panels were "false, counterproductive and unnecessarily severe."

The group used as ammunition an OMB analysis of the House committee cuts, detailing what that agency deemed faulty spending reductions.

President Reagan joined the attack at his June 16 press conference, saying there "is now a clear danger of congressional backsliding and a return to spending as usual."

The collective prodding brought results. To counter the criticism about phony cuts in social programs, the House Education and Labor Committee reworked its spending reductions — lopping off a huge chunk from Comprehensive Employment and Training Act (CETA) jobs programs and putting that money back into popular programs such as student loans and feeding programs for the elderly.

But many Democrats bristled at the notion that Congress was supposed to fall into lock step and not deviate from the president's plan. Panetta, chairman of the House reconciliation task force, contended that if the committees did everything the way OMB and the president wanted, they would be "kissing off" the budget process. "We're stretching the budget process to the breaking point," he said.

The Democrats continued to stress that 250 programs were touched by the reconciliation package, and 85 percent of the cuts in these programs were either recommended by the administration or approved by the House.

The Democratic tactics forced the Republicans to reassess their plan to offer a total alternative spending cut package. "Let's face it," said Michel June 18, "we've come quite a long way from where we were a few weeks ago."

In the end, however, the administration, House Republicans and dissident Democrats decided it was necessary to make the fight over major program changes.

Said a GOP briefing document: "[B]uried within the massive House reconciliation bill and the large score-keeping savings reported for authorized programs is a critical and glaring defect: The reform and hold-down of automatic spending programs has not been achieved."

GOP Proposal

The sponsors of the Republican alternative claimed that the first fiscal 1982 budget resolution required $8.5 billion in savings in entitlement programs, but the committees came up with only $3 billion.

The most important GOP changes in the committees' package were:

- Tighter controls on food stamp and school lunch spending.
- Further tightening of welfare programs.
- A phase-out of student Social Security benefits and elimination of minimum Social Security benefits.
- Further cuts in subsidized housing.
- A means test for guaranteed student loans.
- Once-a-year cost-of-living increases (COLAs) for both military and civilian government retirees and a lower civilian pay cap.
- Minority substitutes for Energy and Commerce and Science and Technology Committee cuts.

House Fight on Rule

In two successive days the Republicans, with the help of a group of 29 hard-core conservative Democrats, engineered a critical procedural victory that paved the way for the ultimate triumph June 26 of the Reagan-backed package of budget cuts known as Gramm-Latta II.

House Democrats thought they had thwarted Republican efforts to overturn the bill reported by the House Budget Committee. They carefully drafted a rule for floor debate under which members would be forced to vote separately on individual spending cuts supported by the administration. Those cuts were deeper than the ones agreed to by 15 House authorizing committees.

The Republicans wanted a single, up-or-down vote on their budget package.

The Democratic leadership believed that members would shrink away from voting to slash an additional $20 billion over the next three years from programs such as Social Security, student loans and Medicaid, and instead would vote for the $37.6 billion package of spending cuts crafted by the committees.

The ground rules upon which the Democratic-controlled Rules Committee agreed made it even more difficult for members to accept further deep cuts, since the rule did not include Gramm-Latta's so-called "sweeteners" — additional funding for popular programs such as the Export-Import Bank and educational impact aid.

The scheme blew up in the Democrats' faces, however, when after several days of intense administration lobbying and a morning of biting rhetoric, the House defeated, 210-217, a procedural motion that would have cleared the way for adoption of the Democrats' ground rules for debate. *(Vote 95, p. 40-H)*

"The Rules Committee came out with a rule that takes two-thirds of the [Gramm-Latta] cuts and throws them in the trash can, and then takes the remaining one-third and rewrites them," said Rep. Gramm, cosponsor of the substitute package. "Don't be deceived, the issue here is not the whole package *vs.* separate cuts. What this rule does is destroy the opportunity for Congress to work the people's will."

Minority Leader Michel said it was "not only a bad rule, it's a rotten rule."

But Majority Leader Jim Wright, D-Texas, told members that they owed themselves the "right to make choices." He characterized the vote on the rule as one by which the House would decide either to vote on a package whose details were determined by OMB Director Stockman and the president, or one that would allow votes on "the hard, tough questions — which programs to cut."

Wright said the House owed the president its

cooperation, but "we do not owe him obeisance, obedience and submissiveness."

Rules Committee Chairman Bolling maintained that voting down the rule would be voting "in a narrow partisan game in support of a narrow, doubtful [economic] program."

"Do we have the guts to stand up for what we believe in?" Bolling asked.

When the votes were in, however, it was evident the Republicans had successfully sold their case: A vote against the rule would allow the House to vote to implement the Gramm-Latta budget adopted earlier in the first budget resolution. Anything less, they maintained, would be denying Reagan his economic program and denying the mandate of the American people.

After the vote, a despondent Speaker Thomas P. O'Neill Jr., D-Mass., told the members, "I've never seen anything like this in my life, to be perfectly truthful."

Following the defeat of the Democratic rule, the House went on to approve a procedure, by a vote of 214-208, that allowed up-or-down votes on the Gramm-Latta package of amendments, plus an amendment — later withdrawn — dealing with cuts in the Energy and Commerce Committee's jurisdiction. *(Vote 98, p. 40-H)*

House Passage

The House June 26 adopted the Gramm-Latta comprehensive amendment by a margin of six votes, 217-211. As on the crucial procedural vote a day earlier, 29 Democrats stood with the administration. Only two Republicans voted against their party: Claudine Schneider, R.I. and Charles F. Dougherty, Pa. *(Vote 102, p. 42-H; Democratic defectors, box, this page)*

Schneider then offered a motion to recommit the bill to the Budget Committee with instructions to reinstate a twice-a-year cost-of-living adjustment for federal employees. Republicans headed off an attempt by Budget Chairman Jones to substitute instructions calling for changes in Social Security, student loans and block grants. The House rejected the Schneider motion by voice vote, after blocking Jones' effort to amend it on a 215-212 vote. *(Vote 103, p. 42-H)*

Passage of the measure followed on a 232-193 vote, with some key Democratic committee leaders voting for passage to assure themselves a role in the conference committee. The House tabled a motion to reconsider the vote on passage, 187-150. As passed, the measure provided $37.3 billion in fiscal 1982 savings. *(Votes 104-105, p. 42-H)*

The Reagan victory followed two days of often acrimonious debate as well as considerable lobbying by the president.

Members from both political parties decried their situation: Most of the details on the Gramm-Latta proposal were not available until hours before the House vote.

"This has been a terrible way to legislate, but we have no alternatives," lamented Barber B. Conable Jr., R-N.Y.

Panetta said, "We are dealing with over 250 programs with no committee consideration, no hearings, no debate and no opportunity to offer amendments."

Before the close of debate, Jones urged his colleagues "not to abandon your legislative responsibility, not to abandon the substantive issues, because of partisan pressures."

But Delbert L. Latta, R-Ohio, a cosponsor of the amendment and ranking GOP member of the House Bud-

Democrats Who Defected

Here is a list of 34 Democrats who voted with President Reagan May 7 on the Latta substitute for first fiscal 1982 budget resolution but who voted with the Democrats June 25 on the key vote on the rule to consider the reconciliation bill. *(Budget resolution, vote 30, p. 20-H; reconciliation rule, vote 95, p. 40-H)*

Albosta, Mich.	Hatcher, Ga.
Andrews, N.C.	Holland, S.C.
Anthony, Ark.	Jacobs, Ind.
Bevill, Ala.	Jenkins, Ga.
Bouquard, Tenn.	Jones, Tenn.
Bowen, Miss.	Levitas, Ga.
Brinkley, Ga.	Long, Md.
Derrick, S.C.	Luken, Ohio
Dyson, Md.	Mazzoli, Ky.
English, Okla.	Mica, Fla.
Evans, Ind.	Natcher, Ky.
Flippo, Ala.	Nelson, Fla.
Fountain, N.C.	Patterson, Calif.
Fuqua, Fla.	Skelton, Mo.
Gibbons, Fla.	Volkmer, Mo.
Ginn, Ga.	Yatron, Pa.
Hall, Ohio	Young, Mo.

Here is a list of 29 Democrats who sided with President Reagan on both the May 7 budget resolution vote and the vote on the rule to consider the reconciliation bill.

Atkinson, Pa.	Ireland, Fla.
Barnard, Ga.	Leath, Texas
Bennett, Fla.	McDonald, Ga.
Breaux, La.	Montgomery, Miss.
Byron, Md.	Mottl, Ohio
Chappell, Fla.	Nichols, Ala.
Daniel, Va.	Roemer, La.
Evans, Ga.	Santini, Nev.
Gramm, Texas	Shelby, Ala.
R. Hall, Texas	Stenholm, Texas
S. Hall, Texas	Stump, Ariz.
Hance, Texas	Tauzin, La.
Hightower, Texas	White, Texas
Huckaby, La.	Wilson, Texas
Hutto, Fla.	

get Committee, framed the vote this way: "It is a question of whether we turn the country around economically or not."

The president, jubilant at the results of the procedural victory June 25, said, "The simple truth is that Congress heard the voice of the people, and they acted to carry out the will of the people."

Reagan himself lobbied by telephone and telegraph the entire group of 63 Democrats who voted with him on the first budget resolution.

Jones said the president used all his powers of persuasion, including promises of sweetening some farm programs. "The Democratic cloakroom had all the earmarks of a tobacco auction," Jones said after the June 25 vote.

When asked if there was anything the Democrats could have done differently or if he saw any future hope of changing the course the Republicans had charted, Jones said that eventually "the substantive issues will be debated, and that's when there will be hope for the Democrats."

Energy-Commerce Provisions

Although the Republicans won the ball game, the Democrats succeeded in retaining at least one important piece of the reconciliation bill: those provisions under the jurisdiction of the Energy and Commerce Committee, the only panel that did not recommend reconciliation savings. After days of maneuvering, the committee deadlocked 21-21 and never took a formal vote.

The House Budget Committee voted to ask for a rule that would give members a choice between a Democratic proposal offered by Energy and Commerce Chairman John D. Dingell, D-Mich., which the Budget Committee had included in its substitute bill, and a minority proposal offered by the panel's ranking Republican, James T. Broyhill, N.C.

According to an aide to Broyhill, Dingell secured the commitment of four conservative Democrats to vote with him when the reconciliation package came to the House floor: Ronald M. Mottl, Ohio; Ralph M. Hall, Texas; W. J. "Billy" Tauzin, La.; and Jack Hightower, Texas.

These four agreed to go with Dingell because his package included provisions repealing sections of the Fuel Use Act, thus allowing plants to burn natural gas after 1989.

When the president called and asked each one for his vote on the crucial procedural motion setting rules for floor debate on reconciliation, these members said they would vote with the Republicans only if they could honor their commitment to Dingell and vote separately on the Energy-Commerce package. The Republican leaders agreed to write their rule so there would be an up-or-down vote on Broyhill. Then the trading began.

The Broyhill amendment contained language, important to the administration, setting a cap on federal payments to the states for Medicaid. These provisions, however, and others on low-income energy assistance, Conrail and Amtrak, proved to be very troublesome to many Republicans from the Northeast.

Bill Green, R-N.Y., led a group of unhappy Frost Belt GOP members in negotiating more favorable Gramm-Latta provisions on these issues, but for some the concessions did not go far enough.

According to accounts by both Democrats and Republicans, the Broyhill package simply was too risky to bring to a vote just before the vote on passage. The GOP leadership finally decided to pull the Broyhill amendment; the Dingell package thus was included in the final bill by default.

Wheeling, Dealing and Accommodation

The administration did not confine its negotiating for votes on the reconciliation measure to the details of the Broyhill amendment. OMB Director Stockman maintained the administration had made accommodations — including changes on education impact aid, food stamps and low-income energy assistance — throughout the weeks following adoption of the reconciliation instructions in May.

"By the time we got to the votes on Thursday and Friday, 98 percent of the compromises were made," Stockman told reporters June 27. "There were a few final adjustments that inevitably occur when you're in this kind of intensely political process. . . ."

Members of the opposition party did not view the administration's negotiations quite so charitably. "They're making deals like crazy in the cloakroom," moaned Jones after the Democrats lost the vote on their rule.

Louisiana Democrat John B. Breaux, when asked if his vote could be bought, replied: "No, it can be rented."

Breaux and a group of others from the Louisiana and Florida delegations were given assurances that the administration would take a second look at sugar price support legislation the White House had opposed as inflationary.

Language also was included in the bill pinpointing money for a pet energy project — a solar electric plant — in the district of Charles W. Stenholm, D-Texas. Stenholm was chairman of the Conservative Democratic Forum, which provided enough Democratic members to give the administration the margin of victory on reconciliation.

There was negotiating on the other side of the aisle, too. Marilyn Lloyd Bouquard, D-Tenn., who voted with the president on the key May vote on the budget resolution, agreed to stick by her party when Jones confirmed on the floor that funding for the Clinch River breeder reactor would be open for discussion in the conference.

Senate Floor Action

In the Senate there never was any doubt that the Republicans had an iron grip on the budget. The Senate approved its version of the reconciliation measure June 25 by an 80-15 vote. *(Vote 182, p. 33-S)*

While the Senate made some minor revisions in its $39.6 billion reconciliation package, the significant elements remained the same as the measure drafted by the Senate authorizing committees and put together by the Budget Committee. Final fiscal 1982 savings tally: $38.1 billion.

Before finally passing the omnibus spending cut package, the Senate agreed to delete many of its extraneous provisions — those having no budgetary impact. But then, on up-or-down votes, the Senate agreed to put some of them back.

This arrangement, arrived at by the leadership of both parties, satisfied the concerns of Minority Leader Robert C. Byrd, D-W.Va. "If we are going to go down this road of including extraneous matter," he said, "I want it to be done here, on this floor — come in the front door and let every senator, with his eyes open, have a chance to vote on it as we now have in connection with adding legislation to an appropriation bill."

The most important provisions to be restored were Banking, Housing and Urban Affairs Committee additions that reauthorized housing and community development programs and denied federal funds to cities with rent control and rent stabilization. The vote on this amendment, offered by Banking Chairman Jake Garn, R-Utah, was 54-42. *(Vote 174, p. 32-S)*

The Senate also restored provisions dealing with programs under the Commerce Committee's jurisdiction that would deregulate radio broadcasting and liberalize television licensing. The vote was 55-40. *(Vote 175, p. 32-S)*

By a vote of 51-47, the Senate also agreed to an amendment to keep Medicare as the primary health insurance provider for federal employees with dual coverage. Sponsors Ted Stevens, R-Alaska, and William V. Roth Jr., R-Del., said that without the amendment, previously rejected 47-50, federal employees' health insurance premi-

ums would be increased, since the burden of providing health insurance would be switched to private health plans. *(Votes 170-72, p. 31-S)*

Other amendments agreed to by the Senate aimed to:

● Restore funds for Indochinese, Cuban and Haitian refugee programs to a level requested by the administration.

● Restore $300 million for impact aid to school districts with large military and other federal installations.

● Restore burial benefits for disabled veterans.

● Authorize the sale of silver from the strategic stockpile.

● Allow the administration to sell Conrail as a single entity after June 1, 1982, and sell Conrail lines after Dec. 1, 1982, if the railroad were determined to be unprofitable. The Senate also authorized $150 million for interim operating expenses and $400 million for labor protection costs.

● Reallocate VHF television stations to New Jersey and Delaware.

● Require the Corporation for Public Broadcasting to pay 50 percent of satellite interconnection costs.

The Senate rejected amendments that would have:

● Restored budget authority for rehabilitation programs for the disabled, 47-50. *(Vote 168, p. 31-S)*

● Reduced fees for consultants and federal travel, 44-52. *(Vote 173, p. 31-S)*

● Reduced funds for the nuclear fission program by $309 million, 25-69. *(Vote 176, p. 32-S)*

● Restored federal assistance for rape victims, 43-52. *(Vote 179, p. 33-S)*

● Barred the Transportation Department from selling Conrail lines before Aug. 1, 1984, if the railroad were determined to be profitable, 34-60. *(Vote 181, p. 33-S)*

Conference Action

The conference on HR 3982 began in mid-July, following unsuccessful efforts by Stockman — and at one point Reagan — to prevail on the GOP Senate leadership simply to accept the House version of the bill.

More than 250 members of Congress participated in the conference, which split up into 58 subgroups to consider various sections of the legislation.

Senate Budget Chairman Domenici and House Chairman Jones agreed that most of the conference issues could be resolved easily. The House-passed Gramm-Latta II was nearly a complete reflection of the Reagan administration's budget-cutting program, and the Senate bill contained only minor differences from the Reagan plan. Domenici predicted that "not more than 20 issues are likely to be difficult."

Rep. Gramm, who described himself as the "major author" of the Reagan-backed House reconciliation bill, was not included in the list of House conferees. Jones explained that "we had to go pretty much on seniority, and we couldn't name [OMB Director] Stockman. Gramm, the most junior Democrat on the Budget Committee, vowed he would watch the conference proceedings closely and would be "actively involved" on an informal basis.

Social Security

As conferees struggled to complete action on reconciliation before Congress' August recess, the Democrats did their best to draw blood from the one domestic issue where the Reagan administration seemed to be vulnerable: the decision to eliminate the $122 minimum benefit for Social

Security recipients. *(Social Security, p. 117)*

On July 21 the House by a 405-13 vote adopted a resolution (H Res 181) urging reconciliation conferees to take steps "to ensure that Social Security benefits are not reduced for those currently receiving them." *(Vote 136, p. 50-H)*

The House resolution was not binding, however.

An effort to save minimum benefits through an amendment to the tax bill was thwarted in the GOP-controlled Senate July 21 by a 52-46 vote. But Majority Leader Baker said that many of his colleagues were troubled by removal of the minimum benefit and that "perhaps it should be restored." *(Vote 207, p. 37-S)*

Despite such reservations, reconciliation conferees from the House Ways and Means and Senate Finance committees abided by the decisions previously reached in each chamber. On July 23, they decided to halt the minimum benefit at the end of February 1982 for all those currently receiving it. Those who became eligible in 1981 would be notified Nov. 1, 1981, of the payment cutoff.

No one, including the Democratic sponsors of the House Social Security resolution, really expected the conferees to reverse the previously adopted House position on minimum benefits.

But the Democrats, with thousands of senior citizens marching on the Capitol to protest changes in the Social Security system, wanted to force Republicans to be counted on the minimum benefits issue.

The Democrats argued that those who would be hurt by eliminating the minimum benefits were mostly elderly women, many of them widows. Patricia Schroeder, D-Colo., told the House, "These women are not living it up as merry widows. . . ."

But the Republicans, armed with data furnished by OMB, contended that only about 300,000 of the three million recipients of minimum benefits would actually be affected by the cutoff. The others would have their regular Social Security benefits or Supplemental Security Income benefits recalculated to make up the difference.

"The truth is that in current form the minimum benefit program does not belong in the Social Security Act," charged House Minority Leader Michel.

Nonetheless, Michel released GOP members to vote for the essentially toothless resolution when it came up July 21 on the House floor. Eager to escape the trap set by the Democrats, Republicans did so in droves.

Final Agreement

Reconciliation conferees finally wound up their negotiations and filed their report (H Rept 97-208) July 29. The conferees had confronted a number of knotty issues, albeit fewer than they would have if the Democratic reconciliation bill had passed in the House. Among the more difficult ones, and the compromises resolving them, were:

Health Block Grants. Nineteen of 25 health programs were combined into four block grants. But family planning — the bone of greatest contention — was retained as a separate program, as the House wanted. Also exempted were immunization, tuberculosis, venereal disease, teen-age pregnancy and migrant health programs.

Medicaid. Conferees rejected the cap on federal contributions to the states for Medicaid sought by the Senate and the administration. However, they agreed to reduce Medicaid costs by 3 percent in fiscal 1982, 4 percent in fiscal 1983 and 4.5 percent in fiscal 1984, for a savings of about $1 billion per year.

Items That Were Dropped

While the final reconciliation package (HR 3982) contained provisions affecting hundreds of programs, conferees dropped some major items that were included in the House or Senate bills.

Items that were dropped included the following:

● An instruction to the Federal Communications Commission (FCC) to allocate the next available VHF television channel, if technically possible, to New Jersey or Delaware.

● A two-year reauthorization of federal noise control programs.

● Reauthorization of the Toxic Substances Control Act.

● Provisions imposing or prohibiting ocean dumping fees.

● An annual $540 million ceiling on Environmental Protection Agency (EPA) non-energy research and pollution control activities.

● A $358.2 million authorization for specified programs of the federal prison system.

● Financing changes in the black lung benefits program.

● Authorization of funds for the Foreign Claims Settlement Commission.

● Authorization of funds for the Community Relations Service.

● Authorization of funds for the National Science Foundation.

● Modification of the law allowing private parties to recover attorneys' fees in specified cases against the government.

● A $100 million, two-year reauthorization for the Legal Services Corporation.

● Transfer of Federal Employees' Compensation Act retirement benefits to the civil service after the beneficiary reaches retirement age.

● Extension of the 1974 Emergency Home Purchase Assistance Act (PL 93-449), known as the "Brooke-Cranston" law.

Communications. The House bill had no provisions for deregulating the radio and television industry, as the Senate proposed. But under the conference agreement, licenses were extended from three to five years for television stations and to seven years for radio licenses.

Food Stamps. Conferees slashed $1.66 billion from the food stamp program for fiscal 1982, almost $200 million more than required by the House bill. However, they resisted still deeper cuts sought by Senate Agriculture Chairman Jesse Helms, R-N.C.

Dairy Price Supports. Conferees accepted House provisions designed to trim $449 million from the $1.8 billion dairy support program, but the savings appeared to be questionable. The dairy support issue was thrashed out during major farm bill consideration later in the year. *(Story, p. 535)*

Energy Assistance. Conferees provided $1.875 billion, $400 million more than the administration had requested, and eliminated a House requirement that states match funds for this assistance.

Conrail. If the freight railroad were deemed profitable, the government could sell Conrail only as a single entity up to June 1, 1984. If Conrail were unprofitable, the railroad could be sold in pieces after Oct. 30, 1983.

Education Block Grants. Conferees decided to lump only 30 education programs, instead of the 44 requested by the administration, into a block grant. However, some of the most expensive programs, such as aid to disadvantaged and handicapped children and vocational education, were kept separate.

Impact Aid and Title I. Impact aid for school districts with many children of military and government employees was cut to $475 million from $707 million, with $3.48 billion provided for the Title I compensatory education program for disadvantaged children. The Senate wanted more for impact aid; the House sought higher funding for Title I.

Student Loans. College students from families with incomes below $30,000 could still borrow up to $2,500 a year in federally backed loans; students from wealthier families would have to meet a needs test to get such loans.

Final Action

The House approved the conference report on the reconciliation bill by voice vote July 31, with the Senate concurring by a vote of 80-14 a few hours later. *(Vote 244, p. 42-S)*

For one frenetic day, however, the fate of the bill had been jeopardized as Democrats staged a last-ditch effort to restore the minimum Social Security benefits eliminated in the conference agreement.

House Rules Committee Chairman Bolling had threatened to refuse to convene his panel to clear the reconciliation bill for floor action unless the conference was reopened to restore the minimum benefits provisions.

But after bipartisan House and Senate leaders met behind closed doors, the issue was resolved by allowing two separate House votes — one on the conference report and one on a bill (HR 4331) that would reinstate the minimum benefits language deleted by the reconciliation report.

The House passed the minimum benefits bill by a 404-20 vote and sent it to the Senate, where an attempt to gain immediate consideration of the measure was rebuffed, 57-30. *(House vote 178, p. 62-H; Senate vote 245, p. 42-S)*

Even though the July 31 vote did not restore the $122 monthly minimum benefit, Democrats felt they had gained some political mileage on the issue and had put the onus for eliminating the payments squarely on President Reagan and his Republican allies in Congress.

During final House debate on HR 3982, Jones called the reconciliation conference report "a true victory for the legislative process."

"The Congress has demonstrated great resiliency," said the Budget Committee chairman, "and those who understand the importance of the legislative process will not desert that process."

Summing up for House Republicans, Latta noted that lawmakers were "about to adopt the largest package of spending cuts in the entire 105-year history of the Congress."

"After years and years and years of talking about controlling federal spending, of giving lip service to the idea of balancing the budget and reducing the national debt," he said, "we are finally being given the opportunity of voting on a bill which will reverse the 25-year trend toward bigger and bigger government." ∎

Second Resolution: Strictly 'Pro Forma'

Congress Dec. 10 adopted what members admitted was a meaningless second budget resolution for fiscal 1982 (S Con Res 50). The resolution simply reaffirmed the first 1982 budget resolution, adopted in May, which called for a combined $57 billion deficit for fiscal 1982 and 1983 and a slight surplus in 1984 — figures totally out of line with current, more pessimistic projections.

The Senate, which in the past had approved budget resolutions by wide margins, narrowly adopted the resolution Dec. 9 by a largely party-line vote of 49-48. The House approved it the following day, 206-200, completing action on the measure. *(Senate vote 451, p. 73-S; House vote 333, p. 108-H; first budget resolution, p. 247)*

The final version of the resolution included "sense of the Senate" language, added on the Senate floor, calling for cuts in all programs and tax increases to achieve a balanced budget in fiscal 1984.

The resolution also called for President Reagan to submit "as soon as possible" his own plan for balancing the budget.

By the time Congress took up the second resolution, the Reagan administration had retreated from its pledge to balance the budget in 1984. And it had resisted attempts to cut too deeply into defense or some entitlements, especially Social Security, or to raise taxes.

However, Reagan had shifted some of the blame for budgetary problems to Congress, which resisted the further budget cuts he requested in September. The resolution was, in part, congressional self-defense.

Background

Congress left Washington for its August recess thinking it had taken care of its economic problems for the year. But a bulging fiscal 1982 deficit, spawned by high interest rates and continuing high inflation, forced members on their return in September to confront a whole new round of tough economic decisions.

Within weeks after enactment of its budget reconciliation bill (HR 3982 — PL 97-35), which chopped $35.2 billion from the fiscal 1982 deficit, and its massive tax cut legislation (HR 4242 — PL 97-34), the Reagan administration was forced to acknowledge that its economic program was not achieving the desired effects. Rather than buoy Wall Street and send the economy on an upward course, approval of the Reagan program seriously shook the financial markets, which feared soaring federal deficits that would perpetuate inflation and high interest rates. *(Reconciliation bill, p. 256; tax cuts, p. 91)*

Thus the administration decided to seek even deeper reductions in fiscal 1982 outlays — including cuts in entitlements and even the sacrosanct defense budget — to hold down the deficit. "The president is determined to show them [investors] that he can balance the budget," said White House Director of Communications David Gergen.

Second Round Cuts

In a nationally televised speech Sept. 24, Reagan outlined his new $16 billion savings package for fiscal 1982 — including $13 billion in spending cuts plus $3 billion in increased taxes — to "lead us out of the economic swamp we've been in so long." *(Text, p. 30-E)*

Despite enactment of his economic recovery plan, Reagan said, further action was needed to keep the deficit from mounting. "And let me be clear that this cannot be the last round of cuts," he warned. "Holding down spending must be a continuing battle for several years to come."

Instead of the $42.5 billion deficit previously projected for fiscal 1982, the White House now estimated a $43.1 billion shortfall. In fiscal 1984, when there was to be a $5 million surplus, the budget would be in balance, according to the administration.

In March, the administration said that in order to reach a balanced budget by fiscal 1984, $30 billion in additional cuts would be needed in 1983 and $44 billion in 1984.

However, according to Office of Management and Budget Director (OMB) David A. Stockman, Congress' failure to enact the president's Social Security reform package added $19 billion in outlays to the budget from fiscal 1982-84, and its failure to include certain entitlement changes in the reconciliation bill added another $13 billion. Thus more than $100 billion in unspecified savings would be needed to balance the budget in fiscal 1984, instead of the $74 billion previously projected.

Stockman said at a press briefing that the new budget cuts would save approximately $80.1 billion over the three fiscal years. That meant that even if the entire program were put in place, additional savings totaling $11.7 billion would be needed in fiscal 1983 and $23 billion in fiscal 1984 to balance the budget.

The administration decided against packaging the new cuts in a single bill and calling for an up-or-down vote on the president's program, as it did in reconciliation. Because Congress was at a "stage of the legislative process right now where there is not a suitable vehicle, we will have to contest [the cuts] one bill at a time," Stockman said.

"We have the threat of a veto," he added, which could be sustained by one-third plus one vote of either house.

Highlights of Reagan's Sept. 24 proposals:

Across-the-Board Cuts. Reagan said he would send Congress revised fiscal 1982 appropriations requests that would reduce discretionary non-defense programs by 12 percent from his March 10 budget plan. These proposed changes would cut budget authority by $18.7 billion in fiscal 1982 and outlays by an estimated $8.4 billion in fiscal 1982, $5.3 billion in fiscal 1983 and $3.8 billion in fiscal 1984. Formal budget requests were sent to Congress Sept. 30.

Several programs were exempted from the 12 percent "pro-rata" cut, the administration said in a fact sheet accompanying the president's speech. They included but were not limited to peace-keeping forces, direct Veterans Administration (VA) hospital care and the Immigration and Naturalization Service. Several law enforcement and criminal justice programs were given partial exemptions.

Social Security. Asking Congress to form a "bipartisan consensus" to address the "pending insolvency" of the Old Age and Survivors Insurance trust fund, Reagan proposed legislation that, not surprisingly, tracked the measure approved by the Senate Finance Committee Sept. 24. *(Story, p. 117)*

Reversing the position he took on reconciliation, the president asked Congress to restore the minimum Social Security benefit to lower-income beneficiaries. And he

backed a stopgap answer to financing problems by proposing temporary interfund borrowing, "to ensure that checks can continue to be issued for the next several years."

To find a permanent solution to Social Security's financial woes, Reagan said he would establish a task force to develop a plan by January 1983. The Speaker of the House and the majority leader of the Senate were asked to name five members each to this task force.

Entitlement Reform. Reagan intended "to forward to Congress this fall a new package of entitlement and welfare reform measures — outside Social Security — to save nearly $27 billion over the next three years." The breakdown for the entitlement savings was to be: $2.6 billion in fiscal 1982; $10 billion in fiscal 1983; and $15 billion in fiscal 1984.

Another task force — this one with representatives from the White House, OMB and the departments of Health and Human Services, Labor and Education — was to be formed to "finalize this legislative proposal" on entitlement savings.

According to Stockman, the changes would involve redefining income in relation to entitlement programs, tightening income eligibility, trimming Medicare and Medicaid payments and doing away with the overindexing of federal retirement programs.

Programs to be reviewed included Medicare, Medicaid, food stamps, subsidized housing, Aid to Families with Dependent Children, railroad retirement, black lung, federal civilian and military retirement and student loans.

Tax Code Revisions. The detailed package of revisions in the Internal Revenue Code — euphemistically called "revenue enhancements" — was still being prepared and would be submitted to Congress "in the very near future," the administration said. The changes would aim to "eliminate abuses, remove obsolete incentives and enhance tax collections." The changes envisioned would add tax revenues totaling $3 billion in fiscal 1982, $8 billion in fiscal 1983 and $11 billion in fiscal 1984.

Defense Spending. Despite indications from GOP members of Congress that Reagan should cut more deeply into the defense budget, the president did not increase the $2 billion reduction planned for fiscal 1982 or the overall $13 billion reduction in outlays for 1982-84. The cuts would reduce budget authority in fiscal 1982 by $7.6 billion, from $220.9 billion to $213.3 billion.

Federal Credit Reductions. Reagan targeted a $21 billion reduction in federal loan guarantee commitments for fiscal 1982, and he instructed OMB to develop added credit reductions for fiscal 1983-84.

User Charges. The president decided to re-offer the same user fee charges he first proposed in his March 10 budget, which Congress refused to adopt. The user fees would add $980 million in revenues during fiscal 1982. *(March 10 budget, p. 19-E)*

Federal Work Force and Reorganization. Keeping a campaign pledge, Reagan proposed to abolish the departments of Energy and Education. According to the administration, dismantling the Department of Energy would save $1.5 billion by fiscal 1984 and reduce the federal work force by 4,400 positions.

Stockman said legislation to abolish the Education Department would be sent to Congress in October, followed by Energy in November. The legislation was never submitted, however.

In addition to doing away with the two Cabinet departments, the administration planned to "abolish, restruc-

ture or realign a number of bureaus, agencies, advisory boards and commissions." The White House, however, did not specify which agencies would be eliminated.

The plan to reduce the federal work force would entail dropping 75,000 non-defense civilian federal employees from the work force, or a 6.5 percent reduction from planned fiscal 1982 levels, by fiscal 1984.

Debt Collection. An "aggressive" debt collection effort was to be developed and implemented by all federal departments. According to the administration, more than $25 billion of the $175 billion in debts owed the federal government were either delinquent or in default. Another $8.4 billion in loans were in some form of rescheduled status because of borrowers' inability to pay.

Retreat

Senate Budget Committee Chairman Pete V. Domenici, R-N.M., and Stockman were the key movers behind the president's decision to ask Congress for another round of fiscal 1982 budget cuts on Sept. 24.

No sooner had Reagan announced his new budget offensive, however, than Congress — including Republicans — began shooting it down.

The Republican members of the Senate Appropriations Committee met soon after the president's speech and decided they could not come up with more than $5 billion in fiscal 1982 appropriations savings — a far cry from the $10.4 billion Reagan had asked for.

House "Gypsy Moths" — a group of Republicans from the Northeast and Midwest — complained that agreements reached during reconciliation not to reduce spending levels for programs crucial to their regions were breached by the new request for cuts.

Senate Republicans who said the president's savings "mix" would not work appeared to coalesce around a plan to raise many billions in revenues by increasing excise taxes and closing a variety of tax loopholes.

But House Republicans balked at the tax hike scheme. There, where Democrats had control, Republicans feared that opening up the tax issue might lead to repeal of the newly passed tax cuts.

Meanwhile, the administration appeared unable to agree upon an entitlements package or a revenue enhancement plan. By early November it had settled on only the appropriations cuts and a package designed to reduce federal loan guarantees by $20.3 billion by Sept. 30, 1982 — primarily by cutting back federal support to the Government National Mortgage Association (Ginnie Mae).

At the very time that the Republicans were tying themselves into knots, bad economic news began confirming that the country had fallen into a recession, one that appeared likely to be longer and deeper than previously anticipated.

The bad economic news reinforced the argument of House Republicans and supply-siders within the administration, such as Treasury Secretary Donald T. Regan, that taxes should not be raised in the midst of a recession. That argument also was offered against making any major economic policy changes for the time being. And balancing the budget became a goal, not a necessity, to Reagan.

On Nov. 6 Reagan acknowledged that he probably would not be able to make good on his campaign promise to balance the budget by 1984.

On Nov. 10 the president retreated from his September call for Congress to trim back the growth in entitlement programs such as Medicare and food stamps, and to in-

crease taxes by "enhancing" revenues.

Instead, he said he would put off decisions on these budget savings until January and focus on holding fiscal 1982 spending to a minimum through the appropriations process. "I stand ready to veto any bill that abuses the limited resources of the taxpayers," Reagan said at a press conference.

Reagan intended his press conference announcement to end the impasse on economic policy that had pitted House Republicans against Senate Republicans and supply-siders against budget-balancers within the administration.

He failed. House Republicans happily agreed to leave any budget fighting until 1982. But Senate Budget Committee Republicans, including many who campaigned on balanced budget platforms, said they felt it was their congressional responsibility to offer some course of direction.

House Committee Action

The House Budget Committee — its members irritated by lack of direction from the White House on specific budget cuts — agreed by voice vote Nov. 12 to adopt a second fiscal 1982 budget resolution that simply reaffirmed the first resolution Congress approved in May. That measure (H Con Res 115) called for deficits of $37.65 billion in fiscal 1982 and $19.05 billion in fiscal 1983, with a $1.05 billion surplus in fiscal 1984.

The committee did not formally report the second resolution until Dec. 8 (H Con Res 230 — H Rept 97-369).

"What this all comes down to is a bid for time," said Leon E. Panetta, D-Calif. "The battleground is not in this session of Congress, but the battleground is clearly next spring."

He and other Democrats argued that they had not received specifics from the administration on how it intended to cut entitlement programs and to raise $3 billion in taxes for fiscal 1982. They added that the committee would be in a better position early in 1982 to assess how well the economy was performing and to decide then what to do about the budget through a third resolution.

Republicans — although less vocal — clearly agreed. The proposal to extend the first resolution was offered by ranking minority member Delbert L. Latta, R-Ohio, as a substitute for a plan by Chairman James R. Jones, D-Okla., to mark up a new resolution by revising the first with more up-to-date economic assumptions. The Jones plan would have resulted in fiscal 1982 outlays totaling $724 billion, $648 billion in revenues and a $76 billion deficit.

Senate Committee Action

Calling it a "sham," a "travesty" and the "height of irresponsibility," the Senate Budget Committee grudgingly followed its House counterpart and voted out a second fiscal 1982 budget resolution that merely reaffirmed the first.

Conceding that its figures were too optimistic, the committee ordered the measure reported without recommendation Nov. 19 by a vote of 13-7.

The resolution was formally reported Nov. 24 (S Con Res 50 — S Rept 97-279).

The panel added to the resolution "sense of Congress" language noting that "large deficits in the range of $76-$92 billion in fiscal 1982, $95-$136 billion in fiscal 1983

and $103-$165 billion in fiscal 1984" would occur if no further action was taken. It called upon the president to "submit a plan as soon as possible" to lower interest rates, decrease unemployment, reduce inflation and balance the budget by 1984.

As reported by the Senate committee, the resolution called for outlays of $695.45 billion, revenues of $657.8 billion and a deficit of $37.65 billion for the fiscal year ending Sept. 30, 1982.

Office of Management and Budget figures showed that without the Sept. 24 budget reductions called for by President Reagan, outlays for fiscal 1982 would reach $722.3 billion, revenues $663.2 billion and the deficit $59.1 billion.

A disheartened Domenici told his colleagues he believed he had done "everything I can do to avoid this situation," but it was obvious there was "not a majority willing to address outyear issues in a mandatory manner."

That consideration did not dissuade senators, including several Republicans, from decrying what they viewed as a dereliction of duty.

"This is a very, very serious blow to the budget process,"said William L. Armstrong, R-Colo. "And it is difficult to see how in difficult [economic] times ahead we can reaffirm that process."

The committee's ranking minority member, Ernest F. Hollings, D-S.C., said what the panel was approving was "just a sham" and "will be dangerous to the committee and the process itself."

The report accompanying the resolution was a long disclaimer for the committee's action. "Approval of the resolution, without recommendation, is a stopgap solution to a problem that the committee found intractable at this time," it explains.

Substantive Proposals Fail

The committee's final action followed a meeting Nov. 16 during which two proposals for substantive budget resolutions were defeated. A Domenici proposal failed 10-12; a Hollings plan lost 5-17.

The Domenici plan, designed to achieve a balanced budget by fiscal 1984, would have saved $160 billion through fiscal 1984, including savings of $26 billion in defense outlays, $39 billion in entitlements and $48 billion in new revenues.

To achieve these reductions, the resolution would have required reconciliation instructions for both revenues and entitlements. The revenue instructions would have directed the Senate Finance and House Ways and Means committees to report legislation raising $48 billion in revenues by March 15, 1982.

The entitlement instructions would have directed four committees with jurisdiction over entitlement programs to report legislation that would save $24 billion over the next three years — also by March 15.

The plan would have limited federal spending growth to 9.3 percent in fiscal 1982, 5.2 percent in fiscal 1983, and 4.5 percent in fiscal 1984 — compared to an average growth of 13.6 percent in fiscal years 1979-81.

On Nov. 13 the committee adopted a set of economic assumptions included in the Domenici proposal. These fiscal 1982 estimates called for real economic growth of 2.5 percent, an increase in the Consumer Price Index (CPI) of 7 percent, an unemployment rate of 7.3 percent and an average interest rate on 91-day Treasury bills of 12.5 percent.

Stockman's 'Loose Talk'

President Reagan's chief budgetary architect, David A. Stockman, offered his resignation Nov. 12 following publication of a magazine article in which the Office of Management and Budget (OMB) director expressed his skepticism about the Reagan administration's supply-side economics. The president asked Stockman to remain on his "team," but both Democrats and Republicans on Capitol Hill questioned Stockman's future credibility on crucial matters.

When the Senate Budget Committee met Nov. 10, the panel's Democrats created an instant commotion with the disclosure of an article in the December issue of *The Atlantic* magazine in which Stockman admitted to a reporter that in his view the supply-side economic theory, on which the administration's economic plan was based, "was the only way to get a tax policy that was really 'trickle down' " — the old Republican economic doctrine.

In the article Stockman said the main objective of the supply-side theory was to reduce the top income tax bracket from 70 to 50 percent — a goal that clearly favored the rich. In order to make the top rate reduction politically acceptable, "you had to bring down all the brackets. But, I mean, Kemp-Roth was always a Trojan horse to bring down the top rate," Stockman said.

Stockman also was quoted as saying that "none of us really understands what's going on with these numbers."

Democrats relished decrying the apparent cynicism of the budget director. "The architect of the administration's economic program is admitting exactly what I and other critics have been saying for six months.... Mr. Stockman misled Congress and the American people as to the consequences of the Reagan economic program," said House Speaker Thomas P. O'Neill Jr., D-Mass. "His credibility and the credibility of the program he supports are in serious doubt."

After meeting with the president Nov. 12, Stockman told a press conference that Reagan was "not happy" and "very chagrined" about his comments in the *Atlantic* article. Stockman admitted that his "poor judgment and loose talk" had done the president's program "a serious disservice." Thus he had offered his resignation, Stockman said, but the president "asked me to stay on the team."

"I absolutely believe that the supply-side theory is workable," the budget director told reporters. But he added he had become "much more realistic about how long it will take."

Senate Floor Action

For Senate Republicans, the Dec. 8-9 debate on S Con Res 50 coincided with some embarrassing developments:

● New Office of Management and Budget estimates showed a $423 billion deficit for fiscal 1982-84 — about $242 billion higher than its September projections.

● Members of President Reagan's Council of Economic Advisers (CEA) told an American Enterprise Institute

gathering Dec. 8 that such large deficits were not necessarily a problem.

"In general, concern about the deficit has been misplaced," CEA member William A. Niskanen was quoted as saying. He added there was no direct evidence that deficits cause inflation or high interest rates.

CEA Chairman Murray L. Weidenbaum and member Jerry Jordan backed Niskanen in playing down the importance of deficits, appearing to contradict years of GOP rhetoric.

Even though White House spokesmen later denied that the remarks reflected administration policy, stunned Senate Republicans took the occasion of debate on the budget resolution to denounce the CEA comments as "incredible," "disheartening" and "foolish."

"The notion that somehow we can have stable or declining interest rates in the face of these massive deficits is preposterous," Armstrong said.

Although unrelated to the previous day's events, Domenici's amendment to add "sense of the Senate" language came at a convenient time for Republicans to disown any indications the party had weakened on deficits. The amendment called for a revised resolution in March 1982 that would achieve a balanced budget in fiscal 1984 by cutting all programs, including defense and entitlement programs, and by increasing taxes. It excluded the individual income tax cuts and business depreciation measures in the 1981 tax law (PL 97-34) from such increases. *(Tax law, p. 91)*

The non-binding amendment, which also called for the 1984 outlays to equal no more than 20.5 percent of the gross national product, was adopted by a largely party-line vote of 50-47. *(Vote 450, p. 73-S)*

An amendment by J. Bennett Johnston, D-La., called for a balanced 1984 budget but did not specify where cuts would be made, and placed some of the burden on Reagan to come up with his own balanced-budget plan. It was rejected 45-52. *(Vote 449, p. 73-S)*

The resolution, as amended by the Domenici amendment, squeaked through the Senate by a 49-48 vote. *(Vote 451, p. 73-S)*

Democrats clearly delighted in the majority's discomfort over the week's events. William Proxmire, D-Wis., called Reagan's recent admissions that the budget could not be balanced in 1984 and the CEA members' remarks "the reversal of the decade."

House Floor Action

As in the Senate, House members had clear disclaimers for the resolution, which they took up Dec. 10.

"There should be no confusion that this will get us through the year," said Budget Committee Chairman James R. Jones, D-Okla. "But this is the only thing upon which we can reach agreement." Congress must adopt a second budget resolution before it can adjourn for the year.

The Senate measure was substituted for the House committee version by unanimous consent as soon as floor debate began.

At the request of Republican leaders, who feared some of their own members might complicate passage with several balance-the-budget amendments, the House adopted, 248-154, a closed rule for floor consideration, barring amendments. The resolution itself was adopted 206-200. *(Votes 332, 333, p. 108-H)*

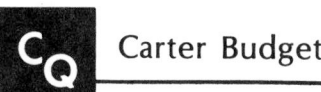

Carter Budget

Final Carter Budget Sets Challenge for Reagan

An unyielding President Carter made his last fiscal stand Jan. 15, facing off Congress and the incoming Reagan administration with a fiscal 1982 budget that would hike taxes and allow funding for most federal programs to continue at current levels.

In submitting his financial blueprint for the budget year beginning Oct. 1, 1981, Carter ignored the election mandate that lost him the presidency by a landslide margin: cut federal spending and return tax dollars to the people.

Instead, he clung to his conviction that income tax cuts would heighten inflation and that spending could not be cut too deeply without hurting needy Americans or weakening the nation's military might.

Carter maintained that his recommendations would "hold down the growth of the budget to the maximum extent, while still meeting the demands of national security and human compassion." *(Text of budget message, p. 5-E)*

Policy Statement

Carter's budget was little more than a final statement of his economic policy, however. Upon taking office Jan. 20, President Reagan planned to revise the Carter proposals "from top to bottom," according to his director-designate of the Office of Management and Budget (OMB), Rep. David A. Stockman, R-Mich. *(Reagan budget, p. 278)*

Speaking to reporters Jan. 15 following an afternoon-long economic policy huddle with Reagan, Stockman said the Carter budget called for "more of the same" — higher spending and higher taxes.

"We have a budget that's obviously out of control," Stockman said, noting that Reagan would make "very, very major cuts" in the fiscal 1982 budget revisions he planned to send Congress in February.

During his campaign, Reagan promised to cut the budget by 2 percent in fiscal 1981 and 1 percent in 1982 and to slash individual income tax rates by 30 percent over three years. He maintained that the current high rate of spending and taxation stifled productivity and produced inflation.

Fiscal 1982 Budget Details

Under the Carter plan, outlays would rise in fiscal 1982 by 11.6 percent to $739.3 billion. Budget authority would go up 11.5 percent, to $809.8 billion. And revenues would increase 17.2 percent to $711.8 billion, for a deficit of $27.5 billion.

Military and energy programs would receive "real" spending increases over the rate of inflation. Funding for such programs as Social Security and unemployment compensation would increase to keep up with the cost of living and to cover new recipients. And a slim .2 percent would be sheared from other domestic programs.

Carter used the budget to make one last plug for a pet initiative — the 10-cent-a-gallon gasoline tax, which was soundly defeated by the 96th Congress. By including the tax in his budget, he was able to reduce the deficit $13.1 billion. *(Background, 1980 Almanac p. 273)*

While acknowledging that federal spending as a percentage of gross national product (GNP) had reached a peacetime high under his administration, Carter blamed the trend on the increasing "uncontrollability" of the budget.

The Budget Totals

(fiscal years, in billions of dollars)

	1980 actual	1981 estimate	1982 estimate
Outlays	$579.6	$662.7	$739.3
Receipts	520.0	607.5	711.8
Deficit	−59.6	−55.2	−27.5
Budget authority	$658.8	$726.5	$809.8

"The reasons for this [growth] are not accurately described by simplistic criticisms of big government or by accusations of wholesale waste, fraud or abuse," the budget said in an apparent reference to Reagan's campaign rhetoric.

Rather, the Carter fiscal plan said, "the momentum of the budget is the product of all past presidential and congressional budgetary decisions."

It noted that such "uncontrollable" programs as retirement benefits, arms contracts and food stamps composed more than three-quarters of federal spending. Only changes in current law would allow the government to cut back on such costs.

To help reduce the entitlement stranglehold on the

Carter Administration Economic Assumptions

(Calendar years; dollar amounts in billions)

Item	Actual 1979	FORECAST			ASSUMPTIONS			
		1980[1]	1981	1982	1983	1984	1985	1986
Major economic indicators:								
Gross national product, percent change, fourth quarter over fourth quarter:								
Current dollars	9.9	9.6	12.3	12.6	12.2	11.5	10.7	9.9
Constant (1972) dollars	1.7	−.3	1.7	3.5	3.7	3.7	3.7	3.7
GNP deflator (percent change, fourth quarter over fourth quarter)	8.1	10.0	10.4	8.8	8.2	7.5	6.7	6.0
Consumer Price Index (percent change, fourth quarter over fourth quarter)[2]	12.8	12.8	12.6	9.6	8.2	7.5	6.7	6.0
Unemployment rate (percent, fourth quarter)	5.9	7.5	7.7	7.4	7.0	6.6	6.2	5.9
Annual economic assumptions:								
Gross national product:								
Current dollars:								
Amount	2,414	2,627	2,928	3,312	3,718	4,156	4,611	5,081
Percent change, year over year	12.0	8.8	11.4	13.1	12.3	11.8	11.0	10.2
Constant (1972) dollars:								
Amount	1,483	1,481	1,493	1,545	1,600	1,659	1,720	1,784
Percent change, year over year	3.2	−.1	.9	3.5	3.5	3.7	3.7	3.7
Incomes:								
Personal income	1,944	2,160	2,420	2,700	3,021	3,360	3,709	4,067
Wages and salaries	1,236	1,344	1,486	1,656	1,850	2,051	2,257	2,466
Corporate profits	255	241	233	269	311	355	404	455
Price level:								
GNP deflator:								
Level (1972 = 100), annual average	162.8	177.4	196.0	214.3	232.4	250.5	268.0	284.8
Percent change, year over year	8.5	9.0	10.5	9.3	8.5	7.8	7.0	6.3
Consumer Price Index:[2]								
Level (1967 = 100), annual average	217.7	247.1	278.1	306.8	333.6	359.5	384.6	408.6
Percent change, year over year	11.4	13.5	12.5	10.3	8.7	7.7	7.0	6.3
Unemployment rates:								
Total, annual average	5.8	7.2	7.8	7.5	7.1	6.7	6.3	6.0
Insured, annual average[3]	3.0	3.9	4.4	4.1	3.8	3.5	3.2	3.0
Federal pay raise, October (percent):[4]					8.5	8.0	7.5	7.0
Civilian	7.0	9.1	5.5	9.0				
Military	7.0	11.7	9.1	9.0				
Interest rate, 91-day Treasury bills (percent)[5]	10.0	11.5	13.5	11.0	9.4	8.5	7.7	6.8

1. Actual data for the 1980 unemployment rate, federal pay raise, and 91-day Treasury bill rate.

2. CPI for urban wage earners and clerical workers. Two versions of the CPI are now published. The index shown here is that currently used, as required by law, in calculating automatic cost-of-living increases for indexed federal programs.

3. This indicator measures unemployment under state regular unemployment insurance as a percentage of covered employment under that program. It does not include recipients of extended benefits under that program.

4. General schedule pay raises become effective in October — the first month of the fiscal year. Thus, the October 1981 pay raise will set new pay scales that will be in effect during fiscal year 1982.

5. Average rate on new issues within period. These projections assume, by convention, that interest rates decline with the rate of inflation. They do not represent a forecast of interest rates.

SOURCE: Fiscal 1982 Budget

budget, Carter proposed $9.4 billion in spending cuts that would require legislative changes in the way certain programs operated.

President-elect Reagan had pledged to cut even deeper into "uncontrollable" spending. By highlighting the multitude of current government financial obligations, Carter's final budget showed just how difficult that task would be.

The Economic Outlook

Carter and his advisers painted a flat picture of the economy in calendar 1981: There would be virtually no improvement in inflation; the economy would grow only modestly; and the jobless rate would climb slightly.

Nor did they see much improvement in the following year. In 1982, they said, the inflation rate would drop to just under 10 percent, unemployment would remain high and the economy, as measured by the GNP, would grow by 3.5 percent. *(Economic assumptions, p. 272)*

"It now appears that the economy has embarked on what is likely to be a relatively slow recovery" from the 1980 recession — the steepest slump since World War II, the budget said.

In January 1980, Carter estimated that the inflation rate, as measured by the Consumer Price Index (CPI), would drop to 10.4 percent at the end of calendar 1980. His fiscal 1982 budget figures showed, however, that inflation was 12.8 percent in the final quarter of 1980 — after reaching a high of almost 20 percent early in the year.

Carter's final budget forecast a 12.6 percent inflation rate in 1981 and a 9.6 percent level in 1982.

The unemployment rate in the final quarter of 1980 equaled what Carter had predicted — 7.5 percent, which meant about 7.5 million Americans were out of work at the end of the year. He saw that rate climbing in fiscal 1981, to 7.7 percent, and easing only slightly the next year to 7.4 percent.

The budget showed that the economy declined .3 percent in the final quarter of calendar 1980. It predicted that 1981 would show only modest improvement, with the GNP increasing to 1.7 percent. But the estimates indicated that in 1982 the economy would expand 3.5 percent in the final months of the year.

Charles L. Schultze, chairman of the Council of Economic Advisers, told reporters that while the economy might decline during the first quarter of 1981, he did not foresee a recession. Some economists had predicted a second downturn during the year.

Carter's Fiscal Policy

In drafting a budget that raised taxes and spared most programs from reductions, Carter stood firm in defense of his economic policy and against the public cry for a scaleback of government and taxes.

He maintained that a continuation of his four-year policy of "prudence and restraint" was the best way to "provide for our security, establish the basis for a strong economy, protect the disadvantaged, build human and physical capital for the future and safeguard this nation's magnificent natural environment."

The budget he sent Congress provided for a 1 percent "real increase" in spending to be applied to three major areas: the military, energy programs and mandatory expenses such as interest on the public debt or Social Security payments. *(Budget by function, next page; by agency, p. 277)*

Budget Terminology

The federal budget is the president's financial plan for the federal government. It accounts for how government funds have been raised and spent, and it proposes financial policies. It covers the **fiscal year.** Fiscal year 1982 began Oct. 1, 1982, and ended Sept. 30, 1982.

The budget discusses **receipts,** amounts the government expects to raise in taxes; **budget authority,** amounts agencies are allowed to obligate or lend; and **outlays,** amounts actually paid out by the government in cash or checks during the year. Examples of outlays are funds spent to buy equipment or property, to meet the government's liability under a contract or to pay the salaries of employees. Outlays also include net lending — the difference between disbursements and repayments under government lending programs.

The purpose of the budget is to establish priorities, and to chart the government's **fiscal policy,** which is the coordinated use of taxes and expenditures to affect the economy.

Congress adopts its own budget in the form of **budget resolutions.** The **first budget resolution,** due May 15, sets overall goals for tax and spending, broken down among major budget categories, called **functions.** The **second budget resolution,** due Sept. 15, sets binding budget figures.

An **authorization** is an act of Congress that establishes government programs. It defines the scope of programs and sets a ceiling for how much can be spent on them. Authorizations do not actually provide the money. In the case of authority to enter contractual obligations, though, Congress authorizes the administration to make firm commitments for which funds must later be provided. Congress also occasionally includes mandatory spending requirements in an authorization in order to ensure spending at a certain level.

An **appropriation** provides money for programs, within the limits established in authorizations. An appropriation may be for a single year, a specified period of years, or an indefinite number of years, according to the restrictions Congress wishes to place on spending for particular purposes.

Appropriations generally take the form of **budget authority.** Budget authority often differs from actual outlays. That is because, in practice, funds actually spent or obligated during a year may be drawn partly from the budget authority conferred in the year in question and partly from budget authority conferred in previous years.

Most other domestic programs would be funded at current levels, after adjustment for inflation. Overall, spending for non-defense programs would drop .2 percent. And the deficit would be reduced from an estimated $55.2 billion in fiscal 1981 to $27.5 billion in 1982.

Carter noted that during his term in office, the budget deficit had dropped from 4 percent of GNP to 2.3 percent in fiscal 1980. In 1982, it would comprise only .9 percent of GNP.

Fiscal 1982 Budget by Function: $739.3 Billion in . . .

(in millions of dollars)†

	BUDGET AUTHORITY‡			OUTLAYS		
	1980	**1981 est.**	**1982 est.**	**1980**	**1981 est.**	**1982 est.**
NATIONAL DEFENSE						
Military Defense	$142,621	$170,305	$195,660	$132,840	$157,600	$180,000
Atomic Energy Defense Activities	2,991	3,658	4,704	2,878	3,587	4,478
Defense-Related Activities	156	−91	−24	142	−96	−76
Deductions#	−4	−3	−3	−4	−3	−3
TOTAL	$145,764	$173,869	$200,337	$135,856	$161,088	$184,399
INTERNATIONAL AFFAIRS						
Foreign Economic and Financial Assistance	$ 7,310	$ 7,306	$ 9,222	$ 5,607	$ 6,664	$ 7,038
Military Assistance	682	363	633	894	854	622
Conduct of Foreign Affairs	1,343	1,553	2,048	1,367	1,494	1,831
Foreign Information and Exchange Activities	518	577	687	534	588	610
International Financial Programs	5,761	15,435	7,129	2,427	1,793	2,131
Deductions#	−96	−81	−79	−96	−81	−79
TOTAL	$ 15,519	$ 25,153	$ 19,639	$ 10,733	$ 11,314	$ 12,152
GENERAL SCIENCE, SPACE AND TECHNOLOGY						
General Science and Basic Research	$ 1,461	$ 1,588	$ 1,966	$ 1,381	$ 1,518	$ 1,787
Space Flight	2,820	3,143	3,802	2,594	2,984	3,679
Space, Science, Applications and Technology	1,425	1,416	1,782	1,346	1,330	1,635
Supporting Space Activities	439	451	558	405	431	494
Deductions#	−3	−4	−4	−3	−4	−4
TOTAL	$ 6,141	$ 6,593	$ 8,104	$ 5,722	$ 6,258	$ 7,590
ENERGY						
Energy Supply	$ 36,813	$ 4,770	$ 6,147	$ 4,574	$ 5,727	$ 6,234
Energy Conservation	736	874	999	568	752	1,067
Emergency Energy Preparedness	−2,000	1,486	3,650	342	1,173	3,412
Energy Information, Policy and Regulation	951	1,217	1,336	882	1,145	1,317
Deductions#	−53	−58	−58	−53	−58	−58
TOTAL	$ 36,447	$ 8,289	$ 12,075	$ 6,313	$ 8,739	$ 11,973
NATURAL RESOURCES AND ENVIRONMENT						
Water Resources	$ 4,157	$ 4,148	$ 4,543	$ 4,294	$ 4,518	$ 4,578
Conservation and Land Management	2,586	2,624	2,471	2,328	2,578	2,425
Recreational Resources	1,672	1,423	1,673	1,707	1,663	1,681
Pollution Control and Abatement	4,672	4,710	5,290	5,510	5,512	5,760
Other Natural Resources	1,401	1,518	1,782	1,412	1,556	1,782
Deductions#	−1,439	−1,717	−2,187	−1,439	−1,717	−2,187
TOTAL	$ 13,051	$ 12,705	$ 13,572	$ 13,812	$ 14,110	$ 14,039
AGRICULTURE						
Farm Income Stabilization	$ 3,637	$ 4,073	$ 3,894	$ 3,459	$ −454	$ 3,148
Agricultural Research and Services	1,402	1,572	1,670	1,398	1,571	1,659
Deductions#	−95	−5	−5	−95	−5	−5
TOTAL	$ 4,945	$ 5,640	$ 5,559	$ 4,762	$ 1,112	$ 4,803
COMMERCE AND HOUSING CREDIT						
Mortgage Credit and Thrift Insurance	$ 6,481	$ 3,347	$ 4,098	$ 3,696	$ −194	$ 1,385
Postal Service	1,677	1,343	1,119	1,677	1,343	1,119
Other Advancement and Regulation of Commerce	2,340	2,290	5,494	2,409	2,307	5,554
Deductions#	—*	—*	—*	—*	—*	—*
TOTAL	$ 10,497	$ 6,979	$ 10,711	$ 7,782	$ 3,456	$ 8,058
TRANSPORTATION						
Ground Transportation	$ 14,019	$ 18,978	$ 18,093	$ 15,079	$ 17,112	$ 14,542
Air Transportation	3,954	4,255	4,571	3,762	3,951	4,171
Water Transportation	2,199	2,965	2,779	2,235	2,939	2,779
Other Transportaton	97	113	122	104	112	115
Deductions#	−60	−60	−56	−60	−60	−56
TOTAL	$ 20,210	$ 26,251	$ 25,509	$ 21,120	$ 24,054	$ 21,551
COMMUNITY AND REGIONAL DEVELOPMENT						
Community Development	$ 4,927	$ 4,911	$ 5,202	$ 4,878	$ 5,061	$ 5,322
Area and Regional Development	2,790	2,826	3,268	3,180	2,835	2,935
Disaster Relief and Insurance	2,426	2,518	739	2,043	3,273	852
Deductions#	−32	−25	−25	−32	−25	−25
TOTAL	$ 10,110	$ 10,230	$ 9,184	$ 10,068	$ 11,144	$ 9,084

... Expenditures, $809.8 Billion in Spending Authority

(in millions of dollars)†

	BUDGET AUTHORITY‡			OUTLAYS		
	1980	1981 est.	1982 est.	1980	1981 est.	1982 est.
EDUCATION, TRAINING, EMPLOYMENT, SOCIAL SERVICES						
Elementary, Secondary and Vocational Education	$ 7,225	$ 7,288	$ 8,505	$ 6,732	$ 6,942	$ 7,366
Higher Education	5,735	7,003	7,121	5,694	6,516	6,927
Research and General Education Aids	1,344	1,456	1,569	1,357	1,473	1,539
Training and Employment	9,623	9,558	11,312	10,345	9,935	10,989
Other Labor Services	572	626	688	551	605	664
Social Services	6,150	5,958	7,173	6,116	6,332	7,058
Deductions#	−28	−30	−32	−28	−30	−32
TOTAL	$ 30,622	$ 31,859	$ 36,336	$ 30,767	$ 31,773	$ 34,511
HEALTH						
Health Care Services	$ 54,300	$ 66,314	$ 80,287	$ 53,019	$ 60,648	$ 68,991
Health Research	3,642	3,795	4,086	3,442	3,563	3,844
Education and Training of Health Care Work Force	923	675	534	719	755	649
Consumer and Occupational Health and Safety	995	1,102	1,172	1,001	1,070	1,156
Deductions#	−17	−3	−3	−17	−3	−3
TOTAL	$ 59,844	$ 71,884	$ 86,075	$ 58,165	$ 66,032	$ 74,636
INCOME SECURITY						
General Retirement and Disability Insurance	$122,262	$137,813	$157,790	$123,684	$145,547	$167,313
Federal Employee Retirement and Disability	24,732	28,263	30,308	14,675	17,591	19,883
Unemployment Compensation	17,703	22,575	24,031	18,023	26,140	21,878
Housing Assistance	27,813	30,870	31,386	5,514	6,861	8,465
Food and Nutrition Assistance	13,774	16,083	18,037	14,015	15,905	17,481
Other Income Security	17,914	19,550	18,000	17,190	19,605	19,987
TOTAL	$224,198	$255,154	$279,551	$193,100	$231,650	$255,006
VETERANS' BENEFITS AND SERVICES						
Income Security	$ 11,770	$ 13,344	$ 14,731	$ 11,688	$ 13,103	$ 14,477
Education, Training and Rehabilitation	2,374	2,041	1,689	2,342	1,956	1,589
Hospital and Medical Care	6,409	7,110	7,851	6,515	6,935	7,737
Housing	—	—	—	−23	−106	−53
Other Benefits and Services	658	702	717	665	706	715
Deductions#	−2	−3	−3	−2	−3	−3
TOTAL	$ 21,208	$ 23,194	$ 24,984	$ 21,183	$ 22,591	$ 24,462
ADMINISTRATION OF JUSTICE						
Federal Law Enforcement Activities	$ 2,214	$ 2,435	$ 2,582	$ 2,237	$ 2,415	$ 2,536
Federal Litigative and Judicial Activities	1,370	1,496	1,641	1,347	1,515	1,620
Federal Correctional Activities	320	355	379	342	367	378
Criminal Justice Assistance	498	183	235	656	501	359
Deductions#	−11	−12	−12	−11	−12	−12
TOTAL	$ 4,391	$ 4,458	$ 4,825	$ 4,570	$ 4,786	$ 4,882
GENERAL GOVERNMENT						
Legislative Functions	$ 1,106	$ 1,114	$ 1,208	$ 1,032	$ 1,174	$ 1,173
Executive Direction and Management	102	114	113	97	113	113
Central Fiscal Operations	2,484	2,820	2,998	2,522	2,820	2,979
General Property and Records Management	406	862	588	364	554	487
Central Personnel Management	145	166	168	154	168	165
Other General Government	583	596	555	559	608	522
Deductions#	−224	−267	−193	−224	−267	−193
TOTAL	$ 4,602	$ 5,405	$ 5,439	$ 4,505	$ 5,170	$ 5,246
GENERAL PURPOSE FISCAL ASSISTANCE						
General Revenue Sharing	$ 6,861	$ 4,577	$ 4,577	$ 6,835	$ 5,163	$ 4,566
Other General Purpose Fiscal Assistance	1,805	1,631	2,310	1,749	1,691	2,336
TOTAL	$ 8,667	$ 6,208	$ 6,887	$ 8,584	$ 6,854	$ 6,902
INTEREST						
Interest on the Public Debt	$ 74,781	$ 94,100	$106,500	$ 74,781	$ 94,100	$106,500
Other Interest	−10,273	−13,700	−16,554	−10,278	−13,695	−16,554
TOTAL	$ 64,508	$ 80,400	$ 89,946	$ 64,504	$ 80,405	$ 89,946
CIVILIAN AGENCY PAY RAISES	—	—	$ 958	—	—	$ 920
CONTINGENCIES	—	—	$ 2,000	—	—	$ 1,000
OFFSETTING RECEIPTS	$−21,933	$−27,796	$−31,863	$−21,933	$−27,796	$−31,863
GRAND TOTAL	$658,790	$726,474	$809,829	$579,613	$662,740	$739,296

*†Figures may not add to totals due to rounding.   ‡Primarily appropriations.   #For offsetting receipts.   *Less than $500 thousand.*

SOURCE: Fiscal 1982 Budget

Federal spending and taxes, however, had taken a larger bite out of the economy during Carter's years in office. In 1976, spending was 22.3 percent of GNP; it was estimated at 23.3 percent in 1981. Tax receipts comprised 18.3 percent of GNP in 1976 and would climb to an estimated 21.4 percent in 1981 and an all-time high of 22.1 percent in 1982.

This large inflation-induced increase in tax revenues had allowed federal spending to boom in recent years while holding the deficit down.

In his final budget, Carter not only rejected calls for a cut in personal income taxes to help offset increases due to inflation, but he also included several proposals — such as the gasoline tax — to raise an additional $5.3 billion in revenue over the current services level.

Already enacted tax increases also would pump up receipts in fiscal 1982. They included the large hike in Social Security assessments, the windfall oil profits tax and various tax changes included in the reconciliation act (HR 7765 — PL 96-499) signed into law Dec. 5. *(Reconciliation act, 1980 Almanac p. 124)*

To partially offset these increases, Carter recommended passage of several tax cut proposals recycled from the "economic revitalization program" he had proposed in August 1980. They would cut revenues by $18.3 billion.

On the spending side of the budget, Carter increased military outlays by $23.3 billion — which represented a 5 percent rate of real growth. Outlays for energy programs would go up $3.2 billion and spending for such entitlement programs as retirement and unemployment would increase by $55.2 billion, due to economic and population changes.

Altogether, the add-ons represented a $3.1 billion rise above the so-called "current services" budget, which measured how much spending would be if the government were left on "automatic pilot."

To accommodate the large increases for military and entitlement programs, Carter proposed $9.4 billion in spending cuts from other domestic programs. Most of the reductions would be made in unemployment benefits, federal employee pay and inflation-indexed programs.

The spending cuts would be achieved by:
● Tightening the conditions that triggered "extended" benefits for the jobless — benefits paid after normal unemployment wages ran out. Savings: $2.1 billion in 1982.
● Reforming federal wage rates to match pay for similar work in private businesses. Savings: $3.5 billion.
● Providing federal workers with a 5.5 percent, rather than an 8.6 percent, wage raise in 1982. Savings: $1.3 bil-

lion.
● Adjusting cost-of-living payments for federal retirees once, rather than twice, each year. Savings: $1.1 billion.
● Adjusting child nutrition, dairy price support and food stamp programs for inflation once a year rather than twice. Savings: $600 million.
● Eliminating the new, more liberal eligibility standards for food stamps; tightening eligibility for child nutrition programs; and reforming the Aid to Families with Dependent Children (AFDC) and railroad retirement programs. Savings: $1 billion.

Fiscal 1981 Revisions

Overshadowed by Carter's full-dress budget proposals for fiscal 1982 were the revised outlay and revenue figures for the current year. They showed in high relief the challenge Reagan would encounter in trying to cut government spending.

In January 1980, Carter proposed a fiscal 1981 budget providing for $615.8 billion in outlays and $600 million in revenues. His new estimate of spending in fiscal 1981 was $662.7 billion — an increase of 7.6 percent over his earlier recommendation. And he proposed that the revenue level be hiked to $607.5 billion.

Behind the rise in spending was a large inflation-induced rise in such government costs as retirement pay and food stamps and higher spending to counter the effect of the 1980 recession.

Natural disasters such as the eruption of Mount St. Helens in Washington; a massive influx of refugees from the Caribbean; and a hike in oil prices also contributed to the surge in expenses.

An increase in military outlays of 10.4 percent over the January 1981 request also helped push the budget totals upward. The new budget included a request for an additional $6.3 billion in defense spending over what Congress already had approved.

Carter applauded lawmakers for enacting the unprecedented reconciliation savings bill, which cut $8.2 billion from the deficit in fiscal 1981 and urged them to "build upon last year's experience."

Current Services

So much of the federal budget had become "uncontrollable" that it "threatens the effectiveness of the budget as an instrument of discretionary national economic policy," the Carter fiscal plan worried.

And nowhere was that threat more apparent than in the "current services" budget prepared by OMB as required under the Congressional Budget Act (PL 93-344).

That analysis of what the budget would look like if all programs were continued at their current levels, as adjusted for inflation, showed that spending would be $736.2 billion in fiscal 1982 and revenues would total $706.5 billion.

Under that projection, spending for welfare-type programs was expected to rise by $27.7 billion in 1982 due to automatic cost-of-living increases and a rise in the number of beneficiaries.

Outlays for the Pentagon automatically would rise nearly $20 billion to cover increases in pay for military and civilian employees, in retirement pay and for arms purchases already under contract.

Other major increases included:
● $21.4 billion for Social Security payments.

The Budget Dollar
Fiscal Year 1982 Estimate

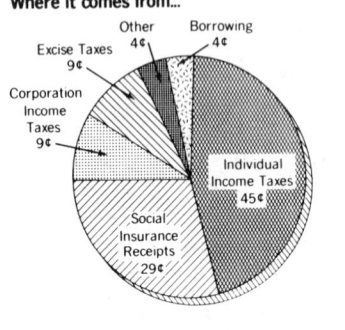

Where it comes from...

Other 4¢
Borrowing 4¢
Excise Taxes 9¢
Corporation Income Taxes 9¢
Individual Income Taxes 45¢
Social Insurance Receipts 29¢

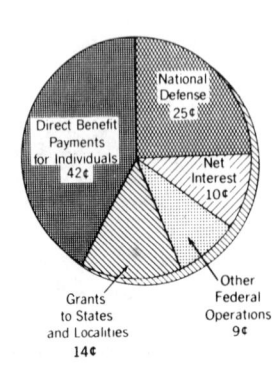

Where it goes...

National Defense 25¢
Direct Benefit Payments for Individuals 42¢
Net Interest 10¢
Grants to States and Localities 14¢
Other Federal Operations 9¢

Budget Authority and Outlays by Agency

(in millions of dollars)

DEPARTMENT OR OTHER UNIT	BUDGET AUTHORITY			OUTLAYS		
	1980 actual	1981 estimate	1982 estimate	1980 actual	1981 estimate	1982 estimate
Legislative branch	$ 1,312	$ 1,327	$ 1,456	$ 1,218	$ 1,448	$ 1,423
The Judiciary	606	670	749	564	673	734
Executive Office of the President	100	110	111	95	108	111
Funds appropriated to the President	12,457	14,657	10,903	7,523	6,212	6,348
Agriculture	24,897	26,654	30,069	24,555	20,897	28,038
Commerce	3,083	2,862	3,064	3,755	2,996	3,222
Defense—Military[1]	142,621	170,305	195,660	132,840	157,600	180,000
Defense—Civil	3,259	3,042	3,367	3,227	3,360	3,383
Education	13,797	15,639	17,031	13,112	14,826	15,713
Energy	10,018	11,663	14,614	6,464	9,726	14,109
Health and Human Services	195,855	225,506	258,406	194,703	227,328	258,180
Housing and Urban Development	35,677	38,391	38,209	12,576	13,305	15,507
Interior	4,579	4,476	4,540	4,377	4,704	4,138
Justice	2,462	2,359	2,557	2,632	2,680	2,658
Labor	28,796	33,608	37,023	29,724	37,588	34,479
State	2,135	2,376	3,024	1,938	2,142	2,596
Transportation	18,243	24,077	23,984	18,963	21,800	19,971
Treasury	90,551	90,901	104,727	76,691	91,166	104,331
Environmental Protection Agency	4,669	4,755	5,325	5,602	5,542	5,799
National Aeronautics and Space Administration	5,240	5,534	6,722	4,850	5,283	6,360
Veterans Administration	21,175	23,160	24,946	21,135	22,500	24,430
Other independent agencies	59,189	52,199	52,247	35,002	38,651	37,708
Allowances[2]	—	—	2,958	—	—	1,920
Undistributed offsetting receipts:						
Employer share, employee retirement	−5,787	−6,561	−6,798	−5,787	−6,561	−6,798
Interest received by trust funds	−12,045	−13,435	−15,165	−12,045	−13,435	−15,165
Rents and royalties on the Outer Continental Shelf lands	−4,101	−7,800	−9,900	−4,101	−7,800	−9,900
Total budget authority and outlays	**$658,790**	**$726,474**	**$809,829**	**$579,613**	**$662,740**	**$739,296**

[1] *Includes allowances for civilian and military pay raises for Department of Defense.* [2] *Includes allowances for civilian agency pay raises and contingencies.*

SOURCE: Fiscal 1982 Budget

● $2.9 billion for federal retirement pay.
● $6.4 billion for housing, food and other welfare programs.
● $8.7 billion for the Medicare and Medicaid programs.
● $8.3 billion for interest on the public debt.
● $3.2 billion for civilian pay raises.
● $3 billion for energy programs.
● $3.5 billion for farm price supports.

CPI Change

In his budget, Carter recommended changing the index currently used to compute cost-of-living adjustments for many entitlement programs. He noted that 30 percent of government spending currently went for programs that were adjusted one or two times a year for inflation.

The index currently used to calculate such adjustments, the CPI, was thought by many experts to be inaccurate because it based the price of shelter on new mortgage rates and house prices.

Carter urged Congress to adopt the new "fixed weight price" index used in figuring his budget. Computed by the Bureau of Labor Statistics, it figured housing costs on the basis of current rental prices.

In 1980, the CPI measured inflation at 12.5 percent while the fixed price index put it at 10.7 percent. However, the budget said program costs would not change in 1982 as a result of the switch.

The Credit Budget

Building on his recommendation of the previous year, Carter again proposed a partial limit on government loan and loan guarantee programs in fiscal 1982.

He requested a $23.6 billion lid on new direct loans and a $73.8 billion ceiling on loan guarantees.

But because many programs were exempted from the limit, total loans would reach $60.2 billion and loan guarantees would be $92.4 billion.

Carter waived the ceiling for such programs as emergency loans but requested that "wherever appropriate," appropriations bills include limits on credit programs.

At the end of 1982, the budget noted, the government would have $97.5 billion in outstanding direct loans on its books, with $302.4 billion in outstanding loan guarantees and another $114 billion in "off-budget" loans. ■

Reagan Seeks Sharp Cut in Federal Role

President Reagan March 10 issued a blunt warning to Congress to adopt his sweeping spending and tax cuts or risk angering voters who instructed Washington in November 1980 to put "America's economic house in order."

In a message accompanying the details of his budget for fiscal 1982, Reagan claimed that his plan to reduce federal spending by $48.6 billion in fiscal 1982 and lower taxes by $53.9 billion would help move America "back toward economic sanity." *(Text, p. 19-E)*

Combined with a "stable" monetary policy and a rollback in regulations, Reagan said the budget reductions would result in a quick drop in inflation and a "return to prosperity."

Reagan recommended that total federal spending be held to $695.3 billion in fiscal 1982, with budget authority of $772.4 billion, revenues of $650.3 billion and a deficit of $45 billion.

In his January budget, President Carter had proposed fiscal 1982 outlays of $739.3 billion, revenues of $711.8 billion and a deficit of $27.5 billion. *(Carter budget, p. 271)*

Reagan's broad spending cuts, which spared only military and so-called "social safety net" programs, would reduce the growth of spending to 6.2 percent in fiscal 1982, compared to the 11.6 percent rate proposed by Carter. *(Budget by function, p. 274)*

His ambitious plan to scale back individual income tax rates by 30 percent over the next three years and speed up depreciation write-offs for businesses would cut revenue growth from 17.2 percent to 8.3 percent.

Because military spending would jump under Reagan's economic program, the broad budget cuts he proposed would reduce dramatically the government's role in hundreds of programs established during the past two decades of social reform.

As the director of the Congressional Budget Office (CBO), Alice M. Rivlin, told the Senate Budget Committee at a hearing March 11, his fiscal plans "represent a radical redirection of the federal budget."

The budget also proposed major changes in how federal funds were distributed. Under Reagan's plan, nearly 100 categorical grant programs would be lumped together into block grants to states and localities.

Under a separate "workfare" proposal, recipients of food stamps or Aid to Families with Dependent Children (AFDC) would be required to "earn back" benefits by working part-time for their local or state government.

Reagan said that enactment of his economic plan — which he described as a "dramatic change" from "business as usual" — would permit him to balance the budget in fiscal 1984.

"I urge the members of Congress to remember that last November the American people's message was loud and clear," Reagan said. "There is nothing more important than putting America's economic house in order."

The budget text was Reagan's third economic message since taking office. He previously had outlined his economic program in a televised speech Feb. 5, followed by an address before a joint session of Congress Feb. 18. *(Texts, pp. 13-E, 15-E)*

Congressional Reaction

Lawmakers of both parties appeared to agree with Reagan's reading of the November election results — and with the need to make major reductions in spending and taxes.

But Democrats criticized many of the proposed outlay cuts, saying they would push for alternatives. They vowed to reshape his tax cut plan to provide more relief for lower-income Americans.

"Congress will disagree in specifics where we think people are being hurt. Congress doesn't give a blank check to any president," said Senate Minority Whip Alan Cranston, D-Calif.

Democratic leaders in both houses also criticized the administration for submitting what they charged were incomplete budget details based on unrealistic economic assumptions.

"We're not going to put out a budget based on mirrors and magic which six months or a year from now will be held up to ridicule," said House Budget Committee Chairman James R. Jones, D-Okla.

Sensitive to Republican charges that they were delaying action on the budget, House Democrats convened an unprecedented caucus with Republican leaders March 10 and agreed to complete action on Reagan's entire economic package by the end of July.

Republicans feared that the longer Reagan's proposals sat on Capitol Hill, the more vulnerable they would be to attack by special interest groups.

Economic Assumptions

Reagan contended that his spending and tax cuts would slash inflation from the current rate of about 12

Budget Totals Compared

(in billions of dollars)

	Budget Authority	Outlays	Revenues	Deficit
Fiscal 1980 actual	$658.8	$579.6	$520.0	$ −59.6
Fiscal 1981				
Congress' 2nd resolution	694.6	632.4	605.0	−27.4
Carter January budget	726.5	662.7	607.5	−55.2
Reagan revised budget	710.1	655.2	600.3	−54.9
Fiscal 1982				
Carter January budget	809.8	739.3	711.8	−27.5
Reagan revised budget	772.4	695.3	650.3	−45.0

Total Outlays, Including Defense

percent to 6 percent by the end of 1983. At the same time, economic growth would jump and productivity would increase.

The administration predicted that inflation would average 11.1 percent in calendar 1981, 8.3 percent in 1982 and 6.2 percent in 1983; unemployment would average 7.8 percent, 7.2 percent and 6.6 percent for the three years; and gross national product (GNP) would rise at real (inflation adjusted) rates of 1.4 percent, 5.2 percent and 4.9 percent.

The new president and his advisers based their predictions on their belief in the as-yet-untested theory of "supply side" economics.

Supply siders held that by returning taxes to businesses and workers and by restricting the growth of government, Americans would work harder and save more. That would lead to increased investment, higher productivity and a decline in inflation.

Advocates of this hypothesis argued that other theories of economic behavior had failed; they said it should be given a chance. Opponents warned it could result in inflation that was even higher than the existing level.

"The economic assumptions used for the administration budget are optimistic, but not impossible," CBO's Rivlin told the Senate Budget Committee. "If the administration's economic scenario is not attained, however, the consequences for the budget are troubling."

Budget Errors

Asked about discrepancies in the budget figures, Office of Management and Budget (OMB) officials acknowledged that their revisions to Carter's budget were compiled so quickly that some numbers were incorrect and many details still were missing.

For instance, several charts in the slim blue budget document were footnoted with an explanation that an error had been found in the data but had not been corrected for lack of time.

Rivlin praised the new administration for the "fantastic job" it had done in drafting such a major budget revision in a few weeks. But she confirmed that some authorizing committees likely were "anguishing for details" on the proposed cuts.

Spending Cuts

The budget figures Reagan sent to Congress March 10 were described

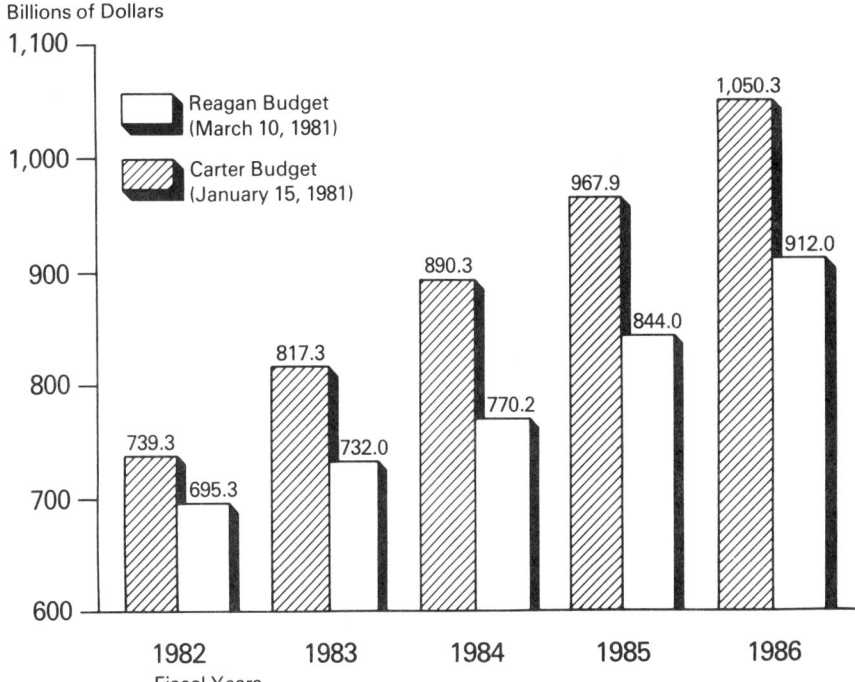

Billions of Dollars

by the OMB as an "update" of the economic "recovery" plan he announced Feb. 18.

The revised figures included $13.8 billion in new outlay savings for fiscal 1982, in addition to the previously announced $34.8 billion in cuts. About half of the new reductions were added to offset a spending error the OMB discovered after release of the Feb. 18 proposals.

The administration claimed that the budget included a total of $48.6 billion in spending cuts. But because the $34.8 billion in cuts was made from the so-called "current policy" budget and the $13.8 billion from Carter's recommendations, adding the two figures provided only a rough estimate of the total reductions.

In addition to the spending cuts, the administration said its package included $7.3 billion in new fees to the users of certain government services and in off-budget reductions. That brought the total savings to $55.9 billion, according to the OMB.

Reagan maintained in his budget document that the cuts would be shared "widely and fairly by different groups and the various regions of the country." And he stressed that the nation's "basic social safety net" of programs for the poorest Americans would be retained.

At a Rose Garden signing ceremony March 9, Reagan pledged to request more cuts if the economy weakened and federal spending rose.

"I am committed to stopping the spending juggernaut," he said.

Savings not detailed in the Feb. 18 speech included:

● $1.1 billion from government personnel and such administrative costs as travel and consultants.

● $1.1 billion from such Agriculture Department programs as nutritional supplements for pregnant women, Puerto Rico food stamps, special milk and the Commodity Credit Corp.

● $400 million from water projects.

● $400 million from new user fees for Energy Department uranium enrichment services.

● $1.2 billion by speeding up certain Medicaid payments, eliminating the lump-sum Social Security death benefit when there were no survivors and making management improvements in the Health and Human Services Department.

● $1.4 billion from Labor Department training grants and reductions in personnel at state employment service offices.

● $700 million from such veterans' programs as education, hospital construction and medical personnel bonuses.

The Defense Department would be exempted from Reagan's belt-tightening exercise. Military programs would get a 31 percent increase in budget authority over the ceiling set by Congress for fiscal 1981.

Reagan described the tax reduction portion of his budget as "essential" to the success of his economic plan. He said the proposed $44.2 billion cut in individual income taxes and the $9.7 billion reduction in business taxes would have an "immediate impact" on the economy. *(Tax bill, p. 91)*

Fiscal 1981 Changes

Reagan's budget for fiscal 1982 also included a recommended increase in spending for the current budget year, which was to end Sept. 30.

Spending in fiscal 1981 would be $655.2 billion, with revenues of $600.3 billion and a deficit of $54.9 billion. That was a spending level $22.8 billion higher and a deficit two times higher than Congress voted in its binding second budget resolution for fiscal 1981 (H Con Res 448). *(Second budget resolution, 1980 Almanac p. 119)*

But Reagan's budget revision for the ongoing fiscal year represented a reduction of $17.5 billion from the spending level Carter recommended in January. Many of the same programs Reagan proposed cutting in fiscal 1982 also would be scaled back in fiscal 1981.

Future Savings

Although Reagan spelled out the details of the spending cuts he was seeking in fiscal 1981 and 1982, he had not yet pinpointed many of the reductions scheduled for fiscal 1983 through 1986.

His fiscal plan assumed that over the next five years, spending would be reduced by a total $409 billion from the "current policy" budget — the cost of continuing all programs at the current funding level with adjustments for inflation.

To reach that level and achieve a surplus of $500 million in 1984, the administration assumed further cuts of $29.8 billion in 1983 and $44.2 billion in 1984.

The Credit Budget

In addition to the spending and tax cuts, Reagan recommended a major scaleback in "off-budget" lending programs, to be accomplished through a lending ceiling for appropriations and changes in authorizing legislation.

He proposed that federal loan guarantee programs be cut by $11 billion in fiscal 1981 and $18.4 billion in 1982 from the level Carter recommended. Direct loans would be cut $2.6 billion in both years.

"Loan guarantees are basically not a business the government ought to be in," OMB Director David A. Stockman told reporters at a briefing. "Every time you do it, you knock someone else out of the pew."

Stockman said the thrust of the cutback, which would produce only "modest" outlay savings, was to reduce the government's role in the credit markets. Currently, about one-third of all credit was extended by the federal government.

Programs that would be affected included: the Export-Import Bank, the Rural Electrification Administration, the Economic Development Administration (EDA), the Federal Housing Administration and the Student Loan Marketing Association.

Under the proposal, the only "off-budget" loan programs slated for an increase would be military and political loans to U.S. allies.

Legislative Status

Most of the 1982 spending and tax cuts proposed by Reagan would require that Congress change current law rather than reduce appropriations.

Stockman said the administration would try to win such legislative changes:

● Through an omnibus reconciliation savings bill making changes in the authorization for many programs.

● Through legislation for such major initiatives as replacing categorical grants to states and localities with block grants.

Funds that already had been appropriated for the current fiscal year would be rescinded or deferred.

Prior to the release of the budget, the administration froze spending in several agencies scheduled for major cuts: the EDA, the Environmental Protection Agency, the Labor Department, the Export-Import Bank.

Stockman said the action — which had been attacked by congressional Democrats — was needed to prevent agencies from rushing to spend funds his office had targeted for reductions.

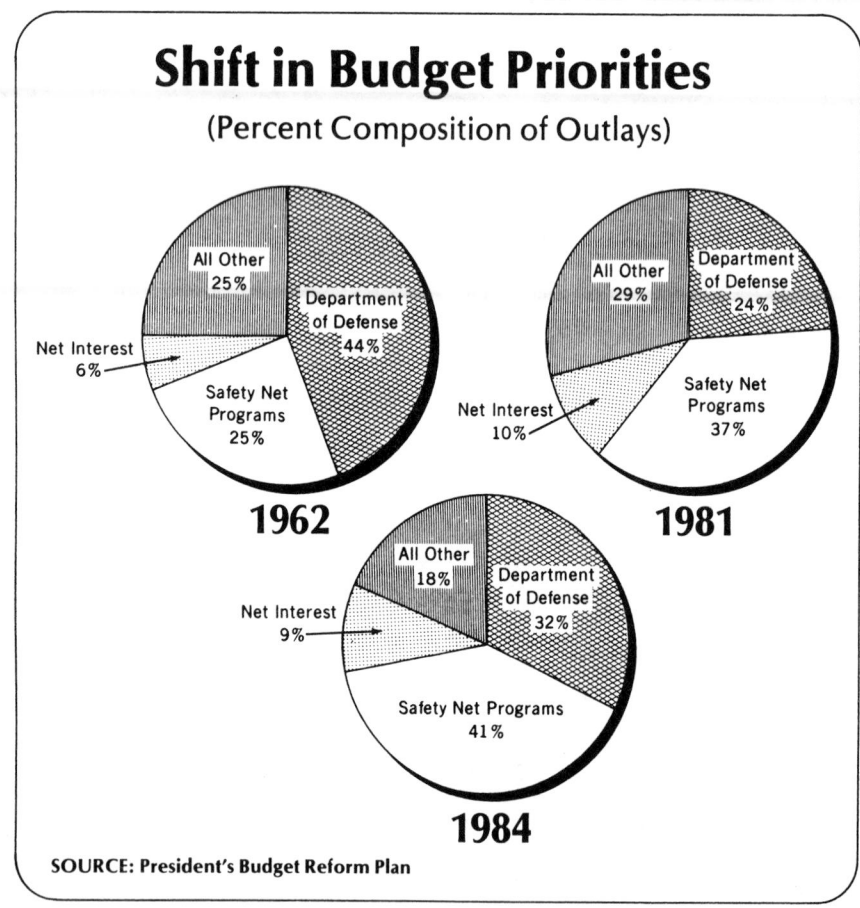

Shift in Budget Priorities
(Percent Composition of Outlays)

All Other 25%
Department of Defense 44%
Net Interest 6%
Safety Net Programs 25%
1962

All Other 29%
Department of Defense 24%
Net Interest 10%
Safety Net Programs 37%
1981

All Other 18%
Department of Defense 32%
Net Interest 9%
Safety Net Programs 41%
1984

SOURCE: President's Budget Reform Plan

Congress Votes Fiscal 1981 Funds, Rescissions

Congress June 4 gave final approval to an omnibus spending bill that provided more money for defense and cut funds for a host of social programs.

The fiscal 1981 supplemental appropriations bill (HR 3512 — PL 97-12), the first spending bill cleared by Congress following the inauguration of President Reagan, conformed in large part to his economic program.

"This is the first major component of the president's program of economic recovery," said Silvio O. Conte, R-Mass., ranking minority member of the House Appropriations Committee.

The bill increased fiscal 1981 spending by $6.6 billion. That was enough to bring total federal spending for the year to within $250 million of the $661.35 billion ceiling set by Congress May 21. *(Story, p. 247)*

The measure contained supplemental appropriations totaling $20.9 billion, of which $7.2 billion was for Defense Department programs and $6 billion was for civilian and military pay increases that took effect Oct. 1, 1980.

Social and environmental programs bore the brunt of the bill's $14.3 billion in rescissions, or cancellations, of previously appropriated funds. Programs that suffered major losses included subsidized housing, Environmental Protection Agency (EPA) waste treatment grants and education.

Reagan had requested $23.5 billion in supplemental appropriations and $15.1 billion in rescissions, for a net spending increase of $8.4 billion. While HR 3512 followed the broad outline of Reagan's request, it did not go as far as he had sought on defense increases or social program cuts.

Congress sustained requests to defer $4.8 billion in spending until fiscal 1982. It rejected deferral requests of $367 million and added $1 billion in deferrals of its own.

Action on HR 3512 provided a striking display of the power of anti-abortion activists in the 97th Congress. The bill contained the toughest-ever congressional limit on Medicaid funding of abortions, allowing them only when needed to save the mother's life.

The bill also extended funding for agencies and programs whose regular fiscal 1981 appropriations bills never became law: foreign aid, the legislative branch, payments to the Postal Service, and the departments of Treasury, Labor, Education, and Health and Human Services (HHS).

HR 3512 extended funding for those agencies from June 5, 1981 — the expiration date of the existing authority provided by a continuing appropriations measure (PL 96-536) passed in 1980 — through Sept. 30, the end of the fiscal year. *(1980 Almanac p. 218)*

Final Provisions

As signed into law June 5, HR 3512 (PL 97-12) included the following supplemental appropriations for fiscal 1981 and rescissions of previous appropriations:

	Budget Request*	Final Action
Agriculture		
Supplementals	$ 1,939,905,000	$ 1,892,030,000
Rescissions	−510,500,000	−505,500,000
Subtotal	1,429,405,000	1,386,530,000
Commerce, Justice, State, the Judiciary		
Supplementals	115,272,000	71,006,000
Rescissions	−483,918,510	−350,947,000
Subtotal	−368,646,510	−279,941,000
Defense		
Supplementals	7,651,859,000	6,936,680,000
District of Columbia		
Supplementals	4,600,000	4,600,000
Energy and Water		
Supplementals	156,000,000	156,000,000
Rescissions	−1,303,315,000	−1,508,038,000
Subtotal	−1,147,315,000	−1,352,038,000
Foreign Assistance		
Supplementals	571,170,000	530,864,000
Rescissions	−27,738,000	−65,370,900
Subtotal	543,432,000	465,493,100
HUD-Independent Agencies		
Supplementals	1,621,057,000	1,719,272,000
Rescissions	−7,441,200,031	−7,475,189,747
Subtotal	−5,820,143,031	−5,755,917,747
Interior		
Supplementals	2,455,379,000	1,561,454,000
Rescissions	−2,103,305,000	−2,158,746,000
Subtotal	352,074,000	−597,292,000
Labor-HHS-Education		
Supplementals	792,234,000	502,705,000
Rescissions	−2,982,644,000	−1,891,369,000
Subtotal	−2,190,410,000	−1,388,664,000
Legislative Branch		
Supplementals	60,873,000	33,378,663
Rescissions	0	−48,208,000
Subtotal	60,873,000	−14,829,337
Military Construction		
Supplementals	334,362,000	227,262,000
Transportation		
Supplementals	772,793,000	645,233,000
Rescissions	−36,200,000	−33,200,000
Subtotal	736,593,000	612,033,000
Treasury, Postal Service, General Government		
Supplementals	963,551,000	697,259,000
Rescissions	−251,710,000	−257,310,000
Subtotal	711,841,000	439,949,000
Increased Pay Costs		
Supplementals	6,075,614,800	5,965,436,000
Grand Total		
Supplementals	$23,514,669,800	$20,943,179,663
Rescissions	−$15,140,530,541	−$14,293,878,647
Net New Budget Authority	$ 8,374,139,259	$ 6,649,301,016

* Included a net of $776,325,000 in budget estimates not considered by the House. Of this amount, $536,124,000 for the food stamp program was not formally transmitted to Congress.

House Committee Action

The House Appropriations Committee May 4 reported the initial version of the supplemental bill (HR 3400 — H Rept 97-29).

All told, the committee recommended $19.1 billion in supplemental appropriations. The bulk of that — $11.2 billion — was for Pentagon spending other than construction of buildings and facilities. Reagan had requested $21.8 billion, with $12.4 billion in defense spending. (*Major funding items, box, this page*)

Along with the spending increases, the panel called for rescission of $12.7 billion in already appropriated fiscal 1981 funds. Most of that amount, which compared with $15.1 billion sought by Reagan, came from domestic social, environmental and energy programs.

In addition, the committee accepted temporary deferral of $5.5 billion in 1981 spending. Unlike rescissions, which required congressional approval, deferrals remained in effect until the end of the fiscal year unless either the House or Senate disapproved them.

Subcommittees Upheld

The committee made virtually no changes in the recommendations that emerged from its subcommittees. Republicans, tempted to push for further spending cuts, agreed to hold off in order to speed action on the bill, according to ranking member Conte.

With one exception, related to defense, the committee rejected efforts to add more funds to the subcommittee recommendations.

Bill Highlights

The biggest changes made by the committee in the administration's requested supplementals and rescissions were in the areas of defense and education.

For defense, the panel cut a total of $1.6 billion from Reagan's request. Much of the difference was due to disagreements over matters such as accounting procedures and fuel price estimates. The committee also rejected a number of weapons requests, including the reactivation of the aircraft carrier *Oriskany* and research on a new ballistic missile defense system.

The committee made a major addition to the defense budget, however, that brought its savings from the Reagan request down to $1.2 billion. Arguing that the administration's 7 percent inflation estimate was too optimistic, the panel added funds to protect the Defense Department from a higher inflation rate. The change was approved on a 6-4 vote in the Defense Subcommittee.

MX Missile

As part of the military construction budget, the committee moved to delay work on the MX missile system. Arguing that work should not go forward until the administration completed its current review of options for the basic design of the system, the panel rejected a requested $26.5 million supplemental for MX planning and design contracts. In addition, it agreed to deferral of $92 million in previously appropriated funds until the president announced his decision on MX design and an environmental impact statement was completed.

While approving most Reagan rescission requests, the committee denied $1.1 billion in rescissions requested for Education Department programs.

Major Funding Items

As approved by the House Appropriations Committee, the fiscal 1981 funding bill included the following major supplemental appropriations, rescissions and deferrals (*in thousands of dollars*):

Supplementals

Mandatory pay costs	$ 1,261,078
Defense Department (other than military construction)	11,180,927
Military construction	221,402
Food stamps (contingent on authorization)	1,204,600
Veterans' entitlements	1,195,840
Civil service retirement	513,007
Conrail	300,000
Strategic Petroleum Reserve purchases	430,000
Strategic Petroleum Reserve purchases (by transfer)	(875,000)
Student aid	661,000
General Services Administration	150,000
Federal crop insurance	192,181

Rescissions

Subsidized housing	5,219,104
EPA waste treatment	1,700,000
Postal Service	250,000
Energy programs	1,757,157
Biomass energy	921,500
Labor programs	234,475
Department of Health and Human Services	533,629
Education programs	785,891
Veterans' construction	162,160
Rehabilitation loan fund	110,857
Economic development program	181,350

Deferrals	5,473,000

Advance Appropriations, 1982

Strategic petroleum reserve	3,883,408

House Floor Action

In the first major test of the fiscal targets set by its budget resolution, the House May 13 voted to cut $3 billion from spending for the Strategic Petroleum Reserve (SPR).

The move to slash fiscal 1982 funding for the petroleum reserve came on an amendment to the second version of the fiscal 1981 supplemental appropriations bill (HR 3512). HR 3512 passed by a 329-70 vote the same day. (*Vote 39, p. 22-H*)

The unexpectedly easy 108-vote margin for the SPR amendment was a victory for Budget Committee efforts to make spending conform to the technically non-binding limits of the budget resolution passed by the House May 7. In addition to the advance appropriation for SPR, which was reduced by the amendment to $883 million from $3.9 billion, HR 3512 contained a potpourri of changes in 1981 spending — supplemental appropriations, rescissions, deferrals. It also extended funding authority, through Sept. 30, 1981, for the five departments and other agencies whose regular 1981 appropriations bills were never cleared.

All told, HR 3512 provided for an increase in spending of $6.8 billion. That was the difference between the bill's $19.5 billion in appropriations and $12.7 billion in rescissions.

Among the hundreds of supplemental items in the bill were funds for defense ($10.7 billion), food stamps ($1.2 billion), and veterans' programs ($1.2 billion). Major rescissions came from subsidized housing programs ($5.2 billion), waste treatment grants ($1.7 billion), and energy programs ($1.8 billion).

The net spending increase ordered by HR 3512 was $787 million less than that requested by President Reagan. The administration had called for $22.7 billion in supplemental appropriations and $15.1 billion in rescissions, for a net spending increase of $7.6 billion.

Along with his request for rescissions of spending, Reagan had asked to defer a total of $5.2 billion in 1981 spending, to be spent in 1982. The House approved a total of $5.7 billion in deferrals.

Budget Maneuvering

After being approved by the House Appropriations Committee April 30, the supplemental bill ran into difficulties in the Rules Committee.

The first version of the bill (HR 3400) went before the Rules Committee May 7. There two problems arose: The bill apparently breached the 1981 budget ceiling, and it intruded on the jurisdiction of the Energy and Commerce Committee.

Under the latest spending estimates, HR 3400 would have brought total federal spending in fiscal 1981 above the limits set by the House-passed budget resolution. The bill contained a $500 million inflation adjustment added by the committee to the defense budget. The administration had not wanted the additional money, on the assumption of a low inflation rate for the year.

Commerce Committee members objected to provisions in the bill that ordered the Nuclear Regulatory Commission (NRC) to speed up the process of licensing new nuclear power plants. Since it already was working on a similar bill, the Commerce Committee asked that the provisions be dropped from HR 3400. *(NRC bill, p. 444)*

The Appropriations Committee met later in the day and reported a new bill (HR 3512) that met both objections. It eliminated both the extra $500 million inflation adjustment and the NRC provisions. The Rules Committee then granted the new bill a rule (H Res 137).

Petroleum Reserve

In H Res 137, the Rules Committee included a waiver of the budget resolution in order to allow the bill to come to the floor with the $3.9 billion for the SPR. Without the waiver, the 1982 appropriation could not have been considered before final congressional approval of the first budget resolution for the year.

Budget Committee Chairman James R. Jones, D-Okla., asked the Rules Committee not to grant the waiver. He argued that the $3.9 billion SPR appropriation violated the spirit of the House's conservative budget resolution, which had assumed an appropriation of only $883 million. When HR 3512 came to the floor, Jones offered an amendment to reduce the SPR funding to the level of the budget resolution's assumptions. Key Democratic leaders opposed his proposal, which was adopted 260-152. *(Vote 35, p. 22-H)*

"This amendment could be called the truth-in-budgeting amendment," Jones said. "This $3.9 billion in funding for the Strategic Petroleum Reserve simply does not conform to the budget resolution that was passed by the House last week," he continued. *(SPR funding, p. 449)*

Supporters of the full $3.9 billion figure stressed the need for immediate funding of the SPR program for the next year. They said current world market conditions, which Interior Appropriations Subcommittee Chairman Sidney R. Yates, D-Ill., described as a "glut of oil on the market," provided a good opportunity to buy oil for the reserve at relatively low prices.

On a more general level, opponents of the Jones amendment pointed out that the first budget resolution was not originally intended to set binding spending limits. In any case, they said, the resolution only set totals for spending under the jurisdiction of each committee, not for individual programs. If the Commerce Committee wanted to meet its savings goals in other programs while preserving the SPR funding, that was it right, they argued.

"It was never intended that [the first resolution] was a final act. All it was was a set of targets, and it was not a straitjacket," said Richard Bolling, D-Mo.

Foreign Trade

Some overnight lobbying by companies and unions involved in foreign trade helped reverse an initial House decision to cut funds for the Export-Import Bank.

The Reagan administration had proposed cutting back on the bank's loans to foreign governments and companies. *(Export-Import Bank, p. 123)*

The administration proposed restricting Ex-Im direct loan authority for 1981 to $5.1 billion from $5.9 billion. The Appropriations Committee set the limit at $5.5 billion and increased the limit on guaranteed loans to $8.1 billion from the administration-backed $7.6 billion.

David R. Obey, D-Wis., offered an amendment to lower the loan limits to the administration levels. With so many programs for the poor being cut, he said, Congress also should cut a program that benefited large corporations, particularly in the aerospace industry.

Obey's amendment was adopted by a 231-166 vote May 12 in the Committee of the Whole. But by the time the House returned to HR 3512 the next day, the aerospace companies and related unions had put heavy pressure on members, according to an Obey aide. The House then rejected the amendment 162-237. *(Votes 33, 38, p. 22-H)*

Earlier, the House voted 272-126 for a John H. Rousselot, R-Calif., amendment to cut the contribution to the International Development Association to $534.6 million from $540 million. *(Vote 32, p. 22-H)*

Other Amendments

In other action on HR 3512, the House accepted amendments by:

● Bobbi Fiedler, R-Calif., to defer $28.5 million for a "people mover" transportation project in Los Angeles; adopted by a 244-156 vote. *(Vote 36, p. 22-H)*

● John M. Ashbrook, R-Ohio, to ban funds for federal employee health insurance policies that provide abortions; adopted by a 242-155 vote. *(Vote 37, p. 22-H)*

● Yates, to cut $1.4 million for the Navajo-Hopi Indian settlement program; adopted by voice vote.

Senate Action

The Senate passed HR 3512 by a 95-0 vote May 21. The bill had been reported by the Appropriations Committee May 14 (S Rept 97-67). *(Vote 134, p. 25-S)*

As passed by the Senate, HR 3512 provided $21.9 billion in appropriations and $15.3 billion in rescissions. The House bill contained appropriations of $19.5 billion and rescissions of $12.7 billion.

The Senate bill called for more defense spending and less social spending than the House measure. There was $13 billion for defense in the Senate version, $2.1 billion above the House level. *(Defense supplemental, p. 352)*

Cuts in education and health programs were deeper than those accepted by the House, although not so deep as requested by Reagan.

One major exception was the food stamp program. The Senate voted to add $538 million to the $1.2 billion provided for the program by the House. The administration supported the full $1.7 billion to keep the program from running out of money during the summer of 1981, although it never made a formal request for the additional $538 million.

During debate May 20, the Senate sent President Reagan a message of unanimous opposition to key parts of his proposed cuts in Social Security benefits.

A 96-0 vote showed the breadth of Senate sentiment against the president's proposals to make immediate reductions in benefits to early retirees and to cut benefits more than some experts considered necessary to make the program solvent. *(Social Security p. 117)*

Before approving the statement of opposition, sponsored by Finance Committee Chairman Robert Dole, R-Kan., senators came within one vote of accepting an even more critical, Democratic-backed attack on the Reagan proposals.

Although the Senate's statement on Social Security was in the form of a non-binding "sense of the Senate" amendment, it came the same day as a similar expression of opposition from House Democrats. And within 24 hours of the Senate action, administration officials seemed to back off from their proposals.

HR 3512 was also the forum for a victory by anti-abortion forces. Members voted to allow funding for abortions for poor women only when needed to save the mother's life. That was a stronger restriction than the Senate has approved in recent years. *(1980 Almanac p. 467)*

Social Security

Making the most of initial unfavorable public reaction to the president's Social Security proposals, Senate Democrats pressed a partisan attack that came within an eyelash of victory.

Meeting May 19, the Senate Democratic Conference approved a resolution that called the proposed reductions "a breach of faith with those aging Americans who have contributed to the Social Security system...."

The resolution went on to vow opposition to any changes that would "precipitously and unfairly deny those men and women approaching retirement age Social Security benefits on which they have planned...."

The text of the resolution was offered as an amendment by Daniel Patrick Moynihan, D-N.Y. After a lengthy debate, it was tabled, 49-48. *(Vote 121, p. 24-S)*

Moynihan and other Democrats focused their strong-

est criticism on the proposed reductions for early retirees. Moynihan said that the proposal to reduce benefits for those retiring at age 62 to 55 percent of full benefits, from 80 percent under current law, would make it "financially impossible to retire at 62."

Minority Leader Robert C. Byrd, D-W.Va., called the proposals a reversal of Reagan's campaign pledge not to tamper with the system. Going back on that promise, Byrd warned, was fraught with political peril. "While he is a popular and well-liked president, I caution his advisers against interpreting the tide of personal popularity as a license to unravel the Social Security system," Byrd said.

Dole and other Republicans expressed reservations about some of Reagan's specific proposals but argued that something had to be done to save the system from its short-term and long-term financial problems. Whatever the political appeal of voting for the Moynihan amendment, Dole said, it would do nothing to save the program from the worst sort of breach of promise — bankruptcy.

The motion to table Moynihan's amendment was offered by Appropriations Committee Chairman Mark O. Hatfield, R-Ore. All 46 Democrats, plus William V. Roth Jr., R-Del., and Lowell P. Weicker Jr., R-Conn., voted against it. Independent Harry F. Byrd Jr., Va., joined 48 Republicans in supporting the tabling motion.

After the vote, Dole offered his amendment, retaining much of the substance of the Moynihan amendment but without some of the partisan rhetoric. The amendment promised that Congress would not approve immediate or inequitable reductions in early retirees' benefits or cut more than necessary to save the system's finances.

Hatfield, who opposed all legislative amendments to appropriations bills, moved to table the Dole amendment. His motion was rejected 4-93, after which the amendment was adopted 96-0. *(Votes 122, 123, p. 24-S)*

Abortion

Efforts by Republican leaders to keep the bill free of controversial legislative amendments were swept aside by a tide of anti-abortion sentiment.

Because of his opposition to legislative riders, Hatfield had deleted the House-passed anti-abortion language in committee. That provision, named for House sponsor Henry J. Hyde, R-Ill., prohibited Medicaid funding of abortions unless needed to save the mother's life. Under current law, Medicaid funds also would pay for abortions in cases of rape or incest.

While stressing his personal opposition to abortion funding, Hatfield argued that the abortion prohibition did not belong on an appropriations bill and should be left to authorizing committees.

Jesse Helms, R-N.C., led the fight for the abortion ban. He moved to strike the Appropriations Committee amendment, which had deleted the House anti-abortion language. Members agreed, 52-43, which in effect restored the ban. *(Vote 132, p. 25-S)*

As in recent years, the abortion fight was waged mostly among Republicans, without much Democratic participation. Opposing Helms were Bob Packwood, R-Ore., and Weicker. Debate reached an unusually emotional level over the issue of the influence of religion on public policy. Catholic and fundamentalist Protestant church groups were among the leading proponents of abortion bans.

"I find growing in this country a spirit of intolerance, of almost religious moralism," Packwood said, warning of a

"Cotton Mather mentality that is trying to impose upon this country a Cotton Mather morality."

Helms said that he did not object to being linked with the 17th century Puritan clergyman, if it was a matter of the "deliberate termination of innocent human life."

Before the vote, Helms warned that the anti-abortion movement would not give excuses to those who voted against the motion on procedural grounds. His motion had the support of 33 Republicans and 19 Democrats; 19 Republicans and 24 Democrats opposed it.

However, the Senate agreed to drop a provision in the House bill that prohibited federal employee health insurance plans from paying for abortions, because it did not allow abortions when needed to save the mother's life.

Other Amendments

In other action, the Senate took roll-call votes on amendments offered by:

● James Abdnor, R-S.D., to add $538 million in fiscal 1981 funds for the food stamp program, and $110 million for child nutrition programs; adopted, 50-45, after a motion to table was rejected, 38-57. *(Votes 131, 133, p. 25-S)*

● Thad Cochran, R-Miss., to delete a proposed rescission of $30 million for the "developing institutions" program aiding traditionally black colleges; adopted by a 76-19 vote. *(Vote 129, p. 25-S)*

● Cochran, to increase by $30 million the proposed rescission of funds for migration and refugee assistance; rejected by a 39-57 vote. *(Vote 130, p. 25-S)*

● Dennis DeConcini, D-Ariz., to prohibit the Education Department from seeking to force school districts to repay funds received under Title I of the Elementary and Secondary Education Act, if the repayment was sought on the basis of an audit that began before 1978; the amendment was ruled out of order, and DeConcini's appeal of the ruling of the chair was tabled, 60-38. *(Vote 127, p. 25-S)*

Conference Action

Despite the vast array of spending changes in HR 3512, covering virtually every agency in government, conference action on the measure proceeded smoothly.

Before passing the bill May 21, the Senate had removed the biggest potential obstacle to quick conference action by agreeing to the House provision banning Medicaid funding for all but life-saving abortions. Senate insistence in past years on less restrictive abortion limits had led to lengthy conference deadlocks.

With the main abortion dispute out of the way, House-Senate conferees June 2 approved a compromise version of the bill in short order, considering that there were 432 differences to be resolved. The conference agreement was reported June 3 (H Rept 97-124).

In the face of Senate opposition, House conferees dropped a provision barring federal employee health insurance plans from paying for abortions. The provision had not allowed an exception for life-threatening situations.

Defense Spending

Along with funding for increases in Defense Department pay and fuel costs, HR 3512 contained provisions affecting three controversial weapons systems.

The most closely fought item was a $20 million appropriation in the bill for development of a new form of chemical weapon. The Senate had agreed by only two votes

to join the House in providing the money to equip a factory to produce an artillery shell that dispensed lethal nerve gas. Conferees on HR 3512 insisted that the administration undertake a study of the long-range costs of the new program and consult with European allies about it.

The bill also contained funds for the reactivation of two mothballed battleships, the *New Jersey* and the *Iowa*.

The bill not only denied a requested $26.5 million supplemental for the MX missile system but also deferred spending of $92 million in already appropriated funds.

The conference agreement deferred the MX funds until Reagan announced his choice for the basic design, or "basing mode," of the system.

Spending Increases

While it reduced funds for a variety of domestic social programs, HR 3512 contained large supplemental appropriations for two quasi-entitlement programs that threatened to run out of money before the end of the fiscal year.

For the food stamp program, the bill provided $1.7 billion, bringing total spending for the program in fiscal 1981 to $11.5 billion. The administration had formally requested a supplemental of only $1.2 billion, although officials had indicated they wanted the additional $536 million in order to prevent benefit reductions to 23 million recipients. The bill made the extra funds available only after the administration submitted an official request.

The measure also included additional funds for the Pell grant program of aid to college students. But it provided only $445 million, compared with the administration's request for $661 million. The bill ordered an $80 cut in the grant for each student recipient.

A similar reduction in the administration request was made in the supplemental appropriation for the U.S. contribution to the International Development Association (IDA). Reagan had sought $540 million, as the first part of a $3.24 billion contribution over three years. However, HR 3512 provided only $500 million.

Another major supplemental appropriation in the bill went for the Strategic Petroleum Reserve (SPR). Conferees approved $1.3 billion for purchase of oil for the reserve. But they rejected an advance 1982 appropriation, sought by the House, of $883 million.

Rescissions

Subsidized housing alone accounted for more than one-third of the rescissions in HR 3512. Fiscal 1981 spending for those programs was cut by $5.1 billion.

Social programs within the departments of Labor, HHS and Education received spending reductions totaling $1.9 billion. The Reagan administration had sought cuts of $3 billion but faced House opposition to reductions in education and health programs, particularly a proposed 25 percent cut in education grants.

Also included in the social program cuts was a $35 million rescission in fiscal 1983 funds for the Corporation for Public Broadcasting. Reagan had requested cuts in advance funding for fiscal 1982-1983 of $95 million.

Another major rescission came from EPA grants for sewage treatment plant construction. The administration sought the $1.7 billion cut in the bill.

Final Action

The House approved the conference report by voice vote June 4. The Senate approved the conference report by voice vote the same day.

Congress Votes Itself New Pay Benefits

Members of Congress used their fiscal 1982 appropriation as the vehicle for enacting several indirect methods of increasing their take-home pay but were able to avoid voting directly on an outright pay increase.

The legislative branch appropriation was included in the continuing appropriations resolution (H J Res 325 — PL 97-51) that was cleared by Congress Oct. 1, the start of the new fiscal year. The legislative branch measure was the only one of the 13 regular 1982 appropriations bills whose text was included in the continuing resolution and it was the only portion of the resolution that did not expire Nov. 20, 1981.

As cleared, the measure gave senators three ways and House members two ways to increase their earnings above their existing official salary of $60,622.50 a year. Members wanted to avoid voting directly on raising salaries — a move they knew would be unpopular because of the fierce budget cutting going on in virtually every federal agency.

Under the bill:

● Starting in 1982, senators and representatives could deduct from their income taxes all "business" expenses they incurred while in Washington. Under a 1952 law repealed by H J Res 325, members could deduct a maximum of only $3,000. *(1952 Almanac p. 110)*

The Joint Committee on Taxation estimated that the change would cost the Treasury $3 million a year and provide a typical member in the 45 percent tax bracket with the equivalent of a $10,500 annual pay raise.

A similar proposal had been pushed earlier in the year by House Appropriations Chairman Jamie L. Whitten, D-Miss., but it never came to a vote in the House. It was pushed though on the Senate floor Oct. 24 by Sen. Ted Stevens, R-Alaska, and then was agreed to by a House-Senate conference committee.

● Starting in fiscal 1983, members were to receive an automatic annual cost-of-living raise equal to the raise given most white-collar federal workers. In 1981 that amounted to 4.8 percent.

In 1975, Congress voted to include itself among federal workers getting the automatic raises, but an annual vote still was required to appropriate the funds. Four times since 1975 — in 1977, 1978, 1980 and 1981 — Congress had voted to block the additional appropriation. So members voted to provide an automatic appropriation that required no annual vote.

● Starting in 1981, the limits were removed on the amount senators could earn by giving speeches or writing articles. Since 1976, they had been limited to up to $25,000 in honoraria income. But the bill did away with the limit, removing all restrictions on senators' outside income.

A Senate rule scheduled to become effective in 1983 established an honoraria limit of about $9,000 a year. *(Background, 1979 Almanac p. 578)*

The change did not affect House members, who were restricted by a separate rule limiting all of their outside earnings, including honoraria, to a maximum of 15 percent of their congressional salary. In 1981, that amount was $9,099.37. Later in the year, an attempt to loosen that restriction failed by a wide margin on the House floor.

Highlights of the Bill

As cleared by Congress, the legislative budget totaled $1.3 billion for fiscal 1982. This was about $40 million more than the previous year but almost $140 million below what was requested.

Major items included $214.4 million for the Senate, $363.8 million for the House, $275.7 million for congressional support and $445.6 million for related legislative branch agencies.

Cut from the budget were 1982 funds for a new Government Printing Office building. Congress also decided against establishing a new Railroad Accounting Principles Board. Tasks assigned to that board by a 1980 railroad deregulation law (PL 96-448) were left to existing agencies. *(1980 Almanac p. 248)*

The bill appropriated a total of $8,000 for creation of $2,000-a-year expense accounts for the Senate secretary, the sergeant-at-arms and the majority and minority secretaries. Previously, only the top elected Senate leaders were provided expense accounts.

The bill also increased the pay of the Senate chaplain to $52,750 from $40,110, making his salary equal to that of the House chaplain.

Final Provisions

As cleared by Congress, H J Res 325 made the following appropriations for fiscal 1982 for the legislative branch *(in thousands of dollars)*:

	Budget Request	Final Amount
Congressional Operations		
Senate	$ 229,992	$ 214,350
House	371,356	363,794
Joint Items	89,776	83,609
Office of Technology Assessment	13,100	12,019
Congressional Budget Office	14,298	12,868
Architect of the Capitol	84,200	52,366
Congressional Research Service	32,288	30,000
Government Printing Office (congressional printing)	91,218	84,843
Subtotal	$ 926,228	$ 853,849
Related Agencies		
Botanic Gardens	2,311	2,311
Library of Congress	165,323	159,827
Architect of the Capitol (library buildings and grounds)	22,718	8,715
Copyright Royalty Tribunal	500	400
Government Printing Office (other than congressional printing)	48,659	45,008
General Accounting Office	244,878	229,300
Railroad Accounting Principles Board	1,000	0
Subtotal	$ 485,389	$ 445,561
Capital Improvements		
New building, Government Printing Office	22,300	0
GRAND TOTAL	$1,433,917	$1,299,410

House Retains Outside Income Restrictions

By a wide margin, the House Oct. 28 turned back an effort to loosen restrictions on the amount of outside income a member could earn.

The action meant House members continued to be bound by a ceiling on their outside earned income of 15 percent of their $60,662.50 official salary, or $9,099.37. The House Dec. 15 boosted the limit to 30 percent, however. *(Story, p. 400)*

The ceiling, which went into effect in January 1979, did not apply to unearned income — such as dividends, interest and rent — or to income from a family-controlled business in which the member was only minimally involved. These types of income remained unlimited.

The House action was in contrast to the Senate, which on Oct. 1 exempted itself from a $25,000 restriction on outside earned income contained in the 1976 Federal Election Campaign Act (PL 94-283). *(Story, p. 286; 1976 act, 1976 Almanac p. 459)*

The House vote to retain its limit was 147-271. With that vote members defeated a proposal (H Res 251) by Rules Committee Chairman Richard Bolling, D-Mo., to raise the outside earned income ceiling to 40 percent of a member's official salary — or $24,265 under the current salary — for 1981 through 1983, when the ceiling was to revert to 15 percent. *(Vote 267, p. 86-H)*

Bolling's proposal also would have increased the limit on each individual honorarium payment for a speech, article or personal appearance to $2,000 from $1,000.

The rule relaxation was supported by House leaders on both sides of the aisle. But the leaders did little in the way of lobbying, and opposition to the resolution crossed party lines: 112 Republicans and 159 Democrats voted against it.

After the vote, Bolling said he had expected his proposal to be approved but was not surprised at its defeat. "It just means people don't want to change things," he said.

Other members cited the difficulty of voting for a "backdoor pay raise" during a time of widespread budget cutting.

'Temporary Solution'

During floor debate, Bolling described the resolution as a compromise between those members seeking no limit on earned income and those trying to retain the existing limit. He said his plan was intended to be only a "temporary solution" to the overall problem of members' pay. Its Dec. 31, 1983, expiration, he said, would virtually assure that the House would return to the issue before then.

Members supporting the resolution argued that the rule change would make it easier for members to meet spiraling expenses and would cost taxpayers nothing.

Opponents cast the debate largely in ethical terms.

Lee H. Hamilton, D-Ind., said passage would "significantly weaken" the House ethics code, adopted in 1977. *(1977 Almanac p. 764)*

Tom Harkin, D-Iowa, said he feared approval would soon have members "tripping over themselves" to seek out speaking fees. And when a member accepts a $2,000 honorarium from an oil industry group, Harkin added, "he's going to tell them what they want to hear."

Before defeating H Res 251, the House rejected by voice vote a Harkin amendment that would have put off the increase until after the 1982 elections and would have limited it to a single year.

H Res 251 was reported (H Rept 97-303) by the Rules Committee Oct. 27 on a voice vote.

The bill also:

● Removed the existing $3,000 ceiling on the amount of business-related tax deductions members of Congress could claim while away from home.

● Removed the existing statutory limit of $25,000 on the amount of outside earned income that could be received by senators. The existing limit of about $9,000, under House rules, would continue to apply to members of the House.

● Established a permanent funding mechanism for salary increases for members of Congress. Under the provision, funds for congressional pay increases, if recommended by the president along with other federal employee pay raises and upheld by Congress, would automatically be appropriated.

● Extended the cap on the salaries of upper-level federal employees through Nov. 20, 1981. The cap froze the salaries of all employees at Executive Level V (currently paid $50,112.50) and above.

House Subcommittee Action

A $1.1 billion budget for fiscal 1982 operations of the legislative branch was approved by the House Legislative Appropriations Subcommittee June 18. The recommenda-

tion was 5.8 percent higher than the comparable appropriation for fiscal 1981, but 6.8 percent below the budget request for fiscal 1982. *(Fiscal 1981 bill, 1980 Almanac p. 176)*

The bill included funding for the House, for congressional support operations such as the Congressional Budget Office, the Congressional Research Service and the architect of the Capitol, and for related agencies, including the General Accounting Office (GAO) and the Library of Congress. It did not include funds for the Senate, which traditionally were added when the measure reached that chamber.

For the most part, the bill allowed only modest increases in the funding of most legislative branch activities. However, the bill provided less in 1982 than in 1981 for the upkeep and maintenance of the Capitol building and the congressional office buildings and grounds, activities performed by the office of the architect of the Capitol. The subcommittee recommended that the budget for that office be cut by $1.9 million to $58.4 million, and it recommended committee report language criticizing the architect's office for frequent cost overruns.

Of the $1.1 billion appropriation, the subcommittee earmarked $363.8 million for the House, $287 million for

congressional support and $450.5 million for related agencies. Those figures compared to fiscal 1981 appropriations of $361 million for the House, $257.1 million for congressional support and $422.7 million for related agencies.

Tax Break for Members

During markup June 18, Whitten said he would ask the full Appropriations Committee to consider an amendment permitting members of Congress to deduct from their taxable income all the money they spend on business-related expenses while in Washington.

His plan would amend a 1952 law (PL 82-471) that imposed a $3,000 ceiling on the amount of money senators and representatives could deduct from their taxable incomes for business expenses while in Washington. That law designated a member's residence within his congressional district as his or her official home for tax purposes, so without the $3,000 ceiling, members could deduct from their taxable incomes all of their living expenses while in Washington. *(Congress and the Nation Vol. I, p. 1429)*

The change, he said, was intended to "put members on the same footing as private businessmen" in their ability to deduct living expenses while away from home. It was backed by Silvio O. Conte of Massachusetts, the ranking Republican on the Appropriations Committee, and by Dan Rostenkowski, D-Ill., chairman of the House Ways and Means Committee.

Congressional Record Subsidy

In other action June 18, the subcommittee decided to eliminate the public subsidy granted the Government Printing Office for the printing of the *Congressional Record*. In order for the Record to remain solvent, said Subcommittee Chairman Vic Fazio, D-Calif., the price of a year's subscription would have to be increased to $195 a year. The current cost of the Record was $135 a year, up from $75 in December 1980.

The subcommittee agreed to add language to the committee report instructing the General Accounting Office to concentrate on eliminating waste and fraud from government activities.

Full Committee Action

The bill reported by the Appropriations Committee July 9 (HR 4120 — H Rept 97-170) provided $1.1 billion for legislative branch operations for fiscal 1982, not including funds for the Senate.

Committee Chairman Whitten attempted to push through the change in members' business expense deductions, but the panel declined to go along.

Members reluctantly approved an amendment continuing a freeze on the salaries of all federal employees earning $50,112.50 a year or more during fiscal 1982 — including members of Congress. The last time those employees got a pay raise was in October 1979, when Congress approved a 5.5 percent cost-of-living increase for fiscal 1980. At that time, the salaries of members of Congress went up from $57,500 to their existing level of $60,662.50 a year. *(1979 Almanac p. 269)*

Tax Break Dropped

During markup, members who chose to speak on the matter of pay generally were supportive of an increase as well as of an additional tax break for themselves.

But when it came to a vote, the support vanished.

During the June 18 subcommittee session, Whitten had been pushing hard for the tax break. But on July 9 he did not even press for a vote, blaming the situation on media publicity.

The pay freeze came in an amendment by John P. Murtha, D-Pa., which was approved by voice vote.

Clair W. Burgener, R-Calif., then predicted that the panel's failure to "do something" about members' pay and allowances would lead to a Congress populated solely by "millionaires and ne'er-do-wells."

Net Staff Reduction Voted

The committee made no changes in the budget authority recommendations of the Legislative Subcommittee. The committee bill called for a net reduction of 83 legislative branch staff positions. Only 22 of 265 new staff positions that had been requested were approved, while 105 existing slots were eliminated.

The committee extended for an additional year a restriction Congress approved in 1980 on the payment of performance awards for superior work to members of the senior executive service (SES). *(1978 Almanac p. 818)*

The restriction required all federal agencies to pay performance bonuses to a maximum of 25 percent of the number of SES employees on their payrolls.

For the second year in a row, the committee turned down a request from the Government Printing Office for $22.3 million for a new printing plant.

The bill also required that all consulting contracts paid for with funds in the bill be made available for public inspection.

In its report, the committee also:

● Warned the office of the Capitol architect to improve its accounting procedures and cost controls and to provide Congress with more accurate cost estimates of its work.

● Told the Office of Technology Assessment (OTA) to pare down its overhead costs, which, the report said, "are approaching 30 percent of the entire OTA budget."

● Told the General Accounting Office to concentrate its efforts "on those areas that are most likely to eliminate waste and fraud and assure the proper use of tax dollars."

Further House Action

By mid-September, as the end of the fiscal year approached, HR 4120 still had not come to the floor. So on Sept. 14, the full Appropriations Committee tacked it onto the continuing resolution (H J Res 315 — H Rept 97-223). The reason a full year rather than a temporary extension was included was because House leaders said they wanted to protect the House budget from Senate interference.

Traditionally, both House and Senate had adopted hands-off attitudes toward each others' budgets. But in 1978, the House deleted from an appropriations bill $54.9 million approved by the Senate for its unfinished Hart Senate Office Building. *(1978 Almanac p. 71)*

In belated retaliation, members of the Senate Legislative Appropriations Subcommittee July 10 deleted from the annual legislative appropriations bill all House budget items, leaving items in both chambers' budgets open to negotiation in conference. The House put their appropriation into the continuing resolution so they could maintain as much leverage as possible in conference.

H J Res 325 was passed by the full House Sept. 16 without amendment. The vote was 281-107. *(Vote 194, p. 66-H)*

Senate Committee Action

The Senate Legislative Branch Appropriations Subcommittee began markup of its fiscal 1982 funding bill July 10. A total of $206.7 million was recommended for Senate operations by Subcommittee Chairman Mack Mattingly, R-Ga. The figure was about 10 percent less than was requested.

Mattingly recommended that the amount approved by the House committee for congressional support be cut by about $18 million and that the amount approved by the House committee for related agencies be cut by about $26 million.

But Ted Stevens, R-Alaska, complained that some of Mattingly's cuts were too severe. He offered a series of amendments restoring about $34 million to the House bill. The amendments were adopted, but because only three subcommittee members were present (Mattingly, Stevens and Appropriations Chairman Mark O. Hatfield, R-Ore.), members agreed to reopen the matter at the full committee level.

However, the full Appropriations Committee wanted to wait until the measure cleared the House before considering it further. And because the funding was tacked onto the continuing resolution, it never was taken up separately by the full Senate committee.

Instead, the Appropriations panel tacked the legislative branch appropriation onto its continuing resolution before reporting it Sept. 23. There was no written report. In committee, a Stevens amendment was adopted, 10-8, removing the $25,000 annual limit on honoraria earnings.

Senate Floor Action

When the continuing resolution reached the floor Sept. 24, senators took the opportunity to vote themselves the additional pay bonuses that appeared in the bill as cleared. The bill was passed the next day, 47-44. *(Vote 284, p. 49-S)*

Like the House version, the Senate bill contained a full-year appropriation for the legislative branch. It provided $934.6 million for functions of the Senate and congressional support services such as the Library of Congress, but did not include funds for the House.

Majority Whip Stevens, who had tried unsuccessfully in 1980 to use a similar continuing resolution as a vehicle for a congressional pay raise, pushed through the two rules changes governing congressional tax deductions and outside income. *(1980 Almanac p. 218)*

Congressional Tax Deduction

One of his amendments eliminated the existing $3,000 limit on job-related tax deductions claimed by members of Congress, allowing members to deduct all the expenses of living away from their home states.

Under the amendment, Stevens said, members of Congress would be treated "the same as all other citizens who are away from home on business." Instead of having a flat $3,000 deduction, with no need for itemization, the amendment allowed members to claim all their expenses, provided they had the same proof required of other taxpayers.

Stevens argued that the $3,000 limit, adopted in 1952, was not nearly enough to cover the high costs of living in or near the capital. He said his amendment would help relieve the heavy burden on members of maintaining homes both in Washington and in their districts.

Proxmire protested that "at a time when we are cutting everything in sight — and then some — it is wrong for us to be generous in this way with our own measure."

The amendment was first ruled out of order on grounds that it was legislation on an appropriations bill. However, Stevens appealed, and the ruling was overturned by the Senate, 44-54. *(Vote 277, p. 47-S)*

The vote on the amendment itself was tied 48-48 at the end of the regulation time for a vote. After a lengthy delay, Majority Leader Howard H. Baker Jr., R-Tenn., and Russell B. Long, D-La., cast their votes for the amendment and it carried, 50-48. *(Vote 278, p. 47-S)*

Honoraria Limit

Proxmire attempted to undo the committee's decision to lift the $25,000 annual limit on senators' honoraria. He offered an amendment deleting the provision, but it was rejected, 43-45. *(Vote 282, p. 48-S)*

Proxmire argued that it was wrong for the Senate to give itself increased income in a year when it was cutting many social programs. But Stevens responded that senators were allowed to have unlimited income from other sources such as book royalties or investments. If they went to the trouble of making a lot of speeches, he said, they had a right to the money.

The amendment retained the existing $2,000 limit on a payment for any one speech.

Other Action. Among other amendments adopted were those:

● By Proxmire, limiting to 8,037 the number of Senate employees and employees of the architect of the Capitol assigned to the Senate and to prohibit use of funds for planning any new Senate office buildings. Adopted 76-15. *(Vote 283, p. 48-S)*

● By Stevens, to remove a "cap" on the pay of federal employees on the executive schedule and upper-level Civil Service employees. Adopted 50-45. *(Vote 279, p. 48-S)*

Conference Action

When the bill got to conference, House conferees offered a deal. They proposed an immediate 4.8 percent pay raise for members of Congress, which had not been in either House or Senate bill, in return for accepting the Senate-passed provisions on honoraria, tax deductions and senior federal employee pay. "The issue that really concerns us is our pay," said Fazio.

House members insisted that if high-ranking federal employees were to get a raise, they wanted one, too. However, Stevens was unable to round up enough votes among Senate conferees for a congressional pay raise. So both the members and the federal executives lost their raises.

However, Stevens was able to get Senate conferees to accept a House proposal establishing a permanent appropriation for future congressional raises. Senate conferees approved the provision by an 11-9 vote. It provided that in the future, members would no longer have to face the politically touchy issue of voting funds for their own raises.

The measure was reported by the conference during the evening of Sept. 30 (H Rept 97-260).

Final Action

The bill then was rushed to the floor of the House and then the Senate chamber in what turned out be a futile

attempt by get it passed by midnight, the end of the fiscal year.

It was approved by voice vote in the House.

In the Senate, the measure was adopted 64-28; the provision on honoraria and permanent appropriations of congressional pay raises was approved 48-44; the removal of the tax deduction limits was approved 48-44. *(Votes 299, 300, 301, pp. 50-S, 51-S)*

President Reagan signed the measure in mid-afternoon Oct. 1.   ∎

District of Columbia Funds

The Senate Nov. 19 cleared by voice vote and sent to the president a compromise bill (HR 4522 — PL 97-91) to appropriate funds for the District of Columbia government in fiscal 1982.

The conference report (H Rept 97-327) had been approved by the House Nov. 18 by a vote of 228-174. *(Vote 295, p. 96-H)*

The measure appropriated $1.9 billion, including revenue raised locally by the District, as well as federal funds.

The conference report, filed Nov. 12, recommended $557.2 million in federal funds. That was the same as the Senate had approved but more than the $520.6 million recommended by the House. The Reagan administration had recommended $570.2 million.

Included in the federal funds total was a $336.6 million federal payment to the city, which was identical to the Senate and administration recommendations but exceeded the House level of $300 million. The federal payment is given to the city as compensation for taxes the city cannot collect on federal property and foreign embassies and for expenses the city incurs as the nation's capital.

The bill also included $628,000 to fund the district's new gaming board, which would run a government lottery. However, conferees stipulated that no federal funds could be used for the board.

The House, when it approved its version of HR 4522 Sept. 22 (H Rept 97-235) by a vote of 299-105, had barred the city from spending money on the lottery. The Senate version, passed Oct. 30 (S Rept 97-254), included funds for the gaming board. *(Vote 204, p. 70-H)*

Federal Funds

Conference agreement, fiscal 1982	$557,170,000
House bill	520,570,000
Senate bill	557,170,000
Budget request	570,170,000
Budget, fiscal 1981	495,382,700

Total D.C. Appropriations

Conference agreement, fiscal 1982	$1,905,258,200
House bill	1,868,658,200
Senate bill	1,905,258,200
Budget request	1,905,258,200
Budget, fiscal 1981	1,765,081,500 ∎

First Continuing Resolution: Oct. 1-Nov. 20

In the early morning hours of Oct. 1, Congress completed action on a continuing appropriations resolution (H J Res 325 — PL 97-51) that extended funding authority for government agencies from Oct. 1, the beginning of fiscal 1982, to Nov. 20, 1981.

The temporary resolution was necessary because none of the 13 fiscal 1982 appropriations bills had been enacted. One of those measures, providing full-year funding for Congress itself, was incorporated in the continuing resolution. *(Legislative branch funds, p. 286)*

The measure was the first of three stopgap funding resolutions to be enacted by Congress in 1981. It subsequently was extended until Dec. 15 after an executive-legislative dispute over funding levels resulted in President Reagan's veto of an alternative measure (H J Res 357). The final continuing resolution (H J Res 370 — PL 97-92) maintained funding through March 1982 for agencies whose appropriations bills did not clear by the time Congress adjourned. *(Subsequent measures, pp. 294, 329)*

Members' Pay

After flirting briefly with an immediate congressional pay raise, members used H J Res 325 to give themselves a tax break and a chance for senators to earn more money.

Beginning in 1982, members of Congress would be able to deduct from their taxable income their expenses of living in the Washington area. In the past, they had been able to deduct no more than $3,000 a year.

The resolution also removed the existing $25,000 limit on the amount of honoraria senators could receive for making speeches.

While the final version of H J Res 325 did not contain a 4.8 percent congressional pay raise — ardently sought by House members but rejected by Senate members of the conference committee on the resolution — it did provide a permanent funding mechanism for subsequent raises. In the future, members no longer would have to face the politically touchy issue of voting funds for their own raises.

A pay raise for senior federal executives and upper-level civil service employees, passed by the Senate, died along with the proposed congressional pay increase.

Beat the Clock

Completion of H J Res 325 came in a last-minute flurry of activity that nevertheless failed to head off a temporary cessation in the government's right to spend money, and big pay raises for federal judges.

Final House and Senate action on the measure showed all the theatrics that a late-night session and an emotional issue like congressional pay can produce. The official Senate clock was stopped. Angry attacks on the press were made. House members pleaded with each other to avoid the political embarrassment of having a roll-call vote on giving themselves more money.

Funding authority for the government expired at midnight Sept. 30, the end of fiscal 1981. Although the House

had passed the resolution Sept. 16, and the Senate had passed it Sept. 24, H J Res 325 did not emerge from the conference committee until the evening of Sept. 30.

Technically, the resolution had to be signed by the president by midnight, or the government would have to shut down, except to protect life and property. But government funding authority had lapsed for 16 hours on Oct. 1, 1980, without any apparent effect. *(Details, 1980 Almanac p. 168)*

However, the existing cap on pay raises for federal employees also expired at midnight. Without it, the salaries of federal judges were to increase by several thousand dollars. Under the Constitution, judicial salaries cannot be lowered. So, even if the cap were to lapse for one minute, the judges' salaries would go up some $3,000-$4,000, and could not be reduced.

As it turned out, Congress failed to meet the deadline. Indeed, President Reagan did not sign H J Res 325 until mid-afternoon Oct. 1.

The House did its part to meet the deadline by refusing to take a roll-call vote on the conference report (H Rept 97-260). Robert S. Walker, R-Pa., and Clarence E. Miller, R-Ohio, tried to force votes on the conference report and its amendments, but could not find enough support among their colleagues. So the resolution was approved by voice vote.

When the conference report got to the Senate, Majority Leader Howard H. Baker Jr., R-Tenn., pushed hard to get it through by midnight. However, he could not prevent roll-call votes that delayed final approval. The conference report was adopted 64-28; the provision on honoraria and permanent appropriations of congressional pay raises was approved 48-44; the removal of the tax deduction limits was approved 48-44. *(Votes 299, 300, 301, pp. 50-S, 51-S)*

According to the Senate clock, final action on the measure came at 11:50 p.m. However, other clocks read 12:27 a.m. when action was completed.

Final Provisions

As signed into law, H J Res 325:

● Extended the funding authority for government agencies whose regular fiscal year 1982 appropriations bills had not been enacted from Oct. 1 to Nov. 20, 1981, or until enactment of the applicable appropriation bill.

● Set the spending rates for individual programs whose 1982 appropriations bills had passed the House as of Oct. 1, but not the Senate, at the lower of the House-approved or fiscal 1981 levels. This provision applied to the following bills: Agriculture (HR 4119); Energy and Water (HR 4144); Commerce, Justice, State and Judiciary (HR 4169); Transportation (HR 4209); Military Construction (HR 4241); and District of Columbia (HR 4522).

● Set spending for programs in bills that had passed the House and been reported or passed in the Senate as of Oct. 1, but not been approved in conference, at the lower of the House or Senate levels. This provision affected only the Treasury bill (HR 4121). The Interior bill (HR 4035), which like the Treasury measure had been reported but not passed by the Senate, was specifically excluded from this provision; it was funded at the lower of the House-passed or fiscal 1981 level.

● Set spending for programs within the Labor-Health and Human Services-Education bill (HR 4560) at the amounts contained in the bill as reported by the Appropriations Committee, or the 1981 level, whichever was less.

● Set spending for programs under the Housing and Urban Development bill (HR 4034) at the level included in the conference report on the bill.

● Set spending for programs in the Defense Department and foreign assistance bills (HR 4559) at the lower of the administration's budget request or the fiscal 1981 level.

● Provided funding during all of fiscal year 1982 for legislative branch operations.

Congressional Pay

● Removed the existing $3,000 ceiling on the amount of business-related tax deductions members of Congress could claim while away from home.

● Removed the existing statutory limit of $25,000 on the amount of outside earned income that could be received by senators. The existing limit of about $9,000, under House rules, would continue to apply to members of the House.

● Established a permanent funding mechanism for salary increases for members of Congress. Under the provision, funds for congressional pay increases, if recommended by the president along with other federal employee pay raises and upheld by Congress, would automatically be appropriated.

● Extended the cap on the salaries of upper-level federal employees through Nov. 20, 1981. The cap froze the salaries of all employees at Executive Level V (currently paid $50,112.50) and above.

Funding Levels

● Provided funds necessary for termination of the Community Services Administration.

● Provided $125 million for the United States' contribution to the multinational force in the Sinai implementing the Israel-Egypt peace treaty; the funds were to be used for purchase of equipment and construction. The provision made clear that no funds were to be used to provide U.S. troops to serve in the multinational force without congressional authorization.

● Provided $250 million for loan guarantees under the Rural Development Insurance fund, for alcohol production facilities.

● Provided $93.2 million for elderly feeding programs.

● Provided $600,000 for support of the Yorktown Bicentennial Celebration.

Other Provisions

● Prohibited agencies from paying performance award bonuses to more than 20 percent of their employees in the Senior Executive Service.

● Excused the Education Department from the requirement in existing law that it provide, during the first month of the fiscal year, impact aid payments to school districts in amounts equal to at least 75 percent of the amount the districts had received in the previous year.

● Allowed the Agriculture Department to make emergency use of department funds to combat the Mediterranean fruit fly and gypsy moth.

● Provided that funds used to buy and store oil for the Strategic Petroleum Reserve not be counted as part of the overall budget. Off-budget status was required by the budget reconciliation bill. *(Reconciliation, p. 256)*

● Directed Amtrak not to terminate rail passenger service on the Washington-to-Chicago *Cardinal* route, during the period of the continuing resolution.

Background

Action on the continuing resolution coincided with the Reagan administration's second assault on the fiscal 1982 budget deficit, in addition to the $35.2 billion in cuts it had achieved through the omnibus budget reconciliation bill (HR 3982), which cleared July 31.

When it became clear that its reconciliation and tax cut measures had failed to buoy the economy, the administration decided to seek another round of cuts to hold the deficit as close as possible to its $42.5 billion goal.

In a televised address to the nation Sept. 24, President Reagan outlined a new, $13 billion round of spending cuts, plus $3 billion in tax increases. As part of the $16 billion savings package, the president requested cuts totaling $10.4 billion in appropriations bills, including $2 billion from defense. *(Text of speech, p. 30-E)*

However, congressional response to the proposals was negative, and the administration asked the Senate Appropriations Committee to hold off its consideration of appropriations measures while it reconsidered its initiatves. Meanwhile, because no appropriations bills had cleared, it became necessary to fund the government by continuing resolution.

House Action

The House Appropriations Committee, including its Republican members, rejected the idea of using the continuing resolution as an appropriations-cutting measure when it voted unanimously Sept. 14 to report a simple 30-day stopgap measure (H Rept 97-223).

The full House passed H J Res 325 Sept. 16 by a vote of 281-107. *(Vote 194, p. 66-H)*

Before approving the resolution, Appropriations Committee Chairman Jamie L. Whitten, D-Miss., said, "It's come to the point now where we've got to see that the government operates in an orderly manner."

The House resolution funded programs under only eight of the 13 regular appropriations bills. Whitten said the Appropriations Committee excluded funding for the five bills passed by the House before the August recess because Congress should be able to clear those bills by Oct. 1.

Silvio O. Conte, R-Mass., the ranking Republican on the Appropriations Committee, told members that each regular appropriations bill should be acted upon before Congress considered "extracurricular actions" on further spending cuts.

The administration joined members of Congress in opposing use of the continuing resolution as a budget-slashing tool.

"This continuing resolution is a ministerial matter," budget director David A. Stockman said after a meeting with House Republicans Sept. 16. "We're more concerned with what gets put into the [appropriations] bills."

Provisions. As passed by the House, H J Res 325 extended the authority for funding of government agencies until enactment of the regular appropriations bills, but no later than Nov. 1, 1981, as follows:
● Provided continuing authority for programs included in five appropriations bills — Commerce, Justice, State and the Judiciary; District of Columbia; Labor, Health and Human Services and Education; Military Construction; and Transportation.

1) Determined the funding level for those agencies whose appropriations had passed both the House and Senate as of Oct. 1, 1981, according to the lesser amount, for each individual line item in the two bills. Where an item was included in only one bill, it would be funded at the lower of the levels in the bill or current law.

2) Determined the funding level for those agencies whose appropriations had passed only the House as of Oct. 1, 1981, according to the rate provided by the House or the current rate, whichever was lower.
● Permitted spending for defense and foreign assistance to proceed at the current rate or the rate of the budget estimate, whichever was lower.
● Allowed legislative branch spending for the full fiscal year as provided in the House-reported bill; extended the federal pay cap to Nov. 1, 1981.
● Continued existing provisions of law prohibiting federally funded abortions and barring voluntary prayer programs in public schools.
● Authorized the secretary of agriculture to exercise emergency authorities to meet financial needs caused by the Mediterranean fruit fly, gypsy moths and other threats from pests and diseases.

Senate Action

The Senate passed its version of the resolution, providing funding authority for government agencies for the first 50 days of the new fiscal year (Oct. 1-Nov. 20), Sept. 25 by a 47-44 vote. *Vote 284, p. 49-S)*

The Senate Appropriations Committee had approved the measure Sept. 23 but had filed no written report.

Senators Sept. 24 added provisions to give themselves a substantial tax break and potentially large increases in income from speechmaking.

Majority Whip Ted Stevens, R-Alaska, pushed through the two changes in rules governing congressional tax deductions and outside income. He also won approval of an amendment that would allow pay increases for high-level government employees — not including members of Congress.

One Stevens amendment would eliminate the existing $3,000 limit on job-related tax deductions claimed by members of Congress. It would allow members to deduct all the expenses of living away from their home states.

The other provision removed the $25,000 limit on the amount of honoraria each senator could receive during a year.

Stopgap Funding

Although the Republican-controlled Senate approved H J Res 325 the day after President Reagan's televised appeal for further reductions in federal spending, the spending authority in its version could exceed that approved by the Democratic House.

The House version set spending levels for programs whose appropriation had passed the House but not the Senate at either the amount contained in the House-passed bill or the fiscal 1981 level, whichever was less. Defense programs were allowed to continue at the lower of the 1981 level or the budget request.

The Senate resolution, however, allowed agencies whose appropriations bills had not been reported by the Senate Appropriations Committee by Oct. 1 to continue operating at the fiscal 1981 level.

That was a crucial difference, argued William Proxmire, D-Wis., ranking Democrat on the Senate Appropriations Committee, because fiscal 1981 spending in many cases was considerably higher than the 1982 figures approved by the House. By allowing spending to continue at the higher 1981 level for 50 days, he said, the Senate was actually increasing spending over the House.

"This continuing resolution reverses what we accomplished ... in cutting spending" in the reconciliation bill approved by Congress in July, Proxmire said.

The Senate resolution also allowed the higher levels of spending to continue for a longer time. It extended funding authority from Oct. 1 through Nov. 20; the House bill went to Nov. 1.

While providing 50-day funding for federal departments, the Senate bill contained a full-year appropriation for the legislative branch. It included $934.6 million for functions of the Senate and congressional support services such as the Library of Congress. It did not include funds for the House.

Congressional Tax Deduction

After trying unsuccessfully in 1980 to use a similar continuing resolution as a vehicle for a congressional pay raise, Stevens won Senate approval of amendments to H J Res 325 that indirectly would increase senators' disposable income. *(1980 pay raise fight, 1980 Almanac p. 218)*

The amendment to remove the $3,000 limit on congressional business deductions was pushed earlier in the year by House Appropriations Committee Chairman Jamie L. Whitten, D-Miss., but was not included in the House bill.

Under the amendment, Stevens said, members of Congress would be treated "the same as all other citizens who are away from home on business." Instead of having a flat $3,000 deduction, with no need for itemization, members would be able under the amendment to claim all their expenses, provided they had the same proof required of other taxpayers.

Stevens argued that the $3,000 limit, adopted in 1952, was not nearly enough to cover the high costs of living in or near the capital. He said his amendment would help relieve the heavy burden on members of maintaining homes both in Washington and their home districts.

Proxmire protested that "at a time when we are cutting everything in sight — and then some — it is wrong for us to be generous in this way with our own measure."

The amendment was first ruled out of order on grounds that it was legislation on an appropriations bill. However, Stevens appealed and the ruling was overturned by the Senate, 44-54. *(Vote 277, p. 47-S)*

The vote on the amendment itself was tied 48-48 at the end of the regulation time for a vote. After a lengthy delay, Majority Leader Howard H. Baker Jr., R-Tenn., and Russell B. Long, D-La., cast their votes for the amendment and it carried 50-48. *(Vote 278, p. 47-S)*

Honoraria Limit

Stevens' amendment to remove the limits on honoraria was included in H J Res 325 by the Appropriations Committee Sept. 23 on a 10-8 vote.

When the resolution came to the floor, Proxmire moved to delete the provision, thus restoring the $25,000 annual limit. His amendment was rejected, 43-45. *(Vote 282, p. 48-S)*

Proxmire argued that it was wrong for the Senate to give itself increased income in a year when it was cutting many social programs. But Stevens responded that senators were allowed to have unlimited income from other sources such as book royalties or investments. If they went to the trouble of making a lot of speeches, he said, they had a right to the money.

The amendment retained the existing $2,000 limit on a payment for any one speech. Moreover, a Senate rule scheduled to become effective in 1983 would establish an honoraria limit of about $9,000 a year. *(Background, 1979 Almanac p. 578)*

Other Amendments

Other amendments included proposals:

● By Stevens, to remove a "cap" on the pay of federal employees on the executive schedule and upper-level Civil Service employees. Adopted 50-45. *(Vote 279, p. 48-S)*

● By Robert W. Kasten Jr., R-Wis., to provide $125 million for U.S. participation in the Sinai peace-keeping force implementing the Egypt-Israel peace treaty. Adopted by voice vote.

● By Jake Garn, R-Utah, to provide $2.4 billion for Environmental Protection Agency wastewater treatment plants, after enactment of authorizing legislation. Adopted by voice vote.

● By Lawton Chiles, D-Fla., to restore the Social Security minimum benefit for current recipients. The amendment was tabled along with the Sasser amendment *(see below)* to which it was attached. *(Minimum benefit, p. 117)*

● By Jim Sasser, D-Tenn., to reduce federal employee travel expenses, other than for defense or law enforcement, by 5 percent. Tabled by a 46-44 vote. *(Vote 281, p. 48-S)*

● By Proxmire, to limit the number of Senate employees and employees of the architect of the Capitol assigned to the Senate to 8,037 and to prohibit use of funds for planning any new Senate office buildings. Adopted 76-15. *(Vote 283, p. 48-S)*

Conference Action

The proposed congressional pay raise, which had not been in either House or Senate versions of H J Res 325, surfaced during conference action Sept. 30.

House members suggested the 4.8 percent raise as part of a package deal, in return for accepting Senate-passed provisions on honoraria, tax deductions and senior federal employee pay. "The issue that really concerns us is our pay," said Vic Fazio, D-Calif., chairman of the House Legislative Appropriations Subcommittee.

House members insisted that if high-ranking federal employees were to get a raise, they wanted one too. However, Sen. Ted Stevens, R-Alaska, was unable to round up enough votes among Senate conferees for a congressional pay raise. So both the members and the federal executives lost their raises.

Stevens was able to get Senate conferees to accept the House proposal establishing a permanent appropriation for future congressional raises. Senate conferees approved the provision by an 11-9 vote.

Sinai Force

Conferees agreed to provide $125 million for peace-keeping activities in the Sinai, but only after making clear

that they were not committing themselves to sending U.S. troops to the peninsula.

After receiving a request from Office of Management and Budget Director David A. Stockman, the Senate had added $125 million to H J Res 325 during floor action Sept. 24. According to Robert W. Kasten Jr., R-Wis., sponsor of the amendment, the money was needed to fulfill the American promise to help set up the Multinational Force and Observers established by the 1979 Egyptian-Israeli peace treaty.

The Reagan administration asked Congress for $135 million to help pay start-up costs for the force. Part of that had already come from a shift of $10 million from fiscal 1981 foreign aid funds. *(Story, p. 151)*

Kasten said the administration wanted the other $125 million immediately, so that the force could begin ordering equipment and construction. Without the additional money, he said, efforts to lay the groundwork for a 1982 Israeli withdrawal from the area would be endangered.

In the conference, however, Kasten's amendment was opposed by Rep. Clarence D. Long, D-Md., chairman of the

Foreign Operations Appropriations Subcommittee. Long argued that Congress had not authorized the money. Moreover, he said, it would be followed by sending American troops, leading to further involvement in the dangerous area.

The administration wanted to send 800 troops to help patrol the Sinai once the Israelis pulled out.

"This is a financial Gulf of Tonkin resolution," Long warned.

Kasten responded that the peace efforts founded by the 1978 Camp David accords were too valuable to jeopardize by withholding U.S. support, even if the money had not been authorized.

"We've got an emergency. The process of peace in the Middle East is more important than committee differences in Congress. The only thing we've got going in the Middle East is the Camp David process," Kasten said.

Long eventually accepted the $125 million, with an amendment to ensure that none of the money would be used to send troops to the area without congressional authorization.   ∎

2nd Continuing Resolution: 1st Reagan Veto

After a dramatic confrontation with President Reagan that forced a temporary shutdown of much of the government, Congress Nov. 23 approved an emergency continuing appropriations measure (H J Res 368 — PL 97-85) to fund federal agencies through Dec. 15.

The three-week extension of funding authority ended a legislative-executive battle over spending that led to Reagan's first use of the presidential veto.

Denouncing Congress for failing to meet his demand for $8.5 billion in spending cuts, Reagan Nov. 23 had vetoed an earlier continuing resolution (H J Res 357), approved by Congress Nov. 22, as "budget-busting." *(Veto text, p. 33-E)*

Funding for the government had run out at midnight Friday Nov. 20 — the expiration date of the first continuing appropriations resolution (H J Res 325 — PL 97-51) for fiscal 1982. *(H J Res 325, p. 290)*

H J Res 368 simply extended the provisions of H J Res 325 until Dec. 15, in order to give Congress and the president more time to reach agreement on fiscal 1982 spending levels.

Approval of H J Res 368 ended a week of intensive action that saw Congress work virtually around the clock, including highly unusual Sunday sessions, in a vain attempt to avoid a spending cutoff.

Action on the resolution was necessary because only one of the 13 regular appropriations bills for fiscal 1982 — the Legislative Branch measure — had been enacted. Two other bills, for the District of Columbia (HR 4522) and energy and water programs (HR 4144), had been cleared by Congress but not signed by the president as of Nov. 25.

When those or other appropriations bills became law, they were no longer covered by H J Res 368. But programs whose appropriations were not enacted before Dec. 15 had to be covered by yet another continuing resolution. *(Third resolution, p. 329)*

H J Res 368 marked another step in the recent trend toward the use of continuing resolutions, once used only as short-term emergency measures, as a primary method for

enacting appropriations. The resolution's awesome size — it provided spending at a total annual rate of $400 billion — was rivaled only by H J Res 325 and the first continuing resolution for fiscal 1981 (PL 96-369). *(PL 96-369, 1980 Almanac p. 168)*

The fiscal 1981 measure, which covered 12 appropriations bills for 10 weeks, remained the all-time champion continuing resolution. But it would have been surpassed by far by the House version of H J Res 357, which could have enacted appropriations for all government agencies except Congress itself for the entire fiscal year.

In all, Congress passed three continuing appropriations resolutions for fiscal 1981. Four regular appropriations bills for that year — Treasury, Legislative Branch, Foreign Assistance and Labor-HHS-Education — never did become law. The third 1981 continuing resolution, which was incorporated in the fiscal 1981 supplemental appropriations measure (HR 3512), extended funding for those programs through the full fiscal year. *(HR 3512, p. 281)*

Veto Message

Reagan's Monday-morning veto of H J Res 357 followed a tense weekend of negotiations between House and Senate members and administration officials, including Office of Management and Budget (OMB) Director David A. Stockman. But despite high initial congressional hopes of a presidential signature, the version of the resolution that cleared Congress Nov. 22 did not cut enough from social programs, or add enough for foreign aid, to be acceptable to Reagan.

The veto of H J Res 357 left government agencies without legal authority to operate, except for essential activities such as defense and law enforcement. Thousands of government workers left their jobs for part of the day; the rest were ordered to prepare to close down their offices. *(Government workers, p. 298)*

Conceding that his action would cause inconvenience and the "possibility of some temporary hardship," Reagan

told a national television audience that a veto was essential to his fight against "excessive government spending."

Senate Republicans — who had voted overwhelmingly for adoption of the conference report on H J Res 357 — vigorously applauded the veto.

But Democrats in both House and Senate charged that the veto was a political tactic aimed at shoring up Reagan's image in the face of mounting economic troubles. "It is a manufactured shoot-out at the OK Corral," said Senate Minority Leader Robert C. Byrd, D-W.Va.

Spending Argument

Spending levels for domestic programs and foreign aid dominated the final stages of congressional action on H J Res 357 and led to the presidential veto.

The argument over spending levels was a highly complex one that revolved in large part around the different assumptions that were fed into computers used by OMB and the House Appropriations Committee.

The fight began when the Senate, in an all-night session that began Nov. 19, approved an amendment to require a 4 percent across-the-board cut in spending for domestic non-entitlement programs.

According to OMB's final estimates, the bill as amended saved a total of $4 billion. Reagan told the amendment sponsor, Majority Leader Howard H. Baker Jr., R-Tenn., he would accept the resolution as passed, even though it saved only about half of his $8.5 billion savings goal.

When House members won conference acceptance of their proposal to cut programs by 2 percent, they thought they had achieved savings comparable to the Senate amendment. According to the House computer, the conference agreement provided budget authority of $427.9 billion, compared with the Senate-passed resolution of $428.5 billion.

But the OMB computer saw things differently. It calculated that the conference report actually saved only $1.7 billion in domestic discretionary programs — less than a quarter of what the president sought.

According to the final OMB calculations, discretionary spending for eight domestic appropriations bills under H J Res 357 was $129.5 billion. Reagan's comparable September budget request totaled $121.7 billion.

Moreover, argued House Minority Leader Robert H. Michel, R-Ill., the conference report on H J Res 357 seriously under-funded certain entitlement programs such as student loans and Medicaid. He predicted that any savings in the conference report would be lost when Congress acted on a supplemental appropriations bill in 1982.

The administration also had pushed for higher levels of foreign aid, particularly for military assistance to nations near the Persian Gulf. *(Foreign aid, p. 339)*

House Committee Action

The House Appropriations Committee approved H J Res 357 (H Rept 97-319) Nov. 12.

Several committee Republicans said the resolution was a prime target for Reagan's promise to "veto any bill that abuses the limited resources of the taxpayers."

"If there is a veto, we'll have payless days and Social Security checks will stop. You're going to be inundated with millions of letters," the Appropriations Committee's ranking Republican, Silvio O. Conte, Mass., warned his colleagues.

"It's creepy. There could be a real showdown. I was up at the White House on Friday for a meeting and [Reagan] said he would do it. Those guys up there are really adamant," Conte said later.

"If we don't hold the bill down, we're going to get that veto," predicted C. W. Bill Young, R-Fla.

Spending Levels

H J Res 357 based funding levels for agencies on regular appropriations bills that in most cases exceeded the administration's September budget requests.

In a televised speech Sept. 24, Reagan asked Congress to reduce discretionary non-defense programs by 12 percent from his March 10 budget plan. *(Text, p. 30-E)*

Congress had slowed final action on individual appropriations bills because of the threat of vetoes.

Under the resolution, spending for individual programs would be set at levels contained in:

● The Defense Department appropriation to be reported by the House Appropriations Committee.

● Conference reports on the Interior (HR 4035), Housing and Urban Development (HR 4034), and Agriculture (HR 4119) appropriations.

● House-passed bills for Military Construction (HR 4241) and Energy and Water (HR 4144).

● House-passed bills or fiscal 1981 levels, whichever was less, for Commerce, Justice, State, Judiciary (HR 4169); District of Columbia (HR 4522); Labor, Health and Human Services (HHS), Education (HR 4560); and Transportation (HR 4209).

● House-passed or Senate-reported bill, whichever was less, for Treasury, Postal Service (HR 4121).

● The fiscal 1981 or budget request levels, whichever was less, for foreign aid (HR 4559).

The resolution would extend funding for agencies through Sept. 30, 1982, the end of fiscal year 1982. However, programs would stop being covered by the resolution as soon as their regular fiscal 1982 appropriations bills were passed.

The measure also extended through Sept. 30 the existing ceiling on salaries for employees of the executive, legislative and judicial branches.

Committee members argued that extending the resolution only through March 1982, as some had advocated, would overburden the congressional schedule. "You can imagine what a chaotic situation we would have next spring. You'll have too much on the platter," Conte said.

Mandated Spending Levels

In an effort to prevent a repetition of secret spending cuts allegedly ordered by OMB under the first fiscal 1982 continuing resolution, the committee mandated spending levels contained in H J Res 357.

The preceding continuing resolution (H J Res 325) had set spending during the period Oct. 1-Nov. 20 at rates "not exceeding" levels in the resolution. Some members, including Senate Appropriations Committee Chairman Mark O. Hatfield, R-Ore., interpreted that language as setting ceilings on spending but not requiring any particular amount of spending below the limits.

House committee member Bob Traxler, D-Mich., argued that OMB was taking advantage of that interpretation by covertly ordering agencies to reduce spending to the September budget amounts, without submitting a formal deferral request. So Jamie L. Whitten, D-Miss., agreed to a

change making clear that funding amounts in the resolution were required spending levels and not upper limits.

OMB spokesman Edwin L. Dale Jr. said that OMB felt it had the authority under the first continuing resolution to order lower spending levels. But, to remove possible ambiguity, it had sent up formal deferral requests when the continuing resolution amounts were above the budget. *(Deferral requests, box, this page)*

"Agencies were ordered to spend at the president's rate, in cases where the continuing resolution would have set it higher. We felt we could have ordered the lower rates anyway, but we sent up deferrals just to be sure," Dale said.

House Floor Action

In the face of a warning from Republican leader Michel that H J Res 357 would be vetoed without further spending cuts, the House Nov. 16 refused to accept an across-the-board reduction in discretionary programs.

The defection of 18 Republicans helped kill Michel's motion to recommit the joint resolution to the Appropriations Committee with instructions to cut 5 percent from each non-entitlement program in the bill. The amendment, which exempted funds for defense, military construction, District of Columbia, Social Security administrative expenses, veterans' health care and food stamps, was rejected 189-201. *(Vote 285, p. 94-H)*

Reagan's Deferrals

President Reagan said at his Nov. 10 press conference that Congress had "enforced spending through a continuing resolution that was above our budget." But, in fact, the president was able to use the deferral process to hold spending within his September budget requests during the first 50 days of fiscal 1982.

Reagan sent Congress a total of 217 deferral requests under the first continuing resolution for fiscal 1982 (H J Res 325). The deferrals ensured that spending levels during the period of H J Res 325, Oct. 1-Nov. 20, were within the rates set by the September budget.

Under the deferral process, the president had authority to postpone spending for programs until the end of the current fiscal year. The deferrals would stand unless either House or Senate disapproved them.

Reagan could use deferrals to hold back spending until Sept. 30, 1982, the end of fiscal 1982. However, the deferrals would not permanently prevent the higher levels of spending. To do that Reagan would have to propose rescissions, which must be approved by Congress in order to go into effect.

Reagan sent five separate deferral messages to Congress during the time covered by H J Res 325. Congress took no action to disapprove any of them. The total amount of deferred funds submitted by Reagan was $2,759,700,000.

Not all of the deferrals came out of the fiscal 1982 continuing resolution appropriations. A total of $640.1 million was deferred from funds that were carried over from fiscal 1981.

Along with the deferral requests, there also were three rescissions totaling $108.7 million.

At the time it came to the floor, the resolution was estimated by the House Budget Committee to contain $439.6 billion in budget authority. Comparisons of that amount with the president's September budget requests, however, proved extremely problematic.

Budget Committee member Les Aspin, D-Wis., said that the resolution was only $1.9 billion over the September budget in discretionary spending for non-defense programs. With a defense reduction of $6.3 billion, the resolution was actually $4.4 billion below the requested budget authority. In outlays, the measure was $2.4 billion below the president's budget, he said.

OMB experts argued, however, that discretionary non-defense spending was $10.3 billion over the budget — an $8 billion estimating difference for which no one had a satisfactory explanation.

Michel estimated that his amendment would reduce outlays in the resolution by $4 billion.

On another crucial vote earlier in the day, the House had adopted a closed rule (H Res 271) barring floor amendments to H J Res 357. If amendments had been allowed, Robert W. Edgar, D-Pa., would have tried to cut the resolution off on March 31, 1982, instead of allowing it to continue through Sept. 30.

However, on a 185-174 vote the House agreed to order the previous question on H Res 271, thus barring changes in the rule. It then adopted H Res 271 by a 197-169 vote. *(Votes 283, 284, p. 94-H)*

After rejecting the Michel motion, the House passed H J Res 357 by a 195-187 vote. *(Vote 286, p. 94-H)*

Senate Committee Action

A proposal to achieve budget savings by giving the president authority to withhold funds was rejected soundly by the Senate Appropriations Committee.

Meeting on H J Res 357 Nov. 17, the committee voted 8-18 against a Mack Mattingly, R-Ga., amendment that would have allowed the president to reduce spending for entitlement programs by up to 1 percent. The amendment also would have cut all discretionary spending by 2 percent.

Under the amendment, entitlement spending for programs such as Social Security could have been cut by reducing mandated cost-of-living increases, or COLAs, by as much as one-third. Congress would have had veto power over the COLA cuts.

The amendment, which required a 2 percent cut in defense spending as well as for domestic programs, would have saved an estimated $8 billion.

Mattingly argued that the amendment would give the president another weapon with which to hold down spending. But Thomas F. Eagleton, D-Mo., responded that the proposal was a revival of the impoundment authority abolished by the 1974 budget act. *(1974 Almanac p. 145)*

Seven Republicans on the committee voted against the amendment; Democrats were unanimous in opposition to it.

The version of H J Res 357 approved by the committee provided total budget authority of $432.5 billion, which according to Hatfield was $800 million above Reagan's total request. Outlays were estimated at $417.4 billion, $2.2 billion over the request.

The committee-approved resolution set spending levels for programs in four bills — Agriculture, Interior, District of Columbia and Transportation — at levels contained in their conference reports.

Four bills — Treasury-Postal Service, Labor-Health and Human Services-Education, Military Construction and Defense — were put at the lower of the House-passed level or the amount approved by the Senate committee.

Programs in two other bills — Foreign Assistance and Energy-Water — were based on amounts contained in bills passed by the Senate. Programs in the Commerce-Justice-State bill were based on the bill as amended on the Senate floor through Nov. 16.

The biggest change made during committee action on the resolution was a $2 billion cut in spending for the Housing and Urban Development (HUD) appropriation bill. The resolution based spending on the conference agreement on the bill, but made cuts in programs such as annual contributions to assisted housing (a $565.8 million cut) and National Aeronautics and Space Administration (NASA) research and development (a $181.2 million cut).

The amendment to cut the HUD bill was offered by subcommittee Chairman Jake Garn, R-Utah. It was subsequently modified by amendments offered by: Alfonse D'Amato, R-N.Y., to restore $224 million of a $440 million cut from community development block grants; Garn, to restore $13 million for Environmental Protection Agency (EPA) water quality programs; and Harrison "Jack" Schmitt, R-N.M., to restore $16 million for NASA research and program management. *(HUD conference report, p. 338)*

Senate Floor Action

In an all-night session that began Nov. 19, the Senate took 23 roll-call votes on H J Res 357, argued over programs covering the whole range of federal government activities, narrowly avoided a filibuster, and finally managed to come up with a compromise spending cut.

Senate Democrats took advantage of the situation to needle the Republicans at length about their reliance on the emergency resolution to fund the whole government. They warned that the Senate was giving up basic control over the budget in order to achieve a relatively small savings and hand the president a victory.

"Why are we doing this for such a small amount? If we want to give [our power] away, let's give it away. Give him a hundred billion. Let him balance the budget," said Joseph R. Biden Jr., D-Del. "Why die on a small cross?"

After agreeing to a 4 percent spending cut and a March 30, 1982, expiration date, the Senate passed H J Res 357 by a 70-26 vote at dawn on Nov. 20, at the end of a 21-hour session. *(Vote 412, p. 68-S)*

Spending Cut

Throughout the long debate on H J Res 357, Republican leaders searched behind the scenes for a spending cut proposal that would win White House support without losing a majority of the Senate.

After running through a series of different ideas — the 5 percent cut proposed in the House, a 3.5 percent cut, cuts including or excluding defense — Majority Leader Baker settled on an amendment to reduce spending on domestic non-entitlement programs by 4 percent.

As proposed, the amendment excluded defense, military construction, foreign aid and food stamp programs from the cuts.

James A. McClure, R-Idaho, outlined on the floor a complex procedure for applying the amendment that narrowed its scope substantially. He said a program would not be affected by the cut if it was in a bill that overall was at or below the president's budget, or in a section of a bill that was at or below the budget, or even in an account listing within a section that was not over budget. Programs that were still eligible for cuts would be reduced 4 percent but not below the level of the budget.

Baker said that the amendment as offered saved $5.3 billion in budget authority and $3.2 billion in outlays.

The key vote on the spending cut issue actually came on a motion by Lawton Chiles, D-Fla., that would have directed the Appropriations Committee to achieve its own 4 percent cut. His amendment was tabled by a 55-42 vote. *(Vote 405, p. 67-S)*

Chiles said Baker's amendment was a "cop-out" that gave away congressional responsibility over government spending by letting the president decide where to make cuts. Under the amendment, Chiles warned, "the only thing we'll have to come down here for is sundown and payday. We probably can keep getting elected, because we won't have to decide what the priorities are."

Baker moved successfully to table the Chiles amendment. Then the Baker amendment with the 4 percent cut was approved 62-35. *(Vote 409, p. 67-S)*

Before adopting the amendment, however, the Senate made two changes in the list of programs that were exempted from cuts. A Chiles amendment to spare federal law enforcement activities was adopted by voice vote. A Proxmire amendment to apply the cut to foreign aid programs, which had been exempted in Baker's original proposal, was adopted 62-35. *(Vote 408, p. 67-S)*

Expiration Date

Democratic opposition to certain Reagan administration defense proposals, especially the B-1 bomber and hardening of missile silos, forced GOP leaders to accept a shortened life for H J Res 357. *(Defense bill p. 311)*

Democrats worried that if the resolution extended for the full fiscal year, there would be no further action on the defense appropriation bill. That would deprive them of a chance to debate issues of weapons policy as important as any since the development of the atomic bomb.

Under the continuing resolution as it came to the floor, the Defense Department had authority to proceed on the new weapons systems for a whole year. Even if Congress were to vote against the B-1 on a defense appropriations bill, Reagan could have vetoed the measure and work on the plane would have continued.

"We are going to be basically giving a blank check to the Pentagon," said David Pryor, D-Ark.

As the Senate worked on H J Res 357 the evening of Nov. 19, Carl Levin, D-Mich., announced that he was prepared to filibuster the resolution because of the defense programs in it. Importantly, Levin was joined in his opposition by Democratic defense authorities such as Sam Nunn, Ga., and Ernest F. Hollings, S.C.

In the face of that threat, Republican leaders accepted an amendment by Minority Leader Robert C. Byrd, D-W.Va., to terminate the resolution March 30, 1982. Combined with a promise from Baker to bring the regular defense bill to the Senate floor Nov. 30, the agreement ensured that the Democrats would have a chance for a full-scale debate on the new weapons programs. Byrd's amendment was adopted 94-3. *(Vote 406, p. 67-S)*

Earlier, Senate Democrats had tried twice on Nov. 18 to shorten the life of the resolution, but failed on straight party-line votes. Byrd proposed amendments to move the

Fund Gap Led to Sweeping Shutdown . . .

Budget brinksmanship shifted many of the cogs of government into an unproductive spin Nov. 23, but the government did not exactly grind to a halt.

The stop-payment shutdown — the second ever of a federal agency, the first of such broad scope — made an impressive show: Thousands of federal workers were sent home on furlough. The Statue of Liberty and Washington Monument were closed. The Constitution and Declaration of Independence were lowered into vaults below their public display cases in the National Archives. Trips, speeches and congressional testimony were canceled. A tape-recorded message at the White House told callers that "the White House is involved in an orderly phase-down. . . . No one is here to answer your call."

At the same time, Uncle Sam continued to patrol borders, brandish missiles, print money, collect taxes, send out Social Security checks, chase and prosecute criminals, put out forest fires, guide airline pilots onto runways and feed the animals at the National Zoo.

When appropriations ran out at midnight Nov. 20, the procedure for shutting down much of the government was governed by a 111-year-old statute called the Antideficiency Act (31 USC § 665) that says the government may not spend money before it is appropriated by Congress.

Rediscovered and extensively analyzed in the Carter administration, that quaintly named statute proved to be newly relevant in an era of stopgap government.

The Antideficiency Act states that "[I]t shall not be lawful for any department of the government to expend in any one fiscal year any sum in excess of appropriations made by Congress for that fiscal year, or to involve the government in any contract for the future payment of money in excess of appropriations."

What it Means

Prior to 1980, the prevailing view was that a lapse in spending authority required suspension of such non-essential activities as travel, grant-making or hiring, but not an actual closing of agencies.

But in 1980, faced with expiration of the appropriation for the Federal Trade Commission (FTC), Attorney General Benjamin R. Civiletti on April 25 issued stricter legal guidelines based on the 1870 law. He said the prevailing practice was "legally insupportable," agencies must begin an orderly shutdown in the absence of appropriations, and his department would prosecute violators.

His interpretation was disputed by some administration lawyers and the General Accounting Office (GAO),

but it became the operating manual for a brief FTC shutdown May 1, 1980. *(1980 Almanac p. 233)*

Later, after Congress had come within hours of a governmentwide appropriations lapse, Civiletti drafted a more flexible version of his memo. Dated Jan. 16, 1981, it said, "The Constitution and the Antideficiency Act itself leave the executive leeway to perform essential functions and make the government 'workable.'"

Endorsed by the Reagan Justice Department, Civiletti's memo became the basis for the Office of Management and Budget (OMB) guidelines governing the Nov. 23 shutdown.

Exemptions

The administration listed three categories of government activities exempt from closing down:

● Presidential activities rooted in the Constitution, especially national security and the related conduct of foreign relations. Thanks to this provision, the Department of Defense was virtually unaffected by the Nov. 23 drama, except that tightened travel budgets prevented Secretary Caspar W. Weinberger from making a speech in Boston.

● Government activities paid by multi-year appropriations or other funds, or authorized by law to be spent in advance of appropriations.

Examples included many government benefit programs. Social Security, for instance, was paid out of trust funds. Aid to Families with Dependent Children, Medicaid and public housing subsidies were paid by the states with federal money that already had been obligated through Dec. 31.

Some other government benefit programs would have been quickly cut short had the hiatus continued. The Agriculture Department, for example, said it would not have issued food stamps on the second day of a shutdown, even to qualified recipients. "It's like you have a check, but the bank is closed," said public information specialist Carol McLaughlin.

● Activities the Antideficiency Act described as "cases of emergency involving the safety of human life or the protection of property." This exemption had been stretched to cover a wide range of functions, including Veterans Administration hospitals, food inspection, air traffic control, law enforcement, tax collection and money printing, building guards and climate control necessary to keep government computers from deteriorating.

Civiletti noted that the law allowed the necessary contingent of employees to carry out the exempted activities, even though they could not receive their paychecks

---

resolution's deadline of Sept. 30, 1982, up to Dec. 18, 1981, or March 30, 1982. The amendments were rejected 46-49 and 46-51, respectively. *(Votes 383, 384, p. 64-S)*

Democrats also said the full-year resolution was a radical change in congressional procedure that would seriously weaken the appropriations process. John C. Stennis, D-Miss., recalled that until recently continuing resolutions had been true emergency measures covering short periods of time. "You would have been laughed out of town if you

had put the whole calendar under the provisions of a continuing resolution," he said.

Appropriations Committee Chairman Mark O. Hatfield, R-Ore., responded that the regular appropriations process would still go forward, with programs dropping off the continuing resolution once their regular funding bills were enacted. He warned that a third continuing resolution would "open a Pandora's box" of changes in all the appropriations bills.

. . .But No Lapse in Essential U.S. Services

until an appropriations bill had passed. It also allowed them to be supplied. "Congress, for example, having allowed the government to hire firefighters must surely have intended that water and fire trucks would be available to them," Civiletti said.

The General Services Administration (GSA), which handles buildings and supplies, thus kept federal phone lines functioning, a bare-bones motor pool operating and needed buildings heated and lighted. GSA did curb some services, however. Sales and acquisitions of strategic metals for the national stockpile were suspended, presidential libraries and federal information centers closed, and temperatures in "non-essential" buildings were ordered dropped to 55 degrees.

GSA spokesman Peter Hickman said he had no idea how many buildings were affected by the order: "If 10 people are working in a building, I suppose you can't let them freeze."

Different Paces

OMB initially told agencies that "non-essential" workers must be sent home within two days of the shutdown order, but Nov. 23 the president decreed that furloughs should be handed out "as soon as possible," according to OMB deputy news director Robin Raborn.

"Generally, the president is taking a harder line than was given out last week," she said.

Individual agency heads moved at widely varying paces in sorting out employees and sending them home.

At the Department of Health and Human Services (HHS), deputy press officer Dick McGowan said, officials decided to wait three days before sending any employees home. McGowan said so much of HHS is related to safety, health and entitlements that "it was difficult to determine who was non-essential."

At the White House, OMB, the departments of Agriculture, Treasury, Education and others, thousands of employees were told to secure their files, cancel appointments, and go home by early afternoon.

The shutdown was carried out with some small theatrical flourishes. Sen. Thad Cochran, R-Miss., said the White House made a special point of calling lawmakers to tell them White House tours for their constituents would be canceled on account of the budget impasse.

Due to the brief duration of the funding hiatus, some agencies managed to duck the effects.

Federal courts, for example, depend on appropriated funds to operate, but court administrators had not determined by late in the day what curtailments might be required of them.

"We are satisfied that the functions of the judiciary are essential to law enforcement," and thus exempt, said William Foley, director of the Administrative Office of the U.S. Courts. He said the constitutional guarantee of a speedy trial would require criminal courts to continue hearing cases, and that civil courts expected to be swamped by federal government motions for delays in pending cases prompted by the funding hiatus.

Foley said an extended appropriations delay might require some cuts in court services, but when it became clear late in the afternoon that funding would soon be reinstated, the administrators decided not to decide. "That's a bridge we haven't crossed yet," Foley said.

One branch of government was funded without interruption throughout the confusion. Congress had passed a $1.8 billion appropriations bill for itself Oct. 1 as part of the first continuing resolution. *(Story, p. 286)*

Costs

When the 1,800 employees of the Federal Trade Commission took their one-day forced holiday in 1980, the GAO estimated that the government lost $700,000, most of it in wasted time.

What the Nov. 23 winding down and the subsequent winding back up may have cost was unknown.

Congressional leaders and the White House agreed that furloughed workers would be paid for a full day, noting that the cost and confusion of deducting a few hours pay would eat up much of the savings. But no one knew exactly how much work-time the government lost.

OMB officials initially estimated that 400,000 workers had been sent home, then revised that to about 200,000. Finally OMB spokesman Edwin Dale told a reporter for *The Washington Post* that, "There is not and never will be an absolute, precise count, and there is no need to [make one]. There's no way to calculate the cost."

Cranston Charge

One Democrat who tried was Sen. Alan Cranston, D-Calif., who initially charged that the shutdown cost the government $1 billion in lost productivity. Later, Cranston aides, admitting the senator's arithmetic was highly questionable, revised the estimate to $700 million, then down to $400 million.

As an employee at GAO, which is funded along with Congress, pointed out, the impact on government productivity extended well beyond the furloughed workers.

"Even here, everybody's standing around talking about it instead of working, and our budget isn't affected at all."

Hatfield later moved successfully to table a third Byrd amendment, setting a Dec. 19 deadline. His motion, adopted 50-47, also killed another Byrd amendment that would have required the president to spell out specific cuts needed to reach a balanced budget by 1984. *(Vote 386, p. 64-S)*

Pay Raise

The Senate reaffirmed its past stand against a congres-

sional pay raise, but agreed to allow a 4.8 percent raise for federal executive employees at all but the highest levels. Amendments to raise both congressional and executive pay were offered by Ted Stevens, R-Alaska, who had championed similar efforts on previous continuing resolutions.

The strong Senate opposition to a congressional pay raise was shown by the 5-90 vote against Stevens' first amendment. However, the executive pay raise was approved by a 54-41 vote. *(Votes 392, 393, p. 65-S)*

The Reagan administration supported the raises, Stevens maintained. He argued that executive pay "compression" caused by the pay cap — some eight employee grade levels currently had the same salaries — was driving good people from the federal service.

Missing Children, Falling Bridges

As was often the case with stopgap spending measures, the senators took full advantage of H J Res 357 as an ideal vehicle for adding amendments on pet projects in diverse areas of government activity.

Paula Hawkins, R-Fla., for example, won an amendment to establish a new nationwide system for locating missing children. Charles McC. Mathias Jr., R-Md., added $60 million for a crumbling bridge in the Washington, D.C., area.

With the help of powerful sponsors, a few domestic programs were pulled from the general inundation of budget cuts. The Job Corps got an additional $10 million, thanks to Orrin G. Hatch, R-Utah. Lowell P. Weicker Jr., R-Conn., won an extra $69.8 million for handicapped education and $44.7 million for vocational rehabilitation. A motion by Harrison "Jack" Schmitt, R-N.M., to table Weicker's amendment was rejected 39-56 and the amendment was subsequently adopted by voice vote.*(Vote 395, p. 65-S)*

Others were not so lucky. The low-income energy assistance program did not get another $200 million, as Weicker had sought. Claiborne Pell, D-R.I., failed in his attempt to add $80 million for the college student aid program that bore his name.

Conference Action

House-Senate conferees began work on H J Res 357 at 5 p.m. Nov. 20, with some seven hours to spare before the formal expiration of the government's spending authority. But it was to take two days of nearly continuous session, stretching to 2 a.m. on Nov. 22, before they reached an agreement.

After settling a host of minor issues, conferees focused on two major differences: the Senate's across-the-board spending cut and its increase in funds for foreign aid.

The basic House proposal, eventually adopted by the conference, called for a 2 percent cut. To achieve savings comparable to the Senate resolution, conferees applied the cut to more programs, including the Defense Department.

The defense cut, which technically amounted to $3.9 billion, was to be applied only to procurement and research programs. It was to extend only until a regular defense appropriation was approved, or the end of the current session of Congress.

Because of the limitations on the defense cut, conferees conceded that it would have an "insignificant" effect on spending, according to Conte, the ranking Republican member of the House Appropriations Committee. So no reductions from defense were included in the final estimate of savings.

On foreign aid, House members adamantly resisted the Senate's level of $7.3 billion, which was $1.6 billion higher than their own. Under pressure from the White House, however, they eventually accepted a compromise that increased the House amount by $500 million, with funds to go for military sales, economic support and Export-Import Bank loan authority.

Conferees expanded the Senate's amendment giving high-ranking federal executives a 4.8 percent raise. They agreed to let House members receive the raise, but not senators.

For the expiration date of the resolution conferees chose July 15, 1982. The House had provided for extension of the resolution through the end of fiscal 1982, Sept. 30, while the Senate had favored March 30, 1982.

House Action

House action on the conference report Nov. 22 was interrupted by the announcement that Reagan would veto the measure.

After reaching the conference agreement (H Rept 97-352) early that morning, House leaders expected, or at least had high hopes, that it would win Reagan's approval. "We had every indication and every reason to believe that the president was satisfied with every one of these figures, except for foreign aid," said Majority Leader Jim Wright, D-Texas.

After talking with Reagan, however, Michel announced on the floor that the resolution faced a certain veto. "There was always a good possibility that the president would veto this resolution," Michel said.

Appropriations Committee Chairman Jamie L. Whitten, D-Miss., rejected Michel's suggestion that the House drop H J Res 357 because of the veto threat and approve a simple extension of H J Res 325. After Michel's motion to recommit failed 184-215, the conference report was adopted 205-194. *(Votes 315, 316, p. 104-H)*

In other action, House members dropped the conference amendment that would have provided a 4.8 percent pay raise for themselves and top-level federal executives.

However, the House accepted a Senate amendment giving a pay raise to air traffic controllers. The amendment, approved on a 213-183 vote, provided a 6.5 percent pay increase for controllers, at an expected cost of $57.5 million. *(Vote 317, p. 104-H)*

Senate Action

Republican leaders found themselves in a somewhat embarrassing position when the Senate took up the conference report.

Knowing that the leader of their party opposed the resolution, Republicans could have voted against the conference report and killed it on the spot. But that would have deprived Reagan of his chance to veto it.

"I intend to vote for the continuing resolution but will do so only as a procedural matter in order to send the resolution to the White House and because we have the assurance of the president that he will veto it," said Charles H. Percy, R-Ill.

Majority Leader Baker gave conflicting signals on how he wanted party members to vote. At first, he announced his support for a vote to approve the conference report in order to get it to the president. But, in a debate that was repeatedly interrupted by laughter, Democrats relentlessly needled Baker about the contradictions of his position.

"Do you vote for or against this conference report if you are trying to be a friend and supporter of the president?" asked J. Bennett Johnston, D-La.

Finally, Baker threw up his hands and urged members to vote however they felt. "All I want to do is make sure we get rid of this thing once and for all. As far as I am concerned, we could have a vote and you can vote it up or

you can vote it down, but just vote it and get it over with," Baker said.

"You're off the hook," Baker told William L. Armstrong, R-Colo., who had said he would vote for the conference report even though he thought it was a "monstrosity."

Armstrong, along with five other Republicans, eventually voted against the conference report. The report was adopted 46-39, with Republicans providing all but two of the "yea" votes. *(Vote 413, p. 68-S)*

Final Action

House Democrats made no attempt to override the veto of H J Res 357. Instead, they hurriedly called up a new resolution, H J Res 368, that simply extended the previous continuing resolution through Feb. 3, 1982.

Democratic leaders argued that a two-month extension would give Congress time to complete action on regular appropriations bills and prevent another government funding crisis. Speaker Thomas P. O'Neill Jr., D-Mass., warned that the House faced another budget crisis before the end of the session if Congress terminated the resolution on Dec. 15, as Reagan asked.

But Michel said Reagan would veto anything but a resolution with a Dec. 15 termination date. He predicted that, after Thanksgiving, members would be in a calmer mood to settle their differences with the White House. "We have a little bit of wine and turkey, and all the rest, and back with the home-folks, and come back here with a fresher view," he said.

O'Neill declined to make a major issue of the date, saying that "if you vote for the 15th of December, I am not going to shed any tears about it." General fatigue and the fear of another veto combined to give a Conte motion to substitute a Dec. 15 termination date a comfortable 221-176 margin of victory. *(Vote 318, p. 104-H)*

Conte also had sweetened the pot by including in his motion special funding for four Public Health Service hospitals that were scheduled to be turned over to local control. That brought along members with the hospitals in their districts, such as Baltimore's Barbara A. Mikulski, D-Md.

H J Res 368 passed the House by a 367-26 vote. *(Vote 319, p. 104-H)*

The Senate then approved the resolution by an 88-1 vote. *(Vote 415, p. 68-S)*

Reagan signed the measure at 6:40 p.m. Nov. 23. ∎

$12.5 Billion Energy-Water Bill Cleared

Congress Nov. 21 cleared the fiscal 1982 energy and water development appropriations bill (HR 4144 — PL 97-88), providing $12.5 billion for energy and water programs.

The legislation included $4.7 billion for nuclear weapons development and production, $3.4 billion for non-defense programs of the Department of Energy (DOE) and $3.7 billion for water projects of the Army Corps of Engineers and the Interior Department's Bureau of Reclamation. No funds were included for starting any new water projects.

Additional funds for fossil energy programs were contained in the Interior Department appropriations bill (HR 4035). *(Story, p. 369)*

Although the bill exceeded his revised September budget request by $375 million, President Reagan signed it into law Dec. 4, expressing his gratitude that it contained nearly three-fourths of the additional savings he had requested. It was $938 million below his initial March budget request of $13.4 billion.

The bill, which Reagan called "a model for a responsible approach to reducing budget deficits," provided less spending than either the House- or Senate-passed version, and the spending for non-defense programs in the bill was lower than in 1981, he noted. The total was $291 million below the amount approved by the Senate Nov. 5 and $718 million below the amount approved by the House July 24, before Reagan revised his budget requests.

Although the largest chunk of money in the bill was for weapons research and manufacturing done by the Energy Department for the Department of Defense, some senators felt that was not enough. The Senate voted to add another $335 million for defense, but conferees deleted the addition. Despite their dissatisfaction, supporters of the increase did not attempt to block the conference agreement.

While the bill provided less than Reagan wanted for military weapons, it gave him more than he requested for energy programs, particularly for solar energy.

Clinch River, Tenn-Tom

HR 4144 continued funding for two costly and controversial projects: the Clinch River (Tenn.) nuclear breeder reactor and the Tennessee-Tombigbee Waterway, a 232-mile-long canal designed to connect the Tennessee and Tombigbee Rivers and provide a direct route to the Gulf Coast for barge traffic.

Efforts to kill the projects failed by narrow margins in both the House and Senate. The votes were the closest opponents had ever come to killing the projects. In past years, opponents relied on environmental and anti-nuclear arguments; in 1981 they based their attack on economic concerns — the high cost of the projects at a time when Congress was trying to cut spending.

The breeder reactor, authorized by Congress in 1970, originally was estimated to cost about $700 million, with industry putting up $250 million. By 1981, the cost was estimated at $3.2 billion; about $1 billion had already been spent and construction still had not begun.

The reactor, to be built on the Clinch River near Oak Ridge, Tenn., would produce more nuclear fuel than it used (hence the term "breeder"), while also providing 350 megawatts of electricity to be distributed by the federal Tennessee Valley Authority. Opponents claimed it would be obsolete before it was finished.

A key supporter of the project was Senate Majority Leader Howard H. Baker, Jr., R-Tenn., who persuaded President Reagan to include funding for it in his budget over the opposition of Office of Management and Budget Director David A. Stockman.

The long dreamed of Tenn-Tom canal, for which cost estimates also ranged up to $3 billion, would be the largest water project in U.S. history. The idea of an inland waterway to give barges a shortcut from Tennessee through Mississippi and Alabama to the port of Mobile, Ala., had been pushed by supporters such as Sen. John C. Stennis, D-Miss., since the 1940s.

Opponents argued that Tenn-Tom's navigational benefits would not outweigh the price tag and the cost in environmental degradation caused by digging the canal. They had tried twice in 1980 to kill the project. *(1980 Almanac pp. 147, 151, 160)*

Provisions

As signed into law, HR 4144 (PL 97-88) appropriated the following amounts for energy and water development programs for fiscal 1982 *(in thousands of dollars)*:

Agency	September Budget Request	Final Amount
Army Corps of Engineers	$ 2,752,992	$ 2,914,666
Interior Department		
Bureau of Reclamation	739,594	760,161
Office of Water Policy	2,200	0
Subtotal, Interior	$ 741,794	$ 760,161
Department of Energy (DOE)		
Energy research, development	1,762,691	1,970,926
Transfer from other accounts	—	−25,000
Uranium enrichment	96,000	1,000
General science, research	381,461	411,060
Nuclear weapons activities	4,847,635	4,673,154
Department administration	208,756	200,468
Construction, capital equipment	409,063	491,463
Federal Energy Regulatory Commission	72,312	76,177
Geothermal resources development	75	2,200
Power marketing administrations	243,318	243,318
Subtotal, DOE	$ 8,021,311	$ 8,044,766
Independent Agencies		
Appalachian Regional Commission	0	152,900
Delaware River Basin Commission	343	390
Potomac River Basin Commission	48	55
Nuclear Regulatory Commission	455,600	465,700
Susquehanna River Basin Commission	297	337
Tennessee Valley Authority	124,162	129,162
Water Resources Council	0	3,888
Subtotal, Independent Agencies	$ 580,450	$ 752,432
GRAND TOTAL	$12,096,547	$12,472,025

House Committee Action

As reported by the House Appropriations Committee July 14 (H Rept 97-177), HR 4144 included $13.2 billion for energy and water projects, $233 million less than the amount requested by the administration in March.

The committee included $228 million for the Clinch River breeder reactor and $189 million for continued construction of the Tenn-Tom canal. The administration had requested $254 million for Clinch River and $201 million for Tenn-Tom.

The panel rejected by a 14-24 show of hands an amendment by Lawrence Coughlin, R-Pa., to delete the Clinch River funding. Coughlin called the project a "turkey" that "simply can't be justified on a cost-benefit basis."

Tom Bevill, D-Ala., chairman of the Appropriations Subcommittee on Energy and Water Development, defended the project, reminding members that $1.2 billion already had been spent on it. Bevill said the government's cost eventually would be repaid by charges for the electricity the plant was expected to produce.

Non-defense Programs. The administration had requested $3.8 billion for the non-defense energy programs in the bill, about $4 million more than the fiscal 1981 amount. The committee provided $3.6 billion, rearranging several of the administration's priorities.

One of its biggest changes was in the funding of solar energy projects. The administration requested $193 million for solar development; the committee provided $304 million. The fiscal 1981 appropriation was $500 million.

The committee also added $24 million to the amount requested for turning sunlight directly into electricity and increased funds for advanced windmills by $20 million. It included $29 million for converting the ocean's temperature differences into electric power, a program the administration wanted to cancel, and set up a $24 million solar account which the administration could spend, with the committee's permission, on a variety of solar projects.

The panel provided $972 million for non-military nuclear fission programs, about $7 million more than the budget request and $52 million more than the 1981 appropriation.

In addition to the funds for the breeder reactor, the committee provided $35 million for research on a gas-cooled nuclear reactor, a program the administration had not sought to fund. The program was supported by Western members of Congress because it could be used in arid regions that did not have enough water to operate water-cooled reactors.

The committee also added $10 million for research at the privately owned Barnwell, S.C., nuclear reprocessing plant. Energy Secretary James B. Edwards had said he would like the government to take over the plant, located in his home state, to begin commercial reprocessing of burned reactor fuel. However, he was unsuccessful in persuading the administration to seek funds for the plant.

The committee provided the $29 million requested to conduct research at the damaged Three Mile Island, Pa., nuclear reactor.

However, the funding request for cleaning up highly radioactive liquid wastes at a defunct nuclear plant at West Valley, N.Y., was reduced by $3 million, to $9.8 million. The committee said it was concerned that, despite a 1980 agreement to do so, the state of New York would not pay 10 percent of the cost of the cleanup, estimated to total at least $254 million. However, the panel agreed to remove language from the committee report that would have blocked any money being spent until the agreement was modified. *(Background, 1980 Almanac p. 488)*

The committee provided $478 million for the Nuclear Regulatory Commission (NRC), about $23 million less than the administration requested. It said it would continue to monitor the speed at which the NRC reduced the backlog

of nuclear power plants awaiting operating licenses, and directed that NRC hearings on specific operating licenses "are not to be used as a forum for discussion of the merits of nuclear power or other issues."

Nuclear Weapons. The largest increase in energy spending requested by the president was for the development and production of nuclear weapons, in keeping with the administration's philosophy of increased military spending. Reagan asked for $5 billion for nuclear weapons — $1.3 billion more than the fiscal 1981 appropriation.

The committee approved $4.7 billion. It cut $51 million from the request for facilities to build the warheads for the MX missile, saying the administration had not yet decided how to base the new missile. It also cut $15 million from the funds requested for facilities to build warheads for cruise missiles, saying the administration's planned production rate was unrealistic. It cut $30 million from the request for funds to build new atomic artillery shells, but doubled the $25 million request for building a facility to develop high-energy laser weapons.

Water Projects. Although no new water project construction starts were recommended in fiscal 1982, the committee voted to increase spending on ongoing projects by 2.9 percent above existing levels and .55 percent above what President Reagan requested.

The bill included $3.99 billion for water projects — $114 million more than the 1981 appropriation and $21.7 million above the budget request. Of the total, $3.15 billion was for Corps of Engineers projects, primarily designed to provide navigation and flood control benefits; $839 million was for Bureau of Reclamation irrigation projects.

The committee cut the $1.54 billion request for Corps of Engineers projects by $31.7 million, including an $11 million reduction in funding for the Tenn-Tom canal. It approved $190 million for the project, 5.5 percent less than requested. The panel felt that because of the huge cost of the waterway and the need for fiscal restraint, it was only fair that the funding be cut, committee staffers said.

The administration wanted to terminate three Corps of Engineers projects: the Red River Waterway in Louisiana, the Yatesville Dam in Kentucky and the Big South Fork National River and Recreation Area along the Kentucky-Tennessee border. The committee went along with deleting funds for the Big South Fork project but provided money to continue the other two.

The Reclamation Bureau's construction budget was cut by $11 million, from $616 million to $605 million.

The committee refused to provide $2.5 million for an Office of Water Policy within the Interior Department, as requested by Interior Secretary James G. Watt. It said no authorization existed for such an office. On the other hand, it provided $2.5 million to continue the Water Resources Council, which Watt wanted to abolish. The council received $19.8 million in fiscal 1981.

House Floor Action

After debating the bill for two days and rejecting amendments to cut funding for the Tenn-Tom and Clinch River projects, the House passed HR 4144 July 24 by a vote of 244-104. *(Vote 152, p. 54-H)*

Although the amendments failed, the relatively close votes showed that House members were less inclined than in the past to go along automatically with funding of costly water and energy projects.

Fiscal conservatives joined environmentalists to mount substantial support for amendments to strip the bill of money for Tenn-Tom, Clinch River and the Garrison Diversion water project in North Dakota. The amendments came within 10 to 20 votes of succeeding. In the past, the Appropriations Committee's recommendations for funding these projects had won easy House approval.

Environmental and taxpayer groups persuaded a majority of House freshmen to vote against the two projects, but enough veteran lawmakers stuck with both to save them.

The House rejected the amendment to delete the Tenn-Tom funding from the bill by a 198-208 vote July 23. Freshman members voted 42-30 for the amendment. *(Vote 147, p. 54-H)*

The following day, the House voted 186-206 against an amendment to delete the funding for Clinch River. The freshmen voted 36-34 for that amendment. *(Vote 150, p. 54-H)*

The new members, who had not previously voted on the projects, were the subjects of extensive lobbying by both sides. The amendments were portrayed by sponsors as taxpayer proposals to end federal funding of expensive, unnecessary and environmentally unsound projects.

Both votes were the closest House opponents had ever come to canceling the projects.

Tenn-Tom Waterway

Joel Pritchard, R-Wash., and Robert W. Edgar, D-Pa., sponsored the amendment to delete the $189 million for Tenn-Tom. Pritchard lost a similar amendment in 1980 by a wider margin — 196-216.

Proponents of the canal argued that it would facilitate the movement of coal for export by allowing barge traffic to flow from the Appalachian coal fields to the seaport of Mobile.

Supporters of the amendment countered by saying there would not be much worldwide demand for the high-sulfur Eastern coal.

Bevill said critics of the canal were misinformed on its total price tag, which he put at $1.8 billion. Critics said the cost would be $3 billion because the lower part of the waterway would have to be straightened to accommodate anticipated barge traffic. That work had not been authorized by Congress.

Although the administration included $201 million in the 1982 budget for the project, it did not lobby substantially against the amendment. The only ammunition canal supporters got from the administration was a letter of support from U.S. Trade Representative William E. Brock III, a former senator from Tennessee.

Much of the debate was clearly aimed at the freshmen. John T. Myers, R-Ind., a Tenn-Tom supporter, said, "New members must realize we have a large investment in it."

But Jim Leach, R-Iowa, said members should vote for the amendment to rectify Congress' past mistake of supporting the waterway. "Clearly it is difficult to bring an end to a project that is half built, but it is better to have half a white elephant than a whole one," he said.

Toby Roth, R-Wis., said completing the waterway would be "throwing good money after bad. The Tenn-Tom is a program whose time has gone." But David R. Bowen, D-Miss., argued that such arguments should have been made 10 years ago, not when the waterway was more than half finished.

After the amendment failed, 198-208, Edgar offered another amendment to limit fiscal 1982 Tenn-Tom spending to $100 million. Since a federal appellate court had blocked construction for environmental reasons on a 40-mile stretch of the waterway, Edgar said the additional $89 million would not be needed right away. That amendment also was defeated, on a 31-67 standing vote.

Other Water Projects

The House also narrowly rejected an amendment by Silvio O. Conte, R-Mass., to delete $4 million in funding for the controversial Garrison Diversion project in North Dakota, which would flood waterfowl breeding areas to provide water for irrigation. Construction of the project, estimated to cost nearly $1 billion, had been blocked by a federal court, and Conte said it would never be built. His amendment was rejected, 188-206. *(Vote 149, p. 54-H)*

An amendment by Buddy Roemer, D-La., to cut $221 million across-the-board from water projects was defeated by voice vote.

The House also rejected, 137-267, an amendment by Barney Frank, D-Mass., to cut out $17.8 million for West Virginia's Stonewall Jackson Dam, which Frank said could not be justified on economic grounds. *(Vote 148, p. 54-H)*

Another amendment by Frank to delete $300,000 for a study of a flood-control project in his district was agreed to by voice vote.

The House also agreed to an amendment by Myers to add $9 million for construction of a recreation area on the Big South Fork River in Kentucky and Tennessee.

Clinch River

The major energy vote was on the amendment by Coughlin to delete the $228 million for the Clinch River breeder reactor.

The nuclear industry, the utilities and the Energy Department lobbied hard to save the funds. Supporters of the facility were put on notice in May that the vote in the House would be close. The Science Committee voted May 7 to deauthorize the project, a decision overturned in June during the budget debate. *(Story, p. 447)*

Coughlin said the reactor was not needed for research purposes and that there was plenty of other money in the bill for work on breeder reactors. Claudine Schneider, R-R.I., who led the revolt against the project in the Science Committee, called it a "total hoax." Judd Gregg, R-N.H., said he supported nuclear power but that Clinch River could not be justified on economic grounds.

Bevill, however, said the project would pay for itself through the sale of electricity. The world's oil supply was running out and the United States must have nuclear power, he said. Added Majority Leader Jim Wright, D-Texas: "We've already spent $1 billion on it. If we stop now, we've wasted $1 billion."

The amendment was defeated, 186-206. Environmental lobbyists said later they were hurt by many members being out of town (the vote was taken on a Friday afternoon) and by defections of members they thought would vote for the amendment.

But in losing by 20 votes, foes of Clinch River came as close as they ever had to killing the project. In 1979, the House defeated a similar amendment, 182-237. *(1979 Almanac, vote 355, p. 104-H)*

Twenty-eight members, mostly conservative Republicans, who supported the reactor in 1979, voted for the amendment to kill it. However, 20 members, 19 of them

---

Clinch River Vote Switchers

Twenty-eight representatives who voted in 1979 for building the Clinch River nuclear breeder reactor voted against the program July 24. They were:

Democrats: Lowry, Wash.; Luken, Ohio; Mineta, Calif.; Williams, Mont.; Yatron, Pa.

Republicans: Bethune, Ark.; Broomfield, Mich.; Clinger, Pa.; Collins, Texas; Daniel, Va.; Dornan, Calif.; Edwards, Okla.; Erdahl, Minn.; Evans, Del.; Gradison, Ohio; Green, N.Y.; Hopkins, Ky.; Hyde, Ill.; Lungren, Calif.; McCloskey, Calif.; Moore, La.; Railsback, Ill.; Ritter, Pa.; Sawyer, Mich.; Snyder, Ky.; Snowe, Maine; Stanton, Ohio; Trible, Va.

Twenty representatives who voted against the project in 1979 voted July 24 to continue the program. They were:

Democrats: Barnard, Ga.; English, Okla.; Ford, Tenn.; Fuqua, Fla.; Hawkins, Calif.; Hefner, N.C.; Huckaby, La.; Ireland, Fla.; Kogovsek, Colo.; Long, La.; Long, Md.; Mavroules, Mass.; Mica, Fla.; Natcher, Ky.; Nelson, Fla.; Pepper, Fla.; Rose, N.C.; Skelton, Mo.; Stokes, Ohio.

Republican: Madigan, Ill.

Democrats, who voted against it in 1979, voted to build it.

Other Amendments

The House rejected on a 157-213 vote an amendment by Butler Derrick, D-S.C., to transfer $10 million from the privately owned Barnwell nuclear reprocessing plant to a federal waste research facility, also in South Carolina. Derrick said he supported reprocessing of nuclear fuel but that it should be done by the private sector, not the government. *(Vote 151, p. 54-H)*

Other amendments agreed to by voice vote were by:

● Samuel S. Stratton, D-N.Y., to prohibit the NRC from developing rules for enforcing standards for cleaning up wastes at uranium mines. Stratton said the Environmental Protection Agency had not written such standards yet.

● Bevill, to provide an additional $3 million for the Tennessee Valley Authority to conduct research on turning wood wastes into alcohol.

● Allen E. Ertel, D-Pa., to prohibit the agencies funded by the bill from hiring personal servants, such as cooks or chauffeurs, for senior officials or from buying passenger cars that got less than 22 miles per gallon.

Senate Committee Action

The Senate Appropriations Committee reported its version of HR 4144 Oct. 28 (S Rept 97-256). It provided $12.4 billion — $322 million more than President Reagan's revised September budget request.

The Energy and Water Subcommittee had approved a $13.3 billion version of the bill Sept. 11. But that figure was scrapped after Reagan issued his revised budget request. The full committee Oct. 22 reduced the total almost $900 million, to $12.4 billion. Chairman Mark O. Hatfield, R-Ore., called it "a bare-bones but equitable bill."

Like the House bill, the Senate measure contained significantly more funds for solar energy programs than Reagan wanted. Reagan's revised budget called for $183

million; the Senate bill provided $244 million. The House-passed bill included $304 million for solar.

Senate Floor Action

After narrowly rejecting amendments to kill the funding for Clinch River and Tenn-Tom, and adding $335 million to the bill for nuclear weapons, the Senate passed HR 4144 Nov. 5 by a vote of 71-22. *(Vote 357, p. 60-S)*

A mixture of senatorial courtesy and political horse-trading saved the two projects. The Senate rejected the amendment to kill Tenn-Tom by a 46-48 vote Nov. 4. Then, by an identical two-vote margin, it tabled an amendment aimed at killing the Clinch River breeder reactor.

Unlike the House freshmen, a majority of new Senate members voted to support both projects.

Nuclear Weapons Spending

As passed by the Senate, HR 4144 appropriated $12.8 billion, about $650 million less than President Reagan requested in March but $667 million more than his revised budget.

Hatfield warned that Reagan might veto the bill because of the Senate's addition of $335 million for nuclear weapons to the $4.7 billion already in the committee bill. He complained that the weapons program was getting too much money — almost twice as much as the amount allotted for energy supply and research.

"I believe our priorities in the energy area are misplaced," Hatfield said. "I submit that energy security and independence is every bit as important to our national strength and security as is our nuclear arsenal and nuclear stockpile."

But Pentagon supporters noted that the committee amount was $170 million less than Reagan's revised request and over $300 million below his original March budget.

By a 49-43 vote Nov. 5, the Senate adopted the amendment by Armed Services Committee Chairman John Tower, R-Texas, to add $335 million to the defense portion of the bill. *(Vote 356, p. 60-S)*

Tower initially wanted to add $509 million but was persuaded to lower it to secure enough votes to pass the amendment. He said the funds were needed to prevent delays in the delivery of new warheads, including the one for the MX missile.

The Senate also agreed to an amendment by Gary Hart, D-Colo., to prohibit the government from using burned fuel from civilian nuclear reactors to make atomic weapons.

Tenn-Tom Debate

Charles H. Percy, R-Ill., sponsored the amendment to delete the $189 million in funding for the Tenn-Tom canal. The amendment was rejected, 46-48. *(Vote 350, p. 59-S)*

Calling the waterway an "economic dinosaur," Percy said the coal companies were not seeking it and that the eventual traffic would not be enough to pay for operating it. Daniel Patrick Moynihan, D-N.Y., called it a perfect example of "pork-barrel" abuse. If Congress did not start "acting responsibly" by killing it, the country would never support any more public works projects, he warned.

J. Bennett Johnston, D-La., leading the debate on behalf of the canal, said no federal project had ever been more misrepresented. He put its total cost at $1.8 billion, not $3 billion, and said there would be enough traffic on

the waterway to generate $145 million a year in commerce. He and others said Tenn-Tom was too far along — 81 percent — to halt work. Opponents said it was no more than 51 percent complete.

Johnston said the basic issue was "an age-old fight" between the railroads and the barges. The railroads "have a monopoly, and they want to keep it," he said. He claimed the railroads had spent thousands of dollars in support of the environmental groups that had fought the project.

An Association of American Railroads spokeswoman confirmed that her group was lobbying hard against Tenn-Tom, which she said would duplicate a privately owned rail system that could handle the traffic.

While Johnston led the floor debate, Stennis patrolled the lobbies off the Senate floor, cornering undecided colleagues to persuade them to support the project.

Backers of Tenn-Tom reportedly reminded other senators that their support was needed to secure votes for other projects, including Clinch River. They also played on affection for Stennis, suggesting that saving Tenn-Tom would help his re-election chances.

Jeremiah Denton, R-Ala., successfully lobbied his fellow freshmen. Senators first elected in 1980 voted 7-11 against Percy's amendment, in contrast to new House members, who voted 42-30 to kill Tenn-Tom.

The freshmen's votes were crucial because seven senators who had supported the project in the past voted for the Percy amendment to kill it. One, Bob Packwood, R-Ore., switched to vote for the project. In 1980 the Senate rejected an amendment to kill Tenn-Tom by a 37-52 vote. *(1980 Almanac p. 160)*

Johnston said the 46-48 vote rejecting Percy's amendment was really not that close because there were six senators who would have supported Tenn-Tom if it proved necessary. He would not reveal their names.

Following the vote supporting the project, the Senate by voice vote adopted an amendment by Carl Levin, D-Mich., expressing the Senate's intention that there be no funding for the section of the waterway south of Demopolis, Ala., the portion that opponents said would cost $1 billion to straighten.

Clinch River Fight

Dale Bumpers, D-Ark., and Gordon J. Humphrey, R-N.H., offered the amendment to kill the Clinch River breeder reactor. Bumpers called it a "technological disaster" that would be obsolete before it was completed. Humphrey, quoting budget director David A. Stockman, called it a white elephant that would not make it in the marketplace.

Paul Tsongas, D-Mass., argued that instead of cutting $180 million from the bill for Clinch River, the Senate should trim $90 million and require the nuclear industry to put up the other half. Tsongas noted that the original intention was that the cost would be split with industry.

The Senate agreed to replace the Bumpers-Humphrey amendment with Tsongas' proposal. But, after considerable parliamentary maneuvering, it voted 48-46 Nov. 4 to table the amendment, thus killing the proposal and keeping funds for the project in the bill. *(Vote 352, p. 59-S)*

Opponents managed to get another vote on the question the next day, but lost 50-45, as Baker persuaded Roger W. Jepsen, R-Iowa, and Richard G. Lugar, R-Ind., to switch their votes. Vice President Bush presided during the vote, ready to break a tie if necessary. *(Vote 353, p. 60-S)*

As Stennis did on Tenn-Tom, Baker relied on Johnston, along with Energy Committee Chairman James A. McClure, R-Idaho, to speak for the project on the floor while he lined up votes. Baker did particularly well with the freshmen, who voted 14-4 for construction of Clinch River.

In the House, new members had voted 36-34 to kill the project.

Conference Action

Conferees reached quick agreement on the bill Nov. 18 and filed their report the next day (H Rept 97-345).

Under the agreement, the administration got less money than it wanted for weapons construction but more than it requested for civilian energy programs and dams and water projects.

It also got $150 million, mostly for road building, for the Appalachian Regional Commission, a favorite of several members of the conference committee. Reagan had not requested any funding for the commission.

The conferees scrapped the Senate provision adding $335 million to the bill for nuclear weapons. The conferees said they agreed with Tower that weapons should not be delayed, but they said the reduction had to made because of "budgetary constraints."

Conferees also deleted the Senate prohibition on the use of spent fuel from civilian nuclear power plants for making military weapons. But in their report they said they supported the continued separation between the military and civilian nuclear programs.

The president had requested $2 billion for energy research and development programs. The conference agreement provided $2.3 billion, including $195 million for Clinch River.

It provided about $83 million more for solar energy programs than Reagan wanted and about $23 million less than he wanted for nuclear fission programs. It contained $189 million for Tenn-Tom.

Final Action

The House approved the conference report by voice vote Nov. 20. The Senate followed suit Nov. 21.

However, the House refused by a separate 67-314 vote to accept a provision reauthorizing the Garrison Diversion water project in North Dakota. The conference committee had retained the Senate language even though it was admittedly legislation on an appropriation bill, which is prohibited by House rules. *(Vote 311, p. 102-H)*

As cleared, the bill did include the $4 million for conducting tests relating to the project.

Opposing the reauthorization on the House floor, John D. Dingell, D-Mich., said the project would have a "more disastrous impact on the migratory waterfowl population and wildlife refuge system of the United States than any single project that has ever been undertaken. . . ."

But Byron L. Dorgan, D-N.D., said the project was promised to North Dakota in 1944 when the state agreed to give up a half million acres of land to create the Garrison Reservoir, which provided flood control benefits downstream on the Missouri River and hydroelectric power. Other proponents of the project said it would enhance wildlife in North Dakota.

The Senate accepted the House deletion of the Garrison Diversion language without a separate vote. ∎

Military Construction

Conferees on the $7.06 billion military construction appropriations bill (HR 4241) called for greater allied burden-sharing in light of U.S. efforts to defend Europe's and Japan's oil supplies.

They also added to the bill a provision expressing the sense of the Congress that the administration should press the allies to increase their defense budgets at an annual rate of at least 3 percent (above the cost of inflation).

NATO agreed in 1978 on the 3 percent annual increase, but most members have not met the goal.

Congress cleared the bill Dec. 15 (PL 97-106).

House Committee Action

The House Appropriations Committee used the $7 billion construction bill to continue the drumfire of congressional demands that U.S. allies in Europe do more to offset the cost of U.S. efforts to defend the continent.

The committee reported the bill (HR 4241) July 23 (H Rept 97-193). The bill provided $6.9 billion for military construction projects in fiscal 1982.

The $1 billion requested for construction in Europe was cut by $79.64 million. That cut was relatively modest because Congress had convinced the Pentagon in 1978-79 that it would make much larger cuts if the Pentagon asked for U.S. funds to build facilities the congressional defense committees thought should be paid for by NATO.

On July 30, West German Chancellor Helmut Schmidt announced that his next budget would include a broad set of austerity measures including restraint of the defense budget that would rescue West German military spending in real terms, after allowing for inflation. Since 1978, NATO members had been committed to annual real growth rates in defense spending of 3 percent, though few consistently met that goal.

Schmidt's decision elicited complaints from the Pentagon and exacerbated congressional unhappiness over the Europeans' unwillingness to pay for defense.

The Appropriations Committee also cut by nearly a third the $541 million request for construction intended to speed the deployment of U.S. forces to the Persian Gulf region.

And the panel refused to approve $522 million requested to continue work related to the MX missile. At the time of the committee markup, the administration had not selected a design of the missile system, and the committee warned that "Congress will require time to review and deliberate on" the eventual recommendation before it would appropriate funds.

Burden-Sharing

Congressional anger over what was seen as allied unwillingness to bear a fair share of the burden of alliance defense was exacerbated by the belief that Western Europe and Japan derived a competitive advantage over U.S. industry as a result. The construction subcommittee's senior Republican, Ralph Regula, R-Ohio, summarized the argument during a March 31 hearing on facilities in the Middle East: "You can build a lot of Toyotas with the money they don't spend on the security of [the Persian Gulf] but we do."

Beyond their relatively small cut in the fiscal 1982 request for construction funds in Europe, House Appropri-

Military Construction Appropriations, Fiscal 1982

HR 4241 appropriated the following amounts for military construction projects in fiscal 1982:

	Revised Reagan Request	House-Passed Amount	Senate-Passed Amount	Final Amount
Army	$ 900,100,000	$1,029,519,000	$ 942,081,000	$ 943,701,000
Navy	1,477,800,000	1,404,883,000	1,475,813,000	1,451,393,000
Air Force	1,709,400,000	1,407,565,000[1]	1,693,426,000	1,545,751,000
Defense Agencies	354,100,000	251,004,000	338,315,000	306,490,000
NATO Infrastructure	385,000,000	385,000,000	345,000,000	345,000,000
Reserve and National Guard	236,200,000	313,342,000	309,733,000	311,371,000
Family Housing[2]	2,236,008,000	2,094,229,000	2,209,648,000	2,153,554,000
Homeowners Assistance Fund	2,000,000	2,000,000	2,000,000	2,000,000
Total[2]	**$7,300,608,000**	**$6,887,542,000**	**$7,316,016,000**	**$7,059,260,000**

[1] MX-related funds totaling $522.3 million were "deferred without prejudice," pending a presidential decision on the specific design of the MX system.

[2] Excludes $128.888 million requested and appropriated but earmarked for debt reduction rather than for new programs. Also excludes $1.992 million transferred to this account from earlier appropriations.

ations staked out three positions that foreshadowed more far-reaching future demands for European support of U.S. deployments abroad:

Pre-Financing. The panel dramatically re-emphasized its reluctance to provide funds for projects eligible for funding by NATO's common kitty for construction projects (the NATO Infrastructure).

The panel refused to provide the $37.12 million requested for ammunition and fuel dumps and aircraft parking spaces at so-called co-located operating bases (COBs). These were facilities at European-owned air bases that would be used by U.S. planes flown to Europe as reinforcements in a time of crisis. The Pentagon assigned a high priority to the COB projects and wanted to build them with U.S. funds that eventually would be recouped from the Infrastructure (a practice called "pre-financing"). The projects could not be funded until after 1985 if they awaited Infrastructure funding.

The committee insisted that the alliance provide up-front money for the COBs.

Personnel Facilities. The committee also declared that it would insist on broadening the categories of facilities for which NATO had agreed to pay.

For instance, the 13 categories of facilities that were eligible for Infrastructure funding did not include barracks, other personnel facilities, or maintenance shops. The committee approved administration requests totaling $75.5 million for such facilities at bases in Italy, Great Britain and the United States for the ground-launched cruise missile (GLCM).

But the panel told the Pentagon to regard that money as pre-financing for NATO projects that it would have to recoup from the NATO Infrastructure. One project was a training base in Arizona for the U.S. crews that were to launch the missile.

German Posts. The committee warned that it might begin ordering the Pentagon unilaterally to demand allied funding for whole new categories of facilities in West Germany and in the Indian Ocean area.

West Germany eventually should cover the whole cost of the so-called Master Re-stationing Plan (MRP) for U.S.

forces, the committee insisted. Over several years, the plan would consolidate U.S. units into modern barracks and maintenance centers near the defensive positions they would take up in case of a Soviet attack. The forces were scattered, many of them in antiquated facilities far behind the East German frontier. For instance, the 8th Infantry Division (headquartered at Bad Kreuznach) would have to cross the Rhine and Main rivers and move through the Frankfurt metropolitan area to reach its planned defensive position.

The land vacated by U.S. forces was to be sold. Since much of it was in heavily developed parts of the country, the plan eventually was to pay for itself. But in November, the Carter administration asked the West German government to consider paying some of the cost of the first set of new facilities.

Pending the outcome of that effort, the Pentagon requested $18 million to begin the project. The Appropriations Committee approved the request but insisted that the funds be recouped from West Germany. And the panel barred any use of the funds until the West German government committed itself to paying for the plan.

In the early 1970s, West Germany built at Garlstedt a base for a U.S. Army brigade that was added to the European force. The German government was particularly eager to locate a U.S. unit in the northern part of the country. In contrast to the southern part of Germany, where U.S. Army units were based, NATO's firepower was spread more thinly and the terrain was more favorable to a Soviet tank lunge in the north.

But some West German officials had warned that it would be politically difficult to find support for the MRP.

Persian Gulf. Japan and U.S. allies in Western Europe depended on Persian Gulf oil far more heavily than did the United States, the committee pointed out. Accordingly, the panel said, those countries should bear some of the burden of defending the region against hostile powers.

In 1980, the committee had recommended two courses toward that end: bases in the region should be eligible for Infrastructure funding, or the U.S. share of the annual Infrastructure payment ought to be reduced to offset the

U.S. expenditures in the Persian Gulf area. The executive branch had pursued neither proposal, the committee complained.

None of the committee's cuts in the Persian Gulf request was linked to the allied burden-sharing argument. But the panel warned that it might be forced to make "adjustments" in the fiscal 1983 appropriations bill if there were no progress on the burden-sharing front.

Rapid Deployment Force

The $541 million request for projects linked to the Rapid Deployment Force (RDF) was cut by nearly 40 percent. The RDF was the umbrella program under which the Pentagon wanted to improve its ability to deploy combat units to distant areas, particularly to the Persian Gulf.

Azores. Following the lead of the House Armed Services Committee, the panel denied the $49.57 million requested for an aerial refueling base at Lajes in the Portuguese-owned Azores Islands. In justifying the deferral, both panels cited continuing uncertainty in negotiating base use rights with Portugal.

Egypt. The panel also disapproved all of the $106.4 million requested to begin construction at a primitive air field at Ras Banas on the Red Sea coast of Egypt. At a total cost of $500 million, the Pentagon hoped to turn the facility into a supply depot for the RDF.

In deference to political sensibilities in the region, the administration described installations at Ras Banas and elsewhere in the region as "facilities" rather than "bases."

The Ras Banas project was denied because of various uncertainties about its future use, including the absence of a formal agreement with Egypt guaranteeing U.S. access to the facility. But the committee did not flatly demand such an agreement as a pre-condition to future appropriations. In January, Egyptian President Anwar Sadat told Sen. Carl Levin, D-Mich., that he would sign an agreement on Ras Banas if Washington insisted. But Sadat warned that such an act would be politically costly to him at home because of lingering resentment of British and Soviet military establishments that had been based in Egypt.

Diego Garcia. The committee also denied $50.3 million of the $237.74 million requested for air and naval facilities at the Indian Ocean island of Diego Garcia. Most of the amount denied was for a runway extension the panel said might be superfluous because of other bases in the region.

American Preference. The committee incorporated into the bill a requirement that in awarding contracts for construction in the Indian Ocean area, the Pentagon use certain procedures intended to give U.S. contractors a bidding advantage. The procedures had been included in the fiscal 1981 military construction appropriations bill (PL 96-436). *(1980 Almanac p. 164)*

Also retained was a provision giving American firms a 20 percent advantage in bidding for dredging contracts in the region. In fiscal 1981, the 20 percent American preference clause for dredging had little effect: a dredging contract at Masirah Island in Oman was awarded to a Japanese firm for $17 million. The low U.S. bid was $42 million.

Other Provisions

Washington Offices. The committee added $2.5 million, not requested by the administration, to plan and design facilities at the Washington Navy Yard to house Navy offices scattered across the Washington, D.C., area. The committee insisted in 1980 that the Pentagon prepare

a long-term plan to consolidate its offices in the Washington area. Members of the Virginia congressional delegation objected to the Navy Yard plan.

Pentagon administrative offices occupied 20 million square feet at 72 locations in the Washington area.

Trident Base. The committee approved the requested $77 million for construction associated with a new base at Kings Bay, Ga., for Trident missile-launching submarines. Plans were to base the first 10 Trident ships at the existing base in Bangor, Wash., and a second group at Kings Bay.

The ultimate size of the Trident fleet was in doubt, because of cost and schedule problems. The first Trident ship, the *Ohio*, began sea trials in June, 1981, more than two years behind schedule. Both Armed Services committees in 1981 refused to fully authorize construction of the 10th Trident ship, because of concern that the Electric Boat division of General Dynamics, the contractor, was not ready to add another contract to the nine behind schedule.

But the Appropriations Committee said military necessity dictated having Trident bases on both coasts, regardless of the ultimate size of the Trident fleet.

Military Construction Subcommittee Chairman Bo Ginn, D-Ga., represented the Kings Bay district.

Refugees. The committee warned the administration against using military construction funds to upgrade inactive military bases to house Cuban, Haitian and other illegal aliens. The administration had considered using several such bases because President Reagan had promised to close down the Cuban entrant program at Fort Chaffee, Ark.

The committee also urged the Pentagon to carry out the long-planned sale of the abandoned Bainbridge Naval Training Center in Maryland, reportedly under consideration as a refugee camp. The district was represented by Roy Dyson, D-Md., who expressed his strong opposition to that use.

House Floor Action

The House Sept. 16 routinely approved a $6.9 billion military construction appropriations bill (HR 4241) for fiscal 1982. The House passed the bill 382-24. *(Vote 195, 66-H)*

When the House took up the bill, senior members of the Military Construction Appropriations Subcommittee expressed disappointment that the West German government had not agreed to fund the U.S. Army's so-called Master Restationing Plan (MRP).

In November, Washington asked Bonn to fund the plan. In August, the West German government expressed its willingness to discuss the program but made no commitment to pay for it.

Rep. Bo Ginn, D-Ga., subcommittee chairman, said it was "essential" that the two governments renew discussions about the base relocation plan.

The House adopted by voice vote an amendment by Jim Coyne, R-Pa., to delete $14,910,000 for a Navy housing project at Horsham, Pa., in Coyne's district. Coyne said the project would unnecessarily erode the local tax base.

An amendment proposed by M. Caldwell Butler, R-Va., to exclude military construction projects in fiscal 1982 from the requirements of the Davis-Bacon Act was ruled out of order. The Davis-Bacon Act required contractors on federal construction projects to pay locally prevailing wages. Butler said his amendment would save $124 million

to $400 million in 1982.

Senate Committee Action

As part of its overall September-October budget cuts, the administration reduced its request for military construction projects by $715.6 million — from the March request of $8,016,209,000 to $7,300,608,000.

Most of the cut — $492 million — came from funds that had been requested for construction related to the MX intercontinental missile. President Reagan in October shelved former President Carter's plan to base the missiles in multiple protective shelters (called MPS).

Carter's January request had included $522.3 million for construction in fiscal 1982 on the multiple-site basing system. Reagan in September cut the MX-related request to $30.3 million.

Reagan also cut $24 million from other Air Force projects and $199.6 million from Army projects.

The Senate Appropriations Committee reported its version of HR 4241 (S Rept 97-271) on Nov. 12. The committee approved $7,287,756,000, which was $12.852 million under the administration's revised request, but $400.214 million above the House-passed version.

MX Missile

The committee approved $11 million of Reagan's revised $30.3 million request for MX missile-related construction. The $11 million was earmarked for construction on an MX headquarters at Norton Air Force Base in California. In its report, the committee said it approved the amount because it had received information that the headquarters "would, in fact, support much more than the MX requirements." The report did not say what the additional support services would be.

Rather than approve the remaining $19.3 million requested by the administration for design of MX facilities, the committee directed the administration to use $92 million in MX funds that had been deferred in the fiscal 1981 military construction appropriation (HR 7592 — PL 96-436). *(1980 Almanac p. 164)*

Rapid Deployment Force

Repeating the pattern of earlier years, the House had proposed a deep reduction of $206.27 million (nearly 40 percent) in the $540.9 million appropriations request for construction projects related to the Rapid Deployment Force (RDF). But the Senate panel restored the money.

The Senate committee said it "strongly supports the administration's position that the national security interests of the United States are directly involved with the flow of oil from that region of the world. The committee further believes that the United States must have the ability to deploy forces rapidly to the area if the oil resources are threatened."

RDF-related facilities for which the administration had requested construction money, and which the committee approved, were:

● Air and naval facilities at Diego Garcia, in the Indian Ocean ($237.74 million; the House had cut $50.3 million).

● Lajes Air Base in the Portuguese-owned Azores Islands ($49.57 million, which the House had eliminated).

● Air and Army facilities at Ras Banas, Egypt ($106.4 million, which the House had eliminated).

● Air and naval facilities in Oman ($78.48 million), Somalia ($24 million) and Kenya ($26 million) — all approved as requested by the House.

● Planning and design work for all facilities ($18.8 million).

The Senate committee approved all those amounts as requested. The committee approved an additional $9 million for dredging of the harbor at Mombasa, Kenya. The committee had deleted that money from the fiscal 1981 supplemental appropriation (HR 3512 — PL 97-12). *(Supplemental, p. 281)*

European Bases

Like the House committee, the Senate panel warned the administration that it wanted more progress in getting European allies to contribute more to their own defense. In particular, the committee repeated past directives to the Pentagon to attempt to recoup money from European nations for NATO projects for which the United States provided advanced financing.

One provision of the committee bill stated the sense of Congress that the administration should call on NATO members and Japan to meet their commitments to increase defense spending. The NATO nations agreed in 1980 to boost their defense spending by 3 percent annually, after inflation, but most of them had not come close to meeting that goal.

The committee made only one major change in European construction programs, slicing $40 million from the $385 million request for the U.S. contribution to the common account for NATO construction projects (called the NATO Infrastructure). The change had been made by the Senate Armed Services Committee in the fiscal 1982 defense authorization bill (S 815), because of the dollar's improved standing in comparison to European currencies. *(Authorization, p. 234)*

The committee also urged the Pentagon to present "a firm plan" to West Germany for the Master Restationing Plan.

Other Issues

On other issues, the Senate committee:

● Agreed to raise the limit on funds the Pentagon could transfer ("reprogram") among accounts. Under the existing limit, the Pentagon could not transfer more than $1 million or 25 percent (whichever was less) from one account to another without getting advance approval from the two Appropriations committees. The House committee raised the dollar limit to $2 million, but kept the 25 percent limit. The Senate panel dropped the dollar limit and kept the 25 percent limit.

● Deleted $2.5 million the House committee had added for design of new facilities at the Washington Navy Yard to consolidate all Navy offices in the Washington, D.C., area. Although expressing concern about the $100 million annual cost of leasing space for the Navy, the committee said the Navy's plans for use of the Navy Yard were incomplete.

● Like the House committee, the Senate panel approved $77 million for construction of a new base at Kings Bay, Ga., for Trident missile-launching submarines.

● The committee added $69 million to the administration's $236.2 million request for various Reserve and National Guard facilities. The largest single addition was $7.4 million for a joint Reserve center in Charleston, S.C.

● Unlike the House committee, the Senate panel approved an administration request for $29 million to begin buying 244,000 acres of grazing land in southeastern Colorado. The Army wanted the land to run large-scale tank

RDF Projects Approved

In the fiscal 1982 military construction appropriations bill (HR 4241), Congress approved the bulk of the administration's requests for projects to bolster the U.S. capacity to respond rapidly to crises in the Indian Ocean/Persian Gulf region. The construction projects were tailored to the needs of the Rapid Deployment Force (RDF).

Most of the funds requested in fiscal 1982 were for ongoing projects that were to be completed in later years. For most of the projects, the first installment was made in fiscal 1981, when Congress appropriated $259.2 million. *(1980 Almanac p. 168)*

The total cost of the projects for fiscal years 1982-85 had been estimated at $1.5 billion, according to the House Appropriations Committee. For example, expansion of air and ground facilities at Ras Banas in Egypt was expected to cost $500 million.

The following amounts were requested and appropriated in fiscal 1982 for RDF-related projects:

Location	Amount Requested	Amount Appropriated
Diego Garcia		
Navy facilities expansion	$122,750,000	$122,750,000
Air Force facilities expansion	114,990,000	114,990,000
Planning and design	2,765,000	2,765,000
Egypt		
RDF bases (Army)	36,000,000	0
RDF facilities (Air Force)	70,400,000	0
Planning and design	14,292,000	14,292,000
Somalia		
Navy facilities expansion	24,000,000	24,000,000
Kenya		
Navy bases support	26,000,000	30,500,000
Planning and design	1,300,000	1,300,000
Oman		
Air Force facilities expansion	78,480,000	78,480,000
Planning and design	1,710,000	1,710,000
Portugal		
Lajes Field (Air Force)	49,570,000	46,570,000
Planning and design	3,344,000	3,344,000
Total	$545,601,000	$440,701,000

maneuvers for the 4th Division, which was stationed at Fort Carson, about 150 miles northwest of the proposed training area.

● The committee rejected requests of $20.4 million for the Army and $43 million for the Navy to make up the "shortfall" in funding for previously approved construction projects. The shortages resulted from inflation, cost overruns and other factors. The committee said the two services could absorb the added costs through various methods, such as transferring money from other accounts. The committee did approve $242.5 million in shortfall funding for

the Air Force, which it said resulted from the "huge cost growth" in the space shuttle program. The committee noted that the cost of building facilities at Vandenberg Air Force Base in California to handle the shuttle could be twice the original $300 million estimate.

● In contrast to the House committee, the Senate panel approved $32 million for a long-term lease of 18,132 acres on parts of three of the Northern Mariana Islands in the western Pacific Ocean. The House panel argued that the United States had no immediate plans to use the lands. But the Senate panel said the islands, along with bases at Guam and Palau islands, could provide a "fallback position for U.S. forces over the next 100 years should our current bases in the western Pacific become unavailable." The Navy and Air Force already used one island, the Farallon de Medinalla, for target practice.

Senate Floor Action

The Senate gave routine consideration to the bill Dec. 4, before passing it by voice vote.

Action on the measure came immediately after the Senate completed five days of debate on the fiscal 1982 defense appropriations bill (HR 4995).

The Senate added $28.26 million to the bill for three programs, on amendments adopted by voice vote:

● By Henry M. Jackson, D-Wash., and Slade Gorton, R-Wash., adding $1.86 million for construction of family service centers at five naval facilities: Puget Sound Naval Shipyard in Bremerton, Wash.; Naval Training Center, Great Lakes, Ill.; Naval Station, Pearl Harbor, Hawaii; Naval Training Center, Orlando, Fla.; and Naval Air Station, Alameda, Calif.

● By Don Nickles, R-Okla., and David L. Boren, D-Okla., adding $23 million for construction of maintenance and crew housing facilities at Tinker Air Force Base in Oklahoma, the home base of Airborne Warning and Control System (AWACS) planes.

● By Robert C. Byrd, D-W.Va., for construction of a new Naval and Marine Corps Reserve Center in Wheeling, W.Va.

Conference Committee

The conference report on the $7.059 billion bill (HR 4241) was filed Dec. 11 (H Rept 97-400). This was $241.35 million less than the administration's October request.

The total in the construction appropriations bill routinely was slightly higher than the authorization bill because some projects did not require annual authorization.

The House adopted the conference report Dec. 15 by voice vote, and the Senate adopted it by a vote of 96-1. *(Vote 474, p. 76-S)*

Acting on the basis of Reagan's original March request for $8.02 billion, the House had passed a version of the bill providing $6.89 billion. By the time the Senate passed its bill, Reagan had cut $715.6 million from his request: $492 million came from the MX missile basing technique he had killed, $24 million from other Air Force projects and $199.6 million from various Army projects.

The Senate version of the bill provided about $15.4 million more than Reagan's $7.3 billion October request.

European Construction

The position of the appropriations conferees on the Army's Master Restationing Plan for forces in West Ger-

many mirrored the position taken by the conference report on the companion authorization bill (HR 3455).

They approved $14.5 million to begin a maintenance and utilities project at Vilseck, but said the funds could not be spent until the West German government entered into "serious negotiations toward" paying for the program.

The conferees also denied the entire request for $37 million to equip European air bases to supply and maintain U.S. reinforcement squadrons. The Senate had approved the $13 million allowed by the authorization bill.

Rapid Deployment Force

Of $120.692 million requested for Army and Air Force construction at Ras Banas, Egypt, the conferees approved only $14.292 million earmarked for planning and design "because of the preliminary nature of the construction program." But they urged the Pentagon to accelerate design work on the projects and said their respective committees would be "receptive" to funding them through supplemental or regular appropriations bills.

The entire $240.5 million requested for Navy and Air Force construction at the Indian Ocean island of Diego Garcia was approved, as was most other RDF-related construction. *(Box, p. 310)*

Both houses had approved $9 million to establish an RDF headquarters at MacDill Air Force Base in Tampa, Fla. Conferees directed the secretary of defense, before spending the funds, to certify that the construction was necessary and that no other existing facilities in the United States were adequate for the headquarters.

MX Missile

The conferees appeared very skeptical of Reagan's proposal to base the first few dozen MX missiles in existing silos that would be "superhardened" against nuclear blasts with additional concrete.

They said $92 million in MX funds appropriated in fiscal 1981 but frozen pending Reagan's MX decision now could be spent on the program. *(1980 Almanac p. 164)*

But the conferees insisted that before any funds were spent for contracts on specific sites, their respective committees be given the following information: a detailed plan identifying the silos to be used and a cost estimate for modifying and operating them; a study of the cost and the survivability of such superhardened silos against Soviet attack; a notice that all environmental requirements had been met; and an audit of the use of previously appropriated MX design and planning funds.

The conferees also approved $28 million of the $29 million requested to buy a 244,000-acre tract of land in southeastern Colorado as a training area for troops stationed at Ft. Carson, 150 miles away. The move had faced heated opposition from local landowners.

The conference report directed the Army, before spending the money, to report to the construction appropriations subcommittees: actions taken to offset any local economic strain; a plan to assure that the price paid by the Army would not be inflated by speculation; and a detailed list of all construction costs involved and a determination of whether or not the tract would have to be fenced.

Other Provisions

In other action, the conferees:

● Refused to provide new appropriations for the $80 million cost-overrun at the Air Force wind tunnel at Tullahoma, Tenn., for testing jet engines. To pay the increased costs, they said, the Air Force should use funds appropriated but not spent in previous years or a so-called "shortfall account" intended to cover such overruns. The conferees approved the $242.5 million requested for the shortfall account. In any case, the Appropriations committees' prior approval would be needed before any of those funds were spent on the Tullahoma overrun.

● Raised the limit on funds the Pentagon could transfer ("reprogram") among accounts to 25 percent of the previous amount or $2 million, whichever was less.

● Rejected a request for $32 million for a long-term lease of 18,132 acres on three of the Northern Mariana Islands in the western Pacific Ocean.

● Directed the Navy to continue planning new facilities at the Washington Navy Yard to consolidate all Navy offices in the Washington, D.C., area. ∎

Reagan Defense Plan Given Final Approval

The day before adjourning, Congress handed President Reagan a $199.7 billion defense appropriations bill (HR 4995 — PL 97-114) that funded essentially the defense program he requested for fiscal 1982.

The House adopted the conference report Dec. 15 by a 334-84 vote, and the Senate concurred a few hours later by a vote of 93-4, clearing the measure for the president. In both houses, liberal Democrats predominated among the "nay" votes. *(House vote 345, p. 112-H; Senate vote 475, p. 76-S)*

The final bill fell just $979 million short of Reagan's request, as revised in October.

In various fiscal 1982 military appropriations bills passed during 1981, Congress appropriated $211.6 billion in new budget authority, which was $1.4 billion less than Reagan's $213 billion request. These figures included the appropriations in HR 4995, the principal Pentagon money bill; HR 4241 (PL 97-106) covering military construction projects; and HR 4144 (PL 97-88), covering nuclear weapons programs in the Department of Energy.

The total defense-related appropriation for fiscal 1982 was expected to include at least another $5 billion in supplemental appropriations that were to be requested in early 1982, largely to pay for annual federal pay hikes.

Reagan originally requested $222 billion in new budget authority for Defense Department programs in fiscal 1982 — almost $26 billion over the January request of President Carter. (These figures included expected supplementals, but did not include the Energy Department's nuclear weapons budget.) But as part of his effort to trim the deficit, Reagan in October reduced his defense request to $214 billion, an $8 billion cut from his March estimates.

The $8 billion cut in budget authority was needed in order to reduce actual defense outlays by $2 billion in fiscal

1982. Reagan decided in September to cut his projections for defense outlays by $13 billion over fiscal years 1982-84: $2 billion in 1982, $5 billion in 1983 and $6 billion in 1984.

The Budget Crunch

House Defense Appropriations Subcommittee Chairman Joseph P. Addabbo, D-N.Y., who frequently charged the Pentagon with profligacy, told the House Dec. 15 that neither Congress nor the White House had been willing to cut "irrelevant and wasteful programs" from the fiscal 1982 budget. But continued budgetary stringency would change that, Addabbo predicted.

"Next year and especially in the following years, a severe shortage of dollars will force pruning of programs that are not cost effective and absolutely essential," Addabbo said.

The managers of the bill in the Senate, though not sharing Addabbo's enthusiasm for cutting the increases planned by the administration, agreed that the buildup begun by HR 4995 cast a massive shadow over future federal budgets.

"The groundwork here is laid ... for the need to appropriate great sums of money that are going to start coming due in a big way the second year, the third year, and the fourth year," the Senate was told by John C. Stennis, D-Miss., senior Democrat on the Defense Appropriations panel.

Defense Subcommittee Chairman Ted Stevens, R-Alaska, agreed with Stennis, saying that the bill portended "funding crises in ... 1983, 1984 and 1985, which will be substantial."

To illustrate the looming problem, Stennis cited the administration's well publicized commitment — which was endorsed by HR 4995 — to build a 600-ship Navy by the 1990s. "To carry out to its ultimate form this 600-ship Navy that we glibly at times talk about," he said, "we are getting up to [annual appropriations of] $22 [billion] and $24 billion to complete that by the year 2000."

The shipbuilding appropriation in HR 4995 was just over one-third that amount ($8.8 billion).

Congressional Challenge

During House and Senate debate on the bill earlier in the year, it had been evident that concern over the defense spending increase was not confined to traditional critics of the military. Senior Republicans in both houses had expressed doubts the Pentagon budget had been subjected to the rigorous scrutiny that was applied during the year to domestic programs.

The Senate Dec. 3 had rejected an amendment that would have cut 2 percent ($1.73 billion) from the procurement and research programs. The vote then was 36-57. But numbered among the "yeas" were 21 Republicans. *(Vote 435, p. 71-S)*

On Nov. 18 the House came within five votes (197-202) of supporting a similar amendment sponsored by Marge Roukema, R-N.J. But that vote was taken on a procedural matter rather than on the amendment itself, and the amendment appeared to be the focus of complex tactical maneuvering. Both factors made it hard to assess the actual breadth of House support for the Roukema amendment. *(Vote 302, p. 98-H)*

When the House voted Dec. 14 to close its conference sessions on HR 4995 to the public, Roukema offered a motion to instruct the House conferees not to increase the bill's funding for procurement or research and develop-

ment above the amounts previously approved by the House. The motion was adopted by voice vote.

For procurement, the bill appropriated $64.84 billion — $881.3 million more than the House-passed amount but $1.285 billion less than the Senate-passed amount. For research and development, the conferees agreed to $19.86 billion, $496.9 million more than the House and $987.2 million less than the Senate.

That wasn't good enough for Roukema, who voted against the conference report.

House Committee Action

As reported by the House Appropriations Committee Nov. 6 (H Rept 97-333), HR 4995 appropriated $196,607,809,000 for defense programs, $4.27 billion less than the administration's October budget request.

Characteristically, the committee's cut was accounted for by hundreds of reductions, many of which involved no

---

Multi-Year Contract Risks

The House Appropriations Committee sounded a cautionary note against the general enthusiasm in the two Armed Services committees for multi-year contracting to procure major weapons systems.

During House debate on the fiscal 1982 defense authorization bill, the Defense Appropriations Subcommittee had failed in an effort to impose tighter congressional controls on the procedure. *(Authorization bill, p. 212)*

Multi-year contracts covered the total number of weapons of a given type the Pentagon expected to buy over a period of several years.

Proponents, notably the House Armed Services Committee, insisted that the multi-year approach would reduce weapons costs by allowing contractors to plan stable, more efficient production runs and by letting them buy raw materials and components in large lots at correspondingly lower prices.

In its report on the defense appropriations bill (HR 4995), the House Appropriations panel warned that the projected savings would not occur automatically, and that they could dissolve into major losses if the cost of inflation far exceeded the contract estimates or if overall budget pressures drove an administration to cut back the size of the contract.

The committee also warned that the total amount of money future Congresses would be committed to appropriate to get the equipment into the field might not be revealed by a multi-year contract. That was because the contract would not cover some equipment — such as engines for airplanes — that would be needed to make the weapons operational.

Like the authorizing committees, the Appropriations panel approved the funds requested to begin a multi-year contract for the F-16 fighter ($249.2 million) and a Navy transport plane ($5 million).

But the committees denied a $126 million request to sign a multi-year contract for the Army's UH-60 troop-carrying helicopter. House Appropriations said the helicopter's price was too unstable to be predictable over several years.

---

more than a few million dollars. None of the changes involved dramatic policy disputes with the administration. Many involved relatively technical issues and some of the largest involved what the committee insisted was "waste, fraud and abuse."

Strategic War

As reported to the floor, HR 4995 essentially approved the Reagan strategic weapons plan, which called for production of the B-1 bomber and an interim basing system for MX intercontinental missiles, announced Oct. 2.

Intercontinental Missiles

The Defense Subcommittee voted Oct. 28 by a one-vote margin to cancel the MX missile. But that decision was narrowly overridden in the full committee Nov. 16, on a 25-23 vote.

The move to restore $1.9 billion for development of the MX missile was led by Jack Edwards, Ala., senior Republican on the Defense Subcommittee. Edwards long had been skeptical about the MX basing plan dropped by Reagan, under which each missile would have been shuttled at random among several hidden launch sites in order to forestall a Soviet missile attack on the MXs. But he urged the committee to support development of the missile itself.

If MX were developed, Reagan's plan to put the first few dozen of the missiles in existing "superhardened" launch silos, while looking for a more effective permanent basing system, made sense, Edwards added.

The amendment was supported by John P. Murtha, D-Pa., who said he had voted against MX in the Defense Subcommittee but had been persuaded by former Defense Secretary Harold Brown to reverse his position. Like Brown — and every senior Air Force officer who had testified on the subject since Reagan's Oct. 2 decision — Murtha still supported the original shuttle version of MX.

But, Murtha told the panel, Brown had convinced him that it was necessary to move toward replacing existing Minuteman ICBMs with new missiles, even if the new technique for basing them was no safer than existing silos.

Jack F. Kemp, R-N.Y., added a diplomatic argument for continuing with MX. If the United States appeared to shrink from developing a new land-based missile for domestic political reasons, he said, some West European governments might yield to strong domestic pressure to cancel the planned deployment on their territory of U.S. missiles able to reach Soviet targets with nuclear warheads.

Only Addabbo argued against the Edwards amendment during the relatively brief debate. It was pointless to fund the program until the administration proposed a basing technique that would protect the missiles against Soviet attack, he maintained.

Addabbo noted that his subcommittee had approved several items aimed at modernizing the U.S. missile force and protecting land-based missiles. Among them, the subcommittee approved the request to develop a larger submarine-launched missile ($240 million).

The subcommittee also added to the bill $89.6 million to modernize the existing Minuteman force. Of that increase, $44.6 million was to continue production of the Mark-12A warhead to replace smaller and less accurate warheads on some Minuteman missiles. The remaining $35 million was earmarked for a program to equip Minuteman silos with long-life batteries so the silos could operate for

days after commercial power was cut off, which might happen in a nuclear war.

Aided by Murtha, who lobbied fellow Democrats, Edwards won on a 25-23 vote, essentially with a coalition of Republicans and Southern Democrats.

Republicans supported the amendment 15-5. Three of the five GOP "no" votes came from members who were associated with the so-called "Gypsy Moths" — moderate Republicans who had complained that the administration was cutting too deeply into domestic programs and funding too large a boost in defense appropriations.

Voting to restore the MX money were:

Democrats (10) — Tom Bevill, Ala.; Bill Chappell Jr., Fla.; John P. Murtha, Pa.; Charles Wilson, Texas.; Lindy (Mrs. Hale) Boggs, La.; Norman D. Dicks, Wash.; Bo Ginn, Ga.; Jack Hightower, Texas; Daniel K. Akaka, Hawaii; Wes Watkins, Okla.

Republicans (15) — Joseph M. McDade, Pa.; Edwards; John T. Myers, Ind.; J. Kenneth Robinson, Va.; Clarence E. Miller, Ohio; C. W. Bill Young, Fla.; Jack F. Kemp, N.Y.; Ralph Regula, Ohio; Clair W. Burgener, Calif.; George M. O'Brien, Ill.; Mickey Edwards, Okla.; Bob Livingston, La.; Tom Loeffler, Texas; Jerry Lewis, Calif.; Carroll A. Campbell Jr., S.C.

Voting not to restore the MX money were:

Democrats (18) — Jamie L. Whitten, Miss.; Edward P. Boland, Mass.; William H. Natcher, Ky.; Neal Smith, Iowa; Joseph P. Addabbo, N.Y.; Clarence D. Long, Md.; Sydney R. Yates, Ill.; David R. Obey, Wis.; Edward R. Roybal, Calif.; Bill Alexander, Ark.; Joseph D. Early, Mass.; Adam Benjamin Jr., Ind.; Matthew F. McHugh, N.Y.; Martin Olav Sabo, Minn.; Julian C. Dixon, Calif.; Les AuCoin, Ore.; Bernard J. Dwyer, N.J.; Bob Traxler, Mich.

Republicans (5) — Lawrence Coughlin, Pa.; Virginia Smith, Neb.; Carl D. Pursell, Mich.; Bill Green, N.Y.; John Edward Porter, Ill.

As a result of that vote, the committee approved the full $1,913,200,000 request for MX research and development. Of that amount, $1.349 billion was for research and development on the MX missile itself and $546.2 million was for research and development on a basing system for the missile.

House Appropriations did not place restrictions on the use of basing research funds.

The panel approved the authorizing committees' proposal to increase to $100 million funds for ballistic missile research not expressly connected with MX. The Appropriations panel gave no reason for the increase, but the intent of the authorizing committees was to use much of the addition to continue research on the kind of mobile missile system President Carter proposed for MX and which Reagan killed Oct. 2.

The Appropriations panel also added to the bill $44.6 million to continue producing more powerful warheads (called Mark 12As) for the existing Minuteman ICBM and $35 million to equip Minuteman silos with a long-enduring emergency power supply.

B-1 Bomber

The committee recommended $2.092 billion of the $2.423 billion requested for the B-1 bomber program. Of the $330.1 million reduction, $151 million in procurement was mandated by the authorization bill.

The Appropriations panel cut an additional $179.1 million from the $471 million requested for development, directing the Air Force to replace the cut with a like amount appropriated but not spent for the B-1 in fiscal 1981.

Ground Combat

The panel approved the $1.348 billion request for 665 M-1 tanks and the $800 million allowed by the authorization bill for 600 M-2 armored infantry carriers, a $9.8 million reduction from the request.

Citing the steadily increasing cost of the M-2 ($11.8 billion for the projected fleet, compared with $1.3 billion estimated in 1977), the committee ordered the Army to conduct "side-by-side field tests" comparing the M-2 with several other armored vehicles that might perform some or all of the missions projected for the fleet of M-2s.

Anti-Aircraft Defense

Like the authorizing committees, House Appropriations disapproved several cutbacks in anti-aircraft missile procurement proposed in October.

For the long-range Patriot missile, it approved the $50 million reduction made in the authorization bill (providing $670 million).

The administration wanted to cancel outright the short-range Roland missile. But the committee added $50 million to the budget request to fund procurement of a limited number of European-designed Roland launchers earmarked to accompany units of the Rapid Deployment Force.

The panel also refused an Air Force proposal to slow procurement of the British-made Rapier short-range missile intended to defend U.S. bases in Britain. It recommended $148.3 million for Rapier procurement, $38.2 million more than the October request.

Remotely Piloted Vehicles

Both the Army and the Air Force were dragging their feet in developing "remotely piloted vehicles" (RPVs), the committee charged. RPVs were very small and relatively inexpensive radio-controlled airplanes — like those flown by hobbyists — that could carry television cameras to spot enemy targets, laser beams to designate targets for guided missiles, or explosive warheads and detectors to home in on enemy radars.

The committee refused an Army proposal to cut in half (to $36.4 million) its March budget request for RPV development. The panel recommended $73.3 million for the program. It also expressed its displeasure with the Air Force's announced intention to drop a RPV program that had begun as a joint venture with West Germany but from which Bonn had withdrawn.

NATO Involvements

As it had previously done, the panel recommended two steps affecting U.S. cooperation with its NATO allies:

● It deleted $39.8 million of the $69.1 million requested to pay claims filed by West German citizens for property damage caused by U.S. units during training maneuvers. This was one more move in the committee's two-year-long campaign to force the executive branch to renegotiate the current claims settlement procedure, which, it believed, accepted claims too readily.

● It added to the bill a provision to block Pentagon plans to store more than the four divisions-worth of tanks and other heavy equipment stockpiled in Europe for Army units that would be flown from the United States in case of a crisis. Two more of these so-called POMCUS stockpiles were planned; that would allow the United States to move six divisions to Europe in less than three weeks.

U.S. forces equivalent to about five divisions were permanently stationed in Europe.

The committee warned that the equipment in the European POMCUS sites might be vulnerable to a sudden Soviet attack. Moreover, it complained, equipment for those stockpiles was drawn from Reserve and National Guard units, thus impairing their combat readiness.

The panel also objected that units with their equipment stored in Europe could not easily be deployed to other areas. It endorsed a fleet of high-speed cargo ships that could quickly deploy divisions with their heavy equipment from the United States to Europe, the Persian Gulf or other areas.

Rapid Deployment Force

In a section of the report approved during full committee action on HR 4995, the panel warned that plans to deploy U.S. forces near the Persian Gulf — the so-called Rapid Deployment Force (RDF) — depended too heavily on uncertain assumptions that countries in the area would allow U.S. use of their facilities.

"We strongly suggest that these assumptions be replaced with formal agreements or appropriate understandings as soon as possible," the panel said.

The administration had been reluctant to attempt to force nations such as Egypt to sign formal agreements that might create political problems for their leaders.

Agreements had been negotiated with Oman, Kenya and Somalia.

Transport Planes

Like the other three congressional defense panels, House Appropriations gave no support to the proposal to develop a new long-range transport plane called the C-17 (formerly the CX) designed to carry heavy combat equipment to poorly equipped airstrips. It denied the $169.7 million request for CX and added $50 million to begin procuring existing transport planes.

The committee rejected a proposal by Bill Alexander, D-Ark., to remove from the report an injunction to kill the C-17. The C-17 would have been built by the St. Louis-based McDonnell-Douglas Corp., which had a plant in Alexander's district.

Alexander's effort to keep the C-17 alive was vigorously opposed by Bo Ginn, D-Ga. The most likely substitute for the C-17 was the Lockheed Corp's C-5A, built in Marietta, Ga. Ginn was a candidate for the 1982 Georgia gubernatorial nomination.

The committee also ordered the Air Force to prepare a $38 million field test in fiscal 1983 of its plans to "surge" the flying tempo of its 77 huge C-5A transport planes in wartime. Plans called for each plane to be flown about 12.5 hours a day for the first 45 days of a crisis instead of the existing daily average of 1.7 hours.

The panel appeared skeptical that the Air Force had enough spare parts, replacement crews and maintenance personnel to increase the big planes' operating tempo by that much.

The committee added $220 million for four KC-10A midair refueling tanker planes — versions of the DC-10 jetliner. The administration had requested eight planes in March, but suggested canceling the program in October.

Transport Ships

The panel approved the amount allowed by the au-

thorization bill to convert a fleet of high-speed cargo ships (called SL-7s) into transports for an Army division — $184 million of the $668.4 million requested.

For more than a year, the committee and the Navy had dueled over how to modify the ships, with the panel favoring a partial conversion that was less costly than the Navy plan to convert the ships to "roll-on, roll-off" (RO-RO) vessels.

The committee said its plan would save money and time; the Navy insisted that the ships would actually deliver combat units to the field much more quickly if tanks and other vehicles could be driven on and off the ships, instead of being hoisted on and off by cranes.

In its report on HR 4995, the committee ordered the Navy to convert one of the eight ships to a partial RO-RO design and to make only slight modifications to four others.

Naval Forces

To buy components for a planned nuclear-powered aircraft carrier, the committee recommended $475 million of the $658 million requested. The $183 million reduction was possible, according to the committee, because the administration decided in October to request the $3.5 billion ship in fiscal 1984 instead of fiscal 1983.

The panel also rejected a request for $22 million to study the possible reactivation of mothballed aircraft carriers. Reactivation of one of the ships — the *Oriskany* — had been proposed by the administration in March, but was abandoned in October, partly because all the congressional defense panels except House Armed Services opposed the move.

The panel approved the request for funds to reactivate two battleships: $237 million to complete reactivation of the *New Jersey* and $90 million to begin work on the *Iowa*.

The committee also funded two ships the authorizing committees had added to the administration request — a third escort frigate, in addition to two requested (for an addition of $178.2 million) and a large amphibious landing ship called an LSD-41 for which the administration had only requested some components (an increase of $267 million).

The panel also cut a total of $143 million from the reserve accounts for future cost growth in ongoing ship contracts.

In a potentially far-reaching decision, the committee told the Navy to cut almost in half the number of ships it planned to equip with LAMPS III anti-submarine helicopters. The committee complained that the cost of modifying existing ships to carry the helicopter and its associated equipment had more than doubled. In HR 4995, the committee's decision meant a reduction of $20 million.

On an amendment by David R. Obey, D-Wis., the committee deleted $34.9 million to develop a radio transmitter (called ELF, for extremely low frequency) designed to communicate with submerged submarines.

The ELF antenna was to consist of more than 100 miles of wire strung from telephone poles in Obey's district and in the district of Bob Traxler, D-Mich., who cosponsored the amendment. Many residents of those two districts had opposed the plan.

Obey and Traxler argued that the proposed sytem would not survive the first blow of a nucler war and that other systems were available for communicating with submarines.

Diesel Submarines

The committee added $2.5 million for the Navy to study the value of relatively small diesel-powered submarines to supplement the $500 million-a-copy nuclear powered subs of the *Los Angeles*-class, which the Navy built to search for enemy submarines.

"While the committee recognizes that for many demanding missions, there is no substitute for nuclear submarines, there may well be missions for which lower cost diesel vessels are capable, thus freeing nuclear submarines for missions to which they are uniquely suited," the committee said.

It expressly ordered the Navy to evaluate the blueprints of a small sub currently built in West Germany.

Tactical Aircraft

For Air Force combat planes, the committee approved essentially the program included in the authorization bill:
- 36 F-15 fighters ($980.2 million), a reduction of 6 planes (and $111.6 million) from the budget request;
- 120 F-16 fighters ($1.27 billion), a reduction of $60.8 million from the request; and
- 20 A-10 anti-tank bombers ($209.7 million), a $40 million cut from the budget.

The panel cut a total of $162.2 million from the $6.2 billion request for Navy combat planes. Most of the reductions came from the purchase of components for planes to be funded in fiscal 1983; the cuts were made because the administration planned to cut back the production rate of several models.

Personnel

The committee's detailed scrutiny of the budget — and its willingness to enforce its judgments by making substantial budget reductions — was evident in its version of the bill's $37 billion military personnel title.

Bonuses

One of the largest single changes in the bill — a cut of $397.9 million — reflected the committee's position that re-enlistment bonuses ought to be paid in installments, rather than in a lump sum at the start of the re-enlistment.

The Pentagon claimed that it got more re-enlistments for a given amount of money with the lump sum techniques used since 1979. The House committee disagreed, saying in its report: "If the bonus is given all at once, it creates a 'what have you done for me lately' syndrome after the first year of re-enlistment, when the individual no longer receives extra pay, but is serving a [longer] tour."

On a similarly detailed judgment, the committee turned down (for the third year in a row) a proposal to pay a cost-of-living allowance to enlisted personnel stationed abroad who lived in barracks.

Such an allowance was paid to overseas personnel who lived off bases and had to provide their own meals. The Pentagon argued that extension of the payment would improve troop morale by enabling troops to afford recreation off the bases.

But House Appropriations refused the proposal, citing the investment in providing recreational facilities on the bases. The reduction amounted to $26 million.

Waste, Fraud and Abuse

The committee cut nearly half a billion dollars from personnel accounts on grounds that the amounts could be saved by reforming various practices that executive branch or congressional auditors had branded as mismanagement, waste, fraud or abuse.

The panel cut $216.5 million from the $3 billion request for travel and transportation costs associated with personnel transfers from one duty station to another.

From the $2.6 billion request for feeding troops who live in barracks and paying subsistence allowances to other military personnel, the committee cut $134.8 million.

From the request for quarters allowances in the Navy alone, the committee cut $111 million.

Recruiting Costs

As it had done for several years since the end of the draft, the committee cut the budget request for recruiting operations (including advertising) on grounds that the Pentagon was looking for manpower in a buyers' market. The $1.3 billion request was cut by $100 million.

The panel explained its action by citing the services' success in meeting their recruitment goals, the shortage of jobs for young men in the private sector, the increased retention of senior enlisted personnel (which reduced the requirement for new recruits) and the recently enacted increases in military pay and benefits.

Guard, Reserves

As traditionally had been the case, the committee added funds to equip Reserve and National Guard units with more modern equipment.

It cut a total of $250 million from various appropriations of each service to fund part of this accelerated modernization. Among the equipment added to the bill for Guard and Reserve use were 12 Cobra anti-tank helicopters ($55 million), eight C-130 transport planes ($109.5 million) and six two-seat trainer versions of the A-7 light bomber ($121.7 million).

Addition of the A-7 funds was conditioned on their being authorized; the 1982 defense authorization bill (S 815) deleted all funds for the plane.

The committee also ordered the Navy to keep in service four minesweepers and two destroyers manned partly by reservists. The ships had been earmarked for retirement in Reagan's October budget cuts ($9.2 million). The authorization bill went along with the administration cuts.

The panel also added $20 million to improve the maintenance of Navy Reserve aircraft and another $20 million to expand the Navy Reserve from 87,600 to 94,000 personnel.

No-Shows. But the Reserves were not immune to the committee's vigilance in searching for waste and inefficiency. The panel cut $34.5 million from Guard and Reserve personnel appropriations, an amount it estimated would otherwise be paid to personnel who did not attend mandatory unit drills.

"While the Appropriations Committee has traditionally been a supporter of a strong Guard and Reserve force, this support does not extend to pay practices which border on outright fraud," the panel declared.

Operations, Maintenance

The committee rejected some of the administration's October budget cuts that would have reduced the number of U.S. combat units (or reduced the number deployed in vital areas).

It restored $100 million of the $173 million cut in October from the Navy's ship operating budget. The October reduction resulted from a decision that only one aircraft carrier would steam near the Persian Gulf at all times, instead of two, as had been the case for nearly two years.

The committee also added $81 million to continue operating the oldest squadrons of B-52 bombers — the "D" models. In its October budget amendment, the administration proposed retiring those planes several years earlier than had been planned.

The committee warned the administration to drop its October proposal to partly demobilize for three years the Army's 7th Infantry Division at Fort Ord, Calif., beginning in fiscal 1983.

Permanent abolition of a division — with its troops and equipment parceled out to beef up other units — might make sense, the panel said, but a temporary cutback would realize no savings over the long-run.

Saudi Support

The panel cut $18.2 million budgeted to pay the cost of operating four U.S. AWACS radar-warning planes in Saudi Arabia.

Though the Saudi government provided fuel for the planes and food and housing for their U.S. crews, extra training in combat operations was needed to make up for time spent in routine patrols. The committee suggested that the Saudis be billed for that cost.

Waste, Fraud, Abuse

The committee recommended several reductions in the Pentagon's operating budget, including the following:

● Arguing that the budget had overestimated fuel price increases, the panel cut $490 million from the $10.5 billion fuel appropriation.

● The panel cut by 50 percent ($86.7 million) the amount requested by the Pentagon to pay "rent" to the General Services Administration (GSA), the federal government's property management office. In its report, the committee charged GSA with gouging the Defense Department — which must ask Congress for funds to build its own facilities — and then using the Pentagon payments to build office space for civilian federal agencies.

● Citing audits critical of various Pentagon supply and logistics programs, the committee cut $54.2 million from the operations accounts.

"Duplication, overlapping and even waste abounds in this area, and attempts by the [office of the secretary of defense] to make improvements in supply management and reduce costs have met with great resistance on the part of the military services," the panel complained.

Medical Programs

The committee used the report to reiterate its complaint that the services spent far too much on medical programs and facilities that did not directly serve troops in the field.

The committee had focused much of its criticism on large military hospitals — such as Letterman Army Hospi-

tal in San Francisco and Fitzsimons Army Hospital in suburban Denver — that had relatively low occupancy rates, particularly for active duty military personnel.

"Department of Defense health officials have stated that the government is wasting money in some of these underutilized areas because of political pressure," the report said.

According to the committee, more than 100 military hospitals had occupancy rates of less than 80 percent; 30 had occupancy rates of less than 67 percent, which was the standard used by the Reagan administration to recommend closure of several Public Health Service hospitals earlier in the year.

"But not a single military hospital is even being considered for closure," the panel protested.

The committee also criticized the services for assigning too many of their physicians to teaching and research positions far removed from active duty military units.

"Five percent of Army hospitals employ or teach 60 percent of Army physicians," the panel said. "Most of these large hospitals ... are located in large cities and are not near posts with major troop concentrations. This results in a significant proportion of the patients treated in these centers being retirees, their dependents, and other secondary beneficiaries."

House Floor Action

President Reagan's Nov. 18 nuclear arms reduction proposal dominated House debate over three nuclear weapons when HR 4995 came to the floor later the same day. *(Text of address, p. 27-E)*

Under that proposal, Reagan offered to cancel U.S. plans to deploy intermediate-range nuclear missiles in Europe if the Soviet Union would dismantle its equivalent missiles. Negotiations on the so-called "theater nuclear force" missiles began in Geneva Nov. 30.

At the outset of the nine-hour-long debate, Jack Edwards summarized the argument that repeatedly prevailed on the House floor: "[Reagan] must go to the bargaining table with chips in his pocket to deal with. We simply cannot at this time consider cutting back or terminating or doing away with or slowing down the MX, ... the B-1, ... the Pershing II's ... and the ground-launched cruise missiles."

Minority Leader Robert H. Michel, R-Ill., made a strong pitch for the weapons: "They are not merely weapons systems," he declared. "They are instruments of peace. They are instruments of negotiation."

Skepticism. Addabbo, who tried to strike production funds for the B-1 bomber and Pershing missiles and research money for the MX, countered that each of them would be seen by Soviet negotiators as a hollow threat because of their respective technical inadequacies.

"What is a bargaining chip?" he demanded. "A bargaining chip is something that can be used. The Russians know what can be used and what cannot be used," Addabbo said. "An MX for which we have no basing mode cannot be used and therefore is not much of a bargaining chip," he concluded.

Ted Weiss, D-N.Y., protested in somewhat stronger terms than Addabbo: "Here we are on the day when the president of the United States is engaging in a peace offensive and in justification of that peace offensive we are asked ... to adopt every worthless, counterproductive, obsolete program in the books."

B-1 Debate

Presenting his amendment to remove $1.8 billion in procurement money for the B-1, Addabbo called the plane "a bummer of a bomber." Not only would it not long be able to penetrate Soviet air defenses, he warned, but it would drain funds from development of a "stealth" bomber that Soviet radar defenses could not intercept. "This country cannot afford to develop both the B-1 and the stealth," he said.

Edwards insisted he would prefer to move directly from the B-52 to stealth, skipping procurement of the B-1, but that he could not guarantee that the radical new plane could be delivered on schedule.

C. W. Bill Young, R-Fla., was more definite: "This paper airplane in my hand is really the only stealth bomber we have now or will have in the near future. We do not know whether it is going to be ready in 1990 or 1995 or ever."

By a vote of 99-307, the House rejected a substitute amendment by Murtha that was similar to Addabbo's but which was designed as part of a strategy to modernize and enlarge 155 F-111 fighters already in service as an alternative to producing B-1s. *(Vote 298, p. 98-H)*

The House then rejected Addabbo's amendment 142-263. Only 21 Republicans supported the amendment, most of them liberals. Liberal Democrats accounted for most of the amendment's supporters. *(Vote 299, p. 98-H)*

Nuclear Missiles

Despite relatively widespread congressional skepticism about the convoluted logic of nuclear war theories that had dominated earlier debates about the MX missile, Addabbo was no more successful in blocking funding for that program.

Addabbo argued that continued work on the missile should await final selection of a basing mode — which Reagan had deferred until 1984 — because the final design of the missile would be affected by whether it was to be dropped from an airplane or stuffed in a silo.

But the bargaining-chip argument pervaded the debate on the amendment. Despite arguments that the proposed interim deployment of MXs in hardened silos would not really be safe from Soviet attack, the program should be funded because of the imminent arms negotiations, argued Ed Bethune, R-Ark.

The silo system "is plausible enough ... that it will be perceived as a viable option when they do go to the [negotiating] table," Bethune maintained. "The question is: What will Congress do today? Is the Congress going to vote for strength or is the Congress going to vote for weakness?" Bethune asked.

Addabbo's MX amendment was rejected by a slightly larger margin than his B-1 amendment: 139-264. *(Vote 300, p. 98-H)*

As with the earlier amendment, only a handful of Republicans supported the MX cut.

Theater Missiles

With the bargaining-chip argument dominating discussion, the House rejected by voice vote another Addabbo amendment that would have deleted $218.9 million to begin procurement of Pershing II missiles. The missile was one of two U.S. weapons at the core of the negotiations on limitations of nuclear missiles in Europe.

Addabbo later announced that he would not offer a planned amendment to delete procurement funds for the

ground-launched cruise missile, the other U.S. weapon at stake in the arms talks.

"No one is listening to the facts," he complained.

Budget-Cutting

The House juggled simultaneously three proposals for across-the-board reductions in the bill:

• Patricia Schroeder, D-Colo., proposed an amendment cutting 5 percent of the amount appropriated by the bill — about $10 billion.

• Toby Moffett, D-Conn., proposed a substitute to Schroeder's amendment cutting 2 percent and limiting the cut to the accounts for procurement and research and development. None of the resulting $1.6 billion spending cut could be taken from accounts for spare parts.

• Marge Roukema, R-N.J., offered a substitute for the Schroeder amendment that was similar to Moffett's proposal but added ammunition and repair parts to the list of accounts that would be protected against any reduction.

Moffett's amendment was rejected 140-256. *(Vote 301, p. 98-H)*

But the motion to substitute Roukema's proposal for Schroeder's failed by only five votes: 197-202. In part, the close vote was accounted for by 46 Republicans who opposed Moffet's amendment but supported Roukema's. *(Vote 302, p. 98-H)*

The Roukema substitute having been rejected, the original Schroeder amendment was rejected by voice vote.

Because of the tactical situation, it was not clear whether the closeness of the Roukema vote indicated widespread support for a slight cutback in defense spending.

On the one hand, one Republican leader who opposed any reduction speculated that much of Roukema's GOP support was "sentimental," a gesture of solidarity by younger Republicans for one of their own. The 46 Republican switchers included 15 members elected in 1980 (including Roukema) and seven elected in 1978. This source speculated that several Republicans had voted so that Roukema's amendment would come close, but would lose.

But on the other hand, the GOP switchers also included several relatively senior members. In a statement inserted in the *Congressional Record*, one of them, Bill Frenzel, R-Minn., said his support for Roukema was intended "to warn the Defense Department that, unless it demonstrates a real commitment to reduce wasteful, unnecessary spending, it will lose the strong coalition that now supports the strengthening of our defense."

Increases

The Appropriations Committee accepted without debate a series of amendments offered by senior members of the Armed Services Committee that added $957.2 million to various accounts in HR 4995. The increases were for programs included in the conference report on the fiscal 1982 defense authorization bill (S 815). The fate of the programs had been doubtful when the Defense Subcommittee marked up the appropriations bill.

Addabbo and Jack Edwards, R-Ala., senior Republican on the Defense Subcommittee, later said that the increase was about half as large as the increases Armed Services members had planned to propose. The lower figure had been negotiated to avoid a floor fight between the two committees.

Among the Appropriations cuts restored by the Armed Services amendments were the following:

• $60 million that had been cut by the Appropriations

Committee from the Army budget for recruitment;

• $83.5 million that had been transferred from various appropriations to speed up the modernization of National Guard and Reserve forces;

• $216 million that had been cut from the shipbuilding account, including $143 million cut from funds given to Navy contract managers to pay for unforeseen cost increases.

The Appropriations panel also accepted an Armed Services amendment dropping a provision that would have limited the effect of the recently enacted military pay raise on military pensions.

And the House adopted by voice vote an amendment by Edwards deleting the $121 million the committee had added for A-7 aircraft for the National Guard. The planes were not included in the final version of the authorization bill.

Other Amendments

The House adopted four other amendments by voice vote:

• By Samuel S. Stratton, D-N.Y., to prohibit the transfer from a government-owned defense plant to a foreign government of any defense equipment or technical data packages to manufacture weapons.

• By Allen E. Ertel, D-Pa., to prohibit the use of funds to provide personal servants, cooks or chauffeurs for Defense Department officials and to prohibit the purchase of passenger cars rated by the Environmental Protection Agency as having a fuel consumption rate of less than 22 miles per gallon.

• By William D. Ford, D-Mich., to delete a provision limiting pay raises for teachers in the schools for military dependents abroad.

• By Patricia Schroeder, D-Colo., raising from 30 to 33 the number of senior civilian executive positions in the Defense Department.

The House rejected two amendments:

• By Ed Weber, R-Ohio, to delete a pay cap on civilian technicians attached to National Guard and Reserve units. Rejected by a standing vote of 55-76.

• By Thomas M. Foglietta, D-Pa., to prohibit for one year contracting out to private firms security and firefighting jobs at defense installations currently held by federal employees. Rejected by standing vote of 83-85.

Senate Committee Action

As reported (S Rept 97-273) by the Senate Appropriations Committee Nov. 17, S 1857 appropriated $208.5 billion for defense. This was $7.641 billion more than Reagan's revised budget and $11.1 billion more than the amount approved Nov. 18 by the House in HR 4995.

Appropriations Committee Chairman Mark O. Hatfield, R-Ore., opened the panel's markup of the defense money bill Nov. 16 by calling it "neither sound nor fiscally responsible."

Reviewing the deep cuts the committee had made in domestic programs, Hatfield protested that nearly three-fourths of the savings would be offset by the defense subcommittee's $7.5 billion addition to the Reagan request.

"That same federal dollar which is deprived from the human services programs is used instead to feed the voracious appetite of the military," Hatfield said.

Subcommittee Chairman Ted Stevens, R-Alaska, countered that most of the increase simply reflected pre-

dictable cost increases not included in the budget. Moreover, he argued, a higher Senate appropriation was needed to give the Senate bargaining leverage against the lower House-passed figure in the conference on the bill.

Different Approaches

As had been the usual case for years, the Senate panel was more hesitant than its House counterpart in enforcing its judgments by deleting money in order to block programs. In many cases, the two panels simply disagreed on the merits of an issue.

As an example, the House committee had deleted $397.9 million to force the services to pay re-enlistment bonuses in increments spread over the term of re-enlistment, rather than in a lump sum at the start of the new tour of duty. The Senate panel restored the amount, arguing that surveys showed larger single bonus payments were more effective inducements to re-enlist.

In other cases, the Senate committee apparently agreed with the House position but challenged the prudence of its tactics.

For instance, as it had done in prior years, the House panel reduced the budget request for claims payments to West German civilians for damage to property caused by U.S. units engaged in NATO exercises. That committee had insisted that the executive branch renegotiate the claims settlement arrangement.

The Senate panel urged the departments of State and Defense to actively pursue "opportunities for greater cost-sharing between the United States and our allies," but restored the money cut by the House.

Research Limits

The Senate panel took as hard a line as its House counterpart on the research and development budget. The committee said it decided to terminate programs that offered "marginal" military advantages or that had the practical effect of absorbing funds that might be spent on more critical projects.

"The committee has chosen to terminate or re-structure ... [such] programs rather than 'nickel and dime' necessary programs across the board," the report said.

The most expensive casualty of this approach was the Air Force's C-17 transport plane (formerly called CX), which received what apparently was the final blow in a two-year-long string of rejections by all four congressional defense committees. The committee denied the entire $169.7 million request for C-17 or CX development.

Also rejected in toto was the $69.8 million request for SOTAS, an Army radar mounted in a helicopter to detect moving vehicles behind enemy lines.

The committee acknowledged the importance of the jobs the two systems were designed to do but concluded that each was far too expensive for the extent to which it improved U.S. combat capability.

'Truth' and Tactics

Three additions that reflected both a budgetary policy and a legislative tactic accounted for much of the committee bill's addition to Reagan's total request.

The policy was "truth-in-budgeting:" the assumption that the budget ought to reflect reasonably foreseeable costs. The tactic, designed by Stevens, was to go into conference with a bill that exceeded Reagan's request by roughly the amount by which the House-passed bill was below the budget.

Pay Raise. To pay for the fiscal 1982 pay raise passed by Congress in October, which averaged 14.3 percent, $4.8 billion was added to the bill.

Traditionally, the pay raise that took effect at the start of each fiscal year was funded in the supplemental appropriations bill adopted the following spring, about halfway through the fiscal year, rather than in the regular defense money bill. The Senate panel argued that funding the pay raise in the regular appropriations bill would clearly display the cost of Reagan's defense buildup and would protect military programs against having to absorb a portion of the pay raise cost in case the supplemental was cut.

Inflation. The committee also boosted the appropriations for operations and maintenance, procurement, and research and development by $1.6 billion. That action was based on the assumption that inflation would increase those costs by 10 percent, an amount the committee called "moderate" but "more realistic" than the 8.4 percent assumed by the Reagan administration.

Administrations routinely were optimistic in their inflation estimates, warning that a public projection of high inflation to come would be self-fulfilling. But the Appropriations panel complained that the fiscal 1981 defense budget had, in effect, cut defense programs by underestimating inflation costs. Since these costs had to be absorbed within existing budget levels, the effect was the same as if the budget had been cut $2 billion below the level enacted.

Cost Growth. The amounts approved for the B-1 and the MX were increased by a total of some $152 million in anticipation that the cost of those projects would increase by 3 percent above and beyond the cost of inflation. This represented the average "cost-growth" (beyond inflation) in a number of major weapons programs studied by the Defense Subcommittee.

When the full Appropriations Committee marked up the bill, this cost-growth allowance came under fire from Hatfield and senior Democrat William Proxmire, D-Wis. — both frequent critics of Pentagon spending practices. They argued that such a cushion would weaken the incentive for Pentagon managers to control costs of the two programs, thus ensuring that the higher costs predicted would in fact occur.

But Stevens prevailed, arguing that the cost increase was a practical certainty. "We can make up our minds to fund it now or fund it later," he said. If the allowance for the predictable increases was deferred, he warned, Congress would wind up paying more in the long run to get a given number of weapons.

Strategic War Forces

Nuclear war programs were funded essentially as requested, with some small but significant additions.

B-1 Fight

The committee fully funded the B-1 request and added 3 percent for higher-than-expected costs. It approved $1.958 billion for procurement and $471 million for B-1 development

In addition, the panel added $18.9 million to continue operating three squadrons of the oldest B-52 version — the "D" model. The administration decided in September to retire these planes in fiscal 1982, several years earlier than had been planned, to pare back the Pentagon budget. The Senate panel noted that the planes recently received expensive modernizations.

The House appropriations bill also restored the $18.9 million for B-52D operations and also restored $62.1 million for additional modifications to the planes.

The committee's B-1 showdown came Nov. 17 on an amendment by Hollings that would have shifted funds from the B-1 to the "stealth" bomber and several programs designed to improve the combat readiness of U.S. conventional forces. The readiness improvements would have restored ammunition procurement, troop strength, and the amount of time the Navy would keep ships at sea to the levels Reagan requested in March. Those items had been pared back in October, to reduce the fiscal 1982 deficit.

Before debating the amendment in public, committee members decided they needed a closed session to discuss secret technical and cost information about the B-1 and stealth radar-evading bombers. Stevens cautioned the panel that only a handful of the members currently were informed of much stealth information.

Cost Estimates. According to one source, the secret discussion then focused on a Pentagon argument that it would cost nearly as much to keep operating the existing B-52 bombers through the year 2000 as it would to build and operate the B-1 and the stealth. In part, the estimate reflected the relatively high operating costs of the B-52, which had eight relatively old jet engines, and its maintenance costs, which were increasing with the plane's age.

According to the estimate, endorsed by Pentagon research chief Richard D. DeLauer, continued operation of the existing force of B-52s and smaller FB-111s through the end of the century would cost $93 billion, counting needed modifications to the bomber.

In July, Lt. Gen. Kelly H. Burke, chief of research and procurement for the Air Force, told the House Defense Appropriations Subcommittee that projected B-52 modifications would cost about $6 billion each for new engines and "hardening" to protect the planes' electronic equipment against the effect of a nuclear blast.

DeLauer said it would cost about $92 billion to buy and operate 200 B-1s to replace the current bomber force — less than the cost of maintaining the old planes.

The total cost for a combined fleet of B-52s and stealth planes would be $114 billion over the same period, while Reagan's proposal to phase-out the B-52s, buy 100 B-1s and later 132 stealth planes would cost $112 billion, according to the estimate.

Debate. When the committee resumed its open meeting, Hollings tried to redefine the issue away from DeLauer's long-term cost comparison. The real questions, he insisted, were whether the B-1 could prevail against Soviet air defenses for very long and whether it would divert money from other defense programs in the next few years, when budgets would be tight.

Hollings cited Defense Secretary Caspar W. Weinberger's Nov. 5 testimony to the Senate Armed Services Committee in which Weinberger repeatedly insisted that the B-1 would be unable to penetrate Soviet defenses after 1990, two years after delivery of the last of the 100 planes in Reagan's plans. Trying to fly into Soviet territory after that date would amount to a suicide mission, Weinberger had said.

Hollings also protested that Reagan's October budget revisions had reduced U.S. readiness to cope with nonnuclear wars that were more likely than a nuclear conflict.

"We're not prepared to fight a war in the Indian Ocean," from which Reagan had removed one aircraft carrier, he declared.

Referring to Congressional Budget Office estimates that the B-1 would cost $40 billion through fiscal 1986, Hollings asked: "Is [the B-1] the best way . . . to allocate this $40 billion?"

But Republicans attacked Hollings' proposal. Stevens noted that Weinberger had backed away from his 1990 estimate and later supported the Air Force position that the bomber could penetrate Soviet defenses well into the 1990s.

And Stevens stressed the long-term cost comparisons: Reagan's plan for both the B-1 and stealth would cost "only slightly more than maintaining the B-52s for the period the Senate would maintain them."

Alfonse D'Amato, R-N.Y., added a diplomatic dimension, arguing that if Reagan's plan were rejected, "we create in the mind of our adversaries [the impression] that this country is incapable of formulating a policy."

Hollings' amendment was rejected 7-21, with all Republicans voting "nay" except Hatfield and Arlen Specter, R-Pa., who voted present. Specter had insisted he needed more information about stealth before he could decide on the B-1.

Voting to delete the B-1 funding were:

Democrats (6) — William Proxmire, Wis.; Robert C. Byrd, W.Va.; Hollings; Thomas F. Eagleton, Mo.; Patrick J. Leahy, Vt.; Dale Bumpers, Ark.

Republicans (1) — Mark O. Hatfield, Ore.;

Voting against deleting the B-1 funding were:

Democrats (8) — John C. Stennis, Miss.; Daniel K. Inouye, Hawaii; Lawton Chiles, Fla.; J. Bennett Johnston, La.; Walter D. Huddleston, Ky.; Quentin N. Burdick, N.D.; Jim Sasser, Tenn.; Dennis DeConcini, Ariz.

Republicans (13) — Ted Stevens, Alaska; Lowell P. Weicker Jr., Conn.; James A. McClure, Idaho; Paul Laxalt, Nev.; Jake Garn, Utah; Harrison "Jack" Schmitt, N.M.; Thad Cochran, Miss.; Mark Andrews, N.D.; James Abdnor, S.D.; Robert W. Kasten Jr., Wis.; Alfonse D'Amato, N.Y.; Mack Mattingly, Ga.; Warren B. Rudman, N.H.

Intercontinental Missile

The committee approved $2.09 billion for MX development, including a $95 million addition to Reagan's request as a buffer against higher costs.

In direct contrast to the defense authorization bill (S 815), Appropriations allowed $10 million for study of an airborne MX launching system. Conferees on the authorization bill had prohibited research on airborne systems.

Like the House bill, S 1857 added funds to improve the existing fleet of Minuteman ICBMs. But the two bills backed different improvement programs.

Both bills added $25 million to equip Minuteman launch silos with an emergency electrical supply that could keep the silos operating for days after commercial power was cut off.

In addition, the Senate panel added $18.8 million to continue developing a system that would let some Minuteman missiles be retargeted and fired by remote control from airborne command posts. And the Senate committee added $5 million to replace 50 single-warhead Minuteman IIs with triple-warhead Minuteman IIIs now in storage. The House committee in 1980 refused to accept an identical Senate proposal. *(1980 Almanac, p. 189)*

The House bill added $44.6 million to continue production of Mark 12A nuclear warheads as larger and more accurate replacements for the warheads already on some Minuteman missiles.

Department of Defense Appropriations, Fiscal 1982

Following are the Department of Defense appropriations in fiscal 1982 under HR 4995, including President Reagan's revised request, the amounts approved by the House and Senate, and the final amount:

Program	Administration Request	House-Passed Amount	Senate-Passed Amount	Final Amount
Personnel	$ 38,659,760,000	$ 37,457,290,000	$ 43,227,673,000	$ 38,098,093,000
Retired personnel	14,981,815,000	14,931,815,000	14,944,815,000	14,938,315,000
Operations and maintenance	62,590,121,000	61,631,465,000	63,428,634,000	61,853,377,000
Procurement	64,225,904,000	63,960,269,000	66,126,988,000	64,841,585,000
Research and development	20,319,388,000	19,362,204,000	20,846,389,000	19,859,148,000
Special foreign currency	3,083,000	3,083,000	3,083,000	3,083,000
Related agencies	98,163,000	97,163,000	98,163,000	97,663,000
Total, new obligational authority	$200,878,234,000	$197,443,289,000	$208,675,745,000	$199,691,264,000
(Transfer from previous appropriations)	——————	(73,900,000)	(192,900,000)	(208,000,000)
Total funding available	$200,878,234,000	$197,517,189,000	$208,868,645,000	$199,899,264,000

Warning and Defense

The Senate bill approved $336.7 million for development of an anti-missile system that could defend U.S. ICBMs from attack, the amount approved by the House and $20 million less than the administration request.

The bill also added $20 million to accelerate development of anti-satellite weapons, which the committee said should include research on laser weapons. A group of Senate conservatives had pressed the administration — with little success — to place more emphasis on developing powerful lasers which, they insisted, could blunt a Soviet missile attack.

Rapid Deployment Force

Like the other defense-funding committees, Senate Appropriations protested that the current command arrangement for the Rapid Deployment Force was too loose. It applauded Weinberger's April 24 announcement that the RDF would evolve over several years into an integrated major command directly under the Joint Chiefs of Staff. But the panel worried that in the interim, the organization would be prey to bureaucratic confusion.

Citing the Marine Corps' traditional role in responding quickly to crises, the committee strongly suggested that the Marines be given the lead in organizing the RDF and planning for its missions.

Transport Ships

Funds were added to speed up the modernization of the Navy's fleet of amphibious assault ships, which were designed to land Marines in the face of opposition. The additions were $264 million to buy a landing ship (called an LSD) that would carry tanks and the small boats that would land them on a beach and $60 million to design and procure components for a larger ship that could carry troop-carrying helicopters.

The committee slightly reduced funds for two kinds of ships designed to transport ground troops to areas where they could land under cover of friendly forces. To begin chartering ships (called T-AKXs) that would store the tanks and other equipment of a Marine division near potential trouble spots, the panel approved $60 million.

Of $668.4 million requested to convert eight fast cargo ships (called SL-7s) so they could load and unload tanks and trucks very quickly, the committee recommended $323 million in new budget authority and $102.4 million appropriated but not spent in prior years. This would convert four of the eight ships.

Naval Warfare

The panel refused the $90 million requested to begin equipping the mothballed battleship *Iowa* with cruise missiles. During floor debate on the fiscal 1981 supplemental appropriations bill (HR 3512 — PL 97-12) May 20, the two committees clashed over Reagan's request for $92 million to modernize the *Iowa*'s sister ship *New Jersey*. Armed Services, which strongly supported the battleship renovation plan, won that round by nearly 2-1.

Most other shipbuilding recommendations conformed to the authorization bill, including the addition of $10 million to design an aircraft carrier weighing less than half as much as the large type currently comprising the bulk of the U.S. carrier fleet.

The Senate panel agreed with its House counterpart that the Navy was letting costs climb too high for the LAMPS III sub-hunting helicopter, which was designed to be carried on surface ships smaller than carriers. But the Senate panel approved the budget request for the continued development of the helicopter and for production of the first 18 planes ($814.7 million).

The House bill cut $64 million from that request and ordered the Navy to reduce by nearly 50 percent the number of ships that would be equipped with the helicopter.

The committee also added $300 million to be transferred to the Coast Guard to modernize its ships and planes, which in time of war would come under Navy control to escort convoys and hunt submarines.

Ground Combat, NATO

Committee recommendations for procurement of tanks and most other Army combat equipment conformed to the authorization bill. Approved were funds for 720 M-1 tanks ($1.686 billion), 600 infantry fighting vehicles ($859 million) and 50 DIVAD anti-aircraft tanks ($335.5 million).

Like the authorizing panels, the committee approved the $545.2 million requested to buy 96 Blackhawk troop-carrying helicopters but deleted $126 million to begin funding a multi-year contract for the helicopters.

To begin procurement of the AH-64 tank-hunting helicopter, the committee recommended $502.8 million, $73.4 million more than the request and the amount agreed to by the other three defense-funding committees. The president had requested 14 helicopters, which the authorizing and House Appropriations committees said could be afforded with the added money.

But Senate Appropriations estimated this would buy only eight of the helicopters because of "substantial cost overruns." The committee told the Army it could not spend the money until it had sent Congress a "full and detailed accounting" of why the costs of the AH-64 program "are out of control."

NATO Plans. One provision dropped by the Senate panel would have limited to four the number of Army divisions for which tanks, trucks, artillery and other equipment could be stored in Europe under a plan called POMCUS. Theoretically, the plan would allow a division to be flown from the United States to Europe in only a few days, since the troops could be carried in civilian airliners and the heavy equipment already would be in place.

Tactical Aircraft

For most fighter planes and light bombers, the committee's recommendations conformed to the authorization conference report.

Funds were recommended for 36 F-15 Air Force fighters ($1.08 billion), 20 A-10 anti-tank planes ($229.7 million) and 30 F-14 Navy fighters ($1.07 billion).

To procure 120 F-16 Air Force fighters and to begin a multi-year contract for future F-16 purchases, the committee recommended $1.75 billion, $126.5 million less than the administration request. But the panel said that about half the cut could be made up by funds appropriated but not spent in prior years and the other half represented savings expected to result from the multi-year contract.

F/A-18. The committee approved the full request to buy 63 F/A-18 fighters ($2.126 billion) but only $190 million of the $224.6 million request for continued development of the plane, planned as an attack bomber for the Navy and Marine Corps and as a fighter for the Marines.

The panel echoed the chorus of criticism of the plane's cost and technical problems. Critics argued that the Navy and Marines could buy other attack bombers that would be more effective and cheaper.

Reserve, National Guard

Most of the equipment added by the authorizing committees to modernize National Guard and Reserve units was funded by the Senate panel. This included $50 million for 36 155mm cannon and more than 100 other armored vehicles, $55 million for 12 AH-1S anti-tank helicopters and $109.5 million for eight C-130 transport planes.

Combat Readiness

The committee rejected two administration proposals to cut the budget by reducing the combat readiness of U.S. forces.

Like the other three defense panels, it restored $100 million of the $173 million the administration proposed to cut for keeping Navy ships underway. The cutback was linked to the administration's reduction in the size of the fleet in the Indian Ocean.

Also rejected was a proposal to reduce the Army's 7th Infantry Division, based at Fort Ord, Calif., to a skeleton force for three years.

The committee also added a total of $400 million to the services' real property maintenance accounts to reduce the backlog of facilities overdue for maintenance projects.

Personnel

To provide overseas cost-of-living payments to troops stationed abroad who live in barracks, the panel approved the $26 million request. The House committee argued that the local cost of living was irrelevant to troops in barracks since food, housing and recreation was provided for them, in contrast to married soldiers who lived outside U.S. bases and received an overseas cost-of-living allowance.

The Pentagon insisted that without the allowance, unmarried soldiers would be unable to afford local entertainment, thus hampering morale. The Senate panel agreed.

Senate Floor Action

Three symbolic battles dominated the Senate's week-long debate over the $208 billion fiscal 1982 defense appropriations bill (HR 4995), which passed Dec. 4 on an 84-5 vote. *(Vote 442, p. 72-S)*

The issues were:

'Superhardening.' Seconding the judgment of most of its defense specialists, the Senate signaled an overwhelming lack of confidence in Reagan's proposal to deploy the first few dozen MX intercontinental missiles in existing silos that would be "superhardened" with additional concrete armor.

That plan was meant as an interim step pending development of a permanent MX basing method that would have a better chance of surviving Soviet attack.

By a vote of 90-4, the Senate adopted an amendment cosponsored by Armed Services Committee members William S. Cohen, R-Maine, and Sam Nunn, D-Ga., that discouraged — but did not flatly prohibit — the proposal to deploy the missiles in superhardened silos. *(Vote 430, p. 70-S)*

But the sponsors' intent — echoed by several of the Senate's defense specialists during debate on the amendment — was to make the administration concentrate its effort on a permanent, more survivable basing method.

Readiness. The Reagan administration came under sustained fire from Democrats for underfunding the combat-readiness of conventional war forces.

In the prolonged partisan maneuvering, several Democratic proposals to add funds were debated twice, but all were disposed of by nearly party-line votes. Only a handful of Democrats — mostly Southerners — joined a solid phalanx of Republicans to block the additions.

The Democrats' charge was led by Minority Leader

Robert C. Byrd, W.Va.; several Armed Services Committee members; and other defense specialists including Nunn; Ernest F. Hollings, S.C.; Carl Levin, Mich.; John Glenn, Ohio; and J. James Exon, Neb.

The Democrats charged Reagan with frittering away the political support for a defense buildup by failing to enunciate a clear strategy linking budget levels to specific military requirements.

Moreover, they said, Reagan's October reductions in his March defense budget request trimmed funds for the combat readiness of conventional war forces for purely budgetary reasons — precisely what candidate Reagan had accused President Carter of doing.

But the Democrats' new-found unity did not bear too close scrutiny, since their amendments did not directly touch on important defense issues — such as nuclear arms policy — over which party members remained in strong disagreement. Several Democrats, for example, joined Republicans in defeating amendments to delete funding for the B-1 bomber.

Nevertheless, the debate marked the first time in more than a decade that most Senate Democrats could coalesce behind a wide range of "pro-defense" proposals.

Republicans opposed the amendments on various grounds, but essentially implied that they were merely an attempt to embarrass the administration. During debate on Dec. 2, Ted Stevens (Alaska), chairman of the Defense Appropriations Subcommittee, declared: "It looks like it is a process of voting to increase military spending, apparently for the record, but it really is not at all."

Budget Levels. The issue of the defense budget's size was nearly submerged by those more prominent battles. But while Democrats were taking potshots at Reagan's defense budget cuts, some influential Republicans were complaining about the Pentagon's relative immunity from the austerity imposed on most domestic programs.

"Perhaps it is unfair to say that we have exempted the Pentagon from all budget scrutiny," said Finance Committee Chairman Robert Dole, R-Kan., "but there is that feeling and that perception by some of us."

Two votes lent some weight to Dole's veiled warning. An amendment by Appropriations Committee Chairman Hatfield to cut the bill's procurement and research titles by 2 percent — $1.73 billion — was rejected 36-57. But among the "yea" votes were 21 Republicans, eight of them freshmen. *(Vote 435, p. 71-S)*

An amendment to cut the bill by $115 million came even closer — within one vote of adoption (46-47). The amendment, by William Proxmire, D-Wis., would have deleted a 3 percent "cushion" the Appropriations Committee added to the MX missile and B-1 bomber appropriations in anticipation that costs would run over the budget. *(Vote 436, p. 71-S)*

Bill Total

As passed by the Senate, the bill appropriated $208.7 billion for defense, close to the amount recommended by the Appropriations Committee. The Senate debated the bill all through the week of Nov. 30, with only minor interruptions.

MX Missile

Drafters of the Cohen-Nunn amendment wanted to dramatize the near-unanimous judgment of defense experts — except for senior political figures in the adminis-

tration — that Reagan's interim MX basing plan would not protect the missiles.

As Cohen put it, "The hardening of missile silos, as has been recommended by the administration on an interim basis, does very little to improve missile survivability."

According to sources involved with the amendment, some backers feared that once hundreds of millions of dollars had been invested in the "interim" solution, pressure might build to rely on superhardened silos for the entire MX force. Both Cohen and Nunn announced they would oppose such a long-term plan because of its military vulnerability.

Supporters of the amendment also hoped to accelerate the selection of a long-term MX basing system and to nudge the administration toward selection of a system combining an anti-missile defense with some mobility features of the MX version killed Oct. 2 by Reagan.

Most military officials who had testified before congressional defense panels had said only such a version of MX would be secure against a surprise Soviet attack.

As adopted 90-4, the amendment provided that, of the $354 million earmarked for development of the interim MX basing mode, $334 million could be used only for development of a method that would put the missiles in "non-superhardened" existing silos. *(Vote 430, p. 70-S)*

It also set a deadline of July 1, 1983, for the selection by the secretary of defense of a long-term MX basing method and stipulated that a "deceptive" system — one in which each missile was shuttled among several possible launch sites — be among the options considered.

The amendment did not flatly block the president's original MX plan, since it did not restrict $20 million for interim basing development and it did not bar use of other funds for the project.

But both Cohen and Nunn professed confidence that the amendment would clearly signal that the Senate wanted a greater emphasis on selection of a long-term option that might be more similar to the Carter version than the administration had insisted in October.

Fund Cutoff. An amendment by David Pryor, D-Ark., to delete the entire $354 million requested to develop an interim MX basing method was rejected 35-60.

Most support for the amendment came from Democrats and liberal Republicans. A dozen Democrats — most of them Southerners or members of the Armed Services Committee — opposed the amendment. *(Vote 431, p. 70-S)*

Bombers

By a vote of 28-66, with no Republicans voting "aye," the Senate rejected a Hollings amendment that would have deleted the entire $2.4 billion in the bill for the B-1 program and would have redistributed $1.8 billion of that amount to a long list of conventional weapons and combat-readiness improvements. Several of the additions previously had been offered by Democrats as independent amendments. *(Vote 434, p. 71-S)*

Proponents of the amendment argued that the B-1 was less essential than improvements in the preparedness of conventional forces and development of other new strategic weapons such as the stealth bomber, which was to be designed to evade radar detection.

Hollings, Nunn and others cited Reagan's October cuts in his earlier defense requests as evidence that the B-1's cost would starve those other programs.

"I believe either the B-1, the MX or the stealth pro-

gram will have to be canceled or significantly delayed, or I believe that our conventional force posture and our readiness will be severely eroded," Nunn warned.

Stevens told reporters Dec. 4 that the Democrats' argument that B-1 funds would come out of other programs was "a legitimate complaint" but that there was "a legitimate choice" of what to fund.

During debate, Stevens and other opponents of the amendment insisted that the B-1 was needed to replace existing B-52 bombers until the stealth bomber could be in service in the 1990s. The stealth design still was too experimental to be confident that the B-52s could be used to penetrate Soviet air space until the radical new plane was in service, they maintained.

Several Democrats who had supported the various "readiness" additions as separate amendments voted against this amendment, including Glenn, Exon and Henry M. Jackson, D-Wash.

Cost Control. The Senate adopted by voice vote a Nunn amendment requiring the president to certify to Congress a baseline cost of the B-1 program against which future cost increases could be measured. It also required the current estimate of the total cost of a fleet of 100 B-1s to be reported in the quarterly report to Congress of major weapons program costs.

Stealth. By an almost pure party-line vote of 51-40, the Senate tabled an amendment by Robert C. Byrd, D-W.Va., that would have added $250 million to the secret amount included in the bill for development of the stealth bomber. All Republicans who voted and Harry F. Byrd Jr., Ind.-Va., voted to table the amendment against the opposition of all Democrats who voted. *(Vote 420, p. 69-S)*

Minority Leader Byrd and his allies argued that the additional money could accelerate the eventual deployment of stealth. Moreover, he said he feared the administration might not fund stealth adequately because of its commitment to the B-1.

Stevens and his allies insisted that the bill funded stealth research at the fastest prudent pace.

On Dec. 4 the Senate rejected 36-53 another Byrd amendment to add $200 million for stealth. *(Vote 441, p. 72-S)*

The Senate did accept by voice vote a Jackson amendment that would force the administration to spend at least the secret amount contained in the bill on stealth development during the fiscal year.

'Readiness' Increases

By nearly identical votes that closely followed party lines, the Senate rejected on Dec. 1-2 several of the Democratic-sponsored amendments. Similar amendments were debated again Dec. 4.

The amendments either would have restored funds cut by the president in October from his original budget or would have restored funds cut from the October request by the Senate Appropriations Committee.

Democrats argued that the programs they wanted to increase would have boosted the combat readiness of forces in the field. Each of the amendments originally had been included in an omnibus amendment by Hollings and Levin that would have canceled the B-1 and used those funds to pay for the "readiness" increases.

On Nov. 30, according to a Democratic aide, the Democrats met and agreed to offer the individual amendments in order to demonstrate that they had an alternative defense policy that emphasized readiness of conventional forces.

The amendments were offered separately — rather than as a single-shot alternative to B-1 funding — in order to attract Democrats such as Glenn who supported the bomber.

The overall shape of the argument on each of the amendments was identical. Democrats attacked each reduction from the original March budget request as inconsistent with Reagan's campaign charges that the Carter administration had let combat-readiness slip.

And they insisted that each of the amendments was being offered on its own merits, not as a package aimed at killing the B-1. Accordingly, they maintained, B-1 supporters could back the "readiness" proposals.

Stevens ruefully complimented the Democrats for coming up with "one of the most delightful and strategic tactics I have seen on the floor in a long time."

In some cases, he said, the Democrats' approach would force him to vote against programs that he supported. The cuts by Reagan and by the Senate committee reflected judgments about the relative priority of defense programs, each of which had merit, but not all of which could be afforded, Stevens argued.

"The Senate has to ask itself," he said while fighting one amendment, "how we put some portion of the reduction in our national expenditures onto the defense bill."

Not a single Republican supported any of the "readiness" amendments on Dec. 1-2. Conversely, only a handful of Democrats — nearly all Southerners — voted against the proposals. Several of the amendments were disposed of by tabling motions offered by Stevens.

Tanker Planes

The legislative minuet began with a Levin amendment to add $220 million to buy four KC-10 tanker planes in addition to four already in the bill. Reagan had requested eight of the planes in March and none in October.

The plane was a version of the DC-10 jetliner adapted to refuel other planes in midair. Because it also could carry a heavy cargo load, the tankers could escort jet fighter squadrons — and carry their ground support equipment — to distant trouble spots non-stop.

Setting the pattern for all subsequent votes on this group of proposals, the Senate rejected the Levin amendment 38-55 on Dec. 1. *(Vote 419, p. 69-S)*

Manpower Levels

By a vote of 54-36 Dec. 2, the Senate tabled a Hollings amendment to add $77 million to increase the Army's manpower ceiling from 780,000 to 786,000 and the Air Force's ceiling from 580,800 to 586,800. In each case, the higher ceiling was the amount requested in March; the lower figure was Reagan's October revised request. *(Vote 423, p. 69-S)*

Hollings complained that the personnel account was being cut because it lacked the pork-barrel constituency of a weapons procurement program and because it cut budget outlays more quickly than a procurement reduction.

Warren B. Rudman, R-N.H., countered that the reduction had been approved by the Senate and House Armed Services panels and that the bill still provided a 10,500-member increase in the Air Force.

Ammunition Stockpile

A Stevens motion to table a Hollings amendment to add $148 million for Army ammunition procurement was

agreed to 55-36 on Dec. 2. *(Vote 424, p. 70-S)*

In addition to leaving the Army short of the stockpiles it planned on to fight a war, Hollings argued, the acknowledged shortage in ammunition curtailed the amount of "live-fire" training and thus eroded troop morale.

Stevens argued that his bill provided a $780 million increase in ammunition funds compared to the fiscal 1981 budget and that too rapid an increase in that budget could not be spent efficiently.

A similar amendment to add $100 million for Army ammunition, sponsored by Exon, was rejected Dec. 4 on a 37-49 vote. *(Vote 440, p. 72-S)*

Equipment Replacement

An amendment by Exon to add $60 million to the Army "force modernization" budget was rejected 37-56. *(Vote 425, p. 70-S)*

The funds were to pay to ship tanks and other weapons from the factory to the field and to equip combat units to operate them. The Appropriations Committee had made the $60 million reduction in the president's request on the grounds that the production of some weapons was running behind schedule.

Exon countered that some other weapons were being manufactured faster than had been planned and that the total requirement for the modernization fund actually was $26.5 million higher than the request — some $86.5 million higher than the amount in the Senate bill.

Indian Ocean Fleet

By a vote of 40-56, the Senate rejected an amendment by Glenn to add $74.6 million to Navy operating funds. *(Vote 426, p. 70-S)*

This amount would allow the Navy to continue operating two aircraft carriers in the Indian Ocean. In October, the administration cut $173 million from the Navy ship operating budget and announced that it would keep only one carrier group in that region full time with a second carrier joining the fleet intermittently. The Senate Appropriations Committee restored $100 million.

Glenn called the carriers "the only non-bluff forces we have" near the Persian Gulf oil fields on which U.S. allies in Europe and Japan depended for their energy supplies.

Stevens conceded the region's importance, but insisted that the change in fleet deployments would not signal a lessening of U.S. commitment to defend its interests in the area. And Stevens asked, "When are the people who produce that oil going to start paying for some of this protection of those [sea] lanes? . . . When are the Japanese going to start paying for it?"

Missile Bases, Economics

Two other Democratic-sponsored amendments, which did not appear to fit into the readiness debate, were rejected by votes nearly identical with those cast on the readiness amendments:

● By Bill Bradley, D-N.J., to require the president to report to Congress on the impact of the domestic economy on his defense program and on his long-term plans to defend the Persian Gulf. Tabled 56-36. *(Vote 421, p. 69-S)*

● By Dennis DeConcini, D-Ariz., expressing the sense of the Senate that the MX missile should not be deployed in areas of high population density. Tabled 57-35. *(Vote 422, p. 69-S)*

Other Amendments

Other amendments adopted by voice vote were:

● By Pryor to prohibit private contractors from directly using money appropriated in the bill to lobby members of Congress or any other legislative body.

● By Levin, adding $62.1 million for spare parts for three squadrons of B-52D bombers. In his September revised budget, Reagan proposed retiring the planes — the oldest model of the B-52. But the Appropriations Committee approved $18.9 million to continue operating the planes in fiscal 1982, and the House defense appropriations bill (HR 4995) also included $62.1 million for the spare parts.

● By Robert Byrd, stating the sense of Congress that achieving the goal of a 600-ship Navy by the end of the 20th century "is highly desirable" and urging the secretary of defense to comply with PL 94-106, which required him to submit a five-year plan for Navy shipbuilding.

● By Stevens, deleting a prohibition on the use of funds to reimburse a defense contractor for the cost of obtaining commercial product liability insurance.

● By Stevens, doubling, to $680,000, the amount of ammunition the Army may issue to the National Board for the Promotion of Rifle Practice for competitive matches.

● By Specter, adding $4 million for long-lead funding for the Army's field artillery ammunition support vehicle.

● By Charles H. Percy, R-Ill., deleting a prohibition on transfers to foreign countries of military equipment or information related to the manufacture of military equipment without prior written approval of the appropriate military service secretary.

● By Percy, deleting a requirement that the service secretaries give advance written notice to the House and Senate Appropriations committees before waiving the requirement that foreign purchasers of U.S. arms pay a portion of the non-recurring research and development costs for those arms.

● By James A. McClure, R-Idaho, mandating a presidential study of the national silver stockpile.

● By Pete V. Domenici, R-N.M., granting the secretary of defense discretionary authority to make certain contracts with American Indians.

● By Stevens, to increase from $5,812,000 to $8,500,000 a contingency fund of the secretary of defense.

● By Robert T. Stafford, R-Vt., to delete a provision transferring from the Education Department to the Defense Department control of certain schools, located on military bases, for military dependents.

Amendments Rejected

The Senate rejected:

● By Patrick J. Leahy, D-Vt., an amendment to cut $201.2 million from the personnel and operations and maintenance accounts, including $39 million for West German damage claims, $60 million in pay for retired personnel. All the items had been cited by various agencies as being waste, fraud or abuse. By 22-72, on Dec. 3. *(Vote 432, p. 71-S)*

● By John C. Danforth, R-Mo., to earmark $150.5 million in the bill to replace engines in KC-135 tanker airplanes with second-hand engines used by some airlines instead of awaiting development of a new engine. By 16-65 on Nov. 30. *(Vote 418, p. 69-S)*

● By Pryor, requiring the secretary of defense to submit a report to Congress on competition in the awarding of defense procurement contracts. Ruled non-germane (and

thus killed) 44-50, on Dec. 2. *(Vote 428, p. 70-S)*

Conference Committee

As reported by the House-Senate conference committee Dec. 15 (H Rept 97-410), HR 4995 appropriated $199.69 billion in new budget authority as well as $208 million appropriated but not spent in previous years.

In terms of new budget authority alone, the bill was $1.187 billion below the president's revised budget submitted in October of $200.878 billion. Counting the money transferred from earlier years, the bill provided $979 million less in funding than the president's request.

'Bookkeeping' Cuts

In new budget authority alone, the conference report was nearly $9 billion below the Senate bill and about $2.25 billion above the House bill. But $7 billion that the Senate conferees "gave up" was covered by four essentially bookkeeping moves which, Stevens said, would have no concrete impact on Pentagon programs.

These four actions were:
● Dropping $4.8 billion included by the Senate to pay for the military pay raise that took effect Oct. 1. The administration planned to request funds for the pay hike in a supplemental appropriation early in 1982, which was the usual practice. Thus total defense spending for fiscal 1982 would climb further through later congressional actions.
● Dropping $1.6 billion added by the Senate on the assumption that inflation during fiscal 1982 would average 10 percent instead of the 8.4 percent assumed in the administration's budget.
● Dropping $115 million added by the Senate to cover a 3 percent price rise (in addition to the cost of inflation) for the B-1 bomber and the MX missile. Such cost increases and unbudgeted inflation also had been covered in previous spring supplemental appropriations bills.
● Accepting a $490 million cut made by the House on grounds that fuel prices had increased more slowly than estimated in the budget. The budget request included more than $10 billion for fuel.

Stevens had labeled the first three provisions a "truth-in-budgeting" package, insisting that they covered foreseeable costs that would have to be funded either through a supplemental appropriation or by diverting money from other defense programs.

Strategic Forces

The conference report provided the $1.913 billion requested for development of the MX missile, but denied $95.5 million added by the Senate in anticipation of a 3 percent increase in costs that was not included in the budget.

The final bill incorporated a Senate floor amendment cosponsored by senators Cohen and Nunn that was designed to discourage the administration from going ahead with its proposal to superharden existing missile silos.

Reagan recommended using the silos to deploy the first few dozen MXs, pending selection of a permanent MX basing technique. With backing from most of the other members of the Senate Armed Services Committee and most Pentagon defense experts, Cohen and Nunn argued that adding extra concrete armor to existing silos would not appreciably improve the chances of their surviving a Soviet missile attack.

The amendment stipulated that $334 million of the $354 million requested for development of the interim basing technique could be used only for existing silos that were not superhardened.

The remaining $20 million was available for the superhardening proposal, but supporters of the provision professed confidence that it would have the effect of pressuring the administration to concentrate on developing a long-term basing technique. The provision also ordered the administration to make a final basing decision by mid-1983, instead of 1984 as had been planned.

MX funds included $10 million to begin development of a system that would launch MXs from large airplanes, one of the candidates for solving the long-term deployment question. The conference report on the defense authorization bill had banned the use of any funds for an air-launched system.

Minuteman Missile

To improve the existing force of Minuteman ICBMs, the conferees added the following funds to the budget request:
● $5 million (as approved by the Senate) to replace 50 single-warhead Minuteman IIs with triple-warhead Minuteman IIIs;
● $22.3 million (half the amount added by the House) to continue production of a larger warhead — called the Mark 12A — for the Minuteman III.

Conferees turned down the Senate addition of $18.8 million to develop a system that would allow 200 Minuteman missiles to be re-targeted and fired from airborne command posts. If the program were sufficiently important, they said, the Air Force should request funding in next year's supplemental appropriation.

Both houses previously had approved $35 million to equip Minuteman silos with long-lasting batteries that could provide electrical power for days after a nuclear attack.

Bombers

As was done with the MX funding, conferees dropped the Senate's 3 percent cost-growth cushion for the B-1 bomber. They also accepted House-approved reductions in B-1 procurement and research funds totaling $329.3 million. For the B-1 program, the conference report appropriated $2,092,900,000.

A Senate floor amendment requiring the president to certify to Congress the estimated cost of a fleet of 100 B-1s was retained.

The total amount appropriated for development of the so-called stealth bomber intended to replace the B-1 in the mid-1990s, was not disclosed in the bill. But the conferees retained a Senate floor amendment prohibiting any reduction in that amount in fiscal 1982. Some Senate Democrats had expressed fears that the administration would divert funds from stealth development to fund the B-1.

Submarines

Conferees approved the higher, Senate-passed amount for components of future Trident missile-launching submarines to be funded in subsequent years. The Senate figure was $330.7 million, of which the Navy was told to provide $15.1 million out of other accounts.

Rejecting a House amendment sponsored by two members in whose districts the facility was to be located, the conferees approved $34.874 million requested for the ELF

radio transmitter designed to communicate with submerged submarines. Reps. Obey and Traxler had opposed the project.

They dropped $71 million added by the Senate to build a third "Pave Paws" radar, the type used to detect submarine-launched missiles. If the program were important enough, according to the conference report, funds should be requested in a supplemental.

Ground Combat Forces

Conferees funded 665 M-1 tanks ($1.348 billion) as requested and approved by the House. The Senate had provided an additional $76.3 million to buy 720 tanks, the number requested by Reagan before the budget cuts submitted in October.

The conference report waived a House requirement that the Army compare its M-2 infantry carrier in "side-by-side" field tests with various less expensive alternative vehicles. But the report urged the Army to test some of the alternative vehicles.

Helicopters

Both houses had approved the $484.6 million requested to buy 96 UH-60 troop-carrying helicopters but denied $126 million to begin a multi-year contract for future procurement of the helicopter. The panels complained that the UH-60's price fluctuated too much to make a multi-year contract feasible. Although conferees did not add any funds for a multi-year UH-60 contract, they did add a provision allowing the Pentagon to sign such a contract after 45 days' advance notice to the Armed Services and Appropriations committees.

Both houses had approved $438 million for AH-64 tank-hunting helicopters. The budget request estimated that 14 planes could be bought for that amount. The Senate panel said it would buy only eight helicopters, but the Army reportedly hoped to buy 11 with that amount.

NATO

Conferees retained two House-passed provisions that could complicate U.S. relations with other NATO members. In providing only $155.7 million for payment of damage claims against the Pentagon, the House denied $39.8 million requested to pay claims filed by West German citizens for damage caused by U.S. units on maneuvers.

The other provision directed the Pentagon to store no more than the four Army divisions-worth of tanks and other equipment stored in Europe to equip U.S. troop reinforcements that would be used on the continent in case of an international crisis. The Pentagon had planned to create two more of these so-called POMCUS sites.

Rapid Deployment Force

Both Appropriations committees had expressly told the Air Force to stop trying to develop a new wide-body, long-range transport plane, the C-17 (formerly called the CX) to haul U.S. ground units to small airstrips near trouble spots. Both versions of the appropriations bill denied the $169.7 million requested for CX and appropriated instead $50 million to begin purchasing existing wide-body transports.

Nevertheless, Defense Secretary Weinberger asked the two Armed Services committees in a letter sent Dec. 7, after HR 4995 had been passed by both houses, not to foreclose eventual development of the C-17.

Storage Ships

The conferees conditionally approved an administration decision to charter, rather than buy, a dozen so-called pre-positioning ships (designated T-AKXs) that would store the tanks, ammunition and other combat gear of a Marine division near foreign trouble spots.

In its October budget cuts, the administration abandoned plans to buy some existing cargo ships for conversion to the role and to build other new T-AKXs for the purpose. In lieu of the $197 million procurement request for three T-AKXs, the administration requested $60 million to begin the contract. The conferees approved the new request, but stipulated that the money be used only to lease the ships, with an option to buy, and that Pentagon money was not to be spent to overhaul or modify such vessels while they were privately owned.

Fast Cargo Ships

For the purchase of two high-speed cargo ships (called SL-7s) and modification of these and six others bought in 1980 to transport an Army division, the conferees approved $307.6 million in new funds plus $102.4 million appropriated but not spent in earlier years. The administration had requested $668.4 million.

The conference report ordered the Navy to make minor modifications in four of the ships, so they could be in service more quickly. The other four were to be redesigned so they could be used as roll-on/roll-off ships. This would allow tanks and other vehicles to be driven directly on and off the vessels instead of having to be loaded and unloaded by cranes.

Amphibious Capability

Like the House and Senate Armed Services committees, the two Appropriations panels apparently placed a higher priority on new Marine amphibious landing ships than did the administration. The SL-7s and pre-positioning ships could be used only if U.S. forces were landing at the invitation of local forces.

To beef up the Navy's shrinking amphibious fleet, the conferees added three items to the budget:

● $301 million for an LSD 41-class landing ship; this already had been approved by both houses. The administration had requested only $34 million for components and planned to fund construction in fiscal 1983.

● $45 million for components of a helicopter carrier that would haul troop-carrying helicopters;

● $15 million to design the new type of helicopter carrier.

New Navy Ships

The two versions of the bill were in basic agreement on the shipbuilding request. In most cases, conferees resolved the relatively minor funding disagreements in favor of the lower House-passed figures. These included:

● $475 million for components for a sixth nuclear-powered aircraft carrier to be funded in a future budget at an approximate cost of $3 billion. The administration had requested and the Senate approved $658 million for carrier components, but the House approved only purchase of the ship's two nuclear reactors, since the administration reportedly had slipped procurement from fiscal 1983 to 1984.

● $2.909 billion for three cruisers equipped with the Aegis missile system designed to protect U.S. carrier task

forces against the large Soviet arsenal of anti-ship cruise missiles. The administration had requested and the Senate approved $2.926 billion for the three ships, but the House committee insisted that the ships did not need a backup radar system.

● $926 million for three missile-armed escort frigates. The administration had requested $748 million for two ships, and both houses had added $224 million for a third. But the House dropped $45.8 million earmarked to shut down the production lines for these ships. The administration later planned to continue frigate production.

Anti-sub Helicopter

For LAMPS III anti-submarine helicopters, the conferees approved $559 million, the amount agreed to by the House, rather than $586 million as requested and approved by the Senate. For components of additional helicopters to be funded in fiscal 1983, the conferees approved $137 million, just about splitting the difference between the House ($118 million) and Senate ($155 million).

Substantial cost increases had bedeviled the Navy's plan to buy 204 of these torpedo-carrying helicopters to serve as the principal anti-submarine weapon of most surface warships in the fleet. (The LAMPS system included powerful computers to help helicopter crews interpret sub-hunting sonars and a complex mechanism to help the helicopter land on the deck of a small ship in rough seas.)

But the helicopter itself — which was a version of the Army's UH-60 troop-carrier — accounted for some of the cost increase. Since the Pentagon had slowed the production rate of the Army version, production overhead costs were spread over a smaller number of planes. In addition, the Navy version required more special components than had been planned.

Citing rising cost estimates, the House had ordered the Navy to drop plans to modify 37 recently built ships to carry the LAMPS III. This would cut by more than one-third the number of ships equipped with the system, which likely would further increase the unit cost of the helicopters.

The conferees rescinded the House action, but directed the Navy to consider alternative approaches to modifying the ships.

Coast Guard

Over the strenuous objection of some House conferees, the compromise bill retained $300 million added by the Senate to buy new ships and equipment for the Coast Guard, including additional 270-foot-long *Bear*-class cutters.

In time of war, when the Coast Guard would be placed under the control of the Navy, the *Bear*-class ships and other large cutters would be equipped with anti-submarine weapons, including the LAMPS III helicopter. Proponents cited this to justify the inclusion of funds for the Coast Guard — an agency of the Transportation Department — in the Defense Department funding bill.

In recent years, Coast Guard budgets had been slashed by the executive branch at a time when the service was saddled with a widening range of responsibilities, including supervision of the expanded U.S. fishing zone from 3 miles to 200 miles, increased maritime drug smuggling and a flood of illegal immigration from Caribbean countries.

Critics of the Senate action, including Rep. Jack Edwards, R-Ala., endorsed the need for heftier Coast Guard budgets but warned that the integrity of the appropriations

process was undermined by bootlegging the funds into the Pentagon bill.

Tactical Aircraft

The two versions of the bill had been in close agreement on funding for most combat aircraft purchases.

For Air Force fighters, both houses had approved $980.2 million for 36 F-15s and $1.27 billion for 120 F-16s. To begin a multi-year contract for the F-16, the conferees approved the $546.8 million requested and approved by the House. The Senate panel had cut that figure by $65.7 million, which, it said, could be made up with funds previously appropriated but not spent.

The final version contained the House-passed amounts for the A-10 tank-hunter: $209.7 million to procure 20 of the planes and $20 million for components of additional planes to be funded in fiscal 1983. The Senate had provided $229.7 million to procure the 20 planes in fiscal 1982 and no money for components.

For Navy carrier-launched planes, both houses had provided $888.7 million for 30 F-14 fighters, $1.89 billion for 63 F-18 fighters and $269 million for 16 A-6E bombers.

The conferees agreed on the House-passed appropriation of $189.2 million to purchase components for F-18s that would be funded in fiscal 1983, instead of $236.4 million requested and approved by the Senate. The House panel said its reduction reflected an administration decision to reduce the number of planes to be purchased in fiscal 1983.

In order to modify existing F-14s, the conferees provided $91 million. The Senate had approved the $107.7 million requested, but the House provided only $34.5 million, denying $71 million for an engine improvement program that was experiencing cost increases. The House committee warned that the Navy, after beginning the modification program, might decide to replace the engines altogether with a new model.

B-52D Bombers

Both houses had rejected an administration proposal in October to cut the budget by retiring the 70-odd oldest B-52s — the D model planes — several years earlier than had been planned. Both chambers had added to the bill $81 million to continue operating the planes.

The B-52Ds had not received some of the modifications given to later B-52s for penetrating Soviet air space in wartime. In many scenarios, the D model planes would be earmarked for non-nuclear missions over Europe or elsewhere. These models could carry more than 100 high-explosive bombs.

Tanker Engines

The conferees approved $85 million — about half the amount recommended by the House — to put used airliner engines on some of the Air Force's more than 600 KC-135 midair refueling planes. But they said this interim program must not delay development of a new and improved engine for the rest of the tanker fleet.

The existing tanker engines (called J-57s) were noisy fuel-guzzlers, with such limited power that the planes could not take off from many bases with a full fuel load. The Air Force planned to replace them with CFM-56 engines that were under development.

The interim step would require the purchase of older commercial jetliners so the Air Force could use the planes'

JT3D engines. The JT3Ds had to be removed from commercial service because they did not meet federal air and noise pollution control standards. The Air Force was exempt from such regulations and the used engines would provide some improvement over the J-57s, in addition to being cheaper than new CFM-56s.

Among the proponents of the interim program were members of Congress from Kansas, home of a Trans World Airlines maintenance depot that was installing the airliner engines on some Air Force planes.

Personnel Costs

Conferees split the difference on funding levels for several personnel programs that had been cut by the House.

The Senate had added to the bill more than $200 million for new bonuses and special pay established by the military pay raise legislation enacted in October. The conferees approved only $44.4 million, which was intended for certain bonuses paid to members of the Army and Navy. The Pentagon should seek specific congressional approval of funds for the other bonuses, the conferees said.

Re-enlistment Bonuses

The House had cut $397.9 million from the request for re-enlistment bonuses and ordered that they be paid in annual installments over the duration of the re-enlistment term. The Senate supported the existing Pentagon policy of paying the bonuses in a lump sum at the start of the re-enlistment.

Conferees agreed to one-half of the House cut and ordered that the bonuses be paid on "a modified lump-sum installment basis." In other words, up to 50 percent of the bonus could be paid in a lump sum and the rest in equal annual installments.

Moving and Travel

The House had cut $216.3 million from the $3 billion request for travel and moving costs associated with personnel transfers. The Senate had concurred in $80.7 million of that reduction.

Conferees approved an additional $61.5 million of the House-passed cut, three-fourths of which was accounted for by a reduction in cost estimates. Rejected by conferees was the House slash of $74.5 million intended to reduce the annual number of transfers.

Food Costs

A House reduction of $134.8 million in the $2.6 billion requested to feed troops who lived in barracks or on ships came in two parts. The conferees denied $34.8 million earmarked to provide an extra subsistence allowance for senior enlisted personnel. But they agreed to only one-fourth of the remaining $100 million cut by the House to trim waste, fraud and abuse.

Navy Quarters Allowance

Similarly, the House cut more than $100 million from the Navy's budget for housing allowances paid to personnel who did not live in government-provided quarters.

The conferees aproved half of the $58.5 million cut linked to allegations of waste, fraud and abuse. But they approved none of an additional $47.4 million cut the House said could be made, assuming improved management of the allowance payments.

Overseas Cost of Living

Rejecting the House position after a three-year-long battle, the conferees allowed $26 million requested to begin paying a cost of living allowance to enlisted personnel stationed abroad and living on U.S. bases.

Recruiting

Of $50 million cut by the House from the recruiting and advertising budgets, the conferees sustained the $25 million cut from operating accounts but provided the $25 million budgeted for personnel costs.

Operations and Maintenance

The conferees dropped a House provision cutting in half (by $86.7 million) the "rent" paid by Pentagon agencies to the General Services Administration (GSA), the agency that managed federal property. But the conference report ordered GSA to provide services commensurate with those provided by private managers for comparable rents.

About one-half of $60 million cut by the Senate from an account for shipping new weapons to Army units was restored by the conferees.

A House reduction of $43.2 million linked to allegations of waste, fraud and abuse in various supply activities was trimmed to an $8 million reduction in the final bill.

Reserves, National Guard

The conferees agreed to an additional $20 million approved by the House to pay for an increase in the size of the Naval Reserve from 87,600 to 94,000.

They cut $17.25 million — one-half the amount proposed by the House — from Reserve personnel accounts to discourage improper payments to reservists who did not attend mandatory drill sessions. ∎

3rd Continuing Resolution

Seeking to avoid another confrontation with President Reagan, Congress Dec. 11 approved a third stopgap funding measure (H J Res 370 — PL 97-92) providing nearly $4 billion in domestic spending reductions.

Negotiations between the White House and congressional Republicans had cleared the way for final action on the fiscal 1982 continuing resolution, which was signed by the president Dec. 15. Agreement on the stopgap measure was followed by resumption of action on long-stalled regular 1982 appropriations bills.

Final action came Dec. 11 when the Senate passed H J Res 370 by a 60-35 vote. The House had approved the identical measure by a 218-197 vote Dec. 10. (Senate vote 468, p. 75-S; House vote 331, p. 108-H)

The resolution contained only about half the spending cuts sought by Reagan in his September budget request. But that was enough to prevent a recurrence of the veto that befell an earlier continuing resolution (H J Res 357) Nov. 23.

Reagan's veto of the previous resolution, which had savings calculated by the Office of Management and Budget (OMB) at less than $2 billion, forced a temporary shutdown in many government functions.

After the veto, Congress hurriedly approved an emer-

gency resolution (H J Res 368 — PL 97-85) providing government funding through Dec. 15. *(Story, p. 294)*

4 Percent Cut

H J Res 370 achieved the minimum amount of savings demanded by Reagan through a 4 percent across-the-board reduction in most domestic programs.

According to congressional estimates, it provided $3.7 billion in outlay savings from seven domestic spending bills. Along with another $400 million or so saved in the Energy-Water bill (HR 4144 — PL 97-88), the total savings reached the $4 billion level required by Reagan.

The measure required a 2 percent cut in certain Defense Department activities, but only until the end of the first session of the 97th Congress.

All told, H J Res 370 provided budget authority at an annual rate estimated at $410.8 billion. Outlays in the resolution were expected to be about $271 billion.

The measure would not cover the remainder of fiscal 1982, however. A last-minute change made by House Republican sponsors ended the resolution on March 31, 1982.

Under pressure from conservative Democrats, Republican leaders also had to cut foreign aid funding to a $9.6 billion level.

H J Res 370 covered all appropriations bills until signed by the president. As of Dec. 11, only the Energy-Water and District of Columbia (HR 4522 — PL 97-91) bills had been enacted. The legislative branch appropriation (HR 4120) was made law as part of an earlier continuing resolution (H J Res 325 — PL 97-51).

Federal Pay Increase

High-level federal workers — whose hopes for a pay raise had been repeatedly raised by earlier continuing resolutions, only to be dashed — were given a substantial pay raise by H J Res 370.

The resolution raised the pay level for federal executives just below Cabinet officials and members of Congress, to $59,500 a year. Other executives and upper-level civil service employees also got increases.

Members of Congress were not covered by the raise. Still, they did not come away empty-handed. H J Res 370 allowed members to receive a new tax break in 1981, instead of having to wait until 1982. The resolution moved up by a year a provision of an earlier continuing resolution (H J Res 325) that removed the existing $3,000 limit on tax deductions taken by members of Congress for expenses related to service in Washington. *(Story, p. 286)*

Air traffic controllers did not fare so well. The House knocked out of H J Res 370 provisions that would have allowed substantial pay increases for non-striking air traffic controllers and other Federal Aviation Administration (FAA) employees.

Republican Compromise

House approval of the Republican version of H J Res 370 saw a revival of the coalition that gave Reagan his major victories earlier in the year.

A week of negotiations between presidential aides and House and Senate Republicans produced a compromise that met Reagan's minimum savings requirement without alienating key GOP moderates such as Silvio O. Conte, Mass., the ranking member of the House Appropriations Committee.

The compromise retained Republican moderate support by protecting funding for certain social programs. For example, the compromise added to the resolution, before application of the 4 percent cut, $175 million for low-income energy assistance, $140 million for education block grants and $45 million for railroad retirement.

According to Marge Roukema, R-N.J., Republican moderates agreed to back the compromise in exchange for the Republican leadership's support of her motion to insist on the lower House levels for the Defense appropriations bill (HR 4995). To win conservative Democratic support — 36 Democrats eventually voted for the Republican plan — the compromise protected funding for law enforcement and reduced spending for foreign aid.

In a last-minute change, Republican sponsors Conte and Minority Leader Robert H. Michel, Ill., changed the termination date of the resolution to March 31 from Sept. 30, 1982. They explained after the vote that some Southern Democrats had objected on principle to providing full-year funding under a continuing resolution. The March date also provided more favorable treatment to Southern states in the distribution of highway funds.

House Floor Action

Going up against the Republican proposal was a Democratic package approved by the Appropriations Committee Dec. 9 (H Rept 97-372).

The Democratic package applied different across-the-board cuts in various bills. Labor-Health and Human Services (HHS)-Education and Treasury-Postal Service programs were cut 2 percent, military construction was cut 3 percent and Interior programs were cut 4 percent.

According to the Congressional Budget Office (CBO), the Democratic package contained $412.5 billion in budget authority and $272.6 billion in outlays.

In offering his compromise substitute, Conte stressed the fact that it would be signed by Reagan, while the Democratic package would not. He said his proposal was "the best possible political compromise under current circumstances."

Appropriations Committee Chairman Jamie L. Whitten, D-Miss., said Congress would be giving up its power if it made legislative decisions solely on the basis of whether or not the president would sign it. "If you support the substitute, you might as well transfer to the executive branch full control and take the legislative branch out of business," he said.

Conte's motion to recommit the resolution to committee with instructions to substitute his proposal was adopted by a 222-194 vote. While picking up three dozen Democrats, Republicans lost only three of their own — Bill Green, N.Y., Harold C. Hollenbeck, N.J., and Charles F. Dougherty, Pa. *(Vote 330, p. 108-H)*

Despite his victory, Michel said after the vote that future spending reductions still faced a difficult time in the House. "I'm not going to delude myself into thinking that any further drastic cuts in discretionary programs are going to fly through," he said.

Senate Action

Once the Republican proposal passed the House, Senate leaders were committed to accepting it without changes, to avoid a conference.

Before passing the resolution, the Senate beat back a series of Democratic amendments restoring funds for various social programs.

Perhaps the most important development during Senate floor action on H J Res 370 was a colloquy that sought

to define how agencies should apply the 4 percent spending cuts.

The resolution contained a provision that allowed the administration to make a cut of up to 6 percent in spending for any individual program, in achieving a 4 percent reduction for a whole appropriations account.

That provision worried Lawton Chiles, D-Fla., who warned that it might be used as a way to revive presidential impoundment, which was barred by the 1974 budget act.

Chiles said that the provision would give OMB officials authority to make deeper cuts than those ordered by Congress, and thus rearrange spending priorities. "My concern is that that provision is going to allow OMB to rewrite some of our appropriations bills," he said.

Appropriations Committee Chairman Mark O. Hatfield, R-Ore., responded, however, that the provision was precisely the opposite of impoundment. Instead of giving more authority to cut funds, he said, the provision sought to protect programs from cuts. He explained that the provision would prevent the administration from eliminating or drastically reducing individual programs, in order to reach the overall 4 percent cut.

Hatfield added that any reductions in excess of 4 percent should be treated like reprogramming requests, which must be reported to congressional appropriations committees.

Major Provisions

As cleared by Congress, H J Res 370 contained the following major provisions:

● Provided funding for government agencies whose regular appropriations bills had not been enacted, but only until enactment of the bills, or March 31, 1982.

● Established base spending rates for programs in the following bills: Agriculture (HR 4119), Housing and Urban Development (HR 4034), Interior (HR 4035), Transportation (HR 4209), according to the conference agreements; Defense (HR 4995), military construction (HR 4241), Labor-HHS-Education (HR 4560), Treasury-Postal Service (HR 4121), according to the lower amount for each program contained in the bill as passed by the House or Senate or reported in the Senate; Commerce-Justice-State-Judiciary (HR 4169), the House level; foreign aid (HR 4559), the lower of the current rate or the budget request.

● Added into the base for HR 4560 funds for certain social programs.

● Reduced by 4 percent, from the base rates set by the bill, spending for programs in HR 4119, HR 4034, HR 4035, HR 4560 and HR 4121.

● Reduced by 2 percent funding in HR 4241 and HR 4995; provided that the reductions in HR 4995 were to come only from defense accounts for procurement and research and development and be applicable only until a conference agreement on the bill was reached, or the first session of the 97th Congress ended.

● Provided that no individual program be cut more than 6 percent.

● Provided specific spending cuts comparable to a 4 percent cut in HR 4209 and HR 4169.

● Exempted from the cuts entitlement programs, food stamps, medical care and certain other veterans' programs, Internal Revenue Service functions and law enforcement activities.

● Provided pay increases for top-level federal executives.

● Allowed members of Congress to take increased business tax deductions in 1981 by advancing the effective date of a provision of H J Res 325 that removed the existing $3,000 limit on tax deductions taken by members for expenses they incurred while in Washington. ∎

Labor-HHS-Education Funds

For the third straight year, Congress did not complete action on the annual appropriations bill for the Departments of Labor, Health and Human Services (HHS) and Education. *(1980 action, 1980 Almanac p. 222)*

An $87.2 billion fiscal 1982 funding bill (HR 4560) passed the House Oct. 6, but the Senate did not act on the slightly less expensive version reported by its Appropriations Committee Nov. 9.

Funding for the three departments and various related agencies covered by the bill was included in the three fiscal 1982 continuing resolutions (PL 97-51, PL 97-85, PL 97-92) passed by Congress in 1981. *(Stories, pp. 290, 294, 329)*

As passed by the House, HR 4560 contained some reductions in spending as requested by President Reagan in his September budget revisions. However, in a defeat for Reagan, the House refused to make further cuts in the bill's popular social programs.

The Senate committee's version of the bill was somewhat closer to Reagan's revised budget, but did not achieve all the savings sought by the administration.

Unlike past Labor-HHS-Education bills, HR 4560 did not get caught up in controversy over the issue of Medicaid funding of abortions for poor women. Both the House and Senate versions prohibited payments for abortions unless needed to save the life of the mother.

House Committee Action

The House Appropriations Committee reported HR 4560 Sept. 23 (H Rept 97-251). As reported, the bill appropriated $87.3 billion for social programs — $871 million above President Reagan's budget request.

Added to permanent appropriations and trust funds for programs such as Social Security, HR 4560 would bring total spending for the three departments to $308.6 billion.

With massive cuts in jobs programs, the bill was $1.2 billion below comparable fiscal 1981 spending.

The committee took only one roll-call vote before approving HR 4560 by voice vote. It rejected, 16-22, a Silvio O. Conte, R-Mass., amendment that would have allowed the National Institute for Occupational Safety and Health (NIOSH) to move its headquarters from Rockville, Md., to Atlanta, Ga.

Labor. Funds for job and job training programs authorized by the Comprehensive Employment and Training Act (CETA), while $104 million above the budget request, were $3.5 billion below the 1981 level. Much of the reduction was due to elimination of funds for the CETA public service jobs programs, as mandated by the budget reconciliation bill (HR 3982 — PL 97-35) cleared in July. *(Reconciliation bill, p. 256)*

The committee approved $1.4 billion for CETA job training, $117 million less than requested. An additional $606 million, deferred from the 1981 appropriation for public service employment, also was available for job training.

Rejecting the administration's plan for consolidating training programs for youths and adults, the committee

provided $400 million for the separate CETA youth employment and training programs. The amount was less than half the 1981 level.

The bill required a total reduction of 734 staff positions in the Occupational Safety and Health Administration (OSHA) and Mine Safety and Health Administration (MSHA).

HHS. HR 4560 provided funds for four new health block grant programs established by PL 97-35. Only one of the programs, for preventive health, got the full amount authorized ($95 million). Primary health care centers, scheduled to become a discretionary block grant in 1983, got $258.8 million; maternal and child health, $331 million; and alcohol/drug abuse/mental health, $485 million.

Other block grants funded by the bill included low-income energy assistance ($1.8 billion), community services ($362 million) and social services ($2.4 billion).

The committee predicted — correctly — that another reconciliation provision, abolition of the Social Security minimum benefit, would not survive future congressional opposition. So it refused to approve $120 million for the administrative costs of eliminating the minimum benefit.

Education. Education programs also were funded at levels below the reconciliation amounts. The new education block grant got $521.5 million, compared with the reconciliation ceiling of $589.4 million. The Title I program of aid for the education of disadvantaged children, modified substantially by reconciliation, got $3.2 billion.

Impact aid for schools educating children whose parents lived or worked on federal property received the full amount allowed by PL 97-35 ($475 million). Pell grants to college students got $2.5 billion and guaranteed student loans, $1.8 billion.

Provisions

As reported by the House Appropriations Committee, HR 4560 appropriated the following amounts:

	Administration Request	Committee Recommendation
Labor Department	$10,965,870,000	$ 8,717,291,000
Health and Human Services Department (HHS)		
Health Services Administration	981,251,000	1,051,916,000
Center for Disease Control	304,193,000	326,590,000
National Institutes of Health	3,762,483,000	3,834,958,000
Alcohol, Drug Abuse and Mental Health Administration	933,890,000	938,590,000
Health Resources Administration	233,685,000	292,746,000
Assistant Secretary for Health	297,710,000	246,211,000
Health Care Financing Administration	33,489,387,000	32,051,378,000
Social Security Administration	19,920,728,000	19,412,111,000
Human Development Services	5,313,307,000	5,388,439,000
Departmental Management	262,061,000	248,610,000
Subtotal, HHS	65,498,695,000	63,791,549,000
Education Department	12,989,366,000	13,941,324,000
Related Agencies	803,913,000	805,086,000
Estimates proposed for later transmittal[1]	— 3,873,105,000	0
Total	$86,384,739,000	$87,255,250,000

[1] *Revised estimates for entitlement programs not transmitted officially to committee.*

House Floor Action

By an 81-vote margin, the House Oct. 6 rejected efforts by the Republican leadership to force Reagan-backed cuts in HR 4560. It was the first test of congressional support for the president's new round of budget cuts.

The House then passed the bill by voice vote.

It made only one reduction from the amounts approved by the Appropriations Committee Sept. 23 — a $74 million cut, backed by the Democratic leadership, that was aimed at bringing the bill within the limit for spending authority set by the first congressional budget resolution.

The defection of 39 Republicans, mostly from the Northeast and Midwest, killed the Republican leadership motion to recommit the bill to the Appropriations Committee for more cuts.

"I don't think we can make the [budget] balancing act by just touching this bill. If we send this bill back to committee, to cut only it, without looking at the defense budget and the water projects, it's unfair," said Carl D. Pursell, R-Mich.

The motion by Ralph Regula, R-Ohio, to recommit the bill was rejected 168-249. Twenty-eight Democrats voted for the recommittal motion. *(Vote 234, p. 76-H)*

Budget Authority and Outlays

The key question during floor debate on HR 4560 was whether it satisfied all of the tests for comparing its spending levels with the targets in the budget resolution. In some ways, the bill reported by the committee was well under the resolution's spending targets; in others, it was substantially over.

The Budget Committee's "early warning" report on the bill found, for example, that it provided $74 million more than the resolution's allocation for budget authority for "discretionary" programs. On the other hand, the report found that HR 4560 was $334 million less than the limit on budget authority for "mandatory" spending.

It was also $844 million under the allocation for discretionary program outlays. Outlay figures reflect actual cash disbursements by government agencies and cannot be controlled directly by the appropriations process.

Spending levels in the Labor-HHS-Education bill were controlled more by mandatory spending for entitlement programs than in most appropriations bills. As reported, HR 4560 contained $57.6 billion for entitlement programs, such as Medicaid, welfare and student loan subsidies, and only $29.7 billion in discretionary spending.

Budget Committee Position

Budget Committee Democrats made clear to the House leadership that they would support a motion to

recommit the bill as reported because it was $74 million over the budget resolution allocation for discretionary spending.

To avoid opposition from the full Budget Committee, Labor-HHS-Education Appropriations Subcommittee Chairman William H. Natcher, D-Ky., developed an amendment to cut budget authority by $74 million. The amendment, which reduced the welfare work incentive program in HHS by $43.8 million and reduced spending for salaries and expenses by all the agencies in the bill by $30.2 million, was adopted by a 383-30 vote. *(Vote 231, p. 76-H)*

Even with the amendment, however, the bill was about $700 million over the budget resolution's limit on combined outlays for discretionary and mandatory programs. For that reason, it faced continued opposition from Budget Committee Chairman James R. Jones, D-Okla.

Jones said the version of the first budget resolution adopted by the House had failed to take into account some $700 million in funds provided by the fiscal 1981 supplemental appropriations bill (PL 97-12) that would actually be spent as outlays in fiscal 1982.

It had been a mistake not to include outlays from the 1981 supplemental in the budget resolution, Jones said. Nevertheless, he said he still felt obliged to oppose the bill for exceeding the outlay limits.

Jones agreed to vote against the Republican motion to recommit the bill but had planned to vote against final passage. After losing on the recommittal motion, however, Republican leaders declined to press for a recorded vote on final passage.

Amendments

In other action on HR 4560, the House adopted the following amendments:

● By Thomas J. Bliley Jr., R-Va., to bar HHS from enforcing a reconciliation bill provision prohibiting Medicaid and Medicare reimbursement for drugs on which the Food and Drug Administration had not made a final determination of efficacy. Adopted 271-148. *(Vote 232, p. 76-H)*

● By John H. Rousselot, R-Calif., to prohibit MHSA enforcement of regulations on surface mining of stone, clay, colloidal phosphate, sand or gravel or the surface construction of facilities relating to coal or other mines. Adopted 254-165. *(Vote 233, p. 76-H)*

● By Paul Simon, D-Ill., to apply to the 1982-83 school year the same family contribution schedule used in 1981-82 for determining awards under the Pell grant program of aid to college students. Adopted by voice vote.

● By Robert S. Walker, R-Pa., to prohibit the use of funds in the bill to enforce regulations requiring quotas related to race or sex in hiring, admissions or contracting. Adopted by voice vote.

● By Elliott H. Levitas, D-Ga., to prohibit the use of funds to carry out regulations that had been vetoed by Congress. Adopted by voice vote.

● By Allen E. Ertel, D-Pa., to prohibit the use of funds to provide a personal cook, chauffeur or other personal servant to agency officials, and to require that autos purchased with funds provided by the bill get at least 22 miles to the gallon. Adopted by voice vote.

● By Dan Daniel, D-Va., to prohibit the use of CETA funds for individuals who advocated violent overthrow of the government. Adopted by voice vote.

Senate Committee Action

The Senate Appropriations Committee approved an $86.7 billion version of HR 4560 on Nov. 5, and filed its report Nov. 9 (S Rept 97-268).

The amount was $472 million below the House-passed total, but still $2.4 billion above President Reagan's September revised budget request. Of the total appropriation, $84.8 billion was for fiscal 1982. The measure also included some advance appropriations for fiscal 1983.

For the most part, the committee did not attempt to comply with Reagan's request for spending reductions, which he made after the Labor-HHS-Education Subcommittee had finished drafting its bill. Subcommittee Chairman Harrison "Jack" Schmitt, R-N.M., tried to get the full committee to make further cuts, but was only partly successful.

Most of the cuts in the House-passed spending levels were in Labor Department training and jobs programs. The cuts were offset in part, however, by higher spending for health programs, particularly Medicaid. The higher Medicaid levels reflected the committee's judgment that changes made in the program by the reconciliation bill would not save as much as the House had assumed.

Labor. The committee cut $839 million from the House-passed amount for the Labor Department, approving $7.9 billion. Most of the cuts came in CETA training and youth employment programs. CETA appropriations were reduced by $557 million below the House level.

CETA's Title II training programs, which remained alive after the reconciliation act eliminated public service employment provisions, were cut by $211 million.

The committee urged that the reduced funds be spread among as many trainees as possible by reducing some individual payments. It estimated the training program still could serve 825,000 people in fiscal 1982, compared to 992,000 in 1981.

The committee cut $320 million from the House-passed amount for CETA youth programs: $200 million from youth employment and training, $92 million from the summer jobs program and $28 million from the Job Corps.

The bill included $208 million less than the House version for community service employment for older Americans. But that savings reflected only an accounting change; the spending rate for the jobs program would not be cut by the bill.

HHS. Appropriations of $64.2 billion were approved for HHS — $421 million above the House level.

The committee allowed more than the House for health programs. The largest increase was an additional $147 million for the Health Services Administration. Within that appropriation, the committee added $20 million for the new maternal and child health care block grant and $53 million for community health services, a program that had been saved from extinction during fiscal 1982 in the reconciliation act.

The panel added $64 million for Public Health Service hospitals and clinics, which were ordered phased out by the reconciliation act. Funds were included to enable several of the hospitals to remain open temporarily so they could be transferred to non-federal operation.

Cuts in other health programs partially offset the committee's increases. The panel cut $29 million from the House-passed appropriation for the Center for Disease Control, $16 million from the National Institutes of Health and $58 million from alcohol, drug abuse and mental health programs.

The committee added $472 million to the House-passed amount for Medicaid, and added another $194 million by "borrowing" from fiscal 1983 spending, for a total addition of $666 million.

The committee said its appropriation, like the House measure, was intended to reflect savings achieved by the 3 percent reduction in Medicaid spending mandated by the reconciliation act. But other factors would offset part of the reduction, the report said, so more funds would have to be appropriated.

Schmitt abandoned an effort to cut the appropriation to force further reductions in Medicaid and other entitlement programs, after encountering opposition from authorizing committees with jurisdiction over the programs.

The Appropriations Committee report, however, said "more action is needed" to reduce entitlement spending.

The committee cut $150 million from the House-passed appropriation for the energy assistance block grant and $63 million from the House figure for the community services block grant. It approved $34 million more for refugee assistance programs than the House did.

Education. The committee approved an appropriation of $13.9 billion for the Department of Education, $82 million less than the House level. Within the relatively close total, however, the committee set different priorities from those set by the House.

The panel cut $403 million from the House appropriation for elementary and secondary education programs, including a $198 million reduction in Title I educational programs for the disadvantaged and a $171 million cut in the new education block grant.

In addition, the committee cut $20 million from the House spending level for impact aid, $52 million from education programs for the handicapped and $17 million from adult and vocational education.

The committee cut the House appropriation for student financial aid, including Pell grants, direct student loans and state grants, by $419 million. But it added $829 million for guaranteed student loans and $47 million for loan programs to support higher education facilities. ∎

HUD, Agencies Funds

Congress Dec. 10 cleared a $60.38 billion appropriations bill for fiscal 1982 for the Department of Housing and Urban Development and 20 independent agencies.

Final action on HR 4034 came when the House adopted a revised conference report (H Rept 97-222) that the Senate had adopted Nov. 21. The bill was signed into law (PL 97-101) by the president Dec. 23.

The final agreement was $1.7 billion in budget authority over the president's revised September budget request of $58.68 billion. But the bill included a provision allowing the administration to cut up to 5 percent from accounts that were over the corresponding amounts in the September request.

Rep. Edward P. Boland, D-Mass., chairman of the Appropriations Committee HUD-Independent Agencies Subcommittee, told colleagues, " I think the bill contains the best that we can presently do for the HUD programs."

The final total was considerably less than originally passed by either chamber. The president originally had requested $63.23 billion. The House July 21 approved $62.60 billion, while the Senate July 30 approved $60.51 billion.

The first conference agreement calling for an appropriation of $60.69 billion was passed by the House Sept. 15, with only 12 votes to spare. (*Vote 191, p. 66-H*)

The September measure had been sent immediately to the Senate, but it languished until Nov. 21 while Senate Republicans attempted to work out an agreement to bring the bill closer to Reagan's September request of $58.68 billion.

The 1981 appropriation had been for $69.57 billion.

Summary of Funding

Housing and Community Development. Housing and community development programs were trimmed in the final bill. The $17.37 billion allotted for additional subsidized housing was expected to support 142,231 units.

The September conference report had recommended funding for 156,000-157,000 units.

That report also had provided $500 million for the popular Urban Development Action Grant (UDAG) program, in which federal money was used to stimulate private development. The final bill trimmed that amount to $439.68 million.

Pressure from congressional supporters and local officials blocked the Reagan administration plan to phase out UDAG.

The Community Development Block Grant program also was trimmed from $3.67 billion to $3.46 billion.

Veterans Administration (VA). Medical care programs for veterans remained at the September conference report level of $6.97 billion. The September budget request was $6.67 billion.

Environmental Protection Agency (EPA). The $540.32 million for EPA salaries and expenses was nearly $28 million above the September request. Boland noted that there had been "considerable concern in Congress and elsewhere" that the administration was reducing EPA personnel so extensively that the agency could not carry out its legislative mandate.

Final Provisions

As signed into law, the Department of Housing and Urban Development-Independent Agencies Appropriations Act of 1982 appropriated the following amounts:

	Budget Request	Final Amount*
Department of Housing and Urban Development		
Housing programs	$18,264,194,040	$18,444,550,120
Community Development	3,666,000,000	3,895,680,000
Policy Development and Research	20,000,000	20,000,000
Fair Housing and Equal Opportunity Assistance	5,016,000	5,016,000
Management and Administration	298,552,000	311,245,440
Total HUD	$22,253,762,040	$22,676,491,560
Independent Agencies		
American Battle Monuments Commission	10,507,000	10,507,000
Cemeterial expenses, Army	4,476,000	4,476,000
Consumer Information Center	1,156,000	1,290,000

Consumer Product Safety Commission	29,025,000	31,663,680
Council on Environmental Quality	919,000	919,000
Treasury Department	4,025,666,000	4,614,950,000
Environmental Protection Agency	1,249,114,000	1,309,783,520
Federal Emergency Management Agency	585,308,000	585,308,000
Federal Home Loan Bank Board	(60,890,000)	(60,890,000)
National Aeronautics and Space Administration	5,755,200,000	5,953,284,000
National Consumer Cooperative Bank	——	4,800,000
National Credit Union Administration	100,000,000	100,000,000
National Institute of Building Sciences	440,000	1,440,000
National Science Foundation	909,480,000	993,800,000
Neighborhood Reinvestment Corporation	13,156,000	13,872,000
Office of Consumer Affairs	1,760,000	1,760,000
Office of Science and Technology	1,578,000	1,578,000
Selective Service System	18,633,000	18,633,000
Veterans Administration	23,725,375,000	24,051,576,520
Grand Total	**$58,685,555,040**	**$60,376,132,280**

* These amounts can vary because the legislation sent to the president gives the administration the discretion to cut up to 5 percent from accounts above the president's September request.

House Committee Action

The House Appropriations Committee voted June 25 to appropriate $63.3 billion in fiscal 1982 for HUD and the agencies.

The committee bill (HR 4034 — H Rept 97-162) was $190.3 million above the total recommended by Reagan in his March budget request. The biggest increase was for the Veterans Administration. The administration had proposed $22.6 billion, but the committee increased that by $276.7 million to $22.9 billion.

HUD Programs

The committee recommended $26.3 billion for HUD programs, compared to Reagan's recommendation of $26.5 billion and 1981 funding of $31.03 billion.

Subsidized Housing. The panel recommended $20.4 billion for the Section 8 rent subsidy program and for public housing. That would support about 179,000 additional subsidized housing units.

Reagan had recommended $19.7 billion, enough for about 175,000 additional units. The committee specifically recommended funding for 4,000 units of Indian housing, which Reagan had proposed eliminating.

Rent Supplements. The committee followed the Reagan recommendation to rescind $1.03 billion in budget authority and $30.5 million in contract authority in the rent supplement program, which gradually was being merged with the Section 8 rental assistance program. Under both, tenants paid 25 percent of their income toward rent, with the government paying the difference between the tenant's contribution and actual cost.

Operating Subsidies. The committee accepted the administration's request for $1.2 billion in operating subsidies for public housing, a $133.8 million increase over fiscal 1981.

Community Development. The committee recommended $3.8 billion for Community Development Block Grants, which provided funds for a range of projects, including housing and improvements in public utilities. Reagan recommended $4.16 billion, but his proposal would have lumped funds for the UDAG program into the block grants. The panel recommended $500 million for UDAG.

Environmental Protection Agency

For EPA, the panel recommended $1.43 billion, a $10 million increase over the Reagan March proposal but $2.6 billion below fiscal 1981 funding.

The panel followed the administration's recommendation against funding local and state construction grants for wastewater treatment facilities.

Reagan said in March that he did not want to spend any more money for sewer grants until the program was overhauled. The subcommittee report on the bill said the panel "has reluctantly recommended no funding" and urged the legislative committees with responsibility for the program to make the necessary legislative reforms.

The committee also accepted the president's recommendation of $200 million for the so-called "superfund," a trust fund created to help defray costs associated with the cleanup of hazardous substance spills and of abandoned hazardous waste sites.

Veterans Administration

The committee recommended $22.9 billion for the VA, an increase of $276.7 million over Reagan's proposal and up $342.6 billion over fiscal 1981.

The panel added $289.8 million over the Reagan budget for medical care, bringing the committee total to $6.96 billion. Reagan had proposed $6.67 billion.

This account included funds to treat servicemen exposed to Agent Orange and other herbicides in Vietnam and to keep open readjustment centers for Vietnam veterans — so-called outreach programs.

Reagan had proposed ending the outreach program, but the House and Senate each passed bills earlier in June to extend it. The bills also backed medical care for medical problems associated with Agent Orange. *(See story, p. 481)*

The committee provided $153.7 million for medical, rehabilitative and health services research, $8 million more than Reagan's proposed $145.7 million.

National Consumer Cooperative Bank

The administration did not recommend new funding for the National Consumer Cooperative Bank, which provided financial and technical assistance to non-profit cooperatives through a Self-Help Development Fund. The fund made repayable interest-bearing capital investment advances to eligible cooperatives.

The committee recommended an additional $5 million for the fund, which had been given $20 million in previous appropriations. It also had provided $58 million to the bank for major loans to eligible co-ops at the market interest rate.

House Floor Action

After trimming funds for subsidized housing, the

House passed a $62.6 billion fiscal 1982 bill July 21 by a vote of 362-54. The total was $522.84 million less than Reagan's March budget request and $713.14 million under the recommendation of the Appropriations Committee. *(Vote 138, p. 52-H)*

An amendment by Lawrence Coughlin, R-Pa., to trim $703,136,000 for subsidized housing was adopted by voice vote July 17. It provided $19.74 billion for assisted housing to fund some 175,000 additional units in fiscal 1982, the same number recommended by Reagan. But it earmarked 3,000 units for Indian housing, which Reagan had wanted to eliminate.

Also, the House adopted 202-162 an amendment by Robin L. Beard, R-Tenn., to cut HUD's Office of Policy Development and Research funds from $30 million to $20 million. *(Vote 134, p. 50-H)*

Beard originally wanted to eliminate $20 million, contending the office was "greatly overfunded." However, after discussion with HUD Subcommittee Chairman Boland and J. William Stanton, R-Ohio, ranking Republican subcommittee member, Beard agreed to a $10 million cut.

EPA Amendments

By a vote July 17 of 177-184, the House rejected an amendment by William E. Dannemeyer, R-Calif., to prevent EPA from spending money to require states to adopt, implement or enforce vehicle emission control inspection and maintenance programs. *(Vote 135, p. 50-H)*

Existing law required 29 states where air quality had been designated substandard to adopt a mandatory annual inspection of motor vehicles if they could not improve their air by 1982.

Other Amendments

By a vote of 152-264 July 21, the House rejected an amendment by Larry Winn Jr., R-Kan., to reduce funds for National Science Foundation research and related activities by $70 million, to $995 million, the amount requested by Reagan. Winn said the committee's funding of $1,103,500,000 for NSF was an increase over the fiscal 1981 appropriation of 8 percent, which he said was "far too large." *(Vote 137, p. 52-H)*

By voice vote July 21, the House adopted an amendment by Elliott H. Levitas, D-Ga., to prevent HUD and the agencies funded under the bill from using money to implement a regulation that had been vetoed by Congress.

By voice vote the same day, the House accepted a proposal by Allen E. Ertel, D-Pa., that he called the "no frills" amendment. It barred the use of funds appropriated under the bill for providing a personal cook, chauffeur or other personal servant to any officer or employee in HUD or the 20 agencies. The amendment also barred money to buy passenger cars with an EPA mileage rating under 22 miles per gallon.

Senate Committee Action

As reported by the Senate Appropriations Committee July 23 (S Rept 97-163), the bill made further cuts in housing and community development. The committee bill appropriated $60.54 billion, $2.06 billion under the House-passed version and $2.71 billion under Reagan's March request.

HUD Programs

Subsidized Housing. The Senate committee provided $17.82 billion, which the report said would cover 156,205 additional housing units in 1982. The House had provided $19.74 billion, the same as the Reagan request, for 175,000 additional housing units.

The panel earmarked funds for 4,000 units of Indian housing, while the House set aside money for 3,000 units. The administration had proposed no new Indian housing for fiscal 1982.

Public Housing Operating Subsidies. The Senate panel provided $1.2 billion for public housing operating subsidies, the same as the House bill and the Reagan request.

Community Development. The committee proposed $4.17 billion for the Community Development Block Grant program, the same as the administration request but $134 million under the House bill. Both bills earmarked $500 million for UDAG.

Policy Development and Research. The committee recommended $30 million, $5 million less than the Reagan request. The House Appropriations Committee had recommended $30 million, but that amount was trimmed by $10 million during floor action.

Solar Energy and Energy Conservation Bank. Following the administration March request, the panel provided no money for the solar energy bank. The House had provided $50 million for the bank, which was created to encourage energy conservation and the application of solar technology in commercial and residential buildings.

Environmental Protection Agency

The committee recommended $1.42 billion, $493,800 less than the administration request and $10.65 million less than the House.

Most of the cut from the House bill — $9,996,300 — came in research and development. The House had proposed $191.25 million, and the Senate committee cut that to $181.25 million.

The administration had requested $190.63 million for research and development.

Reagan had requested $413.93 million for abatement, control and monitoring of pollution. The Senate committee raised that request to $421.84 million, an increase of $7.91 million over the administration proposal. The House provided $422.55 million.

Federal Emergency Management Agency

The committee proposed $654.61 million for FEMA, which supervised federal efforts to prepare for and respond to major civil emergencies. FEMA also administered three national insurance programs covering floods, crime and riots.

The recommendation was $10.5 million less than the Reagan request and $119.15 million more than the House request. The Senate committee decided to provide money for civil defense programs. The House had deferred funding pending an administration review of the programs.

The House did not include the administration estimate of $125.66 million for civil defense in comparing its overall appropriations bill to the Reagan request. The Senate committee included the civil defense request for purposes of comparison.

NASA

The committee's total recommendation for NASA was

$6.21 billion, $91.4 million more than the Reagan request and $79.7 million above the House proposal.

The major increase was the appropriation for research and development. The Senate panel recommended $4.99 billion, an increase of $91.4 million over the administration proposal and $56.4 million more than the House bill.

National Science Foundation

The committee recommended $1.05 billion for the foundation, $14 million more than the budget request and $56 million less than the House.

Veterans Administration

The committee recommended $22.92 billion for the VA, which was $249.6 million more than the Reagan proposal and $27.1 million less than the House bill.

Like the House, the Senate panel included a substantial increase over the administration proposal for medical care. The Senate committee proposed $6.97 billion for medical care — a $291.53 million hike over the administration's request and $1.76 million more than the House bill.

For compensation and pensions payable to disabled veterans, the Senate recommended $12.86 billion. This was a $99.4 million cut from the House proposal and a $57.4 million drop from the administration request.

Co-Op Bank

The Senate committee recommended no additional funding for the bank, adhering to the administration request.

The House had provided $5 million for the bank's self-help development fund, which provided small loans to eligible co-ops, generally with interest below the market rate. The House also had provided $58 million to the bank for major loans to eligible co-ops at the market interest rate.

Senate Floor Action

HR 4034 as approved by the Senate July 30 provided $60.51 billion for HUD and the agencies, while the House version provided $62.60 billion. Reagan had proposed $63.23 billion. The fiscal 1981 appropriation was $69.57 billion.

Before passing the bill by a vote of 87-6, the Senate considered several amendments, including the following *(Vote 242, p. 41-S):*

● By Howard W. Cannon, D-Nev., to add $272 million for subsidized housing, to provide 159,000 additional units for fiscal 1982. Rejected by voice vote.

● By Jake Garn, R-Utah, to cut $46.18 million from a program to help multifamily housing projects experiencing financial difficulties. Adopted by voice vote.

Garn said the cut from the original level of $50.18 million was necessary to meet the level approved in the budget reconciliation package (HR 3982).

● By John Heinz, R-Pa., to add $10 million to the congregate housing services program, which provided aid, including meals and some medical services, to low-income elderly and handicapped persons living at home. Adopted by voice vote.

● By William L. Armstrong, R-Colo., to restrict to 30 days the amount of time funds under the bill could be used to pay rent for any unoccupied housing unit built or subsidized through the Section 8 rental program. Adopted by voice vote.

Under current law, HUD was permitted to pay a landlord market rent up to 60 days for any vacant unit.

● By William Proxmire, D-Wis., to reduce funds for the NASA research and development programs by $86.4 million. Rejected by voice vote.

● By Proxmire, to bar NASA from using federal funds to search for "extraterrestrial intelligence." Adopted by voice vote.

● By Slade Gorton, R-Wash., to add $500,000 to the appropriation for the Council on Environmental Quality (CEQ). Adopted by voice vote.

● By Garn, to trim $500,000 from research and development programs for the Environmental Protection Agency (EPA). Adopted by voice vote.

Garn said this amendment was to offset the increase for the CEQ.

● By Alan Cranston, D-Calif., to disapprove the deferral of $12.6 million previously appropriated for construction of a research and education building at the Long Beach, Calif., Veterans Administration Medical Center. Adopted by voice vote.

Provisions Compared

	House-passed Appropriation	Senate-passed Appropriation
Department of Housing and Urban Development		
Housing programs	$20,968,381,500	$18,954,660,000
Community Development	4,300,000,000	4,166,000,000
Policy Development and Research	20,000,000	30,000,000
Fair Housing and Equal Opportunity Assistance	5,700,000	5,700,000
Management and Administration	324,264,000	324,264,000
Total, HUD	$25,618,345,500	$23,480,624,000
Independent Agencies		
American Battle Monuments Commission	10,507,000	10,507,000
Cemeterial expenses, Army	5,086,000	5,086,000
Consumer Information Center	1,314,000	1,344,000
Consumer Product Safety Commission	32,983,000	32,983,000
Council on Environmental Quality	1,044,000	1,544,000
Treasury Department	4,632,620,000	4,574,620,000
Environmental Protection Agency	1,429,606,000	1,418,453,000
Federal Emergency Management Agency	535,463,000	654,614,000
Federal Home Loan Bank Board	(60,890,000)	(60,890,000)
National Aeronautics and Space Administration	6,133,900,000	6,213,600,000
National Commission on Air Quality	—	—
National Consumer Cooperative Bank	5,000,000	—
National Credit Union Administration	100,000,000	100,000,000
National Institute of Building Sciences	500,000	1,500,000

National Science Foundation	1,103,500,000	1,047,500,000
Neighborhood Reinvestment Corporation	13,950,000	14,950,000
Office of Consumer Affairs	2,000,000	2,000,000
Office of Science and Technology	1,793,000	1,793,000
Selective Service System	20,000,000	20,000,000
Veterans Administration	22,952,347,000	22,925,224,000
Grand Total	**$62,599,958,500**	**$60,506,342,200**

First Conference Report

Housing and Community Development. The first conference report reconciled a number of differences between the House and Senate, with most changes ending up as cuts from the House level.

● For annual contract authority, the amount expended each year to build or rehabilitate housing, conferees agreed on $916.23 million. The House had provided $987.44 million, while the Senate had provided $891.5 million.

● For new budget authority, the amount to be spent over the life of contracts for new or rehabilitated housing, conferees agreed on $17.94 billion, which would cover 156,000-157,000 additional units in fiscal 1982. The House had provided $19.74 billion, the same as the president requested, while the Senate had provided $17.82 billion.

● Conferees stipulated that $2.35 billion in budget authority should be allocated for new public housing construction other than low-income Indian housing.

● The Senate figure of $4 million for housing projects experiencing financial difficulties was accepted. The House had appropriated $50.18 million.

● Conferees deleted a Senate provision that provided $75.96 million for a year-old temporary mortgage assistance payment program. The conference report said that HUD had not approved regulations yet for the new program.

● On the mortgage limitation for the Federal Housing Administration, conferees settled at $40 billion, splitting the difference between the House figure of $39 billion and the Senate figure of $41 billion.

● The mortgage purchase authority for the Government National Mortgage Association was set at the Senate figure of $1.97 billion. The House bill had set the limit at $3.6 billion.

● Conferees agreed to appropriate $25 million for a solar energy and energy conservation bank. The House had provided $50 million, but the Senate, following the Reagan administration, had provided no money.

● For Community Development Block Grants, conferees agreed to appropriate $3.67 billion. The House had proposed $3.8 billion, while the Senate had provided $4.17 billion. However, conferees agreed to a House provision providing $500 million for a separate Urban Development Action Grant program.

● For research and development, conferees appropriated $23 million, instead of $20 million as proposed by the House and $30 million as proposed by the Senate.

● Dropped was a Senate provision prohibiting the use of funds to assist beyond 30 days any unoccupied Section 8 unit.

Independent Agencies

Environmental Protection Agency (EPA). The research and development budget was set at $181.25 mil-

lion — trimmed from the $191.25 million in the House bill but $500,000 more than the Senate proposal of $180.75 million.

For implementing federal pollution control laws, conferees agreed on the Senate figure of $421.84 million. The House had recommended $422.55 million.

Federal Emergency Management Administration. For state and local assistance, conferees agreed on the Senate proposal of $134.79 million. The House had provided $54.08 million. Conferees agreed on $65.46 million for emergency planning and assistance, instead of $29 million as proposed by the House and $67.46 million as proposed by the Senate.

They agreed to restore language inserted by the House to provide $373 million for the national flood insurance fund, to be used to retire fund indebtedness.

Consumer Information Center. Conferees took the Senate figure of $1,344,000 rather than the House figure of $1,314,000.

National Aeronautics and Space Administration. For research and development, conferees appropriated $4.97 billion. The House proposed $4.94 billion and the Senate, $4.99 billion.

The report said conferees agreed to add $70 million above the Reagan request of $4.90 billion only for 10 specified items including solar electric propulsion systems, international solar polar mission, shuttle/spacelab payload development and upper atmospheric research satellites.

For construction, they accepted $99.8 million, up from $95.8 million proposed by the House but a cut from the $104.8 million recommended by the Senate.

Conferees agreed on $1.11 billion for research and program management as proposed by the Senate. The House proposed $1.1 billion.

National Consumer Cooperative Bank. Conferees restored $5 million proposed by the House and deleted by the Senate for the bank's self-help development fund. Conferees also restored House language — stricken by the Senate — establishing a loan limitation of $14 million for the self-help development fund.

National Science Foundation. For research and related activities, conferees appropriated $1.04 billion. The House had proposed $1.06 billion while the Senate had provided $1.02 billion. Conferees accepted Senate language limiting money for biological, behavioral and social sciences to $184.6 million.

For science education activities, conferees agreed on $27.45 million instead of $35 million proposed by the House and $19.9 million proposed by the Senate.

Neighborhood Reinvestment Corporation. Conferees settled on an appropriation of $14.45 million for the corporation. The Senate had proposed $14.95 million while the House had proposed $13.95 million.

Veterans Administration. For compensation and pensions, conferees agreed on $12.88 billion, instead of $12.91 billion proposed by the House and $12.86 billion proposed by the Senate.

Conferees set the appropriation for medical care at $6.97 billion, as proposed by the Senate. The House had proposed $6.96 billion.

They provided $150.7 million for medical and prosthetic research, instead of $153.7 million in the House bill and $145.7 million in the Senate bill.

For medical administration and miscellaneous operating expenses, conferees provided $62.4 million as proposed by the Senate. The House had provided $62.57 million.

Conferees disagreed with the administration on deferring two projects that had been funded in an earlier appropriations bill. Conferees decided that a nursing home and garage project in Washington, D.C., and an education addition to a VA facility in Long Beach, Calif., should proceed.

House Action

With only 12 votes to spare and the threat of a presidential veto in the air, the House Sept. 15 adopted a $60.69 billion appropriations conference report by a vote of 209-197. *(Vote 191, p. 66-H)*

The compromise was $1.91 billion less than the fiscal 1982 bill approved by the House, but $183.63 million above the Senate bill. It was $8.89 billion less than the fiscal 1981 appropriation.

The main reason for the close vote was the threat of a veto. Administration officials contended the bill was too costly and would adversely affect the 1982 budget deficit.

The dispute involved different ways of accounting for the budget.

In debate, Minority Leader Robert H. Michel, R-Ill., said the outlays for fiscal 1982 — the money that actually would be spent during the year — were $620 million over the president's budget. For that reason, Michel said, the report should be rejected.

But Boland, HUD Appropriations Subcommittee chairman, disagreed. He called the $620 million a "false figure," complaining that Michel was engaging in dubious accounting. In particular, Boland said Michel was taking outlays based on fiscal 1981 appropriations and adding them into outlays stemming from the new appropriations bill.

He said the 1982 outlays were only $373 million over the Reagan request and that was largely due to restoring $292 million for veterans' medical services that the administration had not opposed when the House passed its bill.

Boland argued that the bill actually was $2.56 billion under President Reagan's proposal of $63.25 billion in budget authority — the amount that may be obligated but not necessarily spent in a year — for HUD and the agencies. ∎

Reagan Backing Helps Foreign Aid Bill

Congress Dec. 16 cleared HR 4559 (PL 97-121) making appropriations for foreign aid programs in fiscal 1982. It was the first regular foreign aid spending bill enacted by Congress since 1978.

The bill contained $7.495 billion in new budget authority for foreign aid programs. In addition, it set $13.6 billion in limits on Export-Import Bank loans and operations (including $4.4 billion for direct loans) and a $3.1 billion limit on arms loans to foreign countries.

The final bill report squeaked through the House on a 217-201 vote. The Senate adopted the report by a 55-34 vote. *(House vote 348, p. 112-H; Senate vote 483, p. 77-S)*

The conflict over arms aid and the International Development Association was one reason Congress had failed to pass a foreign aid appropriations bill in each of the previous two years. Foreign aid programs had been funded instead under continuing resolutions that also funded a multitude of other programs. *(1980 Almanac p. 197)*

Aid Bill Politics

Along with the foreign aid authorization (S 1196), the aid spending bill was enmeshed all year in partisan disputes that threatened to kill them. But the bills were rushed through Congress in the final days before it adjourned after President Reagan rallied GOP support for them.

Reagan put his prestige on the line when it appeared Congress would fail again to pass an aid appropriations bill, leaving him without increases he wanted in the arms aid so integral to his foreign policy.

Deep partisan and philosophical divisions over the proper ratio of military-to-development assistance kept Congress from passing a regular aid appropriations bill for fiscal 1980 or 1981. The same lack of consensus threatened the fiscal 1982 bill.

Simultaneously, previous Republican attacks on Democrats who backed foreign aid — plus the unpleasant specter of voting to spend money abroad after making deep cuts in the domestic budget — led the Democratic House majority to await GOP leadership on the aid authorization bill.

The situation was turned around when Reagan and Secretary of State Alexander M. Haig Jr. issued personal appeals to their party the week of Dec. 7 to get the Reagan foreign aid program, as embodied in both bills, through Congress.

Reagan and Haig got their way after key Republicans — including some harsh critics of foreign aid — resigned themselves to the necessity of accommodating the desires of House Democrats seeking to hold military aid to a minimum and preserve U.S. development aid donations.

Republicans generally favored military and bilateral economic aid over development assistance funneled through multilateral lending institutions such as the World Bank. Many Democrats took the opposite position.

A central issue in the House struggles of the summer over HR 4559 was an $850 million donation to the International Development Association (IDA) for the second installment on a U.S. pledge to give $3.24 billion to IDA's sixth replenishment (called IDA VI).

The U.S. pledge to IDA, an arm of the World Bank that made no-interest loans to the globe's poorest nations, was fought by GOP conservatives but authorized in the omnibus budget reconciliation bill (HR 3982 — PL 97-35).

Democrats had managed to provide for IDA's funding in the House Appropriations Committee and successfully resisted GOP efforts to increase arms aid, but that led to a stalemate.

The situation changed after a late-November fight between Reagan and Congress over a measure (H J Res 357) to continue government funding in lieu of various fiscal 1982 spending bills.

Reagan vetoed that resolution and challenged Congress to pass the appropriations bills required by regular order.

House Speaker Thomas P. O'Neill Jr., D-Mass., responded that the House had passed all of its appropriations bills except foreign aid.

O'Neill said he would get HR 4559 to the floor before Dec. 15, and he challenged Reagan in turn to round up enough GOP votes to pass the bill.

O'Neill did, and Reagan did.

Provisions

Legislative provisions of HR 4559 *(for funding levels, see box, p. 350)*:

Military Aid

● Earmarked $550 million for Israel and $200 million for Egypt for Foreign Military Sales loans that did not have to be repaid.

Multilateral Aid

● Limited the salaries of U.S. representatives to the international development banks to no more than level IV of the federal Executive Schedule ($52,750 per year in 1981, $58,500 as of Jan. 1, 1982).

● Instructed the U.S. representative to the International Development Association (IDA) to press for a "more efficient distribution" of IDA lending, including a reduction in the maximum loans provided to any individual nation.

● Prohibited U.S. donations to the World Health Organization Special Programme of Research, Development, and Research Training in Human Reproduction.

● Prohibited the use of funds for the United Nations Fund for Science and Technology.

● Prohibited the use of funds for the United Nations Decade for Women.

● Earmarked $126,750,000 for the United Nations Development Program.

● Limited contributions to the United Nations Childrens Fund to $41.5 million.

● Limited contributions to the United Nations Environment Program to $7,850,000.

Bilateral Aid

● Earmarked $10 million of the $27 million international disaster assistance account for the relief of earthquake victims in southern Italy.

● Prohibited expenditure of money under the Special Requirements Fund of the Economic Support Fund without the prior written approval of the House and Senate Appropriations committees.

● Earmarked the following amounts under the Economic Support Fund: $806 million for Israel, $771 million for Egypt, $100 million for the Sudan, $20 million for Costa Rica, $15 million for Cyprus, $5 million for Poland, $5 million for Tunisia.

● Earmarked $30 million in the migration and refugee assistance account for use by the Agency for International Development for resettlement services and facilities for refugees and displaced persons in Africa.

● Limited administrative expenses for the Office of Refugee Programs to $7,426,000.

General Provisions

● Prohibited the use of any funds in the bill to "lobby for abortion."

● Added Libya, Iraq and South Yemen to a list of nations barred from directly receiving "any assistance or reparations" from the United States. Nations previously on the list were Angola, Cambodia, Cuba, Laos, Vietnam and Syria.

House, Senate Committee Action

The House Appropriations Committee reported HR 4559 (H Rept 97-245) on Sept. 22 after weeks of dispute within its Foreign Operations Subcommittee over the IDA VI and military aid questions.

The Senate Appropriations Committee normally would await House action on an appropriations bill before taking up such a measure itself. However, acknowledging that House action on HR 4559 was unlikely, the Senate panel reported its own bill, S 1802 (S Rept 97-266), on Nov. 3.

The bills dramatized the fundamental philosophical and partisan divisions in Congress on how U.S. aid should be spent.

The two bills provided similar amounts for U.S. aid programs in fiscal 1982: $7,594,280,064 under the House bill (HR 4559) and $7,250,083,804 under the Senate measure (S 1802).

But that similarity masked basic disputes over how much of the foreign aid budget should go for military aid given directly to U.S. allies and how much should go toward underwriting IDA. *(IDA background, p. 142)*

Most Democrats generally favored less military aid than did most Republicans. Thus, with Democrats in the majority, the House committee approved $923.5 million for military aid spending in HR 4559 — $172.9 million less than the $1.096 billion the Republican-controlled Senate panel approved in S 1802.

Conservatives in Congress — mainly Republicans — had been waging a campaign to stretch out scheduled U.S. donations to IDA VI. Liberals — most of them Democrats — had been fighting to maintain a Reagan administration plan for graduated IDA VI payments.

Reflecting this division, the Senate committee approved only $532 million for the fiscal 1982 payment to IDA VI while the House committee approved $850 million — the amount President Reagan requested in March. Reagan revised his budget requests in September and reduced his fiscal 1982 IDA VI request to $820 million.

Officially, the Reagan administration was caught in the middle in the fights over IDA and arms aid, resisting cuts in each. As a result, the administration got a little of what it wanted from each bill. In HR 4559, it got full funding — under the original March budget request — for the fiscal 1982 payment to IDA VI in HR 4559; in S 1802, it got its full revised request for military aid.

Reagan originally requested $8.756 billion for foreign aid in fiscal 1982, including $1.668 billion for a military aid program that would have financed $4.054 billion in loans to other nations to buy arms and other military equipment. The administration revised its foreign aid request in September to $7.588 billion, preserving the size of the arms loan program, but cutting economic and development aid.

The House bill included $7.594 billion, slightly above the September request, and financed arms loans of only $3.496 billion rather than the $4.054 billion Reagan wanted. The Senate bill included $7.25 billion, down $338 million from the amended Reagan request, but allowed the $4.054 billion arms loan program.

The fiscal 1981 foreign aid budget was $6.375 billion, not counting a one-time appropriation of $5.516 billion for a subscription to the International Monetary Fund. Thus the House bill would increase foreign aid spending by $1.220 billion in fiscal 1982, and the Senate bill would increase aid spending by $875 million.

Development Banks

IDA VI was only the most controversial of various Reagan requests for multilateral aid, which included U.S. donations to development banks that provided

concessional loans to underdeveloped nations and donations to the United Nations and other international organizations.

The Senate committee dealt more severely with Reagan's revised request for $1.619 billion for multilateral aid, cutting it to $1.296 billion. For all multilateral development banks, the Senate committee approved $1.08 billion — approximately the amount President Carter had proposed to pay the IDA alone in fiscal 1982.

The House committee gave Reagan less than his original request but more than his amended one, approving $1.662 billion for the multilateral aid.

Inter-American Bank

Reagan asked in his revised request for $221 million for donations to the Inter-American Development Bank (IADB) and its "concessional" loan arm, the Fund for Special Operations (FSO). Concessional agencies, such as the FSO, made long-term loans, with little or no interest charges, to the poorest nations.

The revised request was almost $23 million less than Reagan originally asked.

The revised request proposed an appropriation of $46 million for a direct payment to the IADB, which lent to developing nations in the Western Hemisphere, and a limit of $645,574,584 million in callable capital — funds that were not appropriated but could be "called" if necessary for the IADB to meet its obligations.

None of the multilateral banks ever had made a call on callable capital. Starting in fiscal 1981, Congress abandoned the practice of appropriating callable capital; instead, the appropriations bills simply placed limits on the amount the president could commit to a given bank.

The administration also requested $175 million for the U.S. share of a replenishment of the Fund for Special Operations. In March, Reagan had asked for an additional $15.7 million to complete an earlier FSO replenishment that Congress had failed to fully fund. But this part of Reagan's request was dropped in September.

The House committee cut 10 percent, or $22 million, from the overall request. But it added about $2 million to the revised request for the U.S. payment to the IADB, making it $48 million, and cut the limit on callable capital to $610 million. It also approved $173.2 million for the FSO but directed that $15.7 million go toward paying off the U.S. pledge to the earlier FSO replenishment, which Reagan had dropped from his revised request.

The Senate panel matched the House committee's action but provided the full $173.2 million Reagan requested for the current FSO replenishment.

World Bank

Reagan's revised budget asked $159 million for the "hard loan" window of the World Bank, the International Bank for Reconstruction and Development (IBRD), and a limit of $1.831 billion on callable capital for the IBRD. The bank made loans at near-commercial interest rates.

Included in the $159 million was $109.7 million for the first of six equal installments on the U.S. share of a general capital increase for the IBRD, with the rest intended for an unpaid portion of a previous capital increase.

The total U.S. share of the general capital increase was $8.8 billion, but only $658.3 million of that amount was to be paid to the bank over six years; the rest was callable capital.

Both committees reduced the Reagan request to $147 million for the fiscal 1982 direct payment and put a limit of $1.678 billion on callable capital for the IBRD in fiscal 1982.

Similarly, both committees approved the Reagan request for $14.5 million for the bank's International Finance Corporation, which lent to the private sector in developing nations.

The total amounts for the World Bank institutions were: $994 million requested by Reagan; $1.011 billion approved by the House committee; $693 million approved by the Senate committee.

Asian Development Bank

Both committees reduced the Reagan requests for the Asian Development Bank and the bank's concessional loan arm, the Asian Development Fund.

Both Reagan budget requests asked $4.9 million for direct payment to the Asian bank and a limit of $44.9 million on callable capital. The House committee approved $4.5 million for the direct payment and $40.4 million for callable capital. The Senate committee approved $4.7 million and $42.6 million for the same purposes.

Reagan originally requested $125.4 million for the Asian Development Fund, with $111.3 million allocated for a new replenishment and $14.1 million for a prior pledge that Congress failed to fully fund. Reagan's revised request dropped the $14.1 million.

The House committee approved $112.8 million for the fund, including the $14.1 million for the previous replenishment. The Senate committee approved $119 million for the fund, $111.3 million — the full Reagan request — for the new replenishment and $7.8 million toward the prior replenishment.

African Fund, Bank

The administration requested $58.3 million for the African Development Fund, a concessional lending facility associated with the African Development Bank. The House committee approved the full request, but the Senate panel reduced it to $41.7 million, the same amount appropriated for the fund in fiscal 1981.

Reagan originally requested $18 million for an initial U.S. subscription to the African Development Bank, plus a limit of $54 million on callable capital. But member nations of the African bank had failed to approve a plan to allow non-African nations to subscribe to the bank's capital, so the administration withdrew the request in September, and neither committee approved a U.S. donation.

International Organizations

The administration first requested $260 million for U.S. voluntary contributions to international organizations such as the United Nations and the Organization of American States, but reduced that to $229 million in September. The House committee approved $254 million for the same accounts, while the Senate committee cut the Reagan request to $216 million.

A major reason for the difference between the two committee figures was the Senate panel's rejection of a revised request for a $39.6 million donation to the International Fund for Agricultural Development (IFAD) as the U.S. share of a $180 million IFAD replenishment. The House, working from an original Reagan request for $45 million, approved $40.5 million.

The IFAD was established after the 1974 World Food Conference to help impoverished nations with basic food

production. Members of the Organization of Petroleum Exporting Countries (OPEC) were to contribute almost half the initial IFAD funding of $1.05 billion.

The Senate committee complained in its report that the OPEC nations had provided only 43 percent, rather than 50 percent, of the IFAD's funding. The panel also said the fund was being transformed into a bureaucracy by hiring too many professional staff members and implementing its own projects rather than relying on existing multilateral organizations to supervise IFAD-funded projects.

Bilateral Aid

Reagan originally requested $5.338 billion in bilateral aid — assistance sent directly from the United States to recipient countries — but reduced that to $4.873 billion in his September request.

The House committee approved $5.008 billion, and the Senate committee approved $4.857 billion.

Economic Support Fund

As in previous years, about half of bilateral aid came under the Economic Support Fund (ESF), which aimed to help friendly nations with their economic troubles so they could spend more on defense.

The original Reagan request for ESF was $2.682 billion, up from $2.105 billion in fiscal 1981. The revised request was for $2.549 billion. The House committee approved $2.464 billion. The Senate panel approved $2.549 billion.

The bulk of ESF aid was for Israel ($806 million) and Egypt ($771 million) — 64 percent under the House committee bill, 62 percent under the Senate committee version.

Those sums included $21 million for each nation to repay funds that were taken away from them in fiscal 1981 and given instead to El Salvador and Liberia.

The House Foreign Affairs and Senate Foreign Relations committees earmarked the same amounts of ESF for Israel and Egypt in their fiscal 1982 foreign aid authorization bills (HR 3566, S 1196).

Other significant ESF allocations requested by Reagan and agreed to by the two committees included: Turkey, $300 million; Sudan, $50 million; Zimbabwe, $75 million; the Philippines, $50 million; El Salvador, $40 million; and Jamaica, $40 million.

The Senate committee bill approved $100 million for Pakistan that the administration requested as part of a five-year, $3.2 billion Pakistan aid package. The aid package was put together after the administration submitted its fiscal 1982 budget.

The proposed aid to Pakistan was controversial, in part, because of Pakistan's suspected attempts to develop nuclear weapons. The House Appropriations Foreign Operations Subcommittee deferred the request, and the full House committee failed to include it in HR 4559.

Contingency Fund. The committees also differed on a Reagan request for an unallocated ESF contingency fund.

The administration originally requested a $250 million ESF contingency fund under the president's control for quick infusions of aid to friendly nations as the need arose. But the proposal met with disfavor in the House and Senate committees that handled foreign aid, so in September the administration cut the request to $75 million.

The Senate committee approved that amount. In its Sept. 17 markup of HR 4559, the House committee reduced

the ESF contingency fund to $72.5 million on an amendment by Clarence D. Long, D-Md., chairman of the Foreign Operations Subcommittee.

The Senate panel said in its report that it was approving the ESF contingency fund only on the condition that it be subject to "reprogramming" procedures. Under reprogramming, the Appropriations Foreign Operations subcommittees received 15 days' notice of administration plans to shift funds from one account to another and could informally veto such plans by expressing their disapproval.

Bilateral Development Aid

Development aid programs run by the U.S. Agency for International Development (AID) accounted for most of the remaining bilateral aid funds.

Reagan originally requested $1.399 billion but reduced that in September to $1.217 billion for AID programs in agriculture, population planning, health, education and other fields. The House committee approved $1.324 billion. The Senate committee approved $1.211 billion.

For AID agriculture programs, Reagan's revised request asked $638 million. The House committee approved $700 million, claiming a reduction of $27.8 million from the first administration request. The Senate committee approved $680 million, characterizing it as an increase of $45 million above the fiscal 1981 level.

The administration originally requested $253 million for population planning programs, but reduced that to $211 million. The House panel approved $240 million. The Senate committee cut the revised Reagan request to $190 million.

The Senate committee cautioned AID against supporting private or other organizations that funded or promoted abortions. It also specifically prohibited donations to the World Health Organization Special Programme of Research, Development and Research Training in Human Reproduction, calling it "active in abortion related matters."

The administration requested $120 million originally and $100 million in September for AID health programs. The House committee boosted that to $133 million, and the Senate committee approved the original request for $120 million.

Reagan originally requested $110 million and later $98 million for education and related AID programs. The House committee approved $104 million, and the Senate committee approved $101 million.

Both committees took large chunks out of the Reagan request for AID programs in technical assistance and energy, research and reconstruction problems. The administration first requested $178 million, then reduced that to $160 million. The House committee approved $137 million, and the Senate committee approved $120 million.

Peace Corps

The administration originally requested $95 million for the Peace Corps but reduced that to $84 million in September. Demonstrating the Peace Corps' reviving political popularity, both committees increased the Reagan request. The House committee approved $100 million for the Peace Corps. The Senate committee approved $105 million.

Refugees

The committees also differed with each other and the administration on how much to spend to help immigrants

and refugees coming to the United States.

The administration originally requested $568 million — $553 million for migration and refugee assistance through the State Department and international organizations, plus $15 million for the U.S. Emergency Refugee and Migration Assistance Fund. The revised Reagan request dropped the latter and reduced the $553 million to $478 million.

The House committee approved $535 million, saying it intended to cut the original Reagan request "because of the uncertainties associated with this program" — an apparent reference to the difficulty of predicting how many refugees will come to the United States.

The Senate committee cut the revised Reagan request to $473 million. The report on S 1802 said the $4.5 million cut was being made because the administration had estimated that 140,000 refugees would be admitted to the United States in fiscal 1982, which the committee said was "doubtful."

The Senate panel also urged the State Department to be more rigorous in determining whether persons applying for admission to the United States were indeed refugees. It said the State Department's program may have "acted as a magnet, drawing in people who are not in fact refugees."

Military Aid

The House bill made a large cut in Reagan's request for military aid even after it was revised downward, but both bills provided large increases in arms aid spending over fiscal 1981.

Reagan Requests. The administration originally requested an appropriation of $1.668 billion in spending, an increase of $1.03 billion over fiscal 1981, to finance a military aid program. That figure would permit $4.054 billion in arms loans to friendly nations, up from $3.046 billion in fiscal 1981.

The first budget included a proposed program of "direct credits" for 15 selected recipients of Foreign Military Sales (FMS) arms loans. The administration asked Congress to appropriate $982 million to finance FMS loans at interest rates as low as 3 percent for those 15 nations. Regular FMS loans were made at market interest rates.

But the House Foreign Affairs and Senate Foreign Relations committees balked at that plan. In the foreign aid authorization bills, both committees reshaped the plan into a blend of grants and regular FMS credits.

In its aid authorization bill, the Senate approved a 50-50 blend of grants and regular FMS loans, offering the 15 nations the same concession on their arms aid as Reagan proposed but requiring only half the federal spending — $491 million.

In its September budget revision, the administration adopted that plan, dropping the proposal for low-interest FMS loans and requesting instead $491 million for arms aid grants to the 15 nations to go with regular FMS loans.

The authorizing committees also objected to a Reagan request for a $100 million contingency fund under the Military Assistance Program (MAP), which made outright grants to selected foreign nations. The administration later reduced that request to $25 million.

Overall, the administration revised its request to $1.096 billion in spending, but preserved the size of the FMS program at $4.054 billion.

Committee Action. Democrats and Republicans on the House Appropriations Foreign Operations Subcommit-

tee were sharply divided on the military aid issue, which along with the dispute over IDA VI held up full committee markup of the aid bill for weeks.

The Democratic-controlled House subcommittee flatly rejected the plan for concessional arms aid and the MAP contingency fund. The full House committee restored $300 million in arms aid at the urging of conservatives led by Jack F. Kemp, R-N.Y., but did not revive the FMS and MAP programs Reagan wanted.

By contrast, the Senate committee approved the revised Reagan request in full.

Foreign Military Sales

The revised request asked $991 million in total spending under the Foreign Military Sales (FMS) loan program: $500 million for an FMS loan to Israel that would not be repaid — an annual practice begun in 1977 — and $491 million for similar forgiven FMS loans to the 15 countries on the Reagan list of key allies.

Since fiscal 1981, Congress had not been required to make appropriations for the remainder of FMS loans, which nations had to repay at near-commercial interest rates.

Israel, Egypt. Continuing a practice begun after Israel and Egypt signed the Camp David peace accords, the administration proposed, and the committees agreed, that those nations receive the bulk of U.S. arms loans.

The administration proposed $1.4 billion in FMS loans for Israel, including the $500 million loan to be forgiven. It requested $900 million in FMS for Egypt, with $200 million of that to be forgiven.

The Senate committee approved the Reagan request. The House committee approved the $1.4 billion for Israel but increased the amount to be forgiven to $550 million, as the House Foreign Affairs Committee had done in HR 3566.

In the Kemp amendment adopted during its Sept. 17 markup of HR 4559, House Appropriations approved $500 million in regular FMS loans for Egypt, another $100 million in forgiven FMS loans for Egypt, and added $100 million to the grant MAP program and earmarked it for Egypt.

Selected Allies. Besides the $200 million for Egypt, the Senate committee approved the Reagan plan to provide another $291 million in forgiven FMS loans for the other 14 allies on Reagan's list.

The House committee rejected that, but under the Kemp amendment added $100 million in MAP grants and stipulated that the funds be divided pro rata among the nations on the Reagan list other than Egypt.

In its report on HR 4559, the House committee said it had rejected the original administration plan because it would be a "serious drain on the Treasury" and "in future years nearly all countries with which the U.S. has a military relationship would expect to receive" the grants rather than the regular FMS loans.

MAP Grants, Military Training

The revised request proposed $63.5 million in MAP grants, with $25 million of that to be a contingency fund and the rest to go toward phasing out the program, which Congress had tried to end for several years. In recent years the program provided aid to nations such as Spain and the Philippines, where U.S. military bases were located.

The Senate committee approved the administration request. The House committee rejected the $25 million

contingency fund, but approved $238.5 million for MAP grants because of the $100 million it added for Egypt and the additional $100 million it added for the other 14 selected allies. The remaining $38.5 million was to complete existing MAP programs.

The administration originally proposed a significant boost, from $28.4 million in fiscal 1981 to $47.7 million in fiscal 1982, in the International Military Education and Training (IMET) program, under which foreign military officers received U.S. training.

The House committee cut that to $35 million. The revised budget asked $42 million for IMET, and the Senate committee approved that amount.

Export-Import Bank

Both committees approved higher limits than Reagan wanted on lending by the Export-Import Bank, which subsidized financing for foreign buyers of American products.

The administration proposed reducing Ex-Im loans as part of its thrust toward cutting federal credit programs, but did not resist congressional moves to restore the money.

Reagan originally requested an Ex-Im limit of $12.635 billion for fiscal 1982, down from $13.535 billion in fiscal 1981, but revised that in September to $12.105 billion.

The September administration figure included a limit of $3.872 billion on direct loans by Ex-Im, a limit of $8.22 billion on loan guarantees and a limit of $13.3 million on Ex-Im administrative expenses.

The House committee increased those amounts to $3.961 billion for direct loans, to $8.651 billion for loan guarantees and to $15.1 million for administrative expenses. Some panel members said they would attempt to put Ex-Im's direct lending authority at $4.4 billion if HR 4559 reached the House floor.

Ex-Im was highly popular in the Senate, and the Senate committee boosted the Reagan request to $4.7 billion in direct loans, $9.22 billion in loan guarantees and $15.1 million in administrative expenses.

Senate Floor Action

The Senate Nov. 17 risked a fight with the House when it broke with tradition and passed a $7.3 billion fiscal 1982 aid appropriations bill the House had not acted on.

The text of the foreign aid bill (S 1802), which the Senate passed by a vote of 57-33, was then inserted Nov. 18 into the Senate version of a continuing resolution (H J Res 357) needed to fund the government after midnight Nov. 20. *(Vote 380, p. 63-S)*

Some House members were angered by the Senate action, regarding it as an attempt to usurp a traditional House prerogative to initiate all appropriations bills.

In 1962, all appropriations bills were delayed by a bitter feud between the Senate and House Appropriations committees over Senate efforts to assume more power over appropriations bills. *(1962 Almanac p. 144)*

"It will not be recognized legislatively by the House," declared Clarence D. Long, D-Md., chairman of the House Appropriations Foreign Operations Subcommittee.

"It has no standing because the leadership won't allow it," Long said. "It's against all the traditions of Congress. There's nothing in the Constitution that forbids it, but the whole history of Congress, the practice accepted which has virtually the force of law, is that the Senate cannot pass an

appropriations bill" first.

But an aide said Senate Majority Leader Howard H. Baker Jr., R-Tenn., led the Senate to act on S 1802 because he expected Congress to fail for the third year running to pass an aid appropriations bill.

Aid programs were funded in fiscal 1980 and 1981 under continuing resolutions based on unenacted aid bills. *(1980 Almanac p. 197)*

Baker, the aide said, saw the maneuver as a way to bring aid programs more up to date and into line with Reagan's requests.

One House aide said the action might cause problems in a House-Senate conference on the continuing resolution if House members set out to defend the tradition, which many mistakenly believed was established in the Constitution.

Long acknowledged that the Senate's passage of S 1802 as its position on foreign aid in the continuing resolution would require the House to deal with the Senate legislation in some way. But he said he hoped the House would refuse to accept any of the Senate numbers on foreign aid.

"I think it's very unsound legislatively to try to pass something like this [foreign aid] through the continuing resolution year after year," Long said. "To try to do this will simply mean we're never going to get a bill."

Despite the fear of a dispute in the conference on H J Res 357, Jamie L. Whitten, D-Miss., chairman of the House Appropriations Committee, said he appreciated the logic of the Senate action and was not antagonized by it.

"I don't think they did it with any idea of usurping or taking over," Whitten said. "I would guess they probably thought they couldn't do it [pass a new foreign aid program] otherwise."

Whitten said the failure to pass an aid bill in recent years, combined with distaste for foreign aid at all in a year of painful domestic budget cuts, argued in favor of Baker's maneuver.

Kasten Defends Action

When the Senate took up S 1802 on Nov. 17, floor manager Robert W. Kasten Jr., R-Wis., chairman of the Senate Appropriations Foreign Operations Subcommittee, acknowledged that the action might insult the House.

But Kasten said it was "beginning to look like fiscal year 1982 will be the third full year of trying to manage and administer U.S. foreign assistance programs under a continuing resolution."

He said it was "against this background that the [Senate] committee took the unusual step of reporting an original appropriation bill. We took this action for several reasons, but I believe we must emphasize that we did not take this action as a slap at the House."

As reported by the Senate Appropriations Committee on Nov. 3, S 1802 would have appropriated $7.250 billion for fiscal 1982 foreign aid programs, compared to $7.594 billion in the House Appropriations Committee bill.

The Senate passed amendments Nov. 17 adding $77.5 million to its bill, increasing it to $7,327,583,804. In its revised September request, the Reagan administration asked for $7,775,098,683 for fiscal 1982 aid programs.

Despite the controversy that normally surrounded foreign aid programs, the Senate acted quickly on S 1802 and made a few changes.

The only roll-call votes came on amendments the Senate readily rejected.

International Development Association

Kasten and Daniel K. Inouye, D-Hawaii, ranking minority member of the Foreign Operations Subcommittee, dealt amicably with the testy issue of IDA funding.

Senate Appropriations stuck by Kasten's recommendation that the U.S. donation to IDA in fiscal 1982 be held to $532 million, down from an original Reagan administration proposal of $850 million and a revised request for $820 million.

Inouye initially offered an amendment to increase the fiscal 1982 payment to $820 million. He said nations participating in IDA VI would reduce their contributions by $815 million if the United States cut its donation to $532 million.

"I would remind skeptics that seven of the top 10 IDA recipients border on the Indian Ocean," he said. "All are of strategic interest to the United States, and all have been courted by the Soviet Union. Our interest in opposing the expansion of Soviet influence dictates our support of IDA."

Inouye also argued that IDA was one sound way to promote economic development leading to political stability, which he said was good for U.S. commerce.

Kasten said of Inouye that he agreed with the "sense of his eloquent statement," but that the Senate should stick with the $532 million figure. He said $532 million was the proper amount under a Senate position adopted in the fiscal 1981 supplemental appropriations bill (HR 3512 — PL 97-12).

"I also point out to the senator from Hawaii that with the number I am recommending and that the committee has approved, there is clearly room to maneuver in conference with the House of Representatives," Kasten said. "Frankly, we need that maneuvering room in order to get our numbers."

Inouye then said that if Kasten would "lead the Senate delegation to conference with an open mind in this matter" he would withdraw the amendment, which he did.

Ex-Im Bank. Similarly, Inouye offered but then withdrew an amendment to increase the limit on direct loans offered by the Export-Import Bank to foreign purchasers of American goods.

Inouye proposed to raise the limit to $5.065 billion from the $4.7 billion ceiling approved by the committee, but dropped the proposal when Kasten pledged to fight for the Senate figure in conference with the House.

Roll Calls

The amendments that had to be dealt with by roll-call votes were offered by Jesse Helms, R-N.C., and Claiborne Pell, D-R.I.

The Helms amendment, rejected by a vote of 26-67, would have prohibited the president from giving Zimbabwe $75 million in Economic Support Fund (ESF) aid provided in S 1802 unless North Korean military advisers in Zimbabwe had left by Jan. 1, 1982. *(Vote 378, p. 63-S)*

The Helms amendment was similar to one Helms offered Oct. 22, and which the Senate defeated, during floor action on the fiscal 1982 foreign aid authorization bill (S 1196).

Pell's amendment, which he said Daniel Patrick Moynihan, D-N.Y., had intended to offer, would have prohibited giving Pakistan $100 million in ESF aid contained in the bill unless the Pakistani government fully compensated the United States for damages to U.S. facilities in Pakistan during attacks by Pakistani mobs Nov. 21, 1979.

The Pell amendment, rejected by a vote of 36-55, also

would have required Pakistan to compensate the families of four persons killed in the attacks, two of them Americans and two Pakistani employees of the United States. *(Vote 379, p. 63-S)*

Kasten and Inouye opposed the amendment because the Reagan administration had embarked on an effort to improve relations with Pakistan and to bolster its defenses against Soviet expansion through Afghanistan.

Other Action

The Senate adopted these other amendments by voice vote:

● By Kasten and Charles H. Percy, R-Ill., adding $50 million in Economic Support Fund for Sudan, $5 million for Poland, $5 million for Tunisia and $15 million for Costa Rica.

● By Percy, to increase the amount for the United Nations Environmental Program to $7.5 million from $5 million.

● By Percy and Paul S. Sarbanes, D-Md., to add $20 million for Foreign Military Sales credit for Greece, increasing the amount of arms loans for Greece to $280 million from $260 million.

● By Nancy Landon Kassebaum, R-Kan., to cut the Agency for International Development's agriculture account by $42.5 million, to $637.5 million, and add that amount to the Sahel Development Program, raising it to $92.5 million, in each case matching Reagan requests.

● By Kasten, providing that, except for the international disaster assistance, U.S. Emergency Refugee and Migration Assistance Fund and contingency funds within the Military Assistance Program and ESF, no more than 15 percent of the funds in any account could be spent in the last month they were available.

● By Kasten, a technical amendment to increase the limit on callable capital pledged by the United States to the World Bank from $1.678 billion to $1.688 billion. Callable capital was a guarantee to give the bank funds if it should default on its obligations to its creditors.

● By Percy, to delete language prohibiting appropriations for international narcotics control from going to the United Nations Fund for Drug Abuse Control, which operated in Pakistan.

● By Helms, as modified by Kassebaum, to prohibit the president from giving funds to the United Nations Institute for Namibia unless the president certified to Congress that such donations "will promote an internationally recognized settlement in Namibia."

House Floor Action

With a handful of Republicans leading the fight for foreign aid, the House passed the fiscal 1982 foreign aid appropriations bill (HR 4559) on Dec. 11 — only a few weeks after the measure seemed dead.

The vote was 199-166, with 115 Democrats and 84 Republicans supporting the politically unpopular bill. *(Vote 338, p. 110-H)*

The key floor action came earlier, when the House accepted, on a 281-114 vote, a Kemp amendment, cutting the fiscal 1982 contribution to the International Development Association (IDA) to $725 million, from the $850 million recommended by the House Appropriations Committee. *(Vote 336, p. 110-H)*

The $725 million was a compromise amount between the $850 million backed by most Democrats and the $520

million level sought by some Republicans who disliked IDA.

The other issue in the bill involved military aid. Key Democratic liberals were unhappy because the $7.5 billion measure contained $300 million more in military aid than they wanted.

But after adoption of the IDA compromise, the Democrats decided not to try to reduce the arms aid.

Reagan had requested a substantial boost in military aid this year to bolster U.S. allies such as Egypt and the Sudan.

IDA Funding

The contribution to IDA was a central issue in the partisan struggles of the summer over HR 4559.

When HR 4559 reached the floor, Mickey Edwards, R-Okla., offered an amendment reducing the IDA contribution to $520 million.

Kemp offered his $725 million substitute, saying that amount was the minimum that some Democrats demanded as the price for their support of the entire bill. Democrats who supported IDA had complained that Reagan and Republicans were trying to load the foreign aid bill with military aid at the expense of development aid.

The debate found Edwards and Kemp — who often agreed on foreign aid issues — on opposite sides.

Edwards responded to Kemp's appeal for a compromise: "You can talk to me about strategy, about conference committees, about coalitions . . . but there is no way you can defend the increase in funding for IDA in this bill."

But Kemp kept up his appeal, saying to Edwards: "Let me say it frankly and candidly, there's not going to be a bill" if the Edwards amendment were adopted and Democrats bolted as a result. "We need their votes and they need our votes," Kemp said.

Following the intra-Republican debate, Matthew F. McHugh, D-N.Y., a leading supporter of IDA funding, said he "reluctantly" supported the Kemp amendment. If that amendment were to pass, he said, "there is a reasonable chance of passing a foreign aid [appropriations] bill with bipartisan support for the first time in three years."

Opening Debate

Led by Kemp, the Republicans took a positive view of foreign aid that sharply contrasted with their negative rhetoric of recent years.

Bob Livingston, R-La., said that even though he was "one who has never been a supporter of foreign aid," he could say "it is not difficult" to support the bill.

In a semantic distinction apparently intended as a hint to foreign aid critics that there was room to rethink the issue, Livingston called HR 4559 a "foreign policy bill" as opposed to a foreign aid bill.

He said 63 percent of the bill was for military or military-related assistance, which he commended to his colleagues as a tool to "help maintain the military balance of power and deter Soviet aggression."

Kemp said supporting foreign aid was "difficult politically" for him, but the bill was "an investment in the freedom and peace of this country and our allies."

McHugh also portrayed the bill as a compromise.

"It's extremely difficult to get a balanced piece of legislation, which any president needs to conduct foreign policy," he said. "I think this bill is about as close as we can get under current conditions."

Export-Import Bank

The House also adopted an amendment by Conte to boost the ceiling on direct loans by the Export-Import Bank from $3.96 billion to $4.4 billion. Direct loans were highly desired by U.S. exporters.

The original Reagan request had been for a limit of $4.4 billion in Ex-Im direct loans, later revised to $3.87 billion. But Conte argued that even at $4.4 billion, Congress would be "reducing Ex-Im Bank direct loan authority by 20 percent from fiscal year 1981 — one of the largest single reductions of any program."

Conte argued that to retain the $3.96 billion level approved by the Appropriations Committee would be "tantamount to unilateral disarmament in international trade."

Kemp, striving to get the bill passed, argued against the Ex-Im Bank but not against the Conte amendment.

Vic Fazio, D-Calif., argued that Ex-Im lending had to be continued because the General Accounting Office had found that, in 1978, Japan and Britain subsidized 35 percent of their exports, France subsidized 20 percent and West Germany 12 percent. He said 6 percent of American exports were sold under Ex-Im subsidies.

Volkmer offered a substitute for Conte's amendment that would have cut the limit on Ex-Im direct loans $500 million, from the $3.96 billion in the bill to $3.46 billion. But he correctly predicted that his amendment would fail.

"Undoubtedly the individual industries that are affected by the Export-Import Bank have sufficient clout on this floor in order to make sure that they win the day whatever the amount. That is quite obvious to me," Volkmer said.

Volkmer's amendment to cut Ex-Im direct loan authority failed on a division, in which members vote by standing and being counted, of 11-43. The Conte amendment to increase Ex-Im direct loan authority to $4.4 billion then passed by voice vote.

Indirect Aid

The final apparent threat to the bill arose when John M. Ashbrook, R-Ohio, offered an amendment to add the phrase "or indirectly" to a provision in the bill barring "direct" payment of aid or reparations to Angola, Cambodia, Cuba, Laos, Vietnam or Syria.

Ashbrook said he wanted to close a "dangerous loophole" through which the nations on the list could still receive U.S. dollars, despite the ban on direct aid, through the United Nations, IDA and other international organizations.

Democrats such as McHugh and David R. Obey, D-Wis., fiercely opposed banning indirect aid to any nation, arguing that the charters of international organizations such as the United Nations and the World Bank prohibited them from accepting funds with such conditions attached.

The danger to the bill stemmed from Kemp's support for the amendment, which he cosponsored and, with Ashbrook's consent, modified by adding Libya to the list.

McHugh reacted angrily. "We have spent . . . literally months to put together a compromise bill," he said. "At literally the eleventh and a half hour, this amendment comes forward which will, in effect, destroy that compromise."

Recalling past debates on the issue, McHugh repeated that "the effect of this amendment is to prevent any of the multilateral institutions from accepting contributions from the United States."

Added McHugh: "I am astonished that the ranking

minority member [Kemp], who wants a bill as I do, would accede to this amendment at this time." He warned later: "If my friends and colleagues on the Republican side want a bill, they had better vote against this amendment."

The Ashbrook amendment failed on a division vote of 22-44.

Other Amendments

The House adopted these other amendments by voice vote:

● By Mark Siljander, R-Mich., providing that none of the funds appropriated under HR 4559 could be used "to lobby for, promote, or recommend abortion or to train any individual to perform abortion."

● By Jerry Lewis, R-Calif., as modified by Kemp, to require the secretary of the Treasury to direct the U.S. representative to IDA to "undertake negotiations to reallocate" loans made with funds provided under IDA VI "to provide a more efficient distribution among recipient nations." The amendment also required the U.S. director to seek a lower limit on IDA loans to any individual nation — language aimed at reducing India's share of IDA credits.

● By Philip M. Crane, R-Ill., to reduce the amount for AID population planning aid by $29 million, down to $211 million, or slightly below Reagan's revised request of $211.3 million.

Conference Committee

Much of the conference committee meeting was consumed by heated arguments and complex negotiations over the central issue that had held up HR 4559 all year: the proper ratio of military to development aid.

The development aid issue fell under two major items in the bill: the fiscal 1982 U.S. payment to IDA and the combined total of bilateral development aid administered by the U.S. Agency for International Development (AID).

The administration wanted the bulk of the military aid in question to provide arms grants to Israel, Egypt and 14 other nations in addition to regular Foreign Military Sales (FMS) loans for those and other countries.

Other military aid programs requiring appropriations included the grant Military Assistance Program (MAP) and the International Military Education and Training (IMET) program. The latter provided U.S. training to foreign military officers.

The key to the conference was striking a balance between the two forms of aid.

The differences between the bills and the final figure for those three items were:

● $532 million in the Senate bill and $725 million in the House bill for IDA, a difference of $193 million. Reagan had requested $820 for the 1982 installment on a $3.24 billion contribution to IDA. Conferees approved $700 million.

● $1.169 billion in the Senate bill and $1.295 billion in the House bill for U.S.-run AID development assistance programs, a difference of $126 million. Conferees approved the House figure.

● $1.096 billion in the Senate bill and $924 million in the House bill for military aid, a difference of $172 million. Conferees approved $965 million.

Kasten, chairman of the Senate Appropriations Foreign Operations Subcommittee, began the debate on the issue by acknowledging the need to preserve the "fragile coalition" of Democrats and Republicans that had gotten HR 4559 through the House.

Kasten then suggested that the conferees begin their negotiations by assuming a split in each of the three differences as a starting point.

Long reacted with alarm, warning the conference in a loud and urgent voice that if it split the differences, "while you might win here, I think you're risking defeat on the House floor — or not even getting it [the bill] onto the House floor."

Long's remarks set the tone for the ensuing debate, in which various proposals drew shrill warnings that the bill would not survive, and Long and other House Democrats threatened more than once to walk out.

Early on, development aid advocate McHugh showed the political hole card the Democrats were relying on to preserve most of the $725 million for IDA and resist arms aid increases.

"The problem is," McHugh said, "we have split a lot of differences to get where we are. The coalition [supporting foreign aid] is very fragile on the House side. If we go up on military, or economic or development, or either, we are shaking the coalition."

Earlier, Rep. Kemp had said that if development aid had to be increased to balance an increase in military aid, he preferred to increase bilateral AID assistance.

Long agreed, saying that approach made sense because Congress could change AID's programs if they were improperly managed, which it could not do with IDA.

Toward A Compromise

The conferees began moving toward the eventual compromise when Rep. William H. Gray III, D-Pa., proposed that they split the difference on military aid 50-50 and reduce the House levels on IDA and AID by one-third of the differences with the Senate on those items.

Gray's proposal would have meant $660.7 million for IDA, $1.253 billion for AID and $1.01 billion for military aid.

While not acceptable to the other conferees, Gray's idea got the negotiations under way, prompting a series of other proposals that juggled the figures in various ways.

Obey, an ardent supporter of foreign aid in the past who had voted against the administration-backed HR 4559 when it passed the House Dec. 11, urged his fellow Democrats to stand firm and let the Republicans make concessions to get Reagan his foreign aid budget.

"They need the bill; we do not," Obey said of the Republicans.

But Rep. Charles Wilson, D-Texas, urged his colleagues to abandon the partisan approach. A bill was needed, he said, to update the nation's foreign aid programs. Those programs had been funded for two years under continuing resolutions based on spending levels dating to 1978.

Wilson also noted that in the continuing resolution in force, IDA was allocated only $520 million for fiscal 1982.

"That does not bother me in the slightest," Obey snapped. "I ain't bleedin' about it."

Then Kemp, pounding the table, declared that it was "absolutely critical" to pass a fiscal 1982 aid appropriation bill and that "those of us who believe in a bipartisan foreign policy" had a responsibility to find a solution to the issue.

Various other formulas for resolving the differences were offered, then Long moved for a vote by House conferees on a proposal of his own: $720 million for IDA, $1.2 billion for AID, $950 million for military aid. Long's proposal failed by a vote of 7-7.

Military, Development Aid Balance Kept

The ratio between spending on U.S. foreign military and development assistance was strikingly static in fiscal years 1978-82, despite fierce battles in Congress between those who sought to shift the balance one way or the other.

Disagreements over the balance held up passage of a foreign aid appropriations bill for several months in 1981. Republican leaders, especially in the House, fought during the year for increased military aid to key allies. Many Democrats and moderate Republicans, on the other hand, emphasized economic and development aid to poor nations.

A compilation of aid totals for the five fiscal years revealed little change in the ratio.

As calculated by Congressional Quarterly, the ratio in those years averaged 49 percent for military and related aid to 51 percent for development aid. This shifted no more than 7 percentage points in either direction in any given year. President Reagan's original 1982 budget would have approximated the average ratio.

CQ included under military aid the Military Assistance Program, International Military Education and Training, appropriations for Foreign Military Sales credits (not including reserves) and the Economic Support Fund (which enabled recipient nations to boost their military spending). Total Foreign Military Sales credits were not included because they were not appropriated funds.

Development aid included bilateral and multilateral programs but not "callable capital" — reserves pledged to development banks that could be called if a bank defaulted on any of its obligations.

It should be noted that a 7 percent shift in an annual aid program averaging $7 billion would be about $490 million. On foreign aid issues, differences of only a few million dollars frequently took on major political significance.

Also, CQ's method of analyzing the aid ratio was only one of many that could have been selected. It was possible, for example, to include FMS guarantees in military aid totals, since they were loans made with "off budget" federal funds. Also, Economic Support Fund monies could be excluded from from military-related aid, since some were spent on development projects.

The consistency in the ratio of military-to-development aid stemmed in part from the fact that Congress failed to pass regular foreign aid appropriations bills for two years before it cleared the fiscal 1982 bill. Aid spending for fiscal 1980 and 1981 was based on levels established in previous years and incorporated into continuing resolutions. *(1980 Almanac p. 197)*

The failure of Congress to pass the aid bills arose largely from the lack of consensus on the proper ratio of military-to-development aid. But the stability of the aid ratio demonstrated that a *de facto* consensus had arisen through the balance of power in Congress: Neither side in the aid debate could get a spending bill through Congress without cooperation from the other side.

Major Categories of Foreign Aid: Fiscal Years 1978-82

(in millions of dollars)

	1978	1979	1980	1981	1982
International Military Education and Training	$ 30	$ 28	$ 25	$ 28.4	$
Military Assistance Program	179.8	83.4	110	110.2	176.5
Appropriated for Foreign Military Sales credits[1]	675.85[2]	1,024.5[3]	645[4]	500	750[5]
Total Foreign Military Sales credits	2,101	5,673.0[6]	1,950	3,046	3,834
Economic Support Fund	2,174	2,282[7]	1,942	2,105	2,576
Bilateral Development Aid[8]	1,274	1,541	1,575	1,700	1,786
Multilateral Development Aid[9]	1,301	1,840	1,633	1,214[10]	1,477

[1] *In fiscal years 1978, 1979 and 1980, amounts appropriated for FMS included a reserve equal to 10 percent of FMS loan guarantees. The reserve requirement was dropped in fiscal 1981 under the foreign aid authorization bill (HR 6942 — PL 96-533).*

[2] *Includes loans of $500 million for Israel and $17.5 million for Zaire not required to be repaid.*

[3] *Includes loans of $500 million for Israel and $8 million for Zaire not required to be repaid. Also includes $370 million for the reserve for special FMS loans to Israel and Egypt in connection with their 1979 peace treaty.*

[4] *Includes loans of $500 million for Israel not required to be repaid.*

[5] *Includes loans of $550 million for Israel and $200 million for Egypt not required to be repaid.*

[6] *Includes one-time loans of $2.2 billion to Israel and $1.5 billion to Egypt in connection with their 1979 peace treaty. In 1979 Israel received an additional $800 million grant (not included in these figures) to relocate its military bases in the Sinai peninsula.*

[7] *Includes $315 million for a one-time Middle East Special Requirements Fund in connection with Israel-Egypt peace treaty.*

[8] *Bilateral aid includes Agency for International Development (AID)*

programs, American Schools and Hospitals Abroad, Sahel Development program, International Disaster Assistance, AID Operating Expenses and Inter-American Foundation.

[9] *Multilateral aid includes donations to the International Bank for Reconstruction and Development, International Development Association, International Finance Corporation, Inter-American Development Bank, Asian Development Bank, African Development Fund, African Development Bank, International Fund for Agriculture Development, and to international organizations and programs. Figures for multilateral development banks exclude callable capital, which served as a guarantee against defaults and which was appropriated prior to fiscal 1981. Callable capital was: $822 million in fiscal 1978; $883 million in 1979; $883 million in 1980; $1,133 million in 1981; and $2,340 million in 1982.*

(For consistency, amounts for the United Nations Works and Relief Administration [UNWRA] prior to fiscal 1982 were subtracted from multilateral aid totals. UNWRA was shifted in fiscal 1982 to the Migration and Refugee account.)

[10] *Does not include a one-time subscription of $5,516 million for the International Monetary Fund.*

Source: Budget of the United States, fiscal 1980, 1981, 1982

Kemp then proposed $690 million for IDA, $1.2 billion for AID and $975 million for military aid. That, too, failed by a House conferees vote of 7-7.

Final Figures

It soon became apparent that the middle ground on IDA and military aid lay between the Long and Kemp proposals, but it took further debate for the conference to get there.

Finally, Sen. Daniel K. Inouye, D-Hawaii, announced with a smile: "When we sat down, I wrote down some figures and told my assistant, 'These will be the final figures.'"

The figures were: $700 million for IDA, $1.295 billion for AID, $965 million for military aid. Those figures represented a cut of $25 million from the House amount for IDA, the full House amount for AID development programs and an increase of $41.5 million over the House military aid figure.

Wilson immediately moved that the House conferees agree to Inouye's figures. They did by voice vote, and the Senate conferees quickly agreed.

Arms Aid Programs

Conferees later agreed to the following breakdown of the $965 million approved for military aid:

● $38.5 million for IMET, a 50-50 split between the $35 million in the House bill and the $41.9 million in the Senate bill.

● $176.5 million in Military Assistance Program (MAP) grants. Of that amount, $38.5 million was to complete previously authorized grants, and $138 million was to be divided among 14 countries for whom Reagan requested concessional arms aid, not including Israel and Egypt. Reagan originally had requested $582 million for special grants to the 14 countries but in September reduced that request to $265 million.

● $750 million in FMS loans that did not have to be repaid: $550 million for Israel and $200 million for Egypt.

In addition, conferees settled on a $3.084 billion limit, the Senate figure, for regular FMS loans to foreign countries that had to be repaid. The House had approved a $2.846 billion limit. The limit on FMS loans did not count as new budget authority in the appropriations bill.

Special FMS Fund

The administration lost one of its priority requests at the last minute when the conference deleted $250 million that had been provided in both bills for a Special Defense Acquisition Fund (SDAF).

Reagan had requested the SDAF to allow the Pentagon to order in advance those items, such as M-16 rifles, most frequently requested by nations buying U.S. military equipment with FMS credits.

The fund was approved under the foreign aid authorization bill (S 1196) but was dropped from the appropriations bill because the Congressional Budget Office had ruled that the $250 million would be charged against the limit on budget authority imposed on that measure under the second fiscal 1982 budget resolution (S Con Res 50).

The SDAF was to have been established using a portion of receipts coming into the FMS program, so the Appropriations committees had considered it an "off budget" item that would not count toward their budget authority limit.

The conference decided to drop the SDAF for fear the

CBO ruling, which effectively added $250 million to the total of HR 4559, might threaten House and Senate approval of the conference report.

Economic Support Fund

The next most contentious debate occurred when House Democrats sought to trade off a high priority Reagan request for $100 million in Economic Support Fund (ESF) aid for Pakistan against another request for an unallocated ESF Special Requirements Fund.

The administration originally requested $250 million in unallocated ESF monies to be available to the president to use at his discretion to give friendly nations quick injections of aid any time during the fiscal year.

As part of a larger effort to further reduce federal spending in fiscal 1982, Reagan revised that request to $75 million in September. The Senate bill contained $75 million; the House bill contained $72.5 million.

McHugh and others wanted to give the administration only enough money for one or the other — Pakistan or the Special Requirements Fund.

The $100 million request for Pakistan was intended as the first installment on a six-year, $3.2 billion economic and military aid to help counter the threat posed by the Soviet Union's occupation of neighboring Afghanistan. It was not submitted with the rest of the Reagan budget in March because the details were unsettled.

"Some of us have a real problem with the Special Requirements Fund because it is essentially a slush fund," McHugh said.

Kasten responded that the administration would have to get congressional approval for any expenditures from the fund under the "reprogramming procedure."

Under reprogramming, the executive branch was required to give the two Foreign Operations subcommittees at least 15 days' notice of proposals to shift money from one nation to another. An informal agreement gave the subcommittees the right to veto the administration's plans.

"It's not just walking-around money," Kasten said of the fund, using the slang term for political slush funds. "They can't spend it without coming to us."

McHugh said he and others also were uneasy about the request for Pakistan because their committee had not held hearings on the request.

Some Democrats had questioned the aid plan because of their distaste for Pakistan's military government under President Mohammad Zia ul-Haq.

Zia's regime was criticized for human rights abuses and its failure to defend the U.S. Embassy in Islamabad from a mob of Islamic zealots who sacked it in November 1979. The critics also disliked Pakistan because of its efforts to develop nuclear weapons.

But Inouye said the proposal to give $100 million in ESF to Pakistan should be seen in light of the fact that Pakistan had become "one of our most important listening posts" for gathering intelligence about the Soviet Union.

"We can scream and yell about the man in charge there today," Inouye said, "but it just so happens he *is* the man in charge at this point in history, and we have to deal with him."

Kasten added that it was important for the administration to get the full $100 million for Pakistan because Saudi Arabia had pledged to match U.S. aid four dollars to one. The full extent of Saudi aid to Pakistan had not been confirmed.

Foreign Aid Appropriations, Fiscal 1982

The following chart shows amounts in new budget authority of the revised Reagan administration request, the House- and Senate-approved amounts, and the final amounts for foreign aid appropriations in fiscal 1982.

(Figures in parentheses show program limitations that do not count toward total new budget authority; figures for development banks include paid-in capital but not callable capital)

Program	Revised Request	House-Passed Amount	Senate-Passed Amount	Final Amount
Inter-American Development Bank	$ 221,251,201	$ 221,230,477	$ 221,230,477	$ 221,230,477
International Bank for Reconstruction and Development	159,458,301	146,889,040	146,889,040	146,889,040
International Finance Corporation	14,447,900	14,447,900	14,447,900	14,447,900
International Development Association	820,000,000	725,000,000	532,000,000	700,000,000
Asian Development Bank	116,211,948	117,295,314	123,811,720	120,811,720
African Development Fund	58,333,333	58,333,333	41,666,667	58,333,333
International Organizations and Programs	189,200,000	213,638,000	218,638,000	215,438,000
International Fund for Agriculture Development	39,600,000	40,500,000	0	0
Subtotal, multilateral aid	$ 1,618,502,683	$ 1,537,334,064	$ 1,298,683,804	$ 1,477,150,470
Agriculture aid	$ 637,485,000	$ 700,000,000	$ 637,485,000	$ 700,000,000
Population aid	211,306,000	211,000,000	190,000,000	211,000,000
Health aid	104,654,000	133,405,000	120,405,000	133,405,000
Education, human resources aid	97,680,000	103,550,000	101,000,000	103,550,000
Energy, technical, selected development	155,715,000	137,200,000	120,000,000	137,200,000
Science and technology	10,000,000	10,000,000	0	10,000,000
American schools and hospitals abroad	6,600,000	20,000,000	12,000,000	20,000,000
International disaster aid	23,760,000	27,000,000	27,000,000	27,000,000
Sahel development	94,600,000	95,000,000	92,515,000	93,757,500
Foreign service retirement, disability	32,552,000	32,552,000	32,552,000	32,552,000
Economic support fund	2,598,500,000	2,463,500,000	2,623,500,000	2,576,000,000
Peace-keeping[1]	19,000,000	19,000,000	14,000,000	14,000,000
AID operating expenses	317,000,000	335,632,000	331,000,000	331,000,000
Trade and development	6,078,000	6,907,000	6,907,000	6,907,000
International narcotics control	36,700,000	37,700,000	34,160,000	36,700,000
Inter-American Foundation	10,560,000	12,000,000	12,000,000	12,000,000
Peace Corps	83,600,000	100,000,000	105,000,000	105,000,000
Migration, refugee aid	477,500,000	535,000,000	473,000,000	503,000,000
Subtotal, bilateral aid	$ 4,923,290,000	$ 4,979,446,000	$ 4,932,524,000	$ 5,053,071,500
Military assistance program	$ 63,500,000	$ 238,500,000[2]	$ 63,500,000	$ 176,512,000
International military education and training	41,976,000	35,000,000	41,976,000	38,488,000
Foreign Military Sales credits	990,900,000	650,000,000	990,900,000	750,000,000
Foreign Military Sales credit limitation[3]	(4,054,400,000)	(3,496,187,000)	(4,074,400,000)	(3,833,500,000)
Subtotal, military aid	$ 1,096,376,000	$ 923,500,000	$ 1,096,376,000	$ 965,000,000
Housing guaranty program	(150,000,000)	(150,000,000)	(150,000,000)	(150,000,000)
Overseas Private Investment Corp.				
Direct loans	(0)	(10,000,000)	(10,000,000)	(10,000,000)
Loan guarantees	(100,000,000)	(100,000,000)	(100,000,000)	(100,000,000)
Export-Import Bank total limitation	(10,885,301,200)	(13,066,115,000)	(13,935,115,000)	(13,635,115,000)
Direct loans	(3,872,000,000)	(4,400,000,000)	(4,700,000,000)	(4,400,000,000)
Loan guarantees	(7,000,000,000)	(8,651,000,000)	(9,220,000,000)	(9,220,000,000)
Administration	(13,301,200)	(15,115,000)	(15,115,000)	(15,115,000)
Total, new budget authority	$ 7,650,098,683[4]	$ 7,440,280,064	$ 7,327,583,804	$ 7,495,221,970
Grand Total, including new budget authority impact of Ex-Im Bank limitations	$11,096,098,683[4]	$11,414,280,064	$11,601,583,804	$11,469,221,970

[1] *Does not include $125 million for the U.S. contribution to the Sinai peace-keeping mission that was appropriated in the first continuing resolution for fiscal 1981 (H J Res 325 — PL 97-51).*

[2] *The House committee shifted $200 million from Foreign Military Sales (FMS) credits to the Military Assistance Program; the final bill* included $138,012,000 in the Military Assistance Program for direct FMS grants and credits.

[3] *Includes the amount under foreign military credit sales.*

[4] *Request includes $11,930,000 for transfer from previous years.*

Rep. Silvio O. Conte, R-Mass., noted that hearings had been held by the House Foreign Affairs and Senate Foreign Relations committees, with both panels approving the Pakistan item, and the House and Senate had approved the Pakistan aid in the foreign aid authorization bill.

Conte moved that the conference approve the full $100 million for Pakistan and only $25 million for the ESF Special Requirements Fund.

McHugh asked that Conte add to his motion that language be put in the conference report to stipulate that the Pakistan aid was to be spent according to an existing AID plan. Conte agreed, and the House conferees voted 8-3 to approve the motion. Senate conferees then accepted the Conte/McHugh compromise.

Export-Import Bank

Another major debate came on the issue of setting ceilings on direct loans and loan guarantees by the federal Export-Import Bank.

The Ex-Im issue was one of the few on which Republican Kemp and Democrat Obey agreed: Kemp opposed Ex-Im on the philosophical premise that the free market should allocate credit; Obey viewed it as discrimination against small American businesses that received no interest subsidies and did not benefit from Ex-Im lending for foreign concerns.

"It's trickle-down economics, and I just can't support it," Kemp said during the conference. "It's a Trojan horse, I would say."

Kemp's comment was a humorous allusion to a controversial December 1981 *Atlantic* magazine article that almost cost budget director David A. Stockman his job.

In the article, Stockman was quoted as confessing that the multi-year, "supply-side economics" tax cut advocated by Kemp and President Reagan and passed by Congress in 1981 was a "Trojan horse" to disguise traditional Republican "trickle-down economics."

Inouye and Conte argued that Ex-Im lending more than paid its way by creating jobs in the United States.

After little more debate, Long suggested a compromise: House conferees would agree to the higher Senate limit of $9.2 billion on Ex-Im loan guarantees if Senate conferees accepted the House limit on direct loans of $4.4 billion, compared to $4.7 billion in the Senate bill.

The House conferees agreed to Long's compromise by a vote of 6-5. Senate conferees accepted it.

Other Issues

One of the lengthiest debates over a secondary issue came on a Senate proposal to delete a requested $39.6 million U.S. donation to the International Fund for Agricultural Development (IFAD). The House bill contained $40.5 million.

The IFAD was established after the World Food Conference in 1974 to help poor nations with basic food production. The Senate had cut the request for IFAD because members of the Organization of Petroleum Exporting Countries (OPEC) were to provide almost half the initial IFAD funding of $1.05 billion but had not done so.

Sen. Patrick J. Leahy, D-Vt., argued for the House position, saying "the United States cannot be the bread basket of the world" and therefore should assist financially in international efforts to feed the hungry.

Kasten proposed a compromise under which the United States would donate only $10 million to IFAD in fiscal 1982, and the bill would condition U.S. participation to the OPEC nations keeping their pledge.

But Sen. Dennis DeConcini, D-Ariz., argued against giving IFAD any money. "I find even $10 million hard to understand when we're cutting [domestic] school lunch programs," he said.

Given that, Inouye suggested the wisest course might be to simply delete IFAD funding in fiscal 1982, as was done in the 1970s to the Asian Development Bank when Congress was displeased with that organization. OPEC "might straighten up and fly right" if that course were chosen, Inouye said.

The conference agreed and deleted all IFAD funding.

Miscellaneous Provisions

Conferees also agreed to:

● A Senate provision earmarking $10 million of the $27 million international disaster assistance account for the relief of earthquake victims in southern Italy.

● Split the difference between the $92.5 million in the Senate bill and the $95 million in the House bill for the Sahel Development Program, appropriating $93.76 million.

● A House provision of $2 million to establish the African Development Foundation. Congress authorized the foundation in the fiscal 1981 foreign aid authorization bill (HR 6942 — PL 96-533) but provided no funding. The $2 million was a limit, not an appropriation.

● Modify a House amendment prohibiting the use of any funds in the bill "to lobby for, promote, or recommend abortion or to train any individual to perform abortion." Under the final version, funds in the bill could not be used by any agency or group to "lobby for abortion."

● House provisions limiting the salaries of U.S. representatives to various international banks to no more than level IV of the federal Executive Schedule ($52,750 per year in 1981, $58,500 as of Jan. 1, 1982), and instructing the U.S. representative to IDA to press for a "more efficient distribution" of IDA lending, including a reduction in the maximum loans provided to any individual nation. Although not stated, the latter provision was directed at India, the largest recipient of IDA loans.

● A compromise of $120.8 million in total contributions to the Asian Development Bank, up from the House figure of $117.3 million and down from the Senate figure of $123.8 million. In addition, the bill pledged $42.6 billion in "callable capital" that did not need to be paid to the bank.

● The House figure of $58.3 million for the African Development Fund, up from the $41.7 million Senate figure.

● A Senate provision barring U.S. donations to the World Health Organization Special Programme of Research, Development, and Research Training in Human Reproduction because of its work on abortion.

● The House figure of $20 million for American Schools and Hospitals Abroad, up from an original administration request for $7.5 million, a revised request for $6.6 million and the $12 million figure in the Senate bill.

● Delete an earmark in the Senate bill limiting the U.S. donation to the United Nations population program to $32 million. The effect was to approve an earmark of $38 million for that program contained in the foreign aid authorization bill (S 1196).

● Add Libya, Iraq and South Yemen to a list of nations barred from directly receiving "any assistance or reparations" from the United States. Other nations on the list are Angola, Cambodia, Cuba, Laos, Vietnam and Syria.

Unlike conferences on aid bills in the late 1970s, the conference committee on the 1982 bill did not have to wrestle with the issue of prohibiting "indirect" aid to countries such as Vietnam because an amendment to ban indi-

rect aid was defeated on the House floor.

The World Bank and other international agencies had said they could not accept U.S. contributions with such strings attached. ∎

Money Bill Adds $9 Billion for Defense

In its fiscal 1981 supplemental appropriations for the Pentagon, Congress accepted about half of the more than $1 billion in budget cuts the administration assumed would follow a rapid drop in inflation in the late months of 1981.

The supplemental appropriations bill (HR 3512 — PL 97-12) added $514.2 million to President Reagan's request to cover higher-than-estimated inflation in defense operations and maintenance, shipbuilding and military pay.

HR 3512, cleared June 4, appropriated $11.801 billion for defense programs. That included $4.7 billion for a military pay raise that took effect Oct. 1, 1980, and $227.3 million for military construction projects. *(Non-defense provisions of HR 3512, legislative history, p. 281)*

House Committee Action

To judge by its treatment of the $12.75 billion fiscal 1981 supplemental defense appropriation request, the House Appropriations Committee supported the kind of defense spending increases planned by President Reagan.

But, as had been the case for years, the panel did not shrink from second-guessing Pentagon requests down to a fine level of detail.

The committee approved $10.92 billion for defense in the overall 1981 supplemental bill, reported May 4 (H Rept 97-29). Accounting for most of the committee's $1.78 billion cut in the Reagan request were dozens of reductions — partly offset by some increases. Only a handful of changes were flat challenges to administration policy. For example, one $322 million cut essentially reflected a disagreement over bookkeeping.

The largest change based on a policy disagreement was the committee's addition of $482 million to offset what it said was the Reagan administration's underestimate of inflation.

In another policy dispute, the committee opposed $139 million to recommission the aircraft carrier *Oriskany.*

Inflation

The panel's rejection of administration inflation forecasts came at the instigation of Republicans on the Defense Subcommittee. The Carter 1981 budget had assumed a 9 percent inflation rate. By assuming that inflation would be only 8 percent during fiscal 1981, Reagan had cut more than $1 billion from 1981 defense programs to offset part of the cost of additions to the Carter budget.

But the committee said inflation in defense programs had averaged 12 percent for the first six months of the fiscal year. To reach an overall average of 8 percent, defense inflation would have to average 4 percent for the last six months of the year, an event which that committee called "most unlikely."

In fact, the panel warned, inflation was likely to continue increasing in the defense industry even if it abated in other parts of the economy, because materials and skilled personnel were in short supply. "When sharply increased dollars begin to chase a limited resource base, increased

inflation is the likely result, not decreasing inflation as this budget assumes," the committee report said.

Pay Raise

The committee made only minor changes in the amount requested for routine military and civilian pay raises, approving $3.185 billion for the military and $1.54 billion for civilians. The Pentagon was the only agency not required by the Reagan administration to absorb some of the cost of the civilian raise.

The committee said its approval of the civilian pay hike would allow the Pentagon to proceed with a planned addition of 27,900 employees to the Defense Department, bringing total Pentagon civilian employment to just over one million. The added civilians were to replace military personnel performing civilian-type jobs.

Fuel Prices

To offset increases in the price of the 180 million barrels of oil bought each year by the Pentagon, President Carter had requested a supplemental appropriation of $739 million. Forecasting further price increases in the wake of oil price decontrol, Reagan increased the supplemental request to $985 million.

The committee approved only the Carter increase, noting that a "mini-glut" in the world oil market was keeping prices below those forecast by Reagan. But the committee added to the bill $123 million to stockpile fuel reserves for wartime use. This was in addition to $600 million requested for wartime fuel reserves.

Rapid Deployment, Indian Ocean

The committee said it fully supported administration plans to increase U.S. ability to put forces into the Indian Ocean and the Persian Gulf region. But on technical grounds, the panel cut $13.4 million from projects related to those goals.

At the recommendation of its Military Construction Subcommittee, the panel also disapproved as premature $35 million requested to begin construction and related design work for facilities in the Indian Ocean region.

The committee cut $5 million from a $70.2 million request to keep two carrier task forces underway in the Indian Ocean almost constantly. The panel said the Navy was pushing its Indian Ocean forces too hard, wearing out men and equipment. The reduction was intended to make those ships spend more time in port.

A $7 million request to pay the increased cost of civilian contractor employees aboard Indian Ocean ships was denied by the committee. Admitting that these maintenance technicians had increased combat readiness, the committee said that it did not want to encourage the Navy to become more dependent on them.

MX Missile

Consistent with its refusal to risk money on any one version of the MX mobile missile until a final version was

Defense Supplemental Appropriations, Fiscal 1981

HR 3512 (PL 97-12) made the following suplemental appropriations for defense programs in fiscal year 1981:

(in thousands of dollars)

Program	Administration Request	House-Passed Amount	Senate-Passed Amount	Final Appropriation
Military personnel	$ 705,686	$ 549,036	$ 615,596	$ 540,596
(Transfers from other accounts)	——	(47,800)	(47,800)	(47,800)
Operations and maintenance	3,034,937	2,224,514	2,820,502	2,738,390
(Liquidation of contract authority)	(620,053)	(620,053)	(620,053)	(620,053)
Procurement	3,312,936	2,814,590	3,830,236	3,094,246
Research and development	598,300	434,704	837,721	507,948
Military construction	334,362	221,402	232,262	227,262
Pay raises	4,717,874	4,675,574	4,692,874	4,692,874
Total	**$12,704,095**	**$10,919,820**	**$13,029,191**	**$11,801,316**

chosen, the committee denied a $36.2 million request to speed development of an anti-ballistic missile defense for MX bases.

The committee also deleted $35.1 million from MX-related design and construction projects and recommended that Congress block further expenditure of $92 million already appropriated for MX construction until the final MX decision was made.

House Floor Action

The House made no changes in the defense provisions of the supplemental appropriations bill. The bill was passed May 13, on a 329-70 vote. *(Vote 39, p. 22-H)*

Senate Committee Action

As reported by the Appropriations Committee May 14 (S Rept 97-67), HR 3512 appropriated $13.075 billion for defense programs, $325 million more than the president's request. The panel recommended $12.84 billion for programs other than construction — $427 million more than Reagan's request and $2.10 billion more than the amount approved May 13 by the House. For military construction, the committee recommended $232.3 million, $102.1 million less than the budget request and $10.9 million more than the House-passed appropriation.

Inflation Estimates

The largest single change in the Reagan request was the addition of $1.656 billion to offset inflation — other than fuel price increases — which the committee argued would be higher than assumed by the administration.

The committee said its action did not reflect a lack of confidence that Reagan's economic program eventually would reduce inflation. But the panel observed that inflation had averaged 11 percent for the first eight months of the fiscal year. In the remaining four months, it said, inflation could not drop far enough to yield an average rate of only 7.9 percent.

For fuel price increases, on the other hand, the Appropriations Committee was slightly more optimistic than the administration. Like the House, the Senate panel cut the

allowance for estimated fuel price hikes by $246 million. The committee allocated half that amount to increase the Pentagon's fuel stockpile for wartime use; the other half was dropped from the bill.

The amount approved by the committee for fuel price hikes was the amount requested by the Carter administration, which assumed that prices would rise to an average of $49.89 per barrel of refined petroleum. Reagan had assumed that prices would go up another $1.35 in the wake of oil price decontrol, but the committee pointed out that no such increase was evident.

Also like the House bill, the Senate committee version made a $311 million cut in the administration request that merely reflected a difference in bookkeeping assumptions.

MX Basing

In addition to the nerve gas weapons and the warship reactivations, the committee's most substantial impact on defense policy was its refusal to approve any funds to construct launch sites for the MX mobile ICBM until the president selected a specific MX design.

President Carter had selected — and the military preferred — a system that would shuttle 200 missiles among 4,600 hidden launch sites in Nevada and Utah. The system was heavily criticized by residents of those two states. During his presidential campaign, Reagan criticized it as unnecessarily complex and costly.

Pending Reagan's decision on a MX basing system, the House denied a $26.5 million request for construction of the Carter basing system. The House also ordered the Pentagon not to spend $92 million appropriated earlier in fiscal 1981 until the president had selected a basing mode and an environmental impact statement for the system had been completed.

The Senate panel endorsed the House action except for the requirement that the environmental statement be filed. It also deleted $3.9 million the House had approved (of $11.9 million requested) for MX planning.

For research projects to provide water in support of MX construction, the Senate panel added $8 million.

Other nuclear weapons projects approved as requested (but rejected by the House bill) were:

● $59.2 million to cover cost increases in the ground-

launched cruise missile designed to hit Soviet targets from European launch sites;

● $36.2 million for development of an anti-ICBM defense to protect MX missiles.

The committee also added $5 million, not requested by Reagan, to deploy 50 multiple-warhead Minuteman missiles in place of 50 earlier, single-warhead versions.

Rapid Deployment

Like the House bill, the Senate committee version approved in general the administration policy of preparing to deploy more U.S. military units to the Middle East; but it disapproved several specific requests.

The committee concurred with House action to cut $5 million from the $70.2 million requested to keep warships operating in the Indian Ocean. And the panel also rejected a $7 million request to pay for more civilian contractor employees aboard those ships. But unlike the House bill, the Senate committee approved $5 million to lease from the British Navy a ship that would be used to supply the Indian Ocean fleet.

For construction of facilities in the Indian Ocean area, the committee approved $43 million of the $68 million request. It told the Army to use previously appropriated funds to design facilities at Ras Banas in Egypt (on the Red Sea), where combat gear would be stored for use by U.S. troops flown to the Middle East in a crisis. The panel also deferred until the 1982 construction bill further funds for dredging the harbor of Mombasa, Kenya.

Senate Floor Action

Two controversial weapons programs were assured of immediate funding by Senate action on the fiscal 1981 supplemental appropriations bill May 20 and 21.

The Senate voted 61-34 to begin modernizing two mothballed battleships — the *New Jersey* and the *Iowa*. (*Vote 125, p. 24-S*)

But the Senate refused to defer the next step toward producing a new type of lethal nerve gas by a margin of only two votes (48-50). (*Vote 128, p. 25-S*)

In all, the Senate version of the supplemental provided just under $13 billion for defense programs and made few substantial changes from President Reagan's request. In one change, the Senate deleted $139 million for reactivation of the mothballed carrier *Oriskany*. This killed the proposal since the House also vetoed the reactivation.

In its various amendments, the Senate made a net cut of $55.6 million from the amount recommended by the Appropriations Committee.

The bill passed May 21 on a 95-0 vote. (*Vote 134, p. 25-S*)

Chemical Warfare

The chemical warfare project was a $20 million appropriation to equip a factory for making a new type of artillery shell to dispense lethal nerve gas. The new weapons (called binary munitions) contained two chemicals which would become lethal only when mixed. The Army argued that binary weapons would be safer for U.S. troops than current nerve gas weapons, since the two chemicals would mix only when the artillery shell was fired.

John W. Warner, R-Va., offered the amendment to add the funds requested by the administration for the plant that was to be located at the Army's arsenal in Pine Bluff, Ark. He and his supporters argued that chemical

weapons were needed to credibly threaten retaliation against any use of what they said was a very large Soviet chemical arsenal. Existing U.S. chemical weapons had leaked lethal fluids while in storage and were as dangerous to U.S. troops as to their targets, it was argued.

Appropriations Committee Chairman Mark Hatfield, R-Ore., and David Pryor, D-Ark., vehemently opposed the amendment, arguing that chemical weapons were peculiarly inhumane, that U.S. European allies would not consent to storing the new shells on their territory and that, to the extent chemical weapons were needed to deter a Soviet attack, existing stocks are adequate.

The vote came on a motion by Hatfield to table, and thus kill, the amendment providing the $20 million. The money would not be used to actually manufacture the weapons.

Warner's amendment did not increase the net amount of the bill, since it deleted $20 million from the operations and maintenance account for the Army.

Late in 1980, Hatfield blocked inclusion of these funds in the conference report on the fiscal 1981 defense appropriations bill by threatening to filibuster the conference report. (*1980 Almanac, p. 191*)

Battleships

An amendment by Armed Services Committee Chairman John Tower, R-Texas, to approve $92 million for the battleships ($89 million for the *New Jersey* and $3 million for the *Iowa*) marked the fourth time in a year that the Senate debated the project. The arguments (and the participants) were almost identical in each case.

Compared to a similar vote on the supplemental defense authorization bill, opposition to the battleship plan appeared to have increased. However, of 14 senators who voted for the project on the authorization bill April 7 and then against it on the appropriation, eight were Appropriations Committee members. (*Previous vote, vote 79, p. 16-S*)

Flight Officer Bonus

The Senate reversed the Appropriations panel on a proposal to pay bonuses to certain military aviators. By a vote of 79-16, the Senate adopted an amendment by Ernest F. Hollings, D-S.C., to transfer $55.5 million from various operations and maintenance accounts to fund the bonuses. They were to be paid to aviation officers who extended their tour of duty on a year-by-year basis. (*Vote 124, p. 24-S*)

Hollings said the bonus was needed to induce more pilots and other flight officers to stay in service.

Stevens said the bonus would help only the Navy solve its pilot shortage. He said it would undermine morale among other aviators who would not get the bonus, including enlisted personnel and some Air Force officers who were not pilots. Stevens' panel had recommended instead an across-the-board increase in flight pay to all air crew members, an approach Stevens said the Air Force favored.

Only five other members of the Defense Appropriations panel joined Stevens in opposing the measure.

Conference Action

Conferees filed their report (H Rept 97-124) on the bill June 3. They recommended $11.801 billion for defense programs — $1.1 billion below the Senate-approved amount and $881 million above the House-passed amount.

Inflation Estimates

In assuming that inflation would be higher than the administration projected, both houses had added money to the bill in order to pay for higher costs due to inflation. The House added $482 million, and the Senate added $1.665 billion.

In a compromise, conferees accepted the Senate's higher inflation estimates for the bill's operations and maintenance accounts, and added $514.2 million for those items.

But conferees accepted the administration's more optimistic inflation estimates for the procurement and research accounts.

In explaining the conference compromise, House Appropriations Defense Subcommittee Chairman Joseph P. Addabbo, D-N.Y., said he accepted administration assurances that it would request another supplemental if more money was needed for procurement and research.

The conferees used the Senate's inflation estimates for the operations and maintenance accounts, he said, because unbudgeted inflation in those day-to-day costs would have the most adverse impact.

MX Missile

Conferees on the bill denied all requests associated with the MX mobile intercontinental missile because Reagan had not yet decided how to base the missile.

The final bill dropped as redundant a House-passed provision barring use of any design funds for MX basing facilities until a final environmental impact statement had been filed. A provision of the 1981 military construction appropriations (PL 96-436) would have the same effect, conferees said.

The conferees also rejected a $36.2 million request to speed development of an anti-ballistic missile system called LoAD. Senate conferee Harrison "Jack" Schmitt, R-N.M., protested that LoAD could be used to defend whatever intercontinental missile system Reagan approved. But House conferees said the proposed acceleration was linked to MX.

Schmitt also protested in vain the conference decision to drop $5 million added by the Senate to replace some single-warhead Minuteman II ICBM missiles with multiple-warhead Minuteman IIIs.

Other Conference Issues

Reactivations. Over the strong objection of Senate Appropriations Defense Subcommittee Chairman Ted Stevens, R-Alaska, the conferees approved the $89 million requested to begin modernizing the battleship *New Jersey*, which was then in mothballs.

But in their report, conferees noted Navy Secretary John Lehman's pledge that the total cost of the project would not exceed $329 million. The Navy should proceed with the project only if it could be done for that amount, conferees said.

Both houses had rejected a request for $139 million to reactivate the mothballed carrier *Oriskany*.

Flight Officers Bonuses. Conferees accepted the Senate proposal to allow $55.5 million in transfers from other accounts to pay special bonuses to flight officers. The House had authorized $50.14 million in transfers.

Cruise Missiles. Conferees approved $59.2 million, the Senate figure, to cover cost increases in the ground-launched cruise missile to be based in Europe. The House had approved $18 million.

Nerve Gas. A request for $20 million to buy equipment for a plant to manufacture the so-called binary nerve gas weapons was not at issue in conference, since both houses accepted it. But the conferees ordered the administration to inform Congress of the total long-term cost of deploying the nerve gas weapons and of the policies of other NATO nations toward those weapons. ∎

Treasury/Post Office Funds

Congress failed to approve a fiscal 1982 appropriations bill for the Treasury, Post Office and several agencies when the Senate became embroiled in controversy over funding federal employee abortions.

The Senate began consideration Dec. 14 but did not complete action on a $9.4 billion fiscal 1982 bill (HR 4121 — S Rept 97-192) for the Treasury Department, presidential executive offices, the United States Postal Service and 10 independent agencies.

The House's $9.7 billion bill, passed July 30, prohibited the use of funds for abortions or administrative expenses associated with them under some 120 federal health plans.

Sen. Jeremiah Denton, R-Ala., tried to add similar anti-abortion language to the Senate bill Dec. 14. Because of parliamentary confusion, the controversial nature of the measure and the end-of-the-session pressure to adjourn, the leadership pulled the bill from the floor.

Because no 1982 appropriations bill cleared before adjournment, agencies under the bill were included in the continuing appropriations resolution (H J Res 370 — PL 95-92) passed by Congress Dec. 11. *(Story, p. 329)*

It was the second year in a row that Congress had failed to clear a Treasury, Post Office appropriations bill. The 96th Congress had adjourned before passing a fiscal 1981 measure because of controversies that included reapportionment. *(1980 Almanac p. 227)*

The Confusion

The Senate Appropriations Committee Sept. 22 rejected an amendment by Dennis DeConcini, D-Ariz., that would have had the same effect as the House anti-abortion language.

Denton's efforts to raise the issue on the floor were aimed at overturning an Oct. 8 federal court decision barring the Office of Personnel Management (OPM) from administratively eliminating abortion coverage.

Donald J. Devine, director of OPM, unilaterally banned the coverage Sept. 24. In a suit brought by the American Federation of Government Employees (AFGE), the court held that Devine acted outside his statutory authority and ordered OPM not to eliminate abortion coverage in the AFGE plan.

Subsequently, Denton said, other employee organizations filed similar suits before the same judge. OPM had permitted those plans to continue abortion coverage, according to an OPM spokesman.

Noting that the court held that Devine's action was not in line with congressional intent, Denton said the Senate should clarify that intent.

Other Highlights. The bill before the Senate was $254.8 million above President Reagan's September budget request, $348,220,000 below the House version and $919,852,000 below the fiscal 1981 funding.

The committee bill had totaled $9,827,130,000, some $38 million below Reagan's March 1981 request. After Reagan revised his figures to $9,142,274,000, the committee Oct. 22 modified its plan, and the Senate by unanimous consent Nov. 17 incorporated the figures into HR 4121.

The Senate Dec. 14 approved amendments to beef up Secret Service protection for presidential candidates and other top officials and to bar the Reagan administration from reorganizing or eliminating the Bureau of Alcohol, Tobacco and Firearms (BATF) before March 31, 1981.

House Committee Action

The House Appropriations Committee reported its $9.8 billion measure for fiscal 1982 July 9 (H Rept 97-171).

The total was $98.9 million below the president's $9.9 billion March request and $551.2 million below the $10.3 billion appropriated in fiscal 1981.

The committee rebuked both the Office of Management and Budget (OMB) for requesting an increase in funds and the White House for refusing to send a representative of the Office of Policy Development (OPD) to testify before the Treasury subcommittee.

Saying that the budget agency "ought to be setting the example for fiscal restraint," the panel recommended $33.4 million for OMB, $4.7 million below Reagan's request and the same as approved in fiscal 1981.

The panel refused to fund the White House OPD, formerly called the Domestic Policy Staff. The administration had requested $3 million for OPD, but it declined to send anyone from OPD to testify before the Treasury-Postal Service Subcommittee May 5.

The administration sent representatives from the White House Office of Administration, but committee Chairman Edward R. Roybal, D-Calif., refused to allow them to speak on OPD's behalf.

In a July 8 letter to Roybal, White House counsel Fred Fielding said, "The president is not subject to questioning as to the manner in which he formulates executive policy." The principle applied equally to senior members of the president's staff, Fielding said.

The major components of the committee bill included:

Treasury Department. The panel recommended $4 billion, $53 million above Reagan's request and $147.8 million above the $3.8 billion fiscal 1981 appropriations.

Bureau of Alcohol, Tobacco and Firearms (BATF). The recommendation of $155.6 million was $5 million more than Reagan wanted and $5.7 million more than the fiscal 1981 appropriation.

Saying it "was strongly opposed" to the administration's proposal to cut 229 employees from the agency, the panel recommended maintaining the April 30, 1981, level of 3,615 full-time workers.

The committee said the additional people were needed to combat the criminal misuse of explosives and firearms.

U.S. Customs Service. The bill provided $498.5 million, an increase of $18.5 million over the administration's request but identical to fiscal 1981 levels.

The panel explained that the extra money was to maintain the number of employees at the April 30, 1981, level of 13,099 to "stem the tide of illicit drugs coming into the United States."

Internal Revenue Service (IRS). The panel recommended $2.6 billion for IRS, $38 million above the administration request and $128.6 million more than the fiscal 1981 appropriation. It said the extra money would fund 1,500 additional positions above the budget request of around 80,000.

Secret Service. The U.S. Secret Service would get $179.2 million, the same as the administration requested but $885,000 more than the fiscal 1981 appropriation.

Despite the March 30 presidential assassination attempt, the panel reduced the 1981 level of personnel by 30. However, on May 6, the administration requested $1.7 million to boost the number of Secret Service personnel by 58 from 3,634. The increase would help augment security at the White House.

U.S. Postal Service. The committee recommended $869 million for the Postal Service, the full amount requested by the administration but $473 million below fiscal 1981 funding levels.

Members followed Reagan's requested cuts for two Postal Service subsidies. One, the public service subsidy, helped maintain postal service in unprofitable areas. The other, the revenue foregone subsidy, made up for income lost through subsidies primarily to non-profit groups.

The panel recommended $300 million for the public service subsidy and $500 million for revenue foregone. Together, that represented $643.9 million in cuts, according to Appropriation Committee estimates.

Executive Office of the President. The committee recommended $84.5 million for the executive office of the president, $8.7 million below the administration's request and $8.3 million below the fiscal 1981 level. The largest chunks came from cutting OPD and OMB.

Independent Agencies

For the Office of Personnel Management and other independent agencies, the panel recommended a total of $4.8 billion in fiscal 1982. That was $143.6 million below the administration request and $216.7 million below fiscal 1981 funding levels.

General Services Administration (GSA). The committee voted $557.3 million, $23.3 million less than the administration's proposal and $145.5 million less than 1981 levels.

Of that amount, $20 million was dropped from Reagan's $120 million request for the national defense strategic stockpile, which contained strategic and critical materials like tin and silver for use in national emergencies.

House Floor Action

After voting to prohibit the use of federal employee health insurance funds for abortions, the House July 30 approved a $9.7 billion appropriation.

As passed by a vote of 323-94, HR 4121 was $119,346,000 below the amount requested by the administration, $20,425,000 under the House Appropriations Committee recommendation and $571,632,000 below fiscal 1981 funding. *(Vote 174, p. 60-H)*

In addition to abortion, other controversial issues surfaced during the two-day debate July 28 and July 30.

They included efforts to ban advertising of the nine-digit ZIP code until after a study of the proposal was completed, to prohibit the Treasury Department from promoting the sale of savings bonds and to cut back funding for the BATF, which licensed firearms dealers.

Abortion Ban

The 253-167 vote July 30 on an anti-abortion amendment surprised pro-abortion forces. The measure, offered

by John M. Ashbrook, R-Ohio, would ban funds for abortions or administrative expenses associated with abortion under the federal employees' health plan, unless the life of the mother was endangered. *(Vote 171, p. 60-H)*

The House twice before had approved similar amendments, but neither became law.

By a 228-170 vote the House had attached the ban to the fiscal 1980 Treasury-Postal Service appropriations bill (HR 7583), but the bill was stalled over other issues. Then, by a 242-155 vote May 13, 1981, it approved the prohibition as part of the supplemental appropriations bill (HR 3512). The amendment was dropped in conference. *(1980 Almanac p. 230)*

Ashbrook contended that it was a "strange paradox" that Congress banned abortions for poor women eligible for Medicaid but not for the roughly 3 million federal employees. He estimated that the health plan helped fund 25,000 abortions annually at an average reimbursement cost of $625 per patient

But opponents said that reducing coverage under the health insurance plan unfairly cut federal employees' compensation. The government paid 60 percent of the premium; employees paid the rest.

Saying the amendment would "make second-class citizens" out of federal employees, Bill Green, R-N.Y., argued that it was "an attempt to dictate to individuals what they can or cannot do with their own pay."

Firearms Debate

The House July 28 also voted 279-141 to adopt an amendment by Delbert L. Latta, R-Ohio, to cut $5 million from the committee recommendation of $155,591,000 for the BATF. The reduction brought the funding down to the administration's request. *(Vote 160, p. 56-H)*

Some members protested that BATF had overstepped its mandate and harassed private gun owners and the amendment was backed by the National Rifle Association.

The amendment reduced by 229 the 3,615 full-time workers the committee had recommended for the agency.

ZIP Code, Savings Bonds

An amendment by Gerald B. H. Solomon, R-N.Y., to ban the U.S. Postal Service (USPS) from advertising the controversial nine-digit ZIP code during fiscal year 1982 was adopted July 30 by voice vote.

Solomon and others argued that the Postal Service should not be allowed to advertise the new system until the GAO had made its report to Congress on whether it would work.

Protesting that the government spent $16 million annually to sell "the equivalent of ice to Eskimos," Patricia Schroeder, D-Colo., offered an amendment to ban the Treasury Department from promoting the sale of U.S. savings bonds.

The amendment, adopted by a 223-190 vote July 28, cut $13.6 million from the $206,625,000 approved by the committee for the Bureau of the Public Debt, which oversaw the savings bond division. The reduction would mean the loss of roughly 400 jobs, Schroeder said. *(Vote 161, p. 58-H)*

She complained that the bonds were a poor investment, yielding only 8 percent if held for 9 years while Treasury notes and money market certificates currently returned 17 percent and 18 percent.

But other members launched an ultimately successful effort to restore the funds.

Saying that without the low-interest bonds, the government would have to pay an additional $420 million in interest. Clarence E. Miller, R-Ohio, offered an amendment July 30 to restore the $13.6 million in funds. It lost on a 203-210 vote. *(Vote 169, p. 60-H)*

But with the Treasury Department launching a vigorous lobbying effort, on July 30 Miller demanded a second vote on the Schroeder amendment, which was finally rejected 182-233. *(Vote 173, p. 60-H)*

Other Amendments

The House considered other amendments by:

● Abraham Kazen Jr., D-Texas, to increase to $499,743,000 from $498,468,000 the funds for the U.S. Customs Service. Adopted by voice vote July 28.

● Silvio O. Conte, R-Mass., to reduce IRS funding from $2,603,649 to $2,586,949. That was still higher than Reagan's request of $2,565,649. Adopted July 30 by voice vote.

● Richard L. Ottinger, D-N.Y., to reduce to the fiscal 1981 level of $92,823,000 funding for the various executive offices of the president. The committee had recommended $84,473,000 but had deleted funds for the Office of Policy Development, accounting partly for the lower figure. The vote July 30 was 164-253. *(Vote 170, p. 60-H)*

● Ashbrook, to prohibit the IRS from implementing or the courts from enforcing IRS regulations to deny tax-exempt status to private schools that discriminate against racial minorities, unless the court order or regulation was in effect prior to Aug. 22, 1978. Adopted July 30 by a 337-83 vote. *(Vote 172, p. 60-H)*

Senate Committee Action

As reported Sept. 22 (S Rept 97-192), the bill provided $9,827,130,000 in fiscal 1982. That was $37,508,000 less than the administration's March request, $489,794,000 less than the fiscal 1981 funding and $81,838,000 more than the House approved.

About $77 million of the $81.8 million increase over the House amount came from adding funds for the Postal Service to avoid a substantial increase in rates, the report said. The total postal recommendation was $946.2 million, as opposed to the $869.2 million recommended by the House and the administration.

The $946.2 million approved by the panel would help assure second- and third-class non-profit mailers "that they will not have to absorb substantial percentage increases in postal rates that in some cases represent 100 percent increases," the committee said.

For example, postage for a third-class non-profit, fund-raising letter would jump 62 percent under the House bill but only 48 percent under the Senate panel's plan, the report stated.

The committee by a vote of 14-7 rejected an amendment by Dennis DeConcini, D-Ariz., to bar the use of health benefit funds for abortions or administrative expenses associated with them .

The panel restored nearly $3 million deleted by the House for the White House Office of Policy Development and added funds for OMB to bring the level to $37.6 million. That was below the $38.1 million the administration had requested but above the $33.4 million the House approved.

Treasury Department

The panel recommended $3.96 billion for the Treasury Department, $284,000 more than the House, $33.3 million

more than the president's March recommendation and $127.7 million more than the current appropriation.

Bureau of Alcohol, Tobacco and Firearms. The panel voted $148.9 million for the firearms control agency, $1.7 million less than the administration request and House-approved figure, and $1 million less than the fiscal 1981 appropriation.

U.S. Customs Service. Some $503.5 million was recommended for fiscal 1982, as opposed to the $499.7 million approved by the House and the $480 million requested by the president. The increase would fund additional job slots throughout the agency. About $18.5 million would support 12,798 positions, 625 more than the administration had wanted.

IRS. The committee recommended $2.6 billion, $2.8 million less than the House, $18.5 million more than the president's request and $109.1 million more than the fiscal 1981 appropriation.

The panel added some $14.8 million for the investigations and collections division, which it said "has perhaps the largest payoff for the federal government per dollar spent of all IRS activities."

Secret Service. The panel recommended $180.3 million, $1.1 million more than the administration request and the House recommendation. It was also $1.9 million more than the fiscal 1981 appropriation.

The committee agreed to a May 6 Secret Service request to increase employees by 58 from 3,634, at a cost of $1.7 million, to provide increased security at the White House.

Postal Service

The committee recommended $946.2 million for the Postal Service, exceeding the administration and the House figures of $869.2 million.

For the public service subsidy, the committee recommended $250 million. The House and administration wanted $300 million.

For the revenue foregone subsidy, the panel provided $696.2 million. The House and the administration had recommended $500 million.

Miscellaneous. The committee prohibited funds from being used to require the implementation of the 9-digit ZIP code in fiscal 1982. It also required the Postal Service to provide six-day mail delivery and banned the wholesale closing of small post offices.

Executive Office

For the executive office of the president, the committee recommended $91.7 million, $7.2 million more than the House had allowed but $1.5 million less than the budget request and $1.2 million less than the fiscal 1981 funding.

Independent Agencies

For the OPM, GSA and other independent agencies, the panel recommended $4.8 billion. That was $2.6 million less than the House figure, $146.3 million less that the administration request and $219 million less than the fiscal 1981 appropriation.

Federal Election Commission. The committee allotted $9.4 million for the agency. The House had voted $9.66 million, the same as the fiscal 1981 appropriation. The administration had recommended $9.75 million.

General Services Administration (GSA). The committee approved $558.1 million, $812,000 more than the House provided. That was also $144.7 million less than

the fiscal 1981 request and $22.5 million less than the budget request.

Office of Personnel Management. For the government's personnel office, the committee provided $117.5 million. The administration and the House had wanted $119.8 million. The agency got $124.1 million in fiscal 1981.

Senate Floor Action

On Dec. 14, the Senate by voice vote adopted the following amendments by:

● DeConcini, to extend so-called "zones of physical protection" to the vice president and to White House staff and other top officials under Secret Service protection while with the president. The amendment would allow the Secret Service to arrest any individual who penetrated the protective area. It also would allow the Secret Service to prosecute any individual who made threats against the lives of presidential candidates receiving Secret Service protection.

● Lawton Chiles, D-Fla., to allow the Treasury Department and the General Services Administration (GSA) to transfer up to 2 percent of their money from one department activity to another. The transfer would be subject to advance approval from the House and Senate Appropriations Committees.

The Chiles measure was an amendment to an amendment by James Abdnor, R-S.D., to provide for a 5 percent transfer authority. The modified Abdnor amendment was subsequently approved by voice vote.

● Abdnor, to bar the Reagan administration from eliminating all but a few of the BATF's functions before March 31, 1982. The amendment would allow the administration to move ahead with its reorganization plan after that date unless the reorganization was disapproved by the House and Senate Appropriations Committees. The administration wanted to shift BATF's responsibilities for regulating the alcohol and tobacco industries to the U.S. Customs Service and its firearms control responsibilities to the Secret Service.

● Abdnor, to earmark $15 million of the BATF's budget for alcohol regulatory functions.

● Mark O. Hatfield, R-Ore., to strike language barring funding for interagency activities and reviews unless the activities were specifically prescribed by statute.

● Hatfield, to allow the GSA to acquire federal surplus lands and exchange such lands of equal value for land held by private owners that was slated to be used for a federal park in Hawaii.

● DeConcini, to bar the Internal Revenue Service from imposing any excise taxes on gunsmiths who produced 50 or less guns annually. ∎

Transportation Funds

Congress Dec. 14 cleared a $10.1 billion fiscal 1982 appropriations bill (HR 4209 — PL 97-102) for the Transportation Department (DOT) and related agencies after cutting almost $500 million from an earlier House-Senate conference compromise.

Although the final bill was about $343 million more than President Reagan requested in September, it conformed to a temporary funding measure (H J Res 370 — PL 97-92) for the government that he signed Dec. 15.

The original compromise (H Rept 97-331) reported Nov. 13 by House and Senate conferees would have appropriated more than $10.6 billion in fiscal 1982 for transportation programs.

The House Dec. 14 adopted the conference report by voice vote and then approved a motion amending the report by cutting some programs to conform with the temporary funding measure. The Senate concurred the same day, clearing the measure for the president, who signed it Dec. 23.

Some major reductions were in mass transit, the Coast Guard and the Federal Aviation Administration (FAA).

Even though the amended conference agreement provided more funding than Reagan had requested in September, it appropriated almost $1 billion less than the president's March budget plan.

Also the final compromise provided about $2.66 billion less than enacted for fiscal 1981. *(1980 Almanac p. 154)*

Some Compromises Unchanged

A number of areas were left unchanged from the original conference agreement. For example, the measure still provided $735 million for Amtrak, the federally subsidized passenger railroad.

Also retained was a compromise $8 billion cap on Highway Trust Fund expenditures for highway construction and related programs.

The administration had requested a limit of $7.172 billion.

The $450 million limit on Airport and Airway Trust Fund obligations for airport development was left unchanged. The administration request was for a $396 million cap.

The airport development funds might not be spent, however, because the program's authorization had expired due to a congressional dispute over the direction and scope of the federal airport program. *(1980 Almanac p. 267)*

New Reductions

Some of the transportation programs that received additional cuts in the appropriations bill included:

● **Mass Transit.** The amended conference agreement provided $1.68 billion in new and previously appropriated funds for urban mass transit capital expenses and $1.365 billion for urban transit operating aid and some capital purchases.

The conferees originally agreed to $1.71 billion for capital expenses and $1.43 billion for operating and capital aid.

Also, the bill appropriated $538 million for mass transit projects substituted for previously planned Interstate highway segments, down from $560 million.

● **Coast Guard.** The appropriation for Coast Guard operating expenses was set at $1.356 billion, down from the $1.4 billion agreed to originally. Vessel and equipment acquisition appropriations were reduced to $384 million from $400 million.

● **Federal Aviation Administration.** The appropriation for FAA operations, including air traffic control, was reduced to $2.095 billion.

The original amount had been $2.22 billion.

● **Highways.** The amount for highway projects that was substituted for planned Interstate highway segments was reduced to $288 million.

In their original agreement the conferees had settled on $325 million.

Provisions

As signed by the president, HR 4209 appropriated the following amounts for fiscal 1982:

	Budget Request	Final Amount
Department of Transportation		
Office of the Secretary	$ 43,516,000	$ 37,850,000
Coast Guard	1,964,418,927	2,100,158,927
Federal Aviation Administration	2,566,954,000	2,477,126,000
Federal Highway Administration	362,253,000	326,588,000
National Highway Traffic Safety Administration	81,948,000	74,900,000
Federal Railroad Administration	738,859,000	916,358,000
Urban Mass Transportation Administration	3,316,676,000	3,494,738,000
Research and Special Programs Administration	26,441,000	17,441,000
Office of the Inspector General	13,047,000	13,047,000
Subtotal	$9,114,112,927	$ 9,458,206,927
Related Agencies		
Architectural and Transportation Barriers Compliance Board	——	1,900,000
National Transportation Safety Board	16,742,000	17,125,000
Civil Aeronautics Board	92,166,000	91,400,000
Interstate Commerce Commission	69,520,000	70,150,000
Panama Canal Commission	420,520,000	420,520,000
U.S. Railway Association	12,320,000	9,000,000
Washington Metropolitan Area Transit Authority	51,586,000	51,586,000
Subtotal	$ 662,854,000	$ 661,681,000
GRAND TOTAL	$9,776,966,927	$10,119,887,927

House Committee Action

As reported by the House Appropriations Committee July 17 (H Rept 97-186), the bill provided about $11.1 billion in new budget authority for DOT and the related agencies in fiscal 1982.

The appropriation was about $1.9 million less than requested by Reagan in March and about $1.7 billion less than appropriated for fiscal 1981.

The bill included $735 million in fiscal 1982 for Amtrak, $122 million more than Reagan requested. Amtrak officials said they could continue about 85 percent of the current service with that amount if they also received legislative approval to take some cost-savings steps. Reagan's $613 million request, they said, would require ending service on all routes outside the Northeast Corridor between Washington, New York and Boston.

The $735 million and some cost-savings measures were authorized in the House and Senate budget reconciliation bills (HR 3982, S 1377). *(Reconciliation, p. 256)*

The appropriations bill also prohibited the transporta-

tion secretary from selling federal stock in Conrail without prior approval by the House and Senate Appropriations committees.

Some Conrail supporters were concerned that the administration would quickly break up the railroad and sell it in pieces, rather than as a single entity. They said that would mean the loss of vital freight service in the Northeast and Midwest.

Committee Recommendations

As reported, HR 4209 included:

Office of the Secretary. The bill provided $36.2 million and 550 staff positions for the transportation secretary's office, the same as appropriated for fiscal 1981. But the committee recommended cutting 53 jobs in the policy office, which it said was three times larger than the average in 10 other major departments.

Coast Guard. The panel approved the March budget request of more than $1.4 billion for operating expenses, almost $66 million more than fiscal 1981. Included were 38,671 military positions and 4,787 civilian positions, an increase of 85 military jobs and a cut of 379 civilian jobs.

Although the committee said it still was worried that the Coast Guard could not meet all its responsibilities, it said it would not recommend more funds until a review of the Coast Guard's activities was completed in 1982.

Included in the recommendation of $391 million for capital acquisition, construction and improvement programs was almost $177 million for three medium endurance cutters that could be used as anti-submarine vessels.

FAA. The panel recommended $2.4 billion for FAA operations and maintenance of the air traffic control system, including $900 million from the Airport and Airway Trust Fund. The fiscal 1981 appropriations act provided $525 million from the trust fund.

The committee bill set a $650 million ceiling on obligations from the trust fund for airport development projects.

Federal Highway Administration (FHWA). The $8.2 billion ceiling on Highway Trust Fund spending did not include emergency relief, which would amount to about $150 million more. The current ceiling was $8.75 billion.

Also, the committee recommended $400 million from the general Treasury for highway projects that states substitute for Interstate Highway segments, $200 million more than requested.

National Highway Traffic Safety Administration (NHTSA). About $85.9 million was recommended for operations and research, about $7.2 million below the March request and the same as the fiscal 1981 level.

No specific appropriation was included for state enforcement of the 55 mph speed limit, although states could use other monies appropriated under the bill for that purpose. Some $10 million was provided in fiscal 1981 for enforcement, but the new administration proposed dropping the specific 1982 appropriation.

Federal Railroad Administration (FRA). The bill appropriated $4.3 million, about $4.2 million less than Reagan requested and $4 million less than fiscal 1981.

But the committee met the March budget request of $29.8 million in new and unused fiscal 1981 funds for railroad safety programs.

Conrail received $80 million in new funds and $15 million in 1981 funds for severance payments of up to $25,000 for each of 4,600 "excess" employees to help reduce the railroad's work force. The appropriation was $30 million more than requested and $70 million more than 1981.

The Northeast Corridor improvement program received the full $200 million the administration requested. But the committee noted that the funding agreement should not be construed as endorsement of the administration's plan to reduce the scope of the program.

Urban Mass Transportation Administration (UMTA). The committee recommended $4.04 billion for mass transit, about $57 million more than the administration request and $170.4 million less than fiscal 1981.

The fiscal 1982 total included $220 million in previously appropriated funds. The bill included almost $1.8 billion for capital grants, almost $1.5 billion for operating subsidies and some capital expenses, $72.5 million for rural transit and $600 million for mass transit alternatives to Interstate Highway projects.

A major difference between the March Reagan request and the committee bill was the urban discretionary program, which provided aid for capital expenses such as bus and rail purchases. The bill's $1.8 billion appropriation was $61 million more than Reagan's proposal, although by excluding previously appropriated funds, the bill provided $624 million less than fiscal 1981.

The committee recommended $211 million for construction and planning of new rail systems, $81.3 million more than Reagan wanted but $181.5 million below fiscal 1981.

It included the full budget request of almost $1.5 billion for urban formula grants, which were used for mass transit operating and capital expenses. The committee estimated that there also would be about $50 million in unused fiscal 1981 funds that could be used. The $1.5 billion was $25 million over fiscal 1981, with the additional funds targeted for bus purchases.

Civil Aeronautics Board (CAB). The bill included about $29.3 million for the CAB, $568,000 less than Reagan's request and $86,000 above fiscal 1981. The appropriation required cutting 71 positions from the fiscal 1981 level. Staff had been reduced by 214 positions, or 27 percent, since the enactment of the 1978 airline deregulation act (PL 95-504), which required the CAB to be phased out by Jan. 1, 1985. *(1978 Almanac p. 496)*

The committee also provided $58 million for two subsidies for airline service to small communities, one enacted in 1938 and another included in the deregulation act. The total allowed was $48.3 million below fiscal 1981. Reagan wanted to eliminate the 1938 subsidy program. *(Congress and the Nation Vol. I, p. 536)*

Interstate Commerce Commission (ICC). The bill included about $74.2 million for the ICC, a reduction of about $8.3 million from fiscal 1981 and about $4.9 million less than Reagan requested.

United States Railway Association (USRA). The committee provided $1 million for USRA, Conrail's monitor and banker, $28 million less than fiscal 1981 and $13 million below the budget request.

No new funds were recommended for Conrail operating subsidies. But the committee said it anticipated that $242 million of the $485 million appropriated for fiscal 1981 would be available for fiscal 1982.

House Floor Action

The House Sept. 10 cut $100 million from the fiscal 1982 funding proposed by its appropriations panel for the FAA because of the reduction in employment caused by an air traffic controllers' strike.

HR 4209, passed by voice vote, provided about $11.09 billion in new budget authority for DOT and related agencies, about $11 million less than proposed by the House Appropriations Committee.

The total was about $12 million less than requested by Reagan in March and about $1.71 billion less than appropriated for fiscal 1981. The administration, however, opposed the bill's increase in funding over its request in several areas, including Amtrak, airports and highways.

The House, for example, approved $735 million for Amtrak, while the administration wanted $613 million. The $735 million amount was included in the budget reconciliation act (PL 97-35).

The bill provided a limit of $650 million on Airport and Airway Trust Fund spending for airport development projects, $200 million more than Reagan wanted.

In addition, the House approved $850 million in trust fund monies for FAA operations, while the administration wanted about $2 billion. Congress traditionally has resisted spending as much trust fund money on FAA operations as administrations have wanted.

Also included was $400 million for highway projects that states might substitute for proposed Interstate Highway segments, $200 million more than Reagan requested.

Adam Benjamin Jr., D-Ind., chairman of the Transportation Appropriations Subcommittee, proposed cutting the panel's recommendation of $2.4 billion for FAA operations because more than 11,000 controllers were fired after a strike began Aug. 3.

He offered an amendment to reduce the FAA funding and to cut the Appropriation Committee's recommendation of $900 million in trust fund monies for FAA operations to $850 million.

The FAA cuts were partially offset by increases of more than $6 million for the Coast Guard and of $72 million for rail programs. The rail increases were required to bring the bill into compliance with the budget reconciliation act.

Benjamin's amendment, approved by voice vote, provided $50 million for the St. Louis Rail Gateway rehabilitation project and $20 million for the financially ailing Regional Transportation Authority, which served the area outside Chicago.

Also included was $2 million for the Amtrak Commuter Services Corp., which was established by the reconciliation act to take over the commuter operations of Conrail.

An amendment by Gerry E. Studds, D-Mass., to add $84 million for the operations of the Coast Guard, was rejected 129-260. Later, by a vote of 283-98, the House adopted a second amendment by Studds to raise Coast Guard funding by $6.188 million, for a total of $1.409 billion. The amendment also prohibited reducing the number of civilian employees below the fiscal 1981 level. *(Votes 185, 187, p. 64-H)*

Studds and other members said the Coast Guard needed additional funds because of its increasing workload.

Other Amendments

In other action, the House:

● Adopted by 204-188 an amendment by Charles Wilson, D-Texas, to block a DOT plan to reduce traffic at National Airport in Washington, D.C., because of complaints of noise. Under the amendment, no funds could be spent enforcing a rule reducing air traffic below the daily levels of July 31, 1981. *(Vote 188, p. 66-H)*

● Adopted by voice vote an amendment by James L. Oberstar, D-Minn., to earmark $1 million in highway safety funds for the National Driver Register, which provided state officials with information on motorists with driving violations. The administration wanted to phase the register out.

● Adopted by 209-172 an amendment by John D. Dingell, D-Mich., to cut more than $1 million from the secretary's office, leaving a total of about $35.2 million. *(Vote 186, p. 64-H)*

● Adopted by voice vote an amendment by Benjamin to increase the $1 million authorization for the U.S. Railway Association (USRA) to $13 million, bringing the total up to the level in the reconciliation act. The administration requested $14 million.

Senate Committee Action

The Senate Appropriations Committee cut the House-approved funding, but it went only half as far as Reagan wanted in his September round of budget-cutting requests.

Mark Andrews, R-N.D., chairman of the Appropriations Transportation Subcommittee, said no more cuts could be made without inflicting substantial damage on necessary federal programs.

"We'd be cutting muscle out of a lot of programs. We've cut the fat," Andrews said in an interview.

As reported Oct. 27 (S Rept 97-253), HR 4209 appropriated more than $10.4 billion in fiscal 1982, or $637.4 million more than Reagan requested Sept. 24, when he proposed 12 percent cuts in non-defense spending. The total was $675.9 million less than the House approved figure.

Even though the Senate panel did not meet the president's September target, the bill was $688.6 million less than Reagan's March budget request and $2.4 billion less than the fiscal 1981 appropriations.

Some of the major reductions made by the Senate committee were for highways, mass transit operating subsidies and airport development. The committee held firm, however, on $735 million for Amtrak.

The committee recommended running a train that Amtrak discontinued because it did not meet the performance criteria specified by Congress. The train, the *Cardinal*, ran from Washington, D.C., to Chicago via West Virginia, home state of Minority Leader Robert C. Byrd. The panel argued that ridership had improved significantly.

Appropriations Highlights

Highlights of the committee's version of HR 4209 included:

● A $7.7 billion limit on obligations from the Highway Trust Fund for highway construction and related programs, down from the House cap of $8.2 billion.

● A $450 million cap on Airport and Airway Trust Fund obligations for airport development, equaling Reagan's original request but $200 million below the House limit.

● An increase in spending for the Coast Guard. The panel provided $2.24 billion for the Coast Guard, $275 million more than the administration wanted and $46 million more than the House amount.

● A total of $750 million for highway and mass transit projects substituted for planned Interstate Highway construction projects, $250 million less than the House and $46 million more than the September administration request.

● Funds for mass transit operating aid and some capital purchases were $1.4 billion, down from the House amount of $1.5 billion.

Committee Recommendations

As reported by the committee:

Office of the Secretary. The bill provided $35 million for salaries and expenses of the transportation secretary's office, $24,000 less than the budget request and $193,000 less than the House bill.

The bill barred the secretary from selling federal stock in Conrail without prior notification of congressional Appropriations committees. The House required prior committee approval.

Coast Guard. The panel said it was "gravely concerned that the ability of the Coast Guard to meet all of its traditional and recently added responsibility may be degraded by inadequate" resources. The Coast Guard enforced immigration policy on the seas, stopped illicit drug traffic, provided military and national emergency backup, and conducted search and rescue services.

The bill included a total of $2.24 billion for the Coast Guard, with increased funding slated for vessels, equipment and navigation aids. The committee said it disagreed with the House's prohibiting any reduction in civilian employees below the level existing at the end of fiscal 1981 because that would unduly restrict management flexibility.

The bill also included $10 million for state recreational boating safety programs from a fund established by a 1980 act (PL 96-451) for that purpose. The panel said revenues from motorboat fuel taxes should benefit the boaters who paid them. The fund's balance exceeded $14 million, the panel said.

FAA. About $2.2 billion was recommended, including funds for the operation, maintenance, communications and logistic support of the air traffic control system. Of that amount, $750 million came from the Airport and Airway Trust Fund.

The $2.2 billion was $106.4 million less than the House approved and $75 million more than Reagan requested. The House covered $850 million of operating expenses from the trust fund.

The bill placed a $450 million cap on trust fund spending for airport development projects, $54 million more than the budget request and $200 million less than the House.

The committee said the agency's fiscal 1982 funding was reduced partly because of the air controllers' strike. The panel directed the FAA to notify the House and Senate Appropriations committees of any additional funds needed to ensure air safety.

The committee said it was prepared to deal with DOT proposals to raise the pay of non-striking air traffic controllers during the House-Senate conference on differences in the two appropriations bills.

In addition, the panel deleted the House provision blocking a DOT plan to reduce traffic at National Airport in Washington, D.C., because of noise and congestion. The DOT policy "correctly recognizes" that there must be a limit on air traffic growth at National, the panel said.

Federal Highway Administration. The $7.7 billion ceiling on Highway Trust Fund spending for highway programs was $500 million less than the House bill and $528 million more than the budget request. The fiscal 1981 ceiling was $8.75 billion.

The committee recommended $200 million for highway construction projects substituted for planned Inter-

state Highway System segments, $24 million more than the budget request and $200 million less than House.

National Highway Traffic Safety Administration (NHTSA). The panel included $79 million for operations and research, almost $3 million less than requested and $6.9 million less than the House provided.

It recommended that at least $1 million be used for the National Driver Register.

The committee did not include a specific appropriation for state enforcement of the national 55 mph speed limit, although states could use other monies appropriated under the bill for that purpose.

Federal Railroad Administration (FRA). About $7.5 million was recommended, the same as the budget request but more than $3 million above the House bill. Also included were new and unused fiscal 1981 funds of $29.6 million for railroad safety programs, about $200,000 less than the House bill.

Conrail received $225 million in funds previously appropriated for labor protection benefits, such as severance payments, retraining and moving expenses. Included were funds for severance payments of up to $25,000 for each of 4,600 firemen and brakemen declared "excess." The House provided $80 million in new funds and $15 million in 1981 monies.

The Northeast Corridor improvement program received $176 million, the same as the budget request and $24 million less than the House bill. The committee agreed with the House that the appropriation should not be considered by the department as an endorsement of its plans to reduce the scope of the project. *(1980 Almanac p. 238)*

The committee provided $50 million for commuter rail services. Also included was $5 million for the Regional Transportation Authority (RTA) serving the area outside Chicago.

The House provided a total of $22 million, including $20 million for the RTA, under the transportation secretary's office account rather than the FRA.

Also, the committee recommended borrowing authority of $60 million to help Midwest railroads with track rehabilitation costs. The report recommended $15 million for the St. Louis Rail Gateway rehabilitation project, while the House provided $50 million.

Urban Mass Transportation Administration. The panel recommended $3.8 billion for mass transit, including $220 million in previously appropriated funds. The total was about $200 million less than the House amount.

The bill included $1.4 billion in new funds for the urban discretionary program, which provided aid for capital expenses, such as bus and rail purchases. The amount was more than $100 million less than the House bill and $100 million more than the budget request. The House and committee plans also added $220 million in previously appropriated funds for this program.

Also recommended was $1.38 billion for urban formula grants for mass transit operating and capital subsidies. That was about $80 million more than Reagan wanted and $100 million less than the House bill.

The panel provided $550 million for mass transit projects substituted for planned Interstate Highway segments, $50 million less than the House and $22 million more than the budget request.

Civil Aeronautics Board (CAB). The bill included about $26.3 million for the CAB, about $3 million less than the House and the same as the budget request.

Interstate Commerce Commission (ICC). The

bill included about $74.2 million, the same as the House and $4.6 million more than the budget request.

The committee also added a general provision prohibiting the ICC from using any of the funds to allow the Burlington Northern Railroad to abandon more than 350 miles of branch lines in North Dakota. The railroad wanted to abandon 1,202 miles of its 2,221 miles of branchlines in the state. The panel said that would be devastating to rural communities and shippers.

United States Railway Association (USRA). Included was $13 million for the USRA, the same as the House bill and $680,000 more than the budget request.

Senate Floor Action

The Senate Nov. 3 accepted the recommendations of its appropriations panel and by a vote of 77-15 approved the bill. *(Vote 349, p. 59-S)*

The Senate also followed the panel's recommendation to direct Amtrak to restore the *Cardinal* train service from Washington, D.C., to Chicago, via Cincinnati.

The House version of HR 4209, passed Sept. 10, appropriated $675.9 million more than the Senate bill and did not include the Amtrak provision.

Differences

Some major differences between the House and Senate versions included:

● **Highway Trust Fund.** The Senate approved a $7.7 billion cap on spending from the trust fund for highway construction and related programs, $500 million less than the House limit.

● **Mass Transit.** The Senate provided $1.4 billion for urban mass transit operating aid and some capital purchases, down from the House amount of $1.5 billion. Also, the Senate amount of about $1.7 billion for urban mass transit capital expenses was $127 million less than the House bill.

● **Airport Development.** The Senate limit of $450 million on spending from the Airport and Airway Trust Fund for airport development projects was $200 million less than the House ceiling.

● **Coast Guard.** The Senate provided $146 million more than the House amount for Coast Guard equipment and navigation aids, but $71.9 million less for operating expenses.

Funding Cuts

Although the bill exceeded Reagan's revised budget, it did provide more than half the total cuts he wanted. The measure was also $2.4 billion less than the fiscal 1981 appropriations.

By a vote of 39-52, the Senate rejected an amendment to reduce the $10.4 billion recommended by the Appropriations Committee (S Rept 97-253) by 4.1 percent. *(Vote 348, p. 58-S)*

Nineteen Republicans joined 33 Democrats in rejecting the amendment offered by Mack Mattingly, R-Ga.

Mattingly said his plan would have saved another $323 million. The amendment provided that no program would be cut by more than 7 percent and that the Coast Guard funds would not be reduced at all.

No other amendments were offered to reduce or increase the amount of spending recommended by the Appropriations Committee.

Provisions Compared

	Senate-Passed Amount	House-Passed Amount
Department of Transportation		
Office of the Secretary	$ 42,250,000*	$ 64,443,204
Coast Guard	2,239,282,927	2,193,021,927
Federal Aviation Administration	2,635,918,000	2,828,263,000
Federal Highway Administration	235,088,000	447,700,000
National Highway Traffic Safety Administration	79,000,000	86,851,308
Federal Railroad Administration	954,427,000*	954,843,000
Urban Mass Transportation Administration	3,516,576,000	3,804,800,000
Research and Special Programs Administration	26,441,000	29,837,000
Office of the Inspector General	13,047,000	14,826,000
Subtotal	$ 9,742,029,927	$10,424,585,439
Related Agencies		
Architectural and Transportation Barriers Compliance Board	1,821,000	2,070,000
National Transportation Safety Board	19,125,000	19,125,000
Civil Aeronautics Board	92,166,000	87,280,000
Interstate Commerce Commission	74,150,000	74,150,000
Panama Canal Commission	420,520,000	418,510,000
U.S. Railway Association	13,000,000	13,000,000
Washington Metropolitan Area Transit Authority	51,586,000	51,586,000
Subtotal	$ 672,368,000	$ 665,721,000
Grand Total	$10,414,397,927	$11,090,306,439

* The Senate included $22 million for commuter rail under the Federal Railroad Administration that the House had put under the Office of the Secretary.

First Conference Report

House and Senate conferees Nov. 12 agreed to a version of HR 4209 that was about $800 million more than Reagan requested.

The possibility of a presidential veto hung over the conferees as they resolved differences between the House-passed $11.09 billion bill and the Senate-passed version of $10.4 billion.

Major Compromises

Some major areas of compromise included:

● **Amtrak.** The conferees accepted the Senate's general bar against Amtrak paying state and local taxes, resulting in a savings of about $14 million for the federally subsidized passenger railroad.

Despite some House objections, conferees also accepted a Senate requirement that Amtrak restore the *Cardinal* train.

● **Highways.** The conferees agreed to an $8 billion cap on Highway Trust Fund expenditures for highway construction and related programs. The House had wanted $8.2 billion, while the Senate favored $7.7 billion.

The conferees voted $325 million for highway projects that substitute for planned Interstate highways and $560 million for substitute mass transit projects. The Senate provided $200 million for substitute highway projects and $550 million for substitute transit projects, while the House provided $400 million and $600 million, respectively.

● **Mass Transit.** The compromise included $1.71 billion in new and previously appropriated funds for urban mass transit capital expenses and $1.43 billion for urban transit operating aid and some capital purchases. The Senate wanted $1.659 billion for capital expenses and $1.38 billion for operating and capital aid, while the House pro-

vided $1.786 billion for capital expenses and $1.48 billion for operating and capital aid.

● **Airports.** The Senate limit of $450 million on Airport and Airway Trust Fund spending for airport development was accepted, $200 million less than the House had wanted.

● **Coast Guard.** The conferees agreed to $1.4 billion for operating expenses and $400 million for equipment and navigation aids. The Senate wanted $537 million for equipment and aids and $1.34 billion for operations; the House supported $391 million and $1.4 billion, respectively.

● **Commuter rail.** The conferees included $60 million for commuter rail, with $15 million for the Regional Transportation Authority outside Chicago, and $45 million for commuter services transfered from Conrail to other authorities. The House provided $22 million, while the Senate wanted $50 million. ∎

State, Justice, Commerce Appropriations

The House passed but the Senate failed to act on an $8.63 billion fiscal 1982 appropriations bill (HR 4169) for the State, Justice and Commerce departments and related agencies.

Although the bill came to the Senate floor Nov. 10, it subsequently became snarled in a filibuster over the issue of voluntary school prayer. An attempt to invoke cloture and limit debate on the measure was made Dec. 11, but the motion failed by one vote, 59-35. *(Vote 469, p. 76-S)*

It was the second year in a row that the funding bill for these agencies ran into trouble in the Senate. The fiscal 1981 bill was vetoed by President Carter because of anti-busing language attached to the measure. *(1980 Almanac, p. 210)*

When it became clear that the fiscal 1982 bill would not pass, funding for the covered agencies was put into the continuing appropriations resolution (H J Res 370 — PL 97-92). *(Continuing resolution, p. 329)*

House Committee Action

The House Appropriations Committee July 16 approved an $8.75 billion version of HR 4169 (H Rept 97-180) that included funding for several programs President Reagan wanted to abolish.

The funding total was $6.47 million less than the amount recommended by President Reagan for these departments and $868.25 million less than the fiscal 1981 appropriations.

Legal Services Corporation

The committee approved $241 million for the Legal Services Corporation (LSC), which Reagan wanted to abolish. The same amount was recommended in a House bill (HR 3480) reauthorizing the LSC. The LSC, which submitted its budget directly to Congress, had asked for $399.7 million, or $78.4 million more than its fiscal 1981 appropriation of $321.3 million. *(LSC, p. 412)*

The Appropriations panel recommended $70 million for juvenile justice programs designed to help states combat juvenile delinquency. These programs, which Reagan wanted to terminate and incorporate into social services block grants, operated under a $100 million fiscal 1981 appropriation. *(Background, 1980 Almanac p. 402)*

The committee recommended $16 million for planning and construction grants for public radio, television and non-broadcast facilities. This was $3.7 million below the amount made available for fiscal 1981.

Reagan wanted to terminate the 20-year-old program, claiming it had accomplished its purpose of developing the public broadcasting system.

The administration did not seek to kill the Economic Development Administration (EDA), but it recommended a drastic cut, from a fiscal 1981 appropriation of $476.5 million to $50 million — $32 million for economic development assistance programs and $18 million for salaries and expenses.

The committee, however, approved $288.5 million for EDA programs, a reduction of $148.3 million from the 1981 appropriation, and $25 million for salaries and expenses.

Department of State

The committee provided $1.78 billion for State Department programs, which was $123.3 million less than the Reagan request but $280.41 million above the fiscal 1981 appropriation.

The panel said the increase over current spending was largely the result of wage and price hikes and of U.S. contributions to international organizations and to international peace-keeping activities.

Surpassed only by a $924.26 million appropriation for department administration, the amount for contributions to international organizations — $470.89 million — was the second largest item in the State appropriation. It was $23.7 million less than the budget request but $73.78 million more than the fiscal 1981 appropriation.

The funds covered the United States' contribution to 45 international organizations. The committee said more than 70 percent of the total was for assessments from the United Nations and specialized agencies, including the World Health Organization and the International Labor Organization.

Related Agencies

Arms Control and Disarmament Agency (ACDA). The panel approved the full $16.77 million requested for ACDA, a $232,000 decrease from current spending.

International Communication Agency (ICA). The committee recommended $499.59 million for ICA activities, $61.82 million less than requested but $41.82 million more than current spending.

Department of Justice

The total amount for Justice Department programs was $2.45 billion, $98.2 million more than Reagan proposed and $121.88 million more than the fiscal 1981 appropriation. The increase was due primarily to juvenile justice programs and to personnel expenditures in the Immigration and Naturalization Service.

FBI. The committee proposed $736.13 million for the FBI, a reduction of $2.88 million from the Reagan request but an increase of $65.93 million above the current appropriation.

Immigration and Naturalization Service (INS). The committee recommended $387.14 million for administration and for enforcing laws concerning immigration, naturalization and alien registration. The committee proposal was $23.76 million above the budget request and $21.79 million above the fiscal 1981 appropriation.

The committee recommended a $25 million increase over the budget request, which was partially offset by reductions elsewhere, to keep 973 positions that were proposed for elimination.

Drug Enforcement Administration (DEA) The committee recommended $230.85 million for DEA, $2.33 million more than the administration's request and $15.55 million more than the fiscal 1981 appropriation. The panel included funds for 26 additional positions for enforcement of domestic drug laws and 10 additional slots for foreign cooperative investigations.

Related Agencies

Commission on Civil Rights. The committee recommended $12.32 million for the commission, as requested by Reagan. This was $165,000 more than the fiscal 1981 funding.

Equal Employment Opportunity Commission. The bill provided $139.39 million, $1 million less than the Reagan request and $1.81 million less than the fiscal 1981 appropriation.

The Judiciary

Unlike executive branch departments, the federal judiciary submitted its budget directly to Congress without revision by the Office of Management and Budget.

The judiciary requested $741.8 million for fiscal 1982 for salaries of judges, judicial officers and employees, and to cover expenses related to operating courthouses. The committee approved $716.16 million — $25.64 million less than the request but $69.52 million above the 1981 appropriation.

Department of Commerce

The committee voted $1.92 billion for Commerce Department programs, $286.73 million more than Reagan proposed, but $334.91 million less than fiscal 1981 funding.

General Administration. The panel recommended $28.41 million for salaries and expenses of the secretary and assistant secretaries of commerce. This was $7.31 million below the administration request and $5.62 million below the fiscal 1981 appropriation.

Bureau of the Census. The committee approved $152.93 million for Census Bureau programs, a reduction of

$3.39 million from the budget request and $82.12 million from fiscal 1981 funding levels. The cutback largely reflected completion of the 1980 decennial census.

National Oceanic and Atmospheric Administration (NOAA). The committee recommended $809.03 million for NOAA, an increase of $37.78 million over the Reagan request and $4.27 million over fiscal 1981 funding.

The panel delayed for six months the elimination of several NOAA activities, including 38 weather station offices, aviation area forecasts and fruit frost forecasts. The House had voted to eliminate the programs, but the committee report said panel members wanted to continue them for six months "to cushion some of the impact of such a sudden termination."

Coastal Zone Management. The committee provided $5.21 million for Coastal Zone Management programs, which provided assistance to states for developing and managing coastal areas. The amount was $3.2 million less than the Reagan budget request and $46.37 million less than provided in fiscal 1981.

Fisheries Loan Fund. The committee approved $17 million for the Fisheries Loan Fund, which was made up of fees collected from foreign fishing vessels. The money would activate an emergency loan program to help domestic fishermen avoid defaults on outstanding mortgages.

Maritime Operating Subsidies. The bill included $417.15 million, the full administration request, to subsidize the operation of U.S.-flag, U.S.-built ships to make them more competitive with foreign ships. No new funds were included for ship construction subsidies, as proposed by the administration.

Related Agencies

Chrysler Corporation Loan Guarantee. The committee recommended $1.36 million for this program, the amount requested by the administration and $7,000 above the fiscal 1981 appropriation. The program was administered by the Treasury Department.

Federal Communications Commission (FCC). The committee recommended $77.35 million, the full Reagan budget request, for the FCC. The sum was $3.71 million below the fiscal 1981 appropriation.

Federal Maritime Commission. The bill provided $11.4 million for the commission, $23,000 less than requested and $700,000 less than fiscal 1981 funding.

Federal Trade Commission (FTC). The committee recommended $71.96 million for the independent FTC, $2.5 million above the budget request and $1.18 million above the fiscal 1981 appropriation. The increase would allow the FTC to maintain its regional offices.

International Trade Commission (ITC). The panel voted $18.2 million for the ITC, $301,000 less than the budget request but $985,000 more than fiscal 1981 spending.

Marine Mammal Commission. The bill included the full $672,000 requested for the commission, a cut of $62,000 from fiscal 1981.

U.S. Trade Representative. The committee approved the full $10 million budget requested for the Office of the U.S. Trade Representative, an increase of $640,000 over fiscal 1981 funding.

Securities and Exchange Commission (SEC). The committee voted $81.71 million for the SEC, $1.13 million less than Reagan requested but $1.51 million more than the fiscal 1981 funding. The panel included language to bar the SEC from using any funds in the bill to relocate

its headquarters pending a review of its space acquisition activities.

Small Business Administration (SBA). The committee included $612.58 million for the SBA. This was $11.5 million less than the Reagan request and $952 million less than the fiscal 1981 appropriation. The committee report said, however, that the committee level was consistent with the House-passed budget reconciliation bill. The major cuts from fiscal 1981 levels were a $337 million reduction in capital for the Business Loan and Investment Fund and a $613 million slash in the Disaster Loan Fund.

U.S. Metric Board. The bill provided $2.71 million for the board, $482,000 less than the budget request and the same amount as the fiscal 1981 funding.

House Floor Action

The House passed HR 4169 Sept. 9 after rejecting an amendment that would have deleted $241 million for the embattled Legal Services Corporation (LSC).

The bill was passed by a vote of 245-145. *(Vote 183, p. 64-H)*

The $8.68 billion funding provided by HR 4169 was $77.1 million below President Reagan's budget request and $938.9 million below fiscal 1981 levels. *(1980 Almanac p. 210)*

Most of the reduction from fiscal 1981 spending came in the budgets of the Census Bureau, the Maritime Administration, the Small Business Administration, the Economic Development Administration and the LSC. Even so, these and other agencies generally fared better than they would have under Reagan's proposed budget, which targeted most of them for huge reductions or outright termination.

Legal Services Corporation

Members rejected, 122-272, an amendment by Rep. F. James Sensenbrenner Jr., R-Wis., to delete the $241 million appropriation for the LSC. *(Vote 182, p. 64-H)*

That amount had been authorized under a separate bill (HR 3480) passed by the House June 18. Reagan wanted to abolish the LSC, leaving legal aid for the poor to be funded through social service block grants to the states, but Congress balked at his plan. *(Story, p. 412)*

Contributions to International Agencies

The House made only one change in the funding levels approved by its Appropriations Committee.

At the urging of Larry P. McDonald, D-Ga., members agreed by voice vote to slash $70.63 million from the $470.89 million recommended as the United States' contribution to the United Nations and a number of other international organizations.

"Are we prepared to ask our constituents ... to expect less in the way of domestic programs and assistance while we vote to increase the number of their tax dollars for international organizations?" McDonald asked. "I think not. ..."

School Prayer

In other action, members adopted, 333-54, an amendment by Robert S. Walker, R-Pa., barring the Justice Department from using funds in the bill to obstruct programs of voluntary prayer and meditation in public schools. *(Vote 181, p. 64-H)*

Refugees in Florida

By voice vote, the House adopted an amendment by Dante B. Fascell, D-Fla., limiting to 525 the number of refugees, "entrants" and other aliens that may be housed at the often overcrowded Krome North detention center on the edge of the Everglades in south Florida. The amendment also prohibited the establishment of any new detention centers for aliens on federal sites in south Florida.

Fair Housing

Members rejected, 188-202, an amendment by Ronald M. Mottl, D-Ohio, that sought to prevent the Justice Department from requiring communities to accept government-subsidized housing as part of the department's enforcement of the 1968 Fair Housing Act (PL 90-284). *(Vote 180, p. 64-H)*

SEC Office Move

Also rejected, by voice vote, was an amendment by John G. Fary, D-Ill., that sought to strike from the bill a provision barring the Securities and Exchange Commission (SEC) from moving any of its offices from their present location in the District of Columbia. Neal Smith, D-Iowa, floor manager of the bill, contended the SEC had not followed proper procedures in seeking to lease new office space.

Provisions

As passed by the House Sept. 9, HR 4169 made the following appropriations for fiscal 1982 *(in thousands of dollars)*:

	Administration Request	House-passed Amount
Department of Commerce	$1,631,390	$1,918,124
Department of Justice	2,348,914	2,447,114
Department of State	1,908,768	1,714,834
The Judiciary	741,803	716,162
Related Agencies:		
Arms Control and Disarmament Agency	16,768	16,768
Board for International Broadcasting	98,317	88,317
Commission on Civil Rights	12,318	12,318
Commission on Security and Cooperation in Europe	468	458
Chrysler Corp. Loan Guarantee Program: Administrative expenses	1,356	1,356
Equal Employment Opportunity Commission	140,389	139,389
Federal Communications Commission	77,351	77,351
Federal Maritime Commission	11,423	11,400
Federal Trade Commission	69,458	71,958
International Communications Agency	561,402	499,586
International Trade Commission	18,501	18,200
Japan-United States Friendship Commission	1,998	1,998

Related Agencies:	Administration Request	House-passed Amount
Legal Services Corp.	399,700	241,000
Marine Mammal Commission	672	672
Office of the United States Trade Representative	10,000	10,000
Securities and Exchange Commission	82,836	81,706
Small Business Administration	624,080	612,580
U.S. Metric Board	3,190	2,708
TOTAL	**$8,761,102**	**$8,683,999**

Senate Committee Action

As approved by the Senate Appropriations Committee Oct. 28 (S Rept 97-265), HR 4169 appropriated $8.63 billion in fiscal 1982 for the departments of State, Justice and Commerce, the federal judiciary and a number of independent agencies.

The total was $449 million above President Reagan's revised September budget request of $8.18 billion.

But the measure was $53 million below the $8.68 billion House version and $130 million below President Reagan's March budget request of $8.76 billion.

The House bill was passed before President Reagan's Sept. 24 budget proposal. The Senate's State, Justice, Commerce Appropriation Subcommittee had approved its version of the bill before the speech, but after the president's remarks, the panel resumed work and made new cuts. Chief among them were:

● A $32 million reduction in budget authority for the Economic Development Administration.

● A total of $15 million trimmed from the Justice Department, with the cuts spread out over several divisions.

● A $20 million reduction in the State Department budget for contributions to international organizations.

One Justice Department division that fared well was the Immigration and Naturalization Service (INS), which was given $388.38 million by the committee, slightly more than the House provision of $387.14 million.

Reagan had proposed $471.51 million, but part of that was a Sept. 30 request for $108 million for detention and deportation of aliens. The committee did not consider the request because it was sent to the Senate so late.

The Legal Services Corporation (LSC) and the Federal Trade Commission (FTC) were the target of unsuccessful budget-cutting amendments in committee.

Legal Services Corporation

Reagan wanted to eliminate the LSC and let states provide legal aid to the poor through federal block grants. Like the House, the Senate subcommittee recommended $241 million for the LSC — a 25 percent cut from the fiscal 1981 appropriation of $321.3 million.

Thad Cochran, R-Miss., offered an amendment to trim the appropriation to $100 million. "I'm in favor of legal services for the poor," Cochran proclaimed, "but the funding level is out of order. It's too high."

Ernest F. Hollings, D-S.C., told Cochran that if he wanted to trim legal services for the poor, he should think about trimming legal services for the rich. Hollings said that corporations, in particular, can take huge tax deductions for many legal fees. "It is far in excess of $241 mil-

lion," Hollings said. "They write all of that off."

Cochran's amendment subsequently was rejected 8-16.

By voice vote the committee accepted four amendments by Lawton Chiles, D-Fla., restricting LSC operations. With one exception, they were almost identical to restrictions the House adopted in its LSC reauthorization bill (HR 3480). *(LSC bill, p. 412)*

One amendment barred LSC lawyers from bringing class action lawsuits against federal, state or local governments except in accordance with regulations adopted by the national LSC board of directors.

Previously, each local program decided whether to file a class action suit, which was brought on behalf of a large number of people who generally had the same grievance.

Chiles' original amendment, like the House authorization bill, would have barred class actions against government units. But at the urging of DeConcini, the committee agreed to allow class actions in accordance with national board rules.

The other amendments:

● Prohibited LSC lawyers from lobbying except in narrowly defined circumstances.

● Prohibited LSC lawyers from representing illegal aliens in matters other than deportation hearings. The amendment set out the types of aliens LSC attorneys could represent.

● Required that 60 percent of the boards of directors of local programs be appointed by an "appropriate state or local bar" association. Chiles said this was intended to provide greater local control of local LSC agencies.

Federal Trade Commission

Robert W. Kasten Jr., R-Wis., offered an amendment to cut the FTC appropriation by $10.8 million, to $61.1 million from $71.9 million. Kasten was chairman of the Commerce Committee's Consumer Subcommittee, which has jurisdiction over the FTC.

Kasten said FTC Chairman James C. Miller III told him some days before the meeting that the agency didn't need a $71.9 million appropriation. Kasten said Miller assured him the FTC would be able to operate effectively with a $61 million appropriation.

Lowell P. Weicker Jr., R-Conn., chairman of the State, Justice, Commerce Subcommittee, complained that he had just heard from Miller about the amendment at 7 p.m. Oct. 27, the night before the full committee markup.

He said the question of a lower budget had not been discussed during subcommittee hearings on the FTC. With evident irritation, Weicker and Hollings both said that Kasten's amendment amounted to "an end-run around" the subcommittee.

Weicker also presented committee members with a staff analysis contending that the $61 million budget would result in the closing of four of the 10 FTC regional offices and would require laying off more than 100 people. Weicker's document also asserted that the amendment "would dramatically curtail antitrust enforcement in general."

The amendment was defeated 8-14.

Senate Floor Action

There was no hint of the trouble that lay ahead when the Senate took up HR 4169 on Nov. 10 and began plowing through a series of amendments to the bill.

Amendments Accepted

On Nov. 12, the Senate adopted, 85-0, an amendment by Strom Thurmond, R-S.C., declaring the sense of the Senate that the Justice Department and the FTC should vigorously enforce antitrust laws. *(Vote 361, p. 61-S)*

Thurmond's proposal was a substitute for one by Howard M. Metzenbaum, D-Ohio, that included a paragraph stating that a current series of mergers was "tying up substantial amounts of credit to the detriment of small business and is contributing to the intolerably high level of interest rates."

Metzenbaum voiced particular concern about the Mobil Corporation's attempt to take over Marathon Oil Company, a move Marathon was resisting.

By voice vote Nov. 13, the Senate accepted an amendment by Kasten trimming FTC funding to $68.1 million from $71.9 million, a much smaller reduction than the $10 million cut Kasten had sought unsuccessfully in committee.

The Senate also agreed 54-23 to add $85.18 million to the $388.38 million appropriation for the Immigration and Naturalization Service (INS), in part to handle the continuing influx of Haitians in south Florida. *(Vote 372, p. 62-S)*

Amendments Defeated

By a 3-82 vote Nov. 12, the Senate rejected an Appropriations Committee amendment that deleted House language prohibiting the Census Bureau from spending money to prosecute persons who failed to return 1978 agricultural census forms or any similar forms in the future. *(Vote 362, p. 61-S)*

Senators tabled, 84-0, another committee amendment deleting language that barred the Commerce Department from spending money to promote or conduct trade relations with Cuba. *(Vote 363, p. 61-S)*

By a 21-61 vote Nov. 13, the Senate rejected an amendment by Jeremiah Denton, R-Ala., to delete the $241 million earmarked for the LSC. *(Vote 367, p. 62-S)*

It also tabled, 48-33, an amendment by Thad Cochran, R-Miss., to provide only $100 million for the corporation. *(Vote 368, p. 62-S)*

School Prayer Debate

The school prayer issue erupted Nov. 16 when the Senate considered an Appropriations Committee amendment to delete House language that would prevent the Justice Department from spending money to block implementation of voluntary school prayer programs.

The Justice Department never was involved in this area of the law. The major Supreme Court rulings on the subject resulted from cases brought by private parties. The high court held that it was unconstitutional to use a non-denominational prayer or to have daily Bible readings in public schools. *(CQ Guide to the U.S. Supreme Court, p. 464)*

The Senate did not vote directly on the committee amendment deleting the House language. Instead, members agreed 70-12 to a motion by Ernest F. Hollings, D-S.C., to table, and thus kill, the committee amendment. *(Vote 373, p. 62-S)*

Following that vote, Lowell P. Weicker Jr., R-Conn., floor manager for HR 4169, offered an amendment specifying that it was only "constitutional" school prayer programs Justice would be barred from trying to block.

Weicker contended that without the addition of the word "constitutional," the House language would "send a

signal and all of a sudden we are going to have everybody trying out their own particular scheme and back we go again as to what is constitutional and what is not. I would hope we would not send that signal."

Jesse Helms, R-N.C., retorted that Weicker was trying to "obfuscate the issue."

"What the senator is doing," Helms charged, "is trying to use a word knowing that it will signal the courts to keep on doing what you are doing, meddling in something that never was the courts' business in the first place. It is just a code word."

Religious Slur?

The debate turned increasingly emotional as Sens. John C. Danforth, R-Mo., and George J. Mitchell, D-Maine, pressed Hollings about just what would constitute a voluntary prayer.

During their exchange, Metzenbaum sought to be recognized. Finally, Hollings turned to him and said he would hear "from the senator from B'nai B'rith."

B'nai B'rith is a Jewish service organization.

Hollings' remark enraged Metzenbaum, who was Jewish. The Ohio Democrat shouted that Hollings was "incorrect."

"I am not the senator from B'nai B'rith," Metzenbaum said. "I am the senator from Ohio."

As several senators shouted for recognition, Alfonse D'Amato, R-N.Y., who was presiding, repeatedly banged his gavel and demanded order.

Moments later, Metzenbaum again sought recognition and in a subdued voice said he rose "in sadness" over what had just happened.

Quick Apology

Hollings asked for the floor and apologized to Metzenbaum. He said he meant no disrespect to his colleague.

"I was not throwing off on his religion. I said it in a moment of levity — I said it only in fun. I was being besieged from all sides. I had no intention to make fun of his religion," Hollings insisted.

"I consider the matter closed," Metzenbaum replied. The Ohio Democrat later said he received a letter of apology from Hollings.

The entire exchange between Metzenbaum and Hollings was expunged from the *Congressional Record*.

Votes for Prayer

Following this debate, the Senate voted 51-34 to table Weicker's amendment. *(Vote 374, p. 63-S)*

Helms then moved to table a motion to reconsider the vote on the Weicker amendment. Helms was successful on a 54-36 tally. *(Vote 375, p. 63-S)*

The Senate took two more votes on the prayer issue.

On Nov. 17, Weicker offered an amendment to the prayer section of HR 4169 that incorporated part of the First Amendment into the bill. It stated that nothing in the legislation should be interpreted to be "the establishment of religion or prohibiting the free exercise thereof."

The amendment was adopted 93-0. *(Vote 377, p. 63-S)*

Helms offered a subsequent amendment to make clear that the Weicker proposal would not limit the restriction the Senate had just approved on Justice Department involvement in school prayer cases.

The Helms amendment was adopted 58-38 on Nov. 18. *(Vote 382, p. 64-S)*

Interior Appropriations Cleared by Congress

Congress avoided a showdown with President Reagan Dec. 10 when it cut 4 percent from a conference report on the fiscal 1982 appropriations bill (HR 4035) for the Department of the Interior and related agencies.

The $7.2 billion bill was then cleared for the president, who signed it Dec. 23 (PL 97-100).

The fate of the bill had been in doubt Nov. 12 when the House adopted a $7.54 billion version, which exceeded by $1.1 billion the revised budget request sent to Congress by the president in September. Reagan had vowed to veto budget-busting bills.

House and Senate conferees had agreed on the $7.54 billion measure Nov. 4. (H Rept 97-315).

The Senate acted on the conference agreement first, cutting $314.3 million from fiscal 1982 expenditures and $5.4 million from deferred fiscal 1981 funds earmarked for a synthetic fuels plant. The $7.2 billion measure then went to the House, which quickly approved it by voice vote.

The cuts amounted to 4 percent, the minimum reduction demanded by President Reagan and included in Congress' third continuing appropriations resolution for fiscal 1982. The resolution (H J Res 370 — PL 97-92) cleared Congress Dec. 11. *(Story, p. 329)*

Among the cuts made on the Senate floor were $145.9 million from the Interior Department, $59.6 million from the Forest Service, $56.9 million from the Energy Department fossil fuels programs, $26.9 million from the Indian Health Service and $3.2 million from Indian education programs.

The House originally voted $11.1 billion and the Senate $7.36 billion. Conferees had reached the $7.54 billion compromise Nov. 4.

Administration Proposals Rejected

As approved by the conferees, the bill rejected administration proposals to halt federal park expansion and to use park acquisition funds to upgrade existing parks.

Congress went along with an administration request that federal grants for state park acquisition be eliminated, but the conference report insisted that the cuts be effective for only one year.

"We expect the administration to submit a budget request for state assistance in fiscal year 1983," said the conferees.

Sen. Joseph R. Biden Jr., D-Del., complained that conferees had agreed to eliminate the Senate's $100 million for the state park program, which benefited states all over the country, but only cut the Payments in Lieu of Taxes (PILT) program, which primarily benefited Western states, by 3 percent.

The final agreement provided $95.5 million for PILT, which was used to compensate counties for the loss of local taxes on federal lands. The Senate had provided $105 million.

The bill also did not go along with the administration's recommendations to abolish state grants for historic preservation and urban parks, consolidate several Indian programs into block grants, require territories to pay 25 percent of federal project construction costs, abolish several energy conservation programs and halve funding for the arts and humanities.

The conference agreement included a provision barring four controversial oil and gas lease sales offshore from California, but did not include an earlier provision blocking a controversial reorganization of the Office of Surface Mining.

As cleared by Congress, HR 4035 appropriated for fiscal 1982 *(in thousands of dollars)*:

Agency	Revised Budget Request	Final Appropriation
Interior Department		
Bureau of Land Management	$ 456,408	$ 542,057
Office of Water Research and Technology	——	10,636
Fish and Wildlife Service	202,381	250,484
National Park Service	623,274	751,150
Geological Survey	473,582	496,741
Bureau of Mines	124,881	145,885
Office of Surface Mining	158,220	160,597
Bureau of Indian Affairs	889,899	971,008
Office of Territorial Affairs	134,952	163,147
Office of the Solicitor	17,307	17,600
Office of the Secretary	51,652	54,916
Total, Interior Dept.	3,132,556	3,564,221
Department of Agriculture		
Forest Service	1,263,103	1,351,228
Department of Energy		
Fossil energy research	358,259	413,032
Fossil energy construction	15,840	3,840
Naval petroleum and oil shale reserves	230,563	213,142
Energy conservation	103,838	145,400
Economic regulation	14,600	21,416
Strategic Petroleum Reserve	199,408	191,432
Energy Information Administration	70,400	78,919
Total, Energy Dept.	992,908	1,067,181
Department of Health and Human Services		
Indian Health	558,729	646,797
Department of Education		
Indian Education	71,364	77,852
Related Agencies		
Navajo and Hopi Indian Relocation Commission	13,254	10,062
Smithsonian Institution	137,486	142,534
National Gallery of Art	28,844	29,815
Woodrow Wilson Int'l Center for Scholars	1,989	1,872
National Endowment for the Arts	77,440	143,040
National Endowment for the Humanities	74,800	130,560

Agency	Revised Budget Request	Final Appropriation
Institute of Museum Services	194	11,520
Commission on Fine Arts	152	291
Advisory Council on Historic Preservation	1,641	1,567
National Capital Planning Commission	2,095	2,267
Franklin D. Roosevelt Memorial Commission	35	29
Pennsylvania Avenue Development Corporation	16,755	18,278
Federal Inspector for Alaska Gas Pipeline	32,180	27,425
Holocaust Memorial Council	704	768
Total, Related Agencies	387,569	520,028
GRAND TOTAL	$6,406,229	$7,227,307

House Committee Action

The House Appropriations Committee June 25 reported HR 4035 (H Rept 97-163) appropriating $11.2 billion in fiscal 1982 for the Interior and Energy departments and several agencies. The total was $6.89 million below President Reagan's March budget request.

The panel refused to use federal park expansion money to upgrade existing national parks, as recommended by Interior Secretary James G. Watt.

The committee also rejected Watt's plan to abolish grants to states and cities for historic preservation and urban parks; barred Watt from using fiscal 1982 funds to reorganize the Office of Surface Mining, a move seen by environmentalists as an effort to relax federal controls on strip mining, and rejected Reagan's proposal to abolish federal water research programs.

Interior Secretary Watt and Energy Secretary James B. Edwards in the spring of 1981 announced plans to accelerate the development of offshore oil and gas reserves, including five areas off the California coast.

But the committee, through an amendment by Rep. Les AuCoin, D-Ore., prohibited the administration from any leasing, exploration or development at the four areas that are most environmentally sensitive — Point Arena, Bodega, Santa Cruz and Eel River, the one closest to AuCoin's state. Development would be permitted at the Santa Maria basin, which is thought to contain 80 percent of the oil and gas in the lease sale area.

California objected to development at these sites. Watt personally lobbied committee members but could not persuade even panel Republicans to overturn the AuCoin provision.

Interior Department

The committee recommended $3.7 billion in new budget authority for the Interior Department, some $166.1 million more than Reagan had requested.

Much of the increase was for parks programs the president sought to eliminate or sharply reduce.

Parks

The committee approved $155.6 million for the Land and Water Conservation Fund and earmarked $100.5 million of it for the purchase of private land surrounded by national parks. Reagan had sought only $45 million and had wanted an indefinite moratorium on park land acquisition while existing parks were upgraded.

To save money, the panel went along with Reagan and provided no grants to states for park acquisition in 1982, although it did not abolish the program.

Reagan and Interior Secretary Watt also had asked Congress to amend the Land and Water Conservation Fund Act of 1965 (PL 88-578) to allow use of $105 million a year from the fund to rehabilitate existing national parks. (*Land and Water Act, Congress and the Nation Vol. I, p. 1087*)

The committee, rejecting that proposal, instead provided $118 million for such activities from National Park Service construction, operations and maintenance funds.

The committee also rejected Watt's plan to eliminate the urban parks program, providing $10 million for those grants. And it recommended $21.9 million for historic preservation grants that Watt wanted eliminated.

Water Research

The committee rejected Watt's plan to abolish the Office of Water Research and Technology. Members voted $9.8 million in fiscal 1982 funds which, with $2.7 million deferred from fiscal 1981, totaled $12.5 million for conservation and desalinization research.

Fish and Wildlife Service

The committee recommended $207.2 million for management of fish and wildlife, some $15.4 million more than Reagan sought but $26.2 million below the fiscal 1981 appropriation.

OSM Reorganization

The committee prohibited the use of any funds appropriated in the bill to reorganize the Office of Surface Mining (OSM). The Interior Subcommittee had voted June 11 to prohibit use of the 1982 funds for the reorganization that Watt proposed in May. To circumvent Congress, Watt immediately ordered a speedup of the reorganization plan.

Indian Programs

The committee recommended a total appropriation of $1.82 billion in new budget authority for Indian programs in fiscal 1982, up $85.19 million from Reagan's budget request but down $77 million from fiscal 1981 appropriations.

The panel refused to approve, pending further study, a Bureau of Indian Affairs proposal to consolidate 10 programs and cut their combined funding by 25 percent.

Energy Department

The committee recommended a total appropriation of $4.5 billion for fossil fuels and conservation programs of the Energy Department, a net decrease of $394.2 million from Reagan's March budget request but a $665.6 million increase over fiscal 1981.

Funding for the department's defense, nuclear energy and research programs was provided in a separate bill. (*Story, p. 301*)

Major components in this bill included:

Conservation

The largest Reagan budget cuts were proposed for conservation programs. The committee disagreed with the administration's premise that higher energy prices would make conservation more attractive to the private sector. It increased the $195 million conservation request by $177 million, not including an additional $68 million it earlier had deferred from fiscal 1981. The panel said energy conservation offered the greatest short-term savings in oil imports and the most long-term help in slowing the depletion of domestic oil and gas supplies.

The administration requested no funds for the federal program of insulating the homes of the poor and elderly, suggesting that the money be included in a block grant program to the states. However, the committee included $150 million for weatherization in the bill. It said about 125,000 homes could be weatherized with the money.

Compliance

The committee added $33 million to Reagan's $12 million request for the compliance program to force major oil companies to refund billions of dollars that they overcharged consumers while federal oil price controls were in effect. The Energy Department had identified more than $10 billion in such overcharges.

Strategic Petroleum Reserve

Although Congress agreed in the budget reconciliation process to put the Strategic Petroleum Reserve out of the federal budget, the committee included $3.4 billion for the reserve.

Agriculture Department

The panel recommended a total budget of $1.7 billion for the management of 190 million acres of public lands by the U.S. Forest Service. The amount was $48.9 million over the administration's request, and $2.9 million above fiscal 1981 appropriations.

The largest single increase over Reagan's budget was for land acquisition and construction of roads, trails and other facilities. The panel recommended a total of $509.7 million for this purpose, up $78.7 million over the president's budget.

The committee also provided $20 million for the Youth Conservation Corps, a summer jobs program for 15-to-18-year-olds. The administration had sought to eliminate the program.

House Floor Action

Three-quarters of all Republican House members joined Democrats July 22 in approving HR 4035 by a 358-46 vote. *(Vote 144, p. 52-H)*

As passed by the House, the measure appropriated $11.1 billion for programs of the Interior and Energy departments and several other agencies.

During floor action July 21 and 22, the House adopted five substantive amendments that reduced by $70 million the total spending recommended by the Appropriations Committee. Of the savings, $69 million was for a proposed coal liquefaction plant in West Virginia.

The strings attached to HR 4035 blocked efforts by Interior Secretary Watt to halt federal park expansion and to open up four areas off the Northern California coast to oil and gas exploration.

The House also voted to prohibit the Interior secretary from using federal land acquisition money for upgrading existing national parks, and to prevent him from reorganizing the Office of Surface Mining (OSM) without first getting permission from Congress.

Reagan Rebuffed

The House bill provided about $600 million more than the budget request for certain park, energy conservation and cultural programs that Reagan had wanted abolished or cut. However, the total amount in the bill was $76.9 million below Reagan's $11.2 billion request.

The Appropriations Committee accomplished that by providing $500 million less than the $3.9 billion the president wanted for the Strategic Petroleum Reserve (SPR) and shifting that money to other programs. Congress voted to take the SPR account out of the budget in the first budget resolution (H Con Res 115) and reconciliation conferees had agreed.

The House-passed bill provided the following for programs that President Reagan wanted abolished:

● $26.5 million for historic preservation grants and $10 million for urban parks grants to states.

● $20 million for the Youth Conservation Corps, a summer work program in the national forests.

● $150 million for weatherizing homes of low-income persons and $15 million for the energy extension service.

The bill also rejected administration plans to impose a moratorium on federal land acquisition while existing parks and refuges were upgraded. HR 4035 included $155.6 million for land acquisition.

In addition, the House ignored Reagan's proposed 50 percent cuts for the National Endowment for the Arts and the National Endowment for the Humanities and refused to consolidate Indian education and health programs into block grants, as the administration requested.

Amendments Adopted

During floor debate, the House adopted a proposal by Elliott H. Levitas, D-Ga., to prohibit expenditures to implement regulations vetoed by Congress, and a "no frills" amendment offered by Allen E. Ertel, D-Pa.

Ertel's amendment barred agencies funded under the bill from hiring cooks, chauffeurs or other personal servants for their officials, and required that federal cars bought with funds in the bill average at least 22 miles per gallon.

Amendments Rejected

The House rejected, on a 3-32 division vote, an amendment by William E. Dannemeyer, R-Calif., to prohibit the Smithsonian Institution from funding exhibits presenting evolution as the "sole explanation of life's origins."

An amendment by Dan Glickman, D-Kan., to delete $30,000 for the Franklin Delano Roosevelt Memorial Commission was rejected by a 201-216 vote. *(Vote 143, p. 52-H)*

Payments in Lieu of Taxes. The bill provided no funds for payments in lieu of taxes (PILT), although the president had sought only to cut the $103 million program to $45 million. An amendment by Rep. Manuel Lujan Jr., R-N.M., to provide $100 million for PILT was rejected on the floor, 96-320, after having been agreed to by a 22-21 division vote. *(Vote 140, p. 52-H)*

The payments were made to cities and counties that lost local tax income because federal lands were located within their borders. The House committee charged that

many states were receiving more in PILT than they would if the federal lands were subject to taxes.

Office of Territorial Affairs. The bill provided $171.4 million for the Office of Territorial Affairs, $18 million more than the administration requested.

The committee rejected an administration recommendation that territories pay 25 percent of the cost of local construction projects built with federal funds. The report argued that it was not fair to add a 25-percent matching requirement since pending tax cut legislation would significantly affect territories, which by law received 100 percent of the federal revenues collected in their borders.

Fossil Energy Programs. The bill recommended spending $463 million for fossil energy research and development, $46 million over the budget. The primary increases were $29 million for magnetohydrodynamics research and $16 million for coal and peat gasification research.

No funds were recommended by the committee for fossil energy construction projects, but design of a solvent refined coal demonstration plant in Newman, Ky., would continue. An amendment offered on the floor by Rep. Vin Weber, R-Minn., would have deleted the $135 million for the project. It was rejected 177-236. *(Vote 142, p. 52-H)*

The bill provided $150 million for weatherizing homes of low-income families, rejecting the administration's request that the money be consolidated into community development block grants. The committee said consolidation would "skew assistance to urban areas" and cause the poor and elderly to suffer because funds could be diverted to other uses.

Other Agencies

The bill provided $151.5 million for the Smithsonian Institution, $4.7 million less than the president sought.

It provided $157.5 million for the National Endowment for the Arts and $144 million for the National Endowment for the Humanities. The total was $128.3 million more than the $173.2 million sought by the administration. The committee said the endowments should not bear a greater share of budget cuts than other agencies.

Senate Committee Action

As reported July 23 by the Senate Appropriations Committee (S Rept 97-166), HR 4035 provided $7,747,174,391 for the Interior Department and related agencies in fiscal 1982 — $3,469,445,609 less than the administration requested and $3,392,552,609 less than the House-passed bill.

The difference was attributable primarily to the Senate committee's decision to put the Strategic Petroleum Reserve off-budget.

The Senate committee concurred with the House in trying to block controversial proposals by Interior Secretary Watt to halt federal park expansion.

However, the Republican-dominated panel did not go along with the House in trying to prevent Watt from reorganizing the Office of Surface Mining and opening up four areas off the Northern California coast to oil and gas leasing.

The Senate panel agreed with the House in rejecting administration proposals to:

● Halt federal park expansion while using $105 million from land acquisition funds to upgrade existing parks.

● Eliminate historic preservation grants to states.

● Abolish several energy conservation programs.

● Slash by half the funds for the arts and humanities.

● Consolidate various Indian programs into block grants.

● Require that territories pay 25 percent of the cost of federally built construction projects.

However, the Senate committee sided with the administration on eliminating several programs that the House wanted continued, including urban park grants, the Youth Conservation Corps and the Office of Water Research and Technology.

Also, the Senate panel provided money for mineral institutes and state park acquisition grants. The House had agreed with the administration that those programs should be not be funded in fiscal 1982.

The Senate bill differed from the House also in providing $105 million for payments to counties for the loss of local taxes on federal lands within their boundaries. The House bill cut those payments out entirely.

The Senate panel provided $500 million less than the House for the Strategic Petroleum Reserve; most of the funding came from sources that would not show up in the federal budget totals. The House, like the administration, had retained the account in the budget, but the budget reconciliation bill, cleared July 31, provided for mostly off-budget financing.

Interior Department

As reported by the Senate committee, HR 4035 provided $3.79 billion for the Interior Department, $286.6 million less than the fiscal 1981 appropriation but $232.7 million more than the president requested. It provided $66.6 million more than the House bill.

The largest increases over the House amount were in the Payments in Lieu of Taxes program and the state grants for park acquisition.

Land and Water Conservation Fund

The Senate committee refused to grant the administration's request to use $105 million from the Land and Water Conservation Fund for rehabilitating public lands. Like the House, it instead provided $105 million for upgrading deteriorating national parks in the operation and maintenance accounts of the National Park Service.

The committee increased from $45 million to $201.5 million the amount authorized to be spent from the Land and Water Conservation Fund.

The fund, derived from the estimated $8.5 billion received each year from Outer Continental Shelf oil and gas leasing, by law had to be used only to buy federal lands such as parks, refuges and national forests. Watt wanted a moratorium on park expansion and sought amendments to allow the fund to be used for upgrading existing parks.

The amendment increasing 1982 land and water fund expenditures, offered by J. Bennett Johnston, D-La., was approved 15-14 after Republican Arlen Specter, Pa., voted with panel Democrats for the amendment. All other committee Republicans voted against it. A similar $204.7 million amendment, also offered by Johnston, was killed 6-8 in subcommittee July 16 on a straight party-line vote.

The committee amendment provided $102.3 million for grants to states for park acquisition — for which the House provided no funds — and $99.2 million for federal land acquisitions. The administration had sought $45 million for federal land purchases and no money for state grants.

Of the $99.2 million provided for federal acquisition, $73.8 million was slated for the National Park Service and for acquiring the Pinelands National Reserve in New Jersey, $8 million for the Fish and Wildlife Service, $2.3 million for the Bureau of Land Management and $15.1 million for the Agriculture Department's Forest Service.

The House bill provided $155.6 million for federal land acquisition, $100.5 million for the National Park Service and the Pinelands, $18 million for the Fish and Wildlife Service, $1.1 million for the Bureau of Land Management and $35.9 million for the Forest Service.

Historic Preservation Grants

Committee Republicans also voted against McClure on historic preservation grants. Five Republicans ignored McClure's pleas that the committee hold the line on the grants in order to have negotiating room in conference with the House. The panel approved, by a 17-7 vote, an amendment by Mack Mattingly, R-Ga., to increase the subcommittee's $15.6 million recommendation to $26.5 million — the amount provided by the House. It was $21.8 million more than the $4.7 million requested by the president, who wanted the grants eliminated.

Republicans who joined Mattingly in voting for the increase were: James Abdnor, S.D.; Robert W. Kasten Jr., Wis.; Warren B. Rudman, N.H. and Specter.

Urban Parks

The committee went along with the president's request to end funding for grants to local communities for urban park acquisition. The House had provided $10 million.

Payments in Lieu of Taxes (PILT)

The committee provided $105 million for payments to counties in lieu of local tax revenue on federal lands located within their jurisdiction. The administration, which wanted to reform the way the money is handed out, sought only $45 million for the payments in 1982. The House voted no funding.

Some $103 million was paid in PILT to the states in 1981.

Water Resources

The committee concurred with the president that the Office of Water Research and Technology (OWRT) should be eliminated. The House disagreed, providing $9.8 million for research on water conservation and desalination.

The Senate committee provided $10.1 million for the new Office of Water Policy within the Interior Department. The committee did not, however, agree with the president and the House that the grants to water research institutes should be terminated. It earmarked $6.2 million of the $10 million for those grants and directed that they be administered by the new water policy office.

The committee clearly specified that the new Office of Water Policy would not be responsible for setting national water policy or planning and coordinating water programs in other agencies. Some members of Congress feared that Watt would use the new office to set policy for non-Interior Department water programs.

Bureau of Mines

The committee recommended $9.6 million to continue funding the 31 state mineral institutes. The House had agreed with the administration that those funds should be terminated.

The Senate panel's report said the nation "faces a minerals crisis the proportions of which make this nation's petroleum problems pale by comparison." The report blamed that crisis in part on the shortage of personnel trained in mineral engineering, citing testimony received by the committee that only six doctoral degrees in mineral disciplines were awarded in the 1979-80 school year.

Office of Surface Mining. The committee provided $178.6 million for the Office of Surface Mining (OSM), of which $114.2 million was earmarked for reclaiming abandoned strip mines, $1 million less than the House had provided.

In addition, $64.4 million was designated for administering federal strip mining controls, for which the House had provided $66 million.

The committee disagreed with the House-passed provision prohibiting Watt from using fiscal 1982 funds to reorganize the OSM, calling the House's action an "apparent breach of executive privilege" and saying the reorganization would improve OSM service and administration.

Indian Programs

The committee recommended $987.5 million for the Bureau of Indian Affairs, $19.9 million below the president's request and $62.8 million below the House.

Like the House, the committee rejected a controversial administration proposal to consolidate 10 Indian programs under a block grant approach. The proposal, when it was unveiled, prompted the National Tribal Governments Conference to call for Secretary Watt's resignation, because he failed to confer with its members. The tribes maintained that under the Indian Self-Determination Act (PL 93-638), interior secretaries must consult with the tribes before making major policy changes. *(Self-Determination Act, Congress and the Nation Vol. IV, p. 810)*

The committee suggested that if the administration wanted to pursue block grants, it should first get the support of the tribes and then try a demonstration project.

The bill also provided $669.7 million for Indian health programs administered by the Department of Health and Human Services and $81.1 million for Indian education programs administered by the Education Department.

Office of Territorial Affairs

The panel provided $167.4 million for territorial affairs, $14 million above the administration request but $4 million less than the House.

Like the House, the committee rejected an administration recommendation that territories pay 25 percent of the cost for federally funded construction projects.

U.S. Forest Service

The committee recommended $1.6 billion for the Forest Service, which is administered by the Agriculture Department. The amount was $7 million less than the administration request and $56 million less than the House bill.

The Senate panel agreed with the administration that the Youth Conservation Corps should not be funded in fiscal 1982, primarily because the program, which provided summer jobs for youths between the ages of 15 and 18, was not targeted at the populations with high unemployment.

Energy Department

The committee provided $1.09 billion for fossil fuel programs at the Energy Department, $3.8 billion less than

the administration sought and $3.3 billion less than the House bill.

The major difference was that the Senate committee provided only $199.4 million on-budget for the Strategic Petroleum Reserve (SPR) but made $3.7 billion available through off-budget financing. Both the House bill — and the administration's budget — had kept the entire SPR account on-budget. The budget reconciliation bill (HR 3982) required all but $260 million for the reserve to be off-budget. *(Reconciliation bill, p. 256)*

The off-budget money provided by the committee would be used to buy oil and ship it to the reserve on the U.S. Gulf Coast. The on-budget funding would be spent mostly on increasing the size of the reserve.

Energy Conservation

The committee recommended that $371 million be spent in fiscal 1982 for energy conservation programs, $176.1 million more than the president's budget. Of that, only $130.3 million was in new budget authority; $172.6 million was to be transferred from funds that had been earmarked for a now-defunct synthetic fuels project and $67.8 million would come from unspent fiscal 1981 funds.

The panel recommended the following amounts for conservation programs that the administration wanted discontinued or funded through block grants to states:

● $18.6 million for building and community services.
● $23.6 million for industrial conservation.
● $21 million for transportation programs.
● $39 million for conservation grants and extension services.
● $112.5 million to weatherize low-income homes. During subcommittee markup July 16, panel Republicans rejected a proposal by Patrick J. Leahy, D-Vt., to provide $150 million for weatherizing the homes of low-income families. The president had recommended no funds for the weatherization program, urging that it be financed through block grants.

The committee also cut conservation assistance to schools and hospitals by half, from $100 million recommended by the president to $50 million.

Other Agencies

The committee recommended $1.2 billion for 16 other agencies, including $233 million for the National Endowments for the Arts and Humanities. The amount for the endowments was $60 million more than the president requested, but $68.6 million less than the amount recommended by the House.

Senate Floor Action

HR 4035 provided the first Senate test of President Reagan's Sept. 24 demand for additional budget cuts, and it was not a happy one for the administration.

The Republican-dominated Senate voted 87-8 Oct. 27 to pass a bill that surpassed the new spending limits by $1 billion. *(Vote 334, p. 56-S)*

However, the $7.36 billion bill provided about the amount recommended by Reagan in his March budget request.

The measure, which had been ready for floor action since it was reported by the Appropriations Committee in July, had been delayed by the Senate leadership until Congress received Reagan's second round of cuts in September.

Limited Cuts Approved

Interior Appropriations Subcommittee Chairman James A. McClure, R-Idaho, recommended cutting about $163 million in budget authority, or 2 percent, from the bill as reported. His amendment was adopted by voice vote.

The $163 million in cuts included $10.4 million from the Bureau of Land Management, $30.4 million from the National Park Service, $21.5 million from the U.S. Geological Survey, $12.5 million from the Office of Surface Mining, $22.2 million from the U.S. Forest Service and $23 million in the Energy Department's fossil fuels research programs.

McClure opposed an amendment by Mack Mattingly, R-Ga., to cut an additional 5 percent from the bill's total. Mattingly's amendment was rejected 35-61. *(Vote 333, p. 56-S)*

McClure argued that the further cuts would have almost no effect on the budget deficit or on interest rates.

McClure also fought off efforts to delete $135 million for a controversial synthetic fuels plant in Kentucky, and to add $37.5 million for insulating homes for the poor.

William Proxmire, D-Wis., failed 40-57 in his fight to delete funding for a synthetic fuels plant in Newman, Ky. that would convert 6,000 tons of coal a day into boiler fuels and coke. *(Vote 332, p. 56-S)*

Noting the federal government was subsidizing 98 percent of the cost of the $4.5 billion plant, Proxmire argued that, "At a time when Congress is forced to make several cuts in many worthwhile programs, there is no excuse to continue to fund a loser like [this]."

An amendment by George Mitchell, D-Maine, to add $37.5 million to the $112.5 million in the bill for weatherizing homes of low-income families was defeated 46-49. *(Vote 331, p. 56-S)*

Cuts made on the floor brought the Senate bill's total to about the same as the House's $11.1 billion version, not counting $3.4 billion in the House bill for the Strategic Petroleum Reserve (SPR). The Senate provided money for SPR, but in an off-budget account.

Amendments

The senators rejected 43-48 an amendment offered by Patrick J. Leahy, D-Vt., to transfer $12.9 million within the bill to beef up an Energy Department investigation of an estimated $8.6 billion in alleged violations of the now-defunct oil price controls. *(Vote 330, p. 56-S*

McClure opposed the amendment, noting that the administration had assured both the authorizing and appropriating committees that it had enough money to pursue the investigations and close the outstanding cases.

McClure said that if the assurances proved untrue, Congress could provide more money later through a supplemental appropriations bill.

During three days of debate, the Senate adopted several other amendments, including proposals:

● By Thad Cochran, R-Miss., to add $7 million in funding for payments to states to make up for local taxes lost because of federal ownership of national wildlife refuges within their borders. The amendment was adopted 89-1. *(Vote 328, p. 56-S)*

● By McClure, limiting to $242.5 million the amount that could be obligated for timber buyers for road construction in national forests.

● By Don Nickles, R-Okla., clarifying that three Indian boarding schools in Oklahoma and one in Nevada could be used for post-secondary programs but not for elementary and secondary programs.

● By Robert W. Kasten Jr., R-Wis., restoring $1,565,000 to build an Indian courthouse complex in Wisconsin.

The senators rejected by voice vote an amendment offered by William S. Cohen, R-Maine, that would have prevented the Interior Department from using Medicare and Medicaid reimbursements to offset the cost of providing Indian health care.

In addition, the senators rejected 17-71, an amendment offered by Robert Dole, R-Kan., that would have eliminated $7 million earmarked for administering a federal program that required large utilities to conduct residential energy audits. Dole wanted the money transferred to the energy policy and conservation grants program, which funded state energy offices. *(Vote 329, p. 56-S)*

House, Senate Bills Compared

As passed by the House and Senate, HR 4035 appropriated the following amounts for fiscal 1982:

	House-passed Appropriation	Senate-passed Appropriation
Interior Department	$3,720,619,000	$3,698,751,000
Energy Department	4,390,057,000	1,061,652,000
Forest Service	1,701,395,000	1,380,705,000
Other agencies	1,327,656,000	1,217,589,000
Total	**$11,139,727,000**	**$7,358,697,000**

Conference Agreement

The original House-passed bill would have provided $11.1 billion and the Senate version $7.36 billion. House and Senate conferees worked out the $7.54 billion compromise Nov. 4.

The major difference between the two bills was that the House had included $3.4 billion for the Strategic Petroleum Reserve, while the Senate provided $3.68 billion off-budget. Following instructions in the budget reconciliation law (PL 97-35), conferees put the money in an off-budget account.

In the conference agreement, Congress rejected several proposals by Interior Secretary Watt, including a plan to halt federal park expansion and use land acquisition funds to upgrade existing parks.

Conferees accepted the House's $155.6 million for federal park land acquisition and dropped a Senate amendment providing $102.3 million for grants to states for park purchases.

Instead of using $105 million in land acquisition funds to upgrade existing parks, as Watt had requested, the bill provided an extra $105 million in maintenance funds.

The administration wanted to abolish grants for historic preservation and urban parks. Both houses provided $26.5 million for historic preservation grants. The conferees voted $8 million for urban park grants; the House had provided $10 million and the Senate no funds.

The conferees accepted one House provision barring four controversial oil and gas lease sales offshore from California, but rejected another to block a controversial reorganization of the Office of Surface Mining.

The conference provided $105.5 million in payments to compensate counties for the loss of local taxes on federal lands within their boundaries; $6 million of it went to states with national wildlife refuges. The House had voted

no funds for the program, but the Senate had earmarked $112 million, $7 million of which was for wildlife refuges.

Congress also ignored administration proposals to abolish several energy conservation programs, slash by half the amount for the arts and humanities, consolidate several Indian programs into block grants and require that territories pay 25 percent of the construction cost for federal projects within their boundaries. ∎

Agriculture Appropriations

Congress voted to spend more than President Reagan wanted for food and farm programs in fiscal 1982, but it kept the agriculture appropriations bill close to his total budget by reducing foreign food aid and certain other accounts.

The House and Senate approved a fiscal 1982 agriculture appropriations bill (HR 4119 — PL 97-103) that provided $20,835,223,000 for price support and other farm programs, school lunches, food stamps and a special nutritional program for pregnant women and young children.

Another $1.8 billion would be available through Section 32 transfers, which were revenues from certain customs fees.

The House adopted the conference report (H Rept 97-313) by voice vote Dec. 15, and the Senate adopted it the same day by a 75-20 vote. *(Vote 473, p. 76-S)*

The House July 27 had approved a $22.7 billion appropriations bill, while the Senate Oct. 30 passed a $22.9 billion measure.

The final 1982 bill provided $2.8 billion less than the 1981 appropriation, according to Jamie L. Whitten, D-Miss., chairman of the House Appropriations Committee.

It was $317 million less in budget authority for programs than conferees had agreed upon Nov. 3. That earlier agreement had exceeded the president's September budget request by nearly $600 million in budget authority, according to the Congressional Budget Office (CBO). Based on the measure's outlays — the amount of money that would actually be paid out during the year — the Office of Management and Budget (OMB) predicted a $1 billion excess.

Congressional farm leaders had delayed final action on the conference agreement until the stopgap continuing resolution (H J Res 370) for all federal programs was completed Dec. 11. That measure mandated a 4 percent cut in all programs from levels agreed upon in conference, exempting certain programs such as school lunches and food stamps.

The agriculture conferees informally decided instead to cut 22 programs, leaving the rest at levels set in conference. The reductions became part of the measure when it finally passed both houses.

Even with those changes, the bill was about $300 million more than Reagan's September request, according to Sen. Thad Cochran, R-Miss., chairman of the Senate Agriculture Appropriations Subcommittee. But its total was the same as provided by the continuing resolution.

Several features that Reagan had objected to earlier survived in the final bill. They included $281 million more than he requested for the special nutritional program for pregnant women, mothers and young children (WIC) and $23.5 million less than he wanted for the Food for Peace (PL 480) program.

The bill also subtracted $53 million from the Federal Crop Insurance Corp. request and allowed $253 million less for reimbursements of the Commodity Credit Corporation (CCC), the financial arm of the Agriculture Department.

Conferees also added to Reagan's request for popular agricultural research and conservation programs.

The measure did include a requested $207 million block grant for food aid to Puerto Rico — to replace its participation in the food stamp program. The funds were included in the $10.3 billion provided for food stamps.

Provisions

As signed into law Dec. 23, HR 4119 made the following appropriations for fiscal 1982:

Request	September Budget	Final Amount
Agriculture Programs		
Office of the Secretary	$ 4,715,000	$ 4,715,000
Departmental Administration	17,560,000	14,468,000
Governmental and Public Affairs	9,687,000	8,628,000
Office of the Inspector General	27,561,000	27,562,000
Office of the General Counsel	12,072,000	12,822,000
Federal Grain Inspection Service	29,274,000	5,600,000
Agricultural Research Service	401,781,000	432,410,000
Cooperative State Research Service	206,085,000	221,216,000
Extension Service	279,293,000	315,702,000
National Agricultural Library	8,158,000	8,750,000
Animal and Plant Health Inspection Service	256,169,000	280,382,000
Food Safety and Inspection Service	288,189,000	323,250,000
Economic Research Service	39,647,000	39,360,000
Statistical Reporting Service	48,448,000	51,636,000
Agricultural Cooperative Service	4,220,000	4,639,000
World Agricultural Outlook Board	1,436,000	1,422,000
Agricultural Marketing Service	21,047,000	26,611,000
Packers and Stockyards Administration	8,244,000	8,806,000
Agricultural Stabilization and Conservation Service	189,798,000	62,176,000
Federal Crop Insurance Corporation	478,133,000	425,056,000
Commodity Credit Corporation	2,295,856,000	2,043,229,000
Subtotal, Agriculture Programs	$ 4,610,008,000	$ 4,329,036,000

Request	September Budget	Final Amount
Rural Development Programs		
Farmers Home Administration	$ 1,682,495,000	$ 1,789,458,000
Rural Electrification Administration	26,112,000	29,673,000
Soil Conservation Service	485,442,000	574,544,000
Agricultural Stabilization and Conservation Service	167,200,000	220,100,000
Subtotal, Rural Development Programs	$ 2,361,249,000	$ 2,613,775,000
Domestic Food Programs		
Child Nutrition Programs	$ 1,077,890,000	$ 1,082,890,000
Special Milk Program	28,100,000	28,100,000
Special Supplemental Food Programs (WIC)	652,608,000	934,080,000
Food Stamp Program	10,086,884,000	10,293,384,000
Nutrition Assistance for Puerto Rico	206,500,000	——
Food Donations Programs	48,220,000	48,220,000
Food Program Administration	81,461,000	86,461,000
Subtotal, Domestic Food Programs	$12,181,663,000	$12,473,135,000
International Programs		
Foreign Agricultural Service	$ 61,331,000	$ 67,694,000
Office of International Cooperation and Development	3,627,000	3,627,000
Food for Peace (PL 480)	1,023,528,000	1,000,000,000
Subtotal, International Programs	$ 1,088,486,000	$ 1,071,321,000
Related and Independent Agencies		
Food and Drug Administration	$ 295,708,000	$ 328,032,000
Commodity Futures Trading Commission	17,533,000	19,924,000
Subtotal, Related and Independent Agencies	$ 313,241,000	$ 347,956,000
Total, Fiscal Year 1982 new budget authority	$20,554,647,000	$20,835,223,000*
Section 32 Transfers	$ 1,769,618,000	$ 1,769,618,000

* Includes rescissions totaling $285,000,000.

Loan Authorizations. HR 4119 also provided the following loan and rent supplement authorizations:

● $9,062,200,000 in direct and insured loans (budget request: $8,577,800,000).

● $481,000,000 in guaranteed loans (budget request: $181,000,000).

● $398,000,000 in rent supplements (budget request: $398,000,000).

House Committee Action

Although the House Appropriations Committee recommendations for fiscal 1982 appeared to be within budget limits, administration critics charged that the committee ignored major Reagan policy requests and claimed false savings.

The $22.7 billion bill reported July 9 (H Rept 97-172) was $2 billion below the levels set by the March budget and $1 billion less than the president requested, according to the committee. Fiscal 1981 appropriations totaled $25.566 billion. *(1980 Almanac p. 205)*

But David A. Stockman, OMB director, insisted that it actually added $380 million more in outlays than Reagan wanted. And Stockman also contended that committee calculations improperly mixed outlays and budget authority, the accounting equivalent of mixing apples and oranges. Budget authority refers to the amount of money reserved for spending on a specific program over a period of years; outlays refer to the amount of money that will be paid out in a given year.

Appropriations Committee Chairman Whitten maintained that his committee simply exercised its constitutional right to legislate. "They forget that this [Congress] is the people's branch of the government. They propose, we dispose," Whitten said.

Stockman and other administration officials were particularly critical of committee decisions that:

● Exceeded by more than $300 million Reagan's request for a special food program for mothers and young children.

● Provided no food stamp funding for the last month and a half of the fiscal year — a $1 billion dollar omission, according to Agriculture Department officials.

● Made the availability of part of the food stamp money contingent on actions by the secretary of agriculture "to curtail fraud, waste and abuse in the program."

● Funded Rural Electrification Administration (REA) loan programs for rural telephone and electrical systems well above administration requests.

● Continued Farmers Home Administration (FmHA) lending to promote business and industrial development in rural areas, despite Reagan's plans to end it.

But Whitten noted that the administration achieved a number of its objectives too, including rescissions in food programs and the elimination of funding for the economic emergency loan program for farmers.

Agriculture Programs. For price support, research, crop insurance and other basic farm programs, the bill provided $4.7 billion, some $635 million less than fiscal 1981 and $245 million below the administration's request.

Included were two rescissions that reflected program changes authorized by the House reconciliation bill (HR 3982). *(Story, p. 256)*

The first rescission of $24.1 million reflected a shift to the private sector of fees for grading and inspecting grain, a cost borne partially by the government. The second rescission of $20.8 million was a similar shift of cotton and tobacco fees. Reagan requested both changes.

Also in keeping with the reconciliation measure, the

committee did not fund the beekeeper indemnity program, a longtime Whitten priority and a target of attacks by prior administrations. *(1980 Almanac p. 207)*

For the newly expanded subsidized federal crop insurance program, the panel provided $120 million for administrative costs, some $15.8 million less than requested and $62.3 million more than last year.

It also sliced $100 million from a $250 million request for working capital to pay claims. The Agriculture Department contended that cut would undermine confidence in the program during a period of major expansion. *(Crop Insurance Expansion, 1980 Almanac p. 95)*

The panel also provided $75.9 million less than the $2.3 million requested for CCC "losses" — direct, non-recoverable payments that the corporation had already made to farmers in physical disaster grants and other programs.

Farmers Home Administration. The panel provided $450 million for loans for rural water and waste disposal systems, $150 million over the budget request. It went along with the administration's $130 million figure for community facilities loans — half the fiscal 1981 total — but provided $300 million for rural industrialization loans, which Reagan wanted to cancel completely.

The committee provided $250 million worth of guaranteed loans for construction of facilities to manufacture alcohol fuels, although Reagan wanted to end the loans immediately. Federal assurances the loans would be made had prompted applicants to spend "considerable sums of their own money" already, the committee said.

Rural Electrification Administration. Reagan sought an end to insured low-interest REA loans to rural telephone systems, but the Appropriations panel approved a floor of $250 million and a cap of $325 million.

The committee also allotted at least $850 million and up to $1.1 billion for insured loans to electrical systems, while Reagan requested no more than $700 million for that program. The panel also approved a $30 million capital stock purchase for the Rural Telephone Bank against the administration's wishes.

Conservation. The panel overrode administration requests for cuts in individual conservation grants administered by the Agriculture Stabilization and Conservation Service. It provided some $40 million more than requested for a program total of $190 million. The funds would be used for tree-planting, terracing and other improvements on individual farms, with costs shared by owners and the federal government.

The panel also added $30 million to the $162 million requested for watershed and flood prevention projects administered by the service. Those were larger-scale projects whose costs were shared with state and local governments.

The committee provided $1.1 billion for the Women's and Infants' Feeding Program, the same amount as the House budget reconciliation bill. Neither that bill nor the appropriations measure adopted eligibility changes that the Reagan administration requested to bring down the cost of the program. Stockman insisted that the eligibility changes and a lower figure of $742 million from Reagan's March budget should be adopted.

Also in accord with the House reconciliation measure, the panel allotted $9.7 billion for food stamps, the same as requested by Reagan but $1.7 billion less than 1981.

The committee stipulated that the funds run only through Aug. 15, not through the full fiscal year ending Sept. 30 as Reagan planned.

Reagan's request did not include food stamps for Puerto Rico because he assumed the Puerto Rico food stamp program would be handled separately in a block grant. The committee did not fund a separate program.

The panel included rescissions of $1.1 billion from child nutrition programs and $95 million from the Special Milk Program.

International Programs and Related Agencies

The committee generally followed the administration lead on PL 480 (Food for Peace) and the Food and Drug Administration (FDA).

As in past years, however, the panel included explicit policy directions to FDA, including a ban on any action to prohibit the use of antibiotics as preventatives in animal feeds. Health officials had objected that the very common practice of using antibiotics contributed to the development of drug-resistant strains of disease in humans.

The committee also banned FDA action against the artificial sweetener, saccharin, and directed the agency to move into developing "orphan drugs" — those that were not developed by commercial drug companies because they did not appear profitable. *(Other saccharin action, p. 495)*

The panel also suggested that there was no legal barrier to the FDA's approving new drugs on the basis that they had been approved for human use by other countries. While European nations generally approved drugs for use faster than in this country, those governments usually had more power to remove troublesome drugs quickly from the market than in the United States.

House Floor Action

House approval of HR 4119 came July 27 on a 343-33 vote after a brief debate in which only one member raised the strong budget objections of the Reagan administration. *(Vote 155, p. 56-H)*

Norman D. Shumway, R-Calif., protested against the food stamp provisions, which were among the most objectionable to Stockman. By funding food stamps for only 10½ months, not the full year, the bill paved the way for a supplemental appropriation later on, Shumway warned.

The annual catch-all supplemental bill had significant budget-busting potential, Shumway said, characterizing the Appropriations Committee recommendations as "sheer deception."

The $9.7 billion allotted by HR 4119 to food stamps was not enough for the full year, according to the Reagan administration. It could get around that problem by reducing benefits to individuals to stretch out the money. But the bill barred that strategy because it set a date — Aug. 15, 1982 — by which the $9.7 billion had to be spent.

Shumway warned the House that "to invite the need for a supplemental appropriation is to continue that seemingly unbreakable cycle of worse inflation and higher unemployment ... to maintain the status quo."

The House by voice vote adopted an amendment by Hank Brown, R-Colo., to waive the $100 limit on Agricultural Research Service land acquisitions to permit the purchase of 160 acres within the Central Plains Experimental Range from the Colorado State University Research Foundation for no more than $115,000.

Also accepted by voice vote was an amendment by Vic Fazio, D-Calif., to earmark $6 million within the bill's total funding to combat the Mediterranean fruit fly (Medfly) infestation of certain California fruit and vegetable crops.

Senate Committee Action

The Senate Appropriations Committee recommended spending half a billion dollars more during fiscal 1982 for farm and food programs than President Reagan requested in his revised September budget.

In its version of HR 4119 reported Oct. 22 (S Rept 97-248), the committee provided $22.9 billion for price support, loan and rural development programs, as well as food stamps and other feeding programs.

That compared with the $22.7 billion version passed by the House and the president's revised September budget request of $22.3 billion.

In defense of its decisions, the committee said it had provided "assistance in the least costly manner, and in only those situations where it is absolutely imperative."

In a departure from earlier years, the committee adopted a venerable House tactic for bringing its bill closer to the president's budget total. It provided several million dollars less than requested to reimburse the CCC.

The administration's request for the CCC reflected the amount needed to pay back the Treasury for CCC losses in 1980, such as disaster payments and costs of various price support programs.

The CCC's ability to borrow from the Treasury would be reduced in fiscal 1982 by any amount that Congress failed to provide for the reimbursement, according to Agriculture Department budget analyst Stephen Dewhurst. The Senate committee allotted $253 million less than requested for this reimbursement.

Agriculture Programs. The panel added $39 million to the budget figure for agricultural research, $42 million for the extension service, $17 million for the Animal and Plant Health Inspection Service and just over $39 million for the Food Safety and Inspection Service.

It reduced Agricultural Stabilization and Conservation Service salaries and expenses by $128 million, compared with the September request. But it also provided a $314 million transfer from CCC funds, more than double the administration request, so that the actual amount of money for salaries and expenses was $31 million more than requested.

Like the House, the panel provided only $250 million compared to the $308 million requested for capital for the newly expanded Federal Crop Insurance Corp. The funds would be used to pay for losses suffered by farmers insured by the corporation.

Farmers Home Administration. The committee exceeded the FmHA request by $215 million, for a total of $1.9 billion.

It provided $325 million for loans for rural water and waste disposal systems — $25 million above the September request but $150 million less than the House. It added $5 million to the $130 million requested by the administration and approved by the House for community facilities loans.

The panel agreed with the House figure of $300 million for lending to finance rural industrialization projects. The administration wanted to cancel that program entirely.

The committee dropped $250 million worth of guaranteed loans for construction of facilities to manufacture alcohol fuels, provided by the House, because this money was included in the fiscal 1982 continuing resolution (PL 97-51). The panel added $28 million to the administration's request for FmHA salaries and expenses.

Rural Electrification Administration. The panel ignored Reagan's request to end insured low-interest REA

loans for rural telephone systems, and approved instead $250 million in lending authority, the same as the House. Also, both the House and committee added $30 million worth of authority for capital stock purchases by the federal government in the Rural Telephone Bank against Reagan's wishes.

Conservation. The committee added a total of $84 million to the September request for the Soil Conservation Service. That included $44 million more for watershed and flood prevention projects for a total of $187 million, compared with a House figure of $192 million. Those were large-scale projects whose costs were shared with state and local governments.

Food Programs. The committee's total of $12.5 billion for food and nutrition assistance was $330 million more than the September request, because of a $320 million addition for the special nutritional program for infants, pregnant women and nursing mothers. The total was $96 million less than the House provided.

The committee said it believed the women and infant feeding program to be the "most effective nutrition assistance program" and reported that the "impact on infant mortality, chronic ill health, birth defects and subnormal development averts major medical expenditures" for Medicaid, disability and special education programs.

The committee included the $206.5 million the administration requested for a food-aid block grant to Puerto Rico, an item the House rejected.

The panel also met the administration request of $10.1 million for food stamps, compared with $9.8 million provided by the House. Like the House, the panel funded the program only through Aug. 15, 1981, and noted that it expected an administration request for an additional $900 million for the remainder of the year.

International Programs, Related Agencies

The panel provided nearly $60 million less for PL 480 (Food for Peace) than the House, for a total of $1.104 billion. The September request was for $1.024 billion.

Like the House, the Senate committee directed the Food and Drug Administration to hold off its long-proposed ban on the use of antibiotic additives in animal feeds.

Senate Floor Action

The Senate passed its $22.9 billion fiscal 1982 appropriations bill by a 69-15 vote on Oct. 30, after rejecting by a 32-51 vote an administration-backed thrift amendment by Mack Mattingly, R-Ga. *(Votes 341, 342, p. 58-S)*

Mattingly maintained that the committee bill exceeded Reagan's budget request by more than $1 billion in budget authority and $1.1 billion in outlays. (Committee estimates showed the bill exceeding the September request by $523 million in budget authority.)

Mattingly said his amendment would bring the bill's spending down to September levels by directing the secretary of agriculture to cut by an average of 2.6 percent all programs whose payments were not mandated by law, but in any event, no more than 6 percent in any single program.

Child nutrition and the women's and infants feeding programs would have been exempt from any cuts, but food stamps would not, according to a Mattingly aide.

Mattingly's opponents, led by Appropriations Subcommittee chairman Cochran, said that in giving the secretary broad discretion to make program cuts, Mattingly was asking Congress to abandon its job of setting priorities for spending.

Cochran noted that the bill had been $600 million below the March budget when it was approved by the subcommittee in July. And after the president's September request arrived, the full appropriations committee sliced an additional $1.1 billion before reporting the bill, he said.

That left minimal funding for programs on which "the poor and the elderly . . . depend . . . for their very survival," Cochran added.

Mattingly's plan also would compromise the FmHA lending programs by greatly reducing the number of people processing loan applications, and it would "absolutely destroy" efforts to expand the federal crop insurance program, Cochran warned.

In other action, the Senate by voice vote accepted amendments by:

● Max Baucus, D-Mont., to earmark $31.9 million of Foreign Agricultural Service funds for development of foreign markets.

● Howell Heflin, D-Ala., to provide $12.5 million for the forestry incentive program, an increase of $1 million over the committee bill. The program provided development funds on a cost-sharing basis for small wood lot owners.

● Pete V. Domenici, R-N.M., to cut FmHA loan authority to levels set by the reconciliation bill (HR 3982), by cutting $5 million from insured community facility loan authority and $25 million from insured water and sewer facility loan authority.

● Cochran, to earmark $65 million of appropriated funds for work registration and job referral activities of the food stamp program. The administration had unilaterally reduced this program to $30 million, Cochran said, "contrary to congressional intent in enacting tougher work registration requirements."

Provisions Compared

	House-Passed Appropriations	Senate-Passed Appropriations
Agriculture Programs	$ 4,728,030	$ 4,335,226
Rural Development Programs	2,753,450	2,714,293
Domestic Food Programs	11,961,686	12,512,055
International Programs	1,236,794	1,172,486
Related and Independent Agencies	355,956	347,956
Section 32 Transfers	1,694,618	1,769,618
Total, fiscal year 1982 new budget authority	**$22,730,534**	**$22,851,634**

Conference Action

House and Senate conferees agreed on a bill that exceeded the president's request by more than one-half billion dollars.

In a 45-minute meeting Nov. 3, they set total fiscal 1982 obligational authority of $22,922,171,000 for price support and other farm programs, school lunches, food stamps and a special nutritional program for pregnant women and young children.

By the calculations of the CBO, the final version exceeded the president's September budget requests by $597.9 million. But OMB, using methods not accepted by congressional estimators, stated that the bill contained outlays that would put it about $1 billion over budget.

Before Congress adopted the conference report Dec. 15, conferees cut $317 million in budget authority to bring the measure into compliance with the stopgap continuing funding resolution.

Reagan signed the bill Dec. 23.   ∎

Congress and Government

Congressional Republicans convened in Washington Jan. 5, 1981, with high hopes for the 97th Congress. But congressional Democrats appeared barely able to conceal their gloom about their prospects for the first session.

Barely two months earlier, Republicans had won the White House and gained control of the Senate for the first time since January 1955. Though the House remained technically under Democratic control, the Republicans were optimistic about prevailing in that chamber as well.

In addition to compiling an ambitious legislative agenda, Republican leaders had formulated goals for reforming Congress' internal operations.

In the Senate, the Republicans stressed their desire to make the chamber operate more efficiently, and at lower cost.

The new Republican committee chairmen overhauled their professional staffs and vowed to reduce administrative costs.

They sought early — and rapid — action on President Reagan's economic program, followed by an orderly procession of fiscal 1982 appropriations bills and concluding with an October adjournment.

In the House, the GOP sought to dramatize its differences with the Democratic leadership, in an effort to split the Democrats' ranks and win the votes of ideologically like-minded Democrats to their side. In the back of the Republicans' minds was the 1982 election, when they hoped to take over the House.

Mixed Results

At year's end, it was clear the Republicans had met with considerable success in both chambers. But the party did not gain everything it desired.

Senate leaders tried to set the floor schedule well in advance and cut down on roll-call votes and late-night and Saturday sessions. The budgets of the Senate's committees and administrative units were cut by 10 percent across the board. Staffs also were reduced.

As a result, the Senate operated on a more predictable schedule and at lower cost.

But legislation nonetheless moved through Congress more slowly than the leaders had hoped. The appropriations process, in particular, bogged down as congressional leaders wrangled with the White House over budget cutting. Congress limped through much of the new fiscal year that started Oct. 1 on a series of stopgap continuing appropriations resolutions.

Instead of adjourning for the year in October, Congress ended up remaining in session until the week before Christmas.

In the House, a coalition of Republicans and conservative Democrats succeeded in pushing through most of the president's legislative goals. In the process, the formal Democratic leadership was made to appear disorganized and ineffective. Two Democrats — Reps. Eugene V. Atkinson, Pa., and Bob Stump, Ariz. — announced a switch to the Republican side of the aisle.

But by the end of the year, the Democrats were nonetheless predicting a net gain in the number of Democratic House seats in the next Congress. The faltering economy had handed to the Democrats what their elected leaders appeared unable to obtain.

Benefits Broadened

The president kept Congress busy until the very end of the first session with his economic program.

But this did not prevent legislators from looking after their own interests, as well.

Members of Congress shied from voting themselves an immediate pay raise, but they did act to provide themselves with several less direct ways to increase their take-home pay and benefits.

Members approved automatic annual cost-of-living pay increases for themselves for future years, lifted limits on their outside earned income and awarded themselves some new tax breaks.

Congress during the year approved legislation permitting senators for the first time to frank statewide mass mailings, a privilege previously granted only to House members.

Senators maintained the new law would save the government money, but critics suggested that an increase in the volume of Senate mail could offset any savings.

As if to hedge its bet, Congress set aside more than $75 million to pay for its franked mailings during 1982, an election year. This represented a nearly 50 percent increase over 1981 funding.

House members during the year won an increase in their official expense allowances. The allowance hike, the first since 1979, was intended to cover inflationary increases in the cost of travel, office supplies and equipment.

House Ends Abscam Probe

Congressional leaders tried during 1981 to put behind them the "Abscam" congressional bribery scandal, but they met with only partial success.

The House succeeded in bringing to a close its two-year investigation of its members implicated in the FBI corruption probe. This occurred in August when the House Committee on Standards of Official Conduct dismissed a recommendation by its attorney that charges of wrongdoing be voted against Rep. John P. Murtha, D-Pa.

Murtha was to have been the seventh House member to come under the committee's formal scrutiny in connection with Abscam.

The committee's attorney, E. Barrett Prettyman Jr., resigned in protest over the panel's decision not to recommend disciplinary action against Murtha, and the panel simply never named a replacement. In this way, the Abscam probe was brought quietly to a close.

Earlier in the year, in another Abscam case, Rep. Raymond F. Lederer, D-Pa., was convicted in federal court on bribery and conspiracy charges in early January. Lederer resigned from the House May 5 in order to stop expulsion proceedings against him.

Senate Probe Continues

The Senate also had wanted to finish up its parallel Abscam probe before the end of the year. Instead, it ended up delaying until 1982 a vote on its sole Abscam disciplinary case.

Senate leaders announced Dec. 1 that a vote on the expulsion of Sen. Harrison A. Williams Jr., D-N.J., would not take place prior to 1982. Their announcement came just two days before a Senate vote had been scheduled.

In two court decisions touching on several Abscam defendants, U.S. District Judge George C. Pratt in Brooklyn, N.Y., upheld the convictions of Sen. Williams and Reps. Lederer, John M. Murphy, D-N.Y. (1963-81), Michael J. "Ozzie" Myers, D-Pa. (1976-80), and Frank Thompson Jr., D-N.J. (1955-81).

Pratt's decisions rejected the five's post-trial motions that their convictions should be thrown out because of government misconduct in Abscam.

In other ethics matters:

● Rep. Jon Hinson, R-Miss., resigned from the House April 13 after his arrest on a morals charge in a Capitol Hill men's room.

● Former Rep. Charles J. Carney, D-Ohio (1970-79), was ordered acquitted by a Washington, D.C., federal judge Nov. 23 of charges that he accepted an illegal gratuity.

(Background, 1980 Almanac p. 525)

Caucus Restrictions, New GAO Chief

The House Administration Committee approved in October a series of new rules restricting the operations on Capitol Hill of special interest caucuses and similar legislative service organizations.

The new rules required that caucuses receiving outside funding for their activities had to relinquish those funds or sever their official ties with Congress by 1983.

The rules were prompted in part by a report by the independent Better Government Association charging that such outside funding violated the spirit of House ethics rules.

The March 3 retirement of Elmer B. Staats as head of the General Accounting Office gave President Reagan the opportunity to name Charles A. Bowsher, formerly a managing partner with the Arthur Andersen & Co. accounting firm, to a 15-year term as comptroller general of the United States.

Master Plan Completed

About four years late and $164,000 over budget, Capitol Architect George M. White submitted to Congress in September his master plan for the development of the Capitol Hill area.

The 100-page report was intended to serve as a blueprint for congressional expansion and improvement over the next 50 to 75 years.

The report did not propose that Congress actually build any new buildings or make improvements in the Capitol grounds. Instead, it was designed to instruct Congress where a new building should go if it were needed.

—By Irwin B. Arieff

Senate Delays Action on Williams' Expulsion

The Senate in late 1981 put off until the second session its debate on a recommendation that Sen. Harrison A. Williams Jr., D-N.J., be expelled from the Senate.

Senate leaders announced Dec. 1 that floor action on a resolution (S Res 204) to expel Williams would not take place until early in 1982. Their announcement came just two days before the Senate had been scheduled to take up Williams' fate.

Williams was the only senator to be convicted for his involvement in the FBI's Abscam corruption probe. The Senate Select Ethics Committee had unanimously recommended his expulsion on Aug. 24, concluding that his conduct in Abscam had been "ethically repugnant."

The decision to delay the debate on the resolution came at the request of Sen. Daniel K. Inouye, D-Hawaii, who agreed at the last minute to act as Williams' lawyer on the Senate floor. He told Majority Leader Howard H. Baker Jr., R-Tenn., and Minority Leader Robert C. Byrd, D-W.Va., that he would need about a month to prepare Williams' defense.

The leaders' decision to grant the request for a delay was "simply a matter of senatorial courtesy," Inouye said later. "I just told them that I wanted to participate in the case and would need some time to prepare."

A smiling Williams told reporters Dec. 1 he was delighted with the delay because it would "give me the opportunity I need to fully develop all of the evidence and present a winning defense against alleged charges of unethical conduct."

The delay had potentially important political consequences for the Senate. It meant that if Williams ultimately were expelled, the Senate likely would end up with one more Republican member for the rest of the second session.

Had Williams been expelled before the end of the first session, the appointment of a successor would have been up to a Democrat, New Jersey Gov. Brendan T. Byrne.

But Byrne's term was expected to end Jan. 19, six days before the beginning of the second session. His successor was to be Republican Thomas H. Kean. For Kean to choose a Republican to succeed Williams would increase the Senate's ratio of Republicans to Democrats from the current 53-47 to 54-46.

Inouye, who as secretary of the Senate Democratic Conference was the third-ranking Democratic leader in the Senate, said he permitted political considerations to play no part in his decision to represent Williams. To have been motivated by politics would have been "gross and crass," the Hawaii Democrat said.

"Here was a man indicted for a capital offense, so far as the United States Senate is concerned," Inouye said. "If you expel him, you are literally killing this person. What is required on the Senate's part is fair play and even-handedness."

He said he took on Williams' case only after learning that no other senator would do so. "I was a bit saddened when I realized no one was stepping forward to defend him," Inouye said. "This good and gentle man is deserving of his day in court."

Williams said he would use the extra time to continue to press the Senate leadership for an opportunity to stage a full rehearing of the case against him before his 99 Senate colleagues. He maintained he needed such a forum to explore the issue of government misconduct in the Abscam investigation, before the people who ultimately would decide his fate in the Senate.

Earlier, on Nov. 23, Williams had tried to stop Senate action on his expulsion by filing suit in U.S. District Court for the District of Columbia. He sought an injunction barring the Senate from taking up the expulsion resolution unless Senate leaders agreed to a rehearing of the case before the full Senate.

However, on Nov. 27, U.S. District Judge Gerhard A. Gesell turned down Williams' request for a temporary restraining order to bar the Senate from beginning its debate.

Williams filed the suit after Senate leaders Nov. 18 refused his request that he be allowed to turn the expulsion proceeding into a replay of his trial held earlier in the year in a Brooklyn, N.Y., court and of Ethics Committee hearings held in July.

Williams had argued that he needed to question witnesses and present evidence on the Senate floor in order to prove his innocence and assure a fair trial in the Senate.

But the leaders responded that the Ethics Committee — rather than the full Senate — was the proper forum for the submission of additional evidence.

However, hours after Williams filed the Nov. 23 suit, the Ethics Committee also turned down his request for an opportunity to present additional testimony, arguing that the evidence was not "new" and did not justify reopening its hearings.

The panel added that it had no objection to permitting Williams to present affidavits from any witnesses or other written evidence directly to the Senate, so that such material could be considered by individual senators.

Committee's Initial Recommendation

The Ethics Commitee's initial expulsion recommendation, announced after a seven-hour, closed-door meeting Aug. 24, wrapped up a four-month committee investigation of whether Williams was guilty of violating Senate rules.

The panel began its formal probe following the senator's May 1 conviction in a Brooklyn, N.Y., federal court on nine counts, including bribery and conspiracy. (Details, below)

The conviction grew out of Williams' involvement in the Abscam political corruption probe, during which undercover FBI agents masqueraded as businessmen and wealthy Arabs in an effort to catch members of Congress and other public officials committing criminal acts.

Although the jury in the Brooklyn proceeding voted to convict Williams, U.S. District Judge George C. Pratt delayed formally entering the verdict until he ruled on a series of post-trial motions filed by Williams' attorneys.

In those motions, Williams had asked the judge either to throw out the conviction, acquit him or grant him a new trial. Williams argued that the government had been overzealous in its pursuit of the Abscam investigation and had deprived him of his due process rights in order to obtain his conviction.

But Pratt in a Dec. 22 decision rejected all of Williams' motions.

Pratt then set sentencing in the case for Feb. 9. Williams said he would appeal.

$6 Million Suit

Left undecided at year's end was a $6 million civil suit filed by Williams Oct. 1 against the Justice Department and federal officials who participated in the Abscam investigation.

In the suit, filed in U.S. District Court for the District of Columbia, Williams sought $1 million in compensatory damages and $5 million in punitive damages. Named as defendants were the Justice Department, former Attorney General Benjamin R. Civiletti, Attorney General William French Smith, FBI operative and convicted swindler Melvin Weinberg and other FBI Abscam personnel and Justice officials.

The suit also asked that a three-judge panel be formed to appoint a special prosecutor, who would investigate alleged FBI abuses in the Abscam probe.

Noting that he had backed Sen. Edward M. Kennedy, D-Mass., for president in 1980, Williams blamed "political factors" for making him a target of the Carter administration Justice Department.

Williams was the last of the congressional Abscam defendants and the sole senator to be snared in the FBI probe. All six House members indicted on Abscam-related offenses were found guilty. *(Background, box, p. 386; 1980 Almanac p. 513)*

He was the first senator to be convicted of a felony while in office since 1920, when Truman H. Newberry, R-Mich. (1919-1922), was convicted of irregular campaign practices. Williams was only the fourth sitting senator to be convicted in Senate history. *(Box, p. 387)*

The last time a senator was expelled was in 1862, when Waldo P. Johnson, D-Mo. (1861-62), and Jesse D. Bright, D-Ind. (1845-62), were removed for support of the Confederacy during the Civil War.

The last time a senator was disciplined by the Senate was in October 1979, when Herman E. Talmadge, D-Ga. (1957-81), was "denounced" for financial misconduct at the conclusion of a 10-month Ethics Committee investigation. *(Talmadge case, previous House and Senate censure proceedings, 1979 Almanac p. 566; previous House and Senate expulsion proceedings, CQ Guide to Congress 2nd edition, pp. 693-94)*

Williams, 61, was at the time of the Ethics Committee investigation a 22-year Senate veteran. The eighth most senior senator, he served one and a half terms in the House before first winning election to the Senate in November 1958.

He was a member of the Banking, Labor, Rules and Joint Library committees, and was chairman of the Senate Labor Committee from 1971 until the Republicans took over the Senate in January 1981. At that time, he chose to become ranking minority member of the Banking Committee.

Court Decision

Williams was found guilty by a federal district court jury in Brooklyn, N.Y., on May 1. Following a five-week trial, the jury voted to convict him on all nine counts on which he had been indicted, including bribery, conspiracy, receipt of an unlawful gratuity, accepting outside compensation for the performance of official duties and interstate travel in aid of a racketeering enterprise. *(Indictment, 1980 Almanac p. 521)*

The Brooklyn jury also convicted Williams' co-defendant, New Jersey attorney Alexander Feinberg, on nine counts of criminal wrongdoing.

The jury deliberated about 28 hours before finding Williams and Feinberg guilty.

Sentencing of the pair was delayed until after all post-trial motions, including a decision on the question of whether Williams was entrapped by overzealous government agents.

Both men said they would appeal their convictions.

"In my heart, I know I did no wrong," Williams told reporters after the verdict was announced.

Boasts or 'Baloney'?

The trial began March 30. The defense alone presented 45 witnesses, including Williams, who testified last.

During the trial, government prosecutors tried to prove that Williams had accepted a hidden 18 percent interest in a titanium mine in Virginia in return for a promise to use his influence to obtain government contracts to buy the mine's output.

As part of the deal, undercover FBI agents posing as wealthy Arabs and their associates promised to loan $100 million to the mining venture, owned by friends of Williams and Feinberg. Prosecutors alleged the loan would have been of direct benefit to Williams, and the senator was aware of this when he accepted the hidden interest in the mine.

Prosecutors further alleged that Williams had promised to use his influence to help an undercover agent posing as a wealthy Arab gain permanent U.S. residency.

As in previous Abscam trials, government-made videotapes played a major role.

In one tape, made in June 1979, Williams was seen saying that obtaining government contracts for the titanium mine would be "no problem.... It will come to pass." In a May 1979 tape, co-defendant Feinberg boasted that Williams "will open up the doors for us, and use his — you know what I'm talking about — to get the contracts."

During an August 1979 meeting, Williams was seen accepting stock in the corporation set up to develop the mine. And in a January 1980 tape, he promised an undercover agent that he would "do everything in my power" to help a supposed Arab gain permanent residency in the United States.

Lawyers for the defendants said the two men thought they were engaging in a legitimate business deal when they were "entrapped" and "fooled" by the undercover agents into making seemingly incriminating but essentially meaningless statements. During his testimony, Williams repeatedly referred to his own statements on the tapes as "baloney."

Helping a Friend

The defense lawyers said the two men agreed to meet with the supposed sheiks to obtain a $100 million loan for the mining venture for their friends.

"The reason I went there was at the basic request of my friends who saw an opportunity here," Williams said. "I never used my office to advance my personal financial interest.... I never said I would arrange for government contracts."

Defense lawyers maintained that convicted swindler Melvin Weinberg, who worked undercover for the government, had put words in their clients' mouths by "coaching"

them to boast of their influence to impress the supposed wealthy Arabs.

Bolstering this claim, Feinberg testified that Weinberg had threatened to withdraw the Arabs' offer of the $100 million loan if Williams did not hide his interest in the mine. "He can't put it in his name," Weinberg told Feinberg in a June 1979 tape. "If he [publicly] reports [his holding], then he can't do nothing for us."

Testimony indicated that Weinberg's role also upset lawyers for the government. Four Justice Department employees involved in the case testified for the defense that they had told Weinberg not to put words in the sting victims' mouths. They said Weinberg responded, "If we don't do that, we won't have no cases."

Senate Action

The Ethics Committee first began looking at Williams in February 1980 after press reports surfaced of his Abscam involvement. But the panel decided at that time to defer a more formal probe until after the Justice Department had completed its investigation.

The formal probe began on May 5, 1981, when members decided that there was "substantial credible evidence" that Williams was guilty of "improper conduct which may reflect upon the Senate" as well as violations of the Senate's rules on public financial disclosure and conflict of interest.

Normally, the committee would hold an "initial review" of the evidence in a case before voting for a full-scale investigation and hearings. But because of the felony conviction, the committee decided to take a shortcut in its own procedures and proceed directly to the investigation.

The panel decided to further expedite its probe by relying on the trial record for evidence rather than scheduling full evidentiary hearings of its own, which presumably would have required presentation of the same evidence that had come out in court.

The House Standards Committee had relied on a similar expedited procedure in its Abscam probe, prompting some criticism that accused members did not receive a fair

Hearings Begin

Formal Ethics Committee hearings into misconduct charges against Williams opened July 14.

The panel's three Republicans and three Democrats spent one-and-a-half days hearing a presentation of the case against Williams by special counsel Robert S. Bennett.

Most of the evidence was in the form of video and audio tapes made by the FBI during its undercover investigation.

In his opening remarks, Ethics Chairman Malcolm Wallop, R-Wyo., called the proceeding "a serious, painful and most difficult task."

"I have never engaged in so difficult, so unpleasant a task as we undertake today," agreed Vice Chairman Howell Heflin, D-Ala.

In his opening statement, special counsel Bennett said evidence would show that Williams had accepted a hidden interest in a Virginia titanium mine in return for a promise to use his influence to obtain government contracts to buy the mine's output. He also said Williams had promised to use his influence to help an undercover agent posing as a wealthy Arab gain permanent U.S. residency.

Hinson Resignation

Rep. Jon C. Hinson, R-Miss. (1979-81), resigned from the House April 13 after his arrest on a morals charge in a Capitol Hill men's room. Under pressure from Mississippi and House Republican leaders, he announced his intention to resign March 13, slightly more than a month after his Feb. 4 arrest on a charge of attempted oral sodomy.

Hinson, who represented Mississippi's 4th District, was replaced by Democrat Wayne Dowdy, who won a runoff election July 7. *(Election results, p. 5-B)*

Hinson initially pleaded not guilty to the charge, a misdemeanor. But on May 28 he changed his plea to no contest and was sentenced to 30 days in jail. Judge David L. Norman of the District of Columbia Superior Court suspended the sentence and placed Hinson on a year's probation, subject to his continuing the medical treatment and counseling he began following his arrest.

Hinson was arrested after Capitol police witnessed him and a Library of Congress clerk in a restroom in a remote corner of a House office building across the street from the Capitol. A team of plainclothes Capitol police had been observing the restroom for about a week following complaints that it was being used as a homosexual meeting place.

Hinson, 39, was first elected to Congress in November 1978. In November 1980 he defeated two opponents to win re-election with just 39 percent of the vote.

During his re-election campaign, Hinson revealed that in September 1976 he had been arrested for committing an obscene act in a homosexual trysting place in Arlington, Va. He added that in 1977 he had been among the survivors of a fire at a Washington movie theater frequented by homosexuals. However, Hinson denied that he was a homosexual.

At the time of the two incidents, Hinson had been administrative assistant to Rep. Thad Cochran, R-Miss., who became a senator in 1978. When Cochran announced for the Senate, Hinson began his own winning campaign to succeed him.

Representing the senator was Washington attorney Kenneth R. Feinberg, a former top aide to Sen. Edward M. Kennedy, D-Mass. He attacked the evidence, noting that the Abscam probe was under review in a separate court proceeding.

If Williams' conviction were thrown out, he asserted, this would taint the Senate proceeding. The evidence, he said, "conveys a terribly misleading impression. It is unreliable. It is incomplete.... This committee should wait and have before it all the available information."

However, Wallop said the court proceeding had little bearing on the Senate action. "It must be emphasized," he said, "that the recommendation of this committee and the final decision of the Senate are in no way dependent upon the ultimate decision of the courts."

Williams' Testimony

Williams himself appeared before the panel July 28, arguing that he should not be punished by the Senate

Lederer Resigns; He and Others Sentenced

Rep. Raymond F. Lederer, D-Pa., (1977-81), the only House member implicated in Abscam to be re-elected in 1980, resigned from the House May 5. *(Background, 1980 Almanac p. 513)*

His decision was disclosed April 29, the day after the House Committee on Standards of Official Conduct recommended that he be expelled for his involvement in the FBI's political corruption probe.

The Standards Committee had begun a disciplinary proceeding against Lederer in March following his Jan. 9 conviction in federal court on bribery and conspiracy charges in connection with Abscam.

In a statement read to reporters in Philadelphia by Lederer's attorney, James Binns, the congressman said his legal defense had become so time-consuming that he could no longer adequately represent his constituents.

"Faced with a choice between serving my constituents and solving my legal problems," he said, "I have . . . decided that it is in the best interests of the people of the 3rd District for me to resign my seat."

Lederer, 42, was first elected to the House from Pennsylvania's 3rd District in November 1976 and was re-elected in 1978 and 1980.

He was replaced by state Sen. Joseph F. Smith, a Democrat running as a Republican, who won a special election July 21. *(Results, p. 5-B)*

Two 'No' Votes

The Standards Committee's April 28 vote in favor of expelling Lederer was 10-2. Don Bailey, D-Pa., and Ken Holland, D-S.C., voted "no."

Holland said he was uncertain whether the House had the constitutional authority to expel a member. And at the time of the meeting, he said, the Standards Committee staff had not yet completed a memo he had requested on the subject.

Bailey had argued frequently that it was wrong for the Standards Committee to judge a member's guilt on the basis of a conviction that still was on appeal.

In the case of Lederer and Rep. Michael "Ozzie" Myers, D-Pa. (1976-80), he asserted, the panel should have held full evidentiary hearings to determine their guilt or innocence instead of relying on court records, an expedited procedure allowed under the committee's rule 14.

Myers was expelled from the House Oct. 2, 1980. Later that day he had filed suit in U.S. district court for the District of Columbia alleging that the House had deprived him of a fair trial before expelling him. The suit was dismissed Jan. 5.

Six Members Convicted

Lederer was one of six House members convicted on charges stemming from Abscam.

Reps. Myers; John W. Jenrette Jr., D-S.C. (1975-80); John M. Murphy, D-N.Y. (1963-81); and Frank Thompson Jr., D-N.J. (1955-81), all were defeated for re-election in the November general election. Richard Kelly, R-Fla. (1975-81), was defeated in the September Florida primary.

Myers' defeat followed by a month his expulsion from the House. He was the first House member to be expelled since 1861, the first ever to be expelled for misconduct other than treason and only the fourth member to be expelled in House history.

Jenrette, convicted Oct. 7, 1980, resigned from the House in early December in order to halt an expulsion proceeding against him.

Kelly, Murphy and Thompson were defeated prior to their convictions and left Congress before disciplinary proceedings could be initiated against them.

On Aug. 13, Lederer, Myers and Murphy each were sentenced to three years in federal prison and fined $20,000 by U.S. District Judge George C. Pratt of Brooklyn, N.Y. Sentencing of Thompson was put off, pending completion of a medical examination, which was to occur after his appeals were exhausted. Myers and three co-defendants were convicted Aug. 30, 1980, of bribery, conspiracy and interstate travel to aid racketeering. Two of those co-defendants — Angelo J. Errichetti, former mayor of Camden, N.J., and Louis C. Johanson, a member of the Philadelphia City Council — also were sentenced Aug. 13. Errichetti received six years and a $40,000 fine. Johanson was sentenced to three years and was fined $20,000.

Murphy and Thompson, the chairmen respectively of the Merchant Marine and Fisheries and House Administration committees at the time they were implicated, were found guilty Dec. 3, 1980, on conspiracy and other charges stemming from the Abscam probe.

The four former congressmen said they would appeal their convictions and were expected to remain free until appeals were exhausted.

On July 24 Judge Pratt ruled that the four had not been entrapped or arbitrarily "targeted" by undercover government agents and that the government's conduct of the Abscam probe was proper and appropriate. The four had charged in post-trial motions that the government had violated their constitutional rights.

Pratt's ruling was at odds with an opinion rendered in late 1980 in another Abscam case that was tried in Philadelphia. In that decision, U.S. District Judge John P. Fullam overturned the convictions of three other Abscam defendants — none of them members of Congress — on grounds they had been entrapped.

In his 135-page opinion, Pratt said the government's need to root out corruption among public officials "more than justifies the investigative techniques employed in these cases. Without question, these convictions were reliable, and no constitutional right of any defendant has been infringed."

Still to be sentenced were Kelly, Jenrette and Sen. Harrison A. Williams Jr., D-N.J.

Kelly was convicted Jan. 26, 1981, in federal district court for the District of Columbia of bribery and bribery conspiracy. Convicted along with him were Eugene Robert Ciuzio, a Longwood, Fla., businessman, and Stanley Weisz, a Smithtown, N.Y., accountant.

Williams Is 4th Senator Convicted in Office

Sen. Harrison A. Williams Jr., D-N.J., was the fourth senator to have been convicted of criminal wrongdoing while in office.

Prior to Williams, the last sitting senator to be convicted was Truman H. Newberry, R-Mich. (1919-22), found guilty in March 1920 of election irregularities.

Newberry's conviction was reversed by the Supreme Court in May 1921. But he resigned his seat in November 1922 after realizing that despite the Supreme Court's finding, "his position could never be other than uncomfortable," according to "Senate Election, Expulsion and Censure Cases" (S Doc 92-7).

The other two sitting senators to have been convicted were:

● John H. Mitchell, R-Ore. (1873-79, 1885-97, 1901-05), convicted in July 1905 on charges of accepting compensation for services rendered before a U.S. department. He died in late 1905 while his conviction was on appeal.

● Joseph R. Burton, R-Kan. (1901-06), convicted in November 1905 for allegedly using the mails for fraudulent purposes and accepting compensation for services rendered before a U.S. department. Burton's conviction was upheld by the Supreme Court in May 1906, and in June he resigned from the Senate and served five months in prison.

Indicted But Not Convicted

Congressional Quarterly found records of four other senators indicted while in office but not convicted. They were:

● John Smith, D-Ohio (1803-08), indicted in 1806 along with Vice President Aaron Burr for treason. He was found not guilty.

● Charles H. Dietrich, R-Neb. (1901-05), indicted in December 1903 on bribery and conspiracy charges in connection with the appointment of a postmaster and the leasing of a post office. The charges were dropped on a technicality in January 1904.

● Burton K. Wheeler, D-Mont. (1923-47), indicted in April 1924 on a bribery charge. Wheeler was acquitted.

● Edward J. Gurney, R-Fla. (House, 1963-69; Senate, 1969-74), indicted in April 1974 for alleged election law violations. The indictment was dismissed in May 1974. Gurney was again indicted in July 1974, this time on charges of perjury and soliciting bribes. He was acquitted on the bribery solicitation charge in August 1975 and on the perjury charge in October 1976.

---

because he had not violated any Senate rules or broken any law.

"I did make mistakes, errors in judgment," Williams told the Ethics panel. "But I tell this committee under oath that ... I never engaged in any illegal conduct, I never corrupted my office, and I never intended to do anything that would bring dishonor to the Senate."

The committee originally had blocked out a four-day period to hear Williams' defense, but it ended up spending only one day on it.

However, members frequently were called away from the hearing room for Senate floor votes, so the panel stayed in session for 13 hours in order to finish.

In all, Williams spent about five hours on the witness stand. Speaking choppily, but betraying no emotion, he first made a statement and then answered questions.

"It's not easy for me to appear here today," he told the panel. "It's never easy to discuss personal problems before one's longstanding colleagues and friends."

Williams denied Bennett's contention that he had agreed to accept a hidden interest in a Virginia titanium mine in return for a promise to use his influence to obtain government contracts to buy the mine's output.

He also denied that he had promised to use his influence to help an undercover agent posing as a wealthy Arab to gain permanent U.S. residency.

Instead, the New Jersey Democrat said, he had intended only to help out some old friends who owned the mine to obtain a loan from a wealthy Arab businessman.

'Wacky' Statements

His acts of friendship had unwittingly involved him in a "stage play for an audience of government officials who were determined to create a crime and create guilt where none had existed," the senator maintained.

He acknowledged that in his relations with his friends he had been "soft when I should have been strong."

"I am not a good judge of friends," he said. "I permitted my feelings of friendship to override my good judgment."

Williams also acknowledged that he had boasted of his influence with high government officials "to an uncomfortable degree" in the presence of the bogus Arab and that he had accepted stock in the mine. But he said he believed the stock certificates to be worthless.

Williams dismissed each video- or audio-taped statement that Bennett hinted might be incriminating. Undercover agents had "coached" him into making some of the statements, he said. Others, he maintained, were taken out of context or were merely "wacky" statements he made in order to impress the supposed Arab.

'Wronged' - Williams

Williams asked the committee either to vindicate him or to delay its proceeding until after Judge Pratt in Brooklyn had ruled on whether the government was guilty of misconduct in the case.

"If I believed that I was guilty of some crime, or if I were convinced that I had violated the Senate rules, the honorable thing to do would be to resign my office, and I would not hesitate to do so," Williams concluded. "But I have been wronged in this case, and that is why I have not resigned."

Feinberg called only one other witness on Williams' behalf, Notre Dame University Law Professor G. Robert Blakey.

Blakey testified as an expert witness that the committee had inadequate evidence to judge Williams' state of mind during Abscam. He said the panel's decision should

Murtha Cleared by Panel

The House Committee on Standards of Official Conduct announced July 28 that it was ending its probe of Rep. John P. Murtha, D-Pa., for official misconduct in connection with the Abscam investigation.

The panel said it "found on the basis of the evidence presented no reason to issue a statement of alleged violation."

Immediately afterward, E. Barrett Prettyman Jr., the attorney conducting the Abscam investigation for the committee, resigned in protest. He had recommended that charges of wrongdoing be voted against Murtha.

However, neither Prettyman nor the committee would make public a letter from the attorney citing the reasons for his resignation.

Prettyman said that only committee members were in the room when the panel voted not to cite Murtha. The committee would not disclose the actual vote. "I've simply resigned," Prettyman told a reporter.

Murtha was an unindicted co-conspirator in the Abscam case. He testified in one Abscam trial that former Rep. Frank Thompson Jr., D-N.J., had mentioned to him on the House floor in October 1979 a business deal with "Arab sheiks" involving $50,000 in "walking around money." An FBI videotape showed Murtha telling FBI undercover agents that he was not interested in taking any cash "at this point."

---

hinge on whether Williams knowingly committed wrongdoing and suggested that the panel call additional witnesses to determine Williams' intent.

However, the committee ended its hearings without further testimony.

Right to Vote Questioned

Williams' conviction threw into question his right to vote on the Senate floor and in committee.

House rules urged — but did not require — a convicted member to refrain from voting in committee and on the floor until the member either was cleared or re-elected. The Senate had no similar requirement.

Ethics Chairman Wallop and Vice Chairman Heflin said May 5 that they thought Williams would have to seek the Senate's permission to withhold his vote.

Mack Mattingly, R-Ga., a member of the Ethics Committee, said in a May 5 statement that until the committee had concluded its probe, Williams "should not be afforded" the opportunity to vote. He called on Senate Democratic leaders to urge Williams to voluntarily refrain from voting.

In the statement, Mattingly went on to say that he had not prejudged the Williams case. However, he later retracted the statement, explaining that he did not wish to appear to prejudice the committee's deliberations.

Williams continued voting throughout the year.

No Clear Precedent

There apparently was no clear precedent in recent Senate history requiring a senator to refrain from voting or performing any other official duties when convicted or indicted.

In the early 1900s, it was the custom for a senator to voluntarily refrain from voting and even from entering the Senate chamber after being indicted. The March 21, 1920, *New York Times*, for example, noted that Sen. Joseph R. Burton, R-Kan. (1901-06), convicted in November 1905 on charges of accepting a fee for services rendered before a U.S. department, chose to remain outside of the Senate chamber because a colleague had threatened to offer a motion to exclude him from the Senate if he tried to enter.

"To draw his salary as a senator," the Times account continued, "Mr. Burton entered the Senate cloakroom and merely stuck his head into the Senate chamber, thus technically complying with the rule requiring the presence of senators on at least one day of the session before they can draw their salaries."

The custom was reversed, however, after the April 1924 indictment of Sen. Burton K. Wheeler, D-Mont. (1923-47), on a bribery charge.

Wheeler at the time headed a special committee investigating the failure of the Warren G. Harding administration to prosecute federal officials suspected of influence-peddling in the Teapot Dome scandal. Wheeler maintained he had been framed by the very officials he was investigating.

Rather than keep off the floor, Wheeler demanded the right to speak to declare his innocence and to ask the Senate to investigate the charge. During the ensuing probe, he continued to vote.

Wheeler subsequently was cleared of any wrongdoing both by the Senate and by a federal jury. Since then, indicted senators have remained active in Senate affairs until they either were cleared or left the Senate. ∎

Members' Tax Exemption

The 4th U.S. Circuit Court of Appeals Jan. 5 upheld a lower court ruling that members of Congress who resided only part-time in Maryland were exempt from Maryland income taxes.

The decision confirmed a March 31 ruling by U.S. District Judge Frank A. Kaufman of Baltimore that the government can exempt its members from such taxes.

The ruling resulted from a suit filed against Maryland by the Justice Department after the state continued to bill members of Congress for back taxes despite a 1977 law (PL 95-67) prohibiting the practice. Under the 1977 law, members were to be subject solely to the taxes levied by the states and localities they represented, even if they spent less time each year in their home district than in the Washington, D.C., area.

Though many out-of-state members reside in the District of Columbia and Virginia as well as in Maryland, only Maryland has attempted to collect income taxes from out-of-state members. ∎

Code Action Delayed

The Senate Select Ethics Committee put off indefinitely its planned revision of the Senate's four-year-old code of conduct after it voted May 5 to begin an investigation of the Abscam role of Harrison A. Williams Jr., D-N.J. *(Williams, p. 383)*

A committee spokeswoman explained that the panel did not want to put itself in the position of recommending changes in its procedures while conducting an investigation.

The revision project was first approved by the Senate in February 1980, and the Ethics panel had been given until May 15 to complete its recommendations.

Any proposed changes ultimately recommended by the Ethics Committee would have to be considered by the Rules Committee before they could be brought to the floor.

Revisions in the code were proposed by Malcolm Wallop, R-Wyo., after he took over chairmanship of the panel in January 1981. The existing code, approved in 1977, "has nothing to do with ethics. It is bad for the morality of the Senate and bad for the public's perception of the Senate," he said.

At the time, he said he wanted to eliminate from the code many of its express prohibitions and limit the financial disclosure requirement to only those interests "that might create conflict." ∎

Senate Subpoena Power

A three-judge panel of the U.S. Court of Appeals for the District of Columbia Circuit May 13 upheld a provision of the 1978 Ethics in Government Act (PL 95-521) giving the Senate a new mechanism to enforce its subpoenas. *(Ethics in Government Act, 1978 Almanac p. 835)*

The mechanism allowed the jailing of recalcitrant witnesses until they provided the Senate or one of its committees with requested information.

According to Sam Nunn, D-Ga., ranking Democrat on the Senate Governmental Affairs Subcommittee on Permanent Investigations, the decision was "of considerable importance ... in [providing] convincing evidence that the U.S. Senate is willing and determined to follow through in its oversight function and investigative powers."

Before 1978 Congress had two less effective ways to enforce subpoenas. *(CQ Guide to Congress 2nd Edition, p. 143)*

Occasionally in congressional history, an individual found in contempt was held in the Capitol building until he agreed to supply requested information.

In 1857, Congress added a new enforcement weapon: the authority to seek criminal charges against an individual found in contempt. However, a criminal fine or imprisonment was only punitive in nature.

By contrast, the civil mechanism provided by the 1978 law was coercive as well as punitive because the prison term ended as soon as the uncooperative witness decided to cooperate. In addition, it allowed the Senate itself to initiate court action rather than relying on the Justice Department, which it had to do under the old system.

Another aspect of the new provision — attractive to civil libertarians — was that it permitted a witness to challenge judicially the legality of the Senate inquiry leading to the subpoena, an action not permitted under the criminal and congressional contempt procedures. ∎

Curbs Imposed on Special-Interest Caucuses

The House Administration Committee voted unanimously Oct. 21 that special-interest caucuses and similar House legislative service organizations (LSOs) had to relinquish all outside funding or sever their official ties with Congress by 1983.

The committee vote constituted final action on the regulations; no House concurrence was needed.

Under the new rules, caucuses that wanted to continue accepting outside funds had to set up separate, non-profit foundations with private offices, staff and facilities.

Beginning in 1982, LSOs also were required to submit to the House clerk more frequent and more detailed financial reports than under existing rules.

LSOs are groups of members of Congress who have banded together to pursue a common legislative goal. In 1981 there were more than 50 such groups operating on Capitol Hill, including the House Democratic Caucus, the House Republican Study Committee, the Congressional Black Caucus, the Congressional Suburban Caucus, the Steel Caucus and the Environmental Study Conference.

Many of the LSOs were informal groups, with no staff and no offices. But 26 of them had officially registered with the House, making them eligible to occupy space in House office buildings, have House telephone numbers and use House office supplies and equipment.

These LSOs also were eligible to receive donations from members' official allowances. These allowances would help pay for dues, staff salaries and subscriptions to LSO publications.

Better Government Association Report

The committee's action was prompted in part by a Sept. 18 report by the independent, Chicago-based Better Government Association (BGA), which argued that allowing private contributions to LSOs violated the spirit of House ethics rules because such contributions were forbidden to individual members.

BGA said that eight of the 26 LSOs supplemented their budgets with direct contributions from outside sources. These were the Congressional Black Caucus, the Hispanic Caucus, the Rural Caucus, the Travel and Tourism Caucus, the Congresswomen's Caucus, Members of Congress for Peace Through Law, the New England Caucus and the New York Bipartisan Congressional Delegation.

LSOs began filing semiannual financial reports in mid-1980 under a requirement set in 1979 by the Administration Committee.

Records on file with the clerk of the House covering the three six-month periods ending June 30, 1981, showed that the Congressional Black Caucus received more than $550,000 in private contributions during 1980. The Congressional Hispanic Caucus received more than $129,000 during the same period. The Travel and Tourism Caucus reported receipt of more than $480,000 in outside funding during the 18 months ending June 30.

Task Force Appointed

To explore the issue, the Administration Committee appointed a three-member task force consisting of Reps.

William R. Ratchford, D-Conn., Gary A. Lee, R-N.Y., and Al Swift, D-Wash.

During Oct. 1 hearings before the task force, Del. Walter E. Fauntroy, D-D.C., chairman of the Congressional Black Caucus, said curbs on outside support would place "an undue burden and disadvantage" on his group.

But Rep. Louis Stokes, D-Ohio, chairman of the House Standards Committee, said that his panel could find no distinctions in House rules between how restrictions should apply to individual members and to groups of members.

After the hearings, the task force drafted a series of proposed new regulations, sought comment on them, and on Oct. 15 approved them for consideration by the full Administration Committee.

Before adopting the rules Oct. 21, the committee rejected by voice vote an alternative proposal by Lee, the lone Republican on the task force, that would have abolished all official support for House caucuses, leaving them to exist only as informal groups of members without their own staffs and offices.

Provisions

As approved by the committee, the new regulations:

● Defined an LSO as "a grouping of members who pool resources to pursue a common legislative goal."

● Authorized qualified LSOs to be funded through contributions, dues or assessments from members' clerk-hire and expense allowances, and to receive office space, furniture, furnishings, telephone service and other support from the House itself.

● Authorized the House Administration Committee to decide whether a group qualified as an LSO under the rules.

● Required LSOs to notify the House clerk by Jan. 1, 1982, whether they intended to receive any income or contributions, either cash or in-kind, from any source other than Congress or its members after Jan. 1, 1983.

● Required LSOs that intended to seek outside support after Jan. 1, 1983, to give up all support from Congress and its members as of that date.

● Required LSOs that intended to rely solely on support from Congress and its members to relinquish all outside support as of Jan. 1, 1982, except that LSOs receiving income from the sale of subscriptions to their research materials could accept such income until Jan. 1, 1983.

● Required that 30 members or two-thirds of an LSO's members — whichever was less — certify each year to the House clerk that their organization provided "bona fide legislative services or assistance which supports them in the performance of their official duties."

● Required members to certify to the House clerk each month the identity of LSOs to which any of their staff were assigned.

● Required LSOs to certify to the House clerk each month the identity of members contributing clerk-hire funds for their staffers' salaries, and to certify that these aides were performing their assigned duties.

● Authorized LSOs to distribute research material to members from any source, so long as the identity of those preparing the material was fully disclosed on it.

● Required each LSO to submit quarterly reports to the House clerk listing the group's total receipts and disbursements; every individual receipt and disbursement aggregating over $200 during the quarter; and the name and salary of each staff member. The reports also had to list LSO activities and publications issued during the quarter. The reports were due 30 days after the end of each calendar quarter, starting with the quarter beginning Jan. 1, 1982. ∎

Expense Allowances Hiked

The House Administration Committee voted May 6 to increase House members' expense allowances effective May 1. The increase was approved on a voice vote and required no further House action before taking effect.

The hike, the first since 1979, was intended to cover inflationary increases in the cost of travel and office supplies, equipment and furnishings, according to the committee staff.

It had been requested by five committee members — Reps. Robert E. Badham, R-Calif., John L. Burton, D-Calif., William L. Dickinson, R-Ala., William R. Ratchford, D-Conn., and Chairman Augustus F. Hawkins, D-Calif.

Expense allowances covered such official costs as telephone, postage, office supplies and equipment, district office rental and travel. The amount of money made available to each individual member was based on a formula that took into account the cost of rental space in the member's district and the cost of travel and telephone service between the district and Washington, D.C.

Though particular sums of money were earmarked for the various types of official expenses, all the money in the allowance actually could be used as each member saw fit, so long as it was spent for official expenses.

The last time a fundamental adjustment was made in members' expense allowances was in March 1977, when the House voted to adopt a new code of conduct. The code banned unofficial office accounts and increased expense allowances by $5,000 a year to compensate for the loss. *(1977 Almanac p. 768)*

In September of that year, the House approved another increase to reflect increased district office rental costs. *(1977 Almanac p. 797)*

In October 1979, the basic allowance and funds allocated for transportation and office equipment were adjusted for inflation. While allowance increases generally require approval by the whole House, adjustments made to compensate for inflation require only a vote of the Administration Committee. *(1979 Almanac p. 597)*

Changes Approved

To cover the increased cost of office supplies and equipment, the committee increased each member's allowance by $4,300 a year.

To offset rising transportation costs, the committee approved mileage increases of 7 cents a mile for members whose districts were 3,000 or more miles away from Washington, to 12 cents a mile for members whose districts were less than 500 miles away.

The changes would mean annual increases ranging from at least $1,950 for members from districts close to Washington to about $24,600 a year for members whose districts were farthest away.

The panel also raised from $27,000 to $35,000 the ceiling on district office furnishings that could be purchased from the General Services Administration during a member's congressional career.

Committee auditor Robert S. McGuire said the panel had made no estimate of how much the allowance hike would cost taxpayers.

However, a Congressional Quarterly estimate put the cost of the increase at $4 million to $5 million a year for travel and office supplies and equipment. In addition, there would be a one-time expenditure of at least $3.5 million because of the increase in the district office furniture allowance.

New GAO Head Named

Accountant Charles A. Bowsher was confirmed Sept. 29 as comptroller general of the United States. The Senate vote was 99-0. *(Vote 288, p. 49-S)*

Bowsher then began a 15-year term as head of the General Accounting Office (GAO), Congress' official "watchdog" over the executive branch. He replaced Elmer B. Staats, who retired March 3.

The new comptroller general was nominated by President Reagan July 9.

Since 1971 Bowsher, 50, had been a managing partner in the government services division of the Arthur Andersen & Co. accounting firm. Located in the company's Washington office with a specialty in federal financial and management problems, Bowsher had a reputation for working well with Democrats and Republicans. He also helped design bookkeeping systems for the 1976 presidential campaigns of both major parties.

From 1967 to 1971, he was assistant secretary of the Navy for financial management. That service coincided with the administrations of Presidents Lyndon B. Johnson, a Democrat, and Richard M. Nixon, a Republican.

While Navy assistant secretary, Bowsher worked closely with the GAO and Comptroller General Staats. During that time, he won two distinguished public service awards from the Navy and a third from the Department of Defense.

A native of Elkhart, Ind., Bowsher graduated from the University of Illinois in 1953 and served in the Army for two years.

In 1956 he earned a Masters of Business Administration degree from the University of Chicago. The same year he went to work for Arthur Andersen in the company's Chicago office.

Selection Procedure

Bowsher was one of eight men recommended for the post of comptroller general by a special bipartisan commission of 10 members of Congress. The formal selection procedure was a new one, set out by Congress in a 1980 law (PL 96-226). The procedure encouraged, but did not require, the president to choose Staats' successor from among the list of those recommended by the commission.

Bowsher's position is one of the most secure in the federal government. In the 1921 law establishing the GAO, Congress went to great lengths to isolate the agency from political influence. The comptroller general was given a single 15-year term, and a lifetime pay and pension plan similar to that provided for federal judges. The job paid $60,662 a year. At the end of his term, he would continue to be paid a full salary plus regular cost-of-living increases for life.

Senate Television

The full Senate took no action in 1981 on a proposal endorsed by its Rules Committee to open the Senate chamber to television cameras and radio broadcast microphones.

Majority Leader Howard H. Baker Jr., R-Tenn., announced Nov. 30 that consideration of the measure would be put off until 1982 so senators could consider it "without the pressures of the clock."

The plan (S Res 20 — S Rept 97-178) was reported by the Rules panel Aug. 13. It was approved by voice vote.

Earlier, Rules Committee members had turned down an alternative plan by the committee's ranking Democrat, Wendell H. Ford, Ky., that would have permitted only radio broadcasts. That plan was rejected 5-7 on a straight party-line vote.

The Senate panel's action followed by more than two years the beginning of gavel-to-gavel broadcast coverage of House proceedings.

After two years of closed circuit broadcasts that provided a television signal of House proceedings only to members' offices, the House went on the air in March 1979. Gavel-to-gavel coverage was produced using a crew and equipment provided by the House itself under the supervision of the Speaker.

A mid-September survey by the Cable-Satellite Public Affairs Network (C-SPAN), which carried the House telecasts, indicated that Senate sentiment was firming up in favor of live television coverage.

The survey reported that 41 senators were firmly in favor, compared to 35 in favor in a similar C-SPAN survey in late February. In the later survey, only 13 senators said they were firmly opposed to Senate broadcast coverage, compared to 19 in the earlier poll.

In all, 58 senators either favored or were leaning toward favoring Senate broadcast coverage, compared to 19 who were either firmly opposed or leaning toward opposing such coverage. The survey found 23 senators undecided.

Committee Action

The debate in the committee centered on the cost of the system and the impact television might have on Senate proceedings.

Baker, who pushed hard for the proposal, argued that letting in the cameras was "neither radical nor novel" but merely "an extension electronically of the public gallery."

Others, however, suggested televising Senate proceedings might alter the historic character of Senate debate and might cost too much during a time of severe budget cutting.

Capitol Architect George M. White estimated the cost of the necessary broadcast equipment at $2.5 million to $3.5 million and the cost of operating and maintaining the system at $500,000 a year.

Ford argued that permitting radio broadcasts alone would reach more homes and cost less.

As approved by the Rules Committee, S Res 20 did not specify whether the system's cameras and microphones would be owned and operated by the Senate — as in the House — or whether they would be under the control of the broadcast media.

During debate, senators sounded as if they preferred to keep the broadcast equipment under their own control, but the resolution left that matter to be worked out at a later date.

Congress Receives Capitol Hill Master Plan

The first master plan for development of the Capitol Hill area was submitted to Congress Sept. 25 by Capitol Architect George M. White.

The 100-page report was intended to serve as a blueprint for Capitol Hill expansion and improvement over the next 50 to 75 years.

It laid out proposed sites for several additional government office buildings and suggested an underground expansion of the Capitol building and numerous improvements in the layout and landscaping of the Capitol area grounds.

The report did not propose that Congress actually construct all the additional buildings. Instead, the master plan was designed to instruct Congress where a new building should go if it were needed.

Long Delays

White first suggested a master plan in 1975, and Congress approved it that July at an estimated cost of $350,000. However, the final price tag was $514,000. The plan originally was to have been completed by late 1977.

White's recommendation that a plan be drawn up came after unexpectedly strong neighborhood resistance foiled a 1975 attempt by House leaders to appropriate $22.5 million for the purchase of land adjacent to the Capitol grounds for a fourth House office building.

White proposed the master plan as a way to smooth ruffled feathers. The final report provided that no homes would have to be destroyed to build any of the buildings suggested. (Background, 1975 Almanac, p. 853)

Senate, House Office Building Recommendations

The new master plan made numerous recommendations for changes to the Capitol building and the surrounding area.

For the area north of the Capitol, the plan suggested sites for three new Senate office buildings. Two would be on park land located behind the existing Russell and Dirksen office buildings. The third would be next to Union Station, a few blocks farther from the Capitol.

The report called the House side of Capitol Hill, to the south, "the most haphazardly built and unfinished section" of the Capitol grounds. For this area, the report set out sites for as many as nine new office buildings, which would be located in clusters behind the existing three buildings.

The report recommended that Congress' first priority in putting the master plan into effect should be construction of a new House office building. The House already needed an additional 1.6 million square feet of office space for existing employees, according to the report.

Move the Supreme Court?

For the Supreme Court, the architect proposed that it remain in its present quarters on the east side of the Capitol for the next 50 to 75 years.

But eventually, the report went on, the court should be moved to "its own enclave in another appropriate location" in order to symbolize the separation of the judiciary from the legislative branch of government.

The court already needed additional space for offices and tourist facilities, the report said, but the ornate domed

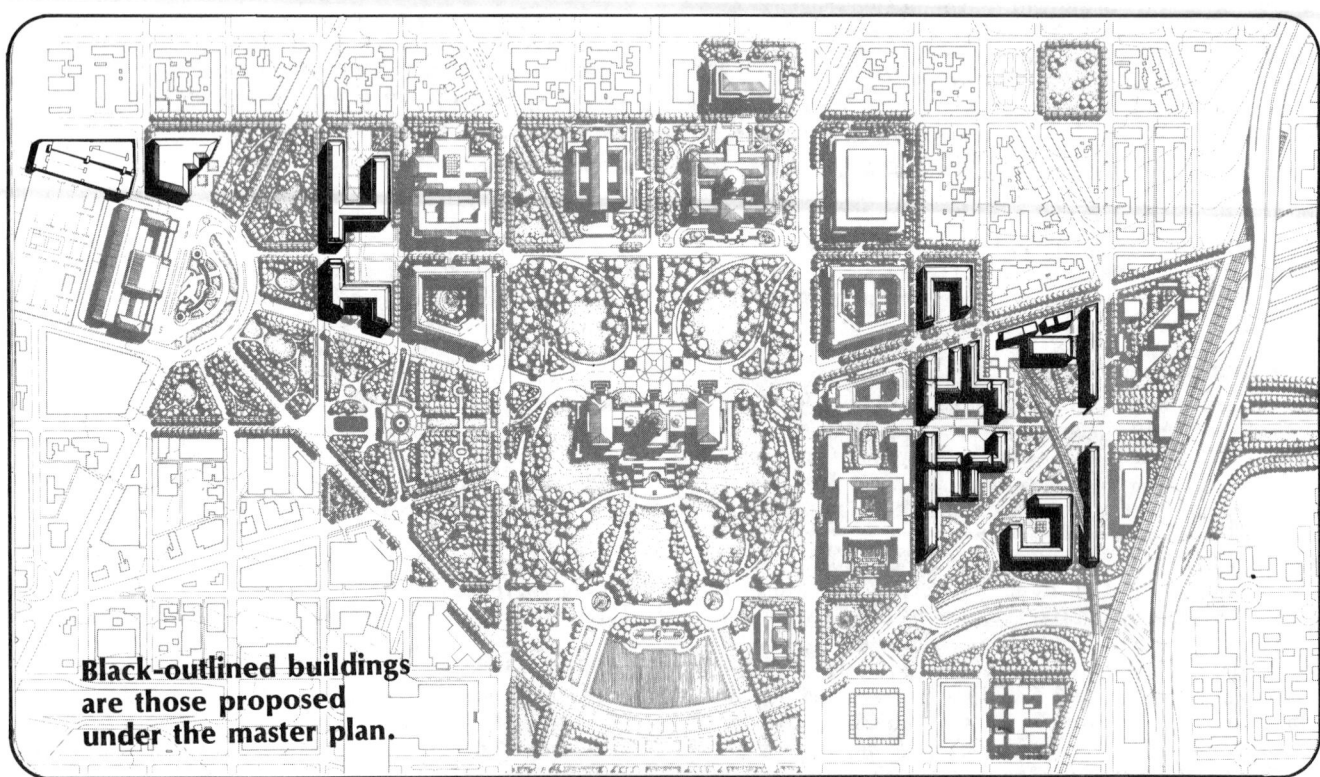

Black-outlined buildings are those proposed under the master plan.

Architect's Proposed Master Plan for Capitol Hill

design of the current court building "does not readily lend itself to additions or alterations."

The report also recommended construction of a second new building near Union Station to house in one location the entire staff of the Administrative Office of the United States Courts, which was housed at eight sites throughout the District of Columbia.

'Transition District'

To set the Capitol grounds off from the surrounding neighborhood, the report suggested creation of a "transition district" around Capitol Hill, featuring new sidewalks and rows of trees. The report said the District of Columbia should create a special district in the strip surrounding the area to protect the fronts of the existing town houses and to impose controls on the use of the adjoining land.

The report also recommended construction of several pedestrian plazas, closing a number of streets and eliminating several congressional parking lots.

To continue providing parking spaces for its employees, the report suggested, Congress probably would have to acquire land around the periphery of the Capitol Hill area. To move congressional staffers from their cars to their offices, the plan recommended that Congress consider building a small-scale rapid transit system.

West Front Question Unresolved

For the Capitol itself, the report suggested that the parking lot to the building's east be turned into a landscaped pedestrian plaza with two large fountains.

Beneath the plaza, the architect said, Congress should construct a three-level underground garage for 500 cars and an additional 86,000 square feet of office space.

However, the report took no position on whether Congress should go ahead with White's controversial proposal to expand the Capitol's crumbling west front. That decision was left to the five-member Commission on the West Central Front of the United States Capitol, which was set up in 1977. However, on March 2 that panel decided to put off a decision for at least a year.

White's plan for the west front, first proposed in 1976, called for a 147,000-square-foot extension.

That area of the Capitol, the last exposed portion of the original building, was constructed of soft Aquia Creek sandstone on the exterior and brick and stone on the interior. The architect's office had said that the wall, which bore a considerable portion of the building's load, had been deteriorating ever since it was built.

Maintenance on the wall had been put off, pending a decision, and it had twice been shored up with timbers. *(West front controversy background, CQ Guide to Congress, 2nd ed., p. 425)*

The House several times agreed to provide the necessary funds for extension, but the Senate each time voted to block the expenditure. ∎

Vets Payment Raise

Legislation providing an 11.2 percent average annual cost-of-living increase in disability payments for veterans with service-connected disabilities was signed by President Reagan Oct. 17.

The final bill (S 917 — PL 97-66) was the result of a compromise worked out by the House and Senate Veter-

GAO Faults Architect

The Capitol architect was taken to task Oct. 30 by the General Accounting Office, which found that inappropriate design and construction methods and inadequate controls had resulted in cost overruns, delays and management problems in all four of the major projects the architect had under way.

The four projects cited were the construction of the Hart Senate Office Building and the James Madison Library of Congress building, and the renovation of House Office Building Annex 2 and the Capitol power plant. All were running behind schedule and had experienced "significant cost overruns," according to the GAO report (PLRD-82-1).

The GAO predicted a total cost for the completed projects of about $326.7 million, about $170.6 million more than what the architect originally estimated.

The report took particular exception to the practice of designing and constructing buildings in "phases," enabling the architect to begin construction before a design was completed. It recommended that projects be completely designed before construction started.

White defended his methods and called the GAO's suggestion "unrealistic."

The project that had traditionally received the most criticism for cost overruns was the Hart Building.

The project was conceived in 1972 when the Senate Public Works Committee determined that "space provided in the two Senate office buildings is no longer adequate for the most effective operation of the Senate." *(1972 Almanac p. 691)*

It was decided to rush an initial appropriation through the Senate, and White was given only a week to estimate the new building's cost, which he put at $47.9 million.

However, within a few weeks, after Senate leaders had had a chance to flesh out what they really wanted, the estimated cost already had almost doubled.

By 1973, the total appropriated for the new building had hit $68.8 million. The next year, it was raised again, to $85.1 million.

In early 1978, White submitted a new estimate for the building's completion — $122.6 million.

Later that year, a small band of senators set out to block the project's completion. But despite their efforts, the Senate in August 1978 raised the total appropriation to $135 million. The House, however, in an unusual breach of congressional comity, refused to approve the additional funds. *(1978 Almanac p. 71)*

During the yearlong delay caused by the House action, inflation continued to push up the building's cost. And by June 1979, White estimated that completion might cost $175 million. *(1979 Almanac p. 227)*

He then was ordered to come up with a way to reduce the cost and by mid-July had found construction economies would result in "a total estimated cost" of $137.7 million.

Congress cleared the additional funds in September 1979, and the last contracts were let in June 1980. *(1980 Almanac p. 568)*

ans' Affairs committees. The Senate approved the compromise by voice vote Oct. 1. The House cleared the measure for the president by voice vote Oct. 2.

The Senate on July 24 by voice vote had approved S 917 providing an 11.2 percent across-the-board boost. S 917 was reported July 16 (S Rept 95-153) by the Veterans' Affairs Committee.

A companion measure (HR 3995 — H Rept 97-179), reported July 16, was passed by voice vote by the House Sept 21. It provided an 11.3 percent average increase. The House amended its language to the Senate bill.

Under the compromise, the 11.2 percent increase, retroactive to Oct. 1, would be for 2,275,969 veterans and 324,206 families of veterans who died of service-connected disabilities. The bill provided an across-the-board 11.2 percent hike for families of severely disabled veterans and families of veterans who died from service-connected causes. The increases would cost $885.7 million in fiscal 1982 outlays, according to a Senate Veterans' Affairs Committee aide.

The compromise bill also increased the maximum grant for disabled veterans who needed automobile adaptations from $3,800 to $4,400. It increased the grant also for housing adaptations from $30,000 to $32,500.

The Senate bill had provided boosts to $5,000 and $35,000, respectively. The House had no similar provisions.

The measure also contained a provision similar to the House language that increased maximum coverage under the servicemen's and veterans' life insurance policy from $20,000 to $35,000.

In addition, the bill provided for a graduated payment mortgage program within the Veterans Administration and extended payment of non-service-connected disability pensions to certain hospitalized veterans undergoing rehabilitation. ∎

Virgin Islands Constitution

A new constitution to be submitted to the voters of the U.S. Virgin Islands was approved by Congress and sent to the president June 16.

The measure (H J Res 238 — PL 97-21) was signed into law July 9.

The resolution was reported April 30 (H Rept 97-25) by the House Interior and Insular Affairs Committee. It was passed by a 408-0 vote under suspension of the rules, a procedure barring amendments and requiring two-thirds approval. *(Vote 24, p. 18-H)*

It was reported May 14 (S Rept 97-66) and passed by voice vote by the Senate June 3. There were only minor changes. The House accepted the Senate version June 16.

The constitution established a republican form of government with a unicameral legislature, an executive branch, an independent judiciary and a bill of rights. In addition, it emphasized continued sovereignty by the United States over the islands.

Congress gave the Virgin Islands the authority in 1976 (PL 94-584) to draw up a constitution, and a constitutional convention finished its work July 31, 1980.

Congress had only 60 days to review the document, following a 60-day presidential review, but when the 96th Congress adjourned without acting, the 60-day period was extended. ∎

Franking Law Revisions

Legislation revising the congressional franking privilege and allowing senators to make franked statewide mass mailings was cleared by Congress Oct. 13.

The franking privilege allowed members of Congress to send letters and packages related to their official duties under a reproduction of their signature in place of a stamp. Congress reimbursed the Postal Service quarterly for the cost of the service.

For fiscal 1982, an election year, Congress set aside $75.1 million for that purpose. For fiscal 1981, $52 million was reserved.

Under a 1973 law (PL 93-191), House members already could send out franked mass mailings to every address in their districts simply by addressing the required number of letters to "postal patron" and turning them over to the Postal Service. *(Congress and the Nation Vol. IV, p. 756)*

But for senators, the same law required that each piece of mail bear a name and address.

The bill (S 1224 — PL 97-69), sponsored by Sen. Ted Stevens, R-Alaska, allowed senators to make statewide mass mailings under their frank if the envelopes bore only a simplified form of address — such as the word "occupant" followed by a street address.

Stevens asserted that changing the law would save the government money, although others suggested that an increase in the volume of senators' mail could offset any savings.

In addition, S 1224 both restricted and expanded the franking privilege. Some of the restrictions it wrote into law already were in effect as provisions of the House and Senate ethics codes. Others went further than existing limits.

For example, the bill barred franked mass mailings less than 60 days before an election if the member making the mailing was a candidate. It also required the government to pay the entire cost of preparing and printing a mass mailing. Both restrictions already were in the House and Senate ethics codes.

The bill went beyond existing restrictions by prohibiting franked letters expressing solely a member's condolences or congratulations and by cutting off a former member's franking privilege 90 days after his term ended.

Two similar bills passed the House in 1977 and 1979 but never cleared the Senate. *(1979 Almanac p. 577)*

A third bill was reported by the Senate Governmental Affairs Committee in 1978 but never came to a floor vote. *(1978 Almanac p. 813)*

Congress established the franking privilege in 1789 — the first year it met. The privilege was intended to make it easy for members to communicate with their constituents on matters of official business.

From the start, members recognized the possibility that the privilege might be abused, and Congress imposed controls on its use. But neither the 1973 statute nor the ethics code restrictions succeeded in quieting criticisms that members used the privilege to promote their re-elections.

The most pressing challenge to the frank was a lawsuit filed in October 1973 by Common Cause, the self-styled citizens' lobby. The suit charged that the frank was unconstitutional because the free mailing privilege promoted the re-election of incumbents and therefore denied challengers equal protection of the law.

At year's end, it was unclear what effect the bill would have on the case. Oral arguments were presented Sept. 30 before a special three-judge panel of the U.S. District Court for the District of Columbia.

Provisions

As cleared by Congress Oct. 13, S 1224:

● Eliminated a member's authority to frank letters expressing solely the member's condolences or congratulations for a "personal" distinction such as a birthday. Letters expressing congratulations for a "public" distinction — such as becoming a citizen or being elected to public office — still were frankable.

● Permitted a member to frank otherwise frankable letters in which the member had added a personal greeting to an individual's wife or family.

● Prohibited any franked mass mailing less than 60 days before any primary or general election in which the member making the mailing was a candidate.

● Prohibited a member who was a candidate for another public office — such as senator, governor or president — from making mass mailings to any area served by that other office that was outside the member's district.

● Permitted a committee chairman who was a candidate in a primary or general election to continue to make mass mailings at any time prior to that election if they related to routine committee business.

● Gave to the Senate Select Ethics Committee and to the House Commission on Congressional Mailing Standards authority to enforce the franking rules and laws and to further regulate use of the franking privilege.

● Defined a "mass mailing" as a mailing of more than 500 pieces of mail of which the content was "substantially identical." Exempted from the definition were letters sent out in response to incoming mail and mailings to the news media, to fellow members of Congress or to state, local or federal government officials.

● Authorized senators to make statewide mass mailings, provided that such mailings were sent "by the most economical means practicable."

● Gave to the Senate Rules Committee and the House congressional mailing commission the authority to impose a limitation on the number of pieces of mail that could be sent each year in districtwide or statewide mailings.

● Required House members to submit to the House congressional mailing commission a sample of each mass mailing in advance, to determine whether it complied with the requirements of the franking law.

● Left it to the Senate Select Ethics Committee to decide whether senators, too, should be required to submit such samples in advance.

● Required that the entire cost of preparing and printing mass mailings be paid from federal funds, except that additional materials could be included in a mailing — even if printed and prepared at private expense — if they were of a "purely instructional or informational" nature.

● Permitted any designated surviving relative of a member who died in office to frank non-political correspondence relating to the member's death.

● Ended the franking privilege for the purpose of mailing official business letters, public documents and agricultural materials 90 days after a member left Congress.

● Extended the House commission's jurisdiction to complaints against former members and House officials.

Action in the Senate

Governmental Affairs Committee

The Senate Governmental Affairs Committee reported S 1224 on July 17 (S Rept 97-155). The original measure had been drafted by Stevens in his capacity as chairman of the Subcommittee on Civil Service and General Services.

The panel said the legislation was intended to "again limit the opportunities for [the frank's] abuse, clarify the privilege and draw a line between what Congress considers primarily official/representative and primarily political."

A brief hearing on the measure was held June 16. At that time, Stevens said the measure was intended to strengthen and clarify the 1973 law and close some loopholes in it.

"There has been some abuse, and even with the enactment of this measure there will probably continue to be some abuse," he said. "However, the few occurrences of abuse must be weighed against the invaluable function the frank plays."

Stevens said the provision allowing statewide franked mass mailings would save the Senate money by eliminating the need to return incorrectly addressed mail and by reducing the computer programming time needed to update senators' computerized mailing lists when constituents moved.

He noted that the Senate paid the Postal Service 25 cents for every piece of incorrectly addressed mail that was returned. A Senate Ethics Committee study found these returns cost the Senate $1.2 million in 1980, almost 6 percent of the $21 million total the Senate spent on mass mailings that year.

In its report, however, the committee acknowledged that the statewide mailing provision could result in "drastic increases" in the volume of franked congressional mail that might wipe out any cost savings.

The panel said it was directing the Senate Rules Committee and the House Commission on Congressional Mailing Standards to establish limits on such districtwide mass mailings in the House and statewide mailings in the Senate. In order to give the Senate Rules Committee time to issue rules, senators could not begin making statewide mass mailings until 120 days after the bill's enactment.

Stevens' draft bill was approved by the panel on July 9 with only minor changes. The vote was 9-1, with only David Durenberger, R-Minn., voting "no." A Durenberger spokesman said the senator was pleased that the bill authorized the Rules Committee to limit the volume of statewide mass mailings but wanted an overall limit on all types of mass mailings a senator could make.

Floor

The bill was approved July 20 by the Senate, which passed it on a voice vote with no debate and no amendments.

House Action

No House committee considered the bill, but it came to the floor anyway on Oct. 13. It was passed by voice vote under suspension of the rules, a procedure barring amendments. Because the identical measure had been approved by the Senate, the House action cleared the measure for the president.   ∎

COLAs, Pay Raises Limited

Congress granted President Reagan his request to limit the paychecks of federal civilian employees and cost-of-living adjustments (COLA) in order to achieve fiscal 1982 savings.

Title XVII of the budget reconciliation bill cleared by Congress July 31 (HR 3982 — PL 97-35) accepted the 4.8 percent ceiling Reagan requested for the pay raises of workers who otherwise would have gotten salary increases of about 13.5 percent in October 1981. By limiting the increase, Congress established savings of $3.7 billion. It was required to save a total of $5.2 billion for federal employee and postal programs. *(Reconciliation, p. 256)*

Although the bill did not set pay levels for fiscal 1982 and 1983, the House Budget and Senate Finance committees allowed conferees to assume pay raises of 7 percent each year and to count savings of $5.2 billion in 1983 and $6.1 billion in 1984.

The bill also included Reagan's proposal to replace the twice-yearly COLAs for federal retirees with an annual adjustment.

The House and Senate reconciliation versions set the same pay and COLA limits. However, earlier both chambers had rejected the president's plan to change the current federal "pay comparability" system to include comparisons with private sector benefits as well as pay.

Executive Service Changes

Conferees generally accepted a House plan setting up procedures for laying off members of the Senior Executive Service (SES) because of reduction-in-force (RIF) requirements caused by funding limits or other reasons. The Senate had no comparable provisions.

The SES, an elite cadre of federal bureaucrats who can receive bonuses and be transferred freely among agencies, was established under the 1978 Civil Service Reform Act (PL 95-454). *(1978 Almanac p. 818)*

Provisions

As cleared by Congress, HR 3982:

Federal Employees

● Placed a 4.8 percent cap on the Oct. 1, 1981, salary increases for civilian employees, achieving a fiscal 1982 $3.7 billion outlay savings.

● Saved $5.2 billion in fiscal 1983 and $6.1 billion in fiscal 1984 outlays by assuming a 7 percent pay raise.

● Continued to permit the president to send to Congress an alternative pay plan calling for a lower raise in times of national emergency or economic distress.

● Reduced COLAs from twice-yearly to annually for civilian and military retirees, with payments made March 1 based on the change in the Consumer Price Index.

Waste, Fraud

● Created employee awards for the disclosure of fraud, waste or mismanagement. Awards could be made from Oct. 1, 1981, to Sept. 30, 1984.

● Limited agency awards to $10,000 each or to one percent of the agency's cost savings, whichever was less.

● Required the comptroller general to review documentation substantiating agency awards.

● Authorized the president to give up to 50 awards a year of $20,000 each.

Senior Executives

● Established procedures by which federal agencies may remove members of the Senior Executive Service (SES) because of a reduction-in-force (RIF) required by reorganization, lack of funds or other reasons.

● Required agencies to establish competitive procedures emphasizing performance to determine who would be removed and, after abolishing positions, to allow employees to compete for remaining jobs.

● Required agency heads to certify to the Office of Personnel Management (OPM) that no job was available.

● Entitled an employee to be placed by OPM in any agency with a vacant SES position, unless the head of that agency determined that the individual was not qualified for that position.

● Allowed the removal of an employee if the individual declined a reasonable SES job offer anywhere in the government or was not placed in a job within 120 days after the agency head first certified that either no position was available, or the employee was not qualified for an opening.

● Allowed the removal of permanent members of the SES on board as of May 31, 1981, only if OPM certified to the House Post Office and Senate Governmental Affairs committees that OPM had taken all reasonable steps to place the individual and that the individual's highly specialized skills made placement impossible. The certification had to be made 30 days prior to removal.

● Permitted an SES career employee to appeal to the Merit Systems Protection Board if the individual believed OPM had not made a reasonable effort to place him or her or had failed to base placement on job performance.

● Required the reinstatement of any removed employee on board as of May 31, 1981, and who had completed his probationary period, to any SES position for which the employee was qualified. The worker had to apply for the job within one year of the agency head's original certification to OPM.

● Allowed employees who applied for reinstatement and who were not selected to appeal to the Merit Systems Protection Board.

● Made the RIF protections effective on June 1, 1981.

Miscellaneous

● Required OPM to enter into agreements with the states to withhold state income taxes from the pension checks of civil service retirees who requested such withholding. The withholdings would be forwarded to the states quarterly. Currently, employees paid directly to the states.∎

Postal Service Reductions

Postal subsidies were cut and the start of the proposed nine-digit ZIP code delayed by the budget reconciliation legislation cleared by Congress July 31.

Title VII of the bill (HR 3982 — PL 97-35) made sharp reductions in two U.S. Postal Service subsidies. The public service subsidy that supported delivery to unprofitable areas was cut by $394 million to a fiscal 1982 level of $250 million. *(Reconciliation, p. 256)*

The other, the revenue foregone subsidy, made up for

income lost through subsidies primarily to charities and other non-profit mailers. Congress limited the subsidy to $696 million in fiscal 1982, a cut of $416 million.

Non-profit third-class bulk mailers faced postage rate increases to make up the difference between what the Postal Service said it needed to fund the revenue foregone subsidy fully and the amount approved under reconciliation, according to a House Post Office Committee aide.

All subsidized classes of mail would face rate hikes if Congress failed to appropriate the full amount of funds authorized for the revenue foregone subsidy, the aide said.

The House had targeted the rate hikes on large charities and other third-class bulk mailers and on newspapers delivered within the county in which they were published. The Senate had no comparable provision.

The bill also delayed the nine-digit ZIP code until Oct. 1, 1983, as the House had wanted. The Postal Service was permitted to advertise, train personnel, buy new sorting machines and take other preliminary steps necessary to start the system.

But the agency specifically was prohibited both from using the new sorting machines to process the expanded code and from offering discounts to businesses until Oct. 1, 1983.

In addition, the General Accounting Office (GAO) must report to Congress by Dec. 1, 1982, on whether the code would work.

Provisions

As cleared by Congress, HR 3982:

● Authorized for the Postal Service a total of $946 million in fiscal 1982, $808 million in fiscal 1983 and $760 million in fiscal 1984, for a savings of $956 million for fiscal 1982, $1.027 billion for fiscal 1983 and $1.087 billion for fiscal 1984.

● Authorized for the public service subsidy $250 million in fiscal 1982, $100 million in fiscal 1983 and zero in fiscal 1984. That resulted in cuts of $394 million in fiscal 1982, $452 million in fiscal 1983 and $460 million in fiscal 1984.

● Authorized for the revenue foregone subsidy, $696 million in fiscal 1982, $708 million in fiscal 1983 and $760 million in fiscal 1984. That resulted in cuts of $416 million in fiscal 1982, $467 million in fiscal 1983 and $542 million in fiscal 1984.

● Established a method for adjusting revenue foregone rates to make up for the cuts: If in any of the three fiscal years covered under the bill, the full amount estimated to be needed by the Postal Service exceeded the ceiling, the Postal Service would adjust the rates for third-class non-profit bulk mail to make up the difference. For example, third-class non-profit bulk mailers would have to make up the difference between the $780 million the Postal Service said it needed to fully fund the revenue foregone subsidies in fiscal 1982 and the $696 million reconciliation ceiling.

If in any of the three fiscal years covered under the bill, the revenue foregone ceiling was greater than the amount actually appropriated, then the Postal Service must make up the difference through rate hikes for all subsidized second-, third- and fourth-class mail users. Rates for materials for the blind and the handicapped were not affected.

● Deferred until fiscal 1985 the fiscal 1982-1984 authorizations for transitional payments to help the Postal Service meet workmen's compensation and other unfunded liabil-ities of the old Post Office Department and required the Postal Service to meet the obligations from other sources. That saved $69 million in fiscal 1982, $69 million in 1983 and $51 million in 1984.

● Provided that public service and other funds apportioned by the Treasury Department to the Postal Service be made quarterly, rather than annually, for savings of $46 million in fiscal 1982, $39 million in fiscal 1983 and $34 million in fiscal 1984.

● Barred the Postal Service during fiscal 1982-1984 from taking any action to reduce or to plan to reduce the number of days for regular mail delivery.

● Barred the Postal Service from implementing the nine-digit ZIP code until Oct. 1, 1983, but allowed the agency to buy sorting machinery, advertise, train personnel and take other preliminary steps aimed at putting the code into effect on Oct. 1, 1983.

● Prohibited the Postal Service from using the new machines to process the longer code until Oct. 1, 1983, although tests could begin in January 1983.

● Barred the Postal Service from offering business mailers a rate discount for using the longer code until Oct. 1, 1983.

● Barred all federal agencies, except the Postal Service and the independent Postal Rate Commission, from converting their mailing lists to nine-digit ZIP codes until Jan. 1, 1983.

● Directed the General Accounting Office (GAO) to conduct a study of the nine-digit code and to report to Congress by Dec. 1, 1982.

● Required the postal provisions to take effect on Oct. 1, 1981, except for the ZIP code provisions, which took effect on the date of the enactment.

SBA Loans

The budget reconciliation legislation (HR 3982 — PL 97-35) cleared by Congress July 31 set higher interest rates on most Small Business Administration (SBA) loans and reduced coverage on disaster loans.

Parren J. Mitchell, D-Md., chairman of the House Small Business Committee, sharply criticized the conference report (H Rept 97-208), saying Congress was "forced to reduce the amount of direct loan assistance even below the low amounts proposed by the president and approved by the House." *(Reconciliation, p. 256)*

The House reconciliation bill had authorized $260 million in fiscal 1982 for direct loans, matching President Reagan's request. The Senate approved $180 million. Conferees settled on $230 million.

For guaranteed loans, conferees approved $3.3 billion, compared to the $3.150 billion sought by the House and the $4 billion provided by the Senate. For disaster loans, conferees accepted the Senate's open-ended authorization. The House had limited the authorization to $693.5 million.

The current authorization (PL 96-302) was for $594 million for direct loans and $4.9 billion for guaranteed loans. *(1980 Almanac p. 547)*

Under HR 3982, interest rates for direct business loans equaled the cost of money to the government, plus up to 1 percent, or around 15.3 percent at current rates. Loans to handicapped individuals remained at 3 percent. Currently, borrowers paid between 3 percent and about 12 percent for business loans.

The legislation also changed the amount of a loan that SBA could guarantee. The current level was 90 percent for all loans. That figure remained for loans of $100,000 or less, but it dropped to 70-90 percent on loans over $100,000.

Interest rates on business disaster loans were also raised, and the amount of the loss covered by the loan was cut from 100 percent to 85 percent.

Businesses unable to obtain credit elsewhere became eligible for disaster loans at an 8 percent interest rate. The current rate was 5 percent. Credit-worthy businesses could get SBA financing at the prevailing market rate. Currently, borrowers paid interest equal to the government's cost of money plus up to one percent.

For homeowners unable to obtain credit elsewhere, the disaster loan rate was set at one-half the cost of money to the government, plus one percent, up to a maximum of 8 percent. Homeowners who could borrow from banks or other lenders would get the loans at a rate equaling the full cost of money to the government, plus up to one percent, or about 15.3 percent at current rates.

Provisions

As signed into law, Title XIX of HR 3982:

Disaster Loans

● Authorized the administration to make direct or guaranteed loans to repair, rehabilitate, or replace real or personal property damaged or destroyed by flood, riot, civil disorder or other catastrophe, if the damage or destruction was not covered by insurance.

● Allowed the administration to refinance a mortgage or lien against a destroyed or damaged business or home.

● Allowed the loans to be made in an area declared a disaster by the president, agriculture secretary or SBA.

● Allowed loans to be made if the governor of a state certified to the SBA that concerns suffered economic injury because of a disaster or if they were in need of assistance not otherwise available in the area, provided they could not obtain credit elsewhere.

Economic injury loans were to be made to small businesses that suffered damage such as the loss of business because they were located in an area struck by a physical disaster.

● Extended the existing "credit elsewhere test" establishing whether an applicant for a disaster loan was able to qualify for privately financed loans to include homeowner as well as business applicants. The test would be used to determine the interest rate on the federal loan.

● Set the interest rate for homeowners unable to obtain credit elsewhere at one-half the cost of money to the government, plus up to one percent at SBA's discretion, but not to exceed 8 percent. Currently, homeowners paid 3 percent on the first $55,000 of the loan.

● Set the interest rate for homeowners able to obtain credit from a bank or other lender at the full cost of money to the government, plus up to one percent.

● Set the interest rate for businesses unable to obtain credit elsewhere at no more than 8 percent. Currently, the interest rate was 5 percent.

● Authorized the SBA administrator to set the interest rate for businesses able to obtain credit elsewhere, but at a level no higher than the prevailing market rate and no higher than the guaranteed business loan rate, whichever was lower. Currently, the rate was based on the government's cost of money, plus up to one percent.

● Set the maximum term of a loan for businesses able to obtain credit elsewhere at three years; current law provided an initial three-year term.

● Limited business disaster loans to 85 percent of the uninsured loss, down from 100 percent.

● Set homeowner loans at 100 percent of the uninsured loss, the same as existing law. SBA had been lowering the percentage administratively.

● Placed a $500,000 limit on loans.

● Continued an open-ended authorization for the disaster loan program.

● Consolidated seven non-physical disaster loan programs, such as regulatory compliance, product disaster and economic dislocation loans, into a new program but provided no funds for fiscal 1982-84. Non-physical disaster loans would be made to businesses, which, for example, would be affected by the closing of an Army base.

Business Loans

● Provided direct and guaranteed business loans to small-business owners for constructing, expanding or converting facilities, including the acquisition of land, purchase of buildings, equipment, or materials; or to obtain working capital; also to finance residential or commercial construction or rehabilitation for sale.

● Provided that small-business owners able to obtain credit elsewhere may not receive SBA business loans.

● Consolidated previously separate business loan programs, such as economic opportunity and solar and energy conservation loans, into a single program.

● Set the maximum term for business loans at 25 years, except that any portion of the loan used to acquire land or to construct, convert or expand facilities may be extended.

● Authorized SBA to set the direct loan interest rate at the cost of money to the government plus one percent, or 15.3 percent at current rates, except that loans to handicapped individuals would continue at 3 percent.

● Provided that SBA guarantee 90 percent of loans of $100,000 or less; 70-90 percent of loans between $100,000 and $714,285; less than 70 percent of loans over $714,285. Currently, SBA guaranteed up to 90 percent of a loan.

● Authorized $230 million for fiscal 1982-84 for SBA direct business loans.

● Provided an annual limit of $3.3 billion for fiscal 1982-84 on the amount of guaranteed loans to businesses. ∎

Travel, Consultants Fees

The reconciliation measure (HR 3982 — PL 97-35) approved by Congress July 31 cut the travel budget for federal employees by $100 million and the consultants' budget by $500 million in fiscal 1982 outlays.

The Senate had originally wanted to slice $500 million from the government's $4 billion consultants' budget and $500 million from its travel budget. The House bill had no similar provisions.

Under Title XVII, HR 3982 set up a two-step process for achieving the $500 million consulting cut. First, it required the president to subtract the amount appropriated by Congress for consultants in fiscal 1982 from his original 1982 budget proposals. That figure would then be subtracted from the $500 million figure, and the president must request a fiscal 1982 rescission for the difference.

It established the same rescissions process for the travel cuts.

Veterans' Benefits Cut

Veterans' educational, dental and burial benefits were reduced as a result of the reconciliation bill cleared by Congress July 31 (HR 3982 — PL 97-35).

The House had voted to end GI Bill benefits for veterans taking flight training and correspondence courses; the Senate bill had no comparable provision.

Conferees on the veterans' provisions of HR 3982 agreed to terminate flight training benefits and to reduce to 55 percent, from 70 percent, the portion of the cost of correspondence training paid by the Veterans Administration (VA). *(Reconciliation, p. 256)*

Also trimmed was an education loan program designed to supplement GI Bill benefits. The House had voted to end the program entirely; the Senate bill continued it in certain cases for Vietnam-era veterans. The conferees essentially went along with the Senate provision.

Burial benefits totaling $450 currently were available to any veteran with wartime service. The House had voted to give the benefits only to veterans with an annual income of $20,000 or less, while the Senate reconciliation bill limited the benefits to veterans with service-connected disabilities of 30 percent or more. The conferees agreed to provide the $300 benefit for funeral expenses only to veterans entitled to receive VA disability compensation or pensions. Eligibility for the $150 burial plot benefit was not changed.

Outpatient dental benefits currently were paid for dental conditions that were service-connected but not disabling, if treatment was sought within a year of discharge. The House voted to eliminate them entirely, while the Senate bill restricted them to veterans with at least six months of service who sought treatment within six months of discharge and who had not been treated for dental conditions immediately before discharge. The conferees decided to limit the benefits to veterans who applied for them within three months of discharge.

Conferees estimated the changes would result in savings of $116.2 million in outlays in fiscal 1982.

Provisions

As signed into law, Title XX of HR 3982:

● Eliminated VA flight training benefits effective Oct. 31, 1981; allowed persons enrolled on Aug. 31, 1981, to continue to receive benefits.

● Reduced to 55 percent, from 70 percent, the portion of the fees the federal government paid for veterans taking education correspondence courses.

● Eliminated education loans supplementing GI Bill education benefits, effective Oct. 1, 1981; continued loan eligibility for certain Vietnam-era veterans.

● Reduced to three months, from one year, the period of time after discharge within which veterans must apply for dental treatment of conditions that were service-connected but not disabling; limited benefits to those who had served at least 180 days.

● Limited funeral benefits, in fiscal 1982-84, to veterans entitled to receive disability or retirement benefits. ∎

Some Arts Funds Restored

Congress voted July 31 to restore about $60 million that President Reagan wanted to cut from the authorizations for the National Endowment for the Arts (NEA) and the National Endowment for the Humanities (NEH).

Reagan had asked for $88 million to be authorized in fiscal 1982 budget authority for NEA and $85 million for NEH, a cut of 50 percent from President Carter's request for each of the endowments. The administration argued the need to cut federal spending required cuts in funding for the two agencies and that the private sector should take more responsibility for supporting NEA and NEH.

But Title V of the reconciliation bill (HR 3982 — PL 97-35) reduced the authorization by 25 percent, providing $119.3 million in fiscal 1982 for NEA and $113.7 million for NEH. *(Reconciliation, p. 256)*

Those were the figures recommended by the Senate. The House had approved a $223 million lump sum for the two agencies for fiscal 1982.

Previous authorizations for fiscal 1982 (PL 96-496) provided $190.5 million for NEA and $187.5 million for NEH. *(1980 Almanac p. 552)* ∎

Pay Hike Rejected

A 16.8 percent pay raise for lawmakers and high-level government employees was rejected by Congress as expected in 1981. *(Subsequent pay raise, p. 329)*

The House March 12 by voice vote approved a resolution (H Res 109) stating "it would be inappropriate at this time" to grant the increases to legislators, senior government executives, judges and others.

After the House vote, the Senate by recorded vote adopted four separate resolutions disapproving salary hikes for the four branches of government.

The votes were: 93-0 disapproving congressional pay raises (S Res 89); 91-3 disapproving legislative branch raises (S Res 90); 87-8 disapproving judicial branch raises (S Res 91); and 86-7 disapproving executive branch raises (S Res 92). *(Votes 29-32, p. 9-S)*

Why should senior government workers get salary hikes "when millions of Americans [are going] to feel the effects of across-the-board budget cuts?" asked Sen. William V. Roth Jr., R-Del., chairman of the Governmental Affairs Committee.

The House and Senate were acting on pay raises recommended by President Carter Jan. 7. Carter's $183.1 million plan would have increased the salary of a member of Congress from $60,662 to $70,853 and a cabinet officer's salary from $69,630 to $81,328.

Carter's proposals were in response to the Dec. 16, 1980, recommendations of the Commission on Executive, Legislative and Judicial Salaries. The nine-member commission, which meets every four years to make recommendations to the president, proposed hikes averaging 40 percent.

President Reagan, who originally supported Carter's plan, switched his postion, citing budgetary considerations.

Members of Congress had not voted themselves a pay raise since 1979 when they approved a 5.5 percent cost-of-living hike. *(1979 Almanac p. 269)* ∎

Members' Benefits

Members of Congress found time in their December pre-adjournment rush to give themselves a couple of last-minute holiday gifts.

In a skillfully executed surprise attack, a handful of House members Dec. 15 won approval of a change in House rules doubling the amount of outside income members were permitted to earn.

The next day — the final day of the session — both House and Senate approved an expansion of a tax break members had voted themselves in October.

Earned Income Rule

The change in the House's earned income rule occurred with surprising swiftness and little warning. During a lull in House business, John P. Murtha, D-Pa., rose and asked for unanimous consent to approve a resolution (H Res 305) increasing the ceiling on House members' outside earnings from 15 percent of their official salary to 30 percent.

When no one objected, Murtha returned to his seat. The entire process took about 10 seconds.

About an hour later, a handful of members opposed to the rules change demanded the floor to complain about the procedure. The action had been "sneaky," charged Millicent Fenwick, R-N.J. "It should not have been done this way," added Sam B. Hall Jr., D-Texas.

But when Robert S. Walker, R-Pa., requested that the rules change be reversed, several of his colleagues loudly voiced their objections, blocking any reconsideration.

"I do agree . . . that maybe this was a little quick, [but] I would have voted for it had I had the chance," commented John H. Rousselot, R-Calif., defending the Murtha proposal.

The Dec. 15 action was in sharp contrast to an earlier House vote on a similar proposal. On Oct. 28, when a recorded vote was forced, the House rejected a resolution that would have raised the earned income limit to 40 percent of a member's salary. But members again pressed the matter out of a desire to catch up with their Senate colleagues, who earlier in 1981 voted to remove the limit on their outside earnings. *(Story, p. 286)*

The principal source of earned income for most members was the payment of honoraria for speeches, articles and personal appearances. The earned income ceiling, which went into effect in January 1979, did not apply to unearned income such as dividends, interest and rent or to income from a family-controlled business in which the member was only minimally involved. Those types of income remained unlimited.

The rules change meant that, beginning in 1981, members would be able to earn up to $18,198.75 a year in outside income at the current congressional salary of $60,662.50. That compared to a ceiling of $9,099.37 a year under the previous rule. But because the ceiling was lifted so late in the year, members had only about two weeks in which to earn the additional income permitted them in 1981 under the rules change.

New Tax Break

Members of Congress depicted the additional tax break they voted themselves Dec. 16 as a clarification and simplification of legislation approved earlier in the year.

On Oct. 1, Congress approved as part of a fiscal 1982 continuing appropriations resolution (H J Res 325) a change in tax law enabling members to deduct from their income taxes the expenses they incurred while in Washington.

Effective Date

The change was to take effect beginning with the 1982 tax year. On Dec. 11, in a subsequent continuing resolution (H J Res 370), the effective date was moved up, to enable members to take the tax break in 1981. *(Third Continuing Resolution, p. 329)*

However, it was discovered later that the new law conflicted with a provision of the 1976 tax law (PL 94-455) which limited the deductibility of second homes which were used in connection with a trade or business. *(1976 Almanac p. 44)*

Under the combined effect of the 1976 and 1981 laws, a member who lived alone while in Washington could depreciate the cost of a second home in the capital area as well as deduct from his taxes his current Washington housing expenses. But a member whose family resided with him in Washington more than 14 days a year was not eligible for those tax breaks.

House Remedy

To remedy that situation, the House Dec. 15 inserted in a miscellaneous tax bill (HR 4961) a provision enabling members living with their families in Washington to claim the same tax benefits as members living alone. The provision applied not only to members of Congress but to any individual whose family resided with him in a second home used in connection with a trade or business. The bill was passed by voice vote.

The next day, the Senate opted for a broader approach. It elaborated on the provision, tacked it onto a black lung benefits bill (HR 5159), and sent the package back to the House, where it was promptly cleared. *(Story, p. 114)*

Senate Action

As drafted in the Senate, the tax provision went beyond simply enabling a member living with his family in Washington to depreciate and claim a deduction for a second home. It also instructed the Treasury secretary to prescribe the "appropriate" business deduction a member could take from his taxes for each day Congress was in session without actually having to substantiate those expenses.

Senate Finance Committee Chairman Robert Dole, R-Kan., said the additional language was necessary to prevent members from taking excessive deductions. He hinted that $75 a day had been suggested as an "appropriate amount for us to deduct," but he said colleagues had asked that the actual figure not be included in the bill "because the press will add up $75 times so many days in session and they will interpret it in some ways as looking like a tax credit or a pay raise."

Dole said members with higher daily expenses could claim the additional amount as long as they were able to substantiate it to the Internal Revenue Service. But because the daily deduction prescribed by the Treasury secretary would be deemed "appropriate" by law, members could claim it even if their actual expenses were less than that amount.

Federal Debt Collection

Congress did not complete action in 1981 on legislation requested by the Reagan administration to speed up the collection of more than $25 billion in overdue federal loans. The legislation was aimed at making it easier for the government to enlist the aid of credit bureaus and collection agencies in tracking down delinquent borrowers.

Credit bureaus, which compiled financial histories on individuals, could list debts owed by students, farmers, businessmen and others who borrowed from the government. But in doing so, the bureaus became subject to the 1974 Privacy Act (PL 93-579), which allowed individuals to inspect, challenge or amend their credit records.

The bureaus already were subject to the 1970 Fair Credit Reporting Act (PL 91-508) disclosure and truth-in-reporting requirements. Not wanting to be subject to two sets of rules, credit bureaus were reluctant to list federal debts. Thus, individuals who failed to pay back federal loans had not had to worry about blemishing their credit records.

A House-passed bill and a measure reported by two Senate committees would exempt bureaus listing federal debts from the Privacy Act requirements. *(Background, 1974 Almanac p. 292; 1970 Almanac p. 624)*

In addition to the Privacy Act exemption, the Senate panels would allow federal agencies to give collection firms the addresses that delinquent borrowers filed with the Internal Revenue Service (IRS). The federal agencies could also send IRS addresses to credit bureaus.

However, credit bureaus, which could use the IRS information to verify an individual's address, could not make the address part of a person's permanent record. The 1976 Tax Reform Act (PL 94-455) prohibited federal agencies from giving the information to private collection firms, credit bureaus or other third parties. *(1976 Almanac p. 49)*

House Action

The House passed its limited debt collection proposal (HR 2811 — H Rept 97-42) May 18. That measure contained the Privacy Act exemption for credit bureaus but did not open the way for private collection agencies to track down delinquent borrowers.

The measure was passed by voice vote under suspension of the rules, a procedure that barred floor amendments.

Senate Action

The Senate Governmental Affairs Committee reported a broader version of the measure July 17 but had not submitted a written report by the end of the year. The Senate Finance Committee Dec. 3 reported only the provisions of S 1249 (S Rept 97-287) that gave private debt collectors and credit bureaus access to IRS and Social Security information.

Those provisions generally agreed with the version reported by Governmental Affairs. In addition to allowing federal agencies to give private collection firms the addresses that delinquent borrowers had filed with the IRS, the Finance Committee bill allowed the IRS to disclose to another federal agency whether a federal loan applicant had outstanding tax liabilities and was therefore a poor credit risk. "The committee believes that it is in the best interest of the federal government and taxpayers that lists of delinquent taxpayers and applicants for loans be cross-

checked to help reduce future defaults on government loans," the Finance Committee report said.

Both Senate committees also required individuals who applied for federal loans to furnish the lending agency with their Social Security numbers. Under existing law, most federal agencies were barred from requiring Social Security numbers on credit applications. ∎

Research Funds

The Senate Dec. 8 approved a bill to give small businesses a chunk of the federal research and development dollar but limited the amount of money an agency could divert from basic research.

The measure (S 881 — S Rept 97-194), debated Dec. 7 and 8 and approved 90-0, would require all federal agencies with research and development budgets exceeding $100 million annually to set aside for small business concerns 1 percent of that portion of the agency's research budget that was contracted out. *(Vote 447, p. 73-S)*

The House Small Business Committee reported a similar bill (HR 4326 — H Rept 97-349 Pt. I) Nov. 20. That bill had been referred to four other committees: Armed Services, Energy and Commerce, Science and Technology and Veterans' Affairs. No further action occurred in 1981.

Sen. Lowell P. Weicker Jr., R-Conn., chairman of the Small Business Committee, said that small businesses were among the most innovative concerns yet received only between 3.5 percent and 4 percent of the $40 billion federal research budget.

But some senators complained that the program would be a drain on the government's $5.5 billion basic research budget, much of which went to university scholars.

"We should ... make sure that basic research is not handicapped," Max Baucus, D-Mont., said.

Representatives of university groups also expressed concern about the loss of basic research funds. The National Association of State Universities and Land Grant Colleges supported an amendment by Harrison "Jack" Schmitt, R-N.M., limiting the basic research money that could be funneled to small businesses. His amendment would stipulate that of the total 1 percent set-aside for small businesses, only 1 percent could be drawn from basic research and from government-owned laboratories. The Senate approved Schmitt's amendment Dec. 7 by voice vote with no opposition.

The Senate rejected an amendment by Minority Leader Robert C. Byrd, D-W.Va., to require the president to nominate an individual with small business background to the next Federal Reserve Board vacancy. Lawmakers instead voted 87-3 Dec. 8 for language offered by Majority Leader Howard H. Baker Jr., R-Tenn., that only put the Senate on record in favor of the president nominating such a person. *(Vote 446, p. 73-S)*

As approved by the Senate, the small business innovation research program would involve two phases.

The first phase would provide $30,000 to $50,000 grants to small businesses. Those firms showing promise could apply for another grant ranging from $100,000 to $500,000. The hope was that federal funding would eventually generate private support for the small business research and development efforts.

The 1 percent set-aside would begin three years after the date of the bill's enactment. ∎

Minority Firm Program

The full House and the Senate Small Business committee approved bills to give a second chance to a pilot program to help minority businesses get government contracts.

As passed by voice vote Nov. 17 under suspension of the rules, the House bill (HR 4500 — H Rept 97-304) would extend for two years, through fiscal year 1983, the so-called 8(a) minority small business pilot program. A similar Senate bill, reported Sept. 28 (S 1620 — S Rept 97-195), extended the pilot effort for 18 months, until March 31, 1983.

Under the regular 8(a) minority program, selected minority businesses received government contracts and special assistance to improve management or other practices so they could compete eventually for contracts without government help. Federal agencies offered contracts to the Small Business Administration (SBA), which then subcontracted the work to firms controlled by economically and socially disadvantaged individuals.

The minority firms had to be full-time, for-profit businesses. No absentee ownership was permitted. In addition, the firms had to submit a specific plan to correct the economic deficiencies that originally qualified them for the assistance. The plan had to contain a "graduation date," after which the firm could no longer qualify for 8(a) aid, a Senate Small Business Committee aide said.

The pilot program was designed to give SBA, rather than the agency offering the contracts, the power to select appropriate contracts. SBA was considered more likely to select contracts demanding more sophisticated manufacturing and other skills than the agencies might offer on their own, the committee staffer explained.

Under the pilot program, the president designated a federal agency to offer the contracts, and SBA actually selected contracts to be awarded to the minority firms. SBA, the firm and the agency negotiated the terms of the contract, but the agency had the final word, the aide said.

Implementation Problems

The program was set up in 1978 (PL 95-507) and was to run for two years. But the pilot effort ran into trouble. It was not until Sept. 27, 1979, that the first contract with the Army, the pilot agency, was signed.

"Part of the difficulty with implementation of the program came from SBA's and Army's differing views on the purpose of the pilot authority," the Senate committee report stated. The report said that the Army felt it already was a strong supporter of the regular 8(a) program and considered the additional demands of the pilot program burdensome.

To assuage the Army, the Senate committee bill provided that the next pilot agency should be a civilian one. The House bill, however, left it up to the president to designate any agency. House Small Business Committee Chairman Parren J. Mitchell, D-Md., said he wanted to abide by a pending SBA report on the most appropriate pilot agency. Mitchell said he would tend to go along with whatever type of agency the SBA recommended.

Though critics charged that the SBA had mismanaged the program, both the House and the Senate committee nevertheless recommended that it be given another chance.

"The track record for this pilot program has left much to be desired — primarily because of SBA's mismanagement of the program [but] the need for this program is as great today as it was in 1978," said Lowell P. Weicker Jr., R-Conn., chairman of the Senate Small Business Committee.

Cost Estimates

The Senate Dec. 16 cleared for the president a bill (HR 1465 — PL 97-108) to require the Congressional Budget Office (CBO) to estimate the cost of major legislation to state and local governments.

The bill would require CBO to prepare cost estimates on bills that would impose at least $200 million in annual costs to local governments. The bill, reported by the House Rules Committee Dec. 3 (H Rept 97-353), was passed by the House by voice vote Dec. 8. The Senate bypassed committee referral.

NASA Authorization

President Reagan Dec. 21 signed a bill (S 1098 — PL 97-96) authorizing $6.172 billion for the National Aeronautics and Space Administration (NASA) in fiscal 1982.

The conference report (H Rept 97-351) was adopted by the Senate Nov. 23 and by the House Dec. 8. The funds the conferees approved compared with the $6.222 billion recommended by the Senate, the $6.122 billion approved by the House and the $5.5 billion authorized in fiscal 1981. The House figure was nearly identical to the administration's request.

The Senate had passed S 1098 (S Rept 97-100) May 21 by voice vote. The House had passed its version of the NASA authorization bill (HR 1257 — H Rept 97-32) June 23 by a 404-13 vote after adopting an amendment to cut $11.2 million from research on the technology needed for a supersonic transport plane. That amendment was approved by voice vote. *(Vote 85, p. 38-H)*

The final measure included a $2.189 billion authorization for the space shuttle, which completed its second orbit Nov. 14. That amount was $5 million less than the administration requested.

S 1098 also included $215.3 million for a planetary exploration program that would include a mission to explore Jupiter. That mission would entail a probe to reach into Jupiter's atmosphere and measure atmospheric temperature and other indicators. Conferees dropped a House provision to provide $5 million for missions to probe Halley's comet, which would make its 75-year periodic appearance at the end of 1985.

Federal Building Policy

House and Senate lawmakers were at odds again over whether to revamp the way Congress approved new federal buildings.

The Senate May 6 unanimously approved a bill (S 533)

that was similar to a measure (S 2080) that died in 1980 when conferees deadlocked. S 533, reported by the Environment and Public Works Committee April 30 (S Rept 97-48), would establish new standards for architectural design and energy efficiency, and set planning requirements. *(Vote 90, p. 19-S; 1980 Almanac p. 537)*

The most controversial provision, and the issue that caused the stalemate in 1980, was the Senate's attempt to change the way Congress approved new buildings.

Under existing procedures, the Senate Environment and House Public Works committees had final authority to authorize General Services Administration (GSA) proposals for new federal buildings costing more than $500,000 and new or renewed leases with annual rents exceeding $500,000. The Office of Management and Budget (OMB) had to approve the construction plans.

But the system allowed lawmakers to get around unsympathetic OMB officials. Members could ask GSA to determine if space should be leased or built in a certain area. GSA could make recommendations to the committee, which then could act without an OMB review.

In both cases, the committee could act without a floor vote. Once authorized by the two committees, the building and leasing projects could be included in the annual appropriations bill, which does require a vote.

Committee Jurisdiction Removed

The Senate bill struck at the heart of the system by removing the committees' exclusive power to authorize new construction and leases.

The bill would require the GSA to prepare one- and five-year plans projecting space needs. The full House and Senate would vote on an annual authorization bill covering all proposed building projects for the year. No rental costs would be detailed because that would weaken GSA's bargaining position with landlords.

In 1980 House conferees objected that the annual authorization would be an open invitation to amendments from members with pet projects. In 1981 members also disagreed on how strongly to push federal construction over leasing.

House and Senate lawmakers generally agreed that GSA should be encouraged to build, rather than lease, office space for federal agencies. However, administration budget officials traditionally favored renting because of the favorable impact on the budget. Rent, which could be listed as an annual expense, showed up as a much lower budget figure than the cost of constructing or purchasing a building. The full cost of construction had to be listed in the annual budget.

Rent paid in fiscal 1981 made up more than 41 percent of the public buildings budget, while construction funds accounted for under 1 percent, according to the Senate Environment Committee.

But because the Reagan administration felt GSA should live within its means, the Senate bill did not include a provision allowing GSA to borrow money from the Treasury to spur federal building. It merely asked OMB and GSA to study the way they computed rental and building costs.

A House subcommittee held hearings on a House bill (HR 1938), introduced by Elliott H. Levitas, D-Ga. Like the Senate bill, it set new architectural design standards and provided for one- and five-year building plans, but it did not change the committee approval system. No further action was taken on the measure in 1981. ∎

King Statue

After sharp debate, the House Sept. 15 by a vote of 386-16 agreed to place a bust or statue of slain civil rights leader the Rev. Dr. Martin Luther King Jr. in the Capitol. The measure, H Con Res 153, limited the cost to $25,000. *(Vote 190, p. 66-H)*

Jonathan B. Bingham, D-N.Y., who first introduced the legislation in the 92nd Congress, said, "This civil rights leader deserves to receive this official recognition and appreciation."

"For too long it has been possible for American schoolchildren who happen to be black" to walk through the Capitol "and not see anyone in this Capitol stand for them," Newt Gingrich, R-Ga., said.

But Larry P. McDonald, D-Ga., and others objected that King's record did not justify the honor. McDonald pointed out tha the FBI's surveillance records on King were sealed for 50 years and suggested Congress not approve a statue until the records could be scrutinized.

The resolution was reported Aug. 4 (H Rept 97-217) by the House Administration Committee.

No further action was taken on the measure in 1981. ∎

FDR Birthday

Congress voted in 1981 to spend $25,000 to commemorate the 100th birthday of the late President Franklin D. Roosevelt.

The measure (H Con Res 220 — H Rept 97-339) to fund a joint session of Congress to honor FDR was approved by the Senate Nov. 24. The House had approved it Nov. 20 by a vote of 344-18. *(Vote 313, p. 102-H)*

H Con Res 220 called for $25,000 in House funds to be used by a special committee to plan a joint session of Congress to commemorate the birthday of FDR, who was born Jan. 30, 1882. The session was to be held Jan. 28.

Rep. Claude Pepper, D-Fla., said that the $25,000 allotted for the celebration was "one of the cheapest" commemorations.

In 1974, Congress established a $30 million scholarship program as a memorial to President Harry S Truman, and $121,000 was spent on a collection of essays to honor the 50th anniversary of President Herbert Hoover's inauguration as president, he said.

The resolution was reported by the House Rules Committee Nov. 17. ∎

NSF Authorization

Although the House agreed Sept. 23 to shave $75 million from a proposed authorization (HR 1520) for the National Science Foundation (NSF), the $1.08 billion total it approved was still $52 million above the president's mark.

The 245-161 vote to cut the authorization was on an amendment by Don Fuqua, D-Fla., chairman of the Science and Technology Committee, to reduce the committee's fiscal 1982 recommendation of $1.16 billion to $1.08 billion. *(Vote 208, p. 70-H)*

Fuqua's measure was an amendment to a proposal by Vin Weber, R-Minn., a member of the Science panel, to reduce the NSF authorization to the $1.03 billion proposed by President Reagan. Weber's amendment, however, would

have restored funds to the foundation's science and engineering education program, which the Reagan administration wanted to cut drastically.

After accepting the Fuqua amendment, the House voted 401-5 to adopt the modified Weber amendment. The House then passed HR 1520 by a 262-149 vote. *(Votes 209 and 210, p. 70-H)*

Funding Levels

As reported by the Science Committee May 13 (H Rept 97-34), the bill authorized $1.16 billion in fiscal 1982 funding for the research agency.

The $1.08 billion figure adopted by the House was $11 million less than the fiscal 1981 authorization level. The $1.08 billion total also exceeded the $1.04 billion authorization recommended by the Senate Labor and Human Resources Committee (S 1200 — S Rept 97-131) and by the Commerce, Science and Transportation Committee May 15 (S 1194 — S Rept 97-72). Both Senate bills were reported May 15 but no futher action was taken in 1981.

Education and Research Cuts

The Reagan administration had requested drastic cuts in the science education, and biological, social and behavioral sciences programs. Weber tried to put more money back into science education.

NSF's social and biological sciences program provided grants to economists, biologists and other scientists to perform research. The education program provided funds for science and engineering programs from the preschool to graduate level.

Under the Reagan proposal, science education would have received $9.9 million; biological, behavioral and social sciences, $172 million.

The Science Committee gave those programs hefty increases, recommending $75 million for science education and $198.1 million for the biological, behavioral and social sciences.

Weber proposed a figure between the administration and committee amounts for science education: $59.9 million. However, the biological and behavioral sciences would have received only $152 million.

As passed, the bill provided $35 million for science education and $184.6 million for the biological and other science research programs. ∎

Freedom of Information Act

Efforts of the Reagan administration and some members of Congress to substantially restrict the use of the Freedom of Information Act (FOIA) drew strong criticism from the press and failed to move beyond the committee stage in 1981.

The Senate Judiciary Constitution Subcommittee Dec. 14 by a 3-2 vote approved a bill (S 1730) borrowing heavily from the administration's sweeping proposals, but no further action took place before adjournment.

Rep. Glenn English, D-Okla., chairman of the Government Operations Information Subcommittee, had introduced a bill (HR 2021) but said he would wait for Senate action before marking it up.

FOIA was enacted in 1966 (PL 20-23) to make previously secret government files available to the public. Amendments in 1974 (PL 93-502), enacted over the veto of President Gerald R. Ford during the post-Watergate re-

form era, broadened access to certain information and were intended to remove bureaucratic obstacles erected to thwart the act. *(Congress and the Nation Vo. IV, p. 805)*

The Reagan administration and Sen. Orrin G. Hatch, R-Utah, chairman of the Constitution Subcommittee, maintained that the law had been misused. They contended that it should be reconstructed to protect vital government documents, national security and law enforcement efforts.

Some business organizations also pushed for changes in the law, charging that information they supplied to federal regulatory agencies was obtained by competitors. They wanted greater protection from the release of what they considered to be sensitive or confidential information.

Groups like the National Association of Manufacturers, for example, pushed for formal notification of requests for information and appeal rights.

Press organizations, however, strongly opposed what they described as efforts to weaken the access of the public to information. They contended that closing some files to public scrutiny could screen official misdeeds.

The administration proposals were revealed Oct. 15 by Assistant Attorney General Jonathan C. Rose during testimony before Hatch's subcommittee and were later incorporated into S 1751 and HR 4805.

The administration called for giving the attorney general the power to exempt all files dealing with organized crime, counterintelligence and terrorism from the disclosure requirements of FOIA.

It also proposed broadening the existing exemption for confidential business information and allowing federal agencies to charge higher fees to cover the estimated $57 million annual cost of meeting requests for information.

As approved by the subcommittee, Hatch's measure (S 1730) incorporated some of the administration's stronger revisions. These included giving broad new powers to the attorney general to exempt all information relating to terrorism, organized crime and foreign counterintelligence investigations.

The measure also made it easier for the Central Intelligence Agency (CIA) to go to court to stop disclosure of information the agency considered to be sensitive and increased protections for information businesses submitted to the government. ∎

Regulatory Reform

Responding to complaints that the federal regulatory machinery had gotten out of hand, committees in both the House and Senate approved bills to rein in rule-making agencies. However, there was no floor action in 1981.

The Senate Judiciary Committee reported its version of S 1080 (S Rept 97-305) July 17; and the Governmental Affairs panel filed its report Sept. 18 (S Rept 97-284). Committee staff and key members reached a compromise on their differences that was expected to go to the floor early in 1982.

In the House, the bill (HR 746) ordered reported Dec. 8 by the Judiciary Committee differed sharply from the Senate committees' compromise. Key issues involved the authority of the president through the Office of Management and Budget (OMB) to oversee the rule-making process, the ability of challengers to find judicial relief and whether Congress should be able to overturn a proposed rule.

Both the House committee measure and the Senate panels' compromise for the first time would require independent and executive branch regulatory agencies to assess the costs and benefits of all proposed major rules.

However, the House panel allowed agencies to remove most of the rules agencies determined to be overly burdensome without a cost-benefit analysis, a provision not included in the Senate committees' plan.

On court review procedures, the Senate compromise contained the so-called Bumpers amendment, named after its chief sponsor, Sen. Dale Bumpers, D-Ark. The Bumpers amendment would make it easier for outside parties to overturn regulations in court and would shift the burden of proof in court suits from outside parties to the agency. The House committee bill had weaker language.

Administration officials said the Bumpers amendment would tie up regulations in the courts for years. But business groups like the National Association of Manufacturers (NAM) and the Chamber of Commerce of the United States supported a strong Bumpers amendment, saying the courts should be the final arbiters of a rule.

The House committee also provided for a legislative veto that would allow both houses of Congress to overturn proposed rules and which would require the president's signature. Administration officials said they would oppose a legislative veto provision that did not require the president's signature.

The Senate proposal as reported did not contain a legislative veto.

Background

Regulatory reform efforts focused on the plethora of regulations issued by old-line independent agencies like the Interstate Commerce Commission (ICC), as well as the newer executive branch regulators like the Occupational Safety and Health Administration (OSHA) and the Environmental Protection Agency (EPA). The regulations have the force of law.

Complaints involved not only how many rules were being promulgated — in 1979 some 40 federal agencies issued 7,900 regulations — but also their rapid increase.

In 1960, the *Federal Register*, which published all proposed and final rules, was 9,562 pages long. By 1980, it contained 74,120 pages.

The 96th Congress took steps towards regulatory reform, with the intensity of feeling perhaps best illustrated by the bitter fight to halt what critics called harassment by the activist Federal Trade Commission (FTC). The drive to clip the wings of the FTC succeeded to some degree. But overall regulatory reform efforts collapsed in controversy. *(FTC, 1980 Almanac p. 233; regulatory reform, p. 526)*

President Reagan moved early administratively to corral the rule-makers. On Jan. 22, he named Vice President George Bush to head a regulatory reform task force to review existing and proposed regulations and to oversee the development of legislative proposals. In addition, he placed a 60-day freeze on many new rules in order to review them.

His agency appointees began to modify or kill numerous rules. For example, the secretary of education Feb. 2 withdrew a proposed rule that would have required school systems to offer bilingual instruction.

A Feb. 17 executive order 12291 required executive branch agencies to examine the costs and benefits of all proposed and existing major rules and to pick the least costly alternative. Major rules were those that would cost businesses $100 million or more to comply with.

Regulators also were told to consider a rule's effect on particular industries and the economy as a whole.

OMB was directed to oversee compliance.

Current Procedures

Regulatory agencies operated under so-called "organic" statutes giving them varying degrees of rule-making authority. The FTC, for example, had one of the broadest mandates.

But some lawmakers complained that Congress had given too much leeway to federal regulators. "We in Congress have practically given carte blanche to the regulators to take the laws we passed and do with them what they choose," William C. Wampler, R-Va., ranking minority member of the House Agriculture Committee, said in a Feb. 21 speech.

Although the breadth of rule-making authority differed by agency, the procedures for establishing rules generally were the same.

Formal rule-making involved a trial-type hearing on such issues as rates and the entry of newcomers into the industry, with witnesses and cross-examination. It was rarely used because it was time-consuming and cumbersome. *(Congress and the Nation Vol. I, p. 1457)*

The more frequently used informal proceeding meant an agency published a description of a proposed rule in the *Federal Register*. Interested parties, including business and public interest groups, could comment within a specific period. The agency could make modifications before publishing the final rule but no formal hearings were held.

Informal rule-making was supposed to be faster, but that was not always the case. Each agency could set its own time limits and could take months reviewing comments or completing other steps, stretching the process out for years.

Groups like the Chamber of Commerce, NAM, the Business Roundtable and the National Federation of Independent Business wanted broad regulatory reform.

They argued that some rules constituted harassment and penalized consumers, that agencies frequently chose the most costly alternative when issuing a rule, driving up the costs of production, and that proceedings were stacked against business, giving them little advance notice of new rules and little chance to help develop them.

On the other side were some labor and public interest groups, like Ralph Nader's Congress Watch and the Natural Resources Defense Council, which countered that while some reforms were necessary, the public needed federal regulations to protect health and safety. Without stringent government regulation of the workplace and environment, businesses would pay little heed to environmental and health concerns, they said.

House Committee Action

The House Judiciary Committee held four markups from Oct. 20 to Dec. 8.

As approved by the Administrative Law Subcommittee, the bill barred OMB from forcing independent agencies to do cost-benefit tests. It required OMB to oversee cost-benefit analyses by executive agencies but stripped OMB of the power to ensure compliance.

The full committee Nov. 17 by voice vote approved an amendment by subcommittee Chairman George E. Danielson, D-Calif., specifically naming all the independent agencies that would be excluded from OMB review.

Earlier the panel had turned back by a 12-15 vote an amendment by Thomas N. Kindness, R-Ohio, that would

have restored OMB's authority to ensure compliance on cost-benefit tests by both independent and executive branch agencies.

But Danielson argued that the amendment would allow OMB to refuse to act on a rule, effectively killing it.

Members also rejected by a 12-15 vote an effort by Tom Railsback, R-Ill., to force OMB to allow the public to comment on the cost-benefit procedures.

On Dec. 8, they approved 16-12 a Danielson amendment that would ensure that the public could scrutinize any exchange of documents between OMB and the agencies, including those that took place before the actual rule-making procedure began.

The Senate committees'compromise would allow OMB to oversee independent agency cost-benefit tests and to ensure compliance with the procedures by all agencies.

The subcommittee version of HR 746 eliminated language that would have shifted the burden of proof from parties bringing suit against regulatory agencies to the agencies. The full House panel Dec. 8 approved by a 17-9 vote a Danielson amendment that weakened the court review provision even further.

The issue involved language that would require courts to take a harder look at agency actions, allowing them to overturn rules more easily. The subcommittee bill allowed courts to overturn any agency action that lacked "substantial" factual support.

Currently, outside parties had to show that an agency's actions were "arbitrary and capricious," a tougher standard to prove. Danielson's amendment essentially struck the substantial support standard, leaving the arbitrary and capricious test in place.

The Senate compromise would shift the burden of proof to regulatory agencies in court suits and contained the substantial support test.

On Oct. 27, the House committee also approved by voice vote a Danielson amendment as amended by Railsback that would allow an agency to remove rules, except for health, safety and environmental rules, that it considered burdensome to business without a time-consuming cost-benefit tests.

Senate Committee Action

The staff compromise ironed out many technical differences between the Governmental Affairs and Judiciary panels.

The agreement would require regulatory agencies to perform cost-benefit studies on all proposed major rules, but the agencies, not OMB, would have final say over the substance of a rule.

The compromise, however, was silent on the legislative veto, leaving that issue to be thrashed out on the floor.

Governmental Affairs

The Governmental Affairs Committee voted to trim the power of the courts to oversee the agencies, thereby setting the stage for conflict with the Judiciary Committee.

First, the Governmental Affairs Committee voted 8-7 Sept. 16 to approve a proposal by Chairman William V. Roth Jr., R-Del., to allow agencies to retain the benefit of the doubt now given agencies in court challenges. In addition, Roth deleted language that effectively would have told the courts to take a harder look at agency actions.

Second, the panel approved 11-3 an amendment by Thomas F. Eagleton, D-Mo., ranking minority member, to bar outside parties from bringing suit if they believed the agency was not designating a rule as "major" under the $100 million standard, thus avoiding the cost-benefit analysis. The amendment in effect left the designation of whether a rule was "major" to the regulatory agencies and the administration.

The Judiciary Committee version contained the Bumpers provision and permitted outside parties to bring suit over the $100 million standard.

The Governmental Affairs Committee rejected by an 8-9 vote an attempt to force OMB to make public all of its significant oral and written communications with agencies and outside parties concerning proposed regulations.

The Judiciary bill limited public access to written comments made by OMB and outside parties.

Judiciary Committee

The bill's approval by the Judiciary Committee was eased by a last-minute agreement by key panel members on who — OMB or the courts — should review the procedures of both independent and executive branch regulatory agencies and decide if a proposed regulation was a "major rule" and thus subject to cost-benefit analysis. Disagreement over the issue had threatened to stall the bill.

As reported by the Judiciary Committee, the bill would give the president the power to establish procedures, subject to public comment, to ensure that regulators properly perform the cost-benefit analysis. But the agencies would still have final say over the substance of the rules; the White House control would be over procedures only.

Both the president and the agencies could designate any rule as "major" that met the $100 million test. In addition, the president could name up to another 75 rules annually as "major" if they met subjective tests such as sparking a substantial increase in costs for workers, businesses and consumers.

Although outside parties could bring suit if they believed that the agency was not designating a rule as major under the $100 million standard, court suits could not be brought if the president or an agency failed to designate a rule as major under the more subjective economic impact tests. ∎

Law Enforcement/Judiciary

The Republican takeover of the Senate in 1981 shifted the focus of domestic legal issues from civil rights and criminal law reform to the divisive subjects of abortion, busing and school prayer.

Even though no legislation on these issues cleared, two Senate Judiciary subcommittees held 23 days of hearings on busing and abortion and sent a total of four measures to the Senate Judiciary Committee for action in 1982.

The proposals had a common thread: all sought to reverse controversial Supreme Court decisions and shift social policy by preventing federal courts from hearing cases on these subjects.

The anti-abortion measures — a proposed constitutional amendment and a bill — were the first such legislation to emerge from a subcommittee since the 1973 Supreme Court decision making abortion legal.

The Senate also made history by confirming the first woman Supreme Court justice — Sandra Day O'Connor, an Arizona appeals court judge.

In the House, where Democrats remained firmly in control of the Judiciary Committee, hardly a word was heard about abortion, busing or school prayer. Instead, the full House approved an extension of the landmark 1965 Voting Rights Act and a reauthorization of the embattled Legal Services Corporation (LSC).

The Committees

The two Judiciary committees in 1981 were ideological opposites.

While the House panel remained solidly liberal — the result of deliberate recruiting efforts by committee veterans — the Senate committee shifted dramatically.

In the 96th Congress, the Senate chairman was Edward M. Kennedy, D-Mass. Three-term liberal Birch Bayh, D-Ind. (1963-81), was next in seniority, and John C. Culver, D-Iowa (House 1965-75; Senate 1975-81), another liberal, also was on the panel.

Kennedy was replaced as chairman by Strom Thurmond, R-S.C., who made his reputation as a states' rights activist and who had voted against every major civil rights bill in Congress.

Thurmond recruited three other conservatives, Jeremiah Denton, R-Ala., Charles E. Grassley, R-Iowa, and John P. East, R-N.C., and one moderate, Arlen Specter, R-Pa. Thurmond broke with the informal tradition of putting lawyers on the panel by asking non-lawyers Grassley and Denton to serve.

In the House, while other committees were taking a conservative turn, Chairman Peter W. Rodino Jr., D-N.J., with help from veterans Don Edwards, D-Calif., and Robert W. Kastenmeier, D-Wis., succeeded in filling vacancies with three liberals. They were Reps. Barney Frank, D-Mass., Harold Washington, D-Ill., and Patricia Schroeder, D-Colo.

The Social Issues

The Senate Judiciary Subcommittee on Separation of Powers jumped into the abortion fray first. In April, freshman Sen. John P. East, R-N.C., began hearings on a bill declaring that human life begins at conception. It would allow states to pass anti-abortion laws to protect life from the moment of conception and would prevent lower federal courts from striking down any new state anti-abortion laws.

After eight hearings, the subcommittee approved the bill 3-2 on July 9.

The Constitution Subcommittee was the other panel to handle the abortion issue. The subcommittee held nine days of hearings, most of them focused on a proposed constitutional amendment offered by Chairman Orrin G. Hatch, R-Utah. The amendment, designed to overturn the 1973 *Roe v. Wade* decision legalizing abortion, declared that no right to abortion was secured by the Constitution. It would give states and Congress joint authority to restrict abortion, and if a state law were more restrictive than any federal law, the state law would govern.

It was approved 4-0 by the panel Dec. 16. Sen. Patrick J. Leahy, D-Vt., did not vote because he was angered that the subcommittee marked up the bill only one hour after hearings were completed. *(Story, p. 425)*

The Separation of Powers and Constitution subcommittees were the two panels that also delved into the busing issue. Both held hearings and sent bills to the full committee that would prevent lower federal courts from ordering busing or pupil assignments for racial balance. One bill sponsored by East also would prevent a judge from ordering school closings or teacher transfers.

Both bills would allow a judge to dissolve an existing busing order, though the procedures for such dissolution differed.

Anti-busing proposals also were appended to the Justice Department authorization, which remained enmeshed in a Senate filibuster at year's end. One proposal, offered by Jesse Helms, R-N.C., would prevent the department from spending money to bring any legal action that could lead, directly or indirectly, to court-ordered busing. The other measure, offered by J. Bennett Johnston, D-La., would permit a judge to order busing only in very narrow circumstances, and it would allow for the dissolution of existing orders.

There was the least action on school prayer. The House approved a rider to the fiscal 1982 State, Justice, Commerce appropriations bill to prevent the Justice Department from blocking any voluntary school prayer program. Senators failed to remove or weaken the provision on the Senate floor, but Sen. Lowell P. Weicker Jr., R-Conn., led a filibuster that prevented the measure from passing in 1981. As a result, funding for the agencies covered in the bill was put into the stopgap funding law.

Other Issues

Voting Rights

With a rejuvenated and united civil rights lobby behind them, House members crushed all weakening amendments and passed an extension of the 1965 Voting Rights Act by a landslide 389-24 vote.

The key enforcement provision — Section Five — required nine states and portions of 13 others to get Justice Department approval for any election law changes. The provision was extended in 1970 and 1975. Without further congressional action, it would have expired Aug. 6, 1982.

The House bill would extend Section Five in its present form until 1984. At that time, the provision would become permanent, but new provisions allowing covered jurisdictions to get out from coverage would take effect. The so-called "bail-out" provisions would require a state or county to meet conditions set out in the bill before getting out from Section Five coverage.

The bill was sent to the Senate where supporters held it at the desk instead of sending it to the Judiciary Committee. Senators said this was a parliamentary precaution, allowing the House bill to come directly to the Senate floor in case a bill stalled in the Senate Judiciary Committee.

In December, senators backing the House version took another precautionary step. They introduced an identical bill (S 1992) and claimed 61 cosponsors — one more than needed to choke off a filibuster. *(Story, p. 415)*

Legal Services Corporation

The House passed a bill to reauthorize the Legal Services Corporation, despite President Reagan's desire to abolish it and let states provide legal aid to the poor in civil cases through social services block grants.

Reagan's plans were thwarted by solid support for the LSC in the House and Senate.

The House bill authorized $241 million for the LSC annually for 1982 and 1983, a 25 percent cut from the fiscal 1981 authorization and appropriation of $321.3 million.

The bill also included new restrictions on the activities of legal aid lawyers, including a ban on any "class action lawsuits" against local, state or federal governments, restrictions on the types of aliens eligible for representation, and tightening up of existing lobbying regulations.

A Senate bill reauthorizing the corporation for three years at $100 million annually was approved by the Senate Labor and Human Resources Committee but was not considered by the full Senate.

The corporation nonetheless survived at least until March 31, 1982, by virtue of a continuing appropriations resolution covering agencies whose regular appropriations had not yet been enacted. The bill included $241 million for the LSC, the amount in the House authorization and in a State, Justice, Commerce appropriations bill approved by the House and by the Senate Appropriations Committee. *(Story, p. 412)*

Criminal Code

For the third time since 1977, the Senate Judiciary Committee approved a massive bill to revise and update federal criminal laws.

However, there was little progress on a similar measure in the House, where a number of members on the Judiciary Committee opposed the idea of a wholesale revision of federal criminal laws.

The 1981 Senate bill, like its predecessors, reorganized federal criminal offenses into chapters divided by subject matter. Currently, offenses were spread through several titles of the U.S. Code. The bill also included a new sentencing structure that virtually abolished parole. Offenses would be graded by seriousness, with sentences and fine levels established according to those grades. In addition, a U.S. Sentencing Commission would be created to develop sentencing guidelines. *(Story, p. 432)*

Immigration

The Senate and House Judiciary subcommittees on refugee affairs held hearings on aspects of the nation's decades-old immigration statutes. The hearings focused on ways to halt the steady stream of illegal aliens into the United States.

Proposals under consideration included hiring more border guards, imposing sanctions against employers who hired illegal aliens and granting amnesty to some of the estimated 3 million to 6 million illegal aliens already in the country.

In addition, an administration proposal sent to Congress would give the president authority to declare an immigration emergency that could last for up to a year and would grant the president broad powers to seal any harbor, port, airport or road. *(Story, p. 422)*

Patent Court

The House and Senate passed bills creating a new federal appeals court primarily to handle patent cases. The bills were virtually identical, but a last-minute Senate amendment to expedite bankruptcy claims for failed farm storage facilities prevented a measure from clearing.

House Judiciary Committee members opposed the Senate bankruptcy amendment.

The bill would create the U.S. Court of Appeals for the Federal Circuit by merging the appellate division of the current U.S. Court of Claims with the U.S. Court of Customs and Patent Appeals.

A new trial court to handle governmental claims cases would be created from the trial division of the existing Court of Claims. *(Story, p. 431)*

Judgeships

In addition to the O'Connor appointment, Reagan appointed 41 judges to lower federal courts — 10 to the U.S. appeals courts and 31 to the federal district courts.

Only one of the 41 judges was a woman and only one was black. None of the Reagan appointees in the president's first year was of Hispanic origin.

Unlike President Carter, who made it clear he wanted to increase the number of women and minorities on the federal bench, the Reagan administration concentrated on candidates' "judicial philosophy."

Officials involved in the selection process said they were looking for nominees who believed that judges should interpret laws, leaving legislatures to make them.

Although Carter's first-year record for appointing women and minorities was only slightly better than Reagan's, interest groups representing women, blacks and Hispanics were upset at the end of 1981. They complained that the atmosphere surrounding judicial nominations had shifted from a broad-based search back to a system of rewarding politicians' friends in the legal community. *(Story, p. 410)*

—By Nadine Cohodas

O'Connor: First Woman on Supreme Court

Sandra Day O'Connor, 51, a former Arizona legislator and state appeals court judge, was sworn in Sept. 25 as the first woman associate justice of the U.S. Supreme Court.

She replaced Potter Stewart, a moderate-to-conservative justice and frequent swing vote, who retired July 3 after nearly 23 years on the court.

The Senate confirmed O'Connor's nomination Sept. 21 by a vote of 99-0. Max Baucus, D-Mont., who had supported the nomination in the Judiciary Committee, was absent the day of the floor vote. *(Vote 271, p. 47-S)*

O'Connor, the 102nd person to serve on the court, was the first new justice since 1975, when John Paul Stevens replaced William O. Douglas. *(1975 Almanac p. 536)*

Her confirmation was never in doubt, despite noisy opposition to her nomination by anti-abortion groups who claimed she had cast some pro-abortion votes while serving in the Arizona state Senate in the early 1970s.

Stewart's Retirement

Stewart's retirement came as a surprise. He said at a June 19 news conference that he wanted to leave the court while he still was in good health and able to enjoy the added time with his family.

"I've always believed that it is better to go too soon than to stay too long," the 66-year-old justice said.

Stewart was named to the Supreme Court in 1958 by President Eisenhower after serving four years on the U.S. Court of Appeals for the Sixth Circuit. At the time of his retirement, he was second in seniority only to William J. Brennan Jr., who has served since 1956. *(CQ Guide to the U.S. Supreme Court p. 860)*

In the 1960s, Stewart found himself in disagreement with a number of the Warren court's most controversial decisions. He was the lone dissenter in the 1962 decision that struck down New York's use of a prescribed prayer in the public schools, and he also dissented from several major rulings expanding the rights of criminal defendants, including *Escobedo v. Illinois* (1964) and *Miranda v. Arizona* (1966).

However, he joined the court majority in other important cases and was responsible for its innovative use of an 1866 civil rights law to ban discrimination in the private sale or rental of housing and to prohibit discrimination by private schools.

After Chief Justice Warren E. Burger took the court's center seat in 1969, Stewart found himself more powerful and more comfortable. He cast the deciding vote in a dozen major rulings in the 1970s on issues ranging from the death penalty to affirmative action.

In the 1972 death penalty case of *Furman v. Georgia,* each justice wrote his own opinion. But it is Stewart's that is most often quoted.

Explaining why all death penalty laws then on the books were unconstitutional, he said, "These death sentences are cruel and unusual in the same way that being struck down by lightning is cruel and unusual." The penalty, he said, was being imposed "wantonly" and "freakishly."

Reagan's Choice

President Reagan announced July 7 that he had chosen O'Connor to succeed Stewart, but her nomination was not formally submitted to the Senate until August 19, after an FBI background investigation had been completed.

Reagan had promised during his 1980 presidential campaign that he would name a woman to the high court, and he wasted no time in fulfilling the campaign pledge.

His choice of O'Connor drew widespread praise from women's groups and from all ends of the ideological spectrum. The only significant opposition to her nomination came from anti-abortion groups, who were singularly unsuccessful in persuading senators to vote against confirmation.

Biographical Background

Unlike her fellow justices, O'Connor, a former majority leader of the Arizona state Senate, brought to the bench some solid political experience. In a court lacking both philosophic "glue" and charismatic leadership, her political background and the skills associated with it offered her the opportunity to exercise unusual influence for a new justice.

A no-nonsense jurist, O'Connor has always excelled — academically and professionally.

She was graduated magna cum laude from Stanford University in 1950 and was near the top of the Stanford law school class of 1952 — like another Arizonan, fellow Justice William H. Rehnquist, who was named to the Supreme Court by President Nixon in 1971.

After moving from California to Arizona with her husband, John Jay O'Connor III, she spent six years in private law practice and then served as assistant state attorney general from 1965 through 1968. She was temporarily appointed to fill a slot in the Arizona Senate in 1969 and then won election to two full terms. She was elected majority leader in 1973.

O'Connor left the Legislature in 1974 to run for superior court judge and remained in that post until Gov. Bruce Babbitt, a Democrat, appointed her to the Arizona Court of Appeals in 1979.

O'Connor's Views

O'Connor deftly maneuvered her way through Senate Judiciary Committee public hearings Sept. 9-11 that focused, as expected, on her abortion views and on votes she cast on the issue between 1970 and 1974 as an Arizona state legislator.

She successfully parried demands by some committee members opposed to abortion that she comment on the 1973 *Roe v. Wade* decision that made abortion legal. "I feel it is improper for me to either endorse or criticize that decision," she said.

O'Connor sought to explain one controversial vote she cast for a bill that would have repealed existing anti-abortion laws. She noted the vote occurred in 1970, when the abortion issue was discussed very little, and said that since that time she had learned more about the issue.

"I would not have voted, I think, Mr. Chairman, for a simple repealer thereafter," she told Judiciary Chairman Strom Thurmond, R-S.C.

O'Connor said she was personally opposed to abortion. "For myself, abortion is simply offensive to me. It is something that is repugnant to me, something in which I would not engage," O'Connor told Sen. Jeremiah Denton, R-Ala., a vehement foe of abortion.

"Obviously there are others who do not share these beliefs," O'Connor added. "I recognize that and I think we are obligated to recognize that others have different views."

O'Connor said her personal views would not be a factor in any case she decided. "Issues that come before the court should be resolved based on the facts ... and the law applicable to those facts," she said.

Several senators questioned O'Connor about the concept of "judicial activism," a term used to describe judges perceived as making social policy through judicial decisions.

"In carrying out the judicial function, I believe in the exercise of judicial restraint. For example, cases should be decided on other than constitutional grounds where that is possible," O'Connor testified.

"... I believe in the importance of the limited role of government generally and in the constitutional restraints on the judiciary, in particular," she said.

"Judges are not only not authorized to engage in executive or legislative functions, they are also ill-equipped to do so," she wrote in response to a committee questionnaire.

Committee Approval

O'Connor's confirmation was all but assured Sept. 15 when the Senate Judiciary Committee voted overwhelmingly to approve her nomination to the high court.

The vote was 17-0, with Denton abstaining. The Alabama Republican said he had not been satisfied with O'Connor's refusal during three days of hearings to state a position on the 1973 Supreme Court decision in *Roe v. Wade.*

Denton said O'Connor's testimony that she found abortion personally offensive was not sufficient to allay his concerns over the issue. He expressed frustration that the hearing process did not yield more information on O'Connor's views about the propriety of the 1973 decision.

Two days after the committee meeting, Denton spoke to President Reagan at the senator's request. A Denton aide said that during the conversation the senator received "some additional information" — which the aide did not specify — concerning O'Connor.

The aide also said O'Connor wrote Denton to clarify her personal views on abortion. The aide said the letter "at least indicated that maybe they were a lot closer on that topic" than Denton might have thought.

For whatever reason, the Alabama freshman voted in favor of confirmation when O'Connor's nomination reached the Senate floor.   ∎

Few Women, Minorities Added to Bench

In his first year as president, Ronald Reagan made good on his Oct. 14, 1980, campaign promise to appoint a woman to the Supreme Court, naming Arizona Appeals Court Judge Sandra Day O'Connor to the high court.

But only one of the 41 judges he had named to the lower federal courts by mid-December 1981 was a woman — Cynthia Holcomb Hall, who already was serving as a U.S. Tax Court judge when Reagan elevated her to a district court seat in California.

One appointee was black — Lawrence W. Pierce — and he, too, already was a sitting federal judge, elevated by Reagan from a district court seat in New York to the 2nd U.S. Circuit Court of Appeals.

None of Reagan's initial judicial appointees was of Hispanic heritage. Thirty-nine were white men.

Comparison With Past Administrations

Although President Carter did only slightly better in his first year, Reagan had a long way to go to match the overall Carter record in broadening the composition of the federal judiciary.

At the outset of his presidency, Carter made clear that he would seek to bring more women and minorities onto the federal bench. He altered public debate on judicial selection and the expectations of the legal profession by deliberately looking for judicial candidates who were neither sitting judges nor white, male lawyers with established corporate careers.

In his first year, Carter appointed blacks to fill two of 10 appeals court vacancies and named a woman to one of the 21 openings on the district court bench, according to the Justice Department.

Aided by the 1978 Omnibus Judgeship Act (PL 95-486) that gave him 152 new federal judgeships, Carter ended his four years in office having appointed 40 women, 38 blacks and 16 Hispanics to the federal bench — more than any other president. *(Judgeship act, 1978 Almanac p. 173)*

In percentage terms, 19.6 percent of Carter's appeals court nominees were women, 16.1 percent were black and 3.6 percent Hispanic. Of Carter's district court appointees, 14.1 percent were women, 14.1 percent black and 6.8 percent Hispanic.

Some 2.5 percent of President Lyndon B. Johnson's appeals court nominees were women and 5 percent were black. Presidents Richard M. Nixon and Gerald R. Ford appointed no blacks and no women to federal appeals courts. No statistics were kept on Hispanic nominees.

At the district court level, 1.6 percent of Johnson's nominees were women, 3.3 percent were black and 2.5 percent Hispanic. For Nixon, the comparable figures were 0.6 percent women, 2.8 percent black and 1.1 percent Hispanic. Of Ford's appointees, 1.9 percent were women, 5.8 percent black and 1.9 percent Hispanic.

Criticism of Reagan Record

Interest groups representing women, blacks and Hispanics were unhappy with the president's selections, notwithstanding the O'Connor appointment. *(O'Connor confirmation, p. 409)*

"His record is absolutely deplorable," said Susan Ness, a lawyer with the National Women's Political Caucus who had watched federal court appointments since 1978. "I'm surprised, because he made a point during the campaign to appoint women to lower courts, and it is not as though he hasn't had ample opportunity."

Elaine Jones, a lawyer with the NAACP Legal Defense and Education Fund in Washington, said:

"They just don't care what blacks think, what black lawyers think ... I would think the administration would

want our input but they made clear they didn't," she said.

For Antonia Hernandez, head of the Washington office of the Mexican American Legal Defense and Educational Fund, the judgeship issue was "a double disappointment."

"When Hispanics met with the president in February, he made a commitment to appoint more Hispanics than any other president including President Carter," she said. "We've been waiting, and there have been no appointments. Sometimes you see the light at the end of the tunnel. Here we don't even see the tunnel, let alone the light. It is a double disappointment."

Administration Position

Not surprisingly, top officials in the Reagan administration vehemently denied that the administration turned a cold shoulder to women and minorities.

"I don't think that it is accurate that we have not sought out and have not considered women and minorities," said Fred Fielding, counsel to the president and one of the key White House officials involved in judicial selections. "But there are some people who think that courts should be staffed, if you will, on a basis of representativeness, and really, we think they should be staffed on the basis of qualifications."

Deputy Attorney General Edward C. Schmults, who coordinated judicial selections for the Justice Department, also disputed suggestions that the administration wanted a white-men-only federal bench.

"We certainly are interested in reaching out and into the applicant pool for well-qualified minorities and women, but I think once people are in that pool, we are looking for the very best judges we can find."

"I don't think one year is a fair test of the administration," Schmults said. "I think those numbers will improve."

Judicial Philosophy

The Reagan administration made clear early in 1981 that the issue of "judicial philosophy" would be important. The Republican Party platform, for example, had called for judges who believed in "the decentralization of the federal government and efforts to return decision-making power to state and local elected officials."

The questionnaire of the Senate Judiciary Committee — which must approve all nominees — included one lengthy question about "judicial activism," a term used to characterize judges perceived as writing legislation from the bench.

To a person, the 41 judicial candidates who were confirmed responded to the question by stating that judges should only interpret the law, leaving legislatures to make it.

The nominees' answers were hardly a surprise to Judiciary members and their staffs. But some senators still considered it useful to get candidates' views in writing.

Candidate Qualifications

Perhaps easier to gauge than judicial philosophy were the basic qualifications of candidates for the bench — years of practice, courtroom experience, variety of legal work.

The American Bar Association (ABA) had been rating federal judges for 33 years.

Of the 41 judges Reagan appointed to the lower courts, three, or 7.3 percent, were given the ABA's highest rating of exceptionally well qualified. This is higher than the percentage for four previous presidents. Nineteen of the

Reagan judges, or 46.3 percent, were given the rating of well qualified, and 19 were given a "qualified" rating. No nominee was rated unqualified.

This was roughly equal to the percentages for the Carter administration.

As was the case in previous administrations, the bulk of Reagan's district court appointments — 23 of 33 — went to lawyers in private practice.

On the appeals court, eight of the 10 new judges had previous judicial experience. The other two were eminent law professors.

This was a change from the Carter administration, which had departed from the informal tradition of elevating federal or state judges to the appeals court. Carter appointed a number of practicing attorneys to appeals court judgeships.

Partisanship

Schmults was particularly critical of the Carter administration's claim that it used "merit selection" in putting judges on the bench. In looking at Carter's appointments, Schmults said Reagan officials found that Carter made the highest percentage of partisan judicial appointments in decades.

A study by the American Judicature Society, a Chicago legal research organization, came up with a different conclusion for Carter's appeals court candidates. The study found that 86 percent of Carter's appointees were Democrats and concluded that this percentage "does not represent any remarkable difference from previous administrations."

According to the Justice Department, at least two of Reagan's appointees were Democrats. However, a spokesman said there may be more. He said the department did not make a special inquiry about candidates' party affiliation.

Appeals Court Selection Process

With no announcement, Reagan on May 6 issued an executive order abolishing the nominating commissions Carter had set up to screen appeals court candidates.

Reagan preferred to select nominees for the appeals court with help from Republican members of Congress, party officials, interest groups and sitting federal judges, sources said.

Jonathan Rose, head of the Justice Department's Office of Legal Policy, which handled judgeships, said the department wanted to make recommendations to the president for appeals courts openings "from the broadest range of people."

"We looked at how the Carter commissions operated, and we were not happy with the results they produced," Rose said, charging that "Carter was prepared to sacrifice quality and merit just to get a particular percentage of people on the bench."

District Court Choices

A memorandum made public March 6 by Attorney General William French Smith suggested that each senator submit three to five candidates for district court seats, and it "encouraged" senators to use a screening process to make sure that "highly qualified candidates are identified and recommended."

Fielding, who chaired an administration "working group" on judgeships, said the process worked roughly like this:

Senators sent names to the White House, which transmitted them to the Justice Department for evaluation. Preliminary selections were made after discussions between White House and Justice officials, with candidates then subjected to a "full field investigation" by the FBI.

Once the FBI probe was completed, and assuming no problems were discovered, names were sent back to the White House for final approval and transmission to the Senate Judiciary Committee.

Consultation between Justice and the White House occured primarily through the "working group," according to Fielding.

Members of the group included Fielding, Smith, presidential counselor Edwin Meese III, chief of staff James A. Baker III, Max L. Friedersdorf, presidential assistant for legislative affairs, Deputy Attorney General Edward C. Schmults, Associate Attorney General Rudy W. Giuliani and Rose.

Carter's Process Different

Reagan did not send his first judicial nomination to the Senate, which must confirm his choices, until the beginning of July, more than five months after he took office.

Michael Egan, an Atlanta lawyer who handled judgeships for former Attorney General Griffin B. Bell, said the Carter administration process was somewhat different and speedier. By the end of April 1977 — three months after Carter took office — two judges had been sworn in, Egan said.

He cited two major reasons for the Carter administration's speed. First, as a former U.S. court of appeals judge, Bell was acutely interested in the federal judiciary and gave appointments to the bench a high priority. Second, the Carter administration left in place much of the Justice Department process and personnel used in the Ford administration.

Rose contended that one reason Carter appointees moved along so quickly was that there was less paperwork for nominees to fill out.

New Senate Questionnaire

At the direction of Judiciary Committee Chairman Strom Thurmond, R-S.C., chief investigator Duke Short prepared a new questionnaire that included questions about each candidate's legal background and asked for a discussion of "judicial activism."

The questionnaire also asked whether the candidate belonged to any clubs that restricted membership on the basis of race, sex or religion. However, in contrast to the committee practice under former Chairman Edward M. Kennedy, D-Mass., the club question was in the confidential rather than the public section of the questionnaire. ∎

Legal Services Corp. Kept Alive Temporarily

The Legal Services Corporation (LSC), slated for extinction by the Reagan administration, survived at least until March 31, 1982, by virtue of a stopgap funding bill signed Dec. 15 by the president.

H J Res 370 (PL 97-92) included $241 million for the LSC. This was the amount included in the State, Justice, Commerce fiscal 1982 appropriations bill (HR 4169), which passed the House but was stalled on the Senate floor at year's end. *(Story, p. 329)*

A House-passed authorization (HR 3480 — H Rept 97-97) also authorized the corporation to spend $241 million annually for two years. That bill was pending in the Senate along with a proposal (S 1533 — S Rept 97-171) authorizing $100 million for the LSC over three years.

The president's aides said they would recommend that Reagan veto the authorization bill.

Reagan wanted to abolish the seven-year-old corporation, which provided legal aid to the poor in civil cases, and allow states to provide such aid through social services block grants. His plan met with strong opposition from LSC supporters in Congress, legal aid lawyers and the influential American Bar Association.

A nationwide coalition of lawyers and judges opposed the Reagan plan and lobbied hard to save the corporation.

Background

Battling to survive was nothing new for the corporation. The LSC was created in 1974 (PL 93-355) and extended in 1977 only after protracted congressional fights over what legal aid programs should do. *(Background, 1977 Almanac p. 587)*

The corporation inherited 257 existing poverty law programs that had been funded by the now-defunct Office of Economic Opportunity. In 1981, LSC provided grants to about 325 programs operating 1,400 offices.

As created by Congress, the corporation operated under a number of restrictions. For example, the Hatch Act's prohibitions against partisan political activity by government employees applied to attorneys in programs funded by LSC. In addition, programs funded through LSC could not provide legal assistance in school desegregation, nontherapeutic abortion and armed forces desertion cases, or in cases involving certain violations of the Selective Service Act.

The corporation's authorization ran out in 1980. The Senate passed a bill that year reauthorizing the LSC for two years. Rep. Robert W. Kastenmeier, D-Wis., chairman of the House Judiciary Courts Subcommittee, offered a companion bill reauthorizing the panel for another three years, but he had to scuttle the effort because of strong opposition. *(1980 Almanac, p. 399)*

Congress, however, did appropriate $321.3 million for the LSC for fiscal 1981, which ended Sept 30.

Saved by Stopgap Funding Bills

The LSC survived the year on temporary appropriations, circumventing the usual rule that no appropriation should be made for a program unless it has been authorized by Congress.

The LSC made it through part of fiscal 1982 on $321 million earmarked in continuing resolutions that ran through Dec. 15, 1981. Then it shifted to the lower funding provided in H J Res 370.

In at least one respect, the LSC was better off with its stopgap funding than if either the appropriations or authorization bill had been enacted.

HR 3480 and HR 4169 each contained a number of new restrictions on legal services lawyers' activities not

contained in the continuing resolutions. These included bans on so-called "class-action" lawsuits against local, state or federal government agencies; restrictions on the types of aliens who could get representation and tightening up of existing lobbying regulations.

House Committee Action

HR 3480 was reported by the House Judiciary Committee May 19 (H Rept 97-97) after the committee approved the reauthorization bill May 13 by a 22-6 vote. It authorized $260 million annually for LSC for fiscal 1982 and fiscal 1983 — about 20 percent less than the corporation's fiscal 1981 appropriation of $321.3 million, which expired Sept. 30.

The bill contained several new restrictions on the activities of legal aid lawyers, including a ban on strikes and a prohibition against their participation in most abortion cases or in cases that sought to legalize homosexuality.

The no-strike provision was rejected 11-15 during a markup session May 12, but sponsor M. Caldwell Butler, R-Va., moved to reconsider the amendment a day later. On the second try, it was adopted 15-11 through a combination of vote switching and the return of members who had been absent May 12.

There had been only nine strikes in the seven-year history of the corporation, with the most recent a New York walkout in 1980.

Restrictive Amendments

During full committee markup, LSC supporters led by subcommittee Chairman Kastenmeier staved off all but three of the 24 amendments offered.

In addition to the no-strike amendment, the committee adopted 14-13 an amendment proposed by Bill McCollum, R-Fla., requiring that local bar groups appoint a majority of the boards of directors for local legal aid programs.

The third amendment, offered by F. James Sensenbrenner Jr., R-Wis., refined an exception to the prohibition on lobbying by legal aid lawyers. It was adopted by voice vote.

Another controversial amendment offered by McCollum but rejected by the panel would have barred LSC lawyers from bringing any "class action" lawsuits. Such suits are filed on behalf of a group of people seeking to resolve the same grievance.

McCollum said LSC class action lawsuits in his district were unpopular.

"Litigation is not a question of popularity," Kastenmeier countered. "Litigation is a question of justice."

House Floor Action

The House passed HR 3480 June 18 after adopting additional restrictions on activities of legal aid lawyers and chopping $19 million from the committee's recommended funding level.

HR 3480 passed 245-137, but the margin did not reflect the intense opposition to the seven-year old organization that surfaced during three days of stormy debate on the bill. *(Vote 83, p. 36-H)*

Final passage came after supporters, by a 165-221 vote, rejected a motion by Robert McClory, R-Ill., to kill the bill by sending it to the Education and Labor and Ways and Means committees for hearings. *(Vote 82, p. 36-H)*

Hovering over the three-day debate was the prospect of a presidential veto should Congress enact the legislation. Before debate started June 16, Minority Leader Robert H. Michel, R-Ill., distributed copies of a letter White House counselor Edwin Meese III sent him reaffirming Reagan's opposition to extending the LSC. Meese said he would recommend a veto of the legislation if it were enacted.

Despite Reagan's opposition, the bill got 59 Republican votes, due largely to the efforts of three veteran GOP members of the House Judiciary Committee — Tom Railsback, Ill., Harold S. Sawyer, Mich., and M. Caldwell Butler, Va.

New Restrictions

A number of major restrictive amendments were added on the House floor, including one that prevented federally funded LSC lawyers from bringing "class action" lawsuits against local, state or federal governments.

A class action suit was one brought on behalf of many clients who generally had the same grievance and were seeking similar judicial relief. While such suits accounted for less than 1 percent of all legal services cases, most had been brought against government agencies — thereby striking sensitive political nerves.

Other amendments imposed tighter bans on cases involving homosexual rights and on lobbying by legal aid lawyers.

HR 3480 originally had provided $260 million annually for the LSC in fiscal 1982 and 1983, but the House cut that to $241 million for each year.

The June 17-18 debates on the class action and homosexuality amendments were lengthy and often acrimonious.

Charles Wilson, D-Texas, sponsor of the class action amendment, said such suits caused "90 percent of the trouble" surrounding the LSC. Barney Frank, D-Mass., argued that the amendment consigned poor people to "second-class legal representation," calling it "the most blatant form of discrimination on the grounds of economics that I have ever heard of."

The amendment was adopted June 17 by a 241-167 vote. *(Vote 75, p. 34-H)*

Larry P. McDonald, D-Ga., proposed an amendment to reword a provision in existing law prohibiting LSC programs from handling cases that seek to "adjudicate the legalization of homosexuality."

The McDonald amendment barred using LSC funds to "promote, defend or protect" homosexuality. "The long and short of the matter is that those who openly profess and promote homosexual conduct do not deserve protection under this amendment," McDonald said.

John L. Burton, D-Calif., one of several members who spoke against the amendment, called it "an outrage." Gerry E. Studds, D-Mass., said the amendment was "wrong and mean-spirited."

Ted Weiss, D-N.Y., offered a substitute to return to existing language but failed, 151-245. The McDonald amendment subsequently was adopted 281-124. *(Votes 76, 77, p. 36-H)*

By voice vote, the House adopted an amendment by John M. Ashbrook, R-Ohio, barring use of LSC money for suits involving the desegregation of any elementary or secondary school system. The amendment was designed to close an exception in a provision of current law prohibiting LSC involvement in desegregation cases.

By voice vote, members adopted an amendment by Bill McCollum, R-Fla., to restrict the use of LSC funds for

representing illegal aliens. His amendment allowed LSC lawyers to represent only specified types of aliens, including those who were admitted as immigrants, married to a U.S. citizen or lawfully admitted as refugees.

The committee version of HR 3480, like existing law, prohibited use of LSC funds to represent a person "known to be an alien" and in the U.S. illegally.

By a 141-262 vote the House rejected an amendment by Hamilton Fish Jr., R-N.Y., to allow representation for aliens in the U.S. "under color of law, " a term used to cover aliens who were in the U.S. legally but were neither citizens nor permanent residents. *(Vote 80, p. 36-H)*

Amendments Rejected

The House rejected 160-242 an amendment by Sensenbrenner to prohibit LSC lawyers from offering legal advice on abortion matters. The Judiciary Committee already had adopted a provision barring lawyers from handling an abortion case unless the mother's life was in danger. *(Vote 78, p. 36-H)*

By a 185-210 vote the House rejected one amendment that would have given the Office of Management and Budget (OMB) authority to review the LSC budget, historically submitted directly to Congress. *(Vote 81, p. 36-H)*

Ken Kramer, R-Colo., argued there was no reason to give the LSC special status. But Railsback and Frank said Kramer's amendment would undercut LSC's independence because OMB could, as Frank put it, "close up the operation" by deferring or withdrawing LSC funds.

The House rejected 176-219 a second Ashbrook amendment that sought to bar LSC participation in cases against local school boards or any of their employees. *(Vote 79, p. 36-H)*

Provisions

As passed by the House, HR 3480 included the following provisions:

• Reauthorized the Legal Services Corporation (LSC) for fiscal 1982 and 1983 at $241 million annually.

• Prevented lawyers in LSC programs from handling any abortion case unless the life of the mother was endangered.

• Prevented LSC lawyers from taking any case to "promote, defend or protect" homosexuality.

• Prevented LSC lawyers from filing any "class action" suits against local, state or federal governments.

• Tightened an existing provision against lobbying activities by preventing LSC lawyers from providing information to local or state elected officials or members of Congress, except in narrow, specified circumstances when officially requested by the official.

• Restricted the types of aliens LSC lawyers could represent.

• Prevented LSC lawyers from striking.

• Tightened an existing ban on political activities to bar the use of legal services money for dissemination of information about political activities or for organizing activities such as picketing, boycotts or strikes.

Conservative Opposition

Some 70 House staffers and a handful of Senate aides met May 28 to discuss the bill (HR 3480) with Michael J. Horowitz, counsel for policy analysis and law at the Office of Management and Budget, and Herbert E. Ellingwood, deputy counsel to the president.

During the meeting, Horowitz pledged the administration's support in fighting the bill. He said President Rea-

gan was committed to abolishing the seven-year-old corporation and to letting the states handle legal aid programs through social services block grants.

Horowitz added that the president's senior advisers unanimously agreed at a meeting in mid-May to recommend that Reagan veto any LSC reauthorization bill.

Bar Support for LSC

As soon as President Reagan announced March 10 that he wanted to eliminate the corporation, ABA President William Reece Smith Jr. and bar leaders from 11 states and cities held a news conference to protest the move.

F. William McCalpin, a St. Louis corporate lawyer who was chairman of the LSC board of directors, sent letters to 152 bar leaders in the country urging them to press their congressmen and senators to support the corporation.

Testifying March 17 before the House subcommittee, McCalpin predicted that Reagan's proposed budget cuts affecting the poor "will raise feelings of alienation and frustration to a level we have not seen in 15 years. In those circumstances . . . we need equal access to justice to keep the controversies in balance, within the system. That's what legal services is all about. I urge you not to retreat from the principle of equal justice under law."

Senate Action

When the Senate considered its fiscal 1982 budget plan May 7, Labor and Human Resources Committee Chairman Orrin G. Hatch, R-Utah, tried to delete $100 million in budget authority for the corporation, but his amendment was rejected 24-72. *(Vote 91, p. 19-S)*

In an interview, Hatch said he believed it was time to dismantle the LSC. "Though I have supported legal services in the vain hope they will concentrate on really helping the poor, personally I have come to the conclusion that they will never do that," Hatch said.

Like other of LSC's detractors, Hatch charged that legal aid lawyers had spent "millions of dollars in what we call lawyer activism for liberal social programs instead of working for the common needs of the poor."

Hatch's committee July 24 approved S 1533, which authorized $100 million for the corporation for fiscal 1982. But the bill never was considered by the full Senate.

Reconciliation Bill

The Senate's version of the budget reconciliation bill (S 1377), passed June 25, incorporated S 1533 by including a two-year reauthorization for the LSC at $100 million annually.

During Senate floor debate, Jeremiah Denton, R-Ala., twice sought to delete the $100 million authorization but failed both times. *(Votes 177, 178, p. 32-S)*

The House reconciliation measure (HR 3982) contained no LSC provision.

House Judiciary Chairman Peter W. Rodino Jr., D-N.J., and Robert W. Kastenmeier, D-Wis., chief proponents of HR 3480, said they were willing to include the LSC in the reconciliation process. But both said they could not accept the $100 million Senate figure. Rodino said Senate conferees offered to hike their amount to $150 million, but he said that amount was too little to make the LSC "a going operation."

Senate and House conferees agreed July 27 to remove the two-year reauthorization from the reconciliation package. ∎

House Passes Bill to Extend Voting Rights Act

The House Oct. 5 overwhelmingly approved a bill to extend enforcement provisions of the landmark 1965 Voting Rights Act, but the Senate failed to act during the 97th Congress.

Final House action on the bill (HR 3112) came on a 389-24 vote after 9½ hours of debate. *(Vote 228, p. 76-H)*

The measure faced tougher sledding in the Senate, where Judiciary Committee Chairman Strom Thurmond, R-S.C., was a longtime foe of the Voting Rights Act.

Sen. Orrin G. Hatch, R-Utah, chairman of the Constitution Subcommittee, scheduled hearings on the act for January 1982. "All of us want to support civil rights," Hatch said, "but we have to have balance."

Supporters of the bill, through a parliamentary maneuver, succeeded in placing HR 3112 directly on the Senate calendar, a "precautionary" step designed to prevent the Judiciary Committee from bottling up the bill. They also introduced a separate, identical bill (S 1992).

Southern Support

In its original form, the Voting Rights Act was aimed squarely at voting rights abuses in the South. When it was passed in 1965, only 33 Southern Democrats in the House voted for it. That number rose to 34 in 1970 and to 56 in 1975 when the enforcement provisions were renewed.

When the House voted in 1981, 71 Southern Democrats — more than double the number in 1965 — voted for HR 3112.

Civil rights supporters in the House easily defeated all proposed amendments that would have weakened the bill. Two were trounced by better than 3-1 margins. Three others were rejected by margins of more than 2-1.

As approved by the Judiciary Committee and passed by the House, HR 3112 would extend the current enforcement provisions in Section Five of the 1965 act for two years. These so-called "pre-clearance" sections required nine states and portions of 13 others to get Justice Department approval for any election law changes. *(1965 Almanac, p. 533)*

Under HR 3112, Section Five would become permanent in 1984. But at that time, a new bail-out procedure would take effect allowing covered states and counties to get out from the pre-clearance requirement once they met certain conditions.

Current law also included a bail-out section, but it was written so tightly that none of the six southern states originally covered in 1965 could get out from coverage.

HR 3112 also would extend for seven years provisions enacted in 1975 requiring certain areas of the country to provide bilingual election materials. *(1975 Almanac p. 521)*

Provisions

As approved by the House, HR 3112:
- Extended until 1984 the existing pre-clearance and bail-out provisions.
- Made the pre-clearance sections permanent in 1984.
- Established a new bail-out procedure as of 1984.
- Allowed a covered jurisdiction to bail out if it could show a three-judge panel in the District of Columbia that it had a clean voting rights record for the preceding 10 years.
- Required that all counties of a covered state be eligible

to bail out before the state could bail out.
- Required as proof of a clean record the following: local authorities had not used any voting test or device in a discriminatory way; there had been no final judgment of a federal court finding a violation of the voting rights law; there had been no consent decree, settlement or agreement entered into concerning voting rights violations; the attorney general had not been required to send in federal examiners to help register voters; local officials had complied with the pre-clearance requirement by making all required submissions to the Justice Department, and had repealed all election law changes the department objected to; and the jurisdiction had made "constructive efforts" to bring minority groups into the election process and to end any intimidation or harassment of prospective voters.
- Extended until 1992 provisions requiring certain areas of the country to provide bilingual election materials.
- Allowed an aggrieved party to prove a voting rights violation by showing that an election law procedure had been imposed "in a manner which results" in voting discrimination. This provision was designed to overturn a 1980 Supreme Court decision that required an aggrieved person to prove that a jurisdiction intended to discriminate through its election laws. *(Mobile (Ala.) v. Bolden, 1980 Almanac p. 9-A)*

Background

Considered the nation's most effective civil rights legislation, the Voting Rights Act (PL 89-110) brought about a dramatic increase in the number of blacks and Hispanics voting in state, local and federal elections.

But unless Congress acted, its key provisions were to expire Aug. 6, 1982.

The 1965 law prohibited the use of literacy tests or similar devices that had been employed to disqualify black voters, gave the Justice Department the power to send federal examiners into areas with low voting participation by blacks and established criminal penalties for interfering with voting rights. All of these protections were a permanent part of the law and needed no renewal. *(1965 Almanac p. 533)*

The act's enforcement provisions had been extended twice, in 1970 and 1975, and the law was expanded to bar discrimination against Hispanics, American Indians and other minorities as well as blacks. *(1970 Almanac p. 192; 1975 Almanac p. 525)*

Although the original act covered only Alabama, Georgia, Louisiana, Mississippi, South Carolina, Virginia and Alaska, the extensions brought in Texas and Arizona plus portions of 13 other states. The areas were selected through a triggering formula based on use of a literacy test and voter registration statistics.

Operation of the Law

Justice Department statistics show that from enactment of the Voting Rights Act in 1965 through 1980, state and local governments submitted 34,798 proposed election law changes to the department. The department objected to only 815 — about 23 percent. *(Chart, p. 416)*

Most of the proposed changes submitted for approval dealt with moving polling places (9,448), changing election

Voting Rights Act in Action

The following chart shows the number of proposed changes in state election laws submitted to the Justice Department as required by the Voting Rights Act of 1965, and the number of changes to which the Justice Department has objected:

	Proposed election law changes				Justice Department objections
	1965-70*	1971-75	1976-80	Total	
Alabama	16	614	1,085	1,715	72
Alaska[3]	0	0	37	37	0
Arizona[4]	0	201	1,537	1,738	8
California[1]	—	12	683	695	5
Colorado[1]	—	0	233	233	0
Connecticut[2]	—	0	0	0	0
Florida[1]	—	1	167	168	0
Georgia	158	935	1,998	3,091	226
Hawaii[1]	0	0	9	9	0
Idaho[1]	0	0	1	1	0
Louisiana	5	882	1,709	2,596	136
Maine[1]	—	0	3	3	0
Massachusetts[2]	—	0	17	17	0
Michigan[2]	—	0	3	3	0
Mississippi	32	503	654	1,189	78
New Hampshire[2]	—	0	0	0	0
New Mexico[1]	—	0	65	65	0
New York[1]	—	166	326	492	5
Oklahoma[1]	—	0	1	1	0
North Carolina[1]	2	485	711	1,198	62
South Carolina	308	834	1,260	2,402	77
South Dakota	—	0	6	6	2
Texas	—	249	15,959	16,208	130
Virginia	57	1,093	1,780	2,930	14
Wyoming[1]	—	1	0	1	0
Total				34,798	815

The pre-clearance requirement, requiring submissions of proposed election law changes to the Justice Department, was enacted in 1965. The provision was continued through the extensions of the act in 1970 and 1975.

[1] *Selected county or counties covered rather than entire state.*

[2] *Selected town or towns covered rather than entire state.*

[3] *Entire state covered 1965-68; selected election districts covered 1970-72; entire state covered since 1975.*

[4] *Selected county or counties covered until 1975; entire state now covered.*

— *Not covered for years indicated.*

Source: U.S. Department of Justice

laws (7,774) and land annexations (7,249). Most of the Justice Department objections were to proposed changes in local election procedures (337), annexations (244) and redistricting (103).

Census Bureau figures for the 1976 election, the most recent available, showed that black voter registration had risen substantially in many states since passage of the act. In Mississippi, for example, only 6.7 percent of the eligible blacks in Mississippi were registered in 1964. By 1976, 67.4 percent had registered. *(Box, next page)*

Since 1975, when bilingual provisions were added to the law, Hispanic voters also made notable registration gains. A study by the Southwest Voter Registration Education Project showed a 29.5 percent increase in Hispanic registration nationwide between 1976 and 1980. In the Southwest, Hispanic registration was up 44 percent.

Pressure on Reagan

On April 7, 1981, Charles McC. Mathias Jr., R-Md., Edward M. Kennedy, D-Mass., and six other senators introduced legislation (S 895) to extend the key provisions until 1992. House Judiciary Chairman Peter W. Rodino Jr., D-N.J., introduced a similar House bill (HR 3112) the same day. Rep. Henry J. Hyde, R-Ill., later introduced his own bill (HR 3948) to extend the enforcement provisions while allowing jurisdictions that met certain requirements to "bail out" from coverage of the act.

Despite pressures from civil rights groups, President Reagan took no position on HR 3112 prior to House passage.

On June 15, Reagan released a letter he sent to Attorney General William French Smith asking Smith for a thorough study of the act and a recommendation by Oct. 1.

Black Voter Registration

Percentage of eligible blacks registered to vote in 1964 and in 1976 in the six Southern states covered by the federal Voting Rights Act since 1965:

	1964	1976
Alabama	23.0%	58.1%
Georgia	44.0	56.3
Louisiana	32.0	63.9
Mississippi	6.7	67.4
South Carolina	38.8	60.6
Virginia	45.7	60.7

SOURCE: 1964 statistics, Voter Education Project of the Southern Regional Council; 1976 statistics, U.S. Census Bureau

When Oct. 1 arrived, Reagan said at a press conference that he supported the Voting Rights Act in principle, but he stopped short of endorsing HR 3112.

Then, on Nov. 6, the president announced that he favored a 10-year extension of the act but believed "as a matter of fairness" that states and localities that have "fully complied" with it should be able to bail out from coverage.

"Toward that end," Reagan said, "I will support amendments which incorporate reasonable 'bail-out' provisions for states and other political subdivisions."

House Committee Action

The Hearings

The House Judiciary Civil and Constitutional Rights Subcommittee on May 6 opened several weeks of hearings on the act's renewal with testimony from such civil rights leaders as Vernon E. Jordan Jr., president of the National Urban League, and Benjamin L. Hooks, executive director of the NAACP.

These and other witnesses urging an extension contended there was still a need for federal protection of minority voting rights. They said that while obvious barriers to voting such as a poll tax may be gone, more subtle methods of discrimination had surfaced, such as the gerrymandering of election districts, at-large elections and city annexations of predominantly white areas to dilute minority voting strength.

Critics of the law — mainly state officials and members of Congress from the South and West — contended the statute was no longer necessary. They said electoral abuses were a thing of the past and that the act's enforcement provisions, which they claimed fell disproportionately on the South, were both burdensome and unfair.

The Bail-Out Battle

A markup on HR 3112 originally was set for July 14. But Don Edwards, D-Calif., chairman of the Civil and Constitutional Rights subcommittee, put off the meeting so that he and Rodino could try to work out a compromise with Hyde, ranking Republican on Edwards' panel.

When subcommittee hearings began, Hyde said he opposed continuing Section Five in its present form. But

after several sessions, the Illinois Republican said he became convinced the enforcement section should be extended — with a provision which would allow covered jurisdictions that made the proper showing to a federal court to "bail out" from coverage.

While talks with Hyde continued, the subcommittee July 21 unanimously approved a simple 10-year extension of the act's enforcement provisions, together with a seven-year extension of provisions which required bilingual elections.

When the negotiations stalled July 30 and no agreement with Hyde appeared possible, Edwards and Rodino enlisted Hamilton Fish Jr., R-N.Y., and F. James Sensenbrenner Jr., R-Wis., to draft a compromise with somewhat tougher bail-out language than Hyde wanted.

Rodino told Hyde about the new bill shortly before the July 31 committee meeting at which the measure was approved 23-1. M. Caldwell Butler, R-Va., cast the lone "nay" vote. HR 3112 was reported Sept. 15 (H Rept 97-227).

During testy debate before the vote, Hyde made clear his disappointment with the manner used to craft the compromise. He voted for the bill but promised sponsors, "I'll see you on the floor" with amendments.

Hyde Objections

At the July 31 committee meeting, Hyde said he was disturbed by three aspects of the compromise bail-out: barring a state from bailing out unless all the counties within it were eligible to bail out; barring bail-out if the county or state had signed a consent decree in a voting rights case within 10 years of the bail-out; and barring a bail-out if there were a case pending against the jurisdiction seeking to get out from coverage.

Hyde said it was unfair to require a state to be responsible for counties' voting rights records when many states, because of home rule laws, did not have power over local governments.

Edwards said he and other members, particularly those in the Black Caucus, believed a state should be held responsible for its jurisdictions and that states could influence local governments to increase minority voting participation.

Hyde contended that barring bail-outs because of consent decrees discouraged settlements of voting rights cases. He said a jurisdiction involved in a suit had little incentive to settle a case with a consent decree if the decree was used against it in a bail-out case.

Armand Derfner, a civil rights lawyer with the Joint Center for Political Studies, a non-profit minority research group, said the consent decree provision was included because cases ending with such decrees could include instances of serious voting rights abuses.

Hyde said that the pending case provision opened the way for frivolous lawsuits filed just to block a bail-out.

John Conyers Jr., D-Mich., told Hyde at the July 31 meeting that his concern about a "daisy chain" of lawsuits was unfounded because there was no record of frivolous lawsuits over voting rights issues.

House Action

The Oct. 5 debate on HR 3112 was often raucous and sometimes humorous. At one point, it was even conducted in Spanish as Mickey Leland, D-Texas, sought to show members how many of his constituents feel when they hear English. As Leland was holding forth, Millicent Fenwick,

R-N.J., rose and began conversing with him in Spanish. Other members broke into laughter and applause, even though most didn't know what the two were saying.

The Bail-Out Issue

Before tackling controversial amendments, the House agreed by voice vote to a committee amendment that made clear that a lawsuit filed after a jurisdiction sought to bail out would not, by itself, bar the bail-out.

Hyde then sought to remove as a bar to bail-out the fact that a jurisdiction had signed a consent decree in a voting rights suit within the 10 years preceding its petition. The amendment was rejected 92-285, a margin that set the pattern for the entire day. *(Vote 223, p. 74-H)*

An amendment offered by M. Caldwell Butler, R-Va., would have changed the forum for hearing bail-out suits. Under the bill, as in current law, any bail-out suit would be heard by a three-judge panel in the District of Columbia.

Butler's proposal called for three-judge federal panels to hear bail-out suits in the jurisdictions seeking to bail out, but it provided that none of the judges could be from the area involved in the suit.

Butler said the existing system resulted in "inconvenience, expense and delay" because all litigants had to come to Washington. Hyde contended that keeping all suits in Washington amounted to a "slap in the face of federal judges." And Sam B. Hall Jr., D-Texas, maintained that "some of the most courageous civil rights decisions were rendered by Southern district judges."

Rodino said Washington should remain the forum to maintain uniformity in voting rights cases. He noted that the District of Columbia was made the site for such cases because litigants with voting rights problems had experienced difficulty getting fair hearings in their states.

After more than two hours of debate, the Butler amendment was rejected 132-277. *(Vote 224, p. 74-H)*

The House rejected 95-313 an amendment by Carroll A. Campbell Jr., R-S.C., to allow a state to bail out if two-thirds of its counties were eligible to do so and the state demonstrated that it had made a reasonable effort to assure that its counties complied with the Voting Rights Act. *(Vote 225, p. 74-H)*

The bill allowed a covered state to bail out only if all of its counties are eligible to bail out. Campbell said it was "unrealistic" to expect a state "to cure every problem, to watch over every local decision."

But Barney Frank, D-Mass., said that states are legally responsible and have "legal power" over their counties. He said the best incentive for states is telling them: "There is no bail-out until you pitch in. . . ."

Bilingual Provisions

Another two-hour debate occurred on a proposal by Robert McClory, R-Ill., to eliminate requirements for bilingual ballots and election materials in some states, requirements McClory called unduly expensive.

McClory said it should be up to each state whether it wanted to have bilingual ballots.

Robert Garcia, D-N.Y., retorted that no one ever said democracy was cheap. He said the bilingual provisions were designed to give non-English speaking voters access to the political process.

And in case anyone questioned the Hispanic contribution to America, Garcia reminded the House that, "It may have been an Italian who discovered America, but it was an Hispanic woman that gave him the money to get here."

His colleagues erupted in laughter at this reference to the financial backing Christopher Columbus received from Spain's Queen Isabella. And the McClory amendment was rejected 128-284. *(Vote 226, p. 74-H)*

By 124-285 the House also rejected an amendment by Dan Lungren, R-Calif., to eliminate the requirement for bilingual ballots while retaining the requirement for bilingual election materials. *(Vote 227, p. 76-H)*

Other Amendments

By voice vote the House rejected several other amendments including the following:

● By Thomas F. Hartnett, R-S.C., to extend the preclearance sections to all states.

● By Thomas J. Bliley Jr., R-Va., to eliminate a provision that allows a violation of the act to be proved by showing that a state or local law was imposed "in a manner which results" in voting discrimination. This provision was designed to overturn a 1980 Supreme Court decision that required an aggrieved party to prove intent to discriminate.

Senate Action

Democratic senators used procedural tactics Oct. 14 to keep HR 3112 from going to the Senate Judiciary Committee.

Negotiations between committee Chairman Thurmond and several senators — Majority Leader Howard H. Baker Jr., R-Tenn.; Charles McC. Mathias Jr., R-Md.; and Democrats Robert C. Byrd, W.Va.; Howard M. Metzenbaum, Ohio; Edward M. Kennedy, Mass.; and Joseph R. Biden Jr., Del. — failed to produce an agreement on a date for committee action.

As a result, moments before HR 3112 would have been sent to Judiciary under normal procedures, Minority Leader Byrd objected. This kept the bill on the Senate calendar, which meant that Baker could call up the measure for consideration at any time.

One Democratic staffer said in mid-October that Byrd's move was a precautionary one and not an attempt to circumvent the Judiciary Committee.

Thurmond was on the floor when Byrd stopped HR 3112 from going to the Judiciary, and he protested mildly.

"I just want to say that I think it is a mistake not to refer the Voting Rights Act to the Judiciary Committee, which normally handles matters of this kind," the chairman said. "However, I will say that hearings will be held by the Judiciary Committee whether the bill is referred to it or not."

Civil rights activists worried that the Senate might not have enough time to consider a voting rights bill.

They recalled what happened in 1980, when the Senate did not consider a fair housing bill until December. The measure fell prey to a filibuster led by Hatch and Thurmond, and the 96th Congress ended before a compromise bill could be enacted. *(1980 Almanac p. 373)*

Ralph Neas, executive director of the Leadership Conference on Civil Rights, said Oct. 15, "I think it is incumbent upon us to ensure that we're in a position to cope with any situation that might come up and make sure that the bill is debated and passed in the Senate before Aug. 6 [the law's expiration date]."

Budget Reconciliation

Only three Justice Department and law-related programs were included in HR 3982 (PL 97-35), the massive budget reconciliation package approved by Congress. *(See story, p. 256)*

However, one of them continued funding for the Office of Juvenile Justice and Delinquency Prevention, which administers programs to help states combat juvenile delinquency. President Reagan had wanted to abolish the programs in favor of wide-ranging social services block grants administered by the states.

In large part because they make up only a small part of the federal budget, the Justice Department's $2.3 billion in programs were relatively untouched by Reagan's budget-cutting proposals and by the reconciliation package approved by Congress.

To meet reconciliation orders from the Budget Committee requiring cuts of $60 million from programs under its jurisdiction, the Senate Judiciary Committee June 9 recommended trimming $17 million from the Office of Justice Assistance Research and Statistics, which oversees department research and statistical programs. The committee also recommended cutting $6 million from the Immigration and Naturalization Service and $1 million from the U.S. Commission on Civil Rights. Members proposed adding $10 million in revenues to the budget by accelerating planned fee increases for the U.S. Patent and Trademark Office.

However, none of these proposals was included in the bill approved by the full Senate or in the final reconciliation package.

The Senate sought to reauthorize the Legal Services Corporation (LSC) in the reconciliation package at $100 million annually for fiscal 1982 and 1983, but dropped that provision in conference with the House. The House had not included the LSC in its reconciliation package; instead, it passed a separate reauthorization. *(LSC reauthorization, p. 412)*

Provisions

As cleared by Congress, the law enforcement provisions of HR 3982 included the following:

● For juvenile justice programs, $77 million for fiscal 1982; $77.5 million for fiscal 1983 and $74.9 million for fiscal 1984.

This was the amount the Senate had proposed in its version of the reconciliation bill. The House had proposed $70 million each in fiscal 1982, 1983 and 1984.

● For administering Indochinese refugee assistance, $583.70 million for fiscal 1982, the amount recommended by the Senate. The House had no provision on this.

● For the U.S. Patent and Trademark Office, $118.96 million for fiscal 1982 for salaries and expenses. This is the amount recommended by the administration and the Senate. The House had no provision on this item. ∎

Federal Death Penalty

Although the Senate Judiciary Committee approved a death penalty bill, the full Senate failed to act in 1981 and similar measures made no progress in the House.

With little debate, the Senate Judiciary Committee June 9 approved a bill (S 114) to re-establish the death penalty for federal crimes such as treason, espionage and killing the president.

The vote was 13-5. Maryland Republican Charles McC. Mathias Jr. joined Democrats Joseph R. Biden Jr., Del., Edward M. Kennedy, Mass., Howard M. Metzenbaum, Ohio, and Patrick J. Leahy, Vt., in opposing the measure (S Rept 97-143).

Currently, the only federal crime carrying the death penalty was homicide during an aircraft hijacking.

In addition to treason, espionage and assassinating the president, S 114 also would cover murders occurring on federal property and deaths resulting from the commission of such felonies as kidnapping.

At the urging of Judiciary Chairman Strom Thurmond, R-S.C., the committee adopted an amendment that would apply the death penalty to certain assassination attempts on the president.

Included would be attempts that seriously injure or come "dangerously close" to killing the president. The amendment grew out of the March 30 shooting that wounded President Reagan and three other persons. *(Gun Control, p. 420; Assassination Attempt, p. 6)*

A written opinion from the Justice Department's Office of Legal Counsel said the amendment would be constitutional and would not be seen by a court as excessively harsh punishment for a crime that did not result in the death of another person.

However, David Landau, a spokesman for the American Civil Liberties Union, contended that the amendment and the entire bill were unconstitutional on the basis of several Supreme Court decisions on the death penalty.

Supreme Court Ruling

The Supreme Court in 1972 invalidated all existing death penalty statutes, although the justices did not find capital punishment per se to be unconstitutional. *(CQ Guide to the Supreme Court, p. 575)*

Since then, 35 states had rewritten their death penalty laws along lines designed to conform with the guidelines set forth in the 1972 and other high court rulings.

To comply with these guidelines, S 114 would require a two-stage trial.

The first part would determine the defendant's guilt or innocence. A defendant found guilty would then face a separate hearing on the issue of punishment. The jury could consider "aggravating" factors, such as the defendant's intention to kill the victim, commission of the crime in an "especially heinous, cruel or depraved manner" or the defendant's prior conviction for a serious crime.

The jury also would be required to consider any "mitigating" factors, such as the young age of a defendant or the fact that the defendant was under substantial duress.

Before imposing the death penalty, the jury would have to determine that the aggravating factors outweighed any mitigating factors it found.

The committee adopted an amendment by Orrin G. Hatch, R-Utah, which required all jurors to agree that aggravating circumstances existed. However, Hatch's amendment would not require that all jurors agree on the same aggravating circumstance.

The committee also adopted several technical amendments suggested by the Justice Department. But the panel rejected a department recommendation that the death penalty be eliminated for peacetime espionage.

With the exception of the Thurmond and Hatch amendments and the technical changes, the bill was virtually the same as one reported by the Judiciary Committee in 1979. That measure never reached the full Senate. *(1979 Almanac p. 369; 1980 Almanac p. 395)*

Although S 114 sailed through the Judiciary Committee, it faced an uncertain fate in the full Senate and in the House, where key members of the Judiciary Committee opposed the measure. ∎

Gun Control Legislation

Despite a March 30 attempt on President Reagan's life, gun control legislation went nowhere in 1981.

Numerous measures were introduced during the year, but none reached the floor in either chamber. For years, the powerful National Rifle Association (NRA), a 1.8-million-member interest group, had been able to prevent any significant action on handgun control legislation.

The chairmen of the Senate and House Judiciary committees wasted little time introducing crime-related legislation after the Reagan shooting.

On April 8, Strom Thurmond, R-S.C., chairman of the Senate panel, introduced three bills (S 907, 908, 909) including one which called for the death penalty for first degree murder committed in the District of Columbia. Edward Zorinsky, D-Neb., cosponsored all three bills.

The other two measures required mandatory sentences for crimes committed with a firearm and made it a felony to kill or assault a Cabinet officer.

Thurmond said he remained opposed to a strict handgun ban: "Criminals will get guns; people have got to be allowed to have guns to protect themselves."

But House Judicary Chairman Peter W. Rodino Jr., D-N.J., and Sen. Edward M. Kennedy, D-Mass., introduced identical bills (HR 3200, S 974) April 9 to ban the manufacture, importation, assembly or sale of small handguns known as "Saturday Night Specials."

Police said it was this type of weapon that wounded the president and three others. *(Story, p. 6)*

Reagan Crime Task Force

A special Justice Department task force on violent crime adopted a package of recommendations Aug. 17 that included proposals for somewhat tighter gun controls and for mandatory prison sentences for the use of a firearm to commit a federal felony.

The task force urged changes in existing gun control laws to:
• Require individuals to report the theft or loss of a handgun to their local law enforcement agency.
• Set a waiting period for the purchase of a handgun to allow for a mandatory records check to make sure the purchaser was not in one of the categories of persons proscribed by existing law from owning a gun.
• Ban the importation of parts for handguns.

Rodino-Kennedy Bills

In addition to banning Saturday Night Specials, the Rodino-Kennedy bills would:
• Require a 21-day waiting period for persons seeking to buy guns so the FBI and local police could check the intended buyer's past.

• Prohibit any person from buying more than two handguns annually without approval from the attorney general.
• Prohibit the sale of handguns by pawnbrokers.
• Transfer enforcement of gun control laws from the Treasury to the Justice Department.

Mandatory Sentences

Perhaps the least controversial of the three Thurmond bills was S 909, which would require mandatory prison sentences for felonies committed with a firearm. If a gun were used, a mandatory sentence, which could not be suspended by a judge, would be imposed on top of the punishment for the original offense.

Even this proposal drew opposition from those who believed that such a law deprived judges of their discretion and also did little good. "It doesn't work. We have that in California, and we still shoot 'em up," said Rep. Don Edwards, D-Calif., a member of the House Judiciary panel.

Later in the year, Sen. Arlen Specter, R-Pa., on Oct. 1 introduced an even tougher bill (S 1688) to provide a mandatory life sentence for "career" criminals, defined as anyone convicted a third time for felony burglary or robbery while using a firearm.

Assaults on Cabinet Officers

Another Thurmond measure (S 907) would make it a federal crime to kill, kidnap or assault a Cabinet officer. Under current law, if a Cabinet member was assaulted on non-federal property, the crime was covered by the laws of the state in which the crime occurred.

Sen. Dan Quayle, R-Ind., introduced a bill (S 904) to make it a federal offense to assault or kill presidential or vice presidential staff members carrying out their official duties.

Death Penalty

Thurmond's bill (S 908) requiring the death penalty for first-degree murder in the District of Columbia was sent to the Governmental Affairs subcommittee that handled District matters.

The subcommittee chairman was Charles McC. Mathias Jr., Md., a moderate Republican who voted against a death penalty bill for specified federal crimes when the matter was considered by the Judiciary Committee in the 96th Congress. *(1979 Almanac p. 369)*

Prior to the assassination attempt, Thurmond and Dennis DeConcini, D-Ariz., had introduced legislation (S 114) to re-establish the death penalty for specified federal crimes, such as murder, treason and espionage, regardless of where they were committed. The Judiciary Committee approved that bill June 9. *(Story, p. 419)*

1968 Laws

In 1968, after the assassinations of Martin Luther King and Robert F. Kennedy, Congress passed two laws dealing with gun control. Title Four of the Omnibus Crime Control and Safe Streets Act (PL 90-351) and the Gun Control Act of 1968 (PL 90-618) together banned the importation of handguns, banned specified interstate transactions involving guns, refined licensing provisions for businesses and collectors and set penalties for crimes committed with a gun. *(1968 Almanac pp. 225, 549)*

However, the laws did not specifically ban importing gun parts — a loophole a number of foreign manufacturers discovered almost immediately.

Since then, many proposals to enact tougher laws had been offered. But in the face of a strong lobby led by the NRA, none emerged from a committee.

Nationwide polls going back to 1938 showed that a majority of Americans favored gun control laws. House Speaker Thomas P. O'Neill Jr., D-Mass., however, suggested that the polls might be misleading.

"People tell you one thing in a poll, but in the privacy of a ballot box they're doing another," he said. ▪

Foreign Bribery Statute

The Senate by voice vote Nov. 23 approved a bill (S 708) to ease the law prohibiting U.S. companies from bribing foreign officials.

Similar legislation (HR 2530) was pending in the House Commerce Subcommittee on Finance, which took no action in 1981.

S 708 would limit prosecutions to companies or corporate officials who "knowingly" falsify records or directly order a bribe offer to be made.

Under the Foreign Corrupt Practices Act of 1977 (PL 95-213), corporate officers could be liable if they had "reason to believe" that bribes were being made. Also, they could be punished if loose accounting standards resulted in bribes going undetected. *(1977 Almanac p. 413)*

Under S 708, entitled the Business Accounting and Foreign Trade Simplification Act, companies could keep less strict records than currently mandated by law.

Background

Congress passed the 1977 act after the Securities and Exchange Commission (SEC) uncovered large-scale foreign bribery involving the secret slush funds of more than 400 U.S. corporations. In 1975 and 1976, for instance, the Lockheed Corp. paid more than $106 million in "commissions" to boost its foreign sales. That included a large payment to Prince Bernhard of the Netherlands to influence his recommendation on Dutch fighter plane purchases. *(Background, 1977 Almanac p. 413)*

Softening the act was a goal of the Reagan administration.

The proponents of S 708 (S Rept 97-209) argued that the existing law discouraged exports, especially by small American companies uneasy about the law's strictness.

"We are not reopening the door to corrupt payments," said Sen. John Heinz, R-Pa. "We are eliminating doubts as to what constitutes a corrupt payment and when a corporation is liable."

Heinz and other proponents of the bill said that some payments were, by custom, necessary in foreign lands.

Outlawing such payments for American firms put this nation at a competitive disadvantage overseas, the bill's advocates contended.

Provisions

As passed by the Senate, S 708 would:

● Strike requirements that a company keep detailed books and records, which the SEC used to track payment of bribes. Instead, companies could devise a "system of internal accounting controls." This was designed to relieve companies from expensive and time-consuming record-keeping to satisfy the SEC.

● Limit criminal liability for keeping false records to those who "knowingly" do so. The 1977 law prohibited even inadvertent accounting errors.

● Establish a separate standard for civil liability; companies would not be liable if they tried "in good faith" to keep true records.

● Exempt from penalties those who made good faith efforts, within their firms, to end illegal payment practices. Sponsors reasoned that those without full control of a company could not be held liable for its actions.

● Prohibit any attempt to "direct or authorize, expressly or by course of conduct" a bribe. The "course of conduct" language referred to winks, shrugs and other non-verbal approval of a bribe offer. Under current law, persons or companies could be held liable if they had "reason to believe" that bribes were being paid.

● Exempt from the law a range of gifts or payments to a foreign official that the bill viewed as not corrupting. Gifts, payments, offers or promises of anything of value were legal if they were lawful in the official's country, constituted a courtesy, were a necessary marketing expense (such as travel or lodging for the official) or were needed to satisfy an existing contract.

● Allow "any facilitating or expediting payment" to an official that accelerated a "routine" government action.

● Keep the present penalties for violating the law: a fine of up to $1 million for a corporation, and a fine of up to $10,000 and/or five years in prison for officers, directors, employees or stockholders of the firm.

● Move all enforcement authority to the Justice Department, which currently shared jurisdiction with the SEC, a setup widely viewed as inefficient. The SEC would continue to police a company's books related to overseas payments.

● Order the attorney general to determine, six months after the bill's enactment, if further clarification of the law was needed and authorized him to issue guidelines to clear up ambiguities.

● Require the president to report to Congress, a year after the bill's enactment, on how it was operating.

● Urge the president to negotiate bilateral and multilateral agreements with other nations to establish standards of conduct for international business.

Senate Committee Action

The Senate Banking Committee approved S 708 by an 11-4 vote on Sept. 16 (S Rept 97-209).

The committee brushed aside complaints by some Democrats that the legislation would open loopholes in the law that would spur corrupt payments overseas. Paul S. Sarbanes, D-Md., warned that easing the law could lead to "resuming practices that have enormous consequences in other countries" and make the United States look bad.

Committee Republicans said current law imposed costly reporting requirements on U.S. companies and inhibited their competitiveness because they were fearful of committing inadvertent violations.

'Materiality'

The biggest dispute centered on the strictness of the accounting standards. Originally, the bill mandated that companies report any overseas payment of a "material" nature — that is, of a sizable amount. William Proxmire, D-Wis., and other Democrats objected that the term was imprecise. As a peace gesture to the Democrats, Republi-

cans deleted it after Proxmire failed, 4-10, in an attempt to knock it out of the bill.

By voice vote, the committee then adopted an amendment by Alfonse D'Amato, R-N.Y., to strike the "materiality" standard and to substitute a requirement that companies keep a "system of internal accounting controls." This was a less exacting standard than the existing accounting methods companies had to adhere to, and it left some Democrats unsatisfied.

Also by voice vote, the committee passed a Heinz amendment prohibiting either verbal or non-verbal approval by a corporate officer of a bribe offer.

Senate Floor Action

To mollify Democrats still concerned about the accounting standards, Alfonse D'Amato, R-N.Y., offered a floor amendment Nov. 23 which toughened the standard for civil liability under the law. It required that a company make a "good faith" effort to keep accurate records.

The D'Amato amendment, approved by voice vote, did not affect the standard for criminal prosecution, which remained knowing falsification of company records.

Chafee Amendment

Also adopted by voice vote was an amendment by John H. Chafee, R-R.I., deleting from the committee bill language which prohibited payments to a foreign official who used his own "judgment" on whether they were legal or not. Chafee said it was unfair to expect U.S. business people to determine whether certain types of payments were customary and legal in another country. ∎

Congress Grapples With Immigration Issues

Spurred by growing political pressure from Southern and Western states, President Reagan and Congress in 1981 began grappling with the problem of overhauling the nation's decades-old immigration laws.

The Senate Judiciary Immigration and Refugee Policy Subcommittee and the House Judiciary Immigration, Refugees and International Law Subcommittee in September held lengthy hearings on various aspects of the decades-old statutes.

The most recent changes in immigration law, which involved only a portion of the statutes, came in 1980, with passage of a bill that revised the laws concerning refugees (PL 96-212). *(1980 Almanac p. 378)*

Concern in the 97th Congress focused on ways to halt the steady stream of illegal aliens into the United States. Proposals under consideration included hiring more border guards, imposing sanctions against employers who hire illegal aliens, granting amnesty to some of the estimated 3 million to 6 million illegal aliens already in the country, and giving the president sweeping new powers to deal with immigration "emergencies."

President's Proposal

After weeks of delays, the Reagan administration unveiled the outlines of its immigration reform plan at a July 30 joint hearing of the House and Senate subcommittees.

Although panels in both houses started hearings in September on key elements of the Reagan plan, bills (HR 4832, S 1765) incorporating the proposals were not introduced until Oct. 22.

The administration proposals resulted from the work of a bipartisan Select Commission on Immigration and Refugee Policy and of a special presidential task force appointed to review the commission's findings. The cornerstones of the administration's policy included:

● Stepped-up enforcement of immigration laws to stem the flow of illegal aliens, including interdicting and seizing U.S.-bound vessels carrying prospective illegal aliens.

This was in part a response to the flood of Cubans and Haitians who came to the United States between April and August 1980. *(1980 Almanac p. 429)*

● Sanctions against employers who knowingly hired illegal aliens, including $500-$1,000 fines for each offense. The Justice Department also would be able to seek injunctions against employers with a "pattern or practice" of hiring illegal aliens. These sanctions would cover employers of at least four workers.

● An experimental, two-year worker program for up to 50,000 Mexican workers. The workers would be admitted for stays of 9 to 12 months.

● Granting legal status to some of the 3 million to 6 million illegal aliens currently in the United States, provided they met certain conditions.

● Empowering the president to declare an immigration "emergency" in certain circumstances and granting him broad powers to deal with such situations. These included power to seal any harbor, port, airport or road; to restrict Americans' travel to named countries, forbidding boats, vehicles or aircraft from going within a certain distance of a designated country; and to restrict sharply illegal aliens' access to federal courts.

Attorney General William French Smith said no U.S. immigration policy could be effective unless it acknowledged that millions of illegal aliens were here and their numbers were growing by 250,000 to 500,000 each year.

The Reagan proposal, which would apply to any alien in the United States prior to Jan. 1, 1980, would allow persons who met certain conditions to apply for status as a "renewable term temporary resident." After a total of 10 years of continuous residency, the person would be eligible to apply for permanent resident status if he or she could demonstrate an ability to communicate in English.

The temporary residents would pay Social Security, income and other taxes but would be ineligible for welfare, federally assisted housing, food stamps or unemployment benefits. In addition, they could not bring spouses and children to this country but could leave the United States for visits to their homeland.

Refugee Resettlement

In addition to seeking curbs on illegal immigration, Congress and the administration were grappling with complaints from state and local officials about the admission and resettling of refugees, who had poured into the country legally by the hundreds of thousands since 1978.

The flood of illegal aliens and refugees had produced a backlash in areas compelled to absorb large numbers of them. Local officials and residents had voiced concern

Refugee Admissions

	Actual admissions fiscal 1981*	Authorized admissions fiscal 1982**
Asia	125,000	100,000
Soviet Union	14,300	20,000
Eastern Europe	6,500	9,000
Near East	4,000	5,000
Africa	2,200	3,000
Latin America and the Caribbean	2,000	3,000
Total	**154,000**	**140,000**

Source: Senate Judiciary Committee
**Source: State Department*

about aliens receiving federal and state assistance, competing for jobs in already strained economies and burdening local services such as schools.

Many also resented newcomers who spoke little English and feared that the nation's growing Spanish-speaking minority would eventually force the United States into bilingualism. In Dade County, Fla., for example, voters in 1980 overwhelmingly approved a countywide law substantially restricting the use of Spanish in local affairs.

The Numbers

The 1980 Refugee Act (PL 96-212) required the president, in consultation with Congress, to set the number of refugees to be admitted each fiscal year. *(Refugee Act, 1980 Almanac p. 378)*

On Oct. 10, President Reagan authorized 140,000 refugee admissions for fiscal 1982, a 35.5 percent reduction from the fiscal 1981 level of 217,000.

This quota was separate from — and in addition to — the 270,000 persons who could be granted visas and admitted as immigrants.

It also did not include another group of immigrants who could come to the United States each year in unlimited numbers — the spouses and minor children of American citizens. In fiscal 1980, the latest year for which figures were available, 155,000 such individuals were admitted, according to Sandra Stevens, a special assistant to Doris Meissner, acting commissioner of the Immigration and Naturalization Service (INS).

Overall during fiscal 1980, Stevens said, more than 700,000 aliens legally came to live in the United States, including 126,000 Cubans and Haitians who arrived between April and June.

During fiscal 1979, Stevens said, there were 526,000 legal immigrants.

Immigration Reforms

Once the refugee consultations were completed for the fiscal year 1982, the Senate and House Judiciary committees turned their attention to immigration reforms.

The House on Oct. 13 passed a bill by voice vote (HR 4327 — H Rept 97-264) designed to streamline existing immigration and naturalization procedures. The Senate revised the bill and Congress cleared it on Dec. 16, the final day of the session. *(Story, next page)*

This measure, however, did not deal with the politically delicate but increasingly urgent problem of illegal immigration.

Alan K. Simpson, R-Wyo., chairman of the Senate immigration subcommittee, planned to combine the administration's immigration bill with a revision drafted by his staff. Both Simpson and House subcommittee Chairman Romano L. Mazzoli, D-Ky., hoped to complete action on immigration reforms in the 97th Congress.

Simpson said any reform package should be a "three-legged stool" — improved enforcement of immigration laws at U.S. borders and internally, sanctions on employers for hiring illegal aliens, and the creation of some type of national identity card not susceptible to counterfeiting.

"If we don't do that," he said, "we won't have solved the problem."

The administration's package did not recommend a national identity card. Instead, the administration suggested that proof of eligibility to work in the United States could be provided through documentation issued by the INS or any two of the following: birth certificate, driver's license, Social Security card and Selective Service System registration certificate.

Employer Sanctions

Among the most controversial proposals was the one calling for sanctions against employers who hired illegal aliens, a move designed to eliminate the work incentive that drew people into the United States.

In Senate testimony Sept. 30, Acting INS Commissioner Meissner contended that "efforts to deter entry of illegal aliens without elimination of the 'pull' effect of high wages [in the United States] is only of minimum value. The border cannot be sealed. Efforts to apprehend and deport aliens in the interior are costly and, at best, partially effective. The only credible enforcement measure remaining is a prohibition on hiring illegal aliens."

Sen. Edward M. Kennedy, Mass., the ranking Democrat on the subcommittee, disagreed, contending that "a more appropriate step" than employer sanctions would be more intensive enforcement of minimum wage, Social Security and labor standards laws.

Hispanic Opposition

Hispanic groups such as the Mexican-American Legal Defense and Education Fund (MALDEF) found little to cheer in the proposals before Congress.

Antonia Hernandez, head of MALDEF's Washington office, said the proposals reflected a hostility in the United States to the Hispanic community in general.

She called the administration's package a "simplistic approach that will not solve the problems and will disproportionately discriminate against Hispanic Americans."

Refugee Admissions

In setting the refugee admissions for fiscal 1982 at 140,000, the administration reduced its initial proposal.

In Senate testimony in September, Attorney General Smith recommended that 173,000 refugees should be admitted in fiscal 1982.

Smith said the largest group — more than 100,000 — would come from Indochina, a number the administration intended to reduce in the future by working with other countries on "humane deterrence" to discourage people from leaving their homelands.

In response to Smith's proposal, both Judiciary com-

mittees recommended lower totals. The Senate panel said only 125,000 refugees should be admitted, noting that actual admissions in fiscal 1981 were 154,000 — well below the 217,000 authorized. The House panel recommended a limit of 140,000 refugees.

The Senate committee observed in its letter that the United States was assuming a new role in the world concerning refugees. Instead of absorbing refugees from countries of "first asylum" — those that accepted refugees directly from their homelands — the United States was itself becoming a country of first asylum.

The panel cited several factors leading to this new role, including government upheaval in Nicaragua, the Cuban "boat-lift" of 1980 and the "continuing flow of Haitians and Salvadoreans" seeking asylum here.

Unlike Indochinese refugees, who were screened by U.S. officials prior to coming to this country, Haitians and others currently seeking asylum entered the United States directly and had to be screened here to ascertain whether they qualified as "refugees" under U.S. law.

The committee said the number of asylum petitions had risen dramatically since 1971, when there were 440 applications. In 1979, the total reached 5,800 and by the fall of 1981, there already were 95,000.

INS estimated that another 50,000 petitions would be filed in 1982, and by the fall of 1982, the Senate letter said, there could be some 145,000 pending applications for asylum from persons already on U.S. soil.

Who Is a 'Refugee'?

Under the 1980 refugee act, a refugee was defined as a person who was outside his or her country and was unable or unwilling to return "because of persecution or a well-founded fear of persecution" based on race, religion, nationality or political views.

The Reagan administration stressed that under existing law, persons who left home solely for economic betterment were not "refugees."

Smith said refugee applications should be analyzed individually. He said the administration would not establish any kind of "presumptive refugee" status for groups of people.

The administration contended that Haitians who left their country by the thousands were not "refugees" under U.S. law, but rather were seeking economic betterment here.

Beginning in July, Haitians who arrived in the United States were sent to detention centers and prisons to await possible deportation. By mid-October, some 2,700 Haitians were in detention, according to Stevens of the INS.

On Sept. 29, Reagan issued an executive order giving U.S. ships the authority to interdict vessels carrying "undocumented aliens" into the United States.

The policy of detaining Haitians stirred political controversy. Lawyers representing the Haitians contended the government was singling them out for harsh treatment while dealing more leniently with the Cubans who surged into the country in 1980.

Resettlement Issues

One of the most controversial aspects of the refugee issue was resettlement. Under the law, resettlement was a federal responsiblity, with the government providing reimbursement to the states for the first three years a refugee was in the United States.

According to a 1981 report by the Office of Refugee

Resettlement in the Health and Human Services Department (HHS), 67 percent of the refugees studied were receiving some type of federal assistance.

Oliver Cromwell, director of public affairs for the HHS resettlement office, said the refugees surveyed were in nine states with high refugee populations and had been in the United States less than three years.

State officials were critical of the resettlement program. In testimony Sept. 22-23 before Senate and House Judiciary panels, Florida Gov. Robert Graham, a Democrat, minced no words on the subject.

"Refugees are a federal responsibility and if Congress cannot or will not provide sufficient funding to meet the basic needs of refugees, then the number being admitted must be decreased," said Graham, chairman of the National Governors' Association Committee on International Trade and Foreign Relations.

"You cannot expect states or their localities, especially in this time of major cuts in other federal domestic assistance programs, to assume any more of the fiscal burden for refugees than we already carry," he said.

Cromwell of the HHS office contended that most resettlement efforts were working smoothly. He said that Florida was an exceptional case because of the unexpected 1980 influx of Cubans and Haitians.

Carol Hecklinger, the State Department's assistant coordinator for domestic refugee programs, conceded there was room for criticism in refugee resettlement.

"People will tell you that domestic resettlement is a patchwork, and indeed it is. There are so many different actors involved," she said, and named nearly a dozen government agencies and private organizations involved in refugee resettlement.

"To some degree we pride ourselves on that, but on the other hand we recognize some of the problems that causes," she added. ∎

Immigration Law Revisions

A bill (HR 4327 — PL 97-116) to make operations of the Immigration and Naturalization Service (INS) more efficient and less costly was cleared Dec. 16, the final day of the first session of the 97th Congress.

Final action came when the House accepted revisions the Senate had made to the bill earlier that day. The House had originally passed HR 4327 by voice vote Oct. 13.

Rep. Romano L. Mazzoli, D-Ky., chairman of Judiciary's Immigration, Refugees and International Law Subcommittee, told the House that reforms in the measure could save "several millions of dollars over the next few years."

The bill (HR 4327 — H Rept 97-264) eliminated a requirement of existing law that permanent resident aliens register each year with the INS.

In the future, such aliens would have to notify the INS only of address changes. Mazzoli said the Congressional Budget Office estimated this would save $800,000 annually.

Mazzoli estimated that a provision eliminating the requirement for two witnesses for naturalization proceedings would save another $1 million annually.

In an effort to reduce the flood of private immigration bills in Congress each year, the measure granted permanent resident status to foreign medical school graduates who had been practicing in this country for several years.

Provisions

As cleared, HR 4327:

• Eliminated a requirement that permanent resident aliens register each year with the INS, but gave the attorney general discretion to order registration of any immigrant or non-immigrant.

• Waived certain proficiency examination requirements for foreign medical graduates fully licensed and practicing in this country on or before Jan. 9, 1978, and extended the time an alien could reside in the United States to study medicine.

• Exempted from numerical limits on immigration certain aliens who made investments in the United States before 1978.

• Authorized the attorney general to waive the exclusion of an alien spouse, parent or child of a U.S. citizen for simple possession of marijuana if such exclusion would result in extreme hardship and permitting entry would not be contrary to the national welfare.

• Eliminated adultery and conviction for possession of no more than 30 grams of marijuana as absolute bars to a finding of "good moral character, " which was necessary for

an alien to become a naturalized U.S. citizen.

• Permitted aliens who were denied entry to the U.S. to be deported to a country other than the one from which they came.

• Limited the current non-immigrant student visa to students in academic institutions and language training programs.

• Created a new non-immigrant classification for students in non-academic and vocational schools. This provision was designed to give INS better control over the abuse and misuse of student visas.

• Eliminated certain requirements in naturalization proceedings, including the need for two witnesses for a naturalization.

• Allowed state courts with jurisdiction to naturalize citizens to retain up to $20,000 in naturalization fees rather than the current $3,000.

• Permitted the INS to recoup funds used to purchase evidence for court cases when such funds were later recovered.

• Repealed certain requirements for reports to Congress by the INS. ∎

Anti-Abortion Measures Begin to Advance

Measures designed to overturn the 1973 Supreme Court decision legalizing abortion moved through the initial phases of the legislative process in 1981.

Two Senate Judiciary Committee subcommittees approved anti-abortion legislation (S 158, S J Res 110), but the full committee did not act on either measure in 1981.

It was the first time that measures designed to overturn the Supreme Court's 1973 *Roe v. Wade* decision legalizing abortion had emerged from a subcommittee in either the Senate or the House.

No action on anti-abortion legislation occurred in the House Judiciary Committee in 1981.

The measures approved by the two Senate Judiciary subcommittees differed significantly in their approach to the abortion issue.

S 158, approved July 9 by the Separation of Powers Subcommittee, declared that human life began at conception and would allow states to enact anti-abortion laws. It also would prevent lower federal courts from striking down any new anti-abortion statutes enacted by the states.

S J Res 110 declared that no right to abortion was secured by the Constitution and would give the states and Congress joint authority to restrict abortion. In a conflict between state and federal law, the more restrictive of the two would govern.

Background

The drive for congressional action to ban abortion began only days after the 1973 Supreme Court decision in *Roe v. Wade*, which struck down state laws banning the procedure. *(CQ Guide to the U.S. Supreme Court p. 645)*

In every Congress since then, some members had tried to overturn the ruling by passing a constitutional amendment to outlaw abortion. All such efforts had failed.

Congress, however, had on numerous occasions restricted federal funding available to the poor for abortions to instances involving rape, incest and danger to the mother's life. The same was true in 1981. *(1980 Almanac p. 467; 1981 action, p. 331)*

The 'Human Life' Bill

Frustrated in efforts to push through Congress a constitutional amendment banning abortion, some "pro-life" forces came up with new tactics in 1981 in their continuing battle to overturn the 1973 Supreme Court decision legalizing abortion.

Sen. Jesse Helms, R-N.C., and Rep. Henry J. Hyde, R-Ill., introduced identical bills (S 158, HR 900) they said would lead to a ban on abortion without a constitutional amendment.

Both bills declared that human life begins at conception and that under the 14th Amendment to the Constitution, states can act to protect unborn fetuses.

The bills also barred federal district and appeals courts from hearing cases that challenged any new state abortion statutes.

Unlike a constitutional amendment — which must be approved by a two-thirds vote of the House and Senate and then ratified by 38 state legislatures — a bill needs only a simple majority of each chamber and the president's signature to become law. *(Amending the Constitution, CQ Guide to Congress 2nd. ed., p. 217)*

In trying a new legislative tactic to ban abortion, Helms and Hyde turned to the private sector for technical aid. The major architect of their bill was Stephen H. Galebach, an attorney from the Washington law firm of Covington & Burling.

Galebach said Congress could step into a void left by *Roe v. Wade* because the Supreme Court, in arriving at its ruling, did not decide when human life began. As a result, he said, there was no way to show that the 14th Amendment "logically extends to unborn children." The 14th Amendment prohibited states from depriving a "person" of life without due process of law.

Anti-abortion leaders expected many states would prohibit abortions if the bill became law, because virtually all had outlawed abortion prior to the 1973 *Roe* ruling.

If Congress passed some type of anti-abortion legislation, the matter almost certainly would end up back at the Supreme Court. A second ruling was unlikely to be any easier for the court to decide than the first.

In *Roe v. Wade*, Justice Harry A. Blackmun, who wrote the decision, conceded as much: "We forthwith acknowledge our awareness of the sensitive and emotional nature of the abortion controversy, of the vigorous opposing views, even among physicians, and of the deep and seemingly absolute convictions that the subject inspires.

"One's philosophy, one's experiences, one's exposure to the raw edges of human existence, one's religious training, one's attitudes toward life and family and their values, and the moral standards one establishes and seeks to observe, are all likely to influence and to color one's thinking and conclusions about abortion."

Constitutional Amendments

Although constitutional amendments are difficult to pass, numerous proposals to ban abortion were introduced in 1981. Many of these "human life amendments" were identical, and most fell into two categories.

In the first were amendments that would prohibit all abortions; in the second, those that would allow abortion if needed to save the mother's life.

The chief sponsors of the no-exception amendment (S J Res 19, H J Res 104) were Helms and Rep. Robert K. Dornan, R-Calif. The chief sponsors of the second type of amendment (S J Res 17, H J Res 125) were Sen. Jake Garn, R-Utah, and Rep. James L. Oberstar, D-Minn.

In September, Sen. Orrin Hatch, R-Utah, introduced yet another type of amendment — one that was procedural, rather than substantive in its approach. And it was this proposal, S J Res 110, that won approval Dec. 16 from the Constitution Subcommittee, which Hatch chaired.

The measure gave Congress and the states joint authority to enact legislation to restrict or prohibit abortion, with the more restrictive law to prevail.

Senate Committee Action

S 158: The Helms Bill

The Senate Judiciary Separation of Powers Subcommittee headed by John P. East, R-N.C., held eight days of hearings on S 158 before approving the measure by a 3-2 vote July 9.

The subcommittee agreed to a request by Hatch for a delay in full committee action on S 158 until Hatch's Constitution Subcommittee could act on proposals for a constitutional amendment on the abortion issue.

The East hearings were marked by repeated clashes among medical and legal experts in sharp disagreement about the bill's factual basis, legality and wisdom.

The North Carolina Republican originally planned only brief and limited hearings focused on the medical question of when life begins. But criticism from Hatch and from Max Baucus, D-Mont., ranking Democrat on East's subcommittee — along with vehement protests from outside groups — forced East to revise his plans and accept testimony on broader issues, including the constitutionality of S 158.

Protesters Convicted

Six women arrested April 23 for causing a disturbance during Senate hearings on an anti-abortion bill (S 158) were convicted Sept. 29 by a Washington, D.C. Superior Court jury and were fined $100 each.

They were the first individuals arrested and convicted for disrupting a congressional hearing since Capitol police record-keeping on such incidents began in 1973.

While there have been arrests and convictions for disturbances on the Capitol grounds, these generally stemmed from outbursts in the House and Senate galleries, according to testimony at a July 6 hearing on a motion to dismiss the charges against the six women.

Defense lawyers claimed their clients were being singled out for prosecution by Sen. John P. East, R-N.C., chairman of the Judiciary subcommittee that conducted the hearings, because of their opposition to S 158 and to East's anti-abortion views.

The attorneys contended the defendants should be compared with other people who had caused disturbances in hearings but were not prosecuted.

Judge Harriet Taylor disagreed, and denied the motion to dismiss the charges. In determining whether there had been discrimination against the women, she said, she considered all those arrested at the Capitol, whether in hearing rooms or in the galleries.

The six defendants, who then went to trial and were convicted, were Karen Zimmerman, Stephanie Roth, Sarah Schulman, Maureen Angelos and Elizabeth Smith, all of New York City, and Tacie Dejanikus, of Washington.

Six former attorneys general said in a letter to Baucus that they considered the bill unconstitutional. Twelve constitutional law specialists of differing political philosophies sent a similar letter to Baucus.

On the other side, John T. Noonan Jr., a law professor at the University of California, Berkeley, contended that S 158 was constitutional and necessary because of biased federal judges. And Galebach, chief author of the proposal, testified that state courts were a proper forum for ruling on new state anti-abortion laws. He said they should be free to operate "without interference" from the federal courts.

The 3-2 subcommittee vote July 9 split along party lines, with Republicans East, Hatch, and Jeremiah Denton, Ala., voting for the measure. Democrats Baucus and Howell Heflin, Ala., voted against it.

Baucus offered an amendment during the markup to delete the ban in S 158 on review by lower federal courts of any state law that might be passed banning abortions, but it was rejected 3-2.

Hatch acknowledged that he had serious reservations about the bill, particularly about the scope of congressional power under the 14th Amendment. But Hatch said he believed the full committee should be allowed to debate the measure.

S J Res 110: The Hatch Proposal

One hour after hearings ended Dec. 16, the Senate Judiciary Constitution approved S J Res 110 by a 4-0 vote, after a markup session that lasted only 15 minutes. Patrick

J. Leahy, D-Vt., who objected to acting so soon after the hearings, did not vote.

In a sharp statement, Leahy said, "I think the precedent the subcommittee sets today does material harm to the tradition of public participation in the lawmaking process." He said the quick action was tantamount to telling the public that senators felt free to ignore testimony.

Orrin G. Hatch, R-Utah, sponsor of the amendment, disagreed. Hatch said there would be ample time to go over the hearing record before full committee markup in 1982.

S J Res 110 surfaced in September as an alternative to S 158 and more restrictive proposed constitutional amendments.

Reaction among anti-abortion groups was mixed at first, but support for the amendment grew in October and November. At hearings Nov. 4, the National Conference of Catholic Bishops endorsed the Hatch proposal as the only one with a realistic chance of passing. In the past, the conference, like most other anti-abortion groups, had backed proposals that would ban abortion outright.

The National Right to Life Committee and the National Pro-Life Political Action Committee also had backed the amendment.

However, other anti-abortion groups opposed the proposal, including the March for Life, a Washington organization operated from the Capitol Hill home of its founder, Nellie Gray, and the Life Amendment Political Action Committee, headed by Paul Brown.

Brown labeled the Hatch proposal "the Catholic bishops' amendment" and called it "nothing short of a sellout of the principles that have motivated the pro-life movement from its very beginning."

Also opposing the amendment were groups that traditionally had taken a pro-choice stand, including the National Abortion Rights Action League, the National Women's Political Caucus, the National Organization for Women, the American Association of University Women and the Religious Coalition for Abortion Rights.

House Committee

Because of the makeup of the House Judiciary Committee, which included Democrats and Republicans opposed to anti-abortion legislation, supporters of HR 900 faced a tougher time moving a bill there.

Early in the year, Hyde said he might circulate a discharge petition to pull the bill from the committee, but he never followed through on the threat.

Under the discharge procedure, a member could file a petition to bring a bill to the floor any time after the bill had been before a legislative committee for 30 days. When 218 members, a majority of the House, had signed the petition, it was put on the Discharge Calendar, where it had to remain for seven legislative days before it could be called up for action.

This seven-day period was intended to allow the committee to act on the bill before a motion to discharge the committee was considered. If the motion to discharge was agreed to by a simple majority, the legislation was considered on the House floor without need for committee action. *(Discharge petition background, CQ Guide to Congress 2nd ed., p. 347)*

Rep. Don Edwards, D-Calif., chairman of the Civil and Constitutional Rights Subcommittee, said he felt no pressure to move on the abortion issue, adding that if members showed an interest in abortion legislation, he would consider holding "serious" hearings on the issue. ∎

Balanced Budget Proposal

Six years after it began, the drive for a constitutional convention on an amendment requiring a balanced federal budget remained four states short of the number needed.

The Senate Judiciary Committee on May 19 approved and July 10 reported a proposed constitutional amendment (S J Res 58 — S Rept 97-151) requiring a balanced budget except in time of war. But the measure moved no further during the first session of the 97th Congress.

The Senate committee vote was 11-5 in favor of the amendment. The panel killed a similar proposal by an 8-9 vote in 1980. *(1980 Almanac p. 304)*

Provisions

As approved by the committee, S J Res 58:
● Required Congress to balance the federal budget each fiscal year except in time of war.
● Allowed budget outlays to exceed receipts for any fiscal year if three-fifths of Congress approved.
● Prohibited federal receipts in any year from increasing at a rate higher than the rate of increase in national income in the previous calendar year. A majority of Congress could vote to allow additional receipts for any one year.

Background

According to the Senate Judiciary Subcommittee on the Constitution, 30 states had passed resolutions by the end of 1981 asking Congress to call a constitutional convention on a balanced budget amendment. Under Article V of the Constitution, two-thirds of the states, or 34, must ask for a convention before Congress is required to call one.

Amendments to the Constitution can also be initiated in Congress, where they must be approved by two-thirds of each house.

An amendment proposed by either procedure then must be approved by three-fourths (38) of the states. None of the 26 amendments adopted so far was added by the convention method. *(CQ Guide to Congress, 2d Ed., p. 217)*

On May 7, the Senate Judiciary Constitution Subcommittee approved S J Res 58. Sponsored by Judiciary Chairman Strom Thurmond, R-S.C., and subcommittee chairman Orrin G. Hatch, R-Utah, the amendment would require a balanced federal budget two years after ratification by the states, except in times of war.

In the House, hearings on a companion measure, H J Res 2, were held in the Judiciary Subcommittee on Monopolies and Commercial Law. However, no markup was undertaken.

Procedural Problems

Although 30 states had passed some type of resolution calling for a convention, many procedural questions remained unanswered.

In 1971 and 1973 the Senate passed bills to establish procedures for calling a convention. But the House took no action in either year. *(1971 Almanac p. 758)*

In 1981, Sens. Orrin G. Hatch, R-Utah, and Dennis DeConcini, D-Ariz., sponsored a bill (S 817) which, like the 1971 and 1973 bills, would establish procedures for calling a constitutional convention. *(Story, p. 435)* ∎

Justice Dept. Authorization

For the second time in three months, the Senate Dec. 10 broke a filibuster against a rider to the Justice Department's fiscal 1982 authorization that would curb court-ordered busing for racial balance.

But the bill (S 951) was still pending as the session ended Dec. 16, with foes of the anti-busing proposal threatening to employ further delaying tactics to prevent its passage.

The House passed its own version (HR 3462) of the authorization June 9 after adopting a different anti-busing rider.

The Justice Department ended the year operating under a temporary authorization (PL 97-76) that was to expire in February 1982. *(Story, next page)*

It was the second year in a row that the department's regular authorization became mired down, requiring enactment of a stopgap measure. *(1980 Almanac, p. 396)*

In the Dec. 10 cloture vote, senators voted 64-35 to limit debate on a proposal by Jesse Helms, R-N.C., to prevent the Justice Department from bringing any legal action that could lead, directly or indirectly, to court-ordered busing. A vote of 60 was needed to invoke cloture. *(Vote 454, p. 74-S)*

The Helms proposal included language added by J. Bennett Johnston, D-La., that would bar courts from ordering busing except in narrowly defined circumstances and that could lead to the overturning of existing busing orders.

Lowell P. Weicker Jr., R-Conn., began a filibuster of the anti-busing riders in June. On Sept. 16, the Senate adopted the Johnston part of the amendment on a 60-39 vote after invoking cloture by a 61-36 margin, one vote more than the 60 needed to limit debate. *(Votes 255, 254, p. 44-S)*

Two anti-busing bills (S 1647, S 1760) were approved in November by the Senate Judiciary's Separation of Powers Subcommittee and its Constitution Subcommittee. *(Story, p. 430)*

Senate Committee Action

As reported May 15 by the Senate Judiciary Committee (S Rept 97-94), S 951 reauthorized Justice Department programs for fiscal 1982 at a funding level of $2.397 billion.

The administration had proposed $2.348 billion for Justice Department programs. However, its request included $61 million for the Office of Justice Assistance, Research and Statistics (OJARS), which was not included in the Senate bill.

OJARS, authorized under separate legislation (PL 96-157), oversees the Bureau of Justice Statistics and the National Institute of Justice, which do research and statistical work for the department. *(1979 Almanac p. 370)*

The GOP-dominated Senate panel rebuffed President Reagan's plan to lump juvenile justice programs into block grants to the states. The Senate bill earmarked $70 million for the Office of Juvenile Justice and Delinquency Prevention.

The juvenile justice office was reauthorized for four years in 1980 under separate legislation (PL 96-509). The 1980 reauthorization permitted $200 million funding annually, although the office in fiscal 1981 operated under a $100 million appropriation. *(1980 Almanac p. 402)*

Through an amendment proposed by Sen. Arlen Specter, R-Pa., the committee reduced the fiscal 1982 authorization under PL 96-509 to $70 million.

House Committee Action

The House Judiciary Committee approved its version of the Justice Department authorization (HR 3462 — H Rept 97-105) on May 13. Ironically, it was leaner than the measure approved by the Republican-led Senate committee.

Furthermore, while the Senate panel rejected Reagan's plan to lump juvenile justice programs into block grants to the states, the House committee remained silent on the subject.

HR 3462 authorized $2.326 billion for Justice Department programs, down from both the Senate bill (S 951), which authorized $2.397 billion, and the $2.348 billion requested by the administration.

Committee Bills and Reagan Request

Following are comparisons of some of the major provisions of the House and Senate bills and the administration proposal.

FBI. The administration and House proposals called for $739 million for the FBI, while the Senate bill gave the FBI $745.1 million. The extra $6.1 million was for foreign counterintelligence and anti-terrorism activities.

U.S. Attorneys and Marshals. The House bill called for $299.56 million for these federal employees while the Senate bill provided $292.59 million. The administration proposal was $291.21 million. The House bill added funds to allow marshals to serve civil court papers, while the Senate bill included money for 65 additional criminal litigators.

Immigration and Naturalization Service (INS). The House bill provided $388.60 million for INS and the Senate bill provided $376.68 million. The administration proposal called for $363.38 million. The House addition of $25.2 million provided for 200 additional inspectors, 160 more border patrol employees, 403 more investigators, 200 adjudicators to handle immigration petitions, 10 additional overseas employees and funds to continue work on tracking illegal aliens in the United States.

The Senate addition of $13.3 million provided for 160 more border patrols and 200 more adjudicators.

Drug Enforcement Administration (DEA). The House bill authorized $231.78 million and the Senate bill $234.44 million, compared to the administration proposal of $228.52 million. Both bills added money for state and local task forces to crack down on drug crimes.

General Administration. The House and administration proposals authorized $37.65 million for general administration in the department, while the Senate figure was $50.23 million. The additional $12.58 million was for state and local law enforcement grants.

House Floor Action

The House passed HR 3462 on June 9 by a vote of 353-42 after adopting an anti-busing rider. *(Vote 63, p. 32-H)*

The bill authorized a total of $2.326 billion for the Justice Department in fiscal 1982, $22 million less than the $2.348 billion requested by the administration.

The vote on the anti-busing amendment offered by

Rep. James M. Collins, R-Texas, was 265-122, a better than 2-1 margin. *(Vote 62, p. 30-H)*

The amendment prohibited the expenditure of funds authorized under the bill for "any sort of action to require directly or indirectly" busing beyond the school nearest a pupil's home. An exception was provided for students needing special education because of a physical or mental handicap.

The amendment would not prohibit a private party from bringing a desegregation lawsuit that could lead to court-ordered busing.

The vote marked the fourth time Collins has succeeded in adding an anti-busing rider to Justice Department legislation.

He began his Justice Department anti-busing efforts in 1978, when the House adopted his amendment to the department's fiscal 1979 authorization. The Senate rejected a similar amendment and the provision was dropped in conference. In 1979, Collins attached an anti-busing rider to the State, Justice, Commerce fiscal 1980 appropriations bill. Again, the Senate rejected a similar provision, and the rider was dropped in conference. *(1978 Almanac p. 182; 1979 Almanac p. 202)*

Collins almost prevailed in 1980, when both the House and Senate adopted anti-busing riders to the State, Justice, Commerce fiscal 1981 appropriations bill. However, President Carter vetoed the measure. *(1980 Almanac p. 210)*

Attorney General William French Smith said he opposed busing as a method of desegregating schools.

In the past, however, the Justice Department played a central role in school cases. Government statistics available in late 1980 showed the department had been responsible for court-ordered desegregation in 544 of the 711 school districts under such orders. Most such court orders required busing.

The debate on the Collins amendment June 9 was brief by comparison to earlier years, largely because there were no new arguments. Collins contended that support for "an end to forced busing has been accelerating" and said Congress "must heed the American people's outcries, and once and for all end this costly and counterproductive forced school busing. . . ."

Peter W. Rodino Jr., D-N.J., Judiciary Committee chairman, and Don Edwards, D-Calif., chairman of the Civil and Constitutional Rights Subcommittee, spoke against the amendment. Both said it would interfere with the Justice Department's ability to meet its responsibility to seek remedies for violations of constitutional rights.

Provisions

As passed by the House, HR 3462 included the following authorizations:

● General department administration, $37.65 million.
● General legal activities, $127.14 million.
● Antitrust division, $49.57 million.
● The FBI, $739.01 million. This was $6.1 million more than the administration asked. The added funds were for foreign counterintelligence and anti-terrorism activities.
● Immigration and Naturalization Service (INS), $388.6 million, which was $25.2 million above the administration request. The additional money was for 160 more border patrol employees, 403 more investigators, 200 adjudicators to handle immigration petitions, 10 additional overseas employees and funds to continue work on tracking illegal aliens.

Senate Floor Action

The Busing Amendment

After a three-month struggle, senators opposed to court-ordered busing succeeded Sept. 16 in attaching an amendment to S 951 to curb busing for racial balance.

The Johnston amendment, which would prevent federal courts from ordering school busing to desegregate schools, was the most far-reaching anti-busing legislation ever passed by either chamber.

The Johnston proposal amended another anti-busing rider offered by Helms to prevent the Justice Department from spending funds for legal actions that could lead, directly or indirectly, to court-ordered busing.

The Johnston amendment was much more extensive than the Helms proposal, however. It would prevent federal courts from ordering a student bused to any school other than the one nearest the student's home, and it would allow the attorney general to file lawsuits on behalf of students who believed they had been subjected to court-ordered busing in violation of this restriction. It could thus result in the overturning of existing busing programs.

The Cloture Votes

The Johnston proposal was adopted after the Senate voted 61-36 to cut off the filibuster Weicker had launched June 16. A vote of 60 was needed to invoke cloture and limit debate on the amendment. *(Vote 254, p. 44-S)*

The cloture vote Sept. 16 was the fifth since Weicker started his filibuster.

The earlier cloture attempts, and the vote by which each failed, were:

● July 10, by 38-48. *(Vote 184, p. 34-S)*
● July 13, by 54-32. *(Vote 185, p. 34-S)*
● July 29, by 59-37. *(Vote 240, p. 41-S)*
● Sept. 10, by 57-33. *(Vote 249, p. 43-S)*

Soon after floor debate began on S 951, the Senate June 19 voted 30-45 against a Weicker proposal aimed at weakening the Helms anti-busing amendment. *(Vote 159, p. 30-S)*

Weicker sought to add language ensuring that the department and any federal court could act to enforce citizens' constitutional rights.

Hatfield took time during debate July 9 to voice concern "that some of us may have lost both our sense of perspective and sense of history.

"To attempt to limit the independence of the federal judiciary as is contemplated in this amendment is not an insignificant matter; yet many in this august body appear to be deaf to the implications of this proposal," he said. ∎

Temporary DOJ Authority

With the Justice Department's regular fiscal 1982 authorization bill snagged in a Senate anti-busing filibuster, Congress for the second year in a row kept the department operating with a temporary extension of an old authorization.

The Senate Oct. 30 cleared for the president a bill (HR 4608) to extend the Justice Department's fiscal 1980 authorization for four months, from Sept. 30, 1981, until Feb. 1, 1982.

President Reagan signed the measure into law (PL 97-76) on Nov. 5.

The House Oct. 27 had amended HR 4608 to provide the four-month extension. As originally passed by the House Sept. 29, the bill extended the department's authorization for six months. The original Senate version, which was passed Sept. 30, provided only a 30-day extension.

Congress never approved a fiscal 1981 authorization for the Justice Department, instead clearing a bill (S 840 — PL 97-7) April 8 that continued the department's authorization from April 6 to Sept. 30. That bill was necessary because the 96th Congress, after failing to complete action on the fiscal 1981 authorization, passed a temporary 180-day authorization Sept. 30, 1980. *(1980 Almanac, p. 396)*

Without the extension, certain types of authority essential to the department's work would have expired. Included, for example, was authority for the FBI to conduct undercover operations, to purchase firearms and ammunitions, and to protect the president and attorney general. ∎

Anti-Busing Bills Advance

Two Senate Judiciary Committee subcommittees approved separate anti-busing bills (S 1760, S 1647) in 1981, but the full committee did not act on the measures before adjournment.

The Constitution Subcommittee Nov. 3 approved a bill (S 1760) sponsored by Chairman Orrin G. Hatch, R-Utah, to prevent federal courts from ordering busing for racial balance. The vote was 4-1.

Joining Hatch in supporting the measure were Strom Thurmond, R-S.C., chairman of the full committee; Charles E. Grassley, R-Iowa, and Dennis DeConcini, D-Ariz. Patrick J. Leahy, D-Vt., voted against the bill.

No hearings were held specifically on S 1760, which Hatch described as the "culmination" of five days of hearings on the subject of school busing. The bill was introduced Oct. 21, just 12 days before subcommittee approval.

On Nov. 16, the Separation of Powers Subcommittee approved a similar bill (S 1647) sponsored by Chairman John P. East, R-N.C. The vote was 3-1.

S 1647 went beyond the Hatch bill. In addition to prohibiting courts from ordering busing, the bill also would prohibit a judge from ordering school closings or the transfer of teachers as a means to desegregate.

The two bills were the first such measures to win approval from congressional subcommittees, although since 1975 anti-busing riders had been attached on the House or Senate floor to spending bills for various departments.

The Hatch Proposal: S 1760

Hatch stressed that S 1760 would not bar federal courts from hearing school discrimination suits. It just would prohibit busing on the basis of race as a remedy.

Remedies still available after a judge finds "unconstitutional segregation" would be:
● Court orders suspending implementation of racially discriminatory laws or other racially discriminatory government action.
● Contempt-of-court proceedings when the court orders were not "scrupulously obeyed."
● Voluntary programs that allowed students to transfer to any school within their school district.

● Advance planning in construction of new facilities to provide non-discriminatory education within students' neighborhoods.

Any school district could have an existing court busing order reopened and vacated unless a reviewing judge found:
● The acts prompting the original order were committed intentionally, specifically caused discrimination and would continue to do so in the absence of the order.
● The totality of circumstances had not changed since the original order was issued.
● No other remedy would preclude "intentional and specific" segregation.
● The economic, social and educational benefits of the order had outweighed the corresponding costs.

The East Bill: S 1647

One version of S 1647 would have dissolved automatically all existing court busing orders. However, the measure adopted by the subcommittee contained a slightly different provision.

As approved, the bill would allow any state or local "educational agency" affected by a court decree ordering busing, school closings or teacher transfers to seek the dissolution of the order in a federal district court.

The bill stated that within one year of receiving such an application, the court "shall dissolve" the order in question.

During discussion of S 1647, Hatch expressed serious doubts about the constitutionality of this dissolution provision.

He said the provision appeared to give the reviewing judge no discretion in looking at the existing desegregration order but simply ordered the judge to dissolve it upon request. Hatch said that amounted to Congress dictating the outcome of a court case.

The senator added that despite his concerns, he voted for the bill so that the full committee would have both options to consider. The third affirmative vote was cast by Jeremiah Denton, R-Ala., while Max Baucus, D-Mont., voted against S 1647. Howell Heflin, D-Ala., was not at the committee meeting.

Other Anti-Busing Proposals

The Hatch and East bills were not the only anti-busing vehicles in the Senate. On Oct. 15 Jesse Helms, R-N.C., introduced a bill (S 1743) that was almost identical to the East proposal. That measure was on the Senate calendar at year's end.

In addition, J. Bennett Johnston, D-La., successfully attached a provision to the Justice Department authorization (S 951) that would prevent federal courts from ordering a student bused to any school other than the one nearest the student's home. *(Story, p. 428)*

No House Action

No separate anti-busing bill moved in the House.

However, a Judiciary subcommittee was holding hearings on the subject — in part to discourage support for a petition that Rep. Ronald M. Mottl, D-Ohio, was circulating in an effort to discharge the Judiciary Committee from considering a proposed anti-busing amendment to the Constitution.

In addition, the full House attached anti-busing language as a rider to the House version of the fiscal 1982 Justice Department authorization (HR 3462), a measure that had not cleared Congress at year's end. ∎

New Federal Appeals Court

Both the House and Senate passed bills (HR 4482, S 1700) to create a new federal appeals court primarily to handle patent cases, but the legislation did not clear Congress in 1981.

The House and Senate passed similar bills in the 96th Congress, but could not agree on a final product before adjournment. *(1979 Almanac p. 400; 1980 Almanac p. 404)*

The House Nov. 18 suspended the rules and passed HR 4482.

HR 4482 was approved Oct. 14 and reported Nov. 4 by the House Judiciary Committee (H Rept 97-312).

The Senate passed S 1700 Dec. 8 by an 83-6 margin. *(Vote 448, p. 73-S)*

The Senate Judiciary Committee approved the bill Oct. 20 by voice vote and reported it Nov. 18 (S Rept 97-275).

Court Provisions

Under both measures, the U. S. Court of Appeals for the Federal Circuit would be formed by merging the appellate division of the current U.S. Court of Claims with the U.S. Court of Customs and Patent Appeals.

Although the new appeals court would be on the same footing as the existing 12 appeals courts, it would differ in its jurisdiction. Where the 12 circuit courts hear cases by region, the new appellate court would take cases by subject matter from all over the country.

The court would hear appeals of cases involving specified suits against the government, appeals from Patent and Trademark Office decisions and from federal district court decisions involving patent and trademark matters.

The bills also would create a new trial court to handle governmental claims cases. This court, to be known as the U.S. Claims Court, would handle cases currently heard by the trial division of the U.S Court of Claims. These primarily were cases in which the government was a defendant, such as suits involving a contract with a government agency.

The new trial court, unlike the existing court, would have the authority to issue injunctions and temporary restraining orders in contract cases.

S 1700: Pros and Cons

Senate proponents of the bill — chiefly Robert Dole, R-Kan., and Dennis DeConcini, D-Ariz., — argued that a specialized patent appeals court was needed to bring uniformity and efficiency to this complicated area of the law.

"The doctrinal confusion in this area, resulting from a dozen different circuits developing a dozen different interpretations of patent law, has handicapped one of our most valued national resources — imaginative and innovative technology," Dole said in remarks on the floor.

Montana Democrat Max Baucus led the opposition to S 1700. He said he opposed creating a federal appeals court that specialized in one subject.

Baucus asserted that the new court "leads to the erosion of our existing regional courts."

Baucus noted that the American Bar Association and the American Trial Lawyers Association opposed the bill.

In the Judiciary Committee markup Oct. 20, Baucus offered an amendment to strip the appeals court of its authority to hear patent cases, but that failed 2-11.

Senate Floor Amendments

After passage of S 1700, chief sponsor Dole called up the House version of the bill (HR 4482 — H Rept 97-312) and amended it to conform with S 1700.

Dole also added an amendment to the bill changing current bankruptcy laws to expedite claims concerning failed farm storage facilities such as grain elevators.

This snagged the progress of the bill because of concern in the House Judiciary Committee over the bankruptcy issue.

Interest Payments

As approved by the Judiciary Committee, S 1700 had allowed federal courts for the first time to order interest payments on claims from the pre-judgment period in specified circumstances.

This provision was stricken on the floor through an amendment by Charles E. Grassley, R-Iowa, who also sponsored another amendment that changed the method of computing interest in certain civil cases.

Currently, the government paid 4 percent interest on claims for which it was found liable. In cases involving state laws, the interest rate was set according to the state laws involved.

The Grassley amendment would have interest computed in accordance with Treasury Department rates that were pegged to the sale of Treasury bills.

The House bill contained no provision on interest payments. ∎

Patent Term Extension

The Senate July 9 passed a bill to extend patent protection for drug manufacturers and others whose products were subject to federal regulatory review. The House failed to act on the measure in 1981.

Final Senate action on S 255 (S Rept 97-138) came by voice vote. The Judiciary Committee approved the bill May 19.

The bill extended the term of a new patent for up to seven years to compensate for the time required for federal review of a new product or manufacturing method.

A patent, which gives the owner certain exclusive marketing rights, generally runs 17 years.

However, drug companies, manufacturers of medical devices and chemical producers needed federal approval before marketing many patented items. Drug companies complained that the federal review process often consumed so many years that less than half the time under the patent remained when an agency finally granted marketing approval.

The companies said that the lost time under the patent reduced their profits and, therefore, the amount of money that could be put back into research on new drugs.

Provisions

S 255 specifically covered new drugs, medical devices, food and color additives subject to the Food, Drug and Cosmetic Act, and pesticides, chemical substances and mixtures subject to the Toxic Substances Control Act.

It required any patent owner seeking an extension to submit a notice requesting the additional time to the Commissioner of Patents and Trademarks. The notice would have to be submitted within 90 days after completion of the regulatory review process.

A similar bill (HR 1937) was pending at year's end in the House Judiciary Subcommittee on Courts, Civil Liberties and Administration of Justice. ∎

Tris Reimbursement Bill

The Senate Dec. 16 sought to spur the House into acting on legislation permitting companies to seek federal reimbursement for losses resulting from the sale of Tris-treated sleepwear.

Six months earlier, on June 18, the Senate passed a bill (S 823) that would help such clothing manufacturers. Similar legislation (HR 161, HR 4011) languished in a House Judiciary subcommittee all year.

At the urging of Judiciary Chairman Strom Thurmond, R-S.C., the Senate committee Dec. 15 attached its Tris bill to a House bill (HR 4755) giving a charter to an organization for former members of Congress. The Senate passed the charter bill Dec. 16.

"The House Judiciary Committee is just fooling around and taking no action," Thurmond complained. The bill was designed to benefit companies who used the chemical Tris in an effort to meet federal regulations requiring that children's sleepwear be made flame-resistant. The Consumer Product Safety Commission in 1977 banned Tris

as a "hazardous substance." Manufacturers were required to repurchase all unsold or unwashed children's garments made from Tris-treated fabric. The reimbursement proposal was approved by the Senate Judiciary Committee May 12 (S Rept 97-130).

1978 Bill Vetoed

Congress passed a similar bill (S 1503) in 1978, but President Carter vetoed the measure. He said it was unwise to indemnify private companies for losses resulting from compliance with a federal standard. *(1978 Almanac p. 520)*

Information about the carcinogenic properties of Tris was available in 1976, and some companies stopped using it then. However, it was not until 1977 that the Consumer Product Safety Commission banned Tris as a "hazardous substance." Manufacturers were required to repurchase all unsold or unwashed children's garments made from Tris-treated fabric.

As passed, S 823 allowed companies to file claims in the U.S. Court of Claims to recover the cost of producing the Tris-treated goods and transportation costs associated with the return of the sleepwear. No recovery would be allowed for lost profits.

The Congressional Budget Office estimated that the bill would require the government to pay between $51 million and $57 million to clothing manufacturers. ∎

Senate Judiciary Approves Criminal Code Bill

For the third time since 1977, the Senate Judiciary Committee approved a wide-ranging bill to revise and update federal criminal laws. But the measure went no further in 1981.

The most recent bill to revise the criminal code (S 1630) was approved Nov. 18 by an 11-5 vote.

Like its predecessors, S 1630 was controversial, drawing sharp criticism from groups ranging from the conservative Moral Majority — which considered the bill too lenient on many crimes — to the American Civil Liberties Union — which argued that the bill included new offenses that threatened civil liberties.

Two criminal code bills (HR 4711, HR 1647) were pending in a House Judiciary Committee subcommittee at the end of 1981. Under a committee agreement, one of the bills was to be sent to the full committee by Jan. 31, 1982.

Past Code Revisions

S 1630 was the third criminal code bill approved by the Senate Judiciary Committee in the last five years.

One version, S 1437, was reported by the panel in 1977 and passed by the Senate in 1978, but it failed to get out of a House subcommittee. *(1978 Almanac p. 165)*

In 1980, both the Senate and House Judiciary committees reported criminal code bills (S 1722, HR 6195), but the measures never were considered by the full House or Senate. *(1980 Almanac p. 383)*

S 1630 had the same chief cosponsors as S 1722 — Judiciary Chairman Strom Thurmond, R-S.C., Edward M. Kennedy, D-Mass., and Orrin G. Hatch, R-Utah. In addition, Joseph R. Biden Jr., D-Del., now the ranking committee Democrat, and Republicans Paul Laxalt, Nev., and Robert Dole, Kan., signed on as cosponsors.

Code Structure

Like its predecessors, S 1630 was divided into five sections.

Part I set forth the definitions to be used throughout the code. It reduced the more than 70 different criminal states of mind in existing law to four — acting "intentionally," "knowingly," "recklessly" or "negligently."

Part II contained the actual offenses, grouping similar ones, such as offenses against a person and offenses against property, in specific sections.

Part III included a new sentencing structure that virtually abolished parole. Offenses would be graded by seriousness, with sentences and fine levels established according to those grades. In addition, a U.S. Sentencing Commission would be created to develop sentencing guidelines.

Part IV contained administrative and procedural provisions, including bail. S 1630 would allow a judge to detain a defendant prior to trial if the judge determined the defendant would be dangerous to the community. These "preventive detention" provisions were identical to those in S 1554, a bail reform bill. *(Story, next page)*

Part V included provisions allowing the federal government to enjoin certain kinds of criminal conduct through civil litigation. It also contained a program for compensating victims of violent federal crimes. Money for the program would come from collected fines.

Different From Past Bills

While S 1630 was similar to past bills, there were important differences, including the following:

● S 1722, the 1980 Senate bill, included the offense of "endangerment" — strongly backed by the Carter adminis-

tration Justice Department — to cover persons or organizations engaged in conduct they knew imperiled another's life. This was dropped in S 1630.

● The 1980 bill expanded the circumstances under which the federal government could bring extortion prosecutions stemming from labor disputes. S 1630 altered this provision and reverted to existing law, which prohibited such federal prosecutions except in narrow circumstances.

● For the offense of contempt for disobeying a court ruling, S 1722 created a specific defense if the order were found to be invalid under the First Amendment. This was stricken from S 1630.

The Opposition

During the committee markup, Sens. Jeremiah Denton, R-Ala., and John P. East, R-N.C., asked that their names be removed from those cosponsoring the bill and then voted against it. Also opposing the measure were Charles McC. Mathias Jr., R-Md., Charles E. Grassley, R-Iowa, and Howell Heflin, D-Ala.

Both Denton and Grassley unsuccessfully offered amendments pushed by the Moral Majority, a conservative lobbying group headed by the Rev. Jerry Falwell.

The Moral Majority lobbied against S 1630, contending that it reduced the seriousness of some crimes, eliminated others and made sentences too lenient.

One amendment favored by the Moral Majority that Denton pushed would have restored immunity from prosecution for raping a spouse. Denton said he considered spousal sexual assault "a hideous crime," but he did not think it should be labeled rape.

Denton said, "Damn it, when you get married, you kind of expect you're going to get a little sex."

East said he believed it was unwise to rework all federal criminal laws in one bill. The North Carolina Republican said so many compromises had been made to get a majority for approval that no one really knew what was in the bill.

House Wrangling

In the House, the Judiciary Committee Oct. 7 set a Jan. 31, 1982 deadline for the completion of Criminal Justice Subcommittee action on a criminal code revision.

Committee Republicans had earlier sought to wrest control of a criminal code bill (HR 1647) from the subcommittee, which was headed by Rep. John Conyers Jr., D-Mich., who opposed a bill in the 96th Congress (HR 1695) that was approved by the full committee. The bill never was considered by the full House.

At a full committee meeting Sept. 22, Harold S. Sawyer, R-Mich., chief sponsor of HR 1647, sought to discharge the subcommittee from handling the bill and let the full committee take over the measure. However, in a 15-11 vote — four short of the two-thirds needed — Sawyer failed on a motion to have the committee consider his request.

The subcommittee held extensive hearings on revision of the criminal laws, with testimony continuing virtually up to adjournment. ∎

Anti-Crime Aid to States

The House Judiciary Committee approved a bill Sept. 22 creating a $150 million grant program to help states combat crime. But the measure went no further in 1981.

The committee vote on HR 4481, sponsored by Wil-

liam J. Hughes, D-N.J., was 22-5. The measure was formally reported Oct. 26 (H Rept 97-293).

As approved by the committee, the bill would create an Office of Justice Assistance to replace the scaled-down Law Enforcement Assistance Administration (LEAA). The new office would distribute block grants to the states on the basis of population and crime rates. States would be required to provide a 50 percent match for any federal funds.

The bill specified 15 categories of programs that could be funded under the legislation, including community and police anti-crime programs; programs to combat arson, white-collar and organized crime; and programs to aid crime victims.

Another $20 million would be authorized for special aid to areas in the country experiencing crime emergencies. The attorney general would coordinate the federal response to a request for federal help. ∎

Pretrial Services Program

The Senate passed a bill (S 923 — S Rept 97-77) June 18 to expand 10 federal demonstration programs aimed at helping judges make pretrial bail decisions.

S 923, passed by voice vote, would require pretrial services programs in all 95 judicial districts within 18 months of the date of enactment.

A similar House bill (HR 3481 — H Rept 97-56) was reported by the Judiciary Committee May 19 but hit a snag June 10 in the House Rules Committee, when several Republican members of the Judiciary Committee sought to attach a tough new bail revision bill to it. *(Bail reform, below)*

After sponsor William J. Hughes, D-N.J., and Judiciary Chairman Peter W. Rodino Jr., D-N.J., objected, Rules Chairman Richard Bolling, D-Mo., said he would not consider a rule for the bill until the dispute was resolved.

The pretrial demonstration programs were created in 1974 as part of the Speedy Trial Act (PL 93-619), which set deadlines for trying those charged with crimes. *(1974 Almanac p. 295; 1979 amendments, 1979 Almanac p. 376)*

Under the programs, pretrial services officers collected information about a defendant and gave it to the judge prior to the bail decision. If bail was granted, the officers supervised those released from custody, alerted the judge of any violation of bail conditions and recommended modifications in release conditions.

A bill identical to S 923 passed the Senate in 1980, but a companion bill died in the House when it failed to pass under suspension of the rules. *(1980 Almanac p. 407)* ∎

Bail Revision Measure

By voice vote Dec. 8, the Senate Judiciary Committee approved a bill (S 1554) to allow federal judges to jail criminal defendants before trial if they believed the defendants were dangerous.

The bill — vigorously opposed by the American Civil Liberties Union (ACLU) — was identical to bail reform provisions included in a wide-ranging criminal code reform bill (S 1630) approved by the committee Nov. 18. *(Criminal code bill, p. 432)*

A similar preventive detention bill (HR 4264) was pending at year's end in a House Judiciary subcommittee.

Both the bail measures and the criminal code proposals were in line with recommendations made in August by a special Justice Department task force on crime and with an anti-crime package proposed by Senate Democrats.

Under current federal law, a judge could detain a defendant only after determining there was a real likelihood the defendant would flee before trial.

Before the committee approved S 1554, Chairman Strom Thurmond, R-S.C., said Chief Justice Warren E. Burger was urging passage of the legislation.

A spokesman for the chief justice said Burger had not actually lobbied for the bill, but was supporting legislation that would give federal judges greater discretion in making bail decisions.

Subcommittee Action

S 1554 was approved 4-0 by the Constitution Subcommittee on Nov. 3. Patrick J. Leahy, D-Vt., abstained.

At the urging of Dennis DeConcini, D-Ariz., the subcommittee adopted an amendment to allow judges to deny bail to persons charged with committing serious drug offenses.

Under DeConcini's proposal, a judge could presume on the basis of the charge alone that no combination of conditions would assure the defendant's appearance at trial and the safety of the community if bail were granted. However, the defendant could attempt to rebut the presumption.

DeConcini said the amendment was necessary because drug smugglers frequently met high bail requirements and then fled before their trials.

S 1554 drew immediate criticism from the American Civil Liberties Union (ACLU), which had been fighting preventive detention proposals for years. David Landau, ACLU legislative counsel, said he believed the bill as a whole would be struck down if enacted because the concept of a defendant's dangerousness to the community was too vague and too hard to predict. He said even the most sophisticated studies that used computers could not show which defendants charged with one crime were likely to commit another offense.

Landau also criticized the DeConcini amendment, saying it amounted to a presumption of guilt for certain suspected drug offenders.

Although Landau said ACLU officials wanted to testify at hearings on bail reform, they were not allowed to do so. A subcommittee aide said no conscious effort was made to exclude the ACLU. He said the subcommittee believed the ACLU's point of view was represented through other witnesses.

Detention Hearing

S 1554 would require a judge to hold a hearing before denying bail. The accused would have the right to a lawyer and the right to testify as well as to present witnesses.

During the hearing the judge would have to consider a number of factors such as the seriousness of the offense, the evidence against the accused, the "history and characteristics" of the person, including his family ties, mental condition, employment, financial resources, and the "danger to the community" that would be created by releasing the defendant.

The judge would have to make written findings of fact and a written statement of why the defendant was held without bail.

The bill would allow a judge to impose money bail to assure a defendant's presence at trial. However, in discussing this provision, Hatch said a judge could not set high bail just to detain a defendant.

Leahy, a former Vermont prosecutor, said he agreed with the need for bail reform, but added he was troubled on two counts. First, Leahy said he was not sure there was evidence that expanded preventive detention was necessary in the federal system.

Second, Leahy said he was concerned about the cumbersome hearing process set up in the bill. Leahy said he could envision defense lawyers using the detention hearing process to prolong criminal proceedings. ∎

Home Video Recording

Several bills were introduced (HR 4783, HR 4808, S 1758) to protect the 3 million Americans with home videotape recorders from being charged with copyright violations for taping their favorite television shows.

The measures were designed to overturn an Oct. 19 decision by the 9th U.S. Circuit Court of Appeals in San Francisco. The court ruled that taping copyrighted shows without permission of the producers violated copyright laws, even if the taping was done solely for home use.

The Senate Judiciary Committee held a hearing Nov. 30 on S 1758, but took no further action.

A House Judiciary subcommittee decided to wait until all court proceedings in the California case were completed before taking up HR 4783 and HR 4808.

All of the bills would make clear that videotape recordings made for home use only, and not for any commercial purpose, did not violate copyright laws. ∎

Pfizer Antitrust Measure

The House Judiciary Committee Dec. 8 approved a bill (HR 5106) eliminating the right of foreign governments to recover treble damages in U.S. antitrust suits.

A companion bill (S 816) was passed by the Senate July 9. However, neither measure cleared Congress before the end of the first session Dec. 16.

HR 5106, which was ordered reported by voice vote, would have allowed foreign governments to collect only their actual damages. This was the same remedy available to the U.S. government in an antitrust suit.

The bill, like its Senate counterpart (S 816), was designed to modify the Supreme Court's 1978 *Pfizer Inc. v. Government of India* decision, which held that foreign governments could sue for triple damages in U.S. courts to recover financial losses resulting from violations of U.S. antitrust law.

As passed, the Senate measure denied recovery to a foreign government unless its laws provided the U.S. with remedies for antitrust violations, but the House bill did not include this provision. Members heeded the objections of the State Department, which said such a provision could be interpreted by U.S. allies as an attempt to impose U.S. antitrust laws on them.

S 816 was passed by the Senate July 9 by voice vote.

The bill was retroactive and covered pending litigation. Arlen Specter, R-Pa., spoke against the bill because this provision could deny relief to foreign countries who had sued U.S. drug companies for price fixing and other alleged antitrust violations that go back 30 years.

S 816 was approved May 12 by voice vote and reported May 15 by the Judiciary Committee (S Rept 97-78).

An antitrust bill (S 300) approved in 1979 by the Senate Judiciary Committee contained provisions similar to S 816, but it died in the 96th Congress. *(1979 Almanac p. 385)*

House Committee Action

A companion bill to S 816 (HR 2812) was approved Nov. 20 by the House Judiciary Monopolies and Commercial Law Subcommittee. It was supplanted by HR 5106.

As approved by the full committee Dec. 8 by voice vote, HR 5106 allowed foreign governments to collect only their actual damages, which was the same remedy available to the U.S. government in an antitrust suit. ∎

Aliens in Virgin Islands

The House Nov. 4 suspended the rules and passed a bill (HR 3517) making some 7,000 to 10,000 Virgin Islanders permanent residents of the United States. The Senate did not act on the measure in 1981, however.

The persons covered by the bill generally had lived in the islands for years as non-immigrant aliens. Virtually all of them went to the islands as temporary workers and stayed on to meet the islands' employment needs.

The bill covered anyone who was admitted to the Virgin Islands as a worker under the immigration laws and had resided there continuously since June 30, 1975.

A Virgin Islander seeking to become a permanent resident would have to make an application to the attorney general within one year of the bill's enactment.

The immediate relatives — spouses and minor children — of any permanent resident would be able to join the resident if they were not already on the islands. But the bill allowed U.S. and Virgin Islands officials to restrict the flow of more distant relatives.

The House Judiciary Committee approved HR 3517 Oct. 27 and reported it Oct. 29 (H Rept 97-307).

Constitutional Convention

Two Democrats staged a mini-filibuster Dec. 8 that delayed Senate Judiciary Committee action on legislation establishing procedures for a constitutional convention.

When it became clear that disagreements over some provisions could not be resolved easily, the committee put off further consideration of S 817.

Chief sponsor Orrin G. Hatch, R-Utah, said he would seek to iron out differences with Democrats Howell Heflin, Ala., and Joseph R. Biden Jr., Del.

S 817 would set up a method for convening a national convention to amend the Constitution.

Article V of the Constitution provides that a convention must be called if two-thirds of the states (34) request one. However, no procedures exist for running such a convention, and questions abound on such matters as how delegates would be selected, who would pay for the convention and what its scope would be.

None of the 26 amendments to the Constitution was added by the convention method. All were adopted through congressional action with subsequent ratification by at least three-fourths of the states. *(Amending the Constitution, CQ Guide to Congress, 2d Ed., p. 217)*

At the end of the year, a six-year-old drive for a convention on an amendment to require a balanced federal budget remained four states short of the 34 necessary to call one. *(Balanced budget amendment, p. 427)*

Provisions

As approved Nov. 3 by the Constitution Subcommittee, S 817 would allow states to pass resolutions calling for a convention. A state could withdraw its call for a convention unless two-thirds or more of the states already had called for a convention.

Convention resolutions would be transmitted to the House and Senate. Congress would have authority only to make sure each resolution actually was passed by the state legislatures. Once 34 valid documents were received, the House and Senate would adopt a resolution calling a convention and stating the general subject of the constitutional amendment or amendments to be considered.

Any state's resolution would be effective for up to seven years, although a state could specify a shorter effective time.

The convention's presiding officer would be the most senior chief justice of the states' highest courts.

The convention would be paid for by the states, with the costs apportioned among them.

Extent of Congressional Power

The major dispute dividing Hatch, Heflin and Biden on Dec. 8 concerned how much authority Congress should have over the convention process.

Biden and Heflin argued that Congress should have more authority than specified in S 817.

For example, they said the federal government should fund the convention and they contended the bill was not clear on how costs would be apportioned among the states. They asked whether a state that opposed the convention but was forced to participate would have to help pay for it.

Hatch said the answer was no, but the two Democrats said they doubted this would be workable.

Biden said he had an amendment to give Congress more authority to investigate the validity of convention resolutions. He said Congress should be able to inquire into the procedures used to pass a resolution to ensure that legislatures followed their own rules. But Hatch said this would give Congress too much power.

Biden had other amendments to give Congress a more active role. He argued that Article V envisioned congressional activity from the beginning of any constitutional convention to the ratification of its amendment.

Biden's amendments were taken verbatim from convention bills the Senate passed in 1971 and 1973. These measures were not considered by the House. *(1971 Almanac p. 758; 1973 Almanac, p. 788)*

Hatch, however, said the main principle of his bill was to make sure Congress could only call a convention and that it would not be "in a position to undermine the convention process." ∎

Service Station Operators

The Senate Judiciary Committee voted 9-6 Nov. 17 to approve a bill (S 326 — S Rept 97-303) preventing 16 major oil refiners from operating service stations. But the measure went no further in the first session of the 97th Congress.

The legislation was sought primarily by service station operators who leased property from the refiners and had

agreements to sell their gas.

These so-called lessee-dealers complained that refiners retailed gas through company-operated stations at the same prices or lower ones than those given to the dealers. This practice, the dealers contended, amounted to an effort to drive them out of business.

The bill still would permit major oil companies to own service stations and lease them to operators.

The major oil companies opposed S 326. They contended the legislation interfered with the free market and would result in burdensome regulations. They argued that the government should not tell refiners how to sell their products.

S 326 also would allow station operators doing business with a particular major refiner to purchase motor fuel from another source if the refiner could not supply the product on competitive terms. However, the dealer would have to tell customers that the gas being pumped was not the advertised refiner's.

A bill similar to S 326 (HR 1362) was pending in the House Small Business and Energy and Commerce committees.

Bankruptcy Bill Vetoed

President Reagan vetoed a bill Dec. 29 that made one change in the 1978 Bankruptcy Reform Act (PL 95-598) because he said it would benefit creditors in a single large bankruptcy case.

As cleared by Congress, HR 4353 would have put a ceiling of $100,000 on administrative fees to be paid in certain bankruptcy cases initiated before the 1978 law took effect but not completed by Sept. 30, 1979. *(1978 law, 1978 Almanac p. 179)*

The 1978 law had imposed a similar ceiling on any Chapter XI reorganization case that had commenced before its enactment but where the plan was not confirmed until after Sept. 30, 1978.

According to the House report on HR 4353 (H Rept 97-414), the $100,000 cap was designed to limit "extraordinarily high fees" in one or more cases pending at the time Congress was writing the 1978 law.

HR 4353 affected one case that fell outside the cap — a Chapter XI proceeding involving Fidelity Mortgage Investors, which filed for reorganization in New York before the 1978 law took effect.

In this case, the plan was confirmed prior to Sept. 30, 1978, but the fees were not determined until after Sept. 30, 1979. It thus fell outside the relevant date in the 1978 law.

Background

Before enactment of the 1978 law, the burden of bankruptcy fees fell on creditors, because the fees were deducted from the assets that otherwise would go to creditors.

Bankruptcy courts were supposed to be self-supporting, getting income from the fees in bankruptcy cases. The 1978 law changed that, as Congress determined that this court system — like the rest of the judicial system — should be funded with general revenues.

Congress abolished administrative fees for all bankruptcy cases initiated after Sept. 30, 1979.

According to the Administrative Office of the U.S. Courts, HR 4353 would have reduced fees of $1.7 million to $100,000 in the case involving Fidelity Mortgage Investors.

Burger Cautions Judges

Chief Justice Warren E. Burger told fellow federal judges in 1981 that he disapproved of their organizing to lobby Congress for higher pay.

In a June 15 letter to San Francisco District Court Judge Spencer Williams, who was spearheading an effort to organize the judges, Burger said he feared that "in the long run, an organization such as you propose will obstruct, rather than advance accomplishment of those things needed by the judiciary."

Burger's letter was in response to a memo Williams sent May 29 to some 800 federal judges. In that memo, Williams said the move to organize was based on responses to the questionnaire Judge Samuel Conti, also of San Francisco, sent to 753 judges in 1980 asking about their interest in "self-help" steps on the pay issue. Williams said that of the 332 responses, 299 favored such a program. "Inflation will continue to erode the purchasing power of compensation and the value of already grossly inadequate fringe benefits," the Williams memo said.

He proposed hiring a "coordinator" in Washington to keep the judges informed about bills affecting the judiciary and to pinpoint members of Congress most closely involved in such legislation. Williams also said judges should inform their "friends in Congress of the dimensions of the problem" and seek "such friends' support for appropriate corrective legislation."

In his letter, Burger said that while he understood "the frustrations of all federal judges, and indeed share them," he disapproved of the action because it could "undercut" efforts of the U.S. Judicial Conference, the policy-making arm of the federal courts authorized to speak for the judiciary.

"I urge all judges to channel these well-intended efforts through that body," Burger concluded.

Prior to a Dec. 15, 1980, Supreme Court decision, federal judges had not received a pay raise since 1976. The 1980 court decision said that two of four appropriation bill riders Congress had enacted between 1976 and 1980 to block authorized pay raises were invalid.

As a result of the decision, federal judges received retroactive pay raises and another in 1981.

The current salaries of federal judges were as follows: Chief Justice Burger, $96,800; associate Supreme Court justices, $93,000; court of appeals judges, $74,300; and district court judges $70,000.

Reduction of the fees payable to the now-defunct Referees' Salary and Expense Fund would have enlarged the sums available to pay creditors.

In a memorandum of disapproval, Reagan said, "I cannot support this effort to confer special relief in the guise of general legislation at a possible loss to the Treasury of $1.6 million." *(Text, p. 33-E)*

Legislative Action

HR 4353 was reported Dec. 15 by the House Judiciary Committee (H Rept 97-414) and passed by the House the following day under suspension of the rules.

The Senate passed the measure by voice vote Dec. 16, clearing it for the president.

Although the bill was never reviewed by the Senate Judiciary Committee, its provisions had been part of a separate bill, S 863, reported July 10 by the Judiciary Committee and passed by the Senate July 17. (S Rept 97-150)

S 863 dealt with a range of technical corrections to the 1978 bankruptcy act. It did not emerge from the House Judiciary Committee, although the panel did consider parts of it in separate bills such as HR 4353. ▪

Drug Abuse Treatment

The House passed a bill (HR 3963 — H Rept 97-283) extending a federal drug abuse treatment program for three years, but the Senate failed to act on the measure.

The bill was passed Oct. 26 under suspension of the rules. It had been reported Oct. 21 by the Judiciary Committee.

As approved by the House, HR 3963 authorized $4.5 million for the program for fiscal 1983, $5.5 million for fiscal 1984 and $6.5 million for fiscal 1985.

Sponsor William J. Hughes, D-N.J., said about 4,300 persons were in the drug program in 1981. He said the Administrative Office of the U.S. Courts estimated that the program would handle 5,300 persons in 1983, 5,600 in 1984 and 6,100 in 1985.

The program covered by the measure was administered by the probation division of the U.S. courts and provided for the examination of all convicted federal offenders released on parole or given probation to determine if they were drug users.

The program also provided drug abuse treatment and monitoring to assure that those receiving treatment stayed off drugs. The monitoring, accomplished largely through urinalysis, accounted for about one-third of the program's budget with the remainder going to counseling. ▪

National Guard Torts

Congress cleared a bill (HR 3799 — PL 97-124) Dec. 16 giving the National Guard and its medical personnel coverage under the Federal Tort Claims Act (PL 79-601) when the guard performs certain authorized training activities.

Final action came when the Senate accepted HR 3799 as passed by the House Dec. 15 under suspension of the rules. A companion Senate measure, S 267, was then shelved. It had been reported Dec. 14 (S Rept 97-297).

HR 3799 was reported from the House Judiciary Committee on Dec. 10 (H Rept 97-384, Part I). The House Armed Services Committee, through a Nov. 3 letter from Chairman Melvin Price, D-Ill., to Judiciary Chairman Peter W. Rodino Jr., D-N.J., also endorsed the bill, although it took no formal action on the measure.

As cleared, the bill extended federal tort claims coverage to acts or omissions of members of the National Guard engaged in federally prescribed training activities. It also made federal tort claims procedures the exclusive remedy in medical malpractice actions involving National Guard members.

The Senate passed a similar measure in 1980, but the House failed to complete action on it. *(1980 Almanac p. 405)*

Background

The federal government funds the training and equipment of National Guard personnel but except when federalized, the Guard is under direct orders of state governments.

Therefore, its activities had not been covered by the Federal Tort Claims Act, even though members of the armed forces and the military reserves — with similar roles in many respects — were protected by that law from liability in damage suits.

Proponents of HR 3799 said that Guard personnel engaged in federally prescribed training activity were at substantial risk of personal liability and that recruitment and morale had suffered as a result. ▪

Record, Tape or Film Piracy

The Senate passed a bill (S 691) sharply increasing the penalties for record, tape and film piracy and counterfeiting, but the House did not act on the legislation.

The bill was reported Nov. 18 by the Judiciary Committee (S Rept 97-274) and passed Dec. 1 by voice vote. There was no debate.

As passed, it provided fines of up to $250,000 or imprisonment for five years, or both, for convictions on charges of trafficking in counterfeit labels for records, films or other audiovisual materials.

Current penalties were fines up to $10,000 or one year in prison, or both, for a first offense and up to $25,000 or a two-year prison term, or both, for any subsequent offense. ▪

Civil Rights Commission

The House Judiciary Committee and a Senate Judiciary subcommittee approved a fiscal 1982 authorization for the Civil Rights Commission, but Congress did not complete action on either measure.

The House committee May 19 reported HR 3275, authorizing $14 million for the commission in fiscal 1982 (H Rept 97-99).

Senate Judiciary's Constitution Subcommittee Nov. 3 approved a similar measure (S 1538) authorizing $12,037,000, but the measure went no further.

The funding level in the Senate bill represented a $563,000 reduction from the fiscal 1981 authorization of $12.6 million and was $281,000 below the Reagan administration's budget request.

The commission was established in the 1957 Civil Rights Act (PL 83-315) to investigate and report to Congress on discrimination based on race, color, religion or national origin. Amendments over the years have added authority for the commission to study discrimination based on sex, age and handicap.

Before approving S 1538, the Senate subcommittee rejected, 2-3, an amendment by Charles E. Grassley, R-Iowa, to cut the commission's funding to $10.84 million.

The panel adopted another Grassley amendment that earmarked up to $4 million of the commission's authorization for studying the economic and social impact of affirmative action and the legal remedies available to those who claim to be hurt by "reverse discrimination." ▪

Energy

In a year without significant energy shortages, the national energy focus shifted from massive government programs to individual initiatives.

The Reagan administration, with congressional approval, scaled back the energy conservation and solar energy programs that had been favored by President Carter. For the first time since the 1973 Arab oil embargo, Congress did not debate any substantial new energy programs.

Instead members fought over which programs of the past would survive in a time of reduced federal energy spending.

But Americans seemed to have learned the lesson that energy would continue to be expensive. Homeowners spent billions of dollars on insulation and wood stoves in an effort to conserve more and spend less on heating and cooling. They installed solar water heaters, and new homes were built with passive solar features. Americans also continued to limit their driving and to buy cars that were more fuel-efficient.

President Reagan and Energy Secretary James B. Edwards promised to drive the government out of the energy business. The marketplace, they said, would allocate resources and determine what new energy technologies, such as solar and synthetic fuels, would be developed by private companies.

The one glaring exception to their philosophy was nuclear power, which they said had been strangled by government red tape. But even though nuclear power was the only energy area in which Reagan increased government spending, the nuclear industry suffered through another rough financial year with not much hope of immediate improvement.

Oil Situation

World oil prices dropped slightly during the year, although substantial increases had been predicted. The $50-a-barrel price that some had predicted for the spring of 1981 never materialized; the average world price at the end of the year was a little over $34 a barrel. Increased conservation around the world helped create a world oil glut that enabled buyers of oil to be more selective with purchases for the first time in several years.

Members of OPEC — the Organization of Petroleum Exporting Countries — fought among themselves over questions of price and production. Two OPEC members — Iraq and Iran — remained at war, although the fighting was sporadic. OPEC lost the stranglehold it had had on world oil prices as its total production slipped to about 20 million barrels of oil a day, down from 31 million barrels a day in 1979.

In September, OPEC raised its official price from $32 to $34 for a 42-gallon barrel of oil. But several OPEC countries that had been selling oil for more than the official rate had to reduce their prices.

U.S. oil imports continued to decrease throughout 1981 as they had in 1980. At the end of 1981, the United States was importing about 5.5 million barrels of oil a day; the 1981 average was about 5.9 million barrels a day, down from 6.8 million barrels in 1980. In 1979, the United States had imported 8.4 million barrels of oil a day.

The government took advantage of the world oil glut and bought oil for its Strategic Petroleum Reserve (SPR). The reserve, held in salt caverns along the Gulf Coast, was doubled in 1981, from about 110 million barrels to more than 220 million barrels by year's end.

One of President Reagan's first acts after taking office was the immediate decontrol of oil prices and supplies. Consumer groups predicted large price hikes in fuel oil and gasoline but these did not materialize.

Gasoline prices increased during 1981 at less than the 10 percent increase in the cost of living. At the beginning of the year, motorists were paying about $1.24 a gallon for regular gasoline. The price was about $1.30 at the end of the year.

Mobil Oil Corp. tried twice in 1981 to "drill for oil on the floor of the New York Stock Exchange," in the words of several members of Congress. It lost multibillion-dollar bidding wars first for Conoco Inc., which finally was bought by E.I. DuPont deNemours & Co., and then for Marathon Oil Co., which was bought by U.S. Steel Corp. The attempted Mobil takeovers angered Congress, and the last act by the House before adjournment was passage of a bill aimed at blocking the acquisition of Marathon by Mobil, which then threatened to buy U.S. Steel to obtain Marathon's oil reserves. *(Story, p. 453)*

But even while part of the industry was obsessed with corporate takeovers, exploratory drilling for new sources of oil and natural gas reached record levels. Some analysts said the increased oil drilling was spurred on by Reagan's decontrol of oil prices and the higher profits that could be realized by producers.

Synthetic Fuels

The combination of the leveling of world oil prices and Reagan's free-market philosophy slowed the government push toward synthetic fuels. In 1980, Congress had created the U.S. Synthetic Fuels Corp., which was given nearly $15 billion to subsidize and encourage the development of synthetic fuels.

But Reagan fired the interim board of directors Carter had installed. It was not until September of 1981 that board members appointed by Reagan were confirmed by the Senate. As 1981 ended, two board vacancies remained as Western Republicans in the Senate scrapped among themselves over who would be the final appointees. *(Story, p. 459)*

The corporation still had not handed out any subsidies by the end of the year, but had narrowed an initial list of companies applying from 63 to 28.

In August, before the corporation became operational,

the administration approved $3.5 billion in loan guarantees and price supports for three projects; one to make natural gas from coal in North Dakota and two to make oil from shale rock in Colorado. The president approved the subsidies, at the urging of Edwards, over the strenuous objections of his budget director, David A. Stockman.

Natural Gas

Producers of natural gas were overjoyed when Reagan was elected president because they believed he would support quick deregulation of natural gas prices. But, although his Cabinet recommended such a move, Reagan put the issue off until 1982.

Under a 1978 law, about half of all gas supplies were to be freed from government regulation in January 1985. But gas producers wanted immediate decontrol of all gas prices. Pipeline companies and utilities that sold gas, however, felt their customers would turn to other fuels if gas were decontrolled. Consumer groups also opposed decontrol, and said residential gas bills could double as a result.

Supplies of natural gas for the next decade appeared abundant in 1981. In the mid-1970s, the fuel had been scarce and thought to be running out. To get more gas, Congress passed a law in 1976 to facilitate bringing gas from Alaska's Prudhoe Bay south to U.S. consumers. In 1981, Congress approved a controversial change in this 1976 law, the effect of which was to assign consumers a portion of the risk that the gas pipeline would be delayed or never finished. As the year ended, the $40 billion project's fate was in the hand of the nation's bankers, who were deciding whether they would put up the financing for the pipeline — which would be by far the largest private construction project ever built. *(Story, next page)*

Also in 1978, Congress had enacted a law that restricted the future use of natural gas. In 1981, Congress repealed the portion of the law that would have prohibited utilities from burning gas to generate electricity. *(Story, p. 449)*

Coal

The U.S. coal industry had a mixed year. Coal production was down slightly from 1980 as a result of a 72-day strike by the United Mine Workers. But consumption of coal was up slightly and exports increased. Utilities continued to use more coal, generating just over half of the nation's electricity from coal.

The coal industry continued its long-time fight with the railroads over the costs of shipping coal and alternative transportation systems. Reagan became the first president to oppose shipping coal mixed with water in slurry pipelines, long a dream of the coal industry, which still hoped to gain congressional approval of such lines in 1982. The industry also fought with Reagan over federal funding for the dredging of U.S. harbors to accept larger coal ships.

Nuclear Power

Reagan gave the nuclear industry a boost in 1981 with a policy statement that overturned his predecessor's ban on the reprocessing of burned nuclear fuel into more fuel, waste and plutonium. He also promised to cut government red tape and increased the nuclear energy budget while cutting all other energy programs. *(Text, p. 24-E)*

But 1981 still was not a good year for nuclear power. While four new atomic plants began operating in 1981 to bring the total running to 72, six plants that had been planned were canceled; 25 others were delayed and might be canceled. Utilities had not placed an order for a nuclear plant since 1978 and no new orders were anticipated for the next few years.

About 30 new plants were expected to begin operating in 1982 and 1983, bringing the percentage of electricity generated by nuclear power to about 15 percent of the nation's total. In 1981, atomic plants generated about 11 percent, down from about 13 percent two years earlier.

The cleanup of the damaged nuclear reactor at Three Mile Island, Pa., went slowly in 1981, with considerable uncertainty over who would pay for the cleanup of the 1979 accident there. Bills introduced in Congress to force nuclear utilities to pay a share of the estimated $1 billion cost went nowhere. And the company that owned the plant was prohibited from restarting the other reactor — which was undamaged — at the site.

In California, more than 1,000 demonstrators were arrested while protesting the government's decision to allow the controversial Diablo Canyon nuclear plant to begin operating. Government approval had been delayed for years because the plant was located near an earthquake fault. Before operations could start, it was learned that part of the earthquake protection for the two-reactor power plant had been built backwards. The license to operate was revoked until changes could be made, perhaps sometime in 1982. The surrounding publicity was a public relations nightmare for the nuclear industry.

The industry appeared on the verge of winning a victory in Congress, with the passage of a provision to allow the Nuclear Regulatory Commission to issue operating licenses to new plants before public hearings were completed. However, the bill to which the provision was attached bogged down in a mire of other issues and was put off until 1982. *(Story, p. 444)*

Supporters of nuclear power also sought legislation that would establish a national plan for disposal of nuclear waste. Although several committees worked on waste bills in 1981, a waste solution was also put off until 1982. *(Story, p. 455)*

—By Andy Plattner

Alaska Gas Pipeline Waivers Approved

Swatting aside last-minute parliamentary tactics by opponents, Congress Dec. 10 cleared a package of waivers (S J Res 115) requested by President Reagan in an attempt to help secure private financing for a 4,800-mile pipeline to bring natural gas from Prudhoe Bay, Alaska, to the continental United States.

The congressional action in effect dumped the fate of the $40 billion project in the lap of the nation's banks and other investors.

The waivers to the 1977 decision to build the pipeline transferred some of the risk of construction delays or noncompletion to 38 million natural gas consumers in 47 states. Opponents called the package "the greatest consumer rip-off in U.S. history."

Under the 1977 law, consumers could not be billed for pipeline construction costs until they actually began to receive Alaskan gas; the waivers allowed billing to start as soon as one of three portions of the pipeline was finished.

The waivers also allowed the oil companies that owned the Alaska gas — Exxon, Standard Oil of Ohio (Sohio) and Atlantic Richfield (ARCO) — to own part of the pipeline; the 1977 law had barred them from doing so.

Project sponsors hoped the waivers would persuade banks and other U.S. and foreign investors to lend them $22.5 billion to build the Alaska segment of the pipeline, which was expected to cost $27 billion.

Funding for the portion going through Canada appeared assured, and the section in the continental United States was nearly completed. If the entire pipeline was built — and there was still considerable doubt, even with the passage of the waivers — it would be the largest project ever built with private financing. *(Pipeline map, p. 442)*

Opponents said the waiver package was contrary to the administration's professed free-market philosophy, as well as unfair to consumers. Supporters said it was a reasonable attempt to open up Alaska's huge supplies of natural gas to help meet the nation's energy needs.

Consumer advocates were outmatched as the pipeline sponsors put on one of the heaviest lobbying campaigns in recent congressional memory. Also working with the sponsors were labor unions whose members would benefit from the jobs pipeline construction would provide.

Provisions

As cleared by Congress, S J Res 115 (PL 97-93):
● Allowed the three major oil companies that owned the Prudhoe Bay, Alaska, gas to also own part of the pipeline. Banks involved in the project had said it was unlikely that private financing could be arranged without the substantial involvement of the oil companies. In testimony supporting the waivers, pipeline sponsors said the oil companies would own 30 percent of the project.
● Allowed a conditioning plant at Prudhoe Bay, needed to prepare the natural gas for shipping in the pipeline, to be included as part of the project that eventually would be charged to consumers. The $6 billion plant originally was to be the responsibility of the oil companies, but they insisted it be included in the system as part of the deal for their assuming ownership.
● Allowed consumers to be billed for part of the project before gas actually was transported. If the entire pipeline was not completed by the date the Federal Energy Regula-

tory Commission (FERC) determined that it should be completed (probably 1987), consumers could begin receiving bills if at least one of the three segments — the pipeline in Alaska, the pipeline in Canada or the conditioning plant — was finished and ready to operate.
● Eliminated the requirement that FERC hold formal hearings on each application for certification that the pipeline required. However, FERC would be allowed to hold such hearings at its discretion.
● Restricted FERC's authority to modify the tariff schedules for billing consumers after it set them. This "regulatory certainty" provision was said to be necessary to assure lenders that the income generated by the project would not be reduced by later FERC changes. Tariffs could be increased by FERC but not lowered.

Background

When 9 billion barrels of recoverable oil was discovered at Prudhoe Bay in 1968, some 26 trillion cubic feet (Tcf) of natural gas also was found. The United States used about 20 Tcf a year of natural gas; Prudhoe Bay represented about 13 percent of known U.S. reserves.

An 800-mile pipeline was completed in 1977 to transport the oil from Prudhoe Bay to Valdez, on Alaska's southern coast, from which the oil was moved by ship to the continental United States. The pipeline, which bisected one of the most environmentally sensitive and pristine regions of the world, was both controversial and expensive. Originally estimated to cost $900 million, it ended up costing more than $9 billion — to date, the largest privately financed project in U.S. history.

While the oil pipeline was being built, several proposals to transport the gas were reviewed by the Federal Power Commission (which later became the Federal Energy Regulatory Commission). But it appeared clear that it would take years to approve a proposal, and then the issue would move into the courts for what could be several more years of litigation.

Legislative Action

In 1976, Congress passed the Alaska Natural Gas Transportation Act (PL 94-586), which directed the president to decide whether such an Alaskan gas transportation system should be built and to pick one of the competing proposals. *(1976 Almanac p. 198)*

Once a decision was made, and approved by Congress, the act authorized federal officials to waive normal procedures to expedite construction. It also restricted review of the project by the courts. The act provided that the president's decision and subsequent modifications to it be approved by Congress within 60 days of submission. Proposed waivers to the decision could be rejected but not modified.

In 1977, when U.S. natural gas supplies were believed to be running out, President Carter decided the Alaska project should go forward. He selected a proposal to build a pipeline that followed the route of the oil pipeline south from Prudhoe Bay past Fairbanks, and then followed the Alaska Highway through Canada to Calgary, Alberta. From there, the line would split, with one section going to the West Coast of the United States, the other to the Midwest. The pipeline would deliver about 2.5 billion cubic feet of Alaskan natural gas a day to the United States.

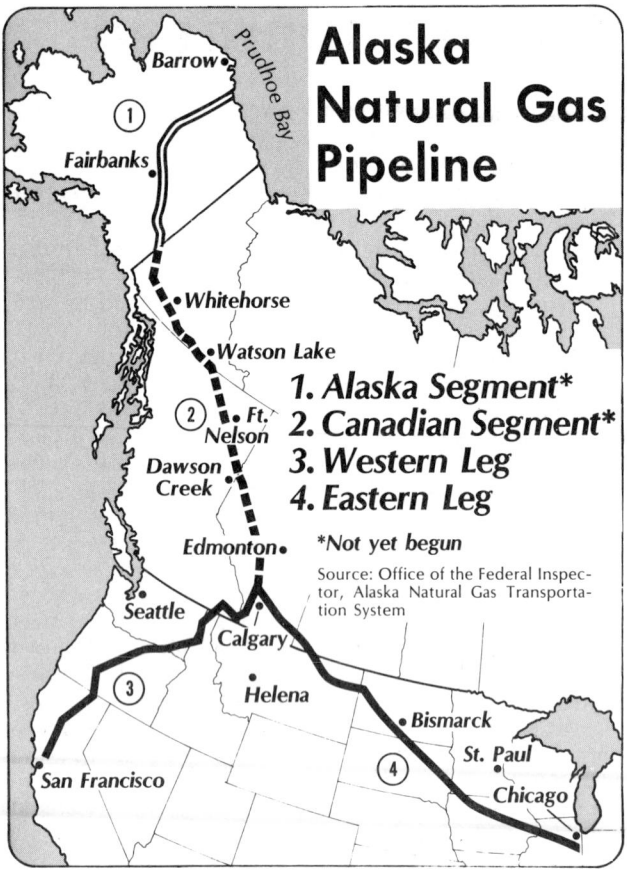

Alaska Natural Gas Pipeline

1. Alaska Segment*
2. Canadian Segment*
3. Western Leg
4. Eastern Leg

*Not yet begun

Source: Office of the Federal Inspector, Alaska Natural Gas Transportation System

The president negotiated a treaty with Canada providing that neither country would discriminate in its tax treatment of the pipeline. The Senate ratified the treaty in November 1977.

Carter's decision stipulated that the pipeline was to be financed by the private sector, not the government. It also specified that gas consumers could not be charged for construction costs until the entire system was finished. And to satisfy Justice Department antitrust concerns, the oil companies that owned the Prudhoe Bay gas were prohibited from owning any part of the pipeline.

Despite reservations by some members, Congress by joint resolution (PL 95-158) in November 1977 approved Carter's decision with all its specifications. *(1977 Almanac p. 675)*

The Senate Energy Committee had voiced skepticism about the project's ability to secure private financing, and members in both chambers warned that the federal government or consumers might end up having to help pay for it.

Cost Estimates Soar

When Congress approved the project in 1977, the cost was estimated at $10 billion, although some members suggested it would be closer to $15 billion. The 745-mile Alaska portion was expected to cost $3.3 billion, and the pipeline was scheduled to be in operation by January 1983.

By 1981, however, cost estimates had soared to around $40 billion, with the Alaska segment alone pegged at $27 billion, and the earliest operating date was estimated to be at least 1987.

The costs of the Alaska segment were huge because of technical problems associated with installing the 48-inch diameter pipe in the frozen tundra. The gas that flowed through the pipeline would have to be cooled to prevent it from thawing the ground and possibly buckling the pipe.

The western leg of the project leading from Alberta to the West Coast of the United States was nearly completed; gas from Canadian wells began flowing in October 1981. The eastern leg to the Midwest was under construction and Canadian gas was expected to flow in fall 1982.

There was only a four-year contract for this Canadian gas, however, creating additional pressure to build the rest of the line in Canada and Alaska to bring the Alaskan gas to the continental United States.

Northwest Energy Co. of Salt Lake City, which headed the consortium of gas companies building the Alaskan segment of the project, had obtained most of the necessary permits to begin construction. But it had not been able to get the $22.5 billion in financing it needed. And the Canadian companies that were to build the line between Calgary and Alaska were waiting to see some progress on the Alaska segment before they began construction.

Sponsors' Proposal

In an effort to get the necessary loans for construction of the pipeline, the consortium asked the Reagan administration in June to seek congressional approval of a package of waivers to the 1977 presidential decision, removing some of the barriers to the financing.

The 1977 decision said the oil companies that owned the Prudhoe Bay gas should help finance the pipeline, but it prohibited them from owning any equity in the pipeline. However, the companies were not interested in putting up money without getting a share of the project, and the banks considering financing the pipeline — Chase Manhattan, Citibank, Morgan Guaranty Trust and Bank of America — felt the oil companies were the only participants with the assets to secure the financing.

So Northwest Energy negotiated an agreement with the oil firms by which they would put up 30 percent of the costs of the pipeline and own a 30 percent share; they also would put up part of the funding for a pool of funds to be used if there were cost overruns. This arrangement required a waiver from the 1977 decision.

The oil companies insisted that the gas conditioning plant needed to treat the gas before it was put in the pipeline be included as part of the project — another demand that required a waiver of existing law.

The banks also insisted on a waiver to allow "prebilling" of consumers for the pipeline's cost. They wanted to start billing natural gas users immediately, not after the gas began to flow, as the 1977 decision stipulated. According to a memorandum written by the House Energy and Commerce Committee staff, that would put consumers in the position of underwriting the pipeline. "The banks have made it quite clear that the financial community will not accept the risk for this project; they want the risk shifted to the consumer to the extent possible," the memo said.

H. Anton Tucher, a vice president at Bank of America, said the deal had to be made "riskless" to lenders because of the amount of money involved, much of which he said would have to come from abroad. "There has never been anything this large financed by the private sector," he said.

Joe Egan, assistant vice president of Merrill Lynch, Pierce, Fenner & Smith investment firm, also noted the risk to investors if gas from the pipeline proved to be too expensive to be marketable, because of the high transportation costs.

Edwin Rothschild, director of Energy Action, a con-

sumer group, called the proposed waivers "a complete betrayal" of the sponsors' promise of private financing. "It makes the Chrysler bail-out look like chicken feed," he said. *(Chrysler loan guarantees, 1980 Almanac p. 144)*

Proposal Modified

Since Congress had to act within 60 days on any waiver package submitted by the president, and could not amend it, administration officials tried to secure agreement from key members before sending the package to Capitol Hill. But no agreement was reached.

In July four senators drafted a more modest set of waivers that would only allow customers to be billed as large portions of the pipeline were completed. The four — James A. McClure, R-Idaho, chairman of the Senate Energy Committee; Henry M. Jackson, D-Wash., the committee's ranking minority member; and Alaska's two Republican senators, Frank H. Murkowski and Ted Stevens — asked Reagan to send their package to Congress right away.

But leaders of two House committees — Energy and Commerce, and Interior — balked. They said the waivers probably would be rejected by the House because they shifted the risk of the pipeline to consumers.

In August the administration gave up efforts to reconcile the two groups. At the urging of the four senators, pipeline sponsors and the Canadian government, Reagan Oct. 15 sent Congress a waiver package similar to what the senators had proposed.

Reagan's letter accompanying the proposal was not effusive in support of the waivers. He noted that that pipeline plan was chosen by President Carter and supported by Congress. He said he favored the project's completion through private financing and that the government should not obstruct development of Alaskan energy resources.

Senate Action

The Senate Energy Committee endorsed the waiver package (S J Res 115 — S Rept 97-272) Nov. 10 by a 14-1 vote, and the full Senate approved it Nov. 19, 75-19. *(Vote 388, p. 65-S)*

Waiver sponsors had been confident of the Senate vote. "This has been one of the finest lobbying jobs Congress has ever seen," said Howard M. Metzenbaum, D-Ohio, who cast the lone vote against the package in the Energy Committee and unsuccessfully led the opposition to the waivers in the Senate. "It's slick, it's been greased, it's all set to roll. The lobbyists have done their job."

"I don't blame the sponsors for bringing in as many lobbyists as they can afford," Stevens retorted.

Metzenbaum said the waivers were "unfair, inequitable and unjust" because they put too much burden on consumers. "This is a bail-out bill for the oil companies, who sure don't need any bail-out," he said.

But Jackson argued that consumers would be hurt more by the failure to bring the gas to market than by the risk put on them by the waivers. Even a year's delay, Jackson said, would cost consumers $3 billion to $6 billion.

Stevens said exploration for the further oil and gas reserves thought to be in Alaska would not occur unless it was demonstrated by building the pipeline that it could be brought to market.

Stevens brushed aside charges by a public interest group, Congress Watch, that companies involved in the pipeline had given more than $82,000 in 1981 in campaign

contributions to members of Congress and campaign committees. He said the contributions would have been made anyway and were not tied to the waivers.

House Committee Action

Two committees had jurisdiction over the resolution in the House. The Interior Committee voted 32-7 for the package (H J Res 341) on Nov. 12; Energy and Commerce gave it its blessing Nov. 19 by a 27-14 vote (H Rept 97-350, Parts I and II). Sponsors had not been sure the Energy Committee would support the waivers.

Energy and Commerce. When the waivers were being considered by the administration in the summer of 1981, the strongest opposition came from the ranking Republicans on the House Energy and Commerce Committee — James T. Broyhill, N.C., and Clarence J. Brown, Ohio. But while both men voted against the waivers, neither led the opposition to them in committee, leaving that to Tom Corcoran, R-Ill., and Richard L. Ottinger, D-N.Y.

As the committee prepared to vote, supporters of the waivers were still not sure they had enough votes. The Fossil Fuels Subcommittee had narrowly approved the package Nov. 17 by a vote of 12-9. But in the full committee, Democrats voted 15-8 for the waiver package, and Republicans backed it 12-6.

Ralph M. Hall, D-Texas, who voted against the waivers in subcommittee, voted for them in committee. He said he was torn between the risk for the consumer and the national need for the gas.

Corcoran called the waivers "the greatest consumer rip-off in history." He proposed instead removing price controls on Alaska gas and letting the oil companies use profits from the higher-priced gas to finance the pipeline.

Interior Committee. The fate of the waivers was never in doubt during Interior Committee consideration. Chairman Morris K. Udall, D-Ariz., supported the package despite some misgivings, particularly about allowing early billing of consumers.

Udall said there was a good chance the pipeline could not be financed even with the waivers, but rejecting them would be "a kick in the teeth" to Canada. Udall noted that at the urging of the United States, Canada agreed to build a large portion of the pipeline and had already completed one part that was delivering gas to U.S. customers. He said Congress should at least give sponsors of the Alaska segment a chance to secure financing.

Several members complained that the burden on consumers would be too great and the price of the Alaska gas too high. John F. Seiberling, D-Ohio, said the initial price of the gas would be $18 to $20 per thousand cubic feet, five times the current price.

House Floor Action

The House passed H J Res 341 by a 233-173 vote Dec. 9. *(Vote 322, p. 106-H)*

However, opponents blocked the resolution from being formally cleared until Dec. 10, when they forced another vote. They hoped the delay would enable them to switch enough votes to kill the waivers.

They did manage to narrow the margin by 18 votes but still lost, 230-188, as the House passed the Senate resolution Dec. 10. Eight members, all Republicans, switched from supporting the resolution to opposing it. There were no defections from the opposition. *(Vote 329, p. 108-H)*

Most of the opposition to the waivers in the House came from members from the Midwest and Northeast, where residential use of natural gas for heat was heaviest. For example, members from Maine, New Hampshire, Vermont, Connecticut, Rhode Island and Massachusetts produced only one vote for the waivers Dec. 9, and 21 against. On the other hand, the gas-producing states of Oklahoma, Texas and Louisiana voted 23-1 for the waivers. Representatives from the 12 Midwest states voted 42-73 on the resolution.

In floor debate Dec. 8, 9 and 10, opponents of the waivers argued that there were cheaper ways to bring the natural gas from Alaska, such as in liquid form by ship. They also warned that the waivers could be the first step toward federal financing of the project.

Sponsors countered that the pipeline was the only viable way to transport the gas. They insisted that the waivers were as far as Congress would go — no federal financing would ever be approved.

Philip R. Sharp, D-Ind., chairman of the Energy Subcommittee on Fossil Fuels, acknowledged that the waivers had problems. "But in my mind the promise of the pipeline is sufficient to outweigh the problems with the waivers," he said, "and you cannot have one without the other." He said failure to go forward with the project would put consumers in danger of not having adequate gas supplies.

Sharp said that even in the worst case, the average gas consumer would have no more than $1.75 a month added to his gas bill under the pre-billing provision if the pipeline were delayed.

While Corcoran again labeled the waivers a consumer rip-off, Don Young, R-Alaska, said "this is a consumer-oriented package of waivers. In return for bearing a small financial risk, consumers will benefit by receiving a secure and economic source of U.S. fuel."

Majority Leader Jim Wright, D-Texas, said approval of the waivers "is one way that we can strike a blow for energy independence for the United States." He said delay of the pipeline would cost consumers more in the long run.

Parliamentary Tactics

After the House passed H J Res 341, Corcoran objected to a routine unanimous consent request to then approve the identical Senate measure. Udall said that in his 20 years in the House he had never seen such an objection.

Aided by consumer advocate Ralph Nader, Corcoran hoped to use the delay to generate additional opposition to the waivers. Nader, noting extensive campaign donations to members of Congress from pipeline sponsors, said after the first House vote that the Democratic Party had "sold its soul and sold its credibility for a few million dollars in campaign contributions."

The Senate could have eased the situation by simply passing H J Res 341, which was identical to S J Res 115, but Metzenbaum promised a filibuster if the issue came up. Instead, sponsors got clearance from the House Rules Committee to bring S J Res 115 to the House floor on Dec. 10.

Metzenbaum and Ottinger challenged the second House vote as illegal and promised a court suit. They said the 1976 law providing for expedited congressional consideration of Alaska pipeline issues prohibited more than one vote in either chamber on the waivers within a 60-day period. Supporters said the vote was legal because it was on an identical resolution. Sharp said opponents were giving a "tortured interpretation" of the 1976 law, which limited debate and barred amendments. ■

NRC Authorization

In the last hours of the session Dec. 16, the promise of a prolonged debate by Henry M. Jackson, D-Wash., blocked Senate consideration of a two-year authorization for the Nuclear Regulatory Commission (NRC).

The House had passed a similar measure (HR 2330) in November.

The Senate bill (S 1207) had been ready for floor action since May. It was expected to be taken up by the Senate soon after Congress returned in 1982.

Both bills contained controversial provisions that would allow nuclear plants to begin operating before the NRC had completed public hearings on them.

Jackson reportedly was unhappy with an amendment that Gary Hart, D-Colo., planned to offer to S 1207, to prohibit the government from using spent fuel from civilian nuclear power plants to make nuclear weapons. Such a plan was being considered by the Reagan administration and some members of Congress.

The Senate had agreed to an identical amendment in November, adding it to the fiscal 1982 energy and water appropriations bill (HR 4144), but the provision was dropped in conference. Hart also added the amendment to a nuclear waste bill (S 1662) reported by the Senate Environment and Energy committees Nov. 30. *(HR 4144, p. 301; S 1662, p. 455)*

Late Dec. 16, with only a few hours left in the session, Jackson informed Hart and Alan K. Simpson, R-Wyo., chairman of the Environment Subcommittee on Nuclear Regulation, that if Hart insisted on offering the amendment, Jackson would need several hours to debate the issue. Hart refused to back down and Simpson, the bill's manager, agreed to wait until 1982.

Interim Licensing Issue

The delay in Senate passage of the bill was particularly disappointing to the nuclear industry. Utilities and makers of nuclear reactors had worked hard for the provision in the legislation that would allow new nuclear plants to begin operating before the NRC had completed public hearings on them.

Electric utilities building nuclear units had complained bitterly about the lengthy NRC hearing process that had to be completed before an operating license could be awarded. Thirteen reactors that were scheduled to be completed in 1981 and 1982 were not expected to be able to start producing electricity when they were finished because the NRC was not ready to issue licenses.

The utilities said the delay between completion of construction and eventual operation resulted in higher costs for consumers because the utilities had to continue to pay the bills for the unused reactors while also providing power from other, usually more expensive, sources.

Congressional committees and individual members had received a large volume of mail from utility customers complaining of the licensing delays. Among the utilities facing delays were companies in California, North Carolina, Texas, New Jersey and Pennsylvania.

In April 1981 the NRC asked Congress for authority to grant interim licenses that would allow reactor testing at low power before the hearing process was completed. That proposal was generally supported by the utilities and the nuclear industry, but was opposed by environmental groups.

Mike Faden, a lobbyist for the Union of Concerned

Scientists, which opposed nuclear power in general, said the hearing process was needed to protect the public safety. He said the licensing delays were a result of NRC staff being diverted to examine safety problems at existing reactors as a result of the 1979 accident at the Three Mile Island (TMI) nuclear reactor in Pennsylvania. *(1979 Almanac p. 694)*

Congress did not pass an NRC authorization for fiscal 1980 until that year was more than half over, and it never passed one at all for fiscal 1981. The main hang-up was nuclear power plant safety and the different ways members sought to address the problem in the wake of the TMI accident.

About half of the NRC's annual budget went for nuclear research, slightly more than one-fourth for regulation, inspection and enforcement at nuclear power plants, and the remainder for developing new standards, safeguarding nuclear materials and for overhead.

House Committee Action

Jurisdiction over the NRC was shared in the House by the Interior and the Energy and Commerce committees.

Interior

The Interior Committee April 10 reported a relatively bland NRC authorization bill (HR 2330 — H Rept 97-22, Part I) that intentionally did not address nuclear policy questions. As reported, the bill authorized $486 million for the NRC in fiscal 1982 and $513 million in fiscal 1983, about 3 percent below the amounts requested by the Reagan administration.

The bill prohibited the NRC from spending any funds on the cleanup or repair of the damaged reactor at Three Mile Island. That ban was offered by James Weaver, D-Ore., who insisted that the nuclear industry, not the taxpayers, should foot the bill for the cleanup, which was estimated to cost at least $1 billion.

Weaver's amendment was adopted by the committee although several members said it was largely symbolic because TMI funding would be included in the authorization bill for the Department of Energy, not the NRC.

The committee rejected two other amendments by Weaver, an opponent of nuclear power. One would have cut the NRC's research budget by 20 percent. The other would have prohibited the NRC from issuing construction permits for nuclear plants until a nuclear waste repository was built, a position identical to one adopted by Oregon voters in 1980. *(Nuclear waste, p. 455; 1980 Almanac p. 494)*

Energy and Commerce

After rejecting a series of amendments promoted by environmental groups, the House Energy and Commerce Committee June 4 approved its version of HR 2330. The panel filed its report June 9 (H Rept 97-22, Part II).

The bill authorized $501 million for the NRC in fiscal 1982 and $530 million in 1983, the amounts requested by President Reagan. It directed the NRC to develop a plan for cutting in half the time (about 12 years) that it took to approve, build and operate a nuclear plant. It also directed the NRC to reach an understanding promptly with the Energy Department specifying each agency's role in the cleanup of the damaged Three Mile Island reactor.

The bill included controversial "interim licensing" provisions that would allow the NRC to issue temporary operating licenses to new atomic plants before public hearings were completed. Under the bill, the NRC could issue operating licenses for fuel loading, low-power testing or full-scale electric power generation before public hearings were completed. The NRC would determine the duration of the temporary licenses.

Environmental lobbyists were surprised in May when Richard L. Ottinger, D-N.Y., chairman of the Subcommittee on Energy Conservation and Power, supported a compromise NRC authorization that he had worked out with subcommittee Republicans. That compromise, approved by the subcommittee May 13, was adopted by the full committee June 4.

Ottinger explained that the subcommittee action had been necessary to prevent the House Appropriations Committee from putting a temporary licensing rider on the fiscal 1981 supplemental appropriations bill. "Under the circumstances," he said, "this is the best we could get." *(Supplemental, p. 281)*

Committee Republicans praised the bill's licensing provisions — the only part of HR 2330 discussed at the markup. Carlos J. Moorhead, Calif., ranking Republican on Ottinger's subcommittee, said the provisions would save consumers more than $2 billion in additional electric charges that could result from licensing delays.

But members who generally did not favor nuclear power, or at least the expansion of nuclear power, were not convinced. Edward J. Markey, D-Mass., warned that allowing temporary full-power licenses would be "excessive and dangerous. This would be to unlearn the lessons of Three Mile Island," he said.

Markey, Mike Synar, D-Okla., and Toby Moffett, D-Conn., separately offered 10 amendments to the subcommittee's licensing provisions. All 10 were rejected, none getting more than 17 votes in the 42-member committee.

House Floor Action

Overriding arguments that public safety would be jeopardized, the House passed HR 2330 by voice vote Nov. 5 with a compromise provision that would allow nuclear plants to operate before the completion of NRC hearings.

The provision, written by leaders of the Interior and Energy and Commerce committees, would allow the NRC to grant temporary operating licenses to nuclear plants before public hearings were completed. The nuclear industry and the administration strongly supported the provision. James T. Broyhill, R-N.C., said it would "save electric consumers over $1 billion in replacement power costs and 63 months of licensing delays at 11 completed power plants by the end of 1983."

Opposing the provision, Markey said the NRC had determined that there would be only 13 months of delays, almost all at the controversial Diablo Canyon, Calif., plant. "Diablo Canyon," Markey noted, "is the power plant that this past month was revealed to have been built using the wrong blueprints in the designing of the support system for the cooling of the core of the reactor."

Markey offered an amendment to eliminate the temporary licensing provision, saying "now is not the time to compromise on nuclear safety. Now is not the time to fuel public skepticism of nuclear power plants."

He was supported by Moffett, whose Government Operations Subcommittee on Environment, Energy and Natural Resources had issued a report concluding that there would be few licensing delays and those that occurred would not be caused by the public hearing process.

But two crafters of the interim licensing provision, Interior Committee Chairman Morris K. Udall, D-Ariz., and Ottinger, neither known as supporters of nuclear power, said the provision was carefully written and would not be used if it were not needed. Several environmental groups said they did not like the provision but accepted it as a reasonable compromise.

The House rejected Markey's amendment by a 90-304 vote. It also voted 100-293 against a second Markey amendment to prohibit the NRC from issuing export licenses for highly enriched uranium, except in cases where the reactor using the fuel could not operate on lower grades of uranium. *(Votes 277, 278, p. 90-H)*

Markey said the latter amendment would help avert the spread of nuclear weapons, since highly enriched uranium "is a vital element in the construction of nuclear bombs." Opponents said it would cause diplomatic problems with European nations that imported enriched uranium.

As passed, the bill authorized $486 million for the NRC in fiscal 1982 and $513 million in 1983.

Senate Committee Action

The Senate Environment and Public Works Committee May 13 unanimously approved a two-year NRC authorization (S 1207) that contained interim licensing provisions for nuclear plants. The panel filed its report May 15 (S Rept 97-113), but floor consideration was postponed over the summer while Pete V. Domenici, R-N.M., and Simpson tried to work out a compromise on the issue of uranium mill wastes, known as tailings.

Domenici wanted to revise and delay NRC regulations that required uranium mills to cover large piles of radioactive tailings with dirt. The regulations were issued in 1980 in response to a law (PL 95-604) enacted by Congress in 1978. *(1978 Almanac p. 750)*

New Mexico state and industry officials had complained that the regulations were excessive and too costly, although other states said they planned to comply. ■

International Energy Agency

Congress in 1981 approved two six-month extensions of an antitrust law exemption for U.S. oil companies that participated in the International Energy Agency (IEA).

The first extension (PL 97-5) was passed in March, the second (PL 97-50) in September, extending until April 1, 1982, the limited antitrust protection granted the oil companies by the 1975 Energy Policy and Conservation Act (PL 94-163). *(1975 Almanac p. 220)*

The Reagan administration had requested a four-year extension. But the Senate said it would make a thorough study of American involvement in the international program before agreeing to a longer extension.

Sen. Howard M. Metzenbaum, D-Ohio, used the first extension bill as a vehicle for an unsuccessful attempt to reimpose price controls on oil and gasoline, which President Reagan had removed on Jan. 28 as one of his first acts in office.

Metzenbaum, questioning the value of U.S. participation in the IEA, also threatened to oppose the second extension bill, but agreed not to in return for a promise of hearings on the issue.

Background

The international energy program was created in 1974 by 18 major oil-consuming nations, including the United States; in 1981 there were 21 member countries. Administered by IEA, the program had three major parts: reducing demand for oil, increasing oil stockpiles and sharing oil in a shortage. This sharing would be triggered by a 7 percent shortage of oil among all the countries or within just one. The agreement never had been triggered.

Because of the complexity of a world oil-sharing plan, the IEA had left the mechanics of operating it to the oil companies. Twenty-two U.S. oil companies were voluntarily participating in the program in 1981. They shared oil supply information with the IEA, which had the power to reroute international oil shipments in case of a shortage.

In the 1975 energy policy act, Congress gave these companies a limited defense from antitrust suits resulting from their participation in the international program. U.S. antitrust laws prohibited information sharing and market allocation activities. The antitrust protection had been extended three times prior to the 1981 extensions. *(1975 Almanac p. 220)*

First Extension

Congress cleared the first extension (HR 2166 — PL 97-5) on March 10 and President Reagan signed it March 13, two days before the previous extension was scheduled to expire.

Without the antitrust exemption, U.S. oil companies would be unwilling to continue their participation in the international energy program, Energy Secretary James B. Edwards said.

HR 2166 extended the exemption until Sept. 30. Sponsors said that would give the Reagan administration enough time to decide whether it wanted to seek changes in the international energy program.

The Senate Energy Committee approved the extension March 5; it did not file a written report. The House Energy and Commerce Committee reported an identical bill March 6 (HR 2166 — H Rept 97-9), and the House passed it March 10 by a vote of 373-0. *(Vote 11, p. 10-H)*

After handily defeating the amendment to reimpose price controls on oil and gasoline, the Senate passed the House version of the bill by voice vote later the same day, clearing it for the president.

Decontrol Challenged

Supporters of the Metzenbaum amendment, mostly liberals, got about as many votes as they expected, but lost 24-68. *(Vote 27, p. 9-S)*

Metzenbaum admitted before the vote that he did not expect to win. But he said he wanted to force every Republican senator to put a "stamp of approval" on Reagan's decontrol of oil prices. He said that would let the voters know that those senators "approve of higher gasoline prices and higher fuel oil prices and that they believe that somehow it is good for the country to add to the inflationary spiral."

Metzenbaum, along with several other members of Congress, labor unions and consumer groups, had filed a lawsuit in an effort to block Reagan's decontrol action, but their challenge was rejected March 4 by a federal court in Washington, D.C. Oil price controls had been scheduled to expire Sept. 30, 1981, without Reagan's decontrol order.

Metzenbaum called the decontrol action "hasty and ill-advised." He said the move would cost U.S. consumers

$10 billion and would kick up inflation by an extra 1.1 to 1.4 percent. He said higher prices had a relatively small effect on demand for gasoline, and that the amount of conservation produced by immediate decontrol would be only an expensive "drop in the bucket."

But James A. McClure, R-Idaho, chairman of the Senate Energy Committee, said higher prices were caused by the increased cost of foreign oil, not by decontrol. He said decontrol would ease U.S. dependence on foreign oil and increase domestic oil production. Recontrolling oil would be a "monumental mistake," he said.

The 24 senators who backed the Metzenbaum amendment were mostly from the Midwest and Northeast, areas that had been hit hard by rising fuel prices. Only three Republicans voted for the amendment: John H. Chafee, R.I., Paula Hawkins, Fla., and William V. Roth Jr., Del.

Second Antitrust Extension

The second extension of the antitrust exemptions was cleared Sept. 29 and signed into law Sept. 30, the day the previous extension expired.

The Senate Energy Committee reported the bill (S 1475) July 29. There was no written report. The Senate passed it Sept. 22 by voice vote. The House Energy and Commerce Committee reported it Sept. 25 (H Rept 97-254), and the House passed it by voice vote Sept. 29 under suspension of the rules.

During Senate debate, Energy Committee Chairman McClure argued that without the antitrust defense, U.S. oil companies would stop participating in the international program. He said the program reduced U.S. vulnerability to "politically inspired" oil embargoes and would limit world oil price increases during a shortage.

But Metzenbaum, a member of the Energy Committee, questioned the value of U.S. participation. "I doubt that IEA can effectively allocate world oil supplies during a severe shortage," he said. Citing a General Accounting Office report, Metzenbaum said the United States probably would be required under the IEA plan to export some of its oil abroad during a worldwide shortage — a "one-sided deal," he said.

In return for Metzenbaum not opposing the bill extending the antitrust provisions, McClure agreed to limit the extension to six months and to hold hearings on U.S. involvement in the IEA. McClure also agreed that future antitrust extensions would be referred to the Senate Judiciary Committee, of which Metzenbaum was also a member.

Energy Reconciliation

Congress included several controversial energy measures in the budget reconciliation bill (HR 3982 — PL 97-35) cleared July 31. *(Reconciliation bill, p. 256)*

The six principal energy sections of the bill were:
- A three-year authorization for the Department of Energy (DOE), the first DOE reauthorization to clear Congress since the department was created in 1977.
- The creation of a new off-budget account to fund the Strategic Petroleum Reserve (SPR).
- A provision allowing utilities to continue generating electricity from natural gas after 1989.
- A provision modifying a 1976 law setting energy efficiency standards for new buildings. When the standards were issued, they would be voluntary guidelines instead of

mandatory requirements.
- A reduction in the government's authorization for funds to subsidize development of alcohol fuels.
- A three-year authorization for the Solar Bank, which the administration wanted eliminated.

DOE Authorization

It took the steamroller of reconciliation to push a DOE authorization bill through Congress.

Previously, DOE bills had bogged down in congressional debates over a variety of energy policy issues, mostly involving nuclear power and energy price controls, and were never completed.

According to the Congressional Budget Office (CBO), HR 3982 authorized $5.65 billion for DOE's civilian programs in fiscal 1982, about $544 million more than the administration requested. The fiscal 1983 authorization was $6.78 billion; for 1984, $7.03 billion. The administration had not submitted budget requests for those years.

The administration's cost estimates for the authorizations were slightly lower — $5.4 billion for fiscal 1982, $6.4 billion for 1983 and $6.5 billion for 1984. The predictions were different because the administration calculated that it would receive more revenue than CBO calculated for uranium enrichment services provided to utilities. Both sets of figures included approximately $40 million in a revolving fund that did not require appropriation.

The fiscal 1982 totals did not reflect the $3.9 billion for the Strategic Petroleum Reserve which was included in the bill but not counted in the final figure. They also did not include about $5 billion for nuclear weapons produced and developed by DOE. *(Strategic Petroleum Reserve, p. 449)*

President Reagan's budget called for increased spending on nuclear power, while cutting funds for solar energy, energy conservation and synthetic fuel demonstration projects. The additions made by Congress were mostly for solar and conservation.

Congress also managed to preserve a number of programs that were popular among members but that the administration had sought to cut or eliminate.

While the changes reflected congressional desires to spend more than the administration wanted on conservation and renewable energy sources, energy spending under the bill would decrease compared with fiscal 1981. Even with the additions, the fiscal 1982 DOE civilian budget was $656 million below the amount Congress had provided for 1981 and $2.4 billion less than President Carter had requested for the same programs before he left office in January.

Clinch River

The bill authorized $228 million for the Clinch River (Tenn.) nuclear breeder reactor. The administration had requested $254 million.

The House Science Committee had voted 22-18 May 7 to terminate the $3 billion project. The vote came on an amendment to the fiscal 1982 DOE authorization bill (HR 3146), which was later included in the reconciliation package. However, with House adoption of the Republican-backed Gramm-Latta substitute, the committee action was overturned.

Controversy over Clinch River during the Carter administration was one of the reasons Congress had never passed a DOE authorization. In previous years, the Science Committee had strongly supported the project, fighting to

have it funded while President Carter repeatedly tried to kill it.

But in 1981, with the Reagan administration firmly behind the project, the committee reversed itself. Ironically, it was the administration's own insistence on a free market in energy that opponents of the project used as their argument for killing the project. That argument apparently appealed to new members on the panel; 10 of the 13 new members voted to terminate the reactor. The vote was viewed as primarily an economic rather than an antinuclear vote.

The committee vote turned out to be only a short-lived blow to Clinch River supporters. The Senate reconciliation measure did not address the issue, but the Senate Energy Committee assumed the project would continue to be funded. And in preparing the substitute reconciliation bill that the House eventually adopted, Clinch River was one of the sweeteners added by the White House to attract the votes of Southern Democrats.

Conservation

HR 3982 authorized $376 million in fiscal 1982 for energy conservation programs run by state and local governments, including $175 million to weatherize the homes of poor families.

The administration had requested only $195 million for these programs and nothing for weatherization, which it said could be funded through a block grant to states from the Department of Housing and Urban Development.

The House reconciliation bill would have killed the weatherization program, but the Senate continued it and the conference committee agreed with the Senate.

States could get additional money for weatherization from a $1.9 billion block grant for low-income energy assistance that also was included in the reconciliation bill. Up to 15 percent of the amount states received for energy aid could be spent on weatherization. *(Block grant, p. 463)*

For these programs run by state and local governments, the bill authorized $387 million in fiscal 1983 and $399 million in 1984.

For conservation programs run by the federal government, the bill authorized $182 million in fiscal 1982, $96 million more than was requested. Congress authorized funding for several programs the administration wanted dropped, including conservation programs for consumer products, industrial efficiency and community energy systems. The programs were authorized at $188 million in fiscal 1983 and $193 million in 1984.

Solar and Fossil Energy

The reconciliation bill authorized $303 million in fiscal 1982 for solar energy programs, $110 million more than was requested by Reagan but $249 million less than the Carter administration asked.

Within the solar accounts, Congress added $38 million to the $56 million request for research on solar cells that turned sunlight directly into electricity; $29 million to the $19 million requested for windmill programs; $17 million to the $43 million requested for solar heating research; and $18 million to create electricity from temperature differences in the oceans, a program the administration wanted killed.

Congress added $44 million to the president's fiscal 1982 request of $435 million for fossil energy programs. The extra money included additions of $8 million to the $106 million requested for producing liquid fuels from coal;

$7 million to the $29 million requested for electrical fuel cells; $29 million for a new method of generating electricity from coal, for which the administration had not requested funding; and $6 million to the $16 million requested for oil shale research. Congress cut $6 million from the $60 million requested for advanced coal research.

The bill authorized $444 million for fossil energy programs in fiscal 1983, and $437 million in 1984.

Other Changes

Further congressional rewriting of the administration's fiscal 1982 energy budget included:

● Adding $55 million to the $28 million requested for regulatory programs, including compliance efforts to recover $10 billion in oil company overcharges of consumers, and for emergency planning.

● Adding $3 million for small-scale hydroelectric programs for which the administration sought no funding.

● Cutting $7 million from the $1.1 billion requested for nuclear fission programs.

● Adding $38 million for research on gas-cooled nuclear reactors, which could be practical in water-short areas of the West. Reagan sought no funding for the program.

● Adding $13 million to the $460 million requested for nuclear fusion research.

● Adding $18 million to the $49 million requested for research on electric batteries and electric energy systems.

● Cutting $26 million from the department's $273 million administrative budget, including a personnel reduction in the secretary's office.

● Directing the department to provide up to $4 million for a solar electric project located in the district of Rep. Charles W. Stenholm, a Texas Democrat who supported the Reagan budget proposals in the House.

● Directing that $135 million deferred from fiscal 1981 be used for finishing the design on a Kentucky demonstration plant to turn coal into synthetic fuel. The administration wanted to kill this project, called SRC-1 (for solvent refined coal). Congress did not authorize any construction money for fiscal 1982, however.

Legislative History

Before the reconciliation process began, three congressional committees had reported bills authorizing civilian programs of the Department of Energy.

The bill reported by the Senate Energy Committee May 15 (S 1021 — S Rept 97-81) was kept relatively free of details and left specific program decisions to the appropriations committees. It provided approximately the funding levels sought by the administration.

The House Science Committee took the opposite path, reporting a bill May 19 (HR 3146 — H Rept 97-94) that went into minute detail in authorizing research and development programs for DOE. The committee stayed within the administration's energy budget totals but rearranged Reagan's energy priorities.

The House Interior Committee, which was responsible for only a small piece of the energy authorization, reported a bill May 19 (HR 3505 — H Rept 97-60, Part I) covering federal power marketing agencies and DOE's nuclear waste programs. Interior, the authorizing committee that most closely shared the views of environmental groups, continued its insistence on a comprehensive nuclear waste disposal program — setting up a confrontation with Senate Energy, House Science and the administration. *(Nuclear waste, p. 455)*

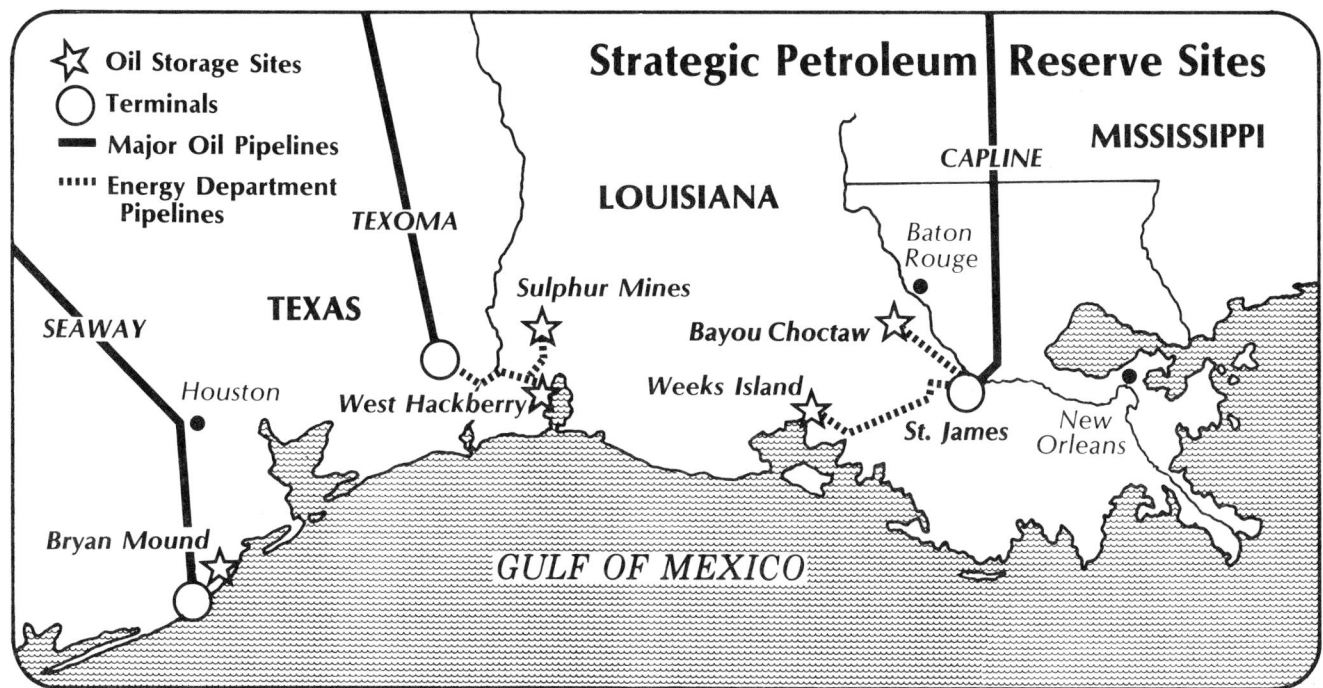

The two House Energy and Commerce subcommittees dealing with energy issues had not begun marking up a DOE authorization before work began on the reconciliation bill.

Strategic Petroleum Reserve

In what members freely admitted was "creative accounting," the reconciliation bill authorized $3.9 billion to buy and store crude oil in the Strategic Petroleum Reserve (SPR) but established a special off-budget account for it so the funding would not be counted in the federal budget.

Another $260 million was included on-budget to administer the program and to expand the storage facilities, located in Louisiana and Texas. The administration had requested all on-budget funding for the reserve.

The SPR enjoyed as much bipartisan support in Congress as any government energy program. But the high cost of filling it caused many members to seek alternative ways of financing the project. The federal government had spent almost $7 billion on the reserve since its inception in the mid-1970s, and it was estimated that another $40 billion would be required during the 1980s. *(SPR background, box, next page)*

Some members, principally on the Budget committees, believed that private funding, such as oil bonds, could be found to pay for the oil, so the funds were knocked out of the budget. But the financial community and the administration opposed private financing, and with no alternative in sight, Congress was faced with either increasing the budget by $3.9 billion or leaving funding for the SPR off-budget. It decided to authorize the spending but simply not count it.

For fiscal 1983 and later, Congress would have to authorize and appropriate money for this off-budget account. Members unhappy with the budgetary gimmick were expected to try to put all SPR funding back into the budget in the future.

The reconciliation bill directed that the SPR be filled at the rate of at least 300,000 barrels of oil a day. It also

directed the administration to determine within six months how much oil the reserve eventually should hold. The original goal was 1 billion barrels; storage of 750 million barrels had already been authorized.

Fuel Use Act

Thanks to some partisan political logrolling in the House Energy and Commerce Committee, the reconciliation bill gave some help to utilities and industrial users of natural gas.

The 1978 Fuel Use Act (PL 95-620) provided that natural gas could not be used after 1989 to fire industrial boilers or to produce electricity. But in an effort to attract votes for the reconciliation measure from key Southern Democrats, whose states were most affected by that provision, the House included repeal of this "off-gas" portion of the 1978 law in the bill. *(1978 Almanac p. 639)*

The Senate Energy Committee did not include such a repeal in its reconciliation package, and the Reagan administration had not yet developed a natural gas policy, but reconciliation conferees agreed to the House provision.

Utilities had complained that, unless the 1978 law was amended, they would have to scrap perfectly good gas-fired generating stations in 1990, even though the facilities could be operated for many more years.

Bolstering their argument was general agreement by experts that more natural gas would be available than was anticipated when Congress passed the 1978 law. That law was passed after a severe winter that saw extensive shortages of natural gas which resulted in industrial and school closings.

To the repeal, the House attached a provision requiring utilities to write conservation plans every five years to save some of the gas they would be allowed to burn. This provision was watered down in conference, however, so that only one initial five-year plan would have to be written.

The reconciliation bill also made several other modifications of the Fuel Use Act. Among other things, it made it easier for utilities to convert voluntarily to coal and still

Strategic Reserve: Insurance Against a Disruption

As insurance against a loss of foreign petroleum imports, the United States in 1981 was pumping about 292,000 barrels of oil a day into salt caverns in Louisiana and Texas. By year's end, this Strategic Petroleum Reserve (SPR) held 220 million 42-gallon barrels of oil; eventually it was to hold 750 million barrels.

If all U.S. oil imports — about 5.5 million barrels a day in 1981 — were cut off, the oil already in the reserve would provide only about 40 days' supply.

If the disruption were smaller — say one million barrels a day — the SPR could replace some seven months of lost supply.

The reserve was authorized by Congress in 1975, in the aftermath of the 1973 Arab oil embargo, in the hope it would reduce the impact of future oil supply disruptions. *(1975 Almanac p. 220)*

Early Problems

Initially, Department of Energy (DOE) officials admitted, the program was plagued by overambitious planning, inept management, schedule delays and large cost overruns. Also, for more than a year between 1979 and 1980, the Carter administration did not put a single drop of oil into the reserve.

The Reagan administration accelerated the volume of crude oil pumped into the SPR, buying it on a plentiful world market. Falling world oil prices also made it easier to buy oil for the reserve, and DOE officials said the program was under control.

The reserve's capacity in 1981 was 250 million barrels. Another 290 million barrels worth of storage was being built, with 210 million barrels more of storage to be constructed later.

The first oil was pumped into the reserve, with much public fanfare, in July 1977. The oil came from Saudi Arabia, at the insistence of James R. Schlesinger, President Carter's energy adviser and later energy secretary. Schlesinger wanted to soften the longstanding Saudi opposition to an American stockpile.

But in March 1979 the Carter administration stopped buying oil because of a world shortage following the Iranian revolution. At that point, there were 91 million barrels in the SPR.

World supplies eased later that year, but the administration did not resume filling the reserve because of quiet Saudi threats to cut production if it did. Administration officials traveled to Saudi Arabia to plead the reserve's case, but were rejected.

Saudi officials complained that they had increased production to stabilize world prices and did not want to push their output close to its limit just to create a reserve in the United States.

Sen. Bill Bradley, D-N.J., who advocated filling the reserve as rapidly as possible, said he was told in 1980 by Saudi oil minister Sheik Ahmed Zaki Yamani that the Saudis would cut production if the SPR was filled. But, Bradley said, Saudi production actually increased after Congress ordered the SPR filled. By mid-1981, he said, there was no longer any concern in Saudi Arabia over the filling of the reserve.

"They now understand that SPR is a life-support system for the U.S. economy, and is not meant to attack them economically," Bradley said.

Richard D. Erb, U.S. executive director of the International Monetary Fund, said the Carter administration should not have asked the Saudis about filling the reserve. He said, "The Saudis I have talked to said that that was stupid. Don't ask, just go ahead and do it, don't make a big thing of it."

No more oil was put in until September 1980, and then only after Congress ordered it.

Fill Rate Increased

President Carter had budgeted to fill the reserve at a rate of 200,000 barrels a day during fiscal 1981, with about 200 million barrels scheduled to be in the reserve at the beginning of fiscal 1982.

The Reagan administration planned to pump 230,000 barrels a day into the SPR in fiscal 1982. Congress in the budget reconciliation bill (HR 3982 — PL 97-35) ordered the reserve filled at a rate of 300,000 barrels a day. *(Story, p. 256)*

---

meet federal air pollution requirements, and allowed homeowners to continue burning natural gas in outdoor lighting fixtures, while requiring utilities to advise homeowners against such use.

Legislative History

Searching for a majority for their opposing reconciliation proposals, both Democrats and Republicans on the House Energy Committee offered three Southern Democrats the gas policy change in return for their votes.

However, neither side managed to muster a majority, and the committee did not send its required reconciliation package to the House Budget Committee. Instead, the Democrats sent a spending reduction package backed by 21 committee Democrats, while the Republicans sent a separate package backed by the committee's 18 Republicans and three Democrats.

While both packages contained the repeal of the off-gas section of the 1978 law, the Democratic version contained provisions to force utilities to save natural gas through conservation. The Democratic package was included in the reconciliation bill approved by the House.

The off-gas repeal was included in both packages solely to win votes. Democrats said the repeal would not generate any budget savings, although the Republicans said it would save about $22 million in enforcement funding. Its inclusion in HR 3982 averted — at least until 1982 — a major battle over the larger issue of gas price decontrol. It had been anticipated that if a bill repealing the off-gas section came to the floor of either chamber, attempts would be made to end natural gas price controls.

Other Energy Changes

Congress also wrote several other energy policy changes into the reconciliation bill.

Energy Efficiency Standards. It made federal energy efficiency standards for new buildings voluntary in-

stead of mandatory, as a 1976 law (PL 94-385) required. New federal buildings would be required to meet the standards, however. *(1976 Almanac p. 95)*

Alcohol Fuels. It reduced funding available for alcohol fuels production.

In 1980, under the omnibus Energy Security Act (PL 96-294), Congress authorized $1.2 billion for the Agriculture and Energy departments to encourage production of alcohol fuels from agricultural and wood products and waste; $600 million was authorized for each agency for loans, loan guarantees, price guarantees and purchase agreements. *(1980 Almanac p. 479)*

HR 3982 reduced the authorization to $460 million for each department.

Solar Bank. In a rebuke to President Reagan, the bill provided a three-year authorization for the Solar Bank administered by the Department of Housing and Urban Development. The bank was authorized to provide $50 million each in fiscal 1982-84 in financial assistance to individuals and businesses that installed conservation or solar equipment.

The bank was created in 1980, also as part of the Energy Security Act, the main purpose of which was to spur development of synthetic fuels. But in March 1981, Reagan requested termination of the program, saying tax credits and high oil prices would encourage solar development without need for federal money.

Emergency Oil Allocation

Both the House and Senate, by lopsided votes, passed bills (S 1503, HR 4700) giving the president authority to allocate oil supplies and set petroleum prices during a severe shortage — authority President Reagan said he did not need or want.

A conference committee met briefly Dec. 15 but did not reach agreement on a compromise measure and planned to meet again after Congress returned in 1982.

The administration insisted the free market could do a better job of allocating oil during a shortage than the government could, and opposed any extension or replacement of the 1973 Emergency Petroleum Allocation Act (EPAA), which expired Sept. 30. Administration officials and others claimed that law exacerbated the effects of past oil shortages, resulting in gasoline lines at service stations and other supply problems.

However, many members of Congress felt standby authority to deal with a severe petroleum supply disruption was needed, and said it should be enacted "dispassionately" before a crisis actually occurred.

Both the House and Senate bills would give the president broad discretionary authority to allocate petroleum supplies and set prices during a severe shortage.

Background

EPAA (PL 93-159) was enacted, over the objections of President Richard M. Nixon, in the midst of the 1973 Arab embargo on oil shipments to the United States. There were long lines at gas stations then, and the administration's voluntary allocation policy was not working. *(1973 Almanac p. 623)*

The law required the president to issue mandatory regulations for allocating and pricing crude oil and oil products. Some oil users, such as independent refiners and farmers, were assured of supplies by the act.

Congress extended the law in 1975, and modified it to make the mandatory controls discretionary beginning in 1979 and to have them expire altogether on Sept. 30, 1981. *(1975 Almanac p. 723)*

At congressional hearings in May and June, witnesses generally agreed that the president should have authority to intervene in the market during a severe petroleum shortage. But there was no general agreement on the definition of such a shortage.

The administration did not testify, saying it was still developing a position.

Tired of waiting, several members of Congress introduced their own legislation. James A. McClure, R-Idaho, chairman of the Senate Energy Committee, introduced S 1503, and Philip R. Sharp, D-Ind., chairman of the House Energy and Commerce Subcommittee on Fossil and Synthetic Fuels, drafted a bill that became HR 4700.

Administration Position

At later hearings July 28, Deputy Energy Secretary W. Kenneth Davis said the administration opposed any legislation as unnecessary. Davis said government management of past petroleum shortages had "seriously hampered the ability of the marketplace to respond to short-term problems and actually contributed to the supply shortage."

In any future disruption of oil supplies, which he said was likely, prices would rise until demand equaled the available oil, Davis said. He shrugged off some members' fears that gasoline could then cost $3 or $4 a gallon.

Davis said the administration had sufficient authority under other laws to allocate fuel for national security needs. And because the Strategic Petroleum Reserve (SPR) was being filled and privately held stocks were high, he said, the nation was in better shape than in the past to weather any disruption of oil imports.

President Reagan, in a Sept. 14 letter to the two top-ranking Republicans on the House Energy and Commerce Committee, said, "I fully share your opposition to any extension of allocation and price control authority."

The administration's determination to let the market handle any oil shortage was criticized by the General Accounting Office (GAO) in a report released Sept. 29. The report said the United States was "grossly unprepared" to cope with a major shortage, and the administration's total reliance on the marketplace was "inappropriate."

Senate Committee Action

Rejecting Reagan's wish to rely on the free market, the Republican-controlled Senate Energy Committee approved a standby petroleum allocation bill (S 1503) by a 13-4 vote Sept. 30, only hours before the president's existing allocation authority expired. The panel filed its report Oct. 1 (S Rept 97-199).

The bill directed Reagan to write within 90 days a plan to allocate oil during a "severe shortage" (undefined). It gave priority to the same list of users that were protected under EPAA, including farmers and refiners. It would override state oil allocation laws and would give Congress 15 days to veto any plan before the president could implement it. Presidential powers under the bill would expire Jan. 1, 1985, just before the end of Reagan's term.

The only strong support for Reagan's approach came from a junior Democrat, Bill Bradley of New Jersey, and a freshman Republican, Don Nickles of Oklahoma. Bradley,

Nickles, John P. East, R-N.C., and Gordon J. Humphrey, R-N.H., cast the four votes against reporting the bill.

When the committee began marking up S 1503 Sept. 22, Nickles predicted the bill would become "a laundry list to protect everybody's friends." Although S 1503 as introduced by McClure was a simple measure with broad discretionary authority for the president, after five voting sessions the committee produced a bill full of the details McClure had hoped to avoid.

Bradley chided committee Republicans, who wore buttons signaling the start of the 1982 fiscal year and the beginning of Reagan's economic programs. "At the verge of a 'new beginning,'" Bradley said, "I'm afraid we're going back to the old ways."

Some committee aides predicted that if Congress cleared anything resembling S 1503, Reagan would veto it. McClure admitted he was not sure he could persuade the administration to accept the bill.

The committee rejected an amendment by Nickles to gut the bill of price controls. It was defeated on a voice vote, supported only by Nickles and Bradley, after senior committee Democrats Henry M. Jackson, Wash., and J. Bennett Johnston, La., insisted that oil allocation authority would not work without strong price controls.

To ease the impact of skyrocketing oil prices, which he acknowledged would occur if the free market were allowed to act in a shortage, Bradley proposed "recycling" to taxpayers extra government revenues from the windfall profits tax on oil. "This would protect individuals while preserving the efficiency of the marketplace," he said. But Bradley could not convince other committee members, and his amendment was defeated 3-10.

Senate Floor Action

Rolling past White House objections by an overwhelming margin, the Senate passed S 1503 on Oct. 29. The vote was 85-7. *(Vote 340, p. 57-S)*

The administration did not actively lobby against the bill.

McClure took pains to emphasize that S 1503 would not extend the mandatory allocation programs of EPAA but would replace that law with discretionary authority for the president. But Bradley said, "Those who say we are not re-enacting EPAA ... have not read the bill." He said S 1503 would extend the "very authorities that have twice in this country caused gasoline lines."

Led by McClure and Johnston, the Senate defeated all hostile amendments offered to the committee bill.

Bradley offered his amendment to "recycle" the additional revenue from the windfall profits tax through reduced personal income taxes, higher Social Security payments and block grants to states. McClure and Johnston said the idea needed more study, McClure calling it a "redistribution of wealth." The amendment was rejected, 8-88. *(Vote 336, p. 57-S)*

Another Bradley amendment would require the president to distribute oil from the Strategic Petroleum Reserve, selling it to the highest bidder, rather than allocating private oil supplies during a shortage. "SPR is our most potent tool for use in an oil supply disruption," Bradley argued. McClure said the committee intentionally did not include SPR in S 1503 but would hold hearings on plans for distributing oil from the reserve during a shortage. The amendment was defeated, 18-76. *(Vote 337, p. 57-S)*

The closest vote came on an amendment by George J.

Mitchell, D-Maine, to allow governors to allocate petroleum products within their states before the president put a national allocation plan into effect. McClure said that could result in a patchwork of laws, varying from state to state. The Senate rejected the amendment, 42-53. *(Vote 339, p. 57-S)*

Also defeated, 22-73, was a proposal by Lowell P. Weicker Jr., R-Conn., to allow the president to ration gasoline and diesel fuel in a shortage. *(Vote 338, p. 57-S)*

By voice vote, the Senate adopted amendments by Bradley, requiring a study of his oil revenue recycling plan; by the Energy Committee, making it clear that the bill's override of state laws did not apply to state energy conservation programs, such as odd-even gasoline sales; and by David Durenberger, R-Minn., allowing Congress to review the president's standby plans as soon as they were written.

Provisions

As passed by the Senate, S 1503:

● Allowed the president to allocate petroleum and set prices when he determined that there was a severe shortage. A severe shortage was not defined.

● Gave priority status to the same list of oil users that had been protected under EPAA, including farmers, refiners, gasoline marketers and local governments.

● Required the president to write a standby version of the old "buy-sell" program that detailed which companies would get oil from other firms and which ones would be forced to share part of their oil.

● Required the president, if he found it necessary to allocate oil, to set aside petroleum for each state government to allocate.

● Required the president to write these standby rules within 90 days of enactment.

● Gave either house of Congress 15 days to veto any allocation plan before the president could put it into effect during a crisis.

● Limited to 150 days the period during which the president could allocate oil and set prices before getting additional congressional approval.

● Provided that the authority in the act would expire Jan. 1, 1985.

House Committee Action

The House Energy and Commerce Committee approved a standby petroleum emergency authority bill (HR 4700) Nov. 18 by a 28-14 vote. It filed its report Dec. 7 (H Rept 97-363).

The bill had been approved Nov. 5 by the Subcommittee on Fossil and Synthetic Fuels, after several weeks of trying. The subcommittee approved the bill while Clarence J. Brown, R-Ohio, the leading opponent of the legislation on the panel, was out of town campaigning for the Ohio governorship.

The bill required the president to write standby plans within six months for allocating oil during a "severe petroleum supply interruption." Sharp said it would provide "great flexibility" to the president to handle an emergency. Congress would have to approve before any allocation plan could go into effect. Sharp said the bill was "not a clone" of the 1973 EPAA.

However, opponents called it simply "a re-creation of EPAA." And, in dissenting views to the committee report, nine Republicans said EPAA was "one of the worst energy statutes ever enacted. It created gasoline lines. It shut

down factories. It subsidized imported oil. And it bailed out the inefficient oil refiners — all at an enormous cost to the average American consumer.''

Several Democrats on the panel felt the authority in HR 4700 gave too much discretion to the president. Timothy E. Wirth, D-Colo., offered an amendment in subcommittee to include much more specific allocation procedures and give greater protection for small refiners and farmers. But the amendment was defeated, 10-14.

Also rejected was a Wirth amendment to require the president to issue specific plans for using the oil in the Strategic Petroleum Reserve in a shortage.

The subcommittee voted 5-12 against an amendment by Phil Gramm, D-Texas, to put a specific "trigger" in the bill. Under Gramm's amendment there would have to be a drop of at least 20 percent in oil imports for 20 days before the president could begin allocating oil.

Sharp had waited to see what standby controls the Senate produced before scheduling action on HR 4700, hoping that passage of a bill by the Republican-controlled Senate would make it easier for House Republicans to support similar legislation.

House Floor Action

The House passed HR 4700 Dec. 14 by a vote of 244-136. *(Vote 344, p. 112-H)*

Once again, the White House made little effort to persuade members to vote against the bill.

Sharp took pains to emphasize that HR 4700 was not an extension of EPAA. Rather, he said, it would be "flexible new standby authority to help meet an oil crisis."

This flexibility drew objections from some liberal Democrats, who complained that the bill was not detailed enough and did not allow rationing of gasoline. But they voted for it anyway.

Tom Corcoran, R-Ill., who led the opposition to the bill on the floor, said the country was better prepared to meet a shortage than in the past because of the SPR, which held about 250 million barrels of oil.

Provisions

As passed by the House, HR 4700:

● Authorized the president to allocate oil supplies and control petroleum prices in a "severe petroleum supply interruption." The bill did not define a severe interruption, leaving it up to the president's discretion.

● Required the president to send Congress an emergency preparedness plan within six months of enactment. This contingency plan would not have to be approved by Congress and could be modified later by the president. It must include a program for sharing crude oil among refiners. Discretionary guidelines were included in the bill, suggesting that priority be given to certain consumers of petroleum, such as farmers and refiners.

● Gave Congress 15 days to disapprove a presidential allocation plan before it could be implemented.

● Limited the implementation of the allocation and price controls to 150 days. After that, the president would have to send Congress another plan, which it could veto.

● Overrode state government price and allocation laws.

● Terminated all authority under the act Dec. 31, 1984.

● Required the president, within six months of enactment, to send Congress a new, more detailed plan for using the oil in the Strategic Petroleum Reserve in an emergency.

● Extended until June 30, 1985, antitrust exemptions for

oil companies that shared information with the International Energy Agency. The existing exemptions were due to expire April 1, 1982. *(Story, p. 446)*

● Required the administration to continue to collect petroleum price and supply information. The Reagan administration had planned to stop collecting such information. ∎

Oil Company Mergers

On the last night of the session, the House agreed to unusual tactics and took a hefty slap at efforts by major oil companies to gobble up smaller oil firms.

By a 233-107 vote Dec. 16, it passed a bill (HR 5274) to put a seven-month moratorium on oil company takeovers. The bill was particularly aimed at blocking Mobil Oil Corp. from buying Marathon Oil Co. *(Vote 353, p. 116-H)*

Senate sponsors were unable to overcome parliamentary obstacles, however, and so the legislation was not considered there.

Squashing protests over its methods, the House passed HR 5274 just minutes before it closed its doors for the year. Sponsors had to defeat a motion to adjourn before they secured House approval for the bill. *(Vote 352, p. 116-H)*

The measure would put a seven-month moratorium, retroactive to Dec. 1, 1981, on takeovers of any of the top 40 oil companies by any of the nine largest firms. The rankings would be based on domestic production of crude oil, not on sales.

Mobil ranked ninth in domestic production. It had been trying for months to acquire Marathon, which ranked 14th. Mobil was locked in a multibillion-dollar bidding war with U.S. Steel Corp. for Marathon. When it appeared that U.S. Steel would win, Mobil threatened to buy both companies to get the oil reserves owned by Marathon.

(The Supreme Court on Jan. 6, 1982, rejected a last-ditch appeal by Mobil to halt the acquisition of Marathon by U.S. Steel, clearing the way for that merger to take place.)

Bill Rammed Through

HR 5274 was introduced Dec. 16, after House sponsors reached a compromise with their Senate counterparts. It was never considered by a House committee. The House passed it the same night under suspension of the rules, a procedure normally reserved for non-controversial bills.

Philip R. Sharp, D-Ind., chairman of the House Energy and Commerce Subcommittee on Fossil and Synthetic Fuels, said he thought the procedure was "obnoxious," but that it was important for the House to make a dramatic statement.

Sharp, whose subcommittee had approved a more stringent measure (HR 4930) Dec. 15, said he hoped the bill would "shake up the administration," which he said had been indifferent toward mergers of large companies.

The bill also would put large energy companies on notice of congressional unhappiness over takeovers before more such efforts occurred, Sharp said. He said members feared such mergers would diminish competition among oil companies, particularly on a regional basis.

Headquartered in Ohio, Marathon sold its products in its own stations and through independent dealers in the Midwest, including Sharp's home state of Indiana.

The bill's sponsor, Clarence J. Brown, Ohio, ranking Republican on Sharp's subcommittee, and John D. Dingell, D-Mich., chairman of the full Energy and Commerce Com-

mittee, rammed the bill through the House Dec. 16.

At one point in the heated debate, Brown offered to yield speaking time to another Republican and was told "take your time and shove it."

Earlier in the week, Brown and Dingell had hoped the Senate would attach the measure to a communications bill (S 271). But supporters of the merger moratorium in the Senate — Bob Packwood, R-Ore., chairman of the Senate Commerce Committee, and the panel's senior Democrat, Howard W. Cannon, Nev. — were blocked by opponents who learned of their plan through press reports.   ∎

Pauley Group Oil Leases

Legislation giving potentially lucrative drilling rights off the California coast back to a consortium of oil companies slid through the House in August, but it ran into controversy in the Senate and remained stalled in the Energy Committee at year's end.

The legislation (S 506, HR 1946) would reinstate two leases for oil exploration in the Santa Barbara Channel once held by a consortium of independent oil companies called the Pauley Group. The leases expired in 1973 while the Pauley Group was suing the U.S. government.

Sponsors said reinstating the leases, which could be worth hundreds of millions of dollars, was a matter of equity for the companies. Opponents said the Pauley Group had had its day in court and lost, and that the tracts should be leased to the highest bidder.

Sen. Dale Bumpers, D-Ark., threatened to filibuster the heavily lobbied bill if it came to the Senate floor. He had blocked enactment of a similar bill in 1980 by threatening an end-of-session filibuster.

Bumpers said that if the legislation passed, the government stood to lose $1 billion in revenues that would come from putting the leases up for bids again. Under the bills, the government would get 50 percent of net profits from the oil exploration venture, instead of its customary royalty — the proceeds from 16.7 percent of the oil produced.

Background

In 1967, 11 independent oil companies formed the Pauley Group, headed by Pauley Petroleum Inc., to bid on offshore leases off the California coast. In March 1968, the consortium paid $74 million in cash and an annual rental of $34,560 for the right to explore and produce oil on two tracts in the Santa Barbara Channel. The leases were for five years or until the oil ran out.

Immediate exploration was begun and eight exploratory wells, all unsuccessful, were drilled by January 1969. As the group was preparing to drill its ninth well in late January 1969, an oil blowout occurred nearby at a well owned by Union Oil Co. The massive spill was among the worst in U.S. history, spoiling beaches and killing waterfowl along the coast.

The government suspended all drilling operations in the channel and then altered the standard of negligence for oil spills. The new standard made drilling companies liable not only for all cleanup costs of an oil spill but also for any damage to a third party, regardless of fault.

With the new standard, the private liability insurance market for offshore oil operations collapsed. The Pauley Group lost its insurance. While the major oil companies had the resources to insure themselves once the drilling ban was lifted, smaller companies such as Pauley did not, and "risked financial disaster by resuming drilling operations," according to the House Interior Committee.

In April 1969, Pauley filed suit against the government, claiming the United States had violated its contract by suspending drilling operations and imposing strict liability requirements. It asked the court to award it the $74 million bonus payment plus drilling costs and as much as $350 million in lost profits.

In 1975, while Pauley's suit was in court and after its leases had expired, Standard Oil Co. of California (Chevron) struck oil on a tract adjacent to Pauley's. According to Bumpers, that renewed Pauley's interest in keeping the tracts. "Pauley wouldn't have given you 10 cents for those leases until after Chevron hit oil," he said.

Bumpers also noted that by 1981 the Pauley Group included several major oil companies, including Standard Oil Co. of Indiana (Amoco) and Gulf Oil Corp., not just small independent companies.

In 1979, the U.S. Court of Claims rejected Pauley's claim against the government. The court suggested that the president or Congress could, "as a matter of grace," extend the lease on the two tracts to allow them to drill.

House Action

The House passed HR 1946 by voice vote, essentially without debate, on Aug. 4, the day before Congress began its August recess. The measure had been reported by the Interior Committee July 13 (H Rept 97-173).

Jerry M. Patterson, D-Calif., the bill's sponsor, said the measure would "provide the federal government with substantial economic benefits."

There was some dispute over that, however. The Congressional Budget Office (CBO) said the bill could cost the government between $250 million and $1.6 billion in fiscal 1982. The Interior Committee, which reported HR 1946 before the CBO estimate was made, said in its report that the bill "will not involve any costs." The estimate was also disputed by the Pauley Group.

CBO Director Alice M. Rivlin sent a clarification letter to the Senate Energy Committee on Sept. 16. She stuck to the estimate on the initial cost of the bill, but she said the government might get as much revenue from reinstating the leases as it would if it resold them. It could be more or it could be less, she said.

The cost estimates varied so widely because of uncertainty over how much would be bid for the tracts if they were resold and how much oil and gas could be produced from them.

The Reagan administration said it was neutral on the measure. The Carter administration had opposed the earlier bill.

Senate Committee Fight

Malcolm Wallop, R-Wyo., led the fight for reinstatement of the leases in the Senate Energy Committee. He said the legislation was needed to ensure that independent oil companies got part of the offshore oil business.

Wallop had hoped the committee, which approved the reinstatement 15-1 in 1980, would report out S 506 Sept. 30, but the markup was called off after Bumpers obtained a letter from the administration saying the bill could cost the government $1 billion in lost revenues. That letter, combined with the CBO cost estimate, led Bumpers' staff to believe that S 506 was as good as dead.

Lobbyists for the Pauley Group did not give up, how-

ever. They drafted an amendment that would put the leases back up for bids. But unless the highest bid was more than $250 million, Pauley would get the leases back for only the cost of the rental payments due since 1973 — about $34,000 a year.

Sponsors believed they had the votes to pass S 506 with this change, and scheduled a markup for Nov. 18. However, Wallop had other business that day and could not attend, so the committee did not take up the bill and the amendment was never offered.

Bumpers, who was sharply critical of the heavy lobbying on the bill, called the amendment "arrogant and insidious." He said other oil companies would be unlikely to bid $250 million because the amendment also would require the successful bidder to give the government a larger royalty payment than normally was made. He said the amendment would result in Pauley getting its leases back. ∎

Naval Oil Reserves

Congress failed to block President Reagan's Oct. 6 proposal to continue pumping oil from the Naval Petroleum Reserve at Elk Hills, Calif., for another three years.

The House Armed Services Committee, with unusual partisanship, voted 19-13 Dec. 9 to block the plan. But the vote proved meaningless because the full House did not act on the disapproval resolution (H Res 287 — H Rept 97-392) before the deadline for congressional consideration (Jan. 6, 1982). The Senate took no action to disapprove Reagan's plan.

The prime beneficiaries of continued production at Elk Hills would be refiners in Reagan's home state of California, and the U.S. Treasury, which got $2 billion a year in revenues from selling the oil. Production also was allowed to continue at the naval reserve at Teapot Dome, Wyo., but it was nearly depleted.

Although the Armed Services Committee traditionally operated in a bipartisan manner, on the resolution of disapproval Democratic members voted 15-4 for it, while the Republicans opposed it 4-9.

The president had told Congress Oct. 6 it was in the national interest to continue production from the reserves at the maximum efficient rate for another three years.

Energy Department (DOE) officials acknowledged the decision was based primarily on economic benefits to the Treasury from sale of the oil. The DOE office that administered the reserves had recommended that Elk Hills be "shut in" (producing at only the minimum level necessary to sustain the field).

Under the 1976 law (PL 94-258) that allowed produc-

tion at the military reserves, Congress had 90 days to block that decision by passage of a resolution of disapproval by either chamber.

House Armed Services thought the oil from Elk Hills should be saved for use by the military in case of emergency. Under H Res 287, oil from the field, the second largest in the United States, would have dried up to a relative trickle, from 180,000 barrels a day to about 25,000 barrels a day.

"There really is no need for Elk Hills production [now]," said Richard C. White, D-Texas, chairman of the Armed Services Investigations Subcommittee, who sponsored the disapproval resolution. "But if we ever get into a national defense emergency, there will be a need for it." White's panel approved the resolution, 6-4, Dec. 8.

Opposing H Res 287 were the administration, California legislators representing refiners that benefited from Elk Hills oil, and Standard Oil Co. of California (Chevron), which owned 20 percent of the reserve.

Background

The reserves at Elk Hills and Teapot Dome were set aside by the government early in the 1900s to ensure that the Navy would have fuel in an emergency. But in 1976 Congress authorized production of oil from these reserves for six years. After that, the president could ask for three-year extensions of production if he certified that it was in the national interest to do so, as Reagan did Oct. 6. *(1976 Almanac p. 105)*

Teapot Dome was producing only about 3,000 barrels of oil a day in 1981, but Elk Hills had proven reserves of over a billion barrels and, in an emergency, could pump nearly 250,000 barrels daily. (The daily peacetime requirement of the Defense Department was about 450,000 barrels a day.)

Elk Hills oil was a light crude that was exceptionally high in quality and low in sulfur content. About 100,000 barrels a day were being sold to California refiners, who mixed it with heavier, lower quality oil in a blend that was piped to West Coast refineries. According to a staff report prepared for the House Energy and Commerce Committee, which studied the issue but did not act on it, "a number of California small refiners have become very dependent on Elk Hills crude oil over the past six years."

Part of the remaining oil went to Chevron, as its share, and part was sold to the Defense Department.

One argument made by Armed Services for shutting in Elk Hills was that a West Coast supply of crude oil was needed in case of a national emergency. Although there were over 200 million barrels of oil in the Strategic Petroleum Reserve on the U.S. Gulf Coast, that oil could only get to the West Coast by ship through the Panama Canal. ∎

Nuclear Waste Disposal Bills Reported

After failing in 1980 to enact a comprehensive national policy for disposing of nuclear waste, Congress tried again in 1981.

The issue was shouldered aside by budget matters early in the year, but pressures for the establishment of a waste program finally spurred action on the controversial legislation.

In late autumn, two Senate committees — Energy and Environment — approved different versions of a bill (S

1662) setting a timetable for locating and approving construction of a permanent nuclear waste repository by the year 2000. The committees filed a joint report Nov. 30 (S Rept 97-282).

One of three House committees with jurisdiction also reported a bill (HR 5016) calling for construction of a waste repository by 1990.

Senate sponsors had hoped for floor action before adjournment, but the bill was put over until 1982. Floor fights

were expected over how to treat nuclear waste from the military weapons program — the issue that killed nuclear waste legislation in 1980 — and over what kind of waste storage to have.

The Environment Committee voted to subject wastes from the production of nuclear weapons to the same requirements as civilian waste. But because of what sponsors admitted was "political expediency," the Energy Committee bill did not apply to military waste.

"We have to keep them [military and civilian wastes] separate if we want to move a bill through Congress," said Energy Committee Chairman James A. McClure, R-Idaho. Senate Armed Services Chairman John Tower, R-Texas, had warned McClure that if military waste was not excluded from the bill, his committee would seek to have the bill referred to it, which could delay or kill the legislation.

The Armed Services committees traditionally had opposed any civilian control over military programs.

As for the type of waste storage to have, senators from Gulf Coast states, who feared nuclear wastes would be stored permanently in underground salt formations in their region, favored long-term, monitored waste storage vaults instead. The Energy Committee supported such monitored storage; Environment called for permanent disposal.

As in the past, the three House committees also took different approaches to the nuclear waste problem, but by year's end they were moving to develop a consensus bill to take to the floor:

● Scrapping a controversial earlier bill (HR 1909) that provided only for an unlicensed test facility, the Science and Technology Committee approved a bill (HR 5016) Nov. 20 to establish a national waste repository by the mid-1990s. The committee filed its report Dec. 15 (H Rept 97-411, Part I).

● The Interior Subcommittee on Energy and the Environment finished work on a comprehensive waste policy bill (HR 3809) introduced by Committee Chairman Morris K. Udall, D-Ariz.

● The Energy and Commerce Committee took no action, but just before adjournment staff members developed a compromise bill they hoped would be agreeable to the Interior Committee. The House bill in 1980 was a compromise between these two committees, while a narrower Science Committee measure was discarded.

Background

Although nuclear waste had been generated in the United States since the 1940s, Congress had never enacted a plan for permanently isolating it from the public. Some waste remained highly radioactive for thousands of years.

The nuclear industry, which had been politically and financially troubled since the 1979 accident at the Three Mile Island nuclear plant in Pennsylvania, said waste legislation was badly needed. Lack of a safe waste disposal plan reduced public confidence in nuclear power, industry officials said. They said the technology existed for disposing of nuclear waste but that a solution had not been adopted largely because of political reasons. *(Three Mile Island, 1979 Almanac p. 694)*

Environmental spokesmen, on the other hand, claimed there were many unresolved technical questions relating to the burial of nuclear waste. They opposed any legislative provisions that would permit accelerated environmental reviews or short-circuit the licensing process of the Nuclear Regulatory Commission (NRC).

The only type of nuclear waste for which Congress had established a disposal policy was low-level radioactive waste. In 1980 Congress gave the states the responsibility for storing that. *(Nuclear waste background, 1980 action, 1980 Almanac p. 494)*

No policy had been enacted for disposing of spent (burned) fuel from nuclear reactors that was piling up at reactor sites around the country, or the millions of gallons of highly radioactive liquid waste that had been generated, mostly in weapons production. It was being stored in tanks in Washington state, Idaho, South Carolina and New York until a waste program was developed.

Controversial Issues

There were a number of thorny issues to be resolved before a national nuclear waste policy could be put into effect. Among them:

Spent Fuel. There were 76 operating nuclear reactors in the United States in 1981, with 80 more under construction. The Department of Energy (DOE) estimated that by 1986 utilities would start running out of room to store spent fuel at reactor sites.

Spent fuel, although not technically classified as waste, was highly radioactive and essentially useless unless it was reprocessed. Originally it was assumed that it would be reprocessed — turned into more uranium fuel, plutonium that could fuel future breeder reactors, and waste for disposal. But the Carter administration banned commercial reprocessing for fear the plutonium produced could be stolen and turned into nuclear weapons.

The Reagan administration supported reprocessing; Deputy Energy Secretary W. Kenneth Davis called it the cornerstone of the administration's waste policy. DOE officials said it would eliminate the need for special storage facilities for spent fuel, would recover the valuable fuel remaining and would put the residue in a more appropriate form for permanent disposal.

But as long as there was no commercial reprocessing, something had to be done to either store or dispose of spent fuel. One idea floated by the administration was to have the government reprocess civilian waste to obtain the plutonium for military weapons. *(Story, box, p. 458)*

The Carter administration had wanted to build a federal facility to store spent fuel after the utilities ran out of room. But the Reagan administration said such away-from-reactor (AFR) storage should be the responsibility of private industry, not the government.

Several bills before Congress — including the Republican Senate proposal — would create a federal AFR funded by utilities with nuclear plants. Environmental groups opposed AFRs as a bail-out for the nuclear industry.

Type of Disposal. Another controversial issue was the question of how to permanently dispose of nuclear waste: in deep, underground geological formations or in monitored, man-made vaults near the earth's surface.

There also were differing estimates of how much time would be needed to examine various sites, design a facility, obtain the necessary permission from regulatory agencies, build the facility and begin putting waste in it.

Some members of Congress wanted to build an unlicensed test and evaluation waste facility, which might or might not eventually become a permanent repository. Supporters of a test facility said it would instill public confidence in the waste program and provide needed experience in handling radioactive material. But environmental groups said it would be of little use and could hamper progress

toward a permanent repository.

Environmental groups also opposed proposals for storing nuclear wastes in man-made, monitored vaults. They said wastes should be permanently isolated from mankind in deep underground formations.

Funding. Another question to be resolved was who should pay for nuclear waste storage. To get around objections to federal funding, most of the bills considered in Congress would put a mandatory surcharge on electricity generated by nuclear power to pay for the costs of waste management by the government. The charges would be paid by the consumers of nuclear-generated electricity.

State Role. One of the biggest problems in formulating a nuclear waste policy was expected to be the reluctance of state or Indian tribal governments to accept a repository within their borders. None of the 30 states with potential storage sites was happy about the thought of having a repository.

As a result of compromises reached in Congress during the 1980 nuclear waste debate, most of the bills considered in 1981 would allow a state or tribe to object to a federal decision to put a waste repository within its borders. The objection would stand if either house of Congress passed a resolution upholding it.

Environmental groups said states should be allowed to veto waste facilities within their borders — or at least be able to object early in the process, such as when a site was first selected for examination. The nuclear industry wanted to require both houses of Congress to uphold a state's objection, not just one.

Military Waste. Radioactive waste from the nuclear weapons program constituted more than 90 percent of the nation's total volume of nuclear waste. Of the more than 77 million gallons of high-level waste produced in the United States, all but a few hundred thousand gallons came from weapons production.

A number of leaks in storage tanks and some intentional releases of waste into the soil had occurred over the years. Environmentalists cited such incidents as reasons why the NRC should regulate military wastes as well as civilian. The hazard to the public was the same regardless of where the waste came from, they said.

But those on the other side of that issue, including some members of Congress, argued that regulation could interfere with weapons production. They also said it would be a bad precedent to allow states to object to the siting of defense facilities — including nuclear storage facilities — within their borders. The 1980 nuclear waste bill died when some members refused to agree to let states object to having waste from the production of nuclear weapons stored within their borders.

Senate Committee Action

S 1662 was introduced Sept. 24 by McClure; Environment Committee Chairman Robert T. Stafford, R-Vt.; Alan K. Simpson, R-Wyo., chairman of the Environment Subcommittee on Nuclear Regulation, and other Republican members of the two committees.

Under a procedure established when the bill was introduced, after one committee approved it, the other had 30 days to act on the measure.

Energy Committee

The bill was rammed through the Energy Committee Oct. 21, at the insistence of McClure. The vote was 11-4.

Several members complained that they were asked to vote on the bill before the committee staff had finished writing it, and said they were unsure of what had been done.

The markup was unusual. A quorum was never present at any one time, and senators were allowed to vote over an extended period. McClure said the haste was necessary to get a bill passed in 1981. He noted that the committee's approval of S 1662 "started the clock" on the Environment Committee.

The bill set a timetable for siting and building a permanent repository for nuclear waste, and provided for building an unlicensed test repository for high-level waste. It also provided for the construction of at least one federal away-from-reactor (AFR) storage facility for spent utility fuel, and a long-term monitored waste storage facility (as opposed to permanent disposal). It authorized a charge on nuclear-generated electricity to fund the waste program and gave states a procedure for objecting to facilities within their borders.

The bill would not cover military wastes. Under a provision added by the staff after the markup, comingling of military and civilian waste was prohibited in effect exempting military waste from the bill.

J. Bennett Johnston, D-La., seeking to block the disposal of nuclear waste in salt domes in his region, argued that the bill should emphasize long-term monitored storage instead of permanent disposal. He said the technology existed for man-made storage, which he said would be the safest. Johnston also said the bill's timetable for siting a permanent repository was too fast. In effect, it would result in the selection of sites in Washington, Nevada and one along the Gulf Coast.

The committee agreed to delete language indicating that man-made storage would be a secondary approach to permanent disposal — in effect putting both ideas on an equal footing. It also required the selection of three sites for a permanent repository by 1984, instead of two in 1982 and one in 1983, as the bill originally provided.

These and other amendments were left to the staff to write into the bill, along with more than 40 technical amendments prepared by the staff that were not discussed in the markup. McClure told members they could propose additional amendments before the bill went to the floor, and those adopted would be presented as committee amendments on the floor.

Environment Committee

The Environment Committee approved a significantly different version of S 1662 Nov. 16 by an 11-0 vote.

The two changes that disturbed Energy Committee members the most were the inclusion of military waste in the bill and the requirement that work on a permanent repository be underway before the government could build a facility for monitored, retrievable waste storage.

The Environment Committee bill called for a unified nuclear waste repository that would accept both military and civilian waste, unless the president certified that national security needs dictated a defense-only facility. It also required the president to submit a plan by January 1983 for the permanent disposal of military waste.

It also provided that the government could not build an interim storage facility — one that could hold nuclear waste for several decades — until after it had applied for a license for a permanent repository. The Energy Committee bill, on the other hand, would allow the government to plan the two facilities simultaneously, or to build either one and

Spent Fuel for Weapons

The Senate Nov. 4 went on record as opposing any plan for making atomic weapons out of the fuel burned by civilian nuclear power plants. A House subcommittee took a similar position in October.

The idea had been floated by the Reagan administration and the House Armed Services Committee. It would be a radical departure from past practice.

What to do with spent fuel was an issue in the nuclear waste debate in Congress. Utilities were not anxious to have it buried as waste, since it still contained hundreds of millions of dollars worth of uranium and plutonium, the key ingredient in making nuclear weapons.

But the Senate, by voice vote with little debate, adopted an amendment by Gary Hart, D-Colo., to prohibit the government from using spent commercial fuel to make nuclear weapons. The amendment was added to the fiscal 1982 energy and water appropriations bill (HR 4144). It was later dropped in conference, although conferees said they supported continued separation of military and civilian nuclear programs. *(Story, p. 301)*

Hart said the use of civilian fuel to make bombs would increase the possibility of other countries doing the same thing. Mark O. Hatfield, R-Ore., agreed that it would undermine the distinction between the peaceful use of nuclear power and the defense weapons program and would be "a public relations nightmare" for the nuclear industry.

The House Interior Subcommittee on Energy and Environment Oct. 13 amended its nuclear waste bill (HR 3809) to prohibit the use of spent civilian fuel for weapons. James Weaver, D-Ore., author of the amendment, said he did not want civilian power plants to become bomb factories."

Manuel Lujan Jr., R-N.M., argued that it made sense to use the plutonium in spent fuel for weapons rather than spend several billion dollars to make it in government reactors, but the subcommittee sided with Weaver.

A senior staff member on the House Science Committee also said that any hope by the military of using spent civilian reactor fuel for bombs is a "pipe dream that Congress will never allow to happen."

Because of the way it was burned in civilian reactors, plutonium that came from reprocessing of spent fuel generally was not pure enough to make weapons. But government scientists were working on a laser process that they believed would be sufficiently developed in two or three years to make a decision to turn spent civilian fuel into the makings of nuclear weapons. Proponents said that would make sense because by the mid-1980s the government would not have enough plutonium to make all the weapons it had planned; unless civilian spent fuel was used, new facilities would have to be built to make plutonium, at a cost of $8 billion to $12 billion.

Energy Secretary James B. Edwards said Oct. 8 his department was considering the issue, but that it would "require considerable debate and a decision at a much higher level than the secretary of energy."

not the other.

Environment Committee members felt long-term, monitored storage could detract from the ultimate goal of a permanent repository, which would not require future generations to maintain and monitor it.

The committee also made other changes in the Energy Committee version of S 1662:

● It allowed, rather than required, the government to build an away-from-reactor (AFR) storage facility for spent fuel from atomic power plants.

● It slowed the timetable for building a repository, requiring the government to choose three potential sites by 1984 and pick one by 1987, and giving the NRC until 1991 to decide whether to issue a license for the repository. The Energy Committee required an NRC decision by 1988.

Environment also included a second repository in its timetable; Energy did not.

● It advanced the point at which the federal government would have to negotiate with a state over the location of a repository, and allowed the government to pay financial inducements to get a state to accept a repository.

Environment's bill also would nullify all agreements that some states, such as Louisiana, had made with the federal government to block or set conditions on putting a repository in their borders. Louisiana had secured a pledge from the Carter administration that in return for accepting the Strategic Petroleum Reserve, the government would not use the state to dispose of nuclear waste.

House Committee Action

Science Committee. Of the three House committees with jurisdiction over nuclear waste, Science spent the most time on the issue in 1981. Its Energy Research and Production Subcommittee July 16 approved a limited bill (HR 1909) that provided for building an unlicensed test repository by 1988. But the panel scrapped that measure after some members suggested more comprehensive legislation was needed, and HR 5016 was reported instead.

Opponents objected to reporting HR 1909 July 16, saying it would only polarize nuclear waste debate in the House. The Interior and Energy committees opposed an unlicensed test facility unless it was included in a larger bill that also would establish a permanent, licensed repository.

Howard Wolpe, D-Mich., said HR 1909 was narrowly written to provide only an unlicensed "research" facility so as to keep sole jurisdiction in the Science Committee.

Subcommittee Chairman Marilyn Lloyd Bouquard, D-Tenn., angrily told Wolpe she had tried to work with the bill's opponents, but "it's July, and we've got to get this bill moving." Bouquard said she felt HR 1909 could pass the House even if the other committees objected to it.

Stanley N. Lundine, D-N.Y., moved to table the bill, but his motion failed, 4-10.

Richard L. Ottinger, D-N.Y., chairman of the Energy and Commerce subcommittee handling nuclear waste legislation, called HR 1909 "ill-advised." He said it could hurt efforts to build a permanent facility because it did not require approval by the NRC, which eventually would have to license a permanent repository. Ottinger said the bill was an attempt to allow DOE to avoid tough NRC safety requirements.

On Oct. 21 the subcommittee agreed 11-0 to report HR 5016 instead, and the full Science Committee spent several hours marking up the bill before voting 37-2 to report it Nov. 20.

As reported, HR 5016 included the fastest timetable for building a waste repository — perhaps as soon as the early 1990s. The schedule was even faster than the pro-nuclear Reagan administration had testified was possible.

The Energy Department would have to identify three potential repository locations within one year of enactment. Detailed research on those sites would have to be completed in another 42 months. After one of the sites was chosen by the president, the NRC would have only two years to issue a construction license. To the dismay of environmental lobbyists, NRC hearings and procedures on the repository license would be more limited than hearing requirements for nuclear plant licenses.

The bill also called for construction of a research repository by the late 1980s. Although this facility would not be licensed by the NRC, the committee directed that the NRC and the Energy Department must reach agreement on it before construction could begin.

The committee also included a provision directing the government to build a plant to demonstrate the dry storage of spent fuel from nuclear power plants. Spent fuel generally had been stored in pools of water.

Interior Committee. The Interior Subcommittee on Energy and the Environment approved HR 3809 Oct. 30, but the full committee did not act on it in 1981.

The bill would require DOE to study several sites, hold public hearings, select a site in accordance with national environmental laws and, with the concurrence of the state, build a repository licensed by the NRC. The repository would not be in operation until about 2000. It would have to be built to allow spent nuclear fuel to be removed for eventual reprocessing.

The bill would allow the government to charge utilities a fee to cover the costs of building and maintaining the repository. It also would allow states to create boards to deal with the federal government on the waste issue, and authorize federal grants to fund the boards.

In addition to dealing with high-level radioactive wastes, the bill would modify existing laws regarding liability insurance for nuclear plants, the safety and siting of nuclear plants, and the disposal of low-level wastes.

The subcommittee adopted an amendment by Manuel Lujan Jr., R-N.M., exempting military facilities from coverage by the bill. Surprising environmental lobbyists, Udall agreed. "It may be a losing battle to take on the Armed Services committees," he said.

The panel also adopted an amendment by James Weaver, D-Ore., to prohibit the use of spent fuel from civilian reactors for making weapons.

Energy and Commerce. The Energy and Commerce Committee held hearings on the waste issue but did not consider specific legislation in 1981.

The panel's ranking Republican, James T. Broyhill, N.C., unsuccessfully urged Chairman John D. Dingell, D-Mich., to act on nuclear waste, and circulated a draft bill that would provide AFR storage under limited circumstances. Dingell and Ottinger, whose Energy Conservation and Power Subcommittee had jurisdiction over nuclear waste, had opposed all AFR proposals in the past.

However, staff members sought to work out a consensus bill with other committee staffs, and shortly before adjournment they came up with a measure they hoped would be acceptable. ∎

Synfuels Directors

President Reagan named five directors to the board of the U.S. Synthetic Fuels Corp., after firing the members appointed by former President Carter in 1980. *(1980 Almanac p. 482)*

Reagan's choice for chairman, Edward E. Noble, a Tulsa manufacturer who lost a 1980 primary bid for the U.S. Senate from Oklahoma, was confirmed by the Senate May 14. The other four directors were not confirmed until Sept. 11. They were Robert A.G. Monks, board chairman of The Boston Company, Inc., a financial holding company; Victor Schroeder, an Atlanta real estate executive; V.M. Thompson Jr., a Tulsa banker, and C. Howard Wilkins, Wichita, Kan., founder of the Pizza Hut chain.

Two board members were still to be named. Republican senators from the West shot down one Reagan selection (Donald E. Santarelli, a Washington, D.C., lawyer) and insisted Westerners should be picked for the last seats. ∎

Executive Privilege Invoked

President Reagan invoked executive privilege for the first time in his presidency Oct. 14 when he refused to allow Interior Secretary James G. Watt to turn over documents that had been subpoenaed by the House Energy and Commerce Oversight and Investigations Subcommittee.

The contested papers dealt with the takeover of U.S. energy companies by Canadian firms, an issue the subcommittee had been investigating. The administration contended that the documents dealt with sensitive foreign policy negotiations then in progress, and included materials prepared for the Cabinet.

Subcommittee Chairman John D. Dingell, D-Mich., said the panel might vote to hold Watt in contempt of Congress. The subcommittee held two days of hearings on the administration's refusal to turn over the documents, but did not take a vote on a contempt citation in 1981. ∎

Health/Education/Welfare

The federal government's social programs — in education, health and welfare — bore the brunt of President Reagan's campaign to cut the federal budget in 1981.

The year saw a radical departure from the expansion of social programs that took place during the 1960s and 1970s.

Congress acted to cut programs for the poor alone by more than $25 billion. Other social programs for the middle class also were cut.

For the Reagan administration, the changes were regarded as only the first step in a more profound revision of national social policy. A key part of Reagan's program, only partially successful in Congress, was to transfer much of the federal role in social programs to state and local governments.

Another element of the Reagan plan was his promise to protect the "truly needy" through a "social safety net" of programs that would be spared from major cuts. Those programs — Social Security retirement benefits, Medicare, Supplemental Security Income, veterans' pensions, school lunches for the poor, Head Start and summer youth jobs — generally escaped the deep budget cuts other programs suffered.

Similarly, other social program benefits for the extremely poor — those with little or no income who were totally dependent on government help — in most cases were not reduced severely.

However, the working poor — families that had some job income but still were near the poverty level — suffered serious losses. Cutbacks in food stamps, welfare, school lunches and other programs fell most heavily on working families. Critics said the cuts would discourage many poor people from holding jobs.

While cutting benefits to the working poor, the administration also sought to require welfare recipients to work in exchange for their benefits. Congress eventually approved provisions allowing states to set up "workfare" programs for Aid to Families with Dependent Children (AFDC) and food stamp recipients.

Reconciliation Bill Effects

The most important legislation affecting social programs passed during 1981 was the budget reconciliation bill (HR 3982 — PL 97-35). That massive measure made hundreds of changes in dozens of different education, welfare and health programs. *(Reconciliation bill, p. 256)*

Some 70 percent of the reconciliation bill's $35.2 billion savings came in programs earmarked for the poor and lower middle-income persons.

The Congressional Budget Office (CBO), various Cabinet departments and outside interest groups attempted to calculate the effects of the reconciliation changes. Their best estimates showed that as a result of that measure alone, not counting further spending cuts achieved through the appropriations process:

● 687,000 households lost all or part of their AFDC benefits. The loss of benefits fell most heavily on households with earnings, and those in states with relatively low benefit levels.

According to some studies, the changes meant that welfare mothers who worked would have little or no more income than those who did not. *(AFDC, p. 473)*

● 1.1 million people lost their food stamps. The largest group thrown off the program was people with incomes over 130 percent of the federal poverty level. Residents of boarding houses and strikers also lost their benefits.

In addition, changes in inflation updates of benefit and deduction levels caused a reduction of $27.50 in the average monthly benefit of a family of four. *(Food stamps, p. 466)*

● Medicaid recipients had less freedom to choose their own doctors, and elderly Medicare beneficiaries would have to pay more out of their own pockets for their health care. *(Medicare, Medicaid, p. 477)*

● Fewer new federally subsidized dwellings were available, and residents of subsidized housing had to pay a larger share of their income as rent. *(Housing subsidies, p. 110)*

● There were 900,000 fewer Comprehensive Employment and Training Act (CETA) job and job training positions than there were in 1981. *(CETA programs, p. 108)*

● School lunch prices were higher and portion sizes were smaller. About 500,000 students who had been getting free meals now had to pay the new reduced-price rate of 40 cents; 450,000 who had been paying the old reduced-price of 20 cents now had to pay the new full-price rate, averaging 75 cents. The average full-price meal in the 1980-81 school year had been 60 cents.

Children from low-income families continued to receive free meals. However, the American School Food Service Association warned that cuts in federal subsidies would force some school districts to close their lunch programs, leaving children without a hot meal in spite of their eligibility. *(Child nutrition, p. 497)*

● Some 1.5 million people lost their extended unemployment benefits. Those losing the additional 13 weeks of benefits, which supplemented the regular 26 weeks of aid, included 46,000 people in Michigan, which was hit severely by unemployment. *(Unemployment benefits, p. 106)*

State Program Cuts

The effects of other social program cuts were more difficult to estimate because they depended to a large extent on decisions made by state and local governments.

Especially under the new block grants, state and local governments had the responsibility for deciding how to distribute federal social program aid, and on whose backs to lay the burden of funding cuts.

The reconciliation bill established seven new block grant programs, with 25 percent reduced federal funding. The programs replaced existing categorical programs in the

areas of health, education, community services and food assistance to Puerto Rico. *(Block grants, next page)*

In addition, state and local governments had control over the allocation of cutbacks in programs such as compensatory education, job training and low-income energy assistance.

Supporters of block grants argued that the savings resulting from the reduction in federal interference and paperwork would help local programs survive with reduced funding.

One program for which savings were predicted was the Title I program of compensatory education for disadvantaged children. While the program was not included in the education block grant, as Reagan had requested, it was revised so as to reduce reporting and other federal requirements.

Block grant critics warned, however, that the loosening of federal standards would dilute the program's focus on the poor. Some feared that the Title I program could be converted into general aid to education under the new legislation.

Similarly, federal rules that had required states to focus the Title XX social services program on the poor were relaxed. Anti-poverty lobbyists said states might move to direct their Title XX funds from programs for the poor to programs serving groups such as the elderly that had more political clout.

School Lunch Controversy

Despite its success in pushing budget cuts in social programs, the Reagan administration was forced into a politically embarrassing retreat when it sought to change school lunch regulations.

Along with its cuts in federal subsidies for school lunches, the reconciliation bill included a provision giving the Agriculture Department authority to revise its regulations. The idea was to enable the department to change its rules so that schools could cope with the reductions in their federal subsidies.

When the regulations came out, they contained a major change in school lunch policy — permitting schools to reduce the size of food portions served to children. The reduced portions meant that in some cases the lunches would no longer meet the longstanding goal of supplying one-third of a child's daily nutritional requirements. The regulations also allowed schools to substitute foods such as soybean curd (tofu) and yogurt for meat and milk, and to count condiments such as pickle relish in meeting the vegetable requirement. Readers of the regulations inferred that ketchup also would be counted toward meeting the vegetable requirement.

That set off a firestorm of criticism. The idea that the Reagan administration was cutting lunches for little children and giving them sugar-laden ketchup instead of spinach stirred many people's anger more than other, bigger budget cuts. Political cartoonists and administration critics had a field day. Senate Democrats were shown on television eating a skimpy lunch of a tiny hamburger on a piece of bread, a few french fries with ketchup and a small glass of milk, which they said would represent a typical school lunch under the new regulations.

In the face of the attacks, the administration withdrew the regulations. Reagan blamed them on "overambitious" bureaucrats and ordered new regulations to be developed. William Hoagland, who as administrator of the Food and Nutrition Service had issued the regulations, eventually lost his job.

—By Harrison Donnelly

Congress Adopts Some Reagan Block Grants

A number of block grants — President Reagan's first step in the redirection of money and power to the state and local levels — were established by Congress in 1981, although not to the extent the president wanted.

The budget reconciliation bill cleared July 31 (HR 3982 — PL 97-35) consolidated 57 existing "categorical" federal programs, mainly in the areas of education, health and community services, into seven new block grants. The programs were abolished as separate programs, and funding for the combined grants was cut by about 25 percent from the funding level for the separate programs.

Congress made substantial changes in the president's proposal, setting federal standards and spending levels for some programs and refusing to include others in the block grants at all.

Block grants are federal payments to state or local governments for generally specified purposes, such as health, education or law enforcement. The money must be spent on programs in the general area, but state or local officials make the decisions on specifically how the money is used.

Categorical grants, on the other hand, can be used only for specific programs as directed by Congress and the federal agencies that write the regulations to implement the laws passed by Congress.

Block grants also differ from general revenue sharing, which is virtually unrestricted.

The concept of block grants had been pushed for years by Republicans and by state and local officials, who said programs could be run better at the local level than from Washington, D.C. However, supporters of many individual programs — Republicans as well as Democrats — fought to retain the separate identity of some programs, fearing they would be funded inadequately or would lose out altogether in competition with other programs. *(History of block grants, box, p. 465)*

Proposals Pared Down

Congress did not go nearly as far in consolidating programs as Reagan had requested.

The Senate Labor and Human Resources Committee, with two Republican members joining the Democratic minority in opposing the president's proposal, deadlocked over the issue for weeks before a compromise was reached. That compromise set the tone for congressional action on the major block grants. It left out some of the biggest categorical programs and provided for some continued federal control over state and local use of block grant money.

The Democratic-controlled House followed a similar pattern in restricting the scope of the block grants. And when the House and Senate bills got to conference, conferees killed what remained of one of Reagan's biggest proposed consolidations, the social services block grant.

Although administration officials from the president on down hailed creation of the block grants as a significant step forward on the road to the "new federalism," conservative critics called the watered-down final version "the worst of both worlds," putting the burden of responsibilities on state and local governments without giving them full authority.

On the other side, a coalition of 100 groups involved with categorical programs labeled the block grants "a step toward abandonment of federal responsibility." The organizations, ranging from the American Association for Retarded Citizens to the United Auto Workers, predicted that block grants would lead to a reduction in help for the needy and to brutal political struggles for funds at the state level.

White House adviser Robert B. Carleson, overseer of the administration's "new federalism" policies, said the congressional block grants were a positive, if insufficient, step forward for its program.

"We're talking about a very revolutionary change," Carleson said. The block grants "move in the direction of Reagan federalism ... (and) show a significant start in reversing the direction of government."

Although the administration agreed to compromises on its original proposals in the reconciliation bill, Carleson indicated it would continue to press for greater decentralization of government functions.

Provisions

As signed into law, HR 3982 (PL 97-35):

● Consolidated 19 existing categorical health programs into four health block grants: preventive health and health services; alcohol, drug abuse and mental health services; primary care; maternal and child health. *(Story, p. 484)*

● Consolidated 13 small education programs into a block grant. *(Story, p. 499)*

● Established a community services block grant, replacing programs administered by the Community Services Administration (CSA). *(Story, p. 490)*

● Established a nutritional assistance block grant for Puerto Rico, to replace food stamps and other federal nutrition programs in the commonwealth. *(Story, p. 466)*

● Required each state to prepare an annual report on its proposed use of block grant funds, including a statement of goals and objectives; information on the types of activities to be supported, geographic areas to be served and categories of individuals to be served; and the criteria and methods to be used for distributing the funds. Beginning in fiscal 1983, the report would describe how the previous year's goals had been met.

● Provided that no state could receive block grant funds until it had prepared and made public a report on its planned use of the funds, allowed for comments on the report from interested parties and conducted a public hearing on it.

● Required each state to certify, in fiscal 1982, that it was in compliance with the public notice rules and that it was ready to use all or part of the block grant funds. The state could begin to administer the programs in the next quarter of the fiscal year.

Reagan Proposal

In his Feb. 18 economic policy address to Congress, President Reagan called for the conversion of 88 categorical programs into seven major block grants. That could save $23.9 billion over five years, Reagan said, by reducing wasteful administrative overhead and program duplication and by targeting programs more effectively through increased local control. *(Text of speech, p. 15-E)*

The specific block grants were outlined in the administration's March 10 budget.

The budget called for a cut of about 25 percent in funding for the consolidated programs, and generally eliminated requirements that states or localities match federal funding or maintain a certain level of expenditures with their own funds.

Because the consolidations would "allow for significant savings in administration and result in more efficient management, the reductions in funding need not cause a comparable reduction in services to the public," the budget said.

Reagan's major block grant proposals were:

● Two education block grants, one to states and one to local education agencies, replacing all or part of 44 separate elementary and secondary education programs.

● Two health block grants (health services and preventive health services) replacing 25 categorical programs.

● A social services block grant composed of 13 programs, including day care, child welfare, foster care and adoption assistance, developmental disabilities, rehabilitation services and community services programs operated by the Community Services Administration (CSA).

● A hardship assistance block grant, consolidating low-income energy assistance and several small emergency aid programs.

● A nutrition assistance block grant for Puerto Rico, replacing food stamps and other nutrition programs there.

The administration also proposed to combine the urban development action grant (UDAG) program with the existing community development block grant; to consolidate 10 programs operated by the Bureau of Indian Affairs as the first step toward an Indian block grant program, and to consolidate a number of employment and training programs and airport programs.

"The federal government in Washington has no special wisdom in dealing with many of the social and educational issues faced at the state and local level," Reagan's budget said. Broad-based block grants "are far more useful than the small categorical grants that are highly regulated and require excessive administrative attention," it added.

For example, the document said, the programs proposed for consolidation into block grants encompassed 616 pages of laws, 1,400 pages of regulations, more than 10,000 separate grants and about 88,000 grant sites. Administering the grants required more than seven million hours of paperwork and several thousand federal employees, the budget said.

The document said there were about 550 different categorical grant programs. Federal grant outlays in fiscal 1982 would total about $86.4 billion under Reagan's budget —$8 billion less than the 1981 total, the budget said.

Congressional Action

Reagan's major block grant proposals were thoroughly rewritten by Congress.

Even the Republican-controlled Senate refused to go along with the proposals as introduced. Key members of the Labor and Human Resources Committee strongly supported several existing education and health programs and feared they would lose funding, or even be eliminated, in the competition with other programs for funds in a block grant. They blocked committee action until Reagan's proposal was modified to protect those programs.

The Senate Finance Committee also made changes in the president's proposal.

In the Democratic-controlled House, the block grant proposals were rejected outright by the Education and Labor and Ways and Means committees, and scaled down by Energy and Commerce. With the adoption of the Republican-backed Gramm-Latta substitute for the committee-reported reconciliation bill, most of the block grants were included in the House bill, but even then, protections for individual programs were added by several key Republican committee members.

Senate Committee Deadlock

The block grant proposal's biggest roadblock in the Senate was the Labor and Human Resources Committee, where two of the nine Republican members — Lowell P. Weicker Jr. of Connecticut and Robert T. Stafford of Vermont — joined the seven Democrats, led by Edward M. Kennedy, Mass., in opposing Reagan's original plan.

They wanted to protect a number of programs by retaining their separate authorizations — in particular, aid to education of the handicapped and compensatory education for economically disadvantaged children under Title I of the Elementary and Secondary Education Act (ESEA), the two largest federal elementary and secondary programs; community and migrant health centers; mental health services; alcohol and drug abuse prevention and treatment programs; family planning and adolescent pregnancy programs.

The committee was deadlocked for weeks. Hatch finally had to call on Senate Majority Leader Howard H. Baker Jr., R-Tenn., for help in ending the stalemate.

To fashion a compromise that would allow the block grants and other stalled legislation to emerge from committee, Senate Republican leaders were forced to give up important parts of Reagan's proposal.

The compromise, written by Stafford at Baker's request, left the two big education programs out of the education block grant. It put the health programs into block grants but included a number of restrictions governing their operation.

Under the compromise, federal funds for major health and energy assistance programs would be disbursed and administered by the states under contracts stipulating certain conditions. While federal agencies would no longer write the rules governing the programs, the secretary of health and human services could revoke the funding if states did not abide by the conditions placed on them by Congress.

Hatch said the deal was the best that could be achieved considering the situation in the committee. He insisted the Senate bill still would make a fundamental shift in government education, health and anti-poverty programs.

"We've come 70 to 80 percent of the way to block grants," Hatch said. "The administration is committed to pure block grants, and so am I. But there was no way we could do that."

To protect himself against conservative complaints that he had "caved in" to the liberals, Hatch refused to sign off on the compromise until he got official White House approval of the deal.

Hatch stressed the new block grants' reliance on contracts between the federal government and the states. "This contractual relationship allows certain program pro-

Block Grants: An Old Republican Idea

President Reagan's call for consolidation of scores of federal categorical grant programs into block grants echoed an old Republican theme.

GOP members of Congress had pushed the block grant approach since the 1960s as a way of turning federal decision-making back to state and local officials. While Congress rejected most of the proposals of Republican Presidents Richard M. Nixon and Gerald R. Ford, the Reagan administration was more successful, benefiting from growing hostility to federal "strings" — the regulations and paperwork that generally accompany federal funds.

History of Block Grants

The block grant concept developed as a reaction against the long trend toward centralization of government authority in the federal government — a trend that accelerated enormously during the Depression and again during President Lyndon B. Johnson's "Great Society" of the 1960s. *(Background, Congress & the Nation Vol. II, p. 164)*

Categorical grant programs had proliferated because the federal government could tap far more revenue sources than states and localities could, and because state and local officials often could not or would not provide funds to deal with certain problems.

The first major block grant was included in the Comprehensive Health Planning and Services Act of 1966 (PL 89-749), replacing a variety of grants to fight certain diseases with a broad comprehensive public health services grant. The only major requirement was that at least 15 percent of the funds had to be spent on mental health. *(Congress & the Nation Vol. II, p. 680)*

In 1967 Republicans almost succeeded in substituting block grants for the traditional categorical aid to education. Only an intensive lobbying campaign by the Johnson administration prevented adoption of the plan. *(Congress & the Nation Vol. II, p. 724)*

In 1968, over the opposition of President Johnson, congressional Republicans did succeed in incorporating block grants in two law enforcement measures — the Omnibus Crime Control and Safe Streets Act (PL 90-351) and the Juvenile Delinquency Prevention and Control Act (PL 90-445). *(Congress & the Nation Vol. II, pp. 317, 319; 1976 Almanac p. 397)*

'New Federalism'

In 1969 President Nixon proposed a "new federalism" in which power, funds and responsibility would be shifted from Washington back to the states. He called for both general revenue sharing and, in 1971, "special revenue sharing" — $11 billion worth of block grants for six general purposes: education, urban development, rural development, transportation, job training and law enforcement. *(1971 Almanac pp. 698, 2-A; 1972 Almanac p. 636; 1973 Almanac p. 769; Congress & the Nation Vol. III, p. 98)*

General revenue sharing was enacted in 1972 (PL 92-512), but except for some law enforcement and manpower training block grants, the Democratic-controlled Congress generally ignored or rejected other block grant proposals from Nixon and his successor, Ford.

Ford proposed four major block grants in 1976, in the areas of health, education, child nutrition and social services. All were rejected. *(1976 Almanac pp. 10, 15, 22)*

Congressional Democrats accused the Republicans of using block grants to try to undo the social programs of Democratic administrations, and there was strong lobbying pressure against the grants by interest groups, many of which had lobbied for creation of the special categorical grants in the first place. They feared their programs would lose funds or be killed altogether if they were lumped in with other programs in a block grant. The same argument was made against Reagan's proposals, but with less success.

tections, while removing the federal bureaucracy from interference with state operations," he said.

Democrats on the committee also defended the compromise for providing protections for vulnerable groups and programs. "We did as well in protecting the major programs as we had the votes to do," said Thomas F. Eagleton, D-Mo.

But conservatives attacked the compromise for retaining too much federal control over the programs.

Dan Quayle, R-Ind., had planned to offer an amendment to reduce federal controls on the block grants during floor action on the reconciliation bill. But Baker and Budget Committee Chairman Pete V. Domenici, R-N.M., joined Hatch in opposing any block grant amendments, and Quayle decided not to make a futile effort. As part of the compromise deal, the administration also had agreed not to support further amendments.

House Bill

Despite the passage of the Gramm-Latta II reconciliation package, a variety of factors worked to hold down the

extent of the block grants approved by the House. Personal influence and tactical maneuvering produced a package that was less extensive than the Senate bill.

The Education and Labor Committee — where Republicans as well as Democrats had generally supported categorical education programs — rejected Reagan's proposal for education block grants. Members worried that the grants would lead to competition between education programs for the disadvantaged and the handicapped for scarce local funds.

The proposal included in the Gramm-Latta substitute was based on a bill (HR 3941) introduced by John M. Ashbrook, R-Ohio, ranking minority member of Education and Labor. Like the Senate measure, Ashbrook's bill continued the separate status of the programs for disadvantaged and handicapped students.

Another restriction on Reagan's block grant proposal was won by John H. Rousselot, R-Calif., a member of the Ways and Means Subcommittee on Public Assistance. According to Brenda Russell of the Child Welfare League of America, Rousselot adamantly resisted administration ef-

forts to include foster care, child welfare and adoption assistance programs in its proposed social services block grant. The final version of Gramm-Latta II continued the separate existence of those programs.

Another major reduction of the Reagan block grants occurred when the House, because of tactical maneuvering, adopted the Democratic reconciliation proposal for programs under the jurisdiction of the Energy and Commerce Committee. That left it with a much smaller version of health block grants than House Republicans had proposed.

The Democratic package consolidated 15 health programs into three block grants: maternal and child health, preventive health services, and alcohol and drug abuse services. The Republican version would have consolidated 24 programs. The Democratic package also left some major health programs, such as community health, migrant and community mental health centers, and family planning, out of the block grants; the Republican package would have included them.

Tacked onto the House reconciliation bill at the last minute was a title setting conditions for block grant recipients. Among other things, it required states to justify any major changes in programs previously administered by the federal government. The title was added by the Republican leadership at the urging of Rep. Charles Pashayan Jr., R-Calif. The Senate bill had no similar title, although the provisions governing several block grants called for public participation in state decisions and for a transition period to state administration of programs.

"I was concerned that recipients, especially those in rural areas, be guaranteed a certain amount of political protection," said Pashayan. The message to states would be that "you cannot decapitate a program in the dark of the night," he said.

Conference Action

Block grant proposals proved to be one of the biggest hurdles in reaching final conference agreement on the reconciliation bill.

After what Hatch called "the toughest reconciliation conference of all," House-Senate conferees agreed July 28 on the health block grant provisions. The stickiest issue in that conference was the family planning program. Both the Senate and the administration wanted to fold the program into a block grant, but the House wanted to protect it at the federal level; supporters, led by Rep. Henry A. Waxman, D-Calif., feared enemies of the program would try to kill it if it were left up to state or local officials.

After a lengthy and bitter dispute, the conferees decided to keep family planning as a separate categorical program run by the federal government. But Hatch refused to sign off on the conference agreement until he received formal White House approval of the decision.

"I just wanted them [White House officials] to stand up and share the burden," Hatch explained later. He said the administration "reluctantly agreed with what had to be done. They don't like family planning, but they understand we don't have the votes in either the House or the Senate."

Although the Senate bill included a number of federal strings on the administration of certain programs placed in its two health block grants, conferees — at the insistence of the House — placed further restrictions on the states and set up a third block grant containing only the community health centers program. They left six programs out of block grants entirely, including health centers for migrant workers, which House members feared states would have little

interest in continuing if funding was rolled into a block grant.

A separate group of conferees approved the fourth health block grant, maternal and child health, on July 23.

Conferees on the education provisions of the reconciliation bill were hung up for a while over who should control the Women's Educational Equity Act (WEEA) program. Following heavy lobbying by Kennedy and women's rights advocates, Senate conferees finally gave up on including the program in a block grant and agreed to maintain it as a separate categorical program.

On July 29 another group of conferees put an end to one of Reagan's biggest block grant proposals — expansion of the existing social services block grant. The House and/or Senate had already rejected his request to add the Community Services Administration, legal services, child welfare, foster care and adoption assistance to the existing program. The conferees dropped the last major remaining additions.

Another sub-conference on the reconciliation bill, made up of members of the Senate Governmental Affairs and House Government Operations committees, July 23 approved several conditions which they said would apply to all the block grants in the bill.

One required states, before they could get block grant funds, to hold public hearings on their plans for distributing the money. Another authorized the federal government to continue operating for up to a year the education, welfare and health programs being consolidated into block grants. States would notify the federal government when they were ready to take over.

The conferees substantially rewrote the title requiring states to justify program changes. That provision had prompted intense opposition from governors and other state officials. They said they would need months to comply, and they feared that vague language about fairness and equity could lead to dozens of lawsuits. The administration also opposed the provision; it objected to any restrictions on the way states used their block grants.

As it turned out, the states turned the House provision to their advantage. The public participation rules were rewritten to the satisfaction of the National Governors' Association and other groups, which also had sought the transition language. Many states had been concerned that they would not be ready to distribute the block grants by Oct. 1, the beginning of the new fiscal year. ∎

Food Stamp Legislation

Congress in 1981 acted on three separate pieces of legislation affecting the food stamp program.

Long a target of attack by congressional conservatives because of alleged waste, fraud and abuse, the program experienced major reductions during the budget-cutting surge of 1981.

Most importantly, the budget reconciliation bill cleared in July made changes in program rules aimed at saving $6 billion over three years. Congress agreed to cut program spending even more sharply than the Reagan administration had requested.

The burden of the reconciliation legislation fell most heavily on the working poor and recipients who were in their first month of the program.

Program defenders managed to provide increased funds for food stamps in fiscal 1981, however, avoiding a

shut-down of the program in the last months of the year.

They also won passage of a fiscal 1982 authorization level that was expected to be adequate to fund the program fully for the entire year. In the past several years the program had run short of money before the year's end and Congress had to provide emergency supplemental funding.

Moreover, Congress rejected an administration proposal to reduce food stamp benefits to families whose children got federally subsidized free lunches at school, and a proposal by Senate Agriculture Committee Chairman Jesse Helms, R-N.C., to restore the purchase requirement for food stamps. That longstanding provision, ended by Congress in 1977, had required recipients to put up some of their own money in order to get a larger value in food stamps. *(1977 Almanac p. 457)*

The three bills affecting the food stamp program were:
● HR 3991 (PL 97-18), which raised the fiscal 1981 spending ceiling on the program to $11.5 billion, from $9.7 billion.
● S 884 (PL 97-98), the omnibus farm bill, which authorized $11.3 billion for the program in fiscal 1982. While other programs in the bill were extended for four years, the food stamp program was extended for only one because of a dispute over the timing of inflation-related increases in benefits.
● HR 3982 (PL 97-35), the budget reconciliation measure, which eliminated more than 1 million people from the program and cut benefits to most of the rest.

Some 23 million persons — one of every 10 Americans — received food stamps in 1981.

Fiscal 1981 Emergency Funding

The first congressional action required on food stamps in 1981 was dealing with a shortage of funds. As in the two preceding years, the existing spending cap proved insufficient to allow full operation of the program until the end of the year. *(1979 Almanac p. 480; 1980 Almanac p. 411)*

The fiscal 1981 ceiling, set by the 1980 food stamp amendments (PL 96-249), was $9.7 billion. Early in 1981, however, it became clear that the cost of the program — pushed up by unexpectedly high unemployment levels and inflation — would far exceed that amount.

Recognizing that $9.7 billion was insufficient, the Reagan administration asked for a supplemental appropriation of $1.2 billion. However, it soon became apparent that even a total appropriation of $10.9 billion would not be enough. Delays in enacting cost-saving provisions, a lengthy coal strike and an unexpected surge in program participation pushed the cost of the program to well over $11 billion.

Because of the potential consequences of the funding shortfall — deep cuts or a total halt in benefits during the last months of the fiscal year — Congress moved, with the support of the administration, to increase the ceiling.

On June 25 it cleared legislation (HR 3991) increasing the fiscal 1981 spending ceiling to $11.5 billion. The House passed the emergency measure by voice vote June 23. The Senate began work on it June 25, but did not complete work until the early morning hours of June 26.

Passage of HR 3991 cleared the way for the Agriculture Department to spend the additional money. The extra $1.7 billion had been included in the fiscal 1981 supplemental appropriations bill (PL 97-12), but the money could not be used until the spending ceiling was increased. *(Supplemental, p. 281)*

Besides increasing the spending cap, HR 3991 cleared

up a problem concerning food stamps for Supplemental Security Income (SSI) recipients living in California.

California provided cash payments to SSI recipients in lieu of food stamps. Under a 1976 law (PL 94-379), those recipients were ineligible for food stamps as long as the state continued to provide them with cost-of-living increases in benefits. On July 1, however, California planned to raise SSI benefits less than the inflation rate, so after that date, the SSI recipients would be eligible for food stamps. While most would have received very small stamp allotments, the administrative costs of dealing with their applications would have been great.

HR 3991 delayed California SSI recipients' eligibility for food stamps until Aug. 1, to give time for a permanent legislative solution to the problem.

Fiscal 1982 Authorization

The legislation extending the authorization for the food stamp program had a complicated history. It started out as a separate measure but ended up as part of the omnibus farm bill.

The Senate passed a separate food stamp bill (S 1007) in June, but in the House, where there traditionally had been political trade-offs between urban supporters of food stamps and rural backers of farm programs, sponsors brought the food stamp provisions to the floor as part of the farm bill. That measure did not clear until Dec. 16, the last day of the session.

Initially, the House and Senate Agriculture Committees included cost-saving amendments in the authorizing legislation, But those provisions were eventually taken out and included in the reconciliation bill.

Committee Action

Tight-fitting "caps" on future food stamp spending were approved by both Agriculture committees May 12 as part of bills extending the program for four years.

Adoption of the ceilings, which would hold program spending below the existing level in fiscal 1982-85, was a victory for the administration.

The committees also accepted many of the administration's proposals for reducing the costs of the program. The Senate bill (S 1007) would save an estimated $1.85 billion in fiscal 1982, the House bill (HR 3109), $1.23 billion, the Congressional Budget Office (CBO) said.

The bills also included provisions raising the fiscal 1981 spending cap to $11.5 billion from $9.7 billion.

In a significant shift in a long-running congressional battle, the House Agriculture Committee voted to prohibit food stamps for strikers. Liberal Democrats, after successfully resisting the amendment for years, could not prevent the committee from joining the Senate committee in support of the ban.

With one important exception, both bills followed the outline of spending cuts sought by the administration. While they preserved the basic structure of the existing food stamp program, the proposed changes saved money by targeting benefits on the most needy and holding down projected increases in benefits due to inflation.

Both panels rejected the administration's biggest single savings proposal, which would have cut about $500 million by reducing food stamp benefits to families whose children got federally subsidized free lunches at school. Nutrition program advocates had concentrated their lobbying efforts on the bill against that proposal in particular.

Nor did the bills contain the provision pushed by Helms to restore the purchase requirement.

Among cost-saving measures accepted by both committees were provisions to exclude from the program all households with incomes in excess of 130 percent of the federal poverty level, provide less generous inflation-based adjustments in benefits and reduce benefits to most recipients during their first month in the program.

Despite the similarity of the bills, the House bill's cuts fell $620 million short of the Senate's.

Flexible Cap Rejected. The biggest fight in either committee came on an attempt by House committee Democrats to establish a flexible cap that would allow some increases in food stamp spending depending on economic conditions.

Dan Glickman, D-Kan., proposed an amendment to set the spending ceilings for each year several hundred million dollars above the administration's proposal. More importantly, the amendment would have increased the annual ceiling by $150 million for each percentage point that the inflation rate exceeded current Office of Management and Budget (OMB) projections and by $650 million for each percentage point increase in the unemployment rate above OMB projections. It also would have allowed appropriations to exceed the ceiling by 2.5 percent each year.

Glickman's amendment was rejected, 20-23. The committee then adopted the administration's spending figures, as proposed by E. Thomas Coleman, R-Mo. Supporters of Glickman's amendment argued that the administration's spending figures were based on unrealistic assumptions about improvements in the economy. Thomas S. Foley, D-Wash., called the administration's economic assumptions "a matrix of fantasy."

But Coleman and others said a flexible cap would not be an effective restraint on food stamp spending. If the administration's figures proved too low in the future, they argued, Congress could come back and raise the ceiling, as it had done several times in recent years.

Spending Ceilings. The House bill set spending ceilings of $10 billion in fiscal 1982, $10.3 billion in 1983, $10.3 billion in 1984 and $10.5 billion in 1985. The Senate bill authorized $10.9 billion in 1982, $11.3 billion in 1983, $11.3 billion in 1984 and $11.8 billion in 1985.

Although they differed in dollar terms, the ceilings would allow approximately the same level of spending in real terms. The reason for the discrepancy was that the Senate bill included funds for the food stamp program in Puerto Rico, while the House bill did not.

The administration proposed to convert food stamps and other nutrition benefits for Puerto Rico into a single nutrition block grant payment. The food stamp program on the island had been costing about $1.1 billion a year.

The Senate bill tightened income eligibility standards for Puerto Rican food stamp recipients, to bring the annual cost of the program down to about $800 million.

Stamps for Strikers. By a 21-19 vote May 11, the House committee approved a ban on food stamps for households involved in labor strikes. Congress had adopted some restrictions on benefits to striking families in both 1979 and 1980.

Supporters of the ban argued that the government should not interfere in strikes by aiding the strikers with food stamps. Opponents said a household should not be penalized because one of its members was on strike, possibly against his will.

The amendment, offered by George Hansen, R-Idaho, provided that households in which a member went on strike would be excluded from food stamp benefits. Households that were already receiving stamps before the strike could continue to get them, but would not receive any additional stamps because of the loss of job income.

Senate Action

The Senate passed S 1007 June 10, agreeing to deep cuts in the food stamp program over the next four years. But it soundly rejected efforts by critics of the program, such as Helms, to make even sharper reductions.

The legislation passed by a vote of 77-17. Helms was joined by 14 other Republicans, William Proxmire, D-Wis., and Harry F. Byrd Jr., Ind-Va., in opposing the measure. *(Vote 147, p. 28-S)*

The cuts made by S 1007 were deeper than President Reagan had requested. The bill's provisions were expected to eliminate at least a million people from the program and reduce future benefits to almost all the rest of the 23 million food stamp recipients.

The defeat of efforts by Helms and others to further restrict the program — including the attempt to restore the purchase requirement — was a victory for Nutrition Subcommittee Chairman Robert Dole, R-Kan. Working with Patrick J. Leahy, D-Vt., Dole put together a package of spending cuts that was substantial enough to forestall further reductions.

The proposal designed by Dole and Leahy, which was reported by the Agriculture Committee June 2 (S Rept 97-128), would reduce fiscal 1982 spending for food stamps by an estimated $1.9 billion. The panel estimated the administration's proposed cuts at about $1.5 billion.

Dole and Leahy's one major defeat was on an attempt to allow some flexibility in the caps on future spending for the program. The administration pushed successfully for strict spending limits.

The caps in the bill would hold food stamp spending at an average of $11.3 billion a year for four years.

Dole and other supporters of the bill said it would hold down the spiraling costs of the program without harming the nutrition of the nation's poorest people. "This bill will target food stamp benefits to the neediest individuals within our society," Dole said.

To Helms, however, the bill's cuts did not go far enough in attacking what he saw as rampant corruption and misuse of the program. "If there has ever been a federal program that cried out for reform, it is this program. Probably more than any other federal program, the food stamp program has been the object of citizen outrage because of perceived waste, abuse and mismanagement," Helms said.

Savings Provisions. As passed by the Senate, S 1007 would reduce food stamp spending by an estimated $8 billion over four years by reducing inflation-related benefit increases, cracking down on alleged waste and fraud and lowering the income eligibility limits for food stamps.

The biggest savings came from reductions in indexing provisions that were aimed at protecting recipients from inflation. For example, a provision to delay the inflation adjustment of the "thrifty food plan," the low-cost diet used as a guide for determining benefit levels, would save an estimated $506 million in 1982. Restrictions on scheduled increases in the income deductions, used in calculating eligibility and benefits, would save over $300 million.

Showing the frequency with which many people moved in and out of poverty — and on and off the food stamp

program, a provision to reduce recipients' benefits in their first month on the program would save $490 million. By contrast, the provision to eliminate the better-off recipients by restricting eligibility to families with total income below 130 percent of the federally defined poverty level would save only $130 million.

The bill would save $118 million by reducing benefits to the working poor by an average of $7 a month. It would do that by reducing the earned income deduction, intended to compensate for work expenses, to 15 percent of job earnings from 20 percent.

Spending Ceilings. Dole and Leahy's amendment to allow the food stamp spending ceiling to rise if inflation and unemployment continued at high levels was rejected, 41-53. *(Vote 145, p. 27-S)*

The spending caps in the bill — $10.9 billion in fiscal 1982, $11.3 billion in 1983, $11.3 billion in 1984 and $11.8 billion in 1985 — were based on the administration's predictions that inflation and unemployment rates would both fall rapidly.

Under the amendment, the annual ceilings would be adjusted according to the degree to which the inflation and unemployment rates diverged from the projections for each year issued by OMB on June 1, 1981. The amount of the adjustments, either up or down, would be $150 million for each percentage point that food price inflation was above or below the OMB projections and $650 million for each percentage point variation in the unemployment rate.

Leahy said the amendment would preserve the concept of a congressional limit on spending while allowing for the fallibility of economic predictions. But opponents, such as Steven D. Symms, R-Idaho, warned that the amendment would turn the program into an entitlement. "Do not turn it closer and closer to an entitlement program, build in indexation, throw away the best estimates, and then wonder why the budget gets out of control," added Budget Committee Chairman Pete V. Domenici, R-N.M.

Purchase Requirement. The most fundamental change in the program considered by the Senate would have restored the requirement that recipients purchase their food stamps. Symms' amendment to restore that pre-1977 provision was rejected 33-66. *(Vote 140, p. 27-S)*

The amendment would have exempted households containing elderly or disabled members from the purchase requirement, as well as extremely poor families.

Symms argued that removal of the purchase requirement was the major cause of the rapid growth in food stamp participation and costs. Helms cited a CBO study attributing 70 to 80 percent of the recent growth of the program to the end of the purchase requirement.

Dole and Leahy said the requirement had been a major source of fraud and administrative headaches and kept cash-short poor people from getting food stamps.

The administration said it did not favor restoration of the requirement, although it would not have favored removing it in 1977, if Reagan had been president then.

Other Amendments. In other action, the Senate:

● Adopted by voice vote a David L. Boren, D-Okla., amendment to exempt households containing elderly or disabled members from the 130 percent of poverty gross income limit.

● Rejected, 30-69, a Helms amendment to freeze through 1985 the income deductions used in calculating eligibility and benefits for the program. *(Vote 141, p. 27-S)*

● Rejected, 25-74, a James A. McClure, R-Idaho, amendment to count energy assistance payments as income in

determining food stamp benefits. *(Vote 142, p. 27-S)*

● Rejected, 24-74, a John Melcher, D-Mont., amendment to allow residents of drug and alcohol rehabilitation centers to continue to receive food stamps if the centers were private, non-profit and got less than 20 percent of their budgets from the federal government. *(Vote 143, p. 27-S)*

● Rejected, 36-56, a Daniel Patrick Moynihan, D-N.Y., amendment to delay until Oct. 1, 1982, from April 1, 1982, the effective date of the provision establishing a nutritional block grant program in Puerto Rico. (Moynihan withdrew an earlier amendment to delete the Puerto Rico block grant provision.) *(Vote 144, p. 27-S)*

● Rejected, 30-64, a Melcher amendment to delete a provision lowering to six years, from 12 in existing law, the age of a child that exempted a parent from the program's work registration requirement. *(Vote 146, p. 27-S)*

Reconciliation Action

The next step in the complicated odyssey of food stamp legislation came in the budget reconciliation bill. Basically, the cost-saving provisions of S 1007 and HR 3109 were taken out of the authorizing bills and put into the reconciliation measures.

With its adoption of the Republican-backed Gramm-Latta II substitute for the committee-reported reconciliation bill, the House added some more cost-savings provisions to those in the Agriculture Committee bill, making the food stamp provisions of the House and Senate reconciliation bills similar. *(Reconciliation bill, p. 256)*

There were some differences, however, that led to a difficult conference. Conferees shaved $199 million more from the food stamp program than the reconciliation bills required them to cut, but they resisted pressure from Helms for still deeper slashes in the program.

In three days of sometimes acrimonious meetings (July 21-23), the conferees approved cuts totaling $1.657 billion in fiscal 1982. Their reconciliation target was $1.458 billion in savings.

Most of the new savings were achieved by a decision to freeze the deduction for excess shelter costs through June 1983, as the Senate bill provided. The House bill permitted annual inflation adjustments; conferees rejected an effort by Rep. James M. Jeffords, R-Vt., to retain that provision.

As the conference sessions moved back and forth between food stamps and agriculture programs, Helms repeatedly urged his colleagues to cut food stamps even more than the reconciliation bills required to leave more money available for farm programs. His insistence on deeper cuts occasionally strained traditional congressional courtesies, particularly during debate on President Reagan's plan to convert Puerto Rico's food stamp program into a food assistance block grant with a lower funding level.

Both houses had gone along with that plan, but the House postponed the effective date until Oct. 1, 1982. The Senate voted to make the change by April 1, 1982, and until then to reduce the eligibility standard for Puerto Ricans to 55 percent of the poverty level.

The plan drew biting criticism from House Agriculture Committee Chairman E. "Kika" de la Garza, D-Texas, who said it discriminated against one group of American citizens — Puerto Ricans.

Conferees finally agreed to begin the block grant on July 1, 1982, and not to lower the eligibility standard in the meantime. Puerto Rico was required to devise a plan by April 1, 1982, for administering the program.

Helms failed to convince conferees that drug and alcohol abuse residential treatment programs were especially corrupt and to exclude them from food stamps for that reason. The conferees refused to accept a Senate provision making residents of such facilities ineligible for food stamps.

The conferees also agreed to exempt households with elderly or disabled persons from the tougher new income eligibility levels for the program. Both reconciliation bills restricted eligibility to households with gross monthly incomes at or below 130 percent of the poverty level, but the conferees accepted the Senate provision exempting households with elderly or disabled members from the new income test.

Conferees also softened the effect of two provisions that opponents said would encourage food stamp recipients working at low-paying jobs to quit and go on welfare instead. They agreed to lower the earned income deduction (the amount subtracted from a household's gross income for purposes of computing its benefit levels) to 18 percent of a household's earnings from the existing level of 20 percent. The Senate bill reduced the figure to 15 percent, while the House bill made no change.

Conferees also dropped a House provision that would have raised the "benefit reduction rate," used to determine benefit levels for individual households.

Conferees also dropped a Senate provision requiring families that were disqualified from the program to repay double the amount of any benefits they had received improperly. Foley objected that imposing such a penalty might violate an individual's constitutional rights to due process. Instead, the bill required disqualified families to repay the actual amount of improperly received benefits. *(Final reconciliation provisions, this page)*

Omnibus Farm Bill

Further legislative action on the food stamp authorization was tied up with the omnibus farm bill (HR 3603 — H Rept 97-106).

Those provisions of the House Agriculture Committee's food stamp bill that had not been included in reconciliation were added to the farm bill and brought to the floor as part of that controversial measure. The bill passed the House Oct. 22. *(Farm bill, p. 535)*

Before HR 3603 came to the floor, food program advocates reached a compromise with administration officials on the funding level for fiscal 1982.

Fred Richmond, D-N.Y., and Coleman, chairman and ranking minority member of the Agriculture Subcommittee on Nutrition, worked together to pressure OMB Director David A. Stockman into accepting a $700 million increase in the authorization level. The administration had favored a $10.6 billion limit.

Richmond, Coleman and Stockman agreed to a figure of $11.3 billion for the authorizing legislation, including money for Puerto Rico. Richmond and Coleman also agreed to offer anti-fraud amendments and an amendment to postpone until Oct. 1, 1983, inflation adjustments for the program.

The compromise was adopted by voice vote on the House floor. It set the authorization levels at $11.3 billion in fiscal 1982, $11.2 billion in 1983, $11.1 billion in 1984 and $11.3 billion in 1985.

The amendment made banks and other food stamp distributors liable for paying food stamp losses if they ignored certain procedures for identifying recipients. It also empowered investigators in the Agriculture Department inspector general's office to carry guns, issue warrants for arresting criminal violators of food stamp and other laws, and to arrest without warrants in certain circumstances. The amendment passed by voice vote after Coleman dropped a section authorizing warrantless searches and seizures of evidence by investigators.

Conference Action

The farm bill conference, which included the food stamp provisions from the House farm bill and the Senate food stamp bill, was a long and difficult one stretching over several months.

While conferees were principally concerned with agricultural issues such as price supports, they also deadlocked over food stamps. They never were able to resolve a House-Senate dispute over the method of making future inflation adjustments in food stamp benefits.

Because of their intractable differences over the inflation adjustments, conferees decided to settle for a one-year reauthorization of the program, at $11.3 billion. That meant Congress would have to act again on the program in 1982, thus reopening the inflation adjustment issue.

Final Provisions

Reconciliation Bill. As cleared by Congress, the food stamp provisions of HR 3982:

● Limited eligibility for the program to households with total incomes below 130 percent of the federally defined poverty level. The bill maintained the "net" eligibility limit for households containing elderly or disabled members at 100 percent of poverty, with various income deductions that in most cases pushed the effective income limit to 130 percent of poverty.

● Required that parents and children living together be treated as one household in determining food stamp eligibility and benefits, but allowed them to be treated as separate households if at least one parent was 60 or older.

● Required that all residents of a house with paying boarders be treated as a single household for benefit calculations.

● Postponed the annual inflation adjustment of the "thrifty food plan" used in calculating benefits. The adjustments would be delayed from the Jan. 1 date in existing law until April 1, 1982, July 1, 1983, and Oct. 1 in each succeeding year.

● Required that inflation adjustments in the standard deduction and in the excess shelter and day care cost deduction be based on a version of the Consumer Price Index that excluded home ownership costs.

● Froze until July 1, 1983, the existing levels for the standard and excess shelter deductions; beginning in 1984, deduction levels would be adjusted on Oct. 1 of each year.

● Reduced to 18 percent, from 20 percent, the portion of earned income to be disregarded in computing income for the purpose of determining benefits.

● Required states to use a system of "periodic retrospective income accounting" to calculate recipients' income. Under the system, benefits would be based on a household's actual income in a preceding period of time, rather than on an estimate of its expected income in the future, as under existing law. In addition, recipients would be required to file periodic reports of their income, instead of only having to report when there had been some change in their circumstances.

● Excluded from the program households with a member

participating in a strike, unless the household was eligible for the program before the strike. Households that were eligible would not receive increased benefits as a result of the loss of the striking worker's income.

● Determined benefit levels for households during their first month on the program according to the day of the month on which they applied. Under existing law, households received a full month's benefits, regardless of when they applied. The new law would provide half-a-month's benefits to recipients who applied on the 15th of the month, for example.

● Prohibited federal funding of outreach programs aimed at informing eligible persons of their rights to receive food stamps.

● Increased penalties for persons found to have engaged in fraud or misrepresentation in applying for or receiving benefits.

● Repealed increases in deductions established by a 1980 law and scheduled to go into effect in fiscal 1982. The provisions would have created a separate dependent care deduction of up to $90 a month and lowered to $25 a month, from $35, the level above which elderly and disabled persons could deduct their medical expenses.

● Established, beginning July 1, 1982, a nutritional block grant program for Puerto Rico, replacing existing federal nutrition programs. The block grant would provide 100 percent of the nutritional assistance given to needy persons on the island, and 50 percent of the related administrative costs, up to a maximum of $825 million a year.

● Extended the provision in existing law that allowed certain states to provide cash payments in lieu of food stamps to SSI recipients.

Farm Bill Provisions

As cleared by Congress, the food stamp provisions of the farm bill (S 884):

● Authorized $11.3 billion for food stamps in fiscal 1982.

● Required the secretary of agriculture to permit towns and other jurisdictions to require food stamp participants to work at public or private-sector jobs, with payment in stamps at the minimum wage rate.

● Permitted Alaska to use a separate thrifty food plan to determine benefits for its rural areas.

● Barred deductions for household expenses paid by a third party in calculating income for eligibility.

● Required that income and resources of sponsors of certain aliens be included in eligibility and benefit determinations.

● Permitted the agriculture secretary to change standards for estimating the value of vehicles for determining eligibility and benefits.

● Made households receiving food stamps ineligible for the program if the wage-earner voluntarily quit a job.

● Made participants who did not comply with either Aid to Families with Dependent Children (AFDC) or unemployment compensation work requirements subject to sanctions if they did not comply with the annual food stamp work registration requirement.

● Made states financially liable for losses of food stamps.

● Repealed the 60-day transfer provision that permitted uninterrupted benefits for a household moving from one political entity to another.

● Permitted states, in certain circumstances, to avoid a requirement that recipients be notified of pending loss of eligibility 30 days before such loss.

● Repealed a requirement that the Agriculture Depart-

ment restore food stamps to households wrongfully denied, if a year had expired before the household applied for restoration.

● Required state agencies to use Social Security and state unemployment wage and benefit information in certifying recipients.

● Required the agriculture secretary to permit political entities to issue food stamps by certified mail.

● Repealed program staffing standards for states.

● Required states to meet federal standards for denials and terminations or lose 55 percent of their federal funds for administrative costs; also required states with error rates exceeding 5 percent to develop corrective plans.

● Required that a participating household provide a Social Security number.

● Continued "cash out" pilot projects, which provided cash instead of stamps, and made AFDC families eligible for such projects.

● Authorized grants and contracts for developing methods of monitoring nutritional status of high-risk groups.

● Set penalties for fraudulent misuse of commodities.

● Authorized pilot projects, for two years, to provide commodities to poor, elderly people and extended through fiscal 1985 commodity distribution programs for poor pregnant women, new mothers and young children.

● Postponed to Oct. 1, 1982, adjustments for inflation in the thrifty food plan, which was used to determine benefit levels; set future annual adjustments for Oct. 1.

● Authorized designated investigators in the Agriculture Department inspector general's office to carry firearms and, in connection with investigations of probable violations of food stamp or other laws under the department's jurisdiction, to execute warrants for searches or seizures of evidence and for arrests, and to arrest without warrants when a criminal violation had occurred in the presence of the investigator or when he had probable cause to believe such a violation had occurred.

● Made banks and other so-called "first endorsers" (distributors of food stamps) liable for paying for food stamp losses if they ignored certain procedures.

● Specified that federal, state or local low-income energy aid could not be counted as income in determining eligibility for food stamps if it was specifically designated as energy aid and if it was provided on a seasonal basis for no more than six months each year.

● Permitted parents living with children to qualify separately for food stamps if one of the parents received disability or certain other forms of aid, and if parents and children bought and prepared food separately.

● Permitted members of federally recognized Indian tribes not living on reservations to qualify for food stamps.

● Authorized pilot projects in which recipients of SSI, Medicaid or AFDC who met food stamp income eligibility requirements would not have to make separate, duplicate applications for stamps.

● Required retail stores accepting food stamps to display instructions for reporting food stamp fraud; also required that program applications state that incorrect information could result in denial of stamps and criminal prosecution.

● Permitted local, state and federal law enforcement officials investigating alleged food stamp violations to inspect information from food stamp applications.

● Required prison sentences for persons convicted of food stamp violations more than once; authorized courts to suspend such violators for up to 18 months, in addition to any other disqualification period. ∎

Foreign Language Grants

The House Education and Labor committee Nov. 10 reported legislation (HR 3231 — H Rept 97-316) aimed at encouraging increased instruction of foreign languages in American schools.

The legislation came in response to worries by chief sponsor Paul Simon, D-Ill., and others that Americans were woefully ignorant of languages other than English. According to testimony before the committee, there were not enough Americans with knowledge of other tongues to meet the nation's defense, intelligence and business needs.

Only 15 percent of U.S. high school students were receiving foreign language instruction, according to the Joint National Committee for Languages. The percentage of college students enrolled in foreign language courses had fallen to 8.8 percent in 1977, from 15.9 percent in 1968.

Committee Action. The Education and Labor Committee approved HR 3231 by a 21-9 vote Oct. 20.

As reported, the bill established four grant programs providing aid for foreign language instruction at all levels. The total authorization was $87 million a year for each of fiscal years 1983-85.

Two programs would aid states that set up model programs for foreign language instruction. Each state could receive $50,000 plus 4 cents times its population, for elementary and secondary school programs, and $30,000 plus 1 cent times its population for community and junior college programs.

Colleges and universities could receive two types of grants. Those with more than 5 percent of their students in first- or second-year foreign language classes would get $30 per student for each student in excess of 5 percent of enrollment. Schools would get $40 for each student receiving advanced language instruction or instruction in less commonly taught languages such as Arabic or Chinese.

Higher education institutions also could get $30 per student if they required two years of high school foreign language for admission or two years of college language classes for graduation. ∎

POW Benefits

Legislation making it easier for former prisoners of war (POWs) to receive compensation and health benefits from the Veterans Administration (VA) was enacted in 1981.

Although the administration had expressed opposition to the legislation (HR 1100) on budgetary grounds, it did not actually lobby against the bill, and President Reagan signed the measure into law Aug. 14 (PL 97-37).

Provisions. As signed into law, the Prisoner of War Benefits and Health Care Services Act of 1981:

● Required the VA administrator to appoint an Advisory Committee on Former Prisoners of War and to seek its advice on the needs of former POWs for compensation, health care and rehabilitation.

● Provided that certain disabilities of veterans who had been prisoners of war for at least 30 days would be presumed to be service-connected, for purposes of receiving VA compensation.

● Allowed VA treatment for psychoses and other mental conditions; eliminated the requirement in existing law that symptoms of such conditions must appear within two years of release for active duty.

● Made former POWs eligible for all types of VA health care; gave them priority over veterans with non-service-connected disabilities.

● Required the VA to maintain records for three years of all POW claims for compensation, and the disposition of such claims.

Legislative History. The House Veterans' Affairs Committee reported HR 1100 on May 4 (H Rept 97-28).

The House passed the bill June 2 by a vote of 394-2 under suspension of the rules. *(Vote 50, p. 28-H)*

As passed by the House, the bill provided monetary compensation to POWs with psychological problems, regardless of when the condition first appeared; reduced from six months to 60 days the minimum time a POW must have been imprisoned to establish an automatic presumption of service-connection for malnutrition-related diseases and disabilities, and provided VA medical treatment on a priority basis to former POWs, regardless of how long they were imprisoned.

The VA said the bill would cost at least $146 million over five years.

The Congressional Budget Office (CBO) estimated the five-year cost at about $64 million. The difference in the estimate, according to CBO, was the assumption of how many former POWs would seek compensation for psychological problems. CBO assumed about 3,500 men would make such claims; the VA assumed the number would be 12,200.

The Senate Veterans' Affairs Committee reported a scaled-down version May 15 (S 468 — S Rept 97-88). It said its bill would not cost more than $25 million. The Senate substituted the text of its bill for HR 1100 and passed it by voice vote June 4.

A compromise was worked out informally by members of the two committees. It was approved by the House and Senate July 30, clearing the bill. ∎

New GI Bill Proposals

The House Veterans' Affairs Committee May 19 reported legislation establishing a new program of educational assistance for veterans (HR 1400 — H Rept 97-80, Part I). However, the Armed Services Committee, which shared jurisdiction, did not act on the proposal. The Senate Veterans' Affairs Committee also took no action on various "new GI Bill" proposals (S 25, S 7, S 417).

Concern about the armed forces' manpower problems prompted the proposals; since the end of the draft in 1973, they had had serious problems attracting and retaining enough qualified personnel. However, fiscal problems dampened enthusiasm for new benefits, which could cost $1 billion a year or more.

The bills would pay living allowances of $400 a month or more to veterans attending college. Some also would pay their tuition. Some proposals would allow personnel to transfer their benefits to their spouse or children.

The first GI Bill was enacted in 1944, later ones in 1952 and 1966. The 1966 benefits expired in 1976; persons who enlisted after 1976 were eligible for the Veterans' Educational Assistance Program (VEAP), which allowed service members to deposit some of their pay in an educational fund, to be matched 2-for-1 by the Veterans Administration when they entered college. That program was not considered very successful. *(Background, Congress and the Nation Vol. I, p. 1335; Vol. II, p. 456; Vol. IV, p. 180)* ∎

Welfare Benefits Cut by Reconciliation

The budget reconciliation bill cleared by Congress July 31 (HR 3982 — PL 97-35) made substantial reductions in assistance to working mothers who received benefits under the core government welfare program, Aid to Families with Dependent Children (AFDC). *(Reconciliation bill, p. 256)*

The reductions were in line with the Reagan administration's policy of making welfare programs a "safety net" for the extremely poor, rather than an income supplement for those with marginal incomes.

The Department of Health and Human Services (HHS) estimated that about 687,000 of the 3.9 million households on the AFDC rolls would lose all or some of their benefits as a result of the legislation. Some 408,000 families would be dropped from the program altogether, while 279,000 would receive reduced benefits.

The Congressional Budget Office estimated the program changes mandated by the bill would save $1.2 billion in fiscal 1982, $1.4 billion in 1983 and $1.4 billion in 1984.

Critics said the changes would discourage many welfare mothers from working. In many states, recipients would have little or no more net income from working than from staying home, they said.

However, the legislation emphasized work by allowing states to set up "workfare" programs under which recipients would do community service work in exchange for their benefits. States were not required to set up such programs, although the administration had favored mandatory workfare programs.

Other provisions of HR 3982 sought to strengthen child support enforcement. That program sought to reduce AFDC costs by collecting child support payments from the absent fathers of low-income children.

Provisions

As signed into law, the welfare provisions of HR 3982 (Title XXIII):

AFDC

Benefit Reductions. Reduced benefits to working AFDC recipients by limiting the "disregards" subtracted from their earnings in calculating eligibility and benefits. Eligibility and benefit calculations would include a standard income disregard of $75 a month, in place of the disregards for itemized work expenses and a disregard for care of dependent children or incapacitated adults of up to $160 a month allowed under existing law. In addition, benefit calculations would use a disregard of $30 a month plus one-third of the remaining earned income, as under existing law; however, the disregard would be used only during the first four months of the recipient's employment.

● Excluded from the program families with property resources (excluding the home and one automobile) whose equity value exceeded $1,000, or a lower amount set by states.

● Allowed states to reduce AFDC payments to families who also received food stamps or housing subsidies by counting those benefits as income.

● Excluded from the program families with total incomes in excess of 150 percent of a state's "standard of need."

● Required that money received by a family in a lump-sum payment (such as a retroactive Social Security payment) be counted as income over a number of months, rather than just during the month it was received, as under existing law.

● Required that benefits to families eligible for earned income tax credits (EITC) be based on the assumption that the family received the payments in the form of monthly advance payments, even if they did not.

● Required states to consider a portion of the income of a stepparent living with a child in determining AFDC eligibility and benefits.

Workfare. Allowed states to establish "community work experience" programs for AFDC recipients. Under the programs, recipients could be required to perform work in such areas as health, social services, education and public safety. The number of hours of work each month could not exceed the number produced by dividing the family's AFDC benefit by the greater of the federal or state minimum wage.

● Allowed states to establish "work supplementation programs." Under the programs, states would be allowed to reduce their regular AFDC grants in order to generate funds for jobs that would be available to recipients on a voluntary basis. The jobs would be with the government, public or private non-profit agencies, or private day-care centers.

● Provided that states operating work supplementation programs could not receive more federal matching funds than they would have if they had continued to operate their AFDC programs in the previous fashion.

● Allowed states to participate in a work incentive demonstration project, aimed at testing alternatives to the existing AFDC work requirements.

Eligibility Restrictions. Prohibited payment of AFDC benefits to families in which the mother or father was participating in a labor strike.

● Limited children's eligibility for AFDC to those 18 or under; allowed states to provide benefits to 18-year-olds who were still enrolled in high school or technical school.

● Allowed states to provide AFDC benefits to pregnant women who had no other children, but only during the final four months of their pregnancy.

● Provided that states that chose to provide AFDC benefits to two-parent families in which one parent was unemployed could do so only if the "principal wage earner" — the parent who had earned more in the preceding two years — was unemployed.

● Continued the existing law's exemption from the program's work requirements for parents with children under age six only if the parent was providing full-time care for the child, with only brief and infrequent absences.

Monthly Retrospective Income Accounting. Required states to establish a system for determining benefit levels known as "monthly retrospective income accounting." Under the system, benefit levels would be determined according to actual recipient income and circumstances in the preceding month; under existing law, most states used a prospective system that estimated client circumstances for the next month. In addition, recipients would be required to file monthly reports on their income; existing practice in most states required only that recipients report changes in their circumstances.

● Barred states from making AFDC payments to families eligible for less than $10 in monthly assistance; however, such families would continue to be eligible for programs, such as Medicaid, that were tied to AFDC.

● Expanded the states' ability to provide benefits in the form of "vendor payments" provided directly to businesses, such as landlords and utility companies, on behalf of AFDC recipients.

● Required that states take action to recover benefit payments made to recipients in excess of the amounts to which they were entitled, and to restore funds to recipients who received less than they were entitled.

● Reduced to 50 percent, from 75 percent, the federal share of state and local costs of training AFDC personnel.

● Limited AFDC eligibility only to persons who were U.S. citizens or legal aliens.

● Required that a portion of the income of the sponsor of an alien applying for AFDC be considered as income and resources of the alien, in determining eligibility and benefits, for three years following the alien's entry into the country.

● Made the effective date of the AFDC provisions Oct. 1, 1981, but allowed delays for states that needed to change their laws in order to comply with the new federal requirements.

Child Support Enforcement. Expanded the states' ability to use the Internal Revenue Service (IRS) to collect overdue child support payments by allowing the IRS to withhold money from a tax refund due to a delinquent parent.

● Allowed state agencies to collect support payments for a parent, as well as for a child.

● Required states to charge a 10 percent fee, to be charged against the absent parent, for collecting child support payments for non-AFDC families.

● Provided that a child support obligation for an AFDC family not be discharged because of the bankruptcy of the absent parent.

● Required state agencies to withhold a portion of unemployment benefits due to persons who owed past due child support payments and forward that money to the state child support agency.

Supplemental Security Income

● Required states to use a retrospective income accounting system for determining Supplemental Security Income (SSI) benefits.

● Limited the existing authority of the Department of HHS to pay state vocational rehabilitation agencies for services provided to blind or disabled SSI recipients.

Legislative History

Reagan Proposal. President Reagan, in his March 10 budget proposal, called for major changes in AFDC, aimed at saving about $1 billion in fiscal 1982. *(Text of message, p. 19-E)* Without changes, federal spending for the program would be about $7.7 billion in 1982, with state governments spending an approximately equal amount on it, according to HHS.

The administration proposed a fundamental shift in the program by establishing a mandatory "workfare" requirement. Reagan had instituted a workfare program in California when he was governor of that state. States would be required to establish workfare programs and AFDC recipients to accept either a private sector job or a service

job in the community, such as school crossing guard or day care center attendant.

Because workfare would not apply to certain recipients, such as those caring for small children, only about 800,000 of the 10 million people on the AFDC rolls would have to work.

The budget also called for changes in AFDC accounting procedures that would reduce benefit eligibility substantially, such as counting a stepparent's income as part of a welfare recipient's resources, which was not done under existing law; limiting income deductions allowed in determining eligibility and benefits, and excluding from the program strikers and children over 18, unless they were still in high school.

The administration also called for strengthening the child support enforcement program, reducing funds for refugee assistance, establishing a central data bank on welfare recipients and requiring states to place liens on the homes of AFDC recipients in certain cases.

Senate Action

The Senate Finance Committee dropped the controversial data bank and home lien proposals when it approved its reconciliation package May 5, and decided to let the states decide whether to operate workfare programs or not. The administration's major savings proposals were left intact, however.

The package, drawn up by Chairman Robert Dole, R-Kan., and ratified by the committee with only a few minor changes, cut $10.3 billion from fiscal 1982 spending for welfare, Social Security, unemployment insurance, Medicare and Medicaid.

Principal welfare savings were achieved by putting lower limits on the amount of income a person could earn and still receive benefits; cutting benefits to persons receiving food stamps or housing subsidies; eliminating payments for children age 18 and over; requiring states to recoup overpayments and correct underpayments; counting the income of stepparents, and reducing to $1,000, from $2,000, the limit on a recipient's assets (excluding a home and automobile).

House Action

The House Ways and Means Committee, in approving its reconciliation package May 19, agreed to tighten welfare eligibility but rejected Reagan's proposal to require "workfare" programs for AFDC recipients. Instead, the panel agreed to make such state programs optional.

The committee approved cuts totaling $720 million in AFDC, considerably less than the administration wanted to cut. It also reduced SSI spending by $170 million by postponing half of a scheduled 1982 cost-of-living increase from July to October and by changing accounting and other administrative procedures.

One of the few protests during committee debate on the welfare cuts came from Thomas J. Downey, D-N.Y. "There are human consequences and economic consequences on a lot of these proposals that just don't make a lot of sense," he said.

Floor Action. With the House adoption of the Republican-sponsored reconciliation substitute known as Gramm-Latta II, the AFDC provisions of the House and Senate bills were virtually identical.

Gramm-Latta II added $450 million in savings to the cuts approved by the Ways and Means Committee, largely by further reducing benefits to AFDC recipients who had

job income. It would not allow an "income disregard" — a part of earned income that is not counted in determining eligibility and benefits — after a recipient had worked for four months; required that the earned income tax credit for the working poor be considered as monthly income, and adopted most of the other cost-saving provisions of the Senate reconciliation bill.

The only significant difference resolved by conferees was acceptance of a House provision limiting AFDC benefits provided to recent immigrants. ■

Health Manpower Programs

Continuing a trend of the past several years, Congress in 1981 substantially reduced federal spending for the education of doctors, nurses and other health professionals.

It made the cuts as part of the budget reconciliation bill cleared July 31 (HR 3982 — PL 97-35). *(Story, p. 256)*

Although Congress reauthorized loans and other aid for health manpower training, it provided less than half the amount spent in fiscal 1980. Total funding for the programs was set at $218.8 million for fiscal 1982, compared to more than $478 million in 1980. That still was almost $100 million more than President Reagan wanted to spend; he requested $125 million for the programs in 1982. *(Authorizations box, p. 476)*

Congress went along with the administration request to end the program of "capitation grants," which had provided per-student payments to medical and nursing schools since 1971. But the president was less successful in his effort to wind down the National Health Service Corps (NHSC). Established in 1972 (PL 92-585), the program provided scholarships for the education of doctors and other health professionals who then served a year in a medically underserved area in return for each year of aid. *(Background, 1980 Almanac p. 445)*

The Senate agreed not to award new NHSC scholarships, but the House reconciliation bill continued the program. The conference compromise (H Rept 97-208) authorized 550 new scholarships for each of fiscal years 1982-84.

Although the changes ended up as part of reconciliation, the Senate Labor and Human Resources Committee had reported legislation May 15 dealing with health manpower programs (S 799 — S Rept 97-124) and the NHSC (S 801 — S Rept 97-125).

As introduced by committee Chairman Orrin G. Hatch, R-Utah, S 799 would have made even deeper cuts in federal aid for medical students. But two moderate Republican members of the panel, Lowell P. Weicker Jr., Conn., and Robert T. Stafford, Vt., joined with the Democratic minority on a number of liberalizing amendments sponsored by Edward M. Kennedy, D-Mass. The final bill still reflected the bulk of Hatch's budget cuts, however.

Dr. John A. D. Cooper, president of the Association of American Medical Colleges (AAMC), said the cuts in health professions student aid meant that in the future, "only those from wealthy families will be able to afford medicine." Although doctors generally have high incomes, the AAMC said the debts many owed for their training would strain almost any budget and discourage potential students with limited financial resources. Tuition in U.S. medical schools averaged over $5,000 a year in 1981.

The administration argued that health professions students could use general student aid programs just as other

students did. However, the reconciliation bill also made deep cutbacks in those programs. *(Story, p. 493)*

Provisions

As cleared by Congress, Title XXVII of HR 3982:

NHSC. Reauthorized the National Health Service Corps (NHSC), providing for continuation of scholarships already awarded for the education of health professionals and for 550 new awards in each of fiscal years 1982-84.

● Directed the secretary of health and human services (HHS) to re-evaluate the method used for defining areas short of health professionals. Members of the NHSC serve in these "health manpower shortage areas."

● Revised rules dealing with private practice to make it more attractive for NHSC recipients to serve their required time as private practitioners rather than as members of the corps. In addition, the bill authorized subsidies to those choosing this option, such as payment of the individual's malpractice insurance or a partial income supplement.

Health Manpower. Authorized $218.8 million for health manpower programs in fiscal 1982, $238.55 million in 1983 and $249.3 million in 1984.

● Extended the Health Professions Student Loans program, which contributes to school loan funds administered by medical school financial aid officers. The ceiling on the interest rate charged was increased to 9 percent, from 7 percent.

● Extended the Health Education Assistance Loan (HEAL) program, which guarantees loans made by private lenders to health professions students. The bill increased to $20,000 the maximum loan guaranteed in each academic year for students enrolled in schools of medicine, osteopathy, dentistry, veterinary medicine, optometry and podiatry, and increased to $12,500 the maximum available to students enrolled in schools of pharmacy, chiropractic or public health, or graduate programs in health administration or clinical psychology.

● Extended the program providing full first-year scholarships in health professions schools to students with exceptional financial need.

● Extended the program aiding medical schools in financial distress, which is directed at four schools with high enrollments of minority-group students.

● Extended funding of area health education centers (AHECs) — training programs located away from schools' major campuses and in a medically underserved area.

● Repealed the authorization for capitation grants for medical and nursing schools, but continued the program for schools of public health, with an authorization of $6.5 million in fiscal 1982, $7 million in 1983 and $7.5 million in 1984.

● Directed the HHS secretary to arrange for a study of physician supply and distribution, with the cost not to exceed $2 million.

Background

Federal aid for the education of health professionals had been dwindling in recent years, as doctor shortages gave way to projected doctor surpluses.

Shortages in the 1960s and 1970s had spurred Congress to give "capitation" grants to medical schools to encourage expansion, with up to $2,100 per student provided. Four major health professions student aid programs

Health Education Aid

HR 3982 authorized the following amounts for health manpower programs in fiscal 1982-84 *(in millions of dollars):*

Program	1982	1983	1984
Health professions			
Construction	$ 4.3	$ 9.3	$ 4.3
Student loans	12	13	14
Scholarships for students with exceptional need	6	6.5	7
Project grants, contracts			
Family medicine	10	10.5	11
Area health education centers	21	22.5	24
Training of physician assistants	5	5.5	6
General internal medicine/pediatrics	17	18	20
Family medicine/ general dentistry	32	34	36
Aid to disadvantaged students	20	21.5	23
Aid to financially distressed medical schools	10	10	10
Curriculum development	6	6.5	7
Public health	12.5	14.3	16
Nurse training	63	67	71
Total	$218.8	$238.6	$249.3

also were established: the Health Professions Student Loan program, the NHSC, scholarships for disadvantaged students and the HEAL program.

Because of these programs and other factors, by 1980 the supply of doctors was considered more than adequate, with surpluses projected by the 1990s.

Support for capitation grants began to erode in the late 1970s. Congress continued the grants in 1976 but, because of concern about overspecialization, required that schools receiving them have a certain percentage of first-year residency positions in primary care.

By the time that authorization expired, in 1980, pressure to trim the budget had increased, and the Carter administration asked Congress to eliminate the capitation grants. The House agreed to a three-year phase-out. The Senate also agreed to cut out the grants but substituted other aid to schools that met certain criteria, such as offering programs in preventive medicine or having a certain percentage of minority students. The two chambers were not able to resolve their differences before the 96th Congress adjourned, and so no reauthorization bill cleared. *(Background, 1980 Almanac p. 445)*

1981 Legislative Action

Continuing health manpower training programs at existing levels, adjusted for inflation, would have required $474 million in fiscal 1982. The Senate reconciliation bill (S 1377) provided only $205 million; the House called for $320 million. Conferees compromised on $218.8 million.

Both chambers refused to include fiscal 1982 funding for capitation grants in their bills, despite pleas from medical colleges. Fiscal 1981 funding already had been re-

scinded under legislation passed in June (HR 3512 — PL 97-12). *(Story, p. 281)*

Although Congress in the past had also provided construction financing to medical schools, both reconciliation bills cut out any new funding for that purpose.

Although the administration wanted no new funding for Health Professions Student Loans, HR 3982 authorized $16.5 million in fiscal 1982. The Senate provided $4.5 million, to go to schools with little or no money in their revolving loan funds. The Senate bill also raised the interest rate ceiling to 9 percent. Conferees agreed to $12 million for loans, at the 9 percent interest rate.

The Senate also agreed to phase out the NHSC scholarship program. The Labor and Human Resources Committee said the expected surplus of doctors in the mid-1980s, and resulting competitive forces, would push doctors into many areas where shortages existed in the past, reducing the need for NHSC personnel. For areas still underserved, the corps could expect to have enough volunteers because of the doctor surplus. So the need for scholarships to draw personnel into the corps would no longer exist, the committee reasoned.

The Senate bill allowed funding only to carry out previous scholarship commitments. The House continued the program at an authorization level of $55 million. Conferees agreed to fund 550 new scholarships in each of fiscal years 1982-84.

The Senate also went along with the administration's request to eliminate the scholarship program for disadvantaged students. The House authorized $10 million for it. Conferees allowed $6 million.

Both bills continued the HEAL program.

While the Senate bill continued aid to nursing students and nursing schools, the funding level was cut to $50 million, about half the amount needed to continue existing programs. The House bill authorized $92 million. The conference compromise was $63 million.

Both bills continued funding for a variety of special projects, including medical schools with an emphasis on primary care, geriatric medicine or preventive medicine; Area Health Education Centers, which coordinate delivery of medical services; programs to recruit disadvantaged students into the health professions and then provide counseling and tutoring, and medical schools in financial distress (four schools educating mainly minority students). The Senate allowed $100 million for project grants, the House, $124 million. ∎

Health Planning System

Although the Reagan administration called for a phase-out of the federal health planning system, Congress decided to continue it for one year at a substantially reduced level of funding.

The reauthorization was included in the budget reconciliation bill cleared July 31 (HR 3982 — PL 97-35). *Story, p. 256)*

Created in 1975 (PL 93-641) and extended in 1979 (PL 96-79), the health planning program was intended to curb unneeded hospital expansions and duplication in the provision of services and purchase of major medical equipment. A hospital must obtain a "certificate of need" from the state before proceeding with major changes. *(Congress and the Nation Vol. IV, p. 335; 1978 Almanac p. 616; 1979 Almanac p. 474)*

The program funded local planning groups, known as health systems agencies (HSAs), which were controlled by locally selected boards made up of consumers and providers of health care. The HSAs, of which there were more than 200 in 1980, were to review any proposed expansion of health services and facilities in their areas and monitor local spending on health by the federal government.

Supporters of the program contended that it helped hold down health care costs, but opponents called it unnecessary federal interference.

In putting together its reconciliation package (S 1377), the Senate went along with Reagan, voting to terminate funding of the local boards in fiscal 1982 and end aid to state planning in fiscal 1983. The House bill continued funding in fiscal 1982 but did not extend the program beyond that.

Conferees provided fiscal 1982 funding of $102 million, but did not address the question of future federal aid.

The authorization represented a substantial reduction compared to fiscal 1980 spending of $157.7 million. Total 1981 funding was $117.4 million, following an $18 million rescission in June. *(Rescission bill, p. 281)*

Provisions

As cleared by Congress, the health planning provisions of HR 3982:

● Provided that no more than $65 million could be spent on HSAs in fiscal 1982.

● Raised the threshold of expenditures subject to review by planning agencies to $600,000 for capital outlays, from $150,000; to $400,000 for major medical equipment, from $150,000, and to $250,000 for the annual operating costs of new services, from $75,000.

● Authorized governors to ask the health and human services secretary to eliminate federal funding of HSAs in their states if they certified that state-level health planning agencies, which also received funding under the program, would take over the functions of the HSAs.

● Reduced the minimum grant for HSAs to $100,000, from $245,000, and allowed HSAs to accept contributions from health insurance companies.

● Extended for one year the deadline by which states must comply with federal planning requirements or face penalties.

Medicaid Spending Cut But 'Cap' Rejected

Congress agreed to cut federal Medicaid spending by about $1 billion a year, but rejected a Reagan administration proposal to set a rigid ceiling on the federal contribution to the state-run health care program for the poor.

The funding cut was included in Title XXI of the reconciliation bill cleared July 31 (HR 3982 — PL 97-35). *(Story, p. 256)*

The reconciliation bill also made numerous other changes in Medicaid and in Medicare, the health care program for the elderly. Among other things, it modified the guarantee that Medicaid recipients be free to choose their health care providers; increased the deductibles that must be paid by Medicare beneficiaries for hospital costs and for supplementary health insurance, and continued the Professional Standards Review Organizations (PSRO) program, which President Reagan wanted to abolish.

Medicaid Controversy

The Medicaid cap was one of the most controversial and bitterly fought proposals in Reagan's fiscal 1982 budget. The administration wanted to avoid continued increases in the federal government's Medicaid bill by placing a cap on the federal share of the program's funding. The federal government pays about 55 percent of Medicaid costs, the states 45 percent. Reagan proposed that in fiscal 1982 the federal government limit its spending on Medicaid to 5 percent more than it spent in 1981.

The Senate agreed to the concept, but set the cap at 9 percent. The House rejected Reagan's approach, voting instead simply to reduce the federal spending level by a given percentage each year; it reduced the amount states would otherwise be entitled to receive by 3 percent in fiscal 1982, 2 percent in 1983 and 1 percent in 1984.

The conference compromise rejected the cap but required higher percentage reductions than voted by the House — 3 percent in 1982, 4 percent in 1983 and 4.5 percent in 1984. States could avoid the full reduction by instituting effective cost-saving measures. In addition,

states suffering from high unemployment could get additional federal dollars to cover persons newly eligible for Medicaid.

Despite the percentage reductions, federal spending for Medicaid still was expected to increase because of rising health care costs. The Congressional Budget Office estimated the federal government would spend about $600 million more for the entitlement program in fiscal 1982 than in 1981, and $2.3 billion more in 1983.

Provisions

As signed into law, HR 3982:

Medicaid

● Reduced the Medicaid payments the states would otherwise be entitled to receive from the federal government by 3 percent in fiscal 1982, 4 percent in 1983 and 4.5 percent in 1984.

● Provided that the cut in the federal payment be reduced by one percentage point if a state had a qualified cost review program; by one percentage point if it had an unemployment rate equal to 150 percent of the national average, and by one percentage point if the total amount of the state's recoveries for fraud and abuse was equal to 1 percent of the federal contribution to that state.

● Provided that a state could win an increase in its federal payment by holding down costs. The supplemental federal payment would be equal to the difference between actual costs and a target figure, but could not exceed the amount by which that year's federal payment had been reduced under the percentage cuts.

The target for fiscal 1982 would be to hold costs to no more than 9 percent above the fiscal 1981 level; fiscal 1983 and 1984 targets would be set by the secretary of health and human services (HHS) based on the medical care expenditure category of the Consumer Price Index.

● Directed the comptroller general to report to Congress

by Oct. 1, 1982, on the existing formula for determining the federal contribution to each state's Medicaid program.

● Loosened federal requirements that states opting to cover the medically needy make eligible for the coverage all medically needy persons.

Under existing law that category included individuals who were aged, blind, disabled or members of families with dependent children, who had too much income to qualify for cash assistance programs but not enough to afford medical care. The revised rule required that coverage apply to pregnant women and that it not discriminate against home health care, but otherwise gave states more flexibility in defining "medically needy."

● Repealed the requirement that hospital reimbursement under Medicaid be based on the determination of "reasonable cost" used by the Medicare program. States still would be required to have reimbursement schedules sufficient to ensure that Medicaid patients had "reasonable access to services of adequate quality."

● Modified the provision guaranteeing "freedom of choice" for Medicaid recipients. The new provision allowed states to arrange through competitive bidding for laboratory services or medical devices for Medicaid patients; restrict the physicians or facilities available to recipients who overutilized services; limit participation in Medicaid by a provider who provided services not considered medically necessary or of poor quality, and implement a case-management system that could require recipients to use only certain providers.

States would have to apply to the secretary of HHS for a waiver from the "freedom of choice" provision in order to impose the above restrictions. A waiver would be considered granted if the secretary had not responded within 90 days with either a denial or a request for additional information.

● Authorized states, subject to approval by the secretary of HHS, to provide Medicaid coverage for certain home or community-based services.

● Repealed a requirement that states not contract with health maintenance organizations (HMOs) in which Medicaid and Medicare enrollees made up more than 50 percent of the membership. The limit was raised to 75 percent.

● Repealed a penalty of 1 percent in federal matching payments for Aid to Families with Dependent Children (AFDC) for states that did not meet certain performance standards for Early and Periodic Screening, Diagnosis and Treatment Services (EPSDT) under Medicaid.

Medicare

● Repealed a provision making eligible for Medicare reimbursement treatment given at alcohol detoxification facilities not connected with hospitals or clinics. The provision took effect April 1, 1981.

● Required "Part A" Medicare beneficiaries to pay for the first $256 of hospital costs in fiscal 1982, instead of $228 as under existing law. The deductible would be increased to $292 in fiscal 1983 and $328 in 1984. The changes were accomplished by changing from $40 to $45 the base figure used in a formula.

● Repealed a provision that allowed Medicare beneficiaries to count expenses incurred in the last quarter of the previous calendar year when determining whether they had met the annual "Part B" deductible for the new year.

● Increased to $75, from $60, the deductible for participants in the optional Part B Medicare coverage, beginning in calendar year 1982.

● Reduced to 5 percent, from 8.5 percent, the differential added to average routine nursing costs to cover what hospitals claimed were the higher costs of caring for elderly Medicare patients.

● Directed the secretary of HHS to issue regulations setting limits on charges for outpatient services for which hospitals could be reimbursed under Medicare and Medicaid.

● Directed the secretary to reimburse hospitals for inpatient services only to the extent that costs did not exceed 108 percent of the mean cost of providing similar services at a comparable group of hospitals.

● Set as the limit on reimbursement for home health agencies the 75th percentile, instead of the 80th, of average per visit costs.

● Provided that private health insurance held by renal dialysis patients provide primary reimbursement for the first year of dialysis services, with Medicare covering any remaining costs.

● Eliminated open enrollment for Medicare and instead allowed enrollment only between Jan. 1 and March 31.

Both Programs

● Allowed federal reimbursement of costs related to the closing or conversion of under-utilized hospital facilities.

● Prohibited payment for drugs determined by the secretary of HHS to be medically ineffective.

● Required that payments be withheld from physicians or other health care providers who had refused to return earlier overpayments or cooperate in investigations.

● Authorized penalties of up to $2,000 for fraudulent claims under Medicare or Medicaid; also authorized the secretary of HHS to assess a recipient for up to twice the amount of a fraudulent claim and to bar from participation in the programs anyone found to have filed a fraudulent claim.

PSROs. Directed the secretary to assess the performance of Professional Standards Review Organizations — groups of physicians that monitor federally provided health care to determine whether the treatment is necessary and of high quality. Upon finding that a PSRO had been ineffective or inefficient, the secretary could refuse to renew the agreement providing federal funding. However, no more than 30 percent of PSROs could be terminated in fiscal 1982. The bill also gave states the option of contracting with PSROs for review of Medicaid services, and cut the federal share of the cost of operating PSROs to 75 percent, from 100 percent.

Background

President Reagan's March 10 budget estimated federal outlays in fiscal 1982 of $47.1 billion for Medicare and $18 billion for Medicaid.

The administration originally said Medicare would be exempt from cuts because it was part of its "social safety net." However, it later proposed about $1 billion in Medicare spending reductions, to be achieved mainly by repealing new benefits enacted in 1980, which had not yet gone into effect, and by changes in hospital reimbursement policies.

The administration proposed to cut about $1 billion from Medicaid spending by limiting federal outlays to 5 percent more than the 1981 level — even though health care costs had been rising at an annual rate of 15 percent.

An estimated 18.3 million low-income people, includ-

ing more than 8 million children, received Medicaid benefits in fiscal 1981. The federal government paid an estimated $16.5 billion, the states about $14.7 billion of the cost. Arizona was the only state that did not participate in the program.

The administration, led by Office of Management and Budget Director David A. Stockman, argued that a cap was the only way to bring Medicaid costs under control. It called for a 5 percent cap the first year; in future years federal spending could rise with the GNP deflator, an inflation measurement that opponents contended was several percentage points behind the actual inflation rate.

State officials, guided by the National Governors' Association (NGA), strongly opposed the cap. They contended that it would only shift millions of dollars in costs to the states, which said they were already overburdened by Medicaid budgets swollen by escalating hospital costs. The states also feared that a cap on Medicaid would set a precedent for caps on federal contributions to other programs, such as welfare.

The states' position prevailed in the House, which rejected the cap and instead agreed to save an equal amount (about $1 billion) by reducing federal Medicaid funding by 3 percent in fiscal 1982, 2 percent in 1983 and one percent in 1984.

A key supporter of that approach was Henry A. Waxman, D-Calif., chairman of the House Energy and Commerce Subcommittee on Health. Waxman called the cap proposal "simplistic" and said it "may well have more tragic consequences than any other administration [budget] proposal."

Waxman noted that high unemployment rates could boost Medicaid rolls and costs even in states with efficient, well-run programs. A cap also failed to deal with the underlying problem of a system that encouraged use of the most expensive services, such as institutional care, instead of those that were more cost-effective, such as preventive programs, he said.

The Republican-controlled Senate agreed to a Medicaid cap, but set it at 9 percent.

Legislative Action

Senate Committee. The Senate Finance Committee, in approving its reconciliation package May 5, made significant changes in the administration proposals for Medicare and Medicaid. The package was proposed by Chairman Robert Dole, R-Kan., and adopted with only minor changes.

The committee nearly doubled Reagan's proposed Medicare savings, cutting an estimated $1.98 billion, compared to Reagan's $1.09 billion cut. Among other things, it voted to raise premiums and deductibles for "Part B;" authorize civil money penalties for Medicare fraud; make Medicare the secondary payor for renal disease if an individual also had a private insurance plan covering the disease, and make changes in hospital reimbursement policies.

The biggest single "saving" was achieved by a budgetary maneuver — shifting back to the fiscal 1981 budget several weeks of Medicare payments to hospitals that Congress in 1980 had shifted to the 1982 budget in order to save money. *(1980 Almanac p. 459)*

The committee agreed to repeal only four of the eight new Medicare benefits passed in 1980. Members argued that the others would save money in the long run. The panel refused to cancel Medicare coverage for vaccinations

against pneumococcal pneumonia, as Reagan asked, but did delay the benefit until 1984. *(1980 Almanac p. 458)*

The committee rejected the administration's proposal to eliminate PSROs. David Durenberger, R-Minn., said the agencies were "the only kind of tool we have out there to deal with [health care] cost containment."

The committee adopted a provision shifting the primary responsibility for the health insurance coverage of certain federal employees and retirees from Medicare to the Federal Employee Health Benefits (FEHB) program. That would reduce Medicare outlays by about $1 billion a year but would increase FEHB spending accordingly. Because a portion of FEHB premiums was paid by the employees, the net savings to the government would be $390 million, the committee said.

The large and influential federal employees' unions were taken by surprise by the proposal and bitterly opposed it. The provision was later dropped.

The Finance Committee changed Reagan's 5 percent cap on the growth of federal Medicaid spending in 1982 to a 9 percent cap. Then, to save money, it adopted a provision reducing the minimum federal match for state Medicaid programs to 40 percent, from 50 percent. Under the provision, 12 states and the District of Columbia, which received the minimum match, would have their Medicaid funds reduced.

(Under existing law, the federal government paid between 50 and 83 percent of a state's Medicaid costs. The exact percentage was based on a complicated formula which provided a higher matching rate to states with lower per capita income, but no state could have a matching rate lower than 50 percent).

Senators whose states would lose money under the change opposed the measure, saying it unfairly shifted the burden of the Medicaid budget cut to a handful of states. Roughly 90 percent of the cut, they said, would come from California, Connecticut, the District of Columbia, Illinois, Michigan and New Jersey. Bill Bradley, D-N.J., fought the provision in committee, but his attempt to lessen the impact of the change was defeated, 2-13.

House Committee Action. The House Ways and Means Committee May 19 agreed to cut more than $1.7 billion from Medicare spending — about $500 million more than Reagan recommended. It adopted the larger cut so that fewer reductions would have to be made in public assistance programs to meet its reconciliation target.

Like the Senate committee, the panel made its largest "saving" by budgetary maneuvering on hospital reimbursements that, in effect, would cut spending in fiscal 1982 by pushing the expenditure back into fiscal 1981.

The committee agreed to shift primary responsibility for the health insurance coverage of some federal employees and retirees from Medicare to the FEHB program, but scaled down the Senate committee's version of the proposal. The Senate version applied to both current and future beneficiaries of both programs. Under great pressure from federal employees' unions, Ways and Means revised the proposal to apply only to FEHB beneficiaries who turned 65 on or after Jan. 1, 1982.

Harold E. Ford, D-Tenn., and Sam Gibbons, D-Fla., tried to kill the proposal altogether, but failed.

The committee agreed to phase out PSROs by Oct. 1, 1983, with half to be eliminated by Oct. 1, 1982; established a reimbursement rate for renal dialysis that would encourage more use of home dialysis; required Medicare inpatients to pay $1 more a day for the first 60 days of acute

care; increased the Part B deductible to $70, and increased the "Part A" (basic benefits) deductible and coinsurance.

The House Energy and Commerce Committee, which had jurisdiction over Medicaid, was unable to reach agreeement on a reconciliation package and sent two rival proposals to the floor.

Floor Action

Senate. The Senate adopted its reconciliation bill (S 1377) June 25.

Recognizing the widespread opposition to the Medicaid cap, Dole planned to offer a compromise amendment to delay any cap for at least three years, with a 2 percent reduction in Medicaid funding in 1982 and a one percent cut in 1983. He also called for a presidential commission to study the advisability of using a cap as a tool for holding down costs. The amendment had bipartisan support and was endorsed by a number of states. But under pressure from the White House, Dole withdrew the proposal and offered instead an amendment simply setting up the commission. It was adopted by voice vote.

The Senate adopted an amendment keeping Medicare as the primary health insurance provider for federal employees with dual coverage. The amendment was first rejected, 47-50, but later adopted, 51-47. Sponsors Ted Stevens, R-Alaska, and William V. Roth Jr., R-Del., said that without the amendment, federal employees' health insurance premiums would be increased, since the burden of providing health insurance would be switched to private health plans. *(Votes 170-172, p. 31-S)*

House. Although the House June 26 adopted the administration-supported Gramm-Latta amendment to its budget reconciliation bill (HR 3982), the Republican substitute did not include health and energy provisions. Instead, the savings package drawn up by Democratic members of the Energy and Commerce Committee remained in the bill.

James T. Broyhill, R-N.C., planned to offer a Republican version of the health and energy provisions, but decided to withdraw his proposal when he found himself short of votes. Unlike the Democratic plan, Broyhill's amendment called for a Medicaid cap. That provision cost Broyhill crucial votes from Republicans representing the Northeast and Midwest, as well as from Southern Democrats who had supported President Reagan earlier. Officials in their states had urged them to oppose the cap.

The inclusion of the Democratic package in the House bill dramatically boosted the chances of those fighting to kill the Senate-passed Medicaid cap in conference.

Conference Action

After bitter disagreement over what to do about Medicaid, reconciliation conferees finally agreed to reject a cap but to cut spending for the program by 3 percent in fiscal 1982, for an estimated saving of $920 million; 4 percent in 1983, saving $944 million, and 4.5 percent in 1984, saving $1 billion.

In other actions the conferees:

● Dropped the Senate proposal to reduce the federal Medicaid contribution to states with above-average per capita income.

● Gave states greater flexibility in applying the "freedom of choice" provision for Medicaid patients, but stopped short of repealing it, as the Senate bill did.

● Dropped the Senate requirement indexing premiums for the optional "Part B" Medicare insurance to inflation.

The annual deductible was raised to $75, as in the Senate bill, however.

● Allowed the secretary of HHS to terminate up to 30 percent of existing PSROs by the end of fiscal 1982, but did not end the entire program, as the House bill did. Conferees also cut the federal share of the cost of operating PSROs to 75 percent, from 100 percent.

● Dropped the House provision making Medicare the secondary payor for certain federal employees and retirees covered by FEHB.

● Accepted a House provision prohibiting Medicare Part B and Medicaid payments for drugs found to be ineffective or not medically necessary. ∎

Federal Aid to HMOs

Rejecting a Reagan administration proposal, Congress continued federal aid to health maintenance organizations (HMOs), which provide health services to members for fixed fees.

The budget reconciliation bill (HR 3982 — PL 97-35) cleared by Congress July 31 authorized $21 million a year in fiscal 1982-84 for grants, loans and loan guarantees to HMOs. That was less than half the amount spent in fiscal 1980. Congress had provided $43.8 million for fiscal 1981, but the June 4 rescission (HR 3512 — PL 97-12) reduced that to $8.8 million. *(Rescission bill, p. 281)*

HMOs had been eligible for federal subsidies since 1973. With the subsidies went federal regulation, guaranteeing members certain basic health services; there were 120 federally qualified HMOs at the end of 1980. Grants, loans and loan guarantees were reauthorized in 1976 (PL 93-222) and 1978 (PL 95-559). The subsidies were scheduled to expire at the end of fiscal 1981. *(Congress and the Nation Vol. IV, p. 327; 1978 Almanac p. 576)*

In its budget proposal, the Reagan administration argued that further federal aid to HMOs was unnecessary. However, because HMOs usually provided health care at lower cost than the traditional fee-for-service approach, legislators seeking to hold down costs were reluctant to end the program.

Legislative Action, Provisions

Although the changes were included in the reconciliation bill, committees in both houses had approved HMO bills earlier in the year.

The House Energy and Commerce Committee reported its bill May 19 (HR 3398 — H Rept 97-88). The text later was included in the House-passed reconciliation measure. The Senate Labor and Human Resources Committee reported its version May 15 (S 1029 — S Rept 97-127) but the bill never reached the Senate floor.

In addition to authorizing $21 million annually over the next three years for HMOs, the reconciliation bill provided for additional funding as needed to maintain $5 million in the loan fund at the end of each fiscal year.

It also modified the requirement that HMOs base their premiums on community-wide, rather than individual, health care costs. The change would permit use of classes of individuals in rate-setting, so that higher-cost groups, such as the elderly, would have to pay higher premiums. Conferees said the revised system would give HMOs "substantial new flexibility" in setting their rates. ∎

Veterans' Health Care

Vietnam veterans in 1981 finally won their long fight to get medical treatment for veterans suffering from ailments attributed to Agent Orange, the toxic chemical used to defoliate jungles in Vietnam.

Legislation directing the Veterans Administration (VA) to provide the care cleared Congress Oct. 16 and was signed into law Nov. 3 (HR 3499 — PL 97-72).

The bill, known as the Veterans' Health Care, Training and Small Business Loan Act, also established and extended several other veterans' programs, including the "storefront" readjustment counseling program, which the Reagan administration wanted to end.

A veto reportedly was considered, primarily on budgetary grounds, but President Reagan contented himself with expressing his concerns about some aspects of the legislation while signing it into law.

House Veterans' Affairs Committee staff estimated the cost of the bill at about $57 million, but that number was based on a guess as to how many veterans would take advantage of the Agent Orange medical care. A senior VA official said he thought the cost would be much higher.

In addition to the Agent Orange coverage and extension of the storefront counseling program, the bill required the VA to maintain a specified number of hospital and nursing home beds — more than the administration wanted; extended the period in which veterans could use certain education benefits, and established a new small-business loan program for veterans.

The House and Senate, by unanimous votes, approved different versions of the legislation in June. Senior members of the Veterans' Affairs committees informally negotiated a compromise version, which the House passed Oct. 2, the Senate Oct. 16.

Shortly before the Senate cleared the bill, Robert W. Edgar, D-Pa., chairman of the House Veterans' Affairs Subcommittee on Education, Training and Employment, charged that Senate Budget Committee Chairman Pete V. Domenici, R-N.M., was giving in to White House pressure and was blocking action on the measure. "Reaganomics is out to get Vietnam vets again," Edgar charged.

As it turned out, Domenici's fiscal objections to the measure were settled by assurances from Alan K. Simpson, R-Wyo., chairman of the Senate Veterans' Affairs Committee, that the Agent Orange health care provision did not create a new automatic entitlement program.

Provisions

As signed into law, HR 3499 (PL 97-72):

● Made veterans who served in Vietnam eligible for VA medical, hospital or nursing home care for problems linked to exposure to Agent Orange or other toxic herbicides or defoliants. Any veteran who served in Vietnam would be presumed to have been exposed. The VA would develop guidelines to determine what disabilities might have been caused by exposure and thus would be treated.

● Also made eligible for VA care veterans exposed to radiation from nuclear weapons testing or during occupation of the Japanese cities of Hiroshima and Nagasaki after World War II. Veterans exposed to Agent Orange or radiation would have priority for care over veterans with non-service-connected disabilities. Authority for care for both groups would expire one year after the completion of a study on the effects of exposure to Agent Orange.

● Expanded the scope of the study mandated by Congress in 1979 (PL 96-151) on the effects of Agent Orange to include other herbicides and defoliants and other factors of Vietnam service, including medications and environmental conditions. *(1979 Almanac p. 518)*

● Extended the readjustment counseling program for Vietnam veterans through Sept. 30, 1984. The VA was directed to prepare to provide similar counseling services at its own medical facilities after that date.

● Allowed the VA to recover the costs of medical treatment for non-service-connected disabilities for which a veteran had insurance coverage.

● Extended through Dec. 31, 1983, the period during which Vietnam-era veterans could use remaining GI Bill eligibility to pursue on-the-job-training programs, vocational courses or a high school diploma.

● Extended through Sept. 30, 1984, the authority for government agencies to hire and train Vietnam-era veterans outside of normal civil service hiring rules.

● Established a small-business loan program to be run by the VA. Loans would be made to disabled and Vietnam-era veterans from a revolving fund authorized at $25 million. Veterans who had received loans from the Small Business Administration (SBA) would be ineligible for the new program. The program would expire Sept. 30, 1986.

● Required the VA to maintain a minimum of 90,000 hospital and nursing home beds, although up to 125,000 beds could be maintained if necessary.

Background

Veterans' groups had been trying for several years to get medical care for veterans exposed to Agent Orange in Vietnam. They blamed the herbicide for a wide range of maladies including cancer, liver damage, depression, sleeplessness, tingling or loss of sensation in limbs, malfunctioning of the body's disease-fighting system, miscarriages, stillbirths and birth defects in their children.

Between 1965 and 1970, when its use was stopped, almost 11 million gallons of Agent Orange were sprayed in Vietnam. Thousands of U.S. servicemen were exposed, although the Defense Department had been unable to determine the precise number.

The VA had refused to allow the claims of veterans suffering from exposure to the chemical except to provide care for chloracne, a skin disease. VA officials said there was not sufficient proof that Agent Orange was the cause of the veterans' problems. Congress ordered a study in 1979 to produce data to make a determination about the herbicide. But that did not satisfy the veterans, who continued to lobby Congress for medical care.

Storefront Counseling. The readjustment counseling program for Vietnam veterans was established in 1979 after years of effort. The authorization expired Sept. 30, 1981. *(1979 Almanac p. 522)*

The outreach program operated out of 91 "storefront" centers around the country — so called because many were located in business districts, away from VA facilities, which many Vietnam veterans did not trust.

Although the program generally was regarded as a success, the administration did not seek to renew it. The administration said the veterans could be treated in VA facilities, at a savings of about $27 million a year.

VA Hospital Beds. Like the Carter administration

before it, the Reagan administration wanted to reduce the number of beds the VA maintained in its hospitals and nursing homes. The Reagan budget called for maintaining only about 80,000 beds.

The House Veterans' Affairs Committee fought the move. It said the VA, against the committee's wishes, had already reduced the number of beds by about 20,000 in the past 10 years, while the number of veterans had doubled.

Legislative Action

House. The House June 2 passed two bills (HR 3499, HR 3423) whose provisions eventually were combined in the final version of HR 3499.

HR 3499 (H Rept 97-79), containing the health care, storefront counseling and minimum hospital beds provisions, passed by a vote of 388-0. HR 3423 (H Rept 97-78), the educational training and business loan act, was approved 352-41. *(Votes 47, 51, p. 28-H)*

The bills, reported by the Veterans' Affairs Committee May 19, were passed under suspension of the rules, which requires a two-thirds majority for passage and precludes any amendments.

The House action on the medical care bill marked the first time either house of Congress had approved legislation calling for treatment of veterans suffering from exposure to Agent Orange.

Although the administration formally notified Congress that it was opposed to the bills, there was no White House or VA lobbying effort to defeat them, and House Republican leaders did not speak against them. In the brief debate June 1 and 2, no one spoke in opposition. A VA spokesman noted that most veterans' bills are passed with such large majorities that lobbying against them would do little good.

As passed by the House, HR 3499 was more liberal than the final version of the bill. It would have provided care to Vietnam veterans for any condition that "may be associated with exposure" to Agent Orange.

Until scientists could determine the cause-and-effect relationship of the herbicide, the VA should do everything possible to provide care to exposed veterans, the Veterans' Affairs Committee said. "When a doubt exists, the doubt should be resolved in favor of the veteran."

The VA said the bill would have the effect of extending hospital care to all Vietnam veterans for almost any medical or psychiatric condition. It said the cost would be "of considerable magnitude."

Thomas A. Daschle, D-S.D., a Vietnam veteran, defended the medical help for veterans exposed to Agent Orange and said he planned to seek separate legislation providing monetary compensation to veterans suffering as a result of exposure.

HR 3499 also extended the storefront counseling centers for three years and required the VA to maintain at least 100,000 beds in its hospitals and nursing homes. It set the minimum number of hospital beds at 82,500 in fiscal 1982-1986. The administration had requested 79,700 beds in fiscal 1982, dropping to 73,300 by 1986. The Congressional Budget Office estimated this provision would add up to $116 million to the Reagan budget in fiscal 1982.

The most controversial provision of HR 3423 was the small-business loan program, to be funded out of a $25 million revolving fund. The Veterans' Affairs Committee said loan guarantees were necessary because the Small

Business Administration had ignored other laws providing special consideration to Vietnam veterans seeking business loans.

Senate Action

Committee. The Senate Veterans' Affairs Committee May 15 reported an omnibus veterans' bill (S 921 — S Rept 97-89) that expanded the VA's Agent Orange study but did not authorize medical coverage for exposed veterans, pending the outcome of the study.

An amendment by Alan Cranston, D-Calif., to provide medical care for Agent Orange- or radiation-related illnesses failed on a 6-6 tie vote. Voting with Cranston were Strom Thurmond, R-S.C.; Jennings Randolph, D-W.Va.; Spark M. Matsunaga, D-Hawaii; Dennis DeConcini, D-Ariz.; and George J. Mitchell, D-Maine. Opposing the proposal were Chairman Alan K. Simpson, R-Wyo., and five other committee Republicans: Robert T. Stafford, Vt.; Robert W. Kasten Jr., Wis.; Jeremiah Denton, Ala.; Frank H. Murkowski, Alaska; and Arlen Specter, Pa.

As reported, the bill extended eligibility for readjustment counseling for only two years.

Floor Action. After reversing the committee's position on providing care for veterans exposed to Agent Orange, the Senate passed the veterans' health care bill June 16 by a vote of 99-0. *(Vote 153, p. 29-S)*

As passed, the bill not only authorized medical care for veterans exposed to Agent Orange but for those exposed to other toxic substances used in Vietnam or to radiation from nuclear weapons tests. And it not only made them eligible for medical care; it also required the VA to give them priority in its outpatient facilities over veterans with non-service-connected ailments.

The administration opposed the bill but did not lobby actively against it. Cranston said its passage would "send a strong, positive signal to Vietnam-era veterans that their concerns have not been lost in the shuffle."

Cranston's amendment to provide medical care to veterans exposed to toxic chemicals or radiation was adopted 98-0 after it was modified in several respects by Simpson. *(Vote 151, p. 29-S)*

Simpson's changes limited the chemicals covered by the bill to herbicides, defoliants and chemicals used to prevent malaria, and continued veterans' eligibility for medical care only until one year after an Agent Orange study mandated by Congress in 1979 was submitted. At that time Congress could develop further legislation as needed, Simpson said.

The Senate also voted to expand the scope of the Agent Orange study. By voice vote it adopted an amendment by Larry Pressler, R-S.D., authorizing the study to cover the psychological and genetic effects of the toxic chemicals used in Vietnam as well as the physical illnesses resulting from exposure to them.

Other amendments adopted by the Senate included:

● By John H. Chafee, R-R.I., to extend eligibility for readjustment counseling services for three years instead of two. Adopted 99-0. *(Vote 152, p. 29-S)*

● By Cranston, to extend for two years the period in which certain educationally disadvantaged, unskilled or unemployed Vietnam-era veterans may use GI Bill benefits. Adopted by voice vote.

Final Action

The compromise version of the bill worked out by senior members of the Veterans' Affairs committees was

approved by the House Oct. 2 and by the Senate Oct. 16, both by voice votes.

President Reagan signed the bill Nov. 3. He said he was doing so, despite several concerns, because of his "strong commitment to the welfare of America's veterans, particularly Vietnam-era veterans."

Reagan said the provisions guaranteeing medical care to veterans exposed to Agent Orange should be "implemented in a manner that will not add to budgetary costs of VA medical care and treatment." He noted that the new eligibility was temporary, pending the outcome of studies of the effects of Agent Orange.

He also expressed concern about the number of VA hospital beds mandated by the bill. The requirement should not preclude the VA from using an "appropriate mix" of health care services, including outpatient care, Reagan said.

Reagan also said that because the small-business loan program created by the bill might duplicate the SBA loan program and would involve the VA in an area in which it had no expertise, he would "weigh carefully any efforts to fund" the new program.   ∎

Health Program Spending Cut by 25 Percent

Congress substantially revised President Reagan's budget proposals for health programs, but the administration still won major reductions in funding under the reconciliation bill cleared July 31 (HR 3982 — PL 97-35). *(Reconciliation bill, p. 256)*

Overall spending on health programs was cut by about 25 percent, for savings averaging about $1 billion a year in fiscal 1982-84. Reduced federal funding of Medicaid was expected to save another $1 billion a year. *(Health program authorizations, box, p. 486; Medicaid, p. 477)*

The reconciliation measure set up four health block grants, which shifted to the states responsibility for 19 health programs formerly run by the federal government. *(Programs included in block grants, box, p. 484)*

But Congress refused to remove from federal control several other programs that Reagan had wanted to include in block grants, including family planning, health centers for migrant workers and venereal disease prevention programs. It also imposed a number of conditions on the states' use of block grant funds, rather than giving them total control over how the money would be spent, as Reagan proposed.

Funding of the block grants was based on the fiscal 1981 appropriation for each of the separate programs, which was adjusted for inflation and then reduced by 25 percent. That substantial cut was expected to require major reductions in services.

Block Grant Controversy

The erosion of Reagan's approach to block grants began in the Senate Labor and Human Resources Committee, where a coalition of Democrats and two Republicans kept Chairman Orrin G. Hatch, R-Utah, from pushing through the proposal. The panel eventually worked out a compromise that set up two health block grants but retained substantial federal authority over spending.

In the House, the Democratic version of health block grants prevailed when Republicans decided not to put their plan to a vote. That meant continuation under federal control of several programs that Reagan had wanted to shift to state responsibility.

After protracted negotiations, conferees agreed to put 19 programs together in four block grants but leave others under federal control. The block grants were for preventive health and health services; alcohol/drug abuse and mental health services; primary health care, and maternal and child health.

The conferees kept a number of restrictions on the states' use of block grant funds. Most restrictive was the primary care block grant, which consisted solely of aid to community health centers. It was essentially a continuation of the federally run program, with qualifying states given the option of taking over administration after a year.

Also as part of the reconciliation bill, Congress reauthorized numerous health programs, including aid for health maintenance organizations (HMOs), the health planning system and training of health professionals. *(Stories, this chapter)*

Also tucked into the bill were provisions setting minimum standards for the training and accreditation of persons operating medical and dental X-ray equipment, and requiring states and federal agencies to adopt radiation guidelines and standards. Sen. Jennings Randolph, D-W.Va., had pushed such a Radiation Health and Safety Act for years.

Provisions

As signed into law, HR 3982 (PL 97-35):

Block Grants

Preventive Health and Health Services. Combined eight existing categorical programs into a preventive health and health services block grant. The combined programs were emergency medical services; health incentive grants; hypertension control; rodent control; fluoridation; health education and risk reduction; home health services, and rape crisis centers. *(Authorizations, box p. 486)*

● Required that in fiscal 1982 states spend an amount equal to 75 percent of fiscal 1981 federal spending on the hypertension program. In fiscal 1983, the figure would be 70 percent, and in fiscal 1984, 60 percent.

● Earmarked $3 million a year for rape crisis centers, to be distributed among the states on the basis of population.

Alcohol/Drug Abuse, Mental Health. Combined existing alcohol abuse, drug abuse and mental health programs into a block grant.

● Required states to continue funding each community mental health center that received federal funds in fiscal 1981 as long as the center was eligible.

● Required a state to divide spending between alcohol and drug abuse and mental health according to the same percentages used by the federal government in the state in fiscal 1980. In fiscal 1982 the restriction applied to 100 percent of funds; in fiscal 1983, 95 percent, and in fiscal 1984, 85 percent.

● Set out a formula for allocation of the share of a state's

Reconciliation's Health Block Grants . . .

Following are the health block grants established by Congress in 1981, and descriptions of the programs to be folded into them:

Preventive Health Services

Congress authorized $95 million for fiscal 1982, $96.5 million for fiscal 1983 and $98.5 million for fiscal 1984.

Emergency Medical Services. Designed to encourage establishment of regional emergency medical systems, this program was responsible for such visible and popular health care improvements as emergency helicopters and ambulances, the 911 emergency telephone number and CPR (cardiopulmonary resuscitation) programs that trained citizens to give emergency aid to heart attack victims. *(1979 Almanac p. 498)*

Set up in 1973 (PL 93-154) and reauthorized in 1976 (PL 94-573) and 1979 (PL 96-142), the program received $30 million in 1981 appropriations. The reconciliation bill (HR 3982 — PL 97-35) required states to continue funding grantees for one year; after that, states could decide whether to continue the program and at what level.

Health Incentive Grants. Established in 1966 and revised in 1978 (PL 95-626), this program provided grants to states for preventive health services. For fiscal 1981, $60 million was authorized. Congress originally appropriated $36 million for fiscal 1981 but reduced that to $9 million in the June 4 rescission (HR 3512). *(1978 Almanac p. 611; rescission bill, p. 281)*

Hypertension Control. In 1975 (PL 94-63) and again in 1978 (PL 95-626), Congress authorized grants to state health authorities for screening, detection, diagnosis and prevention of hypertension, particularly among high-risk and hard-to-reach populations. An estimated 60 million persons in the United States had elevated blood pressure, 35 million of them having a problem severe enough to increase their chances of death or illness from heart attack, heart failure, stroke or kidney failure. The fiscal 1981 authorization was $29 million; $20 million was appropriated. *(1978 Almanac p. 611)*

PL 97-35 required states in fiscal 1982 to spend on hypertension an amount equal to 75 percent of 1981 federal spending in the state for hypertension control; in fiscal 1983, 70 percent, and in fiscal 1984, 60 percent.

Rodent Control. Concerned about control of disease spread by rats and other rodents in urban areas, Congress authorized this program in 1967 (PL 90-174) at the request of President Johnson. It was reauthorized in 1978 (PL 95-626). In fiscal 1981 $17 million was authorized, $13.5 million appropriated. *(1978 Almanac p. 611)*

Fluoridation. Authorized in 1978, this program helped communities fluoridate their water and aided fluoridation treatment provided in schools. The 1981 authorization was $5 million, as was the appropriation.

Health Education and Risk Reduction. These

programs were established in 1978 (PL 95-626). In fiscal 1981 Congress authorized $8 million for demonstration projects to evaluate methods of organizing and delivering comprehensive preventive health services, and $15 million to help states and localities deter smoking and the use of alcoholic beverages among children and adolescents. *(1978 Almanac p. 611)*

Home Health Services. In 1978 (PL 95-626), Congress authorized demonstration grants to help set up new home health agencies or expand those in areas with inadequate medical services. For fiscal 1981 $15.5 million was authorized, but no funds were appropriated.

Rape Crisis Centers. Although the Mental Health Systems Act of 1980 (PL 96-398) set up grants for services to victims of rape, no funds were authorized until fiscal 1982. For that year, $9 million was authorized, with $12 million authorized in both 1983 and 1984. The reconciliation bill earmarked $3 million annually for the program in fiscal 1982-84, to be distributed among the states on the basis of population. *(1980 Almanac p. 430)*

Alcohol and Drug Abuse, Mental Health

Congress authorized $491 million in fiscal 1982; $511 million in fiscal 1983, and $532 million in fiscal 1984.

Mental Health. As part of the nationwide trend away from institutional care of the mentally ill, Congress in 1963 first provided funding to community centers designed to treat mental illness primarily on an outpatient basis. Since the program's inception, the number of institutionalized persons had dropped from 500,000 to 148,000. In contrast, more than 2.4 million persons received some type of service from mental health centers in 1980. Under the program, more than 750 local mental health centers were established; as of 1980, about 20 percent of these were no longer receiving federal support.

In 1980 Congress extended the program through fiscal 1981 (PL 96-398) but revamped it starting in fiscal 1982, when grants were to be targeted toward certain populations, such as the chronically mentally ill and the elderly. In addition, states were given more responsibility for distributing grant funds. *(1980 Almanac p. 430)*

The reconciliation bill required states in fiscal 1982-84 to continue funding each community mental health center that received federal funds in fiscal 1981, as long as it met certain qualifications and had received federal funding for less than eight years. The same percentage of funds would have to be spent on mental health as was spent when the funds were under federal control. For example, if a state in fiscal 1981 got $5 million for alcohol and drug abuse and another $5 million for mental health, then its fiscal 1982 block grant would have to be divided, 50-50, between the two areas. In fiscal 1982, this restriction would apply to 100 percent of the block grant; in fiscal 1983, to 95 percent; in fiscal 1984, to 85 percent.

funds directed toward alcohol and drug abuse, with 35 percent required to be spent on alcohol abuse programs, 35 percent on drug abuse and the remaining 30 percent as the state chose.

Primary Care. Set up a primary care block grant

consisting solely of a program to fund community health centers. The program would provide grants to government and private non-profit entities providing health care services to medically underserved populations. State responsibility was to be increased gradually.

. . . Ease Federal Control of 19 Programs

Alcohol, Drug Abuse. Congress in 1970 began funding programs to help prevent and treat alcohol and drug abuse. The programs were reauthorized in 1979 (PL 96-180, PL 96-181) after Congress rejected President Carter's proposal to fold them into block grants along with mental health programs. In 1981, $180 million was authorized and $101 million appropriated for alcohol abuse grants. For drug abuse, $230 million was authorized, $178 million appropriated. *(1979 Almanac pp. 526, 528)*

Of the amount allotted for the two programs, a state would have to spend 35 percent on alcoholism and 35 percent on drug abuse, with use of the remaining 30 percent up to the state. Twenty percent of a state's funds would have to be used for early intervention programs designed to discourage alcohol and drug abuse.

Primary Care Block Grant

Congress authorized $280 million for fiscal 1982; $302.5 million for fiscal 1983, and $327 million for fiscal 1984. Only one program, community health centers, was included in the block grant.

Community Health Centers. Congress first authorized grants for community health centers in 1966 (PL 89-749). In 1978 (PL 95-626) the program was extended through fiscal 1981. *(1978 Almanac p. 611)*

The program provided grants to state and local governments and to non-profit private groups for delivery of primary health care services to medically underserved populations. In 1981, about 571 rural and 291 urban grantees participated, serving 5.2 million people. The fiscal 1981 authorization was $472 million; the appropriation was $325 million.

The reconciliation bill ensured continued federal spending for community health care by giving the program its own block grant. The transition to state control was carefully spelled out. In fiscal 1982, the federal government would continue to distribute grants and operate the program. States could ask to take over the program, but the secretary of health and human services (HHS) would have to approve the requests. If a state took over the program in fiscal 1983, it would be required to fund all of those who received grants in the previous year. The federal government would continue running the program through fiscal 1984 if a state did not request control.

Maternal and Child Health

Congress authorized $373 million in each of fiscal years 1982, 1983 and 1984. Fifteen percent of that funding in fiscal 1982 and 10 to 15 percent in fiscal 1983 and 1984 would be retained by the HHS secretary for special projects of regional and national significance, for genetic disease testing and counseling, and for hemophilia diagnostic and treatment centers.

Maternal and Child Health and Crippled

Children's Services. Under Title V of the Social Security Act, Congress since 1935 had been providing funds to states to reduce infant mortality, to promote maternal and child health and to treat crippled children. To receive funds, states had to have approved allocation plans. The most recent changes were enacted in 1967 (PL 90-24). The program had a permanent $399.8 million authorization; $357.4 million was appropriated in fiscal 1981.

SSI Disabled Children. Under the Social Security Act, $30 million was authorized annually to provide services to disabled children receiving Supplemental Security Income (SSI) benefits. The fiscal 1981 appropriation was $30 million.

Lead-Based Paint Poisoning Prevention. Administered by the Center for Disease Control, this program screened children for exposure to lead poisoning, which usually occurred when children in older homes ate chips of paint made with lead. Consumption of lead can cause blindness, seizures, mental retardation, behavioral disorders and death. The program also sought to prevent poisoning through education and identification of hazards. In 1980, about 490,000 children were screened; about 35,900 were found to have excessive amounts of lead in their systems. In fiscal 1981, $15 million was authorized; $10.8 million was appropriated.

Sudden Infant Death Syndrome. Established in 1974 (PL 93-270) as part of the Public Health Service Act, this program required the HHS secretary to develop and disseminate information related to Sudden Infant Death Syndrome (SIDS) — the sudden death of an apparently healthy infant. The program, authorized at $7 million and funded at $2.8 million in fiscal 1981, also provided counseling for parents. In 1980, 42 projects received grants. *(Congress and the Nation Vol. III, p. 347)*

Hemophilia. In 1975 (PL 94-63), Congress established this program to provide grants to set up hemophilia diagnosis and treatment centers. It was reauthorized in 1978 (PL 95-626). Hemophilia is a genetic deficiency in blood clotting that is transmitted from mothers to sons. Under the Public Health Service Act, $6 million was authorized in fiscal 1981; $3.3 million was appropriated.

Genetic Diseases. Sickle cell anemia, Cooley's anemia, Tay-Sachs, cystic fibrosis and other genetic diseases were the target when Congress in 1972 (PL 92-294, PL 92-414) first authorized funding for genetic testing and counseling centers. The most recent reauthorization was in 1978 (PL 95-626). In fiscal 1981, $26 million was authorized, $16.4 million appropriated.

Adolescent Pregnancy. Though authorized as a categorical program, aid to pregnant teen-agers also was made an eligible use of funds in the maternal and child health block grant. Congress established the program in 1978 (PL 95-626). In fiscal 1981, $75 million was authorized, $10 million appropriated. *(1978 Almanac p. 611)*

● Provided that, starting in fiscal 1983, a state could request to take over administration of its share of the funding, subject to approval by the secretary of health and human services (HHS). Otherwise, the federal government would continue to administer the program.

● Required that states in fiscal 1983 fund all centers that received federal grants in fiscal 1982.

● Required that states provide matching funds or in-kind services in fiscal 1983 and 1984 in order to receive federal funds. The match was set at 20 percent in 1983 and

Authorizations

The reconciliation bill (HR 3982 — PL 97-35) authorized the following amounts for health programs in fiscal 1982-84 *(in millions of dollars):*

	1982	1983	1984
Block grants			
Preventive health, health services	$ 95	$ 96.5	$ 98.5
Alcohol/drug abuse, mental health services	491	511	532
Primary care	280	302.5	327
Maternal, child health	373	373	373
Childhood immunization	29.5	32	34.5
Tuberculosis prevention	9	10	11
Venereal disease prevention, control	40	46.5	50
Migrant health centers	43	47.5	51
Family planning	130	143	156
Adolescent pregnancy, sexuality program	30	30	30
Primary care research	3	—	—
Developmental disabilities	61.1	61.1	61.1
Health services research	20	22	24
Health statistics	39	39	39
Health care technology	3	4	5
Medical libraries	7.5	—	—
National research service awards	182	195	—
Health planning	102	—	—
Health maintenance organizations	21	21	21
Alcohol, drug abuse prevention, treatment, rehabilitation grants	30	—	—
Alcohol, drug abuse research	70	—	—
Secretary of Health and Human Services	4.1	4.5	4.9
Health manpower programs	218.8	238.6	249.3

33.33 percent in 1984. No federal funds could be used for administrative expenses.

Maternal and Child Health Services. Combined seven categorical programs into a maternal and child health block grant. Eligible services under the block grant were those dealing with maternal and child health and services for crippled children; disabled children receiving Supplemental Security Income; prevention of lead-based paint poisoning; Sudden Infant Death Syndrome; hemophilia; genetic diseases and adolescent pregnancy.

● Required the HHS secretary to retain 15 percent of available funding in fiscal 1982 (and 10 to 15 percent in 1983 and 1984) for special projects of regional and national significance, genetic disease testing and counseling programs, and hemophilia diagnostic and treatment centers.

Categorical Programs

● Reauthorized as categorical programs the childhood immunization, venereal disease control, tuberculosis prevention and control, migrant health centers, family planning and adolescent pregnancy programs.

● Added to the list of services to be provided under the

adolescent pregnancy program the counseling of teen-agers to discourage premarital sexual activity.

● Stipulated that of the $30 million authorized for the adolescent pregnancy program in each of fiscal years 1982-84, $10 million would be used for research and $20 million for services. No more than one-third of the latter could be used for the new sexual counseling program.

● Also reauthorized the following health programs: developmental disabilities, which provided services to handicapped persons; the National Centers for Health Services Research, Health Statistics and Health Care Technology; assistance to medical libraries; the National Research Service Awards, which provided training in biomedical research; health planning; assistance to HMOs; health manpower, and alcohol and drug abuse prevention, treatment and rehabilitation.

Radiation Safety

● Required the secretary of HHS to establish minimum accreditation standards for programs training individuals to perform radiological procedures and for certification of such persons (other than physicians, dentists and certain other practitioners). The secretary was also directed to draft a model statute setting out safe radiological procedures. States were given three years to adopt the standards and safety rules; if they had not done so by the end of fiscal 1984, the secretary was directed to report to Congress on the legislation necessary to ensure their compliance.

● Required the secretary to establish guidelines for safe radiological procedures and directed each department of the federal government to comply with the guidelines.

Legislative History

President Reagan in his March 10 budget proposed to lump 25 categorical health programs into two block grants and cut their funding by 25 percent, for a savings of about $500 million in fiscal 1982 budget authority. *(Block grant background, p. 465)*

The largest block grant, for general health services, would be funded at $1.1 billion in 1982; the second, for preventive health services, would get $260 million.

Senate Action

After weeks of deadlock, with two Republican members siding with the Democratic minority to tie up committee action, the Senate Labor and Human Resources Committee June 10 approved a watered-down version of Reagan's block grant proposal.

The committee approved two health block grants, but refused to include a number of the programs Reagan wanted included. It approved cuts in funding, but insisted on keeping some federal "strings" on the money.

The compromise authorized a new funding arrangement under which federal funds would be disbursed and administered by the states under contracts stipulating certain conditions. For example, states would be required to spend at least 85 percent of the federal funds they received in 1981 for migrant and community health centers on those services in 1982, and 75 percent of the 1981 funding level for community mental health centers. The percentages would decline in future years.

The contracts also would bar for two years the closing of any federal health centers without federal approval, require states to impose performance criteria like those in

existing laws and require them to draw up plans for spending block grant funds.

In effect, the procedure would permit the federal government to look over the shoulders of state administrators, withholding funds if contract terms were violated, committee staffers said. But federal agencies would be explicitly forbidden to write regulations elaborating on the legislation or to require states to produce more information than was "readily available."

The compromise did not require states to match federal funds.

The compromise, required to win the votes of Lowell P. Weicker Jr., R-Conn., and Robert T. Stafford, R-Vt., did not please the most conservative committee Republicans because it strayed too far from Reagan's plan. Gordon J. Humphrey, R-N.H., called it "the worst of both worlds," since states would get less money but still "be burdened by red tape and directions from Washington."

Chairman Orrin G. Hatch, R-Utah, was forced to call in Majority Leader Howard H. Baker Jr., R-Tenn., to help break the committee stalemate. Because of the deadlock, the panel failed to meet the May 15 congressional deadline for reporting authorization bills.

The principal issue in the dispute was who should administer health programs. Under existing law, some, such as the community health center program, were run almost entirely by HHS. Others were administered by state agencies, but under strict HHS regulations.

The administration wanted to give the states complete control of the programs and let them allocate funds among them as they saw fit. The only requirement would be that funds in a block grant be spent on programs within that block.

But committee Democrats, joined by Weicker and Stafford, insisted that the federal government had a responsibility for providing "quality health care for all Americans," as ranking Democrat Edward M. Kennedy, Mass., put it.

Reagan's block grant proposals, Kennedy complained, "contain no assurance that federal dollars will be spent to meet key health needs . . . no assurance that funds will be targeted to the poor and the undeserved . . . no assurance that services provided by the states with federal funds meet minimum quality standards."

Kennedy wanted to protect community and migrant health centers, mental health, drug and alcohol abuse programs, family planning and adolescent pregnancy programs by leaving them out of the block grants altogether, leaving only a group of small programs to be consolidated. And to ensure a smooth transition from federal to state administration, Kennedy wanted to require a minimum level of funding for each program over the next few years.

Like Kennedy, Stafford and Weicker were particularly concerned about the fate of community health centers and mental health services. At the request of Baker, Stafford drafted his own compromise. It included community health centers and mental health programs in the block grants but required states to continue funding them and included a number of restrictions governing their operation.

The Senate Finance Committee approved a separate maternal and child health block grant as part of its reconciliation package May 5.

The committee was unwilling to lump maternal and child health programs in its jurisdiction into a block grant with programs under the jurisdiction of Labor and Human Resources.

Both committees' proposals were adopted as part of the Senate reconciliation bill (S 1377) June 25.

House Action

The House Energy and Commerce Committee, which has jurisdiction over health programs, was unable to agree on a reconciliation package, so Chairman John D. Dingell, D-Mich., forwarded the version backed by a majority of committee Democrats to the Budget Committee for inclusion in the reconciliation bill.

Although the Republican-backed Gramm-Latta substitute replaced most of the Budget Committee's reconciliation provisions, the Energy and Commerce package remained in the measure. James T. Broyhill, R-N.C., had planned to offer an amendment replacing the Democratic provisions with Reagan's health proposals, but came up short of votes. As a result, the House bill differed sharply from the Senate measure.

If Broyhill's amendment had been included in the House bill, the administration would have been in a strong position in conference. As it was, the administration had to work to uphold the Senate position, which was weaker than Reagan's original health proposals.

The House bill left intact separate funding for such programs as community, migrant and mental health centers, the controversial family planning program and venereal disease control. Supporters of family planning charged that the administration was trying to eliminate family planning by putting it into a block grant, and waged a vigorous fight to keep the program's separate identity.

The House bill did consolidate 15 programs into three block grants (maternal and child health, preventive health services, alcohol and drug abuse), but attached federal "strings" to the grants.

The House cut spending for health programs, but by less than 25 percent in most cases. Mental health spending was cut 30 percent, however.

Conference Action

Conferees July 28 agreed to put a variety of health programs into three block grants, to be run by the states according to certain guidelines. (The fourth health block grant, on maternal and child health, was approved by a different set of conferees July 23.)

The new block grant, not considered by the Senate, included only one program — community health centers. States would gradually take over operation of the centers but could shift funding to other unrelated programs.

Conferees retained separate funding for family planning, migrant health centers and several other programs. Funding for health programs was reduced by 25 percent.

Hatch called the conference on health block grants "the toughest reconciliation conference of all." Uncomfortable with elements of the compromise, he refused to agree to it until he got formal White House approval of the decision to keep family planning as a separate categorical program.

"I just wanted them [White House officials] to stand up and share the burden," he explained later. "They reluctantly agreed with what had to be done," he said. "They don't like family planning, but they understand we don't have the votes in either the House or the Senate."

Family Planning Provisions

As part of the compromise on family planning, Hatch won conference approval of a teen-age sexuality program

that had been reported by his committee July 21 (S 1090 — S Rept 97-161).

The program, funded at $30 million a year for three years, continued an existing program, authorized in 1978 (PL 95-626), that provided pregnant teen-agers with prenatal care and counseling. *(1978 Almanac p. 611)*

But it also would fund "prevention services" to discourage sexual activity among teen-agers. It contained controversial restrictions on abortion counseling and required parental consent before teen-agers could participate.

(As originally drafted by freshman Sen. Jeremiah Denton, R-Ala., S 1090 also called for the promotion of teen-age "chastity" as a solution to "the problem of adolescent promiscuity," but that language was dropped.)

Reconciliation conferees modified S 1090 to prohibit any references to abortion during counseling sessions funded under the program, unless such information was requested by the teen-ager and her parents. Counseling about adoption and contraception was allowed, but contraceptives could not be provided under the program unless they were not available elsewhere in a community.

The restrictions on abortion counseling would not apply to the use of $130 million authorized by the conferees for general family planning, a program directed at low-income women and teen-agers under Title X of the Public Health Service Act. In fiscal 1981, the program helped fund more than 5,000 clinics.

Rep. Henry A. Waxman, D-Calif., chairman of the House Energy and Commerce Subcommittee on Health, agreed to accept the teen-age sexuality program in return for keeping the family planning program under federal control. ∎

Infant Formula Marketing

Both houses of Congress in June overwhelmingly approved resolutions criticizing the Reagan administration's stand against a voluntary international code to restrict the promotion of infant formula.

The United States was the only one of 119 countries to vote against the code at the World Health Organization (WHO) assembly May 21 in Geneva, Switzerland.

Infant formulas are powdered-milk substitutes used instead of breast-feeding. The code was aimed at preventing marketing techniques such as salespeople dressing as nurses and ads suggesting that good health depended on formula, as opposed to breast milk. The code, which suggested rules for each nation to adopt individually, was directed primarily at developing countries where unsanitary practices such as preparation of formula with contaminated water had contributed, health experts said, to as many as a million infant deaths a year.

Although the Reagan administration agreed that breast-feeding was preferable to formula, officials argued that the code would infringe on the constitutional guarantees of freedom of speech. However, the emotionalism associated with "motherhood" issues, combined with the isolation of the U.S. position, prompted even administration supporters to question whether principle was being applied too rigidly. Sen. Robert Dole, R-Kan., suggested that an abstention would have been more appropriate.

Administration critics were more forceful. "How often have we placed the profits of the giant international drug firms above saving the lives of dying children?" asked Sen. Edward M. Kennedy, D-Mass. "The answer is never — until this administration's vote in Geneva."

Republicans were as eager as Democrats to distance themselves from the unpopular administration stand. However, the slap at President Reagan was tempered by the mild wording of the two different, non-binding resolutions. The House expressed "dismay" at the action; the Senate voiced "concern."

Almost half the Republicans in the House and most of the Democrats June 16 voted for a sense-of-Congress resolution (H J Res 287) opposing the administration's stand. The resolution was approved 301-100; 85 Republicans and all but seven Democrats voted for it. *(Vote 69, p. 34-H)*

Only two senators — John P. East, R-N.C., and Steven D. Symms, R-Idaho — voted against the resolution, offered June 18 as an amendment to the State Department authorization bill (S 1193) by David Durenberger, R-Minn. The vote was 89-2. *(Vote 157, p. 29-S)*

The lopsided passage of the resolutions, particularly in the Republican-controlled Senate, was evidence that members needed a stand to report to angry constituents.

Formula makers, testifying June 16 and 17 at a joint hearing of two House Foreign Affairs subcommittees, insisted there was no evidence that their promotional methods had encouraged women to choose formula over breast-feeding. They also argued that formula was superior to other alternatives to breast milk, such as corn meal, melon or sugar and water, which were available in developing countries.

The most celebrated spokesman for the administration position was former Sen. Sam Ervin, D-N.C. (1954-74), a constitutional expert who called the code "totalitarian." Ervin testified June 16 on behalf of the Grocery Manufacturers of America. ∎

Social Services, Energy Aid

Congress balked at the Reagan administration's proposals for two new block grant programs in the areas of social services and emergency assistance.

Instead, the budget reconciliation bill approved July 31 (HR 3982 — PL 97-35) extended the existing social service block grant and low-income energy assistance programs, with some changes. *(Reconciliation bill, p. 256)*

The social services program, authorized by Title XX of the Social Security Act, was slightly expanded by consolidation with programs for U.S. territories and for training of social service workers. Funding for the program was reduced, however, and states were no longer required to match their share of federal money with their own funds.

The social services program, already a block grant under existing law, provides funds to states for a variety of programs such as day care, family planning, counseling and aid to the mentally retarded.

Congress refused to include legal services, community services and child welfare programs in the block grant as the administration proposed. Legal services and child welfare programs were continued as categorical programs, and community services programs were put into their own block grant.

The energy assistance block grant was a simplification of the existing program of aid for the heating and cooling

needs of the poor. It did not include the administration's requested transfer of short-term aid to welfare families in emergencies.

Provisions

As signed into law, the social service and energy assistance provisions of HR 3982 (Titles XXIII and XXVI):

Social Services

● Continued the existing program providing funds to states for a variety of social services to individuals and families, authorized by Title XX of the Social Security Act.

● Authorized states to use their funds for programs such as child care, foster care, meal delivery, legal aid, training of social service workers and delinquency prevention, but placed no specific requirements on the types of programs.

● Required states to develop and make public a report on how their Title XX funds would be used, including information about activities to be supported and characteristics of individuals to be served.

● Authorized $2.4 billion in fiscal 1982, $2.45 billion in 1983, $2.5 billion in 1984, $2.6 billion in 1985 and $2.7 billion in 1986 and succeeding years; made the program an appropriated entitlement.

● Repealed the requirement in existing law that states match a portion of their federal Title XX allocation with their own funds.

● Gave each state a share of the funds based on its share of the national population; allotted part of the total funds, under a separate formula, to social service programs in the territories.

● Allowed a state to transfer up to 10 percent of its allocation to other block grant programs.

● Repealed the requirements in existing law that states use at least 50 percent of their social service funds to provide services to welfare recipients, and that they provide services only to persons with incomes below 115 percent of the state's median income.

● Prohibited states from using the funds for purchase of buildings, room and board costs, wage payments other than for hiring welfare recipients to work in day-care centers, medical care, institutional or educational services, or for cash payments.

● Required day-care programs using Title XX funds to meet applicable state and local standards.

● Continued to allow funds to go to day-care centers for payment of the wages of welfare recipients hired as day-care workers.

● Required the secretary of health and human services to conduct a one-year study aimed at helping states assess the effectiveness and efficiency of their Title XX social services programs. The study would include consideration of the use of federal incentive payments to reward states for high performance.

Home Energy Assistance

● Authorized $1.875 billion for each of fiscal years 1982-84 to help low-income families meet home energy costs.

● Allowed states to transfer up to 10 percent of their funds under this program to other block grant programs.

● Allowed states to use federal funds to provide benefits only to recipients of welfare, food stamps or veterans' pensions, or to households with incomes below either 150 percent of the poverty level or 60 percent of the state's median income.

● Provided for reallocation of funds not used by a state.

● Provided for direct transfer of funds to Indian tribes.

● Gave states the option of having the federal government make energy assistance payments directly to qualified Supplemental Security Income recipients.

● Distributed funds to states in the same ratio as in fiscal 1981; reserved a variable portion of funds for aid to territories.

● Required states to provide the highest levels of assistance to households with the lowest incomes and the highest energy costs in relation to income.

● Required states to reserve funds to meet energy crises.

● Imposed on states requirements for public participation, an appeals process, coordination with other federal programs, outreach to eligible households and financial controls.

● Allowed states to spend up to 15 percent of their funds on "weatherization" — home improvements aimed at reducing energy consumption — for low-income households.

● Authorized withholding of funds to states that did not meet the requirements of the law.

● Required states to conduct an annual audit of expenditures under the program, and to repay to the federal government sums spent in violation of the act.

● Provided that assistance supplied under the program should not be considered as income in determining eligibility and benefits under other federal and state programs.

● Allowed states to make payments directly to energy suppliers; also allowed use of funds to provide state tax credits to companies that supply energy to low-income households at reduced rates.

● Prohibited use of grants for the purchase or improvement of land, or for construction or improvement of buildings except for low-cost residential weatherization and other energy-related home repairs.

● Required the secretary of health and human services to submit an annual report to Congress on the operation of the program.

Legislative Action

Senate. The Senate Finance Committee, in its reconciliation package approved May 5, adopted a hybrid form of block grant for social service programs in its jurisdiction. Chairman Robert Dole, R-Kan., referred to the proposal as a "targeted block grant."

It lumped seven programs together in a block grant (social services, day care, state and local social services training, child welfare services, child welfare services training, foster care and adoption assistance), but required states to maintain spending for three of them (child welfare, foster care, adoption assistance) at a minimum of 75 percent of the existing level.

The child welfare program was aimed at preventing the breakup of disadvantaged families; the foster care program paid part of the upkeep of poor children who could not continue to live at home, and the adoption assistance program subsidized the adoption of low-income children with special problems, such as handicaps.

The committee cut 25 percent from the funding of the programs, as requested by the president, for a savings of $1.07 billion.

A few members expressed displeasure with portions of the committee's reconciliation package, but only Daniel Patrick Moynihan, D-N.Y., and Bill Bradley, D-N.J., voted

against it. Moynihan was highly critical of a provision changing foster care and adoption assistance from entitlements to regular appropriations programs. Entitlement programs guarantee a certain level of benefits to all who meet the eligibility requirements; Congress thus has no discretion as to how much money to appropriate for them.

"This constitutes an enormous change of social policy," Moynihan protested. "In the pressures of this reconciliation process, to take away from children an entitlement they have had for 45 years seems to me a very doubtful thing to do."

The Senate adopted its reconciliation bill June 25.

House Action

The House Ways and Means Committee May 19 rejected the administration's social services and emergency assistance block grant proposals, but agreed to cut spending for low-income energy assistance by almost 40 percent ($850 million).

However, in adopting the administration-backed Gramm-Latta substitute instead of the committee-reported reconciliation package, the House agreed to a block grant combining social services, community services and some other small programs. The block grant did not include the child welfare, foster care or adoption assistance programs, however.

Brenda Russell of the Child Welfare League of America credited Rep. John H. Rousselot, R-Calif., a member of the Ways and Means Public Assistance Subcommittee, with saving the programs' separate status. "Rousselot was the champion of the child welfare programs," she said. "He withstood pressure from the administration in order to protect the children and keep the reforms [made by Congress in 1980] in place." *(1980 Almanac p. 417)*

Conference Action

Conferees had two major differences to resolve on the social services program: funding levels and the fate of the child welfare, foster care and adoption assistance programs.

They dropped the three child welfare programs from the block grant, as well as some smaller programs for abused children and runaway youth the House had included. The House provision including community services programs in the block grant was deleted by a different set of reconciliation conferees, who established the community services block grant.

The funding level accepted by conferees for social services was $2.4 billion in fiscal 1982, rising to $2.7 billion by fiscal 1986. Those amounts did not include funding for the community services or child welfare programs, which would have separate funding authorities. Fiscal 1981 funding was $3 billion.

The Senate bill cut social services funding by 25 percent, authorizing a permanent $2.639 billion for the program. The House bill authorized $3.123 billion for each of fiscal years 1982-85, a 16 percent cut. ∎

Anti-Poverty Programs

Some federal anti-poverty programs came up losers and others winners in the budget reconciliation bill cleared by Congress July 31 (HR 3982 — PL 97-35).

The principal anti-poverty agency, the Community Services Administration (CSA), was abolished and replaced by a new community services block grant to the states, with reduced funding. *(Reconciliation bill, p. 256)*

Funding of $389.4 million was authorized for the block grant in each of fiscal years 1982-86. CSA's fiscal 1981 appropriation was $537.8 million.

CSA, successor to the 1960s' Office of Economic Opportunity (OEO), financed local community action agencies and community economic development programs. The Reagan administration had proposed to include community services as part of a much larger social services block grant, but Congress rejected that proposal. *(Story, p. 488)*

Congress also refused to fold the Legal Services Corporation, which provided free legal services to the poor, into a block grant, but did cut its funding. *(Story, p. 412)*

Another holdover from President Lyndon B. Johnson's War on Poverty — VISTA (Volunteers In Service To America) — retained its separate identity but was severely cut back. President Reagan proposed to cut VISTA's 1982 funding to $20.7 million, from $42.8 million in President Carter's budget. Congress earmarked only $16 million for the program in 1982, dropping to $8 million in 1983. VISTA volunteers worked in poverty areas; they were paid a federal stipend.

Volunteer programs for the elderly, including Foster Grandparents, a favorite of First Lady Nancy Reagan, were funded at much higher levels.

In contrast to the other programs, the Head Start preschool program for children from low-income families — probably the most popular legacy of the War on Poverty — emerged from the reconciliation process with an increase in its funding level — one of the few social programs to do so. The reconciliation bill authorized $950 million for it in fiscal 1982, up from $820 million in 1981.

Provisions

As cleared by Congress, Title VI of HR 3982:

Community Services Block Grant. Established a community services block grant, replacing programs formerly administered by the Community Services Administration (CSA).

● Terminated the CSA and created instead an Office of Community Services within the Department of Health and Human Services (HHS).

● Authorized $389.4 million for the block grants in each of fiscal years 1982-86.

● Distributed funds to states in the same ratio as funds were distributed in 1981 under the existing CSA programs; guaranteed each state at least .25 percent of the total distributed to states; set aside .5 percent of funds for the territories.

● Required states to use the block grant funds for programs with a measurable effect on the causes of poverty, and to help people with problems such as jobs, education and housing.

● Provided for annual revisions by the secretary of HHS of the "poverty line" established by the Office of Management and Budget, according to changes in the Consumer Price Index.

● Required states in fiscal 1982 to provide at least 90 percent of their allotments to community action agencies (CAAs) and migrant farm worker organizations. Beginning in fiscal 1983, states would have to provide at least 90

percent of their allotments to local governments, which would either use the funds directly or give them to CAAs.

● Established procedures for planning, public participation, applications and coordination which states would have to meet in order to qualify for block grant assistance.

● Required that existing CAAs be given special consideration as grant recipients.

● Allowed states to transfer up to 5 percent of their allotments to Older Americans, Head Start or energy crisis intervention programs.

● Authorized HHS to withhold funds from states found to have misused funds.

● Prohibited the use of block grant funds for political activities or construction.

● Set aside 9 percent of the funds for discretionary programs of HHS; allowed funding of existing community economic development programs as part of the HHS discretionary programs.

● Established transition provisions allowing HHS to operate the existing programs in fiscal 1982, at state option.

Head Start. Authorized funds for Head Start at the following levels: $950 million in fiscal 1982, $1.007 billion in 1983 and $1.058 billion in 1984.

● Revised the formula for distribution of Head Start funds to states and territories.

● Set aside 13 percent of the funds for Head Start programs for Indians, migrants and children in the territories.

● Required that at least 10 percent of children served by the program in each state be handicapped children.

● Set fiscal, planning and administrative standards for Head Start agencies; authorized HHS to establish regulations concerning eligibility and hearing procedures, and to provide training, technical and research assistance to local agencies.

● Required Head Start agencies to provide for parental participation in decision-making.

● Limited participation in Head Start programs to children from families with incomes below the poverty level, but allowed for participation by other children in certain circumstances.

Other Programs. Authorized funds for domestic volunteer activities at the following levels: $25.8 million in fiscal 1982 and $15.4 million in 1983.

● Reserved for the Volunteers in Service to America (VISTA) program, from the funds available for domestic volunteer programs, $16 million in fiscal 1982 and $8 million in 1983.

● Authorized $28.7 million in fiscal 1982 and $30.4 million in 1983 for retired senior volunteer programs; $49.7 million in fiscal 1982 and $52.7 million in 1983 for foster grandparent programs; $16.6 million in fiscal 1982 and $17.6 million in 1983 for senior companions programs; $30.1 million in fiscal 1982 and $29.3 million in 1983 for administration of domestic volunteer programs.

● Authorized $715 million in fiscal 1982 and $793.3 million in 1983 for Older Americans programs.

● Provided a separate authorization for community service employment for the aged, at $277.1 million in fiscal 1982 and $293.7 million in 1983; provided for additional funding in case the authorized levels were insufficient to maintain 54,000 jobs slots of 20 hours per week.

● Authorized $1.009 billion in fiscal 1982 and $1.054 billion in 1983 for vocational rehabilitation programs.

● Authorized $7 million in each of fiscal years 1982-84 for child abuse prevention and treatment programs.

Who Defines Poverty?

The official "poverty line," used to determine who is eligible for food stamps, free school lunches and other federal assistance, is established by the Office of Management and Budget (OMB) and shall be revised annually (or more often, if necessary) by the secretary of health and human services (HHS) according to changes in the Consumer Price Index.

So stated the final version of the budget reconciliation bill (HR 3982 — PL 97-35) after a brief but bitter debate over who should define poverty.

The debate, which some called a tempest in a teapot, began when a provision was inserted in the House-passed version of the bill — the administration-backed Gramm-Latta substitute — authorizing OMB to define poverty and to revise the definition annually.

Although backers insisted the provision simply restated law that had been in effect for years, it set off a bitter partisan fight in the House. Majority Leader Jim Wright, D-Texas, and other Democrats who opposed President Reagan's budget package objected strenuously to the provision. They said it would give extraordinary power to OMB, and perhaps signal a sweeping change in how the government decided who was poor enough to qualify for food stamps and other assistance programs.

"We will probably in this administration do away with poverty ... because [OMB Director] David Stockman will be defining" it, Thomas J. Downey, D-N.Y., told the House sarcastically June 25.

Donald W. Moran, OMB associate director, said OMB already had the authority outlined in the provision and denied that it contemplated any Draconian changes of the sort predicted by the Democrats. OMB would simply continue to make inflation adjustments in "poverty level" income figures derived from Census Bureau data, he said.

The Senate reconciliation bill had no comparable provision. The final version was a compromise.

The poverty income figure was used by government agencies for several purposes, such as counting the number of poor people living in an area to determine how funding for programs targeted on low-income populations should be distributed, and determining who qualified for certain federal benefits.

In 1981 the official poverty-level income for a non-farm family of four was $8,450 a year. That figure reflected only cash income. Democratic critics feared the Reagan administration would use the reconciliation bill provision to begin counting the dollar value of food stamps, Medicaid and other benefits as "income," as some administration officials wanted to do.

The original poverty index was developed in 1963 by Social Security Administration statistician Mollie Orshansky. The Office of Economic Opportunity adopted it as an eligibility guideline for many of the anti-poverty programs it administered during the 1960s. In 1969 the Budget Bureau (OMB's predecessor) established a revised version as "the standard data series on poverty for the statistical use of all executive agencies."

● Authorized the use of community services block grant funds for community economic development grants and loans in urban and rural low-income areas, formerly authorized under Title VII of the Economic Opportunity Act.

Legislative Action

President Reagan included Head Start in his "social safety net" of seven programs he said were immune from budget cuts. He requested $950 million for the program in fiscal 1982, $130 million more than the 1981 funding level.

The program provided education, health and social services to low-income and handicapped children aged 3-5. About 375,000 children were enrolled in 1,262 local Head Start programs in 1981.

The Senate reconciliation bill, passed June 25, authorized only $820 million for Head Start in 1982. But on July 14 the Senate instructed its conferees on the bill to support a $950 million authorization.

Through a staff error, the Head Start authorization was dropped from the "Gramm-Latta" reconciliation substitute passed by the House June 26, causing momentary concern about the program's fate. But there was no opposition in the conference committee to the higher funding levels. The conferees approved Head Start spending of $950 million in fiscal 1982, $1.007 billion in 1983 and $1.058 billion in 1984.

The other main issue in the conference was the fate of community services programs. The Senate, while abolishing CSA, had at least preserved the separate status of community services programs as part of a new block grant. The Gramm-Latta bill, by contrast, lumped community services programs into the social services block grant, ending their separate status.

House Democrats on the conference committee had little enthusiasm for including the community services programs in the social services block grant, and readily agreed to the Senate's separate block grant proposal. The only remaining dispute concerned protections for existing community action agencies previously funded by CSA. Conferees adopted a provision requiring states to turn over at least 90 percent of their fiscal 1982 community services block grant funds to the local anti-poverty groups. ■

Koop Nomination

Dr. C. Everett Koop, President Reagan's choice to be surgeon general and director of the U.S. Public Health Service (PHS), was confirmed by the Senate Nov. 16 after months of controversy. The nomination was approved by a 68-24 vote. *(Vote 376, p. 63-S)*

The surgeon general is head of the PHS commissioned corps, an elite, quasi-military group of about 7,000 medical service personnel who staff the eight PHS hospitals, Indian Health Service facilities and other federal health posts.

Koop, a prominent Philadelphia pediatric surgeon noted for a 1977 operation to separate Siamese twins and for his outspoken anti-abortion views, had to overcome a number of obstacles to his appointment to the nation's top public health position.

First, his nomination was delayed for months because by law the surgeon general had to be a member of the PHS commissioned corps and under the age of 64. Koop was 64

and not in the corps. Congress eventually changed the requirements, but Koop still had to undergo close scrutiny of his views and experience.

Although his critics focused their attack on his alleged lack of experience in the public health field, it was Koop's views on abortion and other women-related issues that underlay much of the opposition to his nomination.

In speeches and writings, Koop had expressed the view that abortion could lead to a cheapening of moral standards, resulting in government persecution of religion, the killing of defective babies and euthanasia for the elderly and the ill. He also had come out against the intrauterine device (IUD), a popular birth control method, and decried the use of amniocentesis, a surgical procedure used to determine whether a fetus was defective. He blamed Planned Parenthood for increased sexual activity among teen-agers and opposed test-tube conceptions.

Koop promised at his confirmation hearings that he would not use the surgeon general's post as a "pulpit" for his anti-abortion beliefs.

Age Limit

Attempting to clear the way for Koop's appointment, Sen. Jesse Helms, R-N.C., March 12 attached an amendment eliminating the age limit for the surgeon general to an unrelated House-passed banking bill (HR 31). The bill passed the Senate by voice vote. Banking Committee Chairman Jake Garn, R-Utah, said Helms had assured him the amendment would have no problems in the House. *(HR 31, p. 105)*

That assurance proved false, however. The House leadership referred the bill to the Energy and Commerce Committee, where Health Subcommittee Chairman Henry A. Waxman, D-Calif., criticized Helms's amendment as a "surreptitious" tactic to install Koop in the office. Waxman asked that Koop testify before his subcommittee, but the administration rejected the request.

The House April 8 refused to accept the Helms amendment, sending HR 31 to a House-Senate conference. The House reversed its position May 20, passing a resolution instructing the conferees to accept the Senate provision. However, the resolution was not binding.

After weeks of deadlock, the House conferees June 17 agreed to accept the Helms amendment, and HR 31 cleared July 14 (PL 97-25). But, as the conferees had realized by then, that still did not clear the way for Koop's appointment because the Public Health Service Act of 1944 (PL 78-410), which contained the age limit, also required that the surgeon general be a member of the PHS Commissioned Corps — and it also had an age limit of 64. *(PL 78-410, Congress and the Nation Vol. I, p. 1129)*

Koop's supporters finally overcame that barrier by attaching to the budget reconciliation bill (HR 3982 — PL 97-35) a repeal of the age limit for all PHS members. At Waxman's insistence, the conferees also inserted a requirement that the surgeon general have "specialized training or significant experience in public health programs." Koop's opponents contended he did not have enough of either. *(Reconciliation bill, p. 256)*

Confirmation Proceedings

President Reagan then appointed Koop to the PHS commissioned corps and officially nominated him to be surgeon general. Koop had been serving as deputy assistant secretary of health in the Department of Health and Human Services, a post that did not require Senate approval.

Committee Action. At a confirmation hearing Oct. 1 before the Senate Labor and Human Resources Committee, Koop defended his public health experience and played down his controversial views. He said he had delivered babies in Harlem in the 1940s, established a medical school in Ghana, set up an international doctor training program and helped end the X-raying of children's feet in shoe stores. As chief surgeon at Children's Hospital in Philadelphia, he added, he gained the administrative experience he would need to head the PHS.

The American Public Health Association, which represented PHS professionals, opposed Koop, as did feminist groups such as the National Organization for Women.

The committee approved the nomination by an 11-5 vote Oct. 28. Opposing Koop were four Democrats — Edward M. Kennedy, Mass.; Howard M. Metzenbaum, Ohio; Harrison A. Williams Jr., N.J., and Donald W. Riegle Jr., Mich. — and one Republican, Lowell P. Weicker Jr., Conn.

Floor Action. In debate on the nomination Nov. 16, opponents stressed what they said was Koop's lack of qualifications to head the PHS. Metzenbaum complained that Koop had no experience in disease control, occupational health issues, environmental protection, behavioral sciences or public administration, while Kennedy deplored his "cruel, outdated, patronizing and discredited stereotype of women in society."

Koop's defenders said he had never displayed any male chauvinist attitudes and had furthered the careers of female physicians. Roger W. Jepsen, R-Iowa, said Koop would bring to the office "a concern for the individual that is all too frequently lost when health professionals deal with populations and not persons."

One of Koop's strongest supporters, Arlen Specter, R-Pa., disagreed with Koop's advocacy of a constitutional amendment banning abortion but said the abortion question was "not relevant. The duties of the surgeon general ... do not affect the administration of the laws related to that subject," Specter said. ▪

College Student Aid

Despite heavy lobbying by higher education interests, federal aid to college students was cut sharply by the budget reconciliation bill cleared by Congress July 31 (HR 3982 — PL 97-35).

The measure included one of the Reagan administration's two main proposals for curbing the spiraling cost of the guaranteed student loan (GSL) program.

As the president requested, the legislation established a "needs test" limiting GSL loans for individual students to the amounts needed to cover their educational costs. However, the new test applied only to students from families with incomes over $30,000 a year; the administration had wanted to apply the test to all students.

The administration's other chief cost-saving proposal — ending the federal interest subsidy of loans to student borrowers while they were in school — had little support in Congress and was not included in the reconciliation bill. In place of that, however, the bill required students to pay an "origination fee" when they got their loan. The fee — 5 percent of the value of the loan — would be applied against the interest subsidy the government paid to banks. The interest rate on student loans is 9 percent.

The reconciliation bill also set spending limits for the

Pell grant program that were well below the estimated cost of full operation of the program in future years. As a result, millions of low- and middle-income students faced reductions in their grants. Pell grants, formerly known as basic educational opportunity grants (BEOGs), were the cornerstone of federal aid to college students. They had covered up to one-half of a student's educational costs.

Some 2.6 million students received Pell grants in the 1980-81 school year, while 2.3 million students got guaranteed loans in 1979-80, the latest year for which figures were available.

The $2-billion-a-year GSL program had come under fire because large numbers of middle- and upper-income students were said to have taken out the low-interest loans even though they did not need help in paying for school, while their families used their resources for investments paying a higher return.

The needs test and other changes made by the reconciliation bill would reduce costs of the GSL program by $2.8 billion through fiscal 1984, according to a tentative estimate from the Congressional Budget Office.

Higher education interests lobbied heavily against the student assistance cuts. The most severe impact of the cuts was not expected to be felt until the 1982-83 school year.

Provisions

As signed into law, the student assistance provisions of HR 3982 (Title V):

Student Loans. Established a "needs test" limiting the amount of individual guaranteed student loans to a student's "remaining need" — the difference between his educational costs (tuition, room and board and other expenses) and his educational resources, including the expected contribution from his family and other forms of financial assistance.

● Applied the needs test only to students from families with incomes over $30,000 a year. Students from families with incomes below $30,000 could continue to borrow up to the $2,500 annual maximum.

● Gave the secretary of education authority to determine the assessment rate applied to discretionary income in determining the expected contribution from the family; made the regulations setting the assessment rate subject to a veto by either House or Senate.

● Allowed students to borrow $1,000 if their remaining need was between $500 and $1,000; those with remaining need of less than $500 could borrow only the amount of need.

● Required ex-students who had received loan repayment deferments while in military or volunteer service to begin repayment immediately at the end of their period of service. However, ex-students would continue to get a six-month grace period from loan repayment requirements after they left school.

● Allowed banks to charge a 5 percent "origination fee," to be deducted from the amount of each loan at the time it was made; reduced the federal subsidies paid to banks by the amount of the origination fee; made the fee effective 10 days after enactment of the bill.

● Required student borrowers to repay at least $600 a year on their GSL debt after they left school. The previous minimum repayment was $360.

● Gave the Education Department authority to collect defaulted loans that had been guaranteed by the states.

● Increased the interest rate on loans to parents to 14 percent, from 9 percent, effective Oct. 1, 1981; provided that if the 12-month average interest rate on 91-day Treasury bills was 14 percent or less, the interest rate would be 12 percent.

● Allowed independent students to borrow under the parental loan program.

● Reduced the annual ceiling on guaranteed loans to independent students to $2,500, from $3,000, with an aggregate loan limit of $12,500.

● Expanded the authority of the Student Loan Marketing Association (Sallie Mae) to engage in loan activities in cases where GSL loans were not sufficiently available.

● Eliminated the $10 "institutional allowance" paid to schools for each student participating in the GSL program and reduced the allowance for each Pell grant recipient to $5, from $10.

● Increased to 5 percent, from 4 percent, the interest rate on National Direct Student Loans (NDSL) processed on or after Oct. 1, 1981.

Pell Grants. Established the following limits on spending for the Pell grant program of basic educational opportunity grants to college students: $2.65 billion in fiscal 1982, $2.8 billion in 1983 and $3 billion in 1984.

● Authorized the Education Department to modify Pell grant regulations to restrict individual grants, so that annual spending would not exceed the cap; made the proposed rules changes subject to congressional approval.

Authorization Levels. Set spending limits for higher education programs during each of fiscal years 1982-1984, including the following major programs:

● Howard University, $145.2 million.

● Aid to developing institutions, $129.6 million.

● Supplemental education opportunity grants, $370 million.

● State student incentive grants, $76.8 million.

● TRIO programs of special help to students from disadvantaged backgrounds, $165 million in fiscal 1982 and $170 million in 1983 and 1984.

● College work-study, $550 million.

● National Direct Student Loans, $286 million.

● International education, $30.6 million.

● Indian education programs of the Bureau of Indian Affairs, including aid to tribal community colleges, $262.3 million in fiscal 1982, $276.1 million in 1983 and $290.4 million in 1984.

● Aid to land-grant colleges for agriculture teaching assistantships, $2.8 million.

Legislative History

In his March 10 budget, President Reagan called for deep cuts in federal aid to higher education, which accounted for nearly half of all federal education spending. He requested outlays of $12.4 billion for higher education in fiscal 1982, $1.2 billion less than the amount appropriated for 1981.

Reagan called for cuts in both Pell grants for low- and middle-income students and in the GSL program.

The administration proposed to require students and their parents to pay a greater share of college costs before becoming eligible for a loan, and to stop subsidizing the interest on loans to parents or pay interest that accrued while the student was in school.

Sen. Claiborne Pell, D-R.I., former chairman of the Senate Education Subcommittee and "father" of the edu-

cational grant program, called the budget cuts "penny-wise and pound-foolish," and Rep. Peter A. Peyser, D-N.Y., led an attack on them in the House. Peyser said up to 700,000 students could be forced to quit college and many small schools could have to shut down as a result of the cuts.

Saying the proposed cuts would be "devastating," state and local school officials, teachers' unions, higher education institutions, college students, their parents and a wide range of special education interest groups vigorously opposed them.

Education Secretary T. H. Bell admitted the reductions would cause "pain" for many, but he said they were a "necessity" if inflation was to be brought under control.

House Action

Despite their opposition to cuts in social programs, House Education and Labor Committee Democrats pushed through a reconciliation package that basically met their target of $12.1 billion in spending reductions for fiscal 1982, including $1.4 billion in cuts in college student aid.

Among other things, the panel restricted eligibility for guaranteed loans to students from families with incomes below $25,000.

The committee sent its package to the Budget Committee by a 24-4 vote June 10, along with a statement of strong disapproval. It took Democratic members almost a week to work out the proposal, which was adopted as a package by the committee. Chairman Carl D. Perkins, D-Ky., said the panel agreed to the cuts because the House leadership promised to allow floor amendments on four or five of the most controversial reductions.

However, when the reconciliation bill came to the floor, separate votes were not permitted on Democratic floor amendments, and the administration-backed Gramm-Latta substitute was adopted. It followed the Reagan proposal by making all students subject to the needs test.

As a way of reducing federal costs, the House bill also required student borrowers to pay an origination fee amounting to 4 percent of the value of their loan, and increased the interest rate on parental loans to 14 percent, from 9 percent.

Senate Action

The Senate Labor and Human Resources Committee approved a compromise reconciliation package June 10 that reduced spending on education and other social programs by about $11 billion.

The committee retained the federal GSL subsidy that Reagan wanted to end, so that loans would continue to be interest-free while students were in school.

The committee also ignored a Reagan request to restrict the amount students could borrow. Instead, it set an eligibility ceiling of $25,000; students whose family income exceeded that figure would have to pass the financial need test to qualify.

The committee imposed a 5 percent fee on student loans, raised interest rates on loans to parents by the same amount as the House and increased the interest rate on National Direct Student Loans to 7 percent, from 4 percent.

The result of these changes was that the committee saved more than its reconciliation instructions required in fiscal 1981 and 1982, but considerably less than required in the two following years for the student loans.

No changes were made in the higher education provisions on the Senate floor.

Student Aid Rules Blocked

Congress Dec. 10 blocked proposed Education Department regulations governing the distribution of Pell grant assistance to college students.

The rules were overturned by a resolution (S Res 256) approved by the Senate by voice vote. They would have barred most students from families with incomes over $15,000 a year from receiving grants.

In addition to passing S Res 256, Congress inserted a provision in the fiscal 1982 continuing appropriations resolution (H J Res 370) setting guidelines for the Education Department to follow in drawing up new regulations.

Higher education groups worried that new regulations might not come soon enough to prevent widespread confusion on college campuses, as students tried to make plans for the 1982-83 school year without knowing how much federal aid they would get.

The original regulations came about because Congress provided only $2.28 billion for Pell grants in fiscal 1982, far less than the nearly $4 billion required for full operation of the program. Pell grants pay up to half the cost of school attendance for lower- and middle-income students.

To cut program costs, the Education Department proposed that parents of students seeking Pell grants be required to contribute a high proportion of their income — 40 to 55 percent of their "discretionary" income after living expenses — to their child's education. The expected family contribution for the 1981-82 school year was 10.5 percent of discretionary income.

Part of the reason for the rigorous new standard was to achieve savings to make up for the additional cost of provisions in the 1980 higher education act. That law (PL 96-374) required the liberalization of rules affecting independent students and the computation of home value and taxes in determining benefit amounts. *(1980 Almanac p. 420)*

H J Res 370 and S Res 256 sought to avoid the high family contribution requirements by putting off the scheduled liberalizations of benefit rules. But even with those savings, S Res 256 still had to recommend family contribution levels ranging from 11 percent to 25 percent of discretionary income in order to keep the program within its appropriated level.

Conference Action

Conferees on the higher education provisions generally settled on GSL provisions that were more generous to students than either the House or Senate bills. In doing so, they lost an estimated $500 million to $600 million in savings.

Under the conference agreement approved July 21, students from families with incomes below $30,000 a year could continue to borrow up to $2,500 a year in federally guaranteed loans. Students from families with higher incomes could get loans only for educational need — the amount of need remaining after the expected parental contribution and other forms of student aid had been taken into account.

Conferees decided to leave with the Education Department the authority to set the portion of income that parents were expected to contribute to their child's education, which would determine the actual effects of the new needs test. If a high family contribution were required, loans for students from families with incomes over $30,000 would be significantly reduced or eliminated. If the expected contribution were relatively low, loan amounts would, be larger.

Either house of Congress could veto the department's GSL needs analysis.

The conferees accepted in modified form a House provision setting a $1,000 minimum loan, which would allow students with a small financial need to borrow $1,000. Many banks were unwilling to make GSL loans under $1,000.

The agreement would allow students whose financial need was between $500 and $1,000 to borrow $1,000. Those whose need was less than $500 could borrow only the amount needed to cover educational costs.

Conferees followed the Senate bill by charging students a 5 percent origination fee on their loans. The fees would be applied against the federal interest subsidy provided to the banks.

In other actions, conferees raised to 14 percent from 9 percent the interest on loans to parents, but provided that the rate would fall to 12 percent if the interest on 91-day Treasury notes was below 14 percent.

For Pell grants, conferees adopted spending limits between the House and Senate levels. The caps of $2.65 billion in fiscal 1982, $2.8 billion in 1983 and $3 billion in 1984 were expected to force substantial reductions in grants to individual students. ∎

Saccharin Use Allowed

Congress July 31 cleared legislation (S 1278 — PL 97-42) extending for two more years the law prohibiting the Food and Drug Administration (FDA) from banning saccharin, the artificial sweetener that has been linked to cancer in laboratory animals.

President Reagan signed the measure Aug. 14.

The existing law (PL 96-273) expired June 30, but the FDA had made no move to remove saccharin from the food supply, pending congressional action.

Both the Reagan administration and key members of Congress supported the two-year extension. Under the law, products still had to be labeled with warnings about possible risks to health from saccharin, and studies on the health effects of the substance would continue.

Drafted by Senate Labor and Human Resources Committee Chairman Orrin G. Hatch, R-Utah, S 1278 had the support of ranking minority member Edward M. Kennedy, D-Mass. It was endorsed June 8 by Health and Human Services Secretary Richard S. Schweiker.

In the House, Henry A. Waxman, D-Calif., chairman of the Energy and Commerce Subcommittee on Health, agreed to expedite the legislation despite his reservations about the continued use of saccharin. His panel planned to undertake a thorough review of all existing food safety laws, he said.

The Labor and Human Resources Committee reported S 1278 June 19 (S Rept 97-140), and the Senate passed it by voice vote June 25. The House agreed to the Senate bill by voice vote July 31.

Saccharin, which has no calories, was widely used in diet foods and drinks, and both consumers and industry objected vehemently when the FDA originally moved to ban it in 1977 after research studies indicated that it caused cancer in rats. Because of those objections, Congress placed an 18-month moratorium on the FDA ban. When that moratorium expired in 1979, it was extended until June 30, 1981. *(1977 Almanac p. 495; 1980 Almanac p. 416)*

While the new two-year extension was non-controversial, considerable debate was expected when Congress got around to considering an overall revision of the nation's food safety laws, possibly in 1982. Particular controversy was expected over efforts to eliminate or water down the "Delaney Clause," the section of the law that required the FDA to ban substances, such as saccharin, found to induce cancer in animals or humans. ∎

Older Americans Programs

Congress Dec. 16 cleared legislation (S 1086 — PL 97-115) extending Older Americans Act programs for three years, through fiscal 1984.

The measure made few major changes in the politically popular programs, which funded local centers providing nutritional and social service assistance to the elderly.

Final action came when the House approved the conference report on the bill (H Rept 97-386) by voice vote. The Senate had adopted the conference report Dec. 11 by a vote of 90-0. *(Vote 470, p. 76-S)*

The bill did not include the Reagan administration's proposal to merge home-delivered and group meal programs into a single authorization providing grants to states.

However, it did provide increased flexibility for state and local aging centers. It allowed them to transfer up to 20 percent of their funds between their nutrition and social service programs, and removed the requirement in existing law that agencies spend at least half of their social service funds on "priority services" such as transportation and legal aid.

S 1086 provided authorizations totaling $1.1 billion in fiscal 1982, $1.2 billion in 1983 and $1.2 billion in 1984.

Congress had last extended the programs, originally authorized by the 1965 Older Americans Act, in 1978 (PL 95-478). *(1978 Almanac p. 583)*

Provisions

As signed into law, S 1086:

● Extended the authorizations for Older Americans Act programs for fiscal years 1982-84.

● Preserved the existing separate authorizations for the congregate and home-delivered meal programs.

● Allowed states to transfer up to 20 percent of federal funds between their nutrition and social service programs.

● Abolished the provision in existing law that required agencies serving the aged to spend at least 50 percent of their social services funds on access, in-home and legal services; however, agencies still were required to spend an "adequate portion" of their funds on these services.

● Allowed congregate meal programs to provide food to handicapped or disabled persons who were under age 60 but who lived in housing facilities occupied primarily by the elderly.

● Allowed state agencies to fund other services, such as crime prevention, employment services and education.

● Required the Labor Department to develop training and placement programs to find private employment for older workers.

● Authorized $1,085,300,000 in fiscal 1982, $1,161,514,000 in 1983 and $1,240,928,000 in 1984 for programs in the bill.

● Within those totals, authorized $277.1 million in fiscal 1982, $296.5 million in 1983 and $317.3 million in 1984 for community service employment of the elderly; allowed higher spending levels if necessary to maintain 54,200 part-time employment positions of at least 20 hours a week.

● Limited the value of federal commodity contributions to nutrition programs for the elderly to $93.2 million in fiscal 1982, $100 million in 1983 and $105 million in 1984; allowed additional funds if needed to maintain the program at its 1981 level.

● Eliminated the authorization for the National Information and Resource Clearing House for the Aging.

Legislative Action

Senate. The Senate passed S 1086 Nov. 2 by a 75-0 vote after reaffirming its unanimous opposition to taxation of Social Security benefits. *(Vote 345, p. 58-S)*

By a vote of 72-0, the Senate approved an amendment offered by Minority Leader Robert C. Byrd, D-W.Va., stating its opposition to Social Security taxation or benefit cuts that were "designed to reduce the federal deficit rather than insure the solvency of the Social Security system." *(Vote 344, p. 58-S)*

The Senate had adopted a similar resolution in July, but Byrd urged that it reiterate its position because taxation of Social Security benefits was included on a list of potential tax policy changes suggested to the Senate Budget Committee for possible inclusion in the second budget resolution. *(Earlier vote, vote 187, p. 34-S)*

Other than tacking on the non-binding statement, the Senate made relatively few changes in S 1086 as reported by the Labor and Human Resources Committee July 20 (S Rept 97-159). As passed, the bill authorized $1.04 billion in fiscal 1982, $1.1 billion in 1983 and $1.17 billion in 1984 for programs for the elderly.

The measure did not contain the administration's proposal for lumping three separate authorizations for programs for the elderly into a block grant, but it did consolidate some programs and loosened requirements imposed on local programs for the elderly by the 1978 extension of the act. In place of the existing separate authorizations for home-delivered meals and "congregate" meals served at senior-citizen centers, for example, the bill provided a combined nutrition authorization.

Under a floor amendment offered by Edward M. Kennedy, D-Mass., however, states would be prohibited from cutting their share of funds spent on home-delivered meals. The amendment was adopted 72-0. *(Vote 343, p. 58-S)*

House. The House passed its version of the bill (HR 3046) Nov. 20 by a vote of 379-4. *(Vote 312, p. 102-H)*

No one spoke in opposition to extension of the Older Americans programs, which in 1980 provided meals to some three million older persons and social services, such as legal aid and counseling, to 9.3 million elderly. The measure also extended the authorization for the Older Americans volunteer programs of the ACTION agency.

The biggest change in the House bill, as reported by the Education and Labor Committee May 19 (H Rept 97-70), was forced by the budget reconciliation measure (HR 3982 — PL 97-35), which limited total spending for Older Americans programs to $992 million in fiscal 1982. *(Reconciliation bill, p. 256)*

The committee bill, reported with a total authorization estimated by the Congressional Budget Office at $1.8 billion, was amended on the floor to conform to the reconciliation limits.

Of the total authorized by the House, $715 million was for all programs except community service employment for the elderly. The jobs program was authorized at $277 million, but higher spending was allowed if needed to maintain employment at 54,000 job slots of 20 hours a week.

Like the Senate bill, HR 3046 retained separate authorizations for the social services, home-delivered meals and group meals programs. Thomas E. Petri, R-Wis., offered an amendment to consolidate the authorizations into a single allotment to states, but the proposal was rejected by voice vote. ■

Child Nutrition Programs

Child nutrition programs suffered major cuts in the budget reconciliation bill cleared by Congress July 31 (HR 3982 — PL 97-35). *(Reconciliation bill, p. 256)*

The legislation made reductions of up to 40 percent in subsidies for meals served to school children from middle- and upper-income families. Cuts in subsidies for the poor were smaller, but eligibility for free and reduced-price meals for children from low-income families was tightened.

Critics predicted that many "paying" children would drop out of the program because of the higher prices they would have to pay for their school meals; as they did, some schools would be forced to close their lunch and breakfast programs, leaving many poor children without meals even though they were eligible for them, the critics said.

Before enactment of the reconciliation bill, the federal government provided subsidies totaling 37 cents (20.25 cents cash, 16.75 cents in commodities) for each school lunch served, with additional cash subsidies of 91.5 cents for each free lunch and 71.5 cents for each reduced-price lunch.

HR 3982 cut the basic subsidy to 21.5 cents (10.5 cents in cash, 11 cents in commodities), plus an additional 2 cents a lunch in so-called "safety net" schools, where 60 percent or more of the students received free or reduced-price lunches. The special subsidy for free lunches was set at 98.75 cents; for reduced-price lunches, 58.75 cents.

Under the new law, children from families making less than 130 percent of the official poverty level (those with an income up to $11,375 for a family of four) were eligible for free lunches. Reduced-price lunches were available to children from families with incomes up to 185 percent of the poverty level (up to $15,630 for a family of four). The reconciliation bill doubled the lunch price for those children, from 20 cents to 40 cents.

The bill also sought to cut federal costs by ensuring that ineligible children did not receive free or reduced-price meals. It called for stepped-up efforts to verify the true incomes of parents applying for the low-cost school meals.

Another provision required the Agriculture Department to review and revise existing school lunch regulations with an eye to reducing the cost of meals. The department subsequently issued new rules, allowing a reduction in the nutritional content of the meals; they proved so controversial that they had to be withdrawn. *(Story, box, p. 498)*

The reconciliation bill eliminated the special milk program, which subsidized milk distribution to school children, except in schools that had no federal feeding programs. It also placed spending ceilings on the supplemental feeding program for women, infants and children (WIC).

The summer feeding program, which had been troubled by allegations of waste and fraud, was sharply restricted under the bill, but Congress did not eliminate it as the administration requested.

Provisions

As signed into law, the child nutrition provisions (Title VIII) of HR 3982 (PL 97-35):

● Reduced federal subsidies, in both cash and commodities, for school meals.

● Provided the following reimbursement rates for each school lunch served during the 1981-82 school year: 10.5 cents in cash and 11 cents worth of commodities.

● Set the additional subsidies to schools at 98.75 cents for each free lunch served and 58.75 cents for each lunch served at a reduced price, during the 1981-82 school year.

● Established a special "safety net" provision to increase by 2 cents the basic cash reimbursement rate for each lunch served in schools in which 60 percent or more of the students received free or reduced-price meals.

● Provided annual, rather than semiannual, inflation adjustments in reimbursement rates.

● Set the following reimbursement rates for each school breakfast served during the 1981-82 school year: paid, 8.25 cents; reduced-price, 28.5 cents; free, 57 cents.

● Prohibited schools from charging more than 30 cents for a reduced-price breakfast.

● Tightened eligibility standards under which schools could receive extra "severe need" assistance for the breakfast programs.

● Lowered the income eligibility limits for students receiving federally subsidized free and reduced-price school meals. The income limit for free meals (under existing law, 125 percent of the federal poverty limit, plus an $80 standard monthly income deduction) would be 130 percent of poverty, without a standard deduction; beginning July 1, 1983, the income limits for free meals would be the same as those applied to the food stamp program. For reduced-price meals, the limit would be 185 percent of poverty, without a standard deduction, in place of the existing law's 195 percent, with a standard deduction.

● Provided for increased efforts to verify the income information supplied by parents in applying for free and reduced-price school meals.

● Provided that the application forms for free and reduced-price meals could not indicate the actual income limit for receipt of free meals.

● Required applicants for free and reduced-price meals to provide the Social Security numbers of all adult members of the household.

● Eliminated federal assistance for school purchase of food service equipment.

● Eliminated the special milk program, which subsidized milk distribution to children in addition to the milk served under other school feeding programs; allowed the program

to continue in schools which participated in no other federal feeding program.

● Excluded private schools with annual tuitions above

School Lunch Regulations

After a barrage of criticism, the Reagan administration backed away from its plans to allow smaller meals in the school lunch program.

The Sept. 4 draft regulations would have allowed schools and day-care centers to reduce the size of the portions they served to children whose meals were subsidized by the school lunch, school breakfast and day-care center meal programs. They also would have given schools new ways to meet requirements for serving meat, vegetables and fruits, bread and milk — substituting the soybean curd tofu for meat, for example, or ketchup or relish for a vegetable.

The proposed regulations caused acute political embarrassment to the administration and were withdrawn by the Agriculture Department Sept. 25. Agriculture Secretary John R. Block said he and the president still believed the intent of the proposed revisions was sound and would give local authorities needed flexibility in administering the program, but he said the regulations would be reconsidered because of the adverse public reaction.

Food and Nutrition Service (FNS) officials said the regulations were intended to help schools cope with the reductions in federal subsidies ordered by the budget reconciliation bill (PL 97-35). *(Story, p. 256)*

But nutrition groups such as the Food Research and Action Center (FRAC) said the changes would violate the longstanding goal of the school lunch program, to provide children with one-third of their minimum daily nutritional requirements. The new meal patterns would provide less than one-third of an elementary schoolchild's need for magnesium, iron, thiamin and vitamin B, according to FNS estimates.

Democratic critics of the Reagan administration jumped on the regulations, which attracted a wave of negative publicity. Among other things, Senate Democrats, in a well-covered media event Sept. 24, sat down to a lunch that they said would be a typical school lunch under the new regulations: a meat-and-soybean patty, a few french fries, ketchup, one slice of white bread and three-fourths of a glass of milk.

"It was awful. . . , absolutely repulsive," said John Melcher, D-Mont.

Melcher later introduced an amendment to the debt limit bill (H J Res 265) to bar the FNS from implementing any regulations to change the program's goal of supplying one-third of a child's nutritional requirements. He eventually withdrew his amendment when the leadership promised to bring a sense-of-the-Senate resolution to that effect to the floor instead.

The Senate adopted such a resolution (S Res 218) Dec. 9 by a vote of 92-0. *(Vote 452, p. 73-S)*

Gary Hart, D-Colo., also offered an amendment to the debt limit bill to provide more money for school lunches by cutting tax deductions for business meals. That amendment was tabled (killed) Sept. 28 by a vote of 58-30. *(Vote 286, p. 49-S; story, p. 104)*

$1,500 from participation in the school lunch or breakfast programs.

● Required states to provide their own funds for school lunches in an amount equal to at least 30 percent of the amount received by schools in the state under the basic federal program of lunch reimbursement during the 1980-81 school year.

● Specified that a state in which the education agency was prohibited by law from disbursing state funds to private schools was not required to match the federal funds made available for meals served in such private schools.

● Limited the summer food service program to areas in which at least 50 percent of the children met the income eligibility standards for free and reduced-price school meals; limited local sponsorship of the program to public or private non-profit schools, local governments and non-profit residential camps.

● Reduced federal subsidies for meals served in child care centers, and determined the amount of subsidy according to the income needs of each child, rather than according to the percentage of low-income children in each center. Under the legislation, child care subsidies for breakfasts, lunches and dinners would be set in accordance with the subsidies provided for meals served in schools; reimbursements for snacks served in centers would be 2.75 cents for paid snacks, 15 cents for reduced-price snacks and 30 cents for free snacks.

● Restricted participation in the child care food program to children aged 12 or younger, handicapped children or the children of migrant workers, up to age 16.

● Required the secretary of agriculture to review existing regulations, including those pertaining to nutritional requirements, to determine ways to reduce the costs of school meals. Within 90 days, the secretary must promulgate new regulations based on this review. These could entail changes in the "meal patterns" that set the minimum amounts of certain types of food required to be included in a school meal.

● Prohibited states in the future from turning over administration of school feeding programs to the department; allowed the department to administer additional programs only when necessary to provide funds to private schools in states that were prohibited by law from providing funds or services to private schools.

● Gave school districts the option to extend to elementary school students the right to refuse to accept food they did not intend to eat.

● Expanded federal assistance to "commodity only" schools, which received commodity support for meal service but did not participate in the regular school lunch program; in return for the increased support, the schools would have to provide meals that met the standards for the regular program.

● Set authorization ceilings for the following programs: for the supplemental feeding program for women, infants and children (WIC), $1.017 billion in fiscal 1982, $1.06 billion in 1983, $1.126 billion in 1984; for nutrition education and training, $5 million in fiscal 1982 and each succeeding year.

Legislative History

In his March budget, President Reagan proposed to cut federal spending for child nutrition programs by $1.8 billion. The biggest savings would come from eliminating

federal subsidies for lunches served to some 14.5 million children from middle- and upper-income families.

That would cut federal costs by more than $9 billion by 1986 and enable the administration to target benefits on the neediest children, according to the budget. As part of Reagan's social "safety net," about 10 million poor children would continue to receive free school lunches and breakfasts, the administration said.

Reagan proposed to end the special milk and summer feeding programs and to cut spending for the WIC program by about 20 percent, to $742 million — a cut that would force one-third of WIC recipients out of the program.

Congressional Action. Neither the House nor the Senate reconciliation bill went as far as the administration requested in cutting the programs. The Senate Agriculture Committee approved reductions of about $1.5 billion; the House Education and Labor Committee reluctantly agreed to $1.1 billion in cuts. However, the Education and Labor Committee provisions were dropped when the House adopted the Republican-backed "Gramm-Latta II" substitute, removing many of the potential conflicts between the House and Senate bills.

Conferees reached agreement on the child nutrition provisions July 21, making cuts totaling $1.5 billion for fiscal 1982.

The conference was a particularly trying one for House Education and Labor Committee Chairman Carl D. Perkins, D-Ky., who had to participate in cutting programs he helped create and expand over 30 years. He vented his frustration even on his allies, such as the American School Food Service Association, when they seemed too willing to agree to cuts.

"To hell with the food service [lobby]. I've kept this program going for 30 years without them," Perkins said. "We're destroying the school lunch program," he warned.

The provisions lowering income eligibility were identical in the House and Senate bills, but there were major differences in the federal subsidy to schools serving meals.

The House-passed bill would have provided less aid for meals served to middle-class children (8.75 cents in cash, 7.75 cents in commodities) than for children receiving free or reduced-priced meals (17.5 cents in cash, 14.5 cents in commodities). The Senate bill, by contrast, set a flat rate of 9.75 cents for the basic payment and 12 cents for commodity assistance, plus an additional 2 cents in cash for each lunch served in "safety" net schools (those where 60 percent or more of the students received free or reduced-price meals).

The conferees rejected the House proposal, retaining flat rates for both cash and commodities, with the addition of the 2-cent "safety-net" supplement. The agreement provided 10.5 cents in basic payments for all students, plus the additional 2 cents for each lunch recipient in safety net schools. Commodities valued at 11 cents would be provided for all students.

The conferees also scaled back the summer feeding program, which provides food to poor children during the summer. The program had been troubled throughout its history by reports of widespread fraud and abuse.

The Senate reconciliation bill would have ended the program after fiscal 1982. The House measure extended it but limited it to public or private non-profit schools, local governments or non-profit summer camps. Studies had found that most of the fraud had occurred in local programs operated by private organizations.

The conferees adopted the House provision, with the

added limitation that the program operate only in areas with more than 50 percent low-income students.

The WIC supplemental feeding program for women, infants and children also took substantial cuts. The House had capped spending for the program at $1.037 billion a year in fiscal 1982-84. The Senate allowed $998 million in 1982, $1.06 billion in 1983 and $1.126 billion in 1984. The conferees allowed $1.017 billion in 1982 and the Senate figures for 1983 and 1984.

Both bills called for elimination of the special milk program, except in schools that had no other federal nutrition program. ∎

Education Programs

President Reagan's proposals to convert existing elementary and secondary education programs into block grants met with only limited success in Congress.

The budget reconciliation bill cleared July 31 (HR 3982 — PL 97-35) included one education block grant, replacing a variety of small categorical education programs. But it left as separate programs the two main programs of federal education aid — the $3.5 billion-a-year program of compensatory education for economically disadvantaged children, known as Title I, and the $1 billion-a-year program of aid for education of the handicapped.

The reconciliation bill did make changes in the Title I program aimed at reducing federal regulation and paperwork imposed on local schools.

It also provided for the eventual elimination of the "B" part of the impact aid program. "B" payments, which went to school districts that educated children whose parents either lived or worked on federal property (but not both), would be ended after fiscal year 1984.

Overall spending levels for impact aid, as for other education programs, were cut.

Block Grant Controversy

President Reagan had sought to lump 44 education programs — including the two big ones — into block grants and cut their combined funding by 25 percent. He said state and local officials knew best what children in their communities needed, and that block grants would give them more control over how federal education funds were spent. Block grants also would end burdensome federal regulations and paperwork, which educators had long complained about, Reagan said. He said the funding cuts would be offset by administrative savings.

But the proposal ran into stiff opposition both in and out of Congress. Arrayed against the education block grant were civil rights groups, parents of handicapped children, groups representing children and the poor, and key members of Congress. Many of these groups had fought for years to get existing education programs enacted and adequately funded. They said the reason federal programs were created in the first place was that states and localities were unable or unwilling to provide the needed services.

The critics feared that without federal safeguards on how funds were used, supporters of the various programs would fight among themselves for a shrinking amount of funds, with poor school districts standing to lose the most. Programs with the least political clout might not survive at all, they warned.

Critics also feared states might use block grant funds

to replace their own spending on education, rather than supplement it, as required by existing laws. And they warned that savings from program consolidation would be nowhere near enough to offset the budget cuts.

The most ardently defended programs were the Elementary and Secondary Education Act (ESEA) (PL 89-10), enacted in 1965, and the Education for All Handicapped Children Act (PL 94-142), which became law 10 years later.

ESEA, the nation's first broad general program of federal aid to education, was enacted during President Lyndon B. Johnson's "war on poverty." The heart of the act, which was last extended in 1978, was Title I. *(1978 Almanac p. 557)*

The landmark Education for All Handicapped Act for the first time required the states to provide "free and adequate" public education for the nation's eight million handicapped children. *(1975 Almanac p. 651)*

Congressional Republicans tried to change ESEA programs into block grants in 1967, but did not succeed. Presidents Nixon and Ford also proposed education block grants during the 1970s, but Congress again refused to go along. *(Congress and the Nation Vol. IV, p. 401)*

Educators and state government officials generally hailed Reagan's block grant proposal, but protested the 25 percent cut in funding. The Congressional Budget Office (CBO) agreed that savings would fall far short of the cuts, and warned that in some cases program administration could actually cost more under block grants than under existing law.

Provisions

As cleared by Congress, the elementary and secondary education provisions of HR 3982 (Title V):

● Revised the compensatory education program for disadvantaged children, authorized by Title I of the Elementary and Secondary Education Act (ESEA), to simplify administration and reduce federal requirements and reporting.

● Required that compensatory education funds continue to be provided for low-income children enrolled in private schools.

● Continued the requirements of existing law that local education agencies provide services for students enrolled in Title I schools that were comparable to the services provided to students in other schools; use Title I funds to supplement, not replace, their own funds, and not reduce substantially their aggregate educational spending.

● Provided for a gradual phase-out, over three years, of the "B" part of the impact aid program; left the amounts going to the different impact aid categories up to the appropriations process, as under existing law.

● Established a consolidated program of assistance for the education of refugee children.

Education Block Grant. Consolidated, for fiscal years 1982 through 1987, a variety of smaller education programs into a single block grant to state and local education agencies; made the new program effective July 1, 1982.

The programs included in the block grant were basic skills, special projects, educational improvement, state leadership, emergency school aid, community schools and additional programs authorized by Titles II-VI, VIII and IX (except women's educational equity) of ESEA; alcohol and drug abuse education; Teacher Corps and Teacher Centers; Follow Through; pre-college science teacher training and career education.

● Provided that block grant funds would be distributed according to school-age population in each state; guaranteed small states at least .5 percent of the total.

● Required states to distribute at least 80 percent of their block grant funds to local education agencies.

● Divided the programs funded under the block grant into three parts: basic skills (reading, writing and computation instruction), educational improvement and support services (libraries, instructional equipment, guidance and counseling, and programs addressing the problems of the concentration or isolation of children from minority groups), and special projects (metric, arts, consumer and environmental education, programs for gifted and talented children, ethnic heritage studies, Follow Through and teacher training).

● Provided for a phased-in transition to the block grant for the Follow Through program, an adjunct to the Head Start preschool program. The transition was to be completed by Oct. 1, 1984. *(Head Start, p. 491)*

● Reserved 6 percent of block grant funds for discretionary programs of the secretary of education; required that the funds first be used for the inexpensive book distribution, arts in education and alcohol and drug abuse education programs.

● Continued existing ESEA requirements that education authorities maintain their levels of spending, use block grant funds to supplement their own activities and provide assistance to children enrolled in private schools as well as public.

● Allowed the Education Department to provide technical assistance and guidelines, but not binding regulations, governing local implementation of programs funded by the block grants.

● Gave the department authority to withhold funds from a state if it failed to meet federal requirements under the block grant.

● Repealed the separate statutory authority for the categorical programs being consolidated into the block grant.

Authorization Levels. Placed ceilings on spending for the following major elementary and secondary education programs in each of fiscal years 1982-1984:

● Title I compensatory education for the disadvantaged, $3.48 billion.

● Impact aid, $475 million, of which $20 million was to be used for construction assistance, $10 million for assistance to schools damaged by natural disasters and $10 million for land acquisition reimbursement.

● The new educational block grant, $589.4 million.

● Education of the handicapped, $1.15 billion in fiscal 1982 and $1.198 billion in fiscal 1983.

● Vocational education, $735 million.

● Adult education, $100 million.

● Education Department functions, $308 million, of which $49.4 million was reserved for the Office of Civil Rights and $13 million for the inspector general's office.

● Bilingual education, $140 million.

● National Institute of Education, $55.6 million.

● Consolidated refugee education, $5 million in fiscal 1982, $7.5 million in 1983 and $10 million in 1984.

● Emergency school aid, $149.3 million.

● Basic skills improvement, $31.5 million.

● Instructional materials and school library resources, $161 million.

● Improving local educational practice, $66.1 million.

● State educational management, $42.1 million.

● Indian education, $81.7 million in fiscal 1982, $88.4

million in 1983 and $95.3 million in 1984.
- Women's educational equity, $6 million.
- Follow Through, $44.3 million in fiscal 1982, $22.2 million in 1983 and $14.8 million in 1984.

Legislative Action

Reagan, in his March budget, first proposed to consolidate more than 50 education programs into two block grants: one to states for improving state and local school programs and serving children in state institutions, and one to local educational agencies (LEAs). The LEA block grant was to include programs for handicapped and disadvantaged children, functionally illiterate adults and children in schools undergoing desegregation.

The administration had planned to include bilingual education in the block grant but backed off under pressure from Hispanic groups. The program's funding, like that of other education programs, was cut by 25 percent, however.

Reagan requested $4.4 billion for the block grants in fiscal 1982, $1.1 billion less than fiscal 1981 funding for the programs.

The block grant proposal was changed somewhat before it was submitted to Congress. The Elementary and Secondary Education Consolidation Act (HR 3645, S 1103) called for consolidation of 44 programs into block grants to state and local educational agencies for two general purposes: meeting special educational needs and improving school programs. Within those general purposes the agencies could distribute the money as they saw fit; they would not be required to fund any particular program or serve any particular group of children. Most sections of ESEA, including Title I, the Education of All Handicapped Act and several other education laws would be repealed.

The proposal did not require any matching of funds by states or localities, nor did it bar them from using the federal funds to supplant their own education spending.

Hostile Reaction

Reagan's proposal was met with reservations or downright hostility by key members of both the House Education and Labor and the Senate Labor and Human Resources Committee, the committees with jurisdiction over education programs. However, to meet budget reconciliation requirements, members eventually were forced to agree to funding cuts, and they adopted a scaled-down block grant.

The Senate committee deadlocked for weeks over Reagan's block grant proposals before agreeing to a compromise that left Title I and handicapped education out of the education block grant. *(Block grant controversy, p. 499)*

The House Education and Labor Committee rejected the block grant proposal entirely, but the House, in adopting the Gramm-Latta substitute for the committee-reported reconciliation measure, agreed to a small education block grant similar to the one approved by the Senate.

The House proposal was based on a bill (HR 3941) by John M. Ashbrook, R-Ohio, ranking minority member of the Education and Labor Committee. Republicans as well as Democrats on the committee generally had supported categorical education programs and had expressed concern about Reagan's proposal. They feared block grants would lead to competition among programs for poor and handicapped children for scarce local funds.

Conference Action

With similar block grants in both the House and Senate bills, the biggest problem that had to be resolved in conference was the relative funding levels for Title I and impact aid.

House Democrats were most concerned about preserving their bill's $3.544 billion for Title I programs, and

Impact Aid Cut

Congress in 1981 finally took a step toward a goal sought by every president since Dwight D. Eisenhower: eliminating the impact aid program of assistance to school districts educating the children of federally connected parents.

But threats that school districts might start charging tuition to children from military bases kept the program from being cut even deeper than it was.

Because some schools in nearly every congressional district got a share of impact aid funds, Congress routinely had rebuffed presidential requests to kill the program. The program was started in 1950 (PL 81-874). *(Congress and the Nation Vol. II, p. 714)*

In 1981, however, under pressure to cut federal spending, Congress provided for a phase-out over three years of category "B" payments, which went to school districts with children whose parents either lived or worked on tax-exempt federal property. The phase-out was included in the budget reconciliation bill cleared July 31 (HR 3982 — PL 97-35). Payments for children whose parents both lived and worked on federal property would continue.

The reconciliation bill cut impact aid funding to $475 million in fiscal 1982, from $757 million in 1981.

President Reagan had sought an even deeper cut; he first requested $401 million for impact aid in 1982, later lowered his request to $353 million.

Congress originally was sympathetic to cutting the program. In an effort to protect funding for other programs it considered more important, particularly compensatory education for disadvantaged children, the House Education and Labor Committee voted to eliminate impact aid funding altogether. It reversed the action later, however, and the Gramm-Latta substitute adopted in place of the committee-reported reconciliation bill included $401 million for impact aid.

In the Senate, the Labor and Human Resources Committee included only $200 million for impact aid in its reconciliation bill. But Armed Services Committee Chairman John Tower, R-Texas, worried that the cut would hurt school districts near military bases, successfully pressed a floor amendment raising the amount to $500 million. Reconciliation conferees compromised on $475 million; $437 million of that was included in the continuing appropriations resolution (H J Res 370) passed in December. *(Story, p. 329)*

Impact aid might have been cut more sharply than it was except for threats that some jurisdictions, if they lost that source of federal support, would begin charging tuition to children of military families. School districts in several states had warned that they would do so, and Virginia had actually done so; the Justice Department was fighting that claim in court at year's end.

wanted to hold impact aid to $401 million. The Senate bill included $196 million less for Title I, and $99 million more for impact aid.

Senate conferees were under pressure to protect the funding for impact aid. Senate conservatives, worried that the cuts would hurt school districts with large numbers of children of military families, had pushed through an amendment to increase impact aid funding to $500 million, from the $200 million approved by the Labor and Human Resources Committee. Senate Armed Services Chairman John Tower, R-Texas, sponsored the amendment, and support for it was so strong that it was accepted on the Senate floor by voice vote. *(Impact aid, box, p. 501)*

The conferees finally compromised on Title I funding of $3.48 billion and $475 million for impact aid.

Once that was resolved, conferees were further delayed by a dispute over the fate of the Women's Educational Equity Act (WEEA) program, which the Senate wanted to turn over to the states as part of the block grant. WEEA, which received $8 million in fiscal 1981, funded projects aimed at helping women overcome sexual discrimination in education.

Both the House and Senate reconciliation bills included WEEA in the education block grant. However, the House bill put spending authority for the program under the 5 percent of funds reserved for the education secretary's discretionary programs. In effect, that meant the program would continue to operate at the national level. The Senate bill left the fate of the program in the hands of state and local educators.

Despite its small size, WEEA had a group of ardent admirers at the conference meeting, including Sen. Edward M. Kennedy, D-Mass., and a corps of lobbyists led by Holly Knox of the Project on Equal Education Rights. It also had backing from Rep. Bobbi Fiedler, R-Calif., who observed that the preponderance of men at the conference table showed the need for improving women's education rights through programs such as WEEA.

A majority of Senate conferees at first insisted on retaining WEEA as part of the regular block grant, but they eventually gave in and agreed to maintain it as a separate categorical authorization of $6 million a year.

The conference compromise also included spending levels for vocational, adult and refugee education and the new education block grant. Fiscal 1982 funding was set at $735 million for vocational education, $100 million for adult education, $7.5 million for a new consolidated refugee education program and $595 million for the block grants.

Conferees accepted the House bill's stronger language aimed at ensuring that children in private schools received educational help under the block grants. ∎

PHS Hospital Funding Ended

Congress in 1981 ended federal funding of the eight hospitals and 27 clinics operated by the U.S. Public Health Service (PHS), and repealed the right of merchant seamen to free medical care — an entitlement that dated back to 1798.

The changes were made as part of the budget reconciliation bill cleared July 31 (HR 3982 — PL 97-35). *(Reconciliation bill, p. 256)*

The PHS facilities originally were established to treat merchant seamen, free of charge, because of fears that they might bring communicable diseases into the country from overseas. Some 400,000 fishermen, oil rig workers, Coast Guardsmen, marine engineers, waterway operators and others also had been made eligible for free care at the facilities. In addition, the hospitals had been used to treat U.S. military personnel, Cuban and Indochinese refugees and victims of hurricanes and other natural disasters.

Many residents of communities in which the hospitals were located also relied on them for health care. Twenty-five to 30 percent of patients at three of the hospitals (in Staten Island, N.Y., Seattle and Baltimore) were local citizens, and they and those communities vigorously fought the cutoff of federal funding.

The other PHS hospitals were in Norfolk, Va.; New Orleans; San Francisco; Boston and Nassau Bay, Texas.

At one time the PHS operated 28 hospitals in addition to its clinics. Twenty had been closed over the years. Presidents since Dwight D. Eisenhower had tried to shut down all or part of the system as an economy move.

In the 1950s and 1960s, public health professionals and the then-strong maritime unions rallied to save the PHS system from threatened budget cuts, although some individual hospitals were closed. When President Nixon tried to shut down the system in 1973, Congress took over the defense itself.

Particularly powerful friends were committee chairmen with hospitals in their districts, principally Senate Appropriations Chairman Warren G. Magnuson, D-Wash. (1944-81) and House Merchant Marine Chairman John M. Murphy, D-N.Y. (1963-81). However, both Magnuson and Murphy were defeated for re-election in 1980.

Like other administrations before it, the Reagan administration argued that the provision of free government health care for merchant seamen and other selected occupational groups was unnecessary and unwarranted. Most of the facilities were under-used, and there were sufficient alternative health care facilities in all of the cities where the PHS hospitals were located, the administration said.

Reconciliation Bill Provisions. The reconciliation bill permitted transfer of the PHS hospitals to state, local or private control and authorized funding to aid in the transition or to pay the costs of shutting down the hospitals. The funding had not been requested by the administration but was added by Congress.

Hospital officials were required to submit their plans — for local takeover or for closure — to the secretary of health and human services by Sept. 1 in order to be eligible for funds to continue operation until the date of transfer to another party, to upgrade to meet local standards or for other purposes.

Congress provided funding for these purposes in an emergency supplemental appropriation in July (H J Res 308) and in the continuing appropriations resolution (H J Res 368) approved in November. *(Story, p. 294)*

The reconciliation bill also authorized funding to continue hospital care through fiscal 1982 for merchant seamen already under treatment.

By the end of November, six of the eight PHS hospitals had been turned over to local authorities to be run or converted to other uses. Two hospitals and all of the clinics were closed. ∎

Environment

After Ronald Reagan was elected president in 1980, Rep. Morris K. Udall, D-Ariz., prophesied that "it will be a long winter" for environmentalists. His prediction proved to be right on target.

Even before Reagan took office, the announcement Dec. 22, 1980, that he was naming Colorado attorney James G. Watt as secretary of the interior sent shock waves through the environmental community that resounded for the next year. Watt was president of the Mountain States Legal Foundation, a conservative Denver public interest law firm specializing in suing the government on behalf of pro-development interests.

Similar shocks followed in rapid succession as Reagan announced other environmental appointments. Anne M. Gorsuch, another conservative Denver attorney and a friend of Watt's, was named to head the Environmental Protection Agency (EPA). Reagan's nominee for assistant secretary of agriculture for natural resources and environment, John B. Crowell Jr., elicited 25 "nay" votes in the Senate, the second highest of any Reagan appointee.

Two other controversial nominations that Reagan was considering were derailed when congressional leaders warned the White House the appointments would run into problems on Capitol Hill. The president backed off from naming former veterinarian and Reagan county campaign chairman Dr. Norman Roberts as director of the U.S. Fish and Wildlife Service. He also decided not to nominate James McAvoy, administrator of the Ohio Environmental Protection Agency, as a member of the Council on Environmental Quality (CEQ).

Watt, Gorsuch and Crowell spearheaded the Reagan administration's efforts to change the pro-environmental stance of the Carter administration. Watt concentrated on opening up more public land for energy development. Crowell wanted increased timber production from national forests, and Gorsuch tried to change EPA's adversary approach towards industry to one of mutual cooperation and to grant the states more responsibility for enforcement of pollution control laws.

Most of the changes were done administratively. No major new legislative initiatives were undertaken, except in connection with reauthorization of the Clean Water Act.

Reagan refused to request sewer grant money for the states for fiscal 1982 until Congress enacted his proposals to revamp the massive federal program. Congress went along with most of Reagan's proposals and cut the amount of money handed out each year from $5 billion to $2.4 billion.

In the face of strong public support for keeping the Clean Air Act intact, Reagan waited until year's end before embracing proposals for major changes in the law. The administration in December announced it would support a bill introduced Dec. 16, the last day of the session, that would relax auto emission standards by half and give states up to 11 more years to meet national clean air standards.

Public Lands Policy

Watt announced early on that he wanted to shift national public lands policy away from preservation and towards resource exploration and development. "I will err on the side of public use vs. preservation," he declared.

Most of his efforts to change the thrust of federal land policy were made out of the congressional limelight. Using budgetary recommendations, administrative and regulatory actions, the secretary shifted money and personnel away from taking stock of the environmental, wilderness and scenic values of federal lands and put them into developing oil, gas, minerals and timber. He brought in a whole new team, which had a decidedly different perspective from that of the pro-environment group assembled under Cecil D. Andrus, Carter's interior secretary.

The citizens' lobby Common Cause issued a report in December claiming that Watt's new leadership team had "a disproportionately industry-oriented perspective." The report, entitled "Who's Minding the Store?", said 11 of the top 16 Interior officials had been employed by or served clients in the five industries — oil, mining, timber, livestock and utilities — whose activities on public lands were regulated by Interior.

Despite the oil industry ties, Watt, in an effort to increase revenues from public lands, set up a special task force to crack down on non-payment of royalties by oil and gas lessees on federal and Indian lands.

A task force audit released in November found that in Wyoming, 11 oil companies had failed to pay $7.85 million in royalties for oil and gas production. The investigators were planning to audit the program in other Western states, where up to $650 million a year was suspected of being lost through theft, illegal accounting maneuvers and ineffective oversight by the Interior Department.

Rep. Edward J. Markey, D-Mass., whose Interior Oversight and Investigations Subcommittee held hearings on the problem in the fall, introduced a bill Dec. 7 to reform the royalty collection system.

Watt's Wrong?

Watt's efforts to reverse public land policy quickly ran into stiff opposition both in and out of Congress.

In Congress, Watt immediately got off on the wrong foot. He clashed frequently with House Democrats who authorize and appropriate money for his department. The House Interior and Insular Affairs Committee twice moved to block Watt's plans to accelerate oil and gas leasing. The House Appropriations Committee took similar action.

Other Watt legislative proposals which were part of the president's budget package also stalled in Congress. Among them were plans to put a moratorium on land acquisitions for parks while using the money to upgrade existing parks, to eliminate funds for the independent Water Resources Council and to reorganize the Office of Surface Mining.

Democrats, sensing that Reagan's environmental policies would make fine political fodder in 1982, began invoking Watt's name in their fund-raising efforts. The Democratic National Committee (DNC) formed a special fund, initiated by Watt's predecessor Cecil D. Andrus, called the Natural Resources Protection Fund. It would be used to elect pro-environment candidates, said the DNC literature, "to make certain that Mr. Watt and the special interests he represents are stopped from irrevocably ruining our lands, water and wildlife."

Ironically, Watt also became a fund-raiser drawing card for Republicans opposed to what they called the "lockup" of federal resources by previous conservation-oriented administrations.

But not all Republicans liked Watt's policies and his often abrasive style. Watt embarrassed several GOP House members when he moved to open up wilderness and offshore areas in their states to oil and gas leasing. They angrily sought to block his efforts by adding a provision to the Interior Department's 1982 money bill prohibiting the offshore leases. And the House Interior Committee invoked an obscure provision of the Federal Land Management and Policy Act of 1976 to declare a Montana wilderness area off limits to oil and gas leasing.

In another instance, when Watt asserted that the environmental debate pitted "liberals against Americans," Republican Rep. Jim Leach of Iowa dashed off an angry press release demanding that the interior secretary apologize to the American people.

Although he had vowed to make the Interior Department a "good neighbor" to the West, Watt alienated some Western governors with his plans to accelerate energy development on public lands in their states. California and Oregon sued to halt Watt's plans to expand offshore drilling along their coastlines, and governors in other Western states opposed the way Watt wanted to speed up coal production in their states.

Environmentalists Respond

Environmentalists responded to the administration's policies with shock, disbelief, dismay and, eventually, mobilization.

Watt's efforts to open up public land to energy and timber production had a lightning-rod effect, drawing public attention to environmental issues that had been out of the limelight for some time. The resultant backlash was a shot in the arm for the environmental movement.

The Sierra Club launched a nationwide petition drive and collected more than a million signatures demanding Watt's ouster. Dozens of mailings went out to prospective members alleging that the administration represented an unprecedented threat to the environment. Membership rolls of environmental organizations skyrocketed.

Watt unwittingly focused more attention on public land issues and wilderness protection than any previous interior secretary. Popular support for environmental programs was galvanized nearly as much as it was in the early 1970s when the environmental movement was born.

EPA Role Change

Gorsuch also gleaned most of her top administrators from the ranks of major corporations. As a result, EPA adopted a less adversarial attitude towards industry.

Indeed, some House members questioned whether EPA's relations with industry were too friendly. Rep. Toby Moffett, D-Conn., chairman of the Government Operations Subcommittee on the Environment, called Gorsuch and other top agency officials on the carpet during oversight hearings to investigate meetings EPA had held with chemical industry representatives to discuss proposed regulatory actions affecting that industry.

Not only did the new leaders of EPA have different philosophical attitudes about the role of EPA, but they had considerably less money to work with. Press reports began surfacing in the late summer that the administration planned to nearly halve EPA's budget in fiscal 1983.

Three other congressional panels joined Moffett's in holding oversight hearings to determine whether EPA was using deep budget cuts and regulatory "reforms" to retreat from its congressionally mandated pollution-control duties. Since Gorsuch refused to comment on fiscal 1983 proposals, the hearings were inconclusive.

Using leaked EPA budget documents, a group comprised largely of former EPA officials formed the "Save EPA Committee." The group kept Congress and the press up-to-date on the administration's 1983 budget proposals, which they claimed would "demolish" the agency.

The group alleged that by mid-1982, Gorsuch would have driven out, fired or demoted roughly 80 percent of the headquarters staff she inherited in 1981.

"Unable to repeal the country's environmental laws because the public would never stand for it," said William Drayton, former EPA assistant administrator for planning and management and a member of Save EPA, "Reagan is gutting them through the personnel and budgetary back doors."

In the regulatory arena, Gorsuch abolished the office of enforcement, preferring to rely primarily on voluntary industry compliance. She reduced the number of enforcement cases earmarked for court action and began reviewing pollution control rules to ease regulatory burdens on industry.

Justice Role Reversal

The Reagan administration also moved to rein in the Justice Department's Land and Natural Resources Division. Under President Carter the agency had played an activist role, prodding other federal agencies and departments into enforcing the nation's environmental protection laws.

Reagan appointed Houston lawyer Carol Dinkins to head the division. She moved to return the agency to its more traditional role of defending the federal government from lawsuits and filing suits for agencies only when asked to. Under Carter, the division had more aggressively urged other agencies to file suits.

Cutbacks at CEQ

The Council on Environmental Quality (CEQ), which advised the president on environmental matters, escaped the executioner's ax but was reduced to a skeleton. The administration first wanted to eliminate the board, created during the Nixon administration, but decided instead to cut its funding 72 percent. The White House claimed much of what the council did was duplicated by the EPA.

The office monitored federal agency compliance with the National Environmental Policy Act, the law that created the three-member Cabinet-level council. It also published an annual report on the state of the environment.

—By Kathy Koch

Congress Begins Rewrite of Clean Air Act

The Senate Environment and Public Works Committee in mid-November began marking up a reauthorization of the Clean Air Act, but the panel made relatively little progress before Congress adjourned Dec. 16.

In the House, the Energy and Commerce Committee's Health and Environment Subcommittee held extensive hearings on the landmark anti-pollution law, but took no action on any of the rewrite proposals (HR 5252, HR 4400, HR 3471) before it.

Authorization for appropriations under the law expired Sept. 30, but funding was provided through continuing appropriations resolutions.

Congress did clear and send to the president a separate bill (HR 3520 — PL 97-23) giving steel companies up to three extra years to comply with the Clean Air Act's 1982 air pollution cleanup deadline. *(Story, p. 514)*

The Reagan administration and industries affected by the act had hoped for speedy action on a rewrite of the entire clean air law, but neither committee was amenable to their wishes.

In the Senate, Environment Committee Chairman Robert T. Stafford, R-Vt., insisted that only a "fine-tuning" of the law could be accomplished quickly, and that only a measure representing a consensus of the committee could move through the Senate.

Despite months of hearings, "seminars" and markup sessions, no such consensus emerged in Stafford's panel.

The Senate committee did decide unanimously to leave unchanged the way health-related air pollution standards are set. And it rejected a proposal to consider economic and social costs in setting secondary standards, those designed to prevent damage to crops, visibility and structures.

But it left unresolved the thorniest issues involved in a rewrite of the Clean Air Act.

On the House side, Henry A. Waxman, D-Calif., chairman of the Health and Environment Subcommittee, was in no hurry to begin a markup.

Fortified by opinion polls showing strong public support for the Clean Air Act, House Democrats figured they could profit politically by pushing the rewrite over to 1982 and then accusing Republicans of seeking to gut the law.

Background

The Clean Air Act (PL 91-604) was enacted in 1970 and extended and amended in 1977 (PL 95-95). Taken together, the act and its 1977 amendments constituted the nation's most complex and far-reaching environmental law.

The original 1970 Clean Air Act required the Environmental Protection Agency (EPA) to establish safe concentrations for seven major air pollutants and set a 1975 deadline for states to meet those national standards. *(1970 Act, Congress and the Nation Vol. III, p. 757; highlights of act, p. 510)*

When it appeared most states would not meet the deadline, Congress in 1977 extended it to 1982 or, for areas with severe auto-related pollution, to 1987. *(1977 Almanac p. 627)*

In its first 10 years, the act resulted in cleaner air, but progress was slower than hoped, partly because some industries resisted compliance, often in court, and partly because EPA was slow in implementing the act. In early 1981, EPA estimated that 93 percent of industry was in

compliance. Those companies that were not were primarily power plants, steel plants and heavy metal industries.

Efforts to control pollutants with dangerous health effects met with varying success. Nitrogen dioxide and ozone proved the most difficult to control.

EPA figures showed particulates decreased 32 percent between 1960 and 1979. In urban areas, sulfur dioxide decreased 67 percent from 1964 to 1979, and carbon monoxide dropped 36 percent from 1972 to 1979.

But ozone remained constant, mostly because while emissions from industrial processes increased, emissions from transportation sources were being controlled.

Nitrogen dioxide levels increased 15 percent from 1975 to 1979, due to higher emissions from vehicles and factories.

Key Issues

As Congress began grappling with the complex act, it found itself confronting a number of significant issues. These included:

National Standards

The single most important question to be resolved — and one of the few the Senate committee addressed head-on — was whether to change the way EPA set national air quality standards. These constituted the heart of the Clean Air Act, because the rest of the law was designed to force states to meet the standards within certain deadlines.

Critics claimed the standards should be set to protect the general population from major risks, rather than being tailored to protect vulnerable groups from any danger, regardless of cost. They also questioned the scientific validity of the data used by EPA to set the standards.

The law required the health standards to be set without regard to costs. However, it directed the states to consider costs when imposing emission limits on individual plants.

A Business Roundtable report released in November 1980 claimed that the law would cost industry $400 billion from 1970 to 1987, and recommended applying cost-benefit analyses in developing the standards. Many business groups said the benefits of environmental control should outweigh or balance the costs of pollution control equipment.

Opponents of the cost-benefit approach charged that it was nearly impossible to put accurate price tags on intangible benefits. Environmentalists said the cost-benefit argument was a smokescreen for cutting the heart out of the act.

Industrial Growth

To control air quality, the act gave the EPA and the states power to review all proposed industrial construction and modernization to make sure major new facilities had the best possible pollution control equipment and would not cause air quality to deteriorate.

That construction permitting process drew fiery industry criticism for being overly slow and duplicative. Before building a new plant in a clean-air area, a company had to obtain a permit from the state air pollution board requiring the best possible pollution control equipment for every emission source at that plant. In the case of a large petro-

leum refinery, the permit could regulate more than 150,000 minor emission sources like pumps, compressors and valves, not only large smokestacks.

In certain dirtier areas, the requirements were even tougher. Owners of new factories had to promise to install the best control equipment and clean up emissions at existing plants.

In addition, all companies had to gather data on existing air quality where they wanted to build, and use computer models to predict how the air would change as a result of the new facility. The company also had to monitor emissions after a plant was built to show they did not exceed projections.

The permit had to be approved by several entities, including the county, regional and state air pollution boards, the regional EPA office and the Washington office of EPA.

Another study commissioned by the Business Roundtable found that the permitting process took three years or more and cost $250 million to $300 million per plant.

Critics said the process had to be streamlined or it would impede industrial growth and modernization and stymie Western synthetic fuels development.

Congress wanted to prevent industries from fleeing to clean-air areas of the South and West to escape the expensive pollution control equipment that would have to be installed to clean up pollution at existing factories in dirtier Midwestern and Northeastern cities. Older Northern industries would have been at a disadvantage to new competitors in clean-air areas.

To implement the non-degradation policy, the 1977 act outlined a highly complex system called the "prevention of significant deterioration" (PSD) program.

By far the most controversial part of the act, the PSD program was so complicated that both environmentalists and industry agreed it needed improvement. But industry wanted far more radical changes than environmentalists.

Industry questioned the need for requiring cleaner air in PSD areas than the national standards, especially since the standards already ensured an "added margin of safety" for vulnerable persons.

Critics of the PSD provisions also claimed the system was designed to limit economic growth in the South and West to protect industries in the Northeast and Midwest. Thus, the PSD debate threatened to turn into a Snow Belt-Sun Belt confrontation in Congress.

Environmentalists said any major changes in the PSD provisions would mean dirtying up the nation's few remaining unsullied areas.

An entirely different set of regulations applied to companies building factories in urban areas not meeting the national standards for the pollutants those firms would emit. These created a complicated system in which companies bought, sold, traded and "banked" permission to pollute.

By creating market incentives for pollution reduction, Congress hoped companies would devise new ways to reduce pollution. But industry complained that the system did not work and urged changes in it.

Acid Rain

Environmentalists wanted Congress to require EPA to force older coal-burning power plants to install pollution control equipment to reduce acid rain.

Acid rain — caused when sulfur dioxide and nitrogen

dioxide mix with rain, sleet or snow — altered the acidity of water and soil. It was suspected of damaging lakes, fish and vegetation and was blamed for reducing visibility and corroding statues and buildings.

Two-thirds of the sulfur dioxide emissions in the country came from coal-burning power plants. EPA set cleanup standards for new coal-fired power plants, but did not require older plants to install pollution control devices. Lack of uniform nationwide emission limits for older plants caused friction between states in the Midwest and those in the Northeast.

Some states claimed that nearby states with weaker emission requirements were sending pollution across their borders, causing them to violate the national standards.

Industry argued that not enough was known about acid rain to start regulating it.

Airborne Toxics

Environmentalists also wanted Congress to put EPA on a "fast track" in controlling cancer-causing pollutants. From 1970, when it was first directed to start regulating hazardous pollutants, to early 1981, EPA had issued regulations for only four, although dozens had been found to cause such diseases as leukemia and lung cancer.

EPA was regulating asbestos, beryllium, mercury, and vinyl chloride; it had proposed regulations for benzene, arsenic and radioactive pollutants.

The agency was more than three years behind schedule in issuing regulations to control polycyclic aromatic hydrocarbons — created when coal and synthetic fuels were burned — and cadmium, emitted by non-ferrous metal smelters.

Other uncontrolled dangerous pollutants included coke oven emissions at steel plants, formaldehyde from chemical plants, chlorinated solvents used in dry cleaning and acrylonitrile released during plastics production.

Fine Particulates

Environmentalists were urging Congress to direct EPA to start controlling fine particulates within one year.

Although larger particulates were controlled by EPA, the agency had not yet issued emission standards for fine particles — those less than 1/1000th of an inch in diameter — which were easily inhaled deep into the lungs. They hampered breathing, caused respiratory disease and aggravated heart and lung disease.

EPA had promised since 1973 to control these pollutants, but only recently set up a 100-station monitoring network to study the problem.

Mobile Sources

The act set limits for automobile emissions of hydrocarbons (HC), carbon monoxide (CO) and oxides of nitrogen (NOx), and required a 90 percent reduction from uncontrolled levels for HC and CO by 1982. NOx was to be reduced by 75 percent. The EPA could waive certain standards if public health did not require the statutory standards or if the technology to meet them did not exist.

The major auto manufacturers wanted the 1981 CO standard of 3.4 grams per mile to be relaxed to 7.0 grams per mile, and the 1.0 gram per mile NOx standard reduced to 2.0 grams per mile.

The proposal was tough to sell to Congress because it would mean removing equipment already on most cars and rolling back standards that already could be met. Nearly all 1981 cars met the NOx standard. For CO, the Carter ad-

Major Air Pollutants and their Health Effects

Pollutant	Major Sources	Characteristics and Effects
Carbon Monoxide (CO)	Vehicle exhausts	Colorless, odorless poisonous gas. Replaces oxygen in red blood cells, causing dizziness, unconsciousness or death.
Hydrocarbons (HC)	Incomplete combustion of gasoline; evaporation of petroleum fuels, solvents and paints	Although some are poisonous, most are not. Reacts with NO_2 to form ozone, or smog.
Lead (Pb)	Anti-knock agents in gasoline	Accumulates in the bone and soft tissues. Affects blood-forming organs, kidneys and nervous system. Suspected of causing learning disabilities in young children.
Nitrogen Dioxide (NO_2)	Industrial processes, vehicle exhausts	Causes structural and chemical changes in the lungs. Lowers resistance to respiratory infections. Reacts in sunlight with hydrocarbons to produce smog. Contributes to acid rain.
Ozone (O_3)	Formed when HC and NO_2 react	Principal constituent of smog. Irritates mucous membranes, causing coughing, choking, impaired lung function. Aggravates chronic asthma and bronchitis.
Total Suspended Particulates (TSP)	Industrial plants, heating boilers, auto engines, dust	Larger visible types (soot, smoke or dust) can clog the lung sacs. Smaller invisible particles can pass into the bloodstream. Often carry carcinogens and toxic metals; impair visibility.
Sulfur Dioxide (SO_2)	Burning coal and oil, industrial processes	Corrosive, poisonous gas. Associated with coughs, colds, asthma and bronchitis. Contributes to acid rain.

SOURCE: Environmental Protection Agency

ministration had granted waivers to 30 percent of the 1981 fleet. When Reagan came into power, his administration granted waivers to 70 percent of the 1982 fleet.

One reason industry wanted a weaker NOx standard was to allow production of more diesels. But environmentalists were concerned about the proliferation of diesels because their emissions were suspected of causing cancer.

Reagan Administration Position

The Reagan administration, after initially promising to send Congress a package of recommended Clean Air Act changes by June 30, first delayed its submission and then switched its strategy entirely.

Instead of proposing specific legislative modifications, President Reagan on Aug. 5 sent Congress only a set of broadly worded principles for revising the law.

The principles were far more modest in scope and tone than the proposals contained in an early draft that leaked to Capitol Hill and was publicized and denounced by Rep. Henry A. Waxman, D-Calif., chairman of the Commerce Committee's Health and Environment Subcommittee.

The shift in strategy was seen by many on Capitol Hill as a shrewd decision by the president not to stake his prestige on a bid for major revisions in the anti-pollution law in the face of polls showing massive public support for the act.

The administration's 11 principles would continue the nation's progress toward cleaner air, but "at a more reasoned pace," said EPA Administrator Anne M. Gorsuch.

The principles — which called for relaxing pollution standards and delaying some cleanup deadlines — were adopted Aug. 4 by Reagan and the Cabinet.

They were met with enthusiasm by industry groups,

but with suspicion from environmental organizations.

The National Clean Air Coalition called them "a sugar-coated prescription for dirty, unhealthy air."

But the National Association of Manufacturers said they would aid air quality by streamlining licensing so new plants could be built with modern pollution controls.

Shrewd Politics

The adoption of principles rather than specific language was tagged a "shrewd political move" by Senate Environment Chairman Stafford. He said they were worded so as to be "pretty hard to criticize."

But members of the Democrat-controlled House found plenty to chastise. Waxman, for example, said the principles advocated a "dangerous retreat" from current progress toward cleaner air.

He specifically criticized proposals to relax emission standards for cars built in the future and to accelerate research on acid rain instead of starting to control it.

Principles

Among the 11 administration principles were:

● Continuing the current method of setting air pollution standards, without applying a cost-benefit test, so they provided an adequate margin of safety for public health. But the administration wanted the standards "based on sound scientific data" demonstrating real health risks.

● Continuing to have the federal government set the secondary standards, which protected crops, visibility and buildings from degradation due to air pollution.

● Continuing to protect the air in national parks from deterioration, but requiring uniform technology for factories in all other clean-air areas.

● Establishing more effective controls on cancer-causing

pollutants in the air.

● Accelerating research on acid rain.

● Adjusting the deadlines for achieving national air quality standards "to reflect realities."

● Adjusting automobile emission standards to "more reasonable" levels, especially for carbon monoxide and nitrogen oxide.

● Eliminating requirements that emissions from new coal-burning power plants be scrubbed to reduce their sulfur content regardless of whether they burn low- or high-sulfur coal.

● Giving states a full partnership in carrying out the act, with the federal government monitoring their performance.

The Background Papers

In a move that embarrassed Republicans on the Senate committee, EPA's congressional liaison office the week of Nov. 2 gave three panel Democrats — but none of the GOP members — background documents spelling out the details of its proposed changes.

The papers proposed 38 specific revisions of the act that generally paralleled recommendations made by the Clean Air Working Group, an industry coalition.

The documents had no signature, date or letterhead. However, Sen. Daniel Patrick Moynihan said EPA Administrator Gorsuch hand-delivered a set to him.

"She didn't hand it to me or the rest of us," complained Sen. John H. Chafee, R-R.I.

"Are we going to have the administration's position through the front door or the back door?" queried Gary Hart, D-Colo., one of the three Democrats who received the documents.

Senate Committee Action

In a series of "seminar" sessions which began Nov. 3, the Senate Environment and Public Works Committee tried to achieve a consensus on a number of issues to form the basis for a draft reauthorization bill.

Although the effort ultimately failed, the early sessions did produce agreement on one key point.

Primary Standards

With almost no discussion, the Senate committee decided unanimously Nov. 3 to leave unchanged the way the health-related air pollution standards were set.

The decision meant the standards would continue to be set — without regard to cost — at levels that provided an "adequate margin of safety" to protect vulnerable segments of the population, such as the elderly and the young.

The action was a setback for industry and the administration, both of which had advocated requiring a "risk assessment" in setting the standards. In addition, industry groups had wanted costs of air pollution control equipment to be considered during standard-setting.

Kathleen Bennett, assistant EPA administrator for air, said later that the administration preferred that the standards be set at levels that could be shown, using "sound scientific data," to pose a significant health risk.

EPA position papers also urged that the committee require an independent scientific peer review of studies on which the health standards were based, as the administration's principles had advocated.

On Nov. 5, there was general agreement that provisions in existing law aimed at preventing deterioration of air quality in clean-air areas should be revised to minimize red tape. But no accord was reached on specifics.

Formal Markup

On Nov. 17, after three seminar sessions failed to produce a consensus on most aspects of the clean air rewrite, the Senate committee moved to a formal markup.

In a departure from normal procedures, the panel did not work from a draft bill, but rather — at Stafford's instigation — decided to review the existing law on a section-by-section basis and to deal with amendments to it as they were proposed by committee members.

This approach drew criticism from some panel members anxious to make significant changes in the act, since it put the onus on them to draft specific amendments and sell each one to the rest of the committee.

Economic Costs

In the first firm test of committee sentiment, the panel Nov. 17 voted 3-12 against considering economic costs in setting certain air pollution limits.

The rejected amendment, offered by Sen. Steven D. Symms, R-Idaho, would have required EPA to consider "social and economic consequences" when setting secondary air pollution standards. Secondary standards, more stringent than those to protect the public health, were designed to prevent damage to crops, visibility and structures.

Voting with Symms were Sens. James Abdnor, R-S.D., and Alan K. Simpson, R-Wyo.

Symms argued that his amendment would "inject a little realism" into the law. At present, he said, a secondary standard designed to protect palm tree growth in Florida might restrict industrial growth in the Northeast.

Sen. George J. Mitchell, D-Maine, replied that considering economics while setting the standards was a "fundamental deviation" from the basic purpose of the law.

"I prefer to leave it as it is and consider economic effects of the standards when setting the control technologies," said Mitchell. The law required that economic factors be considered when states set guidelines for the kinds of pollution control equipment companies must install.

Economist on Advisory Committee

Symms withdrew another amendment when it was clear the committee would reject the proposal. That amendment would have added an economist to EPA's Clean Air Science Advisory Committee, which reviewed the scientific studies on which pollution standards were based.

It also would have allowed the panel to "approve or disapprove" of the studies, but disapproval would not necessarily prevent EPA from issuing a standard based on the studies.

Sen. Slade Gorton, R-Wash., said the purpose of the amendment was unclear, but that it apparently was to "provide a source for a lawsuit."

"I disapprove of that kind of proposal," Gorton said.

Sen. John H. Chafee, R-R.I., concurred, and said the amendment might be a precedent for adding energy, public health, public welfare and social experts to the panel.

Controls for Trucks

In a rebuff to the Reagan administration, the committee Nov. 24 adopted two clean air amendments that would limit the EPA's authority to relax pollution controls for small and large trucks.

By a 10-3 vote, the committee approved an amendment to the law that would require heavy trucks to have catalytic converters by 1984.

The amendment was designed to block an EPA pro-

posal to exempt trucks from having to install converters.

In another action, the panel voted 13-0 for an amendment that would prevent EPA from rolling back 1984 hydrocarbon and carbon monoxide standards for pickup trucks and vans.

The amendments — which were opposed by the administration — clearly indicated the panel's concern about EPA Administrator Gorsuch's enforcement of the landmark anti-pollution law.

The amendments were sponsored by Sen. Gary Hart, D-Colo., who called the heavy trucks proposal "one of the most important votes this committee will pass."

That amendment would eliminate EPA's authority to defer the 1983 deadline for removing 90 percent of the hydrocarbons and carbon monoxide emitted by heavy trucks. To achieve the 90 percent reduction, manufacturers would have to install catalytic converters in heavy trucks.

Under existing law, EPA could delay that deadline for one year and weaken the 90 percent reduction requirement if the agency determined it was not feasible.

Hart said he was offering the amendment to prevent EPA from doing that. The administration had announced plans to revise carbon monoxide standards so that truck emissions would have to be reduced by 60 percent by 1984, not 90 percent. The agency also was reviewing the hydrocarbon standard for heavy trucks, Hart said.

Hart noted that even if the 90 percent reduction provision were retained, trucks would still contribute a third of the carbon monoxide produced by vehicles in 1985.

Flexibility Reduced

Sen. Alan K. Simpson, R-Wyo., argued that Hart's proposal would limit the administration's flexibility under the law. "Therefore I will not support the amendment," he said, "but I do indeed support the emission standards for heavy-duty trucks."

Also voting against the amendment were Sens. Frank H. Murkowski, R-Alaska, and Steven D. Symms, R-Idaho.

Hart claimed the administration's only argument for relaxing the 90 percent requirement was based on a new economic analysis issued since President Reagan took office. A Carter administration analysis, he said, found that requiring catalytic converters on trucks was technologically and economically feasible.

Kathleen Bennett, assistant EPA administrator for air, said the agency's most recent economic analysis showed the 90 percent reduction requirement would cost the automobile industry $450 million, a figure Hart said "sounded as if it had been plucked right out of the air."

The second Hart amendment inserted into the statute the current standards for hydrocarbon and carbon monoxide emissions from pickups and vans. Those standards, which required a three-way catalytic converter, were set administratively after the law was amended in 1977.

By inserting the standards into the law, the amendment would prevent EPA from relaxing them, Hart said.

The amendment was adopted unanimously after it was changed to exempt trucks used primarily on farms and ranches. Overheated catalytic converters had been blamed for starting fires when pickup trucks equipped with them were driven across fields with high grass.

Notice Requirement

Also adopted was an amendment by Sen. Lloyd Bentsen, D-Texas, requiring EPA to give heavy-truck manufacturers four years' notice before promulgating new or re-

vised emission standards for oxides of nitrogen or particulates. Such standards would have to remain in effect for at least four years under the amendment.

In promulgating those standards, the agency would have to take into account how particulate emissions were affected by controls on nitrogen oxide emissions.

Secondary Standards

Also adopted by voice vote Nov. 24 was a Symms amendment that deleted the word "any" from a provision requiring that secondary air pollution standards be set at levels designed to protect the public welfare from "any known or anticipated adverse effects" associated with the pollutants.

Staffers said the amendment would allow EPA to set secondary standards adequate to protect against minimal adverse effects, but not necessarily all adverse effects.

Auto Emissions: Carbon Monoxide

At its last markup session Dec. 11, the committee voted 9-7 to delay a decision on perhaps the thorniest issue relating to automobile pollution: whether to relax carbon monoxide emission standards, a change sought by automakers and the Reagan administration.

An amendment by Symms would allow 1983-86 model cars to emit 7 grams of carbon monoxide per mile, rather than the 3.4 grams per mile currently required.

After 1986, EPA could determine whether the 7-gram standard should be retained, changed, or returned to the 3.4 gram level, based on new studies of the probable effects of carbon monoxide emissions on public health.

Action on the Symms amendment was delayed at the request of Pete V. Domenici, R-N.M., who wanted the panel to evaluate new information released by environmentalists Dec. 9 about the effects of relaxing the standard. Vice President George Bush called Chairman Robert T. Stafford, R-Vt., during the meeting to urge delay also.

Symms, admitting he lacked the votes to adopt his amendment, supported the delay.

Background: Title II

Title II of the law required new automobiles, trucks, buses and motorcycles to emit fewer pollutants each year — using catalytic converters and other devices — so that cities could meet the national clean air standards by 1982.

The act set limits for hydrocarbons (HC), carbon monoxide (CO) and oxides of nitrogen (NOx), and required a 90 percent reduction from uncontrolled levels for all auto-related pollutants except NOx, which was to be reduced by 75 percent.

The EPA was authorized to waive certain standards, if public health did not require a particular statutory standard and if the technology to meet it did not exist.

Industry Objectives

The Symms amendment was only one of several changes in the act sought by the beleaguered U.S. auto industry, which saw new car sales slump to their lowest levels in 23 years.

The other industry proposals were included in a House measure (HR 4400), introduced by Reps. Bob Traxler, D-Mich., and Elwood Hillis, R-Ind., that auto companies admitted was an industry "wish list." No similar bill was introduced in the Senate.

The Senate committee considered only a handful of the items covered in HR 4400, the most controversial of

The Clean Air Act in a Nutshell

The primary goal of the Clean Air Act was to control the seven most common air pollutants.

It also sought to limit toxic pollutants that caused death or serious illness, but the government only recently began to implement that part of the law.

To control the seven pollutants, the act directed the Environmental Protection Agency (EPA) to determine maximum concentrations of each that should be allowed nationwide. EPA set those limits — called **national ambient air quality standards (NAAQS)** — for the seven pollutants: carbon monoxide, hydrocarbons, lead, nitrogen dioxide, ozone, particulates and sulfur dioxide.

The act directed EPA to set two types of these standards — primary and secondary — without considering the cost of compliance. **Primary standards** were to protect human health with an added margin of safety for vulnerable segments of the population like the elderly and infants. **Secondary standards** were to prevent damage to such things as crops, visibility, buildings, water and materials. The act set Dec. 31, 1982, as the deadline for the nation to meet the primary standards. Five-year extensions were available for regions with severe automobile-related pollution. No specific deadline was set for meeting the secondary standards.

EPA Responsibilities

Besides issuing national air quality standards for the seven basic pollutants, EPA was to set maximum emission limits for plants and factories, called **new source performance standards (NSPS)**. These standards were to be set on an industry-by-industry basis for states to use as guidelines in setting more specific emission restrictions for individual factories. The state limits could be the same as or stronger than EPA's new source standards, but could not be weaker.

EPA's guidelines were to cover any new or expanding plant that potentially could emit 100 tons or more of pollution a year. EPA was to take into account the costs, energy required and environmental effects the guidelines would have on industry. By early 1981, EPA had issued new source standards for 34 industries ranging from coal-fired power plants to grain elevators.

For existing factories, EPA was to issue **control technique guidelines (CTG)**, which told states what types of pollution control equipment could be economically retrofitted on existing plants. By 1981, EPA had issued 23 such guidelines, mostly dealing with hydrocarbons.

EPA was also to monitor compliance by motor vehicle manufacturers with the act's deadlines for new vehicles to meet tailpipe emission standards. The standards were designed to clean up 90 percent of the hydrocarbons and carbon monoxide, and 75 percent of the nitrogen oxides emitted from vehicles.

State Responsibilities

Taking into account the federally set emission standards for new factories and vehicles, states were directed to develop **state implementation plans (SIPs)** outlining how they intended to clean up the air within their borders by the 1982 deadline.

EPA was to approve state plans by July 1, 1979; plans not approved were to be revised by the state or EPA. The agency could ban construction of large new polluting industries in areas that violated the federal standards, if the state did not have an approved SIP.

The act divided the country into 257 regional air basins, called **air quality control regions (AQCRs)**.

Regions that violated standards for one or more of the seven pollutants were designated **non-attainment areas** for those pollutants. States had to limit new construction of pollution sources until the air in these "dirty" areas was brought up to federal standards.

Regions that met the standards for specific pollutants were called **attainment areas** for those pollutants. States could not allow the air in these areas to deteriorate beyond certain levels, and were to enforce a complex set of **prevention of significant deterioration (PSD)** rules. A region could be a non-attainment area for one pollutant and a PSD area for others. States were to impose different emission cleanup requirements for factories depending on whether they were located in non-attainment or PSD areas.

Existing factories in non-attainment areas were required by states to retrofit their plants with pollution control equipment representing **reasonably available control technology (RACT)**.

Companies wanting to expand or build new plants in these dirty-air areas were required to install equipment that limited pollution to the least amount emitted by any similar factory anywhere in the country. States were to set these **lowest achievable emission rate (LAER)** requirements without regard to cost.

New plants could not be built in dirty-air areas unless pollution from existing factories or plants was reduced enough to *more than compensate* for the pollution expected from the new plant.

Thus a company wanting to build in a non-attainment area not only had to install the best possible pollution control equipment, but also had to purchase **emission offsets** from existing companies. Companies could obtain offsets by buying new pollution control equipment for an existing polluter or buying and closing down an old plant.

States in non-attainment areas could have until 1987 to meet the carbon monoxide and ozone standards if they required annual inspection and maintenance of catalytic converters on cars. Federal sewer and highway construction funds could be withheld from states that did not initiate such programs.

In PSD areas, the act mandated that new plants install the **best available control technology (BACT)**, defined by states on a factory-by-factory basis. Companies also had to conduct one-year computer modeling and monitoring tests to show that the proposed plant would not degrade the air quality beyond the specific levels, or **increments,** outlined in the act.

which was the relaxation of carbon monoxide standards for automobiles.

The panel refused to consider another major relaxation sought by the industry: changing the 1.0 gram per mile standard for NOx to 2.0 grams per mile.

The automakers claimed the nation's air quality would continue to improve, and most U.S. cities could still meet the national air pollution standards, even if both the CO and NOx standards were relaxed. As old cars wore out, auto officials argued, the air would improve enough to make up the difference.

The Reagan administration agreed, noting that relaxing the standards would save the industry $1 billion a year.

However, the proposals were tough to sell to Congress because they meant removing equipment already on most cars and rolling back standards that already could be met.

The auto officials never argued that changing the standards would make a sufficient difference in cost to sell enough cars to save the ailing industry. But it would spare car buyers needless expense, they said, because the tighter controls were not necessary to meet the national standards.

The manufacturers argued that if both standards were relaxed they could remove about $360-worth of pollution control equipment — $60-worth of equipment for controlling CO and $300 for equipment to control NOx.

General Motors (GM) Chairman Roger B. Smith promised Congress his company would lower sticker prices on new cars, passing on to consumers "dollar for dollar" any savings realized from removing the equipment.

"The air will keep getting cleaner and cleaner, and car prices will go down," said Smith. "That's the best way I know of affecting sticker shock right now."

Carbon Monoxide Arguments

Although the Senate panel balked at changing the NOx standard, it considered the CO relaxation mainly because it was recommended by the National Commission on Air Quality (NCAQ). The NCAQ said the NOx standard should not be changed. *(NCAQ report, p. 513)*

Symms said relaxing the CO requirements would save $30-$60 per car and improve fuel economy by up to 1 percent. Public health would be adequately protected, he said, yet the action would "help a depressed industry at an environmental cost which is at most infinitesimal."

Sen. Hart, who was chairman of the NCAQ, opposed Symms' amendment because it did not incorporate other NCAQ recommendations proposed as part of a total vehicle pollution control package. Only if all the vehicle recommendations were included in the law, Hart said, could the CO standard be relaxed without causing U.S cities to exceed the national standards.

The NCAQ package included:

● Retaining the CO emission standards for heavy duty trucks scheduled to go into effect in 1984.

● Retaining the requirement that autos sold in high-altitude areas comply with national emission standards.

● Requiring that pickup trucks met the national emission standards in high altitude areas.

● Retaining the requirement that cities with the most severe auto-related pollution problems establish mandatory programs to inspect and maintain pollution control equipment on cars already on the road.

What the Opponents Said

The National Clean Air Coalition — a collection of environmental, labor and citizen action organizations —

disputed the claim that the national standards could still be met even if the CO standard was relaxed.

In a Dec. 9 press conference, the coalition released a study showing that at least 16 cities — containing more than 40 million people — might never meet the national standard for CO if the 3.4-gram standard was relaxed.

"We think it is very important that the myth that we don't need this level of control be dispelled," said David Hawkins, coalition counsel and the former head of EPA's air pollution program. "We believe that relaxing the standard would have a very adverse affect on public health."

Using internal EPA documents, Hawkins said assertions that the standards could still be met with relaxed CO standards were based on over-optimistic predictions about on-the-road performance of pollution control equipment.

In addition, he said, EPA's predictions ignored the increased carbon monoxide emitted by cars at high altitudes and in cold-weather cities.

The same day, seven health organizations, including the American Lung Association and the American Public Health Association, wrote the Senate panel urging rejection of the Symms amendment.

They said carbon monoxide, 83 percent of which comes from motor vehicles, could aggravate angina and could be dangerous to persons with cardiovascular disease and pregnant women.

They noted that the NCAQ suggestion that the CO standard be relaxed was based on the assumption that mandatory inspection and maintenance programs would be retained.

"We question the validity of these assumptions," the groups said, noting that some members of Congress wanted to eliminate mandatory inspection requirements. Without inspection programs, the groups said, violations of the national carbon monoxide standard were projected to double between 1984 and 1990.

NOx Standard Retained

The Senate panel did not even consider relaxing the NOx standard, primarily because it was a precursor to acid rain and contributed to ozone, another pollutant regulated by the act. Further, national levels of NOx were expected to increase over the long term, as more factories and power plants shifted from oil to coal. Coal emissions contain NOx.

Some Senate staffers said one reason the industry wanted to relax the NOx standard was to allow manufacturers to switch to diesel-powered cars.

Diesels might not meet the current 1.0 gram per mile standard for NOx until 1985. All 1981 and most 1982 diesels were granted waivers allowing them to emit up to 1.5 grams per mile.

But because diesels achieved about 35 percent better mileage than gasoline engines, auto companies, particularly GM, planned to start manufacturing diesels on a large scale. It was estimated that diesels could represent 20 to 25 percent of the auto and pickup truck sales by 1995.

Since Ford and Chrysler were not prepared to make the diesel switch as quickly as GM, changing the NOx standard would give GM a competitive advantage over the other two companies, according to a Congressional Research Service study.

Other Unresolved Issues

The Senate committee did not resolve several other vehicle emission issues, including what to do about emissions at high altitudes and in cold climates — where certain

pollutants were more difficult to control — and what kind of manufacturer guarantees should be required for pollution control equipment.

In addition, the panel still had to decide whether to retain a requirement that cities unable to meet national clean air standards had to impose inspection and maintenance programs for pollution control equipment on cars already on the road.

Also held over until 1982 were most non-automobile issues, such as whether to retain the act's strict requirements to protect pristine air and what kind of pollution control measures to require in dirty-air areas.

House Committee Action

Although House Energy and Commerce Committee Chairman John D. Dingell, D-Mich., pressed all year for action by the Health and Environment Subcommittee, that panel took no action. Chairman Henry A. Waxman, D-Calif., held extensive hearings but went no further in 1981.

Automobile manufacturers were seeking quick action in order to avoid installing $1 billion worth of pollution control equipment on 1983-model cars.

HR 4400, introduced by Traxler and Hillis, would give the industry the relief it wanted, and Dingell, whose Detroit district is the principal home of the auto industry, championed the industry's cause in the House.

Dingell pushed for a meeting Oct. 22 of the principal congressional players with Vice President George Bush. At the meeting, Dingell reportedly threatened to yank the bill out of Waxman's subcommittee if he didn't move soon. Waxman, however, stood pat.

Republicans on the House committee, who were mostly interested in getting changes in the act to help electric utilities and manufacturers, did not jump to Dingell's aid.

If Congress eased up on auto emissions, it would have to clamp down on the manufacturers and utilities if clean air standards were to be met.

Some House Democrats, convinced clean air would be a good campaign issue in 1982, were upset at Dingell's push for action in 1981. They asked House Speaker Thomas P. O'Neill Jr., D-Mass., to get Dingell to quit pressuring Waxman.

Environmentalists also favored waiting, believing the closer it got to Election Day, the less willing Congress would be to weaken the law — an opinion shared by some industry spokesmen. "The polls show clean air is a sacred cow," said one industry lobbyist. "And it will be even more sacred next year than this year."

The Polls: Clean Air a Sacred Cow

The polls bolstering Democrats and giving Congress second thoughts about changing the act were conducted in September and October by pollster Louis Harris, the Associated Press-NBC News and *The New York Times*-CBS News.

The Associated Press-NBC poll found that 61 percent of the public thought Reagan was doing only a fair or poor job on environmental issues. His environmental rating was well below his overall rating, where 51 percent said he was doing a good or excellent job as president.

The New York Times-CBS News poll found nearly two-thirds of adult Americans wanted to keep clean air laws "as tough as they are now" even if "some factories might have to close."

And the Harris poll — which Stafford called "the most extraordinary poll I've ever read" — found deep, widespread support for the Clean Air Act across all age and political groups.

Harris outlined his results before Waxman's subcommittee Oct. 15. In an exchange with Rep. Don Ritter, R-Pa., Harris said, "Mess around with the Clean Air and Clean Water acts, and you are going to get into the deepest kind of trouble. The Republican Party is at a crossroads on this. . . .

"I am saying to you just as clear as can be, that clean air happens to be one of the sacred cows of the American people, and the suspicion is afoot that there are interests in the business community and among Republicans and some Democrats who want to keelhaul that legislation.

"And people are saying, 'Watch out. We will have your hide if you do it.' That is the only message that comes out of this as clear-cut as anything I have ever seen in my professional career," Harris said.

Harris found that 80 percent of the American public wanted no relaxation in existing federal regulation of air pollution. The largest single group, 51 percent, wanted no changes in the act, while 29 percent would make it even stricter.

Harris also found that overwhelming majorities opposed six amendments being considered that would:

● Relax pollution standards so that power plants could burn higher sulfur oil and coal.

● Postpone current deadlines for electric companies to meet pollution standards.

● Relax national air quality standards.

● Relax regulations that protect national park and wilderness areas from air pollution.

● Relax current automobile pollution standards.

● Relax pollution standards designed to protect human health if the cost of achieving them is too high.

By a slightly smaller majority, 54-42 percent, respondents opposed postponing deadlines for meeting auto standards.

HR 5252: The Comprehensive Revision

On Dec. 16, the last day of the session, six leading players in the House clean air debate introduced the first major measure in the 97th Congress that addressed air pollution from both vehicles and factories.

The bill (HR 5252) was introduced by Rep. Thomas A. Luken, D-Ohio, a member of both the full House Energy and Commerce Committee and its Subcommittee on Health and the Environment, which was reviewing the reauthorization of the Clean Air Act.

The two earlier bills, HR 4400 and HR 3471, targeted the two types of pollution separately. HR 4400 dealt with automobile emissions, while HR 3471, introduced by James T. Broyhill, R-N.C., ranking full committee Republican, and Edward R. Madigan, R-Ill., ranking minority member of the subcommittee, focused on air pollution from factories.

'Shotgun Marriage'

HR 5252 included many provisions of the earlier bills and was cosponsored by Traxler, Hillis, Broyhill, Madigan and Energy Committee Chairman Dingell.

"It's a shotgun marriage of the Broyhill and Traxler-Hillis bills," said one House subcommittee staffer.

EPA Administrator Gorsuch said the bill represented "excellent progress" and generally reflected the 11 princi-

ples the president wanted to see Congress follow in rewriting the law.

Several House committee staffers described HR 5252 as a bipartisan starting point for House discussion.

Reaction Mixed

Luken predicted labor and industry support for the bill, and said he hoped it would allay environmentalists' fears that Congress might gut the law. Initial returns showed he was right about industry and some unions, but wrong about the environmentalists.

John Brown, legislative director of the International Union of Operating Engineers, said his union was "100 percent behind it."

John Quarles, chairman of the National Environmental Development Association's Clean Air Act Project (NEDA/CAAP), called HR 5252 "the right approach at the right time." NEDA/CAAP was a coalition of more than 35 industrial companies and 17 building and construction trade unions lobbying for revisions of the act.

The bill drew mixed reviews from the National Governors' Association (NGA) and from state air pollution control officials, and outright hostility from environmental groups.

At a joint press conference Dec. 23, the Natural Resources Defense Council (NRDC), and the National Audubon Society dubbed HR 5252 a "sweetheart deal" for industries that want to drastically weaken the law.

The two groups objected to provisions that would delay from 1982 until 1993 the deadline for meeting various clean-air standards and to other provisions they said would seriously undermine the program for controlling automobile emissions.

They asserted the bill could result in five to 10 times more air pollution near national parks and wilderness areas, would do nothing to speed control of airborne toxic substances and would eliminate most of the program to protect air that is already clean. It also would do nothing to curtail acid rain, and could in fact worsen the problem, they contended.

HR 5252 also would block for at least two years any action to control fluorocarbons, the environmental groups said. Fluorocarbons were suspected of destroying the stratospheric ozone layer that protected humans from cancer-causing ultraviolet radiation.

Outlook

Subcommittee Chairman Waxman, D-Calif., was not happy with the bill and reportedly was peeved at Dingell for collaborating with Broyhill without telling him about it in advance.

Waxman told Dingell he was "very displeased" that Dingell drafted a bill behind his back, one staffer said. ∎

Commission on Air Quality

The 97th Congress kicked off its consideration of the Clean Air Act March 2, when the National Commission on Air Quality (NCAQ) released a $9.5 million study on the landmark law and its implementation.

The 643-page report was ordered by Congress in the 1977 amendments (PL 95-95) to the 1970 act (PL 91-604) as a means of dispelling some of the controversy surrounding the law. *(1970 act, Congress and the Nation Vol. III, p.*

757; 1977 amendments, 1977 Almanac, p. 627)

But the report touched off its own controversy, since its recommendations offended both environmentalists and business groups.

Three of the 13 commission members, joined by a fourth on some issues, filed dissenting views because they felt the recommendations would weaken environmental safeguards in the act.

One commission member representing industry disagreed with some recommendations.

Nevertheless, leaders of the two congressional committees working on a reauthorization of the act — the Senate Environment and Public Works Committee and the Health and Environment Subcommittee of the House Energy and Commerce Committee — said they would give the report credence. The commission — made up of Republican and Democratic members of Congress and representatives from business, environmental, labor and scientific groups — presented its report at a joint session of the two panels. *(Clean Air Act reauthorization, p. 505)*

Consensus or Compromise?

The report contained 433 findings and 109 recommendations on how Congress should amend the act.

The most controversial recommendation was a suggestion that Congress scrap the nationwide deadlines for cleaning up cities with polluted air. A recommendation to change the way pollution was controlled in cities with clean air was almost as controversial.

Those two revisions would represent a "serious weakening of the Clean Air Act," charged David Hawkins, an attorney for the National Clean Air Coalition, an environmental group.

The business community objected just as strenuously to other recommendations, including those to require that national standards continue to be set without considering cost, to control acid rain by reducing sulfur dioxide and to speed up the control of cancer-causing air pollutants and fine particles.

NCAQ Chairman Sen. Gary Hart, D-Colo., who had tried to get unanimous approval so that the report would carry more weight with Congress, said the recommendations reflected a "general consensus" on most issues.

Dissenters objected to recommendations to:
- Eliminate the national deadlines.
- Change pollution regulations in clean-air areas.
- Eliminate requirements that new plants in dirty-air areas install the tightest possible emission controls.
- Mandate automatic approval of state air pollution control plans not reviewed by the Environmental Protection Agency (EPA) within 90 days of submittal.

In supplemental views, Commissioner Edwin Dodd, chairman of the board of Owens-Illinois Inc., challenged the finding that the law did not impede energy development. Dodd, who complained he was the panel's only industry representative, said the finding did "not reflect all of the problems the Clean Air Act creates for the energy industry."

Rep. James T. Broyhill, R-N.C., a member of the commission and of the House panel that was reviewing the act, disagreed with the conclusion that cost-benefit analyses should not be used in setting the national air standards.

Findings

Major commission findings were that:
- The nation's air was "measurably better" and was

continuing to improve. By the mid-1980s, probably only eight metropolitan areas would fail to meet the national standards.

● Improved air quality had brought benefits worth from $4.6 billion to $51.2 billion per year, while costs of installing, maintaining and operating pollution equipment were estimated to have been $16.6 billion in 1978.

● Air pollution controls had added about 0.2 percent to the annual inflation rate.

● Costs for air pollution control were likely to rise in the future. One estimate was that about $37 billion (in 1978 dollars) would be spent in 1987 for construction, operation and maintenance of pollution controls.

● The act had not been an important obstacle to energy development, and "substantial increases in domestic energy production" could occur without changes in the act.

● The law had not significantly inhibited economic growth.

Recommendations

Hart said the commission proposed to retain provisions of the current act that worked, streamline or eliminate those not working and expand the act to meet new problems.

Standards. The commission recommended continuing the present method of establishing national air quality standards to protect the health of vulnerable populations, with an added margin of safety.

The panel specifically rejected suggestions of some industry groups that the standards be based on cost-benefit analyses. The report recommended that EPA publish an analysis of the costs and benefits of a proposed standard, but that the study should not be used to set the standard.

The commission also recommended that EPA review its standards to determine whether fine particles should be controlled, whether there should be a standard for long-term exposure to ozone and whether there should be a separate carbon monoxide standard for high altitude areas.

Deadlines. The panel recommended eliminating the 1982 and 1987 deadlines for states to comply with the national standards. Instead all new factories, no matter where they were located, would have to install the best possible pollution control equipment. Every three years EPA would review individual states' progress in meeting the standards. States would set their own dates for compliance, but these would not be federally enforceable.

Henry A. Waxman, D-Calif., chairman of the House Environment Subcommittee, objected to scrapping the deadlines. "Without deadlines, compliance will be slow," Waxman told the Environment Industry Council Feb. 27. "The purpose of deadlines is simple: to force the development of better technology to control air pollution."

Hart said the deadlines largely were being ignored or were serving as excuses for industry to delay installing the best possible control equipment.

PSD. Although the commission found that the program to prevent the significant deterioration (PSD) of the air in regions that were cleaner than the national standards had not affected energy development, the report said the program had imposed more regulatory complexity on industry than could be justified by the benefits being achieved. Thus the panel recommended that Congress:

● Retain requirements that all new plants install the best available pollution control technology.

● Eliminate the system that allowed pollution to in-

crease only up to certain preset "increments," except in national parks and wilderness areas where both air quality and visibility would be protected.

● Retain slightly less restrictive controls on 168 million acres of wildlife refuges, national monuments, national recreation areas, national seashores, wild and scenic rivers, and new national parks and wilderness areas.

Hawkins, of the clean air coalition, charged that the commission had overreacted to complaints about the complexity of the PSD system, and vowed that environmentalists would push for "simplification, not elimination."

He cited a National Academy of Sciences report released Feb. 27 that showed the PSD system "basically sound," although too narrowly interpreted. The academy's report, also mandated by the 1977 amendments, said the present system gave states flexibility to adjust for local conditions and to balance economics with clean air needs.

Non-attainment Areas. For areas that had not attained the national standards, the commission recommended:

● Eliminating requirements that new industries achieve the lowest possible emission rate. Instead they would have to install slightly less stringent pollution control equipment (called "best available control technology"), the same equipment required on similar plants in clean-air regions.

● Requiring inspection and maintenance of automobile pollution control devices only in large cities where the peak 1981 ozone or carbon monoxide levels were 50 percent higher than the national standards.

● Allowing new industries to pay a fee rather than obtain emission "offsets" from existing polluters, if the state used the fees to reduce emissions at existing plants.

Mobile Sources. The commission recommended that Congress relax the carbon monoxide emission standard from 3.4 grams per mile to 7 grams per mile. Hart said devices that achieved the 3.4 standard were unreliable and, if they failed, pollute more than devices that emitted 7 grams.

Acid Rain. The commission recommended an immediate moratorium on state efforts to relax controls on the burning of high-sulfur coal in the Eastern United States, while requiring a "significant reduction" of sulfur dioxide emissions over the next 10 years.

Indoor Air. The panel recommended that Congress establish an interagency task force to study the health risks posed by indoor air pollution. ▮

Steel Industry Wins Delay

Congress on June 26 sent the president a bill (HR 3520) giving the steel industry another three years to meet air pollution cleanup deadlines. President Reagan signed the measure into law July 17 (PL 97-23).

The legislation allowed steel companies to negotiate on a case-by-case basis extensions until Dec. 31, 1985, of the 1982 deadline for cleaning up air pollution emissions. Money saved by deferring pollution control expenditures must be used to modernize older plants.

The extension measure grew out of an agreement developed in the fall of 1980 by a federal advisory board comprised of representatives of the steel industry, the United Steel Workers of America and the federal government.

The bill cleared June 26 when the House voted 412-4

to adopt a conference committee report (H Rept 97-161) that the Senate had approved by voice vote June 25. *(Vote 101, p. 42-H)*

The bill was approved May 13 and reported May 22 by the House Energy and Commerce Committee (H Rept 97-121). It passed the House May 28 under suspension of the rules by a 322-3 vote. *(Vote 46, p. 26-H)*

James T. Broyhill, R-N.C., the only House member to speak against the bill on the floor, objected to granting special treatment to the steel industries. He noted many other industries also were seeking relief from various provi-

sions of the Clean Air Act (PL 95-95).

The Senate passed its version (S 63) by voice vote June 11, substituted its language for the House-passed bill (HR 3520) and adopted the House number.

Conferees dropped one Senate provision giving states veto power over deadline extensions and a second designed to prevent job losses due to plant shutdowns in areas where plants are granted extensions. A third Senate provision, which granted third parties the right to intervene in a judicial proceeding stemming from any deadline extension, was retained in the final measure.   ∎

Congress Clears Sewer Grant Legislation

Congress Dec. 16 cleared legislation (HR 4503 — PL 97-117) that significantly reduced the scope and cost of the huge federal sewage treatment grant program — although more slowly than President Reagan had wanted.

Both the Senate and House adopted the conference agreement for the bill (H Rept 97-408) Dec. 16 by voice vote.

President Reagan signed the measure into law Dec. 29.

House-Senate conferees reached agreement Dec. 10 on the four-year reauthorization. Both the House and Senate had passed separate versions of the measure Oct. 27.

As cleared, HR 4503 not only eliminated federal funding for certain growth-oriented sewage treatment equipment but also reduced the program's annual authorization from $5 billion to $2.4 billion.

The bill also authorized $200 million, starting in fiscal 1983, to correct storm and sanitary sewer overflows in marine bays.

Although no fiscal 1982 funding for the program had been provided pending enactment of HR 4503, Reagan was expected to request — and Congress to approve — a $2.4 billion supplemental appropriation for fiscal 1982.

The formula for distributing federal sewer construction grants under the Clean Water Act (PL 92-500) expired Sept. 30. By then, more than 30 states had exhausted their federal funds. *(Background, Congress and the Nation Vol. III, p. 792)*

HR 4503 continued the existing formula for one year, but changed it for fiscal 1983-1985. Under the new formula, no state would lose more than 10 percent of what it received in 1982.

All treatment plants and equipment remained eligible for 75 percent federal funding until fiscal 1985. After that, only sewage treatment plants, large sewer lines and repairs for leaky pipes would be funded, and those at a 55 percent federal share. However, governors could use up to 20 percent of a state's money for items otherwise ineligible.

Provisions

As cleared by Congress, HR 4503:

● Reduced the annual authorization ceiling for federal sewer grants from $5 billion to $2.4 billion for fiscal 1982-1985, and established a $200 million fund, beginning in fiscal 1983, to correct storm and sanitary sewer overflows into marine bays and estuaries.

● Extended the existing grant allotment formula through fiscal 1982, and used a combination of the existing formula and a new Senate allotment formula in fiscal 1983-

1985, ensuring that no state would receive less than 90 percent of what it would have received under the 1982 formula.

● Retained the 75 percent federal share until Oct. 1, 1984, after which the federal share was to be reduced to 55 percent, except that if a construction grant was awarded prior to that date for a primary, secondary or advanced treatment plant and related interceptors, or for correcting leaks, all subsequent segments and phases of that facility relating to interceptors and leak repairs were to be funded at the 75 percent level.

● Repealed the industrial cost exclusion provision of the Clean Water Act. The House May 28 passed a separate bill (HR 2957) to repeal the provision, but the Senate never acted on that measure. *(Story, p. 520)*

● Retained existing reserve capacity rules until Oct. 1, 1984, except that reserve capacity for any construction grant approved prior to Oct. 1, 1984, for a phase or segment of a treatment plant or interceptor, could be eligible for federal funding.

● Provided that beginning Oct. 1, 1984, no grant could be made for reserve treatment plant capacity in excess of population needs existing as of the date the construction grant was awarded, and in no event for needs in excess of those as of Oct. 1, 1990.

● Retained assistance for all projects currently eligible for federal funds until Oct. 1, 1984; for new projects, allowed up to 20 percent of a state's yearly allotment to be used, at the discretion of the governor, for categories such as correction of combined storm and sanitary sewer overflows, sewer rehabilitation and construction of collector systems; retained eligibility for correcting underground leaks.

● Deleted "grandfather" restrictions allowing only certain communities to discharge wastes that have not received full secondary treatment into deep ocean waters, provided that the cities meet environmental safeguards in the act, and provided that applications were received within one year from date of enactment. No waivers could be granted for the discharge of sewage sludge.

● Deleted a requirement that cities with construction grant funds that later received permission to discharge into the ocean must nonetheless use their funds to provide secondary treatment.

● Extended through fiscal 1982 the provision that no state shall receive less than one-half of 1 percent of the total national allotment.

● Directed the Environmental Protection Agency (EPA) administrator to help states develop capital financing plans

projecting state sewage treatment needs and capital financing plans for at least 10 years.

● Provided that fiscal 1982 grants be allotted no later than the 10th day after enactment of the bill.

● Changed from 2 percent to 4 percent the portion of the authorization available for state administrative costs.

● Extended a provision allowing cities to receive 85 percent federal funding — rather than the normal 75 percent — for plants that use innovative and alternative technologies. Made innovative unit processes of a treatment system eligible for the higher federal funding. After Oct. 1, 1984, the innovative and alternative technologies shall be eligible for 75 percent federal funds. Increased from 4 percent to 7.5 percent the amount that could be set aside by states for increasing the federal share for such technologies.

● Removed a prohibition against federal funding for innovative technologies used for collectors, sewer rehabilitation, and combined storm and sanitary sewers.

● Directed EPA's administrator to reserve at least $100,000 annually for water quality management planning grants per state, which could be used to identify cost-effective ways to curb pollution from urban and agricultural runoff.

● Required the EPA administrator, before approving a construction-phase grant, to find that the project was the most cost-effective method of cleaning up a state's pollution. Water conservation measures and devices had to be considered in determining cost-effectiveness.

● Allotted to New York whatever amount was necessary to transfer sewage temporarily from a new convention center in New York City to a plant in Brooklyn.

● Required the EPA to approve or disapprove a grant application within 45 days if a state had won authority to administer the grant program and had authority to certify that the grant would comply with applicable laws. •

● Stated that it was the policy of Congress that federal sewer grants be used for projects most needed to improve water quality.

● Stated that it was the sense of Congress that courts should consider reduced federal funding levels when requiring cities to complete plant construction by certain court-ordered dates.

● Directed EPA to provide Congress by Dec. 31, 1982, with a new "needs" survey, taking into account the changes made in the law by HR 4503, identifying treatment works that did not comply with the law and assessing the impact of the 1981 amendments to the act on the cost of completing the federal program.

● Directed the administrator to require value engineering review for treatment works before any grant was awarded in excess of $10 million, in order to identify unnecessarily high costs in a project.

● Extended the July 1, 1983, deadline for cities acting in good faith to achieve secondary treatment to July 1, 1988.

● Defined secondary treatment as including oxidation ponds, lagoons and ditches and trickling filters if it could be proven that water quality would not be harmed through use of such processes.

● Provided that as of Oct. 1, 1981, federal grants for planning and design be made only retroactively, after construction grants had been awarded, except that, in the case of small communities that would otherwise be unable to perform such work, the state had to advance money for planning and design.

● Allowed combined design and construction grants to communities of 25,000 population or less for plants costing up to $8 million.

● Required that the prime engineering consultant remain on the site of a sewage treatment project for one year after start-up to certify that the project complies with its permit.

● Modified the requirement that two brand names be listed in bid specifications by providing that, when it was impractical or uneconomical to make a clear description of the technical requirements, one brand name or equal description could be used.

● Amended the definition of "construction" in Section 212 of the act to include as grant-eligible the field testing of innovative and alternative wastewater treatment processes and techniques meeting certain guidelines. The provision was not intended to become a means for any delay in compliance with the effluent limitations outlined in Section 301 of the act.

● Specified that no state could receive a grant unless it had adopted new water quality standards within three years of enactment of the bill.

Background

The multibillion-dollar sewage treatment plant construction program was second only to the federal highway system in expense. Yet the program had been bitterly criticized by nearly everyone involved in it — the states that received federal construction grants, the engineers who built the plants, the General Accounting Office (GAO), congressional investigators and the EPA, which administered the program.

The ambitious program to build thousands of sewage treatment plants was launched in 1972 with enactment of the Federal Water Pollution Control Act (PL 92-500). The act was amended in 1977 when Congress passed the Clean Water Act (PL 95-217). *(1972 Act, Congress and the Nation Vol. III, p. 792; 1977 amendments, 1977 Almanac p. 697)*

The 1972 act, which replaced water pollution control laws dating back to 1899, set two goals: fishable and swimmable waters by 1983 and elimination of all polluted discharges into navigable waters by 1985.

It required industries to install certain equipment by July 1, 1977, and more stringent technology by July 1, 1983. Cities were to provide "secondary treatment" — removing 85 percent of pollutants — by July 1, 1977, and to use the "best practicable" technology by mid-1983. EPA was to define each of the technologies.

One persistent complaint about the 1972 law was that it required high-technology equipment nationwide — in order to achieve zero discharges by 1985 — regardless of how clean or dirty the water was where the treated water was being dumped.

Recognizing the need for more flexibility, Congress in 1977 allowed for "innovative and alternative" technologies — such as using treated sewage water for irrigation or recycling it for other uses.

The 1977 amendments, which authorized $5 billion a year through fiscal 1982, also gave industry until 1984 to clean up toxic and conventional pollutants, and until 1987 to clean up other pollutants. Cities won an additional six years, until 1983, to clean up their discharges if they had not received promised federal funds, as did industries tying into those plants.

In 1980 the act was amended again (PL 96-483) to

repeal a requirement that industries discharging wastes into city-owned plants pay some of the cost of building those plants and to allow states to assume more than their normal 25 percent share. *(1980 Almanac p. 607)*

Progress and Problems

Since 1972, $38.98 billion had been authorized and $33.3 billion appropriated for construction grants. Of the 13,000 grants awarded by 1981, about 3,200 plants were operating.

There was, however, very little reliable data on whether the nation's water was getting cleaner. In April 1981, the GAO reported that the water quality sampling methods of the EPA and the U.S. Geological Survey were "highly questionable" and could not provide sound data for such assessments.

The GAO, in 18 studies of the construction grants program in the last three years, found that:

● Secondary treatment was often unnecessary and could be replaced by cheaper alternative technologies.

● Expensive advanced treatment facilities, which removed all pollutants from wastewater, often did not improve water quality but could cost five times more than secondary plants.

● Non-point sources of pollution such as agricultural and urban runoff might prevent many areas from meeting the 1983 cleanup deadline, yet they had received only 1 percent of the total water pollution control funds.

● Up to 87 percent of the treatment plants surveyed violated their discharge permits at least once a year, and 31 percent were in "serious" violation. The failures were caused by design and equipment deficiencies, overloads from storms and leaks, toxic effluents from industries, and lack of operator training.

● "Staggering" operation and maintenance costs, which could reach $30 billion by 1990, created a heavy financial burden on low-income families in small communities.

● Enforcement by EPA and the states varied from none to minimal, and virtually no one was held legally responsible for the failure of treatment plants.

Escalating costs were a major problem. Initial estimates were that the program would require a total investment of $63 billion in 1972 dollars. But because of inflation, bureaucratic delays and population growth, EPA estimated that by the year 2000 it could cost $120 billion to reach the cleanup goals, with the federal share approaching $90 billion.

The Reagan Proposal

President Reagan announced in March that he did not want to spend another penny on sewage construction grants until the program was overhauled. He asked for and got a $1.7 billion rescission in fiscal 1981 grant funds and said if Congress made the program more cost-effective he would seek $2.4 billion in fiscal 1982 grants.

In proposals sent to Congress in April, Reagan sought to reduce the federal government's future potential obligation from a projected $90 billion to $23 billion. The administration wanted to eliminate federal funding for new collection systems, for "reserve" treatment capacity to serve future population growth, for replacing or repairing existing sewers or leaking pipes and for storing overflows from combined storm and sanitary sewer systems.

The budget reconciliation package that Reagan signed into law Aug. 13 (HR 3982 — PL 97-35) barred any fiscal 1982 spending for the sewer program until and unless Con-

gress reformed the grants, after which it stipulated that no more than $2.4 billion be spent.

Reagan's plan — which would have shifted federal sewer spending from rural and high-growth areas in the South and West to older cities in the Northeast — set off a bitter Sun Belt-Frost Belt struggle in Congress.

Duration of Reauthorization

The administration wanted the construction grants program authorized only through fiscal 1982.

State water program administrators sought a six-year reauthorization to provide funding predictability.

Environmentalists also wanted more than a one-year reauthorization so that Congress could review other parts of the act in 1982 without the threat of changes in the construction grants allotment formula hanging over it.

Coming up for review in 1982 were the national water quality standards and the deadlines for meeting them. The administration was also under pressure from business to relax a controversial provision giving the federal government authority to regulate local dredging projects in wetlands.

But EPA told Congress the administration wanted a one-year reauthorization simply to make the timing of the construction grants consistent with the rest of the act.

Senate Committee Action

The Senate Environment and Public Works Committee, in drafting S 1716 (originally S 1274), adopted far more of Reagan's proposed changes than the House Public Works and Transportation Committee.

The administration wanted to reduce the federal government's potential future obligation under the program from an estimated $90 billion to $23 billion. As approved Sept. 23 by the Senate committee, S 1716 (S Rept 97-204) reduced that potential obligation to about $24 billion, according to EPA.

The House version cut it only to about $53 billion, according to EPA.

The Distribution Formula

The Senate committee bill also reduced the federal share of the grants from the 75 percent level to 55 percent by 1985, and it revamped the formula under which the grants were distributed.

As originally introduced by Sen. John H. Chafee, R-R.I., the bill prohibited federal dollars from being used for either reserve treatment plant capacity to serve future populations or collection lines that reached into residential neighborhoods. Thus, most of the money would have gone to older cities in the Northeast, where secondary sewage treatment plants — which would still be eligible for federal funds — were the top priority.

Under the original Chafee formula, 16 states — mostly in the North and East — and the District of Columbia would have received more sewer money in fiscal 1982 than previously.

Under Reagan's distribution formula, 20 states would have received more money in 1982, while 29 — mostly in the Sun Belt — would have lost funds. One would have received the same amount.

Chafee realized that the "loser" states, located primarily in the Sun Belt where the population was growing, could have killed the bill in the full Senate.

So the Environmental Pollution Subcommittee, which

he chaired, amended the measure July 15 to ensure that no state would receive less than 90 percent of what it would have gotten under the old formula. Under the new formula, 23 states would receive more, and Sun Belt losses would be considerably less than under the original formula.

Sun Belt States Gain

During full committee markup Sept. 11 and 23, Sun Belt members led by Pete V. Domenici, R-N.M., elicited further compromises that continued funding for some currently approved collector and reserve treatment projects.

Domenici, chairman of the Senate Budget Committee, was in a tough position. He represented one of the Southwestern states where federal sewage treatment grants had been a crucial catalyst for growth. Yet he spent most of the year browbeating his colleagues to exercise budgetary restraint.

Domenici repeatedly noted that his amendments authorized no expenditures beyond the $2.4 billion per year Reagan sought. But they gave governors flexibility to spend the grants on the most cost-effective projects, he said, and would prevent cities from having to scrap half-completed projects.

To ensure that only those projects already well on their way to construction would be funded, Domenici's amendments included several restrictions.

One allowed funding for collectors only if the projects had received construction grants as of Oct. 1, 1981. The collectors also had to be necessary to protect the public health from existing discharges into ground or surface water and be preferable to alternative treatment methods.

Earlier, the committee approved a similar amendment by Sen. Jennings Randolph, D-W.Va., that allowed funding of collectors in towns of less than 3,500 persons if they were necessary for public health reasons.

A more controversial Domenici amendment continued federal funding for reserve capacity at treatment plants, but only for plants that had received design grants as of Oct. 1, 1981, and that would receive construction grants by Oct. 1, 1983.

Domenici initially recommended that cities be eligible only if they would receive construction grants by Oct. 1, 1982. But the deadline was extended one year at the urging of Sen. Lloyd Bentsen, D-Texas, who said many Texas cities had done substantial work in anticipation of federal funds for reserve capacity.

By extending the eligibility one year, the amendment could obligate the federal government to pay for up to $1.5 billion more in equipment than if the 1982 deadline had been retained, according to EPA.

Funding Levels

The Senate committee bill authorized $2.4 billion in fiscal 1982, but $2.6 billion in the subsequent three years.

Starting in fiscal 1983, the bill authorized $200 million annually to build storage facilities for sewage overflow during storms, if those overflows would affect marine bays and estuaries. That amendment was aimed specifically at cities surrounding areas such as Rhode Island's Narragansett Bay and the Chesapeake, San Francisco and Galveston bays.

Industrial Cost Exclusion

The Senate panel also inserted a compromise provision, introduced by Sen. Daniel Patrick Moynihan, D-N.Y., that changed the industrial cost exclusion (ICE) amend-

ment attached to the Clean Water Act in 1980.

The 1980 ICE amendment, sponsored by committee Chairman Robert T. Stafford, R-Vt., banned the use of federal grants to build plant capacity to treat industrial discharges greater than 50,000 gallons a day. *(1980 Almanac p. 607)*

Moynihan's amendment repealed the ICE and replaced it with a requirement that after Nov. 15, 1981, no construction grants be used to treat industrial discharges "in excess of existing flows." Any plant that had received a design grant before the preceding May 15 was grandfathered in by the provision.

Senate Floor Action

The Senate passed S 1716 by voice vote Oct. 27 after only minimal discussion.

Before acting, it adopted — also by voice vote — an amendment by Majority Leader Howard H. Baker Jr., R-Tenn., that permitted use of funds in the bill to finance construction of a greenhouse and skills development center as part of a San Francisco sewage treatment plant expansion project.

Baker's amendment also specified that nothing in the law would "displace, restrict, limit, affect, or modify in any way the obligations or liabilities of any person, or the right to seek abatement or damages, under other federal or state law, including common law."

House Committee Action

The House Public Works Committee approved HR 4503 Sept. 30 after agreeing to halt federal funding for the planning of treatment plants designed to accommodate long-term future growth, a less stringent step than the action taken by the Senate committee.

The Water Resources Subcommittee Sept. 17 had approved sweeping "grandfather" provisions designed to protect sewage treatment construction programs already under way.

The subcommittee approved continued federal funding for any project currently receiving federal assistance, including collectors, rehabilitation of leaky pipes and correction of storm overflows.

States also could use up to 30 percent of their yearly allocations for new projects designed to correct such problems as leaky pipes or storm overflows.

Reserve Capacity

In direct defiance of Reagan's wishes, the bill authorized funding of new reserve capacity projects, although these could only provide for 10 years of projected growth.

Subcommittee Chairman Robert A. Roe, D-N.J., argued strongly that the federal government should not change the rules for the sewer grant program midstream. Many states had assumed large debts, he said, based on the assumption that the federal government would continue paying for equipment eligible under the existing law.

At the full committee Sept. 30, Roe offered the amendment to discontinue federal planning grants for "reserve" sewage treatment plant capacity to accommodate 20 years of population growth. Cities that already had received a design or construction grant for such 20-year plants would remain eligible for funds.

Grants to build plants with reserve capacity had been sought primarily by growing Sun Belt cities. "If we didn't

take future growth into consideration," said E. Clay Shaw Jr., R-Fla., "it would be like trying to build a one-bedroom house when your wife is pregnant."

Prior to the committee's Sept. 30 action, the House bill reduced the potential obligation to about $53 billion. Deleting funds for 20-year reserve capacity planning grants cut that obligation "by several billion dollars" more, said Rep. John Paul Hammerschmidt, R-Ark., ranking minority member of the subcommittee.

Ocean Dumping

The committee stuck to an earlier decision to let more seaside towns discharge nominally treated sewage into the ocean.

Rep. James L. Oberstar, D-Minn., sought to reinstate the discharge restrictions, which the committee bill lifted for cities that could show discharges would not harm the marine environment.

Congress in 1977 allowed cities to dump sewage offshore instead of providing secondary treatment, but only if outfall lines already existed or if a city applied for a permit within nine months of Congress' action.

The waivers were intended primarily for cities off the Pacific Coast, where currents were strong and the waters deep. However, under regulations developed by the Environmental Protection Agency (EPA), Atlantic Coast cities were also eligible.

EPA approved the first six ocean discharge waivers, all for Pacific Coast cities, in September 1981. Some 60 cities, including Boston, Los Angeles and San Francisco, were seeking permission to dump sewage offshore instead of providing secondary treatment.

In other action, the committee adopted an amendment introduced by Rep. Geraldine A. Ferraro, D-N.Y., urging courts that had ordered cities to meet certain water cleanup deadlines to re-examine those orders because of the federal cutbacks.

The panel also adopted an amendment by Buddy Roemer, D-La., to allow federal grants to be used for correcting leaky underground pipes.

House Floor Action

The House on Oct. 27 approved HR 4503 by a 382-18 margin. *(Vote 266, p. 86-H)*

As passed by the House, the bill included fewer of Reagan's proposals than S 1716, the Senate version. The administration announced Oct. 19 that Reagan opposed HR 4503 as it had been reported by the Public Works and Transportation Committee.

Despite the announcement, 163 Republicans joined 219 Democrats in voting for final passage.

House members claimed Reagan's plan to halt funding for projects designed to accommodate population growth would cause "total disruption" among cities with plants already under way.

The House bill, which "grandfathered" in plants already under way, provided more of a transition period for cities to adjust to the federal cutbacks.

In addition, the House bill gave cities more flexibility than Reagan's plan, allowing the federal money to be used for such items as conservation measures, correcting leaky pipes and storm overflow problems.

Although both HR 4503 and S 1716 authorized $2.4 billion for the program in fiscal 1982, the Senate bill also authorized expenditures of $2.6 billion annually in fiscal

1983-85.

S 1716 changed the grant allotment formula, while HR 4503 did not.

Conference

The administration announced Oct. 19 that the president opposed HR 4503, casting the shadow of a veto threat over the conference, which lasted for several weeks.

House conferees said Reagan's plan would cause "total disruption" among cities that had plants already under way. By grandfathering in most plants already under construction, they said, the House bill provided a transition period for cities to adjust to the federal cutbacks.

In addition, they said, the House bill would give cities more flexibility than Reagan's plan, allowing the federal money to be used for such items as conservation measures, correcting leaky pipes and storm overflow problems.

Nonetheless, Sen. John H. Chafee, R-R.I., warned that unless the House provisions were cut back significantly, the administration might veto the bill.

"I think we run a danger here in that dangling out here is $2.4 billion. The administration is searching for money. I don't think it's any secret that the administration would be glad to pick up $2.4 billion if they could find a good excuse," said Chafee.

House conferees were concerned about a news report that the Office of Management and Budget (OMB) would only seek $1 billion for sewer grants in fiscal 1983, despite previous indications that if Congress enacted the administration's reform package, it would provide $2.4 billion.

"There's been no indication to us that the administration does not support the $2.4 billion level," said Chafee.

Jennings Randolph, D-W.Va., ranking minority member of the Senate Environment and Public Works Committee, said if the conferees could not reach an agreement, "the legislation might be permanently foreclosed," resulting in a program shutdown.

Rep. Robert A. Roe, D-N.J., chairman of the House Public Works Committee's Water Resources Subcommittee, complained that, "We're afraid the administration wants to 'reform' the program completely out of existence."

Obstacles to Agreement

One major obstacle to a conference agreement was the fact that S 1716 was a four-year bill while HR 4503 was a one-year measure. The House panel wanted to consider other clean-water issues in 1982, and feared that if a multiyear authorization were enacted, the Senate would not consider other amendments to the act then.

But Chafee said, "We feel very strongly it has to be a multi-year authorization. We'd be very pleased to consider other changes next year. You don't need the single-year authorization as bait to get us to come back next year."

Another obstacle for the conferees was that S 1716 contained a new grant distribution formula that would fund only treatment plants and interceptors needed for the 1980 population. The House wanted to continue the existing formula, which allowed funding for certain types of growth-oriented plants and equipment not covered in the Senate bill.

"There's nothing in here that prevents a community from doing whatever it wants. If your town wants to put in a 20-inch pipe [to accommodate] future growth, go do it," said Chafee. "But we're not going to pay for it.

"We're trying to get the water cleaned up," Chafee

continued. "We'll do what we can to get you up to the starting line and anything beyond that in terms of growth is up to you. We're not in the water supply business."

The final formula represented a compromise between the Senate and House versions.

Another sticking point in the negotiations was a $200 million fund in the Senate bill — but not the House measure — that would help primarily Providence, R.I., in Chafee's home state, to correct runoff from combined storm and sanitary sewer systems that dump into marine bays.

Still another major point of contention was the House's desire to allow the federal government to help pay for repairing leaky pipes. Buddy Roemer, D-La., said, "We feel deeply on our side that it is a major and important issue."

The final agreement provided for both Chafee's $200 million fund and federal funds for repairing leaky pipes. ∎

Industrial Cost Exclusion

The House May 28 passed a bill (HR 2957) to allow industries to send their sewage to city treatment plants without having to pay extra for construction of those facilities.

The Senate failed to act on the bill, instead including its provisions in separate legislation (HR 4503 — PL 97-117) overhauling the entire federal sewage treatment grant program. *(Story, p. 515)*

The House passed HR 2957 under suspension of the rules. As passed, it repealed a provision added to the Clean Water Act (PL 92-500) in 1980 prohibiting the use of federal construction grant money to treat industrial discharges of more than 50,000 gallons a day. *(1980 action, 1980 Almanac p. 607; Clean Water Act, Congress and the Nation Vol. III, p. 792)*

Environmentalists charged the action could result in damage to public health and water quality by overloading inadequate public treatment systems with industrial wastes. They also argued that it constituted a special subsidy for industry.

HR 2957 also extended for a year the formula for distributing construction grants to states and a provision encouraging innovative sewage treatment methods.

In addition, it provided funds to temporarily connect a New York City convention center to a nearby sewage treatment plant. Otherwise, the center's wastes would have been dumped into the Hudson River until another treatment plant was built.

Committee Action

HR 2957 was approved May 12 and reported May 19 by the Public Works and Transportation Committee (H Rept 97-90).

In approving the bill May 6, the Water Resources Subcommittee also voted one-year extensions for two expiring portions of the construction grants program — the formula for distributing those grants to states and a provision that encouraged development of innovative sewage treatment technologies.

The extensions were needed to meet the May 15 reporting deadline for committee action on fiscal 1982 authorizations.

A third subcommittee amendment, added at the request of committee Chairman James J. Howard, D-N.J.,

provided 100 percent federal funding for temporarily connecting a New York City convention center to a nearby sewage treatment plant. ∎

Marine Sanctuaries Act

Congress Dec. 14 cleared a bill (S 1003 — PL 97-109) to continue for two years the federal program for designating environmentally sensitive offshore areas as marine sanctuaries, where oil and resource development was strictly controlled.

Final action came in the House, which agreed to Senate amendments to S 1003 and then sent the measure to the White House for the president's signature.

As cleared, S 1003 authorized funding at $2,235,000 annually for fiscal 1982 and fiscal 1983.

Before it finally cleared Congress, the marine sanctuaries bill bounced back and forth between the chambers four times.

The Senate started the process May 4, passing its version of the bill (S Rept 97-44), which provided $2.2 million for the program in fiscal 1982 and 1983.

Then the House July 13 passed its version (HR 2449 — H Rept 97-52), which provided $2.2 million in fiscal 1982 and "such sums as may be necessary" in fiscal 1983. The House adopted the S 1003 number, substituted its language for the Senate bill and sent the measure back to the Senate.

The Senate Dec. 11 amended the measure by inserting a $2.2 million cap on fiscal 1983 expenditures. The House, reluctantly, finally accepted the Senate language Dec. 14 and cleared the bill.

Background

The measure reauthorized Title III of the Marine Protection, Research and Sanctuaries Act of 1972 (PL 92-532). *(Congress and the Nation Vol. III, p. 798)*

The marine sanctuary program was similar to such on-land programs as the National Park System and the National Forest System. To date, six areas had been designated as marine sanctuaries — two off the Florida coast, two offshore of California, and one each off the North Carolina and Georgia coasts. ∎

Timber on Military Lands

The House Nov. 4 passed a bill (HR 4543) establishing a standard of payments to state and local governments for timber harvested on federal military lands.

The Senate did not act on the measure.

As passed under suspension of the rules, HR 4543 entitled state and local governments to receive 25 percent of net receipts from timber harvests on military lands. The money was to be used for school and road needs created by the presence of the military installations.

State and local governments already received 25 percent of gross receipts from timber harvested from national forest lands within their borders.

The Department of Defense controlled approximately 2.5 million acres of productive forest land. More than 150 military installations in 38 states and the District of Columbia had active forest management programs.

HR 4543 was reported Oct. 27 by the House Armed Services Committee (H Rept 97-299). ∎

Reconciliation and Environmental Programs

In its budget reconciliation package (HR 3982 — PL 97-35), Congress blocked President Reagan's plans to halt the expansion of federal park lands and to use acquisition funds for upgrading existing parks.

However, the lawmakers acceded to a second major Reagan request and agreed to stop sending money to the states for building sewage treatment plants while the multibillion-dollar program — the largest civilian construction program other than federal highways — was revamped. *(Sewer grant legislation, p. 515)*

The reconciliation measure, which was sent to the president July 31 and signed into law Aug. 13, included a statement that it was the "sense of Congress" that the expansion of federal parks, forests and refuges through new land acquisitions should be continued, using money from the Land and Water Conservation Fund. *(Reconciliation story, p. 256)*

Interior Secretary James G. Watt had wanted to use the fund to upgrade existing parks instead, which would have required an amendment to the law authorizing the fund. Congress in 1981 was unwilling to amend the act.

The reconciliation law recommended that at least $105 million be spent each year for upgrading parks, but the money would come from the National Park Service's operation and maintenance accounts, not from the land and water fund, which is derived from revenues from offshore oil and gas leasing.

In addition, the measure recommended the continuation of federal grants to the states for historic preservation and acquisition of urban parks. The administration wanted them eliminated.

In the final reconciliation package, Congress also attached a provision — not initiated by the administration — that prohibited federal subsidies after 1983 for commercial development on barrier islands, which are highly susceptible to coastal erosion and flooding.

On another issue, the bill recommended that the federal government continue the Payments in Lieu of Taxes program (PILT) at approximately current levels. Under the program, the federal government reimburses counties — mostly in the West where the bulk of federal land is located — for local taxes they cannot collect on federal lands within their boundaries.

The administration wanted the $103 million program cut back to $45 million in fiscal 1982. Congress recommended that $100 million be appropriated for the payments annually.

For the first time, Congress voted a cap on appropriations for Army Corps of Engineers water projects, setting a fiscal 1982 ceiling of $1.55 billion and limits of $1.69 billion and $1.58 billion in fiscal 1983-84.

An effort to authorize a new national water policy board in the budget reconciliation bill was thwarted during conference when four Western senators raised objections.

The idea of creating a national board resulted from a bipartisan movement in Congress to prevent water policy from being dominated by Watt. The interior secretary opposed creation of the board, preferring instead to coordinate federal water programs in the president's Cabinet Council on Natural Resources and the Environment, which he headed. *(Water Policy reform, p. 528)*

Although both the House and Senate reconciliation bills provided for a new water policy board, conferees dropped the authorization after Sens. James A. McClure, R-Idaho, William L. Armstrong, R-Colo., Alan K. Simpson, R-Wyo., and Malcolm Wallop, R-Wyo., objected to attaching it to the spending cut package.

Aides to the four said the senators felt that the reconciliation bill was not the proper vehicle for making a major policy decision like creating the board.

Provisions

As cleared by Congress, HR 3982 (H Rept 97-208) contained the following major provisions affecting environmental programs:

Barrier Islands (Title III)

● Prohibited after Oct. 1, 1983, the sale of federal flood insurance for new construction or substantial improvements in existing structures on "undeveloped coastal barriers" as designated by the secretary of the interior.

● Defined "coastal barriers" to include areas subject to waves and "tidal and wind energies;" areas that protect "landward aquatic habitats from direct wave attack," and habitats such as wetlands, marshes, estuaries and inlets.

● Specified that a coastal barrier would be treated as undeveloped only if there were few man-made structures and if human activities did not interfere with ecological processes.

● Directed the interior secretary to study the definitions and to make recommendations to Congress within one year for any changes in the coastal barrier definition.

● Allowed federally insured financial institutions to make loans for structures that would become ineligible for the flood insurance.

● Specified that lands set aside as wildlife refuges, sanctuaries, or for recreational or natural resource conservation purposes by a federal, state, or local law or non-profit organization shall not be prohibited from receiving federal flood insurance.

Interior Department Programs (Title XIV)

● Limited appropriations for certain Interior Department programs to $4,095,404,000 for fiscal 1981, $3,970,267,000 for fiscal 1982, $4,680,223,000 for fiscal 1983 and $4,797,281,000 for fiscal 1984.

● Specified that the above spending caps apply only to those programs administered under the Alaska Native Fund, the Bureau of Land Management, the Bureau of Mines, the National Park Service (other than the John F. Kennedy Center for the Performing Arts), offices of the solicitor and the secretary, the Office of Surface Mining Reclamation, the Office of Territorial Affairs, the U.S. Geological Survey, and the Bureau of Reclamation, and do not apply to amounts required for emergency firefighting and for increased pay costs authorized by law.

● Stated the "sense of Congress" that annual appropriation targets for fiscal 1981-1984 should be at least $275 million for the Land and Water Conservation Fund; $30 million for historic preservation grants; $10 million for urban parks grants; $105 million for restoration and rehabilitation of units of the National Park system; $239 million for the Office of Territorial and International Affairs

(including amounts for the Trust Territory of the Pacific Islands); $6.2 million to carry out provisions of Title III of the Surface Mining Control and Reclamation Act of 1977 (PL 95-87), and $100 million for the Payments in Lieu of Taxes program. *(Surface Mining, 1977 Almanac p. 617)*

● Stated the "sense of the Congress" that the expansion of national parks, forests and refuges through new land acquisitions should be continued, using funds from the Land and Water Conservation Fund.

● Limited authorizations for the Advisory Council on Historic Preservation to no more than $1,590,000 in fiscal 1981, $1,865,000 in fiscal 1982, $1,920,000 in fiscal 1983 and $2 million in fiscal 1984.

● Limited authorizations for the Office of Federal Inspector for the Alaska Natural Gas Transportation System to not more than $21,038,000 in fiscal 1981, $36,568,000 for fiscal 1982, $45,532,000 in fiscal 1983 and $46,908,000 in fiscal 1984.

● Limited authorizations for the Pennsylvania Avenue Development Corporation to not more than $31,612,000 in fiscal 1981, $19,040,000 in fiscal 1982, $19,500,000 in fiscal 1983 and $19,300,000 in fiscal 1984.

● Limited authorizations for the U.S. Holocaust Memorial Council to not more than $900,000 in fiscal 1982, $950,000 in fiscal 1983 and $1 million in fiscal 1984.

● Set $25 as a minimum application fee for non-competitive oil and gas leases on federal land after Oct. 1, 1981.

● Required the interior secretary to conduct a one-year study of the impact of raising the $1-per-acre rental fee for oil and gas leases.

● Barred appropriations of funds to carry out the Youth Conservation Corps Act of 1970 (PL 91-378) in fiscal 1982-1984. *(Corps Act, Congress and the Nation Vol. III p. 718)*

Water Programs (Title XVIII)

● Authorized not more than $2,548,837,000 for sewer construction grants in fiscal 1981, and no fiscal 1982 funds unless legislation was enacted reforming the program, in which case the authorization shall not exceed $2.4 billion.

● Authorized up to $40 million in fiscal 1982 for grants to the states for managing their sewer grant programs.

● Authorized for U.S. Army Corps of Engineers' construction projects not more than $1,546,755,000 in fiscal 1982, $1,688,948,000 in fiscal 1983 and $1,575,750,000 in fiscal 1984.

● Limited authorizations for special recreational user fees at U.S. Army Corps of Engineers' projects to not more than $5 million in fiscal 1981, $5.2 million in fiscal 1982, $6 million in fiscal 1983 and $6 million in fiscal 1984.

● Provided that if legislation were enacted establishing a national water policy board, $12.5 million would be authorized annually in fiscal 1982-1984 for water program coordination and water planning grants, and that all unobligated funds for the Water Resources Council would shift to the board. *(Water policy reform, p. 528)*

● Authorized up to $23,650,000 annually in fiscal 1982-1984 for water research.

House-Senate Differences

Although the House and Senate reconciliation bills (HR 3982, S 1377) were in accord on certain key environmental questions, such as the park acquisition issue, they differed in regard to other programs. Those differences, and the conference actions resolving them, were:

Barrier Islands

Conferees from House and Senate banking committees agreed to a House provision to cut off federal flood insurance for new construction on undeveloped barrier islands. The Senate bill had no similar language.

Oil and Gas Lease Fees

Conferees voted to raise from $10 to $25 the application fee for non-competitive oil and gas leases on federally owned land. They rejected a House provision raising the annual rental fee for oil and gas leases from $1 to $3 per acre in favor of a Senate provision requiring a one-year study of the proposal.

Sewer Grants

Conferees from the public works committees agreed with the president that no money should be spent in fiscal 1982 for sewer construction grants unless the program was reformed. The House bill provided $100 million in 1982 for federal aid to states agreeing to assume certain program management responsibilities; the Senate bill contained no funds for such aid. Conferees agreed to spend $40 million.

Corps of Engineers Water Projects

The Senate voted a $1.51 billion limit on fiscal 1982 spending for Army Corps of Engineers' water project construction; the House set a $1.59 billion cap. The Senate also limited expenditures to $1.69 billion in fiscal 1983 and $1.58 billion in 1984.

House and Senate public works conferees agreed to a $1.55 billion cap in fiscal 1982 and accepted the Senate amounts for 1983 and 1984.

Water Policy Board

The Senate bill provided $36 million for the new water board, plus water planning grants to states. The House bill provided $12.5 million. The conferees agreed to provide up to $12.5 million annually in fiscal 1982-1984 for the board and water planning grants, if the authorizing legislation passed. In addition, $23.65 million was provided annually in fiscal 1982-1984 for water research activities administered by the Interior Department.

Ocean Dumping

Conferees dropped a House provision imposing fees on ocean dumping, instead adopting report language stating that in 1982 the budget committees would not direct the authorizing committees to impose Coast Guard user fees as part of reconciliation.

Noise

House Energy and Commerce conferees dropped a provision reauthorizing the federal noise control program for two years at $7.3 million a year. The language was not in the reconciliation bill cleared by the Senate, which passed a separate measure (S 1204) on July 14 retaining federal authority to regulate noise from trucks and railroads. *(Noise control bill, p. 529)*

EPA Research

Conferees dropped a provision adopted in both bills setting a $540 million cap on Environmental Protection Agency research and regulatory programs in fiscal 1982. ∎

Fur Seal Treaty Extended

The Senate June 11 ratified a four-year extension of a treaty limiting the number of fur seals that can be killed on islands offshore of Alaska and the Soviet Union to levels considered consistent with wildlife management.

The 1980 Protocol amending the Interim Convention on Conservation of North Pacific Fur Seals (Exec S, 96th Cong, 2nd Sess) was ratified by a 94-0 vote. *(Vote 148, p. 28-S)*

Originally signed in 1957 by the United States, the Soviet Union, Japan and Canada, the convention was designed to stop the harvesting of fur seals on the high seas, called "pelagic sealing," in the North Pacific Ocean. Pelagic sealing was decimating the seal population because many injured or killed seals were lost at sea.

The convention assured each country a certain percentage of the land harvest. The United States and Soviet Union, where the seal rookeries are located, agreed to share with Canada and Japan in exchange for a halt to pelagic sealing. The United States receives 70 percent — about 17,000 — of the sealskins harvested in Alaska's Pribilof Islands, and Japan and Canada split the remaining 30 percent. The Soviet Union receives 70 percent of the sealskins harvested off its northeast coast, sharing the rest with Japan and Canada.

There has been a persistent public outcry against the seal harvest, with wildlife protection groups arguing that the government should not subsidize the slaughter.

The Department of Commerce pays 80 Aleut Indians in Alaska $250,000 to harvest the skins during the five-week summer breeding season, and about $4 million is paid each year to support the tribe under the Fur Seal Act of 1966 (PL 89-702). The skins are sent to the Fouke Company in South Carolina, under an exclusive contract, for processing and sale at a government auction.

Committee Action

The Senate Foreign Relations Committee by a 6-9 vote on May 14 rejected a reservation proposed by Christopher J. Dodd, D-Conn., to prohibit the United States from taking its share of the sealskins. The Reagan administration opposed the Dodd reservation; the Carter administration had favored it.

Carl Levin, D-Mich., another foe of the seal slaughter, planned to offer a similar amendment on the Senate floor that would have phased out U.S. participation in the harvest over four years. But Alaska's Republican senators, Majority Whip Ted Stevens and Frank H. Murkowski, opposed it.

After negotiations with Stevens and Murkowski, Levin proposed a new amendment that required studies of alternative sources of employment for the Aleuts, of seal feeding and migration habits, and of the impact adjustments in harvest levels would have on the Aleuts, the ecosystem and the seals.

The amendment, which also declared that the United States may initiate adjustments in its share of the harvest if consistent with the convention, the seals' welfare and the interests of the Aleuts, was agreed to by a voice vote.

Sen. Claiborne Pell, D-R.I., noted that because the demand for seal furs has decreased, the United States spent $3.3 million more in 1979 subsidizing the Aleuts and the harvest than it received from the sale of the skins. He also said the treaty is no longer needed to protect seals on the high seas because adoption of the 200-mile fishing zone has brought most of the seals' migration path under the protective provisions of the 1972 Marine Mammal Protection Act (PL 92-522). *(Marine Mammal Act, Congress and the Nation Vol. III, p. 812)*

Marine Mammal Protection

Congress Sept. 29 cleared for the president a bill (HR 4084) that reauthorized the federal marine mammal protection program while modifying existing law to deal with the accidental killing of porpoises by tuna fishermen.

Final action came when the Senate approved the measure by voice vote. The House Sept. 21 had suspended the rules and passed the bill, a three-year reauthorization of the 1972 Marine Mammal Protection Act (PL 92-522).

President Reagan signed the measure into law Oct. 9 (PL 97-58).

The 1972 act required the departments of Interior and Commerce to conserve and manage such marine mammals as polar bears, sea otters, whales and porpoises. *(Background, Congress and the Nation Vol. III, p. 812)*

Since the law was enacted, the number of porpoises taken in tuna fishing operations had dropped from an estimated 368,000 in 1972 to 15,303 in 1980.

Provisions

As approved by Congress, HR 4084 retained the 1972 act's goal of reducing accidental porpoise deaths to "insignificant levels approaching a zero mortality and serious injury rate."

However, it specified that yellowfin tuna fishermen can satisfy this objective through the use of the best equipment and techniques "that are economically and technologically practicable," a clarification designed to spare fishermen from continuing entanglement in litigation as a result of accidental porpoise kills.

The measure allowed other commercial fishermen, deep seabed mining groups, oceanographic researchers and oil and gas drillers to kill accidentally small numbers of marine mammals as long as there is a "negligible" impact on the species.

It also made it easier for states to take over the management of marine mammals within their borders, a provision sought by Alaska, where the greatest numbers of marine mammals are found.

HR 4084 authorized $9.45 million in fiscal 1982, $10.8 million in fiscal 1983 and $11.9 million in fiscal 1984 for funding under the act to the departments of Commerce and Interior, and to the Marine Mammal Commission.

The bill included a provision requiring federal support for research aimed at developing new methods of locating and catching yellowfin tuna that could reduce the porpoise kills still further.

House Action

The House Merchant Marine Committee May 13 approved a one-year reauthorization (HR 2948 — H Rept 97-53) providing $9.5 million for fiscal 1982. This dollar figure was later incorporated, as a committee amendment, into HR 4084, which contained the new provisions on accidental porpoise kills and funding authorizations for fiscal 1983 and fiscal 1984.

After the one-year reauthorization was approved, weeks of negotiations on amendments to the existing law were conducted with all interested parties — environmentalists, fishing industry representatives, Alaskan officials, and others.

The compromise hammered out in these talks was incorporated in HR 4084, which was officially reported on Sept. 16 (H Rept 97-228).

Senate Action

The Senate Commerce Committee May 14 reported a simple two-year reauthorization at $9.5 million annually (S 1186 — S Rept 97-63).

As in the House, negotiations then began over the substantive changes in the 1972 law, and the resulting compromise was incorporated into HR 4084. The bill was passed without opposition on Sept. 29. ■

Illegal Wildlife Trafficking

The House Nov. 4 sent to the president a bill (S 736) strengthening federal controls over illegal imports or trafficking in protected fish and wildlife.

President Reagan signed the measure into law Nov. 16 (PL (97-79).

The bill combined two existing wildlife control laws — the Lacy and Black Bass acts — and stiffened the penalties for illegal importation or interstate trafficking of protected wildlife.

It was designed to crack down on a lucrative illegal trade in fish, wildlife and wild plants that nets as much as $100 million a year in illegal profits and that can subject domestic livestock, fish and pets to deadly exotic diseases.

A similar bill passed the House and was approved by the Senate Environment Committee in 1980, but never cleared Congress. *(1980 Almanac p. 612)*

The Senate passed S 736 July 24. The measure had been reported May 21 from the Environment and Public Works Committee (S Rept 97-123).

The House version of the measure (HR 1638) was reported by the Merchant Marine and Fisheries Committee Oct. 19 (H Rept 97-276). It was passed by the House under suspension Nov. 4 and then replaced with S 736.

Provisions

The bill consolidated the nation's two wildlife smuggling laws, the Lacey Act of 1900 and the Black Bass Act of 1926. Those laws made it illegal to import or possess fish, wildlife or animal products that are taken, transported or sold in violation of a foreign, state or federal law.

S 736 increased the status of a criminal violation from a misdemeanor to a felony for anyone involved in international and commercial trafficking who knew they were violating a foreign, state or federal law. Those violators would be liable for up to $20,000 in fines and five years in jail, instead of $10,000 and one year in jail as previously.

A provision making any second offense a felony was deleted on the Senate floor by voice vote at the urging of John H. Chafee, R-R.I., James A. McClure, R-Idaho, and Howard H. Baker Jr., R-Tenn.

The maximum civil penalty would be increased from $5,000 to $10,000. In addition, the bill extended protection to plants illegally imported or taken across state lines. ■

California Wilderness Bill

For the second year in a row, the House passed a bill designating millions of acres in California as protected wilderness, only to see the measure bog down in the Senate.

The House on July 17 passed a bill (HR 4083) to designate as wilderness 2.1 million acres of California national forests and 1.4 million acres of national park land in the state.

The wilderness designation would restrict commercial development such as road building, mining or construction of resort facilities.

The measure, reported by the House Interior and Insular Affairs Committee July 16 (H Rept 97-181), was virtually identical to a bill (HR 7702) that was passed by the House in 1980 but died in the Senate. *(1980 Almanac p. 617)*

No similar measure was introduced in the Senate in 1981, although Sen. S. I. "Sam" Hayakawa, R-Calif., introduced a bill (S 842) that would establish a 1985 deadline for congressional action on wilderness proposals and prohibit any future considerations of wilderness designations within the national forests.

The Senate Energy Committee held hearings on S 842 but took no action on it in 1981.

Background

The wilderness designations were spawned by the Carter administration's second roadless area review and evaluation program, commonly called RARE II.

Carter in 1979 recommended that 15.4 million acres of national forest land nationwide be designated as wilderness. Since then, Congress — which had exclusive power to set land aside as wilderness — enacted a number of individual measures designating wilderness areas in various states.

President Carter recommended that 1.3 million acres of national forest land in California be set aside as wilderness — 800,000 acres fewer than HR 4083 would cover. Carter also recommended that 2.6 million acres be reviewed further, and that 2.4 million acres be recommended for non-wilderness management.

The Reagan administration proposed designating 1.2 million acres of California forest land as wilderness.

Opposition Biding Time

Although HR 4083 was controversial, there were no votes against it either in committee or on the House floor.

In minority views expressed in the committee report, opponents in the California delegation said the bill's "excessive" wilderness designations would adversely affect the California economy by restricting logging, mining and recreational use of the federal lands.

However, they decided to hold their fire in order to get the measure before the Senate, where they hoped to find a more receptive atmosphere for amendments.

They said another important reason for not opposing the bill in the House was the need to speed enactment of a so-called "release" provision contained in the House bill.

This provision would release from further wilderness consideration some 2.2 million acres of national forest lands in California until the next round of wilderness reviews, sometime in the 1990s. It also would prohibit further wilderness-related lawsuits on national forest lands in Cali-

fornia, and would remove a court injunction against development on 590,000 acres of disputed wilderness land.

The provision reflected a 1980 compromise between environmentalists and the timber industry. But after the election of a Republican-controlled Senate, the industry refused to support the California compromise, preferring to take its chances on enactment of a national release bill like Hayakawa's S 842, which would prohibit any further wilderness designations after 1985.

Burton's Ploy

The release provision was added to HR 4083 on the House floor at the request of Rep. Phillip Burton, D-Calif., who shepherded the bill through the Interior Committee.

In a unique parliamentary maneuver, Burton convinced the committee to order two California wilderness bills reported out, HR 4083 and HR 4043. They were identical, except for the release language of HR 4043.

The House Agriculture Committee could have sought sequential referral of HR 4043 because the release language mentioned the National Forest Management Act of 1976 (PL 94-588). The Agriculture Committee had jurisdiction over that act. *(Congress and the Nation Vol. IV, p. 313)*

However, before introducing HR 4083 on the floor, Burton got assurances that Agriculture had no objections to the release provisions of HR 4043, and the language was then added to HR 4083 on the floor. ∎

Wilderness Leasing

The House Interior and Insular Affairs Committee Nov. 20 voted 41-1 to ask the Reagan administration not to issue any oil and gas leases on the nation's 80 million acres of wilderness until June 1, 1982.

Interior Secretary James G. Watt agreed to go along with the six-month moratorium, thereby avoiding an immediate confrontation with the House committee, which opposed leasing in wilderness areas except as a last resort.

The delay was requested so that Congress could have adequate time to weigh legislation to protect wilderness areas from such leasing.

The committee resolution was prompted by concern over the leasing of 700 acres in New Mexico's Capitan Mountain Wilderness area, an action taken by the Interior Department without conducting environmental studies or notifying Congress.

The Moratorium Request

The Nov. 20 vote showed the committee had little confidence in a Nov. 19 promise by Watt not to issue wilderness-area leases until environmental studies had been completed and Congress and the public notified.

Watt announced the new policy following a meeting with ranking Interior Committee Republican Manuel Lujan Jr., R-N.M., and panel members Dick Cheney, R-Wyo., and Don Young, R-Alaska. The meeting was called after Lujan introduced a resolution that would have prevented Watt from issuing oil and gas leases on the 23.4 million acres of wilderness in the lower 48 states.

Montana Wilderness Test

Earlier in the year, the panel voted May 21 to order Watt to close three popular Montana wilderness areas to oil and gas drilling.

The secretary reluctantly bowed to the committee's wishes and complied a month later. But the Mountain States Legal Foundation, the conservative group Watt headed before taking the Interior post, filed suit challenging the constitutionality of the action and the legislative provision on which it was based.

The committee's resolution was based on a little-used provision of the Federal Land Policy and Management Act of 1976 (FLPMA — PL 94-579). The act allowed the secretary to order the immediate withdrawal of specific land if either the secretary or the House Interior or Senate Energy committees determined that an emergency existed requiring the land to be protected from development. At the time the 1976 law was being considered, the attorney general said the provision might be unconstitutional. *(FLPMA, Congress and the Nation Vol. IV, p. 314)*

The provision was used by the committee once before, when it voted in 1979 to protect water wells in Ventura, Calif., from uranium mine tailings. In addition, former Interior Secretary Cecil D. Andrus used it Nov. 16, 1978, to withdraw 110 million acres of Alaskan land after the 95th Congress failed to pass legislation to protect them. *(Alaska withdrawals, 1978 Almanac p. 741)*

Justice Department Balks

In an August 6 letter to House Speaker Thomas P. O'Neill Jr., D-Mass., Attorney General William French Smith said the Justice Department would not defend the land withdrawal.

Instead, Smith said the department would side with the plaintiffs in challenging the constitutionality of the FLPMA provision used by the House committee to order the closing.

The provision, Smith said, amounted to a one-house veto of the sort the Justice Department had consistently opposed as an intrusion into powers of the executive branch.

Both the House and the Senate subsequently appointed legal counsel to defend the committee's action.

The First Confrontation

The May 21 vote was the first major confrontation between the Democratic-dominated Interior Committee and Watt, who wanted to open up more federal lands to oil and mineral development.

"It's a test vote," committee Chairman Morris K. Udall, D-Ariz., said of the 23-18 vote. "It shows there is strong support for wilderness and the idea of conservation."

Pat Williams, D-Mont., who introduced the resolution to withdraw the wilderness from development, said he acted because "the oil companies are physically poised 20 yards from this great wilderness complex" awaiting the approval of 343 pending lease applications.

Public Lands Subcommittee Chairman John F. Seiberling, D-Ohio, a strong wilderness advocate, said he hoped the committee's action would signal President Reagan that Congress should be consulted before Watt made decisions to open up public lands.

Committee Republicans questioned the constitutionality of the panel's action and claimed it would destroy the committee's credibility.

Republican Ron Marlenee, Montana's other representative on the panel, charged that the resolution was being used "as a club over Watt's head."

The only defectors among the 25 Democrats on the 42-member committee were James D. Santini, D-Nev., and Jerry Huckaby, D-La., who voted with the Republicans.

Background

Williams' resolution ordered Watt to withdraw from mineral leasing the entire 1.5 million acres of the Bob Marshall, Scapegoat and Great Bear national forest wilderness areas, all located south of the Glacier National Park in Montana. The land would be off-limits until Jan. 1, 1984, when all wilderness areas would be closed to further leasing under the 1964 Wilderness Act (PL 88-577). *(Wilderness act, Congress and the Nation Vol. I, p. 1063)*

The resolution called the popular wilderness area, which forms the headwaters of the Columbia and Missouri rivers, the "flagship of America's wilderness fleet" because of its outstanding wildlife and scenic vistas.

However, it was also located above part of the oil-rich Western Overthrust Belt, believed to contain the largest potential oil and gas reserves in the United States. When the committee acted, some 343 leasing applications from oil companies seeking to drill in the area were pending before the Department of Agriculture, which had oversight over national forests.

Proponents said the resolution was also prompted by fear that the Agriculture Department would approve a request from the Denver-based Consolidated Georex Geophysics, which wanted to detonate 5,400 separate seismic charges in and around the wilderness.

Agriculture's Forest Service made non-binding recommendations to the interior secretary on whether to allow mineral leasing in national forest areas.

An Agriculture Department official said after the vote it was uncertain whether the committee's action would in fact prohibit the seismic exploration by Consolidated Georex, because the committee's resolution ordered the land withdrawn under "all laws pertaining to mineral leasing." The department regulated seismic exploration under the 1897 Organic Administration Act, said Howard Banta, director of minerals and geology at the Agriculture Department.

A committee staffer said the question of whether seismic drilling was prohibited was unimportant because, "If an area is not available for leasing, its attractiveness for exploration is reduced." ∎

Ocean Dumping Sites

Congress June 11 approved an administration request to double the funds available in fiscal 1982 for identifying possible sites for the ocean dumping of dredged material, sewage sludge and industrial wastes.

The House cleared the bill (S 1213) for the president by voice vote. The Senate had passed it nine days earlier, on June 2.

President Reagan signed the bill into law (PL 97-16) on June 23.

The measure increased from $2 million to $4.2 million the amount authorized for carrying out Title I of the Marine Protection, Research and Sanctuaries Act (PL 92-532).

The extra funds were needed to meet a Jan. 1, 1982, deadline for phasing out ocean dumping of sewage sludge and industrial wastes. In addition, the U.S. Army Corps of Engineers had reported a growing need for ocean dumping sites for the disposal of dredged material.

Congress in 1980 voted $2 million a year for those activities in fiscal 1981 and 1982 (PL 96-572), and prohibited the dumping of industrial wastes after Dec. 31, 1981, the deadline previously set for halting sewage dumping. *(Marine Sanctuaries Act, Congress and the Nation Vol. III, p. 798; 1980 action, 1980 Almanac p. 609)*

The law directed the Environmental Protection Agency (EPA) to evaluate potential dumping sites and applications from cities or companies seeking to dump wastes in those sites.

S 1213 was reported May 15 by the Senate Environment and Public Works Committee (S Rept 97-119). A companion measure was reported by the House Merchant Marine and Fisheries Committee May 19 (HR 3319 — H Rept 97-65), but it was tabled June 11 in favor of the Senate version. ∎

Water Board Authorization

Legislation (S 1095, HR 3432) to create an independent board to coordinate national water policy was approved by committees in both the House and Senate but did not reach the floor of either chamber.

S 1095 was reported May 15 by the Senate Environment and Public Works Committee (S Rept 97-120).

In the House, HR 3432 was reported May 19 by the Public Works and Transportation Committee and July 17 by the Interior and Insular Affairs Committee and the Agriculture Committee (H Rept 97-104, Parts I, II and III).

An effort to insert the legislation into the budget reconciliation package (HR 3982) was thwarted during a House-Senate conference in late July when four Western senators raised objections. *(Reconciliation, p. 521)*

Provisions

S 1095 and HR 3432 would replace the Water Resources Council (WRC) with a national water resources board, which would include most members of the existing WRC. Both the board and its chairman would be independent of any of the water agencies. The WRC was largely under Interior's control.

Both bills would continue federal grants to states for water planning. The Senate bill would continue the water research grants currently distributed by the Office of Water Research and Technology (OWRT), but would abolish the office, as Reagan proposed.

Both measures would continue authorizations for the six regional river basin commissions which develop water management plans for river basins that cross state lines. Reagan proposed eliminating the commissions.

Reagan's budget proposed saving $111.5 million in fiscal 1981 and 1982 by eliminating the WRC, the OWRT and the river basin commissions, all of which were under Interior Department jurisdiction.

S 1095 would authorize $36.5 million a year for fiscal 1982-1985 to continue water planning and research programs, or roughly half the $71.8 million previously spent annually by the OWRT and WRC. HR 3432 would authorize $12,050,000 a year for fiscal 1982-1984 for water planning activities.

Background

The bills were designed to improve the planning and operation of federal water pollution and supply programs.

Poor coordination between federal water agencies had been blamed for the waste of billions of dollars and cited as one of the causes of an impending water crisis.

Both the WRC and OWRT were established in the mid-1960s to improve coordination of federal and state water planning and research efforts. However, the WRC had been criticized as ineffectual, largely because it lacked control over important agencies outside the Interior Department that were responsible for water supply and pollution-control projects.

The WRC, a six-member Cabinet-level panel authorized by the Water Resources Planning Act of 1965 (PL 89-80), was responsible for overseeing the distribution of federal water planning grants to states and the six river basin commissions. *(Planning act, Congress and the Nation Vol. II, p. 498)*

The OWRT, which provided grants to universities for water research, was established by the Water Resources Research Act of 1964 (PL 88-379) and the Water Research and Development Act of 1978 (PL 95-467). *(Research act, Congress and the Nation Vol. I, p. 897; 1978 act, 1978 Almanac p. 721)*

Congress vs. Watt

The bills also were part of a bipartisan movement in Congress to prevent water policy from being dominated by Interior Secretary James G. Watt.

Congress clashed repeatedly with former President Carter over who would make the final decision on water projects. Several of Watt's proposals sparked fears that the new administration also would try to dominate water policy. *(Carter policy, 1980 Almanac p. 596)*

In his fiscal 1982 budget, President Reagan proposed abolishing the WRC and giving most of its policy-making duties to the Cabinet Council on Natural Resources and the Environment, of which Watt was chairman. The Cabinet council set up a "working group on water resources" to advise the council and the president on water policy and to establish guidelines for determining which water projects should be built.

Many in Congress strongly opposed having water policy drafted by the Cabinet council or its working group, where meetings were closed to the public and there was no opportunity for Congress or the states to offer recommendations.

"I'm sure Mr. Watt is well-intentioned," said House Interior Committee Chairman Morris K. Udall, D-Ariz. "But the Cabinet council will block the Congress out until the decisions have been made."

In an effort to alleviate the fears of many on Capitol Hill, Watt said he favored congressional control of national water policy.

"The primary responsibility for developing the nation's water policy should be vested in the Congress," Watt said in a July 8 letter to Udall. He said the administration opposed establishing the independent water policy board called for by HR 3432 "because Congress might lose its control."

Budget Reconciliation

Both the Senate and House versions of the budget reconciliation bill (HR 3982 — PL 97-35) included provisions to create a new water policy board. However, conferees were unable to reach agreement on such a move and in late July, the language was dropped from the bill.

Four senators objected to attaching S 1095 to the reconciliation measure. They were Energy Committee Chairman James A. McClure, R-Idaho, William L. Armstrong, R-Colo., Alan K. Simpson, R-Wyo., and Malcolm Wallop, R-Wyo.

Aides to the four said the senators felt that the reconciliation bill was not the proper vehicle for making a major policy decision like creating the board.

In exchange for dropping the authorization language, the four agreed not to seek or support a presidential veto if the S 1095 later passed, according to aides for Sen. James Abdnor, R-S.D.

The conferees then limited their negotiations to the differences in the House and Senate reconciliation bills.

The Senate bill provided $36 million for the new board and for water planning and research grants. The House bill provided $12.5 million for the board and planning grants.

The conferees finally agreed to provide up to $12.5 million annually in fiscal 1982-1984 for the board and water planning grants, if the authorizing legislation passed. In addition, $23.65 million would be provided annually in fiscal 1982-1984 for water research activities administered by the Interior Department.

Senate Bill: S 1095

S 1095 was approved May 13 and reported May 15 by the Environment and Public Works Committee (S Rept 97-120).

It would establish a new five-member National Board of Water Policy to replace the WRC. The new board would be independent of the Interior Department and would report directly to the president and Congress. The board could act by majority vote, rather than the unanimous decision required of the WRC.

Sen. James Abdnor, R-S.D., chairman of the Senate Environment and Public Works Committee's Water Resources Subcommittee, said S 1095 was a start towards a "strong, comprehensive water policy for this nation."

Although witnesses at three subcommittee hearings in April agreed that the WRC and OWRT had failed to carry out their mandates, the committee decided Reagan's proposal to abolish them completely was "too precipitous."

Senators also were reluctant to give the Interior Department sole power over national water policy, traditionally carried out by a variety of federal agencies ranging from the Environmental Protection Agency (EPA) to the U.S. Army Corps of Engineers.

The proposed policy board would be composed of the secretaries of the Army, Interior and Agriculture Departments and the administrator of the EPA, with an independent chairman appointed by the president and confirmed by the Senate. In selecting a chairman, the president would give preference to persons not employed by one of the four federal water agencies within the five years prior to the appointment.

"I believe it is essential that Congress be involved in the development of national water policy," Abdnor said in a May 4 Senate speech. "An independent chairman is more likely to ensure that involvement."

The board would be advised on national water problems by a five-member state advisory committee composed of persons recommended by the National Governors Association. The bill authorized $50,000 annually for that panel.

Within the Interior Department, the bill would authorize $3 million a year for an Office of Water Programs to

oversee Interior Department water projects and prepare periodic assessments of national water needs. The office would administer the state water planning grants formerly handled by the WRC and the operation of the river basin commissions — which would be retained under the bill. It also would dispense the research grants formerly handed out by the OWRT.

S 1095 would authorize $32.5 million annually in fiscal 1982 and 1983 to continue planning and research grants. But those grants would be distributed on a competitive basis after 1983, and only $15 million would be available per year in fiscal 1984 and 1985.

The bill also authorized $12 million a year in fiscal 1982-1985 for additional water research activities by institutes, private firms or river basin commissions.

All of the grants would be distributed on a 50-50 matching basis, except that universities willing to pay a higher share would have preference for the competitive grants. The federal government could pick up the tab for 100 percent of the cost of essential "high risk" water research if no state, university or corporation were willing to pay matching funds.

House Bill: HR 3432

The House Public Works and Transportation Committee reported HR 3432 May 19. It was also referred to the Agriculture and Interior Committees, which reported it July 17.

HR 3432 was similar to S 1095, but called for seven members, rather than five, on the national water policy board. The two extra members would be appointed by the president from persons nominated by the House and Senate. Also, the state advisory board in HR 3432 would consist of 21 members.

The House bill required that recommendations and plans adopted by the national board and the states stress coordination of federal and state water pollution and water supply programs, and coordinate ground and surface water programs. S 1095 was silent on those issues.

The House bill also directed the national board to develop regulations for evaluating the costs and benefits of proposed water projects. The rules could be vetoed by one house of Congress within 60 days after promulgation.

House Interior Committee Changes

Before approving HR 3432 July 15, the House Interior Committee voted to create a 21-member blue-ribbon commission — including 12 members of Congress — to advise the president and Congress on what kind of water policy the country should have.

The proposed Commission on Federal Water Policy, which also would include four Cabinet-level members and five members appointed by the president, would have one year to publish its water policy recommendations and then would disband.

The commission would operate separately from the water policy board, which would coordinate often-conflicting federal water programs, develop guidelines for evaluating water projects and disburse water planning grants to states.

Congressional Participation

The other versions of HR 3432 did not include the Interior Committee provision for a congressionally dominated water commission but left development of water policy to the proposed national water resources board.

Interior Committee members argued that without congressional participation and sponsorship, the board's recommendations would be largely ignored, as were numerous studies by earlier water policy commissions.

"Those previous commissions never had this combination of representatives from Congress and the executive branch," said Rep. Don H. Clausen, R-Calif., ranking minority member of the Interior Committee.

Rep. Charles Pashayan Jr., R-Calif., author of the amendment, said, "We want Congress involved in the planning process. I see no better way than to have members sit on the commission." ∎

Water Projects Scrapped

The Senate Dec. 16 cleared for the president a bill (S 1493) to deauthorize some $2 billion worth of water projects, including half of the controversial Dickey-Lincoln Dam in northern Maine. The measure was signed into law Dec. 29 (PL 97-128).

The 13 projects deauthorized by the measure represented only a modest portion of the $58.6 billion backlog of water projects authorized by past Congresses.

S 1493 was approved Oct. 20 and reported Nov. 12 by the Senate Environment and Public Works Committee (S Rept 97-270). The Senate passed the bill Nov. 18.

The House Nov. 23 amended the measure to allow houseboats, cabins and docks located on Army Corps of Engineers lake-front property to remain until Dec. 31, 1989. The corps had been trying to force owners of such structures to remove them. The Senate concurred in the amendments Dec. 16. ∎

Water Problems Have Long History

Management problems in water programs and the lack of coordination among federal water agencies were studied since 1908.

At that time, the Inland Waterways Commission in the administration of Theodore Roosevelt recommended coordinating all federal agencies involved in building waterways. A National Waterways Commission was authorized by Congress to coordinate the various water-related departments, but its members never were appointed, and in 1920 the authorization was repealed.

Since then there had been dozens of studies, commissions and reports, all calling for a unified national water policy. None prompted congressional action, mostly because states feared federal encroachment upon their water rights, and Congress resisted turning over water planning to the executive branch.

Then, in 1961 the Senate Select Committee on Water Resources made five broad recommendations calling for:

● Comprehensive management plans for all the nation's river basins.

- Increased state involvement in water planning.
- Periodic assessment of regional water supplies.
- More federal water research.
- More federal emphasis on conservation.

Although the committee made no legislative proposals, most of its suggestions later were incorporated into two laws — the Water Resources Research Act of 1964 (PL 88-379) and the Water Resources Planning Act of 1965 (PL 89-80). *(Research act, Congress and the Nation Vol. I, p. 897; Planning act, Congress and the Nation Vol. II, 498)*

The laws were touted as the long-sought answer to the coordination problem. Sponsors said they would put an end to the fragmented, project-oriented approach to water planning.

In signing the 1965 act, President Lyndon B. Johnson said, "The day is past when the nation can afford to listen to, or laugh smugly with, those who have gone about slandering our water resources projects as pork barrel and boondoggle."

But the acts failed to achieve that goal. The nation's water program continued to be criticized by environmentalists as being riddled with economically unjustifiable projects built at the behest of politically powerful constituents or members of Congress.

The 1964 law set up an Office of Water Research and Technology, which provided grants to universities to develop better water conservation methods.

The 1965 act established the Water Resources Council (WRC), which was to be the focal point for national water planning. It was to encourage conservation and coordinate water quantity and quality programs. The law also established six river basin commissions to manage rivers on a regional basis.

But the council and the river basin commissions proved ineffective largely because neither had authority to enforce planning efforts. The WRC was unable to coordinate quantity and quality programs, mostly because it could not control the two most powerful water agencies — the Army Corps of Engineers and the Environmental Protection Agency. In addition, the council was chaired by the secretary of the interior, whose agency concentrated on Western water issues. That led states and other federal agencies to distrust the council's objectivity.

President Carter tried unsuccessfully to establish a national water policy and to strengthen the WRC. The plan sparked a bitter confrontation between Carter and Congress, which refused to relinquish water policy-making to the executive branch. *(Background, 1977 Almanac p. 650)*

As a result of the standoff between Carter and Congress, no water project authorization bill was enacted during his administration. ∎

Federal Noise Controls

The Senate and House faced a conference early in 1982 over differing versions of a bill to retain federal authority to regulate certain types of noise.

The House passed its version of the legislation (HR 3071 — H Rept 97-85) Dec. 16 by voice vote under suspension of the rules. The Senate had passed its version (S 1204) July 14.

Both houses decided to continue some form of federal noise control program, even though President Reagan had asked that it be phased out by 1982.

The major difference between the two bills was that the House measure retained federal regulations controlling noise from railroads, trucks and motorcycles. The Senate bill made the regulatory system largely discretionary, and it did not continue federal control over motorcycle noise.

Although the Noise Control Act (PL 92-574) was enacted in 1972, only a few products had been regulated under it — railroads, motor carriers, truck-mounted garbage compactors, air compressors and motorcycles. *(Noise Act, 1972 Almanac p. 979)*

Under S 1204, states and cities could issue their own noise standards for all except trucks and railroads, over which the Environmental Protection Agency (EPA) would retain regulatory discretion.

The bill also authorized $3.3 million for the noise control program in fiscal 1982, $1 million more than the administration wanted but $10 million less than the 1981 appropriation.

The extra $1 million was taken from EPA's toxic substances control budget and was earmarked to continue two programs Reagan had sought to eliminate — the "Each Community Helps Others" (ECHO) and "Buy Quiet" programs.

ECHO helped local officials with successful noise control programs to share their expertise with other localities. In the "Buy Quiet" program, participating state and local governments agreed to include noise limits in the specifications for products they purchased.

HR 3071, reported by the House Energy and Commerce Committee May 19 (H Rept 97-85), would authorize $7.3 million annually for the program for fiscal 1982 and 1983.

Reagan Proposal

During his 1980 presidential campaign, Reagan repeatedly promised to abolish regulations that were hampering U.S. businesses, or to turn their enforcement over to the states. One of his first such actions was a March 10 budget proposal to phase out the EPA's federal noise control program by 1982.

Under Reagan's plan, federal regulations issued under the 1972 law would be left on the books, but there would be no money for federal enforcement.

The Reagan proposal produced a flurry of opposition from manufacturers of railroad and trucking equipment, who lobbied Republicans in Congress to retain the federal rules for trucks and trains. Without them, the manufacturers argued, carriers could be subject to noise standards that could vary from state to state and city to city.

A similar argument was offered in the Senate by Robert W. Kasten Jr., R-Wis., and William Proxmire, D-Wis., on behalf of the motorcycle industry. But their amendment to retain federal noise standards for motorcycle manufacturers was rejected, 40-55. *(Vote 186, p. 34-S)*

House Committee Action

Action on the noise control reauthorization began in the House, where the Commerce, Transportation and Tourism Subcommittee of the Energy and Commerce Committee on April 1 decided to give Reagan what he asked for — and then some.

The panel approved the bill (HR 3071) to repeal the federal noise regulations. If EPA's noise control office was to be abolished, so should the regulations it was set up to administer, said Chairman James J. Florio, D-N.J.

"Our bill is in response to the needs for fiscal restraint," said Florio, his tongue tucked firmly in cheek.

Florio's bill would have authorized only $4.1 million per year — a 70 percent reduction from fiscal 1981 funding levels — for fiscal 1982 and 1983.

Industry Rallies

As soon as they learned of the subcommittee action, the railroad and trucking industries began scrambling to save the federal noise control standards.

Industry lobbyists first went to the administration, which refused to back down from its proposal. Then they turned to Republicans on the Energy and Commerce Committee, beseeching them to restore the regulations.

Their pleas found a sympathetic audience. When HR 3071 was taken up by the full committee May 12, the Republicans were ready with a substitute.

This measure, introduced by Norman F. Lent, R-N.Y., retained the federal noise standards for interstate railroads and motor carriers, and for motorcycle manufacturers.

It also provided $7.3 million annually for fiscal 1982 and 1983 for EPA's noise program — $3.2 million more than the Florio bill, and more than triple the $2.3 million Reagan sought for fiscal 1982.

"It's only logical and economic that there be a single uniform federal standard nationwide," said Lent. "There would be great confusion and chaos if carriers were subjected to a variety of standards."

Florio and his fellow Democrats said not a word in protest as the committee reported the Lent substitute by voice vote.

Senate Action

The Republican-dominated Senate Environment and Public Works Committee took a different tack.

On May 15, it reported a bill that eliminated all federal noise regulations except those for railroads and interstate motor carriers, which become discretionary (S 1204 — S Rept 97-110).

Under the bill, the EPA administrator could decide to keep the existing railroad and motor carrier regulations, eliminate them or make them stricter. If the federal standards were retained, they would pre-empt local and state regulations governing those vehicles.

When S 1204 reached the Senate floor, most of the debate centered on the amendment by Proxmire and Kasten to retain federal controls over motorcycle noise.

The two Wisconsin senators said abolishing the 1980 federal regulation on motorcycle noise would be "devastating" to the Harley-Davidson Motorcycle Co., America's last remaining motorcycle manufacturer, which is located in their home state.

"This [amendment] is so that the manufacturer will not be manufacturing essentially in 50 different ways for 50 different states," said Kasten, noting that the House bill (HR 3071) on noise control retained federal standards for motorcycles for this very reason.

He said states or cities could still adopt laws governing the time, place and manner of motorcycle use.

Thunder on the Road

Opponents led by Slade Gorton, R-Wash., argued that motorcycles did not travel interstate as much as trains and trucks. Thus, they said, motorcycles should be treated the same as power boats and snowmobiles, which would be regulated by state and local governments.

"There is simply no reason," Gorton said, "to exempt from complete state regulation a . . . consumer item which probably annoys more people than any other single one."

He said the Kasten amendment would do precisely that "on behalf of one manufacturer, whose current advertising slogan is 'Make your own thunder.'"

Others disputed Kasten's claim that continued federal regulation would cost nothing because motorcycle manufacturers certified that their products met the standards.

"Self-certification is not self-supporting," said Robert T. Stafford, R-Vt., chairman of the Environment and Public Works Committee. He predicted it would cost $250,000 for the EPA to continue enforcing federal motorcycle noise controls. ∎

Toxic Substances Control

Congress Dec. 16 cleared for the president a bill (S 1211 — PL 97-129) to extend the Toxic Substances Control Act for two years.

The measure provided $60.1 million for fiscal 1982 and $63.5 million for fiscal 1983 — the funding requested by President Reagan in his March 1981 budget, but $7.2 million more than Reagan wanted in his revised budget of September.

Some $1.5 million of the total was earmarked each of those years for grants to states for toxic substances control programs.

The bill made no substantive changes in the Toxic Substances Control Act (TSCA — PL 94-469), which required pre-marketing testing of chemicals to be sure that they were safe. *(TSCA background, 1976 Almanac p. 120)*

Conferees reached agreement on S 1211 Dec. 10 (H Rept 97-373).

The House had suspended the rules and passed it Sept. 29 after amending the measure to conform with its own version, HR 3495.

HR 3495 was ordered reported by the House Energy and Commerce Committee May 12 (H Rept 97-86).

The Senate passed its version of the bill (S 1211) on June 2.

As reported May 15 by the Environment and Public Works Committee (S Rept 97-117), it authorized $59,646,000 for implementation of TSCA during fiscal 1982 — $500,000 less than President Reagan requested. The $500,000 was earmarked instead for the Council on Environmental Quality (CEQ), for which the president had recommended a 72 percent budget cut. *(CEQ, p. 531)* ∎

Pollution Research Funds

Despite the concerns voiced by some members, the House July 27 suspended the rules and passed a bill cutting pollution research funds by 18 percent. A similar measure was pending in the Senate at year's end.

The bill (HR 3115 — H Rept 97-93) authorized $306.2 million for fiscal 1982 for research at the Environmental Protection Agency (EPA). The total was the amount sought by President Reagan in his March budget request, but it was $68.8 million less than the $375 million authorized in fiscal 1981. *(1980 Almanac p. 603)*

HR 3115 also slashed by one-third the amount that had been authorized in fiscal 1981 for research on the environmental effects of developing synthetic fuels and burning more coal.

The president June 8 asked that Congress rescind $56.3 million in EPA's 1981 research funds, but there was no action on that request.

Rep. George E. Brown Jr., D-Calif., who filed a dissenting view in the House committee report on HR 3115, charged during floor debate that it was "irresponsible" to cut EPA research funds at a time when environmental regulations were under fire by industry.

"It is the very lack of an adequate data base that opponents of responsible regulation use to justify elimination of [environmental] standards and regulations," said Brown.

As passed by the House, HR 3115 provided $9 million for research on acid rain, $2 million more than the $7 million appropriated in fiscal 1981, and it authorized a study on how environmental research could be better coordinated.

The measure also prohibited the use of any funds authorized in the bill to release radioactive waters into Pennsylvania's Susquehanna River from the damaged nuclear reactor at Three Mile Island. Residents near the reactor feared the government might propose such a plan.

The House Science and Technology Committee reported the measure May 19.

The Senate Environment and Public Works Committee May 15 reported a similar bill (S 1205 — S Rept 97-111) to provide $305.2 million for fiscal 1982 for environmental research. The full Senate was expected to act on that measure within the first few weeks of the 1982 session. ∎

CEQ Funding Reductions

Congress failed to complete action on a three-year reauthorization for the Council on Environmental Quality (CEQ) that slashed its fiscal 1982 budget by almost three-quarters.

The House Sept. 22 suspended the rules and passed its bill (HR 1953) by a margin of 360-42. *(Vote 202, p. 68-H)*

The Senate's $44,000 version of the bill (S 1210), as amended, was then substituted for the House measure, but it went no further.

The measure was considered to have a low priority because most funding for the council already was authorized in other legislation .

The council, a three-member Cabinet-level panel, advised the president on environmental issues, monitored compliance with the National Environmental Policy Act (NEPA — PL 91-190) and issued an annual report on the state of the environment. *(NEPA, Congress and the Nation Vol. III, p. 748)*

Funding Cutback

As approved by the House, the bill provided just $44,000 in fiscal year 1982 and such sums as might be necessary for fiscal 1983-84.

The authorization dealt only with funds authorized under the Water and Environmental Quality Improvement Act of 1970 (PL 91-224). It did not include $1 million automatically authorized each year under NEPA, which brought the CEQ total to $1,044,000. *(Background, Congress and the Nation Vol. III, p. 765)*

The combined funding total authorized for the CEQ in fiscal 1982 represented a 72 percent cut from the agency's

$3.6 million budget and was the level requested by President Reagan.

The version of HR 1953 originally reported by the House Merchant Marine and Fisheries Committee on May 18 (H Rept 97-49) provided $500,000 annually for the CEQ under the environmental quality improvement law. But panel members later revised the total downward to the $44,000 per year recommended by Reagan and included in the HUD-independent agencies appropriations bill for fiscal 1982.

Administration Reversal

The administration originally sought $1,044,000 for CEQ under PL 91-224, which would have produced a total of $2,044,000 when the NEPA authorization was added.

But the Office of Management and Budget had overlooked the NEPA reauthorization, and later told Congress it had intended CEQ's total authorization under the two acts to be only $1,044,000.

The Senate Environment and Public Works Committee initially refused to cut as much as President Reagan wanted from the CEQ budget.

The panel May 15 reported one-year reauthorization (S 1210 — S Rept 97-116) providing $1,544,000 for the CEQ under the environmental quality law. The extra $500,000 was taken from funds earmarked to carry out a federal program requiring pre-manufacture testing of new chemicals.

Combined with the continuing $1 million NEPA authorization, this would have given the council a $2.5 million authorization for fiscal 1982. ∎

Florida Wilderness Measure

The House Dec. 15 passed a bill to designate as wilderness 49,150 acres in three Florida national forests and to resolve a longstanding dispute over phosphate mining in the Osceola National Forest.

The measure (HR 9), passed under suspension of the rules, was reported Dec. 11 (H Rept 97-402, Part 1) by the Committee on Interior and Insular Affairs. The House Agriculture Committee, to which HR 9 was also referred, took no action.

HR 9 was one of several bills resulting from the Interior Committee's review of 600 national forest wilderness recommendations made to Congress by the Carter administration. *(1979 Almanac p. 688)*

Carter proposed that a total of 55,000 acres in Florida be designated for wilderness.

Phosphate Mining

Besides designating the seven wilderness areas in the Osceola, Ocala and Apalachicola national forests, HR 9 would ban phosphate mining in the Osceola.

At the time the bill was under consideration, four companies had filed 41 lease applications to mine on 52,000 acres — about a third of the entire Osceola National Forest. The state opposed such mining because of fears that it would impair recreational and wildlife values of the forest.

Legislation was introduced in the last three Congresses to ban phosphate mining in the Osceola.

Rep. John F. Seiberling, D-Ohio, chairman of the Interior Committee's Public Lands Subcommittee, said that since the development of land reclamation techniques was

still in its infancy, allowing mining in the Osceola would be using the forest as a "guinea pig" for perfecting that technology.

Under HR 9, leases would be banned unless the president determined that mining was necessary for the national security. Congress would then have 90 days to block such action by approving a concurrent resolution.

HR 9 would give the Interior secretary a year to determine the fair market value of the leases and then three years to acquire the rights to the leases.

A similar bill (S 1873) was pending before the Senate Energy and Natural Resources Committee, as were two other measures (S 1633, S 1138) dealing only with the ban on phosphate mining. No hearings were held in 1981. ∎

Bandon Marsh, Ohio Falls

Congress cleared a bill (HR 2241 — PL 97-137) establishing a national wildlife refuge at Bandon Marsh in Coos County, Ore., and a national wildlife conservation area at the falls of the Ohio River near Louisville, Ky.

Final action came when the Senate passed the measure by voice vote Dec. 16. The House had suspended the rules and done likewise Dec. 15.

As cleared, HR 2241 designated as a wildlife refuge Bandon Marsh, a salt marsh of about 300 acres on the Coquille River estuary along the coast of southern Oregon. The refuge was established to protect numerous migratory waterfowl, shorebirds and fish, including Chinook and silver salmon dependent on the marsh.

The bill authorized expenditures of $270,000 in fiscal 1983 for the acquisition of land for the Bandon Marsh refuge.

Falls of the Ohio

HR 2241 also directed the secretary of interior to designate as a wildlife conservation area about 1,000 acres of land and water around the falls of the Ohio River near Louisville.

The site is not only rich in wildlife but also contains a 300-million-year-old fossilized coral reef which had been studied by geologists and other scientists for more than a century.

Under the bill, the U.S. Army Corps of Engineers — which already managed the McAlpine locks and dam system on part of the site — would be responsible for management of the area, in consultation with the Interior Department.

The measure authorized expenditures of $300,000 in fiscal 1983. ∎

Agriculture

Ronald Reagan's first year as president brought stormy debates in Congress over his insistence on low-cost farm programs and major reductions in lending programs for farmers and rural communities.

Reagan's appointments, his massive tax and budget bills, his deregulation policies and his cancellation of the unpopular embargo on the sale of grain to the Soviet Union generally pleased the agricultural community. *(Embargo, p. 548)*

Still, the "profits" Reagan had promised farmers during his 1980 presidential campaign continued to be elusive.

Reagan had told farmers that during Jimmy Carter's presidency, net farm income dropped to "the lowest level since the. . . depths of the Great Depression."

Yet as Reagan's first year came to an end, the Agriculture Department predicted that net farm income would slide below the level of Carter's last full year in office. Before adjustments for the value of unsold commodities, net farm income for 1981 was expected to total $19 billion, some $2.9 billion less than the 1980 total, according to department forecasts.

That made 1981 the third consecutive year that U.S. farmers' income declined below the previous year's level. Parity, the decades-old measure of farmers' purchasing power, stood at 56 percent in December, perilously close to the all-time low of 53 percent in June, 1932. (One-hundred percent of parity would give farmers the same purchasing power they had had during the prosperous 1910-1914 period.)

Parity, however, was an imperfect measure because it did not reflect major gains in farm productivity since the depression. Nor did net farm income figures reflect the greatly reduced number of farmers among whom the total was divided.

Income per farm for 1981 was expected to average approximately $24,000, nearly $1,000 less than 1979. Of the 1981 figure, only $7,950 was earned on the farm, with the remainder gleaned from outside jobs and other non-farm sources of income.

Production Costs Increased

As in earlier years, farmers found that market prices for their commodities rose less rapidly than the prices they had to pay for fertilizer, credit, machinery and similar items.

Their cash expenses and total production costs increased about 9 percent in 1981, compared to a 5 percent increase in cash receipts. Interest rates reached record highs in August — 20 percent for commercial loans in some regions.

The Farmers Home Administration reported a sharp upsurge in delinquencies on farm loans. Private lenders voiced worries that unless farm income improved signficantly, they too might have trouble collecting on their loans in 1982.

Farm Price Depressants

The chronic imbalance between market prices and farm expenses was worsened by several developments during the year.

Bumper crops, particularly in wheat and corn, depressed prices; crop production was up 14 percent.

Foreign sales of U.S. farm commodities hit a record high of $43.5 billion, but gloomy farm leaders said the total should should have been even higher and did not adequately offset low prices to individual farmers. A stronger U.S. dollar and inflation abroad had eroded the purchasing power of foreign buyers.

At the same time, Australia, Argentina and other U.S. agricultural competitors had increased their production and taken a larger share of the market during the 15 months of Carter's grain embargo.

Yet another depressant on farm prices was administration talk, at the end of the year, of new economic reprisals against the Soviet Union if that nation intervened in the troubled political situation in Poland.

Reagan had pledged to promote farm exports, and administration officials announced Oct. 1 that they had extended the expired U.S.— U.S.S.R grain agreement for one year.

The extension nearly tripled the quantity of U.S wheat and corn that the Russians would be permitted to buy to 23 million metric tons. By the year's end, however, Soviet purchasers had committed themselves to just about half that amount, and they were not expected to buy much more. The Russian buyers ordered American grain only after they had bought as much as they could from other suppliers.

Reagan's cancellation of the grain embargo was one of a number of moves that filled campaign pledges and pleased farmers. He also kept his promise to rid the Agriculture Department of "activists," an apparent reference to Carter's controversial appointments from consumer and environmental groups.

Bureaucratic Changes

Reagan's choice of an Illinois hog farmer, John R. Block, as Secretary of Agriculture, was popular. Block's chief deputy, Richard E. Lyng, was former president of the American Meat Institute; his assistant secretary for marketing and transportation services, C. W. McMillan, had been a vice president of the National Cattlemen's Association; his assistant secretary for natural resources and environment, John B. Crowell, had been chief officer for Louisiana-Pacific Corp., a major forest product company.

Other top department slots went to congressional aides such as William G. Lesher, chief department economist, and Mary Jarratt, assistant secretary for food and consumer services. Jarratt's low-key approach contrasted markedly with that of her combative predecessor Carol Tucker Foreman, who had once led the Consumer Feder-

ation of America.

Block split or combined a number of department agencies and functions in June, and in the process, Carter's special offices for environmental quality and human nutrition disappeared.

Critics complained that those issues would get little attention without the visibility that the special offices had provided. But Block declared that the functions of the offices would be redistributed to the appropriate departmental agencies, thus assuring efficiency.

The department, having distributed some 7 million copies of its controversial 1980 pamphlet *Dietary Guidelines*, decided not to pay for more reprints. Budget pressures dictated the move, a department spokesman said. The pamphlet had offended egg, meat and dairy producers.

On another front, the Interior Department under Secretary James G. Watt did not enforce new regulations that would have severely limited the size of farms that could benefit from federally subsidized irrigation projects. Some owners of massive Western farms that depended on cheap federal water said the new rules, derived from a 1902 act, were out of step with modern agriculture. Watt pushed Congress to step in with a new statute, but the issue was not resolved by the end of the year.

Regulations Scrutinized

As part of Reagan's government wide review of regulations, about a half-dozen Agriculture Department rules came under scrutiny.

Standards for grading beef and labeling processed meat that included pulverized bone fragments were changed in accord with the wishes of producer groups.

The most controversial review, of marketing orders for fruits and vegetables, was not completed during the year. Farm groups defending the rules said that they assured consumer quality while permitting farmers to share the costs of promoting their produce.

But Reagan's Office of Management and Budget was exerting strong pressures against the use of such orders to control prices by restricting the volume of a crop that could come to the market.

Reagan's landmark tax bill included rate reductions and liberalized depreciation allowances that were expected to benefit farmers.

Its provisions permitted tax-free transfer of farm assets between spouses, by gift or by will, and thus ended the so-called "widow's tax" that had been a sore point in the farm community.

The new law also eased transfer of farms within families by tripling the value of gifts that could be made without tax penalties and by revising rules for determining the value of farmland for calculating estate taxes. *(Tax bill, p. 91)*

Congress did not act on another legislative goal of farmers, to provide special treatment under federal bankruptcy laws for producers affected by failures of grain elevators or other farm storage facilities.

The Senate added the bankruptcy exemptions to the omnibus farm bill (S 884), but House and Senate conferees dropped them because of objections from House Judiciary Committee Chairman Peter W. Rodino Jr., D-N.J.

—By Elizabeth Wehr

New Farm Bill Clears by Two-Vote Margin

Just before adjournment Dec. 16, a reluctant House by a two-vote margin cleared the four-year farm bill (S 884 — PL 97-98) the administration wanted.

Conflicting demands from a divided farm community, the Reagan administration, consumer advocates and food processors had kept the outcome in doubt until the final 205-203 vote adopting the $11 billion conference agreement (H Rept 97-377; S Rept 97-290). *(Vote 351, p. 114-H)*

President Reagan signed the measure Dec. 22. The Senate had adopted it by a vote of 68-31 on Dec. 10. *(Vote 453, p. 74-S)*

The final bill renewed basic food and farm programs for four years, replacing the 1977 law (PL 95-113) that had expired Sept. 30. *(1977 Almanac, p. 417)*

The House action on the Agriculture and Food Act of 1981 capped a long and painful process. It was the first year that legislators had to craft farm programs to fit within a total dollar amount specified by the budget. That constraint forced commodity groups to compete directly for shares of a smaller federal pie and shattered their vote-trading relationships.

At critical points during the year, many farm-state members abandoned their log-rolling habits and voted against programs — such as dairy or sugar or peanuts — that were of minimal interest to their own constituents.

The resentment spawned by those votes meant that there was rarely a smoothly functioning coalition to move the farm bill along. Nor was there a united farm front against administration pressures to keep spending levels down.

Stirring up the long-standing rivalries within the farm coalition was a deliberate administration tactic, according to budget director David A. Stockman. It enabled Reagan to block what he viewed as budget-busting farm demands.

The well-financed dairy lobby was isolated early in the year when Reagan persuaded Congress to cancel a scheduled price support increase. *(Dairy support, p. 550)*

Later, when the administration dropped its objections to peanut and sugar programs in vote-bargaining for its budget and tax legislation votes, other commodity groups were displeased.

Other sources of pressure on farm groups during the year were record high interest rates and sagging commodity prices caused by bumper crops and rumors of renewed economic sanctions against the Soviet Union.

The Republican Senate reluctantly complied with Reagan's demands for price support increases that were less generous than the commodity groups wanted. House farm interests shepherded a far more costly bill all the way to conference, and the conference itself dragged on for six weeks until House members bowed to administration pressures for cost reductions.

The House and Senate positions reversed the well-established pattern of Senators being more generous to farmers than urban and suburban House members.

Total outlays for farm programs in the final version of S 884 were estimated at about $11 billion for the life of the bill, according to Agriculture Department officials. That compared with a $16.6 billion estimate for the version passed by the House and $10.6 billion for the Senate bill.

The $8.65 billion conference subtotal for commodity programs was about $400 million more than the Senate-passed level.

Major Changes

The agreement generally continued the price support, research, Food for Peace and other farm programs. It included an $11.3 billion one-year extension of the food stamp program. *(Box, p. 537; food stamps, p. 466)*

Except for the dairy program, whose minimum support level was significantly reduced from existing law, the final agreement increased major crop price supports, but it did not permit those supports to rise as rapidly in future years as many farmers wanted.

It also made substantial changes in the tightly regulated peanut program and created a new sugar price support program.

The bill set minimum support levels for dairymen in dollars instead of linking them to a parity index as in the past. That controversial inflation index would come into play only if government purchases of dairy products, as required by law, exceeded certain levels.

The bitterness within the House was reflected by the unusual action of two Agriculture subcommittee chairmen in urging members to vote against a farm bill. Ed Jones, D-Tenn., and Tom Harkin, D-Iowa, respective chairmen of the Conservation, Credit and Rural Development, and Livestock, Dairy and Poultry subcommittees, argued that farmers needed more help from the government.

Moreover, seven House conferees, including Majority Whip and former Agriculture Committee Chairman Thomas S. Foley, D-Wash., refused to approve the compromise in conference. Foley objected to the grain provisions and withheld his support from the bill until two days before the final House vote.

His late decision to canvass for votes for the bill was essential to the narrow administration victory, according to Agriculture Secretary John R. Block.

Block said that another important element was the realization that the alternatives to S 884 would be much worse for farmers.

Administration lobbyists argued that if congress failed in 1981 to replace the expired 1977 act, farmers would get even less in 1982 because tighter budget constraints were sure to be in force. The other alternative, allowing the permanent farm statutes dating from 1938 and 1949 to take effect, would be too costly for the government and too confusing for farmers, according to the administration.

House Agriculture Committee Chairman E. "Kika" de la Garza, D-Texas, in an emotional speech before the final vote, said, "This [bill] is nothing but a blood transfusion." But he said nothing more for farmers could be wrung from the administration.

Provisions

As signed into law, S 884:

Dairy

● Set dairy price supports at these minimums: for fiscal 1982, the existing level of $13.10 per hundredweight; for the following three fiscal years, $13.25, $14.00 and $14.60 respectively.

However, beginning in 1983, the minimum support would be 70 percent of parity in any year in which anticipated federal purchases of dairy products, as required by the program, would be less than $1 billion. (According to

USDA estimates at the time of passage, 70 percent of parity would be $13.97 per hundredweight in fiscal 1983, $15.53 in 1984 and $17.40 in 1985.)

Or, the minimum would be 75 percent of parity if net purchases were estimated to be less than 4 billion pounds in fiscal 1983, 3.5 billion pounds in 1984 or 2.69 billion pounds in 1985.

Parity is the index comparing prices farmers pay and receive; it is meant to reflect farmers' purchasing power during the prosperous 1910-1914 period.

● Continued milk marketing authority and the indemnity program that reimbursed dairymen for milk that could not be sold because of contamination by pesticides, toxic chemicals or nuclear fallout.

● Directed the secretary, using existing authority, to reduce the volume of dairy products owned by the Commodity Credit Corporation (CCC) so that outlays for the program did not exceed dairy spending levels assumed in budget legislation.

Wool and Mohair

● Set the wool support level at 77.5 percent of a statutory formula. (The 1981 rate was 85 percent.)

Wheat, Feed Grains, Cotton, Rice

● Set commodity loans for wheat at no less than $3.55 a bushel. (The 1981 rate was $3.20.)

When the previous year's market price averaged not more than 105 percent of the loan rate, the secretary could lower the loan rate by no more than 10 percent and not below $3 per bushel.

● Set the wheat target price program minimum rate at $4.05 per bushel for the 1982 crop and $4.30, $4.45 and $4.65 respectively for the following three crop years. (The 1981 rate was $3.81.)

● Established commodity loans for feed grains at no less than $2.55 a bushel for corn. (The 1981 rate was $2.40.) Rates for barley, oats, rye and grain sorghum would be pegged to the corn rate.

In a year when the previous year's market price averaged not more than 105 percent of the loan rate, the secretary could lower the loan rate by no more than 10 percent and not below $2 per bushel.

● Established feed grain target prices at no less than $2.70 per bushel for the 1982 corn crop and $2.86, $3.03 and $3.18 respectively for the following three crop years, with rates for other grains pegged to corn. (The 1981 corn rate was $2.40.)

● **Cotton.** Set commodity loans for cotton by formulas based on market prices, with a minimum of 55 cents a pound.

● Set cotton target prices at whichever of the following was the higher price for a given year: 120 percent of the cotton loan level, or 71 cents a pound for the 1982 crop, 76 cents for 1983, 81 cents for 1984 and 86 cents for 1985.

● Reduced the loan level for extra long staple ("pima") cotton to 75 to 125 percent of upland cotton, from 85 to 135 percent, and eliminated direct payments to producers.

● **Rice.** Repealed authority for rice acreage allotments and marketing quotas, thereby making loans and other program benefits available to all rice growers.

● Established commodity loans for rice at 75 percent of the target price but no lower than $8 per hundredweight.

● Continued the rice target price program at no less than $10.85 per hundredweight for 1982, $11.40, $11.90 and $12.40 respectively for the following three crop years.

Disaster Payments

● Continued disaster payments for damage to wheat, feed grains, cotton and rice, but only for producers for whom federal crop insurance was not available; however, authorized such payments, at the discretion of the secretary, if a disaster created an economic emergency too serious to be relieved by crop insurance or other federal aid.

Production Controls

● Continued authority for wheat and feed grain set-aside and for acreage reduction programs for those crops and cotton and rice. Permitted the secretary, in years of anticipated surplus, to require participation in those programs as a condition of eligibility for price supports.

(In their report, conferees also urged the secretary to raise wheat and feed grain loan rates for farmers participating in set-aside or direct acreage reduction programs.)

● Also continued authority for wheat, feed grain, cotton, and rice paid acreage diversion but without authority to require participation.

● Canceled authority for normal crop acreage planting requirements for cotton, which restricted a producer's acreage to what he had planted in previous years.

● Barred "cross-compliance" — compliance with other commodity program restrictions — as a condition for rice price supports.

Grain Reserves

● Continued the farmer-owned reserve program for wheat and feed grains, with loan rates at not less than those for commodity loans.

● Authorized the secretary to determine the terms under which farmers could sell grain from the reserve without penalty and the terms under which the secretary could encourage such withdrawals by ending storage payments or increasing interest rates.

For the 1981 crop year, loan rates for crops in the reserve were higher than basic price support loans, and the terms under which grain could be withdrawn or forced out of the reserve were tied to market prices and were explicitly stated by law.

● Permitted the secretary to restrict the size of the reserve but specified that a wheat reserve could not be less than 700 million bushels and feed grains not less than one billion bushels.

● Barred USDA sales of federally owned grain, when a reserve was in effect, for less than 110 percent of the "release" price (the market price selected by the secretary at which farmers could sell their grain out of the reserve).

● Set interest rates for reserve loans at not less than the USDA cost of borrowing money from the Treasury, except that the secretary could adjust rates or waive interest.

Peanuts

● Repealed the peanut acreage allotment system, thus allowing farmers without the allotments to grow so-called "additional" peanuts. Additional peanuts, grown in excess of the national peanut poundage quota, could be sold abroad and could be sold for domestic use in years when domestic demand exceeded a national quota. They qualified for the lower of two federal price support loans.

● Continued the poundage quota system, setting the national quota at 1.2 million tons in 1982, down from the 1981 level of 1.4 million tons, and reducing the quota by steps to 1.1 million tons in 1985. Reductions in the quota were, to the extent feasible, to be applied to quota holders who did

Farm Income, Price Support Programs

Permanent farm law, including major statutes passed in 1938 and 1949 and the charter of the Commodity Credit Corporation (CCC), gave the federal government broad authority to increase farm income, including establishing price supports at 100 percent of parity.

Parity referred to an index that related farm income to the purchasing power of farmers during 1910-14, a time when farm earnings were unusually high. Many economists criticized the parity index because it did not accurately reflect the dramatic increases in agricultural productivity.

Beginning in the 1960s, Congress reworked many of the more complex and costly provisions of the permanent statutes, substituting an assortment of devices to bolster farm income, some optional, some mandatory, known collectively as "price supports."

Both Republicans and Democrats backed the general proposition that farm policy should expose American agriculture to market forces, while preventing massive bankruptcies. That meant relatively low price-supports.

For the most part, Congress also abandoned parity as an index for the price supports, choosing instead to link them to market prices, costs of production and similar factors.

Major forms of price supports included:

Commodity Loans. The basic mechanism to stabilize farm income was the commodity loan, whose level acted as a floor for market prices. The loans, administered by the CCC, permitted farmers to borrow from the government at a level pegged to a statutory per-bushel price of whatever crop the farmer offered as collateral. Farmers generally did not market their crops if prices fell below the loan levels; instead, they held them, or defaulted on their loans and let the government keep the crops.

A variation on the basic price-support loan was the "farmer-held reserve" program under which farmers borrowed against crops while retaining ownership and managing storage of them.

In 1980, Congress voted to give participants in the farmer-held reserve higher loan rates than those for basic commodity loans. Farmers in the reserve could not sell the stored crops for three years unless certain market conditions occurred. If a predetermined "release"

market price was reached, farmers could sell their grain and repay their loans; if a higher "call" price was reached, they had to sell. *(PL 96-494; 1980 Almanac, p. 94)*

Target Prices. To provide a supplement for farm income in years when market prices were low, Congress in 1973 added target prices to the basic loan system. Target prices, calculated on the national average cost of producing a crop, were set above the loan levels for major commodities. If market prices failed to reach the target-price level, farmers could collect "deficiency payments." *(1973 Almanac, p. 287)*

Set Asides, Disaster Payments. The government could limit production by requiring farmers to set aside — not plant — a portion of their customary acreage. In the years when the secretary announced a set aside, only the farmers participating became eligible for other farm aid programs, including commodity loans.

There were also special grants — disaster payments — for such physical problems as drought, and a newly-expanded, subsidized crop insurance plan to protect against damage from natural causes.

Miscellaneous. In addition to the price-support loans, there were loans to cover damage from physical disasters and so-called "economic emergencies." The FmHA lent money for a variety of projects broadly construed as rural development and also provided start-up financing and loans covering operating costs for farmers unable to qualify for credit elsewhere. There also was an independent system of farm lending institutions that competed successfully with private banks.

Dairy. The dairy program was still based on the parity index. Existing legislation set dairy price supports at 80 percent of parity with an adjustment every six months to reflect changes in costs.

Under the program, the government was required to purchase, in the form of butter, dried milk and cheese, all the milk that dairy farmers could not sell at a market price equivalent to the price support level. The government paid storage costs.

The dairy program was singled out for special legislation. Reagan pushed through Congress a bill (S 509) canceling a scheduled April 1 adjustment in the price support level. Reagan argued that the scheduled hike would be too costly for consumers and the government. *(Story, p. 550)*

---

not themselves produce peanuts.

(Individual farm quotas, as before, would be held only by those who had had acreage allotments; peanuts grown within the quota would be sold for domestic use and could qualify for the higher of two federal price support loans. These peanuts are referred to as "quota" or "edible" peanuts.)

● Set quota peanut price support loans at $550 a ton for the 1982 crop and additional peanut price support loans at a rate set by the secretary to recognize market conditions and to avoid net cost to the federal government.

(The loan rate in 1981 for quota peanuts was $455 a ton.)

Soybeans

● Set commodity loans at 75 percent of the national five-year average market price (omitting high and low years) but at no less than $5.02 a bushel. In a year when the previous year's market price averaged not more than 105 percent of the loan rate, the secretary could lower the loan rate by no more than 10 percent and not below $4.05 per bushel.

● Barred the secretary from making participation in any production control program a condition of eligibility for soybean loans.

● Barred storage reserve programs and payments to producers for storage of 1982-85 crops.

Sugar

• Required the secretary to support the price of sugar through duties and fees on imported sugar or other means, at 17 cents a pound for the 1982 crop and for the following three crop years, at 17.5 cents, 17.75 cents and 18 cents a pound. Also established a sugar purchase price of 16.75 cents a pound from the date of enactment to Oct. 1, 1982, when the loans would become available.

Establishing the purchase price had the effect of permitting the government to set duties and fees, thereby raising domestic sugar prices and making purchases unnecessary, according to USDA officials.

Miscellaneous

• Continued random inspection of imported meat on entry for cleanliness, quality, species verification and chemical residues; such authority had not been spelled out in statutes previously. Required also that such meat undergo random sampling and testing of internal organs and fat for chemical residues where it was slaughtered, by methods approved by the secretary.

• Expressed the sense of Congress that the tobacco program should operate at no net cost to taxpayers other than administrative expenses. Directed the secretary to determine if new authority was needed to do so and to request such authority from Congress.

• Authorized the secretary to seize, quarantine and treat crops, as well as physical premises, to eliminate infestations of plant pests, such as the Medfly, in emergencies but only if state or other efforts were inadequate. Authorized warrantless inspections of persons and vehicles moving between states that may be infested with plant pests and authorized compensation for losses caused by federal pest control activities.

• Continued existing limits on total payments so that individual farmers could receive no more than $50,000 in any year for all programs except disaster payments and no more than $100,000 in disaster payments.

• Continued the grazing and hay, and emergency feed programs, changing them from mandatory for the secretary to discretionary, and made poultry producers eligible for the feed program.

• Permitted the Federal Grain Inspection Service to transfer export grain inspection functions to state agencies that were doing such inspections at export ports before July 1, 1976, that were designated to conduct other types of grain inspection, and that had grain exports of 5 percent or less of total U.S. grain exports.

• Authorized donation to local food banks for the needy and to nutrition programs for the elderly and children, of surplus food, such as dairy products, that have been bought by federal price support programs. Only commodities not committed to sales or other programs could be donated.

• Required various studies and reports to Congress, by the secretary unless otherwise stated, on these subjects: 1) the relationship of the dairy program and federal milk marketing orders to regional availability of dairy products and self-sufficiency, within a year after enactment; 2) the feasibility of trading rice futures, by July 31, 1983; 3) the feasibility of creating and implementing a new type of farm insurance program to replace existing loan and other farm income programs, to be studied by a 13-member task force and reported 18 months after enactment; 4) the effect on U.S. agricultural exports of policies and practices of foreign governments, with recommendations for action to protect U.S. trade interests, by 180 days after enactment; 5) de-

partment methods for determining farmers' costs of production, with annual reports to Congress, to be conducted by a new board.

• Authorized a new, industry-financed research and promotion program for flower and plant producers, to be established if agreed to by a referendum among producers. Exempted producers or importers with annual sales of less than $100,000.

Export, Embargo, PL 480

• Required compensation to farmers affected by an embargo of U.S. commodity sales abroad for national security or foreign policy reasons but only if the embargo was limited to agricultural commodities and only if the affected nation bought more than 3 percent of U.S. exports of the affected commodity. Farmers would receive either or both: direct payments, based on the difference between 100 percent of parity and the average post-embargo market price of the affected commodity; commodity loans at 100 percent of parity. This was a permanent addition to farm law.

• Authorized set-aside or acreage limitation programs for 1982-85 crops, regardless of prior policy announcements, in the event of an embargo.

• Established a CCC revolving loan fund through Sept. 30, 1985, to promote export sales of commodities, with funds appropriated as needed.

• Authorized commodity export subsidies, at the discretion of the president, to offset subsidies used by other nations.

• Encouraged the president to consult congressional Agriculture committees before making bilateral agreements on exports of farm products.

• Continued the Food for Peace (PL 480) program through Dec. 31, 1985, and raised to $1 billion, from $750 million, the annual ceiling for food donations to foreign nations. Permitted the domestic distilled spirits industry to participate in the PL 480 foreign market development program on the same basis as the beer and wine industries.

Research, Extension and Teaching

• Continued various agricultural research and extension activities, also the Joint Council on Food and Agricultural Sciences and the National Agricultural Research and Extension Users Advisory Board.

• Added aquaculture, range land management, and small farm and rural development to research priorities and authorized $10 million annually through fiscal 1986 for upgrading research facilities at predominantly black land-grant colleges, including Tuskegee Institute.

• Repealed authority to develop and distribute food and nutrition educational materials for elementary and secondary schools.

Credit and Rural Development

• Continued economic emergency loans through Sept. 30, 1982, but restricted new lending in fiscal 1982 to a total of $600 million. (Conference report language stipulated that the program was discretionary for the secretary.)

• Required the secretary to make farm storage facility loans in areas with facility shortages.

• Continued for 10 years the $30-million-per-year authorization for federal purchases of capital stock in the Rural Telephone Bank.

• Made small farm production cooperatives eligible for Farmers Home Administration (FmHA) operating and

ownership loans and dropped restrictions of FmHA loans to unmarried persons.

Conservation

● Authorized a new soil conservation program for areas found by the secretary to have significant erosion problems. Farmers contracting to establish approved conservation projects could qualify for technical aid and payments for part of the cost of such projects.

● Authorized matching federal grants to local governments for conservation projects and authorized loans, to the extent provided by appropriations bills, to individual producers for conservation projects.

● Established a test program for curbing soil erosion and reducing sedimentation affecting publicly owned reservoirs.

● Permitted local soil and water conservation boards to disapprove individual farmers' choices of acreage to use to comply with set-aside or paid land diversion programs.

● Directed the secretary to develop standards for monitoring the role of federal programs in converting farm land to non-farm uses and directed federal agencies to evaluate their programs by those standards, to seek alternatives to proposals that would hasten conversion and to try to avoid conflict with state, local or private farm land protection programs.

● Authorized a test program for improving water quality in areas that have been surface-mined.

● Authorized compensation for taking land out of production and converting it to conservation use, also for promoting conservation tillage.

(For food stamp provisions, see story, p. 466)

Background

As Congress began deliberating the renewal of farm programs that had survived since the 1930s, the situation resembled that of four years ago: Farm interest groups clamored for financial relief in a troubled economy, and the new administration signaled that it wanted low spending levels. *(1977 Almanac p. 417)*

In 1977, Congress demanded substantially higher price-support levels than the new president, Jimmy Carter, wanted. Congress won after a difficult struggle that permanently soured relations between farm-state members and Carter and his Agriculture Secretary, Bob Bergland.

Reagan's Agriculture Secretary, Block, told farm leaders and their congressional allies early in 1981 that the era of subsidized low-interest farm loans was ending.

Reagan's economic message to Congress urged hefty cuts in such deeply entrenched programs as the FmHA and the Rural Electrification Administration (REA). The reductions were in line with the belief of Reagan's economic advisers that federal lending, including federal guarantees of private loans, distorted the economy. *(Text of message, p. 15-E)*

Jesse Helms, R-N.C., new chairman of the Senate Agriculture Committee, and de la Garza at first predicted that committee members and their constituencies would be willing to make do with less.

"Farmers understand that unless this inflation is cured, they don't stand a chance no matter what kind of farm bill we pass," Helms said.

However, as the extent of the revisions the president had in mind became clear, both committees rebelled. Senate Democrats and Republicans — including Helms — introduced competing bills departing markedly from key administration proposals (S 943, HR 3180).

Reagan had asked Congress to eliminate target prices, a major price support, and to drop a number of production control programs. For the basic price support loans, whose minimum levels were traditionally fixed in law, the president asked for discretion to set loan rates as supply and demand dictated.

The versions brought to the floor largely ignored those requests. Both committees chafed under the new restraints required by the budget process. *(Budget resolution, p. 247)*

At one point, the Senate draft was $1.5 billion more than the budget limits. However, last minute revisions just before the bill was reported brought the levels to from $50 million to $150 million more in fiscal 1982.

A second committee compromise accepted on the Senate floor reduced the totals even further, and before passage, a third round of administration-backed reductions in target prices and dairy price supports was adopted also.

The Farm Alliance

As Block was sounding the threat in August of a presidential veto of the developing farm bill because of budget constraints and objections to dairy and certain grain provisions, there were signs that the farm alliances were so shaky that the president's cost-cutting drive might prevail.

The atmosphere of mutual accommodation evident in the spring when the committees began marking up legislation had changed dramatically by the time the bills reached the floor in the fall.

The pressures of the budget sent farm interests scrambling to protect their shrinking shares of the federal pie. An every-man-for-himself attitude threatened years of mutual accommodation in which lobbyists and members were inclined to look after each other's interests.

"It used to be that everybody could get their piece of the pie, and if the pie was too small, they [Congress] could just make it bigger," one lobbyist explained.

In 1981, he added, "There's not enough to go around."

Sen. Robert Dole, R-Kan., remarked that farm coalitions were always unstable but that in 1981, "It's worse. It's sort of dog-eat-dog."

The peanut and tobacco programs were in particular trouble in both chambers, and the sugar price support program drew strong opposition in the House.

Part of the opposition to the tightly controlled peanut and tobacco programs was attributed to an anti-regulation mood. Both programs operated under rigid allotments and quotas that limited growing rights to a select few. Critics called the system "feudalistic."

However, part of the opposition was traced to anti-Helms sentiment. Tobacco and peanuts were critical to the economy of North Carolina. Helms had alienated many members of Congress with his outspoken views on social issues, including abortion, mandatory school busing for desegregation and what he called excessive spending on food stamps and other social programs.

Another factor, particularly in the House, was Northern Democrats' anger at the defections of conservative Southern Democrats to the Reagan budget and tax bills.

All three programs survived, but the tobacco program narrowly missed extinction in the Senate, the peanut program was modified against the wishes of peanut producers, and the sugar program came through with somewhat lower support prices than those approved in committee.

One potentially explosive issue was defused April 24 when Reagan ended the embargo of sales of U.S. grain to

Russia. Farmers had chafed under the embargo ever since it was instituted by Carter in January 1980 to express disapproval of the Soviet invasion of Afghanistan. *(1980 Almanac p. 94)*

Even without the embargo, the 1981 crops were so large that farm prices fell far short of predicted highs. Pressures built quickly for higher price supports. In September, in a move to strengthen prices, Block announced that the government would ask wheat farmers to cut back their acreage. The authority that Block proposed to use was one of the production controls that Reagan had asked Congress to cancel six months earlier.

Reagan Proposals

Block aired the basic thrust of the Reagan farm policy March 31 and April 1 at hearings of the House and Senate Agriculture committees.

He asked for broad, discretionary authority to set commodity loan levels, which generally had been fixed by law, and requested substantial changes in the farmer-held grain reserve.

Block also outlined Reagan proposals for food stamps, and asked that Congress consider the food program as part of Reagan's broad economic package, although four years ago it was included in omnibus farm legislation.

Some committee members said they would reserve judgment until they had had a chance to study a detailed proposal. But others quickly criticized features of Block's outline.

A proposal to overhaul the peanut program, for instance, caused Rep. Charlie Rose, D-N.C., to tell Block tartly, "I look forward to educating you and your staff." Rose chaired the House Agriculture Subcommiteee on Tobacco and Peanuts.

Block began his testimony with a description of the administration loan rates for 1981 crops, calculated under existing law. The modest increases he proposed pleased conservatives like the American Farm Bureau Federation (AFBF). But other groups were expected to press for significantly higher rates to offset the impact of the grain embargo, both in 1981 and in the future.

Rep. Paul Findley, R-Ill., warned that the embargo and the lack of a new Soviet grain agreement would "inevitably influence, to the disadvantage of the American people, the farm legislation."

Findley, an influential representative of conservative farm interests, also questioned the wisdom of eliminating deficiency payments. The payments traditionally deflected pressures for higher loan rates.

Reagan's specific proposals included:

Wheat, Feed Grains, Soybeans, Cotton and Rice

- Terminate target prices and deficiency payments.
- Terminate authority for set asides, a production control used to avoid surpluses in wheat, corn and feed grains, cotton and rice.
- Terminate the "normal crop acreage" program that could be invoked whenever a set-aside was in effect, as a condition of eligibility in some programs. This barred farmers from expanding plantings beyond their customary acreage.
- Terminate disaster payments.
- Continue basic price support loans for wheat, corn and feed grains, soybeans and rice, as well as a related loan program for wheat and feed grains that producers kept in the farmer-held reserve, with loan rates set at the discre-

tion of the secretary instead of rates fixed in law.
- Continue the reserve system but with much broader discretion for the secretary to use financial incentives such as higher or lower loan and interest rates to transfer grain into the reserve or into the market.

Dairy

- Authorize the secretary to set dairy price supports, with periodic adjustments as needed, between 70 and 90 percent of parity and cancel the dairy indemnity program.

Peanuts

- Revise the peanut program so that any farmer could grow additional peanuts and receive the lower price support loan rate. Farmers who, under the existing program, received the higher price support loans could continue to do so, but that level of support would decline significantly.

To accomplish that, the administration proposed to eliminate peanut acreage allotments and reduce the national quota by 10 percent annually over a four-year period. The administration also wanted to continue existing price support levels and the financial penalties for disregarding system regulations.

Other Provisions

- Terminate the indemnity program that reimbursed beekeepers for losses of swarms caused by exposure to pesticides.
- Terminate the grazing and hay program that provided discretionary authority for payments to wheat farmers converting part of their acreage to grazing or hay production.
- Terminate the program that financed feed shipments to livestock producers in regions affected by drought or other physical disasters.
- Convert a program requiring the secretary of agriculture to lend producers money to finance storage facilities, to one permitting such loans.
- Reauthorize the Food for Peace program for four years and raise to $1 billion, from $750 million, the authorization for credit sales abroad under Title II of the program. The administration also proposed to raise to $10 million, from $5 million, the ceiling for emergency non-food relief under Title I.
- Require the secretary, by December 1982, to recommend new soil and water conservation legislation, if needed; also add language encouraging federal agencies to weigh the impact of their actions on conversion of farm land to non-farm uses.

Senate Committee Action

The Senate Agriculture Committee disregarded most of the Reagan requests in its first week of voting and instead tentatively added several billion dollars for programs over the next four years.

Few members of either party spoke of the budget strictures they were breaching.

But after the Senate panel agreed by a 10-5 vote April 27 to include a dairy price support plan favored by the industry and opposed by the administration, Dole warned, "The president won't stand for it."

The committee had chosen a 75 percent of parity minimum, not the 70 percent floor that the administration requested.

The following day, the panel by a vote of 5-11 rejected the administration plan for discretion to set wheat loan rates. It then endorsed a Dole wheat and feed grain pro-

gram that was, as Dole noted, "not supported" by the president.

More than once, Chairman Helms warned members that they would have to "march back down the hill" — that is, reduce the cost of programs — before reporting a bill. "We've already broken the bank," Helms said after one session.

Then, acknowledging to committee members that he, too, had his "special interests," Helms sat quietly while the committee endorsed his proposal to retain the peanut program without the changes that Reagan requested.

The downward march began May 8 in closed-door sessions with committee Republicans, Senate Majority Leader Howard H. Baker Jr., Tenn., Budget Committee Chairman Pete V. Domenici, N.M., and Richard E. Lyng, deputy secretary of agriculture.

After a round of private caucuses, the committee scrapped its budget-breaking draft and reported a measure that merely bent the upper spending limits imposed on it.

The bill (S 884 — S Rept 126) approved May 13 by a 12-1 vote, with two members voting "present," would cost from $50 million to $150 million more in fiscal 1982 than the budget limits.

In its first run-through, however, the committee had endorsed programs that would have totaled at least $1.5 billion more.

On the final day of deliberations, the panel adopted a cost-cutting amendment sponsored by Dole that had been worked out in private caucuses.

Senate Bill Troubles Administration

While the committee bill was not a clear victory for the president, "it certainly isn't a loss," Lyng said.

But several features of the committee bill did trouble the Reagan administration, Lyng explained.

There was a new sugar price support program that Reagan had not asked for and a peanut program without his requested changes.

The committee created new restrictions on the president's authority to embargo farm sales abroad and made embargos very expensive by mandating special payments to affected farmers. It retained the deficiency payments that Reagan wanted to end.

The committee bill would cost an estimated $2 billion to $2.5 billion in fiscal 1982, compared with $1.9 billion for Reagan's plan, according to chief Agriculture Department economist William G. Lesher.

The final changes made by the committee included one that, according to USDA and Congressional Budget Office (CBO) officials, effectively would lower the dairy price support to 70 percent of parity.

Dairy representatives had said a 70 percent level was so far from meeting increasing production costs that many dairymen would go out of business.

However, at the current 80 percent level, the government expected to acquire more than 13 billion pounds of butter, cheese and dry milk. That was more than 10 percent of total dairy production and probably more than the government could store, according to USDA.

The committee originally settled on a 75 to 90 percent range for dairy supports, and Dole's thrift package had reduced that to a 70 percent minimum.

The committee adopted an amendment by Rudy Boschwitz, R-Minn., that moved the minimum back up to 75 percent but allowed the secretary to go down to 70 percent in years when the cost of the dairy program was expected to exceed a certain level or when government

purchases rose to a certain level. One or both conditions would almost certainly pertain for the next four years, according to USDA dairy program officials.

Boschwitz explained to the committee that the $2.1 billion fiscal 1981 cost of the existing program was more than "the entire amount that the Budget Committee, in its wisdom, decided we should spend on all" farm programs in fiscal 1982.

The key vote on the dairy program came when the panel rejected by 7-9 an alternative of Walter D. Huddleston, D-Ky. He suggested a 70 percent minimum in the first two years of the bill and 75 percent for the latter two years.

Dole's cost-cutting package also:

● Shaved 10 cents a bushel from corn price-support loan rates and 5 cents a bushel from wheat loan rates.

● Fixed dollar-and-cents figures for rice loan rates, instead of indexing them to assure increases in future years.

● Fixed a 19.6 cent-per-pound support rate for sugar, instead of calculating the support by a parity base.

● Reduced by $19 the committee's original $650 per-ton price support for peanuts.

John Melcher, D-Mont., was the only committee member to vote against reporting the bill. Two other Democrats, Patrick J. Leahy, Vt., and Edward Zorinsky, Neb., voted "present."

Major Committee Decisions

Major committee decisions:

Wheat, Feed Grains, Soybeans, Cotton, Rice. Continue target prices and deficiency payments at the following per-bushel rates: for wheat, $4.20 in crop year 1982, $4.40 in 1983, $4.60 in 1984 and $4.80 in 1985; for corn, $2.80, $2.95, $3.10 and $3.25 respectively, with feed grain rates pegged to the corn rate as under existing law. Cotton target prices were set at 71 cents a pound in crop year 1982, 76 cents in 1983, 85 cents in 1984 and 93 cents in 1985.

The panel dropped an earlier plan to "trigger" mandatory target prices in years when carry-over stocks reached certain levels. USDA officials had said that the trigger was set so that they would have to make deficiency payments every year; removing the trigger meant that the payments were much less likely to be made.

● Cancel set aside and normal crop acreage programs, as requested by Reagan, but authorized the secretary to require compliance with an acreage reduction program as a condition of eligibility for deficiency payments and price support loans. The provision differed little from existing law, although it revised the method for calculating affected acreage.

● Continue authority for disaster payments, but only for farmers for whom federal crop insurnce was not available.

● Continue basic price support loans at these rates: for wheat in all four years, $3.50 per bushel; for corn in all four years, $2.60 per bushel with feed grains pegged to the corn rate; for cotton, 71 cents a pound in crop year 1982, 76 cents in 1983, 85 cents in 1984 and 93 cents in 1985; for rice, $11.23 per hundred pounds in crop year 1982, $12.14 in 1983, $12.70 in 1984 and $13.50 in 1985. Cotton loans would be calculated by a formula based on market prices, as under existing law.

● Establish the loan rate for soybeans at 75 percent of the average cash price for beans at the Chicago market. The rate derived by the formula could not go below the existing loan rate of $5.02 per bushel.

The bill also stipulated that soybeans could not be included in any production control program and made soybeans ineligible for the reserve program. It barred the secretary from restricting producers' eligibility for price support loans and loans for storage facilities.

● Revise the farmer-held reserve program. The bill continued interest rates for loans at the cost of money to the government and stipulated that grain could not be released from storage and sold until market prices equaled the average cost of production for the preceding three years.

It authorized payments to farmers for storage costs until the market price reached 115 percent of the "release" price.

It permitted a "call" — mandatory sales of reserve grain — only in emergency conditions and only with prior notice to the president and congressional Agriculture committees. And it permitted the secretary to restrict the quantity of wheat going into reserve to 700 million bushels and of feed grains to 1 million bushels.

● Suspend acreage allotments for rice, as requested by Reagan. Existing law limited program benefits to farmers holding the allotments.

● **Dairy.** Authorize the secretary to set dairy price supports between 75 to 90 percent of parity. The secretary could lower the support level to 70 percent in any year when the department expected to spend more than $500 million on the program or to acquire dairy products that would amount to more than 3.52 billion pounds worth of milk.

● **Peanuts.** Raise to $631 per ton, from $420 per ton, the price support for quota peanuts and reduce to 1.3 million tons, from 1.4 million tons, the national quota for peanuts.

● **Sugar.** Require the secretary to support the price of sugar at 19.6 cents a pound through purchases or other steps.

Other Provisions

● Prohibit partial restriction of U.S. exports under the 1979 Export Administration Act (PL 96-72) unless both the House and Senate approved such an embargo by concurrent resolution. *(1979 Almanac p. 300)*

The 1979 act specified conditions for such trade restrictions and authorized congressional veto of trade restrictions on agricultural commodities for foreign policy or short-supply reasons.

The committee also required that Congress approve such a trade embargo and that affected producers must either receive interest-free commodity loans at 100 percent of parity or payments calculated on market prices before the embargo.

● Establish a revolving loan fund to finance exports of farm commodities but without the $15 billion authorization for fiscal years 1982-84 originally approved.

● Remove the $1.9 billion ceiling on the concessional sales program under Food for Peace and raise to $1 billion, from $750 million, the ceiling for donations.

● Establish a new conservation program under which the secretary would designate erosion-prone regions and share costs with producers in those regions for projects to stem erosion.

Senate Floor Action

The bill passed by the Senate Sept. 18 conformed more to Reagan administration demands than the committee bill and gave many farmers less than they wanted for price

support programs.

Bowing to the threat of a presidential veto, the Senate twice reduced the original committee levels. First, it accepted a compromise that was reached by key members and administration representatives just before the bill was brought to the floor; second, it accepted other administration cuts sponsored by Dole. The Senate passed the bill by 49-32. *(Vote 270, p. 46-S)*

Earlier in the evening of Sept. 18, the Senate had adopted, by a vote of 46-39, an amendment sponsored by Dole that substituted the target price levels sought by the administration for those that had been approved previously by the Agriculture panel in its compromise effort and revised by a series of floor amendments Sept. 14. *(Vote 267, p. 46-S)*

Dole said his amendment cutting the target price levels for wheat, rice and feed grains reduced the outlays by an estimated $360 million through fiscal 1986.

Dole, who in 1978 spearheaded a drive to raise grain price supports sharply, in 1981 was a leader in brokering the bill downward for the White House. He frequently reminded colleagues that "there's no money to shovel out of the Treasury" for more generous farm programs.

Before adopting the Dole amendments, the Senate had:

● Adopted a committee compromise trimming rates the panel had approved earlier for target prices for wheat, feed grains, rice and cotton.

● Accepted an amendment by Roger W. Jepsen, R-Iowa, cutting back dairy price supports.

● Rejected amendments Sept. 17 to kill or reduce a new price support program for sugar, ignoring warnings of Paul E. Tsongas, D-Mass., and Dan Quayle, R-Ind., that it would largely benefit wealthy corporations and add hundreds of millions of dollars to food bills.

● Rejected attempts by Richard G. Lugar, R-Ind., Mark O. Hatfield, R-Ore., and Thomas F. Eagleton, D-Mo., to crack the peanut and tobacco programs open so that any farmer could grow the lucrative crops.

The divisions among farm groups were dramatically evident during the voting, such as when some dairy and wheat state members voted against killing an amendment by Lugar to dismantle the peanut program.

Committee Compromise

Floor action had been delayed while Congress completed Reagan's budget and tax bills. In the vote-bargaining over those measures, the administration reversed its opposition to the sugar and peanut programs, thus winning votes from conservative Southern House Democrats.

When the Senate began debate Sept. 14, members agreed without objection to substitute the committee-approved changes and then trimmed the dairy program to fit the administration specifications.

Committee Revisions. The committee changes, before being altered by Dole's final amendment:

● Set wheat target prices at $4.10 per bushel for 1982, with annual 20-cent-per-bushel increases for crop years 1983-85.

● Set corn target prices at $2.75 per bushel with 15-cent-per-bushel increases for the following three years.

● Set cotton target prices at 71 cents and 76 cents a pound for crop years 1982 and 1983 respectively, 83 cents in 1984 and 89 cents in 1985.

● Set rice target prices at $10.98 per hundredweight for 1982, $11.63 for 1983, $12.28 for 1984 and $12.93 for 1985 crop years.

• Set new sugar price supports, to be maintained with loans and/or duties on imported sugar, at 18 cents per pound in 1982, rising to 19.5 cents by 1985. The committee compromise also changed the peanut provision, lowering its price support, shrinking the national quota and loosening the acreage allotment system.

Dairy Program. Jepsen, arguing for the administration, said the expiring 80 percent of parity support was so high that it caused massive surpluses to pile up in government warehouses.

In Spring, Congress had canceled a scheduled April 1 readjustment in dairy payment rates, and without that compensation for inflation, the actual payment of $13.10 per hundredweight worked out to about 73 percent of parity. Dairymen wanted 75 percent but settled in the Senate committee for language that would have dropped the level to 70 percent for at least several years.

However, Jepsen insisted that the administration should be able to go below that level by forgoing scheduled readjustments in years when anticipated spending for the program would top $750 million.

Jepsen's amendment would not permit the actual payment rates to dip below $13.10 or the rate of the preceding year, if that was higher. By 1983 that would be less than 60 percent of parity.

After rejecting two substitutes more favorable to dairymen offered by Boschwitz, the Senate Sept. 15 agreed to Jepsen's amendment by a voice vote. *(Boschwitz amendments, votes 251 and 252, p. 44-S)*

Peanuts. Lugar called the peanut system "feudal" and asked the Senate to eliminate the allotment and quota system, leaving only price supports at a rate set by the secretary.

Although the Senate rejected a motion to table Lugar's plan Sept. 16 by a vote of 42-56, it did not adopt his proposal, voting instead 51-47 for a compromise by Mack Mattingly, R-Ga. *(Votes 253, 256, p. 44-S)*

The compromise raised the quota support price to $596 per ton from the existing $455, with annual adjustments after 1982 to reflect production costs. It also set a national quota of 1.24 million tons and permitted any farmer to grow peanuts for the "additional" market but without the backing of price support loans unless the secretary of agriculture chose to offer loans.

Tobacco. Hatfield Sept. 17 urged the Senate to "Let the tobacco farmer stand on his own feet, as we are asking the poor, the needy and the minorities to do" with budget cuts in social programs.

Hatfield was chairman of the Appropriations Committee.

Helms, Huddleston and others from tobacco-producing states argued that the tobacco subsidy kept small farm families from poverty, financed college education for children and cost the government little.

The Senate tabled Hatfield's amendment to repeal the entire tobacco program by 53-42 and subsequently tabled by 48-45 an amendment by Eagleton that would have scrapped the fixed tobacco support price and given the secretary of agriculture authority to lower support prices. The next day, the Senate narrowly rejected another Eagleton effort to revamp the tobacco program by agreeing to table his plan 41-40. *(Votes 259, 260, p. 45-S; Vote 269, p. 46-S)*

The first tobacco vote occurred at night, the second late on a Friday afternoon; anti-tobacco members believed that they could have won narrowly if the two votes had occurred earlier with more members present.

House Committee Action

The House Agriculture Committee began markup April 30 and on May 19 reported a budget-busting farm bill (HR 3603 — H Rept 97-106) that it said it intended to rewrite before seeking House approval.

The panel clearly felt the pressure to make reductions. But exasperated with confusing information about the budget process itself, it put off cost-cutting decisions until after the Memorial Day recess.

The basic programs renewed by HR 3603 for four years would cost approximately $3.5 billion in fiscal 1982, while the budget (H Con Res 115) set a $2.135 billion limit.

At the May 19 meeting, committee Republicans floated a substitute, which the minority counsel said exceeded the budget by only $86 million.

But Democrats testily objected to the last-minute appearance of the 235-page draft. They complained about what they called confusing CBO cost estimates and language that obscured a major change in the peanut program.

The panel rejected the GOP plan 17-25 and agreed by voice vote to report its original bill.

Earlier, the committee had adopted a package of credit provisions, including extension of the economic emergency program that Reagan wanted to end and a new conservation program designed to target loans and direct payments to farmers in regions most threatened by erosion.

The panel also decided to:

• Authorize dairy price supports at 75 to 90 percent of parity, with adjustments Oct. 1 and April 1.

• Raise peanut price supports to $600 a ton from $420 a ton and reduce the national acreage allotment to 1.3 million tons, from 1.4 million tons.

• Authorize a sugar price support program at 44 percent of parity or about 19.6 cents for 1982.

• Continue the economic emergency and farm storage facility loans that Reagan had wanted to cancel.

House Floor Action

After seven days of often-acrid debate beginning Oct. 2, the House Oct. 22 passed a bill that left none of the interested parties unscathed.

The heavily-amended committee bill passed by voice vote after members rejected by 180-193 a Republican amendment to convert the four-year reauthorization to a two-year measure. The House then voted 192-160 to substitute its text for the Senate version (S 884). *(Vote 263, p. 84-H; Vote 264, p. 86-H)*

E. Thomas Coleman, R-Mo., urged restricting the bill to two years to limit the damage to the budget. But Democrats complained that Coleman simply wanted to force House conferees to accept lower Senate figures for the latter two years.

When floor action was over, the self-styled "tobacco boys" — members from North Carolina and other tobacco-growing Southern states — had blocked a strong drive to end their highly-regulated program.

Most other commodity groups suffered losses, either real or in their expectations. The bill raised grain loan rates and other financial programs for farmers but not as high as many farmers wanted.

Dairy farmers had hoped to keep the 80 percent of parity price support level they had had for the past four years. But the House fixed the fiscal 1982 dairy support at the current dollar level of $13.10 per hundredweight, which worked out to about 73 percent of parity. That could rise to

a 75 percent minimum in later years.

In addition, the House canceled its committee's sugar program and voted to end the peanut program.

The Reagan administration was displeased with the House action. "It is unacceptable," Deputy Agriculture Secretary Lyng said.

The bill was within Reagan budget limits for fiscal 1982 but not for the next three years. The CBO estimated that the four-year costs of the bill would total $53.4 billion.

Of that, $44.9 billion would be for food stamps, with $8.5 billion for farm programs. The four-year total for the administration-backed Senate bill (S 884), which did not include food stamps, was $6.732 billion.

Food Stamps, Dairy Windfall

In missing the Sept. 30 deadline for rewriting the farm programs, the House triggered a windfall for dairymen and a threat of consumer price-hikes for butter, cheese and milk.

But the delay also provided time for a successful bipartisan effort to wring a $700 million increase in food stamp spending for next year from the administration.

"We held up the whole farm bill to get this," said Rep. Fred Richmond, D-N.Y., who with Coleman had pressured Stockman for more money.

On Sept. 22, Agriculture Secretary Block had written Richmond, who chaired the House subcommittee with jurisdiction over food stamp authorizations. Block said that the new estimates placed the full cost of the program for fiscal 1982 at $12.1 billion. He also noted that the administration's budget request was for only $10.6 billion and that request "has not changed."

Block's new figures reflected more people coming into the food stamp program because of cuts in welfare and other social programs. The increase had not been included in S 1007, the food stamp bill passed by the Senate, which set $10.9 billion for the program. Nor was it foreseen by the $10 billion figure included by the House Agriculture Committee in HR 3603.

Richmond, Coleman and budget director Stockman agreed to a figure of $11.3 billion for both authorizing and appropriations legislation, including money for Puerto Rico that had been excluded by the House committee. Richmond and Coleman agreed to offer anti-fraud amendments favored by the administration and an amendment to postpone inflation adjustments until Oct. 1, 1983.

The dairy windfall came about because the expiration of the existing farm law allowed higher price supports mandated by the 1949 farm law and the budget reconciliation bill to take effect. The existing price support of $13.10 per hundredweight went to $13.49 on Oct. 1.

The missed deadline set off a legislative scramble to block the price hike. On Oct. 1 by a vote of 328-58, the House approved HR 4612 (PL 97-67) to delay the increase until Nov. 15. The Senate passed the bill Oct. 19. *(Vote 219, p. 74-H)*

However, when it became clear a new farm bill would not be completed by Nov. 15, the Senate Nov. 9 amended an unrelated bill (S 1322 — PL 97-77) to postpone the increase and to delay two national votes for wheat and cotton farmers until the end of 1981. The House cleared the measure Nov. 11.

Floor Details

Cost Compromise. The frayed farm coalition regrouped and showed its strength Oct. 7 when the House, by a 400-14 vote, accepted a compromise package of amend-

ments cutting the cost of the over-budget committee bill. It then rejected two efforts to tinker with the compromise's dairy section. *(Vote 239 p. 78-H)*

Any change in the compromise would have threatened delicate vote-trading agreements among regional commodity interests and urban food-stamp advocates.

During the first day of House voting, "you could see the peanut and grain and cotton and rice people all working the floor for dairy," according to Farm Bureau lobbyist Mike Durando.

Having won food-stamp concessions from the administration with the backing of his Agriculture Committee colleagues, Richmond told the House, "I want to support sugar ... tobacco, rice, cotton, dairy, every one of these other commodities."

The New York Democrat's statement was notable for several reasons. With his sizable constituency of urban poor, he might have been expected to side with consumer groups such as the Community Nutrition Institute, which feared the sugar and dairy sections would hike supermarket prices.

The $1 billion cost-cutting compromise offered by Berkley Bedell, D-Iowa, fixed dairy price supports for fiscal 1982 at the existing dollar level of $13.10 per hundredweight, almost 73 percent of parity, the index meant to ensure farmers' purchasing power.

In 1983, the minimum would be 72.5 percent of parity. In 1984-85, it would drop to 70 percent, unless federal purchases of surplus dairy goods were estimated to be less than the equivalent of 3.5 billion pounds of milk in either year. Then, the minimum would rise to 75 percent.

The committee bill originally provided 75 percent of parity for four years, while S 884 set a 70 percent or $13.10 minimum under certain circumstances.

Dairymen argued that by 1983 or 1984, the $13.10 figure could represent supports as low as 60 percent of parity.

Bedell's amendment also:

● Lowered to 18 cents a pound, from 19.6 cents, the 1982 sugar support price of the committee bill, with annual half-cent increases thereafter.

● Made the following programs optional for the secretary of agriculture, instead of mandatory: a new price support program for sunflowers and the emergency feed program and farm storage facility loans, except in areas of storage facility shortages. Also, new conservation loans would be optional and subject to appropriations.

Those changes, Bedell said, brought the total fiscal 1982 cost of HR 3603 to $2.165 billion, compared with $2.139 billion for S 884, as calculated under the assumptions of the first budget resolution. That meant the bill complied with the first budget resolution levels for 1982.

However, totals for the subsequent years, summed up by Rep. William C. Wampler, R-Va., showed cost overruns: fiscal 1983, budget resolution, $1.671 billion in new entitlement authority, compared with $1.903 billion for HR 3603 as amended by Bedell; fiscal 1984, budget resolution, $1.407 billion, compared with $2.237 billion for the amended bill.

He added that since the numbers were based on re-estimates of the resolution, they could not "determine whether the bills are over or under."

Further Reductions Defeated. The attack on the compromise came from Barney Frank, D-Mass., who lost by 153-243 in his attempt to insert Reagan's dairy section as approved by the Senate. James M. Jeffords, R-Vt., also sought unsuccessfully to fix a 70 percent or $13.10 mini-

mum for one year only and then to let the dairy program revert to 75 percent as provided by the 1949 farm law. Jeffords' amendment lost 123-277. *(Votes 240 and 241, p. 78-H).*

While Jeffords' plan had more surface appeal for dairymen, it was Bedell who had the backing of most of the industry because his compromise assured votes from other commodity interests.

Frank acknowledged that he had been caught in a maneuver designed to favor Bedell by making himself and Jeffords both appear to be extremists.

Patrick B. Healy, secretary of the National Milk Producers Federation and a key coalition engineer, said afterward that "we're very well pleased" with the House dairy votes.

Peanuts: By a 250-159 vote Oct. 15, the House scrapped the elaborate apparatus that for decades had prohibited all but a select group of farmers from growing peanuts for market. While canceling the acreage allotment and poundage quota system, the House retained peanut price support loans. But it allowed the secretary of agriculture to set the lending rate, rather than specifying a dollar amount in the bill. *(Vote 246, p. 80-H)*

Stanley N. Lundine, D-N.Y., who with Findley had written the amendment, characterized the system as "near feudalistic."

Sugar. The House also Oct. 15 agreed 213-190 to cancel the new price support program for sugar. *(Vote 247, p. 80-H)*

Sponsors Peter A. Peyser, D-N.Y., and Margaret Heckler, R-Mass., declared that creating a new program for sugar growers was unthinkable while the elderly, the poor and students were forced by budget cuts to lose federal benefits.

In addition, other members said privately that the votes against the programs involved personal and political animosity. Northern Democrats had been angered by the votes of conservative Southern Democrats for Reagan's budget and tax measures. In addition, there was some resentment against Senate Agriculture Committee Chairman Helms, whose stringent social views irritated some. Others cited Helms' insistence on trimming dairy and other farm programs while protecting peanuts and tobacco, both prime North Carolina crops.

House leaders were visibly shaken by the two unexpected losses on sugar and peanuts and put off further voting until Oct. 20.

Tobacco. The House Oct. 21 rejected by 184-231 an amendment by Bob Shamansky, D-Ohio, to repeal the tobacco program. *(Vote 257, p. 84-H)*

Defenders of the program, led by North Carolina's Rose, said it was critically important to thousands of small Southern farmers who counted on tobacco profits to stay off city welfare rolls. Neal Smith, D-Iowa, argued that by limiting the quantity of tobacco and propping up its price, the program discouraged smoking.

Shamansky contended that wealthy allotment-owners, not the farmers who pay as much as $1,000 an acre to rent the allotments, profited from the program. "It is a classic case of self-interest," he said.

Later, Shamansky said that he had lost because the vote became a partisan contest for control of the N.C. House delegation in the 1982 elections.

House Speaker Thomas P. O'Neill Jr., D-Mass., acknowledged that "we've been working very, very hard" for Rose and company.

Since the Republican Senate had narrowly agreed to save the program, the Democratic House, O'Neill said, had to avoid blame for its loss. Otherwise, O'Neill added, Helms "would very definitely blame it on the Democrats."

The Republican leadership, also anxious to win political credit in Southern tobacco regions, lobbied with the Reagan administration against Shamansky.

After defeating Shamansky's amendment, the House adopted by 412-0 a Foley substitute for an amendment by Findley, directing the secretary of agriculture to use existing authority to eliminate on-budget program costs. *(Vote 258, p. 84-H)*

Food Stamps. On Oct. 22, the House by voice vote adopted a series of amendments by Richmond and Coleman to set food stamp authorizations at levels negotiated with Stockman and to add further anti-fraud provisions to the bill. The ceilings were $11.3 billion for fiscal 1982; $11.2 billion, 1983; $11.1 billion, 1984; $11.3 billion, 1985. The adjustment for inflation for the thrifty food plan that determined benefit levels was postponed until Oct. 1.

The compromise also made banks and other so-called "first endorsers" (distributors of food stamps) liable for paying for food stamp losses if they ignored certain procedures for identifying recipients.

The measure empowered fraud investigators in the Agriculture Department inspector general's office to carry guns, issue warrants for arresting criminal violators of food stamp and other laws, and to make arrests without warrants in certain circumstances.

Peter W. Rodino Jr., D-N.J., chairman of the House Judiciary Committee, warned against proliferation of police powers. Coleman responded that USDA investigators encountered threats to their lives when pursuing organized crime involvement in the food stamp program.

The amendments passed by voice vote but only after Coleman dropped a section authorizing warrantless searches and seizures of evidence by the investigators.

Separate amendments were also adopted by voice vote specifying that government low-income energy aid could not be counted as income in determining eligibility for food stamps, allowing members of federally recognized Indian tribes not living on reservations to qualify for food stamps and permitting parents living with children to qualify separately for food stamps if one of the parents received disability or certain other aid, and if parents and children bought and prepared food separately.

An amendment by Robert S. Walker, R-Pa., that would have partially restored the requirement eliminated in 1977 to require food stamp recipients to pay for part of the value of food stamps in cash was rejected by 147-251. *(Vote 260, p. 84-H)*

Other Amendments

The House debated HR 3603 Oct. 2, 7, 14, 15, 20, 21 and 22. Action on other amendments included:

Oct. 15:

● Adopted by voice vote an amendment by Glenn English, D-Okla., to require the secretary, in years when stocks of wheat remaining from the previous year were 6 percent or more of world need, to provide a set-aside and raise commodity loan rates. Participants would be required to idle at a minimum, 15 percent of acreage planted in the preceding year, and loan rates for them would rise 5 percent above the established level for that year. The secretary also would be required to provide loans at 15 percent above the established level for producers choosing to idle 30 percent of their acreage.

The House also adopted by voice vote a similar

amendment by Charles W. Stenholm, D-Texas, for feed grains, for years when carryover stocks exceeded 18 percent of world use. The minimum set aside would be 15 percent with a 5 percent loan increase; and loan rates would increase 10 percent for producers idling 25 percent. The House refused Stenholm's plan for a mandatory cotton set aside.

● Adopted by voice vote an amendment by Ron Marlenee, R-Mont., to bar the secretary from requiring more than 60 percent of land to be idled for farmers who had left their land in summer fallow for three out of five years.

● Adopted by voice vote an amendment by David R. Bowen, D-Miss., reducing the loan rate for extra long staple cotton at 75 to 125 percent of the loan rate for upland cotton. (Existing law set the rate at 85 to 130 percent of the upland cotton loan rate.)

Oct. 20:

● Rejected by a 138-270 vote an amendment by James Weaver, D-Ore., to permit the secretary of agriculture to establish a bank for financing U.S. grain exports and to permit the secretary to set prices for such exports. *(Vote 255, p. 82-H)*

● Adopted by voice vote an amendment by Jeffords, permitting free distribution of government-owned surplus dairy products to school children, the poor and the elderly through child nutrition, food bank and older Americans act programs.

Oct. 21:

● Adopted by voice vote an amendment by Dan Glickman, D-Kan., to authorize, through Oct. 1, 1985, a new revolving loan fund in the CCC to finance U.S. commodity exports.

● Rejected by voice vote an amendment by Smith to bar the secretary from requiring feed grain producers to participate in acreage reduction or reserve programs to be eligible for price support and other aid.

● Adopted by voice vote an amendment by William M. Thomas, R-Calif., to authorize the secretary to seize, quarantine and treat crops, as well as physical premises, to eliminate infestations of plant pests in emergencies but only if state or other efforts to combat such infestations were inadequate. Further authorized warrantless inspections of persons and vehicles moving between states that may be infested with plant pests, such as the Medfly that had damaged some California crops.

● Adopted by voice vote an amendment by Arlan Stangeland, R-Minn., to require the secretary to support the price of sunflower seeds with commodity loans at a minimum of $8 per hundredweight.

● Adopted by voice vote an amendment by James L. Oberstar, D-Minn., barring exports of CCC-owned commodities worth more than $5 million, and which were to be sold at less than 85 percent of their value, unless such sales were reported to Congress and were not disapproved by concurrent resolution within 30 days of notification. The amendment reflected congressional hostility to the August sale to New Zealand of some 220 million pounds of CCC-owned surplus butter at 35 cents a pound below the market price. New Zealand, itself a major butter producer, was expected to pass butter on to the Soviet Union. That nation tried to buy American butter directly at the market price of $1.05, but was barred by a Reagan administration "selective embargo," Oberstar said. The deal meant a $77 million loss.

Oct. 22:

● Adopted by voice vote a de la Garza amendment to

authorize $10 million annually, for fiscal years 1982-86, for grants to upgrade research facilities at predominantly black land-grant colleges, including Tuskegee Institute.

● Rejected by voice vote an English amendment that would have permitted the secretary, in regions experiencing economic difficulties, to defer until Sept. 30, 1982, repayment and interest on certain Farmers Home Administration (FmHA) loans and to forego foreclosure.

● Adopted by voice vote an amendment by George E. Brown, D-Calif., that directed the secretary to develop standards for monitoring the role of federal programs in conversion of farmland to non-farm uses, and directed federal agencies to evaluate their programs by those standards and seek alternatives for plans that would hasten conversion or conflict with state, local or private farmland protection programs. Required a report on the program to Congress within a year.

● Rejected by voice vote an amendment by Harold L. Volkmer, D-Mo., lowering to 50 percent of parity, from 60 percent, the minimum federal support price for honey.

● Adopted by voice vote an amendment by Cooper Evans, R-Iowa, to maintain through 1985 a pilot program for selling federal crop insurance through county offices of the Agricultural Stabilization and Conservation Service.

● Adopted by a vote of 211-168 an amendment by Thomas A. Daschle, D-S.D., as amended by English, to bar imports of meat that failed to meet U.S. inspection standards or that was produced with agricultural chemicals or medications that were not approved for U.S. use. The amendment also permitted the president, with 10 days prior notice to Congress, to waive this prohibition in any case where U.S. farm exports were threatened. *(Vote 262, p. 84-H)*

Conference Action

Block urged conferees to ignore the more expensive House version and adopt the Senate plan.

While the administration did not directly threaten a veto, spokesmen warned that Reagan considered the House bill unacceptable.

Reagan had invited key conferees to the Oval Office just before the first conference session Nov. 4 and also sent a letter urging conferees to stick to the Senate plan.

But by Nov. 5, conferees had begun crafting a bill that risked rejection by both the House and the administration.

By agreeing Nov. 5 to include a new sugar price support program that the House had rejected, conferees risked House rebellion. Peyser, who helped engineer the House revolt, warned he would construct another coalition against the compromise bill.

And, because the bill appeared sure to cost hundreds of millions of dollars more during the next four years than Reagan wanted to spend, conferees also risked a veto.

Sugar. Conferees agreed 15-1 on Nov. 5 to keep the Senate's sugar price support program maintaining sugar prices at 18 cents per pound for the 1982 crop, with annual half-cent per pound increases thereafter.

Dairy. On Nov. 6, a new dairy program was adopted. The House bill had allotted about $400 million more to dairy price supports over four years than the Senate. Dairy industry spokesmen insisted that they had already absorbed such severe cuts below the 1977 farm bill level that they could take no more this year.

Dole produced a compromise that would put the four-year cost of the bill about $150 million above the Senate level.

Dairy advocate Harkin still protested that the plan was inadequate because it gave producers only 70 percent of parity at a minimum.

Compared to the 80 percent of parity level of the 1977 bill, the compromise was a precipitous drop. But the Reagan administration had insisted that Congress give the secretary of agriculture discretion to go below 70 percent.

The Dole proposal was to keep the existing dollar figure for 1982 supports of $13.10 per hundredweight and to set minimum supports at 70 percent thereafter. However, the support could go to 75 percent of parity if the federal purchases of dairy products as mandated by law were less than 4 billion pounds in 1983, 3.5 billion pounds in 1984, and 2.69 billion in 1985.

The House version had kept the current support level for 1982 but allowed it to reach 75 percent if 3.5 billion pounds of milk products had been purchased by the government. The Senate plan allowed the secretary to keep the $13.10 level for all four years in the likely event that federal dairy purchases exceeded $750 million annually.

Grain. A key point of disagreement continued to be the grain supports, with the Reagan administration urging thrift and a group of House conferees, led by Foley, insisting they could compromise no more.

"We've done 100 percent of the adjusting," Foley told conferees. "Nothing seems to satisfy this administration except an absolute capitulation" by the House, he said.

Wheat and feed grains price supports passed by the House would have cost some $4 billion more in the next four years than those approved by the Senate. But Foley and his allies Nov. 11 made an offer that would have cost about $100 million more than the Senate version Reagan favored.

Dole said talks with "a high policy official at the White House" led him to believe Reagan would sign a bill raising the costs about $400 million above the Senate version, but no more.

Foley's offer stayed within that total, but the administration objected to an indexing feature that would raise future price supports as production costs rose.

Foley objected that the administration had not opposed indexing in dairy, peanut and other programs. And he was visibly outraged by USDA's Lesher's willingness to accept a Senate provision that could provide farmers as much as $30 billion in one year in the event of an embargo on farm commodities.

That provision, which the conferees agreed to Nov. 13, would raise price supports to 100 percent of parity for commodities whose sales abroad were restricted for reasons of foreign policy or national security. The higher prices would not go into effect if non-farm goods also were embargoed.

Foley offered a minimum wheat loan of $3.50 a bushel and a minimum corn loan of $2.55 a bushel for 1983-85 crops. The wheat target price would be $4.05 a bushel for 1982 crops, with adjustments thereafter for rising costs of production, up to 7 percent each year or no more than $4.85 a bushel. For corn, the target price would be $2.75 a bushel in 1982, and rising thereafter with costs of production, up to 7 percent a year.

Conference Stand-Off

Stalemated on spending levels for farm programs and on a special exemption from bankruptcy laws for farmers, House and Senate conferees broke off negotiations Nov. 20.

They had tentatively agreed Nov. 19 on a bill totaling $681 million more than the administration wanted.

But Lesher, pushing for the administration, sought lower rates for wheat and feed grain price-support loans, a fixed rate of increase instead of inflation indexing for target pricing — a second type of support — and a cheaper dairy program.

Foley flatly refused to support any further changes in the conference agreement. Dole acknowledged in an interview that by squeezing spending further, conferees risked losing farm-state members' votes. "We already know a lot of city members will vote against it," he observed.

A Dole compromise on wheat and feed grain programs — accepted by Foley Nov. 18 with a stipulation that it be the conferees' final decision — turned a significant number of grain-state members against the agreement.

In addition, bankruptcy provisions that applied to grain elevators and other farm commodity storage facilities, would assure that a point of order would be brought against the whole bill on the House floor, according to House Agriculture Committee Chairman de la Garza. He said that Judiciary Committee Chairman Rodino objected because his committee had been bypassed.

Conference Decisions

Before breaking off deliberations at the end of the third week, conferees had made these decisions:

●**Wheat and Feed Grains.** The conferees accepted the Dole compromise for the dual system of price supports — loans for which farmers put up their crops as collateral — and target prices, which provided direct cash payments to farmers.

The agreement called for wheat loans at $3.60 a bushel and corn loans at $2.60 a bushel for crop years 1982-85, with other feed grain loans set in relation to corn. Wheat target prices would be set at $4.05 a bushel and corn target prices at $2.70 a bushel for the 1982 crop year, with adjustments later for rising production costs up to 6 percent a year.

They also agreed on grain reserve programs and dropped two House provisions that would have forced the administration to adopt grain production controls in years when leftover stocks threatened to cause a surplus.

●**Sugar.** Conferees revised an earlier decision to support sugar at 18 cents a pound in 1982, agreeing instead to lower the beginning rate to 17.5 cents a pound, with annual half-cent increases thereafter.

●**Peanuts.** Conferees reduced to $550 a ton, from $580 a ton, the price support they had approved earlier for so-called "quota peanuts" — those grown by farmers who own, inherit or rent acreage allotments. They also decided that the size of the quota would be reduced by 100 million tons over the next four years.

●**Rice and Cotton.** Conferees adopted 6 percent-a-year caps on future increases in price supports for these crops.

●**Food Stamps.** Unable to resolve a dispute over the timing of benefit increases to accommodate rising food prices, the conferees decided to reauthorize the program for only one year and delay a benefit increase until Oct. 1, 1982.

The Last Steps

Senate conferees Dec. 3 accepted a package of changes drafted under strong pressure from the administration. With that compromise, the bill would cost $428 million more over four years than the version passed by the Senate and backed by Reagan.

That was $253 million less than the version tentatively accepted by conferees Nov. 19, when negotiations stalled.

The new plan was negotiated privately by de la Garza and Helms, with certain other conferees and Agriculture Secretary Block. It won the first explicit administration approval of the bill.

But the compromise so angered prominent House conferees who had already retreated from their more expensive version of the bill that several vowed not to sign the conference agreement. That unusual step signaled strong disapproval to members.

Jones, departing from his usual amiability, declared the bill so flawed that he would seek its defeat. Jones warned, "Folks like me are going to do all they can to kill it."

After the meeting, Jones said that the bill ignored the worsening financial problems of farmers. USDA had forecast net farm income for 1982 at $16 billion to $19 billion, a 42 percent drop from the 1979 total of $27.4 billion.

The dairy compromise also prompted Jeffords to predict that dairy allies would seek defeat of the conference agreement.

Not all farm groups objected to the bill. Representatives for cotton, corn and soybean growers endorsed Reagan's position after a Dec. 2 meeting between the president and representatives of 16 farm groups.

House Conferees Balk

Although Senate conferees Dec. 3 took two steps to ease potential House objections to the bill, House conferees did not accept it until Dec. 8.

Senate conferees had lowered the sugar price support to 17 cents a pound in 1982, from 17.5 cents and set increases for 1983-85 at one-fourth of a cent a pound each year, instead of one-half of a cent.

They also dropped the package of bankruptcy law changes that were meant to aid farmers who stored grain in elevators that failed. Rodino had objected that the bankruptcy sections had not gone through his Judiciary Committee.

Agreement Details

The compromise dropped the inflation indexing, strongly opposed by the administration, from target prices for wheat and feed grains. It also set minimum dairy price supports for the next four years in dollars, rather than the inflation-related parity index.

Dairy. The minimum support for 1982 would be the current level of $13.10 per hundredweight and for the following three years, $13.25, $14.00 and $14.60 respectively. However, beginning in 1983, the minimum support could rise to 70 percent of parity in any year in which anticipated federal purchases of dairy products, as required by the program, would be less than $1 billion. That, according to USDA, would work out to $13.97 per hundredweight in fiscal 1983, $15.53 in 1984 and $17.40 in 1985.

Or, the minimum could rise to 75 percent of parity if net purchases were less than 4 billion pounds in fiscal 1983, 3.5 billion pounds in 1984 or 2.69 billion pounds in 1985.

Wheat, Feed Grains, Rice. The compromise dealt with two forms of price supports: loans, for which farmers put up crops as collateral; and target prices, which provide direct cash payments when market prices fall below target price levels established by law.

The compromise set wheat loans at $3.55 a bushel and corn loans at $2.55 a bushel for crop years 1982-85, with other feed grain loans set in relation to corn.

Wheat target prices for the four years would be $4.05,

$4.30, $4.45 and $4.65 a bushel respectively; corn target prices would be $2.70, $2.86, $3.03 and $3.18; rice target prices would be $10.85, $11.40, $11.90 and $12.40.

In the House bill, target prices had been indexed to costs of production; conferees first had capped the price increases at 7 percent and later at 6 percent a year.

Conferees set wool price supports at 77.5 percent of a statutory formula and agreed to make the economic emergency loan program discretionary for the secretary. ∎

Embargo Loans Ended

Less than a year after approving certain interest-free loans for farmers to compensate for the embargo of grain sales to Russia, Congress reinstated the charges. President Reagan signed the legislation (S 1395 — PL 97-24) July 23.

The legislation was passed without separate committee reports; both chambers had already approved the interest change in their budget reconciliation legislation. The Senate approved S 1395 by voice vote June 25, and the House followed suit July 9. *(Reconciliation, p. 256)*

The bill ended a mandatory interest waiver established in December 1980 (PL 96-494) on loans for 1980 and 1981 grain crops stored in the farmer-held reserve. The 1980 legislation was intended to aid farmers adversely affected by President Carter's Jan. 4, 1980 announcement establishing the embargo. *(1980 Almanac p. 94)*

In that program, farmers borrowed from the government, using their crops as collateral and could not sell them to repay the loan until certain market prices were reached. The program was intended to stabilize grain prices by keeping potential surpluses off the market. *(1980 Almanac, p. 94)*

Reagan lifted the embargo April 24. The administration asked Congress to end the interest waiver, and the Agriculture Department refused to admit 1981 grain into the reserve program and make loans until Congress approved the request. The cancellation was expected to save the government $165 million in fiscal 1982. *(Embargo statement, p. 21-E)*

The grain reserve was opened the same day the president signed the bill.

The bill also postponed a mandatory producer referendum on whether to impose acreage restrictions on individual growers. Omnibus farm bills, beginning in 1970, have suspended the requirement, which was mandated by the 1949 agriculture act. ∎

Crop Insurance

President Reagan May 22 signed an uncontroversial bill (PL 97-11) to provide emergency financing to expand the subsidized crop insurance program mandated by Congress in 1980. *(1980 Almanac p. 95)*

The measure (S 730 — S Rept 97-38) passed the Senate by voice vote May 5 and the House by a vote of 384-5 May 19. It allowed the Federal Crop Insurance Corporation (FCIC) to spend up to $14 million from funds normally reserved for indemnity payments to insured farmers, for administrative expenses. *(Vote 41, p. 24-H)*

The bill was reported by the Senate Agriculture Committee April 10. The House Agriculture Committee May 1 had reported a bill without the spending limit (HR 3020 — H Rept 97-27). ∎

Federal Farm Loan Interest Rates Raised

Budget reconciliation revisions brought higher interest rates for many federal farm loans and new charges for grading and inspecting cotton, tobacco and grain.

The bill (HR 3982 — PL 97-35) passed July 31 by Congress also gave dairymen price supports at least 5 percentage points above the 70 percent level the Reagan administration wanted.

The legislation explicitly stated that the dairy program would be reconsidered during deliberations on the farm bill reauthorizing agricultural programs for four years. But controversy delayed enactment of the farm bill, and separate measures were passed to prevent dairymen from reaping a bonus throughout the year. *(Farm bill, p. 535)*

The reconciliation cuts were felt through much of the Agriculture Department (USDA). E. "Kika" de la Garza, D-Texas, chairman of the House Agriculture Committee, noted that USDA programs were cut by $8.8 billion in fiscal years 1982-84, some $3 billion more than was required.

Conferees completed work July 24 after four days of negotiations. Key bargaining revolved around the Senate's refusal to accept the House provision for more liberal dairy price supports, while House conferees resisted Senate interest rate increases and other changes in farm lending programs. *(Reconciliation action, p. 256)*

The conference report (H Rept 97-208) included both the dairy program and lending revisions.

The Dairy Program

The House-passed dairy program that the reconciliation conferees retained was strongly opposed by the administration.

Because Reagan believed that the statutory support price of 80 percent of parity encouraged farmers to produce more milk than Americans could consume, he had already persuaded Congress to cancel a scheduled April 1 adjustment in the payment rate for dairymen. *(Story, p. 550)*

That action left payments at $13.10 per hundredweight — a figure that was about 75 percent of parity in the spring, and which dropped to about 72 percent of parity by the end of the year.

Parity is an index of prices farmers pay and receive, meant to approximate the earning power of farmers in 1910-14. The periodic adjustments were meant to reflect inflationary pressures.

Under the dairy program, if a farmer was not able to sell his dairy products at a price equivalent to the percentage of parity set by law, the government must buy the excess stocks at that price and store them.

In 1980, the government bought 579 million pounds of butter, cheese and non-fat dry milk, at a cost of $1.2 billion, excluding interest and storage charges.

Lowering the stipulated percentage of parity would decrease the government's costs, but dairy interests pushed for higher levels to protect their incomes.

Reagan wanted Congress to give the agriculture secretary broad discretion to set the support level at 70 percent of parity, or even less, to discourage production.

The reconciliation dairy section set a 75 percent minimum price support but postponed semiannual adjustments until fiscal 1983. Legislators intended that the dairy program be reappraised during consideration of the four-year reauthorization of farm programs.

But the House and Senate became embroiled in controversy over the farm bill and the 1977 law (PL 95-113) setting the current level of supports expired on Sept. 30. With that expiration, the reconciliation provision came into play, raising the price support from the current $13.10 per hundredweight to $13.49. *(1977 Almanac p. 417)*

The missed deadline set off a legislative scramble to block the price support hike. On Oct. 1, by a 328-58 vote, the House approved HR 4612 delaying the increase until Nov. 15, by which time the new farm bill with lower price supports was to have been enacted. *(Vote 219, p. 74-H)*

Senate action was blocked by William Proxmire, D-Wis., until he received pledges that Senate conferees on the omnibus farm bill would push for higher supports. The Senate by voice vote Oct. 19 cleared HR 4612 for the president, who signed it into law Oct. 20 (PL 97-67).

When it became clear that farm bill conferees would not reach agreement by Nov. 15, an unrelated bill was amended to postpone the increase until the end of 1981. The bill (S 1322) was cleared for the president when it was passed by the House Nov. 11. The Senate had passed it Nov. 9.

Provisions

As signed into law, Title I of HR 3982 (PL 97-35):

● Set ceilings on authorizations for USDA programs for fiscal years 1982-1984. The limits effectively canceled the indemnity program for beekeepers whose swarms have been damaged by pesticides or other toxic chemicals.

Funding for both titles (loans and donations) of the Food for Peace program (PL 480) was set at combined totals of $1.304 billion, $1.320 billion and $1.402 billion respectively for fiscal years 1982-84.

Authorization limits on other USDA programs were:

Dairy and Beekeeper Indemnity. No more than $200,000 each year.

Agricultural Marketing Service, Payments to States and Possessions. Fiscal year 1982, $1.571 million; 1983, $1.651 million; 1984, $1.723 million.

Farmers Home Administration (FmHA) Rural Community Fire Protection Grants. Fiscal year 1982, $3.565 million; 1983, $3.821 million; 1984, $4.038 million.

Rural Development Planning Grants. Fiscal 1982, $4.767 million; 1983, $4.959 million; 1984, $5.155 million.

Rural Development Grants. Fiscal 1982, $5.007 million; 1983, $5.280 million; 1984, $5.553 million.

Soil Conservation Service. Fiscal 1982, $588.875 million; 1983, $596.767 million; 1984, $602.865 million.

Agricultural Stabilization and Conservation Service (ASCS), Agricultural Conservation Program. Fiscal 1982, $201.325 million; 1983, $209.647 million; 1984, $218.216 million.

Forestry Incentives. Fiscal 1982, $15.090 million; 1983, $16.913 million; 1984, $18.314 million.

Water Bank Program. Fiscal 1982, $10.876 million; 1983, $10.854 million; 1984, $10.813 million.

Emergency Conservation Program. Fiscal 1982, $10.069 million; 1983, $10.507 million; 1984, $10.958 million.

Water and Waste Grants. No more than $154.9 million each year.

Forest Service. Fiscal year 1981, $1.575 billion; 1982, $1.498 billion; 1983, $1.560 billion; 1984, $1.620 billion. (Construction of a proposed road in a Washington state national forest was also barred.)

Personnel

● Placed a ceiling on USDA staff of no more than 117,000 "staff years" for each of the three years, compared to the current level of 121,000 and the department request of 124,000.

Dairy Programs

● Set dairy price supports for fiscal years 1982-1985 at a minimum of 75 percent of parity, an index based on farmers' costs and prices. Reconciliation required program changes only through fiscal 1984, but the bill included a four-year change in the dairy program. The conference statement declared that the dairy program would be reconsidered, along with support prices of other commodities, when Congress took up pending four-year reauthorizations of farm programs.

● Stipulated that the support level could rise to a maximum of 90 percent of parity and established a formula, based on government dairy stocks and anticipated purchases of dairy products under the program, for determining the actual parity support level each year.

● Required adjustments to reflect any increases in dairy imports.

● Provided also for semiannual adjustments in the actual payments, beginning in fiscal 1983, to offset changes in the parity index and thus keep the payments at the minimum 75 percent.

Commodity Credit Programs

● Set a $52 million-per-year ceiling on administrative expenses for the Commodity Credit Corporation.

● Gave the secretary of agriculture discretion to make loans for farm storage facilities, eliminating the current requirement that the loans must be made available. This permitted the administration to cease offering the loans, as it had requested.

● Authorized federal collection of fees, with penalties for non-payment, for costs of official grading and/or inspections of grain, tobacco, cotton, "naval stores" (turpentine and resin) and inspecting warehouses in which agricultural commodities were stored. The effect was to shift the cost from the federal budget to purchasers of the commodities or other sources in the private sector.

The bill limited the total amounts that could be collected.

FmHA Loans

● Raised the interest for FmHA loans for water and waste disposal and community facility projects to a level comparable to rates for municipal bonds. Retained the existing 5 percent rate for hardship cases.

● Increased interest by 2 percent on certain FmHA loans for projects that would convert prime farmland to non-farm uses, unless alternative sites were unavailable.

● Raised the interest for FmHA farm ownership loans to no more than half the cost of money to the government, and no less than 5 percent.

● Raised the interest for farm operating loans to 3 percentage points below the cost of money to the government.

● Set an overall ceiling of $700 million for fiscal 1982 for insured farm ownership loans.

● Set a ceiling of $1.325 billion for fiscal 1982 insured farm operating loans.

● Earmarked 20 percent of the operating loans for low-income, limited-resource borrowers, down from the current 25 percent.

● Set a ceiling of $300 million for insured water and waste disposal loans and $130 million for insured community facility loans.

● Stipulated that FmHA emergency loans for physical disasters be made only to farmers who have lost 30 percent or more of their crop, and for up to 80 percent of their losses. This affirmed an administrative action which had changed earlier figures of 20 and 90 percent respectively.

● Raised interest rates on disaster loans from 5 percent to no more than 8 percent for borrowers without other sources of credit and to commercial rates for others.

Rural Electrification Administration (REA)

● Fixed interest rates at 5 percent for REA insured loans for telephone and electric systems instead of permitting the loan rates to range between 2 percent and 5 percent.

● Allowed loans at less than 5 percent, but no less than 2 percent, for hardship cases.

● Required the REA administrator, at the request of the borrower, to secure REA guaranteed loans from the Federal Financing Bank at interest rates comparable to similar loans in that bank.

Gasohol

● Reduced to $460 million, from $600 million, funds administered by USDA for loans, loan guarantees, price guarantees and purchase agreements to promote production of alcohol and other fuels from biomass, such as crops and crop residues. (The conference agreement included an identical reduction for the separate biomass fuels promotion program in the Department of Energy.) ∎

Dairy Raise Blocked

An administration bill (S 509 — PL 97-6) to cancel a scheduled April 1 increase in the dairy price support provided President Reagan with one of his first legislative victories on Capitol Hill.

The legislation, cleared by Congress March 27, was the first piece of Reagan's ambitious economic program to go before Congress, and its passage was a significant victory. The president's allies and tacticians managed to blunt strong efforts by the dairy industry and some Democrats to make changes that were unacceptable to the president.

The measure canceled an April 1 increase of 90 cents per hundredweight in the federal price support for dairy products. The increase was required by a provision in the 1977 farm law (PL 95-113), which was extended for two years by Congress in 1979 (PL 96-127). *(1977 Almanac p. 417; 1979 Almanac p. 333)*

Administration officials contended that the increase would cost consumers an additional 8 cents per gallon for milk. They also maintained that the dairy program stimulated overproduction of milk and that eliminating the April 1 increase would save the federal government $147 million in 1981 in purchase and storage costs for dairy products.

The program required the government to buy, in the form of butter, dried milk and cheese, all the milk that dairy farmers cannot sell at the price support level. If the

April 1 adjustment were not blocked, the price support level would rise from the current level of $13.10 to $14.00 per hundredweight.

Dairy spokesmen, however, argued that inflation had so increased the expenses of dairymen that they needed the April 1 adjustment badly.

They said low feed-grain prices and relatively low beef prices — not the federal program — had prompted high dairy production. Without the adjustment, they warned, small- to moderate-sized dairy operations would simply fold.

Industry officials, divided on tactics, generally did not attack the basic bill and instead pressed for changes that could have delayed passage beyond the April 1 deadline.

In the Senate, dairymen backed an amendment to sharply curtail the imports of casein, a milk protein that is not produced in the United States. Enacting the limit could have meant jurisdictional complications in the House that could have delayed enactment of the bill.

In the House, the industry secured the approval of the House Agriculture Livestock, Dairy and Poultry Subcommittee for a four-year dairy bill instead of the administration's one-year plan.

Both efforts failed.

The Senate defeated the casein amendments and passed the bill (S 509 — S Rept 97-24) by an 88-5 vote March 25. It added two non-binding amendments expressing objections to the continuing embargo on sales of U.S. grain to the Soviet Union. The bill had been reported March 10 by the Senate Agriculture Committee. *(Senate Vote 40, p. 11-S)*

The House Agriculture Committee in reporting its bill March 24 (HR 2594 — H Rept 97-12) overruled its subcommittee. The bill was considered under a rule designating the bill as HR 1986. After passing the bill by voice vote March 26, the House substituted its language for that of S 509.

The Senate accepted the House version deleting the embargo language and cleared the measure for the president by voice vote March 27. The President signed it March 31.

Senate Action

The president won the first skirmish March 4 when the Senate Agriculture Committee voted 14-2 to cancel the scheduled increase.

The administration pushed hard for the legislation in an effort one congressional aide called a "full-court press."

Reagan personally telephoned some members of the Senate panel prior to the vote. Agriculture Secretary John R. Block, armed with milk production statistics from members' districts, met with Rep. Tom Harkin, D-Iowa, chairman of the House Agriculture Subcommittee on Livestock, Dairy and Poultry, and subcommittee members the day the Senate panel acted.

Members of the full Senate panel clearly were uncomfortable with the choice of opposing dairy interests or of appearing to thwart the president's economic recovery package. Rudy Boschwitz, R-Minn., whose state was the nation's fourth largest dairy producer, said, "I told the people of Minnesota to hang in there with President Reagan — and I hope they hang in with me."

Only Patrick J. Leahy, D-Vt., and Mark Andrews, R-N.D., voted against reporting the bill. John Melcher, D-Mont., voted "present."

The Casein Connection

The committee narrowly rejected, by an 8-8 tie vote, a controversial industry-backed amendment offered by Melcher to restrict imports of casein, an inexpensive milk protein used in manufacturing synthetic cheese, non-dairy "creamer" and certain other foods.

Committee Republicans, except for Boschwitz and Andrews, voted against the amendment, while Democrats, except for Alan J. Dixon, D-Ill., voted for it. Melcher vowed to bring it up on the floor.

Andrews and Leahy characterized the amendment as an essential anti-inflation measure. "Heavily subsidized imports," they said, competed unfairly with domestic dairy products. An import restriction would force food manufacturers to turn to American milk products, they argued. That would lessen the amount of surplus milk bought by the government, saving a third of a million dollars annually, they said.

Senate Floor Action

The Senate considered the bill March 17, 19, 23 and 24.

On March 17, Melcher resurrected the casein amendment. The administration objected that the limitation would invite trade retaliation from other nations and that casein imports had not been shown to damage the American dairy industry.

Senate debate ended abruptly March 17 after the Republican leadership lost a motion 45-53 to table — and thus kill — Melcher's amendment. Votes were postponed several times while the Republican leadership marshaled its troops. *(Vote 33, p. 10-S)*

Industrial users of dairy products and casein, joined by consumer groups and the self-styled citizens' lobby, Common Cause, also fought the casein amendment. When the matter came up again on March 24, Melcher's amendment lost 38-60. *(Senate Vote 34, p. 11-S)*

A complicated series of votes on embargo amendments followed on March 24. Anti-embargo amendments also could have caused problems in the House, which in 1980 voted strongly against an appropriations rider meant to end the embargo. *(1980 Almanac p. 212)*

The first vote in the series had the effect of rejecting, 33-65, an amendment by Edward Zorinsky, D-Neb., to cancel the embargo in April. Zorinsky's amendment would have allowed the embargo to continue if Reagan certified to Congress that it was needed for foreign policy reasons or if the president took other specified actions.

The key vote was on a secondary Zorinsky amendment to change the date of the deadline. *(Vote 35, p. 11-S)*

The Senate then adopted, 58-36, a substitute by Roger W. Jepsen, R-Iowa, declaring the "sense of the Senate" that the embargo should end. *(Senate Vote 36, p. 11-S)*

It then approved by an 80-14 vote an amendment by Majority Leader Howard H. Baker Jr., R-Tenn., expressing the "sense of the Senate" that Soviet agricultural imports should be barred from the United States until the embargo ended.

Baker's amendment was a substitute for an amendment proposed by David L. Boren, D-Okla., that would have ended the Soviet imports April 1. *(Vote 37, p. 11-S)*

House Action

At the March 18 meeting of the House Agriculture subcommittee, Tony Coelho, D-Calif., and James M.

Jeffords, R-Vt., said the panel gave Reagan a "victory" by approving a bill that would save only $20 million less than the president wanted.

In fact, the winner was the dairy industry, since the panel approved a four-year plan that appeared to lock in higher price supports, with less flexibility than Reagan wanted.

The subcommittee bill, adopted by a 7-6 vote, set the dairy price support at 75 to 80 percent of parity through 1985, with semiannual adjustments, depending on how much surplus milk, cheese and butter the government owned.

Nothing in the bill prevented the support level from going higher than 80 percent. The bill was a modified version of a proposal drafted by the milk producers.

Because the rate currently was about 74 per cent, backers of the bill argued that raising dairy price supports by one percent in the next six months would mean savings approaching those sought by Reagan.

The full Agriculture Committee reversed that decision one day later (March 19) partly at the urging of the House leadership not to be obstructionist and to allow the president "a clear shot at his bill."

The bill had been reported as a "clean bill," HR 2594, but it came to the floor under a rule designating it HR 1986, the original administration number.   ∎

Transportation/Commerce/Consumers

President Reagan's efforts to reshape national transportation policy ran into heavy resistance in Congress in 1981.

He sought to reduce federal support sharply for transportation programs and to shift many federal costs to states, local governments and transportation users.

But congressional critics argued that federally aided programs — such as Amtrak, Conrail, highway construction and mass transit — were important to the nation's economy and would be crippled by some of the administration's proposals.

Instead of accepting the full scope of Reagan's plans for the demise or restructuring of many programs, Congress fashioned compromises providing for reduced funding and in some cases more restrictions. That was the case in both rail and highway programs; while the administration did not obtain all the funding cuts it wanted, it did win some curtailment.

Part of the administration's plan to balance the budget involved new or increased user fees for aviation, port development, inland waterways and Coast Guard services. Reagan said federal services should be financed by groups that especially benefited from them and not by the general taxpayers.

Congress generally put off action on user-fee proposals until 1982. Many members and interest groups said the plans would result in excessive fees that did not properly account for public benefits from the services, such as the economic gains that a community received from a busy airport.

The administration also sought to cut back spending for commerce programs. However, consumer advocates found support on Capitol Hill to head off attacks that they felt might devastate the Consumer Product Safety Commission (CPSC) and the National Consumer Cooperative Bank.

Congress and the administration moved on separate tracks to deregulate the telecommunications industry and restructure the American Telephone and Telegraph Co. (AT&T). The Senate passed a landmark bill revising the technologically outdated Communications Act of 1934 and freeing AT&T to enter previously closed unregulated markets like data processing by creating a separate subsidiary. It was the first such bill to reach the floor in the five years that Congress had been working on a telecommunications bill.

The administration through the Justice Department reached a proposed agreement in an antitrust suit giving AT&T access to the lucrative unregulated markets but requiring it to divest its 22 local telephone companies.

Railroads

After several rocky years, the financial picture for both Amtrak and Conrail began to improve in 1981. But spokesmen for the passenger and freight systems said they still needed more federal help.

Administration officials argued that Amtrak was inefficient and general taxpayers should not subsidize railroad passengers. Reagan proposed reducing funding to $613 million in fiscal 1982.

Amtrak supporters cited improvements in ridership and service and charged that the proposed cuts would shut down passenger service outside the Northeast Corridor, which linked Washington, New York and Boston. Truncating the network did not make sense when many communities were finding themselves with less airline service as a result of airline deregulation and motorists were facing higher gasoline costs, they said.

While authorizing the $735 million that rail officials said was necessary to operate a national system, Congress also required Amtrak to do whatever was necessary to operate within its available resources. That could include raising fares and eliminating routes. Amtrak was directed to recover at least 50 percent of its operating costs from the fare box or other non-federal sources.

The administration wanted to phase out all funding for Conrail by the end of 1982 and sell or transfer its lines to other railroads. Several billion dollars in federal subsidies had been spent over the years on Conrail, which had been plagued by management problems, expensive labor agreements and other difficulties.

Some members of Congress feared that breaking up the railroad would result in the loss of freight service, which would have a ripple effect on the entire economy.

Congress reached a solution that gave Conrail more time and money to become successful and thereby more attractive for sale as a single entity. It permitted Conrail to spin off expensive commuter operations inherited when the system was formed in 1976 and to sell unprofitable subsidiaries. Major changes were made in legislated labor protection benefits to reduce spending.

Other Major Transportation Changes

Reagan wanted to realign the partnership of the federal, state and local governments for many major road programs.

The Republican Senate agreed to the general concept of a comprehensive multi-year highway bill as sought by the administration. However, it did not reduce Interstate costs as much as proposed nor did it approve the president's plan to phase out funds for urban and rural roads.

The House agreed to some changes in the Interstate program but passed a more limited bill. Key members wanted to delay comprehensive legislation until 1982 when they would have a better estimate of available revenue. Some also wanted to tie the popular highway program to mass transit legislation in an effort to fight administration attacks on mass transit aid.

A compromise on a limited Interstate bill was reached partly because the states needed legislation to free up previously approved Interstate monies.

The final measure reduced spending by eliminating the eligibility of some projects for Interstate construction funds. It also increased aid for highway repairs, beginning to shift the focus from new construction to repairing the roads already built.

Mass transit authorizations were reduced in the budget reconciliation legislation, but the measure did not address Reagan's plan to phase out operating aid by 1985.

Efforts to revitalize the financially ailing maritime industry continued to flounder, although some industry officials were optimistic that the 1981 move of the Maritime Administration to the Transportation Department from the Commerce Department would focus more government attention on their problems.

There were some major changes in national maritime policy in the 1981 reconciliation bill. Congress supported an administration request to end maritime construction subsidies. Also, owners of U.S.-flag ships were allowed under limited conditions to buy or to build foreign vessels in fiscal 1982 and 1983 and still be eligible for operating subsidies for their ships. The subsidies were designed to help make U.S. ships competitive with foreign vessels.

The House continued efforts to ease government regulation of transportation when it passed a bill that would reduce the restraints on the intercity bus industry.

Supported by the industry, the bill would provide more competition by allowing bus companies to establish new routes and to drop unprofitable ones more easily. They also would be able to raise and lower rates with less government review.

Communications Rewrite

Congress continued to grapple with communications issues in 1981, with the prospect of resolving some of the most important issues likely in 1982.

A Senate bill revising the 1934 Communications Act would allow AT&T to enter unregulated and computer-oriented markets, such as data processing, that were barred to it by a 1956 consent decree settling a Justice Department antitrust suit. AT&T would be required to establish a subsidiary with separate accounting to enter those markets.

A bill was introduced in the House that also would require a separate subsidiary for some activities, but its proponents argued it would go further than the Senate measure to protect existing and potential competitors of AT&T from being overwhelmed by the giant firm.

However, the futures of both measures were left in doubt by a new Justice Department pact with AT&T to revise the 1956 decree and allow the firm to proceed with unregulated ventures. In exchange, AT&T was required to divest itself of its 22 local telephone companies, or two-thirds of its assets.

Some members said they would continue to pursue legislation because they feared the agreement would result in high local telephone rate hikes and possibly grant AT&T certain competitive advantages. The issues raised by the

agreement should be clarified by Congress, they said.

Congress increased broadcasting license terms to seven years for radio and five years for television, both up from three years, as part of the reconciliation measure.

But House and Senate conferees dropped Senate provisions that would have codified Federal Communications Commission actions to drop programming rules for radio. Another bill that would eliminate some rules on radio and television operators remained pending in the Senate.

Some consumer, religious, labor and other groups argued that deregulation would make it more difficult for citizens to protest poor local broadcasting.

Public broadcasting met with mixed results. Congress approved $80 million more for fiscal 1984-1986 for the Corporation for Public Broadcasting (CPB) than Reagan wanted and allowed some public radio and television stations to experiment with advertising to help raise funds.

However, CPB's advance funding, designed by Congress to protect public broadcasting from political pressures and to help long-range planning, was violated when Congress agreed to some of Reagan's cuts in funds already appropriated for fiscal 1983.

Consumers

Consumer legislation was marked more by what was avoided than what was gained.

The administration preferred to abolish the independent CPSC but then sought to clip its wings by putting it under the Commerce Department. Some critics contended that CPSC over-regulated businesses.

Consumer advocates said the agency protected the public from unsafe products, and they argued that the CPSC would be buried in the larger department.

House supporters slipped language into the reconciliation bill retaining the CPSC's independent status. The agency, however, was forced to lay off many employees because of budget cuts, and its regulations became subject to a congressional veto.

The Co-op Bank was targeted for extinction by the administration, but some Republican House members saved it by threatening to vote against a GOP budget proposal if the plan did not include bank funds. But in exchange for fiscal 1982 funding, the bank would have to end its government-backed status and become a private institution sooner than originally planned.

A Federal Trade Commission (FTC) rule requiring used-car dealers to disclose information about known major defects almost became the first test of the congressional veto power established in 1980. But Sen. Bob Packwood, R-Ore., blocked veto resolutions with a parliamentary maneuver, postponing action until 1982 and giving consumer advocates more time to try to reverse the strong sentiment in Congress for the veto.

Car dealers said the regulation would require expensive inspections. Supporters of the rule argued that inspections were specifically not required. Some feared that if the used-car rule was overturned, any regulation opposed by an industry group could be vetoed easily.

—By Judy Sarasohn

Telecommunications Pace Interrupted

Congressional momentum to deregulate much of the telecommunications industry and restructure the American Telephone & Telegraph Co. (AT&T) was interrupted by the announcement of a proposed settlement of an antitrust suit.

The Senate Oct. 7 by a vote of 90-4 passed a far-reaching telecommunications measure (S 898 — S Rept 97-170), the first bill to reach the floor in the five years that Congress had been considering revisions to the 1934 Communications Act. *(Vote 308, p. 52-S)*

A substantially different bill (HR 5158) was introduced Dec. 10 in the House, and hearings by the Energy and Commerce Telecommunications Subcommittee were scheduled for the second session.

However, serious questions about the legislation were raised by an announcement Jan. 8, 1982, by the Justice Department and AT&T of a proposed antitrust consent decree modification that went beyond the pending telecommunications legislation.

The agreement would allow the firm to enter unregulated and computer-oriented fields, such as data processing, if it divested itself of its 22 local telephone operating companies.

Furthermore, it would give AT&T relatively free rein to use its research and manufacturing arms — Bell Laboratories and Western Electric — to enter the new markets and allow AT&T to retain its long-distance operations.

AT&T initially had opposed divestiture but acquiesced because the plan contained fewer restrictions on non-regulated activities than the pending legislation, according to AT&T Chairman Charles Brown.

Both bills required AT&T to establish a separate subsidiary to enter unregulated markets but neither called for divestiture.

Key members of Congress said they would continue to pursue legislation to supplement the agreement and soften any potentially adverse impact.

Without legislation, the plan to split up the AT&T network could result in substantial hikes in local telephone rates because the local rates would no longer be subsidized by AT&T's long-distance service, they said. Other questions were raised about future state regulation of the divested telephone companies and the quality of local service.

There were also concerns about the degree of competition within the telecommunications industry and the possible funneling of funds from AT&T's regulated long-distance telephone service into the new unregulated businesses AT&T would be allowed to enter, they said.

Further, officials of the Federal Communications Commission (FCC) were not sure how the AT&T-Justice Department plan would affect the FCC's administrative attempts to allow AT&T to provide unregulated services. The FCC earlier had announced its own plan to allow AT&T to provide unregulated service if it set up a separate subsidiary.

As congressional committees prepared for hearings on the agreement, U.S. District Judge Harold H. Greene of Washington, D.C., announced Jan. 21 that he would not approve the plan without a court determination of whether it was in the public interest, as required by the 1974 Tunney Act (PL 93-528). Greene had presided over the year-long trial of a Justice Department antitrust suit against

AT&T. *(1974 Almanac, p. 291)*

The Agreement

The Justice Department-AT&T plan would modify a 1956 consent decree that settled a 1949 antitrust suit and barred AT&T from unregulated activities, in effect restricting the firm to providing regulated telephone service. The agreement also called for the dismissal of the Justice Department's antitrust suit, which had been filed in 1974.

The modification permitted AT&T, in addition to retaining Bell Labs and Western Electric, to continue to provide long-distance service under government economic regulation through its Long Lines Department. AT&T would provide telephones, rather than the local companies supplying them.

The agreement did not specify how AT&T must divest itself of the operating companies. There could be one new giant company to provide local service, a prospect critics said would not promote competition. Or there could be many separate firms.

The local companies would provide regulated local telephone service and would allow access to long-distance carriers, such as AT&T or MCI.

The local companies would not be allowed to favor AT&T in granting access to the local telephone network, in providing service quality, or in purchasing products and services. They would charge a fee to connect long-distance carriers with the network.

Until Sept. 1, 1987, however, the local company could require AT&T to provide any service needed to allow the company to fulfill the requirements of the agreement.

Legislation

Many critics of AT&T believed HR 5158, introduced by Timothy E. Wirth, D-Colo., chairman of the House Telecommunications Subcommittee, would provide more safeguards than the Senate bill or the FCC plan against the possibility of AT&T unfairly overwhelming competing firms.

All three would modify the 1956 decree and allow AT&T to go into unregulated and computer-oriented markets. But they required AT&T to establish a subsidiary with separate accounting to do so.

S 898 and HR 5158 also would limit AT&T's entry into electronic mass media services — such as providing newspaper-type information by wire — a restriction sought by the American Newspaper Publishers Association (ANPA) and other media groups.

The FCC plan was not clear on the electronic issue. Assistant Attorney General William F. Baxter said the proposed consent decree would allow AT&T to provide electronic mass media services and cable television.

Sen. Bob Packwood, R-Ore., chairman of the Commerce Committee, said that Congress should ensure that local telephone rates did not greatly increase as a result of the plan. S 898 continued the long-distance service subsidy to prevent local rates from increasing more than 10 percent.

Wirth called for supplemental legislation. He contended that the agreement and the Senate bill would result in local rate increases of 46 percent because local companies would lose the long-distance subsidy and other aid.

Local operating companies would lose revenue from the abrupt transfer of "Yellow Pages" and customer terminal equipment to the new AT&T, Wirth said.

HR 5158 provided for a fund to be fed by charges on long-distance carriers that could be used to prevent big hikes in local rates.

But AT&T's Brown disputed that rates would rise substantially and contended an increase of about 10 percent a year would be necessary even without the agreement because of inflation and increased competition in the long-distance service market.

Justice Department officials said the access fees under the AT&T plan could be used to subsidize local rates.

Background

The Communications Act of 1934 was enacted at a time when one out of every three homes had a telephone, and policy makers believed a monopoly was the key to creating a nationwide network.

Without competitive pressures during the early years, AT&T grew to become the largest corporation in the world. Eventually virtually every home and business became wired into an interlocking network the spanned the country. There are almost 1,500 independent telephone companies that connect with AT&T to form the nationwide telephone network.

But the nature of telephones began to change; telephone lines could be used to transmit high-speed data as well as human conversation, and telephone calls could be transmitted by microwave and satellite. Other firms entered the scene and chipped at the monopoly.

The FCC's Carterfone decision, upheld by the U.S. Supreme Court in 1968, allowed another firm to hook up its car radio phones to the Bell System, breaking the equipment monopoly. Later, specialized carriers providing long-distance service by microwave were allowed to connect to the AT&T local lines.

Some of those firms, however, complained that AT&T unfairly restricted their access to the network and the equipment sales field. AT&T still made most of the telephone equipment, bought most of the equipment and provided most of the telephone service.

AT&T argued that the network would be damaged by improper equipment and complained of the restrictions on its use of new technologies. Among its chief targets was the 1956 consent decree stemming from a 1949 antitrust lawsuit brought by the Justice Department to separate Western Electric.

The consent decree, AT&T officials said, had no place in a competitive environment. AT&T argued that since it already employed the new technology, it should be allowed to compete with other firms. The company's telephone switching equipment was basically a computer operation that could be used to manage the transmissions that currently were sent along unchanged.

The increased opportunities of telecommunications led to mounting pressure to revise the 1934 law and resulting regulations and to clarify who could provide the new services and under what circumstances.

Congressional Efforts

Early congressional efforts to rewrite the telecommunications law progressed no further than committees, with most of the action on the House side.

A bill (HR 12323) drafted and pushed by AT&T in

1976 garnered a lot of support but died at the end of the session. A 1977 version (HR 8), nicknamed the "Bell Bill," was blocked by congressional leaders, who argued that the measure would have essentially outlawed competition and would not have helped consumers. *(1977 Almanac p. 566)*

In 1978, a bill (HR 13015) introduced in the House would have required AT&T to give up Western Electric, something AT&T hotly opposed. A 1979 proposal (HR 3333) required AT&T to deal with its affiliated companies at arms-length, a concept also opposed by AT&T. The bill also contained broadcast provisions that were opposed by segments of the television industry.

Both plans died without being reported by committees.

On Jan. 29, 1980, telecommunications deregulation won its first approval by the House Commerce Communications Subcommittee.

Markup of the bill (HR 6121) by the full committee, however, was delayed for months because of controversy over how AT&T should conduct business with a separate subsidiary.

Revised legislation approved by the subcommittee in June required more restructuring of the firm than the earlier version.

The legislation generally continued to regulate the basic phone service offered by AT&T and other carriers. But it ended regulation in other services, such as the manufacture and sale of telephone equipment and some special long-distance phone services. Companies could enter those unregulated areas with little government interference.

AT&T would be allowed to enter data processing and other computer markets that were closed to it, but any unregulated activities that AT&T entered would have to be handled by a subsidiary with separate accounting for unregulated services.

AT&T was concerned that too much restructuring and too many restrictions would prevent it from properly maintaining the nationwide telephone network and from competing in the new fields.

Critics of AT&T charged that the subsidiary would be massive and could drive competitors out of business unless there were enough safeguards written into the bill.

Later in the summer, critics launched a drive for new hearings on both the House committee bill and legislation pending in the Senate Commerce Committee (S 2827).

Journalists and consumer advocates were worried that AT&T could control the origin, flow and content of information the public normally received from a variety of independent sources. Their concern involved the production of news and advertising. Several companies had been experimenting with the electronic delivery of reading material to home television sets.

The ANPA was concerned that AT&T would begin to produce and distribute news over its wires. Many publishers also were concerned that a computerized "Yellow Pages" would take classified advertising from newspapers.

The House committee bill barred AT&T from originating mass media services, but the measure before the Senate panel had no similar provision.

Disagreement over antitrust implications and the lateness of the session led to the death of the House bill.

Although the Commerce Committee Aug. 25 reported the bill (H Rept 96-1252), the Judiciary Committee Sept. 30 ordered it reported "adversely, without prejudice." That signaled the opposition of a powerful committee, and the complex legislation was not brought to the floor before the

96th Congress adjourned Dec. 16.

The Judiciary Committee indicated it was concerned about not having time to study the complex bill thoroughly and to assess its impact on the pending Justice Department antitrust suit.

S 2827, which died without coming to a committee vote, was similar in some respects regarding restructuring, but a basic difference was the issue of FCC authority. The House panel wanted to bar the FCC from making any further structural changes in AT&T, while the Senate wanted to retain FCC authority to intervene.

FCC Acts on its Own

In April, 1980, the FCC moved administratively to deregulate telecommunications.

After a four-year study, it proposed a rule that would deregulate the manufacture and sale of terminal equipment — everything from household telephones to high-speed computer terminals.

It drew a line between basic telephone service and "enhanced services." The latter combined basic telephone service with computer processing that retrieved or changed information. The FCC held that only basic telephone service was subject to regulation.

AT&T would be required to create a separate subsidiary, if it wanted to sell unregulated products and services.

The FCC order also restricted the information flow between the parent company and the subsidiary to prevent the subsidiary from having an unfair advantage over its competitors. In addition, the subsidiary would be barred from owning transmission facilities.

AT&T took preliminary steps to meet the FCC proposals.

1981 Senate Committee Action

The Senate Commerce Committee began hearings in June with its new chairman, Packwood, sharply criticizing the Reagan administration and industry lobbyists.

The administration, like its predecessor, was finding it difficult to secure Justice Department endorsement of the legislation. Although S 898 disavowed any intent of affecting pending antitrust suits, the Justice Department was still concerned that the legislation would somehow interefere.

Packwood said internal administration bickering over policy led to Commerce Secretary Malcolm Baldrige canceling an appearance before the panel.

He also charged that lobbyists had distorted the bill.

On July 16, the committee ordered S 898 reported by a vote of 16-1.

The sole negative vote was cast by Ernest F. Hollings, D-S.C., ranking minority member and former chairman of the Communications Subcommittee. Hollings contended that the bill would not adequately prevent AT&T from overwhelming its competition.

"It is a cut and paste and patch job . . . of what Bell is willing to accept," Hollings asserted.

As reported, the bill continued federal regulation of ordinary telephone service but deregulated most other telecommunications products and services, such as the sale of telephone equipment. AT&T was allowed to enter unregulated markets only through a fully separated subsidiary.

Significant opposition to the bill from the newspaper publishers was removed when the committee restricted AT&T's entry into electronic publishing.

The bill also got a boost from the cable television industry, which won restraints on local regulation of cable rates. Those provisions, however, touched off a round of heavy lobbying by municipalities and counties, which objected to the loss of authority over cable TV.

Although the approach of S 898 was similar to the 1980 measures and to the proposed FCC reorganization of AT&T, the bill placed fewer restrictions on AT&T's relationship with its subsidiaries. Also, it was less radical than the divestiture sought by the Justice Department in the antitrust suit.

Meanwhile, Packwood had told the Reagan administration, which eventually endorsed the thrust of S 898, that the Justice Department suit would impede House action. The administration considered requesting that the suit be dropped, but it did not do so.

Support, Opposition

AT&T spokesman Pic Wagner said Bell still had reservations about parts of S 898, but it was pleased that the committee moved the bill along.

Many of AT&T's existing and potential competitors, however, continued to oppose S 898 because of what they termed a lack of safeguards concerning the separate subsidiary.

Critics claimed the subsidiary — dubbed "Baby Bell" — would not really be separate but would be a "giant clone" of AT&T.

Herbert N. Jasper, executive vice president of the Ad Hoc Committee for Competitive Telecommunications (ACCT), which opposed the bill, pointed to the panel's specific restrictions on AT&T's entry into electronic publishing and the home alarm industry as proof of the members' lack of confidence in the bill's general safeguards. ACCT represented several companies that provided special long-distance telecommunications services.

Other Committee Action

Before the committee marked up the bill, it reached a compromise with ANPA to restrict AT&T's entry into electronic publishing. AT&T would be allowed to provide the transmission lines to home video terminals and produce weather, time and some sports information, but it could not originate other news.

AT&T, through a second separate subsidiary, would be allowed to provide electronic "Yellow Pages," with addresses and telephone numbers transmitted over telephone lines. But it could not include special advertising and prices.

ANPA officials had complained about First Amendment issues in the original provision that would have required the FCC to determine what was "news" and, therefore beyond AT&T's realm. But many publishers also feared AT&T could update electronic "Yellow Pages" with special sales information and compete with their classified advertising. The bill still allowed the FCC to decide if a proposed service was a mass media service.

The committee by a vote of 8-9 rejected a Hollings amendment that would have required AT&T to sell at least 10 percent of the separated subsidiary's stock to the public.

Hollings said the stock requirement would help ensure public review of AT&T's relationships with the subsidiary and make it difficult for either firm to give preferential treatment to the other.

Communications Subcommittee Chairman Barry Goldwater, R-Ariz., said the amendment would break up

AT&T and lead to the destruction of the basic telephone network.

Slade Gorton, R-Wash., agreed with Hollings that the intended safeguards against potential AT&T anti-competitive behavior were not clear.

"It's an awfully small sea and a large whale. We want to make sure the other fish can swim around," Gorton said.

By a 9-8 vote, the committee approved an amendment offered by Ted Stevens, R-Alaska, that would prevent AT&T from entering the home alarm industry unless there were alternative delivery systems. The industry depended on telephone lines to conduct the alarm signals, and companies feared that AT&T, which provided most of those lines, would woo away their customers.

The bill was reported July 27.

Senate Floor Action

A major issue during three days of debate Oct. 5, 6 and 7 was whether S 898 sufficiently protected AT&T competitors.

The Senate actually began skirmishing Oct. 1 with Hollings preventing floor action by objecting to a unanimous consent request to consider the measure.

While Hollings said he did not intend to filibuster, he said he wanted to delay floor consideration until more senators could learn more about the complex legislation.

Hollings argued that Senators needed more time to understand both the basic legislation and the amendments that had been proposed to strengthen safeguards against possible anti-competitive activities by AT&T.

"Without meaningful separation between the regulated parent and the unregulated affiliate — subsidiary — competition will not develop, and deregulation will merely permit AT&T to re-monopolize outside the protection of regulation," he said Oct. 5 after debate began.

Packwood insisted that the separate subsidiary requirement and other safeguards were sufficient.

In response to concerns about competition and antitrust implications, a number of amendments were worked out between the Judiciary and Commerce committees and Assistant Attorney General Baxter to help ensure adequate separation between AT&T and the subsidiary and to foster competition. They included a guarantee that AT&T competitors have adequate access to the local networks.

The package was approved by voice vote Oct. 6.

But some critics were not satisfied. The amendments, offered by Judiciary Chairman Strom Thurmond, R-S.C., made S 898 "simply atrocious rather than outrageous," said ACCT's Jasper.

However, AT&T Chairman Brown said the bill was "doubly tough" on AT&T and called it "the most significant milestone yet in congressional efforts" to establish a modern telecommunications policy.

Amendments

Several other amendments were adopted Oct. 6. After heavy lobbying by the National League of Cities, the Senate adopted 59-34 an amendment offered by Goldwater to delete language restricting local governments' authority to regulate basic cable television rates. Goldwater said he had promised the cities that hearings would be held before any vote on cable legislation. *(Vote 304, p. 52-S)*

In approving the Goldwater measure, the Senate negated an earlier amendment adopted 52-40 that would have restored most of local governments' authority over cable.

The earlier amendment, supporters said, was a symbolic show of support for cable operators. *(Vote 303, p. 52-S)*

In other action, the Senate:

Adopted 86-4 an amendment by Bill Bradley, D-N.J., that would require the FCC, when it revokes or declines to renew a VHF television station license in a state with more than one station, to reallocate the channel, if technically possible, to a state that does not have one. New Jersey does not have a VHF station. *(Vote 305, p. 52-S)*

Rejected 26-68 a Hollings amendment that would require at least 10 percent of the subsidiary's stock to be sold to persons other than AT&T and its affiliates. *(Vote 306, p. 52-S)*

On Oct. 7, the Senate rejected 38-54 an amendment by Rudy Boschwitz, R-Minn., to eliminate a provision that would allow telephone companies to provide cable service in rural areas possibly under FCC rules. *(Vote 307, p. 52-S)*

Provisions

As passed by the Senate, S 898:

● Established the promotion of competition in the telecommunications industry as national policy.

● Continued regulation of basic telephone and telecommunications services. Federal regulation would pre-empt state regulation of long-distance telephone service within the state. Before basic telephone and telecommunications services may be deregulated, the FCC must determine that there was effective competition and the services would continue to be universally and reasonably available.

Basic telecommunications service generally referred to minimum, two-way service provided on a universal basis. This might include some computer uses of local telephone service and in the future might involve uses not now considered essential, such as electronic home banking.

● Directed the FCC to reduce or eliminate regulation of telecommunications services as competition develops, unless the change would damage national security.

● Provided that the FCC could take limited regulatory steps to prevent AT&T, Western Electric and Bell Labs from engaging in anti-competitive practices with a separated subsidiary. For example, the FCC might act to prevent cross subsidization, which would be the use of AT&T revenues and resources derived from regulated services to give the subsidiary an unfair advantage over competitors.

● Allowed AT&T to provide overall management policy for a separated subsidiary as long as costs were properly allocated between AT&T and the subsidiary.

● Directed the FCC to prevent unreasonable rate hikes for basic telephone service. The FCC would be allowed to set surcharges on connection rates for long-distance service to subsidize rural telephone service.

● Directed the FCC within 30 days of enactment of the bill to identify the carriers to be regulated, based on the kinds of services provided. Regulated carriers generally would be the larger telephone companies currently fully subject to FCC regulation. Unregulated carriers would include some smaller telephone companies and carriers that provide microwave, satellite and other services.

● Classified AT&T as a dominant-regulated carrier, which subjects the firm to additional restrictions not applicable to other regulated carriers. Included within the AT&T classification was its Long Lines Department, which supplied long-distance service, and the local Bell System telephone companies.

● Allowed the FCC under certain conditions to reclassify carriers after the initial determination.

● Barred a carrier that sells regulated services to a second company from prohibiting the second company from reselling the service to other customers. This meant that the second company could market a regulated service, such as long distance, combined with other special services, or it might offer regulated services at a discount to a group of small users at one location like an industrial park.

The FCC would be barred generally from regulating the resale of services.

● Required that if the Postal Service became involved in electronic mail service, and the FCC determined that such activity was a telecommunications service, the Postal Service must provide the electronic mail service through a separate division within the agency that had its own employees and accounting.

● Allowed the FCC to exempt regulated carriers from its rules when consistent with the public interest.

● Required carriers and the Postal Service, if applicable, upon reasonable request to provide connections and facilities for regulated services on a non-discriminatory basis. Telecommunications facilities involved the equipment that allowed for the transmission of information, such as wire, cable, microwave, satellite and fiber optics.

● Authorized the FCC to specify or approve regulated carriers' rates, terms and conditions for regulated telecommunications services, facilities and interconnections.

Local telephone carriers by Sept. 1, 1984, must begin to provide all long-distance carriers with access to local networks equal in type and quality to the access provided by the local carrier for its own long-distance services and any affiliated long-distance carrier. This would prevent the carrier from requiring customers of the second company to dial more digits for long distance than its own customers.

Violation of any rule or order promulgated under this provision would be subject to a $250,000 fine.

Revenues and Tariffs

● Required carriers to file with the FCC tariffs, (schedules of rates and terms of service); contracts and technical information for regulated services. To avoid potential cross subsidization, all tariffs must be accompanied by cost data establishing their reasonableness.

● Barred the FCC or any state commission from considering revenues derived from unregulated activities in reviewing rates for regulated services. However, a state commission for four years may take into account revenues derived from printed "Yellow Pages."

● Allowed the FCC to bar a regulated carrier from discontinuing or reducing a regulated service unless it certified that the change would serve the public.

AT&T would not be allowed to disclose to a separated subsidiary, or any affiliate providing support, components or subassemblies to the subsidiary, any information on equipment and the telephone network prior to release to any other firm or in different form.

● Authorized the FCC to prescribe the form of accounts, records and memorandums to be kept by regulated carriers and directed the FCC within one year of enactment to prescribe guidelines for allocating costs and revenues between regulated and unregulated goods and services.

● Established a board to determine the costs of long-distance carriers' interconnections to local telephone networks. The FCC would create a method for apportioning the costs of access to local telephone networks. Board decisions would be binding on the FCC unless the commission determined that they were arbitrary or inconsistent with the legislation. The FCC may consider establishing interconnection rates that would provide at least as much revenue to the local carrier as it received during 1980.

● Barred regulated local telephone carriers from discontinuing local service to enforce the collection of long-distance service charges owed by a customer.

Separated Subsidiary

● Set rules for the establishment by AT&T (or any other dominant-regulated carrier) of one or more separated subsidiaries. No more than one member of the subsidiary's governing board may be a member of the AT&T governing board or an officer or employee of AT&T or its affiliates. There may not be common employees and officers.

Any business between a separated subsidiary and AT&T must be done by contract on a fully auditable and compensatory basis and in the same manner as with any non-affiliate. There must be separate financial records.

AT&T or its affiliates may not disclose to the subsidiary any commercial information acquired in the provision of regulated services which would give an unfair competitive advantage to the subsidiary.

Any marketing, sales, manufacturing, research and development for unregulated services and products must be done by a separated subsidiary within six years of enactment. The bill would allow common institutional advertising under some conditions if each party paid a fair share. The subsidiary may not offer transmission facilities similiar to AT&T's for four years following enactment.

There may be no joint property except for international telecommunications property. There may be no joint ventures except during times of public peril, national emergency or for international undertakings.

The separation requirements would not apply to the provision of facilities, services or equipment for national defense during public peril or national emergency. The section may not be used to allow anti-competitive actions.

Violation of rules issued under this section would be subject to a $1 million fine.

● Prohibited AT&T from offering any telecommunications service, equipment, customer premises equipment or information services, such as data processing, on an unregulated basis until the FCC approved its proposal for complying with the requirements to establish a separated subsidiary.

● Required that within four years of enactment, the final assembly of equipment for AT&T must be provided by a separated subsidiary or non-affiliate. Within four years, research and development activity relating to equipment used in final assemblies or to software programming must be performed by a separated subsidiary or non-affiliate.

Within six years, any subassembly and related research and development must be performed by a separated subsidiary or non-affiliate. Within six years, the manufacturing of basic components must be performed by a separated subsidiary or non-affiliate. After receiving FCC approval, the subsidiary may acquire subassemblies or components from AT&T, or Western Electric, if the company offered to sell the same type of equipment to non-affiliates at the same charges and terms.

● Created a board to establish the fair value of assets transferred from AT&T to the separated subsidiary. The board's decisions would be binding, unless the FCC determined that they were arbitrary or inconsistent. This provi-

sion was designed to help ensure that the property was not undervalued in order to subsidize the subsidiary.

Consent Decree Modified

● Modified a 1956 consent decree in a Justice Department suit to allow AT&T to enter unregulated markets through a separated subsidiary.

● Prohibited AT&T from transferring to a separated subsidiary any patents or related technical information, although it may license patents and related technical information to the subsidiary on the same terms as it would offer them to anyone else.

Mass Media Services

● Barred AT&T from providing cable or mass media services. AT&T would be allowed to lease facilities like transmission lines to other companies to provide those services. Mass media included television and radio broadcasting, printed or electronic publications and any service similar to the traditional functions of a newspaper.

Using a fully separated subsidiary distinct from the one established for telecommunications services, AT&T could provide weather, time and some sports news. The subsidiary also could provide electronic directory information, including general business and product categories, addresses and phone numbers but not prices or advertising. The subsidiary could not offer transmission services.

● Barred AT&T from providing fire and burglar alarm service over telephone lines.

● Required AT&T by the second year after enactment to purchase up to 20 percent of its telecommunications equipment from non-affiliates for five years, and then there would be a phased reduction in the required percentage.

● Prohibited federal or state regulation of the production, marketing or other provision of customer premises equipment, such as telephone receivers, or information services, such as data processing.

Within 180 days of enactment, the rates for all customer premises equipment, information services and cable service offered along with a regulated service must be provided separately according to FCC rules.

Continuing Service

● Authorized the FCC for two years following enactment to require any unregulated carrier, such as Western Union, to continue to interconnect its facilities with any firm using the service, or to continue services that were offered under regulation at enactment, for a reasonable time, if withdrawal of the interconnection or service would result in hardship or when there was no competition.

● Required a regulated carrier to provide service existing under tariff at the time of enactment for at least two years, by which time the FCC would determine if the service should be deregulated, based on whether there was effective competition.

● Provided that any customer premises equipment provided by AT&T under regulation at the time of enactment must be continued under regulation for three years, a period that may be extended by the FCC for another two years. Once deregulated, the equipment must be provided by the separated subsidiary.

● Authorized the FCC to determine what telecommunications service should be regulated to be universally available at reasonable charges and conditions, whether or not competition existed.

Cable, Miscellaneous

● Barred a regulated carrier from providing cable television in its operating area unless the FCC determined that it would provide significant media diversity and competition.

● Allowed carriers serving rural areas with low population densities to provide cable television in those areas.

● Allowed the FCC to require carriers to coordinate operations to ensure maintenance of telecommunications networks adequate for national security and emergency preparedness purposes.

● Required the FCC when it revoked or declined to renew the license of a VHF television station in a state which had more than one to reallocate the VHF channel, if technically possible, to a state without one.

● Authorized the FCC to establish policies and rules regarding the entry of foreign telecommunications carriers or information service suppliers into U.S. markets in order to ensure that U.S. companies had fair access to foreign markets. The president may veto such FCC decisions.

● Stated that the law did not express a sense of Congress in regard to any antitrust suit.

● Required any affiliate or separated subsidiary of AT&T within two years of enactment to sell some of its telecommunications products to non-affiliates.

Wirth Proposal

Wirth said HR 5158, which he introduced Dec. 10, would promote the development of competition in telecommunications markets before they were freed from government regulation.

Generally, HR 5158 also continued federal regulation of basic telephone service but provided for some deregulation of other telecommunications services, including the sale of customer premises equipment.

It also would remove legal barriers preventing AT&T from entering unregulated markets and require AT&T to establish a separate subsidiary with separate accounting to do so.

The Wirth bill would require some outside ownership of a separated subsidiary formed by AT&T to enter unregulated fields. Public ownership would be intended to help ensure that the subsidiary looks after its own interests and not those of AT&T.

His bill would provide for two types of subsidiaries with varying amounts of outside ownership. One subsidiary would be required to handle services that would compete with AT&T services, such as the leasing of private telephone lines. Other subsidiaries with less public ownership and with closer ties to the parent company would be allowed to provide other telecommunications services.

AT&T also would be barred from engaging in electronic publishing, except for limited directory information. Another subsidiary would be required for the electronic directory information.

Any other large, regulated telephone company that became involved with electronic information publishing would be required to make its facilities available to other electronic publishers.

One provision designed to help ratepayers, Wirth said, would create a National Telecommunications Fund to help prevent large increases in local telephone rates. The fund would be financed by part of the charges that long-distance carriers would pay for connecting to local telephone networks.

Congress Grants Conrail A Reprieve

Congress rejected an administration plan for the quick sale of segments of Conrail, the federally subsidized freight railroad, and gave the troubled rail system a second chance to be returned to the private sector as a single system.

The reprieve, contained in the budget reconciliation legislation (HR 3982 — PL 97-35), established a timetable for ending federal subsidies and set out conditions governing the sale of Conrail, either in segments or as a single system. *(Reconciliation, p. 256)*

Conrail had been created by Congress in the early 1970s out of the Penn Central Railroad and six other bankrupt lines in an attempt to preserve freight rail service in the Northeast and Midwest. The original projections of financial independence in 1979 were dashed by management problems, expensive labor agreements and other difficulties. *(PL 93-236, 1973 Almanac p. 465)*

By 1981, Conrail had received about $6 billion in federal aid, and its administrators believed that under certain conditions and with additional limited federal aid, it could become profitable.

But the Reagan administration called for an end to federal subsidies by fiscal 1983 and wanted to give the transportation secretary a free hand in selling portions of the system to private enterprise.

The timing of the sale was important to many members of Congress, particularly those from the Northeast and Midwest who were afraid that quick, piecemeal sale would result in the loss of vital freight rail service. Their concern eventually led to revisions that protected the Conrail system from what some members considered abrupt sale.

The House and Senate Commerce Committees worked on separate reauthorization legislation (HR 3559 — H Rept 97-153, S 1100 — S Rept 97-101). But before floor action could take place, the committees were required by the budget reconciliation process to revise their measures. New authorization figures eventually were included in each chamber's reconciliation proposal and differences settled in conference.

The conference report (H Rept 97-208) stated that if Conrail's banker and monitor, the U.S. Railway Association (USRA), determined June 1, 1983, that Conrail would not be profitable, then Conrail could be sold piecemeal. But if it were deemed profitable, then Conrail could be sold only as a single system up until Oct. 31, 1983.

There would be a second profitability test then, and if Conrail were deemed profitable, it could be sold only as a single system up until June 1, 1984. If it were deemed not profitable, needed additional subsidies or buyers could not be found for an intact system by that date, the transportation secretary would be allowed to sell Conrail piecemeal.

The House bill had allowed the sale of a profitable Conrail as a single entity up to Dec. 31, 1983, while the Senate set the date at Aug. 1, 1983.

The reconciliation agreement authorized $262 million for operating subsidies through Aug. 1, 1983, and $400 million for labor protection benefits, such as severance pay.

The Senate had called for $150 million for operations and $400 million for labor protection. The House had provided $475 million and $315 million respectively.

Congress also tried to help Conrail become profitable and more attractive to potential buyers. For example, the

new legislation allowed the passenger commuter operations that Conrail inherited in the Northeast to be spun off to a new Amtrak commuter subsidiary.

Provisions

As signed into law, Title XI of HR 3982 (PL 97-35):

● Set goals for Conrail to help it become profitable, including reducing non-union wages and benefits and making layoffs comparable to the reductions and layoffs for union workers contained in a new collective bargaining agreement. The collective bargaining agreement was to save $200 million a year, beginning April 1, 1981, through reduced wage increases, benefits or other labor costs.

● Ended Conrail's obligation to operate short-haul passenger commuter service, which it inherited when Congress established Conrail, on Jan. 1, 1983.

● Directed Amtrak to establish by Nov. 1, 1981, the Amtrak Commuter Services Corp. The subsidiary would operate commuter service for authorities that previously contracted with Conrail. The subsidiary would not have a common carrier obligation to operate either passenger or freight service.

The commuter authorities referred to in the legislation included those in the New York City area, Connecticut, Maryland, southeastern Pennsylvania, New Jersey and Massachusetts.

● Established a board for the commuter subsidiary with the following members: the subsidiary's president, a member of the Amtrak board who was selected to represent commuter authorities on the Amtrak board, two members selected by the Amtrak board and two from commuter authorities.

● Authorized the commuter subsidiary to own, manage or contract for the operation of commuter service. The subsidiary was authorized to operate commuter service only for full reimbursement.

● Directed the subsidiary to provide access to rail tracks to a commuter authority that operated its own service or contracted from someone else.

● Prohibited the use by the commuter subsidiary of federal subsidies authorized for Amtrak's inter-city operations.

● Authorized $20 million in fiscal 1982 for the financially ailing Regional Transportation Authority, which served the area outside Chicago.

● Authorized $50 million in fiscal 1982 for the Amtrak subsidiary and for commuter authorities that operate service. The funds would be available until Oct. 1, 1986.

Conrail Sale

● Authorized $262 million through Aug. 1, 1983, for Conrail operating subsidies.

● Exempted Conrail from state taxes until Conrail's property was sold.

● Directed the transportation secretary to hire a financial institution to arrange for the sale of Conrail common stock owned by the federal government.

● Allowed the transportation secretary any time after enactment to submit to Congress a plan for the sale of federal stock in Conrail. The plan could be vetoed by both chambers of Congress. Sale of the stock rather than Conrail

properties would maintain the railroad as a single system.

● Directed the secretary to offer Conrail stock for sale first to employees.

● Established a framework for the sale of Conrail. On June 1, 1983, the U.S. Railway Association (USRA) board must determine whether Conrail would be a profitable railroad. If it was determined that Conrail would not be profitable, the secretary could sell Conrail piecemeal. The USRA was Conrail's monitor and banker.

If Conrail were deemed profitable, the secretary could sell it only as a single entity until Oct. 31, 1983, when there would be a second profitability test.

If determined to be profitable, the railroad could only be sold as a system until June 1, 1984. If unprofitable, the railroad could be sold in pieces.

The secretary also could sell Conrail piecemeal if the railroad required more subsidies than authorized in the legislation.

After June 1, 1984, the secretary could notify the USRA that he had been unable to sell Conrail as a single entity. If USRA concurred, Conrail employees would have 90 days to submit a purchase plan. If the secretary disapproved the plan, he could begin to sell off Conrail in pieces.

If USRA did not concur with the secretary on the piecemeal sale, he must try to sell Conrail as a system.

● Directed the secretary within one year after selling Conrail properties to arrange for the formation by railroads of one or more terminal companies to be operated as private corporations to provide switching and terminal services in the Northeast Corridor. The new companies would not be required if the secretary certified that the acquiring railroads were capable of assuring adequate freight terminal operations in the corridor. The Northeast Corridor links Washington, New York and Boston.

● Required the secretary to consolidate the sales of Conrail properties for purposes of review and approval. All agreements for sale of properties must include a common transfer date.

● Required that 75 percent of the total rail service operated by Conrail be maintained if the railroad were sold piecemeal.

● Allowed either chamber of Congress to veto the piecemeal sale of Conrail.

● Directed Conrail by Jan. 1, 1982, to determine which of its subsidiaries was not profitable the previous year and to try to sell any that were unprofitable, unless the USRA determined that the benefits of ownership outweighed the financial loss.

Labor Protection Benefits

● Required the labor secretary and labor union representatives within 90 days of enactment to work out a new labor protection agreement for employees who had been covered by the statutory "Title V" Conrail labor protection program. If no agreement were reached, then the secretary within 30 days must prescribe a benefit program. *(Conrail, 1980 Almanac p. 249; 1976 Almanac p.660)*

The agreement might provide for the use of funds for severance, moving expenses, retraining expenses, insurance and other costs. No more than $20,000 might be paid to any individual employee. Eligibility for benefits would terminate two years after enactment.

● Allowed Conrail to pay brakemen and firemen up to $25,000 in severance to reduce the railroad's work force by 4,600.

● Gave laid-off employees right of first hire by other

railroads under certain conditions.

● Provided for a register of laid-off employees and notice by other railroads of vacancies.

● Allowed Conrail to contract for work that could not be done by existing or furloughed employees.

● Barred new collective bargaining agreements from including additional labor protection benefits before April 1, 1984.

● Barred state laws or regulations from requiring Conrail, Amtrak or Amtrak Commuter to employ a certain number of persons.

● Directed Conrail to enter into collective bargaining agreements that provide for the creation of a fact-finding panel to recommend changes in operating practices that result in greater productivity.

● Authorized $400 million for labor protection benefits to remain available until expended.

● Repealed Conrail's existing Title V labor protection benefits program as of Oct. 1, 1981.

● Provided for the transfer of some Conrail employees to Amtrak Commuter, commuter authorities and railroads that acquired Conrail properties.

Board Changes

● Reconstituted the USRA board so that its members included the USRA chairman, the transportation secretary, the U.S. comptroller general, the Interstate Commerce Commission chairman and the Conrail chairman. The legislation eliminated representation of cities, states, labor, railroads and shippers.

● Authorized $13 million for fiscal 1982 for USRA activities and $4 million for fiscal 1983.

● Expedited the sale of some or all Conrail properties and freight service obligations in Connecticut, Rhode Island and Massachusetts. The sale of Conrail lines in Connecticut and Rhode Island must be under a plan that provided for continued rail freight service on all the lines for at least four years.

● Expedited Conrail applications to the Interstate Commerce Commission for abandonment of lines under certain conditions.

● Provided for a presidentially-appointed emergency board to investigate and settle disputes between a publicly funded and operated carrier providing commuter service and its employees.

● Barred strikes by Amtrak Commuter or commuter authority employees against Conrail or vice versa.

● Authorized up to $25 million to pay Title V labor protection benefits that accrued before repeal of the program.

● Gave highest priority for rail rehabilitation funding to carriers in bankruptcy, such as the Milwaukee and Rock Island railroads, and to the St. Louis Rail Gateway project.

● Expedited the review and decision process for applications to acquire the Delaware & Hudson and the Boston & Maine railroads.

● Relieved Conrail of any responsibility after Jan. 1, 1983, for providing crews for inter-city passenger service on the Northeast Corridor.

Background

Sharply different scenarios for the future of Conrail were presented in 1981 by the Reagan administration, Conrail and the USRA.

The administration in its March budget announced that it wanted to end federal aid to Conrail by fiscal 1983. It said it wanted to sell Conrail lines to private railroads and substantially scale back expensive employee benefits, a proposal that some union leaders warned could lead to a nationwide strike.

In announcing additional details in April, Transportation Secretary Drew Lewis said Conrail had already cost U.S. taxpayers almost $6 billion in operating and capital aid since it was created and that it could cost another $4 billion by 1985 if the Department of Transportation's (DOT) recommendations were not adopted.

The DOT proposal, Lewis said, would preserve 95 percent of the Conrail freight service currently provided throughout the region. The railroad at the time operated over about 17,000 miles of track in 17 states and had about 80,000 employees.

The Conrail and USRA assessments of the railroad were in the form of reports on the railroad's prospects, as required by the 1980 railroad deregulation act (PL 96-448). *(1980 Almanac p. 248)*

Conrail, USRA and DOT all agreed that the railroad was beset by high operating costs, an expensive employee protection program and declining traffic caused by the region's poor economy.

But USRA and Conrail said that under certain conditions and with additional limited federal aid, Conrail could begin turning a profit by 1985.

Lewis argued that even if Conrail could earn a profit, the government should get out of the railroad business.

A top rail labor official contended that the DOT plan could result in 50,000 workers being put out of work. Labor would strike all railroads, he said, if Congress approved DOT plans to repeal the protection benefits mandated by law (PL 93-236) and replaced them with a a vastly reduced program. *(Congress and the Nation Vol. IV, p. 513)*

The existing benefits were designed to compensate workers for wages, benefits or jobs lost when Conrail was created. They covered some 11,000 Conrail employees until age 65. Some employees had been receiving $50 to $1,800 a month under the program.

The DOT plan was sharply criticized by Rep. James J. Florio, D-N.J., chairman of the House Energy and Commerce Transportation Subcommittee. He said it did not adequately indicate who would take over Conrail operations or how employee protection benefits could be changed legally and politically.

"I almost don't take it seriously," Florio said, adding that he found the Conrail and USRA reports to be more reasonable.

Administration Plans

The DOT plan called for legislation providing for the following:

● Voluntary acquisition of Conrail lines by other railroads.

● Repeal of the labor protection benefits allowed by the 1973 act that led to Conrail's creation and modified by the 1980 rail deregulation act. The benefits would be replaced by reduced provisions similar to those in the 1979 law (PL 96-101) for the bankrupt Milwaukee Railroad and the 1980 law for the bankrupt Rock Island Railroad (PL 96-254). *(1979 Almanac p. 352; 1980 Almanac p. 238)*

● Transfer of passenger commuter operations that Conrail had been required by law to maintin. Local transit authorities would take over the commuter operations.

Lewis said the DOT plan could result in the loss of 10,000-20,000 rail jobs and the termination of 2,700 to 3,500 miles of lines. Some interim federal funding would be required, as well as additional labor protection funds, but Lewis said firm figures were not available.

USRA, Conrail Alternatives

Under the plan Conrail offered, about 10,000 employees would lose their jobs and 2,400 miles of lines would be abandoned. The USRA report was not specific on job and route loss.

Both Conrail and USRA said the railroad had to be relieved of responsibility for the labor benefits, whose costs negated the economies obtained by job reductions. USRA also suggested that Congress consider reducing the amount of benefits.

According to law, once the $485 million federal subsidy authorized for labor protection benefits was exhausted, Conrail would be responsible for making the payments itself. About $305 million had already been spent, even though the fund was supposed to last past the year 2000.

Conrail and USRA recommended changes in work rules and other concessions to be sought from employees to help bring operating costs down. USRA was also critical of management costs.

USRA said Conrail could operate profitably by 1985 if the recommended changes were made and if it received a total of from $400 million to $600 million more in federal aid, including aid authorized in the 1980 deregulation act.

The funds would cover operating losses in fiscal 1982 and capital costs in fiscal 1983. Conrail said it needed $342 million more through 1984.

Senate Action

Senate Commerce Committee Democrats May 6 temporarily blocked Republican efforts to approve a bill (S 1100) that accepted Reagan's basic plan to return Conrail to private ownership as quickly as possible.

The Democrats said they doubted that the lines could be sold without seriously damaging freight service and the economies of states and communities depending on Conrail. They also objected that the president's bill had not been sent to Congress until a few days before the committee markup.

Although the bill was reported May 15 (S Rept 97-101), Chairman Bob Packwood, R-Ore., agreed to hold hearings before asking the Senate to vote on the bill. He said the committee could offer a substitute bill after the hearings.

Key members, however, continued to oppose the measure, and a compromise was worked out with Lewis to allow the sale of Conrail lines throughout the Northeast and Midwest after Dec. 1, 1982, if the railroad were determined by a special committee to be unprofitable.

The original committee bill would have allowed the immediate sale of the lines, as requested by the administration.

As announced June 9, the compromise:

● Barred sales of Conrail lines before June 1, 1982.

● Allowed the sale of Conrail as a single entity after June 1, 1982.

● Created a review committee to determine if Conrail had become profitable. The committee would include the transportation and Treasury secretaries, the USRA chairman, the comptroller general and Conrail's chief executive.

• Allowed the transportation secretary to sell Conrail only as a single entity until Aug. 1, 1983, if the review committee determined by Dec. 1, 1982, that Conrail was profitable. After the August date, it could be broken up and the pieces sold at one time.

• Allowed the secretary to sell Conrail as a package of parcels anytime after Dec. 1, 1982, if Conrail was deemed by the review committee to be unprofitable.

• Allowed Congress to veto proposed sales.

• Replace Conrail's labor protection plan with one providing a lump sum payment of up to $25,000 to laid-off workers.

• Authorized "such sums as are necessary" during the sale process for the continuation of essential rail service.

The compromise was offered by Packwood as a floor amendment to the Senate reconciliation bill (S 1377) June 25 and was accepted by voice vote.

House Action

The bill (HR 3559 — H Rept 97-153) reported June 18 by the House Energy and Commerce Committee would have prevented the administration from offering parcels of Conrail lines for sale until after Dec. 31, 1983.

The White House opposed the bill, arguing that it unduly delayed returning the subsidized railroad to the private sector.

The bill as originally approved by the Energy and Commerce Transportation Subcommittee would have prevented the transportation secretary from selling parcels of Conrail until April 1983. It would have authorized $500 million in new funds and continued an existing $100 million authorization for operating subsidies during the transition period to private ownership.

After the subcommittee approved the bill, Conrail supporters continued working on the legislation, with New York Republicans Norman F. Lent, ranking minority member of the subcommittee, and Gary A. Lee taking the lead. The eventual compromise approved June 10 by the full committee was backed by subcommittee Chairman Florio.

The new version authorized $375 million in new money and continued the $100 million authorization for operating subsidies during the transition period. It also made Conrail more attractive for sale by relieving it of the financial drain of Northeast commuter service and by revising its expensive labor protection program.

However, James T. Broyhill of North Carolina, ranking minority member, said the transportation secretary's hands would be tied for too long. He proposed an amendment to provide $275 million in new operating subsidies and to allow the secretary to sell the lines a year earlier.

The Broyhill amendment failed 13-28. The Lent-Lee substitute to the subcommittee bill was passed by voice vote, and the bill was ordered reported by a 30-12 vote.

As reported, HR 3559:

• Relieved Conrail within 18 months of enactment of its obligation to run Northeast commuter rail service and created a subsidiary of Amtrak within eight months of enactment to operate the service if Amtrak was adequately reimbursed. It authorized $50 million for a working capital fund for commuter services.

• Authorized $375 million in new funds and continued an existing $100 million authorization to subsidize Conrail operations.

• Required that operating subsidies be provided according to a timetable from Oct. 1, 1981, to Oct. 1, 1983, depending on the railroad's meeting certain conditions, including union and non-union employee wage and benefit concessions and the development of a financial plan for becoming profitable.

• Exempted Conrail from state and local taxes until it was sold.

• Allowed the transportation secretary after July 1, 1982, to sell Conrail common stock up to Dec. 31, 1983, so that the railroad remained a single entity. But USRA must have determined that Conrail was profitable.

• Allowed the secretary to sell Conrail in pieces after Dec. 31, 1983, if USRA determined Conrail was not profitable. The sales must result in preserving at least 75 percent of the service and was subject to congressional veto.

• Revised the current labor protection plan and authorized a total of $315 million in fiscal 1982 and 1983 for termination allowances, retraining and other expenses for employees adversely affected by the new act.

Reconciliation

When the June 12 deadline for revising authorizations as required by the reconciliation process had passed, the Energy and Commerce Committee was the only committee that did not comply. After days of maneuvering, the committee appeared deadlocked 21-21 and never took a formal vote on recommended cuts.

The House Budget Committee accepted a Democratic proposal offered by Committee Chairman John D. Dingell, D-Mich. However, it also voted to ask for a rule that would give members a chance to vote on a minority proposal offered by Broyhill that was included in the GOP reconciliation proposals.

The Broyhill provisions on Conrail, Amtrak and other issues proved to be troublesome to many Republicans from the Northeast. The GOP leadership decided that a vote on the Broyhill package would be too risky just before the vote on its reconciliation plan and decided to pull the Broyhill amendment from its so-called Gramm-Latta II package. The Dingell proposals thus were included in the reconciliation bill approved by the House June 26. ∎

Mass Transit Programs

In its massive budget reconciliation package, Congress authorized up to $3.792 billion in fiscal 1982 for mass transit programs.

The figure represented a reduction of $1.321 billion from the Congressional Budget Office baseline of $5.09 billion. President Reagan had requested a similar cut.

Title XI of the reconciliation measure (HR 3982 — PL 97-35) approved by Congress July 31 reduced capital subsidies to $1.515 billion from $1.6 billion; formula grants, which include operating and some capital subsidies, to $1.480 billion from $1.755 billion; and rural transit aid to $75 million from $120 million.

The conference agreement (H Rept 97-208) did not address Reagan's plan to phase out mass transit operating subsidies by 1985.

Amtrak Saves Routes But Must Trim Costs

The budget reconciliation legislation (HR 3982 — PL 97-35) spared Amtrak from having to make immediate major cuts in its routes in 1982, but Congress put the railroad on notice it must keep a tight watch on its budget.

The conference agreement (H Rept 97-208) authorized $735 million for Amtrak in fiscal 1982 and $788 million in fiscal 1983. The 1982 figure was $122 million more than President Reagan had requested and about $400 million less than President Carter had sought. The current authorization for fiscal 1982 was $329 million for just capital expenses. *(1979 Almanac p. 346)*

But the agreement also required Amtrak to recover at least 50 percent of its operating costs from the fare box or other non-federal source in fiscal 1982, which raised the prospect of higher fares. Some cost-saving steps were mandated that might help Amtrak hold down fare increases, such as deferring interest on Amtrak's federal debt and exempting it from certain state taxes.

According to the bill, Amtrak must operate only trains that meet performance criteria established by Congress in 1979 (PL 96-73). The 1979 law's intent was to stop uneconomical "political" trains that ran through the districts of important members. *(1979 Almanac p. 346)*

Senate conferees had sought to repeal the criteria and let Amtrak decide how best to operate the system. They argued that the standards could be interpreted in different ways and thus require cutting some Western trains, even though they were performing well.

As a compromise, Amtrak was allowed to modify some routes so that they could meet the performance standards.

The legislation also shortcut an administration plan to leave the Northeast Corridor improvement project unfinished. The bill directed the transportation secretary to complete the project as outlined in current law. *(1980 Almanac p. 238)*

Provisions

As signed into law, Title XI of HR 3982:

●**Commuter Service.** Included a policy statement that Amtrak should be available to operate commuter service through a new subsidiary under contract with commuter agencies.

●**Improvement Goal.** Set the goal of a 30 percent improvement in the number of passenger-miles per train-miles by Oct. 1, 1983.

●**New Board.** Reconstituted the Amtrak board of directors to include nine members: the transportation secretary or a representative, the Amtrak president and seven members appointed by the president.

The presidential appointees would include two federal officials representing the government's preferred stockholdings in Amtrak, two persons representing commuter authorities and three representing rail labor, governors of states with an interest in rail transportation and businesses with an interest in rail. The current board included the Amtrak president, transportation secretary, three representatives of railroads and eight members appointed by the president, including three consumer representatives.

●**Debt Conversion.** Converted Amtrak's federal debt to preferred stock to be held by the government beginning Oct. 1, 1981.

●**Fee Exemption.** Exempted the railroad from paying custom and immigration fees.

●**Food Service.** Required Amtrak to reduce the deficit from its on-board food and beverage operations by 50 percent in fiscal 1982 and to eliminate the deficit by Sept. 30, 1982.

●**Tax, Labor Exemptions.** Exempted Amtrak from certain property taxes.

●Exempted Amtrak from state or local requirements that set minimum crew numbers.

●**State Trains.** Allowed Amtrak to run special state train routes if the state paid at least 45 percent of the operating costs in the first year and 65 percent in each year thereafter. Also the state must pay 50 percent of the capital costs each year. Under existing law, the program provided an 80 percent federal share of operating costs in the first year, decreasing to 50 percent by the third year.

●**Changing Standards.** Required Amtrak to submit proposed changes to the performance criteria to Congress. The changes would become effective unless either chamber disapproved them.

●**Cost Recovery.** Required Amtrak to recover at least 50 percent of its operating costs from non-federal sources.

●**Annual Review.** Required Amtrak to conduct an annual review of each route to determine if it would meet congressionally mandated performance criteria. If Amtrak projected that a route would not meet the criteria, the railroad must discontinue, modify or adjust the operation of service over the route.

●**Cutting Costs.** Required Amtrak to take whatever actions necessary to stay within its available funding. Such actions might include changes in service frequency, fare hikes, reduction in on-board service costs such as sleeper and dining cars and restructuring or discontinuing routes.

●Required Amtrak by Oct. 1, 1983, to reduce management costs by at least 10 percent of the administrative costs incurred during the year prior to June 1, 1981.

●Required Amtrak beginning Oct. 1, 1981, to continue existing service if it met the performance criteria after the railroad took into account projected fare increases and any state or local contributions.

●**Authorizations.** Authorized $735 million for fiscal 1982, of which no more than $24 million might be spent on special state service.

●Authorized $788 million for fiscal 1983, of which no more than $26 million might be spent for state service.

●**Loan Guarantees.** Increased the loan guarantee level for Amtrak to $930 million from $900 million to cover the final payment on the purchase of the Northeast Corridor.

●**Interest Deferred.** Deferred Amtrak's interest payment to the federal government until Sept. 30, 1983. By Feb. 1, 1982, the Transportation Department in consultation with the General Accounting Office, Amtrak and the Treasury Department must submit legislative recommendations to Congress for ways of relieving Amtrak of its federal debt. The interest deferral would amount to $82 million in fiscal 1982 and $100 million in fiscal 1983.

●**High-Speed Corridors.** Required Amtrak by June 1, 1982, to submit to Congress recommendations for development of high-speed passenger rail corridors that would serve densely populated areas.

● **Local Rail Aid.** Authorized $40 million in fiscal 1982 for local rail assistance, $44 million for 1983 and $48 million for 1984. The federal share of the local rail assistance program was reduced to 70 percent from 80 percent.

Completing Improvements

● **Northeast Corridor.** Required the transportation secretary to complete the Northeast Corridor improvement project in accordance with the goals set out in existing law.

The conferees said it was their intent that all funds authorized for the project be used to complete improvements, while Reagan planned to cut total project authorizations by $310 million.

The total amount previously authorized by Congress was $2.5 billion. *(1980 Almanac p. 238)*

● Authorized $200 million in fiscal 1982 for the Northeast Corridor improvement project and $185 million for fiscal 1983. These authorizations are part of the $2.5 billion total authorization.

Reagan also proposed authorizations of $200 million in fiscal 1982 and $185 million in 1983.

Miscellaneous

● Authorized $40 million in fiscal 1982 for railroad research and development.

● Authorized $27.65 million for railroad safety programs.

● Authorized $79 million in fiscal 1982 for the Interstate Commerce Commission and $80.4 million annually each for 1983 and 1984.

● Authorized $30.047 million in fiscal 1982 for transportation research and special programs in the Transportation Department, $32.2 million in fiscal 1983 and $33.3 million for fiscal 1984.

Legislative History

The Senate bill incorporated most of a measure reported May 15 by the Commerce Committee that initially went along with the administration cuts. The committee initially approved a $613 million subsidy for fiscal 1982 (S 1199 — S Rept 97-96).

Amtrak contended that the figure would mean eliminating all passenger service outside the Northeast Corridor, which linked Washington, New York and Boston. The administration disputed the claim and argued that taxpayers should not subsidize rail service.

As hometown newspapers churned out editorials protesting the threat to local service and hundreds of letters from constituents supporting Amtrak started pouring into members' offices, lawmakers began to get uneasy.

The Committee June 10 agreed to raise the funding to $735 million, matching the authorization approved May 19 by the House Energy and Commerce Committee (HR 3568 — H Rept 97-81).

The increase was included in the budget cuts recommended to the Budget Committee and included in the Senate reconciliation measure. *(Reconciliation, p. 256)*

The House committee agreed to cut the transportation subcommittee recommendation of $792 million for fiscal 1982. The panel rejected attempts by some Republican members to revert to Reagan's request.

Conference

Both House and Senate bills authorized $735 million in fiscal 1982 for Amtrak. The House authorized $842

million for fiscal 1983, while the Senate provided $735 million.

A major sticking point was a House requirement that Amtrak operate only trains that met performance criteria. The Senate bill repealed the criteria. Senate conferees said the standards could be interpreted in different ways and thus require cutting some Western trains, even though they were performing well.

Sen. Bob Packwood, R-Ore., chairman of the Commerce Committee, said Amtrak should be told how much aid it would get and how much it must recover from fares and then be allowed to decide to operate. Oregon's Seattle-to-Salt Lake City *Pioneer* might not qualify under one reading of the criteria, although Amtrak officials said they planned to continue it.

The standards were retained, but conferees allowed Amtrak to modify some routes to allow some marginal trains to qualify for continuance.

Another point of contention was the makeup of the Amtrak board of directors. The current board included the Amtrak president, the transportation secretary, three members representing railroads and eight members appointed by the president, including three consumer representatives.

Senate conferees contended that the House plan was tilted against the administration. Some House members believed the Senate board was loaded against Amtrak.

"You're going to get a board that doesn't care a darn about costs," Packwood asserted.

The compromise called for a presidentially-appointed board including two members representing the federal stockholdings, one rail labor representative, two members from regional transit authorities, a governor from a state interested in rail and a representative of business interested in rail. Other members would be the Amtrak president and the transportation secretary.

Conferees also accepted a House plan requiring food and beverage losses to be cut by 50 percent in fiscal 1982, for a $31 million savings, and a House plan to defer Amtrak's payment of $82 million interest on its federal debt for two years.

They accepted a Senate proposal exempting Amtrak to a more limited degree than the House from state and local taxes, for a savings of $6.5 million.   ■

Co-Op Bank Funds

Congress rejected President Reagan's proposal to eliminate the National Consumer Cooperative Bank and reauthorized fiscal 1982 funds for the bank in the budget reconciliation legislation (HR 3982 — PL 97-35).

However, the bill also stipulated that the Co-Op Bank sever its ties with the government and become a private financial institution by Dec. 31, 1982, several years sooner than originally planned. *(Reconciliation, p. 256)*

The conference agreement (H Rept 97-208) authorizing $47 million for the bank's market-rate loans to co-ops in fiscal 1982 was a compromise between a Senate position of no new funds for bank loans and a House authorization of $61 million.

The Senate had allowed the bank only to service existing loans. The House bill authorized $47 million for the market-rate loans and $14 million for low-interest loans and technical assistance for low-income co-ops in 1982. In

addition, the House provided for $25 million for both 1983 and 1984 for low-interest loans.

Under current law (PL 95-351), the bank would have been required beginning in 1990 to move toward private status by retiring federally owned stock on a regular basis. *(1978 Almanac p. 521)*

While the reconciliation measure could not guarantee appropriations, the conferees said "... fiscal 1981 and 1982 funding is essential if the bank is to have an adequate, if limited, capital base for the conversion to private status and the ability to meet the act's requirements for mandatory repayments of the government's debt." *(Appropriations, p. 334)*

The bank was created to promote the cooperative movement. Co-ops provide housing, food, health care and marketing services at lower costs to members than if they individually sought those services on the private market. The bank actually opened in 1980.

Co-ops sought help from the federal government because they have trouble securing loans from private sources. Supporters said commercial banks do not want to loan funds to co-ops because they do not understand co-op management.

The administration, however, contended that sound co-ops could secure private financing and should not be subsidized by taxpayers. President Reagan's budget proposed eliminating funds for the bank.

However, before the House voted on the Republican alternative budget, Gramm-Latta II, 18 Republicans informed Minority Leader Robert H. Michel, R-Ill., in a letter that they would vote against the package if the bank funding were dropped. Because the president needed every GOP vote to pass Gramm-Latta II, the GOP House leadership included an authorization for the Co-Op bank in the package.

Provisions

As signed into law, Title III of HR 3982:

● Set the date by which the Treasury must convert its bank stock to notes as Dec. 31, 1981, or 10 days after enactment of fiscal 1982 appropriations legislation for the bank, whichever was later. The bank must repay the notes by Dec. 31, 2020.

● Continued the bank's exemption from state and local taxes, except for real estate taxes.

● Provided that the president appoint three of the bank board's 15 members. The presidential appointees must include a representative of small business, a representative of low-income co-ops and a federal official. The other members would be elected by bank stockholders.

● Directed the Farm Credit Administration and the General Accounting Office to audit the bank's records.

● Made a non-profit housing co-op in existence March 21, 1980, eligible for bank aid even if its organization did not meet the specific one-person, one-vote structure required by law.

● Directed the bank to spin off the Office of Self-Help Development and Technical Assistance, which provided low-interest loans and technical aid to low-income co-ops. The office would become a non-profit corporation, whose directors would be named by the bank board. The bank might provide staff support and financial aid to the corporation. Contributions to the corporation would be tax deductible.

● Authorized $14 million for fiscal 1982 for the low interest loans and technical assistance and $47 million for the bank's basic market-rate loans.

Legislative History

The Co-op bank provisions became involved in budget reconciliation during the battle between the House and Senate Banking Committees over reauthorizing programs of the Department of Housing and Urban Development (HUD) and several independent agencies. The Co-Op authorization normally was contained in the HUD bill. *(HUD authorization, p. 110)*

The House Banking, Finance and Urban Affairs Committee June 9 attached the provisions of its HUD authorization bill (HR 3534) to its reconciliation measure. The Senate June 3 had approved a HUD authorization bill (S 1197 — S Rept 97-87). But, angered by the House action, on June 10 the Senate Banking, Finance and Urban Affairs Committee added S 1197 to its reconciliation proposals. ∎

Congress Overrides Reagan's Public TV Cuts

President Reagan's plan to cut public broadcast subsidies was rejected by Congress, which authorized $80 million more than he requested for fiscal 1984-86.

The final budget reconciliation bill (HR 3982 — PL 97-35) approved by Congress July 31 authorized $130 million annually for fiscal 1984-1986 for the Corporation for Public Broadcasting (CPB), which disburses federal aid to public stations. *(Reconciliation, p. 256)*

The Carter administration had requested authorizations of $183 million in fiscal 1984, $198 million in 1985 and $210 million in fiscal 1986. Reagan had sought levels of $110 million for fiscal 1984 and $100 million annually for 1985 and 1986.

The Senate had accepted the administration levels in a bill reported by the Commerce Committee (S 720 — S Rept 97-98) and included in the Senate reconciliation measure. The House reconciliation bill contained no similiar language but in a previously passed public broadcasting measure (HR 3238), the House approved authorizations of $160 million, $145 million and $130 million.

The agreement reached by reconciliation conferees (H Rept 97-208) provided less than the current appropriations (PL 95-567). Unlike most other federal programs, public broadcasting receives advance funding, and Congress had approved $162 million for fiscal 1981, $172 million for 1982 and $137 million for 1983. The intent of the advance funding was to protect the system from political pressure. *(1978 Almanac p. 492)*

Reagan contended that general taxpayers should not be required to subsidize the entertainment of others.

CPB backers countered that public broadcasting deserved government support because it provided a special cultural service to the nation.

The conference agreement generally followed the more

generous provisions contained in HR 3238. While cutting the money request, Congress did give public broadcasters the ability to raise funds by allowing it for the first time to air sponsor logos and lease facilities.

Also, Congress agreed to permit several public television and radio licensees to experiment with advertisements to find out if stations could raise revenue through advertising without reducing the quality of public broadcasting.

The final legislation also set a mandatory formula for allocating the subsidies. Public television and radio stations supported the formula because it assured them for the first time of a certain amount of money. CPB officials opposed the formula, arguing it would remove the flexibility they needed.

The formula was intended to end the traditional fighting between CPB and the stations over who would control the federal funds.

Provisions

As signed into law, Title XII of HR 3982 (PL 97-35):
● Authorized $20 million in fiscal 1982 for public telecommunications facilities development under the Commerce Department's National Telecommunications and Information Administration (NTIA), $15 million for fiscal 1983 and $12 million for fiscal 1984.
● Required that the use of public broadcasting facilities for other purposes not interfere with public broadcasting services.
● Reduced the size of the CPB board to 11 members from 15, with membership to include 10 presidential appointees and the CPB president. No more than six members may belong to the same political party. One member must represent public television stations and one must represent public radio stations. Members' terms would be reduced to five years from six years.
● Authorized $130 million annually for fiscal 1984-1986 for public broadcasting.
● Directed the Treasury to disburse the fiscal year's appropriated funds on an annual basis, rather than quarterly.
● Established a mandatory formula to allocate federal funds: 10 percent would go for CPB administration, program royalties, interconnection services, debt payment and other costs. Also, 75 percent of the remainder of the funds would go to public television and 25 percent to public radio. Of the television funds, 75 percent would go directly to the stations, and the remainder would be for national programming. The radio funds would be split equally between grants to stations and funds for national programming.

The television and radio stations would pick up some of CPB's costs if certain expenses amounted to more than 60 percent of the corporation's allocated funds.
● Directed CPB and the stations to split equally the cost of interconnection facilities and operations, which link the stations in a type of "network" to share programs.
● Allowed only non-commercial stations that receive no CPB grants to editorialize. But the stations would not be allowed to support or oppose candidates. Public stations that do receive CPB grants may not editorialize or endorse candidates.
● Allowed public television and radio stations to air business logos of program sponsors as long as the announcements did not interrupt regular programming.
● Allowed public broadcast stations to lease their facili-

ties but barred the broadcast of advertisements.
● Required a temporary commission to study alternatives available for public broadcasters to raise additional revenue without reducing the quality or diversity of public broadcasting. The study must be submitted to Congress by July 1, 1982.
● Allowed the temporary commission to establish an experiment permitting several public television and radio licensees to air advertisements under limited conditions.

The test would be for 18 months. CPB, in consultation with the commission, would select up to 10 public television licensees and 10 public radio licensees to participate. The advertising could not interrupt regular programs, and consecutive advertisements could not exceed two minutes.
● Authorized $16.5 million for the administration of the NTIA, which is the chief executive agency responsible for developing national telecommunications policy.

Legislative History

House. HR 3238 (H Rept 97-82) was passed by the House June 24 by a vote of 323-86. *(Vote 93, p. 40-H)*

It provided for the following:
● Authorized $160 million in fiscal 1984 for public broadcasting, $145 million in fiscal 1985 and $130 million in fiscal 1986.
● Authorized $25 million in fiscal 1982 for NTIA's public broadcasting facilities and equipment program, $20 million in fiscal 1983 and $15 million in fiscal 1984.
● Established a mandatory formula for CPB to use for allocating funds, including 90 percent for television and radio and 10 percent for CPB activities and costs. Of the 90 percent, 75 percent would go to television and 25 percent to radio. Of the television funds, 80 percent would be passed directly to local stations and 20 percent would be allocated by CPB for national program production. Of the radio funds, at least 50 percent would go directly to local stations and no more than 50 percent would go for national program production, or National Public Radio (NPR).
● Allowed only non-commercial broadcasting stations that did not receive federal grants to editorialize.
● Allowed stations to broadcast the business logos of sponsors to raise revenue. The logo broadcasts could not interrupt regular programming. The FCC had begun to allow logos to be used. Public broadcasting stations were not otherwise allowed to broadcast advertisements.
● Directed the FCC to study the options available to public broadcasting entities to raise revenue and report to Congress within one year of enactment.
● Allowed the CPB to receive its appropriation annually rather than quarterly.
● Required local stations to assume the cost from the CPB of interconnection.
● Allowed stations to lease their facilities to raise funds, as long as such activities did not interfere with public broadcasting, and allowed other non-advertising income-producing activities.

Senate. As reported (S Rept 97-98) by the Commerce Committee May 15, S 720 included the authorization levels requested by the administration. In addition, S 720:
● Authorized $16 million in fiscal 1982 for NTIA grants for public broadcasting facilities and equipment; $11 million, fiscal 1983; and $7 million, fiscal 1984.
● Required that no less than 60 percent of the federal contribution to public broadcasting be passed by CPB on to stations.

● Eliminated CPB direct support for satellite hookup among public broadcasting stations.

● Allowed public broadcasters who did not receive CPB dollars to editorialize and make political endorsements.

● Directed the FCC to study its rules restricting a station's ability to give on-air credit to sponsors with an eye toward eliminating restrictions where possible. This could provide stations an opportunity to raise more revenue. ∎

Broadcast Licenses

Commercial broadcasters won a partial victory when Congress agreed in 1981 to permit longer radio and television license terms, but the legislators refused to provide as much federal deregulation as the industry wanted.

The trade-off made by House and Senate conferees on the budget reconciliation bill (HR 3982 — PL 97-35) was to continue the general regulation of broadcasting but to drop a plan to require the Federal Communications Commission (FCC) to charge fees for services to broadcasters. The industry had objected to the fees. *(Reconciliation, p. 256)*

The Senate reconciliation bill included the provisions of separate Senate legislation involving the deregulation of radio broadcasting, some limited deregulation of television and establishing fees for FCC services (S 821 — S Rept 97-73).

The House did not include similar provisions in its reconciliation bill, but it passed separate legislation (HR 3239 — H Rept 97-84) authorizing funds for the FCC and requiring fees.

Senate supporters said that federal regulation of broadcasting, which was originally designed to ensure diversity of programming, should be relaxed because industry competition and program variety existed. The industry backed the Senate plan, contending that broadcasters were hampered by over-regulation.

Critics contended the conference agreement (H Rept 97-208) would seriously limit the ability of citizens to challenge broadcasters' licenses.

The reconciliation conferees dropped some of the more controversial Senate provisions such as ending the FCC requirement that radio stations provide news and public affairs programming and that they survey the public regularly to determine audience concerns.

The final agreement also repealed the FCC's permanent authorization and provided for a two-year authorization period. Conferees said the change was designed to give Congress the opportunity for regular oversight of FCC actions.

Conferees dropped a Senate provision that would have required the FCC to allocate the next available VHF commercial channel, if technically feasible, to New Jersey or Delaware. Those were the only states without a VHF television channel.

Provisions

As signed into law, Title XII of HR 3982 (PL 97-35):

● **Licenses.** Increased television license terms to five years from three years. The terms would be extended for new licenses or renewals.

● Increased radio license terms to seven years from three years. The terms would be extended for new licenses or renewals. The conferees said that extending the license term would not affect the citizen complaint procedure that allows the FCC to monitor performance.

● Allowed the FCC the discretion of granting new broadcast licenses by a system of random selection, or lottery, from applicants deemed to be qualified, or of continuing the current comparative hearings on applications.

● Directed the FCC to give "significant preference" to groups under-represented in broadcasting when it used a lottery system for granting new licenses.

● Made it unlawful for a license applicant, without FCC approval, to withdraw his application in exchange for payment from another applicant.

● Changed the FCC's permanent authorization to a two-year period and authorized $76.9 million annually in fiscal 1982 and 1983.

● Required the FCC to appoint a managing director for overall commission management and to report its goals and priorities to Congress annually. The FCC's executive director had some management responsibilities but not the authority to direct the activities of the commission's bureaus and offices. The bureaus and offices operated under the general policies of the commission.

● Required the FCC to complete as soon as possible the pending rule-making proceeding on revising the uniform system of accounts for telephone companies. The legislation said the system must ensure proper allocation of all of the telephone carriers' costs for telecommunications services, facilities and products.

Legislative History

FCC. The Senate reconciliation provisions authorizing $76.9 million annually for fiscal 1982-1984 and establishing fees for FCC services originally were contained in a bill reported May 15 by the Commerce Committee (S 821 — S Rept 97-73).

The House did not have similar language in its reconciliation measure, but it had passed separate legislation (HR 3239) by a 360-21 vote June 9 authorizing $77.4 million for fiscal 1982 for the FCC and allowing the agency to impose fees for services. *(Vote 60, p. 30-H)*

Radio and Television. The Senate Commerce Com-

Broadcast Deregulation

The Senate Commerce Committee Dec. 10 for the second time approved a bill that would significantly reduce federal controls on broadcasters.

The full Senate had passed similar legislation as part of the budget reconciliation measure (PL 97-35) but lost much of it in conference negotiations.

The committee Dec. 10 ordered a bill (S 1629) reported that would bar the Federal Communications Commission (FCC) from setting requirements for radio news and public affairs programming and advertising. Also, the bill would eliminate the current radio and television license renewal procedure of comparing the license holder with other applicants.

Broadcasters complained that regulation should be relaxed because there was industry competition and program variety. Critics argued that the legislation would repeal measures that protected the public interest.

mittee also included controversial provisions of bills (S 270, S 601) on radio and television in its reconciliation recommendations. No similar provisions were approved by the House.

The radio provisions (S 270) would eliminate the current radio license renewal procedure of comparing the license-holder with other applicants. It would establish a lottery to award new licenses and extend the current three-year life of a license to an indefinite period. Stations no longer would be required to determine audience concerns, and most FCC news and public affairs requirements would be lifted.

Although not so sweeping, the television provisions (S 601) would extend licenses to five years from three years. ▮

Maritime Subsidy Programs

Major changes in federal maritime policy were included in the omnibus budget reconciliation bill (HR 3982 — PL 97-35) passed by Congress July 31.

One change allowed owners of U.S.-flag ships under limited circumstances to buy or to build foreign vessels in fiscal 1982 and 1983 and still be eligible for federal operating subsidies for their ships.

Under current law, ships had to be built in American yards to qualify for operating subsidies, and an American operator accepting subsidies must own only American-built ships.

Operating subsidies were intended to help make U.S. shipping competitive with foreign operators.

U.S. shipbuilders were afraid that the provision, included in the House reconciliation bill but not the Senate version, would lead to the further deterioration of the financially ailing maritime industry. *(Reconciliation p. 256)*

The conferees agreed to allow the purchase of foreign ships in fiscal 1982 if there were no funds available to subsidize the construction in American yards and in fiscal 1983 if the president requested at least $100 million for construction subsidies or an equivalent alternative shipbuilding program.

Both House and Senate reconciliation bills accepted President Reagan's plan for eliminating new construction subsidies for fiscal 1982.

Reagan wanted to eliminate the $107 million for subsidies requested by President Carter and to defer $92 million from fiscal 1981 to fiscal 1982.

But the requirement for the fiscal 1983 subsidies was designed to ensure that the president proposed funding construction subsidies for that year or accepted the responsibility for eliminating construction subsidies.

The other major policy change removed an existing legal prohibition and allowed an ocean freight forwarder, who arranged for shipments, to ship property that the forwarder or a business associate owned if he did not receive compensation from the vessel selected for the job.

The change would be in effect until Dec. 31, 1983.

Some smaller freight forwarders contended the change could lead to illegal rebates for shipments, which would give competitors an advantage.

The House included the provision to help diversified transportation companies whose operations included freight forwarding. Some legal interpretations had cast doubt on the legality of those forwarders' operations.

Provisions

Title XVI of HR 3982 for fiscal 1982:
- Authorized $417,148,000 for operating subsidies.
- Authorized $10,491,000 for research and development and $8,005,000 for reserve fleet expenses.
- Authorized $33,684,000 for maritime education and training expenses, including $19,205,000 for the U.S. Merchant Marine Academy at Kings Point, N.Y., and $12,599,000 for state maritime academies.
- Authorized $33,209,000 for other operating and training expenses.
- Allowed a vessel owner receiving operating subsidies to suspend the vessel's subsidy contract for at least one year under certain conditions.
- Allowed new trade routes, services or lines to be established that take into account the seasonal closure of the Saint Lawrence Seaway and provide for an alternate routing of ships to maintain year-round service.
- Barred vessels from receiving operating or construc-

Airport Aid

The federally supported airport development program that expired in 1980 was revived in the omnibus budget reconciliation bill (HR 3982 — PL 97-35) approved by Congress July 31.

House and Senate reconciliation conferees included a bill (HR 4182 — H Rept 97-198) passed by the House by voice vote July 27 authorizing $450 million for airport development in fiscal 1981, which ended Sept. 30.

The original House reconciliation bill did not include a fiscal 1981 authorization, and the Senate version simply set a ceiling on the Airport and Airway Trust Fund spending.

The fiscal 1981 supplemental appropriations act (PL 97-12) provided $450 million for airport development, but no money had been spent because the authorization expired Sept. 30, 1980, due to disputes over the direction of the program. *(1980 Almanac p. 159)*

The reconciliation measure made no substantive changes in the program. There also were no changes in the passenger ticket taxes or other levies that previously fed the trust fund but had gone to the Treasury's general fund since the program expired.

Aviation Provisions

As signed into law, Title XI of HR 3982:
- Authorized $450 million in fiscal 1981 for airport development, planning and noise compatibility projects. The funds would come from the Airport and Airway Trust Fund. At least $25 million of the funds would be used for noise compatibility projects.
- Made projects begun during the program's lapse in fiscal 1981 eligible for fiscal 1981 funding.
- Directed the transportation secretary to obligate $15 million of the fiscal 1981 funds for carrying out noise compatibility programs at Cannon International Airport in Reno, Nev.
- Set a ceiling of $600 million on airport development spending out of the trust fund in fiscal 1982.

tion subsidies unless they are registered in an emergency sealift readiness program approved by the defense secretary.

● Set a ceiling of $1.65 billion on loan guarantees for the commercial demonstration ocean thermal energy conversion program.

● Set a ceiling of $850 million on loan guarantees for fishing vessels and fishery facilities.

● Allowed a freight forwarder to arrange a shipment in which he or a related company or official had an interest as long as the forwarder did not receive compensation. The provision would be in effect until Dec. 31, 1983. The Federal Maritime Commission by June 1, 1983, must submit a report to Congress evaluating the provision.

● Allowed an operator receiving or applying for operating subsidies to build or acquire vessels in a foreign shipyard until Sept. 30, 1983, if the administration determined that the application for subsidy could not be approved due to the unavailability of construction subsidies.

The provision was effective for fiscal 1983 only if the president requested at least $100 million in construction subsidies or proposed an alternative program that would create equivalent merchant shipbuilding activity in privately owned domestic shipyards.

Legislative History

The House provisions were similar to those contained in HR 2526 reported May 19 (H Rept 97-63) by the House Merchant Marine and Fisheries Committee.

An authorization bill was reported May 14 by the Senate Commerce Committee (S 1017 — S Rept 97-64).∎

Maritime Transfer

Congress cleared legislation July 29 to move the Maritime Administration (MarAd) from the jurisdiction of the Commerce Department to the Transportation Department.

Enactment of the bill (HR 4074 — PL 97-31) meant that a single department, Transportation (DOT), would be responsible for coordinating all transportation programs.

That was the intent of President Lyndon B. Johnson when he proposed creating DOT in 1966, but opposition from the maritime industry led to MarAd's being excluded from the new department. Industry officials, however, accepted the proposal when it was renewed by President Reagan in 1981 because they believed maritime issues would receive strong support from Transportation Secretary Drew Lewis. *(Congress and the Nation Vol. II, p. 232)*

MarAd is responsible for programs aiding the development and operation of the Merchant Marine and includes the administration of vessel construction and operation subsidy programs.

The House July 27 agreed by voice vote to suspend the rules and pass the bill (HR 4074 — H Rept 97-199). The measure had been reported by the Merchant Marine and Fisheries Committee July 24.

The Senate did not refer the bill to committee but approved it July 29 by voice vote. The president signed it Aug. 6. ∎

Highway Funds

Congress provided for more federal spending on highway construction and related programs in fiscal 1982 and

1983 than President Reagan wanted, although the totals were only modestly higher.

Title XI of the omnibus budget reconciliation legislation (HR 3982 — PL 97-35) passed by Congress July 31 established a limit of $8.2 billion on obligations, excluding emergency relief, from the Highway Trust Fund in fiscal 1982. The bill set an $8.8 billion limit on trust fund spending in fiscal 1983. *(Reconciliation, p. 256)*

Reagan had requested ceilings of $8.15 billion and $8.675 billion for the two years.

The fiscal 1982 limit on trust fund spending was down from the fiscal 1981 cap of $8.75 billion.

The conferees said the obligational limits would restrict highway and highway safety construction programs "severely below known needs." They said the ceilings would be reviewed when multi-year highway legislation was considered by Congress (HR 3210 — H Rept 97-92, S 1208 — S Rept 97-114). *(Story, p. 583)*

The president's plan to eliminate specific funding for state enforcement of the controversial national 55 mph speed limit also was dealt a blow by House and Senate reconciliation conferees, although they did agree to reduce the authorized funding.

The final bill required at least $20 million of the funds annually authorized for highway safety programs under the National Highway Traffic Safety Administration (NHTSA) to be used for enforcing the 55 mph speed limit. Existing law (PL 95-599) authorized $67.5 million for enforcement of the speed limit. *(1978 Almanac p. 540)*

Also, the legislation continued funding penalties for states that failed to meet minimum compliance standards for enforcement of the speed limit. The compliance level for fiscal 1982 and 1983 was dropped back to 50 percent of the motorists driving 55 mph, from 60 percent and 70 percent, respectively.

Provisions

As signed into law, Title XI of HR 3982 (PL 97-35):

● Set a limit of $8.2 billion on obligations from the Highway Trust Fund in fiscal 1982 for highway programs, excluding emergency relief, and a ceiling of $8.8 billion in fiscal 1983.

● Prohibited the obligation of more than 25 percent of the total federal highway funds available for fiscal 1982 or 1983 during the first quarter of those years. Also, it barred a state from obligating more than 35 percent of its highway funding allocation during the first quarter.

● Authorized $100 million annually for fiscal 1982-1984 for NHTSA highway safety programs.

● Repealed the 1978 highway act's specific authorization of $67.5 million for enforcement of the 55 mph speed limit, and required at least $20 million of the NHTSA highway safety funds to be used for enforcement aid.

● Continued a requirement that each state spend 2 percent of its annual highway safety fund allotment for programs to encourage use of safety belts.

● Authorized up to $10 million annually for fiscal 1982-1984 for highway safety programs administered by the Federal Highway Administration.

● Barred the transportation secretary from repealing 18 standards required of state highway safety programs before Oct. 1, 1982. The standards included those that provide for improved driver performance, accident record keeping, vehicle registration and inspection, and highway design and maintenance.

The legislation required the secretary to begin a rule-making process to determine safety programs that were most effective in reducing accidents, injuries and deaths. Only those programs established by the final rule as most effective would be eligible to receive federal aid.

The rule developed by the secretary would take effect Oct. 1, 1982, if it was submitted to Congress by April 1 of that year and neither chamber vetoed the rule. If the rule was submitted after April 1, it would become final Oct. 1, 1983, unless either the House or Senate vetoed it.

● Required the secretary to reduce a state's apportionment of federal highway funds by up to 5 percent in fiscal 1982 and 1983 and by up to 10 percent in later years if more than 50 percent of the state's motorists violated the 55 mph speed limit. The 1978 law had provided the 10 percent penalty for fiscal 1983. ∎

CPSC Authorization

Congress reauthorized the independent Consumer Product Safety Commission (CPSC) for two years, despite the administration's request to abolish it. But budget cuts would mean staff reductions and new requirements were set for rule-making.

The administration wanted to shift the CPSC's duties to other agencies or, in lieu of that, to reduce funding by 30 percent from Carter's plan, for a total of $33 million in 1982. The final budget reconciliation legislation (HR 3982 — PL 97-35) approved by Congress July 31 included the 1982 figure for the agency and added $35 million for 1983. *(Reconciliation, p. 256)*

Initially there was support in both the House and Senate to clip the CPSC's wings by transferring it to the Commerce Department, where critics said it would be subject to greater supervision and accountability.

Critics complained that CPSC did not understand manufacturing and product use and that it ended up over-regulating in its efforts to protect consumers. Businesses maintained that CPSC rules were overly burdensome. *(1978 Almanac p. 525)*

The CPSC was the first major independent regulatory agency to come before the 97th Congress for renewal. Its detractors were bolstered by the anti-regulatory mood left from the 1980 fight that left the Federal Trade Commission (FTC) bruised and by the general budget-cutting atmosphere. *(1980 Almanac p. 233)*

But consumer advocates successfully argued that folding the agency into the Commerce Department, which was responsible primarily for business promotion, would blunt the CPSC's effectiveness. Although small, the agency had had wide-ranging impact since its creation in 1973 because it could make independent judgments about product safety, they said. *(Congress and the Nation Vol. III., p. 685)*

For example, its regulations and standards had resulted in banning hair dryers with asbestos and requiring that toys not have small parts that can be swallowed by children.

The reconciliation conference agreement (H Rept 97-208) maintained the CPSC's independence but made budget cuts that were expected to result in layoffs of 25-30 percent of the staff.

In addition, new requirements were added on developing consumer product safety rules, including a cost-benefit analysis, and restrictions were placed on the release of information businesses considered confidential.

Also, one chamber of Congress was allowed to veto CPSC regulations if the other chamber did not object.

The authorization levels of $33 million in fiscal 1982 and $35 million in fiscal 1983 were the same as those included in the bill approved by the House Energy and Commerce Subcommittee on Health and Environment. Not included was the subcommittee's third-year funding of $37 million.

CPSC was authorized to receive $65 million in fiscal 1981 but had received only about $44 million.

A bill reported May 15 by the Senate Commerce Committee (S 1155 — S Rept 97-102) would have authorized $33 million annually for fiscal 1982 and 1983, encouraged the use of voluntary industry-imposed product standards over CPSC standards and set guidelines for cost-benefit analysis of industry regulations. The provisions, however, were not included in the Senate reconciliation measure.

Provisions

As signed into law, Title XII of HR 3982 (PL 97-35):

● **Developing Standards.** Directed the CPSC to rely on voluntary safety standards developed by industry groups or individuals, rather than mandatory standards, when compliance would eliminate or adequately reduce risk of injury and when it was likely that there would be substantial compliance with the voluntary standards.

● Eliminated CPSC authority to issue safety standards containing product design requirements and required the agency to express standards in terms of performance requirements.

● **Public Participation.** Allowed the CPSC to pay some expenses of persons who helped develop commission safety standards.

● **Rule-Making Analysis.** Provided detailed guidelines for rule-making proceedings, which required cost-benefit analyses of proposed mandatory standards and advance notice of the proceedings. During the proceeding, the agency must invite proposals for voluntary standards. The CPSC must end a proceeding if a voluntary standard developed in response to the request was likely to reduce the risk adequately and compliance was likely to be substantial.

The legislation also required three findings before the CPSC could issue mandatory safety rules. First, when industry had adopted a voluntary rule dealing with a risk of injury, the commission must find that compliance with the voluntary standard was not likely to result in adequate reduction of the risk or that it was unlikely that there would be substantial compliance. Second, the benefits of the rule must bear a reasonable relationship to the costs. Third, the rule must impose the least burdensome requirement in preventing or adequately reducing the risk of injury.

● **Information Disclosure.** Prohibited the CPSC from disclosing business information marked confidential by the manufacturer that would cause him substantial competitive market damage if released. Prior to the release of information considered confidential, the agency must notify the manufacturer, thereby giving him the opportunity to seek a temporary restraining order in U.S. district court to stop the release.

Prior to the release of business information, the agency must give the manufacturer a chance to mark the information confidential.

The agency could expedite the release of certain information in cases of emergency and other situations, such as imminent health hazards.

● Prohibited the agency from disclosing confidential commercial information through a request made under the Freedom of Information Act (FOIA). Previously, the agency was exempted from being compelled to release the information.

● Barred the CPSC from disclosing information submitted by a manufacturer that a new product might include a hazard unless the CPSC had issued a complaint alleging that the product presented a substantial hazard, the commission had accepted a settlement agreement from the manufacturer or the manufacturer agreed to disclosure.

● Required the CPSC to establish procedures to ensure that inaccurate information was not released.

● **Advisory Panels.** Directed the CPSC to appoint Chronic Hazard Advisory Panels to advise on cancer, birth defects and gene mutations associated with substances in consumer products. The CPSC could not issue a notice of advance proposed rule-making relating to chronic hazards unless a panel reported on the substance of concern.

● **Congressional Veto.** Allowed one chamber of Congress to veto safety standards and regulations if the other chamber did not object.

● **Information Gathering.** Limited the gathering of information to that which was necessary to carry out a specific regulatory or enforcement function of the agency.

● **Lawn Mowers.** Directed the CPSC to amend its lawn mower safety standard, which required mowers to stop when the user took his hand off the handle and to restart automatically. The CPSC was required to provide an alternative that would allow the engine to be started manually.

● **Amusement Rides.** Removed CPSC jurisdiction over amusement rides that were operated by a fixed-location amusement park.

● **Authorizations.** Authorized $33 million for the commission in fiscal 1982 and $35 million in fiscal 1983. President Carter requested $45 million for each year.

● Authorized such amounts as necessary for severance pay for laid-off employees. ∎

Product Liability Insurance

Legislation designed to make it easier for businesses to obtain insurance against claims for damages involving their products was signed into law by the president Sept. 25 (HR 2120 — PL 97-45).

The Product Liability Risk Retention Act of 1981 was cleared for the president Sept. 11, when the Senate accepted the House bill by voice vote.

The legislation generally pre-empted state statutes that restricted the formation of business "risk retention groups" for self-insurance or "purchasing groups" to buy product liability insurance jointly at favorable rates.

The House had overwhelmingly approved a bill (HR 6152) in 1980 that would have eased the creation of risk retention groups, but Senate floor action was blocked by opponents.

The insurance industry fought the legislation partly because the proposals required Commerce Department approval of risk retention groups. The industry said that would be an unwarranted federal intrusion into an area generally regulated by the states. *(Background, 1980 Almanac p. 265)*

The 1981 legislation, however, did not provide for federal regulation, and the industry dropped its active opposition. The bill required risk retention groups to be chartered under state law. Robert W. Kasten Jr., R-Wis., chairman of the Senate Commerce Consumer Subcommittee, noted that the bill involved no new federal bureaucracy or expenditures.

Business associations and consumer groups actively pushed for the legislation because they contended product liability insurance was virtually unobtainable for many businesses because of its spiraling costs. A company could go bankrupt if it were subject to a large court judgment and did not have product liability insurance, or if it had a high deductible charge, they argued.

Also, consumer advocates backed the proposal because of their fear that consumers would not be able to collect in court if businesses were not covered.

Among the supporters of the measure were the National Association of Wholesaler-Distributors, the National Association of Manufacturers, the National Federation of Independent Business and the National Tool Builders Association.

Provisions

As signed into law, HR 2120 (PL 97-45):

● Allowed businesses to form risk retention groups for assuming and sharing the liability risk for either products or completed operations. Completed operations were those which involved product installation or repairs by a firm outside its own premises.

A group could not exclude anyone from membership to obtain a competitive advantage over that person or business.

● Allowed an offshore risk retention group licensed in Bermuda or the Cayman Islands before Jan. 1, 1985, to continue operating if it certified to the insurance commissioner of at least one state that the group satisfied that state's capitalization requirements.

This provision was designed to encourage states to reform laws restricting operations of risk retention groups and thus encourage the formation of groups in those states. Offshore groups had been established because of favorable operating conditions and tax benefits.

● Exempted risk retention groups and persons who provided services to those groups from restrictive state laws and orders except under certain circumstances. For example, a state might require a group to pay premium taxes, submit reports required of licensed insurers relating to product liability insurance losses and expenses, and submit to a state examination if there was reason to believe that the group was in a "financially impaired condition."

● Exempted purchasing groups generally from restrictive state laws and orders.

Legislative History

HR 2120, reported July 21 by the House Energy and Commerce Committee (H Rept 97-190), was approved by the House by voice vote under suspension of the rules July 28.

The Senate accepted the House bill by voice vote Sept. 11 after indefinitely postponing action on its own similiar measure (S 1096). The Senate bill was reported (S Rept 97-

172) by the Commerce, Science and Transportation Committee July 30. ∎

Tourism Promotion

Legislation beefing up the federal role in promoting foreign tourism to the United States (S 304 — PL 97-63) was cleared by Congress Oct. 1 after the Reagan administration withdrew its objections.

Final congressional action on S 304 came when the House voted 288-112 to suspend the rules and agree to the conference report (H Rept 97-252). The Senate by voice vote had agreed to the report Sept. 29. *(Vote 213, p. 72-H)*

The compromise replaced the Commerce Department's U.S. Travel Service (USTS) with an upgraded agency to be called the U.S. Travel and Tourism Administration (USTTA) and generally followed the original House plan (HR 1311). The Senate plan to create an independent agency drew strong criticism from the administration.

Congress in 1980 had cleared a bill (S 1097) similar to the Senate measure, but it was pocket-vetoed by President Carter, who objected to creating a separate agency beyond presidential review. *(1980 Almanac p. 269)*

Although the administration eventually agreed to the upgraded agency within the Commerce Department, some members of Congress continued to oppose the bill. Critics said the government should not promote private industry, and the federal bureaucracy should not be increased during a time of budget constraints.

The conference report contained a typographical error in that it authorized $8.6 million for federal tourism activities in fiscal 1981, instead of fiscal 1982. The correct date was inserted before the bill was sent to the president.

Aiding the Economy

Many members of Congress had contended that the USTS had not aggressively promoted foreign travel to the United States. They pointed out that the tourism industry was a major employer in most states and accounted for more than $140 billion annually in consumer expenditures.

Backers of the Senate bill said an independent agency would be more effective because it would be free of budget and bureaucratic limitations set by an administration.

An earlier version of the House bill did call for an independent agency, but the Energy and Commerce Committee reported a compromise in an attempt to avoid a confrontation with the administration.

Administration officials argued that a new bureaucracy was not necessary and that trade matters should be consolidated within the Commerce Department. The administration originally wanted the tourism office to come under the International Trade Administration within the Commerce Department but accepted the plan to make it a separate office within the department.

Rep. William E. Dannemeyer, R-Calif., a committee member, said he opposed the conference report partly because the $8.6 million authorization came "at a time when we are asking those much less well off than the tourism industry to absorb additional budget cuts." No opposition was expressed in the Senate when the bill was considered.

Another major difference between the House and Senate versions was the funding. The House authorized a total of $7.6 million in fiscal 1982, while the Senate approved $8.6 million in fiscal 1981.

Provisions

As signed into law Oct. 16, S 304 (PL 97-63):

● Established a national policy to promote foreign travel to the United States.

● Created the U.S. Travel and Tourism Administration within the Commerce Department to replace the U.S. Travel Service (USTS). The agency would be headed by an under secretary of commerce for travel and tourism, appointed by the president and confirmed by the Senate. There also would be an assistant secretary responsible for developing the tourism marketing plan.

● Required the new Commerce Department under secretary for travel and tourism to establish facilitation services at major ports-of-entry; consult with foreign governments on travel and tourism matters; develop and administer a program to gather travel and tourism industry data and provide technical assistance; encourage travel on U.S. carriers; and submit annually to Congress, within six weeks of the president's recommended tourism budget, a detailed marketing plan, including funding and staff levels, to promote travel.

● Authorized the commerce secretary to provide aid to a region of not less than portions of two states to assist in the implementation of a regional tourism promotion plan.

● Barred the secretary from reducing the number of foreign offices of the USTTA or the number of employees assigned to those offices to a number less than the number of USTS foreign office employees in fiscal 1979.

● Required that in any fiscal year, the amount of funds available from appropriations for the USTTA foreign offices may not be less than the amount obligated in fiscal 1980.

● Established a policy council, to be known as the Tourism Policy Council, to coordinate policies and programs relating to tourism, recreation or national heritage resources. The council would represent the commerce secretary, other Cabinet members and federal officials.

● Created a Travel and Tourism Advisory Board, to be composed of 15 members appointed by the secretary, to advise on implementation of the act. The board must include members representing different geographical regions, varied segments of the tourism industry, states and consumers.

● Authorized $8.6 million in fiscal 1981 for federal tourism activities.

Legislative Action

Senate. Bypassing the Commerce Committee, the Senate passed S 304 Jan. 27, the same day it was introduced. The action caught the Reagan administration by surprise, with Commerce Secretary Malcolm Baldrige issuing a statement indicating his displeasure at not being consulted.

The Senate bill created an independent agency, the U.S. Travel and Tourism Administration, to prepare a detailed tourism development plan. The agency would be headed by an administrator, who would be appointed by the president and confirmed by the Senate.

It also provided that no federal official or agency could require the tourism unit to submit budget requests, legislative recommendations or testimony for approval before submitting them to Congress. An advisory board dominated by industry representatives would review the activities of the new agency.

The bill directed the USTS to provide the new agency

with $1 million for fiscal 1981 and provided for the transfer of all USTS activities and assets to the new agency within 180 days of enactment.

House. The House approved the Energy and Commerce Committee's compromise bill (HR 1311 — H Rept 97-107) July 28 by a vote of 321-98 after the Reagan administration withdrew its opposition. The House then amended its language to S 304. *(Vote 157, p. 56-H)*

As reported May 19 by the Energy and Commerce Committee, HR 1311 created the U.S. Travel and Tourism Administration (USTTA) within the Commerce Department, replacing the U.S. Travel Service (USTS).

The bill authorized $6.5 million for fiscal 1982 and about $1.1 million in other departmental monies for tourism programs .

The administration first contended that HR 1311 would create bureaucratic difficulties. But David A. Stockman, director of the Office of Management and Budget, informed Rep. James D. Santini, D-Nev., chairman of the U.S. Congressional Travel and Tourism Caucus, in a July 24 letter of the administration's reversal.

Stockman said S 304 would create "an unnecessary and counterproductive independent agency," while HR 1311 was "a reasonable, middle-of-the-road position." ∎

Transportation Safety Board

Congress Oct. 21 cleared legislation authorizing funds for the National Transportation Safety Board (NTSB) in fiscal 1981-1983 and clarifying the board's authority to conduct investigations of transportation accidents.

President Reagan signed the legislation (S 1000 — PL 97-74) Nov. 3.

The measure authorized more than $60 million for fiscal 1981-1983 and gave NTSB accident investigations priority over those conducted by other federal agencies. Members of Congress said they wanted to ensure that one agency was responsible for coordinating accident investigations.

The legislation also made clear that the board had authority to examine vehicles, rolling stock, tracks and pipeline facilities involved in transportation accidents.

The board's authorization lapsed in 1980 when it was tied to hazardous materials legislation (HR 7103, S 1141) that died because of a House dispute over an unrelated provision. *(1980 Almanac p. 266)*

However, NTSB received an appropriation through the fiscal 1981 appropriations act (PL 96-400) for the Transportation Department and related agencies. *(1980 Almanac p. 154)*

In 1981, the board's authorization was in separate legislation from the hazardous materials transportation bill (HR 3403). *(Hazardous Materials Transportation story, p. 577)*

The Senate Commerce Committee April 23 reported the Independent Safety Board Act Amendments of 1981 (S 1000 — S Rept 97-41), which was passed by the Senate by voice vote May 4.

The House Energy and Commerce Committee and the Public Works Committee May 19 reported similar legislation (HR 3404 — H Rept 97-108, Parts I and II). The House passed the measure by voice vote Oct. 13 and substituted the text for S 1000. The Senate Oct. 21 accepted the House version, clearing it for the president's signature.

Provisions

As cleared by Congress, S 1000:

● Authorized $18.54 million in fiscal 1981 for National Transportation Safety Board activities, $19.925 million in fiscal 1982 and $22.1 million in fiscal 1983.

● Gave NTSB investigations of accidents priority over those conducted by other federal agencies, except in the marine area. Other agencies could still conduct accident investigations under their own authority.

● Clarified NTSB authority to require reports for aviation "incidents," as well as accidents.

● Clarified the board's authority to examine vehicles, rolling stock, track and pipeline facilities involved in transportation accidents. The board was directed to preserve the evidence to the maximum extent possible and not to interfere unnecessarily with the transportation services of the equipment's owner or operator.

The NTSB examination was to be conducted with the cooperation of the owner or operator. But the board still would have the authority to secure a court order to obtain evidence and conduct tests if there was no cooperation.

● Required the transportation secretary to submit annual reports to Congress on his responses to NTSB recommendations regarding transportation safety. ∎

Coast Guard Authorizations

President Reagan Dec. 29 signed legislation (S 831 — PL 97-136) authorizing about $1.99 billion in fiscal 1982 for the Coast Guard.

Some members of Congress had expressed concern that the Coast Guard was inadequately funded, and the final measure exceeded the authorizations contained in earlier versions passed by the House and the Senate. The compromise was worked out by members and staff without going to conference.

The House Dec. 14 had passed a $1.9 billion version (HR 2559 — H Rept 97-62), while the Senate measure (S 831 — S Rept 97-45) had authorized $1.83 billion. Also, the final bill exceeded the funds included in separate appropriations legislation (HR 4209 — PL 97-102).

Members agreed to the higher authorization because the Coast Guard might need supplemental appropriations, and because $300 million was included for Coast Guard equipment in a defense appropriations bill (HR 4995 — PL 97-114).

Provisions

As signed by the president, PL 97-136 authorized:

● $1,404,800,000 in fiscal 1982 for Coast Guard operations and maintenance.

● $537,200,000 for acquisition and improvements of aids to navigation, facilities, vessels and aircraft.

● $17,500,000 for alteration or removal of bridges constituting obstructions to navigation.

● $29,730,000 for research and development.

● An end-of-year strength for active duty personnel of 42,224, and an end-of-year strength for civilian personnel of at least 5,484.

Also, the measure:

● Amended the fiscal 1981 Coast Guard authorization (PL 96-376) by increasing the authorization for operating expenses by $88.8 million to $1,337,207,000. That was nec-

essary because supplemental appropriations (PL 97-12) and military pay increases resulted in the Coast Guard appropriations exceeding the authorization. *(Coast Guard authorization, 1980 Almanac p. 258; PL 97-12, p. 281)*

● Removed a requirement that reserve officers on limited active duty be placed on the active duty promotion list, thereby freeing them from having to compete with career officers for promotion.

● Allowed the transportation secretary to delegate some Coast Guard responsibilities for vessel inspections to the American Bureau of Shipping or other similar group, which inspects vessels for insurance and other purposes.

The secretary was required to report to Congress on the implementation of the new policy within six months of enactment and then annually for three years.

● Directed the Coast Guard to deploy at least one helicopter for search and rescue as well as other missions at each of the following sites: Newport, Ore.; Cordova, Alaska; and Charleston, S.C.

Legislative History

HR 2559, reported by the Merchant Marine and Fisheries Committee May 19, was considered by the House on Dec. 8 and passed Dec. 14 by a 391-2 vote. The House then vacated the action and passed S 831, after amending that bill to conform with the language of HR 2559. *(Vote 342, p. 112-H)*

S 831, reported by the Commerce, Science and Transportation Committee April 23, was passed by the Senate May 4. The Senate Dec. 16 amended S 831 to reflect the informal compromise reached by members and staff and returned the bill to the House, which cleared it for the president by voice vote. ∎

New Western Union Service

Congress in 1981 cleared legislation allowing Western Union to provide international telegraph and telex service and to allow international telegraph and telex carriers to compete against Western Union in the United States.

A compromise between Senate and House versions of the bill (S 271 — PL 97-130) was worked out informally. The Senate Dec. 16 passed the compromise by voice vote. The House concurred the same day, suspending the rules and passing the bill by voice vote, thereby clearing it for the president.

Western Union had been prevented from entering the international market when Congress sanctioned the merger of the firm with a failing company in 1943. That bar was designed to prevent Western Union from using its domestic monopoly status to establish an international monopoly.

However, supporters of the bill argued that some international carriers had begun limited operations in the United States, and Western Union should be allowed access to the international market. They also contended that international carriers were able to charge high prices because of the lack of competition.

The original Senate bill was relatively simple, eliminating the prohibition against Western Union's entry into international markets after giving international carriers a four-month head start. The House version added a detailed transition period for deregulation. The compromise followed the general lines of the House measure.

Under the compromise, all carriers would be required

to provide interconnections with their facilities to other carriers upon reasonable request. The Federal Communications Commission (FCC) for three years would be able to oversee carriers' agreements for rates and the conditions of the interconnections.

Also included was an unrelated provision to ensure continued rail service on the bankrupt Rock Island Railroad until May 15, 1982. The provision was designed to clarify a 1980 law (PL 96-254) to maintain service during disposition of the rail lines. It had been in a Senate bill (S 1879 — S Rept 97-299) reported by the Commerce Committee Dec. 14. *(1980 Almanac p. 238)*

Provisions

As cleared by Congress, S 271:

● Directed the FCC to promote the development of competitive domestic and international telex and telegraph markets. The FCC was directed to reduce regulation as competition developed among carriers.

● Directed the FCC to require each carrier to provide facility interconnections to any other carrier upon reasonable request.

● Provided for a formula for sharing interconnecting service by domestic and foreign international carriers.

● Required that if any major carrier engaged in both domestic and international service, then the firm had to be treated separately by the FCC as a domestic carrier and an international carrier for the purposes of interconnection requirements.

If the separated domestic and international services provided interconnections to each other, the interconnections had to be made available at the same rates, conditions and quality to other carriers.

● Provided that after the FCC convened a meeting of carriers regarding interconnections, if carriers could not reach an agreement about interconnections within a 45-day period, the FCC could order an agreement establishing conditions and rates for interconnections. This provision would terminate three years following enactment of the legislation.

● Barred the FCC from approving a Western Union application to provide international service for four months following the company's entering into an agreement with other carriers for interconnections.

● Released carriers seeking to provide domestic service from a requirement to submit an application to the FCC. The commission would have the authority under limited circumstances to require an application, however.

● Allowed the FCC for one year to continue its oversight of the establishment of formulas for Western Union to use for allocating outbound telegraph traffic to international carriers when the sender did not specify a carrier.

● Permitted the Interstate Commerce Commission until May 15, 1982, to authorize temporary rail service over the lines of the Rock Island Railroad until the final disposition of the railroad's properties.

Legislative Action

The Senate passed S 271 (S Rept 97-25) June 22 by voice vote and without debate. That action was in marked contrast to the floor fight that occurred June 2 over committee jurisdiction over the bill.

That battle was over a motion to refer the bill reported by the Senate Commerce Committee to the Judiciary Committee to review antitrust implications. Commerce Committee Chairman Bob Packwood, R-Ore., argued the refer-

ral was a masked attempt to kill the bill. The motion was rejected, 28-59. *(Vote 136, p. 26-S)*.

The House Dec. 8 suspended the rules and adopted its version of the bill (HR 4927 — H Rept 97-356) by voice vote. It then substituted the language of HR 4927 for that of S 271.

The compromise measure was adopted by voice votes in both houses Dec. 16. ∎

Daylight-Saving Time

The House passed legislation to extend daylight-saving time (DST) for an additional two months each year, despite opposition from farmers and members of Congress representing rural areas.

The bill (HR 4437), passed Oct. 28 by a 243-165 vote, would extend the current six-month daylight-saving time to eight months by starting DST on the first Sunday of March. No further action was taken in 1981. *(Vote 270, p. 86-H)*

Under existing law, DST ran from the last Sunday of April to the last Sunday of October. Clocks were set ahead one hour in April and back again in October. Supporters said the bill would allow people more daylight hours for work and recreation during the extra two months, as well as provide a significant energy savings because of the reduced need for electricity.

Opponents said energy savings would be minimal and that the change could increase traffic dangers for school-children in rural areas in the western part of time zones. The sun rises later in those areas, so children would be traveling to school in the dark.

The bill also would cause difficulties for farmers, who would have to tend their animals in morning darkness, said members representing rural areas. The American Farm Bureau Federation opposed the bill.

Pat Roberts, R-Kan., called the measure the "Urban Convenience Act of 1981." He said it would help only urban dwellers who wanted more daylight for shopping and recreation. "In New York or in other metropolitan areas, if you want to play golf, if you want to walk your dog, if you want to go jogging, fine. But do not do it at the expense of our rural areas," Roberts said.

Supporters said a Department of Transportation (DOT) study showed that starting DST on the first Sunday of March would not result in an increase in traffic fatalities among schoolchildren. It also indicated that the longer DST would save about 100,000 barrels of oil a day during the extra two months because of the reduced need for electricity.

"This is a savings which we can get year after year in a painless manner, and reduce our costly dependence on imported oil," said Richard L. Ottinger, D-N.Y., chief sponsor of the bill and chairman of the House Energy and Commerce subcommittee that considered the measure. The committee reported HR 4437 Sept. 22 (H Rept 97-243).

Supporters said opinion polls indicated that the public favored longer DST by a 2-1 margin. Backing the bill were the Retinitis Pigmentosa Foundation, which aids people with night blindness; the National Association of Conve-nience Stores; the International Assocation of Amusement Parks; the International Council of Shopping Centers; and DOT.

The future of the Senate version (S 49) was uncertain

because opponents had blocked action in the Commerce Committee.

Background

The United States first went on daylight time during World War I to conserve fuel and increase national efficiency, and returned to it during World War II. Between the wars and from 1945 to 1966, states and cities passed individual laws and ordinances establishing daylight time. *(Congress and the Nation Vol. II, p. 972)*

In 1966, Congress enacted the Uniform Time Act (PL 89-387) and imposed a six-month DST from April to October. Only Arizona, Hawaii and part of Indiana chose to remain on standard time. *(1966 Almanac p. 585)*

Following the 1973 Arab oil embargo, Congress passed an emergency act (PL 93-182) instituting year-round DST in an effort to save energy. However, a storm of public complaints ensued about children traveling to school in the darkness. Congress in 1974 restored standard time (PL 93-434) for the months of November, December, January and February. Daylight-saving time eventually reverted to six months. *(1976 Almanac p. 507; 1974 Almanac p. 751; 1973 Alamanac, p. 631)*

Provisions

In addition to setting the beginning of daylight-saving time on the first Sunday of March, HR 4437:

● Authorized the Federal Communications Commission to change its regulations on the operating times and power levels of radio stations that broadcast only during daylight hours.

● Continued to allow states to exempt the whole state or a portion in a different time zone than the rest of the state.

However, by a vote of 170-242, the House rejected an amendment by Thomas F. Hartnett, R-S.C., that would have allowed states to exempt themselves from the additional two months of DST. *(Vote 269, p. 86-H)*

Ottinger said the amendment would result in confusion for the nation's commerce because of the need to adjust airline, railroad, radio and television schedules.

Ottinger said extending DST to the beginning of March would result in sunrises no later than those now occurring in October. "The bill will enable the nation to realize the additional benefits of later sunsets without facing any mornings darker than we now face under current daylight-saving time," he asserted. ∎

Hazardous Transport

The House Oct. 20 overwhelmingly passed legislation to improve the safety of transporting hazardous materials after striking language that would have banned large shipments of radioactive substances through New York City.

Approved by a vote of 410-2, the bill (HR 3403 — H Rept 97-87, Pts. I and II) authorized $8.3 million annually for fiscal 1982 and 1983 for federal programs relating to the safe shipment of hazardous materials and for new regional centers to improve the training of state and local personnel. *(Vote 252, p. 82-H)*

A similar bill (HR 7103) died in 1980 because of a dispute over delaying a federal rule establishing a routing system for transporting radioactive material on highways. *(1980 Almanac p. 266)*

The Transportation Department (DOT) rule was op-

posed by New York City officials concerned about shipments from Long Island nuclear facilities. They said that when the rule went into effect Feb. 1, 1982, it would override cities that wanted to prohibit the movement of nuclear waste through their boundaries.

As reported by the House Public Works Committee May 19, HR 3403 prohibited transporting large quantities of radioactive materials by motor vehicle or railroad through New York City, except under limited conditions. It was also reported by the Energy and Commerce Committee.

Geraldine A. Ferraro, D-N.Y., who represented part of New York City, pushed the committee language, but because of the strong opposition by the administration and others, she agreed to a floor compromise offered by Public Works Chairman James J. Howard, D-N.J.

Howard's amendment, accepted by voice vote, directed the transportation secretary to devise a method for analyzing risks and costs associated with transporting radioactive materials by highway, railroad, and barge or other vessel.

The Ferraro provision was criticized for possibly exposing smaller communities to potentially greater risks because of inadequate roads. Norman F. Lent, R-N.Y., who represented part of Long Island, said it "prematurely and arbitrarily" rejected the rule that "seeks to balance national and local interests by providing a uniform national highway routing plan."

The bill, without the Ferraro provision, was reported by the House Energy and Commerce Committee May 19. Similar legislation (S 960 — S Rept 97-99) was reported May 15 by the Senate Commerce Committee.

Provisions

As passed by the House, HR 3403:

●Directed the transportation secretary to establish regional training centers to help improve state and local personnel's response to accidents involving the transportation of hazardous materials and enforcement of state and local regulations governing the shipments.

The secretary would establish centers in agreement with a state, group of states, local government or non-profit group, which had to provide the facility for the center and at least 60 percent of the training costs in the first year and at least 75 percent in the second and third years.

●Allowed the secretary to contract for a supplemental reporting system and data center operated and maintained by a private entity. This would allow DOT to continue to rely on the Chemical Transportation Emergency Center (CHEMTREC), a project of the Chemical Manufacturers Association that provided information on emergency techniques for hazardous materials shipments.

●Authorized $8,332,000 annually for fiscal 1982 and 1983 for federal hazardous materials transportation activities. Not more than $2 million could be used in each year for the regional training centers.

●Required the secretary within one year to report to Congress on the feasibility and cost of implementing systems for notifying state and local governments about shipments of hazardous materials through their jurisdictions.

●Directed the secretary, in consultation with the energy secretary and the Nuclear Regulatory Commission, to develop a method for analyzing the comparative risks and costs associated with transporting a large quantity of radioactive materials by highway, railroad, barge or other vessel. At the request of a state, the secretary would arrange a demonstration of the method. Within one year, the secre-

tary had to report to Congress on the method and demonstration results.

Coal Slurry Pipelines

Legislation to promote the construction of coal slurry pipelines as an alternative to shipping Western coal by rail was approved by one vote by the House Interior and Insular Affairs Committee.

The bill (HR 4230), ordered reported by a 21-20 vote Dec. 8, would allow federally approved pipeline firms to use the power of eminent domain to obtain rights of way across private lands after private negotiation had failed.

Similar legislation was reported during the 96th Congress, but opposition from railroads and some Western states kept it from reaching the House floor or moving out of a Senate committee. In 1982 proponents also faced resistance from President Reagan.

Coal slurry is pulverized coal mixed with water transported through a pipeline. At the end of the line, the water is removed and the coal burned to generate energy.

The only operating pipeline in 1981 was the Black Mesa Pipeline, which connected the Black Mesa coal mine in northeastern Arizona with a power plant in southern Nevada. Others were planned but had been blocked by the refusal of railroads to grant rights of way.

Utilities, other coal interests and some consumer advocates argued that the bill would help bring down energy costs by providing competition to railroads. they said railroads could charge unduly high rates because there was no alternative transportation available.

The railroads, credited with the 1978 House defeat of a pipeline bill, contended that it would be unfair to give competitors the power of eminent domain over rail lands and allow them to siphon off needed revenue. Also, some Western states were concerned that the pipelines would divert scarce water supplies. *(1978 Almanac p. 675)*

Administration officials said that allowing the federal government to grant eminent domain powers to pipeline companies would be a blow to states' rights. President Carter had supported coal slurry legislation.

"We were dealt a severe blow by the administration. I can't believe a Republican administration that believes in competition would be against this," Interior Committee Chairman Morris K. Udall, D-Ariz., said.

Despite Reagan's opposition, HR 4230 drew bipartisan support from committee members.

The House Public Works Committee began hearings on the bill Dec. 8. Another coal pipeline measure (S 1844) was pending in the Senate Energy and Natural Resources Committee.

Provisions. The bill as ordered reported required the Interstate Commerce Commission (ICC), which regulates surface transportation, to issue a certificate to a pipeline company if the commission determined that "public convenience and necessity" required or would be enhanced by the operation of the proposed coal pipeline.

Once a company received the certificate, it then could go to federal or state court to exercise the power of eminent domain and secure rights of way through private lands. The court would set the compensation due the property owner.

However, the eminent domain authority would not give pipeline companies rights to water except as allowed

by the state. That provision was included by the bill's sponsors to help assure Western states that scarce water needed for farming and other uses would not be diverted to coal slurry pipelines against their will.   ∎

Port User Fees

House and Senate committees approved legislation that could for the first time require commercial vessels to pay a share of the cost of federal port dredging projects. There was no floor action in 1981.

The bill (S 1692) ordered reported Dec. 2 by the Senate Environment and Public Works Committee went further than a House committee measure (HR 4627) towards meeting President Reagan's user-fee proposals. Reagan wanted local port authorities to pay 100 percent of both new port construction and maintenance.

Currently the federal government completely funded improvements and maintenance of deep-draft channels and harbors by the Corps of Engineers.

S 1692 would require local authorities to pay the full cost of new port improvements and up to 25 percent of routine port dredging costs.

HR 4627 as ordered reported Oct. 21 by the House Merchant Marine and Fisheries Committee would require local authorities to pay a share of the costs of maintenance and improvements for depths beyond 45 feet.

Both bills allowed port authorities to levy fees on port users to recover their share of the costs.

Representatives of ports were split on the cost-sharing legislation. Smaller ports feared they would be unable to raise the necessary funds. Some larger ports believed they could manage the financing, but they wanted to reduce the time required to complete projects.

Both bills contained provisions designed to reduce the completion time for projects from the current estimate of 26 years, partly by speeding approval of federal permits for projects.

HR 4627 also contained a cargo preference provision that would require that U.S.-flag ships carry a portion of American exports and imports of dry-bulk commodities, such as coal and grain.

House Committee Action

HR 4627 was expected to run into opposition from the administration and from special interests that would be affected by the user fee and cargo preference provisions. The measure also was to be considered by the Public Works Committee before the House acted.

Port Fees. The bill would require the federal government to continue paying 100 percent of the costs of operations and maintenance for ports up to 45 feet deep. Those activities involve periodic dredging to maintain the port's depth.

But if a local port authority or other governmental entity wanted a port deepened beyond 45 feet to handle the larger coal vessels, it would have to pay at least 50 percent of the cost of dredging beyond that depth. It also would have to reimburse the federal government for 75 percent of the operating and maintenance costs made necessary by dredging a port beyond 45 feet.

The bill would authorize a port authority to recover its dredging costs by levying user fees on vessels engaged in foreign commerce that used the port. The fees would have to comply with rules set by the secretary of the Army.

However, many members of Congress as well as special interests said Reagan's proposal to recover all the costs of port dredging and operations through user fees went too far. They argued that the fees would be excessive and that the plan did not properly account for public benefits, such as an improved economy resulting from deeper ports that could handle the large vessels necessary for coal trade.

One aspect of the bill that drew support was a limit on procedural challenges to port deepening projects that could help speed completion of projects.

Currently, projects were delayed because of bureaucratic rules and challenges resulting from environmental concerns, committee staffers said. Coal interests predicted such delays would result in American coal producers losing expected new foreign orders for coal because there were not enough U.S. ports to handle the larger ships.

Cargo Preference. The last significant attempt to pass a cargo preference bill was in 1977, when President Carter supported a measure guaranteeing U.S.-flag ship owners that they could carry 9.5 percent of the nation's oil imports. However, the House defeated the bill after Republicans charged that it would be a political payoff to maritime interests. *(1977 Almanac p. 534)*

Under HR 4627, bilateral agreements would be negotiated with many U.S. trading partners that would result in non-subsidized U.S.-flag ships, built in domestic yards, carrying about 40 percent of American imports and exports of dry-bulk commodities in 10 years. The trading partners' vessels would also carry about 40 percent of the goods; a third party would carry the remainder.

U.S.-flag vessels currently carried only about 4 percent of the U.S. dry-bulk trade.

Gene Snyder, R-Ky., ranking minority member of the Merchant Marine Committee and sponsor of the cargo preference provision, said the bill would help wean American shipbuilding and vessel operations from federal subsidies, an idea that he said should be attractive to the administration. *(Maritime subsidies, p. 570)*

But shippers were concerned that their costs would increase with the forced use of American vessels.

Senate Committee Action

S 1692 as reported by the Environment and Public Works Committee (S Rept 97-301) would allow the local authorities to levy fees on commercial vessels to recover any local funds spent.

Although the plan was closer to Reagan's proposal, David A. Stockman, director of the Office of Management and Budget, wrote to Senate panel members urging them to increase the local share of maintenance costs.

S 1692 would require most local authorities to pay up to 25 percent of the cost of maintenance, which involved periodic dredging to maintain a port's depth.

However, the bill would establish a formula based on national average maintenance costs and the tonnage shipped through the ports that would result in a cap limiting the amount a port would have to pay.

The cap, plus some other restrictions in the bill, would result in an average local share of only 15 percent, rather than 25 percent. A port would pay 25 percent of the costs or the equivalent of 6.9 cents per ton shipped through the port, which ever was less.

The total national cost was estimated by the committee at $337 million, with the local share being $46 million because of the cap and other limiting provisions, rather than $84 million.

Administration User Fees Draw Skepticism

While agreeing generally that people who benefit from special services should help defray the costs, few members of Congress or special interest groups fully supported President Reagan's plans for new or increased user fees.

Reagan contended that user fees would return equity to both taxpayers and the marketplace. The plan would reduce the subsidies paid by general taxpayers for special programs and shift the costs to groups — such as barge operators and boaters — that receive economic benefits from the services, he said.

"When the federal government provides a service directly to a particular industry or to a group of citizens, I believe that those who receive benefits should bear the cost," Reagan said Sept. 24 in renewing his call for new or increased aviation, inland waterway, port development and Coast Guard user fees.

However, his earlier plans were not well received. None was enacted in 1981, the Coast Guard plan was withdrawn for more work and others were expected to be modified in 1982.

Arguments against the proposals were basically the same as those put forth in the past when other administrations sought user fees.

Special interests said the fees were excessive and did not give enough weight to the benefits the general public received from the special services, such as the economic boost an area received from a busy airport.

Others argued that their members would be charged whether or not they actually used the services. Boaters, for example, might never need the search and rescue services of the Coast Guard, they said.

Another issue involved trust funds established to finance certain activities such as airport development.

Some members of Congress believed that the user fee revenues would be used to help balance the budget and not to provide the services to the groups paying for them. Still others backed the trust fund concept, arguing, for example, that the Coast Guard fees might find greater acceptance if there were a trust fund earmarked to receive and expend the monies.

Another point raised in favor of user fees was the contention that special interests would be less likely to lobby for low priority or marginal projects if they had to pay the entire bill. That could mean a reduction in federal spending, proponents said.

Sen. Pete V. Domenici, R-N.M., Budget Committee chairman, claimed that the barge industry, for example, supported all waterway projects whether or not they would produce much in the way of economic benefits.

Who Should Pay?

Reagan's policy was to recover, as much as possible, those costs that could be attributed to a specific group.

He said Sept. 24 that yacht owners, commercial vessels and the airlines would receive $2.8 billion in services from the federal government that year. The government also would spend $525 million to maintain river harbors, channels, locks and dams for the barge and maritime industries.

He said his user-fee plans would recover $980 million, about one-third of the $3.3 billion total.

Following were his transportation proposals:
• **Aviation.** He called for a 12-cent-per-gallon tax for general aviation fuel in fiscal 1982, increasing to 36 cents in 1986, and a 20-cent-per-gallon tax for jet fuel, increasing to 65 cents in 1986. The current 4-cent-per-gallon charge applied to both jet and non-jet fuel. The passenger ticket tax would be hiked to 6.5 percent from 5 percent.

Federal Aviation Administrator J. Lynn Helms said the combined hike in general aviation fuel taxes and airline ticket taxes (HR 2930) would result in aviation users as a whole eventually paying their full share of the operations, maintenance and equipment costs of the air traffic control system, as well as meeting airport capital needs.

Not recovered would be those costs associated with government use of the airway system and federally owned airports.
• **Ports.** The Reagan plan (S 809) would allow local authorities to charge user fees to recover full federal operations and maintenance costs for ports and new construction. Bills were approved by committees (S 1692, HR 4627) setting fees to partly recover the costs.
• **Barges.** The administration's inland waterway proposal (S 810) would more than double the current 6-cent-a-gallon fuel tax for barges, industry spokesmen said. The fuel tax and other new user fees in combination would result in full recovery of operations, maintenance and new construction costs that can be attributed to barges, an administration spokesman said.
• **Coast Guard.** The administration agreed to rework its Coast Guard user fee proposals after the original draft was opposed in Congress. The first provided for fees to recover amounts increasing up to $500 million in fiscal 1986, or 33 percent of the costs of services to boats, commercial vessels and seamen. The fees would cover licenses, inspections, navigation aids, and search and rescue services. The services currently were supported by the general Treasury.

While Reagan called for full local reimbursement of maintenance costs, Stockman said the administration would support a cap limiting charges to about 23 cents per ton.

Pete V. Domenici, R-N.M., who offered the administration plan during the committee meeting, said the limitation would recover less than 50 percent of the federal costs. A committee aide said the proposal would raise the local share to $165 million.

Domenici withdrew his amendment but indicated that he might offer it on the floor.

Provisions

As ordered reported, S 1692 would:
• Require a port authority or other appropriate non-federal entity, beginning Oct. 1, 1982, to pay 25 percent of the total federal cost of maintaining ports to dimensions authorized by Congress as of Jan. 1, 1981.

● Require authorities beginning Oct. 1, 1982, to pay for 50 percent of maintenance costs for improvements authorized after Jan. 1, 1981.

● Authorize $250 million annually for fiscal 1983-1987 for the federal share of maintenance costs.

● Require a local authority to reimburse the federal government within 50 years of enactment of the legislation for the cost of improvements already approved. The federal government would pay for work actually started prior to Sept. 30, 1982.

● Require a local authority to finance any new construction beginning Oct. 1, 1982.

● Allow a local authority to levy fees on commercial vessels using deep-draft channels and harbors to pay for construction and maintenance costs.

● Establish a two-year limit on the process for securing federal permits for port projects. ∎

Bus Deregulation

The House Nov. 19 overwhelmingly passed legislation that would significantly relax the tight government regulation of the intercity bus industry and give companies more freedom to determine their own routes and rates.

The Senate did not act on bus deregulation in 1981.

The ease with which the House passed its measure (HR 3663 — H Rept 97-334) — by a 305-83 vote, after less than an hour of debate and without substantive amendments — contrasted with the controversy over 1980 transportation deregulation measures. *(Vote 308, p. 100-H)*

The bus bill was the fourth in a line of transportation measures considered by Congress designed to increase competition and give industries more flexibility in the marketplace.

Congress enacted trucking and railroad deregulation laws (PL 96-296 and PL 96-448) in 1980 and an airline deregulation measure (PL 95-504) in 1978. *(Trucking, 1980 Almanac p. 242; railroads, 1980 Almanac p. 248; airlines, 1978 Almanac p. 496)*

Summary

The bill would give bus firms flexibility to raise rates up to 10 percent or lower them by 20 percent without review by the Interstate Commerce Commission (ICC).

But it would limit companies' ability to set rates collectively since it would narrow their exemption from antitrust laws.

The bill would eliminate the antitrust immunity after Jan. 1, 1984, for single-line rates and some joint rates. Single-line rates were charges for service handled by one carrier, while joint rates were charges for service handled by more than one carrier.

It would also allow bus companies to enter the industry or expand their operations with less government involvement. Persons objecting to the new service would bear the burden of proving to the ICC that the proposal was not in the public interest.

Currently, a company must show not only that it was fit and able to provide the new service, but that the transportation was required for "public convenience and necessity."

The legislation also would make it easier for bus firms to drop unprofitable routes.

The ICC would be authorized under certain conditions to pre-empt state restrictions on the operations of companies within a state.

The bill covered to varying degrees regular-route service, which was the usual type of scheduled service authorized over specific routes, and charter service, which provided exclusive use of a vehicle to a group at a single charge. Also covered was a catchall category which included special services at per capita rates, such as day trips to casinos or sporting events.

Background

Intercity bus industry officials said federal and state regulations were unnecessarily restrictive. Regulations needed to be loosened, they said, to allow companies to operate more efficiently and compete more vigorously — both with each other and with airlines and private cars.

Some regulations had forbidden buses to pick up or drop off passengers on intermediate points along routes. And, some industry officials contended, state regulators had kept rates for service within states unduly low.

Industry ridership and profits had declined during the last decade because of competition from automobiles and airlines. But both measures of the industry's health had improved during 1979 and 1980.

According to the American Bus Association (ABA), intercity ridership declined from 401 million passenger trips in 1970 to 373 million in 1980. Net operating revenue for the industry fell from $94 million in 1969 to $54 million in 1978, but the revenue increased to $90.2 million in 1979 and $133.5 million in 1980.

Supporters of the House legislation said it was needed to revise the law governing intercity buses to meet contemporary market conditions.

"What we've been working under is a 1930s law, which is not bad, except it's 1981," said Glenn M. Anderson, D-Calif., chairman of the House Public Works Surface Transportation Subcommittee and floor manager of the bill.

Compromise Legislation

The bill was able to move so quickly through the Public Works Committee, which reported the measure Nov. 17 without debate, and the full House two days later because it was a compromise, members said.

The measure was worked out with various segments of the industry, labor, consumer advocates and others. All the interests supported the bill, although no one was happy with all provisions, committee members said.

Some of the small bus companies had been concerned about deregulation, fearing they would be swamped by Greyhound Lines Inc. or Trailways Inc., which dominated the industry. Greyhound, particularly, would have preferred full deregulation.

Labor was concerned that some jobs would be lost when companies left markets. The compromise included provisions to give laid-off employees priority for new bus jobs.

The final bill was "something the industry can live with," ABA President Arthur D. Lewis said. The ABA, which represented small and large bus companies, supported the bill.

The Reagan administration did not take a formal position.

Transportation Secretary Drew Lewis told the committee during hearings in the spring that the administration supported bus deregulation. Administration officials were expected to seek further deregulatory provisions in the Senate.

House Debate

House Public Works Committee Chairman James J. Howard, D-N.J., who manuevered the trucking deregulation measure through the House in 1980, and other supporters emphasized in floor debate that the bus bill did not totally deregulate the industry.

Some members were concerned that loosening government controls would result in a loss of service for small communities. They complained that small towns had lost transportation service with the deregulation of airlines and budget cutbacks in Amtrak, the federally subsidized passenger railroad.

The bill's supporters noted that its statement of national policy called for maintaining service to small communities.

Anderson said provisions in the legislation making it easier for a firm to start up bus service would promote competition, thus increasing service. In addition, he said, the provisions allowing easier reduction of unprofitable service still would require the ICC to consider whether there were reasonable transportation alternatives. ∎

FTC Veto Blocked

A congressional drive to overturn a Federal Trade Commission (FTC) used-car regulation was blocked by a parliamentary maneuver in 1981.

The rule, which would have required used-car dealers to disclose certain information to buyers, would provide the first test of congressional veto power over the FTC since Congress gave itself the authority in 1980 (PL 96-252). The 1980 FTC authorization allowed both chambers to overturn a rule by adopting a resolution of disapproval. The president's signature would not be required. *(1980 Almanac p. 233)*

The rule demanded that dealers disclose to potential buyers known defects in cars and whether a car carried a warranty. Auto dealers opposed the rule, contending that it would require them to make expensive inspections to protect themselves against possible lawsuits.

FTC officials said the rule did not require inspections.

The strength of the sentiment to veto the rule was reflected in there being 47 Senate cosponsors and more than 200 House cosponsors for resolutions (S Con Res 33, H Con Res 178) to disapprove the rule.

The Senate Commerce Committee Dec. 10 had voted 12-4 to approve S Con Res 33. The House Energy and Commerce Committee Dec. 11 voted 27-14 for H Con Res 178.

Senate Commerce Committee Chairman Bob Packwood, R-Ore., who opposed the veto resolution in committee, launched the parliamentary manuever Dec. 11 to sidetrack the resolutions. He said he wanted "a further airing" of the issues.

The Block. The Senate was under a unanimous consent agreement to consider cloture — a move to limit debate — on two issues not related to the FTC. Majority Leader Howard H. Baker Jr., R-Tenn., tried to change the agreement, again a step not related to the FTC veto resolution, but to do so required the unanimous consent of the Senate.

But Packwood objected because the change would have had the effect of allowing the S Con Res 33 to be brought to the floor.

Packwood's objection, for a number of technical reasons, also meant the Senate would be in session beyond the Dec. 20 deadline for action on the FTC resolution. If Congress were in session beyond Dec. 20 and neither chamber had voted, the rule would have gone into effect.

To avoid letting the rule go into effect, opponents of the rule, led by Larry Pressler, R-S.D., and Robert W. Kasten Jr., R-Wis., agreed to postpone action until 1982 if Packwood would withdraw his objection. Packwood agreed.

After the Senate postponed action on the resolution, key House members also decided against a vote until 1982. Once the FTC re-submitted the rule to Congress, members would have 90 days to act before it went into effect. ∎

Pipeline Safety Stalled

Congress adjourned without final action on a bill authorizing funds for federal and state safety programs for gas pipelines.

The House June 1 by voice vote passed a bill (HR 3420 — H Rept 97-89) authorizing more than $8 million in fiscal 1982 for the programs. It included more than $3.6 million in grants to states to regulate natural gas pipeline safety and $3.4 million for federal government safety activities.

The programs involved setting minimum federal standards for the construction and operation of pipelines and related facilities, inspections and enforcement of the standards.

The Public Works and Energy and Commerce committees reported the bill (Parts I and II) May 19.

The Senate Commerce Committee May 15 reported a similar bill (S 1099 — S Rept 97-74), which would have authorized more than $8 million in both fiscal 1982 and 1983. The Senate passed the bill by voice vote June 2, but then invalidated the action in an effort to reach a compromise with the House.

In acting on a compromise version July 17 authorizing about $9 million annually through fiscal 1983, the Senate added a provision allowing states to issue permits allowing trucks 102 inches wide to use interstate highways under limited conditions. Truck widths had been limited to 96 inches.

The House did not act on the revised version before adjournment. The Senate Commerce Committee Dec. 14 reported another measure (S 1402) on truck size. *(Story, below)*

Congress in 1979 toughened pipeline safety regulations because of accidents involving exploding liquefied natural gas (LNG) and liquefied petroleum gas (LPG). The gases were used for home heating, cooking, industrial activities and other purposes. *(1979 Almanac p. 352)* ∎

Truck Size

Legislation (S 1402 — S Rept 97-298) designed to bring some uniformity to conflicting state regulations regarding commercial truck size was reported Dec. 14 by the Senate Commerce Committee.

The bill would bar a state from imposing length limitations of less than 48 feet for certain trailers and from regulating the overall length of the entire truck. States could continue to regulate the size of the cargo units.

Also, states could permit 102-inch-wide trucks on Interstate highways. Federal law currently limited truck widths to 96 inches in most states. The timber industry had pushed for wider trucks because of loading problems.

Committee members contended S 1402 would allow greater cargo capacity without jeopardizing safety.

The bill did not deal with weight limitations on trucks.

The primary lobbying group was the timber industry, which was important to the economies of Oregon and other states. The industry contended that it needed the wider trucks for more efficient shipping. Another interested party was the American Trucking Associations (ATA) representing regulated trucking firms.

The key opponent had been the International Brotherhood of Teamsters, which contended the bill would lead to unsafe trucks for drivers. However, a spokesman said the union was pleased with the committee bill.

The 1956 highway act (PL 84-627) generally prohibited trucks wider than 96 inches from using interstate highways. Rhode Island, Connecticut and Hawaii currently allowed wider trucks on interstates because of laws predating the federal act. Some states allowed 102 inches- wide trucks with special permits. *(1956 Almanac p. 398)*

A truck-width provision had been included in the Senate version of the 1981 budget reconciliation legislation but was taken out before floor consideration because of concerns about including issues not directly related to the budget.

It had also been attached to HR 3420 authorizing funds for pipeline safety programs. *(Story, p. 582)* ∎

Highway Compromise Cleared by Congress

A compromise highway bill reached in the waning days of the session gave the Reagan administration some of the Interstate cost-savings and repair program revisions it requested.

But the legislation (HR 3210 — PL 97-134) was neither as comprehensive as the administration had proposed nor did it grant key requests such as phasing out federal funding for the urban and rural road systems.

The bill, designed to complete the Interstate Highway System at a $15 billion savings, resolved an impasse between the House and Senate over the scope of the legislation that had prevented states from obligating Interstate construction funds.

The House Dec. 15 by voice vote approved the compromise, which had been reached informally by key members without a conference. The Senate concurred by voice vote Dec. 16, clearing the measure for the president.

The bill affected only Interstate programs, tightening eligibility for construction funds and expanding a major repair program, as President Reagan requested. It also reduced previously authorized construction funds (PL 95-599) for fiscal 1983 to $3.1 billion from $3.2 billion. *(PL 95-599, 1978 Almanac p. 536)*

However, the compromise also represented a victory for the House because of its narrow scope.

The president and the Senate wanted comprehensive multi-year legislation dealing with both Interstate and non-Interstate highway programs that reduced federal spending over a period of years and allowed states to target scarce funds.

The House, while agreeing to some of the Interstate program changes, wanted only a one-year bill, with comprehensive legislation postponed until 1982 when more would be known about potential revenue. Also, some members wanted to tie the popular highway program to mass transit legislation in an effort to protect transit from expected administration-backed cuts.

Neither chamber went along with Reagan's requests to phase out aid for urban and rural highways and to allow the transportation secretary to drop some proposed Interstate segments.

Some legislation was required in 1981 to direct the transportation secretary to apportion the fiscal 1983 Interstate construction funds, which states normally obligate a year in advance.

Maryland Gov. Harry R. Hughes, D, on behalf of the National Governors' Association had urged Congress to resolve the impasse because fiscal 1983 obligations had been held up since Oct. 1.

HR 3210 did provide for the fiscal 1983 apportionment.

Completing the Interstate

About 95 percent of the 42,500-mile Interstate System had been completed at a cost of more than $70 billion since the program began in 1956. The federal government paid 90 percent of the construction costs, and the states paid the rest.

Without changes in the law, completing the remaining segments would require $53.8 billion in federal and state funds largely because of escalating construction costs.

In limiting eligibility for construction funds, HR 3210 reduced the estimated total cost to complete the system to $38.9 billion. Projects no longer eligible for construction money — such as providing extra lanes — could be financed under the expanded repair program.

Provisions

As cleared by Congress, HR 3210:

● Authorized $800 million annually for fiscal 1983 and 1984 for an expanded Interstate repair program. The fiscal 1983 level was previously $275 million.

● Directed the transportation secretary to apportion the fiscal 1983 Interstate construction funds based on an estimated cost to complete the system of $38.9 billion.

● Limited obligations for Highway Trust Fund spending to $8 billion in fiscal 1982, excluding emergency relief.

● Reduced the fiscal 1983 Interstate construction authorization to $3.1 billion from $3.2 billion.

● Limited eligibility for Interstate Highway construction funds. The bill generally allowed funding for no more than six lanes in rural areas or in urban areas under 400,000 population, and no more than eight lanes in urban areas over 400,000. Some special lanes for high occupancy vehicles also would be eligible.

Generally ineligible for funding would be weigh stations, pedestrian and bikeway facilities and features not essential to meet safety or environmental requirements.

● Expanded the "3R" repair program — resurfacing, restoration and rehabilitation — to a "4R" program that would include reconstruction. The federal match for 4R projects was increased to 90 percent from 75 percent, with the state paying the rest. Projects no longer eligible for

Interstate construction money could be financed with 4R funds.

● Authorized $60 million out of the trust fund for repairing the federally owned Woodrow Wilson Bridge spanning the Potomac River in Maryland, Virginia and the District of Columbia.

● Authorized $55 million in fiscal 1983 to complete a highway to divert traffic from the Redwood National Park in California. The project's total authorization was raised to $105 million.

Background

The Reagan administration adopted the general course set by the 1978 highway act (PL 95-599) and the Carter administration: Finish the 42,500-mile Interstate Highway System and repair the deteriorating highways. But some of Reagan's methods differed significantly from the past. *(1978 Almanac p. 536)*

He proposed realigning the financial partnership of the federal, state and local governments for many major road and safety programs. In an effort to balance the federal budget, Reagan wanted to shift more responsibility to states and localities, a change that congressional and other critics said could drain local finances and delay needed projects and repairs.

The 1978 act authorized highway aid through fiscal 1982 and the Highway Trust Fund through fiscal 1984. Major changes contained in the administration bill (HR 3197) included provisions that:

● Ended funds in fiscal 1984 for many urban and rural road and safety programs and dropped funds in fiscal 1982 to enforce the 55 mph speed limit. *(Congress and the Nation, Vol. IV, pp. 231, 211)*

● Allowed the transportation secretary to drop some proposed Interstate segments, leaving gaps to be financed by non-federal sources or left undone.

● Encouraged timely completion of the Interstate by tightening eligibility for construction money and required some work such as noise control features and landscaping to compete under other programs for funding.

● Increased federal funds for Interstate repairs from $275 million in fiscal 1982 to $2.7 billion in fiscal 1987 and increased the federal share from 75 percent to 90 percent.

● Extended the Highway Trust Fund, which financed federal highway programs, through fiscal 1990. Highway user taxes would be extended through fiscal 1989 without change.

House Committee Action

The House Public Works Committee rebuffed much of Reagan's request, although it did agree to a modified plan to reduce the cost of completing the Interstate system.

The committee May 19 reported a bill (HR 3210 — H Rept 97-92) that would limit the eligibility for Interstate construction funds to unstarted segments that would be built to a new minimum standard.

By not allowing funds for some special features and for already-opened Interstate segments, the federal-state cost to complete the system would be reduced to $37 billion, according to Bud Shuster, R-Pa., who proposed the change.

Shuster and Committee Chairman James J. Howard, D-N.J., were among the cosponsors of HR 3210.

Reagan's plan (HR 3197, S 841) would have tightened eligibility further, resulting in an estimated cost of about $31.5 billion, with a federal share of about $28.7 billion.

As reported, HR 3210 authorized $3.1 billion in fiscal 1983 for Interstate construction, down from the $3.2 billion previously authorized for that year. Reagan requested $3.3 billion for fiscal 1983 and Interstate construction authorizations totaling $28.7 billion in federal funds through 1990.

The committee also approved an amendment offered by Howard that would make it more difficult for states to circumvent the national 55 mph speed limit.

The amendment barred the transportation secretary from approving highway projects in "any state whose laws do not constitute a substantial deterrent to violations" of the speed limit. Under current law, highway aid would be withheld from a state with a higher limit, and aid would be reduced if the 55 mph limit was not adequately enforced. *(Congress and the Nation Vol. IV, pp. 231, 211)*

The committee retained federal aid to states to enforce the limit, while Reagan wanted it eliminated.

In addition the committee bill limited eligibility for Interstate construction funds, expanded the repair program and established an $8.3 billion limit on obligations from the Highway Trust Fund, including $100 million in emergency projects.

House Floor Action

The House passed HR 3210 by a vote of 377-25 on Sept. 24, the day Reagan in a televised speech called for additional budget cuts. *(Vote 211, p. 72-H; text of speech, p. 20-E)*

There was little disagreement to the bill, although some members were concerned that legislative formulas might result in less funds for their states.

As passed by the House, HR 3210:

● Increased to $1.55 billion from $1.5 billion the fiscal 1982 authorization for Primary System roads.

● Authorized $800 million in fiscal 1983 for 4R projects.

● Increased the fiscal 1982 authorization of $900 million for bridge replacement and repairs to $1 billion.

● Directed the transportation secretary to apportion Interstate funds for fiscal 1983 and 1984 according to factors included in H Rept 97-92 and an estimated cost to complete the system of about $37 billion.

● Set a ceiling of $8.2 billion on trust fund spending in fiscal 1982, not including funds for emergency projects.

● Provided that no more than 25 percent of the total $8.2 billion could be obligated during the first quarter of fiscal 1982.

● Limited obligations to $100 million in fiscal 1982 for National Highway Traffic Safety Administration safety programs and $10 million for Federal Highway Administration safety programs.

● Authorized $3.1 billion for Interstate construction in fiscal 1983.

● Tightened the eligibility for Interstate construction funds. For example, the bill would allow funding for no more than four lanes in rural areas and all urban areas under 400,000 population, six lanes in urban areas of 400,000 to 1 million, and eight lanes in urban areas of more than 1 million. Additional high occupancy vehicle lanes would be eligible for funds.

● Expanded the 3R program to include reconstruction (4R). Projects no longer eligible for construction money would be eligible for 4R funds. The federal share for 4R projects was increased to 90 percent from 75 percent.

● Changed the 4R apportionment formula to one based

on 50 percent lane miles and 50 percent vehicle miles.
- Prohibited the secretary from approving highway projects in a state whose laws do not constitute a substantial deterrent to violations of the 55 mph speed limit.

Senate Committee Action

Highway legislation proposed by key Republican and Democratic senators met Reagan part way, but it also substantially altered some of his major proposals.

S 1024 accepted the concepts of tightening eligibility for Interstate construction funds, expanding repair programs for deteriorating Interstate highways and a multi-year approach, all major points in Reagan's program.

But it continued funding for urban and rural highways and excluded the proposal to allow the transportation secretary to drop proposed Interstate segments under certain conditions without previous recommendation from state and local officials.

S 1024 was introduced by Robert T. Stafford, R-Vt., chairman of the Senate Environment and Public Works Committee, which has jurisdiction over most highway issues; Steven D. Symms, R-Idaho, chairman of the Transportation Subcommittee; Jennings Randolph, D-W.Va., ranking minority member of the committee; and others.

Committee Plan Trimmed

Before reporting the bill Oct. 7 (S Rept 97- 202), the committee answered Reagan's call for a 12 percent cut in federal spending and sliced $1 billion from the $8.6 billion it had planned to authorize for highway programs in fiscal 1982.

But the panel reserved the right to restore the funds on the floor if other committees did not cut their programs.

The bill as reported authorized a total of $7.6 billion in fiscal 1982, including an advance authorization for fiscal 1983, and limited Highway Trust Fund obligations to $7.2 billion in fiscal 1982, not including emergency relief.

It reduced the cost of completing the Interstate System by 1990 to about $35 billion, down from the current estimate of about $53.8 billion. Those changes would make some projects, such as noise control measures, ineligible for construction funds.

As reported, S 1024 also:
- Authorized $3.1 billion for Interstate construction in fiscal 1983, $3.5 billion in 1984, $3.4 billion in 1985, $3.4 billion in 1986, $3.5 billion in 1987.
- Tightened eligibility for new Interstate construction funds.
- Directed the secretary to apportion Interstate funds for fiscal 1983 and 1984 based on an estimated cost to complete the Interstate System of about $35 billion.
- Authorized $400 million in fiscal 1982 for the federal-aid rural highway program, $500 million annually in 1983-1985 and $400 million in 1986. The program would consolidate Secondary System and other rural road projects.
- Authorized $600 million in fiscal 1982 for the federal-aid urban highway program, $700 million annually in 1983-1985 and $600 million in 1986. This would be a consolidation of the Urban System and other urban road projects.
- Authorized $700 million in fiscal 1982 for bridges, $1.1 billion in 1983, $1.3 billion annually in 1984-1986.
- Authorized $100 million annually in fiscal 1982 and 1983 for highway safety programs and $50 million annually in 1984-1986.
- Expanded the 3R program to include reconstruction

(4R). Projects no longer eligible for Interstate construction money would be eligible for 4R funds.
- Changed the apportionment formula for 4R funds to one based on 60 percent lane miles and 40 percent vehicle miles from 75 percent and 25 percent, respectively.
- Authorized $800 million in fiscal 1983 for 4R projects, $1.3 billion in 1984, $1.7 billion annually in 1985 and 1986 and $2.2 billion in 1987.
- Authorized $200 million in trust fund monies in fiscal 1982 for highway projects that states chose as replacement for proposed Interstate projects, $225 million in 1983, $250 million annually in 1984 and 1985, and $300 million in 1986. Currently the funds came from general Treasury revenues.
- Limited obligations for trust fund spending to $7.2 billion in fiscal 1982, not including emergency relief.
- Continued requirements that states meet compliance standards for enforcement of the national 55 mph speed limit but altered the compliance level for fiscal 1982 to requiring 50 percent of the motorists driving 55 mph, down from 60 percent.
- Required states to allow trucks weighing 80,000 pounds on Interstates, up from 73,280 pounds.

Senate Floor Action

The Senate Nov. 16 passed a bill by voice vote authorizing about $28 billion for Interstate construction for fiscal 1982-1990.

The Senate substituted the text of its bill (S 1024 — S Rept 97-202) for the House-passed version of HR 3210, which it passed by voice vote.

As reported Oct. 7 by the Senate Environment and Public Works Committee, S 1024 would have provided for $7.6 billion for Interstates and other highway programs in fiscal 1982. The figures had been reduced in line with Reagan's call for a 12 percent cut in non-defense spending.

The panel's reductions generally were in Interstate construction, bridge repair and replacement, and urban and rural highways.

But the committee offered an amendment on the floor — which was accepted by voice vote — to restore $500 million because Congress had not cut other programs similarly, a committee aide said.

For example, rural highway aid was raised to $525 million in fiscal 1982, up $125 million from the reported bill; urban highway aid was raised to $725 million, up $125 million; and bridge replacement and repair was raised to $775 million, up $75 million.

The amendment also raised the limit on obligations from the Highway Trust Fund to $7.7 billion, from the committee bill's $7.2 billion.

Unchanged by the floor amendment was the $3.1 billion fiscal 1983 authorization for Interstate construction, down from the $3.3 billion that the panel originally wanted and the $3.2 billion already authorized.

The Senate amendment also eliminated a provision that would have required states to allow trucks weighing 80,000 pounds on Interstates, up from 73,280 pounds in current law.

Provisions

As passed by the Senate, HR 3210:
- Authorized $3.1 billion for Interstate construction in fiscal 1983, $3.5 billion in 1984, $3.4 billion in 1985, $3.4 billion in 1986 and $3.5 billion in 1987. The bill also contin-

ued previous authorizations of $3.625 billion annually for fiscal 1988-1990.

● Limited eligibility for Interstate construction funds. It allowed funding for no more than six lanes in rural areas or urban areas under 400,000 population, and no more than eight lanes in urban areas over 400,000. (The Senate panel had agreed to limits of four and six lanes, but changed the limits before reporting the bill.)

Generally ineligible for funding would be weigh stations, pedestrian and bikeway facilities, and features not essential to meet safety or environmental requirements.

● Directed the secretary to apportion Interstate construction funds for fiscal 1983 and 1984 based on an estimated cost to complete the system of $35.8 billion.

● Authorized $1.5 billion annually for Primary highways in fiscal 1982-1983 and $1.6 billion annually for fiscal 1984-1986.

● Authorized $525 million for the federal-aid rural highway program in fiscal 1982, $500 million annually in 1983-1985, and $400 million in 1986. This program would combine the Secondary System with other rural road projects.

● Authorized $725 million for the federal-aid urban highway program in fiscal 1982, $700 million annually in 1983-1985 and $600 million in 1986. The Urban System and other urban road projects would be combined.

● Authorized $775 million in fiscal 1982 for bridge replacement and repair, $1.1 billion in 1983 and $1.3 billion annually in 1984-1986.

● Authorized $100 million annually in fiscal 1982 and 1983 for highway safety programs and $50 million annually in 1984-1986.

● Expanded the 3R program to include reconstruction (4R). Projects no longer eligible for Interstate construction money would be eligible for 4R funds.

● Authorized $875 million for 4R projects in fiscal 1983, $1.3 billion in 1984, $1.7 billion annually in 1985-1986 and $2.2 billion in 1987. The bill also provided a $100 million "hold harmless" Interstate authorization in fiscal 1983 to ensure that states have enough funds for 4R projects because of legislative changes in the highway program.

● Authorized $225 million in trust fund money in fiscal 1983 for highway projects that states chose as replacements for planned Interstate projects, $250 million annually in 1984-1985 and $300 million in 1986.

● Eliminated the priority Primary route program that funded projects with special difficulties. The projects would be eligible for Primary road funds.

● Combined several highway safety programs, including rail highway crossings and implementation of federal safety requirements. They could be funded under the urban and rural programs or under the $100 million highway safety authorization. Specific authorizations for those projects, estimated at $400 million, were eliminated.

● Authorized $60 million out of the trust fund for repairing the Woodrow Wilson Bridge, which is owned by the federal government and spans the Potomac River in Maryland, Virginia and the District of Columbia.

● Reduced the federal share of urban and rural highway projects to 50 percent from 75 percent. States pay the remaining amount.

● Limited obligations for trust fund spending to $7.7 billion in fiscal 1982, not including emergency relief.

● Continued requirements that states meet compliance standards for enforcing the national 55 mph speed limit. But the bill dropped the compliance level for fiscal 1982, requiring that only 50 percent of the motorists drive 55 mph, down from 60 percent in current law. *(1978 Almanac p. 540)* ∎

SPECIAL REPORTS

CQ

Supreme Court Term (1980-81)

Stand-Pat Supreme Court Defers to Others

Intent upon preserving the status quo, the Supreme Court increasingly seemed determined to leave innovation and dramatic changes in national policy to Congress, the executive branch and the states.

In the last major decision of the court's 1980-81 term, Justice William H. Rehnquist wrote: "Our decision today will not dramatically alter this situation, for the framers 'did not make the judiciary the overseer of our government.' "

Rehnquist's comment prefaced an announcement that the court had unanimously upheld the deal struck by President Carter in January 1981 to win the release of 52 Americans held hostage by Iran.

But his words could stand as a summary of the court's entire term, which began in October 1980 and ended July 2.

Some of the court's rulings appeared "conservative," such as its decision upholding the male-only military draft. Others seemed "liberal," such as those endorsing stringent workplace health and safety standards imposed by the Occupational Safety and Health Administration (OSHA).

But all found their origins in the court's cautious and restrictive view of its own role in the American federal system, a view that generated a long string of decisions upholding laws and practices already in effect.

This judicial caution, characteristic of the high court under Chief Justice Warren E. Burger, also produced an unusually long list of cases in which the justices — after agreeing to review a controversy and hearing formal arguments about it — backed off and declined to decide the issue presented.

Judicial Deference

Two of the court's most important decisions came at the end of the term. On June 25, the justices upheld the power of Congress to exclude women from the military draft. And on July 2, they backed President Carter's power to use frozen Iranian assets as a "bargaining chip" in negotiations for release of the Americans held hostage by Iran.

Rehnquist, the most conservative justice, spoke for the court in both cases. And central to both opinions was the majority's view that the court had only a limited role in reviewing acts of Congress and actions of the president — particularly in the areas of national security and foreign policy.

Courts should show a "healthy deference" to Congress when reviewing its decisions on military matters, Rehnquist said in the draft case, *Rostker v. Goldberg.* "Not only is the scope of Congress' constitutional power in this area broad, but the lack of competence on the part of the courts is marked," he wrote for the 6-3 majority.

The dissenters sharply disputed this view, with Justice Thurgood Marshall arguing that "deference to congressional judgments cannot be allowed to shade into an abdication of this court's ultimate responsibility to decide constitutional questions."

In the case of *Dames & Moore v. Regan,* which challenged the constitutionality of Carter's deal with Iran, Rehnquist emphasized the limitations on the court's pow-

ers and the narrow gauge of its decision. He said Congress, in several laws, had given the president powers broad enough to cover his actions in the Iran accord. Beyond that, the court would not go.

"We attempt to lay down no general 'guidelines' covering other situations not involved here and attempt to confine the opinion only to the very questions necessary to decision of the case," he wrote.

Although the draft case and the hostage accord involved issues of national security and foreign policy, the court's deference to Congress was evident in other areas as well.

During the 1980-81 term, the justices reviewed a dozen head-on challenges to the constitutionality of various laws enacted by Congress. Only once did they decree that Congress had overstepped constitutional limits.

That instance involved an issue near and dear to the justices themselves. In a December 1980 decision, the court held that Congress had improperly denied federal judges cost-of-living increases in pay.

The result was a hefty pay raise for all sitting judges, including members of the Supreme Court.

Backing the Regulators

In the controversial sphere of federal regulation, the court's narrow view of its own role produced an unbroken string of decisions upholding existing laws and regulations. These rulings ran directly counter to the Reagan administration's attempts to limit the scope of federal regulations and their cost to industry.

Pleas of economic hardship from industries affected by federal regulations received scant sympathy from the court.

In one of its first decisions of the term, the court on Dec. 2, 1980, brushed aside arguments that some coal, sand and gravel, and crushed-stone companies would be forced out of business if they had to comply with the clean water standards set by the Environmental Protection Agency.

The court said that Congress, in enacting the Federal Water Pollution Control Act Amendments of 1972 (PL 92-500), called for the tough standards with full knowledge of the economic costs of compliance.

More than six months later, the court not only upheld OSHA's tough cotton dust standards for the textile industry but also explicitly rejected the major argument used by business to combat all such standards. By a 5-3 vote, the justices on June 17 dismissed the contention that OSHA should weigh the costs of its standards against the benefits. In deciding the case, the court rebuffed the Reagan administration's plea that it defer a ruling until the cotton dust rules could be called back for a cost-benefit analysis.

The justices also let stand OSHA's stringent standards limiting worker exposure to lead.

The cotton dust decision came just two days after the court unanimously upheld the constitutionality of the sweeping federal strip mining control law of 1977, one of the landmark environmental protection laws of the past decade.

Early in its term, the court endorsed the Federal Com-

munications Commission's (FCC) refusal to consider changes in radio program formats when deciding whether to renew a station's license.

And on July 1, the justices said Congress had given candidates for federal office a broad right of access to radio and television air time, access which the FCC was empowered to enforce.

When eight major oil companies sought a court order halting an investigation of their practices by the Federal Trade Commission (FTC), the justices said that the probe could continue free of judicial interference.

The court upheld the Securities and Exchange Commission's (SEC) practice of relying on a preponderance of the evidence, rather than the stricter test of clear and convincing evidence, in determining whether an individual had violated anti-fraud provisions of federal securities law.

And it held that the Interstate Commerce Commission (ICC) had the final say on whether a railroad may shut down a part of its operations.

The Rest of the Record

There was no consistently liberal or conservative pattern to the court's decisions in other areas.

However, rulings on criminal law, individual rights, First Amendment freedoms and business law demonstrated the same respect for the status quo as those in the regulatory sphere. They required little if any change in current practices and procedures.

Criminal Law. The court unanimously ruled that states may experiment with television coverage of criminal trials. The justices rejected the argument that Florida was denying defendants a fair trial by permitting such coverage of trial proceedings.

The justices ruled that placing two inmates in a prison cell built for one does not necessarily constitute cruel and unusual punishment. The Constitution, the court said, "does not mandate comfortable prisons."

The court also upheld the special sentences that Congress provided for drug pushers and career criminals, and supported the right of federal prosecutors to appeal sentences they regard as too lenient.

In another victory for law enforcement officers, the court ruled in *Michigan v. Summers* that police may detain the owner of a house while they search the dwelling.

But 15 years after the Warren court stirred furious public controversy with its landmark criminal rights decision in *Miranda v. Arizona,* the Burger court reaffirmed and enlarged the application of that ruling.

The 1966 *Miranda* ruling required that before questioning suspects in custody, police must advise them of their right to a lawyer and their right to remain silent.

Burger, then a federal appeals court judge, was one of the leading critics of the decision. In 1981, however, Burger wrote the court's opinion in *Estelle v. Smith* affirming the continuing validity of *Miranda* and extending its required warnings to defendants who are facing court-ordered psychiatric interviews. In a second *Miranda* decision, the justices in *Edwards v. Arizona* held that once a suspect invokes his right to counsel, police must halt their interrogation and may not resume communications with him unless the suspect initiates the additional conversation.

In 1965 the court held that the right to remain silent includes the right not to testify in one's own defense and that neither the prosecutor nor the judge may make any adverse comment when a defendant does not take the witness stand.

In March 1981, the court extended this ruling by declaring that if requested to do so by the defense, a judge must instruct a jury that the defendant's failure to testify is not to be considered evidence of guilt.

Individual Rights. The court was notably unsympathetic to claims that individual rights were being abridged by various governmental actions.

In the final days of its term, the court ruled that the secretary of state may revoke the passport of any citizen whose activities abroad are deemed a serious threat to national security or to U.S. foreign policy.

Abortion rights were narrowed slightly when the court upheld a Utah law requiring doctors to notify the parents of an unmarried minor before performing an abortion on her.

The justices by a 5-4 vote upheld the constitutionality of statutory rape laws that allow prosecution of a man for having sexual relations with a minor but exempt the girl involved from criminal liability.

In another split decision, the court ruled 6-3 that states do not have to move mentally retarded individuals out of institutions in order to receive federal grants to help those persons.

The court term produced a mix of victories and defeats for feminists. The military draft decision was regarded by many as a setback to women's rights, as was the decision in *McCarty v. McCarty* that divorced spouses have no right to share in a veteran's military retirement pay.

But the court did pave the way for women to sue their employers for sex discrimination even if they could not point to a man earning more for exactly the same job. By a 5-4 vote, the justices ruled women may sue under the Civil Rights Act of 1964 without having to prove they were denied "equal pay for equal work" as required by the 1963 Equal Pay Act.

First Amendment Freedoms. The court held that Indiana infringed upon religious freedom when it refused to pay unemployment benefits to a Jehovah's Witness who quit his job with a machinery company after being transferred to a department engaged in arms production.

But the justices ruled that Minnesota did not abridge either religious freedom or freedom of speech when it required members of the Hare Krishna sect and others wishing to solicit funds and sell or distribute literature at the state fair to do so from a fixed location.

The court held that Wisconsin could continue its "open" primary elections in which voters may participate regardless of party allegiance. But the court said the national Democratic Party is free to disregard the results of such primaries, which conflict with its rules requiring that participation be limited to Democrats.

Business Law. In its major business ruling of the term, the court ruled 5-4 that inventions and discoveries may be patentable even if they involve the use of computer programs. The increasing use of computers in all aspects of business and industry had made this a major issue of patent law.

The court decided in the case of *First National Maintenance Corp. v. National Labor Relations Board* that a company need not engage in collective bargaining with unions representing its workers before closing part of its operations for economic reasons.

And finally, the justices ruled that Congress, not the courts, should determine whether to permit companies charged with antitrust violations to force their co-conspirators to share in financial penalties for their misdeeds.

MAJOR DECISIONS, 1980-1981 TERM

CRIMINAL LAW

Search and Seizure

United States v. Cortez, decided by a 9-0 vote, Jan. 21, 1981. Burger wrote the opinion.

Facts that may seem insignificant to an untrained person can properly be used by law enforcement officers — in this case, border patrol officers in Arizona — to justify stopping a vehicle near the border and questioning its occupants.

Steagald v. United States, decided by a 7-2 vote, April 21, 1981. Marshall wrote the opinion; Rehnquist and White dissented.

Police with a warrant for the arrest of a suspect may not enter and search the home of another person without obtaining a warrant for that search — even if they believe that the suspect may be at that home. "Warrantless searches of a home are impermissible absent consent or exigent circumstances," stated the majority.

Michigan v. Summers, decided by a 6-3 vote, June 22, 1981. Stevens wrote the opinion; Stewart, Brennan and Marshall dissented.

Police did not act improperly when they detained a homeowner while searching his home for narcotics, even though they had a warrant only for the search — not for his arrest. Such a detention is a limited intrusion on personal security justified by substantial law enforcement interests in preventing flight, minimizing risk to police and facilitating the orderly completion of the search of the home.

New York v. Belton, decided by a 6-3 vote, July 1, 1981. Stewart wrote the opinion; Brennan, Marshall and White dissented.

When the occupant of an automobile is lawfully arrested, police may, incident to his arrest and without a warrant, search the passenger compartment of the auto in which he was riding. Any evidence uncovered in that search, even in the closed pocket of clothing found within the passenger compartment, is admissible in court.

Robbins v. California, decided by a 6-3 vote, July 1, 1981. Stewart wrote an opinion joined by three other justices; Powell and Burger concurred; Blackman, Rehnquist and Stevens dissented.

Police may not, without a search warrant, open a closed piece of luggage or other container found in a lawfully searched car. If police open such a container without a warrant, its contents may not be used as evidence in court.

Double Jeopardy

United States v. DiFrancesco, decided by a 5-4 vote, Dec. 9, 1980. Blackmun wrote the opinion; Brennan, White, Marshall and Stevens dissented.

The Fifth Amendment guarantee against double jeopardy is not violated by the provisions of the 1970 Organized Crime Control Act that permit federal prosecutors to appeal sentences which they consider too lenient for dangerous special offenders.

Hudson v. Louisiana, decided by a 9-0 vote, Feb. 24, 1981. Powell wrote the opinion.

The double jeopardy clause forbids a state to retry a defendant for a crime if he has already been tried and convicted and the first verdict has been set aside for lack of evidence.

Albernaz v. United States, decided by a 9-0 vote, March 9, 1981. Rehnquist wrote the opinion.

Congress did not violate the double jeopardy clause when it approved provisions of the Drug Abuse Prevention and Control Act of 1970 that allowed the imposition of consecutive prison sentences on persons found guilty of conspiring to import and to distribute marijuana, even if there was only a single conspiracy for the two purposes.

Bullington v. Missouri, decided by a 5-4 vote, May 4, 1981. Blackmun wrote the opinion; Powell, Burger, White and Rehnquist dissented.

A state cannot have a second chance to try to convince a jury to impose the death sentence on a particular defendant. Once a jury has decided that a particular defendant should not be sentenced to die for his crime, that defendant's right to be protected against double jeopardy forbids the state — even if a new trial is granted — to seek the death penalty.

Self-Incrimination

Carter v. Kentucky, decided by an 8-1 vote, March 9, 1981. Stewart wrote the opinion; Rehnquist dissented.

Whenever a defendant does not wish to take the witness stand in his own defense — and requests the judge to instruct the jury that his failure to testify is not to be viewed as evidence of guilt — the judge is constitutionally obligated to give those instructions to protect the defendant's right to remain silent and not to be forced to incriminate himself.

Due Process

Watkins v. Sowders, Summitt v. Sowders, decided by a 7-2 vote, Jan. 13, 1981. Stewart wrote the opinion; Brennan and Marshall dissented.

The due process guarantee does not require a state judge to hold a hearing out of the jury's presence every time a defendant challenges a witness' identification of him as improperly obtained.

Chandler v. Florida, decided by an 8-0 vote, Jan. 26, 1981. Burger wrote the opinion; Stevens did not participate in the decision.

Nothing in the Constitution — neither the guarantee of due process nor the promise of a fair trial — forbids states to experiment with television coverage of criminal trials.

Connecticut Board of Pardons v. Dumschat, decided by a 7-2 vote, June 17, 1981. Burger wrote the opinion; Stevens and Marshall dissented.

Even though the Connecticut Board of Pardons grants about three of every four applications it receives for commutation of a life sentence, the due process guarantee does not require the board to provide a written statement of the reasons for its action to every inmate denied commutation.

Fair Trial

Rosales-Lopez v. United States, decided by a 6-3 vote, April 21, 1981. White wrote an opinion joined by three

justices; Rehnquist and Burger concurred in the result; Stevens, Brennan and Marshall dissented.

A Mexican-American defendant was not denied his right to trial by an impartial jury when the trial judge refused to question prospective jurors about possible prejudice against Mexicans although he did question them about prejudice against aliens.

Right to Counsel

United States v. Morrison, decided by a 9-0 vote, Jan. 13, 1981. White wrote the opinion.

Without any showing that a defendant's right to the aid of counsel was infringed by the actions or remarks of federal agents, dismissal of the charges against her is too drastic a remedy for the misconduct of the federal agents.

Upjohn Company v. United States, decided by a 9-0 vote, Jan. 13, 1981. Rehnquist wrote the opinion.

The attorney-client privilege protects from disclosure virtually all communications involving legal matters between a corporation's counsel and its officers and employees. The court rebuffed the government's argument for a narrower privilege, protecting communications between only the attorney and a "control group" of officers and managers, the persons who in fact determine company policy.

Wood v. Georgia, decided by a 5-4 vote, March 4, 1981. Powell wrote the opinion; White, Brennan, Marshall and Stewart dissented.

Because of a possible conflict of interest on the part of the lawyer who was paid by an employer to represent his employees who were charged with distributing obscene materials in an "adult" theater and bookstore, this case is not the appropriate one in which to decide the question it presents — whether it is constitutional, under the guarantee of equal protection, to imprison a probationer solely because he is unable to make the required installment payments on his fine. The state court that heard this case should reconsider it, looking at the conflict-of-interest situation.

Estelle v. Smith, decided by a 9-0 vote, May 18, 1981. Burger wrote the opinion.

It is unconstitutional for a state to impose a sentence of death on a defendant, basing that sentence in part on psychiatric testimony derived from an interview of the defendant by a state-appointed psychiatrist, when the defendant was not warned, prior to the interview, that he had the right to have his attorney present during the interview and to remain silent during the interview.

Edwards v. Arizona, decided by a 9-0 vote, May 18, 1981. White wrote the opinion.

Once a defendant has invoked his right to have his attorney present during police questioning, all interrogation by police must cease and may not resume until the attorney is present or the defendant initiates a new conversation.

Cruel and Unusual Punishment

Rhodes v. Chapman, decided by an 8-1 vote, June 15, 1981. Powell wrote the opinion; Marshall dissented.

The constitutional ban on cruel and unusual punishment is not invariably offended by the practice, in a state maximum security prison, of placing two inmates in a cell for one.

Organized Crime

United States v. Turkette, decided by an 8-1 vote, June 17, 1981. White wrote the opinion; Stewart dissented.

Title IX of the Organized Crime Control Act of 1970 (PL 91-452) — Racketeer Influenced and Corrupt Organizations (RICO) — was intended to reach both legitimate and illegitimate enterprises, allowing prosecution of persons who conduct the affairs of an enterprise in interstate commerce through a pattern of racketeering activities, whether that enterprise is completely illegitimate or was initially legitimate and has been taken over by organized crime.

CIVIL RIGHTS

City of Memphis v. Greene, decided by a 6-3 vote, April 20, 1981. Stevens wrote the opinion; Marshall, Brennan and Blackmun dissented.

The decision by the city council of Memphis, Tenn., to close off part of a street to reduce traffic and noise and to protect the safety of resident children — all of whom were white — did not infringe on property rights of nearby black residents who were forced to use other streets through the now-closed area nor did this action constitute a "badge of slavery" forbidden by the 13th Amendment abolishing slavery.

The only "injury" that resulted from the action was too trivial to constitute a violation of the law or the Constitution. Without any evidence that the closing was racially motivated, it could not be successfully challenged as a "badge of slavery."

Paratt v. Taylor, decided by an 8-1 vote, May 18, 1981. Rehnquist wrote the opinion; Marshall dissented.

A prison inmate's right to due process was not violated when state prison officials lost a $23.50 hobby kit he ordered in the mail. State laws provide an adequate remedy for such a loss; a suit under the Civil Rights Act of 1871 — Section 1983 in modern form — is not justified by such a trivial "injury."

Jobs

Equal Employment Opportunity Commission (EEOC) v. Associated Dry Goods Corp., decided by votes of 5-2 and 6-1, Jan. 26, 1981. Stewart wrote the opinion; Blackmun dissented in part; Stevens dissented. Powell and Rehnquist did not participate in the decision.

Federal law forbids the EEOC to disclose to the public information it obtains from a defendant employer in the course of investigating job bias charges, but that law does not prevent the EEOC from disclosing such information to the person who filed the complaint against the employer.

Texas Department of Community Affairs v. Burdine, decided by a 9-0 vote, March 4, 1981. Powell wrote the opinion.

An employer charged with job discrimination must prove that he had legitimate non-discriminatory reasons for his challenged actions, but it is then up to the person bringing the charge to show that the explanation is only a pretext for discrimination. The court reversed a lower court's order requiring an employer charged with a dis-

criminatory promotion to prove that the person promoted was better qualified than the one passed over.

Northwest Airlines v. Transport Workers Union of America, decided by an 8-0 vote, April 20, 1981. Stevens wrote the opinion; Blackmun did not take part in the decision.

Neither statutory nor common law gives an employer, found guilty of discriminating against women employees in wage matters, the right to force the union — with whom the employer had agreed on the contested wage scale — to contribute to the monetary settlement that the employer must make with the discriminated-against employees.

Lehman v. Nakshian, decided by a 5-4 vote, June 26, 1981. Stewart wrote the opinion; Brennan, Marshall, Blackmun and Stevens dissented.

A federal employee suing the United States government for violating the Age Discrimination in Employment Act of 1967 is not entitled to a jury trial on those charges. When Congress waives the government's immunity from suit, as it did in this law, the person bringing the suit has the right to trial by jury only if Congress affirmatively grants that right in such cases.

Sex Discrimination

Kirchberg v. Feenstra, decided by a 9-0 vote, March 23, 1981. Marshall wrote the opinion.

Louisiana's law (no longer in effect) that gave a husband the right to dispose of community property without a wife's consent violated the constitutional guarantee of equal protection.

Michael M. v. Superior Court of Sonoma County, Calif., decided by a 5-4 vote, March 23, 1981. Rehnquist wrote an opinion joined by three other justices; Stewart and Blackmun concurred; Brennan, White, Marshall and Stevens dissented.

A state does not discriminate unconstitutionally against men by allowing a man to be prosecuted for having sexual relations with a girl under 18 to whom he is not married but exempting the girl involved from criminal liability. The court upheld California's statutory rape laws against a constitutional challenge, finding that the distinction between its treatment of men and women was justified as an appropriate means of preventing illegitimate teen-age pregnancies.

County of Washington v. Gunther, decided by a 5-4 vote, June 8, 1981. Brennan wrote the court's opinion; Rehnquist, Burger, Stewart and Powell dissented.

Women workers may sue their employers under the 1964 Civil Rights Act for discriminating against them on the basis of sex without first proving that they were denied "equal pay for equal work," a violation of the Equal Pay Act. A violation of the Civil Rights Act ban on sex discrimination in the workplace can be shown initially by simply demonstrating that a woman's sex was used against her in determining how much she was paid, the court held.

Rostker v. Goldberg, decided by a 6-3 vote, June 25, 1981. Rehnquist wrote the opinion; White, Marshall and Brennan dissented.

Congress did not violate the Constitution when it decided to exclude women from the military draft. Because women are barred by law and policy from combat, they are not "similarly situated" with men for purposes of draft registration and thus Congress may properly treat the sexes differently.

Affirmative Action

Minnick v. California Department of Corrections, decided by an 8-1 vote, June 1, 1981. Stevens wrote the opinion; Stewart dissented.

The court dismissed a challenge to California's corrections department's affirmative action plan, which allowed use of race or sex as an affirmative factor in job assignment and promotion decisions. The court dismissed the case because the record was ambiguous and required clarification by the state courts.

INDIVIDUAL RIGHTS

Abortion

H. L. v. Matheson, decided by a 6-3 vote, March 23, 1981. Burger wrote the opinion; Marshall, Brennan and Blackmun dissented.

Utah law, which requires a doctor to notify the parents of a minor upon whom he is to perform an abortion, does not violate the minor's right of privacy in deciding whether to have the abortion, at least, when it is applied as in this case to an immature minor who is still dependent upon her parents. The law does not allow the parents to veto the abortion decision, but simply requires that they be notified beforehand.

Citizenship

Fedorenko v. United States, decided by a vote of 7-2, Jan. 21, 1981. Marshall wrote the opinion; White and Stevens dissented.

A Russian native who concealed from immigration and naturalization officials the fact that he had served as a concentration camp guard must be stripped of his U.S. citizenship, acquired by naturalization in 1970. The concealment of his wartime activities more than 20 years earlier — when he obtained a visa to enter the United States under the Displaced Persons Act — rendered his eventual naturalization invalid because his admission to the United States was not lawful.

Consumers

Anderson Bros. Ford and Ford Motor Credit Co. v. Valencia, decided by a 5-4 vote, June 8, 1981. White wrote the opinion; Stewart, Burger, Brennan and Marshall dissented.

The Truth in Lending Act does not require a creditor to disclose to a consumer who is borrowing money to buy a car that the consumer may forfeit certain insurance premiums to the creditor if the physical damage insurance on the car is canceled.

American Express Co. v. Koerner, decided by a 9-0 vote, June 8, 1981. Blackmun wrote the opinion.

The procedures set out in the Truth in Lending Act for correcting credit card billing errors do not apply when the cardholder is a business rather than an individual.

Equal Protection

United States Railroad Retirement Board v. Fritz, decided by a 7-2 vote, Dec. 9, 1980. Rehnquist wrote the opinion; Brennan and Marshall dissented.

The Railroad Retirement Act of 1974 does not violate the guarantee of equal protection by allowing some retired railroad workers to receive both Social Security and railroad retirement benefits and allowing others to receive only the railroad retirement benefits. Congress had plausible reasons for making that distinction, and that is sufficient to justify it.

Schweiker v. Wilson, decided by a 5-4 vote, March 4, 1981. Blackmun wrote the opinion; Powell, Brennan, Marshall and Stevens dissented.

Congress did not violate the guarantee of equal protection by granting a small supplemental security income allowance for the purchase of "comforts" to residents of public mental institutions whose care is funded by Medicaid but not providing such an allowance to residents whose care is not paid for by Medicaid.

Jones v. Helms, decided by a 9-0 vote, June 15, 1981. Stevens wrote the opinion.

A state does not act unconstitutionally when it provides a more severe punishment for parents who leave the state after abandoning their children than for those who remain in the state after the abandonment.

Handicapped Rights

University of Texas v. Camenisch, decided by a 9-0 vote. Stewart wrote the opinion.

Before the Supreme Court resolves the issue, a lower court first must consider the contention of a deaf graduate student that he is entitled, under the Rehabilitation Act of 1973, to have a sign-language interpreter with him in class paid for by the university he was attending.

Mentally Ill

Pennhurst State School and Hospital v. Terri Lee Halderman, Mayor of City of Philadelphia v. Halderman, Pennsylvania Association for Retarded Citizens v. Pennhurst State School and Hospital, Commissioners and Mental Health/Mental Retardation Administrators for Bucks County v. Halderman, Pennhurst Parents-Staff Association v. Halderman, decided by votes of 9-0 and 6-3, April 20, 1981. Rehnquist wrote the opinion; White, Brennan and Marshall dissented in part.

The Developmentally Disabled Assistance and Bill of Rights Act of 1975 (PL 94-103) did not grant to mentally retarded persons an enforceable right to be treated in the least restrictive situation. The statement in the law that persons have a right to receive treatment and housing in a setting "that is least restrictive of . . . personal liberty" was a general "finding" by Congress — not an obligation imposed upon states receiving federal funds for treatment of the mentally retarded.

Parents

Little v. Streater, decided by a 9-0 vote, June 1, 1981 Burger wrote the opinion.

Connecticut denies a putative father his due process rights when it compels a mother receiving public assistance to file a paternity proceeding against the putative father of her child, but denies the putative father requested blood tests — which could show that he is not the father — unless he can pay for them.

Lassiter v. Department of Social Services of Durham County, decided by a 5-4 vote, June 1, 1981. Stewart wrote

the opinion; Blackmun, Brennan, Marshall and Stevens dissented.

An indigent mother does not have a constitutional right to the aid of free legal counsel when the state moves to terminate her legal relationship with her child. The court has generally held that due process requires that counsel be appointed for an indigent only when he is threatened with the loss of his physical personal liberty. It is his interest in his personal freedom that triggers the right to appointed counsel.

Prisoners

Cuyler v. Adams, decided by a 6-3 vote, Jan. 21, 1981. Brennan wrote the opinion; Rehnquist, Burger and Stewart dissented.

A prisoner held in a state that had adopted the uniform extradition act is entitled to the protections of that act, including the right to a hearing before he is transferred to another jurisdiction. Such a prisoner has the right, under the Interstate Agreement on Detainers, to a hearing in which he can contest the request of a state for his transfer to it.

Weaver v. Graham, decided by a 9-0 vote, Feb. 24, 1981. Marshall wrote the opinion.

A state is forbidden by the Constitution's ban on ex post facto laws from changing the rules for computing a prisoner's time off for good behavior and applying those new rules to prisoners whose crime was committed before the law was changed, at least when the change slows the rate at which "time off" can be accumulated.

Howe v. Smith, decided by an 8-1 vote, June 17, 1981. Burger wrote the opinion; Stewart dissented.

Under federal law, states may transfer prisoners to the federal prison system for a variety of reasons including, but not limited to, special treatment in programs that are not available in state prisons.

Veterans

Monroe v. Standard Oil Company, decided by a 5-4 vote, June 17, 1981. Stewart wrote the opinion; Burger, Brennan, Blackmun and Powell dissented.

The Vietnam Era Veterans' Readjustment Assistance Act of 1974 (PL 93-508) does not require an employer to provide preferential scheduling of work hours for an employee who must be absent from work to fulfill his military reserve obligations.

FIRST AMENDMENT

Right of Association

Democratic Party of the United States v. LaFollette, decided by a 6-3 vote, Feb. 25, 1981. Stewart wrote the opinion; Powell, Blackmun and Rehnquist dissented.

Wisconsin may hold an "open primary" in which voters participate without declaring their allegiance to the party whose primary it is, but it cannot constitutionally compel the national party to recognize those primary results, when to do so would violate the party's rules and infringe upon its protected right of political association.

Freedom of Expression

Flynt v. Ohio, decided by a 5-4 vote, May 18, 1981. Per

curiam (unsigned) opinion; Stevens, Brennan, Stewart and Marshall dissented.

Because there is no final state court ruling in this case — in which the publisher of a "men's magazine," *Hustler,* argues that he was unfairly singled out for prosecution under a state obscenity law by politicians angered by his publication of a non-obscene political cartoon — it should not be considered at this time by the Supreme Court and is dismissed.

Schad v. Borough of Mount Ephraim, decided by a 7-2 vote, June 1, 1981. White wrote the opinion; Burger and Rehnquist dissented.

A borough may not, without infringing upon the rights guaranteed by the First Amendment, enact a zoning ordinance forbidding all live entertainment from the borough. Such a ban prohibits a wide range of expression long held to be within the protection of the First Amendment.

United States Postal Service v. Council of Greenburgh Civic Association, decided by a 7-2 vote, June 25, 1981. Rehnquist wrote the opinion; Marshall and Stevens dissented.

Congress did not violate the guarantees of the First Amendment when it passed a law forbidding persons or groups to place unstamped letters, notices and other "mailable matter" in post boxes used by the U.S. Postal Service for delivering mail to private homes.

Haig v. Agee, decided by a 7-2 vote, June 29, 1981. Burger wrote the opinion; Brennan and Marshall dissented.

Congress, in passing the Passport Act of 1926 authorizing the secretary of state to grant and issue passports, authorized the secretary also to revoke a citizen's passport. If the secretary may deny an application for a passport, he may revoke a passport for the same reasons.

Revocation of the passport in this case did not violate the freedom to travel outside the United States, the First Amendment freedom of expression of the individual who lost his passport or the guarantee of due process.

Metromedia Inc. v. City of San Diego, decided by a 6-3 vote, July 2, 1981. White wrote an opinion joined by three other justices; Brennan and Blackmun concurred; Stevens dissented in part; Burger and Rehnquist dissented in part.

San Diego violated the First Amendment guarantee of freedom of expression when it enacted an ordinance banning most billboards within the city.

Freedom of Religion

Thomas v. Review Board of the Indiana Employment Security Division, decided by an 8-1 vote, April 6, 1981. Burger wrote the opinion; Rehnquist dissented.

Indiana impermissibly burdened the right to free exercise of one's religion when it denied unemployment compensation benefits to a man who quit his job because his religious beliefs forbade his participation in the production of weapons.

St. Martin Evangelical Lutheran Church and Northwestern Lutheran Academy v. State of South Dakota, decided by a 9-0 vote, May 26, 1981. Blackmun wrote the opinion.

Elementary and secondary schools that are controlled by a church and are not separate legal entities are exempt from the requirement that employers pay federal or state unemployment taxes.

Heffron v. International Society for Krishna Consciousness, decided by votes of 5-4 and 9-0, June 22, 1981. White wrote the opinion; Brennan, Marshall, Stevens and Blackmun dissented in part.

Minnesota did not abridge the freedom of members of the Hare Krishna sect to exercise their religion when it made and enforced a rule that persons seeking to sell literature or solicit funds at the state fair must do so from a fixed booth. The state was also acting within constitutional limits when it restricted the free distribution of literature to a particular place on the fair grounds. Those rules were reasonable in light of the state's interest in maintaining order and avoiding congestion in a crowded public place.

Communications

Federal Communications Commission (FCC) v. WNCN Listeners Guild, Insilco Broadcasting Corporation v. WNCN Listeners Guild, American Broadcasting Companies v. WNCN Listeners Guild, National Association of Broadcasters v. WNCN Listeners Guild, decided by a 7-2 vote, March 24, 1981. White wrote the opinion; Marshall and Brennan dissented.

The Federal Communications Commission is not obligated to consider changes in the entertainment format of a radio station when it reviews an application for the renewal or transfer of the station's broadcast license.

CBS Inc. v. Federal Communications Commission (FCC), American Broadcasting Companies Inc. v. FCC, National Broadcasting Company Inc. v. FCC, decided by a vote of 6-3, July 1, 1981. Burger wrote the opinion; White, Rehnquist and Stevens dissented.

Title I of the Federal Election Campaign Act of 1971 (PL 92-225) gives candidates for federal offices a right of access to the air waves once their campaigns are underway. Title I gives the Federal Communications Commission the authority to revoke a broadcaster's license for "willful or repeated failure to allow reasonable access to or to permit purchase of reasonable amounts of time for the use of a broadcasting station by a legally qualified candidate for federal elective office...."

It is up to the FCC, not the networks, to decide when a campaign has begun and when a particular candidate may exercise this right in order to air political broadcasts on behalf of his candidacy.

ELECTION LAWS

Voting Rights

Ball v. James, decided by a 5-4 vote, April 29, 1981. Stewart wrote the opinion; White, Brennan, Marshall and Blackmun dissented.

Arizona did not violate the constitutional guarantee of equal protection when it restricted the right to vote for directors of a water district to landowners in the district. The water district is not the sort of general governmental unit whose officials must be elected by the general populace under the "one person, one vote" rule. Instead, it had functions of a narrow special sort, more like a business than a government.

McDaniel v. Sanchez, decided by a vote of 7-2, June 1, 1981. Stevens wrote the opinion; Stewart and Rehnquist dissented.

Even a reapportionment plan for a county's government developed by local officials under orders from a federal district court is subject to the federal pre-clearance requirements of the Voting Rights Act and must receive such federal approval before being put into effect.

Campaign Finance

California Medical Association v. Federal Election Commission, decided by a 5-4 vote, June 26, 1981. Marshall wrote the opinion; Stewart, Burger, Powell and Rehnquist dissented.

The Federal Election Campaign Act (PL 96-187), which limits to $5,000 per year the amount that one individual or unincorporated association can contribute to one political action committee (PAC), does not violate the guarantee of equal protection or the First Amendment rights of the contributor.

PROPERTY RIGHTS

Webb's Fabulous Pharmacies Inc. v. Beckwith, decided by a 9-0 vote, Dec. 9, 1980. Blackmun wrote the opinion.

A county violates the constitutional ban on the taking of private property for public use without just compensation when it takes for itself interest earned on an interpleader fund, that is private, deposited in the county court registry, at least when there is a separate state law authorizing a fee — to the county — for services rendered with regard to the fund.

San Diego Gas & Electric Co. v. City of San Diego, decided by a 5-4 vote, March 24, 1981. Blackmun wrote the opinion; Brennan, Stewart, Marshall and Powell dissented.

Utility's appeal of a state court ruling denying utility power to recover damages for the "taking" of its land for public use through its rezoning is dismissed because ruling by state court was not "final judgment" by that court on this case.

McCarty v. McCarty, decided by a 6-3 vote, June 26, 1981. Blackmun wrote the opinion; Rehnquist, Brennan and Stewart dissented.

State courts, dividing a couple's property pursuant to a divorce, may not consider the retirement pay of a retired military officer as community property. Thus the court effectively denied the divorced wife of a retired military officer any right to share in that retirement pay.

BUSINESS LAW

Antitrust

Texas Industries v. Radcliff Materials Inc., decided by a 9-0 vote, May 26, 1981. Burger wrote the opinion.

Neither federal statute nor common law allows federal judges to permit companies charged with antitrust violations to force their co-conspirators to share in the financial penalties for their misdeeds. Congress, not the courts, must decide such a policy question.

H. A. Artists & Associates Inc. v. Actors' Equity Assn., decided by votes of 6-3 and 9-0, May 26, 1981. Stewart wrote the opinion; Brennan, Burger and Marshall dissented in part.

Actor's Equity, the union that represents most actors and actresses in the United States, operates a licensing system for the regulation of theatrical agents. In general the creation and maintenance of this system is exempt from the federal antitrust laws under their provisions exempting labor unions from challenge. The fees that Equity levies upon agents applying for licenses, however, are not justified and are not a permissible element of the exempt regulatory system.

National Gerimedical Hospital and Gerontology Center v. Blue Cross of Kansas City and Blue Cross Assn., decided by a 9-0 vote, June 15, 1981. Powell wrote the opinion.

Health insurance companies are not immune from antitrust charges brought by hospitals that were refused permission to participate in the insurance companies' insurance systems — even though the insurance companies based their denial on the fact that the applicant hospital had not received approval for its construction from the local health systems agency as required by the National Health Care Planning and Resources Development Act (PL 93-641).

Banking

Board of Governors of the Federal Reserve System v. Investment Company Institute, decided by a vote of 6-0, Feb. 24, 1981. Stevens wrote the opinion; Stewart, Rehnquist and Powell did not participate in the decision.

The Federal Reserve Board acted within the authority granted it by the Bank Holding Company Act when it allowed bank holding companies and their non-banking subsidiaries to act as investment advisers to closed-end investment companies. Such investment advisory services are closely related to the kind of services long provided by bank trust departments.

Patents

Diamond v. Diehr, decided by a 5-4 vote, March 3, 1981. Rehnquist wrote the opinion; Stevens, Brennan, Blackmun and Marshall dissented.

Inventions and discoveries that involve computer programs may be patentable. Mathematical formulas are not patentable; computer programs are essentially mathematical formulas; but an industrial process does not become unpatentable just because it includes a formula or a program.

Price Discrimination

J. Truett Payne Co. v. Chrysler Motors Corp., decided by votes of 9-0 and 5-4, May 18, 1981. Rehnquist wrote the opinion; Powell, Brennan, Marshall and Blackmun dissented in part.

Businesses which prove that they faced price discrimination — in violation of the ban of the Robinson-Patman Act — must also prove that they were actually injured by that discrimination before they can be awarded damages.

Railroads

Chicago and North Western Transportation Co. v. Kalo Brick & Tile Co., decided by a 9-0 vote, March 9, 1981. Marshall wrote the opinion.

A decision by the Interstate Commerce Commission (ICC) to approve abandonment of certain railroad service may not be challenged in state courts.

Securities

Rubin v. United States, decided by a 9-0 vote, Jan. 21, 1981. Burger wrote the opinion.

When an executive pledges corporate stock as collateral for a bank loan, his pledge is an "offer of sale" of that stock within the meaning of the anti-fraud provisions of federal securities law.

Steadman v. Securities and Exchange Commission, decided by a 7-2 vote, Feb. 25, 1981. Brennan wrote the opinion; Powell and Stewart dissented.

The Securities and Exchange Commission (SEC) properly uses the standard of a preponderance of the evidence — rather than the stricter standard of clear and convincing evidence — in determining whether an individual or firm has violated the anti-fraud provisions of federal securities law.

Shipping

Scindia Steam Navigation Co. Ltd. v. De Los Santos, decided by a 9-0 vote, April 21, 1981. White wrote the opinion.

A shipowner, within limits, is entitled to rely on the stevedore to detect problems in a ship and its equipment that may develop during the stevedore's use. The shipowner is not liable to longshoremen for injuries caused by dangers about which he did not know and about which he had no duty to inform himself. If a shipowner knows that a stevedore is continuing to use malfunctioning equipment at the risk of harm to longshoremen, the shipowner then has the duty to intervene and repair the equipment.

Rodriguez v. Compass Shipping Co., decided by a 9-0 vote, May 18, 1981. Stevens wrote the opinion.

A longshoreman may not prosecute a personal injury action against a negligent shipowner after his right to recover damages for his injury has been assigned to his employer through the provisions of the Longshoremen's and Harbor Workers' Compensation Act.

Taxation

Commissioner of Internal Revenue v. Portland Cement Company of Utah, decided by a 9-0 vote, March 3, 1981. Powell wrote the opinion.

A cement miner and manufacturer must treat cement sold in bulk *and* in bags as his "first marketable product" for the purpose of determining his gross income from mining for figuring his depletion deduction.

United States v. Swank, decided by a 7-2 vote, May 18, 1981. Stevens wrote the opinion; White and Stewart dissented.

A coal mine operator is entitled to claim a mineral depletion deduction on his federal income tax return, even if the person from whom he leases his mine can terminate the lease on short notice.

Rowan Companies Inc. v. United States, decided by a 6-3 vote, June 8, 1981. Powell wrote the opinion; White, Brennan and Marshall dissented.

The Internal Revenue Service may not require an employer to include certain fringe benefits — the value of meals and lodging provided to workers while on the job, for example — in the wage base upon which it pays Social Security and unemployment taxes. Those fringe benefits do not count as wages for the purposes of income tax withholding and thus should not be counted "wages" for these other purposes.

LABOR LAW

Potomac Electric Power Company v. Director, Office of Workers' Compensation Programs, U.S. Department of Labor, decided by an 8-1 vote, Dec. 15, 1980. Stevens wrote the opinion; Blackmun dissented.

Compensation for a permanent partial disability suffered by a worker covered by the Longshoremen's and Harbor Workers' Compensation Act must be determined in accord with a formula set out in that law if the injury is one of those specifically identified in the law. The alternative formula provided in the law for "all other cases" may not be used for injuries specifically identified in the law.

Barrentine v. Arkansas-Best Freight System, decided by a 7-2 vote, April 6, 1981. Brennan wrote the opinion; Burger and Rehnquist dissented.

An employee may bring a federal suit charging his employer with violating the minimum wage provisions of the Fair Labor Standards Act even after he has unsuccessfully made the same claim to a joint grievance committee set up by his union's collective-bargaining agreement.

Universities Research Association Inc. v. Coutu, decided by a 9-0 vote, April 6, 1981. Blackmun wrote the opinion.

The Davis-Bacon Act does not give an employee the right to sue for back wages under a contract that had been determined not to call for Davis-Bacon work and that does not contain any stipulation concerning the payment of the prevailing wage.

United Parcel Service v. Mitchell, decided by an 8-1 vote, April 20, 1981. Rehnquist wrote the opinion; Stevens dissented in part.

A state statute of limitations for actions to vacate arbitration awards was properly applied to an employee's effort to sue in federal court his union and his former employer on the basis that he had been wrongfully discharged. This was the appropriate statute of limitations because the employee had initially contested his firing through the grievance and arbitration procedures set up by the agreement between his union and his employer.

Complete Auto Transit v. Reis, decided by a 7-2 vote, May 4, 1981. Brennan wrote the opinion; Burger and Rehnquist dissented.

Employers may not sue individual employees for damages after the employees strike in violation of a provision of their collective bargaining agreement. Congress deliberately limited the situations in which such a damages remedy might be used, allowing damage suits against unions, but not against individuals, for such violations of collective bargaining agreements.

Alessi v. Raybestos-Manhattan, Buczynski v. General Motors, decided by an 8-0 vote, May 18, 1981. Marshall wrote the opinion; Brennan did not take part in the decision.

Employers are free, under the Employee Retirement Income Security Act of 1974 (ERISA), to reduce benefits to

a retiree in an amount equal to the workers' compensation benefits he receives. Federal law permits such "offsets" and to that extent, pre-empts state laws forbidding them.

Clayton v. United Auto Workers, decided by a vote of 5-4, May 26, 1981. Brennan wrote the opinion; Burger, Powell, Rehnquist and Stewart dissented.

A union member who lost his job for violating a rule set out by his employer did not have to exhaust the internal union appeals procedure (after the union withdrew its pursuit of his grievance) before filing suit against his union in federal court, charging it with breaching its duty to represent him fairly, and against the employer for dismissing him.

Plumbers and Pipefitters, AFL-CIO v. Local # 334, decided by a 6-3 vote, June 22, 1981. Brennan wrote the opinion; Stevens, Rehnquist and Burger dissented.

Federal courts have jurisdiction to hear a suit brought by a local union against its parent international union, charging the parent union with violating its constitution by requiring the consolidation of certain locals.

First National Maintenance Corp. v. National Labor Relations Board, decided by a 7-2 vote, June 22, 1981. Blackmun wrote the opinion; Brennan and Marshall dissented.

A company's management is not required by federal labor law to bargain with the union representing its employees over a decision to terminate a portion of its operations — and put some workers out of a job.

National Labor Relations Board v. Amax Coal Co., decided by an 8-1 vote, June 29, 1981. Stewart wrote the opinion; Stevens dissented.

A trustee of an employee benefit trust, appointed by management, is not a representative of the employer for purposes of collective bargaining or grievance adjustment within the meaning of the National Labor Relations Act (NLRA). But the NLRA does not limit the freedom of a union to try to persuade an employer to choose a particular person as trustee. Nor does union pressure, such as a strike, to induce an employer to contribute to a multiemployer trust fund, amount to an unfair labor practice of dictating to an employer who shall represent him in collective bargaining or grievance adjustments because employee benefit trustees do not engage in such activities.

Occupational Safety

American Textile Manufacturers Institute v. Donovan, National Cotton Council v. Donovan, decided by a 5-3 vote, June 17, 1981. Brennan wrote the opinion; Rehnquist, Burger and Stewart dissented; Powell did not participate in the decision.

Congress in passing the 1970 Occupational Safety and Health Act (PL 91-596) struck the balance between the costs and the benefits of new health and safety standards for American workers. That balance — in favor of the health benefits — is reflected in the language of the law that directs the Occupational Safety and Health Administration (OSHA) to set standards which assure "to the extent feasible" that no worker will suffer "material impairment of health" from exposure to a hazardous substance during his working life.

Therefore the court rebuffed the arguments of the business community — in particular the textile industry facing stringent new cotton dust standards — that the costs and benefits of those standards should be more carefully weighed. And the court upheld those new standards, in spite of arguments that the cost of implementing them could put some manufacturers out of business.

Donovan v. Dewey, decided by an 8-1 vote, June 17, 1981. Marshall wrote the opinion; Stewart dissented.

Federal mine inspectors need not obtain search warrants before conducting routine inspections of mines, authorized by the Federal Mine Safety and Health Act of 1977 (PL 95-164). The "notorious history" of mine accidents and unhealthy conditions and the regular schedule of federal inspections make a warrant unnecessary.

ENERGY AND ENVIRONMENT

Environmental Protection Agency (EPA) v. National Crushed Stone Assn., decided by an 8-0 vote, Dec. 2, 1980. White wrote the opinion; Powell did not participate in the decision.

Congress, in adopting 1977 standards for clean water, in the Federal Water Pollution Control Act Amendments of 1972, did not intend for the EPA to concern itself with the economic impact of compliance with those standards. The court rebuffed the argument that variances from such standards could be justified for plants for whom the cost of compliance might be so great as to force their closing.

Watt v. Alaska, Kenai Peninsula Borough v. Alaska, decided by a 6-3 vote, April 21, 1981. Powell wrote the opinion; Stewart, Burger and Marshall dissented.

Revenues from oil and gas leases of federal land in the Kenai National Moose Range in Alaska, a wildlife refuge, should be distributed according to the formula set out in the Mineral Leasing Act of 1920 — 90 percent to the state and 10 percent to the U.S. Treasury, not the 25-75 percent split between county and federal government set out in the later Wildlife Refuge Revenue Sharing Act.

California v. Sierra Club, Kern County Water Agency v. Sierra Club, decided by a 9-0 vote, April 28, 1981. White wrote the opinion.

Private citizens or groups are not authorized to bring suits to enforce the provisions of the Rivers and Harbors Act of 1899. Only the federal government may sue to enforce that law.

City of Milwaukee v. Illinois and Michigan, decided by a vote of 6-3, April 28, 1981. Rehnquist wrote the opinion; Blackmun, Marshall and Stevens dissented.

A federal court lacks the power to impose more stringent water pollution control standards on a city than Congress has imposed under the Federal Water Pollution Control Act Amendments of 1972. That law set up a comprehensive system of standards and left no room for federal judges to set stricter ones.

Hodel v. Virginia Surface Mining and Reclamation Assn., Virginia Surface Mining and Reclamation Assn. v. Hodel, decided by a 9-0 vote, June 15, 1981. Marshall wrote the opinion.

Congress did not exceed its authority to regulate interstate commerce when it enacted the Surface Mining Control and Reclamation Act of 1977 (PL 95-87). On its face,

the strip mining law — which imposes severe land use restrictions and strict reclamation requirements — does not violate the Constitution.

Hodel v. Indiana, decided by a 9-0 vote, June 15, 1981. Marshall wrote the opinion.

Congress did not act unconstitutionally when it enacted the Surface Mining Control and Reclamation Act of 1977. On its face, the provisions of that law are not unconstitutional.

Middlesex County Sewerage Authority v. National Sea Clammers Assn., Joint Meeting of Essex and Union Counties v. National Sea Clammers Assn., City of New York v. National Sea Clammers Assn., Environmental Protection Agency v. National Sea Clammers Assn., decided by votes of 9-0 and 7-2, June 25, 1981. Powell wrote the opinion; Stevens and Blackmun dissented in part.

Congress, in passing the Federal Water Pollution Control Act (PL 92-500) and the Marine Protection, Research and Sanctuaries Act (PL 92-532), did not authorize citizens to sue violators of those laws for money damages. Citizens may sue under those laws to halt pollution, but not to win damages compensating them for past pollution damage.

Arkansas Louisiana Gas Co. v. Hall, decided by a 5-3 vote, July 2, 1981. Marshall wrote the opinion; Powell, Stevens and Rehnquist dissented; Stewart did not participate in the decision.

Congress has granted the Federal Energy Regulatory Commission exclusive jurisdiction over the rate at which natural gas may be sold and a state court may not award damages to natural gas producers that are tantamount to a retroactive rate increase.

POWERS OF THE PRESIDENT

Dames & Moore v. Regan, decided by a 9-0 vote, July 2, 1981. Rehnquist wrote the opinion.

President Jimmy Carter acted within his statutory power to conduct foreign affairs when he reached the financial agreement with Iran that resulted in the release of 52 Americans held hostage in that country for more than 14 months. Carter was within his power when he agreed to nullify all federal court orders attaching the assets of Iranian businesses and the Iranian government in the United States and to transfer those assets back to Iran. It was also within the president's power to agree that all pending claims against Iran would be transferred to an international tribunal and would be heard and resolved there, not in U.S. courts. Congress, in the International Emergency Economic Powers Act of 1977 (PL 95-223) and a number of other earlier laws, gave the president powers broad enough to take these actions.

STATE POWERS

State of Minnesota v. Clover Leaf Creamery Co., decided by a 7-1 vote, Jan. 21, 1981. Brennan wrote the opinion; Stevens dissented; Rehnquist did not take part in the decision.

The Minnesota legislature did not violate the Constitution's guarantee of equal protection or infringe upon the values protected by the Commerce Clause — granting to the federal government the power to regulate commerce

among the states — when it banned plastic non-returnable milk containers while allowing the use of other non-returnable milk containers such as paperboard cartons. The legislature had a rational basis for making this distinction, and that is all the Constitution requires.

Kassel v. Consolidated Freightways Corporation, decided by a 6-3 vote, March 24, 1981. Powell wrote an opinion joined by three justices; Brennan and Marshall concurred; Rehnquist, Burger and Stewart dissented.

Iowa impermissibly burdened interstate commerce when it banned the use of 65-foot double trailer trucks within its borders, ostensibly for safety reasons.

Montana v. United States, decided by a 6-3 vote, March 24, 1981. Stewart wrote the opinion; Blackmun, Brennan and Marshall dissented.

Title to the bed of the Big Horn River, which flows through an Indian reservation in Montana, passed to Montana when it was admitted to the Union; the tribe may regulate hunting and fishing by non-tribe members on tribal land, but not on land within the reservation that does not belong to the Indians.

Taxation

Rosewell v. LaSalle National Bank, decided by a 5-4 vote, March 24, 1981. Brennan wrote the opinion; Stevens, Stewart, Marshall and Powell dissented.

Federal courts should not intervene in property tax disputes in Illinois but should adhere to the Tax Injunction Act, which forbids such intervention as long as state law provides a "plain, speedy and efficient remedy" for the dispute. Illinois' property tax refund procedure, which requires the taxpayer to pay the protested tax before challenging it in state courts and which pays no interest on any amount refunded, is such a remedy for the purposes of the law.

Western and Southern Life Insurance Co. v. State Board of Equalization of California, decided by a 7-2 vote, May 26, 1981. Brennan wrote the opinion; Stevens and Blackmun dissented.

Because Congress has given the states the freedom to regulate and to tax the insurance business, California does not act unconstitutionally when it imposes a "retaliatory" tax on some out-of-state insurance companies doing business in California. The contested tax is designed to ensure that such "foreign" insurance companies pay as much tax to California as California companies pay to the homestates of those companies.

Maryland v. Louisiana, decided by a vote of 7-1, May 26, 1981. White wrote the opinion; Rehnquist dissented; Powell did not participate in the decision.

Louisiana acts unconstitutionally when it imposes a "first use" tax on gas from offshore wells that passes through the state on the way to out-of-state customers. Such a tax discriminates unfairly against out-of-state customers and thus violates the intent of the Constitution's grant to the federal government of the power to regulate interstate commerce.

Commonwealth Edison Co. v. Montana, decided by a 6-3 vote, July 2, 1981. Marshall wrote the opinion; Blackmun, Powell and Stevens dissented.

Montana's severance tax on each ton of coal mined in the state — which varies up to as much as 30 percent of the sales price of the coal — does not violate the underlying principle of the Constitution's grant to the federal government of the power to regulate interstate commerce, nor the Constitution's clause declaring federal law supreme over state law. The tax does not discriminate against out-of-state customers or consumers and it does not conflict with federal law or national energy policy.

FEDERAL COURTS

Imperial Count v. Munoz, decided by a vote of 6-3, Dec. 2, 1980. Stewart wrote the opinion; Brennan, Stevens and Marshall dissented.

The Anti-Injunction Act forbids a federal district court from issuing an order restraining a county from enforcing a restriction, contained in a land use permit, on the sale of water for use outside the county. The federal court should not issue such an order unless the persons seeking it were "strangers" not bound by state court orders concerning the water dispute.

Allen v. McCurry, decided by a 6-3 vote, Dec. 9, 1980. Stewart wrote the opinion; Brennan, Blackmun and Marshall dissented.

Once a state court considers and rejects a defendant's claim that state police violated his constitutional rights in seizing evidence from him, that claim may not serve as the basis of a federal damage suit against those policemen.

Federal Trade Commission v. Standard Oil Company of California, decided by an 8-0 vote, Dec. 15, 1980. Powell wrote the opinion; Stewart did not participate in the decision.

Federal courts must await the completion of investigatory proceedings by the Federal Trade Commission before intervening in such matters. The ruling was a defeat for eight oil companies that had sought a federal court order halting an FTC investigation of charges of unfair competition and deceptive practices.

Delaware State College v. Ricks, decided by a 5-4 vote, Dec. 15, 1980. Powell wrote the opinion; Stewart, Brennan, Marshall and Stevens dissented.

A faculty member who charges that he was denied academic tenure because of his national origin, a violation of the 1964 Civil Rights Act, has 180 days from that denial in which to file a complaint with the Equal Employment Opportunity Commission and three years from that date in which to file a federal lawsuit based on that charge. The court held that such complaints were filed too late by a man who believed that these time limits began to run only after he terminated his employment relationship with the school, a year after he was denied tenure.

Firestone Tire & Rubber Co. v. Risjord, decided by a 9-0 vote, Jan. 13, 1981. Marshall wrote the opinion.

A federal district court order denying a motion by one party to disqualify counsel for the opposing party in a civil case is not a "final" decision that can be appealed to a higher court.

Sumner v. Mata, decided by a vote of 6-3, Jan. 21, 1981. Rehnquist wrote the opinion; Brennan, Marshall and Stevens dissented.

Congress has made clear that federal courts considering the petitions of state prisoners for writs of habeas corpus must defer to state court decisions on matters of fact unless there is substantial reason to question the correctness of those decisions. If a federal court considering such a petition does decide that a state court erred on a matter of fact, it must set out its reasons for that decision in writing.

Carson v. American Brands Inc., decided by a 9-0 vote, Feb. 25, 1981. Brennan wrote the opinion.

The refusal of a federal district court to approve a consent decree agreed to by both sides in a job discrimination case is an action that can be appealed to a higher court.

Delta Air Lines Inc. v. August, decided by a 6-3 vote, March 9, 1981. Stevens wrote the opinion; Rehnquist, Burger and Stewart dissented.

Under the Federal Rules of Civil Procedure, a plaintiff who refuses a defendant's offer to settle a job discrimination case — and then loses the case — cannot be required to pay the defendant's litigation costs.

Arizona v. Manypenny, decided by a 7-2 vote, April 21, 1981. Blackmun wrote the opinion; Brennan and Marshall dissented.

The state of Arizona may appeal a federal court's acquittal of a federal border patrol agent on charges of assault. The assault occurred on federal land and in the course of the federal agent's duties so his trial, on state charges, took place in federal court. The state retained its right, under state law, to appeal the acquittal as if he had been tried in state court.

Gulf Oil Co. v. Bernard, decided by a 9-0 vote, June 1, 1981. Powell wrote the opinion.

A federal judge lacks the power to bar parties and lawyers in a class action civil rights suit from communicating with other actual or potential members of the class without obtaining prior court approval.

Federated Department Stores v. Moitie, decided by an 8-1 vote, June 15, 1981. Rehnquist wrote the opinion; Brennan dissented.

A group of customers seeking damages from two department store companies that allegedly engaged in price-fixing can no longer pursue their claims because they failed to appeal an earlier court decision dismissing their cases.

Gulf Offshore Company v. Mobil Oil Corp., decided by an 8-0 vote, July 1, 1981. Powell wrote the opinion; Stewart did not take part in the decision.

Federal courts do not have exclusive jurisdiction over personal injury and indemnity cases arising under the Outer Continental Shelf Lands Act; state courts also may hear such cases.

FEDERAL JUDGES

United States v. Will, decided by an 8-0 vote, Dec. 15, 1980. Burger wrote the opinion; Blackmun did not participate.

Congress may not rescind cost-of-living adjustments in the salaries of federal judges after those increases actually

take effect; such an after-the-fact rescission violates the Constitution's guarantee that judicial salaries "shall not be diminished during their Continuance in Office." Congress may rescind such adjustments if it acts before the beginning of the fiscal year in which they take effect.

The court thus held that Congress had properly rescinded cost-of-living increases for fiscal 1978 and 1979 — acting before the first day of the new fiscal year, but had improperly tried to cancel those increases for fiscal 1977 and 1980, when the rescissions were not enacted until after Oct. 1. The effect of this ruling was an increase of about 12 percent in the salaries of all federal judges, including members of the Supreme Court.

STATE COURTS

Allstate Insurance Company v. Hague, decided by a 5-3 vote, Jan. 13, 1981. Brennan wrote an opinion for himself and three justices; Stevens concurred in the judgment; Powell, Burger and Rehnquist dissented; Stewart did not participate in the decision.

Minnesota is not constitutionally required to apply Wisconsin law in an insurance case involving benefits to be paid to a widow, currently residing in Minnesota, of a Wisconsin man who worked in Minnesota and was killed in an accident in Wisconsin.

INTERSTATE RELATIONS

Webb v. Webb, decided by an 8-1 vote, May 18, 1981. White wrote the opinion; Marshall dissented.

The court dismissed a custody dispute case because no federal point of law had been raised during the proceedings in the state courts. The Supreme Court lacks jurisdiction over a case from state courts unless a federal question was raised and ruled upon by those courts.

United States v. Maine, report of special master approved by an 8-0 vote, June 15, 1981. No opinion, simply issuance of a supplemental decree. Marshall did not participate in this case.

The decree specified the boundary line between the submerged lands belonging to the United States and those belonging to the state of Massachusetts.

California v. Arizona and the United States, report of special master approved without dissent June 15, 1981. No opinion, simply a decree.

The decree described the ownership of certain parts of the bed of the former channel of the Colorado River.

United States v. Louisiana, supplemental report of special master received and ordered filed without dissent, June 22, 1981. No opinion, simply entry of final decree. Marshall did not participate in this case.

The decree defined the boundary between the offshore submerged lands belonging to Louisiana and those belong-

ing to the United States. It also required each government to make a full accounting of the revenues it derived from exploitation of the submerged lands belonging to the other.

OFFICIAL IMMUNITY

Dennis v. Sparks, decided by a vote of 9-0, Nov. 17, 1980. White wrote the opinion.

A judge's immunity from a damage suit brought by someone injured by an improperly issued judicial order does not extend to protect from such a suit a private individual who bribed the judge to issue the protested order.

Kissinger v. Halperin, decided by a vote of 4-4, June 22, 1981. No opinion. Rehnquist did not participate in the consideration of this case.

The court without opinion left standing the ruling of a lower court that former President Richard Nixon, former Secretary of State Henry A. Kissinger and former Attorney General John N. Mitchell were liable to a damage suit brought by an individual whose home they had illegally wiretapped.

City of Newport v. Fact Concerts Inc., decided by a 6-3 vote, June 26, 1981. Blackmun wrote the opinion; Brennan, Marshall and Stevens dissented.

A city may not be ordered to pay punitive damages as a result of a civil rights damage suit brought by persons who charge that the city violated their constitutional rights.

MEDICAID

Beltran v. Myers, decided by a 9-0 vote, May 18, 1981. Per curiam (unsigned) opinion.

A federal appeals court should reconsider its decision backing California's denial of Medicaid benefits to persons who have recently disposed of their assets for less than full value. The appeals court should examine that ruling in light of a new law (PL 96-611) barring benefit payments for two years after a person transfers more than $12,000 in assets to family members or friends in order to become eligible for Medicaid or supplemental security income.

Schweiker v. Gray Panthers, decided by a vote of 6-3, June 25, 1981. Powell wrote the opinion; Stevens, Brennan and Marshall dissented.

The Department of Health and Human Services was within its authority, under the Social Security Act, when it issued regulations for the Medicaid program that govern the extent to which states may consider the income of an applicant's spouse in determining eligibility for Medicaid. Under those regulations states may assume that spousal income is always available to pay for the needs of an institutionalized spouse.   ∎

CQ Nominations and Confirmations

Few Reagan Nominees Meet Serious Trouble

Few of President Ronald Reagan's nominees to Cabinet, sub-Cabinet and other executive branch posts ran into any serious opposition to their confirmation by the Senate. Most of the Reagan appointees were white male conservatives, although Reagan named one black, Samuel R. Pierce Jr., and one woman, Jeane J. Kirkpatrick, who was also a Democrat, to Cabinet-level positions. In July Reagan fulfilled a campaign promise — and made history — when he nominated a woman, Sandra Day O'Connor, as associate justice of the Supreme Court of the United States.

Among Reagan's Cabinet appointments there was substantial government experience. For instance, Caspar W. Weinberger, tapped to be defense secretary, headed the Department of Health, Education and Welfare, the Office of Management and Budget and the Federal Trade Commission under Presidents Nixon and Ford.

Others, such as Reagan's choice for attorney general, William French Smith, were wholly new to Washington and to the programs they would oversee.

Reagan supporters on the far right were generally disappointed that more of his nominees did not reflect their political views. One nominee the far right did support — Ernest W. Lefever to be assistant secretary of state for human rights — withdrew his nomination after the Senate Foreign Relations Committee voted to disapprove his confirmation. Another nominee supported by the far right — Dr. C. Everett Koop — won confirmation as surgeon general after Congress changed the law setting an age limit for that position.

Cabinet Nominees

The Republican-dominated Senate gave rapid approval to Reagan's Cabinet, overwhelmingly confirming within two days of his Jan. 20 inauguration all but one of the men he had chosen to head federal departments. Allegations that Labor Secretary-designate Raymond J. Donovan was linked to labor racketeers and organized crime postponed action on his nomination. However, Donovan was confirmed Feb. 3.

Two other Cabinet nominations — those of Alexander M. Haig Jr. to be secretary of state and James G. Watt to be interior secretary — caused more strife than Donovan's. Nonetheless both men were confirmed with little dissent. Although several senators expressed serious reservations about these and other nominations, they voted for confirmation saying they felt Reagan was entitled to the Cabinet he wanted.

Haig. Even before his Dec. 16 appointment, Democratic leaders said they would use Haig's Senate confirmation hearings to examine his past as a top aide in the Nixon White House. During five days of hearings, the Senate Foreign Relations Committee closely probed the retired Army general's foreign policy views and expertise, questioned his morality and judgment and tested the limits of his composure to a degree rare in confirmation hearings.

Haig forcefully defended his conduct under Nixon. Most of his actions during Watergate "have been thoroughly investigated," he said, and "none of these investigations has found any culpability on my part." As White House staff chief, Haig said he protected Nixon "within the boundaries of the law and the advice of lawyers."

That explanation did not satisfy committee Democrats who insisted that the committee subpoena an index of tape recordings made in Nixon's office between May 4 and July 18, 1973, a crucial time during the Watergate affair. However, the former president raised objections and the National Archives refused to comply with the subpoena. The committee voted to drop the inquiry Feb. 24, more than a month after Haig had been confirmed.

But Haig won his confirmation battle not on the strength of his rebuttal of implications about his Nixon ties, but by demonstrating a broad, studied grasp of dozens of foreign policy issues and, in many cases, setting forth firm convictions on how to deal with them. The Foreign Relations Committee recommended his confirmation by a 15-2 vote Jan. 15. The full Senate confirmed the nomination Jan. 21, 93-6. *(Vote 3, p. 2-S)*

Watt. Reagan's nominee for interior secretary stirred up almost as much controversy as Haig's appointment. Watt, who as interior secretary would administer 519 million acres of publicly owned lands, had spent the previous three years as president and chief executive officer of a conservative law foundation that had spent much of its time challenging the Interior Department's use of that land.

Under Watt, the Mountain States Legal Organization fought attempts by the Bureau of Land Management to limit access to public lands by a number of industries. The organization was funded partly by oil, gas, timber and mining companies. Watt's organization also challenged the government's authority to limit grazing on over-grazed land, to review national forest lands for wilderness potential and to prohibit motorized rafts on the Colorado River in the Grand Canyon.

During his confirmation hearings, Watt sought to convince senators that environmentalists were unduly concerned and that he would take more moderate positions on environmental issues than his foundation. Watt promised not to try to change environmental and land-use laws but to better implement them to allow orderly development of coal, oil, gas and minerals on federal lands. In an effort to deflect conflict-of-interest charges, Watt agreed not to participate in current or future suits brought by the foundation involving department policies.

Despite continued objections from environmentalists, Watt was confirmed Jan. 22, 83-12. *(Vote 13, p. 3-S)*

Donovan. Senate action on Donovan's nomination was delayed for nearly two weeks while the FBI and the Senate Labor and Human Resources Committee investigated Donovan and his firm, the Schiavone Construction Co.

The investigation looked into charges, made by FBI informer Ralph Picardo, that Donovan and Schiavone had provided illegal payoffs to corrupt union officials to maintain "labor peace." Other informants said the company had

close ties with organized crime.

But an intensive FBI investigation did not uncover any evidence to substantiate the various charges. On the other hand, the FBI said it could not disprove some of the allegations. After questioning FBI agents and Donovan Jan. 27, the Labor Committee approved the nomination by an 11-0 vote Jan. 29. Five committee Democrats voted "present."

During Senate debate Donovan's supporters stressed that he was entitled to a presumption of innocence if a detailed investigation could not produce any hard evidence of wrongdoing. The vote to confirm Donovan was 80-17; the negative votes were cast by Democrats. *(Vote 19, p. 5-S)*

In early December 1981, it was revealed that the FBI had begun another examination of Donovan as a result of new allegations about the labor secretary's conduct as head of Schiavone. Later that month a special prosecutor was appointed to investigate those charges.

Other Cabinet Nominees. No significant controversy surrounded any of Reagan's other Cabinet appointments. They were:

● Malcolm Baldrige, secretary of commerce. Last position held: chairman of the board and chief executive officer of Scovill Inc. of Waterbury, Conn., a manufacturing conglomerate, since 1969. Confirmed Jan. 22, 97-1. *(Vote 10, p. 3-S)*

● Terrel H. Bell, secretary of education. Last position held: Utah commissioner of higher education since 1976; also U.S. commissioner of education, 1974-76. Confirmed Jan. 22, 90-2. *(Vote 15, p. 4-S)*

● John R. Block, secretary of agriculture. Last position held: director, Illinois Department of Agriculture since 1977. Confirmed Jan. 22, 98-0. *(Vote 9, p. 3-S)*

● James B. Edwards, secretary of energy. Last position held: oral surgeon; also governor of South Carolina, 1975-79. Confirmed Jan. 22, 93-3. *(Vote 14, p. 3-S)*

● Drew Lewis, secretary of transportation. Last position held: Lewis and Associates, a financial and management consulting firm in Plymouth Meeting, Pa.; also Republican National Committeeman from Pennsylvania since 1976. Confirmed Jan. 22, 98-0. *(Vote 12, p. 3-S)*

● Samuel R. Pierce Jr., secretary of housing and urban development. Last position held: partner in the New York City labor law firm of Battle, Fowler Stokes and Kheel; also served as general counsel of the Treasury Department, 1970-73. Confirmed Jan. 22, 98-0. *(Vote 11, p. 3-S)*

● Donald T. Regan, secretary of the Treasury. Last position held: chairman of Merrill Lynch, Pierce, Fenner & Smith, Inc. Confirmed Jan. 21, 98-0. *(Vote 6, p. 2-S)*

● Richard S. Schweiker, secretary of health and human services. Last position held: U.S. senator from Pennsylvania, 1969-81; also U.S. representative from Pennsylvania's 13th District, 1961-69. Confirmed Jan. 21, 99-0. *(Vote 4, p. 2-S)*

● William French Smith, attorney general. Last position held: partner in the California law firm of Gibson, Dunn and Crutcher; also personal lawyer to Reagan. Confirmed Jan. 22, 96-1. *(Vote 8, p. 3-S)*

● Caspar W. Weinberger, secretary of defense. Last position held: general counsel, Bechtel Corp., a San Francisco-based engineering and construction firm; also secretary of health, education and welfare, 1973-75; director, Office of Management and Budget, 1972-73; chairman, Federal Trade Commission, 1970. Confirmed Jan. 20, 97-2. *(Vote 1, p. 2-S)*

The Senate easily confirmed four other officials of

Cabinet-level rank. The nomination of William J. Casey to be CIA director raised questions in the press about Casey's handling of documents sought by a House subcommittee while he was chairman of the Securities and Exchange Commission and about a meeting he had in 1972 with a lawyer for fugitive financier Robert L. Vesco. However, the Senate was apparently satisfied with its background investigation of Casey and confirmed him Jan. 27, 95-0. *(Vote 16, p. 4-S)*

The other three officials were:

● William E. Brock III, head of the Office of U.S. Trade Representative. Last position held: chairman, Republican National Committee, 1977-81; also U.S. senator from Tennessee, 1970-77; U.S. representative from Tennessee's 3rd District, 1962-70. Confirmed Jan. 21, 99-0. *(Vote 5, p. 2-S)*

● Jeane J. Kirkpatrick, U.S. ambassador to the United Nations. Last position held: professor, Georgetown University, 1967-81. Confirmed Jan. 29, 81-0. *(Vote 18, p. 4-S)*

● David A. Stockman, director of the Office of Management and Budget. Last position held: U.S. representative from Michigan's 4th District, 1977-81. Confirmed Jan. 27, 93-0. *(Vote 17, p. 4-S)*

Sub-Cabinet Appointments

Several of Reagan's sub-Cabinet-level appointments, particularly to the Interior, State and Health and Human Services departments, also caused controversy and confirmation delays.

One appointee, **Ernest W. Lefever,** withdrew his nomination as assistant secretary of state for human rights after the Foreign Relations Committee voted against his confirmation. It was the first time within memory that the committee had disapproved a presidential nominee.

Opponents questioned Lefever's commitment to human rights and to its role in foreign policy, citing his opposition to the Carter administration's human rights policies. Lefever testified that he opposed cutting foreign aid assistance to nations whose governments violated human rights, as the Carter administration had done with Argentina, Guatemala and others.

Lefever's credibility was also damaged by his testimony on the relationship between the Ethics and Public Policy Center, a non-profit think tank headed by Lefever, and the Nestlé Corp., a maker and exporter of infant formula. The foundation had received $25,000 from Nestlé and later reprinted and distributed an article favoring infant formula exports. Lefever denied any connection between the Nestlé donations and his foundation's position on the infant formula issue but his disavowals were contradicted by a Nestlé official. Lefever's involvement in the issue was especially controversial because on May 21 the United States cast the lone dissenting vote against a World Health Organization code calling for a worldwide ban on advertising and promotion of baby formula because of its adverse health implications in poor nations. *(Lefever nomination, p. 153)*

Several other State Department appointees were challenged by Sen. Jesse Helms, R-N.C., who objected to the political and foreign policy views of **Chester A. Crocker,** designated to be assistant secretary of state for African affairs, **Myer Rashish,** designated under secretary of state for economic affairs, and **Robert D. Hormats,** designated assistant secretary of state for economic and business affairs. Helms claimed the three men did not share President Reagan's conservatism and might not carry out his policies.

Membership of Federal Regulatory Agencies, 1981

Civil Aeronautics Board

(Five members appointed for six-year terms; not more than three members from one political party; agency due to expire Jan. 1, 1985.)

Member	Party	Term Expires	Nominated	Confirmed by Senate
Clinton D. McKinnon (C)	R	12/31/85	10/6/81	10/26/81
George A Dalley	D	12/31/82	8/3/79	3/6/80
Elizabeth E. Bailey	R	12/31/83	7/8/77	7/28/77
Gloria Schaffer	D	12/31/84	7/13/78	9/13/78
James R. Smith	I	12/31/86	7/25/80	8/27/80

Commodity Futures Trading Commission

(Five members appointed for five-year terms; not more than three members from one political party.)

Philip F. Johnson (C)	R	4/13/84	5/12/81	6/4/81
Robert L. Martin	R	6/19/81	6/3/76	6/17/76
James M. Stone	D	4/15/83	1/15/79	4/10/79
David G. Gartner	D	5/19/83	5/10/78	5/17/78
Susan M. Phillips	R	4/13/85	9/10/81	10/27/81
One vacancy				

Consumer Product Safety Commission

(Five members appointed for seven-year terms; not more than three members from one political party.)

Nancy H. Steorts (C)	R	10/26/84	7/13/81	7/27/81
R. David Pittle	D	10/26/82	1/20/78	2/1/78
Edith B. Sloan	D	10/26/83	1/20/78	2/28/78
Samuel D. Zagoria	R	10/26/85	9/29/78	10/10/78
Stuart M. Statler	R	8/26/86	6/14/79	7/26/79

Federal Communications Commission

(Seven members appointed for seven-year terms; not more than four members from one political party.)

Mark S. Fowler (C)	R	6/30/86	4/27/81	5/14/81
Abbott Washburn	R	6/30/82	6/18/75	9/26/75
Joseph R. Fogarty	D	6/30/83	6/21/76	9/8/76
James H. Quello	D	6/30/84	7/8/81	7/31/81
Anne P. Jones	R	6/30/85	1/15/79	3/21/79
Henry M. Rivera	D	6/30/87	7/8/81	7/31/81
Mary Ann Weyforth-Dawson	R	6/30/88	5/12/81	6/4/81

Federal Election Commission

(Six members appointed for six-year terms; not more than three members from one political party.)

John W. McGarry (C)	D	4/30/83	1/15/79	2/21/79
Robert O. Tiernan	D	4/30/81	5/17/76	5/18/76
Joan D. Aikens	R	4/30/81	5/17/76	5/18/76
Thomas E. Harris	D	4/30/85	5/1/79	6/19/79
Frank P. Reiche	R	4/30/85	5/1/79	7/25/79
One vacancy				

Federal Energy Regulatory Commission

(Five members appointed to staggered four-year terms; not more than three members from one political party.)

Charles M. Butler III (C)	R	10/20/83	5/12/81	6/4/81
John D. Hughes	D	10/20/83	5/1/80	8/27/80
Georgianna Sheldon	R	10/20/84	5/14/81	6/4/81
Anthony G. Sousa	R	10/20/84	6/30/81	7/27/81
One vacancy				

Federal Reserve System Governors

(Seven members appointed for 14-year terms; no statutory limitation on political party membership.)

Paul A. Volcker (C)	D	1/31/92	8/17/79	8/2/79
Frederick H. Schultz	D	1/31/82	4/12/79	7/18/79
Nancy H. Teeters	D	1/31/84	8/28/78	9/15/78
J. Charles Partee	I	1/31/86	12/8/75	12/19/75
Emmett J. Rice	D	1/31/90	4/12/79	6/12/79
Henry C. Wallich	R	1/31/90	4/12/79	6/12/79
Lyle E. Gramley	D	1/31/94	3/21/80	5/15/80

Federal Trade Commission

(Five members appointed for seven-year terms; not more than three members from one political party.)

James C. Miller III (C)	R	9/25/88	7/16/81	9/21/81
David A. Clanton	R	9/25/83	7/20/76	7/26/76
Michael J. Pertschuk	D	9/25/84	3/25/77	4/6/77
Patricia P. Bailey	R	9/25/87	6/10/80	6/26/80
One vacancy				

Interstate Commerce Commission

(Eleven members appointed for seven-year terms; not more than six members from one political party. President Carter decided to cut the commission's size by not filling vacancies.)

Reese H. Taylor Jr. (C)	R	12/31/84	5/5/81	6/16/81
Robert C. Gresham	R	12/31/81	6/3/74	9/19/74
Reginald E. Gilliam Jr.	I	12/31/82	12/12/79	4/2/80
Eight vacancies				

Nuclear Regulatory Commission

(Five members appointed for five-year terms; not more than three members from one political party.)

Nunzio J. Palladino (C)	R	6/30/86	6/11/81	6/19/81
Peter A. Bradford	D	6/30/82	6/12/77	8/3/77
John F. Ahearne	D	6/30/83	5/18/78	7/21/78
Victor Gilinsky	D	6/30/84	5/15/79	6/27/79
Thomas M. Roberts	R	6/30/85	7/9/81	7/31/81

Securities and Exchange Commission

(Five members appointed for five-year terms; not more than three members from one political party.)

John S. R. Shad (C)	R	6/5/82	4/1/81	4/8/81
Bevis Longstreth	D	6/5/82	6/25/81	7/17/81
John R. Evans	R	6/5/83	6/11/79	9/18/79
Philip A. Loomis Jr.	R	6/5/84	6/11/79	9/18/79
Barbara S. Thomas	D	6/5/85	7/29/80	9/8/80

In public defiance of Helms, the Senate Foreign Relations Committee reported the three nominations favorably April 28. Helms then dropped his opposition to Hormats but placed a "hold" on Crocker and Rashish. By tradition such holds obligate the leadership to delay bringing the nominations to the floor until the holds are dropped. Although holds are generally honored only for a day or two, Senate Majority Leader Howard H. Baker Jr., R-Tenn., declined to override Helms' holds. After many behind-the-scenes negotiations, Helms finally agreed to drop his hold on Crocker, who was confirmed June 9, 84-7. The Senate confirmed Rashish June 11, 91-4, after the nominee had been recalled for a further hearing demanded by Helms. *(Votes 139, p. 27-S, 149, p. 28-S)*

Reagan's nomination of **William P. Clark**, an acknowledged foreign policy novice, as deputy secretary of state proved to be more embarrassing than controversial. Clark, Reagan's executive secretary in 1967 and 1968 and later a California Supreme Court judge, confessed his lack of foreign policy expertise but pointed out his primary task would be to manage the complex State Department bureaucracy. Opponents argued that Clark could hardly avoid becoming involved in policy making and that he occasionally would be required to serve as acting secretary of state. The Senate confirmed Clark Feb. 24 on a 70-24 vote. *(Vote 24, p. 7-S)*

Although she was widely opposed by environmental organizations, **Anne McGill Gorsuch** won easy Senate approval; she was confirmed May 5 by unanimous consent. Environmentalists charged that Gorsuch had neither an administrative background nor a history of concern for environmental protection.

Another appointment to an environmentally sensitive position generated more opposition in the Senate. The nomination of **John B. Crowell Jr.** as assistant secretary of agriculture for natural resources and environment sparked conflict-of-interest charges. Crowell was general counsel for the Louisiana-Pacific Corp., parent company of an Alaskan subsidiary, the Ketchikan Pulp Co. On March 5 a Seattle federal judge found the subsidiary guilty of conspiring to fix prices and control the timber market in southeastern Alaska's Tongass National Forest.

Crowell denied any previous knowledge of the price-fixing and said he would not become involved in the department's handling of the Ketchikan case. The Senate Agriculture Committee approved Crowell's nomination April 1. But Democrats Edward M. Kennedy, Mass., and Patrick J. Leahy, Vt., delayed floor action on the nomination, claiming that, despite his denials, they had new evidence that directly linked Crowell with the price-fixing activities of the Ketchikan Pulp Co. Kennedy and Leahy requested another hearing, which the Agriculture Committee refused. They then took their evidence to the Senate, which confirmed Crowell May 20, 72-25. All 25 dissenting votes were cast by Democrats. *(Vote 120, p. 24-S)*

Several legal technicalities had to be cleared out of the way before the Senate could consider the nomination of Dr. **C. Everett Koop** as surgeon general of the United States. Koop, a Philadelphia surgeon noted for his operations to separate Siamese twins, was an outspoken opponent of abortion, Planned Parenthood and test-tube babies.

It was not his conservative views that got him into trouble but his age. Koop was 64 years old and, under existing law, the surgeon general had to be under 64. The Senate added an amendment to a non-related House-passed bill eliminating the age requirement. The House

eventually agreed to that rider, but House opponents of Koop then succeeded in adding language to the budget reconciliation bill requiring that the surgeon general have "specialized training or significant experience in public health programs," a qualification Koop's opponents said the surgeon could not meet. A majority of the Senate disagreed, however, voting to confirm Koop Nov. 16 by a 68-24 vote. *(Details, HEW chapter)*

Another Reagan health appointee withdrew in the face of charges that he was anti-Semitic. From 1969 to 1973, **Warren Richardson**, nominated as assistant secretary of health and human services, had served as general counsel of the extremely conservative Liberty Lobby, which frequently has been criticized for its racist and anti-Jewish sentiments. Richardson denied that he shared these views but said "political realism" was forcing him to withdraw his name.

Federal Judges

President Reagan made instant history in 1981 when he nominated Sandra Day O'Connor as the first woman associate justice of the Supreme Court of the United States. The Senate unanimously confirmed O'Connor Sept. 21. The 51-year-old Arizona appeals court judge was sworn in Sept. 25 to replace Potter Stewart, a moderate-to-conservative swing vote on the court who retired July 3. Relatively little controversy surrounded O'Connor's appointment. She was opposed primarily by anti-abortion groups concerned about her views on abortion.

From what was known about her judicial philosophy, it appeared that O'Connor would fit in comfortably with the court as it functioned under Chief Justice Warren E. Burger. As a state trial and appellate court justice, she was inclined to defer to the legislative and executive branches on most questions, practicing what has come to be known as "judicial restraint." She was also known as a serious student of the law who liked to keep her courtroom running smoothly and displayed little patience with unprepared attorneys. *(Details, Law Enforcement/Judiciary chapter)*

Reagan's nomination of O'Connor made good on his campaign pledge to appoint a woman to the Supreme Court. But in his first year, Reagan fell short on his promise to seek out women for federal district and appeals courts seats. Only one of the 41 judges the president named to the lower federal courts in 1981 was a woman — Cynthia Holcomb Hall, who already was serving as a U.S. Tax Court judge when Reagan elevated her to a district court seat in California.

One appointee was black — Lawrence Q. Pierce — and he, too, already was a sitting federal judge, elevated by Reagan from a district court seat in New York to the 2nd U.S. Circuit Court of Appeals. None of Reagan's judicial appointees in 1981 were of Hispanic heritage. Thirty-nine were white men.

Agency Nominees

Opposition from labor and civil rights groups stalled two of Reagan's nominations to independent agencies in the Senate Labor and Human Resources Committee in 1981 and the nominations faced serious obstacles if they were considered in 1982. A third nomination was stalled in the Senate Commerce Committee.

The nomination of **John R. Van de Water** to be chairman of the National Labor Relations Board (NLRB) was opposed by the AFL-CIO, which argued that Van de

Water was an anti-labor partisan who could not serve as an impartial judge in settling labor-business disputes. Van de Water was a California labor lawyer whose business was to advise companies on how to cope with unionization drives of their employees.

Despite its 9-7 Republican majority, the Labor Committee rejected the nomination by an 8-8 vote Nov. 19. Lowell P. Weicker Jr., R-Conn., joined all committee Democrats in opposing Van de Water. Chairman Orrin G. Hatch, R-Utah, then tried to have the nomination reported unfavorably, but that motion also was rejected 8-8.

Senate Majority Leader Howard H. Baker Jr., R-Tenn., tried Nov. 23 to discharge the committee from consideration of the nomination so it could be brought directly to the Senate floor. But his effort was blocked on the floor by an objection from Minority Leader Robert C. Byrd, D-W.Va. Baker could move in 1982 to discharge the nomination, but it faced certain filibuster on the floor.

Van de Water received an interim appointment as NLRB chairman in August while Congress was in recess. He could stay on under that appointment, without Senate confirmation, until the end of the 97th Congress. Senate Democratic staff argued, however, that the law prohibited paying Van de Water his salary unless the nomination was resubmitted in 1982.

The nomination of **William M. Bell** to head the Equal Employment Opportunity Commission (EEOC) led to the unusual situation of a black man being opposed by civil rights groups. Bell was a Detroit businessman who was an unsuccessful Republican candidate for the House in 1980. He received 5 percent of the vote against Rep. John Conyers, D.

Opposition to Bell's nomination grew after an October hearing in which it was revealed that he had little experience in government, had never managed more than four employees and ran a job placement firm that had not found anyone a job in the preceding year. That record worried civil rights and women's groups, because Bell would be in charge of an agency with more than 3,000 employees and a budget of over $100 million.

When groups such as the National Association for the Advancement of Colored People and the National Organization for Women announced their opposition to Bell, concern spread among Labor Committee members. Support for Bell was so weak that the administration asked the committee to postpone its vote on the nomination, which had been scheduled for Nov. 12.

The Senate Commerce Committee Dec. 15 halted action on the nomination of **F. Keith Adkinson** to the Federal Trade Commission (FTC) after the ranking minority member accused the nominee of lying to the panel.

Adkinson, a Washington lawyer, was national director of Democrats for Reagan-Bush during the 1980 campaign. Most of the controversy surrounding his nomination centered on allegations that he used his former position as a staff member of the Senate Permanent Subcommittee on Investigations to further his financial interests. Sen. Howard W. Cannon, D-Nev., said Adkinson had lied about the details of his book and movie contract with Gary Bowdach, a convicted felon who had provided testimony on organized crime to the panel.

Cannon asked that the committee meet in private to discuss confidential information. The committee rejected that request but then adjourned. Committee Chairman Bob Packwood, R-Ore., said he expected the panel to vote on the nomination in 1982.

1981 Confirmations

Listed below are 355 persons appointed by President Reagan to major federal posts and confirmed by the Senate in 1981. Information is given in the following order: name of office, salary, appointee, legal residence, last occupation before appointment, selected political or public policy posts held, date of birth, party affiliation (where available) and confirmation date.

LEGISLATIVE BRANCH

Government Printing Office

Public Printer, $52,750 — **Danford L. Sawyer;** Sarasota, Fla.; president, Sawyer and Associates Advertising Inc. and Area Guide Inc. (1964-80); Nov. 11, 1939; Rep.; July 31.

General Accounting Office

Comptroller general, $60,662.50 — **Charles A. Bowsher;** Bethesda, Md.; managing partner, Arthur Andersen & Co. (1971-81); assistant secretary of the Navy (1967-71); May 30, 1931; Ind.; Sept. 29.

EXECUTIVE OFFICE OF THE PRESIDENT

Central Intelligence Agency

Director, $60,662.50 — **William J. Casey;** Roslyn Harbor, N.Y.; campaign director, Reagan-Bush general election campaign (1980); counsel, Rogers & Wells (1976-81); president, Export-Import Bank (1974-76); under secretary for economic affairs, State Dept. (1973-74); chairman, Securities and Exchange Commission (1971-73); March 13, 1913; Rep.; Jan. 27.

Deputy director, $55,387.50 — **Adm. Bobby R. Inman;** Rhonesboro, Texas; director, National Security Agency (NSA) (1977-81); NSA vice director (1976-77); director of naval intelligence (1974-76); assistant chief of staff intelligence, U.S. Pacific Fleet (1973-74); April 4, 1931; Ind.; Feb. 5.

Council of Economic Advisers

Member and chairman, $52,750 — **Murray L. Weidenbaum;** Creve Coeur, Mo.; director, Center for the Study of American Business, and Mallinckrodt Distinguished University Professor, Washington Univ. (1971-81); assistant secretary for economic policy, Treasury Dept. (1969-71); Feb. 10, 1927; Rep.; Feb. 24.

Member, $52,750 — **William A. Niskanen Jr.;** Washington, D.C.; director of economics, Ford Motor Co. (1975-80); assistant director, Office of Management and Budget (1970-72); March 13, 1933; Rep.; June 11.

Member, $52,750 — **Jerry L. Jordan;** Albuquerque, N.M.; dean, Robert O. Anderson Schools of Management, Univ. of N.M. (1980-81); Dec. 12, 1941; Rep.; July 10.

Council on Environmental Quality

Chairman and member, $60,662.50 — **A. Alan Hill;** San Rafael, Calif.; president, Hill Building Specialties Inc. (1976-81); deputy secretary, Calif. Agriculture and Services Agency (1969-74); state information officer, Republican State Central Committee of Calif. (1965-69); Feb. 1, 1938; Rep.; July 8.

Member, $52,750 — **W. Ernst Minor;** Cincinnati; member, Environmental Protection Agency transition team (1981); director

of family scheduling, Reagan-Bush Committee (1980); director, Cincinnati Environmental Research Center (1972-80); April 25, 1931; Rep.; July 8.

Office of Management and Budget

Director, $60,662.50 — **David A. Stockman;** St. Joseph, Mich.; U.S. representative, 4th Congressional District, Mich. (1977-81); executive director, U.S. House Republican Conference Committee (1972-76); special assistant to U.S. Rep. John B. Anderson (1970-72); Nov. 10, 1946; Rep.; Jan. 27.

Deputy director, $55,387.50 — **Edwin L. Harper;** St. Louis; vice president, Emerson Electric Co. (1978-81); assistant director, domestic council for President Nixon (1969-73); Nov. 13, 1941; Rep.; March 3.

Administrator, Office of Federal Procurement Policy, $52,750 — **Donald E. Sowle;** McLean, Va.; president, Don Sowle Associates Inc. (1974-81); May 27, 1915; Rep.; June 16.

Office of Science and Technology Policy

Director, $60,662.50 — **George A. Keyworth II;** McLean, Va.; various positions leading to physics division leader, Los Alamos National Laboratory (1968-81); Nov. 30, 1939; Rep.; July 24.

Office of U.S. Trade Representative

U.S. trade representative, $69,630 — **William E. Brock III;** Lookout Mountain, Tenn.; chairman, Republican National Committee (1977-81); U.S. senator, Tenn. (1971-77); U.S. representative, 3rd Congressional District, Tenn. (1963-71); Nov. 23, 1930; Rep.; Jan. 21.

Deputy trade representative, $55,387.50 — **David R. MacDonald;** Winnetka, Ill.; partner, Baker and McKenzie (1962-74, 1977-81); member of policy board of economic affairs council, Republican National Committee (1979-81); under secretary, Navy Dept. (1976-77); Nov. 1, 1930; Rep.; June 1.

CABINET DEPARTMENTS

Department of Agriculture

Secretary, $69,630 — **John R. Block;** Springfield, Ill.; farmer; state agriculture director, Ill. (1977-81); Feb. 15, 1935; Rep.; Jan. 22.

Deputy secretary, $60,662.50 — **Richard E. Lyng;** Arlington, Va.; consultant on food and agriculture (1979-81); assistant secretary for marketing and consumer activities, Agriculture Dept. (1969-73); June 29, 1918; Rep.; Feb. 24.

Assistant secretary for marketing and transportation services, $52,750 — **C. W. McMillan;** Alexandria, Va.; executive vice president for Washington affairs, American National Cattlemen's Assn. (1970-81); Feb. 9, 1926; March 17.

Under secretary for international affairs and commodity programs, $55,387.50 — **Seeley Lodwick;** Wever, Iowa; co-director, farm and food division, Reagan-Bush Committee (1980); Iowa administrator, office of U.S. Sen. Roger W. Jepsen (1979-80); Oct. 19, 1920; Rep.; April 8.

Assistant secretary for economics, $52,750 — **William G. Lesher;** Burke, Va.; director of economics, policy analysis and budget, Agriculture Dept. (Jan. 27-April 8, 1981); economist, U.S. Senate Agriculture, Nutrition and Forestry Committee (1978-81); March 21, 1946; Rep.; April 8.

Under secretary for small community and rural development, $55,387.50 — **Frank W. Naylor Jr.;** Shingle Springs, Calif.; senior vice president, Calif. 11th farm credit district (1976-81); Feb. 7, 1939; Rep.; May 19.

Assistant secretary for food and consumer services, $52,750 — **Mary Claiborne Jarratt;** Alexandria, Va.; professional staff member, U.S. House Agriculture Committee (1975-81); executive assistant to U.S. Rep. Richard H. Poff (1967-72); Oct. 29, 1942; Rep.; May 19.

General counsel, $52,750 — **A. James Barnes;** Washington, D.C.; partner, Beveridge and Diamond (1975-81); assistant to deputy attorney general, Justice Dept. (1973); Aug. 30, 1942; Rep.; May 19.

Assistant secretary for natural resources and environment, $52,750 — **John B. Crowell;** Oswego, Ore.; general counsel, Louisiana-Pacific Corp. (1972-81); March 18, 1930; Rep.; May 20.

Inspector general, $52,750 — **John V. Graziano;** Annandale, Va.; assistant inspector general, Commerce Dept. (1979-81); special coordinator for grain elevator safety, Agriculture Dept. (1978-79); director, office of investigation, Agriculture Dept. (1974-79); July 3, 1927; Rep.; July 30.

Federal Grain Inspection Service

Administrator, $52,750 — **Kenneth A. Gilles;** Fargo, N.D.; various educational and administrative positions, Univ. of N.D. (1961-81); March 6, 1922; Rep.; June 4.

Department of Commerce

Secretary, $69,630 — **Malcolm Baldrige;** Woodbury, Conn.; chairman and chief executive officer, Scovill Inc. (1962-81); chairman, Conn. Bush for President Committee (1980); member, Conn. delegation to Republican National Convention (1968, 1972 and 1976); Oct. 4, 1922; Rep.; Jan. 22.

Deputy secretary, $60,662.50 — **Joseph F. Wright Jr.;** New York City; president, Citicorp Retail Services and Retail Consumer Services Inc. (1976-81); assistant secretary for administration, Agriculture Dept. (1973-76); Sept. 24, 1939; Rep.; April 8.

Assistant secretary for trade development, $52,750 — **William H. Morris Jr.;** Nashville, Tenn.; president, William Morris and Associates (1980-81); deputy state commissioner of economic and community development, Tenn. (1979-80); Jan. 5, 1929; Rep.; April 8.

Under secretary for international trade, $55,387.50 — **Lionel H. Olmer;** Rockville, Md.; director of international programs, Motorola Inc. (1977-81); member, President's Foreign Intelligence Advisory Board (1972-77); Nov. 11, 1934; Rep.; May 4.

Assistant secretary for administration, $52,750 — **Arlene Triplett;** Falls Church, Va.; controller and director of administrative services, Republican National Committee (1977-81); deputy controller, President Ford Committee (1976-77); controller, Citizens for Reagan (1975-76); Jan. 21, 1942; Rep.; May 4.

Assistant secretary for congressional affairs, $52,750 — **Paul A. Vander Myde;** Alexandria, Va.; minority staff director, U.S. House Science and Technology Committee (1977-81); deputy assistant secretary, Agriculture Dept. (1973-77); Feb. 9, 1937; Rep.; May 4.

Assistant secretary for international economic policy, $52,750 — **Raymond J. Waldmann;** Bethesda, Md.; of counsel, Shiff Hardin and Waite (1979-81); special counsel to President Ford (1975-76); deputy assistant secretary, State Dept. (1973-75); Nov. 28, 1938; Rep.; May 4.

General counsel, $52,750 — **Sherman E. Unger;** Cincinnati; lawyer (1972-81); general counsel, Housing and Urban Development Dept. (1969-70); Oct. 9, 1927; Rep.; May 4.

Assistant secretary for tourism, $52,750 — **Frederick M. Bush;** Houston; staff assistant, Reagan-Bush Committee (1980); national finance director, George Bush for President Committee (1979-80); finance director, Ill. Republican Party (1977-79); Feb. 6, 1949; Rep.; June 8.

Assistant secretary for communications and information, $52,750 — **Bernard J. Wunder Jr.;** Dumfries, Va.; associate minority counsel, U.S. House Committee on Energy and Commerce (1975-81); legislative assistant and then administrative assistant to U.S. Rep. James M. Collins (1969-70); Dec. 13, 1943; Rep.; June 10.

Assistant secretary for trade administration, $52,750 — **Lawrence J. Brady;** Bedford, N.H.; Republican primary candidate for U.S. Senate (1980); acting director and deputy director, office of export administration, Commerce Dept. (1974-80); senior staff member and special adviser on international economic policy,

White House (1971-74); April 22, 1939; Rep.; June 11.

Assistant secretary for economic affairs, $52,750 — **Robert G. Dederick;** Hinsdale, Ill.; senior vice president and chief economist, Northern Trust Co. (1970-81); member, economic advisory board, Commerce Dept. (1968-70 and 1975-76); Nov. 18, 1929; Rep.; July 31.

Assistant secretary, economic development administration, $52,750 — **Carlos C. Campbell;** Reston, Va.; management consultant (1976-81); July 19, 1937; Rep.; Nov. 4.

Under secretary for travel and tourism, $55,387.50 — **Peter McCoy;** Los Angeles; deputy assistant to the President, White House (1981); staff director to Nancy Reagan (1980-81); Oct. 25, 1942; Rep.; Dec. 16.

National Oceanic and Atmospheric Administration

Administrator, $55,387.50 — **John V. Byrne;** Corvallis, Ore.; various educational and administrative positions, Ore. State Univ. (1960-81); May 9, 1928; Rep.; June 10.

Director of National Oceanic Survey, $52,750 — **Herbert R. Lippold Jr.;** Darnestown, Md.; various positions with National Oceanic Survey (formerly Coast and Geodetic Survey) (1950-81); April 9, 1926; Ind.; July 31.

Deputy administrator, $52,750 — **Anthony J. Calio;** Bethesda, Md.; various positions leading to associate administrator for space and terrestrial applications, NASA (1963-81); Oct. 27, 1929; Rep.; Dec. 16.

Department of Defense

Secretary, $69,630 — **Caspar W. Weinberger;** Hillsborough, Calif.; general counsel, vice president and director, Bechtel Power Corp. (1975-81); secretary, Health, Education and Welfare Dept. (1973-75); counselor to President Nixon (1973); director, Office of Management and Budget (OMB) (1972-73); OMB deputy director (1970-72); chairman, Federal Trade Commission (1970); state finance director, Calif. (1968-70); Aug. 18, 1917; Rep.; Jan. 20.

Deputy secretary, $60,662.50 — **Frank C. Carlucci III;** Va.; deputy director, Central Intelligence Agency (1978-81); U.S. ambassador to Portugal (1975-78); under secretary, Health, Education and Welfare Dept. (1974-75); deputy director, Office of Management and Budget (1972-74); Oct. 18, 1930; Rep.; Feb. 3.

Under secretary for policy, $55,387.50 — **Fred C. Ikle;** Bethesda, Md.; senior foreign policy adviser, Reagan-Bush Committee (1980); president, Transat Energy Corp. (1977-81); director, U.S. Arms Control and Disarmament Agency (1973-77); Aug. 21, 1924; Rep.; March 27.

General counsel, $52,750 — **William H. Taft IV;** Lorton, Va.; attorney, Leva, Hawes, Symington, Martin and Oppenheimer (1977-81); general counsel, Health, Education and Welfare Dept. (1976-77); Sept. 13, 1945; Rep.; March 27.

Assistant secretary for manpower, reserve affairs and logistics, $52,750 — **Lawrence J. Korb;** Reston, Va.; director of defense policy studies, American Enterprise Institute (1980-81); adviser, Reagan-Bush Committee (1980); July 9, 1939; Rep.; April 27.

Assistant secretary for public affairs, $52,750 — **Henry E. Catto Jr.;** McLean, Va.; chairman, IBIS Corp. (1977-81); U.S. permanent representative to the European office of the United Nations (1976-77); U.S. chief of protocol (1974-76); national finance director, Citizens for Nixon (1968); Dec. 6, 1930; Rep.; May 4.

Assistant secretary for legislative affairs, $52,750 — **Russell A. Rourke;** Annapolis, Md.; administrative assistant to U.S. Rep. Harold S. Sawyer (1977-81); special assistant to President Ford (1976-77); unsuccessful Republican-Conservative candidate, 36th Congressional District, N.Y. (1974); Dec. 30, 1931; Rep.; May 4.

Under secretary for research and engineering, $55,387.50 — **Richard D. De Lauer;** Arlington, Va.; executive vice president, TRW Inc. (1970-81); Sept. 23, 1918; Rep.; May 6.

Assistant secretary for international security affairs, $52,750 — **Francis J. West;** Newport, R.I.; dean, Strategic Research Center, Naval War College (1976-81); May 2, 1940; Rep.; June 25.

Assistant secretary for international security planning, $52,750 — **Richard N. Perle;** Chevy Chase, Md.; consultant (1980-81); professional staff member, U.S. Senate Governmental Affairs Select Permanent Subcommittee on Investigations, and staff member, Subcommittee on Arms Control, U.S. Senate Armed Services Committee (1972-80); adviser to U.S. Sen. Henry M. Jackson (1972); Sept. 16, 1941; Aug. 3.

Air Force

Secretary, $60,662.50 — **Verne Orr;** Pomona, Calif.; adjunct professor, Univ. of Southern Calif. (1975-81); state finance director, Calif. (1970-75); Nov. 12, 1916; Rep.; Feb. 6.

Assistant secretary for manpower, reserve affairs and installations, $52,750 — **Tidal W. McCoy;** McLean, Va.; assistant for national security affairs to U.S. Sen. Jake Garn (1979-81); April 25, 1945; Rep.; June 4.

Assistant secretary for financial management, $52,750 — **Russell D. Hale;** Arlington, Va.; professional staff member, U.S. House Armed Services Committee (1978-81); professional staff member, U.S. House Budget Committee (1975-78); Aug. 8, 1944; Rep.; June 15.

Under secretary, $52,750 — **Edward C. Aldridge Jr.;** Vienna, Va.; vice president, System Planning Corp. (1977-81); director, planning and evaluation, Defense Dept. (1976-77); Aug. 18, 1938; July 30.

Assistant secretary for research, development and logistics, $52,750 — **Alton G. Keel Jr.;** Washington, D.C.; staff member and then senior professional staff member, U.S. Senate Armed Services Committee (1979-81); defense and technical adviser to U.S. Sen. Howard W. Cannon (1977-79); Sept. 8, 1943; July 30.

Army

Secretary, $60,662,50 — **John O. Marsh Jr.;** Strasburg, Va.; partner, Mays, Valentine, Davenport & Moore (1977-81); counselor to President Ford (1974-77); assistant secretary for legislative affairs, Defense Dept. (1973-74); U.S. representative, 7th Congressional District, Va. (1962-70); Aug. 7, 1926; Dem.; Jan. 29.

Assistant secretary for installations, logistics and financial management, $52,750 — **Joel E. Bonner Jr.;** Alexandria, Va.; majority staff director, U.S. Senate Defense Appropriations Subcommittee (1981); professional staff member, U.S. Senate Appropriations Committee (1972-81); March 23, 1922; Rep.; June 4.

Assistant secretary for civil works, $52,750 — **William R. Gianelli;** Monterey, Calif.; consulting civil engineer (1973-81); member, National Commission on Water Quality (1973-76); Feb. 19, 1919; Rep.; June 4.

Assistant secretary for manpower and reserve affairs, $52,750 — **Harry N. Walters;** Hannawa Falls, N.Y.; president, Potsdam Paper Corp. (1977-81); June 4, 1936; Rep.; June 4.

Under secretary, $52,750 — **James R. Ambrose;** Tryon, N.C.; vice president for technical affairs, Ford Aerospace & Communications Corp. (1955-79); Aug. 16, 1922; Oct. 7.

Assistant secretary for research, development and acquisition, $52,750 — **Jay R. Sculley;** Arlington, Va.; various positions leading to head, civil engineering dept., Virginia Military Institute (1969-74 and 1975-81); Aug. 6, 1940; Rep.; Oct. 7.

Navy

Secretary, $60,662.50 — **John F. Lehman Jr.;** Glenside, Pa.; president, Abingdon Corp. (1977-81); chairman, defense advisory committee, Republican National Committee (1977-80); deputy director, U.S. Arms Control and Disarmament Agency (1975-77); Sept. 14, 1942; Rep.; Jan. 29.

Assistant secretary for shipbuilding and logistics, $52,750 — **George A. Sawyer;** Red Bank, N.J.; president, John J. McMullen Associates Inc. (1976-81); April 20, 1931; Rep.; June 15.

Under secretary, $52,750 — **James F. Goodrich;** Portland, Maine; various positions leading to president and chairman of the board, Bath Iron Works (1964-78); Jan. 24, 1913; Rep.; Sept. 25.

Assistant secretary, $52,750 — **John S. Herrington;** Walnut

Creek, Calif.; deputy assistant to the president for presidential personnel (1981); president, Quail Hill Ranch Co. (1968-81); partner, Herrington, Herrington & Herrington (1967-81); May 31, 1939; Rep.; Sept. 25.

Assistant secretary for research, engineering and systems, $52,750 — **Melvyn R. Paisley;** McLean, Va.; various management and engineering positions leading to vice president, Boeing International (1954-81); Oct. 9, 1924; Rep.; Nov. 23.

Department of Education

Secretary, $69,630 — **T. H. Bell;** Salt Lake City; state commissioner of higher education and chief executive officer of state board of regents, Utah (1976-81); U.S. commissioner of education (1974-76); Nov. 11, 1921; Rep.; Jan. 22.

Under secretary, $55,387.50 — **William C. Clohan Jr.;** Washington, D.C.; minority education counsel, U.S. House Education and Labor Committee (1978-81); chief legislative assistant to U.S. Rep. John Buchanan (1977-78); July 29, 1948; Rep.; June 19.

Assistant secretary for elementary and secondary education, $52,750 — **Vincent E. Reed;** Washington, D.C.; acting superintendent and then superintendent of public schools, Washington, D.C. (1975-81); March 1, 1928; Rep.; June 19.

Assistant secretary for vocational and adult education, $52,750 — **Robert M. Worthington;** Salt Lake City; associate commissioner, Utah State Board of Regents (1979-81); associate U.S. commissioner of education, Health, Education and Welfare Dept. (1971-73); May 31, 1922; Rep.; June 19.

Assistant secretary for civil rights, $52,750 — **Clarence Thomas;** Bethesda, Md.; legislative assistant to U.S. Sen. John C. Danforth (1979-81); June 23, 1948; Rep.; June 25.

Inspector general, $52,750 — **James B. Thomas Jr.;** McLean, Va.; inspector general, Education Dept. (1980-81); director, Interstate Commerce Commission (1977-80); inspector general, Housing and Urban Development Dept. (1975-77); March 13, 1935; July 17.

Assistant secretary for legislation and public affairs, $52,750 — **Anne Graham;** McLean, Va.; deputy special assistant for communication to President Reagan (1981); assistant press secretary, Reagan-Bush Committee (1980); press secretary to U.S. Sen. Harrison "Jack" Schmitt (1976-79); Dec. 28, 1949; Rep.; July 28.

Assistant secretary for postsecondary education, $52,750 — **Thomas P. Melady;** Fairfield, Conn.; president, Sacred Heart Univ. (1976-81); U.S. ambassador to Uganda (1972-73); U.S. ambassador to Burundi (1969-72); March 4, 1927; Rep.; July 28.

Assistant secretary for educational research and improvement, $52,750 — **Donald J. Senese;** Alexandria, Va.; senior research associate, U.S. House Republican Study Committee (1976-81); chief legislative assistant to U.S. Rep. Bill Archer (1973-76); April 6, 1942; Rep.; July 28.

General counsel, $52,750 — **Daniel Oliver;** Greenwich, Conn.; president, Rincon Communications Corp. (1980-81); April 10, 1939; July 31.

Assistant secretary for special education and rehabilitative services, $52,750 — **Jean Tufts;** Exeter, N.H.; president, National School Boards Assn. (1980-81); Oct. 7, 1927; Rep.; Oct. 26.

Department of Energy

Secretary, $69,630 — **James B. Edwards;** Charleston, S.C.; oral surgeon; governor, S.C. (1975-79); June 24, 1927; Rep.; Jan. 22.

Assistant secretary for management and administration, $52,750 — **William S. Heffelfinger;** McLean, Va.; director of administration, Energy Dept. (1977-81); Jan. 31, 1925; Rep.; May 13.

Assistant secretary for congressional, intergovernmental and public affairs, $52,750 — **Robert C. Odle Jr.;** Alexandria, Va.; Washington corporate affairs representative, International Paper Co. (1976-81); deputy assistant secretary, Housing and Urban Development Dept. (1973-76); director of administration, Committee to Re-elect the President (1971-73); Feb. 15, 1944; Rep.; May 13.

Deputy secretary, $60,662.50 — **Willard K. Davis;** San Raphael, Calif; vice president, Bechtel Power Corp. (1958-81); July

26, 1918; Rep.; May 14.

Assistant secretary for conservation and renewable energy, $52,750 — **Joseph J. Tribble;** Savannah, Ga.; various positions leading to energy coordinator, Union Camp Corp. (1946-81); chairman, Ga. Reagan for President Campaign (1980); state senator, Ga. (1963-66); member, Ga. delegation to Republican National Convention (1968, 1976 and 1980); Aug. 30, 1920; Rep.; May 14.

General counsel, $52,750 — **R. Tenney Johnson;** Bethesda, Md.; partner, Sullivan & Beauregard (1978-81); member, Civil Aeronautics Board (1976-77); March 24, 1930; Rep.; June 2.

Assistant secretary for defense programs, $52,750 — **Herman E. Roser;** Albuquerque, N.M.; deputy manager and then manager of operations-Albuquerque, Energy Dept. (1972-81); Aug. 5, 1922; Rep.; June 15.

Assistant secretary for nuclear energy, $52,750 — **Shelby T. Brewer;** Gaithersburg, Md.; director, office of program planning and evaluation, Energy Dept. (1977-81); Feb. 19, 1937; Rep.; June 19.

Assistant secretary for fossil energy, $52,750 — **Jan W. Mares;** New Canaan, Conn.; various positions leading to vice president and general manager, Union Carbide Corp. (1963-81); Dec. 12, 1936; Rep.; July 27.

Under secretary, $55,387.50 — **Guy W. Fiske;** McLean, Va.; executive vice president, General Dynamics Corp. (1977-81); Sept. 28, 1924; Rep.; Sept. 18.

Assistant secretary, $52,750 — **William A. Vaughan;** Oakton, Va.; director of energy management, General Motors Corp. (1976-81); April 19, 1935; Rep.; Sept. 18.

Inspector general, $52,750 — **James R. Richards;** Arlington, Va.; general counsel and vice president, National Legal Center for the Public Interest (1980-81); director, office of hearings and appeals, Interior Dept. (1973-77); legislative assistant to U.S. Sen. Peter H. Dominick (1963-65); Nov. 21, 1933; Rep.; Sept. 21.

Assistant secretary for international affairs, $52,750 — **Henry E. Thomas IV;** Alexandria, Va.; senior policy officer and then director, standards and regulations division, Environmental Protection Agency (1973-81); director, cost of living council, White House (1971-73); Oct. 15, 1937; Rep.; Oct. 1.

Economic Regulatory Administration

Administrator, $52,750 — **Rayburn D. Hanzlik;** Pasadena, Calif.; attorney, Darling, Roe & Gute (1979-80); associate director, White House office of intergovernmental relations (1976-77); June 7, 1938; Rep.; Sept. 18.

Energy Information Administration

Administrator, $52,750 — **J. Erich Evered;** Arlington, Va.; petroleum engineer and geologist, CER Corp. (1978-81); energy adviser to U.S. Sen. Dewey F. Bartlett (1976-78); Aug. 27, 1953, Rep.; June 19.

Federal Energy Regulatory Commission

Chairman and member for term expiring Oct. 20, 1983, $55,387.50 — **Charles M. Butler III;** Bethesda, Md.; administrative assistant to U.S. Sen. John Tower (1979-81); Feb. 6, 1943; Rep.; June 4.

Member for term expiring Oct. 20, 1984, $52,750 — **Georgianna Sheldon;** Arlington, Va.; member, Federal Emergency Regulatory Commission (1977-81); acting chairman and vice chairman, U.S. Civil Service Commission (1976-77); Dec. 2, 1923; Rep.; June 4.

Member for term expiring Oct. 20, 1984, $52,750 — **Anthony G. Sousa;** Honolulu; vice president and general counsel, Hawaiian Telephone Co. (1973-81); various positions leading to administrative law judge, Calif. Public Utilities Commission (1968-73); Aug. 8, 1927; Rep.; July 27.

Office of Alcohol Fuels

Director, $52,750 — **James G. Sterns;** Reno, Nev.; director,

Calif. Conservation Dept. (1975-81); secretary, Calif. Agriculture and Services Agency, and member, Gov. Ronald Reagan's Cabinet (1972-75); Jan. 29, 1922; Rep.; July 24.

Office of Energy Research

Director, $52,750 — **Alvin W. Trivelpiece;** La Jolla, Calif.; physicist; corporate vice president, Science Applications Inc. (1978-81); assistant director for research, Atomic Energy Commission (1973-75); March 15, 1931; Rep.; July 27.

Department of Health and Human Services

Secretary, $69,630 — **Richard S. Schweiker;** Worcester, Pa.; U.S. senator, Pa. (1969-81); U.S. representative, 13th Congressional District, Pa. (1961-69); June 1, 1926; Rep.; Jan. 21.

Under secretary, $55,387.50 — **David B. Swoap;** Fairfax, Va.; legislative director, office of U.S. Sen. William L. Armstrong (1979-81); professional staff member, U.S. Senate Finance Committee (1976-79); Aug. 12, 1937; Rep.; March 17.

Assistant secretary for health, $52,750 — **Edward N. Brandt Jr.;** Austin, Texas; vice chancellor for health affairs, Univ. of Texas (1977-81); July 3, 1933; Rep.; May 4.

Assistant secretary for human development services, $52,750 — **Dorcas R. Hardy;** Washington, D.C.; associate director, Center for Health Services Research, Univ. of Southern Calif. (1974-81); state assistant director for health, Calif. (1973-74); July 18, 1946; Rep.; May 4.

Assistant secretary for public affairs, $52,750 — **Pamela Needham Bailey;** Annandale, Va.; member of Reagan-Bush Campaign advisory task force on welfare reform (1981); director of government relations, American Hospital Supply Corp. (1979-81); various staff positions, White House (1970-75); May 24, 1948; Rep.; June 1.

Inspector general, $52,750 — **Richard P. Kusserow;** Aurora, Ill.; special agent, FBI (1969-81); intelligence officer, CIA (1967-68); Dec. 9, 1940; Rep.; June 1.

Assistant secretary for planning and evaluation, $52,750 — **Robert J. Rubin;** Lexington, Mass.; physician; consultant, U.S. Senate Labor and Human Resources Committee (1979-81); Feb. 7, 1946; Rep.; June 2.

Assistant secretary for legislation, $52,750 — **Thomas R. Donnelly Jr.;** Springfield, Va.; partner, Lewis C. Kramp and Associates (1974-81); May 23, 1939; Rep.; July 30.

General counsel, $52,750 — **Juan A. del Real;** Potomac, Md.; assistant general counsel, Health and Human Services Dept. (1980-81); Nov. 4, 1939; July 30.

Alcohol, Drug Abuse, and Mental Health Administration

Administrator, $52,750 — **William E. Mayer;** Coronado, Calif.; medical director, San Diego County Health Services Dept. (1980-81); director, Calif. Health Dept. (1973-75); Sept. 24, 1923; Rep.; July 28.

Social Security Administration

Commissioner, $52,750 — **John A. Svahn;** Severna Park, Md.; private consultant for public policy management (1976-81); administrator, social and rehabilitation service, Health, Education and Welfare Dept. (1975-76); May 13, 1943; Rep.; May 4.

Department of Housing and Urban Development

Secretary, $69,630 — **Samuel R. Pierce Jr.;** Long Island, N.Y.; senior partner, Battle, Fowler, Jaffin, Pierce & Kheel (1961-81); general counsel, Treasury Dept. (1970-73); Sept. 8, 1922; Rep.; Jan. 22.

Under secretary, $55,387.50 — **Donald I. Hovde;** Madison, Wis.; national senior vice president, Partners Real Estate Inc. (1980-81); president, National Assn. of Realtors (1979); March 6, 1931; Rep.; March 23.

Assistant secretary for housing and federal housing commis-sioner, $52,750 — **Philip D. Winn;** Englewood, Colo.; chairman, Philip D. Winn and Associates (1976-81); chairman, Colo. Republican Party (1979-81); Feb. 1, 1925; Rep.; April 2.

Assistant secretary for policy development and research, $52,750 — **Emanuel S. Savas;** New York City; professor and director, Center for Government Studies, Columbia Univ. (1973-81); first deputy city administrator, New York (1970-72); June 8, 1931; Rep.; April 2.

Assistant secretary for community planning and development, $52,750 — **Stephen J. Bollinger;** Columbus, Ohio; executive director, Columbus Metropolitan Housing Authority (1977-81); legislative assistant to U.S. Rep. Gene Snyder (1970-71); April 11, 1948; Rep.; June 11.

Assistant secretary for legislation, $52,750 — **Stephen May;** Rochester, N.Y.; lawyer, Branch, Turner and Wise (1974-81); commissioner and chairman, New York Board of Elections (1975-79); mayor of Rochester (1970-73); executive assistant to U.S. Rep. and then U.S. Sen. Kenneth B. Keating (1955-64); July 30, 1931; Rep.; June 11.

Assistant secretary for fair housing and equal opportunity, $52,750 — **Antonio Monroig;** Alexandria, Va.; administrator, Puerto Rico Municipal Services Administration (1977-81); special assistant to mayor of San Juan (1977); Feb. 7, 1944; Rep.; June 11.

Assistant secretary for administration, $52,750 — **Judith L. Tardy;** Arlington, Va.; member of transition team for Export-Import Bank (1980); director, administrative programs and services, Labor Dept. (1979-80); director, executive secretary, Labor Dept. (1976-79); Feb. 7, 1944; Rep.; June 11.

General counsel, $52,750 — **John J. Knapp;** Garden City, N.Y.; chief legal officer, National Kinney Corp. (1971-81); Sept. 15, 1934; Rep.; June 22.

Inspector general, $52,750 — **Charles L. Dempsey;** Arlington, Va.; inspector general, Housing and Urban Development Dept. (1977-81); June 7, 1928; July 31.

Government National Mortgage Association

President, $52,750 — **Robert W. Karpe;** Bakersfield, Calif.; president and then chairman of the board, Karpe Real Estate Center (1959-81); commissioner, Calif. Real Estate Dept. (1971-75); Nov. 3, 1930; Rep.; July 24.

New Community Development Corporation

General manager, $52,750 — **Warren T. Lindquist;** New York City; chairman, SCETAM Inc. (1978-81); June 18, 1919; Rep.; July 13.

Department of the Interior

Secretary, $69,630 — **James G. Watt;** Englewood, Colo.; president and chief legal officer, Mountain States Legal Foundation (1977-81); member, Federal Power Commission (1975-77); Jan. 31, 1938; Rep.; Jan. 22.

Under secretary, $55,387.50 — **Donald P. Hodel;** Lake Oswego, Ore.; natural resource and energy consultant (1977-81); deputy administrator and then administrator, Bonneville Power Administration (1969-77); May 23, 1935; Rep; Feb. 5.

Assistant secretary for land and water resources, $52,750 — **Garrey E. Carruthers;** Las Cruces, N.M.; professor, N.M. State Univ. (1979-81); chairman, N.M. Republican Party (1977-79); special assistant to secretary, Agriculture Dept. (1974-75); Aug. 29, 1939; Rep.; May 6.

Solicitor, $52,750 — **William H. Coldiron;** Butte, Mont.; various positions leading to director and vice chairman, Montana Power Co. (1953-81); Aug. 12, 1916; Rep.; May 6.

Assistant secretary for fish and wildlife and parks, $52,750 — **G. Ray Arnett;** Stockton, Calif.; executive vice president, International Beefalo Assn. (1980-81); director, state game and fish dept., Calif. (1969-75); June 14, 1924; Rep.; May 13.

Assistant secretary for Indian affairs, $52,750 — **Kenneth L. Smith;** Warm Springs, Ore.; acting general manager and then general manager, Warm Springs Confederated Tribe (1969-81);

member, state board of education, Ore. (1973-79); March 30, 1935; Rep.; May 13.

Assistant secretary for energy and minerals, $52,750 — **Daniel N. Miller Jr.**; Laramie, Wyo.; state geologist and executive director, Geological Survey of Wyo. (1969-81); Aug. 22, 1924; Rep.; June 19.

Assistant secretary for policy, budget and administration, $52,750 — **J. Robinson West**; Unionville, Pa.; member, presidential personnel transition staff (1981); vice president, Blyth, Eastman, Dillon and Co. (1977-80); deputy assistant secretary, Defense Dept. (1976-77); Sept. 16, 1946; Rep.; July 31.

Assistant secretary for territorial and international affairs, $52,750 — **Pedro A. Sanjuan**; Washington, D.C.; resident fellow and director, Hemispheric Center, American Enterprise Institute (1979-81); policy coordinator of transition team for State Dept. (1981); public affairs adviser, U.S. Arms Control and Disarmament Agency (1975-78); Aug. 10, 1930; Rep.; Dec. 3.

Department of Justice

Attorney general, $69,630 — **William French Smith**; Los Angeles; partner, Gibson, Dunn & Crutcher (1946-81); member, Calif. delegation to the Republican National Convention (1968, 1972 and 1976); member, board of regents, Univ. of Calif. (1968-81); Aug. 26, 1917; Rep.; Jan. 22.

Deputy attorney general, $60,662.50 — **Edward C. Schmults**; Greenwich, Conn.; partner, White & Case (1977-81); deputy counsel to President Ford (1975-77); Feb. 6, 1931; Rep.; Feb. 6.

Assistant attorney general, antitrust division, $52,750 — **William F. Baxter**; Atherton, Calif.; law professor, Stanford Univ. (1960-81); July 13, 1929; Rep.; March 26.

Assistant attorney general, land and resources division, $52,750 — **Carol E. Dinkins**; Houston; partner, Vinson and Elkins (1973-81); Nov. 9, 1945; Rep.; April 2.

Assistant attorney general, criminal division, $52,750 — **D. Lowell Jensen**; Castro Valley, Calif.; state district attorney, Oakland, Calif. (1969-81); June 3, 1928; Rep.; April 2.

Assistant attorney general, office of legal counsel, $52,750 — **Theodore Bevry Olson**; Palos Verdes Estates, Calif.; partner, Gibson, Dunn and Crutcher (1965-81); member, Calif. delegation to Republican National Convention (1976 and 1980); Sept. 11, 1940; Rep.; April 2.

Associate attorney general, $55,387.50 — **Rudolph W. Giuliani**; New York City; lawyer, Patterson, Belknap, Webb and Tyler (1977-81); associate deputy attorney general, Justice Dept. (1975-77); May 28, 1944; Rep.; April 27.

Assistant attorney general, $52,750 — **Jonathan C. Rose**; Alexandria, Va.; lawyer, Jones, Day, Reavis and Pogue (1978-81); special assistant to the attorney general, Justice Dept. (1977-78); June 8, 1941; Rep.; May 19.

Assistant attorney general, $52,750 — **Robert A. McConnell**; Tempe, Ariz.; partner, Steiger, Helm, Kyle and McConnell (1978-81); legislative assistant to U.S. Rep. John J. Rhodes (1970-75); Aug. 29, 1944; Rep.; June 10.

Assistant attorney general for civil rights, $52,750 — **William B. Reynolds**; Potomac, Md.; partner, Shaw, Pittman, Potts and Trowbridge (1973-81); assistant to solicitor general, Justice Dept. (1970-73); June 21, 1942; Rep.; July 24.

Solicitor general, $55,387.50 — **Rex E. Lee**; McLean, Va.; dean, Brigham Young Univ. (1977-81); assistant attorney general, Justice Dept. (1975-77); Feb. 27, 1935; Rep.; July 31.

Assistant attorney general, civil division, $52,750 — **J. Paul McGrath**; Potomac, Md.; attorney, then partner, Dewey, Ballantine, Bushby, Palmer & Wood (1965-81); Sept. 9, 1940; Rep.; Sept. 25.

Assistant attorney general, tax division, $52,750 — **Glenn L. Archer**; Falls Church, Va.; partner, Hamel, Park, McCabe & Saunders (1956-81); March 21, 1929; Rep.; Dec. 16.

Department of Labor

Secretary, $69,630 — **Raymond J. Donovan**; Short Hills,

N.J.; vice president and then executive vice president, Schiavone Construction Co. (1969-81); Aug. 31, 1930; Rep.; Feb. 3.

Assistant secretary for employment and training, $52,750 — **Albert Angrisani**; Bernardsville, N.J.; vice president, Chase Manhattan Bank (1972-81); Aug. 26, 1949; Rep.; March 12.

Solicitor, $52,750 — **T. Timothy Ryan Jr.**; Arlington, Va.; lawyer, Pierson, Ball & Dowd (1978-81); deputy general counsel, President Ford Committee (1975-76); June 13, 1945; Rep.; March 12.

Assistant secretary for occupational safety and health, $52,750 — **Thorne G. Auchter**; Jacksonville, Fla.; executive vice president, Auchter Co. (1975-81); March 6, 1945; Rep.; March 17.

Assistant secretary for labor-management relations, $52,750 — **Donald L. Dotson**; Pittsburgh; chief labor counsel, Wheeling-Pittsburgh Steel Corp. (1976-81); Oct. 8, 1938; Rep.; July 8.

Inspector general, $52,750 — **Thomas F. McBride**; Washington, D.C.; inspector general, Agriculture Dept. (1977-81); director, Civil Aeronautics Board (1975-77); associate special prosecutor, Watergate Task Force (1973-75); deputy chief counsel, U.S. House Select Committee on Crime (1969-70); Feb. 8, 1929; July 17.

Under secretary, $55,387.50 — **Malcolm R. Lovell Jr.**; Washington, D.C.; president, Rubber Manufacturers Assn. (1973-81); assistant secretary, Labor Dept. (1970-73); Jan. 1, 1921; Rep.; Sept. 29.

Assistant secretary for policy evaluation and research, $52,750 — **John F. Cogan**; McLean, Va.; senior research fellow, Hoover Institution (1975-80); April 6, 1947; Dem.; Oct. 26.

Assistant secretary for mine safety and health, $52,750 — **Ford B. Ford**; Woodbridge, Va.; vice president, California Institute for Industrial and Governmental Relations (1978-81); chairman, state occupational safety and health appeals board, Calif. (1973-78); Nov. 19, 1922; Dem.; Oct. 26.

Assistant secretary for veterans' employment, $52,750 — **William C. Plowden Jr.**; Alexandria, Va.; director, veterans employment and services, S.C. (1976-81); July 15, 1918; Rep.; Dec. 9.

Department of State

Secretary, $69,630 — **Alexander M. Haig Jr.**; Hartford, Conn.; president and chief operating officer, United Technologies Corp. (1979-81); commander in chief, U.S. European Command (1974-78); chief of staff for President Nixon (1973-74); Dec. 2, 1924; Rep.; Jan. 21.

Deputy secretary, $60,662.50 — **William P. Clark**; Paso Robles, Calif.; associate justice, state supreme court, Calif. (1973-81); chief of staff for Calif. Gov. Ronald Reagan (1967-69); Oct. 23, 1931; Rep.; Feb. 24.

Under secretary for management, $55,387.50 — **Richard T. Kennedy**; Washington, D.C.; member, Nuclear Regulatory Commission (1975-80); Dec. 24, 1919; Rep.; Feb. 26.

Under secretary for political affairs, $55,387.50 — **Walter J. Stoessel Jr.**; Washington, D.C.; U.S. ambassador to the Federal Republic of Germany (1976-81); U.S. ambassador to the Soviet Union (1974-76); Jan. 24, 1920; Rep.; Feb. 26.

Under secretary for coordination of security assistance programs, $55,387.50 — **James L. Buckley**; Norwich, Conn.; business consultant (1977-81); U.S. senator, N.Y. (1971-77); March 9, 1923; Rep.; Feb. 26.

Assistant secretary for congressional relations, $52,750 — **Richard Fairbanks**; Washington, D.C.; partner, Beveridge, Fairbanks and Diamond (1974-81); associate director, domestic council for President Nixon (1971-74); Feb. 10, 1941; Rep.; Feb. 26.

Counselor, $52,750 — **Robert C. McFarlane**; Bethesda, Md.; professional staff, U.S. Senate Armed Services Committee (1979-81); special assistant for national security affairs for President Ford (1976-77); July 12, 1937; Rep.; Feb. 26.

Assistant secretary for international organizations, $52,570 — **Elliott Abrams**; Washington, D.C.; attorney, Verner, Lupert, Bernhard and McPherson (1979-81); special counsel to U.S. Sen. Daniel Patrick Moynihan (1977-79); special counsel to U.S. Sen. Henry M. Jackson (1975-76); Jan. 24, 1948; May 5.

Assistant secretary for economic and business affairs, $52,750 — **Robert D. Hormats**; Chevy Chase, Md.; deputy U.S. trade

representative (1979-81); deputy assistant secretary, State Dept. (1977-79); senior staff member, National Security Council (1974-77); April 13, 1943; Rep.; May 5.

Assistant secretary for Near Eastern and South Asian affairs, $52,750 — **Nicholas A. Veliotes;** San Mateo, Calif.; U.S. ambassador to Jordan (1978-81); deputy assistant secretary, State Dept. (1977-78); Oct. 28, 1928; Rep.; May 7.

Assistant secretary for European affairs, $52,750 — **Lawrence S. Eagleburger;** Daytona Beach, Fla.; U.S. ambassador to Yugoslavia (1977-81); deputy under secretary, State Dept. (1975-77); executive assistant to secretary, State Dept. (1973-75); Aug. 1, 1930; Rep.; May 8.

Assistant secretary for East Asian and Pacific affairs, $52,750 — **John H. Holdridge;** Bethesda, Md.; national intelligence officer, Central Intelligence Agency (1978-81); U.S. ambassador to Republic of Singapore (1975-78); Aug. 24, 1924; Rep.; May 19.

Assistant secretary for oceans and international environmental and scientific affairs, $52,750 — **James L. Malone;** McLean, Va.; lawyer, Doub and Muntzing (1978-81); U.S. ambassador and representative to Conference of the Committee on Disarmament (1976-77); Dec. 22, 1931; Rep.; May 21.

Assistant secretary for African affairs, $52,750 — **Chester Crocker;** Washington, D.C.; associate professor, Georgetown Univ. (1977-81); director, African Studies Program, Center for Strategic and International Studies, Georgetown Univ. (1976-81); Oct. 29, 1941; Rep.; June 9.

Under secretary for economic affairs, $55,387.50 — **Myer Rashish;** Washington, D.C.; private economic consultant (1963-81); chairman, Advisory Committee for Trade Negotiations (1980); consultant, Joint Economic Committee (1967-71); assistant to the president (1961-63); Nov. 10, 1924; Rep.; June 11.

Assistant secretary for inter-American affairs, $52,750 — **Thomas O. Enders;** Hartford, Conn.; U.S. ambassador and representative to the European Communities (1979-81); U.S. ambassador to Canada (1976-79); Nov. 28, 1931; Rep.; June 19.

Inspector general, $52,750 — **Robert L. Brown;** Arlington, Va.; minister-counselor and political adviser to Supreme Allied Commander-Europe (1975-81); foreign service officer, State Dept. (1945-81); July 21, 1920; June 22.

Assistant secretary for public affairs, $52,750 — **Dean E. Fischer;** McLean, Va.; correspondent and then news editor, *Time* magazine (1964-81); Oct. 27, 1936; July 24.

Legal adviser, $52,750 — **Davis R. Robinson;** Washington, D.C.; partner, Leva, Hawes, Symington, Martin and Oppenheimer (1971-81); U.S. foreign service officer (1961-69); July 11, 1940; Rep.; July 24.

Assistant secretary for international narcotics matters, $52,750 — **Dominick L. Di Carlo;** Brooklyn, N.Y.; attorney (1954-81); member, N.Y. state assembly (1964-81); March 11, 1928; Rep.; Sept. 16.

Assistant secretary for human rights and humanitarian affairs, $52,750 — **Elliott Abrams;** Washington, D.C.; assistant secretary for international organizations, State Dept. (1981); attorney, Verner, Liipfert, Bernhard and McPherson (1979-81); special counsel to U.S. Sen. Daniel Patrick Moynihan (1977-79); special counsel to U.S. Sen. Henry M. Jackson (1975-76); Jan. 24, 1948; Nov. 20.

Agency for International Development

Administrator, $60,662.50 — **M. Peter McPherson;** Chevy Chase, Md.; partner, Vorys, Sater, Seymour and Pease (1977-81); special assistant to President Ford (1975-77); Oct. 27, 1940; Rep.; Feb. 26.

Ambassadors

United Nations, U.S. representative to, $60,662.50 — **Jeane J. Kirkpatrick;** Bethesda, Md.; professor, Georgetown Univ. (1967-81); Nov. 19, 1926; Dem.; Jan. 29.

United Nations, alternate representative for special political affairs, $60,662.50 — **Charles M. Lichenstein;** Washington, D.C.; independent consultant (1979-81); special assistant to Presi-

dent Nixon (1974); free-lance writer for Republican National Committee (1963-65); Sept. 20, 1926; Rep.; March 27.

Great Britain and Northern Ireland, $60,662.50 — **John J. Louis Jr.;** Winnetka, Ill.; chairman, Combined Communications Corp. (1968-81); June 10, 1925; Rep.; May 5.

Mexico, $60,662.50 — **John A. Gavin;** Los Angeles; actor; president, Gamma Services Corp. (1968-81); April 8, 1931; Rep.; May 5.

Australia and the Republic of Nauru, $55,387.50 — **Robert D. Nesen;** Thousand Oaks, Calif.; chairman, Nesen Leasing Corp. (1971-72, 1974-81); chairman, R. D. Nesen Oldsmobile-Cadillac Inc. (1948-72, 1974-81); assistant secretary, Navy Dept. (1972-74); Jan. 22, 1918; Rep.; May 19.

Saudi Arabia, $60,662.50 — **Robert G. Neumann;** Culver City, Calif.; senior associate and then vice chairman, Center for Strategic and International Studies, Georgetown Univ. (1976-81); U.S. ambassador to Morocco (1973-76); Jan. 2, 1916; Rep.; May 19.

Organization of American States, $55,387.50 — **J. William Middendorf II;** McLean, Va.; partner, Middendorf, Colgate and Co. (1962-81); secretary of the Navy (1974-76); U.S. ambassador to the Netherlands (1969-74); Sept. 22, 1924, Rep.; June 11.

Austria, $52,750 — **Theodore E. Cummings;** Beverly Hills, Calif.; philanthropist; member, President's Committee on the Health Services Industry, Cost of Living Council (1971); Dec. 25, 1907; Rep.; June 19.

Belgium, $52,750 — **Charles H. Price II;** Kansas City, Mo.; president, Price Candy Co. (1955-81); April 1, 1931; Rep.; June 19.

Italy, $60,662.50 — **Maxwell M. Rabb;** New York City; senior partner, Stroock, Stroock and Lavan (1958-81); secretary of the Cabinet and associate counsel to the president (1953); Sept. 28, 1910; Rep.; June 19.

At-large for cultural affairs, $60,662.50 — **Daniel J. Terra;** Kenilworth, Ill.; chairman and chief executive officer, Lawter Chemicals Inc. (1964-81); June 9, 1911; Rep.; June 22.

Federal Republic of Germany, $60,662.50 — **Arthur F. Burns;** Washington, D.C.; scholar-in-residence, American Enterprise Institute (1978-81); chairman, Federal Reserve System (1970-78); counselor to President Nixon (1969-70); chairman, President's Council of Economic Advisers (1953-56); April 27, 1904; Rep.; June 25.

United Nations (economic and social council), $52,750 — **Jose S. Sorzano;** Arlington, Va.; associate professor, Georgetown Univ. (1969-76 and 1979-81); director of the Peace Corps in Bogota, Colombia (1976-79); Nov. 9, 1940; June 25.

Canada, $60,662.50 — **Paul H. Robinson Jr.;** Lake Bluff, Ill.; president, Robinson Inc. (1960-81); June 22, 1930; Rep.; July 10.

At large, $60,662.50 — **Vernon A. Walters;** Palm Beach, Fla.; senior adviser to the secretary, State Dept. (1981); consultant, lecturer and author (1976-81); deputy director, CIA (1972-76); Jan. 3, 1917; Rep.; July 17.

Korea, $60,662.50 — **Richard L. Walker;** Columbia, S.C.; professor, Univ. of S.C. (1957-81); April 13, 1922; Rep.; July 17.

Liberia, $55,387.50 — **William L. Swing;** Lexington, N.C.; U.S. ambassador, People's Republic of the Congo (1979-81); Sept. 11, 1934; July 17.

New Zealand, $52,750 — **H. Monroe Browne;** San Francisco; president, Institute for Contemporary Studies (1975-81); chairman, Reagan Small Business Task Force (1981); May 9, 1917, Rep.; July 17.

Organization for Economic Cooperation and Development, U.S. representative, $55,387.50 — **Abraham Katz;** Hollywood, Fla.; deputy assistant secretary and then assistant secretary, Commerce Dept. (1978-81); Dec. 4, 1926; July 29.

Turkey, $55,387.50 — **Robert Strausz-Hupé;** Newtown Square, Pa.; diplomat in residence and consultant, Foreign Policy Research Institute, Univ. of Pa. (1977-81); U.S. permanent representative to NATO (1976-77); U.S. ambassador to Sweden (1974-76); U.S. ambassador to Belgium (1972-74); U.S. ambassador to Sri Lanka and Republic of Maldives (1970-72); March 23, 1903; Rep.; July 24.

United Nations, U.S. deputy representative, $55,387.50 — **Kenneth L. Adelman;** Arlington, Va.; senior political scientist, SRI International (1977-81); assistant to the secretary, Defense

Dept. (1976-77); June 9, 1946; July 29.

Asian Development Bank, U.S. director, $55,387.50 — **John A. Bohn Jr.;** Belvedere, Calif.; various positions leading to vice president, Wells Fargo International Banking Group (1972-81); Oct. 31, 1937; Sept. 25.

Morocco, $52,750 — **Joseph V. Reed Jr.;** Greenwich, Conn.; various positions leading to vice president, Chase Manhattan Bank (1963-81); Dec. 17, 1937; Sept. 25.

Tanzania, $52,750 — **David C. Miller Jr.;** Baltimore; special assistant to assistant secretary for African affairs, State Dept. (1981); July 15, 1942; Rep.; Oct. 21.

France, $60,662.50 — **Evan G. Galbraith;** Greenwich, Conn.; managing director, Dillon, Read & Co. (1980-81); special assistant to the secretary, Commerce Dept. (1960-61); July 2, 1928; Rep.; Nov. 6.

United Nations, U.S. representative, European office, $52,750 — **Geoffrey Swaebe;** Los Angeles; business and management consultant (1972-81); March 23, 1911; Rep.; Nov. 6.

Norway, $52,750 — **Mark E. Austad;** Scottsdale, Ariz.; vice president for public affairs, Metromedia Inc. (1960-75 and 1977-81); U.S. ambassador to Finland (1975-77); April 1, 1917; Dec. 10.

Sweden, $52,750 — **Franklin S. Forsberg;** Greenwich, Conn.; president, Forsberg Associates Inc. (1972-81); Oct. 21, 1905; Dec. 10.

Department of Transportation

Secretary, $69,630 — **Andrew L. Lewis Jr.;** Schwenksville, Pa.; deputy chairman, Republican National Committee (1976-81); consultant, Lewis & Associates (1974-81); Nov. 3, 1931; Rep.; Jan. 22.

Deputy secretary, $60,662.50 — **Darrell M. Trent;** Portola Valley, Calif.; senior research fellow and associate director, Hoover Institution, Stanford Univ. (1974-81); deputy assistant for domestic affairs to President Nixon (1969-74); Aug. 2, 1938; Rep.; Jan. 29.

Assistant secretary for policy and international affairs, $52,750 — **Judith C. Connor;** New York City; international affairs director, Pan American World Airways (1977-81); assistant secretary for environment, safety and consumer affairs, Transportation Dept. (1975-77); March 6, 1939; Rep.; March 10.

Assistant secretary for governmental affairs, $52,750 — **Lee L. Verstandig;** Providence, R.I.; administrative assistant and legislative director to U.S. Sen. John H. Chafee (1977-81); Sept. 11, 1937; Rep.; March 10.

General counsel, $52,750 — **John M. Fowler;** Philadelphia; vice president and chief financial officer, Reading Co. (1979-81); April 12, 1949; Rep.; March 10.

Assistant secretary for budget and programs, $52,750 — **Donald A. Derman;** Washington, D.C.; deputy associate director, Office of Management and Budget (1976-81); May 27, 1933; Rep.; May 4.

Inspector general, $52,750 — **Joseph P. Welsch;** Arlington, Va.; vice president, U.S. Railway Assn. (1978-81); deputy assistant secretary, Defense Dept. (1971-78); Oct. 2, 1928; Ind.; July 17.

Federal Aviation Administration

Administrator, $60,662.50 — **J. Lynn Helms;** Westport, Conn.; president and chief executive officer and then chairman of the board, Piper Aircraft Corp. (1974-81); March 1, 1925; Rep., April 8.

Deputy administrator, $52,750 — **Michael J. Fenello;** Eustis, Fla.; various positions leading to vice president, Eastern Airlines (1943-81); Jan. 22, 1916; Rep.; July 24.

Federal Highway Administration

Administrator, $55,387.50 — **Ray A. Barnhart;** Pasadena, Texas; commissioner, state highways and public transportation dept., Texas (1979-81);chairman, Texas Republican Party (1977-79); state representative, Texas (1973-75); Jan. 12, 1928; Rep.; Feb. 6.

Federal Railroad Administration

Administrator, $55,387.50 — **Robert W. Blanchette;** Bethesda, Md.; managing partner, Alston, Miller and Gaines (1976-81); July 7, 1932; Rep.; March 10.

Maritime Administration

Administrator, $55,387.50 — **Harold E. Shear;** Arlington, Va.; vice president, Norton Lilly Co. (1980-81); retired admiral, U.S. Navy (1941-80); commander-in-chief, allied forces, southern Europe (1977-80); Dec. 6, 1918; Rep.; Oct. 7.

National Highway Traffic Safety Administration

Administrator, $55,387.50 — **Raymond A. Peck Jr.;** Washington, D.C.; vice president and director of regulatory affairs, National Coal Assn. (1977-81); deputy assistant secretary for energy and minerals, Interior Dept. (1975-77); Jan. 16, 1940; Rep.; April 8.

Urban Mass Transportation Administration

Administrator, $55,387.50 — **Arthur E. Teele Jr.;** Tallahassee, Fla.; transition team leader, Transportation Dept. (1980-81); national director of voter groups division, Reagan-Bush Committee (1980); lawyer in own firm (1976-80); May 14, 1946; Rep.; April 2.

Department of the Treasury

Secretary, $69,630 — **Donald T. Regan;** Colts Neck, N.J.; various positions leading to chairman and chief executive officer, Merrill Lynch and Co. (1946-81); Dec. 21, 1918; Rep.; Jan. 21.

Deputy secretary, $60,662.50 — **R. T. McNamar;** Los Angeles; executive vice president, Beneficial Standard Corp. (1977-81); executive director, Federal Trade Commission (1973-77); April 21, 1939; Rep.; Feb. 16.

Deputy under secretary for legislative affairs, $52,750 — **W. Dennis Thomas;** Bethesda, Md.; administrative assistant to U.S. Sen. William V. Roth Jr. (1976-81); administrative assistant to U.S. Sen. J. Glenn Beall Jr. (1974-76); Dec. 8, 1943; Rep.; Feb. 16.

Assistant secretary for tax policy, $52,750 — **John E. Chapoton;** Houston; partner, Vinson & Elkins (1972-81); legislative counsel, Treasury Dept. (1970-72); May 18, 1936; Rep.; March 10.

Assistant secretary for economic policy, $52,750 — **Paul Craig Roberts;** Alexandria, Va.; senior fellow, Center for Strategic and International Studies, Georgetown Univ. (1980); associate editor, *Wall Street Journal* (1978-80); economic counsel to U.S. Sen. Orrin G. Hatch (1977-78); chief economist, minority staff, U.S. House Budget Committee (1976); economic counsel to U.S. Rep. Jack F. Kemp (1975-76); April 13, 1937; Rep.; March 10.

Under secretary for monetary affairs, $55,387.50 — **Beryl W. Sprinkel;** Flossmoor, Ill.; executive vice president and economist, Harris Trust and Savings Bank (1952-81); consultant, U.S. Senate Banking, Housing and Urban Affairs Committee (1975); Nov. 20, 1923; Rep.; March 27.

Under secretary for tax policy, $55,387.50 — **Norman B. Ture;** Alexandria, Va.; president, Norman B. Ture Inc. (1971-81); president, Institute for Research on the Economics of Taxation (1977-81); professional staff, U.S. Congress Joint Economic Committee (1955-61); Sept. 8, 1923; Rep.; March 27.

Deputy under secretary for international affairs, $52,750 — **Marc E. Leland;** San Francisco; London resident partner, Proskauer Rose Goetz and Mendelsohn (1978-81); senior adviser, U.S. delegation to Mutual and Balanced Force Reduction negotiations (1972-73); April 20, 1938; Rep.; May 4.

Assistant secretary for domestic finance, $52,750 — **Roger W. Mehle Jr.;** New York City; senior vice president and member of board, Dean Witter Reynolds Inc. (1979-81); Dec. 28, 1941; Rep.; May 4.

Assistant secretary for public affairs, $52,750 — **Ann Dore**

McLaughlin; Washington, D.C.; president, McLaughlin and Co. (1977-81); Nov. 16, 1941; Rep.; June 19.

General counsel, $52,750 — **Peter J. Wallison;** Scarsdale, N.Y.; partner, Rogers and Wells (1977-81); counsel to the vice president (1974-77); special assistant to Gov. Nelson A. Rockefeller (1972-73); June 6, 1941; Rep.; June 19.

Assistant secretary for enforcement and operations, $52,750 — **John M. Walker Jr.;** New York City; partner, Carter, Ledyard and Milburn (1975-81); assistant U.S. attorney, southern district of N.Y., Justice Dept. (1970-75); Dec. 26, 1940; Aug. 1.

Comptroller of the currency for term expiring Dec. 15, 1986, $55,387.50 — **C.T. Conover;** Lafayette, Calif.; partner, Edgar, Dunn & Conover Inc. (1978-81); Oct. 13, 1939; Rep.; Dec. 14.

Internal Revenue Service

Commissioner, $55,387.50 — **Roscoe L. Egger Jr.;** Washington, D.C.; partner, Price Waterhouse and Co. (1956-81); Sept. 19, 1920; Rep.; March 10.

Office of the Treasurer of the United States

Treasurer, $52,750 — **Angela M. Buchanan;** Arlington, Va.; national treasurer, Reagan-Bush general election campaign and Reagan for president primary campaign (1979-81); controller, Citizens for the Republic (1977-79); Dec. 10, 1948; Rep.; March 17.

INDEPENDENT AGENCIES

ACTION

Director, $55,387.50 — **Thomas W. Pauken;** Mesquite, Texas; attorney (1974-81); unsuccessful Republican candidate, 5th Congressional District, Texas (1978 and 1980); Jan. 11, 1944; Rep.; May 7.

Director of the Peace Corps, $55,387.50 — **Loret M. Ruppe;** Potomac, Md.; co-chairman, Mich. Reagan-Bush Committee (1980); chairman, Mich. George Bush for President Committee (1979-80); Jan. 3, 1936; Rep.; May 7.

Deputy director, $52,750 — **Winifred Ann Pizzano;** Arlington, Va.; director of health care practice, Arthur Young & Co. (1975-81); executive administrator, public health dept., Ill. (1972-75); assistant to Gov. Richard B. Ogilvie (1971-72); legislative assistant to U.S. Rep. Robert H. Michel (1966-70); March 24, 1942; Rep.; Sept. 9.

Deputy director of the Peace Corps, $52,750 — **Everett Alvarez Jr.;** Rockville, Md.; commander (last rank), U.S. Navy (1960-80); Dec. 23, 1937; Rep.; July 24.

Administrative Conference of the United States

Chairman for term expiring July 7, 1986, $60,662.50 — **Loren A. Smith;** Yorklyn, Del.; chief counsel, Reagan for President Committee (1979-80); associate professor, Widener Univ. (1976-81); Dec. 22, 1944; Rep.; June 25.

Civil Aeronautics Board

Chairman and member for term expiring Dec. 31, 1985, $55,387.50 — **Clinton D. McKinnon;** Washington, D.C.; owner, various radio and television stations (1962-81); Jan. 27, 1934; Rep.; Oct. 26.

Commodity Futures Trading Commission

Chairman and commissioner for term expiring April 13, 1984, $55,387.50 — **Philip F. Johnson;** Arlington, Va.; partner, Kirkland and Ellis (1962-81); June 18, 1938; Rep.; June 4.

Commissioner for term expiring April 13, 1985, $52,750 — **Susan M. Phillips;** Iowa City, Iowa; associate professor and then associate vice president of finance, Univ. of Iowa (1978-81); Dec. 23, 1944; Rep.; Oct. 27.

Commissioner for term expiring June 19, 1986, $52,750 — **Kalo A. Hineman;** Dighton, Kan.; member, house of representatives, Kansas (1974-81); March 4, 1922; Rep.; Dec. 16.

Community Services Administration

Director, $60,662.50 — **Dwight A. Ink;** Washington, D.C.; vice president, National Consumer Cooperative Bank (1980-81); deputy administrator, General Services Administration (1973-76); Sept. 9, 1922; Rep.; June 25.

Assistant director for community action, $52,750 — **Clarence E. Hodges;** Indianapolis; staff member for U.S. Sen. Richard G. Lugar (1977-81); Oct. 1, 1939; Sept. 15.

Assistant director for external affairs, $52,750 — **Lawrence Y. Goldberg;** Bethesda, Md.; president, Lawrence Y. Goldberg Associates Inc. (1977-81); executive director for coalition, Reagan-Bush Committee (1980); assistant director, Federal Preparedness Agency (1974-77); July 21, 1931; Rep.; Sept. 15.

Deputy director, $55,387.50 — **Samuel J. Cornelius;** Silver Spring, Md.; director, Economic Development Assistance Center (1979-81); deputy director, office of minority business enterprise, Commerce Dept. (1974-77); April 14, 1928; Sept. 30.

Consumer Product Safety Commission

Chairman and member for term expiring Oct. 26, 1984, $55,387.50 — **Nancy H. Steorts;** Bethesda, Md.; consultant to special consumer assistant to President Reagan (1981); Nov. 28, 1936; Rep.; July 27.

Environmental Protection Agency

Administrator, $60,662.50 — **Anne McGill Gorsuch;** Denver; attorney, The Mountain States Telephone and Telegraph Co. (1975-81); state representative, Colo. (1976-80); April 21, 1942; Rep.; May 5.

Deputy administrator, $55,387,50 — **John Whitlock Hernandez;** Las Cruces, N.M.; professor, N.M. State Univ. (1968-81); Aug. 8, 1929; Rep.; May 5.

Assistant administrator for air, noise and radiation, $52,750 — **Kathleen M. Bennett;** Alexandria, Va.; lobbyist, Crown Zellerbach (1977-81); May 11, 1948; Rep.; July 31.

Assistant administrator for administration, $52,750 — **John P. Horton;** Bernardsville, N.J.; president, Danline Inc. (1957-81); Feb. 16, 1925; July 31.

Assistant administrator for toxic substances, $52,750 — **John A. Todhunter;** Silver Spring, Md.; chairman and professor, biochemistry department, Catholic Univ. (1978-81); Oct. 9, 1949; Rep.; Nov. 4.

Export-Import Bank of the United States

President, $55,387.50 — **William H. Draper III;** Atherton, Calif.; partner, Sutter Hill Ventures (1970-81); Jan. 1, 1928; Rep.; July 13.

Federal Communications Commission

Chairman and member for term expiring June 30, 1986, $55,387.50 — **Mark S. Fowler;** Arlington, Va.; senior partner, Fowler and Meyers (1975-81); communications counsel, Citizens for Reagan (1975-76 and 1979-80); Oct. 6, 1941; Rep.; May 14.

Member for term expiring June 30, 1988, $52,750 — **Mary Ann Weyforth-Dawson;** Washington, D.C.; various positions leading to chief of staff to U.S. Sen. Bob Packwood (1973-81); legislative assistant to U.S. Rep. Richard Ichord (1973); Aug. 31, 1944; Rep.; June 4.

Member for term expiring June 30, 1987, $52,750 — **Henry M. Rivera;** Albuquerque, N.M.; attorney, Sutin, Thayer and Browne (1973-81); Sept. 25, 1946; Dem.; July 31.

Member for term expiring June 30, 1984, $52,750 — **James H. Quello;** Alexandria, Va.; member, Federal Communications Commission (1974-80); April 21, 1914; Dem.; July 31.

Federal Emergency Management Agency

Director, $60,662.50 — **Louis O. Giuffrida;** San Luis Obispo, Calif.; director, Calif. Specialized Training Institute (1971-81); Oct. 2, 1920; Rep.; May 19.

Deputy director, $52,750 — **Fred J. Villella;** Pismo Beach, Calif.; chief, academic division, Calif. Specialized Training Institute (1978-81); June 21, 1933; Rep.; June 9.

Associate director, $52,750 — **Charles M. Girard;** Fairfax, Va.; director of human resources, Public Technology Inc. (1980-81); president, International Training, Research and Evaluation Council (1971-80); Feb. 3, 1943; Sept. 29.

Associate director for state and local programs and support, $52,750 — **Lee M. Thomas;** Fairfax, Va.; director, division of public safety, S.C. governor's office (1980-81); June 13, 1944; Rep.; Oct. 6.

Administrator, U.S. Fire Administration, $52,750 — **Bobby Jack Thompson;** Cazenovia, N.Y.; superintendent, National Fire Academy (1980-81); March 26, 1930; Dec. 14.

Administrator, Federal Insurance Administration, $52,750 — **Jeffrey S. Bragg;** Columbus, Ohio; director, public affairs, Ohio Medical Indemnity Corp., Blue Cross & Blue Shield (1976-81); clerk, house of representatives, Ohio (1972-73); Jan. 21, 1949; Nov. 13.

Federal Home Loan Bank Board

Chairman and member for term expiring June 30, 1981, $52,750 — **Richard T. Pratt;** Salt Lake City; president, Richard T. Pratt Associates Inc. (1970-81); partner, Johnson, Pratt & Stewart (1975-81); Feb. 5, 1937; Rep.; April 8.

Federal Maritime Commission

Commissioner for term expiring June 30, 1984, $55,387.50 — **Alan Green Jr.;** Portland, Ore.; president and commissioner, Port of Portland (1974-81); May 1, 1925; Rep.; June 19.

Commissioner for term expiring June 30, 1985, $52,750 — **James J. Carey;** Alexandria, Va.; business development manager, Telemedia Inc. (1980-81); April 9, 1939; Rep.; Oct. 7.

Federal Mine Safety and Health Review Commission

Commissioner for term expiring Aug. 31, 1986, $52,750 — **Rosemary M. Collyer;** Denver; attorney, Sherman & Howard (1977-81); Nov. 19, 1945; Rep.; Oct. 26.

Federal Trade Commission

Chairman and commissioner for term expiring Sept. 25, 1988, $55,387.50 — **James C. Miller III;** Washington, D.C.; administrator, office of information and regulatory affairs, Office of Management and Budget (1981); executive director, Presidential Task Force on Regulatory Relief (1981); resident scholar, American Enterprise Institute (1977-81); June 25, 1942; Rep.; Sept. 21.

General Services Administration

Administrator, $55,387.50 — **Gerald P. Carmen;** Manchester, N.H.; director of political programs, Reagan-Bush Committee (1980); N.H. delegate to Republican National Conventions (1964 and 1980); July 8, 1930; Rep.; May 12.

International Communication Agency

Director, $60,662.50 — **Charles Z. Wick;** Los Angeles; independent businessman; president and chief executive officer of Wick Financial Corp. (1960-81); Oct. 12, 1917; Rep.; June 8.

Associate director, $52,750 — **James B. Conkling;** Sherman Oaks, Calif.; president, BEI Productions (1978-81); March 1, 1915; Rep.; June 25.

Associate director, $52,750 — **James T. Hackett;** Sterling, Va.; administrative director, U.S. Arms Control and Disarmament

Agency (1973-81); deputy executive secretary, National Security Council (1971-73); March 26, 1931; Rep.; June 25.

Deputy director, $55,387.50 — **Gilbert A. Robinson;** Carmel, N.Y.; chairman, Gilbert A. Robinson Inc. (1960-81); consultant, Peace Corps (1971-72); special assistant to the secretary, Commerce Dept. (1955-59); May 25, 1928; Rep.; July 24.

Associate director for programs, $52,750 — **Robert J. Hughes;** Orleans, Mass.; president, publisher and editor, Hughes Newspapers Inc. (1979-81); April 28, 1930; Ind.; July 29.

International Development Cooperation Agency

Agency for International Development

Assistant administrator for food for peace and voluntary assistance, $52,750 — **Julia C. Bloch;** Washington, D.C.; fellow, Institute of Politics, Harvard Univ. (1980-81); deputy director, International Communication Agency (1977-80); professional staff member and then chief minority counsel, U.S. Senate Select Committee on Nutrition and Human Needs (1971-77); March 2, 1942; July 29.

Assistant administrator for private and development cooperation bureau, $52,750 — **Elise R. W. du Pont;** Rockland, Del.; attorney, Montgomery, McCracken, Walker and Rhoads (1978-80); Dec. 27, 1935; Rep.; July 29.

Assistant administrator for the Near East, $52,750 — **W. Antoinette Ford;** Detroit; production supervisor, General Motors Corp. (1978-81); Dec. 14, 1941; Rep.; July 29.

Assistant administrator for the bureau of Asia, $52,750 — **Jon D. Holstine;** Alexandria, Va.; minority staff consultant, U.S. House Foreign Affairs Committee (1975-81); Sept. 23, 1937; Rep.; July 29.

Assistant administrator for external affairs, $52,750 — **Jay F. Morris;** Adelphi, Md.; executive recruiter, office of presidential personnel, White House (1981); member, Reagan-Bush planning task force (1980); regional finance director, Reagan for President Committee (1979-80); legislative assistant to U.S. Sen. James B. Pearson (1967-71); Feb. 21, 1941; Rep.; July 29.

Assistant administrator for African affairs, $52,750 — **Francis S. Ruddy;** Houston; counsel, Exxon Corp. (1978-81); Sept. 15, 1937; July 29.

Assistant administrator, $52,750 — **Nyle C. Brady;** Ithaca, N.Y.; director general, International Rice Research Institute (1973-81); Oct. 25, 1920; Rep.; Sept. 25.

International Trade Commission

Member for term expiring Dec. 16, 1982, $52,750 — **Eugene J. Frank;** Pittsburgh; investment banker, economist and financial consultant; Oct. 13, 1927; Rep.; July 30.

Member for term expiring June 16, 1990, $52,750 — **Albert E. Eckes Jr.;** Alexandria, Va.; executive director, U.S. House Republican Conference (1979-81); July 11, 1942; Rep.; Sept. 16.

Interstate Commerce Commission

Chairman and member for term expiring Dec. 31, 1984, $55,387.50 — **Reese H. Taylor Jr.;** Carson City, Nev.; lawyer, Allison, Brunetti, MacKenzie and Taylor Ltd. (1978-81); May 6, 1928; Rep.; June 16.

Merit Systems Protection Board

Special counsel for term expiring June 5, 1986, $52,750 — **Alex Kozinski;** Washington, D.C.; deputy legal counsel, office of the president-elect (1980-81); associate, Covington and Burling (1979-81); July 23, 1950; Rep.; June 2.

National Aeronautics and Space Administration

Administrator, $55,387.50 — **James M. Beggs;** St. Louis; executive vice president, General Dynamics Corp. (1974-81); under secretary, Transportation Dept. (1969-73); Jan. 9, 1926; June 25.

Deputy administrator, $55,387.50 — **Hans M. Mark;** Alexandria, Va.; secretary of the Air Force (1979-81); under secretary of the Air Force (1977-79); June 17, 1929; July 8.

National Credit Union Administration Board

Chairman and member for term expiring Oct. 21, 1987, $55,387.50 — **Edgar F. Callahan;** Springfield, Ill.; director, state financial institutions dept., Ill. (1977-81); deputy secretary of state, Ill. (1975-77); March 23, 1928; Rep.; Oct. 21.

National Foundation on the Arts and the Humanities

National Endowment for the Arts

Chairman, $55,387.50 — **Francis S. M. Hodsoll;** McLean, Va.; deputy chief of staff, White House (1981); executive director, White House transition, office of president-elect (1980-81); debate staff coordinator, Reagan-Bush Committee (1980); deputy U.S. representative for non-proliferation, State Dept. (1978-80); deputy assistant secretary, Commerce Dept. (1976-77); May 1, 1938; Rep.; Nov. 10.

National Labor Relations Board

Member for term expiring Aug. 25, 1985, $52,750 — **Robert P. Hunter;** Vienna, Va.; chief counsel and chief of staff, U.S. Senate Labor and Human Resources Committee (1981); legislative director to U.S. Sen. Orrin G. Hatch (1977-81); Aug. 23, 1940; Rep.; Sept. 15.

National Transportation Safety Board

Chairman and member for term expiring Dec. 31, 1985, $55,387.50 — **James E. Burnett Jr.;** Clinton, Ark.; juvenile judge, Van Buren county, Ark. (1973-81); city judge, Damascus, Ark. (1980-81); Sept. 20, 1947; Rep.; Dec. 14.

Nuclear Regulatory Commission

Chairman and member for term expiring June 30, 1986, $60,662.50 — **Nunzio J. Palladino;** State College, Pa.; dean, college of engineering, Pa. State Univ. (1966-81); Nov. 10, 1916; Rep.; June 19.

Member for term expiring June 30, 1985, $55,387.50 — **Thomas M. Roberts;** Washington, D.C.; president and chief executive officer, Boiler and Tank Works Inc. (1969-78); April 14, 1937; Rep.; July 31.

Occupational Safety and Health Review Commission

Member for term expiring April 27, 1987, $52,750 — **Robert A. Rowland;** Austin, Texas; private law practice (1962-81); state vice chairman, Reagan-Bush Committee (1980); March 23, 1932; Rep.; July 31.

Office of Personnel Management

Director, $60,662.50 — **Donald J. Devine;** Wheaton, Md.; presidential transition team leader, Office of Personnel Management (1980-81); regional political director, Reagan-Bush Committee (1980); government and politics associate professor, Univ. of Md. (1967-81); April 14, 1937; Rep.; March 23.

Deputy director, $55,387.50 — **Loretta Cornelius;** Warrenton, Va.; various positions leading to vice president, PRC Data Services Co. (1967-81); April 1, 1936; Rep.; Sept. 29.

Overseas Private Investment Corp.

President and chief executive officer, $55,387.50 — **Craig A. Nalen;** Ocean Ridge, Fla.; director, Barnett Bank (1978-81); April 17, 1930; Rep.; June 10.

Securities and Exchange Commission

Chairman and member for term expiring June 5, 1982, $52,750 — **John S. R. Shad;** New York City; vice-chairman of the board, E. F. Hutton Group Inc. (1963-81); chairman, Reagan-Bush New York Finance Committee (1980); June 27, 1923; Rep.; April 8.

Member for term expiring June 5, 1982, $52,750 — **Bevis Longstreth;** New York City; lawyer and then partner, Debevoise, Plimpton, Lyons and Gates (1962-81); Jan. 29, 1934; Dem.; July 17.

Selective Service System

Director, $52,750 — **Maj. Gen. Thomas K. Turnage;** Alexandria, Va.; special assistant to the deputy assistant secretary, Defense Dept. (1979-81); June 27, 1923; Rep.; Sept. 25.

Small Business Administration

Administrator, $55,387.50 — **Michael Cardenas;** Fresno, Calif.; partner, Fox and Co. (1979-81); July 14, 1933; Rep.; March 26.

Chief counsel for advocacy, $52,750 — **Frank S. Swain;** Washington, D.C.; legal counsel, National Federation of Independent Business (1977-81); Jan. 4, 1951; Rep.; July 31.

Tennessee Valley Authority

Chairman and member for term expiring May 5, 1990, $55,387.50 — **Charles H. Dean Jr.;** Knoxville, Tenn.; various positions with Knoxville Utilities Board (1959-81); director, American Public Power Assn. (1977-80); Oct. 22, 1925; June 19.

U.S. Arms Control and Disarmament Agency

Director, $60,662.50 — **Eugene V. Rostow;** New Haven, Conn.; Sterling professor, Yale Law School (1968-81); chairman, Committee on the Present Danger (1976-81); under secretary, State Dept. (1966-69); Aug. 25, 1913; Dem.; June 25.

Special representative, $52,750 — **Edward L. Rowny;** Arlington, Va.; fellow, Wilson Center, Smithsonian Institution (1979-81); joint chiefs of staff representative, Strategic Arms Limitation Talks (1973-79); April 3, 1917; Rep.; July 27.

U.S. Synthetic Fuels Corp.

Chairman for term expiring May 25, 1988, salary to be set by Synthetic Fuels Corp. board — **Edward E. Noble;** Tulsa, Okla.; chairman, Noble Inns Corp.; March 19, 1928; Rep.; May 14.

Veterans Administration

Administrator, $60,662.50 — **Robert P. Nimmo;** Atascadero, Calif.; member, Calif. state Senate (1976-81); member, Calif. state Assembly (1973-76); Feb. 5, 1922; Rep.; July 10.

Inspector general, $52,750 — **Frank S. Sato;** Annandale, Va.; inspector general, Transportation Dept. (1979-81); deputy assistant secretary, Defense Dept. (1974-79); March 16, 1929; July 30.

Deputy administrator for veterans' affairs, $55,387.50 — **Charles T. Hagel;** Washington, D.C.; manager, government affairs, Firestone Tire and Rubber Co. (1978-81); administrative assistant, U.S. Rep. John Y. McCollister (1971-77); Oct. 4, 1946; Rep.; Dec. 7.

JUDICIARY

U.S. Supreme Court

Associate justice, $93,000 — **Sandra Day O'Connor;** Paradise Valley, Ariz.; superior court judge, Maricopa County, Ariz. (1975-81); majority leader, Ariz. senate (1973-75); member, Ariz. senate (1969-73); assistant attorney general, Ariz. (1955-69);

March 26, 1930; Rep.; Sept. 21.

U.S. Circuit Courts

Judge, 4th circuit, $74,300 — **Robert F. Chapman;** Camden, S.C.; U.S. district judge, S.C. (1971-81); chairman, S.C. Republican Party (1961-63); April 24, 1926; Rep.; Sept. 16.

Judge, 5th circuit, $74,300 — **William L. Garwood;** Austin, Texas; partner, Graves, Dougherty, Hearon, Moody and Garwood (1981); associate justice, Texas supreme court (1979-80); Oct. 29, 1931; Rep.; Oct. 21.

Judge, 2nd circuit, $74,300 — **Richard J. Cardamone;** New Hartford, N.Y.; associate justice, N.Y. state supreme court, appellate division (1971-81); trial judge, N.Y. state supreme court (1963-71); Oct. 10, 1925; Rep.; Oct. 29.

Judge, 2nd circuit, $74,300 — **Lawrence W. Pierce;** New York City; judge, U.S. district court, southern district of N.Y. (1971-81); Dec. 31, 1924; Rep.; Nov. 18.

Judge, 7th circuit, $74,300 — **Jesse E. Eschbach;** Fort Wayne, Ind.; judge, U.S. district court, northern district of Indiana (1962-81); Oct. 26, 1920; Nov. 24.

Judge, 7th circuit, $74,300 — **Richard A. Posner;** Chicago; law professor, Univ. of Chicago Law School (1969-81); president, Lexecon Inc. (1977-81); Jan. 11, 1939; Nov. 24.

Judge, 3rd circuit, $74,300 — **Edward R. Becker;** Philadelphia; judge, U.S. district court, eastern district of Pennsylvania (1970-81); May 4, 1933; Rep.; Dec. 3.

Judge, 2nd circuit, $74,300 — **Ralph K. Winter Jr.;** Woodbridge, Conn.; law professor, Yale Univ. (1978-81); July 30, 1935; Dec. 9.

U.S. District Courts

Judge, district of South Carolina, $70,300 — **William W. Wilkins Jr.;** Greenville, S.C.; solicitor, S.C. 13th Judicial Circuit (1975-81); March 29, 1942; Rep.; July 20.

Judge, northern district of Indiana, $70,300 — **William C. Lee;** Fort Wayne, Ind.; partner, Hunt, Swedhoff, Borror, Eilbacker and Lee (1973-81); Feb. 2, 1938; July 27.

Judge, eastern and western districts of Missouri, $70,300 — **Joseph E. Stevens Jr.;** Kansas City, Mo.; partner, Lathrop, Koontz, Righter, Clagett, Parker & Norquist (1962-81); June 23, 1928; Rep.; Sept. 16.

Judge, western district of Missouri, $70,300 — **D. Brook Bartlett;** Kansas City, Mo.; partner, Blackwell, Sanders, Matheny, Weary & Lombardi (1977-81); Feb. 22, 1937; Rep.; Sept. 16.

Judge, western district of Missouri, $70,300 — **John R. Gibson;** Kansas City, Mo.; partner, Morrison, Hecker, Curtis, Kuder & Parrish (1952-81); Dec. 20, 1925; Rep.; Sept. 16.

Judge, eastern district of Kentucky, $70,300 — **Henry R. Wilhoit Jr.;** Grayson, Ky.; attorney, Wilhoit & Wilhoit (1960-81); Feb. 11, 1935; Rep.; Sept. 25.

Judge, district of Maine, $70,300 — **Conrad K. Cyr;** Winterport, Maine; U.S. bankruptcy judge, Maine (1961-81); Dec. 9, 1931; Sept. 25.

Judge, eastern district of New York, $70,300 — **Joseph M. McLaughlin;** Jamaica Estates, N.Y.; dean of law, Fordham Univ. (1971-81); March 20, 1933; Sept. 25.

Judge, northern district of New York, $70,300 — **Roger J. Miner;** Hudson, N.Y.; justice, supreme court, N.Y. (1976-81); April 14, 1934; Rep.; Sept. 25.

Judge, southern district of New York, $70,300 — **John E. Sprizzo;** New York City; partner, Curtis, Mallet-Prevost, Colt & Mosle (1973-81); Dec. 23, 1934; Dem.; Sept. 25.

Judge, western district of Washington, $70,300 — **John C. Coughenour;** Seattle; partner, Bogle & Gates (1966-70 and 1971-81); July 27, 1941; Sept. 25.

Judge, western district of Arkansas, $70,300 — **H. Franklin Waters;** Springdale, Ark.; partner, Blair, Cypert, Waters & Roy (1966-81); July 20, 1932; Rep.; Oct. 21.

Judge, southern district of Texas, $70,300 — **Hayden W. Head Jr.;** Corpus Christi, Texas; partner, Head, Kendrick & Head (1972-81); Nov. 12, 1944; Rep.; Oct. 21.

Judge, western district of Texas, $70,300 — **James R. Nowlin;** San Antonio, Texas; attorney (1969-81); member, state

house of representatives, Texas (1967-71 and 1973-81); Nov. 21, 1937; Rep.; Oct. 21.

Judge, district of Minnesota, $70,300 — **Paul A. Magnuson;** Lake Elmo, Minn.; partner, LeVander, Gillen, Miller and Magnuson (1963-81); Feb. 9, 1937; Rep.; Oct. 29.

Judge, western district of North Carolina, $70,300 — **Robert D. Potter;** Charlotte, N.C.; attorney (1957-81); April 4, 1923; Rep.; Oct. 29.

Judge, southern district of Alabama, $70,300 — **Emmett R. Cox;** Mobile, Ala.; partner, Nettles, Cox & Barker (1969-81); Feb. 13, 1935; Rep.; Nov. 18.

Judge, central district of California, $70,300 — **Cynthia H. Hall;** Pasadena, Calif.; judge, U.S. tax court (1972-81); Feb. 19, 1929; Nov. 18.

Judge, district of Nebraska, $70,300 — **Clarence A. Beam;** Lincoln, Neb.; partner, Knudsen, Berkheimer, Beam, Richardson & Endacott (1971-81); Jan. 14, 1930; Rep.; Nov. 18.

Judge, district of South Dakota, $70,300 — **John B. Jones;** Presho, S.D.; judge, state circuit court, S.D. (1967-81); March 30, 1927; Nov. 18.

Judge, middle district of Florida, $70,300 — **John H. Moore II;** Boynton Beach, Fla.; judge, state district court of appeals, Fla. (1977-81); Aug. 5, 1929; Nov. 24.

Judge, district of South Carolina, $70,300 — **Clyde H. Hamilton;** Spartanburg, S.C.; partner, Butler, Means, Evins & Browne (1966-81); Feb. 8, 1934; Nov. 24.

Judge, eastern district of Virginia, $70,300 — **James C. Cacheris;** Fairfax, Va.; judge, state circuit court, Va. (1972-81); March 30, 1933; Nov. 24.

Judge, district of the Virgin Islands, $70,300 — **David V. O'Brien;** St. Croix, V.I.; partner, O'Brien & Moore (1978-81); June 19, 1932; Nov. 24.

Judge, eastern district of Virginia, $70,300 — **Robert H. Doumar;** Norfolk, Va.; partner, Doumar, Pincus, Knight & Harlan (1958-81); Feb. 17, 1930; Dec. 3.

Judge, western district of Virginia, $70,300 — **Jackson L. Kiser;** Martinsville, Va.; partner, Young, Kiser, Haskins, Mann, Gregory & Young, Ltd. (1961-81); June 24, 1929; Dec. 3.

Judge, northern district of Georgia, $70,300 — **J. Owen Forrester;** Atlanta; U.S. magistrate, northern district of Georgia (1976-81); assistant U.S. attorney, northern district of Georgia (1969-76); April 27, 1939; Dec. 9.

Judge, district of Kansas, $70,300 — **Sam A. Crow;** Topeka, Kan.; U.S. magistrate, Kansas (1975-81); May 5, 1926; Dec. 9.

Judge, eastern district of New York, $70,300 — **Israel L. Glasser;** Brooklyn, N.Y.; various teaching positions leading to dean, Brooklyn Law School (1948-81); April 6, 1924; Dec. 9.

Judge, northern district of Ohio, $70,300 — **Alvin I. Krenzler;** Beechwood, Ohio; judge, 8th district court of appeals, Ohio (1970-81); assistant attorney general, Ohio (1951-56); April 8, 1921; Rep.; Dec. 9.

Judge, western district of Wisconsin, $70,300 — **John C. Shabaz;** New Berlin, Wis.; member, house of representatives, Wis. (1964-81); June 25, 1931; Rep.; Dec. 9.

Judge, district of Idaho, $70,300 — **Harold L. Ryan;** Weiser, Idaho; partner, Ryan, Sweet & Masingill (1978-81); June 17, 1923; Dec. 16.

Judge, northern, eastern and western districts of Oklahoma, $70,300 — **David L. Russell;** Oklahoma City; U.S. attorney, western district of Oklahoma (1981); chief legislative assistant, U.S. Sen. Dewey F. Bartlett (1973-75); assistant attorney general, Okla. (1968-69); July 7, 1942; Dec. 16.

U.S. Tax Court

Judge, $70,300 — **Jules G. Korner III;** Chevy Chase, Md.; partner, Pope, Ballard & Loos (1970-81); July 27, 1922; Rep.; Dec. 3.

Judge, $70,300 — **Perry Shields;** Knoxville, Tenn.; partner, Shields, Rainwater & Humble (1974-81); Jan. 12, 1925; Rep.; Dec. 3.

Judge, $70,300 — **Meade Whitaker;** Franklin, Mich.; federal tax director, office of general counsel, Ford Motor Co. (1978-81); March 22, 1919; Rep.; Dec. 3.   ∎

POLITICAL REPORT

CQ

Off-Year Contests Focus on Reaganomics

Voter uneasiness over President Reagan's economic program helped Democrats in several 1981 off-year elections, although Republican losses were too few to be considered a significant trend.

Of the five House special elections, there was a switch of a GOP seat to the Democrats in only one. Democrat Wayne Dowdy triumphed by getting a large black vote in a Mississippi district that was almost half non-white. He did it through his support for renewing the Voting Rights Act, which his opponent wanted to terminate.

The Democrats also were cheered in midsummer when their candidate almost won an Ohio rural district with Republican ties. Although Republican Michael Oxley took pains to disassociate himself from Reagan's plans to cut back Social Security benefits, his opponent used the issue with unexpected effect.

The outcomes of elections to fill seats in Michigan, Maryland and Pennsylvania surprised no one. The Michigan seat was firmly Republican, the other two were just as Democratic, and traditional voting patterns remained unaltered.

The Pennsylvania contest had an odd wrinkle. This was a fight between factions of the Philadelphia Democratic Party. Joseph F. Smith lost his party's nomination, then ran as a Republican and won. But he made clear before the voting that he would caucus with the Democrats.

At year's end, the partisan breakdown in the House stood at 242 Democrats and 192 Republicans. The one vacancy, a longtime Democratic seat in Connecticut, stayed with the Democrats in early 1982 voting.

November's squeaker election for New Jersey governor showed that Reagan policies were disliked by many blue-collar Democrats who had voted Republican in the 1980 presidential race. But two factors helped the Republicans pull through in the Garden State: the unpopularity of the outgoing Democratic gubernatorial administration and the ability of Republican Thomas H. Kean to distance himself from parts of the Reagan plan New Jerseyans believed threatening to them.

In Virginia's gubernatorial balloting, animosity toward Reaganomics produced a sizable black turnout that helped sweep Democrat Charles S. Robb into office. Yet at the same time, Robb was able to attract conservative whites who previously had deserted Democrats. His conservative positions on a number of issues, however, did not keep the blacks home.

Robb's triumph ended the 12-year Republican occupancy of the Virginia governor's chair. Nationally, the parties traded New Jersey for Virginia. The nationwide tally remained as before, 27 Democratic governors and 23 Republican ones.

While Republicans scored gains in both the Virginia and New Jersey legislatures, Democrats still controlled both.

Gubernatorial Results

New Jersey

Winning an extremely close election that was decided only after a recount, Republican Thomas H. Kean overcame an assault on Reaganomics by an opponent who sounded traditional Democratic themes.

Former Assembly Speaker Kean, 46, had to wait until the last day in November for U.S. Rep. James J. Florio, his Democratic foe, to concede. The statewide recount of the Nov. 3 election showed that Kean's margin of fewer than 2,000 votes remained virtually intact. It was the closest New Jersey gubernatorial contest since 1880, when Democrat George C. Ludlow beat Republican Frederic C. Potts by 651 votes out of 242,000 cast.

Kean's strategy was to embrace the job-generating promise of supply-side theory while opposing specific Reagan cuts in social spending that would hit hard at New Jersey. He proposed state tax reductions that he said would help New Jersey's sour economy.

Four-term Rep. Florio happily made national GOP policy an issue. As a product of the working class running against an "old money" millionaire like Kean, he had the surface credentials to mobilize the blue-collar Democrats who had deserted their party in 1980. And the closeness of the vote did reflect some public doubt about the Reagan policies.

After the recount showed Kean's lead holding up, Florio conceded Nov. 30.

Official results:

Thomas H. Kean	1,145,999	49.5%
James J. Florio	1,144,202	49.4
11 Others	27,038	1.1

Kean ran impressively in diverse areas of the state. He managed to hold onto the usual Republican counties and to keep Florio's urban totals below the level polls had predicted. Kean did not do nearly as well among blue-collar voters as Reagan did in 1980, but he denied Florio the lopsided margins Democrats had counted on in many blue-collar areas — even in Florio's South Jersey home base, where the Democrat had expected to romp.

New Party Chairmen

Both parties chose new national chairmen in early 1981. The Republicans elected a political technician who they hoped would consolidate their gains. The Democrats tapped an experienced fund-raiser, needed to help them overcome their severe financial disadvantage.

The Republican National Committee Jan. 17 named President Reagan's choice as party leader, former Utah GOP Chairman Richard Richards. Richards, 47, a lawyer, served as western coordinator for Reagan in the 1980 campaign. He was Reagan's choice for chairman in 1977, but the job went to Tennessean Bill Brock, who had just been defeated for re-election to a second Senate term.

On Feb. 27, the Democratic National Committee selected Charles T. Manatt of California as its new chairman. He replaced John C. White, after two other aspirants for the job — former New York State Chairman Joseph Crangle and former Arkansas Gov. Bill Clinton — dropped out of contention. A millionaire banker and lawyer, Manatt set about revitalizing the committee financially, starting a elaborate direct mail fund-raising operation.

A resident of the Camden area, Florio used big votes from the southern counties to win the 13-way Democratic primary June 2. But Kean did well in the south in the general election; he took the shore counties of Ocean, Atlantic and Cape May, and came close to Florio in Burlington, Cumberland and Salem. Florio's only wide margin in South Jersey came in the two counties within his 1st Congressional District, Camden and Gloucester.

Kean also surprised Florio by holding down the Democratic vote in Middlesex, a blue-collar stronghold in the northern part of the state. Kean received a good vote from the areas where he had to run well, Republican Morris and Bergen counties.

Florio, who captured nine of the 21 counties overall, turned in solid votes from the banner Democratic counties of Hudson (Jersey City) and Essex (Newark).

The GOP nominee played on voter dissatisfaction with the eight-year tenure of outgoing Democratic Gov. Brendan T. Byrne. While Byrne and Florio never were close, Kean argued that a partisan change was needed in the governor's office. Byrne legally could not seek a second term.

Florio blasted President Reagan's federal budget reductions as harmful to blue-collar New Jersey and scored Kean's tax plan, a local version of the massive Kemp-Roth tax cut, as fiscal folly. Kean claimed that job creation would be spurred by lopping a penny off the 5-cent sales tax, halving the 9 percent state corporate levy and scrapping the graduated corporate net worth tax.

Virginia

Charles S. Robb's "something for everyone" campaign worked beautifully in Virginia Nov. 3, boosting him and the Democratic Party to gubernatorial control in a state Republicans had dominated for the past decade.

Robb, 42, Virginia's lieutenant governor and son-in-law of the late Lyndon B. Johnson, defeated GOP state Attorney General J. Marshall Coleman by more than 100,000 votes and swept in his Democratic running mates for lesser statewide offices.

Robb's conservative platform included support for the Reagan budget cuts and the state's right-to-work law. That combination held the "Byrd Democrats" who had been defecting to the Republicans on the statewide level since 1969. But Robb was careful not to offend blacks and labor, the core Democratic constituency. He offered black voters symbolic stands such as endorsement of a legal holiday in memory of Martin Luther King Jr.

His fragile coalition never unraveled, even when Reagan campaigned for Coleman and insisted on television that a Republican victory was essential to the administration's national program. While private polls showed that Reagan's Oct. 27 visit helped Coleman among some conservatives, it also galvanized blacks, resentful over federal social program cuts, to put aside their doubts and vote for Robb in unexpected numbers. Some heavily black precincts in Richmond gave the Democrat 97 percent of their vote.

Official returns:

Charles S. Robb	760,357	53.5%
J. Marshall Coleman	659,398	46.4
Write-Ins	856	0.1

Robb showed impressive strength in winning areas that had been favoring Republicans consistently. He carried nine of the state's 10 congressional districts, losing only the staunchly conservative 7th, in the Shenandoah Valley, and that by a mere 3,000 votes. In 1980, Reagan prevailed in every district.

The black vote in Richmond allowed Robb to take the 3rd District, which Republicans had been counting on. His 2-1 vote in the city offset the Republican vote in the suburbs.

But Robb built his widest leads in the industrial Tidewater, in the towns that supported populist Democrat Henry E. Howell's losing campaign for governor in 1977. Robb carried the 2nd District (Norfolk) and the 4th (Portsmouth) with about 60 percent of the vote. Organized labor was a boon to Robb in the Tidewater area, although its efforts were quiet. The state AFL-CIO had denied him its official backing, which made it difficult for Republicans to paint Robb as a labor liberal.

Coleman tried to make an issue out of Robb's Johnson connection by repeatedly saying, "I made it on my own." He characterized the Democrat as a closet liberal in the Johnson mold.

Coleman had won the attorney general's office in 1977 by campaigning as a moderate Republican, and this record caused him problems. Despite his strongly pro-Reagan approach, he had a hard time persuading the Richmond "Main Street" business elite that he was a true conservative.

The Republican benefited from the active support of outgoing GOP Gov. John Dalton, who could not legally seek a second term. But many conservatives, who had been supporting Republicans in recent years, found Robb more to their liking.

Special House Elections

Michigan

State Rep. Mark Siljander, a conservative Republican and Christian fundamentalist, kept Michigan's 4th District in GOP hands April 21 by winning a special election to succeed David A. Stockman (1977-81), who had become President Reagan's budget director.

Siljander, a 29-year-old full-time state legislator, swamped the Democratic candidate, Cass County Commissioner Johnie Rodebush. The winner took all the counties in the largely rural district, even Rodebush's home county, Cass.

It was the first special election during the Reagan presidency, but it was not regarded as a test of Reagan's popularity because the 4th is solidly Republican under virtually any circumstances.

The real competition for the seat took place in the March 24 special primary, when Siljander edged attorney John Globensky, a longtime Stockman ally whom the budget director favored as his replacement. Although Globensky had Stockman's organization working for him, the fundamentalists made the difference for Siljander by transporting their adherents to the polls.

Official returns:

Mark Siljander (R)	36,046	72.6%
Johnie Rodebush (D)	12,461	25.1
Bette Irwin (Lib)	658	1.4
Robert Drenkhahn (AIP)	452	0.9

Maryland

Former Maryland Senate President Steny H. Hoyer retained the state's 5th District seat for the Democrats May 19.

He defeated Republican Audrey Scott, mayor of Bowie, to succeed Democrat Gladys Noon Spellman (1975-81), who had been semi-conscious since she suffered a heart attack in late 1980. The House declared her suburban Washington seat vacant Feb. 24.

The victory of Hoyer, 41, came despite a major effort by national Republican groups and the White House. But it was not strictly a referendum on Reagan. The district, composed of northern Prince George's County and a small piece of Montgomery County, was 3-1 Democratic and had a large population of federal employees.

Scott supported the Reagan economic program except for proposals that would hurt federal workers. Hoyer endorsed Reagan's general inflation-fighting goals but criticized his cuts in social programs.

The victory marked a political comeback for Hoyer, who lost a 1978 primary bid for lieutenant governor. Hoyer captured Hyattsville, in the district's western end; District Heights, in the south near his home (he lived four blocks outside the district); and largely black Seat Pleasant. Scott carried Bowie, her home, and Laurel, a mostly Republican town filled with military people from nearby Ft. Meade.

Official returns:

Steny H. Hoyer (D)	42,573	55.2%
Audrey Scott (R)	33,708	43.5
Tom Mathers (Lib)	960	1.3

Ohio

Republican Michael Oxley barely beat Democrat Dale Locker June 25 in the normally GOP 4th District. Locker criticized Reagan's proposed Social Security cuts and stressed that he would "not be a rubber stamp for Ronald Reagan." Oxley also came out against the cuts.

Oxley, 37, replaced the late Republican Rep. Tennyson Guyer (1973-81), who died of a heart attack April 12. He ran as an ardent supporter of Reagan and his economic plan, with the exception of the Social Security proposal.

Both Oxley and Guyer were state representatives. Locker was an outstanding candidate for the farming district. A farmer himself, he chaired the state House Agriculture and Natural Resources Committee.

Lawyer Oxley won six of the district's 12 counties, including his home of Hancock and Allen (Lima), the most populous. Locker's vote was concentrated in the 4th's southern end, where he lived. Because the vote was so close, Locker asked for a recount, which confirmed Oxley's victory.

Official returns:

Michael Oxley (R)	41,987	50.2%
Dale Locker (D)	41,646	49.8

Mississippi

In a July 7 upset that returned Mississippi's 4th District to the Democrats after eight years of GOP control, McComb Mayor Wayne Dowdy edged Republican Liles B. Williams. Democrats claimed the results showed that Reagan's political clout was waning.

The Dowdy-Williams runoff election filled the seat of Republican Jon Hinson (1979-81), who resigned April 13 after being charged with attempted oral sodomy.

Dowdy, 37, placed second behind Williams in the June 23 non-partisan special election. Because Williams failed to clear 50 percent of the vote, the runoff was held between the top two finishers.

Although far outspent by Williams, who received well-publicized support from Reagan, Dowdy won by forging a tricky coalition of blacks and rural whites.

Blacks, who comprised almost 45.4 percent of the 4th's population, came out in large numbers, attracted by Dowdy's backing of the Voting Rights Act. Williams opposed renewing the statute, arguing that it discriminated against the South. In previous elections, independent black candidates had siphoned off votes from white Democratic nominees, giving the district to the Republicans. This time, no black candidate ran.

At the same time, Dowdy's rural populist approach and country-boy manner appealed to rural whites. He came from rural Pike County, while Williams was from metropolitan Hinds County (Jackson), which was suspect elsewhere in the district.

Williams won only three of the district's 12 counties — his home of Hinds, Warren (Vicksburg) and rural Lincoln.

Official returns:

Wayne Dowdy (D)	55,656	50.4%
Liles Williams (R)	54,744	49.6

Pennsylvania

State Sen. Joseph F. Smith, a Democrat running as a Republican, defeated Philadelphia Democratic Chairman David B. Glancey in a July 21 election for the 3rd District.

As he promised during the campaign, Smith, 61, caucused with the Democrats upon entering Congress. He replaced Democrat Raymond F. Lederer (1977-81), who resigned May 5 following his conviction on Abscam bribery and conspiracy charges.

Smith lost the Democratic nomination to Glancey in a vote of ward leaders May 28 and the next day accepted the GOP nomination. He also ran on a separate independent line to attract voters in the 4-1 Democratic district. As the two differed little on issues, the election turned on local political considerations.

The Smith victory was seen as a setback for Philadelphia Mayor William J. Green III, Glancey's mentor, and his "reform" forces. Former Mayor Frank Rizzo, a Smith ally and hero of the party regulars, took partial credit for Glancey's defeat. Seven Democratic ward leaders defected to Smith, who also had most of the labor endorsements.

Smith carried nine of the district's 19 wards, all in the blue-collar area near the Delaware River, by 3-1 margins or better. Glancey won 10 wards, but his margin was smaller.

Official returns:

Joseph F. Smith (R,I)	29,907	52.5%
David B. Glancy (D)	24,390	42.8
Charles L. Duncan (Consumer)	2,283	4.0
David Dorn (Lib)	375	0.7

Connecticut

Democrat Barbara Bailey Kennelly, Connecticut's secretary of the state, easily defeated Republican Ann P. Uccello in the Hartford-based 1st District Jan. 12, 1982.

Former Hartford Mayor Uccelo was the underdog for the seat held by six-term Democrat William R. Cotter until his death of pancreatic cancer Sept. 8.

Kennelly, 45, had a distinguished Democratic pedigree. Her father was the late John Bailey, the longtime state party boss and Democratic national chairman.

Official returns:

Barbara B. Kennelly (D)	51,431	58.8%
Ann P. Uccello (R)	36,085	41.2

VOTING STUDIES

CQ

 Key Votes

Reagan Victories Dominate Key Votes of 1981

Key House and Senate votes in 1981 provided clear evidence of President Reagan's extraordinary success in shepherding his programs through Congress.

The president's top goals of reducing spending, cutting taxes and bolstering defense were at stake in many of 32 important votes selected by Congressional Quarterly. In most cases, Reagan's position prevailed.

Both House and Senate, for example, supported the administration line on each key vote on the president's economic plan, including votes in both chambers on shaping Reagan's package of budget and tax cuts.

Both houses also supported the president's request for an increase in the federal debt limit. In the Senate, a Democratic challenge to the Reagan tax plan was rejected by a wide margin.

Both chambers supported the president's decision to resume production of the B-1 bomber that President Carter had canceled four years before. The House turned back an effort to block funding for the MX missile.

Although Reagan fared quite well in both chambers, the Democratic-controlled House did not give him everything he wanted. A resolution blocking the sale to Saudi Arabia of sophisticated radar planes and other military equipment was approved in the House by an overwhelming vote, although the Senate later cleared the sale.

Similarly, the House rebuked the president on his proposals to eliminate the minimum monthly Social Security benefit and to do away with the Legal Services Corporation.

And while the White House was still wrestling with its formal position on an extension of the 1965 Voting Rights Act, the House sent the president a clear signal of its own strong support for that measure.

In other key votes, the Senate indicated its leanings on two controversial social issues with its votes in favor of far-reaching curbs on abortions and court-ordered school busing for the purpose of racial integration.

Members of both houses shied from voting to approve a congressional pay raise for the year, opting instead for less direct ways to increase their take-home pay.

Senate Key Votes

1. Anti-Busing Rider

The Senate Sept. 16 invoked cloture and approved the most far-reaching anti-busing curb to date when it adopted an amendment to the Justice Department authorization bill (S 951).

The 61-36 cloture vote cut off a filibuster led by Lowell P. Weicker Jr., R-Conn. The vote was the first successful cloture effort out of five attempts since Weicker launched his filibuster in June, meeting the requirement of three-fifths of total Senate membership (60) needed to cut off debate. The breakdown on the vote was: R 36-16; D 25-20 (ND 11-19, SD 14-1).

The Senate then adopted the anti-busing amendment of J. Bennett Johnston, D-La., by a vote of 60-39.

The Johnston amendment would bar federal judges from ordering busing except in very narrow circumstances. It also would allow the attorney general to file lawsuits on behalf of students who believed they had been bused in violation of the standards set out in the Johnston proposal,

opening the way for overturning existing busing orders.

The Johnston proposal was attached to another amendment to S 951, sponsored by Jesse Helms, R-N.C. This proposal would prevent the Justice Department from spending money to bring any legal action that could lead, directly or indirectly, to court-ordered busing.

With outnumbered opponents of the anti-busing proposals employing delaying tactics, the Senate did not pass S 951 before the first session of the 97th Congress ended.

2. Saudi AWACS

The Reagan administration based its Middle East policy on what it called a "strategic consensus" among nations there that the Soviet Union posed the primary threat to them, notwithstanding their regional disputes.

To improve U.S. relations with oil giant Saudi Arabia, in part to nurture the Middle East consensus it perceived, the administration decided in the spring of 1981 to sell Saudi Arabia five sophisticated Airborne Warning and Control System (AWACS) radar planes and other military equipment.

The decision posed the first major test in Congress of President Reagan's authority in foreign policy.

Israel strongly opposed the AWACS sale, viewing it as a threat to Israeli air superiority in the Middle East, and the American Jewish community began to campaign against it from the moment the administration acknowledged its plans.

Critics in Congress said it was unwise to entrust the secrets of the computer-assisted AWACS surveillance system to a nation that often had opposed U.S. policy in the Middle East and whose ruling royal family was seen as vulnerable to being overthrown.

Saudi Arabia cast the deal as a test of U.S.-Saudi relations. The administration argued that Saudi air defenses must be bolstered to protect Saudi oil fields along the eastern coast of the Arabian Peninsula — the source of much of the industrial West's oil supplies.

Reagan's problem was that Congress could veto the AWACS sale under a law giving it the right to block major arms deals by passing a concurrent resolution within 30 days of receiving formal notice.

Formal notice of the deal was delivered on Oct. 1, giving Congress until Oct. 30 to veto the sale.

The House passed a resolution of disapproval (H Con Res 194) on Oct. 14 by an overwhelming vote of 301-111. *(House key vote 4)*

But Reagan won on the issue after he put his personal prestige on the line. He argued that a congressional veto would undermine his authority to conduct foreign policy, and the Senate rejected H Con Res 194 on Oct. 28 by a dramatic vote of 48-52: R 12-41; D 36-11 (ND 28-4, SD 8-7).

3. MX Missile

In its first vote on the issue since 1979, the Senate April 7 tabled an amendment that would have made a symbolic reduction in funds for the MX mobile intercontinental missile.

At the time of the vote, the administration was reviewing alternative approaches to keeping the new missile hidden from Soviet observation.

Critics of the missile saw that review as the ideal time to force a reconsideration of the basic premise behind deploying the MX: that a new, more accurate U.S. missile was needed because existing land-based missiles were vulnerable to a Soviet first strike.

Most Armed Services Committee members and senior Air Force officers favored the mobile basing technique proposed by President Carter, under which each MX would be shuttled among nearly two dozen hidden launch sites.

During Senate consideration of a fiscal 1981 defense supplemental authorizations bill (S 694), Larry Pressler, R-S.D., offered an amendment that would have deleted $7 million for research related to MX.

Pressler said the amendment would be a "clear signal" to the Pentagon and the administration that Congress was concerned about the missile and wanted to know how it would be based before voting funds for it.

Opponents of the amendment said that it would, instead, send a signal to the Soviet Union that the United States was not serious about modernizing its nuclear forces.

The Senate tabled (killed) the Pressler amendment on a 79-15 vote: R 44-6; D 35-9 (ND 20-9, SD 15-0).

4. Tenn-Tom Waterway

Since the 1940s, powerful members of Congress had fought first to authorize and then to appropriate money for the Tennessee-Tombigbee Waterway.

By 1981 about $1 billion had already been spent on the 232-mile inland canal, designed to connect the Tennessee River with the Tombigbee River and enable barges to navigate from Appalachian coal fields to the seaport of Mobile, Ala.

Environmentalists opposed the project as damaging and taxpayer organizations said it was too costly. They warned that "Tenn-Tom," as it was called, would cost $3 billion by the time it was finished.

When the Senate considered the fiscal 1982 energy and water appropriations bill (HR 4144) Nov. 4, a bipartisan group of senators tried to delete the $189 million in the bill for the canal.

Led by Charles H. Percy, R-Ill., and Daniel Patrick Moynihan, D-N.Y., they argued that the project was consuming too much of the money available for water projects. They said supporters of the project were overstating the benefits, and called it an "economic dinosaur."

Supporters said the canal was too near finished to be abandoned. They said it was needed to get coal to the sea for export, and estimated that it would generate $145 million a year in commerce.

The supporters insisted the total cost of the project would be only $1.8 billion, and charged that opponents were misrepresenting it. They said the railroads were behind efforts to kill the waterway to stifle competition for coal transportation.

J. Bennett Johnston, D-La., led the floor debate against Percy's amendment while 80-year-old John C. Stennis, D-Miss., the waterway's principal supporter over the years, twisted arms for votes. Percy's amendment to delete the funding for the waterway was defeated 46-48: R 27-21; D 19-27 (ND 17-14, SD 2-13).

The vote was the closest opponents of the project had ever come to winning, although Johnston said the vote was not as close as it appeared because six senators who voted against Tenn-Tom had promised to switch their votes if necessary to save the project.

Senators said after the vote that backers of the project had suggested to uncommitted senators that they support Tenn-Tom if they wanted support for other projects in which they were interested. They also played on affection for Stennis, suggesting that saving Tenn-Tom would help his re-election chances.

While a majority of House freshmen voted to kill Tenn-Tom *(House key vote 7)*, senators first elected in 1980 opposed Percy's amendment 7-11. The new members' votes were crucial because seven senators who had supported the project in the past voted to kill it in 1981.

5. Clinch River Breeder Reactor

In the 1970s the proposed Clinch River (Tenn.) breeder reactor had become a symbol in the fight over the future of nuclear power.

Anti-nuclear groups had long fought the reactor, and President Carter tried for four years to kill the project, which was designed to generate electricity while producing more plutonium fuel than it used. Carter worried that the plutonium could be stolen and used to make nuclear weapons.

But Congress continued to fund the program. By 1981 more than $1 billion had been spent of a total cost then estimated to be at least $3.2 billion, and construction had not even begun.

President Reagan's budget director, David A. Stockman, had strenuously opposed the project as uneconomical when he was a member of Congress, and left funding for Clinch River out of the president's fiscal 1982 budget. But Senate Majority Leader Howard H. Baker Jr., R-Tenn., persuaded Reagan to request $254 million for it.

The Senate Appropriations Committee included $180 million for the reactor in the fiscal 1982 energy and water appropriations bill (HR 4144).

When the measure came to the Senate floor Nov. 4, Dale Bumpers, D-Ark., and Gordon J. Humphrey, R-N.H., tried to kill the project. They called it an economic white elephant that would be technologically obsolete by the time it was completed.

But their amendment to delete the $180 million was first amended to cut only $90 million and then tabled (killed) by a vote of 48-46: R 36-14; D 12-32 (ND 4-26, SD 8-6). It was the closest Clinch River opponents had ever come to killing the project.

While budget-conscious freshman House members voted 36-34 to kill the project *(House key vote 8)*, Baker managed to persuade 14 of the 18 new Senate members to vote with him to support it.

Opponents managed a second vote the next day, but lost again by a five-vote margin. That day Baker had Vice President George Bush standing by to vote to save the project in case of a tie.

6. Abortion

The long-running fight over government funding of abortions for poor women was effectively ended when the Senate voted to bar such abortions except when needed to save a mother's life.

The vote was crucial because the Senate, over the years, had been a bastion of support for abortion funding. The House long had backed the so-called Hyde amendment (named for its sponsor, Rep. Henry J. Hyde, R-Ill.) to bar Medicaid funding of abortions in non-life-threatening situations.

Past House-Senate disputes over the Hyde amendment had produced lengthy deadlocks in conference. Compromises between the two bodies had allowed payment for abortions when the pregnancy was caused by rape or incest.

The new Senate Republican majority, including many members who were elected on strong anti-abortion platforms, moved decisively against abortion funding.

Despite attempts by Republican leaders to keep a supplemental appropriations bill (HR 3512) free from controversial legislative provisions, the Senate restored the Hyde amendment May 21 by a 52-43 vote: R 33-19; D 19-24 (ND 12-18, SD 7-6).

Debate on the amendment opened old wounds within the Republican Party, which had been deeply divided over the abortion funding issue.

Bob Packwood, R-Ore., a leading spokesman for abortion funding, accused Hyde amendment supporters of seeking to impose a "Cotton Mather mentality" on the country. But Jesse Helms, R-N.C., said the anti-abortion movement would not forgive those who voted against the Hyde amendment.

7. Debt Limit Increase

An increase in the federal debt limit was an unlikely candidate for fiscally conservative President Reagan's first legislative victory. But on Feb. 6 the Senate approved a measure (HR 1553) that raised the debt ceiling to $985 billion through Sept. 30, 1981, thus providing President Reagan with his maiden Capitol Hill success.

The Senate vote was 73-18: R 46-3; D 27-15 (ND 20-7, SD 7-8).

The vote cleared the bill for the president's signature since the House had approved it a day earlier by a 305-104 margin. *(House key vote 9)*

Had Congress failed to act, the outstanding debt would have hit the existing $935.1 billion ceiling by mid-February, leaving the government unable to meet its borrowing needs.

Just before the Senate vote on the measure, Finance Committee Chairman Robert Dole, R-Kan., joked that there had "been a lot of rapid conversion around here on this issue."

Republicans who in the past had opposed debt limit increases, charging that they were "fiscally irresponsible," acceded to the request of their president and voted for the bill. It was really leftover business from the Carter administration, they claimed.

8. Budget Cut Instructions

Budget reconciliation was the vehicle that moved President Reagan's philosophy of fiscal austerity from rhetoric to reality. And Senate action on April 2 to instruct Senate committees to cut $36.9 billion from fiscal 1982 spending was the first major step toward enactment of his budget-cutting proposals.

Under reconciliation, the spending cut instructions went to 14 authorizing and appropriations committees, where members were required to change existing programs to make the required savings.

Without waiting for action on the first fiscal 1982 budget resolution, the Senate adopted separate reconciliation instructions (S Con Res 9) by an 88-10 vote: R 51-1; D 37-9 (ND 22-9, SD 15-0).

Senate leaders — including Majority Leader Howard H. Baker Jr., R-Tenn., and Senate Budget Committee Chairman Pete V. Domenici, R-N.M. — and budget director David A. Stockman agreed that using reconciliation would put the administration's budget-cutting efforts on the fast track.

Together they were able to keep most Republicans united behind the spending reductions. On the final vote only one GOP senator — Lowell P. Weicker Jr., R-Conn., voted "no."

The Democrats, however, were deeply divided. Because many of the more conservative members of the party frequently voted with the Republicans, liberal Democrats did not come close to winning adoption of the more than 20 amendments they introduced.

9. Social Security

When President Reagan May 12 announced proposals to cut Social Security benefits, congressional Democrats saw a political opportunity they could not pass up.

Congress was in the midst of one of the biggest budget battles ever and the minority party, buoyed by public outrage at the proposed cuts in Social Security, repeatedly charged the administration with balancing its budget on the backs of the elderly.

For Republicans, the issue proved to be an embarrassing one.

The first major rebuff of the administration's plans came only a week after they were announced. On May 20 Sen. Daniel Patrick Moynihan, D-N.Y., offered a "sense of the Senate" amendment to a fiscal 1981 supplemental appropriations bill (HR 3512) condemning Reagan's plans as "a breach of faith" with the American elderly. It also stated that Congress would not "precipitously and unfairly" cut Social Security benefits.

The amendment was tabled (killed) by a vote of 49-48: R 48-2; D 1-46 (ND 0-32, SD 1-14).

Almost immediately after that vote, however, the Senate unanimously adopted a toned-down version of the amendment that promised Congress would not make any more cuts in the financially troubled program than were necessary to keep it solvent.

Reagan eventually withdrew his proposals and Congress passed a stopgap measure (HR 4331) to keep Social Security's largest trust fund, Old-Age and Survivors' Insurance, from going broke in 1982. At the end of the session, Senate Minority Leader Robert C. Byrd, D-W.Va., labeled the defeat of the administration's Social Security plans "a victory where victories, for Democrats, appear to be scarce."

10. Tax Indexing

During floor debate on President Reagan's individual and business tax cut package (H J Res 266), Senate Republicans added a provision intended to put an automatic cap on the growth of government spending for years to come.

The Finance Committee amendment, requiring that individual income taxes be indexed annually beginning in 1985 to offset the effects of inflation, was adopted July 16 by a vote of 57-40: R 43-8, D 14-32 (ND 11-20, SD 3-12).

The measure was vigorously opposed by Democrats and some Republicans who charged it would tie the hands of both the administration and Congress in making future budget and tax decisions.

But proponents argued that the government unfairly received a tax "bonus" each year as inflation pushed individuals into higher and higher tax brackets. They said such built-in revenue growth made it too easy for Congress to spend more taxpayers' money.

While lauded at the time as a major victory for fiscal conservatism, indexing soon appeared to be a possible victim of the government spending it was designed to contain. By the end of the year, projections of annual budget deficits approaching $200 billion made some economists and politicians skeptical that indexing would ever take effect.

11. Targeting Tax Cuts

One of the two major components of President Reagan's tax cut program — accelerated write-offs for capital investment — enjoyed fairly broad Senate support. But his proposed 23 percent across-the-board cut in individual income taxes became the primary target for Democratic opposition to the bill — and to the administration's entire economic philosophy.

Many Democrats charged that because income taxes were progressive the bulk of the reduction would be enjoyed by the wealthy, while the poor and middle class would hardly benefit at all. In addition, they said, the cut would mean a loss of $196 billion in tax revenues over the following three years, seriously jeopardizing the goal of a balanced budget in 1984.

The administration and its Republican defenders said the tax cuts would spur enough economic growth to solve many of the country's fiscal problems.

Sen. Ernest F. Hollings, D-S.C., July 23 offered an amendment to the tax bill (H J Res 266) that included a one-year, 10 percent cut in individual income taxes, with much of the relief targeted to those earning under $50,000. He said his cut was more likely than the president's to result in a balanced 1984 budget.

However, public and congressional support was strong for giving the new administration and its revolutionary supply-side tax policies a chance. The amendment was rejected 26-71: R 0-51; D-26-20 (ND 20-12, SD 6-8).

12. Congressional Pay Raise

Seeking to avoid politically embarrassing votes in the future, the Senate approved a permanent funding mechanism for pay raises for members of Congress. The action made it much more likely, although not certain, that members would get future pay raises along with other federal employees.

Congressional salaries had risen very slowly in recent years because members of Congress had been extremely reluctant to go on record in favor of giving themselves more money. Amendments to annual legislative appropriations bills had frozen the pay at $60,622.50 a year since 1979.

During conference action on a continuing appropriations resolution (H J Res 325), the House proposed that members get a 4.8 percent pay raise. That was rejected by Senate conferees. However, conferees agreed to establish a permanent appropriation for congressional pay increases.

When the conference report came to the Senate Sept. 30, the permanent appropriation provision was approved by a 48-44 vote: R 37-13; D 11-31 (ND 7-22, SD 4-9).

As under existing law, the president in the future would propose annual cost-of-living increases for federal employees, including members of Congress. Congress still could reject those proposals.

If the presidential pay proposal were approved, however, the money for increased congressional salaries would automatically be spent from the Treasury. There would no longer be a need to include funds for the raise in the legislative appropriations measure.

13. Oil Decontrol

One of President Reagan's first actions after taking office was his Jan. 28 decontrol of oil prices. Under a plan proposed by his predecessor, President Carter, some controls would have remained in effect until Sept. 30, 1981.

Reagan said allowing the free market to determine oil

prices would stimulate production and encourage conservation. The administration predicted only a moderate rise in oil and gasoline prices as a result of deregulation, but critics of the action were outraged.

Sen. Howard M. Metzenbaum, D-Ohio, other members of Congress, labor unions and consumer groups filed suit to block the decontrol order, but their effort was rejected by a federal court March 4.

Metzenbaum admitted he did not have the votes to overturn Reagan's order, but he insisted on a vote to force Republican senators to put a "stamp of approval" on the action. He said that would let the voters know which senators supported higher prices for gasoline and fuel oil.

When the Senate March 10 considered a bill (S 573) extending antitrust exemptions for oil companies participating in the International Energy Agency, Metzenbaum offered an amendment to nullify Reagan's decontrol order. Although floor debate was one-sided in support of the amendment (opponents knew they had the votes to kill it and did not bother to speak at length on the issue), the amendment was rejected 24-68: R 3-47; D 21-21 (ND 18-10, SD 3-11).

Senators supporting the amendment were mostly liberals from the Midwest and Northeast, areas that had been hit hard by rising fuel prices.

14. Tobacco Price Supports

For the first time in decades, Congress voted on whether tobacco price supports and strict marketing regulations should continue. The politically powerful program survived, but only by a few votes in the Senate.

President Reagan's budget-cutting and deregulation drives provided new arguments and new allies in Congress for the health groups and liberal members who had attacked the tobacco program before. A further embarrassment for the program was testimony, at an International Trade Commission hearing, that government-owned tobacco stocks were deteriorating in warehouses, at considerable cost to taxpayers.

Tobacco's opponents said that when the White House stressed a free-market approach, it was time to end what amounted to a federal monopoly for certain farmers to grow the crop.

Food stamp reductions and cost-cutting in farm and other programs prompted some members to say that tobacco also should bear its share of the budget cuts.

Tobacco's advocates declared the program was essential to the economy of the rural South. They suggested that without the program, cigarette smoking and its related health problems might grow because cheap tobacco would flood the market. The problem with deteriorating stocks could be cured, they said, by discouraging tobacco imports.

Tobacco's opponents thought they had just enough votes to kill or substantially change the program when the Senate considered the omnibus farm bill (S 884). But when tobacco votes were pushed into evening hours Sept. 17 during debate on the farm bill, their slender margins of victory vanished.

First the Senate refused to kill the program outright by 53-42. Then it narrowly rejected, by a 48-45 vote, an amendment by Sen. Thomas F. Eagleton, D-Mo., that would have replaced the fixed support price with discretionary authority for the agriculture secretary to lower support prices. The fixed price support was one of the program's most attractive features for growers.

On Sept. 18, Eagleton tried again with a similar amendment but lost when the amendment was tabled (killed) by a vote of 41-40: R 28-17; D 13-23 (ND 6-20, SD 7-3). The Senate then passed the farm bill.

The House later defeated an anti-tobacco amendment but added a recommendation to the farm bill that the program should be run without cost to taxpayers.

15. Dairy Price Supports

President Reagan prevailed in an early test of his policy proposals March 27 when Congress canceled a scheduled increase in dairy price supports.

Under the dairy program, the government was required to buy in the form of dry milk, butter and cheese, all the dairy products farmers were unable to sell at a price equal to the support price. The support price was due to be increased April 1 from its current level of $13.10 per hundredweight to $14.00.

The Reagan administration argued that the existing support price was so high that it stimulated dairymen to produce more milk, butter and cheese than Americans would buy. The scheduled increase would raise consumer prices and feed inflation, administration officials said.

Opponents insisted that low feed and livestock prices, not the federal program, had boosted production. They held that forgoing the April 1 price increase would mean small- to moderate-sized dairy operations would have to fold.

Dairy lobbyists disagreed on whether to fight the cancellation directly, but they coalesced around amendments that would have delayed congressional action.

A key amendment by Sen. John Melcher, D-Mont., to sharply curtail imports of a milk protein called casein would have caused serious jurisdictional problems and delays in the House. Melcher argued that imports of casein contributed to overproduction by disrupting the domestic market.

The administration objected that Melcher's amendment would invite trade retaliation from foreign purchasers of American farm products.

The Republican leadership initially lost a motion to table (kill) Melcher's amendment and kept the dairy bill (S 509) off the Senate floor for a week.

But by March 24, the administration had mustered enough support to defeat the amendment on a 38-60 vote: R 7-45; D 31-15 (ND 19-12, SD 12-3), and the bill later passed by 88-5.

16. B-1 Bomber

By a wider than expected margin, the Senate Dec. 3 turned down an amendment to the fiscal 1982 defense appropriations bill (HR 4995) that would have shifted funds from production of the B-1 bomber to a long list of conventional weapons and combat-readiness improvements.

Criticism of President Carter's 1977 decision to cancel the B-1 program long had been a staple of Republican political oratory. But by Oct. 2, when President Reagan announced his decision to buy 100 of the planes, some Republicans voiced second thoughts about the program because of its cost — estimated by some at $40 billion — and skyrocketing predictions of the fiscal 1982 deficit.

Some critics charged that existing B-52s could penetrate Soviet defenses for nearly as long as the B-1s and that a radical new kind of bomber called "stealth" could be in service by 1990 to replace the B-52. The stealth plane would be designed to avoid Soviet detection gear.

The administration won over Republican skeptics in mid-November by arguing that the cost of modernizing and operating the B-52s would almost equal the cost of buying and operating the B-1s.

Intertwined with the B-1 issue on this vote was an effort by Senate Democrats to forge a party alternative to Reagan's defense program. Defense specialists spanning a broad band of the party's political spectrum used the defense bill to attack the administration for funding exotic nuclear weapons by diverting funds from the combat readiness of conventional forces.

On a series of votes on amendments to the bill, the Senate split along nearly straight party lines, with most Democrats backing various "readiness" increases.

When several of those efforts were linked to an attack on the B-1, the consolidated amendment lost the support of many Democrats who supported the new bomber, and was rejected 28-66: R 5-43; D 23-23 (ND 18-13, SD 5-10).

House Key Votes

1. Earned Income Limit

The House rejected by a wide margin Oct. 28 a proposal to relax a restriction in the House ethics code on the amount of outside income House members could earn in addition to their official salaries.

The proposal (H Res 251), drafted by House Rules Committee Chairman Richard Bolling, D-Mo., would have raised the ceiling on a member's outside earned income from 15 percent to 40 percent of the member's official salary. The increase would have applied to members' earnings for 1981 through 1983, after which the ceiling would have reverted to 15 percent.

The vote to reject the proposal meant that at their current annual salary of $60,662.50, members continued to be bound by a cap of $9,099.37 a year in outside earned income. Under the Bolling proposal, the ceiling would have risen to $24,265 a year.

The relaxation of the rule appeared to enjoy widespread support and was backed by House leaders on both sides of the aisle. Spurring supporters on was the Senate's total elimination of similar restrictions on senators' outside earned income.

But in an emotional debate, opponents cited the difficulty of voting for a "backdoor pay raise" during a time of widespread budget cutting and argued that the move would weaken the ethics code.

Finally, defeat of Bolling's proposal was assured when opponents forced a recorded vote on the matter. The resolution was rejected 147-271: R 73-112; D 74-159 (ND 49-107, SD 25-52).

But less than two months later, when a recorded vote was avoided, the House reversed itself and approved a similar relaxation of the outside income rule.

On Dec. 15, the day before the end of the first session, the House approved by unanimous consent a request by Rep. John P. Murtha, D-Pa., that the earned income ceiling be raised from 15 percent to 30 percent, beginning in 1981. That proposal (H Res 305) sailed through in about 10 seconds.

2. Legal Services Corporation

The House ignored a proposal by the Reagan administration to abolish the Legal Services Corporation and on June 18 voted 245-137 to reauthorize the agency for two years at $241 million annually.

HR 3480 passed with some Republican support, although GOP members voted overwhelmingly against reauthorization: R 59-116; D 186-21 (ND 137-3, SD 49-18).

President Reagan wanted to abolish the 7-year-old corporation and let states provide legal services to the poor through social services block grants.

That plan met with strong opposition from LSC supporters inside and outside Congress. They argued that states — even with help from the private bar — would be unable to provide meaningful legal representation to the poor.

The vote on final passage did not reflect the intensity of the three-day debate on the bill. A number of amendments were adopted restricting the activities of LSC lawyers. These included a ban on so-called "class action" lawsuits against local, state or federal government agencies, restrictions on the type of aliens who could be represented and a tougher ban on lobbying activities.

3. Voting Rights Act

Signaling its support for a strong bill (HR 3112) to extend the 1965 Voting Rights Act, the House Oct. 5 rejected an amendment that would have changed the forum for hearing certain voting discrimination cases.

The amendment sponsored by M. Caldwell Butler, R-Va., would have required that cases involving jurisdictions covered by key enforcement provisions of the act be heard by three-judge federal panels in those jurisdictions. The amendment specified that none of the judges could be from the jurisdiction involved in the suit.

Under current law, such suits are heard by a three-judge panel in the District of Columbia.

Proponents of the amendment contended that it was burdensome and unnecessary to hear voting cases in Washington, D.C. They argued that there were good federal judges all over the country who were capable of properly handling a voting discrimination case.

Opponents of the amendment contended that it was important to have uniformity in voting-rights decisions and that all cases should be heard by one court. They noted further that the D.C. court had developed expertise in this area of the law.

Supporters of a strong extension bill knew that HR 3112 was out of danger when the Butler amendment was defeated handily by a 132-277 vote: R 102-75; D 30-202 (ND 4-153, SD 26-49).

4. Saudi AWACS

The Reagan administration based its Middle East policy on what it called a "strategic consensus" among nations there that the Soviet Union posed the primary threat to them, notwithstanding their regional disputes.

To improve U.S. relations with oil giant Saudi Arabia, in part to nurture the Middle East consensus it perceived, the administration decided in the spring of 1981 to sell Saudi Arabia five sophisticated Airborne Warning and Control System (AWACS) radar planes and other military equipment.

The decision posed the first major test in Congress of President Reagan's authority in foreign policy.

Israel strongly opposed the AWACS sale, viewing it as a threat to Israeli air superiority in the Middle East, and the American Jewish community began to campaign against it from the moment the administration acknowledged its plans.

Critics in Congress said it was unwise to entrust the secrets of the computer-assisted AWACS surveillance system to a nation that often had opposed U.S. policy in the Middle East and whose ruling royal family was seen as vulnerable to being overthrown.

Saudi Arabia cast the deal as a test of U.S.-Saudi relations. The administration argued that Saudi air defenses must be bolstered to protect Saudi oil fields along the eastern coast of the Arabian Peninsula — the source of much of the industrial West's oil supplies.

Reagan's problem was that Congress could veto the AWACS sale under a law giving it the right to block major arms deals by passing a concurrent resolution within 30 days of receiving formal notice.

Formal notice of the deal was delivered on Oct. 1, giving Congress until Oct. 30 to veto the sale.

The House passed a resolution of disapproval (H Con Res 194) on Oct. 14 by an overwhelming vote of 301-111: R 108-78; D 193-33 (ND 149-5, SD 44-28).

But Reagan won on the issue after he put his personal prestige on the line. He argued that a congressional veto would undermine his authority to conduct foreign policy, and the Senate failed by a dramatic 48-52 vote on Oct. 28 to pass H Con Res 194. *(Senate key vote 2)*

5. B-1 Bomber

After a narrow victory in the Defense Appropriations Subcommittee, House critics of the B-1 bomber were swamped 3-1 on Nov. 18 when they tried to delete $1.8 billion in B-1 procurement funds from the defense appropriations bill (HR 4995).

B-1 critics argued that the plane would not long be able to penetrate Soviet air defenses and that it would drain funds from development of a new "stealth" bomber, designed to evade Soviet radar.

But supporters of the B-1 — which President Carter had canceled in June 1977 and President Reagan revived in October 1981 — cited much more optimistic assessments of the B-1's effectiveness against Soviet defenses. And they warned that the technical feasibility of a stealth bomber remained uncertain.

What likely would have been a victory for B-1 supporters in any case became a cinch when Reagan announced a nuclear arms-control proposal to Moscow a few hours before the B-1 vote. B-1 supporters insisted that a vote against the plane would undermine the U.S. bargaining position in arms control talks with the Russians.

The amendment to delete B-1 funds was rejected 142-263: R 21-157; D 121-106 (ND 111-42, SD 10-64).

6. MX Missile

What might have been a much closer fight became a 2-1 rout when House critics of the MX missile tried Nov. 18 to delete the program from the defense appropriations bill (HR 4995) hours after President Reagan made his nuclear arms reduction proposal to the Soviet Union.

Republicans and conservative House Democrats stampeded to support both the MX and the B-1 bomber as a symbol of their backing for the president's initiative and to ensure that he would have "bargaining chips" in dealing with Moscow.

MX opponents insisted that continued work on the missile should await selection of a final basing technique, which Reagan had deferred until 1984. The final design of the missile would be affected by whether it was launched from an airplane or from deep underground, they said,

citing two possible basing techniques.

But the bargaining-chip argument pervaded the debate on an amendment to delete some $1.9 billion for the MX from the defense bill, and the amendment was rejected 139-264: R 27-151; D 112-113 (ND 103-48, SD 9-65).

7. Tenn-Tom Waterway

Serving notice that they were less inclined than in the past to go along automatically with funding of costly water projects, House members came closer to killing funding for the 232-mile Tennessee-Tombigbee Waterway than ever before.

With budgetary concerns added to longstanding environmental objections, opponents of the canal managed to come within 20 votes of killing it.

Concentrating on fiscally conservative freshman members, lobbyists from environmental and taxpayer groups worked for several weeks lining up votes against "Tenn-Tom," the costliest water project in the nation's history.

When the fiscal 1982 energy and water appropriations bill (HR 4144) came to the House floor July 23, freshman members helped lead the move to delete the $189 million in funding for Tenn-Tom from the bill.

Although the freshmen voted 42-30 for the amendment, enough veteran members stuck with the project to save it, and the amendment failed, 198-208: R 108-70; D 90-138 (ND 82-70, SD 8-68).

As in the Senate *(Senate key vote 4)*, opponents of Tenn-Tom argued that the waterway would cost $3 billion and produce few economic benefits. They said it would be better to kill the canal and have "half a white elephant" than a whole one. Supporters countered that the project would cost only $1.8 billion and claimed the benefits would be substantial.

8. Clinch River Breeder Reactor

Just as on the Tenn-Tom Waterway vote, economy-minded House freshmen came closer to killing the funding for the Clinch River (Tenn.) breeder reactor than ever before.

Freshman members had persuaded the House Science Committee to deauthorize the project in May, but that decision was overturned in the massive budget reconciliation bill (HR 3982) in June. The freshmen tried again July 24 when funding for Clinch River came to the House floor in the fiscal 1982 energy and water appropriations bill (HR 4144).

While proponents argued that the project would pay for itself through the sale of electricity and that the $1 billion already spent on it would be wasted if it were killed, opponents insisted the breeder reactor could not be justified on economic grounds.

Freshman members voted 36-34 for an amendment to delete the $228 million for the project from the bill, but the rest of the House was not persuaded and the amendment was rejected 186-206: R 70-104; D 116-102 (ND 107-38, SD 9-64).

Twenty-eight members, mostly conservative Republicans, who had voted for the project in 1979 voted against it July 24; however, 20 members (19 of them Democrats) who had voted to kill the project in 1979 voted July 24 to continue it.

9. Debt Limit Increase

For the first time in many of their careers, House Republicans joined Democrats on Feb. 5 to approve a mea-

sure (HR 1553) raising the public debt limit to $985 billion through Sept. 30, 1981. The vote was 405-104: R 150-36; D 155-68 (ND 112-37, SD 43-31).

The Senate passed the bill a day later, clearing the bill. *(Senate key vote 7)*

It was President Reagan's first legislative victory.

Without an increase in the debt ceiling, the outstanding debt would have hit the existing $935.1 billion limit by mid-February, thus preventing the government from meeting its borrowing needs.

GOP members, who often had called a vote to increase the debt limit "fiscally irresponsible," argued that this was merely leftover business from the Carter administration. Marjorie S. Holt, R-Md., justified fiscal conservatives' support for the debt limit increase by noting: "I see for the first time some glimmer of hope that we will bring federal spending under control."

10. Budget Cut Instructions

The May 7 House vote to accept the administration-backed Gramm-Latta budget-cutting plan was both a political and a budget milestone.

It was the first formal endorsement in the Democratic-controlled House of Reagan's campaign mandate to slash federal spending.

With the help of 63 Democrats, the House voted 253-176 — R 190-0; D 63-176 (ND 17-144, SD 46-32) — to order its authorizing committees to come up with $36.6 billion in spending cuts for fiscal 1982.

These reconciliation instructions were included in the first budget resolution (H Con Res 115) that set a fiscal 1982 spending target of $688.8 billion, contemplated a $31 billion deficit and provided room for the president's proposed $51.3 billion tax cut.

The cuts made under reconciliation would be permanent cuts in authorizations, and signaled a shift in power from the traditional purse-string stronghold — the Appropriations Committee — to the Budget and authorizing committees.

In accepting the Gramm-Latta substitute to the budget resolution, the House turned aside the product of its own Budget Committee, which had called for slightly higher spending but a smaller tax cut.

The chief difference between the two measures, however, was that the Budget Committee's reconciliation plan followed the more traditional use of reconciliation. It called for authorizing committees to cut $15.8 billion in fiscal 1982 spending and $23.6 billion in cuts from programs funded by appropriations, which could be changed in future years.

11. Reconciliation Budget Cuts

In a stunning victory for the Reagan administration, the House voted on June 26 to overturn the work of its authorizing and Budget committees and instead accept an administration-backed package of $37.3 billion in budget cuts known as Gramm-Latta II.

The narrow 217-211 victory on the GOP alternative to the budget reconciliation bill (HR 3982) was achieved with the help of 29 hard-core conservative Democrats, thus solidifying the coalition that would put into place the entire Reagan economic program. The complete vote breakdown: R 188-2; D 29-209 (ND 3-157, SD 26-52).

Before the vote to substitute the Gramm-Latta provisions, Delbert L. Latta, R-Ohio, a cosponsor of the amendment and ranking GOP member of the House Budget Committee, framed the vote this way: "It is a question of whether we can turn the country around economically or not."

Members of both political parties, however, were upset with the almost complete lack of details about the Gramm-Latta proposal before the vote was taken. The package of cuts covered the entire spectrum of federal programs — save defense.

"This has been a terrible way to legislate, but we have no alternatives," lamented Barber B. Conable Jr., R-N.Y.

There were two reasons the administration felt it necessary to draft a substitute for the $37.6 billion package agreed to by the authorizing committees and compiled by the Budget Committee. First, the Republicans claimed, the committees had failed to cut back entitlement programs. In addition, they said, the authorizing panels had not gone far enough to fold many categorical social programs together into block grants.

12. Tax Cuts

The Democratic-controlled House proved the major battleground for the administration's controversial plans to reduce individual income and business investment taxes.

The Ways and Means Committee attempted to fashion an alternative to Reagan's tax-cut proposals that would appeal to both waivering conservative Democrats — who had defected to back the administration on an earlier budget vote — and party liberals.

Their package (HR 4242) called for a two-year, 15 percent cut in individual income taxes skewed to help those earning below $50,000 a year. An additional 10 percent cut during the third year would have been triggered if the economy performed well. The bill also would have cut corporate income tax rates, as well as provided for accelerated depreciation.

The administration proposed a 23 percent across-the-board cut in individual income taxes and accelerated depreciation for business.

But in a fierce bidding war for votes, special tax breaks were added to both packages, making it increasingly difficult to distinguish between the two. With a heavy, last-minute lobbying effort by the administration, a number of crucial Democratic votes were wooed to the Republican side.

The administration-backed substitute to the committee bill, offered by Barber B. Conable Jr., R-N.Y., and conservative Democrat Kent Hance, Texas, was adopted July 29 by a vote of 238-195: R 190-1; D 48-194 (ND 12-151, SD 36-43).

13. Social Security Minimum

After President Reagan told a joint session of Congress Feb. 18 that "the full retirement benefits" of 36 million Social Security recipients would "be continued," Democrats sought to hold him to his word. They condemned his proposal three weeks later to eliminate the $122 minimum monthly benefit for some 3 million Social Security recipients as a cruel reversal of policy.

Despite the public furor over the cut and growing Republican apprehension, both houses went ahead and separately agreed to cut the benefit as part of a budget reconciliation bill (HR 3982). But when it came time for final approval of the conference agreement, House members balked.

As a result of negotiations between House and Senate leaders eager to resolve the budget issue, House Rules

Committee Chairman Richard Bolling, D-Mo., proposed a rule July 31 to allow consideration of both the reconciliation conference agreement and a bill (HR 4331) to restore the full minimum benefit.

By a vote of 271-151: R 166-21; D 105-130 (ND 56-101, SD 49-29), the House agreed to end debate and the possibility of further amendment on the rule, thus paving the way for passage of the rule, HR 4331, and the conference report.

Although most Democrats expressed support for the minimum benefit, many voted against ending debate because they opposed the entire reconciliation package.

The Senate voted Oct. 15 to restore the minimum payment for some current recipients, and after a lengthy conference Congress agreed to keep the benefit for all current recipients. However, it extended the Social Security payroll tax to the first six months of sick pay to cover most of the $6.1 billion cost for 1982-86 of restoring the benefit.

14. Social Program Spending

The House coalition that had passed President Reagan's economic program cracked on the issue of direct spending cuts in social programs.

More than three dozen Republicans deserted their party leadership to oppose a motion to cut spending in the $87.2 billion appropriations bill for the departments of Labor, Health and Human Services and Education (HR 4560). Reagan Sept. 24 had called for new cuts in fiscal 1982 spending.

On Oct. 6, Ralph Regula, R-Ohio, offered a motion to recommit the bill to the Appropriations Committee to make reductions in spending. His motion — the first test of congressional support for Reagan's revised budget — was rejected 168-249: R 140-39; D 28-210 (ND 3-157, SD 25-53).

The vote showed the potential power of the "Gypsy Moths," a group of moderate House GOP members, mostly from the Northeast and Midwest. These Frost Belt Republicans opposed cuts in programs, such as job training and fuel assistance to the poor, that were particularly helpful to their districts, many of which were facing economic hard times.

Gypsy Moth Carl D. Pursell, R-Mich., said the group did not want further social spending cuts without accompanying reductions in other areas. "I don't think we can make the [budget] balancing act by just touching this bill," he told the House. "We want to see a quid pro quo on cuts in [such programs as] defense, water projects and tobacco."

15. Foreign Aid Appropriations

Always an unpopular program, foreign aid was the subject of especially rancorous disputes in a year when domestic spending was being cut deeply.

Congress was hamstrung in trying to fashion a foreign aid program by a fundamental disagreement in the House between conservative Republicans and liberal Democrats over the ratio of military-to-development aid.

The Reagan administration asked Congress to substantially increase U.S. military aid while stringing out contributions to some international development banks to reduce federal spending.

The House Appropriations Committee reported its aid appropriations bill (HR 4559) on Sept. 22. But the dispute over military *vs.* development aid made Democrats reluctant to bring the measure to the floor.

The stalemate was broken after a fight between President Reagan and Congress in late November over a stopgap funding measure for most of the federal government.

Reagan challenged Congress to accept its responsibility to pass the appropriations bills. House Speaker Thomas P. O'Neill Jr., D-Mass., responded that the House had passed all its appropriations bills except for HR 4559. O'Neill promised to get HR 4559 to the floor if Reagan would round up enough GOP votes to pass it.

Reagan and Secretary of State Alexander M. Haig Jr. then made personal appeals to House Republicans to get the aid bill through Congress.

The House finally took up HR 4559 on Dec. 11 and handled it in whirlwind fashion, with key Republicans leading the fight for it by stressing the national security role of foreign aid.

The House passed the bill by a vote of 199-166. GOP members voted 84-87 against it. But enough of them supported the measure to get it through the House with the help of a majority of Democrats, who voted for it 115-79 (ND 95-36, SD 20-43).

Both houses cleared the conference report on HR 4559 on Dec. 16, marking the first time Congress had cleared a foreign aid appropriations bill since 1978.

16. Omnibus Farm Bill

Fierce competition for a share of the federal pie shattered the historic coalition of farm groups and slowed work on the four-year renewal of farm programs (S 884). The Senate passed a bill meeting President Reagan's stringent budget specifications, but the House passed a far more costly version.

The conference dragged on for six weeks while the administration adamantly held out for revisions and unhappy House members choked down substantial cuts in their bill.

The final conference agreement was approved amid such bitterness that some key House members like Thomas S. Foley, D-Wash., Democratic whip and former Agriculture Committee chairman, withheld support until the last.

The Senate adopted the conference report Dec. 10 by a vote of 68-31.

But the painful process continued in the House until the last night of the session on Dec. 16, when the House narrowly cleared the bill for the president by a vote of 205-203: R 125-59; D 80-144 (ND 27-121, SD 53-23).

The two-vote margin reflected the strong pressures on members. Many wanted the bill to pass because the alternatives — having to revert to antiquated and expensive permanent farm laws or to face the 1982 elections with a farm bill rewrite — were worse. But they also wanted the record to show they opposed it because consumer groups, food processors and certain farm interests objected strenuously.

Dairymen opposed provisions that expressed their minimum supports in dollars instead of percentages of parity, the controversial farm inflation index. Wheat growers also were disturbed by support levels that some felt did not protect them from inflation.

Consumer groups objected that peanut and sugar provisions would cost American families billions of dollars. But sugar, peanut, corn, cotton, rice and soybean groups all backed the bill.

The administration had successfully followed a strategy, according to budget director David A. Stockman, of dividing the farm coalition to hold down program increases that farmers wanted. ∎

State / Senator	1	2	3	4	5	6	7	8
ALABAMA								
Denton	Y	N	Y	N	Y	Y	Y	Y
Heflin	Y	Y	Y	N	Y	?	N	Y
ALASKA								
Murkowski	Y	N	Y	N	Y	Y	Y	Y
Stevens	N	N	Y	X	?	N	?	Y
ARIZONA								
Goldwater	Y	N	Y	?	?	Y	Y	Y
DeConcini	Y	Y	Y	N	Y	N	Y	N
ARKANSAS								
Bumpers	N	Y	Y	N	N	N	Y	Y
Pryor	Y	Y	Y	N	N	N	N	Y
CALIFORNIA								
Hayakawa	Y	N	Y	N	Y	N	Y	Y
Cranston	N	Y	Y	N	N	?	Y	N
COLORADO								
Armstrong	Y	N	Y	Y	N	Y	N	Y
Hart	N	Y	Y	Y	N	N	Y	Y
CONNECTICUT								
Weicker	N	Y	N	?	?	N	Y	N
Dodd	N	Y	N	N	N	N	N	N
DELAWARE								
Roth	Y	Y	?	Y	N	Y	Y	Y
Biden	Y	Y	?	Y	N	Y	Y	Y
FLORIDA								
Hawkins	Y	Y	Y	#	Y	Y	Y	Y
Chiles	Y	Y	Y	Y	N	Y	Y	Y
GEORGIA								
Mattingly	Y	N	Y	N	Y	Y	N	Y
Nunn	Y	N	Y	N	N	N	N	Y
HAWAII								
Inouye	N	Y	Y	N	N	X	Y	Y
Matsunaga	N	Y	N	N	N	N	N	Y
IDAHO								
McClure	Y	N	Y	N	Y	Y	Y	Y
Symms	Y	N	Y	N	Y	Y	Y	Y
ILLINOIS								
Percy	N	N	Y	Y	N	N	Y	Y
Dixon	Y	Y	Y	Y	N	Y	N	Y
INDIANA								
Lugar	Y	N	Y	N	Y	N	Y	Y
Quayle	Y	N	Y	Y	N	Y	Y	Y
IOWA								
Grassley	Y	N	Y	Y	Y	Y	Y	Y
Jepsen	Y	N	Y	Y	N	Y	Y	Y
KANSAS								
Dole	Y	N	Y	N	Y	Y	Y	Y
Kassebaum	Y	N	N	Y	N	N	Y	Y
KENTUCKY								
Ford	Y	Y	Y	N	Y	N	Y	N
Huddleston	Y	N	Y	N	Y	Y	N	Y
LOUISIANA								
Johnston	Y	N	Y	N	Y	Y	Y	Y
Long	Y	N	Y	N	Y	#	Y	Y
MAINE								
Cohen	N	N	Y	Y	N	N	?	Y
Mitchell	N	Y	Y	N	N	Y	Y	Y
MARYLAND								
Mathias	N	N	?	Y	Y	?	?	+
Sarbanes	N	Y	Y	Y	N	N	Y	N
MASSACHUSETTS								
Kennedy	X	Y	N	Y	N	N	Y	Y
Tsongas	N	Y	N	Y	N	N	?	N
MICHIGAN								
Levin	N	Y	Y	N	N	N	Y	N
Riegle	N	Y	N	Y	N	N	Y	Y
MINNESOTA								
Boschwitz	N	N	Y	N	Y	Y	Y	Y
Durenberger	N	Y	?	Y	N	Y	Y	Y
MISSISSIPPI								
Cochran	Y	N	Y	N	Y	Y	Y	Y
Stennis	Y	N	Y	N	Y	N	Y	Y
MISSOURI								
Danforth	Y	Y	Y	Y	N	Y	N	Y
Eagleton	N	Y	N	Y	N	Y	Y	N
MONTANA								
Baucus	N	Y	Y	N	N	N	N	Y
Melcher	Y	N	Y	N	N	Y	-	Y
NEBRASKA								
Exon	Y	N	Y	N	N	Y	N	Y
Zorinsky	Y	N	?	Y	Y	Y	N	Y
NEVADA								
Laxalt	Y	N	Y	?	Y	Y	Y	Y
Cannon	Y	Y	Y	?	+	Y	?	Y
NEW HAMPSHIRE								
Humphrey	Y	N	Y	N	Y	N	Y	Y
Rudman	N	N	Y	Y	N	Y	Y	Y
NEW JERSEY								
Bradley	N	Y	Y	Y	N	N	Y	Y
Williams	N	Y	?	Y	N	N	Y	?
NEW MEXICO								
Domenici	Y	N	Y	Y	Y	Y	Y	Y
Schmitt	Y	N	Y	N	Y	N	Y	Y
NEW YORK								
D'Amato	Y	Y	Y	Y	N	Y	Y	Y
Moynihan	N	Y	Y	Y	?	N	?	Y
NORTH CAROLINA								
East	Y	N	Y	N	Y	N	Y	N
Helms	Y	N	Y	Y	Y	Y	Y	Y
NORTH DAKOTA								
Andrews	N	N	Y	N	Y	Y	Y	Y
Burdick	N	Y	N	Y	N	Y	N	Y
OHIO								
Glenn	N	Y	Y	N	N	?	?	Y
Metzenbaum	N	Y	N	Y	N	N	N	N
OKLAHOMA								
Nickles	Y	N	Y	N	N	Y	Y	Y
Boren	Y	N	Y	N	?	Y	N	Y
OREGON								
Hatfield	N	N	N	N	N	N	Y	Y
Packwood	N	Y	Y	N	Y	N	?	Y
PENNSYLVANIA								
Heinz	N	Y	Y	Y	Y	Y	Y	Y
Specter	N	Y	Y	Y	Y	N	Y	Y
RHODE ISLAND								
Chafee	N	N	Y	N	Y	N	Y	Y
Pell	#	Y	N	Y	N	N	Y	N
SOUTH CAROLINA								
Thurmond	Y	N	Y	N	Y	Y	Y	Y
Hollings	Y	Y	Y	N	N	N	Y	Y
SOUTH DAKOTA								
Abdnor	Y	N	Y	N	Y	Y	Y	Y
Pressler	N	N	N	Y	Y	Y	Y	Y
TENNESSEE								
Baker	Y	N	N	N	Y	N	Y	Y
Sasser	Y	Y	Y	N	Y	Y	N	Y
TEXAS								
Tower	Y	N	Y	N	Y	N	Y	Y
Bentsen	Y	Y	Y	N	Y	Y	Y	Y
UTAH								
Garn	Y	N	Y	Y	Y	Y	Y	Y
Hatch	Y	N	Y	N	Y	Y	Y	Y
VERMONT								
Stafford	?	N	Y	Y	N	Y	Y	Y
Leahy	N	Y	Y	Y	N	N	Y	Y
VIRGINIA								
Warner	Y	N	Y	N	Y	N	Y	Y
Byrd*	Y	N	Y	Y	N	N	N	Y
WASHINGTON								
Gorton	N	N	Y	N	Y	Y	Y	Y
Jackson	Y	Y	Y	N	Y	Y	Y	Y
WEST VIRGINIA								
Byrd	Y	Y	Y	N	Y	N	Y	Y
Randolph	Y	N	Y	N	Y	Y	Y	Y
WISCONSIN								
Kasten	Y	Y	Y	N	Y	Y	Y	Y
Proxmire	Y	Y	N	Y	N	Y	N	Y
WYOMING								
Simpson	Y	N	Y	Y	Y	N	Y	Y
Wallop	Y	N	Y	Y	Y	N	Y	Y

Democrats   *Republicans*

* Byrd elected as an independent.

KEY

- Y Voted for (yea).
- # Paired for.
- + Announced for.
- N Voted against (nay).
- X Paired against.
- - Announced against.
- P Voted "present".
- C Voted "present" to avoid possible conflict of interest.
- ? Did not vote or otherwise make a position known.

1. S 951. Justice Department Authorization. Johnston, D-La., motion to invoke cloture (thus limiting debate) on the Helms, R-N.C.-Johnston amendment to prohibit federal courts in most instances from ordering school busing for racial balance. Motion agreed to 61-36: R 36-16; D 25-20 (ND 11-19, SD 14-1), Sept. 16, 1981. A three-fifths vote (60) of the full Senate is required to invoke cloture.

2. H Con Res 194. Saudi AWACS. Adoption of the concurrent resolution disapproving the proposal by President Reagan to sell Saudi Arabia an $8.5 billion package of military equipment consisting of five E-3A Airborne Warning and Control System (AWACS) radar planes, 1,177 AIM-9L Sidewinder air-to-air missiles, 101 sets of conformal fuel tanks for F-15 fighter planes and six to eight KC-707 tanker aircraft. Rejected 48-52: R 12-41; D 36-11 (ND 28-4, SD 8-7), Oct. 28, 1981. A "nay" was a vote supporting the president's position.

3. S 694. Fiscal 1981 Supplemental Defense Authorization. Tower, R-Texas, motion to table (kill) the Pressler, R-S.D., amendment to delete $7 million for research related to the MX missile. Motion agreed to 79-15: R 44-6; D 35-9 (ND 20-9, SD 15-0), April 7, 1981.

4. HR 4144. Energy and Water Development Appropriations, Fiscal 1982. Percy, R-Ill., amendment to delete $189 million for the continued construction of the Tennessee-Tombigbee Waterway. The effect would be to cancel the project. Rejected 46-48: R 27-21; D 19-27 (ND 17-14, SD 2-13), Nov. 4, 1981. A "nay" was a vote supporting the president's position.

5. HR 4144. Energy and Water Development Appropriations, Fiscal 1982. Johnston, D-La., motion to table (kill) the Bumpers, D-Ark., amendment as amended by the Tsongas, D-Mass., amendment, to reduce by half ($90 million) the appropriation for the Clinch River (Tenn.) nuclear breeder reactor. Motion agreed to 48-46: R 36-14; D 12-32 (ND 4-26, SD 8-6), Nov. 4, 1981. A "yea" was a vote supporting the president's position.

6. HR 3512. Fiscal 1981 Supplemental Appropriations. Helms, R-N.C., motion to table (kill) the Appropriations Committee amendment to delete House-passed language prohibiting Medicaid funding of abortions except when needed to save the mother's life. (The effect of the motion was to restore the House prohibition to the bill.) Motion agreed to 52-43: R 33-19; D 19-24 (ND 12-18, SD 7-6), May 21, 1981. A "yea" was a vote supporting the president's position.

7. HR 1553. Debt Limit Increase. Passage of the bill to increase the public debt limit to $985 billion through Sept. 30, 1981. Passed (thus cleared for the president) 73-18: R 46-3; D 27-15 (ND 20-7; SD 7-8), Feb. 6, 1981. A "yea" was a vote supporting the president's position.

8. S Con Res 9. Budget Reconciliation Instructions. Adoption of the concurrent resolution to instruct 14 Senate authorizing and appropriations committees to cut $36.9 billion from fiscal 1982 spending. Adopted 88-10: R 51-1; D 37-9 (ND 22-9, SD 15-0), April 2, 1981. A "yea" was a vote supporting the president's position.

KEY

Y	Voted for (yea).
#	Paired for.
+	Announced for.
N	Voted against (nay).
X	Paired against.
-	Announced against.
P	Voted "present".
C	Voted "present" to avoid possible conflict of interest.
?	Did not vote or otherwise make a position known.

	9	10	11	12	13	14	15	16
ALABAMA								
Denton	Y	Y	N	Y	N	Y	N	?
Heflin	N	Y	N	N	N	Y	Y	N
ALASKA								
Murkowski	Y	Y	N	Y	N	?	N	N
Stevens	Y	Y	?	Y	N	Y	?	N
ARIZONA								
Goldwater	Y	Y	N	Y	N	Y	N	-
DeConcini	N	Y	N	N	N	N	Y	-
ARKANSAS								
Bumpers	N	N	Y	N	Y	?	Y	Y
Pryor	N	Y	N	N	N	N	Y	Y
CALIFORNIA								
Hayakawa	Y	?	N	Y	N	Y	N	?
Cranston	N	N	Y	Y	?	?	N	N
COLORADO								
Armstrong	Y	Y	N	N	N	Y	N	N
Hart	N	Y	Y	N	?	N	Y	Y
CONNECTICUT								
Weicker	N	N	N	?	N	?	N	N
Dodd	N	N	Y	Y	Y	?	?	Y
DELAWARE								
Roth	N	Y	N	Y	Y	N	N	N
Biden	N	N	Y	N	Y	N	N	Y
FLORIDA								
Hawkins	?	Y	N	Y	Y	Y	N	N
Chiles	N	N	Y	N	N	?	Y	N
GEORGIA								
Mattingly	Y	Y	N	N	N	Y	N	N
Nunn	N	N	Y	N	N	Y	N	Y
HAWAII								
Inouye	N	N	Y	Y	Y	?	N	N
Matsunaga	N	N	Y	?	Y	Y	N	Y
IDAHO								
McClure	Y	Y	N	Y	N	Y	N	N
Symms	Y	Y	N	Y	N	Y	N	N
ILLINOIS								
Percy	Y	Y	N	Y	N	N	N	N
Dixon	N	Y	N	N	N	N	N	N
INDIANA								
Lugar	Y	Y	N	Y	N	Y	N	N
Quayle	Y	Y	N	Y	N	N	N	N
IOWA								
Grassley	Y	Y	N	N	N	Y	Y	N
Jepsen	Y	Y	N	Y	N	Y	N	N
KANSAS								
Dole	Y	Y	N	Y	X	Y	N	N
Kassebaum	Y	Y	N	Y	N	N	N	Y
KENTUCKY								
Ford	N	N	Y	N	N	Y	Y	Y
Huddleston	N	N	Y	Y	Y	Y	Y	N
LOUISIANA								
Johnston	N	N	N	Y	N	?	Y	Y
Long	N	N	N	?	N	Y	Y	N
MAINE								
Cohen	Y	Y	N	N	N	Y	N	N
Mitchell	N	N	N	N	Y	X	Y	Y
MARYLAND								
Mathias	?	N	?	Y	N	N	N	Y
Sarbanes	N	N	N	N	Y	Y	Y	Y
MASSACHUSETTS								
Kennedy	N	N	Y	Y	?	N	N	Y
Tsongas	N	?	Y	Y	N	?	N	Y
MICHIGAN								
Levin	N	Y	Y	N	Y	N	Y	Y
Riegle	N	Y	N	N	Y	N	Y	Y
MINNESOTA								
Boschwitz	Y	N	N	Y	N	Y	N	N
Durenberger	Y	Y	N	Y	N	N	Y	N
MISSISSIPPI								
Cochran	Y	N	N	Y	N	Y	N	N
Stennis	N	N	N	Y	N	#	Y	N
MISSOURI								
Danforth	Y	Y	N	N	N	Y	N	N
Eagleton	N	N	Y	Y	Y	N	Y	Y
MONTANA								
Baucus	N	Y	N	N	N	N	Y	Y
Melcher	N	Y	N	N	N	Y	Y	N
NEBRASKA								
Exon	N	Y	Y	N	N	N	Y	N
Zorinsky	N	Y	N	N	N	N	Y	N
NEVADA								
Laxalt	Y	Y	N	Y	N	?	N	N
Cannon	N	N	N	?	Y	N	Y	N
NEW HAMPSHIRE								
Humphrey	Y	Y	N	N	N	N	N	N
Rudman	Y	Y	N	?	N	Y	N	N
NEW JERSEY								
Bradley	N	N	Y	N	N	-	N	Y
Williams	N	N	Y	Y	Y	N	N	Y
NEW MEXICO								
Domenici	Y	?	N	Y	N	Y	N	N
Schmitt	Y	Y	N	N	N	Y	N	N
NEW YORK								
D'Amato	Y	Y	N	Y	-	+	N	N
Moynihan	N	Y	N	?	Y	N	N	N
NORTH CAROLINA								
East	Y	Y	N	?	N	Y	N	N
Helms	Y	Y	N	N	N	Y	N	N
NORTH DAKOTA								
Andrews	Y	Y	N	N	N	Y	Y	N
Burdick	N	N	N	N	N	Y	Y	N
OHIO								
Glenn	N	N	Y	N	N	N	N	N
Metzenbaum	N	N	Y	N	Y	N	Y	N
OKLAHOMA								
Nickles	Y	Y	N	N	N	Y	N	N
Boren	N	Y	N	N	N	N	Y	N
OREGON								
Hatfield	Y	Y	N	N	N	N	N	Y
Packwood	Y	Y	N	Y	N	N	N	N
PENNSYLVANIA								
Heinz	Y	N	Y	N	Y	N	?	N
Specter	Y	Y	N	Y	N	X	N	N
RHODE ISLAND								
Chafee	Y	N	N	Y	Y	N	N	Y
Pell	N	N	Y	N	Y	N	N	Y
SOUTH CAROLINA								
Thurmond	Y	Y	N	Y	N	Y	N	N
Hollings	N	N	Y	Y	Y	#	N	Y
SOUTH DAKOTA								
Abdnor	Y	Y	N	N	N	Y	Y	N
Pressler	?	Y	N	N	N	Y	Y	Y
TENNESSEE								
Baker	Y	N	N	Y	#	Y	N	N
Sasser	N	N	N	N	+	Y	Y	N
TEXAS								
Tower	Y	Y	N	Y	N	+	N	N
Bentsen	N	N	-	N	N	N	Y	N
UTAH								
Garn	Y	Y	N	Y	N	N	N	N
Hatch	Y	Y	N	Y	N	N	N	N
VERMONT								
Stafford	Y	Y	N	N	N	?	Y	N
Leahy	N	N	Y	N	Y	N	Y	Y
VIRGINIA								
Warner	Y	Y	N	Y	N	N	N	N
Byrd*	Y	N	N	?	N	Y	N	N
WASHINGTON								
Gorton	Y	Y	N	Y	N	N	N	N
Jackson	N	N	Y	N	Y	N	Y	N
WEST VIRGINIA								
Byrd	N	N	Y	N	Y	Y	Y	Y
Randolph	N	N	Y	N	-	Y	Y	N
WISCONSIN								
Kasten	Y	Y	N	N	N	N	Y	N
Proxmire	N	Y	N	N	Y	N	Y	Y
WYOMING								
Simpson	Y	Y	N	Y	N	N	N	N
Wallop	Y	N	N	Y	N	Y	N	-

Democrats   *Republicans*

* Byrd elected as an independent.

9. HR 3512. Fiscal 1981 Supplemental Appropriations. Hatfield, R-Ore., motion to table (kill) the Moynihan, D-N.Y., amendment stating the sense of the Senate in opposition to President Reagan's proposed reductions on Social Security benefits. Motion agreed to 49-48: R 48-2; D 1-46 (ND 0-32, SD 1-14), May 20, 1981. A "yea" was a vote supporting the president's position.

10. H J Res 266. Tax Cuts. Finance Committee amendment to require, beginning in 1985, that individual income taxes be adjusted, or indexed, annually to offset the effects of inflation. Adopted 57-40: R 43-8; D 14-32 (ND 11-20, SD 3-12), July 16, 1981.

11. H J Res 266. Tax Cuts. Hollings, D-S.C., amendment to the Finance Committee bill limiting the size of personal tax reductions and targeting them to middle-income taxpayers in order to achieve a balanced budget by 1984. Rejected 26-71: R 0-51; D 26-20 (ND 20-12, SD 6-8), July 22, 1981. A "nay" was a vote supporting the president's position.

12. H J Res 325. Fiscal 1982 Continuing Appropriations. Hatfield, R-Ore., motion to accept language proposed by House-Senate conferees to provide for a permanent appropriation of funds for congressional pay increases, when recommended by the president and upheld by Congress. Motion agreed to 48-44: R 37-13; D 11-31 (ND 7-22, SD 4-9), Sept. 30, 1981.

13. S 573. Oil Industry Antitrust Exemption. Metzenbaum, D-Ohio, amendment to nullify President Reagan's Jan. 28 order terminating immediately all remaining controls on oil and gasoline. Rejected 24-68: R 3-47; D 21-21 (ND 18-10; SD 3-11), March 10, 1981. A "nay" was a vote supporting the president's position. (The bill, to extend through Sept. 30, 1981, antitrust exemptions for oil companies participating in the programs of the International Energy Agency, subsequently was passed by voice vote.)

14. S 884. Agriculture and Food Act of 1981. Huddleston, D-Ky., motion to table (kill) the Eagleton, D-Mo., amendment to allow the agriculture secretary to establish price support levels for certain grades of tobacco deemed by the secretary to be in excessive supply and non-competitive, except that the level may not go below 75 percent of the level established for the 1982 crop of that kind of tobacco. Motion agreed to 41-40: R 28-17; D 13-23 (ND 6-20, SD 7-3), Sept. 18, 1981.

15. S 509. Milk Price Supports. Melcher, D-Mont., amendment to establish a quota on the importation of casein products into the United States. Rejected 38-60: R 7-45; D 31-15 (ND 19-12, SD 12-3), March 24, 1981. A "nay" was a vote supporting the president's position.

16. HR 4995. Defense Appropriations, Fiscal 1982. Hollings, D-S.C., amendment to delete from the bill $2.429 billion for research on and procurement of the B-1B bomber, and to distribute the money among other accounts. Rejected 28-66: R 5-43; D 23-23 (ND 18-13, SD 5-10), Dec. 3, 1981. A "nay" was a vote supporting the president's position.

1. H Res 251. House Earned Income Limit. Adoption of the resolution to increase the limitation on House members' outside earned income from 15 percent to 40 percent of their official salary, and to increase the limit on each individual honorarium payment for a speech, article or personal appearance from $1,000 to $2,000, for calendar years 1981 through 1983. Rejected 147-271: R 73-112; D 74-159 (ND 49-107, SD 25-52), Oct. 28, 1981.

2. HR 3480. Legal Services Corporation. Passage of the bill to reauthorize the Legal Services Corporation for fiscal 1982-83, at $241 million annually. Passed 245-137: R 59-116; D 186-21 (ND 137-3, SD 49-18), June 18, 1981. A "nay" was a vote supporting the president's position.

3. HR 3112. Voting Rights Act Extension. Butler, R-Va., amendment to allow three-judge federal district courts to hear petitions by jurisdictions seeking to bail out from coverage of the Voting Rights Act. Rejected 132-277: R 102-75; D 30-202 (ND 4-153, SD 26-49), Oct. 5, 1981.

4. H Con Res 194. Disapproving AWACS Sale. Adoption of the concurrent resolution disapproving the sale to Saudi Arabia of Airborne Warning and Control System (AWACS) radar planes, conformal fuel tanks for F-15 aircraft, AIM-9L Sidewinder missiles and KC-707 aerial refueling aircraft. Adopted 301-111: R 108-78; D 193-33 (ND 149-5, SD 44-28), Oct. 14, 1981. A "nay" was a vote supporting the president's position.

5. HR 4995. Defense Department Appropriations, Fiscal 1982. Addabbo, D-N.Y., amendment to delete $1.801 billion from Air Force procurement intended for the B-1 bomber. Rejected 142-263: R 21-157; D 121-106 (ND 111-42, SD 10-64), Nov. 18, 1981. A "nay" was a vote supporting the president's position.

6. HR 4995. Defense Department Appropriations, Fiscal 1982. Addabbo, D-N.Y., amendment to delete $1,913,200,000 in Air Force research, development, test and evaluation funds for the MX missile and basing system. Rejected 139-264: R 27-151; D 112-113 (ND 103-48, SD 9-65), Nov. 18, 1981. A "nay" was a vote supporting the president's position.

7. HR 4144. Energy and Water Development Appropriations, Fiscal 1982. Pritchard, R-Wash., amendment, to the Myers, R-Ind., amendment, to delete $189 million for the Tennessee-Tombigbee Waterway. Rejected 198-208: R 108-70; D 90-138 (ND 82-70, SD 8-68), July 23, 1981. A "nay" was a vote supporting the president's position.

8. HR 4144. Energy and Water Development Appropriations, Fiscal 1982. Coughlin, R-Pa., amendment to delete $228 million for the Clinch River (Tenn.) nuclear breeder reactor. Rejected 186-206: R 70-104; D 116-102 (ND 107-38, SD 9-64), July 24, 1981. A "nay" was a vote supporting the president's position.

1. Rep. William R. Cotter, D-Conn., died Sept. 9, 1981.

2. Rep. Wayne Dowdy, D-Miss., sworn in July 9, 1981, to succeed Jon Hinson, R, who resigned April 13, 1981.

3. Rep. Michael G. Oxley, R-Ohio, sworn in July 21, 1981, to succeed Tennyson Guyer, R, who died April 12, 1981.

4. Rep. Joseph F. Smith, D-Pa., sworn in July 28, 1981, to succeed Raymond F. Lederer, D, who resigned May 5, 1981.

5. Rep. Eugene V. Atkinson, Pa., switched his party affiliation from Democrat to Republican on Oct. 14, 1981.

KEY

Y	Voted for (yea).
#	Paired for.
+	Announced for.
N	Voted against (nay).
X	Paired against.
-	Announced against.
P	Voted "present".
C	Voted "present" to avoid possible conflict of interest.
?	Did not vote or otherwise make a position known.

Democrats *Republicans*

	1	2	3	4	5	6	7	8
ALABAMA								
1 *Edwards*	Y	N	Y	Y	N	N	N	N
2 *Dickinson*	Y	X	Y	N	N	N	N	N
3 Nichols	N	N	Y	N	N	N	N	N
4 Bevill	N	N	Y	N	N	N	N	N
5 Flippo	N	N	Y	N	N	N	N	?
6 *Smith*	N	N	Y	N	N	N	N	N
7 Shelby	N	N	Y	N	N	N	N	N
ALASKA								
AL *Young*	Y	N	N	Y	N	N	N	N
ARIZONA								
1 *Rhodes*	Y	N	Y	N	?	X	N	N
2 Udall	Y	Y	N	Y	Y	N	N	Y
3 *Stump*	N	N	Y	N	N	N	N	N
4 *Rudd*	Y	X	Y	N	N	N	N	N
ARKANSAS								
1 Alexander	Y	Y	N	N	N	N	N	N
2 *Bethune*	N	N	Y	N	N	N	N	Y
3 *Hammerschmidt*	Y	N	N	N	N	N	N	N
4 Anthony	N	Y	N	N	N	N	N	N
CALIFORNIA								
1 *Chappie*	N	X	Y	Y	N	N	?	?
2 *Clausen*	N	Y	Y	Y	N	N	N	N
3 Matsui	Y	Y	N	Y	N	N	N	Y
4 Fazio	Y	Y	N	Y	N	N	N	Y
5 Burton, J.	?	P	?	?	Y	Y	Y	Y
6 Burton, P.	N	Y	N	?	Y	Y	#	Y
7 Miller	N	Y	N	Y	Y	Y	Y	Y
8 Dellums	Y	Y	N	Y	Y	Y	Y	Y
9 Stark	?	Y	N	Y	Y	Y	Y	Y
10 Edwards	N	Y	N	Y	Y	Y	Y	#
11 Lantos	N	+	N	Y	Y	Y	Y	Y
12 *McCloskey*	Y	Y	N	N	?	?	Y	Y
13 Mineta	N	Y	N	Y	Y	Y	Y	Y
14 *Shumway*	Y	N	Y	N	N	N	N	N
15 Coelho	Y	Y	N	Y	N	N	N	N
16 Panetta	N	Y	N	Y	Y	Y	Y	Y
17 *Pashayan*	N	?	?	Y	N	N	N	N
18 *Thomas*	Y	X	#	N	N	N	N	N
19 *Lagomarsino*	N	N	Y	N	N	N	N	N
20 *Goldwater*	Y	N	Y	?	?	?	N	N
21 *Fiedler*	N	N	?	Y	N	N	N	N
22 *Moorhead*	N	N	N	N	N	N	N	N
23 Beilenson	N	Y	N	Y	Y	Y	Y	Y
24 Waxman	Y	Y	N	Y	Y	Y	Y	Y
25 Roybal	Y	Y	N	Y	Y	Y	Y	Y
26 *Rousselot*	Y	N	Y	N	N	Y	N	?
27 *Dornan*	Y	N	Y	?	?	#	#	Y
28 Dixon	N	Y	N	Y	X	#	N	Y
29 Hawkins	N	?	N	Y	N	Y	N	N
30 Danielson	N	Y	N	Y	N	Y	Y	Y
31 Dymally	Y	Y	N	Y	N	?	?	?
32 Anderson	N	Y	N	Y	N	N	N	N
33 Grisham	Y	N	Y	N	-	-	Y	N
34 Lungren	Y	N	Y	N	N	N	Y	Y
35 *Dreier*	N	N	Y	N	N	Y	N	N
36 Brown	N	Y	N	Y	N	Y	N	Y
37 *Lewis*	Y	N	?	Y	N	N	N	X
38 Patterson	Y	Y	N	Y	N	Y	N	?
39 *Dannemeyer*	Y	N	#	N	N	N	N	N
40 *Badham*	Y	X	Y	?	N	N	N	N
41 *Lowery*	?	N	Y	Y	N	N	N	N
42 *Hunter*	N	Y	N	Y	N	N	N	Y
43 *Burgener*	Y	N	Y	?	N	N	X	X
COLORADO								
1 Schroeder	N	Y	N	Y	Y	Y	Y	Y
2 Wirth	N	Y	N	Y	Y	Y	Y	Y
3 Kogovsek	N	?	N	Y	Y	N	N	Y
4 *Brown*	N	N	Y	N	N	Y	N	Y

	1	2	3	4	5	6	7	8
5 *Kramer*	N	N	Y	Y	N	N	N	N
CONNECTICUT								
1 Cotter[1]	?						?	?
2 Gejdenson	N	Y	N	Y	Y	Y	Y	Y
3 *DeNardis*	N	Y	N	Y	Y	Y	Y	Y
4 *McKinney*	Y	Y	N	Y	Y	Y	Y	Y
5 Ratchford	N	Y	N	Y	Y	Y	Y	Y
6 Moffett	N	#	X	Y	Y	Y	Y	Y
DELAWARE								
AL *Evans*	N	Y	Y	N	N	N	Y	Y
FLORIDA								
1 Hutto	N	N	Y	N	N	N	N	N
2 Fuqua	N	Y	N	N	N	N	N	N
3 Bennett	N	Y	Y	N	N	N	N	N
4 Chappell	Y	N	Y	N	N	N	N	N
5 *McCollum*	N	Y	Y	N	N	N	N	N
6 *Young*	N	N	Y	N	N	N	N	N
7 Gibbons	Y	?	N	Y	Y	N	N	?
8 Ireland	N	N	N	N	N	N	N	N
9 Nelson	N	N	Y	N	N	N	N	N
10 *Bafalis*	N	N	Y	N	N	N	N	N
11 Mica	N	Y	N	Y	N	Y	N	N
12 *Shaw*	Y	N	Y	N	N	N	Y	Y
13 Lehman	N	?	N	Y	Y	Y	N	Y
14 Pepper	#	Y	N	#	X	X	N	N
15 Fascell	N	Y	N	Y	Y	Y	N	Y
GEORGIA								
1 Ginn	N	Y	Y	N	N	N	N	N
2 Hatcher	N	Y	Y	N	N	N	N	N
3 Brinkley	N	Y	Y	N	N	N	N	N
4 Levitas	N	Y	Y	?	N	N	N	Y
5 Fowler	N	Y	N	#	Y	N	Y	Y
6 *Gingrich*	Y	N	Y	N	N	N	N	N
7 McDonald	Y	X	N	N	X	X	X	N
8 Evans	Y	Y	Y	N	N	N	N	N
9 Jenkins	N	Y	Y	N	N	N	N	?
10 Barnard	N	Y	Y	X	N	N	N	N
HAWAII								
1 Heftel	N	Y	N	Y	N	Y	N	Y
2 Akaka	Y	Y	N	Y	N	N	N	N
IDAHO								
1 *Craig*	Y	N	Y	N	N	N	N	N
2 *Hansen*	Y	N	Y	N	N	N	X	N
ILLINOIS								
1 Washington	N	Y	N	Y	Y	Y	Y	Y
2 Savage	Y	Y	N	?	Y	Y	?	?
3 Russo	Y	Y	N	Y	Y	Y	N	N
4 *Derwinski*	N	N	Y	N	N	N	N	N
5 Fary	Y	Y	N	Y	N	N	N	N
6 *Hyde*	Y	N	Y	N	N	N	Y	N
7 Collins	Y	Y	N	Y	Y	Y	N	N
8 Rostenkowski	Y	Y	N	Y	Y	N	N	N
9 Yates	N	Y	N	Y	Y	Y	Y	Y
10 *Porter*	Y	Y	N	Y	N	Y	Y	Y
11 Annunzio	Y	Y	N	N	N	N	N	N
12 *Crane, P.*	Y	N	#	?	N	N	N	N
13 *McClory*	N	N	N	N	N	N	N	N
14 *Erlenborn*	Y	Y	N	N	N	N	N	N
15 *Corcoran*	X	N	N	N	N	N	N	N
16 *Martin*	N	Y	N	Y	N	N	N	?
17 *O'Brien*	N	Y	Y	N	N	N	N	N
18 *Michel*	Y	N	Y	N	N	N	N	N
19 *Railsback*	Y	N	Y	N	N	Y	Y	Y
20 *Findley*	Y	Y	N	N	Y	Y	Y	Y
21 *Madigan*	Y	N	Y	N	Y	?	?	Y
22 *Crane, D.*	Y	N	Y	N	N	Y	Y	Y
23 Price	Y	?	N	N	N	N	N	N
24 Simon	Y	?	N	Y	Y	Y	N	Y
INDIANA								
1 Benjamin	N	Y	N	Y	N	N	N	Y
2 Fithian	N	Y	N	Y	N	Y	N	Y
3 *Hiler*	N	N	N	N	N	N	N	Y
4 *Coats*	N	N	N	N	N	N	N	N
5 *Hillis*	N	N	N	N	N	N	N	N
6 Evans	N	Y	N	Y	Y	N	N	N
7 *Myers*	Y	N	N	N	N	N	N	N
8 *Deckard*	N	Y	N	Y	N	Y	Y	Y
9 Hamilton	N	Y	N	Y	N	Y	N	Y
10 Sharp	N	Y	N	Y	Y	Y	N	Y
11 Jacobs	N	Y	N	Y	Y	Y	Y	Y
IOWA								
1 *Leach*	N	Y	N	Y	Y	Y	Y	Y
2 *Tauke*	N	Y	N	N	Y	Y	Y	N
3 *Evans*	N	Y	N	Y	N	Y	Y	N
4 Smith	N	Y	N	Y	Y	Y	Y	Y
5 Harkin	N	?	N	Y	Y	Y	N	Y
6 Bedell	N	?	N	Y	?	?	N	Y

	1 2 3 4 5 6 7 8		1 2 3 4 5 6 7 8		1 2 3 4 5 6 7 8		1 2 3 4 5 6 7 8
KANSAS		4 Skelton	N ? N Y N N N N	9 *Martin*	Y Y Y Y N N Y ?	7 Jones	N Y N Y N N N N
1 *Roberts*	N N Y N N N Y N	5 Bolling	Y Y N ? ? ? Y ?	10 *Broyhill*	N N Y N N N Y N	8 Ford	Y ? N Y Y Y N N
2 *Jeffries*	N N Y N N N Y N	6 *Coleman*	N Y Y N N N Y ?	11 *Hendon*	N N N Y N N N ?	**TEXAS**	
3 *Winn*	N N Y Y N N N N	7 *Taylor*	Y N Y N N N N N	**NORTH DAKOTA**		1 Hall, S.	N N Y N N N N N
4 Glickman	N Y Y Y Y Y Y Y	8 *Bailey*	N N N N Y N N ? N	AL Dorgan	N Y N Y + + N Y	2 Wilson	Y Y N N N N N N
5 *Whittaker*	N N Y Y N N Y N	9 Volkmer	N Y N Y N N N N	**OHIO**		3 *Collins*	N N Y Y N N Y Y
KENTUCKY		10 *Emerson*	N N Y N N N N N	1 *Gradison*	Y Y N Y N N Y Y	4 Hall, R.	N Y Y Y N N N N
1 Hubbard	N Y ? N N N N N	**MONTANA**		2 Luken	Y ? N Y N N N Y	5 Mattox	Y Y N Y # ? # #
2 Natcher	N Y N Y N N N N	1 Williams	N Y N Y Y Y N Y	3 Hall	N Y N Y N N Y Y	6 *Gramm*	Y N Y N N N N N
3 Mazzoli	N + N Y Y Y + N	2 *Marlenee*	N Y Y N N ? Y Y	4 *Oxley*[3]	N N N N N N N	7 *Archer*	N N Y Y N N Y N
4 *Snyder*	Y N Y N N N N Y	**NEBRASKA**		5 *Latta*	Y N Y N N N X N	8 *Fields*	Y N Y N N N N N
5 *Rogers*	N N Y N N N N N	1 *Bereuter*	N N Y N N N Y N	6 *McEwen*	N N Y N N N N N	9 Brooks	Y # ? ? Y Y N N
6 *Hopkins*	N Y N Y N N N Y	2 *Daub*	N N N N N N Y N	7 *Brown*	N ? N Y N N N ?	10 Pickle	N Y N Y N N N N
7 Perkins	N Y N Y N N N N	3 *Smith*	N N Y N N Y N N	8 *Kindness*	N N N N N N N N	11 Leath	Y N Y N N N N N
LOUISIANA		**NEVADA**		9 *Weber*	N Y N Y N N N Y	12 Wright	Y # N Y N N N N
1 *Livingston*	Y X X Y N N N N	AL Santini	N N Y N N N Y ?	10 *Miller*	N N Y N N N N N	13 Hightower	N Y N N N N N N
2 Boggs	Y Y Y N N N N N	**NEW HAMPSHIRE**		11 *Stanton*	Y Y N N N N Y N	14 Patman	N Y N Y N N N N
3 Tauzin	Y Y Y Y N N N N	1 D'Amours	N Y N Y Y N ? Y	12 Shamansky	N Y N Y N N N Y	15 de la Garza	N Y N Y N N N N
4 Roemer	N Y Y N N N N N	2 *Gregg*	N N N Y N Y Y Y	13 Pease	N Y N Y Y Y Y Y	16 White	Y Y N N N N N N
5 Huckaby	N Y N N N N N N	**NEW JERSEY**		14 Seiberling	N Y Y Y Y Y Y Y	17 Stenholm	N N Y N N N N N
6 *Moore*	Y Y Y Y N N Y Y	1 Florio	? ? N Y # ? Y #	15 *Wylie*	N Y N N N N ? Y	18 Leland	Y Y Y Y Y Y Y Y
7 Breaux	Y ? Y Y X X N N	2 Hughes	N Y N Y Y N N Y	16 *Regula*	N Y N N N N N N	19 Hance	Y N N N N N N N
8 Long	N + N Y N N N N	3 Howard	Y Y N Y Y Y N Y	17 *Ashbrook*	N N ? N N N N N	20 Gonzalez	Y Y N Y N N N P
MAINE		4 *Smith*	N N N Y N Y Y Y	18 Applegate	N Y Y N N N Y N	21 *Loeffler*	N N Y Y N N N N
1 *Emery*	N Y N Y N N Y Y	5 *Fenwick*	N Y N Y Y Y Y Y	19 *Williams*	N Y X N N N Y N	22 *Paul*	Y N # Y Y ? Y Y
2 *Snowe*	N N N Y N N Y Y	6 *Forsythe*	N Y N Y ? ? Y N	20 Oakar	N Y ? Y N N Y N	23 Kazen	N Y N N N N N N
MARYLAND		7 *Roukema*	N N N Y N N N N	21 Stokes	Y Y N Y Y Y Y N	24 Frost	N Y N Y N N ? ?
1 Dyson	N N N Y N N Y N	8 Roe	Y Y N Y N N N N	22 Eckart	N Y N Y Y Y Y Y	**UTAH**	
2 Long	N Y N Y Y Y Y N	9 *Hollenbeck*	N Y N Y Y Y Y N	23 Mottl	N Y Y N N Y N ?	1 *Hansen*	N X Y N N X X ?
3 Mikulski	N Y N Y Y Y Y Y	10 Rodino	Y Y N Y Y Y Y Y	**OKLAHOMA**		2 *Marriott*	N N N N N N N N
4 *Holt*	N N N N N N N N	11 Minish	N Y N Y Y Y Y Y	1 Jones	Y Y N Y N N N N	**VERMONT**	
5 Hoyer	Y Y N Y N N N Y	12 *Rinaldo*	N Y N Y Y Y Y N	2 Synar	N Y N Y N N Y Y	AL *Jeffords*	N ? Y Y Y Y Y Y
6 Byron	N Y N Y N N N N	13 *Courter*	N Y N Y N N Y N	3 Watkins	N Y N Y N N N N	**VIRGINIA**	
7 Mitchell	Y Y Y Y Y Y ? Y	14 Guarini	Y Y N Y Y Y Y Y	4 McCurdy	N Y N N N N N Y	1 *Trible*	N N Y N N N N N
8 Barnes	N Y N Y Y Y Y Y	15 Dwyer	N Y N Y N Y N N	5 *Edwards*	Y N Y N N N N N	2 *Whitehurst*	N Y Y ? N N N N
MASSACHUSETTS		**NEW MEXICO**		6 English	Y Y N Y N N N N	3 *Bliley*	? N Y Y N N N N
1 *Conte*	Y Y N Y Y Y Y Y	1 *Lujan*	Y Y N N N N N N	**OREGON**		4 *Daniel, R.*	Y N Y N N N Y Y
2 Boland	N Y N Y Y Y Y Y	2 *Skeen*	N Y Y N N N N N	1 AuCoin	N Y N Y Y Y Y Y	5 Daniel, D.	Y N Y N N N N N
3 Early	Y ? N Y Y Y Y Y	**NEW YORK**		2 *Smith*	Y N Y N N Y Y Y	6 *Butler*	N Y N N N N N N
4 Frank	N Y N Y Y Y Y Y	1 *Carney*	N N Y N N N N N	3 Wyden	N Y N Y Y Y Y Y	7 *Robinson*	Y N N N N N N N
5 Shannon	N Y N Y Y Y Y Y	2 Downey	N Y N Y Y Y ? ?	4 Weaver	N Y N Y Y Y Y Y	8 *Parris*	N N Y N N N N N
6 Mavroules	N Y N Y Y Y Y N	3 *Carman*	Y Y N Y N N Y Y	**PENNSYLVANIA**		9 *Wampler*	Y Y Y N N N N N
7 Markey	N Y N Y Y Y Y Y	4 *Lent*	Y Y N Y N N N Y	1 Foglietta	Y Y N Y Y Y N Y	10 *Wolf*	N N Y N N Y Y N
8 O'Neill		5 *McGrath*	N N N Y N N N Y	2 Gray	Y ? N Y Y Y N ?	**WASHINGTON**	
9 Moakley	Y ? N Y # # ? Y	6 *LeBoutillier*	N N N Y N N N N	3 *Smith*[4]	Y N Y N N	1 *Pritchard*	N Y ? N ? ? Y ?
10 *Heckler*	N Y Y N Y Y N Y	7 Addabbo	Y Y N Y Y Y Y N	4 *Dougherty*	? N Y N N N Y N	2 Swift	N Y N Y Y Y Y Y
11 *Donnelly*	N ? N Y # ? N Y	8 Rosenthal	N Y N Y Y Y ? ?	5 *Schulze*	Y N N N N N N N	3 Bonker	N Y - ? Y Y ? Y
12 Studds	N Y N Y Y Y Y Y	9 Ferraro	N Y N Y Y Y Y Y	6 Yatron	N Y N N N N Y N	4 *Morrison*	N N Y N N N N N
MICHIGAN		10 Biaggi	Y Y N Y Y N N X	7 Edgar	N Y N Y Y Y Y Y	5 Foley	Y Y N N N N N N
1 Conyers	# # N Y Y Y N Y	11 Scheuer	Y Y N Y Y Y Y Y	8 *Coyne, J.*	N N N N N N N N	6 Dicks	N Y N Y Y Y Y Y
2 *Pursell*	N Y Y Y Y Y Y Y	12 Chisholm	Y Y N Y # # N Y	9 *Shuster*	Y N Y N N N N N	7 Lowry	N Y N ? Y Y Y Y
3 Wolpe	N Y N Y Y Y Y Y	13 Solarz	N Y N Y Y Y Y Y	10 *McDade*	Y # N ? N N N Y	**WEST VIRGINIA**	
4 *Siljander*	Y N Y N N N N N	14 Richmond	Y Y N Y N Y N #	11 *Nelligan*	N N N Y N N N N	1 Mollohan	? # N N N N N N
5 *Sawyer*	N Y Y N N N Y N	15 Zeferetti	Y # N Y N Y N N	12 Murtha	Y Y N Y Y N N N	2 *Benedict*	Y N # Y N N N Y
6 *Dunn*	N N Y N ? N Y Y	16 Schumer	N Y N Y Y Y Y Y	13 *Coughlin*	? Y N Y Y Y Y Y	3 *Staton*	Y N Y N. N N N Y
7 Kildee	N Y N Y Y Y Y Y	17 *Molinari*	Y ? Y N Y N Y Y	14 *Coyne, W.*	N Y N Y Y Y Y N	4 Rahall	Y Y N Y N N N N
8 Traxler	N Y N Y Y Y Y N	18 *Green*	Y Y N Y Y Y Y Y	15 Ritter	N N N Y N N + N	**WISCONSIN**	
9 *Vander Jagt*	Y N Y N N N Y N	19 Rangel	Y Y N Y Y Y Y N	16 *Walker*	N N N N N N N N	1 Aspin	N Y N Y Y Y Y Y
10 Albosta	N ? N Y N N Y Y	20 Weiss	N Y N Y Y Y Y Y	17 Ertel	N Y N Y Y Y Y Y	2 Kastenmeier	N Y N Y Y Y Y Y
11 *Davis*	N N Y N N X N N	21 Garcia	N Y N ? Y ? N ?	18 Walgren	N Y N Y Y Y Y Y	3 *Gunderson*	N N N N N N N N
12 Bonior	N Y N Y Y Y Y Y	22 Bingham	N Y N Y Y Y Y Y	19 *Goodling*	N N Y N N Y N N	4 Zablocki	Y Y N N N N N N
13 Crockett	N Y N Y Y Y Y Y	23 Peyser	Y # ? Y Y N Y Y	20 Gaydos	N Y N Y N Y ? ?	5 Reuss	Y Y N Y # # Y ?
14 Hertel	N Y N Y Y Y Y N	24 Ottinger	Y Y N Y Y Y Y Y	21 Bailey	Y Y Y N N N N N	6 Petri	N N Y Y Y Y Y Y
15 Ford	Y Y N Y Y Y Y N	25 *Fish*	Y Y N Y N N Y Y	22 Murphy	N Y N Y N N N N	7 Obey	N Y Y Y Y Y Y Y
16 Dingell	N Y X Y Y Y Y Y	26 *Gilman*	N Y N Y N N - Y	23 *Clinger*	N Y N Y N Y N N	8 *Roth*	N N ? Y Y Y Y Y
17 Brodhead	N Y N Y Y Y Y Y	27 McHugh	N Y N Y Y Y Y Y	24 *Marks*	N Y N N N N N N	9 *Sensenbrenner*	N N N Y Y Y Y Y
18 Blanchard	N Y N Y Y Y Y Y	28 Stratton	N Y N X N N N N	25 *Atkinson*[5]	N Y N ? N N Y N	**WYOMING**	
19 *Broomfield*	N N N Y N N Y Y	29 *Solomon*	N N Y N N N Y N	**RHODE ISLAND**		AL *Cheney*	Y N Y N N N N X
MINNESOTA		30 *Martin*	Y N Y N ? ? Y ?	1 St Germain	N Y N Y Y Y N Y		
1 *Erdahl*	N Y N Y N ? ? N	31 *Mitchell*	N ? N N N N Y Y	2 *Schneider*	N Y N Y Y Y Y Y		
2 *Hagedorn*	Y Y Y N ? ? N N	32 *Wortley*	Y N N Y N N Y N	**SOUTH CAROLINA**			
3 *Frenzel*	Y # Y Y N N Y ?	33 Lee	N N Y N N N N N	1 *Hartnett*	Y N Y N N N Y N		
Vento	N Y N Y Y Y N Y #	34 *Horton*	N Y X Y Y Y N ?	2 *Spence*	N N Y N N N N N		
5 Sabo	N Y N Y Y Y Y Y	35 *Conable*	Y N Y N N N Y N	3 Derrick	Y N N Y N N Y N		
6 *Weber*	N N N N N N N N	36 LaFalce	N ? N Y Y Y Y Y	4 *Campbell*	Y N Y N N N N N		
7 *Stangeland*	N N N N N N N N	37 Nowak	N Y N Y N Y N N	5 Holland	Y N N ? N N N N		
8 Oberstar	N Y N Y Y Y N Y	38 *Kemp*	Y N Y N N ? ? ?	6 *Napier*	N N Y N N N N N		
MISSISSIPPI		39 Lundine	N Y N Y Y Y Y Y	**SOUTH DAKOTA**			
1 Whitten	N Y Y N N N N N	**NORTH CAROLINA**		1 Daschle	N Y N Y N N N Y		
2 Bowen	N Y Y N N N N N	1 Jones	X Y X ? ? ? N N	2 *Roberts*	N N Y Y N N + -		
3 Montgomery	N N N Y N N N N	2 Fountain	N Y N Y N N N N	**TENNESSEE**			
4 Dowdy[2]	N N Y N N N N	3 Whitley	N Y N N N N N N	1 *Quillen*	Y N Y N N N N X		
5 Lott	Y N Y N N N N N	4 Andrews	N Y N N N N N N	2 *Duncan*	N Y N Y X ? N N		
MISSOURI		5 Neal	N Y N Y N N Y Y	3 Bouquard	N Y N Y N N N N		
1 Clay	Y Y N Y Y Y Y Y	6 *Johnston*	# X Y N ? ? Y Y	4 Gore	N Y N Y N N N N		
2 Young	N Y N Y N N N N	7 Rose	Y ? N N N N N N	5 Boner	N ? N Y N N N N		
3 Gephardt	N Y N Y N N Y Y	8 Hefner	N Y N Y N N N N	6 Beard	X Y ? Y N N N N		

9. HR 1553. Debt Limit Increase. Passage of the bill to increase the public debt limit to $985 billion through Sept. 30, 1981. Passed 305-104: R 150-36; D 155-68 (ND 112-37, SD 43-31), Feb. 5, 1981. A "yea" was a vote supporting the president's position.

10. H Con Res 115. Fiscal 1982 Budget Targets. Latta, R-Ohio, substitute, to the resolution as reported by the Budget Committee, to decrease budget authority by $23.1 billion, outlays by $25.7 billion and revenues by $31.1 billion, resulting in a $31 billion deficit for fiscal 1982. Adopted 253-176: R 190-0; D 63-176 (ND 17-144, SD 46-32), May 7, 1981. A "yea" was a vote supporting the president's position.

11. HR 3982. Budget Reconciliation. Latta, R-Ohio, amendments, considered *en bloc*, to strike parts of six titles of the bill recommended by the following committees — Agriculture; Banking, Finance and Urban Affairs; Education and Labor; Post Office and Civil Service; Science and Technology; and Ways and Means — and to substitute provisions endorsed by President Reagan. Adopted 217-211: R 188-2; D 29-209 (ND 3-157, SD 26-52), June 26, 1981. A "yea" was a vote supporting the president's position.

12. HR 4242. Tax Cuts. Conable, R-N.Y., substitute amendment to the bill to reduce individual income tax rates by 25 percent across-the-board over three years, to index tax rates beginning in 1985 and to provide business and investment tax incentives. Adopted 238-195: R 190-1; D 48-194 (ND 12-151, SD 36-43), July 29, 1981. A "yea" was a vote supporting the president's position.

13. HR 4331/HR 3982. Minimum Social Security Benefits/Budget Reconciliation. Bolling, D-Mo., motion to order the previous question (thus ending debate and the possibility of amendment) on the rule (H Res 203) providing for consideration of 1) the bill (HR 4331) to amend the Omnibus Budget Reconciliation Act of 1981 (HR 3982) to restore minimum Social Security benefits and 2) the reconciliation act conference report. Motion agreed to 271-151: R 166-21; D 105-130 (ND 56-101, SD 49-29), July 31, 1981.

14. HR 4560. Labor-HHS-Education Appropriations, Fiscal 1982. Regula, R-Ohio, motion to recommit the bill to the Appropriations Committee. Rejected 168-249: R 140-39; D 28-210 (ND 3-157; SD 25-53), Oct. 6, 1981. (The bill, appropriating $87,181,250,000 for the departments of Labor, Health and Human Services, and Education, and related agencies, subsequently was passed by voice vote.) A "yea" was a vote supporting the president's position.

15. HR 4559. Foreign Aid Appropriations, Fiscal 1982. Passage of the bill to appropriate $7,440,280,064 for foreign aid and related programs in fiscal 1982. Passed 199-166: R 84-87; D 115-79 (ND 95-36, SD 20-43), Dec. 11, 1981. (The president had requested $7,775,098,683.)

16. S 884. Agriculture and Food Act of 1981. Adoption of the conference report on the bill to reauthorize for four years price support and other farm programs and, for one year, food stamps. Adopted 205-203: R 125-59; D 80-144 (ND 27-121, SD 53-23), Dec. 16, 1981. A "yea" was a vote supporting the president's position.

1. Rep. William R. Cotter, D-Conn., died Sept. 8, 1981.

2. Rep. Steny Hoyer, D-Md., sworn in June 3, 1981, to succeed Gladys Noon Spellman, D, whose seat the House declared vacant on Feb. 24, 1981, due to her illness.

3. Rep. Mark Siljander, R-Mich., sworn in April 28, 1981, to succeed David A. Stockman, R, who resigned Jan. 27, 1981.

4. Rep. Wayne Dowdy, D-Miss., sworn in July 9, 1981, to succeed Jon Hinson, R, who resigned April 13, 1981.

5. Rep. Michael G. Oxley, R-Ohio, sworn in July 21, 1981, to succeed Tennyson Guyer, R, who died April 12, 1981.

6. Rep. Joseph F. Smith, D-Pa., sworn in July 28, 1981, to succeed Raymond F. Lederer, D, who resigned May 5, 1981.

7. Rep. Eugene V. Atkinson, Pa., switched his party affiliation from Democrat to Republican on Oct. 14, 1981.

KEY

Y Voted for (yea).
Paired for.
+ Announced for.
N Voted against (nay).
X Paired against.
- Announced against.
P Voted "present".
C Voted "present" to avoid possible conflict of interest.
? Did not vote or otherwise make a position known.

	9	10	11	12	13	14	15	16
ALABAMA								
1 *Edwards*	Y	Y	Y	Y	Y	Y	Y	Y
2 *Dickinson*	Y	Y	Y	Y	Y	Y	?	Y
3 Nichols	N	Y	Y	N	N	N	N	Y
4 Bevill	N	Y	N	N	N	N	N	Y
5 Flippo	N	Y	Y	N	N	N	?	Y
6 *Smith*	Y	Y	Y	Y	Y	Y	?	Y
7 Shelby	N	Y	Y	Y	Y	Y	N	Y
ALASKA								
AL *Young*	Y	Y	Y	Y	Y	N	N	Y
ARIZONA								
1 *Rhodes*	Y	Y	Y	Y	Y	Y	Y	Y
2 Udall	Y	N	N	N	Y	N	Y	Y
3 *Stump*	N	Y	Y	Y	Y	N	Y	N
4 *Rudd*	Y	Y	Y	Y	Y	Y	N	Y
ARKANSAS								
1 Alexander	Y	N	N	N	N	N	?	Y
2 *Bethune*	Y	Y	Y	Y	?	?	N	Y
3 *Hammerschmidt*	Y	Y	Y	Y	Y	Y	N	Y
4 Anthony	Y	Y	N	N	Y	N	?	Y
CALIFORNIA								
1 *Chappie*	N	Y	Y	Y	Y	Y	?	Y
2 *Clausen*	Y	Y	Y	Y	Y	Y	Y	Y
3 Matsui	Y	N	N	N	Y	N	Y	Y
4 Fazio	N	N	N	N	Y	N	Y	Y
5 Burton, J.	?	N	?	N	N	?	?	#
6 Burton, P.	Y	N	N	N	N	N	Y	Y
7 Miller	N	N	N	N	N	N	Y	N
8 Dellums	N	N	N	N	N	N	N	N
9 Stark	Y	N	N	N	N	N	Y	Y
10 Edwards	Y	N	N	N	N	N	Y	N
11 Lantos	N	N	N	N	N	Y	N	N
12 *McCloskey*	Y	Y	Y	Y	Y	Y	?	Y
13 Mineta	Y	N	N	N	Y	N	Y	Y
14 *Shumway*	Y	Y	Y	Y	Y	Y	N	Y
15 Coelho	Y	N	N	N	Y	N	Y	Y
16 Panetta	Y	N	N	N	Y	N	Y	Y
17 *Pashayan*	N	Y	Y	Y	Y	?	N	Y
18 *Thomas*	Y	Y	Y	Y	?	Y	Y	Y
19 *Lagomarsino*	Y	Y	Y	Y	Y	Y	Y	Y
20 *Goldwater*	?	Y	Y	Y	?	Y	X	Y
21 *Fiedler*	Y	Y	Y	Y	?	Y	Y	Y
22 *Moorhead*	N	Y	Y	Y	Y	Y	N	?
23 Beilenson	Y	N	N	N	Y	N	Y	?
24 Waxman	Y	N	N	N	N	N	Y	N
25 Roybal	?	N	N	N	N	N	N	N
26 *Rousselot*	N	Y	Y	Y	Y	N	Y	N
27 *Dornan*	Y	Y	Y	Y	?	Y	?	Y
28 Dixon	Y	N	N	N	N	N	Y	N
29 Hawkins	Y	N	N	N	N	N	Y	N
30 Danielson	Y	N	-	N	Y	N	Y	Y
31 Dymally	Y	N	?	N	N	Y	Y	Y
32 Anderson	N	N	N	N	N	N	N	N
33 *Grisham*	Y	Y	Y	Y	Y	Y	N	Y
34 *Lungren*	Y	Y	Y	Y	Y	Y	N	Y
35 *Dreier*	N	Y	Y	Y	Y	Y	N	Y
36 Brown	Y	N	N	N	N	N	?	Y
37 *Lewis*	Y	Y	Y	Y	Y	Y	Y	Y
38 Patterson	Y	N	Y	N	Y	N	Y	N
39 *Dannemeyer*	N	Y	Y	Y	Y	Y	?	Y
40 *Badham*	N	Y	Y	Y	Y	Y	N	Y
41 *Lowery*	Y	Y	Y	Y	Y	Y	Y	Y
42 *Hunter*	Y	Y	Y	Y	Y	Y	N	Y
43 *Burgener*	Y	Y	Y	Y	Y	Y	Y	#
COLORADO								
1 Schroeder	N	N	N	N	N	N	N	N
2 Wirth	Y	N	N	N	N	N	N	N
3 Kogovsek	Y	N	N	N	N	N	N	N
4 *Brown*	Y	Y	Y	Y	Y	Y	N	Y

	9	10	11	12	13	14	15	16
5 *Kramer*	Y	Y	Y	Y	Y	Y	?	N
CONNECTICUT								
1 Cotter[1]	?	?	?	?	?			
2 Gejdenson	Y	N	N	N	Y	N	Y	N
3 *DeNardis*	N	Y	Y	N	N	Y	N	N
4 *McKinney*	Y	Y	Y	Y	Y	N	Y	N
5 Ratchford	Y	N	N	N	N	N	Y	N
6 Moffett	Y	N	N	N	N	N	Y	?
DELAWARE								
AL *Evans*	Y	Y	Y	Y	Y	Y	Y	N
FLORIDA								
1 Hutto	Y	Y	Y	Y	Y	Y	?	Y
2 Fuqua	?	Y	N	N	Y	N	Y	Y
3 Bennett	N	Y	N	N	N	N	N	Y
4 Chappell	N	Y	Y	Y	Y	N	N	Y
5 *McCollum*	?	Y	Y	Y	Y	Y	N	Y
6 *Young*	Y	Y	Y	Y	Y	Y	N	#
7 Gibbons	Y	Y	N	N	Y	N	N	Y
8 Ireland	Y	Y	Y	Y	Y	Y	Y	Y
9 Nelson	Y	Y	Y	Y	Y	N	Y	Y
10 *Bafalis*	Y	Y	Y	Y	Y	Y	N	Y
11 Mica	Y	Y	Y	N	Y	N	Y	Y
12 *Shaw*	Y	Y	Y	Y	Y	Y	N	Y
13 Lehman	Y	N	N	N	N	N	Y	Y
14 Pepper	Y	N	N	N	Y	N	Y	Y
15 Fascell	Y	N	N	N	?	N	Y	N
GEORGIA								
1 Ginn	Y	Y	N	Y	Y	N	N	Y
2 Hatcher	Y	Y	Y	Y	N	?	Y	Y
3 Brinkley	Y	Y	N	Y	Y	N	N	Y
4 Levitas	N	Y	N	N	N	N	Y	Y
5 Fowler	Y	N	N	N	N	N	N	Y
6 *Gingrich*	Y	Y	Y	Y	?	Y	Y	Y
7 McDonald	N	Y	Y	Y	Y	Y	?	?
8 Evans	N	Y	N	Y	Y	N	?	Y
9 Jenkins	Y	N	N	Y	Y	?	Y	Y
10 Barnard	Y	Y	Y	Y	Y	Y	?	Y
HAWAII								
1 Heftel	N	N	N	?	N	Y	Y	Y
2 Akaka	N	N	N	N	Y	N	Y	Y
IDAHO								
1 *Craig*	N	Y	Y	Y	Y	Y	N	Y
2 *Hansen*	N	Y	Y	Y	Y	N	Y	N
ILLINOIS								
1 Washington	Y	N	N	N	N	N	Y	N
2 Savage	Y	N	N	?	N	N	N	N
3 Russo	Y	N	N	N	N	N	X	X
4 *Derwinski*	Y	Y	Y	Y	Y	?	?	Y
5 Fary	Y	N	N	N	Y	N	N	N
6 *Hyde*	Y	Y	Y	Y	Y	Y	Y	Y
7 Collins	Y	N	N	N	N	N	#	N
8 Rostenkowski	Y	N	N	N	N	N	?	Y
9 Yates	N	N	N	N	N	N	Y	N
10 *Porter*	Y	Y	Y	Y	Y	Y	Y	N
11 Annunzio	Y	N	N	N	Y	N	Y	Y
12 *Crane, P.*	N	Y	Y	Y	Y	Y	N	N
13 *McClory*	Y	Y	Y	Y	Y	Y	Y	Y
14 *Erlenborn*	Y	Y	Y	Y	Y	Y	Y	Y
15 *Corcoran*	Y	Y	Y	Y	Y	Y	N	Y
16 *Martin*	Y	Y	Y	Y	Y	?	N	Y
17 *O'Brien*	Y	Y	Y	Y	Y	Y	Y	Y
18 *Michel*	Y	Y	Y	Y	Y	Y	Y	Y
19 *Railsback*	Y	Y	Y	Y	Y	Y	?	Y
20 *Findley*	Y	Y	Y	Y	Y	Y	Y	Y
21 *Madigan*	Y	Y	Y	Y	Y	Y	Y	Y
22 *Crane, D.*	N	Y	Y	Y	Y	Y	N	Y
23 Price	Y	N	N	N	Y	N	Y	Y
24 Simon	Y	N	N	N	?	N	?	Y
INDIANA								
1 Benjamin	Y	N	N	N	N	N	N	N
2 Fithian	X	N	N	N	N	N	N	N
3 *Hiler*	Y	Y	Y	Y	Y	Y	N	Y
4 *Coats*	Y	Y	Y	Y	Y	Y	N	Y
5 *Hillis*	Y	Y	Y	Y	Y	Y	Y	Y
6 Evans	N	Y	N	N	N	N	?	N
7 *Myers*	N	Y	Y	Y	N	Y	N	Y
8 *Deckard*	Y	Y	Y	Y	Y	Y	N	Y
9 Hamilton	Y	N	N	N	N	N	Y	Y
10 Sharp	Y	N	N	N	N	N	N	Y
11 Jacobs	N	N	N	N	N	N	N	N
IOWA								
1 *Leach*	Y	Y	Y	Y	N	Y	Y	Y
2 *Tauke*	Y	Y	Y	Y	N	Y	Y	Y
3 *Evans*	N	Y	Y	Y	Y	Y	N	Y
4 Smith	Y	N	N	N	N	N	Y	N
5 Harkin	N	N	N	N	Y	N	?	N
6 Bedell	Y	N	N	N	Y	N	?	N

Democrats   *Republicans*

	9	10	11	12	13	14	15	16
KANSAS								
1 ***Roberts***	Y	Y	Y	Y	Y	Y	N	N
2 ***Jeffries***	N	Y	Y	Y	Y	Y	N	Y
3 ***Winn***	Y	Y	Y	Y	Y	Y	Y	Y
4 Glickman	Y	N	N	Y	N	N	Y	N
5 ***Whittaker***	Y	Y	Y	Y	Y	Y	N	Y
KENTUCKY								
1 Hubbard	N	N	N	Y	Y	N	N	N
2 Natcher	Y	Y	N	N	N	N	N	Y
3 Mazzoli	Y	Y	N	Y	Y	N	Y	Y
4 ***Snyder***	Y	Y	Y	Y	N	N	N	Y
5 ***Rogers***	Y	Y	Y	Y	N	N	N	Y
6 ***Hopkins***	Y	Y	Y	Y	N	N	N	Y
7 Perkins	Y	N	N	N	N	N	N	Y
LOUISIANA								
1 ***Livingston***	Y	Y	Y	Y	Y	N	Y	Y
2 Boggs	Y	N	N	N	Y	N	Y	Y
3 Tauzin	N	Y	Y	N	Y	Y	N	Y
4 Roemer	Y	Y	N	Y	Y	Y	N	Y
5 Huckaby	N	Y	Y	Y	Y	Y	N	Y
6 ***Moore***	N	Y	Y	Y	Y	Y	N	Y
7 Breaux	N	Y	Y	N	Y	Y	Y	Y
8 Long	Y	N	N	N	Y	N	Y	Y
MAINE								
1 ***Emery***	Y	Y	Y	Y	Y	Y	N	Y
2 ***Snowe***	Y	Y	Y	Y	Y	N	Y	Y
MARYLAND								
1 Dyson	N	Y	N	Y	N	N	N	Y
2 Long	Y	Y	N	N	N	N	Y	Y
3 Mikulski	N	N	N	N	N	N	Y	N
4 ***Holt***	Y	Y	Y	Y	Y	N	N	Y
5 Hoyer [2]			N	N	Y	N	Y	N
6 Byron	N	Y	Y	Y	Y	N	N	N
7 Mitchell	Y	N	N	N	N	N	Y	N
8 Barnes	Y	N	N	N	N	N	Y	N
MASSACHUSETTS								
1 ***Conte***	Y	Y	Y	Y	Y	N	Y	?
2 Boland	Y	N	N	N	Y	N	#	N
3 Early	N	N	N	N	N	N	?	N
4 Frank	Y	N	N	N	Y	N	Y	N
5 Shannon	Y	N	N	N	Y	N	?	N
6 Mavroules	Y	N	N	N	Y	N	Y	N
7 Markey	Y	N	N	N	Y	N	Y	N
8 O'Neill			N	N				
9 Moakley	Y	N	N	N	Y	N	Y	N
10 ***Heckler***	Y	Y	Y	Y	N	N	Y	N
11 Donnelly	Y	N	N	N	Y	N	N	N
12 Studds	Y	N	N	N	N	N	Y	N
MICHIGAN								
1 Conyers	Y	N	N	N	N	N	N	N
2 ***Pursell***	Y	Y	Y	Y	Y	N	#	N
3 Wolpe	Y	N	N	N	N	N	Y	N
4 ***Slijander*** [3]		Y	Y	Y	Y	Y	Y	N
5 ***Sawyer***	Y	Y	Y	Y	Y	Y	Y	Y
6 ***Dunn***	N	Y	Y	Y	Y	Y	N	Y
7 Kildee	Y	N	N	N	N	N	Y	N
8 Traxler	Y	N	N	N	N	N	?	N
9 ***Vander Jagt***	Y	Y	Y	Y	Y	Y	Y	Y
10 Albosta	Y	Y	N	N	N	N	?	N
11 ***Davis***	Y	Y	Y	Y	N	N	N	N
12 Bonior	Y	N	N	N	N	N	Y	N
13 Crockett	Y	N	N	N	N	N	?	N
14 Hertel	N	N	N	N	N	N	Y	N
15 Ford	Y	N	N	N	N	N	N	?
16 Dingell	Y	N	N	N	Y	N	Y	Y
17 Brodhead	Y	N	N	N	Y	N	N	N
18 Blanchard	Y	N	N	N	N	N	Y	?
19 ***Broomfield***	Y	Y	Y	Y	Y	Y	Y	X
MINNESOTA								
1 ***Erdahl***	Y	Y	Y	Y	Y	N	Y	Y
2 ***Hagedorn***	Y	Y	Y	Y	Y	Y	Y	Y
3 ***Frenzel***	Y	Y	Y	Y	Y	Y	Y	Y
4 Vento	Y	N	N	N	N	N	N	?
5 Sabo	Y	N	N	N	N	N	Y	N
6 ***Weber***	Y	Y	Y	Y	Y	Y	N	N
7 ***Stangeland***	Y	Y	Y	Y	Y	Y	Y	Y
8 Oberstar	Y	N	N	N	N	N	Y	N
MISSISSIPPI								
1 Whitten	Y	N	N	N	N	N	N	Y
2 Bowen	Y	Y	N	Y	N	N	Y	Y
3 Montgomery	Y	Y	Y	Y	Y	Y	N	Y
4 Dowdy [4]				N	N	Y	N	N
5 ***Lott***	Y	Y	Y	Y	Y	Y	N	Y
MISSOURI								
1 Clay	N	N	N	N	N	N	?	N
2 Young	N	Y	N	N	?	N	N	?
3 Gephardt	Y	N	N	N	Y	N	N	N

	9	10	11	12	13	14	15	16
4 Skelton	Y	Y	N	N	Y	N	N	N
5 Bolling	Y	N	N	N	Y	N	?	?
6 ***Coleman***	Y	Y	Y	Y	Y	Y	N	Y
7 ***Taylor***	Y	Y	Y	Y	Y	Y	N	Y
8 ***Bailey***	Y	Y	Y	Y	Y	Y	N	Y
9 Volkmer	X	Y	N	N	N	N	N	N
10 ***Emerson***	Y	Y	Y	Y	Y	Y	N	Y
MONTANA								
1 Williams	Y	N	N	N	N	N	N	N
2 ***Marlenee***	Y	Y	Y	Y	Y	Y	N	N
NEBRASKA								
1 ***Bereuter***	Y	Y	Y	Y	Y	Y	Y	N
2 ***Daub***	Y	Y	Y	Y	Y	Y	N	N
3 ***Smith***	Y	Y	Y	Y	Y	Y	N	N
NEVADA								
AL Santini	N	Y	Y	Y	Y	N	N	X
NEW HAMPSHIRE								
1 D'Amours	N	N	N	N	N	N	N	N
2 ***Gregg***	#	Y	Y	Y	Y	Y	Y	N
NEW JERSEY								
1 Florio	Y	N	N	N	N	?	Y	N
2 Hughes	N	N	N	N	N	N	N	N
3 Howard	#	N	N	N	N	N	Y	N
4 ***Smith***	Y	Y	Y	Y	N	N	Y	Y
5 ***Fenwick***	Y	Y	Y	Y	Y	N	Y	N
6 ***Forsythe***	Y	Y	Y	Y	Y	Y	Y	Y
7 ***Roukema***	Y	Y	Y	Y	Y	N	Y	N
8 Roe	Y	N	N	N	N	N	Y	N
9 ***Hollenbeck***	Y	Y	Y	Y	N	N	Y	Y
10 Rodino	Y	N	N	N	N	N	N	N
11 Minish	Y	N	N	?	N	N	Y	N
12 ***Rinaldo***	Y	Y	Y	Y	N	N	Y	N
13 ***Courter***	Y	Y	Y	Y	Y	Y	Y	N
14 Guarini	Y	N	N	N	N	N	N	N
15 Dwyer	Y	N	N	N	N	N	Y	X
NEW MEXICO								
1 ***Lujan***	N	Y	Y	Y	Y	Y	N	N
2 ***Skeen***	Y	Y	Y	Y	Y	Y	N	Y
NEW YORK								
1 ***Carney***	N	Y	Y	Y	Y	N	Y	N
2 Downey	Y	N	N	N	N	N	Y	N
3 ***Carman***	N	Y	Y	Y	N	Y	Y	N
4 ***Lent***	Y	Y	Y	Y	N	Y	Y	N
5 ***McGrath***	N	Y	Y	Y	N	Y	Y	N
6 ***LeBoutillier***	Y	Y	Y	Y	Y	Y	Y	N
7 Addabbo	Y	N	N	N	Y	N	Y	N
8 Rosenthal	?	N	N	N	N	N	?	N
9 Ferraro	N	N	N	N	N	N	Y	N
10 Biaggi	Y	N	N	Y	N	N	?	N
11 Scheuer	Y	N	N	N	N	N	Y	N
12 Chisholm	Y	N	N	N	Y	?	?	N
13 Solarz	Y	N	N	N	N	N	Y	N
14 Richmond	Y	N	N	N	?	N	#	Y
15 Zeferetti	X	N	N	N	Y	N	Y	N
16 Schumer	Y	N	N	N	N	N	Y	N
17 ***Molinari***	N	Y	Y	Y	Y	Y	Y	N
18 ***Green***	Y	Y	Y	Y	Y	N	Y	Y
19 Rangel	#	N	N	N	N	N	Y	N
20 Weiss	Y	N	N	N	N	N	Y	N
21 Garcia	Y	N	N	N	N	N	?	N
22 Bingham	Y	N	N	N	N	N	Y	N
23 Peyser	Y	N	N	N	N	N	Y	N
24 Ottinger	N	N	N	N	N	N	Y	N
25 ***Fish***	Y	Y	Y	Y	N	N	#	N
26 ***Gilman***	Y	Y	Y	Y	N	N	Y	N
27 McHugh	Y	N	N	N	Y	N	Y	N
28 Stratton	Y	N	N	N	N	N	Y	Y
29 ***Solomon***	X	Y	Y	Y	Y	Y	N	N
30 ***Martin***	Y	Y	Y	Y	Y	Y	N	N
31 ***Mitchell***	Y	Y	Y	Y	Y	N	Y	N
32 ***Wortley***	Y	Y	Y	Y	Y	Y	Y	N
33 ***Lee***	Y	Y	Y	Y	Y	Y	N	N
34 ***Horton***	Y	Y	Y	Y	Y	N	Y	N
35 ***Conable***	Y	Y	Y	Y	Y	Y	Y	Y
36 LaFalce	Y	N	N	N	Y	N	Y	?
37 Nowak	Y	N	N	N	N	N	?	N
38 ***Kemp***	Y	Y	Y	Y	Y	Y	Y	Y
39 Lundine	?	N	N	Y	N	N	Y	N
NORTH CAROLINA								
1 Jones	Y	N	N	N	Y	?	N	Y
2 Fountain	N	Y	N	Y	Y	Y	N	Y
3 Whitley	Y	N	N	N	Y	Y	?	Y
4 Andrews	?	Y	N	N	Y	Y	N	Y
5 Neal	N	N	N	N	N	N	N	Y
6 ***Johnston***	N	Y	Y	Y	Y	?	Y	Y
7 Rose	?	N	N	N	Y	N	?	Y
8 Hefner	Y	N	N	N	Y	N	X	Y

	9	10	11	12	13	14	15	16
9 ***Martin***	Y	Y	Y	Y	N	Y	N	Y
10 ***Broyhill***	Y	Y	Y	Y	Y	Y	N	Y
11 ***Hendon***	N	Y	Y	Y	Y	Y	N	Y
NORTH DAKOTA								
AL Dorgan	Y	N	N	N	Y	N	Y	N
OHIO								
1 ***Gradison***	Y	Y	Y	Y	Y	Y	Y	N
2 Luken	Y	Y	N	Y	N	N	Y	N
3 Hall	?	Y	N	N	Y	N	Y	N
4 ***Oxley*** [5]				Y	Y	Y	Y	Y
5 ***Latta***	Y	Y	Y	Y	Y	Y	N	Y
6 ***McEwen***	Y	Y	Y	Y	Y	Y	N	Y
7 ***Brown***	Y	Y	Y	Y	Y	?	?	Y
8 ***Kindness***	Y	Y	Y	Y	Y	Y	N	N
9 ***Weber***	Y	Y	Y	Y	Y	Y	Y	Y
10 ***Miller***	N	Y	Y	Y	Y	Y	N	N
11 ***Stanton***	Y	Y	Y	Y	Y	Y	Y	Y
12 Shamansky	Y	N	N	N	N	N	Y	N
13 Pease	Y	N	N	N	N	N	?	N
14 Seiberling	Y	N	N	N	N	N	Y	N
15 ***Wylie***	Y	Y	Y	Y	Y	Y	Y	Y
16 ***Regula***	Y	Y	Y	Y	Y	Y	Y	N
17 ***Ashbrook***	N	Y	Y	Y	Y	Y	N	Y
18 Applegate	N	N	N	N	N	N	N	N
19 ***Williams***	Y	Y	Y	Y	Y	N	?	N
20 Oakar	Y	N	N	N	N	N	?	N
21 Stokes	Y	N	N	N	N	N	Y	N
22 Eckart	N	N	N	N	N	N	Y	N
23 Mottl	N	Y	N	Y	N	Y	?	N
OKLAHOMA								
1 Jones	Y	N	N	N	Y	N	N	Y
2 Synar	Y	N	N	N	N	N	Y	N
3 Watkins	N	N	N	N	Y	N	N	N
4 McCurdy	N	N	N	Y	Y	N	N	N
5 ***Edwards***	Y	Y	Y	Y	Y	Y	N	Y
6 English	N	Y	N	Y	Y	N	N	N
OREGON								
1 AuCoin	N	N	N	N	N	N	?	?
2 ***Smith***	N	Y	Y	Y	Y	Y	N	Y
3 Wyden	N	N	N	N	N	N	Y	N
4 Weaver	N	N	N	N	N	N	N	N
PENNSYLVANIA								
1 Foglietta	Y	N	N	N	N	N	Y	N
2 Gray	Y	N	N	N	N	N	Y	N
3 Smith [6]				N	Y	N	Y	N
4 ***Dougherty***	Y	Y	N	Y	Y	N	Y	N
5 ***Schulze***	Y	Y	Y	Y	Y	Y	N	Y
6 Yatron	N	Y	N	Y	N	N	?	N
7 Edgar	N	N	N	N	N	N	Y	N
8 ***Coyne, J.***	Y	Y	Y	Y	Y	Y	Y	N
9 ***Shuster***	Y	Y	Y	Y	Y	Y	N	Y
10 ***McDade***	Y	Y	Y	Y	Y	N	N	?
11 ***Nelligan***	Y	Y	Y	Y	Y	N	N	Y
12 Murtha	Y	N	N	N	Y	N	Y	N
13 ***Coughlin***	Y	Y	Y	Y	Y	Y	Y	N
14 Coyne, W.	Y	N	N	N	N	N	Y	N
15 ***Ritter***	Y	Y	Y	Y	Y	Y	N	N
16 ***Walker***	Y	Y	Y	Y	Y	Y	N	N
17 Ertel	Y	N	N	N	N	N	?	N
18 Walgren	Y	N	N	N	N	N	?	N
19 ***Goodling***	Y	Y	Y	Y	Y	N	N	N
20 Gaydos	N	N	N	N	Y	N	N	?
21 Bailey	Y	N	N	N	Y	N	N	Y
22 Murphy	N	N	N	N	N	N	?	N
23 ***Clinger***	Y	Y	Y	Y	Y	N	Y	Y
24 ***Marks***	Y	Y	Y	Y	Y	Y	?	Y
25 ***Atkinson*** [7]	N	Y	N	Y	N	Y	N	Y
RHODE ISLAND								
1 St Germain	Y	N	N	N	N	N	?	N
2 ***Schneider***	Y	Y	N	Y	N	N	Y	N
SOUTH CAROLINA								
1 ***Hartnett***	Y	Y	Y	Y	Y	Y	#	Y
2 ***Spence***	N	Y	Y	Y	Y	Y	N	Y
3 Derrick	N	Y	N	N	Y	N	N	Y
4 ***Campbell***	Y	Y	Y	Y	Y	Y	Y	Y
5 Holland	Y	Y	Y	N	Y	N	?	?
6 ***Napier***	Y	Y	Y	Y	N	?	N	Y
SOUTH DAKOTA								
1 Daschle	N	N	N	N	N	N	N	N
2 ***Roberts***	N	Y	Y	Y	Y	?	N	N
TENNESSEE								
1 ***Quillen***	Y	Y	Y	Y	Y	Y	X	#
2 ***Duncan***	Y	Y	Y	Y	Y	Y	?	Y
3 Bouquard	N	Y	N	Y	N	N	N	N
4 Gore	Y	N	N	N	N	N	Y	N
5 Boner	N	N	N	Y	Y	N	N	N
6 ***Beard***	Y	Y	Y	Y	Y	?	?	Y

	9	10	11	12	13	14	15	16
7 Jones	N	Y	N	Y	Y	N	X	N
8 Ford	Y	N	N	N	N	N	Y	P
TEXAS								
1 Hall, S.	N	Y	Y	Y	Y	Y	N	N
2 Wilson	Y	Y	Y	N	N	N	Y	N
3 ***Collins***	N	Y	Y	Y	Y	Y	N	Y
4 Hall, R.	N	Y	N	Y	N	Y	N	N
5 Mattox	N	N	N	N	N	N	Y	N
6 Gramm	Y	Y	Y	Y	Y	Y	N	Y
7 ***Archer***	Y	Y	Y	Y	Y	Y	N	N
8 ***Fields***	N	Y	Y	Y	Y	Y	N	Y
9 Brooks	N	N	N	N	N	N	?	Y
10 Pickle	Y	N	N	N	Y	Y	Y	Y
11 Leath	N	Y	Y	Y	Y	Y	N	N
12 Wright	Y	N	N	N	N	N	?	Y
13 Hightower	Y	Y	Y	Y	N	N	N	N
14 Patman	N	N	N	N	N	N	N	N
15 de la Garza	N	N	N	Y	Y	N	N	Y
16 White	Y	Y	Y	N	N	N	N	Y
17 Stenholm	Y	Y	Y	Y	Y	Y	N	N
18 Leland	?	N	N	N	N	N	Y	N
19 Hance	Y	Y	Y	Y	Y	Y	?	N
20 Gonzalez	Y	N	N	N	N	N	N	N
21 ***Loeffler***	Y	Y	Y	Y	Y	Y	Y	Y
22 ***Paul***	N	Y	Y	Y	Y	Y	N	N
23 Kazen	N	N	N	N	N	N	N	Y
24 Frost	Y	N	N	N	Y	N	Y	N
UTAH								
1 ***Hansen***	N	Y	Y	Y	Y	Y	N	Y
2 ***Marriott***	Y	Y	Y	Y	Y	?	N	Y
VERMONT								
AL ***Jeffords***	Y	Y	Y	N	N	N	Y	N
VIRGINIA								
1 ***Trible***	Y	Y	Y	Y	Y	Y	N	Y
2 ***Whitehurst***	Y	Y	Y	Y	Y	Y	?	?
3 ***Bliley***	Y	Y	Y	Y	Y	Y	Y	Y
4 ***Daniel, R.***	Y	Y	Y	Y	Y	Y	N	Y
5 Daniel, D.	Y	Y	Y	Y	Y	Y	N	Y
6 ***Butler***	Y	Y	Y	Y	Y	Y	Y	Y
7 ***Robinson***	Y	Y	Y	Y	Y	Y	N	Y
8 ***Parris***	Y	Y	Y	Y	Y	?	N	Y
9 ***Wampler***	Y	Y	Y	Y	Y	N	N	Y
10 ***Wolf***	Y	Y	Y	Y	N	Y	Y	Y
WASHINGTON								
1 ***Pritchard***	Y	Y	Y	Y	Y	N	Y	N
2 Swift	Y	N	N	N	Y	N	Y	N
3 Bonker	Y	N	N	N	Y	N	Y	Y
4 ***Morrison***	Y	Y	Y	Y	Y	Y	Y	Y
5 Foley	Y	N	N	N	Y	N	Y	Y
6 Dicks	Y	N	N	Y	Y	N	Y	Y
7 Lowry	Y	N	N	N	Y	N	Y	N
WEST VIRGINIA								
1 Mollohan	Y	N	N	N	Y	N	Y	N
2 ***Benedict***	Y	Y	Y	Y	Y	Y	N	Y
3 ***Staton***	N	Y	Y	Y	Y	Y	X	Y
4 Rahall	#	N	N	N	N	N	N	N
WISCONSIN								
1 Aspin	Y	N	N	N	N	N	?	N
2 Kastenmeier	N	N	N	N	N	N	N	N
3 ***Gunderson***	N	Y	Y	Y	Y	Y	N	N
4 Zablocki	Y	N	N	N	Y	N	Y	N
5 Reuss	Y	N	N	N	N	N	Y	N
6 ***Petri***	Y	Y	Y	Y	Y	Y	N	N
7 Obey	N	N	N	N	N	N	N	N
8 ***Roth***	N	Y	Y	Y	Y	Y	N	N
9 ***Sensenbrenner***	N	Y	Y	Y	Y	Y	N	N
WYOMING								
AL ***Cheney***	Y	Y	Y	Y	Y	Y	Y	Y

Democrats ***Republicans***

Voting Record of '81 Shows The Romance and Fidelity of Reagan Honeymoon on Hill

The blush of President Reagan's honeymoon with Congress shines brightly from Congressional Quarterly's annual study of presidential support — a measure of how often congressional votes matched the president's announced positions in 1981.

On roll-call votes where the president declared an opinion, he and the House agreed 72.4 percent of the time, he and the Senate 88.3 percent of the time.

Thanks to the fact that the Republican-run Senate staged many more roll calls than the House in 1981, Reagan's overall score was 82.4 percent. Not since the administration of Lyndon B. Johnson (who had a 93 percent score in 1965) had the CQ study registered such harmony.

But while the study reflects Reagan's first-year success on Capitol Hill, it is not a measure of how much of his program was approved. And as a measure of an individual lawmaker's loyalty to the White House, the study should be used with caution.

First, the study counts only issues that reach a roll-call vote on the House or Senate floor. Elements of the White

House agenda that are abandoned or defeated before they reach the floor, that are quietly compromised, or that breeze through on a voice vote are not counted.

Second, the study counts only votes where the president has indicated clear, personal support or opposition, usually in messages to Congress, press conference remarks or other public statements. In some cases, an executive branch department or White House lobbyists may work actively on legislation without the president expressing a public position.

Third, all votes are given equal weight. The study does not distinguish major votes from minor ones, close calls from lopsided decisions, or administration initiatives from proposals born on Capitol Hill. *(Ground rules, box, p. 20-C)*

Thus the Senate's narrow approval of Reagan's decision to sell advanced weapons to Saudi Arabia (H Con Res 335), his most hotly contested foreign policy initiative, counted the same as the unanimous, pro forma ratification of the U.S.-Canadian Maritime Boundary Treaty.

Thirty-three of the 128 Senate votes counted in the study were to confirm Reagan nominations, most of them non-controversial. All of the nominations that were brought to a floor vote were confirmed, contributing more than 4 percentage points to Reagan's Senate support score.

Many Roll Calls

Finally, issues that Congress took many roll calls to resolve may influence the study more than issues settled by a single vote. The classic recent example was in 1978, when President Carter's Senate support score was dramatically enhanced by winning 55 roll calls — mostly procedural — related to ratification of the Panama Canal treaties.

In 1981, some issues were so thorny that Congress took several roll calls to find a winning formula. For example, 11 of the roll calls counted here related to government treatment of dairy farmers, giving that subject extra importance in the calculation of Reagan's support score.

A reporter or researcher interested in how an individual member of Congress voted on the administration's program is advised to look at the specifics of the member's legislative behavior, including his or her record on CQ's selection of 1981 key votes. *(Key votes, p. 3-C)*

Background

The presidential support score is a rough measure of the comity between Congress and the president — how often Congress voted the way the president wanted or, conversely, how often he endorsed what Congress did.

Over a period of time, the score reflects numerically the rises and dips in relations between the two branches of government, and individual scores show how members of Congress generally fit the trends. *(Individual senators' 1981 scores, p. 24-C; House members' scores, pp. 22-C, 23-C)*

The study, begun in 1953, was long billed as an indicator of the president's success on Capitol Hill. The first study, of Dwight D. Eisenhower's maiden year in the White House, was advertised as "testing congressional support for his program and leadership" and measuring acceptance of "the chief executive's proposals."

Success Rate

Following are the annual percentages of presidential victories since 1953 on congressional votes where the presidents took a clear-cut position:

Eisenhower		Nixon	
1953	89.0%	1969	74.0%
1954	82.8	1970	77.0
1955	75.0	1971	75.0
1956	70.0	1972	66.0
1957	68.0	1973	50.6
1958	76.0	1974	59.6
1959	52.0		
1960	65.0	**Ford**	
		1974	58.2%
Kennedy		1975	61.0
1961	81.0%	1976	53.8
1962	85.4		
1963	87.1	**Carter**	
		1977	75.4%
Johnson		1978	78.3
1964	88.0%	1979	76.8
1965	93.0	1980	75.1
1966	79.0		
1967	79.0	**Reagan**	
1968	75.0	1981	82.4%

A closer reading of the study's ground rules showed its limitations as a measure of executive clout, but not all readers have been discriminating in using the figures.

During the 1980 presidential campaign, President Carter's supporters, citing his 77 percent support score in 1979, claimed that Congress had passed four-fifths of the Carter agenda. A Carter aide later conceded that CQ's statistics had been "mistranslated or misused." The aide claimed, however, that the study itself was "reasonably misleading." *(Carter claims, 1980 Weekly Report p. 3098; Carter 1980 score, 1980 Almanac p. 17-C)*

Until 1975 CQ also published an annual "boxscore" of presidential victories and losses, tallying all specific legislative requests from the White House and computing the percentage passed by Congress. That practice was ended because CQ editors decided it was a dubious measure of a president's record.

Reagan and Predecessors

In his maiden year, Reagan and Congress were in agreement on 55 of 76 votes in the House and 113 of 128 votes in the Senate, by CQ's count.

The highest score since CQ began its study was Johnson's 93 percent in 1965, the lowest Richard M. Nixon's 50.6 percent in 1973, during the Watergate era.

It is usual, but not always true, that presidents fare better in the first years of their terms than at the end. Eisenhower, Johnson, Nixon and Ford all showed declining presidential support scores late in their terms.

In Carter's case, however, the scores remained fairly steady for all four years, though the popular wisdom held that his relations with Congress had deteriorated.

In 1981, the study was heavily weighted toward budget votes — an indicator of the year's legislative obsession.

The process of reconciliation alone, just one crucial step in Reagan's attempt to force budgetary discipline, accounted for 33 of the 204 votes. Reagan's position prevailed on all but four of them.

Tax cut legislation contributed another 13 roll calls to the study, all of which went Reagan's way. Budget resolutions, appropriations bills, spending authorizations and the debt limit added to the list of economic roll calls.

Party Support

Republicans, predictably, agreed with Reagan more often than Democrats did. What was unusual, however, was the degree of fealty to Reagan in the GOP-led Senate.

Senate Republicans, on average, voted with Reagan on 80 percent of the roll calls counted. No other president had commanded such loyalty from members of his own party in either house since CQ began its study 29 years earlier.

Even Democrat Lyndon Johnson, renowned for his command of Congress in the early years of his presidency, never had more than 77 percent support from House Democrats or 63 percent from Senate Democrats.

With 2-to-1 majorities in both houses, Johnson could be more tolerant of stragglers than Reagan, with his scant 53-47 Senate majority.

The Republican discipline in 1981 was even more evident among the crew of senators elected in 1980. The average support score for the 16 new Republicans in the Senate was 82 percent.

Newcomers Mack Mattingly, R-Ga. (88 percent support), Slade Gorton, R-Wash., and Dan Quayle, R-Ind., (both 87 percent) were among the top 10 Senate loyalists. None of the Republican Senate newcomers agreed with Reagan less than 76 percent of the time.

Majority Leader Howard H. Baker Jr., R-Tenn., who was responsible for much of that discipline, voted with the president on 89 percent of the votes studied, a figure surpassed only by Sen. Strom Thurmond, R-S.C., and Richard G. Lugar, R-Ind.

Sen. Paul Laxalt, R-Nev., often described as the president's closest confidant in Congress, voted with his White

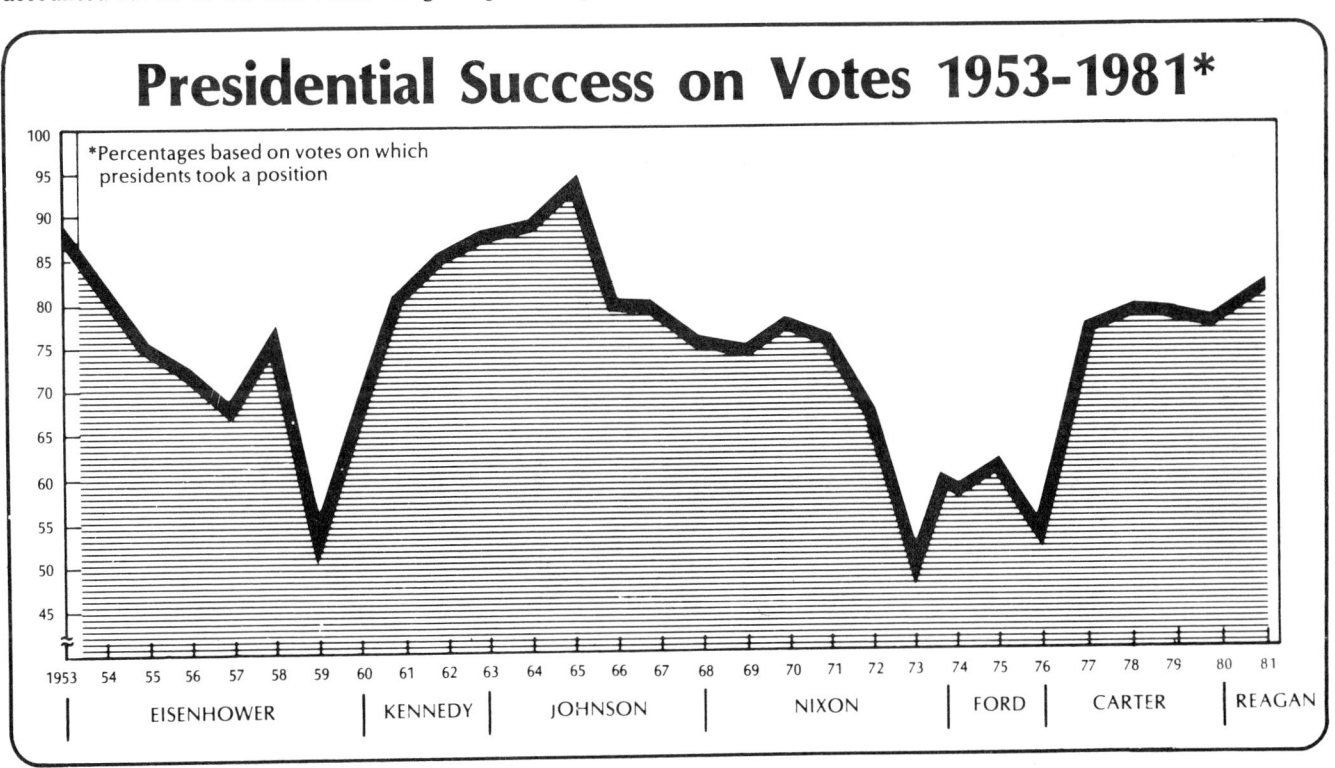

Presidential Success on Votes 1953-1981*

*Percentages based on votes on which presidents took a position

EISENHOWER | KENNEDY | JOHNSON | NIXON | FORD | CARTER | REAGAN

Ground Rules for CQ Presidential Support-Opposition

Presidential Issues — CQ tries to determine what the president personally, as distinct from other administration officials, does and does not want in the way of legislative action by analyzing his messages to Congress, press conference remarks and other public statements and documents.

Borderline Cases — By the time an issue reaches a vote, it may differ from the original form in which the president expressed himself. In such cases, CQ analyzes the measure to determine whether, on balance, the features favored by the president outweigh those he opposed or vice versa. Only then is the vote classified.

Some Votes Excluded — Occasionally, important measures are so extensively amended on the floor that it is impossible to characterize final passage as a victory or defeat for the president.

Procedural Votes — Votes on motions to recommit, to reconsider or to table often are key tests that govern the legislative outcome. Such votes are necessarily included in the presidential support tabulations.

Appropriations — Generally, votes on passage of appropriations bills are not included in the tabulations, since it is rarely possible to determine the president's position on the overall revisions Congress almost invariably makes in the sums allowed. Votes on amendments to cut or increase specific funds requested in the president's budget, however, are included.

Failure to Vote — In tabulating the support or opposition scores of members on the selected presidential-issue votes, CQ counts only "yea" and "nay" votes on the ground that only these affect the outcome. Most failures to vote reflect absences because of illness or official business. Failures to vote lower both support and opposition scores equally.

Weighting — All presidential-issue votes have equal statistical weight in the analysis.

Changed Positions — Presidential support is determined by the position of the president at the time of a vote, even though that position may be different from an earlier position, or may have been reversed after the vote was taken.

House friend three times out of four — not exactly the behavior of a maverick, but below average for his party's senators in general and Western Republicans in particular.

'Weevils, Moths'

Broken down by region, the presidential support scores illustrate the widely reported growth of two intra-party factions, the conservative Southern "Boll Weevils," and the Republican moderate "Gypsy Moths" of the Northeast and Midwest.

Reagan drew his strongest Democratic support from the Boll Weevils. Of the 10 Senate Democrats most often in agreement with the president, eight came from the South (the other two from Nebraska). In the House, 21 of the 22 most supportive Democrats came from the South.

The top Democratic defectors included Texans Charles W. Stenholm, coordinator of the Conservative Democratic Forum (75 percent with Reagan); Phil Gramm, cosponsor of Reagan's reconciliation bill (75 percent); and Kent Hance, cosponsor of Reagan's tax bill (71 percent).

Reagan's Republican opponents tended to be from the ranks of the Gypsy Moths. The 21 House Republicans and the 12 Senate Republicans who most often voted in opposition to him all came from the Northeast or Midwest.

Among them were the co-chairmen of the House Gypsy Moths, Carl D. Pursell, Mich. (45 percent opposition), and Bill Green, N.Y. (39 percent).

State Scores

The average scores for each state show, not surprisingly, that the Republican delegations were most inclined to vote with the president, the Democratic delegations most likely to vote against him.

The most consistent support came, in the Senate, from the all-Republican delegations of Indiana (88 percent), Utah (87 percent), Wyoming (86 percent), Iowa, Kansas,

New Mexico and North Carolina (all 84 percent).

In the House, the highest average support scores were in Idaho (76 percent; two Republicans), Virginia (75 percent; one Democrat, nine Republicans), Utah (72 percent; two Republicans), Nebraska (70 percent; three Republicans) and South Carolina (70 percent; two Democrats, four Republicans). But Alabama's House delegation, with four Democrats and three Republicans, had one of the highest levels of support, 70 percent.

Average Scores

Following are composites of Democratic and Republican scores for 1981 and 1980:

	1981		1980	
	Dem.	**Rep.**	**Dem.**	**Rep.**
	SUPPORT			
Senate	49%	80%	62%	45%
House	42	68	63	40
	OPPOSITION			
Senate	45	15	25	45
House	50	26	26	50

Regional Averages

SUPPORT

Regional presidential support scores for 1981; scores for 1980 are in parentheses:

	East		West		South		Midwest	
DEMOCRATS								
Senate	40%	(64)	46%	(60)	60%	(61)	46%	(63)
House	35	(65)	38	(65)	56	(57)	36	(66)
REPUBLICANS								
Senate	74	(53)	82	(40)	85	(43)	81	(48)
House	64	(47)	70	(35)	73	(37)	67	(41)

OPPOSITION

Regional presidential opposition scores for 1981; scores for 1980 are in parentheses:

	East		West		South		Midwest	
DEMOCRATS								
Senate	52%	(21)	44%	(21)	35%	(28)	49%	(27)
House	57	(23)	54	(23)	37	(33)	57	(24)
REPUBLICANS								
Senate	21	(36)	11	(50)	11	(51)	16	(44)
House	31	(44)	21	(51)	22	(56)	29	(49)

High Scorers — Support

Highest individual scorers in presidential support — those who voted for the president's position most often in 1981:

SENATE

Democrats		Republicans	
Byrd, Va.*	79%	Thurmond, S.C.	90%
Stennis, Miss.	70	Lugar, Ind.	90
Bentsen, Texas	70	Baker, Tenn.	89
Heflin, Ala.	68	Mattingly, Ga.	88
Johnston, La.	68	Garn, Utah	88
Long, La.	66	Hatch, Utah	87
Zorinsky, Neb.	61	Gorton, Wash.	87
Boren, Okla.	60	Quayle, Ind.	87
Nunn, Ga.	59	Warner, Va.	87
		Jepsen, Iowa	87

Elected as an independent, but caucuses with Democrats.

HOUSE

Democrats		Republicans	
Montgomery, Miss.	78%	Lott, Miss.	84%
Daniel, Va.	78	Cheney, Wyo.	83
Shelby, Ala.	76	Shumway, Calif.	83
Stenholm, Texas	75	Daniel, Va.	82
Gramm, Texas	75	Lagomarsino, Calif.	82
Hutto, Fla.	74	Robinson, Va.	80
Ireland, Fla.	74	Hansen, Idaho	80
Stump, Ariz.	74	Michel, Ill.	80
Chappell, Fla.	71	Smith, Ala.	80
Hance, Texas	71		

1981 Presidential Position Votes

Following is a list of all Senate and House recorded votes in 1981 on which President Reagan took a position. The votes, listed by CQ vote number, appear in the vote charts in the 1981 Weekly Reports.

Senate Votes (128)

Presidential Victories (113) — 1, 3, 4, 5, 6, 8, 9, 10, 11, 12, 13, 14, 15, 16, 17, 18, 19, 20, 21, 22, 23, 24, 25, 27, 29, 30, 31, 32, 34, 40, 43, 44, 47, 49, 50, 54, 55, 56, 57, 59, 60, 61, 62, 63, 69, 72, 74, 77, 84, 85, 86, 87, 89, 120, 121, 125, 128, 132, 135, 139, 145, 149, 156, 160, 162, 164, 182, 189, 190, 201, 211, 212, 213, 239, 243, 244, 245, 247, 248, 251, 252, 258, 262, 267, 270, 271, 272, 273, 287, 288, 290, 291, 295, 302, 309, 321, 326, 335, 350, 352, 353, 371, 376, 388, 403, 417, 431, 432, 434, 453, 468, 472, 473.

Presidential Defeats (15) — 33, 45, 46, 58, 66, 151, 152, 153, 157, 275, 314, 340, 341, 342, 351.

House Votes (76)

Presidential Victories (55) — 7, 11, 27, 28, 30, 31, 33, 41, 46, 52, 95, 96, 97, 98, 101, 102, 104, 118, 128, 147, 148, 149, 150, 157, 159, 160, 165, 166, 167, 179, 192, 193, 198, 205, 207, 219, 240, 255, 257, 260, 263, 277, 278, 298, 299, 300, 301, 302, 322, 329, 330, 331, 347, 350, 351.

Presidential Defeats (21) — 32, 38, 47, 48, 50, 51, 69, 83, 87, 234, 239, 241, 243, 244, 258, 261, 262, 264, 266, 285, 344.

High Scorers — Opposition

Highest individual scorers in presidential opposition — those who voted most often against his position in 1981:

SENATE

Democrats		Republicans	
Levin, Mich.	63%	Weicker, Conn.	30%
Eagleton, Mo.	63	Mathias, Md.	27
Sarbanes, Md.	61	Roth, Del.	24
Riegle, Mich.	60	Durenberger, Minn.	24
Kennedy, Mass.	60	Pressler, S.D.	24
Leahy, Vt.	60	Chafee, R.I.	23
Dodd, Conn.	59	Specter, Pa.	22
Metzenbaum, Ohio	59	Heinz, Pa.	20
Hart, Colo.	57	Kasten, Wis.	20
Biden, Del.	54		

HOUSE

Democrats		Republicans	
Gejdenson, Conn.	76%	Jeffords, Vt.	55%
Kastenmeier, Wis.	75	Schneider, R.I.	50
Ottinger, N.Y.	74	Erdahl, Minn.	46
Brodhead, Mich.	74	Pursell, Mich.	45
Bonior, Mich.	74	Heckler, Mass.	43
Kildee, Mich.	74	Conte, Mass.	42
Wolpe, Mich.	72	Leach, Iowa	42
Edgar, Pa.	72		
Yates, Ill.	71		

Presidential Support and Opposition: House

1. Reagan Support Score, 1981. Percentage of 76 Reagan-issue recorded votes in 1981 on which representative voted "yea" or "nay" *in agreement* with the president's position. Failures to vote lower both Support and Opposition scores.

2. Reagan Opposition Score, 1981. Percentage of 76 Reagan-issue recorded votes in 1981 on which representative voted "yea" or "nay" *in disagreement* with the president's position. Failures to vote lower both Support and Opposition scores.

1. Rep. William R. Cotter, D-Conn., died Sept. 9, 1981.

2. Rep. Steny Hoyer, D-Md., sworn in June 3, 1981, to succeed Gladys Noon Spellman, D, whose seat the House declared vacant on Feb. 24, 1981. Spellman was not eligible for any presidential-issue votes in 1981.

3. Rep. Thomas P. O'Neill Jr., D-Mass., as Speaker, votes at his own discretion.

4. Rep. Mark Siljander, R-Mich., sworn in April 28, 1981, to succeed David A. Stockman, R, who resigned Jan. 27, 1981. Stockman was not eligible for any presidential-issue votes in 1981.

5. Rep. Wayne Dowdy, D-Miss., sworn in July 9, 1981, to succeed Jon Hinson, R, who resigned April 13, 1981. Hinson did not vote on either of the two presidential-issue votes for which he was eligible in 1981.

6. Rep. Michael G. Oxley, R-Ohio, sworn in July 21, 1981, to succeed Tennyson Guyer, R, who died April 12, 1981. Guyer's 1981 presidential support score was 100%. Opposition was zero.

7. Rep. Joseph F. Smith, D-Pa., sworn in July 28, 1981, to succeed Raymond F. Lederer, D, who resigned May 5, 1981. Lederer did not vote on either of the two presidential-issue votes for which he was eligible in 1981.

8. Rep. Eugene V. Atkinson, Pa., switched from the Democratic to the Republican Party on Oct. 14, 1981.

KEY

† Not eligible for all recorded votes in 1981 (sworn in after Jan. 5, died or resigned during session, or voted "present" to avoid possible conflict of interest).

	1	2
ALABAMA		
1 *Edwards*	76	24
2 *Dickinson*	72	16
3 Nichols	68	24
4 Bevill	54	42
5 Flippo	59	32
6 *Smith*	80	17
7 Shelby	76	21
ALASKA		
AL *Young*	67	17
ARIZONA		
1 *Rhodes*	68	12
2 Udall	51	41
3 Stump	74	18
4 *Rudd*	71	17
ARKANSAS		
1 Alexander	49	42
2 *Bethune*	70	24
3 *Hammerschmidt*	79	21
4 Anthony	61	38
CALIFORNIA		
1 *Chappie*	74	18
2 *Clausen*	72	26
3 Matsui	45	53
4 Fazio	41	57
5 Burton, J.	18	45
6 Burton, P.	29	62
7 Miller	28	70
8 Dellums	21	66
9 Stark	29	64
10 Edwards	29	63
11 Lantos	46	50
12 *McCloskey*	46	20
13 Mineta	50	47
14 *Shumway*	83	16
15 Coelho	47	49
16 Panetta	50	50
17 *Pashayan*	68	13
18 *Thomas*	76	14
19 *Lagomarsino*	82	18
20 *Goldwater*	49	21
21 *Fiedler*	75	20
22 *Moorhead*	75	18
23 Beilenson	30	64
24 Waxman	25	63
25 Roybal	34	64
26 *Rousselot*	64	21
27 *Dornan*	57	26
28 Dixon	37	54
29 Hawkins	34	59
30 Danielson	41	42
31 Dymally	29	43
32 Anderson	46	50
33 *Grisham*	68	14
34 *Lungren*	72	18
35 *Dreier*	78	21
36 Brown	38	57
37 *Lewis*	72	20
38 Patterson	39	54
39 *Dannemeyer*	74	24
40 *Badham*	63	13
41 *Lowery*	74	24
42 *Hunter*	74	25
43 *Burgener*	66	18
COLORADO		
1 Schroeder	29	70
2 Wirth	38	51
3 Kogovsek	37	61
4 *Brown*	66	34

	1	2
5 *Kramer*	71	28
CONNECTICUT		
1 Cotter [1]	3†	0†
2 Gejdenson	22	76
3 *DeNardis*	57	41
4 *McKinney*	57	38
5 Ratchford	33	66
6 Moffett	21	64
DELAWARE		
AL *Evans*	70	29
FLORIDA		
1 Hutto	74	25
2 Fuqua	54	29
3 Bennett	59	41
4 Chappell	71	24
5 *McCollum*	67	28
6 *Young*	72	24
7 Gibbons	62	34
8 Ireland	74	16
9 Nelson	62	25
10 *Bafalis*	76	17
11 Mica	66	34
12 *Shaw*	78	22
13 Lehman	39	53
14 Pepper	30	43
15 Fascell	41	54
GEORGIA		
1 Ginn	51	41
2 Hatcher	59	36
3 Brinkley	62	37
4 Levitas	47	43
5 Fowler	42	45
6 *Gingrich*	64	24
7 McDonald	66	16
8 Evans	59	32
9 Jenkins	58	34
10 Barnard	67	18
HAWAII		
1 Heftel	46	53
2 Akaka	46	54
IDAHO		
1 *Craig*	72	24
2 *Hansen*	80	18
ILLINOIS		
1 Washington	24	63
2 Savage	14	49
3 Russo	38	54
4 *Derwinski*	68	24
5 Fary	47	37
6 *Hyde*	79	20
7 Collins	28	70
8 Rostenkowski	50	49
9 Yates	26	71
10 *Porter*	68	32
11 Annunzio	55	45
12 *Crane, P.*	64	28
13 *McClory*	66	30
14 *Erlenborn*	71	22
15 *Corcoran*	70	22
16 *Martin*	57	41
17 *O'Brien*	63	24
18 *Michel*	80	17
19 *Railsback*	55	41
20 *Findley*	70	29
21 *Madigan*	68	20
22 *Crane, D.*	66	29
23 Price	51	37
24 Simon	36	59
INDIANA		
1 Benjamin	42	58
2 Fithian	32	50
3 *Hiler*	78	21
4 *Coats*	74	26
5 *Hillis*	68	24
6 Evans	38	58
7 *Myers*	75	25
8 *Deckard*	53	36
9 Hamilton	47	51
10 Sharp	43	57
11 Jacobs	34	64
IOWA		
1 *Leach*	58	42
2 *Tauke*	62	38
3 *Evans*	62	30
4 Smith	42	55
5 Harkin	25	70
6 Bedell	29	61

Democrats   ***Republicans***

	1	2
KANSAS		
1 Roberts	67	30
2 *Jeffries*	74	24
3 *Winn*	74	25
4 Glickman	47	53
5 *Whittaker*	70	30
KENTUCKY		
1 Hubbard	58	41
2 Natcher	54	46
3 Mazzoli	47	43
4 *Snyder*	66	34
5 *Rogers*	72	28
6 *Hopkins*	68	29
7 Perkins	41	57
LOUISIANA		
1 *Livingston*	76	21
2 Boggs	53	45
3 Tauzin	67	28
4 Roemer	68	30
5 Huckaby	67	25
6 *Moore*	70	30
7 Breaux	61	24
8 Long	49	38
MAINE		
1 *Emery*	64	36
2 *Snowe*	67	33
MARYLAND		
1 Dyson	61	39
2 Long	47	53
3 Mikulski	32	68
4 *Holt*	75	21
5 Hoyer [2]	40†	55†
6 Byron	62	33
7 Mitchell	30	66
8 Barnes	33	67
MASSACHUSETTS		
1 *Conte*	55	42
2 Boland	34	62
3 Early	25	62
4 Frank	29	64
5 Shannon	33	66
6 Mavroules	36	63
7 Markey	34	66
8 O'Neill [3]		
9 Moakley	36	47
10 Heckler	54	43
11 Donnelly	33	55
12 Studds	33	67
MICHIGAN		
1 Conyers	32	59
2 *Pursell*	49	45
3 Wolpe	26	72
4 *Siljander* [4]	66†	27†
5 *Sawyer*	61	36
6 Dunn	58	41
7 Kildee	26	74
8 Traxler	39	57
9 *Vander Jagt*	64	21
10 Albosta	46	49
11 *Davis*	59	36
12 Bonior	25	74
13 Crockett	22	47
14 Hertel	25	64
15 Ford	26	58
16 Dingell	36	55
17 Brodhead	24	74
18 Blanchard	34	61
19 *Broomfield*	63	26
MINNESOTA		
1 *Erdahl*	54	46
2 *Hagedorn*	62	29
3 *Frenzel*	64	25
4 Vento	29	61
5 Sabo	29	70
6 *Weber*	55	41
7 *Stangeland*	71	28
8 Oberstar	33	67
MISSISSIPPI		
1 Whitten	50	49
2 Bowen	62	37
3 Montgomery	78	21
4 Dowdy [5]	66†	34†
5 *Lott*	84	16
MISSOURI		
1 Clay	22	68
2 Young	54	42
3 Gephardt	54	43

	1	2
4 Skelton	58	39
5 Bolling	20	38
6 *Coleman*	70	28
7 *Taylor*	71	25
8 *Bailey*	75	22
9 Volkmer	43	51
10 *Emerson*	78	22
MONTANA		
1 Williams	34	62
2 *Marlenee*	66	24
NEBRASKA		
1 *Bereuter*	68	30
2 *Daub*	71	26
3 *Smith*	70	30
NEVADA		
AL Santini	47	30
NEW HAMPSHIRE		
1 D'Amours	34	59
2 *Gregg*	68	29
NEW JERSEY		
1 Florio	20	37
2 Hughes	41	58
3 Howard	38	54
4 Smith	64	36
5 Fenwick	63	37
6 Forsythe	62	24
7 Roukema	66	32
8 Roe	39	39
9 *Hollenbeck*	50	41
10 Rodino	30	68
11 Minish	30	62
12 *Rinaldo*	63	33
13 *Courter*	63	32
14 Guarini	33	57
15 Dwyer	41	57
NEW MEXICO		
1 Lujan	70	25
2 *Skeen*	75	24
NEW YORK		
1 *Carney*	71	20
2 Downey	29	63
3 *Carman*	70	29
4 *Lent*	68	30
5 *McGrath*	64	34
6 *LeBoutillier*	75	21
7 Addabbo	32	64
8 Rosenthal	16	58
9 Ferraro	32	67
10 Biaggi	37	47
11 Scheuer	32	61
12 Chisholm	28	54
13 Solarz	36	58
14 Richmond	22	68
15 Zeferetti	42	50
16 Schumer	30	67
17 *Molinari*	68	30
18 *Green*	55	39
19 Rangel	33	63
20 Weiss	36	64
21 Garcia	25	50
22 Bingham	33	66
23 Peyser	43	54
24 Ottinger	24	74
25 *Fish*	57	38
26 *Gilman*	51	29
27 McHugh	32	68
28 Stratton	47	42
29 *Solomon*	70	24
30 *Martin*	63	25
31 *Mitchell*	57	34
32 *Wortley*	67	30
33 *Lee*	61	33
34 *Horton*	50	34
35 *Conable*	76†	20†
36 LaFalce	36	61
37 Nowak	38	61
38 *Kemp*	75	18
39 Lundine	28	57
NORTH CAROLINA		
1 Jones	37	30
2 Fountain	61	38
3 Whitley	62	37
4 Andrews	53	41
5 Neal	42	55
6 *Johnston*	57	20
7 Rose	49	43
8 Hefner	53	41

	1	2
9 *Martin*	71	20
10 *Broyhill*	70	22
11 *Hendon*	75	24
NORTH DAKOTA		
AL Dorgan	37	55
OHIO		
1 *Gradison*	68	29
2 Luken	55	42
3 Hall	47	46
4 *Oxley* [6]	67†	29†
5 *Latta*	79	20
6 *McEwen*	76	24
7 *Brown*	64†	19†
8 *Kindness*	72	25
9 *Weber*	68	28
10 *Miller*	72	28
11 *Stanton*	71	28
12 Shamansky	42	55
13 Pease	32	64
14 Seiberling	30	70
15 *Wylie*	64	29
16 *Regula*	72	28
17 *Ashbrook*	68	21
18 Applegate	45	53
19 *Williams*	57	26
20 Oakar	34	59
21 Stokes	29	66
22 Eckart	33	63
23 Mottl	41	53
OKLAHOMA		
1 Jones	58	41
2 Synar	37	61
3 Watkins	57	43
4 McCurdy	57	42
5 *Edwards*	75	24
6 English	55	43
OREGON		
1 AuCoin	29	55
2 *Smith*	71	25
3 Wyden	26	68
4 Weaver	25	70
PENNSYLVANIA		
1 Foglietta	25	58
2 Gray	29	59
3 Smith [7]	55†	41†
4 *Dougherty*	54	30
5 *Schulze*	70	14
6 Yatron	49	50
7 Edgar	22	72
8 *Coyne, J.*	68	29
9 *Shuster*	76	22
10 *McDade*	62	30
11 *Nelligan*	64	32
12 Murtha	45	50
13 *Coughlin*	66	32
14 Coyne, W.	38	62
15 *Ritter*	71	24
16 *Walker*	72	18
17 Ertel	37	57
18 Walgren	41	57
19 *Goodling*	59	36
20 Gaydos	43	45
21 Bailey	51	46
22 Murphy	38	53
23 *Clinger*	63	37
24 *Marks*	64	30
25 *Atkinson* [8]	63	32
RHODE ISLAND		
1 St Germain	34	61
2 *Schneider*	47	50
SOUTH CAROLINA		
1 *Hartnett*	79	17
2 *Spence*	74	26
3 Derrick	50	45
4 *Campbell*	79	11
5 Holland	58	22
6 *Napier*	78	20
SOUTH DAKOTA		
1 Daschle	42	57
2 *Roberts*	64	28
TENNESSEE		
1 *Quillen*	63	17
2 *Duncan*	66	26
3 Bouquard	57	36
4 Gore	39	59
5 Boner	57	38
6 *Beard*	67	17

	1	2
7 Jones	58	41
8 Ford	34	59
TEXAS		
1 Hall, S.	66	32
2 Wilson	57	34
3 *Collins*	71	24
4 Hall, R.	61	34
5 Mattox	29	51
6 *Gramm*	75	22
7 *Archer*	67	30
8 *Fields*	76	18
9 Brooks	42	33
10 Pickle	61	36
11 Leath	68	28
12 Wright	49	43
13 Hightower	67	30
14 Patman	50	43
15 de la Garza	57	39
16 White	67	21
17 Stenholm	75	24
18 Leland	30	53
19 Hance	71	26
20 Gonzalez	34	64
21 *Loeffler*	79	21
22 *Paul*	59	36
23 Kazen	58	39
24 Frost	34	38
UTAH		
1 *Hansen*	71	16
2 *Marriott*	74	20
VERMONT		
AL *Jeffords*	41	55
VIRGINIA		
1 *Trible*	75	18
2 *Whitehurst*	70	25
3 *Bliley*	75	25
4 *Daniel, R.*	82	18
5 Daniel, D.	78	20
6 *Butler*	75	21
7 *Robinson*	80	18
8 *Parris*	74	21
9 *Wampler*	64	28
10 *Wolf*	76†	24†
WASHINGTON		
1 *Pritchard*	55	26
2 Swift	43	55
3 Bonker	37	57
4 *Morrison*	74	26
5 Foley	54	45
6 Dicks	50	42
7 Lowry	33	64
WEST VIRGINIA		
1 Mollohan	50	38
2 *Benedict*	74	25
3 *Staton*	79	21
4 Rahall	37	53
WISCONSIN		
1 Aspin	26	67
2 Kastenmeier	22	75
3 *Gunderson*	70	30
4 Zablocki	46	42
5 Reuss	32	58
6 *Petri*	57	41
7 Obey	29	70
8 *Roth*	64	33
9 *Sensenbrenner*	59	41
WYOMING		
AL *Cheney*	83	14

Democrats   *Republicans*

	1	2		1	2		1	2
ALABAMA			**IOWA**			**NEW HAMPSHIRE**		
Denton	85	9	*Grassley*	81	16	*Humphrey*	82	16
Heflin	68	30	*Jepsen*	87	12	*Rudman*	83	14
ALASKA			**KANSAS**			**NEW JERSEY**		
Murkowski	82	11	*Dole*	85	7	Bradley	44	48
Stevens	76	14	*Kassebaum*	82	17	Williams	38	41
ARIZONA			**KENTUCKY**			**NEW MEXICO**		
Goldwater	63	11	Ford	56	44	*Domenici*	84	13
DeConcini	51†	38†	Huddleston	54	44	*Schmitt*	84	9
ARKANSAS			**LOUISIANA**			**NEW YORK**		
Bumpers	39	52	Johnston	68	26	*D'Amato*	82	14
Pryor	47	48	Long	66	24	Moynihan	41	47
CALIFORNIA			**MAINE**			**NORTH CAROLINA**		
Hayakawa	84	5	*Cohen*	76	19	*East*	84	13
Cranston	38	48	Mitchell	45	51	*Helms*	84	16
COLORADO			**MARYLAND**			**NORTH DAKOTA**		
Armstrong	84	13	*Mathias*	58	27	*Andrews*	77	19
Hart	35	57	Sarbanes	38	61	Burdick	52	46
CONNECTICUT			**MASSACHUSETTS**			**OHIO**		
Weicker	59	30	Kennedy	31	60	Glenn	53	42
Dodd	33	59	Tsongas	38	49	Metzenbaum	30	59
DELAWARE			**MICHIGAN**			**OKLAHOMA**		
Roth	75	24	Levin	35	63	*Nickles*	85	13
Biden	44	54	Riegle	34	60	Boren	60	35
FLORIDA			**MINNESOTA**			**OREGON**		
Hawkins	84	14	*Boschwitz*	82	18	*Hatfield*	76	19
Chiles	55	37	*Durenberger*	73	24	*Packwood*	86	13
GEORGIA			**MISSISSIPPI**			**PENNSYLVANIA**		
Mattingly	88	12	*Cochran*	82	9	*Heinz*	74	20
Nunn	59	31	Stennis	70	27	*Specter*	77	22
HAWAII			**MISSOURI**			**RHODE ISLAND**		
Inouye	47	44	*Danforth*	85	13	*Chafee*	75	23
Matsunaga	47	49	Eagleton	33	63	Pell	42	52
IDAHO			**MONTANA**			**SOUTH CAROLINA**		
McClure	79	15	Baucus	45	50	*Thurmond*	90	7
Symms	80	13	Melcher	43	41	Hollings	54	38
ILLINOIS			**NEBRASKA**			**SOUTH DAKOTA**		
Percy	84	9	Exon	56	41	*Abdnor*	79	19
Dixon	57	41	Zorinsky	61	31	*Pressler*	61	24
INDIANA			**NEVADA**			**TENNESSEE**		
Lugar	90	9	*Laxalt*	76	8	*Baker*	89	10
Quayle	87	13	Cannon	55	29	Sasser	57	40

KEY

† Not eligible for all recorded votes in 1981 (sworn in after Jan. 5, died or resigned during session, or voted "present" to avoid possible conflict of interest).

	1	2
TEXAS		
Tower	76	9
Bentsen	70	24
UTAH		
Garn	88	9
Hatch	87	11
VERMONT		
Stafford	72	17
Leahy	34	60
VIRGINIA		
Warner	87	13
Byrd*	79	21
WASHINGTON		
Gorton	87	13
Jackson	55	43
WEST VIRGINIA		
Byrd	47	48
Randolph	45	48
WISCONSIN		
Kasten	80	20
Proxmire	52	48
WYOMING		
Simpson	86	11
Wallop	85	9

Democrats   *Republicans*

* Byrd elected as an independent.

Presidential Support and Opposition: Senate

1. Reagan Support Score, 1981. Percentage of 128 Reagan-issue recorded votes in 1981 on which senator voted "yea" or "nay" *in agreement* with the president's position. Failures to vote lower both Support and Opposition scores.

2. Reagan Opposition Score, 1981. Percentage of 128 Reagan-issue recorded votes in 1981 on which senator voted "yea" or "nay" *in disagreement* with the president's position. Failures to vote lower both Support and Opposition scores.

Highest Score Since 1951:

Congress Establishes Record For Participation in Votes

Conservatives trying to adopt President Reagan's economic program, liberals attempting to stave off deep cuts in social programs and a sharp drop in the number of votes taken combined to push participation in recorded floor votes in Congress to new highs in 1981.

Congressional Quarterly's study of 1981 voting participation showed that members of Congress on average voted on 92 percent of the votes taken, the highest score since CQ began keeping such records in 1951.

The previous high was 91 percent, established in 1975. The 1981 score was 5 percentage points higher than in 1980. Scores are traditionally lower in election years, when members must campaign for re-election. In the previous non-election year, 1979, the average for all members was 89 percent.

The voting participation study is the closest approach to an attendance record for Congress, but it is only an approximation. *(Definition, box, p. 26-C)*

As is traditional, Republicans voted more often than Democrats in 1981. Senate Democrats had outscored their Republican counterparts in only four of the last 30 years; House Democrats only twice. One senator and seven representatives had perfect scores for voting participation, and six representatives voted less than 60 percent of the time. The lowest Senate score was 62 percent.

Chamber, Party Scores

A total of 836 recorded votes was taken in the House and Senate in 1981, 514 fewer than the record 1,350 votes in 1978 and 299 fewer than in 1980. The 836 votes were the fewest since 1971, when 743 votes were recorded. There were 483 Senate votes in 1981, 48 fewer than in 1980 and 205 fewer than the record 688 in 1976.

The House took 353 votes in 1981, 481 fewer than the record 834 in that chamber in 1978 and 251 fewer than in 1980.

Senators voted more consistently than representatives. The average score for senators in 1981 was 93 percent; for representatives, 91 percent.

House members scored 88 percent in 1980, senators 87 percent.

House Republicans on average voted 92 percent of the time in 1981, compared to 89 percent in 1980. Democratic House members scored 90 percent in 1981, 87 percent in 1980.

In the Senate, Republicans scored 94 percent, Democrats 92 percent. In 1980, Senate Republicans scored 89 percent, Democrats 85 percent.

For the two chambers together, the 1981 scores were 93 percent for Republicans and 91 percent for Democrats. In 1980 Republicans led Democrats 89 percent to 87 percent.

Midwestern Republican senators led members from all regions in both chambers, voting 97 percent of the time.

The lowest regional scores came from Democratic and Republican House members from the West and from Western Democratic senators, all 89 percent.

Individual Highs and Lows

One senator, Democrat William Proxmire of Wisconsin, answered every roll call in 1981. Proxmire last missed a vote in 1966 and extended his record of consecutive votes to 7,507. Six other senators, two Democrats and four Republicans, scored 99 percent.

There were seven perfect scores in the House in 1981, recorded by Democrats Charles E. Bennett of Florida, Adam Benjamin Jr. of Indiana, William H. Natcher of Kentucky and Dale E. Kildee of Michigan, and Republicans Robert J. Lagomarsino of California, William F. Clinger Jr. of Pennsylvania and Frank R. Wolf of Virginia. Natcher, who has not missed a vote since his election to the House in 1954, extended his record to 8,554 consecutive votes.

The lowest scoring senator was Republican Barry Goldwater of Arizona, 62 percent. He suffered from a hip ailment in 1981. The lowest scoring Democratic senator was Howard W. Cannon of Nevada, 72 percent.

The lowest scoring House member was freshman Democrat Gus Savage of Illinois, 50 percent.

State Delegations

The Senate delegations with the highest voting participation scores in 1981 were Indiana, Washington and Wisconsin, all 99 percent; Iowa, Kansas and North Dakota, all

---

Absences

Failure to vote often is due to illness or conflicting duties. Members frequently have to be away from Washington on official business. Leaves of absence are granted members for these purposes.

Among those absent for a day or more in 1981 because they were sick or because of illness or death in their families were:

Senate Democrats: Randolph, W.Va.; Sasser, Tenn.; Leahy, Vt.; Levin, Mich.; Heflin, Ala.

Senate Republicans: Dole, Kan.; Domenici, N.M.; Garn, Utah; Denton, Ala.; Stevens, Alaska; Goldwater, Ariz.

House Democrats: Addabbo, N.Y.; AuCoin, Ore; Barnard, Ga.; Bevill, Ala.; Bolling, Mo.; Brooks, Texas; John L. Burton, Calif.; Chisholm, N.Y.; Danielson, Calif.; Derrick, S.C.; Frost, Texas; Gibbons, Fla.; Gray, Pa.; Hall, Ohio; Jones, N.C.; Montgomery, Miss.; Nelson, Fla.; Patman, Texas; Rangel, N.Y.; Rodino, N.J.; Rosenthal, N.Y.; Russo, Ill.; Savage, Ill.

House Republicans: Bafalis, Fla.; Beard, Tenn.; Broyhill, N.C.; Carman, N.Y.; Clausen, Calif.; Derwinski, Ill.; Duncan, Tenn.; Edwards, Ala.; Frenzel, Minn.; Hagedorn, Minn.; Jeffords, Vt.; Lee, N.Y.; Madigan, Ill.; Marks, Pa.; Martin, Ill.; Mitchell, N.Y.; Molinari, N.Y.; Quillen, Tenn.; Roberts, S.D.; Rudd, Ariz.; Siljander, Mich.

---

98 percent; and Georgia, New Hampshire and North Carolina, all 97 percent.

In the House, the highest-scoring delegations with two or more members were Nebraska, 98 percent; and Kansas, Kentucky, Maine and Oklahoma, all 97 percent.

The lowest-scoring Senate delegations were Arizona, 73 percent; Nevada, 82 percent; and California, Massachusetts and New Jersey, all 87 percent.

The House delegations that voted least often were those of Connecticut, 81 percent; Utah, 87 percent; and Arizona, California, Missouri and North Carolina, all 88 percent.

Party Scores

Composites of Democratic and Republican voting participation scores for 1981 and 1980:

	1981		1980	
	Dem.	**Rep.**	**Dem.**	**Rep.**
Senate	92%	94%	85%	89%
House	90	92	87	89

Regional Averages

Regional voting participation breakdowns for 1981 with 1980 scores in parentheses:

	East	**West**	**South**	**Midwest**
DEMOCRATS				
Senate	91% (83)	89% (81)	94% (86)	95% (88)
House	90 (86)	89 (86)	91 (88)	90 (88)
REPUBLICANS				
Senate	93% (88)	92% (88)	96% (91)	97% (90)
House	93 (90)	89 (84)	93 (92)	93 (88)

Highest Scorers

SENATE

Democrats		**Republicans**	
Proxmire, Wis.	100%	Helms, N.C.	99%
Jackson, Wash.	99	Gorton, Wash.	99
Burdick, N.D.	99	Quayle, Ind.	99
Ford, Ky.	98	Lugar, Ind.	99
Mitchell, Maine[1]	98	Grassley, Iowa	99
Sarbanes, Md.	98		

HOUSE

Democrats		**Republicans**	
Kildee, Mich.	100%	Wolf, Va.[1]	100%
Benjamin, Ind.	100	Clinger, Pa.[1]	100
Bennett, Fla.	100	Lagomarsino, Calif.	100
Natcher, Ky.	100	Brown, Colo.	99
English, Okla.	99	Spence, S.C.	99
Annunzio, Ill.	99	Gunderson, Wis.	99
Panetta, Calif.	99	Findley, Ill.	99

> ## Definition
>
> **Voting Participation.** Percentage of recorded votes on which a member voted "yea" or "nay." Failures to vote "yea" or "nay" lower scores — even if the member votes "present," enters a live pair or announces his stand in the *Congressional Record*. Only votes of "yea" or "nay" directly affect the outcome of a vote. Voting participation is the closest approach to an attendance record, but it is only an approximation. A member may be present and nevertheless decline to vote "yea" or "nay" — usually because he has entered a live pair with an absent member.

Hamilton, Ind.	99	Smith, Neb.	99
Ratchford, Conn.	99	Sensenbrenner, Wis.[1]	99
Glickman, Kan.	99	Hiler, Ind.	99
Gore, Tenn.	99	Coats, Ind.	99
Yatron, Pa.	99	Smith, N.J.	99
Kastenmeier, Wis.	99	Daniel, Va.	99
Oberstar, Minn.	99	Whittaker, Kan.	99
Wolpe, Mich.	99	McEwen, Ohio	99
Yates, Ill.	99	Robinson, Va.	99
Kazen, Texas	99	Dunn, Mich.	99
Dyson, Md.	99	Shaw, Fla.	99
Studds, Mass.	99	Hopkins, Ky.	99
Brinkley, Ga.	99	Moore, La.	99
		Hammerschmidt, Ark.	99
		Miller, Ohio	99
		Rogers, Ky.	99
		Snowe, Maine	99

Lowest Scorers

SENATE

Democrats		**Republicans**	
Cannon, Nev.	72%	Goldwater, Ariz.	62%
Williams, N.J.	84	Mathias, Md.	78
DeConcini, Ariz.[1]	85	Tower, Texas	84
Tsongas, Mass.	85	Hayakawa, Calif.	86
Moynihan, N.Y.	86	Pressler, S.D.	89
Leahy, Vt.	86	Weicker, Conn.	89

HOUSE

Democrats[2]		**Republicans**[3]	
Savage, Ill.	50%	McCloskey, Calif.[1]	57%
Bolling, Mo.	53	Goldwater, Calif.	58
Jones, N.C.	59	Brown, Ohio[1]	70
Florio, N.J.	59	Dornan, Calif.	72
John Burton, Calif.	63	Dougherty, Pa.	76
Crockett, Mich.	63	Young, Alaska	76
Chisholm, N.Y.	66	Beard, Tenn.	76
Pepper, Fla.	68	Quillen, Tenn.	76

[1] *Not eligible for all recorded votes in 1981.*
[2] *Other Democrats with low scores were not members for the entire session: Spellman, Md., zero; Lederer, Pa., 4%; Cotter, Conn., 4%.*
[3] *Other Republicans with low scores were not members for the entire session: Stockman, Mich., zero; Hinson, Miss., 22%.*

					KEY

ALABAMA		**IOWA**		**NEW HAMPSHIRE**		
Denton	94#	*Grassley*	99	*Humphrey*	98	† Not eligible for all recorded votes in 1981 (sworn in after Jan. 5, died or resigned during session, or voted "present" to avoid possible conflict of interest).
Heflin	95#	*Jepsen*	97	*Rudman*	97	
ALASKA		**KANSAS**		**NEW JERSEY**		
Murkowski	94	*Dole*	98#	Bradley	90	
Stevens	90#	*Kassebaum*	98	Williams	84	
ARIZONA		**KENTUCKY**		**NEW MEXICO**		# Member absent a day or more in 1981 due to illness or illness or death in family.
Goldwater	62†#	Ford	98	*Domenici*	95#	
DeConcini	85†	Huddleston	94	*Schmitt*	93	
ARKANSAS		**LOUISIANA**		**NEW YORK**		
Bumpers	90	Johnston	95	*D'Amato*	94	
Pryor	95	Long	87	Moynihan	86	
CALIFORNIA		**MAINE**		**NORTH CAROLINA**		
Hayakawa	86	*Cohen*	94	*East*	95	
Cranston	88	Mitchell	98†	*Helms*	99	
COLORADO		**MARYLAND**		**NORTH DAKOTA**		
Armstrong	95	*Mathias*	78	*Andrews*	97	
Hart	92	Sarbanes	98	Burdick	99	
CONNECTICUT		**MASSACHUSETTS**		**OHIO**		**TEXAS**	
Weicker	89	Kennedy	89	Glenn	94	*Tower*	84
Dodd	88	Tsongas	85	Metzenbaum	87	Bentsen	94
DELAWARE		**MICHIGAN**		**OKLAHOMA**		**UTAH**	
Roth	98	Levin	96#	*Nickles*	98	*Garn*	96#
Biden	93	Riegle	93	Boren	95	*Hatch*	97
FLORIDA		**MINNESOTA**		**OREGON**		**VERMONT**	
Hawkins	97	*Boschwitz*	98	*Hatfield*	94	*Stafford*	92
Chiles	94	*Durenberger*	93	*Packwood*	95	Leahy	86#
GEORGIA		**MISSISSIPPI**		**PENNSYLVANIA**		**VIRGINIA**	
Mattingly	98	*Cochran*	96	*Heinz*	92	*Warner*	96
Nunn	96	Stennis	92	*Specter*	98	Byrd*	96
HAWAII		**MISSOURI**		**RHODE ISLAND**		**WASHINGTON**	
Inouye	87	*Danforth*	98	*Chafee*	97	*Gorton*	99#
Matsunaga	91	Eagleton	94	Pell	96	Jackson	99
IDAHO		**MONTANA**		**SOUTH CAROLINA**		**WEST VIRGINIA**	
McClure	92	Baucus	96	*Thurmond*	98	Byrd	95
Symms	96	Melcher	88	Hollings	94	Randolph	96#
ILLINOIS		**NEBRASKA**		**SOUTH DAKOTA**		**WISCONSIN**	
Percy	95	Exon	97	*Abdnor*	98	*Kasten*	98
Dixon	97	Zorinsky	93	*Pressler*	89	Proxmire	100
INDIANA		**NEVADA**		**TENNESSEE**		**WYOMING**	
Lugar	99	*Laxalt*	92	*Baker*	97	*Simpson*	97
Quayle	99	Cannon	72	Sasser	91#	*Wallop*	93

Democrats   *Republicans*   * *Byrd elected as an independent.*

Voting Participation Scores: Senate

Voting Participation, 1981. Percentage of 483 roll calls in 1981 on which senator voted "yea" or "nay."

KEY

†   Not eligible for all recorded votes in 1981 (sworn in after Jan. 5, died or resigned during session, or voted "present" to avoid possible conflict of interest).

\#   Member absent a day or more in 1981 due to illness or illness or death in family.

Voting Participation Scores: House

Voting Participation, 1981. Percentage of 353 recorded votes in 1981 on which representative voted "yea" or "nay."

ALABAMA		
1 *Edwards*	93#	
2 *Dickinson*	86	
3 Nichols	91	
4 Bevill	94#	
5 Flippo	88	
6 *Smith*	93	
7 Shelby	94	
ALASKA		
AL *Young*	76	
ARIZONA		
1 *Rhodes*	79	
2 Udall	90	
3 Stump	95	
4 *Rudd*	87#	
ARKANSAS		
1 Alexander	93	
2 *Bethune*	94	
3 *Hammerschmidt*	99	
4 Anthony	90	
CALIFORNIA		
1 *Chappie*	88	
2 *Clausen*	94#	
3 Matsui	95	
4 Fazio	95	
5 Burton, J.	63#	
6 Burton, P.	86	
7 Miller	92	
8 Dellums	82	
9 Stark	87	
10 Edwards	93	
11 Lantos	88	
12 *McCloskey*	57†	
13 Mineta	96	
14 *Shumway*	98	
15 Coelho	94	
16 Panetta	99	
17 *Pashayan*	82	
18 *Thomas*	86	
19 *Lagomarsino*	100	
20 *Goldwater*	58	
21 *Fiedler*	92	
22 *Moorhead*	95	
23 Beilenson	90	
24 Waxman	87	
25 Roybal	96	
26 *Rousselot*	86	
27 *Dornan*	72	
28 Dixon	84	
29 Hawkins	89	
30 Danielson	84#	
31 Dymally	75	
32 Anderson	96	
33 *Grisham*	87	
34 *Lungren*	95	
35 *Dreier*	98	
36 Brown	87	
37 *Lewis*	90	
38 Patterson	93	
39 *Dannemeyer*	94	
40 *Badham*	81	
41 *Lowery*	91	
42 *Hunter*	98	
43 *Burgener*	87	
COLORADO		
1 Schroeder	97	
2 Wirth	86	
3 Kogovsek	96	
4 *Brown*	99	

5 *Kramer*	96	
CONNECTICUT		
1 Cotter [1]	4†	
2 Gejdenson	97	
3 *DeNardis*	87	
4 *McKinney*	86	
5 Ratchford	99	
6 Moffett	75	
DELAWARE		
AL *Evans*	94	
FLORIDA		
1 Hutto	95	
2 Fuqua	83	
3 Bennett	100	
4 Chappell	89	
5 *McCollum*	96†	
6 *Young*	95	
7 Gibbons	90#	
8 Ireland	86	
9 Nelson	88#	
10 *Bafalis*	91#	
11 Mica	96	
12 *Shaw*	99	
13 Lehman	89	
14 Pepper	68	
15 Fascell	91	
GEORGIA		
1 Ginn	84#	
2 Hatcher	90	
3 Brinkley	99	
4 Levitas	95	
5 Fowler	91†	
6 *Gingrich*	89	
7 McDonald	79	
8 Evans	86	
9 Jenkins	94	
10 Barnard	84#	
HAWAII		
1 Heftel	88	
2 Akaka	97	
IDAHO		
1 *Craig*	94	
2 *Hansen*	97	
ILLINOIS		
1 Washington	78	
2 Savage	50#	
3 Russo	92#	
4 *Derwinski*	91#	
5 Fary	87	
6 *Hyde*	95	
7 Collins	88	
8 Rostenkowski	94	
9 Yates	99	
10 *Porter*	95	
11 Annunzio	99	
12 *Crane, P.*	86	
13 McClory	97	
14 Erlenborn	91	
15 Corcoran	92	
16 Martin	93#	
17 O'Brien	87†	
18 *Michel*	91†	
19 Railsback	89	
20 Findley	99	
21 *Madigan*	82#	
22 *Crane, D.*	93	
23 Price	93	
24 Simon	85	
INDIANA		
1 Benjamin	100	
2 Fithian	77	
3 *Hiler*	99	
4 *Coats*	99	
5 *Hillis*	87†	
6 Evans	94	
7 *Myers*	96	
8 *Deckard*	88	
9 Hamilton	99	
10 Sharp	98	
11 Jacobs	96	
IOWA		
1 Leach	98	
2 *Tauke*	95	
3 *Evans*	95	
4 Smith	96	
5 Harkin	91	
6 Bedell	85†	

1. Rep. William R. Cotter, D-Conn., died Sept. 9, 1981.

2. Rep. Steny Hoyer, D-Md., sworn in June 3, 1981, to succeed Gladys Noon Spellman, D, whose seat the House declared vacant on Feb. 24, 1981. Spellman did not vote on the one vote for which she was eligible in 1981.

3. Rep. Thomas P. O'Neill Jr., D-Mass., as Speaker, votes at his own discretion.

4. Rep. Mark Siljander, R-Mich., sworn in April 28, 1981, to succeed David A. Stockman, R, who resigned Jan. 27, 1981. Stockman did not vote on any of the three votes for which he was eligible in 1981.

5. Rep. Wayne Dowdy, D-Miss., sworn in July 9, 1981, to succeed Jon Hinson, R, who resigned April 13, 1981. Hinson's 1981 voting participation score was 22 percent.

6. Rep. Michael G. Oxley, R-Ohio, sworn in July 21, 1981, to succeed Tennyson Guyer, R, who died April 12, 1981. Guyer's 1981 voting participation score was 78 percent.

7. Rep. Joseph F. Smith, D-Pa., sworn in July 28, 1981, to succeed Raymond F. Lederer, D., who resigned May 5, 1981. Lederer's 1981 voting participation score was 4 percent.

8. Rep. Eugene V. Atkinson, Pa., switched from the Democratic to the Republican Party on Oct. 14, 1981.

Democrats   *Republicans*

KANSAS
1 *Roberts* 96
2 *Jeffries* 98
3 *Winn* 95
4 Glickman 99
5 *Whittaker* 99

KENTUCKY
1 Hubbard 96
2 Natcher 100
3 Mazzoli 90
4 *Snyder* 98
5 *Rogers* 99
6 *Hopkins* 99
7 Perkins 98

LOUISIANA
1 *Livingston* 94
2 Boggs 91
3 Tauzin 95
4 Roemer 97
5 Huckaby 92
6 *Moore* 99
7 Breaux 77
8 Long 88

MAINE
1 *Emery* 96
2 *Snowe* 99

MARYLAND
1 Dyson 99
2 Long 95
3 Mikulski 94
4 *Holt* 86
5 Hoyer [2] 96†
6 Byron 89
7 Mitchell 87
8 Barnes 97

MASSACHUSETTS
1 *Conte* 95
2 Boland 93
3 Early 86
4 Frank 93
5 Shannon 95
6 Mavroules 92
7 Markey 95
8 O'Neill [3]
9 Moakley 89
10 *Heckler* 93
11 Donnelly 87
12 Studds 99

MICHIGAN
1 Conyers 84
2 *Pursell* 88
3 Wolpe 99
4 *Siljander* [4] 91†#
5 Sawyer 93
6 Dunn 99
7 Kildee 100
8 Traxler 91
9 *Vander Jagt* 78†
10 Albosta 90
11 *Davis* 93
12 Bonior 93
13 Crockett 63
14 Hertel 96
15 Ford 75
16 Dingell 80
17 Brodhead 95
18 Blanchard 91
19 *Broomfield* 93

MINNESOTA
1 *Erdahl* 96
2 *Hagedorn* 82#
3 *Frenzel* 89#
4 Vento 94
5 Sabo 98
6 *Weber* 97
7 *Stangeland* 96
8 Oberstar 99

MISSISSIPPI
1 Whitten 97
2 Bowen 94
3 Montgomery 93#
4 Dowdy [5] 93†
5 *Lott* 93

MISSOURI
1 Clay 76
2 Young 92
3 Gephardt 94

---

4 Skelton 93
5 *Bolling* 53#
6 *Coleman* 93
7 *Taylor* 93
8 *Bailey* 95
9 Volkmer 91
10 *Emerson* 98

MONTANA
1 Williams 88
2 *Marlenee* 91

NEBRASKA
1 *Bereuter* 98
2 *Daub* 97
3 *Smith* 99

NEVADA
AL Santini 73

NEW HAMPSHIRE
1 D'Amours 91
2 *Gregg* 97

NEW JERSEY
1 Florio 59
2 Hughes 97
3 Howard 90
4 *Smith* 99
5 *Fenwick* 97
6 *Forsythe* 85
7 *Roukema* 98
8 Roe 83
9 *Hollenbeck* 85
10 Rodino 97#
11 Minish 94
12 *Rinaldo* 95
13 *Courter* 93
14 Guarini 92
15 Dwyer 98

NEW MEXICO
1 *Lujan* 94
2 *Skeen* 96

NEW YORK
1 *Carney* 92
2 Downey 93
3 *Carman* 94#
4 *Lent* 96
5 *McGrath* 97
6 *LeBoutillier* 95
7 Addabbo 89
8 Rosenthal 76#
9 Ferraro 93
10 Biaggi 80
11 Scheuer 93
12 Chisholm 66#
13 Solarz 90†
14 Richmond 80
15 Zeferetti 90
16 Schumer 90
17 *Molinari* 97†#
18 *Green* 96
19 Rangel 88#
20 Weiss 97
21 Garcia 76
22 Bingham 96
23 Peyser 94
24 Ottinger 82
25 *Fish* 91
26 *Gilman* 88
27 McHugh 97
28 Stratton 92
29 *Solomon* 97
30 *Martin* 88
31 *Mitchell* 92#
32 *Wortley* 97
33 *Lee* 92#
34 *Horton* 82
35 *Conable* 94†
36 LaFalce 94†
37 Nowak 97
38 *Kemp* 82
39 Lundine 84

NORTH CAROLINA
1 Jones 59#
2 Fountain 94
3 Whitley 93
4 Andrews 85†
5 Neal 92
6 Johnston 86†
7 Rose 81
8 Hefner 92

---

9 *Martin* 91
10 *Broyhill* 93#
11 *Hendon* 97†

NORTH DAKOTA
AL Dorgan 97

OHIO
1 *Gradison* 95
2 Luken 93
3 Hall 91#
4 *Oxley* [6] 94†
5 *Latta* 93
6 *McEwen* 99
7 *Brown* 70†
8 *Kindness* 93
9 Weber 96
10 *Miller* 99
11 *Stanton* 96
12 Shamansky 96
13 Pease 95
14 Seiberling 95
15 *Wylie* 92
16 *Regula* 98
17 *Ashbrook* 87
18 Applegate 83
19 Williams 80
20 Oakar 88
21 Stokes 94
22 Eckart 98
23 Mottl 92

OKLAHOMA
1 Jones 96
2 Synar 98
3 Watkins 97
4 McCurdy 97
5 *Edwards* 95
6 English 99

OREGON
1 AuCoin 76
2 *Smith* 97
3 Wyden 95
4 Weaver 90

PENNSYLVANIA
1 Foglietta 80
2 Gray 86#
3 *Smith* [7] 94†
4 *Dougherty* 76
5 *Schulze* 88
6 Yatron 99
7 Edgar 92
8 *Coyne, J.* 95
9 *Shuster* 98
10 *McDade* 90
11 *Nelligan* 95
12 Murtha 97
13 Coughlin 94
14 Coyne, W. 96
15 Ritter 97
16 *Walker* 92
17 Ertel 94†
18 Walgren 97
19 *Goodling* 87
20 Gaydos 91
21 Bailey 97
22 Murphy 89
23 *Clinger* 100†
24 *Marks* 92#
25 *Atkinson* [8] 93

RHODE ISLAND
1 St Germain 88
2 Schneider 94

SOUTH CAROLINA
1 *Hartnett* 93
2 *Spence* 99
3 Derrick 89#
4 *Campbell* 92
5 Holland 79
6 *Napier* 95

SOUTH DAKOTA
1 Daschle 90
2 *Roberts* 92#

TENNESSEE
1 *Quillen* 76#
2 *Duncan* 90†
3 Bouquard 92
4 Gore 99
5 Boner 94
6 *Beard* 76#

---

7 Jones 94
8 Ford 91

TEXAS
1 Hall, S. 97
2 Wilson 86
3 *Collins* 98
4 Hall, R. 90
5 Mattox 76
6 Gramm 95
7 *Archer* 98
8 *Fields* 94
9 Brooks 78#
10 Pickle 94
11 Leath 95
12 Wright 88
13 Hightower 96
14 Patman 94#
15 de la Garza 90
16 White 91
17 Stenholm 97
18 Leland 80
19 Hance 88
20 Gonzalez 97
21 *Loeffler* 98
22 *Paul* 90
23 Kazen 99
24 Frost 87#

UTAH
1 *Hansen* 83
2 *Marriott* 92

VERMONT
AL *Jeffords* 92†#

VIRGINIA
1 *Trible* 90
2 *Whitehurst* 93
3 *Bliley* 97
4 *Daniel, R.* 99
5 Daniel, D. 97
6 *Butler* 93
7 *Robinson* 99
8 *Parris* 95
9 Wampler 87
10 *Wolf* 100†

WASHINGTON
1 *Pritchard* 83†
2 Swift 97
3 Bonker 85
4 *Morrison* 98
5 Foley 96
6 Dicks 91
7 Lowry 97

WEST VIRGINIA
1 Mollohan 84
2 *Benedict* 93
3 *Staton* 98
4 Rahall 92

WISCONSIN
1 Aspin 90
2 Kastenmeier 99
3 *Gunderson* 99
4 Zablocki 93
5 Reuss 84
6 Petri 93
7 Obey 94
8 *Roth* 90
9 *Sensenbrenner* 99†

WYOMING
AL *Cheney* 91

Democrats *Republicans*

 Party Unity

Senate Scores Up, House Down:

Partisan Voting Averages Increased in 97th Congress

Partisan voting increased during the first session of the 97th Congress, with the most striking gain in solidarity achieved by Senate Republicans taking advantage of their newly acquired role as the majority party.

Congressional Quarterly's annual study of party unity shows that overall in Congress, a majority of Democrats voted against a majority of Republicans on 43 percent of the recorded votes. The figure for 1980 was 41 percent.

Senate Republicans, on average, voted the party line 81 percent of the time, compared to 65 percent in 1980.

A noticeable increase in Northern Republicans' party loyalty also was recorded in the Senate. They scored 79 percent support, compared to 64 percent the previous year.

Despite their reputation for disarray, Senate Democrats in general raised their party unity score in 1981 by voting with their own majority on 71 percent of the partisan votes, compared to 64 percent in 1980.

But in the House, the key battleground for President Reagan's program, partisan voting as measured by CQ actually declined slightly. The percentage of party unity votes there, where major policy issues were settled on a few roll calls, dropped to 37 percent from 38 percent in 1980.

In the Senate, by contrast, the percentage of partisan votes increased from 46 to 48, the highest level since 1975. The relatively high score in 1981 reflected attempts by Democrats — who as the Senate minority had little chance of defeating Reagan's proposals in floor votes — to establish a record of opposition to social program cuts.

Congressional Democrats on average voted with the party majority 69 percent of the time, while Republicans scored a 76 percent support level.

Average Scores

In the House, the average Democrat voted with the party majority 69 percent of the time, compared to a 74 percent party unity score for Republicans. The figures for House Democrats were identical to 1980's, while Republicans increased their unity score by 3 percentage points.

Overall in Congress, scores for opposition to party majorities increased slightly for Democrats and decreased somewhat for Republicans. Democrats voted against the party line 23 percent of the time, Republicans 18 percent. In 1980, the figures were 20 percent for both parties.

The most noticeable change was among Senate Republicans, who went from 23 percent opposition in 1980 to 14 percent. House Democrats' opposition score rose 3 points to 23 percent.

Party Unity Scoreboard

The following table shows the proportion of Party Unity recorded votes in recent years:

Definitions

Party Unity Votes. Recorded votes in the Senate and House that split the parties, a majority of voting Democrats opposing a majority of voting Republicans.

Party Unity Scores. Percentage of Party Unity votes on which a member votes "yea" or "nay" *in agreement* with a majority of his party. Failure to vote, even if a member announced his stand, lowers his score.

Opposition-to-Party Scores. Percentage of Party Unity votes on which a member votes "yea" or "nay" *in disagreement* with a majority of his party. A member's Party Unity and Opposition-to-Party scores add up to 100 percent only if he voted on all Party Unity votes.

	Total Recorded Votes	Party Unity Recorded Votes	Percentage of Total
1981			
Both Chambers	836	363	43
Senate	483	231	48
House	353	132	37
1980			
Both Chambers	1,135	470	41
Senate	531	243	46
House	604	227	38
1979			
Both Chambers	1,169	550	47
Senate	497	232	47
House	672	318	47
1978			
Both Chambers	1,350	510	38
Senate	516	233	45
House	834	277	33
1977			
Both Chambers	1,341	567	42
Senate	635	269	42
House	706	298	42
1976			
Both Chambers	1,349	493	37
Senate	688	256	37
House	661	237	36
1975			
Both Chambers	1,214	584	48
Senate	602	288	48
House	612	296	48
1974			
Both Chambers	1,081	399	37
Senate	544	241	44
House	537	158	29

Victories, Defeats

	Senate	House	Total
Democrats won, Republicans lost	39	73	112
Republicans won, Democrats lost	192	59	251
Democrats voted unanimously	7	2	9
Republicans voted unanimously	39	12	51

Party Scores

Party Unity and Opposition-to-Party scores below are composites of individual scores and show the percentage of time the average Democrat and Republican voted with his party majority in disagreement with the other party's majority. Failures to vote lower both Party Unity and Opposition-to-Party scores. Averages are closer to House figures because individual votes are counted and the House has more members.

	1981		1980	
	Dem.	Rep.	Dem.	Rep.
Party Unity	69%	76%	68%	70%
Senate	71	81	64	65
House	69	74	69	71
Opposition to Party	23%	18%	20%	20%
Senate	21	14	20	23
House	23	19	20	19

Sectional Support, Opposition

SENATE	Support	Opposition
Northern Democrats	76%	15%
Southern Democrats	60	34
Northern Republicans	79	16
Southern Republicans	88	8

HOUSE	Support	Opposition
Northern Democrats	76%	15%
Southern Democrats	53	40
Northern Republicans	72	21
Southern Republicans	81	14

Party Unity History

Composite Party Unity scores showing the percentage of time the average Democrat and Republican voted with his party majority in partisan votes in recent years:

Year	Democrats	Republicans
1981	69%	76%
1980	68	70
1979	69	72
1978	64	67
1977	67	70
1976	65	66
1975	69	70
1974	63	62

Individual Scores

Highest Party Unity Scores. Those who in 1981 most consistently voted with their party majority against the majority of the other party:

SENATE

Democrats		Republicans	
Sarbanes, Md.	93%	Dole, Kan.	94%
Levin, Mich.	92	Laxalt, Nev.	93
Riegle, Mich.	88	Quayle, Ind.	93
Mitchell, Maine	88	Lugar, Ind.	93
Eagleton, Mo.	85	Jepsen, Iowa	92
Biden, Del.	84	East, N.C.	92
Baucus, Mont.	84	Garn, Utah	92
Ford, Ky.	84	Wallop, Wyo.	91
Hart, Colo.	84	Mattingly, Ga.	91
		Thurmond, S.C.	91

HOUSE

Democrats		Republicans	
Seiberling, Ohio	94%	Daniel, Va.	95%
Stokes, Ohio	93	Dreier, Calif.	95
Dwyer, N.J.	93	Lagomarsino, Calif.	95
Bingham, N.Y.	92	Shaw, Fla.	94
Rodino, N.J.	92	Archer, Texas	93
Wolpe, Mich.	92	Solomon, N.Y.	92
Roybal, Calif.	92	Shumway, Calif.	92
Scheuer, N.Y.	92	Smith, Ore.	92
Gejdenson, Conn.	92	Dannemeyer, Calif.	92
Studds, Mass.	91	Spence, S.C.	92
Ferraro, N.Y.	91	Jeffries, Kan.	91
Markey, Mass.	91	Craig, Idaho	91
Ratchford, Conn.	91	Moorhead, Calif.	91

Highest Opposition-to-Party Scores. Those who in 1981 most consistently voted against their party majority:

SENATE

Democrats		Republicans	
Byrd, Va.[1]	70%	Weicker, Conn.	38%
Long, La.	54	Specter, Pa.	34
Stennis, Miss.	48	Mathias, Md.	34
Proxmire, Wis.	47	Heinz, Pa.	33
Johnston, La.	45	Pressler, S.D.	32

[1] *Byrd, Va., elected as an independent, but caucuses with Democrats.*

HOUSE

Democrats		Republicans	
Daniel, Va.	81%	Green, N.Y.	58%
Stump, Ariz.	81	Jeffords, Vt.[2]	55
Gramm, Texas	77	Conte, Mass.	54
McDonald, Ga.	75	Schneider, R.I.	53
Shelby, Ala.	71	Heckler, Mass.	52
Montgomery, Miss.	68	McKinney, Conn.	51
Stenholm, Texas	67	Hollenbeck, N.J.	50
Leath, Texas	65	DeNardis, Conn.	50
Roemer, La.	65	Pursell, Mich.	50

[2] *Not eligible for all votes in 1981.*

Party Unity and Party Opposition: House

1. Party Unity, 1981. Percentage of 132 House Party Unity recorded votes in 1981 on which representative voted "yea" or "nay" *in agreement* with a majority of his party. (Party unity roll calls are those on which a majority of voting Democrats opposed a majority of voting Republicans. Failures to vote lower both Party Unity and Party Opposition scores.)

2. Party Opposition, 1981. Percentages of 132 House Party Unity recorded votes in 1981 on which representative voted "yea" or "nay" *in disagreement* with a majority of his party.

---

1. Rep. William R. Cotter, D-Conn., died Sept. 9, 1981.

2. Rep. Steny Hoyer, D-Md., sworn in June 3, 1981, to succeed Gladys Noon Spellman, D, whose seat the House declared vacant on Feb. 24, 1981. Spellman did not vote on the one vote for which she was eligible in 1981.

3. Rep. Thomas P. O'Neill Jr., D-Mass., as Speaker, votes at his own discretion.

4. Rep. Mark Siljander, R-Mich., sworn in April 28, 1981, to succeed David A. Stockman, R, who resigned Jan. 27, 1981. Stockman did not vote on any of the three votes for which he was eligible in 1981.

5. Rep. Wayne Dowdy, D-Miss., sworn in July 9, 1981, to succeed Jon Hinson, R, who resigned April 13, 1981. Hinson's 1981 party unity score was 67 percent; opposition was zero.

6. Rep. Michael G. Oxley, R-Ohio, sworn in July 21, 1981, to succeed Tennyson Guyer, R, who died April 12, 1981. Guyer's 1981 party unity score was 67 percent; opposition was zero.

7. Rep. Joseph F. Smith, D-Pa., sworn in July 28, 1981, to succeed Raymond F. Lederer, D., who resigned May 5, 1981. Lederer's 1981 party unity score was 17 percent; opposition was zero.

8. Rep. Eugene V. Atkinson, Pa., switched from the Democratic to the Republican Party on Oct. 14, 1981. His party unity score as a Democrat was 65 percent; opposition was 35 percent.

KEY

† Not eligible for all recorded votes in 1981 (sworn in after Jan. 5, died or resigned during session, or voted "present" to avoid possible conflict of interest).

	1	2
ALABAMA		
1 *Edwards*	63	33
2 *Dickinson*	77	14
3 Nichols	36	58
4 Bevill	54	42
5 Flippo	53	39
6 *Smith*	89	8
7 Shelby	25	71
ALASKA		
AL *Young*	61	14
ARIZONA		
1 *Rhodes*	64	15
2 Udall	76	16
3 *Stump*	17	81
4 *Rudd*	78	11
ARKANSAS		
1 Alexander	67	24
2 *Bethune*	77	19
3 *Hammerschmidt*	80	20
4 Anthony	61	30
CALIFORNIA		
1 *Chappie*	80	5
2 *Clausen*	80	16
3 Matsui	80	17
4 Fazio	81	17
5 Burton, J.	59	5
6 Burton, P.	83	5
7 Miller	89	8
8 Dellums	83	6
9 Stark	84	8
10 Edwards	88	5
11 Lantos	69	14
12 McCloskey	40†	24†
13 Mineta	84	13
14 *Shumway*	92	7
15 Coelho	81	17
16 Panetta	78	22
17 *Pashayan*	75	13
18 *Thomas*	69	11
19 *Lagomarsino*	95	5
20 *Goldwater*	56	6
21 *Fiedler*	80	15
22 *Moorhead*	91	4
23 Beilenson	79	8
24 Waxman	79	5
25 Roybal	92	7
26 *Rousselot*	78	7
27 *Dornan*	67	9
28 Dixon	85	5
29 Hawkins	80	8
30 Danielson	78	7
31 Dymally	66	4
32 Anderson	77	21
33 Grisham	83	8
34 *Lungren*	88	8
35 *Dreier*	95	5
36 Brown	77	10
37 *Lewis*	75	15
38 Patterson	80	14
39 *Dannemeyer*	92	5
40 *Badham*	78	9
41 *Lowery*	85	11
42 *Hunter*	89	11
43 *Burgener*	76	13
COLORADO		
1 Schroeder	76	21
2 Wirth	78	14
3 Kogovsek	85	11
4 *Brown*	77	23

	1	2
5 *Kramer*	85	11
CONNECTICUT		
1 Cotter ¹	5†	0†
2 Gejdenson	92	7
3 *DeNardis*	44	50
4 *McKinney*	44	51
5 Ratchford	91	7
6 Moffett	79	6
DELAWARE		
AL *Evans*	69	27
FLORIDA		
1 Hutto	46	53
2 Fuqua	55	33
3 Bennett	48	52
4 Chappell	38	55
5 *McCollum*	83	14
6 *Young*	83	12
7 Gibbons	46	45
8 Ireland	29	56
9 Nelson	48	42
10 *Bafalis*	85†	6†
11 Mica	57	39
12 *Shaw*	94	6
13 Lehman	77	8
14 Pepper	70	9
15 Fascell	83	10
GEORGIA		
1 Ginn	54	37
2 Hatcher	50	40
3 Brinkley	45	55
4 Levitas	63	36
5 Fowler	60†	31†
6 *Gingrich*	75	17
7 McDonald	6	75
8 Evans	36	49
9 Jenkins	42	53
10 Barnard	26	61
HAWAII		
1 Heftel	71	22
2 Akaka	81	17
IDAHO		
1 *Craig*	91	5
2 *Hansen*	89	8
ILLINOIS		
1 Washington	80	7
2 Savage	57	5
3 Russo	64	25
4 *Derwinski*	76	16
5 Fary	72	22
6 *Hyde*	77	19
7 Collins	83	7
8 Rostenkowski	77	18
9 Yates	90	9
10 *Porter*	65	33
11 Annunzio	77	22
12 *Crane, P.*	81	9
13 *McClory*	75	25
14 *Erlenborn*	67	24
15 *Corcoran*	77	16
16 *Martin*	67	27
17 *O'Brien*	65	27
18 *Michel*	82†	11†
19 *Railsback*	52	44
20 *Findley*	64	34
21 *Madigan*	70	12
22 *Crane, D.*	85	9
23 Price	73	23
24 Simon	76	11
INDIANA		
1 Benjamin	88	12
2 Fithian	60	18
3 *Hiler*	87	13
4 *Coats*	86	14
5 *Hillis*	72†	18†
6 Evans	80	17
7 *Myers*	77	21
8 *Deckard*	58	30
9 Hamilton	71	27
10 Sharp	70	27
11 Jacobs	73	24
IOWA		
1 *Leach*	54	45
2 *Tauke*	65	30
3 *Evans*	72	23
4 Smith	76	20
5 Harkin	81	14
6 Bedell	68†	18†

Democrats   *Republicans*

Member	1	2
KANSAS		
1 *Roberts*	86	11
2 *Jeffries*	91	5
3 *Winn*	80	14
4 Glickman	70	30
5 *Whittaker*	84	14
KENTUCKY		
1 Hubbard	49	48
2 Natcher	69	31
3 Mazzoli	62	29
4 *Snyder*	77	23
5 *Rogers*	81	18
6 *Hopkins*	79	20
7 Perkins	76	23
LOUISIANA		
1 *Livingston*	71	20
2 Boggs	71	27
3 Tauzin	36	60
4 Roemer	33	65
5 Huckaby	33	61
6 *Moore*	79	20
7 Breaux	35	42
8 Long	70	22
MAINE		
1 *Emery*	74	23
2 *Snowe*	68	32
MARYLAND		
1 Dyson	52	48
2 Long	74	21
3 Mikulski	84	9
4 *Holt*	75	14
5 Hoyer[2]	86†	11†
6 Byron	38	56
7 Mitchell	82	5
8 Barnes	86	12
MASSACHUSETTS		
1 *Conte*	45	54
2 Boland	80	15
3 Early	73	13
4 Frank	85	11
5 Shannon	86	9
6 Mavroules	84	14
7 Markey	91	8
8 O'Neill[3]		
9 Moakley	81	8
10 *Heckler*	45	52
11 Donnelly	81	10
12 Studds	91	9
MICHIGAN		
1 Conyers	78	9
2 *Pursell*	42	50
3 Wolpe	92	8
4 *Siljander*[4]	83†	11†
5 Sawyer	61	33
6 Dunn	61	38
7 Kildee	90	10
8 Traxler	79	14
9 *Vander Jagt*	68†	13†
10 Albosta	62	31
11 *Davis*	69	26
12 Bonior	86	8
13 Crockett	67	4
14 Hertel	80	12
15 Ford	84	3
16 Dingell	73	11
17 Brodhead	87	11
18 Blanchard	86	7
19 *Broomfield*	77	19
MINNESOTA		
1 *Erdahl*	57	39
2 *Hagedorn*	71	11
3 *Frenzel*	71	17
4 Vento	86	9
5 Sabo	89	8
6 *Weber*	79	20
7 *Stangeland*	83	14
8 Oberstar	89	8
MISSISSIPPI		
1 Whitten	63	36
2 Bowen	62	36
3 Montgomery	26	68
4 Dowdy[5]	50†	45†
5 *Lott*	90	6
MISSOURI		
1 Clay	86	2
2 Young	60	36
3 Gephardt	64	33
4 Skelton	45	45
5 Bolling	50	7
6 *Coleman*	74	18
7 *Taylor*	86	13
8 *Bailey*	85	11
9 Volkmer	65	31
10 *Emerson*	90	10
MONTANA		
1 Williams	86	10
2 *Marlenee*	72	21
NEBRASKA		
1 *Bereuter*	75	23
2 *Daub*	85	13
3 *Smith*	84	15
NEVADA		
AL Santini	30	45
NEW HAMPSHIRE		
1 D'Amours	76	19
2 *Gregg*	80	17
NEW JERSEY		
1 Florio	52	10
2 Hughes	64	31
3 Howard	86	7
4 *Smith*	65	35
5 *Fenwick*	58	40
6 *Forsythe*	60	26
7 *Roukema*	70	29
8 Roe	70	16
9 *Hollenbeck*	36	50
10 Rodino	92	6
11 Minish	82	11
12 *Rinaldo*	58	39
13 *Courter*	77	19
14 Guarini	85	5
15 Dwyer	93	5
NEW MEXICO		
1 Lujan	68	27
2 Skeen	83	15
NEW YORK		
1 *Carney*	77	20
2 Downey	84	7
3 *Carman*	83	14
4 *Lent*	75	23
5 *McGrath*	78	20
6 *LeBoutillier*	80	17
7 Addabbo	88	7
8 Rosenthal	73	1
9 Ferraro	91	4
10 Biaggi	68	13
11 Scheuer	92	5
12 Chisholm	70	2
13 Solarz	82†	6†
14 Richmond	78	4
15 Zeferetti	70	21
16 Schumer	83	11
17 *Molinari*	74†	22†
18 *Green*	39	58
19 Rangel	83	6
20 Weiss	89	10
21 Garcia	81	3
22 Bingham	92	8
23 Peyser	82	10
24 Ottinger	89	7
25 *Fish*	48	46
26 *Gilman*	42	48
27 McHugh	89	11
28 Stratton	59	38
29 *Solomon*	92	5
30 *Martin*	80	8
31 *Mitchell*	61	30
32 *Wortley*	76	22
33 *Lee*	79	13
34 *Horton*	45	37
35 *Conable*	79†	13†
36 LaFalce	78†	15†
37 Nowak	87	10
38 *Kemp*	72	11
39 Lundine	73	14
NORTH CAROLINA		
1 Jones	47	20
2 Fountain	46	52
3 Whitley	52	42
4 Andrews	56†	32†
5 Neal	66	27
6 *Johnston*	76†	8†
7 Rose	54	22
8 Hefner	57	33
9 *Martin*	77	14
10 *Broyhill*	83	11
11 *Hendon*	83	15
NORTH DAKOTA		
AL Dorgan	80	18
OHIO		
1 *Gradison*	67	27
2 Luken	58	33
3 Hall	69	24
4 *Oxley*[6]	85†	13†
5 *Latta*	84	8
6 *McEwen*	90	8
7 *Brown*	56†	12†
8 *Kindness*	82	15
9 *Weber*	72	24
10 *Miller*	86	14
11 *Stanton*	72	23
12 Shamansky	81	15
13 Pease	83	9
14 Seiberling	94	5
15 *Wylie*	68	22
16 *Regula*	75	25
17 *Ashbrook*	77	7
18 Applegate	45	50
19 *Williams*	55	25
20 Oakar	80	11
21 Stokes	93	4
22 Eckart	82	17
23 Mottl	39	52
OKLAHOMA		
1 Jones	62	33
2 Synar	90	10
3 Watkins	57	43
4 McCurdy	55	43
5 Edwards	84	15
6 English	54	46
OREGON		
1 AuCoin	67	11
2 *Smith*	92	7
3 Wyden	83	10
4 Weaver	76	17
PENNSYLVANIA		
1 Foglietta	80	8
2 Gray	87	2
3 *Smith*[7]	82†	15†
4 *Dougherty*	61	24
5 *Schulze*	87	6
6 Yatron	58	39
7 Edgar	83	10
8 *Coyne, J.*	73	24
9 *Shuster*	89	11
10 *McDade*	55	34
11 *Nelligan*	77	19
12 Murtha	70	27
13 *Coughlin*	62	34
14 Coyne, W.	89	10
15 *Ritter*	82	17
16 *Walker*	84	12
17 Ertel	69†	25†
18 Walgren	77	21
19 *Goodling*	74	17
20 Gaydos	65	25
21 Bailey	70	27
22 Murphy	58	30
23 *Clinger*	69	31
24 *Marks*	48	43
25 *Atkinson*[8]	74	26
RHODE ISLAND		
1 St Germain	73	14
2 *Schneider*	44	53
SOUTH CAROLINA		
1 *Hartnett*	83	9
2 *Spence*	92	8
3 Derrick	62	30
4 *Campbell*	84	11
5 Holland	43	39
6 *Napier*	79	17
SOUTH DAKOTA		
1 Daschle	77	17
2 *Roberts*	82	10
TENNESSEE		
1 *Quillen*	70	14
2 *Duncan*	68	20
3 Bouquard	55	41
4 Gore	80	17
5 Boner	57	34
6 *Beard*	71	10
7 Jones	58	37
8 Ford	89	4
TEXAS		
1 Hall, S.	39	61
2 Wilson	54	36
3 *Collins*	87	10
4 Hall, R.	40	54
5 Mattox	69	6
6 *Gramm*	20	77
7 *Archer*	93	5
8 *Fields*	88	8
9 Brooks	55	23
10 Pickle	58	39
11 Leath	30	65
12 Wright	60	23
13 Hightower	48	50
14 Patman	50	45
15 de la Garza	62	31
16 White	45	48
17 Stenholm	28	67
18 Leland	80	5
19 Hance	37	50
20 Gonzalez	81	15
21 *Loeffler*	86	14
22 *Paul*	69	22
23 Kazen	59	40
24 Frost	70	17
UTAH		
1 *Hansen*	80	4
2 *Marriott*	80	15
VERMONT		
AL *Jeffords*	35†	55†
VIRGINIA		
1 *Trible*	88	8
2 *Whitehurst*	85	12
3 *Bliley*	88	11
4 *Daniel, R.*	95	4
5 Daniel, D.	15	81
6 *Butler*	80	17
7 *Robinson*	89	9
8 *Parris*	83	14
9 *Wampler*	66	21
10 *Wolf*	83	17
WASHINGTON		
1 *Pritchard*	49†	38†
2 Swift	86	14
3 Bonker	70	16
4 *Morrison*	83	17
5 Foley	80	17
6 Dicks	68	24
7 Lowry	89	11
WEST VIRGINIA		
1 Mollohan	58	27
2 *Benedict*	75	19
3 *Staton*	89	10
4 Rahall	77	17
WISCONSIN		
1 Aspin	80	11
2 Kastenmeier	89	11
3 *Gunderson*	75	25
4 Zablocki	71	27
5 Reuss	80	9
6 *Petri*	71	23
7 Obey	83	11
8 *Roth*	77	14
9 *Sensenbrenner*	77	21
WYOMING		
AL *Cheney*	83	13

Democrats   *Republicans*

	1	2
ALABAMA		
Denton	89	5
Heflin	64	34
ALASKA		
Murkowski	83	11
Stevens	81	10
ARIZONA		
Goldwter	55	5
DeConcini	59†	24†
ARKANSAS		
Bumpers	81	8
Pryor	80	15
CALIFORNIA		
Hayakawa	84	3
Cranston	77	10
COLORADO		
Armstrong	88	8
Hcrt	84	10
CONNECTICUT		
Weicker	48	38
Dodd	80	8
DELAWARE		
Roth	72	26
Biden	84	12
FLORIDA		
Hawkins	80	16
Chiles	70	25
GEORGIA		
Mattingly	91	7
Nunn	59	39
HAWAII		
Inouye	74	13
Matsunaga	76	12
IDAHO		
McClure	85	7
Symms	90	7
ILLINOIS		
Percy	79	16
Dixon	73	26
INDIANA		
Lugar	93	7
Quayle	93	6

	1	2
IOWA		
Grassley	84	15
Jepsen	92	7
KANSAS		
Dole	94	5
Kassebaum	77	20
KENTUCKY		
Ford	84	14
Huddleston	76	19
LOUISIANA		
Johnston	49	45
Long	35	54
MAINE		
Cohen	69	25
Mitchell	88	10
MARYLAND		
Mathias	44	34
Sarbanes	93	6
MASSACHUSETTS		
Kennedy	80	9
Tsongas	69	14
MICHIGAN		
Levin	92	5
Riegle	88	4
MINNESOTA		
Boschwitz	78	21
Durenberger	68	25
MISSISSIPPI		
Cochran	87	11
Stennis	39	48
MISSOURI		
Danforth	84	15
Eagleton	85	9
MONTANA		
Baucus	84	14
Melcher	66	23
NEBRASKA		
Exon	69	27
Zorinsky	49	43
NEVADA		
Laxalt	93	1
Cannon	48	21

	1	2
NEW HAMPSHIRE		
Humphrey	84	13
Rudman	82	16
NEW JERSEY		
Bradley	80	10
Williams	74	11
NEW MEXICO		
Domenici	86	8
Schmitt	85	8
NEW YORK		
D'Amato	81	13
Moynihan	71	14
NORTH CAROLINA		
East	92	4
Helms	88	11
NORTH DAKOTA		
Andrews	76	22
Burdick	81	17
OHIO		
Glenn	74	21
Metzenbaum	82	5
OKLAHOMA		
Nickles	87	11
Boren	54	40
OREGON		
Hatfield	71	26
Packwood	80	16
PENNSYLVANIA		
Heinz	57	33
Specter	64	34
RHODE ISLAND		
Chafee	68	29'
Pell	82	14
SOUTH CAROLINA		
Thurmond	91	6
Hollings	58	35
SOUTH DAKOTA		
Abdnor	82	17
Pressler	58	32
TENNESSEE		
Baker	90	6
Sasser	72	17

KEY

† Not eligible for all recorded votes in 1981 (sworn in after Jan. 5, died or resigned during session, or voted "present" to avoid possible conflict of interest).

	1	2
TEXAS		
Tower	83	4
Bentsen	55	42
UTAH		
Garn	92	4
Hatch	89	8
VERMONT		
Stafford	72	21
Leahy	76	8
VIRGINIA		
Warner	88	8
Byrd*	26	70
WASHINGTON		
Gorton	86	13
Jackson	82	18
WEST VIRGINIA		
Byrd	78	14
Randolph	81	15
WISCONSIN		
Kasten	84	15
Proxmire	53	47
WYOMING		
Simpson	90	7
Wallop	91	3

Democrats   *Republicans*

* Byrd elected as an independent.

Party Unity and Party Opposition: Senate

1. Party Unity, 1981. Percentage of 231 Senate Party Unity votes in 1981, on which senator voted "yea" or "nay" *in agreement* with a majority of his party. (Party Unity roll calls are those on which a majority of voting Democrats opposed a majority of voting Republicans. Failures to vote lower both Party Unity and Party Opposition scores.)

2. Party Opposition, 1981. Percentage of 231 Senate Party Unity votes in 1981, on which senator voted "yea" or "nay" *in disagreement* with a majority of his party.

Conservative Coalition

92 Percent Success:

Conservatives Hit New High In Showdown Vote Victories

The conservative coalition of Republicans and Southern Democrats — the backbone of President Reagan's support in both House and Senate during the 97th Congress — in 1981 showed a strength unequaled in the 25 years Congressional Quarterly had measured the coalition's muscle.

Overall, the voting alliance of Republicans and Southern Democrats outpolled Northern Democrats on 92 percent of the recorded votes in both houses in which the two groups faced off.

As defined by CQ in analyzing House and Senate votes, the conservative coalition refers to a voting alliance of a majority of Republicans and Southern Democrats against a majority of Northern Democrats. *(See definitions, box, this page)*

The coalition's previous high score was 89 percent, recorded in 1957, the first year CQ began studying the conservative coalition's voting patterns.

20 Percent Jump

The 1981 success rate represented a jump of 20 percentage points over the coalition's 1980 score of 72 percent, and marked the third straight year the coalition had gained in strength over the previous year. The coalition's 1981 score was even more striking when compared to the average of its annual success scores of the previous 10 years, which was 64.2 percent.

Boosting the coalition's strength was the greater number of coalition members elected to the 97th Congress.

Although the number of Southern Democrats actually declined in both House and Senate from the 96th Congress to the 97th, the greater number of Republicans elected in November 1980 more than made up for the losses in the Southern Democrats' ranks.

There were 68 Republicans and Southern Democrats in the Senate at the beginning of the 97th Congress compared to 60 at the beginning of the 96th. In the House, there were 270 compared to 243 the previous Congress.

Recent Upswing

In 1981, the alliance appeared on 21 percent of the recorded votes held in both houses — up 1 percentage point from 1980 but significantly below the CQ study's high of 30 percent reached in 1971.

On those votes in which the coalition appeared in 1981, it was slightly more successful in the Senate than in the House, which is not surprising considering the coalition's greater proportional strength in the Senate.

The conservative coalition won 95 percent of the recorded votes in which it emerged in the Senate, and 88 percent of the votes in which it emerged in the House.

The sole year studied by CQ during which the coalition enjoyed comparable success was in 1957, when it won 100 percent of the Senate votes in which it emerged and 81 percent of the House votes, for a total score of 89 percent.

Definitions

Conservative Coalition. As used in this study, the term "conservative coalition" means a voting alliance of Republicans and Southern Democrats against the Northern Democrats in Congress. This meaning, rather than any philosophic definition of the "conservative" position, provides the basis for CQ's selection of coalition votes.

Conservative Coalition Vote. Any vote in the Senate or the House on which a majority of voting Southern Democrats and a majority of voting Republicans opposed the stand taken by a majority of voting Northern Democrats. Votes on which there is an even division within the ranks of voting Northern Democrats, Southern Democrats or Republicans are not included.

Southern States. The Southern states are Alabama, Arkansas, Florida, Georgia, Kentucky, Louisiana, Mississippi, North Carolina, Oklahoma, South Carolina, Tennessee, Texas and Virginia. The other 37 states are grouped as the North in the study.

Conservative Coalition Support Score. Percentage of conservative coalition votes on which a member votes "yea" or "nay" *in agreement* with the position of the conservative coalition. Failures to vote, even if a member announces a stand, lower the score.

Conservative Coalition Opposition Score. Percentage of conservative coalition votes on which a member votes "yea" or "nay" *in disagreement* with the position of the conservative coalition.

After 1957, the trend of the coalition's success was downward until 1965, when the victory rate hit bottom at 33 percent. The rate peaked again in 1971, after which it declined to 50 percent in 1975.

Since 1978 there had been a gradual upswing in the coalition's annual success rate.

Support for the coalition increased in 1981 in both House and Senate, among both Republicans and Democrats and in every region of the country compared with 1980, except for Eastern Senate Democrats and Southern House Republicans, whose composite support scores remained about the same.

Reagan Strength

An important factor behind the coalition's 1981 success rate appeared to have been the Reagan presidency. *(Presidential support vote study, p. 18-C)*

To a significant degree, the coalition's extraordinary success during 1981 merely reflected the number of votes held in both chambers on the various components of Reagan's economic program. Throughout the year in both chambers, numerous votes occurred on the Reagan program and most of them went the president's — and the conservatives' — way.

This was particularly true in the Senate, where the Republicans were in the majority. Voting as a bloc on

Reagan's key proposals ensured a victory for the White House, with or without the votes of Southern Democrats.

Though under these circumstances Northern Democrats had little chance of altering the president's proposals, they nonetheless offered amendment after amendment to establish a record of opposition.

In addition to giving the White House a hand on its economic program, the conservative coalition also helped ease through Congress the president's defense proposals as well as several of his most controversial appointments.

In the Senate, the coalition was victorious in votes on cutting back the food stamp program, preserving tobacco price supports, curbing federal abortion funding and limiting school busing to achieve racial balance — though the coalition initially was rebuffed on a series of attempts to cut off a filibuster blocking an anti-busing amendment.

In the House, the coalition won votes reining in the Legal Services Corporation as well as curbing abortion and busing. The coalition also was victorious on a series of five votes disapproving an attempt by the District of Columbia government to ease criminal penalties for certain sex-related offenses.

Supporting the coalition on 100 percent of its Senate votes during 1981 was Strom Thurmond, R-S.C. Among Southern Democrats, the most loyal coalition supporter was J. Bennett Johnston, La. Two Northern Senate Democrats up for re-election in 1982 showed marked increases in their level of coalition support compared to 1980. The score of John Melcher, Mont., leaped 28 points while that of William Proxmire, Wis., went up 20 points.

Coalition Appearances, 1962-81

Following is the percentage of the recorded votes for both houses of Congress on which the coalition appeared:

1962	14%	1972	27%
1963	17	1973	23
1964	15	1974	24
1965	24	1975	28
1966	25	1976	24
1967	20	1977	26
1968	24	1978	21
1969	27	1979	20
1970	22	1980	18
1971	30	1981	21

Coalition Victories, 1962-81

Year	Total	Senate	House
1962	62%	71%	44%
1963	50	44	67
1964	51	47	67
1965	33	39	25
1966	45	51	32
1967	63	54	73
1968	73	80	63
1969	68	67	71
1970	66	64	70
1971	83	86	79
1972	69	63	79
1973	61	54	67
1974	59	54	67
1975	50	48	52
1976	58	58	59
1977	68	74	60
1978	52	46	57
1979	70	65	73
1980	72	75	67
1981	92	95	88

Average Scores

Following are the composite conservative coalition support and opposition scores for 1981 (scores for 1980 are in parentheses):

	Southern Democrats	Republicans	Northern Democrats
Coalition Support			
Senate	71% (61)	80% (67)	27% (22)
House	70 (61)	77 (73)	28 (24)
Coalition Opposition			
Senate	23% (24)	15% (23)	66% (62)
House	23 (28)	17 (17)	65 (65)

Regional Scores

Following are the parties' coalition support and opposition scores by region for 1981 (scores for 1980 are in parentheses):

SUPPORT

	East	West	South	Midwest
DEMOCRATS				
Senate	15% (15)	33% (22)	71% (61)	37% (27)
House	25 (22)	26 (23)	70 (61)	31 (27)
REPUBLICANS				
Senate	59% (47)	84% (76)	93% (81)	82% (66)
House	67 (61)	82 (73)	86 (87)	77 (73)

OPPOSITION

	East	West	South	Midwest
DEMOCRATS				
Senate	76% (68)	57% (58)	23% (24)	60% (60)
House	67 (65)	67 (65)	23 (28)	61 (63)
REPUBLICANS				
Senate	35% (42)	10% (15)	4% (8)	15% (25)
House	29 (30)	9 (14)	9 (6)	19 (17)

Individual Scores

SUPPORT

Highest Coalition Support Scores. Those who voted with the conservative coalition most consistently in 1981:

SENATE

Southern Democrats		Republicans	
Johnston, La.	93%	Thurmond, S.C.	100%
Byrd, Va.[1]	89	East, N.C.	97
Stennis, Miss.	88	Mattingly, Ga.	97
Boren, Okla.	86	Warner, Va.	97
Nunn, Ga.	84	Laxalt, Nev.	95

Northern Democrats

Zorinsky, Neb.	79%
Exon, Neb.	67
DeConcini, Ariz.[2]	63
Proxmire, Wis.	60
Melcher, Mont.	59

[1] *Byrd, Va., elected as an independent, but caucuses with Democrats.*
[2] *Not eligible for all votes in 1981.*

HOUSE

Southern Democrats		Republicans	
Gramm, Texas	99%	Daniel, Va.	99%
Montgomery, Miss.	97	Emerson, Mo.	99
Shelby, Ala.	93	Shuster, Pa.	99
Daniel, Va.	93	Jeffries, Kan.	97
Hutto, Fla.	93	Skeen, N.M.	96
Jenkins, Ga.	91	Lagomarsino, Calif.	96
Tauzin, La.	91	Hammerschmidt, Ark.	96
Leath, Texas	91	Spence, S.C.	96
Stenholm, Texas	91	Fields, Texas	96

Northern Democrats

Stump, Ariz.	97%
Byron, Md.	93
Dyson, Md.	92
Skelton, Mo.	91
Young, Mo.	76
Stratton, N.Y.	75
Applegate, Ohio	72
Yatron, Pa.	72
Albosta, Mich.	71

OPPOSITION

Highest Coalition Opposition Scores. Those who voted against the conservative coalition most consistently in 1981:

SENATE

Southern Democrats		Republicans	
Bumpers, Ark.	69%	Weicker, Conn.	51%
Pryor, Ark.	42	Mathias, Md.	48
Ford, Ky.	41	Specter, Pa.	47
Huddleston, Ky.	40	Chafee, R.I.	47
Hollings, S.C.	30	Heinz, Pa.	41

Northern Democrats

Sarbanes, Md.	93%

1981 Coalition Votes

Following is a list of all 1981 Senate and House votes on which the conservative coalition appeared. The votes are listed by CQ vote number and may be found in the 1981 Almanac vote charts.

SENATE VOTES (104)

Coalition Victories (99) — 24, 27, 28, 42, 46, 51, 54, 55, 56, 58, 59, 60, 61, 62, 69, 70, 72, 73, 74, 75, 79, 80, 81, 82, 97, 98, 99, 101, 103, 105, 107, 111, 112, 113, 117, 120, 125, 126, 128, 132, 138, 143, 144, 145, 146, 159, 163, 165, 176, 179, 181, 182, 190, 201, 206, 211, 213, 222, 224, 247, 254, 255, 256, 258, 260, 269, 273, 291, 296, 302, 306, 307, 309, 321, 323, 331, 352, 353, 374, 375, 376, 382, 387, 397, 401, 402, 409, 412, 417, 431, 434, 453, 454, 456, 458, 459, 461, 464, 465.

Coalition Defeats (5) — 133, 185, 240, 249, 469.

HOUSE VOTES (75)

Coalition Victories (66) — 28, 30, 31, 32, 33, 34, 35, 37, 44, 55, 56, 62, 66, 71; 74, 75, 76, 77, 80, 108, 111, 112, 115, 119, 120, 122, 123, 125, 126, 129, 134, 150, 151, 160, 164, 165, 167, 170, 171, 176, 179, 192, 199, 203, 205, 214, 215, 216, 217, 218, 232, 233, 255, 277, 278, 296, 298, 299, 300, 301, 302, 322, 329, 331, 333, 351.

Coalition Defeats (9) — 109, 130, 135, 180, 269, 270, 295, 338, 348.

Levin, Mich.	93
Riegle, Mich.	87
Moynihan, N.Y.	87
Kennedy, Mass.	87

HOUSE

Southern Democrats		Republicans	
Ford, Tenn.	85%	Jeffords, Vt.	68%
Leland, Texas	79	Schneider, R.I.	67
Fascell, Fla.	73	DeNardis, Conn.	64
Synar, Okla.	72	McKinney, Conn.	64
Lehman, Fla.	71	Green, N.Y.	63
Mattox, Texas	63	Pursell, Mich.	60
Gonzalez, Texas	63	Fish, N.Y.	56
Gore, Tenn.	53	Heckler, Mass.	55
Pepper, Fla.	49	Conte, Mass.	53
Fowler, Ga.	41	Fenwick, N.J.	53
Frost, Texas	41	Hollenbeck, N.J.	53

Northern Democrats

Weiss, N.Y.	96%
Rodino, N.J.	95
Edwards, Calif.	95
Edgar, Pa.	95
Yates, Ill.	95
Kastenmeier, Wis.	95
Seiberling, Ohio	93
Studds, Mass.	93
Miller, Calif.	93

Conservative Coalition
Support and Opposition: House

1. Conservative Coalition Support, 1981. Percentage of 75 conservative coalition recorded votes in 1981 on which representative voted "yea" or "nay" *in agreement* with the position of the conservative coalition. Failures to vote lower both support and opposition scores.

2. Conservative Coalition Opposition, 1981. Percentage of 75 conservative coalition recorded votes in 1981 on which representative voted "yea" or "nay" *in disagreement* with the position of the conservative coalition. Failures to vote lower both support and opposition scores.

KEY

† Not eligible for all recorded votes in 1981 (sworn in after Jan. 5, died or resigned during session, or voted "present" to avoid possible conflict of interest).

	1	2
ALABAMA		
1 Edwards	69	29
2 *Dickinson*	81	7
3 Nichols	88	8
4 Bevill	79	11
5 Flippo	79	11
6 *Smith*	93	1
7 Shelby	93	4
ALASKA		
AL *Young*	89	1
ARIZONA		
1 *Rhodes*	64	11
2 Udall	39	59
3 *Stump*	97	0
4 *Rudd*	95	0
ARKANSAS		
1 Alexander	60	28
2 *Bethune*	85	9
3 *Hammerschmidt*	96	4
4 Anthony	76	15
CALIFORNIA		
1 Chappie	81	4
2 *Clausen*	92	5
3 Matsui	32	63
4 Fazio	33	64
5 Burton, J.	1	76
6 Burton, P.	5	88
7 Miller	0	93
8 Dellums	8	87
9 Stark	11	83
10 Edwards	3	95
11 Lantos	39	53
12 *McCloskey*	44	21
13 Mineta	25	71
14 *Shumway*	95	4
15 Coelho	47	52
16 Panetta	45	55
17 *Pashayan*	75	5
18 *Thomas*	75	11
19 *Lagomarsino*	96	4
20 *Goldwater*	49	7
21 *Fiedler*	80	17
22 *Moorhead*	92	4
23 Beilenson	8	80
24 Waxman	4	88
25 Roybal	12	87
26 *Rousselot*	80	5
27 *Dornan*	63	8
28 Dixon	11	71
29 Hawkins	8	80
30 Danielson	20	71
31 Dymally	11	65
32 Anderson	47	51
33 *Grisham*	79	5
34 *Lungren*	89	8
35 *Dreier*	93	7
36 Brown	19	75
37 *Lewis*	81	15
38 Patterson	24	71
39 *Dannemeyer*	85	11
40 *Badham*	80	4
41 *Lowery*	85	9
42 *Hunter*	95	5
43 *Burgener*	73	15
COLORADO		
1 Schroeder	12	85
2 Wirth	23	61
3 Kogovsek	27	72
4 *Brown*	71	29

	1	2
5 *Kramer*	85	11
CONNECTICUT		
1 Cotter[1]	0†	0†
2 Gejdenson	8	92
3 *DeNardis*	33	64
4 *McKinney*	36	64
5 Ratchford	9	89
6 Moffett	4	81
DELAWARE		
AL *Evans*	72	25
FLORIDA		
1 Hutto	93	5
2 Fuqua	79	12
3 Bennett	80	20
4 Chappell	84	11
5 *McCollum*	85	12
6 *Young*	88	7
7 Gibbons	80	15
8 Ireland	87	7
9 Nelson	75	12
10 *Bafalis*	95†	3†
11 Mica	76	23
12 *Shaw*	95	5
13 Lehman	19	71
14 Pepper	28	49
15 Fascell	19	73
GEORGIA		
1 Ginn	81	11
2 Hatcher	80	13
3 Brinkley	89	11
4 Levitas	64	33
5 Fowler	55	41
6 *Gingrich*	76	15
7 McDonald	77	5
8 Evans	65	12
9 Jenkins	91	4
10 Barnard	84	1
HAWAII		
1 Heftel	52	44
2 Akaka	52	48
IDAHO		
1 *Craig*	91	4
2 *Hansen*	93	7
ILLINOIS		
1 Washington	3	77
2 Savage	5	49
3 Russo	39	57
4 *Derwinski*	64	27
5 Fary	55	39
6 *Hyde*	81	16
7 Collins	4	85
8 Rostenkowski	44	52
9 Yates	5	95
10 *Porter*	61	36
11 Annunzio	59	41
12 *Crane, P.*	80	13
13 *McClory*	72	28
14 *Erlenborn*	65	27
15 *Corcoran*	75	15
16 *Martin*	72	24
17 *O'Brien*	71	21
18 *Michel*	83	13
19 *Railsback*	55	37
20 *Findley*	63	36
21 *Madigan*	71	12
22 *Crane, D.*	81	16
23 Price	53	41
24 Simon	28	64
INDIANA		
1 Benjamin	40	60
2 Fithian	36	37
3 *Hiler*	85	15
4 *Coats*	91	9
5 *Hillis*	89	5
6 Evans	40	55
7 *Myers*	91	9
8 *Deckard*	57	31
9 Hamilton	56	44
10 Sharp	52	47
11 Jacobs	25	75
IOWA		
1 Leach	48	51
2 *Tauke*	67	29
3 *Evans*	79	17
4 Smith	40	55
5 Harkin	21	73
6 Bedell	21	67

1. Rep. William R. Cotter, D-Conn., died Sept. 9, 1981.

2. Rep. Steny Hoyer, D-Md., sworn in June 3, 1981, to succeed Gladys Noon Spellman, D, whose seat the House declared vacant on Feb. 24, 1981. Spellman did not vote on the one vote for which she was eligible in 1981.

3. Rep. Thomas P. O'Neill Jr., D-Mass., as Speaker, votes at his own discretion.

4. Rep. Wayne Dowdy, D-Miss., sworn in July 9, 1981, to succeed Jon Hinson, R, who resigned April 13, 1981. Hinson was not eligible for any conservative coalition votes in 1981.

5. Rep. Michael G. Oxley, R-Ohio, sworn in July 21, 1981, to succeed Tennyson Guyer, R, who died April 12, 1981. Guyer was not eligible for any conservative coalition votes in 1981.

6. Rep. Joseph F. Smith, D-Pa., sworn in July 28, 1981, to succeed Raymond F. Lederer, D., who resigned May 5, 1981. Lederer was not eligible for any conservative coalition votes in 1981.

7. Rep. Eugene V. Atkinson, Pa., switched from the Democratic to the Republican Party on Oct. 14, 1981.

Democrats   *Republicans*

Member	1	2
KANSAS		
1 Roberts	91	5
2 Jeffries	97	1
3 Winn	88	8
4 Glickman	48	51
5 Whittaker	91	9
KENTUCKY		
1 Hubbard	87	13
2 Natcher	75	25
3 Mazzoli	49	36
4 Snyder	77	23
5 Rogers	88	9
6 Hopkins	80	16
7 Perkins	56	40
LOUISIANA		
1 Livingston	76	17
2 Boggs	59	39
3 Tauzin	91	7
4 Roemer	84	15
5 Huckaby	83	9
6 Moore	81	17
7 Breaux	63	7
8 Long	61	37
MAINE		
1 Emery	81	15
2 Snowe	69	31
MARYLAND		
1 Dyson	92	8
2 Long	32	63
3 Mikulski	11	87
4 Holt	84	3
5 Hoyer [2]	32†	67†
6 Byron	93	4
7 Mitchell	3	92
8 Barnes	13	87
MASSACHUSETTS		
1 Conte	44	53
2 Boland	27	64
3 Early	24	64
4 Frank	9	87
5 Shannon	12	85
6 Mavroules	28	72
7 Markey	8	88
8 O'Neill [3]		
9 Moakley	23	63
10 Heckler	45	55
11 Donnelly	25	63
12 Studds	7	93
MICHIGAN		
1 Conyers	9	85
2 Pursell	31	60
3 Wolpe	8	91
4 Siljander	83	12
5 Sawyer	73	25
6 Dunn	56	43
7 Kildee	15	85
8 Traxler	37	56
9 Vander Jagt	76	12
10 Albosta	71	23
11 Davis	84	12
12 Bonior	9	85
13 Crockett	7	65
14 Hertel	27	73
15 Ford	12	68
16 Dingell	27	55
17 Brodhead	11	87
18 Blanchard	19	73
19 Broomfield	73	24
MINNESOTA		
1 Erdahl	52	47
2 Hagedorn	73	9
3 Frenzel	61	23
4 Vento	9	84
5 Sabo	7	92
6 Weber	76	24
7 Stangeland	93	7
8 Oberstar	16	81
MISSISSIPPI		
1 Whitten	67	31
2 Bowen	84	13
3 Montgomery	97	3
4 Dowdy [4]	85†	11†
5 Lott	95	3
MISSOURI		
1 Clay	4	89
2 Young	76	15
3 Gephardt	69	27
4 Skelton	91	5
5 Bolling	12	47
6 Coleman	85	12
7 Taylor	91	4
8 Bailey	89	8
9 Volkmer	67	29
10 Emerson	99	1
MONTANA		
1 Williams	21	73
2 Marlenee	79	12
NEBRASKA		
1 Bereuter	79	19
2 Daub	89	9
3 Smith	89	11
NEVADA		
AL Santini	64	13
NEW HAMPSHIRE		
1 D'Amours	39	60
2 Gregg	72	25
NEW JERSEY		
1 Florio	16	41
2 Hughes	41	59
3 Howard	19	71
4 Smith	67	33
5 Fenwick	47	53
6 Forsythe	55	33
7 Roukema	56	41
8 Roe	36	51
9 Hollenbeck	31	53
10 Rodino	5	87
11 Minish	25	69
12 Rinaldo	71	28
13 Courter	80	13
14 Guarini	16	77
15 Dwyer	16	83
NEW MEXICO		
1 Lujan	81	15
2 Skeen	96	4
NEW YORK		
1 Carney	77	17
2 Downey	12	81
3 Carman	87	13
4 Lent	80	17
5 McGrath	75	23
6 LeBoutillier	81	15
7 Addabbo	12	76
8 Rosenthal	1	79
9 Ferraro	16	80
10 Biaggi	32	52
11 Scheuer	13	83
12 Chisholm	3	69
13 Solarz	13	77
14 Richmond	1	81
15 Zeferetti	59	36
16 Schumer	12	83
17 Molinari	72	24
18 Green	35	63
19 Rangel	4	92
20 Weiss	4	96
21 Garcia	3	76
22 Bingham	9	91
23 Peyser	19	81
24 Ottinger	3	92
25 Fish	40	56
26 Gilman	48	51
27 McHugh	19	80
28 Stratton	75	23
29 Solomon	93	4
30 Martin	75	7
31 Mitchell	71	23
32 Wortley	83	16
33 Lee	80	13
34 Horton	37	44
35 Conable	76	21
36 LaFalce	27	68
37 Nowak	17	77
38 Kemp	71	11
39 Lundine	23	67
NORTH CAROLINA		
1 Jones	40	15
2 Fountain	84	13
3 Whitley	84	9
4 Andrews	75	15
5 Neal	64	29
6 Johnston	72	9
7 Rose	63	25
8 Hefner	76	23
9 Martin	80	13
10 Broyhill	83	12
11 Hendon	87	9
NORTH DAKOTA		
AL Dorgan	37	53
OHIO		
1 Gradison	64	33
2 Luken	64	29
3 Hall	51	44
4 Oxley [5]	88†	12†
5 Latta	91	5
6 McEwen	91	7
7 Brown	67	8
8 Kindness	88	11
9 Weber	73	21
10 Miller	91	9
11 Stanton	77	20
12 Shamansky	37	63
13 Pease	16	77
14 Seiberling	5	93
15 Wylie	79	20
16 Regula	79	21
17 Ashbrook	80	9
18 Applegate	72	25
19 Williams	76	15
20 Oakar	23	65
21 Stokes	5	91
22 Eckart	25	68
23 Mottl	47	43
OKLAHOMA		
1 Jones	72	25
2 Synar	27	72
3 Watkins	89	11
4 McCurdy	88	12
5 Edwards	88	11
6 English	80	20
OREGON		
1 AuCoin	15	67
2 Smith	93	4
3 Wyden	12	85
4 Weaver	11	83
PENNSYLVANIA		
1 Foglietta	13	73
2 Gray	4	88
3 Smith [6]	56†	44†
4 Dougherty	72	17
5 Schulze	93	4
6 Yatron	72	25
7 Edgar	1	95
8 Coyne, J.	69	31
9 Shuster	99	1
10 McDade	63	25
11 Nelligan	88	9
12 Murtha	64	33
13 Coughlin	59	39
14 Coyne, W.	16	84
15 Ritter	76	19
16 Walker	80	15
17 Ertel	51	47
18 Walgren	28	71
19 Goodling	65	21
20 Gaydos	61	29
21 Bailey	67	32
22 Murphy	52	40
23 Clinger	72	28
24 Marks	64	35
25 Atkinson [7]	67	32
RHODE ISLAND		
1 St Germain	35	51
2 Schneider	33	67
SOUTH CAROLINA		
1 Hartnett	92	4
2 Spence	96	4
3 Derrick	55	35
4 Campbell	95	4
5 Holland	72	11
6 Napier	95	3
SOUTH DAKOTA		
1 Daschle	37	60
2 Roberts	88	8
TENNESSEE		
1 Quillen	67	3
2 Duncan	87	1
3 Bouquard	83	12
4 Gore	47	53
5 Boner	75	17
6 Beard	75	4
7 Jones	84	11
8 Ford	9	85
TEXAS		
1 Hall, S.	84	15
2 Wilson	68	24
3 Collins	89	11
4 Hall, R.	80	15
5 Mattox	21	63
6 Gramm	99	0
7 Archer	92	7
8 Fields	96	1
9 Brooks	57	35
10 Pickle	75	24
11 Leath	91	7
12 Wright	63	28
13 Hightower	81	16
14 Patman	72	20
15 de la Garza	68	27
16 White	87	8
17 Stenholm	91	5
18 Leland	8	79
19 Hance	81	13
20 Gonzalez	31	63
21 Loeffler	93	7
22 Paul	59	36
23 Kazen	85	15
24 Frost	52	41
UTAH		
1 Hansen	83	4
2 Marriott	89	7
VERMONT		
AL Jeffords	24	68
VIRGINIA		
1 Trible	85	5
2 Whitehurst	91	7
3 Bliley	89	9
4 Daniel, R.	99	1
5 Daniel, D.	93	4
6 Butler	84	11
7 Robinson	93	4
8 Parris	83	13
9 Wampler	87	7
10 Wolf	88†	12†
WASHINGTON		
1 Pritchard	48	35
2 Swift	31	69
3 Bonker	37	57
4 Morrison	92	8
5 Foley	51	45
6 Dicks	60	35
7 Lowry	11	89
WEST VIRGINIA		
1 Mollohan	59	31
2 Benedict	85	8
3 Staton	93	5
4 Rahall	37	53
WISCONSIN		
1 Aspin	25	68
2 Kastenmeier	5	95
3 Gunderson	75	25
4 Zablocki	57	37
5 Reuss	13	75
6 Petri	67	32
7 Obey	13	81
8 Roth	80	12
9 Sensenbrenner	75	24
WYOMING		
AL Cheney	84	11

Democrats　　**Republicans**

	1	2		1	2		1	2
ALABAMA			**IOWA**			**NEW HAMPSHIRE**		
Denton	92	3	*Grassley*	91	7	*Humphrey*	85	15
Heflin	81	15	*Jepsen*	93	4	*Rudman*	70	25
ALASKA			**KANSAS**			**NEW JERSEY**		
Murkowski	85	9	*Dole*	92	5	Bradley	11	77
Stevens	79	13	*Kassebaum*	80	18	Williams	11	66
ARIZONA			**KENTUCKY**			**NEW MEXICO**		
Goldwater	70	3	Ford	58	41	*Domenici*	94	4
DeConcini	63†	24†	Huddleston	52	40	*Schmitt*	88	6
ARKANSAS			**LOUISIANA**			**NEW YORK**		
Bumpers	20	69	Johnston	93	3	*D'Amato*	78	17
Pryor	54	42	Long	83	6	Moynihan	8	87
CALIFORNIA			**MAINE**			**NORTH CAROLINA**		
Hayakawa	86	6	*Cohen*	59	36	*East*	97	2
Cranston	10	74	Mitchell	24	75	*Helms*	94	6
COLORADO			**MARYLAND**			**NORTH DAKOTA**		
Armstrong	88	7	*Mathias*	26	48	*Andrews*	83	13
Hart	13	83	Sarbanes	7	93	Burdick	41	58
CONNECTICUT			**MASSACHUSETTS**			**OHIO**		
Weicker	42	51	Kennedy	4	87	Glenn	34	66
Dodd	3	85	Tsongas	8	78	Metzenbaum	7	81
DELAWARE			**MICHIGAN**			**OKLAHOMA**		
Roth	75	24	Levin	6	93	*Nickles*	89	10
Biden	24	74	Riegle	7	87	Boren	86	10
FLORIDA			**MINNESOTA**			**OREGON**		
Hawkins	90	6	*Boschwitz*	71	29	*Hatfield*	58	39
Chiles	74	21	*Durenberger*	59	33	*Packwood*	71	25
GEORGIA			**MISSISSIPPI**			**PENNSYLVANIA**		
Mattingly	97	2	*Cochran*	88	7	*Heinz*	51	41
Nunn	84	15	Stennis	88	6	*Specter*	51	47
HAWAII			**MISSOURI**			**RHODE ISLAND**		
Inouye	20	69	*Danforth*	83	16	*Chafee*	50	47
Matsunaga	17	78	Eagleton	10	86	Pell	10	82
IDAHO			**MONTANA**			**SOUTH CAROLINA**		
McClure	89	5	Baucus	29	66	*Thurmond*	100	0
Symms	91	4	Melcher	59	34	Hollings	67	30
ILLINOIS			**NEBRASKA**			**SOUTH DAKOTA**		
Percy	72	25	Exon	67	31	*Abdnor*	92	5
Dixon	57	38	Zorinsky	79	16	*Pressler*	63	27
INDIANA			**NEVADA**			**TENNESSEE**		
Lugar	90	10	*Laxalt*	95	1	*Baker*	89	6
Quayle	88	8	Cannon	48	28	Sasser	57	29

KEY

† Not eligible for all recorded votes in 1981 (sworn in after Jan. 5, died or resigned during session, or voted "present" to avoid possible conflict of interest).

	1	2
TEXAS		
Tower	87	1
Bentsen	83	11
UTAH		
Garn	89	6
Hatch	91	7
VERMONT		
Stafford	63	29
Leahy	4	84
VIRGINIA		
Warner	97	2
Byrd*	89	9
WASHINGTON		
Gorton	77	21
Jackson	41	59
WEST VIRGINIA		
Byrd	43	53
Randolph	39	52
WISCONSIN		
Kasten	88	11
Proxmire	60	40
WYOMING		
Simpson	89	8
Wallop	93	1

Democrats   **Republicans**

* *Byrd elected as an independent.*

Conservative Coalition
Support and Opposition: Senate

1. Conservative Coalition Support, 1981. Percentage of 104 conservative coalition votes in 1981 on which senator voted "yea" or "nay" *in agreement* with the position of the conservative coalition. Failures to vote lower both support and opposition scores.

2. Conservative Coalition Opposition, 1981. Percentage of 104 conservative coalition votes in 1981 on which senator voted "yea" or "nay" *in disagreement* with the position of the conservative coalition. Failures to vote lower both support and opposition scores.

LOBBY
REGISTRATIONS

CQ

Late October 1980 Registrations

MUNIR P. BENJENK, Washington, D.C. Lobbyist — Obermayer, Rebmann, Maxwell & Hippel, Washington, D.C. Filed 10/23/80. Legislative interest — "S 1227 and HR 4706 — Legislation concerning immigration status of international organization employees."

NATIONAL CONSUMER FINANCE ASSOCIATION, Washington, D.C. Filed for self 10/31/80. Legislative interest — "All bills pertaining to ... the consumer finance industry, including ... Bankruptcy (S 658), Privacy (S 2465), Bank Holding Company Amendments (HR 2255, HR 2856, S 380), Rule of 70's Usury Preemption (HR 7735)." Lobbyist — Frank M. Salinger, Washington, D.C.

PUGET SOUND POWER & LIGHT CO., Bellevue, Wash. Lobbyist — Cary & Baron, Seattle, Wash. Filed 10/31/80. Legislative interest — "Pacific Northwest Electric Planning and Conservation Act (S 885, HR 8157)."

November Registrations

Citizens' Groups

AMERICAN ISRAEL PUBLIC AFFAIRS COMMITTEE, Washington, D.C. Filed for self 11/12/80. Legislative interest — "Foreign assistance authorization acts for FY 1981 and FY 1982; general legislation to maintain and strengthen the friendship between the United States and Israel." Lobbyist — Michael R. Gale, Washington, D.C.

THE COMMITTEE FOR FREEDOM OF ACCESS TO LEGAL LOTTERIES, Guilford, Maine. Filed for self 11/7/80. Legislative interest — "...initiate legislation ... that would allow out of state residents to purchase lottery tickets through the mail from state authorized lotteries." Lobbyist — Matthew William Troy, Guilford, Maine.

NATIONAL PARKS AND CONSERVATION ASSOCIATION, Washington, D.C. Lobbyist — Laura L. Beaty, Arlington, Va. Filed 11/3/80. Legislative interest — "...archeology, historic preservation and cultural resource protection and national historic sites ... National Park and Recreation Act of 1980 (HR 3), National Heritage Policy Act of 1979 (S 1842, S 3116), bill to revise boundary of Chaco Canyon National Monument (S 3091), National Heritage Policy Act of 1980 (HR 6805, HR 5496)."

UTE MOUNTAIN UTE TRIBE, Towaoc, Colo. Lobbyist — John J. D'Onofrio, Denver, Colo. Filed 11/6/80. Legislative interest — "Legislative matters affecting the Ute Mountain Ute Tribe, specifically and Indian tribes generally, including funding and continuation of various government programs ... a bill to require the Secretary of the Interior to convey a parcel of land located in Colorado to the Ute Mountain Ute Tribe and to pay an amount to such tribe for economic development."

THE WILDERNESS SOCIETY, Washington, D.C. Filed for self 11/5/80 and 11/14/80. Legislative interest — "California Wilderness Bill (HR 7702), Big Sur Scenic Area Legislation (HR 7380), River of No Return Bill (S 2009), Eastern Wilderness Omnibus Bill, Rattlesnake Wilderness Bill (HR 5898), Mount St. Helens Bill, Cranberry Wilderness Bill." Lobbyists — Larry E. Moss, Trinidad, Calif., and Peter C. Kirby, Washington, D.C.

Businesses and Corporations

AVON PRODUCTS INC., New York, N.Y. Filed for self 11/19/80. Legislative interest — "All legislation related to employer's business, including government regulation of the manufacture and distribution of products, the environment and taxation. Specifically ... witholding federal income taxes and witholding and paying taxes of the Federal Insurance Contributions Act and the Federal Unemployment Tax Act." Lobbyist — Janice Zarro, New York, N.Y.

THE CHASE MANHATTAN BANK, New York, N.Y. Lobbyist — Mary Clare Fitzgerald, Washington, D.C. Filed 11/17/80. Legislative interest — "Any legislation affecting the interest of Chase Manhattan Bank."

CONTINENTAL MATERIALS, Washington, D.C. Lobbyist — The Keefe Co., Washington, D.C. Filed 11/24/80. Legislative interest — "General legislative interest impacting on precious metals mining."

THE EL PASO CO., Houston, Texas. Filed for self 11/17/80. Legislative interest — "...Pending and on-going congressional actions relative to the concerns of the ... company." Lobbyist — Jerald E. Hobson, Washington, D.C.

ENSEARCH CORP., Dallas, Texas. Lobbyist — Timothy L. Donohoe, Washington, D.C. Filed 11/17/80. Legislative interest — "Legislation of interest to the energy industry including Divestiture (S 382), Windfall Profits Tax (HR 3919), Synthetic Fuels Program (S 932), Regulatory Reform (S 262), Taxation of Americans Abroad (HR 7811)."

FIRST BANK AND TRUST CO., Ashland, Ky. Lobbyist — Cook, Purcell, Hansen & Henderson, Washington, D.C. Filed 11/6/80. Legislative interest — "All legislation affecting commercial banking ... implementation of Monetary Policy Control Act (Title I of PL 96-221)."

FIRST CITY BANCORPORATION, Washington, D.C. Lobbyist — Vinson & Elkins, Washington, D.C. Filed 11/5/80. Legislative interest — "In support of grandfather amendment to HR 2255."

FREE THE EAGLE, McLean, Va. Lobbyist — Neal Blair, McLean, Va. Filed 11/20/80. Legislative interest — "...to circumscribe major legislation designed to expand the power of the federal government in both domestic and foreign relations ... interested in the curtailment of federal regulation of the American economy and banking industry ... advocate a return to the gold standard and favor disclosure of government borrowing (HR 2997 and S 1843)."

GENERAL TIRE & RUBBER CO., Akron, Ohio. Lobbyist — Charles H. Crutchfield, Charlotte, N.C. Filed 11/7/80. Legislative interest — "All legislation affecting client's business."

THE GREAT WESTERN SUGAR CO., Denver, Colo. Lobbyist — Arnold & Porter, Washington, D.C. Filed 11/10/80. Legislative interest — "...increase the amount of loan guarantees available for alcohol fuel projects and ... Title II of the Energy Security Act of 1980."

INTERNATIONAL PAPER CO., New York, N.Y. Lobbyist — Dawson, Riddell, Fox, Holroyd & Wilson, Washington, D.C. Filed 11/19/80. Legislative interest — "To provide technical amendment of section 103 (b) of the Internal Revenue Code to require that it be interpreted consistent with congressional intent and environmental policy."

KORF INDUSTRIES INC., Charlotte, N.C. Filed for self 11/7/80. Legislative interest — "Incremental pricing under the Natural Gas Policy Act of 1978, Capital Cost Recovery Act, unemployment compensation, lobby law reform, export trading companies, trigger price mechanism, and all other legislation pertinent to the steel industry, with special regard to the manufacture of wire rod." Lobbyist — Margaret Renken Hudson, Washington, D.C.

MERRILL LYNCH & CO. INC., New York, N.Y. Lobbyist — Allan L. Sher, Washington, D.C. Filed 11/12/80. Legislative interest — "Banking and finance legislation."

MIDAMERICA COMMODITY EXCHANGE, Chicago, Ill. Lobbyist — John V. Rainbolt, Washington, D.C. Filed 11/3/80.

Legislative interest — "Legislation amending or related to the Commodity Exchange Act as amended (S 2604, HR 7541)."

MURRAY OHIO MANUFACTURING CO., Brentwood, Tenn. Lobbyist — Collier, Shannon Hill & Scott, Washington, D.C. Filed 11/25/80. Legislative interest — "Matters affecting lawn mower industry."

NORRIS INDUSTRIES, Los Angeles, Calif. Lobbyist — Collier, Shannon, Hill & Scott, Washington, D.C. Filed 11/25/80. Legislative interest — "Matters concerning Army projectiles in Defense Appropriations Bill."

NORTH AMERICAN SOCCER LEAGUE, New York, N.Y. Lobbyist — Vorys, Satar, Seymour & Pease, Washington, D.C. Filed 11/21/80. Legislative interest — "Generally, as their interests may appear."

NISSAN MOTOR CORP., Carson, Calif. Lobbyist — Verner, Liipfert, Bernhard & McPherson, Washington, D.C. Filed 11/26/80. Legislative interest — "...matters relating to automobile trade legislation (H J Res 598 and S J Res 198)."

NORTHERN SOLAR SYSTEMS INC., Hingham, Mass. Lobbyist — Alston, Miller & Gaines, Washington, D.C. Filed 11/4/80. Legislative interest — "To amend the tax code to provide credits for ground water solar energy systems."

PENNZOIL CO., Houston, Texas. Lobbyist — W. Lee Rawls, Washington, D.C. Filed 11/5/80. Legislative interest — "Energy Mobilization Board and related legislation; Energy Security Corporation and related legislation; S 300, HR 2060 and related legislation; and S 2424, S 1637 and related matters."

PUGET SOUND POWER & LIGHT CO., Bellevue, Wash. Lobbyist — Cary & Baron, Seattle, Wash. Filed 11/20/80. Legislative interest — "Pacific Northwest Electric Planning and Conservation Act (S 885 and HR 8157)."

SALMON RIVER ELECTRIC COOPERATIVE, Challis, Idaho. Lobbyist — Ted C. Springer, Idaho Falls, Idaho. Filed 11/14/80. Legislative interest — "Pacific Northwest Power Planning Conservation Act (S 885 and HR 8157)."

STANDARD OIL CO., Cleveland, Ohio. Lobbyist — Steve A. Villas, Washington, D.C. Filed 11/18/80. Legislative interest — "General legislative matters pertaining to the interests of the company respecting petroleum production, refining and distribution, petrochemicals and coal."

STANDARD & POOR'S CORP., New York, N.Y. Lobbyist — Booth & Baron, New York, N.Y. Filed 11/13/80. Legislative interest — "General legislative focus on bills, resolutions, etc., affecting the investment advisory industry. Current specific legislative interests are S 658 and S 3023, amendments to the U.S. Bankruptcy Code."

SOUTHERN PACIFIC COMMUNICATIONS CO., Burlingame, Calif. Filed for self 11/17/80. Legislative interest — "Legislation affecting common carrier communications (HR 6121, HR 2827, S 611 and S 622)." Lobbyist — Jeanne P. Kowalski, Washington, D.C.

TARGET INC., San Ramon, Calif. Lobbyist — Neal Blair, McLean, Va. Filed 11/20/80. Legislative interest — "...to seek the limitation of federal regulation of newsletters and media commentaries."

TIGER INTERNATIONAL INC., Los Angeles, Calif. Lobbyist — Gary B. Reimer, Washington, D.C. Filed 11/10/80. Legislative interest — "...in general, legislation affecting transportation by rail, truck, and air is of interest as well as some legislation relating to corporation taxes ... Extension of Aviation Taxes (HR 6571); Railroad Rehabilitaion (S 2486); Coal Slurry Pipeline (HR 4370); Airport and Airway Development Act (S 1648)."

TOSCO CORP., Los Angeles, Calif. Lobbyist — Sisk, Foley, Hultin & Driver, Washington, D.C. Filed 11/7/80. Legislative interest — "In support of legislation providing reasonable and effective incentives for synthetic fuels development, energy impact assistance and energy tax laws."

TOYOTA MOTOR SALES U.S.A. INC., Torrance, Calif. Lobbyist — Daniel J. Edelman Inc., Washington, D.C. Filed 11/21/80. Legislative interest — "Legislation concerning Japanese automotive imports (H J Res 598 and S J Res 193)."

TRANSAMERICA LIFE INSURANCE & ANNUITY CO. & OCCIDENTAL LIFE INSURANCE CO., Los Angeles,

Calif. Lobbyist — McCandless & Barrett, Washington, D.C. Filed 11/4/80. Legislative interest — "To obtian equitable treatment of client regarding any legislation resulting from hearings in House Subcommitte on Government Information and Individual Rights."

WASHINGTON GAS LIGHT CO., Washington, D.C. Filed for self 11/26/80. Legislative interest — "General legislation affecting Washington Gas Light Company and the natural gas industry." Lobbyist — Charles G. Krautler, Washington, D.C.

Labor Groups

ALL UNIONS COMMITTEE TO SHORTEN THE WORK WEEK, Detroit, Mich. Filed for self 11/6/80. Legislative interest — "...all statutes and bills related to the length of the work week." Lobbyists — Fred Gaboury and Frank Runnels, Detroit, Mich.

BROTHERHOOD OF RAILWAY, AIRLINE & STEAMSHIP CLERKS, FREIGHT HANDLERS, EXPRESS & STATION EMPLOYEES, Rockville, Md. Filed for self 11/3/80. Legislative interest — "...all legislation affecting labor, especially railroad and airline labor." Lobbyists — C.R. Duggan and Donald R. Sweitzer, Washington, D.C.

INTERNATIONAL LONGSHOREMEN'S & WAREHOUSEMEN'S UNION, San Francisco, Calif. Filed for self 11/10/80. Legislative interest — "Legislative issues affecting unions and their members, particularly with respect to the maritime and transportation industries." Lobbyist — Michael R. Lewis, Washington, D.C.

TEAMSTER LOCAL 959 EMPLOYEE PENSION TRUST, Anchorage, Alaska. Lobbyist — Birch, Horton, Bittner & Monroe, Washington, D.C. Filed 11/7/80. Legislative interest — "Interior Appropriations bill; Indian Health Service."

State and Local Governments

GUAM GROWTH COUNCIL, Agana, Guam. Lobbyist — Cook, Purcell, Hansen & Henderson, Washington, D.C. Filed 11/7/80. Legislative interest — "Visa waiver legislation (S 2727) ... State Department supplemental authorization bill, visa waiver provision amendment."

Trade Associations

AMERICAN GAS ASSOCIATION, Arlington, Va. Filed for self 11/17/80. Legislative interest — "Cogeneration (S 2470); Conservation/RCS Program (HR 7262, S 2719, S 932, S 2862); Department of Energy Research and Development Budget (HR 7724, HR 7449, S 2332); Lobby Reform Legislation; Regulatory Reform (HR 1776, S 262); Superfund Legislation (S 1480); Helium Legislation (HR 2523); Safe Drinking Water Act Amendments (S 4509); Underground Storage Legislation (HR 6094); Outdoor Lighting Legislation (HR 4576); Methane Fleet Vehicle Legislation (HR 6889)." Lobbyists — James W. McCarthy and C. Kyle Simpson, Arlington, Va.

AMERICAN HEALTH PLANNING ASSOCIATION, Washington, D.C. Filed for self 11/13/80. Legislative interest — "Health Planning and Resources Development Act of 1974." Lobbyists — Deborah M. Schechter and Ann C. Scheiner, Washington, D.C.

COUNSELORS FOR MANAGEMENT INC., Washington, D.C. Filed for self 11/3/80. Legislative interest — "Deletion of zinc from S 1480." Lobbyist — Janice C. Lipsen, Washington, D.C.

COUNCIL FOR AMERICAN PRIVATE EDUCATION, Washington, D.C. Lobbyist — Shaw, Pittman, Potts & Trowbridge, Washington, D.C. Filed 11/17/80 and 11/18/80. Legislative interest — "Repeal of Dornan Amendment to current Department of Treasury Appropriation legislation and/or continuing resolution."

THE ESOP ASSOCIATION OF AMERICA, San Francisco, Calif. Lobbyist — Sheldon I. London, Washington, D.C. Filed 11/7/80. Legislative interest — "Supporting legislation to

encourage the establishment and growth of employee stock ownership plans, particularly in the areas of tax pension law and access to capital credit (S 2982)."

FLEXIBLE PACKAGING ASSOCIATION, Washington, D.C. Filed for self 11/5/80. Legislative interest — "General legislation of interest to or affecting the flexible packaging industry." Lobbyist — Richard A. Lillquist, Washington, D.C.

HELICOPTER ASSOCIATION OF AMERICA INC., Washington, D.C. Filed for self 11/5/80. Legislative interest — "ADAP (HR 6721, S 1649); Union Station (HR 3927); Contracting out (HR 4717); Airway Trust Fund Amendments (HR 7477); Air Safety Violations Penalties (HR 4788); Extension of Airport and Airway Trust Fund Taxes (HR 6571); other legislation which may substantially impact the helicopter industry." Lobbyist — Robert A. Richardson, Washington, D.C.

KOREA LEATHER & FUR EXPORTER'S ASSOCIATION, Washington, D.C. Lobbyist — Daniels, Houlihan & Palmeter, Washington, D.C. Filed 11/4/80. Legislative interest — "To oppose adoption of S Con Res and H Con Res which would have disapproved of the president's determination not to impose import restrictions on leather wearing apparel."

NATIONAL ASSOCIATION OF MANUFACTURERS, Washington, D.C. Filed for self 11/3/80. Legislative interest — "Environmental legislation, Enviromental Emergency Response Act, S 1480, Hazardous Waste Containment Act, HR 7020." Lobbyist — Mark N. Griffiths, Washington, D.C.

NATIONAL ASSOCIATION OF POLICE ORGANIZATIONS, Sacramento, Calif. Lobbyist — Seifman & Lechner, Washington, D.C. Filed 11/20/80. Legislative interest — "HR 2141, amendment of PSOB; HR 2748, Federal Hour Reduction; HR 6525, PERISA."

NATIONAL ASSOCIATION OF RETAIL DRUGGISTS, Washington, D.C. Filed for self 11/13/80. Legislative interest — "Professional and business interests of independent retail druggists. Specific interests include national health insurance, drug regulation reform legislation, and small business legislation." Lobbyist — John M. Rector, Washington, D.C.

NATIONAL BUSINESS AIRCRAFT ASSOCIATION, Washington, D.C. Lobbyist — Thevenot, Murray & Scheer, Washington, D.C. Filed 11/12/80. Legislative interest — "...Specifically legislation affecting general aviation with particular emphasis on taxes, airport and airways development and utilization and regulation."

TRAVEL INDUSTRY ASSOCIATION OF AMERICA, Washington, D.C. Filed for self 11/4/80. Legislative interest — "...S 1097 and HR 7321, the National Tourism Policy Act." Lobbyists — Paul A. Equale, J. William Hudson, Washington, D.C.

Miscellaneous

DONALD C. EVANS, Sarasota, Fla. Filed for self 11/20/80. Legislative interest — "None presently (bills relating to private investigation field)."

GREGORY W. FRAZIER, Englewood, Colo. Filed for self 11/17/80. Legislative interest — "Ongoing activities of a various nature related to social and economic self-sufficiency of potential corporations and business interests. Legislation targeted to assist or hinder groups identified [above]."

WASHINGTON OFFICE OF AFRICA, Washington, D.C. Lobbyist — Jean Sindab, Washington, D.C. Filed 11/5/80. Legislative interest — "Legislation concerning U.S. policy towards southern Africa."

DAVID A. WITTS, Dallas, Texas. Lobbyist — Hill and Knowlton Inc., New York, N.Y. Filed 11/14/80. Legislative interest — "...Matters relating to the business interests of the firms employing Hill and Knowlton Inc...."

December 1980 Registrations

Citizens' Groups

SIERRA CLUB, San Francisco, Calif. Filed for self 12/18/80. Legislative interest — "General legislative interest in all land, water and air pollution legislation...." Lobbyist — Karen A. Doherty, New York, N.Y.

WOMEN'S EQUITY ACTION LEAGUE, Washington, D.C. Filed for self 12/17/80. Legislative interest — "...statutes and bills affecting women." Lobbyist — Patricia Blau Reuss, Washington, D.C.

Corporations and Businesses

AGRI-BUSINESS INC., Salina, Kan. Lobbyist — Martin Ryan Haley & Associates Inc., Washington, D.C. Filed 12/8/80. Legislative interest — not specified.

AVON PRODUCTS INC., New York, N.Y. Lobbyist — Janice Zarro, New York, N.Y. Filed 12/19/80. Legislative interest — "All legislation related to employer's business including government regulation of the manufacture and distribution of products, the environment, and taxation...."

BENEFICIAL MANAGEMENT CORP., Morristown, N.J. Lobbyist — Craig Hackler, Washington, D.C. Filed 12/16/80. Legislative interest — "Federal usury legislation."

BOWATER NORTH AMERICA CORP., Old Greenwich, Conn. Lobbyist — Lord, Day & Lord, New York, N.Y. Filed 12/12/80. Legislative interest — "Possible changes in United States taxation of foreign investment in United States real property."

CONTINENTAL MATERIALS CORP., Chicago, Ill. Lobbyist — The Keefe Co., Washington, D.C. Filed 12/10/80. Legislative interest — "General legislative interest impacting precious metals mining."

ENTEX INC., Houston, Texas. Lobbyist — Cogeneration Coalition Inc., Washington, D.C. Filed 12/3/80. Legislative interest — "...the provision of necessary financial or tax incentives for cogeneration, and the removal of federal barriers to the development of cogeneration."

KONA COAST CO., Los Angeles, Calif. Lobbyist — Latham, Watkins & Hills, Washington, D.C. Filed 12/8/80. Legislative interest — "To clarify the authority of the Secretary of the Interior to receive surplus lands from the General Services Administration to use in an exchange with the owners of lands authorized to be converted into a park pursuant to the Omnibus National Parks and Recreation Act, PL 95-625; Interior Appropriations bill HR 7724."

KORF INDUSTRIES INC., Charlotte, N.C. Filed for self 12/4/80. Legislative interest — "Energy — incremental pricing under the Natural Gas Policy Act of 1976. Tax — Capital Cost Recovery Act. Labor — unemployment compensation. Government relations — lobby law reforms. Trade — export trading companies. Commerce — trigger pricing mechanism." Lobbyist — Margaret Renken Hudson, Washington, D.C.

MERRILL LYNCH & CO. INC., New York, N.Y. Lobbyist — Allan L. Sher, Washington, D.C. Filed 12/2/80. Legislative interest — "Banking and finance legislation."

MUSTANG FUEL CORP., Oklahoma City, Okla. Lobbyist — Williams & Jensen, Washington, D.C. Filed 12/21/80. Legislative interest — "Legislation regarding energy investment tax credits."

OCEAN SPRAY CRANBERRIES INC., Plymouth, Mass. Lobbyist — Schlossberg-Cassidy & Associates Inc., Washington, D.C. Filed 12/4/80. Legislative interest — "Laws and regulations pertaining to food labeling."

POTLATCH CORP., Washington, D.C. Lobbyist — Cogeneration Coalition Inc., Washington, D.C. Filed 12/3/80. Legislative interest — "...the provision of necessary financial or tax incentives for cogeneration, and the removal of federal barriers to the development of cogeneration."

RASCH ELEKTRONIK, Rodermark, West Germany. Lobbyist — Paul M. Tendler, Washington, D.C. Filed 12/3/80. Legislative interest — "Legislation regarding trade with European countries."

RONAN TELEPHONE CO., Ronan, Mont. Lobbyist — Preston, Thorgrimson, Ellis & Holman, Washington, D.C. Filed 12/9/80. Legislative interest — "Possible legislative solution to dispute over compliance with section 46 (f) of Internal Revenue Code. HR 6806 and other miscellaneous tax bills."

STICHTING PHILIPS PENSIOENFONDS A AND B, Eindhoven, The Netherlands. Lobbyist — Craig Hackler, Washington, D.C. Filed 12/19/80. Legislative interest — "Exemption from U.S. taxation of foreign pension plans."

TENNECO OIL CO., Houston, Texas. Lobbyist — Davis, Graham & Stubbs, Denver, Colo., and Washington, D.C. Filed 12/1/80. Legislative interest — "Advocating passage of a private bill reinstating a federal oil and gas lease."

TRW INC., Cleveland, Ohio. Filed for self 12/19/80. Legislative interest — "General legislation of broad interest to TRW Inc., including that related to taxes, pension, health insurance, trade, patent, etc." Lobbyist — John J. Castellani, Washington, D.C.

VISA U.S.A. INC., San Mateo, Calif. Filed for self 12/10/80. Legislative interest — "...legislation and regulations affecting bank cards." Lobbyist — Beverly L. Hines, Washington, D.C.

Trade Associations

AMERICAN BANKERS ASSOCIATION, Washington, D.C. Lobbyist — Lloyd G. Ator Jr., Silver Spring, Md. Filed 12/12/80. Legislative interest — "Tax legislation affecting the banking industry."

AMERICAN CHIROPRACTIC ASSOCIATION, Des Moines, Iowa. Filed for self 12/3/80. Legislative interest — "Any legislation affecting the interests of the American Chiropractic Association including supporting portions of HR 3990 — Medicare and Medicaid Amendments of 1980; HR 7765 — Omnibus Reconciliation Act of 1980; HR 1242 — inclusion of chiropractic care under CHAMPUS." Lobbyist — David S. O'Bryon, Washington, D.C.

AMERICAN COUNCIL OF LIFE INSURANCE INC., Washington, D.C. Filed for self 12/9/80. Legislative interest — "Proposed legislation which would affect the life insurance industry." Lobbyists — Marvin Collins, Phyllis H. Gerstell and Julia J. Norrell, Washington, D.C.

AMERICAN FROZEN FOOD INSTITUTE, McLean, Va. Filed for self 12/10/80. Legislative interest — "...proposed measures particularly affecting the frozen food industry, such as: ...the Agricultural Marketing and Bargaining Act, HR 3535; Clean Water Act Amendments, HR 6667; Food Labeling Legislation, S 1651, S 1652." Lobbyist — Susan A. Boolukos, McLean, Va.

AMERICAN PAPER INSTITUTE INC., New York, N.Y. Filed for self 12/21/80. Legislative interest — "Legislative interests are those affecting the pulp, paper and paperboard industry, its operation, practices and properties; tax legislation and environmental legislation — air, water and energy; and legislation to amend Federal Food Drug and Cosmetic Act." Lobbyist — Frederick S. Benson III, Washington, D.C.

AMERICAN PSYCHOANALYTIC ASSOCIATION, New York, N.Y. Lobbyist — Kaye, Scholar, Fierman, Hays & Handler, Washington, D.C. Filed 12/1/80. Legislative interest — "General in nature of legislative proposals affecting the practice of psychoanalysis and health."

THE FERTILIZER INSTITUTE, Washington, D.C. Filed for self 12/5/80. Legislative interest — "...hazardous substances ... inactive waste disposal sites ... Clean Water Act ... standby gasoline rationing authority ... railroad deregulation ... freight car duty suspension ... Resource Conservation and Recovery Act ... Motor Carrier Reform Act ... truck safety ... non-fuels minerals ... incremental pricing ... Natural Gas Policy Act ... agricultural issues...." Lobbyist — David E. Whitten, Washington, D.C.

INTERNATIONAL ASSOCIATION OF AMUSEMENT PARKS AND ATTRACTIONS, North Riverside, Ill. Filed for self 12/19/80. Legislative interest — "Labor, energy, tourism, safety, tax, and other matters involving or affecting the amusement industry." Lobbyist — John R. Graff, Washington, D.C.

INTERNATIONAL COMMUNICATIONS ASSOCIATION, Houston, Texas. Lobbyist — Peabody, Rivlin, Lambert & Meyers, Washington, D.C. Filed 12/8/80. Legislative interest — "HR 3333, S 6121, S 611, S 622, S 2827. In favor of modifications to such bills if they are to be enacted."

NATIONAL ASSOCIATION OF ROYALTY OWNERS INC., Ada, Okla. Lobbyist — Pierson, Ball & Dowd, Washington, D.C. Filed 12/8/80. Legislative interest — "(a) Support Boren-Dole amendment to Budget Reconciliation affecting windfall profits tax (HR 3919). (b) Generally participate in legislative process on windfall profits tax and other legislation affecting ... Association...."

OKLAHOMA MINERAL OWNERS AND SURFACE OWNERS ASSOCIATION, Sayre, Okla. Lobbyist — Pierson, Ball & Dowd, Washington, D.C. Filed 12/8/80. Legislative interest — "(a) Support Boren-Dole amendment to Budget Reconciliation affecting windfall profits tax (HR 3919). (b) Generally participate in legislative process on windfall profits tax and other legislation affecting ... Association...."

OPERATION INDEPENDENCE, Austin, Texas. Lobbyist — Martin Ryan Haley and Associates, Washington, D.C. Filed 12/21/80. Legislative interest — "Legislation of interest to the malt beverage industry."

PROFESSIONAL INSURANCE AGENTS, Washington, D.C. Filed for self 12/30/80. Legislative interest — "...insurance matters and any bills related to the welfare of local fire and casualty insurance agents." Lobbyist — Richard M. Charlton, Washington, D.C.

SHEET METAL AND AIR CONDITIONING CONTRACTORS' NATIONAL ASSOCIATION INC., Vienna, Va. Filed for self 12/12/80. Legislative interest — "...includes any and all issues directly or indirectly affecting the sheet metal and air conditioning trade in particular, and the construction industry in general." Lobbyist — Vincent R. Sandusky, Vienna, Va.

TRAVEL INDUSTRY ASSOCIATION OF AMERICA, Washington, D.C. Filed for self 12/8/80. Legislative interest — "A continued interest is maintained in legislation affecting the welfare of the travel industry." Lobbyists — Paul A. Equale, J. William Hudson, Washington, D.C.

Miscellaneous

PRIEST & FINE INC., Washington, D.C. Filed for self 12/31/80. Legislative interest — "The general legislative interest will vary, depending on the client's interest but will be mainly in tax area." Lobbyist — Daniel B. Priest, Washington, D.C.

GEORGE C. STEINER, Silver Spring, Md. Filed for self 12/30.80. Legislative interest — "At this date none specific."

January 1981 Registrations

Citizens' Groups

BARRIER ISLANDS COALITION, New York, N.Y. Filed for self 1/20/81. Legislative interest — "...legislation to protect barrier islands ... HR 5891 and S 2686...."

CHRISTIAN VOICE MORAL GOVERNMENT FUND, Washington, D.C. Filed for self 1/15/81. Legislative interest — "For school prayer. Against IRS attack on private schools. Against national gay rights legislation." Lobbyist — L. Philip Sheldon Jr., Washington, D.C.

CITIZENS FOR TAX JUSTICE, Washington, D.C. Filed for self 1/12/81. Legislative interest — "General legislation con-

cerning the Internal Revenue Code and federal tax policy." Lobbyist — Robert S. McIntyre, Washington, D.C.

FIVE TRIBES CONFEDERACY OF NORTH CENTRAL OKLA., Ponca City, Okla. Lobbyist — Abourezk, Shack & Mendenhall, Washington, D.C. Filed 1/29/81. Legislative interest — "Matters relating to Indian Affairs."

NATIONAL ENERGY EFFICIENCY COALITION, Washington, D.C. Filed for self 1/19/81. Legislative interest — "Energy efficiency investment incentives, including residential and commercial tax credits, solar and energy conservation bank." Lobbyists — Jerry Brady and David Hurd Moulton, Washington, D.C.

NATIONAL LEGAL AID & DEFENDER ASSOCIATION, Washington, D.C. Filed for self 1/28/81. Legislative interest — "Reauthorization of the Legal Services Corporation ... establishment of a National Center for Defense Services...." Lobbyist — Julie Clark, Washington, D.C.

NATIONAL ORGANIZATION FOR THE REFORM OF MARIJUANA LAWS, Washington, D.C. Filed for self 1/31/81. Legislative interest — "NORML favors the elimination of criminal penalties for marijuana smoking under the Controlled Substances Act of 1970." Lobbyists — George L. Farnham, James N. Hall, and Kevin B. Zeese.

NATIONAL RIFLE ASSOCIATION OF AMERICA, Washington, D.C. Filed for self 1/7/81. Legislative interest — "...all aspects of the acquisition, possession, and use of firearms and ammunition, as well as legislation relating to hunting and wildlife conservation." Lobbyist — Susan M. Rogers, Washington, D.C.

NAVAJO NATION, Window Rock, Ariz. Lobbyist — Hill and Knowlton Inc., New York City. Filed 1/10/81. Legislative interest — unspecified.

SIERRA CLUB, San Francisco, Calif. Filed for self 1/16/81. Legislative interest — "general pollution legislation; specifically reauthorization of the Clean Air Act (PL 95-95)." Lobbyist — David McLane Gardiner, Washington, D.C.

SOLAR LOBBY, Washington, D.C. Filed for self 1/23/81. Legislative interest — "...renewable energy and energy conservation legislation." Lobbyist — Samuel E. Enfield, Washington, D.C.

THE WILDLIFE LEGISLATIVE FUND OF AMERICA, Columbus, Ohio. Lobbyist — Stephen S. Boynton, Arlington,Va. Filed 1/12/81. Legislative interest — "Alaska Lands legislation; anti-trapping proposals, RARE II proposals, fur seal treaty."

Corporations and Businesses

AETNA LIFE & CASUALTY, Hartford, Conn. Lobbyist — Nossaman, Krueger & Marsh, Washington, D.C. Filed 1/13/81. Legislative interest — "Taxation, fringe benefits, insurance and related areas."

ASARCO INC., New York, N.Y. Filed for self 1/7/81. Legislative interest — "Measures affecting production of nonferrous metals and minerals and associated products...." Lobbyist — Robert J. Muth, New York, N.Y.

ASHLAND OIL INC., Ashland, Ky. Filed for self 1/28/81. Legislative interest — "All legislation concerning the petroleum industry, including but not limited to energy, taxes, coal, mining, marine transportation, synthetic fuels, and environment." Lobbyist — Doris J. Dewton, Washington, D.C.

BECHTEL FINANCING SERVICES INC., Washington, D.C. Lobbyist — Charles W. Snyder, Bethesda, Md. Filed 1/22/81. Legislative interest — "...all matters which may be of special interest to an international engineering and construction enterprise."

BLUE CROSS AND BLUE SHIELD ASSOCIATIONS, Washington, D.C. Filed for self 1/8/81, 1/28/81. Legislative interest — "Health legislation." Lobbyists — James D. Isbister, Stanley B. Jones, Mary Nell Lehnhard, and Molly J. Pierce, Washington, D.C.

BLUE RIBBON SPORTS INC., Beaverton, Ore. Lobbyist — David H. Smith, Washington, D.C. Filed 1/9/81. Legislative

interest — "...international trade; customs; and the footwear industry."

BULOVA SYSTEMS & INSTRUMENTS CORP., Valley Stream, N.Y. Lobbyist—Cook, Purcell, Hanson & Henderson, Washington, D.C. Filed 1/15/81. Legislative interest — "...Appropriations for military equipment and procurement."

BURLINGTON INDUSTRIES INC., Washington, D.C. Filed for self 1/8/81. Legislative interest — "Legislation affecting, or of interest to, the textile industry...." Lobbyist — Donna Lee McGee, Washington, D.C.

CHEVRON U.S.A. INC., Washington, D.C. Filed for self 1/10/81. Legislative interest — "Legislation affecting Chevron U.S.A. Inc.; its parent, Standard Oil Company of California; and other subsidiaries of Standard Oil Company of California." Lobbyist — Phil M. Bitter, Washington, D.C.

THE CLEVELAND ELECTRIC ILLUMINATING CO., Cleveland, Ohio. Filed for self 1/10/81. Legislative interest — "Legislation affecting privately-owned utilities." Lobbyist — James R. Smircina, Cleveland, Ohio.

DATAPOINT CORP., San Antonio, Texas. Lobbyists — Gerard L. Cullen, San Antonio, Texas; Sharon L. Messinger, Arlington, Va. Filed 1/12/81. Legislative interest — "To urge that proposed communications legislation (HR 6121 and S 2827) insure continued competition in the data processing field."

ELI LILLY INC., Indianapolis, Ind. Lobbyist — Crowell & Moring, Washington, D.C. Filed 1/16/81. Legislative interest — "Legislation affecting product liablility tort rules and product liability insurance."

ENI COMPANIES, Belleview, Wash. Lobbyist — Morris J. Amitay, Washington, D.C. Filed 1/12/81. Legislative interest — "Legislation pertaining to energy with emphasis on tax laws affecting oil and gas."

FORD MOTOR CO., Dearborn, Mich. Filed for self 1/13/81. Legislative interest — "...federal laws, policies and trends and proposed legislation and regulations in relation to the interests of the Company...." Lobbyist — J. Barry Coughlin, Washington, D.C.

HALEM INDUSTRIES INC., Cocoa, Fla. Filed for self 1/19/81. Legislative interest — unspecified. Lobbyist — Beverly Halem, Cocoa, Fla.

HAMILTON TECHNOLOGY INC., Lancaster, Pa. Lobbyist — Cook, Purcell, Hansen & Henderson, Washington, D.C. Filed 1/15/81. Legislative interest — "...Appropriations for military equipment and procurement."

HOME OWNERS WARRANTY CORP., Washington, D.C. Lobbyist — Brownstein, Zeidman and Schomer, Washington, D.C. Filed 1/12/81. Legislative interest — "Product Liability Risk Retention Act, HR 6152 and related legislation."

INTERNATIONAL TELEPHONE AND TELEGRAPH CORP., New York, N.Y. Filed for self 1/9/81. Legislative interest — "...matters which affect multi-product and services international company." Lobbyist — Christine M. Bangert, Washington, D.C.

KELLOGG CO., Battle Creek, Mich. Lobbyist — Williams & Jensen, Washington, D.C. Filed 1/22/81. Legislative interest — "...antitrust legislation."

LONG ISLAND LIGHTING CO., Mineola, N.Y. Filed for self 1/15/81. Legislative interest — "...all legislation directly or indirectly affecting the operations of a regulated public utility." Lobbyist — William A. Edwards, Mineola, N.Y.

THE LTV CORP., Dallas, Texas. Filed for self 1/16/81. Legislative interest — "...legislation relating to steel and ferrous metal materials and fabrications, meats and foods, and aerospace and ground transportation vehicles and equipment, including energy, tax, procurement and regulatory matters." Lobbyist — John K. Meagher, Washington, D.C.

METROPOLITAN WATER DISTRICT OF SOUTHERN CALIFORNIA, Los Angeles, Calif. Lobbyist — Robert P. Will, Washington, D.C. Filed 1/12/81. Legislative interest — "All matters relating to water and energy within California and the Colorado River Basin."

NATIONAL BANK OF ALASKA, Anchorage, Alaska. Lobbyist — Metzger, Shadyac & Schwarz, Washington, D.C. Filed

1/27/81. Legislative interest — "...to advise the Bank regarding the application of 12 U.S.C. section 29 to the Bank's assets...."

NATIONAL BANK OF DETROIT, Detroit, Mich. Lobbyist — Stuart A. Lewis, Washington, D.C. Filed 1/19/81. Legislative interest — "Financial legislation HR 2255, HR 5625."

NEW YORK LIFE INSURANCE CO., New York, N.Y. Lobbyist — Nossaman, Krueger & Marsh, Washington, D.C. Filed 1/13/81. Legislative interest — "Legislation affecting life insurance companies."

NORTHROP CORP., Arlington, Va. Lobbyist — Morris J. Amitay, Washington, D.C. Filed 1/12/81. Legislative interest — "Defense authorization and appropriations bills and budgetary legislation affecting procurement of Northrop products."

PARTNERSHIP PLACEMENTS INC., Los Angeles, Calif. Lobbyist — Barnett, Alagia & Carey, Washington, D.C. Filed 1/16/81. Legislative interest — "Tax reform legislation ... securities legislation ... particularly any legislation pertaining to Rule 146 of the Securities Act of 1933."

PETROLEUM HEAT AND POWER CO., Philadelphia, Pa. Lobbyist — Barnett, Alagia & Carey, Washington, D.C. Filed 1/16/81. Legislative interest — "Energy matters, particularly those affecting small oil distribution companies."

PHILADELPHIA GAS WORKS, Philadelphia, Pa. Lobbyist — Barnett, Alagia & Carey, Washington, D.C. Filed 1/16/81. Legislative interest — "Energy legislation, specifically that affecting natural gas, Natural Gas Policy Act, incremental pricing sections and amendments thereto; legislative efforts to provide energy assistance to the poor; and, disposition of energy trust fund monies."

PHILADELPHIA STOCK EXCHANGE, Philadelphia, Pa. Lobbyist — Barnett, Alagia & Carey, Washington, D.C. Filed 1/16/81. Legislative interest — "Securities legislation, particularly any and all legislative activity pertaining to trading in options."

PHILLIPS PETROLEUM CO., Bartlesville, Okla. Lobbyist — Covington & Burling, Washington, D.C. Filed 1/9/81. Legislative interest — "Legislation relating to excise taxes on crude oil."

PHILLIPS PETROLEUM CO., Bartlesville, Okla. Filed for self 1/14/81. Legislative interest — "Legislation affecting integrated oil, gas, chemicals and energy industries." Lobbyists — Don R. Duncan and Richard F. Phillips, Washington, D.C.

PHOENIX MUTUAL LIFE INSURANCE CO., Hartford, Conn. Lobbyist — Nossaman, Krueger & Marsh, Washington, D.C. Filed 1/13/81. Legislative interest — "Legislation affecting life insurance companies."

PUBLIC SERVICE CO. OF NEW HAMPSHIRE, Manchester, N.H. Lobbyist — Donald E. Sinville, Manchester, N.H. Filed 1/7/81. Legislative interest — "Legislation affecting electric utilities."

SAFETRAN SYSTEMS CORP., Louisville, Ky. Lobbyist — Arthur E. Cameron, Washington, D.C. Filed 1/18/81. Legislative interest — "In support of federal aid highway legislation, more specifically: 23 U.S.C. 120 (d); energy related traffic control legislation and rail-highway grade crossing legislation."

SCA SERVICES, Boston, Mass. Lobbyist — Mintz, Levin, Cohn, Glovsky and Popeo, Washington, D.C. Filed 1/30/81. Legislative interest — "Legislation concerning hazardous waste and solid waste."

SHAWMUT CORP., Boston, Mass. Lobbyists — Joseph A. Bruno, Cambridge, Mass., John J. Gould, Waltham, Mass. Filed 1/12/81. Legislative interests — "...banking."

SPERRY CORP., Washington, D.C. Filed for self 1/13/81. Legislative interest — "...taxes, communications, agriculture, international affairs, and regulations." Lobbyist — Elisabeth Hanlin, Washington, D.C.

STANDARD OIL CO. OF INDIANA, Chicago, Ill. Lobbyist — Keith A. Pretty, Southfield, Mich. Filed 1/26/81. Legislative interest — "...legislation of concern to the energy industry, general business interests, the environment and the Great Lakes Basin."

ST. GEORGE/HIGHLY CORP., Anchorage, Alaska. Lobbyist — Birch, Horton, Bittner & Monroe, Washington, D.C. Filed 1/10/81. Legislative interest — "Senate fisheries bill."

SUN CO. INC., Radnor, Pa. Filed for self 1/26/81. Legisla-

tive interest — "...Natural gas legislation.... Legislation affecting development of alternative energy resources.... Energy and general business tax reform." Lobbyist — William F. Whitsitt, Washington, D.C.

TARTARIC CHEMICALS CORP., New York, N.Y. Lobbyist — Barnes, Richardson & Colburn, Washington, D.C. Filed 1/14/81. Legislative interest — "Activities supporting legislation to reduce customs tariffs on imports of tartaric chemicals."

TELEPHONE AND DATA SYSTEMS INC., Chicago, Ill. Lobbyist — Taft, Stettinius & Hollister, Cincinnati, Ohio. Filed 1/10/81. Legislative interest — "To advise on legislative matters relating to amendments of Federal Communications Commission Act affecting rural telephone exchanges."

TRW INC., Cleveland, Ohio. Filed for self 1/27/81. Legislative interest — "General legislation of interest to TRW Inc., including aerospace, electronics, transportation, energy, foreign trade ... taxes, pension, health insurance, patent...." Lobbyists — Laranie Faith McNamara, Brenda J. Gore, Washington, D.C.

TWENTIETH CENTURY FOX FILM CORP., Los Angeles, Calif. Lobbyist — Tuvin Associates, Washington, D.C. Filed 1/26/81. Legislative interest — "Copyright, telecommunications, international trade."

UNION OIL CO. OF CALIFORNIA, Los Angeles, Calif. Filed for self 1/8/81. Legislative interest — "Legislation affecting the petroleum industry." Lobbyist — Barbara J. Haugh, Washington, D.C.

UTAH INTERNATIONAL INC., San Francisco, Calif. Filed for self 1/23/81. Legislative interest — "Measures affecting mining, oil and gas and land development." Lobbyists — Claudia R. Spady, Barbara W. Steiner, Washington, D.C.

WEST ALABAMA GRAIN PRODUCTS COOPERATIVE INC., Uniontown, Ala. Lobbyist — Martin Ryan Haley & Associates, Washington, D.C. Filed 1/12/81. Legislative interest — "Affairs of legislative interest."

ZALE CORP., Dallas, Texas. Lobbyist — Akin, Gump, Strauss, Hauer & Feld, Washington, D.C. Filed 1/21/81. Legislative interest — "Hearings and any legislation relating to amendments to the Securities Exchange Act of 1934...."

Labor Groups

AMERICAN FEDERATION OF TEACHERS, Washington, D.C. Filed for self 1/8/81. Legislative interest — "All matters relating to the welfare of the country generally, especially those relating to teachers and education." Lobbyist — Judy Bardacke, Washington, D.C.

PROFESSIONAL AIR TRAFFIC CONTROLLERS ORGANIZATION, Washington, D.C. Filed for self 1/23/81. Legislative interest — "...revision of the Hatch Act; restoration of 'second career' training for Air Traffic Controllers and the introduction of an 'omnibus bill' on behalf of Air Traffic Controllers...." Lobbyist — Patrick L. Doyle, Washington, D.C.

TEAMSTERS FOR A DEMOCRATIC UNION, Washington, D.C. Filed for self 1/9/81. Legislative interest — "Enactment of truck safety, pension reform, and labor reform legislation (e.g., S 1390, HR 4971, S 1076, HR 3904)." Lobbyist — Michael J. Goldberg, Washington, D.C.

Trade Associations

AD HOC GROUP ON LIFE INSURANCE COMPANY TAXATION OF PENSION FUNDS, Washington, D.C. Lobbyist — Groom and Nordberg, Washington, D.C. Filed 1/9/81. Legislative interest — "Federal legislation affecting Title 26 of U.S.C. and Title 29 of the U.S.C."

THE AMERICAN ALLIANCE OF SMALL BUSINESSES, Dallas, Texas. Filed for self 1/27/81. Legislative interest — "To lobby for or against legislation affecting small businesses...." Lobbyist — Susan Drew Hutcheson, Dallas, Texas.

AMERICAN HOSPITAL ASSOCIATION, Chicago, Ill. Filed for self 1/16/81. Legislative interest — "...all legislation

which may affect the ability of hospitals to render good care or which may affect the health care of the American people." Lobbyist — Dwight M. Geduldig, Washington, D.C.

AMERICAN INSTITUTE OF ARCHITECTS, Washington, D.C. Filed for self 1/13/81. Legislative interest — "Issues of interest to the architectural profession...." Lobbyists — Elizabeth Prewitt Chalmers, Sharon Allen Currens and Alan Stover, Washington, D.C.

AMERICAN INSURANCE ASSOCIATION, Washington, D.C. Filed for self 1/12/81. Legislative interest — "...property/casualty insurance and suretyship, together with those matters that will indirectly impact the markets, costs, regulation, etc. of such business." Lobbyist — Penelope S. Farthing, Washington, D.C.

AMERICAN MEAT INSTITUTE, Washington, D.C. Filed for self 1/12/81. Legislative interest — "Legislation affecting the food industry in general and particularly the livestock and meat industry." Lobbyist — Marilee Menard, Washington, D.C.

AMERICAN MEDICAL ASSOCIATION, Chicago, Ill. Filed for self 1/19/81. Legislative interest — "...all federal legislation of a health or medical nature." Lobbyist — Carla Neuschel, Washington, D.C.

AMERICAN MINING CONGRESS, Washington, D.C. Filed for self 1/15/81. Legislative interest — "Measures affecting mining such as income taxation, social security, mine safety, monetary policy, public lands, stockpiling, environmental quality control, etc." Lobbyist — Thomas C. Nelson, Washington, D.C.

AMERICAN SOCIETY OF INTERNAL MEDICINE, Washington, D.C. Filed for self 1/12/81. Legislative interest — "...Medicare/Medicaid, health planning, health manpower, cost containment and related issues." Lobbyist — Richard L. Trachtman, Washington, D.C.

ASPHALT ROOFING MANUFACTURERS ASSOCI-ATION, Washington, D.C. Lobbyist — Cadwalader, Wickersham & Taft, Washington, D.C. Filed 1/31/81. Legislative interest — "Nomination of commissioners to the United States International Trade Commission."

THE ASSOCIATED GENERAL CONTRACTORS OF AMERICA, Washington, D.C. Filed for self 1/16/81. Legislative interest — not specified. Lobbyists — Daniel F. Knise, Mark R. Misiorowski, Gary D. Simms, and Susan Woodard, Washington, D.C.

ASSOCIATED THIRD CLASS MAIL USERS, Washington, D.C. Filed for self 1/13/81. Legislative interest — "All legislation pertaining to postal laws and regulations." Lobbyist — William G. Mallen, Washington, D.C.

ASSOCIATED THIRD CLASS MAIL USERS, Washington, D.C. Lobbyist — J. Edward Day (U.S. Postmaster General, 1961-63), Washington, D.C. Filed 1/19/81. Legislative interest — "Any legislation relating to postal matters and to business users of the mail and mail advertisers."

ASSOCIATION FOR THE ADVANCEMENT OF PSY-CHOLOGY, Washington, D.C. Filed for self 1/19/81. Legislative interest — "All legislation concerning psychology." Lobbyists — Sarah Wells Duffy, Clarence J. Martin, Anne Marie O'Keefe, and Charlotte Voorde, Washington, D.C.

ASSOCIATION OF CALIFORNIA WATER AGEN-CIES, Sacramento, Calif. Lobbyist — Robert P. Will, Washington, D.C. Filed 1/12/81. Legislative interest — "All matters relating to water and energy within California."

AUTOMOBILE IMPORTERS OF AMERICA INC., Arlington, Va. Lobbyist — Busby, Rehm and Leonard, Washington, D.C. Filed 1/15/81. Legislative interest — "Legislation affecting importation, distribution, and sale of foreign automobiles."

THE BUSINESS ROUNDTABLE, New York, N.Y. Filed for self 1/15/81. Legislative interest — "Legislative matters, generally, which may affect business and industry operations — including ... the production and utilization of energy, and proposals in the fields of taxation and antitrust...." Lobbyist — David R. Toll, Washington, D.C.

CIGAR ASSOCIATION OF AMERICA INC., Washington, D.C. Lobbyist — Charls E. Walker Associates Inc., Washing-

ton, D.C. Filed 1/12/81. Legislative interest — "...matters relating to changes in the excise tax on cigars."

CONFERENCE OF STATE BANK SUPERVISORS, Washington, D.C. Filed for self 1/14/81. Legislative interest — "Legislation affecting state banking segment of the dual banking system." Lobbyist — Keith H. Ellis, Washington, D.C.

COUNCIL ON FOUNDATIONS INC., Washington, D.C. Lobbyist — Caplin & Drysdale, Washington, D.C. Filed 1/14/81. Legislative interest — "Support adjustment of private foundation distribution rules to permit appropriate defenses against inflation."

COUNCIL OF POLLUTION CONTROL FINANCING AGENCIES, Washington, D.C. Lobbyist — Linton, Mields, Reisler & Cottone, Ltd., Washington, D.C. Filed 1/31/81. Legislative interest — not specified.

DIVIDEND SUPPORT GROUP, Minneapolis, Minn. Lobbyist — Nossaman, Krueger & Marsh, Washington, D.C. Filed 1/13/81. Legislative interest — "Supporting enactment of legislation amending the Life Insurance Company Tax Act concerning dividends of subsidiaries."

ELECTRONIC INDUSTRIES ASSOCIATION, Washington, D.C. Lobbyist — J. Edward Day, Washington, D.C. Filed 1/24/81. Legislative interest — "Any legislation affecting manufacturers of consumer electronics products including consumer legislation, legislation relating to advertising and trade legislation."

THE FARMERS EDUCATIONAL AND CO-OPERA-TIVE UNION OF AMERICA (NATIONAL FARMERS UNION), Denver. Colo. Filed for self 1/20/81. Legislative interest — "...American agriculture...." Lobbyist — Paul R. Sacia, Washington, D.C.

HEALTH INSURANCE ASSOCIATION OF AMER-ICA INC., Washington, D.C. Filed for self 1/16/81. Legislative interest — "All matters pertaining to business of health and accident insurance companies and their policyholders." Lobbyist — Edward A. Lenz, Washington, D.C.

HICKORY ASSOCIATION, Hicksville, N.Y. Lobbyist — Morris J. Amitay, Washington, D.C. Filed 1/12/81. Legislative interest — "Legislation pertaining to travel, tourism, transportation, airline deregulation."

INDEPENDENT REFINERS ASSOCIATION OF AMERICA, Washington, D.C. Lobbyist — Foley, Lardner, Hollabaugh & Jacobs, Washington, D.C. Filed 1/27/81. Legislative interest — "Aspects of legislation generally which may have special impact upon independent refiners, including refining policy, price and allocation controls, import tariffs and fees and import policy, oil and gas development on federal lands, taxation, antitrust and small business legislation."

INSURANCE ASSOCIATION OF CONNECTICUT, Hartford, Conn. Lobbyist — Nossaman, Krueger & Marsh, Washington, D.C. Filed 1/12/81. Legislative interest — "Insurance, taxation and pension legislation."

NATIONAL AGRICULTURAL CHEMICALS ASSO-CIATION, Washington, D.C. Filed for self 1/27/81. Legislative interest — "All legislation affecting pesticides." Lobbyist — Luther W. Shaw, Washington, D.C.

NATIONAL ASSOCIATION OF CREDIT MANAGE-MENT, New York, N.Y. Lobbyist — David Vienna & Associates, Washington, D.C. Filed 1/12/81. Legislative interest — "For revisions of Section 543 and 1103(b) of the Bankruptcy Reform Act of 1978. General interest in issues affecting the extension of commercial credit."

NATIONAL ASSOCIATION OF MANUFACTURERS, Washington, D.C. Filed for self 1/12/81. Legislative interest — "...HR 7291 — Product Liability Act of 1980; HR 6152 — Risk Retention Act; HR 8146 — Federal Supplemental Unemployment Benefits; and HR 4007 — pertains to the repayment of federal loans borrowed by states to meet their unemployment benefit obligations." Lobbyist — Daniel W. Vannoy, Washington, D.C.

NATIONAL ASSOCIATION OF URBAN FLOOD MANAGEMENT AGENCIES, Washington, D.C. Lobbyist — Linton, Mields, Reisler & Cottone Ltd., Washington, D.C. Filed 1/31/81. Legislative interest — not specified.

NATIONAL ASSOCIATION OF WHOLESALER-DISTRIBUTORS, Washington, D.C. Lobbyist — Crowell & Moring, Washington, D.C. Filed 1/16/81. Legislative interest — "Legislation affecting product liability tort rules and product liability insurance."

NATIONAL CABLE TELEVISION ASSOCIATION, Washington, D.C. Filed for self 1/10/81. Legislative interest — "Legislation affecting cable television: specifically S 2827, HR 6121 (Communications Act of 1980)...." Lobbyist — James P. Mooney, Washington, D.C.

NATIONAL COMMITTEE FOR RESEARCH IN NEUROLOGICAL & COMMUNICATIVE DISORDERS, Washington, D.C. Filed for self 1/20/81. Legislative interest — "...improvement and expansion of research in neurological and communicative disorders through increased federal funding for such research." Lobbyist — Jan Pittman Liebman, Washington, D.C.

NATIONAL COMMUNITY ACTION AGENCY EXECUTIVE DIRECTORS ASSOCIATION, Washington, D.C. Lobbyist — Michael C. Normile, Alexandria, Va. Filed 1/4/81. Legislative interest — "General: Social welfare interests; Specific: Labor/Health and Human Resources/ Education appropriations ... Economic Opportunity Act Amendments of 1981; Energy Management Partnership Act; State and Community Energy Planning Assistance Act."

NATIONAL EDUCATION ASSOCIATION, Washington, D.C. Filed for self 1/30/81. Legislative interest — "Bills pending before Congress relating to public education." Lobbyist — Linda Tarr-Whelan, Washington, D.C.

NATIONAL FARMERS ORGANIZATION, Corning, Iowa. Filed for self 1/21/81. Legislative interest — "Legislation pertaining to family farms, farm income, agricultural bargaining, farm bill, biomass and alternative fuels, and related matters." Lobbyists — Ann L. Bornstein, Bert E. Henningson, Washington, D.C.

THE NATIONAL GRANGE, Washington, D.C. Filed for self 1/12/81. Legislative interest — unspecified. Lobbyist — Susan K. McDowell, Washington, D.C.

NORTH AMERICAN TELEPHONE ASSOCIATION, Washington, D.C. Lobbyist — Tuvin Associates, Washington, D.C. Filed 1/26/81. Legislative interest — "Telecommunications, international trade."

PHARMACEUTICAL MANUFACTURERS ASSOCIATION, Washington, D.C. Lobbyist — Randall, Bangert & Thelen, Washington, D.C. Filed 1/29/81. Legislative interest — "Patent legislation...."

RECORDING INDUSTRY ASSOCIATION OF AMERICA INC., New York, N.Y. Lobbyist — DeHart Associates Inc., Washington, D.C. Filed 1/12/81. Legislative interest — "Copyright and other legislation of interest to the recording industry."

RESEARCH ANIMAL ALLIANCE, Waltham, Mass. Filed for self 1/23/81. Legislative interest — "Legislative matters affecting biomedical research and testing utilizing laboratory animals; Research Modernization Act, Humane Methods of Research Act, Proposed Amendments to the Animal Welfare Act...." Lobbyist — Francine L. Trull, Waltham, Mass.

SERVICE STATION DEALERS OF AMERICA INC., Washington, D.C. Lobbyist — Georgia Association of Petroleum Retailers Inc., Washington, D.C. Filed 1/12/81. Legislative interest — "The Small Business Motor Fuel Marketer Preservation Act of 1980 ... HR 6722, S 2798...."

SIX AGENCY COMMITTEE, Los Angeles, Calif. Lobbyist — Robert P. Will, Washington, D.C. Filed 1/12/81. Legislative interest — "All matters relating to water and energy within California and the Colorado River Basin."

SLURRY TRANSPORT ASSOCIATION, Washington, D.C. Lobbyist — Barnett, Alagia & Carey, Washington, D.C. Filed 1/18/81. Legislative interest — "Legislation to provide imminent [sic] domain authority for coal slurry pipeline."

TENNESSEE HOME MEDICAL PROVIDERS ASSOCIATION INC., Knoxville, Tenn. Filed for self 1/16/81. Legisla-tive interest — "Any legislation pertaining to Part B Medicare coverage...." Lobbyist — Tom B. Holbert, Knoxville, Tenn.

TRUCK TRAILER MANUFACTURERS ASSOCIATION, Washington, D.C. Filed for self 1/12/81. Legislative interest — "...transportation issues, energy policy, labor and general government regulation." Lobbyist — Daniel R. Miller, Washington, D.C.

Miscellaneous

HAUCK & ASSOCIATES, Washington, D.C. Filed for self 1/5/81. Legislative interest — "All legislation affecting proprietary day care centers and/or hearing aid manufacturers...." Lobbyists — Dinah D. McElfish, Carole M. Rogin, Washington, D.C.

ROBERT R. HUMPHREYS, Washington, D.C. Filed 1/14/81. Legislative interest — "Health, labor, employment, taxation, disability, aging, civil rights issues...."

ROBERT D. LANGE, Knoxville, Tenn. Lobbyist — Reynolds & Pitt, Ashland, Ky. Filed 1/28/81. Legislative interest — "In support of HR 751 and S 366, 95th Congress, and their successor bills in order to amend 10 U.S.C. 1331 and thereby obtain Reserve retirement benefits for Dr. Robert D. Lange, Col. USAR, and all members of a class of reservists similarly situated."

JOHN ROCHA, Goleta, Calif. Filed 1/23/81. Legislative interest — "...questions of militarily oriented problems or interests; direction of motions to resolve international conflict...."

RAY ROBERTS & ASSOCIATES, Washington, D.C. Filed 1/30/81. Legislative interest — "Corps of Engineers and reclamation water projects and appropriations for same. Petroleum products and refining affecting U.S. military and territory of Guam. Construction projects such as hospitals, highways, etc."

Late January Registrations

ASSOCIATION FOR THE ADVANCEMENT OF PSYCHOLOGY, Washington, D.C. Filed for self 1/19/81. Legislative interest — "All legislation concerning psychology." Lobbyist — Clarence J. Martin, Washington, D.C.

GLOBAL EXPLORATION & DEVELOPMENT CORP., Lakeland, Fla. Lobbyists — Hoffman, Hendry, Stoner, Sims & Sawicki, Orlando, Fla., and Cramer and Cramer, Washington, D.C. Filed 1/13/81. Legislative interest — "...phosphate mining, the Osceola National Forest, Florida ... HR 1020, HR 5341 and HR 5898...."

February Registrations

Citizens' Groups

CITIZENS OF THE NATIONAL COMMITTEE TO EXONERATE RICHARD NIXON, Norwich, N.Y. Filed for self 2/2/81. Legislative interest — "To urge congressional resolution which will exculpate President Nixon from Watergate."

CITIZEN VICTIMS OF CHRYSLER, Tahlequah, Okla. Filed for self 2/6/81. Legislative interest — "...stopping any further use of taxpayer funds to finance or aid Chrysler Corporation in any way ... supporting a congressional investigation of Chrysler Corporation operations."

CONSUMER FEDERATION OF AMERICA, Washington, D.C. Filed for self 2/13/81. Legislative interest — "Consumer protection; economy; budget; energy; banking; credit; food; regulation." Lobbyists — James G. Boyle and David I. Greenberg, Washington, D.C.

ENVIRONMENTAL ACTION INC., Washington, D.C. Filed for self 2/27/81. Legislative interest — "Any and all acts of Congress affecting the environment of this and future generations...." Lobbyists — Richard J. Kinane, Sandie Nelson and Marchant Wentworth, Washington, D.C.

FRIENDS OF ANIMALS, New York, N.Y. Lobbyist — Finley, Kumble, Wagner, Heine, Casey & Underberg, Washington, D.C. Filed 2/17/81. (The firm listed as agents for this client former U.S. Sen. Joseph D. Tydings, D-Md., 1965-71; former U.S. Rep. Frank N. Ikard, D-Texas, 1951-61; Cory M. Amron and Anne V. Bryan.) Legislative interest — "HR 374 — to prohibit the use of the steel-jaw leghold trap. In favor of passage."

GAY RIGHTS NATIONAL LOBBY INC., Washington, D.C. Lobbyist — Kerry Woodward, Berkeley, Calif. Filed 2/17/81. Legislative interest — "In favor of civil rights for lesbians and gay men; HR 2074."

NATIONAL EDUCATION ASSOCIATION, Washington, D.C. Filed for self 2/3/81. Legislative interest — "Bills pending before Congress relating to public education." Lobbyists — Patsy B. Dix, Washington, D.C., and George Roberts, St. Paul, Minn.

THE NAVAJO NATION, Window Rock, Ariz. Lobbyist — Hill and Knowlton Inc., New York, N.Y., and Washington, D.C. Filed 2/13/81. Legislative interest — unspecified.

THE WILDERNESS SOCIETY, Washington, D.C. Filed for self 2/26/81. Legislative interest — "...all matters affecting the management and use of federal public lands and wild rivers...." Lobbyist — Gaylord Nelson (U.S. senator, D-Wis., 1963-81), Washington, D.C.

THE WILDERNESS SOCIETY, Washington, D.C. Filed for self 2/26/81. Legislative interest — "Appropriations for the Department of Interior ... Department of Agriculture ... legislation relating to the establishment and management of wilderness areas." Lobbyists — Peter Coppelman, Rebecca Wodder, Washington, D.C.

Corporations and Businesses

AIR FLORIDA, Miami, Fla. Lobbyist — Morris J. Amitay, Washington, D.C. Filed 2/20/81. Legislative interest — "...regulation of the airline industry, travel, airport access, and related matters."

AMERICAN FAMILY LIFE INSURANCE CO., Washington, D.C. Lobbyist — The Keefe Company, Washington, D.C. Filed 2/20/81. Legislative interest — "Support for bills relating to the interim treatment of controversies involving whether certain individuals are employees for purposes of employment taxes."

ASHLAND OIL INC., Ashland, Ky. Filed for self 2/13/81. Legislative interest — "All legislation concerning the petroleum industry...." Lobbyist — Doris J. Dewton, Washington, D.C.

BACHE GROUP INC., New York, N.Y. Lobbyist — Akin, Gump, Strauss, Hauer & Feld, Washington, D.C. Filed 2/20/81. Legislative interest — "...amendments to the Security Exchange Act of 1934, including but not limited to application of U.S. margin requirements to certain transactions involving borrowers or lenders with U.S. operations."

BACHE GROUP INC., New York, N.Y. Lobbyist — Sullivan & Cromwell, New York, N.Y., and Washington, D.C. Filed 2/12/81. Legislative interest — "...the securities and insurance industries...."

BROWNING-FERRIS INDUSTRIES INC., Houston, Texas. Lobbyist — Wilmer, Cutler & Pickering, Washington, D.C. Filed 2/4/81. Legislative interest — "...the solid waste industry."

THE COASTAL CORP., Houston, Texas. Filed for self 2/9/81. Legislative interest — "Reinstatement of Santa Barbara leases." Lobbyist — Mitchel Stanfield, Washington, D.C.

CONNECTICUT GENERAL LIFE INSURANCE CO., Hartford, Conn. Lobbyist — Califano, Ross & Heineman, Washington, D.C. Filed 2/2/81. Legislative interest — "Bills to amend the Internal Revenue Code of 1954 to permit an individual to establish a separate limited employee retirement account."

CONSOLIDATED RAIL CORP., Washington, D.C. Lobbyist — William B. Newman Jr., Arlington, Va. Filed 2/2/81. Legislative interest — "...railroads, corporation taxation and regulation, industrial safety and environmental control. Amendments to PL 94-210, PL 96-448, PL 93-236."

THE CONTINENTAL GROUP INC., Stamford, Conn. Filed for self 2/3/81. Legislative interest — "...corporate business activities, particularly HR 6418 — trucking deregulation bill, and S 2445 — Motor Carrier Reform Act."

CONTINENTAL RESOURCES CO., Winter Park, Fla. Lobbyist — George and George, Washington, D.C. Filed 2/13/81. Legislative interest — "...matters relating to energy, tax and labor."

CONTINENTAL RESOURCES CO., Winter Park, Fla. Lobbyist — Kirby & Gillick, Washington, D.C. Filed 2/12/81. Legislative interest — "energy legislation."

ELI LILLY AND CO., Indianapolis, Ind. Filed for self 2/3/81. Legislative interest — "...regulation of business corporations with particular emphasis in the health care, agricultural and cosmetic fields...." Lobbyist — William L. Wright, Washington, D.C.

GENERAL ELECTRIC CO., Daytona, Fla. Lobbyist — R. Q. Old and Associates Inc., Alexandria, Va. Filed 2/17/81. Legislative interest — "Fiscal year 1982 defense authorization bill."

GENERAL INSTRUMENT CORP., Washington, D.C. Lobbyist — Vorys, Sater, Seymour & Pease, Washington, D.C. Filed 2/26/81. Legislative interest — "...District of Columbia and other matters."

GENERAL MILLS RESTAURANT GROUP INC., Orlando, Fla. Filed for self 2/6/81. Legislative interest — "Miscellaneous legislative matters...." Lobbyist — Jean McKee, Washington, D.C.

THE GHK COMPANIES, Oklahoma City, Okla. Lobbyist — Wexler and Associates, Washington, D.C. Filed 2/11/81. Legislative interest — "...to repeal certain portions of the 'Powerplant' and Industrial Fuel Use Act of 1978, PL 95-620."

GOULD INC., Arlington, Va. Lobbyist — R. Q. Old and Associates Inc., Alexandria, Va. Filed 2/17/81. Legislative interest — "Fiscal year 1982 defense authorization bill."

GRUMMAN AEROSPACE CORP., Arlington, Va. Lobbyist — R. Q. Old and Associates Inc., Alexandria, Va. Filed 2/17/81. Legislative interest — "Fiscal year 1982 defense authorization bill."

GULF POWER CO., Pensacola, Fla. Filed for self 2/13/81. Legislative interest — "...electric utilities, energy and the environment." Lobbyist — O. L. Dixon III, Pensacola, Fla.

HOBART CORP., Troy, Ohio. Lobbyist — Hill and Knowlton Inc., New York, N.Y., and Washington, D.C. Filed 2/13/81. Legislative interest — unspecified.

HUGHES AIRCRAFT CO., Arlington, Va. Lobbyist — R. Q. Old and Associates Inc., Alexandria, Va. Filed 2/17/81. Legislative interest — "Fiscal year 1982 defense authorization bill."

INTERNATIONAL TELECOMMUNICATIONS SATELLITE ORGANIZATION, Washington, D.C. Lobbyist — Arnold & Porter, Washington, D.C. Filed 2/27/81. Legislative interest — "Amendments to PL 90-553."

INTERNATIONAL TELEPHONE AND TELEGRAPH CORP., New York, N.Y. Filed for self 2/13/81. Legislative interests — "...may include government regulation, capital formation, communications, environmental matters, miscellaneous tax matters, and other topics...." Lobbyist — Christine M. Bangert, Washington, D.C.

JOHNSON OIL CO. INC., LaBarge, Wyo. Lobbyist — John M. Baines, Washington, D.C. Filed 2/11/81. Legislative interest — "...crude oil supply and price stability for small refiners...."

KELLOGG CO., Battle Creek, Mich. Filed for self 2/4/81. Legislative interest — "HR 914, antitrust issues, issues of general concern to food manufacturers." Lobbyist — Ronald A. Kitlas, Battle Creek, Mich.

LEE WAY MOTOR FREIGHT INC., Oklahoma City, Okla. Lobbyist — Patton, Boggs & Blow, Washington, D.C. Filed 2/17/81. Legislative interest — "Favor amendment of the Internal Revenue Code to permit a deduction for the decline in value of motor carrier operating authorities caused by trading deregulation...."

LITTON INDUSTRIES INC., Beverly Hills, Calif. Lobbyist — Patton, Boggs & Blow, Washington, D.C. Filed 2/17/81. Legislative interest — "Title XI and Title V of the Merchant Marine Act."

LONE STAR INDUSTRIES INC., Greenwich, Conn. Lobbyist — Akin, Gump, Strauss, Hauer & Feld, Washington, D.C. Filed 2/20/81. Legislative interest — "...U.S. tax policy, including but not limited to tax credits for energy efficient industrial processes."

LONG ISLAND LIGHTING CO., Mineola, N.Y. Filed for self 2/27/81. Legislative interest — "...all legislation directly or indirectly affecting the operations of a regulated public utility." Lobbyist — William A. Edwards, Mineola, N.Y.

MARYLAND SAVINGS-SHARE INSURANCE CORP., Baltimore, Md. Lobbyist — Powell, Goldstein, Frazer & Murphy, Washington, D.C. Filed 2/24/81. Legislative interest — "...26 U.S.C. section 501 (c)(14)(B)."

NORANDA MINING INC., Salt Lake City, Utah. Filed for self 2/24/81. Legislative interest — "...government support under the Defense Production Act, Title III for cobalt." Lobbyist — Richard J. Fiorini, Sandy, Utah.

NORANDA MINING INC., Salt Lake City, Utah. Lobbyist — Garvey, Schubert, Adams & Barer, Washington, D.C. Filed 2/27/81. Legislative interest — "Matters involving domestic cobalt production."

NORTHROP CORP., Arlington, Va. Filed for self 2/17/81. Legislative interest — "...authorization and appropriations for programs of the Department of Defense and foreign military sales...." Lobbyists — Albert E. Brewster and M. Diane O'Toole, Arlington, Va.

PHILLIPS PETROLEUM CO., Bartlesville, Okla. Lobbyist — Covington & Burling, Washington, D.C. Filed 2/12/81. Legislative interest — "...excise taxes on crude oil."

PHILLIPS PETROLEUM CO., Bartlesville, Okla. Filed for self 2/5/81. Legislative interest — "...integrated oil, gas, chemicals and energy industries." Lobbyist — Allan D. Hill, Washington, D.C.

PORTMAN PROPERTIES, Atlanta, Ga. Filed for self 2/17/81. Legislative interest — "...the authorization of or appropriations for the Urban Development Action Grant program ... the authorization of or appropriations for the Economic Development Administration." Lobbyist — Glen Isaacson, Atlanta, Ga.

PORTMAN PROPERTIES, Atlanta, Ga. Lobbyist — Hansell, Post, Brandon & Dorsey, Washington, D.C. Filed 2/17/81. Legislative interest — "...the authorization of or appropriations for the Urban Development Action Grant program ... the authorization of or appropriations for the Economic Development Administration."

SANTA ANA VALLEY IRRIGATION CO., Orange, Calif. Lobbyist — Jensen, Sanders & McConnell, Santa Ana, Calif. and Washington, D.C. Filed 2/5/81. Legislative interest — "Legislation authorizing the Army Corps of Engineers to continue with the Santa Ana River Flood Control Project."

SILVER EAGLE OIL CO. INC., LaBarge, Wyo. Lobbyist — John M. Baines, Washington, D.C. Filed 2/11/81. Legislative interest — "...seeking crude oil supply and price stability for small refiners...."

SPERRY DIVISION, Arlington, Va. Lobbyist — R. Q. Old and Associates Inc., Alexandria, Va. Filed 2/17/81. Legislative interest — "Fiscal year 1982 defense authorization bill."

TOSCO OIL CORP., Washington, D.C. Lobbyist — The Hannaford Co. Inc., Washington, D.C. Filed 2/23/81. Legislative interest — "...federal loan guarantee for the Colony Shale Oil Project, re the Defense Production Act. General interest in energy legislation."

URBAN AMERICA DEVELOPMENT GROUP LTD., Baltimore, Md. Filed for self 2/19/81. Legislative interest — unspecified. Lobbyists — Anthony Armstrong and Mel De Rutledge Jr., Baltimore, Md.

UNITED STATES STEEL CORP., Pittsburgh, Pa. Filed for self 2/25/81. Legislative interest — "Any legislation affecting interests of United States Steel Corporation." Lobbyist — Terrence D. Straub, Washington, D.C.

WARNER COMMUNICATIONS INC., New York, N.Y. Filed for self 2/4/81. Legislative interest — "...telecommunications policy ... legislation to amend the current tax treatment of qualified and non-qualified stock options. Legislation to amend the tax on personal capital gains." Lobbyist — Donald Penny, Washington, D.C.

WESTERN UNION TELEGRAPH CO., Washington, D.C. Lobbyist — Cook, Purcell, Hansen & Henderson, Washington, D.C. Filed 2/25/81. Legislative interest — "...Communications law ... favor repeal of section 222 of the Communications Act of 1934 (S 271)."

WESTERN UNION TELEGRAPH CO., Washington, D.C. Lobbyist — Patton, Boggs & Blow, Washington, D.C. Filed 2/27/81. Legislative interest — "S 271; section 222 of the Communications Act of 1934...."

WHITNEY NATIONAL BANK OF NEW ORLEANS, New Orleans, La. Lobbyist — Hill, Christopher and Phillips, Washington, D.C. Filed 2/9/81. Legislative interest — "...the holding of real estate by national banks...."

WHITNEY NATIONAL BANK OF NEW ORLEANS, New Orleans, La. Lobbyist — Eggers & Greene, Dallas, Texas. Filed 2/10/81. Legislative interest — "Legislation relating to banking."

Labor

AMERICAN FEDERATION OF STATE, COUNTY AND MUNICIPAL EMPLOYEES, AFL-CIO, Washington, D.C. Filed for self 2/17/81. Legislative interest — "All bills affecting the welfare of the country generally and state, county and municipal workers specifically...." Lobbyist — Chris Burch, Washington, D.C.

AMERICAN POSTAL WORKERS UNION, AFL-CIO, Washington, D.C. Filed for self 2/9/81. Legislative interest — "...Postal and Federal employee welfare and the Postal Service; namely, HR 14, 79, 677, 733, 826, and 2480." Lobbyist — Roy Braunstein, Washington, D.C.

PROFESSIONAL AIR TRAFFIC CONTROLLERS ORGANIZATION, Washington, D.C. Filed for self 2/18/81. Legislative interest — "...legislation and actual laws which affect or could actually affect employees of the Federal Aviation Administration who are non-supervisory personnel ... revision of the Hatch Act; restoration of 'Second Career' training...." Lobbyist — Patrick L. Doyle, Washington, D.C.

Trade Associations

AIR TRANSPORT ASSOCIATION, Washington, D.C. Lobbyist — Black, Manafort and Stone, Alexandria, Va. Filed 2/26/81. Legislative interest — "General interests."

AMERICAN BUS ASSOCIATION, Washington, D.C. Lobbyist — Kirby & Gillick, Washington D.C. Filed 2/12/81. Legislative interest — "Energy legislation and other general legislation of interest to the bus industry."

THE AMERICAN HUMANE ASSOCIATION, Englewood, Colo. Filed for self 2/2/81. Legislative interest — "...the prevention of cruelty to animals and children." Lobbyist — Robert D. Scott, Englewood, Colo.

AMERICAN LEAGUE FOR EXPORTS AND SECURITY ASSISTANCE INC., Washington, D.C. Filed for self 2/17/81. Legislative interest — "Matters dealing with U.S. export policy, legislation and procedures to include taxes, incentives, Ex-Im Bank, DISC, tax policy, licensing procedures, and other matters relating to the interests of ALESA." Lobbyist — Armistead I. Selden Jr. (U.S. rep., D-Ala., 1953-69), Washington, D.C.

AMERICAN SOCIETY OF TRAVEL AGENTS INC., New York, N.Y. Filed for self 2/13/81. Legislative interest — "Visa waiver, HR 7321, small business taxes and tourists, out-of-country convention taxes, national tourism policy legislation." Lobbyist — Barbara E. O'Hara, Washington, D.C.

AUTOMOTIVE MATERIALS INDUSTRY COUNCIL OF THE U.S., Washington, D.C. Lobbyist — Collier, Shannon, Rill & Scott, Washington, D.C. Filed 2/20/81. Legislative interest — "Any legislation affecting the automotive industry."

COGENERATION COALITION INC., Washington, D.C. Lobbyist — Wickwire, Gavin & Gibbs, Washington, D.C. Filed 2/13/81. Legislative interest — "...the provision of necessary financial or tax incentives for cogeneration development."

CREDIT UNION NATIONAL ASSOCIATION INC., Washington, D.C. Filed for self 2/25/81. Legislative interest — "Issues which impact upon credit unions as corporations and impact upon the services which they offer their members." Lobbyist — Douglas F. Duerr, Washington, D.C.

DEALER BANK ASSOCIATION, Washington, D.C. Lobbyists — Charls E. Walker Associates Inc.; Coan, Couture, Lyon and Moorhead; and Wilmer and Pickering, Washington, D.C. Filed 2/17/81. Legislative interest — "Bills dealing with public finance and banking regulation generally and bills to assist state and local governments by authorizing commercial banks to underwrite revenue bonds."

DREDGING INDUSTRY SIZE STANDARDS COMMITTEE, Washington, D.C. Lobbyist — Patton, Boggs & Blow, Washington, D.C. Filed 2/24/81. Legislative interest — "Support HR 5612 to amend section 8A of the Small Business Act (section 6) PL 96-481...."

THE FERTILIZER INSTITUTE, Washington, D.C. Filed for self 2/23/81. Legislative interest — unspecified. Lobbyist — James D. Massie, Washington, D.C.

HAWAIIAN SUGAR PLANTERS' ASSOCIATION, Honolulu, Hawaii. Filed for self 2/13/81. Legislative interest — "The Food and Agriculture Act and all other legislation affecting the sugar industry in Hawaii." Lobbyist — Eiler C. Ravnholt, Washington, D.C.

HEALTH INDUSTRY MANUFACTURERS ASSOCIATION, Washington, D.C. Filed for self 2/5/81. Legislative interest — "...health and business issues ... any proposal to extend the authorization of the National Center for Health Care Technology beyond the current fiscal year." Lobbyist — Ted R. Mannen, Washington, D.C.

INDEPENDENT REFINERS ASSOCIATION OF AMERICA, Washington, D.C. Lobbyist — Foley, Lardner, Hollabaugh & Jacobs, Washington, D.C. Filed 2/12/81. (The firm listed among the agents for this client former U.S. Rep. John W. Byrnes, R-Wis., 1945-73.) Legislative interest — "...refining policy, price and allocation controls, import tariffs and fees and import policy, oil and gas development on federal lands, taxation, antitrust and small business legislation."

INTERNATIONAL ASSOCIATION OF DRILLING CONTRACTORS, Washington, D.C. Filed for self 2/23/81. Legislative interest — "To amend the Longshoremen's and Harbor Workers' Compensation Act.... To provide a comprehensive system of liability and compensation for oil spill damage and removal costs.... To amend the Internal Revenue Code of 1954 to increase the competitiveness of American firms operating abroad ... to exempt from taxation the earned income of certain individuals working outside the U.S...." Lobbyist — Jon Charles Bednerik, Washington, D.C.

INTERNATIONAL ASSOCIATION OF FISH AND WILDLIFE AGENCIES, Washington, D.C. Lobbyist — Wesley F. Hayden, Alexandria, Va. Filed 2/26/81. Legislative interest — "Legislation concerning fish and wildlife conservation and related matters."

THE LEAGUE OF NEW YORK THEATRES AND PRODUCERS INC., New York, N.Y. Lobbyist — Fisher, Gelband, Sinick & Lamberton, Washington, D.C. Filed 2/17/81. Legislative interest — "Legislation which affects the well-being, conduct or prospects of the legitimate theatre generally ... possible amendments to the Internal Revenue Code and other federal laws which would have the effect of stimulating investment in theatrical productions."

LIVESTOCK MARKETING ASSOCIATION, Kansas City, Mo. Filed for self 2/17/81. Legislative interest — "Livestock

Marketing Reform Act." Lobbyist — Dennis R. Braddock, Alexandria, Va.

NATIONAL ASSOCIATION OF MANUFACTURERS, Washington, D.C. Filed for self 2/19/81. Legislative interest — "...tax, budget, energy, regulatory, international, labor, natural resources and related matters. Specific interests will include but not be limited to: HR 746, 1051, 1321; S 144, 287." Lobbyist — Jerry J. Jasinowski, Washington, D.C.

NATIONAL ASSOCIATION OF PENSION FUNDS, Croyden, England. Lobbyist — Fried, Frank, Harris, Shriver and Kampelman, Washington, D.C. Filed 2/17/81. Legislative interest — "Lobby for the passage of legislation to amend the Internal Revenue Code of 1954, section 503(c), as amended, to permit foreign pension plans to invest in the United States on a non-taxable basis (formerly S 3088)."

NATIONAL ASSOCIATION OF SMALL BUSINESS INVESTMENT COMPANIES, Washington, D.C. Lobbyist — Patton, Boggs & Blow, Washington, D.C. Filed 2/17/81. Legislative interest — "Amendments to section 851 of the Internal Revenue Code to allow subchapter M treatment for business development companies and SBIC's. In favor."

NATIONAL ASSOCIATION OF URBAN FLOOD MANAGEMENT AGENCIES, Washington, D.C. Lobbyist — Linton, Mields, Reisler & Cottone Ltd., Washington, D.C. Filed 2/27/81. Legislative interest — unspecified.

NATIONAL COMMUNITY ACTION AGENCY EXECUTIVE DIRECTORS ASSOCIATION, Washington, D.C. Lobbyist — Michael C. Normile, Alexandria, Va. Filed 2/9/81. Legislative interest — "...Labor/HHS/Education appropriations; continuing appropriation resolutions; Economic Opportunity Act Amendments of 1981; Energy Management Partnership Act; State and Community Energy Planning Assistance Act."

NATIONAL COUNCIL OF FARMER COOPERATIVES, Washington, D.C. Lobbyist — Kirby & Gillick, Washington, D.C. Filed 2/12/81. Legislative interest — "Energy legislation."

NATIONAL COUNCIL ON SYNTHETIC FUELS PRODUCTION, Washington, D.C. Filed for self 2/27/81. Legislative interest — "...the synthetic fuels industry (may include tax, environmental and consumer issues)...." Lobbyists — Michael S. Koleda and R. D. Folsom, Washington, D.C.

NATIONAL FOOD PROCESSORS ASSOCIATION, Washington, D.C. Filed for self 2/25/81. Legislative interest — "All legislation directly affecting fruit, vegetable, seafood and meat processing for human consumption including but not limited to food surveillance, food labeling, fish inspection and development, and the Clean Water Act." Lobbyists — Richard W. Murphy, Claude D. Alexander, Claudia R. Fuquay, Mary Sophos, and Douglas Gordon, Washington, D.C.

NATIONAL LIMESTONE INSTITUTE INC., Fairfax, Va. Filed for self 2/11/81 and 2/23/81. Legislative interest — "All legislation which directly or indirectly affects the interests of limestone producers." Lobbyists — Oneida L. Darley and James H. Williams, Fairfax, Va.

NATIONAL MACHINE TOOL BUILDERS' ASSOCIATION, McLean, Va. Filed for self 2/23/81. Legislative interest — "Industrial preparedness issues." Lobbyist — Charles P. Downer, McLean, Va.

NATIONAL MULTI HOUSING COUNCIL, Washington, D.C. Filed for self 2/23/81. Legislative interest — "All housing legislation and tax legislation as it relates to housing." Lobbyist — Virginia A. Hoy.

NATIONAL OIL JOBBERS COUNCIL, Washington, D.C. Lobbyist — Burson-Marsteller, Washington, D.C. Filed 2/12/81. Legislative interest — "Natural gas deregulation; no statutes or bills at present."

POTATO CHIP/SNACK FOOD ASSOCIATION, Arlington, Va. Filed for self 2/17/81. Legislative interest — "All legislation affecting the flexibly packaged, surface salted snack food industry, including energy, agricultural, and nutritional legislation." Lobbyist — Rodney E. Haugh, Arlington, Va.

ROCKY MOUNTAIN OIL AND GAS ASSOCIATION, Denver, Colo. Filed for self 2/11/81. Legislative interest — "...the

petroleum industry and synthetic fuels development, including S 60, HR 1362, S 326, S 29." Lobbyist — Jess Cooper, Washington, D.C.

SEARCH GROUP INC., Sacramento, Calif. Lobbyist — Hill, Christopher and Phillips, Washington, D.C. Filed 2/27/81. Legislative interest — "...the authorization and appropriations process for the Department of Justice for fiscal year 1982 and fiscal year 1983."

Miscellaneous

AMERICAN COUNCIL ON ALCOHOL PROBLEMS INC., Des Moines, Iowa. Filed for self 2/2/81. Legislative interest — "Bills by Rep. George E. Brown Jr., D-Calif., on alcoholic beverage advertising and labels."

COOPERATIVE LEAGUE OF THE U.S.A., Washington, D.C. Filed for self 2/17/81. Legislative interest — "Legislation affecting cooperative organization, operations, and financing in the USA and in foreign countries, general consumer interests, improvement of agriculture production and marketing, and community development." Lobbyist — Martha McCabe, Washington, D.C.

CORNING ASSOCIATES, Corning, N.Y. Lobbyist — Shearman & Sterling, New York, N.Y. Filed 2/6/81. Legislative interest — "...support of amendment to section 2518 of the Internal Revenue Code of 1954, as amended."

DR. MARTIN LUTHER KING JR. JANUARY 15th NATIONAL HOLIDAY LOBBY COMMITTEE. Filed for self 2/2/81. Legislative interest — "To designate the birthday of Dr. Martin Luther King Jr. as a legal public holiday." Lobbyist — Suhkara Abdul Yahweh.

HARLEY M. FRANKEL, Arlington, Va. Filed for self 2/13/81. Legislative interest — "Head Start re-authorization, HHS appropriation bills, and other legislation affecting human services...."

THE FRANKLIN INSTITUTE, Philadelphia, Pa. Lobbyist — Ballard, Spahr, Andrew & Ingersoll, Washington, D.C. Filed 2/24/81. Legislative interest — "...energy and scientific research, funding for national memorial and museum activities for non-profit organization."

HAUCK & ASSOCIATES, Washington, D.C. Filed for self 2/25/81. Legislative interest — "All legislation affecting proprietary day-care centers and/or hearing aid manufacturers...."

RULE OF LAW COMMITTEE, Washington, D.C. Filed for self 2/17/81. Legislative interest — "Business Accounting and Foreign Trade Simplification Act. 15 USC sec. 78l, 15 USC sec. 78dd-2. For bill with amendments." Lobbyist — Steptoe & Johnson, Washington, D.C.

March Registrations
Citizens' Groups

AMERICAN INDIAN SCHOLARSHIPS INC., Taos, N.M. Lobbyist — Karl A. Funke & Associates Inc., Washington, D.C. Filed 3/18/81. Legislative interest — "...Bureau of Indian Affairs, Department of Interior appropriations to assure that funds for AIS Indian graduate scholarships are not cut."

CITIZENS COMMITTEE FOR THE RIGHT TO KEEP AND BEAR ARMS, Bellevue, Wash. Lobbyist — John M. Snyder, Washington, D.C. Filed 3/12/81. Legislative interest — "Conservation, recreation and firearms legislation."

COMMUNITY NUTRITION INSTITUTE, Washington, D.C. Filed for self 3/30/81. Legislative interest — "...consumer, agriculture, nutrition, food and drug, inflation and budget issues ... proposed legislation relating to commodity price supports, food safety, farm policy, food labeling, food assistance programs, and general consumer protection issues." Lobbyists — Thomas Blaisdell Smith and Myron Zeitz, Washington, D.C.

COMMUNITY SERVICE SOCIETY, New York, N.Y. Filed for self 3/10/81. Legislative interest — "Domestic legislation relating to improving the welfare of the economically disadvantaged." Lobbyists — Anjean Carter, Peggy Chin, Margaret Kerry, New York, N.Y.

THE CONFEDERATED TRIBES OF WARM SPRINGS, Warm Springs, Ore. Lobbyist — Edwards Associates Inc., Washington, D.C. Filed 3/9/81. Legislative interest — "Legislation relating to Indian Affairs, Bureau of Indian Affairs; Department of Interior and related agencies."

CONGRESS WATCH, Washington, D.C. Filed for self 3/11/81. Legislative interest — "Nuclear waste legislation; bills regarding OSHA; The Clean Air Act." Lobbyist — Caroline Mills LeGette, Washington, D.C.

JAPANESE-AMERICAN CITIZENS LEAGUE, San Francisco, Calif. Filed for self 3/2/81. Legislative interest — "...District of Columbia full representation ... internment credit bill ... Pacific Asian American Heritage Week ... U.S. atomic bomb survivors medical payment bill...." Lobbyist — Ronald K. Ikejiri, Washington, D.C.

KEWEENAW BAY CHIPPEWA TRIBE, Baraga, Mich. Lobbyist — Karl A. Funke & Associates Inc., Washington, D.C. Filed 3/18/81. Legislative interest — "Bureau of Indian Affairs, Department of Interior appropriations ... decommercialization of Lake Trout or abrogation of Indian treaty fishing rights in Great Lakes.... Indian land inheritance and fractionated heirship legislation...."

MAKAH INDIAN TRIBE, Neah Bay, Wash. Lobbyist — Fried, Frank, Harris, Shriver & Kampelman, Washington, D.C. Filed 3/20/81. Legislative interest — "All legislation which affects the Economic Development Administration...."

NATIONAL COMMUNITY ACTION FOUNDATION, Boston, Mass. Lobbyist — O'Connor & Hannan, Washington, D.C. Filed 3/19/81. (Among the agents listed for this client was former U.S. Sen. Edward W. Brooke, R-Mass., 1967-79.) Legislative interest — "Continuance of the Community Action Program as a function of the Community Services Administration.

NATIONAL RIGHT TO WORK COMMITTEE, Springfield, Va. Filed for self 3/11/81. Legislative interest — "...compulsory unionism in private industry, farm labor, public sector employees." Lobbyist — William A. Wilson III, Springfield, Va.

PENOBSCOT INDIAN NATION, Indian Island, Maine. Lobbyists — Karl A. Funke & Associates Inc. and Webster & Sheffield, Washington, D.C. Filed 3/18/81 and 3/23/81. Legislative interest — "Fiscal year 1982 Department of Interior appropriations affecting the funding of certain Bureau of Indian Affairs programs."

SHOSHONE-BANNOCK TRIBES, Fort Hall, Idaho. Lobbyist — Karl A. Funke & Associates Inc., Washington, D.C. Filed 3/18/81. Legislative interest — "Sagebrush rebellion legislation ... reauthorization of the Native American Programs Act ... nuclear waste repository legislation ... hunting and fishing regulatory jurisdiction over non-Indians within the Fort Hall Reservation...."

STOCKHOLDERS OF AMERICA INC., Washington, D.C. Filed for self 3/13/81. Legislative interest — "...amendments to the Internal Revenue Code." Lobbyist — Margaret Cox Sullivan, Washington, D.C.

VIRGINIA ASSOCIATION OF RAILWAY PATRONS, Richmond, Va. Filed for self 3/5/81. Legislative interest — "...any legislation providing, preserving, expanding or improving railway freight, passenger, express and mail service, to include commuter and urban rail mass transit, or protecting consumers of railway services. Also interested in other legislation affecting other forms of transportation."

THE WILDERNESS SOCIETY, Washington, D.C. Filed for self 3/18/81. Legislative interest — "All issues related to public lands administered by the Bureau of Land Management; all wilderness issues; issues related to mineral activities on the public lands." Lobbyist — Terry Sopher, Washington, D.C.

YAKIMA INDIAN NATION, Toppenish, Wash. Lobbyist — Karl A. Funke & Associates Inc., Washington, D.C. Filed 3/18/81. Legislative interest — "Decommercialization of steelhead fish in the Columbia River ... Indian land inheritance and fractionated heirship of trust allotments...."

Corporations and Businesses

AMERICAN HONDA MOTOR CO. INC., Gardena, Calif. Lobbyist — Barbara S. Dudeck, Washington, D.C. Filed 3/2/81. Legislative interest — "All legislation affecting products imported and sold by the company."

AMERICAN LIFE AND CASUALTY CO., Fargo, N.D. Lobbyist — Vorys, Sater, Seymour & Pease, Washington, D.C. Filed 3/20/81. Legislative interest — "...certain changes in the Internal Revenue Code relating to individual annuity taxation."

BLUE RIBBON SPORTS INC., Beaverton, Ore. Lobbyist — Edwards Associates Inc., Washington, D.C. Filed 3/9/81. Legislative interest — "Legislation relating to international trade, customs and the footwear industry."

THE BOEING CO., Seattle, Wash. Filed for self 3/5/81. Legislative interest — "Authorizations and appropriations of all departments of government; tax and revenue issues; regulation and control of transportation, air, water and land; labor and management issues; international trade regulation and control." Lobbyist — Elizabeth Nash Schwartz, Arlington, Va.

CARE CABS INC., West Allis, Wis. Lobbyist — Foley, Lardner, Hollabaugh & Jacobs, Washington, D.C. Filed 3/5/81. Legislative interest — "Matters relating to urban mass transportation authority section 16 program."

CENTEX CORP., Dallas, Texas. Lobbyist — Ray Roberts & Associates, Washington, D.C. Filed 3/4/81. Legislative interest — "Corps of Engineers and reclamation water projects ... petroleum products and refining affecting U.S. military and territory of Guam. Construction projects ... powerplants and power transmission line utility rates."

THE CLEVELAND ELECTRIC ILLUMINATING CO., Cleveland, Ohio. Filed for self 3/23/81. Legislative interest — "Legislation affecting privately-owned utilities...." Lobbyists — John R. Bruch and James A. Smircina, Cleveland, Ohio.

COLT INDUSTRIES, Washington, D.C. Lobbyist — Shannon, Heffernan, Moseman & Goren, Washington, D.C. Filed 3/11/81. Legislative interest — "...Capital Cost Recovery Act...."

COLUMBIA GAS DISTRIBUTION COMPANIES, Columbus, Ohio. Lobbyist — Kathleen O'Leary, Washington, D.C. Filed 3/10/81. Legislative interest — "...legislation affecting natural gas industry."

CSX CORP., Richmond, Va. Lobbyist — Charls E. Walker Associates Inc., Washington, D.C. Filed 3/6/81. Legislative interest — "Legislative interests may concern refundability of the investment tax credit."

DEAK NATIONAL BANK, Fleischmanns, N.Y. Lobbyist — O'Connor & Hannan, Washington, D.C. Filed 3/1/81. Legislative interest — "...student loans, including the Education Amendments of 1980, S 1839, amending section 430(a) of the Higher Education Act."

EASTERN AIR LINES INC., Miami, Fla. Lobbyist — Timmons and Co. Inc., Washington, D.C. Filed 3/6/81. Legislative interest — "...commercial aviation and scheduled air carriers, including matters relating to the use of airports...."

EDS CORP., Washington, D.C. Filed for self 3/4/81. Legislative interest — "...matters affecting the business of designing, installing and operating business information systems...." Lobbyist — Richard M. Charlton, Washington, D.C.

ENCYCLOPAEDIA BRITANNICA INC., Chicago, Ill. Lobbyist — Wickham & Craft, Washington, D.C. Filed 3/18/81. Legislative interest — "For legislation to terminate enforcement of discriminatory, anticompetitive, affirmative requirements of Federal Trade Commission orders."

FALLBROOK PUBLIC UTILITY DISTRICT, Washington, D.C. Filed for self 3/20/81. Legislative interest — "HR 1527." Lobbyist — Jack T. Ford, Washington, D.C.

FOOD POLICY CENTER, Washington, D.C. Lobbyist — Jones, Day, Reavis & Pogue, Washington, D.C. Filed 3/30/81. Legislative interest — "...food aid (PL 480), bilateral and multilateral development assistance, domestic food aid and agricultural policy."

FOSS LAUNCH & TUG CO./FOSS ALASKA LINE, Seattle, Wash. Lobbyist — Jack Ferguson Associates Inc., Washington, D.C. Filed 3/6/81. Legislative interest — "Merchant marine policy; Jones Act, Merchant Marine Act."

GENERAL MOTORS CORP., Detroit, Mich. Filed for self 3/16/81. Legislative interest — unspecified. Lobbyist — Stephen E. O'Toole, Washington, D.C.

GEOTHERMAL KINETICS INC., Phoenix, Ariz. Lobbyist — Charls E. Walker, Washington, D.C. Filed 3/6/81. Legislative interest "...grant or loan assistance or other governmental policies pertaining to the development of geothermal resources."

THE GHK COS., Oklahoma City, Okla. Lobbyist — Casey, Lane & Mittendorf, Washington, D.C. Filed 3/5/81. Legislative interest —"...repeal certain portions of the Powerplant and Industrial Fuel Use Act of 1978, PL 95-620."

GUAM OIL & REFINING CO. INC., Dallas, Texas. Lobbyist — Ray Roberts & Associates, Washington, D.C. Filed 3/4/81. Legislative interest — "Corps of Engineers and reclamation water projects and appropriations ... petroleum products and refining affecting U.S. military and territory of Guam. Construction projects ... powerplants and power transmission line utility rates."

GULF & WESTERN MANAGEMENT CO., Washington, D.C. Filed for self 3/4/81. Legislative interest — "...international and domestic commerce and other legislation affecting private industry." Lobbyist — Karen C. Hontz, Washington, D.C.

JOSEPH E. SEAGRAM & SONS INC., New York, N.Y. Lobbyist — O'Connor & Hannan, Washington, D.C. Filed 3/23/81. Legislative interest — "Legislation affecting corporate acquisitions. Filed for self 3/6/81. Legislative interest — "Any legislation affecting Joseph E. Seagram & Sons Inc. or its parent company The Seagram Company Ltd...." Lobbyist — Kenneth S. Levine, New York, N.Y.

LITCHSTREET CO., Northport, N.Y. Lobbyist — Schwabe, Williamson, Wyatt, Moore and Roberts, Washington, D.C. Filed 3/6/81. Legislative interest — "Air traffic control — collision avoidance."

MARATHON OIL CO., Findlay, Ohio. Lobbyist — Wilkinson, Cragun & Barker, Washington, D.C. Filed 3/11/81. Legislative interest — "...crude oil and gas controls and allocation; divorcement of motor fuel retail outlets, and similar legislation (S 409, S 326, HR 1362)."

MILLER COAL SYSTEMS INC., Baton Rouge, La. Lobbyist — Abadie and Hudson, Baton Rouge, La. Filed 3/10/81. Legislative interest — "In support of legislation providing for dredging of ports and waterways."

MONTGOMERY WARD CO. INC., Chicago, Ill. Lobbyist — Patton, Boggs & Blow, Washington, D.C. Filed 3/12/81. Legislative interest — "Cash Discount Act.... "

NORANDA MINING INC., Salt Lake City, Utah. Filed for self 3/17/81. Legislative interest — "...mining, public lands and appropriations...."

NORTON SOUND HEALTH CORP., Nome, Alaska. Lobbyist — Fried, Frank, Harris, Shriver & Kampelman, Washington, D.C. Filed 3/20/81. Legislative interest — "Fiscal year 1982 appropriation for Indian Health Service programs."

NORTHROP CORP., Arlington, Va. Filed for self 3/9/81. Legislative interest — "...authorization and appropriations for programs of the Department of Defense and Foreign Military Sales. Specific areas of interest include the F/A-18 and F-5 series aircraft, plus other Northrop Corp. programs." Lobbyists — Albert E. Brewster and M. Diane O'Toole, Arlington, Va.

OGDEN CORP., New York, N.Y. Lobbyist — Constantine G. Caras, Arlington, Va. Filed 3/2/81. Legislative interest — "...primarily maritime, metals and food service...."

PACIFIC NORTHERN OIL, Seattle, Wash. Lobbyist — Jack Ferguson Associates Inc., Washington, D.C. Filed 3/6/81. Legislative interest — "Export policy; Export Administration Act of 1979."

PACIFIC RESOURCES INC., Honolulu, Hawaii. Filed for self 3/12/81. Legislative interest — unspecified. Lobbyist — Richard P. Woods, Washington, D.C.

PALO VERDE IRRIGATION DISTRICT, Blythe, Calif. Lobbyist — Robert P. Will, Washington, D.C. Filed 3/9/81. Legislative interest — "HR 1333."

PHH GROUP INC., Hunt Valley, Md. Lobbyist —

Wickham & Craft, Washington, D.C. Filed 3/30/81. Legislative interest — "For legislation assuring depreciation tax deductions and investment tax credits on leased property."

RJR INDUSTRIES INC., Winston-Salem, N.C. Filed for self 3/19/81. Legislative interest — "Any legislation affecting the general business community, especially the tobacco industry, the transportation industry, the oil industry, and the foods industry...." Lobbyist — LeAnn Hensche, Washington, D.C.

RYDER SYSTEMS INC., Miami, Fla. Lobbyist — Wickham & Craft, Washington, D.C. Filed 3/18/81. Legislative interest — "For tax legislation to eliminate or reduce the discrimination against business investors in shorter-lived assets under investment tax credit or tax depreciation and similar capital formation allowances."

SCA SERVICES INC., Boston, Mass. Lobbyist — Mintz, Levin, Cohn, Glovsky and Popeo, Washington, D.C. Filed 3/2/81. Legislative interest — "Legislation concerning hazardous waste and solid waste."

SOLMECS CORP., London, England and Jerusalem, Israel. Lobbyist Arent, Fox, Kintner, Plotkin & Kahn, Washington, D.C. Filed 3/19/81. Legislative interest — "Solar energy, conservation and alternative fuels research, development, demonstration and commercialization."

STANDARD OIL CO. (INDIANA), Chicago, Ill. Filed for self 3/6/81. Legislative interest — "...legislation of concern to the energy industry, general business interests, the environment and the Great Lakes Basin." Lobbyist — Keith A. Pretty, Southfield, Mich.

ST. JOE MINERALS CORP., New York, N.Y. Lobbyist — Akin, Gump, Strauss, Hauer & Feld, Washington, D.C. Filed 3/17/81. Legislative interest — " Hearings and any legislation relating to U.S. energy and mineral policy."

TEXAS UTILITIES SERVICES INC., Dallas, Texas. Lobbyist — Ray Roberts & Associates, Washington, D.C. Filed 3/4/81. Legislative interest — "Corps of Engineers and reclamation water projects and appropriations ... petroleum products and refining affecting U.S. military and territory of Guam. Construction projects ... powerplants and power transmission line utility rates."

TRAILER TRAIN CO., Chicago, Ill. Lobbyist — Wickham & Craft, Washington, D.C. Filed 3/30/81. Legislative interest — "For enactment of legislation to provide for refund of investment tax credits, or which would otherwise assure the availability of investment tax credits."

UNITED STATES AUTOMOBILE ASSOCIATION, San Antonio, Texas. Filed for self 3/31/81. Legislative interest — "An amendment to the Internal Revenue Code of 1954 to increase the allowable contributions to individual retirement plans and to allow employees a deduction for savings contributions to employer retirement plans — or to individual retirement accounts, HR 1250 and S 243."

UNIVERSAL FOODS INC., Milwaukee, Wis. Lobbyist — Williams & Jensen, Washington, D.C. Filed 3/16/81. Legislative interest — "Agriculture, import, and tax legislation."

UTAH INTERNATIONAL INC., San Francisco, Calif. Filed for self 3/16/81. Legislative interest — "Measures affecting mining, oil and gas and land development." Lobbyist — Claudia R. Spady, Washington, D.C.

WESTINGHOUSE ELECTRIC CORP., Washington, D.C. Lobbyist — Powell, Goldstein, Frazer & Murphy, Washington, D.C. Filed 3/16/81. Legislative interest — "...export subsidy issues."

International Relations

AMERICAN ISRAEL PUBLIC AFFAIRS COMMITTEE, Washington, D.C. Filed for self 3/18/81. Legislative interest — "Support foreign assistance authorization and appropriations legislation for fiscal year 1982, with full funding for administration request for Israel, and resettlement funds for Soviet and Eastern European refugees in Israel...." Lobbyist — Marla F. Gilson, Washington, D.C.

ARAB REPUBLIC OF EGYPT, Cairo, Egypt. Lobbyists — Surrey & Morse, Washington, D.C. and Moery and Co., McLean, Va. Filed 3/6/81. Legislative interest — "Promoting passage of the administration's military and economic assistance program insofar as they may related to the Arab Republic of Egypt...."

CHINA EXTERNAL TRADE DEVELOPMENT COUNCIL, Taipei, Taiwan. Lobbyist — The Hannaford Co. Inc., Washington, D.C. Filed 3/30/81. Legislative interest — "...to promote mutually beneficial trade, economic and other relationships between the Republic of China and the U.S...."

GOVERNMENT OF HONDURAS. Lobbyist — Inter American Associates Inc., Washington, D.C. Filed 3/17/81. Legislative interest — "...in relation to U.S.-Honduran trade and other matters."

MINISTRY OF FOREIGN AFFAIRS OF THE KINGDOM OF SAUDI ARABIA, Riyadh, Saudi Arabia. Lobbyist — Crawford Cook and Co., Columbia, S.C. Filed 3/30/81. Legislative interest — unspecified.

Labor Groups

AMERICAN POSTAL WORKERS UNION (AFL-CIO), Washington, D.C. Filed for self 3/19/81. Legislative interest — "...all legislation for postal and federal employees' welfare and the Postal Service; namely HR 14, 79, 677, 733, 826 and 2400." Lobbyist — Roy Braunstein, Washington, D.C.

ORGANIZATION FOR THE PRESERVATION OF THE PUBLIC EMPLOYEE RETIREMENT INDUSTRY & OPPOSITION TO SOCIAL SECURITY EXPANSION, Denver, Colo. Lobbyist — Peabody, Rivlin, Lambert & Meyers, Washington, D.C. Filed 3/2/81. Legislative interest — "Opposed to mandatory coverage of state and local employees under the Social Security program. HR 1018, S 484."

UNITED BROTHERHOOD OF CARPENTERS & JOINERS OF AMERICA, Washington, D.C. Filed for self 3/12/81. Legislative interest — "...the general welfare of the working man, in particular that affecting our members." Lobbyist — Kevin B. Campbell, Washington, D.C.

State and Local Governments

CITY OF SOUTH LAKE TAHOE, South Lake Tahoe, Calif., Lobbyist — A-K Associates Inc., Sacramento, Calif. Filed 3/2/81. Legislative interest — unspecified.

GOVERNMENT OF THE FEDERATED STATES OF MICRONESIA, Kolonia, Ponape, Eastern Caroline Islands. Lobbyist — Clifford & Warnke, Washington, D.C. Filed 3/30/81. Legislative interest — "All matters pertaining to the Government of the Federated States of Micronesia including Omnibus Territories Acts, Territories Appropriation Acts."

METRO-METROPOLITAN SERVICE DISTRICT, TRI-COUNTY METROPOLITAN TRANSPORTATION DISTRICT, STATE OF OREGON/CITY OF PORTLAND, ORE. Lobbyist — Schwabe, Williamson, Wyatt, Moore and Roberts, Washington, D.C. Filed 3/6/81. Legislative interest — "Transportation (mass transit); Commuter Transportation Energy Efficiency Act (S 239), intrastate transfer/highway funds."

METROPOLITAN DISTRICT COMMISSION, Hartford, Conn. Lobbyist — Van Ness, Feldman & Sutcliffe, Washington, D.C. Filed 3/17/81. Legislative interest — "Wild and Scenic River study designation for the Farmington River ... Wild and Scenic Rivers Act, 16 U.S.C. section 1271 et seq...."

Trade Associations

THE AMERICAN BUSINESS CONFERENCE, Washington, D.C. Filed for self 3/30/81. Legislative interest — "...tax and regulatory reform, legislation for high-growth, mid-range business organizations ... S 75." Lobbyists — John M. Albertine, Catherine S. Smith, Washington, D.C.

AMERICAN BUSINESS CONFERENCE, Washington, D.C. Lobbyist — Brownstein, Zeidmann and Schomer, Washington, D.C. Filed 3/30/81. Legislative interest — "...tax and regulatory reform legislation for high-growth, mid-range business organizations."

AMERICAN CONSULTING ENGINEERS COUNCIL, Washington, D.C. Filed for self 3/17/81. Legislative interest — "Matters relating to public works, transportation, the environment, pollution control, housing, equal employment opportunity, public health and safety, economy and efficiency in government, and energy legislation." Lobbyist — William J. Birkhofer, Washington, D.C.

AMERICAN HEALTH PLANNING ASSOCIATION, Washington, D.C. Filed for self 3/19/81. Legislative interest — "National Health Planning and Resource Development Act...." Lobbyist — Ann C. Scheiner, Washington, D.C.

AMERICAN HOSPITAL ASSOCIATION, Chicago, Ill. Filed for self 3/2/81. Legislative interest — "...legislation which may affect the ability of hospitals to render good care or which may affect the health of the American people." Lobbyist — Dwight M. Geduldig, Washington, D.C.

AMERICAN INSTITUTE OF ARCHITECTS, Washington, D.C. Filed for self 3/4/81. Legislative interest — unspecified. Lobbyists — Mary Ann Eichenberger, Washington, D.C., and Mary Jo Malone, Alexandria, Va.

AMERICAN IRON AND STEEL INSTITUTE, Washington, D.C. Lobbyist — Charls E. Walker Associates Inc., Washington, D.C. Filed 3/6/81. Legislative interest — "...refundability of the investment tax credit."

AMERICAN OPTOMETRIC ASSOCIATION, Antioch, Ill. Filed for self 3/20/81. Legislative interest — unspecified. Lobbyists — Noel Brazil, David Lewis, Timothy Redman Sr., William W. Reinertson and Stephanie Whyche, Washington, D.C.

AMERICAN PAPER INSTITUTE INC., New York, N.Y. Filed for self 3/13/81. Legislative interest — "...affecting the pulp, paper and paperboard industry, its operation, practices and properties, tax legislation and environmental legislation — air, water and energy." Lobbyists — Robert T. McKernan, Marc D. Yacker, Washington, D.C.

AMERICAN PETROLEUM REFINERS ASSOCIATION, Washington, D.C. Filed for self 3/9/81. Legislative interest — "...the small and independent refining industry. Any legislative issue pertaining to domestic refining policy including but not limited to S 409." Lobbyist — Van R. Boyette, Washington, D.C.

AMERICAN PUBLIC TRANSIT ASSOCIATION, Washington, D.C. Filed for self 3/2/81. Legislative interest — unspecified. Lobbyist — John H. Ingram, Washington, D.C.

AMERICAN TRUCKING ASSOCIATIONS, Washington, D.C. Lobbyist — William H. Harsha & Associates Inc. (former U.S. Rep. William H. Harsha, R-Ohio, 1961-81) Washington, D.C. Filed 3/2/81. Legislative interest — "Tax legislation, HR 1964 tax deductions, truck safety."

ASSOCIATED BUILDERS AND CONTRACTORS INC., Washington, D.C. Filed for self 3/9/81. Legislative interest — "All activities in the U.S. Congress affecting labor-management relations...." Lobbyists — Hubert L. Harris, Richard P. Markey, Susan R. Meisinger, Richard D. Morgan, John C. Runyan and David L. Shapiro, Washington, D.C.

ASSOCIATION OF GOVERNMENT ACCOUNTANTS, Arlington, Va. Filed for self 3/16/81. Legislative interest — "All legislation concerning the accounting profession and government employees engaged in accounting and financial management and the principles of governmental accounting and financial management." Lobbyist — John P. Abbadessa, Arlington, Va.

THE BUSINESS ROUNDTABLE, Washington, D.C. Lobbyist — Hughes Hubbard & Reed, Washington, D.C. Filed 3/4/81. Legislative interest — "To bring to the attention of relevant committees, members and staff of the Senate and House various constitutional, policy and factual issues regarding possible antitrust legislation."

CALIFORNIA SOCIETY OF PATHOLOGISTS, Sacramento, Calif. Lobbyist — A-K Associates Inc., Sacramento, Calif.

Filed 3/2/81. Legislative interest — "All health legislation."

CHAMBER OF COMMERCE OF THE UNITED STATES, Washington, D.C. Filed for self 3/31/81. Legislative interest — "Renewable and nonrenewable resources, environmental issue areas." Lobbyist — Harvey Alter, Washington, D.C.

CHEMICAL MANUFACTURERS ASSOCIATION, Washington, D.C. Filed for self 3/9/81. Legislative interest — "General interest in environmental legislation affecting the chemical manufacturing industry, such as air pollution control." Lobbyist — Karen J. Neale, Washington, D.C.

CORN REFINERS ASSOCIATION, Washington, D.C. Lobbyist — Kirby & Gillick, Washington, D.C. Filed 3/10/81. Legislative interest — "Energy legislation and other general legislation of interest to the Corn Refiners."

EDISON ELECTRIC INSTITUTE, Washington, D.C. Filed for self 3/12/81. Legislative interest — "...Internal Revenue Act, TVA Act, Atomic Energy Act, Federal Power Act, Rural Electrification Act, Bonneville Power Act ... Clean Air Act, Occupational Health and Safety Act, Equal Employment Opportunity Act, Employee Retirement Income Security Act, Wild and Scenic Rivers Act, National Energy Act." Lobbyist — Fred G. Davis, Washington, D.C.

FLORIDA STATE HOSPICE ORGANIZATION INC., Miami, Fla. Lobbyist — Hogan & Hartson, Washington, D.C. Filed 3/4/81. Legislative interest — "Bill to amend Title 18 of the Social Security Act to include hospice care as a covered benefit."

HEALTH INSURANCE ASSOCIATION OF AMERICA INC., Washington, D.C. Filed for self 3/9/81. Legislative interest — "All matters pertaining to business of health and accident insurance companies and their policyholders." Lobbyist — Geza Kadar Jr., Washington, D.C.

HELICOPTER LOGGERS ASSOCIATION, Wilsonville, Ore. Lobbyist — Schwabe, Williamson, Wyatt, Moore and Roberts, Washington, D.C. Filed 3/6/81. Legislative interest — "Allocation of sales by Forest Service between helicopter and conventional services."

HOSPITAL ASSOCIATION OF NEW YORK STATE, Albany, N.Y. Lobbyist — Hogan & Hartson, Washington, D.C. Filed 3/20/81. Legislative interest — "...amend the Medical Assistance Program, Title 19 of the Social Security Act."

INDEPENDENT PRODUCERS GROUP, Wichita, Kan. Lobbyist — Casey, Lane & Mittendorf, Washington, D.C. Filed 3/5/81. Legislative interest — "...amendment of the Crude Oil Windfall Profit Tax Act of 1980, PL 96-233."

INSURANCE ASSOCIATION OF CONNECTICUT, Hartford, Conn. Lobbyist — Robert N. Giaimo (former U.S. Rep. Robert Giaimo, D-Conn., 1959-81), Washington, D.C. Filed 3/18/81. Legislative interest — "Insurance, taxation and pension legislation."

LEAGUE OF CALIFORNIA MILK PRODUCERS, Sacramento, Calif. Filed for self 3/10/81. Legislative interest — "S 509 — against, HR 1986 — against." Lobbyist — Jay F. Goold.

MOTOR VEHICLE MANUFACTURERS ASSOCIATION OF THE U.S. INC., Detroit, Mich. Filed for self 3/6/81. Legislative interest — "All legislation affecting the motor vehicle industry." Lobbyist — Stephen J. Collins, Washington, D.C.

NATIONAL ASSOCIATION OF BUSINESS AND EDUCATIONAL RADIO INC., Washington, D.C. Lobbyist — Newrath, Meyer and Faller, Washington, D.C. Filed 3/11/81. Filed for self 3/11/81. Legislative interest — "...legislation to amend the Communications Act involving matters relating to and affecting private land mobile radio and business radio users...." Lobbyist — Emmett Jay Kitchen Jr., Washington, D.C.

NATIONAL ASSOCIATION OF CATALOG SHOWROOM MERCHANDISERS INC., New York, N.Y. Filed for self 3/19/81. Legislative interest — "...amend Sherman Act to prohibit restricted distribution...." Lobbyists — Michael Goldstein, Richard B. Kelly, New York, N.Y.

NATIONAL ASSOCIATION OF MANUFACTURERS' FTC-ANTITRUST SUBCOMMITTEE, Washington, D.C. Lobbyist — Mayer, Brown & Platt, Washington, D.C. Filed 3/18/81. Legislative interest — "Support an amendment to section 4 of the Clayton Act (15 USC section 15) to clarify the standing of

foreign governments to sue under that section."

NATIONAL CONSTRUCTORS ASSOCIATION, Washington, D.C. Filed for self 3/30/81. Legislative interest — "Legislation affecting the NCA membership ... taxation, labor law, international finance and safety and health law...." Lobbyists — William W. Beddow, Richard F. Guay, Jane McPike, Washington, D.C.

NATIONAL FAMILY PLANNING AND REPRODUCTIVE HEALTH ASSOCIATION INC., Washington, D.C. Filed for self 3/16/81. Legislative interest — "...reauthorization of Title X, Public Health Service Act, the Family Planning Services & Population Research Act and all legislation affecting family planning services." Lobbyist — Scott R. Swirling, Washington, D.C.

NATIONAL HEALTH ACTION COMMITTEE, Columbus, Ohio. Lobbyist — Mary Louise Findley Dennis, Sands Point, N.Y. Filed 3/6/81. Legislative interest — "...water fluoridation."

NATIONAL PORK PRODUCERS COUNCIL, Des Moines, Iowa. Filed for self 3/9/81. Legislative interest — "Agriculture and public health." Lobbyist — Stafford Michael Mishoe, Washington, D.C.

ORGANIZATION FOR THE PROTECTION AND ADVANCEMENT OF SMALL TELEPHONE COMPANIES, Wheaton, Ill. Lobbyist — Preston, Thorgrimson, Ellis, Holman & Fletcher, Washington, D.C. Filed 3/31/81. Legislative interest — "... legislation affecting the telephone industry."

U.S. & OVERSEAS TAX FAIRNESS COMMITTEE, Washington, D.C. Filed for self 3/30/81. Legislative interest — "Legislation affecting TFC membership ... taxation of U.S. citizens at work in foreign countries; Foreign Earned Income Act of 1981...." Lobbyist — Ben Jarratt Brown, Washington, D.C.

WINE AND SPIRITS WHOLESALERS OF AMERICA INC., Washington, D.C. Lobbyist — O'Connor & Hannan, Washington, D.C. Filed 3/23/81. Legislative interest — "Introduction and passage of primary source legislation/provision to the Federal Alcohol Act."

Miscellaneous

ACTION COMMITTEE ON TECHNOLOGY, Charlottesville, Va. Filed for self 3/18/81. Legislative interest — "...education, energy, basic research and space." Lobbyists — Thomas McCrystal, James Muncy, Charlottesville, Va.

AD HOC COMMITTEE ON INDIVIDUAL ANNUITY TAXATION INC., Westport, Conn. Lobbyist — Vorys, Sater, Seymour & Pease, Washington, D.C. Filed 3/12/81. Legislative interest — "...certain changes in the Internal Revenue Code relating to individual annuity taxation."

COHEN & URETZ, Washington, D.C. Lobbyist — Wildman, Harrold, Allen, Dixon & McDonnell, Memphis, Tenn. File 3/9/81. Legislative interest — "Amendment of [IRS Code] relating to estate tax alternative valuation date election (S 3381)."

COVE ASSOCIATES, Washington, D.C. Filed for self 3/18/81. Legislative interest — "Authorizations and appropriations for the Department of Defense and the Department of Energy." Lobbyist — John F. Cove, Washington, D.C.

ELY, GUESS & RUDD, Washington, D.C. Filed for self 3/12/81. Legislative interest — "...natural resources, Alaskan matters, telecommunications, Indian affairs."

THE FRANKLIN INSTITUTE, Philadelphia, Pa. Lobbyist — Ballard, Spahr, Andrews & Ingersoll, Washington, D.C. Filed 3/6/81. Legislative interest — "...energy and scientific research, funding for national memorial and museum activities...."

JAMES A. GOODMAN, Mahanoy City, Pa. Filed for self 3/12/81. Legislative interest — "Uncertain — whatever legislation would affect interests of client."

HAUK & ASSOCIATES, Washington, D.C. Filed for self 3/10/81. Legislative interest — "...proprietary day-care centers and/or hearing aid manufacturers....child welfare, finance and welfare, tax, small business and some health legislation...." Lobbyist — Dinah D. McElfresh, Washington, D.C.

ROBERT R. HUMPHREYS, Washington, D.C. Filed for self 3/13/81. Legislative interest — "Health, labor, employment, taxation, disability, aging, civil rights issues...."

LASKER, STONE & STERN, New York, N.Y. Lobbyist — Breed, Abbott & Morgan, Washington, D.C. Filed 3/20/81. Legislative interest — "...Commodity Straddles Tax Act of 1981...."

NATIONAL PUBLIC RADIO, Washington, D.C. Lobbyist — Pepper, Hamilton & Scheetz, Washington, D.C. Filed 3/30/81. Legislative interest — "...legislative proposals affecting National Public Radio." Filed for self 3/23/81. Legislative interest — "...legislation which is consistent with the public interest, First Amendment, and full development goals of public radio...rescission of the Corporation for Public Broadcasting's fiscal year 1982 funds." Lobbyist — Leslie Sewell, Washington, D.C.

PRIEST & FINE INC., Washington, D.C. Filed for self 3/12/81. Legislative interest — "...will vary depending on the client's interests but will be mainly in the tax area." Lobbyist — Daniel B. Priest, Washington, D.C.

HENRY SCHEIN INC., Port Washington, N.Y. Filed for self 3/30/81. Legislative interest — "...pharmaceutical manufacture and distribution, including patent provisions such as S 255 and HR 1937, Patent Term Restoration Act of 1981."

April Registrations

Citizens' Groups

AD HOC COMMITTEE TO PRESERVE FEDERALLY ASSISTED SHORT LINE RAILROADS, Washington, D.C. Lobbyist — Wald, Harkrader & Ross, Washington, D.C. Filed 4/27/81. Legislative interest — "...passage of an impoundment resolution restoring fiscal year 1981 funds for the [Local Rail Services Assistance] program, and the continuation of program funding for fiscal year 1982 and beyond."

AVIATION CONSUMER ACTION PROJECT, Washington, D.C. Filed for self 4/20/81. Legislative interest — "...HR 902...." Lobbyist — C. F. Hitchcock, Washington, D.C.

C. P. REHAB CORP., New York, N.Y. Lobbyist — Califano, Ross & Heineman, Washington, D.C. Filed 4/21/81. Legislative interest — "Matters affecting cardiac rehabilitation...."

COMMUNITY SERVICE SOCIETY OF NEW YORK INC., New York, N.Y. Filed for self 4/24/81. Legislative interest — "Domestic legislation relating to improving the welfare of the economically disadvantaged." Lobbyists — Anjean Carter, Peggy Chin, Linda Wolf Jones, New York, N.Y.

ENVIRONMENTAL POLICY CENTER, Washington, D.C. Filed for self 4/2/81. Legislative interest — "...energy conservation." Lobbyist — Harriet Holtzman-Parcells, Washington, D.C.

FOR LOVE OF CHILDREN INC., Washington, D.C. Filed for self 4/6/81. Legislative interest — "PL 96-272, Federal Adoption Assistance and Child Welfare Act of 1980...." Lobbyist — Ellen B. Griffith, Washington, D.C.

FRIENDS COMMITTEE ON NATIONAL LEGISLATION, Washington, D.C. File for self 4/10/81. Legislative interest — Not specified. Lobbyist — Ruth Flower, Washington, D.C.

INUPIAT COMMUNITY OF THE ARCTIC SLOPE, Barrow, Alaska. Lobbyist — Ziontz, Pirtle Law Firm, Seattle, Wash. Filed 4/3/81. Legislative interest — "...Native American rights, oil and gas leasing in the Beaufort and Chukchi seas...."

NATIONAL CLEAN AIR COALITION, Washington, D.C. Filed for self 4/11/81. Legislative interest — "...to preserve, restore and insure rational use of the ecosphere, particularly legislation dealing with clean air issues." Lobbyist — Tom Cosgrove, Washington, D.C.

NATIONAL COMMUNITY ACTION FOUNDATION INC., Washington, D.C. Filed for self 4/15/81. Legislative interest — "... reauthorization of programs operated by Community Services Administration; full funding of CSA; full funding and construction of all programs designed to assist the poor and minorities." Lobbyists — David Bradley; O'Connor & Hannan; Pepper, Hamilton & Scheetz, Washington, D.C.

NATIONAL CONGRESS OF AMERICAN INDIANS, Washington, D.C. Lobbyist — Action Inc., Washington, D.C. Filed 4/9/81. Legislative interest — "...maximum Indian access to

federal programs."

NATIONAL FEDERATION OF PARENTS FOR DRUG FREE YOUTH, Silver Spring, Md. Filed for self 4/15/81. Legislative interest — "Legislation concerning drug controls and drug use educational programs." Lobbyists — Susan Silverman; Patricia Burch, Potomac, Md.

NATIONAL RIFLE ASSOCIATION OF AMERICA, Washington, D.C. Filed for self 4/13/81. Legislative interest — "...all aspects of the acquisition, possession, and use of firearms and ammunition as well as legislation relating to hunting and wildlife conservation." Lobbyist — James Jay Baker, Washington, D.C.

NATIONAL RIGHT TO WORK COMMITTEE, Springfield, Va. Filed for self 4/1/81. Legislative interest — "...compulsory unionism in private industry, farm labor, public sector employees." Lobbyist — William A. Wilson III, Springfield, Va.

NATURAL RESOURCES DEFENSE COUNCIL, Washington, D.C. Filed for self 4/13/81. Legislative interest — "Clean Air Act...." Lobbyist — David G. Hawkins, Washington, D.C.

NEIGHBORHOOD SCHOOL COUNSEL, TURNER ELEMENTARY SCHOOL, Washington, D.C. Lobbyist — Pierson, Ball & Dowd, Washington, D.C. Filed 4/17/81. Legislative interest — "All legislation affecting the appropriations to the District of Columbia schools and the conditions of the Turner Elementary School."

PROTECT THE INNOCENT INC., Mooresville, Ind. Filed for self 4/10/81. Legislative interest — "S 114...." Lobbyist — Ros Stovall, Mooresville, Ind.

PUBLIC CITIZEN INC., Washington, D.C. Lobbyist — Richard P. Pollock, Washington, D.C. Filed 4/13/81. Legislative interest — "HR 1993, S 637."

RELIGIOUS COALITION FOR ABORTION RIGHTS INC., Washington, D.C. Filed for self 4/13/81. Legislative interest — "All federal legislation which impacts on a woman's right to choose abortion...." Lobbyists — Brenda I. Bregman, Pamela H. Barnett, Washington, D.C.

SIERRA CLUB, San Francisco, Calif. Filed for self 4/6/81. Legislative interest — "...conservation...." Lobbyist — Douglas W. Scott, San Francisco, Calif.

TULARE LAKE WATER USERS COMMITTEE, Corcoran, Calif. Lobbyist — William B. Hopkins, Roanoke, Va. Filed 4/10/81. Legislative interest — "S 14 and HR 6520, Reclamation Reform Act of 1902...."

UKPEAGVIK INUPIAT CORP., Barrow, Alaska. Lobbyist — Ziontz, Pirtle Law Firm, Seattle, Wash. Filed 4/3/81. Legislative interest — "...Native American rights, oil and gas leasing in the Beaufort and Chukchi seas...."

U.S. OVERSEAS TAX FAIRNESS COMMITTEE INC., Washington, D.C. Lobbyist — The Keefe Co., Washington, D.C. Filed 4/27/81. Legislative interest — "...overseas personal income tax regulations, specifically HR 911 and 913."

Corporations and Businesses

AMERICAN EXPRESS CO., New York, N.Y. Filed for self 4/20/81. Legislative interest — "...Service Industries Development Act, Cash Discount Act, Airline Deregulation Act Amendments." Lobbyist — Susan Clark, Washington, D.C.

AMERICAN GUARANTY FINANCIAL CORP., Portland, Ore. Lobbyist — Ullman Consultants Inc., Washington, D.C. Filed 4/22/81. (Former U.S. Rep. Al Ullman, D-Ore., 1957-81.) Filed for self 4/20/81. Legislative interest — "Legislation affecting the insurance industry."

AMERICAN INTERNATIONAL GROUP, New York, N.Y. Filed for self 4/16/81. Legislative interest — "All commercial insurance related issues." Lobbyist — Michael Cohen, Washington, D.C.

BENEFICIAL MANAGEMENT CORP. OF AMERICA, Wilmington, Del. Filed for self 4/2/81. Legislative interest — "Legislation concerning the consumer finance industry, savings and loan, banks, retailing and insurance." Lobbyist — Valerie M. Riggins, Arlington, Va.

BEST CHEVROLET, Washington, D.C. Lobbyist — Butler, Binion, Rice, Cook & Knapp, Washington, D.C. Filed 4/20/81. Legislative interest — "H J Res 598 and S J Res 193 concerning auto imports."

BOEING CO., Seattle, Wash. Lobbyist — Washington Industrial Team Inc., Washington, D.C. Filed 4/10/81. (Among the agents listed for this client were former U.S. Reps. Richard H. Ichord, D-Mo., 1961-81 and Bob Wilson, R-Calif., 1953-81.) Legislative interest — "...defense issues."

BROWN & ROOT INC., Washington, D.C. Filed for self 4/9/81. Legislative interest — "...engineering and construction industry ... tax reform, regulatory reform, Davis-Bacon, Foreign Corrupt Practices Act and trade issues." Lobbyist — Wyll W. Pleger, Washington, D.C.

CALIFORNIA PORTLAND CEMENT CO., Los Angeles, Calif. Lobbyist — Fred B. Rooney, Washington, D.C. Filed 4/13/81. (Former U.S. rep., D-Pa., 1963-79) Legislative interest — "Legislation under Department of Interior and Public Works Committee...."

COFFEE, SUGAR & COCOA EXCHANGE INC., New York, N.Y. Filed for self 4/14/81. Legislative interest — "Legislation regarding the Commodity Futures Trading Commission and sugar legislation." Lobbyist — Howard C. Katz, New York, N.Y.

COMARK, Newport Beach, Calif. Lobbyist — Edward N. Delaney, Washington, D.C. Filed 4/29/81. Legislative interest — "...S 626 — Commodity Straddles Tax Act of 1981; HR 1293; HR 1338; Internal Revenue Code of 1954, seek modification of proposals."

CONYERS FORD INC., Washington, D.C. Lobbyist — Butler, Binion, Rice, Cook & Knapp, Washington, D.C. Filed 4/20/81. Legislative interest — "H J Res 598 and S J Res 193 concerning auto imports."

COURTESY PONTIAC-AMC JEEP, Washington, D.C. Lobbyist — Butler, Binion, Rice, Cook & Knapp, Washington, D.C. Filed 4/20/81. Legislative interest — "H J Res 598 and S J Res 193 concerning auto imports."

TOM COWARD FORD, Washington, D.C. Lobbyist — Butler, Binion, Rice, Cook & Knapp, Washington, D.C. Filed 4/20/81. Legislative interest — "H J Res 598 and S J Res 193 concerning auto imports."

DIAMOND SHAMROCK CORP., Dallas, Texas. Filed for self 4/13/81. Legislative interest — "...legislation affecting ... business areas ... and corporations generally." Lobbyists — Patti Jo Baber, Dan R. Harlow, William J. Hotes, Charles R. Smith, Washington, D.C.

DUTCHER INDUSTRIES, San Diego, Calif. Lobbyist — Manatt, Phelps, Rothenberg & Tunney, Washington, D.C. Filed 4/17/81. Legislative interest — "...appropriations and authorizations for the Department of Transportation."

EMERSON ELECTRIC CO., St. Louis, Mo. Filed for self 4/13/81. Legislative interest — "...electrical devices." Lobbyist — Robert W. Staley, St. Louis, Mo.

EXXON CORP., New York, N.Y. Filed for self 4/14/81. Legislative interest — "...Emergency Petroleum Allocation Act, Outer Continental Shelf Lands Act, the Mining Law of 1872 and all aspects of the Natural Energy Act of 1978." Lobbyist — Bev D. Blackwood, Washington, D.C.

FEDERATED CASH MANAGEMENT SYSTEMS, Pittsburgh, Pa. Lobbyist — Dickstein, Shapiro & Morin, Washington, D.C. Filed 4/10/81. Legislative interest — "Legislation connected with banks, banking, investment companies and securities, including HR 1916, HR 2591 and HR 2980."

FORD MOTOR CO., Washington, D.C. Lobbyist — Butler, Binion, Rice, Cook & Knapp, Washington, D.C. Filed 4/20/81. Legislative interest — "H J Res 598 and S J Res 193 concerning auto imports."

GENERAL DYNAMICS CORP., St. Louis, Mo. Lobbyist — Washington Industrial Team Inc., Washington, D.C. Filed 4/10/81. (Among the agents listed for this client were former U.S. Reps. Richard H. Ichord, D-Mo., 1961-81 and Bob Wilson, R-Calif., 1953-81.) Legislative interest — "...defense issues."

GENERAL ELECTRIC CO., Fairfield, Conn. Filed for self 4/13/81. Legislative interest — "...aerospace and defense matters, labor law, regulation of trade, interstate and foreign commerce,

government procurement, environmental and customer items, etc." Lobbyist — Thomas L. Fagan, Washington, D.C.

GENERAL MOTORS CORP., Detroit, Mich. Filed for self 4/20/81. Legislative interest — Not specified. Lobbyist — Mark L. Kemmer, Washington, D.C.

GIC FINANCIAL SERVICES CORP., Rosemont, Ill. Lobbyist — Winston & Strawn, Washington, D.C. Filed 4/29/81. Legislative interest — "HR 2400 — the Economic Recovery Tax Act of 1981."

GREAT NATIONAL CORP., Dallas, Texas Lobbyist — Akin, Gump, Strauss, Hauer & Feld, Washington, D.C. Filed 4/27/81. Legislative interest — "...proposed budget rescissions, S Con Res 9, the revised second concurrent resolution on the fiscal year 1981 budget."

GRUMMAN AEROSPACE CORP., Bethpage, N.Y. Lobbyist — Washington Industrial Team Inc., Washington, D.C. Filed 4/10/81. (Among the agents listed for this client were former U.S. Reps. Richard H. Ichord, D-Mo., 1961-81 and Bob Wilson, R-Calif., 1953-81.) Legislative interest — "...defense issues."

GTE TELENET INC., Stamford, Conn. Filed for self 4/9/81. Legislative interest — "...amendments to Communications Act of 1934, amendments to Postal Reorganization Act, U.S. representation in international communications matters. S 271, HR 2813, HR 1957." Lobbyist — Kathleen Casey, Vienna, Va.

GULF OIL CORP., Pittsburgh, Pa. Filed for self 4/14/81. Legislative interest — "...matters pertaining to the oil and gas industry." Lobbyist — Kevin J. Riordan, Washington, D.C.

HELICOPTER ASSOCIATION INTERNATIONAL, Washington, D.C. Lobbyist — Crowell & Moring, Washington, D.C. Filed 4/21/81. Legislative interest — "Legislation affecting the helicopter industry."

HELIONETICS INC., Irvine, Calif. Lobbyist — Nossaman, Krueger & Marsh, Los Angeles, Calif. and Washington, D.C. Filed 4/10/81. Legislative interest — "Alternative energy bills...."

HOLDING AND CUSTOMER DEVELOPMENT PROGRESS INC., Oxon Hill, Md. Filed for self 4/10/81. Legislative interest — HR 2319, Kemp-Garcia bill." Lobbyist — Charles L. Marshall II, Oxon Hill, Md.

J. M. HUBER CORP., Edison, N.J. Filed for self 4/6/81. Legislative interest — "...bills dealing with safety, environment, product safety and energy." Lobbyist — H. R. Balikov, Edison, N.J.

HUGHES AIRCRAFT CO., Culver City, Calif. Lobbyist — Washington Industrial Team Inc., Washington, D.C. Filed 4/10/81. (Among the agents listed for this client were former U.S. Reps. Richard H. Ichord, D-Mo., 1961-81 and Bob Wilson, R-Calif., 1953-81.) Legislative interest — "...defense issues."

JONES, LOYD & WEBSTER INC., Houston, Texas. Lobbyist — Lillick, McHose & Charles, Washington, D.C. Filed 4/11/81. Legislative interest — "Maritime authorization bill, HR 2526."

KANKAKEE, BEAVERVILLE & SOUTHERN RAILROAD CO., Momence, Ill. Lobbyist — Witkowski, Weiner, McCaffrey, and Brodsky, Washington, D.C. Filed 4/13/81. Legislative interest — "...shortline railroad operation, acquisition and financing ... support for 1981 funding of the Local Rail Service Assistance Act."

KLINE IRON & STEEL CO. INC., Columbia, S.C. Lobbyist — Crowell & Moring, Washington, D.C. Filed 4/13/81. Legislative interest — "...installment sales legislation under the Internal Revenue Code."

KNOLL FINE CHEMICALS INC., New York, N.Y. Lobbyist — Morgan, Lewis & Bockius, Washington, D.C. Filed 4/24/81. Legislative interest — "...to reduce the tariff rate for caffeine."

M & M PLASTICS, Chattanooga, Tenn. Lobbyist — Patton, Boggs & Blow, Washington, D.C. Filed 4/14/81. Legislative interest — "For reauthorization of the Consumer Product Safety Commission, particularly as it relates to dual purpose packaging."

McDONNELL DOUGLAS CORP., St. Louis, Mo. Lobbyist — Washington Industrial Team Inc., Washington, D.C. Filed 4/10/81. (Among the agents listed for this client were former U.S. Reps. Richard H. Ichord, D-Mo., 1961-81 and Bob Wilson, R-Calif., 1953-81.) Legislative interest — "...defense issues."

MALLON MOTORS INC., Washington, D.C. Lobbyist — Butler, Binion, Rice, Cook & Knapp, Washington, D.C. Filed 4/20/81. Legislative interest — "H J Res 598 and S J Res 193 concerning auto imports."

MANUFACTURERS HANOVER CORP., New York, N.Y. Lobbyist — Stuart A. Lewis, Washington, D.C. Filed 4/14/81. Legislative interest — "Financial legislation."

MERCK & CO. INC., Rahway, N.J. Lobbyist — Ullman Consultants Inc., Washington, D.C. Filed 4/22/81. (Former U.S. Rep. Al Ullman, D-Ore., 1957-81.) Legislative interest — "Tax legislation affecting the pharmaceutical industry."

MERRELL DOW PHARMACEUTICALS INC., Cincinnati, Ohio. Filed for self 4/8/81. Legislative interest — Not specified. Lobbyist — Paul F. Burdett, Severna Park, Md.

MERRILL LYNCH LEASING INC., New York, N.Y. Lobbyist — Rogers & Wells, Washington, D.C. Filed 4/20/81. Legislative interest — "Taxes generally and HR 2400 specifically."

MONSANTO CO., St. Louis, Mo. Filed for self 4/10/81. Legislative interest — "...the agrochemical and agriculture industries." Lobbyists — John T. Richardson, Chester T. Dickerson Jr., Washington, D.C.

MONTGOMERY WARD & CO. INC., Chicago, Ill. Filed for self 4/28/81. Legislative interest — "...the retail industry, including relations with federal agencies, manufacturers, suppliers, employees and customers." Lobbyist — Thomas E. Grace, Washington, D.C.

MOORE McCORMACK RESOURCES INC., Stamford, Conn. Filed for self 4/20/81. Legislative interest — "...coal, oil, gas, iron ore and cement production, ... domestic and international shipping." Lobbyist — Robert N. Thompson, Stamford, Conn.

MOUNTAIN STATES ENERGY INC., Butte, Mont. Lobbyist — Schwabe, Williamson, Wyatt, Moore and Roberts, Washington, D.C. Filed 4/10/81. (Former U.S. Rep. Robert B. Duncan, D-Ore., 1963-67, 1975-81, was the agent listed for this client.) Legislative interest — "MHD (Magnetohydrodynamics) — low cost, clean electric power derived from coal."

MOWSAFE PRODUCTS INC., Columbus, Ohio Lobbyist — Vorys, Sater, Seymour & Pease, Washington, D.C. Filed 4/2/81. Legislative interest — "...regulations of the Consumer Product Safety Council."

NABISCO INC., East Hanover, N.J. Filed for self 4/17/81. Legislative interest — Not specified. Lobbyist — Laurie L. Michel, Washington, D.C.

NATIONAL BANK OF DETROIT, Detroit, Mich. Lobbyist — Stuart A. Lewis, Washington, D.C. Filed 4/14/81. Legislative interest — "Financial legislation."

NATIONAL INVESTMENT DEVELOPMENT CORP., Los Angeles, Calif. Lobbyist — Manatt, Phelps, Rothenberg & Tunney, Washington, D.C. Filed 4/28/81. (Former U.S. Rep. James C. Corman, D-Calif., 1961-81, was listed as the agent for this client.) Legislative interest — "Various legislative proposals affecting the real estate industry."

NATIONAL PUBLIC RADIO, Washington, D.C. Lobbyist — Miller, Cassidy, Larroca & Lewin, Washington, D.C. Filed 4/28/81. Legislative interest — "...revision of the Copyright Act of 1976 as it relates to cable royalty distribution."

NEIGHBORHOOD TV CO. INC., Washington, D.C. Lobbyist — O'Connor & Hannan, Washington, D.C. Filed 4/14/81. Legislative interest — not specified.

NEW ENERGY CORP. OF INDIANA, Washington, D.C. Lobbyist — Edward A. Merlis, Washington, D.C. Filed 4/13/81. Legislative interest — "Alcohol fuels loan guarantees."

NORANDA MINING INC., Salt Lake City, Utah. Filed for self 4/13/81. Legislative interest — "...mining, public lands, appropriations ... funding of Defense Production Act." Lobbyist — Douglas S. Smith, Salt Lake City, Utah.

NORTH PLAINS GRAIN PRODUCTS COOPERATIVE, Canby, Minn. Lobbyist — Federal Services Co., Washington, D.C. Filed 4/13/81. Legislative interest — "Matters related to the production of alcohol fuels and protein."

NORTHRUP CORP., Los Angeles, Calif. Lobbyist — Manatt, Phelps, Rothenberg & Tunney, Washington, D.C. Filed 4/17/81. Legislative interest — "...appropriations and authoriza-

tions for the Department of Defense. Resolution relating to approval of foreign military sales."

OASIS PETROLEUM CO., Culver City, Calif. Lobbyist — Cotton, Day & Doyle, Washington, D.C. Filed 4/16/81. Legislative interest — "All legislation dealing with alcohol fuels, including the fiscal year 1981 and fiscal year 1982 budgets."

OCCIDENTAL PETROLEUM CORP., Los Angeles, Calif. Lobbyist — Bricker & Eckler, Washington, D.C. Filed 4/2/81. (Listed as agent for this client was former U.S. Rep. Samuel L. Devine, R-Ohio, 1959-81.) Legislative interest — "Any and all legislation affecting the production, development and marketing of natural resources and chemicals."

OTIS ELEVATOR CO., Denver, Colo. Lobbyist — Schwabe, Williamson, Wyatt, Moore and Roberts, Washington, D.C. Filed 4/10/81. (Listed as agent for this client was former U.S. Rep. Robert Duncan, D-Ore., 1963-67, 1975-81.) Legislative interest — "AGRT — Advanced Group Rapid Transit."

PACOR CORP., Philadelphia, Pa. Lobbyist — Crowell & Moring, Washington, D.C. Filed 4/10/81. Legislative interest — "...product liability and compensation systems."

J. C. PENNEY CO. INC., Washington, D.C. Lobbyist — O'Connor & Hannan, Washington, D.C. Filed 4/14/81. Legislative interest — "...Capital Costs Recovery Act, HR 4646 and S 1435."

PEOPLE EXPRESS AIRLINES INC., Newark, N.J. Lobbyist — Butler, Binion, Rice, Cook & Knapp, Washington, D.C. Filed 4/20/81. Legislative interest — "Transportation Appropriations Act for fiscal year 1981, budget resolution for fiscal year 1981, transportation rescission bill."

PFIZER INC., New York, N.Y. Lobbyist — Burt Rosen, Washington, D.C. Filed 4/8/81. Legislative interest — "...chemicals, cosmetics and allied products."

PHELPS DODGE CORP., Washington, D.C. Lobbyist — Charls E. Walker Associates Inc., Washington, D.C. Filed 4/9/81. Legislative interest — "...refundability of the investment tax credit."

PHILLIPS PETROLEUM, Bartlesville, Okla., Lobbyist — Groom and Nordberg, Washington, D.C. Filed 4/10/81. Legislative interest — "Federal legislation affecting Title 26 of U.S.C."

THE PILLSBURY CO., Minneapolis, Minn. Filed for self 4/14/81. Legislative interest — "The Agricultural Act of 1981." Lobbyists — Dan A. Gunderson, Gerald L. Olson, Minneapolis, Minn.

POQUOSON MOTORS INC., Washington, D.C. Lobbyist — Butler, Binion, Rice, Cook & Knapp, Washington, D.C. Filed 4/20/81. Legislative interest — "H J Res 598 and S J Res 193 concerning auto imports."

RAYTHEON CO., Lexington, Mass. Lobbyist — Washington Industrial Team Inc., Washington, D.C. Filed 4/10/81. (Among the agents listed for this client were former U.S. Reps. Richard H. Ichord, D-Mo., 1961-81 and Bob Wilson, R-Calif., 1953-81.) Legislative interest — "...defense issues."

RENEWED ENERGY CORP., Salt Lake City, Utah. Filed for self 4/17/81. Legislative interest — "Synfuels act, gasohol and synfuels loan guarantees...." Lobbyist — Frances L. Babb, Washington, D.C.

REPUBLIC AIRLINES INC., Minneapolis, Minn. Lobbyist — Cook, Purcell, Hansen & Henderson, Washington, D.C. Filed 4/10/81. Legislative interest — "Against termination of section 406 subsidy as authorized by Airline Deregulation Act of 1978."

RIVIANA FOODS INC., McLean, Va. Lobbyist — Surrey & Morse, Washington, D.C. Filed 4/10/81. Legislative interest — "Legislation relating to agriculture, especially rice."

RMI INC., National City, Calif. Lobbyist — Robert C. Wilson, Washington, D.C. Filed 4/10/81. (Former U.S. rep., R-Calif., 1953-81.) Legislative interest — "Military authorization and appropriation."

ROTAN MOSLE INC., Houston, Texas. Lobbyist — Lillick, McHose & Charles, Washington, D.C. Filed 4/11/81. Legislative interest — "Maritime authorization bill, HR 2526."

RUHRKOHLE A. G., Essen, West Germany. Lobbyist — Prather Seeger Doolittle & Farmer, Washington, D.C. Filed 4/9/81. Legislative interest — "...All matters regarding synthetic fuels and other energy issues."

ST. JOE MINERALS CORP., Washington, D.C. Lobbyist — Camp, Carmouche, Palmer, Barsh & Hunter, Washington, D.C. Filed 4/7/81. Legislative interest — "Seeking amendment to Mineral Lands Leasing Act of 1920 (30 U.S.C. 181, et seq.), placing moratorium on foreign acquisition and control of mineral resources on lands."

SCHOLASTIC MAGAZINES INC., Englewood Cliffs, N.J. Lobbyists — Elizabeth Jane Robbins, Roger Tilles, Washington, D.C. Filed 4/23/81. Legislative interest — "...postal operations and school reading programs."

SCOTT PAPER CO., Philadelphia, Pa. Lobbyist — Charls E. Walker Associates Inc., Washington, D.C. Filed 4/9/81. Legislative interest — "...refundability of the investment tax credit."

JOSEPH E. SEAGRAM & SONS INC., New York, N.Y. Lobbyists — Thevenot, Murray & Scheer, Washington, D.C., filed 4/9/81; Van Ness, Feldman & Sutcliffe, Washington, D.C., filed 4/1/81. Legislative interest — "...Mineral Lands Leasing Act of 1981, HR 2826."

SEARS, ROEBUCK AND CO., Chicago, Ill. Lobbyist — Brenda M. Girton, Brian F. Kelly, Washington, D.C. Filed 4/6/81. Legislative interest — "...labor relations, employee benefits and personnel matters ... antitrust, competition, regulatory reform...."

SEATTLE FIRST NATIONAL BANK, Seattle, Wash. Lobbyist — Stuart A. Lewis, Washington, D.C. Filed 4/1/81. Legislative interest — "Financial legislation."

HENRY SCHEIN INC., Port Washington, N.Y. Lobbyist — Botein, Hays, Sklar & Herzberg, New York, N.Y. Filed 4/3/81. Legislative interest — "Legislation concerning pharmaceutical manufacture and distribution...."

SHAMROCK FORD, Washington, D.C. Lobbyist — Butler, Binion, Rice, Cook & Knapp, Washington, D.C. Filed 4/20/81. Legislative interest — "H J Res 598 and S J Res 193 concerning auto imports."

SOUTHDOWN/PELTO OIL CO., Houston, Texas. Lobbyist — Bracewell & Patterson, Washington, D.C. Filed 4/8/81. Legislative interest — "Legislation relating to tight sands gas, waterway user charges and depreciation."

SOUTHERN PACIFIC COMMUNICATIONS CO., Burlingame, Calif. Filed for self 4/8/81. Legislative interest — "Legislation affecting common carrier communications, e.g., HR 6121, HR 2827, S 611, S 622." Lobbyist — Jeanne P. Kowalski, Washington, D.C.

SPERRY DIVISION, Arlington, Va. Lobbyist — R. Q. Old & Associates Inc., Alexandria, Va. Filed 4/9/81. Legislative interest — "fiscal year 1982 defense authorization bill."

THE STANDARD OIL COMPANY (OHIO), Cleveland, Ohio. Filed for self 4/13/81. Legislative interest — "...petroleum production, refining and distribution, petro-chemicals and coal." Lobbyist — John R. Miller, Cleveland, Ohio.

P. L. THOMAS & CO. INC., Barnardsville, N.J. Lobbyist — Harris, Berg & Creskoff, Washington, D.C. Filed 4/29/81. (Former U.S. Rep. Herbert E. Harris II, D-Va., 1975-81, was listed as agent for this client.) Legislative interest — "...assure that carob powder may enter the United States without duty."

TIGER INTERNATIONAL INC., Los Angeles, Calif. Filed for self 4/9/81. Legislative interest — "HR 1053 — Capital Cost Recovery — support; S 508 — Airport & Airway Development Act — support; HR 1964 — Deductability, Government Motor Carrier Operation Rights — support; S 681 — Oil Spill Liability — modify." Lobbyist — Jack Reiter, Washington, D.C.

TOYOTA MOTOR SALES USA INC., Torrance, Calif. Lobbyist — Hogan & Hartson, Washington, D.C. Filed 4/17/81. Legislative interest — "Legislation affecting the importation of motor vehicles into the United States."

TRW INC., Washington, D.C. Lobbyist — Washington Industrial Team Inc., Washington, D.C. Filed 4/10/81. (Among the agents listed for this client were former U.S. Reps. Richard H. Ichord, D-Mo., 1961-81 and Bob Wilson, R-Calif., 1953-81.) Legislative interest — ...defense issues." Filed for self 4/8/81. Legislative interest — "...aerospace, electronics, transportation, energy, foreign trade ... taxation, finance, pension, health insurance...." Lobbyists — John R. Carter Jr., Brenda J. Gore, Raymond R.

Krause, Washington, D.C.

20th CENTURY FOX FILM CORP., Beverly Hills, Calif. Lobbyist — Manatt, Phelps, Rothenberg & Tunney, Washington, D.C. Filed 4/28/81. (Listed as agent for this client was former U.S. Rep. James C. Corman, D-Calif., 1961-81.) Legislative interest — "Various legislative proposals affecting the film industry."

UNITED AIR LINES, Chicago, Ill. Filed for self 4/22/81. Legislative interest — not specified. Lobbyist — James P. Linse, Washington, D.C.

UNITED STATES LEASING INTERNATIONAL INC., San Francisco, Calif. Lobbyist — Cohen & Uretz, Washington, D.C. Filed 4/21/81. Legislative interest — "Capital cost recovery tax legislation proposals."

U.S. WINDPOWER ASSOCIATION, Burlington, Mass. Lobbyist — Benjamin Wolff, Washington, D.C. Filed 4/10/81. Legislative interest — "Crude Oil Windfall Profit Tax Act (PL 96-223) and other legislation and regulations relating to energy."

UNITED TECHNOLOGIES CORP., Hartford, Conn. Lobbyist — Washington Industrial Team Inc., Washington, D.C. Filed 4/10/81. (Among the agents listed for this client were former U.S. Reps. Richard H. Ichord, D-Mo., 1961-81 and Bob Wilson, R-Calif., 1953-81.) Legislative interest — "...defense issues."

VALERO ENERGY CORP., San Antonio, Texas Lobbyist — Bracewell & Patterson, Washington, D.C. Filed 4/8/81. Legislative interest — "Energy legislation ... such as fuel-use act amendments and pricing of natural gas."

VOLKSWAGEN OF AMERICA INC., Warren, Mich. Filed for self 4/1/81. Legislative interest — "Amendments to the Clean Air Act. S 396, to impose quotas on the importation of automobiles from Japan during 1981, 1982 and 1983." Lobbyist — Joseph W. Kennebeck, Washington, D.C.

WARNER COMMUNICATIONS INC., New York, N.Y. Filed for self 4/20/81. Legislative interest — "Legislation dealing with telecommunications policy and other legislative matters of interest to a diversified entertainment company...." Lobbyist — George L. Murphy, Washington, D.C. (Former U.S. sen., R-Calif., 1965-71.)

WESTERN SOLAR UTILIZATION NETWORK, Portland, Ore. Lobbyist — Rob Wallace, Washington, D.C. Filed 4/8/81. Legislative interest — "Appropriations, budget legislation."

WESTERN UNION INTERNATIONAL, New York, N.Y. Lobbyist — Randall, Bangert & Thelen, Washington, D.C. Filed 4/23/81. Legislative interest — "International Record Carrier Competition Act, S 271, against."

WESTERN UNION TELEGRAPH CO., Washington, D.C. Lobbyist — Nossaman, Krueger & Marsh, Washington, D.C. Filed 4/20/81. Legislative interest — "Repeal of Section 222 of the 1934 Communications Act."

WESTINGHOUSE ELECTRIC CORP., Pittsburgh, Pa. Lobbyist — Washington Industrial Team Inc., Washington, D.C. Filed 4/10/81. (Among the agents listed for this client were former U.S. Reps. Richard H. Ichord, D-Mo., 1961-81 and Bob Wilson, R-Calif., 1953-81.) Legislative interest — "...defense issues."

WIEN AIRLINES, Anchorage, Alaska. Lobbyist — Birch, Horton, Bittner and Monroe, Washington, D.C. Filed 4/7/81. Legislative interest — "Airline subsidy issues."

WISCONSIN BARGE LINE INC., St. Louis, Mo. Lobbyist — Lillick McHose & Charles, Washington, D.C. Filed 4/1/81. Legislative interest — "Maritime authorization bill, HR 2526."

WOOD ENTERPRISES INC., Abilene, Texas. Lobbyist — Richard W. Bliss, Washington, D.C. Filed 4/27/81. Legislative interest — "All geothermal energy-related legislation, including S 669."

International Relations

REPUBLIC OF ZAIRE. Lobbyist — Surrey & Morse, Washington, D.C. Filed 4/13/81. Legislative interest — "Promoting passage of the Administration's military and economic assistance program insofar as they may relate to the Republic of Zaire, including foreign assistance authorization and appropriations bills."

SULTANATE OF OMAN. Lobbyist — Patton, Boggs and Blow, Washington, D.C. Filed 4/16/81. Legislative interest — "...foreign assistance and military construction."

Labor Groups

AMERICAN POSTAL WORKERS UNION, AFL-CIO, Washington, D.C. Filed for self 4/21/81. Legislative interest — "...postal and federal employees' welfare and the Postal Service. Lobbyist — Moe Biller, Washington, D.C.

BROTHERHOOD OF RAILROAD SIGNALMEN, Mount Prospect, Ill. Filed for self 4/9/81. Legislative interest — "...matters of interest to railroad workers." Lobbyist — W. D. Pickett, Washington, D.C.

INTERNATIONAL BROTHERHOOD OF TEAMSTERS, CHAUFFEURS, WAREHOUSEMEN AND HELPERS OF AMERICA, LOCAL 959, Anchorage, Alaska. Lobbyist — Birch, Horton, Bittner and Monroe, Washington, D.C. Filed 4/7/81. Legislative interest — "Transportation excise tax bill — S 2075."

NATIONAL EDUCATION ASSOCIATION, Washington, D.C. Filed for self 4/14/81. Legislative interest — "...public education." Lobbyist — George Roberts, Washington, D.C.

NFL PLAYERS ASSOCIATION, Washington, D.C. Lobbyist — Landis, Cohen, Singman and Rauh, Washington, D.C. Filed 4/10/81. Legislative interest — "All matters of legislative concern including HR 823, HR 2263 and other bills affecting professional sports."

OIL, CHEMICAL AND ATOMIC WORKERS INTERNATIONAL UNION, Denver, Colo. Filed for self 4/9/81. Legislative interest — "...opposing oil decontrol, emergency preparedness the Administration is preparing to adopt that is based on the free market concept and the president's budget." Lobbyist — Gary C. Thompson, Washington, D.C.

SEAFARERS INTERNATIONAL UNION, Washington, D.C. Filed for self 4/20/81. Legislative interest — "...maritime authorization, Public Health Service, accelerated tax depreciation, port development, coal exports, DOD budget, SPR." Lobbyist — Elizabeth A. Coker, Mark Reihl, Washington, D.C.

Military and Veterans

VIETNAM VETERANS OF AMERICA, New York, N.Y. Lobbyist — John F. Terzano, Washington, D.C. Filed 4/3/81. Legislative interest — "...legislation affecting war veterans, their dependents and survivors."

State and Local Governments

CANAVERAL PORT AUTHORITY, Cape Canaveral, Fla. Lobbyist — Cramer & Cramer, Washington, D.C. Filed 4/9/81. (Former U.S. Rep. William C. Cramer, R-Fla., 1955-71, was among the agents listed for this client.) Legislative interest — "Legislation relating to federal assistance to ports or railways for enhanced coal transportation or processing facilities...."

CITY OF GARDENA, Gardena, Calif. Lobbyist — Charles H. Wilson, Washington, D.C. Filed 4/10/81. (Former U.S. rep., D-Calif., 1963-81.) Legislative interest — "...Gardena Waste to Energy Resource Recovery Facility ... assist the City of Gardena in obtaining federal funding for the project."

CITY OF PHILADELPHIA, Philadelphia, Pa. Lobbyist — Judith A. Winchester, Washington, D.C. Filed 4/6/81. Legislative interest — "Legislative proposals and regulations affecting the general operations of the City."

CITY AND COUNTY OF SAN FRANCISCO, San Francisco, Calif. Lobbyist — Morrison & Foerster, Washington, D.C. Filed 4/22/81. Legislative interest — "Legislation to amend the Federal Water Pollution Control Act...."

DAYTON-MONTGOMERY COUNTY PARK DISTRICT, Dayton, Ohio. Lobbyist — Duncan, Weinberg & Miller,

Washington, D.C. Filed 4/10/81. Legislative interest — "The Land and Water Conservation Fund, 16 U.S.C., section 4601-5; Interior Appropriations Act...."

EUGENE WATER AND ELECTRIC BOARD, Eugene, Ore. Lobbyist — Schwabe, Williamson, Wyatt, Moore and Roberts, Washington, D.C. Filed 4/10/81. (Listed as agent for this client was former U.S. Rep. Robert Duncan, D-Ore., 1963-67, 1975-81.) Legislative interest — "Geothermal energy generation."

LOS ANGELES COMMUNITY REDEVELOPMENT AGENCY, Los Angeles, Calif. Lobbyist — Manatt, Phelps, Rothenberg & Tunney, Washington, D.C. Filed 4/17/81. Legislative interest — "...appropriations and authorizations for the Department of Transportation."

Trade Associations

AGRICULTURAL PRODUCERS, Los Angeles, Calif. Lobbyist — Seyfarth, Shaw, Fairweather & Geraldson, Washington, D.C. Filed 4/20/81. Legislative interest — "...employment of migratory workers, such as Fair Labor Contractor Registration Act Amendments of 1981 (S 922)...."

AIR TRANSPORT ASSOCIATION, Washington, D.C. Lobbyist — Black, Manafort and Stone, Alexandria, Va. Filed 4/1/81. Legislative interest — not specified.

AMERICAN ASSOCIATION OF CROP INSURERS, Chicago, Ill. Filed for self 4/2/81. Legislative interest — "Legislation to provide funds for implementation of the Federal Crop Insurance Act of 1980."

AMERICAN BOILER MANUFACTURERS ASSOCIATION INC., Arlington, Va. Lobbyist — Wyman, Bautzer, Rothman, Kuchel & Silbert, Washington, D.C. Filed 4/28/81. Legislative interest — "Fuel Use Act of 1978, PL 95-620." Filed for self 4/10/81. Lobbyists — William H. Axtman, Russell N. Mosher, Arlington, Va.

AMERICAN BUSINESS COALITION, Baltimore, Md. Lobbyist — Thompson & Crawford, Washington, D.C. Filed 4/17/81. Legislative interest — "...in support of maintaining the present funding level for the Urban Development Action Grant Program."

AMERICAN CONSULTING ENGINEERS COUNCIL, Washington, D.C. Filed for self 4/10/81. Legislative interest — "Matters relating to public works, transportation, the environment, pollution control, housing, equal employment opportunity, public health and safety, economy and efficiency in government and energy legislation." Lobbyist — Constance E. R. Corbino, Washington, D.C.

AMERICAN COUNCIL OF LIFE INSURANCE INC., Washington, D.C. Filed for self 4/14/81. Legislative interest — "Proposed legislation which would affect the life insurance industry." Lobbyist — Robert F. Froehlke, Washington, D.C.

AMERICAN FARM BUREAU FEDERATION, Park Ridge, Ill. Filed for self 4/22/81. Legislative interest — "Farm price support and adjustment legislation, agricultural marketing and services, surplus disposal, market expansion, monopoly, agricultural research and extension, commodity market regulation, agricultural credit, rural electrification, labeling and standards and grades." Lobbyist — Stuart Proctor, Washington, D.C.

AMERICAN FROZEN FOOD INSTITUTE, McLean, Va. Filed for self 4/17/81. Legislative interest — "...consumer legislation, farm labor legislation, agricultural bargaining legislation, marketing order legislation, FLSA amendments...."

AMERICAN HOME ECONOMICS ASSOCIATION, Washington, D.C. Lobbyist — Action Inc., Washington, D.C. Filed 4/9/81. Legislative interest — "...supporting the Vocational Education Act as it pertains to consumer homemaking...."

AMERICAN HOT DIP GALVANIZERS ASSOCIATION, Washington, D.C. Lobbyists — Taft, Stettinius & Hollister, Cincinnati, Ohio; Robert Taft Jr., Washington, D.C. (Former U.S. rep., R-Ohio, 1963-65; 1967-71; U.S. sen. 1971-77); Robert J. Stayin, Washington, D.C. Filed 4/10/81. Legislative interest — "...matters relating to federal highway standards."

AMERICAN INDIAN HIGHER EDUCATION CONSORTIUM, Denver, Colo. Lobbyist — Action Inc., Washington,

D.C. Filed 4/9/81. Legislative interest — "...in support of PL 95-471, the Tribally Controlled Community College Assistance Act of 1978...."

AMERICAN INSTITUTE OF ARCHITECTS, Washington, D.C. Lobbyist — Thevenot, Murray & Scheer, Washington, D.C. Filed 4/13/81. Legislative interest — "In support of legislation affecting professional liability (HR 248)."

AMERICAN PAPER INSTITUTE INC., New York, N.Y. Filed for self 4/6/81. Legislative interest — "...those affecting the pulp, paper, and paperboard industry, its operation, practices and properties; tax legislation and environmental legislation, air, water and energy." Lobbyists — Robert T. McKernan, Marc D. Yacker, Washington, D.C.

AMERICAN PETROLEUM REFINERS ASSOCIATION, Washington, D.C. Lobbyist — Bracewell & Patterson, Washington, D.C. Filed 4/8/81. Legislative interest — "Legislation relating to refinery policy, such as emergency allocation of crude oil, import tariffs and foreign tax credits."

AMERICAN SOCIETY OF COMPOSERS, AUTHORS AND PUBLISHERS, New York, N.Y. Lobbyist — Landis, Cohen, Singman and Rauh, Washington, D.C. Filed 4/10/81. Legislative interest — "Amendments to Copyright Act, 17 U.S.C., including HR 20, HR 1805, HR 2006, HR 2007, HR 2108 and S 603."

AMERICAN SOCIETY OF TRAVEL AGENTS INC., New York, N.Y. Filed for self 4/29/81. Legislative interest — "Visa waver, HR 7321; small business taxes and tourism, out-of-country convention taxes, national tourism policy legislation." Lobbyist — Barbara E. O'Hara, Washington, D.C.

AMERICAN WAREHOUSEMEN'S ASSOCIATION, Chicago, Ill. Lobbyist — Patrick C. O'Connor, Washington, D.C. Filed 4/20/81. Legislative interest — "Tax legislation, HR 2400."

APARTMENT AND OFFICE BUILDING ASSOCIATION, Washington, D.C. Filed for self 4/7/81. Legislative interest — "S 2080, HR 7579, HR 6075, Public Buildings Act of 1980, S 533."

ASSOCIATED BUILDERS AND CONTRACTORS INC., Washington, D.C. Lobbyist — Hansell, Post, Brandon & Dorsey, Washington, D.C. Filed 4/20/81. Legislative interest — "...the authorization of and appropriations for programs affecting or impacting the construction industry." Filed for self 4/13/81. Legislative interest — "All activities in the U.S. Congress affecting labor-management relations...." Lobbyist — James P. Schlicht, Washington, D.C.

THE ASSOCIATED GENERAL CONTRACTORS OF AMERICA, Washington, D.C. Filed for self 4/9/81. Legislative interest — "MSHA-OSHA clarification — S 351." Lobbyists — John Heffner, Susan J. Loomis, James Thompson Jr., Washington, D.C.

ASSOCIATION OF FOOD DISTRIBUTORS INC., New York, N.Y. Lobbyist — Harris, Berg & Creskoff, Washington, D.C. Filed 4/29/81. (Listed as agent for this client was former U.S. Rep. Herbert E. Harris II, D-Va., 1975-81.) Legislative interest — "To support legislation to assure that tuna packed in U.S. insular possessions is not included in the tabulations made for purposes of the applicable tariff quota."

THE BUSINESS ROUNDTABLE, New York, N.Y. Lobbyist — Leva, Hawes, Symington, Martin & Oppenheimer, Washington, D.C. Filed 4/15/81. Legislative interest — "...amendments to the Clean Air Act." Filed for self 4/8/81. Legislative interest — "...labor relations, employment, antitrust and consumerism...." Lobbyist — Gayle Randol, Washington, D.C.

CHAMBER OF COMMERCE OF THE UNITED STATES, Washington, D.C. Filed for self 4/6/81. Legislative interest — "Energy matters of interest to the business community...." Lobbyist — Susan C. DeMarr, Washington, D.C.

CHEMICAL MANUFACTURERS ASSOCIATION, Washington, D.C. Filed for self 4/11/81. Legislative interest — "...Federal tax and patent legislation affecting the chemical industry." Lobbyist — Robert B. Hill, Washington, D.C.

COAL OIL PRODUCERS ASSOCIATION, Washington, D.C. Lobbyist — Ginsburg, Feldman, Weil and Bress, Washington, D.C. Filed 4/21/81. Legislative interest — "Promoting federal

programs and policies which facilitate the development and demonstration of technologies for the production and use of coal oil mixtures."

COMMITTEE FOR EQUITABLE ACCESS TO CRUDE OIL, Washington, D.C. Filed for self 4/9/81. Legislative interest — "Standby program for crude oil access." Lobbyist — James A. Gavin, Washington, D.C.

COUNCIL OF CREATIVE ARTISTS, LIBRARIES AND MUSEUMS, New York, N.Y. Lobbyist — Landis, Cohen, Singman and Rauh, Washington, D.C. Filed 4/28/81. Legislative interest — "...S 649 and HR 444."

COUNCIL OF INDUSTRIAL BOILER OWNERS, Fairfax, Va. Lobbyist — Sutherland, Asbill & Brennan, Washington, D.C. Filed 4/10/81. Legislative interest — "Energy legislation."

COUNCIL FOR RURAL HOUSING AND DEVELOPMENT, Washington, D.C. Lobbyist — Lane and Edson, Washington, D.C. Filed 4/30/81. Legislative interest — "Housing legislation affecting rural rental housing."

COUNCIL OF STATE CHAMBERS OF COMMERCE, Washington, D.C. Filed for self 4/11/81. Legislative interest — "Federal taxation, federal expenditures, social legislation, labor relations and proposed legislation regulating state taxation of interstate commerce." Lobbyists — William R. Brown, Mark Cahoon, Washington, D.C.

THE EDISON ELECTRIC INSTITUTE, Washington, D.C. Filed for self 4/29/81. Legislative interest — "...Internal Revenue Code, TVA Act, Atomic Energy Act, Federal Power Act...." Lobbyist — Paul C. Bailey, Washington, D.C.

FEDERATION OF AMERICAN CONTROLLED SHIPPING, New York, N.Y. Lobbyist — Steven M. Moodie, Washington, D.C. Filed 4/13/81. Legislative interest — "...foreign flag shipping operations...."

FLEXIBLE PACKAGING ASSOCIATION, Washington, D.C. Filed for self 4/15/81. Legislative interest — "Legislation affecting the flexible packaging industry." Lobbyist — Mary E. Bernhard, Washington, D.C.

FOOD MARKETING INSTITUTE, Washington, D.C. Filed for self 4/10/81. Legislative interest — "...item pricing legislation and beverage container legislation." Lobbyists — Lex J. Byers, Dagmar T. Farr, and John M. Martin Jr., Washington, D.C.

GENERAL AVIATION MANUFACTURERS ASSOCIATION, Washington, D.C. Filed for self 4/13/81. Legislative interest — "Interest in HR 2643, legislation to improve the nation's Airport/Airway system...." Lobbyist — James D. Gormley, Washington, D.C.

GEORGIA ASSOCIATION OF PETROLEUM RETAILERS INC., Decatur, Ga. Filed for self 4/14/81. Legislative interest — "The Small Business Motor Fuel Marketer Preservation Act of 1981, identified as HR 1362 and S 326...." Lobbyist — Jack W. Houston, Decatur, Ga.

GLASS PACKAGING INSTITUTE, Washington, D.C. Lobbyist — O'Connor & Hannan, Washington, D.C. Filed 4/14/81. Legislative interest — "...federal bottle deposit legislation and Clean Air Act, including S 709."

HEALTH INSURANCE ASSOCIATION OF AMERICA INC., Washington, D.C. Filed for self 4/14/81. Legislative interest — "All matters pertaining to business of health and accident insurance companies and their policyholders." Lobbyist — Geza Kadar Jr., Washington, D.C.

INDEPENDENT BANKERS ASSOCIATION OF AMERICA, Sauk Centre, Minn. Filed for self 4/28/81. Legislative interest — "S 388/S 446 — taxation annuities (for); H Con Res 82/84 — capital adequacy (for); farm bill of 1981 (for); money market mutual funds — reserve requirements — HR 2591, et al. (for)." Lobbyist — Jeanne Marie Murphy, Washington, D.C.

INDEPENDENT CATTLEMEN ASSOCIATION, Austin, Texas. Lobbyist — Larry Meyers, Washington, D.C. Filed 4/5/81. Legislative interest — "General farm bill."

INDUSTRIAL OIL CONSUMERS GROUP, Washington, D.C. Lobbyist — Sutherland, Asbill & Brennan, Washington, D.C. Filed 4/10/81. Legislative interest — "Legislation and regulations pertaining to petroleum matters."

INSTITUTE OF ELECTRICAL & ELECTRONIC ENGINEERS, Washington, D.C. Lobbyist — Manatt, Phelps, Rothenberg & Tunney, Washington, D.C. Filed 4/14/81. Legislative interest — "For protection of wages of engineers in government service contracts."

INVESTMENT COMPANY INSTITUTE, Washington, D.C. Lobbyist — Robert C. Eckhardt, Washington, D.C. Filed 4/17/81. (Former U.S. rep., D-Texas, 1967-81.) Legislative interest — "...legislation affecting money market funds."

JOINT MARITIME CONGRESS, Washington, D.C. Filed for self 4/11/81. Legislative interest — "Transportation and maritime-related legislation." Lobbyists — Theresa M. Brady, Gloria Cataneo Rudman, Washington, D.C.

MACHINERY DEALERS NATIONAL ASSOCIATION, Silver Spring, Md. Lobbyist — Virginia E. Hopkins, Washington, D.C. Filed 4/28/81. Legislative interest — "...matters dealing with tax issues ... investment tax credit and depreciation reform."

MASSACHUSETTS ASSOCIATION OF CONTRIBUTORY RETIREMENT SYSTEMS INC., Norwood, Mass. Lobbyist — Seifman & Lechner, Washington, D.C. Filed 4/23/81. Legislative interest — "Social Security, pension legislation."

NATIONAL ASSOCIATION OF MANUFACTURERS, Washington, D.C. Filed for self 4/9/81. Legislative interest — "General product liability, workers' compensation and unemployment compensation legislation...." Lobbyist — Daniel W. Vannoy, Washington, D.C.

NATIONAL ASSOCIATION OF MUTUAL SAVINGS BANKS, New York, N.Y. Lobbyist — Michael T. Kinsella, Washington, D.C. Filed 4/14/81. Legislative interest — "Legislation directly or indirectly affecting mutual savings banks, such as S 243 and HR 1250...."

NATIONAL ASSOCIATION OF PUBLIC HOSPITALS, Washington, D.C. Filed for self 4/1/81. Legislative interest — "All matters pertaining to health care laws and regulations, including Medicare, Medicaid and all titles of the Public Health Service Act...." Lobbyist — Larry S. Gage, Washington, D.C.

NATIONAL ASSOCIATION OF REALTORS, Washington, D.C. Filed for self 4/14/81. Legislative interest — "Any and all legislation affecting the real estate industry, including specifically, tax relief; independent contractor; S 31 ... fair housing, alternative mortgage instruments, public lands management ... energy, environmental and land use legislation affecting all facets of the real estate industry." Lobbyists — David A. Bockorny, Gerard Giovaniello, Thane A. Young, Washington, D.C.

NATIONAL CABLE TELEVISION ASSOCIATION, Washington, D.C. Filed for self 4/13/81. Legislative interest — "Amendments to the Communications Act of 1934 and other legislation affecting cable television generally." Lobbyist — Patricia Carroll, Washington, D.C.

NATIONAL COAL ASSOCIATION, Washington, D.C. Filed for self 4/7/81. Legislative interest — "All measures affecting bituminous coal industry." Lobbyist — Bruce H. Watzman, Washington, D.C.

NATIONAL COUNCIL OF FARMER COOPERATIVES, Washington, D.C. Lobbyist — Victoria R. Calvert, Washington, D.C. Filed 4/14/81. Legislative interest — "U.S. Petroleum policy and priority for agriculture under contingency energy plans; S 409, Standby Petroleum Authority Act of 1981, for."

THE NATIONAL MANAGEMENT ASSOCIATION, Dayton, Ohio Lobbyist — Chappell Communications Management; Penny/Ohlmann/Neiman Inc., Dayton, Ohio Filed 4/30/81. Legislative interest — "For commemorative legislation recognizing the profession of management."

NATIONAL MULTI HOUSING COUNCIL, Washington, D.C. Lobbyist — Powell, Goldstein, Frazer & Murphy, Washington, D.C. Filed 4/9/81. Legislative interest — "...HR 2400 and related bills."

NATIONAL PARKING ASSOCIATION, Washington, D.C. Filed for self 4/28/81. Legislative interest — not specified. Lobbyist — Robin Alan Rhodes, Washington, D.C.

NATIONAL POTATO COUNCIL, Denver, Colo. Lobbyist — Robert W. Porter, Washington, D.C. Filed 4/22/81. Legislative interest — "HR 2160, S 862."

NATIONAL RURAL ELECTRIC COOPERATIVE AS-SOCIATION, Washington, D.C. Filed for self 4/30/81. Legislative interest — "All legislative interests affecting the Rural Electrification Act of 1936, as amended." Lobbyist — Cliff Ouse, Washington, D.C.

NATIONAL SOFT DRINK ASSOCIATION, Washington, D.C. Lobbyists — Hogan & Hartson; Patton, Boggs & Blow, Washington, D.C. Filed 4/14/81. Legislative interest — ". . .Federal Food, Drug & Cosmetic Act . . . relating to food safety."

NATIONAL TELEPHONE COOPERATIVE ASSOCI-ATION, Washington, D.C. Filed for self 4/28/81. Legislative interest — "All legislation affecting the rural telephone program provided for in the Rural Electrification Act of 1936, as amended, all legislation affecting telecommunications and amendments to the Communications Act of 1934. . . ." Lobbyist — T. Michael Barry, Washington, D.C.

NEWSPAPER-BROADCASTER COMMITTEE, San Francisco, Calif. Lobbyist — Hogan & Hartson, Washington, D.C. Filed 4/2/81. Legislative interest — ". . .legislation to amend the Communications Act, including S 270 and S 601."

OUTDOOR ADVERTISING ASSOCIATION OF AMERICA INC., Washington, D.C. Filed for self 4/13/81. Legislative interest — ". . .business interests of the owners of standard outdoor advertising signs." Lobbyist — Richard R. Roberts, Washington, D.C.

OUTDOOR POWER EQUIPMENT INSTITUTE, Washington, D.C. Lobbyist — Collier, Shannon, Rill & Scott, Washington, D.C. Filed 4/29/81. Filed for self 4/23/81. Legislative interest — "Any legislation affecting outdoor power equipment manufacturers including the reauthorization of the Consumer Product Safety Commission." Lobbyist — Dennis Dix, Washington, D.C.

PROFESSIONAL INSURANCE AGENTS, Alexandria, Va. Filed for self 4/9/81. Legislative interest — "insurance matters and legislation related to the welfare of local fire and casualty insurance agents. Lobbyists — John S. Hoyt, Alexandria, Va.; Charles Wegner Jr., Washington, D.C.

RENEWABLE FUELS ASSOCIATION, Washington, D.C. Filed for self 4/20/81. Legislative interest — "All legislation affecting renewable fuels." Lobbyist — David E. Hallberg, Washington, D.C.

SECURITIES INDUSTRY ASSOCIATION, Washington, D.C. Lobbyist — Sullivan & Cromwell, New York, N.Y. Filed 4/27/81. Legislative interest — "Bills to amend the Internal Revenue Code of 1954 with respect to straddles. . . ."

SERVICE STATION DEALERS OF AMERICA INC., Washington, D.C. Filed for self 4/15/81. Legislative interest — "HR 1362 and S 326, Small Business Motor Fuel Marketer Preservation Act of 1981 (for)." Lobbyist — Robert C. Lohse, Washington, D.C.

SOUTHWESTERN PEANUT GROWERS, Gorman, Texas. Lobbyist — Larry Meyers, Washington, D.C. Filed 4/14/81. Legislative interest — "General farm bill."

STOCKHOLDERS OF AMERICA INC., Washington, D.C. Filed for self 4/13/81. Legislative interest — ". . .amendments to the Internal Revenue Code." Lobbyist — Margaret Cox Sullivan, Washington, D.C.

TRANSPORTATION INSTITUTE, Washington, D.C. Filed for self 4/13/81. Legislative interest — "General educational functions concerning maritime authorization legislation." Lobbyists — William Barclift, Jill Finsen, Maryann Kilduff, Mary Beth Sullivan, Washington, D.C.

UNITED EGG PRODUCERS, Decatur, Ga. Filed for self 4/29/81. Legislative interest — "Matters affecting the shell egg industry and nutrition." Lobbyist — Cathy McCharen, Washington, D.C.

UNITED STATES SKI ASSOCIATION, La Canada, Calif. Filed for self 4/16/81. Legislative interest — "Public land issues." Lobbyist — Nancy J. Ingalsbee, La Canada, Calif.

WESTERN FOREST INDUSTRIES ASSOCIATION, Portland, Ore. Lobbyist — Schwabe, Williamson, Wyatt, Moore and Roberts, Washington, D.C. Filed 4/10/81. (Listed as agent for this client was former U.S. Rep. Robert Duncan, D-Ore., 1963-67, 1975-81.) Legislative interest — "Forest Service." Lobbyist — Ullman Consultants Inc., Washington, D.C. Filed 4/1/81. (Former U.S. Rep. Al Ullman, D-Ore., 1957-81, was listed among agents for this client.) Legislative interest — "Estate and gift tax reform, especially as it relates to small businesses, farms, and small timber lots." Lobbyist — Burson-Marsteller, Washington, D.C. Filed 4/29/81. Legislative interest — ". . .amendment of estate tax provisions of the U.S. Internal Revenue Code. . . ."

Miscellaneous

CANADIAN COALITION ON ACID RAIN, Toronto, Ontario, Canada. Filed for self 4/13/81. Legislative interest — ". . .Clean Air Act of 1970 as amended." Lobbyist — Adele M. Hurley, Toronto, Ontario, Canada.

CENTRAL CALIFORNIA EDUCATIONAL TELEVI-SION, Sacramento, Calif. Lobbyist — Dow, Lohnes & Albertson, Washington, D.C. Filed 4/3/81. Legislative interest — "Revision of Communications Act of 1934, S 720, HR 2774. . . ." Registrant also filed for the following organizations, all with the same legislative interest: **KANSAS PUBLIC TELECOMMUNICATIONS SERVICE INC.**, Wichita, Kan.; **LEHIGH VALLEY PUBLIC TELECOMMUNICATIONS CORP.**, Bethlehem, Pa.; **NORTHEAST NEW YORK EDUCATIONAL TELEVI-SION ASSOCIATION**, Plattsburgh, N.Y.; **THE OHIO STATE UNIVERSITY**, Columbus, Ohio; **SOUTHERN TIER ETV ASSOCIATION**, Endwell, N.Y.

COHEN & URETZ, Lobbyist — Wildman, Harrold, Allen, Dixon & McDonnell, Memphis, Tenn. Filed 4/9/81. Legislative interest — "Amendment of Internal Revenue Code relating to estate tax alternate valuation date election (S 3381)."

COMMITTEE TO PRESERVE THE PATENT JURIS-DICTION OF THE U.S. COURTS OF APPEALS, Chicago, Ill. Lobbyist — Landis, Cohen, Singman and Rauh, Washington, D.C. Filed 4/28/81. Legislative interest — "All matters of legislative concern including S 21 and HR 2405."

CONSULTANTS RESEARCH SERVICE, Cold Spring Harbor, N.Y. Filed for self 4/24/81. Legislative interest — "DOD legislation, FAA legislation, training and education legislation. . . ." Lobbyist — Hans Kaehler, Cold Spring Harbor, N.Y.

CRAWFORD COOK AND CO., Columbia, S.C. Filed for self 4/14/81. Legislative interest — Not specified. Lobbyist — Milton F. Capps, Columbia, S.C.

ENERGY CONVERSION GROUP, Washington, D.C. Filed for self 4/13/81. Legislative interest — ". . .increasing certain portions of budget authority for: Office of Fossil Energy and Office of Conservation and Renewable Energy." Lobbyist — Jerry M. Brady, Washington, D.C.

KBS ASSOCIATES INC., Washington, D.C. Lobbyist — Joseph E. Karth, Phoenix, Ariz. Filed 4/13/81. (Former U.S. rep., D-Minn., 1959-79, was listed among agents for this client.) Legislative interest — "Repeal of Section 620B of the Foreign Assistance Act of 1961 as amended (Humphrey-Kennedy amendment of 1977)."

FRANK G. KINGSLEY, New Caanan, Conn. Lobbyist — Corcoran, Youngman & Rowe, Washington, D.C. Filed 4/27/81. Legislative interest — "Tax legislation."

LOS ANGELES OLYMPIC COMMEMORATIVE COIN COMMITTEE, New York, N.Y. Lobbyist — Timmons and Co. Inc., Washington, D.C. Filed 4/9/81. Legislative interest — ". . .issuance and sale of precious metals United States Olympic Coins in honor of the 1984 Olympic Games." Lobbyist — Patton, Boggs & Blow, Washington, D.C. Filed 4/14/81. Legislative interest — ". . .issuance and sale of precious metal U.S. Olympic coins

in honor of the 1984 Olympic Games."

LOS ANGELES OLYMPIC ORGANIZING COMMITTEE, Los Angeles, Calif. Lobbyist — Timmons and Co. Inc., Washington, D.C. Filed 4/9/81. Legislative interest — "...issuance and sale of precious metals United States Olympic Coins in honor of the 1984 Olympic Games." Lobbyist — Patton, Boggs & Blow, Washington, D.C. Filed 4/14/81. Legislative interest — "...issuance and sale of precious metal U.S. Olympic coins in honor of the 1984 Olympic Games."

PARALYSIS CURE RESEARCH FOUNDATION, Washington, D.C. Lobbyist — Janet S. Reed, Potomac, Md. Filed 4/16/81. Legislative interest — "...government funding for National Institutes of Health (NINCDS) for spinal cord regeneration research...."

POPULATION CRISIS COMMITTEE, Washington, D.C. Lobbyist — Finley, Kumble, Wagner, Heine, Underberg & Casey, Washington, D.C. Filed 4/9/81. Legislative interest — "...efforts to increase U.S. population aid in both multilateral and bilateral global efforts to address this problem."

LANCE WELLS, Anchorage, Alaska. Filed for self 4/14/81. Legislative interest — "Airline subsidies...."

WYMAN FAMILY, New York, N.Y. Filed 4/9/81. Lobbyist — Seymour Sheriff, Washington, D.C. Legislative interest — "Czechoslovak claims legislation, HR 2352, HR 2631, S 754. For such bills with amendments."

May Registrations

Citizens' Groups

AMERICAN ASSOCIATION OF PRIVATE RAILROAD CAR OWNERS INC., Baywood Park, Calif. Lobbyist — Smith & Pepper, 1776 K St. N.W., Washington, D.C. 20006. Filed 5/28/81. Legislative interest — "...continuation of maximum funding for a nationwide Amtrak system...."

ARTHRITIS FOUNDATION, Atlanta, Ga. Lobbyist — Hoffheimer, Johnson & Peterson, 1120 20th St. N.W., Washington, D.C. 20036. Filed 5/28/81. Legislative interest — "Biomedical research, services and benefits for persons with arthritis ... fiscal year 1982 appropriations and fiscal year 1981 rescissions/supplementals, National Arthritis Act, Social Security Act, Rehabilitation Act, Older Americans Act ... block grant proposals, various health issues."

FRIENDS COMMITTEE ON NATIONAL LEGISLATION, Washington, D.C. Filed for self 5/22/81. Legislative interest — "...support steps toward world disarmament, reduction of hostilities in Middle East and reconciliation of Indochina ... expansion of food for peace and international development and assistance programs...." Lobbyist — Ruth Flower, Washington, D.C.

NATIONAL CLEAN AIR COALITION, 530 7th St. S.E., Washington, D.C. 20003. Filed for self 6/15/81. Legislative interest — "...to provide legislation to preserve, restore and insure rational use of the ecosphere, particularly legislation dealing with clean air issues; S 63, Steel Industry Compliance Extension Act ... HR 3471, amendments to the Clean Air Act...." Lobbyist — Patricia Senner. Filed for self 5/18/81. Legislative interest — "preserve, restore and insure rational use of the ecosphere, particularly legislation dealing with clean air issues." Lobbyist — Tom Cosgrove, Washington, D.C.

NATIONAL RIFLE ASSOCIATION, 1600 Rhode Island Ave. N.W., Washington, D.C. 20036. Filed for self 5/29/81. Legislative interest — "...all aspects of the acquisition, possession and use of firearms and ammunition as well as legislation relating to hunting and wildlife conservation." Lobbyist — Kenneth D. Schloman.

NATIONAL TAXPAYERS LEGAL FUND, Washington, D.C. Filed for self 5/12/81. Legislative interest — Not specified. Lobbyist — Michael S. Burch, Washington, D.C.

PEOPLE OPPOSED TO ENERGY LOBBY (POTEL), Washington, D.C. Filed for self 5/12/81. Legislative interest — Not specified. Lobbyist — Albert E. Lane, Washington, D.C.

PEOPLE ORGANIZED IN NEIGHBORHOODS TOGETHER (POINT), Detroit, Mich. Filed for self 5/11/81. Legislative interest — Not specified. Lobbyist — Ervin B. Johnson, Detroit, Mich.

PROTECT THE INNOCENT INC., Mooresville, Ind. Filed for self 5/12/81. Legislative interest — "...any and all legislation or appropriations which has any impact on the criminal justice system." Lobbyist — Ros Stovall, Mooresville, Ind.

TANADGUSIX CORP., St. Paul Island, Alaska. Lobbyist — Cook, Purcell, Hansen & Henderson, Washington, D.C. Filed 5/19/81. Legislative interest — "All matters affecting the Aleut citizens of St. Paul Island, Alaska. Funding extension of wildlife refuges in western Alaska; ratification of protocol to North Pacific Fur Seal Convention and all fisheries development legislation."

THE WILDERNESS SOCIETY, Washington, D.C. Lobbyist — Joe Walicki, Portland, Ore. Filed 5/14/81. Legislative interest — "Washington State Omnibus bill - for; Oregon State Omnibus bill - for."

Corporations and Businesses

A-C VALLEY CORP., Emlenton, Pa. Lobbyist — Coan, Couture, Lyons & Moorhead, 1625 I St. N.W., Washington, D.C. 20006. Filed 5/29/81. (Former U.S. Rep. William S. Moorhead, D-Pa., 1959-81, was listed as agent for this client.) Legislative interest — "Synthetic fuel matters."

AG-ENERGY RESOURCES INC., Englewood, Calif. Lobbyist — Akin, Gump, Strauss, Hauer & Feld, Washington, D.C. Filed 5/4/81. Legislative interest — "...budget reconciliation, S Con Res 9, the revised Second Concurrent Resolution on the fiscal year 1981 budget."

ALARM DEVICE MANUFACTURING CO., Syosset, N.Y. Lobbyist — Pepper, Hamilton & Scheetz, Washington, D.C. Filed 5/13/81. Legislative interest — "Legislative provisions affecting the alarm industry."

AMERICAN CAN CO., Greenwich, Conn. Filed for self 5/21/81. Legislative interest — "Beverage Container Reuse & Recycling Act, S 709, HR 2498, against; Foreign Corrupt Practices Act Amendments, S 708, HR 2530, for; Capital Cost Recovery Act of 1981, HR 1053, for; Public Financing of Congressional Elections, against; Social Security Financing, for; Lobby Law Reform, against; Political Action Committee Restrictions, S 9, against." Lobbyist — Edward DeW. Kratovil, Washington, D.C.

AMERICAN INTERNATIONAL GROUP INC., New York, N.Y. Lobbyist — Sullivan & Cromwell, New York, N.Y. Filed 5/11/81. Legislative interest — "Federal income tax legislation affecting the insurance and insurance brokerage businesses and employee benefits...."

AMERICAN INVSCO CORP., Chicago, Ill. Lobbyist — Thomas Ludlow Ashley, Washington, D.C. Filed 5/7/81. (Former U.S. rep., D-Ohio, 1955-81.) Legislative interest — "Public policy consequences of the national condominium and cooperative conversion trend."

AMFAC GARDEN PRODUCTS INC., Burlingame, Calif. Lobbyist — Jim Casey, Falls Church, Va. Filed 5/21/81. Legislative interest — "Amendments to acreage limitation provisions of reclamation law."

BAKER INTERNATIONAL, Orange, Calif. Lobbyist — Sutherland, Asbill & Brennan, Washington, D.C. Filed 5/14/81. Legislative interest — "In support of S 639, the Stock Option bill."

BENEFICIAL MANAGEMENT CORP. OF AMERICA, 1300 Market St., Wilmington, Del. 19899. Filed for self 5/27/81. Legislative interest — "...consumer finance industry, savings and loan, banks, retailing and insurance." Lobbyist — Gary J. Perkinson, 1700 N. Moore St., Arlington, Va. 22209.

BOSTON EDISON CO., Boston, Mass. Lobbyist — Leva, Hawes, Symington, Martin & Oppenheimer, Washington, D.C. Filed 5/4/81. Legislative interest — "Legislation affecting fuel use

by electric utilities, including coal conversion funding."

BRASWELL SHIPYARDS INC., Mt. Pleasant, S.C. Lobbyist — Foley, Hoag & Eliot, Washington, D.C. Filed 5/19/81. Legislative interest — "Amending the Longshoremen's and Harbor Workers' Compensation Act, including HR 25."

BRIDGESTONE TIRE CO. LTD., Tokyo, Japan. Lobbyist — Tanaka Walders & Ritger, 1919 Pennsylvania Ave. N.W., Washington, D.C. 20006. Filed 5/28/81. Legislative interest — "All legislation which might affect marketing of tires in the U.S."

BROADCAST MUSIC INC., New York, N.Y. Lobbyist — Samuel E. Stavisky & Associates Inc., Washington, D.C. Filed 5/20/81. Legislative interest — "Against HR 2006, HR 2007, HR 2108, HR 3392, HR 3408 and S 603 exempting educational, fraternal and other organizations from royalty under Copyright Act of 1976."

THE BROOKLYN UNION GAS CO., Brooklyn, N.Y. Lobbyist — Crowell & Moring, Washington, D.C. Filed 5/5/81. Legislative interest — "Legislation affecting the natural gas distribution industry."

BROWN & ROOT INC., Washington, D.C. Filed for self 5/14/81. Legislative interest — "...those areas which affect the engineering and construction industry ... tax reform, regulatory reform, Davis-Bacon, Foreign Corrupt Practices Act and trade issues." Lobbyist — Wyll W. Pleger, Washington, D.C.

CARGILL INC., Minneapolis, Minn. Lobbyist — Patton, Boggs & Blow, Washington, D.C. Filed 5/1/81. Legislative interest — "Economic Recovery Tax Act of 1981. Favor HR 1053 and favor, subject to technical amendment, HR 2400 and S 683 relating to Economic Recovery Tax Act."

CARNEGIE CORP. OF NEW YORK, New York, N.Y. Lobbyist — Sutherland, Asbill & Brennan, Washington, D.C. Filed 5/14/81. Legislative interest — "In support of HR 1364 and S 464."

THE WILLIAM CARTER CO., Needham Heights, Mass. Lobbyist — Ropes and Gray, Washington, D.C. Filed 5/13/81. Legislative interest — "Enactment of legislation to compensate manufacturer of garments containing TRIS, e.g. S 823 and HR 161...."

CHEVRON U.S.A. INC., Washington, D.C. Filed for self 5/14/81. Legislative interest — Not specified. Lobbyist — Thomas L. Linton, Washington, D.C.

CHICAGO BOARD OF TRADE CLEARING CORP., Chicago, Ill. Lobbyist — Hopkins & Sutter, Chicago, Ill. Filed 5/13/81. Legislative interest — "...amendments to Internal Revenue Code...."

CHICAGO MERCANTILE EXCHANGE, Chicago, Ill. Lobbyist — Charles M. Seeger III, Washington, D.C. Filed 5/14/81. Legislative interest — "Legislation affecting the commodity futures industry."

CHRYSLER CORP., Highland Park, Mich. Filed for self 5/20/81. Legislative interest — Not specified. Lobbyist — Charles T. Cudlip, Washington, D.C.

CITGO SYNFUELS INC., Tulsa, Okla. Lobbyist — Latham, Watkins & Hills, Washington, D.C. Filed 5/13/81. Legislative interest — "Authorization/appropriations legislation affecting synthetic fuel development and business energy property investment tax credit."

COMDISCO INC., Rosemont, Ill. Lobbyist — Mayer, Brown & Platt, Washington, D.C. Filed 5/14/81. Legislative interest — "...amendments to the Internal Revenue Code, including the adoption of a capital cost recovery system."

COMMODITY EXCHANGE INC., New York, N.Y. Filed for self 5/19/81. Legislative interest — "All legislation affecting commodities futures markets, with specific interest in matters relating to the metals markets, including HR 1293, HR 1338 and S 626...." Lobbyist — Joan A. Piccolo, Washington, D.C.

COMMONWEALTH EDISON CO., Chicago, Ill. Lobbyist — Hopkins & Sutter, Chicago, Ill. Filed 5/13/81. Legislative interest — "...amendments to Internal Revenue Code...."

CONOCO INC., Washington, D.C. Lobbyist — Cummings & Lockwood, Washington, D.C. Filed 5/15/81. Legislative interest — "Mineral Lands Leasing Amendment of 1981, HR 2826...."

CONSOLIDATED EDISON CO. OF NEW YORK, New York, N.Y. Lobbyist — Leva, Hawes, Symington, Martin &

Oppenheimer, Washington, D.C. Filed 5/4/81. Legislative interest — "Legislation affecting fuel use by electric utilities, including coal conversion funding."

CONTINENTAL AIRLINES, Los Angeles, Calif. Lobbyist — Thomas F. Baston, Washington, D.C. Filed 5/11/81. Legislative interest — "Legislative oversight of the Civil Aeronautics Board, possible amendments to the Airline Deregulation Act."

CONTINENTAL OIL CO., Stamford, Conn. Lobbyist — Skadden, Arps, Slate, Meagher & Flom, 1775 Pennsylvania Ave. N.W., Washington, D.C. Filed 5/28/81. Legislative interest — "Foreign acquisition of American firms, particularly natural resources companies."

CORE INTERNATIONAL, Alexandria, Va. Lobbyist — Paul H. Cooksey, Alexandria, Va. Filed 5/21/81. Legislative interest — "Defense authorization and appropriations bills."

ELECTRONIC DATA SYSTEMS, Washington, D.C. Lobbyist — Capital Counselors Inc., Washington, D.C. Filed 5/4/81. Legislative interest — "Legislation affecting telecommunications."

EMERSON ELECTRIC CO., St. Louis, Mo. Filed for self 5/18/81. Legislative interest — "...labor reform, anti-trust, energy and deregulation of natural gas, defense and security assistance, tax and revenue measures including HR 1054...." Lobbyist — William E. Peacock, St. Louis, Mo.

FIRST CHICAGO CORP., Chicago, Ill. Lobbyist — Hopkins & Sutter, Chicago, Ill. Filed 5/13/81. Legislative interest — "...amendments to Internal Revenue Code...."

FOREMOST INSURANCE CO., Grand Rapids, Mich. Lobbyist — Witkowski, Weiner, McCaffrey & Brodsky, Washington, D.C. Filed 5/19/81. Legislative interest — "Housing and banking legislation impacting on the insurance industry. Housing and Community Development Amendments of 1981, and the bank holding company bill."

GATX CORP., Chicago, Ill. Lobbyist — Manatt, Phelps, Rothenberg & Tunney, Washington, D.C. Filed 5/11/81. (Former U.S. Rep. James C. Corman, D-Calif., 1961-81, was listed as agent for this client.) Legislative interest — "HR 2400 as it relates to depreciation of railroad tank cars."

GENERAL ELECTRIC CO., Fairfield, Conn. Lobbyist — Washington Industrial Team, Washington, D.C. Filed 5/19/81. (Former U.S. Reps. Richard H. Ichord, D-Mo., 1961-81, and Bob Wilson, R-Calif., 1953-81, were among the agents listed for this client.) Legislative interest — "General legislative matters dealing with defense issues."

GENERAL MILLS INC., Minneapolis, Minn. Lobbyist — Patton, Boggs & Blow, Washington, D.C. Filed 5/1/81. Legislative interest — "Economic Recovery Tax Act of 1981 ... HR 1053 ... HR 2400 and S 683 relating to Economic Recovery Tax Act."

GENERAL PUBLIC UTILITIES CORP., Parsippany, N.J. Lobbyist — Charls E. Walker Associates Inc., Washington, D.C. Filed 5/11/81. Legislative interest — "...the nuclear accident which occurred at Three Mile Island located in Pennsylvania." Lobbyist — Kline, Knopf & Wojdak Inc., Harrisburg, Pa. Filed 5/26/81. Legislative interest — "...Three Mile Island ... and matters relating to GPU." Lobbyist — Thomas Ludlow Ashley, Washington, D.C. Filed 5/7/81. (Former U.S. rep., D-Ohio, 1955-81.) Legislative interest — "Public utility and nuclear power generation financial matters; National Nuclear Property Insurance Act of 1981, HR 2512."

GEORGIA-PACIFIC CORP., Washington, D.C. Lobbyist — King & Spalding, Washington, D.C. Filed 5/6/81. Legislative interest — "...S 995 or similar legislation."

GREAT NATIONAL CORP., Dallas, Texas. Lobbyist — O'Connor & Hannan, Washington, D.C. Filed 5/4/81. Legislative interest — "Energy/synfuels legislation, including proposal to rescind grant funding."

GRUMMAN FLEXIBLE CORP., Washington, D.C. Lobbyist — William H. Harsha, McLean, Va. Filed 5/13/81. (Former U.S. rep., R-Ohio, 1961-81.) Legislative interest — "Mass transportation."

HEDGED PORTFOLIO ADVISORS, New York, N.Y. Lobbyist — Barnett, Alagia & Carey, Washington, D.C. Filed 5/8/81. Legislative interest — "Commodity Straddles Tax Act of

1981 (S 626), HR 1338, Internal Revenue Code, section 1092. . . ."

GEORGE A. HORMEL & CO., Austin, Minn. Lobbyist — C.D. Nyberg, Austin, Minn. Filed 5/18/81. Legislative interest — ". . .food safety, nutrition, labor, transportation and matters relating to business interests generally."

JOHN M. HUBER CORP., Edison, N.J. Filed for self 5/8/81. Legislative interest — ". . .bills dealing with safety, environment, product safety and energy." Lobbyist — H.R. Balikov, Edison, N.J.

HUTHNANCE DRILLING CO., Houston, Texas. Lobbyist — Lillick McHose & Charles, Washington, D.C. Filed 5/18/81. Legislative interest — "Maritime authorization bills. . . ."

INLAND STEEL CO., Chicago, Ill. Lobbyist — Hopkins & Sutter, Chicago, Ill. Filed 5/13/81. Legislative interest — ". . .amendments to Internal Revenue Code. . . ."

INTERGRAPH CORP., Huntsville, Ala. Lobbyist — Powell, Goldstein, Frazer & Murphy, Washington, D.C. Filed 5/4/81. Legislative interest — ". . .Section 103(b) (6) (D) of the Internal Revenue Code."

INTERNATIO INC., New York, N.Y. Lobbyist — Coan, Couture, Lyons & Moorhead, 1625 I St. N.W., Washington, D.C. 20006. Filed 5/29/81. Legislative interest — Not specified.

INTERNATIONAL PAPER CO., 77 West 45th St., New York, N.Y. 10036. Filed for self 5/28/81. Legislative interest — ". . .antitrust contribution." Lobbyist — Byron E. Kabot.

INTERNATIONAL PAPER CO., New York, N.Y. Lobbyist — Davis Polk & Wardwell, New York, N.Y. and Washington, D.C. Filed 5/7/81. Legislative interest — "Legislation relating to antitrust contributions."

KAISER ALUMINUM & CHEMICAL CORP., Washington, D.C. Lobbyist — Leighton Conklin Lemov Jacobs & Buckley, Washington, D.C. Filed 5/7/81. Legislative interest — "Consumer Product Safety Act Amendments, HR 3216, S 833."

KIAWAH ISLAND CO., Charleston, S.C. Lobbyist — Steptoe & Johnson, Washington, D.C. Filed 5/4/81. Legislative interest — "Housing and Community Development Amendments of 1981; other flood insurance legislation. HR 3018."

KOPPERS SYNFUELS CORP., Pittsburgh, Pa. Lobbyist — Latham, Watkins & Hills, Washington, D.C. Filed 5/13/81. Legislative interest — "Authorization/appropriations legislation affecting synthetic fuel development and business energy property investment tax credit."

LIFETIME COMMUNITIES INC., Jacksonville, Fla. Lobbyist — Sutherland, Asbill & Brennan, Washington, D.C. Filed 5/21/81. Legislative interest — ". . .S 863 and similar legislation to amend the Bankruptcy Code. . . ." Lobbyist — Sutherland, Asbill & Brennan, 1666 K St. N.W. Washington, D.C. 20006. Filed 5/21/81. Legislative interest — "Amendments to S 863 and similar legislation to amend the Bankruptcy Code . . . to limit fees paid under Chapter 11 into referee's salary and expense fund under the old act."

MacMILLAN BLOEDEL INC., Pine Hill, Ala. Lobbyist — Kendall P. Dexter, Mobile, Ala. Filed 5/26/81. Legislative interest — ". . .S 995, contribution of damages to an agreement by two or more persons to fix, maintain, or stabilize prices under Section 4, 4A or 4C of the Clayton Act."

MARCONI SPACE & DEFENSE SYSTEMS, Alexandria, Va. Lobbyist — Paul H. Cooksey, Alexandria, Va. Filed 5/21/81. Legislative interest — "Defense authorization and appropriations bills."

MERRILL LYNCH, HUBBARD INC., New York, N.Y. Lobbyist — Brownstein Zeidman and Schomer, Washington, D.C. Filed 5/21/81. Legislative interest — "All matters relating to legislation affecting hospitals, including tax exempt bond financing, HR 3018."

MISSOURI TERMINAL OIL CO. INC., St. Louis, Mo. Lobbyist — Akin, Gump, Strauss, Hauer & Feld, Washington, D.C. Filed 5/4/81. Legislative interest — ". . .proposed budget rescission, S Con Res 9. . . ."

MONTGOMERY WARD CO. INC., Chicago, Ill. Lobbyist — Patton, Boggs & Blow, Washington, D.C. Filed 5/1/81. Legislative interest — "Cash Discount Act, S 414, HR 39."

MULTIFAMILY FINANCE ACTION GROUP, Wash-

ington, D.C. Lobbyist — Brownstein Zeidman and Schomer, Washington, D.C. Filed 5/21/81. Legislative interest — "All matters relating to legislation affecting housing, including HR 3018."

MULTI-STATE COMMUNICATIONS INC., New York, N.Y. Lobbyist — Cummings & Lockwood, 1090 Vermont Ave. N.W., Washington, D.C. 20005. Filed 5/29/81. Legislative interest — ". . .S 601 and other legislation which may impact on Multi-State Communications interests vis-à-vis broadcasting rights. . . ."

MFA MUTUAL INSURANCE CO., Columbia, Mo. Lobbyist — Arnold & Porter, Washington, D.C. Filed 5/27/81. Legislative interest — "HR 3245 and HR 5460."

NATIONAL TECHNICAL SCHOOLS OF LOS ANGELES, Los Angeles, Calif. Lobbyist — Priest & Fine Inc., 1725 K St. N.W., Washington, D.C. 20006. Filed 5/27/81. Legislative interest — "GI Benefits and Veterans Administration Budget, S 918 and HR 1903, having to do with eliminating home study course tuition for veterans. . . ."

NATIONWIDE INSURANCE CO., Columbus, Ohio. Lobbyist — Williams & Jensen, Washington, D.C. Filed 5/5/81. Legislative interest — "Federal income tax matters concerning the insurance industry."

NORTHEAST UTILITIES SERVICE CO., Berlin, Conn. Lobbyist — Leva, Hawes, Symington, Martin & Oppenheimer, Washington, D.C. Filed 5/4/81. Legislative interest — "Legislation affecting fuel use by electric utilities, including coal conversion funding."

NORTHROP CORP., Los Angeles, Calif. Lobbyist — Washington Industrial Team Inc., 499 S. Capitol St. S.W., Washington, D.C. 20003. Filed 5/29/81. (Former U.S. Reps. Richard H. Ichord, D-Mo., 1961-81, and Bob Wilson, R-Calif., 1953-81, were listed among agents for this client.) Legislative interest — ". . .Defense issues."

NORTHWEST INDUSTRIES INC., Chicago, Ill. Lobbyist — Hopkins & Sutter, Chicago, Ill. Filed 5/13/81. Legislative interest — ". . .amendments to Internal Revenue Code. . . ."

OASIS PETROLEUM CO., Culver City, Calif. Lobbyist — Richard W. Bliss, Washington, D.C. Filed 5/16/81. Legislative interest — "All legislation dealing with alcohol fuels, including the fiscal year 1981 and 1982 budgets."

OLIN CORP., Stamford, Conn. Lobbyist — Leighton Conklin Lemov Jacobs & Buckley, Washington, D.C. Filed 5/7/81. Legislative interest — "Consumer Product Safety Act Amendments, HR 3216, S 833."

PARAHO DEVELOPMENT CORP., Grand Junction, Colo. Lobbyist — O'Connor & Hannan, Washington, D.C. Filed 5/4/81. Legislative interest — "Energy-synfuels legislation, including proposal to rescind grant funding."

PENN CENTRAL CORP., Washington, D.C. Lobbyist — Patton, Boggs & Blow, Washington, D.C. Filed 5/20/81. Legislative interest — ". . .continuing group life insurance coverage for former railroad employees who retired prior to April 1, 1976. . . ."

J. C. PENNEY CO. INC., Washington, D.C. Lobbyist — O'Connor & Hannan, Washington, D.C. Filed 5/1/81. Legislative interest — ". . .Capital Costs Recovery Act, HR 4646 and S 1435."

PEOPLES ENERGY CORP., Chicago, Ill. Lobbyist — Hopkins & Sutter, Chicago, Ill. Filed 5/13/81. Legislative interest — ". . .amendments to Internal Revenue Code. . . ."

PEPSICO INC., Purchase, N.Y. Lobbyist — Bricker & Eckler, Washington, D.C. Filed 5/19/81. (Former U.S. Rep. Samuel L. Devine, R-Ohio, 1959-81, was listed as agent for this client.) Legislative interest — "Legislation relating to nutrition."

THE PILLSBURY CO., Minneapolis, Minn. Lobbyist — Patton, Boggs & Blow, Washington, D.C. Filed 5/1/81. Legislative interest — "Economic Recovery Tax Act of 1981 . . . HR 1053 . . . HR 2400 . . . S 683 relating to the Economic Recovery Tax Act."

PLM INC., San Francisco, Calif. Lobbyist — Camp, Carmouche, Palmer, Barsh & Hunter, 2550 M St. N.W., Washington, D.C. 20037. Filed 5/27/81. Legislative interest — "Amendment to Internal Revenue Code section 48 (a) (2)."

PORTEC INC., Oak Brook, Ill. Lobbyist — Camp, Carmouche, Palmer, Barsh & Hunter, 2550 M St. N.W., Washington, D.C. 20037. Filed 5/27/81. Legislative interest — "Amendment to Internal Revenue Code section 48 (a) (2)."

PUGET SOUND POWER & LIGHT CO., Bellevue, Wash. Lobbyist — Michael E. Steward, Washington, D.C. Filed 5/26/81. Legislative interest — "Legislation affecting electric utilities."

REPUBLIC AIRLINES INC., Minneapolis, Minn. Lobbyist — Cook, Purcell, Hansen & Henderson, Washington, D.C. Filed 5/8/81. Legislative interest — "Against termination of Section 406 subsidy as authorized by Airline Deregulation Act of 1978."

REPUBLIC GEOTHERMAL INC., Santa Fe Springs, Calif. Lobbyist — Latham, Watkins & Hills, Washington, D.C. Filed 5/13/81. Legislative interest — "Proposed rescissions of geothermal loan guarantee program and geothermal research funds."

RICHMOND LEASING, Houston, Texas. Lobbyist — Camp, Carmouche, Palmer, Barsh & Hunter, 2550 M St. N.W., Washington, D.C. 20037. Filed 5/27/81. Legislative interest — "Amendment to Internal Revenue Code section 48 (a) (2)."

ROCKWELL INTERNATIONAL, El Segundo, Calif. Lobbyist — Washington Industrial Team Inc., Washington, D.C. Filed 5/26/81. (Former U.S. Reps. Richard H. Ichord, D-Mo., 1961-81, and Bob Wilson, R-Calif., 1953-81, were among the agents listed for this client.) Legislative interest — "General legislative matters dealing with defense issues."

ROTAN MOSLE INC., Houston, Texas. Lobbyist — Baker & Botts, Washington, D.C. Filed 5/14/81. Legislative interest — "Miscellaneous tax matters, including but not limited to the Administration's Economic Recovery Tax Act of 1981 (HR 2400) and related matters."

JOSEPH E. SEAGRAM & SONS INC., New York, N.Y. Lobbyist — Thevenot, Murray & Scheer, 1120 Connecticut Ave. N.W., Washington, D.C. 20036. Filed 5/28/81. Legislative interest — "...Mineral Lands Leasing Act of 1981, HR 2826."

SEARS, ROEBUCK & CO., Chicago, Ill. Lobbyist — Christine A. Edwards, Washington, D.C. Filed 5/4/81. Legislative interest — "...credit, privacy, savings and loan issues." Lobbyist — Hopkins & Sutter, Chicago, Ill. Filed 5/13/81. Legislative interest — "...amendments to Internal Revenue Code...."

SECURITY PACIFIC NATIONAL BANK, Los Angeles, Calif. Lobbyist — Debbie Shannon, Washington, D.C. Filed 5/19/81. Legislative interest — "Any legislation relating to or affecting financial institutions: Export Trading Co., S 734."

SEWARD & KISSEL, Washington, D.C. Filed for self 5/4/81. Legislative interest — "Legislation affecting money market funds."

TAFT BROADCASTING CO., Cincinnati, Ohio. Lobbyist — Taft, Stettinius & Hollister, Dixie Terminal Building, Cincinnati, Ohio. 45202 and 1800 Massachusetts Ave. N.W., Washington, D.C. Filed 5/28/81. Legislative interest — "...Consumer Product Safety Commission reauthorization bill, performer royalty legislation, and copyright/cable legislation."

TENNESSEE GAS PIPELINE CO., Houston, Texas. Filed for self 5/19/81. Legislative interest — "General education functions concerning natural gas pricing and deregulation, revisions to the Internal Revenue Code related to depreciation and tax credits, amendments to the Fuel Use Act, and relocations of transmission facilities. HR 2019, H Con Res 77, HR 2017, S 29, HR 2400, S 683, HR 2032, S 590, HR 55 and S 828." Lobbyist — Clive Seymour, Houston, Texas.

TOLEDO MINING CO., Salt Lake City, Utah. Lobbyist — Joseph Browder, 1015 18th St. N.W., Washington, D.C. 20036. Filed 5/27/81. Legislative interest — "...extension of terms of non-competitive oil and gas leases owned by Toledo Mining Co."

TOSCO CORP., Los Angeles, Calif. Lobbyist — Harry K. Schwartz, Washington, D.C. Filed 5/18/81. Legislative interest — "...Clean Air Act of 1970 as amended, with particular reference to provisions affecting refining and marketing of petroleum and development of oil shale reserves." Lobbyist — John P. Foley Jr., Washington, D.C. Filed 5/12/81. Legislative interest — "...synthetic fuels development, energy impact assistance and energy tax laws including HR 2133 and S 750." Lobbyist — Coan, Couture, Lyons & Moorhead, 1625 I St. N.W., Washington, D.C. 20006. Filed 5/29/81. (Former U.S. Rep. William S. Moorhead, D-Pa., 1959-81, was listed as agent for this client.) Legislative interest — "Synthetic fuel matters."

TRAILER TRAIN CO., Chicago, Ill. Lobbyist — Camp, Carmouche, Palmer, Barsh & Hunter, 2550 M St. N.W., Washington, D.C. 20037. Filed 5/27/81. Legislative interest — "Amendment to Internal Revenue Code section 48 (a) (2)."

TRAILWAYS, Washington, D.C. Lobbyist — Garvey, Schubert, Adams & Barer, Washington, D.C. Filed 5/4/81. Legislative interest — "Bus Regulatory Modernization and Improvement Act of 1981, S 926, and Motor Bus Act of 1981, S 927...."

TRANS UNION CORP., Lincolnshire, Ill. Lobbyist — Hopkins & Sutter, Chicago, Ill. Filed 5/13/81. Legislative interest — "...amendments to Internal Revenue Code...."

UNDERWOOD NEUHAUS, Houston, Texas. Lobbyist — Fulbright & Jaworski, Washington, D.C. Filed 5/21/81. Legislative interest — "Legislation affecting Title 26 of the U.S. Code."

UNION TANK CAR CO., Chicago, Ill. Lobbyist — Camp, Carmouche, Palmer, Barsh & Hunter, 2550 M St. N.W., Washington, D.C. 20037. Filed 5/27/81. Legislative interest — "Amendment to Internal Revenue Code section 48 (a) (2)."

UNITED STATES LEASING INTERNATIONAL INC., San Francisco, Calif. Lobbyist — Fulbright & Jaworski, Washington, D.C. Filed 5/12/81. Legislative interest — "Legislation affecting Title 26 of the U.S. Code." Lobbyist — Cohen and Uretz, Washington, D.C. Filed 5/26/81. Legislative interest — "Capital cost recovery tax legislation proposals."

UNITED STATES RAIL SERVICE INC., San Francisco, Calif. Lobbyist — Camp, Carmouche, Palmer, Barsh & Hunter, 2550 M St. N.W., Washington, D.C. 20037. Filed 5/27/81. Legislative interest — "Amendment to Internal Revenue Code section 48 (a) (2)."

U.S. LINES, Cranford, N.J. Lobbyist — Patton, Boggs & Blow, Washington, D.C. Filed 5/1/81. Legislative interest — "...Merchant Marine Act of 1936, Sections 905 and 1101 (b), HR 2526 and S 877."

VOUGHT CORP., Dallas, Texas. Lobbyist — Washington Industrial Team Inc., Washington, D.C. Filed 5/19/81. (Former U.S. Reps. Richard H. Ichord, D-Mo., 1961-81, and Bob Wilson, R-Calif., 1953-81, were among the agents listed for this client.) Legislative interest — "General legislative matters dealing with defense issues."

WALSH, CLEARY, HAMSHER & DAVIS, Washington, D.C. Filed for self 5/12/81. Legislative interest — Not specified.

WESTINGHOUSE ELECTRIC CORP., Pittsburgh, Pa. Lobbyist — Coan, Couture, Lyons & Moorhead, 1625 I St. N.W., Washington, D.C. 20006. Filed 5/29/81. (Former U.S. Rep. William S. Moorhead, D-Pa., 1959-81, was listed as agent for this client.) Legislative interest — "Energy-related matters."

WEYERHAEUSER CO., Tacoma, Wash. Lobbyist — Patton, Boggs & Blow, Washington, D.C. Filed 5/1/81. Legislative interest — "Economic Recovery Tax Act of 1981. HR 1053 ... HR 2400 ... S 683 relating to Economic Recovery Tax Act."

ZANTOP INTERNATIONAL AIRLINES, Ypsilanti, Mich. Lobbyist — William H. Harsha, McLean, Va. Filed 5/13/81. (Former U.S. rep., R-Ohio, 1961-81.) Legislative interest — "Airline legislation."

International Relations

REPUBLIC OF ZAIRE. Lobbyist — Surrey & Morse, Washington, D.C. Filed 5/14/81. Legislative interest — "...foreign assistance authorization and appropriations bills."

Labor Groups

AMALGAMATED TRANSIT UNION, AFL-CIO, Washington, D.C. Filed for self 5/8/81. Legislative interest — Not specified. Lobbyist — Joseph N. Jaquay, Washington, D.C.

INTERNATIONAL LONGSHOREMEN'S ASSOCIATION, AFL-CIO, 17 Battery Place, New York, N.Y. 10004. Filed for self 5/28/81. Legislative interest — "...the shipping industry and labor relations.... Shipping Act of 1916, the Na-

tional Labor Relations Act, the Labor-Management Relations Act, the Labor-Management Reporting and Disclosure Act and the Longshoremen's and Harbor Workers' Compensation Act." Lobbyists — Robert Gleason, Amy Schmidt, Patrick J. Sullivan, 815 16th St. N.W., Washington, D.C. 20006.

INTERNATIONAL UNION OF OPERATING ENGINEERS, Washington, D.C. Filed for self 5/12/81. Legislative interest — Not specified. Lobbyist — John J. Flynn, Washington, D.C.

PUBLIC EMPLOYEE DEPARTMENT, AFL-CIO, Washington, D.C. Filed for self 5/18/81. Legislative interest — "S Con Res 9 . . . HR 1018 . . . The Finance Plan for Social Security." Lobbyist — John F. Leyden, Washington, D.C.

State and Local Governments

BELLE FOURCHE IRRIGATION DISTRICT, Newell, S.D. Lobbyist — Jim Casey, Falls Church, Va. Filed 5/12/81. Legislative interest — "Legislation to reauthorize Belle Fourche project."

CENTRAL CITY ASSOCIATION OF LOS ANGELES, Los Angeles, Calif. Lobbyist — Latham, Watkins & Hills, Washington, D.C. Filed 5/15/81. (Former Secretary of Housing and Urban Development Carla A. Hills was listed as agent for this client.) Legislative interest — "HR 3512."

COMMONWEALTH OF PUERTO RICO. Lobbyist — Latham, Watkins & Hills, Washington, D.C. Filed 5/13/81. Legislative interest — "1981 and 1982 budgets. . . ."

COUNTY OF SUFFOLK, Hauppauge, N.Y. Lobbyist — Jerome A. Ambro Associates, Arlington, Va. Filed 5/14/81. (Former U.S. rep., D-N.Y., 1975-81.) Legislative interest — Not specified.

DISTRICT OF COLUMBIA DEPARTMENT OF TRANSPORTATION, Washington, D.C. Lobbyist — Brown & Roady, Washington, D.C. Filed 5/22/81. Legislative interest — ". . .completion, repair and development of Union Station/Visitors Center."

MAHONING VALLEY ECONOMIC DEVELOPMENT CORP., Youngstown, Ohio. Lobbyist — O'Neill, Forgotson, Roncalio & Haase, Washington, D.C. Filed 5/18/81. Legislative interest — "Legislation affecting economic development."

NEW YORK STATE DEPARTMENT OF TRANSPORTATION, Albany, N.Y. Lobbyist — Jerome A. Ambro Associates, Arlington, Va. Filed 5/11/81. (Former U.S. rep., D-N.Y., 1975-81.) Legislative interest — Not specified.

NEW YORK STATE MORTGAGE LOAN ENFORCEMENT AND ADMINISTRATION CORP., New York, N.Y. Lobbyist — Barrett Smith Schapiro Simon & Armstrong, New York, N.Y. Filed 5/11/81. Legislative interest — ". . .accelerated depreciation and other tax benefits to encourage investment in low-income housing . . . HR 2400 (The Economic Recovery Tax Act of 1981), HR 2053 (The Real Estate Construction and Rehabilitation Tax Incentives Act of 1981), and HR 1580 (The Residential Rental Housing Tax Incentive Act of 1981)."

NEW YORK STATE URBAN DEVELOPMENT CORP., New York, N.Y. Lobbyist — Barrett Smith Schapiro Simon & Armstrong, New York, N.Y. Filed 5/11/81. Legislative interest — ". . .accelerated depreciation and other tax benefits to encourage investment in low-income housing . . . HR 2400 (The Economic Recovery Tax Act of 1981), HR 2053 (The Real Estate Construction and Rehabilitation Tax Incentives Act of 1981), and HR 1580 (The Residential Rental Housing Tax Incentive Act of 1981)."

PORT AUTHORITY OF GUAM, Agana, Guam. Lobbyist — Cook, Purcell, Hansen & Henderson, Washington, D.C. Filed 5/4/81. Legislative interest — "Economic development assistance funds in House/Senate appropriations rescission bill."

Trade Associations

AIR TRANSPORT ASSOCIATION, Washington, D.C.

Filed for self 5/20/81. Legislative interest — ". . .HR 2643, S 951, HR 3403, S 1100." Lobbyist — Brendon Kenny, Washington, D.C.

ALARM INDUSTRY TELECOMMUNICATIONS COMMITTEE OF THE NATIONAL BURGLAR & FIRE ALARM ASSOCIATION, Washington, D.C. Lobbyist — Pepper, Hamilton & Scheetz, Washington, D.C. Filed 5/15/81. Legislative interest — ". . .proposals affecting the alarm industry, particularly domestic common carrier provisions."

AMERICAN AUTOMOBILE LEASING ASSOCIATION INC., Milwaukee, Wis. Lobbyist — Piper & Marbury, 1050 17th St. N.W., Washington, D.C. 20036. Filed 5/1/81. Legislative interest — ". . .legislation assuring depreciation tax deductions and investment tax credits on leased property."

AMERICAN BANKERS ASSOCIATION, Washington, D.C. Filed for self 5/4/81. Legislative interest — "Tax legislation affecting the banking industry." Lobbyist — Paula D. Porpilia, Washington, D.C.

AMERICAN BUSINESS COALITION, Baltimore, Md. Lobbyist — Thompson & Crawford, 1575 I St. N.W., Washington, D.C. 20005. Filed 5/27/81. Legislative interest — "Support of maintaining the present funding level for the Urban Development Action Grant Program."

AMERICAN HEALTH PLANNING ASSOCIATION, Washington, D.C. Filed for self 5/8/81. Legislative interest — "Health Planning and Resources Development Act of 1974." Lobbyist — Deborah M. Schechter, Washington, D.C.

AMERICAN MINING CONGRESS, Washington, D.C. Filed for self 5/4/81. Legislative interest — "Measures affecting mining such as income taxation, social security, mine safety, monetary policy, public lands, stockpiling, environmental quality control, etc." Lobbyist — Toni McCrary, Washington, D.C.

AMERICAN MOVERS CONFERENCE, Arlington, Va. Filed for self 5/11/81. Legislative interest — "All legislation affecting movers." Lobbyist — Charles C. Irions, Arlington, Va.

AMERICAN NUCLEAR ENERGY COUNCIL, Washington, D.C. Filed for self 5/26/81. Legislative interest — ". . .development and use of nuclear energy . . . HR 29, HR 485, HR 508, HR 751, HR 830, HR 872, HR 942, HR 972, HR 1106, HR 1645, HR 1720." Lobbyist — Thom B. Miranda, Washington, D.C.

AMERICAN PAPER INSTITUTE INC., New York, N.Y. Filed for self 5/11/81. Legislative interest — ". . .the pulp, paper and paperboard industry, its operation, practices and properties and including Power Plant and Industrial Fuel Use Act, Natural Gas Policy Act, National Energy Tax Act, Energy Security Act, Public Utility Regulatory Policies Act." Lobbyist — Sara Hamric, New York, N.Y.

AMERICAN PETROLEUM INSTITUTE, Washington, D.C. Lobbyist — King and Spalding, Washington, D.C. Filed 5/12/81. Legislative interest — ". . .divorcement of motor fuel service stations from operation by certain producers and refiners of motor fuels. . . ." Filed for self 5/12/81. Legislative interest — "HR 3471, HR 3404, HR 3071, HR 3420 and other bills affecting the petroleum industry." Lobbyist — Robert Lamb, Washington, D.C.

AMERICAN PSYCHIATRIC ASSOCIATION, Washington, D.C. Filed for self 5/14/81. Legislative interest — "All health legislation affecting psychiatry." Lobbyist — Phyllis Greenberger, Washington, D.C.

AMERICAN RETAIL FEDERATION, Washington, D.C. Lobbyist — Patton, Boggs & Blow, Washington, D.C. Filed 5/1/81. Legislative interest — ". . .energy tax credit for automatic-energy control systems.

AMERICAN SMALL AND RURAL HOSPITAL ASSOCIATION, Bellevue, Ohio. Lobbyist — Bricker & Eckler, 1301 Pennsylvania Ave. N.W., Washington, D.C. 20515. Filed 5/27/81. (Former U.S. Rep. Samuel L. Devine, R-Ohio, 1959-81, was listed as agent for this client.) Legislative interest — Not specified.

AMERICAN WAREHOUSEMEN'S ASSOCIATION, Chicago, Ill. Lobbyist — J. H. Kent, Washington, D.C. Filed 5/6/81. Legislative interest — "Tax legislation, HR 2400."

ASSOCIATION OF BANK HOLDING COMPANIES, Washington, D.C. Lobbyist — Bernard Moss, Washington, D.C. Filed 5/11/81. Legislative interest — ". . .Regional Banking Dereg-

ulation Act."

ASSOCIATION OF DATA PROCESSING SERVICE ORGANIZATIONS INC., Arlington, Va. Filed for self 5/18/81. Legislative interest — "...regulation of telecommunications." Lobbyist — Olga Grkavac, Arlington, Va.

ASSOCIATION OF UNIVERSITY PROGRAMS IN OCCUPATIONAL HEALTH & SAFETY, Houston, Texas. Lobbyist — D.C. Associates Inc., Washington, D.C. Filed 5/11/81. Legislative interest — "All legislation affecting Educational Resource Centers...."

CALIFORNIA CANNERS AND GROWERS, San Francisco, Calif. Filed for self 5/11/81. Legislative interest — Not specified. Lobbyist — Richard C. Cunan, San Francisco, Calif.

CELLULOSE MANUFACTURERS' ASSOCIATION, Arlington, Va. Filed for self 5/26/81. Legislative interest — "Reauthorization of Consumer Product Safety Commission." Lobbyist — William M. Mackenzie, Arlington, Va.

COMMUTER AIRLINE ASSOCIATION OF AMERICA, Washington, D.C. Lobbyist — William H. Harsha & Associates Inc., Washington, D.C. Filed 5/20/81. (Former U.S. rep., R-Ohio, 1961-81.) Legislative interest — "Airline legislation."

EDISON ELECTRIC INSTITUTE, 1111 19th St. N.W., Washington, D.C. 20036. Filed for self 5/29/81. Legislative interest — "...Internal Revenue Code, TVA Act, Atomic Energy Act, Federal Power Act, REA, Bonneville Power Act, Reclamation Act, Flood Control Act...." Lobbyist — Elvira Orly.

GENERIC PHARMACEUTICAL INDUSTRY ASSOCIATION, New York, N.Y. Lobbyist — Lobel, Novins & Lamont, Washington, D.C. Filed 5/14/81. Legislative interest — "Matters of interest to the generic pharmaceutical industry including patent extension (e.g. S 255)."

GROCERY MANUFACTURERS OF AMERICA INC., Washington, D.C. Lobbyist — Bricker & Eckler, Washington, D.C. Filed 5/19/81. (Former U.S. Rep. Samuel L. Devine, R-Ohio, 1959-81, was listed as agent for this client.) Legislative interest — "The Reagan administration's budget and tax programs."

INTELLECTUAL PROPERTY OWNERS INC., Washington, D.C. Filed for self 5/18/81. Legislative interest — "S 255 — Patent Term Restoration and HR 1937; HR 2405 — Court of Appeals for the Federal Circuit; legislation to amend the Freedom of Information Act; S 881 — Small Business Innovation." Lobbyist — Joseph P. Allen, Washington, D.C.

MASSACHUSETTS ASSOCIATION OF CONTRIBUTORY RETIREMENT SYSTEMS INC., Norwood, Mass. Lobbyist — Seifman & Lechner, 1000 Potomac St. N.W., Washington, D.C. 20007. Filed 5/27/81. Legislative interest — "Social Security legislation, pension legislation (HR 889, HR 903, HR 1018, HR 224, HR 91)."

MASSACHUSETTS HOSPITAL ASSOCIATION, Boston, Mass. Lobbyist — O'Neill, Forgotson, Roncalio & Haase, 1333 New Hampshire Ave. N.W., Washington, D.C. 20036. Filed 5/29/81. Legislative interest — Not specified.

MOTORCYCLE INDUSTRY COUNCIL INC., Washington, D.C. Lobbyist — Hogan & Hartson, Washington, D.C. Filed 5/21/81. Legislative interest — "...Noise Control Act of 1972." Filed for self 5/18/81. Legislative interest — "...HR 3071...." Lobbyists — Melvin R. Stahl, John F. Wetzel, Washington, D.C.

NATIONAL AIR TANKERS ASSOCIATION, Chandler, Ariz. Lobbyist — O'Neal & Claassen, Washington, D.C. Filed 5/8/81. Legislative interest — "Legislation affecting aerial firefighting services privately contracted to the federal government...."

NATIONAL ASSOCIATION OF CONVENIENCE STORES, Falls Church, Va. Lobbyist — Collier, Shannon, Rill & Scott, Washington, D.C. Filed 5/4/81. Legislative interest — "Legislation affecting the distribution of food stamps and other legislation affecting the convenience store industry." Filed for self 5/4/81. Lobbyists — Kerley LeBoeuf, Harry Hunter, Washington, D.C.

NATIONAL ASSOCIATION OF FURNITURE MANUFACTURERS, Washington, D.C. Filed for self 5/18/81. Legislative interest — "Legislation directly affecting the household furniture

manufacturing industry. S 1400, S 1435." Lobbyist — Michael S. Sherman, Washington, D.C.

NATIONAL ASSOCIATION OF INDEPENDENT INSURERS, Des Plaines, Ill. Lobbyist — Hopkins & Sutter, Chicago, Ill. Filed 5/13/81. Legislative interest — "..amendments to Internal Revenue Code...."

NATIONAL CABLE TELEVISION ASSOCIATION INC., Washington, D.C. Filed for self 5/21/81. Legislative interest — "Amendments to the Communications Act of 1934 and other legislation affecting cable television generally." Lobbyist — Patricia Carroll, Washington, D.C.

NATIONAL COUNCIL OF FARMER COOPERATIVES, Washington, D.C. Lobbyist — Victoria R. Calvert, Washington, D.C. Filed 5/22/81. Legislative interest — "U.S. petroleum policy and priority for agriculture under contingency energy plans, S 409 Standby Petroleum Authority Act of 1981."

NATIONAL FEDERATION OF INDEPENDENT BUSINESS, Washington, D.C. Filed for self 5/20/81. Legislative interest — Not specified. Lobbyist — Susan Bingham, Washington, D.C.

NATIONAL FOREST PRODUCTS ASSOCIATION, Washington, D.C. Filed for self 5/19/81. Legislative interest — "...Forest Service appropriations, federal land management policies, wilderness proposals, housing and mortgage finance, public financing, lobby law reform, RARE II Review Act of 1981, regulatory reform and taxation." Lobbyists — John F. Hall, Edlu J. Thom, Washington, D.C.

NATIONAL MULTI HOUSING COUNCIL, Washington, D.C. Lobbyist — Seyfarth, Shaw, Fairweather & Geraldson, Washington, D.C. Filed 5/11/81. Legislative interest — "...tax incentives for rental housing production...."

NATIONAL POTATO COUNCIL, Denver, Colo. Lobbyist — Robert W. Porter, 888 17th St. N.W., Washington, D.C. 20006. Filed 5/27/81. Legislative interest — "HR 2160, S 862."

NATIONAL RURAL ELECTRIC COOPERATIVE ASSOCIATION, Washington, D.C. Lobbyist — Cliff Ouse, Washington, D.C. Filed 5/21/81. Legislative interest — "...Rural Electrification Act of 1936."

OUTDOOR POWER EQUIPMENT INSTITUTE, 1901 L St. N.W., Washington, D.C. 20036. Filed for self 5/28/81. Legislative interest — "Reauthorization legislation for Consumer Product Safety Commission." Lobbyist — Frederick P. Stratton Jr., President, Briggs & Stratton Corp., P.O. Box 702, Milwaukee, Wis. 53201.

SHIPBUILDERS COUNCIL OF AMERICA, Washington, D.C. Lobbyists — Seyfarth, Shaw, Fairweather & Geraldson, Washington, D.C. Filed 5/26/81; Sullivan & Beauregard, Washington, D.C. Filed 5/21/81. Legislative interest — "...Longshoremen's and Harbor Workers' Compensation Act...."

SLURRY TRANSPORT ASSOCIATION, Washington, D.C. Lobbyist — William H. Harsha, McLean, Va. Filed 5/13/81. (Former U.S. rep., R-Ohio, 1961-81.) Legislative interest — "Slurry pipeline legislation."

SOUTHERN FURNITURE MANUFACTURERS ASSOCIATION, High Point, N.C. Filed for self 5/26/81. Legislative interest — "...CPSC reauthorization legislation, tax legislation, budget legislation, FTC proposed care labeling regulations." Lobbyists — Betty-Grace Terpstra, Joseph G. Gerard, Washington, D.C.

UNITED EGG PRODUCERS, Decatur, Ga. Filed for self 5/15/81. Legislative interest — Matters affecting the shell egg industry and nutrition." Lobbyist — Cathy McCharen, Washington, D.C.

UNITED STATES INDUSTRIAL COUNCIL, Nashville, Tenn. Lobbyist — Gregory N. Jonsson, Bellevue, Tenn. Filed 5/8/81. Legislative interest — "Business issues affecting small- and medium-sized businesses, e.g. HR 298, HR 1053, HR 911, HR 2911, HR 1784, S 398, HR 1648, HR 1037, HR 565, S 360, HR 964, HR 1083."

U.S. INDUSTRIAL & BUSINESS COUNCIL, Realtor's Building, Nashville, Tenn. 37201. Filed for self 5/28/81. Legislative interest — "...legislation affecting small and medium-size busi-

nesses and business professionals." Lobbyist — Gregory N. Jonsson.

WESTERN FOREST INDUSTRIES ASSOCIATION, Portland, Ore. Lobbyist — Burson-Marsteller, 1800 M St. N.W., Washington, D.C. 20036. Filed 5/18/81. Legislative interest — "...estate tax provisions of the U.S. Internal Revenue Code...."

Miscellaneous

ADVOCATES TO SAVE LEGAL SERVICES INC., Washington, D.C. Filed for self 5/18/81. Legislative interest — "...Legal Services Corp. and ... legal services to poor people." Lobbyist — Ann K. Macrory, Washington, D.C.

AMERICAN UNIVERSITY OF BEIRUT, New York, N.Y. Lobbyist — William L. Hoffman, Washington, D.C. Filed 5/19/81. Legislative interest — "...federal funding programs for the American University of Beirut ... foreign assistance authorization and appropriations bills."

ASSOCIATED UNIVERSITIES, Upton, N.Y. Lobbyist — Jerome A. Ambro Associates, Arlington, Va. Filed 5/11/81. (Former U.S. rep., D-N.Y., 1975-81.) Legislative interest — Not specified.

CAMPAIGN FOR COMMUNITY-BASED ECONOMIC DEVELOPMENT, Washington, D.C. Lobbyist — James Pickman, Washington, D.C. Filed 5/5/81. Legislative interest — "...HR 3045, to extend authorization of Economic Opportunity Act, amend Housing and Community Development Act of 1981." Lobbyist — Hill, Christopher and Phillips, Washington, D.C. Filed 5/13/81. (Former U.S. Rep. Garry Brown, R-Mich., 1967-79, was listed as agent for this client.) Legislative interest — "Funding of community development corporations by reauthorization and funding of Title VII of the Economic Opportunity Act...."

CAMPAIGN FOR COMMUNITY-BASED ECONOMIC DEVELOPMENT, Washington, D.C. Lobbyist — Patton, Boggs & Blow, 2550 M St. N.W., Washington, D.C. 20036. (Former U.S. Rep. James G. O'Hara, D-Mich., 1959-77, was listed as agent for this client.); Hill, Christopher and Phillips, 1900 M St. N.W., Washington, D.C. 20036. (Former U.S. Rep. Garry Brown, R-Mich., 1967-79, was listed as agent for this client.) James Pickman, 1200 New Hampshire Ave. N.W., Washington, D.C. 20036. Filed 5/13/81. Legislative interest — "Preserve Title VII of the Economic Opportunity Act. Support HR 3045, to extend authorization of Economic Opportunity Act; amend Housing and Community Development Act of 1981. Robert Greenstein, Washington, D.C. Filed 5/1/81. Legislative interest — "Federal food and nutrition programs, such as food stamps, and women, infants and children (WIC); federal public assistance programs (Aid to Families with Dependent Children)."

COALITION FOR LEGAL SERVICES, Washington, D.C. Filed for self 5/18/81. Legislative interest — "All legislation concerning the reauthorization of and appropriations to the Legal Services Corp. and all other legislation regarding the provisions of legal services to poor persons." Lobbyist — Charles Bosley, Washington, D.C.

COMMITTEE FOR 806.30 AND 807 INC., Arlington, Va. Lobbyist — Charles E. Chamberlain, Washington, D.C. Filed 5/21/81. (Former U.S. rep., R-Mich., 1957-74.) Legislative interest — "HR 660 and HR 3033."

CONSUMERS UNION OF U.S. INC., Mt. Vernon, N.Y. Filed for self 5/7/81. Legislative interest — "FTC budget ... telecommunications reform legislation ... regulatory reform legislation ... Consumer Product Safety Commission authorization...." Lobbyist — Robert W. Nichols, Washington, D.C.

COOPERATIVE LEAGUE OF THE USA, Washington, D.C. Lobbyist — E. A. Jaenke & Associates Inc., Washington, D.C. Filed 5/18/81. Legislative interest — "...National Consumer Cooperative Bank."

COUNCIL FOR A COMPETITIVE ECONOMY, Washington, D.C. Lobbyist — Cobb Green & Associates Ltd., Chicago, Ill. Filed 5/26/81. Legislative interest — "Free trade, deregulation, tax cuts, gold standard. Free Market Gold Coinage Act."

JOE H. GALIS, Avon Park, Fla. Filed for self 5/22/81. Legislative interest — "Prisoner rights, prison reform, prison law libraries."

FRANK G. KINGSLEY, New Canaan, Conn. Lobbyist — Corcoran, Youngman & Rowe, Washington, D.C. Filed 5/4/81. Legislative interest — "Legislation relating to non-fuel minerals and metals."

GLENN KNAPP, San Carlos, Calif. Filed for self 5/20/81. Legislative interest — "Bill to amend Internal Revenue Code of 1954 (HR 1700), Home Ownership Opportunity Act of 1981 (HR 3221), Bill to amend Internal Revenue Code, income tax credit retirement savings (HR 3395), Investment Incentive Act of 1981 (S 75), Estate and Gift Tax Equity Act (S 395), Research and Development Act of 1981 (S 98), Capital Gains Rollover Account Act (S 457)."

THE MEDICAL COLLEGE OF PENNSYLVANIA, Philadelphia, Pa. Lobbyist — Kline, Knopf & Wojdak Inc., Harrisburg, Pa. Filed 5/6/81. Legislative interest — "Legislative matters that arise in the health care field that impact on the financial stability of MCP."

NATIONAL COMMUNITY ACTION FOUNDATION INC., Washington, D.C. Lobbyist — David A. Bradley, Washington, D.C. Filed 5/18/81. Legislative interest — "...reauthorization of programs operated by Community Services Administration; full funding of CSA, full funding and construction for all programs designed to assist the poor and minorities."

NATIONAL TECHNICAL SCHOOLS OF LOS ANGELES, Los Angeles, Calif. Lobbyist — Amanda Simmons, Washington, D.C. Filed 5/19/81. Legislative interest — "HR 1903, S 918..."

ELIZABETH NESS, 3024 Wisconsin Ave. N.W., Washington, D.C. 20016. Filed for self 5/21/81. Legislative interest — "...advance the development of agricultural or energy-related technologies...."

SEWARD & KISSEL, 1050 17th St. N.W., Washington, D.C. 20036. Filed for self 5/4/81. Legislative interest — "Legislation affecting money market funds."

RICHARD SUMAN, Houston, Texas. Lobbyist — Akin, Gump, Strauss, Hauer & Feld, Washington, D.C. Filed 5/4/81. Legislative interest — "...budget rescissions, S Con Res 9, the revised second concurrent resolution on the fiscal year 1981 budget."

TURNER ELEMENTARY SCHOOL, Washington, D.C. Lobbyist — Pierson, Ball & Dowd, Washington, D.C. Filed 5/19/81. Legislative interest — "All legislation affecting the appropriations to the District of Columbia schools and the conditions of the Turner Elementary School."

June Registrations

Citizens' Groups

AMERICANS FOR DEMOCRATIC ACTION, 1411 K St. N.W., Washington, D.C. 20005. Filed for self 6/8/81. Legislative interest — "Foreign affairs, defense." Lobbyist — William J. Adler Jr.

AMERICANS FOR NUCLEAR ENERGY, P.O. Box 28371, Washington, D.C. 20005. Filed for self 6/12/81. Legislative interest — "...expansion of nuclear power for generation of electricity." Lobbyist — Douglas O. Lee.

CONGRESS WATCH, 215 Pennsylvania Ave. S.E., Washington, D.C. 20003. Filed for self 6/29/81. Legislative interest — "Foreign Corrupt Practices Act, Social Security, telecommunications." Lobbyist — Gene Kimmelman.

CONSUMER ENERGY COUNCIL OF AMERICA, 2000 L St. N.W., Washington, D.C. 20036. Filed for self 6/26/81. Legislative interest — Not specified. Lobbyist — Julie Mencher.

G-4 CHILDREN'S COALITION, Washington, D.C. Lobbyist — Wilmer, Cutler & Pickering, 1666 K St. N.W., Washington, D.C. 20006. Filed 6/17/81. Legislative interest — "Legislation amending 8 U.S.C. section 1101 (a) to secure rights of G-4 visa

holders who are children, surviving spouses and retirees, to obtain permanent U.S. resident status."

NATIONAL ASSOCIATION OF ARAB AMERICANS, 1825 Connecticut Ave. N.W., Washington, D.C. 20009. Filed for self 6/17/81. Legislative interest — "Middle East related legislation ... fiscal 1982 foreign assistance act, amendments to the Internal Revenue Code sections 911 and 913; S 409, HR 911." Lobbyist — Jean Anne Courey.

NATIONAL TAX LIMITATION COMMITTEE, 1523 L St. N.W., Washington, D.C. 20005. Filed for self 6/26/81. Legislative interest — "Constitutional amendments limiting federal spending, S J Res 54, S J Res 58, H J Res 169." Lobbyists — William R. Worthen, John S. Buckley.

PLANNED PARENTHOOD FEDERATION OF AMERICA INC., 1220 19th St. N.W., Washington, D.C. 20036. Filed for self 6/22/81. Legislative interest — "General health legislation as it pertains to family planning and reproductive health matters; also legislation pertaining to regulations or restrictions upon the rights of individuals to exercise choice and individual discretion on matters of personal health and reproduction. Also tax, budget and appropriations matters affecting the operations of non-profit 501 (c)(3) corporations; HR 2807; HR 900; HR 867; HR 3225; and S 158." Lobbyists — William Gilmartin, William W. Hamilton Jr. and Charlotte Holloman.

U.S. & OVERSEAS TAX FAIRNESS COMMITTEE, Washington, D.C. Lobbyist — Jaffe, Squires & Foote, 1000 Potomac St. N.W., Washington, D.C. 20007. Filed 6/30/81. Legislative interest — "Taxation of foreign-earned income, HR 911, HR 913."

Corporations and Businesses

ACUREX SOLAR CORP., 1725 Jefferson Davis Hwy., Arlington, Va. 22202. Filed for self 6/15/81. Legislative interest — "Legislation impacting development of electric energy from photovoltaic technology, including HR 3146, S 1021." Lobbyist — Joel A. Weiss.

AMAX INC., Greenwich, Conn. Lobbyist — Brown & Roady, 1333 New Hampshire Ave. N.W., Washington, D.C. 20036. Filed 6/8/81. Legislative interest — "...Clean Air Act...."

AMERICAN TANKSHIPS INC., New Orleans, La. Lobbyist — Kominers, Fort, Schlefer & Boyer, 1776 F St. N.W., Washington, D.C. Filed 6/1/81. Legislative interest — "Maritime Administration authorization bills, HR 2526, S 877 and S 1017...."

J. ARON & CO. INC., New York, N.Y. Lobbyist — Dickinson, Wright, McKean, Cudlip & Moon, 1901 L St. N.W., Washington, D.C. 20036. Filed 6/18/81. Legislative interest — "Future contract straddles."

BLUEJAY OIL CO., Wilmington, Del. Lobbyist — Shipley Smoak & Akerman, 1108 National Press Building, Washington, D.C. 20045. Filed 6/23/81. Legislative interest — "Energy, taxes, antitrust, environmental, interstate commerce, real estate."

BOISE CASCADE CORP., Boise, Idaho. Lobbyist — Bell, Boyd & Lloyd, 70 West Madison St., Chicago, Ill. 60602. Filed 6/11/81. Legislative interest — "Antitrust Equal Enforcement Act of 1981, S 995...."

BOWERY SAVINGS BANK, New York, N.Y. Lobbyist — Vorys, Sater, Seymour & Pease, 1828 L St. N.W., Washington, D.C. 20036. Filed 6/24/81. Legislative interest — "...savings and loan industry, specifically HR 3953."

BURNS AND ROE INC., Washington, D.C. Lobbyist — Ernest B. Tremmel Inc., 5908 Rossmore Drive, Bethesda, Md. 20014. Filed 6/8/81. Legislative interest — "...energy legislation ... Department of Energy authorization and appropriations bills for each fiscal year and similar bills for Nuclear Regulatory Commission."

CITIES SERVICE CO., Tulsa, Okla. Lobbyists — Jones, Day, Reavis & Pogue, 1735 I St. N.W., Washington, D.C., 20006; (Former Secretary of Housing and Urban Development James T. Lynn, 1973-75. was listed as agent for this client.) Charls E. Walker Associates Inc., 1730 Pennsylvania Ave. N.W., Washington, D.C. 20006. Filed 6/24/81. Legislative interest — "...discriminatory advantages which have the effect of favoring foreign

corporations seeking to acquire significant interests in domestic corporations."

CLC OF AMERICA INC., Houston, Texas. Lobbyist — Bracewell & Patterson, 1850 K St. N.W., Washington, D.C. 20006. Filed 6/1/81. Legislative interest — "...waterway user proposals."

COMMERCIAL UNION LEASING CORP., New York, N.Y. Lobbyist — White & Case, 1747 Pennsylvania Ave. N.W., Washington, D.C. 20006. Filed 6/26/81. Legislative interest — "...HR 3849, Economic Recovery Tax Act of 1981...."

COMSAT CORP., Washington, D.C. Lobbyist — John Chwat, 5301 Inver-Chapel Road, Springfield, Va. 22151. Filed 6/18/81. Legislative interest — "Communications, telecommunications, science, space; Communications Satellite Act, PL 87-624 ... Communications Act of 1934; FCC Authorization Act. HR 564, HR 1013, HR 1257, HR 1801, HR 1891, HR 1957, HR 2774, HR 3137, HR 3239, HR 3712, S 270, S 708, S 821, S 898...."

CONSUMERS POWER CO., 212 West Michigan Ave., Jackson, Mich. 49201. Filed for self 6/8/81. Legislative interest — "...national energy policy in general and electric utilities in particular ... Emergency Petroleum Allocation Act, Fuel Use Act, Natural Gas Policy Act, Clean Air Act, Clinch River breeder reactor legislation, Price-Anderson Act, Nuclear Regulatory Reform." Lobbyist — H. B. W. Schroeder, 1050 17th St. N.W., Washington, D.C. 20036.

CONTAINER TRANSPORT INTERNATIONAL, New York, N.Y. Lobbyist — Gary N. Freeman, 3340 Peachtree Road N.E., Atlanta, Ga. 30026. Filed 6/11/81. Legislative interest — "...HR 2454 — to modify tariff on certain freight containers...."

COEUR D'ALENE MINES, Wallace, Idaho. Lobbyist — Wagner and Baroody, 1100 17th St. N.W., Washington, D.C. 20036. Filed 6/24/81. Legislative interest — "...silver stockpile."

DATAPOINT CORP., Arlington, Va. Lobbyist — Lipsen & Hamberger, 1725 DeSales St. N.W., Washington, D.C. 20036. Filed 6/26/81. Legislative interest — "Legislation affecting competition in communications."

DEAK NATIONAL BANK, Fleischmanns, N.Y. Lobbyist — O'Connor & Hannan, 1919 Pennsylvania Ave. N.W., Washington, D.C. 20006. Filed 6/22/81. Legislative interest — "Budget reconciliation recommendations related to education."

E. G. G. INDUSTRIES, Wellesley, Mass. Lobbyist — Patton, Boggs & Blow, 2550 M St. N.W., Washington, D.C. 20037. Filed 6/5/81. Legislative interest — "...hydroelectric and other forms of energy development, including the Economic Recovery Tax Act. Includes S 639 and HR 2400...."

ELSEVIER SCIENTIFIC PUBLISHERS, Slotervaart, The Netherlands. Lobbyist — Kaye, Scholer, Fierman, Hays & Handler, 1575 I St. N.W., Washington, D.C. 20005. Filed 6/1/81. Legislative interest — "...government policies regarding the dissemination of published medical and scientific literature ... S 800 and HR 2562...."

EVANS TRANSPORTATION CO., Rolling Meadows, Ill. Lobbyist — Camp, Carmouche, Palmer, Barsh & Hunter, 2550 M St. N.W., Washington, D.C. 20037. Filed 6/2/81. Legislative interest — "Amendment to Internal Revenue Code section 48 (a) (2)."

FACET ENTERPRISES INC., Tulsa, Okla. Lobbyist — Covington & Burling, 888 16th St. N.W., Washington, D.C. 20006. Filed 6/11/81. Legislative interest — "Legislation affecting the application of the termination insurance program under the Employee Retirement Income Security Act of 1974 to single-employer pension plans...."

FEDERATED DEPARTMENT STORES INC., Cincinnati, Ohio. Lobbyist — Shipley Smoak & Akerman, 1108 National Press Building, Washington, D.C. 20045. Filed 6/23/81. Legislative interest — "Taxes, antitrust, environmental, interstate commerce, foreign relations, energy, broadcasting, real estate."

THE FIRST BOSTON CORP., New York, N.Y. Lobbyist — Williams & Jensen, 1101 Connecticut Ave. N.W., Washington, D.C. 20036. Filed 6/24/81. Legislative interest — "Banking and related issues."

FLANIGAN'S ENTERPRISES INC., Miami, Fla. Lobbyist — Shipley Smoak & Akerman, 1108 National Press Building, Washington, D.C. 20045. Filed 6/23/81. Legislative interest — "Taxes, antitrust, environmental, interstate commerce, foreign

relations, energy, broadcasting, real estate."

FORT SILL GARDENS INC., Lawton, Okla. Lobbyist — Shipley Smoak & Akerman, 1108 National Press Building, Washington, D.C. 20045. Filed 6/23/81. Legislative interest — "Taxes, antitrust, environmental, interstate commerce, energy, real estate."

FOSS ALASKA LINE, Seattle, Wash. Lobbyist — Lillick McHose & Charles, 1333 New Hampshire Ave. N.W., Washington, D.C. 20036. Filed 6/25/81. Legislative interest — "HR 3577, Merchant Marine Act of 1920; Merchant Marine Act of 1936...."

FOSS LAUNCH & TUG CO., Seattle, Wash. Lobbyist — Lillick McHose & Charles, 1333 New Hampshire Ave. N.W., Washington, D.C. 20036. Filed 6/25/81. Legislative interest — "HR 3577, Merchant Marine Act of 1920; Merchant Marine Act of 1936...."

GENERAL PUBLIC UTILITIES, Parsippany, N.J. Lobbyist — Van Ness, Feldman, Sutcliffe, Curtis & Levenberg, 1050 Thomas Jefferson St. N.W., Washington, D.C. 20007. Filed 6/15/81. (Former U.S. Rep. Thomas L. Ashley, D-Ohio, 1955-81, was listed as the employer, in his capacity as consultant to General Public Utilities.) Legislative interest — "Public utility and nuclear power generation financial matters; National Nuclear Property Insurance Act of 1981, HR 2512."

GEORGIA-PACIFIC CORP., 900 S.W. Fifth Ave., Portland, Ore. 97204. Filed for self 6/3/81. Legislative interest — "...forest products industry as well as matters relating to gypsum, coal, natural gas and chemicals." Lobbyist — John T. Ferguson II, 1875 I St. N.W., Washington, D.C. 20006.

GREAT NATIONAL CORP., Dallas, Texas. Lobbyist — Mountain West Associates, 1229 19th St. N.W., Washington, D.C. 20036. Filed 6/25/81. Legislative interest — "HR 3975...."

GULF RESOURCES & CHEMICAL CORP., Houston, Texas. Lobbyist — McClure & Trotter, 1100 Connecticut Ave. N.W., Washington, D.C. 20036. Filed 6/24/81. Legislative interest — "...HR 3849-Economic Recovery Act of 1981 and S 1140, HR 3718 and HR 3460 dealing with incentive stock options."

GULF + WESTERN INDUSTRIES INC., New York, N.Y. Lobbyist — McClure & Trotter, 1100 Connecticut Ave. N.W., Washington, D.C. 20036. Filed 6/24/81. Legislative interest — "...HR 3849 — Economic Recovery Act of 1981 and S 1140, HR 3718 and HR 3460 dealing with incentive stock options."

HANDY AND HARMAN, New York, N.Y. Lobbyist — Breed, Abbott & Morgan, 1875 I St. N.W., Washington, D.C. 20006. Filed 6/23/81. Legislative interest — "LIFO inventory accounting concept as found in S 1180 and HR 3606."

HARBISON FORD INC., Morrisville, Pa. Lobbyist — Johnson, Swanson & Barbee, 4700 First International Building, Dallas, Texas 75270. Filed 6/17/81. Legislative interest — "...amendment to Energy Tax Act of 1978 to permit a refund to certain taxpayers of excise taxes paid on buses."

ICI AMERICAS INC., Wilmington, Del. 19897. Filed for self 6/5/81. Legislative interest — "...chemical industry in general." Lobbyists — Robert E. Hampton, Charles L. Hebner, Ellen E. Eves.

INDUSTRIAS QUIMICAS Y TARTARICAS, Gerona, Spain. Lobbyist — Barnes, Richardson & Colburn, 1819 H St. N.W., Washington, D.C. 20006. Filed 6/15/81. Legislative interest — "...Customs tariffs on imports of tartaric chemicals, tartaric chemical duty suspension bill, HR 1910...."

INGRAM TANKSHIPS INC., New Orleans, La. Lobbyist — Kominers, Fort, Schlefer & Boyer, 1776 F St. N.W., Washington, D.C. 20006. Filed 6/1/81. Legislative interest — "Maritime Administration authorization bills, HR 2526, S 877 and S 1017...."

INTERNATIONAL PAPER CO., New York, N.Y. Lobbyist — Patterson, Belknap, Webb & Tyler, 30 Rockefeller Plaza, New York, N.Y. 10112. Filed 6/18/81. Legislative interest — "Antitrust contribution bills...."

K MART CORP., Troy, Mich. Lobbyist — Dickinson, Wright, McKean, Cudlip & Moon, 1901 L St. N.W., Washington, D.C. 20036. Filed 6/18/81. Legislative interest — "Industrial development bonds."

LONE STAR INDUSTRIES INC., One Greenwich Plaza,

Greenwich, Conn. 06830. Filed for self 6/26/81. Legislative interest — "...highway legislation and public works bills; the Antitrust Contribution bills (S 995 and HR 1242) ... tax and environmental bills...." Lobbyists — Nancy L. Parke, F. Eugene Purcell, 1919 Pennsylvania Ave. N.W., Washington, D.C. 20006.

LOUISIANA PACIFIC CORP., Portland, Ore. Lobbyist — Wilkinson, Cragun & Barker, 1735 New York Ave. N.W., Washington, D.C. 20006. Filed 6/2/81. Legislative interest — "...HR 2688 — Redwood National Park - National Park Service rescission request...."

LUZ INTERNATIONAL LTD., Burlingame, Calif. Lobbyist — Manatt, Phelps, Rothenberg & Tunney, 1200 New Hampshire Ave. N.W., Washington, D.C. 20005. Filed 6/19/81. Legislative interest — "HR 3849 and related legislation to exempt solar energy 'property' from the proposed 'at risk' limitation on investment and energy tax credits."

MEAD CORP., Dayton, Ohio. Lobbyist — Skadden, Arps, Slate, Meagher & Flom, 919 Third Ave., New York, N.Y. 10022 and 1775 Pennsylvania Ave. N.W., Washington, D.C. 20006. Filed 6/1/81. Legislative interest — "S 995." Lobbyists — William J. Hunter Jr., Alan M. Wiseman, 1730 Pennsylvania Ave. N.W., Washington, D.C. 20006. Filed 6/16/81. Legislative interest — "Antitrust legislation, including S 995, S 1068, HR 1242."

MORTGAGE GUARANTY INSURANCE CORP., Milwaukee, Wis. Lobbyist — Carl F. Arnold, 1100 Connecticut Ave. N.W., Washington, D.C. 20036. Filed 6/19/81. Legislative interest — "...housing industry ... rates and availability of mortgage money."

NATIONAL TECHNICAL SCHOOLS OF LOS ANGELES, Los Angeles, Calif. Lobbyist — Priest & Fine Inc., 1725 K St. N.W., Washington, D.C. 20006. Filed 6/10/81. Legislative interest — "...saving home study courses for veterans under S 918, HR 1903 and HR 1400."

HUGO NEU & SONS INC., New York, N.Y. Lobbyist — Barrett Smith Schapiro Simon & Armstrong, 26 Broadway, New York, N.Y. 10004. Filed 6/23/81. Legislative interest — "Estate tax, gift tax and income tax revisions benefiting family businesses...."

NEWCOMB SECURITIES CO., New York, N.Y. Lobbyist — Charles M. Seeger III, 2000 L St. N.W., Washington, D.C. 20036. Filed 6/12/81. Legislative interest — "...broker-dealers of government securities and/or affecting financial futures markets."

NORTHWEST ALASKAN PIPELINE CO., Washington, D.C. Lobbyist — Manatt, Phelps, Rothenberg & Tunney, 1200 New Hampshire Ave. N.W., Washington, D.C. 20036. Filed 6/17/81. Legislative interest — "...Internal Revenue Code of 1954."

THE NORTHWESTERN MUTUAL LIFE INSURANCE CO., Milwaukee, Wis. Lobbyist — Charls E. Walker Associates Inc., 1730 Pennsylvania Ave. N.W., Washington, D.C. 20006. Filed 6/17/81. Legislative interest — "...construction and operation of plants designed to produce synthetic fuels."

PAYCO AMERICAN CORP., Columbus, Ohio. Lobbyist — Bricker & Eckler, 1301 Pennsylvania Ave. N.W., Washington, D.C. 20004. Filed 6/1/81. (Former U.S. Rep. Samuel L. Devine, R-Ohio, 1959-81, was listed as agent for this client. Legislative interest — "...collection of debts owed to the federal government."

PLATEAU INC., Albuquerque, N.M. Lobbyist — O'Connor & Hannan, 1919 Pennsylvania Ave. N.W., Washington, D.C. 20006. Filed 6/11/81. Legislative interest — "Energy/synfuels legislation, including proposal to rescind grant funding."

PEN INC., St. Petersburg, Fla. Lobbyist — Lipsen & Hamberger, 1725 DeSales St. N.W., Washington, D.C. 20036. Filed 6/11/81. Legislative interest — "Health legislation."

POPHAM, HAIK, SCHNOBRICH, KAUFMAN & DOTY LTD.; Minneapolis, Minn. Lobbyist — Charles M. Seeger III, 2000 L St. N.W., Washington, D.C. 20036. Filed 6/12/81 Legislative interest — "...broker-dealers of government securities and/or affecting financial futures markets."

PULLMAN STANDARD, Chicago, Ill. Lobbyist — Camp, Carmouche, Palmer, Barsh & Hunter, 2550 M St. N.W., Washington, D.C. 20037. Filed 6/26/81. Legislative interest — "Amend-

ment to Internal Revenue Code section 48 (a) (2)."

REICHHOLD ENERGY CORP., Tacoma, Wash. Lobbyist
— Covington & Burling, 888 16th St. N.W., Washington, D.C.
20006. Filed 6/29/81. Legislative interest — ". . .seeks private relief
legislation for the reinstatement of federal oil and gas lease
OR 13713. . . ."

TOM REIDY INC., Houston, Texas. Lobbyist — Akin,
Gump, Strauss, Hauer & Feld, 1333 New Hampshire Ave. N.W.,
Washington, D.C. 20036. Filed 6/29/81. Legislative interest —
". . .imposition of a statute of limitations on actions enforcing
compliance with federal regulatory programs, including but not
limited to HR 316 (the Limitation of Government Recordkeeping
Requirements and Actions Act of 1981); S 961 . . . HR 4035. . . ."

REPUBLIC AIRLINES INC., Minneapolis, Minn. Lobbyist — Zuckert, Scoutt & Rasenberger, 888 17th St. N.W., Washington, D.C. 20006. Filed 6/26/81. Legislative interest — ". . .subsidies
for small city airline service, Airline Subsidy Reduction Act of
1981, HR 3901 and S 1376. . . ."

RIVIANA FOODS INC., Houston, Texas. Lobbyist —
Surrey & Morse, 1156 15th St. N.W., Washington, D.C. 20005.
Filed 6/16/81. Legislative interest — ". . .agriculture, especially
rice."

SECURITY PACIFIC NATIONAL BANK, Los Angeles,
Calif. Lobbyist — Alfred M. Pollard, 1901 L St. N.W., Washington, D.C. 20036. Filed 6/30/81. Legislative interest — "All legislation affecting financial institutions, including specific banking
legislation, housing, agricultural and other financial matters."

SOUTHERN CALIFORNIA GAS, Washington, D.C. Lobbyist — Peabody, Rivlin, Lambert & Meyers, 1150 Connecticut
Ave. N.W., Washington, D.C. 20036. Filed 6/12/81. (Former Gov.
Endicott Peabody, D-Mass., 1963-65, was listed as agent for this
client.) Legislative interest — "Repeal of the Fuel Use Act. . . ."

SPERRY CORP., 2000 L St. N.W., Washington, D.C. 20036.
Filed for self 6/11/81. Legislative interest — ". . .taxes, communications, agriculture, international affairs, and regulations." Lobbyist — Gerald R. Jones.

STEADMAN MUTUAL FUNDS, Washington, D.C. Lobbyist — Shipley Smoak & Akerman, 1108 National Press Building,
Washington, D.C. 20045. Filed 6/23/81. Legislative interest —
"Taxes, antitrust, environmental, interstate commerce, foreign
relations, energy, broadcasting, real estate."

STEADMAN SECURITY CORP., Wilmington, Del. Lobbyist — Shipley Smoak & Akerman, 1108 National Press Building,
Washington, D.C. 20045. Filed 6/23/81. Legislative interest —
"Taxes, antitrust, environmental, interstate commerce, foreign
relations, energy, broadcasting, real estate."

STEPHENS OVERSEAS SERVICES INC., 1101 Con-
necticut Ave. N.W., Washington, D.C. 20036. Filed for self 6/26/81.
Legislative interest — "Banking, small business, international and
corporate regulatory issues." Lobbyists — Vernon Weaver, E.
Vernon Markham III.

STERN BROTHERS INC., Parkersburg, W. Va. Lobbyist
— Eugene M. Trisko, 9817 Rosensteel Ave., Silver Spring, Md.
20910. Filed 6/3/81. Legislative interest — ". . .Clean Air Act. . . ."

STEWART ENVIRONMENTAL SYSTEMS INC., New
York, N.Y. Lobbyist — Finley, Kumble, Wagner, Heine,
Underberg & Casey, 1120 Connecticut Ave. N.W., Washington,
D.C. 20036. Legislative interest — ". . .opposes the
inclusion of certain materials in S 622 proposed as an amendment
to the Export Administration Act."

TELE-PRESS ASSOCIATES, 342 East 79th St., New
York, N.Y. 10021. Filed for self 6/17/81. Legislative interest —
". . .fishing and whaling." Lobbyist — Michela S. Mago.

TESORO PETROLEUM CORP., 8700 Tesoro Dr., San
Antonio, Texas 78286. Filed for self 6/8/81. Legislative interest —
Not specified. Lobbyist — Perry W. Woofter, 1775 K St. N.W.,
Washington, D.C. 20006.

TEXAS OIL & GAS CORP., Dallas, Texas. Lobbyist —
Edward H. Forgotson, 1627 K St. N.W., Washington, D.C. 20006.
Filed 6/8/81. Legislative interest — "National Energy Policy."

TRACOR INC., Austin, Texas. Lobbyist — Charls E.
Walker Associates Inc., 1730 Pennsylvania Ave. N.W., Washington, D.C. 20006. Filed 6/18/81. Legislative interest — ". . .matters

relating to tax treatment of qualified stock options or other forms
of executive compensation." Lobbyist — McClure & Trotter, 1100
Connecticut Ave. N.W., Washington, D.C. 20036. Filed 6/24/81.
Legislative interest — "In favor of HR 3849 — Economic Recovery
Act of 1981 and S 1140, HR 3718 and HR 3460 dealing with
incentive stock options."

TRANS AMERICA ICS, New York, N.Y. Lobbyist — Gary
N. Freeman, 3340 Peachtree Rd. N.E., Atlanta, Ga. 30026. Filed
6/11/81. Legislative interest — "HR 2454 — To modify tariff on
certain freight containers."

TRANS-LUX CORP., Norwalk, Conn. Lobbyist — Verner,
Liipfert, Bernhard and McPherson, 1660 L St. N.W., Washington,
D.C. 20036. Filed 6/24/81. Legislative interest — ". . .telecommuni-
cations, particularly as it relates to Telex terminal equipment."

TRANS OCEAN LEASING CORP., New York, N.Y.
Lobbyist — Gary N. Freeman, 3340 Peachtree Rd. N.E., Atlanta,
Ga. 30026. Filed 6/11/81. Legislative interest — "HR 2454 — To
modify tariff on certain freight containers."

TRANSCO COMPANIES INC., P.O. Box 1396, Houston,
Texas. 77001. Filed for self 6/5/81. Legislative interest — ". . .natu-
ral gas. . . ." Lobbyist — Lawrence H. Gall.

TRANSPORT MUTUAL SERVICES INC., New York,
N.Y. Lobbyist — O'Connor & Hannan, 1919 Pennsylvania Ave.
N.W., Washington, D.C. 20006. Filed 6/22/81. Legislative interest
— "S 1182 — A bill to amend the Longshoremen's and Harbor
Workers' Compensation Act."

**TWIN COASTS NEWSPAPER INC. (THE JOURNAL
OF COMMERCE),** New York, N.Y. Lobbyist — Blum & Nash,
1015 18th St. N.W., Washington, D.C. 20036. Filed 6/26/81.
Legislative interest — ". . .HR 3637, a bill to amend the Shipping
Act of 1916 . . . legislation affecting amendments to the Freedom of
Information Act. . . ."

UBA INC., 1800 M St. N.W., Washington, D.C. 20036. Filed
for self 6/22/81. Legislative interest — ". . .all bills which deal with
unemployment compensation and workers' compensation. . . ."
Lobbyist — Charles B. Little.

VALERO ENERGY CORP., San Antonio, Texas. Lobbyist
— Akin, Gump, Strauss, Hauer & Feld, 1333 New Hampshire Ave.
N.W., Washington, D.C. 20036. Filed 6/29/81. Legislative interest
— ". . .tax reform, including but not limited to S 639, amendments
to Internal Revenue Code to provide favorable tax treatment for
stock options; and S 683, the Economic Recovery Tax Act of 1981."

WATERMAN STEAMSHIP CORP., New York, N.Y.
Lobbyist — Windels, Marx, Davies & Ives, 51 West 51st St., New
York, N.Y. 10019. Filed 6/30/81. Legislative interest — ". . .ship-
ping industry . . . Department of Defense authorization statutes
and appropriations bills."

WESTERN PIONEER INC., Seattle, Wash. Lobbyist —
Lillick McHose & Charles, 1333 New Hampshire Ave. N.W.,
Washington, D.C. 20036. Filed 6/25/81. Legislative interest —
"Merchant Marine Act of 1936. . . ."

WESTINGHOUSE ELECTRIC CORP., Washington,
D.C. Lobbyist — Lipsen & Hamberger, 1725 DeSales St. N.W.,
Washington, D.C. 20036. Filed 6/11/81. Legislative interest —
"Energy and Economic legislation."

WESTVACO CORP., New York, N.Y. Lobbyist — Skadden,
Arps, Slate, Meagher & Flom, 919 Third Ave., New York, N.Y.
10022, and 1775 Pennsylvania Ave. N.W., Washington, D.C. 20006.
Filed 6/1/81. Legislative interest — "S 995."

WBNO RADIO, Bryan, Ohio. Lobbyist — Shipley Smoak &
Akerman, 1108 National Press Building, Washington, D.C. 20045.
Filed 6/23/81. Legislative interest — "Taxes, broadcasting, antitrust, environmental, interstate commerce, foreign relations, energy, real estate."

WLKM RADIO, Three Rivers, Mich. Lobbyist — Shipley
Smoak & Akerman, 1108 National Press Building, Washington,
D.C. 20045. Filed 6/23/81. Legislative interest — "Taxes, broadcasting, antitrust, environmental, interstate commerce, foreign
relations, energy, real estate."

International Relations

U.S.-SOUTH WEST AFRICA TRADE AND CULTURAL COUNCIL, Washington, D.C. Lobbyist — Shipley, Smoak & Akerman, 1108 National Press Building, Washington, D.C. 20045. Filed 6/23/81. Legislative interest — "Taxes, antitrust, environmental, interstate commerce, foreign relations, energy, broadcasting, real estate."

Labor Groups

MUNICIPAL LABOR COMMITTEE, 140 Park Place, New York, N.Y. 10007. Filed for self 6/29/81. Legislative interest — "General labor law, general cities issues, budget matters." Lobbyist — Brenda White.

NATIONAL EDUCATION ASSOCIATION, Washington, D.C. Lobbyist — Dr. Joseph S. Smolen, 9412 Old Mount Vernon Road, Alexandria, Va. 22309. Filed 6/23/81. Legislative interest — "...to increase congressional appropriations for section 6 schools and Department of Defense Dependents' Schools."

OVERSEAS EDUCATION ASSOCIATION, Washington, D.C. Lobbyist — Dr. Joseph S. Smolen, 9412 Old Mount Vernon Road, Alexandria, Va. 22309. Filed 6/23/81. Legislative interest — "...to increase congressional appropriations for section 6 schools and Department of Defense Dependents' Schools."

SERVICE EMPLOYEES INTERNATIONAL UNION, AFL-CIO, CLC, 2020 K St. N.W., Washington, D.C. 20006. Filed for self 6/16/81. Legislative interest — "...ERA bill, hospital cost containment bill, Humphrey-Hawkins full employment bill, youth subminimum wage, and the CETA bill...." Lobbyist — Geri Palast.

State and Local Governments

CITY OF MIAMI, Miami, Fla. Lobbyist — Cramer & Cramer, 1320 19th St. N.W., Washington, D.C. 20036. Filed 6/17/81. (Former U.S. Rep. William C. Cramer, R-Fla., 1955-71, was listed among agents for this client.) Legislative interest — "Any legislation, including budget, authorization or appropriation, which may affect federal funding or federal programs for the City of Miami, Fla."

CITY OF PAINESVILLE, Painesville, Ohio. Lobbyist — Squire, Sanders & Dempsey, 21 Dupont Circle N.W., Washington, D.C. 20036. Filed 6/22/81. Legislative interest — "To seek an amendment to Section 111 of the Clean Air Act by adding to subsection (a) a proviso making sulfur dioxide standards for new fossil-fuel fired steam generators inapplicable to boilers the construction or modification of which was commenced before Sept. 10, 1975."

DADE COUNTY, Miami, Fla. Lobbyist — Cramer & Cramer, 1320 19th St. N.W., Washington, D.C. 20036. Filed 6/17/81. (Former U.S. Rep. William C. Cramer, R-Fla., 1955-71, was listed among agents for this client.) Legislative interest — "Any legislation, including budget, authorization, or appropriation, which may affect federal funding of federal programs of Dade County, Florida."

ERIE COUNTY INDUSTRIAL DEVELOPMENT AGENCY, Buffalo, N.Y. Lobbyist — Walsh, Cleary, Hamsher & Davis, 1301 Pennsylvania Ave. N.W., Washington, D.C. 20004. Filed 6/17/81. Legislative interest — "Legislation relating to Industrial Revenue Bonds, HR 3461; EDA rescissions and deferrals, HR 3512; and transportation matters."

STATE OF CALIFORNIA OFFICE OF THE COMPTROLLER, Sacramento, Calif. Lobbyist — David Vienna & Associates, 510 C St. N.E., Washington, D.C. 20002. Filed 6/10/81. Legislative interest — "To promote fiscal responsibility, equity and efficiency and economy in government program management."

Trade Associations

AMERICAN ASSOCIATION OF CROP INSURERS, 209 W. Jackson Blvd., Chicago, Ill. 60606. Filed for self 6/28/81. Legislative interest — "Legislation to provide funds for implementation of the Federal Crop Insurance Act of 1980." Lobbyist — M. K. Felt, Chicago, Ill.

AMERICAN BUSINESS COUNCIL, Washington, D.C. Lobbyist — The Dobbs Corp., 2626 Pennsylvania Ave. N.W., Washington, D.C. 20037. Filed 6/29/81. Legislative interest — Not specified.

AMERICAN ELECTRONICS ASSOCIATION, Palo Alto, Calif. Lobbyist — Warren S. Richardson, 325 Pennsylvania Ave. S.E., Washington, D.C. 20003. Filed 6/18/81. Legislative interest — "...tax matters, import, stock options, research and development, labor law ... incentive stock options, HR 822, HR 2797, HR 3460, HR 3718 and S 639...."

AMERICAN GAS ASSOCIATION, 1515 Wilson Blvd., Arlington, Va. 22209. Filed for self 6/15/81. Legislative interest — "...helium, HR 3877; military construction authorization, HR 3455; Metric Conversion Act; HR 1660, HR 1704, HR 2940; Public Lands Reform Act, S 1245." Lobbyist — Forest S. Schmeling.

AMERICAN NEWSPAPER PUBLISHERS ASSOCIATION, Box 17407, Washington, D.C. 20041. Filed for self 6/15/81. Legislative interest — "...all legislation affecting the newspaper business, ranging from First Amendment considerations to business ... Communications Act of 1934...." Lobbyist — W. Terry Maguire.

AMERICAN OSTEOPATHIC ASSOCIATION, 499 South Capitol St. S.W., Washington, D.C. 20003. Filed for self 6/29/81. Legislative interest — "...health, including health manpower, health planning, HMOs, Medicare reimbursement reform and national health insurance." Lobbyist — Brian J. Donadio.

AUTOMOTIVE PARTS REBUILDERS ASSOCIATION, 6849 Old Dominion Dr., McLean, Va. 22101. Filed for self 6/11/81. Legislative interest — "Clean Air Act, as amended August 1977, HR 2310...." Lobbyists — Lawrence P. Mutter, Richard F. Turney, McLean, Va.; Richard A. Mehler, 1225 Connecticut Ave. N.W., Washington, D.C. 20036.

BOARD OF TRADE OF THE CITY OF CHICAGO, Chicago, Ill. Lobbyist — Alston, Miller & Gaines, 35 Broad St., Atlanta, Ga. 30335. Filed 6/3/81. Legislative interest — "...tax treatment of commodity spreads or straddles, under HR 1338, HR 1293...."

THE BUSINESS ROUNDTABLE, New York, N.Y. Lobbyist — Shearman & Sterling, 153 East 53rd St., New York, N.Y. 10022. Filed 6/3/81. Legislative interest — "Amendments to Export Administration Act of 1979...."

DAYTIME BROADCASTERS ASSOCIATION, Mattoon, Ill. Lobbyist — Blum & Nash, 1015 18th St. N.W., Washington, D.C. 20036. Filed 6/17/81. Legislative interest — "...9 kilohertz legislation."

DIRECT MAIL MARKETING ASSOCIATION, 1730 K St. N.W., Washington, D.C. 20006. Filed for self 6/8/81. Legislative interest — "...postal, communications, tax and privacy legislation." Lobbyists — Jonah Gitlitz, Anne P. Werner.

GENERAL AVIATION MANUFACTURERS ASSOCIATION, Washington, D.C. Lobbyist — Schwabe, Williamson, Wyatt, Moore and Roberts, 1000 Potomac St. N.W., Washington, D.C. 20007. Filed 6/26/81. (Former U.S. Rep. Robert Duncan, D-Ore., 1963-67, 1975-81, was listed as agent for this client.) Legislative interest — "International trade."

GENERIC PHARMACEUTICAL INDUSTRY ASSOCIATION, 600 Third Ave., New York, N.Y. 10016. Filed for self 6/29/81. Legislative interest — "...patent extension (S 255)."

INDEPENDENT REFINERS ASSOCIATION OF AMERICA, Washington, D.C. Lobbyist — Foley, Lardner, Hollabaugh & Jacobs, 1775 Pennsylvania Ave. N.W., Washington, D.C. 20006. Filed 6/2/81. Legislative interest — "...refining policy, price and allocation controls, import tariffs and fees and import policy, oil and gas development on federal lands, taxation, antitrust and small business legislation."

MASSACHUSETTS CONSTRUCTION INDUSTRY

COUNCIL, Milford, Mass. Lobbyist — Mintz, Levin, Cohn, Ferris, Glovsky and Popeo, One Center Plaza, Boston, Mass. 02108, and 1015 15th St. N.W., Washington, D.C. 20005. Filed 6/27/81. Legislative interest — "...Federal Aid Highway Act, specifically maximum truck weights."

MOTOR AND EQUIPMENT MANUFACTURERS ASSOCIATION, 1120 19th St. N.W., Washington, D.C. 20036. Filed for self 6/26/81. Legislative interest — "...issues concerning the Clean Air Act." Lobbyist — Paul T. Haluza.

NATIONAL ASSOCIATION OF HOME BUILDERS, Washington, D.C. Lobbyist — John M. Martin Jr., 6909 Fort Hunt Road, Alexandria, Va. 22307. Filed 6/22/81. Legislative interest — "Tax incentives for housing."

NATIONAL ASSOCIATION OF INDEPENDENT IN-SURERS, 2600 River Road, Des Plaines, Ill. 60018. Filed for self 6/3/81. Legislative interest — "Any and all legislation affecting casualty and property insurance...." Lobbyist — Harry G. Wiles II, 499 South Capitol St. S.W., Washington, D.C. 20003.

NATIONAL ASSOCIATION OF MANUFACTURERS, 1776 F St. N.W., Washington, D.C. 20006. Filed for self 6/16/81. Legislative interest — "...labor-management relations, including such issues as amendments to the Walsh-Healey Act (S 398); the Davis-Bacon Act (HR 1034); The National Employment Priorities Act of 1981 (HR 565); and The Sales Representatives Protection Act (HR 3496)." Lobbyist — Geri Colombaro. Legislative interest — "Tax and budget legislation; HR 3849, etc." Lobbyist — Paul R. Huard.

NATIONAL ASSOCIATION OF OPTOMETRISTS AND OPTICIANS INC., Cleveland, Ohio. Lobbyist — James E. Ritchie & Associates, 499 South Capitol St. S.W., Washington, D.C. 20003. Filed 6/5/81. Legislative interest — "...legislation affecting the FTC appropriations."

NATIONAL ASSOCIATION OF REALTORS, 777 14th St. N.W., Washington, D.C. 20005. Filed for self 6/19/81. Legislative interest — "...subsidized housing issues and housing authorizations legislation. Consumer and regulatory matters, including fair housing proposals, changes in federal securities laws, and condominium legislation." Lobbyist — Lee B. Holmes.

NATIONAL COMMITTEE OF DISCOUNT SECURI-TIES BROKERS, Memphis, Tenn. Lobbyist — Shipley, Smoak & Akerman, 1108 National Press Building, Washington, D.C. 20045. Filed 6/23/81. Legislative interest — "Taxes, antitrust, environmental, interstate commerce, foreign relations, energy, broadcasting, real estate."

NATIONAL OFFICE MACHINE DEALERS ASSOCI-ATION, Elk Grove Village, Ill. Lobbyist — Stephens Overseas Services Inc., 1101 Connecticut Ave. N.W., Washington, D.C. 20036. Filed 6/26/81. Legislative interest — "Small business, corporate regulatory and related issues."

PACIFIC SEAFOOD PROCESSORS ASSOCIATION, Seattle, Wash. Lobbyist — Bogle & Gates, The Bank of California Center, Seattle, Wash. 98164. Filed 6/16/81. Legislative interest — "Amendments to Fisheries Conservation and Management Act and other legislation regarding seafood processing issues."

PATHOLOGIST PRACTICE ASSOCIATION, Sacramento, Calif. Lobbyist — A-K Associates Inc., 1225 8th St., Sacramento, Calif. 95814. Filed 6/11/81. Legislative interest — "Any and all health legislation pertaining to the interests of the pathologist profession."

PHARMACEUTICAL MANUFACTURERS ASSOCI-ATION, Washington, D.C. Lobbyist — Manatt, Phelps, Rothenberg & Tunney, 1200 New Hampshire Ave. N.W., Washington, D.C. 20036. Filed 6/15/81. Legislative interest — "...HR 1937, to amend the patent law to restore the term of the patent grant for the period of time that nonpatent regulatory requirements prevent the marketing of a patented product."

SHIPBUILDERS' COUNCIL OF AMERICA, Washington, D.C. Lobbyist — Patton, Boggs & Blow, 2550 M St. N.W., Washington, D.C. 20037. Filed 6/17/81. Legislative interest —

"...HR 25 and S 1182 amending the Longshoremen's and Harbor Workers' Compensation Act."

SHIPPERS NATIONAL FREIGHT CLAIM COUNCIL INC., 200 Main St., Huntington, N.Y. 11743. Filed for self 6/17/81. Legislative interest — "Freight claims aspects of transportation deregulation legislation...." Lobbyist — Robert E. Redding.

THE SHRIMP HARVESTERS COALITION OF THE GULF COAST AND SOUTH ATLANTIC STATES, Washington, D.C. Lobbyist — Dickstein, Shapiro & Morin, 2101 L St. N.W., Washington, D.C. 20037. Filed 6/1/81. Legislative interest — "All treaties and legislation concerning fisheries, particularly shrimp."

UNITED STATES CHAMBER OF COMMERCE, 1615 H St. N.W., Washington, D.C. 20002. Filed for self 6/22/81. Legislative interest — "Tax legislation, HR 3849." Lobbyist — David E. Franasiak, 237 Chatham Lane, Annapolis, Md. 21407.

WEST MEXICO VEGETABLE DISTRIBUTORS AS-SOCIATION, Nogales, Ariz. Filed for self 6/30/81. Legislative interest — "S 729, HR 2487 and HR 2496." Lobbyist — T. Albert Yamada, 900 17th St. N.W., Washington, D.C. 20006.

Miscellaneous

AD HOC COMMITTEE TO PRESERVE FEDERALLY ASSISTED SHORT LINE RAILROADS, Washington, D.C. Lobbyist — Wald, Harkrader & Ross, 1300 19th St. N.W., Washington, D.C. 20036. Filed 6/5/81. Legislative interest — "...support for continuation of funding for the local rail service assistance program ... passage of an impoundment resolution restoring FY 1981 funds for the program, and the continuation of program funding for FY 1982 and beyond."

AMERICAN AGRICULTURE MOVEMENT INC., 100 Maryland Ave. N.E., Washington, D.C. 20002. Filed for self 6/12/81. Legislative interest — "All issues dealing with agriculture; 1981 farm bill." Lobbyist — David Senter.

ASHCRAFT & GEREL, 2000 L St. N.W., Washington, D.C. 20037. Filed for self 6/23/81. Legislative interest — "Labor legislation — Longshoremen's and Harbor Workers' Compensation Act, S 1182, HR 25...." Lobbyist — Mark L. Schaffer.

ASSOCIATION OF AMERICAN FOREIGN SERVICE WOMEN, Washington, D.C. Lobbyist — Edith U. Fierst, 1140 Connecticut Ave. N.W., Washington, D.C. 20036. Filed 6/1/81. Legislative interest — "Hope to obtain survivor protection for divorced widows of foreign service officers."

COMMITTEE FOR COMMERCIAL ENERGY CON-SERVATION, Washington, D.C. Lobbyist — Robert R. Statham & Associates, 1000 Vermont Ave. N.W., Washington, D.C. 20005. Filed 6/22/81. Legislative interest — "Energy conservation legislation as it relates to the commercial sector, including ... S 1288 (Commercial Business Energy Tax Credit Act of 1981)."

GERALD R. CONNOR, 6500 Wisconsin Ave., Chevy Chase, Md. 20015. Filed for self 6/19/81. Legislative interest — "Omnibus Reconciliation Bill ... Social Security Act ... Public Health Service Act."

EMPLOYEE RELOCATION COUNCIL, Washington, D.C. Lobbyist — Eric R. Fox, 1700 Pennsylvania Ave. N.W., Washington, D.C. 20006. Filed 6/3/81. Legislative interest — "Taxation of reimbursed moving expenses of transferred employees."

FINLINSON AND FINLINSON, Salt Lake City, Utah. Lobbyist — Mountain West Associates, 1229 19th St. N.W., Washington, D.C. 20036. Filed 6/25/81. Legislative interest — Not specified.

NATIONAL CONSUMER LAW CENTER, 238 Massachusetts Ave. N.E., Washington, D.C. 20002. Lobbyist — Thomas H. Moore, 2301 Horseferry Court, Reston, Va. Filed 6/4/81. Legislative interest — "HR 3480, Legal Services Corp. Act Amend-

ments of 1981 and any related legislation intended to reauthorize and/or provide funding for the Legal Services Corp. . . ." Filed for self 6/18/81. Legislative interest — "Low-income Energy Assistance Act of 1981, S 1165. . . ."

HERBERT E. RUSSELL, Magnolia, Ark. Lobbyist — Vester T. Hughes Jr., 1000 Mercantile Dallas Building, Dallas, Texas 75201. Filed 6/8/81. Legislative interest — "To obtain legislation reducing the income tax rate on capital gains effective prior to July 1981. Specifically, in favor of HR 2400, the Economic Recovery Tax Act of 1981."

July Registrations

Citizens' Groups

THE AMERICAN WAY, 915 15th St. N.W., Washington, D.C. 20005. Filed for self 7/9/81. Legislative interest — Not specified. Lobbyist — Lloyd V. Temme.

AMERICANS FOR NUCLEAR ENERGY, P.O. Box 28371, Washington, D.C. 20005. Filed for self 7/1/81. Legislative interest — ". . .legislation favoring the expansion of nuclear power for generation of electricity." Lobbyist — Douglas O. Lee.

BARRIER ISLANDS COALITION, 122 East 42nd St., New York, N.Y. Filed for self 7/7/81. Legislative interest — ". . .HR 5981 and S 2686. . . ."

CANADIAN COALITION ON ACID RAIN, 105 Davenport Road, Toronto, Canada M5R-1H6. Filed for self 7/23/81. Legislative interest — ". . .legislation revising and extending authorizations under the Clean Air Act of 1970, as amended." Lobbyist — Adele M. Hurley.

CHILDREN'S DEFENSE FUND, 1520 New Hampshire Ave. N.W., Washington, D.C. 20036. Filed for self 7/10/81. Legislative interest — "Child health, including Title V of the Social Security Act and Medicaid. . .HR 3964 and Senate budget Reconciliation Act of 1981." Lobbyists — Sara Rosenbaum; Fran Eizenstat, Chevy Chase, Md. Filed 7/23/81. Legislative interest — "Reauthorizing legislation for Headstart program."

COMMITTEE FOR HUMANE LEGISLATION INC., New York, N.Y. Lobbyist — Finley, Kumble, Wagner, Heinz, Underberg & Casey, 1120 Connecticut Ave. N.W., Washington, D.C. 20036. Filed 7/15/81. Legislative interest — "HR 374 - to prohibit the use of the steel-jaw leghold trap. . . ."

COMMUNITIES FOR AN EFFECTIVE AIR TRANSPORTATION SYSTEM, Washington, D.C. Lobbyist — Kirby & Gillick, 1625 K St. N.W., Washington, D.C. 20006. Filed 7/8/81. Legislative interest — ". . .HR 902, HR 3562, HR 4065, S 1495, S 1426."

THE CONFEDERATED TRIBES OF THE WARM SPRINGS RESERVATION OF OREGON, Warm Springs, Ore. Lobbyist — Ullman Consultants Inc., 1000 Potomac St. N.W., Washington, D.C. 20007. Filed 7/28/81. (Former U.S. Rep. Al Ullman, D-Ore., 1957-81, was listed as an agent for this client.) Legislative interest — Not specified.

CONSERVATIVES AGAINST LIBERAL LEGISLATION, 5707 Seminary Rd., Falls Church, Va. 22041. Filed for self 7/20/81. Legislative interest — ". . .the Reagan tax package and budget. . . ." Lobbyists — Kris James Kolesnik, Mark A. Florio.

ENVIRONMENTAL POLICY CENTER, 317 Pennsylvania Ave. S.E., Washington, D.C. 20003. Filed for self 7/30/81. Legislative interest — ". . .hazardous materials, nuclear waste, nuclear transportation." Lobbyist — Fred Millar.

FRIENDS OF THE EARTH, 530 7th St. S.E., Washington, D.C. 20003. Filed for self 7/10/81. Legislative interest — ". . .legislation to preserve, restore and insure rational use of the ecosphere." Lobbyist — Geoffrey Webb.

NATIONAL COMMUNITY ACTION FOUNDATION INC., 2101 L St. N.W., Washington, D.C. 20037. Filed for self 7/13/81. Legislative interest — ". . .full funding of Community

Services Administration, full funding and construction of all programs designed to assist the poor and minorities." Lobbyist — Margaret Power.

NATIONAL CONGRESS OF AMERICAN INDIANS INC., Washington, D.C. Lobbyist — Wilkinson, Cragun & Barker, 1735 New York Ave. N.W., Washington, D.C. 20006. Filed 7/10/81. Legislative interest — ". . .S 1298 - Indian Tribal Governmental Tax Status Act of 1981 and HR 3760. . . ."

NATIONAL ORGANIZATION FOR WOMEN, 425 13th St. N.W., Washington, D.C. 20004. Filed for self 7/13/81. Legislative interest — ". . .HR 900, HR 3325 and S 158 in particular (anti-abortion bills and amendments). . . ." Lobbyist — Jessma Blockwick.

NATIONAL RIFLE ASSOCIATION OF AMERICA, 1600 Rhode Island Ave. N.W., Washington, D.C. 20036. Filed for self 7/23/81. Legislative interest — ". . .all aspects of the acquisition, possession and use of firearms and ammunition. . .hunting and wildlife conservation. . . ." Lobbyist — William P. McGuire.

NATURAL RESOURCES DEFENSE COUNCIL INC., 1725 I St. N.W., Washington, D.C. 20006. Filed for self 7/19/81. Legislative interest — ". . .Freedom of Information Act, Nuclear Nonproliferation Act, Clinch River Breeder Reactor, National Environmental Policy Act." Lobbyist — Barbara Finamore.

PLAINTIFFS' ANTI-TRUST LIAISON SOCIETY, Washington, D.C. Lobbyist — Nussbaum & Owen, 1800 M St. N.W., Washington, D.C. 20036. Filed 7/1/81. Legislative interest — "S 1068 - Small Business Innovation and Simplification Act of 1981; S 995 - Amendment to Clayton Act, 15 U.S.C. 12 et seq., new section 4I, and HR 1242 - Amendment to Clayton Act, 15 U.S.C. 12 et seq., new section 4I. . . ."

SHERIDAN-KALORAMA NEIGHBORHOOD COUNCIL, Washington, D.C. Lobbyist — Patton, Boggs & Blow, 2550 M St. N.W., Washington, D.C. 20037. Filed 7/6/81. Legislative interest — ". . .HR 3518, against location of chanceries in residential neighborhoods in the District of Columbia."

Corporations and Businesses

AIRCO INC., Montvale, N.J. Lobbyist — Leva, Hawes, Symington, Martin & Oppenheimer, 815 Connecticut Ave. N.W., Washington, D.C. 20006. Filed 7/30/81. Legislative interest — ". . .patent reform legislation to protect existing patents (S 255)."

AMERICAN GENERAL CORP., Washington, D.C. Lobbyist — Vinson & Elkins, 1101 Connecticut Ave. N.W., Washington, D.C. 20036. Filed 7/17/81. Legislative interest — ". . .HR 3982."

AMERICAN INTERNATIONAL GROUP INC., New York, N.Y. Lobbyist — Thomas Ludlow Ashley, 1730 Pennsylvania Ave. N.W., Washington, D.C. 20006. Filed 7/28/81. (Former U.S. rep., D-Ohio, 1955-81) Legislative interest — ". . .establishment of a Federal earthquake reinsurance role."

AMERICAN RICE INC., Houston, Texas. Lobbyist — Cook, Purcell, Hansen & Henderson, 1015 18th St. N.W., Washington, D.C. 20036. Filed 7/24/81. (Former U.S. Rep. Graham B. Purcell, D-Texas, 1962-73, was listed as agent for this client.) Legislative interest — "Rice provisions of S 884 - Agriculture and Food Act of 1981, HR 3603 - Food and Agriculture Act of 1981."

ANTAEUS ENTERPRISES INC., Stamford, Conn. Lobbyists — James B. Kenin, 2033 M St. N.W., Washington, D.C. 20036. Filed 7/29/81; Zuckert, Scoutt & Rasenberger, 888 17th St. N.W., Washington, D.C. 20006. Filed 7/1/81; Winston & Strawn, 2550 M St. N.W., Washington, D.C. 20037. Filed 7/7/81. Legislative interest — "Tax legislation including HR 3849."

ARMCO, 1747 Pennsylvania Ave. N.W., Washington, D.C. 20006. Filed for self 7/16/81. Legislative interest — ". . .S 1274, Clean Water Act; transportation legislation; HR 3210, Surface Transportation Assistance. . . ." Lobbyist — Glenn R. Van Schooneveld. Legislative interest — "Tax legislation, trade legislation, steel legislation and defense legislation." Lobbyist — Kempton B. Jenkins.

J. ARON & CO. INC., New York, N.Y. Lobbyist — Stroock & Stroock & Lavan, 1150 17th St. N.W., Washington, D.C. 20036.

Filed 7/9/81. Legislative interest — "...S 1432, Straddles Tax Act of 1981."

ATLANTIC RICHFIELD CO., Los Angeles, Calif. Lobbyist — J. James Hur, 1333 New Hampshire Ave. N.W., Washington, D.C. 20036. Filed 7/19/81. Legislative interest — Not specified.

AUSTRALIAN MEAT & LIVESTOCK CORP., New York, N.Y. Lobbyist — Clifford & Warnke, 815 Connecticut Ave. N.W., Washington, D.C. 20006. Filed 7/7/81. Legislative interest — "...S 524 (Meat & Labeling Inspection) and HR 2889 (Lamb Meat Quota Act)...S 905 (Inspection of Foreign Meat Plants), S 884 (1981 Farm Bill), HR 463 (Consumer Food Labeling Act) and HR 631 (Small Business Preservation Act)...."

BANK OF NEW YORK, New York, N.Y. Lobbyist — Charls E. Walker Associates Inc., 1730 Pennsylvania Ave. N.W., Washington, D.C. 20006. Filed 7/29/81. Legislative interest — "...geographic restraints on the trust operations of registered bank-holding companies."

BENCH AD CO., Maywood, Calif. Lobbyist — Surrey & Morse, 1156 15th St. N.W., Washington, D.C. 20005. Filed 7/19/81. Legislative interest — "...Urban Mass Transportation Administration policy and procedure...."

BENEFICIAL CORP., Morristown, N.J. Lobbyist — Dewey, Ballantine, Bushby, Palmer & Wood, 1775 Pennsylvania Ave. N.W., Washington, D.C. 20006. Filed 7/6/81. Legislative interest — "Tax legislation."

PIETRO BERETTA, S.P.A., Gardone, Italy. Lobbyist — Surrey & Morse, 1156 15th St. N.W., Washington, D.C. 20005. Filed 7/13/81. Legislative interest — "...equitable and fair consideration of a potential procurement of equipment by the U.S. Army...."

BLYTH EASTMAN PAINE WEBBER, New York, N.Y. Lobbyist — O'Connor & Hannan, 1919 Pennsylvania Ave. N.W., Washington, D.C. 20006. Filed 7/13/81. Legislative interest — "...industrial development bonds."

BRISTOL-MYERS CO., Washington, D.C. Lobbyist — Hughes, Hubbard & Reed, 1660 L St. N.W., Washington, D.C. 20036. Filed 7/6/81. Legislative interest — "...antitrust legislation."

CADILLAC FAIRVIEW U.S. INC., Wilmington, Del. Lobbyist — Marshall, Bratter, Greene, Allison & Tucker, 430 Park Ave., New York, N.Y. 10022. Filed 7/1/81. Legislative interest — "Amendments to the Internal Revenue Code...more flexibility in depreciation schedules."

CALLERY-JUDGE GROVE, West Palm Beach, Fla. Lobbyist — Patton, Boggs & Blow, 2550 M St. N.W., Washington, D.C. 20037. Filed 7/6/81. Legislative interest — "HR 3900."

CAST NORTH AMERICAN LTD., Montreal, Canada. Lobbyist — Richard H. Streeter, 1729 H St. N.W., Washington, D.C. 20006. Filed 7/31/81. Legislative interest — "...HR 3637, the so-called 'Canadian Diversion Bill.'"

CENTRAL POWER AND LIGHT CO., P.O. Box 2121, Corpus Christi, Texas 78403. Filed for self 7/13/81. Legislative interest — "...dividend reinvestment, repeal of section 301 of Fuel Use Act." Lobbyist — B.J. Durham.

CENTURY 21, Irvine, Calif. Lobbyist — The Hannaford Co. Inc., 1225 19th St. N.W., Washington, D.C. 20036. Filed 7/10/81. Legislative interest — "...Lanham Trademark Act...."

CHEMOLIMPEX, Budapest, Hungary. Lobbyist — Stroock & Stroock & Lavan, 1150 17th St. N.W., Washington, D.C. 20036. Filed 7/28/81. Legislative interest — "...extension of presidential waiver authority pursuant to the Trade Act of 1974...."

CHICAGO MERCANTILE EXCHANGE, 444 West Jackson Blvd., Chicago, Ill. 60606. Filed for self 7/14/81. Legislative interest — "...futures industry." Lobbyists — James M. Copeland, 1101 Connecticut Ave., Washington, D.C. 20036; Popham, Haik, Schnobrich, Kaufman & Doty Ltd., 4344 IDS Center, Minneapolis, Minn. 55402.

CHINOIN, Budapest, Hungary. Lobbyist — Stroock & Stroock & Lavan, 1150 17th St. N.W., Washington, D.C. 20036. Filed 7/28/81. Legislative interest — "...presidential waiver authority pursuant to the trade Act of 1974...."

CHRIS-CRAFT INDUSTRIES INC., New York, N.Y. Lobbyist — O'Neill and Haase, 1333 New Hampshire Ave. N.W.,

Washington, D.C. 20036. Filed 7/31/81. Legislative interest — "Amendments to the Economic Recovery Tax Act of 1981."

THE COASTAL CORP., Houston, Texas. Lobbyist — John C. White, 1333 New Hampshire Ave. N.W., Washington, D.C. 20036. Filed 7/9/81. Legislative interest — "Reinstatement of Santa Barbara leases, commodity straddles and rollovers." Lobbyist — Damrell, Damrell & Nelson, 911 13th St., Modesto, Calif. 95353. Filed 7/16/81. Legislative interest — "...HR 1946 and S 506 (lease reinstatement legislation)." Filed for self 7/22/81. Legislative interest — "...windfall profits tax law 26 U.S.C....standby authority for petroleum supply interruptions, S 409, tax cut bill." Lobbyist — Carla J. Bishop, 9 Greenway Plaza, Houston, Texas 77046.

COMMUTER AIRLINE ASSOCIATION OF AMERICA, Washington, D.C. Lobbyist — Jim Lloyd, 3240 Whitebirch Dr., West Covina, Calif. 91791. Filed 7/15/81. (Former U.S. rep., D-Calif., 1975-81) Legislative interest — "Armed Services Authorization bill, public works aviation bill, appropriations bill pertaining to aviation and transportation systems."

COMPREHENSIVE CARE CORP., Newport Beach, Calif. Lobbyist — Cook, Purcell, Hansen & Henderson, 1015 18th St. N.W., Washington, D.C. 20036. Filed 7/13/81. (Former U.S. Rep. David E. Satterfield III, D-Va., 1965-81, was listed as agent for this client.) Legislative interest — "Improving certificate of need procedures especially with regard to alcoholism treatment and alcoholism treatment facilities as contained in Title XV Public Health Service Act."

CONOCO INC., Washington, D.C. Lobbyist — Camp, Carmouche, Palmer, Barsh & Hunter, 2550 M St. N.W., Washington, D.C. Filed 7/6/81. Legislative interest — "...moratorium on foreign acquisition and control of mineral resources on lands." Lobbyist — Patton, Boggs & Blow, 2550 M St. N.W., Washington, D.C. 20037. Filed 7/6/81. Legislative interest — "...S 1429 and HR 4033 Margin Requirements Fairness Act and Foreign Energy Investment Act of 1981 amending the Securities Exchange Act of 1934." Lobbyist — Richard W. Bliss, 1899 L St. N.W., Washington, D.C. 20036. Filed 7/1/81. Legislative interest — "All legislation relating to foreign investment in U.S. energy and mineral companies; all legislation relating to U.S. mineral policy, including HR 2826, HR 4033, S 1429 and S 1436."

CONTAINER CORP. OF AMERICA, Washington, D.C. Lobbyist — Charls E. Walker Associates Inc., 1730 Pennsylvania Ave. N.W., Washington, D.C. 20006. Filed 7/10/81. Legislative interest — "...incentives for energy conservation projects."

THE CONTINENTAL GROUP, Stamford, Conn. Lobbyist — Weil, Gotshal & Manges, 767 Fifth Ave., New York, N.Y. 10153. Filed 7/7/81. Legislative interest — "S 995...."

CONTINENTAL RESOURCES CO., Winter Park, Fla. Lobbyist — Corcoran, Hardesty, Ewart, Whyte & Polito, 1575 I St. N.W., Washington, D.C. 20005. Filed 7/15/81. Legislative interest — "Support of coal slurry pipeline legislation."

CPC INTERNATIONAL INC., Englewood Cliffs, N.J. Lobbyist — Wilmer, Cutler & Pickering, 1666 K St. N.W., Washington, D.C. 20006. Filed 7/31/81. Legislative interest — "Economic Recovery Act of 1981, HR 4260, H J Res 266...."

CREAMER DICKSON BASFORD INC., 1633 Broadway, New York, N.Y. 10019. Filed for self 7/20/81. Legislative interest — "All matters pertaining to antitrust, banking." Lobbyist — Mark Brand, 1625 K St. N.W., Washington, D.C. 20006.

CROWLEY MARITIME CORP., San Francisco, Calif. Lobbyists — Capitol Advocates, 1127 11th St., Sacramento, Calif.; John H. Hodgson II, 1225 8th St., Sacramento, Calif. Filed 7/24/81. Legislative interest — "Jones Act, Maritime bills and Title 11 (loan guarantee funding)."

DATAPOINT CORP., San Antonio, Texas. Lobbyists — Jack Menache, Harold E. O'Kelley, 7900 Callaghan Rd., San Antonio, Texas 78229. Filed 7/10/81. Legislative interest — "...insure continued competition in the data processing field."

DELTA STEAMSHIP LINES INC., New Orleans, La. Lobbyist — Bowman, Conner, Touhey & Thornton, 1800 M St. N.W., Washington, D.C. 20036. Filed 7/13/81. Legislative interest — "...Omnibus budget reconciliation bill and other matters

relating to shipping."

DOLLAR SAVINGS BANK, Pittsburgh, Pa. Lobbyist — Sullivan & Worcester, 1025 Connecticut Ave. N.W., Washington, D.C. 20036. Filed 7/6/81. Legislative interest — "...financially distressed depository institutions."

EDS CORP., 229 Pennsylvania Ave. S.E., Washington, D.C. 20003. Filed for self 7/27/81. Legislative interest — "...health care, National Health Insurance, banking, insurance, retailing and utilities." Lobbyist — Rodney L. Armstrong.

EMERSON ELECTRIC CO., 8000 W. Florissant, St. Louis, Mo. 63136. Filed for self 7/29/81. Legislative interest — "...labor reform, antitrust, energy and deregulation of natural gas, defense and security assistance, tax and revenue measures including HR 1053...." Lobbyist — William E. Peacock.

EXXON CORP., 1251 Avenue of the Americas, New York, N.Y. Filed for self 7/21/81. Legislative interest — "...administration economic package and international trade matters." Lobbyist — Guenther O. Wilhelm, 1899 L St. N.W., Washington, D.C. 20036.

FMC CORP., Chicago, Ill. Lobbyist — Charls E. Walker Associates Inc., 1730 Pennsylvania Ave. N.W., Washington, D.C. 20006. Filed 7/10/81. Legislative interest — "...Internal Revenue Code as it relates to the minimum tax on corporations."

FORD MOTOR CO., Dearborn, Mich. Lobbyist — Hughes, Hubbard & Reed, 1660 L St. N.W., Washington, D.C. 20036. Filed 7/17/81. Legislative interest — "...product liability law reform."

GANZ MAVAG, Budapest, Hungary. Lobbyist — Lillian Liburdi, 1300 N. 17th St., Arlington, Va. 22209. Filed 7/8/81. Legislative interest — "Authorizing and appropriating legislation relating to trade, public transit and railroad issues."

GENERAL INSTRUMENT CORP., New York, N.Y. Filed for self 7/16/81. Legislative interest — "...communications, copyright...." Lobbyist — Deborah M. Minnich, 1200 New Hampshire Ave. N.W., Washington, D.C. 20036.

GENERAL TELEPHONE CO. OF CALIFORNIA, Santa Monica, Calif. Lobbyist — Manatt, Phelps, Rothenberg & Tunney, 1200 New Hampshire Ave. N.W., Washington, D.C. 20036. Filed 7/17/81. Legislative interest — "Tax legislation relating to normalization of investment tax credit."

GENERAL TIRE & RUBBER CO., Akron, Ohio. Lobbyist — Califano, Ross & Heineman, 1575 I St. N.W., Washington, D.C. 20005. Filed 7/22/81. Legislative interest — Not specified.

GEORGIA-PACIFIC, Portland, Ore. Lobbyist — Bayh, Tabbert & Capehart, 1575 I St. N.W., Washington, D.C. 20005. Filed 7/30/81. Legislative interest — "S 995, Antitrust Equal Enforcement Act of 1981 and related matters."

GEORGIA POWER CO., Atlanta, Ga. Lobbyist — John G. Richardson, 2774 North Hills Drive N.E., Atlanta, Ga. 30305. Filed 7/22/81. Legislative interest — Not specified.

GLENROCK REFINERY INC., Casper, Wyo. Lobbyist — John P. Connolly, 2000 L St. N.W., Washington, D.C. 20036. Filed 7/29/81. Legislative interest — "...small and independent petroleum refiners."

GRAY AND CO., 3255 Grace St. N.W., Washington, D.C. 20007. Filed for self 7/31/81. Legislative interest — "Retention of American cargo preference provisions in budget resolutions." Lobbyist — Jeffrey B. Trammell.

GREAT ATLANTIC & PACIFIC TEA CO. INC., Montvale, N.J. Lobbyist—Patton, Boggs & Blow, 2550 M St. N.W., Washington, D.C. 20037. Filed 7/6/81. Legislative interest— "Economic Recovery Tax Act of 1981, HR 3849, HR 2400, S 683."

GULF OIL CORP., Pittsburgh, Pa. Filed for self 7/15/81. Legislative interest — "Legislative matters pertaining to oil, gas, windfall profits, toxic substances, hazardous waste, synfuels and marketing." Lobbyist — Charlotte Rush, 1025 Connecticut Ave. N.W., Washington, D.C. 20036.

HALLAC ASSOCIATES INC., New York, N.Y. Lobbyist — Seward & Kissel, 1050 17th St. N.W., Washington, D.C. 20036. Filed 7/22/81. Legislative interest — "Legislation relating to the securities industry."

WALTER E. HELLER INTERNATIONAL CORP., Chicago, Ill. Lobbyist—Surrey & Morse, 1156 15th St. N.W., Washington, D.C. 20005. Filed 7/2/81. Legislative interest—"...export

trading company legislation, including S 734 and HR 2326."

HIGH PLAINS GRAIN PRODUCTS COOPERATIVE, Muleshoe, Texas. Lobbyist — Federal Services Co., 1015 15th St. N.W., Washington, D.C. 20005. Filed 7/13/81. Legislative interest — "Matters related to the production of alcohol fuels and related by-products."

HUBBARD BROADCASTING CO., St. Paul, Minn. Lobbyist — The Hannaford Co. Inc., 1225 19th St. N.W., Washington, D.C. 20036. Filed 7/10/81. Legislative interest — "...direct broadcast satellite matters...."

HUDSON BAY MINING & SMELTING CO. LTD., Toronto, Canada. Lobbyist — Feilders Associates Inc., 4909 Rodman St. N.W., Washington, D.C. 20016. Filed 7/20/81. Legislative interest — "Mineral Lands Leasing Amendments of 1981, HR 2826."

HUGHES HELICOPTER, Culver City, Calif. Lobbyist — Jim Lloyd, 3240 Whitebirch Dr., West Covina, Calif. 91791. Filed 7/15/81. (Former U.S. rep., D-Calif., 1975-81) Legislative interest — "Armed services authorization bill, public works aviation bill, appropriations bill pertaining to aviation and transportation systems."

HUNT OIL CO., Dallas Texas. Lobbyist — Johnson, Swanson & Barbee, 4700 First International Building, Dallas, Texas 75270. Filed 7/28/81. Legislative interest — "Modification in the application of at risk rules in the tax area...."

ICI AMERICAS INC., Wilmington, Del. 19897. Filed for self 7/8/81. Legislative interest — "...chemical industry in general." Lobbyists — Ellen Egan Eves, Robert E. Hampton, Charles L. Hebner, Christine M. Waisanen.

IRVING TRUST CO., New York, N.Y. Lobbyist — Thomas Ludlow Ashley, 1730 Pennsylvania Ave. N.W., Washington, D.C. 20006. Filed 7/28/81. (Former U.S. rep., D-Ohio, 1955-81) Legislative interest — Not specified. Lobbyist — Barrett, Smith, Schapiro, Simon & Armstrong, 26 Broadway, New York, N.Y. 10004. Filed 7/20/81. Legislative interest — "...HR 1293 and HR 1338 'To Prohibit tax-motivated commodity straddles, S 626, The Commodity Straddle Tax Act of 1981. S 1432, The Straddles Tax Act of 1981, Internal Revenue Code of 1954...."

KAISER ALUMINUM & CHEMICAL CORP., 900 17th St. N.W., Washington, D.C. 20006. Filed for self 7/17/81. Legislative interest — Not specified. Lobbyist — Robert E. Cole.

KIDDER, PEABODY & CO. INC., New York, N.Y. Lobbyist — Webster & Sheffield, 1200 New Hampshire Ave. N.W., Washington, D.C. 20036. Filed 7/9/81. Legislative interest — "North Alabama coal gasification project and fiscal year 1982 appropriation and authorization legislation."

KOPPERS CO. INC., Pittsburgh, Pa. Lobbyist — Miller & Chevalier, 1700 Pennsylvania Ave. N.W., Washington, D.C. 20006. Filed 7/14/81. Legislative interest — "Economic Recovery Tax Act of 1981...."

LASCO SHIPPING CO., Portland, Ore. Lobbyist — Patton, Boggs & Blow, 2550 M St. N.W., Washington, D.C. 20037. Filed 7/6/81. Legislative interest — "...subpart F of the Internal Revenue Code, 26 U.S.C. 33951 & F...."

LIBERTY CORP., Greenville, S.C. Lobbyist — Sutherland, Asbill & Brennan, 1666 K St. N.W., Washington, D.C. 20006. Filed 7/31/81. Legislative interest — "H J Res 266 and HR 4242. Support amendments to estate tax provisions."

LINCOLN PROPERTY CO., Las Vegas, Nev. Lobbyist — Powell, Goldstein, Frazer and Murphy, 1333 New Hampshire Ave. N.W., Washington, D.C 20036. Filed 7/16/81. Legislative interest — "...federal housing programs."

L.P. MANAGEMENT CORP., Houston, Texas. Lobbyist — C.H. Mayer Inc., 3421 N. Causeway Blvd., Metairie, La. 70002. Filed 7/22/81. Legislative interest — "...Crude Oil Windfall Profits Tax Act."

LUZ INTERNATIONAL LTD., Burlingame, Calif. Lobbyist — Morris J. Amitay, 400 N. Capitol St. N.W., Washington, D.C. 20001. Filed 7/15/81. Legislative interest — "Amendment to tax bill - H J Res 266."

MATLACK INC., Wilmington, Del. Lobbyist — Camp, Carmouche, Palmer, Barsh & Hunter, 2550 M St. N.W., Washington, D.C. 20037. Filed 7/27/81. Legislative interest — "...H J Res

266 and HR 3849."

MAYFLOWER CORP., Indianapolis, Ind. Lobbyist — Bayh, Tabbert & Capehart, 1575 I St. N.W., Washington, D.C. 20005. Filed 7/15/81. Legislative interest — "House Hold Goods Transportation Act of 1980, Motor Carrier Act of 1980, tax legislation impacting upon independent contractors."

THE MEAD CORP., Washington, D.C. Lobbyist — Charls E. Walker Associates Inc., 1730 Pennsylvania Ave. N.W., Washington, D.C. 20006. Filed 7/16/81. Legislative interest — "...treatment of contribution of damages in antitrust litigation, such as HR 4072." Lobbyist — Jones, Jones, Bell, Close & Brown, 700 Valley Bank Plaza, Las Vegas, Nev. Filed 7/10/81. Legislative interest — "...HR 4072, HR 1242 and S 995...."

MILIKEN RESEARCH CORP., Spartanburg, S.C. Lobbyist — Johnson, Smith & Hibbard, 220 N. Church St., Spartanburg, S.C. 29304. Filed 7/20/81. Legislative interest — "...S 995...." Lobbyist — Corcoran, Youngman & Rowe, 1511 K St. N.W., Washington, D.C. 20005. Filed 7/9/81. Legislative interest — "...section 4, 4A or 4C of the Clayton Act...."

MITCHELL ENERGY & DEVELOPMENT CORP., 1925 K St. N.W., Washington, D.C. 20006. Filed for self 7/22/81. Legislative interest — "...HR 3236, HR 2416." Lobbyists — B. Melvin Hurwitz; Vinson & Elkins, 1101 Connecticut Ave. N.W., Washington, D.C. 20036. Filed 7/17/81. Legislative interest — "...HR 3982."

MONSANTO CO., St. Louis, Mo. Filed for self 7/6/81. Legislative interest — "Florida phosphate leasing exchange legislation, HR 9 and S 1138." Lobbyist — George L. Atwood, 700 S. Colorado Blvd., Denver, Colo. 80222. Lobbyist — Dennis M. Olsen, 485 E St., Idaho Falls, Idaho 83402. Filed 7/27/81. Legislative interest — "Florida phosphate leasing exchange legislation, HR 9 and S 1138."

NATIONAL CON-SERV INC., Rockville, Md. Lobbyist — Roger Tilles, 1111 19th St. N.W., Washington, D.C. 20036. Filed 7/21/81. Legislative interest — "Reauthorization of the Federal Crime Insurance Program and related matters."

NCR CORP., Dayton, Ohio. Filed for self 7/22/81. Legislative interest — "Telecommunications, taxation, labor, consumer interests." Lobbyist — Alfred S. Frank Jr., 1612 K St. N.W., Washington, D.C. 20006.

HUGO NEU & SONS INC., New York, N.Y. Lobbyist — Barrett, Smith, Schapiro, Simon & Armstrong, 26 Broadway, New York, N.Y. 10004. Filed 7/17/81. Legislative interest — "H J Res 266, the Economic Recovery Tax Act of 1981."

NEWCOMB SECURITIES CO., New York, N.Y. Lobbyist — John P. Connolly, 2000 L St. N.W., Washington, D.C. 20036. Filed 7/29/81. Legislative interest — "Legislation affecting broker-dealers of government securities and/or affecting financial futures markets."

NISSAN MOTOR CORP. IN U.S.A., Washington, D.C. Lobbyist — Manatt, Phelps, Rothenberg & Tunney, 1200 New Hampshire Ave. N.W., Washington, D.C. 20036. Filed 7/28/81. (Former U.S. Rep. James C. Corman, D-Calif., 1961-81, was listed as agent for this client.) Legislative interest — Not specified.

NORTHERN VIRGINIA SAVINGS & LOAN ASSOCIATION, Arlington, Va. Lobbyist — Richard W. Bliss, 1899 L St. N.W., Washington, D.C. 20036. Filed 7/30/81. Legislative interest — "All legislation affecting the operating practices or mergers of savings and loan institutions, including HR 4050, HR 3456, S 1413 and S 1276."

NORTHROP CORP., Los Angeles, Calif. Lobbyist — Jim Lloyd, 3240 Whitebirch Dr., West Covina, Calif. 91791. Filed 7/15/81. (Former U.S. rep., D-Calif., 1975-81) Legislative interest — "Armed Services Authorization bill, public works aviation bill, appropriations bill pertaining to aviation and transportation systems."

NORTHWEST ALASKAN PIPELINE CO., Washington, D.C. Lobbyist — The Hannaford Co. Inc., 1225 19th St. N.W., Washington, D.C. 20036. Filed 7/10/81. Legislative interest — "...waiver of provisions in accordance with PL 94-586."

NORTHWEST BANCORPORATION, 1200 Northwestern Bank Building, Minneapolis, Minn. 55480. Filed for self 7/31/81. Legislative interest — "All matters directly affecting bank-holding companies, banks." Lobbyist — Richard J. Lovett.

NORTHWEST MARINE IRON WORKS, Portland, Ore. Lobbyist — Garvey, Schubert, Adams & Barer, 1000 Potomac St. N.W., Washington, D.C. 20007. Filed 7/29/81. Legislative interest — "...ocean vessel construction and repair industry."

NORTHWEST TEXAS GRAIN PRODUCTS COOPERATIVE, Dumas, Texas. Lobbyist — Federal Services Co., 1015 15th St. N.W., Washington, D.C. 20005. Filed 7/13/81. Legislative interest — "Matters related to the production of alcohol fuels and related byproducts."

OWENS-ILLINOIS, Toledo, Ohio. Lobbyist — Wilmer, Cutler & Pickering, 1666 K St. N.W., Washington, D.C. 20006. Filed 7/16/81. Legislative interest — "Clean Air Act and other environmental legislation."

OY WARTSILA AB, Helsinki, Finland. Lobbyist — Parrish & Chambers Inc., 1011 Arlington Blvd., Arlington, Va. 22209. Filed 7/8/81. Legislative interest — "All legislation relating to trade, merchant marine/Coast Guard legislation."

PACIFIC GAS AND ELECTRIC, San Francisco, Calif. Lobbyist — Francis Associates Ltd., 316 Pennsylvania Ave. S.E., Washington, D.C. 20003. Filed 7/31/81. Legislative interest — Not specified.

PELICAN TERMINAL, Galveston, Texas. Lobbyist — Vinson & Elkins, 1101 Connecticut Ave. N.W., Washington, D.C. 20036. Filed 7/8/81. Legislative interest — "...legislation authorizing local cost-sharing of costs and construction, operation and maintenance of deepdraft channel for Port of Galveston."

PFIZER INC., Washington, D.C. Lobbyist — Hughes, Hubbard & Reed, 1660 L St. N.W., Washington, D.C. 20036. Filed 7/9/81. Legislative interest — "...antitrust legislation."

PHILLIPS PETROLEUM CO., Bartlesville, Okla. Lobbyist — Clifford & Warnke, 815 Connecticut Ave. N.W., Washington, D.C. 20006. Filed 7/7/81. Legislative interest — "creditability of foreign taxes and specifically the U.S.-Norwegian Protocol now pending before the Senate."

PIEDMONT AIRLINES, Winston-Salem, N.C. Lobbyist — Cook, Purcell, Hansen & Henderson, 1015 18th St. N.W., Washington, D.C. 20036. Filed 7/15/81. Legislative interest — "S 508...HR 2643...."

PLANNING RESEARCH CORP., 7600 Old Springhouse Road, McLean, Va. 22102. Filed for self 7/1/81. Legislative interest — "...the professional service industry...." Lobbyist — Barbara Brendes Thies.

PUBLIC SERVICE COMPANY OF OKLAHOMA, P.O. Box 201, Tulsa, Okla. 74102. Filed for self 7/6/81. Legislative interest — "...the electric utility industry." Lobbyist — Lee W. Paden.

RALSTON PURINA GOVERNMENT AFFAIRS INC., 2000 L St. N.W., Washington, D.C. 20036. Filed for self 7/13/81. Legislative interest — "...corporate, agricultural and consumer legislation." Lobbyists — Claude D. Alexander, Charles E. Ehrhart.

RJR INDUSTRIES INC., P.O. Box 2959, Winston-Salem, N.C. 27102. Filed for self 7/9/81. Legislative interest — "...the tobacco...transportation...oil...and the foods industry...." Lobbyist — LeAnn R. Hensche, 2550 M St. N.W., Washington, D.C. 20037.

ROLM CORP., Santa Clara, Calif. Filed for self 7/28/81. Legislative interest — "...HR 3519...S 898." Lobbyist — Linda Meyer Johnson, 9700 Little River Turnpike, Annandale, Va. 22003.

ST. REGIS PAPER CO., New York, N.Y. Lobbyist — John T. Gould Jr., 1625 I St., N.W., Washington, D.C. Filed 7/27/81. Legislative interest — "...taxation, energy, international, natural resources, environment, transportation and corporate governance."

SAN DIEGO GAS AND ELECTRIC CO., 101 Ash St., San Diego, Calif. 92101. Filed for self 7/13/81. Legislative interest —"...HR 1765, S 1080 and S 988...."

SEA COLONY INC., Potomac, Md. Lobbyist — Fried, Frank, Harris, Shriver & Kampelman, 600 New Hampshire Ave. N.W., Washington, D.C. 20037. Filed 7/10/81. Legislative interest — "...S 1018 and HR 3252...protection of the Barrier Islands."

JOSEPH E. SEAGRAM & SONS INC., New York, N.Y. Lobbyist — O'Connor & Hannan, 1919 Pennsylvania Ave. N.W., Washington, D.C. 20006. Filed 7/6/81. Legislative interest — "...HR 4033, H J Res 801, S 1429, S 1436."

THE SECURITIES GROUP, New York, N.Y. Lobbyist — Carl F. Arnold, 1100 Connecticut Ave. N.W., Washington, D.C. 20036. Filed 7/10/81. Legislative interest — "...indebtedness of the United States... interest rates, inflation rates and the general economy." Lobbyist — Cladouhos & Brashares, 1750 New York Ave. N.W., Washington, D.C. 10022. Filed 7/13/81. Legislative interest — "...S 626, HR 1338 and HR 1293...."

SECURITY PACIFIC NATIONAL BANK, 333 S. Hope St., Los Angeles, Calif. 90071. Filed for self 7/10/81. Legislative interest — "...banking legislation, housing, agricultural and other financial matters." Lobbyist — Alfred M. Pollard, 1901 L St. N.W., Washington, D.C. 20036.

SIERRA PACIFIC POWER CO., Reno, Nev. Lobbyist — Crowell & Moring, 1100 Connecticut Ave. N.W., Washington, D.C. 20036. Filed 7/16/81. Legislative interest — "...HR 3982."

J.R. SIMPLOT CO., Box 27, Boise, Idaho 83707. Filed for self 7/13/81. Legislative interest — "Agricultural interests." Lobbyist — Larry Grupp, Box 8032, Moscow, Idaho 83843.

SOLAR POWER CORP., 20 Cabot Road, Woburn, Mass. 01810. Filed for self 7/2/81. Legislative interest — "...PL 95-590." Lobbyist — Sylvester L. Farrell, 500 E. Poplar Road, Sterling, Va. 22120.

SOUTHERN INDIANA SHALE OIL CO. INC., Shelbyville, Ind. Lobbyist — O'Connor & Hannan, 1919 Pennsylvania Ave. N.W. 20006. Filed 7/13/81. Legislative interest — "Energy/synfuels legislation, including proposal to rescind grant funding."

THE SPERRY AND HUTCHINSON CO., 330 Madison Ave., New York, N.Y. 10017. Filed for self 7/6/81. Legislative interest — "HR 3849...." Lobbyist — Edward A. Hynes, 425 13th St. N.W., Washington, D.C. 20004.

SPRUELL DEVELOPMENT CORP., Hyattsville, Md. Lobbyist — Ullman Consultants Inc., 1000 Potomac St. N.W., Washington, D.C. 20007. Filed 7/28/81. (Former U.S. Rep. Al Ullman, D-Ore., 1957-81, was listed as agent for this client.) Legislative interest — "...Subchapter S corporations."

STATE FARM MUTUAL AUTOMOBILE INSURANCE CO., Bloomington, Ill. Lobbyist — Dennis M. Olsen, 485 E St., Idaho Falls, Idaho 83402. Filed 7/27/81. Legislative interest — "...Introduction of legislation for congressional reference to Court of Claims on claims arising out of the failure of the Teton Dam in Idaho."

STERN BROS. INC., Parkersburg, W.Va. Lobbyist — Eugene M. Trisko, 9817 Rosensteel Ave., Silver Spring, Md. 20910. Filed 7/13/81. Legislative interest — "...Clean Air Act...."

TEACHERS INSURANCE AND ANNUITY ASSOCIATION OF AMERICA, New York, N.Y. Lobbyist — Dewey, Ballantine, Bushby, Palmer & Wood, 1775 Pennsylvania Ave. N.W., Washington, D.C. 20006. Filed 7/23/81. Legislative interest — "Tax legislation."

TELEPHONE AND DATA SYSTEMS INC., Chicago, Ill. Lobbyist — Taft, Stettinius & Hollistar, First National Bank Center, Cincinnati, Ohio 45202 and 1800 Massachusetts Ave. N.W., Washington, D.C. 20036. Filed 7/21/81. Legislative interest — "...amendments to Federal Communications Commission Act affecting rural telephone exchanges... S 898." Lobbyist — Federal Services Co. Inc., 1015 15th St. N.W., Washington, D.C. 20005. Filed 7/31/81. Legislative interest — "Rural telecommunications legislation."

TENNESSEE SYNFUELS ASSOCIATES. Lobbyist — Charls E. Walker Associates Inc., 1730 Pennsylvania Ave. N.W., Washington, D.C. 20006. Filed 7/2/81. Legislative interest — "Authorization/appropriations legislation affecting synthetic fuel development and business energy property investment tax credit."

TEXAS AIR CORP., Houston, Texas. Lobbyist — Manatt, Phelps, Rothenberg & Tunney, 1200 New Hampshire Ave. N.W., Washington, D.C. 20036. Filed 7/30/81. (Former U.S. Rep. James C. Corman, D-Calif., 1961-81, was listed as agent for this client.) Legislative interest — "Opposing Senate unprinted amendment 320 to H J Res 266." Lobbyist — Akin, Gump, Strauss, Hauer & Feld, 1333 New Hampshire Ave. N.W., Washington, D.C. 20036. Filed 7/24/81. Legislative interest — "...transportation policy... HR 4209."

TEXAS EASTERN TRANSMISSION CORP., Houston, Texas. Lobbyist — John M. Monley, 1090 Vermont Ave. N.W., Washington, D.C. 20005. Filed 7/13/81. Legislative interest — "...Fuel Use Act amendments/coal conversion... HR 85 and S 681... HR 3420... HR 3471... HR 3849."

TEXAS INTERNATIONAL AIRLINES INC., Houston, Texas. Lobbyist — Skadden, Arps, Slate, Meagher & Flom, 1775 Pennsylvania Ave. N.W., Washington, D.C. 20006. Filed 7/30/81. Legislative interest — "...HR 4260." Lobbyist — Hughes Hubbard & Reed, 1660 L St. N.W., Washington, D.C. 20036. Filed 7/29/81. Legislative interest — "...tax legislation." Lobbyist — Baker & Botts, 1701 Pennsylvania Ave. N.W., Washington, D.C. 20006. Filed 7/31/81. Legislative interest — "...airline industry."

TEXASGULF INC., Stamford, Conn. Lobbyist — Baker & Botts, 1701 Pennsylvania Ave. N.W., Washington, D.C. 20006. Filed 7/1/81. Legislative interest — "United States policy towards international business transactions."

THE TOLEDO TRUST CO., Toledo, Ohio. Lobbyist — Vorys, Sater, Seymour & Pease, 1828 L St. N.W., Washington, D.C. 20036. Filed 7/13/81. Legislative interest — "...Urban Jobs and Enterprise Zone Act of 1981."

TOSCO CORP., Boulder, Colo. Lobbyist — Wexler and Associates, 1616 H St. N.W., Washington, D.C. 20006. Filed 7/1/81. Legislative interest — "...synthetic fuels programs...."

TWIN COASTS NEWSPAPER INC. (THE JOURNAL OF COMMERCE), New York, N.Y. Lobbyist — Blum & Nash, 1015 18th St. N.W., Washington, D.C. 20036. Filed 7/10/81. Legislative interest — "...HR 3637... amendments to the Freedom of Information Act...."

UNION CARBIDE CORP., 270 Park Ave., New York, N.Y. 10017. Filed for self 7/13/81. Legislative interest — "International trade and investment legislation...." Lobbyist — Richard M. Brennan, 1730 Pennsylvania Ave. N.W., Washington, D.C. 20006.

UNION PACIFIC CORP., New York, N.Y. Lobbyist — Patton, Boggs, and Blow, 2550 M St. N.W., Washington, D.C. 20037. Filed 7/6/81. Legislative interest — "...HR 3849...."

USAIR INC., Washington, D.C. Lobbyist — Cook, Purcell, Hansen & Henderson, 1015 18th St. N.W., Washington, D.C. 20036. Filed 7/15/81. Legislative interest — "S 508... HR 2643... amendment to Internal Revenue Code of 1954 regarding industrial development bonds." Lobbyist — Piper & Marbury, 1050 17th St. N.W., Washington, D.C. 20036. Filed 7/31/81. Legislative interest — "Tax treatment of stock options."

U.S. ETHANOL CORP., New York, N.Y. Lobbyist — Van Ness, Feldman, Sutcliffe, Curtis & Levenberg, 1050 Thomas Jefferson St. N.W., Washington, D.C. 20007. Filed 7/8/81. Legislative interest — "...incentives for production of fuel alcohol and tax credits for alternative fuels... HR 3849."

U.S. INDUSTRIES INC., New York, N.Y. Lobbyist — Leva, Hawes, Symington, Martin & Oppenheimer, 815 Connecticut Ave. N.W., Washington, D.C. 20006. Legislative interest — "Clean Water Act."

WASHINGTON MUTUAL SAVINGS BANK, Seattle, Wash. Lobbyist — Sullivan & Worcester, 1025 Connnecticut Ave. N.W., Washington, D.C. 20036. Filed 7/6/81. Legislative interest — "...federal regulation and supervision of depository institutions...."

WESTINGHOUSE ELECTRIC CORP., Pittsburgh, Pa. Lobbyist — Groom and Nordberg, 1775 Pennsylvania Ave. N.W., Washington, D.C. 20006. Filed 7/10/81. Legislative interest — "Federal legislation affecting Title 26 of U.S. Code." Lobbyist — Lillian Liburdi, 1300 N. 17th St., Arlington, Va. 22209. Filed 7/8/81. Legislative interest — "...public transportation and railroad issues." Lobbyist — National Public Affairs Corp., 1120 Connecticut Ave. N.W., Washington, D.C. 20036. Filed 7/6/81. Legislative interest — "...S 1021, HR 3505 and Export-Import Bank bill."

WESTMORELAND COAL CO., Philadelphia, Pa. Lobbyist — John A.C. Gibson, 1815 Corcoran St. N.W., Washington,

D.C. 20009. Filed 7/24/81. Legislative interest — "Black Lung legislation."

WESTVACO CORP., 299 Park Ave., New York, N.Y. 10171. Filed for self 7/7/81. Legislative interest — "S 995 . . . HR 1242. . . ." Lobbyists — Thomas R. Long and John C. Callihan.

ZIMPRO INC., Rothschild, Wis. Lobbyist — Crowell & Moring, 1100 Connecticut Ave. N.W., Washington, D.C. 20036. Filed 7/13/81. Legislative interest — ". . .Clean Water Act. . . ."

International Relations

PROVINCE OF ONTARIO, CANADA, MINISTRY OF THE ENVIRONMENT, Toronto, Ontario, Canada. Lobbyist — Genesee Public Affairs Inc., 36 W. Main St., Rochester, N.Y. 14614. Filed 7/9/81. Legislative interest — "Legislation extending and amending the Clean Air Act of 1970, as amended - for adequate consideration of trans-boundary pollution."

Labor Groups

AMERICAN FEDERATION OF STATE, COUNTY AND MUNICIPAL EMPLOYEES, AFL-CIO, 1625 L St. N.W., Washington, D.C. 20036. Filed for self 7/24/81. Legislative interest — Not specified. Lobbyist — Carol Jackson.

COMMUNICATIONS WORKERS OF AMERICA, 1925 K St. N.W., Washington, D.C. 20006. Filed for self 7/30/81. Legislative interest — ". . .HR 3982, Omnibus Reconciliation Act; Social Security financing and benefit reduction proposals; HR 3112, Voting Rights Act extension; personal and business tax cut proposals." Lobbyist — Leslie Loble.

CONTINENTAL EMPLOYEES ASSOCIATION, El Segundo, Calif. Lobbyist — Powell, Goldstein, Frazer & Murphy, 1110 Vermont Ave. N.W., Washington, D.C. Filed 7/30/81. Legislative interest — Not specified.

NATIONAL EDUCATION ASSOCIATION, 1201 16th St. N.W., Washington, D.C. 20036. Filed for self 7/13/81. Legislative interest — ". . .20 U.S.C. 901-907 and 20 U.S.C. 921-932. Lobbyists — Jack Rollins, Ronald R. Austin. Legislative interest — "Education and education-related issues such as: HR 777, collective bargaining; HR 27, school lunch; HR 3282, asbestos hazards; HR 67, mobile teacher retirement . . . HR 3181 and S 360, higher education programs; HR 83 and S 200 CETA extension of programs . . . HR 9, HR 35, S 1095, tuition tax credits . . . HR 371, minimum competency testing; S 103 private school taxation. . . ." Lobbyist — Debra Diener.

OVERSEAS EDUCATION ASSOCIATION, 1201 16th St. N.W., Washington, D.C. 20036. Filed for self 7/13/81. Legislative interest — ". . .20 U.S.C. 901-907 and 20 U.S.C. 921-932." Lobbyists — Ronald R. Austin, Jack Rollins.

UNITED AUTOMOBILE, AEROSPACE AND AGRICULTURAL IMPLEMENT WORKERS OF AMERICA, INTERNATIONAL UNION, 8000 E. Jefferson Ave., Detroit, Mich. 48214. Filed for self 7/27/81. Legislative interest — "Congressional budget resolution, reconciliation, trade policy, OSHA and regulatory policy, unemployment compensation, other income support programs, social security, tax legislation." Lobbyist — William H. Dodds, 1735 N St. N.W., Washington, D.C. 20036.

State and Local Governments

ALASKA INDUSTRIAL DEVELOPMENT AUTHORITY, Anchorage, Alaska. Lobbyist — Ballard, Spahr, Andrews & Ingersoll, 1875 I St. N.W., Washington, D.C. 20006. Filed 7/2/81. Legislative interest — ". . .to preserve the present authority for issue of Industrial Development Bonds."

COUNCIL OF STATE HOUSING AGENCIES, Washington, D.C. Lobbyist — Powell, Goldstein, Frazer & Murphy, 1333 New Hampshire Ave. N.W., Washington, D.C. 20036. Filed 7/9/81. Legislative interest — ". . .Mortgage Subsidy Bond Tax Act of 1968."

DADE COUNTY AVIATION DEPARTMENT, Miami, Fla. Lobbyist — Alcalde, Henderson, O'Bannon & Bracy, 1901 N. Fort Myer Dr., Rosslyn, Va. Filed 7/7/81. Legislative interest — ". . .HR 2540 and S 1202."

DADE COUNTY FARM BUREAU, Homestead, Fla. Lobbyist — Barnett, Alagia & Carey, 1627 K St. N.W., Washington, D.C. 20006. Filed 7/29/81. Legislative interest — ". . .renewing farming in the Everglades National Park."

DADE COUNTY SEAPORT AUTHORITY, Miami, Fla. Lobbyist — Alcalde, Henderson, O'Bannon & Bracy, 1901 N. Fort Myer Dr., Rosslyn, Va. Filed 7/7/81. Legislative interest — ". . .HR 3197."

DELAWARE RIVER PORT AUTHORITY, Philadelphia, Pa. Lobbyist — Butler, Binion, Rice, Cooke, Knapp, 1747 Pennsylvania Ave. N.W., Washington, D.C. 20006. Filed 7/20/81. Legislative interest — "Customs Authorization Acts, S 1202 and HR 2540; Treasury Appropriations Act, fiscal year 1982, HR 4121."

NATIONAL ASSOCIATION OF STATE AGENCIES FOR FOOD DISTRIBUTION, Albany, N.Y. Lobbyist — Purcell, Hansen & Henderson, 1015 19th St. N.W., Washington, D.C. 20036. Filed 7/24/81. (Former U.S. Rep. Graham B. Purcell, D-Texas, 1962-73, was listed as an agent for this client.) Legislative interest — "Child nutrition provisions of S 1254, S 1377 and HR 3982."

NORTH TEXAS MUNICIPAL WATER DISTRICT, Wylie, Texas. Lobbyist — Ray Roberts & Associates, 499 S. Capitol St. S.W., Washington, D.C. 20003. Filed 7/9/81. (Former U.S. Rep. Ray Roberts, D-Texas, 1962-81, was listed as an agent for this client.) Legislative interest — "Corps of Engineers and reclamation water projects and appropriations. . . ."

PENNSYLVANIA ASSOCIATION OF INDUSTRIAL DEVELOPMENT AUTHORITIES, Erie, Pa. Lobbyist — Ballard, Spahr, Andrews & Ingersoll, 1875 I St. N.W., Washington, D.C. 20006. Filed 7/9/81. Legislative interest — ". . .to preserve the present authority for issue of Industrial Development Bonds."

POWER AUTHORITY OF THE STATE OF NEW YORK, New York, N.Y. Lobbyist — Federal Services Co., 1015 15th St. N.W., Washington, D.C. 20005. Filed 7/31/81. Legislative interest — Not specified.

Trade Associations

AD HOC COMMITTEE OF FLOOR BROKERS, Washington, D.C. Lobbyist — Cadwalader, Wickersham & Taft, 1333 New Hampshire Ave. N.W., Washington, D.C. 20036. Filed 7/7/81. Legislative interest — "Tax Straddle Act of 1981, S 1432."

AGRICULTURAL TRADE COUNCIL, 750 13th St. S.E., Washington, D.C. 20003. Filed for self 7/27/81. Legislative interest — "Legislation affecting agricultural exporters, including agricultural, commerce and trade barriers, international banking."

AIR CONDITIONING & REFRIGERATION INSTITUTE, 1815 N. Fort Myer Dr., Arlington, Va. 22209. Filed for self 7/9/81. Legislative interest — "Legislation affecting the air conditioning industry, including bills related to regulation of chlorofluorocarbons (HR 1853, S 517, HR 2296), the Clean Air Act (HR 1817, S 63) and budget measures affecting the Department of Energy." Lobbyists — Raymond Durazo, Kevin J. Fay, David A. Hunt.

ALABAMA FARM BUREAU FEDERATION, Montgomery, Ala. Lobbyist — Dale Sherwin, 1735 I St. N.W., Washington, D.C. 20006. Filed 7/15/81. Legislative interest — ". . .commodity interest of peanuts, soybeans, cotton, dairy, poultry and livestock."

AMERICAN ACADEMY OF OPHTHALMOLOGY, San Francisco, Calif. Lobbyist — Cook, Purcell, Hansen & Henderson, 1015 18th St. N.W., Washington, D.C. 20036. Filed 7/13/81. (Former U.S. Rep. David E. Satterfield III, D-Va., 1965-81, was listed as agent for this client.) Legislative interest — "Matters pertaining to ophthalmology and ophthalmologists, including delivery of health services relating to the human eye and use of medical devices. . . ."

AMERICAN ASSOCIATION OF ADVERTISING AGENCIES, Washington, D.C. Lobbyist — O'Connor & Hannan, 1919 Pennsylvania Ave. N.W., Washington, D.C. 20006. Filed 7/3/81. Legislative interest — ". . .legislation to repeal the investment interest expense limitation of the Internal Revenue Code."

AMERICAN BANKERS ASSOCIATION, 1120 Connecticut Ave. N.W., Washington, D.C. 20036. Filed for self 7/15/81. Legislative interest — "Tax legislation affecting the banking industry." Lobbyist — Marian S. Urnikis.

AMERICAN BUS ASSOCIATION, 1025 Connecticut Ave. N.W., Washington, D.C. 20036. Filed for self 7/13/81. Legislative interest — "All legislation affecting inter-city bus industry, including highway regulatory and tax." Lobbyist — Susan Perry.

AMERICAN BUSINESS COALITION, Baltimore, Md. Lobbyist — Thompson & Crawford, 1575 I St. N.W., Washington, D.C. 20005. Filed 7/1/81. Legislative interest — ". . .maintaining the present funding level for the Urban Development Action Grant Program."

AMERICAN CONSULTING ENGINEERS COUNCIL, 1015 15th St. N.W., Washington, D.C. 20005. Filed for self 7/9/81. Legislative interest — "Matters relating to public works: transportation, the environment, pollution control, housing, equal employment opportunity, public health and safety, economy and efficiency in government, and energy legislation." Lobbyist — Waldon L. Baker.

AMERICAN ELECTRONICS ASSOCIATION, Washington, D.C. Lobbyist — Hogan & Hartson, 815 Connecticut Ave. N.W., Washington, D.C. 20006. Filed 7/16/81. Legislative interest — "Legislation to provide tax incentives for high technology companies."

THE AMERICAN INSTITUTE OF ARCHITECTS, 1735 New York Ave. N.W., Washington, D.C. 20006. Filed for self 7/10/81. Legislative interest — Not specified. Lobbyist — Joseph S. Crane.

AMERICAN IRON AND STEEL INSTITUTE, Washington, D.C. Lobbyist — Fred B. Rooney, 1300 19th St. N.W., Washington, D.C. 20036. Filed 7/10/81. (Former U.S. rep., D-Pa., 1963-79) Legislative interest — Not specified.

AMERICAN MEAT INSTITUTE, Arlington, Va. Lobbyist — Collier, Shannon, Rill & Scott, 1055 Thomas Jefferson St. N.W., Washington, D.C. 20007. Filed 7/17/81. Legislative interest — ". . .measures involving regulatory reform (HR 746 and S 1080) and food safety (S 1442 and HR 4014)." Filed for self 7/15/81. Legislative interest — ". . .livestock production and feeding, animal diseases, meat inspection, food additives, labeling, transportation, environmental protection, safety, trade practices, consumer protection, energy, food safety, regulatory reform." Lobbyist — Cynthia L. Thornburg, P.O. Box 3556, Washington, D.C. 20007.

AMERICAN MINING CONGRESS, 1920 N St. N.W., Washington, D.C. 20036. Filed for self 7/13/81. Legislative interest — ". . .income taxation, social security, public lands, monetary policy, mine safety, stockpiling, environmental quality control, etc." Lobbyist — William Echols.

AMERICAN PARATRANSIT INSTITUTE, Coral Gables, Fla. Lobbyist — Webster, Chamberlain & Bean, 1747 Pennsylvania Ave. N.W., Washington, D.C. 20006. Filed 7/10/81. Legislative interest — "S 8, Independent contractor legislation, S 1160, transit legislation, bills providing a gas tax rebate for taxicabs, minimum wage legislation."

AMERICAN PETROLEUM INSTITUTE, 2101 L St. N.W., Washington, D.C. 20037. Filed for self 7/9/81. Legislative interest — ". . .HR 1362, S 1326 (retain marketing divorcement), Clean Air Act amendments, Superfund (HR 85, S 68)." Lobbyist — Angela G. Skelton, P.O. Box 167, Raleigh, N.C. 27602.

AMERICAN PUBLIC POWER ASSOCIATION, 2600 Virginia Ave. N.W., Washington, D.C. 20037. Filed for self 7/13/81. Legislative interest — Not specified. Lobbyist — Ted Handel.

AMERICAN TEXTILE MANUFACTURERS INSTITUTE, 1101 Connecticut Ave. N.W., Washington, D.C. 20036. Filed for self 7/14/81. Legislative interest — ". . .domestic and foreign trade policy, tax policy, consumer issues, environmental control, energy and lobbying legislation." Lobbyist — Christine M. Warnke.

THE ASSOCIATED GENERAL CONTRACTORS OF AMERICA, 1957 E St. N.W., Washington, D.C. 20006. Filed for self 7/10/81. Legislative interest — Not specified. Lobbyist — Edmond Graber.

CALIFORNIA SOCIETY OF PATHOLOGISTS, Sacramento, Calif. Lobbyist — A-K Associates Inc., 1225 8th St., Sacramento, Calif. 95814. Filed 7/24/81. Legislative interest — "HR 3982. . . ."

CHAMBER OF COMMERCE OF THE UNITED STATES, 1615 H St. N.W., Washington, D.C. 20062. Filed for self 7/10/81. Legislative interest — Not specified. Lobbyists — Jane B. Esterly, Ann K. Hall.

COMMITTEE OF DOMESTIC STEEL WIRE ROPE AND SPECIALTY CABLE MANUFACTURERS, Washington, D.C. Lobbyist — Harris, Berg & Creskoff, 2033 M ST. N.W., Washington, D.C. 20036. Filed 7/8/81. Legislative interest — Not specified.

COMPUTER AND BUSINESS EQUIPMENT MANUFACTURERS ASSOCIATION, Washington, D.C. Lobbyist — Hogan & Hartson, 815 Connecticut Ave. N.W., Washington, D.C. 20006. Legislative interest — ". . .tax incentive for high technology companies."

CONGRESS OF COUNTY MEDICAL SOCIETIES, Shawnee, Okla. Lobbyist — Cook, Purcell, Hansen & Henderson, 1015 18th St. N.W., Washington, D.C. 20036. Filed 7/13/81. Legislative interest — ". . .private practice of medicine."

CROP INSURANCE RESEARCH BUREAU, Indianapolis, Ind. Lobbyist — Collier, Shannon, Rill & Scott, 1055 Thomas Jefferson St. N.W., Washington, D.C. 20007. Filed 7/8/81. Legislative interest — Not specified.

DELTA DENTAL PLANS ASSOCIATION, Chicago, Ill. Lobbyist — Joseph M. Rees, 1625 Massachusetts Ave. N.W., Washington, D.C. 20036. Filed 7/23/81. Legislative interest — ". . .legislation affecting prepaid dental plans."

DISTILLED SPIRITS COUNCIL OF THE U.S. INC., 1300 Pennsylvania Ave. N.W., Washington, D.C. 20004. Filed for self 7/16/81. Legislative interest — Not specified. Lobbyist — Debra K. Shelton.

EDISON ELECTRIC INSTITUTE, 1111 19th St. N.W., Washington, D.C. 20036. Filed for self 7/24/81. Legislative interest — "Nuclear legislation." Lobbyist — Jan E. McKenzie.

ELECTRONICS INDUSTRIES ASSOCIATION, Washington, D.C. Lobbyist — Hogan & Hartson, 815 Connecticut Ave. N.W., Washington, D.C. 20036. Filed 7/16/81. Legislative interest — "Legislation to provide tax incentives for high technology companies."

FAIR OPPORTUNITIES FOR COMPETITION IN THE U.S. (FOCUS), Washington, D.C. Lobbyist — Pepper, Hamilton & Scheetz, 1776 F St. N.W., Washington, D.C. 20006. Filed 7/7/81. Legislative interest — ". . .communications common carrier industry, specifically S 898. . . ."

FLEXIBLE PACKAGING ASSOCIATION, 1090 Vermont Ave. N.W., Washington, D.C. 20005. Filed for self 7/9/81. Legislative interest — Not specified. Lobbyist — Mary E. Barnhard.

INDEPENDENT LUBRICANT MANUFACTURERS ASSOCIATION, Washington, D.C. Lobbyist — Collier, Shannon, Rill & Scott, 1055 Thomas Jefferson St. N.W., Washington, D.C. 20007. Filed 7/24/81. Legislative interest — Not specified.

INTERNATIONAL FRANCHISE ASSOCIATION, 1025 Connecticut Ave. N.W., Washington, D.C. Filed for self 7/8/81. Legislative interest — ". . .HR 460 and S 8. . . ." Lobbyist — William B. Cherkasky.

THE LEAGUE OF NEW YORK THEATRES AND PRODUCERS INC., New York, N.Y. Lobbyist — Proskauer, Rose, Goetz & Mendelsohn, 300 Park Ave., New York, N.Y. 10022. Filed 7/8/81. Legislative interest — ". . .amendments to the Internal Revenue Code (such as tax credits to persons investing in theatrical productions). . . ."

MANUFACTURERS OF EMISSION CONTROLS ASSOCIATION, Washington, D.C. Lobbyist — John Adams Associates Inc., 1825 K St. N.W., Washington, D.C. 20006. Filed 7/8/81. Legislative interest — "Clean Air Act reauthorization."

MARITIME INSTITUTE FOR RESEARCH AND INDUSTRIAL DEVELOPMENT, 1133 15th St. N.W., Washington, D.C. 20005. Filed for self 7/28/81. Legislative interest — Not specified.

MILITARY ACCESSORIES SERVICE ASSOCIATION INC., New York, N.Y. Lobbyist — Akin, Gump, Strauss, Hauer & Feld, 1133 New Hampshire Ave. N.W., Washington, D.C. 20036. Filed 7/16/81. Legislative interest — "...Department of Defense appropriations for fiscal year 1982."

NATIONAL ASSOCIATION OF BROADCASTERS, 1771 N St. N.W., Washington, D.C. 20036. Filed for self 7/11/81. Legislative interest — "...Communications Act of 1934...Copyright Law of 1909...Communications Satellite Act of 1962...Regulation of advertising, taxation, appropriations, public broadcasting, newsmen's privilege and consumer protection." Lobbyist — Carol Randles.

NATIONAL ASSOCIATION OF CHAIN DRUG STORES INC., P.O. Box 1417-D49, Alexandria, Va. 22313. Filed for self 7/14/81. Legislative interest — "...capital cost recovery, budget reconciliation (S 1377 and HR 3982) and pharmacy protection (HR 2034)." Lobbyist — James A. Whitman.

NATIONAL ASSOCIATION OF INDUSTRIAL & OFFICE PARKS, Arlington, Va. Lobbyist — Stanford, Williams and Briggs, 1825 K St. N.W., Washington, D.C. 20006. Filed 7/1/81. Legislative interest — Not specified.

NATIONAL ASSOCIATION OF MANUFACTURERS, 1776 F St. N.W., Washington, D.C. 20006. Filed for self 7/9/81. Legislative interest — Not specified. Lobbyist — Charles Argyll Campbell. Lobbyist — Patton, Boggs & Blow, 2550 M St. N.W., Washington, D.C. 20006. Filed 7/5/81. Legislative interest — "Economic Recovery Tax Act of 1981, Capital Cost Recovery Act of 1981, HR 3849, HR 1053, H J Res 266, S 287."

NATIONAL ASSOCIATION OF TRUCK STOP OPERATORS, 700 N. Fairfax St., Alexandria, Va. 22314. Filed for self 7/14/81. Legislative interest — "...HR 31, S 414, S 348, HR 3197, S 841, S 1988, HR 1508, S 1142." Lobbyists — Ronald L. Ziegler, Thomas H. Gorey.

NATIONAL CABLE TELEVISION ASSOCIATION, Washington, D.C. Lobbyist — Mintz, Levin, Cohn, Ferris, Glovsky & Popeo, 1015 15th St. N.W., Washington, D.C. 20005. Filed 7/14/81. Legislative interest — "Legislation affecting the copyright law and the effect of any proposed changes upon the cable industry."

NATIONAL COAL ASSOCIATION, 1130 17th St. N.W., Washington, D.C. 20036. Filed for self 7/6/81. Legislative interest — Not specified. Lobbyist — Susan B. Carver.

NATIONAL CONFERENCE OF BANKRUPTCY JUDGES, Oakland, Calif. Lobbyist — Francis C. Rosenberger, 6809 Melrose Dr., McLean, Va. 22101. Filed 7/24/81. Legislative interest — "...bankruptcy legislation."

NATIONAL FOOD PROCESSORS ASSOCIATION, 1133 20th St. N.W., Washington, D.C. 20036. Filed for self 7/31/81. Legislative interest — "All legislation directly affecting fruit, vegetable, seafood and meat processing for human consumption, including, but not limited to, food surveillance, food labeling, fish inspection and development, and the Clean Water Act." Lobbyists — Peter B. Summerville, Leigh Ann Zunke.

NATIONAL MILK PRODUCERS FEDERATION, 30 F St. N.W., Washington, D.C. 20001. Filed for self 7/13/81. Legislative interest — Not specified. Lobbyist — M. Elizabeth Stotler.

NATIONAL OCEAN INDUSTRIES ASSOCIATION, 1100 17th St. N.W., Washington, D.C. Filed for self 7/28/81. Legislative interest — "...oceanography, conservation and development of natural resources and environmental quality." Lobbyist — Richard A. Legatski.

NATIONAL OIL JOBBERS COUNCIL, 1707 H St. N.W., Washington, D.C. 20006. Filed for self 7/10/81. Legislative interest — Not specified. Lobbyist — Linda S. Rearick.

THE NEW ENGLAND COUNCIL INC., Boston, Mass. Lobbyist — Federal Services Co., 1015 15th St. N.W., Washington, D.C. 20005. Filed 7/26/81. Legislative interest — Not specified.

PACIFIC SEAFOOD PROCESSORS ASSOCIATION, Seattle, Wash. Lobbyist — Bogle & Gates, The Bank of California Center, Seattle, Wash. 98164. Filed 7/9/81. Legislative interest — "Amendments to the Fisheries Conservation and Management Act and other legislation regarding seafood processing issues."

PATHOLOGIST PRACTICE ASSOCIATION, Sacramento, Calif. Lobbyist — A-K Associates Inc., 1225 8th St., Sacramento, Calif. 95814. Filed 7/24/81. Legislative interest — "HR 3982...."

THE PUBLIC UTILITY TAX COMMITTEE, Washington, D.C. Lobbyist — Ullman Consultants Inc., 1000 Potomac St. N.W., Washington, D.C. 20007. Filed 7/10/81. (Former U.S. Rep. Al Ullman, D-Ore., 1957-81, was listed as agent for this client.) Legislative interest — "Tax legislation affecting public utilities."

RISK AND INSURANCE MANAGEMENT SOCIETY INC., 205 East 42nd St., New York, N.Y. 10017. Filed for self 7/14/81. Legislative interest — "seeking amendments to sections 461 and 165 of the Internal Revenue Code of 1954...."

RURAL BUILDERS COUNCIL OF CALIFORNIA, Newport Beach, Calif. Lobbyist — Nooley Reinheardt & Associates, P.O. Box 23190, Washington, D.C. 20024. Filed 7/14/81. Legislative interest — "Housing and tax legislation, particularly related to rural areas."

SCIENTIFIC APPARATUS MAKERS ASSOCIATION, Washington, D.C. Lobbyist — Hogan & Hartson, 815 Connecticut Ave. N.W., Washington, D.C. 20006. Filed 7/18/81. Legislative interest — "Legislation to provide tax incentives for high technology companies."

SENIOR EXECUTIVES ASSOCIATION, P.O. Box 7610, Washington, D.C. 20044. Filed for self 7/31/81. Legislative interest — "...S 1130 and HR 3743...." Lobbyist — G. Jerry Shaw.

SHIPBUILDERS COUNCIL OF AMERICA, 600 New Hampshire Ave. N.W., Washington, D.C. 20037. Filed for self 7/13/81. Legislative interest — Not specified. Lobbyist — Jed L. Babbin, 4910 N. 27th St., Arlington, Va. 22207.

TRAVEL INDUSTRY ASSOCIATION OF AMERICA, 1899 L St. N.W., Washington, D.C. 20036. Filed for self 7/19/81. Legislative interest — "...S 304 and HR 1311, the National Tourism Policy Act." Lobbyist — Anthi K. Jones.

WESTERN FOREST INDUSTRIES ASSOCIATION, Portland, Ore. Lobbyist — Burson-Marsteller, 1800 M St. N.W., Washington, D.C. 20036. Filed 7/9/81. Legislative interest — "Estate and gift tax relief, HR 3882."

WESTERN GROWERS ASSOCIATION, 888 17th St. N.W., Washington, D.C. 20006. Filed for self 7/13/81. Legislative interest — "S 922 and HR 3636." Lobbyist — Robert W. Porter.

WESTERN PENNSYLVANIA COAL MINING ASSOCIATION, Philadelphia, Pa. Lobbyist — Dilworth, Paxson, Kalish & Levy, 1819 H St. N.W., Washington, D.C. 20006. Filed 7/16/81. Legislative interest — "Coal use tax provision in HR 3982...."

Miscellaneous

JAMES BALTON III, 305 Normandy Drive, Silver Spring, Md. 20801. Filed for self 7/22/81. Legislative interest — Not specified.

CH2M HILL INC., Corvallis, Ore. Lobbyist — Richard L. Corrigan, 1090 Vermont Ave. N.W., Washington, D.C. 20005. Filed 7/10/81. Legislative interest — "Matters relating to the environment, public health and safety, public works, transportation, energy, military construction and government procurement."

CLADOUHOS & BRASHARES, 1750 New York Ave. N.W., Washington, D.C. 20006. Filed for self 7/13/81. Legislative interest — "...S 396, which would impose a quota on Japanese auto imports and S 626, HR 1338 and HR 1293, bills involving the tax consequences of commodity tax straddles...."

COALITION OF INDEPENDENT COLLEGE AND UNIVERSITY STUDENTS (COPUS), 1730 Rhode Island Ave. N.W., Washington, D.C. 20036. Filed for self 7/23/81. Legislative interest — Not specified. Lobbyist — Miriam Ann Rosenberg.

COUNCIL FOR LANGUAGES AND OTHER INTERNATIONAL STUDIES, 11 DuPont Circle N.W., Washington, D.C. 20037. Filed for self 7/28/81. Legislative interest — "...HR 3231, HR 2043 as amended, HR 2868 and S 386...." Lobbyist — J. David Edwards.

ROY CULLEN, Washington, D.C. Lobbyist — Vinson & Elkins, 1101 Connecticut Ave. N.W., Washington, D.C. 20036. Filed 7/19/81. Legislative interest — "...national flood insurance and opposing the House Budget Reconciliation Act's prohibition on national flood insurance for undeveloped coastal areas...."

LEANDER J. FOLEY III, 1434 A St. S.E., Washington, D.C. 20003. Filed for self 7/24/81. Legislative interest — "...community development credit unions, community development corporations, National Rural Development & Finance Corp...."

FRANCIS ASSOCIATES LTD., 316 Pennsylvania Ave. S.E., Washington, D.C. 20003. Filed for self 7/31/81. Legislative interest — not specified. Lobbyist — Leslie C. Francis.

FRED T. & CENUS N. FRANZIA, JOHN G. JR. & MARY L. FRANZIA, JOSEPH S. & MARILYN L. FRANZIA, Whittier, Calif. Lobbyist — Leighton, Conklin, Lemov, Jacobs & Buckley, 2033 M St. N.W., Washington, D.C. 20036. Filed 7/24/81. Legislative interest — "Amendment to Section 83 of the Internal Revenue Code of 1954, as amended."

GENERAL ELECTRIC PENSION TRUST, Stamford, Conn. Lobbyist — Dewey, Ballantine, Bushby, Palmer & Wood, 1775 Pennsylvania Ave. N.W., Washington, D.C. 20006. Filed 7/23/81. Legislative interest — "Tax legislation."

GOVERNMENT RELATIONS ASSOCIATES INC., 1629 K St. N.W., Washington, D.C. 20006. Filed for self 7/13/81. Legislative interest — "Trade matters, coal leasing, domestic preference, export trading companies, shipping...." Lobbyists — Christie K. Bohner, John W. Feist.

GREATER BOSTON REAL ESTATE BOARD, Boston, Mass. Lobbyist — Leighton, Conklin, Lemov, Jacobs & Buckley, 2033 M St. N.W., Washington, D.C. 20036. Filed 7/6/81. Legislative interest — "...legislation to provide tax incentives for home buyers."

LISBON ASSOCIATES INC., 515 Madison Ave., New York, N.Y. 10022. Filed for self 7/13/81. Legislative interest — Not specified.

LOYAL TRUST, Dallas, Texas. Lobbyist —Sutherland, Asbill & Brennan, 1666 K St. N.W., Washington, D.C. 20006. Filed 7/31/81. Legislative interest — "H J Res 266 and HR 4242. Support amendments to estate tax provisions."

A. LESTER MARX (MRS.), Honolulu, Hawaii. Lobbyist — Sutherland, Asbill & Brennan, 1666 K St. N.W., Washington, D.C. 20006. Filed 7/31/81. Legislative interest — "H J Res 266 and HR 4242. Support amendments to estate tax provisions."

SANTERELLI AND GIMER, Washington, D.C. Lobbyist — O'Neill and Haase, 1333 New Hampshire Ave. N.W., Washington, D.C. Filed 7/13/81. Legislative interest — "...provisions of the Internal Revenue Code pertaining to the Investment Tax Credit."

JAMES SCHNEIDER, San Diego, Calif. Lobbyist — Manatt, Phelps, Rothenberg & Tunney, 1200 New Hampshire Ave. N.W., Washington, D.C. 20036. Filed 7/17/81. (Former U.S. Rep. James C. Corman, D-Calif., 1961-81, was listed as an agent for this client.) Legislative interest — "...tax legislation relating to investment tax credit for restoration of historical sites."

NORMAN D. SHUTLER, 1607 New Hampshire Ave. N.W., Washington, D.C. 20009. Filed for self 7/13/81. Legislative interest — "Environmental and energy." Lobbyists — Matthew A. Low, Benjamin R. Jackson.

LOUIS H. STRAUSS, Washington, D.C. Lobbyist — Sutherland, Asbill & Brennan, 1666 K St. N.W., Washington, D.C. 20006. Filed 7/31/81. Legislative interest — "H J Res 266 and HR 4242. Support amendments to estate tax provisions."

EDNA WINSTON, New York, N.Y. Lobbyist — Sutherland, Asbill & Brennan, 1666 K St. N.W., Washington, D.C. 20006. Filed 7/31/81. Legislative interest — "H J Res 266 and HR 4242. Support amendments to estate tax provisions."

August Registrations
Citizens' Groups

AD HOC COMMITTEE ON INDIVIDUAL ANNUITY TAXATION, 10 Post Office Square, Boston, Mass. 02109. Filed for self 8/1/81. Legislative interest — "...changes in Internal Revenue Code relating to individual annuities taxation."

AMERICAN CONSERVATIVE UNION, 316 Pennsylvania Ave. S.E., Washington, D.C. 20003. Filed 8/21/81. Legislative interest — "...Economic Recovery Act." Lobbyist — Don Todd.

AMERICAN LUNG ASSOCIATION, New York, N.Y. Filed for self 8/27/81. Legislative interest — "...TB project grants, reauthorization of Clean Air Act, pending reauthorization of NHLBI, appropriations for federal lung research, deregulation of tobacco support program, and postal rates for non-profit organizations." Lobbyist — Robert G. Weymueller, 1629 K St. N.W., Washington, D.C. 20006.

BALTIC AMERICAN FREEDOM LEAGUE, Los Angeles, Calif. Lobbyist — The Hannaford Co. Inc., 1225 19th St. N.W., Washington, D.C. 20036. Filed 8/7/81. Legislative interest — "...the continuing plight of the captive peoples of the Baltic states and ... appropriate congressional action for their relief."

CITIZENS HOUSING & PLANNING ASSOCIATION INC., Boston, Mass. Lobbyist — Roisman, Reno & Cavanaugh, 1016 16th St. N.W., Washington, D.C. 20036. Filed 8/7/81. Legislative interest — "...operating subsidies for low income housing, authorized under U.S. Housing Act of 1937...."

HANDGUN CONTROL INC., 810 18th St. N.W., Washington, D.C. 20006. Filed for self 8/7/81. Legislative interest — "...Handgun Crime Control Act of 1981, S 974 and HR 3200." Lobbyist — David Cohen.

LOS ANGELES OLYMPIC COMMEMORATIVE COIN, Los Angeles, Calif. Lobbyist — Robert E. Juliano Associates, 1101 New Hampshire Ave. N.W., Washington, D.C. 20036. Filed 8/17/81. Legislative interest — "...legislation to provide for issuance and sale of precious metals United States Olympic coins in honor of the 1984 Olympic games."

LOS ANGELES OLYMPIC ORGANIZING COMMITTEE, New York, N.Y. Lobbyist — Robert E. Juliano Associates, 1101 New Hampshire Ave. N.W., Washington, D.C. 20036. Filed 8/17/81. Legislative interest — "...legislation to provide for issuance and sale of precious metals United States Olympic coins in honor of the 1984 Olympic games."

NATIONAL AUDUBON SOCIETY, 950 Third Ave., New York, N.Y. Filed for self 8/7/81. Legislative interest — "...environment, population, natural resources issues." Lobbyists — Russell W. Peterson, New York; Hope M. Babcock, William A. Butler, Leslie Dach, Charlene Dougherty, Maureen K. Hinkle, Christopher N. Palmer, 645 Pennsylvania Ave. S.E., Washington, D.C. 20003.

NATIONAL COMMUNITY ACTION FOUNDATION INC., 2101 L St. N.W., Washington, D.C. 20037. Filed for self 8/24/81. Legislative interest — "...reauthorization of programs operated by Community Services Administration, full funding of CSA, full funding and construction of all programs designed to assist the poor and minorities." Lobbyist — Margaret Power.

NATIONAL RIGHT TO LIFE COMMITTEE INC., 341 National Press Building, Washington, D.C. 20045. Filed for self 8/13/81. Legislative interest — "...Ashbrook amendment to Treasury-Postal appropriations bill (HR 4121); Hyde amendment to fiscal 1982 Department of Health and Human Services appropriations bill; abortion-related amendments to Internal Security and Development Cooperation Act of 1981 (S 1196); confirmation of C. Everett Koop as Surgeon General; HR 1337, HR 1596 and S 99, relating to income tax deductions for adoption-related expenses; S J Res 17 and H J Res 125, Human Life amendment ... opposition to nomination of Sandra D. O'Connor to the United States

Supreme Court." Lobbyist — Douglas Johnson.

NATIONAL TAX LIMITATION COMMITTEE, Washington, D.C. Lobbyist — David A. Keene, 1000 Connecticut Ave. N.W., Washington, D.C. 20036. Filed 8/6/81. Legislative interest — "...S J Res 54, S J Res 58, H J Res 169."

THE WILDERNESS SOCIETY, Washington, D.C. Lobbyist — Fletcher Shives, 3110 Maple Dr. N.E., Atlanta, Ga. 30305. Filed 8/5/81. Legislative interest — "Appropriations for Land and Water Conservation Fund; wilderness designation for Cumberland Island National Seashore; wilderness designation for Great Smokey National Park."

Corporations and Businesses

AIR PRODUCTS AND CHEMICALS INC., Allentown, Pa. 18105. Filed for self 8/4/81. Legislative interest — "...energy, the environment, product distribution and procurement, research and development...." Lobbyists — Lewis I. Dale, Beth Gordon, 1800 K St. N.W., Washington, D.C. 20006.

AIRBUS INDUSTRIE, Blagnac, France. Lobbyist — DGA International Inc., 1225 19th St. N.W., Washington, D.C. 20036. Filed 8/6/81. Legislative interest — "Legislation affecting noise, ADAP (S 508 and HR 2643), any legislation affecting commercial aircraft manufacturing and legislation affecting the U.S. Export-Import Bank...."

AMERICAN EXPRESS CO., Washington, D.C. Lobbyist — Thaxter, Lipez, Stevens, Broder & Micoleau, 1825 K St. N.W., Washington, D.C. 20006. Filed 8/28/81. Legislative interest — "Cash Discount Act, HR 31...."

AMERICAN INLAND WATERWAYS COMMITTEE, St. Louis, Mo. Lobbyist — Thompson & Mitchell, One Mercantile Center, St. Louis, Mo. 63101. Filed 8/4/81. Legislative interest — "...S 810, HR 2384, S 621 and S 484 and bills dealing with water resources planning."

AMERICAN TELEPHONE & TELEGRAPH CO., Washington, D.C. Lobbyist — Akin, Gump, Strauss, Hauer & Feld, 1333 New Hampshire Ave. N.W., Washington, D.C. 20036. Filed 8/25/81. Legislative interest — "...legislation affecting the communications industry, including general corporate, financial and tax issues."

BLUEJAY OIL CO., Wilmington, Del. Lobbyist — Shipley, Smoak & Akerman, 1108 National Press Bldg., Washington, D.C. 20045. Filed 8/4/81. Legislative interest — "Energy, taxes, antitrust, environmental, interstate commerce, real estate."

THE BUDD CO., Troy, Mich. Lobbyist — Gray and Co., 3255 Grace St., Washington, D.C. 20007. Filed 8/3/81. Legislative interest — "HR 3568, S 1199."

BURLINGTON INDUSTRIES INC., Washington, D.C. Lobbyist — Patton, Boggs & Blow, 2550 M St. N.W., Washington, D.C. 20037. Filed 8/26/81. Legislative interest — "...S 995, HR 1242, HR 4072 and related bills."

BURLINGTON NORTHERN, Billings, Mont. Lobbyist — Nossaman, Krueger & Marsh, 1140 19th St. N.W., Washington, D.C. 20036. Filed 8/17/81. Legislative interest — "...section of the Mineral Leasing Act of 1920 concerning federal coal lease ownership."

CATERPILLAR TRACTOR CO., 100 N.E. Adams St., Peoria, Ill. 61629. Filed for self 8/20/81. Legislative interest — "HR 4016 — for, S 708 — for, HR 3136 — for." Lobbyist — Donald H. Defoe. Lobbyist — Bernard J. Cooney, 1730 Pennsylvania Ave. N.W., Washington, D.C. 20006. Filed 8/31/81. Legislative interest — "Clean Air Act legislation, including HR 4400."

CHAMPION INTERNATIONAL CORP., One Champion Plaza, Stamford, Conn. 06921. Filed for self 8/12/81. Legislative interest — Not specified. Lobbyists — James M. Quigley, Merribel Symington, Nick L. Van Nelson, 1875 I St. N.W., Washington, D.C. 20006.

THE CHARTER CO., Jacksonville, Fla. Filed for self 8/26/81. Legislative interest — Not specified. Lobbyist — Ginger Gardner, 2550 M St. N.W., Washington, D.C. 20037.

CHEVRON U.S.A. INC., 1700 K St. N.W., Washington, D.C. 20006. Filed for self 8/28/81. Legislative interest — "...HR 31, HR 85, HR 299, HR 859, HR 1362 and HR 8232." Lobbyist — Kathy J. Cooper.

CHICAGO BOARD OF TRADE, Chicago, Ill. Lobbyists — Theodore L. Jones, 1140 19th St. N.W., Washington, D.C. 20036; Murphy & Boyle, 221 N. La Salle St., Chicago, Ill. 60601. Filed 8/4/81. (Former U.S. Rep. Morgan F. Murphy, D-Ill., 1971-81, was listed among agents for this client.) Legislative interest — "Economic Recovery Act of 1981, HR 4242."

COLUMBIA PICTURES INDUSTRIES INC., New York, N.Y. Lobbyist — Hill, Christopher and Phillips, 1900 M St. N.W., Washington, D.C. 20036. Filed 8/4/81. Legislative interest — "Removal of compulsory license on retransmission of broadcast signals by cable systems. HR 3528, HR 3560."

COMPUTER SCIENCES CORP., El Segundo, Calif. Lobbyist — Hoffheimer, Johnson & Peterson, 1120 20th St. N.W., Washington, D.C 20036. Filed 8/10/81. Legislative interest — "Health legislation, specifically relating to data processing/computer related activities...."

CROWLEY MARITIME CORP., San Francisco, Calif. Lobbyists — Donald K. Brown, 1127 11th St., Sacramento, Calif. 95814; John H. Hodgson II, 1225 8th St., Sacramento, Calif. 95814. Filed 8/20/81. Legislative interest — "Jones Act, maritime legislation and Title II (loan guarantee funding)."

CSX CORP., Richmond, Va. Filed for self 8/5/81. Legislative interest — "S 828 — Ports and Navigation Act of 1981 ... S 739 — Rail Investment Incentive Act of 1981 ... HR 1647 — Criminal Code Revision Act of 1981 ... HR 3982 — Budget Reconciliation Act ... HR 4242 — Economic Recovery Tax Act of 1981." Lobbyist — James T. Glenn, 15th St. & New York Ave. N.W., Washington, D.C. 20005.

CUMMINS ENGINE CO., Columbus, Ind. Lobbyist — Bayh, Tabbert & Capehart, 1575 I St. N.W., Washington, D.C. 20005. Filed 8/10/81. Legislative interest — "Amendments to the Clean Air Act and related matters."

DAMSON OIL CORP., Houston, Texas. Lobbyist — Gerard, Byler & Associates Inc., 1100 17th St. N.W., Washington, D.C. 20036. Filed 8/24/81. Legislative interest — "Promote legislation to facilitate non-lease agreements between Indian tribes and energy firms."

DATAPOINT CORP., San Antonio, Texas. Lobbyist — Harold E. O'Kelley, 7900 Callaghan Rd., San Antonio, Texas. 78229. Filed 8/3/81. Legislative interest — "To urge that any proposed communications legislation insure continued competition in the data processing field."

DELTA STEAMSHIP LINES INC., New Orleans, La. Lobbyist — Bowman, Conner, Touhey & Thornton, 2828 Pennsylvania Ave. N.W., Washington, D.C. 20007. Filed 8/6/81. Legislative interest — "...Omnibus Budget Reconciliation bill and other matters relating to shipping."

DREXEL BURNHAM LAMBERT INC., New York, N.Y. Lobbyist — Marshall, Bratter, Greene, Allison & Tucker, 1140 Connecticut Ave. N.W., Washington, D.C. 20036. Filed 8/28/81. Legislative interest — "Tax legislation affecting profits from trading in foreign and domestic futures and forward markets...."

ECONOPURE, Denver, Colo. Lobbyist — Benoit, Smith & Laughlin, 2001 Jefferson Davis Hwy., Arlington, Va. 22202. Filed 8/31/81. Legislative interest — "Clean Air Act."

FEDERAL NATIONAL MORTGAGE ASSOCIATION, Washington, D.C. Lobbyist — Califano, Ross & Heineman, 1575 I St. N.W., Washington, D.C. 20005. Filed 8/3/81. Legislative interest — Not specified.

FEDERATED DEPARTMENT STORES INC., Cincinnati, Ohio. Lobbyist — Shipley, Smoak & Akerman, 1108 National Press Bldg., Washington, D.C. 20045. Filed 8/4/81. Legislative interest — "Taxes, antitrust, environmental, interstate commerce, foreign relations, energy, broadcasting, real estate."

FIRST CENTRUM CORP., East Lansing, Mich. Lobbyist — Roisman, Reno & Cavanaugh, 1016 16th St. N.W., Washington, D.C. 20036. Filed 8/7/81. Legislative interest — "Seeking increased appropriations for the rural rental housing program...."

FLANIGAN'S ENTERPRISES INC., Miami, Fla. Lobbyist — Shipley, Smoak & Akerman, 1108 National Press Bldg., Washington, D.C. 20045. Filed 8/4/81. Legislative interest — "Taxes, antitrust, environmental, interstate commerce, energy, real estate."

FORT SILL GARDENS INC., Lawton, Okla. Lobbyist — Shipley, Smoak & Akerman, 1108 National Press Bldg., Washington, D.C. 20045. Filed 8/4/81. Legislative interest — "Taxes, antitrust, environmental, interstate commerce, energy, real estate."

GATES LEARJET CORP., Wichita, Kan. Filed for self 8/8/81. Legislative interest — Not specified. Lobbyist — William R. Edgar, 815 Connecticut Ave. N.W., Washington, D.C. 20006.

GENERAL DYNAMICS CORP., St. Louis, Mo. Lobbyist — Miller & Chevalier, 1700 Pennsylvania Ave. N.W., Washington, D.C. 20006. Filed 8/13/81. Legislative interest — "...H J Res 266, HR 4260, HR 4242, S 639, HR 822 and HR 2797."

GENERAL INSTRUMENT CORP., New York, N.Y. Filed for self 8/14/81. Legislative interest — "...communications, copyright...." Lobbyist — Deborah M. Minnich, 1200 New Hampshire Ave. N.W., Washington, D.C. 20036.

GENERAL TELEPHONE & ELECTRONICS CORP., Washington, D.C. Lobbyist — Gray and Co., The Power House, Washington, D.C. 20007. Filed 8/19/81. Legislative interest — "S 63, S 898."

GEOPRODUCTS CORP., Oakland, Calif. Lobbyist — F. H. Hutchison & Co., 1744 R St. N.W., Washington, D.C. 20009. Filed 8/3/81. Legislative interest — "Geothermal energy tax provisions of Internal Revenue Code; HR 4091...."

GRAY AND CO., The Power House, Washington, D.C. 20007. Filed for self 8/3/81. Legislative interest — Not specified. Lobbyists — Robert K. Gray, James C. Jennings, Elizabeth S. Weltner.

GULF OIL CORP., Pittsburgh, Pa. Lobbyist — K. R. Murphy, 1025 Connecticut Ave. N.W., Washington, D.C. 20036. Filed 8/7/81. Legislative interest — "...Clean Air Act, natural gas policy, Tar Sands and Oil Shale Omnibus bill."

HAGAN INDUSTRIES INC., Montgomery, Ala. Lobbyist — Sutherland, Asbill & Brennan, 1666 K St. N.W., Washington, D.C. 20006. Filed 8/7/81. Legislative interest — "H J Res 266 and HR 4242."

HARTFORD FIRE INSURANCE CO., Hartford, Conn. Lobbyist — Alston, Miller & Gaines, 1800 M St. N.W., Washington, D.C. 20036. Filed 8/11/81. Legislative interest — "...comprehensive revision of subchapter L of the Internal Revenue Code."

HYDROTHERMAL ENERGY CORP., Los Angeles, Calif. Lobbyist — F. H. Hutchison & Co., 1744 R St. N.W., Washington, D.C. 20009. Filed 8/3/81. Legislative interest — "Energy and Water Development Appropriations measures, appropriations for User-Coupled Confirmation Drilling Program (geothermal)."

INTERNATIONAL PAPER CO., New York, N.Y. Lobbyist — Miller, Canfield, Paddock & Stone, 2500 Detroit Bank & Trust Bldg., Detroit, Mich. 48226. Filed 8/24/81. Legislative interest — "...S 995, HR 1242." Lobbyist — Powell, Goldstein, Frazer & Murphy, 1110 Vermont Ave. N.W., Washington, D.C. 20005. Filed 8/17/81. Legislative interest — "...antitrust contribution legislation."

KOCH INDUSTRIES, Wichita, Kan. Lobbyist — Venners and Co. Ltd., 1899 L St. N.W., Washington, D.C. 20036. Filed 8/12/81. Legislative interest — "...energy legislation, specifically crude oil and petroleum products, energy transportation matters."

LP MANAGEMENT CORP., 11 Greenway Plaza, Houston, Texas 77046. Filed for self 8/21/81. Legislative interest — "...Crude Oil Windfall Profits Tax Act."

MANAGEMENT INSIGHTS INC., Dallas, Texas. Lobbyist — Gray and Co., 3255 Grace St. N.W., Washington, D.C. 20007. Filed 8/4/81. Legislative interest — "HR 4242."

MATLACK INC., Wilmington, Del. Lobbyist — Camp, Carmouche, Palmer, Barsh & Hunter, 2550 M St. N.W., Washing-

ton, D.C. 20037. Filed 8/20/81. Legislative interest — "...H J Res 266 and HR 3849."

MCDERMOTT INC., New Orleans, La. Lobbyist — David P. Stang, 1629 K St. N.W., Washington, D.C. 20006. Filed 8/12/81. Legislative interest — "HR 2530 Foreign Corrupt Practices Act, S 708...."

MIDLAND ENTERPRISES INC., Cincinnati, Ohio. Lobbyist — Thompson & Mitchell, One Mercantile Center, St. Louis, Mo. 63101. Filed 8/8/81. Legislative interest — "...Locks and Dam 26 ... Water Resources Development Act of 1976."

NATIONAL CON-SERV INC., Rockville, Md. Lobbyist — Roger Tilles, 1111 19th St. N.W., Washington, D.C. 20036. Filed 8/6/81. Legislative interest — "Reauthorization of the Federal Crime Insurance Program...."

NATIONAL RURAL DEVELOPMENT & FINANCE CORP., 1300 19th St. N.W., Washington, D.C. 20036. Filed for self 8/5/81. Legislative interest — "Rural loan programs and rural community development programs in Department of Agriculture, CSA, and EDA; their authorizations and appropriations." Lobbyist — Leander S. Foley III.

NEWMONT MINING CORP., 1090 Vermont Ave. N.W., Washington, D.C. 20005. Filed for self 8/3/81. Legislative interest — "...Clean Air Act, regulatory reform." Lobbyists — Mary Beth O'Brien, David C. Ridinger.

NORTHROP CORP., 1000 Wilson Blvd., Arlington, Va. 22209. Filed for self 8/31/81. Legislative interest — "F/A-18 and F-5 series aircraft...." Lobbyist — M. Douglas Todd.

NORTHWEST INLAND WATERWAYS COMMITTEE, Portland, Ore. Lobbyist — Schwabe, Williamson, Wyatt, Moore & Roberts, 1200 Standard Plaza, Portland, Ore. 97204. Filed 8/24/81. (Former U.S. Rep. Wendell Wyatt, R-Ore., 1964-75, was listed as an agent for this client.) Legislative interest — "HR 2962 and HR 2384."

NORTON SIMON INC., New York, N.Y. Lobbyist — Bregman, Abell & Kay, 1900 L St. N.W., Washington, D.C. 20036. Filed 8/4/81. Legislative interest — Not specified.

OCEAN MINERALS CO., Mountain View, Calif. Lobbyist — David P. Stang, 1629 K St. N.W., Washington, D.C. 20006. Filed 8/12/81. Legislative interest — "Law of the Sea Treaty."

OILFIELD INDUSTRIAL LINES INC., Big Spring, Texas. Filed for self 8/7/81. Legislative interest — Not specified. Lobbyist — Gwen Pharo, 1101 S. Arlington Ridge Rd., Arlington, Va. 22202.

PHH GROUP INC., Hunt Valley, Md. Lobbyist — Himes & Ketchey, 100 Twiggs St., Tampa, Fla. 33602. Filed 8/4/81. Legislative interest — "...depreciation tax deductions and investment tax credits on leased property."

PHILADELPHIA BELT LINE RAILROAD, Philadelphia, Pa. Lobbyist — Pepper & Corazzini, 1776 K St. N.W., Washington, D.C. 20006. Filed 8/14/81. Legislative interest — "Conrail provisions of budget reconciliation bills of 1981...."

RENEWABLE ENERGY INC., Denver, Colo. Lobbyist — F. H. Hutchison & Co., 1744 R St. N.W., Washington, D.C. 20009. Filed 8/3/81. Legislative interest — "Energy and Water Development appropriations bills, appropriations for User-Coupled confirmation drilling program."

SCOTT PAPER CO., Scott Plaza, Philadelphia, Pa. 19113. Filed for self 8/5/81. Legislative interest — "...HR 3471, Clean Air Act amendments; HR 2957, Industrial Cost Exclusion Repeal, HR 7 and S 75, Capital Gains Tax Reduction; HR 2269, Yankee Dryer Duty Exemption; HR 4242, tax legislation." Lobbyists — Jeffrey P. Eves, James A. Morrill.

SHEARSON LOEB RHOADES INC., New York, N.Y. Lobbyist — Stroock & Stroock & Lavan, 1150 17th St. N.W., Washington, D.C. 20036. Filed 8/7/81. Legislative interest — "Amendments to HR 4242, Economic Recovery Tax Act of 1981."

J. R. SIMPLOT CO., Boise, Idaho. Lobbyist — Larry Grupp, Box 8032, Moscow, Idaho. 83843. Filed 8/24/81. Legislative interest — Not specified.

STEADMAN MUTUAL FUNDS, Washington, D.C. Lobbyist — Shipley, Smoak & Akerman, 1108 National Press Bldg., Washington, D.C. 20045. Filed 8/4/81. Legislative interest — "Taxes, antitrust, environmental, interstate commerce, foreign

relations, energy, broadcasting, real estate."

STEADMAN SECURITY CORP., Wilmington, Del. Lobbyist — Shipley, Smoak & Akerman, 1108 National Press Bldg., Washington, D.C. 20045. Filed 8/4/81. Legislative interest — "Taxes, antitrust, environmental, interstate commerce, foreign relations, energy, broadcasting, real estate."

TALISMAN FUND, Marina Del Rey, Calif. Lobbyist — Donald C. Lubick, 1776 F St. N.W., Washington, D.C. 20006. Filed 8/4/81. Legislative interest — "Economic Recovery Tax Act of 1981 — HR 4242...."

TEXAS INTERNATIONAL AIRLINES INC., Houston, Texas. Lobbyist — Baker & Botts, 1701 Pennsylvania Ave. N.W., Washington, D.C. 20006. Filed 8/3/81. Legislative interest — Not specified. Lobbyist — Nossaman, Krueger & Marsh, 1140 19th St. N.W., Washington, D.C. 20036. Filed 8/5/81. Legislative interest — "Economic Recovery Tax Act of 1981, HR 4242...."

TOSCO CORP., Washington, D.C. Lobbyist — Robert C. Farber, 4600 Duke St., Alexandria, Va. 22304. Filed 8/21/81. Legislative interest — Not specified.

TRANSOL SUNBELT INC., San Francisco, Calif. Lobbyist — Cole & Corette, 1200 17th St. N.W., Washington, D.C. 20036. Filed 8/5/81. Legislative interest — "...HR 4242, 4260 and H J Res 266."

TURNER BROADCASTING SYSTEM INC., Atlanta, Ga. Filed for self 8/21/81. Legislative interest — "...Communications Act of 1934, Copyright (S 898) and legislation affecting professional sports." Lobbyist — George W. Breece, 2133 Wisconsin Ave. N.W., Washington, D.C. 20007.

UNION CARBIDE CORP., 270 Park Ave., New York, N.Y. Filed for self 8/6/81. Legislative interest — "Export Trading company bill, Export-Import Bank funding bills, foreign aid bills, modifications to the Foreign Corrupt Practices Act." Lobbyist — Richard M. Brennan, 1730 Pennsylvania Ave. N.W., Washington, D.C. 20006.

UTAH POWER AND LIGHT CO., Salt Lake City, Utah. Lobbyist — Mountain West Associates, 2000 L St. N.W., Washington, D.C. 20036. Filed 8/27/81. Legislative interest — "Clean Air Act..."

THE VALLEY LINE CO., Clayton, Mo. Lobbyist — Thompson & Mitchell, One Mercantile Center, St. Louis, Mo. 63101. Filed 8/9/81. Legislative interest — "...Locks and Dam 26 ... Water Resources Development Act of 1976."

WBNO RADIO, Bryan, Ohio. Lobbyist — Shipley, Smoak & Akerman, 1108 National Press Bldg., Washington, D.C. 20045. Filed 8/4/81. Legislative interest — Taxes, broadcasting, antitrust, environmental, interstate commerce, foreign relations, energy, real estate."

WESTEC SERVICES INC., San Diego, Calif. Lobbyist — F. H. Hutchison & Co., 1744 R St. N.W., Washington, D.C. 20009. Filed 8/3/81. Legislative interest — "Energy and Water Development appropriations bills, geothermal energy appropriations."

WESTVACO CORP., 299 Park Ave., New York, N.Y. Filed for self 8/21/81. Legislative interest — "S 995, antitrust revision ... HR 1242, antitrust revisions...." Lobbyist — Thomas R. Long.

WLKM RADIO, Three Rivers, Mich. Lobbyist — Shipley, Smoak & Akerman, 1108 National Press Bldg., Washington, D.C. 20045. Filed 8/4/81. Legislative interest — Taxes, broadcasting, antitrust, environmental, interstate commerce, foreign relations, energy, real estate."

ZAPATA CORP., Houston, Texas. Lobbyist — David P. Stang, 1629 K St. N.W., Washington, D.C. 20006. Filed 8/12/81. Legislative interest — "HR 25, Longshoremen's and Harborworkers' Compensation Act Amendments of 1981, Oil Spill Liability and Compensation Act of 1981."

International Relations

THE UNITED KINGDOM MUTUAL STEAM SHIP ASSURANCE ASSOCIATION LTD., Hamilton, Bermuda. Lobbyist — O'Connor and Hannan, 1919 Pennsylvania Ave. N.W., Washington, D.C. 20006. Filed 8/5/81. Legislative interest — "S 1182...."

U.S.-SOUTH WEST AFRICA TRADE & CULTURAL COUNCIL, Washington, D.C. Lobbyist — Shipley, Smoak & Akerman, 1108 National Press Bldg., Washington, D.C. 20045. Filed 8/4/81. Legislative interest — "Taxes, antitrust, environmental, interstate commerce, foreign relations, energy, broadcasting, real estate."

THE WEST OF ENGLAND SHIP OWNERS MUTUAL PROTECTION AND INDEMNITY ASSOCIATION, Luxembourg, Luxembourg. Lobbyist — O'Connor & Hannan, 1919 Pennsylvania Ave. N.W., Washington, D.C. 20006. Filed 8/5/81. Legislative interest — "S 1182...."

Labor Groups

AMERICAN FEDERATION OF TEACHERS/AFL-CIO, Washington, D.C. Filed for self 8/7/81. Legislative interest — Not specified. Lobbyist — Gerald A. Morris.

INTERNATIONAL FEDERATION OF PROFESSIONAL & TECHNICAL ENGINEERS, AFL-CIO, Washington, D.C. Filed for self 8/13/81. Legislative interest — Not specified. Lobbyists — Kathryn JoAnn Hawes, Steve Aaron Schwartz.

UNITED BROTHERHOOD OF CARPENTERS AND JOINERS OF AMERICA, Washington, D.C. Filed for self 8/19/81. Legislative interest — Not specified. Lobbyist — Charles E. Nichols.

Military and Veterans'

NATIONAL MILITARY WIVES ASSOCIATION INC., 2666 Military Rd., Arlington, Va. 22207. Filed 8/18/81. Legislative interest — Not specified.

State and Local Governments

MASSACHUSETTS BAY TRANSIT AUTHORITY, Boston, Mass. 02110. Lobbyist — William W. Nickerson, 10955 Trotting Ridge Way, Columbia, Md. 21044. Filed 8/18/81. Legislative interest — "...financing, operation or regulation of public mass transit."

STATE OF MONTANA, Helena, Mont. Lobbyist — Leon G. Billings Inc., 1660 L St. N.W., Washington, D.C. 20036. Filed 8/11/81. Legislative interest — "Legislation limiting state severance taxes."

Trade Associations

AIR CONDITIONING & REFRIGERATION INSTITUTE, 1815 N. Fort Myer Dr., Arlington, Va. 22209. Filed for self 8/11/81. Legislative interest — "...HR 1853, S 517, HR 2296; the Clean Air Act (HR 1817, S 63), and budget measures affecting the Department of Energy." Lobbyists — Raymond Durazo, Kevin J. Fay, David A. Hunt.

ALABAMA FARM BUREAU FEDERATION, Montgomery, Ala. Lobbyist — Dale Sherwin, 1735 I St. N.W., Washington, D.C. 20006. Filed 8/21/81. Legislative interest — Not specified.

AMERICAN ACADEMY OF FEDERAL CIVIL SERVICE PHYSICIANS, Washington, D.C. Lobbyist — Harris, Berg & Creskoff, 2033 M St. N.W., Washington, D.C. 20036. Filed 8/15/81. Legislative interest — "...improve recruitment and retention of doctors in the federal service."

AMERICAN ACADEMY OF PHYSICIAN ASSISTANTS, 2341 Jefferson Davis Hwy., Arlington, Va. 22202. Filed for self 8/24/81. Legislative interest — "...continued authorization and appropriation for health manpower training and education programs...." Lobbyists — Nicole Gara, Peter Rosenstein.

AMERICAN BOILER MANUFACTURERS ASSOCIATION, 1500 Wilson Blvd., Arlington, Va. 22209. Filed for self 8/20/81. Legislative interest — Not specified. Lobbyists — William H. Axtman, Russell N. Mosher.

AMERICAN IRON AND STEEL INSTITUTE, Washington, D.C. Lobbyist — Gray and Co., The Power House, Washington, D.C. 20007. Filed 8/19/81. Legislative interest — "S 63, S 898."

AMERICAN NEWSPAPER PUBLISHERS ASSOCIATION, Reston, Va. Lobbyist — Black, Manafort & Stone, 435 North Lee St., Alexandria, Va. 22314. Filed 8/4/81. Legislative interest — "S 898."

AMERICAN SOCIETY OF COMPOSERS, AUTHORS AND PUBLISHERS, New York, N.Y. Lobbyist — The Hannaford Co. Inc., 1225 19th St. N.W., Washington, D.C. 20036. Filed 8/7/81. Legislative interest — "...copyright matters...."

COLORADO SKI COUNTRY USA INC., 1410 Grant St., Denver, Colo. 80203. Filed for self 8/15/81. Legislative interest — "...legislation covering recreational use of public lands." Lobbyists — Robert L. Knous Jr., Brenda J. Michaud.

CONFERENCE OF STATE BANK SUPERVISORS, 1015 18th St. N.W., Washington, D.C. 20036. Filed for self 8/27/81. Legislative interest — Not specified. Lobbyist — Michael J. DeLoose.

CONSUMER BANKERS ASSOCIATION, Washington, D.C. Lobbyist — Bingham, Dana & Gould, 1724 Massachusetts Ave. N.W., Washington, D.C. 20036. Filed 8/5/81. Legislative interest — "...S 1406."

COOPERATIVE LEAGUE OF THE USA, Washington, D.C. Lobbyist — E. A. Jaenke & Associates Inc., 1575 I St. N.W., Washington, D.C. 20036. Filed 8/28/81. Legislative interest — "Legislation which would revoke the charter of the National Consumer Cooperative Bank."

DISTILLED SPIRITS COUNCIL OF THE U.S. INC., 1300 Pennsylvania Building, Washington, D.C. 20004. Filed for self 8/12/81. Legislative interest — Not specified. Lobbyist — Richard J. Connor Jr.

GENERIC PHARMACEUTICAL INDUSTRY ASSOCIATION, New York, N.Y. Lobbyist — William F. Haddad, 322 W. 57th St., New York, N.Y. 10019. Filed 8/20/81. Legislative interest — "...HR 1937."

INTERNATIONAL CONFERENCE INDUSTRY ASSOCIATION, 2021 K St. N.W., Washington, D.C. 20006. Filed for self 8/11/81. Legislative interest — "...deductibility of overseas conventions of section 274(h) of the tax code." Lobbyist — John C. Vickerman.

NATIONAL ASSOCIATION OF AIRCRAFT AND COMMUNICATIONS SUPPLIERS INC., 7360 Laurel Canyon Blvd., North Hollywood, Calif. 91605. Filed for self 8/12/81. Legislative interest — "Small Business Act, section 8 (e)...."

NATIONAL ASSOCIATION OF CHAIN DRUG STORES INC., P.O. Box 1417-D49, Alexandria, Va. 22313. Filed for self 8/25/81. Legislative interest — "...capital cost recovery, budget reconciliation (S 1377 and HR 3982) and pharmacy protection (HR 2034)." Lobbyist — James A. Whitman.

NATIONAL ASSOCIATION OF MANUFACTURERS, 1776 F St. N.W., Washington, D.C. 20006. Filed for self 8/4/81. Legislative interest — "Regulatory Reform legislation ... tax cuts and budget reductions...." Lobbyists — Ann Anderson Duff, 222 S. Prospect Ave., Park Ridge, Ill. 60068; Donnae Sutherlin, 17 W. Market St., Indianapolis, Ind. 46204.

NATIONAL BEER WHOLESALERS ASSOCIATION, Falls Church, Va. Lobbyist — Thaxter, Lipez, Stevens, Broder & Micoleau, 1825 K St. N.W., Washington, D.C. 20006. Filed 8/28/81. Legislative interest — "Malt Beverage Interbrand Competition Act, HR 3269."

NATIONAL CABLE TELEVISION ASSOCIATION, Washington, D.C. Lobbyist — Patton, Boggs & Blow, 2550 M St. N.W., Washington, D.C. 20037. Filed 8/26/81. Legislative interest — "...S 898 Telecommunication Competition and Deregulation Act."

NATIONAL COMMITTEE OF DISCOUNT SECURITIES BROKERS, Memphis, Tenn. Lobbyist — Shipley, Smoak & Akerman, 1108 National Press Building, Washington, D.C. 20045. Filed 8/4/81. Legislative interest — "Taxes, antitrust, environmental, interstate commerce, foreign relations, energy, broadcasting, real estate."

NATIONAL COTTON COUNCIL OF AMERICA, P.O. Box 12285, Memphis, Tenn. 38112. Filed for self 8/1/81. Legislative interest — Not specified. Lobbyist — Gaylon B. Booker.

NATIONAL COUNCIL OF FARMER COOPERATIVES, 1800 Massachusetts Ave. N.W., Washington, D.C. 20036. Filed for self 8/26/81. Legislative interest — "Energy and natural resources." Lobbyist — James P. Howell.

NATIONAL FEDERATION OF COMMUNITY DEVELOPMENT CREDIT UNIONS, 16 Court St., Brooklyn, N.Y. 11201. Filed for self 8/10/81. Legislative interest — Not specified. Lobbyist — Leander J. Foley III.

NATIONAL MULTI HOUSING COUNCIL, 1800 M St. N.W., Washington, D.C. 20036. Filed for self 8/6/81. Legislative interest — "...opposition to rent control and condo conversion regulation and support for tax incentives." Lobbyist — Steven F. Stockmeyer.

NATIONAL OFFICE MACHINE DEALERS ASSOCIATION, Elk Grove Village, Ill. Filed for self 8/26/81. Legislative interest — "Small business, regulatory and taxation issues."

NATIONAL TELEPHONE COOPERATIVE ASSOCIATION, 2626 Pennsylvania Ave. N.W., Washington, D.C. 20037. Filed for self 8/10/81. Legislative interest — "...Rural Electrification Act of 1936 ... amendments to the Communications Act of 1934...." Lobbyist — Andrew Brown.

ORGANIZATION FOR THE PROTECTION AND ADVANCEMENT OF SMALL TELEPHONE COMPANIES, 1200 New Hampshire Ave. N.W., Washington, D.C. 20036. Filed for self 8/10/81. Legislative interest — "...rural and small-company independent telephone companies." Lobbyist — James G. Mercer.

SHRIMP HARVESTERS COALITION OF THE GULF AND SOUTH ATLANTIC STATES, 2101 L St. N.W., Washington, D.C. 20037. Filed for self 8/29/81. Legislative interest — "...HR 4041, HR 3816, HR 3668 and fiscal year 1982 NOAA appropriations." Lobbyist — Laura Jo Katz.

SPORTING ARMS AND AMMUNITION MANUFACTURERS INSTITUTE, New York, N.Y. Lobbyist — Cleary, Gottlieb, Steen & Hamilton, 1250 Connecticut Ave. N.W., Washington, D.C. 20036. Filed 8/25/81. Legislative interest — "...measures which would extend the date for payment of excise taxes on the sale of ammunition, pistols, or firearms."

WEST TEXAS LAND AND ROYALTY OWNERS ASSOCIATION, P.O. Box 67, Synder, Texas. 79549. Filed for self 8/24/81. Legislative interest — Not specified.

Miscellaneous

CENTER FOR SCIENCE IN THE PUBLIC INTEREST, 1755 S St. N.W., Washington, D.C. Filed for self 8/4/81. Legislative interest — "...Food Safety Amendments of 1981, Food and Drug Act, Alcoholic beverage labeling, food labeling (sodium)." Lobbyist — Bruce A. Silverglade.

HANCOCK/DIKEWOOD SERVICES INC., Albuquerque, N.M. Lobbyist — Hoffheimer, Johnson & Peterson, 1120 20th St. N.W, Washington, D.C. 20036. Filed 8/10/81. Legislative interest — "...Health Maintenance Organization Act of 1973 and HMO issues."

BENJAMIN J. AND HUGH MCMASTER TARBUTTON, Sandersville, Ga. Lobbyist — Sutherland, Asbill & Brennan, 1666 K St. N.W., Washington, D.C. 20006. Filed 8/7/81. Legislative interest — "...H J Res 266 and HR 4242...."

NATIONAL HOUSING LAW PROJECT, Washington, D.C. Lobbyist — Roisman, Reno & Cavanaugh, 1016 16th St. N.W., Washington, D.C. 20036. Filed 8/7/81. Legislative interest — "...legal rights and responsibilities of homeowners and low income tenants."

NATIONAL PEACE ACADEMY CAMPAIGN, 1625 I St. N.W., Washington, D.C. 20006. Filed for self 8/31/81. Legislative interest — "...establish a National Academy of Peace...."

PLAINTIFFS' ANTITRUST LIAISON SOCIETY, 1776 K St. N.W., Washington, D.C. 20006. Filed for self 8/20/81. Legislative interest — "S 1068 — Small Business Innovation and

Simplification Act of 1981, S 995 — Amendment to Clayton Act ... HR 1242...." Lobbyist — Terry S. Cohen.

STATE BAR OF TEXAS, Austin, Texas. Lobbyist — Cain & Smith, 402 Scarbrough Building, Austin, Texas. 78701. Filed 8/31/81. Legislative interest — "...amend section 457 of the Internal Revenue Code...."

September Registrations

Citizens' Groups

THE AMERICAN HUMANE ASSOCIATION, 9725 E. Hampden, Denver, Colo. 80231. Filed for self 9/8/81. Legislative interest — "...the prevention of cruelty to animals and children including H J Res 305, HR 4406, HR 666, HR 3823/S 1053." Lobbyist — Mary G. Knopke, 1828 L St. N.W., Washington, D.C. 20036.

AMERICAN LIFE LOBBY, 6 Library Court S.E., Washington, D.C. 20003. Filed for self 9/9/81. Legislative interest — "Support reduction in funding of the non-research programs of Title X of the Public Health Service Act." Lobbyist — Gary L. Curran, 328 F St. N.E., Washington, D.C. 20002.

COMMUNITY SERVICE SOCIETY, 105 East 22nd St., New York, N.Y. 10010. Filed for self 9/21/81. Legislative interest — "Domestic legislation relating to improving the welfare of the economically disadvantaged." Lobbyists — Adelin Cobden, Paul DuBrul, Eleanor Stier.

CONSUMERS FOR WORLD TRADE, 1346 Connecticut Ave. N.W., Washington, D.C. 20036. Filed for self 9/10/81. Legislative interest — "...against quotas on imported automobiles, shoes, textiles, etc., and in support of bills that encourage U.S. exports." Lobbyists — Doreen L. Brown, Lori Consadori.

LIBERTY LOBBY, 300 Independence Ave. S.E., Washington, D.C. 20003. Filed for self 9/2/81. Legislative interest — "...Genocide Treaty, Executive Treaty O (against); Monetary Control Act, HR 3599 (for) repeal; Freedom of Information Act S 587 (for); capital punishment S 114 (for)." Lobbyist — Patricia L. Katson.

NATIONAL AUDUBON SOCIETY, 645 Pennsylvania Ave. S.E., Washington, D.C. 20003. Filed for self 9/2/81. Legislative interest — "... S 342 - RARE II review bill — against; HR 3364 — National Minerals Security Act — against; HR 3252/S 1018 — Barrier Islands — for; HR 4057 — Mono Lake — for; Interior appropriations." Lobbyist — Alison Horton.

NATIONAL BOARD OF YOUNG MEN'S CHRISTIAN ASSOCIATIONS, 291 Broadway, New York, N.Y. 10007. Filed for self 9/29/81. Legislative interest — "...the Fisher-Conable above-the-line charitable contribution bill, CETA appropriations, Juvenile Justice & Delinquency Prevention Act appropriations, and the Urban Parks and Recreation Recovery Act appropriations." Lobbyist — Patty Bankson, 1725 K St. N.W., Washington, D.C. 20006.

NATIONAL CONGRESS OF PARENTS AND TEACHERS, 700 N. Rush St., Chicago, Ill. 60611. Filed for self 9/1/81. Legislative interest — "...welfare of children and youth in education, world understanding, social and economic well-being, health, child labor, juvenile protection, homemaking, consumer protection and environmental concerns...." Lobbyist — Manya S. Ungar, 10 Brandywine Court, Scotch Plains, N.J. 07076.

NATIONAL FAMILY PLANNING & REPRODUCTIVE HEALTH ASSOCIATION INC., 1110 Vermont Ave. N.W., Washington, D.C 20005. Filed for self 9/23/81. Legislative interest — "...reauthorization of Title X, Public Health Service Act, the Family Planning Services & Population Research Act, and all legislation affecting family planning services." Lobbyist — Scott R. Swirling.

PUEBLO DE COCHITI, Cochiti, N.M. Lobbyist — Wilkinson, Cragun & Barker, 1735 New York Ave., Washington, D.C. 20006. Filed 9/30/81. Legislative interest — "...Seeking legislative return of the Santa Cruz Spring Tract (a 24,000-acre parcel in New Mexico which abuts the Pueblo de Cochiti on the east)."

U.S.O. INC., Washington, D.C. Lobbyist — Gray and Co., 3255 Grace St. N.W., Washington, D.C. 20007. Filed 9/25/81. Legislative interest — "Including but not limited to legislation to permit erection of a statue in the District of Columbia."

WILDLIFE LEGISLATIVE FUND OF AMERICA, Columbus, Ohio. Lobbyist — Randal R. Bowman, 1050 17th St. N.W., Washington, D.C. 20036. Filed 9/23/81. Legislative interest — "Any legislation affecting hunting, fishing, trapping and wildlife management."

Corporations and Businesses

ALLIED FIDELITY CORP., Indianapolis, Ind. Lobbyist — Bayh, Tabbert & Capehart, 1575 I St. N.W., Washington, D.C. 20005. Filed 9/16/81. Legislative interest — "S 1554, S 1455...."

AMAX INC., Golden, Colo. Lobbyist — J. Michael Morgan, 2000 L St. N.W., Washington, D.C. 20036. Filed 9/11/81. Legislative interest — "Legislation affecting the leasing, mining and transportation of minerals."

AMERICAN RICE INC., Houston, Texas. Lobbyist — Cook, Purcell, Hansen & Henderson, 1015 18th St. N.W., Washington, D.C. 20036. Filed 9/23/81. (Former U.S. Rep. Graham Purcell, D-Texas, 1962-73, was listed as agent for this client.) Legislative interest — "Rice provisions of S 884 — Agriculture and Food Act of 1981, HR 3603 — Food and Agriculture Act of 1981, favor passage."

ANHEUSER-BUSCH COMPANIES INC., Washington, D.C. Lobbyist — Sam J. Ervin Jr., P.O. Box 69, Morganton, N.C. 28655. Filed 9/18/81. (Former U.S. sen., D-N.C., 1954-74; U.S. rep., 1946-47.) Legislative interest — "...S 995...."

ARCHER-DANIELS-MIDLAND CO., Decatur, Ill. Lobbyist — Mark A. Siegel & Associates Inc., 400 North Capitol St. N.W., Washington, D.C. 20001. Filed 9/3/81. Legislative interest — "Agriculture bill(s) and alcohol tariff." Lobbyist — Akin, Gump, Strauss, Hauer & Feld, 1333 New Hampshire Ave. N.W., Washington, D.C. 20036. Filed 9/12/81. Legislative interest — "...HR 1989, repeal of graduated duties on imported ethyl alcohol."

AVIS ENTERPRISES, Washington, D.C. Lobbyist — Gray and Co., 3255 Grace St. N.W., Washington, D.C. 20007. Filed 9/28/81. Legislative interest — "Including but not limited to tax legislation."

BENCO INC., 1625 I St. N.W., Washington, D.C. 20006. Filed for self 9/23/81. Legislative interest — "Amendments to HR 4242." Lobbyists — Nicholas A. Rizzo Jr., Moon Landrieu.

H & R BLOCK INC., 4410 Main St., Kansas City, Mo. 64111. Filed for self 9/30/81. Legislative interest — Not specified. Lobbyist — A. James Golato.

THE BOWERY SAVINGS BANK, 110 E. 42nd St.,New York, N.Y. 10007. Filed for self 9/14/81. Legislative interest — "...all-savers legislation (S 1279 and HR 3456) and the Regulatory Flexibility and Expanded Powers Act of 1981 (S 1413)."

J. C. BROCK CORP., Buffalo, N.Y. Lobbyist — Hodgson, Russ, Andrews, Woods & Goodyear, 1776 F St. N.W., Washington, D.C. 20006. Filed 9/11/81. Legislative interest — "In favor of HR 4075, S 1588 to suspend duty on imports of fresh and chilled carrots."

BROYHILL FURNITURE INDUSTRIES, Lenoir, N.C. Lobbyist — Dan Kuykendall, P.O. Box 40841, Washington, D.C. 20016. Filed 9/2/81. (Former U.S. rep., R-Tenn., 1967-75.) Legislative interest — "Economic recovery program."

BROYHILL MANAGEMENT CORP., Lenoir, N.C. Lobbyist — Dan Kuykendall, P.O. Box 40841, Washington, D.C. 20016. Filed 9/2/81. (Former U.S. rep., R-Tenn., 1967-75.) Legislative interest — "Economic recovery program."

BRUNSWICK CORP., Skokie, Ill. Lobbyist — Mayer, Brown & Platt, 888 17th St. N.W., Washington, D.C. 20006. Filed 9/30/81. Legislative interest — "Amendments to the Clayton Act and the Federal Trade Commission Act."

BUDD CO., Washington, D.C. Lobbyist — Gray and Co., 3255 Grace St. N.W., Washington, D.C. 20007. Filed 9/25/81.

Legislative interest — "Including but not limited to environmental and transportation legislation."

BURLINGTON INDUSTRIES INC., 1800 M St. N.W., Washington, D.C. 20036. Lobbyist — Anderson, Hibey, Nauheim & Blair, 1605 New Hampshire Ave. N.W., Washington, D.C. 20009. Filed 9/11/81. Legislative interest — "...S 995 and other legislation concerning antitrust contribution."

BURLINGTON NORTHERN INC., 413 New Jersey Ave. S.E., Washington, D.C. 20003. Filed for self 9/1/81. Legislative interest — "...railroad industry, trucking industry, air freight industry, timber industry, logging industry, lumber industry, natural resources, coal industry, gas industry, oil industry, real estate industry...." Lobbyist — Robin J. Carpenter.

CARGILL INC., Minneapolis, Minn. Lobbyist — Lord, Day & Lord, 1120 20th St. N.W., Washington, D.C. 20036. Filed 9/30/81. Legislative interest — "International tax and trade considerations."

CARGILL LEASING CORP., Minnetonka, Minn. Lobbyist — Lord, Day & Lord, 1120 20th St. N.W., Washington, D.C. 20036. Filed 9/30/81. Legislative interest — "United States income tax consideration."

CATERPILLAR TRACTOR CO., 100 N.E. Adams St., Peoria, Ill. 61629. Filed for self 9/14/81. Legislative interest — "S 1182 — for, HR 25 — for, HR 4016 — for, S 708 — for, HR 3136 — for." Lobbyists — Lawrence W. Carroll, Donald H. Defoe.

CHANCELLOR CORP., Boston, Mass. Lobbyist — Shea & Gould, 330 Madison Ave., New York, N.Y. 10017. Filed 9/1/81. Legislative interest — "Legislation regarding depreciation of leased equipment."

CHEVRON U.S.A. INC., 1700 K St. N.W., Washington, D.C. 20006. Filed for self 9/29/81. Legislative interest — "S Con Res 9, S 19, S 21, S 29, S 40, S 60, S 75, S 85, S 87 ... HR 5, HR 31, HR 45, HR 70, HR 85, HR 94, HR 215...." Lobbyist — Jane N. Scherer.

CONTINENTAL GRAIN CO., New York, N.Y. Lobbyist — Lord, Day & Lord, 1120 20th St. N.W., Washington, D.C. 20036. Filed 9/30/81. Legislative interest — "International tax and trade consideration."

COTTON BELT INSURANCE CO., New Orleans, La. Lobbyist — George L. Will, P.O. Box 010781, Miami, Fla. 33101. Filed 9/21/81. Legislative interest — "...S 1554 ... S 1853."

DEFENSE LOGISTICS SUPPLY CORP., Lobbyist — Gray and Co., 3255 Grace St. N.W., Washington, D.C. 20007. Filed 9/28/81. Legislative interest — "Including but not limited to defense and rules legislation."

DEKALB AGRESEARCH INC., Dekalb, Ill. Lobbyist — Sidley & Austin, 1730 Pennsylvania Ave. N.W., Washington, D.C. 20006. Filed 9/29/81. Legislative interest — "Tax legislation concerning single purpose agriculture structures, Farm Labor Contractor Registration Act Amendments (FLCRA)."

DOLLAR SAVINGS BANK, Washington, D.C. Lobbyist — Sullivan & Worcester, 1025 Connecticut Ave. N.W., Washington, D.C. 20036. Filed for self 9/11/81. Legislative interest — "...Bill proposed by the Federal financial regulatory agencies to deal with financially distressed depository institutions."

DOW CHEMICAL CO., Midland, Mich. Lobbyist — Kaye, Scholer, Fierman, Hays & Handler, 1575 I St. N.W., Washington, D.C. 20005. Filed 9/29/81. Legislative interest — "...section 991 of the Internal Revenue Code of 1954 (The Domestic International Sales Corporation)...."

ECONOPURE, Denver, Colo. Lobbyist — Benoit, Smith & Laughlin, 2001 Jefferson Davis Highway, Arlington, Va. 22202. Filed 9/23/81. Legislative interest — "Clean Air Act."

EL PASO NATURAL GAS CO., El Paso, Texas. Lobbyist — Gray and Co., 3255 Grace St. N.W., Washington, D.C. 20007. Filed 9/30/81. Legislative interest — "Including but not limited to natural gas legislation."

FTC COMMUNICATIONS INC., New York, N.Y. Lobbyist — Gardner, Carton & Douglas, 1875 I St. N.W., Washington, D.C. 20006. Filed 9/17/81. Legislative interest —"Revision of Communications Act; S 898, Telecommunications Competition and Deregulation Act of 1981."

GATES LEARJET CORP., 8220 West Harry, Wichita,

Kan. 67266. Filed for self 9/9/81. Legislative interest — Not specified. Lobbyist — William R. Edgar, 815 Connecticut Ave. N.W., Washington, D.C. 20006.

GENERAL TELEPHONE & ELECTRONICS CORP., Washington, D.C. 20036. Lobbyist — McNair, Glenn, Kondouras, Corley, Singletary, Porter & Dibble, P.O. Box 11390, Columbia, S.C. 29211. Filed 9/24/81. Legislative interest — "Patents S 255, antitrust, foreign trade, communications...." Lobbyist — Gray and Co., 3255 Grace St. N.W., Washington, D.C. 20007. Filed 9/30/81. Legislative interest — "Including but not limited to communications legislation." Lobbyist — Garvey, Schubert, Adams & Barer, 1000 Potomac St. N.W., Washington, D.C. 20007. Filed 9/4/81. Legislative interest — "S 898, Telecommunications Competition and Deregulation Act of 1981...."

GUAM OIL & REFINING CO. INC., Dallas, Texas. Lobbyist — Hogan & Hartson, 815 Connecticut Ave. N.W., Washington, D.C. 20006. Filed 9/5/81. Legislative interest — "...legislation to extend federal authority to allocate petroleum supplies during a supply disruption, including S 1503, S 409, S 1354." Lobbyist — Craig Hackler, 115 D St. S.E., Washington, D.C. 20003. Filed 9/21/81. Legislative interest — "Emergency Energy Allocation (S 409, S 445, S 1354, S 1476, S 1503, HR 4313)."

HAMILTON BROTHERS OIL & GAS CORP., Denver, Colo. Lobbyist — Arnold & Porter, 1200 New Hampshire Ave. N.W., Washington, D.C. 20036. Filed 9/28/81. Legislative interest — "...amendments to proposed U.S.-Canada tax convention (Exec T, 96th Congress, 2nd Session)."

HUGHES AIRCRAFT CO., Los Angeles, Calif. Lobbyist — Benoit, Smith & Laughlin, 2001 Jefferson Davis Highway, Arlington, Va. 22202. Filed 9/23/81. Legislative interest — "Revision of the Paris Convention of 1883 for the protection of industrial property and associated treaties and implementing federal legislation."

INTERNATIONAL PAPER CO., New York, N.Y. Lobbyist — Miller, Canfield, Paddock & Stone, 2500 Detroit Bank & Trust Bldg., Detroit, Mich. 48226. Filed 9/30/81. Legislative interest — "...S 995, HR 1242." Lobbyist — Steptoe & Johnson, 1250 Connecticut Ave. N.W., Washington, D.C. 20036. Filed 9/8/81. Legislative interest — "...S 995."

KIMBERLY-CLARK CORP., Arlington, Va. Lobbyist — O'Connor & Hannan, 1919 Pennsylvania Ave. N.W., Washington, D.C. 20006. Filed 9/14/81. Legislative interest — "A bill to amend the tariff schedules of the United States by creating an *eo nomine* classification for certain items."

LINCOLN PROPERTY CO., Las Vegas, Nev. Lobbyist — Shuffett, Kenton, Curry & Karem, 109 N. Mill St., Lexington, Ky. 40507. Filed 9/23/81. Legislative interest — "...apartment development and management."

MANAGEMENT INSIGHTS INC., Dallas, Texas. Lobbyist — Gray and Co., 3255 Grace St. N.W., Washington, D.C. 20007. Filed 9/16/81. Legislative interest — "HR 4242."

MCI TELECOMMUNICATIONS INC., Washington, D.C. Lobbyist — Patton, Boggs & Blow, 2550 M St. N.W., Washington, D.C. 20037. Filed 9/14/81. Legislative interest — "...S 898...."

MEAD CORP., Dayton, Ohio. Lobbyist — Miller, Cassidy, Larroca & Lewin, 2555 M St. N.W., Washington, D.C. 20037. Filed 9/15/81. Legislative interest — "S 995, a bill to amend the Clayton Act, 15 U.S.C., section 12...." Lobbyist — Sam J. Ervin Jr., P.O. Box 69, Morganton, N.C. 28655. Filed 9/18/81. (Former U.S. sen., D-N.C., 1954-74; U.S. rep., 1946-47.) Legislative interest — "...S 995...."

MOTOROLA INC., Schaumburg, Ill. Lobbyist — Gray and Co., 3255 Grace St. N.W., Washington, D.C. 20007. Filed 9/30/81. Legislative interest — "Including but not limited to communications legislation."

MUSIC CORPORATION OF AMERICA INC., Universal City, Calif. Lobbyist — Manatt, Phelps, Rothenberg & Tunney, 1200 New Hampshire Ave. N.W., Washington, D.C. 20036. Filed 9/17/81. (Former U.S. Rep. James C. Corman, D-Calif., 1961-81, was listed as agent for this client.) Legislative interest — "Tax and copyright legislation as it affects the movie industry."

NATIONAL MEDICAL ENTERPRISES INC., Los An-

geles, Calif. Lobbyist — Barrett, Hanna, Daly & Gaspar, 2550 M St. N.W., Washington, D.C. 20037. Filed 9/3/81. Legislative interest — "Tax allowances for the depreciation of buildings and equipment. Provisions affecting reimbursement of health care facilities. Operation and construction of health care facilities in foreign countries."

NATIONAL RURAL DEVELOPMENT & FINANCE CORP., 1300 19th St. N.W., Washington, D.C. 20036. Filed for self 9/17/81. Legislative interest — "Rural loan programs and rural community development programs in Department of Agriculture, CSA and EDA, their authorizations and appropriations." Lobbyist — Leander S. Foley III.

NORTHWEST ALASKAN PIPELINE CO., Washington, D.C. Lobbyist — Mayer, Brown & Platt, 888 17th St. N.W., Washington, D.C. 20006. Filed 9/11/81. Legislative interest — "Waivers of provisions of law as applied to the Alaskan natural gas transportation system that may be proposed to the Congress by the president, pursuant to section 8 of the Alaskan Natural Gas Transportation Act...." Lobbyist — Dilworth, Paxson, Kalish & Levy, 1819 H St. N.W., Washington, D.C. 20006. Filed 9/18/81. Legislative interest — "Congressional waivers pursuant to the Alaskan Natural Gas Transportation Act...."

OIL COUNTRY TUBULAR GOODS, Midland, Texas. Lobbyist — Dan Kuykendall, P.O. Box 40841, Washington, D.C. 20016. Filed 9/2/81. (Former U.S. rep., R-Tenn., 1967-75.) Legslative interest — "...the shortage of steel necessary for oil and gas exploration...."

PHILADELPHIA NATIONAL BANK, Philadelphia, Pa. Lobbyist — Metzger, Shadyac & Schwarz, One Farragut Square South, Washington, D.C. 20006. Filed 9/30/81. Legislative interest — "...general banking legislation." Filed for self 9/30/81. Legislative interest — Not specified. Lobbyist — Leslie F. Newcomer, 226 W. Rittenhouse Square, Philadelphia, Pa. 19101.

PIZZA HUT INC., Wichita, Kan. Lobbyist — Miles & Stockbridge, 1701 Pennsylvania Ave. N.W., Washington, D.C. 20006. Filed 9/30/81. Legislative interest — "...1981 Omnibus Farm bill, tax matters, labor (minimum wage legislation)."

PLANTERS PEANUTS, Suffolk, Va. Lobbyist — Cook, Purcell, Hansen & Henderson, 1015 18th St. N.W., Washington, D.C. 20036. Filed 9/23/81. (Former U.S. Rep. Graham Purcell, D-Texas, 1962-73, was listed as agent for this client.) Legislative interest — "Peanut provisions of S 884 — Agriculture and Food Act of 1981, HR 3603 — Food and Agriculture Act of 1981...."

ROCKY MOUNTAIN ENERGY CO., Broomfield, Colo. Lobbyist — J. Michael Morgan, 2000 L St. N.W., Washington, D.C. 20036. Filed 9/11/81. Legislative interest — "Legislation affecting the leasing, mining, and transportation of minerals."

THE SCOTT CO., 8 Jacana Road, Hilton Head, S.C. 29928. Filed for self 9/25/81. Legislative interest — "Legislation affecting coastal development — oppose restrictions on coastal development."

SHAKLEE CORP., 444 Market St., San Francisco, Calif. 94111. Filed for self 9/21/81. Legislative interest — "...Independent Contractor bill — S 8 (in support of); IRS Home Business Deduction — S 31 (in support of)." Lobbyist — Evelyn Jarvis-Ferris.

SOUTHERN PACIFIC COMMUNICATIONS CO., Burlington, Conn. Lobbyist — Davis, Wright, Todd, Riese & Jones, 1050 Thomas Jefferson St. N.W., Washington, D.C. 20007. Filed 9/21/81. Legislative interest — "S 898, Telecommunications Competition and Deregulation Act of 1981...."

SOUTHLAND-ARIZONA COLLEGES, Los Angeles, Calif. Lobbyist — Roger Tilles, 1111 19th St. N.W., Washington, D.C. 20036. Filed 9/17/81. Legislative interest — Not specified.

STERN ELECTRONICS INC., Chicago, Ill. Lobbyist — Sidley & Austin, 1730 Pennsylvania Ave. N.W., Washington, D.C. 20006. Filed 9/29/81. Legislative interest — "HR 1805 — copyright royalties."

TALISMAN FUND, Marina Del Rey, Calif. Lobbyist — Breed, Abbott & Morgan, 1875 I St. N.W., Washington, D.C. 20006. Filed 9/21/81. Legislative interest — "To permit forward contracts in foreign currencies to be marked mark to market for income tax purposes."

TEXAS AIR CORP., Houston, Texas. Lobbyist — Anderson, Hibey, Nauheim & Blair, 1605 New Hampshire Ave. N.W., Washington, D.C. 20009. Filed 9/11/81. Legislative interest — "...air carrier regulation, including but not limited to Washington Metropolitan Airports policy and acquisition of airlines."

THERAPEDIC, Rock Island, Ill. Lobbyist — Hill and Knowlton Inc., 1425 K St. N.W., Washington, D.C. 20005. Filed 9/25/81. Legislative interest — "Any legislation providing tax credits for purchase of fire resistant sleep products or otherwise promoting the use of such products."

TOSCO CORP., Los Angeles, Calif. Lobbyists — William J. Robinson, Frank Verrastro, 2000 L St. N.W., Washington, D.C. 20036. Filed 9/20/81. Legislative interest — "...reasonable and effective incentives for synthetic fuels development, energy impact assistance and energy tax laws...."

TRANS WORLD AIRLINES INC., Washington, D.C. Lobbyist — The Hannaford Co. Inc., 1225 19th St. N.W., Washington, D.C. 20036. Filed 9/28/81. Legislative interest — "...Warsaw convention, Montreal protocol and supplemental compensation plan."

TWIN CITY BARGE INC., South St. Paul, Minn. Lobbyist — Mark A. Siegel and Associates Inc., 400 North Capitol St. N.W., Washington, D.C. 20001. Filed 9/3/81. Legislative interest — "Proposed user fee charges for inland waterways."

UNION CARBIDE CORP., 270 Park Ave., New York, N.Y. 10017. Filed for self 9/2/81. Legislative interest — "International trade and investment legislation — Export trading company bill, Export-Import funding bills, foreign aid bills, modifications to the Foreign Corrupt Practices Act." Lobbyist — Richard M. Brennan.

WASHINGTON MUTUAL SAVINGS BANK, Washington, D.C. Lobbyist — Sullivan & Worcester, 1025 Connecticut Ave. N.W., Washington, D.C. 20036. Filed for self 9/11/81. Legislative interest — "...Bill proposed by the federal financial regulatory agencies to deal with financially distressed depository institutions."

WESTERN DEVELOPMENT, Washington, D.C. Lobbyist — Gray and Co., 3255 Grace St. N.W., Washington, D.C. 20007. Filed 9/28/81. Legislative interest — "Including but not limited to legislation concerning federally owned buildings in the District of Columbia."

WESTINGHOUSE BROADCASTING CO., New York, N.Y. Lobbyist — Gray and Co., 3255 Grace St. N.W., Washington, D.C. 20007. Filed 9/25/81. Legislative interest — "Including but not limited to communication legislation."

WESTVACO CORP., 299 Park Ave., New York, N.Y. 10171. Filed for self 9/18/81. Legislative interest — "...S 995...." Lobbyist — Sam J. Ervin Jr., P.O. Box 69, Morganton, N.C. 28655. (Former U.S. sen., D-N.C., 1954-74; U.S. rep. 1946-47.) Filed for self 9/24/81. Legislative interest — "S 995, Antitrust revision ... HR 1242, Antitrust revision...." Lobbyist — Thomas R. Long.

International Relations

REPUBLIC OF HAITI EMBASSY, Washington, D.C. Lobbyist — Anderson, Hibey, Nauheim & Blair, 1605 New Hampshire Ave. N.W., Washington, D.C 20009. Filed 9/11/81. Legislative interest — "...foreign aid, immigration and international agreements."

State and Local Governments

THE CITY OF KANSAS CITY, Kansas City, Mo. Lobbyist — Mark A. Siegel & Associates Inc., 400 N. Capitol St. N.W., Washington, D.C. 20001. Filed 9/3/81. Legislative interest — "Federal domestic assistance — urban mass transportation, community development block grants...."

GOVERNMENT OF AMERICAN SAMOA, Pago Pago, American Samoa. Lobbyist — Richard W. Bliss, 1899 L St. N.W., Washington, D.C. 20036. Filed 9/28/81. Legislative interest — "Clean Air Act, all legislation affecting environmental issues."

MIAMI CONSERVANCY DISTRICT, Dayton, Ohio. Lobbyist — Taft, Stettinius & Hollister, First National Bank

Center, Cincinnati, Ohio 45202 and 1800 Massachusetts Ave. N.W., Washington, D.C. 20036. Filed 9/23/81. Legislative interest — "...Rivers and Harbors Act and HR 777."

NATIONAL ASSOCIATION OF STATE AGENCIES FOR FOOD DISTRIBUTION, Albany, N.Y. Lobbyist — Cook, Purcell, Hansen & Henderson, 1015 18th St. N.W., Washington, D.C. 20036. Filed 9/23/81. (Former U.S. Rep. Graham Purcell, D-Texas, 1962-73, was listed as an agent for this client.) Legislative interest — Not specified.

SENATE OF PUERTO RICO, San Juan, Puerto Rico. Lobbyist — Richard M. Millman, 1730 M St. N.W., Washington, D.C. 20036. Filed 9/16/81. Legislative interest — "HR 3982...."

Trade Associations

AMERICAN BAKERS ASSOCIATION, 2020 K St. N.W., Washington, D.C. 20006. Filed for self 9/23/81. Legislative interest — "...S 1503 and related legislation." Lobbyist — Ira Dorfman.

AMERICAN BOILER MANUFACTURERS ASSOCIATION, 1500 Wilson Blvd., Arlington, Va. 22209. Filed for self 9/8/81. Legislative interest — "Energy and environmental issues...." Lobbyists — William H. Axtman, Russell N. Mosher.

AMERICAN BUSINESS COALITION, Baltimore, Md. Lobbyist — Thompson & Crawford, 1575 Eye St. N.W., Washington, D.C. 20005. Filed 9/21/81. Legislative interest — "...maintaining the present funding level for the Urban Development Action Grant Program."

AMERICAN NEWSPAPER PUBLISHERS ASSOCIATION, Washington, D.C. Lobbyist — Terese C. D'Alessio, 2020 N. 14th St., Arlington, Va. 22201. Filed 9/28/81. Legislative interest — "...S 898."

AMERICAN PUBLIC HEALTH ASSOCIATION, 1015 15th St. N.W., Washington, D.C. 20005. Filed for self 9/8/81. Legislative interest — "...national health policy ... effective public and private health and environmental health programming at federal, state and local levels." Lobbyists — Barbara W. Levine, Katherine S. McCarter.

AMERICAN WATERWAYS OPERATORS INC., Arlington, Va. Lobbyist — Lipsen & Hamberger, 1725 DeSales St. N.W., Washington, D.C. 20036. Filed 9/2/81. Legislative interest — Not specified.

ASSOCIATION OF AMERICAN PHYSICIANS AND SURGEONS, Burke, Va. Lobbyist — Fraser Associates, 1800 K St. N.W., Washington, D.C. 20006. Filed 9/25/81. Legislative interest — "...Medicare and Medicaid; general health legislation affecting the private practice of medicine."

COASTAL PROPERTIES INSTITUTE INC., P.O. Box 6255, Hilton Head, S.C. 29938. Filed for self 9/25/81. Legislative interest — "Legislation affecting coastal development — oppose restrictions on coastal development."

COMMITTEE OF PUBLICLY OWNED COMPANIES, New York, N.Y. Lobbyist — Vorys, Sater, Seymour & Pease, 1828 L St. N.W., Washington, D.C. 20036. Filed 9/14/81. Legislative interest — "...securities legislation, particularly amendments to the Williams Act."

ENERGY CONSUMERS AND PRODUCERS ASSOCIATION, Seminole, Okla. Lobbyist — Barrett, Hanna, Daly & Gaspar, 2550 M St. N.W., Washington, D.C. 20037. Filed 9/3/81. Legislative interest — "Taxation of domestic oil production regarding royalty interests and independent producers, including the Windfall Profits Tax. Against."

FLORIDA STATE HOSPICE ORGANIZATION INC., Miami, Fla. Lobbyist — Hogan & Hartson, 815 Connecticut Ave. N.W., Washington, D.C. 20006. Filed 9/4/81. Legislative interest — "...to amend Title 18 of the Social Security Act to include hospice care as a covered benefit."

HEALTH INSURANCE ASSOCIATION OF AMERICA, Washington, D.C. Lobbyist — Gray and Co., 3255 Grace St. N.W., Washington, D.C. 20007. Filed 9/28/81. Legislative interest — "Including but not limited to health insurance legislation."

INDEPENDENT TELECOMMUNICATIONS SUP-

PLIERS' COUNCIL, Washington, D.C. Lobbyist — Pierson, Ball & Dowd, 1200 18th St. N.W., Washington, D.C. 20036. Filed 9/17/81. Legislative interest — "Telecommunications Competition and Deregulation Act of 1981, S 898."

THE INSTITUTE OF INTERNAL AUDITORS INC., 249 Maitland Ave., Altamone Springs, Fla. 32701. Filed for self 9/15/81. Legislative interest — "...bills affecting the practice of internal auditing in either business or government." Lobbyist — Stanley C. Gross.

NATIONAL ASSOCIATION OF CHAIN DRUG STORES, Alexandria, Va. Lobbyist — Rogers, Hoge & Hills, 1111 19th St. N.W., Washington, D.C. 20036. Filed 9/25/81. Legislative interest — "...the practice of pharmacy and the operation of chain drug stores."

NATIONAL ASSOCIATION OF HOME BUILDERS, Washington, D.C. Lobbyist — Gray and Co., 3255 Grace St. N.W., Washington, D.C. 20007. Filed 9/25/81. Legislative interest — "Including but not limited to Job Corps and housing legislation."

NATIONAL ASSOCIATION OF NUMISMATIC PROFESSIONALS, Dallas, Texas. Lobbyist — O'Connor & Hannan, 1919 Pennsylvania Ave. N.W., Washington, D.C. 20006. Filed 9/30/81. Legislative interest — "...HR 4418 and S 1645."

NATIONAL ASSOCIATION OF REALTORS, 777 14th St. N.W., Washington, D.C. 20005. Filed for self 9/18/81. Legislative interest — "...fair housing legislation, depreciation revision, tax incentive for savings, condominium legislation, federal budget for fiscal years 1981 and 1982." Lobbyist — Micah S. Green.

NATIONAL FARM AND POWER EQUIPMENT DEALERS ASSOCIATION, St. Louis, Mo. Lobbyist — Smathers, Symington & Herlong, 1700 K St. N.W., Washington, D.C. 20006. Filed 9/9/81. Legislative interest — "Inventory tax matters, supporting S 1276, income tax matters."

NATIONAL GASOHOL COMMISSION, Lincoln, Neb. Lobbyist — Marilyn J. Herman, 2550 M St. N.W., Washington, D.C. 20037. Filed 9/16/81. Legislative interest — "Use and production of alcohol fuels, oppose HR 1989...."

NATIONAL OCEAN INDUSTRIES ASSOCIATION, 1100 17th St. N.W., Washington, D.C. 20036. Filed for self 9/30/81. Legislative interest — "...laws relative to oceanography, conservation and development of natural resources and environmental quality." Lobbyist — Richard A. Legatski.

NATIONAL OIL JOBBERS COUNCIL, 1707 H St. N.W., Washington, D.C. 20006. Filed for self 9/28/81. Legislative interest — "...deregulation of natural gas." Lobbyist — Mark O. Decker.

NATIONAL RESTAURANT ASSOCIATION, 311 First St. N.W., Washington, D.C. 20002. Filed for self 9/8/81. Legislative interest — "...legislation involving small business, labor laws, wages and hours, taxation, consumer protection, food marketing and economic stabilization." Lobbyists — Robert E. Bradford, J. Ballad Everett, Elizabeth E. Hendrix, James T. Rogers, Patrick A. Davis.

NORTHWEST INLAND WATERWAYS COMMITTEE, Portland, Ore. Lobbyist — Schwabe, Williamson, Wyatt, Moore & Roberts, 1200 Standard Plaza, Portland, Ore. 97204. Filed 9/14/81. (Former U.S. Rep. Wendell Wyatt, R-Ore., 1964-75, was listed as agent for this client.) Legislative interest — "To oppose HR 2962 and HR 2384...."

OFFSHORE INDUSTRY COMMITTEE, Washington, D.C. Lobbyist — David P. Stang, 1629 K St. N.W., Washington, D.C. 20006. Filed 9/28/81. Legislative interest — Not specified.

STEAMSHIP CONFERENCES, Washington, D.C. Lobbyist — Billig, Sher & Jones, 2033 K St. N.W., Washington, D.C. 20006. Filed 9/23/81. Legislative interest — "...S 1593, S 125, HR 4374."

TELE-CAUSE, Washington, D.C. Lobbyist — O'Connor & Hannan, 1919 Pennsylvania Ave. N.W., Washington, D.C. 20006. Filed 9/14/81. Legislative interest — "Seek amendments to S 898...." Lobbyist — Pierson, Ball & Dowd, 1200 18th St. N.W., Washington, D.C. Filed 9/4/81. Legislative interest — "... Telecommunications Competition and Deregulation Act of 1981, S 898."

UNI-BELL PLASTIC PIPE ASSOCIATION, 2655 Villa Creek Drive, Dallas, Texas 75234. Filed for self 9/18/81. Legislative interest — "Legislation affecting the plastic pipe industry." Lobbyist — William D. Nesbeitt.

UTILITY GROUP, Washington, D.C. Lobbyist — Reid & Priest, 1111 19th St. N.W., Washington, D.C. 20036. Filed 9/24/81. Legislative interest — "Revision of section 3 of the Public Utility Holding Company Act of 1935."

WASHINGTON PSYCHIATRIC SOCIETY, Washington, D.C. Lobbyist — Roger Tilles, 1111 19th St. N.W., Washington, D.C. 20036. Filed 9/17/81. Legislative interest — "...Federal Employee Health Benefits Program."

Miscellaneous

CENTER FOR LAW AND EDUCATION INC., 6 Appian Way, Cambridge, Mass. 02138. Filed for self 9/18/81. Legislative interest — "...HR 1079, HR 4410, S 1361, HR 1662, S J Res 41, S 528, HR 3480, S 1533." Lobbyists — Diana Pullin, 236 Massachusetts Ave. N.W., Washington, D.C. 20002; Paul Weckstein.

RUDOLPH N. D'AGARIS, 15 W. Montgomery Ave., Rockville, Md. 20850. Filed for self 9/21/81. Legislative interest — Not specified.

NATHAN FRED MARKS, 685 8th St., Gresham, Ore. 97030. Filed for self 9/22/81. Legislative interest — "Transportation, Interstate Commerce Act ... Motor Carriers Act...."

October Registrations

Citizens' Groups

ALLIANCE TO SAVE ENERGY, 1925 K St. N.W., Washington, D.C. 20006. Filed for self 10/15/81. Legislative interest — "Promotion of energy efficiency. Authorizations, appropriations, tax credits, depreciation provisions and other financial incentives promoting energy efficiency...." Lobbyists — Edward Lyle, Robert Rauch.

CAMPAIGN FOR COMMUNITY ECONOMIC DEVELOPMENT, Washington, D.C. Lobbyist — Leander J. Foley III, 267 Cape St. John Rd., Cape St. John, Md. 21401. Filed 10/14/81. Legislative interest — "Community Services Block Grant Act of 1981."

COMMITTEE FOR HUMANE LEGISLATION, New York, N.Y. Lobbyist — Sanford D. Horwitt, 5935 N. 5th Rd., Arlington, Va. 21203. Filed 10/14/81. Legislative interest — "Wildlife conservation and animal protection, reform of Pittman-Robertson Act, leg-hold trap reform."

FRIENDS OF ANIMALS INC., New York, N.Y. Lobbyist — Sanford D. Horwitt, 5935 N. 5th Rd., Arlington, Va. 21203. Filed 10/14/81. Legislative interest — "Wildlife conservation and animal protection, reform of Pittman-Robertson Act, leg-hold trap reform."

HEALTH RESEARCH GROUP, 2000 P St. N.W, Washington, D.C. 20036. Filed for self 10/15/81. Legislative interest — "All health care legislation, and particularly that pertaining to medical devices." Lobbyist — Allen Greenberg.

NATIONAL AUDUBON SOCIETY, 645 Pennsylvania Ave. S.E., Washington, D.C. 20003. Filed for self 10/5/81. Legislative interest — "...wildlife and management of public lands and waters...Endangered Species Act (for), Clean Water Act, HR 3252/S 1018 Barrier Islands (for)." Lobbyist — Amos S. Eno.

NATIONAL ORGANIZATION FOR WOMEN, 425 13th St. N.W., Washington, D.C. 20004. Filed for self 10/13/81. Legislative interest — "Women's rights legislation in general and especially anti-abortion bills and amendments...." Lobbyist — Ellen Griffee.

RENEWABLE ENERGY INSTITUTE, 1050 17th St. N.W., Washington, D.C. 20036. Filed for self 10/15/81. Legislative interest — "Generally, in support of renewable energy technology development and utilization." Lobbyist — John W. Wilson.

SIERRA CLUB, 530 Bush St., San Francisco, Calif. 94108. Filed for self 10/6/81. Legislative interest — "Energy matters...." Lobbyist — Brooks B. Yeager, 330 Pennsylvania Ave. S.E., Washington, D.C. 20003.

UPPER HUMBOLDT RIVER WATER USERS ASSOCIATION, Elko, Nev. Lobbyist — Leva, Hawes, Symington, Martin & Oppenheimer, 815 Connecticut Ave. N.W., Washington, D.C. 20006. Filed 10/13/81. Legislative interest — "Appropriations bill - energy and water projects, fiscal year 1982."

Corporations and Businesses

ADVANCED HEALTH SYSTEMS INC., Irvine, Calif. Lobbyist — Perito, Duerk, Carlson & Pinco, 1140 Connecticut Ave. N.W., Washington, D.C. 20036. Filed 10/13/81. Legislative interest — "Legislation which may affect Medicare coverage and reimbursement for alcoholism treatment."

AMERADA HESS CORP., New York, N.Y. Lobbyist — Akin, Gump, Strauss, Hauer & Feld, 1333 New Hampshire Ave. N.W., Washington, D.C. 20036. Filed 10/1/81. Legislative interest — "...S 1503, the Standby Petroleum Allocation Act of 1981."

AMERICAN PACIFIC INTERNATIONAL INC., Los Angeles, Calif. Lobbyist — Manatt, Phelps, Rothenberg & Tunney, 1200 New Hampshire Ave. N.W., Washington, D.C. 20036. Filed 10/8/81. (Former U.S. Rep. James C. Corman, D-Calif., 1961-81, was listed as agent for this client.) Legislative interest — "Change in the Windfall Profits Tax for independent producers."

AVON PRODUCTS INC., 9 West 57th St., New York, N.Y. 10019. Filed for self 10/15/81. Legislative interest — "...government regulation of the manufacture and distribution of products, the environment and taxation." Lobbyist — Robert R. McMillan.

BENEFICIAL MANAGEMENT CORPORATION OF AMERICA, Morristown, N.J. Lobbyist — Wexler and Associates Inc., 1616 H St. N.W., Washington, D.C. 20006. Filed 10/9/81. Legislative interest — "...legislation affecting the bankruptcy code...." Lobbyist — Daniel A. Dutko, 412 First St. S.E., Washington, D.C. 20003. Filed 10/8/81. Legislative interest — "Consumer financing issues, i.e. Bankruptcy Act amendments; federal usury legislation, HR 2501, generally for."

THE BROOKLYN UNION GAS CO., 195 Montague St., Brooklyn, N.Y. 11201. Filed for self 10/9/81. Legislative interest — "...tax legislation relating to the natural gas industry, in particular S 765." Lobbyist — Fred J. Gentile.

BRUNSWICK CORP., One Brunswick Plaza, Skokie, Ill. 60077. Filed for self 10/5/81. Legislative interest — "Taxation, international trade, antitrust and regulatory matters pertaining to recreation, medical supply, transportation, defense and energy industries." Lobbyist — Ralph A. Biedermann.

BURLINGTON INDUSTRIES, Washington, D.C. Lobbyist — Willkie, Farr & Gallagher, 818 Connecticut Ave. N.W., Washington, D.C. 20036. Filed 10/2/81. Legislative interest — "Antitrust contribution bill, S 995...."

CABOT CORP., Boston, Mass. Lobbyist — Vorys, Sater, Seymour & Pease, 1828 L St. N.W., Washington, D.C. 20036. Filed 10/15/81. Legislative interest — "...Public Utility Companies Holding Act."

CINCINNATI MILACRON, Cincinnati, Ohio. Lobbyist — Shea & Gould, 330 Madison Ave., New York, N.Y. 10017. Filed 10/10/81. Legislative interest — "Section 904 (f) Internal Revenue Code."

THE COASTAL CORP., 9 Greenway Plaza, Houston, Texas 77046. Filed for self 10/13/81. Legislative interest — "...Windfall profits tax law 26 U.S.C., sec. 4994, et seq.; standby authority for petroleum supply interruptions, S 409; tax cut bill." Lobbyist — Carla J. Bishop.

CROWLEY MARITIME CORP., Seattle, Wash. Lobbyist — Preston, Thorgrimson, Ellis & Holman, 1776 G St. N.W., Washington, D.C. 20006. Filed 10/13/81. Legislative interest — "...support of HR 4278 and related legislation affecting the Alaska Railroad."

CUMMINS ENGINE CO. INC., Columbus, Ind. Lobbyist — Winston & Strawn, 2550 M St. N.W., Washington, D.C. 20037.

Filed 10/1/81. Legislative interest — "Clean Air Act (including HR 4400)."

DILWORTH, PAXSON, KALISH & LEVY, Washington, D.C. Lobbyist — Bricker & Eckler, 1301 Pennsylvania Ave. N.W., Washington, D.C. 20004. Filed 10/10/81. (Former U.S. Rep. Samuel L. Devine, R-Ohio, 1959-81, was listed as agent for this client.) Legislative interest — "Financing of the Alaskan natural gas transportation system."

DOW CHEMICAL CO., Midland, Mich. Lobbyist — Cole & Corette, 1200 17th St. N.W., Washington, D.C. 20036. Filed 10/13/81. Legislative interest — "...26 U.S.C. 991-999 (Internal Revenue Code of 1954)...Domestic International Sales Corporation provisions."

EATON ASSOCIATES INC., 1750 K St. N.W., Washington, D.C. 20006. Filed for self 10/15/81. Legislative interest — "...energy programs, space programs and national defense." Lobbyist — Charles H. S. Eaton.

EDS CORP., 229 Pennsylvania Ave. S.E., Washington, D.C. 20003. Filed for self 10/10/81. Legislative interest — "...health care, national health insurance, banking, insurance, retailing and utilities." Lobbyist — Julia A. Turner.

ETHYL CORP., 1155 15th St. N.W., Washington, D.C. 20005. Filed for self 10/8/81. Legislative interest — "Clean Air Act amendments, superfund amendments, export of hazardous substances policy, Toxic Substances Control Act amendments, Coal Conversion Act, natural gas policy, capital cost recovery, tax reform, Food, Drug & Cosmetic Act amendments, Federal Insecticide, Fungicide & Rodenticide Act." Lobbyist — Barbara A. Little.

FLUOR CORP., Irvine, Calif. Lobbyist — Califano, Ross & Heineman, 1575 Eye St. N.W., Washington, D.C. 20005. Filed 10/9/81. Legislative interest — "Bills to amend the Internal Revenue Code of 1954 with respect to the treatment of foreign construction activities...."

GENENTECH INC., South San Francisco, Calif. Lobbyist — Pierson, Ball & Dowd, 1200 18th St. N.W., Washington, D.C. 20036. Filed 10/9/81. Legislative interest — "Recombinant DNA issues and patent restoration legislation (S 255, HR 1937)."

GENERAL TELEPHONE AND ELECTRONICS CORP., Stamford, Conn. Lobbyist — Mayer, Brown & Platt, 888 17th St. N.W., Washington, D.C. 20006. Filed 10/1/81. Legislative interest — "S 898."

GEORGIA PACIFIC CORP., Portland, Ore. Lobbyist — Venable, Baetjer, Howard & Civiletti, 1301 Pennsylvania Ave. N.W., Washington, D.C. 20004. Filed 10/2/81. Legislative interest — "...S 995, HR 1242, HR 4072."

GPU SERVICE CORP., 100 Interpace Parkway, Parsippany, N.J. 07054. Filed for self 10/8/81. Legislative interest — "Nuclear Regulatory Commission, fiscal year 1982 authorization; Department of Energy, fiscal year 1982 authorization; nuclear waste disposal, Three Mile Island federal aid, Clean Air Act." Lobbyist — Cynthia Mansfield, 1800 M St. N.W., Washington, D.C. 20036.

HOBBS CONSTRUCTION & DEVELOPMENT CO. INC., Panama City, Fla. Lobbyist — Cramer & Cramer, 1320 19th St. N.W., Washington, D.C. 20036. Filed 10/8/81. (Former U.S. Rep. William C. Cramer, R-Fla., 1955-71, was listed among agents for this client.) Legislative interest — "General oversight activities regarding S 533 and its application to the construction of federal buildings."

HOOKER INVESTMENTS LTD., Nashville, Tenn. Lobbyist — Pepper, Hamilton & Scheetz, 1776 F St. N.W., Washington, D.C. 20006. Filed 10/13/81. Legislative interest — "Tax legislation affecting enhanced oil recovery. Economic Recovery Tax Act of 1981...."

HUGHES HELICOPTERS INC., Culver City, Calif. Lobbyist — Jim Lloyd, 3240 Whitebirch Dr., West Covina, Calif. 91793. Filed 10/14/81. (Former U.S. rep., D-Calif., 1975-81.) Legislative interest — "All legislation involving AAH and AHIP in authorization and appropriation committees."

HWL PROPERTIES, Tarzana, Calif. Lobbyist — Silverstein and Mullens, 1776 K St. N.W., Washington, D.C. 20006. Filed 10/13/81. Legislative interest — Not specified.

INGERSOLL JOHNSON STEEL CO., P.O. Box 370, New Castle, Ind. 47362. Filed for self 10/14/81. Legislative interest — "...oppose passage of HR 2485...." Lobbyist — George W. Stamm.

LEONARD, KOEHN, ROSE AND HURT, 1025 Connecticut Ave. N.W., Washington, D.C. 20036. Filed for self 10/2/81. Legislative interest — "...Voting Rights Act of 1964, 42 U.S.C. 1973." Lobbyist — Jay D. Terry.

THE LTV CORP., Dallas, Texas. Filed for self 10/13/81. Legislative interest — "...steel and ferrous metal materials and fabrications and aerospace and ground transportation vehicles and equipment, including energy, tax, procurement and regulatory matters." Lobbyist — Gael M. Sullivan, 1155 15th St. N.W., Washington, D.C. 20005.

MCI COMMUNICATIONS CORP., 1133 19th St. N.W., Washington, D.C. 20036. Filed for self 10/9/81. Legislative interest — "...S 898...." Lobbyist — Robert S. Jackson.

THE MEAD CORP., Dayton, Ohio. Lobbyist — Jones, Jones, Bell, Close & Brown, 1000 Potomac St. N.W., Washington, D.C. 20007. Filed 10/8/81. Legislative interest — "...HR 4072, HR 1242 and S 995." Lobbyist — Venable, Baetjer, Howard & Civiletti, 1301 Pennsylvania Ave. N.W., Washington, D.C. 20004. Filed 10/2/81. Legislative interest — "...S 995, HR 1242, HR 4072."

WILLIAM M. MERCER INC., New York, N.Y. Lobbyist — Peter Small & Associates Inc., 400 Madison Ave., New York, N.Y. 10017. Filed 10/9/81. Legislative interest — "...income tax legislation, Social Security, executive compensation, etc."

MERRILL LYNCH WHITE WELD CAPITAL MARKETS GROUP, New York, N.Y. Lobbyist — The Hannaford Co. Inc., 1225 19th St. N.W., Washington, D.C. 20036. Filed 10/15/81. Legislative interest — "...government assets redeployment, alternate financing of quasi-government agencies and matters involving leasing of government facilities."

MILLIKEN & CO., Spartanburg, S.C. Lobbyist — Kirkland & Ellis, 1776 K St. N.W., Washington, D.C. 20006. Filed 10/28/81. Legislative interest — "...amend S 995...."

MUTUAL SAVINGS CENTRAL FUND INC., Boston, Mass. Lobbyist — Leighton, Conklin, Lemov, Jacobs & Buckley, 2033 M St. N.W., Washington, D.C. 20036. Filed 10/9/81. Legislative interest — "...proposals affecting deposit insurance."

NATIONAL BROADCASTING CO. INC., 1825 K St. N.W., Washington, D.C. 20006. Filed for self 10/8/81. Legislative interest — "...HR 1805, HR 3528, S 601, S 270 and S 821." Lobbyist — Dan C. Tate.

NLT CORP., Nashville, Tenn. Lobbyist — Davis, Polk & Wardwell, 1575 Eye St. N.W., Washington, D.C. 20005. Filed 10/13/81. Legislative interest — "Legislation relating to management interlocks."

NORTHWEST ALASKAN PIPELINE CO., Washington, D.C. Lobbyist — White, Fine & Verville, 1156 15th St. N.W., Washington, D.C. 20005. Filed 10/14/81. Legislative interest — "For certain waivers of law pursuant to the Alaska Natural Gas Transportation Act of 1976 (PL 94-586)."

O'CONNOR & HANNAN, Washington, D.C. Lobbyist — Bricker & Eckler, 1301 Pennsylvania Ave. N.W., Washington, D.C. 20004. Filed 10/10/81. (Former U.S. Rep. Samuel L. Devine, R-Ohio, 1959-81, was listed as agent for this client.) Legislative interest — "Coal severance tax legislation, HR 1313 and S 178."

PERPETUAL AMERICAN FEDERAL SAVINGS AND LOAN ASSOCIATION, Washington, D.C. Lobbyist — Capital Counselors Inc., 1700 K St. N.W., Washington, D.C. 20006. Filed 10/7/81. Legislative interest — "Legislation affecting interstate branching of savings and loans."

PETRO-LEWIS CORP., Denver, Colo. Lobbyist — Fulbright & Jaworski, 1150 Connecticut Ave. N.W., Washington, D.C. 20036. Filed 10/13/81. Legislative interest — "...HR 4626 and S 1660...."

ROHM AND HAAS CO., Philadelphia, Pa. Lobbyist — Geoffrey B. Hurwitz, 1899 L St. N.W., Washington, D.C. 20036. Filed 10/9/81. Legislative interest — "...manufacture, use and sale of chemicals and allied products."

SAENZ INTERNATIONAL INC., P.O. Box 1556, Springfield, Va. 22151. Filed for self 10/5/81. Legislative interest —

"...educational benefits given to those [who] have served in the armed forces of the U.S.A."

SNELLING AND SNELLING INC., Sarasota, Fla. Lobbyist — Collier, Shannon, Rill & Scott, 1055 Thomas Jefferson St. N.W., Washington, D.C. 20007. Filed 10/8/81. Legislative interest — "Enactment of legislation to encourage the use of private sector employment services by federal and state agencies."

SOUTHERN PACIFIC COMMUNICATION CO., Washington, D.C. Lobbyist — Pepper, Hamilton & Scheetz, 1776 F St. N.W., Washington, D.C. 20006. Filed 10/13/81. Legislative interest — "S 898...."

SOUTHERN PACIFIC COMMUNICATIONS CO., Burlington, Calif. Lobbyist — Davis, Wright, Todd, Riese & Jones, 1050 Thomas Jefferson St. N.W., Washington, D.C. 20007. Filed 10/5/81. Legislative interest — "S 898...."

SPERRY CORP., 2000 L St. N.W., Washington, D.C. 20036. Filed for self 10/15/81. Legislative interest — "...taxes, communications, agriculture, international affairs and regulations." Lobbyist — Elizabeth W. Pierson.

STANDARD OIL COMPANY OF INDIANA, Chicago, Ill. Filed for self 10/13/81. Legislative interest — "...national energy policy - natural gas; public lands - Outer Continental Shelf; environmental; antitrust and monopoly." Lobbyist — Don J. Zeller, 1000 16th St. N.W., Washington, D.C. 20036.

STANDARD OIL COMPANY OF OHIO, Cleveland, Ohio. Filed for self 10/9/81. Legislative interest — "...petroleum products, refining and distribution, petro-chemicals, coal and metal/non-metal minerals." Lobbyist — Marshall E. Whitenton, 1050 17th St. N.W., Washington, D.C. 20036.

TEXACO INC., White Plains, N.Y. Filed for self 10/10/81. Legislative interest — Not specified. Lobbyist — James C. Pruitt, 1050 17th St. N.W., Washington, D.C. 20036.

TIME INC., Washington, D.C. Lobbyist — Blum & Nash, 1015 18th St. N.W., Washington, D.C. 20036. Filed 10/8/81. Legislative interest — "Legislation affecting the cable television industry, including S 898."

U.S. TELEPHONE COMMUNICATIONS INC., Dallas, Texas. Lobbyist — Coudert Brothers, One Farragut Square South, Washington, D.C. 20006. Filed 10/9/81. Legislative interest — "...S 898...."

VGS CORP., Washington, D.C. Lobbyist — Foley, Lardner, Hollabaugh & Jacobs, 1775 Pennsylvania Ave. N.W., Washington, D.C. 20006. Filed 10/30/81. Legislative interest — "Energy-related legislation, including S 1503 and HR 4700."

WESTVACO CORP., New York, N.Y. Lobbyist — Venable, Baetjer, Howard & Civiletti, 1301 Pennsylvania Ave. N.W., Washington, D.C. 20004. Filed 10/2/81. Legislative interest — "...S 995, HR 1242, HR 4072."

WIEN AIR ALASKA, Washington, D.C. Lobbyist — Jim Lloyd, 3240 Whitebirch Dr., West Covina, Calif. 91793. Filed 10/14/81. (Former U.S. rep., D-Calif., 1975-81.) Legislative interest — "All legislation involving air transportation regulations 406/419."

Labor Groups

AMALGAMATED CLOTHING AND TEXTILE WORKERS UNION, New York, N.Y. Filed for self 10/7/81. Legislative interest — "Trade adjustment assistance, OSHA, Clean Air Act, Hobbs Act, natural gas deregulation, child care." Lobbyist — Paul J. Mignini Sr., 815 16th St. N.W., Washington, D.C. 20006.

INDUSTRIAL UNION DEPARTMENT, AFL-CIO, 815 16th St. N.W, Washington, D.C. 20006. Filed for self 10/10/81. Legislative interest — "...trade, OSHA, pension and employment legislation." Lobbyist — Mark Finkelstein.

State and Local Governments

BRAZOS RIVER AUTHORITY, Waco, Texas. Lobbyist — Ray Roberts & Associates, 499 S. Capitol St. S.W., Washington,

D.C. 20003. Filed 10/9/81. (Former U.S. Rep. Ray Roberts, D-Texas, 1962-81, was listed as agent for this client.) Legislative interest — "Corps of Engineers and reclamation water projects and appropriations for same."

FLATHEAD JOINT BOARD OF CONTROL, Moiese, Mont. Lobbyist — Sutherland, Asbill & Brennan, 1666 K St. N.W., Washington, D.C. 20006. Filed 10/1/81. Legislative interest — "...HR 4035 (Interior Department appropriation bill) to increase the $75,000 limitation that section 6 of the Act of May 25, 1948 (62 Stat. 269, 273) places upon the use of net power revenues standing to the credit of the Flathead Irrigation Project, Montana."

Trade Associations

AMERICAN COUNCIL OF LIFE INSURANCE INC., 1850 K St. N.W., Washington, D.C. 20006. Filed for self 10/9/81. Legislative interest — Not specified. Lobbyist — Carl B. Wilkerson.

AMERICAN GREYHOUND TRACK OPERATORS ASSOCIATION, North Miami, Fla. Lobbyist — Arthur E. Cameron, 499 S. Capitol St. S.W., Washington, D.C. 20003. Filed 10/13/81. Legislative interest — "HR 4592."

AMERICAN MEAT INSTITUTE, P.O. Box 3556, Washington, D.C. 20007. Filed for self 10/13/81. Legislative interest — "...livestock production and feeding, animal diseases, meat inspection, food additives, labeling, transportation, environmental protection, safety, trade practices, consumer protection, energy, food safety, regulatory reform." Lobbyist — Stephen E. Eure.

AMERICAN MINING CONGRESS, 1920 N St. N.W., Washington, D.C. 20036. Filed for self 10/10/81. Legislative interest — "...income taxation, social security, public lands, monetary policy, mine safety, stockpiling, environmental quality control, etc." Lobbyist — Edward Johnson.

AMUSEMENT DEVICE MANUFACTURERS ASSOCIATION, Des Plaines, Ill. Lobbyist — Rufus King, 910 17th St. N.W., Washington, D.C. 20006. Filed 10/10/81. Legislative interest — Not specified.

ANIMAL HEALTH INSTITUTE, Alexandria, Va. Lobbyist — Frederick A. Kessinger, 1201 4th St. S.W., Washington, D.C. 20024. Filed 10/14/81. Legislative interest — "Amendments to the Federal Food, Drug & Cosmetic Act and other legislation affecting producers of animal health and nutrition products."

CIGAR ASSOCIATION OF AMERICA INC., 1120 19th St. N.W., Washington, D.C. 20036. Filed for self 10/5/81. Legislative interest — "...changes in the excise taxes on cigars." Lobbyist — Norman F. Sharp.

COLORADO SKI COUNTRY U.S.A., 1410 Grant St., Denver, Colo. 80203. Filed for self 10/8/81. Legislative interest — "...recreational use of public lands." Lobbyist — Robert L. Knous Jr.

COMMUTER AIRLINE ASSOCIATION OF AMERICA, Washington, D.C. Lobbyist — Jim Lloyd, 3240 Whitebirch Dr., West Covina, Calif. 91793. Filed 10/14/81. (Former U.S. rep., D-Calif., 1975-81.) Legislative interest — "All legislation involving joint fares for commuter airlines."

COMPUTER AND COMMUNICATIONS INDUSTRY ASSOCIATION, Arlington, Va. Lobbyist — Cohen & White, 1218 16th St. N.W., Washington, D.C. 20036. Filed 10/9/81. Legislative interest — "Federal ADP procurement legislation. HR 2580 - oppose; PL 89-306 - support; HR 3915 - oppose."

THE CONSUMER BANKERS ASSOCIATION, 1300 N. 17th St., Arlington, Va. 22209. Filed for self 10/13/81. Legislative interest — "HR 2501, S 1406." Lobbyist — Maryann M. Kaswell.

ELECTRONIC INDUSTRIES ASSOCIATION OF JAPAN, Tokyo, Japan. Lobbyist — Edelman International Corp., 1730 Pennsylvania Ave. N.W., Washington, D.C. 20006. Filed

10/9/81. Legislative interest — "Unitary tax legislation. HR 1983, S 655."

INFECTIOUS DISEASES SOCIETY OF AMERICA, Rochester, N.Y. Lobbyist — Pierson, Ball & Dowd, 1200 18th St. N.W., Washington, D.C. 20036. Filed 10/9/81. Legislative interest — "Legislation (substantive and appropriations) relating to biomedical research."

LEGISLATIVE ALLIANCE OF PHILATELISTS AND HARD ASSET DEALERS AND COLLECTORS, New York, N.Y. Lobbyist — O'Neill and Haase, 1333 New Hampshire Ave. N.W., Washington, D.C. 20036. Filed 10/13/81. Legislative interest — "...repeal of section 314(b) of the Economic Recovery Tax Act of 1981."

NATIONAL ASSOCIATION OF BROADCASTERS, 1771 N St. N.W., Washington, D.C. 20036. Filed for self 10/13/81. Legislative interest — "...amendments relating to Communications Act of 1934...Copyright Law of 1909...Communications Satellite Act of 1962...regulation of advertising, taxation, appropriations, public broadcasting, newsmen's privilege and consumer protection." Lobbyist — James J. Popham.

NATIONAL BEER WHOLESALERS' ASSOCIATION, 5205 Leesburg Pike, Falls Church, Va. 22041. Filed for self 10/8/81. Legislative interest — "Passage of the Malt Beverage Interbrand Competition Act (HR 3269 and S 1215)...." Lobbyist — Richard B. Thornburg.

NATIONAL CATTLEMEN'S ASSOCIATION, Denver, Colo. Lobbyist — Thomas M. Cook, 425 13th St. N.W., Washington, D.C. 20004. Filed 10/13/81. Legislative interest — "Appropriations acts: Department of Agriculture, Department of Interior and independent agencies...1981 Farm bill...HR 3603, HR 2561 and S 884.... school lunch program: supported continuing the present food commodity purchase and distribution program while pilot project on alternate cash system is studied - HR 3077, et al...."

NATIONAL COTTON COUNCIL OF AMERICA, P.O. Box 12285, Memphis, Tenn. 38112. Filed for self 10/29/81. Legislative interest — Not specified. Lobbyist — Jesse P. Brown Jr.

NATIONAL MUSIC PUBLISHERS' ASSOCIATION, New York, N.Y. Lobbyist — Paskus, Gordon & Hyman, 1919 Pennsylvania Ave. N.W., Washington, D.C. 20006. Filed 10/9/81.

Legislative interest — "...Copyright Act (Title 17 U.S.C.) and in favor of amendments to HR 3530 and S 691, bills to amend the copyright laws to strengthen the penalties for record and tape piracy...."

NATURAL GAS SUPPLY ASSOCIATION, 1025 Connecticut Ave. N.W., Washington, D.C. 20036. Filed for self 10/5/81. Legislative interest — "...oversight of the Natural Gas Policy Act of 1978...." Lobbyist — Eliza Demetree. Lobbyist — Camp, Carmouche, Palmer, Barsh & Hunter, 2550 M St. N.W., Washington, D.C. 20037. Filed 10/2/81. Legislative interest — "...legislation affecting the production, transportation, distribution and marketing of natural gas...."

SECURITIES INDUSTRY ASSOCIATION, New York, N.Y. Lobbyist — Mintz, Levin, Cohn, Ferris, Glovsky & Popeo, 1015 15th St. N.W., Washington, D.C. 20005. Filed 10/9/81. Legislative interest — "Bills related to revenue bond underwriting, including HR 2828."

SLURRY TRANSPORT ASSOCIATION, Washington, D.C. Lobbyist — Vinson & Elkins, 1101 Connecticut Ave. N.W., Washington, D.C. 20036. Filed 10/9/81. Legislative interest — "...natural gas industry and supporting eminent domain for coal slurry pipelines."

TELOCATOR NETWORK OF AMERICA, 1800 M St. N.W., Washington, D.C. 20036. Filed for self 10/13/81. Legislative interest — "Matters pertaining to the radio common carrier industry and telecommunications. Specifically, S 898 and S 929." Lobbyist — Grace H. Smith.

Miscellaneous

CHURCH WORLD SERVICE, New York, N.Y. Lobbyist — Hoffheimer, Johnson & Peterson, 1120 20th St. N.W., Washington, D.C. 20036. Filed 10/8/81. Legislative interest — "International development legislation and funding for foreign aid accounts, including loans and Food for Peace. Refugee and immigration policy as regards third world countries."

RICHARD ROSEN, 5010 Wisconsin Ave. N.W., Washington, D.C. 20016. Filed for self 10/15/81. Legislative interest — Not specified. ∎

LOBBY REGISTRATION INDEX

Bitter, Phil M. - 7-D
Black, Manafort and Stone
    Air Transport Association - 12-D, 23-D
    American Newspaper Publishers Association - 50-D
Blackwood, Bev D. - 19-D
Blair, Neal - 3-D, 4-D
Bliss, Richard W. - 22-D, 28-D, 39-D, 41-D, 53-D
H & R Block Inc. - 51-D
Blockwick, Jessma - 38-D
Blue Cross and Blue Shield Associations - 7-D
Blue Ribbon Sports Inc. - 7-D, 15-D
Bluejay Oil Co. - 33-D, 47-D
Blum & Nash
    Daytime Broadcasters Association - 36-D
    Time Inc. - 57-D
    Twin Coasts Newspaper Inc. (The Journal of Commerce) - 35-D, 42-D
Blyth Eastman Paine Webber - 39-D
Bockorny, David A. - 24-D
Boeing Co., The - 15-D, 19-D
Bogle & Gates
    Pacific Seafood Processors Association - 37-D, 45-D
Bohner, Christie K. - 46-D
Boise Cascade Corp. - 33-D
Booker, Gaylon B. - 50-D
Boolukos, Susan A. - 6-D
Booth & Baron
    Standard & Poor's Corp. - 4-D
Bornstein, Ann L. - 10-D
Bosley, Charles - 32-D
Boston Edison Co. - 26-D
Botein, Hays, Sklar & Herzberg
    Henry Schein Inc. - 21-D
Bowater North America Corp. - 5-D
Bowery Savings Bank - 33-D, 51-D
Bowman, Conner, Touhey & Thornton
    Delta Steamship Lines Inc. - 39-D, 47-D
Bowman, Randal R. - 51-D
Boyd & Lloyd
    Boise Cascade Corp. - 33-D
Boyette, Van R. - 17-D
Boyle, James G. - 10-D
Bosley, Charles - 32-D
Boynton, Stephen S. - 7-D
Bracewell & Patterson
    American Petroleum Refiners Association - 23-D
    CLC of America Inc. - 33-D
    Southdown/Pelto Oil Co. - 21-D
    Valero Energy Corp. - 22-D
Braddock, Dennis R. - 13-D
Bradford, Robert E. - 54-D
Bradley, David - 18-D, 32-D
Brady, Jerry M. - 7-D, 25-D
Brady, Theresa M. - 24-D
Brand, Mark - 39-D
Braswell Shipyards Inc. - 27-D
Braunstein, Roy - 12-D, 16-D
Brazil, Noel - 17-D
Brazos River Authority - 57-D
Breece, George W. - 49-D
Breed, Abbott & Morgan
    Handy and Harman - 34-D
    Lasker, Stone & Stern - 18-D
    Talisman Fund - 53-D
Bregman, Abell & Kay
    Norton Simon Inc. - 48-D
Bregman, Brenda I. - 19-D
Brennan, Richard M. - 42-D, 49-D, 53-D
Brewster, Albert E. - 12-D, 15-D
Bricker & Eckler
    American Small and Rural Hospital Association - 30-D
    Dillworth, Paxson, Kalish & Levy - 56-D
    Grocery Manufacturers of America Inc. - 31-D
    Occidental Petroleum Corp. - 21-D
    O'Connor & Hannan - 56-D

Payco American Corp. - 34-D
Pepsico Inc. - 28-D
Bridgestone Tire Co. Ltd. - 27-D
Bristol-Myers Co. - 39-D
Broadcast Music Inc. - 27-D
J. C. Brock Corp. - 51-D
Brooklyn Union Gas Co., The - 27-D, 55-D
Brotherhood of Railroad Signalmen - 22-D
Brotherhood of Railway, Airline & Steamship Clerks, Freight Handlers, Express & Station Employees - 4-D
Browder, Joseph - 29-D
Brown, Andrew - 50-D
Brown & Roady
    Amax Inc. - 33-D
    District of Columbia Department of Transportation - 30-D
Brown & Root Inc. - 19-D, 27-D
Brown, Ben Jarratt - 18-D
Brown, Donald K. - 47-D
Brown, Doreen L. - 51-D
Brown, Jesse P. Jr. - 58-D
Brown, William R. - 24-D
Browning-Ferris Industries Inc. - 11-D
Brownstein, Zeidman & Schomer
    American Business Conference - 17-D
    Home Owners Warranty Corp. - 7-D
    Merrill Lynch, Hubbard Co. - 28-D
    Multifamily Finance Action Group - 28-D
Broyhill Furniture Industries - 51-D
Broyhill Management Corp. - 51-D
Bruch, John R. - 15-D
Bruno, Joseph A. - 8-D
Brunswick Corp. - 51-D, 55-D
Buckley, John S. - 33-D
Budd Co. - 47-D, 51-D
Bulova Systems & Instruments Corp. - 7-D
Burch, Chris - 12-D
Burch, Michael S. - 26-D
Burch, Patricia - 19-D
Burdett, Paul F. - 20-D
Burlington Industries Inc. - 7-D, 47-D, 52-D, 55-D
Burlington Northern Inc. - 47-D, 52-D
Burns and Roe Inc. - 33-D
Burson-Marsteller
    National Oil Jobbers Council - 13-D
    Western Forest Industries Association - 25-D, 32-D, 45-D
Busby, Rehm and Leonard
    Automobile Importers of America, Inc. - 9-D
Business Roundtable - 9-D, 17-D, 23-D, 36-D
Butler, Binion, Rice, Cook & Knapp
    Best Chevrolet - 19-D
    Conyers Ford Inc. - 19-D
    Courtesy Pontiac-AMC Jeep - 19-D
    Delaware River Port Authority - 43-D
    Ford Motor Co. - 19-D
    Mallon Motors Inc. - 20-D
    People Express Airlines Inc. - 21-D
    Poquoson Motors Inc. - 21-D
    Shamrock Ford - 21-D
    Tom Coward Ford - 19-D
Butler, William A. - 46-D
Byers, Lex J. - 24-D

C

Cabot Corp. - 55-D
Cadillac Fairview U.S. Inc. - 39-D
Cadwalader, Wickersham & Taft
    Ad Hoc Committee of Floor Brokers - 43-D
    Asphalt Roofing Manufacturers Association - 9-D
Cahoon, Mark - 24-D

Cain & Smith
    State Bar of Texas - 51-D
Califano, Ross and Heineman
    Connecticut General Life Insurance Co. - 11-D
    C.P. Rehab Corp. - 18-D
    Federal National Mortgage Association - 47-D
    Fluor Corp. - 56-D
    General Tire & Rubber Co. - 40-D
California Canners and Growers - 31-D
State of California Office of the Comptroller - 36-D
California Portland Cement Co. - 19-D
California Society of Pathologists - 17-D, 44-D
Callery-Judge Grove - 39-D
Callihan, John C. - 43-D
Calvert, Victoria R. - 24-D, 31-D
Cameron, Arthur E. - 8-D, 57-D
Camp, Carmouche, Palmer, Barsh & Hunter
    Conoco Inc. - 39-D
    Evans Transportation Co. - 33-D
    Matlack Inc. - 40-D, 48-D
    Natural Gas Supply Association - 58-D
    PLM Inc. - 28-D
    Portec Inc. - 28-D
    Pullman Standard - 34-D
    Richmond Leasing - 29-D
    St. Joe Minerals Corp. - 21-D
    Trailer Train Co. - 29-D
    Union Tank Car Co. - 29-D
    United States Rail Service Inc. - 29-D
Campaign for Community-Based Economic Development - 32-D
Campaign for Community Economic Development - 55-D
Campbell, Charles Argyll - 45-D
Campbell, Kevin B. - 16-D
Canadian Coaliton on Acid Rain - 25-D, 38-D
Canaveral Port Authority - 22-D
Capital Counselors Inc.
    Electronic Data Systems - 27-D
    Perpetual American Federal Savings and Loan Association - 56-D
Capitol Advocates - 39-D
Caplin & Drysdale
    Council on Foundations Inc. - 9-D
Capps, Milton F. - 25-D
Caras, Constantine G. - 15-D
Care Cabs Inc. - 15-D
Cargill Inc. - 27-D, 52-D
Cargill Leasing Corp. - 52-D
Carnegie Corp. of New York - 27-D
Carpenter, Robin J. - 52-D
Carroll, Lawrence W. - 52-D
Carroll, Patricia - 24-D, 31-D
Carter, Anjean - 14-D, 18-D
Carter, John R. Jr. - 21-D
William Carter Co., The - 27-D
Carver, Susan B. - 45-D
Cary & Baron
    Puget Sound Power & Light Co. - 3-D, 4-D
Casey, Jim - 26-D, 30-D
Casey, Kathleen - 20-D
Casey, Lane & Mittendorf
    GHK Cos., The - 15-D
    Independent Producers Group - 17-D
Cast North American Ltd. - 39-D
Castellani, John J. - 6-D
Caterpillar Tractor Co. - 47-D, 52-D
Cellulose Manufacturers' Association - 31-D
Center for Law and Education Inc. - 55-D
Center for Science in the Public Interest - 50-D
Centex Corp. - 15-D
Central California Educational Television - 25-D

Central City Association of Los Angeles - 30-D
Central Power and Light Co. - 39-D
Century 21 - 39-D
CH2M Hill Inc. - 45-D
Chalmers, Elizabeth Prewitt - 9-D
Chamber of Commerce of the United States - 17-D, 23-D, 37-D, 44-D
Chamberlain, Charles E. - 32-D
Champion International Corp. - 47-D
Chancellor Corp. - 52-D
Chappell Communications Management - 24-D
Charlton, Richard M. - 6-D
    EDS Corp. - 15-D
Charter Co. - 47-D
Chase Manhattan Bank, The - 3-D
Chemical Manufacturers Association - 17-D, 23-D
Chemolimpex - 39-D
Cherkasky, William B. - 44-D
Chevron U.S.A. Inc. - 7-D, 27-D, 47-D, 52-D
Chicago Board of Trade, City of Chicago - 36-D, 47-D
Chicago Board of Trade Clearing Corp. - 27-D
Chicago Mercantile Exchange - 27-D, 39-D
Children's Defense Fund - 38-D
Chin, Peggy - 14-D, 18-D
China External Trade Development Council - 16-D
Chinoin - 39-D
Chris-Craft Industries Inc. - 39-D
Christian Voice Moral Government Fund - 6-D
Chrysler Corp. - 27-D
Church World Service - 58-D
Chwat, John - 33-D
Cigar Association of America Inc. - 9-D, 57-D
Cincinnati Milacron - 55-D
Citgo Synfuels Inc. - 27-D
Cities Service Co. - 33-D
Citizen Victims of Chrysler - 10-D
Citizens Committee for the Right to Keep and Bear Arms - 14-D
Citizens for Tax Justice - 6-D
Citizens Housing & Planning Association Inc. - 46-D
Citizens of the National Committee to Exonerate Richard Nixon - 10-D
Cladouhos & Brashares - 45-D
    Securities Group, The - 42-D
Clark, Julie - 7-D
Clark, Susan - 19-D
CLC of America Inc. - 33-D
Cleary, Gottlieb, Steen & Hamilton
    Sporting Arms and Ammunition Manufacturers Institute - 50-D
Cleveland Electric Illuminating Co. - 7-D, 15-D
Clifford & Warnke
    Australian Meat & Livestock Corp. - 39-D
    Government of the Federated States of Micronesia - 16-D
    Phillips Petroleum Co. - 41-D
Coal Oil Producers Association - 23-D
Coalition for Legal Services - 32-D
Coalition of Independent College and University Students (COPUS) - 45-D
Coan, Couture, Lyons & Moorhead
    A-C Valley Corp. - 26-D
    Internatio Inc. - 28-D
    Tosco - 29-D
    Westinghouse Electric Corp. - 29-D
Coastal Corp., The - 11-D, 39-D, 55-D
Coastal Properties Institute Inc. - 54-D
Cobden, Adelin - 51-D
Coeur D'Alene Mines - 33-D
Coffee, Sugar & Cocoa Exchange Inc. - 19-D

Dilworth, Paxson, Kalish, & Levy
Bricker & Eckler - 56-D
Northwest Alaskan Pipeline Co. - 53-D
Western Pennsylvania Coal Mining Association - 45-D
Direct Mail Marketing Association - 36-D
Distilled Spirits Council of the U.S. Inc. - 44-D, 50-D
District of Columbia Department of Transportation - 30-D
Dividend Support Group - 9-D
Dix, Dennis - 25-D
Dix, Patsy B. - 11-D
Dixon, O.L. III - 11-D
Dobbs Corp., The - 36-D
Dodds, William H. - 43-D
Doherty, Karen A. - 5-D
Dollar Savings Bank - 40-D, 52-D
Donadio, Brian J. - 36-D
D'Onofrio, John J. - 3-D
Donohoe, Timothy L. - 3-D
Dorfman, Ira - 54-D
Dougherty, Charlene - 46-D
Dow Chemical Co. - 52-D, 56-D
Dow, Lohnes & Albertson
Central California Educational Television - 25-D
Kansas Public Telecommunications Service Inc. - 25-D
Lehigh Valley Public Telecommunications Corp. - 25-D
Northeast New York Educational Television Association - 25-D
Ohio State University - 25-D
Southern Tier ETV Association - 25-D
Downer, Charles P. - 13-D
Doyle, Patrick L. - 8-D, 12-D
Dr. Martin Luther King Jr. January 15th National Holiday Lobby Committee - 14-D
Dredging Industry Size Standards Committee - 13-D
Drexel Burnham Lambert Inc. - 47-D
DuBrul, Paul - 51-D
Dudeck, Barbara S. - 15-D
Duerr, Douglas F. - 13-D
Duff, Ann Anderson - 50-D
Duffy, Sarah Wells - 9-D
Duggan, C.R. - 4-D
Duncan, Don R. - 8-D
Duncan, Weinberg & Miller
Dayton-Montgomery County Park District - 22-D
Durazo, Raymond - 43-D, 49-D
Durham, B.J. - 39-D
Dutcher Industries - 19-D
Dutko, Daniel A. - 55-D

E

E.G.G. Industries - 33-D
Eastern Airlines Inc. - 15-D
Eaton Associates Inc. - 56-D
Eaton, Charles H. S. - 56-D
Echols, William - 44-D
Eckhardt, Robert C. - 24-D
Econopure - 47-D, 52-D
Daniel J. Edelman Inc.
Toyota Motor Sales U.S.A. Inc. - 4-D
Edelman International Corp. - 57-D
Edgar, William R. - 48-D, 52-D
Edison Electric Institute - 17-D, 24-D, 31-D, 44-D
EDS Corp. - 15-D, 40-D, 56-D
Edwards Associates Inc.
Blue Ribbon Sports - 14-D
Confederated Tribes of Warm Springs, The - 14-D
Edwards, Christine A. - 29-D
Edwards, J. David - 45-D
Edwards, William A. - 7-D, 12-D

Eggers & Greene
Whitney National Bank of New Orleans - 12-D
Ehrhart, Charles E. - 41-D
Eichenberger, Mary Ann - 17-D
Eizenstat, Fran - 38-D
Electronic Data Systems - 27-D
Electronic Industries Association - 9-D, 44-D
Electronics Industries Association of Japan - 57-D
Eli Lilly and Co. - 7-D, 11-D
Ellis, Keith H. - 9-D
El Paso Co., The - 3-D
El Paso Natural Gas Co. - 52-D
Elsevier Scientific Publishers - 33-D
Ely, Guess & Rudd - 18-D
Emerson Electric Co. - 19-D, 27-D, 40-D
Employee Relocation Council - 37-D
Encyclopaedia Britannica Inc. - 15-D
Energy Consumers and Producers Association - 54-D
Energy Conversion Group - 25-D
Enfield, Samuel E. - 7-D
ENI Companies - 7-D
Eno, Amos S. - 15-D
Ensearch Corp. - 3-D
Entex Inc. - 5-D
Environmental Action Inc. - 10-D
Environmental Policy Center - 18-D, 38-D
Equale, Paul A. - 5-D, 6-D
Erie County Industrial Development Agency - 14-D
Ervin, Sam J. Jr. - 51-D, 52-D, 53-D
Esop Association of America, The - 4-D
Esterly, Jane B. - 44-D
Ethyl Corp. - 56-D
Eugene Water and Electric Board - 23-D
Eure, Stephen E. - 57-D
Evans, Donald C. - 5-D
Evans Transportation Company - 33-D
Everett, J. Ballad - 54-D
Eves, Ellen E. - 34-D, 40-D
Eves, Jeffrey P. - 48-D
Exxon Corp. - 19-D, 40-D

F

Facet Enterprises Inc. - 33-D
Fagan, Thomas L. - 20-D
Fair Opportunities for Competition in the U.S. (FOCUS) - 44-D
Fallbrook Public Utility District - 15-D
Farber, Robert C. - 49-D
Farmers Educational and Co-operative Union of America (National Farmers Union) - 9-D
Farnham, George L. - 7-D
Farr, Dagmar T. - 24-D
Farrell, Sylvester L. - 42-D
Farthing, Penelope S. - 9-D
Fay, Kevin J. - 43-D, 49-D
Federal National Mortgage Association - 47-D
Federal Services Co.
High Plains Grain Products Cooperative - 40-D
New England Council Inc., The - 45-D
North Plains Grain Products Coopertive - 20-D
Northwest Texas Grain Products Cooperative - 41-D
Power Authority of the State of New York - 43-D
Telephone and Data Systems Inc. - 42-D
Federated Cash Management Systems - 19-D
Federated Department Stores Inc. - 33-D, 47-D
Federated States of Micronesia, Government of - 16-D

Federation of American Controlled Shipping - 24-D
Feilders Associates Inc.
Hudson Bay Mining & Smelting Co. Ltd. - 40-D
Feist, John W. - 46-D
Felt, M.K. - 36-D
Jack Ferguson Associates Inc.
Foss Launch & Tug Co./Foss Alaska Line - 15-D
Pacific Northern Oil - 15-D
Ferguson II, John T. - 34-D
Fertilizer Institute - 6-D, 13-D
Fierst, Edith U. - 37-D
Finamore, Barbara - 38-D
Finkelstein, Mark - 57-D
Finley, Kumble, Wagner, Heine, Casey & Underberg
Committee for Humane Legislation Inc. - 38-D
Friends of Animals - 11-D
Population Crisis Committee - 26-D
Stewart Environmental Systems Inc. - 35-D
Finlinson and Finlinson - 37-D
Finsen, Jill - 25-D
Fiorini, Richard J. - 12-D
First Bank and Trust Co. - 3-D
First Boston Corp. - 33-D
First Centrum Corp. - 47-D
First Chicago Corp. - 27-D
First City Bancorporation - 3-D
Fisher, Gelband, Sinick & Lamberton
League of New York Theaters and Producers Inc. - 13-D
Fitzgerald, Mary Clare - 3-D
Five Tribes Confedercy of North Central Okla. - 7-D
Flanigan's Enterprises Inc. - 33-D, 48-D
Flathead Joint Board of Control - 57-D
Flexible Packaging Association - 5-D, 24-D, 44-D
Florida State Hospice Organization Inc. - 17-D, 54-D
Florio, Mark A. - 38-D
Flower, Ruth - 18-D, 26-D
Fluor Corp. - 56-D
Flynn, John J. - 30-D
FMC Corp. - 40-D
Foley, Hoag & Eliot
Braswell Shipyards Inc. - 27-D
Foley, John P. Jr. - 29-D
Foley III, Leander J. - 46-D, 48-D, 50-D, 53-D, 55-D
Foley, Lardner, Hollabaugh & Jacobs
Care Cabs Inc. - 15-D
Independent Refiners Association of America - 9-D, 13-D, 36-D
VGS Corp. - 57-D
Folsom, R.D. - 13-D
Food Marketing Institute - 24-D
Food Policy Center - 15-D
For Love of Children Inc. - 18-D
Ford, Jack T. - 15-D
Ford Motor Co. - 7-D, 19-D, 40-D
Foremost Insurance Co. - 27-D
Forgotson, Edward H. - 35-D
Fort Sill Gardens Inc. - 34-D, 48-D
Foss Alaska Line - 34-D
Foss Launch & Tug Co./Foss Alaska Line - 15-D, 34-D
Fox, Eric R. - 37-D
Franasiak, David E. - 37-D
Francis Associates Ltd. - 41-D, 46-D
Francis, Leslie C. - 46-D
Frank, Alfred S. Jr. - 41-D
Frankel, Harley M. - 14-D
Franklin Institute, The - 18-D
Franzia, Fred T., Cenus N. John G. Jr., Mary L., Joseph S., Marilyn L. - 46-D
Fraser Associates
Association of American Physicians and Surgeons - 54-D

Frazier, Gregory W. - 5-D
Free the Eagle - 3-D
Freeman, Gary N. - 33-D, 35-D
Fried, Frank, Harris, Shriver and Kampelman
Makah Indian Tribe - 14-D
National Association of Pension Funds - 13-D
Norton Sound Health Corp. - 15-D
Sea Colony Inc. - 41-D
Friends Committee on National Legislation - 18-D, 26-D
Friends of Animals - 11-D, 55-D
Friends of the Earth - 38-D
Froehlke, Robert F. - 23-D
FTC Communications Inc. - 52-D
Fulbright & Jaworski
Petro-Lewis Corp. - 56-D
Underwood Neuhaus - 29-D
United States Leasing International Inc. - 29-D
Karl A. Funke & Associates Inc.
American Indian Scholarships Inc. - 14-D
Keweenaw Bay Chippewa Tribe - 14-D
Penobscot Indian Nation - 14-D
Shoshone-Bannock Tribes - 14-D
Yakima Indian Nation - 14-D
Fuquay, Claudia R. - 13-D

G

G-4 Children's Coalition - 32-D
Gaboury, Fred - 4-D
Gage, Larry S. - 24-D
Gale, Michael R. - 3-D
Galis, Joe H. - 32-D
Gall, Lawrence H. - 35-D
Ganz Mavag - 40-D
Gara, Nicole - 49-D
Gardena, City of - 22-D
Gardiner, David McLane - 7-D
Gardner, Carton & Douglas
FTC Communications Inc. - 52-D
Gardner, Ginger - 47-D
Garvey, Schubert, Adams & Barer
General Telephone & Electronics Corp. - 52-D
Noranda Mining Inc. - 12-D
Northwest Marine Iron Works - 41-D
Trailways - 29-D
Gates Learjet Corp. - 48-D, 52-D
Gatx Corp. - 27-D
Gavin, James A. - 24-D
Gay Rights National Lobby Inc. - 11-D
Gedulig, Dwight M. - 9-D, 17-D
Genentech Inc. - 56-D
General Aviation Manufacturers Association - 24-D, 36-D
General Dynamics Corp. - 19-D, 48-D
General Electric Co. - 11-D, 19-D, 27-D
General Electric Pension Trust - 46-D
General Instrument Corp. - 11-D, 40-D, 48-D
General Mills Inc. - 27-D
General Mills Restaurant Group Inc. - 11-D
General Motors Corp. - 15-D, 20-D
General Public Utilities Corp. - 27-D, 34-D
General Telephone & Electronics Corp. - 48-D, 52-D, 56-D
General Telephone Co. of California - 40-D
General Tire & Rubber Co. - 3-D, 40-D
Generic Pharmaceutical Industry Association - 31-D, 36-D, 50-D
Genesee Public Affairs Inc.
Province of Ontario, Canada, Minisry of the Environment - 43-D
Gentile, Fred J. - 55-D
Geoproducts Corp. - 48-D

George and George
  Continental Resources Co. - 11-D
Georgia Association of Petroleum Retailers Inc. - 24-D
  Service Station Dealers of America - 10-D
Georgia-Pacific Corp. - 27-D, 33-D, 40-D, 56-D
Georgia Power Co. - 40-D
Geothermal Kinetics Inc. - 15-D
Gerard, Byler & Associates Inc.
  Damson Oil Corp. - 47-D
Gerard, Joseph G. - 31-D
Gerstell, Phyllis H. - 6-D
GHK Companies, The - 11-D, 15-D
Giaimo, Robert N. - 17-D
Gibson, John A.C. - 42-D
GIC Financial Services Corp. - 20-D
Gilmartin, William - 33-D
Gilson, Marla F. - 16-D
Ginsburg, Feldman, Weil and Bress
  Coal Oil Producers Association - 23-D
Giovaniello, Gerard - 24-D
Girton, Brenda M. - 21-D
Gitlitz, Jonah - 36-D
Glass Packaging Institute - 24-D
Gleason, Robert - 30-D
Glenn, James T. - 47-D
Glenrock Refinery Inc. - 40-D
Global Exploration and Development Corp. - 10-D
Golato, A. James - 51-D
Goldberg, Michael J. - 8-D
Goldstein, Michael - 17-D
Goodman, James A. - 18-D
Goold, Jay F. - 17-D
Gordon, Beth - 47-D
Gordon, Douglas - 13-D
Gore, Brenda J. - 8-D, 21-D
Gormley, James D. - 24-D
Gory, Thomas H. - 45-D
Gould Inc. - 11-D
Gould, John J. - 8-D
Gould, John T. Jr. - 41-D
Government Relations Associates Inc. - 46-D
GPU Service Corp. - 56-D
Graber, Edmond - 44-D
Grace, Thomas E. - 20-D
Graff, John R. - 6-D
Gray and Co. - 40-D, 48-D
  American Iron and Steel Institute - 50-D
  Avis Enterprises - 51-D
  Budd Co. - 47-D, 51-D
  Defense Logistics Supply Corp. - 52-D
  El Paso Natural Gas Co. - 52-D
  General Telephone and Electronics Corp. - 48-D, 52-D
  Health Insurance Association of America - 54-D
  Management Insights Inc. - 48-D, 52-D
  Motorola Inc. - 52-D
  National Association of Home Builders - 54-D
  U.S.O. Inc. - 51-D
  Western Development - 53-D
  Westinghouse Broadcasting Co. - 53-D
Gray, Robert K. - 48-D
Great Atlantic and Pacific Tea Co. Inc. - 40-D
Great National Corp. - 20-D, 27-D, 34-D
Great Western Sugar Co., The - 3-D
Greater Boston Real Estate Board - 46-D
Green, Micah S. - 54-D
Cobb Green & Associates Ltd.
  Council for a Competitive Economy - 32-D
Greenberg, Allen - 55-D
Greenberg, David I. - 10-D
Greenberger, Phyllis - 30-D
Greenstein, Robert - 32-D
Griffee, Ellen - 55-D

Griffith, Ellen B. - 18-D
Griffiths, Mark N. - 5-D
Grkavac, Olga - 31-D
Grocery Manufacturers of America Inc. - 31-D
Groom and Nordberg
  Ad Hoc Group on Life Insurance Company Taxation of Pension Funds - 8-D
  Phillips Petroleum - 21-D
  Westinghouse Electric Corp. - 42-D
Gross, Stanley C. - 54-D
Grumman Aerospace Corp. - 11-D, 20-D
Grumman Flxible Corp. - 27-D
Grupp, Larry - 42-D, 48-D
GTE Telenet Inc. - 20-D
Guam Growth Council - 4-D
Guam Oil & Refining Co. Inc. - 15-D, 52-D
Guam, Port Authority of - 30-D
Guay, Richard T. - 54-D
Gulf & Western Industries Inc. - 34-D
Gulf & Western Management Co. - 15-D
Gulf Oil Corp. - 20-D, 40-D, 48-D
Gulf Power Co. - 11-D
Gulf Resources & Chemical Corp. - 34-D
Gunderson, Dan A. - 21-D

H

Hackler, Craig - 5-D, 6-D, 52-D
Haddad, William F. - 50-D
Hagan Industries Inc. - 48-D
Haiti Embassy, Republic of - 53-D
Halem, Beverly - 7-D
Halem Industries Inc. - 7-D
Hall, Ann K. - 44-D
Hall, James N. - 7-D
Hall, John F. - 31-D
Hallac Associates Inc. - 40-D
Hallberg, David E. - 25-D
Haluza, Paul T. - 37-D
Hamilton Brothers Oil & Gas Corp. - 52-D
Hamilton, William W. Jr. - 33-D
Hamilton Technology Inc. - 7-D
Hampton, Robert E. - 34-D, 40-D
Hamric, Sara - 30-D
Hancock/Dikewood Services Inc. - 50-D
Handel, Ted - 44-D
Handgun Control Inc. - 46-D
H & R Block - 51-D
Handy and Harman - 34-D
Hanlin, Elisabeth - 8-D
Hannaford Co. Inc., The
  American Society of Composers, Authors and Publishers - 50-D
  Baltic American Freedom League - 46-D
  Century 21 - 39-D
  China External Trade Development Council - 16-D
  Hubbard Broadcasting Co. - 40-D
  Merrill Lynch White Weld Capital Markets Group - 56-D
  Northwest Alaskan Pipeline Co. - 41-D
  Tosco Oil Corp. - 12-D
  Trans World Airlines Inc. - 53-D
Hansell, Post, Brandon & Dorsey
  Associated Builders and Contractors Inc. - 23-D
  Portman Properties - 12-D
Harbison Ford Inc. - 34-D
Harlow, Dan. R. - 19-D
Harris, Berg & Creskoff
  American Academy of Federal Civil Service Physicians - 49-D
  Association of Food Distributors Inc. - 23-D
  Committee of Domestic Steel Wire Rope and Specialty Cable Manufacturers - 44-D

P.L. Thomas & Co. Inc. - 21-D
Harris, Hubert L. - 17-D
William H. Harsha & Associates
  American Trucking Associations - 17-D
  Commuter Airline Association of America - 31-D
  Grumman Flexible Corp. - 27-D
  Slurry Transport Association - 31-D
  Zantop International Airlines - 29-D
Hartford Fire Insurance Co. - 48-D
Hauck & Associates - 10-D, 14-D, 18-D
Haugh, Barbara J. - 8-D
Haugh, Rodney E. - 13-D
Hawaiian Sugar Planters' Association - 13-D
Hawes, Kathryn JoAnn - 49-D
Hawkins, David G. - 19-D
Hayden, Wesley F. - 13-D
Health Industry Manufacturers Association - 13-D
Health Insurance Association of America - 9-D, 17-D, 24-D, 54-D
Health Research Group - 55-D
Hebner, Charles L. - 34-D, 40-D
Hedged Portfolio Advisors - 27-D
Heffner, John - 23-D
Helicopter Association International - 20-D
Helicopter Association of America Inc. - 5-D
Helicopter Loggers Association - 17-D
Helionetics Inc. - 20-D
Walter E. Heller International Corp. - 40-D
Hendrix, Elizabeth E. - 54-D
Henningson, Bert E. - 10-D
Hensche, LeAnn R. - 16-D, 41-D
Herman, Marilyn J. - 54-D
Hickory Association - 9-D
High Plains Grain Products Cooperative - 40-D
Hill, Allan D. - 12-D
Hill & Knowlton
  Hobart Corp. - 11-D
  Navajo Nation - 7-D, 11-D
  Therapedic - 53-D
  Witts, David A. - 5-D
Hill, Christopher and Phillips
  Campaign for Community-Based Economic Development - 32-D
  Columbia Pictures Industries Inc. - 47-D
  Search Group Inc. - 14-D
  Whitney National Bank of New Orleans - 12-D
Hill, Robert B. - 23-D
Himes & Ketchey
  PHH Group Inc. - 48-D
Hines, Beverly L. - 6-D
Hinkle, Maureen K. - 46-D
Hitchcock, C.F. - 18-D
Hobart Corp. - 11-D
Hobbs Construction & Development Co. - 56-D
Hobson, Jerald E. - 3-D
Hodgson, John H. III - 47-D
Hodgson, Russ, Andrewa, Woods & Goodyear
  J.C. Brock Corp. - 51-D
Hoffheimer, Johnson & Peterson
  Arthritis Foundation - 26-D
  Church World Service - 58-D
  Computer Sciences Corp. - 47-D
  Hancock/Dikewood Services Inc. - 50-D
Hoffman, Hendry, Stoner, Sims & Sawicki
  Global Exploration & Development Corp. - 10-D
Hoffman, William L. - 32-D
Hogan & Hartson
  American Electronics Association - 44-D
  Computer and Business Equipment Manufacturers Association - 44-D
  Electronics Industries Association - 44-D

Florida State Hospice Organization Inc. - 17-D, 54-D
Guam Oil & Refining Co. Inc. - 52-D
Hospital Association of New York State - 17-D
Motorcycle Industry Council Inc. - 31-D
National Soft Drink Association - 25-D
Newspaper-Broadcaster Committee - 25-D
Scientific Apparatus Makers Association - 45-D
Toyota Motor Sales USA Inc. - 21-D
Holbert, Tom B. - 10-D
Holding and Customer Development Progress Inc. - 20-D
Holloman, Charlotte - 33-D
Holmes, Lee B. - 37-D
Holtzman-Parcells, Harriet - 18-D
Home Owners Warranty Corp. - 7-D
Honduras, Government of - 16-D
Hontz, Karen C. - 15-D
Hooker Investments Ltd. - 56-D
Hopkins & Sutter
  Chicago Board of Trade Clearing Corp. - 27-D
  Commonwealth Edison Co. - 27-D
  First Chicago Corp. - 27-D
  Inland Steel Co. - 28-D
  National Association of Independent Insurers - 31-D
  Northwest Industries Inc. - 28-D
  Peoples Energy Corp. - 28-D
  Trans Union Corp. - 29-D
Hopkins, Virginia E. - 24-D
Hopkins, William B. - 19-D
George A. Hormel & Co. - 28-D
Horton, Alison - 51-D
Horwitt, Sanford D. - 55-D
Hospital Association of New York State - 17-D
Hotes, William J. - 19-D
Houston, Jack W. - 24-D
Howell, James P. - 50-D
Hoy, Virginia A. - 13-D
Hoyt, John S. - 25-D
Huard, Paul R. - 37-D
Hubbard Broadcasting Co. - 40-D
J.M. Huber Corp. - 20-D, 28-D
Hudson Bay Mining and Smelting Co. Ltd. - 40-D
Hudson, J. William - 5-D, 6-D
Hudson, Margaret Renken - 3-D, 5-D
Hughes Aircraft Co. - 11-D, 20-D, 52-D
Hughes Helicopters Inc. - 40-D, 56-D
Hughes Hubbard & Reed
  Bristol-Myers Co. - 39-D
  Business Roundtable, The - 17-D
  Ford Motor Co. - 40-D
  Pfizer Inc. - 41-D
  Texas International Airlines - 42-D
Hughes Jr., Vester T. - 38-D
Hugo Neu & Sons Inc. - 34-D, 41-D
Humphreys, Robert R. - 10-D, 18-D
Hunt, David A. - 43-D, 49-D
Hunt Oil Co. - 40-D
Hunter, Harry - 31-D
Hunter, William J. Jr. - 34-D
Hur, J. James - 39-D
Hurley, Adele M. - 25-D, 38-D
Hurwitz, B. Melvin - 41-D
Hurwith, Geoffrey B. - 56-D
Hutcheson, Susan Drew - 8-D
F.H. Hutchison & Co.
  Geoproducts Corp. - 48-D
  Hydrothermal Energy Corp. - 48-D
  Renewable Energy Inc. - 48-D
  Westec Services Inc. - 49-D
Huthnance Drilling Co. - 28-D
HWL Properties - 56-D
Hydrothermal Energy Corp. - 48-D
Hynes, Edward A. - 42-D

I

Ichord, Richard H. - 20-D
ICI Americas Inc. - 34-D, 40-D
Ikejiri, Ronald K. - 14-D
Independent Bankers Association of America - 24-D
Independent Cattlemen Association - 24-D
Independent Lubricant Manufacturers Association - 44-D
Independent Producers Group - 17-D
Independent Refiners Association of America - 9-D, 13-D, 36-D
Independent Telecommunications Suppliers' Council - 54-D
Industrial Oil Consumers Group - 24-D
Industrial Union Department, AFL-CIO - 57-D
Industrias Quimacas Y Tartaricas - 34-D
Infectious Diseases Society of America - 58-D
Ingalsbee, Nancy J. - 25-D
Ingersoll Johnson Steel Co. - 56-D
Ingram, John H. - 17-D
Ingram Tankships Inc. - 17-D
Inland Steel Co. - 28-D
Institute of Electrical & Electronic Engineers - 24-D
Institute of Internal Auditors Inc. - 54-D
Insurance Association of Connecticut - 9-D, 17-D
Intellectual Property Owners Inc. - 31-D
Inter-American Associates Inc.
    Government of Honduras - 16-D
Intergraph Corp. - 28-D
Internatio Inc. - 28-D
International Association of Amusement Parks and Attractions - 6-D
International Association of Drilling Contractors - 13-D
International Association of Fish and Wildlife Agencies - 13-D
International Brotherhood of Teamsters, Chauffeurs, Warehousemen and Helpers of America, Local 959 - 22-D
International Communications Association - 6-D
International Conference Industry Association - 50-D
International Federation of Professional & Technical Engineers, AFL-CIO - 49-D
International Franchise Association - 44-D
International Longshoremen's & Warehousemen's Union - 4-D
International Longshoremen's Association, AFL-CIO - 29-D
International Paper Co. - 3-D, 28-D, 34-D, 48-D, 52-D
International Telecommunications Satellite Organization - 11-D
International Telephone and Telegraph Corp. - 7-D, 11-D
International Union of Operating Engineers - 30-D
Inupiat Community of the Arctic Slope - 18-D
Investment Company Institute - 24-D
Irions, Charles C. - 30-D
Irving Trust Co. - 40-D
Isaacson, Glen - 12-D
Isbister, James D. - 7-D

J

J. Aron & Co. Inc. - 33-D, 38-D
J.C. Brock Corp. - 51-D
J.C. Penny Co. Inc. - 21-D, 28-D
J.M. Huber Corp. - 20-D, 28-D
Jackson, Benjamin R. - 46-D
Jackson, Carol - 43-D
Jackson, Robert S. - 56-D
E.A. Jaenke & Associates Inc.
    Cooperative League of the USA - 32-D, 50-D
Jaffe, Squires & Foote
    U.S. & Overseas Tax Fairness Committee - 33-D
Japanese-American Citizens League - 14-D
Jaquay, Joseph N. - 29-D
Jarvis-Ferris, Evelyn - 53-D
Jasinowski, Jerry J. - 13-D
Jenkins, Kempton B. - 38-D
Jennings, James C. - 38-D
Jensen, Sanders & McConnell
    Santa Ana Valley Irrigation Co. - 12-D
Johnson, Douglas - 47-D
Johnson, Edward - 57-D
Johnson, Ervin B. - 26-D
Johnson, Gregory N. - 31-D
Johnson, Linda Meyer - 41-D
Johnson Oil Co. Inc. - 11-D
Johnson, Smith & Hibbard
    Miliken Research Corp. - 41-D
Johnson, Swanson & Barbee
    Harbison Ford Inc. - 34-D
    Hunt Oil Co. - 40-D
Joint Maritime Congress - 24-D
Jones, Anthi K. - 45-D
Jones, Day, Reavis & Pogue
    Cities Service Co. - 33-D
    Food Policy Center - 15-D
Jones, Gerald R. - 35-D
Jones, Jones, Bell, Close & Brown
    The Mead Corp. - 41-D, 56-D
Jones, Loyd & Webster Inc. - 20-D
Jones, Lynda Wolf - 18-D
Jones, Stanley B. - 7-D
Jones, Theodore L. - 47-D
Jonsson, Gregory N. - 31-D, 32-D
Robert E. Juliano Associates
    Los Angeles Olympic Commemorative Coin - 46-D
    Los Angeles Olympic Organizing Committee - 46-D

K

Kabot, Byron E. - 28-D
Kadar, Geza Jr. - 17-D, 24-D
Kaehler, Hans - 25-D
Kaiser Aluminum & Chemical Corp. - 28-D, 40-D
Kankakee, Beaverville & Southern Railroad Company - 20-D
Kansas City, City of - 53-D
Kansas Public Telecommunications Service Inc. - 25-D
Karth, Joseph E. - 25-D
Kaswell, Maryann M. - 57-D
Katson, Patricia L. - 51-D
Katz, Howard C. - 19-D
Katz, Laura Jo - 50-D
Kaye, Scholar, Fierman, Hays & Handler
    American Psychoanalytic Association - 6-D
    Dow Chemical Co. - 52-D
    El Sevier Scientific Publishers - 33-D
KBS Associates Inc. - 25-D
Keefe Co., The
    American Family Life Insurance Co. - 11-D
    Continental Materials - 3-D, 5-D
    U.S. Overseas Tax Fairness Committee Inc. - 19-D
Keene, David A. - 47-D
Kellogg Co. - 7-D, 11-D
Kelly, Brian F. - 21-D

Kelly, Richard B. - 17-D
Kemmer, Mark L. - 20-D
Kenin, James B. - 38-D
Kennebeck, Joseph W. - 22-D
Kenny, Brendon - 30-D
Kent, J.H. - 30-D
Kerry, Margaret - 14-D
Kessinger, Frederick A. - 57-D
Keweenaw Bay Chippewa Tribe - 14-D
Kiawah Island Co. - 28-D
Kidder, Peabody & Co. Inc. - 40-D
Kilduff, Maryann - 25-D
Kimberly-Clark Corp. - 52-D
Kimmelman, Gene - 32-D
Kinane, Richard J. - 10-D
King & Spalding
    American Petroleum Institute - 30-D
    Georgia Pacific Corp. - 27-D
King, Rufus - 57-D
Kingsley, Frank G. - 25-D, 32-D
Kinsella, Michael T. - 24-D
Kirby and Gillick
    American Bus Association - 12-D
    Communities for an Effective Air Transportation System - 38-D
    Continental Resources Co. - 11-D
    Corn Refiners Association - 17-D
    National Council of Farmer Cooperatives - 13-D
Kirby Co., Peter - 3-D
Kirkland & Ellis
    Milliken & Co. - 56-D
Kitchen, Emmett Jay Jr. - 17-D
Kitlas, Ronald A. - 11-D
Kline Iron & Steel Co., Inc. - 20-D
Kline, Knopf & Wojdak Inc.
    General Public Utilities Corp. - 27-D
    Medical College of Pennsylvania, The - 32-D
K Mart Corp. - 34-D
Knapp, Glenn - 32-D
Knise, Daniel F. - 9-D
Knoll Fine Chemicals Inc. - 20-D
Knopke, Mary G. - 51-D
Knous, Robert L. Jr. - 50-D, 57-D
Koch Industries - 48-D
Koleda, Michael S. - 13-D
Kolesnik, Kris James - 38-D
Kominers, Fort, Schlefer & Boyer
    American Tankships Inc. - 33-D
    Ingram Tankships Inc. - 34-D
Kona Coast Co. - 5-D
Koppers Co. Inc. - 40-D
Koppers Synfuels Corp. - 28-D
Korea Leather & Fur Exporter's Association - 5-D
Korf Industries Inc. - 3-D, 5-D
Kowalski, Jeanne P. - 4-D, 21-D
Kratovil, Edward DeW. - 26-D
Krause, Raymond R. - 22-D
Krautler, Charles G. - 4-D
Kuykendall, Dan - 51-D, 53-D

L

L.P. Manangement Corp. - 40-D, 48-D
LTV Corp. - 7-D
Lamb, Robert - 30-D
Landis, Cohen, Signman and Rauh
    American Society of Composers, Authors and Publishers - 23-D
    Committee to Preserve the Patent Jurisdiction of the U.S. Court of Appeals - 25-D
    Council of Creative Artists, Libraries and Museums - 24-D
    NFL Players Association - 22-D
Landrieu, Moon - 51-D
Lane, Albert E. - 26-D
Lane and Edson

Council for Rural Housing and Development - 24-D
Lange, Robert D. - 10-D
Lasco Shipping Co. - 40-D
Lasker, Stone & Stern - 18-D
Latham, Watkins & Hills
    Central City Association of Los Angeles - 30-D
    Citgo Synfuels Inc. - 27-D
    Commonwealth of Puerto Rico - 30-D
    Kona Coast Co. - 5-D
    Koppers Synfuels Corp. - 28-D
    Republic Geothermal Inc. - 29-D
League of California Milk Producers - 17-D
League of New York Theatres and Producers Inc., The - 13-D, 44-D
LeBoeuf, Kerley - 31-D
Lee, Douglas O. - 32-D, 38-D
Lee Way Motor Freight Inc. - 11-D
Legatski, Richard A. - 45-D, 54-D
LeGette, Caroline Mills - 14-D
Legislative Alliance of Philatelists and Hard Asset Dealers and Collectors - 58-D
Lehigh Valley Public Telecommunications Corp. - 25-D
Lehnhard, Mary Nell - 7-D
Leighton Conklin Lemov Jacobs & Buckley
    Fred T. & Cenus N. Franzia, John G. Jr. & Mary L. Franzia, Joseph S. & Marilyn L. Franzia - 46-D
    Greater Boston Real Estate Board - 46-D
    Kaiser Aluminum & Chemical Corp. - 28-D
    Mutual Savings Central Fund Inc. - 56-D
    Olin Corp. - 28-D
Lenz, Edward A. - 9-D
Leonard, Koehn, Rose and Hurt - 56-D
Leva, Hawes, Symington, Martin & Oppenheimer
    Airco Inc. - 38-D
    Boston Edison Co. - 26-D
    Business Roundtable - 23-D, 36-D
    Consolidated Edison Co. of New York - 27-D
    Northeast Utilities Service Co. - 28-D
    Upper Humboldt River Water Users Association - 55-D
    U.S. Industries Inc. - 42-D
Levine, Barbara W. - 54-D
Levine, Kenneth S. - 15-D
Lewis, David - 17-D
Lewis, Michael R. - 4-D
Lewis, Stuart A. - 8-D, 20-D, 21-D
Leyden, John F. - 30-D
Liberty Corp. - 40-D
Liberty Lobby - 51-D
Liburdi, Lillian - 40-D, 42-D
Liebman, Jan Pittman - 10-D
Lifetime Communities Inc. - 28-D
Lillick, McHose & Charles
    Foss Alaska Line - 34-D
    Foss Launch & Tug Co. - 34-D
    Huthnance Drilling Co. - 28-D
    Jones, Loyd & Webster Inc. - 20-D
    Rotan Mosle Inc. - 21-D
    Western Pioneer Inc. - 35-D
    Wisconsin Barge Line Co. - 22-D
Lillquist, Richard A. - 5-D
Lincoln Property Co. - 40-D, 52-D
Linse, James P. - 22-D
Linton, Mields, Reisler & Cottone Ltd.
    Council of Pollution Control Financing Agencies - 9-D
    National Association of Urban Flood Management Agencies - 13-D
Linton, Thomas L. - 27-D
Lipsen & Hamberger
    American Waterways Operators Inc. - 54-D

Datapoint Corp. - 33-D
Pen Inc. - 34-D
Westinghouse Electric Corp. - 35-D
Lipsen, Janice C. - 4-D
Lisbon Associates Inc. - 46-D
Litchstreet Co. - 15-D
Little, Barbara A. - 56-D
Little, Charles B. - 35-D
Litton Industries Inc. - 12-D
Livestock Marketing Association - 13-D
Lloyd, Jim - 39-D, 40-D, 41-D, 56-D, 57-D
Loble, Leslie - 43-D
Lobel, Novins & Lamont
Generic Pharmaceutical Industry Association - 31-D
Lohse, Robert C. - 25-D
London, Sheldon I. - 4-D
Lone Star Industries Inc. - 12-D, 34-D
Long Island Lighting Co. - 7-D, 12-D
Long, Thomas R. - 43-D, 49-D, 53-D
Loomis, Susan J. - 23-D
Lord, Day & Lord
Bowater North America Corp. - 5-D
Cargill Inc. - 52-D
Cargill Leasing Corp. - 52-D
Continental Grain Co. - 52-D
Los Angeles Community Redevelopment Agency - 23-D
Los Angeles Olympic Commemorative Coin Committee - 25-D, 46-D
Los Angeles Olympic Organizing Program - 26-D, 46-D
Louisiana Pacific Corp. - 34-D
Lovett, Richard J. - 41-D
Low, Matthew A. - 46-D
Loyal Trust - 46-D
LTV Corp. - 7-D, 56-D
Lubick, Donald C. - 49-D
Luz International LTD. - 34-D, 40-D
Lyle, Edward - 55-D

M

M & M Plastics - 20-D
Machinery Dealers National Association - 24-D
Mackenzie, William M. - 31-D
MacMillan Bloedel Inc. - 28-D
Macrory, Ann K. - 32-D
Mago, Michela S. - 35-D
Maguire, W. Terry - 36-D
Mahoning Valley Economic Development Corp. - 30-D
Makah Indian Tribe - 14-D
Mallen, William G. - 9-D
Mallon Motors Inc. - 20-D
Malone, Mary Jo - 17-D
Management Insights Inc. - 48-D, 52-D
Manatt, Phelps, Rothenberg & Tunney
American Pacific International Inc. - 55-D
Dutcher Industries - 19-D
Gatx Corp. - 27-D
General Telephone Co. of California - 40-D
Institute of Electrical & Electronic Engineers - 24-D
Los Angeles Community Development Agency - 23-D
Luz International Ltd. - 34-D
Music Corporation of America Inc. - 52-D
National Investment Development Corp. - 20-D
Nissan Motor Corp. in U.S.A. - 41-D
Northrup Corp. - 20-D
Northwest Alaska Pipeline Co. - 34-D
Pharmaceutical Manufacturers Association - 37-D
Schneider, James - 46-D
Texas Air Corp. - 42-D

20th Century Fox Film Corp. - 22-D
Mannen, Ted R. - 13-D
Mansfield, Cynthia - 56-D
Manufacturers Hanover Corp. - 20-D
Manufacturers of Emission Controls Association - 44-D
Marathon Oil Co. - 15-D
Marconi Space & Defense Systems - 28-D
Maritime Institute for Research and Industrial Development - 45-D
Markey, Richard P. - 17-D
Markham III, Vernon - 35-D
Marks, Nathan Fred - 55-D
Marshall, Bratter, Greene, Allison & Tucker
Cadillac Fairview U.S. Inc. - 39-D
Drexel Burnham Lambert Inc - 47-D
Marshall, Charles L. - 20-D
Martin, Clarence J. - 9-D, 10-D
Martin, John M. Jr. - 24-D, 37-D
Martin Ryan Haley & Associates Inc.
Agri-Business Inc. - 5-D
Operation Independence - 6-D
West Alabama Grain Products Cooperative Inc. - 8-D
Marx, Mrs. A. Lester - 46-D
Maryland Savings-Share Insurance Corp. - 12-D
Massachusetts Association of Contributory Retirement Systems Inc. - 24-D, 31-D
Massachusetts Bay Transit Authority - 49-D
Massachusetts Construction Industry Council - 36-D
Massachusetts Hospital Association - 31-D
Massie, James D. - 13-D
Matlack Inc. - 40-D, 48-D
C.H. Mayer Inc.
L.P. Management Corp. - 40-D
Mayer, Brown & Platt
Brunswick Corp. - 51-D
Comdisco Inc. - 27-D
General Telephone and Electronics Corp. - 56-D
National Association of Manufacturers' FTC-Antitrust Subcommittee - 17-D
Northwest Alaskan Pipeline Co. - 53-D
Mayflower Corp. - 41-D
McCabe, Martha - 14-D
McCandless & Barrett
Transamerica Life Insurance & Annuity Co. & Occidental Life Insurance Co. - 4-D
McCarter, Katherine S. - 54-D
McCarthy, James W. - 4-D
McCharen, Cathy - 25-D, 31-D
McClure & Trotter
Gulf & Western Industries Inc. - 34-D
Gulf Resources & Chemical Corp. - 34-D
Tractor Corp. - 35-D
McCrary, Toni - 30-D
McCrystal, Thomas - 18-D
McDermott Inc. - 48-D
McDonnell Douglas Corp. - 20-D
McDowell, Susan K. - 10-D
McElfresh, Dinah D. - 10-D, 18-D
McGee, Donna Lee - 7-D
McGuire, William P. - 38-D
MCI Communications Corp. - 56-D
MCI Telecommunications Inc. - 52-D
McIntyre, Robert S. - 7-D
McKee, Jean - 11-D
McKenzie, Jan E. - 44-D
McKernan, Robert T. - 17-D, 23-D
McMillan, Robert R. - 55-D
McNair, Glenn, Kondouras
General Telephone & Electronics Corp. - 52-D
McNamara, Faith - 8-D

McPike, Jane - 18-D
Mead Corp. - 34-D, 41-D, 52-D, 56-D
Meagher, John K. - 7-D
Medical College of Pennsylvania, The - 32-D
Mehler, Richard A. - 36-D
Meisinger, Susan R. - 17-D
Menache, Jack - 39-D
Menard, Marilee - 9-D
Mencher, Julie - 32-D
Mercer, James G. - 50-D
Mercer, William M. Inc. - 56-D
Merck & Co. Inc. - 20-D
Merlis, Edward A. - 20-D
Merrell Dow Pharmaceuticals Inc. - 20-D
Merrill Lynch & Co. Inc. - 3-D, 5-D
Merrill Lynch, Hubbard Inc. - 28-D
Merrill Lynch Leasing Inc. - 20-D
Merrill Lynch White Weld Capital Markets Group - 56-D
Messinger, Sharon L. - 7-D
Metro-Metropolitan Service District, Tri-County Metropolitan Transportation District, State of Oregon, City of Portland, Ore. - 16-D
Metropolitan District Commission - 16-D
Metropolitan Water District of Southern California - 7-D
Metzger, Shadyac & Schwarz
National Bank of Alaska - 7-D
Philadelphia National Bank - 53-D
Meyers, Larry - 24-D, 25-D
MFA Mutual Insurance Co. - 28-D
Miami, City of - 36-D
Miami Conservancy District - 53-D
Michaud, Brenda J. - 50-D
Michel, Laurie L. - 20-D
Midamerica Commodity Exchange - 3-D
Midland Enterprises Inc. - 48-D
Mignini, Paul J. Sr. - 57-D
Miles & Stockbridge
Pizza Hut Inc. - 53-D
Milliken & Co. - 56-D
Miliken Research Corp. - 41-D
Military Accessories Service Association Inc. - 45-D
Millar, Fred - 38-D
Miller & Chevalier
General Dynamics Corp. - 48-D
Koppers Co. Inc. - 40-D
Miller, Canfield, Paddock & Stone
International Paper Co. - 48-D, 52-D
Miller, Cassidy, Larroca & Lewin
Mead Corp. - 52-D
National Public Radio - 20-D
Miller Coal Systems Inc. - 15-D
Miller, Daniel R. - 10-D
Miller, John R. - 21-D
Millman, Richard M. - 54-D
Ministry of Foreign Affairs of the Kingdom of Saudi Arabia - 16-D
Minnich, Deborah M. - 40-D, 48-D
Mintz, Levin, Cohn, Glovsky and Popeo
Massachusetts Construction Industry Council - 37-D
National Cable Television Association - 45-D
SCA Services - 8-D, 16-D
Securities Industry Association - 58-D
Miranda, Thom B. - 30-D
Mishoe, Stafford Michael - 18-D
Misiorowski, Mark R. - 9-D
Missouri Terminal Oil Co. Inc. - 28-D
Mitchell Energy & Development Corp. - 41-D
Monley, John M. - 42-D
Monsanto Co. - 20-D, 41-D
Montana, State of - 49-D
Montgomery Ward Co. Inc. - 15-D, 20-D, 28-D

Moodie, Steven M. - 24-D
Mooney, James P. - 10-D
Moore McCormack Resources Inc. - 20-D
Moore, Thomas H. - 37-D
Morgan, J. Michael - 51-D, 53-D
Morgan, Lewis & Bockius
Knoll Fine Chemicals Inc. - 20-D
Morgan, Richard D. - 17-D
Morrill, James A. - 48-D
Morris, Gerald A. - 49-D
Morrison & Foerster
City and County of San Francisco - 22-D
Mortgage Guaranty Insurance Corp. - 34-D
Mosher, Russell N. - 23-D, 49-D, 54-D
Moss, Bernard - 30-D
Moss, Larry E. - 3-D
Motor and Equipment Manufacturers Association - 37-D
Motorcycle Industry Council Inc. - 31-D
Motorola Inc. - 52-D
Motor Vehicle Manufacturers Association of the U.S. Inc. - 17-D
Moulton, David Hurd - 7-D
Mountain States Energy Inc. - 20-D
Mountain West Associates - 34-D, 37-D, 49-D
Mowsafe Products Inc. - 20-D
Multifamily Finance Action Group - 28-D
Multi-state Communications Inc. - 28-D
Muncy, James - 18-D
Municipal Labor Committee - 36-D
Murphy & Boyle
Chicago Board of Trade - 47-D
Murphy, George L. - 22-D
Murphy, Jeanne Marie - 24-D
Murphy, K.R. - 48-D
Murphy, Richard W. - 13-D
Murray Ohio Manufacturing Co. - 4-D
Music Corporation of America Inc. - 52-D
Mustang Fuel Corp. - 5-D
Muth, Robert J. - 7-D
Mutter, Lawrence P. - 36-D
Mutual Savings Central Fund Inc. - 56-D

N

Nabisco Inc. - 20-D
National Agricultural Chemicals Association - 9-D
National Air Tankers Association - 31-D
National Association of Aircraft and Communications Suppliers Inc. - 50-D
National Association of Arab Americans - 33-D
National Association of Broadcasters - 45-D, 58-D
National Association of Business and Educational Radio Inc. - 17-D
National Association of Catalog Showroom Merchandisers Inc. - 17-D
National Association of Chain Drug Stores - 45-D, 50-D, 54-D
National Association of Convenience Stores - 31-D
National Association of Credit Management - 9-D
National Association of Furniture Manufacturers - 31-D
National Association of Home Builders - 37-D, 54-D
National Association of Independent Insurers - 31-D, 37-D
National Association of Industrial & Office Parks - 45-D
National Association of Manufacturers - 5-D, 9-D, 13-D, 24-D, 37-D, 45-D, 50-D

National Association of Manufacturers' FTC-Antitrust Subcommittee - 17-D

National Association of Mutual Savings Banks - 24-D

National Association of Numismatic Professionals - 54-D

National Association of Optometrists and Opticians Inc. - 37-D

National Association of Pension Funds - 13-D

National Association of Police Organizations - 5-D

National Association of Public Hospitals - 24-D

National Association of Realtors - 24-D, 37-D, 54-D

National Association of Retail Druggists - 5-D

National Association of Royalty Owners Inc. - 6-D

National Association of Small Business Investment Companies - 13-D

National Association of State Agencies for Food Distribution - 43-D, 54-D

National Association of Truck Stop Operators - 45-D

National Association of Urban Flood Management Agencies - 9-D, 13-D

National Association of Wholesaler-Distributors - 10-D

National Audubon Society - 46-D, 51-D, 55-D

National Bank of Alaska - 7-D

National Bank of Detroit - 8-D, 20-D

National Beer Wholesalers Association - 50-D, 58-D

National Board of Young Men's Christian Associations - 51-D

National Broadcasting Co. Inc. - 56-D

National Business Aircraft Association - 5-D

National Cable Television Association - 10-D, 24-D, 31-D, 45-D, 50-D

National Cattlemen's Association - 58-D

National Clean Air Coaliton - 18-D, 26-D

National Coal Association - 24-D, 45-D

National Committee of Discount Securities Brokers - 37-D, 50-D

National Committee for Research in Neurological & Communicative Disorders - 10-D

National Community Action Agency Executive Directors Association - 10-D, 13-D

National Community Action Foundation Inc. - 14-D, 18-D, 32-D, 38-D, 46-D

National Conference of Bankruptcy Judges - 45-D

National Congress of American Indians - 18-D, 38-D

National Congress of Parents and Teachers - 51-D

National Con-Serv Inc. - 41-D, 48-D

National Constructors Association - 18-D

National Consumer Finance Association - 3-D

National Consumer Law Center - 37-D

National Cotton Council of America - 50-D, 58-D

National Council of Farmer Cooperatives - 13-D, 24-D, 31-D, 50-D

National Council on Synthetic Fuels Production - 13-D

National Education Association - 10-D, 11-D, 22-D, 36-D, 43-D

National Energy Efficiency Coalition - 7-D

National Family Planning and Reproductive Health Association Inc. - 18-D, 51-D

National Farm and Power Equipment Dealers Association - 54-D

National Farmers Organizations - 10-D

National Federation of Community Development Credit Unions - 50-D

National Federation of Independent Business - 31-D

National Federation of Parents for Drug Free Youth - 19-D

National Food Processors Association - 13-D, 45-D

National Forest Products Association - 31-D

National Gasohol Commission - 54-D

National Grange - 10-D

National Health Action Committee - 18-D

National Housing Law Project - 50-D

National Investment Development Corp. - 20-D

National Legal Aid & Defenders Association - 7-D

National Limestone Institute Inc. - 13-D

National Machine Tool Builders' Association - 13-D

National Management Association, The - 24-D

National Medical Enterprises Inc. - 52-D

National Military Wives Association Inc. - 49-D

National Milk Producers Federation - 45-D

National Multi Housing Council - 13-D, 24-D, 31-D, 50-D

National Music Publishers' Association - 58-D

National Ocean Industries Association - 45-D, 54-D

National Office Machine Dealers Association - 37-D, 50-D

National Oil Jobbers Council - 13-D, 45-D, 54-D

National Organization for the Reform of Marijuana Laws - 7-D

National Organization for Women - 38-D, 55-D

National Parking Association - 24-D

National Parks and Conservation Association - 3-D

National Peace Academy Campaign - 50-D

National Pork Producers Council - 18-D

National Potato Council - 25-D, 31-D

National Public Affairs Corp. - 42-D

National Public Radio - 18-D, 20-D

National Restaurant Association - 54-D

National Rifle Association of America - 7-D, 19-D, 26-D, 38-D

National Right to Life Committee Inc. - 46-D

National Right to Work Committee - 14-D, 19-D

National Rural Development and Finance Corp. - 48-D, 53-D

National Rural Electric Cooperative Association - 25-D, 31-D

National Soft Drink Association - 25-D

National Tax Limitation Committee - 33-D, 47-D

National Taxpayers Legal Fund - 26-D

National Technical Schools of Los Angeles - 28-D, 32-D, 34-D

National Telephone Cooperative Association - 25-D, 50-D

Nationwide Insurance Co. - 28-D

Natural Gas Supply Association - 58-D

Natural Resources Defense Council - 19-D, 38-D

Navajo Nation, The - 7-D, 11-D

NCR Corp. - 41-D

Neale, Karen J. - 17-D

Neighborhood School Counsel, Turner Elementary School - 19-D, 20-D

Neighborhood TV Co. Inc. - 20-D

Nelson, Gaylord - 11-D

Nelson, Nick L. Van - 47-D

Nelson, Sandie - 10-D

Nelson, Thomas C. - 9-D

Nesbeitt, William D. - 55-D

Ness, Elizabeth - 32-D

Hugo Neu & Sons Inc. - 34-D, 41-D

Neuschel, Carla - 9-D

New Energy Corp. of Indiana - 20-D

New England Council Inc., The - 45-D

New York Life Insurance Co. - 8-D

New York State Department of Transportation - 30-D

New York State Mortgage Loan Enforcement and Administration Corp. - 30-D

New York State Urban Development Corp. - 30-D

Newcomb Securities Co. - 34-D, 41-D

Newcomer, Leslie F. - 53-D

Newman, William B. Jr. - 11-D

Newmont Mining Corp. - 48-D

Newrath, Meyer and Faller
  National Association of Business and Educational Radio Inc. - 17-D

Newspaper-Broadcaster Committee - 25-D

NFL Players Association - 22-D

Nichols, Charles E. - 49-D

Nichols, Robert W. - 32-D

Nickerson, William W. - 49-D

Nissan Motor Corp. - 4-D, 41-D

NLT Corp. - 56-D

Nooley Reinheardt & Associates
  Rural Builders Council of California - 45-D

Noranda Mining Inc. - 12-D, 15-D, 20-D

Normile, Michael C. - 10-D, 13-D

Norrell, Julia J. - 6-D

Norris Industries - 4-D

North American Soccer League - 4-D

North American Telephone Association - 10-D

North Plains Grain Products Cooperative - 20-D

North Texas Municipal Water District - 43-D

Northeast New York Educational Television Association - 25-D

Northeast Utilities Service Co. - 25-D

Northern Solar Systems Inc. - 4-D

Northern Virginia Savings & Loan Association - 41-D

Northrop Corp. - 8-D, 12-D, 15-D, 20-D, 28-D, 41-D, 48-D

Northwest Alaskan Pipeline Co. - 34-D, 41-D, 53-D, 56-D

Northwest Bancorporation - 41-D

Northwest Industries Inc. - 28-D

Northwest Inland Waterways Committee - 48-D, 54-D

Northwest Marine Iron Works - 41-D

Northwest Texas Grain Products Cooperative - 41-D

Northwestern Mutual Life Insurance Co. - 34-D

Norton Simon Inc. - 48-D

Norton Sound Health Corp. - 15-D

Nossaman, Krueger & Marsh
  Aetna Life & Casualty - 7-D
  Burlington Northern - 47-D
  Dividend Support Group - 9-D
  Helionetics Inc. - 20-D
  Insurance Association of Connecticut - 9-D
  New York Life Insurance Co. - 8-D
  Phoenix Mutual Life Insurance Co. - 8-D
  Texas International Airlines Inc. - 49-D
  Western Union Telegraph Co. - 22-D

Nussbaum & Owen
  Plaintiffs' Antitrust Liaison Society - 38-D

Nyberg, C.D. - 28-D

O

Oasis Petroleum Co. - 21-D, 28-D

Obermayer, Rebmann, Maxwell & Hippel
  Munir P. Benjenk - 3-D

O'Brien, Mary Beth - 48-D

O'Bryon, David S. - 6-D

Occidental Petroleum Corp. - 21-D

Ocean Spray Cranberries Inc. - 5-D

Ocean Minerals Co. - 48-D

O'Connor & Hannan
  American Association of Advertising Agencies - 56-D
  Blyth Eastman Paine Webber - 39-D
  Bricker & Eckler - 56-D
  Deak National Bank - 15-D, 33-D
  Glass Packaging Institute - 24-D
  Great National Corp. - 27-D
  Kimberly-Clark Corp. - 52-D
  National Association of Numismatic Professionals - 54-D
  National Community Action Foundation - 14-D, 18-D
  Neighborhood TV Co. Inc. - 20-D
  Paraho Development Corp. - 28-D
  J.C. Penny Co. Inc. - 21-D, 28-D
  Plateau Inc. - 34-D
  Joseph E. Seagram & Sons Inc. - 15-D, 32-D
  Southern Indiana Shale Oil Co. Inc. - 42-D
  Tele-Cause - 54-D
  Transport Mutual Services Inc. - 35-D
  United Kingdom Mutual Steam Ship Assurance Association LTD. - 49-D
  West of England Ship Owners Mutual Protection and Indemnity Association - 49-D
  Wine and Spirits Wholesalers of America Inc. - 18-D

O'Connor, Patrick C. - 23-D

Offshore Industry Committee - 54-D

Ogden Corp. - 15-D

O'Hara, Barbara E. - 12-D, 23-D

Ohio State University - 25-D

Oil, Chemical and Atomic Workers International Union - 22-D

Oil Country Tubular Goods - 53-D

Oilfield Industrial Lines Inc. - 48-D

O'Keefe, Anne Marie - 9-D

O'Kelley, Harold E. - 39-D, 47-D

Oklahoma Mineral Owners and Surface Owners Association - 6-D

Old, R.Q. and Associates, Inc.
  General Electric Co. - 11-D
  Gould Inc. - 11-D
  Grumman Aerospace Corp. - 11-D
  Hughes Aircraft Co. - 11-D
  Sperry Division - 12-D, 21-D

O'Leary, Kathleen - 15-D

Olin Corp. - 28-D

Olsen, Dennis M. - 41-D, 42-D

Olson, Gerald L. - 21-D

Oman, Sultanate of - 22-D

O'Neal & Claassen
  National Air Tankers Association - 31-D

O'Neill & Haase
  Chris-Craft Industries Inc. - 39-D
  Legislative Alliance of Philatelists and Hard Asset Dealers and Collectors - 58-D
  Santerelli and Gimer - 46-D

O'Neill, Forgotson, Roncalio & Haase
  Mahoning Valley Economic Development Corp. - 30-D
  Massachusetts Hospital Association - 31-D

Operation Independence - 6-D

Organization for the Preservation of the Public Employee Retirement Industry & Opposition to Social Security Expansion - 16-D
Organization for the Protection and Advancement of Small Telephone Companies - 18-D, 50-D
Orly, Elvira - 31-D
Otis Elevator Corp. - 21-D
O'Toole, M. Diane - 12-D, 15-D
O'Toole, Stephen E. - 15-D
Ouse, Cliff - 25-D, 31-D
Outdoor Advertising Association of America Inc. - 25-D
Outdoor Power Equipment Institute - 25-D, 31-D
Overseas Education Association - 36-D, 43-D
Owens-Illinois - 41-D
Oy Wartsila Ab - 41-D

P

P.L. Thomas & Co. Inc. - 21-D
Pacific Gas and Electric - 41-D
Pacific Northern Oil - 15-D
Pacific Resources Inc. - 15-D
Pacific Seafood Processors Association - 37-D, 45-D
Pacor Corp. - 21-D
Paden, Lee W. - 41-D
Painesville, City of - 36-D
Palast, Geri - 36-D
Palmer, Christopher N. - 46-D
Palo Verde Irrigation District - 15-D
Paraho Development Corp. - 28-D
Paralysis Cure Research Foundation - 26-D
Parke, Nancy L. - 34-D
Partnership Placements Inc. - 8-D
Parrish & Chambers Inc.
  Oy Wartsila Ab - 41-D
Paskus, Gordon & Hyman
  National Music Publishers' Association - 58-D
Pathologist Practice Association - 37-D, 45-D
Patterson, Belknap, Webb & Tyler
  International Paper Co. - 34-D
Patton, Boggs & Blow
  American Retail Federation - 30-D
  Burlington Industries Inc. - 47-D
  Callery Judge Grove - 39-D
  Campaign for Community Based Economic Development - 32-D
  Cargill Inc. - 27-D
  Conoco Inc. - 39-D
  Dredging Industry Size Standards Committee - 13-D
  E.G.G. Industries - 33-D
  General Mills Inc. - 27-D
  Great Atlantic & Pacific Tea Co. Inc. - 40-D
  Lasco Shipping Co. - 40-D
  Lee Way Motor Frieght Inc. - 11-D
  Litton Industries Inc. - 12-D
  Los Angeles Olympic Commemorative Coin Committee - 25-D
  Los Angeles Olympic Organizing Committee - 26-D
  M & M Plastics - 20-D
  MCI Telecommunications Inc. - 52-D
  Montgomery Ward Co. Inc. - 28-D
  National Association of Manufacturers - 45-D
  National Association of Small Business Investment Companies - 13-D
  National Association of Truck Stop Operators - 45-D
  National Cable Television Association - 50-D
  National Soft Drink Association - 25-D

Penn Central Corp. - 28-D
The Pillsbury Co. - 28-D
Sheridan-Kalorama Neighborhood Council - 38-D
Shipbuilders' Council of America - 37-D
Sultanate of Oman - 22-D
Union Pacific Corp. - 42-D
U.S. Lines - 29-D
Western Union Telegraph Company - 12-D
Weyerhaeuser Co. - 29-D
Payco American Corp. - 34-D
Peabody, Rivlin, Lambert & Meyers
  International Communications Association - 6-D
  Organization for the Preservation of the Public Employee Retirement Industry & Opposition to Social Security Expansion - 16-D
  Southern California Gas - 35-D
Peacock, William E. - 27-D, 40-D
Pelican Terminal - 41-D
Pen Inc. - 34-D
Penn Central Corp. - 28-D
J.C. Penney Co. Inc. - 21-D, 28-D
Pennsylvania Association of Industrial Development Authorities - 43-D
Penny, Donald - 12-D
Pennzoil Co. - 4-D
Penobscot Indian Nation - 14-D
People Express Airlines Inc. - 21-D
People Opposed to Energy Lobby (POTEL) - 26-D
People Organized in Neighborhoods Together (POINT) - 26-D
Peoples Energy Corp. - 28-D
Pepper & Corazzini
  Philadelphia Belt Line Railroad - 48-D
Pepper, Hamilton & Scheetz
  Alarm Device Manufacturing Co. - 26-D
  Alarm Industry Telecommunications Committee of the National Burglar & Fire Alarm Association - 30-D
  Fair Opportunities for Competion in the U.S. (FOCUS) - 44-D
  Hooker Investments Ltd. - 56-D
  National Community Action Foundation - 18-D
  National Public Radio - 18-D
  Southern Pacific Communication Co. - 57-D
Pepsico Inc. - 28-D
Perito, Duerk, Carlson & Pinco
  Advanced Health Systems Inc. - 55-D
Perkinson, Gary J. - 26-D
Perpetual American Federal Savings and Loan Association - 56-D
Perry, Susan - 44-D
Peter Small & Associates Inc.
  William M. Mercer Inc. - 56-D
Peterson, Russell W. - 46-D
Petroleum Heat and Power Co. - 8-D
Petro-Lewis Corp. - 56-D
Pfizer Inc. - 21-D, 41-D
Pharmaceutical Manufacturers Association - 10-D, 37-D
Pharo, Gwen - 48-D
Phelps Dodge Corp. - 21-D
PHH Group Inc. - 15-D, 48-D
Philadelphia Belt Line Railroad - 48-D
Philadelphia, City of - 8-D
Philadelphia Gas Works - 8-D
Philadelphia National Bank - 53-D
Philadelphia Stock Exchange - 8-D
Phillips Petroleum Co. - 8-D, 12-D, 21-D, 41-D
Phillips, Richard F. - 8-D
Phoenix Mutual Life Insurance Co. - 8-D
Piccolo, Joan A. - 27-D
Pickett, W.D. - 22-D
Pickman, James - 32-D

Piedmont Airlines - 41-D
Pierce, Molly J. - 7-D
Pierson, Ball & Dowd
  Genentech Inc. - 56-D
  Independent Telecommunications Suppliers' Council - 54-D
  Infectious Diseases Society of America - 58-D
  National Association of Royalty Owners Inc. - 6-D
  Neighborhood School Counsel, Turner Elementary School - 19-D
  Oklahoma Mineral Owners and Surface Owners Association - 6-D
  Tele-Cause - 54-D
  Turner Elementary School - 32-D
Pierson, Elizabeth W. - 57-D
Pillsbury Co. - 21-D, 28-D
Piper & Marbury
  American Automobile Leasing Association Inc. - 30-D
  USAir Corp. - 42-D
Pizza Hut Inc. - 53-D
Plaintiffs' Anti-Trust Liaison Society - 38-D, 50-D
Planned Parenthood Federation of America, Inc. - 33-D
Planning Research Corp. - 41-D
Planters Peanuts - 53-D
Plateau Inc. - 34-D
Pleger, Wyll W. - 19-D, 27-D
PLM Inc. - 28-D
Pollock, Richard P. - 19-D
Pollard, Alfred M. - 35-D, 42-D
Popham, Haik, Schnobrich, Kaufman & Doty Ltd. - 34-D
  Chicago Mercantile Exchange - 39-D
Popham, James J. - 58-D
Population Crisis Committee - 26-D
Poquoson Motors Inc. - 21-D
Porpilia, Paula D. - 30-D
Portec Inc. - 28-D
Porter, Robert W. - 25-D, 31-D, 45-D
Portland, Oregon, City of - 16-D
Portman Properties - 12-D
Potato Chip/Snack Food Association - 13-D
Potlatch Corp. - 5-D
Powell, Goldstein, Frazer & Murphy
  Continental Employees Association - 43-D
  Council of State Housing Agencies - 43-D
  Intergraph Corp. - 28-D
  International Paper Co. - 48-D
  Lincoln Property Co. - 40-D
  Maryland Savings-Share Insurance Corp. - 12-D
  National Multi Housing Council - 24-D
  Westinghouse Electric Corp. - 16-D
Power Authority of the State of New York - 43-D
Power, Margaret - 38-D, 46-D
Prather Seeger Doolittle & Farmer
  Ruhrkohle A.G. - 21-D
Preston, Thorgrimson, Ellis & Holman
  Crowley Maritime Corp. - 55-D
  Organization for the Protection and Advancement of Small Telephone Companies - 18-D
  Ronan Telephone Co. - 6-D
Pretty, Keith A. - 8-D, 16-D
Priest & Fine Inc. - 6-D, 18-D
  National Technical Schools of Los Angeles - 28-D, 34-D
Priest, Daniel B. - 6-D, 18-D
Proctor, Stuart - 23-D
Professional Air Traffic Controllers Organization - 8-D, 12-D
Professional Insurance Agents - 6-D, 25-D
Proskauer, Rose, Goetz & Mendelsohn
  The League of New York Theatres and Producers Inc. - 44-D

Protect the Innocent Inc. - 19-D, 26-D
Province of Ontario, Canada, Ministry of the Environment - 43-D
Pruitt, James C. - 57-D
Public Citizen Inc. - 19-D
Public Employee Department, AFL-CIO - 30-D
Public Service Co. of New Hampshire - 8-D
Public Service Co. of Oklahoma - 41-D
Public Utility Tax Committee, The - 45-D
Pueblo De Cochiti - 51-D
Puerto Rico, Commonwealth of - 30-D
Puerto Rico, Senate of - 54-D
Puget Sound Power & Light Co. - 3-D, 4-D, 29-D
Pullin, Diana - 55-D
Pullman Standard - 34-D
Purcell, F. Eugene - 34-D
Purcell, Graham - 53-D, 54-D
Purcell, Hansen & Henderson
  National Association of State Agencies for Food Distribution - 43-D

Q

Quigley, James M. - 47-D

R

Rainbolt, John V. - 3-D
Ralston Purina Government Affairs Inc. - 41-D
Randall, Bangert & Thelen
  Pharmaceutical Manufacturers Association - 10-D
  Western Union International - 22-D
Randles, Carol - 45-D
Randol, Gayle - 23-D
Rasch Elecktronik - 6-D
Rauch, Robert - 55-D
Ravnholt, Eiler C. - 13-D
Rawls, W. Lee - 4-D
Ray Roberts & Associates - 10-D
  Centex Corp. - 15-D
  Guam Oil & Refining Co. Inc. - 15-D
  Texas Utilities Services Inc. - 16-D
Raytheon Co. - 21-D
Rearick, Linda S. - 45-D
Recording Industry Association of America Inc. - 10-D
Rector, John M. - 5-D
Redding, Robert E. - 37-D
Redman, Timothy Sr. - 17-D
Reed, Janet S. - 26-D
Rees, Joseph M. - 44-D
Reichhold Energy Corp. - 35-D
Reid & Priest
  Utility Group - 55-D
  Tom Reidy Inc. - 35-D
Reihl, Mark - 22-D
Reimer, Gary B. - 4-D
Reinertson, William W. - 17-D
Reiter, Jack - 21-D
Religious Coalition for Abortion Rights Inc. - 19-D
Renewable Energy Inc. - 48-D
Renewable Energy Institute - 55-D
Renewable Fuels Association - 25-D
Renewed Energy Corp. - 21-D
Republic Airlines Inc. - 21-D, 29-D, 35-D
Republic Geothermal Inc. - 29-D
Research Animal Alliance - 10-D
Reuss, Patricia Blau - 5-D
Reynolds & Pitt
  Robert D. Lange - 10-D
Rhodes, Robin Alan - 24-D
Richardson, John G. - 40-D
Richardson, John T. - 20-D
Richardson, Robert A. - 5-D
Richardson, Warren S. - 36-D

Richmond Leasing - 29-D
Ridinger, David C. - 48-D
Riggins, Valerie M. - 19-D
Riordan, Kevin J. - 20-D
Risk and Insurance Management Society Inc. - 45-D
James E. Ritchie & Associates - 37-D
Riviana Foods Inc. - 21-D, 35-D
Rizzo, Nicholas A. - 51-D
RJR Industries Inc. - 16-D, 41-D
RMI Inc. - 21-D
Ray Roberts & Associates - 10-D
   Brazos River Authority - 57-D
   Centex & Corp. - 15-D
   Guam Oil & Refining Co. Inc. - 15-D
   North Texas Municipal Water District - 43-D
   Texas Utilities Services Inc. - 16-D
Robbins, Elizabeth Jane - 21-D
Roberts, George - 11-D, 22-D
Roberts, Richard R. - 25-D
Robinson, William J. - 53-D
Rocha, John - 10-D
Rockwell International - 28-D
Rocky Mountain Energy Co. - 53-D
Rocky Mountain Oil and Gas Association - 13-D
Rogers & Wells
   Merrill Lynch Leasing Inc. - 20-D
Rogers, Hoge & Hills
   National Association of Chain Drug Stores - 54-D
Rogers, James T. - 54-D
Rogers, Susan M. - 7-D
Rogin, Carole M. - 10-D
Rohm and Haas Co. - 56-D
Roisman, Reno & Cavanaugh
   Citizens Housing & Planning Association Inc. - 46-D
   First Centrum Corp. - 47-D
   National Housing Law Project - 50-D
Rollins, Jack - 43-D
Rolm Corp. - 41-D
Ronan Telephone Co. - 6-D
Rooney, Fred B. - 19-D
Ropes and Gray
   The William Carter Co. - 27-D
Rosen, Burt - 21-D
Rosen, Richard - 58-D
Rosenbaum, Sara - 38-D
Rosenberg, Francis C. - 45-D
Rosenberg, Miriam Ann - 45-D
Rosenstein, Peter - 49-D
Rotan Mosle Inc. - 21-D, 29-D
Rudman, Gloria Cataneo - 24-D
Ruhrkohle A.G. - 21-D
Rule of Law Committee - 14-D
Runnels, Frank - 4-D
Runyan, John C. - 17-D
Rural Builders Council of California - 45-D
Rush, Charlotte - 40-D
Russell, Herbert E. - 38-D
Ryder Systems Inc. - 16-D

S

Sacia, Paul R. - 9-D
Saenz International Inc. - 56-D
Safetran Systems Corp. - 8-D
Salinger, Frank M. - 3-D
Salmon River Electric Cooperative - 4-D
San Diego Gas and Electric Co. - 41-D
San Francisco, City and County of - 22-D
Sandusky, Vincent R. - 6-D
Santa Ana Valley Irrigation Co. - 12-D
Santerelli and Gimer - 46-D
SCA Services Inc. - 8-D, 16-D
Schaffer, Mark L. - 37-D
Schechter, Deborah M. - 4-D, 30-D
Henry Schein Inc. - 18-D, 21-D

Scheiner, Ann C. - 4-D, 21-D
Scherer, Jane N. - 52-D
Schlicht, James P. - 23-D
Schloman, Kenneth D. - 26-D
Schlossberg-Cassidy & Associates Inc.
   Ocean Spray Cranberries Inc. - 5-D
Schmeling, Forest S. - 36-D
Schmidt, Amy - 30-D
Schneider, James - 46-D
Scholastic Magazines Inc. - 21-D
Schroeder, H.B.W. - 33-D
Schwabe, Williamson, Wyatt, Moore and Roberts
   Eugene, Water and Electric Board - 23-D
   General Aviation Manufacturers Association - 36-D
   Helicopter Loggers Association - 17-D
   Litchstreet Co. - 15-D
   Los Angeles Community Redevelopment Agency - 23-D
   Mountain States Energy Inc. - 20-D
   Northwest Inland Waterways Committee - 48-D, 54-D
   Otis Elevator Co. - 21-D
   Portland, Oregon, City of - 16-D
   Western Forest Industries Association - 25-D
Schwartz, Elizabeth Nash - 15-D
Schwartz, Harry K. - 29-D
Schwartz, Steve Aaron - 49-D
Scientific Apparatus Makers Association - 45-D
Scott Co., The - 53-D
Scott, Douglas W. - 19-D
Scott Paper Co. - 21-D, 48-D
Scott, Robert D. - 12-D
Sea Colony Inc. - 41-D
Seafarers International Union - 22-D
Joseph E. Seagram & Sons Inc. - 15-D, 21-D, 29-D, 42-D
Search Group Inc. - 14-D
Sears, Roebuck & Co. - 21-D, 29-D
Seattle First National Bank - 21-D
Securities Group, The - 42-D
Securities Industry Association - 25-D, 58-D
Security Pacific National Bank - 29-D, 35-D, 42-D
Seeger, Charles M. III - 27-D, 34-D
Seifman & Lechner
   Massachusetts Association of Contributory Retirement Systems Inc. - 24-D, 31-D
   National Association of Police Organizations - 5-D
Selden, Armistead I. Jr. - 12-D
Senior Executives Association - 45-D
Senner, Patricia - 26-D
Senter, David - 37-D
Service Employees International Union, AFL-CIO, CLC - 36-D
Service Station Dealers of America Inc. - 10-D, 25-D
Seward & Kissel - 29-D, 32-D, 40-D
Sewell, Leslie - 18-D
Seyfarth, Shaw, Fairweather & Geraldson
   Agricultural Producers - 23-D
   National Multi Housing Council - 31-D
   Shipbuilders Council of America - 31-D
Seymour, Clive - 29-D
Shaklee Corp. - 53-D
Shamrock Ford - 21-D
Shannon, Debbie - 29-D
Shannon, Heffernan, Moseman & Goren
   Colt Industries - 15-D
Shapiro, David L. - 17-D
Sharp, Norman F. - 57-D
Shaw, G. Jerry - 45-D
Shaw, Luther W. - 9-D

Shaw, Pittman, Potts & Trowbridge
   Council for American Private Education - 4-D
Shawmut Corp. - 8-D
Shea & Gould
   Chancellor Corp. - 52-D
   Cincinnati Milacron - 55-D
Shearman & Sterling
   The Business Roundtable - 36-D
   Corning Associates - 14-D
Shearson Loeb Rhoades Inc. - 48-D
Sheet Metal and Air Conditioning Contractors' National Association Inc. - 6-D
Sheldon, L. Philip Jr. - 6-D
Shelton, Debra K. - 44-D
Sher, Allan L. - 3-D, 5-D
Sheridan-Kalorama Neighborhood Council - 38-D
Sheriff, Seymour - 26-D
Sherman, Michael S. - 31-D
Sherwin, Dale - 43-D, 49-D
Shipbuilders' Council of America - 31-D, 37-D, 45-D
Shipley, Smoak & Akerman
   Bluejay Oil Co. - 33-D, 47-D
   Federated Department Stores Inc. - 33-D, 47-D
   Flanigan's Enterprises Inc. - 33-D, 48-D
   Fort Sill Gardens Inc. - 34-D, 48-D
   National Committee of Discount Securities Brokers - 37-D, 50-D
   Steadman Mutual Funds - 35-D, 48-D
   Steadman Security Corp. - 35-D, 49-D
   U.S.-South West Africa Trade and Cultural Council - 36-D, 49-D
   WBNO Radio - 35-D, 49-D
   WLKM Radio - 35-D, 49-D
Shippers National Freight Claim Council Inc. - 37-D
Shives, Fletcher - 47-D
Shoshone-Bannock Tribes - 14-D
Shrimp Harvesters Coalition of the Gulf Coast and South Atlantic States - 37-D, 50-D
Shuffett, Kenton, Curry & Karem
   Lincoln Property Co. - 52-D
Shutler, Norman D. - 46-D
Sidley & Austin
   Dekalb Agresearch Inc. - 52-D
   Stern Electronics Inc. - 53-D
Mark A. Siegel & Associates
   Archer-Daniels-Midland Co. - 51-D
   City of Kansas City - 53-D
   Twin City Barge Inc. - 53-D
Sierra Club - 5-D, 12-D, 19-D, 55-D
Sierra Pacific Power Co. - 42-D
Silver Eagle Oil Co. Inc. - 12-D
Silverglade, Bruce A. - 50-D
Silverman, Susan - 19-D
Silverstein and Mullens
   HWL Properties - 56-D
Simmons, Amanda - 32-D
Simms, Gary D. - 9-D
J.R. Simplot Co. - 42-D, 48-D
Simpson, C. Kyle - 4-D
Sindab, Jean - 5-D
Sinville, Donald E. - 8-D
Sisk, Foley, Hultin & Driver
   Tosco Corp. - 4-D
Six Agency Committee - 10-D
Skadden, Arps, Slate, Meagher & Flom
   Continental Oil Co. - 27-D
   Mead Corp. - 34-D
   Texas International Airlines Inc. - 42-D
   Westvaco Corp. - 52-D
Skelton, Angela G. - 44-D
Slurry Transport Association - 10-D, 31-D, 58-D
Smircina, James R. - 7-D, 15-D
Smathers, Symington & Herlong
   National Farm and Power Equipment Dealers Association - 54-D

Smith & Pepper
   American Association of Private Railroad Car Owners Inc. - 25-D
Smith, Catherine S. - 16-D
Smith, Charles R. - 19-D
Smith, David H. - 7-D
Smith, Douglas S. - 20-D
Smith, Grace H. - 58-D
Smith, Thomas Blaisdell - 14-D
Smolen, Joseph S. - 36-D
Snelling and Snelling Inc. - 57-D
Snyder, Charles W. - 7-D
Snyder, John M. - 14-D
Solar Lobby - 7-D
Solar Power Corp. - 42-D
Solmecs Corp. - 16-D
Sopher, Terry - 14-D
Sophos, Mary - 13-D
South Lake Tahoe, City of - 16-D
Southdown/Pelto Oil Co. - 21-D
Southern California Gas - 35-D
Southern Furniture Manufacturers Association - 31-D
Southern Indiana Shale Oil Co. Inc. - 42-D
Southern Pacific Communications Co. - 4-D, 21-D, 53-D, 57-D
Southern Tier ETV Association - 25-D
Southland-Arizona Colleges - 53-D
Southwestern Peanut Growers - 25-D
Spady, Claudia R. - 8-D, 16-D
Sperry and Hutchinson Co., The - 42-D
Sperry Corp. - 8-D, 35-D, 57-D
Sperry Division - 12-D, 21-D
Sporting Arms and Ammunition Manufacturers Institute - 50-D
Springer, Ted C. - 4-D
Spruell Development Corp. - 42-D
Squire, Sanders & Dempsey
   City of Painesville - 36-D
St. George/Highly Corp. - 8-D
St. Joe Minerals Corp. - 16-D, 21-D
St. Regis Paper Co. - 41-D
Stahl, Melvin R. - 31-D
Stamm, George W. - 56-D
Staley, Robert W. - 19-D
Standard & Poor's Corp. - 4-D
Standard Oil Co. (Indiana) - 8-D, 16-D, 57-D
Standard Oil Co. (Ohio) - 4-D, 21-D, 57-D
Stanfield, Mitchel - 11-D
Stanford, Williams and Briggs
   National Association of Industrial & Office Parks - 45-D
Stang, David P. - 48-D, 49-D, 54-D
State Farm Mutual Automobile Insurance Co. - 42-D
Statham & Associates, Robert R. - 37-D
Samuel E. Stavisky & Associates Inc. - 27-D
Stayin, Robert J. - 23-D
Steadman Mutual Funds - 35-D, 48-D
Steadman Security Corp. - 49-D
Steamship Conferences - 54-D
Steiner, Barbara W. - 8-D
Steiner, George C. - 6-D
Stephens Overseas Services Inc. - 35-D, 37-D
Steptoe & Johnson
   International Paper Co. - 52-D
   Kiawah Island Co. - 28-D
   Rule of Law Committee - 14-D
Stern Brothers Inc. - 35-D, 42-D
Stern Electronics Inc. - 53-D
Steward, Michael E. - 29-D
Stewart Environmental Systems Inc. - 35-D
Stichting Philips Pensioenfonds A And B - 6-D
Stier, Eleanor - 51-D
Stockholders of America Inc. - 14-D, 25-D

Stockmeyer, Steven F. - 50-D
Stotler, M. Elizabeth - 45-D
Stovall, Ros - 19-D, 26-D
Stover, Alan - 9-D
Stratton, Frederick P. - 31-D
Straub, Terence D. - 12-D
Strauss, Louis H. - 46-D
Streeter, Richard H. - 39-D
Stroock & Stroock & Lavan
    J. Aron & Co. Inc. - 38-D
    Chemolimpex - 39-D
    Chinoin - 39-D
    Shearson Loeb Rhoades Inc. - 48-D
Suffolk, County of - 30-D
Sullivan & Cromwell
    American International Group Inc. - 26-D
    Bache Group Inc. - 11-D
    Securities Industry Association - 25-D
Sullivan & Worcester
    Dollar Savings Bank - 40-D, 52-D
    Washington Mutual Savings Bank - 42-D, 53-D
Sullivan, Gael M. - 56-D
Sullivan, Margaret Cox - 14-D, 25-D
Sullivan, Mary Beth - 25-D
Sullivan, Patrick J. - 30-D
Suman, Richard - 32-D
Summerville, Peter B. - 45-D
Sun Co. Inc. - 8-D
Surrey & Morse
    Arab Republic of Egypt - 16-D
    Bench Ad Co. - 39-D
    Walter E. Heller International Corp. - 40-D
    Pietro Beretta S.P.A. - 39-D
    Republic of Zaire - 22-D, 29-D
    Riviana Foods Inc. - 21-D, 35-D
Sutherland, Asbill & Brennan
    Baker International - 26-D
    Benjamin J. and Hugh McMaster Tarbutton - 50-D
    Carnegie Corp. of New York - 27-D
    Council of Industrial Boiler Owners - 24-D
    Flathead Joint Board of Control - 57-D
    Hagan Industries Inc. - 48-D
    Industrial Oil Consumers Group - 24-D
    Liberty Corp. - 40-D
    Lifetime Communities Inc. - 28-D
    Loyal Trust - 46-D
    Mrs. A. Lester Marx - 46-D
    Strauss, Louis H. - 46-D
    Winston, Edna - 46-D
Sutherlin, Donnae - 50-D
Sweitzer, Donald R. - 4-D
Swirling, Scott R. - 18-D, 51-D
Symington, Merribel - 47-D

T

Taft Broadcasting Co. - 29-D
Taft, Robert Jr. - 23-D
Taft, Stettinius & Hollister
    American Hot Dip Galvanizers Association - 23-D
    Miami Conservancy District - 53-D
    Taft Broadcasting Co. - 29-D
    Telephone and Data Systems Inc. - 8-D, 42-D
Talisman Fund - 49-D, 53-D
Tanadgusix Corp. - 26-D
Tanaka, Walders & Ritger
    Bridgestone Tire Co. Ltd. - 27-D
Tarbutton, Benjamin J. and Hugh McMaster - 50-D
Target Inc. - 4-D
Tarr-Whelan, Linda - 10-D
Tartaric Chemicals Corp. - 8-D
Tate, Dan C. - 56-D
Teachers Insurance and Annuity Association of America - 42-D

Teamster Local 959 Employee Pension Trust - 4-D
Teamsters for a Democratic Union - 8-D
Tele-Cause - 54-D
Telephone and Data Systems Inc. - 8-D, 42-D
Tele-Press Associates - 35-D
Telocator Network of America - 58-D
Temme, Lloyd V. - 38-D
Tendler, Paul M. - 6-D
Tenneco Oil Co. - 6-D
Tennessee Gas Pipeline Co. - 29-D
Tennessee Home Medical Providers Association Inc. - 10-D
Tennessee Synfuels Associates - 42-D
Terpstra, Betty-Grace - 31-D
Terry, Jay D. - 56-D
Terzano, John F. - 22-D
Tesoro Petroleum Corp. - 35-D
Texaco Inc. - 57-D
Texas Air Corp. - 42-D, 53-D
Texas Eastern Transmission Corp. - 42-D
Texas International Airlines Inc. - 42-D, 49-D
Texas Oil & Gas Corp. - 35-D
Texas, State Bar of - 51-D
Texas Utilities Services Inc. - 16-D
Texasgulf Inc. - 42-D
Thaxter, Lipez, Stevens, Broder & Micoleau
    American Express Co. - 47-D
    National Beer Wholesalers Association - 50-D
Therapedic - 53-D
Thevenot, Murray & Scheer
    American Institute of Architects - 23-D
    National Business Aircraft Association - 5-D
    Joseph E. Seagram & Sons Inc. - 21-D, 29-D
Thies, Barbara Brendes - 41-D
Thom, Edlu J. - 31-D
P.L. Thomas & Co. Inc. - 21-D
Thompson & Crawford
    American Business Coalition - 23-D, 30-D, 44-D, 54-D
Thompson & Mitchell
    American Inland Waterways Committee - 47-D
    Midland Enterprises Inc. - 48-D
    Valley Line Co., The - 49-D
Thompson, Gary C. - 22-D
Thompson, James Jr. - 23-D
Thompson, Robert N. - 20-D
Thornburg, Cynthia L. - 44-D
Thornburg, Richard B. - 58-D
Tiger International Inc. - 4-D, 21-D
Tilles, Roger - 21-D, 48-D, 53-D, 55-D
Time Inc. - 57-D
Timmons and Co. Inc.
    Eastern Air Lines Inc. - 15-D
    Los Angeles Commemorative Coin Committee - 25-D
    Los Angeles Olympic Organizing Committee - 26-D
Todd, Don - 46-D
Todd, M. Douglas - 48-D
Toledo Mining Co. - 29-D
Toledo Trust Co., The - 42-D
Toll, David R. - 9-D
Tom Reidy Inc. - 35-D
Tosco Corp. - 4-D, 29-D, 42-D, 49-D, 53-D
Tosco Oil Corp. - 12-D
Toyota Motor Sales U.S.A. Inc. - 4-D, 21-D
Trachtman, Richard L. - 9-D
Tracor Inc. - 35-D
Trailer Train Co. - 16-D, 29-D
Trailways - 29-D
Trammell, Jeffrey B. - 40-D
Trans America ICS - 35-D

Transamerica Life Insurance & Annuity Co. & Occidental Life Insurance Co. - 4-D
Transco Companies Inc. - 35-D
Trans-Lux Corp. - 35-D
Trans Ocean Leasing Corp. - 35-D
Transol Sunbelt Inc. - 49-D
Transportation Institute - 25-D
Transport Mutual Services Inc. - 35-D
Trans Union Corp. - 29-D
Trans World Airlines Inc. - 53-D
Travel Industry Association of America - 5-D, 6-D, 45-D
Ernest B. Tremmel Inc. - 33-D
Trisko, Eugene M. - 35-D, 42-D
Troy, Matthew William - 3-D
Truck Trailer Manufacturers Association - 10-D
Trull, Francine L. - 10-D
TRW Inc. - 6-D, 8-D, 22-D
Tulare Lake Water Users Committee - 19-D
Turner Broadcasting System Inc. - 49-D
Turner Elementary School - 32-D
Turner, Julia A. - 56-D
Turney, Richard F. - 36-D
Tuvin Associates
    North American Telephone Association - 10-D
    Twentieth Century Fox Film Corp. - 8-D
20th Century Fox Film Corp. - 21-D
Twin City Barge Inc. - 53-D
Twin Coasts Newspaper Inc. (The Journal of Commerce) - 35-D, 42-D

U

UBA Inc. - 35-D
Ukpeagvik Inupiat Corp. - 19-D
Ullman Consultants Inc.
    American Guaranty Financial Corp. - 19-D
    Confederated Tribes of the Warm Springs Reservation of Oregon - 38-D
    Merck & Co. Inc. - 20-D
    Public Utility Tax Committee - 45-D
    Spruell Development Corp. - 42-D
    Western Forest Industries Association - 25-D
Underwood Neuhaus - 29-D
Ungar, Manya S. - 51-D
Uni-Bell Plastic Pipe Association - 55-D
Union Carbide Corp. - 42-D, 49-D, 53-D
Union Oil Co. of California - 8-D
Union Pacific Corp. - 42-D
Union Tank Car Co.1 - 29-D
United Air Lines - 22-D
United Automobile, Aerospace and Agricultural Implement Workers of America, International Union - 43-D
United Brotherhood of Carpenters & Joiners of America - 16-D, 49-D
United Egg Producers - 25-D, 31-D
United Kingdom Mutual Steam Ship Assurance Association LTD. - 49-D
United States Automobile Association - 16-D
United States Industrial Council - 31-D
United States Leasing International Inc. - 22-D, 29-D
United States Rail Service Inc. - 29-D
United States Ski Association - 25-D
United States Steel Corp. - 12-D
United Technologies Corp. - 22-D
Universal Foods Inc. - 16-D
Upper Humboldt River Water Users Association - 55-D
Urban America Development Group Ltd. - 12-D
Urnikis, Marian S. - 44-D
USAir Inc. - 42-D
U.S. Ethanol Corp. - 42-D

U.S. Industrial & Business Council - 31-D
U.S. Industries Inc. - 42-D
U.S. Lines - 29-D
U.S. & Overseas Tax Fairness Committee - 18-D, 19-D, 33-D
U.S.- South West Africa Trade and Cultural Council - 36-D, 49-D
U.S. Telephone Communications Inc. - 57-D
U.S. Windpower Association - 22-D
U.S.O. Inc. - 51-D
Utah International Inc. - 6-D, 16-D
Utah Power and Light Co. - 49-D
Ute Mountain Ute Tribe - 3-D
Utility Group - 55-D

V

Valero Energy Corp. - 22-D, 35-D
Valley Line Co. - 49-D
Van Ness, Feldman & Sutcliffe
    General Public Utilities - 34-D
    Metropolitan District Commission
    U.S. Ethanol Corp. - 42-D
Van Schooneveld, Glenn R. - 38-D
Vannoy, Daniel W. - 9-D, 24-D
Venable, Baetjer, Howard & Civiletti
    Georgia Pacific Corp. - 56-D
    Mead Corp. - 56-D
    Westvaco Corp. - 57-D
Venners and Co. Ltd. - 48-D
Verner, Liipfert, Bernhard & McPherson
    Nissan Motor Corp. - 4-D
    Trans-Lux Corp. - 35-D
Verrastro, Frank - 53-D
VGS Corp. - 57-D
Vickerman, John C. - 50-D
Vienna, David & Associates
    National Association of Credit Management - 9-D
    State of California Office of the Comptroller - 36-D
Vietnam Veterans of America - 22-D
Villas, Steve A. - 4-D
Vinson & Elkins
    American General Corp. - 38-D
    Cullen, Roy - 46-D
    First City Bancorporation - 3-D
    Mitchell Energy & Development Corp. - 41-D
    Pelican Terminal - 41-D
    Slurry Transport Association - 58-D
Virginia Association of Railway Patrons - 14-D
Visa U.S.A. Inc. - 6-D
Volkswagen of America Inc. - 22-D
Voorde, Charlotte - 9-D
Vorys, Sater, Seymour & Pease
    Ad Hoc Committee on Individual Annuity Taxation Inc. - 18-D
    American Life and Casualty Co. - 15-D
    Bowery Savings Bank - 33-D
    Cabot Corporation - 55-D
    Committee of Publicly Owned Companies - 54-D
    General Instrument Corp. - 11-D
    Mowsafe Products Inc. - 20-D
    North American Soccer League - 4-D
    Toledo Trust Co., The - 42-D
Vought Corp. - 29-D

W

Wagner & Baroody
    Coeur D'Alene Mines - 33-D
Waisaman, Christine M. - 40-D
Wald, Harkrader & Ross
    Ad Hoc Committee to Preserve Federally Assisted Short Line Railroads - 18-D, 37-D
    Geothermal Kinetics Inc. - 15-D

Walicki, Joe - 26-D

Charls E. Walker & Associates
American Iron and Steel Institute - 17-D
Bank of New York - 39-D
Cigar Association of America Inc. - 9-D
Container Corp. of America - 39-D
CSX Corp. - 15-D
Dealer Bank Association - 13-D
FMC Corp. - 40-D
General Public Utilities Corp. - 27-D
Geothermal Kinetics Inc. - 15-D
Mead Corp., The - 41-D
Northwestern Mutual Life Insurance Co., The - 34-D
Phelps Dodge Corp. - 21-D
Scott Paper Co. - 21-D
Tennessee Synfuels Associates - 42-D
Tracor Inc. - 35-D

Wallace, Rob - 22-D

Walsh, Cleary, Hamsher & Davis - 29-D
Erie County Industrial Development Agency - 36-D

Walter E. Heller International Corp. - 40-D

Warner Communications Inc. - 12-D, 22-D

Warnke, Christine M. - 44-D

Washington Gas Light Co. - 4-D

Washington Industrial Team Inc.
Boeing Co. - 19-D
General Dynamics - 19-D
General Electric Co. - 27-D
Grumman Aerospace Corp. - 20-D
Hughes Aircraft Co. - 20-D
McDonnell Douglas Corp. - 20-D
Northrop Corp. - 28-D
Raytheon Co. - 21-D
Rockwell International - 29-D
TRW Inc. - 21-D
United Technologies Corp. - 22-D
Vought Corp. - 29-D
Westinghouse Electric Corp. - 22-D, 29-D

Washington Mutual Savings Bank - 42-D, 53-D

Washington Office of Africa - 5-D

Washington Psychiatric Society - 55-D

Waterman Steamship Corp. - 35-D

Watzman, Bruce H. - 24-D

WBNO Radio - 35-D, 49-D

Weaver, Vernon - 35-D

Webb, Geoffrey - 38-D

Webster & Sheffield
Kidder, Peabody & Co. Inc. - 40-D
Penobscot Indian Nation - 14-D

Webster, Chamberlain & Bean
American Paratransit Institute - 44-D

Weckstein, Paul - 55-D

Wegner, Charles Jr. - 25-D

Weil, Gotshal & Manges
The Continental Group - 39-D

Weiss, Joel A. - 33-D

Wells, Lance - 26-D

Weltner, Elizabeth S. - 48-D

Wentworth, Marchant - 10-D

Werner, Anne P. - 36-D

West Alabama Grain Products Cooperative Inc. - 8-D

West Mexico Vegetable Distributors Association - 37-D

West of England Ship Owners Mutual Protection and Indemnity Association - 49-D

West Texas Land and Royalty Owners Association - 50-D

Westec Services Inc. - 49-D

Western Development - 53-D

Western Forest Industries Association - 25-D, 31-D, 45-D

Western Growers Association - 45-D

Western Pennsylvania Coal Mining Association - 45-D

Western Pioneer Inc. - 35-D

Western Solar Utilization Network - 22-D

Western Union International - 22-D

Western Union Telegraph Co. - 12-D, 22-D

Westinghouse Broadcasting Co. - 53-D

Westinghouse Electric Corp. - 16-D, 22-D, 35-D, 42-D

Westmoreland Coal Co. - 42-D

Westvaco Corp. - 35-D, 43-D, 49-D, 53-D, 57-D

Wetzel, John F. - 31-D

Wexler and Associates
Beneficial Management Corporation of America - 55-D
GHK Companies, The - 11-D
Tosco Corp. - 42-D

Weyerhaeuser Co. - 29-D

Weymueller, Robert G. - 46-D

White & Case
Commercial Union Leasing Corp. - 33-D

White, Brenda - 36-D

White, Fine & Verville
Northwest Alaskan Pipeline Co. - 56-D

White, John C. - 39-D

Whitenton, Marshall E. - 57-D

Whitman, James A. - 45-D, 50-D

Whitney National Bank of New Orleans - 12-D

Whitsitt, William F. - 8-D

Whitten, David E. - 6-D

Whyche, Stephanie - 17-D

Wickham & Craft
Encyclopaedia Britannica Inc. - 15-D
PHH Group Inc. - 16-D
Ryder Systems Inc. - 16-D
Trailer Train Co. - 16-D

Wickwire, Gavin & Gibbs
Cogeneration Coalition Inc. - 13-D

Wien Air Alaska - 57-D

Wien Airlines - 22-D

Wilderness Society, The - 3-D, 11-D, 14-D, 26-D, 47-D

Wildlife Legislative Fund of America - 7-D, 51-D

Wildman, Harrold, Allen, Dixon & McDonnell
Cohen & Uretz - 18-D, 25-D

Wiles, Harry G. - 37-D

Wilhelm, Guenther O. - 40-D

Wilkerson, Carl B. - 57-D

Wilkinson, Cragun & Barker
Louisiana Pacific Corp. - 34-D
Marathon Oil Co. - 15-D
National Congress of American Indians Inc. - 38-D

Will, George L. - 52-D

Will, Robert P. - 7-D, 9-D, 10-D, 15-D

Williams & Jensen
The First Boston Corp. - 33-D
Kellogg Co. - 7-D
Mustang Fuel Corp. - 5-D
Nationwide Insurance Co. - 28-D
Universal Foods Inc. - 16-D

Williams, James H. - 13-D

Willkie, Farr & Gallagher
Burlington Industries - 55-D

Wilmer, Cutler & Pickering
Browning-Ferris Industries Inc. - 11-D
CPC International Inc. - 39-D
G-4 Children's Coalition - 32-D
Owens Illinois - 41-D

Wilson, Bob - 20-D

Wilson, Charles H. - 22-D

Wilson, John W. - 55-D

Wilson, Robert C. - 21-D

Wilson, William A. III - 14-D, 19-D

Winchester, Judith A. - 22-D

Windels, Marx, Davies & Ives
Waterman Steamship Corp. - 35-D

Wine and Spirits Wholesalers of America Inc. - 18-D

Winston & Strawn
Cummins Engine Co. Inc. - 55-D
GIC Financial Services Corp. - 20-D

Winston, Edna - 46-D

Wisconsin Barge Line Inc. - 22-D

Wiseman, Alan M. - 34-D

Witkowski, Weiner, McCaffrey and Brodsky
Foremost Insurance Co. - 27-D
Kankakee, Beaverville & Southern Railroad Co. - 20-D

Witts, David A. - 5-D

WLKM Radio - 35-D, 49-D

Wodder, Rebecca - 11-D

Wolff, Benjamin - 22-D

Women's Equity Action League - 5-D

Wood Enterprises Inc. - 22-D

Woodard, Susan - 9-D

Woods, Richard P. - 15-D

Woodward, Kerry - 11-D

Woofter, Perry W. - 35-D

Worthen, William R. - 33-D

Wright, William L. - 11-D

Wyman, Bautzer, Rothman, Juchel & Silbert
American Boiler Manufacturers Association Inc. - 23-D

Wyman Family - 26-D

X,Y,Z

Yacker, Marc D. - 17-D, 23-D

Yahweh, Suhkara Abdul - 14-D

Yakima Indian Nation - 14-D

Yamada, T. Albert - 37-D

Yeager, Brooks B. - 55-D

Young, Thane A. - 24-D

Zaire, Republic of - 22-D, 29-D

Zale Corp. - 8-D

Zantop International Airlines - 29-D

Zapata Corp. - 49-D

Zarro, Janice - 3-D, 5-D

Zeese, Kevin B. - 7-D

Zeitz, Myron - 14-D

Zeller, Don J. - 57-D

Ziegler, Ronald L. - 45-D

Zimpro Inc. - 43-D

Ziontz, Pirtle Law Firm
Inupiat Community of the Arctic Slope - 18-D
Ukpeagvik Inupiat Corp. - 19-D

Zuckert, Scoutt & Rasenberger
Antaeus Enterprises Inc. - 38-D
Republic Airlines Inc. - 35-D

Zunke, Leigh Ann - 45-D

PRESIDENTIAL MESSAGES

Jimmy Carter Recommends Federal Pay Raise

Following is President Carter's Jan. 7 message to Congress urging approval of the pay increases recommended by the Commission on Executive, Legislative and Judicial Salaries:

TO THE CONGRESS OF
THE UNITED STATES:

If the Federal Government is to meet successfully the enormous challenges it faces in these difficult times, it must be able to attract and retain men and women of outstanding ability and experience for its highest posts.

Monetary awards are not the principal attractions offered by the public service, and complete parity with private sector salaries is neither desirable nor possible. Those who serve at the highest levels of the Federal Government expect and are willing to make some financial sacrifice to serve their country. Nevertheless, compensation levels today have fallen below the point at which they provide adequate monetary recognition of the complexity and importance of top Federal jobs.

The financial sacrifice demanded of top Federal officials is becoming far too great. Since the last quadrennial adjustment in 1977, the salaries of those officials have increased only 5.5 percent. During that same period, the CPI has risen by about 45 percent, which means that the purchasing power of these salaries has declined by about 28 percent.

I fully recognize that the salaries already being paid these officials look very large to the average taxpayer. But when we are seeking to fill an Assistant Secretary position, a Bureau Chief position, or one of the other top level policymaking positions in the Executive Branch, we want people who know the specialized field involved and who have had extensive experience and success in it. Usually, these people are already being highly paid, and there is a limit to the financial sacrifices they can afford to make.

Not only is the discrepancy between private sector executive pay large now; it is continuing to widen. Since 1977, for example, while Federal executive pay has risen only 5.5 percent, private sector executive pay has gone up about 25 percent. If this gap continues to widen, government service will be so unattractive that increasing numbers of the best qualified will refuse to serve.

These observations apply equally to the selection of judges. The Federal judiciary has traditionally drawn a substantial number of appointees from the top echelons of the legal profession. These individuals are mature, experienced, and often at the height of their career earnings. When they become judges, it is usually at a financial sacrifice. If the sacrifice we ask becomes too great, increasing numbers of those best qualified will refuse consideration for appointment. The Attorney General tells me we are already receiving many declinations from lawyers of the quality we desire. We must not allow that trend to accelerate.

In addition to the recruiting problem, there are important considerations of retention and of equity. Resignations from the Federal bench show a disturbing tendency: only seven Federal judges resigned in the 1950s, and eight in the 1960s; but 24 resigned in the 1970s. Three resigned in 1980 alone.

The Constitution wisely provided that Federal judges would be appointed for life. The founders believed, and experience has confirmed, that lifetime service enhance the integrity and independence of a judge's performance. It also strengthens public confidence that judges possess these qualities, and increases public respect for their decisions. When lifetime judges leave the bench because of inadequate salaries, the public loses more than their experience and efficiency. The public also loses the confidence in the judicial process that is central to the success of our Constitutional system.

Obviously, many judges will not leave the bench even for the much larger salaries they could earn by returning to private practice. But the devotion of these judges should not be rewarded by unfair treatment. Something must be done to encourage and reward continuous judicial service.

Turning now to career executives, you know that Executive Levels IV and V are by law the ceiling for career salaries. You know also that General Schedule salaries have risen by 3.9 percent over the period in which executive salaries rose by only 5.5 percent. As a result, more and more GS employees each year reach the executive pay ceiling.

Consequently, we now have a salary system in which up to seven levels of career executives and managers are all receiving the same pay. Career executives who are promoted to more responsible and demanding positions often receive no pay increase whatsoever to compensate them for taking on heavier responsibilities. Agencies with field organizations, which need to advance successful managers from district offices to regional offices to headquarters offices, find it increasingly difficult to persuade capable employees to move their families for "promotions" that carry no pay increase.

One result of this compression is that many experienced and valuable career executives are retiring as quickly as they become eligible for retirement. For the twelve month period ending last March, a startling 75 percent of career executives in the 55-59 age bracket who were at the executive pay ceiling and were eligible to retire, did so. The result is that talented, experienced and creative public servants are leaving when they are of maximum value to their agencies. Unless these trends are reversed, the nation cannot expect to retain a high quality senior career group.

Congress shares many of these salary problems. We all know that people do not run for office because of the salaries involved, and that many people would run for Congress even if the member drew no pay at all. But it is of vital importance to have Congressional salaries high enough to attract a broad range of people, including those who want their families to enjoy the same standard of living they would if they were carrying even moderately comparable responsibilities in other occupations.

Congressional salaries have experienced the same loss of purchasing power as those already discussed. Yet, Congressmen face even greater expense than the other groups because they must maintain two residences and have other expenses stemming from their unique responsibilities. So they, too, need pay increases.

As the law provides, a Commission on Executive, Legislative and Judicial Salaries has considered these and related salary issues. This Commission, which was composed of distinguished private citizens with no selfish interests in Federal pay scales, made the findings I have summarized above. To correct them, it has unanimously recommended salary increases averaging about 40 percent.

I have no doubt that the facts fully justify those recommendations. Nevertheless, I continue to be concerned that we balance compensation needs against Federal Government leadership in fighting inflation and in minimizing the overall costs of government. Consequently, I am recommending to you in my budget for FY 1982 that smaller increases be allowed at this time, but — just as importantly — that we commit ourselves to allowing future increases annually to prevent these salary problems from continuing to worsen.

As you know, General Schedule employees received increases in FY 1979 and FY 1980 that totaled 16.8 percent. By operation of PL 94-82, the legal salaries of top level officials also increased by these same amounts. Congress, with my concurrence, enacted appropriation language that temporarily prohibited the *payment* of those increases to the top officials. Consequently, their payable salaries are now 16.8 percent below their legal salaries. Several judges sued over the application of that appropriation limitation to the judiciary and recently won a Supreme Court decision that means many judges will receive the 16.8 percent in question.

I believe the least we can do at this point is to give the Executive and Legislative branch officials the 16.8 percent already received by most General Schedule employees and already won by the judges. Just as important as the immediate in-

crease, however, is adoption of the principle that we will allow whatever increase is granted in General Schedule employees in October of 1981 and in subsequent years to be paid also to the top level officials, as PL 94-82 provides. Only by following this principle can we prevent the salary muddle from becoming worse every year. Experience has shown that if we wait four years to make salary adjustments in a time of rapid inflation, the needed catch-up will be so large as to be unacceptable to our citizens.

Because the case for a significant increase in the salaries of Federal judges is especially strong, I urge also that Congress give consideration to a salary scale for judges that would explicitly recognize the public importance of continuous judicial service; for example, by an annual or periodic increase for longevity in addition to the cost of living adjustments that are made from time to time.

In addition, I urge that Congress give careful consideration to the five non-salary recommendations made by the commission, especially their proposal for a special two year study of the complex and harmful compensation problems that now exist.

The Commission concluded that the conditions I have outlined constitute ". . . a quiet crisis, unperceived by most citizens of the nation but requiring an immediate response by the President and the Congress to safeguard the high quality of its senior officials." I agree with that conclusion and urge you to act favorably upon my recommendations. President-elect Reagan has authorized me to say that he fully supports these recommendations.

PL 95-19 provides that each House must within 60 days conduct a separate recorded vote on my recommendations for each branch of government. In addition, if you wish to accept my recommendation to make the current legal rates payable now, you should amend section 101(c) of PL 96-536 accordingly.

In the event that you decide you do not wish to approve increases for your own Members, I strongly urge that you allow them for officials of the Executive and Judicial branches. The gravity of the "quiet crisis" those branches face requires you to do no less.

JIMMY CARTER

The White House
Jan. 7, 1981 ∎

President Carter's Farewell Address

Following is the text of President Carter's farewell address broadcast to the nation Jan. 14:

Good evening. In a few days, I will lay down my official responsibilities in this office — to take up once more the only title in our democracy superior to that of president, the title of citizen.

Of Vice President Mondale, my Cabinet and the hundreds of others who have served with me during the last four years, I wish to say publicly what I have said in private: I thank them for the dedication and competence they have brought to the service of our country.

But I owe my deepest thanks to you, the American people, because you gave me this extraordinary opportunity to serve. We have faced great challenges together. We know that future problems will also be difficult, but I am now more convinced than ever that the United States — better than any other country — can meet successfully whatever the future might bring.

These last four years have made me more certain than ever of the inner strength of our country — the unchanging value of our principles and ideals, the stability of our political system, the ingenuity and the decency of our people.

Tonight I would like first to say a few words about this most special office, the presidency of the United States.

This is at once the most powerful office in the world — and among the most severely constrained by law and custom. The president is given a broad responsibility to lead — but cannot do so without the support and consent of the people, expressed formally through the Congress and informally in many ways through a whole range of public and private institutions.

This is as it should be. Within our system of government every American has a right and a duty to help shape the future course of the United States. Thoughtful criticism and close scrutiny of all government officials by the press and the public are an important part of our democratic society. Now as in the past, only the understanding and involvement of the people through full and open debate can help to avoid serious mistakes and assure the continued dignity and safety of the nation.

Today we are asking our political system to do things of which the Founding Fathers never dreamed. The government they designed for a few hundred thousand people now serves a nation of almost 230 million people. Their small coastal republic now spans beyond a continent, and we also now have the responsibility to help lead much of the world through difficult times to a secure and prosperous future.

Dangers

Today, as people have become ever more doubtful of the ability of the government to deal with our problems, we are increasingly drawn to single-issue groups and special interest organizations to ensure that whatever else happens our own personal views and our private interests are protected.

This is a disturbing factor in American political life. It tends to distort our purposes because the national interest is not always the sum of all our single or special interests. We are all Americans together — and we must not forget that the common good is our common interest and our individual responsibility.

Because of the fragmented pressures of these special interests, it's very important that the office of the president be a strong one, and that its constitutional authority be preserved. The president is the only elected official charged with the primary responsibility of representing all the people. In the moments of decision, after the different and conflicting views have been aired, it is the president who then must speak to the nation and for the nation. I understand after four years in office, as few others can, how formidable is the task the president-elect is about to undertake. To the very limits of conscience and conviction, I pledge to support him in that task. I wish him success, and Godspeed.

I know from experience that presidents have to face major issues that are controversial, broad in scope, and which do not arouse the natural support of a political majority.

Nuclear Threat

For a few minutes now, I want to lay aside my role as leader of one nation, and speak to you as a fellow citizen of the world about three issues, three difficult issues: The threat of nuclear destruction, our stewardship of the physical resources of the planet, and the pre-eminence of the basic rights of human beings.

It's now been 35 years since the first atomic bonb fell on Hiroshima. The great majority of the world's people cannot remember a time when the nuclear shadow did not hang over the earth. Our minds have adjusted to it, as after a time our eyes adjust to the dark.

Yet the risk of a nuclear conflagration has not lessened. It has not happened yet, thank God, but that can give us little comfort — for it only has to happen once.

The danger is becoming greater. As the arsenals of the superpowers grow in size and sophistication and as other governments — perhaps, even in the future, dozens of governments — acquire these weapons, it may only be a matter of time before madness, desperation, greed or miscalculation lets loose this terrible force.

In an all-out nuclear war, more destructive power than in all of World War II would be unleashed every second during the long afternoon it would take for all the missiles and bombs to fall. A World War II every second — more people killed in the first few hours than all of the wars of history put together. The survivors, if any, would live in despair amid the poisoned ruins of a civilization that had committed suicide.

National weakness — real or perceived — can tempt aggression and thus cause war. That's why the United States can never neglect its military strength. We must and we will remain strong. But with

equal determination, the United States and all countries must find ways to control and to reduce the horrifying danger that is posed by the world's enormous stockpiles of nuclear arms.

This has been a concern of every American president since the moment we first saw what these weapons could do. Our leaders will require understanding and our support as they grapple with this difficult but crucial challenge. There is no disagreement on the goals or the basic approach to controlling this enormous destructive force. The answer lies not just in the attitudes or actions of world leaders, but in the concern and the demands of all of us as we continue our struggle to preserve the peace.

Nuclear weapons are an expression of one side of our human character. There is another side. The same rocket technology that delivers nuclear warheads has also taken us peacefully into space. From that perspective, we see our Earth as it really is — a small and fragile and beautiful blue globe, the only home we have. We see no barriers of race or religion or country. We see the essential unity of our species and our planet; and with faith and common sense, that bright vision will ultimately prevail.

Quality of World

Another major challenge, therefore, is to protect the quality of this world within which we live. The shadows that fall across the future are cast not only by the kinds of weapons we have built, but by the kind of world we will either nourish or neglect.

There are real and growing dangers to our simple and our most precious possessions: The air we breathe; the water we drink; the land which sustains us. The rapid depletion of irreplaceable minerals, the erosion of topsoil, the destruction of beauty, the blight of pollution, the demands of increasing millions of people, all combine to create problems which are easy to observe and predict but difficult to resolve. If we do not act, the world of the year 2000 will be much less able to sustain life than it is now.

But there is no reason for despair. Acknowledging the physical realities of our planet does not mean a dismal future of endless sacrifice. In fact, acknowledging these realities is the first step in dealing with them. We can meet the resource problems of the world — water, food, minerals,

farmlands, forests, overpopulation, pollution — if we tackle them with courage and foresight.

I have just been talking about forces of potential destruction that mankind has developed, and how we might control them. It is equally important that we remember the beneficial forces that we have evolved over the ages, and how to hold fast to them.

Human Freedoms

One of those constructive forces is the enhancement of individual human freedoms through the strengthening of democracy, and the fight against deprivation, torture, terrorism and the persecution of people throughout the world. The struggle for human rights overrides all differences of color, or nation or language.

Those who hunger for freedom, who thirst for human dignity, and who suffer for the sake of justice — they are the patriots of this cause.

I believe with all my heart that America must always stand for these basic human rights — at home and abroad. That is both our history and our destiny.

America did not invent human rights. In a very real sense, it is the other way around. Human rights invented America.

Ours was the first nation in the history of the world to be founded explicitly on such an idea. Our social and political progress has been based on one fundamental principle — the value and importance of the individual. The fundamental force that unites us is not kinship or place or origin or religious preference. The love of liberty is a common blood that flows in American veins.

The battle for human rights — at home and abroad — is far from over. We should never be surprised nor discouraged because the impact of our efforts has had, and will always have, varied results. Rather, we should take pride that the ideals which gave birth to our nation should inspire the hopes of oppressed people around the world. We have no cause for self-righteousness or complacency. But we have every reason to persevere, both within our own country and beyond our borders.

American Values

If we are to serve as a beacon for human rights, we must continue to perfect

here at home the rights and the values which we espouse around the world: A decent education for our children, adequate medical care for all Americans, an end to discrimination against minorities and women, a job for all those able to work and freedom from injustice and religious intolerance.

We live in a time of transition, an uneasy era which is likely to endure for the rest of the century. It will be a period of tensions both within nations and between nations — of competition for scarce resources, of social, political and economic stresses and strains. During this period we may be tempted to abandon some of the time-honored principles and commitments which have been proven during the difficult times of past generations.

We must never yield to this temptation. Our American values are not luxuries but necessities — not the salt in our bread but the bread itself. Our common vision of a free and just society is our greatest source of cohesion at home and strength abroad — greater even than the bounty of our material blessings.

Remember these words:

"We hold these truths to be self-evident, that all men are created equal; that they are endowed by their creator with certain inalienable rights; that among these are life, liberty and the pursuit of happiness."

Carter's Vision

This vision still grips the imagination of the world. But we know that democracy is always an unfinished creation. Each generation must renew its foundations. Each generation must rediscover the meaning of this hallowed vision in the light of its own modern challenges. For this generation, ours, life is nuclear survival; liberty is human rights; the pursuit of happiness is a planet whose resources are devoted to the physical and spiritual nourishment of its inhabitants.

During the next few days I will work hard to make sure that the transition from myself to the next president is a good one so that the American people are served well. And I will continue as I have the last 14 months to work hard and to pray for the lives and the well-being of the American hostages held in Iran. I can't predict yet what will happen, but I hope you will join me in my constant prayer for their freedom.... ∎

Carter's Fiscal 1982 Budget Message

Following is the text of President Carter's fiscal 1982 budget message sent to Congress Jan. 15.

My administration has faced a wide range of challenges at home and abroad, challenges stemming from our strengths, not our weaknesses: our strengths as a

world leader, as a developed industrial nation, and as a heterogeneous democracy with high goals and great ambitions. Meeting these challenges satisfactorily requires that we establish priorities, recognizing the limits to even our Nation's enormous resources. We cannot do all that we wish at the same time. But we must provide

for our security, establish the basis for a strong economy, protect the disadvantaged, build human and physical capital for the future, and safeguard this Nation's magnificent natural environment.

This budget provides for meeting these needs, while continuing a 4-year policy of prudence and restraint. While our budget

deficits have been higher than I would have liked, their size has been determined for the most part by economic conditions. Even so, the trend has been downward. In 1976, the budget deficit equalled 4.0% of gross national product. This was reduced to 2.3% in the budget year that ended 3 months ago. The 1982 budget deficit is estimated to equal only 0.9% of gross national product.

The rate of growth in budget outlays has been held to a minimum. In spite of significant increases in indexed programs, outlays for nondefense programs — after adjusting for inflation — decrease slightly.

The 1982 budget calls for outlays of $739 billion, an increase of 1.0% when adjusted for inflation. Nondefense spending is projected to decline by 0.2% in real terms. The tax reductions I proposed as part of the economic revitalization program have been retained, but some have been delayed or phased in over a longer period in recognition of the continued high inflation rate. The budget deficit — which is now projected at $55.2 billion in 1981 — is estimated to decline to $27.5 billion in 1982.

In planning this budget, I have considered four major issues:

● What is the economic policy that will ensure prosperity for all while minimizing inflation?

● How much of our Nation's wealth should be used by the Federal Government?

● What are desirable spending proposals and strategies for defense, human resources, and investment?

● How can the management of Government be improved?

The Economy

During the last decade we withstood a series of economic shocks unprecedented in peacetime. The most dramatic of these were the explosive increases of OPEC oil prices. But we have also faced world commodity shortages, natural disasters, agricultural shortages, and major challenges to world peace and security. Our ability to deal with these shocks has been impaired by slower productivity growth and persistent, underlying inflationary forces built up over the past 15 years.

Nevertheless, the economy has proved remarkably resilient. Real output has grown at an average annual rate of 3% since I took office, and employment has grown by 2-1/2%. Nearly 8 million productive private sector jobs have been added to the economy. However, unacceptably high inflation remains our most difficult economic problem. This inflation requires that we hold down the growth of the budget to the maximum extent, while still meeting the demands of national security and human compassion. I have done so, as I did in my earlier budgets.

While budget restraint is essential to any appropriate economic policy, high inflation cannot be attributed solely to Government spending. The growth in budget outlays has been more the result of economic factors than the cause of them. For fiscal year 1981 alone, budget outlays must be increased by $9 billion over last year's estimate as a result of higher interest rates. Yet this increase results not only from inflation but from the monetary policies undertaken to combat it. Nearly $18 billion for 1981 reflects higher defense costs and higher automatic inflation adjustments than were anticipated a year ago.

We are now in the early stages of economic recovery following a short recession. Typically, post-recessionary periods have been marked by vigorous economic growth abetted by stimulative policies such as large tax cuts or spending programs. I am not recommending such actions, because persistent inflationary pressures dictate a restrained fiscal policy. However, I continue to recommend specific tax reductions that contribute directly to increased productivity and long-term growth.

The Size and Role of Government

We allocate about 23% of our Nation's output through the Federal budget. (Including all levels of government, the total government share of our gross national product is about one-third.) We must come close to matching Federal outlays with tax receipts if we are to avoid excessive and inflationary Federal borrowing. This means either controlling our appetite for spending or accepting the burden of higher taxes.

The growth of budget outlays is puzzling to many Americans, but it arises from valid social and national security concerns. Other developed countries face similar pressures. We face a threat to our security, as events in Afghanistan, the Middle East, and Eastern Europe make clear. We have a steadily aging population; as a result, the biggest single increase in the Federal budget is the rising cost of retirement programs, particularly social security. We must meet other important domestic needs: to assist the disadvantaged; to provide the capital needed by our cities and our transportation systems; to protect our environment; and to revitalize American industry.

I have been concerned with the proper role of the Federal Government in designing and providing such assistance. The Federal Government must not usurp functions that are best left to the private sector or to State and local governments. My administration has sought to make the proper assignments of responsibility, to resolve problems in the most efficient manner.

We have also recognized the need to simplify the system of Federal grants to State and local governments. Once again, I am proposing several grant consolidations in the 1982 budget, including a new proposal that would consolidate several highway programs. Previous consolidation proposals of my administration have been in the areas of youth training and employment, environment, energy conservation, airport development, and rehabilitation services. These consolidations are essential to improving our intergovernmental system. However, the Congress has so far agreed to consolidate only rehabilitation services grants. Therefore, I am proposing again the consolidations recommended earlier.

Major Budget Priorities

Spending growth can be constrained; not easily, not quickly, but it is possible. My budget priorities have been established, once again, to achieve this goal in a responsible manner.

Three years ago, in my 1979 budget message, I outlined the following principles:

● The Nation's armed forces must always stand sufficiently strong to deter aggression and to assure our security.

● An effective national energy plan is essential to reduce our increasingly critical dependence upon diminishing supplies of oil and gas, to encourage conservation of scarce energy resources, to stimulate conversion to more abundant fuels, and to reduce our large trade deficit.

● The essential human needs of our citizens must be given high priority.

● The Federal Government must lead the way in investment in the Nation's technological future.

● The Federal Government has an obligation to nurture and protect our environment — the common resource, birthright, and sustenance of the American people.

My 1982 budget is again based on these principles.

Tax policy and economic revitalization. — I continue to believe that large inflationary individual income tax cuts are neither appropriate nor possible today, however popular they might appear in the short run. My economic revitalization program stresses tax reductions on a timetable that we can afford, and that will fight inflation by encouraging capital formation and increasing industrial productivity. This program stresses:

● simplification and liberalization of depreciation allowances;

● modification of the investment tax credit to encourage investment by temporarily depressed firms and by growing new firms;

● an income tax credit to offset increases in social security taxes;

● a liberalized earned income credit to also offset social security taxes and to encourage low-income earners to work;

● a working-spouse deduction to make more equitable the way working husbands and wives are taxed; and

● more favorable tax treatment for Americans in certain areas overseas to help American exports and strengthen the dollar.

Defense. — Maintaining a strong defense has been a primary objective of this administration. In order to meet the security needs of the Nation, real spending for defense increased in 1979 and 1980 by more than the 3% target I set at the NATO

ministerial meeting in 1977. This real growth rate in defense spending has been maintained despite the adverse effects of higher than anticipated inflation, and restrained budgets.

To meet critical remaining needs, this budget includes a $6.3 billion supplemental request for 1981, largely for military pay increases and combat readiness. Together with congressional add-ons to my earlier 1981 request, this supplemental will increase defense programs almost 8% in real terms over 1980. For 1982 and beyond, the budget charts a course of sustained and balanced improvements in defense programs that will require real annual increases in funding of about 5% per year.

The budget request reflects a careful balance between the need to meet all critical defense needs, while maintaining fiscal restraint. There will be advocates for higher defense levels, but after careful review I do not believe that higher spending would add significantly to our national security. My budget already provides for the three major defense requirements:

● *Personnel recruitment and retention.* — Our armed forces can be no better than the quality of the people who serve in them. Accordingly, I recently approved the largest pay and benefits increase in history — a $4.5 billion compensation package that provides for an average compensation increase of 16%. This increase in base pay, plus better housing allowances, expanded enlistment and reenlistment bonuses, and special pay enhancements for submariners and other specialists, will help attract and retain highly qualified men and women.

● *Improving combat readiness.* — Increased compensation will be a key factor in overcoming key personnel shortages, which are the major source of readiness problems. In addition, there have been shortages in critical spare parts and, in a few cases, inadequate funds for training. The funds recommended by this budget should alleviate these problems.

● *Modernizing our forces.* — I also propose major investments to enhance substantially the capabilities of our forces: Strategic forces are being upgraded through continued procurement of Trident submarines and missiles, procurement of cruise missiles, modification of the B-52 bomber, and development of the MX missile. Army equipment, including tanks, armored vehicles, helicopters, and air defense and other missile systems, is being modernized. Fighter and attack planes are being added to Navy and Marine forces, and a continuing major shipbuilding program will add over 80 ships to our growing fleet between 1982 and 1986. The rapid deployment of our forces is being improved through the acquisition of more cargo ships and modification of airlift aircraft.

Foreign aid. — Foreign assistance remains crucial in achieving our country's international political and economic goals. From the start of my administration, I have stressed the need for substantial increases in assistance to friendly nations, many of whom are drastically harmed by constantly increasing oil prices and other external economic and security pressures. At the same time, I have insisted upon improved management of both our security and development assistance programs.

In the first 2 years of this administration, the Congress reduced my foreign aid requests but permitted some program growth. For the past 2 years, however, the Congress has failed to pass regular foreign aid appropriations. Assistance programs in 1981 are being funded under a continuing resolution that provides amounts slightly above the 1979 levels in nominal terms, and substantially below them in real terms.

I believe in the need for higher levels of aid to achieve foreign policy objectives, promote economic growth, and help needy people abroad. Foreign aid is not politically popular and represents an easy target for budget reduction. But it is not a wise one. For 1982, therefore, I am requesting a foreign assistance program level that is higher by 14% in real terms than the amount currently available for 1981. This request would reverse the recent real decline in aid and demonstrate that the United States retains its commitment to a world of politically stable and economically secure nations.

The bilateral development aid budget includes a U.S. response to the 1980 Venice Summit agreement that the major industrial countries should increase bilateral aid for food production, energy production and conservation, and family planning in the developing countries. Such an effort to increase the availability of resources on which the industrial countries depend will serve U.S. national security, and will stimulate additional actions by the private sector in the recipient countries. This U.S. effort is planned in the expectation that the other Summit countries will also increase aid in these sectors, in response to the Venice Summit agreement. We hope this initiative will lead to agreement on arrangements for increased consultation and cooperation among the major industrial countries providing increased bilateral aid to these three vital sectors.

Energy. — My administration, working with the Congress, has established fundamental new policies that will profoundly change the way the Nation produces and uses energy. They have already led to more domestic exploration and to substantial energy conservation. This energy program represents a major long-range national commitment to meeting one of our most pressing problems. It includes:

● Deregulation and decontrol of oil prices to be completed by October of this year.

● Establishment of the Synthetic Fuels Corporation, which will share with the private sector the risk in producing oil and natural gas substitutes that directly reduce U.S. oil imports.

● Support for energy research and development in technologies, such as solar and fusion energy, that the private sector would not finance.

● Development of the strategic petroleum reserve to reduce the impact of disruptions in world oil supplies.

● Energy conservation in public and nonprofit enterprises.

● Research on the environmental effects of energy production and use to assure that adverse effects on environmental quality are minimized.

Continuation of a sound energy policy is essential to the Nation's well-being in the coming decades. Such a policy must include the pricing of energy at its true cost, mechanisms to stimulate conservation, incentives for the continued development of our own domestic sources of energy, encouragement for longer-run renewable forms of energy, and equity for all our citizens as we adjust to this new reality.

Basic science and space technology. — Basic research is essential to the long-term vitality of the Nation's economy. Because the benefits of such investments cannot be fully realized by individual companies, the Federal Government plays a key role in supporting such research.

My budgets have reversed a long period of decline in Federal support for basic research. The 1982 budget continues that policy by providing for 4% real growth in support for the conduct of basic research across all Federal agencies. The budget also provides for greater efforts to foster cooperation among government, business, and universities in research.

In addition, we have recognized the growing importance of improving scientific technology in the Nation's universities as critical to the advancement of science and to the training of scientific and engineering manpower.

My administration's comprehensive space policy encourages the practical, effective use of information obtained from orbiting satellites and the coordinated use of the Space Shuttle, now nearing completion. Successful resolution of development problems is expected to lead to the first manned orbital flight of the Shuttle in 1981.

With these increases, Federal support for basic research will have increased by almost 58% over 1978.

Social programs. — This budget supports my deep commitment to programs that help our citizens develop their full potential, and to programs assisting the poor, the unemployed, the elderly, and the sick.

The most extensive such programs are *social security* and *medicare*. Parts of this system are expected to experience short-run financing problems because higher than expected unemployment has decreased payroll taxes below previous forecasts, and high inflation has increased benefit payments. Therefore, the administration continues to urge the passage of legislation that would permit the three major social security trust funds to borrow from each other. In addition, it is essential that the Congress and the American people

give early consideration to medium-term financing concerns.

The reports of the Commission on Pension Policy, which I established 2 years ago, and the National Commission on Social Security should stimulate constructive debate on these issues. These Commissions will complete their final reports during the coming months.

My administration has consistently maintained a strong commitment to remedying *youth unemployment* and the problems it causes. This budget includes an increase of $1.2 billion in 1982 and an additional increase of $0.8 billion in 1983 for the youth initiative I proposed last year. This initiative emphasizes the mastery of basic arithmetic and literacy skills, as well as the link between the classroom and the workplace.

The Job Corps would be continued at this year's level, serving twice as many youth as when my administration took office. In addition, my budget provides 240,000 public service jobs for low-income, long-term unemployed persons in 1982. This program is designed for the hard-core structurally unemployed, and includes substantial training in order to place men and women in permanent jobs. At the same time, the budget continues the countercyclical public service employment program through 1982 at the 100,000 level set by the Congress for 1981. The budget also provides a slight increase for the administration's private sector jobs initiative and essentially maintains the 1980 level of summer youth employment.

I am again proposing to augment medicaid with a *child health assurance* program effective by the end of 1982. This proposal, which the House of Representatives passed last year, would extend medicaid coverage to an additional 2 million children and pregnant women.

I am also proposing a number of changes in existing programs. For example, I am again proposing that retirement benefits for government employees be adjusted for inflation once, rather than twice, a year. This change would make these adjustments comparable to those for social security and most private sector automatic adjustment practices. The Congress approved a similar administration initiative last year for the food stamp program. This proposal would save $1.1 billion in 1982.

Benefits that are adjusted by statute for inflation will comprise nearly one-third of total Federal spending in 1981. During the last year, my administration has been assessing whether these adjustments are fair and equitable. We have concluded that the Consumer Price Index has several deficiencies as a measure of the true cost of living, particularly because of the manner in which it represents housing costs. I am therefore proposing, in this budget, that future benefits be based on an alternative, more representative index. The alternative index is already calculated and published by the Bureau of Labor Statistics. This proposal is designed to improve the technique of indexing these programs,

not to reduce benefits. Therefore, no cost savings are assumed in the budget.

The budget also includes legislation to make unemployment benefits more nearly uniform among the States and to coordinate benefits more precisely with unemployment rates. Although this proposal would save about $2 billion in 1982 under the unemployment rates being projected for this budget, a slightly higher rate of unemployment would trigger extended benefits nationally. In such a case, unemployment benefits would be very close to those under current law. Even with the projected change, under current economic projections $1.5 billion would be paid in 1982 for extended benefits in States where the program is triggered.

I remain committed to a national health plan that would assure basic and catastrophic medical coverage for all Americans, as well as for prenatal and infant care. An estimated 22 million Americans lack any private or public health insurance coverage. Another 60 million people lack adequate basic coverage or protection against catastrophic medical expenses. Given the fact that adequate cost containment does not exist and the need for overall budgetary constraints, the budget does not include specific amounts for this plan. However, it is important that our Nation attempt to meet these needs and that the incentives in our health care system be restructured. A clear demonstration of success in restraining medical care costs is an essential prerequisite to the enactment of a national health plan.

My proposals to reform our welfare system should also be enacted as soon as possible. Such a program is essential to ensuring that no American goes hungry or lacks a reasonable income, and to provide needed fiscal relief to States, counties, and cities.

Improving Government Management

This budget reinforces my commitment to use resources not only wisely, but efficiently. During my administration we have:

● installed new Offices of Inspectors General in 15 major agencies to combat waste, fraud, and abuse;

● carried out a major Government-wide reform of the civil service system;

● reorganized important areas of the Federal Government, particularly those concerned with education and energy;

● reduced permanent Federal civilian employment by 45,000;

● achieved budgetary savings directly through improved cash management; and

● reduced paperwork and established a paperwork budget.

Such efforts to streamline the way the Government conducts its business are rarely dramatic. Improved efficiency is not the product of a simple sweeping reform but, rather, of diligent, persistent attention to many aspects of Federal program management.

One important aspect of improved management has been in the budget pro-

cess itself. *Zero-base budgeting* is now an integral part of the decisionmaking system, providing a more systematic basis for making decisions. We have also instituted a 3-year budget planning horizon so that the longer range consequences of short-term budget decisions are fully considered and understood.

In 1978 I made a major commitment to establish a system of controlling *Federal credit* since, in the past, the very large Federal loan guarantee programs had largely escaped the discipline of the budget process. This system is now in place.

I am gratified that the Congress has supported these efforts to improve budget control. Appropriations bills now include limits on many credit programs. The congressional budget resolutions place significantly greater emphasis on longer range budget trends and set overall credit targets.

While the credit control system provides a means of assessing and limiting Federal credit programs, I believe Federal credit programs have become unduly complex and pose an increasing threat to the effective and efficient operation of private capital markets. In particular, the Federal Financing Bank has become a major and rapidly growing source of off-budget funds for direct loans to a wide range of borrowers.

Therefore, I am recommending that a panel of outstanding financial and budget experts should be established to examine these issues. Such a panel should consider the treatment of credit activities in the budget, the adequacy of program administration, uniform rules and procedures for Federal credit programs, the role of the Federal Financing Bank, and the relationship of tax-exempt financing to overall credit and tax policies.

Conclusion

My budget recommendations reflect the major changes that have taken place in our country over recent decades. In 1950, social security and railroad retirement benefits accounted for less than 3% of budget outlays. Last year they accounted for more than one-fifth of the total. Mandatory outlays for entitlement programs, the levels of which are fixed by law, for interest on the public debt, and for payments under binding contracts account for three-fourths of total budget outlays. Because so much of the budget is committed under current law before either the President or the Congress begins the annual budget formulation process, controlling budget growth has been difficult, and the results uneven. It has been difficult because benefit payments and other legal obligations have too often been spared from annual budget scrutiny. The results have been uneven because budget restraint has fallen disproportionately on programs subject to the annual appropriations process.

My administration and the Congress began to redress this imbalance in the 1981 budget. The Congress passed, and I signed into law, a reconciliation bill that for the

first time was used as a mechanism for changing a variety of entitlement and tax programs. I do not propose that we break faith with the American people by arbitrarily or unfairly reducing entitlement programs. However, these programs developed independently, and they should be made less duplicative, more consistent, and more equitable. The size of these programs, and our need for budget restraint, requires that we address these problems. I urge the Congress to build upon last year's experience and review all aspects of the budget with equal care.

The allocation of one-fifth of our Nation's resources through the Federal budget is a complex, difficult, and contentious process. Restraint on any program, small or large, is usually subject to heated debate. At a time when there is broad consensus that the size of the Federal budget is too large, we can no longer — as individuals

or groups — make special pleas for exceptions to budget discipline. Too often we have taken the attitude that individual benefits or particular programs or specific tax measures are not large enough to require restraint. Too often we have taken the attitude that there must be alternative sources for reductions in programs that benefit our particular group. This attitude is in part responsible for the rapid budget growth we have experienced — and can no longer afford.

Given our Nation's needs and our economic constraints, my recommendations meet the fundamental demands of our society: a strong defense, adequate protection for the poor and the disadvantaged, support for our free enterprise economy, and investment in the Nation's future.

JIMMY CARTER

January 15, 1981.

Carter State of the Union Message

Following is the introduction to President Carter's 76-page State of the Union Message sent to Congress Jan. 16.

TO THE CONGRESS
OF THE UNITED STATES:

The State of the Union is sound. Our economy is recovering from a recession. A national energy plan is in place and our dependence on foreign oil is decreasing. We have been at peace for four uninterrupted years.

But, our Nation has serious problems. Inflation and unemployment are unacceptably high. The world oil market is increasingly tight. There are trouble spots throughout the world, and 52 American hostages are being held in Iran against international law and against every precept of human affairs.

However, I firmly believe that, as a result of the progress made in so many domestic and international areas over the past four years, our Nation is stronger, wealthier, more compassionate and freer than it was four years ago. I am proud of that fact. And I believe the Congress should be proud as well, for so much of what has been accomplished over the past four years had been due to the hard work, insights and cooperation of Congress. I applaud the Congress for its efforts and its achievements.

In this State of the Union Message I want to recount the achievements and progress of the last four years and to offer recommendations to the Congress for this year. While my term as President will end before the 97th Congress begins its work in earnest, I hope that my recommendations will serve as a guide for the direction this country should take so we build on the record of the past four years.

RECORD OF PROGRESS

When I took office, our Nation faced a number of serious domestic and international problems:

● no national energy policy existed, and our dependence on foreign oil was rapidly increasing;

● public trust in the integrity and openness of the government was low;

● the Federal government was operating inefficiently in administering essential programs and policies;

● major social problems were being ignored or poorly addressed by the Federal government;

● our defense posture was declining as a result of a defense budget which was continuously shrinking in real terms;

● the strength of the NATO Alliance needed to be bolstered;

● tensions between Israel and Egypt threatened another Middle East war; and

● America's resolve to oppose human rights violations was under serious question.

Over the past 48 months, clear progress has been made in solving the challenges we found in January of 1977:

● almost all of our comprehensive energy program have *[sic]* been enacted, and the Department of Energy has been established to administer the program;

● confidence in the government's integrity has been restored, and respect for the government's openness and fairness has been renewed;

● the government has been made more effective and efficient: the Civil Service system was completely reformed for the first time this century; 14 reorganization initiatives have been proposed to the Congress, approved, and implemented; two new Cabinet departments have been created to consolidate and streamline the government's handling of energy and educa-

tion problems; inspectors general have been placed in each Cabinet department to combat fraud, waste and other abuses; the regulatory process had been reformed through creation of the Regulatory Council, implementation of Executive Order 12044 and its requirement for cost-impact analyses, elimination of the unnecessary regulation, and passage of the Regulatory Flexibility Act; procedures have been established to assure citizen participation in government; and the airline, trucking, rail and communications industries are being deregulated;

● critical social problems, many long ignored by the Federal government, have been addressed directly; an urban policy was developed and implemented to reverse the decline in our urban areas; the Social Security System was refinanced to put it on a sound financial basis; the Humphrey-Hawkins Full Employment Act was enacted; Federal assistance for education was expanded by more than 75 percent; the minimum wage was increased to levels needed to ease the effects of inflation; affirmative action has been pursued aggressively — more blacks, Hispanics and women have been appointed to senior government positions and to judgeships than at any other time in our history; the ERA ratification deadline was extended to aid the ratification effort; and minority business procurement by the Federal government has more than doubled;

● the Nation's first sectoral policies were put in place, for the auto and steel industries, with my Administration demonstrating the value of cooperation between the government, business and labor;

● reversing previous trends, real defense spending has increased every year since 1977; the real increase in FY 1980 defense spending is well above 3 percent and I expect FY 1981 defense spending to be even higher; looking ahead, the defense program I am proposing is premised on a real increase in defense spending over the next five years of 20 percent or more;

● the NATO Alliance has proven its unity in responding to the situations in Eastern Europe and Southwest Asia and in agreeing on the issues to be addressed in the review of the Helsinki Final Act currently underway in Madrid;

● the peace process in the Middle East established at Camp David and by the Peace Treaty between Egypt and Israel is being buttressed on two fronts: steady progress in the normalization of Egyptian-Israeli relations in many fields, and the commitment of both Egypt and Israel, with United States' assistance, to see through to successful conclusion the autonomy negotiations for the West Bank and Gaza;

● the Panama Canal treaties have been put into effect, which has helped to improve relations with Latin America.

● we have continued this Nation's strong commitment to the pursuit of human rights throughout the world, evenhandedly and objectively; our commitment to a worldwide human rights policy has remained

firm; and many other countries have given high priority to it;

• our resolve to oppose aggression, such as the illegal invasion by the Soviet Union into Afghanistan, has been supported by tough action.... ■

U.S.-Iran Agreement on Release of the American Hostages

Following is President Carter's Jan. 19 message to Congress reporting on his actions regarding the agreement with Iran prior to the Jan. 20 release of U.S. hostages held in Tehran:

TO THE CONGRESS OF THE UNITED STATES:

Pursuant to Section 204(b) of the International Emergency Economic Powers Act, 50 U.S.C. 1703, I hereby report to the Congress that I have today exercised the authority granted by this Act to take certain measures with respect to property of the government of Iran and its controlled entities and instrumentalities.

1. On November 14, 1979, I took the step of blocking certain property and interests in property of the government of Iran and its controlled entities and instrumentalities. This action was taken in response to a series of aggressive actions by Iran, including the attack on the United States Embassy in Tehran, the holding of U.S. citizens and diplomats as hostages, and threats to withdraw assets from United States banks, and otherwise seek to harm the economic and political interests of the United States. Subsequently, on April 7, 1980, and April 17, 1980, I took further action restricting various kinds of transactions with Iran by persons subject to the jurisdiction of the United States.

2. Agreement has now been reached with Iran concerning the release of the hostages and the settlement of claims of U.S. nationals against Iran. Among other things this agreement involves the payment by Iran of approximately $3.67 billion to pay off principal and interest outstanding on syndicated loan agreements in which a U.S. bank is a party. This includes making all necessary payments to the foreign members of these syndicates. An additional $1.418 billion shall remain available to pay all other loans as soon as any disputes as to the amounts involved are settled and to pay additional interest to banks upon agreement or arbitration with Iran. In addition, there will be established an international tribunal to adjudicate various disputed claims by U.S. nationals against Iran; and the deposit of $1 billion by Iran from previously blocked assets as released, which will be available for payments of awards against Iran. Iran has committed itself to replenish this fund as necessary.

This tribunal, among other things, will also hear certain disputes between Iranian nationals and the United States Government and contractual disputes between Iran and the United States.

In connection with this agreement, and to begin the process of normalization of relations between the two countries, I have issued and will issue, a series of Orders.

3. First, I have signed an Executive Order authorizing the Secretary of the Treasury to enter into or to direct the Federal Reserve Bank of New York to enter into escrow and depositary agreements with the Bank of England.

Under these agreements, assets in the escrow account will be returned to the control of Iran upon the safe departure of the United States hostages from Iran. I have also by this Order instructed the Federal Reserve Bank of New York, as fiscal agent of the United States, to receive other blocked Iranian assets, and, as further directed to the Secretary of the Treasury, to transfer these assets to the escrow account.

4. Second, I have signed an Executive Order directing the Federal Reserve Bank of New York to transfer to its account at the Bank of England and then to the escrow account referred to in the preceding paragraph, the assets of the Government of Iran, both transfers to take place as and when directed by the Secretary of the Treasury.

In order to assure that this transaction can be executed, and having considered the claims settlement agreement described above, I have exercised my authority to nullify, and barred the exercise of, all rights, powers or privileges acquired by anyone; I have revoked all licenses and authorizations for acquiring any rights, powers, or privileges; and I have prohibited anyone from acquiring or exercising any right, power, or privileges, all with respect to these properties of Iran. These prohibitions and nullifications apply to rights, powers, or privileges whether acquired by court order, attachment, or otherwise. I have also prohibited any attachments or other like proceeding or process affecting these properties.

5. Third, I have signed an Executive Order which directs branches and offices of United States banks located outside the United States to transfer all Iranian government funds, deposits and securities held by them on their books on or after November 14, 1979 at 8:10 a.m. EST to the account of the Federal Reserve Bank of New York at the Bank of England in London. These assets will be transferred to the account of the Central Bank of Algeria, an escrow agent. The transfer is to include interest from the date of the blocking order at commercially reasonable rates. In addition, any banking institution that has executed a set-off subsequent to the date of the blocking order against Iranian deposits covered by this order is directed to cancel the set-off and to transfer the funds that had been subject to the set-off in the same manner as the other overseas deposits.

This Order also provides for the revocation of licenses and the nullifications and bars described in paragraph 4 of this report.

6. Fourth, I will have signed an Executive Order directing American banks located within the United States which hold Iranian deposits to transfer those deposits, including interest from the date of entry of the blocking order at commercially reasonable rates, to the Federal Reserve Bank of New York, to be held or transferred as directed by the Secretary of the Treasury. Half of these funds will be transferred to Iran and the other half (up to a maximum of $1 billion) will be placed in a security account as provided in the Declaration and the Claims Settlement Agreement that are part of the agreement we have reached with Iran. This fund will be maintained at a $500 million level until the claims program is concluded. While these transfers should take place as soon as possible, I have been advised that court actions may delay it. This Order also provides for the revocation of licenses and the nullifications and bars described in paragraph 4 of this report.

7. Fifth, I have signed an Executive Order directing the transfer to the Federal Reserve Bank of New York by nonbanking institutions of funds and securities held by them for the Government of Iran, to be held or transferred as directed by the Secretary of the Treasury. This transfer will be accomplished at approximately the same time as that described in paragraph 6.

This Order also provides for the revocation of licenses and the nullifications and bars described in paragraph 4 of this report.

8. Sixth, I will sign, upon release of the hostages, an Executive Order directing any person subject to the jurisdiction of the United States who is in possession or control of properties owned by Iran, not including funds and securities, to transfer the property as directed by the Government of Iran acting through its authorized agent. The Order recites that it does not relieve persons subject to it from existing legal requirements other than those based on the International Emergency Economic Powers Act. This Order does not apply to contingent liabilities. This Order also provides for the revocation of licenses and the nullifications and bars described in paragraph 4 of this report.

9. Seventh, I will sign, upon release of the hostages, an Executive Order revoking prohibitions previously imposed against transactions involving Iran. The Executive Order revokes prohibitions contained in Executive Order No. 12205 of April 7, 1980; and Executive Order No. 12211 of April 17, 1980; and the amendments contained in Proclamation No. 4702 of November 12, 1979. The two Executive Orders limited trade and financial transactions involving Iran and travel to Iran. The proclamation restricted oil imports. In revoking these sanctions I have no intention of superseding other existing controls relating to ex-

ports including the Arms Export Control Act and the Export Administration Act.

10. Eighth, I will sign, upon release of the hostages, an Executive Order providing for the waiver of certain claims against Iran. The Order directs that the Secretary of the Treasury shall promulgate regulations: (1) prohibiting any person subject to U.S. jurisdiction from prosecuting in any court within the United States or elsewhere any claim against the Government of Iran arising out of events occurring before the date of this Order arising out: (1) the seizure of the hostages on November 4, 1979; (2) their subsequent detention; (3) injury to the United States property or property of United States nationals within the United States Embassy compound in Tehran after November 1979; (4) or injury to United States nationals or their property as a result of popular movements in the course of the Islamic Revolution in Iran which were not an act of the government of Iran; (b) prohibiting any person not a U.S. national from prosecuting any such claim in any court within the United States; (c)

ordering the termination of any previously instituted judicial proceedings based upon such claims; and (d) prohibiting the enforcement of any judicial order issued in the course of such proceedings.

The Order also authorizes and directs the Attorney General of the United States immediately upon the issuance of such a Treasury regulation to notify all appropriate courts of the existence of the Executive Order and implementing regulations and the resulting termination of relevant litigation. At the same time, I will create a commission to make recommendations on the issue of compensation for those who have been held as hostages.

11. Finally, I will sign, upon release of the hostages, an Executive Order invoking the blocking powers of the International Emergency Economic Powers Act to prevent the transfer of property located in the United States and controlled by the estate of Mohammed Reza Pahlavi, the former Shah of Iran, or by any close relative of the former Shah served as a defendant in litigation in United States courts brought by

Iran seeking the return of property alleged to belong to Iran. This Order will remain effective as to each person until litigation concerning such person or estate is terminated. The Order also requires reports from private citizens and Federal agencies concerning this property so that information can be made available to the Government of Iran about this property.

The Order would further direct the Attorney General to assert in appropriate courts that claims of Iran for recovery of this property are not barred by principles of sovereign immunity or the act of state doctrine.

12. In addition to these actions taken pursuant to the International Economic Emergency Powers Act, other relevant statutes, and my powers under the Constitution, I will take the steps necessary to withdraw all claims now pending against Iran before the International Court of Justice. Copies of the Executive Orders are attached.

JIMMY CARTER

Jan. 19, 1981

President Reagan's Inaugural Address

Following is the text of President Reagan's inaugural address as delivered Jan. 20.

To a few of us here today this is a solemn and most momentous occasion. And, yet, in the history of our nation it is a commonplace occurrence.

The orderly transfer of authority as called for in the Constitution routinely takes place as it has for almost two centuries and few of us stop to think how unique we really are. In the eyes of many in the world, this every-four-year ceremony we accept as normal is nothing less than a miracle.

Mr. President, I want our fellow citizens to know how much you did to carry on this tradition. By your gracious cooperation in the transition process you have shown a watching world that we are a united people pledged to maintaining a political system which guarantees individual liberty to a greater degree than any other, and I thank you and your people for all your help in maintaining the continuity which is the hallmark of our Republic.

The business of our nation goes forward. These United States are confronted with an economic affliction of great proportions. We suffer from the longest and one of the worst sustained inflations in our national history. It distorts our economic decisions, penalizes thrift and crushes the struggling young and the fixed-income elderly alike. It threatens to shatter the lives of millions of our people.

Idle industries have cast workers into unemployment, human misery and per-

sonal indignity. Those who do work are denied a fair return for their labor by a tax system which penalizes successful achievement and keeps us from maintaining full productivity.

But great as our tax burden is, it has not kept pace with public spending. For decades we have piled deficit upon deficit, mortgaging our future and our children's future for the temporary convenience of the present. To continue this long trend is to guarantee tremendous social, cultural, political, and economic upheavals.

You and I, as individuals, can, by borrowing, live beyond our means, but for only a limited period of time. Why should we think that collectively, as a nation, we are not bound by that same limitation? We must act today in order to preserve tomorrow. And let there be no misunderstanding — we are going to begin to act beginning today.

The economic ills we suffer have come upon us over several decades. They will not go away in days, weeks, or months, but they will go away. They will go away because we as Americans have the capacity now, as we have had in the past, to do whatever needs to be done to preserve this last and greatest bastion of freedom.

In this present crisis, government is not the solution to our problem. Government is the problem.

From time to time we have been tempted to believe that society has become too complex to be managed by self-rule, that government by an elite group is superior to government for, by and of the people. But, if no one among us is capable of governing himself, then who among us has the capacity to govern someone else.

All of us together — in and out of government — must bear the burden. The solutions we seek must be equitable with no one group singled out to pay a higher price.

We hear much of special interest groups, but our concern must be for a special interest group that has been too long neglected. It knows no sectional boundaries, crosses ethnic and racial divisions and political party lines. It is made up of men and women who raise our food, patrol our streets, man our mines and factories, teach our children, keep our homes and heal us when we're sick. Professionals, industrialists, shopkeepers, clerks, cabbies and truck drivers. They are, in short, "We the people," this breed called Americans.

Well, this administration's objective must be a healthy, vigorous, growing economy that provides equal opportunities for all Americans with no barriers born of bigotry or discrimination. Putting America back to work means putting all Americans back to work. Ending inflation means freeing all Americans from the terror of runaway living costs. All must share in the productive work of this "new beginning," and all must share in the bounty of a revived economy. With the idealism and fair play which are the core of our system and our strength, we can have a strong, prosperous America at peace with itself and the world.

So as we begin, let us take inventory. We are a nation that has a government — not the other way around. And this makes us special among the nations of the Earth. Our government has no special power except that granted it by the people. It is time to check and reverse the growth

of government which shows signs of having grown beyond the consent of the governed.

It is my intention to curb the size and influence of the Federal establishment and to demand recognition of the distinction between the powers granted to the Federal government and those reserved to the states or to the people. All of us need to be reminded that the Federal government did not create the states; the states created the Federal government.

Now so there will be no misunderstanding, it is not my intention to do away with government. It is rather to make it work — work with us, not over us; to stand by our side, not ride on our back. Government can and must provide opportunity, not smother it; foster productivity, not stifle it.

If we look to the answer as to why for so many years we achieved so much, prospered as no other people on earth, it was because here in this land we unleashed the energy and individual genius of man to a greater extent than had ever been done before. Freedom and the dignity of the individual have been more available and assured here than in any other place on earth. The price for this freedom at times has been high, but we have never been unwilling to pay that price.

It is no coincidence that our present troubles parallel and are proportionate [to] the intervention and intrusion in our lives that have resulted from unnecessary and excessive growth of government.

It is time for us to realize that we are too great a nation to limit ourselves to small dreams. We are not, as some would have us believe, doomed to an inevitable decline. I do not believe in a fate that will fall on us no matter what we do. I do believe in a fate that will fall on us if we do nothing.

So, with all the creative energy at our command, let us begin an era of national renewal. Let us renew our determination, our courage, and our strength and let us renew our faith and our hope. We have every right to dream heroic dreams.

Those who say we are in a time when there are no heroes, they just don't know where to look. You can see heroes every day going in and out of factory gates. Others, a handful in number, produce food enough to feed all of us and much of the world beyond.

You meet heroes across a counter. And they're on both sides of that counter. There are entrepreneurs with faith in themselves and faith in an idea who create new jobs, new wealth and opportunity. They are individuals and families whose taxes support the government and whose voluntary gifts support church, charity, culture, art, and education. Their patriotism is quiet but deep. Their values sustain our national life.

Now, I have used the words "they" and "their" in speaking of these heroes. I could say "you" and "your" because I am addressing the heroes of whom I speak — you, the citizens of this blessed land. Your dreams, your hopes, your goals are going to be the dreams, the hopes and goals

of this administration, so help me God.

We shall reflect the compassion that is so much a part of your makeup. How can we love our country and not love our countrymen? And loving them reach out a hand when they fall, heal them when they are sick and provide opportunity to make them self-sufficient so they will be equal in fact and not just in theory.

Can we solve the problems confronting us? Well, the answer is an unequivocal and emphatic yes. To paraphrase Winston Churchill, I did not take the oath I have just taken with the intention of presiding over the dissolution of the world's strongest economy.

In the days ahead I will propose removing the roadblocks that have slowed our economy and reduced productivity. Steps will be taken aimed at restoring the balance between the various levels of government. Progress may be slow — measured in inches and feet, not miles — but we will progress. It is time to reawaken this industrial giant, to get government back within its means, and to lighten our punitive tax burden. And these will be our first priorities, and on these principles, there will be no compromise.

On the eve of our struggle for independence a man who might have been one of the greatest among the Founding Fathers, Dr. Joseph Warren, President of the Massachusetts Congress, said to his fellow Americans, "Our country is in danger, but not to be despaired of . . . On you depend the fortunes of America. You are to decide the important questions on which rests the happiness and liberty of millions yet unborn. Act worthy of yourselves."

Well, I believe we the Americans of today are ready to act worthy of ourselves, ready to do what must be done to ensure happiness and liberty for ourselves, our children, and our children's children.

And as we renew ourselves here in our own land, we will be seen as having greater strength throughout the world. We will again be the exemplar of freedom and a beacon of hope for those who do not now have freedom.

To those neighbors and allies who share our ideal of freedom, we will strengthen our historic ties and assure them of our support and firm commitment. We will match loyalty with loyalty. We will strive for mutually beneficial relations. We will not use our friendship to impose on their sovereignty, for our own sovereignty is not for sale.

As for the enemies of freedom, to those who are potential adversaries, they will be reminded that peace is the highest aspiration of the American people. We will negotiate for it, sacrifice for it; we will not surrender for it — now or ever.

Our forbearance should never be misunderstood. Our reluctance for conflict should not be misjudged as a failure of will. When action is required to preserve our national security, we will act. We will maintain sufficient strength to prevail if need be, knowing that if we do so we have

the best chance of never having to use that strength.

Above all we must realize that no arsenal or no weapon in the arsenals of the world is so formidable as the will and moral courage of free men and women. It is a weapon our adversaries in today's world do not have. It is a weapon that we as Americans do have. Let that be understood by those who practice terrorism and prey upon their neighbors.

I am told that tens of thousands of prayer meetings are being held on this day. For that I am deeply grateful. We are a nation under God, and I believe God intended for us to be free. It would be fitting and good, I think, if each Inaugural Day in future years it should be a day of prayer.

This, as you've been told, is the first time in our history that this ceremony has been held on the West Front of the Capitol Building. Standing here, we face a magnificent vista, opening up on this city's special beauty and history. At the end of this open mall are those shrines to the giants on whose shoulders we stand.

Directly in front of me, the monument to a monumental man. George Washington, Father of our country. A man of humility who came to greatness reluctantly. He led America out of revolutionary victory into infant nationhood.

Off to one side, the stately memorial to Thomas Jefferson. The Declaration of Independence flames with his eloquence.

And then beyond the reflecting pool, the dignified columns of the Lincoln Memorial. Whoever would understand in his heart the meaning of America will find it in the life of Abraham Lincoln.

Beyond these monuments to heroism is the Potomac River, and on the far shore the sloping hills of Arlington National Cemetery with its row upon row of simple white markers bearing crosses or Stars of David. They add up to only a tiny fraction of the price that has been paid for our freedom.

Each one of those markers is a monument to the kind of hero I spoke of earlier. Their lives ended in places called Belleau Wood, The Argonne, Omaha Beach, Salerno and halfway round the world on Guadalcanal, Tarawa, Pork Chop Hill, The Chosin Reservoir, and in a hundred rice paddies and jungles of a place called Vietnam.

Under such a marker lies a young man — Martin Treptow — who left his job in a small town barber shop in 1917 to go to France with the famed Rainbow Division. There, on the Western front, he was killed trying to carry a message between battalions under heavy artillery fire.

We are told that on his body was found a diary. On the flyleaf under the heading, "My Pledge," he had written these words: "America must win this war. Therefore I will work, I will save, I will sacrifice, I will endure, I will fight cheerfully and do my utmost, as if the issue of the whole struggle depended on me alone."

The crisis we are facing today does not require of us the kind of sacrifice that

Martin Treptow and so many thousands of others were called upon to make. It does, however, require our best effort, and our willingness to believe in ourselves and to believe in our capacity to perform great deeds; to believe that together and with God's help we can and will resolve the problems which confront us.

And after all, why shouldn't we believe that? We are Americans.

God bless you.   ▪

Oil Deregulation

Following is President Reagan's Jan. 28 statement describing his action (executive order 12287) on removing federal controls on oil production:

I am ordering — effective immediately — the elimination of remaining Federal controls on U.S. oil production and marketing.

For more than nine years, restrictive price controls have held U.S. oil production below its potential, artificially boosted energy consumption, aggravated our balance of payments problems and stifled technological breakthroughs. Price controls have also made us more energy-dependent on the OPEC nations — a development that has jeopardized our economic security and undermined price stability at home.

Fears that the planned phase-out of controls would not be carried out for political reasons have also hampered production. Ending these controls now will erase this uncertainty.

This step will also stimulate energy conservation. At the same time, the elimination of price controls will end the entitlements system, which has been, in reality, a subsidy for the importation of foreign oil.

This order also ends the gasoline allocation regulations which the Departments of Energy and Justice cite as important causes of the gas lines and shortages which have plagued American consumers on and off since 1974.

In order to provide for the orderly termination of petroleum controls, certain minor provisions of the current regulatory program will not end until March 31, 1981. . . .   ▪

President Reagan's Economic Policy Address

Following is the text of President Reagan's report to the nation on the economy, as broadcast Feb. 5.

Good evening. I am speaking to you tonight to give you a report on the state of our Nation's economy. I regret to say that we are in the worst economic mess since the Great Depression. A few days ago I was presented with a report I had asked for — a comprehensive audit if you will of our economic condition. You won't like it, I didn't like it, but we have to face the truth and then go to work to turn things around. And make no mistake about it, we can turn them around.

I'm not going to subject you to the jumble of charts, figures, and economic jargon of that audit but rather will try to explain where we are, how we got there, and how we can get back.

First, however, let me just give a few "attention getters" from the audit. The Federal budget is out of control and we face runaway deficits, of almost $80 billion for this budget year that ends September 30. That deficit is larger than the entire Federal budget in 1957 and so is the almost $80 billion we will pay in interest this year on the national debt.

Twenty years ago in 1960 our Federal Government payroll was less than $13 billion. Today it is $75 billion. During these twenty years, our population has only increased by 23.3 percent. The Federal budget has gone up 528 percent.

Now, we've just had two years of back-to-back double digit inflation, 13.3 percent in 1979 — 12.4 percent last year. The last time this happened was in World War I.

In 1960 mortgage interest rates averaged about 6 percent. They are 2-1/2 times as high now, 15.4 percent. The percentage of your earnings the Federal Government took in taxes in 1960 has almost doubled. And finally there are 7 million Americans caught up in the personal indignity and human tragedy of unemployment. If they stood in a line — allowing 3 feet for each person — the line would reach from the Coast of Maine to California.

Inflation Impact

Well, so much for the audit itself. Let me try to put this in personal terms. Here is a dollar such as you earned, spent, or saved in 1960. Here is a quarter, a dime, and a penny — 36¢. That's what this 1960 dollar is worth today. And if the present inflation rate should continue three more years, that dollar of 1960 will be worth a quarter. What initiative is there to save? And if we don't save we are short of the investment capital needed for business and industry expansion. Workers in Japan and West Germany save several times the percentage of their income than Americans do.

What's happened to that American dream of owning a home? Only ten years ago a family could buy a home and the monthly payment averaged little more than a quarter — 27¢ out of each dollar earned. Today it takes 42¢ out of every dollar of income. So, fewer than 1 out of 11 families can afford to buy their first new home.

Regulations adopted by government with the best of intentions have added $666 to the cost of an automobile. It is estimated that altogether regulations of every kind, on shopkeepers, farmers, and major industries add $100 billion or more to the cost of the goods and services we buy. And then another $20 billion is spent by government handling the paperwork created by those regulations.

I'm sure you are getting the idea that the audit presented to me found government policies of the last few decades responsible for our economic troubles. We forgot or just overlooked the fact that government — any government — has a built-in tendency to grow. Now, we all had a hand in looking to government for benefits as if government had some sources of revenue other than our earnings. Many if not most of the things we thought of or that government offered to us seemed attractive.

In the years following the Second World War it was easy (for awhile at least) to overlook the price tag. Our income more than doubled in the 25 years after the War. We increased our take-home pay in those 25 years by more than we had amassed in all the preceding 150 years put together. Yes, there was some inflation, 1 or 1-1/2 percent a year, that didn't bother us. But if we look back at those golden years we recall that even then voices had been raised warning that inflation, like radioactivity, was cumulative and that once started it could get out of control. Some government programs seemed so worthwhile that borrowing to fund them didn't bother us.

By 1960 our national debt stood at $284 billion. Congress in 1971 decided to put a ceiling of $400 billion on our ability to borrow. Today the debt is $934 billion. So-called temporary increases or extensions in the debt ceiling have been allowed 21 times in these 10 years and now I have been forced to ask for another increase in the debt ceiling or the government will be unable to function past the middle of February and I've only been here 16 days. Before we reach the day when we can reduce the debt ceiling we may in spite of our best efforts see a national debt in excess of a trillion dollars. Now this is a figure literally beyond our comprehension.

We know now that inflation results from all that deficit spending. Government has only two ways of getting money other than raising taxes. It can go into the money market and borrow, competing with its own citizens and driving up interest rates, which it has done, or it can print money, and it's done that. Both methods are inflationary.

We're victims of language, the very word "inflation" leads us to think of it as

just high prices. Then, of course, we resent the person who puts on the price tags forgetting that he or she is also a victim of inflation. Inflation is not just high prices, it is a reduction in the value of our money. When the money supply is increased but the goods and services available for buying are not, we have too much money chasing too few goods.

Wars are usually accompanied by inflation. Everyone is working or fighting but production is of weapons and munitions not things we can buy and use.

Taxes

One way out would be to raise taxes so that government need not borrow or print money. But in all these years of government growth we've reached — indeed surpassed — the limit of our people's tolerance or ability to bear an increase in the tax burden.

Prior to World War II, taxes were such that on the average we only had to work just a little over one month each year to pay our total Federal, state, and local tax bill. Today we have to work four months to pay that bill.

Some say shift the tax burden to business and industry but business doesn't pay taxes. Oh, don't get the wrong idea, business is being taxed — so much so that we are being priced out of the world market. But business must pass its costs of operation and that includes taxes, onto the customer in the price of the product. Only people pay taxes — all the taxes. Government just uses business in a kind of sneaky way to help collect the taxes. They are hidden in the price and we aren't aware of how much tax we actually pay. Today, this once great industrial giant of ours has the lowest rate of gain in productivity of virtually all the industrial nations with whom we must compete in the world market. We can't even hold our own market here in America against foreign automobiles, steel, and a number of other products.

Japanese production of automobiles is almost twice as great per worker as it is in America. Japanese steel workers out-produce their American counterparts by about 25 percent.

Now this isn't because they are better workers. I'll match the American working man or woman against anyone in the world. But we have to give them the tools and equipment that workers in the other industrial nations have.

We invented the assembly line and mass production, but punitive tax policies and excessive and unnecessary regulations plus government borrowing have stifled our ability to update plant and equipment. When capital investment is made it's too often for some unproductive alterations demanded by government to meet various of its regulations.

Excessive taxation of individuals has robbed us of incentive and made overtime unprofitable.

We once produced about 40 percent of the world's steel. We now produce 19 percent.

We were once the greatest producer of automobiles, producing more than all the rest of the world combined. That is no longer true, and in addition, the big 3, the major auto companies, in our land have sustained tremendous losses in the past year and have been forced to lay off thousands of workers.

All of you who are working know that even with cost-of-living pay raises you can't keep up with inflation. In our progressive tax system as you increase the number of dollars you earn you find yourself moved up into higher tax brackets, paying a higher tax rate just for trying to hold your own. The result? Your standard of living is going down.

Over the past decades we've talked of curtailing government spending so that we can then lower the tax burden. Sometimes we've even taken a run at doing that. But there were always those who told us taxes couldn't be cut until spending was reduced. Well, you know, we can lecture our children about extravagance until we run out of voice and breath. Or we can cure their extravagance by simply reducing their allowance.

Turning Point

It is time to recognize that we have come to a turning point. We are threatened with an economic calamity of tremendous proportions and the old business as usual treatment can't save us.

Together, we must chart a different course. We must increase productivity. That means making it possible for industry to modernize and make use of the technology which we ourselves invented; that means putting Americans back to work. And that means above all bringing government spending back within government revenues which is the only way, together with increased productivity that we can reduce and, yes, eliminate inflation.

In the past we've tried to fight inflation one year and then when unemployment increased turn the next year to fighting unemployment with more deficit spending as a pump primer. So again, up goes inflation. It hasn't worked. We don't have to choose between inflation and unemployment — they go hand in hand. It's time to try something different and that's what we're going to do.

I've already placed a freeze on hiring replacements for those who retire or leave government service. I have ordered a cut in government travel, the number of consultants to the government, and the buying of office equipment and other items. I have put a freeze on pending regulations and set up a task force under Vice President Bush to review regulations with an eye toward getting rid of as many as possible. I have decontrolled oil which should result in more domestic production and less dependence on foreign oil. And I am eliminating that ineffective Council on Wage and Price Stability.

But it will take more, much more and we must realize there is no quick fix. At the same time, however, we cannot delay in implementing an economic program aimed at both reducing tax rates to stimulate productivity and reducing the growth in government spending to reduce unemployment and inflation.

On February 18th, I will present in detail an economic program to Congress embodying the features I have just stated. It will propose budget cuts in virtually every department of government. It is my belief that these actual budget cuts will only be part of the savings. As our Cabinet Secretaries take charge of their departments, they will search out areas of waste, extravagance, and costly administrative overhead which could yield additional and substantial reductions.

Now at the same time we're doing this, we must go forward with a tax relief package. I shall ask for a 10 percent reduction across the board in personal income tax rates for each of the next three years. Proposals will also be submitted for accelerated depreciation allowances for business to provide necessary capital so as to create jobs.

Now, here again, in saying this, I know that language, as I said earlier, can get in the way of a clear understanding of what our program is intended to do. Budget cuts can sound as if we are going to reduce total government spending to a lower level than was spent the year before. This is not the case. The budgets will increase as our population increases and each year we'll see spending increases to match that growth. Government revenues will increase as the economy grows, but the burden will be lighter for each individual because the economic base will have been expanded by reason of the reduced rates.

Balanced Budget

Now let me show you a chart I've had drawn to illustrate how this can be. Here you see two trend lines. The bottom line shows the increase in tax revenues. The red line on top is the increase in government spending. Both lines turn upward reflecting the giant tax increase already built into the system for this year 1981, and the increases in spending built into the '81 and '82 budgets and on into the future.

As you can see, the spending line rises at a steeper slant than the revenue line. And that gap between those lines illustrates the increasing deficits we've been running including this year's $80 billion deficit.

Now, in the second chart, the lines represent the positive effects when Congress accepts our economic program. Both lines continue to rise allowing for necessary growth but the gap narrows as spending cuts continue over the next few years, until finally the two lines come together meaning a balanced budget.

I am confident that my Administration can achieve that. At that point tax revenues in spite of rate reductions will be increasing faster than spending which means we can look forward to further reductions in the tax rates.

Now, in all of this we will of course work closely with the Federal Reserve System toward the objective of a stable monetary policy.

Our spending cuts will not be at the expense of the truly needy. We will, however, seek to eliminate benefits to those who are not really qualified by reason of need.

As I've said before, on February 18th, I will present this economic package of budget reductions and tax reform to a joint session of Congress and to you in full detail.

Our basic system is sound. We can, with compassion, continue to meet our responsibility to those who through no fault of their own need our help. We can meet fully the other legitimate responsibilities of government. We cannot continue any longer our wasteful ways at the expense of the workers of this land or of our children.

Since 1960 our government has spent $5.1 trillion; our debt has grown by $648 billion. Prices have exploded by 178 percent. How much better off are we for all that? We all know, we are very much worse off.

When we measure how harshly these years of inflation, lower productivity, and uncontrolled government growth have affected our lives, we know we must act and act now.

We must not be timid.

We will restore the freedom of all men and women to excel and to create. We will unleash the energy and genius of the American people — traits which have never failed us.

To the Congress of the United States, I extend my hand in cooperation and I believe we can go forward in a bipartisan manner.

I found a real willingness to cooperate on the part of Democrats and members of my own Party.

To my colleagues in the Executive Branch of government and to all Federal employees I ask that we work in the spirit of service.

I urge those great institutions in America — business and labor — to be guided by the national interest and I'm confident they will. The only special interest that we will serve is the interest of all the people.

We can create the incentives which take advantage of the genius of our economic system — a system, as Walter Lippmann observed more than 40 years ago, which for the first time in history gave men "a way of producing wealth in which the good fortune of others multiplied their own."

Our aim is to increase our national wealth so all will have more not just redistribute what we already have which is just a sharing of scarcity. We can begin to reward hard work and risk-taking, by forcing this government to live within its means.

Over the years we've let negative economic forces run out of control. We've stalled the judgment day. We no longer have that luxury. We're out of time.

And to you my fellow citizens, let us join in a new determination to rebuild the foundation of our society; to work together to act responsibly. Let us do so with the most profound respect for that which must be preserved as well as with sensitive understanding and compassion for those who must be protected.

We can leave our children with an unrepayable massive debt and a shattered economy or we can leave them liberty in a land where every individual has the opportunity to be whatever God intended us to be. All it takes is a little common sense and recognition of our own ability. Together we can forge a new beginning for America.

Thank you and good night. ∎

President Reagan's Economic Proposals Text

Following is the text of the address as delivered by President Reagan to a joint session of Congress on Feb. 18. President Reagan presented his proposals to cut government spending in all areas, except defense. But he reassured the truly needy who depend on social security and welfare programs that the government would fulfill its obligations.

Mr. Speaker, Mr. President, distinguished Members of Congress, honored guests, and fellow citizens. Only a month ago, I was your guest in this historic building and I pledged to you my cooperation in doing what is right for this Nation that we all love so much.

I am here tonight to reaffirm that pledge and to ask that we share in restoring the promise that is offered to every citizen by this, the last, best hope of man on earth.

All of us are aware of the punishing inflation which has, for the first time in some 60 years, held to double digit figures for 2 years in a row. Interest rates have reached absurd levels of more than 20 percent and over 15 percent for those who would borrow to buy a home. All across this land one can see newly built homes standing vacant, unsold because of mortgage interest rates.

Almost eight million Americans are out of work. These are people who want to be productive. But as the months go by, despair dominates their lives. The threats of layoffs and unemployment hang over other millions, and all who work are frustrated by their inability to keep up with inflation.

One worker in a Midwest city put it to me this way: He said, "I'm bringing home more dollars than I thought I ever believed I could possibly earn, but I seem to be getting worse off." And he is. Not only have hourly earnings of the American worker, after adjusting for inflation, declined 5 percent over the past 5 years, but in these 5 years, Federal personal taxes for the average family increased 67 percent.

We can no longer procrastinate and hope that things will get better. They will not. Unless we act forcefully, and now, the economy will get worse.

National Debt

Can we who man the ship of state deny it is somewhat out of control? Our national debt is approaching $1 trillion. A few weeks ago I called such a figure — a trillion dollars — incomprehensible. I've been trying ever since to think of a way to illustrate how big a trillion is. The best I could come up with is that if you had a stack of $1,000 bills in your hand only four inches high you would be a millionaire. A trillion dollars would be a stack of $1,000 bills 67 miles high.

The interest on the public debt this year we know will be over $90 billion. And unless we change the proposed spending for the fiscal year beginning October 1, we'll add another almost $80 billion to the debt.

Adding to our troubles is a mass of regulations imposed on the shopkeeper, the farmer, the craftsman, professionals and major industry that is estimated to add $100 billion to the price of things we buy and it reduces our ability to produce. The rate of increase in American productivity, once one of the highest in the world, is among the lowest of all major industrial nations. Indeed, it has actually declined in the last 3 years.

I have painted a pretty grim picure but I think that I have painted it accurately. It is within our power to change this picture and we can act with hope. There is nothing wrong with our internal strengths. There has been no breakdown in the human, technological, and natural resources upon which the economy is built.

Four-point Proposal

Based on this confidence in a system which has never failed us — but which we have failed through a lack of confidence, and sometimes through a belief that we could fine tune the economy and get a tune to our liking — I am proposing a comprehensive four-point program. Let me outline in detail some of the principal parts of this program. You will each be provided with a completely detailed copy of the entire program.

This plan is aimed at reducing the growth in Government spending and tax-

ing, reforming and eliminating regulations which are unnecessary and unproductive or counterproductive, and encouraging a consistent monetary policy aimed at maintaining the value of the currency.

If enacted in full, this program can help America create 13 million new jobs, nearly 3 million more than we would have without these measures. It will also help us gain control of inflation.

Tax Increase Rate Reduction

It is important to note that we are only reducing the rate of increase in taxing and spending. We are not attempting to cut either spending or taxing levels below that which we presently have. This plan will get our economy moving again, increase productivity growth, and thus create the jobs our people must have.

And I am asking that you join me in reducing direct Federal spending by $41.4 billion in fiscal year 1982, along with another $7.7 billion user fees and off-budget savings for a total savings of $49.1 billion.

This will still allow an increase of $40.8 billion over 1981 spending.

Full Funding for Truly Needy

I know that exaggerated and inaccurate stories about these cuts have disturbed many people, particularly those dependent on grant and benefit programs for their basic needs. Some of you have heard from constituents, I know, afraid that social security checks, for example, were going to be taken away from them. I regret the fear that these unfounded stories have caused and I welcome this opportunity to set things straight.

We will continue to fulfill the obligations that spring from our national conscience. Those who through no fault of their own must depend on the rest of us, the poverty stricken, the disabled, the elderly, all those with true need, can rest assured that the social safety net of programs they depend on are exempt from any cuts.

The full retirement benefits of the more than 31 million social security recipients will be continued along with an annual cost of living increase. Medicare will not be cut, nor will supplemental income for the blind, aged, and disabled, and funding will continue for veterans' pensions.

School breakfasts and lunches for the children of low income families will continue, as will nutrition and other special services for the aging. There will be no cut in Project Head Start or summer youth jobs.

All in all, nearly $216 billion worth of programs providing help for tens of millions of Americans — will be fully funded. But government will not continue to subsidize individuals or particular business interests where real need cannot be demonstrated.

And while we will reduce some subsidies to regional and local governments, we will at the same time convert a number of categorical grant programs into block grants to reduce wasteful administrative overhead and to give local government enti-

ties and States more flexibility and control. We call for an end to duplication in Federal programs and reform of those which are not cost effective.

Restore Programs to States and Private Sector

Already, some have protested that there must be no reduction in aid to schools. Let me point out that Federal aid to education amounts to only eight percent of the total educational funding. For this eight percent the Federal Government has insisted on a tremendously disproportionate share of control over our schools. Whatever reductions we've proposed in that eight percent will amount to very little in the total cost of education. They will, however, restore more authority to States and local school districts.

Historically the American people have supported by voluntary contributions more artistic and cultural activities than all the other countries in the world put together. I wholeheartedly support this approach and believe that Americans will continue their generosity. Therefore, I am proposing a savings of $85 million in the Federal subsidies now going to the arts and humanities.

There are a number of subsidies to business and industry that I believe are unnecessary. Not because the activities being subsidized aren't of value but because the marketplace contains incentives enough to warrant continuing these activities without a government subsidy. One such subsidy is the Department of Energy's synthetic fuels program. We will continue support of research leading to development of new technologies and more independence from foreign oil, but we can save at least $3.2 billion by leaving to private industry the building of plants to make liquid or gas fuels from coal.

We are asking that another major industry, business subsidy I should say, the Export-Import Bank loan authority, be reduced by one-third in 1982. We are doing this because the primary beneficiaries of tax payer funds in this case are the exporting companies themselves — most of them profitable corporations.

High Cost of Government Borrowing

This brings me to a number of other lending programs in which Government makes low-interest loans. Some of them at an interest rate as low as 2 percent. What has not been very well understood is that the Treasury Department has no money of its own. It has to go into the private capital market and borrow the money. So in this time of excessive interest rates the government finds itself borrowing at an interest rate several times as high as the interest rate it gets back from those it lends the money to. This difference, of course, is paid by your constituents, the taxpayers. They get hit again if they try to borrow because Government borrowing contributes to raising all interest rates.

By terminating the Economic Development Administration we can save hundreds

of millions of dollars in 1982 and billions more over the next few years. There is a lack of consistent and convincing evidence that EDA and its Regional Commissions have been effective in creating new jobs. They have been effective in creating an array of planners, grantsmen and professional middlemen. We believe we can do better just by the expansion of the economy and the job creation which will come from our economic program.

Wefare and Unemployment Programs

The Food Stamp program will be restored to its original purpose, to assist those without resources to purchase sufficient nutritional food. We will, however, save $1.8 billion in fiscal year 1982 by removing from eligibility those who are not in real need or who are abusing the program.

Even with this reduction, the program will be budgeted for more than $10 billion.

We will tighten welfare and give more attention to outside sources of income when determining the amount of welfare an individual is allowed. This plus strong and effective work requirements will save $520 million in the next year.

I stated a moment ago our intention to keep the school breakfast and lunch programs for those in true need. But by cutting back on meals for children of families who can afford to pay, the savings will be $1.6 billion in fiscal year 1982.

Let me just touch on a few other areas which are typical of the kinds of reductions we have included in this economic package. The Trade Adjustment Assistance program provides benefits for workers who are unemployed when foreign imports reduce the market for various American products causing shutdown of plants and layoff of workers. The purpose is to help these workers find jobs in growing sectors of our economy. There is nothing wrong with that. But because these benefits are paid out on top of normal unemployment benefits, we wind up paying greater benefits to those who lose their jobs because of foreign competition than we do to their friends and neighbors who are laid off due to domestic competition. Anyone must agree that this is unfair. Putting these two programs on the same footing will save $1.15 billion in just 1 year.

Federal Regulation Burden

Earlier I made mention of changing categorical grants to States and local governments into block grants. We know, of course, that the categorical grant programs burden local and State governments with a mass of Federal regulations and Federal paperwork.

Ineffective targeting, wasteful administrative overhead — all can be eliminated by shifting the resources and decision-making authority to local and State government. This will also consolidate programs which are scattered throughout the Federal bureaucracy, bringing government closer to the people and saving $23.9 billion over the next 5 years.

Our program for economic renewal deals with a number of programs which at present are not cost-effective. An example is Medicaid. Right now Washington provides the States with unlimited matching payments for their expenditures. At the same time we here in Washington pretty much dictate how the States are going to manage these programs. We want to put a cap on how much the Federal Government will contribute but at the same time allow the States much more flexibility in managing and structuring the programs. I know from our experience in California that such flexibility could have led to far more cost-effective reforms. This will bring a savings of $1 billion next year.

Space and Postal Agencies

The space program has been and is important to America and we plan to continue it. We believe, however, that a reordering of priorities to focus on the most important and cost-effective NASA programs can result in a savings of a quarter of a billion dollars.

Coming down from space to the mailbox — the Postal Service has been consistently unable to live within its operating budget. It is still dependent on large Federal subsidies. We propose reducing those subsidies by $632 million in 1982 to press the Postal Service into becoming more effective. In subsequent years, the savings will continue to add up.

The Economic Regulatory Administration in the Department of Energy has programs to force companies to convert to specific fuels. It has the authority to administer a gas rationing plan, and prior to decontrol it ran the oil price control program. With these and other regulations gone we can save several hundreds of millions of dollars over the next few years.

Defense Spending

I'm sure there is one department you've been waiting for me to mention, the Department of Defense. It is the only department in our entire program that will actually be increased over the present budgeted figure.

But even here there was no exemption. The Department of Defense came up with a number of cuts which reduced the budget increase needed to restore our military balance. These measures will save $2.9 billion in 1982 outlays and by 1986 a total of $28.2 billion will have been saved. Perhaps I should say will have been made available for the necessary things that we must do. The aim will be to provide the most effective defense for the lowest possible cost.

I believe that my duty as President requires that I recommend increases in defense spending over the coming years.

I know that you are aware but I think it bears saying again that since 1970, the Soviet Union has invested $300 billion more in its military forces than we have. As a result of its massive military buildup, the Soviets have made a significant numerical advantage in strategic nuclear delivery sys-

tems, tactical aircraft, submarines, artillery and antiaircraft defense. To allow this imbalance to continue is a threat to our national security.

Notwithstanding our economic straits, making the financial changes beginning now is far less costly than waiting and having to attempt a crash program several years from now.

We remain committed to the goal of arms limitation through negotiation. I hope we can persuade our adversaries to come to realistic balanced and verifiable agreements.

But, as we negotiate, our security must be fully protected by a balanced and realistic defense program.

New Inspectors General

Let me say a word here about the general problem of waste and fraud in the Federal Government. One government estimate indicated that fraud alone may account for anywhere from 1 to 10 percent — as much as $25 billion — of Federal expenditures for social programs. If the tax dollars that are wasted or mismanaged are added to this fraud total, the staggering dimensions of this problem begin to emerge.

The Office of Management and Budget is now putting together an interagency task force to attack waste and fraud. We are also planning to appoint as Inspectors General highly trained professionals who will spare no effort to do this job.

No administration can promise to immediately stop a trend that has grown in recent years as quickly as Government expenditures themselves. But let me say this: waste and fraud in the Federal budget is exactly what I have called it before — an unrelenting national scandal — a scandal we are bound and determined to do something about.

Tax Proposals

Marching in lockstep with the whole program of reductions in spending is the equally important program of reduced tax rates. Both are essential if we are to have economic recovery. It's time to create new jobs. To build and rebuild industry, and to give the American people room to do what they do best. And that can only be done with a tax program which provides incentive to increase productivity for both workers and industry.

Our proposal is for a 10-percent across-the-board cut every year for three years in the tax rates for all individual income taxpayers, making a total cut in tax rates of 30 percent. This 3-year reduction will also apply to the tax on unearned income, leading toward an eventual elimination of the present differential between the tax on earned and unearned income.

I would have hoped that we could be retroactive with this, but as it stands the effective starting date for these 10-percent personal income tax rate reductions will be called for as of July 1st of this year.

Again, let me remind you that while this 30 percent reduction will leave the taxpayers with $500 billion more in their pockets over the next five years, it's actually only a reduction in the tax increase already built into the system.

Unlike some past "tax reforms," this is not merely a shift of wealth between different sets of taxpayers. This proposal for an equal reduction in everyone's tax rates will expand our national prosperity, enlarge national incomes, and increase opportunities for all Americans.

Some will argue, I know, that reducing tax rates now will be inflationary. A solid body of economic experts does not agree. And tax cuts adopted over the past three-fourths of a century indicate these economic experts are right. They will not be inflationary. I have had advice that in 1985 our real production of goods and services will grow by 20 percent and will be $300 billion higher than it is today. The average worker's wage will rise (in real purchasing power) 8 percent, and this is in after-tax dollars and this, of course, is predicated on a complete program of tax cuts and spending reductions being implemented.

The other part of the tax package is aimed directly at providing business and industry with the capital needed to modernize and engage in more research and development. This will involve an increase in depreciation allowances, and this part of our tax proposal will be retroactive to January 1st.

The present depreciation system is obsolete, needlessly complex, and is economically counterproductive. Very simply, it bases the depreciation of plant, machinery, vehicles, and tools on their original cost with no recognition of how inflation has increased their replacement cost. We are proposing a much shorter write-off time than is presently allowed: a 5-year write-off for machinery; 3 years for vehicles and trucks; and a 10-year write-off for plant.

In fiscal year 1982 under this plan business would acquire nearly $10 billion for investment. By 1985 the figure would be nearly $45 billion. These changes are essential to provide the new investment which is needed to create millions of new jobs between now and 1985 and to make America competitive once again in the world market.

These won't be make-work jobs, they are productive jobs, jobs with a future.

I'm well aware that there are many other desirable and needed tax changes such as indexing the income tax brackets to protect taxpayers against inflation; the unjust discrimination against married couples if both are working and earning; tuition tax credits; the unfairness of the inheritance tax, especially to the family-owned farm and the family-owned business, and a number of others. But our program for economic recovery is so urgently needed to begin to bring down inflation that I am asking you to act on this plan first and with great urgency. Then I pledge I will join with you in seeking these additional tax changes at the earliest date possible.

Overregulation

American society experienced a virtual explosion in Government regulation during the past decade. Between 1970 and 1979, expenditures for the major regulatory agencies quadrupled, the number of pages published annually in the *Federal Register* nearly tripled, and the number of pages in the *Code of Federal Regulations* increased by nearly two-thirds.

The result has been higher prices, higher unemployment, and lower productivity growth. Overregulation causes small and independent businessmen and women, as well as large businesses, to defer or terminate plans for expansion, and since they are responsible for most of our new jobs, those new jobs just aren't created.

We have no intention of dismantling the regulatory agencies — especially those necessary to protect [the] environment and to ensure the public health and safety. However, we must come to grips with inefficient and burdensome regulations — eliminate those we can and reform the others.

I have asked Vice President Bush to head a Cabinet-level Task Force on Regulatory Relief. Second, I asked each member of my Cabinet to postpone the effective dates of the hundreds of regulations which have not yet been implemented. Third, in coordination with the task force, many of the agency heads have already taken prompt action to review and rescind existing burdensome regulations. Finally, just yesterday, I signed an executive order that for the first time provides for effective and coordinated management of the regulatory process.

Much has been accomplished, but it is only a beginning. We will eliminate those regulations that are unproductive and unnecessary by executive order, where possible, and cooperate fully with you on those that require legislation.

The final aspect of our plan requires a national monetary policy which does not allow money growth to increase consistently faster than the growth of goods and services. In order to curb inflation, we need to slow the growth in our money supply.

We fully recognize the independence of the Federal Reserve System and will do nothing to interfere with or undermine that independence. We will consult regularly with the Federal Reserve Board on all aspects of our economic program and will vigorously pursue budget policies that will make their job easier in reducing monetary growth.

A successful program to achieve stable and moderate growth patterns in the money supply will keep both inflation and interest rates down and restore vigor to our financial institutions and markets.

'Economic Recovery' Proposed

This, then, is our proposal. "America's New Beginning: A Program for Economic Recovery." I don't want it to be simply the plan of my Administration — I'm here tonight to ask you to join me in making it our plan. [Applause, members rising]

I should have arranged to quit right there.

Well, together we can embark on this road, not to make things easy, but to make things better.

Our social, political and cultural as well as our economic institutions can no longer absorb the repeated shocks that have been dealt them over the past decades.

Can we do the job? The answer is yes, but we must begin now.

We are in control here. There is nothing wrong with America that we can't fix. I'm sure there will be some who will raise the familiar old cry, "Don't touch my program — cut somewhere else."

I hope I've made it plain that our approach has been evenhanded; that only the programs for the truly deserving needy remain untouched.

The question is, are we simply going to go down the same path we've gone down before — carving out one special program here, another special program there. I don't think that is what the American people expect of us. More important, I don't think that is what they want. They are ready to return to the source of our strength.

The substance and prosperity of our Nation is built by wages brought home from the factories and the mills, the farms and the shops. They are the services provided in 10,000 corners of America; the interest on the thrift of our people and the returns for their risk-taking. The production of America is the possession of those who build, serve, create and produce.

For too long now, we've removed from our people the decisions on how to dispose of what they created. We have strayed from first principles. We must alter our course.

The taxing power of government must be used to provide revenues for legitimate government purposes. It must not be used to regulate the economy or bring about social change. We've tried that and surely must be able to see it doesn't work.

Proper Province of Government

Spending by Government must be limited to those functions which are the proper province of Government. We can no longer afford things simply because we think of them.

Next year we can reduce the budget by $41.4 billion, without harm to Government's legitimate purposes or to our responsibility to all who need our benevolence. This, plus the reduction in tax rates, will help bring an end to inflation.

In the health and social services area alone the plan we are proposing will substantially reduce the need for 465 pages of law, 1,400 pages of regulations, 5,000 Federal employees who presently administer 7,600 separate grants in about 25,000 separate locations. Over 7 million man and woman hours of work by State and local officials are required to fill out government forms.

I would direct a question to those who have indicated already an unwillingness to accept such a plan. Have they an alternative which offers a greater chance of balancing the budget, reducing and eliminating inflation, stimulating the creation of jobs, and reducing the tax burden? And if they haven't, are they suggesting we can continue on the present course without coming to a day of reckoning?

If we don't do this, inflation and the growing tax burden will put an end to everything we believe in and our dreams for the future. We don't have an option of living with inflation and its attendant tragedy, millions of productive people willing and able to work but unable to find a buyer for their work in the job market.

We have an alternative, and that is the program for economic recovery.

True, it will take time for the favorable effects of our proposal to be felt. So we must begin now.

The people are watching and waiting. They don't demand miracles. They do expect us to act. Let us act together.

Thank you and good night. ∎

Iran Claims Settlement

Following is the text of President Reagan's Feb. 24 message to Congress outlining actions taken to implement the Jan. 19 agreement with Iran:

TO THE CONGRESS
OF THE UNITED STATES:

Pursuant to Section 204(b) of the International Emergency Economic Powers Act (IEEPA), 50 U.S.C. 1703(b), I have today exercised the authority granted by this Act to suspend certain litigation against Iran.

1. The circumstance necessitating the exercise of this authority is the implementation of the Claims Settlement Agreement between the United States and Iran. After a complete review of the agreements with Iran leading to the release of the hostages held by Iran I have decided to implement them.

This order is part of a series of actions necessary to resolve the national emergencies declared in Executive Order 12170 of November 14, 1979, and in Executive Order 12211 of April 17, 1980, and described in reports submitted to Congress under the IEEPA by President Carter on November 14, 1979; April 7, 1980; April 17, 1980; and January 19, 1981.

2. Although the hostages have been released, financial and diplomatic aspects of the crisis have not yet been resolved and continue to present an unusual and ex-

traordinary threat to the national security, foreign policy and economy of the United States.

3. Thus claims which may be presented to the Iran-United States Claims Tribunal are suspended in accordance with the terms of the attached Executive Order pursuant to the terms of the Claims Settlement Agreement, and my powers under Article II of the Constitution, Section 1732 of Title 22, known as the Hostage Act, and Section 203 of IEEPA.

I am also ratifying earlier Executive Orders signed by President Carter on Jan-

uary 19, 1981, to remove any doubt as to their effect, an issue that has been raised in recent litigation challenging them. In this connection I note that Executive Orders 12276 through 12285 were all signed by President Carter and made effective while he was still in office. The Report to Congress required by IEEPA dated January 19, 1981, indicates that some of the Executive Orders were not signed until the release of the hostages, an event that did not occur until after the end of his term. The report, which was prepared in advance, did not, because of the press of circumstances, re-

flect events precisely as they occurred and to that extent it stands corrected.

4. The present Executive Order is necessary for the United States to meet its obligations under the Claims Settlement Agreement to peacefully arbitrate certain claims.

5. The action is taken with respect to Iran for the reasons outlined above.

RONALD REAGAN

The White House
Feb. 24, 1981   ∎

Text of Reagan FY '82 Budget Revisions

Following is the text of President Reagan's March 10 message to Congress transmitting revisions to the fiscal 1982 budget:

TO THE CONGRESS OF
THE UNITED STATES:

On February 18, I spoke to a Joint Session of Congress about the economic crisis facing America. I pledged then to take the action necessary to alleviate the grievous economic plight of our people. The plan I outlined will stop runaway inflation and revitalize our economy if given a chance. There is nothing but politics — as — usual standing in the way of lower inflation, increased productivity, and a return to prosperity.

Economic Recovery Program

Our program for economic recovery does not rely upon complex theories or elaborate Government programs. Instead, it recognizes basic economic facts of life and, as humanely as possible, it will move America back toward economic sanity. The principles are easily understood, but it will take determination to apply them. Nevertheless, if inflation and unemployment are to be curtailed, we must act.

First, we must cut the growth of Government spending.

Second, we must cut tax rates so that once again work will be rewarded and savings encouraged.

Third, we must carefully remove the tentacles of excessive Government regulation which are strangling our economy.

Fourth, while recognizing the independence of the Institution, we must work with the Federal Reserve Board to develop a monetary policy that will rationally control the money supply.

Fifth, we must move, surely and predictably, toward a balanced budget.

The budget reform plan announced on February 18 includes 83 major cuts resulting in $34.8 billion outlay savings for 1982,

with greater future savings. With this message, over 200 additional reductions are proposed. An additional $13.8 billion in savings are now planned. Further, I am proposing changes in user charges and off — budget payments that will bring total fiscal savings to $55.9 billion. This compares with $49.1 billion in fiscal savings announced on February 18.

In terms of appropriations and other budget authority that will affect future spending, we are proposing elimination of $67 billion in 1982 and over $475 billion in the period 1981 to 1986.

These cuts sound like enormous sums — and they are — until one considers the overwhelming size of the total budget. Even with these cuts, the 1982 budget will total $695.3 billion, an increase of 6.1 percent over 1981.

'Dramatic Change' Needed

The budget reductions we are proposing will, undoubtedly, face stiff opposition from those who are tied to maintaining the status quo. But today's status quo is nothing more than economic stagnation coupled with high inflation. Dramatic change is needed or the situation will simply get worse, resulting in even more suffering and misery, and possibly the destruction of traditional American values.

While recognizing the need for bold action, we have ensured that the impact of spending reductions will be shared widely and fairly by different groups and the various regions of the country. Also, we have, as pledged, maintained this society's basic social safety net, protecting programs for the elderly and others who rely on Government for their very existence.

Budget cuts alone, however, will not turn this economy around. Our package includes a proposal to reduce substantially the personal income tax rates levied on our people and to accelerate the recovery of business with capital investment. These rate reductions are essential to restoring strength and growth to the economy by

reducing the existing tax barriers that discourage work, saving, and investment. Individuals are the ultimate source of all savings and investment. Lasting economic progress, which is our goal, depends on our success in encouraging people to involve themselves in this kind of productive behavior.

Our tax proposal will, if enacted, have an immediate impact on the economic vitality of the Nation, where even a slight improvement can produce dramatic results. For example, a 2 percent increase in economic growth will add $60 billion to our gross national product in one year alone. That $60 billion adds to the state and local tax base, to the purchasing power of the American family, and to the resources available for investment.

Nov. 4 Mandate

When considering the economic recovery package, I urge the Members of Congress to remember that last November the American people's message was loud and clear. The mandate for change, expressed by the American people, was not my mandate; it was our mandate. Together we must remember that our primary responsibility is to the Nation as a whole and that there is nothing more important than putting America's economic house in order.

The next steps are up to Congress. It has not been easy for my administration to prepare this revised budget. I am aware that it will not be easy for the Congress to act upon it. I pledge my full cooperation. It is essential that, together, we succeed in again making this Nation a land whose expanding economy offers an opportunity for all to better themselves, a land where productive behavior is rewarded, a land where one need not fear that economic forces beyond one's control will, through inflation, destroy a lifetime of savings.

RONALD REAGAN

The White House
March 10, 1981   ∎

President Reagan's Address on Economy

Following is the text of a speech made by President Reagan April 28 to a joint session of Congress. It was Reagan's first public appearance since the assassination attempt on March 30.

The PRESIDENT. Mr. Speaker, Mr. President, distinguished Members of the Congress, honored guests and fellow citizens.

I have no words to express my appreciation for that greeting.

I have come to speak to you tonight about our economic recovery program and why I believe it is essential that the Congress approve this package which I believe will lift the crushing burden of inflation off of our citizens and restore the vitality to our economy, and our industrial machine.

Acknowledgment of Get Well Wishes

First, however, and due to events of the past few weeks, will you permit me to digress for a moment from the all important subject of why we must bring Government spending under control and reduce tax rates. I would like to say a few words directly to all of you and to those who are watching and listening tonight. Because this is the only way I know to express to all of you on behalf of Nancy and myself our appreciation for your messages, your flowers, and most of all, your prayers, not only for me, but for those others who fell beside me.

The warmth of your words, the expression of friendship and, yes, love, meant more to us than you can ever know. You have given us a memory that we will treasure forever. And you have provided an answer to those few voices that were raised saying that what happened was evidence that ours is a sick society.

The society we heard from is made up of millions of compassionate Americans and their children from college age to kindergarten.

As a matter of fact, as evidence of that I have a letter with me. The letter came from Peter Sweeney. He is in the second grade in the Riverside School in Rockville Center. And he said, "I hope you get well quick or you might have to make a speech in your pajamas." [Laughter.]

He added a postscript. "P.S. If you have to make a speech in your pajamas, I warned you." [Laughter.]

Well, sick societies do not produce men like the two who recently returned from outer space. Sick societies do not produce young men like Secret Service Agent Tim McCarthy, who placed his body between mine and the man with the gun simply because he felt that is what his duty called for him to do. Sick societies do not produce dedicated police officers like Tom

Delahanty or able and devoted public servants like Jim Brady.

Sick societies do not make people like us so proud to be Americans and so very proud of our fellow citizens.

'Economic Mess'

Now, let us talk about getting spending and inflation under control and cutting your tax rates.

Mr. Speaker and Senator Baker, I want to thank you for your cooperation in helping to arrange this joint session of the Congress. I won't be speaking to you very long tonight, but I asked for this meeting because the urgency of our joint mission has not changed.

Thanks to some very fine people, my health is much improved. I would like to be able to say that with regard to the health of the economy. It has been half a year since the election that charged all of us in this Government with the task of restoring our economy. Where have we come in these 6 months? Inflation as measured by the Consumer Price Index has continued at a double-digit rate. Mortgage interest rates have averaged almost 15 percent for these 6 months, preventing families across America from buying homes. There are still almost 8 million unemployed. The average worker's hourly earnings after adjusting for inflation are lower today than they were 6 months ago, and there have been over 6,000 business failures.

Six months is long enough. The American people now want us to act, and not in half measures. They demand, and they have earned, a full and comprehensive effort to clean up our economic mess.

Because of the extent of our economy's sickness, we know that the cure will not come quickly, and that even with our package, progress will come in inches and feet, not in miles. But to fail to act will delay even longer, and more painfully, the cure which must come.

And that cure begins with the Federal budget. And the budgetary actions taken by the Congress over the next few days will determine how we respond to the message of last November 4.

That message was very simple. Our Government is too big and it spends too much.

Budget Timetable

For the past few months you and I have enjoyed a relationship based on extraordinary cooperation. Because of this cooperation we have come a long distance in less than 3 months. I want to thank the leadership of the Congress for helping in setting a fair timetable for consideration of our recommendations, and committee chairmen on both sides of the aisle have called prompt and thorough hearings.

We have also communicated in a spirit of candor, openness, and mutual respect.

Tonight, as our decision day nears, and as the House of Representatives weighs its alternatives, I wish to address you in that same spirit.

The Senate Budget Committee, under the leadership of Pete Domenici, has just today voted out a budget resolution supported by Democrats and Republicans alike that is in all major respects consistent with the program that we have proposed.

Now we look forward to favorable action on the Senate floor. But an equally crucial test involves the House of Representatives.

Approves House Bipartisan Plan

The House will soon be choosing between two different versions or measures to deal with the economy. One is the measure offered by the House Budget Committee. The other is a bipartisan measure, a substitute introduced by Congressmen Phil Gramm of Texas and Del Latta of Ohio.

On behalf of the Administration, let me say that we embrace and fully support that bipartisan substitute.

It will achieve all the essential aims of controlling Government spending, reducing the tax burden, building a national defense second to none, and stimulating economic growth and creating millions of new jobs.

At the same time, however, I must state our opposition to the measure offered by the House Budget Committee.

It may appear that we have two alternatives. In reality, however, there are no more alternatives left. The committee measure quite simply falls far too short of the essential actions that we must take. For example, in the next 3 years:

● The Committee measure projects spending $141 billion more than does the bipartisan substitute.

● It regrettably cuts over $14 billion in essential defense funding — funding required to restore America's national security.

● It adheres to the failed policy of trying to balance the budget on the taxpayers' back. It would increase tax payments by over a third — adding up to a staggering quarter of a trillion dollars. Federal taxes would increase 12 percent each year. Taxpayers would be paying a larger share of their income to Government in 1984 than they do at present.

● In short, that measure reflects an echo of the past rather than a benchmark for the future. High taxes and excess spending growth created our present economic mess; more of the same will not cure the hardship, anxiety, and discouragement it has imposed on the American people.

Let us cut through the fog for a moment. The answer to a Government that is too big is to stop feeding its growth. Government spending has been growing faster than the economy itself. The massive national debt which we accumulated is the

result of the Government's high spending diet. Well, it is time to change the diet and to change it in the right way.

Tax Proposal

I know the tax portion of our package is of concern to some of you. Let me make a few points that I feel have been overlooked. First of all, it should be looked at as an integral part of the entire package, not something separate and apart from the budget reductions, the regulatory relief, and the monetary restraints.

Probably the most common misconception is that we are proposing to reduce Government revenues to less than what the Government has been receiving. This is not true. Actually, the discussion has to do with how much of a tax increase should be imposed on the taxpayer in 1982.

Now, I know that over the recess in some informal polling some of your constituents have been asked which they would rather have, a balanced budget or a tax cut. And with the common sense that characterizes the people of this country, the answer of course has been a balanced budget. But may I suggest with no inference that there was wrong intent on the part of those who asked the question, the question was inappropriate to the situation. Our choice is not between a balanced budget and a tax cut. Properly asked, the question is, do you want a great big raise in your taxes this coming year, or at the worst a very little increase with the prospect of tax reduction and a balanced budget down the road a ways.

With the common sense that the people have already shown, I am sure we all know what the answer to that question would be. A gigantic tax increase has been built into the system. We propose nothing more than a reduction of that increase. The people have a right to know that even with our plan they will be paying more in taxes, but not as much more as they will without it.

The option I believe offered by the House Budget Committee will leave spending too high and tax rates too high. At the same time, I think it cuts the defense budget too much. And by attempting to reduce the deficit through higher taxes, it will not create the kind of strong economic growth and the new jobs that we must have.

Let us not overlook the fact that the small, independent business man or woman creates more than 80 percent of all the new jobs and employs more than half of our total work force. Our across-the-board cut in tax rates for a 3-year period will give them much of the incentive and promise of stability they need to go forward with expansion plans calling for additional employees.

Asks for Cooperation

Tonight I renew my call for us to work as a team, to join in cooperation so that we find answers which will begin to solve all our economic problems and not just some of them. The economic recovery package

that I have outlined to you over the past few weeks is, I deeply believe, the only answer that we have left. Reducing the growth of spending, cutting marginal tax rates, providing relief from over-regulation, and following a noninflationary and predictable monetary policy are interwoven measures which will ensure that we have addressed each of the severe dislocations which threaten our economic future. These policies will make our economy stronger and the stronger economy will balance the budget which we are committed to do by 1984.

When I took the oath of office, I pledged loyalty to only one special interest group — "We the people." Those people — neighbors and friends, shopkeepers and laborers, farmers and craftsmen — do not have infinite patience. As a matter of fact, some 80 years ago Teddy Roosevelt wrote these instructive words in his first message to the Congress: "The American people are slow to wrath, but when their wrath is once kindled, it burns like a consuming flame."

Calls for New Solutions

Well, perhaps that kind of wrath will be deserved if our answer to these serious problems is to repeat the mistakes of the past. The old and comfortable way is to shave a little here and add a little there. Well, that is not acceptable any more. I think this great and historic Congress knows that way is no longer acceptable. [applause] Thank you very much. Thank you.

I think you have shown that you know the one sure way to continue the inflationary spiral is to fall back into the predictable patterns of old economic practices.

Isn't it time that we tried something new?

When you allowed me to speak to you here in these Chambers a little earlier, I told you that I wanted this program for economic recovery to be ours, yours and mine. I think the bipartisan substitute bill has achieved that purpose. It moves us toward an economic vitality.

Praises Shuttle Astronauts

Just 2 weeks ago you and I joined millions of our fellow Americans in marveling at the magical historical moment that John

Young and Bob Crippen created in their space shuttle Columbia.

The last manned effort was almost 6 years ago, and I remembered on this more recent day over the years how we had all come to expect technological precision of our men and machines. And each amazing achievement became commonplace, until the next new challenge was raised.

With the Space Shuttle, we tested our ingenuity once again, moving beyond the accomplishments of the past into the promise and uncertainty of the future. Thus we not only planned to send up a 122-foot aircraft, 170 miles into space, but we also intended to make it maneuverable and return it to Earth landing 98 tons of exotic metals delicately on a remote dry lake bed.

The Space Shuttle did more than prove our technological abilities. It raised our expectations once more. It started us dreaming again. The poet Carl Sandburg wrote, "The Republic is a dream. Nothing happens unless first a dream."

And that is what makes us as Americans different. We have always reached for a new spirit and aimed at a higher goal. We have been courageous and determined, unafraid and bold. Who among us wants to be first to say we no longer have those qualities, that we must limp along doing the same things that have brought us our present misery?

I believe that the people you and I represent are ready to chart a new course. They look to us to meet the great challenge, to reach beyond the commonplace and not fall short for lack of creativity or courage.

Someone, you know, has said that he who would have nothing to do with thorns must never attempt to gather flowers.

But we have much greatness before us. We can restore our economic strength and build opportunities like none we have ever had before.

As Carl Sandburg said, all we need to begin with is a dream that we can do better than before.

All we need to have is faith, and that dream will come true.

All we need to do is act, and the time for action is now.

Thank you and good night.   ∎

Soviet Grain Embargo Lifted

Following is the text of President Reagan's April 24 statement lifting the prohibition of grain sales to the Soviet Union:

I am today lifting the U.S. limitation on additional agricultural sales to the Soviet Union as I promised to do during last year's Presidential campaign. My Administration has made a full and complete study of this sales limitation, and I reached my decision after weighing all options carefully and conferring fully with my advisers, including members of the Cabinet and the National Security Council. We have also

been consulting with our allies on this matter.

As a Presidential candidate, I indicated my opposition to the curb on sales because American farmers had been unfairly singled out to bear the burden of this ineffective national policy. I also pledged that when elected President I would "fully assess our national security, foreign policy and agricultural needs to determine how best to terminate" the decision made by my predecessor.

This assessment began as soon as I entered office and has continued until now. In the first few weeks of my Presidency, I

decided that an immediate lifting of the sales limitation could be misinterpreted by the Soviet Union. I therefore felt that my decision should be made only when it was clear that the Soviets and other nations would not mistakenly think it indicated a weakening of our position.

I have determined that our position now cannot be mistaken: The United States, along with the vast majority of nations, has condemned and remains opposed to the Soviet occupation of Afghanistan and other aggressive acts around the world. We will react strongly to acts of aggression wherever they take place. There will never be a weakening of this resolve. ∎

Veterans' Education Assistance

Following is the text of President Reagan's June 1 message to Congress requesting extension of PL 94-502 providing education aid for veterans:

TO THE CONGRESS OF
THE UNITED STATES:

In 1976, the Congress established, in P.L. 94-502, a new contributory education program under which individuals entering military service on and after January 1, 1977, would, on a voluntary basis, have funds withheld from their military pay for their future education. These contributions would, under the law, be matched by the Veterans Administration on a $2 for $1 basis.

The law provides for this Veterans' Education Assistance Program (VEAP) to be conducted on a test basis and requires termination of new enrollments by service personnel after December 31, 1981, unless I recommend continuation of the program before June 1, 1981.

Last year, the Congress enacted the Department of Defense Authorization Act, 1981, and the Veterans' Rehabilitation and Education Amendments of 1980. These two laws included revisions to the VEAP program and established a new, second test program under which service personnel, who enlist or reenlist after September 30, 1980, and before October 1, 1981, may be eligible for education benefits after serving for a specified period of time.

The conference report on the Department of Defense Authorization Act, 1981, recommended that the VEAP program be extended to June 30, 1982, in order to provide sufficient time for the Department of Defense to test and evaluate the new pilot program. That program is currently undergoing testing and evaluation.

As of the end of February 1981, a total of 3,872 individuals had commenced education training under the VEAP program. The relatively low training rate reflects, in part, the fact that under the law an individual may not begin to use his or her educational entitlement until the completion of the first obligated period of active duty or 6 years of active duty, whichever period is less. Since the law did not become effective until January 1, 1977, the number of persons eligible to pursue training has thus far been minimal.

Over the next several months the Administration will be continuing its evaluation and review of both the VEAP and Department of Defense test programs, with a view towards developing legislative recommendations regarding education programs for service members and veterans. In view of this effort, I am recommending that the VEAP program be continued beyond its current termination date of December 31, 1981. This will permit the Administration to complete its review and will provide time for submission of legislative recommendations that I anticipate will be submitted in early 1982.

Recently, the Veterans Administration submitted legislation to the Congress that would authorize a 1-year extension of the Veterans' Educational Assistance Program and make certain other adjustments in Public Law 94-502. I urge the Congress to enact this legislation.

Ronald Reagan

The White House
May 30, 1981 ∎

Reagan Immigration/Refugee Policy

President Reagan released the following statement July 30 setting out his proposal to reorganize federal immigration and refugee policy and procedures.

Our Nation is a nation of immigrants. More than any other country, our strength comes from our own immigrant heritage and our capacity to welcome those from other lands. No free and prosperous nation can by itself accommodate all those who seek a better life or flee persecution. We must share this responsibility with other countries.

The bipartisan select commission which reported this spring concluded that the Cuban influx to Florida made the United States sharply aware of the need for more effective immigration policies and the need for legislation to support those policies.

For these reasons, I asked the Attorney General last March to chair a Task Force on Immigration and Refugee Policy. We discussed the matter when President

López Portillo visited me last month, and we have carefully considered the views of our Mexican friends. In addition, the Attorney General consulted with those concerned in Congress and in affected States and localities and with interested members of the public.

The Attorney General is undertaking administrative actions and submitting to Congress, on behalf of the administraton, a legislative package, based on eight principles. These principles are designed to preserve our tradition of accepting foreigners to our shores, but to accept them in a controlled and orderly fashion:

● We shall continue America's tradition as a land that welcomes peoples from other countries. We shall also, with other countries, continue to share in the responsibility of welcoming and resettling those who flee oppression.

● At the same time, we must ensure adequate legal authority to establish control over immigration: to enable us, when sudden influxes of foreigners occur, to decide to whom we grant the status of refugee or asylee; to improve our border control; to expedite (consistent with fair procedures and our Constitution) return of those coming here illegally; to strengthen enforcement of our fair labor standards and laws; and to penalize those who would knowingly encourage violation of our laws. The steps we take to further these objectives, however, must also be consistent with our values of individual privacy and freedom.

● We have a special relationship with our closest neighbors, Canada and Mexico. Our immigration policy should reflect this relationship.

● We must also recognize that both the United States and Mexico have historically benefited from Mexicans obtaining employment in the United States. A number of our States have special labor needs, and we should take these into account.

● Illegal immigrants in considerable numbers have become productive members of our society and are a basic part of our work force. Those who have established equities in the United States should be recognized and accorded legal status. At the same time, in so doing, we must not encourage illegal immigration.

● We shall strive to distribute fairly, among the various localities of this country, the impacts of our national immigration and refugee policy, and we shall improve the capability of those agencies of the Federal Government which deal with these matters.

● We shall seek new ways to integrate refugees into our society without nurturing their dependence on welfare.

● Finally, we recognize that immigration and refugee problems require international solutions. We will seek greater international cooperation . . . . ∎

Reagan Pay Raise Proposal

Following is the text of President Reagan's Aug. 31 message to Congress proposing a 4.8 percent pay raise for federal white-collar employees, effective in October 1981.

TO THE CONGRESS
OF THE UNITED STATES:

Under the Pay Comparability Act of 1970, an adjustment in Federal white collar pay will be required in October, 1981.

That Act requires that calculations be made annually of the adjustments that would be required in Federal statutory pay systems to achieve comparability with private sector pay for the same levels of work. My pay advisers have made those calculations and indicated that an average 15.1 percent increase would be required to achieve comparability as the concept and process were defined in the Pay Comparability Act of 1970.

While I fully support the comparability principle as the best basis for determining Federal pay, I believe that significant changes are required in the way that principle is currently defined and implemented. Therefore, last March we transmitted to the Congress proposed legislation to revise and strengthen the comparability process. At that time, we estimated that the revised process would result in an average increase in Federal pay of 4.8 percent in October, 1981.

The reform proposal has not yet been acted upon in Congress, but in accordance with our economic recovery program, the Congress included in the Omnibus Budget Reconciliation Act of 1981 (P.L. 97-35) a provision which limits this October's Federal white collar pay adjustment to the same 4.8 percent. Accordingly, I am submitting to the Congress an alternative plan which would implement that limitation on Federal white collar increases.

Current law provides that the annual increase for the military be the same as the average Federal white collar increase. This year, however, the Congress is expected to provide for larger military pay increase as a part of the Defense Authorization Act for FY 82. The larger increases proposed under that legislation will supersede the increases that military personnel would otherwise receive under the alternative plan.

RONALD REAGAN

The White House
August 31, 1981   ■

President Reagan Announces Nuclear Arms Decisions

Following is the text of President Reagan's Oct. 2 announcement of his strategic arms policy.

As President, it's my solemn duty to insure America's national security while vigorously pursuing every path to peace. Toward this end I've repeatedly pledged to halt the decline in America's military strength and restore that margin of safety needed for the protection of the American people and the maintenance of peace.

During the last several years a weakening in our security posture has been particularly noticeable in our strategic nuclear forces — the very foundation of our strategy for deterring foreign attacks.

A window of vulnerability is opening, one that would jeopardize not just our hopes for serious productive arms negotiations, but our hopes for peace and freedom. Shortly after taking office, I directed the Secretary of Defense to review our strategy for deterrence and to evaluate the adequacy of the forces now available for carrying out that strategy. He and his colleagues in consultation with many leaders outside the executive branch have done that job well. And after one of the most complex, thorough, and carefully conducted processes in memory, I am announcing today a plan to revitalize our strategic forces and maintain America's ability to keep the peace well into the next century.

Our plan is a comprehensive one. It will strengthen and modernize the strategic triad of land-based missiles, sea-based missiles and bombers. It will end longstanding delays in some of these programs and introduce new elements into others and just as important, it will improve communications and control systems that are vital to these strategic forces.

This program will achieve three objectives. It will act as a deterrent against any Soviet actions directed against the American people or our allies. It will provide us with the capability to respond at reasonable cost and within adequate time to any further growth in Soviet forces. It will signal our resolve to maintain the strategic balance and this is the keystone to any genuine arms reduction agreement with the Soviets.

Let me point out here that this is a strategic program that America can afford. It fits within the revised fiscal guidelines for the Department of Defense that I announced last week. And during the next five years, the entire cost of maintaining and rebuilding our strategic forces will take less than 15 percent of our defense expenditures. This is considerably below the 20 percent of our defense budget spent on strategic arms during the 1960s when we constructed many of the forces that exist today. It is fair to say that this program will enable us to modernize our strategic forces, and at the same time meet our many other commitments as a nation.

Now, let me outline the five main features of our program. First, I have directed the Secretary of Defense to revitalize our bomber forces by constructing and deploying some 100 B-1 bombers as soon as possible, while continuing to deploy cruise missiles on existing bombers.

We will also develop an advanced bomber with stealth characteristics for the 1990s.

Second, I have ordered the strengthening and expansion of our sea-based forces. We will continue the construction of Trident submarines at a steady rate. We will develop a larger and more accurate sea-based ballistic missile. We will also deploy nuclear cruise missiles in some existing submarines.

Third, I've ordered completion of the MX missiles. We have decided, however, not to deploy the MX in the racetrack shelters proposed by the previous administration or in any other scheme for multiple protective shelters. We will not deploy 20 missiles in 4600 holes nor will we deploy 100 missiles in 1000 holes.

We have concluded that these basing schemes would be just as vulnerable as the existing minuteman silos. The operative factor here is this: No matter how many shelters we might build, the Soviets can build more missiles, more quickly, and just as cheaply.

Instead, we will complete the MX missile which is much more powerful and accurate than our current minuteman missiles, and we will deploy a limited number of the MX missiles in existing silos as soon possible.

At the same time, we will pursue three promising long-term options for basing the MX missile and choose among them by 1984 so that we can proceed promptly with full deployment.

Fourth, I have directed the Secretary of Defense to strengthen and rebuild our communications and control system — a much neglected factor in our strategic deterrent. I consider this decision to improve our communications and control system as important as any of the other decisions announced today.

This system must be foolproof in case of any foreign attack. Finally, I have directed that we end our long neglect of strategic defenses. This will include cooperation with Canada on improving North American air surveillance in defense and as part of this effort I have also directed that we devote greater resources to improving our civil defenses.

This plan is balanced and carefully

considered — a plan that will meet our vital security needs and strengthen our hopes to peace. It's my hope that this program will prevent our adversaries from making the mistake others have made and deeply regretted in the past. The mistake of underestimating the resolve and the will of the American people to keep their freedom and protect their homeland and their allies.

Now, I can only remain here for a few minutes. And I will do so for just a few questions that might deal with the statement or with policy. But for all the technical matters, I am going to turn you over to Secretary Cap Weinberger.

Questions from Reporters

Q. On that, would we be ready to use these new systems as bargaining chips in arms talks with the Soviets?

P. Well, I think everything having to do with arms, Helen, would have to be on the table.

Q. Mr. President, when exactly is the "window of vulnerability"? We heard yesterday the suggestion that it exists now. Earlier this morning a defense official indicated that it was not until '84 or '87. Are we facing it right now?

P. Well, I think in some areas we are, yes. I think the imbalance of forces, for example, in the Western front — in the NATO line, we are vastly outdistanced there. I think the fact that right now they have a superiority at sea.

Q. Mr. President, if there is or will be a "window of vulnerability", why is the MX any less vulnerable if it's in silos the location of which the Soviets presumably already know unless we were going to launch on their attack?

P. I don't know but what maybe you haven't gotten into the area that I'm going to turn over to the Secretary of Defense. I could say this. The plan also includes the hardening of silos so that they are protected against nuclear attack. Now, we know that is not permanent. We know that they can then improve their accuracy, their power, and their ability, but it would take them some time to do that and they would have to devote a decided effort to doing that.

Q. So this is a way then of buying time, is it?

P. In a way of narrowing that "window of vulnerability."

Q. Mr. President, some people already are saying that your decisions are based to a large extent on politics, domestic politics so let me ask you about two points. One, that you never considered the racetrack system because it was proposed by Jimmy Carter and you didn't want to have anything to do with something that he had proposed. And, two, that you are not basing the MX in Utah and Nevada because of opposition from the Mormon church and your good friend Senator Paul Laxalt.

P. Sam, I can tell you now, no, the entire study of the basis for basing — I got tangled up there with two words that

sounded so much alike — the MX missile was a very thorough study of all those proposals that had been made and, actually, I could refer you to the Town's Commission, their study and their report that we would not have an invulnerable missile basing by doing that. That all they would have to do is increase the number of targeted warheads on that particular area and take out the whole area. And, while it would force them to build additional missiles, we would be just as vulnerable as we are in the present Minutemen.

Q. Laxalt didn't persuade you, sir?

P. No, no.

Q. Mr. President, your predecessor killed the B-1 manned bomber because he said it couldn't penetrate Soviet air defenses. The Soviets can make a lot of progress in radar between now and 1986. Can you guarantee that the B-1 could penetrate Soviet air defenses and is it the best plane as a cruise missile launch platform?

P. I think again — you are getting — I think that my few minutes are up and I am going to turn that question over to Cap. I know the answer to it, but I do believe that you are getting in to the kind of questions that he is properly —

Q. Could you tell us why you decided to build the B-1 as opposed to your predecessors' decision not to build it? Do you think it can penetrate Soviet air space?

P. We have to have it because between the aging B-52 and the bomber we are developing, a newer bomber, there is too long a time gap in there. It would leave us a lengthy, vulnerable period. And the B-1 is designed not just to fill that gap, but it will then have a cruise missile-carrying capacity later in which it will still be worth the cost of building and worth having.

Now, I am going to turn it over to Cap here for the rest of the questions. ∎

Nuclear Policy Text

Following is the official White House text of President Reagan's Oct. 8 policy statement on nuclear power:

A more abundant, affordable, and secure energy future for all Americans is a critical element of this Administration's economic recovery program. While homeowners and business firms have shown remarkable ingenuity and resourcefulness in meeting their energy needs at lower cost through conservation, it is evident that sustained economic growth over the decades ahead will require additional energy supplies. This is particularly true of electricity, which will supply an increasing share of our energy.

If we are to meet this need for new energy supplies, we must move rapidly to eliminate unnecessary government barriers to efficient utilization of our abundant, economical resources of coal and uranium. It is equally vital that the utilities — inves-

tor-owned, public, and co-ops — be able to develop new generating capacity that will permit them to supply their customers at the lowest cost, be it coal, nuclear, hydro, or new technologies such as fuel cells.

One of the best potential sources of new electrical energy supplies in the coming decades is nuclear power. The U.S. has developed a strong technological base in the production of electricity from nuclear energy. Unfortunately, the Federal Government has created a regulatory environment that is forcing many utilities to rule out nuclear power as a source of new generating capacity, even when their consumers may face unnecessarily high electric rates as a result. Nuclear power has become entangled in a morass of regulations that do not enhance safety but that do cause extensive licensing delays and economic uncertainty. Government has also failed in meeting its responsibility to work with industry to develop an acceptable system for commercial waste disposal, which has further hampered nuclear power development.

To correct present government deficiencies and to enable nuclear power to make its essential contribution to our future energy needs, I am announcing today a series of policy initiatives:

(1) I am directing the Secretary of Energy to give immediate priority attention to recommending improvements in the nuclear regulatory and licensing process. I anticipate that the Chairman of the Nuclear Regulatory Commission will take steps to facilitate the licensing of plants under construction and those awaiting licenses. Consistent with public health and safety, we must remove unnecessary obstacles to deployment of the current generation of nuclear power reactors. The time involved to proceed from the planning stage to an operating license for new nuclear power plants has more than doubled since the mid-1970s and is presently some 10-14 years. This process must be streamlined, with the objective of shortening the time involved to 6-8 years, as is typical in some other countries.

(2) I am directing that government agencies proceed with the demonstration of breeder reactor technology, including completion of the Clinch River Breeder Reactor. This is essential to ensure our preparedness for longer-term nuclear power needs.

(3) I am lifting the indefinite ban which previous Administrations placed on commercial reprocessing activities in the United States. In addition, we will pursue consistent, long-term policies concerning reprocessing of spent fuel from nuclear power reactors and eliminate regulatory impediments to commercial interest in this technology, while ensuring adequate safeguards.

It is important that the private sector take the lead in developing commercial reprocessing services. Thus I am also requesting the Director of the Office of Science and Technology Policy, working with the Secretary of Energy, to undertake a

study of the feasibility of obtaining economical plutonium supplies for the Department of Energy by means of a competitive procurement. By encouraging private firms to supply fuel for the breeder program at a cost that does not exceed that of government-produced plutonium, we may be able to provide a stable market for private sector reprocessing, and simultaneously reduce the funding needs of the U.S. breeder demonstration program.

(4) I am instructing the Secretary of Energy, working closely with industry and state governments, to proceed swiftly toward deployment of means of storing and disposing of commercial high-level radioactive waste. We must take steps now to accomplish this objective and demonstrate to the public that problems associated with

management of nuclear waste can be resolved.

(5) I recognize that some of the problems besetting the nuclear option are of a deep-seated nature and may not be quickly resolved. Therefore, I am directing the Secretary of Energy and the Director of the Office of Science and Technology Policy to meet with representatives from the universities, private industry and the utilities, and requesting them to report to me on the obstacles which stand in the way of increased use of nuclear energy and the steps needed to overcome them in order to assure the continued availability of nuclear power to meet America's future energy needs not later than September 30, 1982.

Eliminating the regulatory problems

that have burdened nuclear power will be of little use if the utility sector cannot raise the capital necessary to fund construction of new generating facilities. We have already taken significant steps to improve the climate for capital formation with the passage of my program for economic recovery. The tax bill contains substantial incentives designed to attract new capital into industry.

Safe, commercial nuclear power can help meet America's future energy needs. The policies and actions that I am announcing today will permit a revitalization of the U.S. industry's efforts to develop nuclear power. In this way, native American genius — not arbitrary federal policy — will be free to provide for our energy future. ∎

Reagan Assures Senate About AWACS Sale

Following is the text of President Reagan's Oct. 28, 1981, letter to Senate Majority Leader Howard H. Baker Jr., R-Tenn., concerning the sale to Saudi Arabia of Airborne Warning and Control System (AWACS) airplanes and other air defense equipment.

Dear Senator Baker:

On October 1, 1981, I formally notified the Congress of our intention to sell AWACS aircraft and F-15 enhancement items to Saudi Arabia. This sale will enhance our vital national security interests by contributing directly to the stability and security of the critical area from the Persian Gulf through the Middle East to North Africa. It will improve significantly the capability of Saudi Arabia and the United States to defend the oilfields and facilities on which the security of the Free World depends, and it will pose no realistic threat to Israel.

When this proposed sale was first announced last spring, the Congress expressed concerns about certain aspects of the sale. After analyzing these concerns in detail, we entered into a series of discussions with the Government of Saudi Arabia over the summer.

The Government of Saudi Arabia has agreed, and I am convinced welcomes the fact, that the United States will have an important, long-term role and will maintain direct involvement in the development of the Saudi air defense system, including the AWACS. We also have reached agreement with the Saudi Government on a number of specific arrangements that go well beyond their firm agreement to abide fully by all the standard terms of the normal Letter of Offer and Acceptance as required by the Arms Export Control Act.

Transfer of the AWACS will take place only on terms and conditions consistent with the Act and only after the Congress has received in writing a Presidential certi-

fication, containing agreements with Saudi Arabia, that the following conditions have been met:

1. Security of Technology

A. That a detailed plan for the security of equipment, technology, information, and supporting documentation has been agreed to by the United States and Saudi Arabia and is in place; and

B. The security provisions are no less stringent than measures employed by the U.S. for protection and control of its equipment of like kind outside the continental U.S.; and

C. The U.S. has the right of continual on-site inspection and surveillance by U.S. personnel of security arrangements for all operations during the useful life of the AWACS. It is further provided that security arrangements will be supplemented by additional U.S. personnel if it is deemed necessary by the two parties;

D. Saudi Arabia will not permit citizens of third nations either to perform maintenance on the AWACS or to modify any such equipment without prior, explicit mutual consent of the two governments; and

E. Computer software, as designated by the U.S. Government, will remain the property of the USG.

2. Access to Information

That Saudi Arabia has agreed to share with the United States continuously and completely the information that it acquires from use of the AWACS.

3. Control Over Third-Country Participation

A. That Saudi Arabia has agreed not to share access to AWACS equipment, technology, documentation, or any information developed from such equipment or technology with any nation other than the

U.S. without the prior, explicit mutual consent of both governments; and

B. There are in place adequate and effective procedures requiring the screening and security clearance of citizens of Saudi Arabia and that only cleared Saudi citizens and cleared U.S. nationals will have access to AWACS equipment, technology, or documentation, or information derived therefrom, without the prior, explicit mutual consent of the two governments.

4. AWACS Flight Operations

That the Saudi AWACS will be operated solely within the boundaries of Saudi Arabia, except with the prior, explicit mutual consent of the two governments, and solely for defensive purposes as defined by the United States, in order to maintain security and regional stability.

5. Command Structure

That agreements as they concern organizational command and control structure for the operation of AWACS are of such a nature to guarantee that the commitments above will be honored.

6. Regional Peace and Security

That the sale contributes directly to the stability and security of the area, enhances the atmosphere and prospects for progress toward peace, and that initiatives toward the peaceful resolution of disputes in the region have either been successfully completed or that significant progress toward that goal has been accomplished with the substantial assistance of Saudi Arabia.

The agreements we have reached with Saudi Arabia on security of technology, access to information, control over third-country participation, and AWACS flight operations will be incorporated into the U.S./Saudi General Security of Military Information Agreement, the Letters of Offer and Acceptance (the government-to-gov-

ernment sales contracts), and related documents. These documents will stipulate that the sale will be cancelled and that no equipment or services will be delivered in the event any of the agreements is breached. I will not authorize U.S. approval of any of these contracts and agreements until I am satisfied that they incorporate fully the provisions that satisfy the concerns that you and I share. I do not foresee any need for changes in these arrangements, but should circumstances arise that might require such changes, they would be made only with Congressional participation.

I believe it is important to look beyond these agreements to their practical consequences, and to the implications of U.S. security assistance and training requested by Saudi Arabia. For example, the agreement we have reached with the Saudi Government to protect the security of equipment also affects the nature, extent, and duration of the U.S. role in the AWACS program. Since skilled Saudi personnel available for this program will remain in short supply, the U.S./Saudi agreement that third-country nationals will not be permitted to operate or maintain the Saudi AWACS will, in practice, extend U.S. involvement in Saudi AWACS operations and activities well into the 1990s. U.S. military and contractor personnel will be required to provide extensive operational training for Saudi AWACS aircrews; it will be 1990 at the earliest before the eight Saudi crews needed to operate all five AWACS aircraft will be trained, and replacement and refresher training of individual Saudi crew members will require USAF Technical Assistance Field Teams during the 1990s. Critical AWACS maintenance, logistics, and support functions, particularly radar and computer software support, will, of necessity, be performed by U.S. personnel in Saudi Arabia and in the United States, for the life of the AWACS.

The Saudi agreement not to share AWACS-gathered information with third countries also has significant practical consequences. This agreement, combined with the standard requirement that U.S.-supplied equipment be used solely for defensive purposes, as well as the agreed-to Saudi AWACS configuration, precludes any possibility that Saudi AWACS could contribute to coordinated operations with other countries' armed forces against any nation in the region without our consent and cooperation.

Concerning the agreement to operate AWACS only inside the Kingdom, it should also be noted that the Saudi Air Force will be trained to operate the AWACS in accordance with standard USAF AWACS doctrine and procedures, which call for AWACS to remain at all times a "safe distance" behind sensitive political borders — normally 100 to 150 nautical miles — to ensure AWACS security and survivability. Given the physical location of the oilfields AWACS is to defend, the vulnerability of AWACS should it

operate near sensitive borders, and the history of Saudi observance of U.S. Air Force tactical doctrine, we are confident that the Saudis will adopt these practices.

In a broader sense, by enhancing the perception of the United States as a reliable security partner, we improve the prospects for closer cooperation between ourselves and the Saudi Government in working toward our common goal of a just and lasting peace in the region. Since assuming the responsibilities of the Presidency, I have been impressed by the increasingly constructive policy of Saudi Arabia in advancing the prospects for peace and stability in the Middle East. The Saudi Government's critical contribution to securing a ceasefire in Lebanon is a striking example. I am persuaded that this growing Saudi influence is vital to the eventual settlement of the differences that continue to divide Israel and most of the Arab world.

I am confident that the Saudi AWACS will pose no realistic threat to Israel. I remain fully committed to protecting Israel's security and to preserving Israel's ability to defend against any combination of potentially hostile forces in the region. We will continue to make available to Israel the military equipment it requires to defend its land and people, with due consideration to the presence of AWACS in Saudi Arabia. We have also embarked on a program of closer security cooperation with Israel. This proposed sale to Saudi Arabia neither casts doubt on our commitment, nor compromises Israeli security.

It is my view that the agreements we have reached with the Government of Saudi Arabia take account of the concerns raised by the Congress. I am persuaded, as I believe the Congress will be, that the proposed Saudi air defense enhancement package makes an invaluable contribution to the national security interests of the United States, by improving both our strategic posture and the prospects for peace in the Middle East. I look forward to continuing to work with you toward these vital goals.

Sincerely,

Ronald Reagan ∎

Reagan Reaction To AWACS Vote

Following is the official White House text of President Reagan's remarks following the Senate vote on the AWACS sale to Saudi Arabia Oct. 28:

I want to express my gratitude to the members of the United States Senate for their approval of the sale of the AWACS defense system to Saudi Arabia. Today I think we've seen the Upper Chamber at its

best. The United States Senate has acted with statesmanship, with foresight, and with courage.

I can't fully express my gratitude to Senator Baker and the other Senate leaders, Democrats as well as Republicans, who played such a crucial role in this decision.

Today's action by the Senate will not only strengthen Saudi-American relations but will also protect our economic lifeline to the Middle East, win favor among moderate Arab nations, and most important, continue the difficult but steady progress toward peace and stability in the Middle East.

We've acted in concert to demonstrate that the United States is indeed a reliable security partner. Our friends should realize that steadfastness to purpose is a hallmark of American foreign policy, while those who would create instability in this region should note that the forces of moderation have our unequivocal support in deterring aggression.

This vote alone doesn't mean that our security problems in that part of the world have been completely solved. This package is but a part of our overall regional security strategy. Our strategy seeks to enhance the capacity of friendly states to defend themselves and to improve our own ability to project our own forces into the region should deterrence fail. We'll continue to pursue efforts in both areas.

Our support for the security of Israel is, of course, undiminished by today's vote. The United States will maintain its unshakeable commitment to the security and welfare of the State of Israel, recognizing that a strong Israel is essential to our basic goals in that area.

Much work still remains ahead. I trust that all of us who disagreed openly and vigorously in recent days can now put aside our honest differences and work together for common goals: Friendship, security, and peace at last in the cradle of our civilization. Because of actions like today's by the Senate, the cause of peace is again on the march in the Middle East. For this, all of us can be grateful.

Questions from Press

Following are some of the questions asked by reporters after the president's statement.

Q: Do you think this will be an inducement to get the Saudis into the Middle East peace process now?

P: Yes, I do. I think that as a matter of fact, the Saudis have shown, by their own introduction of a peace proposal, that they are willing to discuss peace in the Middle East.... They submitted a plan. We could not agree with all the points, nor could the Israelis, but it was the first time that they had recognized Israel as a nation and it is a beginning point for negotiations.

Q: What do you think this vote means for your ability to conduct the arms...

P: I think that it's going to be — it's going to have a very good effect. We had heard from many leaders who had ex-

pressed their concern about what this could mean in the whole world scene, if it had not turned out the way it did.

Q: What aspect of what you told the senators did you think was the convincing aspect and what final thing do you think turned the tide in the last few days?

P: Contrary to some of things that have been said, there have been no deals made. None were offered. I talked strictly on the merits of the proposal and basically I tried to point out in every instance, the progress that has been made so far in the Middle East towards stability and peace

and the part that was played in that by Saudi Arabia, Prince Fahd, beginning with the cease fire that we were able to secure in Lebanon, in which they played a major role. And I simply played on that that this, I felt, was essential for the security of Israel, for the entire Middle East and for ourselves on the world scene.

Q: Do you foresee any circumstance under which by 1985 this sale might be cancelled if the Saudis aren't cooperating with the lease?

P: I would think that the only thing that could happen to make us not fulfill that would be if by some chance the radical

elements that we know are there and that have made themselves tragically evident in the last few weeks, that if they should gain control in the Middle East and gain control of all of those governments we are talking about, I think the very fact of what we have done and the knowledge now that the United States and our allies are not walking away from the Middle East is going to contribute to the stability and make it very unlikely that the other can happen.

Photographer: A big smile, Mr. President.

P: I'm trying to smile with dignity. I don't want to look jubilant. (Laughter.) ■

Text of Reagan Address on Foreign Policy

Following is the White House text of President Reagan's address as delivered before the National Press Club Nov. 18, 1981.

THE PRESIDENT: Officers, ladies and gentlemen of the National Press Club and, as of a very short time ago, fellow members, — (applause) — back in April while in the hospital I had, as you can readily understand, a lot of time for reflection. And one day I decided to send a personal handwritten letter to Soviet President Leonid Brezhnev reminding him that we had met about ten years ago in San Clemente, California, as he and President Nixon were concluding a series of meetings that had brought hope to all the world. Never had peace and goodwill seemed closer at hand.

I'd like to read you a few paragraphs from that letter. "Mr. President, when we met, I asked if you were aware that the hopes and aspirations of millions of people throughout the world were dependent on the decisions that would be reached in those meetings. You took my hand in both of yours and assured me that you were aware of that and that you were dedicated with all your heart and soul and mind to fulfilling those hopes and dreams."

I went on in my letter to say, "The people of the world still share that hope. Indeed, the peoples of the world despite differences in racial and ethnic origin have very much in common. They want the dignity of having some control over their individual lives — their destiny. They want to work at the craft or trade of their own choosing and to be fairly rewarded. They want to raise their families in peace without harming anyone or suffering harm themselves. Government exists for their convenience, not the other way around.

"If they are incapable, as some would have us believe, of self-government, then where among them do we find any who are capable of governing others?

"Is it possible that we have permitted ideology, political and economic philosophies and governmental policies to keep us from considering the very real everyday problems of our peoples? Will the average Soviet family be better off or even aware that the Soviet Union has imposed a government of its own choice on the people of Afghanistan? Is life better for the people of Cuba because the Cuban military dictate who shall govern the people of Angola?"

"It is often implied that such things have been made necessary because of territorial ambitions of the United States, that we have imperialistic designs, and they thus constitute a threat to your own security and that of the newly emerging nations. Not only is there no evidence to support such a charge, there is solid evidence that the United States, when it could have dominated the world with no risk to itself, made no effort whatsoever to do so.

"When World War II ended, the United States had the only undamaged industrial power in the world. Our military might was at its peak, and we alone had the ultimate weapon, the nuclear weapon, with the unquestioned ability to deliver it anywhere in the world. If we had sought world domination — and who could have opposed us? — but the United States followed a different course, one unique in all the history of mankind. We used our power and wealth to rebuild the war-ravished economies of the world, including those of the nations who had been our enemies. May I say, there is absolutely no substance to charges that the United States is guilty of imperialism or attempts to impose its will on other countries, by use of force."

I continued my letter by saying — or concluded my letter — I should say, by saying, "Mr. President, should we not be concerned with eliminating the obstacles which prevent our people, those you and I represent, from achieving their most cherished goals?"

It is in the same spirit that I want to speak today to this audience and the people of the world about America's program for peace and the coming negotiations which begin November 30th in Geneva, Switzerland.

North Atlantic Treaty Alliance

Specifically, I want to present our program for preserving peace in Europe and our wider program for arms controls. Twice in my lifetime, I have seen the peoples of Europe plunged into the tragedy of war. Twice in my lifetime Europe has suffered destruction and military occupation in wars that statesmen proved powerless to prevent, soldiers unable to contain and ordinary citizens unable to escape. And twice in my lifetime, young Americans have bled their lives into the soil of those battlefields, not to enrich or enlarge our domain, but to restore the peace and independence of our friends and allies.

All of us who lived through those troubled times share a common resolve that they must never come again. And most of us share a common appreciation of the Atlantic Alliance that has made a peaceful, free and prosperous Western Europe in the post-war era possible. But today, a new generation is emerging on both sides of the Atlantic. Its members were not present at the creation of the North Atlantic Alliance. Many of them don't fully understand its roots in defending freedom and rebuilding a war-torn continent.

Some young people question why we need weapons, particularly nuclear weapons to deter war and to assure peaceful development. They fear that the accumulation of weapons itself may lead to conflagration.

Some even propose unilateral disarmament. I understand their concerns. Their questions deserve to be answered. But we have an obligation to answer their questions on the basis of judgment and reason and experience. Our policies have resulted in the longest European peace in this century. Wouldn't a rash departure from these policies, as some now suggest, endanger that peace?

From its founding, the Atlantic Alliance has preserved the peace through unity, deterrence and dialogue. First, we and our allies have stood united by the firm commitment that an attack upon any one of us would be considered an attack upon

us all. Second, we and our allies have deterred aggression by maintaining forces strong enough to insure that any aggressor would lose more from an attack than he could possibly gain. And third, we and our allies have engaged the Soviets in a dialogue about mutual restraint and arms limitations, hoping to reduce the risk of war and the burden of armaments and to lower the barriers that divide East from West.

These three elements of our policy have preserved the peace in Europe for more than a third of a century. They can preserve it for generations to come, so long as we pursue them with sufficient will and vigor.

Today, I wish to reaffirm America's commitment to the Atlantic Alliance and our resolve to sustain the peace. And from my conversations with allied leaders, I know that they also remain true to this tried and proven course.

Soviet Military Buildup

NATO's policy of peace is based on restraint and balance. No NATO weapons, conventional or nuclear, will ever be used in Europe except in response to attack. NATO's defense plans have been responsible and restrained. The allies remain strong, united and resolute. But the momentum of the continuing Soviet military buildup threatens both the conventional and the nuclear balance.

Consider the facts. Over the past decade, the United States reduced the size of its armed forces and decreased its military spending. The Soviets steadily increased the number of men under arms, they now number more than double those of the United States. Over the same period the Soviets expanded their real military spending by about one-third. The Soviet Union increased its inventory of tanks to some 50,000 compared to our 11,000. Historically a land power, they transformed their navy from a coastal defense force to an open ocean fleet, while the United States, a sea power with trans-oceanic alliances, cut its fleet in half.

During a period when NATO deployed no new intermediate range nuclear missiles and actually withdrew 1,000 nuclear warheads, the Soviet Union deployed more than 750 nuclear warheads on the new SS-20 missiles alone.

Our response to this relentless buildup of Soviet military power has been restrained but firm. We have made decisions to strengthen all three legs of the strategic triad: Sea, land and airbase. We have proposed a defense program in the United States for the next five years which will remedy the neglect of the past decade and restore the eroding balance on which our security depends.

Threat to Western Europe

I would like to discuss more specifically the growing threat to Western Europe which is posed by the continuing deployment of certain Soviet intermediate range nuclear missiles.

The Soviet Union has three different type such missile systems: The SS-20, the SS-4, and the SS-5, all with a range capable of reaching virtually all of Western Europe. There are other Soviet weapons systems which also represent a major threat.

The only answer to these systems is a comparable threat to Soviet threats, to Soviet targets. In other words, a deterrent preventing the use of these Soviet weapons by the counter-threat of a like response against their own territory. At present, however, there is no equivalent deterrent to these Soviet intermediate missiles. And the Soviets continue to add one new SS-20 a week.

To counter this the Allies agreed in 1979, as part of a two-track decision to deploy as a deterrent land-based cruise missiles and Pershing II missiles capable of reaching targets in the Soviet Union. These missiles are to be deployed in several countries of Western Europe. This relatively limited force in no way serves as a substitute for the much larger strategic umbrella spread over our NATO allies. Rather, it provides a vital link between conventional shorter-range nuclear forces in Europe and intercontinental forces in the United States.

Deployment of these systems will demonstrate to the Soviet Union that this link cannot be broken. Deterring war depends on the perceived ability of our forces to perform effectively. The more effective our forces are, the less likely that we'll have to use them. So we and our allies are proceeding to modernize NATO's nuclear forces of intermediate range to meet increased Soviet deployments of nuclear systems threatening Western Europe.

Arms Control Negotiations

Now, let me turn now to our hopes for arms control negotiations. There is a tendency to make this entire subject overly complex. I want to be clear and concise.

I told you of the letter I wrote to President Brezhnev last April. I've just sent another message to the Soviet leadership. It's a simple, straightforward yet historic message. The United States proposes the mutual reduction of conventional intermediate range nuclear and strategic forces. Specifically, I have proposed a four-point agenda to achieve this objective in my letter to President Brezhnev.

1 - Nuclear Forces

The first and most important point concerns the Geneva negotiations. As part of the 1979 two-track decision, NATO made a commitment to seek arms control negotiations with the Soviet Union on intermediate range nuclear forces. The United States has been preparing for these negotiations through close consultation with our NATO partners.

We're now ready to set forth our proposal. I have informed President Brezhnev that when our delegation travels to the negotiations on intermediate range land based nuclear missiles in Geneva on the 30th of this month, my representatives will present the following proposal: The United States is prepared to cancel its deployment of Pershing II and ground launch cruise missiles if the Soviets will dismantle their SS-20, SS-4 and SS-5 missiles. This would be an historic step. With Soviet agreement, we could together substantially reduce the dread threat of nuclear war which hangs over the people of Europe.

This, like the first footstep on the moon would be a giant step for mankind. And we intend to negotiate in good faith and go to Geneva willing to listen to and consider the proposals of our Soviet counterparts. But let me call to your attention the background against which our proposal is made.

During the past six years while the United States deployed no new intermediate range missiles and withdrew 1,000 nuclear warheads from Europe, the Soviet Union deployed 750 warheads on mobile accurate ballistic missiles. They now have 1100 warheads on the SS-20s, SS-4s and 5s. And the United States has no comparable missile. Indeed, the United States dismantled the last such missile in Europe over 15 years ago.

As we look to the future of the negotiations, it's also important to address certain Soviet claims which left unrefuted could become critical barriers to world progress and arms control.

The Soviets assert that a balance of intermediate range nuclear forces already exist. That assertion is wrong. By any objective measure, as this chart indicates, the Soviet Union has developed an increasing overwhelming advantage. They now enjoy a superiority on the order of six-to-one. The red is the Soviet build-up. The blue is our own — that is 1975 and that is 1981.

A Soviet spokesman has suggested that moving their SS-20s beyond the Ural Mountains will remove the threat to Europe. As this map demonstrates, the SS-20s, even if deployed behind the Urals, will have a range that puts almost all of Western Europe — the great cities — Rome, Athens, Paris, London, Brussels, Amsterdam, Berlin, and so many more, all of Scandinavia, all of the Middle East, all of Northern Africa, all within range of these missiles which incidentally are mobile and can be moved on shorter notice.

2 - Strategic Weapons

These little images marked the present location which would give them a range clear out into the Atlantic. The second proposal that I've made to President Brezhnev concerns strategic weapons. The United States proposes to open negotiations on strategic arms as soon as possible next year.

I've instructed Secretary Haig to discuss the timing of such meetings with Soviet representatives. Substance, however, is far more important than timing. As our

proposal for the Geneva talks this month illustrates we can make proposals for genuinely serious reductions, but only if we take the time to prepare carefully.

The United States has been preparing carefully for resumption of strategic arms negotiations because we don't want a repetition of past disappointments. We don't want an arms control process that sends hopes soaring only to end in dashed expectations.

Now, I have informed President Brezhnev that we will seek to negotiate substantial reductions in nuclear arms which would result in levels that are equal and verifiable. Our approach to verification will be to emphasize openness and creativity, rather than the secrecy and suspicion which have undermined confidence in arms control in the past.

While we can hope to benefit from work done over the past decade in strategic arms negotiations, let us agree to do more than simply begin where these previous efforts left off. We can and should attempt major qualitative and quantitative progress. Only such progress can fulfill the hopes of our own people and the rest of the world. And let us see how far we can go in achieving truly substantial reductions in our strategic arsenals.

To symbolize this fundamental change in direction, we will call these negotiations START — Strategic Arms Reduction Talks.

3 - Conventional Forces in Europe

The third proposal I've made to the Soviet Union is that we act to achieve equality at lower levels of conventional forces in Europe. The defense needs of the Soviet Union hardly call for maintaining more combat divisions in East Germany today than were in the whole allied invasion force that landed in Normandy on D-Day.

The Soviet Union could make no more convincing contribution to peace in Europe and in the world than by agreeing to reduce its conventional forces significantly and constrain the potential for sudden aggression.

4 - Conference on Disarmament

Finally, I have pointed out to President Brezhnev that to maintain peace we must reduce the risks of surprise attack and the chance of war arising out of uncertainty or miscalculation.

I am renewing our proposal for a conference to develop effective measures that would reduce these dangers. At the current Madrid meeting, the Conference on Security and Cooperation in Europe, we're laying the foundation for a Western proposed Conference on Disarmament in Europe. This conference would discuss new measures to enhance stability and security in Europe. Agreement in this conference is within reach. I urge the Soviet Union to join us and the many other nations who are ready to launch this important enterprise.

All of these proposals are based on the same fair-minded principles — substantial militarily significant reductions in forces, equal feelings for similar types of forces, and adequate provisions for verification.

My administration, our country, and I are committed to achieving arms reductions agreements based on these principles. Today, I have outlined the kinds of bold equitable proposals which the world expects of us. But we cannot reduce arms unilaterally. Success can only come if the Soviet Union will share our commitment — if it will demonstrate that its often repeated professions of concern for peace will be matched by positive action.

Preservation of peace in Europe and the pursuit of arms reductions talks are of fundamental importance. But we must also help to bring peace and security to regions now torn by conflict, external intervention and war.

American Concept of Peace

The American concept of peace goes well beyond the absence of war. We foresee a flowering of economic growth and individual liberty in a world at peace.

At the economic summit conference in Cancún, I met with the leaders of 21 nations and sketched out our approach to global economic growth. We want to eliminate the barriers to trade and investment which hinder these critical incentives to growth. And we're working to develop new programs to help the poorest nations achieve self-sustaining growth. And terms like "peace" and "security" we have to say have little meaning for the oppressed and the destitute. They also mean little to the individual whose state has stripped him of

human freedom and dignity.

Wherever there is oppression, we must strive for the peace and security of individuals as well as states. We must recognize that progress and the pursuit of liberty is a necessary complement to military security. Nowhere has this fundamental truth been more boldly and clearly stated than in the Helsinki Accords of 1975. These accords have not yet been translated into living reality.

Today I am announcing an agenda that can help to achieve peace, security, and freedom across the globe. In particular, I have made an important offer to forego entirely deployment of new American missiles in Europe if the Soviet Union is prepared to respond on an equal footing.

There is no reason why people in any part of the world should have to live in permanent fear of war or expect it. I believe the time has come for all nations to act in a responsible spirit that doesn't threaten other states. I believe the time is right to move forward on arms control and the resolution of critical regional disputes at the conference table. Nothing will have a higher priority for me and for the American people over the coming months and years.

Addressing the United Nations 20 years ago, another American President described the goal we still pursue today. He said, "If we all can persevere, if we can look beyond our shores and ambitions, then surely the age will dawn in which the strong are just and the weak secure and the peace preserved."

He didn't live to see that goal achieved. I invite all nations to join with America today in the quest for such a world. Thank you. (Applause.) ∎

Remarks on Strategic Nuclear Weapons

Following are excerpts from remarks made by President Reagan at a meeting with a group of editors Oct. 16:

Q. Do you believe that there could be a limited exchange of nuclear weapons between us and the Soviet Union, or that it would simply escalate inevitably?

P. I don't honestly know....I know that all over the world there's research going on to try and find the defensive weapon against strategic nuclear weapons. There never has been a weapon that someone hasn't come up with a defense. But except in this one, the only defense is, "Well, if you shoot yours, we'll shoot ours." And if you still had that kind of stalemate, I could see where you could have the exchange of tactical weapons against troops in the field without it bringing either one of the major powers to pushing the button.

The intermediate thing — and this is to call your attention to where SALT was so much at fault — is that we have our allies there who don't have an ocean between them [and the Soviet Union], so it

doesn't take intercontinental ballistic missiles, it just takes ballistic missiles of the SS-20 type. Well, the SS-20's [Soviet missiles] will have, with what they're adding, 750 warheads — one of them capable of pretty much leveling a city. And they can sit right there and that's got all of Europe, including England and all, targeted. And the only comparable thing that has come along is now our proposal ... to provide and put on European soil the Pershings and the cruise missiles, so that, again, you've got this same kind of a stalemate....

The SS-20's were not even considered a strategic weapon, because they didn't cross an ocean. In that SALT treaty there was no restriction on them, just as there was no restriction where they called our old B-52's strategic bombers, they didn't call their Backfire bombers, and we agreed to that in that treaty. But these are the weapons ... what I call strategic, these theatre weapons ... that we want to limit.

Q. Do you think there could be a battlefield exchange without having buttons pressed all the way up the line?

P. Well, ... if they realized that ... our retaliatory power would be so destructive that they couldn't afford it, that would hold them off. ...Everything that has been said and everything in their manuals indi- cates that, unlike us, the Soviet Union believes that a nuclear war is possible. And they believe it's winnable, which means that they believe that [if] you could achieve enough superiority, then your opponent wouldn't have retaliatory strike capacity.

Now, there is a danger to all of us in the world as long as they think that. And this, again, is one of the things that we just want to disabuse them of. ∎

Text of President Reagan's Address to Nation

Following is the text of President Reagan's Sept. 24 televised address to the nation reporting on the country's economic situation and requesting public support for further budget cuts and adjustments in Social Security payments.

THE PRESIDENT: Good evening. Shortly after taking office I came before you to map out a four-part plan for national economic recovery: tax cuts to stimulate more growth and more jobs, spending cuts to put an end to continuing deficits and high inflation, regulatory relief to lift the heavy burden of government rules and paperwork, and, finally, a steady, consistent, monetary policy.

We've made strong, encouraging progress on all four fronts. The flood of new governmental regulations, for example, has been cut by more than a third. I was especially pleased when a bipartisan coalition of Republicans and Democrats enacted the biggest tax cuts and the greatest reduction in federal spending in our nation's history. Both will begin to take effect a week from today. These two bills would never have passed without your help. Your voices were heard in Washington and were heeded by those you've chosen to represent you in government. Yet, in recent weeks we've begun to hear a chorus of other voices protesting that we haven't had full economic recovery. These are the same voices that were raised against our program when it was first presented to Congress. Now that the first part of it has been passed, they declare it hasn't worked. Well, it hasn't. It doesn't start until a week from today.

Inflation Easing Up

There have been some bright spots in our economic performance these past few months. Inflation has fallen and pressures are easing on both food and fuel prices. More than a million more Americans are now at work than a year ago, and recently there has even been a small crack in interest rates. But let me be the first to say that our problems won't suddenly disappear next week, next month, or next year. We're just starting down a road that I believe will lead us out of the economic swamp we've been in for so long. It'll take time for the effect of the tax rate reductions to be felt in increased savings, productivity, and new jobs. It will also take time for the budget cuts to reduce the deficits which have brought us near runaway inflation and ru- inous interest rates.

The important thing now is to hold to a firm, steady, course. Tonight I want to talk with you about the next steps that we must take on that course, additional reductions in federal spending that will help lower our interest rates, our inflation, and bring us closer to full economic recovery.

I know that high interest rates are punishing many of you, from the young family that wants to buy its first home to the farmer who needs a new truck or tractor. But all of us know that interest rates will only come down and stay down when government is no longer borrowing huge amounts of money to cover its deficits.

These deficits have been piling up every year and some people here in Washington just throw up their hands in despair. Maybe you'll remember that we were told in the spring of 1980 that the 1981 budget, the one we have now, would be balanced. Well, that budget, like so many in the past, hemorrhaged badly and wound up in a sea of red ink.

More Cuts in Federal Spending

I have pledged that we shall not stand idly by and see that same thing happen again. When I presented our economic recovery program to Congress, I said we were aiming to cut the deficit steadily to reach a balance by 1984.

The budget bill that I signed this summer cut $35 billion from the 1982 budget and slowed the growth of spending by $130 billion over the next three years. We cut the government's rate of growth nearly in half.

Now we must move on to a second round of budget savings — to keep us on the road to a balanced budget.

Our immediate challenge is to hold down the deficit in the fiscal year that begins next week. A number of threats are now appearing that will drive the deficit upward if we fail to act. For example, in the euphoria just after our budget bill was approved this summer, we didn't point out immediately as we should that while we did get most of what we'd asked for, most isn't all. Some of the savings in our proposal were not approved; and since then, the Congress has taken actions that could add even more to the cost of government.

The result is that without further reductions, our deficit for 1982 will be increased by some $16 billion. The estimated deficit for '83 will be increased proportionately. And without further cuts, we can't achieve our goal of a balanced budget by 1984.

Now, it would be easy to sit back and say, "Well, it will take longer than we thought. We got most of what we proposed, so let's stop there." But that's not good enough.

Must 'Face Up' to Cuts

In meeting to discuss this problem a few days ago, Senator Pete Domenici of New Mexico, Chairman of the Senate Budget Committee, recalled the words of that great heavy-weight champion and great American Joe Louis just before he stepped into the ring against Billy Conn. There had been some speculation that Billy might be able to avoid Joe's lethal right hand. Joe said, "Well, he can run but he can't hide."

Senator Domenici said to me, "That's just what we're facing on runaway federal spending. We can try to run from it but we can't hide. We have to face up to it."

He's right, of course. In the last few decades we started down a road that led to a massive explosion in federal spending. It took about 170 years for the federal budget to reach $100 billion. That was in 1962. It took only eight years to reach the $200 billion mark and only five more to make it $300 billion. And in the next five we nearly doubled that.

It would be one thing if we'd been able to pay for all the things government decided to do, but we've only balanced the budget once in the last 20 years.

$1 Trillion National Debt

In just the past decade, our national debt has more than doubled. And in the next few days it will pass the trillion dollar mark. One trillion dollars of debt — if we as a nation needed a warning, let that be it.

Our interest payments on the debt alone are now running more than $96 million a year. That's more than the total combined profits last year of the 500 biggest companies in the country; or to put it another way, Washington spends more on interest than on all of its education, nutrition and medical programs combined.

In the past, there have been several methods used to fund some of our social experiments. One was to take it away from national defense. From being the strongest nation on earth in the post World War II years, we've steadily declined, while the Soviet Union engaged in the most massive military buildup the world has ever seen.

Now, with all our economic problems, we're forced to try to catch up so that we can preserve the peace. Government's first responsibility is national security and we're determined to meet that responsibility. In-

deed, we have no choice.

Well, what all of this is leading up to is — what do we plan to do? Last week I met with the Cabinet to take up this matter. I'm proud to say there was no hand-wringing, no pleading to avoid further budget cuts. We all agreed that the "tax and tax, spend and spend," policies of the past few decades lead only to economic disaster. Our government must return to the tradition of living within our means and must do it now. We asked ourselves two questions — and answered them: "If not us — who? If not now — when?"

Let me talk with you now about the specific ways that I believe we ought to achieve additional savings — savings of some $16 billion in 1982 and a total of $80 billion when spread over the next three years. I recognize that many in Congress may have other alternatives and I welcome a dialogue with them. But let there be no mistake: We have no choice but to continue down the road toward a balanced budget — a budget that will keep us strong at home and secure overseas. And let me be clear that this cannot be the last round of cuts. Holding down spending must be a continuing battle for several years to come.

Here is what I propose. First, I'm asking Congress to reduce the 1982 appropriation for most government agencies and programs by 12 percent. This will save $17.5 billion over the next several years. Absorbing these reductions will not be easy, but duplication, excess, waste and overhead is still far too great and can be trimmed further.

Defense Budget to be Cut

No one in the meeting asked to be exempt from belt-tightening. Over the next three years, the increase we had originally planned in the defense budget will be cut by $13 billion. I'll confess, I was reluctant about this because of the long way we have to go before the dangerous window of vulnerability confronting us will be appreciably narrowed. But the Secretary of Defense assured me that he can meet our critical needs in spite of this cut.

Reduce Federal Staff

Second, to achieve further economies, we'll shrink the size of the non-defense payroll over the next three years by some 6½ percent, some 75,000 employees. Much of this will be attained by not replacing those who retire or leave. There will, however, be some reductions in force simply because we're reducing our administrative overhead. I intend to set the example here by reducing the size of the White House staff and the staff of the Executive Office of the President.

As a third step, we propose to dismantle two Cabinet departments, Energy and Education. Both secretaries are wholly in accord with this. Some of the activities in both of these departments will, of course, be continued either independently or in other areas of government. There's only one way to shrink the size and cost of big government and that is by eliminating agencies that are not needed and are getting in the way of a solution. Now, we don't need an Energy Department to solve our basic energy problem. As long as we let the forces of the marketplace work without undue interference, the ingenuity of consumers, business, producers and inventors will do that for us.

Similarly, education is the principal responsibility of local school systems, teachers, parents, citizen boards and state governments. By eliminating the department of education less than two years after it was created, we cannot only reduce the budget, but insure that local needs and preferences rather than the wishes of Washington determine the education of our children. We also plan the elimination of a few smaller agencies and a number of boards and commissions, some of which have fallen into disuse or which are not being duplicated.

Loan Guarantee Reductions

Fourth, we intend to make reductions of some $20 billion in federal loan guarantees. These guarantees are not funds that the government spends directly. They're funds that are loaned in the private market and insured by government at subsidized rates. Federal loan guarantees have become a form of back door, uncontrolled borrowing that prevent many small businesses that aren't subsidized from obtaining financing of their own. They are also a major factor in driving up interest rates. It's time we brought this practice under control.

Welfare and Entitlement Reform

Fifth, I intend to forward to Congress this fall a new package of entitlement and welfare reform measures, outside Social Security, to save nearly $27 billion over the next three years. In the past two decades we've created hundreds of new programs to provide personal assistance. Many of these programs may have come from a good heart but not all have come from a clear head. And the costs have been staggering.

In 1955 these programs cost $8 billion. By 1965 the cost was $79 billion. Next year it will be $188 billion. Let there be no confusion on this score. Benefits for the needy will be protected, but the black market in food stamps must be stopped, the abuse and fraud by beneficiaries and providers alike cannot be tolerated, provision of school loans and meal subsidies to the affluent can no longer be afforded.

In California when I was Governor and embarked upon welfare reform, there were screams from those who claimed that we intended to victimize the needy. But in a little over three years we saved the taxpayer some $2 billion at the same time we were able to increase the grants for the deserving and truly needy by an average of more than 40 percent. It was the first cost of living increase they'd received in 13 years. I believe progress can also be made at the national level.

We can be compassionate about human needs without being complacent about budget extravagance.

Tax Reform

Sixth, I will soon urge Congress to enact new proposals to eliminate abuses and obsolete incentives in the tax code. The Treasury Department believes that the deficit can be reduced by $3.0 billion next year and $22 billion over the next three years with prompt enactment of these measures.

Now that we've provided the greatest incentives for saving, investment, work and productivity ever proposed, we must also ensure that taxes due the government are collected and that a fair share of the burden is borne by all.

Finally, I am renewing my plea to Congress to approve my proposals for user fees — proposals first suggested last spring, but which have been neglected since.

When the federal government provides a service directly to a particular industry or to a group of citizens, I believe that those who receive benefits should bear the cost. For example, this next year the federal government will spend $525 million to maintain river harbors, channels, locks, and dams for the barge and maritime industries. Yacht owners, commercial vessels and the airlines will receive services worth $2.8 billion from Uncle Sam.

My spring budget proposals included legislation that would authorize the federal government to recover a total of $980 million from the users of these services through fees. Now, that's only a third of the $3.3 billion it will cost the government to provide those same services.

None of these steps will be easy. We're going through a period of difficult and painful readjustment. I know that we're asking for sacrifices from virtually all of you. But there is no alternative. Some of those who oppose this plan have participated over the years in the extravagance that has brought us inflation, unemployment, high interest rates and an intolerable debt. I grant they were well intentioned but their costly reforms didn't eliminate poverty or raise welfare recipients from dependence to self-sufficiency, independence and dignity. Yet in their objections to what we've proposed they offer only what we know has been tried before and failed.

I believe we've chosen a path that leads to an America at work, to fiscal sanity, to lower taxes and less inflation. I believe our plan for recovery is sound and it will work.

Tonight I'm asking all of you who joined in this crusade to save our economy to help again. To let your representatives know that you'll support them in making the hard decisions to further reduce the cost and size of government.

Social Security

Now, if you'll permit me, I'd like to turn to another subject which I know has

many of you very concerned and even frightened. This is an issue apart from the economic reform package that we've just been discussing, but I feel I must clear the air. There has been a great deal of misinformation and for that matter pure demagoguery on the subject of Social Security.

During the campaign I called attention to the fact that Social Security had both a short and a long range fiscal problem. I pledged my best to restore it to fiscal responsibility without in any way reducing or eliminating existing benefits for those now dependent on it.

To all of you listening and particularly those of you now receiving Social Security, I ask you to listen very carefully: First to what threatens the integrity of Social Security and then to a possible solution.

Some thirty years ago, there were 16 people working and paying the Social Security payroll tax for every one retiree. Today that ratio has changed to only 3.2 workers paying in for each beneficiary.

For many years we've known that an actuarial imbalance existed and that the program faced an unfunded liability of several trillion dollars.

Now, the short range problem is much closer than that. The Social Security retirement fund has been paying out billions of dollars more each year than it takes in and it could run out of money before the end of 1982 unless something is done.

Some of our critics claim new figures reveal a cushion of several billions of dollars which will carry the program beyond 1982. I'm sure it's only a coincidence that 1982 is an election year.

The cushion they speak of is borrowing from the Medicare fund and the disability fund. Of course doing this would only postpone the day of reckoning. Alice Rivlin of the Congressional Budget Office told a congressional committee the day before yesterday that such borrowing might carry us to 1990, but then we'd face the same problem. And as she put it, we'd have to cut benefits or raise the payroll tax. Well, we're not going to cut benefits and the payroll tax is already being raised.

In 1977, Congress passed the largest tax increase in our history. It called for a payroll tax increase in January of 1982, another in 1985, and again in 1986 and in 1990.

When that law was passed we were told it made Social Security safe until the year 2030. But we're running out of money 48 years short of 2030.

For the nation's work force, the Social Security tax is already the biggest tax they pay. In 1935 we were told the tax would never be greater than 2% of the first $3,000 of earnings. It is presently 13.3% of the first $29,700 and the scheduled increases will take it to 15.3% of the first $60,600. And that's when Mrs. Rivlin says we would need an additional increase.

Some have suggested reducing benefits. Others propose an income tax on benefits, or that the retirement age should be moved back to age 68 and there are some

who would simply fund Social Security out of general tax funds as welfare is funded. I believe there are better solutions. I am asking the Congress to restore the minimum benefit for current beneficiaries with low incomes. It was never our intention to take this support away from those who truly need it.

Possible Solutions

There is, however, a sizable percentage of recipients who are adequately provided for by pensions or other income and should not be added to the financial burden of Social Security.

The same situation prevails with regard to disability payments. No one will deny our obligation to those with legitimate claims. But there's widespread abuse of the system which should not be allowed to continue.

Since 1962, early retirement has been allowed at age 62 with 80 percent of full benefits. In our proposal we ask that early retirees in the future receive 55 percent of the total benefit, but, and this is most important, those early retirees would only have to work an additional 20 months to be eligible for the 80 percent payment. I don't believe very many of you were aware of that part of our proposal.

The only change we proposed for those already receiving Social Security had to do with the annual cost of living adjustment. Now, those adjustments are made on July 1st each year, a hangover from the days when the fiscal year began in July. We proposed a one-time delay in making that adjustment, postponing it for three months until October 1st. From then on it would continue to be made every 12 months. That one time delay would not lower your existing benefits but would, on the average, reduce your increase by about $86 one time next year.

By making these few changes, we would have solved the short and long range problems of Social Security funding once and for all. In addition, we could have cancelled the increases in the payroll tax by 1985. To a young person just starting in the work force, the savings from cancelling those increases would, on the average, amount to $33,000 by the time he or she reached retirement, and compound interest, add that, and it makes a tiny nest egg to add to the Social Security benefits.

However, let me point out, our feet were never imbedded in concrete on this proposal. We hoped it could be a starting point for a bipartisan solution to the problem. We were ready to listen to alternatives and other ideas which might improve on or replace our proposals. But, the majority leadership in the House of Representatives has refused to join in any such cooperative effort.

I therefore am asking, as I said, for restoration of the minimum benefit and for interfund borrowing as a temporary measure to give us time to seek a permanent solution. To remove Social Security once and for all from politics I am also asking

Speaker Tip O'Neill of the House of Representatives and Majority Leader in the Senate Howard Baker to each appoint five members and I will appoint five to a task force which will review all the options and come up with a plan that assures the fiscal integrity of Social Security and that Social Security recipients will continue to receive their full benefits. . . .

Well now, in conclusion, let me return to the principal purpose of this message, the budget and the imperative need for all of us to ask less of government, to help to return to spending no more than we take in, to end the deficits and bring down interest rates that otherwise can destroy what we've been building here for two centuries.

Requests Volunteer Help

I know that we're asking for economies in many areas and programs that were started with the best of intentions and the dedication to a worthwhile cause or purpose, but I know also that some of those programs have not succeeded in their purpose. Others have proven too costly, benefiting those who administer them rather than those who were the intended beneficiaries. This doesn't mean we should discontinue trying to help where help is needed. Government must continue to do its share. But I ask all of you, as private citizens, to join this effort too. As a people we have a proud tradition of generosity.

More than a century ago a Frenchman came to America and later wrote a book for his countrymen telling them what he had seen here. He told them that in America when a citizen saw a problem that needed solving he would cross the street and talk to a neighbor about it and the first thing you know a committee would be formed and before long the problem would be solved. And then he added, "You may not believe this, but not a single bureaucrat would ever have been involved." . . . I believe the spirit of volunteerism still lives in America. We see examples of it on every hand, the community charity drive, support of hospitals and all manner of nonprofit institutions, the rallying around whenever disaster or tragedy strikes.

The truth is we've let government take away many things we once considered were really ours to do voluntarily out of the goodness of our hearts and a sense of community pride and neighborliness. I believe many of you want to do those things again, want to be involved if only someone will ask you or offer the opportunity. Well, we intend to make that offer.

We're launching a nationwide effort to encourage our citizens to join with us in finding where need exists and then to organize volunteer programs to meet that need. We've already set the wheels of such a volunteer effort in motion.

As Tom Paine said 200 years ago, "We have it within our power to begin the world over again."

What are we waiting for?

God bless you, and good night. ∎

Continuing Appropriations Veto

Following is the Congressional Record *text of President Reagan's Nov. 23 message accompanying his veto of H J Res 357, providing funding authority through Sept. 30, 1982, for government agencies whose regular fiscal 1982 appropriations bills had not been enacted. It was Reagan's first veto of a public bill during the 97th Congress.*

To the House of Representatives:

I am returning to the Congress without my signature H.J. Res. 357, the Continuing Resolution providing appropriations for Fiscal Year 1982.

This Resolution presented me with a difficult choice:

● Either to sign a budget-busting appropriations bill that would finance the entire Government at levels well above my recommendations, and thus set back our efforts to halt the excessive Government spending that has fueled inflation and high interest rates, and destroyed investments for new jobs;

● Or, to hold the line on spending with a veto, but risk interruption of Government activities and services.

I have chosen the latter. The failure to provide a reasonable Resolution means that some citizens may be inconvenienced and that there is a possibility of some temporary hardship. Nevertheless, a far greater threat to all Americans is the sustained hardship they will suffer by continuing the past budget-busting policies of big spending and big deficits.

When reports came to us in September that spending and the deficit for Fiscal Year 1982 were rising, we took action to stem the tide.

On September 24, I asked for a reduction of 12 percent in the appropriations for nearly all non-defense discretionary programs and a modest reduction in our planned program to strengthen the national defense. The 12 percent cut would have saved $8.5 billion — a significant contribution to reducing the deficit, but a modest sum in a budget which will total more than $700 billion.

By refusing to make even this small saving to protect the American people against overspending, the Congress has paved the way for higher interest rates and inflation, and a continued loss of investment, jobs and economic growth. At the same time, the Continuing Resolution fails to provide sufficient security assistance to allow America to meet its obligations.

The practice of loading the budget with unnecessary spending — and then waiting until after the eleventh hour to pass a Continuing Resolution on the assumption that it was safe from a Presidential veto — has gone on much too long. It is one of the principal reasons why the growth of Government spending is still not under control.

For much of the past fiscal year, most of the domestic budget was funded in this manner — through a Continuing Resolution, without regular appropriations bills subject to Presidential approval or disapproval. These so-called stop-gap resolutions are actually budget-busters that can last for an entire year and create the kind of economic mess we inherited last year.

A few days ago I offered to meet the Congress half-way. But the Continuing Resolution the Congress has now passed provides less than one-quarter of the savings I requested. This represents neither fair compromise nor responsible budget policy.

In the hours ahead the Congress has the opportunity to reconsider, and I urgently request that it do so. In the meantime, we are making every effort to avoid unnecessary dislocations and personal hardship. I can give assurance that:

● Social Security and most other benefit checks will be paid on schedule.

● The national security will be protected.

● Government activities essential to the protection of life and property, such as the treatment of patients in veterans hospitals, air traffic control and the functioning of the Nation's banks, will also continue.

But in order to prevent unnecessary inconvenience and hardship as Thanksgiving approaches, I must urge the Congress to act promptly and responsibly.

RONALD REAGAN.

The White House
November 23, 1981. ∎

Bankruptcy Bill Veto

Following is the White House text of President Reagan's Dec. 29, 1981, memorandum of disapproval (pocket veto) on HR 4353, establishing a uniform law on the subject of bankruptcies. It was Reagan's second veto of a public bill during the 97th Congress.

I am withholding my approval of H.R. 4353, to amend the Act entitled "An Act to Establish a Uniform Law on the Subject of Bankruptcies."

This bill would benefit the creditors of a single large asset bankruptcy. The debtor's estate has disputed the amount which it must pay to the Referees' Salary and Expense Fund. While I am aware that the Fund has been abolished with respect to recent cases, nothing except this debtor's dispute of the assessment distinguishes this one case from all others where the plan of arrangement was confirmed prior to September 30, 1978. I cannot support this effort to confer special relief in the guise of general legislation at a possible loss to the Treasury of $1.6 million. I believe the judicial process should be allowed to run its course.

RONALD REAGAN

The White House
December 29, 1981 ∎

PUBLIC LAWS

C
Q

Public Laws, 97th Congress, 1st Session

PL 97-1 (S J Res 16) Proclaim Jan. 29, 1981 as a "Day of Thanksgiving To Honor Our Safely Returned Hostages." HATFIELD, R-Ore. — 1/22/81 — Senate passed Jan. 22. House passed Jan. 23. President signed Jan. 26, 1981.

PL 97-2 (HR 1553) Allow a temporary increase in the public debt ceiling. ROSTENKOWSKI, D-Ill. — 2/3/81 — House Ways and Means Committee reported Feb. 3 (H Rept 97-1). House passed Feb. 5. Senate passed Feb. 6. President signed Feb. 6, 1981.

PL 97-3 (S 253) Increase the number of members of the Commission on Wartime Relocation and Internment of Civilians. STEVENS, R-Alaska — 1/27/81 — Senate passed Jan. 27. House Judiciary Committee discharged Jan. 28. House passed Jan. 28. President signed Feb. 10, 1981.

PL 97-4 (S 272) Increase the number of members of the Joint Committee on Printing. MATHIAS, R-Md. — 1/27/81 — Senate Rules Committee reported Jan. 27 (S Rept 97-2). Senate passed Feb. 3. House passed Feb. 5. President signed Feb. 17, 1981.

PL 97-5 (HR 2166) Extend the antitrust exemption for oil companies that participate in the agreement on an international energy program. SHARP, D-Ind. — 2/25/81 — House Energy and Commerce reported March 6 (H Rept 97-9). House passed, under suspension of the rules, March 10. Senate passed March 10. President signed March 13, 1981.

PL 97-6 (S 509) Repeal authority for a semi-annual increase in dairy price supports. HELMS, R-N.C. — 2/20/81 — Senate Agriculture, Nutrition and Forestry reported March 10 (S Rept 97-24). Senate passed, amended, March 25. House passed, amended, March 26. Senate agreed to House amendments March 27. President signed March 31, 1981.

PL 97-7 (S 840) Continue in effect any authority provided under the fiscal 1980 Justice Department authorization, through Sept. 30, 1981. THURMOND, R-S.C. — 3/31/81 — Senate passed March 31. House Judiciary discharged April 7. House passed, amended, April 7. Senate agreed to House amendment April 8. President signed April 9, 1981.

PL 97-8 (S J Res 61) Authorize and request the president to issue a proclamation designating April 9, 1981, as "African Refugee Relief Day." KASSEBAUM, R-Kan. — 4/7/81 — Senate passed April 7. House passed April 7. President signed April 9, 1981.

PL 97-9 (H J Res 182) Designate April 26, 1981, as "National Recognition Day for Veterans of the Vietnam Era." ALBOSTA, D-Mich. — 2/23/81 — House Post Office and Civil Service discharged March 26. House passed March 26. Senate passed March 31. President signed April 14, 1981.

PL 97-10 (H J Res 155) Authorize and request the president to issue a proclamation designating May 3-10, 1981, as "Jewish Heritage Week." ADDABBO, D-N.Y. — 2/3/81 — House Post Office and Civil Service discharged March 26. House passed March 26. Senate Judiciary reported April 10. Senate passed April 27. President signed May 1, 1981.

PL 97-11 (S 730) Provide for the use of the funds of the Commodity Credit Corporation in implementing the Federal Crop Insurance Act of 1980. HUDDLESTON, D-Ky. — 3/17/81 — Senate Agriculture, Nutrition and Forestry reported April 1 (S Rept 97-38). Senate passed, amended, May 5. House passed, under suspension of the rules, May 19. President signed May 22, 1981.

PL 97-12 (HR 3512) Appropriate supplemental funds for the fiscal year ending Sept. 30, 1981, and rescind certain budget authority. WHITTEN, D-Miss. — 5/8/81 — House passed, amended, May 13. Senate Appropriations reported May 14 (S Rept 97-67). Senate passed, amended, May 21. House agreed to conference report June 4 (H Rept 97-124). Senate agreed to conference report June 4. President signed June 5, 1981.

PL 97-13 (S J Res 50) Designate July 17, 1981, as "National P.O.W.-M.I.A. Recognition Day." DeCONCINI, D-Ariz. — 3/19/81 — Senate Judiciary reported May 5. Senate passed May 6. House Post Office and Civil Service discharged May 28. House passed May 28. President signed June 12, 1981.

PL 97-14 (S 1070) Authorize funds for fiscal year 1982 for youth employment/demonstration programs. QUAYLE, R-Ind. — 4/30/81 — Senate Labor and Human Resources reported May 6 (S Rept 97-56). Senate passed May 12. House passed June 2. President signed June 16, 1981.

PL 97-15 (HR 2156) Extended by 12 months the period during which funds appropriated for grants by the Veterans Administration for the establishment and support of new state medical schools may be expended. MOTTL, D-Ohio — 2/25/81 — House Veterans' Affairs reported May 19 (H Rept 97-77). House passed, amended, June 2. Senate passed June 3. President signed June 17, 1981.

PL 97-16 (S 1213) Authorize funds for fiscal year 1982 for the Marine Protection Research and Sanctuaries Act. CHAFEE, R-R.I. — 5/15/81 — Senate Environment and Public Works reported (S Rept 97-119). Senate passed June 2. House passed June 11. President signed June 23, 1981.

PL 97-17 (H J Res 288) Correct PL 97-12 due to an error in the enrollment of HR 3512. WHITTEN, D-Miss. — 6/15/81 — House passed June 15. Senate passed June 15. President signed June 29, 1981.

PL 97-18 (HR 3991) Amend the Food Stamp Act of 1977 to increase the authorization for appropriations for fiscal year 1981 and amend PL 93-233 to continue, through Aug. 1, 1981, the cash-out of food stamp program benefits of certain recipients of Supplemental Security Income. DE LA GARZA, D-Texas — 6/23/81 — House Agriculture discharged June 23. House Ways and Means discharged June 23. House passed June 23. Senate passed June 26. President signed June 30, 1981.

PL 97-19 (S 1123) Permit rental, lease or purchase of office equipment for use in District of Columbia and state Senate offices. MATHIAS, R-Md. — 5/6/81 — Senate Rules and Administration reported May 6 (S Rept 97-50). Senate passed May 14. House Administration discharged June 24. House passed June 24. President signed July 6, 1981.

PL 97-20 (S 1124) Authorize the Senate sergeant-at-arms and doorkeeper to enter into contracts which provide for the making of advanced payments for computer programming services. MATHIAS, R-Md. — 5/6/81 — Senate Rules and Administration reported May 6 (S Rept 97-51). Senate passed May 12. House Administration discharged June 24. House passed June 24. President signed July 6, 1981.

PL 97-21 (H J Res 238) Approve the Constitution of the Virgin Islands. DE LUGO, R-Virgin Islands. — 4/28/81 — House Interior and Insular Affairs reported April 30 (H Rept 97-25). House passed May 5. Senate Energy and Natural Resources reported May 14 (S Rept 97-66). Senate passed, amended, June 3. House agreed to Senate amendments June 16. President signed July 9, 1981.

PL 97-22 (HR 3807) Make technical corrections in the Defense Officer Personnel Management Act. NICHOLS, D-Ala. — 6/4/81 — House Armed Services reported June 11 (H Rept 97-141). House passed June 16. Senate Armed Services discharged June 25. Senate passed June 25. President signed July 10, 1981.

PL 97-23 (HR 3520) Provide environmental compliance date extensions for steelmaking facilities on a case-by-case basis to facilitate modernization. WAXMAN, D-Calif. — 5/12/81 — House Energy and Commerce reported May 22 (H Rept 97-121). House passed May 28. Senate Environment and Public Works discharged June 11. Senate passed, amended, June 11. Senate agreed to conference report June 25 (H Rept 97-161). House agreed to conference report June 26. President signed July 17, 1981.

PL 97-24 (S 1395) Extend the time for conducting the referendum with respect to the national marketing quota for wheat for the marketing year beginning June 1, 1982, and eliminate the requirement that the secretary of agriculture waive interest on loans made on 1980 and 1981 crops of wheat and feed grains placed in the farmer-held grain reserve. HELMS, R-N.C. — 6/19/81 — Senate Agriculture discharged June 25. Senate passed June 25. House passed July 9. President signed July 23, 1981.

PL 97-25 (HR 31) Permit merchants to offer unlimited discounts to cash-paying customers and provide a three-year extension of law prohibiting imposition of surcharges on purchases made by credit card. ANNUNZIO, D-Ill. — 1/5/81 — House Banking, Finance and Urban Affairs reported, Feb. 24. House passed, amended, Feb. 24. Senate passed, amended, March 12. House agreed to conference report June 24 (H Rept 97-159). Senate agreed to conference report July 14. President signed July 27, 1981.

PL 97-26 (H J Res 308) Appropriate supplemental amounts for the Department of Health and Human Services for fiscal year 1981. NATCHER, D-Ky. — 7/21/81 — House Appropriations reported July 23 (H Rept 97-192). House passed July 23. Senate passed July 23. President signed July 29, 1981.

PL 97-27 (H J Res 84) Request the president to designate the week of Oct. 4 through Oct. 11, 1981, as "National Diabetes Week." FORSYTHE, R-N.J. — 1/16/81 — House Post Office and Civil Service discharged March 26. House passed March 26. Senate Judiciary discharged July 24. Senate passed July 24. President signed Aug. 4, 1981.

PL 97-28 (S J Res 28) Request the president to designate the week beginning March 7, 1982, as "Women's History Week." HATCH, R-Utah — 2/6/81 — Senate Judiciary reported March 6. Senate passed March 10. House Post Office and Civil Service discharged July 15. House passed, amended, July 15. Senate agreed to House amendments July 24. President signed Aug. 4, 1981.

PL 97-29 (H J Res 191) Request the president to designate Aug. 8, 1981, as "National Children's Day." GUYER, R-Ohio — 2/25/81 — House Post Office and Civil Service discharged July 23. House passed July 23. Senate passed July 24. President signed Aug. 6, 1981.

PL 97-30 (S 1040) Amend the District of Columbia Self-Government and

Governmental Reorganization Act to increase the amount authorized to be appropriated as the annual federal payment to the District of Columbia. MATHIAS, R-Md. — 4/29/81 — Senate Governmental Affairs reported May 15 (S Rept 97-80). Senated passed June 2. House passed July 27. President signed Aug. 6, 1981.

PL 97-31 (HR 4074) Transfer all functions, powers, duties, assets and liabilities of the Maritime Administration from the Commerce Department to the Transportation Department. JONES, D-N.C. — 7/8/81 — House Merchant Marine and Fisheries reported July 24 (H Rept 97-199). House passed, amended, July 27. Senate passed July 29. President signed Aug. 6, 1981.

PL 97-32 (S J Res 64) Request the president to designate Aug. 13, 1981, as "National Blinded Veterans Recognition Day." SIMPSON, R-Wyo. — 4/8/81 — Senate Judiciary reported June 24. Senate passed June 25. House Post Office and Civil Service discharged July 30. House passed July 30. President signed Aug. 6, 1981.

PL 97-33 (S 1104) Amend the International Investment Survey Act of 1976 to provide an authorization for further appropriations, to avoid unnecessary duplication of certain surveys and for other purposes. PRESSLER, R-S.D. — 5/4/81 — Senate Commerce reported May 15 (S Rept 97-68). Senate passed, amended, June 2. House passed July 27. President signed Aug. 7, 1981.

PL 97-34 (HR 4242) Amend the Internal Revenue Code of 1954 to encourage economic growth through reductions in individual income tax rates, the expensing of depreciable property, incentives for small businesses and incentives for savings and for other purposes. ROSTENKOWSKI, D-Ill. — 7/23/81 — House Ways and Means reported July 24 (H Rept 97-201). House passed, amended, July 29. Senate passed, amended, July 31. Senate agreed to conference report Aug. 3 (H Rept 97-215). House agreed to conference report Aug. 4. President signed Aug. 13, 1981.

PL 97-35 (HR 3982) Provide for reconciliation pursuant to section 301 of the First Concurrent Resolution on the Budget for fiscal year 1982. JONES — D-Okla. — 6/19/81 — House Budget reported June 19 (H Rept 97-158). House passed, amended, June 26. Senate passed, amended, July 13. House agreed to conference report July 31 (H Rept 97-208). Senate agreed to conference report July 31. President signed Aug. 13, 1981.

PL 97-36 (H J Res 141) Request the president to designate the week of Oct. 4 through Oct. 10, 1981, as "National Schoolbus Safety Week." EVANS, D-Ga. — 1/28/81 — House Post Office and Civil Service discharged July 15. House passed July 15. Senate Judiciary reported July 30. Senate passed July 31. President signed Aug. 14, 1981.

PL 97-37 (HR 1100) Amend title 38, U.S. Code, to expand eligibility of former prisoners of war for certain health-care benefits provided by the Veterans Administration and for other purposes. MONTGOMERY, D-Miss. — 1/22/81 — House Veterans' Affairs reported May 4 (H Rept 97-28). House passed, amended, June 2. Senate passed, amended, June 4. House agreed to Senate amendments with amendments July 30. Senate agreed to House amendments to Senate amendments July 30. President signed Aug. 14, 1981.

PL 97-38 (S 547) Enable the secretary of the interior to erect permanent improvements on land acquired for the Confederated Tribes of Siletz Indians of Oregon. HATFIELD, R-Ore. — 2/24/81 — Senate Select Indian Affairs reported May 15 (S Rept 97-108). Senate passed, amended, May 21. House passed Aug. 4. President signed Aug. 14, 1981.

PL 97-39 (S 694) Authorize supplemental appropriations for fiscal year 1981 for procurement of aircraft, missiles, naval vessels and tracked combat vehicles and for research development, tests, evaluation and increase the authorized personnel strength for military and civilian personnel of the Defense Department and for other purposes. TOWER, R-Texas — 3/12/81 — Senate Armed Services reported April 1 (S Rept 97-35). Senate passed, amended, April 7. House passed, amended, June 23. Senate agreed to conference report July 30 (H Rept 97-204). House agreed to conference report Aug. 4. President signed Aug. 14, 1981.

PL 97-40 (S 640) Amend the District of Columbia Self-Government and Governmental Reorganization Act with respect to the borrowing authority of the District of Columbia. MATHIAS, R-Md. — 3/6/81 — Senate Governmental Affairs reported May 15 (S Rept 97-79). Senate passed, amended, June 3. House passed, amended, July 27. Senate agreed to House amendments Aug. 3. President signed Aug. 14, 1981.

PL 97-41 (S 875) Authorize the generation of electrical power at Palo Verde Irrigation District Diversion Dam, Calif. HAYAKAWA, R-Calif. — 4/2/81 — Senate Energy and Natural Resources reported May 8 (S Rept 97-60). Senate passed, amended, May 14. House Interior and Insular Affairs reported July 30 (H Rept 97-209). House passed Aug. 4. President signed Aug. 14, 1981.

PL 97-42 (S 1278) Amend the Saccharin Study and Labeling Act to extend until 24 months after the date of enactment of this Act the period during which the secretary of health and human services may

not take certain actions to restrict the continued use of saccharin or any food, drug or cosmetic containing saccharin. HATCH, R-Utah — 5/21/81 — Senate Labor and Human Resources reported June 19 (S Rept 97-140). Senate passed June 25. House passed July 31. President signed Aug. 14, 1981.

PL 97-43 (S J Res 87) Authorize and request the president to designate Sept. 13, 1981, as "Commodore John Barry Day." MATHIAS, R-Md.— 6/9/81 — Senate Judiciary reported July 30. Senate passed July 31. House passed Aug. 4. President signed Aug. 20, 1981.

PL 97-44 (S J Res 62) Designate the week of Sept. 20-26, 1981, as "National Cystic Fibrosis Week." DOLE, R-Kan. — 4/7/81 — Senate Judiciary reported July 30. Senate passed July 31. House passed Sept. 15. President signed Sept. 17, 1981.

PL 97-45 (HR 2120) Facilitate the ability of product sellers to establish product liability risk retention groups, facilitating the ability of such sellers to purchase product liability insurance on a group basis. FLORIO, D-N.J. — 2/25/81 — House Energy and Commerce reported July 21 (H Rept 97-190). House passed, under suspension of the rules, July 28. Senate passed Sept. 11. President signed Sept. 25, 1981.

PL 97-46 (HR 4416) Enable the secretary of agriculture to assist, on an emergency basis, in the eradication of plant pests and contagious or infectious animal and poultry diseases. DE LA GARZA, D-Texas — 9/9/81 — House Agriculture discharged. House passed Sept. 9. Senate passed Sept. 11. President signed Sept. 25, 1981.

PL 97-47 (HR 2903) Extend by one year the expiration date of the Defense Production Act. BLANCHARD, D-Mich. — 3/31/81 — House Banking, Finance and Urban Affairs reported May 18 (H Rept 97-48). House passed, under suspension of the rules, July 13. Senate passed, amended, Sept. 22. House agreed to Senate amendments Sept. 24. President signed Sept. 30, 1981.

PL 97-48 (H J Res 266) Increase the temporary public debt for the period from May 21, 1981, through Sept. 30, 1981. WRIGHT, D-Texas — 5/21/81 — House passed May 21. Senate Finance reported July 6 (S Rept 97-144). Senate passed Sept. 29. President signed Sept. 30, 1981.

PL 97-49 (H J Res 265) Provide for a temporary increase in the public debt. WRIGHT, D-Texas — 5/21/81 — House passed May 21. Senate Finance reported Sept. 15. Senate passed Sept. 29. President signed Sept. 30, 1981.

PL 97-50 (S 1475) Extend until April 1, 1982, the authority of section 252 of the Energy Policy and Conservation Act, authorizing U.S. oil companies to participate in voluntary agreements for implementing the allocation and information provisions of the agreement on an international energy program. McCLURE, R-Idaho — 7/14/81 — Senate Energy and Natural Resources reported July 29. Senate passed Sept. 22. House Energy and Commerce reported Sept. 25 (H Rept 97-254). House passed, under suspension of the rules, Sept. 29. President signed Sept. 30, 1981.

PL 97-51 (H J Res 325) Make continuing appropriations for the period from Oct. 1 to Nov. 20, 1981, for programs of the federal government, and for all of fiscal 1982 for the legislative branch. WHITTEN, D-Miss. — 9/9/81 — House Appropriations reported Sept. 14 (H Rept 97-223). House passed Sept. 16. Senate Appropriations reported Sept. 23. Senate passed, amended, Sept. 25. House agreed to conference report Sept. 30 (H Rept 97-260). Senate agreed to conference report Sept. 30. President signed Oct. 1, 1981.

PL 97-52 (S J Res 78) Designate Oct. 2, 1981, as "American Enterprise Day." COCHRAN, R-Miss. — 5/6/81 — Senate Judiciary reported July 14. Senate passed July 17. House Post Office and Civil Service discharged. House passed Sept. 30. President signed Oct. 2, 1981.

PL 97-53 (S J Res 103) Request the president to designate the week beginning Oct. 4, 1981, as "National Port Week." HOLLINGS, D-S.C. — 7/30/81 — Senate Judiciary reported Sept. 15. Senate passed Sept. 16. House Post Office and Civil Service discharged. House passed Sept. 30. President signed Oct. 2, 1981.

PL 97-54 (S J Res 65) Proclaim Raoul Wallenberg an honorary citizen of the United States, and request further information from the Soviet Union on his whereabouts. PELL, D-R.I. — 4/8/81 — Senate Foreign Relations and Judiciary reported jointly July 27 (S Rept 97-169). Senate passed Aug. 3. House passed Sept. 22. President signed Oct. 5, 1981.

PL 97-55 (HR 618) Convey certain interest in public lands to the city of Angels, Calif. SHUMWAY, R-Calif. — 1/5/81 — House Interior and Insular Affairs reported March 24 (H Rept 97-13). House passed April 6. Senate Energy and Natural Resources reported Aug. 27 (S Rept 97-185). Senate passed Sept. 22. President signed Oct. 6, 1981.

PL 97-56 (HR 2218) Convey certain National Forest Systems lands to Douglas County, Nev. SANTINI, D-Nev. — 2/26/81 — House Interior and Insular Affairs reported July 9 (H Rept 97-169). House passed July 20. Senate Environment and Natural Resources reported Aug. 27 (S Rept 97-186). Senate passed Sept. 22. President signed Oct. 6, 1981.

PL 97-57 (H J Res 263) Designate May 6, 1982, as "National Recognition Day for Nurses." LUJAN, R-N.M. — 5/20/81 — House Post

Office and Civil Service discharged. House passed July 30. Senate Judiciary reported Sept. 23. Senate passed Sept. 25. President signed Oct. 9, 1981.

PL 97-58 (HR 4084) Amend the Marine Mammal Protection Act of 1972 to exempt pure seine yellow-fin tuna fishing from the zero-mortality goals of such Act. Require the continuation of the best marine mammal safety techniques that are economically and technologically practical for tuna fishing in lieu of such zero-mortality goals, and allow management of marine mammals by state agencies under specified circumstances. BREAUX, D-La. — 7/9/81 — House Merchant Marine and Fisheries reported Sept. 16 (H Rept 97-228). House passed, under suspension of the rules, Sept. 21. Senate Commerce, Science and Transportation discharged. Senate passed Sept. 29. President signed Oct. 9, 1981.

PL 97-59 (S 1033) Establish a lateral seaward boundary between the states of North Carolina and South Carolina. HOLLINGS, D-S.C. — 4/29/81 — Senate Judiciary reported June 3 (S Rept 97-129). Senate passed June 9. House Judiciary discharged. House passed Sept. 29. President signed Oct. 9, 1981.

PL 97-60 (S 1181) Increase the pay allowances and benefits for members of the uniformed services. JEPSEN, R-Iowa — 5/14/81 — Senate Armed Services reported July 8 (S Rept 97-146). Senate passed Sept. 11. House passed, amended, Sept. 15. House agreed to conference report Oct. 7 (H Rept 97-265). Senate agreed to conference report Oct. 7. President signed Oct. 14, 1981.

PL 97-61 (S J Res 98) Designate Oct. 16, 1981, as "World Food Day." LEAHY, D-Vt. — 7/15/81 — Senate Judiciary reported July 30. Senate passed July 31. House Post Office and Civil Service discharged. House passed Sept. 30. President signed Oct. 14, 1981.

PL 97-62 (S 1712) Extend the time for conducting the referendum with respect to the national marketing quota for wheat for the marketing year beginning June 1, 1982, from Oct. 15, 1981, to Nov. 15, 1981. DOLE, R-Kan. — 10/7/81 — Senate passed Oct. 7. House passed Oct. 7. President signed Oct. 14, 1981.

PL 97-63 (S 304) Establish a national tourism policy and an independent government agency to carry out the national tourism policy. PRESSLER, R-S.D. — 1/27/81 — Senate passed Jan. 27. House Energy and Commerce discharged. House passed, amended, July 28. Senate agreed to conference report Sept. 29 (H Rept 97-252). House agreed to conference report, under suspension of the rules, Oct. 1. President signed Oct. 16, 1981.

PL 97-64 (HR 4048) Grant the consent of Congress to the agreement between the states of Kansas and Missouri establishing their mutual boundary in the vicinity of the French Bottoms near Saint Joseph, Mo. and Elwood, Kan. JEFFRIES, R-Kan. — 6/26/81 — House Judiciary reported Sept. 22 (H Rept 97-239). House passed, under suspension of the rules, Sept. 29. Senate passed Oct. 1. President signed Oct. 16, 1981.

PL 97-65 (HR 3136) Amend the Foreign Assistance Act of 1961, with repect to the activities of the Overseas Private Investment Corp. BINGHAM, D-N.Y. — 4/8/81 — House Foreign Affairs reported July 23 (H Rept 97-195). House passed Sept. 22. Senate passed, amended, Sept. 25. House agreed to Senate amendment, with an amendment, Sept. 28. Senate agreed to House amendment, with amendments, Sept. 30. House agreed to Senate amendments Oct. 2. President signed Oct. 16, 1981.

PL 97-66 (S 917) Increase the rates of disability compensation for disabled veterans and the rates of dependency and indemnity compensation for their survivors. SIMPSON, R-Wyo. — 4/8/81 — Senate Veterans' Affairs reported July 16 (S Rept 97-153). Senate passed July 24. House passed, amended, Sept. 21. Senate agreed to House amendments, with amendments, Oct. 1. House agreed to Senate amendments Oct. 2. President signed Oct. 17, 1981.

PL 97-67 (HR 4612) Temporarily delay the Oct. 1, 1981, increase in the price support level for milk and extend the time for conducting the referendum with respect to the national marketing quota for wheat for the marketing year beginning July 1, 1982. DE LA GARZA, D-Texas — 9/29/81 — House passed Oct. 1. Senate Agriculture, Nutrition and Forestry reported Oct. 6. Senate passed Oct. 19. President signed Oct. 20, 1981.

PL 97-68 (S 1191) Reimburse commercial fishermen of the United States for certain losses incurred as the result of the seizure of their vessels by foreign nationals. PACKWOOD, R-Ore. — 5/18/81 — Senate Commerce, Science and Transportation reported May 15 (S Rept 97-69). Senate passed Aug. 3. House passed, amended, Sept. 21. Senate agreed to House amendments, with amendments, Sept. 30. House agreed to Senate amendments Oct. 7. President signed Oct. 26, 1981.

PL 97-69 (S 1224) Strengthen and clarify the congressional franking law. STEVENS, R-Alaska — 5/19/81 — Senate Governmental Affairs reported July 17 (S Rept 97-155). Senate passed July 20. House passed, under suspension of the rules, Oct. 13. President signed Oct. 26, 1981.

PL 97-70 (S 1687) Make a technical amendment to the International

Investment Survey Act of 1976. BAKER, R-Tenn. — 9/30/81 — Senate passed Sept. 30. House Foreign Affairs discharged. House passed Oct. 14. President signed Oct. 26, 1981.

PL 97-71 (H J Res 268) Designate Oct. 23, 1981, as "Hungarian Freedom Fighters Day." FENWICK, R-N.J. — 5/28/81 — House Post Office and Civil Service discharged. House passed Oct. 14. Senate Judiciary reported Oct. 20. Senate passed Oct. 20. President signed Oct. 26, 1981.

PL 97-72 (HR 3499) Improve certain programs provided by the federal government to veterans. MOTTL, D-Ohio — 5/7/81 — House Veterans' Affairs reported May 19 (H Rept 97-79). House passed, under suspension of the rules, June 2. Senate passed, amended, June 16. House agreed to Senate amendments, with amendments, Oct. 2. Senate agreed to House amendments Oct. 16. President signed Nov. 3, 1981.

PL 97-73 (S 1209) Authorize funds for the United States Park Service for non-performing arts functions of the John F. Kennedy Center for the Performing Arts. STAFFORD, R-Vt. — 5/18/81 — Senate Environment and Public Works reported May 15 (S Rept 97-115). Senate passed June 2. House passed Oct. 20. President signed Nov. 3, 1981.

PL 97-74 (S 1000) Authorize funds through fiscal year 1983 and supplemental funds for fiscal year 1981 for the National Transportation Safety Board. PACKWOOD, R-Ore. — 4/23/81 — Senate Commerce, Science and Transportation reported April 23 (S Rept 97-41). Senate passed May 4. House passed, amended, Oct. 13. Senate agreed to House amendments Oct. 21. President signed Nov. 3, 1981.

PL 97-75 (S J Res 4) Request the president to designate that week in November which includes Thanksgiving Day as National Family Week. BURDICK, D-N.D. — 1/5/81 — Senate Judiciary reported Sept. 15. Senate passed Sept. 16. House Post Office and Civil Service discharged. House passed Oct. 20. President signed Nov. 3, 1981.

PL 97-76 (HR 4608) Continue in effect any authority provided under the Department of Justice Authorizations Act, 1980, until Feb. 1, 1982. RODINO, D-N.J. — 9/28/81 — House Judiciary discharged. House passed Sept. 29. Senate passed, amended, Sept. 30. House disagreed to Senate amendment Oct. 6. Senate insisted on its amendment Oct. 7. House receded and concurred in Senate amendment, with an amendment, Oct. 27. Senate agreed to House amendment Oct. 30. President signed Nov. 5, 1981.

PL 97-77 (S 1322) Designate the Department of Agriculture Boll Weevil Research Laboratory building located adjacent to the campus of Mississippi State University, Starkville, Miss., as the Robey Wentworth Harned Laboratory. COCHRAN, R-Miss. — 6/3/81 — Senate Agriculture, Nutrition and Forestry reported Oct. 28 (S Rept 97-255). Senate passed Nov. 9. House passed Nov. 12. President signed Nov. 13, 1981.

PL 97-78 (HR 3975) Create a procedure for issuance of a combined hydrocarbon lease in special tar sand areas. SANTINI, D-Nev. — 6/18/81 — House Interior and Insular Affairs reported July 13 (H Rept 97-174). House passed, under suspension of the rules, July 14. Senate Energy and Natural Resources reported Oct. 23 (S Rept 97-250). Senate passed Oct. 29. President signed Nov. 16, 1981.

PL 97-79 (S 736) Make it illegal to import or trade in live fish or wildlife or animal products which are taken, transported, or sold in violation of state or foreign laws. CHAFEE, R-R.I. — 3/19/81 — Senate Environment and Public Works reported May 21 (S Rept 97-123). Senate Judiciary discharged. Senate passed July 24. House Merchant Marine and Fisheries discharged. House passed Nov. 4. President signed Nov. 16, 1981.

PL 97-80 (S 999) Authorize funds for fiscal years 1982, 1983 and 1984 for the U.S. Fire Administration. PACKWOOD, R-Ore. — 4/23/81 — Senate Commerce, Science and Transportation reported April 23 (S Rept 97-39). Senate passed April 29. House passed, amended, Oct. 13. Senate agreed to House amendments, with an amendment, Oct. 16. House agreed to Senate amendment, with amendments, Nov. 5. Senate agreed to House amendments Nov. 5. President signed Nov. 20, 1981.

PL 97-81 (HR 4792) Amend Title 10, United States Code, to improve the military justice system. NICHOLS, D-Ala. — 10/20/81 — House Armed Services reported Oct. 29 (H Rept 97-306). House passed, under suspension of the rules, Nov. 4. Senate passed Nov. 5. President signed Nov. 20, 1981.

PL 97-82 (HR 4734) Grant a federal charter to Italian-American War Veterans of the United States. ANNUNZIO, D-Ill. — 10/14/81 — House Judiciary reported Oct. 22 (H Rept 97-287). House passed, under suspension of the rules, Oct. 26. Senate Judiciary reported Nov. 10. Senate passed Nov. 10. President signed Nov. 20, 1981.

PL 97-83 (S 195) Grant a federal charter to United States Submarine Veterans of World War II. GOLDWATER, R-Ariz. — 1/22/81 — Senate Judiciary reported April 10 (S Rept 97-37). Senate passed April 27. House Judiciary discharged. House passed, amended, Oct. 26.

Senate agreed to House amendments Nov. 9. President signed Nov. 20, 1981.

PL 97-84 (S 1672) Increase the membership of the United States Holocaust Memorial Council. BOSCHWITZ, R-Minn. — 9/28/81 — Senate Judiciary reported Oct. 6. Senate passed Oct. 7. House Interior and Insular Affairs reported Nov. 2 (H Rept 97-308, Part I). House Administration and Post Office and Civil Service discharged. House passed, amended, Nov. 4. Senate agreed to House amendment Nov. 13. President signed Nov. 20, 1981.

PL 97-85 (H J Res 368) Make further continuing appropriations for fiscal year 1982. WHITTEN, D-Miss. — 11/23/81 — House passed Nov. 23. Senate passed Nov. 23. President signed Nov. 23, 1981.

PL 97-86 (S 815) Authorize funds for fiscal year 1982 for the military procurement programs of the Department of Defense. TOWER, R-Texas — 3/26/81 — Senate Armed Services reported May 6 (S Rept 97-58). Senate passed May 14. House passed, amended, July 16. Senate agreed to conference report Nov. 5 (H Rept 97-311). House agreed to conference report Nov. 17. President signed Dec. 1, 1981.

PL 97-87 (S 1133) Authorize funds for fiscal year 1982 for the National Advisory Committee on Oceans and Atmosphere. PACKWOOD, R-Ore. — 5/7/81 — Senate Commerce, Science and Transportation reported May 7 (S Rept 97-59). Senate passed May 14. House passed Nov. 17. President signed Dec. 1, 1981.

PL 97-88 (HR 4144) Appropriate funds for fiscal year 1982 for energy and water development programs. BEVILL, D-Ala. — 7/14/81 — House Appropriations reported July 14 (H Rept 97-177). House passed July 24. Senate Appropriations reported Oct. 28 (S Rept 97-256). Senate passed, amended, Nov. 5. House agreed to conference report Nov. 20 (H Rept 97-345). Senate agreed to conference report Nov. 21. President signed Dec. 4, 1981.

PL 97-89 (HR 3454) Authorize funds for fiscal year 1982 for the intelligence activities of the United States government. BOLAND, D-Mass. — 5/6/81 — House Intelligence reported May 19 (H Rept 97-101, Part I). House Armed Services reported May 19 (H Rept 97-101, Part II). House passed under suspension of the rules, July 13. Senate passed, amended, July 16. House agreed to conference report Nov. 18 (H Rept 97-332). Senate agreed to conference report Nov. 18. President signed Dec. 4, 1981.

PL 97-90 (HR 3413) Authorize funds for fiscal years 1982 and 1983 for national security programs of the Department of Energy. STRATTON, D-N.Y. — 5/4/81 — House Armed Services reported May 15 (H Rept 97-45). House passed June 11. Senate Armed Services discharged. Senate passed, amended, Nov. 3. House agreed to conference report Nov. 19 (H Rept 97-342). Senate agreed to conference report Nov. 19. President signed Dec. 4, 1981.

PL 97-91 (HR 4522) Appropriate funds for fiscal year 1982 for the District of Columbia government. DIXON, D-Calif. — 9/17/81 — House Appropriations reported Sept. 17 (H Rept 97-235). House passed Sept. 22. Senate Appropriations reported Oct. 27 (S Rept 97-254). Senate passed, amended, Oct. 30. House agreed to conference report Nov. 18 (H Rept 97-327). Senate agreed to conference report Nov. 19. President signed Dec. 4, 1981.

PL 97-92 (H J Res 370) Make further continuing appropriations for fiscal year 1982. WHITTEN, D-Miss. — 12/9/81 - House Appropriations reported Dec. 9 (H Rept 97-372). House passed Dec. 10. Senate passed Dec. 11. President signed Dec. 15, 1981.

PL 97-93 (S J Res 115) Approve the president's recommendation waiver of law to expedite the construction and initial operation of the Alaska Natural Gas Transportation System. McCLURE, R-Idaho — 10/19/81 — Senate Energy and Natural Resources reported Nov. 16 (S Rept 97-272). Senate passed Nov. 19. House passed Dec. 10. President signed Dec. 15, 1981.

PL 97-94 (HR 4591) Amend the mineral leasing laws of the U.S. to provide for uniform treatment of certain receipts under such laws. HAMMERSCHMIDT, R-Ark. — 9/24/81 — House Armed Services reported Oct. 27 (H Rept 97-296). House passed, under suspension of the rules, Nov. 4. Senate Energy and Natural Resources discharged. Senate passed Dec. 1. President signed Dec. 17, 1981.

PL 97-95 (S J Res 136) Validate the effectiveness of a plan for the use or distribution of funds appropriated to pay a judgment awarded to the San Carlos Tribe of Arizona. DeCONCINI, D-Ariz. — 12/15/81 — Senate passed Dec. 15. House passed Dec. 16. President signed Dec. 17, 1981.

PL 97-96 (S 1098) Authorize fiscal 1982 appropriations for the National Aeronautics and Space Administration for research and development, construction of facilities, and research and program management. PACKWOOD, R-Ore. — 5/4/81 — Senate Commerce, Science and Transportation reported May 15 (S Rept 97-100). Senate passed May 21. House passed, amended, June 23. Senate agreed to conference

report Nov. 23 (H Rept 97-351). House agreed to conference report Dec. 8. President signed Dec. 21, 1981.

PL 97-97 (HR 4845) Designate the building known as the Lincoln Federal Building and Courthouse in Lincoln, Nebraska, as the "Robert V. Denney Federal Building and Courthouse." HOWARD, D-N.J. — 10/27/81 — House Public Works and Transportation reported Nov. 12 (H Rept 97-325). House passed Nov. 16. Senate passed Dec. 11. President signed Dec. 21, 1981.

PL 97-98 (S 884) Revise and extend programs to provide price support and production incentives for farmers to assure an abundance of food and fiber. HELMS, R-N.C. — 4/7/81 — Senate Agriculture, Nutrition and Forestry reported May 27 (S Rept 97-126). Senate passed Sept. 18. House passed, amended, Oct. 22. Senate agreed to conference report Dec. 10 (H Rept 97-377). House agreed to conference report Dec. 16. President signed Dec. 22, 1981.

PL 97-99 (HR 3455) Authorize certain construction at military installations for fiscal year 1982. BRINKLEY, D-Ga. — 5/6/81 — House Armed Services reported May 15 (H Rept 97-44). House passed June 4. Senate Armed Services discharged. Senate passed, amended, Nov. 5. House agreed to conference report Dec. 8 (H Rept 97-362). Senate agreed to conference report Dec. 8. President signed Dec. 23, 1981.

PL 97-100 (HR 4035) Make appropriations for the Department of Interior and related agencies for fiscal year 1982. YATES, D-Ill. — 6/25/81 — House Appropriations reported June 25 (H Rept 97-163). House passed July 22. Senate Appropriations reported July 23 (S Rept 97-166). Senate passed, amended, Oct. 27. House agreed to conference report Nov. 12 (H Rept 97-315). Senate agreed to conference report Dec. 10. President signed Dec. 23, 1981.

PL 97-101 (HR 4034) Make appropriations for the Department of Housing and Urban Development, and for sundry independent agencies for fiscal year 1982. BOLAND, D-Mass. — 6/25/81 — House Appropriations reported June 25 (H Rept 97-162). Senate Appropriations reported July 23 (S Rept 97-163). Senate passed, amended, July 30. House agreed to conference report Sept. 15 (H Rept 97-222). Senate agreed to conference report Nov. 21. House agreed to Senate amendment to House amendment to Senate amendment Dec. 10. President signed Dec. 23, 1981.

PL 97-102 (HR 4209) Make appropriations for the Department of Transportation and related agencies for fiscal year 1982. BENJAMIN, D-Ind. — 7/17/81 — House Appropriations reported July 17 (H Rept 97-186). House passed Sept. 10. Senate Appropriations reported Oct. 27 (S Rept 97-253). Senate passed, amended, Nov. 3. House agreed to conference report Dec. 14 (H Rept 97-331). Senate agreed to conference report Dec. 14. President signed Dec. 23, 1981.

PL 97-103 (HR 4119) Make appropriations for Agriculture, Rural Development and related agencies programs for fiscal year 1982. WHITTEN, D-Miss. — 7/9/81 — House Appropriations reported July 9 (H Rept 97-172). House passed July 27. Senate Appropriations reported Oct. 22 (S Rept 97-248). Senate passed, amended, Oct. 30. House agreed to conference report Dec. 15 (H Rept 97-313). Senate agreed to conference report Dec. 15. President signed Dec. 23, 1981.

PL 97-104 (HR 3484) Provide for the minting of half dollars with a design emblematic of the 250th anniversary of the birth of George Washington. BARNARD, D-Ga. — 5/7/81 — House passed, under suspension of the rules, May 19. Senate Banking, Housing and Urban Affairs reported Nov. 20 (S Rept 97-277). Senate passed Dec. 9. President signed Dec. 23, 1981.

PL 97-105 (HR 4910) Amend the District of Columbia Self-Government and Governmental Reorganization Act and the charter of the District of Columbia with respect to the provisions allowing the District of Columbia to issue general obligation bonds and notes and revenue bonds, notes and other obligations. BLILEY, R-Va. — 11/5/81 — House District of Columbia reported Dec. 4 (H Rept 97-361). House passed Dec. 14. Senate passed Dec. 15. President signed Dec. 23, 1981.

PL 97-106 (HR 4241) Make appropriations for military construction for the Department of Defense for fiscal year 1982. GINN, D-Ga. — 7/23/81 — House Appropriations reported July 23 (H Rept 97-193). House passed Sept. 16. Senate Appropriations reported Nov. 12 (S Rept 97-271). Senate passed, amended, Dec. 4. House agreed to conference report Dec. 15 (H Rept 97-400). Senate agreed to conference report Dec. 15. President signed Dec. 23, 1981.

PL 97-107 (HR 5273) Allow the George Washington University Higher Education Facilities Revenue Bond Act of 1981 of the District of Columbia to take effect immediately. BARNES, D-Md. — 12/16/81 — House passed Dec. 16. Senate passed Dec. 16. President signed Dec. 23, 1981.

PL 97-108 (HR 1465) Require the Congressional Budget Office to prepare a cost estimate of House and Senate reported legislation which has certain economic consequences to state and local governments in compliance with such legislation. ZEFERETTI, D-N.Y. — 1/28/81 — House Rules reported Dec. 3 (H Rept 97-353). House passed, under suspension of the rules, Dec. 8. Senate Budget discharged. Senate

passed Dec. 16. President signed Dec. 23, 1981.

PL 97-109 (S 1003) Amend Title III of the Marine Protection and Research Sanctuaries Act of 1972 to authorize appropriations for such title for fiscal years 1982 and 1983. PACKWOOD, R-Ore. — 4/23/81 — Senate Commerce, Science and Transportation reported April 23 (S Rept 97-44). Senate passed May 4. House Merchant Marine and Fisheries discharged. House passed, amended, July 13. Senate agreed to House amendments, with an amendment Dec. 11. House agreed to Senate amendment to House amendments, Dec. 14. President signed Dec. 26, 1981.

PL 97-110 (HR 4879) Amend the Federal Deposit Insurance Act to clarify the treatment of international banking facility deposits for purposes of deposit insurance assessments. SCHUMER, D-N.Y. — 11/2/81 — House Banking, Finance and Urban Affairs discharged. House passed, under suspension of the rules, Nov. 17. Senate Banking, Housing and Urban Affairs reported Dec. 15. Senate passed, amended, Dec. 15. House agreed to Senate amendments Dec. 16. President signed Dec. 26, 1981.

PL 97-111 (S 1948) Permit certain Farm Credit Administration regulations to become effective which expand the authority of financing institutions other than farm credit institutions, to borrow from and discount with federal intermediate credit banks. BAKER, R-Tenn. 12/11/81 — Senate passed Dec. 11. House passed Dec. 14. President signed Dec. 26, 1981.

PL 97-112 (HR 4894) Authorize the Secretary of the Interior to disburse certain trust funds of the Lac Courte Oreilles Band of Lake Superior Chippewa Indians of Wisconsin. OBEY, D-Wis. — 11/4/81 — House Interior and Insular Affairs reported Nov. 20 (H Rept 97-348). House passed Dec. 15. Senate passed, amended, Dec. 15. House agreed to Senate amendments Dec. 16. President signed Dec. 29, 1981.

PL 97-113 (S 1196) Amend the Foreign Assistance Act of 1961 and the Arms Export Control Act to authorize appropriations for development and security assistance programs for fiscal year 1982. PERCY, R-Ill. — 5/18/81 — Senate Foreign Relations reported May 15 (S Rept 97-83). Senate passed Oct. 22. House passed, amended, Dec. 9. Senate agreed to conference report Dec. 15 (H Rept 97-413). House agreed to conference report Dec. 16. President signed Dec. 29, 1981.

PL 97-114 (HR 4995) Make appropriations for the Department of Defense for fiscal year 1982. ADDABBO, D-N.Y. — 11/16/81 — House Appropriations reported Nov. 6 (H Rept 97-333). House passed Nov. 18. Senate passed, amended, Dec. 4. House agreed to conference report Dec. 15 (H Rept 97-410). Senate agreed to conference report Dec. 15. President signed Dec. 29, 1981.

PL 97-115 (S 1086) Extend and revise the Older Americans Act of 1965. DENTON, R-Ala. — 4/30/81 — Senate Labor and Human Resources reported July 20 (S Rept 97-159). Senate passed Nov. 2. House passed, amended, Nov. 20. Senate agreed to conference report Dec. 11 (H Rept 97-386). House agreed to conference report Dec. 16. President signed Dec. 29, 1981.

PL 97-116 (HR 4327) Amend the Immigration and Nationality Act. MAZZOLI, D-Ky. — 7/29/81 — House Judiciary reported Oct. 2 (H Rept 97-264). House passed, under suspension of the rules, Oct. 13. Senate passed, amended, Dec. 16. House agreed to Senate amendments Dec. 16. President signed Dec. 29, 1981.

PL 97-117 (HR 4503) Amend the Federal Water Pollution Control Act to authorize funds for fiscal year 1982. ROE, D-N.J. — 9/16/81 — House Public Works and Transportation reported Oct. 9 (H Rept 97-270). House passed Oct. 27. Senate passed, amended, Oct. 29. House agreed to conference report Dec. 16 (H Rept 97-408). Senate agreed to conference report Dec. 16. President signed Dec. 29, 1981.

PL 97-118 (HR 4506) Name the lock and dam authorized to replace locks and dam 26, Mississippi River, Alton, Ill., as "Melvin Price Lock and Dam." ANNUNZIO, D-Ill. — 9/17/81 — House Public Works and Transportation reported Nov. 12 (H Rept 97-322). House passed Nov. 16. Senate Environment and Public Works discharged. Senate passed Dec. 16. President signed Dec. 29, 1981.

PL 97-119 (HR 5159) Amend the Internal Revenue Code of 1954 to provide a temporary increase in the tax imposed on producers of coal, in order to restore the Black Lung Disability Trust Fund. ROSTENKOWSKI, D-Ill. — 12/10/81 — House Ways and Means reported Dec. 14 (H Rept 97-406, Part I). House passed, under suspension of the rules, Dec. 15. Senate passed, amended, Dec. 16. House agreed to Senate amendments Dec. 16. President signed Dec. 29, 1981.

PL 97-120 (S 657) Designate the Department of Commerce Building in Washington, D.C. as the "Herbert Clark Hoover Department of Commerce Building." HATFIELD, R-Ore. — 3/10/81 — Senate Environment and Public Works reported Dec. 3 (S Rept 97-286). Senate passed Dec. 4. House Public Works and Transportation discharged. House passed Dec. 16. President signed Dec. 29. 1981.

PL 97-121 (HR 4559) Make appropriations for Foreign Assistance and related programs for fiscal year 1982. LONG, D-Md. — 9/22/81 — House Appropriations reported Sept. 22 (H Rept 97-245). House passed Dec. 11. Senate passed, amended, Dec. 11. Senate agreed to

conference report Dec. 16 (H Rept 97-416). House agreed to conference report Dec. 16. President signed Dec. 29, 1981.

PL 97-122 (HR 4431) Provide for the designation of the E. Michael Roll Post Office in Forestville, Md. HOYER, D-Md. — 9/9/81 — House Post Office and Civil Service discharged. House passed Sept. 23. Senate Environment and Public Works discharged. Senate Governmental Affairs reported Dec. 9. Senate passed Dec. 15. President signed Dec. 29, 1981.

PL 97-123 (HR 4331) Amend the Omnibus Reconciliation Act of 1981 to restore minimum benefits under the Social Security Act. BOLLING, D-Mo. — 7/30/81 — House passed July 31. Senate passed, amended, Oct. 15. Senate agreed to conference report Dec. 15 (H Rept 97-409). House agreed to conference report Dec. 16. President signed Dec. 29, 1981.

PL 97-124 (HR 3799) Provide that the federal tort claims procedure be the exclusive remedy in medical malpractice actions and proceedings resulting from federally authorized National Guard training activities. KASTENMEIER, D-Wis. — 6/4/81 — House Judiciary reported Dec. 10 (H Rept 97-384, Part I). House Armed Services discharged. House passed Dec. 15. Senate Judiciary discharged. Senate passed Dec. 16. President signed Dec. 29. 1981.

PL 97-125 (S 1192) Amend the National Visitor Center Facilities Act of 1968 to provide for the rehabilitation and completion of Union Station in Washington, D.C., as primarily a transportation center. PACKWOOD, R-Ore. — 5/18/81 — Senate Commerce, Science and Transportation reported May 15 (S Rept 97-70). Senate Environment and Public Works reported Nov. 10 (S Rept 97-269). Senate passed Nov. 23. House passed Dec. 16. President signed Dec. 29, 1981.

PL 97-126 (HR 2494) Designate the John Archibald Campbell Federal Building-United States Courthouse in Mobile, Ala. EDWARDS, R-Ala. — 3/12/81 — House Public Works and Transportation reported Nov. 12 (H Rept 97-321). House passed Nov. 16. Senate Environment and Public Works discharged. Senate passed Dec. 16. President signed Dec. 29, 1981.

PL 97-127 (S 1946) Provide for the final settlement of certain claims against Czechoslovakia. MOYNIHAN, D-N.Y. — 12/11/81 — Senate passed Dec. 11. House passed, amended, Dec. 15. Senate agreed to House amendments, with amendments, Dec. 16. House agreed to Senate amendments to House amendments Dec. 16. President signed Dec. 29, 1981.

PL 97-128 (S 1493) Deauthorize several projects within the jurisdiction of the Army Corps of Engineers. ABDNOR, R-S.D. — 7/16/81 — Senate Environment and Public Works reported Nov. 12 (S Rept 97-270). Senate passed Nov. 18. House passed, amended, Nov. 23. Senate agreed to House amendments Dec. 16. President signed Dec. 29, 1981.

PL 97-129 (S 1211) Extend the Toxic Substance Control Act for one year. GORTON, R-Wash. — 5/18/81 — Senate Environment and Public Works reported May 15 (S Rept 97-117). Senate passed June 2. House passed, amended, Sept. 29. Senate agreed to conference report Dec. 16. (H Rept 97-373). House agreed to conference report Dec. 16. President signed Dec. 29, 1981.

PL 97-130 (S 271) Repeal section 222 of the Communications Act of 1934. GOLDWATER, R-Ariz. — 1/27/81 — Senate Commerce, Science and Transportation reported March 12 (S Rept 97-25). Senate passed June 22. House Energy and Commerce discharged. House passed, amended, Dec. 8. Senate agreed to House amendments, with amendments, Dec. 16. House agreed to Senate amendments to House amendments Dec. 16. President signed Dec. 29, 1981.

PL 97-131 (S J Res 34) Provide for the designation of the week of Feb. 15, 1982, as National Patriotism Week. GOLDWATER, R-Ariz. — 2/24/81 — Senate Judiciary reported Nov. 10. Senate passed Nov. 16. House Post Office and Civil Service discharged. House passed Dec. 16. President signed Dec. 29, 1981.

PL 97-132 (S J Res 100) Authorize the participation of the United States in a multinational force and observers to implement the Treaty of Peace between Egypt and Israel. PERCY, R-Ill. — 7/22/81 — Senate Foreign Relations reported Sept. 30 (S Rept 97-197). Senate passed Oct. 7. House Foreign Affairs discharged. House passed, amended, Nov. 19. Senate agreed to House amendments, with an amendment, Dec. 16. House agreed to Senate amendment to House amendments Dec. 16. President signed Dec. 29, 1981.

PL 97-133 (H J Res 377) Provide for the convening of the second session of the 97th Congress. FOLEY, D-Wash. — 12/15/81 — House passed Dec. 15. Senate passed Dec. 16. President signed Dec. 29, 1981.

PL 97-134 (HR 3210) Amend the Surface Transportation Assistance Act of 1978, to establish obligation limitations for fiscal year 1982. ANDERSON, D-Calif. — 4/10/81 — House Public Works and Transportation reported May 19 (H Rept 97-92). House passed Sept. 24. Senate passed, amended, Nov. 16. House agreed to Senate amendment, with amendment, Dec. 15. Senate agreed to House amendment to Senate amendment Dec. 16. President signed Dec. 29, 1981.

PL 97-135 (S J Res 57) Provide for the designation of Feb. 7-13, 1982, as "National Scleroderma Week." SYMMS, D-Idaho — 3/26/81 — Sen-

PUBLIC LAWS

ate Judiciary reported Nov. 17. Senate passed Nov. 18. House Post Office and Civil Service discharged. House passed Dec. 16. President signed Dec. 29, 1981.

PL 97-136 (S 831) Authorize appropriations for the Coast Guard for fiscal year 1982. PACKWOOD, R-Ore. — 3/31/81 — Senate Commerce, Science and Transportation reported April 23 (S Rept 97-45). Senate passed May 4. House passed, amended, Dec. 14. Senate agreed to House amendments, with amendments, Dec. 16. House agreed to Senate amendments to House amendments Dec. 16. President signed Dec. 29, 1981.

PL 97-137 (HR 2241) Provide for the establishment of the Bandon Marsh National Wildlife Refuge, Coos County, Oregon. WEAVER, D-Ore. — 3/2/81 — House Merchant Marine and Fisheries reported Dec. 9 (H Rept 97-376). House passed, under suspension of the rules, Dec. 15. Senate Energy and Natural Resources discharged. Senate passed Dec. 16. President signed Dec. 29, 1981.

PL 97-138 (S J Res 84) Proclaim March 19, 1982, as "National Energy Education Day." DeCONCINI, D-Ariz. — 5/21/81 — Senate Judiciary reported July 21. Senate passed July 24. House Post Office and Civil Service discharged. House passed Dec. 16. President signed Dec. 29, 1981.

PL 97-139 (S J Res 121) Provide for the designation of the year 1982 as the "Bicentennial Year of the American Bald Eagle" and the designation of June 20, 1982, as "National Bald Eagle Day." CHAFEE, R-R.I. — 11/9/81 — Senate Judiciary reported Dec. 8. Senate passed Dec. 15. House Post Office and Civil Service discharged. House passed Dec. 16. President signed Dec. 29, 1981.

PL 97-140 (HR 779) Authorize the Secretary of the Army to contract with the Tarrant County Water Control and Improvement District Number One and the city of Weatherford, Texas, for the use of water supply storage in Benbrook Lake. WRIGHT, D-Texas — 1/6/81 — House Public Works and Transportation reported May 19 (H Rept 97-95). House passed June 1. Senate Environment and Public Works discharged. Senate passed, amended, Dec. 16. House agreed to Senate amendments Dec. 16. President signed Dec. 29, 1981.

PL 97-141 (S 1551) Amend Title 5, United States Code, to extend the period within which physicians comparability contracts may be entered into. MATHIAS, R-Md. — 7/30/81 — Senate Governmental Affairs reported Oct. 29 (S Rept 97-257). Senate passed Nov. 9. House passed, amended, Nov. 17. Senate agreed to House amendments Dec. 15. President signed Dec. 29, 1981.

PL 97-142 (HR 4926) Authorize the Secretary of the Army to acquire, by purchase or condemnation, such interests in oil, gas, coal, and other minerals owned or controlled by the Osage Tribe of Indians as are needed for construction of the Skiatook Lake, Osage County, Okla. JONES, D-Okla. — 11/6/81 — House Interior and Insular Affairs reported Dec. 10 (H Rept 97-382, Part I). House Public Works and Transportation discharged. House passed, under suspension of the rules, Dec. 15. Senate passed Dec. 15. President signed Dec. 29, 1981.

PL 97-143 (S 1976) Clarify the authority of U.S. Capitol police to extend protection beyond the Capitol grounds, subject to the direction of the Capitol Police Board. STEVENS, R-Alaska — 12/16/81 — Senate passed Dec. 16. House passed Dec. 16. President signed Dec. 29, 1981.

PL 97-144 (S J Res 117) Authorize and request the president to designate the week of Jan. 17-23, 1982, as "National Jaycee Week." BOREN, D-Okla. — 10/28/81 — Senate Judiciary reported Dec. 15. Senate passed Dec. 16. House passed Dec. 16. President signed Dec. 29, 1981.

PL 97-145 (HR 3567) Authorize appropriations for fiscal years 1982 and 1983 to carry out the purposes of the Export Administration Act of 1979. BINGHAM, D-N.Y. — 5/13/81 — House Foreign Affairs reported May 19 (H Rept 97-57). House passed, under suspension of the rules, June 8. Senate passed, amended, Nov. 12. Senate agreed to conference report Dec. 15 (H Rept 97-401). House agreed to conference report Dec. 16. President signed Dec. 29, 1981. ∎

SENATE ROLL-CALL VOTES

CQ Senate Votes 1 - 6

Corresponding to Congressional Record Votes 1, 2, 3, 4, 5, 6

	1	2	3	4	5	6
ALABAMA						
Denton	Y	Y	Y	Y	Y	Y
Heflin	Y	Y	Y	Y	Y	Y
ALASKA						
Murkowski	Y	Y	Y	Y	Y	Y
Stevens	Y	Y	Y	Y	Y	Y
ARIZONA						
Goldwater	Y	N	Y	Y	Y	Y
DeConcini	Y	Y	Y	Y	Y	Y
ARKANSAS						
Bumpers	Y	Y	Y	Y	Y	Y
Pryor	Y	Y	Y	Y	Y	Y
CALIFORNIA						
Hayakawa	Y	Y	Y	Y	Y	Y
Cranston	Y	Y	Y	Y	Y	Y
COLORADO						
Armstrong	Y	Y	Y	Y	Y	Y
Hart	Y	Y	Y	Y	Y	Y
CONNECTICUT						
Weicker	Y	Y	N	Y	Y	Y
Dodd	Y	Y	Y	Y	Y	Y
DELAWARE						
Roth	Y	Y	Y	Y	Y	Y
Biden	Y	Y	Y	Y	Y	Y
FLORIDA						
Hawkins	Y	Y	Y	Y	Y	Y
Chiles	Y	Y	Y	Y	Y	Y
GEORGIA						
Mattingly	Y	Y	Y	Y	Y	Y
Nunn	?	?	?	?	?	?
HAWAII						
Inouye	Y	?	Y	Y	Y	Y
Matsunaga	Y	Y	Y	Y	Y	Y
IDAHO						
McClure	Y	Y	Y	Y	Y	Y
Symms	Y	?	Y	Y	Y	Y
ILLINOIS						
Percy	Y	Y	Y	Y	Y	Y
Dixon	Y	Y	Y	Y	Y	Y
INDIANA						
Lugar	Y	Y	Y	Y	Y	Y
Quayle	Y	Y	Y	Y	Y	Y
IOWA						
Grassley	Y	Y	Y	Y	Y	Y
Jepsen	Y	Y	Y	Y	Y	Y
KANSAS						
Dole	Y	Y	Y	Y	Y	Y
Kassebaum	Y	Y	Y	Y	Y	Y
KENTUCKY						
Ford	Y	Y	Y	Y	Y	Y
Huddleston	Y	Y	Y	Y	Y	Y
LOUISIANA						
Johnston	Y	Y	Y	Y	Y	Y
Long	Y	N	Y	Y	Y	Y
MAINE						
Cohen	Y	Y	Y	Y	Y	Y
Mitchell	Y	Y	Y	Y	Y	Y
MARYLAND						
Mathias	Y	Y	Y	Y	Y	Y
Sarbanes	Y	Y	N	Y	Y	Y
MASSACHUSETTS						
Kennedy	Y	Y	Y	Y	Y	Y
Tsongas	Y	Y	N	Y	Y	Y
MICHIGAN						
Levin	Y	Y	N	Y	Y	+
Riegle	Y	Y	N	Y	Y	Y
MINNESOTA						
Boschwitz	Y	Y	Y	Y	Y	Y
Durenberger	Y	Y	Y	Y	Y	Y
MISSISSIPPI						
Cochran	Y	Y	Y	Y	Y	Y
Stennis	Y	Y	Y	Y	Y	Y
MISSOURI						
Danforth	Y	Y	Y	Y	Y	Y
Eagleton	Y	Y	Y	Y	Y	Y
MONTANA						
Baucus	Y	Y	Y	Y	Y	Y
Melcher	Y	Y	Y	Y	Y	Y
NEBRASKA						
Exon	Y	Y	Y	Y	Y	Y
Zorinsky	Y	Y	Y	Y	Y	Y
NEVADA						
Laxalt	Y	Y	Y	Y	Y	Y
Cannon	Y	Y	Y	Y	Y	Y
NEW HAMPSHIRE						
Humphrey	Y	Y	Y	Y	Y	Y
Rudman	Y	Y	Y	Y	Y	Y
NEW JERSEY						
Bradley	Y	Y	Y	Y	Y	Y
Williams	Y	Y	Y	Y	Y	Y
NEW MEXICO						
Domenici	Y	Y	Y	Y	Y	Y
Schmitt	Y	Y	Y	Y	Y	Y
NEW YORK						
D'Amato	Y	Y	Y	Y	Y	Y
Moynihan	Y	Y	Y	Y	Y	Y
NORTH CAROLINA						
East	N	Y	Y	Y	Y	Y
Helms	N	Y	Y	Y	Y	Y
NORTH DAKOTA						
Andrews	Y	Y	Y	Y	Y	Y
Burdick	Y	Y	Y	Y	Y	Y
OHIO						
Glenn	Y	Y	Y	Y	Y	Y
Metzenbaum	Y	Y	Y	Y	Y	Y
OKLAHOMA						
Nickles	Y	Y	Y	Y	Y	Y
Boren	Y	Y	Y	Y	Y	Y
OREGON						
Hatfield	Y	Y	Y	Y	Y	Y
Packwood	Y	Y	Y	Y	Y	Y
PENNSYLVANIA						
Heinz	Y	Y	Y	Y	Y	Y
Specter	Y	Y	Y	Y	Y	Y
RHODE ISLAND						
Chafee	Y	Y	Y	Y	Y	Y
Pell	Y	Y	Y	Y	Y	Y
SOUTH CAROLINA						
Thurmond	Y	Y	Y	Y	Y	Y
Hollings	Y	Y	Y	Y	Y	Y
SOUTH DAKOTA						
Abdnor	Y	Y	Y	Y	Y	Y
Pressler	Y	Y	Y	Y	Y	Y
TENNESSEE						
Baker	Y	Y	Y	Y	Y	Y
Sasser	Y	Y	Y	Y	Y	Y
TEXAS						
Tower	Y	Y	Y	Y	Y	Y
Bentsen	Y	Y	Y	Y	Y	Y
UTAH						
Garn	Y	Y	Y	Y	Y	Y
Hatch	Y	Y	Y	Y	Y	Y
VERMONT						
Stafford	Y	Y	Y	Y	Y	Y
Leahy	Y	Y	v	Y	Y	Y
VIRGINIA						
Warner	Y	Y	Y	Y	Y	Y
Byrd*	Y	Y	Y	Y	Y	Y
WASHINGTON						
Gorton	Y	Y	Y	Y	Y	Y
Jackson	Y	Y	Y	Y	Y	Y
WEST VIRGINIA						
Byrd	Y	Y	N	Y	Y	Y
Randolph	Y	?	Y	Y	Y	Y
WISCONSIN						
Kasten	Y	Y	Y	Y	Y	Y
Proxmire	Y	Y	Y	Y	Y	Y
WYOMING						
Simpson	Y	Y	Y	Y	Y	Y
Wallop	Y	Y	Y	Y	Y	Y

KEY

Y	Voted for (yea).
#	Paired for.
+	Announced for.
N	Voted against (nay)
X	Paired against.
-	Announced against.
P	Voted "present."
C	Voted "present" to avoid possible conflict of interest.
?	Did not vote or otherwise make a position known.

Democrats   *Republicans*

*Byrd elected as an independent.

1. Weinberger Nomination. Confirmation of President Reagan's nomination of Caspar W. Weinberger of California to be secretary of defense. Confirmed 97-2: R 51-2; D 46-0 (ND 32-0; SD 14-0), Jan. 20, 1981. A "yea" was a vote supporting the president's position.

2. Haig Nomination. Baker, R-Tenn., motion to instruct the sergeant-at-arms to request the attendance of absent senators. Motion agreed to 94-2: R 51-1; D 43-1 (ND 30-0; SD 13-1), Jan. 21, 1981.

3. Haig Nomination. Confirmation of President Reagan's nomination of Alexander M. Haig Jr. of Connecticut as secretary of state. Confirmed 93-6: R 52-1; D 41-5 (ND 27-5; SD 14-0), Jan. 21, 1981. A "yea" was a vote supporting the president's position.

4. Schweiker Nomination. Confirmation of President Reagan's nomination of Richard S. Schweiker of Pennsylvania to be secretary of health and human services. Confirmed 99-0: R 53-0; D 46-0 (ND 32-0; SD 14-0), Jan. 21, 1981. A "yea" was a vote supporting the president's position.

5. Brock Nomination. Confirmation of President Reagan's nomination of William E. Brock III of Tennessee to be U.S. trade representative. Confirmed 99-0: R 53-0; D 46-0 (ND 32-0; SD 14-0) Jan. 21, 1981. A "yea" was a vote supporting the president's position.

6. Regan Nomination. Confirmation of President Reagan's nomination of Donald T. Regan of New Jersey to be secretary of the Treasury. Confirmed 98-0: R 53-0; D 45-0 (ND 31-0; SD 14-0), Jan. 21, 1981. A "yea" was a vote supporting the president's position.

	7	8	9	10	11	12	13	14
ALABAMA								
Denton	Y	Y	Y	Y	Y	Y	Y	Y
Heflin	Y	Y	Y	Y	Y	Y	Y	Y
ALASKA								
Murkowski	Y	Y	Y	Y	Y	Y	Y	Y
Stevens	Y	Y	Y	Y	Y	Y	Y	Y
ARIZONA								
Goldwater	N	Y	Y	Y	Y	Y	Y	Y
DeConcini	Y	Y	Y	Y	Y	Y	Y	Y
ARKANSAS								
Bumpers	Y	Y	Y	Y	Y	Y	N	Y
Pryor	Y	Y	Y	Y	Y	Y	Y	Y
CALIFORNIA								
Hayakawa	Y	Y	Y	Y	Y	Y	Y	Y
Cranston	Y	Y	Y	Y	Y	N	Y	Y
COLORADO								
Armstrong	Y	Y	Y	Y	Y	Y	Y	Y
Hart	Y	Y	Y	Y	Y	Y	Y	Y
CONNECTICUT								
Weicker	N	Y	Y	Y	Y	Y	Y	Y
Dodd	Y	Y	Y	Y	Y	Y	N	N
DELAWARE								
Roth	Y	Y	Y	Y	Y	Y	Y	Y
Biden	Y	Y	Y	Y	Y	Y	N	Y
FLORIDA								
Hawkins	Y	Y	Y	Y	Y	Y	Y	Y
Chiles	Y	Y	Y	Y	Y	Y	Y	Y
GEORGIA								
Mattingly	Y	Y	Y	Y	Y	Y	Y	Y
Nunn	?	?	?	?	?	?	?	?-
HAWAII								
Inouye	?	Y	Y	Y	Y	Y	Y	Y
Matsunaga	?	Y	Y	Y	Y	Y	Y	Y
IDAHO								
McClure	Y	Y	Y	Y	Y	Y	Y	Y
Symms	Y	Y	Y	Y	Y	Y	Y	Y
ILLINOIS								
Percy	Y	Y	Y	Y	Y	Y	Y	Y
Dixon	Y	Y	Y	Y	Y	Y	Y	Y
INDIANA								
Lugar	Y	Y	Y	Y	Y	Y	Y	Y
Quayle	Y	Y	Y	Y	Y	Y	Y	Y
IOWA								
Grassley	Y	Y	Y	Y	Y	Y	Y	Y
Jepsen	Y	Y	Y	Y	Y	Y	Y	Y
KANSAS								
Dole	Y	Y	Y	Y	Y	Y	Y	Y
Kassebaum	Y	Y	Y	Y	Y	Y	Y	Y
KENTUCKY								
Ford	Y	Y	Y	Y	Y	Y	Y	Y
Huddleston	Y	Y	Y	Y	Y	Y	Y	Y
LOUISIANA								
Johnston	Y	Y	Y	Y	Y	Y	Y	Y
Long	Y	Y	Y	Y	Y	Y	Y	Y
MAINE								
Cohen	Y	Y	Y	Y	Y	Y	Y	Y
Mitchell	Y	Y	Y	Y	Y	Y	Y	Y
MARYLAND								
Mathias	?	Y	Y	Y	Y	Y	?	?
Sarbanes	Y	Y	Y	Y	Y	Y	N	Y
MASSACHUSETTS								
Kennedy	Y	Y	Y	Y	Y	Y	N	N
Tsongas	Y	Y	Y	Y	Y	Y	Y	Y
MICHIGAN								
Levin	Y	Y	Y	Y	Y	Y	N	Y
Riegle	Y	P	Y	Y	Y	Y	N	Y
MINNESOTA								
Boschwitz	Y	Y	Y	Y	Y	Y	Y	Y
Durenberger	Y	Y	Y	Y	Y	Y	Y	Y
MISSISSIPPI								
Cochran	Y	Y	Y	Y	Y	Y	Y	Y
Stennis	Y	Y	Y	Y	Y	Y	Y	Y
MISSOURI								
Danforth	Y	Y	Y	Y	Y	Y	Y	Y
Eagleton	Y	Y	Y	Y	Y	Y	Y	Y
MONTANA								
Baucus	Y	Y	Y	Y	Y	Y	Y	Y
Melcher	Y	Y	Y	Y	Y	Y	Y	Y
NEBRASKA								
Exon	Y	Y	Y	Y	Y	Y	Y	Y
Zorinsky	N	Y	Y	Y	Y	Y	Y	Y
NEVADA								
Laxalt	?	+	+	+	+	+	+	+
Cannon	Y	Y	Y	Y	Y	Y	Y	Y
NEW HAMPSHIRE								
Humphrey	Y	Y	Y	Y	Y	Y	Y	Y
Rudman	Y	Y	Y	Y	Y	Y	Y	Y
NEW JERSEY								
Bradley	Y	Y	Y	Y	Y	Y	Y	Y
Williams	Y	Y	Y	Y	Y	Y	+	Y
NEW MEXICO								
Domenici	Y	Y	Y	Y	Y	Y	Y	Y
Schmitt	Y	Y	Y	Y	Y	Y	Y	Y
NEW YORK								
D'Amato	Y	Y	Y	Y	Y	Y	Y	Y
Moynihan	Y	Y	Y	Y	Y	Y	N	Y
NORTH CAROLINA								
East	Y	Y	Y	Y	Y	Y	Y	Y
Helms	?	Y	Y	Y	Y	Y	Y	Y
NORTH DAKOTA								
Andrews	Y	Y	Y	Y	Y	Y	Y	Y
Burdick	Y	Y	Y	Y	Y	Y	Y	Y
OHIO								
Glenn	Y	Y	Y	Y	Y	Y	Y	Y
Metzenbaum	Y	Y	Y	Y	Y	Y	N	Y
OKLAHOMA								
Nickles	Y	Y	Y	Y	Y	Y	Y	Y
Boren	?	Y	Y	Y	Y	Y	Y	Y
OREGON								
Hatfield	Y	Y	Y	Y	Y	Y	Y	Y
Packwood	Y	Y	Y	Y	Y	Y	Y	Y
PENNSYLVANIA								
Heinz	Y	Y	Y	Y	Y	Y	Y	Y
Specter	Y	Y	Y	Y	Y	Y	Y	Y
RHODE ISLAND								
Chafee	Y	Y	Y	Y	Y	Y	Y	Y
Pell	Y	Y	Y	Y	Y	Y	Y	Y
SOUTH CAROLINA								
Thurmond	Y	Y	Y	Y	Y	Y	Y	Y
Hollings	Y	Y	Y	Y	Y	Y	Y	Y
SOUTH DAKOTA								
Abdnor	Y	Y	Y	Y	Y	Y	Y	Y
Pressler	Y	Y	Y	Y	Y	Y	Y	Y
TENNESSEE								
Baker	Y	Y	Y	Y	Y	Y	Y	Y
Sasser	Y	Y	Y	Y	Y	Y	Y	Y
TEXAS								
Tower	Y	Y	Y	Y	Y	Y	Y	Y
Bentsen	Y	Y	Y	Y	Y	Y	Y	Y
UTAH								
Garn	Y	Y	Y	Y	Y	Y	Y	Y
Hatch	+	Y	Y	Y	Y	Y	Y	Y
VERMONT								
Stafford	Y	Y	Y	Y	Y	Y	+	+
Leahy	Y	Y	Y	Y	Y	Y	N	Y
VIRGINIA								
Warner	Y	Y	Y	Y	Y	Y	Y	Y
Byrd*	Y	Y	Y	Y	Y	Y	Y	Y
WASHINGTON								
Gorton	Y	Y	Y	Y	Y	Y	Y	Y
Jackson	Y	Y	Y	Y	Y	Y	Y	Y
WEST VIRGINIA								
Byrd	Y	Y	Y	Y	Y	Y	Y	Y
Randolph	Y	Y	Y	Y	Y	Y	Y	Y
WISCONSIN								
Kasten	Y	Y	Y	Y	Y	Y	Y	Y
Proxmire	Y	N	Y	N	Y	Y	N	N
WYOMING								
Simpson	Y	Y	Y	Y	Y	Y	Y	Y
Wallop	Y	Y	Y	Y	Y	Y	Y	Y

KEY

Y	Voted for (yea).
#	Paired for.
+	Announced for.
N	Voted against (nay)
X	Paired against.
-	Announced against.
P	Voted "present."
C	Voted "present" to avoid possible conflict of interest.
?	Did not vote or otherwise make a position known.

Democrats   *Republicans*

*Byrd elected as an independent.

---

7. Smith Nomination. Baker, R-Tenn., motion that the sergeant-at-arms be instructed to request the attendance of absent senators. Motion agreed to 89-3: R 47-2; D 42-1 (ND 29-1; SD 13-0), Jan. 22, 1981.

8. Smith Nomination. Confirmation of President Reagan's nomination of William French Smith of California as attorney general. Confirmed 96-1: R 52-0; D 44-1 (ND 30-1; SD 14-0), Jan. 22, 1981. A "yea" was a vote supporting the president's position.

9. Block Nomination. Confirmation of President Reagan's nomination of John R. Block of Illinois to be secretary of agriculture. Confirmed 98-0: R 52-0; D 46-0 (ND 32-0; SD 14-0), Jan. 22, 1981. A "yea" was a vote supporting the president's position.

10. Baldrige Nomination. Confirmation of President Reagan's nomination of Malcolm Baldrige of Connecticut to be secretary of commerce. Confirmed 97-1: R 52-0; D 45-1 (ND 31-1; SD 14-0), Jan. 22, 1981. A "yea" was a vote supporting the president's position.

11. Pierce Nomination. Confirmation of President Reagan's nomination of Samuel R. Pierce Jr. of New York to be secretary of housing and urban development. Confirmed 98-0: R 52-0; D 46-0 (ND 32-0; SD 14-0), Jan. 22, 1981. A "yea" was a vote supporting the president's position.

12. Lewis Nomination. Confirmation of President Reagan's nomination of Andrew L. Lewis Jr. of Pennsylvania to be transportation secretary. Confirmed 98-0: R 52-0; D 46-0 (ND 32-0; SD 14-0), Jan. 22, 1981. A "yea" was a vote supporting the president's position.

13. Watt Nomination. Confirmation of President Reagan's nomination of James G. Watt of Colorado to be secretary of the interior. Confirmed 83-12: R 50-0; D 33-12 (ND 20-11; SD 13-1), Jan. 22, 1981. A "yea" was a vote supporting the president's position.

14. Edwards Nomination. Confirmation of President Reagan's nomination of James B. Edwards of South Carolina to be secretary of energy. Confirmed 93-3: R 50-0; D 43-3 (ND 29-3; SD 14-0), Jan. 22, 1981. A "yea" was a vote supporting the president's position.

CQ Senate Votes 15 - 18

Corresponding to Congressional Record Votes 15, 16, 17, 18

	15 16 17 18		15 16 17 18		15 16 17 18
ALABAMA		**IOWA**		**NEW HAMPSHIRE**	
Denton	Y Y Y ?	*Grassley*	Y Y Y Y	*Humphrey*	Y Y Y Y
Heflin	Y Y Y Y	*Jepsen*	Y ? ? Y	*Rudman*	Y Y Y Y
ALASKA		**KANSAS**		**NEW JERSEY**	
Murkowski	Y Y Y Y	*Dole*	Y Y Y Y	Bradley	Y ? ? Y
Stevens	? Y Y Y	*Kassebaum*	Y Y Y Y	Williams	Y Y Y Y
ARIZONA		**KENTUCKY**		**NEW MEXICO**	
Goldwater	Y Y Y ?	Ford	Y Y Y Y	*Domenici*	Y Y Y Y
DeConcini	N Y Y ?	Huddleston	Y Y Y ?	*Schmitt*	Y Y Y Y
ARKANSAS		**LOUISIANA**		**NEW YORK**	
Bumpers	Y Y Y Y	Johnston	Y Y Y ?	*D'Amato*	Y Y Y Y
Pryor	Y Y Y ?	Long	Y Y Y Y	Moynihan	Y Y Y Y
CALIFORNIA		**MAINE**		**NORTH CAROLINA**	
Hayakawa	Y Y Y Y	*Cohen*	Y Y Y Y	*East*	Y Y Y Y
Cranston	Y Y Y Y	Mitchell	Y Y Y ?	*Helms*	Y Y Y Y
COLORADO		**MARYLAND**		**NORTH DAKOTA**	
Armstrong	Y Y Y Y	*Mathias*	? Y Y Y	*Andrews*	Y Y Y Y
Hart	Y Y Y Y	Sarbanes	Y Y Y Y	Burdick	Y Y Y Y
CONNECTICUT		**MASSACHUSETTS**		**OHIO**	
Weicker	Y Y Y ?	Kennedy	Y Y Y Y	Glenn	Y Y Y Y
Dodd	Y Y Y Y	Tsongas	Y Y Y Y	Metzenbaum	Y Y Y Y
DELAWARE		**MICHIGAN**		**OKLAHOMA**	
Roth	Y Y Y Y	Levin	Y Y Y Y	*Nickles*	Y Y Y Y
Biden	Y Y Y Y	Riegle	Y Y Y Y	Boren	Y Y Y Y
FLORIDA		**MINNESOTA**		**OREGON**	
Hawkins	Y Y Y Y	*Boschwitz*	Y Y Y Y	*Hatfield*	Y Y Y Y
Chiles	Y Y Y ?	*Durenberger*	Y Y Y Y	*Packwood*	Y Y Y Y
GEORGIA		**MISSISSIPPI**		**PENNSYLVANIA**	
Mattingly	Y Y Y Y	*Cochran*	Y ? ? ?	*Heinz*	Y Y Y Y
Nunn	? Y Y Y	Stennis	Y Y Y Y	*Specter*	Y Y Y Y
HAWAII		**MISSOURI**		**RHODE ISLAND**	
Inouye	Y Y Y Y	*Danforth*	Y Y Y Y	*Chafee*	Y Y Y Y
Matsunaga	Y Y Y Y	Eagleton	Y Y Y Y	Pell	+ Y Y Y
IDAHO		**MONTANA**		**SOUTH CAROLINA**	
McClure	Y Y Y Y	Baucus	Y Y Y Y	*Thurmond*	Y Y Y Y
Symms	Y Y Y Y	Melcher	Y Y Y ?	Hollings	Y Y Y ?
ILLINOIS		**NEBRASKA**		**SOUTH DAKOTA**	
Percy	+ Y Y +	Exon	Y Y Y Y	*Abdnor*	Y Y Y Y
Dixon	Y Y Y Y	Zorinsky	Y Y Y ?	*Pressler*	Y Y Y ?
INDIANA		**NEVADA**		**TENNESSEE**	
Lugar	Y Y Y Y	*Laxalt*	+ + + +	*Baker*	Y Y Y Y
Quayle	Y Y Y Y	Cannon	Y Y Y Y	Sasser	Y Y Y Y

KEY

- Y Voted for (yea).
- # Paired for.
- + Announced for.
- N Voted against (nay)
- X Paired against.
- - Announced against.
- P Voted "present."
- C Voted "present" to avoid possible conflict of interest.
- ? Did not vote or otherwise make a position known.

	15 16 17 18
TEXAS	
Tower	Y Y ? Y
Bentsen	Y ? ? Y
UTAH	
Garn	Y Y Y Y
Hatch	Y Y Y Y
VERMONT	
Stafford	+ Y Y +
Leahy	Y Y Y Y
VIRGINIA	
Warner	Y Y Y Y
Byrd*	Y Y Y Y
WASHINGTON	
Gorton	Y Y Y Y
Jackson	Y Y Y Y
WEST VIRGINIA	
Byrd	Y Y Y Y
Randolph	Y Y Y Y
WISCONSIN	
Kasten	Y Y Y Y
Proxmire	N Y Y Y
WYOMING	
Simpson	Y Y + +
Wallop	? Y Y ?

Democrats *Republicans*

*Byrd elected as an independent.

15. Bell Nomination. Confirmation of President Reagan's nomination of Terrel H. Bell of Utah to be secretary of education. Confirmed 90-2: R 47-0; D 43-2 (ND 29-2; SD 14-0), Jan. 22, 1981. A "yea" was a vote supporting the president's position.

16. Casey Nomination. Confirmation of President Reagan's nomination of William J. Casey of New York to be director of central intelligence. Confirmed 95-0: R 50-0; D 45-0 (ND 31-0; SD 14-0), Jan. 27, 1981. A "yea" was a vote supporting the president's position.

17. Stockman Nomination. Confirmation of President Reagan's nomination of David A. Stockman of Michigan to be director of the Office of Management and Budget. Confirmed 93-0: R 48-0; D 45-0 (ND 31-0; SD 14-0), Jan. 27, 1981. A "yea" was a vote supporting the president's position.

18. Kirkpatrick Nomination. Confirmation of President Reagan's nomination of Jeane J. Kirkpatrick of Maryland as United States representative to the United Nations. Confirmed 81-0: R 43-0; D 38-0 (ND 28-0; SD 10-0), Jan. 29, 1981. A "yea" was a vote supporting the president's position.

	19 20 21		19 20 21		19 20 21	KEY
ALABAMA		**IOWA**		**NEW HAMPSHIRE**		Y Voted for (yea).
Denton	Y Y Y	*Grassley*	Y Y Y	*Humphrey*	Y Y Y	# Paired for.
Heflin	Y Y Y	*Jepsen*	Y Y Y	*Rudman*	Y Y Y	+ Announced for.
ALASKA		**KANSAS**		**NEW JERSEY**		N Voted against (nay).
Murkowski	Y Y Y	*Dole*	Y Y Y	Bradley	Y Y Y	X Paired against.
Stevens	Y Y ?	*Kassebaum*	Y Y Y	Williams	Y Y Y	- Announced against.
ARIZONA		**KENTUCKY**		**NEW MEXICO**		P Voted "present."
Goldwater	Y Y Y	Ford	Y Y Y	*Domenici*	Y Y Y	C Voted "present" to avoid possible conflict of interest.
DeConcini	N Y Y	Huddleston	N Y Y	*Schmitt*	Y Y Y	
ARKANSAS		**LOUISIANA**		**NEW YORK**		? Did not vote or otherwise make a position known.
Bumpers	Y Y Y	Johnston	Y Y Y	*D'Amato*	Y Y Y	
Pryor	Y Y Y	Long	Y Y Y	Moynihan	Y Y Y	
CALIFORNIA		**MAINE**		**NORTH CAROLINA**		
Hayakawa	Y Y Y	*Cohen*	Y Y Y	*East*	Y N Y	
Cranston	Y Y Y	Mitchell	Y Y Y	*Helms*	Y N Y	
COLORADO		**MARYLAND**		**NORTH DAKOTA**		
Armstrong	Y Y ?	*Mathias*	Y Y Y	*Andrews*	Y Y Y	
Hart	N Y Y	Sarbanes	Y Y Y	Burdick	Y Y Y	
CONNECTICUT		**MASSACHUSETTS**		**OHIO**		
Weicker	Y Y Y	Kennedy	N Y Y	Glenn	Y Y Y	
Dodd	N Y ?	Tsongas	N Y Y	Metzenbaum	N Y Y	
DELAWARE		**MICHIGAN**		**OKLAHOMA**		
Roth	Y Y Y	Levin	Y Y Y	*Nickles*	Y Y Y	
Biden	Y Y Y	Riegle	N Y ?	Boren	Y Y Y	
FLORIDA		**MINNESOTA**		**OREGON**		
Hawkins	Y Y Y	*Boschwitz*	Y Y Y	*Hatfield*	Y Y Y	
Chiles	N Y Y	*Durenberger*	Y Y Y	*Packwood*	Y Y Y	
GEORGIA		**MISSISSIPPI**		**PENNSYLVANIA**		
Mattingly	Y Y Y	*Cochran*	? ? Y	*Heinz*	Y Y Y	
Nunn	N Y Y	Stennis	Y Y Y	*Specter*	Y Y Y	
HAWAII		**MISSOURI**		**RHODE ISLAND**		
Inouye	Y Y Y	*Danforth*	Y Y Y	*Chafee*	Y Y Y	
Matsunaga	Y Y Y	Eagleton	N Y Y	Pell	N Y Y	
IDAHO		**MONTANA**		**SOUTH CAROLINA**		
McClure	Y N Y	Baucus	N Y Y	*Thurmond*	Y Y Y	
Symms	Y N Y	Melcher	? ? ?	Hollings	N Y Y	
ILLINOIS		**NEBRASKA**		**SOUTH DAKOTA**		
Percy	Y Y Y	Exon	Y Y Y	*Abdnor*	Y Y Y	
Dixon	Y Y Y	Zorinsky	Y Y Y	*Pressler*	Y Y Y	
INDIANA		**NEVADA**		**TENNESSEE**		
Lugar	Y Y Y	*Laxalt*	Y Y Y	*Baker*	Y Y Y	
Quayle	Y Y Y	Cannon	? + +	Sasser	Y Y Y	

	19 20 21
TEXAS	
Tower	Y Y Y
Bentsen	Y Y Y
UTAH	
Garn	Y Y Y
Hatch	Y N Y
VERMONT	
Stafford	Y Y Y
Leahy	N Y Y
VIRGINIA	
Warner	Y Y Y
Byrd*	Y Y Y
WASHINGTON	
Gorton	Y Y Y
Jackson	Y Y Y
WEST VIRGINIA	
Byrd	N Y Y
Randolph	Y Y Y
WISCONSIN	
Kasten	Y N Y
Proxmire	N Y Y
WYOMING	
Simpson	Y Y Y
Wallop	Y Y Y

Democrats   *Republicans*

Byrd elected as an independent.

19. Donovan Nomination. Confirmation of President Reagan's nomination of Raymond J. Donovan of New Jersey to be secretary of labor. Confirmed 80-17: R 52-0; D 28-17 (ND 17-13; SD 11-4), Feb. 3, 1981. A "yea" was a vote supporting the president's position.

20. Carlucci Nomination. Confirmation of President Reagan's nomination of Frank C. Carlucci of Virginia as deputy secretary of defense. Confirmed 91-6: R 46-6; D 45-0 (ND 30-0; SD 15-0), Feb. 3, 1981. A "yea" was a vote supporting the president's position.

21. Inman Nomination. Confirmation of President Reagan's nomination of Adm. Bobby R. Inman as deputy director of central intelligence. Confirmed 94-0: R 51-0; D 43-0 (ND 28-0; SD 15-0), Feb. 5, 1981. A "yea" was a vote supporting the president's position.

CQ Senate Votes 22 - 23

Corresponding to Congressional Record Votes 22, 23

	22 23			22 23			22 23	KEY
ALABAMA			**IOWA**			**NEW HAMPSHIRE**		Y Voted for (yea).
Denton	Y Y		*Grassley*	Y Y		*Humphrey*	Y Y	# Paired for.
Heflin	N N		*Jepsen*	Y Y		*Rudman*	Y Y	+ Announced for.
ALASKA			**KANSAS**			**NEW JERSEY**		N Voted against (nay)
Murkowski	Y Y		*Dole*	Y Y		Bradley	N Y	X Paired against.
Stevens	# ?		*Kassebaum*	Y Y		Williams	N Y	- Announced against.
ARIZONA			**KENTUCKY**			**NEW MEXICO**		P Voted "present."
Goldwater	Y Y		Ford	N N		*Domenici*	Y Y	C Voted "present" to avoid possible conflict of interest.
DeConcini	N N		Huddleston	N N		*Schmitt*	Y Y	
ARKANSAS			**LOUISIANA**			**NEW YORK**		? Did not vote or otherwise make a position known.
Bumpers	N Y		Johnston	N Y		*D'Amato*	Y Y	
Pryor	N N		Long	Y Y		Moynihan	? ?	
CALIFORNIA			**MAINE**			**NORTH CAROLINA**		
Hayakawa	Y Y		*Cohen*	? ?		*East*	Y N	
Cranston	N Y		Mitchell	N Y		*Helms*	Y Y	
COLORADO			**MARYLAND**			**NORTH DAKOTA**		
Armstrong	X N		*Mathias*	Y ?		*Andrews*	Y Y	
Hart	N Y		Sarbanes	N Y		Burdick	N Y	22 23
CONNECTICUT			**MASSACHUSETTS**			**OHIO**		
Weicker	Y Y		Kennedy	N Y		Glenn	? ?	**TEXAS**	
Dodd	N Y		Tsongas	N ?		Metzenbaum	N N	*Tower*	Y Y
DELAWARE			**MICHIGAN**			**OKLAHOMA**		Bentsen	N Y
Roth	Y Y		Levin	N Y		*Nickles*	Y Y	**UTAH**	
Biden	N Y		Riegle	N Y		Boren	N N	*Garn*	Y Y
FLORIDA			**MINNESOTA**			**OREGON**		*Hatch*	Y Y
Hawkins	Y Y		*Boschwitz*	Y Y		*Hatfield*	Y Y	**VERMONT**	
Chiles	N Y		*Durenberger*	Y Y		*Packwood*	Y ?	*Stafford*	Y Y
GEORGIA			**MISSISSIPPI**			**PENNSYLVANIA**		Leahy	N Y
Mattingly	Y N		*Cochran*	Y Y		*Heinz*	Y Y	**VIRGINIA**	
Nunn	N N		Stennis	N Y		*Specter*	Y Y	*Warner*	Y Y
HAWAII			**MISSOURI**			**RHODE ISLAND**		Byrd*	Y N
Inouye	N Y		*Danforth*	Y Y		*Chafee*	Y Y	**WASHINGTON**	
Matsunaga	N Y		Eagleton	N Y		Pell	N Y	*Gorton*	Y Y
IDAHO			**MONTANA**			**SOUTH CAROLINA**		Jackson	N Y
McClure	Y Y		Baucus	N N		*Thurmond*	Y Y	**WEST VIRGINIA**	
Symms	Y Y		Melcher	- -		Hollings	N Y	Byrd	N Y
ILLINOIS			**NEBRASKA**			**SOUTH DAKOTA**		Randolph	N Y
Percy	Y Y		Exon	N N		*Abdnor*	Y Y	**WISCONSIN**	
Dixon	N N		Zorinsky	N N		*Pressler*	Y Y	*Kasten*	Y Y
INDIANA			**NEVADA**			**TENNESSEE**		Proxmire	N N
Lugar	Y Y		*Laxalt*	Y Y		*Baker*	Y Y	**WYOMING**	
Quayle	Y Y		Cannon	? ?		Sasser	N N	*Simpson*	Y Y
								Wallop	Y Y

Democrats *Republicans*

*Byrd elected as an independent.

22. HR 1553. Debt Limit Increase. Baker, R-Tenn., motion to table (kill) the Byrd, D-W.Va., amendment to increase the public debt limit to $963 billion through Sept. 30, 1981. Motion agreed to 52-41: R 50-0; D 2-41 (ND 0-28; SD 2-13), Feb. 6, 1981. A "yea" was a vote supporting the president's position.

23. HR 1553. Debt Limit Increase. Passage of the bill to increase the public debt limit to $985 billion through Sept. 30, 1981. Passed (thus cleared for the president) 73-18: R 46-3; D 27-15 (ND 20-7; SD 7-8), Feb. 6, 1981. A "yea" was a vote supporting the president's position.

	24 25			24 25			24 25		KEY
ALABAMA			**IOWA**			**NEW HAMPSHIRE**			Y Voted for (yea).
Denton	Y Y		*Grassley*	Y Y		*Humphrey*	Y Y		# Paired for.
Heflin	Y Y		*Jepsen*	Y Y		*Rudman*	Y Y		+ Announced for.
ALASKA			**KANSAS**			**NEW JERSEY**			N Voted against (nay)
Murkowski	Y Y		*Dole*	? ?		Bradley	? ?		X Paired against.
Stevens	Y Y		*Kassebaum*	Y Y		Williams	Y Y		- Announced against.
ARIZONA			**KENTUCKY**			**NEW MEXICO**			P Voted "present."
Goldwater	Y Y		Ford	N Y		*Domenici*	Y Y		C Voted "present" to avoid pos-
DeConcini	Y Y		Huddleston	N Y		*Schmitt*	Y Y		sible conflict of interest.
ARKANSAS			**LOUISIANA**			**NEW YORK**			? Did not vote or otherwise
Bumpers	N Y		Johnston	Y Y		*D'Amato*	Y Y		make a position known.
Pryor	N Y		Long	Y Y		Moynihan	Y Y		
CALIFORNIA			**MAINE**			**NORTH CAROLINA**			
Hayakawa	Y Y		*Cohen*	? ?		*East*	Y Y		
Cranston	Y Y		Mitchell	N Y		*Helms*	Y Y		
COLORADO			**MARYLAND**			**NORTH DAKOTA**			24 25
Armstrong	Y Y		*Mathias*	Y Y		*Andrews*	Y Y		
Hart	N Y		Sarbanes	N Y		Burdick	Y Y		**TEXAS**
CONNECTICUT			**MASSACHUSETTS**			**OHIO**			*Tower*	Y Y
Weicker	Y Y		Kennedy	N Y		Glenn	N Y		Bentsen	Y Y
Dodd	N Y		Tsongas	? ?		Metzenbaum	Y Y		**UTAH**
DELAWARE			**MICHIGAN**			**OKLAHOMA**			*Garn*	Y Y
Roth	Y Y		Levin	N Y		*Nickles*	Y Y		*Hatch*	Y Y
Biden	N Y		Riegle	N Y		Boren	N Y		**VERMONT**
FLORIDA			**MINNESOTA**			**OREGON**			*Stafford*	Y Y
Hawkins	Y Y		*Boschwitz*	Y Y		*Hatfield*	Y Y		Leahy	N Y
Chiles	? ?		*Durenberger*	Y Y		*Packwood*	Y Y		**VIRGINIA**
GEORGIA			**MISSISSIPPI**			**PENNSYLVANIA**			*Warner*	Y Y
Mattingly	Y Y		*Cochran*	Y Y		*Heinz*	Y Y		Byrd*	Y Y
Nunn	Y Y		Stennis	Y Y		*Specter*	Y Y		**WASHINGTON**
HAWAII			**MISSOURI**			**RHODE ISLAND**			*Gorton*	Y Y
Inouye	N Y		*Danforth*	Y Y		*Chafee*	Y Y		Jackson	Y Y
Matsunaga	N Y		Eagleton	N Y		Pell	Y Y		**WEST VIRGINIA**
IDAHO			**MONTANA**			**SOUTH CAROLINA**			Byrd	N Y
McClure	Y Y		Baucus	N Y		*Thurmond*	Y Y		Randolph	Y Y
Symms	Y Y		Melcher	N Y		Hollings	Y Y		**WISCONSIN**
ILLINOIS			**NEBRASKA**			**SOUTH DAKOTA**			*Kasten*	Y Y
Percy	Y Y		Exon	Y Y		*Abdnor*	Y Y		Proxmire	N Y
Dixon	N Y		Zorinsky	P Y		*Pressler*	Y Y		**WYOMING**
INDIANA			**NEVADA**			**TENNESSEE**			*Simpson*	Y Y
Lugar	Y Y		*Laxalt*	Y Y		*Baker*	Y Y		*Wallop*	Y Y
Quayle	Y Y		Cannon	Y Y		Sasser	N Y		

Democrats   *Republicans*

*Byrd elected as an independent.

24. Clark Nomination. Confirmation of President Reagan's nomination of William P. Clark of California to be deputy secretary of state. Confirmed 70-24: R 51-0; D 19-24 (ND 11-18; SD 8-6), Feb. 24, 1981. A "yea" was a vote supporting the president's position.

25. Weidenbaum Nomination. Confirmation of President Reagan's nomination of Murray L. Weidenbaum of Missouri to be a member of the Council of Economic Advisers. Confirmed 95-0: R 51-0; D 44-0 (ND 30-0; SD 14-0), Feb. 24, 1981. A "yea" was a vote supporting the president's position.

	26		26		26	KEY	
ALABAMA		**IOWA**		**NEW HAMPSHIRE**		Y	Voted for (yea).
Denton	Y	*Grassley*	Y	*Humphrey*	Y	#	Paired for.
Heflin	Y	*Jepsen*	Y	*Rudman*	Y	+	Announced for.
ALASKA		**KANSAS**		**NEW JERSEY**		N	Voted against (nay)
Murkowski	Y	*Dole*	+	Bradley	Y	X	Paired against.
Stevens	Y	*Kassebaum*	Y	Williams	Y	-	Announced against.
ARIZONA		**KENTUCKY**		**NEW MEXICO**		P	Voted "present."
Goldwater	Y	Ford	Y	*Domenici*	Y	C	Voted "present" to avoid pos-
DeConcini	Y	Huddleston	Y	*Schmitt*	Y		sible conflict of interest.
ARKANSAS		**LOUISIANA**		**NEW YORK**		?	Did not vote or otherwise
Bumpers	Y	Johnston	Y	*D'Amato*	Y		make a position known.
Pryor	Y	Long	?	Moynihan	Y		
CALIFORNIA		**MAINE**		**NORTH CAROLINA**			
Hayakawa	?	*Cohen*	Y	*East*	Y		26
Cranston	Y	Mitchell	Y	*Helms*	Y		
COLORADO		**MARYLAND**		**NORTH DAKOTA**			
Armstrong	Y	*Mathias*	Y	*Andrews*	Y	**TEXAS**	
Hart	Y	Sarbanes	Y	Burdick	Y	*Tower*	Y
CONNECTICUT		**MASSACHUSETTS**		**OHIO**		Bentsen	Y
Weicker	Y	Kennedy	Y	Glenn	Y	**UTAH**	
Dodd	Y	Tsongas	Y	Metzenbaum	Y	*Garn*	Y
DELAWARE		**MICHIGAN**		**OKLAHOMA**		*Hatch*	Y
Roth	Y	Levin	Y	*Nickles*	Y	**VERMONT**	
Biden	Y	Riegle	Y	Boren	Y	*Stafford*	Y
FLORIDA		**MINNESOTA**		**OREGON**		Leahy	Y
Hawkins	Y	*Boschwitz*	Y	*Hatfield*	Y	**VIRGINIA**	
Chiles	Y	*Durenberger*	+	*Packwood*	Y	*Warner*	Y
GEORGIA		**MISSISSIPPI**		**PENNSYLVANIA**		Byrd*	Y
Mattingly	Y	*Cochran*	Y	*Heinz*	Y	**WASHINGTON**	
Nunn	Y	Stennis	Y	*Specter*	Y	*Gorton*	Y
HAWAII		**MISSOURI**		**RHODE ISLAND**		Jackson	Y
Inouye	Y	*Danforth*	Y	*Chafee*	Y	**WEST VIRGINIA**	
Matsunaga	Y	Eagleton	?	Pell	Y	Byrd	Y
IDAHO		**MONTANA**		**SOUTH CAROLINA**		Randolph	Y
McClure	Y	Baucus	Y	*Thurmond*	Y	**WISCONSIN**	
Symms	Y	Melcher	Y	Hollings	Y	*Kasten*	?
ILLINOIS		**NEBRASKA**		**SOUTH DAKOTA**		Proxmire	Y
Percy	?	Exon	Y	*Abdnor*	Y	**WYOMING**	
Dixon	Y	Zorinsky	Y	*Pressler*	Y	*Simpson*	Y
INDIANA		**NEVADA**		**TENNESSEE**		*Wallop*	Y
Lugar	Y	*Laxalt*	Y	*Baker*	Y		
Quayle	Y	Cannon	Y	Sasser	Y		

Democrats   *Republicans*   *Byrd elected as an independent.*

26. S Res 25, 34, 39, 43, 45, 49-57, 60-62, 75. Senate Committee Funding. Adoption, *en bloc*, of 18 separate resolutions to authorize a total of $40,425,099 for 18 Senate committees for the period March 1, 1981 to Feb. 28, 1982: $1,322,000 for the Agriculture Committee, $3,791,203 for Appropriations, $1,554,400 for Armed Services, $1,583,411 for Banking, Housing and Urban Affairs, $2,693,632 for Budget, $3,171,746 for Commerce, Science and Transportation, $2,029,259 for Energy and Natural Resources, $2,166,000 for Environment and Public Works, $2,063,200 for Finance, $2,333,100 for Foreign Relations, $4,672,526 for Governmental Affairs, $4,272,722 for Judiciary, $4,004,000 for Labor and Human Resources, $748,630 for Veterans' Affairs, $901,946 for Special Aging, $902,000 for Select Small Business, $1,648,000 for Select Intelligence and $567,324 for Select Indian Affairs. Adopted 93-0: R 48-0; D 45-0 (ND 31-0; SD 14-0), March 3, 1981.

	27 28 29 30 31 32		27 28 29 30 31 32		27 28 29 30 31 32	KEY
ALABAMA		**IOWA**		**NEW HAMPSHIRE**		Y Voted for (yea).
Denton	N Y Y Y Y Y	*Grassley*	N N Y Y Y Y	*Humphrey*	N Y Y Y Y Y	# Paired for.
Heflin	N N Y Y Y Y	*Jepsen*	N N Y Y Y N	*Rudman*	N N Y Y Y Y	+ Announced for.
ALASKA		**KANSAS**		**NEW JERSEY**		N Voted against (nay).
Murkowski	N N Y Y Y Y	*Dole*	X ? + + + +	Bradley	N Y Y Y Y Y	X Paired against.
Stevens	N N Y N N N	*Kassebaum*	N N Y Y Y Y	Williams	Y N Y Y Y Y	- Announced against.
ARIZONA		**KENTUCKY**		**NEW MEXICO**		P Voted "present."
Goldwater	N N + + + +	Ford	N N Y Y Y Y	*Domenici*	N N Y Y Y Y	C Voted "present" to avoid possible conflict of interest.
DeConcini	N Y Y Y Y Y	Huddleston	Y N Y Y Y Y	*Schmitt*	N N Y Y Y Y	? Did not vote or otherwise make a position known.
ARKANSAS		**LOUISIANA**		**NEW YORK**		
Bumpers	Y N Y Y Y Y	Johnston	N Y Y Y Y Y	*D'Amato*	- N Y Y N Y	
Pryor	N N Y Y N Y	Long	N ? ? ? ? ?	Moynihan	Y Y Y Y Y Y	
CALIFORNIA		**MAINE**		**NORTH CAROLINA**		27 28 29 30 31 32
Hayakawa	N N Y Y Y Y	*Cohen*	N Y Y Y Y Y	*East*	N Y Y Y Y Y	
Cranston	? N + - - -	Mitchell	Y N Y Y Y Y	*Helms*	N Y Y Y Y Y	
COLORADO		**MARYLAND**		**NORTH DAKOTA**		**TEXAS**	
Armstrong	N Y Y Y Y Y	*Mathias*	N Y Y Y N N	*Andrews*	N N Y Y Y Y	*Tower*	N N ? ? N N
Hart	? Y Y Y Y Y	Sarbanes	Y Y Y Y Y Y	Burdick	N Y Y Y Y Y	Bentsen	N Y Y Y Y Y
CONNECTICUT		**MASSACHUSETTS**		**OHIO**		**UTAH**	
Weicker	N Y Y Y N Y	Kennedy	? Y ? ? ? ?	Glenn	N Y Y Y Y Y	*Garn*	N N Y Y Y Y
Dodd	Y Y Y Y Y Y	Tsongas	N Y Y Y Y Y	Metzenbaum	Y Y Y Y Y Y	*Hatch*	N N Y Y Y Y
DELAWARE		**MICHIGAN**		**OKLAHOMA**		**VERMONT**	
Roth	Y N Y Y Y Y	Levin	Y N Y Y Y Y	*Nickles*	N Y Y Y Y Y	*Stafford*	N Y Y Y Y Y
Biden	Y N Y Y Y Y	Riegle	Y N Y Y Y Y	Boren	N ? + Y Y Y	Leahy	Y Y Y Y Y Y
FLORIDA		**MINNESOTA**		**OREGON**		**VIRGINIA**	
Hawkins	Y N Y Y Y Y	*Boschwitz*	N Y Y Y Y Y	*Hatfield*	N N Y Y Y Y	*Warner*	N N Y Y Y Y
Chiles	N N Y Y Y Y	*Durenberger*	N Y Y Y Y Y	*Packwood*	N N Y Y Y Y	Byrd*	N Y Y Y Y Y
GEORGIA		**MISSISSIPPI**		**PENNSYLVANIA**		**WASHINGTON**	
Mattingly	N N Y Y Y Y	*Cochran*	N N Y Y Y Y	*Heinz*	N N Y Y Y Y	*Gorton*	N N Y N N N
Nunn	N Y Y Y Y Y	Stennis	N N Y Y Y Y	*Specter*	N N Y Y Y Y	Jackson	Y Y Y Y Y Y
HAWAII		**MISSOURI**		**RHODE ISLAND**		**WEST VIRGINIA**	
Inouye	Y N Y Y Y Y	*Danforth*	N N Y Y Y Y	*Chafee*	Y N Y Y Y Y	Byrd	Y Y Y Y Y Y
Matsunaga	Y N Y Y Y Y	Eagleton	Y N Y Y Y Y	Pell	Y Y Y Y Y Y	Randolph	- N Y Y Y Y
IDAHO		**MONTANA**		**SOUTH CAROLINA**		**WISCONSIN**	
McClure	N N Y Y Y Y	Baucus	N Y Y Y Y Y	*Thurmond*	N N Y Y Y Y	*Kasten*	N Y Y Y Y Y
Symms	N Y Y Y Y ?	Melcher	N Y Y N N N	Hollings	Y Y Y Y Y Y	Proxmire	Y Y Y Y Y Y
ILLINOIS		**NEBRASKA**		**SOUTH DAKOTA**		**WYOMING**	
Percy	N Y Y Y Y Y	Exon	N Y Y Y Y Y	*Abdnor*	N N Y Y Y ?	*Simpson*	N Y Y Y Y N
Dixon	N N Y Y Y Y	Zorinsky	N N Y Y Y Y	*Pressler*	N N Y Y Y Y	*Wallop*	N N Y Y Y Y
INDIANA		**NEVADA**		**TENNESSEE**			
Lugar	N N Y Y Y Y	*Laxalt*	N N Y Y Y Y	*Baker*	# N Y Y Y Y		
Quayle	N Y Y Y Y Y	Cannon	Y N Y Y Y Y	Sasser	+ N Y Y Y Y		

Democrats *Republicans*

*Byrd elected as an independent.

27. S 573. Oil Industry Antitrust Exemption. Metzenbaum, D-Ohio, amendment to nullify President Reagan's Jan. 28 order terminating immediately all remaining controls on oil and gasoline. Rejected 24-68: R 3-47; D 21-21 (ND 18-10; SD 3-11), March 10, 1981. A "nay" was a vote supporting the president's position. (The bill, to extend through Sept. 30, 1981, antitrust exemptions for oil companies participating in the programs of the International Energy Agency, subsequently was passed by voice vote.)

28. S 414. Cash Discounts. Proxmire, D-Wis., amendment to allow merchants to impose a surcharge on purchases by customers who use credit cards. Rejected 41-56: R 17-35; D 24-21 (ND 19-13; SD 5-8), March 12, 1981. (The Senate subsequently passed by voice vote the bill to repeal the existing 5 percent maximum limit on discounts merchants may offer customers for cash purchases and to extend an earlier prohibition on surcharges for purchases by credit card.)

29. S Res 89. Pay Raise for Members of Congress. Adoption of the resolution of disapproval on salary increases for members of Congress. Adopted 93-0: R 50-0; D 43-0 (ND 30-0; SD 13-0), March 12, 1981. A "yea" was a vote supporting the president's position.

30. S Res 90. Pay Raise for Legislative Branch Officials. Adoption of the resolution of disapproval on salary increases for certain members of the legislative branch. Adopted 91-3: R 48-2; D 43-1 (ND 29-1; SD 14-0), March 12, 1981. A "yea" was a vote supporting the president's position.

31. S Res 91. Pay Raise for Judicial Branch Officials. Adoption of the resolution of disapproval on salary increases for certain members of the judicial branch. Adopted 87-8: R 45-6; D 42-2 (ND 29-1; SD 13-1), March 12, 1981. A "yea" was a vote supporting the president's position.

32. S Res 92. Pay Raise for Executive Branch Officials. Adoption of the resolution of disapproval on salary increases for senior-level executive branch employees. Adopted 86-7: R 43-6; D 43-1 (ND 29-1; SD 14-0), March 12, 1981. A "yea" was a vote supporting the president's position.

	33		33		33	KEY
ALABAMA		**IOWA**		**NEW HAMPSHIRE**		Y Voted for (yea).
Denton	Y	*Grassley*	N	*Humphrey*	Y	# Paired for.
Heflin	N	*Jepsen*	Y	*Rudman*	Y	+ Announced for.
ALASKA		**KANSAS**		**NEW JERSEY**		N Voted against (nay)
Murkowski	Y	*Dole*	Y	Bradley	Y	X Paired against.
Stevens	Y	*Kassebaum*	Y	Williams	N	- Announced against.
ARIZONA		**KENTUCKY**		**NEW MEXICO**		P Voted "present."
Goldwater	Y	Ford	N	*Domenici*	Y	C Voted "present" to avoid pos-
DeConcini	N	Huddleston	N	*Schmitt*	Y	sible conflict of interest.
ARKANSAS		**LOUISIANA**		**NEW YORK**		? Did not vote or otherwise
Bumpers	N	Johnston	N	*D'Amato*	Y	make a position known.
Pryor	N	Long	N	Moynihan	Y	
CALIFORNIA		**MAINE**		**NORTH CAROLINA**		
Hayakawa	Y	*Cohen*	Y	*East*	Y	
Cranston	N	Mitchell	N	*Helms*	Y	
COLORADO		**MARYLAND**		**NORTH DAKOTA**		
Armstrong	Y	*Mathias*	Y	*Andrews*	N	

	33
TEXAS	
Tower	Y
Bentsen	N
UTAH	
Garn	Y
Hatch	Y
VERMONT	
Stafford	N
Leahy	N
VIRGINIA	
Warner	Y
Byrd*	
WASHINGTON	
Gorton	Y
Jackson	N
WEST VIRGINIA	
Byrd	N
Randolph	N
WISCONSIN	
Kasten	N
Proxmire	N
WYOMING	
Simpson	Y
Wallop	Y

CONNECTICUT		**MASSACHUSETTS**		**OHIO**	
Weicker	Y	Kennedy	N	Glenn	N
Dodd	N	Tsongas	N	Metzenbaum	N
DELAWARE		**MICHIGAN**		**OKLAHOMA**	
Roth	Y	Levin	N	*Nickles*	Y
Biden	N	Riegle	N	Boren	N
FLORIDA		**MINNESOTA**		**OREGON**	
Hawkins	Y	*Boschwitz*	N	*Hatfield*	Y
Chiles	N	*Durenberger*	N	*Packwood*	Y
GEORGIA		**MISSISSIPPI**		**PENNSYLVANIA**	
Mattingly	?	*Cochran*	Y	*Heinz*	?
Nunn	N	Stennis	N	*Specter*	Y
HAWAII		**MISSOURI**		**RHODE ISLAND**	
Inouye	N	*Danforth*	Y	*Chafee*	Y
Matsunaga	N	Eagleton	N	Pell	N
IDAHO		**MONTANA**		**SOUTH CAROLINA**	
McClure	Y	Baucus	N	*Thurmond*	Y
Symms	Y	Melcher	N	Hollings	N
ILLINOIS		**NEBRASKA**		**SOUTH DAKOTA**	
Percy	Y	Exon	N	*Abdnor*	N
Dixon	N	Zorinsky	N	*Pressler*	N
INDIANA		**NEVADA**		**TENNESSEE**	
Lugar	Y	*Laxalt*	Y	*Baker*	Y
Quayle	Y	Cannon	N	Sasser	N

Democrats *Republicans*

*Byrd elected as an independent.

33. S 509. Milk Price Supports. Baker, R-Tenn., motion to table (kill) the Melcher, D-Mont., amendment *(see vote 34, p. 11-S)* to establish a quota on the importation of casein products into the United States. Motion rejected 45-53: R 43-8; D 2-45 (ND 2-30; SD 0-15), March 17, 1981. A "yea" was a vote supporting the president's position.

	34	35	36	37	38	39	40	41
ALABAMA								
Denton	N	N	Y	Y	Y	Y	Y	Y
Heflin	Y	Y	P	P	Y	Y	Y	Y
ALASKA								
Murkowski	N	N	Y	Y	Y	Y	Y	Y
Stevens	?	?	?	?	?	?	?	Y
ARIZONA								
Goldwater	N	N	N	Y	Y	N	Y	N
DeConcini	Y	Y	N	Y	Y	Y	Y	Y
ARKANSAS								
Bumpers	Y	N	N	N	Y	Y	Y	Y
Pryor	Y	Y	Y	P	Y	Y	Y	Y
CALIFORNIA								
Hayakawa	N	N	Y	Y	Y	Y	Y	Y
Cranston	N	N	N	N	N	Y	Y	Y
COLORADO								
Armstrong	N	N	Y	Y	Y	?	Y	Y
Hart	Y	Y	Y	Y	Y	Y	Y	Y
CONNECTICUT								
Weicker	N	N	N	Y	Y	N	Y	N
Dodd	?	?	?	?	?	?	?	Y
DELAWARE								
Roth	N	N	Y	Y	Y	Y	Y	Y
Biden	N	N	N	Y	Y	Y	Y	Y
FLORIDA								
Hawkins	N	N	Y	Y	Y	Y	+	Y
Chiles	Y	Y	N	Y	Y	Y	Y	Y
GEORGIA								
Mattingly	N	N	Y	Y	Y	Y	Y	Y
Nunn	N	N	N	Y	Y	Y	Y	?
HAWAII								
Inouye	N	Y	N	Y	Y	Y	Y	Y
Matsunaga	N	N	N	N	N	Y	Y	?
IDAHO								
McClure	N	Y	N	Y	Y	Y	Y	Y
Symms	N	Y	Y	Y	Y	Y	Y	Y
ILLINOIS								
Percy	N	N	Y	Y	Y	Y	Y	Y
Dixon	N	Y	Y	Y	Y	Y	Y	Y
INDIANA								
Lugar	N	N	Y	Y	Y	?	Y	Y
Quayle	N	N	N	N	N	Y	Y	Y

	34	35	36	37	38	39	40	41
IOWA								
Grassley	Y	Y	Y	Y	Y	Y	Y	Y
Jepsen	N	N	Y	Y	Y	Y	Y	Y
KANSAS								
Dole	N	Y	Y	Y	Y	Y	Y	Y
Kassebaum	N	N	Y	Y	Y	Y	Y	Y
KENTUCKY								
Ford	Y	Y	N	Y	Y	Y	Y	Y
Huddleston	Y	Y	N	N	Y	Y	Y	Y
LOUISIANA								
Johnston	Y	Y	N	Y	Y	Y	Y	Y
Long	Y	N	N	N	Y	Y	?	?
MAINE								
Cohen	N	N	N	Y	Y	Y	Y	Y
Mitchell	Y	N	N	Y	Y	Y	Y	Y
MARYLAND								
Mathias	N	N	N	Y	Y	Y	Y	Y
Sarbanes	Y	Y	N	Y	Y	Y	Y	Y
MASSACHUSETTS								
Kennedy	N	Y	Y	N	Y	Y	Y	Y
Tsongas	N	Y	N	Y	Y	Y	Y	Y
MICHIGAN								
Levin	Y	Y	N	N	Y	Y	Y	Y
Riegle	Y	Y	P	Y	Y	Y	Y	Y
MINNESOTA								
Boschwitz	N	N	Y	Y	Y	Y	Y	Y
Durenberger	Y	N	Y	Y	Y	Y	Y	Y
MISSISSIPPI								
Cochran	N	N	Y	Y	Y	Y	Y	Y
Stennis	Y	N	Y	Y	Y	Y	Y	Y
MISSOURI								
Danforth	N	N	N	Y	Y	Y	Y	Y
Eagleton	Y	Y	Y	Y	Y	Y	Y	Y
MONTANA								
Baucus	Y	Y	Y	Y	Y	Y	Y	Y
Melcher	Y	Y	Y	Y	Y	Y	Y	Y
NEBRASKA								
Exon	Y	Y	P	P	Y	Y	Y	Y
Zorinsky	Y	Y	P	P	Y	Y	Y	Y
NEVADA								
Laxalt	N	N	Y	Y	Y	?	Y	Y
Cannon	Y	N	N	Y	Y	Y	Y	Y

	34	35	36	37	38	39	40	41
NEW HAMPSHIRE								
Humphrey	N	N	N	Y	Y	Y	+	?
Rudman	N	N	Y	Y	Y	Y	Y	Y
NEW JERSEY								
Bradley	N	Y	N	N	Y	Y	Y	Y
Williams	N	N	N	Y	Y	Y	?	Y
NEW MEXICO								
Domenici	N	N	Y	Y	Y	Y	Y	Y
Schmitt	N	N	Y	Y	Y	Y	Y	Y
NEW YORK								
D'Amato	N	N	Y	Y	Y	Y	Y	Y
Moynihan	N	N	N	N	N	Y	Y	Y
NORTH CAROLINA								
East	N	N	Y	Y	Y	Y	Y	?
Helms	N	N	Y	Y	Y	Y	Y	Y
NORTH DAKOTA								
Andrews	Y	Y	Y	Y	Y	Y	Y	Y
Burdick	Y	Y	Y	Y	Y	Y	N	Y
OHIO								
Glenn	N	N	N	N	Y	Y	Y	Y
Metzenbaum	Y	N	N	Y	Y	Y	Y	Y
OKLAHOMA								
Nickles	N	N	Y	Y	Y	Y	Y	Y
Boren	Y	Y	N	Y	Y	Y	Y	Y
OREGON								
Hatfield	N	N	Y	Y	Y	Y	Y	Y
Packwood	N	N	N	N	N	Y	Y	Y
PENNSYLVANIA								
Heinz	N	N	Y	?	Y	Y	Y	Y
Specter	N	N	Y	Y	Y	Y	Y	Y
RHODE ISLAND								
Chafee	N	N	N	Y	Y	Y	Y	Y
Pell	N	Y	N	Y	Y	Y	Y	Y
SOUTH CAROLINA								
Thurmond	N	N	Y	Y	Y	Y	Y	Y
Hollings	N	N	N	Y	Y	Y	Y	Y
SOUTH DAKOTA								
Abdnor	Y	Y	Y	Y	Y	Y	Y	Y
Pressler	Y	Y	Y	Y	Y	Y	Y	Y
TENNESSEE								
Baker	N	N	Y	Y	Y	Y	Y	Y
Sasser	Y	Y	Y	Y	Y	Y	Y	Y

KEY

Y	Voted for (yea).
#	Paired for.
+	Announced for.
N	Voted against (nay)
X	Paired against.
-	Announced against.
P	Voted "present."
C	Voted "present" to avoid possible conflict of interest.
?	Did not vote or otherwise make a position known.

	34	35	36	37	38	39	40	41
TEXAS								
Tower	N	N	Y	Y	Y	?	Y	?
Bentsen	Y	Y	N	Y	Y	Y	Y	Y
UTAH								
Garn	N	N	Y	Y	Y	Y	Y	Y
Hatch	N	N	Y	Y	Y	Y	Y	Y
VERMONT								
Stafford	Y	N	Y	Y	Y	Y	N	Y
Leahy	Y	Y	Y	Y	Y	Y	N	Y
VIRGINIA								
Warner	N	N	Y	Y	Y	Y	Y	Y
Byrd*	N	N	Y	N	Y	Y	Y	Y
WASHINGTON								
Gorton	N	N	Y	Y	Y	Y	Y	Y
Jackson	Y	N	N	Y	Y	Y	Y	Y
WEST VIRGINIA								
Byrd	Y	N	N	N	Y	Y	Y	Y
Randolph	Y	N	N	Y	Y	Y	Y	Y
WISCONSIN								
Kasten	Y	N	Y	Y	Y	N	Y	Y
Proxmire	Y	N	Y	Y	Y	Y	N	Y
WYOMING								
Simpson	N	N	Y	Y	Y	Y	Y	Y
Wallop	N	N	Y	Y	Y	Y	Y	Y

Democrats   *Republicans*

*Byrd elected as an independent.

34. S 509. Milk Price Supports. Melcher, D-Mont., amendment to establish a quota on the importation of casein products into the United States. Rejected 38-60: R 7-45; D 31-15 (ND 19-12; SD 12-3), March 24, 1981. A "nay" was a vote supporting the president's position.

35. S 509. Milk Price Supports. Zorinsky, D-Neb., amendment, to the Zorinsky amendment (see vote 36, below), to change to April 15, 1981, from April 30, 1981, the date by which the president would have to make a decision regarding the embargo on sales of U.S. grain to the Soviet Union. Rejected 33-65: R 7-45: D 26-20 (ND 18-13; SD 8-7), March 24, 1981. (The original Zorinsky amendment would have repealed the embargo on April 30, unless the president certified to Congress that U.S. foreign policy required its continuation and that the embargo would not have an "undue adverse effect" on "the agricultural economy" and on American farmers.)

36. S 509. Milk Price Supports. Jepsen, R-Iowa, substitute amendment, to the Zorinsky, D-Neb., amendment (see vote 35, above), that it was the "sense of the Senate" that the embargo on sales of U.S. grain to the Soviet Union be terminated. Adopted 58-36: R 44-8; D 14-28 (ND 9-19; SD 5-9), March 24, 1981. (The Zorinsky amendment, as amended, was adopted subsequently by voice vote.)

37. S 509. Milk Price Supports. Baker, R-Tenn., substitute amendment to the Boren, D-Okla., amendment (see vote 38, below), that it was the "sense of the Senate" that no agricultural commodities produced in the Soviet Union enter the United States when the president has restricted sales of U.S. grain or other agricultural commodities to the Soviet Union. The amendment applied to the existing embargo, as well as to future embargoes. Adopted 80-14: R 50-2; D 30-12 (ND 21-8; SD 9-4), March 24, 1981. (The Boren amendment would have barred Soviet agricultural imports as of April 1 and during future agricultural trade restrictions.)

38. S 509. Milk Price Supports. Boren, D-Okla., amendment, as amended by the Baker, R-Tenn., amendment (see vote 37, above). Adopted 90-6: R 48-2; D 42-4 (ND 28-3; SD 14-1), March 24, 1981.

39. S 509. Milk Price Supports. Baker, R-Tenn., motion to instruct the sergeant-at-arms to invite the attendance of absent senators. Adopted 94-2: R 48-2; D 46-0 (ND 31-0; SD 15-0), March 24, 1981.

40. S 509. Milk Price Supports. Passage of the bill to eliminate the April 1, 1981, adjustment in the parity price support for dairy products. Passed 88-5: R 47-2; D 41-3 (ND 27-3; SD 14-0), March 25, 1981. A "yea" was a vote supporting the president's position.

41. S Con Res 9. Budget Reconciliation Instructions. Baker, R-Tenn., motion that the sergeant-at-arms be instructed to direct the attendance of absent senators. Motion agreed to 92-2: R 48-2; D 44-0 (ND 31-0; SD 13-0), March 26, 1981.

CQ Senate Votes 42 - 49

Corresponding to Congressional Record Votes 42, 43, 44, 45, 46, 47, 48, 49

	42	43	44	45	46	47	48	49
ALABAMA								
Denton	N	N	N	Y	Y	N	Y	N
Heflin	N	Y	Y	Y	Y	Y	Y	Y
ALASKA								
Murkowski	N	N	N	Y	Y	N	Y	N
Stevens	N	N	N	Y	Y	N	Y	N
ARIZONA								
Goldwater	N	N	N	Y	Y	N	Y	N
DeConcini	Y	Y	Y	Y	Y	+	+	+
ARKANSAS								
Bumpers	Y	Y	Y	N	N	Y	Y	N
Pryor	Y	Y	?	Y	Y	Y	Y	Y
CALIFORNIA								
Hayakawa	N	N	N	N	N	?	Y	?
Cranston	Y	Y	Y	Y	N	Y	Y	+
COLORADO								
Armstrong	N	N	N	Y	Y	N	Y	N
Hart	Y	Y	Y	Y	N	Y	Y	Y
CONNECTICUT								
Weicker	N	Y	Y	Y	Y	N	N	Y
Dodd	Y	Y	Y	Y	N	N	Y	Y
DELAWARE								
Roth	N	N	N	Y	N	Y	N	Y
Biden	Y	Y	Y	N	Y	Y	Y	Y
FLORIDA								
Hawkins	N	N	N	Y	N	Y	N	N
Chiles	N	Y	Y	Y	Y	Y	Y	Y
GEORGIA								
Mattingly	N	N	N	Y	Y	N	Y	N
Nunn	N	N	N	Y	Y	Y	Y	N
HAWAII								
Inouye	N	Y	Y	?	?	?	?	?
Matsunaga	Y	Y	Y	Y	N	Y	N	Y
IDAHO								
McClure	N	N	N	N	Y	N	Y	N
Symms	N	N	N	N	Y	N	Y	N
ILLINOIS								
Percy	N	N	N	N	N	N	Y	N
Dixon	N	Y	Y	Y	Y	Y	Y	N
INDIANA								
Lugar	N	N	N	N	N	N	Y	N
Quayle	N	N	N	Y	Y	N	Y	N

	42	43	44	45	46	47	48	49
IOWA								
Grassley	N	N	N	Y	Y	N	Y	N
Jepsen	N	N	N	Y	Y	N	Y	N
KANSAS								
Dole	N	N	N	Y	Y	N	Y	N
Kassebaum	N	N	N	Y	Y	N	Y	N
KENTUCKY								
Ford	Y	Y	Y	Y	Y	Y	Y	Y
Huddleston	Y	Y	Y	Y	Y	Y	Y	?
LOUISIANA								
Johnston	N	N	N	Y	Y	N	Y	N
Long	N	Y	Y	Y	Y	Y	Y	Y
MAINE								
Cohen	N	N	N	Y	Y	N	Y	N
Mitchell	Y	Y	Y	Y	Y	Y	Y	Y
MARYLAND								
Mathias	N	N	Y	N	Y	N	N	N
Sarbanes	Y	Y	Y	Y	N	Y	Y	Y
MASSACHUSETTS								
Kennedy	Y	Y	Y	Y	N	Y	Y	Y
Tsongas	Y	Y	Y	Y	N	Y	Y	Y
MICHIGAN								
Levin	Y	Y	Y	Y	N	Y	Y	Y
Riegle	Y	Y	Y	Y	N	Y	Y	Y
MINNESOTA								
Boschwitz	N	N	N	Y	Y	N	Y	N
Durenberger	N	N	N	Y	Y	N	Y	N
MISSISSIPPI								
Cochran	N	N	N	?	?	?	?	?
Stennis	N	Y	Y	Y	Y	Y	Y	Y
MISSOURI								
Danforth	N	N	N	Y	N	N	N	N
Eagleton	Y	Y	Y	Y	Y	Y	Y	Y
MONTANA								
Baucus	Y	Y	Y	Y	Y	Y	Y	Y
Melcher	Y	Y	Y	Y	Y	Y	Y	Y
NEBRASKA								
Exon	Y	Y	Y	Y	Y	Y	Y	Y
Zorinsky	N	Y	Y	Y	Y	Y	Y	?
NEVADA								
Laxalt	N	N	N	Y	Y	N	Y	N
Cannon	N	Y	Y	+	+	+	+	+

	42	43	44	45	46	47	48	49
NEW HAMPSHIRE								
Humphrey	N	N	N	Y	Y	Y	Y	N
Rudman	N	N	N	+	Y	N	Y	N
NEW JERSEY								
Bradley	Y	Y	Y	Y	N	Y	Y	Y
Williams	Y	Y	Y	Y	N	Y	Y	Y
NEW MEXICO								
Domenici	N	N	N	Y	Y	N	Y	N
Schmitt	N	N	N	Y	Y	N	Y	N
NEW YORK								
D'Amato	N	N	N	Y	Y	N	Y	N
Moynihan	Y	Y	Y	Y	N	N	Y	Y
NORTH CAROLINA								
East	N	N	N	Y	Y	N	Y	N
Helms	Y	N	N	Y	Y	Y	Y	N
NORTH DAKOTA								
Andrews	N	N	N	Y	Y	?	Y	N
Burdick	Y	Y	Y	Y	Y	Y	Y	Y
OHIO								
Glenn	Y	Y	Y	Y	N	Y	Y	Y
Metzenbaum	Y	Y	Y	Y	N	Y	Y	Y
OKLAHOMA								
Nickles	Y	N	N	N	Y	N	Y	N
Boren	Y	Y	Y	Y	Y	Y	Y	N
OREGON								
Hatfield	N	N	N	Y	Y	N	Y	N
Packwood	N	N	N	Y	Y	N	Y	N
PENNSYLVANIA								
Heinz	N	N	N	Y	Y	N	Y	N
Specter	N	N	N	Y	N	?	Y	N
RHODE ISLAND								
Chafee	N	N	N	Y	Y	N	Y	N
Pell	Y	Y	Y	Y	N	Y	Y	Y
SOUTH CAROLINA								
Thurmond	N	N	N	Y	Y	N	Y	N
Hollings	N	Y	Y	Y	Y	Y	Y	?
SOUTH DAKOTA								
Abdnor	N	N	N	Y	Y	N	Y	?
Pressler	N	N	N	Y	Y	N	Y	?
TENNESSEE								
Baker	N	N	N	Y	Y	N	Y	N
Sasser	N	Y	Y	Y	Y	Y	Y	Y

KEY

Y Voted for (yea).
Paired for.
+ Announced for.
N Voted against (nay)
X Paired against.
- Announced against.
P Voted "present."
C Voted "present" to avoid possible conflict of interest.
? Did not vote or otherwise make a position known.

	42	43	44	45	46	47	48	49
TEXAS								
Tower	N	N	N	Y	?	?	Y	N
Bentsen	Y	Y	Y	Y	Y	Y	Y	N
UTAH								
Garn	N	N	N	Y	Y	N	Y	N
Hatch	N	N	N	Y	Y	N	Y	N
VERMONT								
Stafford	N	N	N	Y	Y	N	Y	N
Leahy	Y	Y	Y	Y	N	Y	N	Y
VIRGINIA								
Warner	N	N	N	Y	Y	N	Y	N
Byrd*	Y	N	N	N	Y	N	Y	N
WASHINGTON								
Gorton	N	N	N	Y	Y	N	Y	N
Jackson	N	Y	Y	Y	Y	Y	Y	Y
WEST VIRGINIA								
Byrd	N	Y	Y	Y	Y	Y	Y	Y
Randolph	Y	Y	Y	Y	Y	Y	Y	Y
WISCONSIN								
Kasten	N	N	N	Y	Y	N	Y	N
Proxmire	Y	N	N	N	Y	N	Y	N
WYOMING								
Simpson	N	N	N	Y	Y	N	Y	N
Wallop	N	N	N	Y	Y	N	Y	N

Democrats *Republicans*

*Byrd elected as an independent.

---

42. S Con Res 9. Budget Reconciliation Instructions. Pryor, D-Ark., amendment to deepen cuts recommended by the Budget Committee by directing the Appropriations Committee to reduce government procurement outlays in fiscal 1982 by $2 billion across-the-board. Rejected 35-65: R 2-51; D 33-14 (ND 26-6; SD 7-8), March 26, 1981.

43. S Con Res 9. Budget Reconciliation Instructions. Chiles, D-Fla., amendment to lessen cuts recommended by the Budget Committee by restoring $300 million in fiscal 1982 budget authority and $270 million in fiscal 1982 outlays for Veterans' Affairs Committee health programs. Rejected 44-56: R 1-52; D 43-4 (ND 31-1; SD 12-3), March 26, 1981. A "nay" was a vote supporting the president's position.

44. S Con Res 9. Budget Reconciliation Instructions. Cranston, D-Calif., amendment to lessen cuts recommended by the Budget Committee by restoring $104 million in fiscal 1982 budget authority and outlays for Veterans' Affairs Committee health programs. Rejected 44-55: R 2-51; D 42-4 (ND 31-1; SD 11-3), March 26, 1981. A "nay" was a vote supporting the president's position.

45. S Con Res 9. Budget Reconciliation Instructions. Helms, R-N.C., amendment, part 1, to lessen cuts recommended by the Budget Committee by restoring $200 million in fiscal 1982 budget authority and outlays for the Agriculture, Nutrition and Forestry Committee's school lunch program. Adopted 87-9: R 44-7; D 43-2 (ND 29-1; SD 14-1), March 27, 1981. A "nay" was a vote supporting the president's position.

46. S Con Res 9. Budget Reconciliation Instructions. Helms, R-N.C., amendment, part 2, to deepen cuts recommended by the Budget Committee by reducing Foreign Relations Committee programs by $900 million in budget authority and $200 million in outlays in fiscal 1982. Adopted 70-26: R 42-9; D 28-17 (ND 14-16; SD 14-1), March 27, 1981. A "nay" was a vote supporting the president's position.

47. S Con Res 9. Budget Reconciliation Instructions. Boren, D-Okla., amendment to deepen cuts recommended by the Budget Committee in Foreign Relations Committee programs by $104 million in fiscal 1982 outlays and restore that sum to the Veterans' Affairs Committee for health programs. Rejected 44-48: R 2-46; D 42-2 (ND 27-2; SD 15-0), March 27, 1981. A "nay" was a vote supporting the president's position.

48. S Res 103. Polish Situation. Adoption of the resolution stating the sense of the Senate that outside intervention in Poland would violate international law and supporting the president's efforts to work with other nations to ease Poland's economic difficulties. Adopted 96-0: R 52-0; D 44-0 (ND 29-0; SD 15-0), March 27, 1981.

49. S Con Res 9. Budget Reconciliation Instructions. Sasser, D-Tenn., amendment to lessen cuts recommended by the Budget Committee by restoring $181 million in fiscal 1982 budget authority and $200 million in fiscal 1982 outlays for the Agriculture, Nutrition and Forestry Committee's school lunch program. Rejected 35-54: R 2-47; D 33-7 (ND 25-2; SD 8-5), March 27, 1981. A "nay" was a vote supporting the president's position.

	50 51 52 53 54 55 56 57		50 51 52 53 54 55 56 57		50 51 52 53 54 55 56 57
ALABAMA		**IOWA**		**NEW HAMPSHIRE**	
Denton	N N N N N N N N	*Grassley*	N N N N N N N N	*Humphrey*	N N N Y N N N N
Heflin	Y N N Y N N N N	*Jepsen*	N N N N N N N N	*Rudman*	N N N N N N N N
ALASKA		**KANSAS**		**NEW JERSEY**	
Murkowski	N Y Y Y N N N N	*Dole*	N N N N N N N N	Bradley	Y Y Y Y Y Y Y Y
Stevens	N Y N N N N N N	*Kassebaum*	N N N N N N N N	Williams	? ? ? ? ? ? ? ?
ARIZONA		**KENTUCKY**		**NEW MEXICO**	
Goldwater	N N N N N N N N	Ford	Y Y Y N Y N Y Y	*Domenici*	N N N N N N N N
DeConcini	+ - N N Y Y N X	Huddleston	Y Y N Y Y N Y Y	*Schmitt*	N N N N N N N N
ARKANSAS		**LOUISIANA**		**NEW YORK**	
Bumpers	+ ? Y N Y Y Y Y	Johnston	Y N N N N N N N	*D'Amato*	N N N N N N N N
Pryor	Y N N N N Y N Y	Long	Y N N N N N N Y	Moynihan	Y Y Y N Y Y Y #
CALIFORNIA		**MAINE**		**NORTH CAROLINA**	
Hayakawa	N Y N N N N N N	*Cohen*	N N N N N N Y Y	*East*	N N N N N N N N
Cranston	Y Y Y N Y Y Y Y	Mitchell	Y N N N N N Y Y	*Helms*	N N N Y N N N N
COLORADO		**MARYLAND**		**NORTH DAKOTA**	
Armstrong	N N N N N N N N	*Mathias*	N N N N N N Y Y	*Andrews*	N N N N N N Y N
Hart	Y N N N Y Y Y Y	Sarbanes	Y Y N Y Y Y Y Y	Burdick	Y N N N Y Y Y Y
CONNECTICUT		**MASSACHUSETTS**		**OHIO**	
Weicker	N N Y N N N Y Y	Kennedy	Y Y Y N Y Y Y Y	Glenn	Y Y Y N Y Y Y Y
Dodd	Y Y Y Y + Y Y Y	Tsongas	? ? ? ? ? ? ? Y	Metzenbaum	Y Y Y N Y Y Y ?
DELAWARE		**MICHIGAN**		**OKLAHOMA**	
Roth	N N N N N N N N	Levin	Y N Y N Y Y Y Y	*Nickles*	N N N N N N N N
Biden	Y Y N Y Y Y Y Y	Riegle	Y N N Y Y Y Y Y	Boren	Y N N N N N N N
FLORIDA		**MINNESOTA**		**OREGON**	
Hawkins	N N N N N N N N	*Boschwitz*	N N N N N N N N	*Hatfield*	N N N N N N N N
Chiles	Y N N N N N N N	*Durenberger*	N Y N N N N Y N	*Packwood*	N N N N N N N N
GEORGIA		**MISSISSIPPI**		**PENNSYLVANIA**	
Mattingly	N N N N N N N N	*Cochran*	? ? N N N N N N	Heinz	N N N N N N N Y
Nunn	Y N N N N N N N	Stennis	N N N N Y Y N Y	*Specter*	N Y N N N N Y Y
HAWAII		**MISSOURI**		**RHODE ISLAND**	
Inouye	Y Y Y Y Y Y Y Y	*Danforth*	N N N N N N Y N	*Chafee*	N N N N N N Y N
Matsunaga	Y Y Y Y Y Y Y Y	Eagleton	Y N N N Y Y Y Y	Pell	Y Y N Y Y Y Y Y
IDAHO		**MONTANA**		**SOUTH CAROLINA**	
McClure	N N N Y N N N N	Baucus	Y N N N Y Y N Y	*Thurmond*	N N N N N N N N
Symms	N N N Y N N N N	Melcher	Y N N Y N Y N Y	Hollings	N N N N N Y N Y
ILLINOIS		**NEBRASKA**		**SOUTH DAKOTA**	
Percy	N N N N N N N Y	Exon	Y N N Y N N N N	*Abdnor*	N N N N N N N N
Dixon	Y N N N Y Y Y Y	Zorinsky	Y Y N Y Y N N N	*Pressler*	? ? N N N N N N
INDIANA		**NEVADA**		**TENNESSEE**	
Lugar	N N N N N N N N	*Laxalt*	N N N N N N N N	*Baker*	N N N N N N N N
Quayle	N N N N N N N N	Cannon	Y Y N N Y N Y Y	Sasser	Y N N N Y Y N Y

	50 51 52 53 54 55 56 57

		50 51 52 53 54 55 56 57
	TEXAS	
	Tower	N N N N N N N N
	Bentsen	Y N N Y N N N N
	UTAH	
	Garn	N N N N N N N N
	Hatch	N N N N N N N N
	VERMONT	
	Stafford	N N N N N N Y N
	Leahy	Y Y N N Y Y Y Y
	VIRGINIA	
	Warner	N N N N N N N N
	Byrd*	N N Y N N N N N
	WASHINGTON	
	Gorton	N N N N N N N N
	Jackson	Y Y Y Y Y Y Y Y
	WEST VIRGINIA	
	Byrd	Y N Y Y Y Y Y Y
	Randolph	Y N N N Y Y Y Y
	WISCONSIN	
	Kasten	N N N N N N N N
	Proxmire	N N N N N N N N
	WYOMING	
	Simpson	N N N N N N N N
	Wallop	N N N Y N N N N

KEY

Y	Voted for (yea).
#	Paired for.
+	Announced for.
N	Voted against (nay).
X	Paired against.
-	Announced against.
P	Voted "present."
C	Voted "present" to avoid possible conflict of interest.
?	Did not vote or otherwise make a position known.

Democrats *Republicans*

*Byrd elected as an independent.

50. S Con Res 9. Budget Reconciliation Instructions. Riegle, D-Mich., amendment to lessen cuts recommended by the Budget Committee in the Finance Committee's Social Security program and increase cuts in Governmental Affairs Committee activities. Fiscal 1982 outlays of $800 million would be restored to permit current recipients of minimum Social Security benefits to continue receiving payments after that program is eliminated. Outlays for fiscal 1982 Governmental Affairs activities would be cut an equal $800 million to offset the restoration. Rejected 39-55: R 0-51; D 39-4 (ND 28-1; SD 11-3), March 30, 1981. A "nay" was a vote supporting the president's position.

51. S Con Res 9. Budget Reconciliation Instructions. Stevens, R-Alaska, amendment to lessen cuts recommended by the Budget Committee by restoring $1.5 billion in fiscal 1982 budget authority and $1.4 billion in fiscal 1982 outlays for the Energy and Natural Resources Committee's Strategic Petroleum Reserve program. Rejected 23-71: R 5-46; D 18-25 (ND 16-13; SD 2-12), March 30, 1981.

52. S Con Res 9. Budget Reconciliation Instructions. Bradley, D-N.J., amendment to lessen cuts recommended by the Budget Committee by restoring $3 billion in fiscal 1982 budget authority and outlays for the Energy and Natural Resources Committee's Strategic Petroleum Reserve program. Rejected 17-81: R 3-50; D 14-31 (ND 12-18; SD 2-13), March 31, 1981.

53. S Con Res 9. Budget Reconciliation Instructions. McClure, R-Idaho, amendment to alter cuts recommended by the Budget Committee by restoring $3 billion in fiscal 1982 budget authority and outlays for the Energy and Natural Resources Committee's Strategic Petroleum Reserve program and offsetting the restoration by cutting spending for all other programs but military by $3 billion across the board. Rejected 22-76: R 9-44; D 13-32 (ND 9-21; SD 4-11), March 31, 1981.

54. S Con Res 9. Budget Reconciliation Instructions. Moynihan, D-N.Y., amendment to lessen cuts recommended by the Budget Committee by restoring $150 million in fiscal 1982 budget authority and $100 million in fiscal 1982 outlays for the Labor and Human Resources Committee's higher education grant program. Rejected 30-67: R 0-53; D 30-14 (ND 25-4; SD 5-10), March 31, 1981. A "nay" was a vote supporting the president's position.

55. S Con Res 9. Budget Reconciliation Instructions. Moynihan, D-N.Y., amendment to lessen cuts recommended by the Budget Committee by restoring $600 million in fiscal 1982 budget authority and $435 million in fiscal 1982 outlays for the Labor and Human Resources Committee's elementary and secondary education programs. Rejected 33-65: R 1-52; D 32-13 (ND 25-5; SD 7-8), March 31, 1981. A "nay" was a vote supporting the president's program.

56. S Con Res 9. Budget Reconciliation Instructions. Chafee, R-R.I., amendment to lessen cuts recommended by the Budget Committee by restoring $1.2 billion in fiscal 1982 budget authority and $973 million in fiscal 1982 outlays to various committees for elementary and secondary education, low-income fuel aid, urban development action grants, urban mass transit, community health centers and the energy weatherization program. Rejected 40-59: R 11-42; D 29-17 (ND 26-5; SD 3-12), March 31, 1981. A "nay" was a vote supporting the president's position.

57. S Con Res 9. Budget Reconciliation Instructions. Mitchell, D-Maine, amendment to lessen cuts recommended by the Budget Committee by restoring $720 million in fiscal 1982 budget authority and $224 million in fiscal 1982 outlays to the Environment and Public Works Committee for Commerce Department Economic Development Administration programs. Rejected 37-59: R 5-48; D 32-11 (ND 24-4; SD 8-7), March 31, 1981. A "nay" was a vote supporting the president's position.

Corresponding to Congressional Record Votes 58, 59, 60, 61, 62, 63, 64, 65

	58	59	60	61	62	63	64	65
ALABAMA								
Denton	N	N	N	N	N	N	N	N
Heflin	N	N	N	N	N	N	N	Y
ALASKA								
Murkowski	N	N	N	N	N	N	N	N
Stevens	N	N	N	N	N	N	N	N
ARIZONA								
Goldwater	N	N	N	N	N	N	?	?
DeConcini	N	Y	Y	N	N	N	Y	Y
ARKANSAS								
Bumpers	N	Y	Y	Y	N	N	N	N
Pryor	N	Y	Y	N	N	N	N	N
CALIFORNIA								
Hayakawa	Y	N	N	N	N	N	N	N
Cranston	Y	Y	Y	Y	Y	N	N	N
COLORADO								
Armstrong	N	N	N	N	N	N	N	N
Hart	Y	Y	Y	Y	Y	N	Y	N
CONNECTICUT								
Weicker	Y	Y	Y	N	Y	N	N	N
Dodd	Y	Y	Y	Y	Y	N	N	N
DELAWARE								
Roth	N	N	N	N	Y	N	N	Y
Biden	N	Y	Y	Y	Y	N	N	N
FLORIDA								
Hawkins	N	N	N	N	N	N	N	N
Chiles	N	Y	N	Y	N	N	N	N
GEORGIA								
Mattingly	N	N	N	N	N	N	N	N
Nunn	Y	N	N	N	N	Y	N	Y
HAWAII								
Inouye	Y	Y	Y	Y	Y	N	N	N
Matsunaga	?	Y	Y	Y	Y	N	N	N
IDAHO								
McClure	N	N	N	N	N	Y	N	N
Symms	N	N	N	N	N	Y	N	N
ILLINOIS								
Percy	N	N	N	N	N	N	N	N
Dixon	N	Y	Y	N	Y	N	N	Y
INDIANA								
Lugar	N	N	N	N	N	N	N	N
Quayle	N	N	N	N	N	Y	N	N

	58	59	60	61	62	63	64	65
IOWA								
Grassley	N	N	N	N	N	N	N	Y
Jepsen	N	N	N	N	N	N	N	N
KANSAS								
Dole	N	N	N	N	N	N	N	N
Kassebaum	N	N	N	N	N	N	N	N
KENTUCKY								
Ford	Y	Y	Y	Y	Y	N	N	N
Huddleston	N	Y	Y	Y	N	Y	N	N
LOUISIANA								
Johnston	N	N	N	N	N	N	N	N
Long	N	N	Y	N	N	N	N	N
MAINE								
Cohen	Y	N	N	N	N	N	N	N
Mitchell	Y	Y	Y	N	N	N	N	Y
MARYLAND								
Mathias	Y	N	Y	N	Y	N	N	?
Sarbanes	Y	Y	Y	Y	Y	N	Y	N
MASSACHUSETTS								
Kennedy	Y	Y	Y	Y	Y	N	Y	N
Tsongas	Y	Y	Y	Y	Y	N	Y	N
MICHIGAN								
Levin	Y	Y	Y	Y	Y	N	Y	N
Riegle	Y	Y	Y	Y	Y	N	Y	N
MINNESOTA								
Boschwitz	N	N	N	N	N	N	N	N
Durenberger	N	N	N	N	N	N	N	N
MISSISSIPPI								
Cochran	N	N	N	N	N	N	N	N
Stennis	N	N	N	N	N	N	N	N
MISSOURI								
Danforth	N	N	N	N	N	N	N	N
Eagleton	N	Y	Y	Y	Y	N	Y	N
MONTANA								
Baucus	Y	Y	Y	N	N	N	N	N
Melcher	N	Y	Y	N	N	N	N	N
NEBRASKA								
Exon	N	Y	N	N	N	N	N	N
Zorinsky	N	Y	N	N	N	N	N	Y
NEVADA								
Laxalt	N	N	N	N	N	N	N	N
Cannon	Y	N	Y	N	N	N	N	N

	58	59	60	61	62	63	64	65
NEW HAMPSHIRE								
Humphrey	N	N	N	N	N	Y	N	Y
Rudman	N	N	N	N	N	Y	N	N
NEW JERSEY								
Bradley	Y	Y	Y	Y	N	Y	N	Y
Williams	?	+	?	?	?	?	?	?
NEW MEXICO								
Domenici	N	N	N	N	N	N	N	N
Schmitt	N	N	N	N	N	N	N	N
NEW YORK								
D'Amato	N	N	N	N	N	N	N	N
Moynihan	Y	Y	Y	Y	Y	N	Y	N
NORTH CAROLINA								
East	N	N	N	N	N	N	N	N
Helms	N	N	N	N	N	Y	N	N
NORTH DAKOTA								
Andrews	N	N	N	N	N	N	N	N
Burdick	N	N	Y	Y	N	N	N	N
OHIO								
Glenn	Y	Y	Y	Y	Y	N	N	N
Metzenbaum	Y	Y	Y	Y	Y	N	Y	N
OKLAHOMA								
Nickles	N	N	N	N	N	N	N	Y
Boren	N	N	N	N	N	N	Y	Y
OREGON								
Hatfield	N	N	N	N	N	N	N	N
Packwood	Y	N	N	N	N	N	N	N
PENNSYLVANIA								
Heinz	Y	N	N	N	N	N	N	N
Specter	Y	N	N	N	N	N	N	N
RHODE ISLAND								
Chafee	N	N	N	N	N	N	N	N
Pell	?	+	Y	Y	Y	N	Y	N
SOUTH CAROLINA								
Thurmond	N	N	N	N	N	N	N	N
Hollings	N	Y	Y	N	N	Y	N	Y
SOUTH DAKOTA								
Abdnor	N	N	N	N	N	N	N	N
Pressler	N	N	N	N	N	N	N	?
TENNESSEE								
Baker	N	N	N	N	N	N	N	N
Sasser	N	N	Y	N	N	N	N	Y

KEY

Y	Voted for (yea).
#	Paired for.
+	Announced for.
N	Voted against (nay)
X	Paired against.
-	Announced against.
P	Voted "present."
C	Voted "present" to avoid possible conflict of interest.
?	Did not vote or otherwise make a position known.

	58	59	60	61	62	63	64	65
TEXAS								
Tower	N	N	N	N	N	N	?	N
Bentsen	N	N	N	N	N	N	N	N
UTAH								
Garn	N	N	N	N	N	N	N	N
Hatch	Y	N	N	N	N	N	N	N
VERMONT								
Stafford	N	N	N	N	N	N	N	N
Leahy	Y	Y	Y	Y	N	N	N	N
VIRGINIA								
Warner	N	N	N	N	N	N	N	N
Byrd*	N	N	N	N	N	N	N	Y
WASHINGTON								
Gorton	N	N	N	N	N	Y	N	N
Jackson	N	Y	N	Y	N	N	N	N
WEST VIRGINIA								
Byrd	Y	Y	Y	Y	N	N	N	N
Randolph	+	+	+	+	+	-	N	N
WISCONSIN								
Kasten	N	N	N	N	N	Y	N	N
Proxmire	N	N	N	N	N	N	Y	Y
WYOMING								
Simpson	N	N	N	N	N	Y	N	N
Wallop	N	N	N	N	N	N	N	N

Democrats   *Republicans*   *Byrd elected as an independent.

58. S Con Res 9. Budget Reconciliation Instructions. Weicker, R-Conn., amendment to lessen cuts recommended by the Budget Committee by restoring $155 million in fiscal 1982 budget authority and $143 million in fiscal 1982 outlays for Small Business Committee loan programs. Rejected 28-68: R 8-45: D 20-23 (ND 18-10; SD 2-13), April 1, 1981. A "yea" was a vote supporting the president's program.

59. S Con Res 9. Budget Reconciliation Instructions. Hart, D-Colo., amendment to alter cuts recommended by the Budget Committee by restoring $2.2 billion in budget authority in fiscal 1981 but deepening 1981 outlay cuts by $34 million and 1982 outlay cuts by $13 million. Energy and Agriculture Committee funds would be shifted from nuclear programs to the solar energy bank and gasohol programs. Rejected 32-65: R 1-52; D 31-13 (ND 25-4; SD 6-9), April 1, 1981. A "nay" was a vote supporting the president's position.

60. S Con Res 9. Budget Reconciliation Instructions. Kennedy, D-Mass., amendment to lessen cuts recommended by the Budget Committee by restoring $150 million in budget authority and $125 million in outlays in fiscal 1982 for the Labor and Human Resources Committee preventive health program. Rejected 36-62: R 2-51; D 34-11 (ND 27-3; SD 7-8), April 1, 1981. A "nay" was a vote supporting the president's program.

61. S Con Res 9. Budget Reconciliation Instructions. Metzenbaum, D-Ohio, amendment to lessen cuts recommended by the Budget Committee by restoring $400 million in budget authority and $300 million in outlays in fiscal 1982 for Labor and Human Resources Committee youth training programs. Rejected 24-74: R 0-53; D 24-21 (ND 20-10; SD 4-11), April 1, 1981. A "nay" was a vote supporting the president's program.

62. S Con Res 9. Budget Reconciliation Instructions. Bradley, D-N.J., amendment to lessen cuts recommended by the Budget Committee by restoring $803 million in budget authority and $264 million in outlays for fiscal 1982 for the National Science Foundation, trade adjustment assistance, Conrail and mass transit programs. Rejected 22-76: R 3-50; D 19-26 (ND 18-12; SD 1-14), April 1, 1981. A "nay" was a vote supporting the president's position.

63. S Con Res 9. Budget Reconciliation Instructions. Hollings, D-S.C., amendment to deepen cuts recommended by the Budget Committee by changing the index used to adjust government retirement programs for inflation, for an outlay savings of $2.6 billion in fiscal 1982. Rejected 12-86: R 9-44; D 3-42 (ND 0-30; SD 3-12), April 1, 1981. A "nay" was a vote supporting the president's position.

64. S Con Res 9. Budget Reconciliation Instructions. Metzenbaum, D-Ohio, motion to waive a section of the Congressional Budget Act (PL 93-344) to permit consideration of his amendment to deepen cuts recommended by the Budget Committee by requiring the Finance Committee to tighten tax loopholes for a savings of $1.3 billion in fiscal 1982. Rejected 15-82: R 0-51; D 15-31 (ND 14-17; SD 1-14), April 1, 1981.

65. S Con Res 9. Budget Reconciliation Instructions. Proxmire, D-Wis., amendment to deepen the cuts recommended by the Budget Committee by reducing Appropriations Committee funds by $2.373 billion in budget authority in fiscal 1982. Rejected 15-81: R 5-45; D 10-36 (ND 4-27; SD 6-9), April 1, 1981.

	66	67	68	69	70	71	72	73
ALABAMA								
Denton	N	N	N	N	N	N	N	N
Heflin	Y	Y	Y	Y	N	N	Y	N
ALASKA								
Murkowski	N	N	N	N	N	N	N	N
Stevens	N	N	N	N	N	N	N	N
ARIZONA								
Goldwater	?	?	N	N	N	N	N	N
DeConcini	Y	Y	Y	N	N	N	Y	N
ARKANSAS								
Bumpers	N	Y	Y	N	Y	Y	Y	Y
Pryor	N	Y	Y	N	N	N	Y	N
CALIFORNIA								
Hayakawa	N	N	N	N	N	N	N	N
Cranston	Y	Y	Y	Y	Y	Y	Y	Y
COLORADO								
Armstrong	N	N	N	N	N	N	N	N
Hart	N	Y	Y	N	Y	N	Y	Y
CONNECTICUT								
Weicker	N	N	N	N	N	N	Y	N
Dodd	Y	Y	Y	Y	Y	Y	Y	N
DELAWARE								
Roth	N	N	N	Y	N	N	N	N
Biden	N	Y	Y	Y	N	N	N	N
FLORIDA								
Hawkins	N	N	Y	N	N	N	N	N
Chiles	N	Y	Y	N	N	N	N	N
GEORGIA								
Mattingly	N	N	N	N	N	N	N	N
Nunn	Y	Y	Y	N	N	N	N	N
HAWAII								
Inouye	N	Y	Y	Y	Y	Y	Y	Y
Matsunaga	N	Y	Y	N	Y	Y	Y	Y
IDAHO								
McClure	N	N	N	N	N	N	N	N
Symms	N	N	N	N	N	N	N	N
ILLINOIS								
Percy	N	N	N	N	N	N	N	N
Dixon	N	Y	Y	Y	N	Y	Y	N
INDIANA								
Lugar	N	N	N	N	N	N	N	N
Quayle	N	N	N	N	N	N	N	N
IOWA								
Grassley	N	N	N	N	N	N	N	N
Jepsen	N	N	N	N	N	N	N	N
KANSAS								
Dole	Y	N	N	N	N	N	N	N
Kassebaum	N	N	N	N	N	N	N	N
KENTUCKY								
Ford	N	Y	Y	Y	Y	N	Y	N
Huddleston	Y	Y	Y	N	N	N	Y	N
LOUISIANA								
Johnston	N	Y	N	N	N	N	N	N
Long	N	N	N	N	N	Y	N	Y
MAINE								
Cohen	Y	N	N	N	N	N	N	N
Mitchell	Y	Y	Y	Y	N	Y	N	N
MARYLAND								
Mathias	?	N	Y	Y	Y	N	Y	N
Sarbanes	N	Y	Y	Y	N	Y	N	Y
MASSACHUSETTS								
Kennedy	N	Y	Y	Y	Y	Y	Y	Y
Tsongas	N	Y	Y	Y	N	Y	N	Y
MICHIGAN								
Levin	N	Y	Y	Y	Y	Y	Y	Y
Riegle	Y	Y	Y	Y	Y	Y	Y	Y
MINNESOTA								
Boschwitz	N	N	N	N	N	N	N	N
Durenberger	N	N	N	N	N	N	N	N
MISSISSIPPI								
Cochran	N	N	N	N	N	N	N	N
Stennis	Y	N	Y	N	N	N	N	N
MISSOURI								
Danforth	N	N	N	N	N	Y	N	N
Eagleton	N	Y	Y	Y	Y	Y	Y	Y
MONTANA								
Baucus	N	Y	Y	N	N	N	Y	N
Melcher	N	Y	Y	Y	N	N	Y	N
NEBRASKA								
Exon	Y	Y	Y	N	N	N	N	N
Zorinsky	Y	Y	Y	N	N	N	N	N
NEVADA								
Laxalt	N	?	N	N	N	N	N	N
Cannon	N	Y	Y	N	N	N	Y	N
NEW HAMPSHIRE								
Humphrey	Y	N	N	N	N	N	N	N
Rudman	N	N	N	N	N	N	N	N
NEW JERSEY								
Bradley	N	Y	Y	Y	Y	Y	Y	Y
Williams	?	?	?	?	+	?	+	?
NEW MEXICO								
Domenici	N	N	N	N	N	N	N	N
Schmitt	N	N	N	N	N	N	N	N
NEW YORK								
D'Amato	N	N	N	N	N	N	N	N
Moynihan	N	Y	Y	Y	Y	Y	Y	Y
NORTH CAROLINA								
East	N	N	N	N	N	N	N	N
Helms	Y	N	N	N	N	N	N	N
NORTH DAKOTA								
Andrews	N	N	N	N	N	N	N	N
Burdick	Y	Y	Y	Y	N	Y	Y	Y
OHIO								
Glenn	N	Y	Y	Y	Y	Y	Y	Y
Metzenbaum	N	Y	Y	Y	N	Y	Y	Y
OKLAHOMA								
Nickles	Y	N	N	N	N	N	N	N
Boren	Y	Y	Y	N	N	N	N	N
OREGON								
Hatfield	N	N	N	N	N	N	N	N
Packwood	N	N	N	N	N	N	N	N
PENNSYLVANIA								
Heinz	N	N	N	Y	N	N	Y	N
Specter	N	N	N	Y	N	Y	N	N
RHODE ISLAND								
Chafee	N	N	N	N	N	N	Y	N
Pell	N	Y	Y	Y	Y	Y	Y	Y
SOUTH CAROLINA								
Thurmond	N	N	N	N	N	N	N	N
Hollings	N	N	Y	N	N	N	N	N
SOUTH DAKOTA								
Abdnor	N	N	N	N	N	N	N	N
Pressler	?	?	N	N	N	N	N	N
TENNESSEE								
Baker	N	N	N	N	N	N	N	N
Sasser	N	Y	Y	Y	N	Y	N	Y
TEXAS								
Tower	N	N	?	?	?	?	?	N
Bentsen	N	Y	Y	N	N	N	N	N
UTAH								
Garn	N	N	N	N	N	N	N	N
Hatch	N	N	N	N	N	N	N	N
VERMONT								
Stafford	N	N	N	N	N	N	N	N
Leahy	N	Y	Y	Y	N	N	Y	Y
VIRGINIA								
Warner	N	N	N	N	N	N	N	N
Byrd*	Y	Y	N	N	N	N	N	N
WASHINGTON								
Gorton	N	N	N	N	N	N	N	N
Jackson	N	Y	Y	Y	N	Y	Y	Y
WEST VIRGINIA								
Byrd	N	Y	Y	Y	N	N	Y	N
Randolph	N	Y	Y	Y	N	Y	N	Y
WISCONSIN								
Kasten	N	N	N	N	N	N	N	N
Proxmire	Y	Y	N	N	N	N	N	N
WYOMING								
Simpson	N	N	N	N	N	N	N	N
Wallop	N	N	N	N	N	N	N	N

KEY

- Y Voted for (yea).
- # Paired for.
- + Announced for.
- N Voted against (nay)
- X Paired against.
- - Announced against.
- P Voted "present."
- C Voted "present" to avoid possible conflict of interest.
- ? Did not vote or otherwise make a position known.

*Byrd elected as an independent.

Democrats Republicans

---

66. S Con Res 9. Budget Reconciliation Instructions. Proxmire, D-Wis., amendment to deepen the cuts recommended by the Budget Committee by reducing $665 million in budget authority and $110 million in outlays in fiscal 1982 for the Banking, Housing and Urban Affairs Committee's Export-Import Bank program. Rejected 20-76: R 5-45; D 15-31 (ND 9-22; SD 6-9), April 1, 1981. A "yea" was a vote supporting the president's position.

67. S Con Res 9. Budget Reconciliation Instructions. DeConcini, D-Ariz., amendment to deepen the cuts recommended by the Budget Committee by requiring the Governmental Affairs Committee to save budget authority of $3.9 billion and outlays of $1.7 billion in fiscal 1982 through reduction of waste, fraud and abuse and through other administrative changes. Rejected 43-53: R 0-50; D 43-3 (ND 31-0; SD 12-3), April 1, 1981.

68. S Con Res 9. Budget Reconciliation Instructions. Bumpers, D-Ark., amendment to lessen cuts recommended by the Budget Committee by restoring $6 million in budget authority and $6 million in outlays in fiscal 1982 for the Labor and Human Resources Committee child immunization program. Rejected 44-54: R 2-50; D 42-4 (ND 30-1; SD 12-3), April 2, 1981.

69. S Con Res 9. Budget Reconciliation Instructions. Eagleton, D-Mo., amendment to lessen cuts recommended by the Budget Committee by restoring $400 million in budget authority and outlays in fiscal 1982 for the Finance Committee trade adjustment assistance program. Rejected 29-69: R 4-48; D 25-21 (ND 22-9; SD 3-12), April 2, 1981. A "nay" was a vote supporting the president's position.

70. S Con Res 9. Budget Reconciliation Instructions. Eagleton, D-Mo., amendment to lessen cuts recommended by the Budget Committee by restoring $78 million in budget authority and $39 million in outlays in fiscal 1982 for National Science Foundation research and education programs under the Labor and Human Resources Committee. Rejected 21-77: R 1-51; D 20-26 (ND 18-13; SD 2-13), April 2, 1981.

71. S Con Res 9. Budget Reconciliation Instructions. Moynihan, D-N.Y., amendment directing committees to distribute budget cuts among states on the principle of "equal sacrifice." Rejected 19-79: R 2-50; D 17-29 (ND 15-16; SD 2-13), April 2, 1981.

72. S Con Res 9. Budget Reconciliation Instructions. Riegle, D-Mich., amendment to lessen cuts recommended by the Budget Committee by restoring $285 million in outlays for fiscal 1983 for the Finance Committee unemployment insurance program. Rejected 38-60: R 4-48; D 34-12 (ND 28-3; SD 6-9), April 2, 1981. A "nay" was a vote supporting the president's position.

73. S Con Res 9. Budget Reconciliation Instructions. Glenn, D-Ohio, amendment to lessen cuts recommended by the Budget Committee by restoring $75 million in budget authority and $83 million in outlays in fiscal 1982 for the Labor and Human Resources Committee Employment Opportunity Pilot Program. Rejected 22-77: R 0-53; D 22-24 (ND 19-12; SD 3-12), April 2, 1981.

	74 75 76 77 78 79 80 81		74 75 76 77 78 79 80 81		74 75 76 77 78 79 80 81	KEY
ALABAMA		**IOWA**		**NEW HAMPSHIRE**		Y Voted for (yea).
Denton	N N N Y Y Y Y Y	*Grassley*	N N N Y Y Y Y Y	*Humphrey*	N N N Y Y Y Y Y	# Paired for.
Heflin	N Y Y Y Y Y Y ?	*Jepsen*	N N N Y Y Y Y Y	*Rudman*	N N N Y Y Y Y Y	+ Announced for.
ALASKA		**KANSAS**		**NEW JERSEY**		N Voted against (nay)
Murkowski	N N N Y Y Y Y Y	*Dole*	N N N Y Y Y Y Y	Bradley	Y Y Y Y Y ? ? ?	X Paired against.
Stevens	N N N Y Y Y Y Y	*Kassebaum*	N N N Y N Y Y Y	Williams	+ ? ? ? ? ? ? ?	- Announced against.
ARIZONA		**KENTUCKY**		**NEW MEXICO**		P Voted "present."
Goldwater	N N N Y Y Y Y Y	Ford	Y Y Y Y Y Y Y Y	*Domenici*	N N N Y Y Y Y Y	C Voted "present" to avoid pos-
DeConcini	N Y Y Y Y Y Y Y	Huddleston	N N Y Y Y Y ? ?	*Schmitt*	N N N Y Y Y Y Y	sible conflict of interest.
ARKANSAS		**LOUISIANA**		**NEW YORK**		? Did not vote or otherwise
Bumpers	Y N Y Y Y N N Y	Johnston	N N N Y Y Y Y Y	*D'Amato*	N N N Y Y Y Y Y	make a position known.
Pryor	Y N Y Y Y N N Y	Long	N N N Y Y Y Y N	Moynihan	Y Y Y Y Y Y N N	
CALIFORNIA		**MAINE**		**NORTH CAROLINA**		
Hayakawa	N N N Y Y Y Y Y	*Cohen*	Y N Y Y Y Y Y Y	*East*	N N N Y Y Y Y Y	
Cranston	Y Y Y N Y N Y N N	Mitchell	Y Y Y Y Y N Y Y	*Helms*	N N N Y Y Y Y Y	
COLORADO		**MARYLAND**		**NORTH DAKOTA**		74 75 76 77 78 79 80 81
Armstrong	N N N Y Y Y Y Y	*Mathias*	? ? ? + ? Y Y N	*Andrews*	N N N Y Y Y Y N	
Hart	Y N Y Y Y Y N N	Sarbanes	Y Y Y N Y N N N	Burdick	Y Y Y Y Y Y N N	**TEXAS**
CONNECTICUT		**MASSACHUSETTS**		**OHIO**		*Tower* N N N Y Y Y Y Y
Weicker	Y N N N N N Y Y	Kennedy	Y Y Y N N N N N	Glenn	Y Y Y Y Y Y Y Y	Bentsen N N Y Y Y Y Y Y
Dodd	Y Y Y N N N N N	Tsongas	Y Y Y N N N Y Y	Metzenbaum	Y Y Y Y N N N Y	**UTAH**
DELAWARE		**MICHIGAN**		**OKLAHOMA**		*Garn* N N N Y Y Y Y Y
Roth	Y N N Y ? N N Y	Levin	Y Y Y N Y N N N	*Nickles*	N N N Y Y Y Y Y	*Hatch* N N N Y Y Y Y Y
Biden	Y Y Y Y ? ? N N	Riegle	Y Y Y N Y N N N	Boren	N N N Y Y Y Y Y	**VERMONT**
FLORIDA		**MINNESOTA**		**OREGON**		*Stafford* Y N Y Y Y Y N Y
Hawkins	N N Y Y Y Y ? Y	*Boschwitz*	N N N Y N Y Y Y	*Hatfield*	N N N Y N N Y Y	Leahy Y Y Y Y Y N Y N
Chiles	Y N Y Y Y Y Y Y	*Durenberger*	Y N N Y ? ? ? Y	*Packwood*	N N Y Y Y ? ? ?	**VIRGINIA**
GEORGIA		**MISSISSIPPI**		**PENNSYLVANIA**		*Warner* N N N Y Y Y Y Y
Mattingly	N N N Y Y Y Y Y	*Cochran*	N N N Y Y Y Y Y	Heinz	Y N N Y Y Y Y N	Byrd* N N N Y Y Y Y Y
Nunn	N N N Y Y Y Y Y	Stennis	N N N Y Y Y Y Y	Specter	Y Y N Y Y Y Y N	**WASHINGTON**
HAWAII		**MISSOURI**		**RHODE ISLAND**		*Gorton* N N N Y Y Y Y Y
Inouye	Y Y Y Y Y N N N	*Danforth*	N N N Y Y Y Y N	*Chafee*	Y N N Y Y N N Y	Jackson Y N Y Y Y Y Y N
Matsunaga	Y Y Y Y N N N N	Eagleton	Y Y Y N N N N Y	Pell	Y Y Y N N N N N	**WEST VIRGINIA**
IDAHO		**MONTANA**		**SOUTH CAROLINA**		Byrd N N Y Y Y Y N Y
McClure	N N N Y Y Y Y Y	Baucus	N Y Y Y Y N N N	*Thurmond*	N N N Y Y Y Y Y	Randolph Y Y Y Y Y N N N
Symms	N N N Y Y Y Y Y	Melcher	Y N Y Y Y Y Y N	Hollings	N N Y Y Y Y N Y	**WISCONSIN**
ILLINOIS		**NEBRASKA**		**SOUTH DAKOTA**		*Kasten* N N N Y Y Y Y Y
Percy	N N N Y Y Y Y Y	Exon	N N Y Y Y N N N	*Abdnor*	N N N Y Y Y Y Y	Proxmire N N N Y N N N Y
Dixon	N N Y Y Y Y ? ?	Zorinsky	N Y Y Y ? ? N Y	*Pressler*	N N N Y N Y Y Y	**WYOMING**
INDIANA		**NEVADA**		**TENNESSEE**		*Simpson* N N N Y Y Y Y Y
Lugar	N N N Y Y Y Y Y	*Laxalt*	N N N Y Y Y Y Y	*Baker*	N N N Y N Y Y Y	*Wallop* N N N Y Y Y Y Y
Quayle	N N N Y Y ? Y Y	Cannon	Y N Y Y Y Y Y Y	Sasser	Y N Y Y Y ? N Y	

Democrats *Republicans*

*Byrd elected as an independent.

---

74. S Con Res 9. Budget Reconciliation Instructions. Biden, D-Del., amendment to lessen cuts recommended by the Budget Committee by restoring $400 million in budget authority and outlays for fiscal 1982 for the Labor and Human Resources Committee fuel subsidy program for low-income Americans. Rejected 37-61: R 8-44; D 29-17 (ND 24-7, SD 5-10), April 2, 1981. A "nay" was a vote supporting the president's position.

75. S Con Res 9. Budget Reconciliation Instructions. Kennedy, D-Mass., amendment to lessen cuts required by the Budget Committee by restoring $116 million in budget authority and $13 million in outlays in fiscal 1982 for the Judiciary Committee juvenile justice program. Rejected 26-72: R 1-51; D 25-21 (ND 23-8, SD 2-13), April 2, 1981.

76. S Con Res 9. Budget Reconciliation Instructions. Chiles, D-Fla., amendment to lessen cuts recommended by the Budget Committee by restoring $100 million in budget authority and $80 million in outlays for fiscal 1982 for the Labor and Human Resources Committee youth training program. Rejected 46-52: R 5-47; D 41-5 (ND 30-1, SD 11-4), April 2, 1981.

77. S Con Res 9. Budget Reconciliation Instructions. Adoption of the concurrent resolution to instruct 14 Senate authorizing and appropriations committees to cut $36.9 billion from fiscal 1982 spending. Adopted 88-10: R 51-1; D 37-9 (ND 22-9, SD 15-0),

April 2, 1981. A "yea" was a vote supporting the president's position.

78. S 694. Fiscal 1981 Supplemental Defense Authorization. Tower, R-Texas, motion to table (kill) the Pressler, R-S.D., amendment to delete $7 million for research related to the MX missile. Motion agreed to 79-15: R 44-6; D 35-9 (ND 20-9, SD 15-0), April 7, 1981.

79. S 694. Fiscal 1981 Supplemental Defense Authorization. Tower, R-Texas, motion to table (kill) the Bumpers, D-Ark., amendment to bar use of funds for reactivation of the battleship *New Jersey*. Motion agreed to 69-23: R 45-5; D 24-18 (ND 12-16, SD 12-2), April 7, 1981.

80. S 734. Export Trading Companies/Natural Gas Decontrol. Heinz, R-Pa., motion to table (kill) the Exon, D-Neb., amendment to express the sense of the Senate that the schedule of phased decontrol of natural gas prices under the National Gas Policy Act of 1978 (PL 95-621) should not be altered. Motion agreed to 66-27: R 48-2; D 18-25 (ND 9-20, SD 9-5), April 8, 1981.

81. S 734. Export Trading Companies. Armstrong, R-Colo., amendment to delete provisions authorizing $2 million annually for a three-year pilot program of Commerce Department grants to small businesses to help absorb first-year costs of hiring export managers. Adopted 68-25: R 46-5; D 22-20 (ND 10-19, SD 12-1), April 8, 1981.

	82 83			82 83			82 83
ALABAMA			**IOWA**			**NEW HAMPSHIRE**	
Denton	Y Y		*Grassley*	Y Y		*Humphrey*	Y Y
Heflin	N Y		*Jepsen*	N Y		*Rudman*	Y Y
ALASKA			**KANSAS**			**NEW JERSEY**	
Murkowski	Y Y		*Dole*	Y Y		Bradley	? ?
Stevens	N Y		*Kassebaum*	Y Y		Williams	? ?
ARIZONA			**KENTUCKY**			**NEW MEXICO**	
Goldwater	Y Y		Ford	Y Y		*Domenici*	Y Y
DeConcini	Y Y		Huddleston	? ?		*Schmitt*	Y Y
ARKANSAS			**LOUISIANA**			**NEW YORK**	
Bumpers	Y Y		Johnston	Y Y		*D'Amato*	N Y
Pryor	Y Y		Long	? ?		Moynihan	Y Y
CALIFORNIA			**MAINE**			**NORTH CAROLINA**	
Hayakawa	Y Y		*Cohen*	N Y		*East*	Y Y
Cranston	N Y		Mitchell	Y Y		*Helms*	Y Y
COLORADO			**MARYLAND**			**NORTH DAKOTA**	
Armstrong	Y Y		*Mathias*	N Y		*Andrews*	N Y
Hart	N Y		Sarbanes	N Y		Burdick	N Y
CONNECTICUT			**MASSACHUSETTS**			**OHIO**	
Weicker	N Y		Kennedy	N Y		Glenn	Y Y
Dodd	N Y		Tsongas	N Y		Metzenbaum	N Y
DELAWARE			**MICHIGAN**			**OKLAHOMA**	
Roth	Y Y		Levin	N Y		*Nickles*	Y Y
Biden	Y Y		Riegle	N Y		Boren	Y Y
FLORIDA			**MINNESOTA**			**OREGON**	
Hawkins	Y Y		*Boschwitz*	Y Y		*Hatfield*	N Y
Chiles	Y Y		*Durenberger*	? +		*Packwood*	? ?
GEORGIA			**MISSISSIPPI**			**PENNSYLVANIA**	
Mattingly	Y Y		*Cochran*	N Y		*Heinz*	N Y
Nunn	Y Y		Stennis	N Y		*Specter*	N Y
HAWAII			**MISSOURI**			**RHODE ISLAND**	
Inouye	N Y		*Danforth*	N Y		*Chafee*	N Y
Matsunaga	N Y		Eagleton	Y Y		Pell	N Y
IDAHO			**MONTANA**			**SOUTH CAROLINA**	
McClure	Y Y		Baucus	Y Y		*Thurmond*	Y Y
Symms	Y Y		Melcher	Y Y		Hollings	Y Y
ILLINOIS			**NEBRASKA**			**SOUTH DAKOTA**	
Percy	Y Y		Exon	Y Y		*Abdnor*	Y Y
Dixon	? ?		Zorinsky	Y Y		*Pressler*	N Y
INDIANA			**NEVADA**			**TENNESSEE**	
Lugar	Y Y		*Laxalt*	N Y		*Baker*	N Y
Quayle	Y Y		Cannon	N Y		Sasser	Y Y

KEY

Y	Voted for (yea).
#	Paired for.
+	Announced for.
N	Voted against (nay)
X	Paired against.
-	Announced against.
P	Voted "present."
C	Voted "present" to avoid possible conflict of interest.
?	Did not vote or otherwise make a position known.

	82 83
TEXAS	
Tower	Y Y
Bentsen	Y Y
UTAH	
Garn	N Y
Hatch	Y Y
VERMONT	
Stafford	Y Y
Leahy	N Y
VIRGINIA	
Warner	Y Y
Byrd*	Y Y
WASHINGTON	
Gorton	N Y
Jackson	N Y
WEST VIRGINIA	
Byrd	N Y
Randolph	N Y
WISCONSIN	
Kasten	Y Y
Proxmire	Y Y
WYOMING	
Simpson	Y Y
Wallop	Y Y

Byrd elected as an independent.

82. S 734. Export Trading Companies. Armstrong, R-Colo., motion to table (kill) the Heinz, R-Pa., substitute to the Proxmire, D-Wis., amendment, to authorize $25 million (rather than $50 million as recommended by the Senate Banking Committee) over five years for loans and loan guarantees to export trading companies by the Economic Development Administration and the Small Business Administration. Motion agreed to 55-38: R 33-18; D 22-20 (ND 11-18, SD 11-2), April 8, 1981. (The Proxmire amendment to delete the authorization entirely was adopted subsequently by voice vote.)

83. S 734. Export Trading Companies. Passage of the bill to encourage the formation of export trading companies to help U.S. firms market their goods abroad. Passed 93-0: R 51-0; D 42-0 (ND 29-0, SD 13-0), April 8, 1981.

Corresponding to Congressional Record Votes 84, 85, 86, 87, 88

	84 85 86 87 88		84 85 86 87 88		84 85 86 87 88	KEY
ALABAMA		**IOWA**		**NEW HAMPSHIRE**		Y Voted for (yea).
Denton	Y N Y Y Y	*Grassley*	Y N N N Y	*Humphrey*	Y N N N Y	# Paired for.
Heflin	Y Y N N Y	*Jepsen*	Y N Y Y Y	*Rudman*	Y N Y Y Y	+ Announced for.
ALASKA		**KANSAS**		**NEW JERSEY**		N Voted against (nay)
Murkowski	Y N Y Y Y	*Dole*	Y N Y Y Y	Bradley	Y N Y Y Y	X Paired against.
Stevens	Y N Y Y Y	*Kassebaum*	Y N Y Y Y	Williams	? ? ? ? ?	- Announced against.
ARIZONA		**KENTUCKY**		**NEW MEXICO**		P Voted "present."
Goldwater	Y N Y N N	Ford	Y N Y Y Y	*Domenici*	Y N N N Y	C Voted "present" to avoid pos-
DeConcini	Y Y N N Y	Huddleston	Y Y N N Y	*Schmitt*	Y N Y Y Y	sible conflict of interest.
ARKANSAS		**LOUISIANA**		**NEW YORK**		? Did not vote or otherwise
Bumpers	Y N Y Y Y	Johnston	Y Y N N Y	*D'Amato*	Y N Y Y Y	make a position known.
Pryor	Y Y N Y Y	Long	Y Y N N Y	Moynihan	+ ? ? ? ?	
CALIFORNIA		**MAINE**		**NORTH CAROLINA**		
Hayakawa	Y N Y Y Y	*Cohen*	Y N Y Y Y	*East*	? Y N N Y	
Cranston	Y N Y Y Y	Mitchell	Y Y N Y Y	*Helms*	Y Y N N Y	
COLORADO		**MARYLAND**		**NORTH DAKOTA**		
Armstrong	Y N Y Y Y	*Mathias*	Y N Y Y Y	*Andrews*	Y N Y N Y	
Hart	? ? ? ? ?	Sarbanes	Y N Y Y Y	Burdick	Y Y N N Y	
CONNECTICUT		**MASSACHUSETTS**		**OHIO**			84 85 86 87 88
Weicker	Y N Y Y Y	Kennedy	Y N Y ? Y	Glenn	Y N ? ? ?	
Dodd	Y N Y Y Y	Tsongas	Y N Y Y Y	Metzenbaum	? ? ? ? Y	**TEXAS**
DELAWARE		**MICHIGAN**		**OKLAHOMA**		*Tower*	? ? ? ? ?
Roth	Y N Y N Y	Levin	Y N Y Y Y	*Nickles*	Y Y N N Y	Bentsen	Y N Y Y Y
Biden	Y N Y Y Y	Riegle	Y Y Y Y Y	Boren	Y ? N N Y	**UTAH**
FLORIDA		**MINNESOTA**		**OREGON**		*Garn*	Y N Y Y Y
Hawkins	Y N Y N Y	*Boschwitz*	Y N Y Y Y	*Hatfield*	Y N Y Y Y	*Hatch*	Y Y N Y Y
Chiles	Y ? ? ? ?	*Durenberger*	Y N Y Y Y	*Packwood*	Y N Y Y Y	**VERMONT**
GEORGIA		**MISSISSIPPI**		**PENNSYLVANIA**		*Stafford*	Y N Y Y Y
Mattingly	Y N Y Y Y	*Cochran*	? N Y Y Y	*Heinz*	Y N Y Y Y	Leahy	Y N Y Y Y
Nunn	Y Y Y Y Y	Stennis	Y Y N N Y	*Specter*	Y N Y Y Y	**VIRGINIA**
HAWAII		**MISSOURI**		**RHODE ISLAND**		*Warner*	Y N N N Y
Inouye	Y N Y Y Y	*Danforth*	Y N Y Y Y	*Chafee*	Y N Y Y Y	Byrd*	Y Y N N Y
Matsunaga	Y N Y Y Y	Eagleton	? ? ? ? ?	Pell	Y N Y Y Y	**WASHINGTON**
IDAHO		**MONTANA**		**SOUTH CAROLINA**		*Gorton*	Y N Y Y Y
McClure	Y Y N N Y	Baucus	Y N Y Y Y	*Thurmond*	Y N Y Y Y	Jackson	Y Y Y N Y
Symms	Y Y N N Y	Melcher	Y Y N N Y	Hollings	Y Y N Y Y	**WEST VIRGINIA**
ILLINOIS		**NEBRASKA**		**SOUTH DAKOTA**		Byrd	Y Y Y N Y
Percy	Y N Y Y Y	Exon	Y Y N N Y	*Abdnor*	Y Y N N Y	Randolph	Y Y Y N Y
Dixon	Y N Y Y Y	Zorinsky	Y Y N N Y	*Pressler*	? ? ? ? ?	**WISCONSIN**
INDIANA		**NEVADA**		**TENNESSEE**		*Kasten*	Y N N N Y
Lugar	Y N Y Y Y	*Laxalt*	Y N Y Y Y	*Baker*	Y N Y Y ?	Proxmire	Y Y N N Y
Quayle	Y N N N Y	Cannon	Y Y Y Y Y	Sasser	Y Y N Y Y	**WYOMING**
						Simpson	Y N N Y Y
						Wallop	Y N Y Y Y

Democrats *Republicans*

Byrd elected as an independent.

84. Exec U, 96th Cong, 1st Sess. U.S.-Canadian Maritime Boundary Treaty. Adoption of the resolution of ratification for the treaty to request World Court arbitration of an East Coast maritime boundary dispute between the United States and Canada. Adopted 91-0: R 49-0; D 42-0 (ND 27-0, SD 15-0), April 29, 1981. A two-thirds majority vote (61 in this case) is required for adoption of resolutions of ratifications of treaties. A "yea" was a vote supporting the president's position.

85. S 786. Development Banks Authorizations. DeConcini, D-Ariz., motion to table (kill) the Percy, R-Ill., substitute, to the DeConcini amendment (*see vote 86, below*), to provide full funding ($3.24 billion) for the International Development Association. Motion rejected 30-61: R 8-43; D 22-18 (ND 12-15, SD 10-3), April 29, 1981. A "nay" was a vote supporting the president's position.

86. S 786. Development Banks Authorizations. Percy, R-Ill., substitute, to the DeConcini, D-Ariz., amendment, to provide full funding ($3.24 billion) for the International Development Association. Adopted 58-33: R 36-15; D 22-18 (ND 18-8, SD 4-10), April

29, 1981. A "yea" was a vote supporting the president's position. (The original DeConcini amendment would have cut funding by $810 million. The DeConcini amendment, as amended by the Percy substitute, was adopted subsequently by voice vote.)

87. S 786. Development Banks Authorizations. Passage of the bill to authorize $3.24 billion for the sixth replenishment to the International Development Association and to authorize U.S. membership in and a contribution of $359,733,570 to the African Development Bank. Passed 58-32: R 35-16; D 23-16 (ND 16-9, SD 7-7), April 29, 1981. A "yea" was a vote supporting the president's position.

88. S Res 115. U.S. Submarine and Japanese Freighter Collision. Adoption of the resolution expressing regret at the loss of life and property resulting from the April 9, 1981, collision between a U.S. submarine and a Japanese freighter and assuring Japan that a complete investigation of the incident would be conducted. Adopted 92-0: R 50-0; D 42-0 (ND 28-0, SD 14-0), April 29, 1981.

	89	90	91	92
ALABAMA				
Denton	Y	Y	Y	N
Heflin	Y	Y	N	Y
ALASKA				
Murkowski	?	?	N	N
Stevens	Y	Y	N	N
ARIZONA				
Goldwater	Y	Y	Y	X
DeConcini	?	Y	N	Y
ARKANSAS				
Bumpers	?	Y	N	Y
Pryor	Y	Y	N	Y
CALIFORNIA				
Hayakawa	Y	Y	Y	N
Cranston	Y	Y	N	Y
COLORADO				
Armstrong	Y	Y	Y	N
Hart	Y	Y	N	Y
CONNECTICUT				
Weicker	Y	Y	N	Y
Dodd	Y	Y	N	Y
DELAWARE				
Roth	Y	Y	N	N
Biden	Y	?	N	Y
FLORIDA				
Hawkins	Y	Y	Y	N
Chiles	Y	Y	?	#
GEORGIA				
Mattingly	Y	Y	Y	N
Nunn	Y	Y	N	N
HAWAII				
Inouye	Y	?	N	Y
Matsunaga	Y	Y	N	Y
IDAHO				
McClure	Y	Y	Y	N
Symms	Y	Y	Y	N
ILLINOIS				
Percy	Y	Y	N	N
Dixon	Y	Y	N	Y
INDIANA				
Lugar	Y	Y	Y	N
Quayle	Y	Y	N	N
IOWA				
Grassley	Y	Y	Y	N
Jepsen	Y	?	Y	N
KANSAS				
Dole	Y	Y	N	N
Kassebaum	Y	Y	N	N
KENTUCKY				
Ford	Y	Y	N	Y
Huddleston	Y	Y	N	Y
LOUISIANA				
Johnston	Y	Y	N	N
Long	Y	Y	N	N
MAINE				
Cohen	Y	Y	N	Y
Mitchell	Y	Y	N	Y
MARYLAND				
Mathias	Y	Y	N	?
Sarbanes	Y	Y	N	Y
MASSACHUSETTS				
Kennedy	Y	Y	N	Y
Tsongas	Y	?	N	Y
MICHIGAN				
Levin	Y	Y	N	Y
Riegle	Y	Y	N	Y
MINNESOTA				
Boschwitz	Y	Y	N	N
Durenberger	Y	Y	N	N
MISSISSIPPI				
Cochran	Y	Y	Y	N
Stennis	Y	Y	Y	N
MISSOURI				
Danforth	Y	Y	N	N
Eagleton	Y	Y	N	Y
MONTANA				
Baucus	Y	Y	N	Y
Melcher	Y	Y	N	?
NEBRASKA				
Exon	Y	Y	N	Y
Zorinsky	Y	Y	Y	Y
NEVADA				
Laxalt	Y	Y	N	N
Cannon	Y	Y	?	?
NEW HAMPSHIRE				
Humphrey	Y	Y	Y	N
Rudman	Y	Y	N	N
NEW JERSEY				
Bradley	Y	Y	N	Y
Williams	?	?	?	?
NEW MEXICO				
Domenici	Y	Y	N	N
Schmitt	Y	Y	N	N
NEW YORK				
D'Amato	Y	+	Y	-
Moynihan	Y	Y	N	Y
NORTH CAROLINA				
East	Y	Y	Y	N
Helms	Y	Y	Y	N
NORTH DAKOTA				
Andrews	Y	Y	N	Y
Burdick	Y	Y	N	Y
OHIO				
Glenn	Y	Y	N	Y
Metzenbaum	Y	Y	N	Y
OKLAHOMA				
Nickles	Y	Y	Y	N
Boren	Y	Y	N	N
OREGON				
Hatfield	Y	Y	N	N
Packwood	Y	Y	N	N
PENNSYLVANIA				
Heinz	Y	Y	N	N
Specter	Y	Y	N	N
RHODE ISLAND				
Chafee	Y	Y	N	N
Pell	Y	Y	N	Y
SOUTH CAROLINA				
Thurmond	Y	Y	Y	N
Hollings	Y	Y	N	Y
SOUTH DAKOTA				
Abdnor	Y	Y	N	Y
Pressler	Y	Y	N	Y
TENNESSEE				
Baker	Y	Y	N	N
Sasser	Y	Y	N	Y
TEXAS				
Tower	Y	Y	N	N
Bentsen	Y	Y	N	N
UTAH				
Garn	Y	Y	Y	N
Hatch	Y	Y	Y	?
VERMONT				
Stafford	Y	Y	N	N
Leahy	Y	Y	N	Y
VIRGINIA				
Warner	Y	Y	?	?
Byrd*	Y	Y	Y	N
WASHINGTON				
Gorton	Y	Y	N	N
Jackson	Y	Y	N	Y
WEST VIRGINIA				
Byrd	Y	Y	N	Y
Randolph	Y	Y	N	Y
WISCONSIN				
Kasten	Y	Y	N	N
Proxmire	Y	Y	Y	N
WYOMING				
Simpson	Y	Y	Y	N
Wallop	Y	Y	N	N

KEY

Y Voted for (yea).
Paired for.
+ Announced for.
N Voted against (nay).
X Paired against.
- Announced against.
P Voted "present".
C Voted "present" to avoid possible conflict of interest.
? Did not vote or otherwise make a position known.

Democrats   **Republicans**

* Byrd elected as an independent.

89. State Department Nominations. Confirmation of President Reagan's nominations of Leonore Annenberg of Pennsylvania to hold the rank of ambassador while serving as chief of protocol for the White House; John J. Louis Jr. of Illinois to be ambassador to Great Britain and Northern Ireland; Arthur H. Woodruff of Florida to be ambassador to the Central African Republic; John A. Burroughs Jr. of Maryland to be ambassador to Malawi; John A. Gavin of California to be ambassador to Mexico; Elliott Abrams of the District of Columbia to be assistant secretary of state for international organizations; and Robert D. Hormats of Maryland to be assistant secretary of state for economic and business affairs. Confirmed 96-0: R 52-0; D 44-0 (ND 30-0, SD 14-0), May 5, 1981. A "yea" was a vote supporting the president's position.

90. S 533. Public Buildings Act of 1981. Passage of the bill to reorganize the General Services Administration's (GSA) public buildings program and to provide for long-range planning for public building needs. Passed 93-0: R 50-0; D 43-0 (ND 28-0, SD 15-0), May 6, 1981.

91. S Con Res 19. Fiscal 1982 Budget Targets. Hatch, R-Utah, amendment to delete $100 million in budget authority and budget outlays for fiscal 1982 from the administration of justice function in order to delete funds for the Legal Services Corp. Rejected 24-72: R 20-32; D 4-40 (ND 2-28, SD 2-12), May 7, 1981.

92. S Con Res 19. Fiscal 1982 Budget Targets. DeConcini, D-Ariz., substitute, to the Thurmond, R-S.C., amendment *(see vote 95, p. 20-S)*, to increase budget authority for the Veterans Administration by $400 million and budget outlays by $250 million in fiscal 1982. Rejected 39-52: R 4-44; D 35-8 (ND 28-1, SD 7-7), May 7, 1981.

CQ Senate Votes 93 - 100

Corresponding to Congressional Record Votes 93, 94, 95, 96, 97, 98, 99, 100

	93 94 95 96 97 98 99 100		93 94 95 96 97 98 99 100		93 94 95 96 97 98 99 100
ALABAMA		**IOWA**		**NEW HAMPSHIRE**	
Denton	Y N Y N N N N Y	*Grassley*	Y N Y N N N Y Y	*Humphrey*	Y N Y N N N Y N
Heflin	Y Y Y Y Y N N N	*Jepsen*	Y N N N ? ? ? Y	*Rudman*	Y N N N ? ? Y
ALASKA		**KANSAS**		**NEW JERSEY**	
Murkowski	Y N Y N N N N Y	*Dole*	Y N N N N N Y Y	Bradley	Y Y N Y Y Y Y Y
Stevens	Y N N N N N N Y	*Kassebaum*	Y Y N N N N N Y	Williams	Y Y N Y Y ? Y Y
ARIZONA		**KENTUCKY**		**NEW MEXICO**	
Goldwater	N N N N N N N Y	Ford	Y Y N Y Y N N Y	*Domenici*	Y N Y N N N N Y
DeConcini	Y Y N Y N N N N	Huddleston	Y N N Y Y ? ? ?	*Schmitt*	? ? ? ? ? N N Y
ARKANSAS		**LOUISIANA**		**NEW YORK**	
Bumpers	Y Y N Y ? ? ? ?	Johnston	Y N Y N N N N Y	*D'Amato*	Y N N N N - N Y
Pryor	Y Y N Y N Y N Y	Long	? ? ? ? ? N N Y	Moynihan	Y Y N Y Y Y Y Y
CALIFORNIA		**MAINE**		**NORTH CAROLINA**	
Hayakawa	Y N Y N N N N Y	*Cohen*	Y N Y N N Y Y Y	*East*	Y N Y N N N N Y
Cranston	Y Y N Y Y N N Y	Mitchell	Y Y Y Y Y Y Y Y	*Helms*	Y N Y N N N Y N
COLORADO		**MARYLAND**		**NORTH DAKOTA**	
Armstrong	Y N Y N N ? N Y	*Mathias*	? ? ? ? ? Y Y Y	*Andrews*	Y N N N N N N Y
Hart	Y Y N Y Y N N Y	Sarbanes	Y Y N Y Y Y N Y	Burdick	Y Y Y Y Y N N Y
CONNECTICUT		**MASSACHUSETTS**		**OHIO**	
Weicker	? ? ? ? ? Y Y Y	Kennedy	Y Y N Y Y ? ? Y	Glenn	Y Y N Y - Y Y Y
Dodd	? Y N Y Y Y Y Y	Tsongas	Y Y N Y Y Y Y Y	Metzenbaum	Y Y N Y ? Y Y Y
DELAWARE		**MICHIGAN**		**OKLAHOMA**	
Roth	Y N Y N Y ? Y Y	Levin	Y Y N Y Y Y Y Y	*Nickles*	Y N Y N N N N Y
Biden	Y Y N Y Y Y Y Y	Riegle	Y Y N Y Y Y Y Y	Boren	Y N Y N N Y N N
FLORIDA		**MINNESOTA**		**OREGON**	
Hawkins	Y N Y N N ? N Y	*Boschwitz*	Y N N N N N N Y	*Hatfield*	Y N N N N N N Y
Chiles	Y Y Y Y N N N Y	*Durenberger*	Y N Y N N Y Y Y	*Packwood*	Y N N N N N N Y
GEORGIA		**MISSISSIPPI**		**PENNSYLVANIA**	
Mattingly	Y N N N N N N Y	*Cochran*	Y N Y N N ? - Y	*Heinz*	Y Y N N ? Y Y Y
Nunn	Y N Y N Y N Y Y	Stennis	Y N N N N N N Y	*Specter*	Y Y Y N N Y Y Y
HAWAII		**MISSOURI**		**RHODE ISLAND**	
Inouye	Y Y N Y Y ? Y Y	*Danforth*	Y N N N N N N Y	*Chafee*	Y Y N N N Y Y Y
Matsunaga	? + ? ? ? Y N Y	Eagleton	Y N Y N Y Y Y Y	Pell	Y Y N Y Y Y Y Y
IDAHO		**MONTANA**		**SOUTH CAROLINA**	
McClure	Y N N N N N N Y	Baucus	Y Y N Y Y N N N	*Thurmond*	Y N Y N N N N Y
Symms	Y N Y N N N N N	Melcher	Y Y N Y Y N N N	Hollings	Y N N N N N N Y
ILLINOIS		**NEBRASKA**		**SOUTH DAKOTA**	
Percy	Y N N N N N N Y	Exon	? ? ? ? ? N N Y	*Abdnor*	Y N Y N N N N Y
Dixon	Y Y Y Y Y Y Y Y	Zorinsky	Y Y Y N N N N N	*Pressler*	? ? ? ? ? N N Y
INDIANA		**NEVADA**		**TENNESSEE**	
Lugar	Y N Y N N Y Y Y	*Laxalt*	Y N Y N N N N Y	*Baker*	Y N N N N N N Y
Quayle	Y N Y N N ? ? ?	Cannon	? ? + ? ? ? ? ?	Sasser	Y Y N Y + - - ?

Democrats **Republicans**

KEY

Y	Voted for (yea).
#	Paired for.
+	Announced for.
N	Voted against (nay).
X	Paired against.
-	Announced against.
P	Voted "present".
C	Voted "present" to avoid possible conflict of interest.
?	Did not vote or otherwise make a position known.

	93 94 95 96 97 98 99 100
TEXAS	
Tower	Y N N N N N N Y
Bentsen	Y Y Y Y N N Y N
UTAH	
Garn	Y N N N N N N Y
Hatch	? - ? - - N N Y
VERMONT	
Stafford	Y N Y N N N N Y
Leahy	Y Y N Y Y Y Y Y
VIRGINIA	
Warner	Y N N N N N N Y
Byrd*	Y Y Y Y N N Y N
WASHINGTON	
Gorton	Y N N N N N N Y
Jackson	Y Y N Y Y N N Y
WEST VIRGINIA	
Byrd	Y Y N Y Y Y Y N
Randolph	Y Y N Y Y Y N Y
WISCONSIN	
Kasten	Y N Y N N N N Y
Proxmire	N Y Y Y N Y N Y
WYOMING	
Simpson	Y N Y N N N N Y
Wallop	Y N N N N N N Y

*Byrd elected as an independent

93. S Con Res 19. Fiscal 1982 Budget Targets. Baker, R-Tenn., motion that the sergeant-at-arms be instructed to request the attendance of absent senators. Motion agreed to 88-2: R 47-1; D 41-1 (ND 27-1, SD 14-0), May 8, 1981.

94. S Con Res 19. Fiscal 1982 Budget Targets. Riegle, D-Mich., amendment, to the Thurmond, R-S.C., amendment *(see vote 95, below)*, to retain the existing system of calculating cost-of-living adjustments (COLAs) in federal retirement programs, thereby reversing a Budget Committee proposal designed to hold down COLA costs. The Riegle amendment proposed to add $7.85 billion in fiscal 1982 outlays for increased COLA costs, to be offset by $7.85 billion in unspecified savings in other areas. Rejected 42-49: R 5-43; D 37-6 (ND 29-0, SD 8-6), May 8, 1981.

95. S Con Res 19. Fiscal 1982 Budget Targets. Thurmond, R-S.C., amendment to add $300 million in budget authority and $150 million in outlays for veterans' programs in fiscal 1982 and make offsetting cuts in health programs. Rejected 36-55: R 24-24; D 12-31 (ND 5-24, SD 7-7), May 8, 1981.

96. S Con Res 19. Fiscal 1982 Budget Targets. DeConcini, D-Ariz., amendment to save $3.9 billion in budget authority and $1.7 billion in outlays in fiscal 1982 by cutting funds for consultant services, travel, audio-visual and filmmaking programs, advertising, public relations, and debt collection activities. Rejected 42-49: R 2-46; D 40-3 (ND 29-0, SD 11-3), May 8, 1981.

97. S Con Res 19. Fiscal 1982 Budget Targets. Kennedy D-Mass., amendment to provide an additional $400 million in budget authority and outlays in fiscal 1982 for school lunch and other child nutrition programs, to be offset by unspecified cuts in other areas. Rejected 29-58: R 1-46; D 28-12 (ND 25-3, SD 3-9), May 8, 1981.

98. S Con Res 19. Fiscal 1982 Budget Targets. Moynihan, D-N.Y., amendment to reduce funding for water projects by $200 million in budget authority and outlays in fiscal 1982, and increase funding for mass transit and guaranteed student loan programs by $100 million in budget authority and outlays each. Rejected 30-55: R 9-36; D 21-19 (ND 19-9, SD 2-10), May 11, 1981.

99. S Con Res 19. Fiscal 1982 Budget Targets. Metzenbaum, D-Ohio, amendment to reduce funding for water projects by $300 million in budget authority and $200 million in outlays in fiscal 1982. Rejected 39-52: R 18-31; D 21-21 (ND 18-12, SD 3-9), May 11, 1981.

100. S Con Res 19. Fiscal 1982 Budget Targets. Domenici, R-N.M., motion to table (kill) the Proxmire, D-Wis., amendment to balance the budget in fiscal 1982. Motion agreed to 81-13: R 47-4; D 34-9 (ND 26-5, SD 8-4), May 11, 1981.

	101	102	103	104	105	106	107	108
ALABAMA								
Denton	N	N	N	N	N	N	N	N
Heflin	N	N	N	N	N	Y	N	N
ALASKA								
Murkowski	N	N	N	N	N	N	N	N
Stevens	N	N	N	N	N	N	N	N
ARIZONA								
Goldwater	N	N	N	N	N	N	N	N
DeConcini	N	N	Y	N	N	Y	Y	N
ARKANSAS								
Bumpers	?	?	?	?	N	Y	Y	Y
Pryor	Y	N	N	N	Y	N	N	N
CALIFORNIA								
Hayakawa	N	N	N	N	N	N	N	N
Cranston	Y	Y	Y	N	Y	N	Y	Y
COLORADO								
Armstrong	N	N	N	N	N	N	N	N
Hart	Y	Y	Y	N	Y	Y	Y	N
CONNECTICUT								
Weicker	N	Y	N	N	N	N	Y	Y
Dodd	Y	Y	Y	Y	Y	N	Y	N
DELAWARE								
Roth	N	N	N	N	N	Y	N	N
Biden	Y	Y	Y	Y	Y	N	Y	N
FLORIDA								
Hawkins	N	N	?	?	N	Y	N	N
Chiles	N	N	Y	N	N	N	Y	N
GEORGIA								
Mattingly	N	N	N	N	N	N	N	N
Nunn	Y	N	Y	N	N	Y	Y	N
HAWAII								
Inouye	Y	Y	Y	N	Y	Y	Y	Y
Matsunaga	Y	N	?	N	Y	Y	Y	Y
IDAHO								
McClure	N	N	N	N	N	Y	N	N
Symms	N	N	N	N	N	Y	N	N
ILLINOIS								
Percy	N	N	N	N	N	N	N	N
Dixon	N	N	N	N	N	N	Y	N
INDIANA								
Lugar	N	N	N	N	N	N	N	N
Quayle	?	?	N	N	N	N	N	N
IOWA								
Grassley	N	N	N	N	N	Y	N	N
Jepsen	N	N	N	N	N	Y	N	N
KANSAS								
Dole	N	N	N	N	N	N	N	N
Kassebaum	N	N	N	N	N	N	N	N
KENTUCKY								
Ford	Y	N	Y	N	N	Y	Y	N
Huddleston	?	N	N	N	N	Y	N	N
LOUISIANA								
Johnston	N	N	N	N	N	Y	N	N
Long	N	?	N	N	N	N	N	N
MAINE								
Cohen	N	N	Y	N	Y	N	Y	N
Mitchell	Y	N	Y	N	N	Y	Y	Y
MARYLAND								
Mathias	N	N	N	N	?	?	?	?
Sarbanes	Y	N	Y	N	Y	Y	Y	Y
MASSACHUSETTS								
Kennedy	Y	?	Y	Y	Y	N	Y	Y
Tsongas	Y	N	Y	Y	Y	N	Y	Y
MICHIGAN								
Levin	Y	N	Y	N	Y	N	Y	Y
Riegle	Y	N	Y	N	Y	Y	Y	Y
MINNESOTA								
Boschwitz	N	N	N	N	N	N	N	N
Durenberger	N	?	?	?	N	N	N	N
MISSISSIPPI								
Cochran	N	N	N	N	N	N	N	N
Stennis	N	N	N	N	N	N	N	N
MISSOURI								
Danforth	N	N	N	N	N	N	N	N
Eagleton	Y	Y	Y	Y	Y	Y	Y	Y
MONTANA								
Baucus	Y	N	Y	N	N	Y	Y	N
Melcher	N	N	N	N	N	Y	N	N
NEBRASKA								
Exon	N	Y	Y	N	N	Y	Y	N
Zorinsky	N	N	N	N	N	Y	N	N
NEVADA								
Laxalt	N	N	N	N	N	N	N	N
Cannon	?	?	?	?	?	?	?	?
NEW HAMPSHIRE								
Humphrey	N	N	N	N	N	N	N	N
Rudman	Y	N	N	N	N	N	N	N
NEW JERSEY								
Bradley	Y	N	Y	Y	Y	N	Y	N
Williams	Y	Y	Y	Y	Y	N	Y	Y
NEW MEXICO								
Domenici	N	N	N	N	N	N	N	N
Schmitt	N	N	N	N	N	N	N	N
NEW YORK								
D'Amato	N	?	N	N	N	N	N	N
Moynihan	Y	N	Y	Y	Y	N	Y	N
NORTH CAROLINA								
East	N	N	N	N	N	N	N	N
Helms	N	N	N	N	N	Y	N	N
NORTH DAKOTA								
Andrews	N	N	N	N	N	Y	N	N
Burdick	N	N	N	N	N	Y	N	N
OHIO								
Glenn	N	Y	Y	N	N	N	Y	N
Metzenbaum	Y	N	Y	Y	Y	N	Y	Y
OKLAHOMA								
Nickles	N	N	N	N	N	N	N	N
Boren	N	?	N	N	N	Y	N	N
OREGON								
Hatfield	N	?	N	N	N	N	N	Y
Packwood	N	N	N	N	N	N	N	N
PENNSYLVANIA								
Heinz	N	N	N	N	N	N	N	N
Specter	N	N	Y	N	N	N	N	N
RHODE ISLAND								
Chafee	N	N	N	N	N	N	N	N
Pell	Y	?	?	Y	Y	N	Y	Y
SOUTH CAROLINA								
Thurmond	N	N	N	N	N	N	N	N
Hollings	N	Y	N	N	N	N	N	N
SOUTH DAKOTA								
Abdnor	N	N	N	N	N	Y	N	N
Pressler	N	Y	Y	N	N	Y	N	N
TENNESSEE								
Baker	N	N	N	N	N	N	?	N
Sasser	?	?	N	N	N	Y	Y	N
TEXAS								
Tower	N	N	N	N	N	N	N	N
Bentsen	N	N	Y	N	Y	Y	N	N
UTAH								
Garn	N	N	N	N	N	Y	N	N
Hatch	N	N	N	N	N	N	N	N
VERMONT								
Stafford	N	N	N	N	N	N	N	N
Leahy	Y	N	Y	N	Y	N	Y	Y
VIRGINIA								
Warner	N	N	N	N	N	N	N	N
Byrd*	N	?	N	N	N	N	N	N
WASHINGTON								
Gorton	N	N	N	N	N	N	N	N
Jackson	N	Y	Y	Y	Y	Y	Y	N
WEST VIRGINIA								
Byrd	Y	Y	Y	N	Y	Y	Y	N
Randolph	N	N	Y	N	Y	Y	Y	N
WISCONSIN								
Kasten	N	N	N	N	N	N	N	N
Proxmire	Y	N	Y	N	Y	N	Y	N
WYOMING								
Simpson	N	N	N	N	N	N	N	N
Wallop	N	N	N	N	N	N	N	N

KEY

- Y Voted for (yea).
- # Paired for.
- + Announced for.
- N Voted against (nay).
- X Paired against.
- - Announced against.
- P Voted "present".
- C Voted "present" to avoid possible conflict of interest.
- ? Did not vote or otherwise make a position known.

Democrats **Republicans**

*Byrd elected as an independent.

101. S Con Res 19. Fiscal 1982 Budget Targets. Bradley, D-N.J., amendment to express the sense of Congress that by Oct. 1, 1981, the president should prepare a report describing the economic impact of a three-year tax cut and projected increases in defense and civilian spending in fiscal 1982-86. Rejected 26-69: R 1-51; D 25-18 (ND 22-9, SD 3-9), May 11, 1981.

102. S Con Res 19. Fiscal 1982 Budget Targets. Hollings, D-S.C., amendment to restrict fiscal 1982 tax cuts to supply-side measures totaling $25.5 billion and put off across-the-board cuts in corporate and individual taxes until fiscal 1983. Rejected 14-74: R 2-47; D 12-27 (ND 11-18, SD 1-9), May 11, 1981.

103. S Con Res 19. Fiscal 1982 Budget Targets. Metzenbaum, D-Ohio, amendment to increase revenues by $1.3 billion in fiscal 1982 by eliminating the use of commodity tax straddles that allow individuals to defer the payment of taxes and convert ordinary income into long-term capital gains. Rejected 32-62: R 3-48; D 29-14 (ND 25-4, SD 4-10), May 12, 1981.

104. S Con Res 19. Fiscal 1982 Budget Targets. Metzenbaum, D-Ohio, amendment to increase revenues by $2.3 billion in fiscal 1982 by eliminating the expensing, or one-year write-off, of intangible oil drilling, and exploration and development costs. Rejected 12-84: R 0-51; D 12-33 (ND 12-19, SD 0-14), May 12, 1981.

105. S Con Res 19. Fiscal 1982 Budget Targets. Bradley, D-N.J., amendment to add $1.8 billion in budget authority and $1 billion in outlays in fiscal 1982 for a variety of education, scientific research, space technology and job training programs. To pay for the package, the amendment proposed to increase fiscal 1982 revenues by $3.1 billion through elimination of the commodity tax straddle and special tax treatment for Domestic International Sales Corporations (DISCs). Rejected 22-76: R 0-52; D 22-24 (ND 21-10, SD 1-14), May 12, 1981.

106. S Con Res 19. Fiscal 1982 Budget Targets. Melcher, D-Mont., amendment to increase fiscal 1982 budget authority and outlays for agriculture programs by $200 million, to be offset by equivalent decreases in foreign aid. Rejected 39-59: R 12-40; D 27-19 (ND 17-14, SD 10-5), May 12, 1981.

107. S Con Res 19. Fiscal 1982 Budget Targets. Moynihan, D-N.Y., amendment to make room for a $51.2 billion tax cut in fiscal 1982 and provide a budget surplus in fiscal 1984 by assuming adoption of a one-year tax cut containing the same elements as the bill approved by the Senate Finance Committee in August 1980. Rejected 34-63: R 1-50; D 33-13 (ND 28-3, SD 5-10), May 12, 1981.

108. S Con Res 19. Fiscal 1982 Budget Targets. Riegle, D-Mich., amendment to add $2.2 billion in budget authority and $1.8 billion in outlays in fiscal 1982 for mass transit, community development, education and training, low income energy assistance, and other social programs, to be offset by equivalent reductions in defense programs. Rejected 17-81: R 2-50; D 15-31 (ND 14-17, SD 1-14), May 12, 1981.

Corresponding to Congressional Record Votes 109, 110, 111, 112, 113, 114, 115

	109 110 111 112 113 114 115		109 110 111 112 113 114 115		109 110 111 112 113 114 115
ALABAMA		**IOWA**		**NEW HAMPSHIRE**	
Denton	N Y Y Y Y N Y	*Grassley*	N Y Y Y Y N Y	*Humphrey*	N Y N N Y N Y
Heflin	Y Y Y Y Y Y Y	*Jepsen*	N Y Y Y Y N Y	*Rudman*	N Y N Y Y N Y
ALASKA		**KANSAS**		**NEW JERSEY**	
Murkowski	N Y Y Y N N Y	*Dole*	N Y Y Y Y N Y	Bradley	Y Y N N N Y ?
Stevens	N Y Y Y Y N Y	*Kassebaum*	N Y N Y N N Y	Williams	Y Y N N N Y Y
ARIZONA		**KENTUCKY**		**NEW MEXICO**	
Goldwater	N Y Y Y Y N Y	Ford	Y Y Y Y N Y Y	*Domenici*	N Y Y Y Y N Y
DeConcini	Y Y Y Y Y Y Y	Huddleston	N Y Y Y Y Y Y	*Schmitt*	N Y Y Y Y N Y
ARKANSAS		**LOUISIANA**		**NEW YORK**	
Bumpers	Y Y N Y N N Y	Johnston	N Y Y Y Y Y ?	*D'Amato*	N Y Y Y Y N ?
Pryor	Y Y Y Y N Y Y	Long	Y Y Y Y Y Y Y	Moynihan	Y Y N N N ? Y
CALIFORNIA		**MAINE**		**NORTH CAROLINA**	
Hayakawa	N Y Y Y Y N Y	*Cohen*	N Y N Y Y N Y	*East*	N Y Y Y Y N Y
Cranston	Y Y Y N N N Y	Mitchell	Y Y N Y N Y Y	*Helms*	N N Y Y Y N Y
COLORADO		**MARYLAND**		**NORTH DAKOTA**	
Armstrong	N Y N Y Y N Y	*Mathias*	? ? ? + ? ? ?	*Andrews*	N Y Y Y Y Y Y
Hart	Y Y N N N N Y	Sarbanes	Y Y Y N N Y Y	Burdick	Y Y Y Y N Y Y
CONNECTICUT		**MASSACHUSETTS**		**OHIO**	
Weicker	N Y N N N N Y	Kennedy	Y Y N N N Y Y	Glenn	Y Y N N Y N Y
Dodd	Y Y N N N Y Y	Tsongas	Y Y N N N N N	Metzenbaum	Y Y N N N ? Y
DELAWARE		**MICHIGAN**		**OKLAHOMA**	
Roth	N Y N Y N N Y	Levin	Y Y N N N Y Y	*Nickles*	N Y N Y Y N Y
Biden	Y Y N Y N Y Y	Riegle	Y Y N N N Y Y	Boren	N Y Y Y Y Y Y
FLORIDA		**MINNESOTA**		**OREGON**	
Hawkins	Y Y N Y Y ? Y	*Boschwitz*	N Y N Y N N Y	*Hatfield*	N N Y N N N N
Chiles	Y Y Y Y Y ? ?	*Durenberger*	N Y N Y Y N Y	*Packwood*	N Y N Y Y N Y
GEORGIA		**MISSISSIPPI**		**PENNSYLVANIA**	
Mattingly	N Y Y Y Y N Y	*Cochran*	N Y Y Y Y N Y	*Heinz*	Y Y N N Y N Y
Nunn	N Y Y Y Y Y Y	Stennis	N Y Y Y Y N Y	*Specter*	Y Y N Y N N Y
HAWAII		**MISSOURI**		**RHODE ISLAND**	
Inouye	Y Y Y Y N Y Y	*Danforth*	N Y N Y N Y Y	*Chafee*	Y Y N N Y N Y
Matsunaga	Y Y Y Y N Y Y	Eagleton	Y Y N N N Y Y	Pell	Y Y N N N Y Y
IDAHO		**MONTANA**		**SOUTH CAROLINA**	
McClure	N Y Y Y N N Y	Baucus	Y Y Y Y N Y Y	*Thurmond*	N Y Y Y Y N Y
Symms	N Y Y Y Y N Y	Melcher	Y Y Y Y Y Y Y	Hollings	N Y N Y N Y Y
ILLINOIS		**NEBRASKA**		**SOUTH DAKOTA**	
Percy	N Y Y Y Y N Y	Exon	N Y Y N Y Y Y	*Abdnor*	N Y Y Y Y N Y
Dixon	Y Y Y Y Y N Y	Zorinsky	Y Y Y Y Y Y Y	*Pressler*	Y Y Y Y N N Y
INDIANA		**NEVADA**		**TENNESSEE**	
Lugar	N Y Y Y Y N Y	*Laxalt*	N Y Y Y Y N Y	*Baker*	N Y Y Y Y N Y
Quayle	N Y N Y Y N Y	Cannon	+ ? ? + ? + ?	Sasser	Y Y Y Y Y Y Y

KEY

Y	Voted for (yea).
#	Paired for.
+	Announced for.
N	Voted against (nay).
X	Paired against.
-	Announced against.
P	Voted ''present''.
C	Voted ''present'' to avoid possible conflict of interest.
?	Did not vote or otherwise make a position known.

	109 110 111 112 113 114 115
TEXAS	
Tower	N Y Y Y Y N Y
Bentsen	Y Y N Y Y Y Y
UTAH	
Garn	N Y N Y Y N Y
Hatch	N Y N Y Y N Y
VERMONT	
Stafford	N Y N Y N N Y
Leahy	Y Y N N N Y Y
VIRGINIA	
Warner	N Y Y Y Y N Y
Byrd*	Y Y Y Y Y N Y
WASHINGTON	
Gorton	N Y N Y Y N Y
Jackson	Y Y Y Y Y Y Y
WEST VIRGINIA	
Byrd	Y Y Y Y N Y Y
Randolph	Y Y Y Y N Y Y
WISCONSIN	
Kasten	N Y N Y Y N Y
Proxmire	Y Y N Y N N N
WYOMING	
Simpson	N Y Y Y N N Y
Wallop	N Y Y Y Y N Y

Democrats   *Republicans*

Byrd elected as an independent

109. S Con Res 19. Fiscal 1982 Budget Targets. Riegle, D-Mich., amendment, to the Stevens, R-Alaska, amendment (see vote 110, below), to add $7.85 billion in fiscal 1982 outlays by retaining the existing system of calculating cost-of-living adjustments (COLAs) for Social Security recipients, federal and military retirees, railroad retirees, and veterans. Rejected 44-54: R 5-47; D 39-7 (ND 30-1, SD 9-6), May 12, 1981.

110. S Con Res 19. Fiscal 1982 Budget Targets. Stevens, R-Alaska, amendment to increase fiscal 1982 outlays by $1.7 billion by exempting federal civilian and military retirees from the delay in annual cost-of-living adjustments prescribed in the budget resolution for other federal pension beneficiaries. Adopted 97-1: R 51-1; D 46-0 (ND 31-0, SD 15-0), May 12, 1981.

111. S Con Res 19. Fiscal 1982 Budget Targets. Huddleston, D-Ky., motion to table (kill) the Metzenbaum, D-Ohio, amendment to reduce outlays for tobacco price supports by $79 million in fiscal 1982. Motion agreed to 56-42: R 29-23; D 27-19 (ND 14-17, SD 13-2), May 12, 1981.

112. H Con Res 115. Fiscal 1982 Budget Targets. Adoption of the resolution, as amended, to set budget targets for the fiscal year ending Sept. 30, 1982, as follows: budget authority, $775.9 billion; outlays $700.8 billion; revenues $650.3 billion; and deficit, $50.5 billion. The resolution also revised binding budget levels for fiscal 1981. Adopted 78-20: R 50-2; D 28-18 (ND 14-17, SD 14-1), May 12, 1981.

113. S 815. Fiscal 1982 Defense Authorization. Tower, R-Texas, motion to table (kill) the Levin, D-Mich., amendment to require advance approval by both houses of Congress before funds authorized in the bill could be spent on a basing mode for the MX missile. Motion agreed to 59-39: R 39-13; D 20-26 (ND 8-23, SD 12-3), May 13, 1981.

114. S Res 132. Federal Reserve Board Monetary Policies. Adoption of the resolution to express the sense of Congress that high interest rates are damaging the nation's economy and to urge the Senate and House Banking committees and the Joint Economic Committee to study the advisability of seeking institutional reforms in the structure and operation of the Federal Reserve System. The resolution stipulated that the study should include the feasibility of implementing a dual prime rate system and the advisability of increasing congressional supervision of policies affecting the nation's monetary system. Rejected 37-57: R 1-50; D 36-7 (ND 25-4, SD 11-3), May 13, 1981.

115. S 815. Fiscal 1982 Defense Authorization. Wallop, R-Wyo., amendment to authorize $50 million for research and development of airborne and space-based laser weapons and to direct the secretary of the Air Force to establish a Program Management Office for those weapons programs. Adopted 91-3: R 50-1; D 41-2 (ND 28-2, SD 13-0), May 13, 1981.

	116	117	118	119
ALABAMA				
Denton	Y	Y	Y	Y
Heflin	Y	Y	Y	Y
ALASKA				
Murkowski	Y	Y	Y	Y
Stevens	Y	Y	Y	Y
ARIZONA				
Goldwater	Y	Y	Y	Y
DeConcini	Y	Y	Y	Y
ARKANSAS				
Bumpers	Y	N	Y	Y
Pryor	Y	N	Y	Y
CALIFORNIA				
Hayakawa	Y	Y	Y	Y
Cranston	Y	Y	Y	Y
COLORADO				
Armstrong	Y	Y	N	Y
Hart	Y	Y	Y	Y
CONNECTICUT				
Weicker	Y	N	Y	Y
Dodd	Y	N	Y	Y
DELAWARE				
Roth	Y	Y	Y	Y
Biden	Y	N	Y	Y
FLORIDA				
Hawkins	Y	Y	N	Y
Chiles	Y	Y	Y	Y
GEORGIA				
Mattingly	Y	Y	Y	Y
Nunn	Y	Y	Y	Y
HAWAII				
Inouye	Y	N	Y	Y
Matsunaga	+	N	Y	Y
IDAHO				
McClure	Y	Y	Y	Y
Symms	Y	Y	Y	Y
ILLINOIS				
Percy	Y	?	Y	Y
Dixon	Y	Y	Y	+
INDIANA				
Lugar	Y	Y	Y	Y
Quayle	Y	Y	N	Y
IOWA				
Grassley	Y	N	Y	Y
Jepsen	Y	Y	Y	N
KANSAS				
Dole	Y	Y	Y	Y
Kassebaum	Y	N	Y	Y
KENTUCKY				
Ford	Y	#	Y	Y
Huddleston	Y	N	Y	Y
LOUISIANA				
Johnston	Y	Y	Y	Y
Long	Y	Y	Y	Y
MAINE				
Cohen	Y	Y	Y	Y
Mitchell	Y	Y	Y	Y
MARYLAND				
Mathias	?	?	?	?
Sarbanes	Y	N	Y	Y
MASSACHUSETTS				
Kennedy	Y	N	?	Y
Tsongas	Y	N	Y	Y
MICHIGAN				
Levin	Y	N	Y	Y
Riegle	Y	X	Y	Y
MINNESOTA				
Boschwitz	Y	Y	Y	Y
Durenberger	Y	Y	Y	Y
MISSISSIPPI				
Cochran	Y	Y	Y	?
Stennis	Y	Y	Y	Y
MISSOURI				
Danforth	Y	Y	Y	Y
Eagleton	Y	N	Y	Y
MONTANA				
Baucus	Y	N	Y	Y
Melcher	Y	Y	Y	Y
NEBRASKA				
Exon	Y	N	Y	Y
Zorinsky	Y	Y	Y	Y
NEVADA				
Laxalt	Y	Y	Y	Y
Cannon	?	?	?	+
NEW HAMPSHIRE				
Humphrey	Y	Y	N	Y
Rudman	Y	Y	Y	Y
NEW JERSEY				
Bradley	Y	N	Y	Y
Williams	Y	N	Y	Y
NEW MEXICO				
Domenici	Y	Y	Y	Y
Schmitt	Y	Y	Y	Y
NEW YORK				
D'Amato	Y	Y	Y	Y
Moynihan	Y	N	Y	Y
NORTH CAROLINA				
East	Y	Y	Y	Y
Helms	Y	Y	N	Y
NORTH DAKOTA				
Andrews	Y	Y	Y	Y
Burdick	Y	Y	Y	Y
OHIO				
Glenn	Y	Y	Y	?
Metzenbaum	Y	N	Y	Y
OKLAHOMA				
Nickles	Y	Y	N	Y
Boren	Y	N	Y	Y
OREGON				
Hatfield	Y	N	Y	N
Packwood	Y	Y	Y	Y
PENNSYLVANIA				
Heinz	Y	Y	Y	Y
Specter	Y	Y	Y	Y
RHODE ISLAND				
Chafee	Y	Y	Y	Y
Pell	Y	N	Y	Y
SOUTH CAROLINA				
Thurmond	Y	Y	Y	Y
Hollings	Y	Y	N	Y
SOUTH DAKOTA				
Abdnor	Y	Y	Y	Y
Pressler	?	N	N	Y
TENNESSEE				
Baker	Y	Y	Y	Y
Sasser	Y	N	Y	Y
TEXAS				
Tower	Y	Y	Y	Y
Bentsen	Y	Y	Y	Y
UTAH				
Garn	Y	Y	Y	Y
Hatch	Y	Y	Y	Y
VERMONT				
Stafford	Y	Y	Y	Y
Leahy	Y	N	Y	?
VIRGINIA				
Warner	Y	Y	Y	Y
Byrd*	Y	Y	Y	Y
WASHINGTON				
Gorton	Y	N	Y	Y
Jackson	Y	Y	Y	Y
WEST VIRGINIA				
Byrd	Y	Y	Y	Y
Randolph	Y	Y	Y	Y
WISCONSIN				
Kasten	Y	Y	Y	Y
Proxmire	Y	N	Y	Y
WYOMING				
Simpson	Y	Y	Y	Y
Wallop	Y	Y	?	+

KEY

Y	Voted for (yea).
#	Paired for.
+	Announced for.
N	Voted against (nay).
X	Paired against.
-	Announced against.
P	Voted "present".
C	Voted "present" to avoid possible conflict of interest.
?	Did not vote or otherwise make a position known.

Democrats   **Republicans**

Byrd elected as an independent.

116. S 815. Fiscal 1982 Defense Authorization. Nunn, D-Ga., amendment to require various reports on weapons cost increases. Adopted 96-0: R 51-0; D 45-0 (ND 30-0, SD 15-0), May 14, 1981.

117. S 815. Fiscal 1982 Defense Authorization. Tower, R-Texas, motion to table (kill) the Levin, D-Mich., amendment to cut $200 million to force consolidation of certain organizations. Motion agreed to 66-29: R 45-6; D 21-23 (ND 12-18, SD 9-5), May 14, 1981.

118. S 815. Fiscal 1982 Defense Authorization. Warner, R-Va., amendment to permit for one year certain Defense Department contracts to be awarded to firms in high-unemployment areas. Adopted 87-9: R 43-8; D 44-1 (ND 30-0, SD 14-1), May 14, 1981.

119. S 815. Fiscal 1982 Defense Authorization. Passage of the bill to authorize $136,521,111,000 for weapons procurement, military research, and operations and maintenance programs of the Defense Department, and for attack-related civil defense programs in fiscal 1982. Passed 92-1: R 49-1; D 43-0 (ND 28-0, SD 15-0), May 14, 1981.

CQ Senate Votes 120 - 126

Corresponding to Congressional Record Votes 120, 121, 122, 123, 124, 125, 126

	120	121	122	123	124	125	126
ALABAMA							
Denton	Y	Y	N	Y	Y	Y	Y
Heflin	Y	N	N	Y	Y	Y	Y
ALASKA							
Murkowski	Y	Y	N	Y	N	Y	Y
Stevens	Y	Y	N	Y	N	N	Y
ARIZONA							
Goldwater	Y	Y	N	Y	Y	N	Y
DeConcini	Y	N	N	Y	Y	Y	N
ARKANSAS							
Bumpers	N	N	N	Y	Y	N	Y
Pryor	Y	N	N	Y	Y	N	Y
CALIFORNIA							
Hayakawa	Y	Y	Y	Y	Y	Y	Y
Cranston	N	N	N	Y	Y	N	N
COLORADO							
Armstrong	Y	Y	N	Y	Y	Y	Y
Hart	N	N	N	Y	Y	Y	N
CONNECTICUT							
Weicker	Y	N	N	Y	Y	N	N
Dodd	N	N	?	?	?	?	X
DELAWARE							
Roth	Y	Y	N	Y	Y	N	Y
Biden	N	N	N	Y	Y	Y	Y
FLORIDA							
Hawkins	Y	?	N	Y	Y	Y	Y
Chiles	Y	N	N	Y	Y	Y	Y
GEORGIA							
Mattingly	Y	Y	N	Y	N	N	Y
Nunn	Y	N	N	Y	Y	Y	Y
HAWAII							
Inouye	N	N	N	Y	Y	Y	Y
Matsunaga	N	N	N	Y	Y	N	Y
IDAHO							
McClure	Y	Y	Y	Y	N	N	Y
Symms	Y	Y	N	Y	Y	Y	Y
ILLINOIS							
Percy	Y	Y	N	Y	Y	Y	Y
Dixon	Y	N	N	Y	Y	Y	Y
INDIANA							
Lugar	Y	Y	N	Y	Y	Y	Y
Quayle	Y	Y	N	Y	Y	Y	Y
IOWA							
Grassley	Y	Y	N	Y	Y	Y	#
Jepsen	Y	Y	N	Y	Y	Y	Y
KANSAS							
Dole	Y	Y	N	Y	N	Y	Y
Kassebaum	Y	Y	N	Y	Y	Y	Y
KENTUCKY							
Ford	N	N	N	Y	Y	Y	Y
Huddleston	Y	N	N	Y	Y	Y	Y
LOUISIANA							
Johnston	Y	N	N	Y	Y	N	Y
Long	Y	N	N	Y	?	?	+
MAINE							
Cohen	Y	Y	N	Y	Y	Y	Y
Mitchell	Y	N	N	Y	Y	N	Y
MARYLAND							
Mathias	?	?	?	?	?	?	?
Sarbanes	N	N	N	Y	Y	N	N
MASSACHUSETTS							
Kennedy	N	N	N	Y	Y	N	N
Tsongas	N	N	N	Y	Y	N	N
MICHIGAN							
Levin	N	N	N	Y	Y	Y	N
Riegle	N	N	N	Y	Y	N	N
MINNESOTA							
Boschwitz	Y	Y	N	Y	Y	Y	Y
Durenberger	Y	Y	N	Y	Y	Y	Y
MISSISSIPPI							
Cochran	Y	Y	N	Y	Y	Y	Y
Stennis	Y	N	N	Y	Y	Y	Y
MISSOURI							
Danforth	Y	Y	N	Y	Y	Y	Y
Eagleton	N	N	N	Y	Y	N	N
MONTANA							
Baucus	Y	N	N	Y	Y	N	Y
Melcher	Y	N	N	Y	Y	Y	Y
NEBRASKA							
Exon	N	N	N	Y	Y	N	N
Zorinsky	Y	N	N	Y	Y	Y	Y
NEVADA							
Laxalt	Y	Y	N	Y	Y	Y	Y
Cannon	Y	N	N	Y	Y	Y	Y
NEW HAMPSHIRE							
Humphrey	Y	Y	N	Y	Y	Y	N
Rudman	Y	Y	N	Y	N	N	Y
NEW JERSEY							
Bradley	N	N	N	Y	Y	Y	N
Williams	N	N	N	Y	Y	Y	N
NEW MEXICO							
Domenici	Y	Y	N	Y	N	N	Y
Schmitt	Y	Y	N	Y	N	N	Y
NEW YORK							
D'Amato	Y	Y	N	Y	Y	Y	Y
Moynihan	N	N	N	Y	Y	N	N
NORTH CAROLINA							
East	Y	Y	N	Y	Y	Y	Y
Helms	Y	Y	N	Y	Y	Y	Y
NORTH DAKOTA							
Andrews	Y	Y	N	Y	N	N	Y
Burdick	Y	N	N	Y	Y	Y	Y
OHIO							
Glenn	N	N	N	Y	Y	Y	N
Metzenbaum	?	N	N	Y	N	N	N
OKLAHOMA							
Nickles	Y	Y	N	Y	Y	Y	Y
Boren	N	N	N	Y	Y	Y	Y
OREGON							
Hatfield	Y	Y	Y	Y	N	N	Y
Packwood	Y	Y	N	Y	N	N	Y
PENNSYLVANIA							
Heinz	Y	Y	N	Y	Y	Y	Y
Specter	Y	Y	N	Y	Y	Y	Y
RHODE ISLAND							
Chafee	Y	Y	N	Y	Y	N	Y
Pell	N	N	N	Y	Y	N	N
SOUTH CAROLINA							
Thurmond	Y	Y	N	Y	Y	Y	Y
Hollings	N	N	N	Y	Y	Y	N
SOUTH DAKOTA							
Abdnor	Y	Y	N	Y	N	N	Y
Pressler	?	?	?	?	?	?	Y
TENNESSEE							
Baker	Y	Y	Y	Y	N	N	Y
Sasser	Y	N	N	Y	Y	Y	Y
TEXAS							
Tower	Y	Y	N	Y	Y	Y	Y
Bentsen	Y	N	N	?	?	?	Y
UTAH							
Garn	Y	Y	N	Y	Y	Y	Y
Hatch	Y	Y	N	Y	Y	Y	Y
VERMONT							
Stafford	Y	Y	N	Y	Y	Y	Y
Leahy	N	N	N	Y	Y	N	N
VIRGINIA							
Warner	Y	Y	N	Y	Y	Y	Y
Byrd*	Y	Y	N	Y	Y	Y	Y
WASHINGTON							
Gorton	Y	Y	N	Y	N	Y	Y
Jackson	Y	N	N	Y	Y	Y	Y
WEST VIRGINIA							
Byrd	N	N	N	Y	Y	Y	Y
Randolph	Y	N	N	Y	Y	N	Y
WISCONSIN							
Kasten	Y	Y	N	Y	N	Y	Y
Proxmire	N	N	N	Y	Y	N	Y
WYOMING							
Simpson	Y	Y	N	Y	Y	Y	Y
Wallop	Y	Y	N	Y	Y	Y	Y

KEY

Y   Voted for (yea).
\#   Paired for.
\+   Announced for.
N   Voted against (nay).
X   Paired against.
-   Announced against.
P   Voted "present".
C   Voted "present" to avoid possible conflict of interest.
?   Did not vote or otherwise make a position known.

Democrats   *Republicans*

* Byrd elected as an independent.

---

120. Crowell Nomination. Confirmation of President Reagan's nomination of John B. Crowell Jr. of Oregon to be assistant secretary of agriculture for natural resources and environment. Confirmed 72-25: R 51-0; D 21-25 (ND 10-21, SD 11-4), May 20, 1981. A "yea" was a vote supporting the president's position.

121. HR 3512. Fiscal 1981 Supplemental Appropriations. Hatfield, R-Ore., motion to table (kill) the Moynihan, D-N.Y., amendment stating the sense of the Senate in opposition to President Reagan's proposed reductions in Social Security benefits. Motion agreed to 49-48: R 48-2; D 1-46 (ND 0-32, SD 1-14), May 20, 1981. A "yea" was a vote supporting the president's position.

122. HR 3512. Fiscal 1981 Supplemental Appropriations. Hatfield, R-Ore., motion to table (kill) the Dole, R-Kan., amendment *(see vote 123, below)* stating the sense of the Senate in opposition to "unfair" reductions in Social Security benefits to early retirees and to benefit reductions in excess of the amount needed to put the Social Security System on a sound financial basis. Motion rejected 4-93: R 4-47; D 0-46 (ND 0-31, SD 0-15), May 20, 1981.

123. HR 3512. Fiscal 1981 Supplemental Appropriations. Dole, R-Kan., amendment stating the sense of the Senate in opposition to "unfair" reductions in Social Security benefits to early retirees and to benefit reductions in excess of the amount needed to put the Social Security System on a sound financial basis. Adopted 96-0: R 51-0; D 45-0 (ND 31-0, SD 14-0), May 20, 1981.

124. HR 3512. Fiscal 1981 Supplemental Appropriations. Hollings, D-S.C., amendment to transfer $55.5 million from Defense Department operations and maintenance accounts to pay for bonuses to certain military pilots. Adopted 79-16: R 36-15; D 43-1 (ND 30-1, SD 13-0), May 20, 1981.

125. HR 3512. Fiscal 1981 Supplemental Appropriations. Tower, R-Texas, amendment to provide $92 million for advanced procurement, and research and development for reactivation of the battleships *New Jersey* and *Iowa*. Adopted 61-34: R 36-15; D 25-19 (ND 15-16; SD 10-3), May 20, 1981. A "yea" was a vote supporting the president's position.

126. H Con Res 115. Fiscal 1982 Budget Targets. Adoption of the conference report on the resolution to set budget targets for the fiscal year ending Sept. 30, 1982, as follows: budget authority, $770.9 billion; outlays, $695.45 billion; revenues, $657.8 billion; and deficit, $37.65 billion. The resolution also revised binding budget levels for fiscal 1981 and included reconciliation instructions requiring House and Senate committees to make approximately $36 billion in spending cuts in fiscal 1982. Adopted 76-20: R 49-2; D 27-18 (ND 14-17, SD 13-1), May 21, 1981.

	127	128	129	130	131	132	133	134
ALABAMA								
Denton	Y	N	Y	N	?	Y	N	Y
Heflin	Y	N	?	?	?	?	?	?
ALASKA								
Murkowski	Y	Y	Y	N	Y	Y	N	Y
Stevens	Y	Y	Y	Y	N	N	Y	Y
ARIZONA								
Goldwater	N	N	N	Y	?	Y	N	Y
DeConcini	N	N	Y	Y	Y	Y	N	Y
ARKANSAS								
Bumpers	N	Y	Y	Y	Y	N	N	Y
Pryor	N	Y	Y	Y	Y	N	N	Y
CALIFORNIA								
Hayakawa	N	N	N	N	Y	Y	N	Y
Cranston	N	Y	Y	N	N	?	?	?
COLORADO								
Armstrong	Y	N	Y	N	Y	Y	N	Y
Hart	Y	Y	Y	N	Y	N	N	Y
CONNECTICUT								
Weicker	Y	Y	Y	N	N	N	Y	Y
Dodd	Y	Y	Y	N	Y	N	N	Y
DELAWARE								
Roth	Y	Y	Y	Y	Y	Y	N	Y
Biden	Y	Y	Y	N	Y	Y	N	Y
FLORIDA								
Hawkins	N	N	+	N	Y	Y	N	Y
Chiles	N	N	Y	N	N	Y	Y	Y
GEORGIA								
Mattingly	Y	N	Y	Y	Y	Y	N	Y
Nunn	Y	N	Y	N	Y	N	N	Y
HAWAII								
Inouye	N	Y	Y	N	N	X	?	?
Matsunaga	N	Y	Y	N	N	N	Y	Y
IDAHO								
McClure	Y	Y	N	Y	Y	Y	N	Y
Symms	Y	N	N	N	Y	Y	N	Y
ILLINOIS								
Percy	N	N	N	N	Y	N	N	Y
Dixon	N	N	Y	Y	N	Y	Y	Y
INDIANA								
Lugar	N	N	Y	N	Y	Y	N	Y
Quayle	Y	N	Y	Y	Y	Y	N	Y
IOWA								
Grassley	Y	Y	Y	N	Y	Y	N	Y
Jepsen	Y	N	Y	N	Y	Y	N	Y
KANSAS								
Dole	Y	N	Y	N	N	Y	Y	Y
Kassebaum	Y	Y	Y	N	Y	N	N	Y
KENTUCKY								
Ford	N	N	Y	Y	N	Y	Y	Y
Huddleston	N	Y	Y	Y	N	Y	N	Y
LOUISIANA								
Johnston	Y	N	Y	Y	N	Y	Y	Y
Long	?	?	?	?	?	#	?	?
MAINE								
Cohen	Y	N	Y	N	N	N	N	Y
Mitchell	Y	Y	Y	Y	N	Y	Y	Y
MARYLAND								
Mathias	?	?	?	?	?	?	?	?
Sarbanes	N	Y	Y	N	N	N	Y	Y
MASSACHUSETTS								
Kennedy	Y	Y	Y	N	N	N	N	Y
Tsongas	N	Y	Y	N	N	N	Y	Y
MICHIGAN								
Levin	N	Y	Y	N	N	N	Y	Y
Riegle	N	Y	Y	N	N	N	Y	Y
MINNESOTA								
Boschwitz	Y	N	N	N	N	Y	Y	Y
Durenberger	Y	Y	Y	N	Y	Y	Y	Y
MISSISSIPPI								
Cochran	N	Y	Y	Y	N	N	Y	Y
Stennis	N	N	Y	Y	Y	N	N	Y
MISSOURI								
Danforth	Y	Y	N	N	Y	Y	Y	Y
Eagleton	N	Y	Y	N	Y	Y	Y	Y
MONTANA								
Baucus	Y	Y	N	N	N	N	Y	Y
Melcher	Y	N	Y	Y	N	Y	Y	Y
NEBRASKA								
Exon	N	N	Y	Y	Y	Y	N	Y
Zorinsky	N	N	Y	Y	Y	Y	N	Y
NEVADA								
Laxalt	N	N	Y	N	Y	N	Y	N
Cannon	N	N	Y	N	N	N	Y	Y
NEW HAMPSHIRE								
Humphrey	Y	N	N	Y	Y	Y	N	Y
Rudman	Y	N	N	N	N	N	Y	Y
NEW JERSEY								
Bradley	N	Y	Y	N	N	N	Y	Y
Williams	N	Y	Y	N	N	N	Y	Y
NEW MEXICO								
Domenici	Y	Y	Y	N	N	Y	Y	Y
Schmitt	Y	N	N	Y	N	N	Y	Y
NEW YORK								
D'Amato	Y	N	Y	N	Y	Y	Y	Y
Moynihan	Y	N	Y	N	N	N	Y	Y
NORTH CAROLINA								
East	Y	N	Y	Y	Y	Y	N	Y
Helms	Y	N	Y	Y	Y	Y	N	Y
NORTH DAKOTA								
Andrews	N	Y	Y	N	N	Y	Y	Y
Burdick	N	Y	Y	N	N	Y	Y	Y
OHIO								
Glenn	Y	N	Y	N	N	N	Y	Y
Metzenbaum	Y	Y	?	N	N	N	Y	Y
OKLAHOMA								
Nickles	Y	N	Y	Y	Y	Y	N	Y
Boren	N	Y	Y	Y	Y	Y	N	Y
OREGON								
Hatfield	Y	Y	N	Y	N	N	Y	Y
Packwood	Y	Y	N	Y	N	N	Y	Y
PENNSYLVANIA								
Heinz	N	Y	Y	N	N	Y	Y	Y
Specter	N	Y	Y	N	N	N	Y	Y
RHODE ISLAND								
Chafee	Y	Y	N	Y	N	N	Y	Y
Pell	Y	Y	Y	N	N	N	Y	Y
SOUTH CAROLINA								
Thurmond	N	N	Y	N	Y	Y	Y	Y
Hollings	N	N	Y	N	N	N	Y	Y
SOUTH DAKOTA								
Abdnor	Y	N	N	Y	N	Y	Y	Y
Pressler	Y	Y	Y	N	N	Y	Y	Y
TENNESSEE								
Baker	Y	Y	Y	Y	N	N	Y	Y
Sasser	N	Y	Y	Y	Y	Y	N	Y
TEXAS								
Tower	Y	N	Y	?	N	N	N	Y
Bentsen	N	N	Y	Y	Y	Y	N	Y
UTAH								
Garn	Y	N	Y	Y	Y	Y	N	Y
Hatch	Y	N	Y	Y	Y	Y	N	Y
VERMONT								
Stafford	Y	Y	Y	Y	N	N	Y	Y
Leahy	Y	Y	Y	N	N	N	Y	Y
VIRGINIA								
Warner	Y	N	Y	N	N	N	N	Y
Byrd*	Y	N	Y	Y	Y	Y	N	Y
WASHINGTON								
Gorton	Y	Y	Y	N	Y	Y	Y	Y
Jackson	Y	N	Y	N	N	N	Y	Y
WEST VIRGINIA								
Byrd	Y	N	Y	Y	Y	Y	N	Y
Randolph	N	Y	Y	Y	N	Y	Y	Y
WISCONSIN								
Kasten	Y	N	N	N	N	Y	Y	Y
Proxmire	Y	Y	N	Y	Y	Y	N	Y
WYOMING								
Simpson	Y	N	N	N	N	N	N	Y
Wallop	Y	N	N	N	N	N	N	Y

KEY

Y Voted for (yea).
Paired for.
+ Announced for.
N Voted against (nay).
X Paired against.
- Announced against.
P Voted "present".
C Voted "present" to avoid possible conflict of interest.
? Did not vote or otherwise make a position known.

Democrats *Republicans*

Byrd elected as an independent.

127. HR 3512. Fiscal 1981 Supplemental Appropriations. Hatfield, R-Ore., motion to table (kill) the DeConcini, D-Ariz., appeal of the ruling of the chair that the DeConcini amendment, to prohibit the Education Department from seeking to recover funds provided to local school districts under Title I of the Elementary and Secondary Education Act if the repayment was based on an audit conducted before 1978, was out of order. Motion agreed to 60-38: R 41-11; D 19-27 (ND 15-17, SD 4-10), May 21, 1981.

128. HR 3512. Fiscal 1981 Supplemental Appropriations. Hatfield, R-Ore., motion to table (kill) the Warner, R-Va., amendment to provide $20 million to equip a factory to produce lethal nerve gas weapons (called binary munitions). Motion rejected 48-50: R 21-31; D 27-19 (ND 22-10, SD 5-9), May 21, 1981. A "nay" was a vote supporting the president's position. (The Warner amendment subsequently was agreed to by voice vote.)

129. HR 3512. Fiscal 1981 Supplemental Appropriations. Cochran, R-Miss., amendment, part 1, to delete from the bill the $30 million rescission from the "developing institutions" program authorized by Title III of the Higher Education Act. Adopted 76-19: R 34-17; D 42-2 (ND 29-2, SD 13-0), May 21, 1981.

130. HR 3512. Fiscal 1981 Supplemental Appropriations. Cochran, R-Miss., amendment, part 2, to increase by $30 million the rescission of funds for migration and refugee assistance. Rejected 39-57: R 18-33; D 21-24 (ND 10-22, SD 11-2), May 21, 1981.

131. HR 3512. Fiscal 1981 Supplemental Appropriations. Helms, R-N.C., motion to table (kill) the Abdnor, R-S.D., amendment to add $538 million for the food stamp program and $110 million for child nutrition programs (see vote 133, below). Motion rejected 38-57: R 22-28; D 16-29 (ND 8-24, SD 8-5), May 21, 1981.

132. HR 3512. Fiscal 1981 Supplemental Appropriations. Helms, R-N.C., motion to table (kill) the Appropriations Committee amendment to delete House-passed language prohibiting Medicaid funding of abortions except when needed to save the mother's life. (The effect of the motion was to restore the House prohibition to the bill.) Motion agreed to 52-43: R 33-19; D 19-24 (ND 12-18, SD 7-6), May 21, 1981. A "yea" was a vote supporting the president's position.

133. HR 3512. Fiscal 1981 Supplemental Appropriations. Abdnor, R-S.D., amendment to add $538 million for the food stamp program and $110 million for child nutrition programs. Adopted 50-45: R 24-28; D 26-17 (ND 22-8, SD 4-9), May 21, 1981.

134. HR 3512. Fiscal 1981 Supplemental Appropriations. Passage of the bill to provide $21,954,381,663 in fiscal 1981 supplemental appropriations and $15,260,551,622 in fiscal 1981 rescissions; and to extend from June 5, 1981, through Sept. 30, 1981, the spending authority of departments whose regular 1981 appropriations never became law. Passed 95-0: R 52-0; D 43-0 (ND 30-0, SD 13-0), May 21, 1981. The president formally had requested $21,795,137,800 in supplemental appropriations and $15,045,530,541 in rescissions.

	135	136	137	138
ALABAMA				
Denton	Y	Y	N	Y
Heflin	Y	P	N	N
ALASKA				
Murkowski	Y	N	N	Y
Stevens	Y	X	N	Y
ARIZONA				
Goldwater	Y	N	N	Y
DeConcini	Y	Y	Y	N
ARKANSAS				
Bumpers	Y	N	Y	N
Pryor	Y	N	Y	Y
CALIFORNIA				
Hayakawa	Y	N	N	Y
Cranston	Y	N	Y	N
COLORADO				
Armstrong	Y	Y	N	Y
Hart	Y	N	Y	N
CONNECTICUT				
Weicker	Y	N	Y	Y
Dodd	N	?	Y	N
DELAWARE				
Roth	Y	N	N	Y
Biden	Y	Y	Y	N
FLORIDA				
Hawkins	Y	N	N	+
Chiles	Y	Y	Y	Y
GEORGIA				
Mattingly	Y	N	?	?
Nunn	Y	N	?	?
HAWAII				
Inouye	Y	N	Y	N
Matsunaga	Y	N	Y	N
IDAHO				
McClure	Y	N	N	Y
Symms	Y	Y	N	Y
ILLINOIS				
Percy	Y	Y	N	Y
Dixon	Y	N	Y	Y
INDIANA				
Lugar	Y	N	N	Y
Quayle	Y	N	N	Y

	135	136	137	138
IOWA				
Grassley	Y	Y	N	Y
Jepsen	Y	N	N	Y
KANSAS				
Dole	Y	Y	N	Y
Kassebaum	Y	N	?	Y
KENTUCKY				
Ford	Y	N	Y	Y
Huddleston	Y	N	?	Y
LOUISIANA				
Johnston	Y	N	Y	Y
Long	Y	N	N	Y
MAINE				
Cohen	?	?	N	Y
Mitchell	Y	N	Y	N
MARYLAND				
Mathias	Y	#	?	?
Sarbanes	Y	N	Y	N
MASSACHUSETTS				
Kennedy	?	?	Y	?
Tsongas	Y	Y	Y	N
MICHIGAN				
Levin	Y	N	Y	N
Riegle	Y	N	Y	N
MINNESOTA				
Boschwitz	Y	N	N	Y
Durenberger	Y	N	N	Y
MISSISSIPPI				
Cochran	Y	N	N	Y
Stennis	Y	Y	N	Y
MISSOURI				
Danforth	Y	N	N	Y
Eagleton	Y	N	Y	N
MONTANA				
Baucus	Y	Y	Y	Y
Melcher	Y	Y	Y	N
NEBRASKA				
Exon	Y	N	N	Y
Zorinsky	Y	Y	N	Y
NEVADA				
Laxalt	Y	Y	N	Y
Cannon	Y	N	Y	Y

	135	136	137	138
NEW HAMPSHIRE				
Humphrey	Y	N	N	Y
Rudman	Y	N	N	Y
NEW JERSEY				
Bradley	?	?	Y	N
Williams	Y	N	Y	N
NEW MEXICO				
Domenici	Y	N	N	Y
Schmitt	?	N	N	Y
NEW YORK				
D'Amato	Y	Y	N	Y
Moynihan	Y	N	Y	N
NORTH CAROLINA				
East	+	#	N	Y
Helms	Y	Y	N	Y
NORTH DAKOTA				
Andrews	Y	N	N	Y
Burdick	Y	N	Y	N
OHIO				
Glenn	Y	N	Y	Y
Metzenbaum	N	Y	?	?
OKLAHOMA				
Nickles	Y	Y	N	Y
Boren	Y	Y	N	Y
OREGON				
Hatfield	Y	N	N	Y
Packwood	Y	N	N	Y
PENNSYLVANIA				
Heinz	Y	N	N	Y
Specter	Y	Y	N	Y
RHODE ISLAND				
Chafee	Y	N	N	Y
Pell	Y	N	Y	N
SOUTH CAROLINA				
Thurmond	Y	Y	N	Y
Hollings	?	?	?	?
SOUTH DAKOTA				
Abdnor	Y	Y	N	?
Pressler	?	?	N	Y
TENNESSEE				
Baker	Y	X	N	Y
Sasser	Y	N	Y	Y

KEY

Y	Voted for (yea).
#	Paired for.
+	Announced for.
N	Voted against (nay).
X	Paired against.
-	Announced against.
P	Voted "present".
C	Voted "present" to avoid possible conflict of interest.
?	Did not vote or otherwise make a position known.

	135	136	137	138
TEXAS				
Tower	+	?	-	+
Bentsen	Y	N	Y	Y
UTAH				
Garn	Y	N	N	Y
Hatch	Y	Y	N	Y
VERMONT				
Stafford	Y	Y	N	Y
Leahy	Y	Y	Y	N
VIRGINIA				
Warner	Y	N	N	Y
Byrd*	Y	N	?	?
WASHINGTON				
Gorton	Y	N	N	Y
Jackson	Y	N	Y	Y
WEST VIRGINIA				
Byrd	Y	N	Y	N
Randolph	Y	N	Y	Y
WISCONSIN				
Kasten	Y	N	N	Y
Proxmire	N	Y	Y	N
WYOMING				
Simpson	Y	Y	N	Y
Wallop	?	?	-	+

Democrats   *Republicans*

Byrd elected as an independent.

135. Johnson Nomination. Confirmation of President Reagan's nomination of R. Tenney Johnson of Maryland as general counsel of the Department of Energy. Confirmed 88-3: R 47-0; D 41-3 (ND 27-3; SD 14-0), June 2, 1981. A "yea" was a vote supporting the president's position.

136. S 271. International Telecommunications Competition Act. Thurmond, R-S.C., motion to refer to the Senate Judiciary Committee for up to seven calendar days the bill that would allow the Western Union Telegraph Co. to compete internationally in the telegraph and telex business. Motion rejected 28-59: R 16-29; D 12-30 (ND 9-20; SD 3-10), June 2, 1981.

137. S 1197. Housing and Community Development Act Amendments. Proxmire, D-Wis., amendment to retain provisions in existing law requiring communities to file a detailed application form for community development block grant funds. Rejected 37-53: R 1-47; D 36-6 (ND 29-2; SD 7-4), June 3, 1981.

138. S 1197. Housing and Community Development Act Amendments. Passage of the bill to reauthorize for two years housing and urban aid programs of the Department of Housing and Urban Development. The bill provided $17.8 billion for an additional 150,000 subsidized housing units annually in fiscal 1982 and 1983. Passed 65-24: R 47-0; D 18-24 (ND 8-22; SD 10-2), June 3, 1981.

KEY

- Y Voted for (yea).
- # Paired for.
- + Announced for.
- N Voted against (nay).
- X Paired against.
- - Announced against.
- P Voted "present".
- C Voted "present" to avoid possible conflict of interest.
- ? Did not vote or otherwise make a position known.

	139	140	141	142	143	144	145	146
ALABAMA								
Denton	N	Y	Y	Y	N	N	N	N
Heflin	Y	N	Y	N	N	N	N	Y
ALASKA								
Murkowski	Y	N	Y	N	N	N	Y	N
Stevens	Y	N	N	Y	N	Y	N	N
ARIZONA								
Goldwater	?	Y	N	Y	N	N	N	N
DeConcini	Y	?	?	?	?	?	?	?
ARKANSAS								
Bumpers	Y	N	N	N	N	N	Y	Y
Pryor	Y	N	N	N	Y	N	N	?
CALIFORNIA								
Hayakawa	?	Y	Y	Y	N	N	N	N
Cranston	Y	N	N	N	Y	+	?	?
COLORADO								
Armstrong	Y	Y	Y	Y	?	?	?	?
Hart	Y	N	N	N	Y	Y	Y	Y
CONNECTICUT								
Weicker	Y	N	N	N	Y	Y	Y	N
Dodd	Y	N	N	N	Y	?	?	?
DELAWARE								
Roth	Y	Y	Y	Y	N	N	N	N
Biden	?	Y	N	N	N	Y	N	Y
FLORIDA								
Hawkins	Y	N	N	N	N	N	N	N
Chiles	Y	N	N	N	Y	N	N	Y
GEORGIA								
Mattingly	Y	Y	Y	Y	N	N	N	N
Nunn	Y	Y	N	N	N	N	N	N
HAWAII								
Inouye	Y	N	N	N	Y	Y	Y	Y
Matsunaga	Y	N	N	N	Y	Y	Y	Y
IDAHO								
McClure	N	Y	Y	Y	N	N	N	N
Symms	N	Y	Y	Y	N	N	N	N
ILLINOIS								
Percy	+	N	N	N	N	N	N	N
Dixon	Y	N	N	N	N	N	N	Y
INDIANA								
Lugar	Y	Y	Y	Y	N	N	N	N
Quayle	Y	Y	Y	Y	N	N	N	N

	139	140	141	142	143	144	145	146
IOWA								
Grassley	Y	Y	Y	N	N	N	N	N
Jepsen	Y	Y	Y	Y	N	N	N	N
KANSAS								
Dole	Y	N	N	N	N	Y	Y	N
Kassebaum	Y	N	N	N	N	N	N	N
KENTUCKY								
Ford	Y	N	N	N	N	N	N	Y
Huddleston	Y	N	N	N	Y	Y	Y	Y
LOUISIANA								
Johnston	Y	N	N	N	?	?	N	?
Long	Y	Y	Y	N	Y	N	Y	N
MAINE								
Cohen	Y	N	N	N	Y	Y	Y	N
Mitchell	?	N	N	N	N	Y	Y	Y
MARYLAND								
Mathias	Y	N	N	N	Y	Y	Y	N
Sarbanes	Y	N	N	N	Y	Y	Y	Y
MASSACHUSETTS								
Kennedy	Y	N	N	N	Y	Y	Y	Y
Tsongas	Y	N	N	N	Y	Y	Y	Y
MICHIGAN								
Levin	Y	N	N	N	Y	?	Y	N
Riegle	Y	N	N	N	Y	?	?	?
MINNESOTA								
Boschwitz	Y	N	N	N	N	N	N	N
Durenberger	Y	N	N	N	N	N	Y	N
MISSISSIPPI								
Cochran	Y	N	N	N	Y	Y	Y	N
Stennis	Y	Y	Y	N	N	N	N	N
MISSOURI								
Danforth	Y	N	N	N	Y	Y	Y	N
Eagleton	Y	N	N	N	Y	Y	Y	N
MONTANA								
Baucus	Y	N	N	N	Y	Y	Y	Y
Melcher	Y	N	N	N	Y	N	Y	Y
NEBRASKA								
Exon	Y	N	N	N	N	N	N	N
Zorinsky	Y	N	Y	Y	N	N	N	N
NEVADA								
Laxalt	?	Y	Y	Y	N	N	N	N
Cannon	Y	N	N	N	Y	N	N	N

	139	140	141	142	143	144	145	146
NEW HAMPSHIRE								
Humphrey	N	Y	Y	N	N	N	N	N
Rudman	Y	N	Y	N	N	N	N	N
NEW JERSEY								
Bradley	Y	N	N	N	Y	N	Y	Y
Williams	Y	N	N	N	Y	N	Y	Y
NEW MEXICO								
Domenici	?	N	N	N	N	N	N	N
Schmitt	?	N	N	N	N	N	N	N
NEW YORK								
D'Amato	Y	N	N	N	N	Y	N	N
Moynihan	Y	N	N	N	Y	Y	Y	Y
NORTH CAROLINA								
East	N	Y	Y	Y	N	N	N	N
Helms	N	Y	Y	Y	N	N	N	N
NORTH DAKOTA								
Andrews	Y	Y	N	N	N	N	Y	N
Burdick	Y	N	N	N	N	N	Y	Y
OHIO								
Glenn	Y	N	N	N	N	Y	N	Y
Metzenbaum	Y	N	N	N	Y	Y	Y	Y
OKLAHOMA								
Nickles	Y	Y	N	N	N	N	N	N
Boren	Y	Y	N	N	N	N	N	N
OREGON								
Hatfield	Y	N	N	N	N	Y	Y	Y
Packwood	Y	N	Y	N	N	N	N	N
PENNSYLVANIA								
Heinz	Y	N	N	N	N	Y	Y	Y
Specter	Y	N	N	N	Y	Y	Y	Y
RHODE ISLAND								
Chafee	Y	N	N	N	Y	Y	Y	N
Pell	?	N	N	N	Y	Y	Y	Y
SOUTH CAROLINA								
Thurmond	Y	Y	Y	Y	N	N	N	N
Hollings	Y	N	N	N	N	Y	Y	Y
SOUTH DAKOTA								
Abdnor	Y	Y	N	Y	N	N	N	N
Pressler	Y	N	N	N	N	N	Y	N
TENNESSEE								
Baker	Y	Y	N	N	?	N	N	
Sasser	Y	N	N	N	Y	N	N	

	139	140	141	142	143	144	145	146
TEXAS								
Tower	Y	Y	Y	Y	N	N	N	N
Bentsen	Y	N	N	N	N	Y	Y	N
UTAH								
Garn	Y	Y	Y	Y	N	N	N	N
Hatch	N	Y	Y	Y	N	Y	N	N
VERMONT								
Stafford	Y	N	N	N	N	Y	Y	N
Leahy	Y	N	N	N	Y	Y	Y	Y
VIRGINIA								
Warner	Y	Y	Y	N	N	N	N	N
Byrd*	Y	Y	Y	Y	N	N	N	N
WASHINGTON								
Gorton	Y	N	N	N	Y	N	Y	N
Jackson	Y	N	N	N	N	Y	Y	Y
WEST VIRGINIA								
Byrd	Y	N	N	N	N	N	Y	N
Randolph	Y	N	N	N	Y	N	Y	Y
WISCONSIN								
Kasten	Y	N	N	N	N	N	N	N
Proxmire	Y	Y	Y	N	N	N	N	N
WYOMING								
Simpson	Y	N	Y	N	N	N	N	N
Wallop	Y	N	N	N	N	N	N	N

Democrats *Republicans*

*Byrd elected as an independent.

139. Crocker Nomination. Confirmation of President Reagan's nomination of Chester A. Crocker of the District of Columbia to be assistant secretary of state for African affairs. Confirmed 84-7: R 40-7; D 44-0 (ND 29-0, SD 15-0), June 9, 1981. A "yea" was a vote supporting the president's position.

140. S 1007. Food Stamps. Symms, R-Idaho, amendment to require households to pay the food stamp issuing agency some of their own money, up to 30 percent of their income, in exchange for a larger value of food stamps. The amendment exempted very poor households and those containing an elderly or disabled member. Rejected 33-66: R 26-27; D 7-39 (ND 2-29; SD 5-10), June 10, 1981.

141. S 1007. Food Stamps. Helms, R-N.C., amendment to eliminate the requirement in existing law that income deductions, used in calculating program eligibility and benefits, be adjusted annually for inflation. Rejected 30-69: R 24-29; D 6-40 (ND 2-29, SD 4-11), June 10, 1981.

142. S 1007. Food Stamps. McClure, R-Idaho, amendment to require that federal energy assistance payments be counted as income in determining a household's eligibility and benefits. Rejected 25-74: R 22-31; D 3-43 (ND 2-29, SD 1-14), June 10, 1981.

143. S 1007. Food Stamps. Melcher, D-Mont., amendment to allow residents of alcohol and drug abuse rehabilitation centers to receive food stamps if the centers were private, non-profit and received less than 20 percent of their funding from federal sources. Rejected 24-74: R 2-50; D 22-24 (ND 19-12, SD 3-12), June 10, 1981.

144. S 1007. Food Stamps. Moynihan, D-N.Y., amendment to delay to Oct. 1, 1982, from April 1, 1982, the effective date of the provision establishing a block grant nutritional program in Puerto Rico. Rejected 36-56: R 15-36; D 21-20 (ND 17-10, SD 4-10), June 10, 1981.

145. S 1007. Food Stamps. Leahy, D-Vt., amendment to provide that the annual ceilings on food stamp spending be adjusted, upward or downward, when food price inflation or unemployment significantly exceeded or was less than the projected rates on which the spending ceilings in the bill were based. Rejected 41-53: R 15-37; D 26-16 (ND 21-7, SD 5-9), June 10, 1981. A "nay" was a vote supporting the president's position.

146. S 1007. Food Stamps. Melcher, D-Mont., amendment to delete from the bill the provision reducing to 6 years old, from 12 under existing law, the age of a child that exempts a parent from the program's work registration requirement. Rejected 30-64: R 3-49; D 27-15 (ND 21-7, SD 6-8), June 10, 1981.

	147 148 149		147 148 149		147 148 149
ALABAMA		**IOWA**		**NEW HAMPSHIRE**	
Denton	N Y Y	*Grassley*	Y Y Y	*Humphrey*	N Y Y
Heflin	Y Y Y	*Jepsen*	Y Y Y	*Rudman*	Y Y Y
ALASKA		**KANSAS**		**NEW JERSEY**	
Murkowski	Y Y Y	*Dole*	Y Y Y	Bradley	Y Y Y
Stevens	Y Y Y	*Kassebaum*	Y Y Y	Williams	Y Y Y
ARIZONA		**KENTUCKY**		**NEW MEXICO**	
Goldwater	N Y Y	Ford	Y Y Y	*Domenici*	Y Y Y
DeConcini	? Y Y	Huddleston	Y Y Y	*Schmitt*	Y Y Y
ARKANSAS		**LOUISIANA**		**NEW YORK**	
Bumpers	Y Y Y	Johnston	Y Y Y	*D'Amato*	Y Y Y
Pryor	? Y Y	Long	Y Y Y	Moynihan	Y Y Y
CALIFORNIA		**MAINE**		**NORTH CAROLINA**	
Hayakawa	N Y Y	*Cohen*	Y Y Y	*East*	N Y N
Cranston	? Y Y	Mitchell	Y Y Y	*Helms*	N Y N
COLORADO		**MARYLAND**		**NORTH DAKOTA**	
Armstrong	? Y N	*Mathias*	Y Y Y	*Andrews*	Y Y Y
Hart	Y Y Y	Sarbanes	Y Y Y	Burdick	Y Y Y
CONNECTICUT		**MASSACHUSETTS**		**OHIO**	
Weicker	Y Y Y	Kennedy	Y Y Y	Glenn	Y Y Y
Dodd	? + Y	Tsongas	Y Y Y	Metzenbaum	Y ? ?
DELAWARE		**MICHIGAN**		**OKLAHOMA**	
Roth	Y Y Y	Levin	Y Y Y	*Nickles*	N Y Y
Biden	Y + ?	Riegle	+ Y Y	Boren	Y Y Y
FLORIDA		**MINNESOTA**		**OREGON**	
Hawkins	Y Y Y	*Boschwitz*	Y Y Y	*Hatfield*	Y ? ?
Chiles	Y Y Y	*Durenberger*	Y Y Y	*Packwood*	Y Y Y
GEORGIA		**MISSISSIPPI**		**PENNSYLVANIA**	
Mattingly	Y Y Y	*Cochran*	Y Y Y	*Heinz*	Y Y Y
Nunn	Y Y Y	Stennis	Y Y Y	*Specter*	Y Y Y
HAWAII		**MISSOURI**		**RHODE ISLAND**	
Inouye	Y Y Y	*Danforth*	Y Y Y	*Chafee*	Y Y Y
Matsunaga	Y Y Y	Eagleton	Y Y Y	Pell	Y Y Y
IDAHO		**MONTANA**		**SOUTH CAROLINA**	
McClure	N Y Y	Baucus	Y Y Y	*Thurmond*	Y Y Y
Symms	N Y N	Melcher	Y Y Y	Hollings	Y Y Y
ILLINOIS		**NEBRASKA**		**SOUTH DAKOTA**	
Percy	Y Y Y	Exon	Y Y Y	*Abdnor*	Y Y Y
Dixon	Y Y Y	Zorinsky	Y ? ?	*Pressler*	Y Y Y
INDIANA		**NEVADA**		**TENNESSEE**	
Lugar	N Y Y	*Laxalt*	N ? ?	*Baker*	Y Y Y
Quayle	Y Y Y	Cannon	Y Y Y	Sasser	Y Y Y

	147 148 149
TEXAS	
Tower	N Y Y
Bentsen	Y Y Y
UTAH	
Garn	N Y Y
Hatch	N Y Y
VERMONT	
Stafford	Y Y Y
Leahy	Y Y Y
VIRGINIA	
Warner	Y Y Y
Byrd*	N Y Y
WASHINGTON	
Gorton	Y Y Y
Jackson	Y Y Y
WEST VIRGINIA	
Byrd	Y Y Y
Randolph	Y Y Y
WISCONSIN	
Kasten	Y Y Y
Proxmire	N Y Y
WYOMING	
Simpson	Y Y Y
Wallop	N Y Y

Democrats   *Republicans*

* Byrd elected as an independent.

147. S 1007. Food Stamps. Passage of the bill to extend the authorization for the food stamp program through fiscal 1985; to set annual spending ceilings of $11.5 billion in fiscal 1981, $10.9 billion in 1982, $11.3 billion in 1983, $11.3 billion in 1984 and $11.8 billion in 1985, and to make numerous changes in order to reduce the cost of the program. Passed 77-17: R 37-15; D 40-2 (ND 27-1, SD 13-1), June 10, 1981.

148. Exec S, 96th Cong, 2nd Sess. North Pacific Fur Seals Conservation. Adoption of the resolution of ratification of the Interim Convention on Conservation of North Pacific Fur Seals, extending for four years the interim convention of 1957 signed by the United States, Japan, Canada and the Soviet Union to prohibit high seas sealing in the North Pacific, to limit land harvesting of fur seals in the area, and to conduct research to conserve and increase the fur seal herds. Adopted 94-0: R 51-0; D 43-0 (ND 28-0, SD 15-0), June 11, 1981. A two-thirds majority vote (63 in this case) is required for adoption of resolutions of ratification.

149. Rashish Nomination. Confirmation of Myer Rashish of the District of Columbia to be under secretary of state for economic affairs. Confirmed 91-4: R 47-4; D 44-0 (ND 29-0, SD 15-0), June 11, 1981. A "yea" was a vote supporting the president's position.

Corresponding to Congressional Record Votes 150, 151, 152, 153, 154, 155, 156, 157

KEY

Y Voted for (yea).
\# Paired for.
\+ Announced for.
N Voted against (nay).
X Paired against.
\- Announced against.
P Voted "present".
C Voted "present" to avoid possible conflict of interest.
? Did not vote or otherwise make a position known.

	150	151	152	153	154	155	156	157
ALABAMA								
Denton	Y	Y	Y	Y	Y	Y	N	Y
Heflin	Y	Y	Y	Y	Y	N	Y	Y
ALASKA								
Murkowski	Y	Y	Y	Y	Y	Y	Y	Y
Stevens	Y	Y	Y	Y	Y	Y	Y	Y
ARIZONA								
Goldwater	Y	Y	Y	Y	Y	Y	N	Y
DeConcini	?	C	Y	Y	Y	N	N	Y
ARKANSAS								
Bumpers	Y	Y	Y	Y	Y	N	Y	?
Pryor	Y	Y	Y	Y	Y	N	Y	Y
CALIFORNIA								
Hayakawa	Y	Y	Y	Y	Y	Y	Y	?
Cranston	Y	Y	Y	Y	Y	N	Y	Y
COLORADO								
Armstrong	Y	Y	Y	Y	Y	Y	Y	Y
Hart	Y	Y	Y	Y	N	Y	?	?
CONNECTICUT								
Weicker	Y	Y	Y	Y	Y	N	Y	Y
Dodd	Y	Y	Y	Y	Y	N	Y	Y
DELAWARE								
Roth	Y	Y	Y	Y	Y	Y	?	Y
Biden	Y	Y	Y	Y	Y	N	Y	Y
FLORIDA								
Hawkins	Y	Y	Y	Y	Y	Y	N	Y
Chiles	Y	Y	Y	Y	Y	N	Y	Y
GEORGIA								
Mattingly	Y	Y	Y	Y	Y	Y	N	Y
Nunn	Y	Y	Y	Y	Y	N	Y	Y
HAWAII								
Inouye	Y	Y	Y	Y	Y	N	Y	Y
Matsunaga	Y	Y	Y	Y	Y	N	Y	Y
IDAHO								
McClure	Y	Y	Y	Y	Y	Y	N	Y
Symms	Y	Y	Y	Y	Y	N	N	N
ILLINOIS								
Percy	?	?	?	?	Y	Y	Y	Y
Dixon	Y	Y	Y	Y	Y	N	Y	Y
INDIANA								
Lugar	Y	Y	Y	Y	Y	Y	Y	Y
Quayle	Y	Y	Y	Y	Y	Y	N	Y
IOWA								
Grassley	Y	Y	Y	Y	Y	Y	N	Y
Jepsen	Y	Y	Y	Y	Y	Y	Y	Y
KANSAS								
Dole	Y	Y	Y	Y	Y	Y	Y	Y
Kassebaum	Y	Y	Y	Y	Y	N	Y	Y
KENTUCKY								
Ford	Y	Y	Y	Y	Y	N	Y	Y
Huddleston	Y	Y	Y	Y	Y	N	Y	Y
LOUISIANA								
Johnston	Y	Y	Y	Y	Y	N	Y	Y
Long	Y	Y	Y	Y	Y	N	?	Y
MAINE								
Cohen	Y	Y	Y	Y	Y	N	Y	Y
Mitchell	Y	Y	Y	Y	Y	N	Y	Y
MARYLAND								
Mathias	Y	Y	Y	Y	Y	N	Y	Y
Sarbanes	Y	Y	Y	Y	Y	N	Y	Y
MASSACHUSETTS								
Kennedy	Y	Y	Y	Y	Y	N	Y	Y
Tsongas	Y	Y	Y	Y	Y	N	Y	Y
MICHIGAN								
Levin	Y	Y	Y	Y	Y	N	Y	Y
Riegle	Y	Y	Y	Y	Y	N	Y	+
MINNESOTA								
Boschwitz	Y	Y	Y	Y	Y	N	Y	Y
Durenberger	Y	Y	Y	Y	Y	Y	Y	Y
MISSISSIPPI								
Cochran	Y	Y	Y	Y	Y	Y	Y	Y
Stennis	Y	Y	Y	Y	Y	N	Y	Y
MISSOURI								
Danforth	Y	Y	Y	Y	Y	N	Y	Y
Eagleton	Y	Y	Y	Y	Y	N	Y	Y
MONTANA								
Baucus	Y	Y	Y	Y	Y	N	Y	Y
Melcher	Y	Y	Y	Y	Y	N	N	Y
NEBRASKA								
Exon	Y	Y	Y	Y	Y	N	Y	Y
Zorinsky	Y	Y	Y	Y	Y	Y	N	Y
NEVADA								
Laxalt	Y	Y	Y	Y	Y	Y	Y	Y
Cannon	Y	Y	Y	Y	Y	Y	Y	Y
NEW HAMPSHIRE								
Humphrey	Y	Y	Y	Y	Y	Y	N	N
Rudman	Y	Y	Y	Y	Y	Y	Y	?
NEW JERSEY								
Bradley	Y	Y	Y	Y	Y	N	Y	Y
Williams	Y	Y	Y	Y	Y	N	Y	Y
NEW MEXICO								
Domenici	Y	Y	Y	Y	Y	Y	Y	Y
Schmitt	Y	Y	Y	Y	Y	Y	?	?
NEW YORK								
D'Amato	Y	Y	Y	Y	Y	Y	+	Y
Moynihan	Y	Y	Y	Y	Y	?	?	?
NORTH CAROLINA								
East	Y	Y	Y	Y	Y	Y	N	N
Helms	Y	Y	Y	Y	Y	Y	N	Y
NORTH DAKOTA								
Andrews	Y	Y	Y	Y	Y	Y	N	Y
Burdick	Y	Y	Y	Y	Y	N	N	Y
OHIO								
Glenn	Y	Y	Y	Y	Y	N	Y	Y
Metzenbaum	Y	Y	Y	Y	Y	N	Y	Y
OKLAHOMA								
Nickles	Y	Y	Y	Y	Y	N	Y	Y
Boren	Y	Y	Y	Y	Y	N	N	Y
OREGON								
Hatfield	Y	Y	Y	Y	Y	N	Y	Y
Packwood	Y	Y	Y	Y	Y	Y	Y	Y
PENNSYLVANIA								
Heinz	Y	Y	Y	Y	Y	?	?	Y
Specter	Y	Y	Y	Y	Y	N	Y	Y
RHODE ISLAND								
Chafee	Y	Y	Y	Y	Y	N	Y	Y
Pell	Y	Y	Y	Y	Y	N	Y	Y
SOUTH CAROLINA								
Thurmond	Y	Y	Y	Y	Y	Y	N	Y
Hollings	Y	Y	Y	Y	Y	N	Y	Y
SOUTH DAKOTA								
Abdnor	Y	Y	Y	Y	Y	Y	N	Y
Pressler	Y	Y	Y	Y	?	?	?	Y
TENNESSEE								
Baker	Y	Y	Y	Y	Y	N	Y	Y
Sasser	Y	Y	Y	Y	Y	N	Y	+
TEXAS								
Tower	Y	Y	Y	Y	Y	Y	Y	?
Bentsen	Y	Y	Y	Y	Y	N	Y	Y
UTAH								
Garn	Y	Y	Y	Y	Y	Y	N	Y
Hatch	Y	Y	Y	Y	Y	Y	N	Y
VERMONT								
Stafford	Y	Y	Y	Y	Y	N	Y	Y
Leahy	Y	Y	Y	Y	Y	N	Y	Y
VIRGINIA								
Warner	Y	Y	Y	Y	Y	Y	N	Y
Byrd*	Y	Y	Y	Y	Y	Y	N	Y
WASHINGTON								
Gorton	Y	Y	Y	Y	Y	Y	N	Y
Jackson	Y	Y	Y	Y	Y	N	Y	Y
WEST VIRGINIA								
Byrd	Y	Y	Y	Y	Y	N	N	Y
Randolph	Y	Y	Y	Y	Y	N	N	Y
WISCONSIN								
Kasten	Y	Y	Y	Y	Y	Y	N	Y
Proxmire	Y	Y	Y	Y	Y	N	N	N
WYOMING								
Simpson	Y	Y	Y	Y	Y	Y	Y	Y
Wallop	Y	Y	Y	Y	Y	Y	Y	Y

Democrats   *Republicans*

* Byrd elected as an independent.

150. S 921. Veterans' Health Care Act. Proxmire, D-Wis., amendment to increase to $25,000, from $20,000, the maximum amount of insurance military personnel and veterans can purchase under the servicemen's and veterans' group life insurance programs (SGLI and VGLI). Adopted 98-0: R 52-0; D 46-0 (ND 31-0, SD 15-0), June 16, 1981.

151. S 921. Veterans' Health Care Act. Cranston, D-Calif., amendment to make veterans exposed to Agent Orange or other toxic substances in Vietnam or to radiation from a nuclear weapons test eligible for Veterans Administration (VA) health care and priority outpatient care for disabilities that medical evidence indicates could have been caused by that exposure. Adopted 98-0: R 52-0; D 46-0 (ND 31-0, SD 15-0), June 16, 1981. A "nay" was a vote supporting the president's position.

152. S 921. Veterans' Health Care Act. Chafee, R-R.I., amendment to extend for three years, through Sept. 30, 1984, the eligibility period for Vietnam-era veterans to request readjustment counseling and other mental health services from the Veterans Administration. Adopted 99-0: R 52-0; D 47-0 (ND 32-0, SD 15-0), June 16, 1981. A "nay" was a vote supporting the president's position.

153. HR 3499. Veterans' Health Care Act. Passage of the bill to provide medical coverage to Vietnam veterans exposed to the herbicide Agent Orange and to continue readjustment counseling centers for Vietnam veterans. Passed 99-0: R 52-0; D 47-0 (ND 32-0, SD 15-0), June 16, 1981. A "nay" was a vote supporting the president's position.

154. S 1193. State Department Authorization. Moynihan, D-N.Y., amendment stating the sense of Congress that none of the funds authorized in the bill for the U.S.-assessed contribution to the United Nations Educational, Scientific and Cultural Organization may be used for projects to license journalists, to restrict the flow of information within or between countries or to impose mandatory codes of journalistic practice. Adopted 99-0: R 52-0; D 47-0 (ND 32-0, SD 15-0), June 17, 1981.

155. S 1193. State Department Authorization. Helms, R-N.C, motion to table (kill) the Cranston, D-Calif., amendment to separate the Peace Corps from the ACTION agency and to establish the Peace Corps as an independent agency. Motion rejected 45-52: R 42-9; D 3-43 (ND 2-29, SD 1-14), June 17, 1981. (The Cranston amendment, as amended, subsequently was adopted by voice vote.)

156. S 1195. Multilateral Development Banks. Passage of the bill to provide for a U.S. subscription of $8.8 billion to an increase in the capital resources of the International Bank for Reconstruction and Development (an agency of the World Bank), with $658 million of that sum to be paid to the bank and the rest to be pledged to cover any loan defaults; and for U.S. contributions of $275 million to the Inter-American Development Bank (IDB), $70 million to the IDB's Fund for Special Operations and $66.8 million to the Asian Development Fund. Passed 65-27: R 30-18; D 35-9 (ND 23-7, SD 12-2), June 17, 1981. A "yea" was a vote supporting the president's position.

157. S. 1193. State Department Authorization/Infant Formula. Durenberger, R-Minn., amendment expressing congressional "concern" at the U.S. vote against the voluntary international code for marketing infant formula adopted May 21 by the World Health Organization. Adopted 89-2: R 47-2; D 42-0 (ND 29-0, SD 13-0), June 18, 1981. A "nay" was a vote supporting the president's position.

CQ Senate Votes 158 - 165

Corresponding to Congressional Record Votes 158, 159, 160, 161, 162, 163, 164, 165

	158	159	160	161	162	163	164	165
ALABAMA								
Denton	Y	N	N	N	N	Y	N	N
Heflin	N	Y	Y	N	N	N	Y	N
ALASKA								
Murkowski	Y	N	N	N	N	Y	N	-
Stevens	Y	?	N	N	N	N	Y	N
ARIZONA								
Goldwater	Y	N	N	-	N	Y	N	N
DeConcini	Y	X	Y	Y	Y	Y	N	Y
ARKANSAS								
Bumpers	?	?	Y	Y	Y	N	Y	Y
Pryor	Y	?	Y	Y	Y	N	Y	Y
CALIFORNIA								
Hayakawa	?	?	N	N	Y	N	N	N
Cranston	Y	Y	Y	Y	Y	N	Y	Y
COLORADO								
Armstrong	Y	N	N	Y	N	Y	N	N
Hart	?	#	Y	Y	Y	Y	N	Y
CONNECTICUT								
Weicker	Y	Y	Y	N	Y	N	Y	Y
Dodd	Y	Y	Y	Y	Y	N	Y	Y
DELAWARE								
Roth	Y	N	N	N	N	Y	N	N
Biden	Y	N	Y	Y	Y	N	Y	Y
FLORIDA								
Hawkins	Y	N	Y	N	N	N	Y	N
Chiles	Y	N	Y	Y	Y	Y	N	Y
GEORGIA								
Mattingly	Y	N	N	N	N	Y	N	N
Nunn	Y	N	N	Y	Y	Y	Y	N
HAWAII								
Inouye	Y	Y	Y	Y	Y	N	Y	Y
Matsunaga	Y	#	Y	Y	Y	N	Y	Y
IDAHO								
McClure	Y	N	N	N	N	Y	N	N
Symms	Y	N	N	N	N	Y	N	N
ILLINOIS								
Percy	Y	Y	N	N	N	Y	N	N
Dixon	Y	Y	Y	Y	Y	N	Y	Y
INDIANA								
Lugar	Y	N	N	N	N	Y	N	N
Quayle	Y	N	N	N	N	Y	N	N

	158	159	160	161	162	163	164	165
IOWA								
Grassley	N	N	N	Y	N	Y	N	N
Jepsen	Y	N	N	N	N	Y	N	N
KANSAS								
Dole	Y	N	N	N	N	Y	N	N
Kassebaum	Y	N	N	N	N	Y	N	N
KENTUCKY								
Ford	Y	N	Y	N	Y	N	Y	Y
Huddleston	Y	?	Y	N	Y	N	Y	Y
LOUISIANA								
Johnston	Y	N	N	Y	Y	N	Y	N
Long	Y	N	N	Y	Y	Y	Y	N
MAINE								
Cohen	Y	#	N	N	N	Y	Y	Y
Mitchell	Y	Y	Y	Y	Y	N	Y	Y
MARYLAND								
Mathias	Y	Y	N	N	Y	N	Y	Y
Sarbanes	Y	Y	Y	Y	Y	N	Y	Y
MASSACHUSETTS								
Kennedy	Y	Y	Y	Y	Y	Y	Y	Y
Tsongas	Y	?	Y	Y	?	?	Y	Y
MICHIGAN								
Levin	Y	Y	Y	Y	Y	N	Y	Y
Riegle	Y	Y	Y	Y	Y	N	Y	Y
MINNESOTA								
Boschwitz	Y	Y	N	N	N	Y	N	N
Durenberger	Y	Y	N	N	Y	Y	Y	N
MISSISSIPPI								
Cochran	Y	?	N	N	N	Y	N	N
Stennis	Y	?	N	Y	Y	N	Y	N
MISSOURI								
Danforth	Y	N	N	N	N	Y	N	N
Eagleton	Y	Y	Y	N	Y	N	Y	Y
MONTANA								
Baucus	Y	Y	Y	Y	Y	N	Y	Y
Melcher	Y	?	Y	N	Y	N	N	Y
NEBRASKA								
Exon	Y	N	Y	Y	Y	N	Y	N
Zorinsky	N	N	Y	N	N	N	N	N
NEVADA								
Laxalt	Y	N	?	?	N	Y	N	N
Cannon	Y	N	+	+	?	?	?	?

	158	159	160	161	162	163	164	165
NEW HAMPSHIRE								
Humphrey	Y	N	N	N	N	Y	N	N
Rudman	?	?	N	N	N	Y	N	N
NEW JERSEY								
Bradley	Y	?	Y	Y	Y	N	Y	Y
Williams	Y	?	Y	Y	Y	N	Y	Y
NEW MEXICO								
Domenici	Y	N	N	N	N	Y	N	N
Schmitt	?	?	N	N	N	Y	N	N
NEW YORK								
D'Amato	Y	N	N	N	N	Y	N	N
Moynihan	?	Y	Y	Y	Y	N	Y	Y
NORTH CAROLINA								
East	Y	N	N	N	N	?	N	N
Helms	Y	N	N	N	N	N	N	N
NORTH DAKOTA								
Andrews	Y	N	N	N	N	Y	N	N
Burdick	Y	Y	Y	Y	Y	N	Y	Y
OHIO								
Glenn	Y	Y	Y	Y	Y	N	Y	Y
Metzenbaum	Y	#	Y	Y	Y	N	Y	Y
OKLAHOMA								
Nickles	Y	?	N	N	N	Y	N	N
Boren	Y	N	Y	Y	Y	Y	Y	N
OREGON								
Hatfield	Y	Y	N	N	N	Y	N	N
Packwood	Y	N	N	N	N	Y	N	N
PENNSYLVANIA								
Heinz	Y	N	N	Y	Y	Y	Y	N
Specter	Y	Y	Y	N	Y	Y	Y	N
RHODE ISLAND								
Chafee	Y	Y	N	N	N	N	N	N
Pell	Y	Y	Y	Y	Y	N	Y	Y
SOUTH CAROLINA								
Thurmond	Y	N	N	N	N	Y	N	N
Hollings	Y	N	N	Y	Y	Y	Y	N
SOUTH DAKOTA								
Abdnor	Y	N	N	N	N	Y	N	N
Pressler	Y	Y	Y	Y	Y	Y	N	N
TENNESSEE								
Baker	Y	N	N	N	N	Y	N	N
Sasser	+	X	Y	N	Y	N	Y	N

KEY

Y	Voted for (yea).
#	Paired for.
+	Announced for.
N	Voted against (nay).
X	Paired against.
-	Announced against.
P	Voted "present".
C	Voted "present" to avoid possible conflict of interest.
?	Did not vote or otherwise make a position known.

	158	159	160	161	162	163	164	165
TEXAS								
Tower	+	X	N	N	N	Y	?	N
Bentsen	Y	N	Y	Y	Y	Y	N	N
UTAH								
Garn	Y	N	N	N	N	Y	N	N
Hatch	Y	N	N	N	N	Y	N	N
VERMONT								
Stafford	Y	?	N	N	N	Y	N	N
Leahy	Y	Y	Y	Y	Y	N	Y	Y
VIRGINIA								
Warner	Y	N	N	N	N	Y	N	N
Byrd*	Y	N	N	N	N	Y	N	N
WASHINGTON								
Gorton	Y	N	N	N	N	Y	N	N
Jackson	Y	Y	Y	N	Y	N	Y	Y
WEST VIRGINIA								
Byrd	Y	X	Y	Y	Y	N	Y	Y
Randolph	Y	N	Y	Y	Y	N	Y	Y
WISCONSIN								
Kasten	Y	N	N	N	N	Y	N	N
Proxmire	N	N	N	Y	N	Y	N	N
WYOMING								
Simpson	Y	?	N	N	N	Y	N	N
Wallop	Y	?	N	N	N	Y	N	N

Democrats   *Republicans*

* Byrd elected as an independent.

158. S 1193. State Department Authorization. Passage of the bill to authorize $3.1 billion in fiscal 1982 and $2.8 billion in fiscal 1983 for State Department programs, including assessed U.S. contributions to the United Nations and operations of the International Communications Agency, the Board for International Broadcasting and the Arms Control and Disarmament Agency. Passed 88-4: R 48-1; D 40-3 (ND 28-2, SD 12-1), June 18, 1981.

159. S 951. Justice Department Authorization. Weicker, R-Conn., amendment, to the Helms, R-N.C., amendment, to ensure that the Justice Department and any federal court could act to enforce citizens' constitutional rights. Rejected 30-45: R 12-30; D 18-15 (ND 17-6, SD 1-9), June 19, 1981.

160. S 1377. Budget Reconciliation. Riegle, D-Mich., amendment to repeal the $122 minimum monthly Social Security payment only for those who would become eligible after July 1981, thus retaining the payment for current beneficiaries. Rejected 45-53: R 4-48; D 41-5 (ND 30-1, SD 11-4), June 23, 1981. A "nay" was a vote supporting the president's position.

161. S 1377. Budget Reconciliation. Metzenbaum, D-Ohio, amendment, to the McClure, R-Idaho, amendment, to stipulate that all funds appropriated to fill the Strategic Petroleum Reserve must be included in the federal budget totals. Rejected 39-58: R 3-48; D 36-10 (ND 27-4, SD 9-6), June 23, 1981. (The McClure amendment, subsequently adopted by voice vote, provided for off-budget financing of the Strategic Petroleum Reserve in fiscal 1982.)

162. S 1377. Budget Reconciliation. Moynihan, D-N.Y., amendment to preserve parts of existing law that provided for separate, categorical programs of aid to states for the maintenance of welfare children placed in foster care, for child welfare services aimed at preventing the breakup of low-income families and for assistance to families adopting welfare children with special needs. Rejected 46-52: R 5-48; D 41-4 (ND 28-2, SD 13-2), June 23, 1981. A "nay" was a vote supporting the president's position.

163. S 1377. Budget Reconciliation. Stafford, R-Vt., amendment to bring the higher education provisions of the bill into compliance with the reconciliation instructions, by providing that fiscal 1984 higher education authorizations not be increased over their 1983 levels; the amendment allowed authorization increases for the Pell grant program of aid to college students, the international education program and grants to Howard University. Adopted 60-37: R 50-2; D 10-35 (ND 2-28, SD 8-7), June 24, 1981.

164. S 1377. Budget Reconciliation. Mitchell, D-Maine, amendment to authorize $200 million in fiscal 1982 to continue Economic Development Administration programs, which would be terminated under the bill. Rejected 45-53: R 6-46; D 39-7 (ND 27-4, SD 12-3), June 24, 1981. A "nay" was a vote supporting the president's position.

165. S 1377. Budget Reconciliation. Bumpers, D-Ark., amendment to provide a $450 million increase in fiscal 1982 funding for energy conservation, solar energy research and development and the Solar Energy and Energy Conservation Bank. Rejected 35-63: R 2-50; D 33-13 (ND 28-3, SD 5-10), June 24, 1981.

CQ Senate Votes 166 - 173
Corresponding to Congressional Record Votes 166, 167, 168, 169, 170, 171, 172, 173

	166	167	168	169	170	171	172	173
ALABAMA								
Denton	N	Y	N	Y	N	Y	Y	N
Heflin	N	Y	N	Y	Y	Y	Y	Y
ALASKA								
Murkowski	Y	N	N	N	Y	Y	Y	N
Stevens	Y	N	N	Y	N	Y	Y	N
ARIZONA								
Goldwater	Y	N	N	N	N	N	N	N
DeConcini	N	Y	N	N	Y	Y	Y	Y
ARKANSAS								
Bumpers	N	N	Y	Y	Y	Y	Y	Y
Pryor	N	N	Y	Y	Y	Y	Y	Y
CALIFORNIA								
Hayakawa	N	Y	N	N	N	N	N	N
Cranston	Y	N	Y	Y	?	?	?	?
COLORADO								
Armstrong	N	Y	N	N	N	N	N	N
Hart	N	N	Y	Y	Y	Y	Y	Y
CONNECTICUT								
Weicker	Y	N	Y	Y	Y	Y	Y	Y
Dodd	Y	N	+	Y	Y	Y	Y	Y
DELAWARE								
Roth	Y	N	Y	Y	Y	Y	Y	Y
Biden	Y	N	Y	Y	Y	Y	Y	Y
FLORIDA								
Hawkins	N	Y	Y	Y	Y	Y	Y	Y
Chiles	Y	N	Y	Y	Y	Y	Y	Y
GEORGIA								
Mattingly	N	Y	N	Y	N	Y	Y	N
Nunn	Y	N	Y	Y	N	Y	Y	Y
HAWAII								
Inouye	Y	N	Y	Y	Y	Y	Y	N
Matsunaga	N	N	Y	Y	Y	Y	Y	N
IDAHO								
McClure	Y	N	N	N	N	N	N	N
Symms	Y	N	N	N	N	N	N	N
ILLINOIS								
Percy	Y	N	N	Y	N	N	N	N
Dixon	N	N	Y	Y	Y	Y	Y	Y
INDIANA								
Lugar	N	Y	N	N	N	N	N	N
Quayle	N	Y	N	N	N	N	N	N
IOWA								
Grassley	N	Y	N	Y	N	N	N	Y
Jepsen	N	Y	N	N	N	N	N	N
KANSAS								
Dole	N	N	N	Y	N	N	N	N
Kassebaum	N	Y	N	N	N	N	N	N
KENTUCKY								
Ford	Y	N	Y	Y	Y	Y	Y	Y
Huddleston	Y	N	Y	Y	Y	Y	Y	Y
LOUISIANA								
Johnston	Y	N	N	Y	N	N	N	Y
Long	Y	N	N	Y	N	N	N	N
MAINE								
Cohen	N	Y	N	Y	Y	Y	Y	N
Mitchell	N	Y	Y	Y	N	Y	Y	Y
MARYLAND								
Mathias	Y	N	Y	N	Y	Y	Y	N
Sarbanes	N	Y	Y	Y	Y	Y	Y	Y
MASSACHUSETTS								
Kennedy	N	N	Y	Y	Y	Y	Y	Y
Tsongas	N	N	Y	Y	Y	Y	Y	Y
MICHIGAN								
Levin	Y	N	Y	Y	Y	Y	Y	Y
Riegle	Y	N	Y	Y	Y	Y	Y	Y
MINNESOTA								
Boschwitz	N	Y	Y	N	N	N	N	N
Durenberger	N	Y	N	N	N	N	N	N
MISSISSIPPI								
Cochran	N	Y	N	N	N	N	N	N
Stennis	Y	N	N	Y	N	N	N	Y
MISSOURI								
Danforth	N	Y	N	N	Y	Y	Y	N
Eagleton	Y	N	Y	Y	Y	Y	Y	Y
MONTANA								
Baucus	N	Y	Y	Y	N	N	N	Y
Melcher	N	Y	Y	Y	Y	Y	Y	Y
NEBRASKA								
Exon	Y	N	Y	Y	N	N	N	Y
Zorinsky	N	Y	Y	Y	Y	Y	Y	Y
NEVADA								
Laxalt	N	Y	N	Y	N	N	N	N
Cannon	-	+	+	?	+	+	+	?
NEW HAMPSHIRE								
Humphrey	N	Y	N	Y	N	N	N	N
Rudman	Y	Y	N	Y	Y	Y	Y	N
NEW JERSEY								
Bradley	N	N	Y	Y	N	N	N	Y
Williams	N	Y	Y	Y	Y	Y	Y	Y
NEW MEXICO								
Domenici	Y	N	N	N	N	Y	N	N
Schmitt	N	Y	N	Y	N	Y	N	N
NEW YORK								
D'Amato	N	Y	N	Y	N	Y	N	N
Moynihan	Y	N	+	?	?	?	Y	N
NORTH CAROLINA								
East	Y	Y	N	N	N	N	N	N
Helms	N	Y	N	N	N	N	N	N
NORTH DAKOTA								
Andrews	N	Y	N	Y	Y	Y	Y	N
Burdick	N	Y	Y	Y	Y	Y	Y	Y
OHIO								
Glenn	Y	N	Y	Y	Y	Y	Y	N
Metzenbaum	Y	N	Y	Y	Y	Y	Y	?
OKLAHOMA								
Nickles	N	Y	N	Y	N	N	N	Y
Boren	N	N	Y	N	Y	N	N	Y
OREGON								
Hatfield	N	Y	N	Y	Y	Y	Y	N
Packwood	N	N	N	Y	N	N	N	N
PENNSYLVANIA								
Heinz	N	Y	Y	Y	N	N	N	N
Specter	N	Y	Y	Y	Y	Y	Y	N
RHODE ISLAND								
Chafee	Y	N	Y	Y	N	N	N	N
Pell	N	N	Y	Y	Y	Y	Y	N
SOUTH CAROLINA								
Thurmond	Y	N	N	Y	N	N	N	N
Hollings	Y	N	Y	N	N	N	N	N
SOUTH DAKOTA								
Abdnor	Y	N	N	N	N	N	N	Y
Pressler	N	Y	Y	N	N	N	N	Y
TENNESSEE								
Baker	N	N	N	Y	N	N	N	N
Sasser	N	Y	Y	Y	Y	Y	Y	Y
TEXAS								
Tower	N	Y	N	N	Y	N	N	?
Bentsen	Y	N	Y	Y	Y	Y	Y	Y
UTAH								
Garn	N	Y	N	Y	N	N	N	N
Hatch	N	Y	N	N	N	N	N	N
VERMONT								
Stafford	N	Y	N	Y	N	N	N	N
Leahy	N	N	Y	Y	Y	Y	Y	Y
VIRGINIA								
Warner	N	Y	N	Y	Y	Y	Y	N
Byrd*	Y	N	N	N	N	Y	N	N
WASHINGTON								
Gorton	Y	N	N	N	N	N	N	N
Jackson	Y	Y	Y	Y	Y	Y	Y	Y
WEST VIRGINIA								
Byrd	Y	N	Y	Y	Y	Y	Y	Y
Randolph	Y	N	Y	Y	Y	Y	Y	Y
WISCONSIN								
Kasten	N	Y	N	N	N	N	N	Y
Proxmire	Y	N	N	N	N	N	N	Y
WYOMING								
Simpson	N	Y	N	N	N	N	N	N
Wallop	N	Y	N	N	N	N	N	N

KEY

Y Voted for (yea).
\# Paired for.
\+ Announced for.
N Voted against (nay).
X Paired against.
\- Announced against.
P Voted "present".
C Voted "present" to avoid possible conflict of interest.
? Did not vote or otherwise make a position known.

Democrats *Republicans*

Byrd elected as an independent.

166. S 1377. Budget Reconciliation. Stevens, R-Alaska, motion to table (kill) the Durenberger, R-Minn., amendment *(see vote 167, below)* to prohibit use of funds authorized by the bill to implement the nine-digit ZIP code. Motion rejected 41-58: R 16-37; D 25-21 (ND 15-16, SD 10-5), June 24, 1981.

167. S 1377. Budget Reconciliation. Durenberger, R-Minn., amendment to prohibit use of funds authorized by the bill to implement the nine-digit ZIP code. Rejected 47-52: R 36-17; D 11-35 (ND 9-22, SD 2-13), June 24, 1981.

168. S 1377. Budget Reconciliation. Cranston, D-Calif., amendment to delete two provisions that would repeal authority for Social Security funding of vocational rehabilitation programs for disabled beneficiaries of disability insurance and Supplemental Security Income. Rejected 47-50: R 10-43; D 37-7 (ND 27-2; SD 10-5), June 25, 1981.

169. S 1377. Budget Reconciliation. Levin, D-Mich., amendment to lower the interest rate on Small Business Administration disaster loans for homeowners. Adopted 67-31: R 25-28; D 42-3 (ND 28-2, SD 14-1), June 25, 1981.

170. S 1377. Budget Reconciliation. Roth, R-Del., amendment to delete a provision in order to retain Medicare as the primary payer of health insurance benefits for federal employees who are also covered by the Federal Employee Health Benefits program. Rejected 47-50: R 14-39; D 33-11 (ND 24-5, SD 9-6), June 25, 1981. (Subsequently, the Roth amendment was adopted *(see vote 172, below)* upon reconsideration.)

171. S 1377. Budget Reconciliation. Stevens, R-Alaska, motion to reconsider the vote *(vote 170, above)* by which the Roth, R-Del., amendment was rejected. Motion agreed to 53-44: R 18-35; D 35-9 (ND 25-4, SD 10-5), June 25, 1981.

172. S 1377. Budget Reconciliation. Roth, R-Del., amendment to delete a provision in order to retain Medicare as the primary payer of health insurance benefits for federal employees who are also covered by the Federal Employee Health Benefits program *(votes 170 and 171, above)*. Adopted 51-47: R 15-38; D 36-9 (ND 26-4, SD 10-5), June 25, 1981.

173. S 1377. Budget Reconciliation. DeConcini, D-Ariz., amendment to reduce fiscal 1982 spending for government consultant and contract services by an additional $500 million and to reduce spending by an additional $200 million for non-defense travel. Rejected 44-52: R 7-45; D 37-7 (ND 24-5, SD 13-2), June 25, 1981.

	174	175	176	177	178
ALABAMA					
Denton	Y	Y	N	N	Y
Heflin	N	Y	N	Y	N
ALASKA					
Murkowski	Y	Y	N	N	Y
Stevens	Y	Y	N	Y	Y
ARIZONA					
Goldwater	Y	Y	N	Y	Y
DeConcini	N	Y	N	Y	-
ARKANSAS					
Bumpers	N	N	Y	N	Y
Pryor	N	N	N	Y	N
CALIFORNIA					
Hayakawa	Y	Y	N	N	Y
Cranston	?	?	?	?	?
COLORADO					
Armstrong	Y	C	N	Y	Y
Hart	N	N	N	Y	N
CONNECTICUT					
Weicker	N	N	N	Y	N
Dodd	N	N	Y	Y	N
DELAWARE					
Roth	Y	Y	N	Y	Y
Biden	N	N	Y	Y	N
FLORIDA					
Hawkins	Y	Y	N	N	Y
Chiles	N	N	N	Y	N
GEORGIA					
Mattingly	Y	Y	N	N	Y
Nunn	N	N	N	Y	N
HAWAII					
Inouye	Y	N	Y	Y	N
Matsunaga	Y	N	Y	Y	N
IDAHO					
McClure	Y	N	N	N	Y
Symms	Y	Y	N	N	Y
ILLINOIS					
Percy	Y	Y	Y	Y	N
Dixon	N	N	N	Y	N
INDIANA					
Lugar	Y	Y	N	Y	Y
Quayle	Y	Y	N	Y	Y
IOWA					
Grassley	Y	Y	N	N	Y
Jepsen	Y	Y	N	N	Y
KANSAS					
Dole	Y	Y	N	Y	Y
Kassebaum	Y	Y	N	Y	N
KENTUCKY					
Y Ford	N	N	N	Y	N
Y Huddleston	Y	N	N	N	N
LOUISIANA					
Johnston	N	N	N	Y	N
Long	N	N	N	Y	N
MAINE					
Cohen	?	?	?	?	?
Mitchell	N	Y	Y	Y	N
MARYLAND					
Mathias	N	Y	N	Y	N
Sarbanes	N	N	Y	Y	N
MASSACHUSETTS					
Kennedy	N	N	Y	Y	N
Tsongas	N	N	Y	Y	N
MICHIGAN					
Levin	N	N	Y	Y	N
Riegle	N	N	Y	Y	N
MINNESOTA					
Boschwitz	Y	Y	Y	Y	N
Durenberger	Y	Y	N	Y	N
MISSISSIPPI					
Cochran	Y	Y	N	N	Y
Stennis	N	N	N	Y	Y
MISSOURI					
Danforth	Y	Y	N	Y	N
Eagleton	N	N	Y	Y	N
MONTANA					
Baucus	N	N	Y	Y	N
Melcher	N	N	?	?	?
NEBRASKA					
Exon	N	Y	N	Y	N
Zorinsky	N	Y	N	Y	Y
NEVADA					
Laxalt	Y	Y	N	N	Y
Cannon	?	?	?	?	?
NEW HAMPSHIRE					
Humphrey	Y	Y	N	N	Y
Rudman	Y	Y	N	Y	N
NEW JERSEY					
Bradley	N	N	Y	Y	N
Williams	N	N	Y	Y	N
NEW MEXICO					
Domenici	Y	Y	N	Y	N
Schmitt	Y	Y	N	Y	N
NEW YORK					
Y *D'Amato*	Y	Y	N	Y	Y
Y Moynihan	N	N	Y	Y	N
NORTH CAROLINA					
East	Y	Y	N	N	Y
Helms	Y	Y	N	N	Y
NORTH DAKOTA					
Andrews	Y	Y	N	Y	N
Burdick	N	N	N	Y	N
OHIO					
Glenn	N	N	N	Y	N
Metzenbaum	?	?	?	?	?
OKLAHOMA					
Nickles	Y	Y	N	N	Y
Boren	N	N	?	?	?
OREGON					
Hatfield	Y	Y	Y	Y	N
Packwood	Y	Y	N	Y	N
PENNSYLVANIA					
Heinz	Y	Y	N	Y	N
Specter	Y	Y	N	Y	N
RHODE ISLAND					
Chafee	Y	Y	Y	Y	N
Pell	N	N	Y	Y	N
SOUTH CAROLINA					
Thurmond	Y	Y	N	N	Y
Hollings	N	N	N	Y	N
SOUTH DAKOTA					
Abdnor	Y	Y	N	Y	N
Pressler	Y	Y	Y	Y	N
TENNESSEE					
Baker	Y	Y	N	Y	Y
Sasser	N	N	N	Y	N
TEXAS					
Tower	Y	Y	N	N	Y
Bentsen	N	N	N	Y	N
UTAH					
Garn	Y	Y	N	N	Y
Hatch	Y	Y	N	N	Y
VERMONT					
Stafford	Y	Y	N	Y	N
Leahy	N	N	Y	Y	N
VIRGINIA					
Warner	Y	Y	N	N	Y
Byrd*	Y	Y	N	Y	Y
WASHINGTON					
Gorton	Y	Y	N	Y	N
Jackson	N	N	N	Y	N
WEST VIRGINIA					
Byrd	N	N	Y	Y	N
Randolph	N	N	Y	Y	N
WISCONSIN					
Kasten	Y	Y	N	Y	N
Proxmire	N	N	Y	N	Y
WYOMING					
Y *Simpson*	Y	Y	N	Y	Y
Y *Wallop*	Y	Y	N	Y	Y

KEY

Y   Voted for (yea).
\#   Paired for.
+   Announced for.
N   Voted against (nay).
X   Paired against.
-   Announced against.
P   Voted "present".
C   Voted "present" to avoid possible conflict of interest.
?   Did not vote or otherwise make a position known.

Democrats   *Republicans*

* Byrd elected as an independent.

174. S 1377. Budget Reconciliation. Garn, R-Utah, amendment to reinstate provisions under the jurisdiction of the Banking, Housing and Urban Affairs Committee relating to community development block grants, Urban Development Action Grants, Federal Housing Administration loan ceilings, mortgage purchase authority, rural housing and rent control. Adopted 54-42: R 50-2; D 4-40 (ND 2-27, SD 2-13), June 25, 1981.

175. S 1377. Budget Reconciliation. Packwood, R-Ore., amendment to reinstate provisions under the jurisdiction of the Commerce, Science and Transportation Committee relating to radio and television broadcasting and communications user fees. Adopted 55-40: R 49-2; D 6-38 (ND 4-25, SD 2-13), June 25, 1981.

176. S 1377. Budget Reconciliation. Kennedy, D-Mass., amendment to reduce the nuclear fission research and development budget by $309 million in fiscal 1982. Rejected 25-69: R 5-47; D 20-22 (ND 19-9, SD 1-13), June 25, 1981.

177. S 1377. Budget Reconciliation. Denton, R-Ala., appeal of the chair's ruling that the Denton amendment, to delete the $100 million authorization for the Legal Services Corporation, was out of order because it was not germane. Ruling of the chair upheld 73-21: R 32-20; D 41-1 (ND 27-1, SD 14-0), June 25, 1981.

178. S 1377. Budget Reconciliation. Denton, R-Ala., amendment to establish a block grant to the states for legal services to the poor. Rejected 35-58: R 31-21; D 4-37 (ND 2-25, SD 2-12), June 25, 1981.

	179 180 181 182		179 180 181 182		179 180 181 182
ALABAMA		**IOWA**		**NEW HAMPSHIRE**	
Denton	N Y Y Y	*Grassley*	N N N Y	*Humphrey*	N N N Y
Heflin	N Y Y Y	*Jepsen*	N N Y Y	*Rudman*	N N N Y
ALASKA		**KANSAS**		**NEW JERSEY**	
Murkowski	Y N N Y	*Dole*	N Y N Y	Bradley	Y N Y N
Stevens	Y N N Y	*Kassebaum*	N N N Y	Williams	Y N Y N
ARIZONA		**KENTUCKY**		**NEW MEXICO**	
Goldwater	N N N Y	Ford	Y Y Y Y	*Domenici*	N Y N Y
DeConcini	+ ? ? #	Huddleston	N N Y Y	*Schmitt*	Y N N Y
ARKANSAS		**LOUISIANA**		**NEW YORK**	
Bumpers	Y Y N Y	Johnston	N N N Y	*D'Amato*	Y Y Y Y
Pryor	Y Y N Y	Long	N N N Y	Moynihan	Y Y Y N
CALIFORNIA		**MAINE**		**NORTH CAROLINA**	
Hayakawa	N Y N Y	*Cohen*	? ? ? ?	*East*	N Y N Y
Cranston	? ? ? X	Mitchell	Y Y N Y	*Helms*	N Y N Y
COLORADO		**MARYLAND**		**NORTH DAKOTA**	
Armstrong	N Y N Y	*Mathias*	Y N Y Y	*Andrews*	N N N Y
Hart	Y N Y N	Sarbanes	Y Y Y N	Burdick	Y N Y Y
CONNECTICUT		**MASSACHUSETTS**		**OHIO**	
Weicker	N N Y Y	Kennedy	Y N Y N	Glenn	N N Y Y
Dodd	Y N Y N	Tsongas	Y N Y N	Metzenbaum	? ? ? ?
DELAWARE		**MICHIGAN**		**OKLAHOMA**	
Roth	N N Y Y	Levin	Y N Y N	*Nickles*	N N N Y
Biden	Y N Y N	Riegle	Y N Y N	Boren	N Y N Y
FLORIDA		**MINNESOTA**		**OREGON**	
Hawkins	N N N Y	*Boschwitz*	Y Y N Y	*Hatfield*	Y N N Y
Chiles	Y N N Y	*Durenberger*	N N N Y	*Packwood*	Y Y N Y
GEORGIA		**MISSISSIPPI**		**PENNSYLVANIA**	
Mattingly	N N N Y	*Cochran*	N N N Y	*Heinz*	Y N Y Y
Nunn	N N N Y	Stennis	N N N Y	*Specter*	Y N Y Y
HAWAII		**MISSOURI**		**RHODE ISLAND**	
Inouye	Y N N Y	*Danforth*	N N N Y	*Chafee*	Y N N Y
Matsunaga	Y N N Y	Eagleton	Y N N Y	Pell	Y N N N
IDAHO		**MONTANA**		**SOUTH CAROLINA**	
McClure	N N N Y	Baucus	Y N N Y	*Thurmond*	N N N Y
Symms	N N N Y	Melcher	Y Y N Y	Hollings	N Y N Y
ILLINOIS		**NEBRASKA**		**SOUTH DAKOTA**	
Percy	N N Y Y	Exon	N Y Y Y	*Abdnor*	N N N Y
Dixon	Y Y Y Y	Zorinsky	N Y N Y	*Pressler*	Y N N Y
INDIANA		**NEVADA**		**TENNESSEE**	
Lugar	N N Y Y	*Laxalt*	N Y N Y	*Baker*	N N N Y
Quayle	N N Y Y	Cannon	? ? ? ?	Sasser	Y Y Y Y

KEY

Y Voted for (yea).
\# Paired for.
+ Announced for.
N Voted against (nay).
X Paired against.
- Announced against.
P Voted "present".
C Voted "present" to avoid possible conflict of interest.
? Did not vote or otherwise make a position known.

	179 180 181 182
TEXAS	
Tower	N Y N Y
Bentsen	Y Y N Y
UTAH	
Garn	N N N Y
Hatch	N N ? Y
VERMONT	
Stafford	N N Y Y
Leahy	Y Y Y N
VIRGINIA	
Warner	N N N Y
Byrd*	N N N Y
WASHINGTON	
Gorton	N N N Y
Jackson	Y Y Y Y
WEST VIRGINIA	
Byrd	Y Y Y Y
Randolph	Y Y Y N
WISCONSIN	
Kasten	N Y N Y
Proxmire	N N N Y
WYOMING	
Simpson	Y N N Y
Wallop	N N N Y

Democrats   **Republicans**

* Byrd elected as an independent.

179. S 1377. Budget Reconciliation. Mathias, R-Md., amendment to restore funds for grants for services to rape victims by striking a section of the bill repealing that section of the Mental Health Services Act. Rejected 43-52: R 13-39; D 30-13 (ND 24-4, SD 6-9), June 25, 1981.

180. S 1377. Budget Reconciliation. Helms, R-N.C., amendment to restore $11.5 million in funding for Gallaudet College and $12.5 million for the National Technical Institute for the Deaf in fiscal 1982-83 by shifting funds from education for the handicapped programs. Rejected 32-63: R 13-39; D 19-24 (ND 11-17, SD 8-7), June 25, 1981.

181. S 1377. Budget Reconciliation. Heinz, R-Pa., amendment to extend the period during which Conrail could be sold as an entity if it were determined to be profitable. Rejected 34-60: R 11-40; D 23-20 (ND 19-9, SD 4-11), June 25, 1981.

182. S 1377. Budget Reconciliation. Passage of the bill to revise existing laws to achieve budget savings in fiscal 1982-84 as ordered by the first budget resolution for fiscal 1982. Passed 80-15: R 52-0; D 28-15 (ND 13-15, SD 15-0), June 25, 1981. A "yea" was a vote supporting the president's position.

CQ Senate Votes 183 - 188

Corresponding to Congressional Record Votes 183, 184, 185, 186, 187, 188

	183 184 185 186 187 188		183 184 185 186 187 188		183 184 185 186 187 188
ALABAMA		**IOWA**		**NEW HAMPSHIRE**	
Denton	Y Y ? N Y Y	*Grassley*	Y N Y N Y Y	*Humphrey*	Y Y Y N Y Y
Heflin	Y N Y Y Y N	*Jepsen*	Y ? ? N Y Y	*Rudman*	Y Y ? N Y Y
ALASKA		**KANSAS**		**NEW JERSEY**	
Murkowski	? ? Y Y Y Y	*Dole*	Y Y Y N Y Y	Bradley	Y N ? N Y N
Stevens	Y Y ? Y Y Y	*Kassebaum*	Y Y N Y Y Y	Williams	Y N ? Y Y N
ARIZONA		**KENTUCKY**		**NEW MEXICO**	
Goldwater	Y Y Y ? Y Y	Ford	Y N Y Y Y N	*Domenici*	Y Y Y N Y ?
DeConcini	Y Y Y Y Y N	Huddleston	Y N Y Y Y N	*Schmitt*	Y Y Y Y Y Y
ARKANSAS		**LOUISIANA**		**NEW YORK**	
Bumpers	Y Y N Y Y N	Johnston	Y N Y N Y N	*D'Amato*	Y Y N Y Y Y
Pryor	? + Y Y Y N	Long	Y N Y Y Y N	Moynihan	Y N X N Y N
CALIFORNIA		**MAINE**		**NORTH CAROLINA**	
Hayakawa	? ? Y ? ? Y	*Cohen*	Y N N N Y Y	*East*	Y Y Y Y Y Y
Cranston	Y N N N Y N	Mitchell	Y N N N Y N	*Helms*	Y Y Y Y Y Y
COLORADO		**MARYLAND**		**NORTH DAKOTA**	
Armstrong	Y Y Y ? Y Y	*Mathias*	Y N N N Y Y	*Andrews*	Y N ? Y Y Y
Hart	Y N ? ? Y N	Sarbanes	Y N N N Y N	Burdick	Y N N Y Y N
CONNECTICUT		**MASSACHUSETTS**		**OHIO**	
Weicker	Y N N N Y Y	Kennedy	Y ? N N Y N	Glenn	Y N N Y Y ?
Dodd	Y X - Y Y N	Tsongas	? X - ? ? ?	Metzenbaum	Y N N N Y N
DELAWARE		**MICHIGAN**		**OKLAHOMA**	
Roth	Y N Y N Y Y	Levin	Y N N N Y N	*Nickles*	Y Y Y N Y Y
Biden	Y N Y N Y N	Riegle	Y N N Y Y N	Boren	Y N Y Y Y N
FLORIDA		**MINNESOTA**		**OREGON**	
Hawkins	Y Y Y Y Y Y	*Boschwitz*	Y N N Y Y Y	*Hatfield*	Y N N N Y Y
Chiles	Y N Y N Y N	*Durenberger*	Y N N N Y Y	*Packwood*	Y Y N Y Y Y
GEORGIA		**MISSISSIPPI**		**PENNSYLVANIA**	
Mattingly	Y Y Y Y Y Y	*Cochran*	Y Y Y Y Y Y	*Heinz*	Y ? N Y Y Y
Nunn	Y N Y N Y N	Stennis	Y N Y N Y N	*Specter*	Y N N Y Y Y
HAWAII		**MISSOURI**		**RHODE ISLAND**	
Inouye	Y N N N Y N	*Danforth*	Y Y Y N Y Y	*Chafee*	Y N N N Y Y
Matsunaga	Y N N Y Y N	Eagleton	Y N N N Y N	Pell	Y # # Y Y N
IDAHO		**MONTANA**		**SOUTH CAROLINA**	
McClure	Y Y Y Y Y Y	Baucus	Y N N N Y N	*Thurmond*	Y Y Y N Y Y
Symms	Y Y Y N Y Y	Melcher	Y ? Y N Y N	Hollings	Y Y Y N Y N
ILLINOIS		**NEBRASKA**		**SOUTH DAKOTA**	
Percy	Y ? N Y Y Y	Exon	Y N Y Y Y N	*Abdnor*	Y Y Y N Y Y
Dixon	Y N N N Y N	Zorinsky	Y Y Y Y Y N	*Pressler*	Y N N Y Y N
INDIANA		**NEVADA**		**TENNESSEE**	
Lugar	Y Y Y N Y Y	*Laxalt*	Y Y Y N Y Y	*Baker*	Y Y Y N Y Y
Quayle	Y Y Y N Y Y	Cannon	Y N Y Y Y -	Sasser	Y ? Y Y Y N

KEY

Y Voted for (yea).
\# Paired for.
\+ Announced for.
N Voted against (nay).
X Paired against.
- Announced against.
P Voted "present".
C Voted "present" to avoid possible conflict of interest.
? Did not vote or otherwise make a position known.

	183 184 185 186 187 188
TEXAS	
Tower	Y Y Y Y Y Y
Bentsen	Y N Y Y Y N
UTAH	
Garn	Y Y Y N Y Y
Hatch	Y Y Y N Y Y
VERMONT	
Stafford	Y N N N Y Y
Leahy	Y # N N Y N
VIRGINIA	
Warner	Y Y ? N Y Y
Byrd*	? ? ? N Y N
WASHINGTON	
Gorton	Y Y Y N Y Y
Jackson	Y N N N Y N
WEST VIRGINIA	
Byrd	Y N Y N Y N
Randolph	Y N Y N Y N
WISCONSIN	
Kasten	Y Y Y Y Y Y
Proxmire	Y N Y N Y N
WYOMING	
Simpson	Y N Y N Y Y
Wallop	Y Y Y N Y Y

Democrats   *Republicans*

* Byrd elected as an independent.

183. S Res 141. Violent Crime in America. Adoption of the resolution expressing the sense of the Senate that taking all appropriate action necessary to combat violent crime should be a national priority. Adopted 95-0: R 51-0; D 44-0 (ND 31-0, SD 13-0), July 9, 1981.

184. S 951. Justice Department Authorization. Baker, R-Tenn., motion to invoke cloture (and thus limit debate) on the bill to authorize programs for the Justice Department in fiscal 1982. Motion rejected 38-48: R 34-14; D 4-34 (ND 2-24, SD 2-10), July 10, 1981. A three-fifths vote of the total Senate membership (60) is required to invoke cloture.

185. S 951. Justice Department Authorization. Johnston, D-La., motion to invoke cloture (and thus limit debate) on the Helms, R-N.C.-Johnston, D-La., amendment to prohibit federal courts in most instances from ordering busing for racial purposes. Motion rejected 54-32: R 32-15; D 22-17 (ND 9-16, SD 13-1), July 13, 1981. A three-fifths vote of the total Senate membership (60) is required to invoke cloture.

186. S 1204. Noise Control Authorization. Kasten, R-Wis., amendment to retain federal noise control standards for newly manufactured motorcycles. Rejected 40-55: R 19-31; D 21-24 (ND 12-18, SD 9-6), July 14, 1981.

187. S Res 87. Taxation of Social Security Benefits. Adoption of the resolution to express the sense of the Senate that Social Security benefits should remain exempt from federal taxation. Adopted 98-0: R 52-0; D 46-0 (ND 31-0, SD 15-0), July 14, 1981.

188. H J Res 266. Tax Cuts/Social Security. Baker, R-Tenn., motion to table (kill) the Moynihan, D-N.Y., amendment, to the Finance Committee amendment *(see vote 191, p. 35-S)*, to permit the Old Age and Survivors Insurance Trust Fund to borrow from the Disability Insurance Trust Fund or the Hospital Insurance Trust Fund if necessary to maintain the solvency of the pension system. Motion agreed to 51-45: R 51-1; D 0-44 (ND 0-29, SD 0-15), July 16, 1981.

KEY

Y Voted for (yea).
Paired for.
+ Announced for.
N Voted against (nay).
X Paired against.
- Announced against.
P Voted "present".
C Voted "present" to avoid possible conflict of interest.
? Did not vote or otherwise make a position known.

	189	190	191	192	193	194	195	196
ALABAMA								
Denton	Y	Y	Y	Y	N	Y	Y	Y
Heflin	Y	N	Y	N	Y	N	N	Y
ALASKA								
Murkowski	Y	Y	Y	Y	N	N	N	Y
Stevens	Y	Y	Y	Y	N	N	N	Y
ARIZONA								
Goldwater	Y	Y	Y	Y	N	Y	N	Y
DeConcini	N	N	Y	N	Y	N	N	Y
ARKANSAS								
Bumpers	Y	N	N	N	N	Y	N	Y
Pryor	N	N	Y	N	Y	N	N	Y
CALIFORNIA								
Hayakawa	Y	?	?	?	?	?	?	?
Cranston	N	N	N	N	Y	N	N	Y
COLORADO								
Armstrong	Y	Y	Y	?	N	Y	Y	N
Hart	Y	N	Y	N	Y	N	N	Y
CONNECTICUT								
Weicker	Y	Y	N	Y	N	N	N	Y
Dodd	N	N	N	N	Y	N	N	Y
DELAWARE								
Roth	Y	Y	Y	Y	N	N	N	Y
Biden	Y	N	N	N	N	N	N	Y
FLORIDA								
Hawkins	Y	N	Y	N	Y	N	Y	Y
Chiles	Y	Y	N	N	Y	N	N	Y
GEORGIA								
Mattingly	Y	Y	Y	Y	N	Y	Y	Y
Nunn	N	Y	N	N	Y	N	N	Y
HAWAII								
Inouye	N	N	N	N	Y	N	N	Y
Matsunaga	N	N	N	N	N	N	N	Y
IDAHO								
McClure	Y	Y	Y	Y	N	Y	Y	Y
Symms	Y	Y	Y	Y	N	Y	Y	Y
ILLINOIS								
Percy	Y	Y	Y	Y	N	Y	Y	Y
Dixon	N	N	Y	N	Y	N	N	Y
INDIANA								
Lugar	Y	Y	Y	Y	N	Y	Y	N
Quayle	Y	Y	Y	Y	N	Y	Y	Y
IOWA								
Grassley	Y	Y	Y	Y	N	N	N	Y
Jepsen	Y	Y	Y	Y	N	Y	Y	N
KANSAS								
Dole	Y	Y	Y	Y	N	Y	Y	N
Kassebaum	Y	Y	Y	N	N	N	N	Y
KENTUCKY								
Ford	Y	Y	N	N	Y	N	N	Y
Huddleston	N	Y	N	N	Y	N	N	Y
LOUISIANA								
Johnston	N	Y	N	N	Y	N	N	Y
Long	N	Y	N	N	Y	N	N	Y
MAINE								
Cohen	Y	Y	Y	Y	N	Y	Y	Y
Mitchell	N	N	N	N	Y	N	N	Y
MARYLAND								
Mathias	N	Y	N	Y	N	Y	Y	N
Sarbanes	N	N	N	N	Y	N	N	Y
MASSACHUSETTS								
Kennedy	Y	Y	N	N	Y	?	N	Y
Tsongas	?	?	?	?	?	?	?	?
MICHIGAN								
Levin	N	N	Y	N	Y	N	N	Y
Riegle	N	N	Y	N	Y	N	N	Y
MINNESOTA								
Boschwitz	Y	Y	N	Y	N	N	N	Y
Durenberger	Y	Y	Y	Y	N	Y	Y	Y
MISSISSIPPI								
Cochran	Y	Y	N	Y	N	N	N	Y
Stennis	N	Y	N	N	Y	N	N	Y
MISSOURI								
Danforth	Y	Y	Y	Y	N	Y	N	Y
Eagleton	Y	N	N	N	Y	N	N	Y
MONTANA								
Baucus	N	N	Y	N	Y	N	N	Y
Melcher	Y	Y	Y	N	Y	N	N	Y
NEBRASKA								
Exon	N	N	Y	Y	N	N	N	Y
Zorinsky	N	N	Y	Y	N	N	N	Y
NEVADA								
Laxalt	Y	Y	Y	Y	N	Y	Y	Y
Cannon	N	N	N	N	Y	N	N	Y
NEW HAMPSHIRE								
Humphrey	Y	Y	Y	Y	N	Y	Y	Y
Rudman	Y	Y	Y	Y	N	Y	Y	Y
NEW JERSEY								
Bradley	N	N	N	Y	N	Y	Y	Y
Williams	N	?	N	N	Y	N	N	Y
NEW MEXICO								
Domenici	?	?	?	?	?	?	?	?
Schmitt	Y	N	Y	N	Y	N	Y	Y
NEW YORK								
D'Amato	Y	N	Y	N	Y	N	Y	N
Moynihan	N	N	Y	Y	?	?	?	?
NORTH CAROLINA								
East	Y	Y	Y	Y	N	Y	Y	Y
Helms	Y	N	Y	N	Y	N	Y	Y
NORTH DAKOTA								
Andrews	Y	Y	Y	Y	Y	N	N	Y
Burdick	N	N	N	N	Y	N	N	Y
OHIO								
Glenn	N	N	N	Y	N	Y	N	Y
Metzenbaum	Y	N	N	N	Y	N	N	Y
OKLAHOMA								
Nickles	Y	N	Y	N	Y	N	Y	N
Boren	N	N	Y	N	Y	N	N	Y
OREGON								
Hatfield	Y	Y	Y	Y	N	N	N	Y
Packwood	Y	Y	Y	N	Y	N	N	Y
PENNSYLVANIA								
Heinz	Y	Y	Y	Y	N	Y	N	Y
Specter	Y	N	Y	Y	N	Y	N	Y
RHODE ISLAND								
Chafee	Y	Y	N	Y	N	Y	Y	Y
Pell	N	N	N	N	Y	N	Y	N
SOUTH CAROLINA								
Thurmond	Y	Y	Y	Y	N	Y	N	Y
Hollings	Y	Y	N	Y	N	N	N	Y
SOUTH DAKOTA								
Abdnor	Y	N	Y	N	Y	N	N	Y
Pressler	Y	Y	Y	Y	N	N	N	Y
TENNESSEE								
Baker	Y	Y	N	Y	N	Y	Y	N
Sasser	N	N	N	N	Y	N	N	Y
TEXAS								
Tower	Y	Y	Y	Y	N	Y	Y	Y
Bentsen	N	Y	N	N	Y	N	N	Y
UTAH								
Garn	Y	Y	Y	Y	N	Y	N	Y
Hatch	Y	Y	Y	Y	N	Y	Y	Y
VERMONT								
Stafford	Y	Y	Y	Y	N	Y	Y	Y
Leahy	N	N	N	N	Y	N	N	Y
VIRGINIA								
Warner	Y	Y	Y	Y	N	Y	Y	Y
Byrd*	N	Y	N	Y	N	Y	N	Y
WASHINGTON								
Gorton	Y	Y	Y	Y	N	Y	Y	Y
Jackson	N	N	N	N	Y	N	N	Y
WEST VIRGINIA								
Byrd	N	N	N	N	Y	N	N	Y
Randolph	N	N	N	N	Y	N	N	Y
WISCONSIN								
Kasten	Y	Y	Y	Y	N	N	N	Y
Proxmire	N	N	Y	N	Y	N	N	Y
WYOMING								
Simpson	Y	Y	Y	Y	N	Y	Y	Y
Wallop	Y	Y	N	Y	N	Y	Y	Y

Democrats *Republicans*

* Byrd elected as an independent.

189. H J Res 266. Tax Cuts. Dole, R-Kan., motion to table (kill) the Bradley, D-N.J., amendment, to the Finance Committee amendment *(see vote 191, below)*, to lower the maximum tax on capital gains to 15 percent from 28 percent under existing law and 20 percent under the bill. Motion agreed to 62-36: R 51-1; D 11-35 (ND 6-25, SD 5-10), July 16, 1981. A "yea" was a vote supporting the president's position.

190. H J Res 266. Tax Cuts. Dole, R-Kan., motion to table (kill) the D'Amato, R-N.Y., amendment to make permanent the current exclusion from taxes of interest and dividend income up to $200 for individuals ($400 for a joint return). Motion agreed to 56-40: R 44-7; D 12-33 (ND 2-28, SD 10-5), July 16, 1981. A "yea" was a vote supporting the president's position.

191. H J Res 266. Tax Cuts. Finance Committee amendment to require, beginning in 1985, that individual income taxes be adjusted, or indexed, annually to offset the effects of inflation. Adopted 57-40: R 43-8; D 14-32 (ND 11-20, SD 3-12), July 16, 1981.

192. H J Res 266. Tax Cuts. Schmitt, R-N.M., amendment, to the Bentsen, D-Texas, amendment *(see vote 196, below)*, to extend to 15 months (from one year under the bill and two years under the Bentsen amendment) the period during which tax-exempt savings certificates could be issued and to provide a 15 percent exclusion from taxation for interest income up to $3,000 for individuals ($6,000 for a joint return), starting in 1984. Adopted 56-40: R 50-0; D 6-40 (ND 5-26, SD 1-14), July 16, 1981.

193. H J Res 266. Tax Cuts. DeConcini, D-Ariz., motion to table (kill) the Garn, R-Utah, amendment, to the Bentsen, D-Texas, amendment *(see vote 196, below)*, to permit targeting of funds from tax-exempt savings certificates to automobile purchase, small-business and student loans as well as home or farm loans. Motion rejected 48-48: R 6-45; D 42-3 (ND 28-2, SD 14-1), July 16, 1981.

194. H J Res 266. Tax Cuts. Garn, R-Utah, amendment, to the Bentsen, D-Texas, amendment *(see vote 196, below)*, to permit targeting of funds from tax-exempt savings certificates to automobile purchase, small-business and student loans as well as home or farm loans. Rejected 36-59: R 33-18; D 3-41 (ND 2-27, SD 1-14), July 16, 1981.

195. H J Res 266. Tax Cuts. Garn, R-Utah, amendment, to the Bentsen, D-Texas, amendment *(see vote 196, below)*, to require that 50 percent, rather than 75 percent, of funds from tax-exempt savings certificates be targeted to home or farm loans. Rejected 33-63: R 31-20; D 2-43 (ND 1-29; SD 1-14), July 16, 1981.

196. H J Res 266. Tax Cuts. Bentsen, D-Texas, amendment, as amended, to require institutions issuing tax-exempt savings certificates to put at least 75 percent of the face amount of the certificates into home or farm loans; to permit issuance of tax-exempt savings certificates over a 15-month period (Oct. 1, 1981, through Dec. 31, 1982); and to provide a 15 percent exclusion from taxation for interest income up to $3,000 for individuals ($6,000 for a joint return), starting in 1984. Adopted 86-10: R 41-10; D 45-0 (ND 30-0, SD 15-0), July 16, 1981.

CQ Senate Votes 197 - 204

Corresponding to Congressional Record Votes 197, 198, 199, 200, 201, 202, 203, 204

	197	198	199	200	201	202	203	204
ALABAMA								
Denton	Y	Y	Y	Y	N	Y	Y	Y
Heflin	N	N	Y	Y	N	Y	Y	Y
ALASKA								
Murkowski	Y	Y	Y	Y	N	Y	Y	Y
Stevens	Y	Y	Y	Y	N	Y	Y	Y
ARIZONA								
Goldwater	Y	Y	Y	Y	N	Y	Y	N
DeConcini	?	N	Y	Y	N	?	Y	Y
ARKANSAS								
Bumpers	N	N	Y	Y	Y	Y	Y	Y
Pryor	N	N	?	?	?	Y	Y	Y
CALIFORNIA								
Hayakawa	?	?	?	?	?	Y	N	Y
Cranston	N	N	Y	Y	Y	Y	Y	Y
COLORADO								
Armstrong	Y	Y	Y	Y	N	Y	Y	Y
Hart	N	N	Y	Y	Y	Y	Y	Y
CONNECTICUT								
Weicker	Y	Y	Y	?	?	Y	Y	N
Dodd	N	N	Y	Y	Y	Y	Y	Y
DELAWARE								
Roth	Y	Y	Y	Y	N	Y	Y	Y
Biden	N	N	Y	Y	Y	Y	Y	Y
FLORIDA								
Hawkins	Y	Y	Y	Y	N	Y	Y	Y
Chiles	N	?	?	?	?	Y	Y	Y
GEORGIA								
Mattingly	Y	Y	Y	Y	N	Y	Y	Y
Nunn	N	N	Y	Y	N	Y	Y	Y
HAWAII								
Inouye	N	N	Y	Y	Y	Y	Y	Y
Matsunaga	N	N	Y	Y	Y	Y	Y	Y
IDAHO								
McClure	Y	Y	Y	Y	N	Y	Y	Y
Symms	Y	Y	Y	Y	-	Y	Y	Y
ILLINOIS								
Percy	?	?	+	+	-	Y	Y	Y
Dixon	N	N	Y	Y	N	Y	Y	Y
INDIANA								
Lugar	Y	Y	Y	Y	N	Y	Y	Y
Quayle	Y	Y	Y	Y	N	Y	Y	N

	197	198	199	200	201	202	203	204
IOWA								
Grassley	Y	Y	Y	?	?	Y	Y	Y
Jepsen	Y	Y	Y	Y	N	Y	Y	Y
KANSAS								
Dole	Y	Y	Y	Y	N	Y	Y	Y
Kassebaum	Y	Y	Y	Y	N	Y	Y	Y
KENTUCKY								
Ford	N	N	Y	Y	N	Y	Y	Y
Huddleston	N	N	Y	Y	Y	Y	Y	Y
LOUISIANA								
Johnston	N	N	Y	Y	N	Y	Y	Y
Long	N	Y	Y	Y	N	Y	Y	Y
MAINE								
Cohen	Y	Y	Y	Y	N	Y	Y	Y
Mitchell	N	N	Y	Y	Y	Y	Y	Y
MARYLAND								
Mathias	Y	Y	Y	Y	N	Y	Y	Y
Sarbanes	N	N	Y	Y	Y	Y	Y	Y
MASSACHUSETTS								
Kennedy	N	N	Y	Y	Y	Y	Y	Y
Tsongas	?	?	?	+	?	?	?	?
MICHIGAN								
Levin	N	N	Y	Y	Y	Y	Y	Y
Riegle	N	N	Y	Y	N	Y	Y	Y
MINNESOTA								
Boschwitz	Y	Y	Y	Y	N	Y	Y	Y
Durenberger	Y	Y	Y	Y	N	Y	Y	Y
MISSISSIPPI								
Cochran	Y	Y	Y	Y	N	Y	Y	Y
Stennis	Y	N	Y	?	?	Y	Y	Y
MISSOURI								
Danforth	Y	Y	Y	Y	N	Y	Y	Y
Eagleton	N	N	Y	Y	Y	Y	Y	Y
MONTANA								
Baucus	N	?	Y	Y	Y	Y	Y	Y
Melcher	N	N	Y	Y	N	Y	Y	Y
NEBRASKA								
Exon	N	N	Y	Y	N	Y	Y	Y
Zorinsky	N	N	Y	Y	N	Y	Y	Y
NEVADA								
Laxalt	Y	Y	Y	Y	N	Y	Y	Y
Cannon	N	N	Y	Y	Y	Y	Y	Y

	197	198	199	200	201	202	203	204
NEW HAMPSHIRE								
Humphrey	Y	Y	Y	Y	N	Y	Y	Y
Rudman	Y	Y	Y	Y	N	Y	Y	Y
NEW JERSEY								
Bradley	N	N	Y	Y	Y	Y	Y	Y
Williams	N	N	Y	Y	Y	Y	Y	Y
NEW MEXICO								
Domenici	?	?	?	?	?	Y	Y	Y
Schmitt	Y	Y	Y	?	?	Y	Y	Y
NEW YORK								
D'Amato	Y	Y	Y	Y	N	Y	Y	Y
Moynihan	?	-	+	+	+	Y	Y	Y
NORTH CAROLINA								
East	Y	Y	Y	Y	N	Y	Y	Y
Helms	Y	Y	Y	Y	N	Y	Y	Y
NORTH DAKOTA								
Andrews	Y	Y	Y	Y	?	Y	Y	Y
Burdick	N	N	Y	Y	N	Y	Y	Y
OHIO								
Glenn	N	N	Y	Y	Y	Y	Y	Y
Metzenbaum	N	N	Y	Y	Y	Y	Y	Y
OKLAHOMA								
Nickles	Y	Y	Y	Y	N	Y	Y	Y
Boren	N	N	Y	Y	N	Y	Y	Y
OREGON								
Hatfield	+	+	+	+	-	+	?	?
Packwood	Y	Y	Y	Y	N	Y	Y	Y
PENNSYLVANIA								
Heinz	Y	Y	Y	Y	N	Y	Y	Y
Specter	Y	Y	Y	Y	N	Y	Y	?
RHODE ISLAND								
Chafee	Y	Y	Y	Y	N	Y	Y	Y
Pell	N	N	Y	Y	Y	Y	Y	Y
SOUTH CAROLINA								
Thurmond	Y	Y	Y	Y	N	Y	Y	Y
Hollings	Y	N	Y	Y	N	Y	Y	Y
SOUTH DAKOTA								
Abdnor	Y	Y	Y	Y	N	Y	Y	Y
Pressler	Y	Y	Y	Y	N	Y	Y	Y
TENNESSEE								
Baker	Y	Y	Y	Y	N	Y	Y	Y
Sasser	N	N	Y	Y	N	Y	Y	Y

	197	198	199	200	201	202	203	204
TEXAS								
Tower	Y	Y	Y	Y	N	Y	Y	Y
Bentsen	N	N	Y	Y	N	Y	Y	Y
UTAH								
Garn	Y	Y	Y	Y	-	Y	Y	N
Hatch	Y	Y	Y	Y	N	Y	Y	Y
VERMONT								
Stafford	Y	Y	Y	Y	N	Y	Y	Y
Leahy	N	N	Y	Y	Y	Y	Y	Y
VIRGINIA								
Warner	Y	Y	Y	Y	N	Y	Y	Y
Byrd*	Y	Y	Y	Y	N	Y	Y	Y
WASHINGTON								
Gorton	Y	Y	Y	Y	N	Y	Y	Y
Jackson	N	N	Y	Y	Y	Y	Y	Y
WEST VIRGINIA								
Byrd	N	N	Y	Y	N	Y	Y	Y
Randolph	N	N	Y	Y	Y	Y	Y	Y
WISCONSIN								
Kasten	Y	Y	Y	Y	N	Y	Y	Y
Proxmire	Y	N	Y	Y	N	Y	Y	N
WYOMING								
Simpson	Y	Y	Y	Y	N	Y	Y	Y
Wallop	Y	Y	Y	Y	N	Y	Y	Y

KEY

- Y Voted for (yea).
- # Paired for.
- + Announced for.
- N Voted against (nay).
- X Paired against.
- - Announced against.
- P Voted "present".
- C Voted "present" to avoid possible conflict of interest.
- ? Did not vote or otherwise make a position known.

Democrats *Republicans*

* Byrd elected as an independent.

197. H J Res 266. Tax Cuts. Dole, R-Kan., motion to table (kill) the Boren, D-Okla., amendment to express the sense of the Senate that President Reagan should assure our allies at the July 19-21 Ottawa economic summit that the United States will take "immediate, direct and affirmative steps to lower significantly our domestic interest rates." Motion agreed to 53-40: R 49-0; D 4-40 (ND 1-28, SD 3-12), July 17, 1981.

198. H J Res 266. Tax Cuts. Durenberger, R-Minn., motion to table (kill) the Riegle, D-Mich., amendment to reduce the corporate income tax rate on small businesses. Motion agreed to 51-41: R 49-0; D 2-41 (ND 0-29, SD 2-12), July 17, 1981.

199. H J Res 266. Tax Cuts. Weicker, R-Conn., amendment to reduce the lowest corporate tax rate for small businesses in two steps — reducing the rate for income up to $25,000 in 1982 from 17 percent to 16 percent and in 1983 to 15 percent; and cutting the rate for income between $25,000-$50,000 in 1982 from 20 percent to 19 percent and in 1983 to 18 percent. Adopted 92-0: R 49-0; D 43-0 (ND 30-0, SD 13-0), July 17, 1981.

200. S Res 179. Nuclear Non-Proliferation Policy. Adoption of the resolution calling on the president to: confer with other nuclear supplier nations to consider such measures as a temporary moratorium on transfers of nuclear enrichment and reprocessing equipment; develop with other nations a program to improve international safeguards on nuclear facilities; formulate a clear U.S. policy for improved international restrictions on nuclear trade; call for a prompt re-evaluation of world nuclear energy policy; and reaffirm U.S. policy to assist other countries, especially developing countries, in meeting their energy needs. Adopted 88-0: R 46-0; D 42-0 (ND 30-0, SD 12-0), July 17, 1981.

201. H J Res 266. Tax Cuts. Bradley, D-N.J., amendment to limit the personal income tax to one year and target the relief to persons with incomes of $50,000 or less. Rejected 24-61: R 0-43; D 24-18 (ND 22-8, SD 2-10), July 17, 1981. A "nay" was a vote supporting the president's position.

202. Treaty Doc 97-13. U.S.-Canada Tuna Vessels Treaty. Adoption of the resolution of ratification of a treaty with Canada delineating the rights of Pacific Coast albacore tuna-fishing vessels from each nation and their port privileges. Adopted 97-0: R 52-0; D 45-0 (ND 30-0, SD 15-0), July 20, 1981. A two-thirds majority vote (65 in this case) is required for adoption of resolutions of ratification.

203. H J Res 266. Tax Cuts. Packwood, R-Ore., amendment to allow individuals who do not itemize deductions to take a deduction for charitable contributions. The deduction would be phased in — in 1982-83, a 25 percent deduction to a maximum of $100; in 1984, a 25 percent deduction with no limit; in 1985, a 50 percent deduction with no limit; in 1986, a 100 percent deduction; and no deductions after 1986. Adopted 97-1: R 51-1; D 46-0 (ND 31-0, SD 15-0), July 20, 1981.

204. H J Res 266. Tax Cuts. Baker, R-Tenn., motion to instruct the sergeant-at-arms to request the attendance of absent senators. Motion agreed to 92-5: R 47-4; D 45-1 (ND 30-1, SD 15-0), July 20, 1981.

KEY

- Y Voted for (yea).
- # Paired for.
- + Announced for.
- N Voted against (nay).
- X Paired against.
- - Announced against.
- P Voted "present".
- C Voted "present" to avoid possible conflict of interest.
- ? Did not vote or otherwise make a position known.

	205	206	207	208	209	210	211	212
ALABAMA								
Denton	Y	Y	Y	Y	Y	-	N	N
Heflin	Y	Y	N	N	N	N	N	N
ALASKA								
Murkowski	Y	Y	Y	Y	Y	N	N	N
Stevens	Y	Y	Y	Y	Y	N	?	N
ARIZONA								
Goldwater	Y	Y	?	Y	Y	N	N	N
DeConcini	Y	N	N	N	N	Y	N	Y
ARKANSAS								
Bumpers	Y	N	N	N	Y	Y	Y	Y
Pryor	Y	Y	N	N	N	N	N	Y
CALIFORNIA								
Hayakawa	Y	Y	Y	Y	Y	N	N	N
Cranston	Y	Y	N	N	N	Y	Y	Y
COLORADO								
Armstrong	Y	Y	Y	Y	Y	N	N	N
Hart	N	N	N	N	N	N	N	Y
CONNECTICUT								
Weicker	Y	N	N	N	Y	Y	N	N
Dodd	Y	Y	N	N	N	Y	Y	Y
DELAWARE								
Roth	Y	N	Y	Y	Y	Y	N	N
Biden	Y	N	N	N	Y	Y	Y	Y
FLORIDA								
Hawkins	Y	Y	Y	N	Y	Y	N	N
Chiles	Y	Y	N	N	N	Y	Y	Y
GEORGIA								
Mattingly	Y	Y	Y	Y	Y	N	N	N
Nunn	Y	Y	Y	N	N	Y	Y	Y
HAWAII								
Inouye	Y	Y	N	N	N	Y	Y	Y
Matsunaga	Y	Y	?	N	N	N	Y	Y
IDAHO								
McClure	Y	N	Y	Y	Y	N	N	N
Symms	Y	N	Y	Y	N	N	N	N
ILLINOIS								
Percy	Y	Y	Y	Y	Y	N	N	N
Dixon	Y	N	N	N	N	Y	N	Y
INDIANA								
Lugar	Y	N	Y	Y	Y	N	N	N
Quayle	Y	Y	Y	Y	Y	N	N	N
IOWA								
Grassley	Y	N	Y	Y	Y	N	N	N
Jepsen	Y	Y	Y	Y	N	N	N	N
KANSAS								
Dole	Y	Y	Y	Y	Y	N	N	N
Kassebaum	Y	N	Y	Y	Y	N	N	N
KENTUCKY								
Ford	Y	N	N	N	N	Y	Y	Y
Huddleston	Y	Y	N	N	N	Y	Y	Y
LOUISIANA								
Johnston	Y	Y	N	N	N	N	N	Y
Long	Y	Y	N	Y	N	N	N	N
MAINE								
Cohen	Y	Y	Y	N	Y	Y	Y	N
Mitchell	Y	N	N	N	Y	Y	N	Y
MARYLAND								
Mathias	Y	Y	Y	N	?	?	?	N
Sarbanes	Y	N	N	N	Y	Y	N	Y
MASSACHUSETTS								
Kennedy	Y	Y	N	N	Y	Y	Y	Y
Tsongas	?	?	N	N	Y	Y	Y	Y
MICHIGAN								
Levin	Y	N	N	N	Y	Y	Y	Y
Riegle	Y	N	N	N	Y	Y	N	Y
MINNESOTA								
Boschwitz	Y	N	Y	Y	Y	N	N	N
Durenberger	Y	N	Y	Y	Y	Y	N	N
MISSISSIPPI								
Cochran	Y	Y	Y	Y	N	N	N	N
Stennis	Y	Y	Y	N	Y	N	N	N
MISSOURI								
Danforth	Y	Y	Y	Y	Y	Y	N	N
Eagleton	Y	N	N	N	Y	Y	Y	Y
MONTANA								
Baucus	Y	N	N	N	N	Y	N	Y
Melcher	Y	Y	N	N	N	N	N	Y
NEBRASKA								
Exon	Y	Y	N	N	N	Y	Y	Y
Zorinsky	Y	N	N	Y	N	N	N	Y
NEVADA								
Laxalt	Y	Y	Y	Y	Y	N	N	N
Cannon	Y	Y	N	N	N	#	N	Y
NEW HAMPSHIRE								
Humphrey	Y	Y	Y	Y	Y	N	N	N
Rudman	Y	Y	Y	N	Y	Y	N	N
NEW JERSEY								
Bradley	Y	Y	N	N	Y	Y	Y	Y
Williams	Y	?	N	N	Y	Y	Y	Y
NEW MEXICO								
Domenici	Y	Y	Y	Y	Y	N	N	N
Schmitt	Y	Y	Y	Y	Y	N	N	N
NEW YORK								
D'Amato	Y	N	Y	Y	Y	N	N	N
Moynihan	Y	N	N	N	Y	Y	N	Y
NORTH CAROLINA								
East	Y	Y	Y	Y	Y	N	N	N
Helms	Y	Y	Y	Y	Y	N	N	N
NORTH DAKOTA								
Andrews	Y	Y	Y	Y	Y	N	N	N
Burdick	Y	N	N	N	N	N	N	Y
OHIO								
Glenn	Y	Y	N	N	N	Y	Y	Y
Metzenbaum	N	N	N	N	Y	Y	Y	Y
OKLAHOMA								
Nickles	Y	Y	Y	Y	Y	N	N	N
Boren	Y	Y	N	Y	N	N	N	Y
OREGON								
Hatfield	+	+	Y	Y	Y	Y	N	N
Packwood	Y	Y	Y	Y	Y	Y	N	N
PENNSYLVANIA								
Heinz	Y	N	Y	Y	Y	N	N	N
Specter	?	?	N	Y	Y	Y	N	N
RHODE ISLAND								
Chafee	Y	Y	Y	N	Y	Y	N	N
Pell	Y	N	N	N	Y	Y	Y	Y
SOUTH CAROLINA								
Thurmond	Y	Y	Y	Y	Y	N	N	N
Hollings	Y	N	N	Y	Y	Y	Y	Y
SOUTH DAKOTA								
Abdnor	Y	Y	Y	Y	Y	N	N	N
Pressler	Y	N	N	Y	Y	N	N	N
TENNESSEE								
Baker	Y	Y	Y	Y	Y	N	N	N
Sasser	Y	N	N	N	N	Y	N	Y
TEXAS								
Tower	Y	Y	Y	Y	N	N	N	N
Bentsen	Y	N	N	N	N	X	-	N
UTAH								
Garn	Y	N	Y	Y	Y	N	N	?
Hatch	Y	N	Y	N	N	N	N	N
VERMONT								
Stafford	Y	Y	Y	Y	Y	Y	Y	N
Leahy	Y	N	N	N	N	Y	Y	Y
VIRGINIA								
Warner	Y	Y	Y	Y	Y	N	N	N
Byrd*	Y	N	Y	Y	Y	Y	N	N
WASHINGTON								
Gorton	Y	Y	Y	Y	Y	N	N	N
Jackson	Y	N	N	N	Y	Y	Y	Y
WEST VIRGINIA								
Byrd	Y	N	N	N	N	Y	Y	Y
Randolph	Y	N	N	N	N	Y	Y	Y
WISCONSIN								
Kasten	Y	Y	Y	Y	Y	N	N	N
Proxmire	N	N	Y	N	Y	Y	N	Y
WYOMING								
Simpson	Y	Y	Y	Y	Y	N	N	N
Wallop	Y	Y	Y	Y	Y	N	N	N

Democrats   *Republicans*

Byrd elected as an independent.

205. H J Res 266. Tax Cuts. Stevens, R-Alaska, amendment to allow closely held corporations to take tax breaks for initiating employee stock ownership plans even if the firms do not give their workers voting shares. Adopted 94-3: R 51-0; D 43-3 (ND 28-3, SD 15-0), July 20, 1981.

206. H J Res 266. Tax Cuts. Dole, R-Kan., amendment to reduce the Finance Committee bill's provisions on depreciation write-offs for investments in real property, including a reduction in the write-offs for the rehabilitation of old buildings. Adopted 56-40: R 37-14; D 19-26 (ND 10-20, SD 9-6), July 20, 1981.

207. H J Res 266. Tax Cuts. Dole, R-Kan., motion to table (kill) the Riegle, D-Mich., amendment to retain minimum Social Security benefits for those who are currently receiving the benefits and those who would be entitled to receive them through the end of 1981. Motion agreed to 52-46: R 48-4; D 4-42 (ND 1-30, SD 3-12), July 21, 1981.

208. H J Res 266. Tax Cuts. Dole, R-Kan., motion to table (kill) the Kennedy, D-Mass., amendment to increase by 5 percent the existing energy conservation tax credit for commercial and industrial energy users. Motion agreed to 54-46: R 48-5; D 6-41 (ND 1-31, SD 5-10), July 21, 1981.

209. H J Res 266. Tax Cuts. Dole, R-Kan., motion to table (kill) the Bentsen, D-Texas, amendment, to the Bentsen amendment, to exempt independent oil producers and certain royalty owners from the windfall profits tax on the first 1,000 barrels of daily oil production. Motion agreed to 61-38: R 43-9; D 18-29 (ND 15-17, SD 3-12), July 21, 1981. (Subsequently, the original Bentsen amendment was withdrawn.)

210. H J Res 266. Tax Cuts. Dole, R-Kan., motion to table (kill) the Dole amendment to phase out the windfall profits tax on new oil and certain hard-to-find oil. Motion rejected 47-49: R 12-39; D 35-10 (ND 26-5, SD 9-5), July 22, 1981. (After the narrow defeat of his tabling motion, which was designed to test support for the phase-out, Dole withdrew the amendment so as to speed consideration of the bill.)

211. H J Res 266. Tax Cuts. Hollings, D-S.C., amendment to the Finance Committee bill limiting the size of personal tax reductions and targeting them to middle-income taxpayers in order to achieve a balanced budget by 1984. Rejected 26-71: R 0-51; D 26-20 (ND 20-12, SD 6-8), July 22, 1981. A "nay" was a vote supporting the president's position.

212. H J Res 266. Tax Cuts. Bradley, D-N.J., amendment to provide a three-year personal tax cut targeted to help individuals earning under $50,000. Rejected 42-57: R 0-52; D 42-5 (ND 32-0, SD 10-5), July 23, 1981. A "nay" was a vote supporting the president's position.

CQ Senate Votes 213 - 220

Corresponding to Congressional Record Votes 213, 214, 215, 216, 217, 218, 219, 220

KEY

- Y Voted for (yea).
- # Paired for.
- + Announced for.
- N Voted against (nay).
- X Paired against.
- - Announced against.
- P Voted "present".
- C Voted "present" to avoid possible conflict of interest.
- ? Did not vote or otherwise make a position known.

State / Senator	213	214	215	216	217	218	219	220
ALABAMA								
Denton	N	N	Y	Y	N	Y	N	Y
Heflin	N	N	Y	Y	N	Y	N	Y
ALASKA								
Murkowski	N	N	Y	Y	N	Y	N	Y
Stevens	N	?	Y	Y	N	Y	N	Y
ARIZONA								
Goldwater	N	N	Y	Y	N	Y	N	Y
DeConcini	N	Y	Y	Y	N	Y	Y	Y
ARKANSAS								
Bumpers	Y	N	Y	Y	N	Y	Y	Y
Pryor	Y	N	Y	Y	N	Y	Y	Y
CALIFORNIA								
Hayakawa	N	N	Y	?	?	?	?	?
Cranston	Y	Y	Y	Y	N	Y	Y	Y
COLORADO								
Armstrong	N	N	Y	Y	N	Y	N	Y
Hart	Y	Y	Y	Y	N	N	Y	Y
CONNECTICUT								
Weicker	N	N	Y	Y	N	N	Y	Y
Dodd	Y	N	Y	Y	Y	Y	Y	Y
DELAWARE								
Roth	N	N	Y	Y	N	Y	Y	Y
Biden	Y	N	Y	Y	N	Y	Y	Y
FLORIDA								
Hawkins	N	N	Y	Y	N	Y	Y	Y
Chiles	N	N	Y	Y	N	Y	Y	Y
GEORGIA								
Mattingly	N	N	Y	Y	N	Y	N	Y
Nunn	N	N	Y	Y	N	Y	Y	Y
HAWAII								
Inouye	Y	N	Y	?	?	Y	Y	Y
Matsunaga	Y	N	Y	Y	N	Y	Y	Y
IDAHO								
McClure	N	N	N	Y	N	N	N	Y
Symms	N	N	Y	Y	N	Y	N	Y
ILLINOIS								
Percy	N	N	Y	Y	N	Y	N	Y
Dixon	N	N	Y	Y	N	Y	Y	Y
INDIANA								
Lugar	N	N	Y	Y	N	Y	N	Y
Quayle	N	N	Y	Y	N	Y	N	Y
IOWA								
Grassley	N	N	Y	Y	N	Y	N	Y
Jepsen	N	N	Y	Y	N	Y	N	Y
KANSAS								
Dole	N	N	Y	Y	N	Y	N	Y
Kassebaum	N	N	Y	Y	N	Y	N	Y
KENTUCKY								
Ford	N	N	Y	Y	N	Y	Y	Y
Huddleston	N	N	Y	Y	N	Y	Y	Y
LOUISIANA								
Johnston	N	N	Y	Y	N	Y	N	Y
Long	N	N	Y	Y	N	Y	N	Y
MAINE								
Cohen	N	N	Y	Y	N	Y	N	Y
Mitchell	Y	N	Y	Y	N	Y	Y	Y
MARYLAND								
Mathias	N	N	Y	Y	Y	Y	Y	Y
Sarbanes	Y	N	Y	Y	Y	Y	Y	Y
MASSACHUSETTS								
Kennedy	Y	N	Y	Y	N	Y	Y	Y
Tsongas	Y	N	Y	Y	N	Y	Y	Y
MICHIGAN								
Levin	Y	Y	Y	Y	N	Y	Y	Y
Riegle	Y	N	Y	Y	N	Y	Y	Y
MINNESOTA								
Boschwitz	N	N	Y	Y	N	Y	N	Y
Durenberger	N	N	Y	Y	N	Y	N	Y
MISSISSIPPI								
Cochran	N	N	Y	Y	N	Y	N	Y
Stennis	N	N	Y	Y	N	?	?	?
MISSOURI								
Danforth	N	N	Y	Y	Y	Y	N	Y
Eagleton	Y	N	Y	Y	Y	Y	Y	Y
MONTANA								
Baucus	Y	N	Y	Y	N	Y	Y	Y
Melcher	N	N	Y	Y	N	Y	Y	Y
NEBRASKA								
Exon	N	N	Y	Y	Y	Y	N	Y
Zorinsky	N	N	Y	Y	N	Y	Y	Y
NEVADA								
Laxalt	N	N	Y	Y	N	Y	N	Y
Cannon	N	N	Y	Y	N	Y	+	+
NEW HAMPSHIRE								
Humphrey	N	N	Y	Y	N	Y	N	Y
Rudman	N	N	Y	Y	N	Y	N	Y
NEW JERSEY								
Bradley	N	N	Y	Y	N	Y	Y	Y
Williams	Y	N	Y	Y	Y	+	Y	Y
NEW MEXICO								
Domenici	N	N	Y	Y	N	Y	N	Y
Schmitt	N	N	Y	Y	N	Y	N	Y
NEW YORK								
D'Amato	N	N	Y	Y	N	Y	N	Y
Moynihan	N	N	Y	Y	N	Y	Y	Y
NORTH CAROLINA								
East	N	N	Y	Y	N	Y	N	Y
Helms	N	N	Y	Y	N	Y	N	Y
NORTH DAKOTA								
Andrews	N	N	Y	Y	N	Y	N	Y
Burdick	N	N	Y	Y	N	Y	Y	Y
OHIO								
Glenn	Y	N	Y	Y	N	Y	Y	Y
Metzenbaum	Y	N	Y	Y	Y	Y	Y	Y
OKLAHOMA								
Nickles	N	N	N	Y	N	Y	N	Y
Boren	N	N	Y	Y	N	Y	N	Y
OREGON								
Hatfield	N	N	Y	Y	N	Y	N	Y
Packwood	N	N	Y	Y	N	Y	N	Y
PENNSYLVANIA								
Heinz	N	N	Y	Y	N	?	?	?
Specter	N	N	Y	Y	N	Y	N	Y
RHODE ISLAND								
Chafee	N	N	Y	Y	N	Y	N	Y
Pell	N	N	Y	Y	N	Y	Y	Y
SOUTH CAROLINA								
Thurmond	N	N	Y	Y	N	Y	N	Y
Hollings	N	N	Y	N	N	N	Y	Y
SOUTH DAKOTA								
Abdnor	N	N	Y	N	Y	N	Y	N
Pressler	N	N	Y	Y	N	Y	Y	Y
TENNESSEE								
Baker	N	N	Y	Y	N	Y	Y	Y
Sasser	N	N	Y	Y	N	Y	Y	Y
TEXAS								
Tower	N	N	Y	Y	N	?	?	?
Bentsen	N	N	Y	Y	N	Y	N	Y
UTAH								
Garn	?	?	?	?	?	?	?	?
Hatch	N	N	Y	Y	N	Y	N	Y
VERMONT								
Stafford	N	N	Y	Y	N	Y	N	Y
Leahy	?	?	+	?	?	Y	Y	Y
VIRGINIA								
Warner	N	N	Y	Y	N	Y	N	Y
Byrd*	N	N	Y	Y	N	Y	N	Y
WASHINGTON								
Gorton	N	N	Y	Y	N	Y	N	Y
Jackson	Y	N	Y	Y	N	Y	Y	Y
WEST VIRGINIA								
Byrd	N	N	Y	Y	N	Y	Y	Y
Randolph	Y	N	Y	Y	N	Y	Y	Y
WISCONSIN								
Kasten	N	N	Y	Y	N	?	N	Y
Proxmire	Y	N	N	Y	N	Y	Y	N
WYOMING								
Simpson	N	N	Y	Y	N	Y	N	Y
Wallop	N	N	Y	Y	N	Y	N	Y

Democrats   *Republicans*

* Byrd elected as an independent.

213. H J Res 266. Tax Cuts. Bumpers, D-Ark.—Kennedy, D-Mass., amendment to provide a three-year personal income tax cut designed to offset increases in Social Security taxes and inflation by increasing the standard deduction, the earned income tax credit and reducing rates for the middle brackets. Rejected 22-76: R 0-52; D 22-24 (ND 20-11, SD 2-13), July 23, 1981. A "nay" was a vote supporting the president's position.

214. H J Res 266. Tax Cuts. Hart, D-Colo., amendment to substitute indexing of personal tax rates for the personal income tax reductions contained in the Finance Committee substitute. Rejected 4-93: R 0-51; D 4-42 (ND 4-27, SD 0-15), July 23, 1981.

215. H J Res 266. Tax Cuts. Heinz, R-Pa., amendment to extend for one year the targeted jobs tax credit program that allows employers to take a tax credit up to $3,000 the first year for hiring the handicapped and disadvantaged. Adopted 95-3: R 50-2; D 45-1 (ND 30-1, SD 15-0), July 23, 1981.

216. H J Res 266. Tax Cuts. Dole, R-Kan., amendment to express the sense of the Senate that Senate conferees on the tax bill should limit the revenue loss in fiscal 1981 to $1.5 billion; in fiscal 1982 to $38.3 billion; in fiscal 1983 to $91.8 billion; and in fiscal 1984 to $150 billion. Adopted 95-1: R 51-0; D 44-1 (ND 30-0, SD 14-1), July 23, 1981.

217. H J Res 266. Tax Cuts. Kennedy, D-Mass., amendment to limit the increase in the estate and gift tax credit to estates and donors with interests in small farms and/or small businesses. Rejected 9-87: R 1-50; D 8-37 (ND 8-22, SD 0-15), July 23, 1981.

218. H J Res 266. Tax Cuts. Sasser, D-Tenn., amendment to express the sense of the Senate that the Finance Committee report to the full Senate by Nov. 15, 1981, a bill authorizing inter-fund borrowing within the Social Security system to alleviate a short-term cash flow problem facing the Old Age and Survivors Trust Fund. Adopted 89-4: R 46-2; D 43-2 (ND 30-l, SD 13-1), July 24, 1981.

219. H J Res 266. Tax Cuts. Kennedy, D-Mass., amendment to increase the base for the tax credit for the elderly of 15 percent of retirement income from $2,500 to $3,000 for single persons and from $3,750 to $4,500 for married couples. The maximum credit would increase from $375 to $450 for single persons and from $562 to $675 for couples. Rejected 44-50: R 6-43; D 38-7 (ND 30-1, SD 8-6), July 24, 1981.

220. H J Res 266. Tax Cuts. Title III, Subtitle C of the Finance Committee substitute to revise the provisions in current law providing tax credits to employers for contributions to employee stock ownership plans (ESOP) and thus encourage the use of ESOPs. Adopted 93-1: R 49-0; D 44-1 (ND 30-1, SD 14-0), July 24, 1981.

KEY

Y Voted for (yea).
\# Paired for.
+ Announced for.
N Voted against (nay).
X Paired against.
- Announced against.
P Voted "present".
C Voted "present" to avoid possible conflict of interest.
? Did not vote or otherwise make a position known.

Senator	221	222	223	224	225	226	227	228
ALABAMA								
Denton	Y	N	N	N	N	Y	Y	Y
Heflin	Y	N	Y	N	N	Y	Y	Y
ALASKA								
Murkowski	Y	N	N	Y	Y	Y	Y	Y
Stevens	Y	N	N	N	Y	Y	Y	Y
ARIZONA								
Goldwater	N	N	N	N	?	?	Y	Y
DeConcini	Y	Y	Y	N	N	Y	Y	Y
ARKANSAS								
Bumpers	Y	Y	Y	Y	N	Y	?	Y
Pryor	Y	Y	Y	Y	N	Y	Y	Y
CALIFORNIA								
Hayakawa	?	N	N	N	N	Y	Y	Y
Cranston	Y	Y	Y	Y	N	Y	Y	Y
COLORADO								
Armstrong	Y	N	N	N	Y	Y	Y	Y
Hart	N	Y	Y	Y	N	Y	Y	Y
CONNECTICUT								
Weicker	Y	N	N	Y	Y	Y	Y	Y
Dodd	+	Y	Y	Y	N	Y	Y	Y
DELAWARE								
Roth	Y	N	N	N	N	Y	Y	Y
Biden	Y	Y	Y	Y	N	Y	N	Y
FLORIDA								
Hawkins	Y	Y	N	N	N	Y	Y	Y
Chiles	Y	N	Y	X	N	Y	+	Y
GEORGIA								
Mattingly	N	N	N	N	N	Y	Y	Y
Nunn	Y	N	Y	N	N	Y	Y	Y
HAWAII								
Inouye	Y	Y	Y	Y	N	Y	Y	Y
Matsunaga	Y	Y	Y	Y	N	Y	Y	Y
IDAHO								
McClure	Y	?	?	?	?	?	?	?
Symms	Y	N	N	N	Y	Y	Y	Y
ILLINOIS								
Percy	Y	N	N	N	N	Y	Y	Y
Dixon	Y	N	Y	Y	N	Y	Y	Y
INDIANA								
Lugar	Y	N	N	N	N	Y	Y	Y
Quayle	Y	N	N	N	Y	Y	Y	Y
IOWA								
Grassley	Y	N	N	N	Y	Y	Y	Y
Jepsen	Y	N	N	N	N	Y	Y	Y
KANSAS								
Dole	Y	N	N	N	Y	Y	Y	Y
Kassebaum	Y	N	N	N	N	Y	Y	Y
KENTUCKY								
Ford	Y	Y	Y	Y	N	Y	Y	Y
Huddleston	Y	Y	Y	Y	N	Y	Y	Y
LOUISIANA								
Johnston	Y	N	N	N	N	Y	Y	Y
Long	Y	N	N	N	N	Y	Y	Y
MAINE								
Cohen	Y	N	N	Y	N	Y	Y	Y
Mitchell	Y	Y	Y	Y	N	Y	Y	Y
MARYLAND								
Mathias	Y	Y	N	Y	Y	Y	Y	Y
Sarbanes	Y	Y	Y	Y	N	Y	Y	Y
MASSACHUSETTS								
Kennedy	Y	Y	Y	Y	?	?	?	Y
Tsongas	Y	Y	Y	Y	N	Y	Y	Y
MICHIGAN								
Levin	Y	Y	Y	Y	N	Y	Y	Y
Riegle	Y	Y	Y	Y	N	Y	Y	Y
MINNESOTA								
Boschwitz	Y	N	N	N	Y	Y	Y	Y
Durenberger	Y	N	N	N	Y	Y	Y	Y
MISSISSIPPI								
Cochran	Y	N	N	N	Y	Y	Y	Y
Stennis	?	?	?	?	N	Y	Y	Y
MISSOURI								
Danforth	Y	N	N	N	N	Y	Y	Y
Eagleton	Y	Y	Y	Y	N	Y	Y	Y
MONTANA								
Baucus	Y	Y	Y	Y	N	Y	Y	Y
Melcher	Y	Y	N	Y	N	Y	Y	Y
NEBRASKA								
Exon	Y	Y	Y	Y	N	Y	Y	Y
Zorinsky	Y	Y	N	N	N	Y	Y	Y
NEVADA								
Laxalt	N	N	N	N	N	Y	Y	Y
Cannon	+	\#	+	\#	-	+	Y	Y
NEW HAMPSHIRE								
Humphrey	Y	N	N	Y	Y	Y	?	Y
Rudman	Y	N	N	Y	N	Y	Y	Y
NEW JERSEY								
Bradley	N	Y	Y	Y	?	?	Y	Y
Williams	Y	Y	Y	Y	Y	Y	Y	Y
NEW MEXICO								
Domenici	Y	N	N	N	N	Y	Y	?
Schmitt	Y	?	?	N	N	Y	Y	Y
NEW YORK								
D'Amato	Y	Y	N	Y	Y	Y	Y	Y
Moynihan	Y	Y	Y	Y	N	Y	Y	Y
NORTH CAROLINA								
East	Y	N	N	N	Y	Y	Y	Y
Helms	Y	N	N	N	N	Y	Y	Y
NORTH DAKOTA								
Andrews	Y	N	N	Y	Y	Y	Y	Y
Burdick	Y	Y	Y	Y	N	Y	Y	Y
OHIO								
Glenn	Y	N	Y	Y	N	Y	Y	Y
Metzenbaum	Y	?	?	?	?	?	Y	Y
OKLAHOMA								
Nickles	Y	N	N	N	N	Y	Y	Y
Boren	Y	X	Y	N	N	Y	Y	Y
OREGON								
Hatfield	Y	N	N	N	Y	Y	Y	Y
Packwood	Y	N	N	N	Y	Y	Y	Y
PENNSYLVANIA								
Heinz	?	N	N	Y	Y	Y	Y	Y
Specter	Y	N	N	Y	Y	Y	Y	Y
RHODE ISLAND								
Chafee	Y	N	N	Y	Y	Y	Y	Y
Pell	Y	Y	Y	Y	N	Y	Y	Y
SOUTH CAROLINA								
Thurmond	Y	N	N	N	N	Y	Y	Y
Hollings	Y	N	Y	N	N	Y	Y	Y
SOUTH DAKOTA								
Abdnor	Y	N	N	N	N	Y	Y	Y
Pressler	Y	N	Y	N	N	Y	Y	Y
TENNESSEE								
Baker	Y	N	N	N	Y	Y	Y	Y
Sasser	Y	Y	N	Y	N	Y	Y	Y
TEXAS								
Tower	?	N	N	N	Y	Y	Y	?
Bentsen	Y	N	N	N	N	Y	Y	Y
UTAH								
Garn	?	N	N	N	Y	Y	Y	Y
Hatch	Y	N	N	N	N	Y	Y	Y
VERMONT								
Stafford	Y	N	N	Y	N	Y	Y	Y
Leahy	Y	Y	Y	N	Y	Y	Y	Y
VIRGINIA								
Warner	Y	N	N	N	Y	Y	Y	Y
Byrd*	Y	N	N	N	N	Y	Y	Y
WASHINGTON								
Gorton	Y	N	N	Y	Y	Y	Y	Y
Jackson	Y	Y	Y	N	Y	Y	Y	Y
WEST VIRGINIA								
Byrd	Y	Y	Y	Y	N	Y	Y	Y
Randolph	Y	Y	Y	N	Y	Y	Y	Y
WISCONSIN								
Kasten	Y	N	N	N	Y	Y	Y	Y
Proxmire	Y	Y	N	Y	N	Y	Y	Y
WYOMING								
Simpson	Y	N	N	N	N	Y	Y	Y
Wallop	Y	?	N	N	Y	Y	Y	Y

Democrats **Republicans**

* Byrd elected as an independent.

221. H J Res 266. Tax Cuts. Kennedy, D-Mass., amendment to increase from 5 percent to 10 percent of taxable income the amount a corporation may deduct for charitable contributions, effective Jan. 1, 1982. Adopted 88-5: R 46-3; D 42-2 (ND 28-2, SD 14-0), July 24, 1981.

222. H J Res 266. Tax Cuts. Riegle, D-Mich., amendment to permit a tax deduction for two-earner married couples equal to the lesser of $3,000 or 10 percent of the earned income of the spouse with the lower wages, effective in 1982 rather than 1983 as provided in the Finance Committee substitute. Rejected 36-57: R 3-47; D 33-10 (ND 28-2, SD 5-8), July 27, 1981.

223. H J Res 266. Tax Cuts. Exon, D-Neb., amendment to make the third year of reductions in individual tax rates contingent upon achievement of certain economic conditions as projected by the Reagan administration. Rejected 37-58: R 1-50; D 36-8 (ND 27-3, SD 9-5), July 27, 1981.

224. H J Res 266. Tax Cuts. Kennedy, D-Mass., amendment to provide a home heating tax credit equal to a family's residential heating bill multiplied by one-half the inflation rate. Rejected 47-48: R 14-38; D 33-10 (ND 28-2, SD 5-8), July 27, 1981.

225. H J Res 266. Tax Cuts. Dole, R-Kan., motion to table (kill) the Nunn, D-Ga., amendment to modify provisions of the Tax Reform Act of 1976 governing disclosure of information by the Internal Revenue Service (IRS) to permit greater IRS cooperation in non-tax criminal law enforcement. Motion rejected 28-66: R 26-25; D 2-41 (ND 2-26, SD 0-15), July 27, 1981. (The Nunn amendment was adopted subsequently by voice vote.)

226. H J Res 266. Tax Cuts. Mitchell, D-Maine, amendment to make the last in, first out (LIFO) method of inventory accounting more attractive for small businesses with annual sales averaging less than $3 million over three successive tax years. Adopted 94-0: R 51-0; D 43-0 (ND 28-0, SD 15-0), July 27, 1981.

227. H J Res 266. Tax Cuts. Long, D-La., motion to table (kill) the Stevens, R-Alaska, motion to reconsider the voice vote by which the Metzenbaum, D-Ohio, amendment was adopted. The Metzenbaum amendment provided an increase of the child-care expense tax credit from the current level of 20 percent of the first $2,000 spent on child-care expenses to 20 percent of the first $2,400 spent. Motion agreed to 94-1: R 51-0; D 43-1 (ND 30-1, SD 13-0), July 28, 1981.

228. H J Res 266. Tax Cuts. Matsunaga, D-Hawaii, amendment to provide that at-risk rules do not apply to solar, wind, hydroelectric, cogeneration, biomass, geothermal and ocean thermal energy projects. Adopted 97-0: R 50-0; D 47-0 (ND 32-0, SD 15-0), July 28, 1981.

CQ Senate Votes 229 - 236

Corresponding to Congressional Record Votes 229, 230, 231, 232, 233, 234, 235, 236

KEY

- Y — Voted for (yea).
- # — Paired for.
- + — Announced for.
- N — Voted against (nay).
- X — Paired against.
- - — Announced against.
- P — Voted "present".
- C — Voted "present" to avoid possible conflict of interest.
- ? — Did not vote or otherwise make a position known.

State / Senator	229	230	231	232	233	234	235	236
ALABAMA								
Denton	Y	Y	N	N	Y	Y	Y	N
Heflin	Y	Y	N	N	N	Y	Y	Y
ALASKA								
Murkowski	Y	Y	N	N	N	Y	Y	N
Stevens	Y	Y	N	N	N	Y	Y	N
ARIZONA								
Goldwater	Y	Y	N	N	?	?	Y	N
DeConcini	Y	Y	N	Y	N	N	?	Y
ARKANSAS								
Bumpers	Y	Y	N	N	N	Y	Y	N
Pryor	Y	Y	N	N	N	Y	Y	Y
CALIFORNIA								
Hayakawa	Y	Y	N	N	N	N	Y	N
Cranston	Y	Y	N	Y	N	N	Y	Y
COLORADO								
Armstrong	Y	Y	N	N	N	Y	Y	N
Hart	Y	Y	Y	Y	N	Y	Y	Y
CONNECTICUT								
Weicker	Y	Y	N	N	N	Y	Y	N
Dodd	Y	Y	N	Y	Y	Y	Y	Y
DELAWARE								
Roth	Y	Y	N	N	N	Y	Y	N
Biden	Y	Y	N	Y	Y	Y	Y	Y
FLORIDA								
Hawkins	Y	Y	N	N	N	Y	Y	N
Chiles	Y	Y	N	N	N	N	Y	Y
GEORGIA								
Mattingly	Y	Y	N	N	N	Y	Y	N
Nunn	Y	Y	N	N	N	N	Y	Y
HAWAII								
Inouye	Y	Y	N	N	Y	?	Y	Y
Matsunaga	Y	Y	N	Y	Y	Y	Y	Y
IDAHO								
McClure	Y	Y	N	N	N	Y	N	Y
Symms	Y	Y	N	N	N	N	Y	N
ILLINOIS								
Percy	Y	Y	N	N	N	Y	Y	N
Dixon	Y	Y	N	N	N	Y	Y	Y
INDIANA								
Lugar	Y	Y	N	N	N	Y	Y	N
Quayle	Y	Y	N	N	N	Y	Y	N
IOWA								
Grassley	Y	Y	N	N	N	Y	Y	N
Jepsen	Y	Y	N	N	N	Y	Y	N
KANSAS								
Dole	Y	Y	N	N	Y	N	Y	N
Kassebaum	Y	Y	N	N	N	Y	Y	N
KENTUCKY								
Ford	Y	Y	Y	N	N	Y	Y	Y
Huddleston	Y	Y	N	Y	N	Y	Y	Y
LOUISIANA								
Johnston	Y	Y	N	N	N	N	N	Y
Long	Y	Y	N	N	N	N	Y	N
MAINE								
Cohen	Y	Y	N	N	N	Y	Y	N
Mitchell	Y	Y	N	N	N	Y	Y	Y
MARYLAND								
Mathias	Y	Y	Y	N	N	Y	Y	N
Sarbanes	Y	Y	N	Y	N	Y	Y	Y
MASSACHUSETTS								
Kennedy	Y	Y	N	Y	N	Y	Y	Y
Tsongas	Y	Y	N	Y	N	Y	Y	Y
MICHIGAN								
Levin	Y	Y	N	Y	N	Y	Y	Y
Riegle	Y	Y	N	N	N	Y	Y	Y
MINNESOTA								
Boschwitz	Y	Y	Y	N	Y	N	Y	N
Durenberger	Y	Y	Y	N	Y	N	Y	N
MISSISSIPPI								
Cochran	Y	Y	N	N	N	N	Y	N
Stennis	Y	Y	N	N	N	N	Y	Y
MISSOURI								
Danforth	Y	Y	N	N	N	N	Y	N
Eagleton	Y	Y	N	N	N	Y	Y	Y
MONTANA								
Baucus	Y	Y	N	N	N	Y	Y	Y
Melcher	Y	Y	N	Y	N	+	Y	Y
NEBRASKA								
Exon	Y	Y	N	N	N	Y	Y	Y
Zorinsky	Y	Y	N	N	N	Y	Y	Y
NEVADA								
Laxalt	Y	Y	N	N	?	?	Y	N
Cannon	Y	Y	N	N	N	Y	Y	Y
NEW HAMPSHIRE								
Humphrey	Y	Y	N	N	N	Y	Y	N
Rudman	Y	Y	N	N	N	Y	Y	N
NEW JERSEY								
Bradley	Y	Y	Y	Y	N	Y	Y	Y
Williams	Y	Y	?	?	N	Y	Y	Y
NEW MEXICO								
Domenici	Y	Y	N	N	N	N	Y	N
Schmitt	Y	Y	N	N	Y	Y	Y	N
NEW YORK								
D'Amato	Y	Y	Y	N	N	Y	Y	N
Moynihan	Y	Y	Y	Y	N	Y	Y	Y
NORTH CAROLINA								
East	Y	Y	N	N	N	Y	Y	N
Helms	Y	Y	N	N	N	Y	Y	N
NORTH DAKOTA								
Andrews	Y	Y	N	N	N	Y	Y	N
Burdick	Y	Y	N	N	N	Y	Y	Y
OHIO								
Glenn	Y	Y	N	N	N	Y	Y	Y
Metzenbaum	Y	Y	N	N	N	Y	Y	Y
OKLAHOMA								
Nickles	Y	Y	N	N	N	N	Y	N
Boren	Y	Y	N	N	N	Y	Y	N
OREGON								
Hatfield	Y	Y	N	N	N	N	Y	N
Packwood	Y	Y	N	N	N	N	Y	N
PENNSYLVANIA								
Heinz	Y	Y	Y	N	N	Y	Y	N
Specter	Y	Y	Y	N	N	Y	Y	N
RHODE ISLAND								
Chafee	Y	Y	N	N	Y	N	N	N
Pell	Y	Y	N	N	N	Y	Y	Y
SOUTH CAROLINA								
Thurmond	Y	Y	N	N	N	Y	Y	N
Hollings	Y	Y	N	Y	N	N	Y	Y
SOUTH DAKOTA								
Abdnor	Y	Y	N	N	N	Y	Y	N
Pressler	Y	Y	N	N	N	Y	Y	Y
TENNESSEE								
Baker	Y	Y	N	N	N	Y	Y	N
Sasser	Y	Y	N	N	N	Y	Y	Y
TEXAS								
Tower	Y	Y	Y	N	N	N	N	N
Bentsen	Y	Y	Y	N	N	N	N	Y
UTAH								
Garn	Y	Y	N	N	N	Y	Y	N
Hatch	Y	Y	N	N	N	Y	Y	N
VERMONT								
Stafford	Y	Y	N	N	N	Y	Y	N
Leahy	Y	Y	N	N	N	Y	Y	Y
VIRGINIA								
Warner	Y	Y	N	N	N	Y	Y	N
Byrd*	Y	Y	N	N	N	N	Y	N
WASHINGTON								
Gorton	Y	Y	N	N	N	Y	Y	N
Jackson	Y	Y	N	N	N	Y	Y	Y
WEST VIRGINIA								
Byrd	Y	Y	N	N	N	Y	Y	N
Randolph	Y	Y	Y	N	N	Y	Y	Y
WISCONSIN								
Kasten	Y	Y	N	N	N	Y	Y	N
Proxmire	Y	Y	N	N	N	Y	Y	Y
WYOMING								
Simpson	Y	Y	N	N	N	Y	Y	N
Wallop	Y	Y	N	N	N	N	Y	N

Democrats   **Republicans**

Byrd elected as an independent.

229. H J Res 266. Tax Cuts. Chiles, D-Fla., amendment to provide that the president should adopt policies to ensure continued availability of credit to small businesses, thrift institutions, small banks and small farms; that the Federal Reserve system exercise its powers to require that loans be made for productive economic purposes; and that the Federal Reserve, the president and the Congressional Budget Office should report to the Congress on actions taken to implement these policies by Jan. 1, 1982. Adopted 100-0: R 53-0; D 47-0 (ND 32-0, SD 15-0), July 28, 1981.

230. H J Res 266. Tax Cuts. Melcher, D-Mont., amendment to keep the maximum interest rate that is imputed in contract sales between buyers and sellers at 7 percent. Adopted 100-0: R 53-0; D 47-0 (ND 32-0, SD 15-0), July 28, 1981.

231. H J Res 266. Tax Cuts. Heinz, R-Pa., amendment to allow the issuance of tax-free industrial development bonds to finance pollution control or waste disposal facilities. Rejected 15-84: R 9-44; D 6-40 (ND 4-27, SD 2-13), July 28, 1981.

232. H J Res 266. Tax Cuts. Bradley, D-N.J., amendment to provide a 20 percent tax credit for net savings up to $2,000 for single taxpayers and $4,000 for joint returns. Rejected 15-84: R 0-53; D 15-31 (ND 13-18, SD 2-13), July 28, 1981.

233. H J Res 266. Tax Cuts. Biden, D-Del., amendment to provide that no credit for child-care expenses will be allowed to any taxpayer when both spouses have a total adjusted gross income in excess of $30,000. Rejected 8-90: R 4-47; D 4-43 (ND 4-28, SD 0-15), July 28, 1981.

234. H J Res 266. Tax Cuts. Rudman, R-N.H., amendment to provide a home heating tax credit of up to $200 that is the product of a family's heating expenditures multiplied by 40 percent of the inflation rate. Adopted 71-25: R 36-15; D 35-10 (ND 28-2, SD 7-8), July 28, 1981.

235. H J Res 266. Tax Cuts. Eagleton, D-Mo., amendment to require the president to submit to Congress each year a separate estimate of the outlays, revenues, surplus or deficit of Social Security trust funds and of all other government functions, along with an explanation of the economic assumptions upon which such estimates were based. Adopted 97-2: R 51-2; D 46-0 (ND 31-0, SD 15-0), July 29, 1981.

236. H J Res 266. Tax Cuts. Baucus, D-Mont., amendment to permit small businesses to write off in one year up to $25,000 of their assets in 1986 instead of $10,000 as provided in the committee bill. Rejected 45-55: R 2-51; D 43-4 (ND 32-0, SD 11-4), July 29, 1981.

Corresponding to Congressional Record Votes 237, 238, 239, 240, 241, 242, 243, 244, 245

	237 238 239 240 241 242		237 238 239 240 241 242		237 238 239 240 241 242
ALABAMA		**IOWA**		**NEW HAMPSHIRE**	
Denton	N Y Y Y Y Y	*Grassley*	N Y Y Y Y N	*Humphrey*	N Y Y Y Y N
Heflin	N Y Y Y ? ?	*Jepsen*	N Y Y Y Y Y	*Rudman*	N Y Y N Y Y
ALASKA		**KANSAS**		**NEW JERSEY**	
Murkowski	N Y Y Y N Y	*Dole*	N Y Y Y Y Y	Bradley	N Y N N Y Y
Stevens	N Y Y N Y Y	*Kassebaum*	Y Y Y N Y Y	Williams	N Y Y N Y Y
ARIZONA		**KENTUCKY**		**NEW MEXICO**	
Goldwater	N Y Y ? Y ?	Ford	N Y Y Y Y Y	*Domenici*	N Y Y Y Y Y
DeConcini	N Y Y Y Y Y	Huddleston	N Y Y Y Y Y	*Schmitt*	N Y Y Y Y Y
ARKANSAS		**LOUISIANA**		**NEW YORK**	
Bumpers	N Y N N Y Y	Johnston	N Y Y Y Y Y	*D'Amato*	N Y Y Y Y Y
Pryor	N Y Y Y Y Y	Long	N Y Y Y Y Y	Moynihan	N Y Y N Y Y
CALIFORNIA		**MAINE**		**NORTH CAROLINA**	
Hayakawa	N Y Y Y Y Y	*Cohen*	N Y Y N Y Y	*East*	N Y Y Y Y Y
Cranston	N Y Y N Y Y	Mitchell	N Y Y N Y Y	*Helms*	N Y Y Y Y N
COLORADO		**MARYLAND**		**NORTH DAKOTA**	
Armstrong	N Y Y Y Y ?	*Mathias*	N Y N N Y Y	*Andrews*	Y Y Y N Y Y
Hart	Y Y N N Y Y	Sarbanes	N Y Y N Y ?	Burdick	N Y Y N Y Y
CONNECTICUT		**MASSACHUSETTS**		**OHIO**	
Weicker	N Y Y N Y ?	Kennedy	Y Y N X Y Y	Glenn	N Y Y N Y Y
Dodd	N Y N N Y Y	Tsongas	Y Y N N Y Y	Metzenbaum	N Y Y N Y Y
DELAWARE		**MICHIGAN**		**OKLAHOMA**	
Roth	N Y Y Y Y Y	Levin	Y Y N N Y Y	*Nickles*	N Y Y Y Y Y
Biden	N Y Y Y Y Y	Riegle	N Y Y N Y Y	Boren	Y Y Y Y Y Y
FLORIDA		**MINNESOTA**		**OREGON**	
Hawkins	N Y Y Y Y Y	*Boschwitz*	N Y Y N Y Y	*Hatfield*	Y Y Y N Y Y
Chiles	N Y Y Y Y Y	*Durenberger*	N Y Y N Y Y	*Packwood*	N Y Y N Y Y
GEORGIA		**MISSISSIPPI**		**PENNSYLVANIA**	
Mattingly	N Y Y Y ? ?	*Cochran*	N Y Y Y Y Y	*Heinz*	N Y Y N Y Y
Nunn	N Y Y Y Y Y	Stennis	N Y Y Y Y Y	*Specter*	Y Y Y N Y Y
HAWAII		**MISSOURI**		**RHODE ISLAND**	
Inouye	N Y Y N Y Y	*Danforth*	N Y Y Y Y Y	*Chafee*	N Y Y N Y Y
Matsunaga	N Y Y N Y Y	Eagleton	N Y N N Y N	Pell	Y Y Y # Y Y
IDAHO		**MONTANA**		**SOUTH CAROLINA**	
McClure	N Y Y Y Y ?	Baucus	N Y Y N Y Y	*Thurmond*	N Y Y Y Y Y
Symms	N Y Y Y Y N	Melcher	N Y Y ? Y Y	Hollings	N Y N Y Y Y
ILLINOIS		**NEBRASKA**		**SOUTH DAKOTA**	
Percy	N Y Y N Y Y	Exon	N Y Y Y Y Y	*Abdnor*	N Y Y Y Y Y
Dixon	N Y Y Y Y Y	Zorinsky	N Y Y Y Y Y	*Pressler*	N Y Y N Y Y
INDIANA		**NEVADA**		**TENNESSEE**	
Lugar	N Y Y Y Y Y	*Laxalt*	N Y Y Y Y Y	*Baker*	N Y Y Y Y Y
Quayle	N Y Y Y Y Y	Cannon	N Y Y Y Y Y	Sasser	N Y Y Y Y Y

KEY

Y Voted for (yea).
Paired for.
+ Announced for.
N Voted against (nay).
X Paired against.
- Announced against.
P Voted "present".
C Voted "present" to avoid possible conflict of interest.
? Did not vote or otherwise make a position known.

	237 238 239 240 241 242
TEXAS	
Tower	? Y Y Y Y Y
Bentsen	N Y Y Y Y Y
UTAH	
Garn	N Y Y Y Y Y
Hatch	N Y Y Y Y Y
VERMONT	
Stafford	N Y Y N Y Y
Leahy	N Y N N Y Y
VIRGINIA	
Warner	N Y Y Y Y Y
Byrd*	N Y Y Y Y Y
WASHINGTON	
Gorton	N Y Y Y Y Y
Jackson	N Y Y Y Y Y
WEST VIRGINIA	
Byrd	Y Y Y Y Y Y
Randolph	N Y Y Y Y Y
WISCONSIN	
Kasten	N Y Y Y Y Y
Proxmire	Y Y Y Y Y N
WYOMING	
Simpson	N Y Y Y Y Y
Wallop	N Y Y Y Y Y

Democrats   *Republicans*

* Byrd elected as an independent.

237. H J Res 266. Tax Cuts. Kennedy, D-Mass., amendment to reduce the allowable deduction for the cost of business meals to 50 percent, from 100 percent, effective Jan. 1, 1982. Rejected 12-87: R 4-48; D 8-39 (ND 7-25, SD 1-14), July 29, 1981.

238. H J Res 266. Tax Cuts. Byrd, D-W.Va., amendment to provide for accelerated depreciation of 10 years for power plants voluntarily converting to coal or replaced by coal-burning generating facilities and depreciation of three years for related pollution-control equipment, instead of the 15 years and five years, respectively, provided in the committee substitute. Adopted 100-0: R 53-0; D 47-0 (ND 32-0, SD 15-0), July 29, 1981.

239. H J Res 266. Tax Cuts. Finance Committee substitute amendment, as amended, to reduce individual income tax rates by 25 percent across-the-board over three years, index tax brackets beginning in 1985, and provide business, savings and investment incentives. Adopted 89-11: R 52-1; D 37-10 (ND 24-8, SD 13-2), July 29, 1981. A "yea" was a vote supporting the president's position.

240. S 951. Justice Department Authorization. Johnston, D-La., motion to invoke cloture (and thus limit debate) on the Helms, R-N.C.—Johnston, D-La., amendment to prohibit federal courts in most instances from ordering busing for racial balance. Motion rejected 59-37: R 35-17; D 24-20 (ND 10-19, SD 14-1), July 29, 1981. A three-fifths vote of the total Senate membership (60) is required to invoke cloture.

241. Treaties. Adoption of the resolutions of ratification for **Exec N, 96th Cong, 2nd Sess,** International Convention Against the Taking of Hostages; **Exec H, 96th Cong, 2nd Sess,** Convention on the Physical Protection of Nuclear Material; **Exec M, 95th Cong, 1st Sess,** Revised Customs Convention on the International Transport of Goods Under Cover of Transport International Routier Carnets; and **Exec K, 96th Cong, 2nd Sess,** Inter-governmental Maritime Consultative Organization Convention. Adopted 98-0: R 52-0; D 46-0 (ND 32-0; SD 14-0), July 30, 1981. A two-thirds majority vote (66 in this case) is required for adoption of resolutions of ratification.

242. HR 4034. HUD-Independent Agencies Appropriations, Fiscal 1982. Passage of the bill to appropriate $60,506,342,000 in fiscal 1982 for the Department of Housing and Urban Development and 20 independent agencies. Passed 87-6: R 44-4; D 43-2 (ND 29-2, SD 14-0), July 30, 1981. The president had requested $63,248,452,500.

	243	244	245	246	247	248
ALABAMA						
Denton	Y	Y	Y	N	N	Y
Heflin	Y	Y	N	Y	N	Y
ALASKA						
Murkowski	Y	Y	Y	N	?	?
Stevens	Y	Y	Y	N	N	Y
ARIZONA						
Goldwater	?	?	?	?	?	?
DeConcini	Y	Y	N	Y	N	Y
ARKANSAS						
Bumpers	?	?	?	?	Y	X
Pryor	Y	Y	N	Y	?	?
CALIFORNIA						
Hayakawa	Y	Y	Y	N	N	Y
Cranston	N	N	N	Y	?	?
COLORADO						
Armstrong	Y	Y	Y	N	N	Y
Hart	N	N	Y	Y	?	?
CONNECTICUT						
Weicker	?	+	?	?	Y	Y
Dodd	N	N	N	Y	Y	N
DELAWARE						
Roth	Y	Y	N	Y	Y	Y
Biden	Y	Y	N	Y	Y	Y
FLORIDA						
Hawkins	Y	Y	Y	N	N	Y
Chiles	Y	Y	N	Y	?	?
GEORGIA						
Mattingly	Y	Y	Y	N	N	Y
Nunn	Y	Y	Y	Y	Y	Y
HAWAII						
Inouye	N	Y	#	Y	X	Y
Matsunaga	N	Y	N	Y	Y	Y
IDAHO						
McClure	?	?	?	?	?	?
Symms	Y	Y	Y	N	-	?
ILLINOIS						
Percy	Y	Y	Y	N	X	+
Dixon	Y	Y	N	Y	-	+
INDIANA						
Lugar	Y	Y	Y	N	N	Y
Quayle	Y	Y	Y	N	N	Y

	243	244	245	246	247	248
IOWA						
Grassley	Y	Y	Y	?	N	Y
Jepsen	Y	Y	Y	N	N	Y
KANSAS						
Dole	Y	Y	Y	N	N	Y
Kassebaum	Y	Y	Y	N	N	Y
KENTUCKY						
Ford	Y	Y	N	Y	N	Y
Huddleston	Y	Y	N	Y	N	Y
LOUISIANA						
Johnston	Y	Y	N	Y	?	?
Long	Y	Y	Y	Y	N	Y
MAINE						
Cohen	Y	Y	?	?	Y	Y
Mitchell	N	Y	?	?	Y	Y
MARYLAND						
Mathias	Y	Y	Y	N	Y	N
Sarbanes	N	N	N	Y	Y	Y
MASSACHUSETTS						
Kennedy	N	N	N	Y	Y	N
Tsongas	N	N	N	Y	Y	N
MICHIGAN						
Levin	Y	N	N	Y	Y	N
Riegle	N	N	N	Y	#	+
MINNESOTA						
Boschwitz	Y	Y	Y	N	N	Y
Durenberger	Y	Y	Y	N	N	Y
MISSISSIPPI						
Cochran	Y	Y	Y	N	N	Y
Stennis	Y	Y	Y	Y	N	Y
MISSOURI						
Danforth	Y	Y	Y	N	?	?
Eagleton	Y	N	N	Y	Y	N
MONTANA						
Baucus	Y	Y	N	Y	?	?
Melcher	?	?	?	?	X	#
NEBRASKA						
Exon	Y	Y	N	Y	-	+
Zorinsky	?	?	?	?	N	Y
NEVADA						
Laxalt	Y	Y	Y	N	?	?
Cannon	Y	Y	?	?	N	Y

	243	244	245	246	247	248
NEW HAMPSHIRE						
Humphrey	Y	Y	Y	N	N	Y
Rudman	Y	Y	Y	N	Y	Y
NEW JERSEY						
Bradley	N	Y	N	Y	N	N
Williams	Y	N	N	Y	N	Y
NEW MEXICO						
Domenici	Y	Y	Y	N	N	Y
Schmitt	Y	Y	Y	N	N	Y
NEW YORK						
D'Amato	Y	Y	Y	N	N	Y
Moynihan	N	Y	N	Y	Y	Y
NORTH CAROLINA						
East	Y	Y	Y	N	N	Y
Helms	Y	Y	Y	N	N	Y
NORTH DAKOTA						
Andrews	Y	Y	Y	N	?	?
Burdick	Y	Y	?	N	N	Y
OHIO						
Glenn	Y	Y	N	Y	N	Y
Metzenbaum	N	N	N	Y	?	?
OKLAHOMA						
Nickles	Y	Y	Y	N	N	Y
Boren	Y	Y	Y	Y	N	Y
OREGON						
Hatfield	Y	Y	Y	N	N	Y
Packwood	Y	Y	Y	N	N	Y
PENNSYLVANIA						
Heinz	Y	Y	Y	N	#	+
Specter	Y	Y	Y	?	N	Y
RHODE ISLAND						
Chafee	Y	Y	Y	N	N	Y
Pell	Y	N	N	Y	Y	Y
SOUTH CAROLINA						
Thurmond	Y	Y	Y	N	N	Y
Hollings	N	Y	?	?	Y	N
SOUTH DAKOTA						
Abdnor	Y	Y	Y	N	N	Y
Pressler	Y	N	Y	N	?	?
TENNESSEE						
Baker	Y	Y	Y	N	N	Y
Sasser	Y	Y	X	+	N	Y

KEY	
Y	Voted for (yea).
#	Paired for.
+	Announced for.
N	Voted against (nay).
X	Paired against.
-	Announced against.
P	Voted "present".
C	Voted "present" to avoid possible conflict of interest.
?	Did not vote or otherwise make a position known.

	243	244	245	246	247	248
TEXAS						
Tower	Y	Y	Y	N	N	Y
Bentsen	Y	Y	N	Y	?	?
UTAH						
Garn	Y	Y	Y	N	N	Y
Hatch	Y	Y	Y	N	N	Y
VERMONT						
Stafford	Y	Y	Y	N	?	?
Leahy	Y	N	N	Y	#	?
VIRGINIA						
Warner	Y	Y	Y	N	N	Y
Byrd*	Y	Y	Y	N	N	Y
WASHINGTON						
Gorton	Y	Y	Y	N	N	Y
Jackson	Y	Y	N	Y	N	Y
WEST VIRGINIA						
Byrd	Y	Y	Y	Y	Y	Y
Randolph	Y	Y	N	Y	N	Y
WISCONSIN						
Kasten	Y	Y	Y	N	N	Y
Proxmire	N	Y	Y	N	N	Y
WYOMING						
Simpson	Y	Y	Y	N	N	Y
Wallop	Y	Y	Y	N	N	Y

Democrats   *Republicans*

* *Byrd elected as an independent.*

243. Lee Nomination. Confirmation of President Reagan's nomination of Rex E. Lee of Utah to be solicitor general of the United States. Confirmed 79-15: R 50-0; D 29-15 (ND 16-14, SD 13-1), July 31, 1981. A "yea" was a vote supporting the president's position.

244. HR 3982. Budget Reconciliation. Adoption of the conference report on the bill to revise existing laws to reduce federal outlays by $35.1 billion in fiscal 1982 and a total of $130.6 billion in fiscal 1982-84. The reconciliation measure affected about 250 federal programs. Adopted (thus clearing the measure for the president) 80-14: R 49-1; D 31-13 (ND 17-13, SD 14-0), July 31, 1981. A "yea" vote was a vote supporting the president's position.

245. HR 4331/HR 3982. Minimum Social Security Benefits/Budget Reconciliation. Judgment of the Senate on the chair's ruling that the Moynihan, D-N.Y., motion to proceed to consideration of the bill (HR 4331) to amend the Omnibus Budget Reconciliation Act of 1981 (HR 3982) to restore minimum Social Security benefits was out of order. Senate rules barred consideration of the bill on the day it was received. Ruling of the chair upheld 57-30: R 49-0; D 8-30 (ND 3-23, SD 5-7), July 31, 1981. A "yea" vote was a vote supporting the president's position.

246. HR 4331/HR 3982. Minimum Social Security Benefits/Budget Reconciliation. Byrd, D-W.Va., motion that the Senate adjourn for one minute, thus changing the legislative day to permit consideration (see vote 245, above) of the bill (HR 4331) to amend the Omnibus Budget Reconciliation Act of 1981 (HR 3981) to restore minimum Social Security benefits. Motion rejected 37-49: R 0-47; D 37-2 (ND 26-1, SD 11-1), July 31, 1981.

247. HR 4242. Tax Cuts. Kennedy, D-Mass., motion to recommit to the conference committee the conference report on the tax cut bill with instructions to the Senate conferees to seek to reduce the revenue loss from certain crude oil windfall profits tax provisions. Motion rejected 20-55: R 5-37; D 15-18 (ND 12-10, SD 3-8), Aug. 3, 1981. A "nay" was a vote supporting the president's position.

248. HR 4242. Tax Cuts. Adoption of the conference report on the bill (known as the "Economic Recovery Tax Act of 1981") to cut individual income tax rates by 25 percent across-the-board over 33 months; require that individual income taxes be adjusted, or indexed, annually to offset the effects of inflation, starting in 1985; allow accelerated depreciation for business investment in new assets; and provide special savings and investment incentives. Adopted 67-8: R 41-1; D 26-7 (ND 17-6, SD 9-1), Aug. 3, 1981. A "yea" was a vote supporting the president's position.

	249		249		249
ALABAMA		**IOWA**		**NEW HAMPSHIRE**	
Denton	Y	*Grassley*	Y	*Humphrey*	Y
Heflin	Y	*Jepsen*	Y	*Rudman*	N
ALASKA		**KANSAS**		**NEW JERSEY**	
Murkowski	Y	*Dole*	Y	Bradley	N
Stevens	N	*Kassebaum*	Y	Williams	N
ARIZONA		**KENTUCKY**		**NEW MEXICO**	
Goldwater	Y	Ford	Y	*Domenici*	Y
DeConcini	Y	Huddleston	Y	*Schmitt*	Y
ARKANSAS		**LOUISIANA**		**NEW YORK**	
Bumpers	N	Johnston	Y	*D'Amato*	Y
Pryor	Y	Long	Y	Moynihan	N
CALIFORNIA		**MAINE**		**NORTH CAROLINA**	
Hayakawa	Y	*Cohen*	N	*East*	Y
Cranston	X	Mitchell	N	*Helms*	Y
COLORADO		**MARYLAND**		**NORTH DAKOTA**	
Armstrong	Y	*Mathias*	N	*Andrews*	Y
Hart	N	Sarbanes	N	Burdick	N
CONNECTICUT		**MASSACHUSETTS**		**OHIO**	
Weicker	N	Kennedy	N	Glenn	N
Dodd	?	Tsongas	N	Metzenbaum	N
DELAWARE		**MICHIGAN**		**OKLAHOMA**	
Roth	Y	Levin	N	*Nickles*	Y
Biden	Y	Riegle	N	Boren	Y
FLORIDA		**MINNESOTA**		**OREGON**	
Hawkins	Y	*Boschwitz*	N	*Hatfield*	N
Chiles	Y	*Durenberger*	N	*Packwood*	N
GEORGIA		**MISSISSIPPI**		**PENNSYLVANIA**	
Mattingly	Y	*Cochran*	Y	*Heinz*	N
Nunn	Y	Stennis	Y	*Specter*	N
HAWAII		**MISSOURI**		**RHODE ISLAND**	
Inouye	N	*Danforth*	Y	*Chafee*	N
Matsunaga	N	Eagleton	?	Pell	Y
IDAHO		**MONTANA**		**SOUTH CAROLINA**	
McClure	Y	Baucus	N	*Thurmond*	Y
Symms	+	Melcher	Y	Hollings	Y
ILLINOIS		**NEBRASKA**		**SOUTH DAKOTA**	
Percy	Y	Exon	Y	*Abdnor*	?
Dixon	Y	Zorinsky	?	*Pressler*	N
INDIANA		**NEVADA**		**TENNESSEE**	
Lugar	Y	*Laxalt*	Y	*Baker*	Y
Quayle	Y	Cannon	#	Sasser	—

	249
TEXAS	
Tower	Y
Bentsen	?
UTAH	
Garn	Y
Hatch	Y
VERMONT	
Stafford	N
Leahy	N
VIRGINIA	
Warner	Y
Byrd*	Y
WASHINGTON	
Gorton	N
Jackson	Y
WEST VIRGINIA	
Byrd	Y
Randolph	Y
WISCONSIN	
Kasten	Y
Proxmire	Y
WYOMING	
Simpson	?
Wallop	Y

KEY

Y   Voted for (yea).
\#   Paired for.
+   Announced for.
N   Voted against (nay).
X   Paired against.
-   Announced against.
P   Voted "present".
C   Voted "present" to avoid possible conflict of interest.
?   Did not vote or otherwise make a position known.

Democrats   **Republicans**

Byrd elected as an independent.

249. S 951. Justice Department Authorization. Johnston, D-La., motion to invoke cloture (thus limiting debate) on the Helms, R-N.C.-Johnston amendment to prohibit federal courts in most instances from ordering busing for racial purposes. Motion rejected 57-33: R 35-15; D 22-18 (ND 10-17, SD 12-1), Sept. 10, 1981. A three-fifths vote of the total Senate membership (60) is required to invoke cloture.

KEY

- Y Voted for (yea).
- \# Paired for.
- \+ Announced for.
- N Voted against (nay).
- X Paired against.
- \- Announced against.
- P Voted "present".
- C Voted "present" to avoid possible conflict of interest.
- ? Did not vote or otherwise make a position known.

State / Senator	250	251	252	253	254	255	256
ALABAMA							
Denton	Y	Y	Y	Y	Y	Y	Y
Heflin	Y	Y	Y	Y	Y	N	
ALASKA							
Murkowski	Y	Y	Y	N	Y	Y	Y
Stevens	Y	Y	Y	Y	N	Y	Y
ARIZONA							
Goldwater	Y	Y	Y	N	Y	Y	N
DeConcini	Y	Y	N	N	Y	Y	N
ARKANSAS							
Bumpers	Y	N	Y	N	N	N	Y
Pryor	Y	N	Y	Y	Y	Y	Y
CALIFORNIA							
Hayakawa	Y	Y	Y	Y	Y	Y	N
Cranston	?	Y	N	N	N	N	N
COLORADO							
Armstrong	?	Y	Y	N	Y	Y	N
Hart	Y	N	N	N	N	N	Y
CONNECTICUT							
Weicker	Y	Y	Y	N	N	N	N
Dodd	+	N	N	N	N	N	N
DELAWARE							
Roth	Y	Y	Y	N	Y	Y	N
Biden	Y	Y	Y	N	Y	Y	N
FLORIDA							
Hawkins	Y	Y	Y	Y	Y	Y	Y
Chiles	Y	N	N	Y	Y	Y	Y
GEORGIA							
Mattingly	Y	Y	Y	N	Y	Y	Y
Nunn	Y	N	Y	Y	Y	Y	Y
HAWAII							
Inouye	Y	N	N	Y	N	N	Y
Matsunaga	Y	?	?	+	N	N	Y
IDAHO							
McClure	Y	Y	Y	Y	Y	Y	Y
Symms	?	Y	Y	N	Y	Y	Y
ILLINOIS							
Percy	Y	Y	Y	N	N	N	N
Dixon	+	Y	N	N	Y	N	N
INDIANA							
Lugar	Y	Y	Y	N	Y	Y	N
Quayle	Y	Y	Y	N	Y	Y	N
IOWA							
Grassley	Y	?	?	N	Y	Y	Y
Jepsen	Y	Y	Y	N	Y	Y	Y
KANSAS							
Dole	Y	Y	Y	Y	Y	Y	Y
Kassebaum	Y	Y	Y	N	Y	Y	N
KENTUCKY							
Ford	?	N	N	Y	Y	Y	Y
Huddleston	Y	N	N	Y	Y	Y	Y
LOUISIANA							
Johnston	Y	N	N	Y	Y	Y	Y
Long	Y	Y	Y	Y	Y	Y	Y
MAINE							
Cohen	Y	N	N	N	N	N	N
Mitchell	Y	Y	N	N	N	N	N
MARYLAND							
Mathias	?	Y	Y	N	N	N	N
Sarbanes	Y	N	N	N	N	N	N
MASSACHUSETTS							
Kennedy	?	?	N	N	X	N	N
Tsongas	Y	Y	Y	N	N	N	N
MICHIGAN							
Levin	Y	N	N	N	N	N	N
Riegle	Y	N	N	N	N	N	N
MINNESOTA							
Boschwitz	Y	N	N	N	N	N	N
Durenberger	Y	N	N	N	N	N	N
MISSISSIPPI							
Cochran	Y	Y	Y	Y	Y	Y	Y
Stennis	Y	N	N	Y	Y	Y	Y
MISSOURI							
Danforth	?	N	N	N	Y	N	N
Eagleton	Y	N	N	N	N	N	N
MONTANA							
Baucus	Y	N	N	Y	N	N	Y
Melcher	Y	N	N	Y	Y	Y	Y
NEBRASKA							
Exon	Y	N	N	N	Y	N	N
Zorinsky	?	N	N	N	Y	N	N
NEVADA							
Laxalt	Y	Y	Y	Y	Y	Y	Y
Cannon	+	Y	Y	Y	Y	Y	Y
NEW HAMPSHIRE							
Humphrey	Y	Y	Y	N	Y	N	N
Rudman	Y	Y	Y	N	N	N	Y
NEW JERSEY							
Bradley	?	N	N	N	N	N	N
Williams	+	?	?	N	N	N	N
NEW MEXICO							
Domenici	Y	Y	Y	Y	Y	Y	Y
Schmitt	Y	Y	Y	Y	Y	Y	Y
NEW YORK							
D'Amato	Y	N	N	N	Y	Y	N
Moynihan	Y	N	?	N	N	N	N
NORTH CAROLINA							
East	Y	Y	Y	Y	Y	Y	Y
Helms	Y	Y	Y	Y	Y	Y	Y
NORTH DAKOTA							
Andrews	Y	N	N	N	Y	N	Y
Burdick	Y	N	N	Y	N	N	Y
OHIO							
Glenn	Y	Y	Y	N	N	N	N
Metzenbaum	Y	N	N	N	N	N	N
OKLAHOMA							
Nickles	?	Y	Y	Y	Y	Y	Y
Boren	Y	N	N	Y	Y	Y	Y
OREGON							
Hatfield	Y	Y	?	N	N	N	N
Packwood	Y	Y	Y	N	N	N	N
PENNSYLVANIA							
Heinz	Y	N	N	N	N	N	N
Specter	Y	N	N	N	N	N	N
RHODE ISLAND							
Chafee	Y	Y	Y	N	N	N	N
Pell	Y	Y	Y	N	#	N	N
SOUTH CAROLINA							
Thurmond	Y	Y	Y	Y	Y	Y	Y
Hollings	Y	Y	Y	Y	Y	Y	Y
SOUTH DAKOTA							
Abdnor	?	N	N	Y	Y	Y	Y
Pressler	?	N	N	N	N	N	Y
TENNESSEE							
Baker	Y	Y	Y	Y	Y	Y	Y
Sasser	+	N	N	Y	Y	Y	Y
TEXAS							
Tower	Y	Y	Y	Y	Y	Y	Y
Bentsen	?	N	N	Y	Y	Y	Y
UTAH							
Garn	Y	Y	Y	N	Y	Y	N
Hatch	+	Y	Y	N	Y	Y	Y
VERMONT							
Stafford	Y	-	?	-	?	-	-
Leahy	Y	N	N	Y	N	N	Y
VIRGINIA							
Warner	Y	Y	Y	N	Y	Y	Y
Byrd*	Y	Y	Y	Y	Y	Y	Y
WASHINGTON							
Gorton	Y	Y	Y	N	Y	Y	N
Jackson	Y	N	N	N	Y	N	N
WEST VIRGINIA							
Byrd	Y	-	-	Y	Y	Y	Y
Randolph	Y	N	N	Y	Y	Y	+
WISCONSIN							
Kasten	Y	N	N	N	Y	N	N
Proxmire	Y	N	N	N	Y	N	N
WYOMING							
Simpson	Y	Y	Y	N	Y	N	N
Wallop	Y	Y	Y	Y	Y	Y	Y

Democrats *Republicans*

* Byrd elected as an independent.

250. S 1181. Military Pay Raise. Passage of the bill to provide basic pay raises of 18-22 percent for senior enlisted personnel and 7-9 percent for junior enlisted personnel. Passed 81-0: R 45-0; D 36-0 (ND 24-0, SD 12-0), Sept. 11, 1981.

251. S 884. Agriculture and Food Act of 1981. Dole, R-Kan., motion to table (kill) the Boschwitz, R-Minn., amendment, to the Jepsen, R-Iowa, amendment *(see vote 252, below)*, to set dairy price supports at 75-90 percent of parity, with an annual readjustment to maintain at least a 75 percent level and a second, semiannual adjustment to 70 percent, and with authority for the annual adjustment also to be as low as 70 percent of parity in years when anticipated outlays for purchases of surplus dairy products would exceed $500 million. Motion agreed to 53-41: R 40-11; D 13-30 (ND 9-19, SD 4-11), Sept. 15, 1981. A "yea" was a vote supporting the president's position.

252. S 884. Agriculture and Food Act of 1981. Dole, R-Kan., motion to table (kill) the Boschwitz, R-Minn., amendment, to the Jepsen, R-Iowa, amendment, to set dairy price supports at 75-90 percent of parity through 1985, with an annual adjustment to maintain at least a 75 percent level and a second, semiannual adjustment to 70 percent, and with authority for the annual adjustment also to be as low as 70 percent when anticipated outlays to buy surplus dairy products would exceed $500 million. Also, the secretary would be authorized to forgo the semiannual readjustment in years when anticipated outlays would exceed $750 million. Motion agreed to 51-42: R 39-11; D 12-31 (ND 5-23, SD 7-8), Sept. 15, 1981. A "yea" was a vote supporting the president's position. (By voice vote the Senate subsequently adopted the Jepsen amendment, which provided supports at 70-90 percent of parity with annual adjustments and with authority for the secretary to forgo the annual adjustment in years when anticipated outlays

would exceed $750 million; however, the actual payment rate for the price supports could not drop below $13.10 per hundredweight.)

253. S 884. Agriculture and Food Act of 1981. Baker, R-Tenn., motion to table (kill) the Lugar, R-Ind., amendment *(see vote 256, below)* to repeal the allotment and quota program for peanuts and to continue peanut price support loans for all peanut producers, with loan rates at the discretion of the secretary of agriculture. Motion rejected 42-56: R 20-32; D 22-24 (ND 8-23, SD 14-1), Sept 16, 1981.

254. S 951. Justice Department Authorization. Johnston, D-La., motion to invoke cloture (thus limiting debate) on the Helms, R-N.C.-Johnston amendment *(see vote 255, below)* to prohibit federal courts in most instances from ordering school busing for racial balance. Motion agreed to 61-36: R 36-16; D 25-20 (ND 11-19, SD 14-1), Sept. 16, 1981. A three-fifths vote of the total Senate membership (60) is required to invoke cloture.

255. S 951. Justice Department Authorization. Helms, R-N.C.-Johnston, D-La., amendment to prohibit federal courts in most instances from ordering school busing for racial balance. Adopted 60-39: R 38-14; D 22-25 (ND 9-23, SD 13-2), Sept. 16, 1981.

256. S 884. Agriculture and Food Act of 1981. Mattingly, R-Ga., amendment, to the Lugar, R-Ind., amendment, to repeal the allotment program for peanuts, retain the poundage quota system and continue peanut price support loans for producers within the quota system. Adopted 51-47: R 27-25; D 24-22 (ND 9-22, SD 15-0), Sept. 16, 1981. (The Lugar amendment was subsequently adopted by voice vote.)

	257	258	259	260	261	262
ALABAMA						
Denton	N	Y	Y	Y	Y	Y
Heflin	Y	N	Y	Y	Y	N
ALASKA						
Murkowski	Y	?	?	?	?	?
Stevens	Y	Y	Y	Y	Y	Y
ARIZONA						
Goldwater	Y	Y	Y	Y	Y	Y
DeConcini	Y	Y	N	N	Y	N
ARKANSAS						
Bumpers	P	N	N	N	Y	N
Pryor	Y	N	Y	Y	Y	N
CALIFORNIA						
Hayakawa	Y	Y	Y	Y	Y	Y
Cranston	?	?	?	?	?	?
COLORADO						
Armstrong	+	Y	N	-	+	Y
Hart	Y	N	Y	N	Y	N
CONNECTICUT						
Weicker	N	Y	N	N	Y	Y
Dodd	Y	N	N	N	N	N
DELAWARE						
Roth	N	Y	N	N	N	Y
Biden	N	Y	N	N	N	Y
FLORIDA						
Hawkins	Y	Y	Y	Y	Y	Y
Chiles	Y	Y	Y	Y	Y	Y
GEORGIA						
Mattingly	N	Y	Y	Y	N	Y
Nunn	Y	Y	Y	Y	Y	N
HAWAII						
Inouye	Y	Y	Y	Y	Y	N
Matsunaga	Y	Y	Y	Y	Y	N
IDAHO						
McClure	Y	N	Y	Y	Y	Y
Symms	Y	N	Y	Y	Y	Y
ILLINOIS						
Percy	N	Y	N	N	N	Y
Dixon	Y	Y	Y	N	N	Y
INDIANA						
Lugar	N	Y	Y	Y	N	Y
Quayle	N	Y	Y	N	N	Y

	257	258	259	260	261	262
IOWA						
Grassley	Y	N	Y	Y	Y	Y
Jepsen	Y	Y	Y	Y	Y	Y
KANSAS						
Dole	Y	Y	Y	Y	Y	Y
Kassebaum	Y	Y	Y	N	Y	Y
KENTUCKY						
Ford	Y	Y	Y	Y	Y	N
Huddleston	Y	Y	Y	Y	Y	Y
LOUISIANA						
Johnston	Y	Y	Y	Y	Y	N
Long	Y	Y	Y	Y	Y	Y
MAINE						
Cohen	Y	Y	N	Y	Y	Y
Mitchell	Y	N	N	N	Y	Y
MARYLAND						
Mathias	N	Y	?	?	Y	Y
Sarbanes	N	N	Y	N	Y	N
MASSACHUSETTS						
Kennedy	N	Y	N	?	?	?
Tsongas	N	Y	N	N	N	Y
MICHIGAN						
Levin	Y	N	Y	N	Y	N
Riegle	Y	N	N	N	Y	N
MINNESOTA						
Boschwitz	Y	N	N	N	Y	N
Durenberger	Y	N	N	N	Y	N
MISSISSIPPI						
Cochran	Y	Y	Y	Y	Y	Y
Stennis	?	Y	Y	Y	Y	Y
MISSOURI						
Danforth	N	Y	N	N	N	Y
Eagleton	N	N	N	N	N	N
MONTANA						
Baucus	Y	N	Y	N	Y	N
Melcher	Y	N	Y	Y	Y	N
NEBRASKA						
Exon	Y	N	Y	Y	Y	N
Zorinsky	Y	N	Y	Y	Y	N
NEVADA						
Laxalt	Y	Y	Y	Y	Y	Y
Cannon	Y	N	N	N	Y	Y

	257	258	259	260	261	262
NEW HAMPSHIRE						
Humphrey	N	Y	N	N	N	Y
Rudman	N	Y	N	N	N	Y
NEW JERSEY						
Bradley	?	?	-	.	?	?
Williams	N	Y	N	N	N	Y
NEW MEXICO						
Domenici	N	Y	Y	Y	N	Y
Schmitt	Y	Y	N	Y	N	Y
NEW YORK						
D'Amato	N	N	N	N	N	Y
Moynihan	N	Y	N	N	N	Y
NORTH CAROLINA						
East	Y	Y	Y	Y	Y	Y
Helms	Y	Y	Y	Y	Y	Y
NORTH DAKOTA						
Andrews	Y	N	Y	Y	Y	N
Burdick	Y	N	Y	Y	Y	N
OHIO						
Glenn	N	Y	Y	N	Y	Y
Metzenbaum	N	N	N	N	N	N
OKLAHOMA						
Nickles	N	Y	N	N	N	Y
Boren	Y	N	Y	Y	Y	N
OREGON						
Hatfield	N	Y	N	N	N	Y
Packwood	N	Y	N	N	N	Y
PENNSYLVANIA						
Heinz	N	Y	N	N	N	Y
Specter	N	N	N	N	N	Y
RHODE ISLAND						
Chafee	N	Y	N	N	N	Y
Pell	N	Y	N	N	N	Y
SOUTH CAROLINA						
Thurmond	Y	Y	Y	Y	Y	Y
Hollings	Y	Y	Y	Y	Y	N
SOUTH DAKOTA						
Abdnor	Y	N	Y	Y	Y	N
Pressler	Y	N	N	N	Y	N
TENNESSEE						
Baker	Y	Y	Y	Y	Y	Y
Sasser	Y	N	Y	Y	Y	N

KEY

Y   Voted for (yea).
\#   Paired for.
+   Announced for.
N   Voted against (nay).
X   Paired against.
-   Announced against.
P   Voted "present".
C   Voted "present" to avoid possible conflict of interest.
?   Did not vote or otherwise make a position known.

	257	258	259	260	261	262
TEXAS						
Tower	Y	?	Y	Y	Y	Y
Bentsen	Y	Y	N	Y	Y	N
UTAH						
Garn	Y	Y	N	N	Y	Y
Hatch	Y	Y	N	N	Y	Y
VERMONT						
Stafford	?	-	.	?	?	?
Leahy	Y	N	Y	N	Y	N
VIRGINIA						
Warner	Y	Y	Y	Y	Y	Y
Byrd*	N	Y	Y	Y	N	Y
WASHINGTON						
Gorton	N	Y	N	N	Y	Y
Jackson	Y	N	N	N	Y	Y
WEST VIRGINIA						
Byrd	Y	N	Y	N	Y	N
Randolph	Y	N	Y	Y	Y	N
WISCONSIN						
Kasten	N	N	N	N	N	Y
Proxmire	N	N	N	N	N	N
WYOMING						
Simpson	Y	Y	N	N	Y	Y
Wallop	Y	Y	N	Y	Y	Y

Democrats   **Republicans**

*Byrd elected as an independent.

---

257. S 884. Agriculture and Food Act of 1981. Helms, R-N.C., motion to table (kill) the Quayle, R-Ind., amendment to eliminate the sugar price support program. Motion agreed to 61-33: R 30-21; D 31-12 (ND 19-11, SD 12-1), Sept. 17, 1981.

258. S 884. Agriculture and Food Act of 1981. Huddleston, D-Ky., motion to table (kill) the Pressler, R-S.D., amendment to limit imports of casein to 50 percent of the average volume of imports over the preceding five years. Motion agreed to 60-35: R 39-11; D 21-24 (ND 11-19, SD 10-5), Sept. 17, 1981. A "yea" was a vote supporting the president's position.

259. S 884. Agriculture and Food Act of 1981. Helms, R-N.C., motion to table (kill) the Hatfield, R-Ore., amendment to repeal tobacco acreage allotment, quota and price support programs. Motion agreed to 53-42: R 25-25; D 28-17 (ND 15-15, SD 13-2), Sept. 17, 1981.

260. S 884. Agriculture and Food Act of 1981. Helms, R-N.C., motion to table (kill) the Eagleton, D-Mo., amendment to authorize the agriculture secretary to adjust tobacco price support loan rates as needed to make various grades of American tobacco competitive with foreign tobacco. Motion agreed to 48-45: R 26-23; D 22-22 (ND 8-21, SD 14-1), Sept. 17, 1981.

261. S 884. Agriculture and Food Act of 1981. Inouye, D-Hawaii, motion to table (kill) the Humphrey, R-N.H., amendment to reduce to 16.5 cents per pound, from 18 cents, the price support for sugar. Motion agreed to 64-30: R 32-18; D 32-12 (ND 18-11, SD 14-1), Sept. 17, 1981.

262. S 884. Agriculture and Food Act of 1981. Dole, R-Kan., motion to table (kill) the Zorinsky, D-Neb., amendment to substitute higher target prices for wheat, feed grains, cotton and rice, and higher price supports for dairy than contained in a committee compromise approved Sept. 15. Motion agreed to 60-35: R 45-6; D 15-29 (ND 10-19, SD 5-10), Sept. 17, 1981. A "yea" was a vote supporting the president's position.

CQ Senate Votes 263 - 270

Corresponding to Congressional Record Votes 266, 267, 268, 269, 270, 271, 272, 273

	263	264	265	266	267	268	269	270
ALABAMA								
Denton	Y	N	Y	Y	Y	P	Y	Y
Heflin	N	Y	Y	N	N	Y	Y	N
ALASKA								
Murkowski	?	?	?	?	?	?	?	?
Stevens	Y	N	N	Y	Y	N	Y	Y
ARIZONA								
Goldwater	Y	N	N	Y	Y	Y	Y	N
DeConcini	Y	N	Y	Y	N	N	N	N
ARKANSAS								
Bumpers	N	?	?	?	-	?	?	?
Pryor	N	Y	Y	N	N	N	N	N
CALIFORNIA								
Hayakawa	Y	N	N	Y	Y	N	Y	Y
Cranston	?	?	?	?	?	?	?	?
COLORADO								
Armstrong	Y	N	N	Y	Y	P	Y	Y
Hart	N	Y	Y	N	N	Y	N	N
CONNECTICUT								
Weicker	?	?	?	?	?	?	?	?
Dodd	?	?	?	?	?	?	?	?
DELAWARE								
Roth	Y	Y	N	Y	Y	N	N	N
Biden	Y	Y	N	Y	Y	N	N	N
FLORIDA								
Hawkins	Y	N	Y	N	Y	N	Y	Y
Chiles	Y	Y	Y	?	?	?	?	?
GEORGIA								
Mattingly	Y	N	N	Y	Y	Y	Y	Y
Nunn	N	Y	Y	Y	N	N	Y	N
HAWAII								
Inouye	?	?	?	?	?	?	?	?
Matsunaga	N	Y	Y	N	N	N	Y	Y
IDAHO								
McClure	Y	N	N	Y	Y	N	Y	Y
Symms	Y	N	N	Y	Y	Y	Y	X
ILLINOIS								
Percy	Y	N	N	Y	Y	Y	N	Y
Dixon	Y	Y	Y	N	N	N	N	Y
INDIANA								
Lugar	Y	N	N	Y	Y	Y	Y	Y
Quayle	Y	N	N	Y	Y	Y	N	Y

	263	264	265	266	267	268	269	270
IOWA								
Grassley	Y	N	Y	Y	N	Y	Y	Y
Jepsen	Y	N	N	Y	Y	N	Y	Y
KANSAS								
Dole	Y	N	N	Y	Y	N	Y	Y
Kassebaum	Y	N	Y	N	N	?	N	Y
KENTUCKY								
Ford	N	Y	Y	N	N	N	Y	Y
Huddleston	N	Y	Y	N	N	N	Y	Y
LOUISIANA								
Johnston	Y	Y	Y	Y	N	?	?	?
Long	Y	N	Y	Y	Y	N	Y	Y
MAINE								
Cohen	Y	N	N	Y	N	Y	N	Y
Mitchell	Y	Y	N	?	?	?	X	?
MARYLAND								
Mathias	Y	Y	N	Y	Y	N	N	N
Sarbanes	Y	Y	Y	Y	N	N	Y	N
MASSACHUSETTS								
Kennedy	?	?	?	Y	N	N	N	N
Tsongas	Y	Y	N	?	?	?	?	?
MICHIGAN								
Levin	?	Y	Y	N	N	N	N	N
Riegle	?	Y	Y	N	N	P	N	N
MINNESOTA								
Boschwitz	Y	N	N	Y	N	Y	Y	Y
Durenberger	Y	Y	Y	N	N	N	N	Y
MISSISSIPPI								
Cochran	Y	N	N	Y	Y	N	Y	Y
Stennis	Y	Y	Y	Y	N	N	#	+
MISSOURI								
Danforth	Y	N	N	Y	Y	N	Y	Y
Eagleton	N	Y	Y	N	N	N	N	N
MONTANA								
Baucus	N	Y	Y	N	Y	N	N	N
Melcher	N	Y	Y	N	N	Y	Y	N
NEBRASKA								
Exon	N	Y	Y	N	N	P	N	N
Zorinsky	N	Y	Y	N	N	N	N	N
NEVADA								
Laxalt	Y	?	?	?	?	?	?	?
Cannon	Y	Y	N	Y	Y	N	N	N

	263	264	265	266	267	268	269	270
NEW HAMPSHIRE								
Humphrey	Y	N	N	N	Y	Y	N	N
Rudman	Y	N	N	Y	Y	Y	Y	Y
NEW JERSEY								
Bradley	?	?	?	?	?	?	-	?
Williams	Y	?	?	Y	N	N	N	N
NEW MEXICO								
Domenici	Y	N	N	Y	Y	N	Y	Y
Schmitt	Y	N	N	Y	N	Y	N	Y
NEW YORK								
D'Amato	Y	N	N	Y	Y	#	+	+
Moynihan	Y	N	N	Y	N	Y	N	N
NORTH CAROLINA								
East	Y	Y	Y	Y	Y	N	Y	Y
Helms	Y	Y	Y	Y	Y	Y	Y	Y
NORTH DAKOTA								
Andrews	N	N	N	Y	N	Y	N	Y
Burdick	N	Y	Y	N	N	N	Y	N
OHIO								
Glenn	N	Y	Y	N	N	N	N	Y
Metzenbaum	N	Y	Y	N	Y	N	N	N
OKLAHOMA								
Nickles	Y	Y	Y	N	N	P	N	Y
Boren	N	Y	Y	N	N	N	N	N
OREGON								
Hatfield	Y	N	N	Y	Y	N	N	Y
Packwood	Y	N	N	Y	Y	N	N	Y
PENNSYLVANIA								
Heinz	Y	N	N	Y	+	?	?	#
Specter	Y	N	N	Y	N	X	Y	X
RHODE ISLAND								
Chafee	Y	N	N	Y	Y	N	N	N
Pell	Y	N	N	Y	Y	N	N	N
SOUTH CAROLINA								
Thurmond	Y	N	N	Y	Y	Y	Y	Y
Hollings	?	?	?	?	?	?	#	?
SOUTH DAKOTA								
Abdnor	N	N	Y	N	N	N	Y	Y
Pressler	N	Y	Y	N	N	N	Y	Y
TENNESSEE								
Baker	?	Y	Y	Y	Y	Y	N	Y
Sasser	N	Y	Y	N	N	N	Y	Y

	263	264	265	266	267	268	269	270
TEXAS								
Tower	Y	N	N	Y	+	X	+	+
Bentsen	Y	Y	Y	Y	N	Y	N	N
UTAH								
Garn	Y	N	N	Y	Y	Y	N	N
Hatch	Y	N	N	Y	Y	Y	N	Y
VERMONT								
Stafford	?	?	?	?	?	?	?	?
Leahy	Y	Y	Y	N	N	N	N	N
VIRGINIA								
Warner	Y	N	N	Y	N	Y	N	Y
Byrd*	Y	N	N	Y	Y	Y	P	Y
WASHINGTON								
Gorton	Y	N	N	Y	N	N	N	N
Jackson	N	Y	Y	N	N	N	N	N
WEST VIRGINIA								
Byrd	Y	Y	Y	Y	N	Y	N	Y
Randolph	N	Y	Y	N	N	N	N	Y
WISCONSIN								
Kasten	Y	N	Y	N	N	Y	N	N
Proxmire	Y	Y	N	Y	Y	Y	N	N
WYOMING								
Simpson	Y	N	N	Y	N	Y	N	N
Wallop	Y	N	N	Y	N	Y	N	Y

KEY

- Y Voted for (yea).
- # Paired for.
- + Announced for.
- N Voted against (nay).
- X Paired against.
- - Announced against.
- P Voted "present".
- C Voted "present" to avoid possible conflict of interest.
- ? Did not vote or otherwise make a position known.

Democrats *Republicans*

* Byrd elected as an independent.

263. S 884. Agriculture and Food Act of 1981. Dole, R-Kan., motion to table (kill) the Melcher, D-Mont., amendment to the Lugar, R-Ind., amendment *(see vote 265, below)*, to raise the loan rate to $4 per bushel for wheat and $2.80 per bushel for corn through the 1985 crop year. Motion agreed to 65-23: R 46-3; D 19-20 (ND 13-12, SD 6-8), Sept. 18, 1981.

264. S 884. Agriculture and Food Act of 1981. Lugar, R-Ind., motion to table (kill) the Dole, R-Kan., amendment to the Lugar, R-Ind., amendment *(see vote 265, below)*, to reduce target prices for wheat, feed grains, rice and cotton. Motion rejected 42-46: R 8-41; D 34-5 (ND 23-3, SD 11-2), Sept. 18, 1981. (Subsequently, the Dole amendment was re-offered as a separate amendment to the bill and was adopted *(see vote 267, below)*.)

265. S 884. Agriculture and Food Act of 1981. Huddleston, D-Ky., motion to table (kill) the Lugar, R-Ind., amendment to change loan rates, land diversion and payment yield for the 1982 through 1985 crops of wheat, feed grains, rice and cotton, and to eliminate target prices. Motion agreed to 45-43: R 14-35; D 31-8 (ND 19-7, SD 12-1), Sept. 18, 1981.

266. S 884. Agriculture and Food Act of 1981. Dole, R-Kan., motion to table (kill) the Baucus, D-Mont., amendment, to the Dole amendment *(see vote 267, below)*, to increase the loan level for wheat for the 1982 crop year to $3.60 per bushel from $3.50 per bushel. Motion agreed to 59-28: R 42-7; D 17-21 (ND 11-15, SD 6-6), Sept. 18, 1981.

267. S 884. Agriculture and Food Act of 1981. Dole, R-Kan., amendment to change loan rates, target prices, disaster payments, reduction program and land diversion for the 1982 through 1985 crops of wheat, feed grains, cotton and rice. Adopted 46-39: R 39-8; D 7-31 (ND 5-21, SD 2-10), Sept. 18, 1981. A "yea" was a vote supporting the president's position.

268. S 884. Agriculture and Food Act of 1981. Moynihan, D-N.Y., amendment to express the sense of Congress that the taxing power of government should not be used to regulate the agricultural economy or bring about social change. Rejected 22-54: R 14-28; D 8-26 (ND 6-18, SD 2-8), Sept. 18, 1981.

269. S 884. Agriculture and Food Act of 1981. Huddleston, D-Ky., motion to table (kill) the Eagleton, D-Mo., amendment to allow the agriculture secretary to establish price support levels for certain grades of tobacco deemed by the secretary to be in excessive supply and non-competitive, except that the level may not go below 75 percent of the level established for the 1982 crop of that kind of tobacco. Motion agreed to 41-40: R 28-17; D 13-23 (ND 6-20, SD 7-3), Sept. 18, 1981.

270. S 884. Agriculture and Food Act of 1981. Passage of the bill to revise and extend commodity price support programs administered by the Department of Agriculture for fiscal years 1982 through 1985. Passed 49-32: R 38-7; D 11-25 (ND 6-20, SD 5-5), Sept. 18, 1981. A "yea" was a vote supporting the president's position.

	271	272	273	274	275	276	277	278
ALABAMA								
Denton	Y	Y	Y	N	Y	N	N	Y
Heflin	Y	Y	Y	N	Y	N	Y	N
ALASKA								
Murkowski	Y	Y	Y	Y	Y	N	N	Y
Stevens	Y	Y	Y	N	Y	N	N	Y
ARIZONA								
Goldwater	Y	Y	Y	N	Y	N	N	Y
DeConcini	Y	Y	N	Y	N	Y	Y	N
ARKANSAS								
Bumpers	Y	Y	N	Y	N	Y	Y	N
Pryor	Y	Y	N	Y	N	Y	N	N
CALIFORNIA								
Hayakawa	Y	Y	Y	N	Y	N	N	Y
Cranston	Y	Y	N	Y	N	Y	N	Y
COLORADO								
Armstrong	Y	Y	Y	N	Y	N	N	Y
Hart	Y	Y	N	Y	N	Y	Y	N
CONNECTICUT								
Weicker	Y	Y	Y	?	N	Y	N	Y
Dodd	Y	Y	N	Y	N	Y	N	Y
DELAWARE								
Roth	Y	Y	Y	N	Y	N	Y	N
Biden	Y	Y	N	?	N	Y	Y	N
FLORIDA								
Hawkins	Y	Y	Y	N	Y	N	N	Y
Chiles	Y	Y	N	Y	N	Y	Y	N
GEORGIA								
Mattingly	Y	Y	Y	N	Y	N	Y	N
Nunn	Y	Y	N	N	Y	N	Y	N
HAWAII								
Inouye	Y	Y	N	?	N	Y	N	Y
Matsunaga	Y	Y	Y	?	?	?	?	?
IDAHO								
McClure	Y	Y	Y	N	Y	N	N	Y
Symms	Y	Y	Y	N	Y	N	N	Y
ILLINOIS								
Percy	Y	Y	Y	Y	N	Y	Y	Y
Dixon	Y	Y	Y	N	Y	N	Y	Y
INDIANA								
Lugar	Y	Y	Y	N	Y	N	N	Y
Quayle	Y	Y	Y	N	Y	N	N	Y

	271	272	273	274	275	276	277	278
IOWA								
Grassley	Y	Y	Y	Y	Y	N	Y	N
Jepsen	Y	Y	Y	N	Y	N	N	Y
KANSAS								
Dole	Y	Y	Y	N	Y	N	N	Y
Kassebaum	Y	Y	Y	N	Y	Y	Y	N
KENTUCKY								
Ford	Y	Y	Y	Y	N	Y	Y	N
Huddleston	Y	Y	N	Y	N	Y	Y	Y
LOUISIANA								
Johnston	Y	Y	Y	Y	N	Y	N	Y
Long	Y	Y	Y	N	Y	Y	Y	Y
MAINE								
Cohen	Y	Y	Y	N	Y	N	N	N
Mitchell	Y	Y	N	Y	N	Y	Y	N
MARYLAND								
Mathias	Y	Y	Y	N	Y	N	Y	N
Sarbanes	Y	Y	N	Y	N	Y	Y	N
MASSACHUSETTS								
Kennedy	Y	Y	N	Y	N	Y	Y	N
Tsongas	Y	Y	N	Y	N	Y	N	Y
MICHIGAN								
Levin	Y	Y	N	Y	N	Y	Y	N
Riegle	Y	Y	N	Y	-	?	?	-
MINNESOTA								
Boschwitz	Y	Y	Y	Y	Y	N	N	N
Durenberger	Y	Y	Y	N	Y	N	Y	N
MISSISSIPPI								
Cochran	Y	Y	Y	N	Y	N	N	N
Stennis	Y	Y	Y	N	Y	Y	Y	N
MISSOURI								
Danforth	Y	Y	Y	N	Y	N	N	N
Eagleton	Y	Y	N	Y	N	Y	N	Y
MONTANA								
Baucus	+	+	-	Y	N	Y	Y	Y
Melcher	Y	Y	Y	N	Y	N	Y	N
NEBRASKA								
Exon	Y	Y	N	Y	N	Y	Y	N
Zorinsky	Y	Y	Y	N	Y	N	Y	N
NEVADA								
Laxalt	Y	Y	Y	N	Y	N	N	Y
Cannon	Y	Y	Y	Y	N	Y	Y	N

	271	272	273	274	275	276	277	278
NEW HAMPSHIRE								
Humphrey	Y	Y	Y	N	Y	N	N	Y
Rudman	Y	Y	Y	Y	Y	N	N	Y
NEW JERSEY								
Bradley	Y	Y	N	Y	N	Y	Y	N
Williams	Y	Y	N	Y	N	Y	N	Y
NEW MEXICO								
Domenici	Y	Y	Y	N	Y	N	N	Y
Schmitt	Y	Y	Y	N	Y	N	Y	N
NEW YORK								
D'Amato	Y	Y	Y	Y	Y	N	N	Y
Moynihan	Y	Y	N	Y	N	Y	Y	N
NORTH CAROLINA								
East	Y	Y	Y	N	Y	N	N	N
Helms	Y	Y	Y	N	Y	N	N	N
NORTH DAKOTA								
Andrews	Y	Y	Y	Y	Y	N	N	Y
Burdick	Y	Y	Y	Y	N	Y	Y	N
OHIO								
Glenn	Y	Y	Y	N	Y	N	Y	N
Metzenbaum	Y	N	N	N	Y	Y	N	N
OKLAHOMA								
Nickles	Y	Y	Y	N	Y	N	N	N
Boren	Y	Y	Y	N	N	Y	Y	N
OREGON								
Hatfield	Y	Y	Y	Y	N	Y	Y	N
Packwood	Y	Y	Y	N	Y	N	N	Y
PENNSYLVANIA								
Heinz	Y	Y	Y	Y	N	Y	Y	N
Specter	Y	Y	Y	Y	N	Y	N	Y
RHODE ISLAND								
Chafee	Y	Y	Y	Y	N	Y	Y	N
Pell	Y	Y	Y	Y	N	Y	Y	N
SOUTH CAROLINA								
Thurmond	Y	Y	Y	N	Y	N	N	N
Hollings	Y	Y	Y	N	N	Y	N	Y
SOUTH DAKOTA								
Abdnor	Y	Y	Y	N	Y	N	N	Y
Pressler	Y	Y	Y	Y	N	Y	Y	N
TENNESSEE								
Baker	Y	Y	Y	Y	N	Y	N	N
Sasser	Y	?	N	Y	N	Y	Y	N

	271	272	273	274	275	276	277	278
TEXAS								
Tower	Y	Y	Y	N	Y	N	N	Y
Bentsen	Y	Y	Y	Y	N	Y	Y	N
UTAH								
Garn	Y	Y	Y	N	Y	N	N	Y
Hatch	Y	Y	Y	N	Y	N	N	Y
VERMONT								
Stafford	Y	Y	Y	N	Y	N	N	Y
Leahy	Y	Y	N	Y	N	Y	Y	Y
VIRGINIA								
Warner	Y	Y	Y	N	Y	N	N	Y
Byrd*	Y	Y	Y	N	Y	N	Y	N
WASHINGTON								
Gorton	Y	Y	Y	Y	N	Y	N	Y
Jackson	Y	Y	Y	Y	N	Y	N	N
WEST VIRGINIA								
Byrd	Y	Y	N	Y	N	Y	Y	N
Randolph	Y	Y	N	N	N	Y	Y	N
WISCONSIN								
Kasten	Y	Y	Y	N	Y	N	N	Y
Proxmire	Y	N	N	Y	N	Y	Y	N
WYOMING								
Simpson	Y	Y	Y	N	Y	N	N	N
Wallop	Y	Y	Y	N	Y	N	N	Y

KEY

- Y Voted for (yea).
- \# Paired for.
- \+ Announced for.
- N Voted against (nay).
- X Paired against.
- \- Announced against.
- P Voted "present".
- C Voted "present" to avoid possible conflict of interest.
- ? Did not vote or otherwise make a position known.

Democrats *Republicans*

* Byrd elected as an independent.

271. O'Connor Nomination. Confirmation of President Reagan's nomination of Sandra Day O'Connor of Arizona to be associate justice of the Supreme Court. Confirmed 99-0: R 53-0; D 46-0 (ND 31-0, SD 15-0), Sept. 21, 1981. A "yea" was a vote supporting the president's position.

272. Miller Nomination. Confirmation of President Reagan's nomination of James C. Miller III of Washington, D.C., to be a commissioner of the Federal Trade Commission. Confirmed 97-2: R 53-0; D 44-2 (ND 29-2, SD 15-0), Sept. 21, 1981. A "yea" was a vote supporting the president's position.

273. Richards Nomination. Confirmation of President Reagan's nomination of James R. Richards of Virginia to be inspector general of the Department of Energy. Confirmed 71-28: R 53-0; D 18-28 (ND 9-22, SD 9-6), Sept. 21, 1981. A "yea" was a vote supporting the president's position.

274. S 1196. Foreign Aid Authorization. Pell, D-R.I., amendment, to the Lugar, R-Ind., amendment, to establish as a requirement, rather than as the sense of the Senate, that for U.S. military or economic aid to the government of El Salvador to continue, the president of the United States must certify every 180 days after enactment of the bill that the Salvadoran junta has met certain conditions aimed at protecting human rights and fostering economic and political reforms. Adopted 54-42: R 17-35; D 37-7 (ND 28-1, SD 9-6), Sept. 23, 1981.

275. S 1196. Foreign Aid Authorization. Helms, R-N.C., substitute amendment, to the Lugar, R-Ind., amendment, as modified by the Pell, D-R.I., amendment *(see vote 274, above)*. The Helms amendment would have transformed proposed conditions on U.S. military aid to El Salvador into a statement of the sense of Congress that U.S. military aid should be used to encourage a peaceful and democratic solution of the civil war there, protect human rights and promote economic and political reforms. Rejected 47-51: R 43-10; D 4-41 (ND 0-30, SD 4-11), Sept. 24, 1981. A "yea" was a vote supporting the president's position. (Subsequently, the Lugar amendment, as amended, was adopted by voice vote.)

276. S 1196. Foreign Aid Authorization. Cranston, D-Calif., motion to table (kill) the Pell, D-R.I., motion to reconsider the vote *(vote 275, above)* by which the Helms, R-N.C., amendment was rejected. Motion agreed to 52-46: R 10-43; D 42-3 (ND 30-0, SD 12-3), Sept. 24, 1981.

277. H J Res 325. Fiscal 1982 Continuing Appropriations. Judgment of the Senate concerning the chair's ruling that the Stevens, R-Alaska, amendment *(see vote 278, below)* (to remove the $3,000 limit on tax deductions for living expenses of members of Congress while away from home) was out of order because it constituted legislation on an appropriations bill. Ruling of the chair rejected 44-54: R 10-43; D 34-11 (ND 22-8, SD 12-3), Sept. 24, 1981.

278. H J Res 325. Fiscal 1982 Continuing Appropriations. Stevens, R-Alaska, amendment to remove the existing $3,000 limit on tax deductions for living expenses for members of Congress while away from home. Adopted 50-48: R 36-17; D 14-31 (ND 10-20, SD 4-11), Sept. 24, 1981.

CQ Senate Votes 279 - 283

Corresponding to Congressional Record Votes 282, 283, 284, 285, 286

	279 280 281 282 283		279 280 281 282 283		279 280 281 282 283
ALABAMA		**IOWA**		**NEW HAMPSHIRE**	
Denton	Y N Y N Y	*Grassley*	N Y Y Y Y	*Humphrey*	? ? ? ? ?
Heflin	N N N Y Y	*Jepsen*	Y Y Y N Y	*Rudman*	Y Y Y Y N
ALASKA		**KANSAS**		**NEW JERSEY**	
Murkowski	Y Y Y N Y	*Dole*	Y Y Y N Y	Bradley	N Y N Y Y
Stevens	Y Y Y N N	*Kassebaum*	N Y Y N Y	Williams	N N N Y Y
ARIZONA		**KENTUCKY**		**NEW MEXICO**	
Goldwater	Y Y ? N N	Ford	N N N Y Y	*Domenici*	N Y Y N N
DeConcini	N Y N Y Y	Huddleston	N N N N Y	*Schmitt*	N Y Y Y N
ARKANSAS		**LOUISIANA**		**NEW YORK**	
Bumpers	N N N Y Y	Johnston	N N N N Y	*D'Amato*	Y Y Y N Y
Pryor	N N N Y Y	Long	Y Y Y Y N	Moynihan	Y Y N Y Y
CALIFORNIA		**MAINE**		**NORTH CAROLINA**	
Hayakawa	Y Y Y N Y	*Cohen*	Y ? ? # ?	*East*	N Y Y N Y
Cranston	Y Y N N N	Mitchell	N N N Y Y	*Helms*	N Y Y Y Y
COLORADO		**MARYLAND**		**NORTH DAKOTA**	
Armstrong	N Y Y N Y	*Mathias*	Y Y Y N N	*Andrews*	N Y Y N Y
Hart	N Y N Y Y	Sarbanes	Y N N Y Y	Burdick	N Y N Y Y
CONNECTICUT		**MASSACHUSETTS**		**OHIO**	
Weicker	Y Y N N Y	Kennedy	Y Y N Y N	Glenn	? ? ? ? Y
Dodd	N N N N Y	Tsongas	Y Y N ? ?	Metzenbaum	N N N Y Y
DELAWARE		**MICHIGAN**		**OKLAHOMA**	
Roth	N Y Y N Y	Levin	N Y N Y Y	*Nickles*	N Y Y N Y
Biden	N N N ? ?	Riegle	- ? - ? +	Boren	N N N Y Y
FLORIDA		**MINNESOTA**		**OREGON**	
Hawkins	N N N N Y	*Boschwitz*	Y Y Y N Y	*Hatfield*	Y Y Y N N
Chiles	N N N Y Y	*Durenberger*	Y Y Y N Y	*Packwood*	Y Y Y N N
GEORGIA		**MISSISSIPPI**		**PENNSYLVANIA**	
Mattingly	N Y Y Y Y	*Cochran*	Y Y Y N N	*Heinz*	N ? ? ? ?
Nunn	Y N N Y Y	Stennis	N N ? N Y	*Specter*	Y Y N N Y
HAWAII		**MISSOURI**		**RHODE ISLAND**	
Inouye	Y N N N N	*Danforth*	Y Y Y N Y	*Chafee*	Y Y Y N Y
Matsunaga	? ? ? ? ?	Eagleton	Y N N N Y	Pell	Y Y N Y Y
IDAHO		**MONTANA**		**SOUTH CAROLINA**	
McClure	Y Y Y N Y	Baucus	Y N N Y Y	*Thurmond*	Y Y Y Y Y
Symms	Y Y Y N Y	Melcher	Y Y N Y Y	Hollings	Y N N N N
ILLINOIS		**NEBRASKA**		**SOUTH DAKOTA**	
Percy	Y Y Y N Y	Exon	N N N Y Y	*Abdnor*	N Y Y Y Y
Dixon	N Y N Y Y	Zorinsky	N N N Y Y	*Pressler*	N Y N Y Y
INDIANA		**NEVADA**		**TENNESSEE**	
Lugar	Y Y Y N Y	*Laxalt*	Y Y Y N Y	*Baker*	Y Y Y N N
Quayle	Y Y Y N Y	Cannon	N N N Y Y	Sasser	N N N Y Y

	279 280 281 282 283
TEXAS	
Tower	Y Y Y X Y
Bentsen	Y N N ? ?
UTAH	
Garn	Y Y Y N Y
Hatch	Y Y Y N Y
VERMONT	
Stafford	Y Y Y Y Y
Leahy	Y N N Y Y
VIRGINIA	
Warner	? ? ? ? ?
Byrd*	N ? ? ? Y
WASHINGTON	
Gorton	Y Y Y Y Y
Jackson	N N N Y Y
WEST VIRGINIA	
Byrd	N N N Y Y
Randolph	Y N N Y Y
WISCONSIN	
Kasten	N Y Y Y Y
Proxmire	N N N Y Y
WYOMING	
Simpson	N Y Y N Y
Wallop	Y Y Y N Y

KEY

Y Voted for (yea).
\# Paired for.
+ Announced for.
N Voted against (nay).
X Paired against.
- Announced against.
P Voted "present".
C Voted "present" to avoid possible conflict of interest.
? Did not vote or otherwise make a position known.

Democrats   **Republicans**

* Byrd elected as an independent.

279. H J Res 325. Fiscal 1982 Continuing Appropriations. Stevens, R-Alaska, amendment to raise the pay caps for senior government employees, not including members of Congress. Adopted 50-45: R 34-17; D 16-28 (ND 12-17, SD 4-11), Sept. 24, 1981.

280. H J Res 325. Fiscal 1982 Continuing Appropriations. Judgment of the Senate concerning the chair's ruling that the Chiles, D-Fla., amendment (to extend for two years the existing moratorium on interstate operation of trust companies by national banks) was out of order because it constituted legislation on an appropriations bill. Ruling of the chair upheld 60-32: R 47-2; D 13-30 (ND 12-17, SD 1-13), Sept. 24, 1981.

281. H J Res 325. Fiscal 1982 Continuing Appropriations. Hatfield, R-Ore., motion to table (kill) the Sasser, D-Tenn., amendment to reduce by 5 percent travel costs of federal agencies, except those involved in defense or law enforcement. Motion agreed to 46-44: R 44-4; D 2-40 (ND 1-28, SD 1-12), Sept. 24, 1981. (The tabling motion also had the effect of killing the Chiles, D-Fla., amendment to the Sasser amendment to restore the Social Security minimum benefit to current recipients.)

282. H J Res 325. Fiscal 1982 Continuing Appropriations. Proxmire, D-Wis., amendment to delete from the resolution the provision eliminating the $25,000 annual ceiling on honoraria received by individual senators. Rejected 43-45: R 12-36; D 31-9 (ND 22-5, SD 9-4), Sept. 24, 1981.

283. H J Res 325. Fiscal 1982 Continuing Appropriations. Proxmire, D-Wis., amendment to limit to 8,037 the number of full-time Senate employees and employees of the Architect of the Capitol assigned to the Senate, and to prohibit use of funds for the planning of any new Senate office building. Adopted 76-15: R 39-10; D 37-5 (ND 25-3, SD 12-2), Sept. 24, 1981.

	284	285	286	287	288	289	290	291
ALABAMA								
Denton	Y	Y	Y	Y	Y	Y	Y	Y
Heflin	N	N	N	Y	Y	Y	N	Y
ALASKA								
Murkowski	Y	Y	Y	Y	Y	Y	Y	Y
Stevens	Y	Y	Y	Y	Y	Y	Y	Y
ARIZONA								
Goldwater	N	?	?	?	Y	Y	Y	Y
DeConcini	?	?	?	?	Y	Y	N	Y
ARKANSAS								
Bumpers	N	N	N	N	Y	Y	N	N
Pryor	N	N	N	Y	Y	Y	N	Y
CALIFORNIA								
Hayakawa	Y	Y	Y	Y	Y	Y	Y	Y
Cranston	N	N	N	N	Y	Y	N	X
COLORADO								
Armstrong	N	Y	Y	Y	Y	N	Y	Y
Hart	N	Y	N	N	Y	Y	N	N
CONNECTICUT								
Weicker	Y	Y	Y	N	Y	Y	Y	Y
Dodd	N	N	N	N	Y	Y	N	N
DELAWARE								
Roth	N	Y	Y	Y	Y	Y	Y	Y
Biden	?	N	N	N	Y	Y	N	N
FLORIDA								
Hawkins	N	Y	Y	Y	Y	Y	Y	Y
Chiles	N	N	N	Y	Y	Y	N	N
GEORGIA								
Mattingly	Y	Y	Y	Y	Y	N	Y	Y
Nunn	N	Y	N	Y	Y	Y	N	N
HAWAII								
Inouye	?	?	?	?	Y	Y	N	N
Matsunaga	?	N	Y	Y	Y	Y	N	Y
IDAHO								
McClure	Y	?	?	?	Y	Y	Y	Y
Symms	N	Y	+	Y	Y	N	Y	Y
ILLINOIS								
Percy	Y	Y	Y	Y	Y	Y	Y	Y
Dixon	N	Y	Y	Y	Y	Y	N	Y
INDIANA								
Lugar	Y	Y	Y	Y	Y	Y	Y	Y
Quayle	Y	Y	Y	Y	Y	N	Y	Y
IOWA								
Grassley	N	Y	Y	Y	Y	N	Y	Y
Jepsen	N	Y	Y	Y	Y	Y	Y	Y
KANSAS								
Dole	Y	Y	Y	Y	Y	Y	Y	Y
Kassebaum	Y	Y	Y	Y	Y	Y	Y	Y
KENTUCKY								
Ford	N	N	N	Y	Y	Y	N	Y
Huddleston	N	N	N	Y	Y	Y	N	N
LOUISIANA								
Johnston	Y	?	?	?	Y	Y	N	Y
Long	Y	Y	Y	Y	Y	Y	Y	Y
MAINE								
Cohen	Y	Y	Y	Y	Y	Y	Y	N
Mitchell	N	N	N	Y	Y	N	N	N
MARYLAND								
Mathias	?	?	Y	N	Y	Y	N	N
Sarbanes	N	N	N	Y	Y	Y	N	N
MASSACHUSETTS								
Kennedy	Y	N	N	N	Y	N	N	N
Tsongas	N	Y	N	N	Y	Y	N	N
MICHIGAN								
Levin	N	N	N	Y	Y	N	N	N
Riegle	N	N	N	Y	Y	Y	N	N
MINNESOTA								
Boschwitz	Y	Y	Y	Y	Y	Y	Y	Y
Durenberger	Y	Y	Y	Y	Y	Y	Y	Y
MISSISSIPPI								
Cochran	Y	Y	Y	Y	Y	Y	Y	Y
Stennis	N	?	?	?	Y	Y	N	Y
MISSOURI								
Danforth	Y	Y	Y	Y	Y	Y	Y	Y
Eagleton	N	N	Y	N	Y	Y	N	N
MONTANA								
Baucus	N	N	N	Y	Y	Y	N	Y
Melcher	N	N	Y	Y	+	+	+	#
NEBRASKA								
Exon	N	N	N	Y	Y	N	N	N
Zorinsky	N	N	Y	Y	Y	N	Y	Y
NEVADA								
Laxalt	Y	Y	Y	Y	Y	Y	Y	Y
Cannon	N	N	Y	Y	Y	Y	N	N
NEW HAMPSHIRE								
Humphrey	Y	Y	Y	?	Y	N	Y	Y
Rudman	Y	Y	Y	?	Y	Y	Y	N
NEW JERSEY								
Bradley	?	Y	N	Y	Y	Y	N	N
Williams	Y	?	?	?	Y	Y	N	N
NEW MEXICO								
Domenici	Y	Y	Y	Y	Y	Y	Y	Y
Schmitt	Y	Y	Y	Y	Y	Y	Y	Y
NEW YORK								
D'Amato	Y	Y	Y	Y	Y	Y	Y	Y
Moynihan	N	N	N	Y	Y	Y	N	N
NORTH CAROLINA								
East	Y	Y	Y	Y	Y	Y	Y	Y
Helms	N	Y	Y	Y	Y	N	Y	Y
NORTH DAKOTA								
Andrews	Y	Y	Y	Y	Y	Y	Y	Y
Burdick	N	N	N	Y	Y	Y	N	Y
OHIO								
Glenn	N	Y	N	Y	Y	N	N	Y
Metzenbaum	N	N	Y	Y	Y	N	N	N
OKLAHOMA								
Nickles	N	Y	N	Y	Y	N	Y	Y
Boren	N	N	N	Y	Y	Y	N	Y
OREGON								
Hatfield	Y	Y	Y	Y	Y	Y	Y	Y
Packwood	Y	Y	Y	Y	Y	Y	Y	Y
PENNSYLVANIA								
Heinz	Y	Y	Y	Y	Y	Y	Y	Y
Specter	Y	Y	Y	Y	Y	Y	Y	Y
RHODE ISLAND								
Chafee	Y	Y	Y	Y	Y	Y	Y	Y
Pell	Y	N	N	N	Y	Y	N	N
SOUTH CAROLINA								
Thurmond	Y	Y	Y	Y	Y	Y	Y	Y
Hollings	Y	N	N	N	Y	Y	N	N
SOUTH DAKOTA								
Abdnor	Y	Y	Y	Y	Y	Y	Y	Y
Pressler	?	?	?	?	Y	N	N	Y
TENNESSEE								
Baker	Y	Y	Y	Y	Y	Y	Y	Y
Sasser	N	N	N	Y	Y	Y	N	N
TEXAS								
Tower	Y	Y	Y	Y	Y	Y	Y	Y
Bentsen	?	Y	Y	Y	Y	Y	Y	Y
UTAH								
Garn	Y	Y	Y	Y	Y	Y	Y	Y
Hatch	N	Y	Y	Y	Y	N	Y	Y
VERMONT								
Stafford	Y	Y	Y	Y	Y	Y	Y	Y
Leahy	N	N	Y	N	Y	Y	N	N
VIRGINIA								
Warner	?	?	?	?	Y	Y	Y	Y
Byrd*	N	Y	Y	Y	Y	N	Y	N
WASHINGTON								
Gorton	Y	Y	Y	Y	Y	N	Y	Y
Jackson	Y	N	Y	Y	Y	Y	N	N
WEST VIRGINIA								
Byrd	N	N	N	Y	Y	Y	N	Y
Randolph	N	N	N	Y	Y	Y	N	Y
WISCONSIN								
Kasten	Y	Y	Y	Y	Y	N	Y	Y
Proxmire	N	Y	N	Y	Y	Y	N	Y
WYOMING								
Simpson	Y	?	?	?	Y	Y	Y	Y
Wallop	Y	+	+	+	Y	Y	Y	Y

Democrats *Republicans*

* Byrd elected as an independent.

KEY

Y	Voted for (yea).
#	Paired for.
+	Announced for.
N	Voted against (nay).
X	Paired against.
-	Announced against.
P	Voted "present".
C	Voted "present" to avoid possible conflict of interest.
?	Did not vote or otherwise make a position known.

284. H J Res 325. Fiscal 1982 Continuing Appropriations. Passage of the joint resolution to provide funding authority during the period Oct. 1 through Nov. 20, 1981, for federal agencies whose regular fiscal 1982 appropriations had not been enacted; to appropriate $934,616,108 for fiscal 1982 for legislative branch operations, excluding the House of Representatives; and to remove certain limits on tax deductions claimed by members of Congress and on honoraria received by senators. Passed 47-44: R 40-10; D 7-34 (ND 4-23; SD 3-11), Sept. 25, 1981.

285. H J Res 265. Debt Limit Increase. Dole, R-Kan., motion to table (kill) the Melcher, D-Mont., amendment to direct the president to consult with the Federal Reserve Board in order to modify the board's monetary policy to significantly reduce interest rates within the next 90 days. Motion agreed to 56-32: R 46-0; D 10-32 (ND 6-23; SD 4-9), Sept. 28, 1981.

286. H J Res 265. Debt Limit Increase. Dole, R-Kan., motion to table (kill) the Hart, D-Colo., amendment to reduce the 100 percent tax deduction for business meals to 70 percent and earmark the 30 percent savings for the school lunch program. Motion agreed to 58-30: R 46-0; D 12-30 (ND 9-20; SD 3-10), Sept. 28, 1981.

287. H J Res 265. Debt Limit Increase. Dole, R-Kan., motion to table (kill) the Hart, D-Colo., amendment to provide that individual tax reductions provided in the Economic Recovery Tax Act of 1981 (PL 97-34) shall not take effect until the federal budget is balanced. Motion agreed to 74-13: R 43-2; D 31-11 (ND 20-9; SD 11-2), Sept. 28, 1981. A "yea" was a vote supporting the president's position.

288. Bowsher Nomination. Confirmation of President Reagan's nomination of Charles A. Bowsher of Maryland to be comptroller general of the United States. Confirmed 99-0: R 53-0; D 46-0 (ND 31-0; SD 15-0), Sept. 29, 1981. A "yea" was a vote supporting the president's position.

289. H J Res 265. Debt Limit Increase. Dole, R-Kan., motion to table (kill) the Armstrong, R-Colo., amendment to make it easier for the president to rescind, or withhold from spending, appropriated funds. Under the amendment, rescissions would stand unless vetoed within 45 days by both houses of Congress through adoption of a concurrent resolution. Under existing law, the money must be spent unless both houses approve the rescissions within 45 days through enactment of legislation. Motion agreed to 84-15: R 41-12; D 43-3 (ND 29-2, SD 14-1), Sept. 29, 1981.

290. H J Res 265. Debt Limit Increase. Dole, R-Kan., motion to table (kill) the Exon, D-Neb., amendment to reduce the third-year, personal income tax cut provided by the Economic Recovery Tax Act of 1981 (PL 97-34) if certain economic goals are not attained. Motion agreed to 56-43: R 51-2; D 5-41 (ND 2-29, SD 3-12), Sept. 29, 1981. A "yea" was a vote supporting the president's position.

291. H J Res 265. Debt Limit Increase. Dole, R-Kan., motion to table (kill) the Eagleton, D-Mo., amendment to establish a trust fund financed from revenues from the reductions in the windfall profits tax contained in the Economic Recovery Tax Act of 1981 (PL 97-34). The money in the trust fund would be used as a reserve for the Social Security trust fund. Motion agreed to 67-31: R 50-3; D 17-28 (ND 9-21, SD 8-7), Sept. 29, 1981. A "yea" was a vote supporting the president's position.

	292	293	294	295	296	297	298	299
ALABAMA								
Denton	Y	Y	Y	Y	Y	Y	Y	Y
Heflin	N	N	N	N	Y	Y	Y	N
ALASKA								
Murkowski	Y	Y	Y	Y	Y	Y	Y	Y
Stevens	Y	Y	Y	Y	Y	Y	Y	Y
ARIZONA								
Goldwater	Y	Y	Y	Y	Y	Y	Y	N
DeConcini	N	Y	N	N	Y	Y	Y	N
ARKANSAS								
Bumpers	N	N	N	N	N	Y	Y	Y
Pryor	Y	N	N	N	N	Y	Y	Y
CALIFORNIA								
Hayakawa	Y	Y	Y	Y	Y	Y	Y	Y
Cranston	N	N	N	Y	N	Y	Y	Y
COLORADO								
Armstrong	N	Y	N	N	Y	Y	Y	N
Hart	Y	N	N	N	N	Y	Y	Y
CONNECTICUT								
Weicker	Y	Y	Y	Y	?	?	?	?
Dodd	Y	N	N	Y	N	Y	Y	Y
DELAWARE								
Roth	Y	Y	Y	Y	Y	Y	Y	N
Biden	N	N	N	Y	N	Y	Y	N
FLORIDA								
Hawkins	Y	Y	Y	Y	Y	Y	Y	Y
Chiles	N	N	N	N	Y	Y	Y	N
GEORGIA								
Mattingly	Y	Y	Y	N	Y	Y	Y	Y
Nunn	N	N	N	N	Y	Y	Y	N
HAWAII								
Inouye	Y	N	N	Y	?	Y	Y	Y
Matsunaga	Y	Y	N	Y	-	?	?	?
IDAHO								
McClure	Y	Y	Y	Y	Y	Y	Y	Y
Symms	N	Y	Y	Y	Y	Y	Y	N
ILLINOIS								
Percy	Y	Y	Y	Y	Y	Y	Y	Y
Dixon	N	Y	N	N	N	Y	Y	Y
INDIANA								
Lugar	Y	Y	Y	Y	Y	Y	Y	Y
Quayle	Y	Y	Y	Y	Y	Y	Y	Y

	292	293	294	295	296	297	298	299
IOWA								
Grassley	N	Y	Y	N	Y	Y	Y	N
Jepsen	Y	Y	Y	Y	Y	Y	Y	N
KANSAS								
Dole	Y	Y	Y	Y	Y	Y	Y	Y
Kassebaum	Y	Y	Y	Y	Y	Y	Y	Y
KENTUCKY								
Ford	N	N	N	N	N	Y	Y	Y
Huddleston	N	N	N	N	N	Y	Y	Y
LOUISIANA								
Johnston	N	N	N	Y	Y	Y	Y	Y
Long	Y	Y	Y	Y	Y	?	?	?
MAINE								
Cohen	Y	Y	Y	Y	Y	Y	Y	Y
Mitchell	N	Y	N	N	N	Y	Y	Y
MARYLAND								
Mathias	Y	Y	Y	N	Y	Y	Y	Y
Sarbanes	Y	N	N	Y	N	Y	Y	N
MASSACHUSETTS								
Kennedy	Y	N	N	Y	N	Y	Y	N
Tsongas	Y	N	N	Y	N	Y	Y	N
MICHIGAN								
Levin	Y	N	N	Y	N	Y	Y	N
Riegle	N	Y	N	N	N	Y	Y	N
MINNESOTA								
Boschwitz	Y	Y	Y	Y	Y	Y	Y	Y
Durenberger	Y	Y	Y	Y	Y	Y	Y	Y
MISSISSIPPI								
Cochran	Y	Y	Y	Y	Y	Y	Y	Y
Stennis	X	X	X	Y	Y	Y	Y	Y
MISSOURI								
Danforth	Y	Y	Y	Y	Y	Y	Y	Y
Eagleton	#	N	N	Y	N	Y	Y	N
MONTANA								
Baucus	N	N	N	N	Y	Y	Y	N
Melcher	X	+	?	-	Y	Y	Y	Y
NEBRASKA								
Exon	N	N	N	N	Y	Y	Y	N
Zorinsky	N	Y	N	N	Y	Y	Y	N
NEVADA								
Laxalt	Y	Y	Y	Y	Y	?	Y	Y
Cannon	N	N	N	N	Y	?	?	?

	292	293	294	295	296	297	298	299
NEW HAMPSHIRE								
Humphrey	Y	Y	Y	N	Y	Y	Y	Y
Rudman	Y	Y	Y	Y	?	?	?	
NEW JERSEY								
Bradley	Y	N	N	Y	N	Y	Y	Y
Williams	N	Y	N	N	N	Y	Y	Y
NEW MEXICO								
Domenici	Y	Y	Y	Y	Y	Y	Y	Y
Schmitt	Y	Y	Y	Y	?	Y	Y	Y
NEW YORK								
D'Amato	Y	Y	Y	Y	Y	Y	Y	Y
Moynihan	Y	N	N	N	N	?	?	?
NORTH CAROLINA								
East	Y	Y	Y	Y	Y	Y	?	+
Helms	Y	Y	Y	Y	Y	Y	Y	N
NORTH DAKOTA								
Andrews	Y	Y	Y	Y	Y	Y	Y	Y
Burdick	Y	N	N	Y	Y	Y	Y	Y
OHIO								
Glenn	Y	N	N	N	N	Y	Y	Y
Metzenbaum	N	Y	N	N	Y	Y	Y	N
OKLAHOMA								
Nickles	Y	Y	Y	N	Y	Y	Y	Y
Boren	N	N	N	N	Y	Y	Y	N
OREGON								
Hatfield	Y	Y	Y	N	Y	Y	Y	Y
Packwood	Y	Y	Y	Y	Y	Y	Y	Y
PENNSYLVANIA								
Heinz	Y	Y	Y	Y	Y	Y	Y	Y
Specter	Y	Y	Y	N	Y	Y	Y	Y
RHODE ISLAND								
Chafee	Y	Y	Y	Y	Y	Y	Y	Y
Pell	N	N	N	Y	N	Y	Y	Y
SOUTH CAROLINA								
Thurmond	#	#	#	?	Y	Y	Y	Y
Hollings	N	N	N	N	Y	Y	Y	Y
SOUTH DAKOTA								
Abdnor	Y	Y	Y	Y	Y	Y	Y	Y
Pressler	Y	Y	Y	Y	Y	Y	Y	N
TENNESSEE								
Baker	Y	Y	Y	Y	Y	Y	Y	Y
Sasser	N	Y	N	N	Y	Y	Y	N

	292	293	294	295	296	297	298	299
TEXAS								
Tower	Y	Y	Y	Y	Y	Y	Y	Y
Bentsen	N	Y	N	Y	Y	Y	Y	N
UTAH								
Garn	Y	Y	Y	Y	Y	Y	Y	Y
Hatch	Y	Y	Y	Y	Y	Y	Y	N
VERMONT								
Stafford	Y	Y	Y	Y	Y	Y	Y	Y
Leahy	N	N	N	N	N	Y	Y	Y
VIRGINIA								
Warner	Y	Y	Y	Y	Y	Y	Y	Y
Byrd*	N	Y	Y	N	Y	?	?	?
WASHINGTON								
Gorton	Y	Y	Y	Y	+	Y	Y	Y
Jackson	N	Y	N	Y	Y	Y	Y	Y
WEST VIRGINIA								
Byrd	N	Y	N	N	N	Y	Y	Y
Randolph	Y	N	N	N	Y	Y	Y	Y
WISCONSIN								
Kasten	N	Y	Y	Y	Y	Y	Y	Y
Proxmire	N	N	N	N	N	Y	Y	N
WYOMING								
Simpson	Y	Y	Y	Y	Y	Y	Y	Y
Wallop	Y	Y	Y	Y	Y	Y	Y	Y

KEY

- Y Voted for (yea).
- # Paired for.
- + Announced for.
- N Voted against (nay).
- X Paired against.
- - Announced against.
- P Voted "present".
- C Voted "present" to avoid possible conflict of interest.
- ? Did not vote or otherwise make a position known.

Democrats *Republicans*

* Byrd elected as an independent.

292. H J Res 265. Debt Limit Increase. Dole, R-Kan., motion to table (kill) the Proxmire, D-Wis., amendment to increase the public debt limit to $995 billion, rather than $1.0798 trillion as provided by the bill. Motion agreed to 63-33: R 48-4; D 15-29 (ND 13-17, SD 2-12), Sept. 29, 1981.

293. H J Res 265. Debt Limit Increase. Dole, R-Kan., motion to table (kill) the Nunn, D-Ga., amendment to reduce the personal income tax reductions provided under the Economic Recovery Tax Act of 1981 (PL 97-34) in 1982 and 1983 so that the total revenue loss from each year's tax cuts is no more than the budget reductions achieved through the reconciliation process in the first budget resolution. Motion agreed to 66-31: R 52-0; D 14-31 (ND 10-21; SD 4-10), Sept. 29, 1981.

294. H J Res 265. Debt Limit Increase. Dole, R-Kan., motion to table (kill) the Moynihan, D-N.Y., amendment to increase the debt limit only through March 31, 1982, rather than Sept. 30, 1982, as provided in the bill. Motion agreed to 53-44: R 51-1; D 2-43 (ND 0-31, SD 2-12), Sept. 29, 1981.

295. H J Res 265. Debt Limit Increase. Passage of the bill to increase the public debt limit to $1,079,800,000,000 through Sept. 30, 1982. Passed 64-34: R 46-6; D 18-28 (ND 14-17, SD 4-11), Sept. 29, 1981. A "yea" was a vote supporting the president's position.

296. S 1196. Foreign Aid Authorization. Percy, R-Ill., motion to table (kill) the Tsongas, D-Mass., amendment to repeal the ban on U.S. aid to military factions on Angola by the earliest of the following dates: the date by which the president determined that an effective cease-fire was in place in Namibia and that preparations for internationally supervised elections in Namibia were in place; or March 31, 1985. Motion agreed to 66-29: R 47-3; D 19-26 (ND 8-22, SD 11-4), Sept. 30, 1981. (Then Senate subsequently adopted, by voice vote, the Kassebaum, R-Kan., amendment repealing the ban on U.S. aid to military factions in Angola, but stating that repeal should not be "construed to be an endorsement by Congress" of covert aid to military factions in Angola.)

297. S 1196. Foreign Aid Authorization. Proxmire, D-Wis., amendment stating the sense of Congress that the president should undertake diplomatic initiatives to persuade the Soviet Union to pay all its outstanding debts to the United Nations. Adopted 92-0: R 50-0; D 42-0 (ND 29-0, SD 13-0), Sept. 30, 1981.

298. S 1196. Foreign Aid Authorization. Humphrey, R-N.H., amendment stating the sense of Congress that the president should seek an explanation from the government of the Soviet Union of the reports that it has used or has prepared to use biological or chemical weapons against the people of Loas, Cambodia, Afghanistan and the Soviet Union. Adopted 92-0: R 50-0; D 42-0 (ND 29-0, SD 13-0), Sept. 30, 1981.

299. H J Res 325. Fiscal 1982 Continuing Appropriations. Adoption of the conference report on the joint resolution to provide funding authority, from Oct. 1 to Nov. 20, 1981, for government agencies whose regular fiscal 1982 appropriations bills had not been enacted. Adopted 64-28: R 41-9; D 23-19 (ND 16-13, SD 7-6), Sept. 30, 1981.

	300 301 302		300 301 302		300 301 302
ALABAMA		**IOWA**		**NEW HAMPSHIRE**	
Denton	Y Y Y	*Grassley*	N N Y	*Humphrey*	N Y Y
Heflin	N N Y	*Jepsen*	Y Y Y	*Rudman*	? ? ?
ALASKA		**KANSAS**		**NEW JERSEY**	
Murkowski	Y Y Y	*Dole*	Y Y Y	Bradley	N N Y
Stevens	Y Y Y	*Kassebaum*	Y N Y	Williams	Y Y Y
ARIZONA		**KENTUCKY**		**NEW MEXICO**	
Goldwater	Y Y Y	Ford	N N Y	*Domenici*	Y Y Y
DeConcini	N N Y	Huddleston	Y Y Y	*Schmitt*	N N Y
ARKANSAS		**LOUISIANA**		**NEW YORK**	
Bumpers	N N N	Johnston	Y Y Y	*D'Amato*	Y Y Y
Pryor	N N Y	Long	? ? Y	Moynihan	? ? ?
CALIFORNIA		**MAINE**		**NORTH CAROLINA**	
Hayakawa	Y Y ?	*Cohen*	N N Y	*East*	? ? Y
Cranston	Y Y N	Mitchell	N N N	*Helms*	N N Y
COLORADO		**MARYLAND**		**NORTH DAKOTA**	
Armstrong	N Y Y	*Mathias*	Y Y Y	*Andrews*	N Y Y
Hart	N N N	Sarbanes	N N N	Burdick	N N Y
CONNECTICUT		**MASSACHUSETTS**		**OHIO**	
Weicker	? ? Y	Kennedy	Y N N	Glenn	N N Y
Dodd	Y Y N	Tsongas	Y Y N	Metzenbaum	N N N
DELAWARE		**MICHIGAN**		**OKLAHOMA**	
Roth	Y N Y	Levin	N N N	*Nickles*	N Y Y
Biden	N N N	Riegle	N N N	Boren	N N Y
FLORIDA		**MINNESOTA**		**OREGON**	
Hawkins	Y Y Y	*Boschwitz*	Y N Y	*Hatfield*	Y Y P
Chiles	N N Y	*Durenberger*	Y N Y	*Packwood*	Y Y Y
GEORGIA		**MISSISSIPPI**		**PENNSYLVANIA**	
Mattingly	N Y Y	*Cochran*	Y Y Y	*Heinz*	Y N Y
Nunn	N N Y	Stennis	Y N Y	*Specter*	Y Y Y
HAWAII		**MISSOURI**		**RHODE ISLAND**	
Inouye	Y Y N	*Danforth*	Y N Y	*Chafee*	Y Y Y
Matsunaga	? ? N	Eagleton	Y Y N	Pell	N N Y
IDAHO		**MONTANA**		**SOUTH CAROLINA**	
McClure	Y Y Y	Baucus	N Y N	*Thurmond*	Y N Y
Symms	Y Y Y	Melcher	N N Y	Hollings	Y Y Y
ILLINOIS		**NEBRASKA**		**SOUTH DAKOTA**	
Percy	Y Y Y	Exon	N N Y	*Abdnor*	N Y Y
Dixon	N Y Y	Zorinsky	N N N	*Pressler*	N N Y
INDIANA		**NEVADA**		**TENNESSEE**	
Lugar	Y Y Y	*Laxalt*	Y Y Y	*Baker*	Y Y Y
Quayle	Y Y Y	Cannon	? ? ?	Sasser	N N Y

KEY

Y Voted for (yea).
\# Paired for.
\+ Announced for.
N Voted against (nay).
X Paired against.
\- Announced against.
P Voted "present".
C Voted "present" to avoid possible conflict of interest.
? Did not vote or otherwise make a position known.

	300 301 302
TEXAS	
Tower	Y Y Y
Bentsen	N N Y
UTAH	
Garn	Y Y Y
Hatch	Y Y Y
VERMONT	
Stafford	N Y Y
Leahy	N Y N
VIRGINIA	
Warner	Y Y Y
Byrd*	? ? Y
WASHINGTON	
Gorton	Y Y Y
Jackson	N N Y
WEST VIRGINIA	
Byrd	N N N
Randolph	N N +
WISCONSIN	
Kasten	N N Y
Proxmire	N N Y
WYOMING	
Simpson	Y N Y
Wallop	Y Y Y

Democrats *Republicans*

* *Byrd elected as an independent.*

300. H J Res 325. Fiscal 1982 Continuing Appropriations. Hatfield, R-Ore., motion to accept language proposed by House-Senate conferees to provide for a permanent appropriation of funds for congressional pay increases, when recommended by the president and upheld by Congress. Motion agreed to 48-44: R 37-13; D 11-31 (ND 7-22, SD 4-9), Sept. 30, 1981.

301. H J Res 325. Fiscal 1982 Continuing Appropriations. Hatfield, R-Ore., motion to accept a technical change in the Senate amendment to remove the existing $3,000 cap on business-related tax deductions claimed by members of Congress while away from home. Motion agreed to 48-44: R 36-14; D 12-30 (ND 9-20, SD 3-10), Sept. 30, 1981.

302. Funderburk Nomination. Confirmation of David B. Funderburk of North Carolina to be ambassador extraordinary and plenipotentiary of the United States to the Socialist Republic of Romania. Confirmed 75-19: R 50-0; D 25-19 (ND 11-18, SD 14-1), Oct. 1, 1981. A "yea" was a vote supporting the president's position.

KEY

- Y Voted for (yea).
- # Paired for.
- + Announced for.
- N Voted against (nay).
- X Paired against.
- - Announced against.
- P Voted "present".
- C Voted "present" to avoid possible conflict of interest.
- ? Did not vote or otherwise make a position known.

	303	304	305	306	307	308
ALABAMA						
Denton	Y	Y	Y	N	Y	Y
Heflin	Y	N	Y	N	N	Y
ALASKA						
Murkowski	Y	Y	Y	N	Y	Y
Stevens	Y	Y	Y	N	N	Y
ARIZONA						
Goldwater	N	Y	Y	N	Y	Y
DeConcini	C	C	Y	N	C	N
ARKANSAS						
Bumpers	Y	N	Y	N	N	Y
Pryor	Y	N	Y	N	N	Y
CALIFORNIA						
Hayakawa	Y	N	?	Y	N	Y
Cranston	Y	N	Y	Y	Y	N
COLORADO						
Armstrong	Y	N	Y	N	Y	Y
Hart	N	Y	Y	Y	Y	N
CONNECTICUT						
Weicker	Y	N	Y	N	N	Y
Dodd	Y	N	Y	Y	Y	Y
DELAWARE						
Roth	N	Y	Y	N	N	Y
Biden	N	Y	Y	N	N	Y
FLORIDA						
Hawkins	Y	Y	Y	N	N	Y
Chiles	N	Y	Y	N	N	Y
GEORGIA						
Mattingly	N	Y	Y	N	N	Y
Nunn	?	Y	Y	Y	N	Y
HAWAII						
Inouye	?	?	?	?	?	?
Matsunaga	Y	N	Y	N	Y	Y
IDAHO						
McClure	Y	Y	Y	N	N	Y
Symms	Y	N	Y	N	N	Y
ILLINOIS						
Percy	?	Y	?	N	Y	Y
Dixon	N	Y	Y	N	Y	Y
INDIANA						
Lugar	Y	N	?	N	Y	Y
Quayle	Y	N	Y	N	N	Y

	303	304	305	306	307	308
IOWA						
Grassley	Y	Y	Y	N	Y	Y
Jepsen	N	?	Y	N	Y	Y
KANSAS						
Dole	Y	Y	Y	N	N	Y
Kassebaum	Y	Y	Y	Y	Y	Y
KENTUCKY						
Ford	Y	N	Y	Y	N	Y
Huddleston	Y	N	Y	N	N	Y
LOUISIANA						
Johnston	N	Y	Y	N	N	Y
Long	N	Y	Y	N	N	Y
MAINE						
Cohen	N	Y	Y	N	Y	Y
Mitchell	N	Y	Y	N	Y	Y
MARYLAND						
Mathias	?	?	?	?	?	Y
Sarbanes	N	Y	Y	N	N	Y
MASSACHUSETTS						
Kennedy	N	Y	Y	Y	N	Y
Tsongas	N	Y	Y	Y	N	Y
MICHIGAN						
Levin	N	Y	Y	Y	N	Y
Riegle	N	Y	Y	Y	N	Y
MINNESOTA						
Boschwitz	N	Y	Y	N	Y	Y
Durenberger	N	Y	Y	Y	Y	Y
MISSISSIPPI						
Cochran	Y	N	Y	N	N	Y
Stennis	N	Y	Y	Y	N	Y
MISSOURI						
Danforth	N	Y	Y	N	N	Y
Eagleton	N	Y	Y	Y	Y	Y
MONTANA						
Baucus	Y	N	Y	N	Y	Y
Melcher	Y	N	Y	N	+	?
NEBRASKA						
Exon	N	Y	Y	N	Y	Y
Zorinsky	Y	N	Y	N	Y	Y
NEVADA						
Laxalt	?	?	?	?	N	Y
Cannon	Y	N	Y	N	Y	Y

	303	304	305	306	307	308
NEW HAMPSHIRE						
Humphrey	Y	Y	Y	N	Y	Y
Rudman	Y	Y	Y	N	Y	Y
NEW JERSEY						
Bradley	Y	N	Y	?	N	Y
Williams	N	Y	Y	N	N	Y
NEW MEXICO						
Domenici	Y	Y	Y	N	N	Y
Schmitt	Y	Y	Y	N	N	Y
NEW YORK						
D'Amato	Y	N	N	N	N	Y
Moynihan	Y	N	N	Y	Y	Y
NORTH CAROLINA						
East	Y	N	Y	N	Y	Y
Helms	Y	N	Y	N	Y	Y
NORTH DAKOTA						
Andrews	Y	Y	Y	N	N	Y
Burdick	N	Y	Y	N	Y	Y
OHIO						
Glenn	Y	N	Y	N	N	Y
Metzenbaum	N	Y	Y	N	N	Y
OKLAHOMA						
Nickles	Y	Y	Y	N	N	Y
Boren	Y	N	Y	N	N	Y
OREGON						
Hatfield	N	Y	Y	N	N	Y
Packwood	Y	N	Y	N	N	Y
PENNSYLVANIA						
Heinz	N	Y	Y	N	N	Y
Specter	N	Y	N	Y	N	Y
RHODE ISLAND						
Chafee	Y	N	Y	N	N	Y
Pell	Y	N	Y	Y	Y	Y
SOUTH CAROLINA						
Thurmond	Y	Y	Y	N	N	Y
Hollings	N	Y	Y	Y	N	N
SOUTH DAKOTA						
Abdnor	N	Y	Y	N	Y	Y
Pressler	N	Y	?	N	Y	Y
TENNESSEE						
Baker	Y	Y	?	N	N	Y
Sasser	N	Y	Y	Y	Y	Y

	303	304	305	306	307	308
TEXAS						
Tower	N	Y	Y	N	?	?
Bentsen	?	?	?	?	?	?
UTAH						
Garn	N	Y	Y	N	N	Y
Hatch	N	Y	Y	N	N	Y
VERMONT						
Stafford	Y	N	Y	N	?	?
Leahy	Y	N	Y	Y	Y	Y
VIRGINIA						
Warner	N	Y	Y	N	N	Y
Byrd*	N	Y	Y	N	N	Y
WASHINGTON						
Gorton	Y	Y	Y	Y	Y	Y
Jackson	Y	Y	Y	Y	Y	Y
WEST VIRGINIA						
Byrd	Y	N	Y	N	Y	Y
Randolph	Y	N	Y	N	Y	Y
WISCONSIN						
Kasten	N	Y	Y	N	N	Y
Proxmire	N	Y	Y	Y	N	Y
WYOMING						
Simpson	Y	N	Y	N	N	Y
Wallop	?	?	?	?	?	?

Democrats   *Republicans*

* Byrd elected as an independent.

303. S 898. Telecommunications Competition and Deregulation. Cannon, D-Nev., amendment to restore local government authority over basic cable television rates. Adopted 52-40: R 31-18; D 21-22 (ND 15-15, SD 6-7), Oct. 6, 1981.

304. S 898. Telecommunications Competition and Deregulation. Goldwater, R-Ariz., amendment to delete provisions relating to cable television rate regulation and utility pole attachments. Adopted 59-34: R 35-14; D 24-20 (ND 16-14, SD 8-6), Oct. 6, 1981.

305. S 898. Telecommunications Competition and Deregulation. Bradley, D-N.J., amendment to provide that if the Federal Communications Commission revokes or declines to renew a VHF television station license in a state with more than one VHF station, it should assign the channel to a state without a VHF station, if technically feasible. Adopted 86-4: R 42-3; D 44-1 (ND 30-1, SD 14-0), Oct. 6, 1981.

306. S 898. Telecommunications Competition and Deregulation. Hollings, D-S.C., amendment to require that at least 10 percent of the stock of a fully separate subsidiary of the American Telephone & Telegraph Co. (AT&T) be sold to persons other than AT&T or its affiliates. Rejected 26-68: R 5-45; D 21-23 (ND 16-14; SD 5-9), Oct. 6, 1981.

307. S 898. Telecommunications Competition and Deregulation. Boschwitz, R-Minn., amendment to delete a provision that would allow telephone companies to provide cable television service in rural areas possibly subject to Federal Communications Commission regulations. Rejected 38-54: R 22-27; D 16-27 (ND 15-14; SD 1-13), Oct. 7, 1981.

308. S 898. Telecommunications Competition and Deregulation. Passage of the bill to deregulate much of the telecommunications industry and allow the American Telephone & Telegraph Co. through the formation of a fully separated subsidiary to enter unregulated markets. Passed 90-4: R 50-0; D 40-4 (ND 27-3; SD 13-1), Oct. 7, 1981.

	309 310 311 312		309 310 311 312		309 310 311 312
ALABAMA		**IOWA**		**NEW HAMPSHIRE**	
Denton	Y Y Y Y	*Grassley*	Y Y Y Y	*Humphrey*	Y Y Y Y
Heflin	Y N Y Y	*Jepsen*	Y Y Y Y	*Rudman*	N Y Y Y
ALASKA		**KANSAS**		**NEW JERSEY**	
Murkowski	? ? ? ?	*Dole*	Y Y Y Y	Bradley	N N Y Y
Stevens	Y Y Y Y	*Kassebaum*	Y Y Y Y	Williams	N N Y Y
ARIZONA		**KENTUCKY**		**NEW MEXICO**	
Goldwater	Y Y Y Y	Ford	Y N Y Y	*Domenici*	Y Y Y Y
DeConcini	Y N Y Y	Huddleston	Y N Y Y	*Schmitt*	Y Y Y Y
ARKANSAS		**LOUISIANA**		**NEW YORK**	
Bumpers	N N Y Y	Johnston	Y N Y Y	*D'Amato*	Y Y Y Y
Pryor	Y N Y Y	Long	Y N Y Y	Moynihan	N N Y Y
CALIFORNIA		**MAINE**		**NORTH CAROLINA**	
Hayakawa	Y Y Y Y	*Cohen*	N Y Y Y	*East*	Y Y Y Y
Cranston	N N Y Y	Mitchell	N N Y Y	*Helms*	Y Y Y Y
COLORADO		**MARYLAND**		**NORTH DAKOTA**	
Armstrong	Y Y Y Y	*Mathias*	N Y Y Y	*Andrews*	Y Y Y Y
Hart	Y N Y Y	Sarbanes	N N Y Y	Burdick	Y N Y Y
CONNECTICUT		**MASSACHUSETTS**		**OHIO**	
Weicker	N Y Y Y	Kennedy	N N Y Y	Glenn	Y N Y Y
Dodd	N N Y Y	Tsongas	N N Y Y	Metzenbaum	N N Y Y
DELAWARE		**MICHIGAN**		**OKLAHOMA**	
Roth	N Y Y Y	Levin	N N Y Y	*Nickles*	Y Y Y Y
Biden	N N Y Y	Riegle	N N Y Y	Boren	Y N Y Y
FLORIDA		**MINNESOTA**		**OREGON**	
Hawkins	Y Y Y Y	*Boschwitz*	Y Y Y Y	*Hatfield*	Y Y Y Y
Chiles	Y N Y Y	*Durenberger*	Y Y Y Y	*Packwood*	Y Y Y Y
GEORGIA		**MISSISSIPPI**		**PENNSYLVANIA**	
Mattingly	Y Y Y Y	*Cochran*	Y Y Y Y	*Heinz*	Y Y Y Y
Nunn	Y N Y Y	Stennis	Y N Y Y	*Specter*	N Y Y Y
HAWAII		**MISSOURI**		**RHODE ISLAND**	
Inouye	? N Y Y	*Danforth*	Y Y Y Y	*Chafee*	Y Y Y Y
Matsunaga	Y N Y Y	Eagleton	N N Y Y	Pell	N N Y Y
IDAHO		**MONTANA**		**SOUTH CAROLINA**	
McClure	? ? ? ?	Baucus	Y N Y Y	*Thurmond*	Y Y Y Y
Symms	+ + + +	Melcher	Y N Y Y	Hollings	N N Y Y
ILLINOIS		**NEBRASKA**		**SOUTH DAKOTA**	
Percy	Y Y Y Y	Exon	Y N Y Y	*Abdnor*	Y Y Y Y
Dixon	Y N Y Y	Zorinsky	Y N Y Y	*Pressler*	N Y Y Y
INDIANA		**NEVADA**		**TENNESSEE**	
Lugar	Y Y ? ?	*Laxalt*	Y Y Y Y	*Baker*	Y Y Y Y
Quayle	Y Y Y Y	Cannon	N N Y Y	Sasser	Y N Y Y

	309 310 311 312
TEXAS	
Tower	Y Y Y Y
Bentsen	Y N Y Y
UTAH	
Garn	Y Y Y Y
Hatch	Y Y Y Y
VERMONT	
Stafford	Y Y Y +
Leahy	N N Y Y
VIRGINIA	
Warner	Y Y Y Y
Byrd*	N N Y Y
WASHINGTON	
Gorton	+ Y Y Y
Jackson	N N Y Y
WEST VIRGINIA	
Byrd	N N Y Y
Randolph	Y N Y Y
WISCONSIN	
Kasten	Y Y Y Y
Proxmire	N N Y Y
WYOMING	
Simpson	Y Y Y Y
Wallop	Y Y Y Y

KEY

Y Voted for (yea).
\# Paired for.
\+ Announced for.
N Voted against (nay).
X Paired against.
- Announced against.
P Voted "present".
C Voted "present" to avoid possible conflict of interest.
? Did not vote or otherwise make a position known.

Democrats   *Republicans*

* *Byrd elected as an independent.*

309. HR 4331. Minimum Social Security Benefits. Dole, R-Kan., motion to table (kill) the Eagleton, D-Mo., amendment to repeal a scheduled reduction in the windfall profits tax on newly discovered oil (PL 97-34) and to put the additional revenues in an emergency reserve fund for Social Security. Motion agreed to 65-30: R 42-7; D 23-23 (ND 11-20; SD 12-3), Oct. 15, 1981. A "yea" was a vote supporting the president's position.

310. HR 4331. Minimum Social Security Benefits. Dole, R-Kan., motion to table (kill) the Byrd, D-W.Va., amendment to the Pressler, R-S.D., amendment *(see vote 311, below)* to require the director of the Office of Management and Budget to submit to Congress no later than Nov. 15, 1981, a detailed list of all budget cuts the administration plans to propose for fiscal years 1982, 1983 and 1984. Motion agreed to 50-47: R 50-0; D 0-47 (ND 0-32; SD 0-15), Oct. 15, 1981.

311. HR 4331. Minimum Social Security Benefits. Pressler, R-S.D., amendment expressing the sense of Congress that no future changes in Social Security will reduce the current dollar amount of monthly benefits received by beneficiaries on the date of enactment of this bill. Adopted 96-0: R 49-0; D 47-0 (ND 32-0; SD 15-0), Oct. 15, 1981.

312. HR 4331. Minimum Social Security Benefits. Passage of the bill to restore the minimum Social Security benefit for most current recipients; to reallocate payroll taxes among the three Social Security trust funds; to apply the payroll tax to the first six months of all sick pay; and to lower the maximum family retirement and survivors benefit. Passed 95-0: R 48-0; D 47-0 (ND 32-0; SD 15-0), Oct. 15, 1981.

	313 314 315 316 317 318 319 320		313 314 315 316 317 318 319 320		313 314 315 316 317 318 319 320	KEY

	313 314 315 316 317 318 319 320
ALABAMA	
Denton	N ? ? ? ? Y N ?
Heflin	N Y N N Y ? N Y
ALASKA	
Murkowski	N N N N Y Y N Y
Stevens	N N Y ? ? ? ? ?
ARIZONA	
Goldwater	N N Y Y Y Y ? ?
DeConcini	N Y N N Y ? ? ?
ARKANSAS	
Bumpers	Y Y N N Y N Y Y
Pryor	Y Y N N Y N Y Y
CALIFORNIA	
Hayakawa	Y N Y Y Y Y N Y
Cranston	N Y N N Y N Y Y
COLORADO	
Armstrong	Y N ? N Y Y N ?
Hart	N Y N N N N Y Y
CONNECTICUT	
Weicker	N Y N N ? ? ? ?
Dodd	N Y N N Y X # +
DELAWARE	
Roth	Y N N Y Y Y N Y
Biden	N Y N N Y N Y Y
FLORIDA	
Hawkins	N N N N Y Y N Y
Chiles	N Y N N Y N Y Y
GEORGIA	
Mattingly	N N P ? ? Y N Y
Nunn	N Y N Y Y N N Y
HAWAII	
Inouye	N ? ? ? ? N Y Y
Matsunaga	N Y N N Y ? Y Y
IDAHO	
McClure	Y N N Y Y N ? ?
Symms	Y N N Y Y Y ? Y
ILLINOIS	
Percy	Y N Y Y Y N Y Y
Dixon	N Y N Y Y N Y Y
INDIANA	
Lugar	Y N Y Y Y Y N Y
Quayle	Y N N N Y Y N Y

	313 314 315 316 317 318 319 320
IOWA	
Grassley	Y N Y Y Y Y N Y
Jepsen	Y N Y Y Y Y N Y
KANSAS	
Dole	Y N Y Y Y Y N Y
Kassebaum	Y Y N N Y N Y Y
KENTUCKY	
Ford	N Y N N Y N Y Y
Huddleston	N Y N N Y N Y Y
LOUISIANA	
Johnston	N Y N N Y N Y Y
Long	N Y N Y Y Y N Y
MAINE	
Cohen	N N N Y Y ? N Y
Mitchell	N Y N N N N Y Y
MARYLAND	
Mathias	N Y N N Y N Y Y
Sarbanes	N Y N N Y N Y Y
MASSACHUSETTS	
Kennedy	N Y N N N N Y Y
Tsongas	N ? N ? ? X # ?
MICHIGAN	
Levin	N Y N N Y N Y Y
Riegle	N Y N N Y N Y Y
MINNESOTA	
Boschwitz	Y Y N N Y N Y Y
Durenberger	Y Y N N Y Y N Y
MISSISSIPPI	
Cochran	N N Y Y Y N Y Y
Stennis	N N Y Y Y N N Y
MISSOURI	
Danforth	Y Y Y Y Y N Y Y
Eagleton	? ? ? ? ? N Y Y
MONTANA	
Baucus	N Y N N Y N Y Y
Melcher	N Y N N Y N Y Y
NEBRASKA	
Exon	Y Y ? ? ? ? Y Y
Zorinsky	N N Y Y Y # Y Y
NEVADA	
Laxalt	N N Y Y Y Y N Y
Cannon	N Y N N Y # + Y

	313 314 315 316 317 318 319 320
NEW HAMPSHIRE	
Humphrey	Y N Y Y Y N N Y
Rudman	N N Y Y Y Y N Y
NEW JERSEY	
Bradley	? Y N N Y N Y Y
Williams	N Y N N Y N Y Y
NEW MEXICO	
Domenici	Y N Y Y Y Y N Y
Schmitt	N N Y Y Y Y N Y
NEW YORK	
D'Amato	N N ? + + Y N Y
Moynihan	N Y N N Y N Y Y
NORTH CAROLINA	
East	N N Y Y Y Y N Y
Helms	N Y Y Y Y Y N Y
NORTH DAKOTA	
Andrews	N N Y Y Y Y N Y
Burdick	N Y N N Y N Y Y
OHIO	
Glenn	N Y N N Y N Y Y
Metzenbaum	N Y N N Y N Y Y
OKLAHOMA	
Nickles	Y N Y Y Y Y N Y
Boren	N Y N N Y Y X Y
OREGON	
Hatfield	N Y N N Y Y N Y
Packwood	N N N N Y Y X Y
PENNSYLVANIA	
Heinz	N Y N N Y N Y Y
Specter	N Y N Y Y N Y Y
RHODE ISLAND	
Chafee	N Y N Y Y ? ? ?
Pell	N Y N Y Y N Y Y
SOUTH CAROLINA	
Thurmond	Y N Y Y Y Y N Y
Hollings	N N N N Y N Y Y
SOUTH DAKOTA	
Abdnor	Y N Y Y Y Y N Y
Pressler	N N Y Y Y ? ? ?
TENNESSEE	
Baker	Y N Y Y Y Y N Y
Sasser	N Y N N Y N Y Y

KEY

Y Voted for (yea).
\# Paired for.
\+ Announced for.
N Voted against (nay).
X Paired against.
\- Announced against.
P Voted "present".
C Voted "present" to avoid possible conflict of interest.
? Did not vote or otherwise make a position known.

	313 314 315 316 317 318 319 320
TEXAS	
Tower	N N N Y Y Y ? ?
Bentsen	N N N Y Y N Y Y
UTAH	
Garn	N N Y Y Y Y N Y
Hatch	Y N Y Y Y Y N Y
VERMONT	
Stafford	N N N Y Y Y Y Y
Leahy	Y Y N N Y N Y Y
VIRGINIA	
Warner	N N Y ? ? Y N Y
Byrd*	N Y N Y Y Y N Y
WASHINGTON	
Gorton	N N Y Y Y N Y Y
Jackson	N Y N N Y N Y Y
WEST VIRGINIA	
Byrd	N Y N N Y N Y Y
Randolph	N Y Y N Y N Y Y
WISCONSIN	
Kasten	N N Y Y Y N Y Y
Proxmire	Y Y N N Y N Y Y
WYOMING	
Simpson	Y N N Y Y Y N Y
Wallop	N N N Y Y Y N Y

Democrats   *Republicans*

* *Byrd elected as an independent.*

313. S 1196. Foreign Aid Authorization. Danforth, R-Mo., amendment to repeal the requirement that 50 percent of all shipments of U.S. food aid under the PL-480 Food for Peace program be carried on U.S. flag ships. Rejected 28-70: R 23-30; D 5-40 (ND 3-27, SD 2-13), Oct. 20, 1981.

314. S 1196. Foreign Aid Authorization. Glenn, D-Ohio, amendment to require that the president cut off aid to Pakistan or India if either should explode a nuclear device in the future. Adopted 51-45: R 11-41, D 40-4 (ND 28-1, SD 12-3), Oct. 21, 1981. A "nay" was a vote supporting the president's position.

315. S 1196. Foreign Aid Authorization. Percy, R-Ill., motion to table (kill) the Hart, D-Colo., amendment imposing a ban on U.S. purchases of Libyan oil within 90 days of enactment of the bill, unless the president chose to delay the ban another 90 days by certifying that the delay was necessary to protect the lives of American citizens in Libya. Motion rejected 33-60: R 30-19; D 3-41 (ND 2-27, SD 1-14), Oct. 21, 1981.

316. S 1196. Foreign Aid Authorization. Percy, R-Ill., substitute amendment for the Hart, D-Colo., amendment (see vote 317, below) to impose a ban on U.S. purchases of Libyan oil within 90 days of enactment of the bill. The substitute declared that Congress condemned the Libyan government for its support of international terrorist movements, its disruption of efforts to establish peace in the Middle East and its attempts to control other North African nations. Further, the substitute stated that the president should review steps the United States might take with its allies to force Libya to stop such activities, including the possibility of prohibiting the importation of Libyan oil. Adopted 47-44: R 39-9; D 8-35 (ND 3-25, SD 5-10), Oct. 21, 1981.

317. S 1196. Foreign Aid Authorization. Hart, D-Colo., amendment, as amended by the Percy substitute (see vote 316, above) condemning Libya and proposing that the president study possible sanctions against that nation. Adopted 87-3: R 47-0; D 40-3 (ND 25-3, SD 15-0), Oct. 21, 1981.

318. S 1196. Foreign Aid Authorization. Hatch, R-Utah, amendment to strike from the bill a section taking the Peace Corps out of the ACTION agency and making the Peace Corps an independent agency. Rejected 39-48: R 36-12; D 3-36 (ND 0-25, SD 3-11), Oct. 22, 1981.

319. S 1196. Foreign Aid Authorization. Mathias, R-Md., motion to table (kill) the Mattingly, R-Ga., amendment to make the separation of the Peace Corps from the ACTION agency effective on Oct. 1, 1982, rather than on the date of enactment of the bill. Motion agreed to 49-37: R 12-32; D 37-5 (ND 28-0, SD 9-5), Oct. 22, 1981.

320. S 1196. Foreign Aid Authorization. Moynihan, D-N.Y., amendment to require the president, in considering whether to provide foreign aid or allow arms sales to a foreign nation represented at the September 1981 meeting of non-aligned nations, to take into account whether that nation had dissociated itself from the communiqué issued following the meeting. Adopted 88-0: R 44-0; D 44-0 (ND 29-0, SD 15-0), Oct. 22, 1981.

	321	322	323	324	325	326	327
ALABAMA							
Denton	?	?	?	?	?	?	?
Heflin	N	Y	Y	N	N	Y	N
ALASKA							
Murkowski	N	Y	N	N	Y	Y	Y
Stevens	?	?	?	?	?	?	?
ARIZONA							
Goldwater	?	?	?	?	?	?	?
DeConcini	?	?	?	?	?	?	?
ARKANSAS							
Bumpers	?	?	?	?	?	?	?
Pryor	Y	Y	Y	N	N	Y	N
CALIFORNIA							
Hayakawa	?	?	?	?	?	?	?
Cranston	Y	Y	Y	N	N	Y	Y
COLORADO							
Armstrong	N	Y	N	Y	Y	N	N
Hart	Y	Y	N	N	?	N	Y
CONNECTICUT							
Weicker	?	?	?	?	?	?	?
Dodd	+	+	+	-	-	-	+
DELAWARE							
Roth	N	Y	N	N	Y	N	N
Biden	Y	Y	Y	N	N	Y	N
FLORIDA							
Hawkins	N	Y	N	Y	Y	Y	Y
Chiles	N	Y	N	N	Y	Y	Y
GEORGIA							
Mattingly	N	Y	N	N	Y	N	N
Nunn	N	Y	N	N	Y	N	N
HAWAII							
Inouye	Y	Y	Y	N	Y	N	Y
Matsunaga	Y	Y	Y	N	N	Y	Y
IDAHO							
McClure	N	Y	N	Y	Y	N	N
Symms	N	Y	?	+	?	-	-
ILLINOIS							
Percy	N	Y	Y	N	N	Y	N
Dixon	N	Y	Y	N	N	Y	Y
INDIANA							
Lugar	N	Y	Y	N	Y	N	Y
Quayle	N	Y	N	N	Y	N	N
IOWA							
Grassley	N	Y	N	Y	Y	N	N
Jepsen	N	Y	N	N	Y	N	N
KANSAS							
Dole	N	Y	N	N	Y	N	Y
Kassebaum	N	Y	Y	N	Y	N	Y
KENTUCKY							
Ford	Y	Y	N	Y	N	Y	N
Huddleston	Y	Y	Y	N	Y	Y	Y
LOUISIANA							
Johnston	N	Y	N	?	?	?	?
Long	N	Y	N	N	N	Y	N
MAINE							
Cohen	N	Y	N	N	Y	N	Y
Mitchell	Y	Y	Y	N	N	Y	Y
MARYLAND							
Mathias	N	Y	Y	N	Y	N	Y
Sarbanes	Y	Y	Y	?	?	?	?
MASSACHUSETTS							
Kennedy	Y	Y	Y	-	?	+	#
Tsongas	?	?	?	?	?	?	?
MICHIGAN							
Levin	Y	Y	N	N	N	Y	Y
Riegle	Y	Y	Y	N	N	Y	Y
MINNESOTA							
Boschwitz	N	Y	Y	N	Y	N	Y
Durenberger	?	?	?	?	?	?	?
MISSISSIPPI							
Cochran	N	Y	N	N	Y	N	Y
Stennis	N	Y	N	N	N	Y	N
MISSOURI							
Danforth	N	Y	Y	N	Y	N	Y
Eagleton	Y	Y	Y	N	N	Y	N
MONTANA							
Baucus	Y	Y	Y	N	N	Y	Y
Melcher	Y	Y	N	N	N	Y	N
NEBRASKA							
Exon	Y	Y	N	N	N	Y	N
Zorinsky	N	Y	Y	N	Y	Y	N
NEVADA							
Laxalt	N	Y	N	N	?	?	?
Cannon	Y	Y	N	N	N	Y	N
NEW HAMPSHIRE							
Humphrey	N	Y	N	Y	Y	N	N
Rudman	N	Y	N	N	Y	N	Y
NEW JERSEY							
Bradley	Y	Y	?	?	?	?	?
Williams	Y	Y	Y	?	?	?	?
NEW MEXICO							
Domenici	N	Y	N	N	Y	N	Y
Schmitt	N	Y	N	N	Y	N	N
NEW YORK							
D'Amato	?	?	?	?	?	?	?
Moynihan	Y	Y	Y	N	Y	Y	Y
NORTH CAROLINA							
East	N	Y	N	Y	Y	N	N
Helms	N	Y	Y	Y	N	N	N
NORTH DAKOTA							
Andrews	N	Y	?	?	?	?	?
Burdick	Y	Y	#	?	?	?	X
OHIO							
Glenn	Y	Y	Y	N	N	N	Y
Metzenbaum	Y	?	?	?	?	?	?
OKLAHOMA							
Nickles	N	Y	N	Y	Y	N	N
Boren	N	Y	N	Y	N	N	N
OREGON							
Hatfield	N	Y	Y	N	Y	Y	N
Packwood	N	Y	N	Y	N	Y	N
PENNSYLVANIA							
Heinz	N	Y	Y	N	Y	N	Y
Specter	N	Y	N	Y	N	Y	N
RHODE ISLAND							
Chafee	?	?	?	N	Y	N	Y
Pell	Y	Y	Y	N	N	Y	Y
SOUTH CAROLINA							
Thurmond	N	Y	N	Y	Y	N	Y
Hollings	N	Y	N	N	Y	N	N
SOUTH DAKOTA							
Abdnor	N	Y	N	N	Y	N	N
Pressler	?	?	?	?	?	?	?
TENNESSEE							
Baker	N	Y	?	N	Y	N	Y
Sasser	N	Y	?	?	-	?	?
TEXAS							
Tower	N	Y	N	N	Y	N	Y
Bentsen	N	Y	N	N	N	N	N
UTAH							
Garn	N	Y	?	?	?	?	?
Hatch	N	Y	N	N	Y	?	-
VERMONT							
Stafford	N	Y	Y	N	Y	N	Y
Leahy	Y	Y	Y	N	Y	N	Y
VIRGINIA							
Warner	N	Y	N	Y	Y	N	N
Byrd*	N	Y	N	Y	N	Y	N
WASHINGTON							
Gorton	N	Y	N	N	Y	N	Y
Jackson	Y	Y	N	N	Y	N	Y
WEST VIRGINIA							
Byrd	Y	Y	?	?	?	?	?
Randolph	Y	Y	X	Y	N	Y	N
WISCONSIN							
Kasten	N	Y	N	N	Y	N	Y
Proxmire	Y	Y	Y	Y	N	Y	N
WYOMING							
Simpson	N	Y	?	?	?	?	?
Wallop	N	Y	N	N	Y	N	N

KEY

Y   Voted for (yea).
\#   Paired for.
\+   Announced for.
N   Voted against (nay).
X   Paired against.
–   Announced against.
P   Voted "present".
C   Voted "present" to avoid possible conflict of interest.
?   Did not vote or otherwise make a position known.

Democrats   **Republicans**

* Byrd elected as an independent.

321. S 1196. Foreign Aid Authorization. Kennedy, D-Mass., motion to table (kill) the Helms, R-N.C., amendment repealing the prohibition on military aid and arms sales to Chile. Motion rejected 30-57: R 0-44; D 30-13 (ND 27-2, SD 3-11), Oct. 22, 1981. A "nay" was a vote supporting the president's position.

322. S 1196. Foreign Aid Authorization. Percy, R-Ill., substitute, to the Helms, R-N.C., amendment, to repeal the prohibition on military-related assistance to Chile but require the president to certify to Congress before doing so that Chile had made significant progress in preserving human rights. The Percy amendment also stated the sense of the Congress that the government of Chile should take steps to bring to justice Chilean officials indicted by a U.S. grand jury in connection with the 1976 assassination in Washington of former Chilean Ambassador to the United States Orlando Letelier. (The Helms amendment, as amended, subsequently was adopted by voice vote.) Adopted 86-0: R 44-0; D 42-0 (ND 28-0, SD 14-0), Oct. 22, 1981.

323. S 1196. Foreign Aid Authorization. Percy, R-Ill., motion to table (kill) the Tower, R-Texas, amendment to reverse the Foreign Relations Committee and retain existing Defense Department authority to lease property to individuals, businesses or other nations without congressional review. Motion rejected 33-43: R 12-27; D 21-16 (ND 18-6, SD 3-10), Oct. 22, 1981. (The Tower amendment subsequently was adopted by voice vote).

324. S 1196. Foreign Aid Authorization. Helms, R-N.C., amendment to prohibit aid to Zimbabwe unless the president certified to Congress that no North Korean military advisers were present in Zimbabwe after Jan. 1, 1982. Rejected 14-61: R 10-31; D 4-30 (ND 2-20, SD 2-10), Oct. 22, 1981.

325. S 1196. Foreign Aid Authorization. Baker, R-Tenn., motion to reconsider the voice vote by which the Senate had rejected the Kasten, R-Wis., amendment to provide that up to $75 million of Economic Support Fund monies could be used by the president as a contingency fund to give economic aid to nations without specific congressional approval so long as the House Foreign Affairs, Senate Foreign Relations and House and Senate Appropriations committees were notified 15 days in advance. Motion agreed to 49-24: R 39-1; D 10-23 (ND 5-16, SD 5-7) Oct. 22, 1981. (The Kasten amendment subsequently was adopted by voice vote).

326. S 1196. Foreign Aid Authorization. Hatfield, R-Ore., amendment to delete from the bill $100 million for economic assistance to Pakistan. Rejected 28-45: R 3-36; D 25-9 (ND 17-5, SD 8-4), Oct. 22, 1981. A "nay" was a vote supporting the president's position.

327. S 1196. Foreign Aid Authorization. Passage of the bill to authorize $5.8 billion for fiscal 1982 foreign aid programs. Passed 40-33: R 23-16; D 17-17 (ND 15-7, SD 2-10), Oct. 22, 1981.

CQ Senate Votes 328 - 335

Corresponding to Congressional Record Votes 331, 332, 333, 334, 335, 336, 337, 338

	328	329	330	331	332	333	334	335
ALABAMA								
Denton	Y	Y	N	N	N	Y	Y	N
Heflin	Y	Y	Y	N	N	Y	N	Y
ALASKA								
Murkowski	Y	Y	N	N	N	N	Y	N
Stevens	Y	N	?	?	N	N	Y	N
ARIZONA								
Goldwater	Y	N	N	N	N	N	?	N
DeConcini	Y	N	Y	N	N	N	Y	Y
ARKANSAS								
Bumpers	Y	N	Y	Y	N	N	Y	Y
Pryor	Y	N	Y	Y	N	N	Y	Y
CALIFORNIA								
Hayakawa	Y	?	N	N	Y	N	Y	N
Cranston	Y	N	Y	Y	N	N	Y	Y
COLORADO								
Armstrong	Y	N	N	N	Y	Y	Y	N
Hart	Y	N	Y	Y	N	N	Y	Y
CONNECTICUT								
Weicker	Y	N	Y	N	Y	Y	Y	Y
Dodd	Y	N	+	Y	Y	N	Y	Y
DELAWARE								
Roth	Y	Y	Y	N	Y	Y	N	Y
Biden	?	?	Y	Y	Y	N	Y	Y
FLORIDA								
Hawkins	Y	N	?	Y	Y	N	Y	Y
Chiles	Y	N	Y	N	N	N	Y	Y
GEORGIA								
Mattingly	Y	Y	N	N	Y	N	Y	N
Nunn	Y	N	Y	N	N	N	Y	N
HAWAII								
Inouye	?	-	+	?	.	?	+	Y
Matsunaga	Y	N	Y	N	N	Y	N	Y
IDAHO								
McClure	Y	N	N	N	N	N	Y	N
Symms	Y	N	N	N	Y	Y	Y	N
ILLINOIS								
Percy	Y	N	N	N	N	Y	Y	N
Dixon	Y	N	Y	N	N	N	Y	Y
INDIANA								
Lugar	Y	Y	N	N	Y	Y	Y	N
Quayle	Y	N	N	N	Y	Y	Y	N
IOWA								
Grassley	Y	N	N	N	Y	N	N	N
Jepsen	Y	Y	N	N	Y	Y	N	N
KANSAS								
Dole	Y	Y	N	N	N	Y	Y	N
Kassebaum	Y	Y	N	N	Y	Y	N	N
KENTUCKY								
Ford	Y	N	?	N	N	N	Y	Y
Huddleston	Y	N	Y	Y	N	N	Y	N
LOUISIANA								
Johnston	Y	N	N	N	N	N	Y	N
Long	?	?	N	N	N	N	Y	N
MAINE								
Cohen	Y	N	Y	Y	N	Y	N	N
Mitchell	?	?	Y	Y	N	N	Y	Y
MARYLAND								
Mathias	Y	N	Y	N	N	N	Y	N
Sarbanes	Y	N	Y	N	N	N	Y	Y
MASSACHUSETTS								
Kennedy	Y	N	Y	Y	N	Y	N	Y
Tsongas	?	?	Y	Y	N	N	Y	Y
MICHIGAN								
Levin	Y	N	Y	Y	N	Y	N	Y
Riegle	Y	-	+	Y	Y	Y	Y	Y
MINNESOTA								
Boschwitz	Y	Y	N	N	Y	Y	N	N
Durenberger	Y	N	Y	Y	N	Y	N	N
MISSISSIPPI								
Cochran	Y	Y	N	N	N	N	Y	N
Stennis	?	?	N	N	N	N	Y	N
MISSOURI								
Danforth	Y	N	N	N	Y	Y	Y	Y
Eagleton	Y	N	?	?	?	?	?	Y
MONTANA								
Baucus	Y	N	Y	Y	N	N	Y	Y
Melcher	Y	N	N	Y	N	N	Y	N
NEBRASKA								
Exon	Y	N	Y	N	N	Y	N	Y
Zorinsky	?	?	?	?	Y	Y	Y	N
NEVADA								
Laxalt	Y	N	N	N	Y	Y	Y	N
Cannon	Y	N	Y	Y	N	N	Y	Y
NEW HAMPSHIRE								
Humphrey	Y	Y	N	Y	Y	Y	N	N
Rudman	Y	N	N	Y	N	N	Y	N
NEW JERSEY								
Bradley	Y	N	Y	Y	N	N	Y	Y
Williams	Y	N	Y	Y	N	N	Y	Y
NEW MEXICO								
Domenici	Y	N	N	N	N	N	Y	N
Schmitt	Y	N	N	?	?	?	+	N
NEW YORK								
D'Amato	Y	N	+	Y	Y	N	Y	Y
Moynihan	Y	N	Y	Y	N	N	Y	Y
NORTH CAROLINA								
East	Y	Y	N	N	Y	Y	Y	N
Helms	Y	Y	N	N	Y	Y	N	N
NORTH DAKOTA								
Andrews	Y	N	N	N	N	N	Y	N
Burdick	Y	N	Y	N	Y	N	Y	Y
OHIO								
Glenn	Y	N	Y	Y	N	Y	N	N
Metzenbaum	?	?	Y	Y	N	N	Y	Y
OKLAHOMA								
Nickles	Y	N	N	N	N	Y	Y	N
Boren	Y	N	N	N	Y	Y	Y	N
OREGON								
Hatfield	Y	N	Y	Y	N	N	Y	Y
Packwood	Y	N	N	N	N	N	Y	Y
PENNSYLVANIA								
Heinz	Y	N	Y	N	Y	N	Y	Y
Specter	Y	?	Y	Y	N	Y	Y	Y
RHODE ISLAND								
Chafee	Y	N	Y	Y	N	N	Y	N
Pell	Y	N	Y	Y	N	N	Y	Y
SOUTH CAROLINA								
Thurmond	Y	N	N	N	N	Y	Y	N
Hollings	?	?	Y	Y	N	N	Y	Y
SOUTH DAKOTA								
Abdnor	Y	N	N	N	N	N	Y	N
Pressler	Y	N	N	N	N	N	Y	N
TENNESSEE								
Baker	Y	N	N	N	N	Y	Y	N
Sasser	Y	N	N	Y	N	Y	Y	Y
TEXAS								
Tower	Y	Y	N	N	N	N	Y	N
Bentsen	?	N	N	N	N	Y	Y	Y
UTAH								
Garn	Y	N	N	N	Y	N	Y	N
Hatch	Y	N	N	Y	N	Y	N	Y
VERMONT								
Stafford	Y	N	Y	N	N	Y	Y	N
Leahy	Y	N	Y	Y	N	Y	N	Y
VIRGINIA								
Warner	Y	N	N	N	N	?	?	N
Byrd*	Y	Y	N	N	Y	Y	N	N
WASHINGTON								
Gorton	Y	N	Y	N	Y	N	Y	N
Jackson	Y	N	Y	Y	N	N	Y	Y
WEST VIRGINIA								
Byrd	Y	N	Y	N	N	Y	N	N
Randolph	Y	N	Y	Y	N	N	Y	N
WISCONSIN								
Kasten	Y	N	N	N	Y	Y	Y	Y
Proxmire	N	N	Y	N	Y	Y	Y	N
WYOMING								
Simpson	Y	N	N	N	Y	Y	Y	N
Wallop	Y	N	N	N	Y	Y	Y	N

KEY

Y Voted for (yea).
Paired for.
+ Announced for.
N Voted against (nay).
X Paired against.
- Announced against.
P Voted "present".
C Voted "present" to avoid possible conflict of interest.
? Did not vote or otherwise make a position known.

Democrats *Republicans*

* *Byrd elected as an independent.*

328. HR 4035. Interior Appropriations, Fiscal 1982. Cochran, R-Miss., amendment to add $7 million in payments to states for local revenues lost due to federal wildlife refuges located within their borders. Adopted 89-1: R 53-0; D 36-1 (ND 25-1, SD 11-0), Oct. 26, 1981.

329. HR 4035. Interior Appropriations, Fiscal 1982. Dole, R-Kan., amendment to transfer to other energy programs $7 million earmarked for a federal program that requires large utilities to conduct residential energy audits. Rejected 17-71: R 15-36; D 2-35 (ND 0-25, SD 2-10), Oct. 26, 1981.

330. HR 4035. Interior Appropriations, Fiscal 1982. Leahy, D-Vt., amendment to provide $12.9 million for Energy Department investigations of alleged oil price control violations. Rejected 43-48: R 11-39; D 32-9 (ND 25-2, SD 7-7), Oct. 27, 1981.

331. HR 4035. Interior Appropriations, Fiscal 1982. Mitchell, D-Maine, amendment to add $37.5 million for weatherizing homes of low-income residents. Rejected 46-49: R 15-36; D 31-13 (ND 26-3, SD 5-10), Oct. 27, 1981.

332. HR 4035. Interior Appropriations, Fiscal 1982. Proxmire, D-Wis., amendment to delete $135 million for a synthetic fuels demonstration plant in Newman, Ky. Rejected 40-57: R 29-23; D 11-34 (ND 9-21, SD 2-13), Oct. 27, 1981.

333. HR 4035. Interior Appropriations, Fiscal 1982. Mattingly, R-Ga., amendment to reduce appropriations in the bill by 5 percent. Rejected 35-61: R 26-25; D 9-36 (ND 4-26, SD 5-10), Oct. 27, 1981.

334. HR 4035. Interior Appropriations, Fiscal 1982. Passage of the bill to appropriate $7,358,697,760 in fiscal 1982 for the Interior Department and related agencies. Passed 87-8: R 45-5; D 42-3 (ND 29-1, SD 13-2), Oct. 27, 1981. The president in September had requested $6,680,895,000.

335. H Con Res 194. Disapproving AWACS Sale. Adoption of the concurrent resolution disapproving the proposal by President Reagan to sell Saudi Arabia an $8.5 billion package of military equipment consisting of five E-3A Airborne Warning and Control System (AWACS) radar planes, 1,177 AIM-9L Sidewinder air-to-air missiles, 101 sets of conformal fuel tanks for F-15 fighter planes and six to eight KC-707 tanker aircraft. Rejected 48-52: R 12-41; D 36-11 (ND 28-4, SD 8-7), Oct. 28, 1981. A "nay" was a vote supporting the president's position.

	336 337 338 339 340		336 337 338 339 340		336 337 338 339 340
ALABAMA		**IOWA**		**NEW HAMPSHIRE**	
Denton	N N N N Y	*Grassley*	N N N Y Y	*Humphrey*	N N N N N
Heflin	N N N Y Y	*Jepsen*	N N N Y Y	*Rudman*	N N N N N
ALASKA		**KANSAS**		**NEW JERSEY**	
Murkowski	N N N N Y	*Dole*	N N N N ?	Bradley	Y Y N Y N
Stevens	N N N N Y	*Kassebaum*	N N N N Y	Williams	N Y Y Y Y
ARIZONA		**KENTUCKY**		**NEW MEXICO**	
Goldwater	N N N N Y	Ford	N N N Y Y	*Domenici*	N N N N Y
DeConcini	N N N Y Y	Huddleston	N N Y N Y	*Schmitt*	- - ? ? +
ARKANSAS		**LOUISIANA**		**NEW YORK**	
Bumpers	N N Y Y Y	Johnston	N N N N Y	*D'Amato*	N N N N Y
Pryor	N Y N Y Y	Long	N N N N Y	Moynihan	Y Y Y Y Y
CALIFORNIA		**MAINE**		**NORTH CAROLINA**	
Hayakawa	N N N N Y	*Cohen*	N N N Y Y	*East*	N N N N Y
Cranston	N N Y Y Y	Mitchell	N N N Y Y	*Helms*	N N N N Y
COLORADO		**MARYLAND**		**NORTH DAKOTA**	
Armstrong	N N N N N	*Mathias*	Y Y Y Y Y	*Andrews*	N N N N Y
Hart	Y Y Y Y Y	Sarbanes	N N Y Y Y	Burdick	N N N N Y
CONNECTICUT		**MASSACHUSETTS**		**OHIO**	
Weicker	N Y Y Y Y	Kennedy	N Y Y Y Y	Glenn	N N Y ? ?
Dodd	N N Y Y Y	Tsongas	Y Y N Y Y	Metzenbaum	N N Y Y Y
DELAWARE		**MICHIGAN**		**OKLAHOMA**	
Roth	N N N Y Y	Levin	N Y Y Y Y	*Nickles*	N N N N N
Biden	Y Y N Y Y	Riegle	N N Y Y Y	Boren	N Y N N Y
FLORIDA		**MINNESOTA**		**OREGON**	
Hawkins	- - - N Y	*Boschwitz*	N Y Y Y Y	*Hatfield*	? ? ? ? ?
Chiles	N N N Y Y	*Durenberger*	N N N Y +	*Packwood*	N - N N Y
GEORGIA		**MISSISSIPPI**		**PENNSYLVANIA**	
Mattingly	N N N N N	*Cochran*	N N N N Y	*Heinz*	N N N N Y
Nunn	N Y N N Y	Stennis	N N N Y Y	*Specter*	N N N Y Y
HAWAII		**MISSOURI**		**RHODE ISLAND**	
Inouye	? ? Y Y Y	*Danforth*	N N N N Y	*Chafee*	N N N Y Y
Matsunaga	N N N N Y	Eagleton	N Y N Y Y	Pell	N Y Y Y Y
IDAHO		**MONTANA**		**SOUTH CAROLINA**	
McClure	N N N N Y	Baucus	N N N Y Y	*Thurmond*	N - - - +
Symms	N N N N ?	Melcher	N N N N Y	Hollings	N N Y Y Y
ILLINOIS		**NEBRASKA**		**SOUTH DAKOTA**	
Percy	Y Y N Y N	Exon	N Y N N Y	*Abdnor*	N N N N Y
Dixon	N N N Y Y	Zorinsky	N N N N Y	*Pressler*	N N N N Y
INDIANA		**NEVADA**		**TENNESSEE**	
Lugar	N N N N Y	*Laxalt*	N N N N Y	*Baker*	N N N N Y
Quayle	N N N N Y	Cannon	Y N N N Y	Sasser	N N N Y Y

	336 337 338 339 340
TEXAS	
Tower	N N ? N Y
Bentsen	N N N N Y
UTAH	
Garn	N N N N Y
Hatch	N N N N Y
VERMONT	
Stafford	N N N N Y
Leahy	N N Y Y Y
VIRGINIA	
Warner	N N N N Y
Byrd*	N N N N Y
WASHINGTON	
Gorton	N N N N Y
Jackson	N N N N Y
WEST VIRGINIA	
Byrd	N N Y N Y
Randolph	N N Y + +
WISCONSIN	
Kasten	N N N N Y
Proxmire	N N N Y Y
WYOMING	
Simpson	N N N N Y
Wallop	N N N N Y

KEY

Y Voted for (yea).
Paired for.
+ Announced for.
N Voted against (nay).
X Paired against.
- Announced against.
P Voted "present".
C Voted "present" to avoid possible conflict of interest.
? Did not vote or otherwise make a position known.

Democrats   **Republicans**

* Byrd elected as an independent.

336. S 1503. Standby Petroleum Allocation Act. Bradley, D-N.J., amendment to prohibit government allocation of oil and recycle government revenue to individuals during an oil shortage. Rejected 8-88: R 2-48; D 6-40 (ND 6-25, SD 0-15), Oct. 29, 1981.

337. S 1503. Standby Petroleum Allocation Act. Bradley, D-N.J., amendment to require the government to sell oil from the Strategic Petroleum Reserve instead of implementing any oil allocation plan during a shortage. Rejected 18-76: R 4-44; D 14-32 (ND 11-20, SD 3-12), Oct. 29, 1981.

338. S 1503. Standby Petroleum Allocation Act. Weicker, R-Conn., amendment to give the president the authority to include plans for rationing gasoline and diesel fuel in a standby oil allocation plan. Rejected 22-73: R 3-45; D 19-28 (ND 16-16, SD 3-12), Oct. 29, 1981.

339. S 1503. Standby Petroleum Allocation Act. Mitchell, D-Maine, amendment to allow states to allocate oil before a national oil allocation plan went into effect. Rejected 42-53: R 12-38; D 30-15 (ND 22-8, SD 8-7), Oct. 29, 1981.

340. S 1503. Standby Petroleum Allocation Act. Passage of the bill to give the president discretionary authority to allocate oil and set prices during a severe oil shortage. Passed 85-7: R 41-6; D 44-1 (ND 29-1, SD 15-0), Oct. 29, 1981. A "nay" was a vote supporting the president's position.

CQ Senate Votes 341 - 348

Corresponding to Congressional Record Votes 344, 345, 346, 347, 348, 349, 350, 351

	341	342	343	344	345	346	347	348
ALABAMA								
Denton	Y	Y	Y	Y	Y	Y	Y	Y
Heflin	N	N	?	?	?	Y	N	Y
ALASKA								
Murkowski	Y	Y	Y	Y	Y	Y	Y	Y
Stevens	N	Y	Y	Y	Y	Y	N	N
ARIZONA								
Goldwater	?	?	?	?	?	?	?	?
DeConcini	Y	N	Y	Y	Y	Y	N	Y
ARKANSAS								
Bumpers	N	Y	Y	Y	Y	Y	N	N
Pryor	N	Y	Y	Y	Y	Y	N	N
CALIFORNIA								
Hayakawa	Y	Y	Y	Y	Y	Y	Y	Y
Cranston	N	Y	Y	Y	Y	Y	N	N
COLORADO								
Armstrong	Y	N	Y	Y	Y	N	Y	Y
Hart	N	Y	?	?	?	?	?	N
CONNECTICUT								
Weicker	?	?	Y	Y	Y	Y	N	N
Dodd	N	Y	Y	Y	Y	Y	N	N
DELAWARE								
Roth	Y	N	?	?	?	Y	N	Y
Biden	N	Y	?	?	?	Y	N	N
FLORIDA								
Hawkins	N	Y	Y	Y	Y	Y	N	N
Chiles	N	Y	?	?	?	Y	N	N
GEORGIA								
Mattingly	Y	Y	Y	Y	Y	Y	Y	Y
Nunn	N	Y	Y	Y	Y	Y	N	Y
HAWAII								
Inouye	N	Y	?	?	?	?	?	?
Matsunaga	N	Y	Y	Y	Y	?	N	N
IDAHO								
McClure	Y	Y	?	?	?	Y	Y	?
Symms	Y	N	Y	Y	Y	N	Y	Y
ILLINOIS								
Percy	Y	Y	Y	Y	Y	Y	Y	N
Dixon	N	Y	Y	Y	Y	Y	N	N
INDIANA								
Lugar	Y	Y	Y	Y	Y	Y	N	Y
Quayle	Y	Y	Y	Y	Y	Y	N	Y

	341	342	343	344	345	346	347	348
IOWA								
Grassley	N	Y	Y	Y	Y	Y	Y	Y
Jepsen	N	Y	?	+	+	Y	Y	Y
KANSAS								
Dole	?	?	Y	Y	Y	Y	Y	Y
Kassebaum	N	Y	Y	Y	Y	Y	Y	N
KENTUCKY								
Ford	N	Y	?	?	?	?	?	N
Huddleston	N	Y	Y	Y	Y	Y	N	N
LOUISIANA								
Johnston	N	?	Y	Y	Y	Y	N	N
Long	N	Y	Y	Y	Y	Y	N	N
MAINE								
Cohen	N	Y	?	?	?	?	?	N
Mitchell	N	Y	Y	Y	Y	Y	N	N
MARYLAND								
Mathias	?	Y	Y	Y	Y	Y	N	N
Sarbanes	N	Y	Y	Y	Y	Y	N	N
MASSACHUSETTS								
Kennedy	N	Y	Y	Y	Y	Y	N	N
Tsongas	Y	Y	?	?	?	Y	N	N
MICHIGAN								
Levin	N	Y	Y	Y	Y	Y	N	N
Riegle	N	Y	Y	Y	Y	Y	N	N
MINNESOTA								
Boschwitz	Y	Y	?	?	?	?	?	+
Durenberger	N	Y	Y	Y	Y	N	Y	N
MISSISSIPPI								
Cochran	N	Y	Y	Y	Y	Y	N	N
Stennis	N	Y	Y	Y	Y	Y	N	N
MISSOURI								
Danforth	Y	Y	Y	Y	Y	N	Y	Y
Eagleton	N	Y	Y	Y	Y	Y	N	Y
MONTANA								
Baucus	N	Y	Y	Y	Y	Y	N	N
Melcher	?	Y	Y	Y	Y	Y	N	N
NEBRASKA								
Exon	N	N	Y	Y	Y	Y	N	N
Zorinsky	?	?	Y	Y	Y	Y	N	Y
NEVADA								
Laxalt	Y	Y	Y	Y	Y	Y	Y	Y
Cannon	Y	Y	+	+	+	?	?	?

	341	342	343	344	345	346	347	348
NEW HAMPSHIRE								
Humphrey	Y	N	Y	Y	Y	N	Y	Y
Rudman	N	Y	Y	Y	Y	Y	N	N
NEW JERSEY								
Bradley	?	Y	Y	Y	Y	Y	N	N
Williams	N	Y	?	?	?	?	?	?
NEW MEXICO								
Domenici	N	Y	?	?	?	N	Y	Y
Schmitt	?	+	Y	Y	Y	Y	Y	Y
NEW YORK								
D'Amato	Y	Y	+	?	?	Y	N	N
Moynihan	Y	Y	Y	Y	Y	Y	N	N
NORTH CAROLINA								
East	Y	N	?	?	?	?	?	?
Helms	Y	N	Y	Y	Y	Y	Y	Y
NORTH DAKOTA								
Andrews	N	Y	Y	Y	Y	Y	N	N
Burdick	N	Y	Y	Y	Y	Y	N	N
OHIO								
Glenn	N	Y	Y	Y	Y	Y	N	N
Metzenbaum	N	Y	Y	Y	Y	?	?	?
OKLAHOMA								
Nickles	?	?	Y	Y	Y	N	Y	Y
Boren	N	N	Y	Y	Y	Y	N	Y
OREGON								
Hatfield	-	+	+	+	+	Y	N	N
Packwood	N	Y	Y	Y	Y	N	Y	N
PENNSYLVANIA								
Heinz	N	Y	Y	Y	Y	Y	N	N
Specter	N	Y	Y	Y	Y	Y	Y	Y
RHODE ISLAND								
Chafee	N	Y	+	+	+	N	Y	Y
Pell	#	X	Y	Y	Y	Y	N	N
SOUTH CAROLINA								
Thurmond	+	+	Y	Y	Y	Y	Y	Y
Hollings	?	?	?	Y	Y	Y	N	N
SOUTH DAKOTA								
Abdnor	N	Y	Y	Y	Y	Y	N	N
Pressler	N	N	Y	Y	Y	Y	Y	N
TENNESSEE								
Baker	Y	Y	Y	Y	Y	Y	Y	Y
Sasser	N	Y	+	+	Y	Y	N	N

	341	342	343	344	345	346	347	348
TEXAS								
Tower	Y	Y	?	?	?	?	?	Y
Bentsen	Y	Y	Y	Y	Y	Y	N	Y
UTAH								
Garn	Y	N	?	?	Y	Y	Y	Y
Hatch	?	+	Y	Y	Y	Y	Y	Y
VERMONT								
Stafford	N	+	Y	Y	Y	Y	Y	N
Leahy	N	Y	Y	Y	Y	Y	N	N
VIRGINIA								
Warner	Y	Y	?	?	?	Y	N	N
Byrd*	Y	N	?	?	?	N	Y	Y
WASHINGTON								
Gorton	Y	Y	Y	Y	Y	Y	Y	Y
Jackson	X	#	Y	Y	Y	Y	N	N
WEST VIRGINIA								
Byrd	?	?	Y	Y	Y	Y	N	N
Randolph	N	Y	Y	Y	Y	?	-	-
WISCONSIN								
Kasten	Y	N	?	?	?	?	?	Y
Proxmire	Y	N	Y	Y	Y	N	Y	Y
WYOMING								
Simpson	Y	Y	?	?	?	Y	Y	Y
Wallop	?	?	Y	Y	Y	N	Y	Y

Democrats   *Republicans*

* Byrd elected as an independent.

341. HR 4119. Agriculture Appropriations, Fiscal 1982. Mattingly, R-Ga., amendment to reduce by an average of 2.6 percent (and no more than 6 percent for any single program) appropriations in the bill except for programs whose payments are required by law. Rejected 32-51: R 25-18; D 7-33 (ND 5-21, SD 2-12), Oct. 30, 1981. A "yea" was a vote supporting the president's position.

342. HR 4119. Agriculture Appropriations, Fiscal 1982. Passage of the bill to appropriate $22,852,634,000 in fiscal 1982 for the Agriculture Department, the Food and Drug Administration and the Commodity Futures Trading Commission. Passed 69-15: R 34-9; D 35-6 (ND 25-3, SD 10-3), Oct. 30, 1981. A "nay" was a vote supporting the president's position.

343. S 1086. Older Americans Act. Kennedy, D-Mass., amendment to prohibit states from reducing their share of nutrition funds for the elderly spent on home-delivered meals. Adopted 72-0: R 37-0; D 35-0 (ND 26-0, SD 9-0), Nov. 2, 1981.

344. S 1086. Older Americans Act. Byrd, D-W.Va., amendment stating the sense of the Senate in opposition to taxation of Social Security benefits and to reduction of benefits aimed at balancing the federal budget. Adopted 72-0: R 37-0; D 35-0 (ND 26-0, SD 9-0), Nov. 2, 1981.

345. S 1086. Older Americans Act. Passage of the bill to extend Older Americans Act programs through fiscal 1984, to consolidate two authorizations for nutrition programs for the elderly and to set spending limits on commodity support for elderly nutrition programs. Passed 75-0: R 38-0; D 37-0 (ND 26-0, SD 11-0), Nov. 2, 1981.

346. HR 4209. Transportation Appropriations, Fiscal 1982. Judgment of the Senate whether the Senate Appropriations Committee amendment to direct Amtrak to provide passenger rail service between Washington, D.C., to Chicago, via Cincinnati, was germane. Ruled germane 75-12: R 37-10; D 38-2 (ND 25-1, SD 13-1), Nov. 3, 1981.

347. HR 4209. Transportation Appropriations, Fiscal 1982. Packwood, R-Ore., amendment to delete the provision requiring Amtrak to provide passenger rail service between Washington, D.C., to Chicago, via Cincinnati. Rejected 34-53: R 32-15; D 2-38 (ND 1-25, SD 1-13), Nov. 3, 1981.

348. HR 4209. Transportation Appropriations, Fiscal 1982. Mattingly, R-Ga., amendment to cut the bill's total appropriations by 4.1 percent. Rejected 39-52: R 30-19; D 9-33 (ND 4-23, SD 5-10), Nov. 3, 1981.

KEY

- Y Voted for (yea).
- # Paired for.
- + Announced for.
- N Voted against (nay).
- X Paired against.
- - Announced against.
- P Voted "present".
- C Voted "present" to avoid possible conflict of interest.
- ? Did not vote or otherwise make a position known.

	349	350	351	352
ALABAMA				
Denton	Y	N	Y	Y
Heflin	N	N	Y	Y
ALASKA				
Murkowski	Y	N	Y	Y
Stevens	Y	X	?	?
ARIZONA				
Goldwater	?	?	?	?
DeConcini	Y	N	N	N
ARKANSAS				
Bumpers	Y	N	N	N
Pryor	Y	N	N	N
CALIFORNIA				
Hayakawa	N	N	Y	Y
Cranston	Y	N	N	N
COLORADO				
Armstrong	N	Y	N	N
Hart	Y	Y	N	N
CONNECTICUT				
Weicker	Y	?	?	?
Dodd	Y	N	N	N
DELAWARE				
Roth	N	Y	N	N
Biden	Y	Y	N	N
FLORIDA				
Hawkins	Y	#	Y	Y
Chiles	Y	Y	N	N
GEORGIA				
Mattingly	Y	N	Y	Y
Nunn	Y	N	N	N
HAWAII				
Inouye	?	N	N	N
Matsunaga	Y	N	N	N
IDAHO				
McClure	Y	N	Y	Y
Symms	N	N	Y	Y
ILLINOIS				
Percy	Y	Y	N	N
Dixon	Y	Y	N	N
INDIANA				
Lugar	Y	Y	N	N
Quayle	Y	Y	N	N

	349	350	351	352
IOWA				
Grassley	N	Y	Y	Y
Jepsen	Y	Y	N	N
KANSAS				
Dole	Y	N	Y	Y
Kassebaum	Y	Y	N	N
KENTUCKY				
Ford	Y	N	N	Y
Huddleston	Y	N	Y	Y
LOUISIANA				
Johnston	Y	N	Y	Y
Long	Y	N	Y	Y
MAINE				
Cohen	Y	Y	N	N
Mitchell	Y	N	N	N
MARYLAND				
Mathias	Y	Y	Y	Y
Sarbanes	Y	Y	N	N
MASSACHUSETTS				
Kennedy	Y	Y	N	N
Tsongas	Y	Y	N	N
MICHIGAN				
Levin	Y	N	N	N
Riegle	Y	Y	N	N
MINNESOTA				
Boschwitz	?	Y	N	N
Durenberger	Y	Y	N	N
MISSISSIPPI				
Cochran	Y	N	Y	Y
Stennis	Y	N	Y	Y
MISSOURI				
Danforth	N	Y	Y	Y
Eagleton	N	Y	N	N
MONTANA				
Baucus	Y	Y	N	N
Melcher	Y	N	N	N
NEBRASKA				
Exon	Y	N	N	N
Zorinsky	Y	Y	Y	Y
NEVADA				
Laxalt	Y	?	Y	Y
Cannon	?	?	?	+

	349	350	351	352
NEW HAMPSHIRE				
Humphrey	N	Y	N	N
Rudman	Y	Y	N	Y
NEW JERSEY				
Bradley	Y	Y	N	N
Williams	?	Y	N	N
NEW MEXICO				
Domenici	Y	Y	Y	Y
Schmitt	Y	N	Y	Y
NEW YORK				
D'Amato	Y	N	Y	Y
Moynihan	Y	Y	?	?
NORTH CAROLINA				
East	?	N	Y	Y
Helms	N	Y	Y	Y
NORTH DAKOTA				
Andrews	Y	N	Y	Y
Burdick	Y	N	Y	Y
OHIO				
Glenn	Y	N	N	N
Metzenbaum	?	Y	N	N
OKLAHOMA				
Nickles	N	N	N	N
Boren	Y	N	?	?
OREGON				
Hatfield	Y	N	N	N
Packwood	Y	N	N	Y
PENNSYLVANIA				
Heinz	Y	Y	Y	Y
Specter	Y	Y	Y	Y
RHODE ISLAND				
Chafee	Y	Y	N	N
Pell	Y	Y	N	N
SOUTH CAROLINA				
Thurmond	Y	N	Y	Y
Hollings	Y	N	N	N
SOUTH DAKOTA				
Abdnor	Y	N	Y	Y
Pressler	Y	Y	Y	Y
TENNESSEE				
Baker	Y	N	Y	Y
Sasser	Y	N	Y	Y

	349	350	351	352
TEXAS				
Tower	Y	N	Y	Y
Bentsen	Y	N	Y	Y
UTAH				
Garn	N	Y	Y	Y
Hatch	N	N	N	Y
VERMONT				
Stafford	Y	Y	Y	Y
Leahy	Y	Y	N	N
VIRGINIA				
Warner	Y	Y	Y	Y
Byrd*	N	Y	N	N
WASHINGTON				
Gorton	Y	Y	Y	Y
Jackson	Y	N	Y	Y
WEST VIRGINIA				
Byrd	Y	N	N	N
Randolph	+	N	N	Y
WISCONSIN				
Kasten	Y	N	Y	Y
Proxmire	N	Y	N	N
WYOMING				
Simpson	Y	Y	Y	Y
Wallop	Y	Y	Y	Y

Democrats *Republicans*

* Byrd elected as an independent.

349. HR 4209. Transportation Appropriations, Fiscal 1982. Passage of the bill to appropriate $10,414,397,927 in fiscal 1982 for the Transportation Department and related agencies. Passed 77-15: R 39-11; D 38-4 (ND 25-2, SD 13-2), Nov. 3, 1981.

350. HR 4144. Energy and Water Development Appropriations, Fiscal 1982. Percy, R-Ill., amendment to delete $189 million for the continued construction of the Tennessee-Tombigbee Waterway. The effect would be to cancel the project. Rejected 46-48: R 27-21; D 19-27 (ND 17-14, SD 2-13), Nov. 4, 1981. A "nay" was a vote supporting the president's position.

351. HR 4144. Energy and Water Development Appropriations, Fiscal 1982. Johnston, D-La., motion to table (kill) the Tsongas, D-Mass., amendment to reduce by half ($90 million) the appropriation for the Clinch River (Tenn.) nuclear breeder reactor. Motion rejected 43-51: R 33-17; D 10-34 (ND 3-27, SD 7-7), Nov. 4, 1981. A "yea" was a vote supporting the president's position.

352. HR 4144. Energy and Water Development Appropriations, Fiscal 1982. Johnston, D-La., motion to table (kill) the Bumpers, D-Ark., amendment as amended by Tsongas, D-Mass., to reduce by half ($90 million) the appropriation for the Clinch River (Tenn.) nuclear breeder reactor. Motion agreed to 48-46: R 36-14; D 12-32 (ND 4-26, SD 8-6), Nov. 4, 1981. A "yea" was a vote supporting the president's position.

	353 354 355 356 357		353 354 355 356 357		353 354 355 356 357
ALABAMA		**IOWA**		**NEW HAMPSHIRE**	
Denton	Y N Y Y Y	*Grassley*	Y N Y Y N	*Humphrey*	N N Y Y N
Heflin	Y Y Y Y Y	*Jepsen*	Y N Y Y Y	*Rudman*	Y N Y N Y
ALASKA		**KANSAS**		**NEW JERSEY**	
Murkowski	Y Y Y Y Y	*Dole*	Y N Y Y Y	Bradley	N Y Y N ?
Stevens	? ? ? ? ?	*Kassebaum*	N N Y N Y	Williams	N Y Y ? Y
ARIZONA		**KENTUCKY**		**NEW MEXICO**	
Goldwater	? ? ? ? ?	Ford	Y Y Y N Y	*Domenici*	Y Y Y Y Y
DeConcini	N Y Y Y Y	Huddleston	Y Y Y N Y	*Schmitt*	Y N Y N Y
ARKANSAS		**LOUISIANA**		**NEW YORK**	
Bumpers	N Y Y N N	Johnston	Y Y Y N Y	*D'Amato*	Y Y Y ? +
Pryor	N N Y N N	Long	Y Y Y N Y	Moynihan	N Y Y + ?
CALIFORNIA		**MAINE**		**NORTH CAROLINA**	
Hayakawa	Y N Y Y Y	*Cohen*	N N Y Y Y	*East*	Y N Y Y Y
Cranston	N Y Y N Y	Mitchell	N Y Y N N	*Helms*	Y N Y Y N
COLORADO		**MARYLAND**		**NORTH DAKOTA**	
Armstrong	N N Y Y N	*Mathias*	Y Y Y N N	*Andrews*	Y Y Y N Y
Hart	N Y Y Y Y	Sarbanes	N Y Y N N	Burdick	Y Y Y N Y
CONNECTICUT		**MASSACHUSETTS**		**OHIO**	
Weicker	Y Y Y N Y	Kennedy	N Y Y N N	Glenn	N Y Y Y Y
Dodd	N Y Y N Y	Tsongas	N Y Y N Y	Metzenbaum	N Y Y N N
DELAWARE		**MICHIGAN**		**OKLAHOMA**	
Roth	N N Y N N	Levin	N Y Y N Y	*Nickles*	N N Y Y N
Biden	N Y Y N N	Riegle	N Y Y N N	Boren	? N Y N Y
FLORIDA		**MINNESOTA**		**OREGON**	
Hawkins	Y N Y Y Y	*Boschwitz*	N N Y Y Y	*Hatfield*	N N N N Y
Chiles	N Y Y Y Y	*Durenberger*	N Y Y Y Y	*Packwood*	Y Y Y Y Y
GEORGIA		**MISSISSIPPI**		**PENNSYLVANIA**	
Mattingly	Y N Y Y Y	*Cochran*	Y N Y Y Y	*Heinz*	Y Y Y N Y
Nunn	N N Y Y Y	Stennis	Y N Y Y Y	*Specter*	Y Y Y N Y
HAWAII		**MISSOURI**		**RHODE ISLAND**	
Inouye	N Y Y N Y	*Danforth*	Y Y Y Y Y	*Chafee*	N Y Y N Y
Matsunaga	N Y Y N Y	Eagleton	N Y N N N	Pell	N Y Y N N
IDAHO		**MONTANA**		**SOUTH CAROLINA**	
McClure	Y Y Y Y Y	Baucus	N Y Y N N	*Thurmond*	Y Y Y Y Y
Symms	Y N Y Y Y	Melcher	N Y Y ? Y	Hollings	N Y Y Y Y
ILLINOIS		**NEBRASKA**		**SOUTH DAKOTA**	
Percy	N Y Y Y N	Exon	N Y Y Y Y	*Abdnor*	Y N Y Y Y
Dixon	N Y Y N N	Zorinsky	Y N Y Y Y	*Pressler*	Y N Y N Y
INDIANA		**NEVADA**		**TENNESSEE**	
Lugar	Y N Y N Y	*Laxalt*	? N Y Y Y	*Baker*	Y Y Y Y Y
Quayle	N N Y Y Y	Cannon	+ + + ? +	Sasser	Y Y Y Y Y

	353 354 355 356 357
TEXAS	
Tower	Y N Y Y Y
Bentsen	Y N Y Y Y
UTAH	
Garn	Y N Y Y Y
Hatch	Y N Y ? ?
VERMONT	
Stafford	Y Y Y N Y
Leahy	N Y Y N N
VIRGINIA	
Warner	Y N Y Y Y
Byrd*	N N Y N N
WASHINGTON	
Gorton	Y N Y Y Y
Jackson	Y Y Y Y Y
WEST VIRGINIA	
Byrd	N Y Y Y Y
Randolph	Y Y Y N Y
WISCONSIN	
Kasten	Y N Y Y Y
Proxmire	N Y Y N N
WYOMING	
Simpson	Y N Y Y Y
Wallop	Y N Y Y Y

KEY

- Y Voted for (yea).
- # Paired for.
- + Announced for.
- N Voted against (nay).
- X Paired against.
- - Announced against.
- P Voted "present".
- C Voted "present" to avoid possible conflict of interest.
- ? Did not vote or otherwise make a position known.

Democrats **Republicans**

* Byrd elected as an independent.

353. HR 4144. Energy and Water Development Appropriations, Fiscal 1982. Johnston, D-La., motion to table the Baker, R-Tenn., motion to reconsider the vote by which the Bumpers, D-Ark., amendment, as amended by the Tsongas, D-Mass., amendment (see votes 351, 352, p. 59-S) was tabled. As amended, the Bumpers amendment would have reduced by half ($90 million) the appropriations for the Clinch River (Tenn.) nuclear breeder reactor. Motion agreed to 50-45: R 38-12; D 12-33 (ND 4-27, SD 8-6), Nov. 5, 1981. A "yea" was a vote supporting the president's position.

354. S 1408. Military Construction Authorization. Jackson, D-Wash., amendment to delete a provision of the bill that exempted military construction projects from the so-called Davis-Bacon Act, which required building contractors on federal construction projects to pay locally prevailing wages. Adopted 55-42: R 16-35; D 39-7 (ND 30-1, SD 9-6), Nov. 5, 1981.

355. HR 3455. Military Construction Authorization. Passage of the bill to authorize $6.5 billion for military construction projects in fiscal 1982. Passed 95-2: R 50-1; D 45-1 (ND 30-1, SD 15-0), Nov. 5, 1981.

356. HR 4144. Energy and Water Development Appropriations, Fiscal 1982. Tower, R-Texas, amendment to increase spending in the bill by $335.5 million for nuclear weapons activities of the Department of Energy. Adopted 49-43: R 35-14; D 14-29 (ND 7-21, SD 7-8), Nov. 5, 1981.

357. HR 4144. Energy and Water Development Appropriations, Fiscal 1982. Passage of the bill appropriating $12,763,636,000 for energy and water development programs. The president in September had requested $12,096,547,000. Passed 71-22: R 41-8; D 30-14 (ND 17-12, SD 13-2), Nov. 5, 1981.

	358	359	360	361	362	363	364	365
ALABAMA								
Denton	?	?	?	?	?	?	N	Y
Heflin	Y	N	Y	Y	N	Y	N	N
ALASKA								
Murkowski	N	Y	N	Y	N	Y	N	Y
Stevens	N	Y	Y	Y	N	Y	N	Y
ARIZONA								
Goldwater	?	?	?	?	?	?	?	?
DeConcini	Y	N	Y	Y	N	Y	Y	?
ARKANSAS								
Bumpers	?	?	Y	Y	N	Y	Y	N
Pryor	Y	N	Y	Y	N	Y	Y	N
CALIFORNIA								
Hayakawa	?	?	Y	Y	N	?	?	?
Cranston	Y	N	Y	Y	N	Y	Y	N
COLORADO								
Armstrong	N	Y	Y	Y	N	Y	Y	Y
Hart	Y	N	Y	Y	N	?	?	?
CONNECTICUT								
Weicker	N	Y	Y	Y	N	Y	Y	Y
Dodd	?	?	Y	Y	N	Y	Y	N
DELAWARE								
Roth	N	Y	Y	Y	N	Y	Y	Y
Biden	Y	N	Y	?	?	Y	Y	N
FLORIDA								
Hawkins	Y	Y	Y	Y	N	Y	Y	Y
Chiles	Y	N	Y	Y	N	Y	N	N
GEORGIA								
Mattingly	N	Y	Y	Y	N	Y	Y	Y
Nunn	Y	N	Y	Y	N	Y	Y	N
HAWAII								
Inouye	?	?	?	Y	N	Y	Y	N
Matsunaga	?	N	Y	Y	N	Y	Y	N
IDAHO								
McClure	?	?	?	Y	N	Y	N	Y
Symms	N	Y	N	Y	N	Y	N	Y
ILLINOIS								
Percy	N	Y	N	Y	N	Y	Y	Y
Dixon	N	N	N	+	?	?	Y	N
INDIANA								
Lugar	N	Y	N	Y	N	Y	Y	Y
Quayle	N	Y	Y	Y	N	Y	Y	Y
IOWA								
Grassley	N	Y	Y	Y	N	Y	Y	Y
Jepsen	N	Y	Y	?	?	Y	N	Y
KANSAS								
Dole	N	Y	Y	Y	N	Y	Y	Y
Kassebaum	?	?	?	Y	N	Y	Y	Y
KENTUCKY								
Ford	Y	N	Y	Y	N	Y	Y	N
Huddleston	Y	N	Y	?	?	?	?	?
LOUISIANA								
Johnston	Y	N	Y	Y	N	Y	Y	N
Long	Y	N	Y	?	?	?	?	?
MAINE								
Cohen	N	Y	Y	Y	N	Y	N	Y
Mitchell	Y	N	Y	Y	N	Y	Y	N
MARYLAND								
Mathias	N	Y	Y	Y	Y	Y	Y	Y
Sarbanes	Y	N	Y	Y	N	Y	Y	N
MASSACHUSETTS								
Kennedy	Y	N	Y	Y	N	Y	Y	N
Tsongas	N	N	Y	Y	N	Y	Y	Y
MICHIGAN								
Levin	Y	N	Y	?	?	?	?	?
Riegle	Y	N	Y	Y	N	Y	Y	N
MINNESOTA								
Boschwitz	N	Y	Y	Y	N	Y	N	Y
Durenberger	N	Y	Y	Y	N	Y	Y	Y
MISSISSIPPI								
Cochran	N	Y	Y	Y	N	Y	Y	Y
Stennis	?	?	?	Y	N	Y	Y	?
MISSOURI								
Danforth	N	Y	Y	?	?	?	?	?
Eagleton	Y	N	Y	Y	N	Y	Y	N
MONTANA								
Baucus	Y	N	Y	Y	N	Y	Y	N
Melcher	Y	N	Y	?	-	?	+	?
NEBRASKA								
Exon	Y	N	Y	Y	N	Y	N	N
Zorinsky	Y	Y	Y	Y	N	Y	Y	N
NEVADA								
Laxalt	N	Y	Y	Y	N	Y	N	Y
Cannon	+	-	?	?	?	?	?	?
NEW HAMPSHIRE								
Humphrey	N	Y	N	Y	N	Y	N	Y
Rudman	N	Y	Y	Y	N	Y	Y	Y
NEW JERSEY								
Bradley	N	N	Y	Y	N	Y	N	N
Williams	Y	N	Y	Y	N	Y	Y	N
NEW MEXICO								
Domenici	N	Y	Y	Y	N	Y	Y	Y
Schmitt	N	Y	N	Y	N	Y	Y	Y
NEW YORK								
D'Amato	+	+	Y	Y	N	Y	Y	Y
Moynihan	N	Y	Y	?	?	?	?	?
NORTH CAROLINA								
East	N	Y	Y	Y	N	+	+	?
Helms	N	Y	Y	Y	N	Y	Y	N
NORTH DAKOTA								
Andrews	N	Y	Y	Y	N	Y	Y	Y
Burdick	Y	N	Y	Y	N	Y	Y	Y
OHIO								
Glenn	N	N	Y	?	?	?	?	?
Metzenbaum	Y	N	Y	Y	N	Y	Y	N
OKLAHOMA								
Nickles	N	Y	N	Y	N	Y	Y	Y
Boren	Y	N	Y	Y	N	Y	Y	N
OREGON								
Hatfield	N	Y	Y	Y	N	Y	N	Y
Packwood	?	?	?	?	?	?	?	?
PENNSYLVANIA								
Heinz	N	Y	Y	Y	N	Y	Y	Y
Specter	N	Y	Y	Y	N	Y	N	Y
RHODE ISLAND								
Chafee	-	+	+	Y	Y	N	Y	
Pell	+	-	+	Y	N	Y	Y	N
SOUTH CAROLINA								
Thurmond	N	Y	Y	Y	N	Y	Y	Y
Hollings	Y	N	Y	Y	N	Y	Y	N
SOUTH DAKOTA								
Abdnor	N	Y	Y	Y	N	Y	Y	Y
Pressler	N	Y	Y	Y	N	Y	Y	Y
TENNESSEE								
Baker	N	Y	Y	Y	N	Y	Y	Y
Sasser	Y	N	Y	Y	N	Y	Y	N
TEXAS								
Tower	N	Y	N	Y	N	Y	Y	Y
Bentsen	N	Y	Y	Y	N	Y	Y	N
UTAH								
Garn	N	Y	N	Y	N	Y	Y	Y
Hatch	N	Y	N	Y	N	Y	Y	Y
VERMONT								
Stafford	N	Y	Y	Y	N	Y	Y	Y
Leahy	+	-	?	?	?	?	?	?
VIRGINIA								
Warner	N	Y	Y	Y	N	Y	Y	Y
Byrd*	N	Y	Y	Y	N	Y	N	N
WASHINGTON								
Gorton	N	Y	Y	Y	Y	Y	Y	Y
Jackson	Y	N	Y	Y	N	Y	Y	N
WEST VIRGINIA								
Byrd	Y	N	Y	Y	N	Y	Y	N
Randolph	Y	N	Y	Y	N	Y	Y	N
WISCONSIN								
Kasten	N	Y	Y	Y	N	Y	N	Y
Proxmire	N	Y	Y	Y	N	Y	N	N
WYOMING								
Simpson	N	Y	Y	Y	N	Y	Y	Y
Wallop	N	Y	N	Y	N	Y	Y	Y

KEY

Y Voted for (yea).
\# Paired for.
\+ Announced for.
N Voted against (nay).
X Paired against.
- Announced against.
P Voted "present".
C Voted "present" to avoid possible conflict of interest.
? Did not vote or otherwise make a position known.

Democrats **Republicans**

*Byrd elected as an independent.

358. S 1112. Export Administration Authorization/Monetary Policy. Chiles, D-Fla., perfecting amendment, to the Chiles amendment *(see vote 359, below)*, to direct the president in cooperation with the Federal Reserve Board of Governors by Dec. 1 to exercise appropriate authorities to ensure an adequate flow of credit to small borrowers at affordable prices and to limit large-scale diversion of credit to corporate takeovers. As originally proposed, the Chiles amendment called for such action by Nov. 25. Rejected 32-52: R 1-44; D 31-8 (ND 20-6, SD 11-2). Nov. 10, 1981.

359. S 1112. Export Administration Authorization/Monetary Policy. Heinz, R-Pa., substitute amendment, to the Chiles, D-Fla., amendment, to direct the administration to emphasize and continue to implement policies necessary to sustain the downward movement of interest rates. Adopted 50-35: R 45-0; D 5-35 (ND 3-24, SD 2-11). Nov. 10, 1981. (The Chiles amendment, as amended, subsequently was adopted by voice vote.)

360. S 1112. Export Administration Authorization/Monetary Policy. Kennedy, D-Mass., amendment to direct the president to take appropriate actions on a voluntary basis to encourage financial institutions to exercise restraint in extending credit for unproductive large-scale corporate takeovers. Adopted 77-12: R 36-11; D 41-1 (ND 27-1, SD 14-0). Nov. 10, 1981.

361. HR 4169. State, Justice, Commerce, Judiciary Appropriations, Fiscal 1982. Thurmond, R-S.C., substitute amendment for the Metzenbaum, D-Ohio, amendment, declaring the sense of the Senate that the Justice Department and the Federal Trade Commission vigorously enforce antitrust laws. Adopted 85-0: R 48-0; D 37-0 (ND 24-0, SD 13-0). Nov. 12, 1981. (The Metzenbaum amendment, as amended, subsequently was adopted by voice vote.)

362. HR 4169. State, Justice, Commerce, Judiciary Appropriations, Fiscal 1982. Appropriations Committee amendment deleting language prohibiting the U.S. Bureau of the Census from prosecuting persons who failed to return agricultural census forms in 1978 or any such forms in the future. Rejected 3-82: R 3-45; D 0-37 (ND 0-24, SD 0-13), Nov. 12, 1981.

363. HR 4169. State, Justice, Commerce, Judiciary Appropriations, Fiscal 1982. Thurmond, R-S.C., motion to table (kill) an Appropriations Committee amendment deleting language prohibiting the Commerce Department from spending money to promote or conduct trade with Cuba. Motion agreed to 84-0: R 47-0; D 37-0 (ND 24-0, SD 13-0), Nov. 12, 1981.

364. S 1112. Export Administration Authorization/Embargo. Percy, R-Ill., amendment, as amended by the Percy substitute, to require as of Jan. 21, 1985, that a selective U.S. embargo on agricultural goods ordered by the president must cease if Congress fails to adopt a joint resolution of approval. Adopted 66-20: R 34-14; D 32-6 (ND 22-3, SD 10-3), Nov. 12, 1981. (Under the original Percy amendment, the embargo provision would have gone into effect immediately upon enactment of the bill.)

365. S 1112. Export Administration Authorization/Embargo. Heinz, R-Pa., perfecting amendment to Byrd, D-W.Va., amendment, stating the sense of the Senate that an embargo should be imposed on all U.S. exports to the Soviet Union if the Soviet Union or its allies engaged in direct military action against Poland, and to provide that the Export Administration Act shall not be construed as prohibiting a total embargo in the event of Soviet or Warsaw Pact military action against Poland. Adopted 49-35: R 47-1; D 2-34 (ND 2-22, SD 0-12). Nov. 12, 1981. (The Byrd amendment would have required a total embargo under certain conditions. As amended, it subsequently was adopted by voice vote.)

	366	367	368	369	370	371	372	373
ALABAMA								
Denton	N	Y	N	N	N	Y	Y	Y
Heflin	Y	N	Y	Y	Y	Y	N	Y
ALASKA								
Murkowski	N	N	Y	?	Y	Y	Y	Y
Stevens	N	N	Y	Y	Y	Y	Y	Y
ARIZONA								
Goldwater	?	?	?	?	?	?	?	?
DeConcini	?	N	Y	Y	Y	Y	Y	Y
ARKANSAS								
Bumpers	Y	N	Y	Y	Y	Y	Y	Y
Pryor	Y	?	?	?	?	?	?	Y
CALIFORNIA								
Hayakawa	?	?	?	?	?	?	?	Y
Cranston	Y	?	?	?	?	?	?	N
COLORADO								
Armstrong	N	Y	N	N	N	Y	N	Y
Hart	?	?	+	?	?	?	?	Y
CONNECTICUT								
Weicker	Y	N	Y	Y	Y	Y	Y	Y
Dodd	Y	N	Y	Y	Y	Y	Y	Y
DELAWARE								
Roth	N	N	N	N	N	Y	N	Y
Biden	Y	N	Y	Y	Y	Y	Y	Y
FLORIDA								
Hawkins	N	Y	N	Y	N	Y	Y	Y
Chiles	Y	N	N	Y	N	Y	Y	Y
GEORGIA								
Mattingly	N	N	N	N	N	Y	?	Y
Nunn	Y	N	N	Y	N	Y	Y	Y
HAWAII								
Inouye	Y	N	Y	Y	Y	Y	Y	N
Matsunaga	Y	N	Y	Y	Y	Y	Y	N
IDAHO								
McClure	N	Y	N	N	N	Y	N	?
Symms	N	Y	N	N	N	Y	N	Y
ILLINOIS								
Percy	N	N	Y	Y	Y	Y	Y	Y
Dixon	Y	N	Y	Y	Y	Y	Y	N
INDIANA								
Lugar	N	N	N	Y	N	Y	Y	Y
Quayle	N	Y	N	N	N	Y	N	Y

	366	367	368	369	370	371	372	373
IOWA								
Grassley	N	Y	N	N	N	Y	N	Y
Jepsen	N	Y	N	N	N	Y	N	Y
KANSAS								
Dole	N	N	N	Y	N	Y	Y	Y
Kassebaum	N	N	N	Y	N	Y	Y	Y
KENTUCKY								
Ford	Y	N	Y	Y	Y	Y	Y	Y
Huddleston	?	N	Y	Y	Y	Y	Y	N
LOUISIANA								
Johnston	Y	N	Y	N	Y	N	Y	Y
Long	?	?	?	?	?	?	?	?
MAINE								
Cohen	N	N	Y	Y	Y	Y	Y	Y
Mitchell	Y	N	Y	Y	Y	Y	Y	Y
MARYLAND								
Mathias	N	?	?	?	?	?	?	N
Sarbanes	Y	N	Y	Y	Y	Y	Y	Y
MASSACHUSETTS								
Kennedy	Y	N	Y	Y	Y	Y	Y	?
Tsongas	Y	N	Y	Y	Y	Y	Y	?
MICHIGAN								
Levin	?	-	+	+	+	?	?	N
Riegle	Y	N	Y	Y	Y	Y	Y	Y
MINNESOTA								
Boschwitz	N	N	Y	Y	Y	Y	Y	N
Durenberger	N	N	Y	Y	Y	Y	Y	?
MISSISSIPPI								
Cochran	N	N	N	Y	Y	Y	Y	Y
Stennis	?	N	N	Y	Y	Y	Y	Y
MISSOURI								
Danforth	?	N	Y	Y	Y	Y	Y	Y
Eagleton	Y	N	Y	Y	Y	Y	Y	?
MONTANA								
Baucus	Y	N	+	?	+	+	+	-
Melcher	+	?	?	?	?	?	?	+
NEBRASKA								
Exon	Y	N	X	N	N	Y	N	Y
Zorinsky	Y	Y	N	N	N	Y	N	Y
NEVADA								
Laxalt	N	Y	N	Y	N	Y	Y	Y
Cannon	?	?	?	?	?	?	?	Y

	366	367	368	369	370	371	372	373
NEW HAMPSHIRE								
Humphrey	N	Y	N	N	N	Y	Y	Y
Rudman	N	N	Y	Y	Y	Y	Y	Y
NEW JERSEY								
Bradley	Y	N	Y	Y	Y	Y	Y	Y
Williams	Y	N	Y	Y	Y	?	?	N
NEW MEXICO								
Domenici	N	N	Y	?	N	Y	N	Y
Schmitt	N	N	Y	?	?	?	?	Y
NEW YORK								
D'Amato	N	N	Y	Y	Y	Y	Y	Y
Moynihan	?	?	+	?	?	+	?	?
NORTH CAROLINA								
East	-	+	-	-	-	+	-	Y
Helms	Y	Y	N	N	N	Y	N	Y
NORTH DAKOTA								
Andrews	N	N	Y	Y	Y	Y	Y	Y
Burdick	Y	N	Y	Y	Y	Y	N	N
OHIO								
Glenn	?	?	?	?	?	?	?	N
Metzenbaum	Y	-	#	+	+	?	?	N
OKLAHOMA								
Nickles	N	Y	N	N	N	Y	Y	Y
Boren	Y	?	?	?	?	?	?	?
OREGON								
Hatfield	N	N	Y	Y	Y	Y	Y	Y
Packwood	?	?	?	?	?	?	?	Y
PENNSYLVANIA								
Heinz	N	N	Y	Y	Y	Y	N	Y
Specter	N	?	Y	Y	Y	Y	N	?
RHODE ISLAND								
Chafee	N	N	Y	Y	Y	Y	Y	?
Pell	Y	N	Y	Y	Y	Y	Y	?
SOUTH CAROLINA								
Thurmond	N	Y	N	N	N	Y	N	Y
Hollings	Y	N	Y	Y	Y	Y	Y	Y
SOUTH DAKOTA								
Abdnor	N	N	Y	N	N	Y	Y	Y
Pressler	Y	N	Y	Y	Y	Y	Y	?
TENNESSEE								
Baker	N	N	Y	Y	Y	Y	?	Y
Sasser	Y	N	Y	Y	Y	Y	?	Y

KEY

Y	Voted for (yea).
#	Paired for.
+	Announced for.
N	Voted against (nay).
X	Paired against.
-	Announced against.
P	Voted "present".
C	Voted "present" to avoid possible conflict of interest.
?	Did not vote or otherwise make a position known.

	366	367	368	369	370	371	372	373
TEXAS								
Tower	N	Y	N	N	N	?	Y	Y
Bentsen	Y	N	Y	Y	N	Y	Y	Y
UTAH								
Garn	N	Y	N	N	N	Y	N	?
Hatch	N	Y	N	N	N	Y	N	Y
VERMONT								
Stafford	N	N	N	Y	?	?	Y	Y
Leahy	?	?	+	?	?	?	?	?
VIRGINIA								
Warner	N	N	Y	N	Y	N	Y	Y
Byrd*	Y	Y	N	N	N	Y	N	Y
WASHINGTON								
Gorton	N	N	Y	Y	Y	Y	Y	Y
Jackson	Y	N	Y	Y	Y	Y	Y	N
WEST VIRGINIA								
Byrd	Y	N	Y	Y	Y	Y	Y	Y
Randolph	Y	N	Y	Y	Y	Y	Y	Y
WISCONSIN								
Kasten	N	N	N	N	N	Y	N	?
Proxmire	Y	Y	N	N	N	Y	N	Y
WYOMING								
Simpson	N	Y	N	N	N	Y	Y	Y
Wallop	N	Y	N	N	N	Y	N	Y

Democrats *Republicans*

Byrd elected as an independent.

366. S 1112. Export Administration Authorization/Embargo. Byrd, D-W.Va., substitute amendment, for the Byrd amendment, as amended *(see vote 365, p. 61-S)*, to require an embargo on all U.S. goods to the Soviet Union, if the Soviet Union or its allies engaged in direct military action against Poland, unless the president certified to Congress within 60 days of the action that the embargo was not in the U.S. national security and foreign policy interests. Rejected 39-45: R 3-45; D 36-0 (ND 24-0, SD 12-0), Nov. 12, 1981.

367. HR 4169. State, Justice, Commerce, Judiciary Appropriations, Fiscal 1982. Denton, R-Ala., amendment to delete the $241 million appropriation for the Legal Services Corporation. Rejected 21-61: R 18-29; D 3-32 (ND 2-21, SD 1-11), Nov. 13, 1981.

368. HR 4169. State, Justice, Commerce, Judiciary Appropriations, Fiscal 1982. Weicker, R-Conn., motion to table (kill) the Cochran, R-Miss., amendment to provide $100 million for the Legal Services Corporation. Motion agreed to 48-33: R 22-26; D 26-7 (ND 18-3, SD 8-4), Nov. 13, 1981.

369. HR 4169. State, Justice, Commerce, Judiciary Appropriations, Fiscal 1982. Judgment of the Senate whether an Appropriations Committee amendment restricting activities of Legal Services Corporation lawyers was germane. Ruled germane 57-23: R 27-19; D 30-4 (ND 19-3, SD 11-1), Nov. 13, 1981.

370. HR 4169. State, Justice, Commerce, Judiciary Appropriations, Fiscal 1982. Appropriations Committee amendment restricting Legal Services Corporation activities concerning representation of aliens, lobbying and filing class action suits. Adopted 47-33: R 22-24; D 25-9 (ND 18-4, SD 7-5), Nov. 13, 1981.

371. Exec I, 95th Cong, 2nd Sess. Prohibition of Nuclear Weapons in Latin America. Adoption of the resolution of ratification for Protocol I to the Treaty of Tlatelolco, under which the United States agreed not to test, use, store or deploy nuclear weapons in the territories of Puerto Rico, the Virgin Islands and Guantanamo Naval Base. Adopted 79-0: R 45-0; D 34-0 (ND 22-0, SD 12-0), Nov. 13, 1981. A two-thirds majority (53 in this case) is required for adoption of resolutions of ratification of treaties. A "yea" was a vote supporting the president's position.

372. HR 4169. State, Justice, Commerce, Judiciary Appropriations, Fiscal 1982. Weicker, R-Conn., amendment to increase the appropriation for the Immigration and Naturalization Service by $85.18 million. Adopted 54-23: R 29-16; D 25-7 (ND 16-5, SD 9-2), Nov. 13, 1981.

373. HR 4169. State, Justice, Commerce, Judiciary Appropriations, Fiscal 1982. Hollings, D-S.C., motion to table (kill) an Appropriations Committee amendment deleting House language to prevent the Justice Department from spending money to block implementation of "voluntary school prayer" programs. Motion agreed to 70-12: R 43-2; D 27-10 (ND 15-9, SD 12-1), Nov. 16, 1981.

CQ Senate Votes 374 - 381

Corresponding to Congressional Record Votes 377, 378, 379, 380, 381, 382, 383, 384, 385, 386, 387, 388, 389, 390, 391, 392

	374	375	376	377	378	379	380	381
ALABAMA								
Denton	Y	Y	Y	Y	Y	N	Y	Y
Heflin	Y	Y	Y	?	?	?	?	Y
ALASKA								
Murkowski	Y	Y	Y	Y	N	-	Y	Y
Stevens	Y	Y	Y	Y	N	N	Y	Y
ARIZONA								
Goldwater	?	?	+	?	?	?	?	?
DeConcini	Y	Y	Y	Y	Y	Y	N	Y
ARKANSAS								
Bumpers	N	N	X	Y	N	Y	Y	Y
Pryor	N	N	Y	?	N	?	?	Y
CALIFORNIA								
Hayakawa	Y	Y	Y	Y	Y	N	Y	Y
Cranston	N	N	N	Y	N	Y	Y	Y
COLORADO								
Armstrong	Y	Y	Y	Y	Y	N	N	Y
Hart	N	N	N	Y	N	N	Y	Y
CONNECTICUT								
Weicker	N	N	N	Y	?	?	?	Y
Dodd	N	N	N	Y	N	Y	N	Y
DELAWARE								
Roth	Y	Y	Y	Y	N	N	N	Y
Biden	N	N	N	Y	N	Y	Y	Y
FLORIDA								
Hawkins	Y	Y	Y	Y	Y	N	Y	Y
Chiles	Y	Y	Y	Y	Y	Y	Y	Y
GEORGIA								
Mattingly	Y	Y	Y	Y	Y	N	Y	Y
Nunn	Y	Y	Y	Y	N	Y	N	Y
HAWAII								
Inouye	N	N	N	Y	N	N	Y	Y
Matsunaga	N	N	N	Y	N	Y	Y	Y
IDAHO								
McClure	?	Y	Y	Y	Y	N	N	Y
Symms	Y	Y	Y	Y	Y	N	N	Y
ILLINOIS								
Percy	N	Y	Y	Y	N	Y	Y	Y
Dixon	Y	#	?	Y	N	Y	Y	Y
INDIANA								
Lugar	Y	Y	Y	Y	N	N	Y	Y
Quayle	Y	Y	Y	Y	N	N	Y	Y
IOWA								
Grassley	Y	Y	Y	Y	Y	N	N	Y
Jepsen	Y	Y	Y	Y	N	Y	Y	Y
KANSAS								
Dole	Y	Y	Y	Y	N	N	Y	Y
Kassebaum	Y	Y	Y	Y	N	N	Y	Y
KENTUCKY								
Ford	Y	Y	Y	Y	Y	Y	N	Y
Huddleston	N	N	Y	Y	N	Y	Y	Y
LOUISIANA								
Johnston	Y	Y	Y	Y	N	N	Y	Y
Long	?	?	?	Y	Y	Y	N	Y
MAINE								
Cohen	N	N	N	Y	N	N	Y	Y
Mitchell	N	N	N	Y	N	Y	Y	Y
MARYLAND								
Mathias	N	N	N	Y	N	N	Y	Y
Sarbanes	N	N	N	Y	N	Y	Y	Y
MASSACHUSETTS								
Kennedy	N	N	N	Y	?	?	?	Y
Tsongas	?	N	N	Y	N	N	Y	Y
MICHIGAN								
Levin	N	N	N	Y	N	Y	Y	Y
Riegle	N	N	N	Y	N	Y	Y	Y
MINNESOTA								
Boschwitz	N	N	Y	N	N	Y	Y	Y
Durenberger	?	?	Y	Y	N	N	Y	Y
MISSISSIPPI								
Cochran	Y	Y	Y	Y	N	N	Y	Y
Stennis	Y	Y	Y	Y	N	Y	?	Y
MISSOURI								
Danforth	N	N	Y	N	N	Y	Y	Y
Eagleton	?	?	#	Y	N	Y	N	Y
MONTANA								
Baucus	-	X	+	Y	N	Y	Y	Y
Melcher	+	+	Y	Y	N	Y	N	Y
NEBRASKA								
Exon	Y	Y	Y	Y	N	Y	N	Y
Zorinsky	Y	Y	Y	Y	N	Y	N	Y
NEVADA								
Laxalt	Y	Y	Y	Y	N	N	N	Y
Cannon	Y	Y	Y	?	Y	Y	N	Y
NEW HAMPSHIRE								
Humphrey	Y	Y	Y	Y	Y	Y	N	Y
Rudman	N	N	Y	Y	N	Y	Y	Y
NEW JERSEY								
Bradley	N	N	N	Y	N	Y	Y	Y
Williams	N	N	N	Y	N	Y	Y	Y
NEW MEXICO								
Domenici	Y	Y	Y	?	Y	N	N	Y
Schmitt	Y	Y	N	Y	N	N	N	Y
NEW YORK								
D'Amato	Y	Y	Y	Y	N	N	Y	Y
Moynihan	N	N	N	Y	?	+	?	Y
NORTH CAROLINA								
East	Y	Y	Y	Y	N	N	N	Y
Helms	Y	Y	Y	Y	Y	N	N	Y
NORTH DAKOTA								
Andrews	Y	Y	Y	Y	N	N	N	Y
Burdick	N	N	N	Y	N	Y	N	Y
OHIO								
Glenn	N	N	N	Y	N	N	Y	Y
Metzenbaum	N	N	N	Y	N	N	Y	Y
OKLAHOMA								
Nickles	Y	Y	Y	Y	Y	N	N	Y
Boren	Y	Y	Y	Y	N	N	N	Y
OREGON								
Hatfield	N	N	Y	N	Y	N	Y	Y
Packwood	N	N	N	Y	N	N	Y	Y
PENNSYLVANIA								
Heinz	?	N	Y	Y	N	N	Y	Y
Specter	N	N	Y	Y	N	N	Y	Y
RHODE ISLAND								
Chafee	?	N	N	Y	N	N	Y	Y
Pell	?	N	Y	Y	N	Y	Y	Y
SOUTH CAROLINA								
Thurmond	Y	Y	Y	Y	Y	N	Y	Y
Hollings	Y	Y	Y	Y	N	Y	N	Y
SOUTH DAKOTA								
Abdnor	Y	Y	Y	Y	N	N	N	Y
Pressler	?	?	?	Y	N	Y	N	Y
TENNESSEE								
Baker	Y	Y	Y	Y	N	N	Y	Y
Sasser	N	Y	Y	?	?	?	?	Y
TEXAS								
Tower	Y	Y	Y	Y	N	N	?	Y
Bentsen	Y	Y	Y	Y	N	N	Y	Y
UTAH								
Garn	?	?	Y	Y	Y	N	Y	Y
Hatch	Y	Y	Y	Y	Y	N	N	Y
VERMONT								
Stafford	N	N	Y	Y	N	N	Y	Y
Leahy	?	?	?	?	?	?	?	?
VIRGINIA								
Warner	Y	Y	Y	Y	Y	Y	N	Y
Byrd*	Y	Y	Y	Y	Y	Y	N	Y
WASHINGTON								
Gorton	N	N	Y	Y	N	N	Y	Y
Jackson	N	N	Y	Y	N	N	Y	Y
WEST VIRGINIA								
Byrd	Y	Y	Y	Y	Y	Y	N	Y
Randolph	Y	Y	Y	Y	Y	Y	N	Y
WISCONSIN								
Kasten	?	Y	Y	Y	N	N	Y	Y
Proxmire	Y	Y	N	Y	Y	Y	N	Y
WYOMING								
Simpson	Y	Y	Y	Y	N	N	Y	Y
Wallop	Y	Y	Y	Y	N	N	Y	Y

KEY

Y	Voted for (yea).
#	Paired for.
+	Announced for.
N	Voted against (nay).
X	Paired against.
-	Announced against.
P	Voted "present".
C	Voted "present" to avoid possible conflict of interest.
?	Did not vote or otherwise make a position known.

Democrats *Republicans*

* Byrd elected as an independent.

374. HR 4169. State, Justice, Commerce, Judiciary Appropriations, Fiscal 1982. Helms, R-N.C., motion to table (kill) the Weicker, R-Conn., amendment to prevent the Justice Department from spending money to block implementation of "constitutional" voluntary school programs. Motion agreed to 51-34: R 33-12; D 18-22 (ND 8-18, SD 10-4), Nov. 16, 1981.

375. HR 4169. State, Justice, Commerce, Judiciary Appropriations, Fiscal 1982. Helms, R-N.C., motion to table (kill) the Helms motion to reconsider the vote by which the Weicker, R-Conn., amendment was tabled *(see vote 374, above)*. Motion agreed to 54-36: R 36-13; D 18-23 (ND 7-20, SD 11-3), Nov. 16, 1981.

376. Koop Nomination. Confirmation of President Reagan's nomination of Dr. C. Everett Koop of Pennsylvania to be surgeon general of the Public Health Service and medical director of the Regular Corps of the Public Health Service. Confirmed 68-24: R 46-5; D 22-19 (ND 9-19, SD 13-0), Nov. 16, 1981. A "yea" was a vote supporting the president's position.

377. HR 4169. State, Justice, Commerce, Judiciary Appropriations, Fiscal 1982. Weicker, R-Conn., amendment to make clear that nothing in the bill shall be interpreted as the establishment of religion or prohibiting the free exercise of religion. Adopted 93-0: R 51-0; D 42-0 (ND 30-0, SD 12-0), Nov. 17, 1981.

378. S 1802. Foreign Aid Appropriations, Fiscal 1982. Helms, R-N.C., amendment to prohibit aid to Zimbabwe after Jan. 1, 1982, if any military adviser or technician or other military personnel of the Democratic People's Republic of Korea (North Korea) were in Zimbabwe. Rejected 26-67: R 17-34; D 9-33 (ND 5-24, SD 4-9), Nov. 17, 1981.

379. S 1802. Foreign Aid Appropriations, Fiscal 1982. Pell, D-R.I., amendment to prohibit aid to any nation where, on Nov. 21, 1979, the United States Embassy and other U.S. government property had been attacked and which had failed to fully compensate the United States for damages done and the families of U.S. employes killed. (The U.S. Embassy in Islamabad, Pakistan, was attacked by a mob on Nov. 21, 1979.) Rejected 36-55: R 6-44; D 30-11 (ND 22-7, SD 8-4), Nov. 17, 1981.

380. S 1802. Foreign Aid Appropriations, Fiscal 1982. Passage of the bill appropriating $7,327,583,804 for fiscal 1982 foreign economic and military aid programs. Passed 57-33: R 32-18; D 25-15 (ND 19-10, SD 6-5), Nov. 17, 1981. (The president had requested $7,775,098,683.)

381. Treaties. Adoption of the resolutions of ratification for the following treaties: **Treaty Doc. No. 97-20,** Agreement Extending for Eight Months the Treaty of Friendship with Spain; **Exec Y, 96th Cong, 2nd Sess,** Tax Treaty with the People's Republic of Bangladesh; **Exec U, 96th Cong, 2nd Sess,** Tax Treaty with the Arab Republic of Egypt; **Treaty Doc. No. 97-1,** 97th Cong, 1st Sess, Tax Treaty with the Federal Republic of Germany; **Exec C, 94th Cong, 2nd Sess,** Tax Convention with the State of Israel; **Exec M, 96th Cong, 2nd Sess,** Tax Treaty and Proposed Protocol with the State of Israel; **Exec E, 96th Cong, 2nd Sess,** Tax Treaty with the Republic of Malta; **Exec H, 95th Cong, 2nd Sess,** Tax Treaty with the Kingdom of Morocco; **Exec Z, 96th Cong, 2nd Sess,** Protocol to the Tax Treaty with the Kingdom of Norway. Adopted 97-0: R 52-0; D 45-0 (ND 30-0, SD 15-0), Nov. 18, 1981. A two-thirds majority vote (65 in this case) is required for adoption of resolutions of ratification of treaties.

CQ Senate Votes 382 - 387

Corresponding to Congressional Record Votes 393, 394, 395, 396, 397, 398

	382	383	384	385	386	387
ALABAMA						
Denton	Y	N	N	Y	Y	N
Heflin	Y	Y	Y	N	N	N
ALASKA						
Murkowski	Y	N	N	Y	Y	N
Stevens	Y	N	N	Y	Y	N
ARIZONA						
Goldwater	?	?	?	?	?	?
DeConcini	Y	Y	Y	N	N	N
ARKANSAS						
Bumpers	N	Y	Y	N	N	N
Pryor	N	Y	Y	N	N	Y
CALIFORNIA						
Hayakawa	Y	N	N	Y	Y	N
Cranston	N	Y	Y	N	N	Y
COLORADO						
Armstrong	Y	?	N	Y	Y	N
Hart	N	Y	Y	N	N	Y
CONNECTICUT						
Weicker	N	N	N	Y	Y	N
Dodd	N	Y	?	?	-	?
DELAWARE						
Roth	Y	N	N	Y	Y	N
Biden	N	Y	Y	N	N	Y
FLORIDA						
Hawkins	Y	N	N	Y	Y	N
Chiles	Y	Y	Y	N	N	Y
GEORGIA						
Mattingly	Y	N	N	Y	Y	N
Nunn	Y	Y	Y	N	N	N
HAWAII						
Inouye	N	Y	Y	N	N	Y
Matsunaga	N	Y	Y	N	N	Y
IDAHO						
McClure	Y	N	N	Y	Y	N
Symms	Y	N	N	Y	Y	N
ILLINOIS						
Percy	N	N	N	Y	Y	N
Dixon	Y	Y	Y	N	N	Y
INDIANA						
Lugar	Y	N	N	N	Y	N
Quayle	Y	N	N	N	Y	Y
IOWA						
Grassley	Y	N	N	Y	Y	N
Jepsen	Y	N	N	Y	Y	N
KANSAS						
Dole	Y	N	N	Y	Y	N
Kassebaum	Y	N	N	Y	Y	?
KENTUCKY						
Ford	Y	Y	Y	N	N	Y
Huddleston	N	Y	Y	N	N	Y
LOUISIANA						
Johnston	Y	Y	Y	N	N	N
Long	Y	Y	Y	N	N	Y
MAINE						
Cohen	N	N	N	Y	Y	N
Mitchell	N	Y	Y	N	N	Y
MARYLAND						
Mathias	N	N	N	N	Y	Y
Sarbanes	N	Y	Y	N	N	Y
MASSACHUSETTS						
Kennedy	?	Y	Y	N	N	Y
Tsongas	N	Y	Y	N	N	Y
MICHIGAN						
Levin	N	Y	Y	N	N	Y
Riegle	N	Y	Y	N	N	Y
MINNESOTA						
Boschwitz	N	?	N	Y	Y	N
Durenberger	Y	N	N	Y	Y	N
MISSISSIPPI						
Cochran	Y	N	N	Y	Y	N
Stennis	Y	Y	Y	N	N	N
MISSOURI						
Danforth	N	N	N	Y	Y	N
Eagleton	N	Y	Y	N	N	Y
MONTANA						
Baucus	N	Y	Y	N	N	Y
Melcher	Y	Y	Y	-	N	Y
NEBRASKA						
Exon	Y	Y	Y	N	N	N
Zorinsky	Y	Y	Y	N	N	N
NEVADA						
Laxalt	Y	N	N	Y	Y	N
Cannon	Y	Y	Y	Y	N	Y
NEW HAMPSHIRE						
Humphrey	Y	Y	Y	Y	N	N
Rudman	N	N	N	Y	Y	N
NEW JERSEY						
Bradley	N	Y	Y	N	N	Y
Williams	N	Y	Y	N	N	Y
NEW MEXICO						
Domenici	Y	N	N	Y	Y	N
Schmitt	Y	N	N	Y	Y	N
NEW YORK						
D'Amato	Y	N	N	Y	Y	N
Moynihan	N	Y	Y	N	N	+
NORTH CAROLINA						
East	Y	N	N	Y	Y	N
Helms	Y	N	N	Y	N	N
NORTH DAKOTA						
Andrews	Y	N	N	N	Y	N
Burdick	N	Y	Y	N	N	Y
OHIO						
Glenn	N	Y	Y	N	N	N
Metzenbaum	N	Y	Y	N	N	Y
OKLAHOMA						
Nickles	Y	N	N	Y	Y	N
Boren	Y	Y	Y	N	N	N
OREGON						
Hatfield	N	N	N	N	Y	N
Packwood	N	N	N	Y	Y	N
PENNSYLVANIA						
Heinz	N	N	N	Y	Y	Y
Specter	N	N	N	Y	Y	Y
RHODE ISLAND						
Chafee	N	N	N	Y	Y	Y
Pell	N	Y	Y	N	N	Y
SOUTH CAROLINA						
Thurmond	Y	N	N	Y	Y	N
Hollings	Y	Y	Y	N	N	Y
SOUTH DAKOTA						
Abdnor	Y	N	N	N	Y	N
Pressler	Y	N	N	Y	Y	N
TENNESSEE						
Baker	Y	N	N	Y	Y	?
Sasser	Y	Y	Y	N	N	Y
TEXAS						
Tower	?	N	N	Y	Y	N
Bentsen	Y	Y	Y	N	N	N
UTAH						
Garn	Y	N	N	Y	Y	N
Hatch	Y	N	N	Y	Y	N
VERMONT						
Stafford	N	N	N	Y	Y	N
Leahy	?	+	?	?	-	?
VIRGINIA						
Warner	Y	N	N	Y	Y	N
Byrd*	Y	N	Y	N	N	N
WASHINGTON						
Gorton	N	-	N	Y	Y	N
Jackson	N	Y	Y	N	N	Y
WEST VIRGINIA						
Byrd	Y	Y	Y	N	N	Y
Randolph	Y	Y	Y	N	N	Y
WISCONSIN						
Kasten	Y	N	N	Y	Y	N
Proxmire	Y	Y	Y	Y	N	N
WYOMING						
Simpson	Y	N	N	Y	Y	N
Wallop	Y	N	N	Y	Y	N

KEY

Y Voted for (yea).
\# Paired for.
\+ Announced for.
N Voted against (nay).
X Paired against.
- Announced against.
P Voted "present".
C Voted "present" to avoid possible conflict of interest.
? Did not vote or otherwise make a position known.

Democrats *Republicans*

* Byrd elected as an independent.

382. HR 4169. State, Justice, Commerce, Judiciary Appropriations, Fiscal 1982. Helms, R-N.C., amendment to make clear that nothing in the Weicker, R-Conn., amendment *(see vote 377, p. 63-S)* should be interpreted as limiting the restriction on Justice Department involvement in voluntary school prayer cases. Adopted 58-38: R 37-14; D 21-24 (ND 9-21, SD 12-3), Nov. 18, 1981.

383. H J Res 357. Continuing Appropriations, Fiscal 1982. Byrd, D-W.Va., amendment to change the expiration date of the resolution to Dec. 18, 1981, from Sept. 30, 1982. Rejected 46-49: R 1-48; D 45-1 (ND 31-0, SD 14-1), Nov. 18, 1981.

384. H J Res 357. Continuing Appropriations, Fiscal 1982. Byrd, D-W.Va., amendment to change the expiration date of the resolution to March 30, 1982, from Sept. 30, 1982. Rejected 46-51: R 1-51; D 45-0 (ND 30-0, SD 15-0), Nov. 18, 1981.

385. H J Res 357. Continuing Appropriations, Fiscal 1982. Packwood, R-Ore., amendment to prohibit the use of funds in the joint resolution for operation of the *Cardinal* Amtrak train route between Washington, D.C., and Chicago. Rejected 47-49: R 45-7; D 2-42 (ND 2-27, SD 0-15), Nov. 18, 1981.

386. H J Res 357. Continuing Appropriations, Fiscal 1982. Hatfield, R-Ore., motion to table the Byrd, D-W.Va., amendment to change the expiration date of the resolution to Dec. 19, 1981, from Sept. 30, 1982. (The amendment carried with it another Byrd amendment to express the sense of the Senate that the administration's fiscal 1983 budget should include specific proposals to attain a balanced budget by fiscal 1984.) Motion agreed to 50-47: R 50-2; D 0-45 (ND 0-30, SD 0-15), Nov. 18, 1981.

387. H J Res 357. Continuing Appropriations, Fiscal 1982. Kennedy, D-Mass., amendment to add $334 million for youth jobs programs under the Comprehensive Employment and Training Act. Rejected 36-58: R 5-45; D 31-13 (ND 24-5, SD 7-8), Nov. 18, 1981.

KEY

Y Voted for (yea).
\# Paired for.
+ Announced for.
N Voted against (nay).
X Paired against.
- Announced against.
P Voted "present".
C Voted "present" to avoid possible conflict of interest.
? Did not vote or otherwise make a position known.

	388	389	390	391	392	393	394	395
ALABAMA								
Denton	Y	Y	Y	Y	N	Y	Y	Y
Heflin	Y	N	N	Y	N	N	Y	N
ALASKA								
Murkowski	Y	Y	Y	Y	Y	Y	Y	Y
Stevens	Y	Y	Y	Y	Y	Y	N	Y
ARIZONA								
Goldwater	?	?	?	?	?	?	?	?
DeConcini	N	Y	Y	Y	N	N	Y	N
ARKANSAS								
Bumpers	Y	N	N	Y	N	N	Y	N
Pryor	Y	N	N	Y	N	N	Y	N
CALIFORNIA								
Hayakawa	Y	Y	Y	Y	N	Y	Y	Y
Cranston	Y	N	N	Y	N	Y	Y	N
COLORADO								
Armstrong	?	Y	Y	Y	N	N	Y	N
Hart	Y	N	N	Y	N	Y	Y	N
CONNECTICUT								
Weicker	Y	N	N	Y	N	Y	N	N
Dodd	N	N	N	Y	N	N	Y	N
DELAWARE								
Roth	Y	N	N	Y	N	N	N	Y
Biden	N	N	N	Y	N	N	N	Y
FLORIDA								
Hawkins	Y	Y	Y	Y	N	N	N	N
Chiles	Y	Y	Y	Y	N	N	Y	N
GEORGIA								
Mattingly	N	Y	Y	Y	N	N	Y	Y
Nunn	Y	N	N	Y	N	Y	Y	N
HAWAII								
Inouye	Y	N	N	Y	Y	Y	Y	Y
Matsunaga	+	?	?	+	-	+	Y	N
IDAHO								
McClure	Y	Y	Y	Y	N	Y	N	Y
Symms	Y	Y	Y	Y	N	Y	Y	Y
ILLINOIS								
Percy	Y	Y	Y	Y	N	N	N	Y
Dixon	Y	N	N	Y	N	N	Y	N
INDIANA								
Lugar	N	Y	Y	Y	N	Y	Y	Y
Quayle	Y	Y	Y	Y	N	Y	Y	Y
IOWA								
Grassley	Y	Y	Y	Y	N	N	N	Y
Jepsen	Y	Y	Y	Y	N	N	N	N
KANSAS								
Dole	Y	N	N	Y	N	Y	N	N
Kassebaum	Y	N	N	Y	N	Y	N	N
KENTUCKY								
Ford	Y	N	N	Y	N	N	Y	N
Huddleston	Y	N	N	Y	N	N	Y	N
LOUISIANA								
Johnston	Y	N	N	Y	N	N	N	Y
Long	Y	N	N	Y	N	Y	Y	N
MAINE								
Cohen	Y	Y	Y	Y	N	Y	Y	Y
Mitchell	Y	N	N	Y	N	N	Y	N
MARYLAND								
Mathias	Y	N	N	Y	Y	Y	N	N
Sarbanes	Y	N	N	Y	N	Y	Y	N
MASSACHUSETTS								
Kennedy	N	N	N	Y	N	Y	Y	N
Tsongas	N	N	N	Y	N	Y	Y	N
MICHIGAN								
Levin	N	N	N	Y	N	N	N	Y
Riegle	N	N	N	Y	N	N	Y	N
MINNESOTA								
Boschwitz	Y	Y	Y	Y	N	N	N	N
Durenberger	N	N	N	Y	N	N	N	N
MISSISSIPPI								
Cochran	Y	Y	Y	Y	N	N	N	N
Stennis	Y	Y	Y	Y	N	N	Y	Y
MISSOURI								
Danforth	Y	N	N	Y	N	N	N	Y
Eagleton	Y	N	N	Y	N	Y	N	N
MONTANA								
Baucus	Y	N	N	Y	N	Y	Y	N
Melcher	Y	N	N	Y	N	Y	Y	N
NEBRASKA								
Exon	Y	Y	Y	Y	N	N	Y	Y
Zorinsky	Y	Y	\#	Y	N	N	Y	N
NEW HAMPSHIRE								
Humphrey	N	Y	Y	Y	N	N	P	N
Rudman	Y	Y	Y	Y	N	Y	N	N
NEW JERSEY								
Bradley	Y	N	N	Y	N	N	Y	-
Williams	N	N	N	Y	N	Y	Y	N
NEW MEXICO								
Domenici	Y	Y	Y	Y	N	N	N	Y
Schmitt	Y	Y	Y	Y	N	N	N	Y
NEW YORK								
D'Amato	Y	Y	Y	Y	Y	Y	N	N
Moynihan	N	Y	N	Y	N	Y	-	-
NORTH CAROLINA								
East	Y	Y	Y	Y	N	N	Y	Y
Helms	Y	Y	Y	Y	N	N	Y	Y
NORTH DAKOTA								
Andrews	Y	Y	Y	Y	N	N	N	Y
Burdick	Y	N	N	Y	N	N	N	N
OHIO								
Glenn	N	N	N	Y	N	Y	Y	N
Metzenbaum	N	N	N	Y	N	Y	Y	N
OKLAHOMA								
Nickles	Y	+	+	+	-	-	Y	Y
Boren	Y	N	N	Y	N	N	N	Y
OREGON								
Hatfield	Y	Y	Y	Y	N	Y	N	Y
Packwood	Y	N	N	Y	N	Y	Y	N
PENNSYLVANIA								
Heinz	Y	N	N	Y	N	N	N	N
Specter	Y	N	N	Y	N	Y	N	N
RHODE ISLAND								
Chafee	?	N	N	Y	N	Y	N	N
Pell	N	N	N	Y	N	Y	Y	N
SOUTH CAROLINA								
Thurmond	Y	Y	Y	Y	N	Y	Y	N
Hollings	Y	Y	Y	Y	N	Y	Y	N
SOUTH DAKOTA								
Abdnor	Y	Y	v	Y	N	N	N	Y
Pressler	N	Y	v	Y	N	N	Y	N
TENNESSEE								
Baker	Y	Y	Y	Y	N	Y	Y	Y
Sasser	Y	N	N	Y	N	N	N	N
TEXAS								
Tower	Y	Y	Y	Y	N	Y	N	Y
Bentsen	Y	N	N	Y	N	Y	Y	N
UTAH								
Garn	Y	Y	Y	Y	N	Y	Y	Y
Hatch	Y	Y	Y	Y	N	Y	N	N
VERMONT								
Stafford	Y	Y	Y	Y	N	Y	N	N
Leahy	?	?	?	+	?	?	?	-
VIRGINIA								
Warner	N	Y	Y	Y	N	Y	N	Y
Byrd*	Y	Y	Y	Y	N	N	Y	Y
WASHINGTON								
Gorton	Y	Y	Y	Y	N	Y	Y	Y
Jackson	Y	N	N	Y	N	N	N	Y
WEST VIRGINIA								
Byrd	?	?	X	+	-	-	?	-
Randolph	Y	N	N	Y	N	Y	N	N
WISCONSIN								
Kasten	Y	Y	Y	Y	N	N	N	Y
Proxmire	N	Y	Y	Y	N	Y	Y	Y
WYOMING								
Simpson	Y	Y	Y	Y	N	N	Y	Y
Wallop	Y	Y	Y	Y	N	Y	N	Y

Democrats *Republicans*

* Byrd elected as an independent.

388. S J Res 115. Alaska Natural Gas Transportation System Waivers. Passage of the joint resolution approving the president's waivers of various stipulations in the 1977 decision to build a pipeline to carry natural gas from Alaska to the continental United States. The waivers were aimed at securing private financing for the pipeline. Passed 75-19: R 44-6; D 31-13 (ND 16-13, SD 15-0), Nov. 19, 1981. A "yea" was a vote supporting the president's position.

389. H J Res 357. Continuing Appropriations, Fiscal 1982. Schmitt, R-N.M., motion to table (kill) the Danforth, R-Mo., amendment to add $98.6 million for trade adjustment assistance. Motion agreed to 49-46: R 40-11; D 9-35 (ND 5-24, SD 4-11), Nov. 19, 1981.

390. H J Res 357. Continuing Appropriations, Fiscal 1982. Schmitt, R-N.M., motion to table (kill) the Moynihan, D-N.Y., motion to reconsider the vote by which the Danforth amendment *(see vote 389, above)* was tabled. Motion rejected 47-47: R 40-11; D 7-36 (ND 3-25, SD 4-11), Nov. 19, 1981.

391. H Con Res 224. Strategic Arms Talks. Adoption of the concurrent resolution expressing congressional support for President Reagan's Nov. 18, 1981, proposals for limiting strategic and intermediate-range weapons. Adopted 95-0: R 51-0; D 44-0 (ND 29-0, SD 15-0), Nov. 19, 1981.

392. H J Res 357. Continuing Appropriations, Fiscal 1982. Stevens, R-Alaska, amendment, to the Stevens amendment *(see vote 393, below)*, to allow a 4.8 percent pay raise, beginning Dec. 1, for the two top federal executive pay levels and for members of Congress. Rejected 5-90: R 4-47; D 1-43 (ND 1-28, SD 0-15), Nov. 19, 1981.

393. H J Res 357. Continuing Appropriations, Fiscal 1982. Stevens, R-Alaska, amendment to allow a 4.8 percent pay raise, beginning Dec. 1, for senior federal executives below the two top levels. Adopted 54-41: R 34-17; D 20-24 (ND 16-13, SD 4-11), Nov. 19, 1981.

394. H J Res 357. Continuing Appropriations, Fiscal 1982. Cannon, D-Nev., amendment to stipulate that funds provided by the joint resolution should not be subject to language in the conference report on the Transportation Department appropriations bill (HR 4209) that barred the Civil Aeronautics Board from prohibiting participation in an international rate-making conference by U.S. airlines. Adopted 60-35: R 22-29; D 38-6 (ND 26-3, SD 12-3), Nov. 19, 1981.

395. H J Res 357. Continuing Appropriations, Fiscal 1982. Schmitt, R-N.M., motion to table (kill) the Weicker, R-Conn., amendment to add $69.8 million for education of the handicapped. Motion rejected 39-56: R 31-21; D 8-35 (ND 4-24, SD 4-11), Nov. 19, 1981. (The amendment subsequently was adopted by voice vote.)

CQ Senate Votes 396 - 403

Corresponding to Congressional Record Votes 407, 408, 409, 410, 411, 412, 413, 414

	396	397	398	399	400	401	402	403
ALABAMA								
Denton	N	N	N	Y	Y	N	N	Y
Heflin	Y	N	Y	N	Y	N	Y	N
ALASKA								
Murkowski	Y	N	N	N	Y	N	N	Y
Stevens	Y	Y	Y	N	Y	N	N	Y
ARIZONA								
Goldwater	?	?	?	?	?	?	?	?
DeConcini	Y	N	Y	N	Y	N	N	Y
ARKANSAS								
Bumpers	Y	Y	Y	N	N	Y	N	N
Pryor	Y	N	Y	N	N	Y	N	N
CALIFORNIA								
Hayakawa	N	N	N	Y	Y	N	N	Y
Cranston	Y	Y	Y	N	N	Y	Y	N
COLORADO								
Armstrong	Y	N	N	Y	Y	N	N	Y
Hart	Y	Y	Y	N	N	Y	Y	N
CONNECTICUT								
Weicker	Y	Y	Y	N	Y	N	Y	N
Dodd	Y	Y	Y	N	N	Y	Y	N
DELAWARE								
Roth	N	N	Y	N	Y	N	N	Y
Biden	Y	Y	Y	N	N	Y	Y	N
FLORIDA								
Hawkins	Y	Y	Y	N	Y	N	N	Y
Chiles	Y	N	Y	Y	N	N	N	N
GEORGIA								
Mattingly	N	N	N	Y	Y	N	N	Y
Nunn	Y	N	Y	N	N	N	N	N
HAWAII								
Inouye	Y	Y	Y	N	N	N	N	N
Matsunaga	Y	Y	Y	N	N	Y	Y	N
IDAHO								
McClure	N	N	N	N	Y	N	N	Y
Symms	N	N	N	Y	Y	N	N	Y
ILLINOIS								
Percy	N	N	N	N	Y	N	Y	Y
Dixon	N	Y	Y	N	N	N	N	N
INDIANA								
Lugar	N	N	N	Y	Y	N	Y	Y
Quayle	N	N	N	Y	Y	N	N	Y

	396	397	398	399	400	401	402	403
IOWA								
Grassley	N	N	Y	Y	Y	N	N	Y
Jepsen	Y	N	Y	N	Y	N	N	Y
KANSAS								
Dole	N	N	N	Y	Y	N	N	Y
Kassebaum	Y	N	Y	N	Y	N	N	Y
KENTUCKY								
Ford	Y	Y	Y	N	Y	N	N	N
Huddleston	Y	Y	Y	N	Y	N	Y	N
LOUISIANA								
Johnston	N	N	Y	Y	N	N	N	Y
Long	X	N	Y	Y	N	N	N	Y
MAINE								
Cohen	N	Y	N	N	Y	N	N	Y
Mitchell	Y	Y	Y	N	N	Y	Y	N
MARYLAND								
Mathias	Y	Y	Y	N	Y	Y	Y	Y
Sarbanes	Y	Y	Y	N	N	Y	Y	N
MASSACHUSETTS								
Kennedy	Y	Y	Y	N	N	Y	Y	?
Tsongas	Y	Y	Y	N	N	Y	N	N
MICHIGAN								
Levin	Y	Y	Y	N	N	Y	Y	N
Riegle	Y	Y	Y	N	N	Y	Y	N
MINNESOTA								
Boschwitz	N	N	N	N	Y	N	N	Y
Durenberger	Y	Y	Y	N	Y	N	Y	Y
MISSISSIPPI								
Cochran	Y	N	N	N	Y	N	N	Y
Stennis	Y	N	Y	N	N	N	N	N
MISSOURI								
Danforth	N	N	N	N	Y	N	N	Y
Eagleton	Y	Y	Y	N	N	Y	Y	N
MONTANA								
Baucus	Y	N	N	N	N	Y	N	Y
Melcher	Y	Y	Y	N	Y	N	N	N
NEBRASKA								
Exon	N	N	N	N	N	N	N	N
Zorinsky	Y	N	N	N	N	N	N	N
NEVADA								
Laxalt	N	N	N	Y	Y	N	N	Y
Cannon	Y	Y	Y	N	N	Y	Y	N

	396	397	398	399	400	401	402	403
NEW HAMPSHIRE								
Humphrey	Y	Y	N	Y	N	N	N	Y
Rudman	N	Y	N	N	Y	N	Y	Y
NEW JERSEY								
Bradley	?	?	+	?	?	Y	Y	N
Williams	Y	Y	Y	N	N	Y	Y	N
NEW MEXICO								
Domenici	N	N	Y	N	Y	N	N	Y
Schmitt	N	N	N	N	Y	N	N	Y
NEW YORK								
D'Amato	Y	Y	Y	N	Y	Y	Y	Y
Moynihan	#	+	?	N	N	Y	Y	N
NORTH CAROLINA								
East	N	N	N	N	Y	N	N	Y
Helms	N	N	N	Y	Y	N	N	Y
NORTH DAKOTA								
Andrews	N	N	Y	N	Y	N	N	Y
Burdick	Y	Y	Y	N	N	Y	Y	N
OHIO								
Glenn	Y	N	Y	N	Y	N	Y	N
Metzenbaum	Y	Y	Y	N	N	Y	Y	N
OKLAHOMA								
Nickles	N	N	N	Y	Y	N	N	Y
Boren	N	N	N	N	N	N	N	N
OREGON								
Hatfield	N	Y	N	N	Y	N	N	Y
Packwood	Y	N	N	N	Y	N	N	Y
PENNSYLVANIA								
Heinz	Y	Y	Y	N	Y	Y	Y	Y
Specter	Y	Y	Y	N	Y	Y	Y	Y
RHODE ISLAND								
Chafee	Y	Y	Y	Y	Y	Y	Y	Y
Pell	Y	Y	Y	N	N	Y	Y	N
SOUTH CAROLINA								
Thurmond	Y	N	N	N	Y	N	N	Y
Hollings	Y	Y	Y	N	N	Y	N	N
SOUTH DAKOTA								
Abdnor	N	N	N	N	Y	N	N	Y
Pressler	Y	N	Y	N	Y	N	N	Y
TENNESSEE								
Baker	N	N	N	N	Y	N	N	Y
Sasser	Y	Y	Y	N	N	Y	Y	N

KEY

- Y Voted for (yea).
- # Paired for.
- + Announced for.
- N Voted against (nay).
- X Paired against.
- - Announced against.
- P Voted "present".
- C Voted "present" to avoid possible conflict of interest.
- ? Did not vote or otherwise make a position known.

	396	397	398	399	400	401	402	403
TEXAS								
Tower	N	N	N	N	Y	N	N	Y
Bentsen	N	N	Y	N	Y	N	N	Y
UTAH								
Garn	N	N	N	Y	Y	N	N	Y
Hatch	Y	N	Y	Y	Y	N	N	Y
VERMONT								
Stafford	Y	Y	N	N	Y	Y	Y	Y
Leahy	+	+	?	?	?	?	?	?
VIRGINIA								
Warner	N	N	N	N	Y	N	N	Y
Byrd*	N	N	N	N	Y	N	N	Y
WASHINGTON								
Gorton	N	N	N	N	Y	N	N	Y
Jackson	Y	Y	Y	N	N	Y	N	N
WEST VIRGINIA								
Byrd	+	?	+	-	-	+	Y	N
Randolph	Y	Y	Y	N	N	Y	N	N
WISCONSIN								
Kasten	N	N	N	N	Y	N	N	Y
Proxmire	N	N	Y	Y	N	N	Y	Y
WYOMING								
Simpson	N	N	N	N	Y	N	N	Y
Wallop	N	N	N	N	Y	N	N	Y

Democrats *Republicans*

* Byrd elected as an independent.

---

396. H J Res 357. Continuing Appropriations, Fiscal 1982. Weicker, R-Conn., amendment to add $44,741,000 for state vocational rehabilitation grants. Adopted 55-39: R 20-32; D 35-7 (ND 25-3, SD 10-4), Nov. 19, 1981.

397. H J Res 357. Continuing Appropriations, Fiscal 1982. Weicker, R-Conn., amendment to add $200 million for low-income energy assistance. Rejected 41-54: R 14-38; D 27-16 (ND 22-6, SD 5-10), Nov. 19, 1981.

398. H J Res 357. Continuing Appropriations, Fiscal 1982. Metzenbaum, D-Ohio, amendment to add $90 million for payment of "windfall" railroad retirement benefits. Adopted 61-34: R 19-33; D 42-1 (ND 28-0, SD 14-1), Nov. 19, 1981.

399. H J Res 357. Continuing Appropriations, Fiscal 1982. Byrd, Ind-Va., amendment to limit funding under the resolution to the level of the president's budget estimates. Rejected 23-73: R 15-37; D 8-36 (ND 2-27, SD 6-9), Nov. 19, 1981.

400. H J Res 357. Continuing Appropriations, Fiscal 1982. Hatfield, R-Ore., motion to table (kill) the Sasser, D-Tenn., amendment to provide for a 3 percent across-the-board cut for payments not required by law, with certain exceptions, provided that no one program could be reduced by more than 1 percent; reduce by 33 percent the total amount paid to political appointees of the federal government; and direct that additional reductions must come from administrative costs such as public relations, consultants and travel. Motion agreed to 52-44: R 51-1; D 1-43 (ND 1-28, SD 0-15), Nov. 19, 1981.

401. H J Res 357. Continuing Appropriations, Fiscal 1982. Pell, D-R.I., amendment to add $160 million for financial assistance to college students. Rejected 38-59: R 8-44; D 30-15 (ND 23-7, SD 7-8), Nov. 19, 1981.

402. H J Res 357. Continuing Appropriations, Fiscal 1982. Specter, R-Pa., amendment to maintain the existing enforcement authority of the Mine Safety and Health Administration over sand, gravel and stone mines. Rejected 35-63: R 10-42; D 25-21 (ND 23-8, SD 2-13), in the session which began Nov. 19, 1981.

403. H J Res 357. Continuing Appropriations, Fiscal 1982. Garn, R-Utah, motion to table (kill) the DeConcini, D-Ariz., amendment to disapprove the president's proposal to defer spending $91.3 million previously appropriated for Veterans Administration construction projects. Motion agreed to 58-39: R 52-0; D 6-39 (ND 2-28, SD 4-11), in the session which began Nov. 19, 1981. A "yea" was a vote supporting the president's position.

	404	405	406	407	408	409	410	411		404	405	406	407	408	409	410	411		404	405	406	407	408	409	410	411
ALABAMA									**IOWA**									**NEW HAMPSHIRE**								
Denton	Y	Y	Y	Y	Y	Y	N	Y	*Grassley*	Y	Y	Y	N	Y	Y	N	Y	*Humphrey*	Y	N	Y	N	Y	Y	N	Y
Heflin	N	N	Y	N	Y	Y	Y	Y	*Jepsen*	Y	Y	Y	Y	Y	Y	N	Y	*Rudman*	Y	Y	Y	N	Y	Y	N	Y
ALASKA									**KANSAS**									**NEW JERSEY**								
Murkowski	Y	Y	Y	N	Y	Y	N	Y	*Dole*	Y	Y	Y	Y	Y	Y	N	Y	Bradley	N	N	Y	N	N	N	Y	N
Stevens	Y	Y	N	Y	Y	Y	N	Y	*Kassebaum*	Y	Y	Y	N	Y	N	Y	Y	Williams	N	N	Y	N	N	N	Y	N
ARIZONA									**KENTUCKY**									**NEW MEXICO**								
Goldwater	?	?	?	?	?	?	?	?	Ford	N	N	Y	N	Y	Y	Y	N	*Domenici*	Y	Y	Y	Y	Y	Y	Y	Y
DeConcini	N	N	Y	N	Y	Y	Y	Y	Huddleston	N	N	Y	N	Y	Y	Y	N	*Schmitt*	Y	Y	Y	N	Y	Y	N	Y
ARKANSAS									**LOUISIANA**									**NEW YORK**								
Bumpers	?	N	Y	N	Y	N	Y	N	Johnston	N	N	Y	N	Y	Y	Y	N	*D'Amato*	Y	Y	Y	N	Y	N	Y	N
Pryor	N	N	Y	N	Y	Y	Y	Y	Long	N	Y	Y	N	Y	Y	Y	Y	Moynihan	N	N	Y	N	N	N	Y	N
CALIFORNIA									**MAINE**									**NORTH CAROLINA**								
Hayakawa	Y	Y	Y	Y	N	Y	N	Y	*Cohen*	Y	Y	Y	Y	N	N	Y	N	*East*	Y	Y	Y	N	Y	N	Y	Y
Cranston	N	N	Y	Y	N	N	Y	N	Mitchell	N	N	Y	N	Y	N	Y	N	*Helms*	Y	Y	Y	N	Y	N	Y	Y
COLORADO									**MARYLAND**									**NORTH DAKOTA**								
Armstrong	Y	Y	Y	N	Y	Y	N	Y	*Mathias*	Y	Y	Y	Y	N	N	Y	N	*Andrews*	Y	Y	Y	N	Y	N	Y	Y
Hart	N	N	Y	Y	Y	N	Y	N	Sarbanes	N	N	Y	N	Y	N	Y	N	Burdick	N	N	Y	N	Y	N	Y	N
CONNECTICUT									**MASSACHUSETTS**									**OHIO**								
Weicker	N	Y	Y	N	N	Y	N	Y	Kennedy	?	?	?	?	?	?	?	?	Glenn	N	N	Y	N	N	N	Y	Y
Dodd	N	N	Y	N	N	Y	N	Y	Tsongas	N	N	Y	N	N	N	Y	N	Metzenbaum	N	N	Y	N	N	N	Y	Y
DELAWARE									**MICHIGAN**									**OKLAHOMA**								
Roth	Y	Y	Y	N	Y	Y	N	Y	Levin	N	N	Y	N	N	N	Y	N	*Nickles*	Y	Y	Y	N	Y	Y	N	Y
Biden	N	N	Y	N	N	Y	N	Y	Riegle	N	N	Y	N	Y	N	Y	N	Boren	N	N	Y	N	Y	Y	Y	Y
FLORIDA									**MINNESOTA**									**OREGON**								
Hawkins	Y	Y	Y	Y	Y	Y	N	Y	*Boschwitz*	Y	Y	Y	Y	N	Y	Y	Y	*Hatfield*	Y	Y	N	N	N	N	Y	Y
Chiles	N	N	Y	N	Y	N	Y	N	*Durenberger*	Y	Y	Y	N	Y	Y	Y	Y	*Packwood*	Y	Y	Y	Y	N	Y	Y	Y
GEORGIA									**MISSISSIPPI**									**PENNSYLVANIA**								
Mattingly	Y	Y	Y	Y	Y	Y	N	Y	*Cochran*	Y	N	Y	N	N	Y	Y	Y	*Heinz*	Y	Y	Y	N	N	Y	Y	Y
Nunn	N	N	Y	N	Y	Y	Y	N	Stennis	N	Y	Y	N	Y	Y	?	?	*Specter*	Y	Y	Y	N	Y	Y	Y	Y
HAWAII									**MISSOURI**									**RHODE ISLAND**								
Inouye	N	N	Y	N	Y	N	Y	N	*Danforth*	Y	Y	Y	N	Y	Y	Y	Y	*Chafee*	Y	Y	Y	N	N	Y	N	N
Matsunaga	N	N	Y	N	Y	N	Y	N	Eagleton	N	N	Y	N	Y	N	Y	N	Pell	N	N	Y	N	N	Y	N	N
IDAHO									**MONTANA**									**SOUTH CAROLINA**								
McClure	Y	Y	Y	N	Y	Y	N	Y	Baucus	N	N	Y	N	Y	N	Y	N	*Thurmond*	Y	Y	Y	N	Y	Y	N	Y
Symms	Y	Y	Y	N	Y	Y	N	Y	Melcher	N	Y	Y	N	Y	Y	Y	Y	Hollings	N	Y	Y	Y	N	N	Y	N
ILLINOIS									**NEBRASKA**									**SOUTH DAKOTA**								
Percy	Y	Y	N	Y	N	Y	N	Y	Exon	N	Y	Y	N	Y	Y	Y	N	*Abdnor*	Y	Y	Y	N	Y	N	Y	Y
Dixon	N	N	Y	N	Y	Y	Y	Y	Zorinsky	N	N	Y	Y	Y	Y	N	Y	*Pressler*	Y	Y	Y	N	Y	N	Y	Y
INDIANA									**NEVADA**									**TENNESSEE**								
Lugar	Y	Y	Y	N	N	Y	Y	Y	*Laxalt*	Y	Y	Y	N	Y	N	N	Y	*Baker*	Y	Y	Y	N	Y	N	Y	Y
Quayle	Y	Y	Y	Y	Y	Y	N	Y	Cannon	N	N	Y	N	Y	N	Y	Y	Sasser	N	N	Y	N	Y	Y	Y	Y

KEY

Y Voted for (yea).
\# Paired for.
\+ Announced for.
N Voted against (nay).
X Paired against.
- Announced against.
P Voted "present".
C Voted "present" to avoid possible conflict of interest.
? Did not vote or otherwise make a position known.

	404	405	406	407	408	409	410	411
TEXAS								
Tower	Y	Y	Y	Y	N	Y	N	Y
Bentsen	N	N	Y	N	Y	Y	Y	N
UTAH								
Garn	Y	Y	Y	Y	Y	Y	N	Y
Hatch	Y	Y	Y	Y	Y	Y	Y	Y
VERMONT								
Stafford	Y	Y	Y	N	Y	N	Y	N
Leahy	?	?	?	?	?	?	?	?
VIRGINIA								
Warner	Y	Y	Y	N	Y	N	Y	Y
Byrd*	Y	N	Y	N	Y	Y	N	Y
WASHINGTON								
Gorton	Y	Y	Y	N	Y	N	Y	N
Jackson	N	N	Y	N	Y	N	Y	N
WEST VIRGINIA								
Byrd	N	N	Y	N	Y	Y	N	Y
Randolph	N	N	Y	N	N	Y	N	Y
WISCONSIN								
Kasten	Y	Y	Y	N	Y	N	Y	Y
Proxmire	Y	N	Y	N	Y	Y	Y	Y
WYOMING								
Simpson	Y	Y	Y	Y	Y	Y	N	Y
Wallop	Y	Y	Y	Y	Y	Y	Y	Y

Democrats *Republicans*

* Byrd elected as an independent.

404. H J Res 357. Continuing Appropriations, Fiscal 1982. Hatfield, R-Ore., motion to table (kill) the DeConcini, D-Ariz., amendment to specify that disapproval of the proposed Veterans Administration deferral *(see vote 403, p. 66-S)* would have the same effect as passage of an impoundment resolution. Motion agreed to 53-43: R 51-1; D 2-42 (ND 1-29, SD 1-13), in the session which began Nov. 19, 1981. (The amendment carried with it a Cranston, D-Calif., amendment to disapprove the administration's plan to study alternative methods of providing veterans' medical care.)

405. H J Res 357. Continuing Appropriations, Fiscal 1982. Baker, R-Tenn., motion to table (kill) the Chiles, D-Fla., motion to recommit the joint resolution to the Appropriations Committee with instructions to report back within five hours specific cuts to achieve a 4 percent reduction. Motion agreed to 55-42: R 50-2; D 5-40 (ND 2-28, SD 3-12), in the session which began Nov. 19, 1981.

406. H J Res 357. Continuing Appropriations, Fiscal 1982. Byrd, D-W.Va., amendment to the Baker, R-Tenn., amendment *(see vote 409, below)* to advance the expiration date of the joint resolution to March 30, 1982, from Sept. 30, 1982. Adopted 94-3: R 49-3; D 45-0 (ND 30-0, SD 15-0), in the session which began Nov. 19, 1981.

407. H J Res 357. Continuing Appropriations, Fiscal 1982. Hatfield, R-Ore., motion to table (kill) the Proxmire, D-Wis., amendment, to the Baker, R-Tenn., amendment *(see vote 409, below)*, to eliminate the exemption of foreign aid programs from the 4 percent cut. Motion rejected 48-49: R 33-19; D 15-30 (ND 14-16, SD 1-14), in the session which began Nov. 19, 1981.

408. H J Res 357. Continuing Appropriations, Fiscal 1982. Proxmire, D-Wis., amendment, to the Baker, R-Tenn., amendment *(see vote 409, below)*, to eliminate the exemption of foreign aid programs from the 4 percent cut. Adopted 62-35: R 30-22; D 32-13 (ND 18-12, SD 14-1), in the session which began Nov. 19, 1981.

409. H J Res 357. Continuing Appropriations, Fiscal 1982. Baker, R-Tenn., amendment, as amended, to reduce by 4 percent the total funds appropriated or otherwise made available by the joint resolution except for veterans' health care, entitlements, food stamps, defense, military construction and law enforcement activities. Adopted 62-35: R 42-10; D 20-25 (ND 8-22, SD 12-3), in the session which began Nov. 19, 1981.

410. H J Res 357. Continuing Appropriations, Fiscal 1982. Cranston, D-Calif., motion to table (kill) the Jepsen, R-Iowa, amendment to bar funding after March 15, 1982, for the Federal Election Commission in the absence of authorizing legislation. Motion agreed to 65-31: R 23-29; D 42-2 (ND 29-1, SD 13-1), in the session which began Nov. 19, 1981.

411. H J Res 357. Continuing Appropriations, Fiscal 1982. Garn, R-Utah, motion to table (kill) the Hart, D-Colo., amendment to provide funds for the Environmental Protection Agency and the Council on Environmental Quality at the amounts provided in the conference report on the HUD-independent agencies appropriations bill. Motion agreed to 59-37: R 45-7; D 14-30 (ND 8-22, SD 6-8), in the session which began Nov. 19, 1981.

CQ Senate Votes 412 - 415

Corresponding to Congressional Record Votes 423, 424, 425, 426

	412 413 414 415		412 413 414 415		412 413 414 415
ALABAMA		**IOWA**		**NEW HAMPSHIRE**	
Denton	Y Y Y Y	*Grassley*	N N Y Y	*Humphrey*	Y N Y Y
Heflin	Y N N Y	*Jepsen*	Y N Y Y	*Rudman*	Y Y Y Y
ALASKA		**KANSAS**		**NEW JERSEY**	
Murkowski	Y Y Y Y	*Dole*	Y Y Y Y	Bradley	N N N Y
Stevens	Y Y Y Y	*Kassebaum*	Y Y Y Y	Williams	N N ? Y
ARIZONA		**KENTUCKY**		**NEW MEXICO**	
Goldwater	? ? ? ?	Ford	Y N N Y	*Domenici*	Y Y Y Y
DeConcini	Y ? ? ?	Huddleston	Y N N Y	*Schmitt*	Y Y Y Y
ARKANSAS		**LOUISIANA**		**NEW YORK**	
Bumpers	N N N ?	Johnston	Y N N Y	*D'Amato*	Y Y Y Y
Pryor	N ? ? Y	Long	Y N N Y	Moynihan	N Y N Y
CALIFORNIA		**MAINE**		**NORTH CAROLINA**	
Hayakawa	Y Y Y Y	*Cohen*	Y Y Y Y	*East*	Y Y Y Y
Cranston	N N N N	Mitchell	N N N Y	*Helms*	Y N Y Y
COLORADO		**MARYLAND**		**NORTH DAKOTA**	
Armstrong	N N Y Y	*Mathias*	Y Y Y Y	*Andrews*	Y Y Y Y
Hart	N ? ? Y	Sarbanes	N N N Y	Burdick	Y N N Y
CONNECTICUT		**MASSACHUSETTS**		**OHIO**	
Weicker	Y Y Y Y	Kennedy	? N N Y	Glenn	N N N Y
Dodd	N N N Y	Tsongas	N N N Y	Metzenbaum	N ? ? Y
DELAWARE		**MICHIGAN**		**OKLAHOMA**	
Roth	N ? ? Y	Levin	N N N Y	*Nickles*	N Y Y Y
Biden	N ? ? ?	Riegle	N N N Y	Boren	Y ? ? +
FLORIDA		**MINNESOTA**		**OREGON**	
Hawkins	Y Y Y Y	*Boschwitz*	Y Y Y Y	*Hatfield*	Y Y Y Y
Chiles	N ? ? ?	*Durenberger*	Y Y Y +	*Packwood*	Y Y Y Y
GEORGIA		**MISSISSIPPI**		**PENNSYLVANIA**	
Mattingly	Y Y Y Y	*Cochran*	Y Y Y Y	*Heinz*	Y Y Y Y
Nunn	Y N N Y	Stennis	? N N Y	*Specter*	Y Y Y Y
HAWAII		**MISSOURI**		**RHODE ISLAND**	
Inouye	Y N N Y	*Danforth*	Y Y Y Y	*Chafee*	Y Y Y Y
Matsunaga	N N N Y	Eagleton	N ? ? Y	Pell	N N N Y
IDAHO		**MONTANA**		**SOUTH CAROLINA**	
McClure	Y Y Y Y	Baucus	Y N N Y	*Thurmond*	Y Y Y Y
Symms	N Y Y Y	Melcher	Y ? ? +	Hollings	N N N Y
ILLINOIS		**NEBRASKA**		**SOUTH DAKOTA**	
Percy	Y Y Y Y	Exon	Y N N Y	*Abdnor*	Y Y Y Y
Dixon	Y N N Y	Zorinsky	Y ? ? Y	*Pressler*	Y N Y Y
INDIANA		**NEVADA**		**TENNESSEE**	
Lugar	Y Y Y Y	*Laxalt*	Y Y Y Y	*Baker*	Y Y Y Y
Quayle	Y Y Y Y	Cannon	Y N N Y	Sasser	Y N N Y

KEY

Y Voted for (yea).
\# Paired for.
+ Announced for.
N Voted against (nay).
X Paired against.
- Announced against.
P Voted "present".
C Voted "present" to avoid possible conflict of interest.
? Did not vote or otherwise make a position known.

	412 413 414 415
TEXAS	
Tower	Y ? ? ?
Bentsen	Y ? ? ?
UTAH	
Garn	Y Y Y Y
Hatch	Y Y Y Y
VERMONT	
Stafford	Y Y Y Y
Leahy	? ? ? ?
VIRGINIA	
Warner	Y Y Y Y
Byrd*	Y N N Y
WASHINGTON	
Gorton	Y Y Y Y
Jackson	Y Y N Y
WEST VIRGINIA	
Byrd	Y N N Y
Randolph	Y N N Y
WISCONSIN	
Kasten	Y Y Y Y
Proxmire	Y N N Y
WYOMING	
Simpson	Y Y Y Y
Wallop	Y Y Y Y

Democrats *Republicans*

* Byrd elected as an independent.

412. H J Res 357. Continuing Appropriations, Fiscal 1982. Passage of the joint resolution to provide funding authority during the period Nov. 20, 1981, through March 30, 1982, for government agencies whose regular fiscal 1982 appropriations bills had not been enacted. Passed 70-26: R 47-5; D 23-21 (ND 13-17, SD 10-4), in the session which began Nov. 19, 1981.

413. H J Res 357. Continuing Appropriations, Fiscal 1982. Adoption of the conference report on the joint resolution to provide funding authority during the period Nov. 20, 1981, through July 15, 1982, for government agencies whose regular fiscal 1982 appropriations bills had not been enacted. Adopted 46-39: R 44-6; D 2-33 (ND 2-22, SD 0-11), Nov. 22, 1981.

414. H J Res 357. Continuing Appropriations, Fiscal 1982. Stevens, R-Alaska, motion to table (kill) the Moynihan, D-N.Y., motion to reconsider the vote *(see vote 413, above)* by which the conference report on the joint resolution was adopted. Motion agreed to 50-34: R 50-0; D 0-34 (ND 0-23, SD 0-11), Nov. 22, 1981.

415. H J Res 368. Continuing Appropriations, Fiscal 1982. Passage of the joint resolution to provide funding authority for the period Nov. 20, 1981, through Dec. 15, 1981, for government agencies whose regular fiscal 1982 appropriations bills had not been enacted. Passed 88-1: R 50-0; D 38-1 (ND 27-1, SD 11-0), Nov. 23, 1981.

	416	417	418	419	420	421	422	423
ALABAMA								
Denton	Y	Y	N	N	Y	Y	Y	Y
Heflin	?	?	?	Y	N	N	N	Y
ALASKA								
Murkowski	?	?	?	N	Y	Y	Y	Y
Stevens	Y	N	N	N	Y	Y	Y	Y
ARIZONA								
Goldwater	?	?	?	?	?	?	?	?
DeConcini	Y	Y	N	Y	N	Y	N	-
ARKANSAS								
Bumpers	Y	N	N	Y	N	N	N	N
Pryor	Y	N	N	Y	N	N	N	N
CALIFORNIA								
Hayakawa	?	?	?	N	Y	Y	Y	Y
Cranston	?	?	?	Y	N	N	N	X
COLORADO								
Armstrong	Y	Y	N	N	Y	Y	Y	Y
Hart	Y	N	N	Y	N	N	N	N
CONNECTICUT								
Weicker	?	N	Y	N	Y	Y	Y	Y
Dodd	?	?	Y	Y	N	N	N	N
DELAWARE								
Roth	Y	N	Y	N	Y	Y	Y	Y
Biden	?	?	?	Y	N	N	Y	N
FLORIDA								
Hawkins	Y	Y	N	N	Y	Y	Y	Y
Chiles	Y	Y	Y	Y	N	N	N	N
GEORGIA								
Mattingly	Y	N	N	N	Y	Y	Y	Y
Nunn	Y	Y	N	Y	N	N	Y	N
HAWAII								
Inouye	Y	Y	Y	Y	N	N	N	N
Matsunaga	Y	N	N	Y	N	N	N	N
IDAHO								
McClure	?	?	?	N	Y	Y	Y	Y
Symms	Y	Y	N	Y	Y	Y	Y	Y
ILLINOIS								
Percy	Y	Y	N	N	Y	Y	Y	Y
Dixon	Y	Y	N	Y	N	N	Y	N
INDIANA								
Lugar	Y	Y	Y	N	Y	Y	Y	Y
Quayle	N	Y	N	N	Y	Y	Y	Y
IOWA								
Grassley	Y	Y	N	N	Y	Y	Y	Y
Jepsen	Y	Y	N	N	Y	Y	Y	Y
KANSAS								
Dole	Y	N	Y	N	Y	Y	N	Y
Kassebaum	?	?	?	N	Y	Y	Y	Y
KENTUCKY								
Ford	Y	Y	N	Y	N	N	N	N
Huddleston	?	?	?	Y	N	N	N	?
LOUISIANA								
Johnston	Y	Y	?	Y	N	N	N	N
Long	?	?	?	?	?	?	?	?
MAINE								
Cohen	Y	Y	Y	N	Y	Y	Y	Y
Mitchell	Y	N	Y	Y	N	N	N	N
MARYLAND								
Mathias	?	?	?	?	?	?	?	?
Sarbanes	?	N	N	Y	N	N	N	N
MASSACHUSETTS								
Kennedy	?	N	N	Y	N	N	N	N
Tsongas	?	?	?	?	?	?	?	N
MICHIGAN								
Levin	Y	N	N	Y	N	N	N	N
Riegle	Y	#	?	Y	N	N	N	N
MINNESOTA								
Boschwitz	Y	Y	Y	N	Y	Y	Y	Y
Durenberger	Y	Y	N	N	Y	Y	Y	?
MISSISSIPPI								
Cochran	?	Y	N	N	Y	Y	Y	Y
Stennis	Y	Y	N	?	?	?	?	#
MISSOURI								
Danforth	Y	Y	Y	N	Y	Y	Y	Y
Eagleton	Y	N	Y	Y	N	N	N	N
MONTANA								
Baucus	Y	N	N	Y	N	N	N	N
Melcher	Y	Y	N	Y	N	N	N	N
NEBRASKA								
Exon	Y	N	N	Y	N	N	N	N
Zorinsky	?	?	?	?	?	?	?	?
NEVADA								
Laxalt	Y	Y	N	N	Y	Y	Y	Y
Cannon	Y	Y	N	Y	N	?	?	?
NEW HAMPSHIRE								
Humphrey	Y	Y	N	N	Y	Y	Y	Y
Rudman	Y	N	N	N	Y	Y	Y	Y
NEW JERSEY								
Bradley	Y	Y	Y	Y	N	N	N	N
Williams	Y	Y	Y	Y	N	N	N	N
NEW MEXICO								
Domenici	Y	N	N	N	Y	Y	Y	Y
Schmitt	Y	Y	N	N	Y	Y	Y	Y
NEW YORK								
D'Amato	Y	Y	N	N	Y	Y	Y	Y
Moynihan	Y	N	N	Y	N	N	N	N
NORTH CAROLINA								
East	Y	Y	N	N	Y	Y	Y	Y
Helms	Y	Y	N	N	Y	Y	Y	Y
NORTH DAKOTA								
Andrews	?	?	?	N	Y	Y	Y	Y
Burdick	Y	N	N	N	Y	N	Y	N
OHIO								
Glenn	Y	Y	N	N	Y	N	Y	N
Metzenbaum	?	?	?	Y	N	N	N	N
OKLAHOMA								
Nickles	Y	Y	N	N	Y	Y	Y	Y
Boren	Y	N	N	Y	N	N	N	N
OREGON								
Hatfield	Y	N	N	-	+	Y	Y	Y
Packwood	Y	Y	N	N	Y	Y	Y	Y
PENNSYLVANIA								
Heinz	Y	Y	N	N	Y	Y	Y	Y
Specter	Y	Y	N	N	Y	Y	Y	Y
RHODE ISLAND								
Chafee	Y	N	N	N	Y	Y	Y	Y
Pell	?	X	Y	N	N	N	N	N
SOUTH CAROLINA								
Thurmond	?	Y	N	N	Y	Y	Y	Y
Hollings	Y	Y	N	Y	N	N	Y	N
SOUTH DAKOTA								
Abdnor	?	+	-	N	Y	Y	Y	Y
Pressler	Y	N	Y	N	Y	Y	Y	Y
TENNESSEE								
Baker	Y	Y	N	N	Y	Y	Y	Y
Sasser	Y	Y	N	Y	X	-	-	N
TEXAS								
Tower	Y	Y	N	N	Y	Y	Y	Y
Bentsen	?	?	?	Y	N	Y	Y	N
UTAH								
Garn	Y	Y	N	N	Y	Y	Y	Y
Hatch	Y	Y	N	N	Y	Y	Y	Y
VERMONT								
Stafford	Y	N	N	N	Y	Y	Y	Y
Leahy	Y	N	N	Y	N	N	N	N
VIRGINIA								
Warner	Y	Y	N	N	Y	Y	Y	Y
Byrd*	?	Y	N	N	#	Y	Y	Y
WASHINGTON								
Gorton	Y	N	N	N	Y	Y	Y	Y
Jackson	Y	Y	N	Y	N	N	N	N
WEST VIRGINIA								
Byrd	Y	Y	N	Y	N	N	N	N
Randolph	Y	N	N	Y	N	Y	N	N
WISCONSIN								
Kasten	Y	Y	N	N	Y	Y	Y	Y
Proxmire	Y	N	N	N	N	N	N	Y
WYOMING								
Simpson	Y	Y	N	N	Y	Y	Y	Y
Wallop	?	Y	N	N	Y	Y	Y	Y

KEY

Y Voted for (yea).
Paired for.
+ Announced for.
N Voted against (nay).
X Paired against.
- Announced against.
P Voted "present".
C Voted "present" to avoid possible conflict of interest.
? Did not vote or otherwise make a position known.

Democrats   *Republicans*

*Byrd elected as an independent.

416. HR 4995. Defense Appropriations, Fiscal 1982. Baker, R-Tenn., motion to instruct the sergeant-at-arms to request the attendance of absent senators. Motion agreed to 73-1: R 40-1; D 33-0 (ND 23-0, SD 10-0), Nov. 30, 1981.

417. HR 4995. Defense Appropriations, Fiscal 1982. Heinz, R-Pa., amendment to add to the bill $90 million (including $88 million for procurement and $2 million for research and development) for reactivation of the battleship *Iowa*. Adopted 51-29: R 33-12; D 18-17 (ND 10-14, SD 8-3), Nov. 30, 1981. A "yea" was a vote supporting the president's position.

418. HR 4995. Defense Appropriations, Fiscal 1982. Danforth, R-Mo., amendment to earmark $103.5 million for procurement of Boeing 707 aircraft to provide engines and parts for KC-135 tanker aircraft, and to earmark $46.8 million for installation of additional engines on the KC-135 tankers. Rejected 16-65: R 8-37; D 8-28 (ND 7-19, SD 1-9), Nov. 30, 1981.

419. HR 4995. Defense Appropriations, Fiscal 1982. Levin, D-Mich., amendment to add $222 million to procure four KC-10A tanker/cargo aircraft. Rejected 38-55: R 0-50; D 38-5 (ND 26-4, SD 12-1), Dec. 1, 1981.

420. HR 4995. Defense Appropriations, Fiscal 1982. Stevens, R-Alaska, motion to table (kill) the Byrd, D-W.Va., amendment to add $250 million for basic and applied research, development, testing and evaluation. Motion agreed to 51-40: R 50-0; D 1-40 (ND 1-29, SD 0-11), Dec. 1, 1981.

421. HR 4995. Defense Appropriations, Fiscal 1982. Stevens, R-Alaska, motion to table (kill) the Bradley, D-N.J., amendment requiring the president to submit to Congress by Jan. 31, 1982, a report explaining the effect of his tax and spending policies on military programs and outlining his plans for protecting U.S. interests in the Middle East. Motion agreed to 56-36: R 51-0; D 5-36 (ND 3-26, SD 2-10), Dec. 1, 1981.

422. HR 4995. Defense Appropriations, Fiscal 1982. Stevens, R-Alaska, motion to table (kill) the DeConcini, D-Ariz., amendment expressing the sense of the Senate that the MX intercontinental missile should not be based near areas of high population density. Motion agreed to 57-35: R 50-1; D 7-34 (ND 3-26, SD 4-8), Dec. 1, 1981.

423. HR 4995. Defense Appropriations, Fiscal 1982. Stevens, R-Alaska, motion to table (kill) the Hollings, D-S.C., amendment to add funding for 6,000 personnel in the Army ($35 million) and 6,000 personnel in the Air Force ($42 million). Motion agreed to 54-36: R 50-0; D 4-36 (ND 2-26, SD 2-10), Dec. 2, 1981.

CQ Senate Votes 424 - 431

Corresponding to Congressional Record Votes 435, 436, 437, 438, 439, 440, 441, 442, 443, 444, 445

	424	425	426	427	428	429	430	431
ALABAMA								
Denton	Y	N	Y	Y	N	Y	Y	?
Heflin	N	N	Y	Y	Y	Y	Y	N
ALASKA								
Murkowski	Y	N	N	Y	N	Y	Y	N
Stevens	Y	N	N	Y	N	Y	Y	N
ARIZONA								
Goldwater	?	?	?	?	?	?	?	?
DeConcini	-	+	+	+	+	+	+	-
ARKANSAS								
Bumpers	N	Y	N	Y	N	Y	Y	N
Pryor	N	Y	Y	Y	Y	Y	Y	Y
CALIFORNIA								
Hayakawa	Y	N	N	Y	N	Y	Y	?
Cranston	X	Y	Y	Y	Y	Y	Y	Y
COLORADO								
Armstrong	Y	N	N	Y	N	Y	Y	N
Hart	N	Y	Y	Y	Y	N	N	Y
CONNECTICUT								
Weicker	Y	N	N	Y	N	Y	Y	N
Dodd	N	Y	Y	Y	Y	Y	Y	Y
DELAWARE								
Roth	Y	N	N	Y	N	N	N	N
Biden	N	Y	Y	Y	Y	Y	Y	Y
FLORIDA								
Hawkins	Y	N	N	Y	N	Y	Y	N
Chiles	N	Y	Y	Y	Y	Y	Y	N
GEORGIA								
Mattingly	Y	N	N	Y	N	Y	Y	N
Nunn	N	Y	Y	Y	Y	Y	Y	N
HAWAII								
Inouye	N	Y	Y	Y	Y	Y	Y	N
Matsunaga	N	Y	Y	Y	Y	Y	Y	Y
IDAHO								
McClure	Y	N	N	Y	N	Y	Y	N
Symms	Y	N	N	Y	N	Y	Y	N
ILLINOIS								
Percy	Y	N	N	Y	N	Y	Y	N
Dixon	N	N	N	Y	Y	Y	Y	Y
INDIANA								
Lugar	Y	N	N	Y	N	Y	Y	N
Quayle	Y	N	N	Y	N	Y	Y	N
IOWA								
Grassley	Y	N	N	Y	Y	Y	Y	N
Jepsen	Y	N	N	Y	N	Y	Y	N
KANSAS								
Dole	Y	N	N	Y	N	Y	Y	N
Kassebaum	Y	N	N	Y	Y	Y	Y	Y
KENTUCKY								
Ford	N	Y	Y	Y	Y	Y	Y	Y
Huddleston	N	Y	N	Y	Y	Y	Y	Y
LOUISIANA								
Johnston	N	Y	Y	Y	Y	Y	Y	N
Long	?	?	N	Y	N	Y	Y	N
MAINE								
Cohen	Y	N	N	Y	N	Y	Y	N
Mitchell	N	Y	Y	Y	Y	Y	Y	Y
MARYLAND								
Mathias	?	?	?	?	?	Y	Y	Y
Sarbanes	N	Y	Y	Y	Y	Y	Y	Y
MASSACHUSETTS								
Kennedy	N	Y	Y	Y	Y	Y	Y	Y
Tsongas	N	Y	Y	Y	Y	Y	Y	Y
MICHIGAN								
Levin	N	Y	Y	Y	Y	Y	Y	Y
Riegle	N	Y	Y	Y	Y	Y	Y	Y
MINNESOTA								
Boschwitz	Y	N	N	Y	N	Y	Y	N
Durenberger	?	?	N	Y	N	Y	Y	Y
MISSISSIPPI								
Cochran	Y	N	N	Y	N	Y	Y	N
Stennis	#	N	N	Y	N	Y	Y	N
MISSOURI								
Danforth	Y	N	N	Y	N	Y	Y	N
Eagleton	N	Y	Y	Y	Y	Y	Y	Y
MONTANA								
Baucus	N	Y	Y	Y	Y	Y	Y	N
Melcher	N	Y	Y	Y	Y	Y	Y	Y
NEBRASKA								
Exon	N	Y	Y	Y	Y	Y	Y	N
Zorinsky	?	?	Y	Y	Y	Y	Y	N
NEVADA								
Laxalt	Y	N	N	Y	N	Y	Y	N
Cannon	?	?	?	+	?	+	+	N
NEW HAMPSHIRE								
Humphrey	Y	N	Y	N	Y	Y	Y	N
Rudman	Y	N	N	Y	N	Y	Y	N
NEW JERSEY								
Bradley	N	Y	Y	Y	Y	Y	Y	N
Williams	N	Y	Y	Y	Y	Y	Y	Y
NEW MEXICO								
Domenici	Y	N	N	Y	N	Y	Y	N
Schmitt	Y	N	N	Y	N	Y	Y	N
NEW YORK								
D'Amato	Y	N	N	Y	N	+	+	N
Moynihan	N	Y	Y	Y	?	?	?	Y
NORTH CAROLINA								
East	Y	N	N	Y	N	Y	Y	N
Helms	Y	N	N	Y	N	Y	Y	N
NORTH DAKOTA								
Andrews	Y	N	N	Y	Y	Y	Y	Y
Burdick	Y	N	N	Y	Y	Y	Y	Y
OHIO								
Glenn	Y	Y	Y	Y	?	?	?	Y
Metzenbaum	N	Y	Y	Y	Y	N	N	Y
OKLAHOMA								
Nickles	Y	N	N	Y	N	Y	Y	N
Boren	N	Y	Y	Y	Y	Y	Y	N
OREGON								
Hatfield	Y	N	N	Y	N	N	N	N
Packwood	Y	N	N	Y	N	Y	Y	N
PENNSYLVANIA								
Heinz	Y	N	N	Y	N	Y	Y	N
Specter	Y	N	N	Y	N	Y	Y	N
RHODE ISLAND								
Chafee	Y	N	N	Y	N	Y	Y	N
Pell	N	Y	Y	Y	Y	Y	Y	Y
SOUTH CAROLINA								
Thurmond	Y	N	N	Y	N	Y	Y	N
Hollings	N	Y	Y	Y	Y	Y	Y	?
SOUTH DAKOTA								
Abdnor	Y	N	N	Y	N	Y	Y	N
Pressler	Y	N	N	Y	N	Y	Y	N
TENNESSEE								
Baker	Y	N	N	Y	N	Y	Y	N
Sasser	N	Y	Y	Y	Y	Y	Y	N
TEXAS								
Tower	Y	N	N	Y	N	Y	Y	N
Bentsen	N	Y	Y	Y	Y	Y	Y	N
UTAH								
Garn	Y	N	N	Y	N	Y	Y	N
Hatch	Y	N	N	Y	N	Y	Y	N
VERMONT								
Stafford	Y	N	N	Y	N	Y	Y	N
Leahy	N	Y	Y	Y	Y	Y	Y	Y
VIRGINIA								
Warner	Y	N	N	Y	N	Y	Y	N
Byrd*	Y	N	N	Y	N	Y	Y	N
WASHINGTON								
Gorton	Y	N	N	Y	N	Y	Y	N
Jackson	N	Y	Y	Y	Y	Y	Y	N
WEST VIRGINIA								
Byrd	N	Y	Y	Y	Y	Y	Y	N
Randolph	Y	Y	Y	Y	Y	Y	Y	Y
WISCONSIN								
Kasten	Y	N	N	Y	N	Y	Y	N
Proxmire	Y	N	N	Y	Y	Y	Y	Y
WYOMING								
Simpson	Y	N	N	Y	N	Y	Y	N
Wallop	Y	N	N	Y	N	Y	Y	N

KEY

Y Voted for (yea).
\# Paired for.
\+ Announced for.
N Voted against (nay).
X Paired against.
- Announced against.
P Voted "present".
C Voted "present" to avoid possible conflict of interest.
? Did not vote or otherwise make a position known.

Democrats *Republicans*

* Byrd elected as an independent.

424. HR 4995. Defense Appropriations, Fiscal 1982. Stevens, R-Alaska, motion to table (kill), the Hollings, D-S.C., amendment to add $148 million for procurement of ammunition for the Army. Motion agreed to 55-36: R 50-0; D 5-36 (ND 4-24, SD 1-12), Dec. 2, 1981.

425. HR 4995. Defense Appropriations, Fiscal 1982. Exon, D-Neb., amendment to add $60 million for the Army force modernization program. Rejected 37-56: R 0-50; D 37-6 (ND 26-3, SD 11-3), Dec. 2, 1981.

426. HR 4995. Defense Appropriations, Fiscal 1982. Glenn, D-Ohio, amendment to add $74.6 million to Navy operating funds to allow the Navy to continue operating two aircraft carriers full time in the Indian Ocean. Rejected 40-56: R 2-49; D 38-7 (ND 27-3, SD 11-4), Dec. 2, 1981.

427. Treaties. Adoption of the resolutions of ratification for the following treaties: **Treaty Doc. No. 97-7**, Treaty of Extradition Between the United States and the Kingdom of the Netherlands; **Treaty Doc. No. 97-8**, Treaty of Extradition Between the United States and the Republic of Colombia; **Treaty Doc. No 97-11**, Treaty of Mutual Legal Assistance Between the United States and the Republic of Colombia; and **Treaty Doc. No. 97-16**, Treaty of Mutual Legal Assistance Between the United States and the Kingdom of the Netherlands. Adopted 96-0: R 51-0; D 45-0 (ND 30-0, SD 15-0), Dec. 2, 1981. A two-thirds majority vote (64 in this case) is required for adoption of resolutions of ratification of treaties.

428. HR 4995. Defense Appropriations, Fiscal 1982. Judgment of the Senate whether the Pryor, D-Ark., amendment requiring the secretary of defense to submit a report to Congress on competition in the awarding of defense procurement contracts was germane. Ruled non-germane 44-50: R 3-48; D 41-2 (ND 28-0, SD 13-2), Dec. 2, 1981.

429. HR 4995. Defense Appropriations, Fiscal 1982. Cohen, R-Maine, amendment to provide that the $354 million in the bill for research and development of an interim basing system for the MX intercontinental missile may be used only for basing the missiles in existing silos that had not been "superhardened" to withstand a nuclear attack. Further, the temporary basing system had to be compatible with a permanent system that might include: using the existing silos with ballistic missile defense, deceptive basing, and/or superhardening of the silos. The president was to recommend the permanent basing system to Congress by July 1, 1983. Adopted 90-4: R 49-2; D 41-2 (ND 26-2, SD 15-0), Dec. 2, 1981. (The Cohen amendment subsequently was modified (see vote 430, below) by another Cohen amendment.)

430. HR 4995. Defense Appropriations, Fiscal 1982. Cohen, R-Maine, amendment to provide that $334 million (of the $354 million in the bill for research and development of an interim basing system for the MX intercontinental missile) may be used for basing the missiles in existing silos that had not been "superhardened" to withstand a nuclear attack. Further, the temporary basing system had to be compatible with a permanent system that might include: using the existing silos with ballistic missile defense, deceptive basing, and/or superhardening of existing silos. The secretary of defense was to recommend the permanent basing system to Congress by July 1, 1983. Adopted 90-4: R 49-2; D 41-2 (ND 26-2, SD 15-0), Dec. 2, 1981.

431. HR 4995. Defense Appropriations, Fiscal 1982. Pryor, D-Ark., amendment to delete $354 million from the bill for research on an interim basing system for the MX intercontinental missile, and to prohibit use of funds appropriated in the bill for research on or deployment of such a basing system. Rejected 35-60: R 7-43; D 28-17 (ND 24-7, SD 4-10), Dec. 3, 1981. A "nay" was a vote supporting the president's position.

	432 433 434 435 436 437		432 433 434 435 436 437		432 433 434 435 436 437
ALABAMA		**IOWA**		**NEW HAMPSHIRE**	
Denton	? ? ? ? ? ?	*Grassley*	N Y N N N Y	*Humphrey*	N Y N N N Y
Heflin	N Y N N Y N	*Jepsen*	N Y N N N Y	*Rudman*	N Y N N N Y
ALASKA		**KANSAS**		**NEW JERSEY**	
Murkowski	N Y N N N Y	*Dole*	N Y N Y N Y	Bradley	N N Y N Y N
Stevens	N Y N N N Y	*Kassebaum*	N ? Y Y Y Y	Williams	N N Y Y Y N
ARIZONA		**KENTUCKY**		**NEW MEXICO**	
Goldwater	? ? - ? ? ?	Ford	N N Y N Y N	*Domenici*	N Y N N N Y
DeConcini	- + - - ? ?	Huddleston	N N N N Y N	*Schmitt*	N Y N N N Y
ARKANSAS		**LOUISIANA**		**NEW YORK**	
Bumpers	Y N Y N Y N	Johnston	N N N N Y ?	*D'Amato*	N Y N N N Y
Pryor	N N Y Y Y N	Long	Y Y N N Y ?	Moynihan	N N N N Y N
CALIFORNIA		**MAINE**		**NORTH CAROLINA**	
Hayakawa	? ? ? ? ? ?	*Cohen*	N Y N N N Y	*East*	N Y N N N Y
Cranston	Y N N N Y N	Mitchell	Y N Y Y Y N	*Helms*	N Y N N N Y
COLORADO		**MARYLAND**		**NORTH DAKOTA**	
Armstrong	N Y N N N Y	*Mathias*	N N Y Y Y Y	*Andrews*	N Y N Y N Y
Hart	N N Y N Y N	Sarbanes	N N Y N Y N	Burdick	N N N Y Y Y
CONNECTICUT		**MASSACHUSETTS**		**OHIO**	
Weicker	Y N N Y N Y	Kennedy	Y N Y Y Y N	Glenn	N N N N Y N
Dodd	N N Y N Y N	Tsongas	N N Y Y Y N	Metzenbaum	N N N Y Y N
DELAWARE		**MICHIGAN**		**OKLAHOMA**	
Roth	Y Y N Y N Y	Levin	Y N Y N Y N	*Nickles*	N Y N Y N Y
Biden	N N Y N Y N	Riegle	Y N Y Y Y N	Boren	Y Y N N Y N
FLORIDA		**MINNESOTA**		**OREGON**	
Hawkins	N N N Y N Y	*Boschwitz*	N Y N N N Y	*Hatfield*	Y Y Y Y Y Y
Chiles	Y N N N N N	*Durenberger*	N Y N Y N Y	*Packwood*	N Y N N N Y
GEORGIA		**MISSISSIPPI**		**PENNSYLVANIA**	
Mattingly	N Y N Y N N	*Cochran*	N Y N ? N Y	*Heinz*	Y N - ? ? ?
Nunn	Y N Y N Y N	Stennis	N Y N N N ?	*Specter*	Y N N Y N Y
HAWAII		**MISSOURI**		**RHODE ISLAND**	
Inouye	Y N N Y Y N	*Danforth*	N Y N Y N Y	*Chafee*	N N Y Y N Y
Matsunaga	Y N Y Y Y N	Eagleton	N N Y Y Y N	Pell	Y N Y Y Y ?
IDAHO		**MONTANA**		**SOUTH CAROLINA**	
McClure	N Y N N N Y	Baucus	N N Y N Y N	*Thurmond*	N Y N N N Y
Symms	N Y N N N Y	Melcher	N N N N Y N	Hollings	? Y Y N ? N
ILLINOIS		**NEBRASKA**		**SOUTH DAKOTA**	
Percy	N N N Y N Y	Exon	N N N N N N	*Abdnor*	N Y N Y N Y
Dixon	Y N N N Y Y	Zorinsky	N Y N N Y Y	*Pressler*	N Y Y Y N Y
INDIANA		**NEVADA**		**TENNESSEE**	
Lugar	N Y N N N Y	*Laxalt*	N Y N N N Y	*Baker*	N Y N N N Y
Quayle	N Y N Y N N	Cannon	N Y N N Y N	Sasser	N N N N N Y

KEY

Y	Voted for (yea).
#	Paired for.
+	Announced for.
N	Voted against (nay).
X	Paired against.
-	Announced against.
P	Voted "present".
C	Voted "present" to avoid possible conflict of interest.
?	Did not vote or otherwise make a position known.

	432 433 434 435 436 437
TEXAS	
Tower	N Y N N N N
Bentsen	N N N N Y N
UTAH	
Garn	N Y N N N Y
Hatch	N Y N N N Y
VERMONT	
Stafford	N N N Y N Y
Leahy	Y N Y N Y N
VIRGINIA	
Warner	N Y N N N Y
Byrd*	Y Y N Y Y N
WASHINGTON	
Gorton	N Y N N N Y
Jackson	N Y N N N Y
WEST VIRGINIA	
Byrd	N N Y N Y N
Randolph	N N N Y Y Y
WISCONSIN	
Kasten	N Y N Y N Y
Proxmire	Y N Y Y Y Y
WYOMING	
Simpson	N Y N Y N Y
Wallop	? ? - ? ? ?

Democrats   *Republicans*

Byrd elected as an independent.

432. HR 4995. Defense Appropriations, Fiscal 1982. Leahy, D-Vt., amendment to cut $201.2 million from the personnel and operations and maintenance accounts, including $39 million for West German damage claims and $60 million in pay for retired personnel. Rejected 22-72: R 5-44; D 17-28 (ND 11-20, SD 6-8), Dec. 3, 1981. A "nay" was a vote supporting the president's position.

433. HR 4995. Defense Appropriations, Fiscal 1982. Baker, R-Tenn., motion to table (kill) the Glenn, D-Ohio, amendment stating the sense of Congress that the United States should not take any action in connection with its defense programs that would undercut existing strategic arms limitation agreements unless the president certified to Congress that the Soviet Union was no longer exercising the same restraint or that such an action would be vital to the U.S. national security interest. Motion agreed to 49-45: R 40-8; D 9-37 (ND 3-28, SD 6-9), Dec. 3, 1981.

434. HR 4995. Defense Appropriations, Fiscal 1982. Hollings, D-S.C., amendment to delete from the bill $2.429 billion for research on and procurement of the B-1B bomber, and to distribute the money among other accounts. Rejected 28-66: R 5-43; D 23-23 (ND 18-13, SD 5-10), Dec. 3, 1981. A "nay" was a vote supporting the president's position.

435. HR 4995. Defense Appropriations, Fiscal 1982. Hatfield, R-Ore., amendment to reduce funds in the bill for procurement and research and development by 2 percent. Rejected 36-57: R 21-26; D 15-31 (ND 13-18, SD 2-13), Dec. 3, 1981.

436. HR 4995. Defense Appropriations, Fiscal 1982. Proxmire, D-Wis., amendment to delete from the bill funds to anticipate a 3 percent "cost growth" in the B-1B bomber ($57 million) and MX intercontinental missile ($58.5 million) programs. Rejected 46-47: R 3-45; D 43-2 (ND 31-0, SD 12-2), Dec. 3, 1981.

437. HR 4995. Defense Appropriations, Fiscal 1982. Stevens, R-Alaska, motion to table (kill) the Nunn, D-Ga., amendment to add $187.5 million for a classified program in the Air Force research and development account. Motion agreed to 49-41: R 44-4; D 5-37 (ND 5-25, SD 0-12), Dec. 3, 1981.

	438	439	440	441	442	443	444	445
ALABAMA								
Denton	Y	Y	N	N	Y	Y	Y	N
Heflin	N	Y	Y	Y	Y	Y	Y	Y
ALASKA								
Murkowski	Y	Y	N	N	Y	Y	Y	N
Stevens	Y	Y	?	N	Y	?	?	?
ARIZONA								
Goldwater	?	?	?	?	?	?	?	?
DeConcini	-	+	+	+	+	?	?	+
ARKANSAS								
Bumpers	?	?	?	?	?	Y	Y	Y
Pryor	N	Y	Y	Y	Y	Y	Y	Y
CALIFORNIA								
Hayakawa	?	?	?	?	?	?	?	N
Cranston	N	Y	Y	Y	Y	Y	Y	Y
COLORADO								
Armstrong	Y	Y	Y	N	Y	?	?	N
Hart	N	Y	Y	Y	Y	?	?	Y
CONNECTICUT								
Weicker	Y	Y	N	N	Y	Y	Y	N
Dodd	N	Y	Y	Y	Y	Y	Y	Y
DELAWARE								
Roth	Y	Y	N	N	Y	Y	Y	N
Biden	?	?	?	?	+	?	?	Y
FLORIDA								
Hawkins	Y	Y	N	N	Y	Y	Y	N
Chiles	N	Y	Y	Y	Y	Y	Y	Y
GEORGIA								
Mattingly	Y	Y	N	N	Y	Y	Y	N
Nunn	N	Y	Y	Y	Y	Y	Y	Y
HAWAII								
Inouye	N	Y	Y	Y	Y	Y	Y	Y
Matsunaga	N	Y	Y	Y	Y	+	+	Y
IDAHO								
McClure	Y	Y	N	N	Y	Y	Y	N
Symms	Y	Y	N	N	Y	Y	Y	N
ILLINOIS								
Percy	Y	Y	N	N	Y	Y	Y	N
Dixon	N	Y	Y	Y	Y	Y	Y	Y
INDIANA								
Lugar	Y	Y	N	N	Y	?	?	N
Quayle	Y	Y	N	N	Y	Y	Y	N
IOWA								
Grassley	Y	Y	N	N	Y	Y	Y	N
Jepsen	Y	Y	N	N	Y	Y	Y	N
KANSAS								
Dole	Y	Y	N	N	Y	Y	Y	N
Kassebaum	Y	Y	N	N	Y	Y	Y	N
KENTUCKY								
Ford	N	Y	Y	Y	Y	Y	Y	Y
Huddleston	N	Y	Y	Y	Y	Y	Y	?
LOUISIANA								
Johnston	?	?	?	?	?	Y	Y	Y
Long	Y	Y	Y	N	Y	Y	Y	Y
MAINE								
Cohen	Y	Y	N	N	Y	Y	Y	N
Mitchell	N	Y	Y	Y	Y	Y	Y	Y
MARYLAND								
Mathias	Y	Y	N	N	Y	Y	Y	N
Sarbanes	N	Y	Y	Y	Y	?	?	?
MASSACHUSETTS								
Kennedy	N	Y	?	Y	Y	Y	Y	Y
Tsongas	N	Y	Y	Y	N	?	?	Y
MICHIGAN								
Levin	N	P	Y	Y	N	Y	Y	Y
Riegle	-	+	+	+	+	Y	Y	Y
MINNESOTA								
Boschwitz	Y	Y	N	N	Y	Y	Y	N
Durenberger	Y	Y	N	N	Y	Y	Y	N
MISSISSIPPI								
Cochran	Y	Y	N	N	Y	Y	Y	N
Stennis	Y	Y	N	N	Y	Y	Y	Y
MISSOURI								
Danforth	Y	Y	N	N	Y	Y	Y	N
Eagleton	N	Y	Y	Y	Y	Y	Y	?
MONTANA								
Baucus	N	Y	Y	Y	Y	?	?	Y
Melcher	N	Y	N	Y	Y	+	+	Y
NEBRASKA								
Exon	N	Y	Y	Y	Y	?	?	Y
Zorinsky	Y	Y	Y	Y	Y	Y	Y	Y
NEVADA								
Laxalt	Y	Y	N	N	Y	Y	Y	N
Cannon	N	Y	Y	Y	Y	?	+	+
NEW HAMPSHIRE								
Humphrey	Y	Y	N	N	Y	N	Y	N
Rudman	Y	Y	N	N	Y	Y	Y	N
NEW JERSEY								
Bradley	N	Y	Y	N	Y	N	Y	Y
Williams	N	Y	Y	Y	Y	Y	Y	Y
NEW MEXICO								
Domenici	-	+	?	-	+	Y	Y	N
Schmitt	Y	Y	N	?	?	Y	Y	N
NEW YORK								
D'Amato	Y	Y	N	N	Y	Y	Y	N
Moynihan	N	Y	Y	Y	Y	Y	Y	Y
NORTH CAROLINA								
East	Y	Y	N	N	Y	Y	Y	N
Helms	Y	Y	N	N	Y	Y	Y	N
NORTH DAKOTA								
Andrews	Y	Y	N	N	Y	Y	Y	N
Burdick	N	Y	N	Y	Y	Y	Y	Y
OHIO								
Glenn	N	Y	Y	N	Y	Y	Y	Y
Metzenbaum	N	Y	Y	Y	Y	?	?	?
OKLAHOMA								
Nickles	Y	Y	N	N	Y	Y	Y	N
Boren	Y	Y	Y	Y	Y	Y	Y	Y
OREGON								
Hatfield	Y	Y	N	N	Y	Y	Y	N
Packwood	Y	Y	N	N	Y	Y	Y	N
PENNSYLVANIA								
Heinz	?	?	?	N	Y	?	?	N
Specter	Y	Y	N	N	Y	Y	Y	N
RHODE ISLAND								
Chafee	Y	Y	N	N	Y	Y	Y	N
Pell	N	Y	Y	Y	N	Y	Y	Y
SOUTH CAROLINA								
Thurmond	Y	Y	N	N	Y	Y	Y	N
Hollings	N	Y	Y	?	?	Y	Y	Y
SOUTH DAKOTA								
Abdnor	Y	Y	N	N	Y	Y	Y	N
Pressler	Y	Y	N	N	Y	Y	Y	N
TENNESSEE								
Baker	Y	Y	?	N	Y	Y	Y	N
Sasser	N	Y	Y	Y	Y	Y	Y	Y
TEXAS								
Tower	Y	?	N	N	Y	Y	Y	N
Bentsen	Y	Y	Y	Y	Y	Y	Y	Y
UTAH								
Garn	Y	Y	N	N	Y	Y	Y	N
Hatch	Y	Y	N	N	Y	Y	Y	N
VERMONT								
Stafford	Y	Y	?	N	Y	?	?	?
Leahy	N	Y	Y	Y	Y	Y	Y	Y
VIRGINIA								
Warner	Y	Y	N	N	Y	Y	Y	N
Byrd*	Y	Y	N	N	Y	Y	Y	N
WASHINGTON								
Gorton	Y	Y	N	N	Y	Y	Y	N
Jackson	N	Y	Y	Y	Y	Y	Y	Y
WEST VIRGINIA								
Byrd	N	Y	Y	Y	Y	Y	Y	Y
Randolph	N	Y	Y	Y	Y	Y	Y	Y
WISCONSIN								
Kasten	Y	Y	N	N	Y	Y	Y	N
Proxmire	N	Y	N	Y	N	N	Y	Y
WYOMING								
Simpson	Y	Y	N	N	Y	Y	Y	N
Wallop	?	?	?	?	+	Y	Y	N

KEY

Y Voted for (yea).
Paired for.
+ Announced for.
N Voted against (nay).
X Paired against.
- Announced against.
P Voted "present".
C Voted "present" to avoid possible conflict of interest.
? Did not vote or otherwise make a position known.

Democrats **Republicans**

Byrd elected as an independent.

438. HR 4995. Defense Appropriations, Fiscal 1982. Dole, R-Kan., motion to table (kill) the Metzenbaum, D-Ohio, amendment to express the sense of the Senate that Congress should give priority attention to recommendations of the White House Conference on Aging. Motion agreed to 54-36: R 48-0; D 6-36 (ND 1-28, SD 5-8), Dec. 4, 1981.

439. HR 4995. Defense Appropriations, Fiscal 1982. Dole, R-Kan., substitute amendment for the Metzenbaum, D-Ohio, amendment *(see vote 438, above)*, to express the sense of the Senate that Congress should commend the delegates to the White House Conference on Aging and that the appropriate committees of Congress should consider the conference recommendations. Adopted 88-0: R 47-0; D 41-0 (ND 28-0, SD 13-0), Dec. 4, 1981. (The Metzenbaum amendment, as modified by the Dole amendment, subsequently was adopted by voice vote.)

440. HR 4995. Defense Appropriations, Fiscal 1982. Exon, D-Neb., amendment to add $100 million to the bill for procurement of ammunition for the Army. Rejected 37-49: R 1-44; D 36-5 (ND 25-3, SD 11-2), Dec. 4, 1981.

441. HR 4995. Defense Appropriations, Fiscal 1982. Byrd, D-W.Va., amendment to add $200 million for development of the so-called "stealth" advanced technology bomber. Rejected 36-53: R 0-48; D 36-5 (ND 27-2, SD 9-3), Dec. 4, 1981.

442. HR 4995. Defense Appropriations, Fiscal 1982. Passage of the bill to appropriate $203,675,745,000 in fiscal 1982 for programs of the Department of Defense. Passed 84-5: R 47-1; D 37-4 (ND 25-4, SD 12-0), Dec. 4, 1981. (The president had requested $200,878,234,000.)

443. S 10. Commission on More Effective Government. Passage of the bill to establish an 18-member Commission on More Effective Government to study the management, operation and organization of the executive branch of government and to recommend to Congress within 30 months of the bill's enactment how to improve these functions; and to authorize $16 million for the commission's activities. Passed 79-4: R 44-2; D 35-2 (ND 20-2, SD 15-0), Dec. 7, 1981.

444. S Res 238. Mortgage Interest Deductions. Adoption of the resolution to express the sense of the Senate that the present home mortgage interest deduction should be retained as an essential component of a fair and equitable tax system. Adopted 83-0: R 46-0; D 37-0 (ND 22-0, SD 15-0), Dec. 7, 1981.

445. S 881. Small Business Innovation Research Act. Byrd, D-W.Va., motion to table (kill) the Baker, R-Tenn.-Jepsen, R-Iowa-Weicker, R-Conn., amendment to the Byrd amendment *(see vote 446, p. 73-S)*, to express the sense of the Senate that the next vacancy on the Board of Governors of the Federal Reserve System be filled by an individual with substantial small-business or agricultural experience. Motion rejected 41-50: R 0-50; D 41-0 (ND 27-0, SD 14-0), Dec. 8, 1981. (The Baker-Jepsen-Weicker amendment subsequently was adopted by voice vote. The original Byrd amendment would have required the appointment of a person with small-business or agricultural background.)

	446	447	448	449	450	451	452
ALABAMA							
Denton	Y	Y	Y	N	Y	Y	Y
Heflin	Y	Y	Y	Y	N	N	Y
ALASKA							
Murkowski	Y	Y	Y	N	Y	Y	Y
Stevens	?	?	?	N	Y	Y	Y
ARIZONA							
Goldwater	?	?	?	?	?	?	?
DeConcini	+	?	+	Y	N	N	Y
ARKANSAS							
Bumpers	Y	Y	Y	Y	N	N	Y
Pryor	Y	Y	Y	Y	N	N	Y
CALIFORNIA							
Hayakawa	Y	Y	Y	N	Y	Y	Y
Cranston	Y	Y	N	Y	N	N	Y
COLORADO							
Armstrong	Y	Y	Y	N	Y	Y	Y
Hart	Y	Y	Y	Y	N	N	Y
CONNECTICUT							
Weicker	Y	Y	Y	?	?	?	?
Dodd	?	?	?	Y	N	N	Y
DELAWARE							
Roth	Y	Y	Y	N	N	N	Y
Biden	Y	Y	Y	Y	N	N	Y
FLORIDA							
Hawkins	Y	Y	Y	N	Y	Y	Y
Chiles	Y	Y	Y	Y	N	N	Y
GEORGIA							
Mattingly	Y	Y	Y	N	Y	Y	Y
Nunn	Y	Y	Y	Y	N	N	Y
HAWAII							
Inouye	N	Y	Y	Y	N	N	Y
Matsunaga	Y	Y	Y	Y	N	N	Y
IDAHO							
McClure	Y	Y	Y	N	Y	Y	Y
Symms	Y	Y	Y	N	Y	Y	Y
ILLINOIS							
Percy	Y	Y	Y	N	Y	Y	Y
Dixon	Y	Y	Y	Y	N	N	Y
INDIANA							
Lugar	Y	Y	Y	N	Y	Y	Y
Quayle	Y	Y	Y	N	Y	Y	Y
IOWA							
Grassley	Y	Y	Y	N	Y	N	Y
Jepsen	Y	Y	Y	N	Y	Y	Y
KANSAS							
Dole	Y	Y	Y	N	Y	Y	Y
Kassebaum	Y	Y	Y	N	Y	Y	Y
KENTUCKY							
Ford	Y	Y	Y	Y	N	N	Y
Huddleston	?	?	?	?	?	?	?
LOUISIANA							
Johnston	Y	Y	Y	N	N	N	Y
Long	Y	Y	Y	Y	N	N	Y
MAINE							
Cohen	Y	Y	Y	N	Y	Y	Y
Mitchell	Y	Y	C	Y	N	N	Y
MARYLAND							
Mathias	Y	Y	N	N	Y	Y	Y
Sarbanes	?	?	?	Y	N	N	Y
MASSACHUSETTS							
Kennedy	Y	Y	Y	Y	N	N	Y
Tsongas	Y	Y	Y	Y	N	N	Y
MICHIGAN							
Levin	Y	Y	Y	Y	N	N	?
Riegle	Y	Y	Y	Y	N	N	Y
MINNESOTA							
Boschwitz	Y	Y	Y	N	Y	Y	Y
Durenberger	Y	Y	Y	N	Y	Y	?
MISSISSIPPI							
Cochran	Y	Y	Y	N	Y	Y	Y
Stennis	Y	Y	Y	Y	N	N	Y
MISSOURI							
Danforth	Y	Y	Y	N	Y	Y	Y
Eagleton	?	?	?	Y	N	N	Y
MONTANA							
Baucus	Y	Y	N	Y	N	N	Y
Melcher	Y	Y	Y	Y	N	N	Y
NEBRASKA							
Exon	Y	Y	Y	Y	N	N	Y
Zorinsky	Y	Y	Y	Y	N	N	Y
NEVADA							
Laxalt	Y	Y	Y	N	Y	Y	Y
Cannon	+	+	?	Y	N	N	Y
NEW HAMPSHIRE							
Humphrey	Y	Y	N	N	Y	N	Y
Rudman	Y	Y	Y	N	Y	Y	Y
NEW JERSEY							
Bradley	N	Y	Y	Y	N	N	?
Williams	Y	Y	Y	Y	N	N	Y
NEW MEXICO							
Domenici	Y	Y	Y	N	Y	Y	Y
Schmitt	Y	Y	Y	N	Y	Y	Y
NEW YORK							
D'Amato	Y	Y	Y	N	Y	Y	Y
Moynihan	Y	Y	?	Y	N	N	?
NORTH CAROLINA							
East	Y	Y	Y	N	Y	Y	Y
Helms	Y	Y	Y	N	Y	Y	Y
NORTH DAKOTA							
Andrews	Y	Y	Y	N	Y	Y	Y
Burdick	Y	Y	Y	Y	N	N	Y
OHIO							
Glenn	N	Y	Y	Y	N	N	?
Metzenbaum	?	?	Y	Y	N	N	Y
OKLAHOMA							
Nickles	Y	Y	Y	N	Y	Y	Y
Boren	Y	Y	Y	Y	N	N	Y
OREGON							
Hatfield	Y	Y	Y	N	Y	Y	Y
Packwood	Y	Y	Y	N	Y	Y	Y
PENNSYLVANIA							
Heinz	Y	Y	Y	N	N	Y	Y
Specter	Y	Y	Y	N	Y	Y	Y
RHODE ISLAND							
Chafee	Y	Y	Y	N	Y	Y	Y
Pell	Y	Y	Y	Y	N	N	Y
SOUTH CAROLINA							
Thurmond	Y	Y	Y	N	Y	Y	Y
Hollings	Y	Y	Y	Y	N	N	Y
SOUTH DAKOTA							
Abdnor	Y	Y	Y	N	Y	Y	Y
Pressler	Y	Y	Y	N	Y	Y	Y
TENNESSEE							
Baker	Y	Y	Y	N	Y	Y	Y
Sasser	Y	Y	Y	Y	N	N	Y
TEXAS							
Tower	Y	Y	Y	N	Y	Y	Y
Bentsen	Y	Y	Y	Y	N	N	Y
UTAH							
Garn	Y	Y	Y	N	Y	Y	Y
Hatch	Y	Y	Y	N	Y	N	Y
VERMONT							
Stafford	?	?	?	N	Y	Y	Y
Leahy	Y	Y	Y	Y	N	N	Y
VIRGINIA							
Warner	Y	Y	Y	N	Y	Y	Y
Byrd*	Y	Y	Y	Y	Y	Y	Y
WASHINGTON							
Gorton	Y	Y	Y	N	Y	Y	Y
Jackson	Y	Y	Y	Y	N	N	Y
WEST VIRGINIA							
Byrd	Y	Y	Y	Y	N	N	Y
Randolph	Y	Y	Y	Y	N	N	Y
WISCONSIN							
Kasten	Y	Y	Y	N	Y	Y	Y
Proxmire	Y	Y	N	N	Y	Y	Y
WYOMING							
Simpson	Y	Y	N	N	Y	Y	Y
Wallop	Y	Y	Y	N	Y	Y	Y

KEY

Y Voted for (yea).
\# Paired for.
+ Announced for.
N Voted against (nay).
X Paired against.
- Announced against.
P Voted "present".
C Voted "present" to avoid possible conflict of interest.
? Did not vote or otherwise make a position known.

Democrats **Republicans**

* Byrd elected as an independent.

446. S 881. Small Business Innovation Research Act. Byrd, D-W.Va., amendment, as amended *(see vote 445, p. 72-S)*, to express the sense of the Senate that the next vacancy on the Board of Governors of the Federal Reserve System be filled by an individual with substantial small-business or agricultural experience. Adopted 87-3: R 50-0; D 37-3 (ND 23-3, SD 14-0), Dec. 8, 1981.

447. S 881. Small Business Innovation Research Act. Passage of the bill to require federal agencies with annual research and development budgets of more than $100 million to set aside 1 percent of their budget for small businesses. Passed 90-0: R 50-0; D 40-0 (ND 26-0, SD 14-0), Dec. 8, 1981.

448. S 1700. Federal Courts Improvement Act of 1981. Passage of the bill to create the U.S. Court of Appeals for the Federal Circuit to handle patent cases. Passed 83-6: R 47-3; D 36-3 (ND 22-3, SD 14-0), Dec. 8, 1981.

449. S Con Res 50. Second Budget Resolution, Fiscal 1982. Johnston, D-La., amendment to the Domenici, R-N.M., amendment *(see vote 450, below)*, to express the sense of the Senate that the Budget Committee, after receiving the president's plan but no later than April 15, 1982, should report a budget resolution to achieve the goals of reduced unemployment and inflation and a balanced federal budget for fiscal 1984. Rejected 45-52: R 0-51; D 45-1 (ND 31-1, SD 14-0), Dec. 9, 1981.

450. S Con Res 50. Second Budget Resolution, Fiscal 1982. Domenici, R-N.M., amendment to express the sense of the Senate that: 1) the Budget Committee report no later than March 31, 1982, a combined revised second fiscal 1982 budget resolution and first fiscal 1983 budget resolution that will also contain a balanced budget for fiscal 1984; 2) the budget should be balanced through spending reductions in all parts of the budget, including entitlement programs, and revenue increases, excluding changes in the Accelerated Cost Recovery System and individual rate reductions provided by the Economic Recovery Tax Act of 1981 (PL 97-34); and 3) the plan to be submitted by the committee should be a balanced plan providing for federal outlays no greater than 20.5 percent of the gross national product in fiscal 1984. Adopted 50-47: R 48-3; D 2-44 (ND 1-31, SD 1-13), Dec. 9, 1981.

451. S Con Res 50. Second Budget Resolution, Fiscal 1982. Adoption of the concurrent resolution to reaffirm the first fiscal 1982 budget resolution and to express the sense of the Senate that: 1) the Budget Committee by March 31, 1982, report a budget resolution containing a balanced budget for fiscal 1984; 2) a balanced budget should be achieved through spending reductions in all parts of the budget, including entitlement programs, and revenue increases, excluding changes in the Accelerated Cost Recovery System and individual rate reductions provided by the Economic Recovery Tax Act of 1981 (PL 97-34); and 3) under the committee plan, federal outlays should not exceed 20.5 percent of the gross national product in fiscal 1984. Adopted 49-48: R 47-4; D 2-44 (ND 1-31, SD 1-13), Dec. 9, 1981.

452. S Res 218. School Lunch Program. Adoption of the resolution to express the sense of the Senate that the school lunch program should retain the goal of providing one-third of the recommended dietary allowances of nutrients for children, as established by the National Academy of Sciences. Adopted 92-0: R 50-0; D 42-0 (ND 28-0, SD 14-0), Dec. 9, 1981.

CQ Senate Votes 453-460

Corresponding to Congressional Record Votes 467, 468, 469, 470, 471, 472, 473, 474

KEY

- Y Voted for (yea).
- # Paired for.
- + Announced for.
- N Voted against (nay).
- X Paired against.
- - Announced against.
- P Voted "present".
- C Voted "present" to avoid possible conflict of interest.
- ? Did not vote or otherwise make a position known.

	453	454	455	456	457	458	459	460
ALABAMA								
Denton	Y	Y	Y	Y	Y	N	Y	N
Heflin	Y	Y	Y	Y	N	N	N	Y
ALASKA								
Murkowski	N	Y	Y	Y	Y	N	Y	N
Stevens	Y	Y	?	Y	Y	N	Y	N
ARIZONA								
Goldwater	?	?	?	?	?	?	?	?
DeConcini	Y	Y	Y	Y	Y	N	Y	Y
ARKANSAS								
Bumpers	Y	N	Y	N	N	Y	N	Y
Pryor	Y	Y	Y	Y	Y	N	Y	Y
CALIFORNIA								
Hayakawa	Y	Y	Y	Y	Y	N	Y	N
Cranston	Y	N	Y	N	N	Y	N	Y
COLORADO								
Armstrong	Y	Y	Y	Y	Y	N	Y	N
Hart	N	N	Y	N	Y	Y	N	Y
CONNECTICUT								
Weicker	Y	N	Y	N	Y	N	N	N
Dodd	N	N	Y	N	N	Y	N	Y
DELAWARE								
Roth	N	Y	Y	Y	Y	N	Y	N
Biden	N	Y	Y	Y	Y	N	Y	Y
FLORIDA								
Hawkins	Y	Y	Y	Y	Y	N	Y	N
Chiles	Y	Y	Y	Y	Y	N	Y	Y
GEORGIA								
Mattingly	Y	Y	Y	Y	Y	N	Y	N
Nunn	Y	Y	Y	Y	Y	N	Y	Y
HAWAII								
Inouye	Y	N	Y	N	N	Y	N	Y
Matsunaga	Y	N	Y	N	N	Y	N	Y
IDAHO								
McClure	Y	Y	Y	Y	Y	N	Y	N
Symms	Y	Y	Y	Y	Y	N	Y	N
ILLINOIS								
Percy	Y	N	Y	Y	Y	Y	Y	N
Dixon	Y	Y	Y	Y	Y	Y	Y	N
INDIANA								
Lugar	Y	Y	Y	Y	Y	N	Y	N
Quayle	Y	Y	N	Y	Y	N	Y	N

	453	454	455	456	457	458	459	460
IOWA								
Grassley	Y	Y	Y	Y	Y	N	Y	N
Jepsen	Y	Y	Y	Y	Y	N	Y	N
KANSAS								
Dole	Y	Y	N	Y	Y	N	Y	N
Kassebaum	Y	Y	Y	Y	Y	N	Y	N
KENTUCKY								
Ford	Y	Y	Y	Y	Y	N	Y	Y
Huddleston	Y	Y	Y	N	Y	N	Y	Y
LOUISIANA								
Johnston	Y	Y	Y	Y	Y	N	Y	Y
Long	Y	Y	N	N	Y	N	Y	N
MAINE								
Cohen	Y	N	Y	Y	N	Y	N	N
Mitchell	Y	N	Y	Y	N	Y	N	Y
MARYLAND								
Mathias	N	N	Y	N	N	?	?	?
Sarbanes	N	N	Y	N	N	Y	N	Y
MASSACHUSETTS								
Kennedy	N	N	Y	N	N	Y	N	Y
Tsongas	N	N	Y	Y	Y	Y	N	Y
MICHIGAN								
Levin	N	N	Y	N	N	Y	N	Y
Riegle	N	N	Y	N	N	Y	N	Y
MINNESOTA								
Boschwitz	Y	N	Y	N	N	Y	N	N
Durenberger	Y	N	Y	N	N	Y	N	N
MISSISSIPPI								
Cochran	Y	Y	Y	Y	Y	N	Y	N
Stennis	Y	Y	Y	Y	Y	N	Y	N
MISSOURI								
Danforth	Y	Y	Y	Y	Y	N	Y	N
Eagleton	N	N	Y	N	N	Y	N	Y
MONTANA								
Baucus	N	N	Y	Y	N	Y	N	Y
Melcher	N	Y	Y	Y	Y	N	Y	Y
NEBRASKA								
Exon	N	Y	Y	Y	Y	N	Y	Y
Zorinsky	N	Y	Y	Y	Y	N	Y	Y
NEVADA								
Laxalt	Y	Y	Y	Y	?	N	Y	N
Cannon	N	Y	Y	Y	Y	N	Y	Y

	453	454	455	456	457	458	459	460
NEW HAMPSHIRE								
Humphrey	N	Y	Y	Y	Y	N	Y	N
Rudman	Y	N	Y	Y	Y	Y	N	N
NEW JERSEY								
Bradley	Y	N	Y	N	N	Y	N	Y
Williams	Y	N	Y	N	N	Y	N	?
NEW MEXICO								
Domenici	Y	Y	Y	Y	Y	N	Y	N
Schmitt	Y	Y	Y	Y	Y	N	Y	N
NEW YORK								
D'Amato	N	Y	Y	Y	Y	N	Y	N
Moynihan	N	N	Y	N	N	Y	N	Y
NORTH CAROLINA								
East	Y	Y	Y	Y	Y	N	Y	N
Helms	Y	Y	Y	Y	Y	N	Y	N
NORTH DAKOTA								
Andrews	Y	Y	Y	Y	Y	N	Y	N
Burdick	Y	Y	Y	Y	Y	Y	N	Y
OHIO								
Glenn	Y	N	Y	N	N	Y	N	Y
Metzenbaum	N	N	Y	N	N	Y	N	Y
OKLAHOMA								
Nickles	Y	Y	Y	Y	Y	N	Y	N
Boren	N	Y	Y	Y	Y	N	Y	Y
OREGON								
Hatfield	Y	N	Y	N	N	Y	N	N
Packwood	Y	N	Y	N	N	Y	N	N
PENNSYLVANIA								
Heinz	Y	N	Y	N	Y	Y	N	?
Specter	Y	N	Y	N	Y	Y	Y	N
RHODE ISLAND								
Chafee	N	N	Y	Y	Y	Y	N	N
Pell	N	Y	Y	Y	Y	Y	N	Y
SOUTH CAROLINA								
Thurmond	Y	Y	Y	Y	Y	N	Y	N
Hollings	Y	Y	Y	Y	Y	N	Y	Y
SOUTH DAKOTA								
Abdnor	Y	Y	Y	Y	Y	N	Y	N
Pressler	N	N	Y	N	N	Y	N	N
TENNESSEE								
Baker	Y	Y	Y	Y	Y	N	Y	N
Sasser	Y	Y	+	+	+	-	?	+

	453	454	455	456	457	458	459	460
TEXAS								
Tower	Y	Y	Y	Y	Y	N	Y	?
Bentsen	Y	Y	Y	Y	Y	N	Y	N
UTAH								
Garn	Y	Y	Y	Y	Y	N	Y	N
Hatch	Y	Y	Y	Y	Y	N	Y	N
VERMONT								
Stafford	N	N	Y	N	Y	N	Y	N
Leahy	N	N	Y	N	Y	Y	N	Y
VIRGINIA								
Warner	Y	Y	N	Y	N	Y	N	N
Byrd*	Y	Y	Y	Y	N	N	Y	N
WASHINGTON								
Gorton	Y	Y	Y	Y	Y	N	Y	N
Jackson	Y	N	Y	N	Y	N	Y	N
WEST VIRGINIA								
Byrd	N	Y	Y	Y	Y	N	Y	Y
Randolph	N	Y	Y	Y	Y	N	Y	Y
WISCONSIN								
Kasten	N	Y	Y	Y	Y	N	Y	N
Proxmire	N	Y	Y	Y	Y	N	Y	N
WYOMING								
Simpson	Y	Y	Y	Y	Y	N	Y	N
Wallop	Y	Y	Y	Y	Y	N	Y	N

Democrats *Republicans*

* Byrd elected as an independent.

453. S 884. Agriculture and Food Act of 1981. Adoption of the conference report on the bill to reauthorize for four years price support and other farm programs and, for one year, food stamps. Adopted 68-31: R 43-9; D 25-22 (ND 11-21, SD 14-1), Dec. 10, 1981. A "yea" was a vote supporting the president's position.

454. S 951. Justice Department Authorization. Helms, R-N.C., motion to invoke cloture (thus limiting debate) on the Helms amendment to prevent the Justice Department from bringing legal action that could lead, directly or indirectly, to busing for racial balance. The amendment also included language proposed by Johnston, D-La., to limit federal courts' authority to order busing. Motion agreed to 64-35: R 38-14; D 26-21 (ND 12-20, SD 14-1), Dec. 10, 1981. A three-fifths majority vote (60) of the total Senate is required to invoke cloture.

455. S 951. Justice Department Authorization. Baker, R-Tenn., motion to instruct the sergeant-at-arms to request the attendance of absent senators. Motion agreed to 93-4: R 48-3; D 45-1 (ND 32-0, SD 13-1), Dec. 10, 1981.

456. S 951. Justice Department Authorization. Baker, R-Tenn., motion to table (kill) the Weicker, R-Conn., motion to extend debate for 124 hours. Motion agreed to 70-28: R 44-8; D 26-20 (ND 15-17, SD 11-3), Dec. 10, 1981.

457. S 951. Justice Department Authorization. Judgment of the Senate affirming the chair's ruling that the Weicker, R-Conn., motion to reconsider the tabling motion *(see vote 456, above)* was dilatory. Ruling of the chair upheld 70-27: R 42-9; D 28-18 (ND 17-15, SD 11-3), Dec. 10, 1981.

458. S 951. Justice Department Authorization. Weicker, R-Conn., motion to table (kill) the Helms, R-N.C.-Johnston, D-La., amendment *(see vote 454, above)*. Motion rejected 36-61: R 12-39; D 24-22 (ND 23-9, SD 1-13), Dec. 10, 1981.

459. S 951. Justice Department Authorization. Johnston, D-La., motion to table (kill) the Weicker, R-Conn., motion to reconsider the previous motion to table *(see vote 458, above)*. Motion agreed to 61-36: R 40-11; D 21-25 (ND 9-23, SD 12-2), Dec. 10, 1981.

460. H J Res 370. Continuing Appropriations, Fiscal 1982. Bumpers, D-Ark., amendment to provide $362 million for the maternal and child health care block grant. Rejected 41-53: R 0-49; D 41-4 (ND 30-1, SD 11-3), Dec. 10, 1981.

KEY

Y Voted for (yea).
\# Paired for.
\+ Announced for.
N Voted against (nay).
X Paired against.
\- Announced against.
P Voted "present".
C Voted "present" to avoid possible conflict of interest.
? Did not vote or otherwise make a position known.

	461	462	463	464	465	466	467	468
ALABAMA								
Denton	N	N	N	N	N	N	N	Y
Heflin	N	Y	N	N	N	Y	Y	N
ALASKA								
Murkowski	N	N	N	N	Y	N	N	Y
Stevens	N	N	N	N	N	N	N	Y
ARIZONA								
Goldwater	?	?	?	?	?	?	?	?
DeConcini	N	Y	Y	N	Y	N	Y	N
ARKANSAS								
Bumpers	Y	Y	Y	Y	Y	Y	Y	N
Pryor	Y	Y	Y	N	Y	Y	Y	N
CALIFORNIA								
Hayakawa	N	N	N	N	N	N	N	Y
Cranston	Y	Y	Y	Y	Y	Y	Y	N
COLORADO								
Armstrong	N	N	N	N	N	N	N	Y
Hart	Y	Y	Y	Y	?	?	Y	N
CONNECTICUT								
Weicker	N	N	N	N	N	N	N	Y
Dodd	Y	Y	Y	Y	Y	Y	Y	N
DELAWARE								
Roth	N	N	N	Y	?	N	N	
Biden	Y	Y	Y	Y	Y	Y	Y	N
FLORIDA								
Hawkins	N	N	N	N	N	N	N	Y
Chiles	N	Y	Y	N	Y	N	Y	N
GEORGIA								
Mattingly	N	N	N	N	N	N	N	Y
Nunn	N	Y	Y	N	N	N	Y	Y
HAWAII								
Inouye	Y	Y	Y	Y	Y	Y	Y	Y
Matsunaga	Y	Y	Y	Y	Y	Y	?	Y
IDAHO								
McClure	N	N	N	N	N	N	N	Y
Symms	N	N	N	N	N	N	N	Y
ILLINOIS								
Percy	N	N	N	N	N	N	N	Y
Dixon	N	Y	Y	N	Y	N	Y	N
INDIANA								
Lugar	N	N	N	N	N	N	N	Y
Quayle	N	N	N	N	N	N	N	Y
IOWA								
Grassley	N	N	N	N	N	N	N	Y
Jepsen	N	N	N	N	N	N	N	Y
KANSAS								
Dole	N	N	N	N	N	N	N	Y
Kassebaum	N	N	N	N	N	N	N	Y
KENTUCKY								
Ford	N	Y	Y	Y	Y	Y	Y	N
Huddleston	Y	Y	Y	Y	Y	Y	Y	Y
LOUISIANA								
Johnston	N	Y	Y	N	N	Y	X	Y
Long	N	N	N	N	N	?	N	Y
MAINE								
Cohen	N	N	N	N	N	N	N	Y
Mitchell	Y	Y	Y	Y	Y	Y	Y	N
MARYLAND								
Mathias	?	?	?	?	?	?	?	?
Sarbanes	Y	Y	Y	Y	Y	Y	Y	N
MASSACHUSETTS								
Kennedy	Y	Y	Y	Y	Y	Y	?	N
Tsongas	Y	Y	Y	Y	Y	Y	Y	N
MICHIGAN								
Levin	Y	Y	Y	Y	Y	Y	Y	N
Riegle	Y	Y	Y	Y	Y	Y	Y	N
MINNESOTA								
Boschwitz	N	N	N	N	N	N	N	Y
Durenberger	N	N	N	N	N	N	N	Y
MISSISSIPPI								
Cochran	N	N	N	N	N	N	N	Y
Stennis	N	N	N	N	N	N	Y	Y
MISSOURI								
Danforth	N	N	N	N	N	N	N	Y
Eagleton	Y	Y	Y	Y	Y	Y	Y	N
MONTANA								
Baucus	Y	Y	Y	Y	Y	Y	Y	N
Melcher	Y	Y	Y	Y	Y	Y	Y	?
NEBRASKA								
Exon	N	Y	Y	Y	Y	N	Y	N
Zorinsky	N	N	N	N	Y	N	N	Y
NEVADA								
Laxalt	N	N	N	N	N	N	N	Y
Cannon	Y	Y	Y	Y	N	Y	?	?
NEW HAMPSHIRE								
Humphrey	N	N	N	N	N	N	N	Y
Rudman	N	N	N	N	N	N	N	Y
NEW JERSEY								
Bradley	Y	Y	Y	Y	Y	Y	Y	N
Williams	Y	Y	Y	Y	Y	Y	Y	N
NEW MEXICO								
Domenici	N	N	N	N	N	N	N	Y
Schmitt	N	N	N	N	N	N	N	Y
NEW YORK								
D'Amato	N	N	N	N	N	N	N	Y
Moynihan	Y	Y	Y	Y	Y	Y	Y	N
NORTH CAROLINA								
East	N	N	N	N	N	N	N	Y
Helms	N	N	N	N	N	N	N	Y
NORTH DAKOTA								
Andrews	N	N	N	N	N	N	N	Y
Burdick	Y	Y	Y	Y	Y	Y	Y	N
OHIO								
Glenn	N	Y	Y	N	Y	N	Y	N
Metzenbaum	Y	Y	Y	Y	Y	Y	?	?
OKLAHOMA								
Nickles	N	N	N	N	N	N	N	Y
Boren	N	N	Y	N	N	N	Y	N
OREGON								
Hatfield	N	N	N	N	N	N	N	Y
Packwood	N	N	N	N	N	N	N	Y
PENNSYLVANIA								
Heinz	?	?	?	?	?	?	Y	Y
Specter	N	N	N	N	N	N	Y	Y
RHODE ISLAND								
Chafee	N	N	N	N	N	N	N	Y
Pell	Y	Y	Y	Y	Y	Y	Y	N
SOUTH CAROLINA								
Thurmond	N	N	N	N	N	N	N	Y
Hollings	Y	Y	Y	Y	Y	Y	Y	N
SOUTH DAKOTA								
Abdnor	N	N	N	N	N	N	N	Y
Pressler	N	Y	N	N	N	Y	N	N
TENNESSEE								
Baker	N	N	N	N	N	N	N	Y
Sasser	+	+	+	+	+	+	#	N
TEXAS								
Tower	?	?	?	?	?	N	N	Y
Bentsen	N	Y	Y	N	N	N	N	N
UTAH								
Garn	N	N	N	N	N	N	N	Y
Hatch	N	N	N	N	N	N	N	Y
VERMONT								
Stafford	N	N	N	N	Y	N	Y	
Leahy	Y	Y	Y	Y	Y	Y	Y	N
VIRGINIA								
Warner	N	N	N	N	N	N	N	Y
Byrd*	N	N	N	N	N	N	N	Y
WASHINGTON								
Gorton	N	N	N	N	N	N	N	Y
Jackson	Y	Y	Y	Y	N	Y	Y	
WEST VIRGINIA								
Byrd	Y	Y	Y	Y	Y	Y	Y	N
Randolph	Y	Y	Y	Y	Y	Y	Y	N
WISCONSIN								
Kasten	N	N	N	N	N	N	N	Y
Proxmire	N	N	N	N	N	N	N	Y
WYOMING								
Simpson	N	N	N	N	N	N	N	Y
Wallop	N	N	N	N	N	N	N	Y

Democrats **Republicans**

* Byrd elected as an independent.

461. H J Res 370. Continuing Appropriations, Fiscal 1982. Kennedy, D-Mass., amendment to restore $120 million for administration of the unemployment insurance program. Rejected 30-65: R 0-49; D 30-16 (ND 26-6, SD 4-10), Dec. 10, 1981.

462. H J Res 370. Continuing Appropriations, Fiscal 1982. Kennedy, D-Mass., amendment to exempt the Older Americans, Head Start and community health center programs from the 4 percent funding cut in the resolution. Rejected 41-54: R 1-48; D 40-6 (ND 30-2, SD 10-4), Dec. 10, 1981.

463. H J Res 370. Continuing Appropriations, Fiscal 1982. Dodd, D-Conn., amendment to express the sense of the Senate in opposition to budget cuts in housing programs. Rejected 40-55: R 0-49; D 40-6 (ND 30-2, SD 10-4), Dec. 10, 1981.

464. H J Res 370. Continuing Appropriations, Fiscal 1982. Eagleton, D-Mo., amendment to provide $300 million for youth employment demonstration programs authorized by the Comprehensive Employment and Training Act (CETA). Rejected 31-64: R 0-49; D 31-15 (ND 27-5, SD 4-10), Dec. 10, 1981.

465. H J Res 370. Continuing Appropriations, Fiscal 1982. Bradley, D-N.J., amendment to provide an additional $30 million for foreign food aid under Public Law 480, to be used for Poland. Rejected 37-57: R 2-47; D 35-10 (ND 29-2, SD 6-8), Dec. 10, 1981.

466. H J Res 370. Continuing Appropriations, Fiscal 1982. Bradley, D-N.J., amendment to provide $76.7 million for the State Student Incentive grant program, and $2.4 billion for Pell grants to college students. Rejected 33-60: R 2-47; D 31-13 (ND 24-7, SD 7-6), Dec. 10, 1981.

467. H J Res 370. Continuing Appropriations, Fiscal 1982. Byrd, D-W.Va., amendment to exempt the Mine Safety and Health Administration from the 4 percent funding cut in the resolution. Rejected 38-54: R 2-49; D 36-5 (ND 26-2, SD 10-3), Dec. 11, 1981.

468. H J Res 370. Continuing Appropriations, Fiscal 1982. Passage of the joint resolution providing fiscal 1982 funding for government agencies whose regular appropriations bills had not been enacted, but only until the regular bill was enacted or March 31, 1982. Passed 60-35: R 49-2; D 11-33 (ND 5-24, SD 6-9), Dec. 11, 1981. A "yea" was a vote supporting the president's position.

KEY

- Y Voted for (yea).
- # Paired for.
- + Announced for.
- N Voted against (nay).
- X Paired against.
- - Announced against.
- P Voted "present".
- C Voted "present" to avoid possible conflict of interest.
- ? Did not vote or otherwise make a position known.

	469	470	471	472	473	474	475	476
ALABAMA								
Denton	Y	Y	Y	Y	Y	Y	Y	Y
Heflin	Y	Y	N	Y	Y	Y	Y	N
ALASKA								
Murkowski	Y	Y	Y	Y	Y	Y	Y	Y
Stevens	N	Y	Y	Y	Y	Y	Y	Y
ARIZONA								
Goldwater	?	?	?	?	?	?	?	?
DeConcini	Y	Y	Y	Y	Y	Y	Y	N
ARKANSAS								
Bumpers	N	?	Y	Y	Y	Y	N	Y
Pryor	Y	Y	N	Y	Y	Y	Y	N
CALIFORNIA								
Hayakawa	Y	Y	Y	Y	Y	Y	Y	Y
Cranston	N	Y	Y	Y	Y	Y	Y	Y
COLORADO								
Armstrong	Y	Y	Y	Y	N	Y	Y	N
Hart	N	Y	Y	Y	N	Y	Y	Y
CONNECTICUT								
Weicker	N	Y	Y	N	Y	Y	Y	Y
Dodd	N	Y	Y	N	Y	Y	Y	Y
DELAWARE								
Roth	Y	Y	N	Y	N	Y	Y	N
Biden	Y	Y	N	Y	N	Y	Y	Y
FLORIDA								
Hawkins	Y	+	Y	Y	Y	Y	Y	Y
Chiles	Y	Y	Y	Y	Y	Y	Y	Y
GEORGIA								
Mattingly	Y	Y	Y	Y	Y	Y	Y	Y
Nunn	Y	Y	N	Y	Y	Y	Y	N
HAWAII								
Inouye	N	Y	Y	Y	Y	Y	Y	Y
Matsunaga	N	Y	Y	Y	Y	Y	Y	Y
IDAHO								
McClure	Y	Y	N	Y	Y	Y	Y	N
Symms	Y	Y	N	Y	N	Y	Y	N
ILLINOIS								
Percy	N	Y	N	Y	Y	Y	Y	Y
Dixon	Y	Y	N	Y	Y	Y	Y	Y
INDIANA								
Lugar	Y	Y	Y	Y	Y	Y	Y	Y
Quayle	Y	Y	Y	Y	Y	Y	Y	Y

	469	470	471	472	473	474	475	476
IOWA								
Grassley	Y	Y	N	Y	Y	Y	Y	N
Jepsen	Y	Y	N	Y	Y	Y	Y	N
KANSAS								
Dole	Y	Y	N	Y	Y	Y	Y	Y
Kassebaum	Y	Y	?	Y	Y	Y	Y	Y
KENTUCKY								
Ford	Y	Y	Y	Y	Y	Y	Y	N
Huddleston	Y	Y	N	Y	Y	Y	Y	Y
LOUISIANA								
Johnston	Y	Y	Y	Y	Y	Y	Y	N
Long	Y	Y	Y	Y	Y	Y	Y	N
MAINE								
Cohen	N	Y	Y	Y	Y	Y	Y	Y
Mitchell	N	Y	Y	Y	Y	Y	Y	Y
MARYLAND								
Mathias	?	?	?	?	?	?	?	?
Sarbanes	N	Y	Y	Y	Y	Y	Y	Y
MASSACHUSETTS								
Kennedy	N	Y	Y	Y	Y	Y	Y	Y
Tsongas	N	Y	Y	Y	N	Y	N	Y
MICHIGAN								
Levin	N	Y	Y	Y	Y	Y	N	Y
Riegle	?	?	Y	Y	Y	Y	Y	Y
MINNESOTA								
Boschwitz	N	Y	Y	Y	Y	Y	Y	Y
Durenberger	Y	Y	Y	Y	Y	Y	Y	Y
MISSISSIPPI								
Cochran	Y	Y	Y	Y	Y	Y	Y	Y
Stennis	Y	Y	Y	Y	Y	Y	Y	N
MISSOURI								
Danforth	N	Y	Y	Y	Y	Y	Y	Y
Eagleton	N	Y	?	Y	N	Y	Y	N
MONTANA								
Baucus	N	Y	Y	Y	Y	Y	Y	N
Melcher	Y	?	+	+	#	Y	Y	N
NEBRASKA								
Exon	Y	Y	N	Y	X	Y	Y	N
Zorinsky	Y	Y	N	Y	Y	Y	Y	N
NEVADA								
Laxalt	Y	Y	Y	Y	Y	Y	Y	Y
Cannon	?	+	Y	Y	Y	Y	Y	N

	469	470	471	472	473	474	475	476
NEW HAMPSHIRE								
Humphrey	Y	Y	N	Y	N	Y	Y	N
Rudman	N	?	Y	Y	Y	Y	Y	Y
NEW JERSEY								
Bradley	N	Y	Y	N	Y	N	Y	Y
Williams	N	Y	Y	Y	N	Y	Y	Y
NEW MEXICO								
Domenici	Y	Y	Y	Y	Y	Y	Y	Y
Schmitt	Y	Y	Y	Y	Y	Y	Y	N
NEW YORK								
D'Amato	Y	Y	Y	Y	N	Y	Y	N
Moynihan	N	Y	Y	Y	N	Y	Y	Y
NORTH CAROLINA								
East	Y	Y	N	Y	Y	Y	Y	N
Helms	Y	Y	N	Y	Y	Y	Y	N
NORTH DAKOTA								
Andrews	Y	Y	Y	Y	Y	Y	Y	N
Burdick	N	Y	N	Y	Y	Y	Y	N
OHIO								
Glenn	N	Y	Y	N	Y	Y	Y	N
Metzenbaum	N	?	Y	Y	N	Y	Y	Y
OKLAHOMA								
Nickles	Y	Y	N	Y	Y	Y	Y	N
Boren	Y	Y	N	Y	Y	Y	Y	N
OREGON								
Hatfield	N	Y	Y	Y	Y	Y	N	Y
Packwood	N	Y	Y	Y	Y	Y	Y	Y
PENNSYLVANIA								
Heinz	N	Y	Y	Y	Y	Y	Y	Y
Specter	N	Y	Y	Y	Y	Y	Y	Y
RHODE ISLAND								
Chafee	N	Y	Y	Y	N	Y	Y	Y
Pell	X	Y	Y	Y	N	Y	Y	Y
SOUTH CAROLINA								
Thurmond	Y	Y	Y	Y	Y	Y	Y	Y
Hollings	Y	Y	Y	Y	Y	Y	Y	N
SOUTH DAKOTA								
Abdnor	Y	Y	N	Y	Y	Y	Y	N
Pressler	Y	Y	N	Y	N	Y	Y	N
TENNESSEE								
Baker	N	Y	Y	Y	Y	Y	Y	Y
Sasser	Y	Y	N	Y	Y	Y	Y	Y

	469	470	471	472	473	474	475	476
TEXAS								
Tower	Y	Y	?	?	?	?	?	?
Bentsen	Y	Y	N	Y	Y	Y	Y	N
UTAH								
Garn	Y	Y	Y	Y	Y	Y	Y	Y
Hatch	Y	Y	Y	Y	Y	Y	Y	N
VERMONT								
Stafford	N	Y	Y	Y	Y	Y	Y	Y
Leahy	#	Y	Y	Y	Y	Y	Y	Y
VIRGINIA								
Warner	Y	Y	Y	Y	Y	Y	Y	N
Byrd*	Y	?	Y	Y	N	Y	Y	N
WASHINGTON								
Gorton	N	Y	Y	Y	Y	Y	Y	Y
Jackson	N	Y	Y	Y	Y	Y	Y	Y
WEST VIRGINIA								
Byrd	Y	Y	Y	Y	Y	Y	Y	N
Randolph	Y	Y	Y	Y	Y	Y	Y	N
WISCONSIN								
Kasten	Y	Y	Y	Y	N	Y	Y	Y
Proxmire	Y	Y	N	Y	N	Y	Y	N
WYOMING								
Simpson	Y	Y	Y	Y	Y	Y	Y	N
Wallop	Y	Y	Y	Y	Y	Y	Y	Y

Democrats *Republicans*

* Byrd elected as an independent.

469. HR 4169. State, Justice, Commerce, Judiciary Appropriations, Fiscal 1982. Helms, R-N.C., motion to invoke cloture (thus limiting debate) on the bill to make appropriations for the State, Justice and Commerce departments and the federal judiciary. Motion rejected 59-35: R 36-15; D 23-20 (ND 9-19, SD 14-1), Dec. 11, 1981. A three-fifths majority vote (60) of the full Senate is required to invoke cloture.

470. S 1086. Older Americans Act. Adoption of the conference report on the bill extending Older Americans Act programs for three years, through fiscal 1984. Adopted 90-0: R 49-0; D 41-0 (ND 28-0, SD 13-0), Dec. 11, 1981.

471. HR 3567. Export Administration Authorization, Fiscal 1982-1983. Adoption of the conference report on the bill to authorize $9,659,000 annually for fiscal 1982 and 1983 for federal export control programs. Adopted 67-27: R 35-14; D 32-13 (ND 24-6, SD 8-7), Dec. 15, 1981.

472. HR 4331. Minimum Social Security Benefits. Adoption of the conference report on the bill to restore the minimum Social Security benefit; to extend the payroll tax to the first six months of sick pay; and to permit borrowing of assets among the three Social Security trust funds through Dec. 31, 1982. Adopted 96-0: R 50-0; D 46-0 (ND 31-0, SD 15-0), Dec. 15, 1981. A "yea" was a vote supporting the president's position.

473. HR 4119. Agriculture Appropriations, Fiscal 1982. Adoption of the conference report on the bill to appropriate $22,604,841,000 in fiscal 1982 for the Agriculture Department, the Food and Drug Administration and the Commodity Futures Trading Commission. Adopted 75-20: R 41-9; D 34-11 (ND 20-10, SD 14-1), Dec. 15, 1981. A "yea" was a vote supporting the president's position.

474. HR 4241. Military Construction Appropriations, Fiscal 1982. Adoption of the conference report on the bill to appropriate $7,059,260,000 for military construction programs in fiscal year 1982. Adopted 96-1: R 49-1; D 47-0 (ND 32-0, SD 15-0), Dec. 15, 1981. (The president had requested $7,300,608,000.)

475. HR 4995. Defense Appropriations, Fiscal 1982. Adoption of the conference report on the bill to appropriate $199,899,264,000 for the Department of Defense in fiscal year 1982. Adopted 93-4: R 49-1; D 44-3 (ND 30-2, SD 14-1), Dec. 15, 1981. (The president had requested $200,878,234,000.)

476. S 1196. Foreign Aid Authorizations. Adoption of the conference report on the bill to authorize $5,901,070,000 in fiscal year 1982 and $5,960,570,000 in fiscal year 1983 for foreign aid and related programs. Adopted 55-42: R 30-20, D 25-22 (ND 21-11, SD 4-11), Dec. 15, 1981. (The president had requested $5,727,854,000 for fiscal year 1982.)

KEY

- **Y** Voted for (yea).
- **#** Paired for.
- **+** Announced for.
- **N** Voted against (nay).
- **X** Paired against.
- **-** Announced against.
- **P** Voted "present".
- **C** Voted "present" to avoid possible conflict of interest.
- **?** Did not vote or otherwise make a position known.

	477	478	479	480	481	482	483
ALABAMA							
Denton	Y	Y	Y	Y	Y	Y	Y
Heflin	Y	N	N	Y	Y	N	N
ALASKA							
Murkowski	Y	Y	Y	Y	Y	Y	Y
Stevens	Y	Y	Y	Y	Y	Y	Y
ARIZONA							
Goldwater	?	?	?	?	?	?	?
DeConcini	Y	N	N	N	N	Y	N
ARKANSAS							
Bumpers	Y	N	N	N	N	Y	Y
Pryor	Y	?	N	N	N	N	N
CALIFORNIA							
Hayakawa	Y	Y	Y	Y	Y	Y	Y
Cranston	Y	Y	?	?	N	Y	Y
COLORADO							
Armstrong	Y	Y	Y	Y	Y	Y	N
Hart	?	Y	Y	Y	N	N	Y
CONNECTICUT							
Weicker	Y	Y	N	N	N	Y	Y
Dodd	Y	Y	Y	Y	N	N	Y
DELAWARE							
Roth	Y	N	N	N	Y	N	N
Biden	?	N	N	N	N	N	?
FLORIDA							
Hawkins	Y	Y	Y	Y	Y	Y	Y
Chiles	Y	N	N	N	N	N	Y
GEORGIA							
Mattingly	Y	N	N	N	Y	Y	N
Nunn	Y	N	N	N	Y	N	N
HAWAII							
Inouye	Y	Y	N	Y	N	N	Y
Matsunaga	Y	?	Y	Y	Y	N	Y
IDAHO							
McClure	Y	?	?	?	?	?	?
Symms	Y	Y	Y	Y	Y	Y	N
ILLINOIS							
Percy	Y	?	?	?	?	?	?
Dixon	Y	N	N	Y	N	N	Y
INDIANA							
Lugar	Y	N	Y	Y	Y	Y	Y
Quayle	Y	Y	Y	Y	N	Y	Y

	477	478	479	480	481	482	483
IOWA							
Grassley	Y	Y	Y	Y	Y	Y	N
Jepsen	Y	Y	Y	Y	Y	N	N
KANSAS							
Dole	Y	Y	Y	Y	Y	Y	Y
Kassebaum	Y	N	N	N	Y	Y	Y
KENTUCKY							
Ford	Y	N	Y	Y	N	N	N
Huddleston	Y	Y	Y	Y	N	Y	Y
LOUISIANA							
Johnston	Y	Y	Y	Y	Y	Y	N
Long	Y	Y	Y	Y	Y	Y	?
MAINE							
Cohen	Y	N	Y	Y	N	Y	Y
Mitchell	Y	N	N	N	N	N	Y
MARYLAND							
Mathias	?	Y	Y	Y	Y	Y	Y
Sarbanes	Y	N	N	N	N	N	Y
MASSACHUSETTS							
Kennedy	Y	?	?	Y	N	N	Y
Tsongas	Y	Y	Y	Y	N	N	Y
MICHIGAN							
Levin	Y	N	N	N	N	N	Y
Riegle	Y	N	N	N	N	N	Y
MINNESOTA							
Boschwitz	Y	Y	Y	Y	Y	Y	Y
Durenberger	Y	-	?	?	?	?	?
MISSISSIPPI							
Cochran	Y	Y	Y	Y	Y	Y	Y
Stennis	Y	N	N	N	?	?	?
MISSOURI							
Danforth	Y	Y	Y	Y	Y	Y	Y
Eagleton	Y	N	N	N	N	N	N
MONTANA							
Baucus	Y	Y	Y	Y	N	N	Y
Melcher	Y	N	N	Y	N	N	N
NEBRASKA							
Exon	Y	N	N	N	N	N	N
Zorinsky	Y	N	N	N	Y	N	N
NEVADA							
Laxalt	Y	Y	Y	Y	Y	Y	N
Cannon	Y	N	N	N	N	Y	N

	477	478	479	480	481	482	483
NEW HAMPSHIRE							
Humphrey	Y	Y	Y	Y	Y	Y	N
Rudman	Y	Y	Y	Y	Y	Y	Y
NEW JERSEY							
Bradley	Y	N	N	N	N	N	Y
Williams	Y	Y	Y	Y	Y	N	Y
NEW MEXICO							
Domenici	Y	N	N	N	Y	Y	N
Schmitt	Y	Y	Y	Y	Y	Y	Y
NEW YORK							
D'Amato	Y	Y	Y	Y	Y	Y	Y
Moynihan	Y	N	N	N	-	?	?
NORTH CAROLINA							
East	Y	Y	Y	Y	Y	Y	Y
Helms	Y	-	Y	Y	Y	Y	N
NORTH DAKOTA							
Andrews	Y	Y	Y	Y	Y	N	N
Burdick	Y	N	Y	Y	Y	N	N
OHIO							
Glenn	Y	N	Y	Y	Y	N	Y
Metzenbaum	Y	N	N	N	N	N	Y
OKLAHOMA							
Nickles	Y	Y	Y	Y	Y	Y	N
Boren	Y	N	N	N	?	?	?
OREGON							
Hatfield	Y	Y	Y	Y	Y	Y	Y
Packwood	Y	Y	Y	Y	Y	Y	Y
PENNSYLVANIA							
Heinz	Y	N	Y	Y	Y	?	?
Specter	Y	N	Y	Y	Y	Y	Y
RHODE ISLAND							
Chafee	Y	N	Y	Y	Y	Y	Y
Pell	Y	Y	Y	Y	N	N	Y
SOUTH CAROLINA							
Thurmond	Y	Y	Y	Y	Y	Y	N
Hollings	Y	Y	Y	Y	N	N	N
SOUTH DAKOTA							
Abdnor	Y	Y	N	N	Y	N	N
Pressler	Y	N	N	N	Y	N	N
TENNESSEE							
Baker	Y	Y	?	+	Y	Y	Y
Sasser	Y	N	N	N	N	N	Y

	477	478	479	480	481	482	483
TEXAS							
Tower	?	?	?	?	?	?	?
Bentsen	Y	N	N	N	Y	Y	N
UTAH							
Garn	Y	Y	Y	Y	Y	Y	N
Hatch	Y	Y	Y	Y	Y	Y	Y
VERMONT							
Stafford	Y	Y	Y	Y	Y	Y	Y
Leahy	Y	?	Y	Y	Y	N	Y
VIRGINIA							
Warner	Y	N	Y	Y	Y	N	N
Byrd*	Y	N	Y	Y	Y	Y	N
WASHINGTON							
Gorton	Y	Y	Y	Y	Y	Y	Y
Jackson	Y	N	N	Y	N	N	Y
WEST VIRGINIA							
Byrd	Y	N	N	Y	N	N	N
Randolph	Y	N	Y	Y	-	N	N
WISCONSIN							
Kasten	Y	N	N	Y	N	Y	Y
Proxmire	Y	N	N	N	N	N	N
WYOMING							
Simpson	Y	N	Y	Y	Y	Y	Y
Wallop	Y	Y	Y	Y	Y	Y	Y

Democrats *Republicans*

* Byrd elected as an independent.

477. S Res 268. Martial Law in Poland. Adoption of the resolution condemning the imposition of martial law in Poland on Dec. 13, 1981, and urging the president and the secretary of state to stress to Polish officials that continued U.S. aid to the Polish government would depend on the avoidance of violence and bloodshed and the Polish government's commitment to a continuation of reforms. Adopted 95-0: R 50-0; D 45-0 (ND 30-0, SD 15-0), Dec. 15, 1981.

478. HR 5159. Black Lung Benefits. Dole, R-Kan., amendment, to the Dole, R-Kan., substitute amendment (see vote 479, below), to instruct the Treasury secretary to prescribe an "appropriate" amount of business tax deductions that can be taken by members of Congress without having to substantiate those expenses. Adopted 46-44: R 34-13; D 12-31 (ND 8-21, SD 4-10), Dec. 16, 1981.

479. HR 5159. Black Lung Benefits. Dole, R-Kan., substitute amendment to temporarily double the excise tax on coal; to liberalize rules governing business tax deductions for the cost of maintaining a second home; to allow business deductions for costs related to the rental of a dwelling to a relative for use as a primary residence; to require businesses involved in the leasing of equipment for tax purposes to report such activities to the Internal Revenue Service within 30 days of the transaction; and to delay for two years the effective date of new limits on how long corporations can carry over net operating losses. Adopted 56-36: R 39-8; D 17-28 (ND 11-19, SD 6-9), Dec. 16, 1981.

480. HR 5159. Black Lung Benefits. Passage of the bill to double temporarily the excise tax on coal; to tighten rules used in determining eligibility for black lung disability benefits; to liberalize rules governing business tax deductions for the cost of maintaining a second home; to allow business deductions for costs related to the rental of a dwelling to a relative for use as a primary residence; to require businesses involved in the leasing of equipment for tax benefits to report such activities to the Internal Revenue Service within 30 days of the transaction; and to delay for two years the effective date of new limits on how long corporations can carry over net operating losses. Passed 63-30: R 39-8; D 24-22 (ND 17-14, SD 7-8), Dec. 16, 1981.

481. HR 4717. Miscellaneous Revenue Act of 1981. Dole, R-Kan., motion to table (kill) the Hart, D-Colo., amendment to express the sense of the Senate that the president should impose a ban on the import of Libyan oil and take steps to coordinate an international ban on such imports. Motion agreed to 57-34: R 45-3; D 12-31 (ND 6-24, SD 6-7), Dec. 16, 1981.

482. HR 4717. Miscellaneous Revenue Act of 1981. Dole, R-Kan., motion to table (kill) the Melcher, D-Mont., amendment to limit to 7 percent or less the interest rate the Internal Revenue Service can impute on the sale of non-depreciable property, such as land. Motion agreed to 48-43: R 39-8; D 9-35 (ND 3-28, SD 6-7), Dec. 16, 1981.

483. HR 4559. Foreign Aid Appropriations, Fiscal 1982. Adoption of the conference report on the bill to appropriate $7,495,221,970 in fiscal 1982 for foreign aid and related programs. Adopted 55-34: R 31-16; D 24-18 (ND 20-10, SD 4-8), Dec. 16, 1981. (The president had requested $7,775,098,683.)

HOUSE ROLL-CALL VOTES

KEY

Y   Voted for (yea).
Paired for.
+   Announced for.
N   Voted against (nay).
X   Paired against.
-   Announced against.
P   Voted "present."
C   Voted "present" to avoid possible conflict of interest.
?   Did not vote or otherwise make a position known.

1. Election of Speaker. For election of the Speaker of the House of Representatives for the 97th Congress, the nominees were Rep. Thomas P. O'Neill Jr., D-Mass, the Speaker since 1977, and Rep. Robert H. Michel, R-Ill., who had been elected the Republican leader in December 1980. O'Neill was elected 234-182: R 0-182; D 234-0 (ND 159-0; SD 75-0), Jan. 5, 1981. A "Y" on the chart represents a vote for O'Neill, an "N" a vote for Michel.

2. H Res 5. House Rules. Wright, D-Texas, motion to order the previous question (thus ending further debate and possibility for amendment) on the resolution to adopt the rules of the House of Representatives for the 97th Congress as proposed by the Democratic Caucus in December 1980. Motion agreed to 216-179: R 0-176; D 216-3 (ND 146-1; SD 70-2), Jan. 5, 1981. (The rules were adopted subsequently by voice vote.)

3. H Res 5. House Rules. Michel, R-Ill., motion to commit to a special select committee the resolution to adopt the rules of the House of Representatives for the 97th Congress with instructions to add language providing that the ratio of members from the majority party to members from the minority party on House committees, subcommittees, task forces and other committee subunits should reflect the ratio of majority to minority party members in the whole House except that the ratio would be 3-to-2 for the Appropriations, Budget and Ways and Means committees, 2-to-1 for the Rules Committee and 1-to-1 for the Committee on Standards of Official Conduct. Motion rejected 180-220: R 179-0; D 1-220 (ND 0-151; SD 1-69), Jan. 5, 1981.

4. H Res 45. Republican Committee Elections. Lott, R-Miss., motion to commit to a special select committee the resolution designating the Republican membership of House committees with instructions to add two Republican members to the Ways and Means committee. Motion rejected 172-221: R 172-0; D 0-221 (ND 0-148; SD 0-73), Jan. 28, 1981. (H Res 45 was subsequently adopted by voice vote.)

	1	2	3	4
ALABAMA				
1 *Edwards*	?	?	?	Y
2 *Dickinson*	N	N	Y	Y
3 Nichols	Y	?	?	N
4 Bevill	Y	Y	N	N
5 Flippo	Y	Y	N	N
6 *Smith*	N	N	Y	Y
7 Shelby	Y	Y	N	N
ALASKA				
AL *Young*	N	?	Y	Y
ARIZONA				
1 *Rhodes*	N	N	Y	Y
2 Udall	Y	Y	N	N
3 *Stump*	Y	Y	N	N
4 *Rudd*	N	N	Y	Y
ARKANSAS				
1 Alexander	Y	Y	N	N
2 *Bethune*	N	N	Y	Y
3 *Hammerschmidt*	N	N	Y	Y
4 Anthony	Y	?	?	N
CALIFORNIA				
1 *Chappie*	N	N	Y	Y
2 *Clausen*	N	N	Y	Y
3 Matsui	Y	Y	N	N
4 Fazio	Y	Y	N	N
5 Burton, J.	Y	Y	N	N
6 Burton, P.	Y	Y	N	?
7 Miller	Y	Y	N	N
8 Dellums	Y	Y	N	N
9 Stark	Y	Y	N	N
10 Edwards	Y	?	N	N
11 Lantos	Y	Y	N	N
12 *McCloskey*†	?			Y
13 Mineta	Y	Y	N	N
14 *Shumway*	N	N	Y	Y
15 Coelho	Y	Y	N	N
16 Panetta	Y	Y	N	N
17 *Pashayan*	N	N	Y	Y
18 *Thomas*	N	N	Y	Y
19 *Lagomarsino*	N	N	Y	Y
20 *Goldwater*	N	N	Y	Y
21 *Fiedler*	N	N	Y	Y
22 *Moorhead*	N	?	Y	Y
23 Beilenson	Y	Y	N	N
24 Waxman	Y	Y	N	N
25 Roybal	Y	Y	N	N
26 *Rousselot*	N	N	Y	Y
27 *Dornan*	N	N	Y	Y
28 Dixon	Y	Y	N	N
29 Hawkins	Y	Y	N	N
30 Danielson	Y	Y	N	N
31 Dymally	Y	?	N	N
32 Anderson	Y	Y	N	N
33 *Grisham*	N	?	Y	?
34 *Lungren*	N	N	Y	Y
35 *Dreier*	N	N	Y	Y
36 Brown	Y	Y	N	?
37 *Lewis*	N	N	Y	Y
38 Patterson	Y	?	N	N
39 *Dannemeyer*	N	N	Y	Y
40 *Badham*	N	N	Y	Y
41 *Lowery*	N	N	Y	?
42 *Hunter*	N	N	Y	Y
43 *Burgener*	N	N	Y	Y
COLORADO				
1 Schroeder	Y	Y	N	N
2 Wirth	Y	Y	N	N
3 Kogovsek	Y	Y	N	N
4 *Brown*	N	N	Y	Y

	1	2	3	4
5 *Kramer*	N	N	Y	Y
CONNECTICUT				
1 Cotter	Y	Y	N	N
2 Gejdenson	Y	?	?	N
3 *DeNardis*	N	N	Y	Y
4 *McKinney*	N	N	Y	Y
5 Ratchford	Y	Y	N	N
6 Moffett	Y	Y	N	N
DELAWARE				
AL *Evans*	N	N	Y	Y
FLORIDA				
1 Hutto	Y	Y	N	N
2 Fuqua	Y	Y	N	N
3 Bennett	Y	Y	N	N
4 Chappell	Y	Y	N	N
5 *McCollum*	N	N	Y	Y
6 *Young*	N	N	Y	Y
7 Gibbons	Y	Y	N	N
8 Ireland	Y	Y	N	N
9 Nelson	Y	Y	N	N
10 *Bafalis*	N	N	Y	Y
11 Mica	Y	Y	N	N
12 *Shaw*	N	N	Y	Y
13 Lehman	Y	Y	N	N
14 Pepper	Y	Y	N	N
15 Fascell	Y	Y	N	N
GEORGIA				
1 Ginn	Y	Y	N	N
2 Hatcher	Y	Y	N	N
3 Brinkley	Y	Y	N	N
4 Levitas	Y	Y	N	N
5 Fowler†	?			?
6 *Gingrich*	N	N	Y	Y
7 McDonald	?	N	Y	?
8 Evans	Y	Y	N	N
9 Jenkins	Y	Y	N	N
10 Barnard	Y	Y	N	N
HAWAII				
1 Heftel	Y	Y	N	N
2 Akaka	Y	Y	N	N
IDAHO				
1 *Craig*	N	N	Y	Y
2 *Hansen*	N	N	Y	Y
ILLINOIS				
1 Washington	Y	Y	N	N
2 Savage	Y	Y	N	N
3 Russo	Y	Y	N	?
4 *Derwinski*	N	N	Y	Y
5 Fary	Y	Y	N	N
6 *Hyde*	N	N	Y	Y
7 Collins	Y	?	?	N
8 Rostenkowski	Y	Y	N	N
9 Yates	Y	Y	N	N
10 *Porter*	N	N	Y	Y
11 Annunzio	Y	Y	N	N
12 *Crane, P.*	N	?	?	?
13 *McClory*	N	N	Y	Y
14 *Erlenborn*	N	N	Y	Y
15 *Corcoran*	N	N	Y	Y
16 *Martin*	N	N	Y	?
17 *O'Brien*	N	N	Y	Y
18 *Michel*	C	N	Y	Y
19 *Railsback*	N	N	Y	Y
20 *Findley*	N	N	Y	Y
21 *Madigan*	N	N	Y	Y
22 *Crane, D.*	N	N	Y	Y
23 Price	Y	Y	N	N
24 Simon	Y	Y	N	N
INDIANA				
1 Benjamin	Y	Y	N	N
2 Fithian	Y	Y	N	N
3 *Hiler*	N	N	Y	Y
4 *Coats*	N	N	Y	Y
5 *Hillis*†	?			Y
6 Evans	Y	Y	N	N
7 *Myers*	N	N	Y	Y
8 *Deckard*	N	N	Y	Y
9 Hamilton	Y	Y	N	N
10 Sharp	Y	Y	N	N
11 Jacobs	Y	N	N	N
IOWA				
1 *Leach*	N	N	Y	Y
2 *Tauke*	N	N	Y	Y
3 *Evans*	N	N	Y	Y
4 Smith	Y	Y	N	N
5 Harkin	Y	Y	N	?
6 Bedell†	?			N

Column headers for all sections: 1 2 3 4

KANSAS

	1	2	3	4
1 Roberts	N	N	Y	Y
2 Jeffries	N	N	Y	Y
3 Winn	N	N	Y	Y
4 Glickman	Y	Y	N	N
5 Whittaker	N	N	Y	Y

KENTUCKY

	1	2	3	4
1 Hubbard	Y	Y	N	N
2 Natcher	Y	Y	N	N
3 Mazzoli	Y	Y	N	N
4 Snyder	N	N	Y	Y
5 Rogers	N	N	Y	Y
6 Hopkins	N	N	Y	Y
7 Perkins	Y	Y	N	N

LOUISIANA

	1	2	3	4
1 Livingston	N	N	Y	Y
2 Boggs	Y	Y	N	N
3 Tauzin	Y	Y	?	N
4 Roemer	Y	N	?	N
5 Huckaby	Y	Y	N	N
6 Moore	N	N	Y	Y
7 Breaux	Y	Y	N	N
8 Long	Y	Y	N	N

MAINE

	1	2	3	4
1 Emery	N	N	Y	Y
2 Snowe	N	N	Y	Y

MARYLAND

	1	2	3	4
1 Dyson	Y	Y	N	N
2 Long	Y	Y	N	N
3 Mikulski	Y	Y	N	?
4 Holt	N	N	Y	Y
5 Spellman††	?			
6 Byron	Y	Y	N	N
7 Mitchell	Y	Y	N	N
8 Barnes	Y	Y	N	N

MASSACHUSETTS

	1	2	3	4
1 Conte	N	N	Y	Y
2 Boland	Y	Y	N	N
3 Early	Y	Y	N	N
4 Frank	Y	Y	N	N
5 Shannon	Y	Y	N	N
6 Mavroules	Y	Y	N	N
7 Markey	Y	Y	N	N
8 O'Neill	C			
9 Moakley	Y	Y	N	N
10 Heckler	N	N	Y	?
11 Donnelly	Y	Y	N	N
12 Studds	Y	Y	N	N

MICHIGAN

	1	2	3	4
1 Conyers	Y	Y	N	N
2 Pursell	N	N	Y	?
3 Wolpe	Y	Y	N	N
4 Stockman†††	?	?	?	
5 Sawyer	N	N	Y	Y
6 Dunn	N	N	Y	Y
7 Kildee	Y	Y	N	N
8 Traxler	Y	Y	N	N
9 Vander Jagt†	?		Y	
10 Albosta	Y	Y	N	N
11 Davis	N	N	?	Y
12 Bonior	Y	Y	N	N
13 Crockett	Y	Y	N	N
14 Hertel	Y	Y	N	N
15 Ford	Y	Y	N	N
16 Dingell	Y	Y	N	N
17 Brodhead	Y	Y	N	N
18 Blanchard	Y	Y	N	N
19 Broomfield	N	N	Y	N

MINNESOTA

	1	2	3	4
1 Erdahl	N	N	Y	Y
2 Hagedorn	N	N	Y	Y
3 Frenzel	N	N	Y	Y
4 Vento	Y	Y	N	N
5 Sabo	Y	Y	N	N
6 Weber	N	N	Y	Y
7 Stangeland	N	N	Y	Y
8 Oberstar	Y	Y	N	?

MISSISSIPPI

	1	2	3	4
1 Whitten	Y	Y	N	N
2 Bowen	Y	Y	N	N
3 Montgomery	Y	Y	N	N
4 Hinson	N	N	Y	Y
5 Lott	N	N	Y	Y

MISSOURI

	1	2	3	4
1 Clay	Y	Y	N	N
2 Young	Y	Y	N	N
3 Gephardt	Y	Y	N	N
4 Skelton	Y	Y	N	N
5 Bolling	Y	Y	N	N
6 Coleman	N	N	Y	?
7 Taylor	N	N	Y	?
8 Bailey	N	N	Y	Y
9 Volkmer	Y	Y	N	N
10 Emerson	N	N	Y	Y

MONTANA

	1	2	3	4
1 Williams	Y	Y	N	N
2 Marlenee	N	N	Y	Y

NEBRASKA

	1	2	3	4
1 Bereuter	N	N	Y	Y
2 Daub	N	N	Y	Y
3 Smith	N	N	Y	Y

NEVADA

	1	2	3	4
AL Santini	Y	Y	N	N

NEW HAMPSHIRE

	1	2	3	4
1 D'Amours	Y	Y	N	N
2 Gregg	N	N	Y	Y

NEW JERSEY

	1	2	3	4
1 Florio	Y	Y	N	N
2 Hughes	Y	Y	N	?
3 Howard	Y	Y	N	N
4 Smith	N	N	Y	Y
5 Fenwick	N	N	Y	Y
6 Forsythe	N	N	Y	Y
7 Roukema	N	N	Y	Y
8 Roe	Y	?	N	?
9 Hollenbeck	N	N	Y	Y
10 Rodino	Y	Y	N	N
11 Minish	Y	Y	N	N
12 Rinaldo	N	N	Y	Y
13 Courter	N	N	Y	Y
14 Guarini	Y	?	N	N
15 Dwyer	Y	Y	N	N

NEW MEXICO

	1	2	3	4
1 Lujan	N	N	Y	Y
2 Skeen	N	N	Y	Y

NEW YORK

	1	2	3	4
1 Carney	N	N	Y	Y
2 Downey	Y	Y	N	N
3 Carman	N	N	Y	Y
4 Lent	N	N	Y	Y
5 McGrath	N	N	Y	Y
6 LeBoutillier	N	N	Y	Y
7 Addabbo	Y	Y	N	N
8 Rosenthal	Y	Y	N	?
9 Ferraro	Y	Y	N	N
10 Biaggi	Y	Y	N	N
11 Scheuer	Y	Y	N	N
12 Chisholm	Y	?	?	?
13 Solarz†	?		Y	
14 Richmond	Y	Y	N	N
15 Zeferetti	Y	Y	N	N
16 Schumer	Y	Y	N	N
17 Molinari†	-			Y
18 Green	N	N	Y	Y
19 Rangel	Y	Y	N	?
20 Weiss	Y	Y	N	N
21 Garcia	Y	Y	N	N
22 Bingham	Y	Y	N	N
23 Peyser	Y	Y	N	N
24 Ottinger	Y	Y	N	N
25 Fish	N	N	Y	Y
26 Gilman	N	N	Y	Y
27 McHugh	Y	Y	N	N
28 Stratton	Y	Y	N	N
29 Solomon	N	N	Y	Y
30 Martin	N	N	Y	Y
31 Mitchell	N	N	Y	?
32 Wortley	N	N	Y	Y
33 Lee	N	N	Y	Y
34 Horton	N	N	Y	Y
35 Conable	N	N	Y	Y
36 LaFalce†	?		N	
37 Nowak	Y	Y	N	N
38 Kemp	N	N	Y	Y
39 Lundine	Y	Y	N	N

NORTH CAROLINA

	1	2	3	4
1 Jones	Y	Y	N	N
2 Fountain	Y	Y	N	N
3 Whitley	Y	Y	N	N
4 Andrews†	?		?	
5 Neal	Y	Y	N	N
6 Johnston	N	N	?	Y
7 Rose	Y	Y	N	N
8 Hefner	Y	Y	N	N
9 Martin	N	N	Y	Y
10 Broyhill	N	N	Y	Y
11 Hendon	N	N	Y	Y

NORTH DAKOTA

	1	2	3	4
AL Dorgan	Y	Y	N	N

OHIO

	1	2	3	4
1 Gradison	N	N	Y	Y
2 Luken	Y	Y	N	N
3 Hall	Y	Y	N	N
4 Guyer	N	N	Y	Y
5 Latta	N	N	Y	?
6 McEwen	N	N	Y	Y
7 Brown†	?		?	
8 Kindness	N	N	Y	Y
9 Weber	N	N	Y	Y
10 Miller	N	N	Y	Y
11 Stanton	N	?	?	Y
12 Shamansky	Y	Y	N	N
13 Pease	Y	Y	N	N
14 Seiberling	Y	Y	N	N
15 Wylie	N	N	Y	Y
16 Regula	N	N	Y	Y
17 Ashbrook	N	N	Y	?
18 Applegate	Y	Y	N	N
19 Williams	N	N	Y	?
20 Oakar	Y	Y	N	N
21 Stokes	Y	Y	?	N
22 Eckart	Y	Y	N	N
23 Mottl	Y	Y	?	N

OKLAHOMA

	1	2	3	4
1 Jones	Y	Y	N	N
2 Synar	Y	Y	N	N
3 Watkins	Y	Y	N	N
4 McCurdy	Y	Y	N	N
5 Edwards	N	N	Y	Y
6 English	Y	Y	N	N

OREGON

	1	2	3	4
1 AuCoin	Y	Y	N	?
2 Smith	N	N	Y	Y
3 Wyden	Y	Y	N	N
4 Weaver	Y	Y	N	N

PENNSYLVANIA

	1	2	3	4
1 Foglietta*		Y	Y	N	N
2 Gray	Y	Y	N	N
3 Lederer	Y	?	?	?
4 Dougherty	N	N	Y	Y
5 Schulze	N	N	Y	Y
6 Yatron	Y	Y	N	N
7 Edgar	Y	Y	N	N
8 Coyne, J.	N	N	Y	Y
9 Shuster	N	N	Y	Y
10 McDade	N	N	Y	Y
11 Nelligan	N	N	Y	Y
12 Murtha	Y	Y	N	N
13 Coughlin	N	N	Y	Y
14 Coyne, W.	Y	Y	N	N
15 Ritter	N	N	Y	Y
16 Walker	N	N	Y	Y
17 Ertel†	?		N	
18 Walgren	Y	Y	N	N
19 Goodling	N	N	Y	Y
20 Gaydos	Y	Y	N	N
21 Bailey	Y	Y	N	N
22 Murphy	Y	Y	N	N
23 Clinger	N	N	Y	Y
24 Marks	N	N	Y	Y
25 Atkinson	Y	?	N	N

RHODE ISLAND

	1	2	3	4
1 St Germain	Y	Y	N	N
2 Schneider	N	N	Y	Y

SOUTH CAROLINA

	1	2	3	4
1 Hartnett	N	-	Y	Y
2 Spence	N	N	Y	Y
3 Derrick	Y	?	N	N
4 Campbell	N	N	Y	Y
5 Holland	Y	Y	N	N
6 Napier	N	N	Y	Y

SOUTH DAKOTA

	1	2	3	4
1 Daschle	Y	Y	N	N
2 Roberts	N	N	Y	Y

TENNESSEE

	1	2	3	4
1 Quillen	N	N	Y	Y
2 Duncan	N	N	Y	Y
3 Bouquard	Y	Y	N	N
4 Gore	Y	Y	N	N
5 Boner	Y	Y	N	?
6 Beard	N	N	Y	Y

TEXAS

	1	2	3	4
7 Jones	Y	Y	N	N
8 Ford	Y	Y	N	N
1 Hall, S.	Y	Y	N	N
2 Wilson	Y	Y	N	N
3 Collins	N	N	Y	Y
4 Hall, R.	Y	?	?	N
5 Mattox	Y	Y	N	N
6 Gramm	Y	Y	N	N
7 Archer	N	N	Y	Y
8 Fields	N	N	Y	Y
9 Brooks	Y	Y	N	N
10 Pickle	Y	Y	N	N
11 Leath	Y	Y	N	N
12 Wright	Y	Y	N	N
13 Hightower	Y	Y	N	N
14 Patman	Y	Y	N	N
15 de la Garza	Y	Y	N	?
16 White	Y	Y	N	N
17 Stenholm	Y	Y	N	N
18 Leland	Y	Y	N	N
19 Hance	Y	Y	N	N
20 Gonzalez	Y	Y	N	N
21 Loeffler	N	N	Y	Y
22 Paul	N	N	Y	Y
23 Kazen	Y	Y	N	N
24 Frost	Y	Y	N	N

UTAH

	1	2	3	4
1 Hansen	N	N	Y	Y
2 Marriott	N	N	Y	Y

VERMONT

	1	2	3	4
AL Jeffords†	?		Y	

VIRGINIA

	1	2	3	4
1 Trible	N	N	Y	Y
2 Whitehurst	N	N	Y	Y
3 Bliley	N	N	Y	Y
4 Daniel, R.	N	N	Y	Y
5 Daniel, D.	Y	Y	N	N
6 Butler	N	N	Y	Y
7 Robinson	N	N	Y	Y
8 Parris	N	N	Y	Y
9 Wampler	N	N	Y	?
10 Wolf	N	N	Y	Y

WASHINGTON

	1	2	3	4
1 Pritchard†	?		Y	
2 Swift	Y	Y	N	N
3 Bonker	Y	Y	N	N
4 Morrison	N	N	Y	Y
5 Foley	Y	Y	N	N
6 Dicks	Y	Y	N	N
7 Lowry	Y	Y	N	N

WEST VIRGINIA

	1	2	3	4
1 Mollohan	Y	Y	N	N
2 Benedict	N	N	Y	Y
3 Staton	N	N	Y	Y
4 Rahall	Y	Y	N	N

WISCONSIN

	1	2	3	4
1 Aspin	Y	Y	N	N
2 Kastenmeier	Y	Y	N	N
3 Gunderson	N	N	Y	Y
4 Zablocki	Y	Y	N	N
5 Reuss	Y	?	?	N
6 Petri	N	N	Y	Y
7 Obey	Y	?	?	N
8 Roth	N	?	Y	?
9 Sensenbrenner	N	N	Y	Y

WYOMING

	1	2	3	4
AL Cheney	N	N	Y	Y

All members-elect are eligible to vote on election of the Speaker.

*Rep. Foglietta, Pa., elected as an independent.

† Not yet sworn in and therefore ineligible for CQ votes 2-3.

†† Rep. Spellman, D-Md., not sworn in and ineligible for CQ votes 2-4.

††† Rep. Stockman, R-Mich., resigned Jan. 27, 1981.

Democrats   *Republicans*

5. Procedural Motion. Walker, R-Pa., motion to approve the House *Journal* of Wednesday, Feb. 4. Motion agreed to 367-10: R 168-6; D 199-4 (ND 130-4; SD 69-0), Feb. 5, 1981.

6. HR 1553. Debt Limit Increase. Adoption of the rule (H Res 54) providing for House floor consideration of the bill to increase the public debt limit to $985 billion through Sept. 30, 1981. Adopted 333-67: R 138-44; D 195-23 (ND 138-9; SD 57-14), Feb. 5, 1981.

7. HR 1553. Debt Limit Increase. Passage of the bill to increase the public debt limit to $985 billion through Sept. 30, 1981. Passed 305-104: R 150-36; D 155-68 (ND 112-37; SD 43-31), Feb. 5, 1981. A "yea" was a vote supporting the president's position.

KEY

Y	Voted for (yea).	
#	Paired for.	
+	Announced for.	
N	Voted against (nay)	
X	Paired against.	
-	Announced against.	
P	Voted "present."	
C	Voted "present" to avoid possible conflict of interest.	
?	Did not vote or otherwise make a position known.	

	5	6	7
ALABAMA			
1 *Edwards*	Y	Y	Y
2 *Dickinson*	N	Y	Y
3 Nichols	Y	Y	N
4 Bevill	Y	Y	N
5 Flippo	Y	Y	N
6 *Smith*	Y	Y	Y
7 Shelby	Y	N	N
ALASKA			
AL *Young*	Y	Y	Y
ARIZONA			
1 *Rhodes*	Y	Y	Y
2 Udall	Y	Y	Y
3 Stump	P	N	N
4 *Rudd*	Y	Y	Y
ARKANSAS			
1 Alexander	P	Y	Y
2 *Bethune*	Y	Y	Y
3 *Hammerschmidt*	Y	Y	Y
4 Anthony	Y	?	Y
CALIFORNIA			
1 *Chappie*	?	Y	N
2 *Clausen*	Y	Y	Y
3 Matsui	Y	Y	Y
4 Fazio	Y	Y	?
5 Burton, J.	?	?	?
6 Burton, P.	Y	Y	Y
7 Miller	Y	?	N
8 Dellums	Y	Y	N
9 Stark	Y	Y	Y
10 Edwards	Y	Y	Y
11 Lantos	Y	Y	N
12 *McCloskey*	Y	N	Y
13 Mineta	Y	Y	Y
14 *Shumway*	Y	Y	Y
15 Coelho	Y	Y	Y
16 Panetta	Y	Y	Y
17 *Pashayan*	Y	N	N
18 *Thomas*	Y	N	Y
19 *Lagomarsino*	Y	Y	Y
20 *Goldwater*	?	?	?
21 *Fiedler*	Y	Y	Y
22 *Moorhead*	Y	Y	N
23 Beilenson	Y	Y	Y
24 Waxman	Y	Y	Y
25 Roybal	?	?	?
26 *Rousselot*	Y	N	N
27 *Dornan*	?	N	Y
28 Dixon	Y	Y	Y
29 Hawkins	Y	Y	Y
30 Danielson	Y	Y	Y
31 Dymally	Y	Y	Y
32 Anderson	Y	N	N
33 *Grisham*	Y	Y	Y
34 *Lungren*	Y	Y	Y
35 *Dreier*	Y	N	N
36 Brown	?	Y	Y
37 *Lewis*	Y	N	Y
38 Patterson	Y	Y	Y
39 *Dannemeyer*	Y	N	N
40 *Badham*	Y	Y	Y
41 *Lowery*	?	N	Y
42 *Hunter*	Y	N	Y
43 *Burgener*	Y	Y	Y
COLORADO			
1 Schroeder	N	N	N
2 Wirth	Y	Y	Y
3 Kogovsek	Y	Y	Y
4 *Brown*	Y	N	Y

	5	6	7
5 *Kramer*	Y	N	Y
CONNECTICUT			
1 Cotter	?	?	?
2 Gejdenson	Y	Y	Y
3 *DeNardis*	Y	Y	N
4 *McKinney*	Y	Y	Y
5 Ratchford	Y	Y	Y
6 Moffett	Y	Y	Y
DELAWARE			
AL *Evans*	Y	Y	Y
FLORIDA			
1 Hutto	Y	Y	Y
2 Fuqua	P	?	?
3 Bennett	Y	Y	N
4 Chappell	Y	Y	N
5 *McCollum*	?	?	?
6 *Young*	Y	N	Y
7 Gibbons	Y	Y	Y
8 Ireland	Y	Y	Y
9 Nelson	?	Y	Y
10 *Bafalis*	P	Y	Y
11 Mica	Y	Y	Y
12 *Shaw*	Y	N	Y
13 Lehman	Y	Y	Y
14 Pepper	?	Y	Y
15 Fascell	Y	Y	Y
GEORGIA			
1 Ginn	Y	Y	Y
2 Hatcher	?	Y	Y
3 Brinkley	Y	Y	Y
4 Levitas	Y	N	N
5 Fowler	Y	Y	Y
6 *Gingrich*	Y	Y	Y
7 McDonald	Y	N	N
8 Evans	Y	N	N
9 Jenkins	Y	Y	Y
10 Barnard	Y	N	N
HAWAII			
1 Heftel	?	N	N
2 Akaka	Y	Y	N
IDAHO			
1 *Craig*	Y	N	N
2 *Hansen*	Y	Y	N
ILLINOIS			
1 Washington	P	Y	Y
2 Savage	Y	Y	Y
3 Russo	Y	Y	Y
4 *Derwinski*	Y	Y	Y
5 Fary	Y	Y	Y
6 *Hyde*	Y	Y	Y
7 Collins	Y	Y	Y
8 Rostenkowski	Y	Y	Y
9 Yates	Y	Y	Y
10 *Porter*	Y	N	Y
11 Annunzio	Y	Y	Y
12 *Crane, P.*	?	?	N
13 *McClory*	Y	Y	Y
14 *Erlenborn*	?	Y	Y
15 *Corcoran*	Y	Y	Y
16 *Martin*	Y	Y	Y
17 *O'Brien*	Y	Y	Y
18 *Michel*	Y	Y	Y
19 *Railsback*	Y	Y	Y
20 *Findley*	Y	Y	Y
21 *Madigan*	?	Y	Y
22 *Crane, D.*	Y	N	N
23 Price	Y	Y	Y
24 Simon	Y	Y	Y
INDIANA			
1 Benjamin	Y	Y	Y
2 Fithian	?	?	X
3 *Hiler*	Y	N	Y
4 *Coats*	Y	Y	Y
5 *Hillis*	Y	Y	Y
6 Evans	Y	Y	N
7 *Myers*	Y	Y	N
8 *Deckard*	Y	Y	Y
9 Hamilton	Y	Y	Y
10 Sharp	Y	Y	Y
11 Jacobs	N	N	N
IOWA			
1 *Leach*	Y	Y	Y
2 *Tauke*	Y	N	Y
3 *Evans*	Y	N	N
4 Smith	Y	Y	Y
5 Harkin	N	N	N
6 Bedell	Y	Y	Y

Democrats   *Republicans*

	5 6 7		5 6 7		5 6 7		5 6 7

KANSAS
1 Roberts — Y N Y
2 Jeffries — Y N N
3 Winn — Y Y Y
4 Glickman — Y Y Y
5 Whittaker — Y Y Y

KENTUCKY
1 Hubbard — Y Y N
2 Natcher — Y Y Y
3 Mazzoli — Y Y Y
4 Snyder — Y Y Y
5 Rogers — Y Y Y
6 Hopkins — Y Y Y
7 Perkins — Y Y Y

LOUISIANA
1 Livingston — Y Y Y
2 Boggs — Y Y Y
3 Tauzin — Y Y N
4 Roemer — Y Y Y
5 Huckaby — Y N N
6 Moore — Y N N
7 Breaux — Y Y N
8 Long — Y Y Y

MAINE
1 Emery — Y ? Y
2 Snowe — Y Y Y

MARYLAND
1 Dyson — Y Y N
2 Long — Y ? Y
3 Mikulski — ? Y N
4 Holt — Y Y Y
5 Spellman* —
6 Byron — Y Y N
7 Mitchell — ? Y Y
8 Barnes — Y Y Y

MASSACHUSETTS
1 Conte — Y Y Y
2 Boland — Y Y Y
3 Early — Y Y N
4 Frank — Y Y Y
5 Shannon — Y Y Y
6 Mavroules — Y Y Y
7 Markey — Y ? Y
8 O'Neill —
9 Moakley — Y Y Y
10 Heckler — Y Y Y
11 Donnelly — Y Y Y
12 Studds — Y Y Y

MICHIGAN
1 Conyers — Y Y Y
2 Pursell — Y Y Y
3 Wolpe — Y Y Y
4 Vacancy
5 Sawyer — Y Y Y
6 Dunn — Y Y N
7 Kildee — Y Y Y
8 Traxler — Y Y Y
9 Vander Jagt — Y Y N
10 Albosta — Y Y Y
11 Davis — Y Y Y
12 Bonior — Y Y Y
13 Crockett — Y Y Y
14 Hertel — Y Y N
15 Ford — ? Y Y
16 Dingell — Y Y Y
17 Brodhead — Y Y Y
18 Blanchard — Y Y Y
19 Broomfield — Y Y Y

MINNESOTA
1 Erdahl — Y N Y
2 Hagedorn — Y Y Y
3 Frenzel — Y Y Y
4 Vento — ? Y Y
5 Sabo — N Y Y
6 Weber — Y Y Y
7 Stangeland — Y Y Y
8 Oberstar — Y Y Y

MISSISSIPPI
1 Whitten — Y Y Y
2 Bowen — Y Y Y
3 Montgomery — Y Y Y
4 Hinson — ? ? ?
5 Lott — Y Y Y

MISSOURI
1 Clay — ? Y N
2 Young — Y Y N
3 Gephardt — Y Y Y

4 Skelton — Y Y Y
5 Bolling — Y Y Y
6 Coleman — Y Y Y
7 Taylor — Y Y Y
8 Bailey — Y Y Y
9 Volkmer — ? ? X
10 Emerson — Y Y Y

MONTANA
1 Williams — ? Y Y
2 Marlenee — Y Y Y

NEBRASKA
1 Bereuter — Y Y Y
2 Daub — Y Y Y
3 Smith — Y Y Y

NEVADA
AL Santini — Y Y N

NEW HAMPSHIRE
1 D'Amours — Y Y N
2 Gregg — ? ? #

NEW JERSEY
1 Florio — Y Y Y
2 Hughes — Y Y N
3 Howard — ? ? #
4 Smith — Y N Y
5 Fenwick — Y Y Y
6 Forsythe — N Y Y
7 Roukema — Y Y Y
8 Roe — Y Y Y
9 Hollenbeck — Y Y Y
10 Rodino — Y Y Y
11 Minish — Y Y Y
12 Rinaldo — Y Y Y
13 Courter — Y Y Y
14 Guarini — Y Y Y
15 Dwyer — Y Y Y

NEW MEXICO
1 Lujan — Y N N
2 Skeen — Y Y Y

NEW YORK
1 Carney — Y N N
2 Downey — Y Y Y
3 Carman — Y Y N
4 Lent — Y ? Y
5 McGrath — ? N N
6 LeBoutillier — Y Y Y
7 Addabbo — Y Y Y
8 Rosenthal — ? ? ?
9 Ferraro — Y Y N
10 Biaggi — Y ? Y
11 Scheuer — Y Y Y
12 Chisholm — ? Y Y
13 Solarz — Y Y Y
14 Richmond — Y Y Y
15 Zeferetti — ? ? X
16 Schumer — Y Y Y
17 Molinari — ? N N
18 Green — Y Y Y
19 Rangel — ? ? #
20 Weiss — Y Y Y
21 Garcia — Y Y Y
22 Bingham — Y Y Y
23 Peyser — Y Y Y
24 Ottinger — P Y N
25 Fish — Y Y Y
26 Gilman — Y Y Y
27 McHugh — Y Y Y
28 Stratton — Y Y Y
29 Solomon — N N X
30 Martin — Y Y Y
31 Mitchell — Y Y Y
32 Wortley — Y ? Y
33 Lee — Y N Y
34 Horton — Y Y Y
35 Conable — Y Y Y
36 LaFalce — Y Y Y
37 Nowak — Y Y Y
38 Kemp — Y Y Y
39 Lundine — ? ? ?

NORTH CAROLINA
1 Jones — Y ? Y
2 Fountain — ? N N
3 Whitley — ? Y Y
4 Andrews — ? ? ?
5 Neal — Y N N
6 Johnston — Y Y N
7 Rose — ? ? ?
8 Hefner — Y Y Y

9 Martin — Y Y Y
10 Broyhill — Y Y Y
11 Hendon — Y Y N

NORTH DAKOTA
AL Dorgan — Y Y Y

OHIO
1 Gradison — Y Y Y
2 Luken — Y Y Y
3 Hall — ? ? ?
4 Guyer — Y Y Y
5 Latta — Y Y Y
6 McEwen — Y Y Y
7 Brown — Y ? Y
8 Kindness — Y N Y
9 Weber — Y Y Y
10 Miller — Y Y N
11 Stanton — Y Y Y
12 Shamansky — Y Y Y
13 Pease — Y Y Y
14 Seiberling — Y Y Y
15 Wylie — Y Y Y
16 Regula — Y Y Y
17 Ashbrook — Y N N
18 Applegate — ? Y N
19 Williams — Y Y Y
20 Oakar — Y Y Y
21 Stokes — Y Y Y
22 Eckart — Y Y N
23 Mottl — Y Y N

OKLAHOMA
1 Jones — Y Y Y
2 Synar — Y Y Y
3 Watkins — Y N N
4 McCurdy — Y Y N
5 Edwards — Y Y Y
6 English — Y Y N

OREGON
1 AuCoin — ? Y N
2 Smith — Y N N
3 Wyden — Y Y N
4 Weaver — Y Y N

PENNSYLVANIA
1 Foglietta — Y Y Y
2 Gray — Y Y Y
3 Lederer — ? ? ?
4 Dougherty — Y Y Y
5 Schulze — Y Y Y
6 Yatron — Y N N
7 Edgar — ? Y N
8 Coyne, J. — Y Y Y
9 Shuster — Y Y Y
10 McDade — Y Y Y
11 Nelligan — Y N Y
12 Murtha — Y Y Y
13 Coughlin — N N Y
14 Coyne, W. — Y Y Y
15 Ritter — Y Y Y
16 Walker — N N Y
17 Ertel — Y Y Y
18 Walgren — Y Y Y
19 Goodling — N Y Y
20 Gaydos — Y Y N
21 Bailey — Y Y Y
22 Murphy — Y N N
23 Clinger — Y Y Y
24 Marks — Y Y Y
25 Atkinson — Y N N

RHODE ISLAND
1 St Germain — Y Y Y
2 Schneider — Y Y Y

SOUTH CAROLINA
1 Hartnett — Y Y Y
2 Spence — Y Y N
3 Derrick — Y ? N
4 Campbell — Y Y Y
5 Holland — Y Y Y
6 Napier — ? Y Y

SOUTH DAKOTA
1 Daschle — Y Y N
2 Roberts — Y N N

TENNESSEE
1 Quillen — Y Y Y
2 Duncan — Y Y Y
3 Bouquard — Y Y N
4 Gore — Y Y Y
5 Boner — Y Y N
6 Beard — Y Y Y

7 Jones — Y Y N
8 Ford — Y Y Y

TEXAS
1 Hall, S. — Y Y N
2 Wilson — Y Y Y
3 Collins — Y N N
4 Hall, R. — Y N N
5 Mattox — Y Y N
6 Gramm — Y ? Y
7 Archer — ? Y Y
8 Fields — Y Y N
9 Brooks — Y Y N
10 Pickle — Y Y Y
11 Leath — Y N N
12 Wright — Y Y Y
13 Hightower — Y Y Y
14 Patman — Y N N
15 de la Garza — Y N N
16 White — Y Y Y
17 Stenholm — Y Y Y
18 Leland — Y Y ?
19 Hance — Y Y Y
20 Gonzalez — Y Y Y
21 Loeffler — Y Y Y
22 Paul — Y N N
23 Kazen — Y N N
24 Frost — Y Y Y

UTAH
1 Hansen — Y Y N
2 Marriott — Y Y Y

VERMONT
AL Jeffords — Y Y Y

VIRGINIA
1 Trible — Y Y Y
2 Whitehurst — ? Y Y
3 Bliley — Y Y Y
4 Daniel, R. — Y N Y
5 Daniel, D. — Y N Y
6 Butler — Y Y Y
7 Robinson — Y N Y
8 Parris — Y Y Y
9 Wampler — Y N Y
10 Wolf — Y Y Y

WASHINGTON
1 Pritchard — Y Y Y
2 Swift — Y Y Y
3 Bonker — Y Y Y
4 Morrison — ? Y Y
5 Foley — Y Y Y
6 Dicks — Y Y Y
7 Lowry — Y Y Y

WEST VIRGINIA
1 Mollohan — Y Y Y
2 Benedict — Y Y Y
3 Staton — Y Y N
4 Rahall — Y Y #

WISCONSIN
1 Aspin — Y Y Y
2 Kastenmeier — Y Y N
3 Gunderson — Y Y N
4 Zablocki — Y Y Y
5 Reuss — ? Y Y
6 Petri — Y Y Y
7 Obey — ? Y N
8 Roth — Y Y N
9 Sensenbrenner — Y N N

WYOMING
AL Cheney — Y Y Y

Rep. Spellman not sworn in and therefore ineligible for CQ votes 5-7.

Democrats   *Republicans*

KEY

Y Voted for (yea).
Paired for.
+ Announced for.
N Voted against (nay).
X Paired against.
- Announced against.
P Voted "present."
C Voted "present" to avoid possible conflict of interest.
? Did not vote or otherwise make a position known.

8. HR 31. Cash Discount Act. Annunzio, D-Ill., motion to suspend the rules and pass the bill to repeal the existing 5 percent maximum limit on discounts merchants may offer customers for cash purchases and to extend for three years, until Feb. 27, 1984, the existing prohibition on surcharges for purchases by credit card. Motion agreed to 372-4: R 167-1; D 205-3 (ND 137-3; SD 68-0), Feb. 24, 1981. A two-thirds majority vote (251 in this case) is required for passage under suspension of the rules.

9. H Res 13. House Select Committee on Narcotics Abuse. Adoption of the resolution to establish a 19-member House Select Committee on Narcotics Abuse and Control for the 97th Congress. Adopted 276-101: R 104-56; D 172-45 (ND 112-34; SD 60-11), Feb. 25, 1981.

	8	9
ALABAMA		
1 Edwards	Y	N
2 Dickinson	Y	Y
3 Nichols	Y	Y
4 Bevill	Y	Y
5 Flippo	Y	Y
6 Smith	?	N
7 Shelby	Y	Y
ALASKA		
AL Young	?	?
ARIZONA		
1 Rhodes	?	Y
2 Udall	?	?
3 Stump	Y	Y
4 Rudd	Y	Y
ARKANSAS		
1 Alexander	Y	N
2 Bethune	Y	N
3 Hammerschmidt	Y	Y
4 Anthony	Y	Y
CALIFORNIA		
1 Chappie	Y	N
2 Clausen	Y	Y
3 Matsui	Y	Y
4 Fazio	Y	Y
5 Burton, J.	Y	Y
6 Burton, P.	Y	?
7 Miller	Y	N
8 Dellums	Y	Y
9 Stark	Y	Y
10 Edwards	Y	Y
11 Lantos	Y	Y
12 McCloskey	Y	N
13 Mineta	Y	Y
14 Shumway	Y	N
15 Coelho	?	Y
16 Panetta	Y	Y
17 Pashayan	Y	?
18 Thomas	Y	Y
19 Lagomarsino	Y	Y
20 Goldwater	Y	Y
21 Fiedler	Y	Y
22 Moorhead	Y	Y
23 Beilenson	Y	N
24 Waxman	Y	Y
25 Roybal	Y	Y
26 Rousselot	Y	?
27 Dornan	Y	Y
28 Dixon	?	Y
29 Hawkins	Y	Y
30 Danielson	Y	Y
31 Dymally	Y	Y
32 Anderson	Y	Y
33 Grisham	Y	?
34 Lungren	Y	Y
35 Dreier	?	Y
36 Brown	Y	Y
37 Lewis	?	?
38 Patterson	Y	N
39 Dannemeyer	Y	Y
40 Badham	?	?
41 Lowery	Y	?
42 Hunter	Y	Y
43 Burgener	?	?
COLORADO		
1 Schroeder	Y	N
2 Wirth	Y	N
3 Kogovsek	Y	Y
4 Brown	Y	N

	8	9
5 Kramer	Y	N
CONNECTICUT		
1 Cotter	?	N
2 Gejdenson	?	Y
3 DeNardis	Y	Y
4 McKinney	Y	Y
5 Ratchford	Y	Y
6 Moffett	Y	N
DELAWARE		
AL Evans	Y	?
FLORIDA		
1 Hutto	?	Y
2 Fuqua	Y	Y
3 Bennett	Y	Y
4 Chappell	Y	Y
5 McCollum	Y	Y
6 Young	Y	Y
7 Gibbons	Y	N
8 Ireland	Y	Y
9 Nelson	Y	Y
10 Bafalis	Y	Y
11 Mica	Y	Y
12 Shaw	Y	Y
13 Lehman	Y	N
14 Pepper	?	Y
15 Fascell	Y	Y
GEORGIA		
1 Ginn	Y	Y
2 Hatcher	Y	Y
3 Brinkley	Y	Y
4 Levitas	Y	Y
5 Fowler	Y	Y
6 Gingrich	Y	N
7 McDonald	Y	Y
8 Evans	Y	Y
9 Jenkins	Y	Y
10 Barnard	Y	Y
HAWAII		
1 Heftel	Y	N
2 Akaka	Y	Y
IDAHO		
1 Craig	?	N
2 Hansen	Y	N
ILLINOIS		
1 Washington	Y	?
2 Savage	?	?
3 Russo	Y	Y
4 Derwinski	Y	?
5 Fary	Y	Y
6 Hyde	Y	?
7 Collins	Y	Y
8 Rostenkowski	Y	Y
9 Yates	Y	N
10 Porter	Y	Y
11 Annunzio	Y	Y
12 Crane, P.	Y	N
13 McClory	Y	Y
14 Erlenborn	Y	N
15 Corcoran	Y	N
16 Martin	Y	N
17 O'Brien	?	Y
18 Michel	Y	Y
19 Railsback	Y	Y
20 Findley	Y	Y
21 Madigan	Y	Y
22 Crane, D.	Y	N
23 Price	Y	Y
24 Simon	?	Y
INDIANA		
1 Benjamin	Y	N
2 Fithian	Y	Y
3 Hiler	Y	X
4 Coats	Y	N
5 Hillis	Y	?
6 Evans	Y	N
7 Myers	Y	N
8 Deckard	Y	Y
9 Hamilton	Y	N
10 Sharp	Y	N
11 Jacobs	Y	N
IOWA		
1 Leach	Y	Y
2 Tauke	Y	N
3 Evans	Y	N
4 Smith	Y	Y
5 Harkin	Y	Y
6 Bedell	Y	N

Democrats   *Republicans*

	8	9			8	9			8	9			8	9
KANSAS			4 Skelton	Y	Y	9 Martin	Y	N	7 Jones	Y	Y
1 Roberts	Y	Y	5 Bolling	Y	Y	10 Broyhill	Y	N	8 Ford	Y	Y
2 Jeffries	Y	Y	6 Coleman	Y	Y	11 Hendon	Y	Y	**TEXAS**		
3 Winn	Y	Y	7 Taylor	Y	Y	**NORTH DAKOTA**			1 Hall, S.	Y	N
4 Glickman	Y	N	8 Bailey	Y	N	AL Dorgan	Y	Y	2 Wilson	?	?
5 Whittaker	Y	N	9 Volkmer	Y	Y	**OHIO**			3 Collins	Y	N
KENTUCKY			10 Emerson	Y	N	1 Gradison	Y	Y	4 Hall, R.	?	?
1 Hubbard	Y	Y	**MONTANA**			2 Luken	Y	Y	5 Mattox	Y	?
2 Natcher	Y	Y	1 Williams	Y	Y	3 Hall	Y	Y	6 Gramm	Y	N
3 Mazzoli	Y	N	2 Marlenee	Y	N	4 Guyer	Y	Y	7 Archer	Y	Y
4 Snyder	Y	Y	**NEBRASKA**			5 Latta	Y	Y	8 Fields	Y	Y
5 Rogers	Y	Y	1 Bereuter	Y	Y	6 McEwen	Y	Y	9 Brooks	Y	Y
6 Hopkins	Y	Y	2 Daub	Y	Y	7 Brown	Y	?	10 Pickle	Y	N
7 Perkins	Y	Y	3 Smith	Y	Y	8 Kindness	Y	N	11 Leath	Y	Y
LOUISIANA			**NEVADA**			9 Weber	Y	N	12 Wright	Y	Y
1 Livingston	Y	Y	AL Santini	Y	N	10 Miller	Y	N	13 Hightower	Y	Y
2 Boggs	Y	#	**NEW HAMPSHIRE**			11 Stanton	Y	Y	14 Patman	?	Y
3 Tauzin	Y	Y	1 D'Amours	Y	N	12 Shamansky	?	N	15 de la Garza	Y	#
4 Roemer	Y	N	2 Gregg	Y	N	13 Pease	Y	Y	16 White	Y	Y
5 Huckaby	Y	Y	**NEW JERSEY**			14 Seiberling	Y	Y	17 Stenholm	Y	Y
6 Moore	Y	N	1 Florio	Y	Y	15 Wylie	Y	?	18 Leland	?	#
7 Breaux	Y	Y	2 Hughes	Y	N	16 Regula	Y	Y	19 Hance	Y	Y
8 Long	?	?	3 Howard	Y	Y	17 Ashbrook	Y	Y	20 Gonzalez	Y	Y
MAINE			4 Smith	Y	Y	18 Applegate	Y	Y	21 Loeffler	Y	Y
1 Emery	Y	Y	5 Fenwick	Y	N	19 Williams	Y	Y	22 Paul	Y	N
2 Snowe	Y	Y	6 Forsythe	Y	N	20 Oakar	Y	Y	23 Kazen	Y	Y
MARYLAND			7 Roukema	Y	N	21 Stokes	Y	Y	24 Frost	Y	Y
1 Dyson	Y	Y	8 Roe	Y	?	22 Eckart	Y	N	**UTAH**		
2 Long	Y	N	9 Hollenbeck	Y	Y	23 Mottl	Y	N	1 Hansen	Y	N
3 Mikulski	Y	?	10 Rodino	Y	Y	**OKLAHOMA**			2 Marriott	?	?
4 Holt	?	N	11 Minish	Y	Y	1 Jones	Y	N	**VERMONT**		
5 Vacancy*			12 Rinaldo	Y	Y	2 Synar	Y	N	AL Jeffords	Y	Y
6 Byron	Y	Y	13 Courter	Y	Y	3 Watkins	Y	Y	**VIRGINIA**		
7 Mitchell	Y	Y	14 Guarini	Y	Y	4 McCurdy	Y	Y	1 Trible	Y	?
8 Barnes	?	Y	15 Dwyer	Y	Y	5 Edwards	?	?	2 Whitehurst	Y	Y
MASSACHUSETTS			**NEW MEXICO**			6 English	Y	Y	3 Bliley	Y	N
1 Conte	Y	Y	1 Lujan	Y	N	**OREGON**			4 Daniel, R.	Y	Y
2 Boland	Y	Y	2 Skeen	Y	N	1 AuCoin	Y	N	5 Daniel, D.	Y	N
3 Early	Y	N	**NEW YORK**			2 Smith	Y	N	6 Butler	Y	Y
4 Frank	N	N	1 Carney	Y	?	3 Wyden	?	N	7 Robinson	Y	N
5 Shannon	N	Y	2 Downey	Y	Y	4 Weaver	?	?	8 Parris	Y	Y
6 Mavroules	?	Y	3 Carman	Y	Y	**PENNSYLVANIA**			9 Wampler	Y	Y
7 Markey	?	Y	4 Lent	Y	Y	1 Foglietta	?	Y	10 Wolf	Y	Y
8 O'Neill			5 McGrath	Y	Y	2 Gray	Y	?	**WASHINGTON**		
9 Moakley	Y	Y	6 LeBoutillier	Y	N	3 Lederer	?	?	1 Pritchard	Y	Y
10 Heckler	?	N	7 Addabbo	Y	Y	4 Dougherty	Y	Y	2 Swift	N	N
11 Donnelly	Y	Y	8 Rosenthal	Y	Y	5 Schulze	?	?	3 Bonker	?	?
12 Studds	Y	N	9 Ferraro	Y	Y	6 Yatron	Y	Y	4 Morrison	Y	Y
MICHIGAN			10 Biaggi	?	Y	7 Edgar	Y	N	5 Foley	Y	Y
1 Conyers	Y	Y	11 Scheuer	Y	Y	8 Coyne, J.	Y	Y	6 Dicks	Y	Y
2 Pursell	?	?	12 Chisholm	?	?	9 Shuster	?	Y	7 Lowry	Y	Y
3 Wolpe	Y	Y	13 Solarz	Y	?	10 McDade	Y	Y	**WEST VIRGINIA**		
4 Vacancy			14 Richmond	Y	Y	11 Nelligan	?	Y	1 Mollohan	Y	Y
5 Sawyer	Y	N	15 Zeferetti	Y	Y	12 Murtha	Y	Y	2 Benedict	Y	Y
6 Dunn	Y	N	16 Schumer	Y	Y	13 Coughlin	Y	Y	3 Staton	Y	Y
7 Kildee	Y	Y	17 Molinari	Y	Y	14 Coyne, W.	Y	Y	4 Rahall	Y	Y
8 Traxler	Y	?	18 Green	?	Y	15 Ritter	Y	Y	**WISCONSIN**		
9 Vander Jagt	Y	?	19 Rangel	?	Y	16 Walker	N	?	1 Aspin	Y	Y
10 Albosta	?	Y	20 Weiss	Y	Y	17 Ertel	Y	Y	2 Kastenmeier	Y	Y
11 Davis	Y	Y	21 Garcia	Y	Y	18 Walgren	Y	N	3 Gunderson	?	N
12 Bonior	Y	Y	22 Bingham	Y	Y	19 Goodling	Y	N	4 Zablocki	Y	Y
13 Crockett	Y	?	23 Peyser	Y	Y	20 Gaydos	Y	Y	5 Reuss	Y	Y
14 Hertel	Y	Y	24 Ottinger	Y	Y	21 Bailey	Y	Y	6 Petri	Y	Y
15 Ford	Y	Y	25 Fish	Y	Y	22 Murphy	Y	Y	7 Obey	?	?
16 Dingell	?	Y	26 Gilman	Y	Y	23 Clinger	Y	N	8 Roth	Y	?
17 Brodhead	Y	N	27 McHugh	Y	Y	24 Marks	Y	Y	9 Sensenbrenner	Y	N
18 Blanchard	Y	Y	28 Stratton	Y	Y	25 Atkinson	Y	Y	**WYOMING**		
19 Broomfield	Y	Y	29 Solomon	Y	?	**RHODE ISLAND**			AL Cheney	?	?
MINNESOTA			30 Martin	Y	Y	1 St Germain	Y	Y			
1 Erdahl	Y	Y	31 Mitchell	Y	Y	2 Schneider	Y	Y			
2 Hagedorn	?	?	32 Wortley	Y	N	**SOUTH CAROLINA**					
3 Frenzel	Y	N	33 Lee	?	Y	1 Hartnett	Y	N			
4 Vento	Y	?	34 Horton	Y	Y	2 Spence	Y	Y			
5 Sabo	Y	Y	35 Conable	Y	Y	3 Derrick	Y	Y			
6 Weber	Y	X	36 LaFalce	Y	Y	4 Campbell	Y	?			
7 Stangeland	Y	Y	37 Nowak	Y	Y	5 Holland	?	Y			
8 Oberstar	Y	N	38 Kemp	Y	Y	6 Napier	Y	Y			
MISSISSIPPI			39 Lundine	Y	Y	**SOUTH DAKOTA**					
1 Whitten	Y	Y	**NORTH CAROLINA**			1 Daschle	Y	N			
2 Bowen	Y	Y	1 Jones	?	?	2 Roberts	Y	N			
3 Montgomery	?	Y	2 Fountain	Y	Y	**TENNESSEE**					
4 Hinson	?	?	3 Whitley	Y	Y	1 Quillen	Y	Y			
5 Lott	Y	N	4 Andrews	Y	Y	2 Duncan	Y	Y			
MISSOURI			5 Neal	Y	Y	3 Bouquard	Y	Y			
1 Clay	?	?	6 Johnston	Y	X	4 Gore	Y	Y			
2 Young	Y	Y	7 Rose	Y	Y	5 Boner	Y	Y			
3 Gephardt	Y	Y	8 Hefner	Y	Y	6 Beard	Y	Y			

The seat held by Rep. Spellman was declared vacant by the House Feb. 24, 1981.

Democrats   **Republicans**

KEY

Y   Voted for (yea).
Paired for.
+   Announced for.
N   Voted against (nay)
X   Paired against.
-   Announced against.
P   Voted "present."
C   Voted "present" to avoid possible conflict of interest.
?   Did not vote or otherwise make a position known.

10. H Res 67. House Abscam Investigation. Adoption of the resolution to authorize the House Committee on Standards of Official Conduct to conduct a complete investigation to determine whether the FBI's "Abscam" investigation of official corruption found improper conduct by House members, officers or employees, and to grant the committee additional powers to conduct its investigation. Adopted 390-1: R 170-0; D 220-1 (ND 151-0; SD 69-1), March 4, 1981.

	10
ALABAMA	
1 *Edwards*	Y
2 *Dickinson*	Y
3 Nichols	Y
4 Bevill	Y
5 Flippo	Y
6 *Smith*	?
7 Shelby	Y
ALASKA	
AL *Young*	Y
ARIZONA	
1 *Rhodes*	Y
2 Udall	Y
3 Stump	Y
4 *Rudd*	?
ARKANSAS	
1 Alexander	Y
2 *Bethune*	Y
3 *Hammerschmidt*	Y
4 Anthony	Y
CALIFORNIA	
1 *Chappie*	Y
2 *Clausen*	Y
3 Matsui	Y
4 Fazio	Y
5 Burton, J.	Y
6 Burton, P.	Y
7 Miller	?
8 Dellums	Y
9 Stark	Y
10 Edwards	Y
11 Lantos	Y
12 *McCloskey*	Y
13 Mineta	Y
14 *Shumway*	Y
15 Coelho	Y
16 Panetta	Y
17 *Pashayan*	Y
18 *Thomas*	Y
19 *Lagomarsino*	Y
20 *Goldwater*	Y
21 *Fiedler*	Y
22 *Moorhead*	Y
23 Beilenson	Y
24 Waxman	Y
25 Roybal	Y
26 *Rousselot*	Y
27 *Dornan*	Y
28 Dixon	Y
29 Hawkins	Y
30 Danielson	Y
31 Dymally	Y
32 Anderson	Y
33 *Grisham*	Y
34 *Lungren*	Y
35 *Dreier*	Y
36 Brown	Y
37 *Lewis*	Y
38 Patterson	Y
39 *Dannemeyer*	Y
40 *Badham*	Y
41 *Lowery*	Y
42 *Hunter*	Y
43 *Burgener*	Y
COLORADO	
1 Schroeder	Y
2 Wirth	Y
3 Kogovsek	Y
4 *Brown*	Y

	10
5 *Kramer*	Y
CONNECTICUT	
1 Cotter	Y
2 Gejdenson	Y
3 *DeNardis*	Y
4 *McKinney*	Y
5 Ratchford	Y
6 Moffett	Y
DELAWARE	
AL *Evans*	?
FLORIDA	
1 Hutto	Y
2 Fuqua	Y
3 Bennett	Y
4 Chappell	Y
5 *McCollum*	Y
6 *Young*	Y
7 Gibbons	Y
8 Ireland	Y
9 Nelson	Y
10 *Bafalis*	Y
11 Mica	Y
12 *Shaw*	Y
13 Lehman	Y
14 Pepper	Y
15 Fascell	Y
GEORGIA	
1 Ginn	Y
2 Hatcher	Y
3 Brinkley	Y
4 Levitas	Y
5 Fowler	Y
6 *Gingrich*	Y
7 McDonald	Y
8 Evans	Y
9 Jenkins	Y
10 Barnard	Y
HAWAII	
1 Heftel	Y
2 Akaka	Y
IDAHO	
1 *Craig*	Y
2 *Hansen*	Y
ILLINOIS	
1 Washington	Y
2 Savage	?
3 Russo	Y
4 *Derwinski*	Y
5 Fary	Y
6 *Hyde*	Y
7 Collins	Y
8 Rostenkowski	Y
9 Yates	Y
10 *Porter*	+
11 Annunzio	Y
12 *Crane, P.*	?
13 *McClory*	Y
14 *Erlenborn*	Y
15 *Corcoran*	Y
16 *Martin*	?
17 O'Brien	+
18 *Michel*	Y
19 *Railsback*	?
20 *Findley*	Y
21 *Madigan*	?
22 *Crane, D.*	Y
23 Price	Y
24 Simon	Y
INDIANA	
1 Benjamin	Y
2 Fithian	Y
3 *Hiler*	Y
4 *Coats*	Y
5 *Hillis*	?
6 Evans	Y
7 *Myers*	Y
8 *Deckard*	Y
9 Hamilton	Y
10 Sharp	Y
11 Jacobs	Y
IOWA	
1 *Leach*	?
2 *Tauke*	Y
3 *Evans*	Y
4 Smith	Y
5 Harkin	Y
6 Bedell	Y

Democrats   *Republicans*

	10			10			10			10
KANSAS			4 Skelton	Y		9 Martin	Y		7 Jones	Y
1 Roberts	Y		5 Bolling	Y		10 Broyhill	Y		8 Ford	Y
2 Jeffries	Y		6 Coleman	Y		11 Hendon	Y		**TEXAS**	
3 Winn	Y		7 Taylor	Y		**NORTH DAKOTA**			1 Hall, S.	Y
4 Glickman	Y		8 Bailey	Y		AL Dorgan	Y		2 Wilson	Y
5 Whittaker	Y		9 Volkmer	Y		**OHIO**			3 Collins	Y
KENTUCKY			10 Emerson	Y		1 Gradison	Y		4 Hall, R.	Y
1 Hubbard	Y		**MONTANA**			2 Luken	Y		5 Mattox	Y
2 Natcher	Y		1 Williams	Y		3 Hall	Y		6 Gramm	Y
3 Mazzoli	Y		2 Marlenee	Y		4 Guyer	Y		7 Archer	Y
4 Snyder	Y		**NEBRASKA**			5 Latta	Y		8 Fields	?
5 Rogers	Y		1 Bereuter	Y		6 McEwen	Y		9 Brooks	Y
6 Hopkins	Y		2 Daub	Y		7 Brown	Y		10 Pickle	Y
7 Perkins	?		3 Smith	Y		8 Kindness	Y		11 Leath	Y
LOUISIANA			**NEVADA**			9 Weber	Y		12 Wright	Y
1 Livingston	Y		AL Santini	Y		10 Miller	Y		13 Hightower	?
2 Boggs	Y		**NEW HAMPSHIRE**			11 Stanton	Y		14 Patman	Y
3 Tauzin	Y		1 D'Amours			12 Shamansky	Y		15 de la Garza	Y
4 Roemer	Y		2 Gregg	Y		13 Pease	Y		16 White	Y
5 Huckaby	?		**NEW JERSEY**			14 Seiberling	Y		17 Stenholm	Y
6 Moore	Y		1 Florio	Y		15 Wylie	Y		18 Leland	Y
7 Breaux	?		2 Hughes	Y		16 Regula	Y		19 Hance	Y
8 Long	?		3 Howard	Y		17 Ashbrook	Y		20 Gonzalez	N
MAINE			4 Smith	Y		18 Applegate	Y		21 Loeffler	Y
1 Emery	Y		5 Fenwick	Y		19 Williams	Y		22 Paul	Y
2 Snowe	Y		6 Forsythe	Y		20 Oakar	Y		23 Kazen	Y
MARYLAND			7 Roukema	Y		21 Stokes	Y		24 Frost	Y
1 Dyson	Y		8 Roe	Y		22 Eckart	Y		**UTAH**	
2 Long	?		9 Hollenbeck	Y		23 Mottl	Y		1 Hansen	Y
3 Mikulski	Y		10 Rodino	Y		**OKLAHOMA**			2 Marriott	Y
4 Holt	Y		11 Minish	Y		1 Jones	Y		**VERMONT**	
5 Vacancy			12 Rinaldo	Y		2 Synar	Y		AL Jeffords	Y
6 Byron	Y		13 Courter	Y		3 Watkins	Y		**VIRGINIA**	
7 Mitchell	Y		14 Guarini	Y		4 McCurdy	?		1 Trible	Y
8 Barnes			15 Dwyer	Y		5 Edwards	Y		2 Whitehurst	Y
MASSACHUSETTS			**NEW MEXICO**			6 English	Y		3 Bliley	Y
1 Conte	Y		1 Lujan	Y		**OREGON**			4 Daniel, R.	Y
2 Boland	Y		2 Skeen	Y		1 AuCoin	Y		5 Daniel, D.	Y
3 Early	Y		**NEW YORK**			2 Smith	Y		6 Butler	Y
4 Frank	Y		1 Carney	Y		3 Wyden	Y		7 Robinson	Y
5 Shannon	Y		2 Downey	Y		4 Weaver	Y		8 Parris	Y
6 Mavroules	Y		3 Carman	Y		**PENNSYLVANIA**			9 Wampler	Y
7 Markey	?		4 Lent	Y		1 Foglietta	Y		10 Wolf	Y
8 O'Neill			5 McGrath	Y		2 Gray	Y		**WASHINGTON**	
9 Moakley	Y		6 LeBoutillier	?		3 Lederer	?		1 Pritchard	?
10 Heckler	Y		7 Addabbo	?		4 Dougherty	?		2 Swift	Y
11 Donnelly	Y		8 Rosenthal	?		5 Schulze	Y		3 Bonker	Y
12 Studds	Y		9 Ferraro	Y		6 Yatron	Y		4 Morrison	Y
MICHIGAN			10 Biaggi	Y		7 Edgar	?		5 Foley	Y
1 Conyers	Y		11 Scheuer	Y		8 Coyne, J.	Y		6 Dicks	Y
2 Pursell	?		12 Chisholm	Y		9 Shuster	Y		7 Lowry	Y
3 Wolpe	Y		13 Solarz	Y		10 McDade	Y		**WEST VIRGINIA**	
4 Vacancy			14 Richmond	Y		11 Nelligan	Y		1 Mollohan	Y
5 Sawyer	Y		15 Zeferetti	Y		12 Murtha	Y		2 Benedict	Y
6 Dunn	Y		16 Schumer	Y		13 Coughlin	Y		3 Staton	Y
7 Kildee	Y		17 Molinari	Y		14 Coyne, W.	Y		4 Rahall	Y
8 Traxler	Y		18 Green	Y		15 Ritter	Y		**WISCONSIN**	
9 Vander Jagt	?		19 Rangel	?		16 Walker	Y		1 Aspin	Y
10 Albosta	?		20 Weiss	Y		17 Ertel	Y		2 Kastenmeier	Y
11 Davis	Y		21 Garcia	Y		18 Walgren	Y		3 Gunderson	Y
12 Bonior	Y		22 Bingham	Y		19 Goodling	Y		4 Zablocki	Y
13 Crockett	Y		23 Peyser	Y		20 Gaydos	Y		5 Reuss	Y
14 Hertel	Y		24 Ottinger	Y		21 Bailey	Y		6 Petri	Y
15 Ford	?		25 Fish	?		22 Murphy	Y		7 Obey	Y
16 Dingell	Y		26 Gilman	Y		23 Clinger	Y		8 Roth	Y
17 Brodhead	Y		27 McHugh	Y		24 Marks	Y		9 Sensenbrenner	Y
18 Blanchard	Y		28 Stratton	Y		25 Atkinson	Y		**WYOMING**	
19 Broomfield	Y		29 Solomon	Y		**RHODE ISLAND**			AL Cheney	Y
MINNESOTA			30 Martin	Y		1 St Germain	Y			
1 Erdahl	Y		31 Mitchell	Y		2 Schneider	Y			
2 Hagedorn	Y		32 Wortley	Y		**SOUTH CAROLINA**				
3 Frenzel	Y		33 Lee	Y		1 Hartnett	Y			
4 Vento	?		34 Horton	Y		2 Spence	Y			
5 Sabo	Y		35 Conable	Y		3 Derrick	Y			
6 Weber	Y		36 LaFalce	Y		4 Campbell	Y			
7 Stangeland	Y		37 Nowak	Y		5 Holland	Y			
8 Oberstar	Y		38 Kemp	Y		6 Napier	Y			
MISSISSIPPI			39 Lundine	Y		**SOUTH DAKOTA**				
1 Whitten	Y		**NORTH CAROLINA**			1 Daschle	Y			
2 Bowen	Y		1 Jones	?		2 Roberts	Y			
3 Montgomery	Y		2 Fountain	Y		**TENNESSEE**				
4 Hinson	?		3 Whitley	Y		1 Quillen	?			
5 Lott	?		4 Andrews	Y		2 Duncan	Y			
MISSOURI			5 Neal	Y		3 Bouquard	Y			
1 Clay	Y		6 Johnston	Y		4 Gore	Y			
2 Young	Y		7 Rose	Y		5 Boner	?			
3 Gephardt	Y		8 Hefner	Y		6 Beard	Y			

Democrats   *Republicans*

KEY		11	

Y Voted for (yea).
Paired for.
+ Announced for.
N Voted against (nay)
X Paired against.
- Announced against.
P Voted "present."
C Voted "present" to avoid possible conflict of interest.
? Did not vote or otherwise make a position known.

11. HR 2166. Oil Industry Antitrust Exemption. Sharp, D-Ind., motion to suspend the rules and pass the bill to extend through Sept. 30, 1981, the limited antitrust exemptions for oil companies that participate in the programs of the International Energy Agency. Motion agreed to 373-0: R 164-0; D 209-0 (ND 141-0; SD 68-0), March 10, 1981. A "yea" was a vote supporting the president's position. A two-thirds majority vote (249 in this case) is required for passage under suspension of the rules.

		11				11
ALABAMA				5 *Kramer*	Y	
1 *Edwards*	Y			**CONNECTICUT**		
2 *Dickinson*	Y			1 Cotter	Y	
3 Nichols	Y			2 Gejdenson	Y	
4 Bevill	Y			3 *DeNardis*	Y	
5 Flippo	Y			4 *McKinney*	?	
6 *Smith*	Y			5 Ratchford	Y	
7 Shelby	Y			6 Moffett	Y	
ALASKA				**DELAWARE**		
AL *Young*	Y			AL *Evans*	Y	
ARIZONA				**FLORIDA**		
1 *Rhodes*	Y			1 Hutto	Y	
2 Udall	Y			2 Fuqua	Y	
3 Stump	Y			3 Bennett	Y	
4 *Rudd*	Y			4 Chappell	Y	
ARKANSAS				5 *McCollum*	Y	
1 Alexander	Y			6 *Young*	Y	
2 *Bethune*	Y			7 Gibbons	Y	
3 *Hammerschmidt*	Y			8 Ireland	Y	
4 Anthony	Y			9 Nelson	Y	
CALIFORNIA				10 *Bafalis*	Y	
1 *Chappie*	Y			11 Mica	Y	
2 *Clausen*	Y			12 *Shaw*	Y	
3 Matsui	Y			13 Lehman	Y	
4 Fazio	?			14 Pepper	Y	
5 Burton, J.	Y			15 Fascell	Y	
6 Burton, P.	Y			**GEORGIA**		
7 Miller	Y			1 Ginn	Y	
8 Dellums	Y			2 Hatcher	Y	
9 Stark	Y			3 Brinkley	Y	
10 Edwards	Y			4 Levitas	Y	
11 Lantos	Y			5 Fowler	Y	
12 *McCloskey*	Y			6 *Gingrich*	?	
13 Mineta	Y			7 McDonald	Y	
14 *Shumway*	Y			8 Evans	Y	
15 Coelho	?			9 Jenkins	Y	
16 Panetta	Y			10 Barnard	Y	
17 *Pashayan*	Y			**HAWAII**		
18 *Thomas*	Y			1 Heftel	Y	
19 *Lagomarsino*	Y			2 Akaka	Y	
20 *Goldwater*	Y			**IDAHO**		
21 *Fiedler*	Y			1 *Craig*	Y	
22 *Moorhead*	Y			2 *Hansen*	Y	
23 Beilenson	Y			**ILLINOIS**		
24 Waxman	?			1 Washington	P	
25 Roybal	Y			2 Savage	?	
26 *Rousselot*	Y			3 Russo	Y	
27 *Dornan*	Y			4 *Derwinski*	Y	
28 Dixon	Y			5 Fary	Y	
29 Hawkins	Y			6 *Hyde*	Y	
30 Danielson	Y			7 Collins	Y	
31 Dymally	P			8 Rostenkowski	Y	
32 Anderson	Y			9 Yates	Y	
33 *Grisham*	Y			10 *Porter*	Y	
34 *Lungren*	Y			11 Annunzio	Y	
35 *Dreier*	?			12 *Crane, P.*	?	
36 Brown	Y			13 *McClory*	+	
37 *Lewis*	?			14 *Erlenborn*	Y	
38 Patterson	Y			15 *Corcoran*	Y	
39 *Dannemeyer*	Y			16 *Martin*	Y	
40 *Badham*	?			17 *O'Brien*	Y	
41 *Lowery*	Y			18 *Michel*	Y	
42 *Hunter*	Y			19 *Railsback*	Y	
43 *Burgener*	Y			20 *Findley*	Y	
COLORADO				21 *Madigan*	?	
1 Schroeder	Y			22 *Crane, D.*	Y	
2 Wirth	Y			23 Price	Y	
3 Kogovsek	Y			24 Simon	Y	
4 *Brown*	Y			**INDIANA**		
				1 Benjamin	Y	
				2 Fithian	Y	
				3 *Hiler*	Y	
				4 *Coats*	Y	
				5 *Hillis*	Y	
				6 Evans	?	
				7 *Myers*	Y	
				8 *Deckard*	Y	
				9 Hamilton	Y	
				10 Sharp	Y	
				11 Jacobs	Y	
				IOWA		
				1 *Leach*	Y	
				2 *Tauke*	Y	
				3 *Evans*	Y	
				4 Smith	Y	
				5 Harkin	Y	
				6 Bedell	?	

Democrats   *Republicans*

	11
KANSAS	
1 *Roberts*	?
2 *Jeffries*	Y
3 *Winn*	Y
4 Glickman	Y
5 *Whittaker*	Y
KENTUCKY	
1 Hubbard	Y
2 Natcher	Y
3 Mazzoli	?
4 *Snyder*	Y
5 *Rogers*	Y
6 *Hopkins*	Y
7 Perkins	Y
LOUISIANA	
1 *Livingston*	Y
2 Boggs	Y
3 Tauzin	?
4 Roemer	Y
5 Huckaby	?
6 *Moore*	Y
7 Breaux	Y
8 Long	?
MAINE	
1 *Emery*	Y
2 *Snowe*	Y
MARYLAND	
1 Dyson	Y
2 Long	Y
3 Mikulski	Y
4 *Holt*	?
5 Vacancy	
6 Byron	Y
7 Mitchell	Y
8 Barnes	Y
MASSACHUSETTS	
1 *Conte*	Y
2 Boland	Y
3 Early	Y
4 Frank	Y
5 Shannon	Y
6 Mavroules	Y
7 Markey	Y
8 O'Neill	
9 Moakley	Y
10 *Heckler*	?
11 Donnelly	Y
12 Studds	Y
MICHIGAN	
1 Conyers	Y
2 *Pursell*	Y
3 Wolpe	Y
4 Vacancy	
5 *Sawyer*	Y
6 *Dunn*	Y
7 Kildee	Y
8 Traxler	Y
9 *Vander Jagt*	?
10 Albosta	Y
11 *Davis*	?
12 Bonior	Y
13 Crockett	Y
14 Hertel	?
15 Ford	Y
16 Dingell	Y
17 Brodhead	Y
18 Blanchard	Y
19 *Broomfield*	Y
MINNESOTA	
1 *Erdahl*	Y
2 *Hagedorn*	Y
3 *Frenzel*	?
4 Vento	Y
5 Sabo	Y
6 *Weber*	Y
7 *Stangeland*	Y
8 Oberstar	Y
MISSISSIPPI	
1 Whitten	Y
2 Bowen	Y
3 Montgomery	Y
4 *Hinson*	?
5 *Lott*	Y
MISSOURI	
1 Clay	Y
2 Young	Y
3 Gephardt	Y

	11
4 Skelton	Y
5 Bolling	Y
6 *Coleman*	Y
7 *Taylor*	Y
8 *Bailey*	Y
9 Volkmer	Y
10 *Emerson*	Y
MONTANA	
1 Williams	Y
2 *Marlenee*	Y
NEBRASKA	
1 *Bereuter*	Y
2 *Daub*	Y
3 *Smith*	Y
NEVADA	
AL Santini	Y
NEW HAMPSHIRE	
1 D'Amours	?
2 *Gregg*	Y
NEW JERSEY	
1 Florio	Y
2 Hughes	Y
3 Howard	Y
4 Smith	Y
5 Fenwick	Y
6 *Forsythe*	Y
7 *Roukema*	Y
8 Roe	Y
9 *Hollenbeck*	Y
10 Rodino	Y
11 Minish	Y
12 *Rinaldo*	Y
13 *Courter*	Y
14 Guarini	?
15 Dwyer	Y
NEW MEXICO	
1 *Lujan*	Y
2 *Skeen*	?
NEW YORK	
1 *Carney*	Y
2 Downey	?
3 *Carman*	Y
4 *Lent*	Y
5 *McGrath*	Y
6 *LeBoutillier*	Y
7 Addabbo	Y
8 Rosenthal	?
9 Ferraro	Y
10 Biaggi	Y
11 Scheuer	?
12 Chisholm	?
13 Solarz	Y
14 Richmond	Y
15 Zeferetti	?
16 Schumer	Y
17 *Molinari*	Y
18 *Green*	Y
19 Rangel	Y
20 Weiss	Y
21 Garcia	Y
22 Bingham	Y
23 Peyser	Y
24 Ottinger	Y
25 *Fish*	Y
26 *Gilman*	Y
27 McHugh	Y
28 Stratton	Y
29 *Solomon*	Y
30 *Martin*	Y
31 *Mitchell*	Y
32 *Wortley*	?
33 *Lee*	Y
34 *Horton*	?
35 *Conable*	?
36 LaFalce	Y
37 Nowak	Y
38 *Kemp*	Y
39 Lundine	Y
NORTH CAROLINA	
1 Jones	?
2 Fountain	Y
3 Whitley	Y
4 Andrews	?
5 Neal	Y
6 *Johnston*	Y
7 Rose	Y
8 Hefner	Y

	11
9 *Martin*	Y
10 *Broyhill*	Y
11 *Hendon*	Y
NORTH DAKOTA	
AL Dorgan	Y
OHIO	
1 *Gradison*	Y
2 Luken	?
3 Hall	Y
4 *Guyer*	Y
5 *Latta*	Y
6 *McEwen*	Y
7 *Brown*	Y
8 *Kindness*	Y
9 *Weber*	Y
10 *Miller*	Y
11 *Stanton*	Y
12 Shamansky	Y
13 Pease	Y
14 Seiberling	Y
15 *Wylie*	Y
16 *Regula*	Y
17 *Ashbrook*	Y
18 Applegate	Y
19 *Williams*	Y
20 Oakar	Y
21 Stokes	?
22 Eckart	Y
23 Mottl	Y
OKLAHOMA	
1 Jones	Y
2 Synar	Y
3 Watkins	Y
4 McCurdy	?
5 *Edwards*	?
6 English	Y
OREGON	
1 AuCoin	Y
2 *Smith*	Y
3 Wyden	Y
4 Weaver	Y
PENNSYLVANIA	
1 Foglietta	?
2 Gray	Y
3 Lederer	?
4 *Dougherty*	Y
5 *Schulze*	Y
6 Yatron	Y
7 Edgar	Y
8 *Coyne, J.*	Y
9 *Shuster*	Y
10 *McDade*	Y
11 *Nelligan*	?
12 Murtha	Y
13 *Coughlin*	Y
14 Coyne, W.	Y
15 *Ritter*	Y
16 *Walker*	Y
17 Ertel	Y
18 Walgren	Y
19 *Goodling*	Y
20 Gaydos	Y
21 Bailey	Y
22 Murphy	Y
23 *Clinger*	Y
24 *Marks*	Y
25 Atkinson	Y
RHODE ISLAND	
1 St Germain	Y
2 *Schneider*	?
SOUTH CAROLINA	
1 *Hartnett*	Y
2 *Spence*	Y
3 Derrick	Y
4 *Campbell*	Y
5 Holland	Y
6 *Napier*	Y
SOUTH DAKOTA	
1 Daschle	Y
2 *Roberts*	?
TENNESSEE	
1 *Quillen*	?
2 *Duncan*	Y
3 Bouquard	Y
4 Gore	Y
5 Boner	Y
6 *Beard*	Y

	11
7 Jones	Y
8 Ford	Y
TEXAS	
1 Hall, S.	Y
2 Wilson	?
3 *Collins*	Y
4 Hall, R.	Y
5 Mattox	Y
6 Gramm	Y
7 *Archer*	?
8 *Fields*	Y
9 Brooks	?
10 Pickle	?
11 Leath	Y
12 Wright	Y
13 Hightower	Y
14 Patman	Y
15 de la Garza	Y
16 White	Y
17 Stenholm	Y
18 Leland	Y
19 Hance	Y
20 Gonzalez	Y
21 *Loeffler*	Y
22 *Paul*	Y
23 Kazen	Y
24 Frost	Y
UTAH	
1 *Hansen*	Y
2 *Marriott*	Y
VERMONT	
AL *Jeffords*	Y
VIRGINIA	
1 *Trible*	Y
2 *Whitehurst*	Y
3 *Bliley*	Y
4 *Daniel, R.*	Y
5 Daniel, D.	Y
6 *Butler*	?
7 *Robinson*	Y
8 *Parris*	Y
9 *Wampler*	Y
10 *Wolf*	Y
WASHINGTON	
1 *Pritchard*	Y
2 Swift	?
3 Bonker	Y
4 *Morrison*	Y
5 Foley	Y
6 Dicks	Y
7 Lowry	Y
WEST VIRGINIA	
1 Mollohan	Y
2 *Benedict*	Y
3 *Staton*	Y
4 Rahall	Y
WISCONSIN	
1 Aspin	?
2 Kastenmeier	Y
3 *Gunderson*	Y
4 Zablocki	Y
5 Reuss	Y
6 *Petri*	Y
7 Obey	Y
8 *Roth*	Y
9 *Sensenbrenner*	Y
WYOMING	
AL *Cheney*	Y

Democrats   *Republicans*

KEY

Y Voted for (yea).
Paired for.
+ Announced for.
N Voted against (nay)
X Paired against.
- Announced against.
P Voted "present."
C Voted "present" to avoid possible conflict of interest.
? Did not vote or otherwise make a position known.

12. H Res 115. House Committee Funds. Wright, D-Texas, amendment to authorize for calendar year 1981 a total of $39,605,373 for investigations and studies to be conducted by House committees (other than the Budget and Appropriations committees) and for computer services, a reduction of 10 percent from the $43,602,118 authorized by the House for 1980. Adopted 407-2: R 178-0; D 229-2 (ND 155-2; SD 74-0), March 25, 1981.

13. H Res 115. House Committee Funds. Frenzel, R-Minn., motion to recommit the resolution to the House Administration Committee with instructions to reduce the amount authorized in 1981 for investigations and studies to be conducted by House committees (other than the Budget and Appropriations committees) and for computer services provided by the House Information Systems (HIS) to 90 percent of what was spent by those committees and by the HIS for these functions in 1980. Motion rejected 184-225: R 179-0; D 5-225 (ND 2-153; SD 3-72), March 25, 1981.

14. H Res 115. House Committee Funds. Adoption of the resolution to authorize for calendar year 1981 a total of $39,605,373 for investigations and studies to be conducted by House committees other than the Budget and Appropriations committees and for computer services — $1,183,680 for the Select Aging Committee, $1,184,840 for Agriculture, $952,223 for Armed Services, $2,414,919 for Banking, $275,187 for District of Columbia, $2,565,448 for Education and Labor, $3,750,000 for Energy and Commerce, $1,800,119 for Foreign Affairs, $2,229,402 for Government Operations, $1,219,000 for House Administration, $938,700 for Permanent Select Intelligence, $1,219,615 for Interior, $1,350,410 for Judiciary, $1,581,241 for Merchant Marine, $540,000 for Select Narcotics Abuse, $902,500 for Post Office, $1,806,373 for Public Works, $530,738 for Rules, $1,820,928 for Science and Technology, $776,000 for Small Business, $450,000 for Standards of Official Conduct, $352,490 for Veterans' Affairs, $2,252,000 for Ways and Means and $7,509,560 for the House Information Systems. Adopted 231-171: R 10-168; D 221-3 (ND 151-1; SD 70-2), March 25, 1981.

15. H J Res 182. Vietnam-Era Veterans Day. Passage of the joint resolution to designate April 26, 1981, as National Recognition Day for Veterans of the Vietnam-Era. Passed 391-0: R 173-0; D 218-0 (ND 147-0; SD 71-0), March 26, 1981.

	12	13	14	15
ALABAMA				
1 *Edwards*	Y	Y	N	Y
2 *Dickinson*	Y	Y	N	?
3 Nichols	Y	N	Y	Y
4 Bevill	Y	N	Y	Y
5 Flippo	Y	N	Y	Y
6 *Smith*	Y	Y	N	Y
7 Shelby	Y	N	Y	Y
ALASKA				
AL *Young*	?	?	?	?
ARIZONA				
1 *Rhodes*	Y	Y	N	Y
2 Udall	Y	N	Y	Y
3 Stump	Y	N	Y	Y
4 *Rudd*	Y	Y	N	Y
ARKANSAS				
1 Alexander	Y	N	Y	?
2 *Bethune*	Y	Y	N	Y
3 *Hammerschmidt*	Y	Y	Y	Y
4 Anthony	Y	N	Y	Y
CALIFORNIA				
1 *Chappie*	Y	Y	?	?
2 *Clausen*	Y	Y	Y	Y
3 Matsui	Y	N	Y	Y
4 Fazio	Y	N	Y	Y
5 Burton, J.	Y	N	Y	Y
6 Burton, P.	N	N	?	Y
7 Miller	Y	N	Y	Y
8 Dellums	Y	N	Y	Y
9 Stark	Y	N	Y	Y
10 Edwards	Y	N	Y	?
11 Lantos	Y	N	Y	?
12 *McCloskey*	Y	Y	N	Y
13 Mineta	Y	N	Y	Y
14 *Shumway*	Y	Y	N	Y
15 Coelho	Y	N	Y	Y
16 Panetta	Y	N	Y	Y
17 *Pashayan*	Y	Y	N	Y
18 *Thomas*	Y	Y	N	Y
19 *Lagomarsino*	Y	Y	N	Y
20 *Goldwater*	Y	Y	Y	Y
21 *Fiedler*	Y	Y	N	Y
22 *Moorhead*	Y	Y	N	Y
23 Beilenson	Y	N	Y	Y
24 Waxman	Y	N	Y	Y
25 Roybal	Y	N	Y	Y
26 *Rousselot*	Y	Y	N	Y
27 *Dornan*	Y	Y	N	Y
28 Dixon	Y	N	Y	Y
29 Hawkins	Y	N	Y	Y
30 Danielson	Y	N	Y	+
31 Dymally	Y	N	Y	Y
32 Anderson	Y	N	Y	Y
33 *Grisham*	Y	Y	N	Y
34 *Lungren*	Y	Y	N	Y
35 *Dreier*	Y	Y	N	Y
36 Brown	Y	N	Y	?
37 *Lewis*	Y	Y	N	?
38 Patterson	Y	N	Y	Y
39 *Dannemeyer*	Y	Y	N	?
40 *Badham*	Y	Y	N	Y
41 *Lowery*	Y	Y	N	Y
42 *Hunter*	Y	Y	N	?
43 *Burgener*	Y	Y	N	Y
COLORADO				
1 Schroeder	Y	N	Y	Y
2 Wirth	Y	N	Y	Y
3 Kogovsek	Y	N	Y	Y
4 *Brown*	Y	Y	N	Y

	12	13	14	15
5 *Kramer*	Y	Y	N	Y
CONNECTICUT				
1 Cotter	?	?	?	?
2 Gejdenson	Y	N	Y	Y
3 *DeNardis*	Y	Y	N	+
4 *McKinney*	Y	Y	N	Y
5 Ratchford	Y	N	Y	Y
6 Moffett	Y	N	Y	?
DELAWARE				
AL *Evans*	Y	Y	N	Y
FLORIDA				
1 Hutto	Y	N	Y	Y
2 Fuqua	Y	N	Y	Y
3 Bennett	Y	N	Y	Y
4 Chappell	Y	N	Y	Y
5 *McCollum*	Y	Y	N	Y
6 *Young*	Y	Y	N	Y
7 Gibbons	?	?	?	?
8 Ireland	Y	N	Y	Y
9 Nelson	Y	N	Y	Y
10 *Bafalis*	Y	Y	N	Y
11 Mica	?	N	Y	Y
12 *Shaw*	Y	Y	N	Y
13 Lehman	Y	N	Y	Y
14 Pepper	Y	N	+	?
15 Fascell	Y	N	Y	Y
GEORGIA				
1 Ginn	Y	N	Y	Y
2 Hatcher	Y	N	Y	Y
3 Brinkley	Y	N	Y	Y
4 Levitas	Y	N	Y	Y
5 Fowler	Y	N	Y	Y
6 *Gingrich*	Y	Y	N	Y
7 McDonald	Y	Y	N	Y
8 Evans	Y	N	Y	Y
9 Jenkins	Y	N	Y	Y
10 Barnard	Y	N	Y	Y
HAWAII				
1 Heftel	Y	N	Y	Y
2 Akaka	Y	N	Y	Y
IDAHO				
1 *Craig*	Y	Y	N	Y
2 *Hansen*	Y	Y	N	Y
ILLINOIS				
1 Washington	Y	N	?	Y
2 Savage	Y	N	Y	Y
3 Russo	Y	N	Y	Y
4 *Derwinski*	Y	Y	N	Y
5 Fary	Y	N	Y	Y
6 *Hyde*	Y	Y	N	Y
7 Collins	Y	N	Y	Y
8 Rostenkowski	Y	N	Y	Y
9 Yates	Y	N	Y	Y
10 *Porter*	Y	Y	N	Y
11 Annunzio	Y	N	Y	Y
12 *Crane, P.*	Y	Y	N	Y
13 *McClory*	Y	Y	N	Y
14 *Erlenborn*	Y	Y	N	Y
15 *Corcoran*	Y	Y	N	Y
16 *Martin*	Y	Y	N	Y
17 *O'Brien*	Y	Y	N	Y
18 *Michel*	Y	Y	N	Y
19 *Railsback*	Y	Y	N	Y
20 *Findley*	Y	Y	N	Y
21 *Madigan*	Y	?	?	?
22 *Crane, D.*	Y	Y	N	Y
23 Price	Y	N	Y	Y
24 Simon	Y	N	Y	Y
INDIANA				
1 Benjamin	Y	N	Y	Y
2 Fithian	Y	N	Y	Y
3 *Hiler*	Y	Y	N	Y
4 *Coats*	Y	Y	N	?
5 *Hillis*	Y	Y	Y	Y
6 Evans	Y	N	Y	Y
7 *Myers*	Y	Y	N	Y
8 *Deckard*	Y	Y	N	Y
9 Hamilton	Y	Y	Y	Y
10 Sharp	Y	N	Y	Y
11 Jacobs	Y	?	Y	Y
IOWA				
1 *Leach*	Y	Y	N	Y
2 *Tauke*	Y	Y	N	Y
3 *Evans*	Y	Y	N	Y
4 Smith	Y	N	Y	Y
5 Harkin	Y	N	Y	Y
6 Bedell	Y	N	Y	Y

Democrats   *Republicans*

	12	13	14	15
KANSAS				
1 *Roberts*	Y	Y	N	Y
2 *Jeffries*	Y	Y	N	Y
3 *Winn*	Y	Y	N	Y
4 Glickman	Y	N	Y	Y
5 *Whittaker*	Y	Y	N	Y
KENTUCKY				
1 Hubbard	Y	N	Y	Y
2 Natcher	Y	N	Y	Y
3 Mazzoli	Y	N	Y	Y
4 *Snyder*	Y	Y	Y	Y
5 *Rogers*	Y	Y	N	Y
6 *Hopkins*	Y	Y	N	Y
7 Perkins	Y	N	Y	Y
LOUISIANA				
1 *Livingston*	Y	Y	N	Y
2 Boggs	Y	N	Y	Y
3 Tauzin	Y	N	Y	Y
4 Roemer	Y	Y	Y	Y
5 Huckaby	Y	N	Y	Y
6 *Moore*	Y	Y	N	Y
7 Breaux	Y	N	Y	Y
8 Long	?	?	?	?
MAINE				
1 *Emery*	Y	Y	N	Y
2 *Snowe*	Y	Y	N	Y
MARYLAND				
1 Dyson	Y	N	Y	Y
2 Long	Y	N	?	Y
3 Mikulski	Y	N	Y	Y
4 *Holt*	?	?	-	Y
5 Vacancy				
6 Byron	Y	N	Y	Y
7 Mitchell	Y	N	Y	Y
8 Barnes	Y	N	Y	Y
MASSACHUSETTS				
1 *Conte*	Y	Y	N	Y
2 Boland	Y	N	Y	Y
3 Early	Y	N	Y	Y
4 Frank	Y	N	Y	Y
5 Shannon	Y	?	?	?
6 Mavroules	Y	N	Y	Y
7 Markey	Y	N	Y	Y
8 O'Neill				
9 Moakley	Y	Y	N	Y
10 *Heckler*	Y	Y	N	Y
11 Donnelly	Y	N	Y	Y
12 Studds	N	N	Y	Y
MICHIGAN				
1 Conyers	Y	N	Y	?
2 *Pursell*	Y	Y	N	Y
3 Wolpe	Y	N	Y	Y
4 Vacancy				
5 *Sawyer*	Y	Y	N	Y
6 *Dunn*	Y	Y	N	Y
7 Kildee	Y	N	Y	Y
8 Traxler	Y	N	Y	Y
9 *Vander Jagt*	?	Y	N	?
10 Albosta	Y	N	Y	Y
11 *Davis*	Y	Y	N	Y
12 Bonior	Y	N	Y	Y
13 Crockett	Y	N	Y	Y
14 Hertel	Y	N	Y	Y
15 Ford	Y	N	Y	Y
16 Dingell	Y	N	Y	Y
17 Brodhead	Y	N	Y	Y
18 Blanchard	Y	N	Y	Y
19 *Broomfield*	Y	Y	N	Y
MINNESOTA				
1 *Erdahl*	Y	Y	N	?
2 *Hagedorn*	Y	N	Y	Y
3 *Frenzel*	Y	Y	N	Y
4 Vento	Y	N	Y	Y
5 Sabo	Y	N	Y	Y
6 *Weber*	Y	Y	N	Y
7 *Stangeland*	Y	Y	N	Y
8 Oberstar	Y	N	Y	Y
MISSISSIPPI				
1 Whitten	Y	N	Y	Y
2 Bowen	Y	N	Y	?
3 Montgomery	Y	N	Y	Y
4 *Hinson*	?	?	?	?
5 *Lott*	Y	Y	N	Y
MISSOURI				
1 Clay	Y	N	Y	Y
2 Young	Y	N	Y	Y
3 Gephardt	Y	N	Y	Y
4 Skelton	Y	N	Y	Y
5 Bolling	Y	N	Y	Y
6 *Coleman*	Y	Y	N	Y
7 *Taylor*	Y	Y	N	Y
8 *Bailey*	Y	Y	N	Y
9 Volkmer	Y	N	Y	Y
10 *Emerson*	Y	Y	N	Y
MONTANA				
1 Williams	Y	N	Y	Y
2 *Marlenee*	Y	Y	N	Y
NEBRASKA				
1 *Bereuter*	Y	Y	N	Y
2 *Daub*	Y	Y	N	Y
3 *Smith*	Y	Y	N	Y
NEVADA				
AL Santini	Y	N	Y	?
NEW HAMPSHIRE				
1 D'Amours	Y	N	Y	?
2 *Gregg*	Y	Y	N	Y
NEW JERSEY				
1 Florio	Y	N	Y	?
2 Hughes	Y	N	?	Y
3 Howard	Y	N	Y	Y
4 *Smith*	Y	Y	N	Y
5 *Fenwick*	Y	Y	N	Y
6 *Forsythe*	Y	Y	Y	Y
7 *Roukema*	Y	Y	N	Y
8 Roe	Y	N	?	Y
9 *Hollenbeck*	Y	Y	N	Y
10 Rodino	Y	N	Y	Y
11 Minish	Y	N	Y	Y
12 *Rinaldo*	Y	Y	N	Y
13 *Courter*	Y	Y	N	Y
14 Guarini	Y	N	Y	Y
15 Dwyer	Y	N	Y	Y
NEW MEXICO				
1 *Lujan*	Y	Y	N	Y
2 *Skeen*	Y	Y	N	Y
NEW YORK				
1 *Carney*	Y	Y	N	Y
2 Downey	Y	N	Y	Y
3 *Carman*	Y	Y	N	Y
4 *Lent*	Y	Y	N	Y
5 *McGrath*	Y	Y	N	Y
6 *LeBoutillier*	Y	Y	N	Y
7 Addabbo	Y	N	Y	Y
8 Rosenthal	Y	N	Y	Y
9 Ferraro	+	-	+	+
10 Biaggi	Y	N	Y	Y
11 Scheuer	Y	N	Y	Y
12 Chisholm	Y	N	Y	Y
13 Solarz	Y	N	Y	Y
14 Richmond	Y	N	Y	Y
15 Zeferetti	Y	N	Y	Y
16 Schumer	Y	N	Y	Y
17 *Molinari*	Y	N	Y	Y
18 *Green*	Y	Y	N	Y
19 Rangel	?	-	+	Y
20 Weiss	Y	N	Y	Y
21 Garcia	Y	N	Y	Y
22 Bingham	Y	N	Y	Y
23 Peyser	Y	N	Y	Y
24 Ottinger	Y	N	Y	Y
25 *Fish*	?	?	?	Y
26 *Gilman*	Y	Y	N	Y
27 McHugh	Y	N	Y	Y
28 Stratton	Y	N	Y	Y
29 *Solomon*	Y	Y	N	Y
30 *Martin*	Y	Y	N	Y
31 *Mitchell*	?	Y	N	Y
32 *Wortley*	Y	Y	N	Y
33 *Lee*	Y	Y	N	Y
34 *Horton*	Y	Y	Y	Y
35 *Conable*	Y	Y	N	Y
36 LaFalce	Y	N	Y	Y
37 Nowak	Y	N	Y	Y
38 *Kemp*	Y	Y	N	Y
39 Lundine	Y	N	Y	Y
NORTH CAROLINA				
1 Jones	Y	N	Y	Y
2 Fountain	Y	N	Y	Y
3 Whitley	Y	N	Y	Y
4 Andrews	Y	N	Y	Y
5 Neal	Y	N	Y	Y
6 *Johnston*	Y	Y	N	Y
7 Rose	?	?	?	Y
8 Hefner	Y	N	Y	Y
9 *Martin*	Y	Y	N	Y
10 *Broyhill*	Y	Y	N	Y
11 *Hendon*	Y	Y	N	Y
NORTH DAKOTA				
AL Dorgan	Y	N	Y	Y
OHIO				
1 *Gradison*	Y	Y	N	Y
2 Luken	Y	N	Y	Y
3 Hall	Y	N	Y	Y
4 *Guyer*	?	?	-	?
5 *Latta*	Y	Y	N	Y
6 *McEwen*	Y	Y	N	Y
7 *Brown*	?	?	-	Y
8 *Kindness*	Y	Y	N	Y
9 *Weber*	Y	Y	N	Y
10 *Miller*	Y	Y	N	Y
11 *Stanton*	Y	Y	N	Y
12 Shamansky	Y	N	Y	Y
13 Pease	Y	N	Y	Y
14 Seiberling	Y	N	Y	+
15 *Wylie*	?	+	?	Y
16 *Regula*	Y	Y	N	Y
17 *Ashbrook*	Y	Y	N	Y
18 Applegate	Y	N	Y	Y
19 *Williams*	Y	Y	N	Y
20 Oakar	Y	N	Y	Y
21 Stokes	Y	N	Y	Y
22 Eckart	Y	N	Y	Y
23 Mottl	Y	Y	N	Y
OKLAHOMA				
1 Jones	Y	N	Y	Y
2 Synar	Y	N	Y	Y
3 Watkins	Y	N	Y	Y
4 McCurdy	Y	N	Y	Y
5 *Edwards*	Y	N	Y	Y
6 English	Y	N	Y	Y
OREGON				
1 AuCoin	?	-	+	?
2 *Smith*	Y	Y	N	Y
3 Wyden	Y	N	Y	Y
4 Weaver	Y	N	Y	Y
PENNSYLVANIA				
1 Foglietta	Y	N	Y	Y
2 Gray	Y	N	Y	Y
3 Lederer	?	?	?	?
4 *Dougherty*	Y	Y	N	Y
5 *Schulze*	Y	Y	N	Y
6 Yatron	Y	N	Y	Y
7 Edgar	Y	N	Y	Y
8 *Coyne, J.*	Y	Y	N	Y
9 *Shuster*	Y	Y	N	Y
10 *McDade*	Y	Y	N	Y
11 *Nelligan*	Y	Y	N	Y
12 Murtha	Y	N	Y	Y
13 *Coughlin*	Y	Y	N	Y
14 Coyne, W.	Y	?	Y	Y
15 *Ritter*	Y	Y	N	Y
16 *Walker*	Y	Y	N	Y
17 Ertel	Y	N	Y	Y
18 Walgren	Y	N	Y	Y
19 *Goodling*	Y	Y	N	Y
20 Gaydos	Y	N	Y	Y
21 Bailey	Y	N	Y	Y
22 Murphy	Y	N	Y	Y
23 *Clinger*	Y	Y	N	Y
24 *Marks*	?	?	?	?
25 Atkinson	Y	N	Y	Y
RHODE ISLAND				
1 St Germain	Y	N	Y	Y
2 *Schneider*	Y	Y	N	Y
SOUTH CAROLINA				
1 *Hartnett*	Y	Y	Y	Y
2 *Spence*	Y	Y	N	Y
3 Derrick	Y	N	Y	?
4 *Campbell*	Y	Y	N	Y
5 Holland	Y	N	Y	Y
6 *Napier*	Y	Y	Y	Y
SOUTH DAKOTA				
1 Daschle	Y	N	Y	Y
2 *Roberts*	Y	Y	N	Y
TENNESSEE				
1 *Quillen*	?	?	?	?
2 *Duncan*	Y	Y	N	Y
3 Bouquard	Y	N	Y	Y
4 Gore	Y	N	Y	Y
5 Boner	Y	N	Y	Y
6 *Beard*	Y	Y	N	Y
7 Jones	Y	N	Y	Y
8 Ford	Y	N	Y	Y
TEXAS				
1 Hall, S.	Y	N	Y	Y
2 Wilson	Y	N	Y	Y
3 *Collins*	Y	Y	N	Y
4 Hall, R.	Y	N	?	Y
5 Mattox	Y	N	Y	Y
6 Gramm	Y	N	Y	Y
7 *Archer*	Y	Y	N	Y
8 *Fields*	Y	Y	N	Y
9 Brooks	Y	N	Y	?
10 Pickle	Y	N	Y	Y
11 Leath	Y	N	Y	Y
12 Wright	Y	N	Y	Y
13 Hightower	Y	N	Y	Y
14 Patman	Y	N	Y	Y
15 de la Garza	Y	N	Y	Y
16 White	Y	N	?	Y
17 Stenholm	Y	N	Y	Y
18 Leland	Y	N	Y	Y
19 Hance	Y	N	Y	Y
20 Gonzalez	Y	N	Y	Y
21 *Loeffler*	Y	Y	N	Y
22 *Paul*	Y	Y	N	Y
23 Kazen	Y	N	Y	Y
24 Frost	Y	N	Y	Y
UTAH				
1 *Hansen*	Y	Y	N	Y
2 *Marriott*	?	+	?	?
VERMONT				
AL *Jeffords*	Y	Y	N	Y
VIRGINIA				
1 *Trible*	Y	Y	N	?
2 *Whitehurst*	Y	Y	N	Y
3 *Bliley*	Y	Y	N	Y
4 *Daniel, R.*	Y	Y	N	Y
5 Daniel, D.	Y	N	Y	Y
6 *Butler*	Y	Y	N	Y
7 *Robinson*	Y	Y	N	Y
8 *Parris*	Y	Y	N	Y
9 *Wampler*	?	?	?	Y
10 *Wolf*	Y	Y	N	Y
WASHINGTON				
1 *Pritchard*	Y	Y	N	Y
2 Swift	Y	N	Y	Y
3 Bonker	Y	N	Y	Y
4 *Morrison*	Y	Y	N	Y
5 Foley	Y	N	Y	Y
6 Dicks	Y	N	Y	Y
7 Lowry	Y	N	Y	Y
WEST VIRGINIA				
1 Mollohan	?	N	Y	Y
2 *Benedict*	Y	Y	N	Y
3 *Staton*	Y	Y	N	Y
4 Rahall	Y	N	Y	Y
WISCONSIN				
1 Aspin	Y	N	Y	Y
2 Kastenmeier	Y	N	Y	Y
3 *Gunderson*	Y	Y	N	Y
4 Zablocki	Y	N	Y	Y
5 Reuss	Y	N	Y	Y
6 *Petri*	Y	Y	N	Y
7 Obey	Y	N	Y	Y
8 *Roth*	Y	Y	N	Y
9 *Sensenbrenner*	Y	Y	N	Y
WYOMING				
AL *Cheney*	Y	Y	N	Y

Democrats *Republicans*

	KEY	16 17 18

KEY

Y Voted for (yea).
\# Paired for.
+ Announced for.
N Voted against (nay).
X Paired against.
- Announced against.
P Voted "present."
C Voted "present" to avoid possible conflict of interest.
? Did not vote or otherwise make a position known.

16. S 840. Justice Department Authorization. Passage of the bill to continue the authorization for the Department of Justice from April 6 to Sept. 30, 1981. Passed 368-2: R 158-2; D 210-0 (ND 140-0, SD 70-0), April 7, 1981.

17. H Con Res 55. International Year of Disabled Persons. Bonker, D-Wash., motion to suspend the rules and adopt the concurrent resolution calling on the president to implement the objectives of the International Year of Disabled Persons (1981), as proclaimed by the United Nations. Motion agreed to 364-2: R 146-1; D 218-1 (ND 148-0, SD 70-1), April 7, 1981. A two-thirds majority vote (244 in this case) is required for adoption under suspension of the rules.

18. S Con Res 17. Congressional Adjournment. Adoption of the concurrent resolution to provide for a recess of both the House and Senate from the close of business on April 10 until noon on April 27, 1981. Adopted 241-73: R 78-62; D 163-11 (ND 113-7, SD 50-4), April 8, 1981.

	16	17	18
ALABAMA			
1 *Edwards*	Y	?	Y
2 *Dickinson*	?	?	?
3 Nichols	Y	Y	Y
4 Bevill	Y	Y	?
5 Flippo	Y	Y	?
6 *Smith*	?	Y	N
7 Shelby	Y	Y	?
ALASKA			
AL *Young*	Y	Y	?
ARIZONA			
1 *Rhodes*	Y	Y	Y
2 Udall	Y	Y	Y
3 Stump	Y	Y	Y
4 *Rudd*	?	?	Y
ARKANSAS			
1 Alexander	Y	Y	Y
2 *Bethune*	Y	Y	N
3 *Hammerschmidt*	Y	Y	N
4 Anthony	Y	Y	Y
CALIFORNIA			
1 *Chappie*	?	Y	Y
2 *Clausen*	Y	Y	N
3 Matsui	Y	Y	?
4 Fazio	Y	Y	Y
5 Burton, J.	Y	Y	Y
6 Burton, P.	Y	Y	Y
7 Miller	Y	Y	?
8 Dellums	Y	Y	Y
9 Stark	Y	Y	Y
10 Edwards	Y	Y	Y
11 Lantos	Y	Y	Y
12 *McCloskey*	?	?	?
13 Mineta	Y	Y	Y
14 *Shumway*	Y	Y	Y
15 Coelho	?	Y	Y
16 Panetta	Y	Y	Y
17 *Pashayan*	?	?	?
18 *Thomas*	Y	Y	Y
19 *Lagomarsino*	Y	Y	Y
20 *Goldwater*	?	Y	Y
21 *Fiedler*	?	Y	Y
22 *Moorhead*	Y	Y	?
23 Beilenson	Y	Y	Y
24 Waxman	Y	Y	Y
25 Roybal	Y	Y	Y
26 *Rousselot*	Y	Y	N
27 *Dornan*	Y	Y	?
28 Dixon	Y	?	Y
29 Hawkins	Y	Y	Y
30 Danielson	Y	Y	+
31 Dymally	?	?	?
32 Anderson	Y	Y	N
33 *Grisham*	Y	Y	Y
34 *Lungren*	Y	+	Y
35 *Dreier*	Y	Y	Y
36 Brown	Y	Y	Y
37 *Lewis*	Y	Y	?
38 Patterson	?	Y	Y
39 *Dannemeyer*	Y	Y	N
40 *Badham*	Y	?	Y
41 *Lowery*	Y	?	Y
42 *Hunter*	Y	Y	Y
43 *Burgener*	Y	?	Y
COLORADO			
1 Schroeder	Y	Y	?
2 Wirth	Y	Y	Y
3 Kogovsek	Y	Y	Y
4 *Brown*	Y	Y	N

	16	17	18
5 *Kramer*	Y	Y	N
CONNECTICUT			
1 Cotter	?	?	?
2 Gejdenson	Y	Y	Y
3 *DeNardis*	Y	Y	?
4 *McKinney*	Y	Y	N
5 Ratchford	Y	Y	Y
6 Moffett	?	?	?
DELAWARE			
AL *Evans*	Y	Y	Y
FLORIDA			
1 Hutto	Y	Y	Y
2 Fuqua	Y	Y	?
3 Bennett	Y	Y	Y
4 Chappell	Y	Y	Y
5 *McCollum*	Y	Y	N
6 *Young*	Y	?	Y
7 Gibbons	Y	Y	Y
8 Ireland	Y	Y	?
9 Nelson	Y	Y	Y
10 *Bafalis*	Y	Y	Y
11 Mica	Y	Y	Y
12 *Shaw*	Y	Y	N
13 Lehman	Y	Y	Y
14 Pepper	Y	Y	?
15 Fascell	Y	Y	Y
GEORGIA			
1 Ginn	Y	Y	Y
2 Hatcher	Y	Y	Y
3 Brinkley	Y	Y	Y
4 Levitas	Y	Y	N
5 Fowler	Y	Y	Y
6 *Gingrich*	?	?	N
7 McDonald	Y	N	Y
8 Evans	Y	Y	?
9 Jenkins	Y	Y	Y
10 Barnard	Y	Y	?
HAWAII			
1 Heftel	Y	Y	Y
2 Akaka	Y	Y	Y
IDAHO			
1 *Craig*	Y	Y	?
2 *Hansen*	Y	Y	N
ILLINOIS			
1 Washington	Y	Y	?
2 Savage	Y	Y	Y
3 Russo	Y	Y	?
4 *Derwinski*	Y	Y	Y
5 Fary	Y	Y	Y
6 *Hyde*	Y	Y	Y
7 Collins	Y	Y	Y
8 Rostenkowski	Y	Y	Y
9 Yates	Y	Y	Y
10 *Porter*	Y	?	?
11 Annunzio	Y	Y	Y
12 *Crane, P.*	Y	Y	Y
13 *McClory*	Y	Y	Y
14 *Erlenborn*	Y	?	?
15 *Corcoran*	Y	Y	N
16 *Martin*	Y	Y	Y
17 *O'Brien*	Y	?	Y
18 *Michel*	Y	?	Y
19 *Railsback*	Y	Y	?
20 *Findley*	Y	Y	Y
21 *Madigan*	?	Y	Y
22 *Crane, D.*	Y	Y	Y
23 Price	Y	Y	Y
24 Simon	?	Y	Y
INDIANA			
1 Benjamin	Y	Y	Y
2 Fithian	Y	Y	?
3 *Hiler*	Y	?	N
4 *Coats*	Y	Y	N
5 *Hillis*	Y	Y	Y
6 Evans	Y	Y	?
7 *Myers*	?	?	Y
8 *Deckard*	?	?	N
9 Hamilton	Y	Y	Y
10 Sharp	Y	Y	Y
11 Jacobs	Y	Y	N
IOWA			
1 *Leach*	Y	Y	?
2 *Tauke*	Y	Y	?
3 *Evans*	Y	Y	N
4 Smith	Y	Y	Y
5 Harkin	Y	Y	Y
6 Bedell	Y	Y	Y

Democrats *Republicans*

	16	17	18		16	17	18		16	17	18		16	17	18
KANSAS				4 Skelton	Y	Y	Y	9 *Martin*	?	Y	?	7 Jones	?	?	?
1 *Roberts*	Y	Y	N	5 Bolling	?	?	Y	10 *Broyhill*	Y	Y	Y	8 Ford	Y	Y	Y
2 *Jeffries*	Y	Y	N	6 *Coleman*	Y	Y	Y	11 *Hendon*	Y	Y	N	**TEXAS**			
3 *Winn*	Y	Y	?	7 *Taylor*	?	?	?	**NORTH DAKOTA**				1 Hall, S.	Y	Y	Y
4 Glickman	Y	Y	Y	8 *Bailey*	?	Y	?	AL Dorgan	Y	Y	Y	2 Wilson	?	?	Y
5 *Whittaker*	Y	Y	Y	9 Volkmer	Y	Y	?	**OHIO**				3 *Collins*	N	Y	Y
KENTUCKY				10 *Emerson*	Y	Y	N	1 *Gradison*	Y	Y	?	4 Hall, R.	?	Y	?
1 Hubbard	Y	Y	N	**MONTANA**				2 Luken	Y	Y	?	5 Mattox	Y	Y	Y
2 Natcher	Y	Y	Y	1 Williams	Y	Y	N	3 Hall	Y	Y	Y	6 Gramm	Y	Y	Y
3 Mazzoli	Y	Y	?	2 *Marlenee*	Y	Y	N	4 *Guyer*	Y	Y	N	7 *Archer*	Y	Y	N
4 *Snyder*	Y	Y	Y	**NEBRASKA**				5 *Latta*	Y	Y	Y	8 *Fields*	Y	Y	?
5 *Rogers*	Y	Y	Y	1 *Bereuter*	Y	Y	?	6 *McEwen*	Y	Y	N	9 Brooks	Y	Y	Y
6 *Hopkins*	Y	Y	N	2 *Daub*	Y	Y	N	7 *Brown*	Y	Y	Y	10 Pickle	Y	Y	?
7 Perkins	Y	Y	Y	3 *Smith*	Y	+	N	8 *Kindness*	Y	Y	N	11 Leath	Y	Y	?
LOUISIANA				**NEVADA**				9 *Weber*	Y	Y	Y	12 Wright	Y	Y	Y
1 *Livingston*	Y	?	Y	AL Santini	?	Y	Y	10 *Miller*	Y	Y	N	13 Hightower	Y	Y	?
2 Boggs	Y	Y	Y	**NEW HAMPSHIRE**				11 *Stanton*	Y	Y	Y	14 Patman	Y	Y	?
3 Tauzin	?	Y	?	1 *D'Amours*	Y	Y	?	12 Shamansky	?	Y	Y	15 de la Garza	Y	Y	Y
4 Roemer	Y	Y	Y	2 *Gregg*	Y	Y	Y	13 Pease	Y	Y	Y	16 White	Y	Y	Y
5 Huckaby	?	?	?	**NEW JERSEY**				14 Seiberling	Y	Y	Y	17 Stenholm	Y	Y	Y
6 *Moore*	Y	Y	N	1 Florio	Y	Y	?	15 *Wylie*	Y	Y	Y	18 Leland	Y	?	Y
7 Breaux	Y	Y	Y	2 Hughes	Y	Y	Y	16 *Regula*	Y	Y	Y	19 Hance	Y	Y	?
8 Long	?	?	?	3 Howard	Y	Y	Y	17 *Ashbrook*	Y	Y	?	20 Gonzalez	Y	Y	Y
MAINE				4 *Smith*	Y	Y	Y	18 Applegate	Y	Y	Y	21 *Loeffler*	Y	?	Y
1 *Emery*	Y	?	?	5 *Fenwick*	Y	Y	?	19 *Williams*	Y	Y	Y	22 *Paul*	N	N	N
2 *Snowe*	Y	Y	Y	6 *Forsythe*	Y	Y	Y	20 Oakar	Y	Y	?	23 Kazen	Y	Y	Y
MARYLAND				7 *Roukema*	Y	Y	Y	21 Stokes	Y	Y	Y	24 Frost	Y	Y	?
1 Dyson	Y	Y	Y	8 Roe	?	?	?	22 Eckart	Y	Y	Y	**UTAH**			
2 Long	Y	Y	Y	9 *Hollenbeck*	Y	?	?	23 Mottl	Y	Y	?	1 *Hansen*	?	?	?
3 Mikulski	Y	Y	Y	10 Rodino	Y	Y	Y	**OKLAHOMA**				2 *Marriott*	?	?	?
4 *Holt*	Y	?	Y	11 Minish	Y	Y	Y	1 Jones	Y	Y	Y	**VERMONT**			
5 Vacancy				12 *Rinaldo*	Y	Y	N	2 Synar	Y	Y	Y	AL *Jeffords*	Y	Y	?
6 Byron	Y	Y	Y	13 *Courter*	Y	Y	N	3 Watkins	Y	Y	Y	**VIRGINIA**			
7 Mitchell	Y	Y	?	14 Guarini	?	Y	Y	4 McCurdy	Y	Y	Y	1 *Trible*	Y	Y	Y
8 Barnes	Y	Y	Y	15 Dwyer	Y	Y	Y	5 *Edwards*	Y	?	N	2 *Whitehurst*	Y	Y	Y
MASSACHUSETTS				**NEW MEXICO**				6 English	Y	Y	Y	3 *Bliley*	?	?	N
1 *Conte*	Y	Y	Y	1 *Lujan*	Y	Y	N	**OREGON**				4 *Daniel, R.*	Y	Y	Y
2 Boland	Y	Y	Y	2 *Skeen*	Y	Y	Y	1 AuCoin	Y	Y	Y	5 Daniel, D.	Y	Y	?
3 Early	Y	Y	Y	**NEW YORK**				2 *Smith*	Y	Y	?	6 *Butler*	Y	Y	N
4 Frank	Y	Y	?	1 *Carney*	Y	Y	Y	3 Wyden	Y	Y	Y	7 *Robinson*	Y	Y	N
5 Shannon	?	?	Y	2 Downey	Y	Y	Y	4 Weaver	?	?	?	8 *Parris*	Y	Y	N
6 Mavroules	Y	Y	?	3 *Carman*	Y	Y	Y	**PENNSYLVANIA**				9 *Wampler*	Y	Y	N
7 Markey	?	Y	?	4 *Lent*	Y	Y	N	1 Foglietta	Y	Y	?	10 *Wolf*	Y	Y	N
8 O'Neill				5 *McGrath*	Y	Y	?	2 Gray	Y	Y	Y	**WASHINGTON**			
9 Moakley	Y	Y	Y	6 *LeBoutillier*	Y	Y	N	3 Lederer	?	?	?	1 *Pritchard*	Y	Y	Y
10 *Heckler*	?	?	?	7 Addabbo	Y	Y	Y	4 *Dougherty*	Y	Y	?	2 Swift	Y	Y	?
11 Donnelly	Y	Y	Y	8 Rosenthal	?	?	?	5 *Schulze*	Y	Y	N	3 Bonker	Y	Y	Y
12 Studds	Y	Y	Y	9 Ferraro	Y	Y	Y	6 Yatron	Y	Y	N	4 *Morrison*	Y	Y	N
MICHIGAN				10 Biaggi	Y	Y	Y	7 Edgar	Y	?	Y	5 Foley	Y	Y	Y
1 Conyers	?	?	Y	11 Scheuer	Y	Y	Y	8 Coyne, J.	Y	Y	N	6 Dicks	Y	Y	Y
2 *Pursell*	?	?	Y	12 Chisholm	Y	Y	?	9 *Shuster*	Y	Y	Y	7 Lowry	Y	Y	Y
3 Wolpe	Y	Y	?	13 Solarz	Y	Y	Y	10 *McDade*	Y	?	Y	**WEST VIRGINIA**			
4 Vacancy				14 Richmond	Y	Y	?	11 *Nelligan*	Y	Y	N	1 Mollohan	Y	Y	Y
5 *Sawyer*	Y	Y	?	15 Zeferetti	?	Y	Y	12 Murtha	Y	Y	Y	2 *Benedict*	Y	Y	?
6 *Dunn*	Y	Y	N	16 Schumer	Y	Y	Y	13 *Coughlin*	Y	?	N	3 *Staton*	Y	Y	N
7 Kildee	Y	Y	Y	17 *Molinari*	Y	Y	Y	14 Coyne, W.	?	Y	?	4 Rahall	Y	Y	?
8 Traxler	Y	Y	Y	18 *Green*	Y	?	Y	15 *Ritter*	Y	Y	Y	**WISCONSIN**			
9 *Vander Jagt*	?	Y	?	19 Rangel	?	?	Y	16 *Walker*	Y	Y	N	1 Aspin	Y	Y	Y
10 Albosta	Y	Y	?	20 Weiss	Y	Y	Y	17 Ertel	Y	Y	Y	2 Kastenmeier	Y	Y	Y
11 *Davis*	Y	Y	Y	21 Garcia	Y	Y	Y	18 Walgren	Y	Y	Y	3 *Gunderson*	Y	Y	Y
12 Bonior	Y	Y	Y	22 Bingham	Y	Y	Y	19 *Goodling*	Y	Y	Y	4 Zablocki	Y	Y	Y
13 Crockett	Y	Y	Y	23 Peyser	Y	Y	Y	20 Gaydos	Y	Y	Y	5 Reuss	Y	Y	Y
14 Hertel	Y	Y	Y	24 Ottinger	Y	Y	?	21 Bailey	Y	Y	Y	6 *Petri*	Y	Y	N
15 Ford	?	Y	?	25 *Fish*	Y	?	?	22 Murphy	Y	Y	Y	7 Obey	Y	Y	N
16 Dingell	Y	Y	?	26 *Gilman*	Y	Y	N	23 *Clinger*	Y	Y	Y	8 *Roth*	Y	Y	?
17 Brodhead	Y	Y	Y	27 McHugh	Y	Y	Y	24 *Marks*	?	?	?	9 *Sensenbrenner*	Y	Y	N
18 Blanchard	Y	Y	Y	28 Stratton	Y	Y	?	25 Atkinson	Y	Y	N	**WYOMING**			
19 *Broomfield*	Y	Y	?	29 *Solomon*	Y	Y	N	**RHODE ISLAND**				AL *Cheney*	Y	Y	?
MINNESOTA				30 *Martin*	Y	Y	Y	1 St Germain	Y	Y	Y				
1 *Erdahl*	Y	Y	?	31 *Mitchell*	?	?	?	2 *Schneider*	+	Y	?				
2 *Hagedorn*	Y	Y	N	32 *Wortley*	Y	Y	N	**SOUTH CAROLINA**							
3 *Frenzel*	Y	Y	Y	33 *Lee*	Y	Y	N	1 *Hartnett*	?	Y	Y				
4 Vento	Y	Y	Y	34 *Horton*	Y	Y	Y	2 *Spence*	Y	Y	Y				
5 Sabo	Y	Y	?	35 *Conable*	?	Y	?	3 Derrick	?	?	?				
6 *Weber*	Y	Y	N	36 LaFalce	Y	Y	Y	4 *Campbell*	Y	?	Y				
7 *Stangeland*	Y	Y	Y	37 Nowak	Y	Y	N	5 Holland	Y	Y	?				
8 Oberstar	Y	Y	Y	38 *Kemp*	Y	Y	Y	6 *Napier*	?	?	N				
MISSISSIPPI				39 Lundine	Y	Y	Y	**SOUTH DAKOTA**							
1 Whitten	Y	Y	Y	**NORTH CAROLINA**				1 Daschle	?	?	?				
2 Bowen	Y	Y	Y	1 Jones	Y	Y	?	2 *Roberts*	Y	Y	?				
3 Montgomery	Y	Y	Y	2 Fountain	Y	Y	Y	**TENNESSEE**							
4 *Hinson*	?	?	?	3 Whitley	Y	Y	Y	1 *Quillen*	?	?	?				
5 *Lott*	Y	?	Y	4 Andrews	Y	Y	?	2 *Duncan*	Y	Y	Y				
MISSOURI				5 Neal	Y	Y	N	3 Bouquard	?	?	?				
1 Clay	?	?	?	6 *Johnston*	?	Y	N	4 Gore	Y	Y	Y				
2 Young	?	Y	?	7 Rose	Y	Y	?	5 Boner	Y	Y	Y				
3 Gephardt	Y	Y	Y	8 Hefner	Y	Y	N	6 *Beard*	?	?	?				

Democrats   *Republicans*

KEY

Y Voted for (yea).
\# Paired for.
+ Announced for.
N Voted against (nay).
X Paired against.
- Announced against.
P Voted "present."
C Voted "present" to avoid possible conflict of interest.
? Did not vote or otherwise make a position known.

19. Procedural Motion. Walker, R-Pa., motion to approve the House *Journal* of Monday, April 27. Motion agreed to 321-7: R 140-4; D 181-3 (ND 121-3, SD 60-0), April 28, 1981.

20. Procedural Motion. Weiss, D-N.Y., motion to approve the House *Journal* of Wednesday, April 29. Motion agreed to 371-12: R 163-7; D 208-5 (ND 135-5, SD 73-0), April 30, 1981.

21. H Con Res 115. Fiscal 1982 Budget Targets. Adoption of the rule (H Res 134) providing for House floor consideration of the resolution to set spending and revenue targets for fiscal 1982, revise binding budget levels for fiscal 1981 and direct House committees to cut back programs within their jurisdictions to save $15.8 billion in outlays in fiscal 1982. Adopted 328-76: R 158-16; D 170-60 (ND 103-51, SD 67-9), April 30, 1981.

	19	20	21
ALABAMA			
1 *Edwards*	Y	Y	Y
2 *Dickinson*	Y	Y	Y
3 Nichols	Y	Y	Y
4 Bevill	Y	Y	Y
5 Flippo	?	Y	Y
6 *Smith*	?	?	Y
7 Shelby	Y	Y	Y
ALASKA			
AL *Young*	Y	Y	Y
ARIZONA			
1 *Rhodes*	Y	Y	Y
2 Udall	P	?	Y
3 Stump	Y	Y	Y
4 *Rudd*	Y	Y	Y
ARKANSAS			
1 Alexander	Y	Y	Y
2 *Bethune*	Y	Y	Y
3 *Hammerschmidt*	Y	Y	Y
4 Anthony	?	Y	Y
CALIFORNIA			
1 *Chappie*	?	Y	Y
2 *Clausen*	?	Y	Y
3 Matsui	Y	Y	Y
4 Fazio	?	Y	Y
5 Burton, J.	?	?	?
6 Burton, P.	?	?	?
7 Miller	Y	?	?
8 Dellums	?	?	N
9 Stark	Y	?	\#
10 Edwards	?	Y	Y
11 Lantos	Y	?	Y
12 *McCloskey*	?	Y	Y
13 Mineta	Y	Y	Y
14 *Shumway*	Y	Y	Y
15 Coelho	Y	Y	Y
16 Panetta	Y	Y	Y
17 *Pashayan*	?	Y	Y
18 *Thomas*	Y	Y	Y
19 *Lagomarsino*	Y	Y	Y
20 *Goldwater*	?	?	Y
21 *Fiedler*	?	Y	Y
22 *Moorhead*	Y	Y	Y
23 Beilenson	Y	Y	Y
24 Waxman	Y	?	Y
25 Roybal	Y	Y	Y
26 *Rousselot*	Y	Y	N
27 *Dornan*	?	?	Y
28 Dixon	Y	Y	Y
29 Hawkins	Y	Y	N
30 Danielson	Y	Y	Y
31 Dymally	Y	Y	Y
32 Anderson	Y	Y	Y
33 *Grisham*	?	Y	Y
34 *Lungren*	?	?	?
35 *Dreier*	Y	Y	Y
36 Brown	Y	Y	Y
37 *Lewis*	Y	Y	Y
38 Patterson	Y	Y	N
39 *Dannemeyer*	Y	Y	N
40 *Badham*	Y	Y	Y
41 *Lowery*	?	Y	Y
42 *Hunter*	Y	Y	Y
43 *Burgener*	Y	Y	Y
COLORADO			
1 Schroeder	?	N	N
2 Wirth	Y	Y	Y
3 Kogovsek	Y	Y	Y
4 *Brown*	Y	Y	Y

	19	20	21
5 *Kramer*	Y	Y	Y
CONNECTICUT			
1 Cotter	?	?	?
2 Gejdenson	Y	Y	Y
3 *DeNardis*	?	?	Y
4 *McKinney*	?	?	Y
5 Ratchford	Y	Y	Y
6 Moffett	?	?	N
DELAWARE			
AL *Evans*	Y	Y	N
FLORIDA			
1 Hutto	?	Y	Y
2 Fuqua	Y	Y	Y
3 Bennett	Y	Y	Y
4 Chappell	Y	Y	Y
5 *McCollum*	Y	Y	Y
6 *Young*	Y	Y	Y
7 Gibbons	Y	Y	Y
8 Ireland	Y	Y	Y
9 Nelson	?	Y	Y
10 *Bafalis*	Y	Y	Y
11 Mica	Y	Y	Y
12 *Shaw*	Y	Y	Y
13 Lehman	Y	Y	N
14 Pepper	Y	?	Y
15 Fascell	?	Y	Y
GEORGIA			
1 Ginn	Y	Y	Y
2 Hatcher	?	Y	Y
3 Brinkley	Y	Y	Y
4 Levitas	Y	Y	N
5 Fowler	Y	Y	N
6 *Gingrich*	Y	Y	?
7 McDonald	Y	Y	N
8 Evans	?	Y	Y
9 Jenkins	Y	Y	Y
10 Barnard	Y	Y	Y
HAWAII			
1 Heftel	Y	Y	N
2 Akaka	?	Y	Y
IDAHO			
1 *Craig*	Y	Y	Y
2 *Hansen*	Y	Y	Y
ILLINOIS			
1 Washington	?	?	N
2 Savage	Y	?	?
3 Russo	Y	Y	Y
4 *Derwinski*	?	Y	N
5 Fary	Y	Y	Y
6 *Hyde*	Y	Y	Y
7 Collins	?	Y	Y
8 Rostenkowski	?	Y	Y
9 Yates	Y	Y	N
10 *Porter*	Y	Y	Y
11 Annunzio	Y	Y	Y
12 *Crane, P.*	Y	Y	Y
13 *McClory*	?	?	?
14 *Erlenborn*	Y	Y	Y
15 *Corcoran*	Y	+	Y
16 *Martin*	?	Y	Y
17 *O'Brien*	Y	Y	?
18 *Michel*	Y	Y	Y
19 *Railsback*	?	?	?
20 *Findley*	Y	Y	Y
21 *Madigan*	Y	Y	Y
22 *Crane, D.*	Y	Y	?
23 Price	Y	Y	Y
24 Simon	Y	Y	Y
INDIANA			
1 Benjamin	Y	Y	Y
2 Fithian	Y	Y	N
3 *Hiler*	Y	Y	Y
4 *Coats*	?	Y	Y
5 *Hillis*	?	Y	Y
6 Evans	?	Y	Y
7 *Myers*	?	?	?
8 *Deckard*	Y	Y	Y
9 Hamilton	Y	Y	Y
10 Sharp	Y	Y	Y
11 Jacobs	N	N	N
IOWA			
1 *Leach*	?	Y	N
2 *Tauke*	Y	Y	N
3 *Evans*	Y	N	Y
4 Smith	?	Y	N
5 Harkin	N	N	N
6 Bedell	Y	Y	N

Democrats   *Republicans*

	19	20	21
ARKANSAS			
1 *Roberts*	?	Y	Y
2 *Jeffries*	Y	Y	Y
3 *Winn*	Y	Y	Y
4 Glickman	?	Y	N
5 *Whittaker*	Y	Y	Y
KENTUCKY			
1 Hubbard	Y	Y	N
2 Natcher	Y	Y	Y
3 Mazzoli	Y	+	+
4 *Snyder*	?	Y	Y
5 *Rogers*	Y	Y	Y
6 *Hopkins*	Y	Y	Y
7 Perkins	Y	Y	N
LOUISIANA			
1 *Livingston*	Y	N	Y
2 Boggs	Y	Y	Y
3 Tauzin	?	Y	Y
4 Roemer	Y	Y	X
5 Huckaby	Y	Y	Y
6 *Moore*	Y	Y	Y
7 Breaux	?	Y	Y
8 Long	Y	Y	Y
MAINE			
1 *Emery*	?	Y	Y
2 *Snowe*	Y	Y	Y
MARYLAND			
1 Dyson	Y	Y	Y
2 Long	Y	Y	Y
3 Mikulski	Y	Y	Y
4 *Holt*	Y	Y	Y
5 Vacancy			
6 Byron	Y	Y	Y
7 Mitchell	?	N	Y
8 Barnes	Y	Y	N
MASSACHUSETTS			
1 *Conte*	Y	Y	Y
2 Boland	Y	Y	Y
3 Early	Y	Y	N
4 Frank	Y	Y	N
5 Shannon	Y	Y	Y
6 Mavroules	Y	Y	N
7 Markey	Y	Y	Y
8 O'Neill			
9 Moakley	?	Y	Y
10 *Heckler*	Y	?	N
11 Donnelly	Y	?	Y
12 Studds	Y	Y	Y
MICHIGAN			
1 Conyers	?	?	#
2 *Pursell*	Y	Y	?
3 Wolpe	Y	Y	Y
4 *Siljander****		Y	Y
5 *Sawyer*	Y	Y	Y
6 *Dunn*	Y	Y	N
7 Kildee	Y	Y	N
8 Traxler	Y	Y	Y
9 *Vander Jagt*	Y	Y	?
10 Albosta	Y	Y	?
11 *Davis*	Y	Y	?
12 Bonior	Y	Y	Y
13 Crockett	?	?	Y
14 Hertel	Y	Y	N
15 Ford	?	?	N
16 Dingell	Y	Y	Y
17 Brodhead	Y	Y	Y
18 Blanchard	?	Y	Y
19 *Broomfield*	Y	Y	Y
MINNESOTA			
1 *Erdahl*	Y	Y	Y
2 *Hagedorn*	?	Y	Y
3 *Frenzel*	Y	?	Y
4 Vento	Y	Y	N
5 Sabo	?	N	N
6 *Weber*	Y	Y	Y
7 *Stangeland*	Y	Y	Y
8 Oberstar	Y	Y	Y
MISSISSIPPI			
1 Whitten	Y	Y	Y
2 Bowen	Y	Y	Y
3 Montgomery	Y	Y	Y
4 Vacancy**			
5 *Lott*	Y	Y	Y
MISSOURI			
1 Clay	?	Y	N
2 Young	Y	Y	Y
3 Gephardt	Y	Y	Y

	19	20	21
4 Skelton	?	Y	Y
5 Bolling	Y	Y	Y
6 *Coleman*	Y	Y	Y
7 *Taylor*	Y	Y	Y
8 *Bailey*	?	Y	Y
9 Volkmer	Y	Y	Y
10 *Emerson*	Y	Y	Y
MONTANA			
1 Williams	Y	Y	Y
2 *Marlenee*	Y	Y	Y
NEBRASKA			
1 *Bereuter*	Y	Y	Y
2 *Daub*	?	Y	Y
3 *Smith*	Y	Y	Y
NEVADA			
AL Santini	?	Y	Y
NEW HAMPSHIRE			
1 D'Amours	Y	Y	Y
2 *Gregg*	Y	Y	Y
NEW JERSEY			
1 Florio	Y	Y	Y
2 Hughes	Y	Y	N
3 Howard	Y	Y	Y
4 *Smith*	Y	Y	Y
5 *Fenwick*	Y	Y	Y
6 *Forsythe*	N	N	?
7 *Roukema*	?	Y	Y
8 Roe	?	Y	X
9 *Hollenbeck*	Y	Y	N
10 Rodino	?	Y	N
11 Minish	Y	Y	Y
12 *Rinaldo*	Y	?	Y
13 *Courter*	Y	Y	Y
14 Guarini	Y	Y	Y
15 Dwyer	Y	Y	Y
NEW MEXICO			
1 *Lujan*	Y	Y	Y
2 *Skeen*	Y	Y	Y
NEW YORK			
1 *Carney*	Y	?	?
2 Downey	Y	Y	Y
3 *Carman*	?	Y	Y
4 *Lent*	Y	Y	Y
5 *McGrath*	Y	Y	Y
6 *LeBoutillier*	Y	Y	Y
7 Addabbo	Y	Y	N
8 Rosenthal	?	Y	Y
9 Ferraro	Y	Y	Y
10 Biaggi	Y	Y	N
11 Scheuer	Y	Y	N
12 Chisholm	?	?	Y
13 Solarz	Y	Y	Y
14 Richmond	Y	Y	Y
15 Zeferetti	Y	Y	Y
16 Schumer	Y	Y	N
17 *Molinari*	Y	Y	Y
18 *Green*	Y	Y	N
19 Rangel	Y	Y	N
20 Weiss	Y	Y	N
21 Garcia	?	Y	N
22 Bingham	Y	Y	N
23 Peyser	Y	Y	Y
24 Ottinger	P	P	N
25 *Fish*	Y	Y	Y
26 *Gilman*	Y	Y	N
27 McHugh	Y	Y	N
28 Stratton	Y	Y	Y
29 *Solomon*	Y	N	Y
30 *Martin*	Y	Y	Y
31 *Mitchell*	?	Y	Y
32 *Wortley*	Y	Y	Y
33 *Lee*	Y	Y	Y
34 *Horton*	Y	Y	Y
35 *Conable*	Y	Y	Y
36 LaFalce	?	Y	N
37 Nowak	Y	Y	N
38 *Kemp*	Y	?	Y
39 Lundine	P	Y	Y
NORTH CAROLINA			
1 Jones	?	?	Y
2 Fountain	Y	Y	Y
3 Whitley	Y	Y	Y
4 Andrews	Y	Y	Y
5 Neal	Y	Y	Y
6 *Johnston*	P	Y	Y
7 Rose	Y	Y	Y
8 Hefner	Y	Y	Y

	19	20	21
9 *Martin*	Y	Y	Y
10 *Broyhill*	Y	Y	Y
11 *Hendon*	Y	Y	Y
NORTH DAKOTA			
AL Dorgan	Y	Y	Y
OHIO			
1 *Gradison*	Y	Y	Y
2 Luken	?	Y	Y
3 Hall	Y	Y	Y
4 Vacancy*			
5 *Latta*	Y	Y	Y
6 *McEwen*	Y	Y	Y
7 *Brown*	Y	?	?
8 *Kindness*	Y	Y	Y
9 *Weber*	Y	Y	Y
10 *Miller*	Y	Y	Y
11 *Stanton*	?	Y	Y
12 Shamansky	Y	Y	Y
13 Pease	Y	Y	N
14 Seiberling	Y	Y	N
15 *Wylie*	?	?	?
16 *Regula*	Y	Y	Y
17 *Ashbrook*	Y	Y	Y
18 Applegate	Y	?	Y
19 *Williams*	?	Y	Y
20 Oakar	Y	Y	Y
21 Stokes	Y	Y	Y
22 Eckart	Y	Y	Y
23 Mottl	Y	Y	Y
OKLAHOMA			
1 Jones	Y	Y	Y
2 Synar	Y	Y	Y
3 Watkins	?	Y	Y
4 McCurdy	Y	Y	Y
5 *Edwards*	N	N	Y
6 English	Y	Y	Y
OREGON			
1 AuCoin	Y	Y	N
2 *Smith*	Y	Y	Y
3 Wyden	Y	Y	Y
4 Weaver	Y	?	N
PENNSYLVANIA			
1 Foglietta	?	Y	N
2 Gray	Y	Y	Y
3 Lederer	?	?	?
4 *Dougherty*	Y	Y	Y
5 *Schulze*	Y	Y	Y
6 Yatron	Y	Y	N
7 Edgar	N	?	Y
8 *Coyne, J.*	?	Y	Y
9 *Shuster*	Y	Y	Y
10 *McDade*	Y	Y	N
11 *Nelligan*	Y	Y	Y
12 Murtha	Y	Y	N
13 *Coughlin*	Y	Y	Y
14 Coyne, W.	Y	Y	Y
15 *Ritter*	Y	Y	Y
16 *Walker*	N	N	N
17 Ertel	Y	Y	N
18 Walgren	Y	Y	N
19 *Goodling*	N	N	Y
20 Gaydos	Y	Y	Y
21 Bailey	Y	Y	Y
22 Murphy	Y	Y	Y
23 *Clinger*	Y	Y	Y
24 *Marks*	Y	Y	Y
25 Atkinson	Y	Y	N
RHODE ISLAND			
1 St Germain	Y	Y	N
2 *Schneider*	Y	Y	Y
SOUTH CAROLINA			
1 *Hartnett*	?	Y	Y
2 *Spence*	Y	Y	Y
3 Derrick	Y	Y	Y
4 *Campbell*	Y	Y	Y
5 Holland	Y	Y	Y
6 *Napier*	?	Y	Y
SOUTH DAKOTA			
1 Daschle	Y	Y	Y
2 *Roberts*	Y	Y	Y
TENNESSEE			
1 *Quillen*	?	?	?
2 *Duncan*	Y	Y	Y
3 Bouquard	Y	Y	N
4 Gore	Y	Y	Y
5 Boner	?	Y	Y
6 *Beard*	Y	Y	Y

	19	20	21
7 Jones	Y	Y	Y
8 Ford	?	Y	N
TEXAS			
1 Hall, S.	Y	Y	Y
2 Wilson	?	Y	Y
3 *Collins*	Y	Y	Y
4 Hall, R.	?	Y	Y
5 Mattox	?	?	Y
6 Gramm	Y	?	Y
7 *Archer*	Y	Y	Y
8 *Fields*	Y	Y	Y
9 Brooks	Y	Y	Y
10 Pickle	Y	Y	Y
11 Leath	Y	Y	Y
12 Wright	Y	Y	Y
13 Hightower	Y	Y	Y
14 Patman	Y	Y	Y
15 de la Garza	Y	Y	Y
16 White	Y	Y	Y
17 Stenholm	Y	Y	Y
18 Leland	?	Y	N
19 Hance	Y	Y	Y
20 Gonzalez	Y	Y	Y
21 *Loeffler*	Y	Y	Y
22 *Paul*	Y	Y	Y
23 Kazen	Y	Y	Y
24 Frost	Y	Y	Y
UTAH			
1 *Hansen*	?	?	Y
2 *Marriott*	Y	Y	Y
VERMONT			
AL *Jeffords*	Y	Y	N
VIRGINIA			
1 *Trible*	Y	Y	Y
2 *Whitehurst*	?	Y	Y
3 *Bliley*	?	Y	Y
4 *Daniel, R.*	Y	Y	Y
5 Daniel, D.	Y	Y	Y
6 *Butler*	Y	Y	Y
7 *Robinson*	Y	Y	Y
8 *Parris*	?	Y	Y
9 *Wampler*	?	Y	N
10 *Wolf*	Y	Y	Y
WASHINGTON			
1 *Pritchard*	?	Y	Y
2 Swift	Y	Y	Y
3 Bonker	Y	Y	Y
4 *Morrison*	Y	Y	Y
5 Foley	Y	Y	Y
6 Dicks	Y	Y	Y
7 Lowry	Y	Y	N
WEST VIRGINIA			
1 Mollohan	Y	Y	Y
2 *Benedict*	Y	?	Y
3 Staton	Y	Y	Y
4 Rahall	Y	Y	N
WISCONSIN			
1 Aspin	Y	Y	Y
2 Kastenmeier	?	Y	N
3 *Gunderson*	Y	Y	Y
4 Zablocki	Y	Y	Y
5 Reuss	Y	?	Y
6 *Petri*	Y	Y	Y
7 Obey	Y	Y	Y
8 *Roth*	Y	Y	Y
9 *Sensenbrenner*	Y	Y	Y
WYOMING			
AL *Cheney*	?	Y	Y

* Rep. Tennyson Guyer, R-Ohio, died April 12, 1981.

** Resignation of Rep. Jon Hinson, R-Miss., became effective at the close of business April 13, 1981.

*** Rep. Mark Siljander, R-Mich., was sworn in April 28, 1981. The first vote for which he was eligible was CQ 20.

Democrats **Republicans**

22. HR 3132. Cash Discount Act. Annunzio, D-Ill., motion to suspend the rules and pass the bill to repeal the existing 5 percent ceiling on discounts merchants may offer customers for cash purchases and to extend for three years, until Feb. 27, 1984, a prohibition on surcharges for purchases by credit card. Motion agreed to 296-43: R 145-5; D 151-38 (ND 86-36, SD 65-2), May 4, 1981. A two-thirds majority vote (226 in this case) is required for passage under suspension of the rules.

23. H Con Res 115. Fiscal 1982 Budget Targets. Jones, D-Okla., motion that the House resolve itself into the Committee of the Whole for further consideration of the resolution to set spending and revenue targets for fiscal 1982, to revise binding budget levels for fiscal 1981 and to direct House committees to cut back programs within their jurisdictions to save $15.8 billion in outlays in fiscal 1982. Motion agreed to 334-2: R 149-0; D 185-2 (ND 119-2, SD 66-0), May 4, 1981.

24. H J Res 238. Constitution for the U.S. Virgin Islands. Won Pat, D-Guam, motion to suspend the rules and pass the joint resolution to approve a constitution for the U.S. Virgin Islands. Motion agreed to 408-0: R 186-0; D 222-0 (ND 151-0, SD 71-0), May 5, 1981. A two-thirds majority vote (272 in this case) is required for passage under suspension of the rules.

25. H Con Res 115. Fiscal 1982 Budget Targets. Jones, D-Okla., motion that the House resolve itself into the Committee of the Whole for further consideration of the resolution (see vote 23, above). Motion agreed to 379-3: R 177-1; D 202-2 (ND 137-2, SD 65-0), May 5, 1981.

26. H Con Res 115. Fiscal 1982 Budget Targets. Simon, D-Ill., motion that the House resolve itself into the Committee of the Whole for further consideration of the resolution (see vote 23, above). Motion agreed to 406-3: R 179-1; D 227-2 (ND 152-2, SD 75-0), May 6, 1981.

27. H Con Res 115. Fiscal 1982 Budget Targets. Fauntroy, D-D.C., substitute, to the resolution as reported by the Budget Committee, to decrease budget authority by $9.7 billion and outlays by $4.7 billion, and increase revenues by $28.8 billion, resulting in a $7.8 billion surplus for fiscal 1982. Rejected 69-356: R 0-188; D 69-168 (ND 64-96, SD 5-72), May 6, 1981. A "nay" was a vote supporting the president's position.

28. H Con Res 115. Fiscal 1982 Budget Targets. Obey, D-Wis., substitute, to the resolution as reported by the Budget Committee, to increase budget authority by $6 billion, outlays by $2 billion and revenues by $28.1 billion, resulting in a $500 million surplus for fiscal 1982. Rejected 119-303: R 1-186; D 118-117 (ND 111-48, SD 7-69), May 6, 1981. A "nay" was a vote supporting the president's position.

KEY

Y	Voted for (yea).
#	Paired for.
+	Announced for.
N	Voted against (nay).
X	Paired against.
-	Announced against.
P	Voted "present".
C	Voted "present" to avoid possible conflict of interest.
?	Did not vote or otherwise make a position known.

	22	23	24	25	26	27	28
ALABAMA							
1 *Edwards*	Y	Y	Y	Y	Y	N	N
2 *Dickinson*	?	?	Y	?	Y	N	N
3 Nichols	Y	Y	Y	Y	Y	N	?
4 Bevill	Y	Y	Y	Y	Y	N	N
5 Flippo	Y	Y	Y	Y	Y	N	N
6 *Smith*	Y	Y	Y	Y	Y	N	N
7 Shelby	Y	Y	Y	Y	Y	N	N
ALASKA							
AL *Young*	Y	Y	Y	Y	Y	N	N
ARIZONA							
1 *Rhodes*	Y	Y	?	Y	Y	N	N
2 Udall	Y	Y	Y	Y	Y	N	Y
3 *Stump*	Y	Y	Y	Y	Y	N	N
4 *Rudd*	Y	Y	Y	Y	Y	N	N
ARKANSAS							
1 Alexander	Y	Y	Y	Y	Y	N	N
2 *Bethune*	?	Y	Y	Y	Y	N	N
3 *Hammerschmidt*	Y	Y	Y	Y	Y	N	N
4 Anthony	Y	Y	Y	?	Y	N	N
CALIFORNIA							
1 *Chappie*	Y	?	Y	?	Y	N	N
2 *Clausen*	?	?	Y	Y	Y	?	N
3 Matsui	Y	Y	Y	Y	Y	N	Y
4 Fazio	Y	Y	?	?	Y	N	Y
5 Burton, J.	N	Y	Y	Y	Y	Y	Y
6 Burton, P.	N	Y	Y	Y	Y	Y	Y
7 Miller	?	?	Y	Y	Y	N	Y
8 Dellums	N	Y	Y	Y	Y	Y	Y
9 Stark	Y	Y	Y	Y	Y	Y	Y
10 Edwards	N	Y	Y	Y	Y	Y	Y
11 Lantos	Y	Y	Y	Y	Y	N	N
12 *McCloskey*	?	?	Y	Y	Y	N	N
13 Mineta	Y	Y	Y	Y	Y	N	Y
14 *Shumway*	Y	Y	Y	Y	Y	N	N
15 Coelho	Y	Y	Y	Y	Y	N	N
16 Panetta	Y	Y	Y	Y	Y	N	N
17 *Pashayan*	Y	Y	Y	Y	?	N	N
18 *Thomas*	Y	Y	Y	Y	Y	N	N
19 *Lagomarsino*	Y	Y	Y	Y	Y	N	N
20 *Goldwater*	Y	Y	Y	Y	Y	N	N
21 *Fiedler*	Y	?	Y	Y	Y	N	N
22 *Moorhead*	Y	Y	Y	Y	Y	N	?
23 Beilenson	N	Y	Y	?	Y	Y	Y
24 Waxman	Y	Y	Y	Y	Y	N	Y
25 Roybal	?	?	Y	?	Y	Y	Y
26 *Rousselot*	Y	Y	Y	Y	Y	N	N
27 *Dornan*	Y	Y	Y	Y	?	N	N
28 Dixon	Y	Y	Y	Y	Y	Y	Y
29 Hawkins	Y	Y	Y	Y	Y	N	Y
30 Danielson	Y	Y	Y	Y	Y	N	Y
31 Dymally	Y	Y	Y	Y	Y	Y	Y
32 Anderson	?	?	Y	Y	Y	N	N
33 *Grisham*	Y	Y	Y	Y	Y	N	N
34 *Lungren*	?	?	Y	Y	Y	N	N
35 *Dreier*	Y	Y	Y	Y	Y	N	N
36 Brown	Y	Y	Y	Y	Y	Y	Y
37 *Lewis*	Y	Y	Y	Y	Y	N	N
38 Patterson	Y	Y	?	?	Y	Y	Y
39 *Dannemeyer*	?	?	Y	Y	Y	N	N
40 *Badham*	?	?	Y	Y	Y	N	?
41 *Lowery*	Y	Y	Y	Y	Y	N	N
42 *Hunter*	Y	Y	Y	Y	Y	N	N
43 *Burgener*	Y	Y	Y	Y	Y	N	?
COLORADO							
1 Schroeder	Y	Y	Y	Y	Y	Y	Y
2 Wirth	?	?	?	Y	Y	N	N
3 Kogovsek	Y	Y	Y	Y	Y	N	N
4 *Brown*	Y	Y	Y	Y	Y	N	N

	22	23	24	25	26	27	28
5 *Kramer*	Y	Y	Y	Y	Y	N	N
CONNECTICUT							
1 Cotter	?	?	?	?	?	?	?
2 Gejdenson	N	Y	Y	Y	Y	N	Y
3 *DeNardis*	Y	Y	Y	Y	Y	Y	N
4 *McKinney*	?	?	Y	?	Y	N	N
5 Ratchford	N	Y	Y	Y	Y	N	Y
6 Moffett	N	?	Y	Y	Y	Y	Y
DELAWARE							
AL *Evans*	Y	Y	Y	Y	Y	N	N
FLORIDA							
1 Hutto	?	?	Y	Y	Y	N	N
2 Fuqua	Y	Y	Y	Y	Y	N	N
3 Bennett	Y	Y	Y	Y	Y	N	N
4 Chappell	Y	Y	Y	Y	Y	N	N
5 *McCollum*	Y	?	Y	Y	Y	N	N
6 *Young*	Y	Y	Y	Y	Y	N	N
7 Gibbons	Y	Y	Y	Y	Y	N	N
8 Ireland	Y	Y	?	?	Y	N	N
9 Nelson	Y	Y	Y	Y	Y	N	N
10 *Bafalis*	Y	Y	Y	Y	Y	N	N
11 Mica	?	?	Y	Y	Y	N	N
12 *Shaw*	Y	Y	Y	Y	Y	N	N
13 Lehman	Y	Y	Y	Y	Y	Y	N
14 Pepper	#	?	Y	Y	Y	Y	Y
15 Fascell	Y	Y	Y	Y	Y	N	N
GEORGIA							
1 Ginn	Y	Y	Y	Y	Y	N	N
2 Hatcher	?	?	Y	Y	Y	N	N
3 Brinkley	Y	Y	Y	Y	Y	N	N
4 Levitas	Y	Y	Y	Y	Y	N	N
5 Fowler	?	?	Y	Y	Y	N	Y
6 *Gingrich*	Y	Y	Y	Y	Y	N	N
7 McDonald	#	?	Y	Y	Y	N	N
8 Evans	Y	Y	Y	Y	Y	?	N
9 Jenkins	Y	Y	Y	Y	Y	N	N
10 Barnard	Y	Y	?	?	Y	N	N
HAWAII							
1 Heftel	?	?	Y	Y	Y	N	N
2 Akaka	Y	Y	Y	Y	Y	N	Y
IDAHO							
1 *Craig*	Y	Y	Y	Y	Y	N	N
2 *Hansen*	Y	Y	Y	Y	Y	N	N
ILLINOIS							
1 Washington	N	Y	Y	?	Y	Y	Y
2 Savage	?	?	Y	?	Y	Y	Y
3 Russo	Y	Y	Y	Y	Y	N	Y
4 *Derwinski*	Y	Y	Y	Y	Y	N	N
5 Fary	Y	Y	Y	Y	Y	N	Y
6 *Hyde*	Y	Y	Y	Y	Y	N	N
7 Collins	N	Y	Y	Y	Y	Y	Y
8 Rostenkowski	?	?	Y	Y	Y	N	N
9 Yates	N	Y	Y	Y	Y	Y	Y
10 *Porter*	Y	Y	Y	Y	Y	N	N
11 Annunzio	Y	Y	Y	Y	Y	N	N
12 *Crane, P.*	?	?	Y	Y	Y	N	N
13 *McClory*	Y	Y	Y	Y	Y	N	N
14 *Erlenborn*	?	?	Y	?	Y	N	N
15 *Corcoran*	Y	Y	Y	Y	Y	N	N
16 *Martin*	Y	Y	Y	Y	Y	N	N
17 *O'Brien*	?	?	Y	Y	Y	N	N
18 *Michel*	Y	Y	Y	Y	Y	N	N
19 *Railsback*	Y	Y	Y	Y	Y	N	N
20 *Findley*	Y	Y	Y	Y	Y	N	N
21 *Madigan*	Y	Y	Y	Y	Y	N	N
22 *Crane, D.*	?	?	Y	Y	Y	N	N
23 Price	Y	Y	Y	Y	Y	Y	Y
24 Simon	?	?	?	?	Y	Y	Y
INDIANA							
1 Benjamin	Y	Y	Y	Y	Y	N	Y
2 Fithian	Y	Y	Y	Y	Y	N	?
3 *Hiler*	Y	Y	Y	Y	Y	N	N
4 *Coats*	Y	Y	Y	Y	Y	N	N
5 *Hillis*	?	?	Y	Y	Y	N	N
6 Evans	Y	Y	Y	Y	Y	N	N
7 *Myers*	Y	Y	Y	Y	Y	N	N
8 *Deckard*	Y	Y	Y	Y	Y	N	N
9 Hamilton	Y	Y	Y	Y	Y	N	N
10 Sharp	Y	Y	Y	Y	Y	N	N
11 Jacobs	Y	Y	Y	Y	Y	N	N
IOWA							
1 *Leach*	Y	Y	Y	Y	Y	N	N
2 *Tauke*	Y	Y	Y	Y	Y	N	N
3 *Evans*	Y	Y	Y	N	N	N	N
4 Smith	Y	Y	Y	Y	Y	N	N
5 Harkin	N	Y	Y	Y	Y	Y	Y
6 Bedell	N	Y	Y	Y	Y	N	N

Democrats *Republicans*

Corresponding to Congressional Record Votes 27, 28, 29, 30, 31, 32, 33

	22	23	24	25	26	27	28
KANSAS							
1 ***Roberts***	Y	Y	Y	Y	Y	N	N
2 ***Jeffries***	Y	Y	Y	Y	Y	N	N
3 ***Winn***	Y	Y	Y	Y	Y	N	N
4 Glickman	Y	Y	Y	Y	Y	N	N
5 ***Whittaker***	Y	Y	Y	Y	Y	N	N
KENTUCKY							
1 Hubbard	?	?	Y	Y	Y	N	N
2 Natcher	Y	Y	Y	Y	Y	N	N
3 Mazzoli	Y	Y	Y	Y	Y	N	N
4 ***Snyder***	?	?	Y	Y	Y	N	N
5 ***Rogers***	Y	Y	Y	Y	?	N	N
6 ***Hopkins***	Y	Y	Y	Y	Y	N	N
7 Perkins	Y	Y	Y	Y	Y	N	Y
LOUISIANA							
1 ***Livingston***	Y	Y	Y	Y	Y	N	N
2 Boggs	Y	Y	Y	Y	Y	N	N
3 Tauzin	Y	Y	+	+	Y	N	N
4 Roemer	N	Y	?	?	Y	N	N
5 Huckaby	Y	Y	?	?	Y	N	N
6 ***Moore***	Y	Y	Y	Y	Y	N	N
7 Breaux	Y	Y	Y	Y	Y	N	N
8 Long	Y	Y	Y	?	Y	N	N
MAINE							
1 ***Emery***	Y	Y	Y	Y	Y	N	N
2 ***Snowe***	Y	Y	Y	Y	Y	N	N
MARYLAND							
1 Dyson	X	?	Y	Y	Y	N	N
2 Long	Y	Y	Y	Y	Y	N	Y
3 Mikulski	Y	Y	Y	Y	Y	Y	Y
4 ***Holt***	Y	Y	Y	Y	Y	N	N
5 Vacancy							
6 Byron	Y	Y	Y	Y	?	?	N
7 Mitchell	N	N	Y	N	N	Y	Y
8 Barnes	Y	Y	Y	Y	Y	N	Y
MASSACHUSETTS							
1 ***Conte***	Y	Y	Y	Y	Y	N	N
2 Boland	Y	Y	?	Y	Y	N	Y
3 Early	Y	Y	Y	Y	Y	N	Y
4 Frank	N	Y	Y	Y	Y	Y	Y
5 Shannon	N	Y	Y	Y	Y	N	Y
6 Mavroules	Y	Y	Y	Y	Y	N	Y
7 Markey	N	Y	Y	Y	Y	N	Y
8 O'Neill							
9 Moakley	Y	Y	Y	Y	Y	Y	Y
10 ***Heckler***	Y	Y	Y	Y	Y	N	N
11 Donnelly	?	?	Y	Y	Y	N	Y
12 Studds	N	Y	Y	Y	Y	Y	Y
MICHIGAN							
1 Conyers	N	Y	Y	Y	Y	Y	Y
2 ***Pursell***	Y	Y	Y	Y	?	N	N
3 Wolpe	N	Y	Y	Y	P	N	N
4 ***Siljander***	Y	Y	Y	Y	Y	N	N
5 ***Sawyer***	Y	Y	Y	Y	Y	N	N
6 ***Dunn***	N	Y	Y	P	Y	N	N
7 Kildee	Y	Y	Y	Y	Y	Y	Y
8 Traxler	?	?	Y	Y	Y	N	N
9 ***Vander Jagt***	Y	Y	?	?	Y	?	N
10 Albosta	Y	Y	Y	Y	Y	N	N
11 ***Davis***	Y	Y	Y	Y	Y	N	N
12 Bonior	Y	Y	Y	Y	Y	Y	Y
13 Crockett	X	Y	?	Y	Y	Y	?
14 Hertel	Y	Y	Y	Y	Y	Y	Y
15 Ford	Y	Y	Y	Y	?	Y	Y
16 Dingell	Y	Y	Y	Y	Y	N	Y
17 Brodhead	Y	Y	Y	Y	Y	Y	Y
18 Blanchard	Y	Y	Y	Y	Y	N	N
19 ***Broomfield***	Y	Y	Y	Y	Y	N	N
MINNESOTA							
1 ***Erdahl***	Y	Y	Y	Y	Y	N	N
2 ***Hagedorn***	Y	?	Y	Y	Y	N	N
3 ***Frenzel***	Y	Y	Y	Y	Y	N	N
4 Vento	Y	?	Y	Y	Y	N	Y
5 Sabo	Y	Y	Y	?	Y	Y	Y
6 ***Weber***	N	Y	Y	Y	Y	N	N
7 ***Stangeland***	Y	Y	Y	Y	Y	N	N
8 Oberstar	Y	Y	Y	Y	Y	Y	Y
MISSISSIPPI							
1 Whitten	Y	Y	Y	Y	?	N	N
2 Bowen	Y	Y	Y	Y	Y	N	N
3 Montgomery	Y	Y	Y	?	Y	N	N
4 Vacancy							
5 ***Lott***	Y	Y	Y	Y	Y	N	N
MISSOURI							
1 Clay	N	?	Y	Y	Y	Y	Y
2 Young	Y	Y	Y	Y	Y	N	N
3 Gephardt	#	?	Y	P	Y	N	N

	22	23	24	25	26	27	28
4 Skelton	Y	Y	?	?	Y	N	N
5 Bolling	Y	Y	Y	?	Y	Y	Y
6 ***Coleman***	Y	Y	Y	Y	Y	N	N
7 ***Taylor***	?	?	Y	Y	Y	N	N
8 ***Bailey***	Y	Y	Y	?	Y	N	N
9 Volkmer	Y	?	Y	Y	Y	N	N
10 ***Emerson***	Y	Y	Y	Y	Y	N	N
MONTANA							
1 Williams	N	Y	Y	Y	Y	N	Y
2 ***Marlenee***	Y	Y	Y	Y	Y	N	N
NEBRASKA							
1 ***Bereuter***	?	?	Y	Y	Y	N	N
2 ***Daub***	Y	Y	Y	Y	Y	N	N
3 ***Smith***	Y	Y	Y	Y	Y	N	N
NEVADA							
AL Santini	?	?	Y	Y	Y	N	N
NEW HAMPSHIRE							
1 D'Amours	?	?	Y	Y	?	N	Y
2 ***Gregg***	Y	Y	Y	Y	Y	N	N
NEW JERSEY							
1 Florio	?	?	Y	Y	Y	N	Y
2 Hughes	Y	Y	Y	Y	Y	N	N
3 Howard	Y	Y	Y	Y	Y	Y	Y
4 ***Smith***	Y	Y	Y	Y	Y	N	N
5 ***Fenwick***	N	Y	Y	Y	Y	N	N
6 ***Forsythe***	Y	Y	Y	?	Y	N	N
7 ***Roukema***	Y	Y	Y	?	Y	N	N
8 Roe	?	?	Y	Y	Y	N	Y
9 ***Hollenbeck***	Y	Y	Y	Y	Y	N	N
10 Rodino	Y	Y	Y	Y	Y	Y	Y
11 Minish	Y	Y	Y	Y	Y	N	Y
12 ***Rinaldo***	Y	Y	Y	Y	Y	N	N
13 ***Courter***	N	Y	Y	Y	Y	N	N
14 Guarini	#	?	Y	?	Y	N	Y
15 Dwyer	Y	Y	Y	Y	Y	N	Y
NEW MEXICO							
1 ***Lujan***	Y	Y	Y	Y	Y	N	N
2 ***Skeen***	Y	Y	Y	Y	Y	N	N
NEW YORK							
1 ***Carney***	Y	Y	Y	Y	Y	N	N
2 Downey	?	?	Y	Y	Y	N	Y
3 ***Carman***	Y	Y	Y	Y	Y	N	N
4 ***Lent***	Y	?	Y	Y	Y	N	N
5 ***McGrath***	Y	Y	Y	Y	?	N	N
6 ***LeBoutillier***	Y	Y	Y	Y	Y	N	N
7 Addabbo	Y	Y	Y	Y	Y	Y	Y
8 Rosenthal	N	Y	Y	Y	Y	Y	Y
9 Ferraro	Y	Y	Y	Y	Y	N	Y
10 Biaggi	#	?	Y	Y	Y	N	Y
11 Scheuer	Y	Y	Y	Y	Y	Y	Y
12 Chisholm	?	?	Y	?	Y	Y	Y
13 Solarz	?	?	Y	Y	Y	N	Y
14 Richmond	Y	Y	Y	Y	Y	Y	Y
15 Zeferetti	#	?	Y	Y	Y	N	Y
16 Schumer	?	?	Y	Y	Y	Y	Y
17 ***Molinari***	Y	Y	Y	Y	Y	N	N
18 ***Green***	Y	Y	Y	Y	Y	N	N
19 Rangel	N	Y	Y	Y	Y	Y	Y
20 Weiss	N	Y	Y	Y	Y	Y	Y
21 Garcia	X	?	Y	Y	Y	Y	Y
22 Bingham	N	Y	Y	Y	Y	Y	Y
23 Peyser	Y	Y	Y	Y	Y	N	Y
24 Ottinger	N	P	Y	P	P	Y	Y
25 ***Fish***	Y	?	Y	Y	Y	N	N
26 ***Gilman***	+	+	Y	Y	Y	N	N
27 McHugh	?	?	Y	Y	Y	N	Y
28 Stratton	Y	Y	Y	Y	Y	N	N
29 ***Solomon***	Y	Y	Y	Y	Y	N	N
30 ***Martin***	Y	Y	Y	Y	Y	N	N
31 ***Mitchell***	?	?	Y	Y	Y	N	N
32 ***Wortley***	Y	Y	Y	Y	?	N	N
33 ***Lee***	Y	?	Y	Y	Y	N	N
34 ***Horton***	?	?	Y	Y	Y	N	N
35 ***Conable***	?	?	Y	Y	Y	N	N
36 LaFalce	N	Y	Y	Y	Y	N	N
37 Nowak	Y	Y	Y	Y	Y	N	N
38 ***Kemp***	Y	Y	Y	Y	?	N	N
39 Lundine	N	?	Y	Y	Y	N	N
NORTH CAROLINA							
1 Jones	Y	?	Y	Y	Y	?	N
2 Fountain	Y	Y	Y	Y	Y	N	N
3 Whitley	Y	Y	Y	Y	Y	N	N
4 Andrews	Y	Y	Y	Y	Y	N	N
5 Neal	Y	Y	Y	Y	Y	N	N
6 ***Johnston***	Y	Y	Y	Y	Y	N	N
7 Rose	Y	Y	Y	Y	Y	N	N
8 Hefner	Y	Y	Y	Y	Y	N	N

	22	23	24	25	26	27	28
9 ***Martin***	?	?	Y	Y	Y	N	N
10 ***Broyhill***	?	?	Y	Y	Y	N	N
11 ***Hendon***	Y	Y	Y	Y	Y	N	N
NORTH DAKOTA							
AL Dorgan	Y	Y	Y	Y	Y	N	Y
OHIO							
1 ***Gradison***	?	?	Y	Y	Y	N	N
2 Luken	Y	Y	Y	Y	Y	N	N
3 Hall	Y	Y	Y	?	Y	N	N
4 Vacancy							
5 ***Latta***	Y	Y	Y	Y	Y	N	N
6 ***McEwen***	Y	Y	Y	Y	Y	N	N
7 ***Brown***	?	?	Y	Y	Y	N	N
8 ***Kindness***	?	Y	Y	Y	Y	N	N
9 ***Weber***	Y	Y	Y	Y	Y	N	N
10 ***Miller***	?	?	Y	Y	Y	N	N
11 ***Stanton***	Y	Y	Y	Y	Y	N	N
12 Shamansky	Y	Y	Y	?	Y	N	N
13 Pease	Y	Y	Y	Y	Y	N	Y
14 Seiberling	Y	Y	Y	Y	Y	Y	Y
15 ***Wylie***	Y	Y	Y	Y	Y	N	N
16 ***Regula***	?	Y	Y	Y	Y	N	N
17 ***Ashbrook***	Y	Y	Y	Y	Y	N	N
18 Applegate	Y	Y	Y	Y	?	N	N
19 ***Williams***	?	?	Y	Y	Y	N	N
20 Oakar	?	?	Y	Y	Y	Y	Y
21 Stokes	N	Y	Y	Y	Y	Y	Y
22 Eckart	N	Y	Y	Y	Y	N	Y
23 Mottl	N	Y	Y	Y	Y	Y	N
OKLAHOMA							
1 Jones	Y	Y	Y	Y	Y	N	N
2 Synar	Y	Y	Y	Y	Y	N	N
3 Watkins	Y	Y	?	Y	Y	N	N
4 McCurdy	Y	Y	Y	Y	Y	N	N
5 ***Edwards***	Y	Y	Y	Y	Y	N	N
6 English	Y	Y	?	Y	Y	N	N
OREGON							
1 AuCoin	Y	Y	?	?	Y	N	N
2 ***Smith***	Y	Y	Y	Y	Y	N	N
3 Wyden	N	Y	Y	Y	Y	N	Y
4 Weaver	Y	Y	Y	Y	Y	N	Y
PENNSYLVANIA							
1 Foglietta	?	?	?	?	Y	Y	Y
2 Gray	?	?	Y	Y	Y	Y	Y
3 Lederer*	?	?	?	?			
4 ***Dougherty***	?	?	Y	Y	Y	N	N
5 ***Schulze***	Y	Y	Y	Y	Y	N	N
6 Yatron	Y	Y	Y	Y	Y	N	Y
7 Edgar	?	?	Y	Y	Y	Y	Y
8 ***Coyne, J.***	?	?	Y	Y	Y	N	N
9 ***Shuster***	Y	Y	Y	Y	Y	N	N
10 ***McDade***	Y	Y	Y	Y	Y	N	N
11 ***Nelligan***	Y	Y	Y	Y	Y	N	N
12 Murtha	N	Y	Y	Y	Y	N	N
13 ***Coughlin***	Y	Y	Y	Y	Y	N	N
14 Coyne, W.	Y	Y	Y	Y	Y	Y	Y
15 ***Ritter***	Y	Y	Y	Y	Y	N	N
16 ***Walker***	N	Y	Y	Y	Y	N	N
17 Ertel	Y	Y	Y	Y	Y	N	N
18 Walgren	Y	Y	Y	Y	Y	N	N
19 ***Goodling***	Y	Y	Y	Y	?	N	N
20 Gaydos	?	?	Y	Y	Y	N	Y
21 Bailey	Y	Y	Y	Y	Y	N	Y
22 Murphy	Y	Y	Y	Y	Y	N	N
23 ***Clinger***	Y	Y	Y	Y	Y	N	N
24 ***Marks***	?	?	Y	Y	Y	N	N
25 Atkinson	Y	Y	Y	Y	Y	N	N
RHODE ISLAND							
1 St Germain	Y	Y	Y	Y	Y	Y	N
2 ***Schneider***	Y	Y	Y	Y	Y	N	N
SOUTH CAROLINA							
1 ***Hartnett***	?	Y	Y	Y	Y	N	N
2 ***Spence***	Y	Y	Y	Y	Y	N	N
3 Derrick	Y	Y	Y	Y	Y	N	N
4 ***Campbell***	?	Y	Y	Y	Y	N	N
5 Holland	Y	Y	Y	Y	Y	N	N
6 ***Napier***	Y	Y	Y	Y	Y	N	N
SOUTH DAKOTA							
1 Daschle	?	?	Y	Y	Y	N	N
2 ***Roberts***	Y	Y	?	Y	?	N	N
TENNESSEE							
1 ***Quillen***	?	?	Y	Y	Y	N	N
2 ***Duncan***	Y	Y	Y	Y	Y	N	N
3 Bouquard	Y	Y	Y	?	Y	N	N
4 Gore	Y	Y	Y	Y	Y	N	Y
5 Boner	Y	Y	Y	Y	Y	N	N
6 ***Beard***	Y	Y	Y	?	Y	N	N

	22	23	24	25	26	27	28
7 Jones	Y	Y	Y	Y	Y	N	N
8 Ford	N	Y	Y	Y	Y	Y	Y
TEXAS							
1 Hall, S.	Y	Y	Y	Y	Y	N	N
2 Wilson	Y	Y	Y	Y	Y	N	N
3 ***Collins***	Y	Y	Y	Y	Y	N	N
4 Hall, R.	Y	Y	Y	?	?	N	N
5 Mattox	Y	Y	Y	Y	Y	N	N
6 Gramm	Y	Y	Y	Y	Y	N	N
7 ***Archer***	Y	Y	Y	Y	Y	N	N
8 ***Fields***	Y	Y	Y	Y	Y	N	N
9 Brooks	Y	Y	Y	Y	Y	N	N
10 Pickle	?	?	Y	Y	Y	N	N
11 Leath	?	?	Y	Y	Y	N	N
12 Wright	?	?	Y	Y	Y	N	N
13 Hightower	Y	Y	Y	?	Y	N	N
14 Patman	Y	Y	Y	Y	Y	N	N
15 de la Garza	Y	Y	Y	?	?	N	N
16 White	Y	Y	Y	Y	Y	N	N
17 Stenholm	Y	Y	Y	Y	Y	N	N
18 Leland	?	?	Y	Y	Y	Y	Y
19 Hance	Y	Y	Y	Y	Y	N	N
20 Gonzalez	Y	Y	Y	Y	Y	Y	Y
21 ***Loeffler***	Y	Y	Y	Y	Y	N	N
22 ***Paul***	?	?	Y	Y	Y	N	N
23 Kazen	Y	Y	Y	Y	Y	N	N
24 Frost	Y	Y	Y	Y	Y	N	N
UTAH							
1 ***Hansen***	?	?	Y	?	?	N	N
2 ***Marriott***	Y	Y	Y	Y	Y	N	N
VERMONT							
AL ***Jeffords***	Y	Y	Y	Y	Y	N	Y
VIRGINIA							
1 ***Trible***	?	?	Y	Y	Y	N	N
2 ***Whitehurst***	Y	Y	Y	Y	Y	N	N
3 ***Bliley***	Y	Y	Y	Y	Y	N	N
4 ***Daniel, R.***	Y	Y	Y	Y	Y	N	N
5 Daniel, D.	Y	Y	Y	?	Y	N	N
6 ***Butler***	Y	Y	Y	Y	Y	N	N
7 ***Robinson***	Y	Y	Y	Y	Y	N	N
8 ***Parris***	Y	Y	Y	Y	Y	N	N
9 ***Wampler***	Y	Y	?	?	Y	N	N
10 ***Wolf***	Y	Y	Y	Y	Y	N	N
WASHINGTON							
1 ***Pritchard***	?	Y	Y	Y	Y	N	N
2 Swift	?	?	Y	Y	Y	N	N
3 Bonker	?	Y	Y	?	?	N	N
4 ***Morrison***	?	?	Y	Y	Y	N	N
5 Foley	Y	Y	Y	Y	Y	N	N
6 Dicks	?	Y	Y	?	Y	N	N
7 Lowry	?	Y	Y	Y	Y	Y	Y
WEST VIRGINIA							
1 Mollohan	Y	Y	Y	Y	Y	N	Y
2 ***Benedict***	Y	Y	Y	Y	Y	N	N
3 ***Staton***	Y	Y	Y	Y	Y	N	N
4 Rahall	N	Y	Y	Y	Y	Y	Y
WISCONSIN							
1 Aspin	?	Y	Y	Y	Y	N	Y
2 Kastenmeier	N	N	Y	N	N	Y	Y
3 ***Gunderson***	Y	Y	Y	Y	Y	N	N
4 Zablocki	?	?	Y	Y	Y	N	Y
5 Reuss	Y	Y	?	?	Y	Y	Y
6 ***Petri***	?	?	Y	Y	Y	N	N
7 Obey	?	?	Y	Y	Y	Y	Y
8 ***Roth***	Y	Y	Y	Y	Y	N	N
9 ***Sensenbrenner***	Y	Y	Y	Y	Y	N	N
WYOMING							
AL ***Cheney***	Y	Y	Y	Y	Y	N	N

** Resignation of Rep. Raymond F. Lederer, D-Pa., became effective at the close of business May 5, 1981. The last vote for which he was eligible was CQ vote 25.*

emocrats ***Republicans***

KEY

Y Voted for (yea).
Paired for.
+ Announced for.
N Voted against (nay).
X Paired against.
- Announced against.
P Voted "present".
C Voted "present" to avoid possible conflict of interest.
? Did not vote or otherwise make a position known.

29. H Con Res 115. Fiscal 1982 Budget Targets. Jones, D-Okla., motion that the House resolve itself into the Committee of the Whole for further consideration of the resolution to set spending and revenue targets for fiscal 1982, to revise binding budget levels for fiscal 1981 and to direct House committees to cut back programs within their jurisdictions to save $15.8 billion in outlays in fiscal 1982. Motion agreed to 400-5: R 184-1; D 216-4 (ND 142-3, SD 74-1), May 7, 1981.

30. H Con Res 115. Fiscal 1982 Budget Targets. Latta, R-Ohio, substitute, to the resolution as reported by the Budget Committee, to decrease budget authority by $23.1 billion, outlays by $25.7 billion and revenues by $31.1 billion, resulting in a $31 billion deficit for fiscal 1982. Adopted 253-176: R 190-0; D 63-176 (ND 17-144, SD 46-32), May 7, 1981. A "yea" was a vote supporting the president's position.

31. H Con Res 115. Fiscal 1982 Budget Targets. Adoption of the resolution, as amended, to set budget targets for the fiscal year ending Sept. 30, 1982, as follows: budget authority, $764.5 billion; outlays, $688.8 billion; revenues, $657.8 billion; and deficit, $31 billion. The resolution also revised binding budget levels for fiscal 1981 and directed House committees to cut back programs within their jurisdictions to save $36.6 billion in outlays in fiscal 1982. Adopted 270-154: R 186-1; D 84-153 (ND 23-136, SD 61-17), May 7, 1981. A "yea" was a vote supporting the president's position.

	29	30	31
ALABAMA			
1 Edwards	Y	Y	Y
2 Dickinson	Y	Y	Y
3 Nichols	Y	Y	Y
4 Bevill	Y	Y	Y
5 Flippo	Y	Y	Y
6 Smith	Y	Y	Y
7 Shelby	Y	Y	Y
ALASKA			
AL Young	?	Y	Y
ARIZONA			
1 Rhodes	Y	Y	Y
2 Udall	Y	N	Y
3 Stump	Y	Y	Y
4 Rudd	Y	Y	Y
ARKANSAS			
1 Alexander	Y	N	Y
2 Bethune	Y	Y	Y
3 Hammerschmidt	Y	Y	Y
4 Anthony	Y	Y	Y
CALIFORNIA			
1 Chappie	Y	Y	Y
2 Clausen	Y	Y	Y
3 Matsui	Y	N	N
4 Fazio	Y	N	N
5 Burton, J.	Y	N	N
6 Burton, P.	Y	N	N
7 Miller	Y	N	N
8 Dellums	Y	N	N
9 Stark	?	N	X
10 Edwards	Y	N	N
11 Lantos	Y	N	N
12 McCloskey	Y	Y	Y
13 Mineta	Y	N	N
14 Shumway	Y	Y	Y
15 Coelho	Y	N	N
16 Panetta	Y	N	N
17 Pashayan	Y	Y	Y
18 Thomas	Y	Y	Y
19 Lagomarsino	Y	Y	Y
20 Goldwater	Y	Y	?
21 Fiedler	Y	Y	Y
22 Moorhead	Y	Y	Y
23 Beilenson	Y	N	N
24 Waxman	Y	N	N
25 Roybal	Y	N	N
26 Rousselot	Y	Y	#
27 Dornan	Y	Y	Y
28 Dixon	?	N	N
29 Hawkins	Y	N	N
30 Danielson	Y	N	N
31 Dymally	Y	N	N
32 Anderson	Y	N	Y
33 Grisham	Y	Y	Y
34 Lungren	Y	Y	Y
35 Dreier	Y	Y	Y
36 Brown	Y	N	N
37 Lewis	Y	Y	Y
38 Patterson	Y	Y	Y
39 Dannemeyer	Y	Y	Y
40 Badham	Y	Y	Y
41 Lowery	Y	Y	Y
42 Hunter	Y	Y	Y
43 Burgener	Y	Y	Y
COLORADO			
1 Schroeder	Y	N	N
2 Wirth	Y	N	N
3 Kogovsek	Y	N	N
4 Brown	Y	Y	Y

	29	30	31
5 Kramer	Y	Y	Y
CONNECTICUT			
1 Cotter	?	?	?
2 Gejdenson	Y	N	N
3 DeNardis	Y	Y	Y
4 McKinney	Y	Y	Y
5 Ratchford	Y	N	N
6 Moffett	Y	N	N
DELAWARE			
AL Evans	Y	Y	Y
FLORIDA			
1 Hutto	Y	Y	Y
2 Fuqua	Y	Y	Y
3 Bennett	Y	Y	Y
4 Chappell	Y	Y	Y
5 McCollum	Y	Y	Y
6 Young	Y	Y	Y
7 Gibbons	Y	Y	Y
8 Ireland	Y	Y	Y
9 Nelson	Y	Y	Y
10 Bafalis	Y	Y	Y
11 Mica	Y	Y	Y
12 Shaw	Y	Y	Y
13 Lehman	Y	N	N
14 Pepper	Y	N	N
15 Fascell	Y	N	Y
GEORGIA			
1 Ginn	Y	Y	Y
2 Hatcher	Y	Y	Y
3 Brinkley	Y	Y	Y
4 Levitas	Y	Y	Y
5 Fowler	Y	N	N
6 Gingrich	Y	Y	Y
7 McDonald	Y	Y	Y
8 Evans	Y	Y	Y
9 Jenkins	Y	Y	Y
10 Barnard	Y	Y	Y
HAWAII			
1 Heftel	?	N	N
2 Akaka	Y	N	N
IDAHO			
1 Craig	Y	Y	Y
2 Hansen	Y	Y	Y
ILLINOIS			
1 Washington	?	N	N
2 Savage	Y	N	N
3 Russo	Y	N	N
4 Derwinski	Y	Y	Y
5 Fary	Y	N	N
6 Hyde	Y	Y	Y
7 Collins	Y	N	N
8 Rostenkowski	Y	N	N
9 Yates	Y	N	N
10 Porter	Y	Y	Y
11 Annunzio	Y	N	N
12 Crane, P.	Y	Y	Y
13 McClory	Y	Y	Y
14 Erlenborn	?	Y	Y
15 Corcoran	Y	Y	Y
16 Martin	Y	Y	Y
17 O'Brien	Y	Y	Y
18 Michel	Y	Y	Y
19 Railsback	Y	Y	Y
20 Findley	Y	Y	Y
21 Madigan	Y	Y	Y
22 Crane, D.	Y	Y	Y
23 Price	Y	N	N
24 Simon	Y	N	N
INDIANA			
1 Benjamin	Y	N	N
2 Fithian	Y	N	N
3 Hiler	Y	Y	Y
4 Coats	Y	Y	Y
5 Hillis	Y	Y	Y
6 Evans	Y	Y	Y
7 Myers	Y	Y	Y
8 Deckard	Y	Y	Y
9 Hamilton	Y	N	N
10 Sharp	Y	N	N
11 Jacobs	Y	Y	N
IOWA			
1 Leach	Y	Y	Y
2 Tauke	Y	Y	Y
3 Evans	N	Y	Y
4 Smith	Y	N	N
5 Harkin	Y	N	N
6 Bedell	Y	N	N

Democrats   *Republicans*

	29	30	31
KANSAS			
1 *Roberts*	Y	Y	Y
2 *Jeffries*	Y	Y	+
3 *Winn*	Y	Y	Y
4 Glickman	Y	N	Y
5 *Whittaker*	Y	Y	Y
KENTUCKY			
1 Hubbard	Y	N	N
2 Natcher	Y	Y	Y
3 Mazzoli	Y	Y	Y
4 *Snyder*	Y	Y	Y
5 *Rogers*	Y	Y	Y
6 *Hopkins*	Y	Y	Y
7 Perkins	Y	N	N
LOUISIANA			
1 *Livingston*	Y	Y	Y
2 Boggs	Y	N	N
3 Tauzin	Y	Y	Y
4 Roemer	Y	Y	Y
5 Huckaby	Y	Y	Y
6 *Moore*	Y	Y	Y
7 Breaux	Y	Y	Y
8 Long	Y	N	Y
MAINE			
1 *Emery*	Y	Y	Y
2 *Snowe*	Y	Y	Y
MARYLAND			
1 Dyson	Y	Y	Y
2 Long	Y	Y	Y
3 Mikulski	Y	N	N
4 *Holt*	Y	Y	Y
5 Vacancy			
6 Byron	Y	Y	Y
7 Mitchell	N	N	N
8 Barnes	Y	N	N
MASSACHUSETTS			
1 Conte	Y	Y	Y
2 Boland	Y	N	N
3 Early	Y	N	N
4 Frank	Y	N	N
5 Shannon	Y	N	N
6 Mavroules	Y	N	N
7 Markey	Y	N	N
8 O'Neill			
9 Moakley	Y	N	N
10 *Heckler*	Y	Y	Y
11 Donnelly	Y	N	N
12 Studds	Y	N	N
MICHIGAN			
1 Conyers	Y	N	N
2 *Pursell*	Y	Y	Y
3 Wolpe	Y	N	N
4 *Siljander*	Y	Y	Y
5 *Sawyer*	Y	Y	Y
6 *Dunn*	Y	Y	Y
7 Kildee	Y	N	N
8 Traxler	Y	N	Y
9 *Vander Jagt*	?	Y	Y
10 Albosta	Y	Y	Y
11 *Davis*	Y	Y	Y
12 Bonior	Y	N	N
13 Crockett	?	N	N
14 Hertel	Y	N	N
15 Ford	?	N	N
16 Dingell	Y	N	N
17 Brodhead	Y	N	N
18 Blanchard	Y	N	N
19 *Broomfield*	Y	Y	Y
MINNESOTA			
1 *Erdahl*	Y	Y	Y
2 *Hagedorn*	Y	Y	Y
3 *Frenzel*	Y	Y	Y
4 Vento	Y	N	N
5 Sabo	N	N	N
6 *Weber*	Y	Y	Y
7 *Stangeland*	Y	Y	Y
8 Oberstar	Y	N	N
MISSISSIPPI			
1 Whitten	Y	N	Y
2 Bowen	Y	Y	Y
3 Montgomery	Y	Y	Y
4 Vacancy			
5 *Lott*	Y	Y	Y
MISSOURI			
1 Clay	?	N	N
2 Young	Y	Y	Y
3 Gephardt	Y	N	N

	29	30	31
4 Skelton	Y	Y	Y
5 Bolling	?	N	N
6 *Coleman*	Y	Y	Y
7 *Taylor*	Y	Y	Y
8 *Bailey*	Y	Y	Y
9 Volkmer	Y	Y	Y
10 *Emerson*	Y	Y	Y
MONTANA			
1 Williams	Y	N	N
2 *Marlenee*	Y	Y	Y
NEBRASKA			
1 *Bereuter*	Y	Y	Y
2 *Daub*	Y	Y	Y
3 *Smith*	Y	Y	Y
NEVADA			
AL Santini	Y	Y	Y
NEW HAMPSHIRE			
1 D'Amours	Y	N	Y
2 *Gregg*	Y	Y	Y
NEW JERSEY			
1 Florio	Y	N	N
2 Hughes	Y	N	N
3 Howard	Y	N	N
4 *Smith*	Y	Y	Y
5 *Fenwick*	Y	Y	Y
6 *Forsythe*	Y	Y	Y
7 *Roukema*	Y	Y	Y
8 Roe	Y	N	N
9 *Hollenbeck*	?	Y	Y
10 Rodino	Y	N	N
11 Minish	Y	N	N
12 *Rinaldo*	Y	Y	Y
13 *Courter*	Y	Y	Y
14 Guarini	Y	N	N
15 Dwyer	Y	N	N
NEW MEXICO			
1 *Lujan*	Y	Y	Y
2 *Skeen*	Y	Y	Y
NEW YORK			
1 *Carney*	Y	Y	Y
2 Downey	?	N	N
3 *Carman*	Y	Y	Y
4 *Lent*	Y	Y	Y
5 *McGrath*	Y	Y	Y
6 *LeBoutillier*	Y	Y	Y
7 Addabbo	Y	N	N
8 Rosenthal	Y	N	N
9 Ferraro	Y	N	N
10 Biaggi	?	N	N
11 Scheuer	Y	N	N
12 Chisholm	Y	N	N
13 Solarz	Y	N	N
14 Richmond	Y	N	N
15 Zeferetti	Y	N	N
16 Schumer	Y	N	N
17 *Molinari*	Y	Y	Y
18 *Green*	Y	Y	Y
19 Rangel	Y	N	N
20 Weiss	Y	N	N
21 Garcia	Y	N	N
22 Bingham	?	N	N
23 Peyser	Y	N	N
24 Ottinger	P	N	N
25 *Fish*	Y	Y	Y
26 *Gilman*	Y	Y	Y
27 McHugh	Y	N	N
28 Stratton	Y	N	N
29 *Solomon*	Y	Y	Y
30 *Martin*	Y	Y	Y
31 *Mitchell*	Y	Y	Y
32 *Wortley*	Y	Y	Y
33 *Lee*	Y	Y	Y
34 *Horton*	Y	Y	Y
35 *Conable*	Y	Y	Y
36 LaFalce	Y	N	N
37 Nowak	Y	N	N
38 *Kemp*	Y	Y	Y
39 Lundine	Y	N	N
NORTH CAROLINA			
1 Jones	Y	N	Y
2 Fountain	Y	Y	Y
3 Whitley	Y	N	Y
4 Andrews	Y	Y	Y
5 Neal	Y	N	Y
6 *Johnston*	Y	Y	Y
7 Rose	?	N	Y
8 Hefner	Y	N	Y

	29	30	31
9 *Martin*	Y	Y	Y
10 *Broyhill*	Y	Y	Y
11 *Hendon*	Y	Y	Y
NORTH DAKOTA			
AL Dorgan	Y	N	Y
OHIO			
1 *Gradison*	Y	Y	Y
2 Luken	Y	Y	Y
3 Hall	Y	Y	Y
4 Vacancy			
5 *Latta*	Y	Y	Y
6 *McEwen*	Y	Y	Y
7 *Brown*	Y	Y	Y
8 *Kindness*	Y	Y	Y
9 *Weber*	Y	Y	Y
10 *Miller*	Y	Y	Y
11 *Stanton*	Y	Y	Y
12 Shamansky	Y	N	N
13 Pease	Y	N	N
14 Seiberling	Y	N	N
15 *Wylie*	Y	Y	Y
16 *Regula*	Y	Y	Y
17 *Ashbrook*	?	Y	Y
18 Applegate	?	N	Y
19 *Williams*	Y	Y	Y
20 Oakar	Y	N	N
21 Stokes	Y	N	N
22 Eckart	Y	N	N
23 Mottl	Y	Y	N
OKLAHOMA			
1 Jones	Y	N	Y
2 Synar	Y	N	N
3 Watkins	Y	N	Y
4 McCurdy	Y	N	Y
5 *Edwards*	Y	Y	Y
6 English	Y	Y	Y
OREGON			
1 AuCoin	?	N	N
2 *Smith*	Y	Y	Y
3 Wyden	Y	N	N
4 Weaver	Y	N	N
PENNSYLVANIA			
1 Foglietta	?	N	N
2 Gray	Y	N	N
3 Vacancy			
4 *Dougherty*	Y	Y	Y
5 *Schulze*	Y	Y	Y
6 Yatron	Y	N	N
7 Edgar	Y	N	N
8 *Coyne, J.*	Y	Y	Y
9 *Shuster*	Y	Y	Y
10 *McDade*	Y	Y	Y
11 *Nelligan*	Y	Y	Y
12 Murtha	Y	N	N
13 *Coughlin*	Y	Y	Y
14 Coyne, W.	Y	N	N
15 *Ritter*	Y	Y	Y
16 *Walker*	Y	Y	Y
17 Ertel	Y	N	Y
18 Walgren	Y	N	N
19 *Goodling*	Y	Y	Y
20 Gaydos	?	N	N
21 Bailey	Y	N	N
22 Murphy	Y	N	N
23 *Clinger*	Y	Y	Y
24 *Marks*	Y	Y	Y
25 Atkinson	Y	Y	Y
RHODE ISLAND			
1 St Germain	Y	N	?
2 *Schneider*	Y	Y	Y
SOUTH CAROLINA			
1 *Hartnett*	Y	Y	Y
2 *Spence*	Y	Y	Y
3 Derrick	Y	Y	Y
4 *Campbell*	Y	Y	Y
5 Holland	Y	Y	Y
6 *Napier*	Y	Y	Y
SOUTH DAKOTA			
1 Daschle	Y	N	N
2 *Roberts*	Y	Y	Y
TENNESSEE			
1 *Quillen*	Y	Y	Y
2 *Duncan*	Y	Y	Y
3 Bouquard	Y	Y	Y
4 Gore	Y	N	N
5 Boner	Y	N	Y
6 *Beard*	Y	Y	Y

	29	30	31
7 Jones	Y	Y	Y
8 Ford	N	N	N
TEXAS			
1 Hall, S.	?	Y	Y
2 Wilson	Y	Y	Y
3 *Collins*	Y	Y	Y
4 Hall, R.	Y	Y	Y
5 Mattox	Y	N	N
6 *Gramm*	Y	Y	Y
7 *Archer*	Y	Y	Y
8 *Fields*	Y	Y	Y
9 Brooks	Y	N	Y
10 Pickle	Y	N	Y
11 Leath	Y	Y	Y
12 Wright	Y	N	N
13 Hightower	Y	N	N
14 Patman	Y	N	N
15 de la Garza	Y	N	N
16 White	Y	Y	Y
17 Stenholm	Y	Y	Y
18 Leland	?	N	N
19 Hance	Y	N	N
20 Gonzalez	Y	N	N
21 *Loeffler*	Y	Y	Y
22 *Paul*	Y	Y	Y
23 Kazen	Y	N	N
24 Frost	Y	N	N
UTAH			
1 *Hansen*	Y	Y	Y
2 *Marriott*	Y	Y	Y
VERMONT			
AL *Jeffords*	Y	Y	Y
VIRGINIA			
1 *Trible*	Y	Y	Y
2 *Whitehurst*	Y	Y	Y
3 *Bliley*	Y	Y	Y
4 *Daniel, R.*	Y	Y	Y
5 Daniel, D.	Y	Y	Y
6 *Butler*	Y	Y	Y
7 *Robinson*	Y	Y	Y
8 *Parris*	Y	Y	Y
9 *Wampler*	Y	Y	Y
10 *Wolf*	Y	Y	Y
WASHINGTON			
1 *Pritchard*	Y	Y	Y
2 Swift	Y	N	N
3 Bonker	Y	N	N
4 *Morrison*	Y	Y	Y
5 Foley	Y	N	N
6 Dicks	Y	N	N
7 Lowry	Y	N	N
WEST VIRGINIA			
1 Mollohan	Y	N	N
2 *Benedict*	Y	Y	Y
3 *Staton*	Y	Y	Y
4 Rahall	Y	N	N
WISCONSIN			
1 Aspin	Y	N	N
2 Kastenmeier	N	N	N
3 *Gunderson*	Y	Y	Y
4 Zablocki	Y	N	N
5 Reuss	Y	N	N
6 *Petri*	Y	Y	Y
7 Obey	Y	N	N
8 *Roth*	Y	Y	Y
9 *Sensenbrenner*	Y	Y	Y
WYOMING			
AL *Cheney*	Y	Y	Y

Democrats   *Republicans*

32. HR 3512. Fiscal 1981 Supplemental Appropriations. Rousselot, R-Calif., amendment to reduce to $534,600,000, from $540,000,000, the U.S. contribution to the International Development Association. Adopted 272-126: R 139-39; D 133-87 (ND 70-79, SD 63-8), May 12, 1981. A "nay" was a vote supporting the president's position.

33. HR 3512. Fiscal 1981 Supplemental Appropriations. Obey, D-Wis., amendment to reduce to $5,148,000,000, from $5,524,000,000, the limit on direct loans and to $7,559,000,000, from $8,059,000,000, the limit on the total commitment to guaranteed loans made by the Export-Import Bank in fiscal 1981. Adopted 231-166: R 110-68; D 121-98 (ND 70-77, SD 51-21), May 12, 1981. A "yea" was a vote supporting the president's position. (The amendment subsequently was rejected after the House rose from the Committee of the Whole, *see vote 38 below.*)

34. H Con Res 115. Fiscal 1982 Budget Targets. Latta, R-Ohio, motion to instruct the House conferees on the first fiscal 1982 budget resolution to insist on the House position on budget authority and outlays for defense programs in fiscal 1982. Motion agreed to 247-162: R 162-22; D 85-140 (ND 28-124, SD 57-16), May 13, 1981.

35. HR 3512. Fiscal 1981 Supplemental Appropriations. Jones, D-Okla., amendment to reduce to $883,408,000, from $3,883,408,000, the fiscal 1982 advance appropriation for the strategic petroleum reserve. Adopted 260-152: R 160-24; D 100-128 (ND 48-105, SD 52-23), May 13, 1981.

36. HR 3512. Fiscal 1981 Supplemental Appropriations. Fiedler, R-Calif., amendment to defer $28.5 million in fiscal 1981 funds appropriated for a "people mover" transportation project in Los Angeles. Adopted 244-156: R 178-2; D 66-154 (ND 32-115, SD 34-39), May 13, 1981.

37. HR 3512. Fiscal 1981 Supplemental Appropriations. Ashbrook, R-Ohio, amendment to prohibit funds for federal employee health insurance policies that provide abortions. Adopted 242-155: R 144-32; SD 98-123 (ND 56-92, SD 42-31), May 13, 1981.

38. HR 3512. Fiscal 1981 Supplemental Appropriations. Obey, D-Wis., amendment to reduce to $5,148,000,000, from $5,524,000,000, the limit on direct loans and to $7,559,000,000, from $8,059,000,000, the limit on the total commitment to guaranteed loans made by the Export-Import Bank in fiscal 1981. Rejected 162-237: R 91-86; D 71-151 (ND 39-110, SD 32-41), May 13, 1981. A "yea" was a vote supporting the president's position. (The amendment had been previously adopted in the Committee of the Whole, *see vote 33 above.*)

39. HR 3512. Fiscal 1981 Supplemental Appropriations. Passage of the bill to provide $18,633,539,663 in fiscal 1981 supplemental appropriations and $12,706,661,747 in fiscal 1981 rescissions; to allow $5,747,000,000 in fiscal 1981 spending deferrals; to extend from June 5, 1981, through Sept. 30, 1981, the spending authority of departments whose regular 1981 appropriations bills never cleared; and to provide $883,408,000 in fiscal 1982 advance funding for the strategic petroleum reserve. Passed 329-70: R 173-4; D 156-66 (ND 88-61, SD 68-5), May 13, 1981. The president had requested $21,754,657,800 in fiscal 1981 supplemental appropriations, $15,140,589,541 in fiscal 1981 rescissions, $5,222,000,000 in fiscal 1981 spending deferrals and $3,883,408,000 in regular fiscal 1982 spending for the strategic petroleum reserve.

KEY

Y	Voted for (yea).
#	Paired for.
+	Announced for.
N	Voted against (nay).
X	Paired against.
-	Announced against.
P	Voted "present".
C	Voted "present" to avoid possible conflict of interest.
?	Did not vote or otherwise make a position known.

	32	33	34	35	36	37	38	39
ALABAMA								
1 *Edwards*	Y	N	Y	Y	Y	N	N	Y
2 *Dickinson*	Y	Y	Y	Y	Y	N	N	Y
3 Nichols	Y	Y	Y	Y	Y	Y	Y	Y
4 Bevill	Y	N	Y	N	Y	N	Y	Y
5 Flippo	Y	Y	Y	Y	Y	Y	N	Y
6 *Smith*	Y	Y	Y	Y	Y	Y	N	Y
7 Shelby	Y	Y	Y	Y	Y	Y	Y	Y
ALASKA								
AL *Young*	Y	?	Y	?	?	#	?	?
ARIZONA								
1 *Rhodes*	N	N	Y	Y	Y	Y	N	Y
2 Udall	Y	Y	Y	Y	N	N	Y	N
3 *Stump*	Y	Y	Y	Y	Y	Y	Y	Y
4 *Rudd*	Y	Y	Y	Y	Y	Y	N	Y
ARKANSAS								
1 Alexander	Y	N	N	Y	N	N	N	Y
2 *Bethune*	Y	Y	Y	Y	Y	Y	Y	Y
3 *Hammerschmidt*	Y	Y	Y	Y	Y	Y	N	Y
4 Anthony	Y	Y	N	Y	N	N	Y	Y
CALIFORNIA								
1 *Chappie*	?	Y	?	Y	Y	Y	N	Y
2 *Clausen*	Y	Y	Y	Y	Y	Y	N	Y
3 Matsui	N	N	Y	N	N	N	N	Y
4 Fazio	N	N	N	N	N	N	N	Y
5 Burton, J.	?	?	?	?	?	?	?	?
6 Burton, P.	N	N	N	N	N	N	N	N
7 Miller	N	N	N	N	N	N	N	N
8 Dellums	N	Y	N	N	N	N	N	N
9 Stark	Y	Y	N	N	N	N	Y	N
10 Edwards	N	Y	N	N	N	N	N	N
11 Lantos	Y	N	N	Y	N	N	N	Y
12 *McCloskey*	Y	Y	N	Y	N	Y	N	Y
13 Mineta	N	Y	N	N	N	N	N	Y
14 *Shumway*	Y	Y	Y	Y	Y	Y	Y	Y
15 Coelho	Y	N	N	N	N	N	N	Y
16 Panetta	Y	N	N	Y	N	N	Y	N
17 *Pashayan*	Y	Y	Y	Y	Y	Y	N	Y
18 *Thomas*	Y	Y	Y	Y	Y	Y	N	Y
19 *Lagomarsino*	Y	Y	Y	Y	Y	Y	N	Y
20 *Goldwater*	Y	N	Y	Y	Y	Y	N	Y
21 *Fiedler*	N	Y	Y	Y	N	Y	N	Y
22 *Moorhead*	Y	Y	Y	Y	Y	Y	N	Y
23 Beilenson	N	N	N	N	Y	N	N	N
24 Waxman	N	N	N	N	N	?	N	N
25 Roybal	Y	N	N	N	N	N	Y	N
26 *Rousselot*	Y	Y	Y	Y	Y	Y	Y	Y
27 *Dornan*	Y	N	Y	Y	N	Y	N	Y
28 Dixon	N	N	N	N	N	N	N	N
29 Hawkins	N	N	N	Y	N	N	N	N
30 Danielson	N	Y	N	N	N	N	N	N
31 Dymally	N	N	?	?	?	?	?	?
32 Anderson	Y	Y	Y	Y	N	N	N	Y
33 *Grisham*	?	?	Y	Y	Y	Y	N	Y
34 *Lungren*	Y	Y	Y	Y	Y	Y	N	Y
35 *Dreier*	Y	Y	Y	Y	Y	Y	Y	Y
36 Brown	N	N	N	N	N	N	N	Y
37 *Lewis*	N	N	Y	Y	Y	Y	N	Y
38 Patterson	N	N	N	N	N	N	N	N
39 *Dannemeyer*	Y	Y	Y	Y	Y	Y	Y	Y
40 *Badham*	Y	?	Y	Y	Y	Y	N	Y
41 *Lowery*	Y	N	Y	Y	Y	Y	N	Y
42 *Hunter*	Y	N	Y	Y	Y	N	N	Y
43 *Burgener*	Y	N	Y	Y	Y	N	N	Y
COLORADO								
1 Schroeder	Y	Y	N	N	N	N	Y	N
2 Wirth	N	Y	Y	N	N	N	N	Y
3 Kogovsek	Y	Y	N	N	N	N	N	Y
4 *Brown*	Y	Y	N	Y	N	Y	N	Y

	32	33	34	35	36	37	38	39
5 *Kramer*	Y	Y	Y	Y	Y	Y	Y	Y
CONNECTICUT								
1 Cotter	?	?	?	?	?	?	?	?
2 Gejdenson	N	N	N	N	N	N	N	N
3 *DeNardis*	N	Y	N	Y	Y	N	Y	Y
4 *McKinney*	Y	N	Y	Y	Y	N	N	Y
5 Ratchford	N	N	Y	N	N	N	N	Y
6 Moffett	N	?	N	N	N	N	N	N
DELAWARE								
AL *Evans*	N	N	Y	Y	N	N	N	Y
FLORIDA								
1 Hutto	Y	N	Y	Y	N	Y	N	Y
2 Fuqua	Y	Y	Y	Y	N	Y	N	Y
3 Bennett	Y	Y	Y	Y	Y	N	Y	Y
4 Chappell	Y	N	Y	N	Y	N	Y	Y
5 *McCollum*	Y	N	Y	Y	Y	Y	N	Y
6 *Young*	Y	Y	Y	Y	Y	Y	Y	Y
7 Gibbons	Y	N	Y	N	Y	N	Y	Y
8 Ireland	Y	Y	?	?	?	?	?	?
9 Nelson	Y	Y	Y	Y	Y	N	N	Y
10 *Bafalis*	Y	Y	Y	Y	Y	Y	Y	Y
11 Mica	Y	Y	Y	N	N	N	N	Y
12 *Shaw*	Y	Y	Y	Y	Y	Y	Y	Y
13 Lehman	N	N	N	N	N	N	N	N
14 Pepper	N	N	N	N	N	N	N	N
15 Fascell	Y	N	N	Y	N	N	Y	Y
GEORGIA								
1 Ginn	Y	N	Y	N	N	N	N	Y
2 Hatcher	Y	Y	Y	Y	N	Y	N	Y
3 Brinkley	Y	Y	Y	Y	N	Y	N	Y
4 Levitas	?	?	Y	N	N	N	Y	Y
5 Fowler	?	?	Y	N	N	N	Y	Y
6 *Gingrich*	?	?	Y	Y	Y	Y	N	Y
7 McDonald	Y	#	Y	Y	Y	Y	Y	Y
8 Evans	?	Y	?	?	?	?	?	?
9 Jenkins	Y	Y	Y	Y	N	Y	N	Y
10 Barnard	Y	N	Y	N	Y	N	Y	Y
HAWAII								
1 Heftel	Y	N	N	N	N	N	N	Y
2 Akaka	Y	N	N	N	N	N	N	Y
IDAHO								
1 *Craig*	Y	Y	Y	Y	Y	Y	N	Y
2 *Hansen*	Y	Y	Y	Y	Y	Y	Y	Y
ILLINOIS								
1 Washington	N	N	N	Y	N	N	N	N
2 Savage	N	N	N	N	N	N	N	N
3 Russo	Y	Y	N	N	N	N	N	Y
4 *Derwinski*	Y	Y	Y	Y	Y	N	N	Y
5 Fary	N	Y	N	N	N	N	N	Y
6 *Hyde*	Y	N	Y	Y	Y	Y	N	Y
7 Collins	N	N	N	N	N	N	N	N
8 Rostenkowski	N	N	N	N	N	N	N	N
9 Yates	N	N	N	N	N	N	N	N
10 *Porter*	N	N	Y	N	Y	N	N	Y
11 Annunzio	N	N	Y	N	N	N	N	Y
12 *Crane, P.*	Y	Y	Y	Y	Y	Y	Y	N
13 *McClory*	Y	N	Y	Y	Y	N	N	Y
14 *Erlenborn*	N	?	Y	Y	?	?	?	?
15 *Corcoran*	Y	Y	Y	Y	Y	Y	N	Y
16 *Martin*	Y	Y	Y	Y	Y	Y	N	Y
17 *O'Brien*	N	N	Y	Y	Y	N	N	Y
18 *Michel*	N	N	Y	Y	Y	N	N	Y
19 *Railsback*	Y	N	N	Y	N	N	N	Y
20 *Findley*	N	N	Y	Y	N	N	N	Y
21 *Madigan*	Y	N	Y	Y	Y	N	N	Y
22 *Crane, D.*	Y	Y	Y	Y	Y	Y	Y	N
23 Price	N	Y	N	Y	N	Y	N	Y
24 Simon	N	N	N	Y	N	Y	N	Y
INDIANA								
1 Benjamin	Y	N	Y	N	Y	N	Y	Y
2 Fithian	N	N	Y	N	Y	Y	Y	Y
3 *Hiler*	Y	Y	Y	Y	Y	Y	Y	Y
4 *Coats*	Y	Y	Y	Y	Y	Y	N	Y
5 *Hillis*	Y	Y	Y	Y	Y	Y	N	Y
6 Evans	?	?	N	Y	N	Y	Y	Y
7 *Myers*	Y	Y	Y	Y	Y	Y	N	Y
8 *Deckard*	Y	Y	Y	N	?	?	Y	Y
9 Hamilton	N	N	N	N	N	N	N	N
10 Sharp	Y	N	Y	N	Y	N	Y	Y
11 Jacobs	Y	N	Y	Y	Y	Y	Y	Y
IOWA								
1 *Leach*	N	Y	Y	Y	Y	Y	Y	Y
2 *Tauke*	N	N	N	Y	N	Y	Y	Y
3 *Evans*	Y	N	Y	Y	Y	Y	N	Y
4 Smith	N	N	N	N	N	N	N	N
5 Harkin	N	N	Y	N	N	N	N	Y
6 Bedell	N	N	N	Y	N	Y	N	Y

Democrats   *Republicans*

Corresponding to Congressional Record Votes 39, 40, 41, 42, 43, 44, 45, 46

	32	33	34	35	36	37	38	39
KANSAS								
1 ***Roberts***	Y	N	Y	Y	Y	?	N	Y
2 ***Jeffries***	Y	Y	Y	Y	Y	Y	Y	Y
3 ***Winn***	Y	N	Y	Y	Y	Y	N	Y
4 Glickman	Y	N	N	Y	Y	N	N	N
5 ***Whittaker***	Y	N	Y	Y	Y	Y	N	Y
KENTUCKY								
1 Hubbard	Y	Y	Y	N	Y	Y	N	Y
2 Natcher	Y	Y	Y	N	N	Y	Y	Y
3 Mazzoli	Y	Y	N	Y	Y	Y	Y	Y
4 ***Snyder***	Y	Y	Y	Y	Y	Y	Y	Y
5 ***Rogers***	Y	Y	Y	Y	Y	Y	Y	Y
6 ***Hopkins***	Y	Y	Y	Y	Y	Y	Y	Y
7 Perkins	Y	N	N	N	N	Y	N	Y
LOUISIANA								
1 ***Livingston***	N	N	Y	Y	Y	Y	N	Y
2 Boggs	N	N	Y	N	N	Y	N	Y
3 Tauzin	Y	Y	Y	Y	?	?	?	?
4 Roemer	Y	Y	Y	Y	Y	Y	Y	Y
5 Huckaby	Y	Y	Y	Y	Y	Y	Y	Y
6 ***Moore***	Y	Y	Y	Y	Y	Y	Y	Y
7 Breaux	?	?	Y	Y	Y	Y	N	Y
8 Long	N	N	N	N	N	Y	N	Y
MAINE								
1 ***Emery***	Y	Y	Y	Y	Y	Y	Y	Y
2 ***Snowe***	Y	Y	Y	Y	Y	N	Y	Y
MARYLAND								
1 Dyson	Y	Y	Y	Y	Y	Y	N	Y
2 Long	Y	N	Y	N	Y	N	N	Y
3 Mikulski	N	N	N	Y	N	N	N	N
4 ***Holt***	Y	Y	Y	Y	Y	Y	N	Y
5 Vacancy								
6 Byron	Y	Y	Y	Y	Y	Y	N	Y
7 Mitchell	N	Y	N	N	N	N	Y	N
8 Barnes	N	N	N	N	N	N	N	N
MASSACHUSETTS								
1 ***Conte***	N	N	N	N	N	Y	N	Y
2 Boland	N	N	N	?	N	Y	N	Y
3 Early	Y	Y	N	N	N	Y	Y	N
4 Frank	N	N	N	N	N	N	N	N
5 Shannon	Y	Y	N	N	N	N	Y	N
6 Mavroules	Y	N	N	N	N	Y	N	Y
7 Markey	N	Y	N	N	N	Y	Y	N
8 O'Neill								
9 Moakley	Y	Y	N	N	N	Y	N	Y
10 ***Heckler***	Y	Y	Y	N	Y	Y	Y	Y
11 Donnelly	Y	Y	N	Y	N	Y	N	N
12 Studds	N	Y	N	N	N	N	Y	N
MICHIGAN								
1 Conyers	N	Y	N	N	N	N	Y	N
2 ***Pursell***	Y	X	N	?	N	N	N	Y
3 Wolpe	N	N	N	Y	N	N	N	N
4 ***Siljander***	Y	Y	Y	Y	Y	Y	Y	Y
5 ***Sawyer***	N	N	Y	N	Y	Y	N	Y
6 ***Dunn***	Y	Y	Y	N	Y	N	Y	Y
7 Kildee	N	Y	N	N	N	Y	Y	N
8 Traxler	Y	Y	N	N	Y	Y	?	Y
9 ***Vander Jagt***	Y	N	Y	Y	Y	Y	?	#
10 Albosta	Y	Y	Y	Y	Y	Y	N	Y
11 ***Davis***	Y	Y	Y	Y	Y	Y	Y	Y
12 Bonior	N	N	N	N	N	Y	Y	Y
13 Crockett	N	Y	N	Y	?	?	?	?
14 Hertel	Y	N	N	N	Y	Y	N	Y
15 Ford	?	?	N	N	?	N	N	Y
16 Dingell	Y	N	N	Y	N	N	N	Y
17 Brodhead	?	?	N	Y	N	N	Y	N
18 Blanchard	N	N	N	N	N	N	N	Y
19 ***Broomfield***	N	N	Y	N	Y	Y	N	Y
MINNESOTA								
1 ***Erdahl***	N	N	N	Y	Y	N	N	Y
2 ***Hagedorn***	Y	Y	Y	Y	Y	Y	Y	Y
3 ***Frenzel***	N	N	Y	Y	Y	N	N	Y
4 Vento	N	N	N	N	N	Y	N	N
5 Sabo	N	N	N	N	?	N	Y	Y
6 ***Weber***	Y	Y	Y	Y	Y	Y	Y	Y
7 ***Stangeland***	Y	N	Y	Y	Y	Y	N	Y
8 Oberstar	N	Y	N	Y	N	Y	N	Y
MISSISSIPPI								
1 Whitten	Y	N	N	N	N	Y	N	Y
2 Bowen	N	N	Y	Y	N	Y	N	Y
3 Montgomery	Y	Y	Y	Y	Y	Y	Y	Y
4 Vacancy								
5 ***Lott***	N	Y	Y	Y	Y	Y	Y	Y
MISSOURI								
1 Clay	N	Y	N	N	N	N	N	N
2 Young	Y	Y	Y	Y	Y	Y	N	Y
3 Gephardt	Y	Y	N	Y	Y	Y	Y	Y
4 Skelton	Y	Y	?	Y	N	Y	N	Y
5 Bolling	N	Y	N	N	?	?	?	?
6 ***Coleman***	Y	Y	Y	Y	Y	Y	Y	Y
7 ***Taylor***	Y	Y	Y	Y	Y	Y	N	Y
8 ***Bailey***	Y	Y	Y	Y	Y	Y	N	Y
9 Volkmer	Y	Y	N	Y	Y	Y	Y	N
10 ***Emerson***	Y	Y	Y	Y	Y	Y	Y	Y
MONTANA								
1 Williams	Y	Y	N	N	N	N	N	Y
2 ***Marlenee***	Y	Y	Y	N	Y	Y	Y	Y
NEBRASKA								
1 ***Bereuter***	N	Y	Y	Y	Y	Y	Y	Y
2 ***Daub***	Y	Y	Y	Y	Y	Y	Y	Y
3 ***Smith***	Y	Y	Y	Y	Y	Y	Y	Y
NEVADA								
AL Santini	Y	Y	Y	Y	Y	Y	N	Y
NEW HAMPSHIRE								
1 D'Amours	Y	Y	N	N	Y	Y	Y	Y
2 ***Gregg***	Y	Y	Y	Y	Y	Y	Y	Y
NEW JERSEY								
1 Florio	Y	N	N	N	N	N	N	N
2 Hughes	Y	Y	N	N	Y	N	Y	Y
3 Howard	Y	Y	N	N	N	N	N	Y
4 ***Smith***	Y	Y	Y	Y	Y	Y	Y	Y
5 ***Fenwick***	N	N	N	Y	Y	N	N	Y
6 ***Forsythe***	N	N	N	Y	Y	N	N	Y
7 ***Roukema***	N	N	N	N	Y	N	N	Y
8 Roe	?	?	N	N	N	?	?	?
9 ***Hollenbeck***	X	#	?	?	?	X	?	#
10 Rodino	N	N	N	N	N	N	N	N
11 Minish	Y	Y	N	N	N	Y	Y	Y
12 ***Rinaldo***	Y	Y	Y	N	Y	Y	N	Y
13 ***Courter***	Y	Y	Y	N	Y	Y	Y	Y
14 Guarini	N	X	N	N	N	N	N	Y
15 Dwyer	Y	Y	N	N	N	Y	N	Y
NEW MEXICO								
1 ***Lujan***	Y	Y	Y	Y	Y	Y	Y	N
2 ***Skeen***	Y	Y	Y	Y	Y	Y	N	Y
NEW YORK								
1 ***Carney***	Y	Y	Y	Y	Y	Y	Y	Y
2 Downey	N	N	?	?	?	?	?	?
3 ***Carman***	Y	N	Y	Y	Y	Y	N	Y
4 ***Lent***	Y	N	Y	Y	Y	Y	N	Y
5 ***McGrath***	Y	N	?	Y	Y	Y	N	Y
6 ***LeBoutillier***	#	N	Y	Y	?	?	?	?
7 Addabbo	Y	N	N	N	N	N	N	Y
8 Rosenthal	?	?	?	?	?	?	?	?
9 Ferraro	Y	N	N	N	N	N	N	Y
10 Biaggi	Y	N	Y	N	N	Y	N	N
11 Scheuer	N	N	N	N	N	N	N	Y
12 Chisholm	N	N	N	N	N	N	N	N
13 Solarz	N	N	N	N	N	N	N	Y
14 Richmond	N	N	N	N	N	N	N	N
15 Zeferetti	Y	Y	Y	N	N	Y	N	Y
16 Schumer	N	N	N	N	N	N	N	N
17 ***Molinari***	Y	Y	Y	Y	Y	Y	Y	Y
18 ***Green***	N	N	N	N	Y	N	N	Y
19 Rangel	N	Y	N	N	N	N	Y	N
20 Weiss	N	Y	N	N	?	N	Y	N
21 Garcia	N	N	N	N	N	N	N	N
22 Bingham	N	N	N	N	N	N	N	N
23 Peyser	N	N	Y	Y	N	N	N	Y
24 Ottinger	N	N	N	N	N	?	N	N
25 ***Fish***	N	N	Y	N	Y	Y	N	Y
26 ***Gilman***	N	N	Y	N	Y	N	N	Y
27 McHugh	N	N	N	N	N	Y	N	N
28 Stratton	Y	N	Y	Y	Y	Y	N	Y
29 ***Solomon***	Y	Y	Y	Y	Y	Y	Y	Y
30 ***Martin***	Y	Y	Y	Y	Y	Y	Y	Y
31 ***Mitchell***	N	Y	Y	Y	Y	?	?	?
32 ***Wortley***	Y	N	Y	Y	Y	Y	N	Y
33 ***Lee***	Y	N	Y	Y	Y	Y	N	Y
34 ***Horton***	N	N	Y	Y	Y	N	N	Y
35 ***Conable***	N	N	Y	N	Y	?	?	?
36 LaFalce	N	N	N	N	N	N	N	X
37 Nowak	N	N	N	Y	N	Y	N	N
38 ***Kemp***	N	Y	Y	Y	Y	Y	Y	Y
39 Lundine	?	N	N	Y	N	N	N	Y
NORTH CAROLINA								
1 Jones	Y	Y	Y	Y	N	N	N	Y
2 Fountain	Y	Y	Y	Y	Y	N	Y	Y
3 Whitley	Y	Y	Y	Y	Y	N	Y	Y
4 Andrews	Y	Y	Y	N	N	N	N	Y
5 Neal	Y	N	Y	N	Y	N	N	Y
6 ***Johnston***	Y	Y	Y	Y	Y	Y	Y	Y
7 Rose	Y	Y	?	Y	N	N	N	Y
8 Hefner	Y	Y	Y	Y	N	N	Y	Y
9 ***Martin***	?	?	Y	Y	Y	N	Y	Y
10 ***Broyhill***	Y	Y	Y	Y	Y	N	Y	Y
11 ***Hendon***	Y	Y	Y	Y	Y	Y	Y	Y
NORTH DAKOTA								
AL Dorgan	Y	?	N	Y	N	Y	N	Y
OHIO								
1 ***Gradison***	Y	Y	Y	Y	Y	Y	Y	Y
2 Luken	Y	N	Y	Y	Y	Y	N	Y
3 Hall	Y	Y	Y	Y	Y	N	Y	Y
4 Vacancy								
5 ***Latta***	Y	Y	Y	Y	Y	Y	Y	Y
6 ***McEwen***	Y	Y	Y	Y	Y	Y	Y	Y
7 ***Brown***	Y	Y	?	?	?	?	?	?
8 ***Kindness***	Y	Y	Y	Y	Y	Y	Y	Y
9 ***Weber***	?	N	Y	Y	Y	Y	N	Y
10 ***Miller***	Y	Y	Y	N	Y	Y	Y	Y
11 ***Stanton***	N	N	Y	Y	Y	Y	N	Y
12 Shamansky	N	Y	N	N	?	N	N	Y
13 Pease	N	N	?	?	?	?	?	?
14 Seiberling	N	Y	N	N	N	N	N	N
15 ***Wylie***	Y	N	Y	Y	Y	Y	N	Y
16 ***Regula***	N	N	Y	N	Y	Y	N	Y
17 ***Ashbrook***	Y	Y	Y	Y	Y	Y	Y	Y
18 Applegate	Y	Y	Y	N	Y	Y	N	Y
19 ***Williams***	Y	Y	Y	Y	Y	Y	N	Y
20 Oakar	?	?	N	N	Y	Y	N	Y
21 Stokes	?	?	N	N	N	N	N	N
22 Eckart	Y	Y	N	Y	Y	N	Y	Y
23 Mottl	Y	N	Y	N	Y	Y	N	Y
OKLAHOMA								
1 Jones	Y	Y	N	Y	N	Y	Y	Y
2 Synar	Y	N	N	N	N	N	N	Y
3 Watkins	Y	Y	Y	Y	N	Y	Y	Y
4 McCurdy	Y	Y	Y	Y	Y	Y	Y	Y
5 ***Edwards***	Y	Y	?	Y	Y	Y	Y	Y
6 English	Y	Y	Y	Y	Y	Y	Y	Y
OREGON								
1 AuCoin	Y	N	N	N	N	N	N	Y
2 ***Smith***	Y	Y	Y	Y	Y	Y	Y	Y
3 Wyden	Y	N	N	Y	Y	N	N	Y
4 Weaver	Y	Y	N	N	Y	N	Y	N
PENNSYLVANIA								
1 Foglietta	?	?	?	N	N	N	N	N
2 Gray	N	N	N	N	N	N	N	N
3 Vacancy								
4 ***Dougherty***	N	N	Y	Y	Y	Y	N	Y
5 ***Schulze***	Y	N	Y	Y	Y	Y	N	Y
6 Yatron	Y	Y	Y	Y	Y	Y	N	Y
7 Edgar	N	N	N	N	?	?	?	?
8 ***Coyne, J.***	N	Y	Y	N	Y	N	Y	Y
9 ***Shuster***	Y	Y	Y	Y	Y	Y	Y	Y
10 ***McDade***	Y	N	Y	N	Y	Y	N	Y
11 ***Nelligan***	Y	N	Y	N	?	?	?	?
12 Murtha	Y	N	Y	N	N	Y	N	Y
13 ***Coughlin***	N	N	N	Y	Y	N	N	Y
14 Coyne, W.	N	N	N	N	N	Y	N	Y
15 ***Ritter***	?	?	N	Y	Y	Y	Y	Y
16 ***Walker***	Y	Y	Y	Y	Y	Y	Y	Y
17 Ertel	Y	N	Y	Y	N	N	N	Y
18 Walgren	Y	Y	N	N	Y	N	Y	Y
19 ***Goodling***	?	?	N	Y	Y	Y	Y	Y
20 Gaydos	?	?	Y	N	N	Y	N	Y
21 Bailey	Y	N	Y	N	N	Y	N	Y
22 Murphy	Y	Y	N	N	Y	Y	N	N
23 ***Clinger***	N	N	Y	Y	Y	N	N	Y
24 ***Marks***	Y	N	Y	Y	Y	N	N	Y
25 Atkinson	Y	Y	Y	Y	Y	Y	N	Y
RHODE ISLAND								
1 St Germain	Y	Y	?	?	?	?	?	?
2 ***Schneider***	N	Y	N	N	Y	N	N	Y
SOUTH CAROLINA								
1 ***Hartnett***	Y	Y	Y	Y	?	?	?	?
2 ***Spence***	Y	Y	Y	Y	Y	Y	Y	Y
3 Derrick	Y	Y	?	Y	Y	N	N	Y
4 ***Campbell***	N	Y	Y	Y	Y	Y	Y	Y
5 Holland	Y	Y	Y	Y	N	N	N	Y
6 ***Napier***	Y	Y	Y	Y	Y	Y	Y	Y
SOUTH DAKOTA								
1 Daschle	Y	Y	Y	N	N	N	N	N
2 ***Roberts***	Y	Y	Y	Y	Y	Y	Y	Y
TENNESSEE								
1 ***Quillen***	?	#	?	?	?	?	?	?
2 ***Duncan***	Y	Y	Y	Y	Y	Y	N	Y
3 Bouquard	Y	Y	Y	N	Y	Y	N	Y
4 Gore	Y	Y	Y	N	N	Y	Y	N
5 Boner	Y	Y	Y	Y	Y	Y	N	Y
6 ***Beard***	?	Y	Y	Y	Y	?	?	?
7 Jones	Y	Y	Y	Y	N	Y	N	Y
8 Ford	N	Y	N	N	N	N	N	Y
TEXAS								
1 Hall, S.	Y	Y	Y	Y	Y	Y	Y	Y
2 Wilson	?	N	Y	Y	N	N	N	Y
3 ***Collins***	Y	Y	Y	Y	Y	Y	Y	Y
4 Hall, R.	?	?	Y	Y	Y	Y	N	Y
5 Mattox	Y	N	N	Y	?	?	?	X
6 Gramm	Y	Y	Y	Y	Y	Y	Y	Y
7 ***Archer***	Y	N	Y	Y	Y	Y	N	Y
8 ***Fields***	Y	Y	Y	Y	Y	Y	Y	Y
9 Brooks	Y	Y	Y	N	N	N	N	N
10 Pickle	Y	Y	Y	Y	N	N	Y	Y
11 Leath	Y	Y	Y	Y	Y	Y	N	Y
12 Wright	Y	N	N	N	N	Y	N	Y
13 Hightower	Y	Y	Y	Y	Y	Y	N	Y
14 Patman	?	?	?	?	?	?	?	?
15 de la Garza	Y	Y	Y	N	Y	Y	Y	Y
16 White	Y	Y	Y	Y	Y	Y	Y	Y
17 Stenholm	Y	Y	Y	Y	Y	Y	Y	Y
18 Leland	N	Y	N	N	N	N	N	N
19 Hance	Y	Y	Y	Y	Y	N	N	Y
20 Gonzalez	N	N	N	Y	N	N	N	N
21 ***Loeffler***	Y	N	Y	Y	Y	Y	N	Y
22 ***Paul***	Y	Y	N	Y	Y	Y	Y	N
23 Kazen	Y	Y	Y	Y	N	Y	Y	N
24 Frost	Y	Y	Y	Y	Y	N	Y	Y
UTAH								
1 ***Hansen***	Y	Y	Y	+	+	+	+	+
2 ***Marriott***	Y	N	Y	Y	Y	Y	N	Y
VERMONT								
AL ***Jeffords***	N	N	N	N	Y	N	N	Y
VIRGINIA								
1 ***Trible***	Y	Y	Y	Y	Y	Y	N	Y
2 ***Whitehurst***	Y	N	Y	Y	Y	Y	N	Y
3 ***Bliley***	Y	N	Y	Y	Y	Y	N	Y
4 ***Daniel, R.***	Y	Y	Y	Y	Y	Y	Y	Y
5 Daniel, D.	Y	N	Y	Y	Y	Y	N	Y
6 ***Butler***	Y	N	Y	N	Y	N	N	Y
7 ***Robinson***	Y	N	Y	Y	Y	Y	N	Y
8 ***Parris***	Y	N	Y	Y	Y	Y	N	Y
9 ***Wampler***	Y	N	Y	Y	Y	Y	N	Y
10 ***Wolf***	Y	Y	Y	Y	Y	Y	Y	Y
WASHINGTON								
1 ***Pritchard***	?	X	Y	Y	Y	N	N	Y
2 Swift	Y	N	N	N	N	N	N	Y
3 Bonker	Y	N	N	Y	N	N	N	Y
4 ***Morrison***	Y	N	Y	Y	Y	Y	N	Y
5 Foley	Y	N	Y	N	N	N	N	Y
6 Dicks	Y	N	Y	N	N	N	N	Y
7 Lowry	N	N	N	N	N	N	N	N
WEST VIRGINIA								
1 Mollohan	Y	N	N	N	N	N	N	Y
2 ***Benedict***	Y	Y	Y	Y	Y	Y	Y	Y
3 ***Staton***	Y	Y	Y	Y	Y	Y	Y	Y
4 Rahall	?	?	?	?	?	?	?	?
WISCONSIN								
1 Aspin	N	Y	N	Y	N	Y	Y	Y
2 Kastenmeier	N	Y	N	N	N	N	Y	N
3 ***Gunderson***	Y	Y	N	Y	Y	Y	Y	Y
4 Zablocki	N	Y	N	N	N	Y	N	Y
5 Reuss	N	Y	N	N	N	N	Y	N
6 ***Petri***	Y	Y	N	Y	Y	Y	Y	Y
7 Obey	N	Y	N	N	N	N	Y	Y
8 ***Roth***	Y	Y	Y	Y	Y	Y	Y	Y
9 ***Sensenbrenner***	Y	Y	Y	Y	Y	Y	Y	Y
WYOMING								
AL ***Cheney***	N	Y	Y	Y	Y	Y	Y	Y

Democrats ***Republicans***

KEY

Y   Voted for (yea).
Paired for.
+   Announced for.
N   Voted against (nay).
X   Paired against.
-   Announced against.
P   Voted "present".
C   Voted "present" to avoid possible conflict of interest.
?   Did not vote or otherwise make a position known.

40. H Res 133. Philippines Martial Law. Solarz, D-N.Y., motion to suspend the rules and adopt the resolution praising the government of the Philippines for lifting martial law and stating the sense of the House that the government of the Philippines should make further progress toward restoring democracy, including the revival of political and civil liberties. Motion agreed to 387-4: R 172-1; D 215-3 (ND 146-3; SD 69-0), May 19, 1981. A two-thirds majority vote (261 in this case) is required for adoption under suspension of the rules.

41. S 730. Federal Crop Insurance Act Funding. De la Garza, D-Texas, motion to suspend the rules and pass the bill to authorize the Federal Crop Insurance Corporation temporarily to use funds intended for payment of crop insurance indemnities for administrative and operating expenses in fiscal year 1981. Motion agreed to (thus cleared for the president) 384-5: R 167-5; D 217-0 (ND 147-0, SD 70-0), May 19, 1981. A two-thirds majority vote (260 in this case) is required for passage under suspension of the rules. A "yea" was a vote supporting the president's position.

42. HR 2098. Inspector General Act Amendments. Brooks, D-Texas, motion to suspend the rules and pass the bill to authorize inspectors general for the Defense, Justice and Treasury departments and for the Agency for International Development. Motion agreed to 334-65: R 130-46; D 204-19 (ND 145-8, SD 59-11), May 19, 1981. A two-thirds majority vote (266 in this case) is required for passage under suspension of the rules.

43. HR 2979. Historical Publications and Records Act. English, D-Okla., motion to suspend the rules and pass the bill to authorize $3 million annually for fiscal years 1982 and 1983 for the National Historical Publications and Records Commission. Motion rejected 165-231: R 19-155; D 146-76 (ND 105-46, SD 41-30), May 19, 1981. A two-thirds majority vote (264 in this case) is required for passage under suspension of the rules.

44. H Con Res 115. Fiscal 1982 Budget Targets. Adoption of the conference report on the resolution to set budget targets for the fiscal year ending Sept. 30, 1982, as follows: budget authority, $770.9 billion; outlays, $695.45 billion; revenues, $657.8 billion; and deficit, $37.65 billion. The resolution also revised binding budget levels for fiscal 1981 and included reconciliation instructions requiring House and Senate committees to make approximately $36 billion in spending cuts in fiscal 1982. Adopted 244-155: R 167-8; D 77-147 (ND 18-135, SD 59-12), May 20, 1981.

	40	41	42	43	44
ALABAMA					
1 Edwards	Y	Y	Y	N	Y
2 Dickinson	Y	Y	N	N	?
3 Nichols	Y	Y	N	N	Y
4 Bevill	Y	Y	Y	Y	Y
5 Flippo	?	Y	Y	N	Y
6 Smith	Y	Y	N	N	?
7 Shelby	Y	Y	Y	N	Y
ALASKA					
AL Young	?	Y	Y	N	Y
ARIZONA					
1 Rhodes	Y	Y	Y	N	Y
2 Udall	Y	Y	Y	Y	Y
3 Stump	Y	Y	N	N	Y
4 Rudd	Y	Y	N	N	Y
ARKANSAS					
1 Alexander	Y	Y	Y	N	Y
2 Bethune	Y	Y	Y	N	Y
3 Hammerschmidt	Y	Y	N	N	Y
4 Anthony	Y	Y	Y	Y	Y
CALIFORNIA					
1 Chappie	Y	Y	Y	N	Y
2 Clausen	Y	Y	N	N	Y
3 Matsui	Y	Y	Y	Y	N
4 Fazio	Y	Y	Y	Y	N
5 Burton, J.	Y	Y	Y	N	N
6 Burton, P.	Y	Y	Y	Y	N
7 Miller	?	Y	Y	N	N
8 Dellums	Y	Y	Y	Y	N
9 Stark	Y	Y	N	N	N
10 Edwards	Y	Y	Y	N	N
11 Lantos	Y	Y	Y	N	N
12 McCloskey	Y	Y	N	N	#
13 Mineta	?	?	Y	Y	N
14 Shumway	Y	Y	Y	N	Y
15 Coelho	Y	Y	Y	Y	N
16 Panetta	Y	Y	Y	N	N
17 Pashayan	Y	Y	Y	N	Y
18 Thomas	Y	Y	Y	N	Y
19 Lagomarsino	Y	Y	Y	N	Y
20 Goldwater	Y	Y	Y	N	Y
21 Fiedler	Y	Y	Y	N	Y
22 Moorhead	Y	Y	Y	N	Y
23 Beilenson	Y	Y	Y	Y	N
24 Waxman	Y	Y	Y	Y	N
25 Roybal	Y	Y	Y	Y	N
26 Rousselot	Y	Y	Y	N	P
27 Dornan	Y	Y	N	?	?
28 Dixon	Y	Y	Y	Y	-
29 Hawkins	?	?	?	?	X
30 Danielson	Y	Y	Y	Y	N
31 Dymally	Y	Y	Y	Y	N
32 Anderson	Y	Y	Y	Y	N
33 Grisham	Y	Y	N	N	#
34 Lungren	Y	Y	Y	N	Y
35 Dreier	Y	Y	N	N	Y
36 Brown	Y	Y	Y	Y	N
37 Lewis	Y	Y	Y	N	Y
38 Patterson	Y	Y	Y	Y	Y
39 Dannemeyer	Y	Y	N	N	Y
40 Badham	Y	Y	N	N	Y
41 Lowery	Y	Y	Y	N	Y
42 Hunter	Y	Y	Y	N	Y
43 Burgener	Y	Y	N	N	?
COLORADO					
1 Schroeder	Y	Y	N	N	N
2 Wirth	Y	Y	Y	Y	N
3 Kogovsek	?	?	?	?	N
4 Brown	Y	Y	Y	N	Y

	40	41	42	43	44
5 Kramer	Y	Y	N	N	Y
CONNECTICUT					
1 Cotter	?	?	?	?	?
2 Gejdenson	Y	?	Y	Y	N
3 DeNardis	Y	Y	Y	N	Y
4 McKinney	Y	Y	Y	N	Y
5 Ratchford	Y	Y	Y	Y	Y
6 Moffett	Y	Y	Y	Y	N
DELAWARE					
AL Evans	?	?	?	?	?
FLORIDA					
1 Hutto	Y	Y	N	Y	Y
2 Fuqua	?	?	?	?	Y
3 Bennett	Y	Y	Y	Y	Y
4 Chappell	Y	Y	N	Y	Y
5 McCollum	Y	Y	N	N	Y
6 Young	Y	N	Y	N	Y
7 Gibbons	Y	Y	Y	N	Y
8 Ireland	Y	Y	Y	Y	Y
9 Nelson	Y	Y	Y	N	Y
10 Bafalis	Y	Y	Y	N	Y
11 Mica	Y	Y	Y	N	Y
12 Shaw	Y	Y	Y	N	Y
13 Lehman	Y	Y	Y	Y	N
14 Pepper	?	?	?	?	Y
15 Fascell	Y	Y	Y	Y	Y
GEORGIA					
1 Ginn	Y	Y	Y	Y	Y
2 Hatcher	Y	Y	Y	Y	Y
3 Brinkley	Y	Y	Y	Y	Y
4 Levitas	Y	Y	Y	Y	Y
5 Fowler	Y	Y	Y	Y	N
6 Gingrich	Y	Y	N	N	#
7 McDonald	-	-	-	-	X
8 Evans	Y	Y	Y	N	Y
9 Jenkins	?	?	?	?	Y
10 Barnard	Y	Y	N	Y	?
HAWAII					
1 Heftel	Y	Y	Y	N	N
2 Akaka	Y	Y	Y	N	N
IDAHO					
1 Craig	Y	Y	N	N	Y
2 Hansen	Y	Y	N	N	Y
ILLINOIS					
1 Washington	Y	?	Y	Y	?
2 Savage	Y	Y	Y	N	N
3 Russo	Y	Y	Y	N	Y
4 Derwinski	Y	Y	Y	N	Y
5 Fary	Y	Y	N	N	N
6 Hyde	Y	Y	N	N	Y
7 Collins	Y	Y	Y	N	N
8 Rostenkowski	Y	Y	Y	N	N
9 Yates	Y	Y	Y	Y	N
10 Porter	Y	Y	Y	N	Y
11 Annunzio	Y	Y	Y	Y	N
12 Crane, P.	Y	N	N	N	Y
13 McClory	N	Y	Y	Y	Y
14 Erlenborn	Y	Y	Y	N	Y
15 Corcoran	Y	Y	N	N	#
16 Martin	Y	Y	Y	N	Y
17 O'Brien	?	?	?	?	Y
18 Michel	?	Y	Y	N	Y
19 Railsback	?	?	?	?	Y
20 Findley	Y	?	Y	N	Y
21 Madigan	Y	Y	Y	N	Y
22 Crane, D.	Y	N	N	N	N
23 Price	Y	Y	N	N	N
24 Simon	Y	Y	Y	Y	N
INDIANA					
1 Benjamin	Y	Y	Y	N	N
2 Fithian	Y	Y	Y	N	Y
3 Hiler	Y	Y	N	N	Y
4 Coats	Y	Y	N	N	Y
5 Hillis	Y	N	Y	N	Y
6 Evans	Y	Y	Y	N	N
7 Myers	Y	Y	Y	N	Y
8 Deckard	Y	Y	N	N	Y
9 Hamilton	Y	Y	Y	N	Y
10 Sharp	Y	Y	Y	N	N
11 Jacobs	Y	Y	Y	N	N
IOWA					
1 Leach	Y	Y	Y	N	#
2 Tauke	Y	Y	Y	N	Y
3 Evans	Y	Y	Y	N	Y
4 Smith	Y	Y	Y	Y	N
5 Harkin	Y	Y	Y	N	N
6 Bedell	Y	Y	Y	N	N

Democrats   *Republicans*

Member	40	41	42	43	44
KANSAS					
1 Roberts	?	?	?	?	Y
2 Jeffries	Y	Y	Y	N	Y
3 Winn	?	?	?	?	Y
4 Glickman	Y	Y	Y	N	Y
5 Whittaker	Y	Y	Y	N	Y
KENTUCKY					
1 Hubbard	Y	Y	Y	N	N
2 Natcher	Y	Y	Y	N	Y
3 Mazzoli	Y	Y	Y	N	Y
4 Snyder	Y	Y	Y	N	Y
5 Rogers	Y	Y	Y	N	Y
6 Hopkins	Y	Y	N	N	Y
7 Perkins	Y	Y	Y	N	N
LOUISIANA					
1 Livingston	Y	Y	Y	N	Y
2 Boggs	Y	Y	Y	Y	Y
3 Tauzin	Y	Y	Y	N	Y
4 Roemer	Y	Y	Y	N	Y
5 Huckaby	Y	Y	Y	N	Y
6 Moore	Y	Y	Y	N	Y
7 Breaux	Y	Y	Y	N	Y
8 Long	Y	Y	Y	Y	Y
MAINE					
1 Emery	Y	Y	Y	N	Y
2 Snowe	Y	Y	Y	N	Y
MARYLAND					
1 Dyson	Y	Y	Y	N	Y
2 Long	Y	Y	Y	Y	Y
3 Mikulski	Y	Y	Y	Y	N
4 Holt	?	?	?	?	Y
5 Vacancy					
6 Byron	Y	Y	Y	Y	Y
7 Mitchell	Y	Y	Y	Y	N
8 Barnes	Y	Y	Y	Y	N
MASSACHUSETTS					
1 Conte	Y	Y	Y	N	Y
2 Boland	?	?	Y	Y	N
3 Early	Y	Y	N	Y	N
4 Frank	Y	Y	Y	Y	-
5 Shannon	Y	Y	Y	Y	N
6 Mavroules	Y	Y	Y	Y	N
7 Markey	Y	Y	Y	Y	N
8 O'Neill					
9 Moakley	Y	Y	Y	Y	N
10 Heckler	Y	Y	Y	N	Y
11 Donnelly	Y	Y	Y	Y	N
12 Studds	Y	Y	Y	Y	N
MICHIGAN					
1 Conyers	Y	Y	Y	N	N
2 Pursell	Y	Y	Y	Y	Y
3 Wolpe	Y	Y	Y	Y	N
4 Siljander	Y	Y	Y	N	Y
5 Sawyer	Y	Y	N	N	Y
6 Dunn	Y	Y	Y	Y	Y
7 Kildee	Y	Y	Y	Y	N
8 Traxler	Y	Y	Y	Y	N
9 Vander Jagt	Y	Y	Y	N	Y
10 Albosta	Y	Y	Y	N	Y
11 Davis	Y	?	?	N	Y
12 Bonior	Y	Y	Y	Y	N
13 Crockett	Y	Y	Y	?	N
14 Hertel	Y	Y	Y	Y	N
15 Ford	Y	Y	Y	Y	N
16 Dingell	?	?	?	?	?
17 Brodhead	Y	Y	Y	Y	N
18 Blanchard	Y	Y	Y	N	N
19 Broomfield	Y	Y	Y	N	Y
MINNESOTA					
1 Erdahl	Y	Y	Y	N	Y
2 Hagedorn	Y	Y	Y	N	Y
3 Frenzel	Y	Y	Y	N	Y
4 Vento	Y	Y	Y	Y	N
5 Sabo	Y	Y	Y	Y	N
6 Weber	Y	Y	Y	N	Y
7 Stangeland	Y	Y	Y	Y	N
8 Oberstar	Y	Y	Y	Y	N
MISSISSIPPI					
1 Whitten	Y	Y	Y	Y	Y
2 Bowen	Y	Y	Y	Y	Y
3 Montgomery	Y	Y	N	N	Y
4 Vacancy					
5 Lott	Y	Y	Y	N	Y
MISSOURI					
1 Clay	Y	Y	Y	Y	N
2 Young	Y	Y	Y	N	Y
3 Gephardt	Y	Y	N	N	N
4 Skelton	Y	Y	N	N	Y
5 Bolling	Y	Y	Y	Y	N
6 Coleman	Y	Y	Y	N	Y
7 Taylor	Y	Y	N	N	Y
8 Bailey	Y	Y	Y	N	Y
9 Volkmer	Y	Y	Y	N	N
10 Emerson	Y	Y	Y	N	Y
MONTANA					
1 Williams	Y	Y	Y	Y	N
2 Marlenee	Y	Y	N	N	Y
NEBRASKA					
1 Bereuter	Y	Y	Y	N	Y
2 Daub	Y	Y	Y	Y	Y
3 Smith	Y	Y	Y	N	Y
NEVADA					
AL Santini	Y	Y	N	N	Y
NEW HAMPSHIRE					
1 D'Amours	?	?	?	?	Y
2 Gregg	Y	Y	Y	N	Y
NEW JERSEY					
1 Florio	?	?	?	?	N
2 Hughes	Y	Y	Y	N	N
3 Howard	Y	Y	Y	N	Y
4 Smith	Y	Y	Y	N	Y
5 Fenwick	Y	Y	Y	N	Y
6 Forsythe	Y	Y	Y	Y	Y
7 Roukema	Y	Y	Y	N	Y
8 Roe	Y	Y	Y	Y	N
9 Hollenbeck	?	?	Y	Y	Y
10 Rodino	Y	Y	N	Y	N
11 Minish	Y	Y	Y	Y	N
12 Rinaldo	Y	Y	Y	N	Y
13 Courter	Y	Y	N	N	Y
14 Guarini	Y	Y	Y	Y	N
15 Dwyer	Y	Y	Y	Y	N
NEW MEXICO					
1 Lujan	Y	Y	Y	N	Y
2 Skeen	Y	Y	Y	N	Y
NEW YORK					
1 Carney	Y	Y	Y	N	Y
2 Downey	Y	Y	Y	Y	N
3 Carman	Y	Y	Y	N	Y
4 Lent	Y	Y	N	N	Y
5 McGrath	Y	Y	Y	Y	Y
6 LeBoutillier	Y	Y	Y	N	Y
7 Addabbo	Y	Y	Y	Y	N
8 Rosenthal	Y	Y	Y	Y	N
9 Ferraro	Y	Y	Y	Y	N
10 Biaggi	Y	Y	Y	N	N
11 Scheuer	Y	Y	Y	Y	N
12 Chisholm	Y	Y	Y	Y	N
13 Solarz	Y	Y	Y	Y	N
14 Richmond	Y	Y	Y	Y	N
15 Zeferetti	Y	Y	Y	Y	N
16 Schumer	Y	Y	Y	Y	N
17 Molinari	Y	Y	N	N	Y
18 Green	?	?	Y	Y	Y
19 Rangel	Y	Y	Y	Y	N
20 Weiss	Y	Y	Y	Y	N
21 Garcia	Y	Y	Y	Y	N
22 Bingham	Y	Y	Y	Y	N
23 Peyser	Y	Y	Y	Y	N
24 Ottinger	Y	Y	Y	Y	N
25 Fish	Y	Y	N	Y	Y
26 Gilman	Y	Y	Y	Y	Y
27 McHugh	Y	Y	Y	Y	N
28 Stratton	N	Y	N	N	Y
29 Solomon	Y	Y	N	N	Y
30 Martin	Y	Y	N	N	Y
31 Mitchell	Y	Y	N	N	Y
32 Wortley	Y	Y	N	Y	N
33 Lee	Y	Y	Y	N	Y
34 Horton	Y	Y	Y	Y	N
35 Conable	Y	Y	Y	Y	Y
36 LaFalce	Y	Y	Y	Y	N
37 Nowak	Y	Y	Y	Y	N
38 Kemp	?	?	?	?	Y
39 Lundine	Y	Y	Y	?	N
NORTH CAROLINA					
1 Jones	Y	Y	Y	N	Y
2 Fountain	Y	Y	Y	N	Y
3 Whitley	Y	?	Y	N	Y
4 Andrews	Y	Y	Y	Y	Y
5 Neal	Y	Y	Y	Y	Y
6 Johnston	Y	Y	N	N	Y
7 Rose	Y	Y	Y	Y	Y
8 Hefner	Y	Y	Y	Y	Y
9 Martin	Y	Y	Y	N	Y
10 Broyhill	Y	Y	Y	N	Y
11 Hendon	Y	Y	Y	N	Y
NORTH DAKOTA					
AL Dorgan	Y	Y	Y	Y	N
OHIO					
1 Gradison	Y	Y	Y	N	Y
2 Luken	Y	Y	Y	N	Y
3 Hall	Y	Y	Y	N	Y
4 Vacancy					
5 Latta	Y	Y	Y	N	Y
6 McEwen	Y	Y	Y	N	Y
7 Brown	?	?	?	?	?
8 Kindness	Y	Y	Y	N	Y
9 Weber	Y	Y	Y	N	Y
10 Miller	Y	Y	Y	N	N
11 Stanton	Y	Y	Y	N	Y
12 Shamansky	Y	+	Y	Y	N
13 Pease	Y	Y	Y	N	N
14 Seiberling	Y	Y	Y	Y	N
15 Wylie	?	?	?	?	Y
16 Regula	Y	Y	Y	N	Y
17 Ashbrook	Y	Y	N	?	N
18 Applegate	Y	Y	Y	N	N
19 Williams	?	?	?	?	?
20 Oakar	Y	Y	Y	N	N
21 Stokes	Y	Y	Y	Y	N
22 Eckart	Y	Y	Y	Y	N
23 Mottl	Y	Y	Y	N	N
OKLAHOMA					
1 Jones	Y	Y	Y	Y	N
2 Synar	Y	Y	Y	Y	N
3 Watkins	Y	Y	Y	Y	Y
4 McCurdy	Y	Y	Y	Y	Y
5 Edwards	Y	Y	Y	N	Y
6 English	Y	Y	Y	Y	Y
OREGON					
1 AuCoin	Y	Y	Y	N	N
2 Smith	Y	Y	Y	N	N
3 Wyden	Y	Y	Y	N	N
4 Weaver	?	?	?	?	?
PENNSYLVANIA					
1 Foglietta	?	?	?	?	X
2 Gray	Y	Y	Y	Y	N
3 Vacancy					
4 Dougherty	?	?	?	?	N
5 Schulze	Y	Y	N	?	Y
6 Yatron	Y	Y	Y	N	Y
7 Edgar	Y	Y	Y	Y	N
8 Coyne, J.	Y	Y	Y	N	Y
9 Shuster	Y	Y	Y	N	Y
10 McDade	Y	Y	Y	N	#
11 Nelligan	Y	Y	Y	N	Y
12 Murtha	N	Y	N	N	Y
13 Coughlin	Y	Y	Y	N	Y
14 Coyne, W.	Y	Y	Y	N	Y
15 Ritter	Y	Y	Y	N	Y
16 Walker	Y	Y	Y	N	Y
17 Ertel	Y	Y	Y	Y	Y
18 Walgren	Y	Y	Y	N	Y
19 Goodling	Y	?	Y	N	Y
20 Gaydos	Y	Y	Y	N	N
21 Bailey	Y	Y	Y	N	N
22 Murphy	Y	Y	Y	N	N
23 Clinger	Y	Y	Y	N	Y
24 Marks	Y	Y	Y	?	Y
25 Atkinson	Y	Y	Y	N	Y
RHODE ISLAND					
1 St Germain	Y	Y	Y	Y	N
2 Schneider	Y	Y	Y	N	Y
SOUTH CAROLINA					
1 Hartnett	Y	Y	N	N	Y
2 Spence	Y	Y	N	N	Y
3 Derrick	Y	Y	Y	Y	+
4 Campbell	Y	Y	N	N	Y
5 Holland	Y	Y	N	Y	Y
6 Napier	Y	Y	N	N	Y
SOUTH DAKOTA					
1 Daschle	Y	Y	Y	Y	N
2 Roberts	Y	Y	Y	N	N
TENNESSEE					
1 Quillen	Y	Y	Y	Y	Y
2 Duncan	Y	Y	Y	N	Y
3 Bouquard	Y	Y	N	N	Y
4 Gore	Y	Y	Y	Y	N
5 Boner	Y	Y	Y	N	Y
6 Beard	Y	Y	Y	N	Y
7 Jones	Y	Y	Y	Y	Y
8 Ford	Y	Y	Y	Y	X
TEXAS					
1 Hall, S.	Y	Y	Y	N	Y
2 Wilson	Y	Y	?	Y	Y
3 Collins	Y	Y	N	N	Y
4 Hall, R.	Y	Y	Y	N	Y
5 Mattox	?	?	?	?	X
6 Gramm	Y	Y	N	N	Y
7 Archer	Y	Y	Y	N	Y
8 Fields	Y	Y	Y	N	Y
9 Brooks	Y	Y	Y	Y	Y
10 Pickle	Y	Y	Y	Y	Y
11 Leath	Y	Y	N	N	Y
12 Wright	?	Y	Y	N	N
13 Hightower	Y	Y	Y	N	Y
14 Patman	?	?	?	?	X
15 de la Garza	Y	Y	Y	N	?
16 White	Y	Y	N	N	Y
17 Stenholm	Y	Y	Y	N	Y
18 Leland	Y	Y	Y	Y	N
19 Hance	?	?	?	?	Y
20 Gonzalez	Y	Y	Y	Y	N
21 Loeffler	Y	Y	Y	N	Y
22 Paul	Y	N	Y	N	N
23 Kazen	Y	Y	Y	N	N
24 Frost	Y	Y	Y	Y	N
UTAH					
1 Hansen	Y	Y	Y	N	+
2 Marriott	?	Y	N	N	Y
VERMONT					
AL Jeffords	Y	Y	Y	N	Y
VIRGINIA					
1 Trible	Y	Y	N	N	Y
2 Whitehurst	Y	Y	N	N	Y
3 Bliley	Y	Y	N	N	Y
4 Daniel, R.	Y	Y	N	N	Y
5 Daniel, D.	Y	Y	N	N	Y
6 Butler	Y	Y	Y	Y	Y
7 Robinson	Y	Y	Y	N	Y
8 Parris	Y	Y	Y	N	Y
9 Wampler	Y	Y	Y	N	Y
10 Wolf	Y	Y	Y	N	Y
WASHINGTON					
1 Pritchard	Y	Y	Y	N	Y
2 Swift	Y	Y	Y	N	N
3 Bonker	Y	Y	Y	Y	N
4 Morrison	Y	Y	Y	N	Y
5 Foley	Y	Y	Y	Y	N
6 Dicks	?	?	?	?	?
7 Lowry	Y	Y	Y	N	N
WEST VIRGINIA					
1 Mollohan	N	Y	Y	N	N
2 Benedict	Y	?	?	N	Y
3 Staton	Y	Y	N	N	Y
4 Rahall	Y	Y	Y	Y	N
WISCONSIN					
1 Aspin	Y	Y	Y	Y	N
2 Kastenmeier	?	?	Y	Y	N
3 Gunderson	Y	Y	Y	N	Y
4 Zablocki	Y	Y	Y	Y	N
5 Reuss	Y	Y	Y	Y	N
6 Petri	Y	Y	Y	N	Y
7 Obey	Y	Y	Y	Y	N
8 Roth	Y	Y	Y	N	Y
9 Sensenbrenner	Y	Y	N	N	Y
WYOMING					
AL Cheney	?	?	?	?	Y

Democrats *Republicans*

KEY

Y Voted for (yea).
Paired for.
+ Announced for.
N Voted against (nay).
X Paired against.
- Announced against.
P Voted "present".
C Voted "present" to avoid possible conflict of interest.
? Did not vote or otherwise make a position known.

45. Procedural Motion. Ashbrook, R-Ohio, motion to approve the House *Journal* of Wednesday, May 27. Motion agreed to 278-8: R 122-4; D 156-4 (ND 103-3, SD 53-1), May 28, 1981.

46. HR 3520. Steel Industry Compliance. Waxman, D-Calif., motion to suspend the rules and pass the bill to grant the steel industry a three-year extension of the 1982 deadline for meeting national clean air standards. Motion agreed to 322-3: R 140-2; D 182-1 (ND 125-0, SD 57-1), May 28, 1981. A two-thirds majority vote (217 in this case) is required for passage under suspension of the rules. A "yea" was a vote supporting the president's position.

	45	46
ALABAMA		
1 *Edwards*	?	Y
2 *Dickinson*	?	?
3 Nichols	Y	Y
4 Bevill	Y	Y
5 Flippo	Y	Y
6 *Smith*	?	Y
7 Shelby	?	?
ALASKA		
AL *Young*	?	?
ARIZONA		
1 *Rhodes*	Y	Y
2 Udall	?	Y
3 *Stump*	?	?
4 *Rudd*	?	?
ARKANSAS		
1 Alexander	Y	Y
2 *Bethune*	Y	Y
3 *Hammerschmidt*	Y	Y
4 Anthony	Y	Y
CALIFORNIA		
1 *Chappie*	?	Y
2 *Clausen*	Y	Y
3 Matsui	Y	Y
4 Fazio	Y	Y
5 Burton, J.	Y	Y
6 Burton, P.	Y	Y
7 Miller	Y	Y
8 Dellums	?	?
9 Stark	?	?
10 Edwards	Y	Y
11 Lantos	Y	Y
12 *McCloskey*	?	?
13 Mineta	Y	Y
14 *Shumway*	Y	Y
15 Coelho	Y	Y
16 Panetta	Y	Y
17 *Pashayan*	?	?
18 *Thomas*	Y	Y
19 *Lagomarsino*	Y	Y
20 *Goldwater*	?	?
21 *Fiedler*	Y	Y
22 *Moorhead*	Y	Y
23 Beilenson	Y	Y
24 Waxman	Y	Y
25 Roybal	Y	Y
26 *Rousselot*	Y	Y
27 *Dornan*	?	?
28 Dixon	?	Y
29 Hawkins	Y	Y
30 Danielson	+	+
31 Dymally	?	?
32 Anderson	Y	Y
33 *Grisham*	?	?
34 *Lungren*	?	?
35 *Dreier*	Y	Y
36 Brown	?	Y
37 *Lewis*	Y	Y
38 Patterson	?	?
39 *Dannemeyer*	?	?
40 *Badham*	?	?
41 *Lowery*	?	Y
42 *Hunter*	Y	Y
43 *Burgener*	Y	Y
COLORADO		
1 Schroeder	N	Y
2 Wirth	Y	Y
3 Kogovsek	Y	Y
4 *Brown*	Y	Y

	45	46
5 *Kramer*	Y	Y
CONNECTICUT		
1 Cotter	?	?
2 Gejdenson	Y	Y
3 *DeNardis*	Y	Y
4 *McKinney*	Y	Y
5 Ratchford	Y	Y
6 Moffett	Y	Y
DELAWARE		
AL *Evans*	Y	Y
FLORIDA		
1 Hutto	Y	Y
2 Fuqua	?	?
3 Bennett	Y	Y
4 Chappell	Y	Y
5 *McCollum*	?	?
6 *Young*	?	?
7 Gibbons	?	Y
8 Ireland	Y	Y
9 Nelson	Y	Y
10 *Bafalis*	?	Y
11 Mica	Y	Y
12 *Shaw*	?	Y
13 Lehman	Y	Y
14 Pepper	Y	?
15 Fascell	Y	Y
GEORGIA		
1 Ginn	?	?
2 Hatcher	?	?
3 Brinkley	Y	Y
4 Levitas	Y	Y
5 Fowler	Y	Y
6 *Gingrich*	?	?
7 McDonald	?	Y
8 Evans	Y	Y
9 Jenkins	Y	Y
10 Barnard	?	?
HAWAII		
1 Heftel	?	?
2 Akaka	Y	Y
IDAHO		
1 *Craig*	Y	Y
2 *Hansen*	?	Y
ILLINOIS		
1 Washington	?	Y
2 Savage	Y	Y
3 Russo	Y	Y
4 *Derwinski*	?	?
5 Fary	?	?
6 *Hyde*	Y	Y
7 Collins	P	Y
8 Rostenkowski	Y	Y
9 Yates	Y	Y
10 *Porter*	?	Y
11 Annunzio	Y	Y
12 *Crane, P.*	?	?
13 *McClory*	Y	Y
14 Erlenborn	Y	Y
15 Corcoran	Y	Y
16 *Martin*	Y	Y
17 *O'Brien*	Y	Y
18 *Michel*	Y	Y
19 *Railsback*	Y	Y
20 *Findley*	?	Y
21 *Madigan*	Y	Y
22 *Crane, D.*	?	?
23 Price	?	?
24 Simon	?	?
INDIANA		
1 Benjamin	Y	Y
2 Fithian	Y	Y
3 *Hiler*	Y	Y
4 *Coats*	Y	Y
5 *Hillis*	?	?
6 Evans	?	Y
7 *Myers*	Y	Y
8 *Deckard*	Y	Y
9 Hamilton	Y	Y
10 Sharp	Y	Y
11 Jacobs	?	Y
IOWA		
1 *Leach*	Y	Y
2 *Tauke*	Y	Y
3 *Evans*	N	Y
4 Smith	?	Y
5 Harkin	N	Y
6 Bedell	Y	Y

Democrats *Republicans*

	45	46
KANSAS		
1 *Roberts*	Y	Y
2 *Jeffries*	Y	Y
3 *Winn*	Y	Y
4 Glickman	Y	Y
5 *Whittaker*	Y	Y
KENTUCKY		
1 Hubbard	Y	Y
2 Natcher	Y	Y
3 Mazzoli	Y	Y
4 *Snyder*	Y	Y
5 *Rogers*	Y	Y
6 *Hopkins*	Y	Y
7 Perkins	Y	Y
LOUISIANA		
1 *Livingston*	Y	Y
2 Boggs	?	Y
3 Tauzin	Y	Y
4 Roemer	?	Y
5 Huckaby	?	?
6 *Moore*	Y	Y
7 Breaux	Y	?
8 Long	?	?
MAINE		
1 *Emery*	Y	Y
2 *Snowe*	Y	Y
MARYLAND		
1 Dyson	Y	Y
2 Long	Y	Y
3 Mikulski	Y	Y
4 *Holt*	N	Y
5 Vacancy		
6 Byron	?	Y
7 Mitchell	?	Y
8 Barnes	Y	Y
MASSACHUSETTS		
1 *Conte*	Y	Y
2 Boland	?	Y
3 Early	Y	Y
4 Frank	?	?
5 Shannon	Y	Y
6 Mavroules	?	?
7 Markey	?	Y
8 O'Neill		
9 Moakley	Y	Y
10 *Heckler*	Y	Y
11 Donnelly	?	?
12 Studds	Y	Y
MICHIGAN		
1 Conyers	Y	Y
2 *Pursell*	?	?
3 Wolpe	?	Y
4 *Siljander*	Y	Y
5 *Sawyer*	Y	Y
6 *Dunn*	Y	Y
7 Kildee	Y	Y
8 Traxler	?	?
9 *Vander Jagt*	?	Y
10 Albosta	?	?
11 *Davis*	Y	Y
12 Bonior	Y	Y
13 Crockett	Y	Y
14 Hertel	Y	Y
15 Ford	Y	?
16 Dingell	Y	Y
17 Brodhead	Y	Y
18 Blanchard	Y	Y
19 *Broomfield*	Y	Y
MINNESOTA		
1 *Erdahl*	Y	Y
2 *Hagedorn*	?	Y
3 *Frenzel*	Y	?
4 Vento	Y	Y
5 Sabo	N	Y
6 *Weber*	?	?
7 *Stangeland*	?	?
8 Oberstar	Y	Y
MISSISSIPPI		
1 Whitten	Y	Y
2 Bowen	Y	?
3 Montgomery	Y	Y
4 Vacancy		
5 *Lott*	Y	Y
MISSOURI		
1 Clay	?	?
2 Young	Y	Y
3 Gephardt	Y	Y
4 Skelton	Y	Y
5 Bolling	Y	Y
6 *Coleman*	?	?
7 Taylor	Y	Y
8 Bailey	Y	Y
9 Volkmer	Y	Y
10 *Emerson*	Y	Y
MONTANA		
1 Williams	Y	Y
2 *Marlenee*	?	?
NEBRASKA		
1 *Bereuter*	Y	Y
2 *Daub*	Y	Y
3 *Smith*	Y	Y
NEVADA		
AL Santini	?	?
NEW HAMPSHIRE		
1 D'Amours	Y	Y
2 *Gregg*	Y	Y
NEW JERSEY		
1 Florio	?	?
2 Hughes	Y	Y
3 Howard	Y	Y
4 *Smith*	?	Y
5 *Fenwick*	Y	Y
6 *Forsythe*	N	Y
7 *Roukema*	Y	Y
8 Roe	?	?
9 *Hollenbeck*	Y	Y
10 Rodino	?	?
11 Minish	Y	?
12 *Rinaldo*	?	Y
13 *Courter*	Y	Y
14 Guarini	Y	Y
15 Dwyer	Y	Y
NEW MEXICO		
1 *Lujan*	?	?
2 *Skeen*	Y	Y
NEW YORK		
1 *Carney*	?	?
2 Downey	Y	Y
3 *Carman*	Y	Y
4 *Lent*	Y	Y
5 McGrath	Y	Y
6 *LeBoutillier*	Y	Y
7 Addabbo	?	?
8 Rosenthal	Y	Y
9 Ferraro	?	Y
10 Biaggi	Y	Y
11 Scheuer	Y	Y
12 Chisholm	Y	Y
13 Solarz	Y	Y
14 Richmond	Y	Y
15 Zeferetti	?	?
16 Schumer	Y	Y
17 *Molinari*	Y	Y
18 *Green*	Y	Y
19 Rangel	Y	Y
20 Weiss	Y	Y
21 Garcia	Y	Y
22 Bingham	?	?
23 Peyser	Y	Y
24 Ottinger	?	Y
25 *Fish*	Y	Y
26 *Gilman*	Y	Y
27 McHugh	Y	Y
28 Stratton	?	?
29 *Solomon*	Y	Y
30 *Martin*	Y	Y
31 *Mitchell*	?	?
32 *Wortley*	Y	?
33 *Lee*	?	Y
34 *Horton*	Y	Y
35 *Conable*	Y	Y
36 LaFalce	Y	Y
37 Nowak	Y	Y
38 *Kemp*	?	?
39 Lundine	?	Y
NORTH CAROLINA		
1 Jones	Y	Y
2 Fountain	?	Y
3 Whitley	Y	Y
4 Andrews	Y	Y
5 Neal	?	Y
6 *Johnston*	Y	Y
7 Rose	Y	Y
8 Hefner	Y	Y
9 *Martin*	Y	Y
10 *Broyhill*	Y	N
11 *Hendon*	Y	Y
NORTH DAKOTA		
AL Dorgan	Y	Y
OHIO		
1 *Gradison*	Y	Y
2 Luken	Y	Y
3 Hall	Y	Y
4 Vacancy		
5 *Latta*	Y	Y
6 *McEwen*	?	Y
7 *Brown*	Y	Y
8 *Kindness*	?	?
9 *Weber*	Y	Y
10 *Miller*	Y	Y
11 Stanton	Y	Y
12 Shamansky	Y	Y
13 Pease	Y	Y
14 Seiberling	?	Y
15 *Wylie*	Y	Y
16 *Regula*	Y	Y
17 *Ashbrook*	Y	Y
18 Applegate	?	Y
19 *Williams*	Y	Y
20 Oakar	Y	Y
21 Stokes	Y	Y
22 Eckart	?	?
23 Mottl	Y	Y
OKLAHOMA		
1 Jones	N	Y
2 Synar	?	?
3 Watkins	Y	Y
4 McCurdy	Y	Y
5 *Edwards*	?	Y
6 English	Y	Y
OREGON		
1 AuCoin	?	?
2 *Smith*	?	?
3 Wyden	Y	Y
4 Weaver	?	?
PENNSYLVANIA		
1 Foglietta	Y	Y
2 Gray	?	?
3 Vacancy		
4 *Dougherty*	?	?
5 *Schulze*	?	?
6 Yatron	?	Y
7 Edgar	Y	Y
8 *Coyne, J.*	Y	Y
9 *Shuster*	Y	Y
10 *McDade*	?	?
11 *Nelligan*	Y	Y
12 Murtha	Y	Y
13 *Coughlin*	?	?
14 Coyne, W.	Y	Y
15 *Ritter*	?	Y
16 *Walker*	?	?
17 Ertel	Y	Y
18 Walgren	Y	Y
19 *Goodling*	N	Y
20 Gaydos	Y	Y
21 Bailey	Y	Y
22 Murphy	Y	Y
23 *Clinger*	Y	Y
24 *Marks*	Y	Y
25 Atkinson	Y	Y
RHODE ISLAND		
1 St Germain	?	Y
2 *Schneider*	Y	Y
SOUTH CAROLINA		
1 *Hartnett*	?	?
2 *Spence*	Y	Y
3 Derrick	Y	Y
4 *Campbell*	?	?
5 Holland	Y	Y
6 *Napier*	Y	Y
SOUTH DAKOTA		
1 Daschle	Y	Y
2 *Roberts*	Y	Y
TENNESSEE		
1 *Quillen*	?	?
2 *Duncan*	Y	Y
3 Bouquard	?	?
4 Gore	Y	Y
5 Boner	Y	Y
6 *Beard*	Y	Y
7 Jones	?	?
8 Ford	Y	?
TEXAS		
1 Hall, S.	?	Y
2 Wilson	?	?
3 *Collins*	Y	Y
4 Hall, R.	?	Y
5 Mattox	?	?
6 *Gramm*	Y	N
7 *Archer*	Y	Y
8 *Fields*	?	?
9 Brooks	Y	Y
10 Pickle	Y	Y
11 Leath	Y	Y
12 Wright	Y	Y
13 Hightower	?	?
14 Patman	?	?
15 de la Garza	Y	Y
16 White	+	+
17 Stenholm	Y	Y
18 Leland	Y	Y
19 Hance	Y	Y
20 Gonzalez	Y	Y
21 *Loeffler*	Y	Y
22 *Paul*	Y	Y
23 Kazen	Y	Y
24 Frost	?	?
UTAH		
1 *Hansen*	?	?
2 *Marriott*	?	?
VERMONT		
AL *Jeffords*	?	?
VIRGINIA		
1 *Trible*	?	?
2 *Whitehurst*	Y	Y
3 *Bliley*	Y	N
4 *Daniel, R.*	Y	Y
5 Daniel, D.	Y	Y
6 *Butler*	?	?
7 *Robinson*	?	?
8 *Parris*	Y	Y
9 *Wampler*	Y	Y
10 *Wolf*	Y	Y
WASHINGTON		
1 *Pritchard*	?	?
2 Swift	Y	Y
3 Bonker	?	?
4 *Morrison*	Y	Y
5 Foley	Y	Y
6 Dicks	?	?
7 Lowry	?	Y
WEST VIRGINIA		
1 Mollohan	?	?
2 *Benedict*	?	?
3 Staton	Y	Y
4 Rahall	Y	Y
WISCONSIN		
1 Aspin	?	?
2 Kastenmeier	Y	Y
3 *Gunderson*	Y	Y
4 Zablocki	?	?
5 Reuss	?	?
6 *Petri*	?	?
7 Obey	Y	Y
8 Roth	Y	Y
9 *Sensenbrenner*	Y	Y
WYOMING		
AL *Cheney*	Y	Y

Democrats *Republicans*

47. HR 3499. Veterans' Health Care Act. Mottl, D-Ohio, motion to suspend the rules and pass the bill to provide medical coverage to Vietnam veterans exposed to the herbicide Agent Orange, to continue readjustment counseling centers for Vietnam veterans and to set minimum requirements for the number of hospital and nursing home beds the Veterans Administration must maintain. Motion agreed to 388-0: R 176-0; D 212-0 (ND 145-0, SD 67-0), June 2, 1981. A two-thirds majority vote (259 in this case) is required for passage under suspension of the rules. A "nay" was a vote supporting the president's position.

48. HR 2136. National Cemetery Construction. Montgomery, D-Miss., motion to suspend the rules and pass the bill to require congressional review and approval of national cemetery construction, alteration and acquisition. Motion agreed to 383-8: R 169-7; D 214-1 (ND 147-1, SD 67-0), June 2, 1981. A two-thirds majority vote (261 in this case) is required for passage under suspension of the rules. A "nay" was a vote supporting the president's position.

49. HR 3337. Youth Employment. Hawkins, D-Calif., motion to suspend the rules and pass the bill to extend youth employment programs authorized by the Comprehensive Employment and Training Act (CETA) through fiscal 1982. Motion agreed to 309-84: R 106-72; D 203-12 (ND 147-1, SD 56-11), June 2, 1981. A two-thirds majority vote (262 in this case) is required for passage under suspension of the rules.

50. HR 1100. Prisoner of War Benefits and Health Care Services Act. Montgomery, D-Miss., motion to suspend the rules and pass the bill to provide monetary compensation and priority medical care to former prisoners of war. Motion agreed to 394-2: R 178-0; D 216-2 (ND 148-1, SD 68-1), June 2, 1981. A two-thirds majority vote (264 in this case) is required for passage under suspension of the rules. A "nay" was a vote supporting the president's position.

51. HR 3423. Veterans' Training and Business Loan Act. Montgomery, D-Miss., motion to suspend the rules and pass the bill to provide business loans and additional educational benefits to Vietnam veterans. Motion agreed to 352-41: D 138-38; D 214-3 (ND 146-1, SD 68-2), June 2, 1981. A two-thirds majority vote (262 in this case) is required for passage under suspension of the rules. A "nay" was a vote supporting the president's position.

52. HR 2039. Veterans' Home Loan Guarantees. Montgomery, D-Miss., motion to suspend the rules and pass the bill to allow the Veterans Administration to guarantee graduated payment home mortgage loans for veterans. Motion agreed to 397-0: R 179-0; D 218-0 (ND 148-0, SD 70-0), June 2, 1981. A two-thirds majority vote (265 in this case) is required for passage under suspension of the rules. A "yea" was a vote supporting the president's position.

53. H Con Res 76. Plaque Honoring Servicemen Who Died In Hostage Rescue Attempt. Montgomery, D-Miss., motion to suspend the rules and adopt the resolution expressing the sense of Congress that the secretary of the Army should place a plaque in Arlington National Cemetery honoring the eight U.S. servicemen who died April 25, 1980, during an unsuccessful attempt to rescue the American hostages in Iran. Motion agreed to 391-0: R 177-0; D 214-0 (ND 146-0, SD 68-0), June 2, 1981. A two-thirds majority vote (261 in this case) is required for adoption under suspension of the rules.

54. HR 3512. Fiscal 1981 Supplemental Appropriations. Conte, R-Mass., motion to concur in the Senate amendment to prohibit reduction of full-time staff positions at the National Oceanic and Atmospheric Administration below 12,580, with an amendment providing that the Commerce Department need not comply with the provision. Motion agreed to 195-178: R 158-1; D 37-177 (ND 13-132, SD 24-45), June 4, 1981.

KEY	
Y	Voted for (yea).
#	Paired for.
+	Announced for.
N	Voted against (nay).
X	Paired against.
-	Announced against.
P	Voted "present".
C	Voted "present" to avoid possible conflict of interest.
?	Did not vote or otherwise make a position known.

	47	48	49	50	51	52	53	54
ALABAMA								
1 *Edwards*	Y	Y	N	Y	Y	Y	Y	Y
2 *Dickinson*	?	?	?	?	?	?	?	?
3 Nichols	Y	Y	Y	Y	Y	Y	Y	Y
4 Bevill	Y	Y	Y	Y	Y	Y	Y	N
5 Flippo	?	?	?	?	?	?	?	?
6 Smith	Y	Y	N	Y	N	Y	Y	Y
7 Shelby	Y	Y-	Y	Y	Y	Y	Y	
ALASKA								
AL *Young*	Y	Y	Y	Y	Y	Y	Y	#
ARIZONA								
1 *Rhodes*	Y	Y	N	Y	Y	Y	Y	Y
2 Udall	Y	Y	Y	Y	Y	Y	Y	N
3 *Stump*	?	?	?	?	?	?	?	?
4 *Rudd*	Y	Y	N	Y	Y	Y	Y	Y
ARKANSAS								
1 Alexander	Y	Y	Y	Y	Y	Y	Y	Y
2 *Bethune*	Y	Y	Y	Y	Y	Y	Y	Y
3 *Hammerschmidt*	Y	Y	N	Y	Y	Y	Y	Y
4 Anthony	Y	Y	Y	Y	Y	Y	Y	Y
CALIFORNIA								
1 *Chappie*	Y	Y	N	Y	Y	Y	Y	Y
2 *Clausen*	Y	Y	Y	Y	Y	Y	Y	Y
3 Matsui	Y	Y	Y	Y	Y	Y	Y	N
4 Fazio	Y	Y	Y	Y	Y	Y	Y	N
5 Burton, J.	Y	Y	Y	Y	Y	Y	Y	N
6 Burton, P.	Y	Y	Y	Y	Y	Y	Y	N
7 Miller	Y	Y	Y	Y	Y	Y	Y	N
8 Dellums	Y	Y	Y	Y	Y	Y	Y	X
9 Stark	Y	Y	Y	Y	Y	Y	Y	N
10 Edwards	Y	Y	Y	Y	Y	Y	Y	N
11 Lantos	Y	Y	Y	Y	Y	Y	Y	N
12 *McCloskey*	Y	Y	Y	Y	Y	Y	Y	Y
13 Mineta	Y	Y	Y	Y	Y	Y	Y	N
14 *Shumway*	Y	Y	N	Y	N	Y	Y	Y
15 Coelho	?	Y	Y	Y	Y	Y	Y	N
16 Panetta	Y	Y	Y	Y	Y	Y	Y	N
17 *Pashayan*	?	?	?	?	?	?	?	Y
18 Thomas	Y	Y	Y	Y	Y	Y	Y	Y
19 *Lagomarsino*	Y	Y	Y	Y	Y	Y	Y	Y
20 *Goldwater*	Y	Y	Y	Y	Y	Y	Y	?
21 *Fiedler*	Y	Y	Y	Y	Y	Y	Y	Y
22 *Moorhead*	Y	Y	N	Y	Y	Y	Y	Y
23 Beilenson	Y	Y	Y	N	N	Y	Y	?
24 Waxman	Y	Y	Y	Y	Y	Y	Y	N
25 Roybal	Y	Y	Y	Y	Y	Y	Y	N
26 *Rousselot*	Y	Y	N	Y	Y	Y	Y	#
27 *Dornan*	Y	Y	Y	Y	Y	Y	Y	Y
28 Dixon	Y	Y	Y	Y	Y	Y	Y	N
29 Hawkins	Y	Y	Y	Y	Y	Y	?	N
30 Danielson	Y	Y	Y	Y	Y	Y	Y	N
31 Dymally	Y	Y	Y	Y	Y	Y	Y	?
32 Anderson	?	?	?	?	?	?	?	?
33 *Grisham*	?	?	?	?	?	?	?	?
34 *Lungren*	Y	Y	N	Y	N	Y	Y	Y
35 *Dreier*	Y	Y	N	Y	Y	Y	Y	Y
36 Brown	Y	Y	Y	Y	Y	Y	Y	N
37 *Lewis*	Y	Y	Y	N	Y	Y	Y	Y
38 *Patterson*	Y	Y	Y	Y	Y	Y	Y	N
39 *Dannemeyer*	Y	Y	N	Y	N	Y	Y	Y
40 *Badham*	?	?	?	?	?	?	?	?
41 *Lowery*	Y	Y	N	Y	Y	Y	Y	Y
42 *Hunter*	Y	Y	Y	Y	Y	Y	Y	Y
43 *Burgener*	Y	Y	N	Y	Y	Y	Y	Y
COLORADO								
1 Schroeder	Y	Y	Y	Y	Y	Y	Y	N
2 Wirth	?	?	?	?	?	?	Y	N
3 Kogovsek	Y	Y	Y	Y	Y	Y	Y	N
4 *Brown*	Y	Y	N	Y	N	Y	Y	Y

	47	48	49	50	51	52	53	54
5 *Kramer*	Y	Y	N	Y	Y	Y	Y	Y
CONNECTICUT								
1 Cotter	?	?	?	?	?	?	?	?
2 Gejdenson	Y	Y	Y	Y	Y	Y	Y	N
3 *DeNardis*	Y	Y	Y	Y	Y	Y	Y	Y
4 *McKinney*	Y	Y	Y	Y	Y	Y	Y	Y
5 Ratchford	Y	Y	Y	Y	Y	Y	Y	N
6 Moffett	Y	Y	Y	Y	Y	Y	Y	N
DELAWARE								
AL *Evans*	Y	Y	Y	Y	Y	Y	Y	Y
FLORIDA								
1 Hutto	Y	Y	Y	Y	Y	Y	Y	N
2 Fuqua	?	?	?	?	?	?	?	X
3 Bennett	Y	Y	Y	Y	Y	Y	Y	N
4 Chappell	+	+	Y	Y	Y	Y	Y	N
5 *McCollum*	Y	Y	N	Y	Y	Y	Y	Y
6 *Young*	Y	Y	N	Y	Y	Y	Y	Y
7 Gibbons	Y	Y	Y	Y	Y	Y	Y	?
8 Ireland	Y	Y	N	Y	N	Y	Y	N
9 Nelson	+	+	+	+	+	+	+	N
10 *Bafalis*	Y	Y	N	Y	Y	Y	Y	?
11 Mica	Y	Y	Y	Y	Y	Y	Y	Y
12 *Shaw*	Y	Y	Y	Y	N	Y	Y	Y
13 Lehman	Y	Y	Y	Y	Y	Y	Y	Y
14 Pepper	Y	Y	Y	Y	Y	Y	Y	N
15 Fascell	Y	Y	Y	Y	Y	Y	Y	N
GEORGIA								
1 Ginn	Y	Y	Y	Y	Y	Y	Y	N
2 Hatcher	Y	Y	Y	Y	Y	Y	Y	N
3 Brinkley	Y	Y	Y	Y	Y	Y	Y	N
4 Levitas	Y	Y	Y	Y	Y	Y	Y	N
5 Fowler	Y	Y	Y	Y	Y	Y	Y	Y
6 *Gingrich*	Y	Y	Y	Y	Y	?	Y	Y
7 McDonald	Y	Y	N	N	N	Y	Y	N
8 Evans	Y	Y	N	Y	Y	Y	Y	Y
9 Jenkins	Y	Y	Y	Y	Y	Y	Y	N
10 Barnard	Y	Y	N	Y	Y	?	N	N
HAWAII								
1 Heftel	Y	Y	Y	Y	Y	Y	Y	?
2 Akaka	Y	Y	Y	Y	Y	Y	Y	N
IDAHO								
1 *Craig*	Y	N	N	Y	N	Y	Y	#
2 *Hansen*	Y	Y	N	Y	N	Y	Y	Y
ILLINOIS								
1 Washington	?	?	?	?	?	?	?	?
2 Savage	Y	Y	Y	Y	Y	?	Y	N
3 Russo	Y	Y	Y	Y	Y	Y	Y	N
4 *Derwinski*	Y	Y	N	Y	N	Y	Y	Y
5 Fary	?	?	?	?	?	?	?	X
6 *Hyde*	Y	Y	N	Y	N	Y	Y	Y
7 Collins	Y	Y	Y	Y	Y	Y	Y	N
8 Rostenkowski	Y	Y	Y	Y	Y	Y	Y	N
9 Yates	Y	Y	Y	Y	Y	Y	Y	N
10 *Porter*	Y	Y	Y	Y	Y	N	Y	Y
11 Annunzio	Y	Y	Y	Y	Y	Y	Y	N
12 *Crane, P.*	Y	Y	N	Y	N	Y	Y	#
13 *McClory*	Y	Y	N	Y	Y	Y	Y	Y
14 *Erlenborn*	Y	Y	Y	Y	Y	N	Y	Y
15 *Corcoran*	Y	Y	N	Y	Y	Y	Y	Y
16 *Martin*	Y	Y	N	Y	N	Y	Y	Y
17 *O'Brien*	Y	Y	Y	Y	Y	Y	Y	Y
18 *Michel*	Y	N	N	Y	N	Y	Y	Y
19 *Railsback*	Y	Y	Y	Y	Y	Y	Y	Y
20 *Findley*	Y	Y	Y	Y	Y	Y	Y	Y
21 *Madigan*	Y	Y	N	Y	Y	Y	Y	Y
22 *Crane, D.*	Y	Y	N	Y	N	Y	Y	#
23 Price	?	?	?	?	?	?	?	?
24 Simon	Y	Y	Y	Y	Y	Y	Y	N
INDIANA								
1 Benjamin	Y	Y	Y	Y	Y	Y	Y	N
2 Fithian	Y	Y	Y	Y	Y	Y	Y	N
3 *Hiler*	Y	Y	N	Y	N	Y	Y	Y
4 *Coats*	Y	Y	Y	Y	Y	Y	Y	Y
5 *Hillis*	?	?	?	?	?	?	?	?
6 Evans	Y	Y	Y	Y	Y	Y	Y	N
7 *Myers*	Y	Y	N	Y	N	Y	Y	Y
8 *Deckard*	?	?	?	?	?	Y	Y	Y
9 Hamilton	Y	Y	Y	Y	Y	Y	Y	N
10 Sharp	Y	Y	Y	Y	Y	Y	Y	N
11 Jacobs	Y	Y	Y	Y	Y	Y	Y	N
IOWA								
1 *Leach*	Y	Y	Y	Y	Y	Y	Y	N
2 *Tauke*	Y	Y	Y	Y	Y	Y	Y	N
3 *Evans*	+	+	+	+	+	+	+	#
4 Smith	Y	Y	Y	Y	Y	Y	Y	N
5 Harkin	Y	Y	Y	Y	Y	?	Y	N
6 Bedell	Y	Y	Y	Y	Y	Y	Y	Y

Democrats *Republicans*

	47	48	49	50	51	52	53	54
KANSAS								
1 ***Roberts***	Y	Y	Y	Y	Y	Y	Y	Y
2 ***Jeffries***	Y	Y	N	Y	N	Y	Y	Y
3 ***Winn***	Y	Y	Y	Y	Y	Y	?	Y
4 Glickman	Y	Y	Y	Y	Y	Y	Y	Y
5 ***Whittaker***	Y	Y	Y	Y	Y	Y	Y	Y
KENTUCKY								
1 Hubbard	Y	Y	Y	Y	Y	Y	Y	N
2 Natcher	Y	Y	Y	Y	Y	Y	Y	N
3 Mazzoli	Y	Y	Y	Y	Y	Y	Y	Y
4 ***Snyder***	Y	Y	N	Y	Y	Y	Y	Y
5 ***Rogers***	Y	Y	Y	Y	Y	Y	Y	Y
6 ***Hopkins***	Y	Y	Y	Y	Y	Y	Y	Y
7 Perkins	Y	Y	Y	Y	Y	Y	Y	N
LOUISIANA								
1 ***Livingston***	Y	Y	N	Y	N	Y	Y	Y
2 Boggs	Y	Y	Y	Y	Y	Y	Y	Y
3 Tauzin	Y	Y	Y	Y	Y	Y	Y	Y
4 Roemer	Y	Y	Y	Y	Y	Y	Y	Y
5 Huckaby	Y	Y	Y	Y	Y	Y	Y	N
6 ***Moore***	Y	Y	Y	Y	Y	Y	Y	+
7 Breaux	Y	Y	Y	Y	Y	Y	Y	N
8 Long	Y	Y	Y	Y	Y	Y	Y	N
MAINE								
1 ***Emery***	Y	Y	Y	Y	Y	Y	Y	Y
2 ***Snowe***	Y	Y	Y	Y	Y	Y	Y	Y
MARYLAND								
1 Dyson	Y	Y	Y	Y	Y	Y	Y	N
2 Long	Y	Y	Y	Y	Y	Y	Y	N
3 Mikulski	Y	Y	Y	Y	Y	Y	Y	N
4 ***Holt***	Y	Y	Y	Y	Y	Y	Y	Y
5 Hoyer*								N
6 Byron	Y	Y	Y	Y	Y	Y	Y	N
7 Mitchell	Y	Y	Y	Y	Y	Y	Y	N
8 Barnes	Y	Y	Y	Y	Y	Y	Y	N
MASSACHUSETTS								
1 ***Conte***	Y	Y	Y	Y	Y	Y	Y	Y
2 Boland	Y	Y	Y	Y	?	Y	Y	N
3 Early	Y	Y	Y	Y	Y	Y	?	N
4 Frank	Y	Y	Y	Y	Y	Y	Y	N
5 Shannon	Y	Y	Y	Y	Y	Y	Y	N
6 Mavroules	Y	Y	Y	Y	Y	Y	Y	N
7 Markey	Y	Y	Y	Y	Y	Y	Y	N
8 O'Neill								
9 Moakley	Y	Y	Y	Y	Y	Y	Y	N
10 ***Heckler***	Y	Y	Y	Y	Y	Y	Y	Y
11 Donnelly	Y	Y	Y	Y	Y	Y	Y	N
12 Studds	Y	Y	Y	Y	Y	Y	Y	N
MICHIGAN								
1 Conyers	Y	Y	Y	Y	Y	Y	?	N
2 ***Pursell***	Y	Y	Y	Y	Y	Y	Y	Y
3 Wolpe	Y	Y	Y	Y	Y	Y	Y	N
4 ***Siljander***	Y	Y	N	Y	Y	Y	Y	Y
5 ***Sawyer***	Y	Y	Y	Y	Y	Y	Y	Y
6 ***Dunn***	Y	Y	Y	Y	Y	Y	Y	Y
7 Kildee	Y	Y	Y	Y	Y	Y	Y	N
8 Traxler	Y	Y	Y	Y	Y	Y	Y	N
9 ***Vander Jagt***	Y	Y	Y	Y	Y	Y	Y	?
10 Albosta	Y	Y	Y	Y	?	Y	?	N
11 ***Davis***	Y	Y	Y	Y	Y	Y	Y	Y
12 Bonior	Y	Y	Y	Y	Y	Y	Y	N
13 Crockett	Y	Y	Y	Y	Y	Y	Y	N
14 Hertel	Y	Y	Y	Y	Y	Y	Y	N
15 Ford	Y	Y	Y	Y	Y	Y	Y	N
16 Dingell	?	?	?	Y	Y	Y	Y	N
17 Brodhead	Y	Y	Y	Y	Y	Y	Y	N
18 Blanchard	Y	Y	Y	Y	Y	Y	Y	N
19 ***Broomfield***	?	?	?	?	?	?	?	Y
MINNESOTA								
1 ***Erdahl***	Y	Y	Y	Y	Y	Y	Y	Y
2 ***Hagedorn***	Y	Y	N	Y	Y	Y	Y	Y
3 ***Frenzel***	Y	Y	Y	Y	Y	Y	Y	?
4 Vento	Y	Y	Y	Y	Y	Y	Y	N
5 Sabo	Y	Y	Y	Y	Y	Y	Y	N
6 ***Weber***	?	?	N	Y	Y	Y	Y	?
7 ***Stangeland***	Y	Y	N	Y	Y	Y	Y	Y
8 Oberstar	Y	Y	Y	Y	Y	Y	Y	N
MISSISSIPPI								
1 Whitten	Y	Y	Y	Y	Y	Y	Y	N
2 Bowen	Y	Y	Y	Y	Y	Y	Y	N
3 Montgomery	Y	Y	N	Y	Y	Y	Y	Y
4 Vacancy								
5 ***Lott***	Y	Y	N	Y	Y	Y	Y	Y
MISSOURI								
1 Clay	Y	Y	Y	Y	Y	Y	Y	N
2 Young	Y	Y	Y	Y	Y	Y	Y	N
3 Gephardt	Y	Y	Y	Y	Y	Y	Y	N

	47	48	49	50	51	52	53	54
4 Skelton	Y	Y	Y	Y	Y	Y	Y	N
5 Bolling	Y	Y	Y	Y	Y	Y	Y	N
6 ***Coleman***	Y	Y	Y	Y	Y	Y	Y	Y
7 ***Taylor***	Y	Y	N	Y	Y	Y	Y	Y
8 ***Bailey***	Y	Y	N	Y	Y	Y	Y	Y
9 Volkmer	Y	Y	Y	Y	Y	Y	Y	N
10 ***Emerson***	Y	Y	Y	Y	Y	Y	Y	Y
MONTANA								
1 Williams	Y	Y	Y	Y	Y	Y	Y	N
2 ***Marlenee***	?	?	?	?	?	?	?	Y
NEBRASKA								
1 ***Bereuter***	Y	Y	Y	Y	Y	Y	Y	Y
2 ***Daub***	Y	Y	Y	Y	Y	Y	Y	Y
3 ***Smith***	Y	Y	N	Y	Y	Y	Y	Y
NEVADA								
AL Santini	Y	Y	N	Y	Y	Y	Y	N
NEW HAMPSHIRE								
1 D'Amours	Y	Y	Y	Y	Y	Y	Y	N
2 ***Gregg***	Y	N	N	Y	Y	Y	Y	Y
NEW JERSEY								
1 Florio	?	?	?	?	?	?	?	?
2 Hughes	Y	Y	Y	Y	Y	Y	Y	Y
3 Howard	Y	Y	Y	Y	Y	Y	Y	N
4 ***Smith***	Y	Y	Y	Y	Y	Y	Y	Y
5 ***Fenwick***	Y	Y	Y	Y	N	Y	Y	Y
6 ***Forsythe***	Y	?	Y	Y	Y	Y	Y	Y
7 ***Roukema***	Y	Y	Y	Y	N	Y	Y	Y
8 Roe	?	?	?	?	?	?	?	?
9 ***Hollenbeck***	Y	Y	Y	Y	Y	Y	Y	#
10 Rodino	Y	Y	Y	Y	Y	Y	Y	N
11 Minish	Y	Y	Y	Y	Y	Y	Y	N
12 ***Rinaldo***	Y	Y	Y	Y	Y	Y	Y	Y
13 ***Courter***	Y	Y	Y	Y	Y	Y	Y	Y
14 Guarini	Y	Y	Y	Y	Y	Y	Y	N
15 Dwyer	Y	Y	Y	Y	Y	Y	Y	N
NEW MEXICO								
1 ***Lujan***	Y	Y	Y	Y	Y	Y	Y	Y
2 ***Skeen***	Y	Y	N	Y	Y	Y	Y	Y
NEW YORK								
1 ***Carney***	?	?	?	?	?	?	?	?
2 Downey	Y	Y	Y	Y	Y	Y	Y	N
3 ***Carman***	Y	Y	Y	Y	Y	Y	Y	Y
4 ***Lent***	Y	Y	Y	Y	Y	Y	Y	Y
5 ***McGrath***	Y	Y	Y	Y	Y	Y	Y	Y
6 ***LeBoutillier***	Y	Y	N	Y	Y	Y	Y	Y
7 Addabbo	Y	Y	Y	Y	Y	Y	Y	N
8 Rosenthal	Y	Y	Y	Y	Y	Y	Y	N
9 Ferraro	Y	Y	Y	Y	Y	Y	Y	?
10 Biaggi	Y	Y	Y	Y	Y	Y	Y	?
11 Scheuer	?	Y	Y	Y	Y	Y	Y	N
12 Chisholm	Y	Y	Y	Y	Y	Y	Y	N
13 Solarz	Y	Y	Y	Y	Y	Y	Y	N
14 Richmond	Y	Y	Y	Y	Y	Y	Y	N
15 Zeferetti	Y	Y	Y	Y	Y	Y	Y	N
16 Schumer	Y	Y	Y	Y	Y	Y	Y	N
17 ***Molinari***	Y	Y	Y	Y	Y	Y	Y	Y
18 ***Green***	Y	Y	Y	Y	Y	Y	Y	Y
19 Rangel	Y	Y	Y	Y	Y	Y	Y	N
20 Weiss	Y	Y	Y	Y	Y	Y	Y	N
21 Garcia	Y	Y	Y	Y	Y	Y	Y	N
22 Bingham	Y	Y	Y	Y	Y	Y	Y	N
23 Peyser	Y	Y	Y	Y	Y	Y	Y	N
24 Ottinger	Y	Y	Y	Y	Y	Y	Y	N
25 ***Fish***	Y	Y	Y	Y	Y	Y	Y	?
26 ***Gilman***	Y	Y	Y	Y	Y	Y	Y	Y
27 McHugh	Y	Y	Y	Y	Y	Y	Y	N
28 Stratton	?	?	?	?	?	?	?	?
29 ***Solomon***	Y	Y	N	Y	Y	Y	Y	Y
30 ***Martin***	Y	Y	Y	Y	Y	Y	Y	Y
31 ***Mitchell***	Y	Y	Y	Y	Y	Y	Y	Y
32 ***Wortley***	Y	Y	Y	Y	Y	Y	Y	Y
33 ***Lee***	Y	Y	N	Y	Y	Y	Y	Y
34 ***Horton***	Y	Y	Y	Y	Y	Y	Y	Y
35 ***Conable***	Y	Y	Y	Y	N	Y	Y	?
36 LaFalce	Y	Y	Y	Y	Y	Y	Y	?
37 Nowak	Y	Y	Y	Y	Y	Y	Y	N
38 ***Kemp***	Y	Y	Y	Y	Y	Y	Y	Y
39 Lundine	Y	Y	Y	Y	Y	Y	Y	N
NORTH CAROLINA								
1 Jones	Y	Y	Y	Y	Y	Y	Y	X
2 Fountain	Y	Y	Y	Y	Y	Y	Y	Y
3 Whitley	Y	Y	Y	Y	Y	Y	Y	N
4 Andrews	Y	Y	Y	Y	Y	Y	Y	N
5 Neal	Y	Y	Y	Y	Y	Y	Y	?
6 ***Johnston***	Y	N	N	Y	N	Y	Y	Y
7 Rose	Y	Y	Y	Y	Y	Y	Y	N
8 Hefner	Y	Y	Y	Y	Y	Y	Y	N

	47	48	49	50	51	52	53	54
9 ***Martin***	Y	Y	Y	Y	Y	Y	Y	?
10 ***Broyhill***	Y	Y	N	Y	Y	Y	Y	Y
11 ***Hendon***	Y	Y	N	Y	Y	Y	Y	Y
NORTH DAKOTA								
AL Dorgan	Y	Y	Y	Y	Y	Y	Y	N
OHIO								
1 ***Gradison***	Y	Y	Y	Y	Y	Y	Y	?
2 Luken	Y	Y	Y	Y	Y	Y	Y	Y
3 Hall	Y	Y	Y	Y	Y	Y	Y	N
4 Vacancy								
5 ***Latta***	Y	N	N	Y	N	Y	Y	Y
6 ***McEwen***	Y	Y	Y	Y	Y	Y	Y	Y
7 ***Brown***	Y	Y	Y	Y	?	Y	Y	?
8 ***Kindness***	Y	Y	Y	Y	Y	Y	Y	Y
9 ***Weber***	Y	Y	Y	Y	Y	Y	Y	Y
10 ***Miller***	Y	Y	Y	Y	Y	Y	Y	Y
11 ***Stanton***	Y	Y	Y	Y	Y	Y	Y	Y
12 Shamansky	Y	Y	Y	Y	Y	Y	Y	N
13 Pease	Y	Y	Y	Y	Y	Y	Y	N
14 Seiberling	Y	Y	Y	Y	Y	Y	Y	N
15 ***Wylie***	Y	Y	Y	Y	Y	Y	Y	Y
16 ***Regula***	Y	Y	Y	Y	Y	Y	Y	Y
17 ***Ashbrook***	Y	Y	N	Y	Y	Y	Y	Y
18 Applegate	Y	Y	Y	Y	Y	Y	Y	Y
19 ***Williams***	Y	Y	Y	Y	Y	Y	Y	Y
20 Oakar	Y	Y	Y	Y	Y	Y	Y	N
21 Stokes	Y	Y	Y	Y	Y	Y	Y	N
22 Eckart	Y	Y	Y	Y	Y	Y	Y	N
23 Mottl	Y	Y	Y	Y	Y	Y	Y	N
OKLAHOMA								
1 Jones	Y	Y	Y	Y	Y	Y	Y	N
2 Synar	Y	Y	Y	Y	Y	Y	Y	N
3 Watkins	Y	Y	Y	Y	Y	Y	Y	N
4 McCurdy	Y	Y	Y	Y	Y	Y	Y	N
5 ***Edwards***	Y	N	N	Y	N	Y	Y	Y
6 English	Y	Y	Y	Y	Y	Y	Y	N
OREGON								
1 AuCoin	Y	Y	Y	Y	Y	Y	Y	?
2 ***Smith***	Y	Y	N	Y	N	Y	Y	Y
3 Wyden	Y	Y	Y	Y	Y	Y	Y	N
4 Weaver	Y	N	Y	Y	Y	Y	Y	N
PENNSYLVANIA								
1 Foglietta	?	?	?	?	?	?	?	?
2 Gray	?	?	?	?	?	?	Y	N
3 Vacancy								
4 ***Dougherty***	Y	Y	Y	Y	Y	Y	Y	Y
5 ***Schulze***	?	?	?	?	?	?	?	#
6 Yatron	Y	Y	Y	Y	Y	Y	Y	Y
7 Edgar	Y	Y	Y	Y	Y	Y	Y	N
8 ***Coyne, J.***	Y	Y	N	Y	Y	Y	Y	Y
9 ***Shuster***	Y	Y	N	Y	Y	Y	Y	Y
10 ***McDade***	Y	Y	Y	Y	Y	Y	Y	Y
11 ***Nelligan***	Y	Y	Y	Y	Y	Y	Y	Y
12 Murtha	Y	Y	Y	Y	Y	Y	Y	Y
13 ***Coughlin***	Y	Y	Y	Y	Y	Y	Y	Y
14 Coyne, W.	Y	Y	Y	Y	Y	Y	Y	N
15 ***Ritter***	Y	Y	Y	Y	Y	Y	Y	Y
16 ***Walker***	?	?	?	?	?	?	?	?
17 Ertel	Y	Y	Y	Y	Y	Y	Y	Y
18 Walgren	Y	Y	Y	Y	Y	Y	Y	Y
19 ***Goodling***	Y	Y	Y	Y	Y	Y	Y	Y
20 Gaydos	Y	Y	Y	Y	Y	Y	Y	N
21 Bailey	Y	Y	Y	Y	Y	Y	Y	N
22 Murphy	Y	Y	Y	Y	Y	Y	Y	N
23 ***Clinger***	Y	Y	Y	Y	Y	Y	Y	Y
24 ***Marks***	Y	Y	Y	Y	Y	Y	Y	Y
25 Atkinson	Y	Y	Y	Y	Y	Y	Y	Y
RHODE ISLAND								
1 St Germain	Y	Y	Y	Y	Y	Y	Y	N
2 ***Schneider***	?	Y	Y	Y	Y	Y	Y	Y
SOUTH CAROLINA								
1 ***Hartnett***	Y	N	N	Y	Y	Y	Y	?
2 ***Spence***	Y	Y	Y	Y	Y	Y	Y	Y
3 Derrick	?	?	?	Y	Y	Y	Y	Y
4 ***Campbell***	Y	Y	Y	Y	Y	Y	Y	Y
5 Holland	Y	Y	Y	Y	Y	Y	Y	Y
6 ***Napier***	Y	Y	Y	Y	Y	Y	Y	Y
SOUTH DAKOTA								
1 Daschle	Y	Y	Y	Y	Y	Y	Y	N
2 ***Roberts***	Y	Y	Y	Y	Y	Y	Y	Y
TENNESSEE								
1 ***Quillen***	Y	Y	N	Y	Y	Y	Y	Y
2 ***Duncan***	Y	Y	N	Y	Y	Y	Y	?
3 Bouquard	?	?	?	?	?	?	?	X
4 Gore	Y	Y	Y	Y	Y	Y	Y	N
5 Boner	Y	Y	Y	Y	Y	Y	Y	N
6 ***Beard***	Y	Y	N	Y	N	Y	Y	Y

	47	48	49	50	51	52	53	54
7 Jones	Y	Y	Y	Y	Y	Y	Y	N
8 Ford	Y	Y	Y	Y	Y	Y	Y	N
TEXAS								
1 Hall, S.	Y	Y	N	Y	Y	Y	Y	N
2 Wilson	?	?	?	?	Y	Y	Y	Y
3 ***Collins***	Y	Y	N	Y	N	Y	Y	Y
4 Hall, R.	Y	Y	Y	Y	Y	Y	Y	Y
5 Mattox	Y	Y	Y	Y	Y	Y	?	N
6 Gramm	Y	Y	N	Y	Y	Y	Y	Y
7 ***Archer***	Y	Y	N	Y	N	Y	Y	?
8 ***Fields***	Y	Y	N	Y	Y	Y	Y	Y
9 Brooks	?	?	?	?	?	?	?	?
10 Pickle	Y	Y	Y	Y	Y	Y	Y	Y
11 Leath	Y	Y	N	Y	Y	Y	Y	N
12 Wright	Y	Y	Y	Y	Y	Y	Y	N
13 Hightower	Y	Y	Y	Y	Y	Y	Y	Y
14 Patman	Y	Y	Y	Y	Y	Y	Y	N
15 de la Garza	Y	Y	Y	Y	Y	Y	Y	N
16 White	+	+	+	+	+	+	+	+
17 Stenholm	Y	Y	N	Y	Y	Y	Y	Y
18 Leland	?	?	?	?	?	?	?	X
19 Hance	Y	Y	N	Y	Y	Y	Y	Y
20 Gonzalez	Y	Y	Y	Y	Y	Y	Y	N
21 ***Loeffler***	Y	Y	N	Y	Y	Y	Y	Y
22 ***Paul***	Y	Y	N	Y	N	Y	Y	Y
23 Kazen	Y	Y	Y	Y	Y	Y	Y	Y
24 Frost	?	?	?	?	?	?	?	N
UTAH								
1 ***Hansen***	Y	Y	N	Y	N	Y	Y	?
2 ***Marriott***	Y	Y	Y	Y	Y	Y	Y	Y
VERMONT								
AL ***Jeffords***	Y	Y	Y	Y	Y	Y	Y	?
VIRGINIA								
1 ***Trible***	Y	Y	Y	Y	Y	Y	Y	Y
2 ***Whitehurst***	Y	Y	Y	Y	Y	Y	Y	Y
3 ***Bliley***	Y	Y	N	Y	Y	Y	Y	Y
4 ***Daniel, R.***	Y	Y	N	Y	Y	Y	Y	Y
5 Daniel, D.	Y	Y	N	Y	Y	Y	Y	Y
6 ***Butler***	Y	Y	N	Y	N	Y	Y	Y
7 ***Robinson***	Y	Y	N	Y	N	Y	Y	Y
8 ***Parris***	Y	Y	Y	Y	Y	Y	Y	Y
9 ***Wampler***	Y	Y	Y	Y	Y	Y	Y	Y
10 ***Wolf***	Y	Y	Y	Y	Y	Y	Y	Y
WASHINGTON								
1 ***Pritchard***	Y	Y	Y	Y	?	Y	Y	Y
2 Swift	Y	Y	Y	Y	Y	Y	Y	Y
3 Bonker	Y	Y	Y	Y	Y	Y	Y	N
4 ***Morrison***	Y	Y	Y	Y	Y	Y	Y	Y
5 Foley	Y	Y	Y	Y	Y	Y	Y	N
6 Dicks	Y	Y	Y	Y	Y	Y	Y	N
7 Lowry	Y	Y	Y	Y	Y	Y	Y	N
WEST VIRGINIA								
1 Mollohan	?	?	?	?	?	?	?	X
2 ***Benedict***	Y	Y	Y	Y	N	Y	Y	Y
3 ***Staton***	Y	Y	N	Y	Y	Y	Y	Y
4 Rahall	Y	Y	Y	Y	Y	Y	Y	N
WISCONSIN								
1 Aspin	Y	Y	Y	Y	Y	Y	Y	N
2 Kastenmeier	+	Y	Y	Y	Y	Y	Y	N
3 ***Gunderson***	Y	Y	Y	Y	N	Y	Y	Y
4 Zablocki	?	?	?	?	?	?	?	N
5 Reuss	Y	Y	Y	Y	Y	Y	Y	N
6 ***Petri***	Y	Y	Y	Y	Y	Y	Y	Y
7 Obey	Y	Y	Y	Y	Y	Y	Y	N
8 ***Roth***	Y	Y	Y	Y	Y	Y	Y	Y
9 ***Sensenbrenner***	Y	Y	N	Y	Y	Y	Y	N
WYOMING								
AL ***Cheney***	Y	Y	N	Y	N	Y	Y	Y

Rep. Steny Hoyer, D-Md., was sworn in June 3, 1981. The first vote for which he was eligible was CQ vote 54.

Democrats ***Republicans***

KEY

Y Voted for (yea).
Paired for.
+ Announced for.
N Voted against (nay).
X Paired against.
- Announced against.
P Voted "present".
C Voted "present" to avoid possible conflict of interest.
? Did not vote or otherwise make a position known.

55. HR 3455. Military Construction Authorization. Kogovsek, D-Colo., amendment to delete $30 million for purchase of land for an Army training area in Colorado. Rejected 175-209: R 16-155; D 159-54 (ND 130-12, SD 29-42), June 4, 1981.

56. HR 3455. Military Construction Authorization. Bonior, D-Mich., amendment to rescind $3.15 million in the fiscal 1981 military construction appropriations (PL 96-436) to construct a manufacturing plant for binary chemical munitions. Rejected 135-220: R 30-129; D 105-91 (ND 96-33, SD 9-58), June 4, 1981.

57. HR 3455. Military Construction Authorization. Passage of the bill to authorize $6,987,497,000 for military construction projects in fiscal 1982. Passed 311-36: R 151-3; D 160-33 (ND 95-33, SD 65-0), June 4, 1981.

58. Procedural Motion. Hartnett, R-S.C., motion to approve the House *Journal* for Monday, June 8. Motion agreed to 344-7: R 150-2; D 194-5 (ND 129-4, SD 65-1), June 9, 1981.

59. HR 3240. National Telecommunications and Information Administration. Wirth, D-Colo., motion to suspend the rules and pass the bill to authorize $16,467,000 in fiscal 1982 for the National Telecommunications and Information Administration. Motion agreed to 369-12: R 157-6; D 212-6 (ND 144-2, SD 68-4), June 9, 1981. A two-thirds majority vote (254 in this case) is required for adoption under suspension of the rules.

60. HR 3239. Federal Communications Commission. Wirth, D-Colo., motion to suspend the rules and pass the bill to authorize $77,351,000 in fiscal 1982 for the Federal Communications Commission (FCC), replace the FCC's permanent authorization with a periodic one and allow the FCC to impose fees for services. Motion agreed to 360-21: R 151-13; D 209-8 (ND 142-4, SD 67-4), June 9, 1981. A two-thirds majority vote (254 in this case) is required for adoption under suspension of the rules.

61. HR 3462. Justice Department Authorization. Rodino, D-N.J., motion that the House resolve itself into the Committee of the Whole to consider the bill to reauthorize Justice Department programs for fiscal 1982. Motion agreed to 357-1: R 156-1 (ND 134-0; SD 67-0), June 9, 1981.

62. HR 3462. Justice Department Authorization. Collins, R-Texas, amendment to prohibit use of funds authorized under the bill to bring any legal action that could lead directly or indirectly to busing, other than to bus a student to the nearest school. Adopted 265-122: R 145-24; D 120-98 (ND 61-87; SD 59-11), June 9, 1981.

	55	56	57	58	59	60	61	62
ALABAMA								
1 Edwards	N	N	Y	Y	Y	Y	Y	Y
2 Dickinson	X	?	?	?	?	?	?	?
3 Nichols	N	N	Y	Y	Y	Y	Y	Y
4 Bevill	N	N	Y	Y	Y	Y	Y	Y
5 Flippo	?	?	?	?	?	?	?	?
6 Smith	N	N	Y	Y	Y	Y	Y	Y
7 Shelby	N	N	Y	Y	Y	Y	Y	Y
ALASKA								
AL Young	N	N	Y	Y	Y	Y	Y	Y
ARIZONA								
1 Rhodes	N	N	Y	Y	Y	Y	Y	#
2 Udall	Y	Y	?	?	?	?	?	?
3 Stump	?	?	?	?	Y	N	Y	Y
4 Rudd	N	N	Y	Y	Y	Y	Y	Y
ARKANSAS								
1 Alexander	Y	X	#	Y	Y	Y	Y	Y
2 Bethune	N	Y	Y	Y	Y	Y	Y	Y
3 Hammerschmidt	N	N	Y	Y	Y	Y	Y	Y
4 Anthony	Y	N	Y	Y	Y	Y	Y	Y
CALIFORNIA								
1 Chappie	N	N	Y	?	Y	Y	?	Y
2 Clausen	N	N	Y	Y	Y	Y	Y	Y
3 Matsui	N	N	Y	Y	Y	Y	Y	N
4 Fazio	Y	N	Y	Y	Y	Y	Y	N
5 Burton, J.	Y	Y	Y	Y	Y	Y	Y	N
6 Burton, P.	Y	#	?	Y	Y	Y	Y	N
7 Miller	Y	Y	Y	Y	Y	Y	Y	N
8 Dellums	Y	Y	N	?	?	?	?	X
9 Stark	Y	Y	Y	Y	Y	Y	Y	N
10 Edwards	Y	X	Y	Y	Y	Y	Y	N
11 Lantos	Y	Y	Y	Y	Y	Y	Y	Y
12 McCloskey	N	Y	Y	Y	Y	Y	Y	N
13 Mineta	Y	Y	Y	Y	Y	Y	Y	N
14 Shumway	N	N	Y	Y	Y	Y	Y	Y
15 Coelho	Y	N	Y	Y	Y	Y	Y	N
16 Panetta	Y	Y	Y	Y	Y	Y	Y	N
17 Pashayan	?	?	?	Y	N	Y	Y	Y
18 Thomas	N	N	Y	Y	Y	Y	Y	Y
19 Lagomarsino	N	N	Y	Y	Y	Y	Y	Y
20 Goldwater	?	?	?	?	?	?	?	?
21 Fiedler	N	N	Y	Y	Y	Y	Y	Y
22 Moorhead	N	N	Y	Y	Y	Y	Y	Y
23 Beilenson	?	?	?	Y	Y	Y	Y	N
24 Waxman	Y	Y	Y	Y	Y	Y	Y	N
25 Roybal	Y	Y	N	Y	Y	Y	Y	N
26 Rousselot	N	N	Y	?	?	?	?	?
27 Dornan	N	N	Y	Y	Y	Y	Y	Y
28 Dixon	?	Y	Y	Y	Y	Y	Y	N
29 Hawkins	Y	Y	N	Y	Y	Y	Y	N
30 Danielson	Y	Y	Y	Y	Y	Y	Y	N
31 Dymally	?	?	?	?	Y	Y	Y	N
32 Anderson	Y	N	Y	Y	Y	Y	Y	Y
33 Grisham	?	?	?	?	?	?	?	?
34 Lungren	N	X	?	Y	Y	Y	Y	Y
35 Dreier	N	N	Y	Y	Y	Y	Y	Y
36 Brown	Y	Y	Y	Y	Y	Y	Y	N
37 Lewis	N	N	Y	Y	Y	Y	Y	Y
38 Patterson	Y	Y	Y	Y	Y	Y	Y	N
39 Dannemeyer	N	N	Y	Y	Y	Y	Y	Y
40 Badham	X	X	?	?	?	?	?	?
41 Lowery	N	X	Y	?	Y	Y	?	Y
42 Hunter	N	N	Y	?	Y	Y	Y	Y
43 Burgener	N	X	?	?	?	?	?	?
COLORADO								
1 Schroeder	Y	?	?	N	Y	Y	N	Y
2 Wirth	Y	?	?	Y	Y	Y	N	Y
3 Kogovsek	Y	Y	Y	Y	Y	Y	N	Y
4 Brown	Y	N	Y	Y	Y	Y	Y	Y

	55	56	57	58	59	60	61	62
5 Kramer	N	N	Y	Y	Y	Y	Y	Y
CONNECTICUT								
1 Cotter	?	?	?	?	?	?	?	?
2 Gejdenson	Y	Y	Y	Y	Y	Y	Y	N
3 DeNardis	Y	Y	Y	Y	?	?	Y	N
4 McKinney	Y	Y	Y	?	Y	N	?	N
5 Ratchford	Y	Y	Y	Y	Y	?	Y	Y
6 Moffett	Y	#	X	Y	Y	Y	Y	N
DELAWARE								
AL Evans	N	N	Y	Y	Y	Y	Y	Y
FLORIDA								
1 Hutto	N	N	Y	Y	Y	Y	Y	Y
2 Fuqua	?	?	?	?	?	?	?	?
3 Bennett	N	N	Y	Y	Y	Y	Y	Y
4 Chappell	N	?	?	?	?	?	?	#
5 McCollum	N	N	Y	Y	Y	Y	Y	Y
6 Young	N	N	Y	Y	Y	Y	Y	Y
7 Gibbons	N	N	Y	Y	Y	Y	Y	Y
8 Ireland	N	N	Y	Y	Y	Y	?	Y
9 Nelson	Y	N	Y	Y	Y	Y	Y	Y
10 Bafalis	N	N	Y	+	+	+	+	+
11 Mica	Y	N	Y	Y	Y	Y	Y	Y
12 Shaw	N	N	Y	Y	Y	Y	Y	Y
13 Lehman	Y	Y	Y	Y	Y	Y	Y	N
14 Pepper	Y	?	#	?	Y	Y	Y	N
15 Fascell	Y	Y	Y	Y	N	N	Y	N
GEORGIA								
1 Ginn	P	N	Y	Y	Y	Y	Y	Y
2 Hatcher	N	N	?	Y	Y	Y	Y	Y
3 Brinkley	N	N	Y	Y	Y	Y	Y	Y
4 Levitas	N	N	Y	Y	Y	Y	Y	Y
5 Fowler	Y	N	Y	Y	Y	Y	Y	Y
6 Gingrich	N	N	Y	Y	Y	Y	Y	Y
7 McDonald	N	N	Y	N	N	Y	N	Y
8 Evans	N	N	Y	N	N	Y	Y	Y
9 Jenkins	N	N	Y	N	N	Y	Y	Y
10 Barnard	N	N	Y	Y	Y	Y	Y	Y
HAWAII								
1 Heftel	Y	Y	Y	Y	Y	Y	Y	Y
2 Akaka	Y	N	Y	Y	Y	Y	Y	Y
IDAHO								
1 Craig	?	?	?	?	Y	N	Y	Y
2 Hansen	N	N	Y	N	N	Y	Y	Y
ILLINOIS								
1 Washington	?	?	?	?	Y	Y	Y	N
2 Savage	Y	Y	N	Y	Y	Y	Y	N
3 Russo	Y	Y	Y	Y	Y	Y	Y	Y
4 Derwinski	Y	Y	Y	Y	Y	Y	Y	Y
5 Fary	#	?	#	?	?	?	?	?
6 Hyde	N	X	?	Y	Y	Y	Y	Y
7 Collins	Y	#	X	?	?	?	?	X
8 Postenkowski	Y	Y	Y	Y	Y	Y	Y	Y
9 Yates	Y	N	N	Y	Y	Y	Y	N
10 Porter	N	Y	Y	Y	Y	Y	Y	Y
11 Annunzio	Y	N	Y	Y	Y	Y	Y	Y
12 Crane, P.	N	N	Y	N	N	Y	Y	Y
13 McClory	N	N	Y	Y	Y	Y	Y	Y
14 Erlenborn	N	N	Y	Y	Y	Y	Y	Y
15 Corcoran	N	N	Y	Y	Y	Y	Y	Y
16 Martin	N	?	?	Y	Y	Y	Y	Y
17 O'Brien	N	N	Y	Y	Y	Y	Y	Y
18 Michel	N	N	Y	?	?	?	?	?
19 Railsback	N	Y	Y	?	?	?	?	?
20 Findley	N	N	Y	Y	Y	Y	Y	Y
21 Madigan	N	N	Y	?	?	?	?	Y
22 Crane, D.	N	N	Y	N	N	Y	Y	Y
23 Price	?	?	?	?	Y	?	?	?
24 Simon	Y	Y	Y	Y	Y	Y	Y	N
INDIANA								
1 Benjamin	Y	N	Y	Y	Y	Y	Y	Y
2 Fithian	Y	Y	Y	Y	Y	Y	Y	Y
3 Hiler	N	N	Y	Y	Y	Y	Y	Y
4 Coats	N	N	Y	Y	Y	Y	Y	Y
5 Hillis	?	?	?	?	?	?	?	?
6 Evans	Y	Y	Y	N	N	Y	Y	Y
7 Myers	N	N	Y	Y	Y	Y	Y	Y
8 Deckard	N	Y	Y	Y	Y	Y	?	Y
9 Hamilton	Y	Y	Y	Y	Y	Y	Y	Y
10 Sharp	?	?	Y	Y	Y	Y	Y	Y
11 Jacobs	Y	Y	Y	N	Y	Y	Y	N
IOWA								
1 Leach	Y	Y	Y	Y	Y	Y	Y	Y
2 Tauke	N	Y	N	Y	Y	Y	Y	N
3 Evans	-	-	+	N	Y	Y	Y	Y
4 Smith	Y	N	Y	Y	Y	Y	Y	Y
5 Harkin	Y	Y	N	?	?	?	?	?
6 Bedell	Y	Y	N	Y	Y	Y	Y	N

Democrats *Republicans*

Corresponding to Congressional Record Votes 62, 63, 64, 65, 66, 67, 68, 69

	55	56	57	58	59	60	61	62
KANSAS								
1 ***Roberts***	N	N	Y	Y	Y	?	Y	Y
2 ***Jeffries***	N	N	Y	Y	Y	Y	Y	Y
3 ***Winn***	N	N	Y	Y	Y	Y	Y	Y
4 Glickman	Y	Y	Y	Y	Y	Y	Y	Y
5 ***Whittaker***	N	Y	Y	Y	Y	Y	Y	Y
KENTUCKY								
1 Hubbard	N	N	?	Y	Y	Y	Y	Y
2 Natcher	Y	N	Y	Y	Y	Y	Y	Y
3 Mazzoli	N	Y	Y	Y	Y	Y	Y	N
4 ***Snyder***	N	N	Y	Y	Y	Y	Y	Y
5 ***Rogers***	N	N	Y	Y	Y	Y	Y	Y
6 ***Hopkins***	N	Y	Y	Y	Y	Y	Y	Y
7 Perkins	Y	N	Y	Y	Y	Y	Y	Y
LOUISIANA								
1 ***Livingston***	N	N	Y	Y	Y	Y	Y	Y
2 Boggs	Y	Y	Y	Y	Y	Y	Y	Y
3 Tauzin	N	N	Y	Y	Y	Y	Y	Y
4 Roemer	Y	N	?	Y	Y	N	Y	Y
5 Huckaby	N	N	Y	Y	Y	Y	Y	Y
6 ***Moore***	N	N	Y	Y	Y	Y	Y	Y
7 Breaux	N	N	Y	Y	Y	Y	Y	Y
8 Long	Y	Y	Y	?	Y	Y	Y	Y
MAINE								
1 ***Emery***	N	X	?	Y	Y	Y	Y	N
2 ***Snowe***	N	N	Y	Y	Y	Y	Y	N
MARYLAND								
1 Dyson	N	N	Y	?	Y	Y	Y	Y
2 Long	N	N	Y	Y	Y	Y	Y	N
3 Mikulski	Y	?	?	Y	Y	Y	Y	N
4 ***Holt***	N	N	Y	Y	Y	Y	Y	Y
5 Hoyer	Y	Y	Y	Y	Y	Y	Y	N
6 Byron	N	N	Y	?	?	?	?	?
7 Mitchell	Y	Y	N	N	Y	Y	Y	N
8 Barnes	Y	Y	Y	Y	Y	Y	Y	N
MASSACHUSETTS								
1 ***Conte***	Y	Y	Y	?	?	?	?	?
2 Boland	#	?	#	Y	Y	Y	Y	N
3 Early	Y	?	?	Y	Y	Y	Y	Y
4 Frank	Y	Y	Y	Y	Y	Y	Y	N
5 Shannon	Y	Y	Y	Y	Y	Y	Y	N
6 Mavroules	Y	Y	Y	Y	Y	Y	?	N
7 Markey	Y	Y	Y	Y	Y	Y	Y	Y
8 O'Neill								
9 Moakley	Y	Y	Y	Y	Y	Y	Y	Y
10 ***Heckler***	Y	Y	Y	?	Y	Y	Y	Y
11 Donnelly	Y	Y	Y	Y	Y	Y	?	Y
12 Studds	Y	Y	N	Y	Y	Y	Y	N
MICHIGAN								
1 Conyers	Y	Y	N	Y	Y	N	Y	N
2 ***Pursell***	?	?	?	?	Y	Y	Y	Y
3 Wolpe	Y	Y	Y	Y	Y	Y	Y	N
4 ***Siljander***	N	N	?	Y	Y	Y	Y	Y
5 ***Sawyer***	N	N	Y	Y	Y	Y	Y	Y
6 ***Dunn***	Y	Y	Y	Y	Y	Y	Y	Y
7 Kildee	Y	Y	Y	Y	Y	Y	Y	N
8 Traxler	Y	?	?	Y	?	?	Y	Y
9 ***Vander Jagt***	N	?	?	Y	Y	Y	?	Y
10 Albosta	Y	?	?	?	?	?	?	?
11 ***Davis***	N	N	Y	Y	Y	Y	Y	Y
12 Bonior	Y	Y	N	Y	Y	Y	Y	Y
13 Crockett	Y	Y	N	Y	Y	Y	Y	N
14 Hertel	Y	N	Y	Y	Y	Y	Y	Y
15 Ford	Y	Y	Y	Y	Y	Y	Y	Y
16 Dingell	?	N	Y	Y	Y	Y	Y	Y
17 Brodhead	Y	Y	Y	Y	N	Y	Y	Y
18 Blanchard	Y	Y	Y	?	Y	Y	Y	Y
19 ***Broomfield***	N	N	Y	Y	Y	Y	Y	?
MINNESOTA								
1 ***Erdahl***	N	Y	Y	Y	Y	Y	Y	N
2 ***Hagedorn***	N	N	Y	Y	Y	Y	Y	?
3 ***Frenzel***	N	Y	?	Y	Y	Y	Y	N
4 Vento	Y	Y	N	Y	Y	Y	Y	N
5 Sabo	Y	Y	N	N	Y	Y	Y	N
6 ***Weber***	Y	Y	Y	Y	Y	Y	Y	Y
7 ***Stangeland***	N	N	Y	Y	Y	N	Y	Y
8 Oberstar	Y	Y	N	Y	Y	Y	Y	N
MISSISSIPPI								
1 Whitten	Y	N	?	Y	Y	Y	Y	?
2 Bowen	N	N	Y	Y	Y	Y	Y	Y
3 Montgomery	N	N	Y	Y	Y	Y	?	Y
4 Vacancy								
5 ***Lott***	N	N	Y	?	?	?	?	Y
MISSOURI								
1 Clay	Y	Y	N	?	Y	Y	Y	N
2 Young	Y	N	Y	Y	Y	Y	Y	Y
3 Gephardt	Y	N	Y	Y	Y	Y	Y	Y
4 Skelton	N	N	Y	Y	Y	Y	Y	Y
5 Bolling	Y	Y	Y	Y	Y	Y	?	?
6 ***Coleman***	N	N	Y	Y	Y	N	Y	Y
7 ***Taylor***	N	N	Y	Y	Y	Y	Y	Y
8 ***Bailey***	N	-	+	Y	Y	Y	Y	Y
9 Volkmer	Y	N	Y	Y	Y	Y	Y	Y
10 ***Emerson***	N	N	Y	Y	Y	N	Y	Y
MONTANA								
1 Williams	Y	Y	Y	Y	Y	Y	?	N
2 ***Marlenee***	N	N	Y	Y	Y	Y	Y	Y
NEBRASKA								
1 ***Bereuter***	Y	N	Y	Y	Y	Y	Y	N
2 ***Daub***	N	N	Y	Y	Y	Y	Y	Y
3 ***Smith***	N	N	Y	?	Y	Y	Y	Y
NEVADA								
AL Santini	?	?	?	?	Y	Y	Y	Y
NEW HAMPSHIRE								
1 D'Amours	N	N	Y	Y	Y	Y	Y	Y
2 ***Gregg***	N	Y	Y	Y	Y	Y	Y	Y
NEW JERSEY								
1 Florio	?	#	#	?	?	?	?	Y
2 Hughes	Y	N	Y	Y	Y	Y	Y	Y
3 Howard	Y	?	?	?	?	?	?	?
4 ***Smith***	Y	Y	Y	Y	Y	Y	Y	Y
5 ***Fenwick***	N	Y	Y	Y	Y	Y	Y	N
6 ***Forsythe***	N	Y	Y	?	?	?	?	?
7 ***Roukema***	N	Y	Y	Y	Y	Y	Y	Y
8 Roe	?	?	?	?	?	?	?	?
9 ***Hollenbeck***	#	Y	N	Y	Y	Y	Y	Y
10 Rodino	Y	Y	Y	Y	Y	Y	Y	N
11 Minish	N	Y	Y	Y	Y	Y	Y	Y
12 ***Rinaldo***	N	N	Y	Y	Y	Y	Y	Y
13 ***Courter***	N	N	Y	?	+	+	?	+
14 Guarini	Y	Y	Y	Y	Y	Y	Y	N
15 Dwyer	Y	Y	Y	Y	Y	Y	Y	Y
NEW MEXICO								
1 ***Lujan***	Y	?	?	Y	Y	Y	Y	Y
2 ***Skeen***	N	N	Y	Y	Y	Y	Y	Y
NEW YORK								
1 ***Carney***	?	?	?	?	?	?	?	?
2 Downey	Y	Y	N	Y	Y	Y	Y	Y
3 ***Carman***	N	N	Y	?	?	Y	Y	Y
4 ***Lent***	N	N	Y	Y	Y	Y	Y	Y
5 ***McGrath***	N	N	Y	Y	Y	Y	Y	Y
6 ***LeBoutillier***	N	N	Y	Y	Y	Y	Y	Y
7 Addabbo	Y	Y	Y	Y	Y	Y	Y	N
8 Rosenthal	Y	Y	N	Y	Y	Y	Y	Y
9 Ferraro	?	?	?	?	?	?	?	?
10 Biaggi	?	?	?	Y	Y	Y	Y	Y
11 Scheuer	Y	Y	N	Y	Y	Y	Y	N
12 Chisholm	Y	Y	N	?	Y	Y	Y	N
13 Solarz	Y	Y	Y	Y	Y	Y	Y	N
14 Richmond	Y	#	X	Y	Y	Y	Y	N
15 Zeferetti	Y	N	Y	?	Y	Y	Y	Y
16 Schumer	Y	Y	N	Y	Y	Y	?	N
17 ***Molinari***	N	N	Y	Y	Y	Y	Y	Y
18 ***Green***	Y	Y	Y	Y	Y	Y	Y	N
19 Rangel	Y	#	X	Y	Y	Y	Y	N
20 Weiss	Y	Y	N	Y	Y	Y	Y	N
21 Garcia	Y	Y	N	Y	Y	Y	Y	N
22 Bingham	N	Y	N	Y	Y	Y	?	N
23 Peyser	Y	N	Y	Y	Y	Y	Y	Y
24 Ottinger	Y	Y	N	P	Y	Y	Y	N
25 ***Fish***	?	?	?	Y	Y	Y	Y	N
26 ***Gilman***	N	N	Y	Y	Y	Y	Y	N
27 McHugh	Y	?	N	Y	Y	Y	Y	N
28 Stratton	?	?	?	?	?	?	?	N
29 ***Solomon***	N	N	Y	Y	N	N	N	Y
30 ***Martin***	N	N	Y	Y	Y	Y	Y	Y
31 ***Mitchell***	X	X	?	Y	Y	Y	Y	Y
32 ***Wortley***	N	N	Y	Y	Y	Y	Y	Y
33 ***Lee***	N	N	Y	?	Y	Y	Y	Y
34 ***Horton***	N	N	Y	Y	Y	Y	?	N
35 ***Conable***	N	N	Y	Y	Y	Y	Y	N
36 LaFalce	?	?	?	Y	Y	Y	Y	N
37 Nowak	Y	Y	Y	Y	Y	Y	Y	N
38 ***Kemp***	?	?	?	?	?	?	?	?
39 Lundine	Y	Y	N	Y	Y	Y	?	N
NORTH CAROLINA								
1 Jones	N	N	Y	?	Y	Y	Y	Y
2 Fountain	N	N	Y	Y	Y	Y	?	Y
3 Whitley	N	N	Y	Y	Y	Y	Y	Y
4 Andrews	Y	N	Y	Y	Y	Y	Y	Y
5 Neal	N	N	Y	Y	Y	Y	Y	Y
6 ***Johnston***	N	X	?	Y	Y	N	Y	Y
7 Rose	N	N	Y	?	Y	Y	Y	N
8 Hefner	N	N	Y	Y	Y	Y	Y	Y
9 ***Martin***	N	N	?	Y	Y	Y	Y	?
10 ***Broyhill***	N	N	?	Y	Y	Y	Y	Y
11 ***Hendon***	N	N	Y	Y	Y	Y	Y	Y
NORTH DAKOTA								
AL Dorgan	Y	Y	Y	Y	Y	Y	Y	N
OHIO								
1 ***Gradison***	Y	N	Y	Y	Y	Y	Y	Y
2 Luken	N	Y	Y	Y	Y	Y	Y	Y
3 Hall	Y	Y	Y	Y	Y	Y	?	Y
4 Vacancy								
5 ***Latta***	N	N	Y	Y	Y	Y	Y	Y
6 ***McEwen***	N	N	Y	Y	Y	Y	Y	Y
7 ***Brown***	?	?	?	?	?	?	?	?
8 ***Kindness***	N	N	Y	Y	Y	Y	Y	Y
9 ***Weber***	N	N	Y	Y	Y	Y	Y	Y
10 ***Miller***	N	N	Y	Y	Y	Y	Y	Y
11 ***Stanton***	N	N	Y	Y	Y	Y	Y	Y
12 Shamansky	Y	Y	Y	Y	Y	Y	Y	N
13 Pease	Y	Y	Y	Y	Y	Y	Y	N
14 Seiberling	Y	Y	N	?	Y	Y	Y	N
15 ***Wylie***	N	Y	Y	Y	Y	Y	Y	Y
16 ***Regula***	N	N	Y	Y	Y	Y	Y	Y
17 ***Ashbrook***	?	?	?	?	?	Y	Y	Y
18 Applegate	Y	N	Y	?	Y	Y	?	Y
19 ***Williams***	N	N	Y	Y	Y	Y	Y	Y
20 Oakar	Y	Y	Y	Y	Y	Y	Y	Y
21 Stokes	Y	Y	N	Y	Y	Y	Y	N
22 Eckart	Y	Y	Y	Y	Y	Y	Y	Y
23 Mottl	Y	N	Y	Y	Y	N	Y	Y
OKLAHOMA								
1 Jones	Y	N	Y	N	Y	Y	Y	Y
2 Synar	Y	N	Y	Y	Y	Y	Y	N
3 Watkins	Y	N	Y	Y	Y	Y	Y	Y
4 McCurdy	N	N	Y	Y	Y	Y	Y	Y
5 ***Edwards***	N	N	Y	Y	?	?	?	Y
6 English	N	N	Y	Y	Y	Y	Y	Y
OREGON								
1 AuCoin	?	#	?	Y	Y	Y	Y	N
2 ***Smith***	N	N	Y	Y	Y	N	Y	Y
3 Wyden	Y	#	?	Y	Y	Y	Y	N
4 Weaver	Y	Y	N	?	Y	Y	Y	?
PENNSYLVANIA								
1 Foglietta	?	?	?	?	?	?	?	Y
2 Gray	Y	Y	Y	Y	Y	Y	?	N
3 Vacancy								
4 ***Dougherty***	N	N	Y	?	Y	Y	?	Y
5 ***Schulze***	?	?	?	?	?	?	?	Y
6 Yatron	Y	N	Y	Y	Y	Y	Y	Y
7 Edgar	Y	Y	N	Y	Y	Y	Y	N
8 ***Coyne, J.***	N	N	Y	?	Y	Y	Y	Y
9 ***Shuster***	N	N	Y	Y	Y	Y	Y	Y
10 ***McDade***	N	N	Y	Y	Y	Y	Y	Y
11 ***Nelligan***	N	N	Y	Y	Y	Y	Y	Y
12 Murtha	Y	N	Y	Y	Y	Y	Y	Y
13 ***Coughlin***	N	Y	Y	Y	Y	Y	?	Y
14 Coyne, W.	Y	Y	Y	Y	Y	Y	Y	N
15 ***Ritter***	N	N	Y	Y	Y	N	Y	Y
16 ***Walker***	?	?	?	?	?	?	?	?
17 Ertel	Y	N	Y	Y	Y	Y	Y	Y
18 Walgren	Y	Y	Y	Y	Y	Y	Y	Y
19 ***Goodling***	Y	N	Y	N	Y	Y	Y	Y
20 Gaydos	Y	N	Y	Y	Y	Y	Y	Y
21 Bailey	N	N	Y	Y	Y	Y	Y	Y
22 Murphy	Y	?	?	Y	Y	Y	Y	Y
23 ***Clinger***	N	N	Y	Y	Y	Y	Y	Y
24 ***Marks***	N	N	Y	Y	Y	Y	Y	Y
25 Atkinson	Y	N	Y	Y	Y	Y	Y	Y
RHODE ISLAND								
1 St Germain	Y	?	?	Y	Y	Y	Y	N
2 ***Schneider***	Y	Y	Y	?	Y	Y	Y	N
SOUTH CAROLINA								
1 ***Hartnett***	N	N	Y	Y	Y	Y	Y	Y
2 ***Spence***	N	N	Y	Y	Y	Y	Y	Y
3 Derrick	Y	N	Y	Y	Y	Y	Y	N
4 ***Campbell***	N	N	Y	Y	Y	Y	Y	Y
5 Holland	N	N	Y	Y	Y	Y	Y	Y
6 ***Napier***	N	N	Y	Y	Y	Y	Y	Y
SOUTH DAKOTA								
1 Daschle	Y	Y	Y	Y	Y	Y	?	N
2 ***Roberts***	N	N	Y	Y	Y	Y	Y	Y
TENNESSEE								
1 ***Quillen***	N	N	Y	?	?	?	?	?
2 ***Duncan***	N	N	Y	Y	Y	Y	Y	Y
3 Bouquard	X	?	?	?	?	?	?	?
4 Gore	Y	N	Y	Y	Y	Y	Y	N
5 Boner	N	N	Y	Y	Y	Y	Y	Y
6 ***Beard***	N	N	Y	Y	Y	Y	?	Y
7 Jones	N	N	Y	Y	Y	Y	Y	Y
8 Ford	Y	Y	Y	Y	Y	Y	Y	N
TEXAS								
1 Hall, S.	N	N	Y	Y	Y	Y	Y	Y
2 Wilson	?	N	Y	Y	Y	Y	Y	Y
3 ***Collins***	N	N	Y	Y	Y	Y	Y	Y
4 Hall, R.	Y	N	?	Y	Y	?	?	Y
5 Mattox	Y	Y	Y	Y	Y	Y	Y	Y
6 Gramm	N	N	Y	Y	Y	Y	Y	Y
7 ***Archer***	N	N	Y	Y	Y	Y	?	Y
8 ***Fields***	N	N	Y	Y	Y	Y	Y	Y
9 Brooks	Y	N	Y	Y	Y	Y	Y	Y
10 Pickle	N	N	Y	?	Y	Y	Y	Y
11 Leath	N	N	Y	Y	Y	Y	Y	Y
12 Wright	Y	?	Y	Y	Y	Y	Y	?
13 Hightower	N	Y	Y	Y	Y	Y	Y	?
14 Patman	N	N	Y	Y	Y	Y	Y	Y
15 de la Garza	Y	N	Y	?	?	?	?	Y
16 White	+	-	+	+	+	+	+	+
17 Stenholm	N	N	Y	?	Y	Y	Y	Y
18 Leland	#	#	X	Y	Y	Y	?	N
19 Hance	Y	?	Y	Y	Y	Y	Y	Y
20 Gonzalez	Y	P	Y	Y	Y	Y	Y	N
21 ***Loeffler***	N	N	Y	Y	?	?	?	Y
22 ***Paul***	Y	Y	N	Y	N	N	Y	Y
23 Kazen	N	N	Y	Y	Y	Y	Y	Y
24 Frost	Y	Y	Y	Y	Y	Y	Y	Y
UTAH								
1 ***Hansen***	N	N	Y	Y	Y	Y	Y	Y
2 ***Marriott***	N	N	?	Y	Y	Y	Y	Y
VERMONT								
AL ***Jeffords***	?	#	?	Y	Y	Y	Y	N
VIRGINIA								
1 ***Trible***	N	N	Y	?	Y	Y	Y	Y
2 ***Whitehurst***	N	N	Y	Y	Y	Y	Y	Y
3 ***Bliley***	N	N	?	Y	Y	Y	Y	Y
4 ***Daniel, R.***	N	N	Y	Y	Y	Y	Y	Y
5 Daniel, D.	N	N	Y	Y	Y	Y	Y	Y
6 ***Butler***	N	N	Y	Y	Y	Y	Y	Y
7 ***Robinson***	N	N	Y	Y	Y	Y	Y	Y
8 ***Parris***	N	N	Y	Y	Y	Y	Y	Y
9 ***Wampler***	N	N	Y	Y	Y	Y	Y	Y
10 ***Wolf***	N	N	Y	Y	Y	Y	Y	Y
WASHINGTON								
1 ***Pritchard***	N	Y	Y	Y	Y	Y	Y	Y
2 Swift	Y	Y	Y	Y	Y	Y	Y	N
3 Bonker	Y	Y	Y	?	Y	Y	Y	Y
4 ***Morrison***	N	N	Y	Y	Y	Y	Y	Y
5 Foley	Y	N	Y	Y	Y	Y	Y	?
6 Dicks	N	N	Y	Y	Y	Y	?	Y
7 Lowry	Y	Y	Y	Y	Y	Y	Y	N
WEST VIRGINIA								
1 Mollohan	?	?	#	?	?	?	?	Y
2 ***Benedict***	N	?	?	Y	Y	Y	Y	Y
3 ***Staton***	N	N	Y	Y	Y	Y	Y	Y
4 Rahall	Y	Y	Y	Y	Y	Y	Y	Y
WISCONSIN								
1 Aspin	Y	Y	Y	Y	Y	Y	Y	N
2 Kastenmeier	Y	Y	N	Y	Y	Y	Y	N
3 ***Gunderson***	N	Y	Y	Y	Y	Y	Y	Y
4 Zablocki	N	N	Y	Y	Y	Y	Y	?
5 Reuss	Y	Y	N	Y	Y	Y	Y	N
6 ***Petri***	N	X	?	?	?	?	Y	N
7 Obey	Y	Y	Y	Y	Y	Y	Y	N
8 ***Roth***	N	N	Y	Y	Y	Y	Y	Y
9 ***Sensenbrenner***	N	?	?	Y	Y	Y	Y	Y
WYOMING								
AL ***Cheney***	N	N	Y	Y	Y	Y	Y	Y

Democrats ***Republicans***

KEY

Y Voted for (yea).
\# Paired for.
\+ Announced for.
N Voted against (nay).
X Paired against.
- Announced against.
P Voted "present".
C Voted "present" to avoid possible conflict of interest.
? Did not vote or otherwise make a position known.

63. HR 3462. Justice Department Authorization. Passage of the bill to reauthorize programs of the Department of Justice for fiscal 1982. Passed 353-42: R 147-26; D 206-16 (ND 140-11, SD 66-5), June 9, 1981.

64. Procedural Motion. Walker, R-Pa., motion to approve the House *Journal* of Wednesday, June 10. Motion agreed to 342-13: R 159-6; D 183-7 (ND 123-6, SD 60-1), June 11, 1981.

65. HR 3480. Legal Services Corporation. Adoption of the rule (H Res 148) providing for House floor consideration of the bill to reauthorize the Legal Services Corporation for two years. Adopted 303-88: R 88-84; D 215-4 (ND 148-1, SD 67-3), June 11, 1981.

66. HR 3413. Department of Energy National Security Programs Authorization. Weiss, D-N.Y., amendment to prohibit use of funds in the bill to develop or produce enhanced radiation (neutron) weapons. Rejected 88-293: R 10-157; D 78-136 (ND 73-71, SD 5-65), June 11, 1981.

67. HR 3413. Department of Energy National Security Programs Authorization. Hightower, D-Texas, amendment to delete a provision barring preparation of any environmental impact statement not already being prepared for an Energy Department military facility, unless the statement is required by law. Adopted 233-122: R 72-89; D 161-33 (ND 112-19, SD 49-14), June 11, 1981.

	63	64	65	66	67
ALABAMA					
1 *Edwards*	Y	Y	?	?	?
2 *Dickinson*	Y	?	N	N	N
3 Nichols	Y	?	Y	N	N
4 Bevill	Y	Y	Y	N	N
5 Flippo	?	Y	Y	N	N
6 *Smith*	N	P	N	N	N
7 Shelby	Y	?	?	X	?
ALASKA					
AL *Young*	Y	N	Y	N	Y
ARIZONA					
1 *Rhodes*	Y	Y	N	N	Y
2 Udall	?	Y	Y	Y	Y
3 *Stump*	Y	Y	Y	N	N
4 *Rudd*	Y	Y	N	N	\#
ARKANSAS					
1 Alexander	N	Y	Y	?	?
2 *Bethune*	Y	Y	N	N	N
3 *Hammerschmidt*	Y	Y	N	N	N
4 Anthony	Y	?	Y	N	Y
CALIFORNIA					
1 *Chappie*	Y	Y	N	?	N
2 *Clausen*	Y	Y	Y	N	Y
3 Matsui	Y	?	Y	N	Y
4 Fazio	Y	Y	Y	?	?
5 Burton, J.	Y	?	?	Y	Y
6 Burton, P.	Y	Y	Y	Y	Y
7 Miller	N	Y	Y	Y	Y
8 Dellums	?	Y	Y	Y	Y
9 Stark	Y	?	Y	N	?
10 Edwards	Y	?	Y	Y	Y
11 Lantos	Y	Y	Y	N	Y
12 *McCloskey*	Y	Y	Y	N	Y
13 Mineta	Y	Y	Y	N	Y
14 *Shumway*	N	Y	N	N	Y
15 Coelho	Y	Y	Y	N	Y
16 Panetta	Y	Y	Y	N	Y
17 *Pashayan*	N	Y	N	N	N
18 *Thomas*	Y	Y	N	N	N
19 *Lagomarsino*	Y	Y	N	N	N
20 *Goldwater*	?	Y	N	N	?
21 *Fiedler*	Y	Y	N	N	N
22 *Moorhead*	N	Y	N	N	Y
23 Beilenson	Y	Y	Y	Y	Y
24 Waxman	Y	Y	N	Y	Y
25 Roybal	Y	Y	Y	Y	Y
26 *Rousselot*	?	?	N	N	N
27 *Dornan*	Y	Y	N	N	N
28 Dixon	Y	Y	Y	Y	Y
29 Hawkins	Y	N	?	Y	Y
30 Danielson	Y	Y	N	Y	+
31 Dymally	N	Y	Y	?	?
32 Anderson	Y	Y	Y	N	N
33 *Grisham*	?	Y	?	N	N
34 *Lungren*	Y	Y	Y	N	N
35 *Dreier*	N	Y	N	N	N
36 Brown	Y	Y	Y	?	N
37 *Lewis*	Y	Y	N	N	N
38 Patterson	Y	Y	Y	Y	N
39 *Dannemeyer*	Y	Y	?	N	N
40 *Badham*	?	Y	N	N	N
41 *Lowery*	Y	?	?	N	Y
42 *Hunter*	Y	Y	Y	N	N
43 *Burgener*	Y	Y	N	N	Y
COLORADO					
1 Schroeder	Y	N	Y	Y	Y
2 Wirth	Y	Y	Y	Y	Y
3 Kogovsek	Y	Y	Y	Y	?
4 *Brown*	N	Y	N	N	N

	63	64	65	66	67
5 *Kramer*	Y	Y	Y	?	X
CONNECTICUT					
1 Cotter	?	?	?	?	?
2 Gejdenson	Y	Y	Y	Y	Y
3 *DeNardis*	Y	?	Y	N	Y
4 *McKinney*	Y	?	?	Y	Y
5 Ratchford	Y	Y	Y	Y	Y
6 Moffett	Y	?	Y	Y	Y
DELAWARE					
AL *Evans*	Y	Y	Y	N	Y
FLORIDA					
1 Hutto	Y	?	Y	N	Y
2 Fuqua	?	Y	Y	N	N
3 Bennett	Y	Y	N	N	N
4 Chappell	\#	?	?	X	?
5 *McCollum*	Y	Y	N	N	N
6 *Young*	Y	Y	Y	N	?
7 Gibbons	Y	Y	N	N	N
8 Ireland	Y	Y	N	N	Y
9 Nelson	Y	Y	N	N	N
10 *Bafalis*	Y	?	N	?	?
11 Mica	Y	Y	N	N	?
12 *Shaw*	Y	Y	N	N	N
13 Lehman	Y	Y	Y	Y	Y
14 Pepper	Y	Y	Y	N	Y
15 Fascell	Y	Y	Y	N	Y
GEORGIA					
1 Ginn	Y	Y	Y	N	Y
2 Hatcher	Y	Y	Y	N	Y
3 Brinkley	Y	Y	Y	N	N
4 Levitas	Y	Y	Y	N	Y
5 Fowler	Y	Y	Y	N	Y
6 *Gingrich*	Y	Y	Y	N	Y
7 McDonald	N	?	N	N	N
8 Evans	?	Y	N	N	N
9 Jenkins	Y	Y	Y	N	Y
10 Barnard	Y	Y	Y	N	Y
HAWAII					
1 Heftel	Y	?	N	N	Y
2 Akaka	Y	Y	Y	N	Y
IDAHO					
1 *Craig*	N	Y	N	N	N
2 *Hansen*	N	Y	N	N	N
ILLINOIS					
1 Washington	Y	?	Y	Y	Y
2 Savage	N	?	Y	Y	Y
3 Russo	Y	Y	Y	N	Y
4 *Derwinski*	Y	?	?	?	X
5 Fary	Y	Y	Y	N	Y
6 *Hyde*	Y	Y	Y	N	N
7 Collins	?	Y	?	Y	Y
8 Rostenkowski	Y	Y	Y	N	Y
9 Yates	Y	Y	Y	Y	Y
10 *Porter*	Y	+	+	-	\#
11 Annunzio	Y	Y	Y	N	Y
12 *Crane, P.*	N	?	N	N	N
13 *McClory*	Y	Y	N	N	Y
14 *Erlenborn*	Y	?	?	?	?
15 *Corcoran*	Y	Y	N	N	N
16 *Martin*	Y	Y	Y	N	?
17 *O'Brien*	Y	Y	Y	N	Y
18 *Michel*	?	Y	N	N	N
19 *Railsback*	?	Y	Y	N	Y
20 *Findley*	Y	Y	Y	N	N
21 *Madigan*	Y	Y	Y	?	N
22 *Crane, D.*	N	Y	N	N	N
23 Price	?	Y	Y	N	N
24 Simon	Y	Y	Y	Y	Y
INDIANA					
1 Benjamin	Y	Y	Y	N	Y
2 Fithian	Y	Y	Y	?	?
3 *Hiler*	Y	Y	Y	N	N
4 *Coats*	Y	Y	Y	N	N
5 *Hillis*	Y	Y	Y	N	?
6 Evans	N	Y	N	Y	Y
7 *Myers*	Y	Y	N	N	N
8 *Deckard*	Y	Y	Y	N	Y
9 Hamilton	Y	Y	Y	N	Y
10 Sharp	Y	Y	Y	N	Y
11 Jacobs	Y	N	Y	Y	Y
IOWA					
1 *Leach*	Y	Y	Y	Y	Y
2 *Tauke*	Y	Y	Y	N	Y
3 *Evans*	Y	N	N	N	N
4 Smith	Y	Y	Y	N	N
5 Harkin	?	N	Y	Y	Y
6 Bedell	Y	?	Y	Y	Y

Democrats *Republicans*

Corresponding to Congressional Record Votes 70, 71, 72, 73, 74

	63	64	65	66	67
KANSAS					
1 *Roberts*	Y	Y	Y	N	N
2 *Jeffries*	N	Y	N	N	N
3 *Winn*	Y	Y	Y	N	N
4 Glickman	Y	Y	Y	Y	Y
5 *Whittaker*	Y	Y	Y	N	N
KENTUCKY					
1 Hubbard	N	Y	Y	N	Y
2 Natcher	Y	Y	N	N	Y
3 Mazzoli	+	Y	Y	Y	N
4 *Snyder*	Y	Y	N	N	Y
5 *Rogers*	Y	Y	N	N	Y
6 *Hopkins*	Y	Y	N	N	Y
7 Perkins	Y	Y	Y	N	Y
LOUISIANA					
1 *Livingston*	Y	Y	Y	N	Y
2 Boggs	Y	Y	Y	N	Y
3 Tauzin	Y	?	Y	N	Y
4 Roemer	Y	?	Y	N	Y
5 Huckaby	Y	Y	?	N	Y
6 *Moore*	Y	Y	Y	N	N
7 Breaux	Y	?	?	N	Y
8 Long	Y	Y	Y	N	Y
MAINE					
1 *Emery*	Y	Y	Y	N	Y
2 *Snowe*	Y	Y	Y	N	Y
MARYLAND					
1 Dyson	Y	Y	Y	N	Y
2 Long	Y	Y	Y	N	Y
3 Mikulski	Y	Y	Y	Y	Y
4 *Holt*	Y	Y	N	N	N
5 Hoyer	Y	Y	Y	N	Y
6 Byron	?	Y	Y	N	N
7 Mitchell	Y	N	Y	Y	Y
8 Barnes	Y	?	Y	Y	?
MASSACHUSETTS					
1 *Conte*	?	Y	Y	N	Y
2 Boland	Y	Y	Y	?	?
3 Early	Y	Y	Y	Y	Y
4 Frank	Y	Y	Y	Y	Y
5 Shannon	Y	Y	Y	Y	Y
6 Mavroules	Y	Y	Y	N	N
7 Markey	Y	Y	Y	Y	Y
8 O'Neill					
9 Moakley	Y	Y	Y	Y	Y
10 *Heckler*	Y	?	Y	Y	Y
11 Donnelly	Y	Y	Y	Y	Y
12 Studds	Y	Y	Y	Y	Y
MICHIGAN					
1 Conyers	Y	?	?	#	?
2 *Pursell*	Y	?	?	?	?
3 Wolpe	N	Y	Y	Y	Y
4 *Siljander*	Y	Y	N	N	N
5 *Sawyer*	Y	Y	Y	N	N
6 *Dunn*	Y	Y	Y	N	N
7 Kildee	Y	Y	Y	Y	Y
8 Traxler	Y	Y	Y	?	?
9 *Vander Jagt*	Y	Y	N	?	X
10 Albosta	?	Y	Y	N	?
11 *Davis*	Y	Y	Y	N	N
12 Bonior	Y	Y	Y	Y	Y
13 Crockett	N	?	Y	Y	Y
14 Hertel	Y	Y	Y	N	Y
15 Ford	Y	?	Y	?	Y
16 Dingell	Y	Y	Y	N	N
17 Brodhead	Y	?	Y	Y	Y
18 Blanchard	Y	?	Y	N	Y
19 *Broomfield*	Y	Y	N	N	N
MINNESOTA					
1 *Erdahl*	Y	Y	Y	Y	Y
2 *Hagedorn*	Y	Y	Y	N	N
3 *Frenzel*	Y	Y	N	N	N
4 Vento	Y	Y	Y	Y	Y
5 Sabo	Y	N	Y	Y	Y
6 *Weber*	Y	Y	N	N	N
7 *Stangeland*	N	Y	N	N	Y
8 Oberstar	Y	Y	Y	Y	Y
MISSISSIPPI					
1 Whitten	Y	Y	Y	N	N
2 Bowen	Y	Y	Y	N	N
3 Montgomery	Y	Y	Y	N	N
4 Vacancy					
5 *Lott*	N	Y	N	N	N
MISSOURI					
1 Clay	Y	?	?	?	?
2 Young	Y	Y	?	N	Y
3 Gephardt	Y	?	Y	N	Y

	63	64	65	66	67
4 Skelton	Y	?	Y	N	?
5 Bolling	Y	Y	Y	?	?
6 *Coleman*	Y	Y	Y	N	N
7 *Taylor*	Y	Y	N	N	N
8 *Bailey*	Y	Y	N	-	N
9 Volkmer	Y	Y	Y	N	Y
10 *Emerson*	Y	Y	N	N	N
MONTANA					
1 Williams	Y	Y	Y	Y	Y
2 *Marlenee*	Y	Y	Y	Y	Y
NEBRASKA					
1 *Bereuter*	N	Y	Y	N	Y
2 *Daub*	Y	Y	Y	N	Y
3 *Smith*	Y	Y	Y	N	Y
NEVADA					
AL Santini	Y	?	Y	N	?
NEW HAMPSHIRE					
1 D'Amours	Y	Y	Y	N	Y
2 *Gregg*	N	Y	N	N	N
NEW JERSEY					
1 Florio	Y	Y	Y	N	Y
2 Hughes	Y	Y	Y	N	Y
3 Howard	?	Y	Y	N	Y
4 *Smith*	Y	Y	Y	Y	Y
5 *Fenwick*	Y	Y	Y	N	Y
6 *Forsythe*	?	N	Y	Y	N
7 *Roukema*	N	?	Y	Y	N
8 Roe	?	?	?	?	?
9 *Hollenbeck*	?	?	Y	?	#
10 Rodino	Y	Y	Y	Y	Y
11 Minish	Y	Y	Y	N	Y
12 *Rinaldo*	Y	Y	Y	N	Y
13 *Courter*	+	Y	N	N	Y
14 Guarini	Y	Y	Y	N	?
15 Dwyer	Y	Y	Y	N	Y
NEW MEXICO					
1 *Lujan*	Y	Y	Y	N	Y
2 *Skeen*	Y	Y	?	N	#
NEW YORK					
1 *Carney*	?	Y	N	N	N
2 Downey	Y	?	Y	N	Y
3 *Carman*	Y	?	N	N	N
4 *Lent*	Y	Y	N	N	N
5 *McGrath*	Y	?	N	N	N
6 *LeBoutillier*	Y	Y	N	N	N
7 Addabbo	Y	Y	?	N	Y
8 Rosenthal	Y	Y	Y	?	?
9 Ferraro	?	?	Y	N	Y
10 Biaggi	Y	Y	Y	N	Y
11 Scheuer	Y	?	Y	N	Y
12 Chisholm	Y	?	Y	Y	Y
13 Solarz	Y	Y	Y	N	Y
14 Richmond	Y	?	Y	#	?
15 Zeferetti	Y	Y	Y	N	Y
16 Schumer	Y	?	Y	Y	Y
17 *Molinari*	Y	Y	Y	N	N
18 *Green*	Y	Y	Y	N	N
19 Rangel	Y	Y	Y	Y	?
20 Weiss	N	Y	Y	Y	Y
21 Garcia	Y	Y	Y	Y	Y
22 Bingham	Y	Y	Y	Y	Y
23 Peyser	Y	Y	Y	N	Y
24 Ottinger	Y	P	Y	Y	Y
25 *Fish*	Y	Y	Y	N	Y
26 *Gilman*	Y	Y	Y	N	Y
27 McHugh	Y	Y	Y	Y	Y
28 Stratton	Y	Y	Y	N	N
29 *Solomon*	N	Y	N	N	N
30 *Martin*	N	Y	N	N	?
31 *Mitchell*	Y	Y	Y	N	Y
32 *Wortley*	Y	Y	Y	N	N
33 *Lee*	Y	Y	Y	N	N
34 *Horton*	Y	Y	Y	N	N
35 *Conable*	Y	Y	Y	N	N
36 LaFalce	Y	Y	Y	N	Y
37 Nowak	Y	Y	Y	Y	Y
38 *Kemp*	?	?	?	N	N
39 Lundine	Y	?	?	?	?
NORTH CAROLINA					
1 Jones	Y	Y	Y	N	Y
2 Fountain	Y	Y	Y	N	N
3 Whitley	Y	?	?	?	?
4 Andrews	Y	Y	Y	N	Y
5 Neal	Y	?	?	?	?
6 Johnston	N	N	N	?	?
7 Rose	Y	?	N	N	?
8 Hefner	Y	Y	Y	N	Y

	63	64	65	66	67
9 *Martin*	N	Y	Y	N	N
10 *Broyhill*	N	Y	?	N	N
11 *Hendon*	Y	Y	N	N	N
NORTH DAKOTA					
AL Dorgan	Y	Y	Y	Y	Y
OHIO					
1 *Gradison*	Y	Y	Y	N	N
2 Luken	Y	Y	Y	N	N
3 Hall	Y	Y	Y	N	N
4 Vacancy					
5 *Latta*	N	Y	N	N	Y
6 *McEwen*	Y ·	Y	N	N	Y
7 *Brown*	?	Y	Y	N	N
8 *Kindness*	Y	Y	Y	N	N
9 *Weber*	Y	?	?	?	?
10 *Miller*	Y	Y	Y	N	N
11 *Stanton*	Y	Y	Y	N	N
12 Shamansky	Y	Y	Y	N	Y
13 Pease	Y	Y	Y	N	Y
14 Seiberling	Y	Y	Y	Y	Y
15 *Wylie*	Y	Y	Y	?	#
16 *Regula*	Y	Y	Y	N	N
17 *Ashbrook*	?	Y	N	?	?
18 Applegate	Y	?	Y	N	Y
19 Williams	Y	Y	Y	N	N
20 Oakar	Y	Y	Y	Y	Y
21 Stokes	Y	?	Y	Y	Y
22 Eckart	Y	Y	Y	Y	Y
23 Mottl	X	Y	Y	?	?
OKLAHOMA					
1 Jones	Y	N	?	?	?
2 Synar	Y	Y	Y	N	Y
3 Watkins	Y	Y	Y	N	Y
4 McCurdy	Y	Y	Y	N	Y
5 *Edwards*	Y	?	N	N	Y
6 English	Y	?	Y	N	Y
OREGON					
1 AuCoin	Y	Y	Y	Y	?
2 *Smith*	Y	Y	N	N	N
3 Wyden	N	Y	Y	Y	?
4 Weaver	N	Y	Y	Y	Y
PENNSYLVANIA					
1 Foglietta	Y	?	Y	Y	Y
2 Gray	Y	Y	Y	Y	Y
3 Vacancy					
4 *Dougherty*	Y	?	Y	N	N
5 *Schulze*	Y	Y	N	N	N
6 Yatron	Y	Y	Y	N	Y
7 Edgar	Y	Y	Y	Y	?
8 *Coyne, J.*	Y	?	N	N	Y
9 *Shuster*	Y	N	N	N	Y
10 *McDade*	Y	Y	Y	N	N
11 *Nelligan*	Y	?	?	?	X
12 Murtha	Y	Y	Y	N	N
13 *Coughlin*	Y	Y	Y	Y	N
14 Coyne, W.	Y	Y	Y	Y	N
15 *Ritter*	N	Y	Y	N	N
16 *Walker*	?	N	N	N	Y
17 Ertel	Y	Y	Y	N	Y
18 Walgren	Y	Y	Y	Y	Y
19 *Goodling*	Y	N	Y	N	?
20 Gaydos	Y	Y	Y	N	N
21 Bailey	Y	Y	Y	N	N
22 Murphy	N	Y	Y	N	N
23 *Clinger*	Y	Y	Y	N	Y
24 *Marks*	Y	?	Y	N	Y
25 Atkinson	Y	Y	Y	N	Y
RHODE ISLAND					
1 St Germain	Y	Y	Y	?	?
2 *Schneider*	Y	?	Y	Y	Y
SOUTH CAROLINA					
1 *Hartnett*	Y	Y	N	?	X
2 *Spence*	Y	Y	N	N	N
3 Derrick	Y	Y	Y	N	Y
4 *Campbell*	Y	Y	N	N	N
5 Holland	Y	?	?	?	?
6 *Napier*	Y	Y	N	N	Y
SOUTH DAKOTA					
1 Daschle	Y	Y	Y	N	Y
2 *Roberts*	Y	Y	N	?	#
TENNESSEE					
1 *Quillen*	?	?	?	?	X
2 *Duncan*	Y	Y	N	N	N
3 Bouquard	?	Y	Y	N	Y
4 Gore	N	Y	Y	N	Y
5 Boner	Y	Y	Y	N	Y
6 *Beard*	Y	Y	Y	?	N

	63	64	65	66	67
7 Jones	Y	Y	Y	N	Y
8 Ford	Y	Y	Y	Y	Y
TEXAS					
1 Hall, S.	Y	Y	Y	N	Y
2 Wilson	Y	?	Y	N	?
3 *Collins*	Y	Y	?	N	Y
4 Hall, R.	Y	Y	Y	N	Y
5 Mattox	Y	Y	Y	Y	Y
6 Gramm	Y	Y	Y	N	Y
7 *Archer*	Y	Y	N	N	N
8 *Fields*	Y	Y	N	N	N
9 Brooks	Y	?	Y	N	Y
10 Pickle	Y	Y	Y	N	Y
11 Leath	Y	Y	Y	N	?
12 Wright	Y	Y	Y	N	?
13 Hightower	?	Y	Y	N	Y
14 Patman	Y	Y	Y	N	Y
15 de la Garza	Y	Y	Y	N	?
16 White	Y	Y	Y	N	Y
17 Stenholm	Y	Y	Y	N	N
18 Leland	N	?	Y	Y	Y
19 Hance	Y	Y	Y	?	?
20 Gonzalez	Y	Y	Y	N	Y
21 *Loeffler*	Y	Y	N	N	N
22 *Paul*	N	Y	N	Y	#
23 Kazen	Y	Y	Y	N	?
24 Frost	Y	Y	Y	N	Y
UTAH					
1 *Hansen*	Y	Y	N	N	N
2 *Marriott*	Y	Y	N	N	N
VERMONT					
AL *Jeffords*	Y	Y	Y	N	Y
VIRGINIA					
1 *Trible*	Y	Y	N	?	X
2 *Whitehurst*	Y	Y	Y	N	N
3 *Bliley*	Y	Y	N	N	N
4 *Daniel, R.*	Y	Y	N	N	N
5 Daniel, D.	Y	Y	Y	N	N
6 *Butler*	Y	Y	Y	N	N
7 *Robinson*	Y	Y	N	N	N
8 *Parris*	Y	Y	?	N	N
9 *Wampler*	Y	Y	Y	N	Y
10 *Wolf*	Y	Y	Y	N	Y
WASHINGTON					
1 *Pritchard*	Y	Y	Y	N	Y
2 Swift	Y	Y	Y	N	Y
3 Bonker	Y	Y	Y	Y	N
4 *Morrison*	Y	Y	N	N	N
5 Foley	Y	Y	Y	N	Y
6 Dicks	Y	Y	Y	N	N
7 Lowry	N	Y	Y	Y	Y
WEST VIRGINIA					
1 Mollohan	Y	Y	Y	N	N
2 *Benedict*	N	Y	?	N	Y
3 *Staton*	Y	Y	N	N	Y
4 Rahall	Y	Y	Y	Y	Y
WISCONSIN					
1 Aspin	Y	?	?	?	?
2 Kastenmeier	Y	Y	Y	Y	Y
3 *Gunderson*	Y	Y	N	N	Y
4 Zablocki	?	?	?	?	?
5 Reuss	Y	?	?	N	Y
6 *Petri*	Y	Y	Y	N	N
7 Obey	Y	Y	Y	Y	Y
8 Roth	Y	Y	Y	N	Y
9 *Sensenbrenner*	N	Y	N	N	?
WYOMING					
AL *Cheney*	?	Y	N	?	?

Democrats   *Republicans*

68. Procedural Motion. Walker, R-Pa., motion to approve the House *Journal* of Monday, June 15. Motion agreed to 366-10: R 164-4; D 202-6 (ND 135-5, SD 67-1), June 16, 1981.

69. H J Res 287. Infant Formula. Zablocki, D-Wis., motion to suspend the rules and pass the joint resolution expressing congressional "dismay" at the U.S. vote at a World Health Organization (WHO) assembly May 21, 1981, against a voluntary international marketing code for infant formula and urging the administration to notify WHO that the United States will cooperate fully in implementation of the code. Motion agreed to 301-100: R 85-93; D 216-7 (ND 151-2, SD 65-5), June 16, 1981. A two-thirds majority vote (268 in this case) is required for passage under suspension of the rules. A "nay" was a vote supporting the president's position.

70. H Res 159. Habib Mission. Adoption of the resolution expressing the support of the House of Representatives for diplomatic efforts to resolve the crisis in Lebanon and congratulating special envoy Philip C. Habib on his peace efforts concerning Lebanon. Adopted 398-1: R 179-1; D 219-0 (ND 148-0, SD 71-0), June 16, 1981.

71. HR 3480. Legal Services Corporation. Kastenmeier, D-Wis., amendment to delete the requirement in the bill that all recipients of LSC grants be organized solely to furnish legal aid to eligible clients and to require a majority of the board of any LSC grantee to be appointed by the bar association or associations in a particular area. Rejected 155-249: R 10-169; D 145-80 (ND 129-24, SD 16-56), June 16, 1981.

72. HR 3480. Legal Services Corporation. Sensenbrenner, R-Wis., to delete a provision in the bill limiting termination or suspension of funding for an LSC grantee to 30 days, unless the grant recipient had been given notice and the opportunity for a hearing. Rejected 152-251: R 136-42; D 16-209 (ND 3-149, SD 13-60), June 16, 1981.

73. HR 3480. Legal Services Corporation. Kastenmeier, D-Wis., motion that the House resolve itself in the Committee of the Whole for further consideration of the bill. Motion agreed to 389-9: R 171-6; D 218-3 (ND 147-2, SD 71-1), June 17, 1981.

74. HR 3480. Legal Services Corporation. Kramer, R-Colo., amendment to prohibit LSC funds from being used for personal services, advertisements, telegrams, telephone calls, letters or other devices to influence any local, state or federal agency decision, except where any of these actions related to a client's legal rights. The amendment also prohibited attempts to influence local, state or federal elected officials on legislation, referenda or initiatives. Adopted 271-141: R 179-3; D 92-138 (ND 35-120, SD 57-18), June 17, 1981.

75. HR 3480. Legal Services Corporation. Wilson, D-Texas, amendment to bar LSC lawyers from bringing class action lawsuits against federal, state or local governments under any circumstances. Adopted 241-167: R 158-23; D 83-144 (ND 24-127, SD 59-17), June 17, 1981.

KEY

Y Voted for (yea).
Paired for.
+ Announced for.
N Voted against (nay).
X Paired against.
- Announced against.
P Voted "present".
C Voted "present" to avoid possible conflict of interest.
? Did not vote or otherwise make a position known.

	68	69	70	71	72	73	74	75
ALABAMA								
1 *Edwards*	Y	N	Y	N	Y	Y	Y	Y
2 *Dickinson*	Y	N	Y	N	Y	Y	Y	Y
3 Nichols	Y	Y	Y	N	Y	Y	Y	Y
4 Bevill	Y	Y	Y	N	N	Y	Y	Y
5 Flippo	Y	Y	Y	N	N	Y	Y	Y
6 *Smith*	Y	N	Y	N	Y	Y	Y	Y
7 Shelby	Y	Y	Y	N	Y	Y	Y	Y
ALASKA								
AL *Young*	Y	Y	Y	N	N	Y	Y	Y
ARIZONA								
1 *Rhodes*	Y	N	Y	N	?	Y	Y	Y
2 Udall	Y	Y	Y	N	Y	N	Y	N
3 *Stump*	Y	N	Y	N	Y	Y	Y	Y
4 *Rudd*	Y	N	Y	N	Y	Y	Y	Y
ARKANSAS								
1 Alexander	Y	Y	Y	Y	N	?	N	Y
2 *Bethune*	Y	Y	Y	N	N	Y	Y	Y
3 *Hammerschmidt*	Y	N	Y	N	N	Y	Y	Y
4 Anthony	Y	Y	Y	N	N	Y	Y	Y
CALIFORNIA								
1 *Chappie*	?	N	Y	X	Y	Y	Y	#
2 *Clausen*	Y	Y	Y	N	Y	Y	Y	Y
3 Matsui	Y	Y	Y	N	Y	N	N	N
4 Fazio	Y	Y	Y	N	?	N	N	N
5 Burton, J.	Y	Y	Y	N	N	N	N	N
6 Burton, P.	Y	Y	Y	N	N	N	N	N
7 Miller	Y	Y	Y	N	N	N	N	N
8 Dellums	Y	Y	Y	N	N	N	N	N
9 Stark	Y	Y	Y	N	N	N	N	N
10 Edwards	Y	Y	Y	N	N	N	N	N
11 Lantos	+	+	+	+	-	Y	N	N
12 *McCloskey*	Y	Y	Y	N	N	Y	Y	N
13 Mineta	Y	Y	Y	N	N	N	N	N
14 *Shumway*	Y	N	Y	N	Y	Y	Y	Y
15 Coelho	Y	Y	Y	N	Y	N	N	Y
16 Panetta	Y	Y	Y	N	N	N	N	N
17 *Pashayan*	Y	N	Y	N	Y	Y	#	?
18 *Thomas*	?	?	?	?	?	?	#	?
19 *Lagomarsino*	Y	N	Y	N	Y	Y	Y	Y
20 *Goldwater*	?	?	Y	N	Y	Y	Y	?
21 *Fiedler*	Y	Y	Y	N	Y	Y	Y	Y
22 *Moorhead*	Y	Y	Y	N	Y	Y	Y	Y
23 Beilenson	Y	Y	Y	N	N	N	N	N
24 Waxman	Y	Y	Y	N	?	N	N	N
25 Roybal	Y	Y	Y	N	N	N	N	N
26 *Rousselot*	Y	N	Y	N	Y	Y	Y	Y
27 *Dornan*	Y	N	Y	N	?	Y	Y	Y
28 Dixon	Y	Y	Y	N	?	N	N	N
29 Hawkins	N	Y	Y	N	?	Y	N	N
30 Danielson	Y	Y	Y	N	N	Y	-	N
31 Dymally	?	Y	Y	Y	Y	N	N	?
32 Anderson	Y	Y	Y	Y	N	N	N	N
33 *Grisham*	Y	N	Y	N	Y	?	?	Y
34 *Lungren*	Y	N	Y	N	Y	Y	Y	Y
35 *Dreier*	Y	N	Y	N	Y	Y	Y	Y
36 Brown	Y	Y	Y	N	N	N	N	N
37 *Lewis*	Y	N	Y	N	Y	Y	Y	Y
38 Patterson	Y	Y	Y	N	N	N	N	N
39 *Dannemeyer*	Y	N	Y	N	Y	Y	N	Y
40 *Badham*	Y	N	Y	N	Y	Y	Y	Y
41 *Lowery*	Y	Y	Y	N	Y	Y	Y	Y
42 *Hunter*	Y	N	Y	N	Y	Y	Y	Y
43 *Burgener*	Y	N	Y	N	Y	Y	Y	Y
COLORADO								
1 Schroeder	N	Y	Y	Y	N	Y	N	N
2 Wirth	Y	Y	Y	N	N	Y	N	N
3 Kogovsek	Y	Y	Y	N	N	Y	Y	N
4 *Brown*	Y	Y	Y	N	Y	Y	Y	Y

	68	69	70	71	72	73	74	75
5 *Kramer*	Y	N	Y	N	Y	Y	Y	Y
CONNECTICUT								
1 Cotter	?	?	?	?	?	?	?	?
2 Gejdenson	Y	Y	Y	Y	N	Y	N	N
3 *DeNardis*	?	Y	Y	N	Y	N	Y	Y
4 *McKinney*	Y	Y	Y	N	?	N	N	Y
5 Ratchford	Y	Y	Y	N	N	Y	N	X
6 Moffett	Y	Y	Y	N	?	N	N	N
DELAWARE								
AL *Evans*	Y	Y	Y	N	Y	Y	Y	Y
FLORIDA								
1 Hutto	Y	Y	Y	N	N	Y	Y	Y
2 Fuqua	Y	Y	Y	N	N	Y	Y	Y
3 Bennett	Y	Y	Y	N	Y	Y	N	Y
4 Chappell	Y	-	Y	N	N	Y	Y	Y
5 *McCollum*	Y	Y	Y	N	Y	Y	Y	Y
6 *Young*	Y	Y	Y	N	Y	Y	Y	Y
7 Gibbons	Y	N	Y	N	N	Y	Y	Y
8 Ireland	?	?	?	?	?	Y	Y	Y
9 Nelson	Y	Y	Y	N	N	Y	Y	Y
10 *Bafalis*	Y	Y	Y	N	Y	Y	Y	Y
11 Mica	Y	Y	Y	N	N	Y	Y	Y
12 *Shaw*	Y	N	Y	N	Y	Y	Y	Y
13 Lehman	?	?	?	#	?	?	X	?
14 Pepper	Y	Y	Y	N	Y	N	N	N
15 Fascell	Y	Y	Y	N	N	Y	N	N
GEORGIA								
1 Ginn	Y	Y	Y	N	N	Y	Y	Y
2 Hatcher	?	?	?	?	?	Y	Y	Y
3 Brinkley	Y	Y	Y	N	Y	Y	Y	Y
4 Levitas	Y	Y	Y	N	Y	N	Y	Y
5 Fowler	Y	Y	Y	N	N	Y	N	N
6 *Gingrich*	Y	N	Y	N	N	Y	Y	Y
7 McDonald	Y	N	Y	N	Y	N	Y	Y
8 Evans	Y	Y	Y	N	Y	Y	?	?
9 Jenkins	?	Y	Y	N	Y	Y	Y	Y
10 Barnard	Y	Y	Y	N	Y	Y	Y	Y
HAWAII								
1 Heftel	Y	Y	Y	N	N	Y	Y	Y
2 Akaka	Y	Y	?	Y	N	Y	N	N
IDAHO								
1 *Craig*	Y	N	Y	N	Y	Y	Y	Y
2 *Hansen*	Y	N	?	N	Y	?	Y	Y
ILLINOIS								
1 Washington	?	?	?	?	?	Y	N	N
2 Savage	?	?	?	P	N	?	N	N
3 Russo	Y	Y	Y	N	N	Y	N	N
4 *Derwinski*	?	?	?	?	?	Y	Y	Y
5 Fary	Y	Y	Y	N	Y	N	N	N
6 *Hyde*	Y	N	Y	N	Y	Y	Y	Y
7 Collins	Y	Y	Y	N	?	X	N	N
8 Rostenkowski	Y	Y	Y	N	N	Y	N	N
9 Yates	Y	Y	Y	N	N	N	N	N
10 *Porter*	Y	Y	Y	Y	Y	Y	Y	Y
11 Annunzio	Y	Y	Y	N	?	Y	N	N
12 *Crane, P.*	Y	N	Y	N	Y	Y	Y	Y
13 *McClory*	Y	N	Y	N	Y	N	Y	Y
14 *Erlenborn*	?	?	?	?	?	?	#	?
15 *Corcoran*	Y	N	Y	N	Y	Y	Y	Y
16 *Martin*	?	Y	Y	Y	N	Y	Y	Y
17 *O'Brien*	Y	Y	Y	N	Y	Y	Y	Y
18 *Michel*	Y	N	Y	N	Y	Y	Y	Y
19 *Railsback*	Y	N	Y	N	N	Y	Y	Y
20 *Findley*	P	Y	Y	N	Y	Y	Y	Y
21 *Madigan*	N	N	Y	N	Y	Y	Y	Y
22 *Crane, D.*	?	N	Y	N	Y	Y	Y	Y
23 Price	Y	Y	Y	N	N	Y	N	N
24 Simon	Y	Y	Y	N	N	Y	N	N
INDIANA								
1 Benjamin	Y	Y	Y	N	N	Y	N	Y
2 Fithian	Y	Y	Y	N	N	Y	N	Y
3 *Hiler*	Y	N	Y	N	Y	Y	Y	Y
4 *Coats*	Y	Y	Y	N	Y	Y	Y	Y
5 *Hillis*	Y	Y	Y	N	N	Y	Y	Y
6 Evans	Y	Y	Y	N	N	Y	Y	N
7 *Myers*	Y	N	Y	N	Y	Y	Y	Y
8 *Deckard*	Y	Y	Y	N	Y	Y	Y	Y
9 Hamilton	Y	Y	Y	N	N	Y	Y	Y
10 Sharp	Y	Y	Y	N	Y	N	Y	N
11 Jacobs	N	Y	Y	N	N	Y	N	N
IOWA								
1 *Leach*	Y	Y	Y	N	Y	Y	N	Y
2 *Tauke*	Y	Y	Y	N	Y	Y	Y	N
3 *Evans*	N	N	Y	N	Y	N	Y	Y
4 *Smith*	Y	Y	Y	N	N	Y	Y	Y
5 Harkin	?	Y	Y	Y	N	Y	N	N
6 Bedell	Y	Y	Y	N	N	Y	N	N

Democrats *Republicans*

	68	69	70	71	72	73	74	75
KANSAS								
1 *Roberts*	Y	Y	Y	N	Y	Y	Y	Y
2 *Jeffries*	?	N	Y	N	Y	Y	Y	Y
3 *Winn*	Y	Y	Y	N	Y	Y	Y	Y
4 Glickman	Y	Y	Y	Y	N	Y	Y	N
5 *Whittaker*	Y	Y	Y	N	Y	Y	Y	Y
KENTUCKY								
1 Hubbard	Y	N	Y	N	N	Y	Y	Y
2 Natcher	Y	Y	Y	N	N	Y	Y	Y
3 Mazzoli	Y	Y	Y	N	N	Y	Y	N
4 *Snyder*	Y	N	Y	N	Y	Y	Y	Y
5 *Rogers*	Y	Y	Y	N	Y	Y	Y	Y
6 *Hopkins*	Y	Y	Y	N	Y	Y	Y	Y
7 Perkins	Y	Y	Y	N	N	Y	N	N
LOUISIANA								
1 *Livingston*	Y	N	?	N	Y	Y	Y	Y
2 Boggs	Y	Y	Y	Y	Y	?	N	Y
3 Tauzin	Y	Y	Y	N	Y	Y	Y	Y
4 Roemer	Y	Y	Y	N	N	Y	Y	Y
5 Huckaby	?	?	?	?	?	Y	Y	Y
6 *Moore*	Y	N	Y	N	Y	Y	Y	Y
7 Breaux	?	?	?	?	?	?	?	?
8 Long	Y	Y	Y	Y	N	Y	N	N
MAINE								
1 *Emery*	Y	Y	Y	N	Y	Y	Y	Y
2 *Snowe*	?	Y	Y	N	Y	Y	Y	Y
MARYLAND								
1 Dyson	Y	Y	Y	N	N	Y	Y	Y
2 Long	Y	Y	Y	N	N	Y	N	N
3 Mikulski	Y	Y	Y	Y	N	Y	N	N
4 *Holt*	Y	Y	?	?	?	N	Y	Y
5 Hoyer	Y	Y	Y	Y	N	Y	N	N
6 Byron	?	?	?	?	?	Y	Y	Y
7 Mitchell	N	Y	Y	Y	N	N	N	N
8 Barnes	Y	Y	Y	Y	N	Y	N	N
MASSACHUSETTS								
1 *Conte*	Y	Y	Y	N	N	Y	Y	N
2 Boland	Y	Y	Y	Y	N	?	Y	N
3 Early	Y	Y	Y	Y	N	Y	Y	N
4 Frank	Y	Y	Y	Y	N	Y	N	N
5 Shannon	Y	Y	Y	Y	N	Y	N	N
6 Mavroules	Y	Y	Y	Y	N	Y	N	N
7 Markey	Y	Y	Y	Y	N	Y	N	N
8 O'Neill								
9 Moakley	?	Y	Y	Y	N	Y	N	N
10 *Heckler*	Y	Y	Y	N	N	Y	Y	N
11 Donnelly	?	Y	Y	Y	N	Y	N	N
12 Studds	Y	Y	Y	Y	N	Y	N	N
MICHIGAN								
1 Conyers	Y	Y	Y	Y	N	?	N	N
2 *Pursell*	Y	Y	Y	P	N	Y	Y	N
3 Wolpe	Y	Y	Y	Y	N	Y	N	N
4 *Siljander*	Y	N	Y	N	Y	Y	?	Y
5 *Sawyer*	Y	Y	Y	Y	N	Y	Y	Y
6 *Dunn*	Y	Y	Y	N	Y	Y	Y	N
7 Kildee	Y	Y	Y	Y	N	Y	N	N
8 Traxler	Y	Y	Y	N	N	Y	Y	N
9 *Vander Jagt*	Y	N	Y	N	Y	Y	Y	?
10 Albosta	Y	Y	Y	N	N	Y	Y	Y
11 *Davis*	Y	Y	Y	N	Y	Y	Y	Y
12 Bonior	Y	Y	Y	Y	N	Y	N	N
13 Crockett	?	Y	Y	Y	N	Y	N	?
14 Hertel	Y	Y	Y	Y	N	Y	N	N
15 Ford	Y	Y	?	Y	N	Y	?	?
16 Dingell	?	?	Y	Y	N	Y	N	N
17 Brodhead	Y	Y	Y	Y	N	Y	N	N
18 Blanchard	Y	Y	Y	Y	N	Y	Y	N
19 *Broomfield*	Y	N	Y	N	Y	Y	Y	Y
MINNESOTA								
1 *Erdahl*	Y	Y	Y	N	N	Y	N	N
2 *Hagedorn*	Y	N	Y	N	N	Y	Y	Y
3 *Frenzel*	Y	N	Y	N	N	Y	Y	Y
4 Vento	Y	Y	Y	Y	N	Y	N	N
5 Sabo	N	Y	Y	Y	N	Y	N	N
6 *Weber*	Y	Y	Y	N	Y	Y	Y	Y
7 *Stangeland*	Y	N	Y	N	Y	Y	Y	Y
8 Oberstar	Y	Y	Y	Y	N	Y	X	X
MISSISSIPPI								
1 Whitten	Y	Y	Y	N	N	Y	Y	Y
2 Bowen	Y	Y	Y	N	N	?	Y	N
3 Montgomery	Y	Y	Y	N	Y	?	Y	Y
4 Vacancy								
5 *Lott*	Y	N	Y	N	Y	Y	Y	Y
MISSOURI								
1 Clay	?	Y	Y	Y	N	N	N	N
2 Young	Y	Y	Y	N	N	Y	Y	N
3 Gephardt	Y	Y	Y	N	N	Y	Y	Y

	68	69	70	71	72	73	74	75
4 Skelton	Y	Y	Y	N	Y	Y	Y	Y
5 Bolling	Y	Y	Y	Y	N	Y	N	N
6 *Coleman*	Y	Y	Y	N	Y	Y	Y	Y
7 *Taylor*	Y	N	Y	N	Y	Y	Y	Y
8 *Bailey*	Y	N	Y	N	Y	Y	Y	Y
9 Volkmer	Y	Y	Y	N	N	Y	N	?
10 *Emerson*	?	Y	Y	N	Y	Y	Y	Y
MONTANA								
1 Williams	Y	Y	?	Y	N	Y	Y	N
2 *Marlenee*	Y	Y	Y	N	Y	Y	Y	Y
NEBRASKA								
1 *Bereuter*	Y	Y	Y	N	Y	Y	Y	Y
2 *Daub*	Y	Y	Y	N	Y	Y	Y	Y
3 *Smith*	Y	Y	Y	N	Y	Y	Y	Y
NEVADA								
AL Santini	Y	?	Y	N	N	Y	Y	Y
NEW HAMPSHIRE								
1 D'Amours	?	?	?	Y	N	Y	Y	N
2 *Gregg*	Y	Y	Y	N	Y	Y	Y	Y
NEW JERSEY								
1 Florio	Y	Y	Y	N	N	Y	?	?
2 Hughes	Y	Y	Y	Y	N	Y	Y	N
3 Howard	Y	Y	Y	Y	N	?	N	N
4 *Smith*	Y	Y	Y	N	Y	Y	Y	Y
5 *Fenwick*	Y	Y	Y	N	N	Y	Y	Y
6 *Forsythe*	?	?	Y	N	Y	Y	Y	Y
7 *Roukema*	Y	Y	Y	N	N	Y	Y	Y
8 Roe	Y	Y	Y	N	N	Y	Y	N
9 *Hollenbeck*	Y	Y	Y	N	N	Y	Y	N
10 Rodino	Y	Y	Y	Y	N	Y	N	N
11 Minish	Y	Y	Y	Y	N	Y	N	N
12 *Rinaldo*	Y	Y	Y	N	N	Y	Y	N
13 *Courter*	Y	Y	Y	N	N	Y	Y	Y
14 Guarini	Y	Y	Y	#	?	Y	N	N
15 Dwyer	Y	Y	Y	Y	N	Y	N	N
NEW MEXICO								
1 *Lujan*	Y	Y	Y	N	Y	Y	Y	Y
2 *Skeen*	Y	N	Y	N	Y	Y	Y	Y
NEW YORK								
1 *Carney*	Y	N	Y	N	Y	Y	Y	Y
2 Downey	Y	Y	Y	Y	N	Y	N	N
3 *Carman*	?	Y	Y	N	Y	Y	Y	Y
4 *Lent*	Y	Y	Y	N	Y	Y	Y	Y
5 *McGrath*	Y	Y	Y	N	?	Y	Y	Y
6 *LeBoutillier*	Y	N	Y	N	Y	?	Y	Y
7 Addabbo	?	Y	Y	Y	N	Y	N	N
8 Rosenthal	?	?	?	?	?	?	N	N
9 Ferraro	Y	Y	Y	Y	N	Y	N	N
10 Biaggi	?	Y	Y	N	N	Y	N	N
11 Scheuer	Y	Y	Y	Y	N	Y	N	N
12 Chisholm	?	Y	Y	Y	N	Y	N	N
13 Solarz	Y	Y	Y	Y	N	Y	X	?
14 Richmond	Y	Y	Y	Y	N	Y	N	N
15 Zeferetti	Y	Y	Y	N	N	Y	Y	Y
16 Schumer	?	Y	Y	Y	N	Y	N	N
17 *Molinari*	Y	Y	Y	N	Y	Y	Y	Y
18 *Green*	Y	?	Y	Y	?	Y	N	N
19 Rangel	Y	Y	Y	Y	N	Y	N	N
20 Weiss	Y	Y	Y	Y	N	Y	N	N
21 Garcia	Y	Y	Y	Y	N	?	N	N
22 Bingham	Y	Y	Y	Y	N	Y	N	N
23 Peyser	Y	Y	Y	Y	N	Y	N	N
24 Ottinger	P	Y	Y	Y	N	Y	N	N
25 *Fish*	Y	Y	Y	Y	N	Y	Y	N
26 *Gilman*	Y	Y	Y	Y	N	Y	Y	N
27 McHugh	Y	Y	Y	Y	N	Y	N	N
28 Stratton	Y	Y	Y	N	N	Y	Y	Y
29 *Solomon*	Y	N	Y	N	Y	N	Y	Y
30 *Martin*	Y	?	Y	N	Y	Y	Y	Y
31 *Mitchell*	Y	Y	Y	N	Y	Y	Y	Y
32 *Wortley*	Y	N	Y	N	Y	Y	Y	Y
33 *Lee*	Y	Y	Y	N	Y	Y	Y	Y
34 *Horton*	Y	Y	Y	N	N	Y	Y	Y
35 *Conable*	Y	C	Y	N	Y	Y	Y	Y
36 LaFalce	Y	Y	Y	Y	N	Y	N	N
37 Nowak	Y	Y	Y	Y	N	Y	N	N
38 *Kemp*	Y	N	Y	N	Y	Y	Y	Y
39 Lundine	Y	Y	?	Y	N	Y	N	?
NORTH CAROLINA								
1 Jones	Y	Y	Y	N	N	Y	N	Y
2 Fountain	Y	Y	Y	N	N	Y	Y	Y
3 Whitley	Y	Y	Y	N	Y	Y	Y	Y
4 Andrews	Y	Y	Y	N	N	Y	Y	Y
5 Neal	Y	Y	Y	?	N	Y	Y	Y
6 *Johnston*	?	?	?	N	Y	N	Y	Y
7 Rose	Y	Y	Y	N	N	Y	Y	Y
8 Hefner	Y	Y	?	N	N	Y	Y	Y

	68	69	70	71	72	73	74	75
9 *Martin*	Y	N	Y	N	Y	Y	Y	Y
10 *Broyhill*	Y	N	Y	N	N	?	?	?
11 *Hendon*	Y	N	Y	N	Y	N	Y	Y
NORTH DAKOTA								
AL Dorgan	Y	Y	Y	Y	N	Y	Y	N
OHIO								
1 *Gradison*	Y	N	Y	N	Y	Y	Y	N
2 Luken	Y	Y	Y	Y	N	Y	Y	Y
3 Hall	Y	Y	?	Y	N	Y	N	N
4 Vacancy								
5 *Latta*	Y	N	Y	N	Y	Y	Y	Y
6 *McEwen*	Y	N	Y	N	Y	Y	Y	Y
7 *Brown*	Y	N	Y	?	?	?	#	?
8 *Kindness*	Y	N	Y	N	Y	N	Y	Y
9 *Weber*	Y	N	Y	N	N	Y	Y	Y
10 *Miller*	Y	N	Y	N	Y	Y	Y	Y
11 *Stanton*	Y	Y	Y	N	N	Y	Y	Y
12 Shamansky	Y	N	Y	Y	N	?	N	N
13 Pease	Y	Y	Y	Y	N	Y	N	N
14 Seiberling	Y	Y	Y	Y	N	Y	N	N
15 *Wylie*	Y	N	Y	N	N	Y	Y	Y
16 *Regula*	Y	N	Y	N	N	Y	Y	Y
17 *Ashbrook*	Y	N	Y	N	Y	Y	Y	#
18 Applegate	?	Y	?	N	N	?	Y	Y
19 *Williams*	Y	Y	Y	?	?	Y	Y	N
20 Oakar	Y	Y	Y	Y	N	Y	N	?
21 Stokes	Y	Y	Y	Y	N	Y	N	N
22 Eckart	Y	Y	Y	Y	N	Y	N	N
23 Mottl	Y	Y	Y	N	Y	Y	N	Y
OKLAHOMA								
1 Jones	N	Y	Y	Y	N	Y	Y	Y
2 Synar	Y	Y	Y	Y	N	Y	N	N
3 Watkins	Y	Y	Y	N	N	Y	Y	Y
4 McCurdy	Y	Y	Y	N	N	Y	Y	Y
5 *Edwards*	Y	N	Y	N	Y	Y	Y	Y
6 English	Y	Y	Y	N	N	Y	Y	Y
OREGON								
1 AuCoin	?	?	?	?	?	?	?	?
2 *Smith*	Y	N	Y	N	Y	Y	Y	Y
3 Wyden	Y	Y	Y	Y	N	Y	N	N
4 Weaver	Y	Y	Y	Y	N	Y	N	N
PENNSYLVANIA								
1 Foglietta	?	Y	Y	Y	N	Y	N	N
2 Gray	Y	Y	Y	Y	N	Y	N	N
3 Vacancy								
4 *Dougherty*	?	Y	Y	N	Y	Y	Y	Y
5 *Schulze*	Y	N	Y	N	Y	Y	Y	Y
6 Yatron	Y	Y	Y	N	N	Y	Y	Y
7 Edgar	Y	Y	Y	Y	N	Y	N	N
8 *Coyne, J.*	Y	Y	Y	N	Y	Y	Y	Y
9 *Shuster*	Y	N	Y	N	Y	Y	Y	Y
10 *McDade*	Y	Y	Y	N	N	Y	Y	N
11 *Nelligan*	Y	Y	Y	N	Y	Y	Y	Y
12 Murtha	Y	Y	Y	Y	N	Y	N	Y
13 *Coughlin*	?	N	Y	N	N	Y	Y	Y
14 Coyne, W.	Y	Y	Y	Y	N	Y	N	N
15 *Ritter*	Y	N	Y	N	Y	Y	Y	Y
16 *Walker*	N	N	Y	N	Y	Y	Y	Y
17 Ertel	Y	Y	Y	Y	N	Y	N	Y
18 Walgren	Y	Y	Y	Y	N	Y	Y	N
19 *Goodling*	N	Y	Y	N	Y	Y	Y	Y
20 Gaydos	Y	Y	Y	N	N	Y	Y	Y
21 Bailey	Y	Y	?	N	N	Y	N	Y
22 Murphy	Y	Y	Y	N	N	Y	Y	Y
23 *Clinger*	Y	Y	Y	N	Y	Y	Y	N
24 *Marks*	Y	Y	Y	N	N	Y	Y	N
25 Atkinson	Y	Y	Y	Y	N	Y	N	N
RHODE ISLAND								
1 St Germain	Y	Y	Y	Y	N	Y	Y	N
2 *Schneider*	Y	Y	Y	N	N	Y	Y	N
SOUTH CAROLINA								
1 *Hartnett*	Y	Y	Y	N	Y	Y	Y	Y
2 *Spence*	Y	Y	Y	N	Y	Y	Y	Y
3 Derrick	?	Y	Y	Y	Y	Y	Y	Y
4 *Campbell*	?	N	Y	N	Y	Y	Y	Y
5 Holland	Y	Y	Y	N	N	Y	Y	Y
6 *Napier*	?	?	?	?	?	Y	Y	Y
SOUTH DAKOTA								
1 Daschle	Y	Y	Y	Y	N	Y	Y	N
2 *Roberts*	?	Y	Y	N	Y	Y	Y	Y
TENNESSEE								
1 *Quillen*	Y	N	Y	N	Y	Y	Y	Y
2 *Duncan*	Y	N	Y	N	Y	P	Y	Y
3 Bouquard	Y	Y	Y	N	N	Y	Y	Y
4 Gore	Y	Y	Y	Y	N	Y	N	N
5 Boner	Y	Y	Y	N	N	Y	Y	N
6 *Beard*	?	?	?	?	?	?	Y	Y

	68	69	70	71	72	73	74	75
7 Jones	?	Y	Y	N	N	Y	Y	Y
8 Ford	Y	Y	Y	Y	N	Y	N	N
TEXAS								
1 Hall, S.	Y	Y	Y	N	N	Y	Y	Y
2 Wilson	Y	Y	Y	N	N	Y	Y	Y
3 *Collins*	Y	N	Y	N	Y	Y	Y	Y
4 Hall, R.	Y	P	Y	N	Y	Y	Y	Y
5 Mattox	Y	Y	Y	Y	N	Y	N	N
6 Gramm	?	N	?	N	N	Y	Y	Y
7 *Archer*	Y	N	Y	N	Y	Y	Y	Y
8 *Fields*	Y	N	Y	N	Y	Y	Y	Y
9 Brooks	Y	Y	Y	N	N	Y	N	Y
10 Pickle	Y	Y	Y	N	N	Y	Y	Y
11 Leath	Y	Y	Y	N	Y	N	Y	Y
12 Wright	Y	Y	Y	N	N	Y	Y	Y
13 Hightower	Y	Y	Y	N	N	Y	Y	Y
14 Patman	Y	Y	Y	N	N	Y	Y	Y
15 de la Garza	Y	Y	Y	N	N	Y	N	Y
16 White	Y	Y	Y	N	N	Y	Y	Y
17 Stenholm	Y	Y	Y	N	N	Y	Y	Y
18 Leland	?	?	Y	Y	N	Y	N	N
19 Hance	Y	Y	Y	N	N	Y	Y	Y
20 Gonzalez	Y	Y	Y	Y	N	Y	N	N
21 *Loeffler*	Y	N	Y	N	Y	Y	Y	Y
22 *Paul*	Y	N	N	N	Y	Y	Y	Y
23 Kazen	Y	Y	Y	N	N	Y	N	Y
24 Frost	Y	Y	Y	Y	N	Y	N	N
UTAH								
1 *Hansen*	Y	N	Y	N	Y	Y	Y	Y
2 *Marriott*	Y	N	Y	N	N	Y	Y	Y
VERMONT								
AL *Jeffords*	Y	Y	Y	Y	N	Y	?	N
VIRGINIA								
1 *Trible*	Y	N	Y	N	Y	Y	Y	Y
2 *Whitehurst*	Y	Y	Y	N	N	Y	Y	Y
3 *Bliley*	Y	Y	Y	X	?	Y	Y	Y
4 *Daniel, R.*	Y	N	Y	N	Y	Y	Y	Y
5 Daniel, D.	Y	N	Y	N	Y	Y	Y	Y
6 *Butler*	Y	N	Y	N	N	Y	Y	Y
7 *Robinson*	Y	N	Y	N	Y	Y	Y	Y
8 *Parris*	Y	?	?	N	Y	Y	Y	Y
9 *Wampler*	Y	Y	Y	N	Y	Y	Y	Y
10 *Wolf*	Y	Y	Y	N	Y	Y	Y	Y
WASHINGTON								
1 *Pritchard*	Y	Y	Y	N	N	Y	Y	Y
2 Swift	Y	Y	Y	Y	N	Y	N	N
3 Bonker	Y	Y	Y	Y	N	Y	N	N
4 *Morrison*	Y	Y	Y	N	Y	?	Y	Y
5 Foley	Y	Y	Y	Y	N	Y	N	N
6 Dicks	Y	Y	Y	Y	N	Y	N	N
7 Lowry	Y	Y	Y	Y	N	Y	N	N
WEST VIRGINIA								
1 Mollohan	?	Y	Y	?	N	Y	N	N
2 *Benedict*	Y	N	Y	N	Y	Y	Y	Y
3 *Staton*	Y	N	Y	N	Y	Y	Y	Y
4 Rahall	Y	Y	Y	Y	N	Y	N	N
WISCONSIN								
1 Aspin	Y	Y	Y	Y	N	Y	N	N
2 Kastenmeier	Y	Y	Y	Y	N	Y	N	N
3 *Gunderson*	Y	Y	Y	N	Y	Y	Y	Y
4 Zablocki	Y	Y	Y	Y	N	Y	Y	Y
5 Reuss	Y	Y	Y	Y	N	Y	N	N
6 *Petri*	Y	Y	Y	N	Y	Y	Y	Y
7 Obey	Y	Y	Y	Y	N	Y	N	N
8 *Roth*	?	Y	Y	N	Y	Y	Y	Y
9 *Sensenbrenner*	Y	Y	Y	N	Y	Y	Y	Y
WYOMING								
AL *Cheney*	Y	N	Y	N	Y	Y	Y	Y

Democrats ***Republicans***

KEY

Y Voted for (yea).
Paired for.
+ Announced for.
N Voted against (nay).
X Paired against.
- Announced against.
P Voted "present".
C Voted "present" to avoid possible conflict of interest.
? Did not vote or otherwise make a position known.

76. HR 3480. Legal Services Corporation. Weiss, D-N.Y., amendment, to the McDonald, D-Ga., amendment (see vote 77, below), to prevent Legal Services Corporation funds from being used in cases that seek the "legalization" of homosexuality. Rejected 151-245: R 35-143; D 116-102 (ND 107-38, SD 9-64), June 18, 1981.

77. HR 3480. Legal Services Corporation. McDonald, D-Ga., amendment to prohibit Legal Services Corporation funds from being used in cases to "promote, defend or protect" homosexuality. Adopted 281-124: R 153-28; D 128-96 (ND 62-87, SD 66-9), June 18, 1981.

78. HR 3480. Legal Services Corporation. Sensenbrenner, R-Wis., amendment to prohibit lawyers in Legal Services Corporation programs from giving legal advice on abortion laws. Rejected 160-242: R 118-60; D 42-182 (ND 24-131, SD 18-51), June 18, 1981.

79. HR 3480. Legal Services Corporation. Ashbrook, R-Ohio, amendment to prohibit Legal Services Corporation funds from being used in lawsuits brought against local school boards or any of their employees. Rejected 176-219: R 129-46; D 47-173 (ND 13-138, SD 34-35), June 18, 1981.

80. HR 3480. Legal Services Corporation. Fish, R-N.Y., amendment (to the McCollum, R-Fla., substitute to the Kazen, D-Texas, amendment) to allow legal aid programs to represent aliens in the United States "under color of law," a term covering aliens who are in the United States legally but who are neither citizens nor permanent residents. Rejected 141-262: R 27-154; D 114-108 (ND 107-42, SD 7-66), June 18, 1981. The McCollum substitute specified certain categories of aliens entitled to LSC representation. The original Kazen amendment prohibited LSC aid to illegal aliens. Both the McCollum substitute and the Kazen amendment, as amended, were adopted by voice vote.

81. HR 3480. Legal Services Corporation. Kramer, R-Colo., amendment to give the Office of Management and Budget (OMB) authority to review the Legal Services Corporation budget. Rejected 185-210: R 149-27; D 36-183 (ND 5-141, SD 31-42), June 18, 1981.

82. HR 3480. Legal Services Corporation. McClory, R-Ill., motion to recommit (thus effectively killing) the bill reauthorizing the Legal Services Corporation to the Education and Labor and Ways and Means committees for hearings on President Reagan's proposal to abolish the corporation. Motion rejected 165-221: R 134-41; D 31-180 (ND 2-140, SD 29-40), June 18, 1981.

83. HR 3480. Legal Services Corporation. Passage of the bill to reauthorize the Legal Services Corporation for fiscal 1982-83, at $241 million annually. Passed 245-137: R 59-116; D 186-21 (ND 137-3, SD 49-18), June 18, 1981. A "nay" was a vote supporting the president's position.

	76	77	78	79	80	81	82	83
ALABAMA								
1 *Edwards*	Y	N	N	N	Y	Y	Y	N
2 *Dickinson*	N	Y	N	#	X	?	#	X
3 Nichols	N	Y	N	Y	N	Y	N	Y
4 Bevill	N	Y	N	Y	N	Y	Y	N
5 Flippo	N	Y	N	N	N	N	Y	N
6 *Smith*	N	Y	Y	N	Y	Y	Y	N
7 Shelby	N	Y	Y	N	Y	Y	Y	N
ALASKA								
AL *Young*	N	Y	Y	Y	N	?	Y	N
ARIZONA								
1 *Rhodes*	N	Y	N	Y	N	Y	N	Y
2 Udall	Y	N	N	N	N	N	N	Y
3 *Stump*	N	Y	Y	Y	N	Y	Y	N
4 *Rudd*	N	Y	Y	Y	N	?	#	X
ARKANSAS								
1 Alexander	N	Y	N	Y	N	N	Y	Y
2 *Bethune*	N	Y	N	Y	N	Y	Y	Y
3 *Hammerschmidt*	N	Y	N	Y	N	Y	Y	N
4 Anthony	N	Y	N	Y	N	N	N	Y
CALIFORNIA								
1 *Chappie*	?	?	?	#	X	?	#	X
2 *Clausen*	N	Y	Y	?	N	Y	Y	Y
3 Matsui	Y	X	N	Y	N	Y	N	Y
4 Fazio	Y	N	N	N	Y	N	N	Y
5 Burton, J.	P	N	N	N	Y	N	N	P
6 Burton, P.	Y	N	N	N	Y	N	N	Y
7 Miller	Y	N	N	N	Y	N	N	Y
8 Dellums	Y	N	N	N	Y	N	N	Y
9 Stark	Y	N	N	N	Y	N	N	Y
10 Edwards	Y	N	N	N	Y	N	N	Y
11 Lantos	?	X	-	-	+	-	-	+
12 *McCloskey*	Y	N	N	N	N	N	N	Y
13 Mineta	Y	N	N	N	Y	N	N	Y
14 *Shumway*	N	Y	Y	Y	N	Y	Y	N
15 Coelho	Y	N	N	N	Y	N	N	Y
16 Panetta	Y	N	N	N	Y	N	N	Y
17 *Pashayan*	?	?	Y	Y	N	Y	?	?
18 *Thomas*	?	?	X	?	X	?	#	X
19 *Lagomarsino*	N	Y	Y	Y	N	Y	Y	N
20 *Goldwater*	Y	N	N	Y	N	?	Y	N
21 *Fiedler*	Y	N	N	N	Y	N	Y	N
22 *Moorhead*	N	Y	Y	N	Y	N	Y	N
23 Beilenson	Y	N	N	N	Y	N	N	Y
24 Waxman	Y	N	N	N	Y	N	N	Y
25 Roybal	Y	N	N	N	Y	N	N	Y
26 *Rousselot*	N	Y	Y	N	Y	Y	Y	N
27 *Dornan*	N	Y	Y	N	Y	N	Y	N
28 Dixon	Y	N	N	N	Y	N	N	Y
29 Hawkins	?	?	N	?	#	?	X	?
30 Danielson	Y	N	N	N	Y	N	N	Y
31 Dymally	Y	N	N	?	Y	N	N	Y
32 Anderson	Y	N	N	N	Y	N	N	Y
33 *Grisham*	N	Y	Y	Y	N	Y	Y	N
34 *Lungren*	N	Y	Y	N	Y	N	Y	N
35 *Dreier*	N	Y	Y	Y	N	Y	Y	N
36 Brown	Y	N	N	N	Y	N	N	Y
37 *Lewis*	Y	N	N	N	Y	N	N	Y
38 Patterson	Y	N	N	N	Y	N	N	Y
39 *Dannemeyer*	N	Y	Y	Y	N	Y	Y	N
40 *Badham*	X	#	?	#	X	?	#	X
41 *Lowery*	N	Y	Y	Y	N	Y	Y	N
42 *Hunter*	N	Y	Y	Y	N	Y	Y	Y
43 *Burgener*	N	Y	N	Y	N	Y	Y	N
COLORADO								
1 Schroeder	Y	N	N	N	Y	N	N	Y
2 Wirth	Y	N	N	N	Y	N	N	Y
3 Kogovsek	Y	N	N	N	Y	?	X	?
4 *Brown*	N	Y	N	N	Y	Y	Y	N

	76	77	78	79	80	81	82	83
5 *Kramer*	N	Y	Y	Y	N	Y	Y	N
CONNECTICUT								
1 Cotter	?	?	?	?	?	?	?	?
2 Gejdenson	Y	N	N	N	Y	N	N	Y
3 *DeNardis*	Y	Y	N	N	N	N	N	Y
4 *McKinney*	Y	N	N	N	Y	N	N	Y
5 Ratchford	Y	N	N	N	Y	N	N	Y
6 Moffett	Y	N	N	N	#	?	X	#
DELAWARE								
AL *Evans*	N	Y	N	Y	Y	Y	Y	N
FLORIDA								
1 Hutto	N	Y	N	Y	N	Y	N	Y
2 Fuqua	N	Y	N	N	N	Y	N	Y
3 Bennett	N	Y	N	N	N	N	N	Y
4 Chappell	N	Y	N	Y	N	Y	N	Y
5 *McCollum*	N	Y	Y	N	Y	N	Y	N
6 *Young*	N	Y	Y	Y	N	Y	Y	N
7 Gibbons	N	Y	Y	Y	N	Y	?	?
8 Ireland	N	Y	Y	Y	N	Y	Y	N
9 Nelson	N	Y	N	N	N	Y	N	Y
10 *Bafalis*	N	Y	Y	Y	N	Y	Y	Y
11 Mica	N	Y	N	N	N	Y	Y	Y
12 *Shaw*	N	Y	Y	N	Y	N	Y	N
13 Lehman	#	X	?	?	#	?	X	?
14 Pepper	Y	N	N	N	N	N	N	Y
15 Fascell	Y	N	N	N	N	N	N	Y
GEORGIA								
1 Ginn	N	Y	N	Y	Y	Y	Y	Y
2 Hatcher	N	Y	N	N	N	Y	Y	Y
3 Brinkley	N	Y	Y	Y	Y	Y	Y	Y
4 Levitas	N	Y	N	Y	Y	Y	Y	Y
5 Fowler	N	N	N	N	N	N	N	Y
6 *Gingrich*	N	Y	N	Y	N	Y	Y	N
7 McDonald	N	Y	Y	N	Y	N	#	X
8 Evans	N	Y	Y	N	?	N	Y	
9 Jenkins	N	Y	N	N	N	Y	Y	Y
10 Barnard	N	Y	Y	N	Y	Y	Y	Y
HAWAII								
1 Heftel	Y	Y	N	N	Y	N	Y	N
2 Akaka	Y	N	N	N	N	N	N	Y
IDAHO								
1 *Craig*	N	Y	Y	Y	N	Y	Y	N
2 *Hansen*	N	Y	Y	N	Y	Y	Y	N
ILLINOIS								
1 Washington	Y	N	N	N	Y	N	N	Y
2 Savage	?	?	N	N	?	?	N	Y
3 Russo	Y	Y	N	N	N	N	N	Y
4 *Derwinski*	N	Y	N	Y	N	Y	Y	Y
5 Fary	N	N	N	N	N	N	N	Y
6 *Hyde*	Y	Y	Y	N	Y	N	Y	N
7 Collins	Y	N	N	N	Y	N	N	Y
8 Rostenkowski	Y	N	N	N	Y	N	N	Y
9 Yates	Y	N	N	N	Y	N	N	Y
10 *Porter*	N	N	X	N	Y	N	N	Y
11 Annunzio	Y	N	N	N	Y	N	N	Y
12 *Crane, P.*	N	Y	Y	N	Y	Y	Y	N
13 *McClory*	Y	N	Y	N	Y	N	Y	N
14 *Erlenborn*	N	Y	N	N	Y	N	Y	N
15 *Corcoran*	N	Y	Y	N	Y	N	Y	N
16 *Martin*	Y	N	N	X	N	X	N	Y
17 *O'Brien*	Y	Y	N	N	N	N	N	Y
18 *Michel*	N	Y	?	N	N	Y	Y	N
19 *Railsback*	N	N	N	N	N	Y	N	Y
20 *Findley*	Y	N	N	N	N	N	N	Y
21 *Madigan*	X	Y	N	N	N	N	N	Y
22 *Crane, D.*	N	Y	Y	N	Y	Y	Y	N
23 Price	N	Y	N	N	N	Y	?	?
24 Simon	N	Y	N	N	Y	N	?	?
INDIANA								
1 Benjamin	Y	N	N	N	N	N	N	Y
2 Fithian	N	Y	N	N	N	N	N	Y
3 *Hiler*	N	Y	Y	N	Y	Y	Y	N
4 *Coats*	N	Y	Y	N	Y	Y	Y	N
5 *Hillis*	N	Y	Y	N	Y	Y	Y	N
6 Evans	Y	Y	N	Y	N	Y	N	Y
7 *Myers*	N	Y	Y	N	Y	Y	Y	N
8 *Deckard*	N	Y	Y	N	Y	Y	Y	N
9 Hamilton	N	Y	N	N	N	Y	N	Y
10 Sharp	Y	N	N	N	N	N	N	Y
11 Jacobs	Y	N	N	N	N	N	N	Y
IOWA								
1 *Leach*	Y	N	N	N	Y	N	N	Y
2 *Tauke*	Y	Y	Y	N	Y	N	N	Y
3 *Evans*	N	Y	Y	N	N	Y	Y	Y
4 Smith	Y	N	N	N	N	N	N	Y
5 Harkin	?	N	N	N	Y	N	?	?
6 Bedell	Y	N	N	N	Y	N	?	?

Democrats *Republicans*

Corresponding to Congressional Record Votes 84, 85, 86, 87, 88, 89, 90, 91

	76	77	78	79	80	81	82	83
KANSAS								
1 ***Roberts***	N	Y	Y	Y	N	Y	Y	N
2 ***Jeffries***	N	Y	Y	Y	N	Y	Y	N
3 ***Winn***	N	#	Y	Y	N	Y	Y	N
4 Glickman	N	Y	N	N	Y	N	N	Y
5 ***Whittaker***	N	Y	N	Y	N	Y	Y	N
KENTUCKY								
1 Hubbard	N	Y	N	Y	N	N	N	Y
2 Natcher	N	Y	Y	Y	N	N	N	Y
3 Mazzoli	N	Y	N	N	Y	N	-	+
4 ***Snyder***	N	Y	Y	Y	N	Y	Y	N
5 ***Rogers***	X	#	Y	Y	N	Y	Y	N
6 ***Hopkins***	N	Y	Y	Y	N	Y	Y	Y
7 Perkins	?	Y	Y	Y	N	N	N	Y
LOUISIANA								
1 ***Livingston***	X	#	#	#	X	?	#	X
2 Boggs	Y	N	Y	N	N	N	N	Y
3 Tauzin	N	Y	Y	Y	N	N	N	Y
4 Roemer	N	N	N	Y	N	Y	N	Y
5 Huckaby	N	Y	N	Y	N	Y	Y	Y
6 ***Moore***	N	Y	Y	Y	N	Y	Y	Y
7 Breaux	?	?	?	?	?	?	?	?
8 Long	Y	Y	Y	Y	N	N	N	+
MAINE								
1 ***Emery***	N	Y	Y	Y	N	Y	N	Y
2 ***Snowe***	N	Y	N	Y	N	Y	Y	N
MARYLAND								
1 Dyson	N	Y	Y	N	N	N	N	N
2 Long	?	?	N	N	N	N	N	Y
3 Mikulski	Y	N	N	N	Y	N	N	Y
4 ***Holt***	N	Y	Y	Y	N	Y	Y	N
5 Hoyer	Y	N	N	N	Y	N	N	Y
6 Byron	N	Y	Y	N	N	N	N	Y
7 Mitchell	Y	N	N	N	Y	N	N	Y
8 Barnes	Y	N	N	N	Y	N	N	Y
MASSACHUSETTS								
1 ***Conte***	Y	N	N	N	Y	N	N	Y
2 Boland	Y	N	N	N	Y	N	N	Y
3 Early	Y	Y	N	N	Y	N	?	?
4 Frank	Y	N	N	N	Y	N	N	Y
5 Shannon	Y	N	N	N	Y	N	N	Y
6 Mavroules	Y	N	Y	N	Y	N	N	Y
7 Markey	?	N	Y	N	Y	N	N	Y
8 O'Neill								
9 Moakley	Y	Y	Y	Y	Y	?	X	?
10 ***Heckler***	Y	Y	Y	N	Y	N	N	Y
11 Donnelly	Y	Y	Y	Y	N	N	?	?
12 Studds	Y	N	N	N	Y	N	N	Y
MICHIGAN								
1 Conyers	?	?	?	?	?	?	X	#
2 ***Pursell***	N	Y	N	N	Y	N	N	Y
3 Wolpe	Y	N	N	N	Y	N	N	Y
4 ***Siljander***	N	Y	Y	Y	N	Y	Y	N
5 ***Sawyer***	Y	Y	N	N	Y	N	N	Y
6 ***Dunn***	Y	N	N	N	Y	Y	N	Y
7 Kildee	Y	N	Y	N	Y	N	N	Y
8 Traxler	Y	Y	Y	Y	N	N	N	Y
9 ***Vander Jagt***	N	Y	Y	Y	N	Y	Y	N
10 Albosta	N	Y	Y	Y	N	N	?	?
11 ***Davis***	N	Y	Y	Y	N	Y	N	Y
12 Bonior	Y	N	N	N	Y	N	N	Y
13 Crockett	Y	N	N	N	Y	N	N	Y
14 Hertel	Y	Y	Y	N	Y	N	N	Y
15 Ford	Y	N	N	N	Y	N	N	Y
16 Dingell	N	Y	N	?	N	N	N	Y
17 Brodhead	Y	N	N	N	Y	N	N	Y
18 Blanchard	Y	Y	N	N	Y	N	N	Y
19 ***Broomfield***	N	Y	#	Y	N	Y	Y	N
MINNESOTA								
1 ***Erdahl***	Y	Y	N	N	N	N	N	Y
2 ***Hagedorn***	N	Y	Y	Y	N	N	Y	Y
3 ***Frenzel***	?	#	X	X	?	?	?	#
4 Vento	Y	N	N	N	Y	N	N	Y
5 Sabo	Y	N	N	N	Y	N	N	Y
6 ***Weber***	N	Y	Y	Y	N	Y	Y	N
7 ***Stangeland***	N	Y	Y	Y	N	Y	Y	N
8 Oberstar	Y	N	Y	N	Y	N	N	Y
MISSISSIPPI								
1 Whitten	N	Y	Y	Y	N	N	N	Y
2 Bowen	N	Y	N	N	N	N	N	Y
3 Montgomery	N	Y	?	?	N	Y	Y	N
4 Vacancy								
5 ***Lott***	N	Y	#	#	N	Y	Y	N
MISSOURI								
1 Clay	Y	N	N	N	Y	N	N	Y
2 Young	N	Y	N	Y	N	N	N	Y
3 Gephardt	N	Y	N	?	Y	N	N	Y
4 Skelton	N	Y	Y	?	?	?	?	?
5 Bolling	Y	N	N	N	?	N	N	Y
6 ***Coleman***	N	Y	N	Y	N	Y	Y	Y
7 ***Taylor***	N	Y	Y	Y	N	Y	Y	N
8 ***Bailey***	N	Y	Y	Y	N	Y	Y	N
9 Volkmer	N	Y	Y	N	Y	N	N	Y
10 ***Emerson***	N	Y	Y	Y	N	Y	Y	N
MONTANA								
1 Williams	Y	N	N	N	Y	N	N	Y
2 ***Marlenee***	N	Y	N	Y	N	N	N	Y
NEBRASKA								
1 ***Bereuter***	N	Y	Y	N	N	Y	Y	N
2 ***Daub***	N	Y	Y	Y	N	Y	Y	N
3 ***Smith***	N	Y	Y	Y	N	Y	Y	N
NEVADA								
AL Santini	N	Y	Y	N	N	Y	Y	N
NEW HAMPSHIRE								
1 D'Amours	Y	Y	N	N	N	N	N	Y
2 ***Gregg***	N	Y	Y	N	N	Y	Y	N
NEW JERSEY								
1 Florio	Y	Y	N	N	?	?	?	?
2 Hughes	Y	N	N	N	N	N	N	Y
3 Howard	Y	N	N	N	Y	N	N	Y
4 ***Smith***	N	Y	Y	Y	Y	Y	Y	N
5 ***Fenwick***	Y	N	N	N	Y	N	N	Y
6 ***Forsythe***	Y	N	N	N	N	Y	Y	Y
7 ***Roukema***	Y	N	N	N	N	N	Y	N
8 Roe	N	Y	N	N	N	N	N	Y
9 ***Hollenbeck***	#	N	N	N	Y	N	N	Y
10 Rodino	Y	N	N	N	Y	N	N	Y
11 Minish	N	Y	N	N	N	N	N	Y
12 ***Rinaldo***	N	Y	Y	N	N	N	N	Y
13 ***Courter***	N	Y	Y	Y	N	Y	Y	Y
14 Guarini	Y	N	N	N	Y	N	N	Y
15 Dwyer	Y	N	N	N	Y	N	N	Y
NEW MEXICO								
1 ***Lujan***	Y	Y	Y	Y	N	N	N	Y
2 ***Skeen***	N	Y	Y	Y	N	Y	Y	Y
NEW YORK								
1 ***Carney***	N	Y	Y	Y	N	Y	Y	N
2 Downey	Y	N	N	N	Y	N	N	Y
3 ***Carman***	N	Y	Y	Y	N	Y	Y	N
4 ***Lent***	N	Y	Y	Y	N	Y	Y	Y
5 ***McGrath***	N	Y	Y	Y	N	Y	Y	N
6 ***LeBoutillier***	N	Y	Y	Y	N	Y	Y	N
7 Addabbo	Y	N	N	X	?	N	N	Y
8 Rosenthal	Y	N	N	N	Y	N	N	Y
9 Ferraro	Y	N	N	N	Y	N	N	Y
10 Biaggi	Y	N	N	N	N	N	N	Y
11 Scheuer	Y	N	N	N	Y	N	N	Y
12 Chisholm	Y	N	N	N	Y	?	N	Y
13 Solarz	#	X	N	N	Y	N	N	Y
14 Richmond	Y	N	?	N	Y	?	N	Y
15 Zeferetti	N	Y	Y	N	?	?	X	#
16 Schumer	?	?	N	N	Y	N	N	Y
17 ***Molinari***	Y	Y	Y	N	?	?	?	?
18 ***Green***	Y	N	N	N	Y	N	N	Y
19 Rangel	Y	N	N	N	Y	N	N	Y
20 Weiss	Y	N	N	N	Y	N	N	Y
21 Garcia	#	X	N	N	Y	N	N	Y
22 Bingham	Y	N	N	N	Y	N	N	Y
23 Peyser	Y	N	N	N	Y	?	X	#
24 Ottinger	Y	N	N	N	Y	N	N	Y
25 ***Fish***	Y	N	N	N	Y	N	N	Y
26 ***Gilman***	Y	N	N	N	Y	N	N	Y
27 McHugh	Y	Y	N	N	Y	N	N	Y
28 Stratton	N	Y	N	N	N	N	N	Y
29 ***Solomon***	X	Y	Y	Y	N	Y	Y	N
30 ***Martin***	N	N	Y	Y	N	Y	Y	N
31 ***Mitchell***	N	Y	Y	Y	N	?	#	?
32 ***Wortley***	N	Y	Y	Y	N	Y	Y	N
33 ***Lee***	N	Y	Y	Y	N	Y	Y	N
34 ***Horton***	N	N	N	X	N	Y	N	Y
35 ***Conable***	N	N	N	Y	N	Y	Y	N
36 LaFalce	N	Y	N	N	Y	N	N	?
37 Nowak	Y	Y	N	N	Y	N	N	Y
38 ***Kemp***	N	Y	?	?	N	Y	Y	N
39 Lundine	Y	Y	N	N	N	N	N	Y
NORTH CAROLINA								
1 Jones	N	Y	N	N	N	N	N	Y
2 Fountain	N	Y	N	Y	N	N	Y	Y
3 Whitley	N	Y	N	N	N	Y	Y	Y
4 Andrews	N	Y	N	N	N	N	Y	Y
5 Neal	?	Y	N	N	N	N	N	Y
6 ***Johnston***	N	Y	Y	Y	N	Y	#	X
7 Rose	N	Y	?	?	?	?	?	?
8 Hefner	N	Y	N	N	N	Y	Y	Y
9 ***Martin***	N	Y	N	Y	N	Y	Y	Y
10 ***Broyhill***	N	Y	N	Y	N	Y	Y	N
11 ***Hendon***	N	Y	Y	Y	N	Y	Y	N
NORTH DAKOTA								
AL Dorgan	Y	Y	N	N	N	N	N	Y
OHIO								
1 ***Gradison***	Y	Y	N	N	Y	Y	N	Y
2 Luken	?	?	?	?	?	?	?	?
3 Hall	Y	N	N	N	N	N	N	Y
4 Vacancy								
5 ***Latta***	N	Y	#	#	N	Y	Y	N
6 ***McEwen***	N	Y	Y	Y	N	Y	Y	N
7 ***Brown***	Y	Y	?	?	?	?	?	?
8 ***Kindness***	N	Y	N	Y	N	Y	Y	N
9 ***Weber***	N	Y	Y	Y	N	Y	Y	Y
10 ***Miller***	N	Y	Y	Y	N	Y	Y	N
11 ***Stanton***	?	Y	Y	Y	N	Y	Y	Y
12 Shamansky	N	Y	N	N	Y	N	N	Y
13 Pease	Y	Y	N	N	Y	N	N	Y
14 Seiberling	Y	N	N	N	Y	N	N	Y
15 ***Wylie***	N	Y	N	?	N	Y	N	Y
16 ***Regula***	N	Y	Y	N	N	Y	Y	Y
17 ***Ashbrook***	N	Y	Y	Y	Y	Y	Y	N
18 Applegate	N	Y	Y	Y	N	N	N	Y
19 ***Williams***	N	Y	N	N	N	N	N	Y
20 Oakar	Y	N	Y	Y	Y	N	N	Y
21 Stokes	Y	N	N	N	Y	N	N	Y
22 Eckart	?	?	N	N	N	N	N	Y
23 Mottl	N	Y	Y	Y	N	Y	N	Y
OKLAHOMA								
1 Jones	N	Y	N	N	N	N	N	Y
2 Synar	Y	Y	N	N	Y	N	N	Y
3 Watkins	N	Y	N	Y	N	Y	N	Y
4 McCurdy	N	Y	N	N	N	N	N	Y
5 ***Edwards***	N	Y	Y	Y	N	Y	Y	N
6 English	N	Y	N	N	N	Y	N	Y
OREGON								
1 AuCoin	?	N	N	N	N	N	N	Y
2 ***Smith***	N	Y	Y	Y	N	Y	Y	N
3 Wyden	Y	N	N	N	N	N	N	Y
4 Weaver	Y	N	N	N	Y	N	N	Y
PENNSYLVANIA								
1 Foglietta	Y	N	N	N	Y	N	N	Y
2 Gray	#	X	X	X	#	?	X	?
3 Vacancy								
4 ***Dougherty***	N	Y	Y	Y	?	Y	Y	N
5 ***Schulze***	N	Y	Y	Y	N	Y	Y	N
6 Yatron	N	Y	Y	Y	N	Y	N	Y
7 Edgar	Y	N	N	N	Y	N	N	Y
8 ***Coyne, J.***	Y	Y	N	Y	N	Y	Y	N
9 ***Shuster***	N	Y	Y	Y	N	Y	Y	N
10 ***McDade***	?	#	Y	Y	N	?	#	#
11 ***Nelligan***	N	Y	Y	Y	N	Y	Y	N
12 Murtha	N	Y	N	Y	N	N	N	Y
13 ***Coughlin***	N	Y	N	N	Y	Y	N	Y
14 Coyne, W.	Y	N	N	N	Y	N	N	Y
15 ***Ritter***	N	Y	Y	Y	N	Y	Y	N
16 ***Walker***	N	Y	Y	Y	N	Y	Y	N
17 Ertel	Y	Y	N	N	Y	N	N	Y
18 Walgren	N	Y	N	N	Y	N	N	Y
19 ***Goodling***	N	Y	Y	Y	N	Y	Y	N
20 Gaydos	N	Y	N	Y	N	N	N	Y
21 Bailey	N	Y	N	N	N	N	N	Y
22 Murphy	Y	Y	Y	Y	N	N	N	Y
23 ***Clinger***	N	Y	N	N	N	Y	Y	Y
24 ***Marks***	Y	Y	N	N	Y	N	N	Y
25 Atkinson	N	Y	Y	N	N	N	N	Y
RHODE ISLAND								
1 St Germain	N	Y	Y	N	Y	N	N	Y
2 ***Schneider***	Y	N	N	N	Y	N	N	Y
SOUTH CAROLINA								
1 ***Hartnett***	N	Y	Y	Y	N	Y	Y	N
2 ***Spence***	N	Y	Y	Y	N	Y	Y	N
3 Derrick	Y	Y	N	N	N	N	Y	N
4 ***Campbell***	N	Y	Y	Y	N	Y	Y	N
5 Holland	N	Y	N	Y	N	Y	N	N
6 ***Napier***	N	Y	Y	Y	N	Y	Y	N
SOUTH DAKOTA								
1 Daschle	Y	Y	?	N	Y	N	N	Y
2 ***Roberts***	N	Y	Y	Y	N	Y	Y	N
TENNESSEE								
1 ***Quillen***	N	Y	Y	Y	N	Y	Y	N
2 ***Duncan***	N	Y	N	Y	N	Y	Y	Y
3 Bouquard	N	Y	Y	N	N	Y	N	Y
4 Gore	N	Y	N	N	N	N	N	Y
5 Boner	N	?	?	?	?	?	?	?
6 ***Beard***	N	Y	N	Y	N	Y	Y	Y
7 Jones	N	Y	N	N	N	N	N	Y
8 Ford	Y	N	N	N	Y	N	N	?
TEXAS								
1 Hall, S.	N	Y	N	Y	N	Y	Y	N
2 Wilson	N	Y	?	?	?	N	N	Y
3 ***Collins***	N	Y	Y	Y	N	Y	Y	N
4 Hall, R.	N	Y	N	Y	N	Y	Y	Y
5 Mattox	Y	N	N	N	N	N	N	Y
6 Gramm	N	Y	?	?	N	Y	Y	N
7 ***Archer***	N	Y	Y	Y	N	Y	Y	N
8 ***Fields***	N	Y	Y	Y	N	Y	Y	N
9 Brooks	N	Y	N	N	N	N	?	#
10 Pickle	N	Y	N	Y	Y	N	N	Y
11 Leath	N	Y	Y	Y	N	Y	Y	N
12 Wright	N	Y	N	N	N	N	X	#
13 Hightower	N	Y	Y	Y	N	Y	N	Y
14 Patman	N	Y	Y	Y	N	Y	Y	N
15 de la Garza	N	Y	N	N	Y	N	N	Y
16 White	N	Y	N	Y	N	Y	N	Y
17 Stenholm	N	Y	?	?	N	Y	Y	N
18 Leland	Y	N	N	N	Y	N	N	Y
19 Hance	N	Y	?	?	N	Y	Y	N
20 Gonzalez	P	N	N	N	Y	N	N	Y
21 ***Loeffler***	N	Y	Y	Y	N	Y	Y	N
22 ***Paul***	N	Y	Y	Y	N	Y	Y	N
23 Kazen	N	Y	N	N	N	N	N	Y
24 Frost	N	Y	N	N	N	N	N	Y
UTAH								
1 ***Hansen***	N	Y	Y	Y	N	?	#	X
2 ***Marriott***	N	Y	Y	Y	N	Y	Y	N
VERMONT								
AL ***Jeffords***	Y	N	N	N	Y	N	?	?
VIRGINIA								
1 ***Trible***	N	Y	Y	Y	N	Y	Y	N
2 ***Whitehurst***	N	Y	Y	Y	N	Y	N	Y
3 ***Bliley***	N	Y	Y	Y	N	Y	Y	N
4 ***Daniel, R.***	N	Y	Y	Y	N	Y	Y	N
5 Daniel, D.	N	Y	Y	Y	N	Y	Y	N
6 ***Butler***	N	Y	N	N	N	Y	N	Y
7 ***Robinson***	N	Y	Y	Y	N	Y	Y	N
8 ***Parris***	N	Y	Y	Y	N	Y	Y	N
9 ***Wampler***	N	Y	Y	Y	N	Y	N	Y
10 ***Wolf***	N	Y	Y	Y	N	Y	Y	N
WASHINGTON								
1 ***Pritchard***	Y	N	N	N	Y	N	N	Y
2 Swift	Y	N	N	N	Y	N	N	Y
3 Bonker	N	Y	N	N	N	N	N	Y
4 ***Morrison***	N	Y	N	Y	N	Y	Y	N
5 Foley	N	Y	N	N	Y	N	N	Y
6 Dicks	?	Y	?	N	N	N	N	Y
7 Lowry	Y	N	N	N	Y	N	N	Y
WEST VIRGINIA								
1 Mollohan	?	Y	N	X	#	?	X	#
2 ***Benedict***	N	Y	Y	Y	N	Y	Y	N
3 ***Staton***	N	Y	Y	Y	N	Y	Y	N
4 Rahall	N	Y	N	N	Y	N	N	Y
WISCONSIN								
1 Aspin	Y	N	N	N	Y	N	N	Y
2 Kastenmeier	Y	N	N	N	Y	N	N	Y
3 ***Gunderson***	N	Y	N	Y	N	Y	Y	N
4 Zablocki	N	Y	Y	N	Y	N	N	Y
5 Reuss	Y	N	N	N	Y	N	N	Y
6 ***Petri***	N	Y	Y	Y	N	Y	Y	N
7 Obey	Y	?	N	N	Y	N	N	Y
8 ***Roth***	N	Y	N	Y	Y	Y	Y	N
9 ***Sensenbrenner***	N	Y	Y	Y	Y	Y	Y	N
WYOMING								
AL ***Cheney***	N	Y	N	Y	N	Y	Y	N

Democrats ***Republicans***

84. HR 1257. NASA Authorization. Adoption of the rule (H Res 161) providing for House floor consideration of the bill to authorize $6.1 billion in fiscal 1982 for the National Aeronautics and Space Administration (NASA). Adopted 399-0: R 182-0; D 217-0 (ND 146-0, SD 71-0), June 23, 1981.

85. HR 1257. NASA Authorization. Passage of the bill to authorize $6.1 billion in fiscal 1982 for the National Aeronautics and Space Administration (NASA). Passed 404-13: R 186-2; D 218-11 (ND 142-11, SD 76-0), June 23, 1981.

86. HR 2614. Fiscal 1981 Defense Supplemental Authorization. Passage of the bill to authorize $2,665,462,000 for defense programs in fiscal 1981. Passed 360-50: R 179-4; D 181-46 (ND 106-46, SD 75-0), June 23, 1981.

87. HR 3238. Public Broadcasting Authorization. Collins, R-Texas, amendment to reduce public broadcasting authorizations to $110 million in fiscal 1984 and $100 million annually in fiscal 1985 and 1986 from the bill's $160 million in fiscal 1984, $145 million in fiscal 1985 and $130 million in fiscal 1986. Rejected 146-265: R 124-64; D 22-201 (ND 2-146, SD 20-55), June 23, 1981. A "yea" was a vote supporting the president's position.

88. Procedural Motion. Walker, R-Pa., motion to approve the House *Journal* of Tuesday, June 23. Motion agreed to 344-16: R 163-8; D 181-8 (ND 123-6, SD 58-2), June 24, 1981.

89. S 1124. Senate Computer Services Contracts. Passage of the bill to allow the Senate sergeant-at-arms and doorkeeper to enter into contracts that provide for the making of advance payments for computer programming services. Passed (clearing the measure for the president) 375-16: R 168-11; D 207-5 (ND 134-4, SD 73-1), June 24, 1981.

90. HR 31. Cash Discount Act/Surgeon General Age Limit. Adoption of the conference report on the bill to repeal the existing 5 percent ceiling on discounts merchants may offer customers for cash purchases; extend until Feb. 27, 1984, an earlier prohibition on surcharges for purchases by credit card; and authorize the appointment of a surgeon general aged 64 or older. Adopted 398-9: R 183-0; D 215-9 (ND 137-9, SD 78-0), June 24, 1981.

91. HR 3238. Public Broadcasting Authorization. Wirth, D-Colo., motion that the House resolve itself into the Committee of the Whole for consideration of the fiscal 1984-86 public broadcasting authorization bill. Motion agreed to 385-16: R 169-14; D 216-2 (ND 143-1, SD 73-1), June 24, 1981.

KEY

Y Voted for (yea).
Paired for.
+ Announced for.
N Voted against (nay).
X Paired against.
- Announced against.
P Voted "present".
C Voted "present" to avoid possible conflict of interest.
? Did not vote or otherwise make a position known.

	84	85	86	87	88	89	90	91
ALABAMA								
1 *Edwards*	Y	Y	Y	Y	Y	Y	Y	Y
2 *Dickinson*	Y	Y	Y	Y	N	Y	Y	Y
3 Nichols	Y	Y	Y	N	Y	Y	Y	Y
4 Bevill	Y	Y	Y	N	Y	Y	Y	Y
5 Flippo	Y	Y	Y	N	Y	Y	Y	Y
6 *Smith*	Y	Y	Y	Y	Y	Y	Y	Y
7 Shelby	Y	Y	Y	Y	Y	Y	Y	Y
ALASKA								
AL *Young*	Y	Y	Y	N	N	N	Y	Y
ARIZONA								
1 *Rhodes*	Y	Y	Y	Y	Y	Y	Y	Y
2 Udall	Y	Y	Y	N	Y	Y	Y	Y
3 Stump	Y	Y	Y	Y	Y	Y	Y	Y
4 *Rudd*	Y	Y	Y	Y	Y	Y	Y	Y
ARKANSAS								
1 Alexander	Y	Y	Y	N	Y	Y	Y	Y
2 *Bethune*	Y	Y	Y	N	Y	Y	Y	Y
3 *Hammerschmidt*	Y	Y	Y	Y	Y	Y	Y	Y
4 Anthony	Y	Y	Y	N	Y	Y	Y	Y
CALIFORNIA								
1 *Chappie*	Y	Y	Y	Y	?	Y	Y	Y
2 *Clausen*	Y	Y	Y	Y	Y	Y	Y	Y
3 Matsui	Y	Y	Y	N	Y	Y	Y	Y
4 Fazio	Y	Y	Y	N	Y	Y	Y	Y
5 Burton, J.	Y	Y	N	N	Y	Y	Y	Y
6 Burton, P.	Y	Y	N	N	Y	Y	N	Y
7 Miller	Y	Y	N	N	Y	Y	Y	Y
8 Dellums	Y	N	N	N	Y	?	Y	Y
9 Stark	Y	Y	N	N	?	Y	Y	Y
10 Edwards	Y	Y	N	N	Y	Y	Y	Y
11 Lantos	Y	Y	Y	N	?	?	+	Y
12 *McCloskey*	Y	Y	Y	N	Y	Y	Y	Y
13 Mineta	Y	Y	Y	N	Y	Y	Y	Y
14 *Shumway*	Y	Y	Y	Y	Y	Y	Y	Y
15 Coelho	Y	Y	Y	N	Y	Y	Y	Y
16 Panetta	Y	Y	Y	N	Y	Y	Y	Y
17 Pashayan	Y	Y	Y	Y	Y	Y	Y	Y
18 Thomas	Y	Y	Y	Y	Y	Y	Y	Y
19 *Lagomarsino*	Y	Y	Y	Y	Y	Y	Y	Y
20 *Goldwater*	Y	Y	Y	Y	Y	Y	Y	N
21 *Fiedler*	Y	Y	Y	Y	Y	Y	Y	Y
22 *Moorhead*	Y	Y	Y	Y	Y	Y	Y	Y
23 Beilenson	Y	Y	N	N	Y	Y	Y	Y
24 Waxman	Y	Y	N	?	Y	Y	Y	Y
25 Roybal	Y	Y	N	N	Y	Y	Y	Y
26 *Rousselot*	Y	Y	Y	Y	Y	Y	Y	Y
27 *Dornan*	Y	Y	Y	Y	Y	Y	Y	Y
28 Dixon	Y	Y	Y	N	?	Y	Y	Y
29 Hawkins	Y	Y	N	N	Y	Y	Y	Y
30 Danielson	+	+	+	-	+	+	+	+
31 Dymally	Y	N	N	N	?	Y	Y	Y
32 Anderson	Y	Y	N	N	Y	Y	Y	Y
33 Grisham	Y	Y	Y	Y	Y	Y	Y	Y
34 Lungren	Y	Y	Y	Y	Y	Y	Y	N
35 *Dreier*	Y	Y	Y	Y	Y	Y	Y	N
36 Brown	Y	?	Y	?	Y	Y	Y	Y
37 *Lewis*	Y	Y	Y	N	Y	Y	Y	Y
38 Patterson	Y	Y	Y	N	Y	Y	Y	Y
39 *Dannemeyer*	Y	Y	Y	N	Y	Y	Y	Y
40 *Badham*	Y	Y	Y	Y	?	Y	Y	Y
41 *Lowery*	Y	Y	Y	Y	Y	Y	Y	Y
42 *Hunter*	Y	Y	Y	Y	Y	Y	Y	Y
43 *Burgener*	Y	Y	Y	N	Y	Y	Y	Y
COLORADO								
1 Schroeder	Y	Y	N	N	N	N	Y	Y
2 Wirth	Y	Y	Y	N	Y	Y	Y	Y
3 Kogovsek	Y	Y	Y	N	Y	Y	Y	Y
4 *Brown*	Y	Y	Y	Y	Y	Y	Y	Y
5 *Kramer*	Y	Y	Y	Y	Y	Y	Y	Y
CONNECTICUT								
1 Cotter	?	?	?	?	?	?	?	?
2 Gejdenson	Y	Y	Y	N	Y	Y	Y	Y
3 *DeNardis*	?	Y	Y	N	?	?	Y	Y
4 *McKinney*	?	Y	Y	Y	Y	Y	Y	Y
5 Ratchford	Y	Y	Y	N	Y	Y	Y	Y
6 Moffett	?	Y	X	?	?	Y	N	Y
DELAWARE								
AL *Evans*	Y	Y	Y	N	Y	Y	Y	Y
FLORIDA								
1 Hutto	Y	Y	Y	N	Y	Y	Y	Y
2 Fuqua	Y	Y	Y	N	Y	Y	Y	Y
3 Bennett	Y	Y	Y	Y	Y	Y	Y	Y
4 Chappell	Y	Y	Y	N	Y	Y	Y	Y
5 *McCollum*	Y	Y	Y	Y	Y	Y	Y	Y
6 *Young*	Y	Y	Y	Y	Y	Y	Y	Y
7 Gibbons	Y	Y	Y	N	Y	Y	Y	Y
8 Ireland	Y	Y	N	?	Y	Y	Y	Y
9 Nelson	Y	Y	Y	N	Y	Y	Y	Y
10 *Bafalis*	Y	Y	Y	N	Y	Y	Y	Y
11 Mica	Y	Y	Y	N	Y	Y	Y	Y
12 *Shaw*	Y	Y	Y	Y	Y	Y	Y	Y
13 Lehman	Y	Y	Y	N	Y	Y	Y	Y
14 Pepper	Y	Y	Y	N	?	Y	Y	?
15 Fascell	Y	Y	Y	N	Y	Y	Y	Y
GEORGIA								
1 Ginn	?	?	#	?	Y	Y	Y	Y
2 Hatcher	Y	Y	Y	N	?	?	Y	Y
3 Brinkley	Y	Y	Y	Y	Y	Y	Y	Y
4 Levitas	Y	Y	Y	N	Y	Y	Y	Y
5 Fowler	Y	Y	Y	N	Y	Y	Y	Y
6 *Gingrich*	Y	Y	Y	N	Y	Y	Y	Y
7 McDonald	?	Y	Y	Y	?	N	Y	N
8 Evans	Y	Y	Y	N	Y	Y	Y	Y
9 Jenkins	?	Y	Y	N	Y	Y	Y	Y
10 Barnard	Y	Y	Y	Y	Y	Y	Y	Y
HAWAII								
1 Heftel	Y	Y	Y	N	Y	Y	Y	Y
2 Akaka	Y	Y	Y	N	Y	Y	Y	Y
IDAHO								
1 *Craig*	Y	Y	Y	Y	Y	Y	Y	Y
2 *Hansen*	Y	Y	Y	Y	N	Y	N	Y
ILLINOIS								
1 Washington	Y	N	N	N	Y	Y	Y	Y
2 Savage	?	Y	N	N	?	?	?	?
3 Russo	Y	N	N	?	Y	Y	Y	Y
4 *Derwinski*	Y	Y	Y	N	Y	Y	N	Y
5 Fary	?	?	?	?	?	?	?	?
6 *Hyde*	Y	Y	Y	Y	Y	Y	Y	Y
7 Collins	Y	Y	N	N	Y	Y	Y	Y
8 Rostenkowski	Y	Y	N	N	Y	Y	Y	Y
9 Yates	Y	N	N	N	Y	Y	Y	Y
10 *Porter*	Y	Y	Y	N	Y	Y	Y	Y
11 Annunzio	Y	Y	Y	N	Y	Y	Y	Y
12 *Crane, P.*	?	Y	Y	Y	?	N	Y	N
13 *McClory*	Y	Y	Y	N	Y	Y	Y	Y
14 *Erlenborn*	Y	Y	Y	Y	Y	Y	Y	Y
15 *Corcoran*	Y	Y	Y	N	Y	Y	Y	Y
16 *Martin*	Y	Y	Y	N	?	Y	Y	Y
17 *O'Brien*	Y	Y	+	Y	Y	Y	Y	Y
18 *Michel*	Y	Y	Y	Y	Y	Y	Y	Y
19 *Railsback*	?	Y	Y	N	Y	Y	Y	Y
20 *Findley*	Y	Y	Y	Y	Y	Y	Y	Y
21 *Madigan*	Y	Y	Y	N	Y	Y	Y	Y
22 *Crane, D.*	Y	Y	Y	Y	Y	Y	N	N
23 Price	Y	Y	Y	N	Y	Y	Y	Y
24 Simon	Y	Y	Y	N	Y	Y	Y	Y
INDIANA								
1 Benjamin	Y	Y	Y	N	Y	Y	Y	Y
2 Fithian	Y	Y	Y	N	?	Y	Y	Y
3 *Hiler*	Y	Y	Y	Y	Y	Y	Y	Y
4 *Coats*	Y	Y	Y	Y	Y	Y	Y	Y
5 *Hillis*	?	Y	Y	N	Y	Y	Y	?
6 Evans	Y	N	Y	N	Y	Y	Y	Y
7 *Myers*	Y	Y	Y	N	Y	Y	Y	Y
8 *Deckard*	Y	Y	Y	Y	Y	Y	Y	?
9 Hamilton	Y	Y	Y	N	Y	Y	Y	Y
10 Sharp	Y	Y	Y	N	Y	Y	Y	Y
11 Jacobs	Y	N	Y	N	N	N	N	Y
IOWA								
1 Leach	Y	Y	Y	N	Y	Y	Y	Y
2 *Tauke*	Y	N	N	N	N	Y	Y	Y
3 *Evans*	Y	Y	Y	N	Y	Y	Y	Y
4 Smith	Y	Y	Y	N	Y	Y	Y	Y
5 Harkin	Y	N	N	N	N	Y	Y	Y
6 Bedell	Y	N	N	N	Y	Y	Y	Y

Democrats *Republicans*

Corresponding to Congressional Record Votes 92, 93, 94, 95, 96, 97, 98, 99

	84 85 86 87 88 89 90 91		84 85 86 87 88 89 90 91		84 85 86 87 88 89 90 91		84 85 86 87 88 89 90 91
KANSAS		4 Skelton	Y Y Y N Y Y Y ?	9 *Martin*	Y Y Y Y Y Y Y N	7 Jones	Y Y Y N Y Y Y Y
1 *Roberts*	Y Y Y Y Y Y Y Y	5 Bolling	? ? ? ? ? ? ? ?	10 *Broyhill*	Y Y Y Y Y Y Y Y	8 Ford	Y Y Y N ? Y Y Y
2 *Jeffries*	Y Y Y Y Y Y Y Y	6 *Coleman*	Y Y Y N Y Y Y Y	11 *Hendon*	Y Y Y Y Y Y Y N	**TEXAS**	
3 Winn	Y Y Y Y Y Y Y Y	7 *Taylor*	Y Y Y Y Y Y Y Y	**NORTH DAKOTA**		1 Hall, S.	Y Y Y N Y Y Y Y
4 Glickman	Y Y Y N Y Y Y Y	8 *Bailey*	Y Y Y N ? Y Y Y	AL Dorgan	Y Y Y N Y Y Y Y	2 Wilson	? Y Y N Y Y Y Y
5 *Whittaker*	Y Y Y Y Y Y Y Y	9 Volkmer	Y Y Y N Y Y Y Y	**OHIO**		3 *Collins*	Y Y Y Y Y N Y Y
KENTUCKY		10 *Emerson*	Y Y Y Y Y Y Y N	1 *Gradison*	Y Y Y N Y Y Y Y	4 Hall, R.	Y Y Y Y ? ? Y Y
1 Hubbard	Y Y Y N Y Y Y Y	**MONTANA**		2 Luken	Y Y Y N Y Y Y Y	5 Mattox	Y Y Y N Y Y Y Y
2 Natcher	Y Y Y N Y Y Y Y	1 Williams	Y Y Y N ? ? Y Y	3 Hall	Y Y Y N Y Y Y Y	6 Gramm	Y Y Y N Y Y Y Y
3 Mazzoli	Y Y Y N Y Y Y Y	2 *Marlenee*	Y Y Y Y Y Y Y Y	4 Vacancy		7 *Archer*	Y Y Y Y Y Y Y Y
4 *Snyder*	Y Y Y Y Y Y Y Y	**NEBRASKA**		5 *Latta*	Y Y Y Y Y Y Y Y	8 *Fields*	Y Y Y Y Y Y Y N
5 *Rogers*	Y Y Y Y Y Y Y Y	1 *Bereuter*	Y Y Y N Y Y Y Y	6 *McEwen*	Y Y Y Y Y Y Y Y	9 Brooks	Y Y # N Y ? Y Y
6 *Hopkins*	Y Y Y Y Y Y Y Y	2 *Daub*	Y Y Y Y Y Y Y Y	7 *Brown*	Y Y ? Y ? ? ? ?	10 Pickle	Y Y Y N ? Y Y Y
7 Perkins	Y Y Y N Y Y Y Y	3 *Smith*	Y Y Y Y Y Y Y Y	8 *Kindness*	Y Y Y Y Y Y Y N	11 Leath	Y Y Y N Y Y Y Y
LOUISIANA		**NEVADA**		9 Weber	Y Y Y N Y Y Y Y	12 Wright	Y Y Y ? Y Y Y Y
1 *Livingston*	Y Y Y Y Y Y Y Y	AL Santini	Y Y ? N Y Y Y Y	10 *Miller*	Y N N Y Y Y Y Y	13 Hightower	Y Y Y Y Y Y Y Y
2 Boggs	Y Y Y N Y Y Y ?	**NEW HAMPSHIRE**		11 *Stanton*	Y Y Y N Y Y Y Y	14 Patman	Y Y Y N Y Y Y Y
3 Tauzin	Y Y Y N Y Y Y Y	1 D'Amours	Y Y Y N ? ? Y Y	12 Shamansky	Y Y Y N Y Y Y Y	15 de la Garza	Y Y Y N Y Y Y Y
4 Roemer	Y Y Y Y ? Y Y Y	2 *Gregg*	Y Y Y Y Y Y Y Y	13 Pease	Y Y N N Y N Y Y	16 White	Y Y Y Y Y Y Y Y
5 Huckaby	Y Y Y Y Y Y Y Y	**NEW JERSEY**		14 Seiberling	Y Y N N Y Y Y Y	17 Stenholm	Y Y Y Y Y Y Y Y
6 *Moore*	Y Y Y Y Y Y Y Y	1 Florio	Y Y Y ? Y Y Y Y	15 *Wylie*	Y Y Y N Y Y Y Y	18 Leland	? Y Y N ? Y Y Y
7 Breaux	? ? ? ? Y Y Y ?	2 Hughes	Y Y Y N Y Y Y Y	16 *Regula*	Y Y Y Y Y Y Y Y	19 Hance	Y Y Y ? Y Y Y Y
8 Long	Y Y Y N Y Y Y Y	3 Howard	Y Y Y N Y Y Y Y	17 *Ashbrook*	Y Y Y Y Y Y Y Y	20 Gonzalez	Y Y Y N Y Y Y Y
MAINE		4 *Smith*	Y Y Y N Y Y Y Y	18 Applegate	Y Y Y Y ? Y Y Y	21 *Loeffler*	Y Y Y Y Y Y Y Y
1 *Emery*	Y Y Y Y Y Y Y Y	5 *Fenwick*	Y Y Y N Y ? Y Y	19 *Williams*	Y Y Y N ? ? ? Y	22 *Paul*	Y N N Y Y N Y N
2 *Snowe*	Y Y Y Y Y ? ? Y	6 *Forsythe*	Y Y N N Y Y Y ?	20 Oakar	Y Y Y N Y Y Y Y	23 Kazen	Y Y Y N Y Y Y Y
MARYLAND		7 *Roukema*	Y Y Y N Y Y Y Y	21 Stokes	Y Y N N Y Y Y Y	24 Frost	Y Y Y N Y Y Y Y
1 Dyson	Y Y Y N Y Y Y Y	8 Roe	Y Y Y N Y Y Y Y	22 Eckart	Y Y Y N Y Y Y Y	**UTAH**	
2 Long	Y Y Y N Y Y Y Y	9 Hollenbeck	Y Y Y N Y Y Y Y	23 Mottl	Y Y Y N Y Y Y Y	1 *Hansen*	Y Y Y Y Y Y Y Y
3 Mikulski	Y Y Y N ? ? ? ?	10 Rodino	Y Y N N Y Y Y Y	**OKLAHOMA**		2 *Marriott*	Y Y Y Y Y Y Y Y
4 *Holt*	Y Y Y Y N Y Y N	11 Minish	Y Y Y N Y Y Y Y	1 Jones	Y Y Y N Y Y Y Y	**VERMONT**	
5 Hoyer	Y Y Y N Y Y Y Y	12 *Rinaldo*	Y Y Y N Y Y Y Y	2 Synar	Y Y Y N Y Y Y Y	AL *Jeffords*	Y Y Y N Y Y Y Y
6 Byron	Y Y Y N ? Y Y Y	13 *Courter*	Y Y Y N Y Y Y Y	3 Watkins	Y Y Y Y Y Y Y Y	**VIRGINIA**	
7 Mitchell	? N N N ? ? ? N	14 Guarini	Y Y Y N Y Y Y Y	4 McCurdy	Y Y Y N Y Y Y Y	1 *Trible*	Y Y Y Y Y Y Y Y
8 Barnes	Y Y Y N Y Y Y Y	15 Dwyer	Y Y Y N Y Y Y Y	5 *Edwards*	Y Y Y ? Y Y Y Y	2 *Whitehurst*	Y Y Y Y Y Y Y Y
MASSACHUSETTS		**NEW MEXICO**		6 English	Y Y Y N Y Y Y Y	3 *Bliley*	Y Y Y Y Y Y Y Y
1 *Conte*	Y Y Y N Y Y Y Y	1 *Lujan*	? Y Y Y Y Y Y Y	**OREGON**		4 Daniel, R.	Y Y Y Y Y Y Y Y
2 Boland	Y Y Y N Y Y Y Y	2 *Skeen*	Y Y Y N ? ? ? ?	1 AuCoin	Y Y Y Y Y Y Y Y	5 Daniel, D.	Y Y Y Y Y Y Y Y
3 Early	Y Y Y N Y Y Y Y	**NEW YORK**		2 *Smith*	Y Y Y Y Y Y Y Y	6 *Butler*	Y Y Y Y Y Y Y Y
4 Frank	Y Y N N Y Y N Y	1 *Carney*	Y Y Y Y Y Y Y Y	3 Wyden	Y N N N Y Y Y Y	7 *Robinson*	Y Y Y Y Y Y Y Y
5 Shannon	Y Y Y N Y Y N Y	2 Downey	Y Y N N Y Y Y Y	4 Weaver	Y N N N Y Y Y Y	8 *Parris*	Y Y Y Y Y Y Y Y
6 Mavroules	Y Y Y N Y Y Y Y	3 *Carman*	Y Y Y ? ? ? Y Y	**PENNSYLVANIA**		9 Wampler	Y Y Y Y ? ? ? ?
7 Markey	Y Y Y N Y Y Y Y	4 *Lent*	Y Y Y N Y Y Y Y	1 Foglietta	? Y Y N ? Y Y Y	10 *Wolf*	Y Y Y N Y Y Y Y
8 O'Neill		5 *McGrath*	Y Y Y N Y Y Y Y	2 Gray	Y Y N N ? ? ? ?	**WASHINGTON**	
9 Moakley	Y Y Y N Y ? Y Y	6 *LeBoutillier*	Y Y Y N Y Y Y N	3 Vacancy		1 *Pritchard*	Y Y Y N ? Y Y Y
10 *Heckler*	Y Y Y N Y Y Y Y	7 Addabbo	Y Y Y N Y Y Y Y	4 *Dougherty*	Y Y Y N Y Y Y Y	2 Swift	Y Y Y N Y Y Y Y
11 Donnelly	? ? ? ? ? ? ? ?	8 Rosenthal	Y Y N N N Y N Y	5 *Schulze*	Y Y ? Y Y Y Y Y	3 Bonker	Y Y Y N Y Y Y Y
12 Studds	Y Y N N Y N Y N	9 Ferraro	Y Y Y N Y Y Y Y	6 Yatron	Y Y Y N Y Y Y Y	4 *Morrison*	Y Y Y N Y Y Y Y
MICHIGAN		10 Biaggi	Y N Y N Y Y Y Y	7 Edgar	Y Y N N Y Y Y Y	5 Foley	Y Y Y N Y Y Y Y
1 Conyers	? ? ? ? ? ? ? ?	11 Scheuer	? ? ? ? ? ? Y Y	8 Coyne, J.	Y Y Y N Y Y Y Y	6 Dicks	Y Y Y N Y Y Y Y
2 *Pursell*	Y Y Y N ? Y Y Y	12 Chisholm	Y Y N N ? Y Y Y	9 *Shuster*	Y Y Y Y Y Y Y Y	7 Lowry	Y Y N N N N Y Y
3 Wolpe	Y Y Y N Y Y N Y	13 Solarz	? Y Y N ? ? ? ?	10 *McDade*	Y Y Y N Y Y Y Y	**WEST VIRGINIA**	
4 *Siljander*	Y Y Y Y Y Y Y Y	14 Richmond	Y Y N N N Y Y Y	11 *Nelligan*	Y Y Y N Y Y Y Y	1 Mollohan	Y ? ? ? Y Y Y Y
5 *Sawyer*	? ? ? ? ? ? ? ?	15 Zeferetti	? Y Y N ? ? ? ?	12 Murtha	Y Y Y N Y Y Y Y	2 *Benedict*	Y Y Y Y ? Y Y Y
6 *Dunn*	Y Y Y N Y Y Y Y	16 Schumer	? Y Y N ? ? ? ?	13 *Coughlin*	Y Y Y N Y Y Y Y	3 *Staton*	Y Y Y Y Y Y Y Y
7 Kildee	Y Y Y N Y Y Y Y	17 *Molinari*	Y Y Y N Y Y Y Y	14 Coyne, W.	Y Y Y N Y ? Y ?	4 Rahall	Y Y Y N Y Y Y Y
8 Traxler	Y Y Y N Y Y Y Y	18 Green	Y Y Y N Y Y Y Y	15 *Ritter*	Y Y Y Y N Y Y Y	**WISCONSIN**	
9 *Vander Jagt*	Y Y Y Y ? ? ? ?	19 Rangel	Y Y N N Y Y N Y	16 *Walker*	Y Y Y Y Y Y Y Y	1 Aspin	Y Y Y N ? ? Y Y
10 Albosta	Y Y Y N Y Y Y Y	20 Weiss	Y Y N N N Y N Y	17 Ertel	Y Y Y N Y Y Y Y	2 Kastenmeier	Y Y N N Y Y Y Y
11 *Davis*	Y Y ? N Y Y Y Y	21 Garcia	? Y N N ? ? ? ?	18 Walgren	Y Y Y N Y Y Y Y	3 *Gunderson*	Y Y Y N Y Y Y Y
12 Bonior	Y Y N N Y Y Y Y	22 Bingham	Y Y Y N Y Y Y Y	19 *Goodling*	Y Y Y N Y Y Y Y	4 Zablocki	Y Y Y N Y Y Y Y
13 Crockett	? ? X ? ? ? Y Y	23 Peyser	Y Y Y N Y Y Y Y	20 Gaydos	Y Y Y N Y Y Y Y	5 Reuss	N N N N Y Y Y Y
14 Hertel	Y Y Y N Y Y Y Y	24 Ottinger	P N N N P Y Y P	21 Bailey	Y Y Y N Y Y Y Y	6 *Petri*	Y Y Y N Y Y Y Y
15 Ford	? Y Y ? ? ? ? ?	25 *Fish*	? ? ? ? Y Y Y Y	22 Murphy	Y Y Y N Y Y Y Y	7 Obey	N Y N Y Y Y Y Y
16 Dingell	Y Y Y N ? Y Y Y	26 *Gilman*	Y Y Y N Y Y Y Y	23 *Clinger*	Y Y Y N Y Y Y Y	8 *Roth*	Y Y Y Y Y Y Y Y
17 Brodhead	Y Y Y N Y Y Y Y	27 McHugh	Y Y Y N Y Y Y Y	24 *Marks*	Y Y Y N Y Y Y Y	9 *Sensenbrenner*	Y Y Y Y Y N Y Y
18 Blanchard	Y Y Y N Y Y Y Y	28 Stratton	Y Y Y N Y Y Y Y	25 Atkinson	Y Y Y N Y Y Y Y	**WYOMING**	
19 *Broomfield*	Y Y Y Y Y Y Y Y	29 *Solomon*	Y Y Y Y Y Y N Y	**RHODE ISLAND**		AL *Cheney*	Y Y Y Y Y Y Y Y
MINNESOTA		30 *Martin*	Y Y Y N Y Y Y Y	1 St Germain	Y Y Y N Y Y Y Y		
1 *Erdahl*	Y Y Y N Y Y Y Y	31 *Mitchell*	Y Y Y N Y Y Y Y	2 *Schneider*	Y Y Y N Y Y Y Y		
2 *Hagedorn*	Y Y Y Y Y Y Y Y	32 *Wortley*	Y Y Y N ? Y Y Y	**SOUTH CAROLINA**			
3 *Frenzel*	Y Y Y Y Y Y Y Y	33 Lee	Y Y Y N Y Y Y Y	1 *Hartnett*	Y Y Y Y Y Y Y Y		
4 Vento	Y Y N N Y Y Y Y	34 *Horton*	Y Y ? N Y Y Y Y	2 *Spence*	Y Y Y Y Y Y Y Y		
5 Sabo	Y Y N N N Y Y Y	35 *Conable*	Y Y Y N Y Y Y Y	3 Derrick	Y Y Y N Y Y Y Y		
6 *Weber*	Y Y Y Y Y N Y Y	36 LaFalce	Y Y Y N Y Y N Y	4 *Campbell*	Y Y Y Y Y Y Y Y		
7 *Stangeland*	Y Y Y N Y Y Y Y	37 Nowak	Y Y Y N Y Y Y Y	5 Holland	Y Y Y N Y Y Y Y		
8 Oberstar	Y Y N N Y Y Y Y	38 *Kemp*	Y Y Y Y Y ? Y Y	6 *Napier*	Y Y Y Y Y Y Y Y		
MISSISSIPPI		39 Lundine	Y Y N N Y Y Y ?	**SOUTH DAKOTA**			
1 Whitten	Y Y Y N Y Y Y ?	**NORTH CAROLINA**		1 Daschle	Y Y Y N Y Y Y Y		
2 Bowen	Y Y Y N ? ? Y Y	1 Jones	? Y Y N ? Y Y Y	2 *Roberts*	Y Y Y Y Y Y Y Y		
3 Montgomery	Y Y Y N ? Y Y Y	2 Fountain	Y Y Y N ? Y Y Y	**TENNESSEE**			
4 Vacancy		3 Whitley	Y Y Y Y ? Y Y Y	1 *Quillen*	Y Y Y Y Y Y Y Y		
5 *Lott*	Y Y Y Y Y Y Y Y	4 Andrews	Y Y Y N Y Y Y Y	2 *Duncan*	Y Y Y Y Y Y Y Y		
MISSOURI		5 Neal	Y Y Y N ? Y Y Y	3 Bouquard	Y Y Y N Y Y Y Y		
1 Clay	Y Y N N ? Y Y Y	6 *Johnston*	Y Y Y Y N N Y N	4 Gore	Y Y Y N Y Y Y Y		
2 Young	Y Y Y N Y Y Y Y	7 Rose	Y Y Y N ? Y Y Y	5 Boner	Y Y Y N Y Y Y Y		
3 Gephardt	Y Y Y N Y Y Y ?	8 Hefner	Y Y Y N Y Y Y Y	6 *Beard*	Y Y Y Y Y Y Y Y		

Democrats *Republicans*

1981 CQ ALMANAC—39-H

92. HR 3238. Public Broadcasting Authorization. Bliley, R-Va., amendment to retain the requirement in existing law for quarterly disbursement of federal funds to the Corporation for Public Broadcasting. Rejected 171-226: R 153-23; D 18-203 (ND 8-138, SD 10-65), June 24, 1981.

93. HR 3238. Public Broadcasting Authorization. Passage of the bill to authorize $160 million in fiscal 1984 for public broadcasting, $145 million in fiscal 1985 and $130 million in fiscal 1986; to establish a formula for allocating the funds; and to allow an 18-month experiment to determine the impact of advertising on public broadcasting. Passed 323-86: R 102-81; D 221-5 (ND 149-1, SD 72-4), June 24, 1981.

94. Procedural Motion. Rousselot, R-Calif., motion to approve the House *Journal* of Wednesday, June 24. Motion agreed to 380-12: R 171-6; D 209-6 (ND 138-6, SD 71-0), June 25, 1981.

95. HR 3982. Budget Reconciliation. Bolling, D-Mo., motion to order the previous question (thus ending debate and the possibility of amendment) on the rule (H Res 169) providing for House floor consideration of the bill to make changes in existing federal programs to achieve budget cuts required by the first fiscal 1982 budget resolution. Motion rejected 210-217: R 1-188; D 209-29 (ND 155-5, SD 54-24), June 25, 1981. A "nay" was a vote supporting the president's position.

96. HR 3982. Budget Reconciliation. Latta, R-Ohio, motion to order the previous question (thus ending debate and the possibility of amendment) on the Latta substitute *(see vote 97, below)* for the rule (H Res 169) providing for House floor consideration of the bill. Motion agreed to 219-208: R 188-0; D 31-208 (ND 5-156, SD 26-52), June 25, 1981. A "yea" was a vote supporting the president's position.

97. HR 3982. Budget Reconciliation. Latta, R-Ohio, substitute for the rule (H Res 169) providing for House floor consideration of the bill. The Latta substitute permitted a single vote on a reconciliation savings package endorsed by President Reagan as an alternative for the package drafted by House committees. The rule as reported required division of the Reagan package into a series of separate amendments. Adopted 216-212: R 189-0; D 27-212 (ND 4-157, SD 23-55), June 25, 1981. A "yea" was a vote supporting the president's position.

98. HR 3982. Budget Reconciliation. Adoption of the rule (H Res 169), as amended by the Latta, R-Ohio, substitute *(see vote 97, above)*, providing for House floor consideration of the reconciliation savings bill making changes in existing federal programs to achieve budget cuts required by the first fiscal 1982 budget resolution. Adopted 214-208: R 188-0; D 26-208 (ND 4-153, SD 22-55), June 25, 1981. A "yea" was a vote supporting the president's position.

KEY

Y Voted for (yea).
Paired for.
+ Announced for.
N Voted against (nay).
X Paired against.
- Announced against.
P Voted "present".
C Voted "present" to avoid possible conflict of interest.
? Did not vote or otherwise make a position known.

	92	93	94	95	96	97	98
ALABAMA							
1 *Edwards*	N	Y	Y	N	Y	Y	Y
2 *Dickinson*	?	N	Y	N	Y	Y	Y
3 Nichols	N	Y	Y	N	Y	Y	Y
4 Bevill	N	Y	Y	Y	N	N	N
5 Flippo	N	Y	Y	Y	N	N	N
6 *Smith*	Y	N	?	N	Y	Y	Y
7 Shelby	Y	Y	Y	N	Y	Y	Y
ALASKA							
AL *Young*	?	Y	Y	Y	N	Y	Y
ARIZONA							
1 *Rhodes*	Y	Y	Y	N	Y	Y	Y
2 Udall	N	Y	Y	Y	N	N	N
3 *Stump*	Y	N	Y	N	Y	Y	Y
4 *Rudd*	Y	N	Y	N	Y	Y	Y
ARKANSAS							
1 Alexander	N	Y	Y	Y	N	N	N
2 *Bethune*	Y	Y	Y	N	Y	Y	Y
3 *Hammerschmidt*	Y	Y	Y	N	Y	Y	Y
4 Anthony	N	Y	Y	Y	N	N	N
CALIFORNIA							
1 *Chappie*	Y	N	Y	N	Y	Y	Y
2 *Clausen*	Y	Y	?	N	Y	Y	Y
3 Matsui	N	Y	Y	Y	N	N	N
4 Fazio	N	?	Y	Y	N	N	N
5 Burton, J.	N	Y	Y	Y	N	N	N
6 Burton, P.	N	Y	Y	Y	N	N	N
7 Miller	N	Y	Y	Y	N	N	N
8 Dellums	N	Y	Y	Y	N	N	N
9 Stark	?	Y	Y	Y	N	N	N
10 Edwards	?	Y	Y	N	N	N	N
11 Lantos	-	+	Y	Y	N	N	N
12 *McCloskey*	N	Y	Y	N	Y	Y	Y
13 Mineta	N	Y	Y	Y	N	N	N
14 *Shumway*	Y	N	Y	N	Y	Y	Y
15 Coelho	N	Y	Y	Y	N	N	N
16 Panetta	N	Y	Y	Y	N	N	N
17 *Pashayan*	N	Y	Y	N	Y	Y	Y
18 *Thomas*	Y	Y	Y	N	Y	Y	Y
19 *Lagomarsino*	Y	N	Y	N	Y	Y	Y
20 *Goldwater*	N	Y	Y	N	Y	Y	Y
21 *Fiedler*	N	N	?	N	Y	Y	Y
22 *Moorhead*	Y	N	Y	N	Y	Y	Y
23 Beilenson	N	Y	Y	Y	N	N	N
24 Waxman	N	Y	Y	Y	N	N	N
25 Roybal	N	Y	Y	Y	N	N	N
26 *Rousselot*	Y	N	Y	N	Y	Y	Y
27 *Dornan*	Y	N	Y	N	Y	Y	Y
28 Dixon	N	Y	Y	Y	N	N	N
29 Hawkins	N	Y	Y	Y	N	N	N
30 Danielson	-	+	+	+	-	-	-
31 Dymally	N	Y	?	Y	N	N	N
32 Anderson	N	Y	Y	Y	N	N	N
33 *Grisham*	Y	N	Y	N	Y	Y	Y
34 *Lungren*	Y	N	Y	N	Y	Y	Y
35 *Dreier*	Y	N	Y	N	Y	Y	Y
36 Brown	N	Y	Y	Y	N	N	N
37 *Lewis*	Y	N	Y	?	Y	Y	Y
38 Patterson	N	Y	Y	Y	N	N	N
39 *Dannemeyer*	Y	N	Y	N	Y	Y	Y
40 *Badham*	Y	N	Y	N	Y	Y	Y
41 *Lowery*	Y	Y	Y	N	Y	Y	Y
42 *Hunter*	Y	N	Y	N	Y	Y	Y
43 *Burgener*	Y	N	Y	N	Y	Y	Y
COLORADO							
1 Schroeder	N	Y	N	Y	N	N	N
2 Wirth	N	Y	Y	Y	N	N	N
3 Kogovsek	N	Y	Y	Y	N	N	N
4 *Brown*	Y	N	Y	N	Y	Y	Y

	92	93	94	95	96	97	98
5 *Kramer*	Y	N	Y	N	Y	Y	Y
CONNECTICUT							
1 Cotter	?	?	?	?	?	?	?
2 Gejdenson	N	Y	Y	Y	N	N	N
3 *DeNardis*	N	Y	?	N	Y	Y	Y
4 *McKinney*	N	Y	?	N	Y	Y	Y
5 Ratchford	N	Y	Y	Y	N	N	N
6 Moffett	N	Y	?	Y	N	N	N
DELAWARE							
AL *Evans*	Y	Y	Y	N	Y	Y	Y
FLORIDA							
1 Hutto	N	Y	Y	N	Y	Y	Y
2 Fuqua	N	Y	Y	Y	N	N	N
3 Bennett	N	Y	Y	N	N	N	N
4 Chappell	N	Y	Y	N	Y	Y	Y
5 *McCollum*	Y	N	Y	N	Y	Y	Y
6 *Young*	Y	Y	Y	N	Y	Y	Y
7 Gibbons	?	?	Y	Y	Y	Y	N
8 Ireland	N	Y	Y	N	Y	Y	Y
9 Nelson	N	Y	Y	Y	N	N	N
10 *Bafalis*	Y	N	Y	N	Y	Y	Y
11 Mica	N	Y	Y	Y	N	N	N
12 *Shaw*	Y	N	Y	N	Y	Y	Y
13 Lehman	N	Y	Y	Y	N	N	N
14 Pepper	N	Y	?	N	Y	N	N
15 Fascell	N	Y	Y	Y	N	N	N
GEORGIA							
1 Ginn	N	Y	Y	N	N	N	N
2 Hatcher	N	Y	Y	Y	N	N	N
3 Brinkley	N	Y	Y	Y	N	N	N
4 Levitas	N	Y	Y	Y	N	N	N
5 Fowler	N	Y	Y	Y	N	N	N
6 *Gingrich*	Y	Y	Y	N	Y	Y	Y
7 McDonald	Y	N	Y	N	Y	Y	Y
8 Evans	N	Y	?	N	Y	Y	Y
9 Jenkins	N	Y	Y	Y	N	N	N
10 Barnard	Y	Y	Y	N	Y	Y	Y
HAWAII							
1 Heftel	N	Y	Y	Y	N	N	N
2 Akaka	N	Y	Y	Y	N	N	N
IDAHO							
1 *Craig*	Y	N	Y	N	Y	Y	Y
2 *Hansen*	Y	N	Y	N	Y	Y	Y
ILLINOIS							
1 Washington	N	Y	Y	Y	N	N	N
2 Savage	N	Y	?	Y	N	N	N
3 Russo	N	Y	Y	Y	N	N	N
4 *Derwinski*	?	N	Y	N	Y	Y	Y
5 Fary	?	?	Y	Y	N	N	N
6 *Hyde*	Y	Y	Y	N	Y	Y	Y
7 Collins	N	Y	Y	Y	N	N	N
8 Rostenkowski	?	Y	Y	Y	N	N	N
9 Yates	N	Y	Y	Y	N	N	N
10 *Porter*	Y	Y	Y	N	Y	Y	Y
11 Annunzio	N	Y	Y	Y	N	N	N
12 *Crane, P.*	Y	N	Y	N	Y	N	Y
13 *McClory*	Y	Y	Y	N	Y	Y	Y
14 *Erlenborn*	Y	Y	Y	N	Y	Y	Y
15 *Corcoran*	Y	Y	Y	N	Y	Y	Y
16 *Martin*	Y	Y	Y	N	Y	Y	Y
17 *O'Brien*	Y	Y	Y	N	Y	Y	Y
18 *Michel*	Y	N	Y	N	Y	Y	Y
19 *Railsback*	Y	Y	Y	N	Y	Y	Y
20 *Findley*	Y	N	Y	N	Y	Y	Y
21 *Madigan*	Y	Y	Y	N	Y	Y	Y
22 *Crane, D.*	Y	N	Y	N	Y	Y	Y
23 Price	N	Y	Y	Y	N	N	N
24 Simon	N	Y	Y	Y	N	N	N
INDIANA							
1 Benjamin	N	Y	Y	Y	N	N	N
2 Fithian	N	Y	Y	Y	N	N	N
3 *Hiler*	Y	N	Y	N	Y	Y	Y
4 *Coats*	Y	N	Y	N	Y	Y	Y
5 *Hillis*	Y	Y	Y	N	Y	Y	Y
6 Evans	N	Y	Y	Y	N	N	N
7 *Myers*	Y	N	Y	N	Y	Y	Y
8 *Deckard*	Y	Y	?	N	-	+	+
9 Hamilton	N	Y	Y	Y	N	N	N
10 Sharp	N	Y	Y	Y	N	N	N
11 Jacobs	N	Y	N	Y	N	N	N
IOWA							
1 *Leach*	Y	Y	Y	N	Y	Y	Y
2 *Tauke*	Y	Y	Y	N	Y	Y	Y
3 *Evans*	Y	Y	N	N	Y	Y	Y
4 Smith	N	Y	Y	Y	N	N	N
5 Harkin	N	Y	Y	Y	N	N	N
6 Bedell	N	Y	Y	Y	N	N	N

Democrats *Republicans*

Corresponding to Congressional Record Votes 101, 102, 103, 104, 105, 106, 107

	92	93	94	95	96	97	98
KANSAS							
1 ***Roberts***	Y	Y	Y	N	Y	Y	Y
2 ***Jeffries***	Y	N	Y	N	Y	Y	Y
3 ***Winn***	Y	Y	Y	N	Y	Y	Y
4 Glickman	Y	Y	Y	Y	N	N	N
5 ***Whittaker***	N	Y	Y	N	Y	Y	Y
KENTUCKY							
1 Hubbard	N	Y	Y	Y	N	N	N
2 Natcher	N	Y	Y	Y	N	N	N
3 Mazzoli	N	Y	Y	Y	N	N	N
4 ***Snyder***	N	Y	Y	N	Y	Y	Y
5 ***Rogers***	Y	Y	Y	N	Y	Y	Y
6 ***Hopkins***	Y	Y	Y	N	Y	Y	Y
7 Perkins	N	Y	Y	Y	N	N	N
LOUISIANA							
1 ***Livingston***	Y	N	Y	N	Y	Y	Y
2 Boggs	N	Y	Y	Y	N	N	N
3 Tauzin	N	Y	?	N	Y	Y	Y
4 Roemer	N	Y	Y	N	Y	Y	N
5 Huckaby	Y	Y	?	N	Y	Y	Y
6 ***Moore***	Y	Y	Y	N	Y	Y	Y
7 Breaux	N	Y	Y	N	Y	Y	Y
8 Long	N	Y	Y	Y	N	N	?
MAINE							
1 ***Emery***	Y	Y	Y	N	Y	Y	Y
2 ***Snowe***	Y	Y	Y	N	Y	Y	Y
MARYLAND							
1 Dyson	N	Y	Y	Y	N	N	N
2 Long	Y	Y	Y	Y	N	N	N
3 Mikulski	N	Y	Y	Y	N	N	N
4 ***Holt***	Y	N	Y	N	Y	Y	Y
5 Hoyer	-	+	Y	Y	N	N	N
6 Byron	N	Y	Y	N	Y	Y	Y
7 Mitchell	N	Y	N	Y	N	N	N
8 Barnes	N	Y	Y	Y	N	N	N
MASSACHUSETTS							
1 ***Conte***	Y	Y	Y	N	Y	Y	Y
2 Boland	N	Y	Y	Y	N	N	N
3 Early	N	Y	Y	Y	N	N	N
4 Frank	N	Y	?	Y	N	N	?
5 Shannon	N	Y	Y	Y	N	N	N
6 Mavroules	N	Y	Y	Y	N	N	N
7 Markey	N	Y	Y	Y	N	N	N
8 O'Neill					N	N	
9 Moakley	N	Y	Y	Y	N	N	N
10 ***Heckler***	Y	Y	Y	N	+	Y	Y
11 Donnelly	?	?	Y	Y	N	N	N
12 Studds	N	Y	Y	Y	N	N	N
MICHIGAN							
1 Conyers	?	?	?	?	?	?	?
2 ***Pursell***	Y	Y	Y	N	Y	Y	Y
3 Wolpe	N	Y	Y	Y	N	N	N
4 ***Siljander***	Y	N	Y	N	Y	Y	Y
5 ***Sawyer***	?	?	Y	N	Y	Y	Y
6 ***Dunn***	Y	Y	Y	N	Y	Y	Y
7 Kildee	N	Y	Y	Y	N	N	N
8 Traxler	N	Y	Y	Y	N	N	N
9 ***Vander Jagt***	?	?	?	N	Y	Y	Y
10 Albosta	N	Y	Y	Y	N	N	N
11 ***Davis***	?	Y	Y	N	Y	Y	Y
12 Bonior	N	Y	Y	Y	N	N	N
13 Crockett	N	Y	?	Y	N	N	N
14 Hertel	N	Y	Y	Y	N	N	N
15 Ford	N	Y	?	Y	N	N	N
16 Dingell	N	Y	?	Y	N	N	N
17 Brodhead	N	Y	Y	Y	N	N	N
18 Blanchard	N	Y	Y	Y	N	N	N
19 ***Broomfield***	Y	Y	Y	N	Y	Y	Y
MINNESOTA							
1 ***Erdahl***	Y	Y	Y	N	Y	Y	Y
2 ***Hagedorn***	Y	N	Y	N	Y	Y	Y
3 ***Frenzel***	Y	Y	Y	N	Y	Y	Y
4 Vento	N	Y	Y	Y	N	N	N
5 Sabo	N	Y	N	Y	N	N	N
6 ***Weber***	Y	N	Y	N	Y	Y	Y
7 ***Stangeland***	Y	Y	Y	N	Y	Y	Y
8 Oberstar	N	Y	Y	Y	N	N	N
MISSISSIPPI							
1 Whitten	N	Y	Y	Y	N	N	N
2 Bowen	N	Y	Y	Y	N	N	N
3 Montgomery	N	Y	Y	N	Y	Y	Y
4 Vacancy							
5 ***Lott***	Y	N	Y	N	Y	Y	Y
MISSOURI							
1 Clay	N	Y	?	Y	N	N	N
2 Young	N	Y	Y	Y	Y	N	N
3 Gephardt	N	Y	Y	Y	N	N	N
4 Skelton	Y	Y	Y	Y	N	N	?
5 Bolling	?	?	Y	Y	N	N	N
6 ***Coleman***	Y	Y	Y	N	Y	Y	Y
7 ***Taylor***	Y	N	Y	N	Y	Y	Y
8 ***Bailey***	Y	N	Y	N	Y	Y	Y
9 Volkmer	Y	Y	Y	Y	N	N	N
10 ***Emerson***	Y	N	Y	N	Y	Y	Y
MONTANA							
1 Williams	N	Y	Y	Y	N	N	N
2 ***Marlenee***	Y	Y	Y	N	Y	Y	Y
NEBRASKA							
1 ***Bereuter***	Y	Y	Y	N	Y	Y	Y
2 ***Daub***	Y	Y	Y	N	Y	Y	Y
3 ***Smith***	Y	Y	Y	N	Y	Y	Y
NEVADA							
AL Santini	?	?	Y	N	Y	Y	Y
NEW HAMPSHIRE							
1 D'Amours	Y	Y	?	Y	N	N	N
2 ***Gregg***	Y	N	Y	N	Y	Y	Y
NEW JERSEY							
1 Florio	N	Y	Y	Y	N	N	N
2 Hughes	Y	Y	Y	Y	N	N	N
3 Howard	N	Y	Y	Y	N	N	N
4 ***Smith***	Y	Y	Y	N	Y	Y	Y
5 ***Fenwick***	N	Y	Y	N	Y	Y	Y
6 ***Forsythe***	Y	Y	?	N	Y	Y	Y
7 ***Roukema***	Y	Y	Y	N	Y	Y	Y
8 Roe	N	Y	Y	Y	N	N	N
9 ***Hollenbeck***	?	?	?	N	Y	Y	Y
10 Rodino	N	Y	Y	Y	N	N	N
11 Minish	N	Y	Y	Y	N	N	N
12 ***Rinaldo***	Y	Y	Y	N	Y	Y	?
13 ***Courter***	Y	Y	Y	N	Y	Y	Y
14 Guarini	N	Y	Y	Y	N	N	N
15 Dwyer	N	Y	Y	Y	N	N	N
NEW MEXICO							
1 ***Lujan***	Y	Y	Y	N	Y	Y	Y
2 ***Skeen***	?	Y	Y	N	Y	Y	Y
NEW YORK							
1 ***Carney***	Y	N	Y	N	Y	Y	Y
2 Downey	N	Y	Y	Y	N	N	N
3 ***Carman***	?	?	?	N	Y	Y	Y
4 ***Lent***	Y	Y	Y	N	Y	Y	Y
5 ***McGrath***	Y	Y	Y	N	Y	Y	Y
6 ***LeBoutillier***	Y	N	Y	N	Y	Y	Y
7 Addabbo	N	Y	Y	Y	N	N	N
8 Rosenthal	N	Y	?	Y	N	N	N
9 Ferraro	N	Y	Y	Y	N	N	N
10 Biaggi	N	Y	Y	Y	N	N	N
11 Scheuer	N	Y	Y	Y	N	N	N
12 Chisholm	N	Y	?	Y	N	N	N
13 Solarz	?	?	Y	Y	N	N	N
14 Richmond	N	Y	?	Y	N	N	N
15 Zeferetti	N	Y	Y	Y	N	N	N
16 Schumer	?	Y	?	Y	N	N	N
17 ***Molinari***	Y	Y	Y	N	Y	Y	Y
18 ***Green***	N	Y	Y	N	Y	Y	Y
19 Rangel	N	Y	Y	Y	N	N	N
20 Weiss	N	Y	Y	Y	N	N	N
21 Garcia	?	?	Y	Y	N	N	N
22 Bingham	N	Y	?	Y	N	N	N
23 Peyser	N	Y	Y	Y	N	N	N
24 Ottinger	N	Y	P	Y	N	N	N
25 ***Fish***	N	Y	Y	N	Y	Y	Y
26 ***Gilman***	N	Y	Y	N	Y	Y	Y
27 McHugh	N	Y	Y	Y	N	N	N
28 Stratton	N	Y	Y	Y	N	N	N
29 ***Solomon***	Y	N	Y	N	Y	Y	Y
30 ***Martin***	?	?	Y	N	Y	Y	Y
31 ***Mitchell***	N	Y	Y	N	Y	Y	Y
32 ***Wortley***	Y	Y	N	N	Y	Y	Y
33 ***Lee***	N	N	Y	N	Y	Y	Y
34 ***Horton***	N	Y	Y	N	Y	Y	Y
35 ***Conable***	?	?	Y	N	Y	Y	Y
36 LaFalce	N	Y	Y	Y	N	N	N
37 Nowak	N	Y	Y	Y	N	N	N
38 ***Kemp***	Y	N	Y	N	Y	Y	Y
39 Lundine	N	Y	Y	Y	N	N	N
NORTH CAROLINA							
1 Jones	?	Y	Y	Y	N	N	N
2 Fountain	N	Y	Y	Y	N	N	N
3 Whitley	N	Y	Y	Y	N	N	N
4 Andrews	N	Y	?	Y	N	N	N
5 Neal	N	Y	?	Y	N	N	N
6 ***Johnston***	Y	N	N	N	Y	Y	Y
7 Rose	N	Y	Y	Y	N	N	N
8 Hefner	N	Y	Y	Y	N	N	N
9 ***Martin***	Y	N	Y	N	Y	Y	Y
10 ***Broyhill***	Y	N	Y	N	Y	Y	Y
11 ***Hendon***	Y	N	Y	N	Y	Y	Y
NORTH DAKOTA							
AL Dorgan	N	Y	Y	Y	N	N	N
OHIO							
1 ***Gradison***	Y	Y	Y	N	Y	Y	Y
2 Luken	N	Y	N	Y	N	N	N
3 Hall	N	Y	Y	Y	N	N	N
4 Vacancy							
5 ***Latta***	Y	N	Y	N	Y	Y	Y
6 ***McEwen***	Y	N	Y	N	Y	Y	Y
7 ***Brown***	?	Y	Y	N	Y	Y	Y
8 ***Kindness***	Y	N	Y	N	Y	Y	Y
9 ***Weber***	Y	Y	Y	N	Y	Y	Y
10 ***Miller***	Y	Y	Y	N	Y	Y	Y
11 ***Stanton***	Y	Y	Y	N	Y	Y	Y
12 Shamansky	N	Y	Y	Y	N	N	N
13 Pease	N	Y	Y	Y	N	N	N
14 Seiberling	N	Y	Y	Y	N	N	N
15 ***Wylie***	N	Y	Y	N	Y	Y	Y
16 ***Regula***	Y	Y	Y	N	Y	Y	Y
17 ***Ashbrook***	Y	N	?	N	Y	Y	Y
18 Applegate	N	Y	?	Y	N	N	N
19 ***Williams***	N	Y	Y	N	Y	Y	Y
20 Oakar	N	Y	Y	Y	N	N	N
21 Stokes	N	Y	Y	Y	N	N	N
22 Eckart	N	Y	Y	Y	N	N	N
23 Mottl	N	Y	Y	N	Y	Y	Y
OKLAHOMA							
1 Jones	N	Y	Y	Y	N	N	N
2 Synar	N	Y	Y	Y	N	N	N
3 Watkins	N	Y	Y	Y	N	N	N
4 McCurdy	N	?	Y	Y	N	N	N
5 ***Edwards***	Y	Y	Y	N	Y	Y	Y
6 English	N	Y	Y	Y	N	N	N
OREGON							
1 AuCoin	N	Y	Y	Y	N	N	N
2 ***Smith***	Y	N	Y	N	Y	Y	Y
3 Wyden	N	Y	Y	Y	N	N	N
4 Weaver	N	Y	Y	Y	N	N	N
PENNSYLVANIA							
1 Foglietta	N	Y	Y	Y	N	N	N
2 Gray	N	Y	Y	Y	N	N	N
3 Vacancy							
4 ***Dougherty***	?	Y	Y	N	Y	Y	Y
5 ***Schulze***	Y	N	Y	N	Y	Y	Y
6 Yatron	N	Y	Y	Y	N	N	N
7 Edgar	N	Y	Y	Y	N	N	N
8 ***Coyne, J.***	Y	Y	Y	N	Y	Y	Y
9 ***Shuster***	N	N	Y	N	Y	Y	Y
10 ***McDade***	Y	Y	Y	N	Y	Y	Y
11 ***Nelligan***	Y	Y	Y	N	Y	Y	Y
12 Murtha	N	Y	Y	Y	N	N	N
13 ***Coughlin***	Y	Y	Y	N	Y	Y	Y
14 Coyne, W.	N	Y	Y	Y	N	N	N
15 ***Ritter***	N	Y	Y	N	Y	Y	Y
16 ***Walker***	Y	N	N	N	Y	Y	Y
17 Ertel	N	Y	Y	Y	N	N	N
18 Walgren	N	Y	Y	Y	N	N	N
19 ***Goodling***	Y	Y	N	N	Y	Y	Y
20 Gaydos	N	Y	Y	Y	N	N	N
21 Bailey	N	Y	Y	Y	N	N	N
22 Murphy	Y	Y	Y	Y	N	N	N
23 ***Clinger***	Y	Y	Y	N	Y	Y	Y
24 ***Marks***	N	Y	?	N	Y	Y	Y
25 Atkinson	N	Y	Y	N	N	N	N
RHODE ISLAND							
1 St Germain	?	Y	Y	Y	N	N	N
2 ***Schneider***	Y	Y	Y	N	Y	Y	Y
SOUTH CAROLINA							
1 ***Hartnett***	Y	N	Y	N	Y	Y	Y
2 ***Spence***	Y	N	Y	N	Y	Y	Y
3 Derrick	N	Y	Y	Y	N	N	N
4 ***Campbell***	Y	N	Y	N	Y	Y	Y
5 Holland	N	Y	Y	Y	Y	N	Y
6 ***Napier***	Y	N	Y	N	Y	Y	Y
SOUTH DAKOTA							
1 Daschle	N	+	Y	Y	N	N	N
2 ***Roberts***	Y	Y	Y	N	Y	Y	Y
TENNESSEE							
1 ***Quillen***	Y	N	Y	N	Y	Y	Y
2 ***Duncan***	Y	Y	Y	N	Y	Y	Y
3 Bouquard	N	Y	Y	Y	N	N	N
4 Gore	N	Y	Y	Y	N	N	N
5 Boner	N	Y	Y	Y	N	N	N
6 ***Beard***	Y	N	Y	N	Y	Y	Y
7 Jones	N	Y	Y	Y	N	N	N
8 Ford	?	Y	Y	Y	N	N	N
TEXAS							
1 Hall, S.	Y	Y	Y	N	Y	Y	Y
2 Wilson	N	Y	Y	N	Y	N	Y
3 ***Collins***	Y	N	N	N	Y	Y	Y
4 Hall, R.	Y	Y	?	N	Y	Y	N
5 Mattox	N	Y	Y	Y	N	N	N
6 Gramm	Y	N	Y	N	Y	Y	Y
7 ***Archer***	Y	N	Y	N	Y	Y	Y
8 ***Fields***	Y	N	Y	N	Y	Y	Y
9 Brooks	N	Y	Y	Y	N	N	N
10 Pickle	N	Y	Y	Y	N	N	N
11 Leath	N	Y	Y	N	Y	Y	Y
12 Wright	N	Y	Y	Y	N	N	N
13 Hightower	N	Y	Y	N	Y	Y	Y
14 Patman	N	Y	Y	Y	N	N	N
15 de la Garza	Y	Y	Y	Y	N	N	N
16 White	N	Y	Y	N	Y	Y	N
17 Stenholm	Y	N	Y	N	Y	Y	Y
18 Leland	N	Y	Y	Y	N	N	N
19 Hance	N	Y	Y	N	Y	Y	Y
20 Gonzalez	N	Y	Y	Y	N	N	N
21 ***Loeffler***	Y	N	Y	N	Y	Y	Y
22 ***Paul***	Y	N	Y	N	Y	Y	Y
23 Kazen	N	Y	Y	Y	N	N	N
24 Frost	N	Y	Y	Y	N	N	N
UTAH							
1 ***Hansen***	Y	N	Y	N	Y	Y	Y
2 ***Marriott***	Y	Y	Y	N	Y	Y	Y
VERMONT							
AL ***Jeffords***	N	Y	Y	N	Y	Y	Y
VIRGINIA							
1 ***Trible***	Y	N	Y	N	Y	Y	Y
2 ***Whitehurst***	Y	N	Y	N	Y	Y	Y
3 ***Bliley***	Y	N	Y	N	Y	Y	Y
4 ***Daniel, R.***	Y	N	Y	N	Y	Y	Y
5 Daniel, D.	Y	N	Y	N	Y	Y	Y
6 ***Butler***	Y	N	Y	N	Y	Y	Y
7 ***Robinson***	Y	N	Y	N	Y	Y	Y
8 ***Parris***	Y	Y	Y	N	Y	Y	Y
9 ***Wampler***	?	?	Y	N	Y	Y	Y
10 ***Wolf***	Y	Y	Y	N	Y	Y	Y
WASHINGTON							
1 ***Pritchard***	N	Y	Y	N	Y	Y	Y
2 Swift	N	Y	Y	Y	N	N	N
3 Bonker	N	Y	Y	Y	N	N	N
4 ***Morrison***	Y	Y	?	N	Y	Y	Y
5 Foley	?	Y	Y	Y	N	N	N
6 Dicks	N	Y	Y	Y	N	N	N
7 Lowry	N	Y	Y	Y	N	N	N
WEST VIRGINIA							
1 Mollohan	N	Y	Y	Y	N	N	N
2 ***Benedict***	Y	Y	Y	N	Y	Y	Y
3 ***Staton***	Y	Y	Y	N	Y	Y	Y
4 Rahall	N	Y	Y	Y	N	N	N
WISCONSIN							
1 Aspin	N	Y	Y	Y	N	N	N
2 Kastenmeier	N	Y	Y	Y	N	N	N
3 ***Gunderson***	Y	Y	Y	N	Y	Y	Y
4 Zablocki	N	Y	Y	Y	N	N	?
5 Reuss	N	Y	Y	Y	N	N	N
6 ***Petri***	Y	Y	Y	N	Y	Y	Y
7 Obey	N	Y	Y	Y	N	N	N
8 ***Roth***	Y	Y	Y	N	Y	Y	Y
9 ***Sensenbrenner***	Y	N	Y	N	Y	Y	Y
WYOMING							
AL ***Cheney***	Y	Y	Y	N	Y	Y	Y

Democrats ***Republicans***

99. Procedural Motion. Walker, R-Pa., motion to approve the House *Journal* of Thursday, June 25. Motion agreed to 346-37: R 172-6; D 174-31 (ND 102-30, SD 72-1), June 26, 1981.

100. HR 3982. Budget Reconciliation. Panetta, D-Calif., motion that the House resolve itself into the Committee of the Whole to consider the budget reconciliation bill. Motion agreed to 316-84: R 182-2; D 134-82 (ND 74-70, SD 60-12), June 26, 1981.

101. HR 3520. Steel Industry Compliance. Adoption of the conference report on the bill to give steel companies, on a case-by-case basis, until Dec. 31, 1985, to meet the 1982 air pollution cleanup deadline. Money saved by deferring pollution control expenditures must be used to modernize older steel plants. Adopted (thus cleared for the president) 412-4: R 185-2; D 227-2 (ND 152-1, SD 75-1), June 26, 1981. A "yea" was a vote supporting the president's position.

102. HR 3982. Budget Reconciliation. Latta, R-Ohio, amendments, considered *en bloc*, to strike parts of six titles of the bill recommended by the following committees — Agriculture; Banking, Finance and Urban Affairs; Education and Labor; Post Office and Civil Service; Science and Technology; and Ways and Means — and to substitute provisions endorsed by President Reagan. Adopted 217-211: R 188-2; D 29-209 (ND 3-157, SD 26-52), June 26, 1981. A "yea" was a vote supporting the president's position.

103. HR 3982. Budget Reconciliation. Jones, D-Okla., motion to order the previous question (thus ending debate and the possibility of amendment) on the Schneider, R-R.I., motion to recommit the bill to the Budget Committee with instructions to provide a twice-a-year, cost-of-living adjustment for federal employees. Motion agreed to 215-212: R 189-1; D 26-211 (ND 3-157, SD 23-54), June 26, 1981. (Jones sought defeat of his own motion in order to open the way for a vote on an alternative Democratic proposal.)

104. HR 3982. Budget Reconciliation. Passage of the bill to revise existing laws to achieve budget savings in fiscal 1982-84 as ordered by the first budget resolution for fiscal 1982. Passed 232-193: R 185-5; D 47-188 (ND 11-148, SD 36-40), June 26, 1981. A "yea" was a vote supporting the president's position.

105. HR 3982. Budget Reconciliation. Campbell, R-S.C., motion to table (kill) the Lott, R-Miss., motion to reconsider the vote *(vote 104, above)* by which the bill was passed. Motion agreed to 187-150: R 153-1; D 34-149 (ND 9-106, SD 25-43), June 26, 1981.

KEY	
Y	Voted for (yea).
#	Paired for.
+	Announced for.
N	Voted against (nay).
X	Paired against.
-	Announced against.
P	Voted "present".
C	Voted "present" to avoid possible conflict of interest.
?	Did not vote or otherwise make a position known.

	99	100	101	102	103	104	105
ALABAMA							
1 Edwards	Y	Y	Y	Y	Y	Y	Y
2 *Dickinson*	N	Y	Y	Y	Y	Y	Y
3 Nichols	Y	Y	Y	Y	Y	Y	?
4 Bevill	Y	Y	Y	N	N	N	N
5 Flippo	Y	Y	Y	Y	Y	Y	Y
6 *Smith*	Y	Y	Y	Y	Y	Y	Y
7 Shelby	Y	Y	Y	Y	Y	Y	Y
ALASKA							
AL *Young*	?	?	Y	Y	Y	Y	Y
ARIZONA							
1 *Rhodes*	Y	Y	Y	Y	Y	Y	Y
2 Udall	?	Y	Y	N	N	N	N
3 Stump	Y	Y	N	Y	Y	Y	Y
4 *Rudd*	Y	Y	Y	Y	Y	Y	Y
ARKANSAS							
1 Alexander	Y	Y	Y	N	N	N	N
2 *Bethune*	Y	Y	?	Y	Y	Y	Y
3 *Hammerschmidt*	Y	Y	Y	Y	Y	Y	?
4 Anthony	Y	N	Y	N	N	N	N
CALIFORNIA							
1 *Chappie*	Y	?	Y	Y	Y	Y	Y
2 *Clausen*	Y	Y	Y	Y	Y	Y	Y
3 Matsui	Y	N	Y	N	N	N	N
4 Fazio	N	Y	Y	N	N	N	N
5 Burton, J.	Y	Y	Y	?	?	?	?
6 Burton, P.	Y	N	Y	N	N	N	N
7 Miller	N	N	Y	N	N	N	N
8 Dellums	Y	N	?	N	N	N	N
9 Stark	Y	Y	Y	N	N	N	?
10 Edwards	Y	N	Y	N	N	N	?
11 Lantos	Y	Y	Y	N	N	N	N
12 *McCloskey*	?	Y	Y	Y	Y	Y	Y
13 Mineta	Y	Y	Y	N	N	Y	N
14 *Shumway*	Y	Y	Y	Y	Y	Y	Y
15 Coelho	?	?	Y	N	N	N	N
16 Panetta	Y	Y	Y	N	N	Y	N
17 Pashayan	Y	Y	Y	Y	Y	Y	Y
18 *Thomas*	Y	Y	Y	Y	Y	Y	Y
19 *Lagomarsino*	Y	Y	Y	Y	Y	Y	Y
20 *Goldwater*	Y	Y	Y	Y	Y	Y	Y
21 *Fiedler*	Y	Y	Y	Y	Y	Y	Y
22 *Moorhead*	Y	Y	Y	Y	Y	Y	?
23 Beilenson	N	N	N	N	N	N	?
24 Waxman	Y	N	Y	N	N	N	N
25 Roybal	Y	Y	Y	N	N	N	N
26 *Rousselot*	Y	Y	Y	Y	Y	Y	Y
27 *Dornan*	Y	Y	Y	Y	Y	Y	Y
28 Dixon	?	?	?	N	N	N	N
29 Hawkins	Y	N	Y	N	N	N	?
30 Danielson	+	+	+	-	-	-	-
31 Dymally	?	?	?	?	?	?	?
32 Anderson	Y	Y	Y	N	N	N	N
33 *Grisham*	Y	Y	Y	Y	Y	Y	Y
34 *Lungren*	Y	Y	Y	Y	Y	Y	Y
35 *Dreier*	Y	Y	Y	Y	Y	Y	Y
36 Brown	Y	Y	Y	N	N	Y	?
37 *Lewis*	Y	Y	Y	Y	Y	Y	Y
38 Patterson	N	N	N	N	N	Y	N
39 *Dannemeyer*	Y	Y	N	Y	Y	Y	Y
40 *Badham*	Y	Y	Y	Y	Y	Y	Y
41 *Lowery*	Y	Y	Y	Y	Y	Y	Y
42 *Hunter*	Y	Y	Y	Y	Y	Y	Y
43 *Burgener*	Y	Y	Y	Y	Y	Y	?
COLORADO							
1 Schroeder	N	N	N	N	N	N	N
2 Wirth	Y	Y	Y	N	N	N	Y
3 Kogovsek	Y	N	Y	N	N	N	N
4 *Brown*	Y	Y	Y	Y	Y	Y	Y

	99	100	101	102	103	104	105
5 *Kramer*	Y	Y	Y	Y	Y	Y	Y
CONNECTICUT							
1 Cotter	?	?	?	?	?	?	?
2 Gejdenson	Y	Y	N	N	N	N	N
3 *DeNardis*	?	Y	Y	Y	Y	Y	Y
4 *McKinney*	Y	Y	Y	Y	Y	Y	Y
5 Ratchford	N	N	Y	N	N	N	N
6 Moffett	N	?	Y	N	N	N	N
DELAWARE							
AL *Evans*	Y	Y	Y	Y	Y	Y	Y
FLORIDA							
1 Hutto	Y	Y	Y	Y	Y	Y	Y
2 Fuqua	Y	Y	N	?	?	?	?
3 Bennett	Y	Y	N	N	Y	N	Y
4 Chappell	Y	Y	Y	Y	Y	Y	Y
5 *McCollum*	Y	Y	Y	Y	Y	Y	Y
6 *Young*	Y	N	Y	Y	Y	Y	Y
7 Gibbons	Y	Y	N	N	Y	N	Y
8 Ireland	Y	Y	Y	Y	Y	Y	?
9 Nelson	Y	Y	Y	N	Y	N	Y
10 *Bafalis*	Y	Y	Y	Y	Y	Y	?
11 Mica	Y	Y	Y	N	Y	N	Y
12 *Shaw*	?	Y	Y	Y	Y	Y	Y
13 Lehman	Y	?	N	N	N	N	?
14 Pepper	Y	?	N	N	N	N	N
15 Fascell	Y	?	N	N	N	N	N
GEORGIA							
1 Ginn	Y	Y	Y	N	N	N	N
2 Hatcher	Y	Y	Y	Y	Y	Y	Y
3 Brinkley	Y	Y	Y	N	N	Y	?
4 Levitas	Y	N	Y	N	N	N	N
5 Fowler	Y	N	Y	N	N	N	?
6 *Gingrich*	Y	Y	Y	Y	Y	Y	Y
7 McDonald	Y	Y	Y	Y	Y	Y	Y
8 Evans	Y	Y	Y	Y	Y	Y	Y
9 Jenkins	Y	Y	N	N	N	N	N
10 Barnard	Y	Y	Y	Y	Y	Y	Y
HAWAII							
1 Heftel	?	Y	Y	N	N	N	N
2 Akaka	Y	Y	N	N	N	N	N
IDAHO							
1 *Craig*	Y	Y	Y	Y	Y	Y	?
2 *Hansen*	Y	Y	Y	Y	Y	Y	Y
ILLINOIS							
1 Washington	Y	N	Y	N	N	N	?
2 Savage	?	?	?	N	N	N	N
3 Russo	Y	Y	N	N	N	N	N
4 *Derwinski*	Y	Y	Y	Y	Y	Y	Y
5 Fary	Y	Y	N	N	N	N	N
6 *Hyde*	Y	Y	Y	Y	Y	Y	Y
7 Collins	Y	N	Y	N	N	N	?
8 Rostenkowski	?	?	Y	N	N	N	N
9 Yates	Y	Y	N	N	N	N	?
10 *Porter*	Y	Y	Y	Y	Y	Y	Y
11 Annunzio	Y	Y	N	N	N	N	N
12 *Crane, P.*	Y	Y	Y	Y	Y	Y	Y
13 *McClory*	Y	Y	Y	Y	Y	Y	Y
14 *Erlenborn*	Y	Y	Y	Y	Y	Y	?
15 *Corcoran*	Y	Y	Y	Y	Y	Y	Y
16 *Martin*	Y	Y	Y	Y	Y	Y	Y
17 *O'Brien*	?	Y	Y	Y	Y	Y	Y
18 *Michel*	Y	Y	Y	Y	Y	Y	Y
19 *Railsback*	Y	Y	Y	Y	Y	Y	Y
20 *Findley*	Y	Y	Y	Y	Y	Y	?
21 *Madigan*	Y	Y	Y	Y	Y	Y	Y
22 *Crane, D.*	Y	Y	Y	Y	Y	Y	Y
23 Price	Y	Y	Y	N	N	N	N
24 Simon	N	Y	Y	N	N	N	N
INDIANA							
1 Benjamin	Y	Y	Y	N	N	N	N
2 Fithian	N	N	Y	N	N	N	N
3 *Hiler*	Y	Y	Y	Y	Y	Y	Y
4 *Coats*	Y	Y	Y	Y	Y	Y	Y
5 *Hillis*	Y	?	Y	Y	Y	Y	?
6 Evans	Y	Y	Y	N	N	Y	Y
7 *Myers*	Y	Y	Y	Y	Y	Y	Y
8 *Deckard*	Y	Y	Y	Y	Y	Y	Y
9 Hamilton	Y	Y	N	N	N	N	?
10 Sharp	Y	Y	N	N	N	N	N
11 Jacobs	N	N	Y	N	N	N	N
IOWA							
1 *Leach*	Y	Y	Y	Y	Y	Y	Y
2 *Tauke*	Y	Y	Y	Y	Y	Y	Y
3 *Evans*	N	Y	Y	Y	Y	Y	Y
4 Smith	Y	N	Y	N	N	N	N
5 Harkin	?	?	?	N	N	N	N
6 Bedell	Y	N	Y	N	N	N	N

Democrats *Republicans*

	99	100	101	102	103	104	105
KANSAS							
1 *Roberts*	Y	Y	Y	Y	Y	Y	Y
2 *Jeffries*	Y	Y	Y	Y	Y	Y	Y
3 *Winn*	Y	Y	Y	Y	Y	Y	?
4 Glickman	Y	Y	Y	N	N	N	Y
5 *Whittaker*	Y	Y	Y	Y	Y	Y	Y
KENTUCKY							
1 Hubbard	Y	Y	Y	N	N	N	N
2 Natcher	Y	Y	Y	N	N	N	N
3 Mazzoli	Y	Y	Y	N	N	N	Y
4 *Snyder*	Y	Y	Y	Y	Y	Y	Y
5 *Rogers*	Y	Y	Y	Y	Y	Y	Y
6 *Hopkins*	Y	Y	Y	Y	Y	Y	Y
7 Perkins	Y	Y	Y	N	N	N	N
LOUISIANA							
1 *Livingston*	Y	Y	Y	Y	Y	Y	Y
2 Boggs	?	?	Y	N	N	N	N
3 Tauzin	Y	Y	Y	Y	Y	Y	Y
4 Roemer	Y	Y	Y	N	Y	N	N
5 Huckaby	Y	Y	Y	Y	Y	Y	?
6 *Moore*	Y	Y	Y	Y	Y	Y	Y
7 Breaux	?	Y	Y	Y	N	Y	Y
8 Long	?	?	?	N	N	N	N
MAINE							
1 *Emery*	Y	Y	Y	Y	Y	Y	?
2 *Snowe*	Y	Y	Y	Y	Y	Y	Y
MARYLAND							
1 Dyson	Y	Y	Y	N	N	Y	N
2 Long	Y	Y	Y	N	N	Y	?
3 Mikulski	Y	Y	Y	N	N	N	?
4 *Holt*	Y	Y	Y	Y	Y	Y	?
5 Hoyer	Y	Y	Y	N	N	N	N
6 Byron	Y	Y	Y	Y	Y	Y	Y
7 Mitchell	N	N	Y	N	N	N	?
8 Barnes	Y	N	Y	N	N	N	N
MASSACHUSETTS							
1 *Conte*	Y	Y	Y	Y	Y	N	Y
2 Boland	Y	Y	Y	N	N	N	N
3 Early	Y	N	Y	N	N	N	N
4 Frank	Y	N	Y	N	N	N	N
5 Shannon	Y	N	Y	N	N	N	N
6 Mavroules	N	N	Y	N	N	N	?
7 Markey	N	N	Y	N	N	N	N
8 O'Neill				N	N		
9 Moakley	Y	N	Y	N	N	N	N
10 *Heckler*	Y	Y	Y	Y	Y	N	Y
11 Donnelly	Y	N	Y	N	N	N	?
12 Studds	Y	N	Y	N	N	N	N
MICHIGAN							
1 Conyers	?	?	Y	N	N	N	N
2 *Pursell*	Y	Y	Y	Y	Y	Y	Y
3 Wolpe	Y	N	Y	N	N	N	N
4 *Siljander*	Y	Y	Y	Y	Y	Y	Y
5 *Sawyer*	Y	Y	Y	Y	Y	Y	Y
6 *Dunn*	N	Y	Y	Y	Y	Y	?
7 Kildee	Y	Y	Y	N	N	N	N
8 Traxler	Y	Y	Y	N	N	N	?
9 *Vander Jagt*	?	Y	Y	Y	Y	Y	Y
10 Albosta	Y	Y	Y	N	N	N	?
11 *Davis*	Y	Y	Y	Y	Y	Y	?
12 Bonior	Y	Y	Y	N	N	N	N
13 Crockett	Y	N	Y	N	N	N	?
14 Hertel	Y	Y	Y	N	N	N	N
15 Ford	?	N	?	N	N	N	N
16 Dingell	?	N	Y	N	N	N	N
17 Brodhead	N	Y	Y	N	N	N	N
18 Blanchard	Y	N	Y	N	N	N	N
19 *Broomfield*	Y	Y	Y	Y	Y	Y	?
MINNESOTA							
1 *Erdahl*	Y	Y	Y	Y	Y	Y	Y
2 *Hagedorn*	Y	Y	Y	Y	Y	Y	?
3 *Frenzel*	P	Y	Y	Y	Y	Y	Y
4 Vento	N	N	Y	N	N	N	N
5 Sabo	N	N	Y	N	N	N	N
6 *Weber*	Y	Y	Y	Y	Y	Y	Y
7 *Stangeland*	Y	Y	Y	Y	Y	Y	Y
8 Oberstar	Y	N	Y	N	N	N	N
MISSISSIPPI							
1 Whitten	Y	Y	Y	N	N	N	N
2 Bowen	Y	Y	Y	N	N	N	N
3 Montgomery	Y	Y	Y	Y	Y	Y	Y
4 Vacancy							
5 *Lott*	Y	Y	Y	Y	Y	Y	Y
MISSOURI							
1 Clay	N	?	Y	N	N	N	?
2 Young	Y	Y	Y	N	N	N	?
3 Gephardt	?	N	Y	N	N	N	N

	99	100	101	102	103	104	105
4 Skelton	Y	?	Y	N	N	Y	N
5 Bolling	Y	N	?	N	N	N	Y
6 *Coleman*	Y	Y	Y	Y	Y	Y	?
7 *Taylor*	Y	Y	Y	Y	Y	Y	Y
8 *Bailey*	Y	Y	Y	Y	Y	Y	Y
9 Volkmer	Y	N	Y	N	N	N	N
10 *Emerson*	Y	Y	Y	Y	Y	Y	Y
MONTANA							
1 Williams	?	?	Y	N	N	N	N
2 *Marlenee*	Y	Y	Y	Y	Y	Y	Y
NEBRASKA							
1 *Bereuter*	Y	Y	Y	Y	Y	Y	Y
2 *Daub*	Y	Y	Y	Y	Y	Y	Y
3 *Smith*	Y	Y	Y	Y	Y	Y	?
NEVADA							
AL Santini	Y	Y	Y	Y	Y	Y	Y
NEW HAMPSHIRE							
1 D'Amours	Y	Y	Y	N	N	N	N
2 *Gregg*	Y	Y	Y	Y	Y	Y	?
NEW JERSEY							
1 Florio	?	?	Y	N	N	N	N
2 Hughes	N	N	Y	N	N	N	N
3 Howard	Y	Y	Y	N	N	N	N
4 *Smith*	Y	Y	Y	Y	Y	Y	Y
5 *Fenwick*	Y	Y	Y	Y	Y	Y	Y
6 *Forsythe*	N	Y	Y	Y	Y	Y	Y
7 *Roukema*	Y	Y	Y	Y	Y	Y	Y
8 Roe	?	Y	Y	N	N	N	?
9 *Hollenbeck*	?	Y	Y	Y	Y	Y	?
10 Rodino	Y	Y	Y	N	N	N	N
11 Minish	Y	Y	Y	N	N	N	N
12 *Rinaldo*	Y	Y	Y	Y	Y	Y	Y
13 *Courter*	Y	Y	Y	Y	Y	Y	Y
14 Guarini	Y	Y	Y	N	N	N	N
15 Dwyer	Y	N	Y	N	N	N	?
NEW MEXICO							
1 *Lujan*	Y	Y	Y	Y	Y	Y	?
2 *Skeen*	Y	Y	Y	Y	Y	Y	Y
NEW YORK							
1 *Carney*	Y	Y	Y	Y	Y	Y	Y
2 Downey	N	N	Y	N	N	N	N
3 *Carman*	Y	Y	Y	Y	Y	Y	Y
4 *Lent*	Y	Y	?	Y	Y	Y	Y
5 *McGrath*	Y	Y	Y	Y	Y	Y	Y
6 *LeBoutillier*	Y	Y	Y	Y	Y	Y	?
7 Addabbo	Y	Y	Y	N	N	N	?
8 Rosenthal	Y	Y	Y	N	N	N	?
9 Ferraro	N	N	Y	N	N	N	?
10 Biaggi	Y	Y	Y	N	N	N	N
11 Scheuer	Y	Y	Y	N	N	N	N
12 Chisholm	Y	N	Y	N	N	N	?
13 Solarz	?	?	Y	N	N	N	N
14 Richmond	?	?	?	N	N	N	?
15 Zeferetti	Y	Y	Y	N	N	N	?
16 Schumer	N	N	Y	N	N	N	?
17 *Molinari*	Y	Y	Y	Y	Y	Y	Y
18 *Green*	Y	Y	Y	Y	N	Y	Y
19 Rangel	Y	Y	Y	N	N	N	N
20 Weiss	N	N	Y	N	N	N	N
21 Garcia	?	N	Y	N	N	N	N
22 Bingham	Y	N	Y	N	N	N	N
23 Peyser	Y	Y	Y	N	N	N	?
24 Ottinger	P	Y	Y	N	N	N	N
25 *Fish*	Y	Y	Y	Y	Y	Y	Y
26 *Gilman*	Y	Y	?	Y	Y	Y	N
27 McHugh	?	N	Y	N	N	N	N
28 Stratton	Y	N	Y	N	N	N	N
29 *Solomon*	Y	Y	Y	Y	Y	Y	Y
30 *Martin*	Y	Y	Y	Y	Y	Y	Y
31 *Mitchell*	Y	Y	Y	Y	Y	Y	Y
32 *Wortley*	Y	Y	Y	Y	Y	Y	Y
33 *Lee*	Y	Y	Y	Y	Y	Y	Y
34 *Horton*	Y	Y	Y	Y	Y	Y	?
35 *Conable*	Y	Y	Y	Y	Y	Y	Y
36 LaFalce	Y	N	Y	N	N	N	N
37 Nowak	Y	?	Y	N	N	N	N
38 *Kemp*	Y	Y	Y	Y	Y	Y	Y
39 Lundine	?	N	Y	N	N	N	?
NORTH CAROLINA							
1 Jones	Y	N	Y	N	N	Y	?
2 Fountain	?	N	Y	N	N	Y	N
3 Whitley	Y	Y	Y	N	N	Y	Y
4 Andrews	?	Y	Y	N	N	N	N
5 Neal	Y	N	Y	N	N	N	N
6 *Johnston*	N	Y	Y	Y	Y	Y	?
7 Rose	Y	N	Y	N	N	?	?
8 Hefner	Y	Y	Y	N	N	N	N

	99	100	101	102	103	104	105
9 *Martin*	Y	Y	Y	Y	Y	Y	Y
10 *Broyhill*	Y	Y	Y	Y	Y	Y	Y
11 *Hendon*	Y	Y	Y	Y	Y	Y	Y
NORTH DAKOTA							
AL Dorgan	N	N	Y	N	N	N	N
OHIO							
1 *Gradison*	Y	Y	Y	Y	Y	Y	?
2 Luken	Y	Y	Y	N	N	N	?
3 Hall	Y	Y	Y	N	N	N	N
4 Vacancy							
5 *Latta*	Y	Y	Y	Y	Y	Y	Y
6 *McEwen*	Y	Y	Y	Y	Y	Y	Y
7 *Brown*	Y	Y	Y	Y	Y	Y	Y
8 *Kindness*	Y	Y	Y	Y	Y	Y	Y
9 *Weber*	Y	Y	Y	Y	Y	Y	?
10 *Miller*	Y	Y	Y	Y	Y	Y	Y
11 *Stanton*	Y	Y	Y	Y	Y	Y	Y
12 Shamansky	Y	Y	Y	N	N	N	?
13 Pease	P	Y	Y	N	N	N	N
14 Seiberling	N	Y	Y	N	N	N	N
15 *Wylie*	Y	Y	Y	Y	Y	Y	Y
16 *Regula*	Y	Y	Y	Y	Y	Y	Y
17 *Ashbrook*	Y	Y	Y	Y	Y	Y	?
18 Applegate	?	?	Y	N	N	N	N
19 *Williams*	Y	Y	Y	Y	Y	Y	?
20 Oakar	Y	Y	Y	N	N	N	N
21 Stokes	Y	N	Y	N	N	N	N
22 Eckart	N	N	Y	N	N	N	N
23 Mottl	Y	Y	Y	N	N	N	?
OKLAHOMA							
1 Jones	N	N	Y	N	N	Y	N
2 Synar	Y	Y	Y	N	N	N	N
3 Watkins	Y	Y	Y	N	N	N	N
4 McCurdy	Y	Y	Y	N	N	N	N
5 *Edwards*	Y	Y	Y	Y	Y	Y	Y
6 English	Y	Y	?	N	N	Y	Y
OREGON							
1 AuCoin	?	?	Y	N	N	N	N
2 *Smith*	Y	Y	Y	Y	Y	Y	Y
3 Wyden	Y	Y	Y	N	N	N	N
4 Weaver	N	N	Y	N	N	N	N
PENNSYLVANIA							
1 Foglietta	?	Y	Y	N	N	N	N
2 Gray	Y	N	Y	N	N	N	?
3 Vacancy							
4 *Dougherty*	?	?	Y	N	Y	N	Y
5 *Schulze*	Y	Y	Y	Y	Y	Y	?
6 Yatron	Y	Y	Y	N	N	N	N
7 Edgar	N	N	Y	N	N	N	N
8 *Coyne, J.*	Y	Y	Y	Y	Y	Y	Y
9 *Shuster*	Y	Y	Y	Y	Y	Y	Y
10 *McDade*	?	Y	Y	Y	Y	Y	Y
11 *Nelligan*	Y	Y	Y	Y	Y	Y	Y
12 Murtha	Y	Y	Y	N	N	N	N
13 *Coughlin*	Y	Y	Y	Y	Y	Y	Y
14 Coyne, W.	Y	N	Y	N	N	N	N
15 *Ritter*	Y	Y	Y	Y	Y	Y	Y
16 *Walker*	N	Y	Y	Y	Y	Y	Y
17 Ertel	Y	N	Y	N	N	N	Y
18 Walgren	Y	Y	Y	N	N	N	N
19 *Goodling*	Y	Y	Y	Y	Y	Y	?
20 Gaydos	Y	N	Y	N	N	N	N
21 Bailey	Y	N	Y	N	N	N	N
22 Murphy	N	Y	Y	N	N	N	?
23 *Clinger*	Y	Y	Y	Y	Y	Y	Y
24 *Marks*	Y	Y	Y	Y	Y	Y	?
25 Atkinson	?	Y	Y	N	N	N	N
RHODE ISLAND							
1 St Germain	N	N	Y	N	N	N	N
2 *Schneider*	?	Y	Y	N	Y	N	?
SOUTH CAROLINA							
1 *Hartnett*	Y	Y	Y	Y	Y	Y	Y
2 *Spence*	Y	Y	Y	Y	Y	Y	Y
3 Derrick	Y	Y	Y	N	N	N	N
4 *Campbell*	Y	Y	Y	Y	Y	Y	Y
5 Holland	Y	Y	Y	Y	N	Y	N
6 *Napier*	Y	Y	Y	Y	Y	Y	Y
SOUTH DAKOTA							
1 Daschle	?	N	Y	N	N	N	?
2 *Roberts*	Y	Y	Y	Y	Y	Y	Y
TENNESSEE							
1 *Quillen*	Y	Y	Y	Y	Y	Y	?
2 *Duncan*	Y	Y	Y	Y	Y	Y	?
3 Bouquard	Y	Y	Y	N	N	Y	N
4 Gore	Y	N	Y	N	N	N	N
5 Boner	Y	Y	Y	N	N	N	N
6 *Beard*	Y	Y	Y	Y	Y	Y	Y

	99	100	101	102	103	104	105
7 Jones	Y	Y	Y	N	N	Y	N
8 Ford	Y	Y	Y	N	N	N	N
TEXAS							
1 Hall, S.	Y	Y	Y	Y	Y	Y	Y
2 Wilson	Y	Y	Y	Y	Y	Y	Y
3 *Collins*	Y	Y	Y	Y	Y	Y	Y
4 Hall, R.	Y	Y	Y	N	N	N	N
5 Mattox	Y	Y	Y	N	N	N	N
6 Gramm	Y	Y	N	Y	Y	Y	Y
7 *Archer*	Y	Y	Y	Y	Y	Y	?
8 *Fields*	Y	Y	Y	Y	Y	Y	Y
9 Brooks	Y	Y	Y	N	N	N	N
10 Pickle	Y	Y	Y	N	N	Y	Y
11 Leath	Y	Y	Y	Y	Y	Y	Y
12 Wright	Y	Y	Y	N	N	N	N
13 Hightower	Y	Y	Y	Y	Y	Y	?
14 Patman	Y	N	Y	N	N	N	N
15 de la Garza	Y	Y	Y	N	N	N	N
16 White	Y	Y	Y	Y	Y	N	N
17 Stenholm	Y	Y	Y	Y	Y	Y	Y
18 Leland	Y	N	Y	N	N	N	N
19 Hance	Y	?	Y	Y	Y	Y	Y
20 Gonzalez	Y	Y	Y	N	N	N	N
21 *Loeffler*	Y	Y	Y	Y	Y	Y	Y
22 *Paul*	Y	Y	Y	Y	Y	N	Y
23 Kazen	Y	Y	Y	N	N	N	N
24 Frost	Y	N	Y	N	N	N	N
UTAH							
1 *Hansen*	?	Y	Y	Y	Y	Y	Y
2 *Marriott*	Y	Y	Y	Y	Y	Y	Y
VERMONT							
AL *Jeffords*	Y	N	Y	Y	Y	Y	Y
VIRGINIA							
1 *Trible*	Y	Y	Y	Y	Y	Y	Y
2 *Whitehurst*	Y	Y	Y	Y	Y	Y	?
3 *Bliley*	Y	Y	N	Y	Y	Y	Y
4 *Daniel, R.*	Y	Y	Y	Y	Y	Y	?
5 Daniel, D.	Y	Y	Y	Y	Y	Y	Y
6 *Butler*	Y	Y	Y	Y	Y	Y	Y
7 *Robinson*	Y	Y	Y	Y	Y	Y	Y
8 *Parris*	Y	Y	Y	Y	Y	Y	Y
9 *Wampler*	Y	Y	Y	Y	Y	Y	Y
10 *Wolf*	Y	Y	Y	Y	Y	Y	Y
WASHINGTON							
1 *Pritchard*	?	Y	Y	Y	Y	Y	Y
2 Swift	Y	Y	Y	N	N	N	Y
3 Bonker	?	Y	Y	N	N	N	?
4 *Morrison*	Y	Y	Y	Y	Y	Y	Y
5 Foley	Y	Y	Y	N	N	N	N
6 Dicks	Y	N	Y	N	N	N	N
7 Lowry	N	N	Y	N	N	N	N
WEST VIRGINIA							
1 Mollohan	Y	Y	Y	N	N	N	?
2 *Benedict*	Y	Y	Y	Y	Y	Y	Y
3 *Staton*	Y	Y	Y	Y	Y	Y	Y
4 Rahall	Y	N	Y	N	N	N	N
WISCONSIN							
1 Aspin	?	Y	Y	N	N	N	N
2 Kastenmeier	Y	N	Y	N	N	N	N
3 *Gunderson*	Y	Y	Y	Y	Y	Y	Y
4 Zablocki	Y	Y	Y	N	N	N	Y
5 Reuss	Y	N	Y	N	N	N	?
6 *Petri*	Y	Y	Y	Y	Y	Y	Y
7 Obey	Y	N	Y	N	N	N	N
8 *Roth*	Y	Y	Y	Y	Y	Y	Y
9 *Sensenbrenner*	Y	Y	Y	Y	Y	Y	Y
WYOMING							
AL *Cheney*	Y	Y	Y	Y	Y	Y	Y

Democrats *Republicans*

KEY

Y Voted for (yea).
Paired for.
+ Announced for.
N Voted against (nay).
X Paired against.
- Announced against.
P Voted "present".
C Voted "present" to avoid possible conflict of interest.
? Did not vote or otherwise make a position known.

106. HR 3519. Defense Department Authorization. Price, D-Ill., motion that the House resolve itself into the Committee of the Whole for consideration of the bill to authorize funds for the Defense Department in fiscal 1982. Motion agreed to 345-2: R 151-2; D 194-0 (ND 129-0, SD 65-0), July 8, 1981.

107. HR 3519. Defense Department Authorization. Price, D-Ill., motion that the House resolve itself into the Committee of the Whole for consideration of the bill to authorize funds for the Defense Department in fiscal 1982. Motion agreed to 385-4: R 177-2; D 208-2 (ND 141-2, SD 67-0), July 9, 1981.

108. HR 3519. Defense Department Authorization. Simon, D-Ill., amendment to the Hansen, R-Utah, amendment, to prohibit the expenditure of funds in the bill for the MX missile system until both houses of Congress have adopted resolutions approving the MX missile system selected by the president. Rejected 201-207: R 48-134; D 153-73 (ND 131-24, SD 22-49), July 9, 1981. (The Hansen amendment, which gave Congress the right to overturn the presidentially selected MX system, was adopted subsequently by voice vote.)

109. HR 3519. Defense Department Authorization. Stratton, D-N.Y., motion to end debate on the Dellums, D-Calif., amendment *(see vote 110, below)* to delete $2.4 billion for development of the MX missile system. Motion rejected 193-213: R 125-55; D 68-158 (ND 30-124, SD 38-34), July 9, 1981.

110. HR 3519. Defense Department Authorization. Dellums, D-Calif., amendment to delete $2.4 billion for development of the MX missile system. Rejected 96-316: R 17-167; D 79-149 (ND 75-81; SD 4-68), July 9, 1981.

111. HR 3519. Defense Department Authorization. Fowler, D-Ga., amendment to make funds specified in the bill for the B-1 bomber available also for research and development of an advanced technology bomber. Rejected 153-254: R 25-155; D 128-99 (ND 116-40, SD 12-59), July 9, 1981.

112. HR 3519. Defense Department Authorization. Schroeder, D-Colo., amendment to reinstate a requirement that the Defense Department reduce the number of civilian employees in grades GS-13 to GS-18. Rejected 142-249: R 25-148; D 117-101 (ND 102-46, SD 15-55), July 9, 1981.

	106	107	108	109	110	111	112
ALABAMA							
1 *Edwards*	Y	?	N	Y	N	N	N
2 *Dickinson*	Y	Y	N	Y	N	N	N
3 Nichols	Y	Y	N	Y	N	N	N
4 Bevill	Y	Y	N	Y	N	N	N
5 Flippo	Y	Y	N	Y	N	N	N
6 *Smith*	?	Y	N	Y	N	N	N
7 Shelby	Y	Y	N	Y	N	N	N
ALASKA							
AL *Young*	N	N	Y	Y	N	N	N
ARIZONA							
1 *Rhodes*	Y	Y	N	Y	N	N	?
2 Udall	Y	Y	Y	N	Y	Y	Y
3 *Stump*	Y	Y	N	Y	N	N	N
4 *Rudd*	Y	Y	N	Y	N	N	N
ARKANSAS							
1 Alexander	Y	Y	N	Y	N	N	N
2 *Bethune*	Y	Y	N	N	N	N	N
3 *Hammerschmidt*	Y	Y	N	N	N	N	N
4 Anthony	Y	Y	N	N	?	?	
CALIFORNIA							
1 *Chappie*	Y	Y	N	Y	N	N	N
2 *Clausen*	Y	Y	N	Y	N	N	N
3 Matsui	Y	Y	N	Y	N	N	N
4 Fazio	?	Y	N	Y	N	N	N
5 Burton, J.	Y	Y	Y	N	Y	Y	Y
6 Burton, P.	Y	Y	Y	N	Y	Y	N
7 Miller	Y	Y	Y	N	Y	Y	Y
8 Dellums	Y	Y	Y	N	Y	Y	Y
9 Stark	?	Y	Y	N	Y	Y	?
10 Edwards	Y	Y	Y	N	Y	Y	Y
11 Lantos	?	Y	Y	N	N	N	N
12 *McCloskey*	Y	Y	Y	Y	N	N	N
13 Mineta	Y	Y	Y	N	Y	Y	Y
14 *Shumway*	Y	Y	N	Y	N	N	N
15 Coelho	Y	Y	Y	Y	N	N	Y
16 Panetta	Y	Y	Y	N	Y	Y	Y
17 *Pashayan*	?	Y	N	Y	N	N	N
18 *Thomas*	?	Y	N	Y	N	N	N
19 *Lagomarsino*	Y	Y	N	Y	N	N	N
20 *Goldwater*	?	?	?	?	?	?	?
21 *Fiedler*	Y	Y	Y	Y	N	N	N
22 *Moorhead*	Y	Y	N	Y	N	N	N
23 Beilenson	Y	Y	Y	N	Y	Y	Y
24 Waxman	Y	Y	Y	N	Y	Y	Y
25 Roybal	Y	Y	Y	N	Y	Y	Y
26 *Rousselot*	Y	Y	N	Y	N	?	Y
27 *Dornan*	Y	Y	N	N	N	N	N
28 Dixon	Y	Y	Y	N	Y	N	?
29 Hawkins	Y	Y	Y	N	Y	Y	Y
30 Danielson	Y	Y	Y	N	N	N	Y
31 Dymally	?	Y	Y	N	Y	Y	Y
32 Anderson	Y	Y	Y	N	Y	Y	Y
33 *Grisham*	Y	Y	N	Y	N	N	N
34 *Lungren*	Y	Y	N	Y	N	N	N
35 *Dreier*	Y	Y	N	Y	N	N	Y
36 Brown	Y	?	Y	N	N	Y	?
37 *Lewis*	?	Y	N	N	N	N	N
38 Patterson	?	?	Y	N	Y	Y	Y
39 *Dannemeyer*	Y	Y	N	Y	N	N	N
40 *Badham*	Y	Y	N	Y	N	N	N
41 *Lowery*	Y	Y	Y	Y	N	N	N
42 *Hunter*	Y	Y	N	Y	N	N	N
43 *Burgener*	?	Y	N	Y	N	N	N
COLORADO							
1 Schroeder	Y	Y	Y	N	Y	Y	Y
2 Wirth	Y	?	#	?	#	?	?
3 Kogovsek	Y	Y	Y	N	Y	N	N
4 *Brown*	Y	Y	N	Y	N	N	N

	106	107	108	109	110	111	112
5 *Kramer*	?	Y	N	N	N	N	N
CONNECTICUT							
1 Cotter	?	?	?	?	?	?	?
2 Gejdenson	Y	Y	Y	N	Y	Y	Y
3 *DeNardis*	Y	Y	Y	N	N	Y	?
4 *McKinney*	?	Y	Y	N	Y	Y	N
5 Ratchford	Y	Y	Y	N	Y	Y	Y
6 Moffett	?	?	Y	N	Y	Y	Y
DELAWARE							
AL *Evans*	?	?	Y	N	N	N	N
FLORIDA							
1 Hutto	Y	?	N	Y	N	N	N
2 Fuqua	?	Y	N	Y	N	N	N
3 Bennett	Y	Y	Y	Y	N	N	N
4 Chappell	?	Y	N	Y	N	N	N
5 *McCollum*	Y	Y	N	N	N	N	N
6 *Young*	Y	Y	N	N	N	N	N
7 Gibbons	Y	?	N	Y	N	N	N
8 Ireland	Y	Y	N	N	N	N	N
9 Nelson	+	+	X	+	X	X	-
10 *Bafalis*	Y	Y	N	Y	N	N	N
11 Mica	Y	Y	N	N	N	N	N
12 *Shaw*	Y	Y	N	N	N	N	N
13 Lehman	Y	Y	Y	N	Y	Y	Y
14 Pepper	?	Y	N	N	N	Y	Y
15 Fascell	Y	Y	Y	N	Y	Y	Y
GEORGIA							
1 Ginn	?	Y	N	Y	N	N	N
2 Hatcher	Y	Y	N	Y	N	N	N
3 Brinkley	Y	Y	N	Y	N	N	N
4 Levitas	Y	Y	N	N	N	N	N
5 Fowler	Y	Y	N	N	N	Y	N
6 *Gingrich*	Y	Y	N	N	N	N	N
7 McDonald	?	Y	N	N	N	N	N
8 Evans	Y	?	N	N	N	N	N
9 Jenkins	Y	Y	N	N	N	N	N
10 Barnard	?	?	?	?	?	?	?
HAWAII							
1 Heftel	?	Y	N	N	N	N	N
2 Akaka	Y	Y	N	N	N	N	N
IDAHO							
1 *Craig*	Y	Y	N	Y	N	N	N
2 *Hansen*	Y	Y	N	N	N	N	N
ILLINOIS							
1 Washington	?	?	#	?	#	#	#
2 Savage	?	?	?	?	?	?	?
3 Russo	?	Y	Y	N	Y	Y	Y
4 *Derwinski*	Y	Y	N	Y	N	N	N
5 Fary	Y	Y	N	N	N	N	N
6 *Hyde*	Y	Y	N	N	N	N	N
7 Collins	Y	Y	Y	N	Y	Y	Y
8 Rostenkowski	Y	Y	N	N	N	N	Y
9 Yates	Y	Y	Y	N	Y	Y	Y
10 *Porter*	Y	Y	Y	N	N	Y	N
11 Annunzio	Y	Y	N	N	N	N	N
12 *Crane, P.*	Y	Y	N	N	N	N	N
13 McClory	Y	Y	Y	N	N	N	N
14 *Erlenborn*	Y	Y	N	Y	N	N	N
15 *Corcoran*	Y	Y	N	Y	N	N	N
16 *Martin*	Y	Y	N	Y	N	N	N
17 *O'Brien*	Y	Y	Y	N	N	N	Y
18 *Michel*	?	Y	N	Y	N	N	N
19 *Railsback*	?	Y	Y	N	?	?	N
20 *Findley*	Y	Y	Y	N	N	N	N
21 *Madigan*	Y	Y	N	Y	N	N	N
22 *Crane, D.*	Y	Y	N	N	N	N	N
23 Price	Y	Y	N	N	N	N	N
24 Simon	Y	Y	Y	N	Y	Y	Y
INDIANA							
1 Benjamin	Y	Y	Y	Y	N	Y	Y
2 Fithian	Y	Y	Y	?	?	?	?
3 *Hiler*	Y	Y	N	N	N	N	N
4 *Coats*	Y	Y	N	Y	N	N	N
5 *Hillis*	Y	Y	N	N	N	N	N
6 Evans	Y	Y	Y	Y	N	Y	Y
7 *Myers*	Y	Y	N	Y	N	N	N
8 *Deckard*	Y	Y	N	Y	N	N	?
9 Hamilton	Y	Y	Y	N	N	Y	N
10 Sharp	Y	Y	Y	N	N	Y	N
11 Jacobs	Y	Y	?	N	Y	Y	Y
IOWA							
1 Leach	Y	Y	Y	N	Y	Y	N
2 *Tauke*	?	Y	Y	N	Y	N	N
3 Evans	N	N	N	Y	N	N	N
4 Smith	?	Y	Y	N	Y	Y	Y
5 Harkin	Y	Y	Y	N	Y	Y	Y
6 Bedell	Y	Y	Y	N	Y	Y	Y

Democrats *Republicans*

Corresponding to Congressional Record Votes 115, 116, 117, 118, 119, 120, 121

	106	107	108	109	110	111	112
KANSAS							
1 ***Roberts***	Y	Y	N	Y	N	N	N
2 ***Jeffries***	Y	Y	N	Y	N	N	N
3 ***Winn***	Y	Y	N	Y	N	N	N
4 Glickman	Y	Y	Y	N	N	Y	Y
5 ***Whittaker***	Y	Y	N	Y	N	N	N
KENTUCKY							
1 Hubbard	Y	Y	N	Y	N	N	N
2 Natcher	Y	Y	N	N	N	N	N
3 Mazzoli	Y	Y	Y	Y	N	Y	?
4 ***Snyder***	Y	Y	N	Y	N	N	Y
5 ***Rogers***	Y	Y	N	Y	N	N	N
6 ***Hopkins***	Y	Y	N	?	N	N	N
7 Perkins	Y	Y	N	Y	N	N	N
LOUISIANA							
1 ***Livingston***	Y	Y	?	N	N	N	N
2 Boggs	Y	Y	N	N	N	N	N
3 Tauzin	Y	Y	N	N	N	N	N
4 Roemer	Y	Y	N	N	N	N	N
5 Huckaby	Y	Y	N	Y	N	?	N
6 ***Moore***	Y	Y	N	N	N	Y	N
7 Breaux	Y	?	?	?	?	?	?
8 Long	Y	Y	Y	Y	N	N	N
MAINE							
1 ***Emery***	Y	Y	N	N	N	N	N
2 ***Snowe***	Y	Y	N	Y	N	N	N
MARYLAND							
1 Dyson	Y	Y	N	Y	N	N	N
2 Long	?	Y	Y	N	N	Y	N
3 Mikulski	Y	Y	Y	N	Y	Y	Y
4 ***Holt***	Y	?	X	?	N	N	N
5 Hoyer	Y	Y	Y	N	N	Y	N
6 Byron	Y	Y	N	Y	N	N	N
7 Mitchell	?	N	Y	N	Y	Y	Y
8 Barnes	Y	Y	Y	N	N	Y	N
MASSACHUSETTS							
1 ***Conte***	Y	Y	Y	N	Y	Y	N
2 Boland	Y	Y	Y	N	N	N	N
3 Early	?	Y	Y	?	?	?	?
4 Frank	Y	Y	Y	N	Y	Y	Y
5 Shannon	Y	Y	Y	N	Y	Y	Y
6 Mavroules	?	Y	Y	N	N	Y	N
7 Markey	Y	Y	Y	N	Y	Y	Y
8 O'Neill							
9 Moakley	Y	Y	Y	N	Y	Y	Y
10 ***Heckler***	Y	Y	Y	N	N	Y	Y
11 Donnelly	Y	Y	Y	N	Y	Y	Y
12 Studds	Y	Y	Y	N	Y	Y	Y
MICHIGAN							
1 Conyers	Y	Y	Y	N	Y	Y	Y
2 ***Pursell***	Y	Y	Y	N	Y	Y	Y
3 Wolpe	Y	Y	Y	N	Y	Y	Y
4 ***Siljander***	Y	Y	N	N	N	N	N
5 ***Sawyer***	Y	Y	N	Y	N	N	Y
6 ***Dunn***	Y	Y	Y	Y	Y	N	N
7 Kildee	Y	Y	Y	N	Y	Y	Y
8 Traxler	Y	Y	Y	N	N	Y	N
9 ***Vander Jagt***	Y	Y	N	Y	N	N	?
10 Albosta	Y	Y	Y	Y	N	N	N
11 ***Davis***	Y	Y	N	N	N	N	N
12 Bonior	Y	Y	Y	N	Y	Y	Y
13 Crockett	?	?	Y	?	Y	Y	Y
14 Hertel	Y	Y	Y	N	Y	Y	Y
15 Ford	Y	?	Y	N	?	Y	Y
16 Dingell	Y	?	Y	N	Y	Y	Y
17 Brodhead	Y	Y	Y	N	Y	Y	Y
18 Blanchard	?	Y	Y	N	N	Y	Y
19 ***Broomfield***	Y	Y	Y	Y	N	N	N
MINNESOTA							
1 ***Erdahl***	Y	Y	Y	N	Y	Y	Y
2 ***Hagedorn***	?	?	?	?	?	?	?
3 ***Frenzel***	?	?	?	?	?	?	?
4 Vento	Y	Y	Y	N	Y	Y	Y
5 Sabo	Y	Y	Y	N	Y	Y	Y
6 ***Weber***	Y	Y	Y	N	Y	Y	N
7 ***Stangeland***	?	Y	N	Y	N	N	N
8 Oberstar	Y	Y	Y	N	Y	Y	Y
MISSISSIPPI							
1 Whitten	Y	Y	N	N	N	N	N
2 Bowen	Y	Y	N	Y	N	N	N
3 Montgomery	Y	Y	N	Y	N	N	N
4 Dowdy*						N	N
5 ***Lott***	?	?	N	Y	N	N	N
MISSOURI							
1 Clay	Y	?	Y	N	Y	Y	?
2 Young	Y	Y	Y	N	Y	N	N
3 Gephardt	?	Y	?	N	N	N	N
4 Skelton	Y	Y	N	Y	N	N	N
5 Bolling	?	Y	Y	N	N	Y	?
6 ***Coleman***	Y	Y	N	N	N	N	N
7 ***Taylor***	?	Y	N	Y	N	N	N
8 ***Bailey***	Y	Y	N	N	N	N	N
9 Volkmer	?	?	N	N	N	Y	Y
10 ***Emerson***	Y	Y	N	Y	N	N	N
MONTANA							
1 Williams	?	Y	Y	N	N	Y	Y
2 ***Marlenee***	?	?	?	?	?	?	?
NEBRASKA							
1 ***Bereuter***	Y	Y	N	Y	N	N	Y
2 ***Daub***	Y	Y	N	Y	N	N	N
3 ***Smith***	Y	Y	N	Y	N	N	N
NEVADA							
AL Santini	Y	Y	Y	N	N	Y	N
NEW HAMPSHIRE							
1 D'Amours	Y	Y	?	N	N	Y	N
2 ***Gregg***	Y	Y	N	N	N	Y	N
NEW JERSEY							
1 Florio	Y	Y	Y	Y	N	Y	?
2 Hughes	Y	Y	Y	N	N	Y	N
3 Howard	Y	Y	Y	N	N	Y	N
4 ***Smith***	?	Y	Y	N	Y	N	N
5 ***Fenwick***	?	Y	Y	N	N	Y	N
6 ***Forsythe***	?	Y	Y	Y	Y	Y	Y
7 ***Roukema***	?	Y	Y	Y	N	N	N
8 Roe	Y	Y	Y	N	N	N	N
9 ***Hollenbeck***	Y	Y	Y	Y	Y	Y	?
10 Rodino	Y	Y	Y	N	Y	Y	Y
11 Minish	Y	Y	Y	N	N	Y	Y
12 ***Rinaldo***	?	Y	Y	N	N	Y	N
13 ***Courter***	Y	Y	N	N	N	N	N
14 Guarini	Y	Y	#	N	N	Y	Y
15 Dwyer	Y	Y	Y	N	N	Y	Y
NEW MEXICO							
1 ***Lujan***	Y	Y	N	Y	N	N	Y
2 ***Skeen***	Y	Y	Y	Y	N	N	N
NEW YORK							
1 ***Carney***	Y	Y	N	N	N	N	N
2 Downey	Y	Y	Y	N	Y	Y	Y
3 ***Carman***	Y	Y	N	N	N	N	N
4 ***Lent***	Y	Y	N	Y	N	N	N
5 ***McGrath***	Y	Y	N	Y	N	N	N
6 ***LeBoutillier***	Y	Y	N	Y	N	N	N
7 Addabbo	Y	Y	Y	Y	Y	Y	Y
8 Rosenthal	Y	Y	Y	N	Y	Y	Y
9 Ferraro	Y	Y	Y	N	N	Y	Y
10 Biaggi	Y	Y	Y	N	N	N	Y
11 Scheuer	Y	Y	Y	N	Y	Y	?
12 Chisholm	?	?	Y	?	Y	#	?
13 Solarz	?	Y	N	N	N	Y	Y
14 Richmond	?	?	Y	?	Y	Y	Y
15 Zeferetti	Y	Y	N	Y	N	N	N
16 Schumer	?	P	Y	N	Y	Y	?
17 ***Molinari***	Y	Y	N	Y	N	N	N
18 ***Green***	Y	Y	Y	Y	Y	Y	Y
19 Rangel	?	Y	#	N	Y	Y	Y
20 Weiss	Y	Y	Y	N	Y	Y	Y
21 Garcia	?	Y	Y	N	Y	Y	Y
22 Bingham	Y	Y	Y	N	Y	Y	Y
23 Peyser	Y	Y	Y	N	N	Y	Y
24 Ottinger	P	P	Y	N	Y	Y	Y
25 ***Fish***	Y	Y	Y	N	N	N	N
26 ***Gilman***	Y	Y	N	N	N	N	N
27 McHugh	Y	Y	Y	N	N	Y	N
28 Stratton	Y	Y	N	Y	N	N	N
29 ***Solomon***	Y	Y	N	Y	N	N	N
30 ***Martin***	?	Y	N	Y	N	N	N
31 ***Mitchell***	Y	Y	N	N	N	N	N
32 ***Wortley***	Y	Y	Y	Y	N	N	N
33 ***Lee***	Y	Y	N	N	N	N	?
34 ***Horton***	?	Y	N	N	N	N	?
35 ***Conable***	Y	Y	N	Y	N	N	Y
36 LaFalce	Y	Y	N	N	N	Y	Y
37 Nowak	Y	Y	Y	N	Y	Y	Y
38 ***Kemp***	?	?	?	?	?	?	?
39 Lundine	?	Y	Y	Y	Y	Y	Y
NORTH CAROLINA							
1 Jones	?	?	X	?	X	X	X
2 Fountain	Y	Y	N	N	N	N	N
3 Whitley	Y	Y	N	Y	N	N	N
4 Andrews	?	?	?	?	?	?	?
5 Neal	?	Y	Y	N	N	N	N
6 ***Johnston***	Y	Y	N	Y	N	N	N
7 Rose	?	?	X	?	?	?	?
8 Hefner	Y	Y	N	N	N	N	Y
9 ***Martin***	Y	Y	N	N	N	N	N
10 ***Broyhill***	Y	Y	N	Y	N	N	N
11 ***Hendon***	Y	Y	N	Y	N	N	N
NORTH DAKOTA							
AL Dorgan	Y	Y	Y	N	N	Y	Y
OHIO							
1 ***Gradison***	?	Y	Y	Y	N	N	N
2 Luken	Y	Y	Y	Y	N	N	N
3 Hall	Y	Y	Y	Y	Y	N	Y
4 Vacancy							
5 ***Latta***	?	Y	N	Y	N	N	N
6 ***McEwen***	Y	Y	Y	Y	N	N	N
7 ***Brown***	Y	Y	N	Y	N	N	N
8 ***Kindness***	Y	Y	N	?	N	N	N
9 ***Weber***	Y	Y	Y	Y	N	N	N
10 ***Miller***	Y	Y	N	Y	N	N	N
11 ***Stanton***	Y	Y	N	Y	N	N	N
12 Shamansky	Y	Y	N	N	N	N	Y
13 Pease	Y	Y	Y	N	Y	Y	Y
14 Seiberling	Y	Y	Y	N	N	Y	Y
15 ***Wylie***	Y	Y	N	Y	Y	N	Y
16 ***Regula***	Y	Y	N	Y	N	N	N
17 ***Ashbrook***	Y	Y	N	Y	N	?	?
18 Applegate	?	?	Y	Y	N	N	N
19 ***Williams***	Y	Y	N	Y	N	N	N
20 Oakar	Y	Y	Y	N	N	N	Y
21 Stokes	Y	?	Y	N	Y	Y	Y
22 Eckart	Y	Y	Y	N	Y	Y	Y
23 Mottl	Y	Y	N	Y	N	N	Y
OKLAHOMA							
1 Jones	Y	Y	Y	Y	N	N	Y
2 Synar	Y	Y	Y	N	N	Y	Y
3 Watkins	Y	Y	N	Y	N	N	Y
4 McCurdy	Y	Y	N	Y	N	Y	N
5 ***Edwards***	?	Y	N	N	N	N	Y
6 English	Y	Y	Y	N	N	N	Y
OREGON							
1 AuCoin	Y	Y	Y	N	Y	Y	Y
2 ***Smith***	Y	Y	N	Y	N	N	N
3 Wyden	Y	Y	Y	N	Y	Y	Y
4 Weaver	Y	N	Y	N	Y	Y	Y
PENNSYLVANIA							
1 Foglietta	Y	Y	Y	Y	N	Y	Y
2 Gray	Y	Y	Y	N	Y	Y	Y
3 Vacancy							
4 ***Dougherty***	Y	?	N	Y	N	N	N
5 ***Schulze***	?	Y	N	Y	N	N	N
6 Yatron	Y	Y	N	N	N	N	Y
7 Edgar	Y	Y	Y	N	Y	Y	Y
8 ***Coyne, J.***	Y	Y	Y	Y	N	N	N
9 ***Shuster***	Y	Y	N	Y	N	N	N
10 ***McDade***	?	?	?	?	?	?	?
11 ***Nelligan***	Y	Y	N	Y	N	N	N
12 Murtha	Y	Y	N	Y	N	N	N
13 ***Coughlin***	Y	Y	N	N	Y	N	N
14 Coyne, W.	Y	Y	Y	N	Y	N	N
15 ***Ritter***	Y	Y	Y	N	N	N	Y
16 ***Walker***	Y	Y	N	Y	N	N	Y
17 Ertel	Y	Y	Y	N	N	Y	Y
18 Walgren	Y	Y	Y	N	Y	Y	Y
19 ***Goodling***	Y	Y	Y	Y	N	N	?
20 Gaydos	Y	Y	Y	N	N	N	N
21 Bailey	Y	Y	N	N	N	N	N
22 Murphy	Y	Y	Y	Y	N	N	N
23 ***Clinger***	Y	Y	Y	Y	N	N	N
24 ***Marks***	Y	Y	Y	N	N	Y	N
25 Atkinson	?	Y	Y	N	N	Y	Y
RHODE ISLAND							
1 St Germain	Y	Y	Y	Y	Y	Y	Y
2 ***Schneider***	Y	Y	Y	Y	Y	Y	Y
SOUTH CAROLINA							
1 ***Hartnett***	Y	Y	N	Y	N	N	N
2 ***Spence***	Y	Y	N	Y	N	N	N
3 Derrick	Y	Y	Y	N	N	N	Y
4 ***Campbell***	Y	Y	N	Y	N	N	N
5 Holland	Y	Y	Y	Y	N	N	N
6 ***Napier***	Y	Y	N	Y	N	N	N
SOUTH DAKOTA							
1 Daschle	?	Y	Y	N	N	N	Y
2 ***Roberts***	Y	Y	N	Y	N	N	N
TENNESSEE							
1 ***Quillen***	Y	Y	N	Y	N	N	?
2 ***Duncan***	Y	Y	N	Y	N	N	N
3 Bouquard	Y	Y	N	Y	N	N	N
4 Gore	Y	Y	Y	N	N	Y	N
5 Boner	Y	Y	Y	Y	N	N	N
6 ***Beard***	Y	Y	N	Y	N	N	N
7 Jones	Y	Y	Y	Y	N	N	N
8 Ford	?	Y	Y	N	Y	Y	Y
TEXAS							
1 Hall, S.	Y	?	N	N	N	N	N
2 Wilson	Y	Y	N	N	N	N	N
3 ***Collins***	Y	Y	N	Y	N	N	N
4 Hall, R.	Y	?	N	N	N	N	N
5 Mattox	Y	Y	Y	N	N	Y	Y
6 Gramm	Y	Y	N	Y	N	N	N
7 ***Archer***	Y	Y	N	Y	N	N	N
8 ***Fields***	Y	Y	N	Y	N	N	N
9 Brooks	Y	Y	Y	N	N	N	Y
10 Pickle	Y	Y	Y	N	N	N	N
11 Leath	?	Y	N	Y	N	N	N
12 Wright	Y	Y	?	Y	N	N	?
13 Hightower	Y	Y	N	Y	N	N	N
14 Patman	Y	Y	N	Y	N	N	N
15 de la Garza	Y	Y	Y	N	N	N	Y
16 White	Y	Y	N	Y	N	N	N
17 Stenholm	Y	Y	N	Y	N	N	N
18 Leland	Y	Y	Y	N	Y	Y	Y
19 Hance	Y	Y	N	Y	N	N	N
20 Gonzalez	Y	Y	N	N	N	N	Y
21 ***Loeffler***	Y	Y	N	Y	N	N	N
22 ***Paul***	Y	Y	Y	N	Y	Y	N
23 Kazen	Y	Y	N	N	N	N	N
24 Frost	Y	Y	N	Y	N	N	N
UTAH							
1 ***Hansen***	Y	Y	N	Y	N	N	N
2 ***Marriott***	Y	Y	N	Y	N	N	N
VERMONT							
AL ***Jeffords***	Y	Y	Y	N	Y	Y	Y
VIRGINIA							
1 ***Trible***	Y	Y	N	Y	N	N	N
2 ***Whitehurst***	?	Y	N	Y	N	N	N
3 ***Bliley***	Y	Y	N	Y	N	N	N
4 ***Daniel, R.***	Y	Y	N	Y	N	N	N
5 Daniel, D.	Y	Y	N	Y	N	N	N
6 ***Butler***	Y	Y	N	Y	N	N	N
7 ***Robinson***	Y	Y	N	Y	N	N	N
8 ***Parris***	Y	Y	N	Y	N	N	N
9 ***Wampler***	?	Y	N	?	N	N	N
10 ***Wolf***	Y	Y	N	N	N	N	N
WASHINGTON							
1 ***Pritchard***	?	Y	Y	Y	N	Y	Y
2 Swift	Y	Y	Y	N	N	Y	N
3 Bonker	Y	?	Y	N	N	Y	N
4 ***Morrison***	?	Y	N	Y	N	N	N
5 Foley	Y	Y	Y	N	N	Y	N
6 Dicks	Y	Y	N	N	N	Y	N
7 Lowry	Y	Y	Y	N	Y	Y	Y
WEST VIRGINIA							
1 Mollohan	Y	Y	N	Y	N	N	N
2 ***Benedict***	Y	Y	Y	N	Y	Y	N
3 ***Staton***	Y	Y	N	Y	N	N	N
4 Rahall	Y	Y	Y	N	Y	Y	N
WISCONSIN							
1 Aspin	Y	Y	Y	N	N	Y	Y
2 Kastenmeier	Y	Y	Y	N	Y	Y	Y
3 ***Gunderson***	Y	Y	N	Y	N	N	Y
4 Zablocki	Y	Y	N	Y	N	N	N
5 Reuss	Y	Y	Y	N	Y	Y	Y
6 ***Petri***	Y	Y	Y	Y	N	Y	Y
7 Obey	?	Y	Y	N	N	Y	Y
8 ***Roth***	Y	Y	N	Y	N	N	?
9 ***Sensenbrenner***	Y	Y	Y	Y	N	N	N
WYOMING							
AL ***Cheney***	?	Y	N	Y	N	N	N

** Rep. Wayne Dowdy, D-Miss., was sworn in July 9, 1981. The first vote for which he was eligible was CQ vote 111.*

Democrats ***Republicans***

113. Procedural Motion. Ashbrook, R-Ohio, motion to approve the House *Journal* of Thursday, July 9. Motion agreed to 345-11: R 156-7; D 189-4 (ND 125-4, SD 64-0), July 10, 1981.

114. HR 3519. Defense Department Authorization. Price, D-Ill., motion that the House resolve itself into the Committee of the Whole for further consideration of the bill to authorize Defense Department funding for fiscal 1982. Motion agreed to 370-2: R 169-1; D 201-1 (ND 136-1, SD 65-0), July 10, 1981.

115. HR 3519. Defense Department Authorization. Government Operations Committee amendment to delete a provision authorizing the Defense Department to use grants (rather than contracts) for research and procurement. Rejected 190-194: R 49-127; D 141-67 (ND 117-26, SD 24-41), July 10, 1981.

116. HR 4034. HUD-Independent Agencies Appropriations, Fiscal 1982. Moakley, D-Mass., motion to adopt the rule (H Res 171) providing for House floor consideration of the Department of Housing and Urban Development appropriations bill. Motion agreed to 336-13: R 155-8; D 181-5 (ND 121-3, SD 60-2), July 10, 1981.

117. HR 4034. HUD-Independent Agencies Appropriations, Fiscal 1982. Boland, D-Mass., motion that the House resolve itself into the Committee of the Whole for consideration of the bill making appropriations for the Department of Housing and Urban Development and independent agencies. Motion agreed to 326-7: R 149-4; D 177-3 (ND 120-2, SD 57-1), July 10, 1981.

118. HR 3975. Production of Oil From Tar Sands. Santini, D-Nev., motion to suspend the rules and pass the bill to facilitate the production of oil from tar sands deposits on federal lands. Motion agreed to 416-0: R 187-0; D 229-0 (ND 155-0, SD 74-0), July 14, 1981. A two-thirds majority vote (278 in this case) is required for passage under suspension of the rules. A "yea" was a vote supporting the president's position.

119. HR 3519. Defense Department Authorization. Government Operations Committee amendment to delete from the bill increases in three thresholds on Defense Department purchases: an increase from $10,000 to $25,000 of the ceiling on the use of simplified small purchase procedures; an increase from $100,000 to $500,000 of the minimum amount of cost and pricing data that must be certified by contractors under the Truth in Negotiations Act; and an increase from $100,000 to $5 million of the maximum contract that can be negotiated by a service secretary for experimental, development or research work. Rejected 109-311: R 11-178; D 98-133 (ND 88-66, SD 10-67), July 14, 1981.

120. HR 3519. Defense Department Authorization. Shaw, R-Fla., amendment, to the Judiciary Committee amendment *(see vote 121, p. 48-H)*, to permit U.S. armed forces personnel to participate, under certain circumstances, in illegal-drug seizures or arrests outside the land area of the United States. Adopted 248-168: R 153-32; D 95-136 (ND 35-118, SD 60-18), July 15, 1981.

KEY

Y Voted for (yea).
Paired for.
+ Announced for.
N Voted against (nay).
X Paired against.
- Announced against.
P Voted "present".
C Voted "present" to avoid possible conflict of interest.
? Did not vote or otherwise make a position known.

	113	114	115	116	117	118	119	120
ALABAMA								
1 *Edwards*	Y	Y	N	Y	Y	Y	N	Y
2 *Dickinson*	N	Y	N	Y	Y	Y	N	Y
3 Nichols	Y	Y	N	Y	Y	Y	N	Y
4 Bevill	Y	Y	N	?	Y	Y	N	Y
5 Flippo	?	?	X	?	?	Y	N	Y
6 *Smith*	Y	Y	N	Y	Y	Y	N	Y
7 Shelby	Y	Y	N	Y	?	Y	N	Y
ALASKA								
AL *Young*	?	?	?	Y	Y	Y	N	Y
ARIZONA								
1 *Rhodes*	Y	Y	N	Y	Y	Y	N	Y
2 Udall	Y	Y	Y	Y	Y	Y	N	N
3 *Stump*	Y	Y	N	Y	Y	Y	N	Y
4 *Rudd*	?	?	?	?	?	Y	N	Y
ARKANSAS								
1 Alexander	Y	Y	N	Y	Y	Y	N	Y
2 *Bethune*	Y	Y	N	Y	Y	Y	N	Y
3 *Hammerschmidt*	Y	Y	N	Y	Y	Y	N	Y
4 Anthony	?	?	?	?	?	Y	N	Y
CALIFORNIA								
1 *Chappie*	Y	Y	N	Y	Y	Y	N	Y
2 *Clausen*	Y	Y	N	Y	Y	Y	N	Y
3 Matsui	Y	Y	Y	Y	Y	Y	Y	N
4 Fazio	Y	Y	Y	Y	Y	Y	N	Y
5 Burton, J.	Y	Y	Y	?	?	Y	Y	N
6 Burton, P.	Y	Y	Y	Y	Y	Y	Y	N
7 Miller	?	?	#	?	?	Y	#	N
8 Dellums	Y	Y	Y	Y	Y	Y	Y	N
9 Stark	Y	Y	Y	?	Y	?	Y	N
10 Edwards	Y	Y	Y	Y	Y	Y	Y	N
11 Lantos	Y	Y	Y	Y	Y	Y	N	-
12 *McCloskey*	?	?	?	?	?	Y	N	N
13 Mineta	Y	Y	Y	Y	Y	Y	N	N
14 *Shumway*	Y	Y	N	Y	Y	Y	N	Y
15 Coelho	Y	Y	Y	Y	Y	Y	N	N
16 Panetta	Y	Y	Y	Y	Y	Y	N	N
17 *Pashayan*	Y	Y	N	Y	Y	Y	N	Y
18 *Thomas*	Y	Y	Y	Y	Y	Y	N	Y
19 *Lagomarsino*	Y	Y	Y	Y	Y	Y	N	Y
20 *Goldwater*	Y	?	?	?	?	Y	N	Y
21 *Fiedler*	Y	Y	N	Y	Y	Y	N	Y
22 *Moorhead*	Y	Y	N	Y	Y	Y	N	Y
23 Beilenson	Y	Y	Y	Y	Y	Y	Y	N
24 Waxman	Y	?	Y	Y	Y	Y	N	Y
25 Roybal	Y	Y	Y	Y	Y	Y	Y	P
26 *Rousselot*	Y	Y	N	Y	Y	Y	N	Y
27 *Dornan*	?	Y	N	Y	Y	Y	N	Y
28 Dixon	?	?	Y	?	Y	Y	Y	N
29 Hawkins	Y	Y	Y	Y	Y	Y	?	N
30 Danielson	Y	Y	Y	Y	Y	Y	Y	N
31 Dymally	Y	Y	Y	Y	?	Y	?	N
32 Anderson	Y	Y	Y	Y	Y	Y	N	N
33 *Grisham*	Y	Y	Y	Y	Y	Y	N	Y
34 *Lungren*	Y	Y	Y	Y	Y	Y	N	Y
35 *Dreier*	Y	Y	N	Y	Y	Y	N	Y
36 Brown	Y	Y	Y	Y	Y	Y	Y	N
37 *Lewis*	Y	Y	N	Y	Y	Y	N	Y
38 *Patterson*	Y	Y	Y	Y	Y	Y	Y	N
39 *Dannemeyer*	Y	Y	Y	Y	Y	Y	Y	Y
40 *Badham*	Y	Y	N	Y	Y	Y	N	Y
41 *Lowery*	Y	Y	N	Y	Y	Y	N	Y
42 *Hunter*	Y	Y	N	Y	Y	Y	N	Y
43 *Burgener*	Y	Y	Y	Y	Y	Y	N	Y
COLORADO								
1 Schroeder	N	Y	Y	+	+	Y	Y	N
2 Wirth	?	?	#	?	?	Y	N	Y
3 Kogovsek	Y	Y	Y	Y	Y	Y	N	Y
4 *Brown*	Y	Y	N	N	Y	Y	N	Y

	113	114	115	116	117	118	119	120
5 *Kramer*	Y	Y	N	Y	Y	Y	N	Y
CONNECTICUT								
1 Cotter	?	?	?	?	?	?	?	?
2 Gejdenson	Y	Y	Y	Y	Y	Y	N	N
3 *DeNardis*	?	?	Y	Y	Y	?	Y	Y
4 *McKinney*	Y	Y	Y	Y	?	Y	N	Y
5 Ratchford	Y	Y	Y	Y	Y	Y	Y	N
6 Moffett	?	?	Y	Y	Y	Y	Y	N
DELAWARE								
AL *Evans*	Y	Y	N	Y	Y	Y	N	N
FLORIDA								
1 Hutto	Y	Y	N	Y	Y	?	N	Y
2 Fuqua	?	?	?	?	?	Y	N	Y
3 Bennett	Y	Y	N	Y	Y	Y	N	Y
4 Chappell	Y	Y	N	Y	Y	Y	N	Y
5 *McCollum*	Y	Y	N	Y	Y	Y	N	Y
6 *Young*	Y	Y	N	Y	Y	Y	N	Y
7 Gibbons	Y	Y	N	Y	Y	Y	N	Y
8 Ireland	Y	Y	N	Y	Y	Y	N	Y
9 Nelson	+	+	-	+	+	Y	N	Y
10 *Bafalis*	Y	Y	N	Y	Y	Y	N	Y
11 Mica	Y	Y	N	Y	Y	Y	N	Y
12 *Shaw*	Y	Y	Y	Y	Y	Y	N	Y
13 Lehman	Y	Y	Y	Y	Y	Y	N	N
14 Pepper	Y	Y	N	Y	Y	Y	N	Y
15 Fascell	Y	Y	Y	Y	Y	Y	Y	Y
GEORGIA								
1 Ginn	?	?	X	?	?	Y	N	Y
2 Hatcher	Y	Y	N	Y	Y	Y	N	Y
3 Brinkley	Y	Y	N	Y	Y	Y	N	Y
4 Levitas	Y	Y	N	Y	Y	Y	N	Y
5 Fowler	Y	Y	N	Y	Y	Y	N	Y
6 *Gingrich*	Y	Y	N	Y	Y	Y	N	Y
7 McDonald	Y	Y	N	N	N	Y	N	Y
8 Evans	Y	Y	N	Y	Y	Y	N	Y
9 Jenkins	Y	Y	N	Y	Y	?	N	Y
10 Barnard	?	?	X	?	?	Y	N	Y
HAWAII								
1 Heftel	Y	Y	Y	Y	Y	Y	N	Y
2 Akaka	Y	Y	N	Y	Y	Y	N	Y
IDAHO								
1 *Craig*	Y	Y	N	N	Y	Y	N	Y
2 *Hansen*	?	Y	N	N	Y	Y	N	Y
ILLINOIS								
1 Washington	?	?	?	?	?	Y	Y	N
2 Savage	?	?	?	?	?	?	?	?
3 Russo	Y	Y	Y	Y	Y	Y	Y	N
4 *Derwinski*	N	Y	N	N	N	Y	N	Y
5 Fary	Y	Y	N	Y	Y	Y	N	N
6 *Hyde*	Y	Y	N	?	?	Y	N	Y
7 Collins	Y	Y	Y	Y	Y	Y	N	N
8 Rostenkowski	Y	Y	Y	Y	Y	Y	N	Y
9 Yates	Y	Y	Y	Y	Y	Y	N	Y
10 *Porter*	Y	Y	Y	+	+	Y	N	Y
11 Annunzio	Y	Y	N	Y	Y	Y	N	N
12 *Crane, P.*	?	Y	N	Y	Y	Y	N	Y
13 *McClory*	Y	Y	Y	Y	Y	Y	N	Y
14 *Erlenborn*	Y	Y	N	Y	Y	Y	N	Y
15 *Corcoran*	Y	Y	Y	Y	Y	Y	N	Y
16 *Martin*	Y	Y	N	Y	Y	Y	N	Y
17 *O'Brien*	Y	Y	N	Y	Y	Y	N	Y
18 *Michel*	Y	Y	N	Y	Y	Y	N	Y
19 *Railsback*	Y	Y	?	?	Y	Y	N	Y
20 *Findley*	Y	Y	N	Y	Y	Y	N	N
21 *Madigan*	Y	Y	N	Y	Y	Y	N	Y
22 *Crane, D.*	Y	Y	N	?	?	Y	N	Y
23 Price	Y	Y	N	Y	Y	Y	N	N
24 Simon	Y	Y	Y	?	Y	Y	N	Y
INDIANA								
1 Benjamin	Y	Y	N	Y	Y	Y	N	Y
2 Fithian	?	?	?	?	?	?	?	Y
3 *Hiler*	Y	Y	N	Y	Y	Y	N	Y
4 *Coats*	Y	Y	N	Y	Y	Y	N	Y
5 *Hillis*	Y	Y	N	?	?	Y	N	Y
6 Evans	?	Y	Y	Y	Y	Y	Y	Y
7 *Myers*	Y	?	N	Y	Y	Y	N	Y
8 *Deckard*	Y	Y	Y	Y	Y	Y	N	?
9 Hamilton	Y	Y	Y	Y	Y	Y	N	Y
10 Sharp	Y	Y	Y	Y	Y	Y	N	N
11 Jacobs	Y	Y	N	Y	Y	Y	N	Y
IOWA								
1 *Leach*	?	Y	Y	Y	Y	Y	N	N
2 *Tauke*	Y	Y	Y	Y	Y	Y	N	N
3 *Evans*	N	N	N	Y	N	Y	N	Y
4 Smith	Y	Y	Y	Y	Y	Y	N	Y
5 Harkin	?	?	?	?	?	?	Y	N
6 Bedell	Y	Y	Y	?	?	Y	N	Y

Democrats *Republicans*

Corresponding to Congressional Record Votes 122, 123, 124, 125, 126, 127, 128, 129

	113	114	115	116	117	118	119	120
KANSAS								
1 ***Roberts***	Y	Y	N	Y	Y	Y	N	Y
2 ***Jeffries***	Y	Y	N	Y	Y	Y	N	Y
3 ***Winn***	Y	Y	N	Y	Y	Y	N	Y
4 Glickman	Y	Y	Y	Y	Y	Y	N	N
5 ***Whittaker***	Y	Y	N	Y	Y	Y	N	Y
KENTUCKY								
1 Hubbard	Y	Y	N	Y	Y	Y	N	Y
2 Natcher	Y	Y	N	Y	Y	Y	N	N
3 Mazzoli	?	+	+	+	+	Y	N	N
4 ***Snyder***	Y	Y	N	Y	Y	Y	N	N
5 ***Rogers***	Y	Y	N	Y	Y	Y	N	Y
6 ***Hopkins***	Y	Y	N	Y	Y	Y	N	Y
7 Perkins	Y	Y	N	Y	Y	Y	N	N
LOUISIANA								
1 ***Livingston***	Y	Y	N	Y	?	Y	N	Y
2 Boggs	Y	Y	Y	Y	Y	Y	N	Y
3 Tauzin	Y	Y	Y	Y	Y	Y	N	Y
4 Roemer	Y	Y	Y	Y	Y	Y	N	Y
5 Huckaby	Y	Y	N	Y	?	Y	N	Y
6 ***Moore***	Y	Y	Y	Y	Y	Y	N	Y
7 Breaux	?	?	?	?	?	?	N	Y
8 Long	Y	Y	Y	Y	Y	Y	N	N
MAINE								
1 ***Emery***	Y	Y	N	Y	Y	Y	N	N
2 ***Snowe***	Y	Y	Y	Y	Y	Y	N	Y
MARYLAND								
1 Dyson	Y	Y	N	Y	Y	Y	N	Y
2 Long	Y	?	Y	?	?	Y	Y	N
3 Mikulski	Y	Y	Y	Y	Y	Y	Y	N
4 ***Holt***	?	?	X	?	?	Y	N	Y
5 Hoyer	Y	Y	N	Y	Y	Y	N	N
6 Byron	?	Y	N	Y	Y	Y	N	Y
7 Mitchell	N	N	Y	Y	N	Y	Y	X
8 Barnes	Y	Y	Y	Y	Y	Y	N	N
MASSACHUSETTS								
1 ***Conte***	Y	Y	N	Y	Y	Y	Y	N
2 Boland	Y	Y	N	Y	Y	Y	N	N
3 Early	?	?	?	?	?	Y	N	Y
4 Frank	?	?	?	Y	Y	Y	Y	N
5 Shannon	Y	Y	Y	Y	Y	Y	N	N
6 Mavroules	Y	Y	N	?	?	Y	N	Y
7 Markey	Y	Y	Y	Y	Y	Y	Y	N
8 O'Neill								
9 Moakley	Y	Y	Y	Y	Y	Y	Y	N
10 ***Heckler***	Y	Y	Y	Y	Y	Y	Y	N
11 Donnelly	Y	Y	Y	Y	Y	Y	N	N
12 Studds	Y	Y	Y	Y	Y	Y	Y	N
MICHIGAN								
1 Conyers	Y	Y	Y	Y	Y	Y	Y	N
2 ***Pursell***	Y	Y	Y	?	?	Y	Y	N
3 Wolpe	Y	Y	Y	Y	Y	Y	Y	N
4 ***Siljander***	?	?	?	?	?	Y	N	Y
5 ***Sawyer***	Y	Y	Y	Y	Y	Y	N	Y
6 ***Dunn***	Y	Y	Y	Y	Y	Y	N	Y
7 Kildee	Y	Y	Y	Y	Y	Y	Y	N
8 Traxler	Y	Y	?	?	?	Y	Y	Y
9 ***Vander Jagt***	?	?	?	?	?	Y	N	?
10 Albosta	Y	Y	N	?	Y	Y	N	Y
11 ***Davis***	?	?	N	Y	Y	Y	N	Y
12 Bonior	Y	Y	Y	Y	Y	Y	Y	?
13 Crockett	?	Y	Y	?	?	?	Y	N
14 Hertel	Y	Y	N	Y	Y	Y	N	N
15 Ford	Y	Y	Y	Y	Y	?	?	N
16 Dingell	?	Y	Y	Y	Y	Y	Y	N
17 Brodhead	Y	Y	Y	?	?	Y	Y	N
18 Blanchard	?	Y	Y	Y	Y	Y	N	N
19 ***Broomfield***	Y	Y	Y	Y	N	Y	N	Y
MINNESOTA								
1 ***Erdahl***	Y	Y	Y	Y	Y	Y	N	Y
2 ***Hagedorn***	Y	Y	N	Y	Y	Y	N	Y
3 ***Frenzel***	?	?	?	?	?	Y	N	Y
4 Vento	Y	Y	Y	Y	Y	Y	Y	N
5 Sabo	N	Y	Y	Y	Y	Y	Y	N
6 ***Weber***	Y	Y	Y	Y	Y	Y	N	Y
7 ***Stangeland***	Y	Y	N	Y	Y	Y	N	Y
8 Oberstar	Y	Y	Y	Y	Y	Y	Y	N
MISSISSIPPI								
1 Whitten	Y	Y	Y	Y	Y	Y	Y	Y
2 Bowen	Y	Y	N	Y	Y	Y	N	Y
3 Montgomery	Y	Y	N	Y	?	Y	N	Y
4 Dowdy	Y	Y	N	Y	Y	Y	N	Y
5 ***Lott***	Y	Y	N	Y	Y	Y	N	Y
MISSOURI								
1 Clay	?	?	?	?	?	Y	Y	N
2 Young	Y	Y	N	?	?	Y	N	Y
3 Gephardt	Y	Y	?	?	?	Y	N	Y
4 Skelton	Y	Y	N	Y	Y	Y	N	Y
5 Bolling	?	?	?	?	?	?	Y	N
6 ***Coleman***	?	?	?	?	?	Y	N	Y
7 ***Taylor***	Y	Y	N	?	?	Y	N	Y
8 ***Bailey***	Y	Y	Y	Y	Y	Y	Y	Y
9 Volkmer	Y	Y	N	Y	Y	Y	N	N
10 ***Emerson***	Y	Y	N	Y	Y	Y	N	Y
MONTANA								
1 Williams	Y	?	Y	?	Y	Y	N	N
2 ***Marlenee***	?	?	?	?	?	Y	N	Y
NEBRASKA								
1 ***Bereuter***	Y	Y	N	Y	Y	Y	N	Y
2 ***Daub***	Y	Y	Y	Y	Y	Y	N	Y
3 ***Smith***	Y	Y	Y	Y	Y	Y	N	Y
NEVADA								
AL Santini	Y	Y	Y	Y	?	Y	?	?
NEW HAMPSHIRE								
1 D'Amours	Y	Y	Y	Y	Y	Y	N	N
2 ***Gregg***	Y	Y	Y	Y	?	Y	N	N
NEW JERSEY								
1 Florio	?	?	#	?	?	Y	Y	Y
2 Hughes	Y	Y	Y	Y	Y	Y	Y	N
3 Howard	?	?	#	?	?	Y	Y	N
4 ***Smith***	Y	Y	N	Y	Y	Y	N	Y
5 ***Fenwick***	Y	Y	Y	Y	Y	Y	N	N
6 ***Forsythe***	N	Y	Y	Y	?	Y	N	N
7 ***Roukema***	Y	Y	Y	Y	Y	Y	N	N
8 Roe	Y	Y	Y	Y	Y	Y	N	N
9 ***Hollenbeck***	?	?	Y	Y	Y	Y	Y	N
10 Rodino	Y	Y	Y	Y	Y	Y	Y	N
11 Minish	Y	Y	Y	Y	Y	Y	Y	Y
12 ***Rinaldo***	Y	Y	N	Y	Y	Y	N	N
13 ***Courter***	Y	Y	N	Y	Y	Y	N	Y
14 Guarini	Y	Y	Y	Y	Y	Y	N	N
15 Dwyer	Y	Y	Y	Y	Y	Y	Y	N
NEW MEXICO								
1 ***Lujan***	Y	Y	Y	Y	Y	Y	N	Y
2 ***Skeen***	Y	Y	N	Y	Y	Y	N	Y
NEW YORK								
1 ***Carney***	Y	Y	N	Y	Y	Y	N	N
2 Downey	Y	Y	Y	Y	Y	Y	N	N
3 ***Carman***	Y	Y	N	Y	Y	Y	N	Y
4 ***Lent***	Y	Y	N	Y	?	Y	N	N
5 ***McGrath***	Y	Y	Y	Y	Y	Y	N	Y
6 ***LeBoutillier***	Y	Y	N	Y	Y	Y	N	Y
7 Addabbo	Y	Y	Y	?	?	Y	Y	N
8 Rosenthal	Y	Y	Y	Y	Y	Y	Y	?
9 Ferraro	Y	Y	Y	Y	Y	Y	Y	N
10 Biaggi	Y	Y	Y	?	Y	Y	N	N
11 Scheuer	?	?	?	?	?	Y	Y	Y
12 Chisholm	?	Y	Y	Y	?	Y	Y	N
13 Solarz	Y	Y	N	Y	Y	?	Y	N
14 Richmond	?	?	Y	?	Y	Y	Y	N
15 Zeferetti	Y	Y	Y	?	?	Y	N	N
16 Schumer	?	?	N	Y	Y	Y	Y	N
17 ***Molinari***	Y	Y	N	Y	Y	Y	N	Y
18 ***Green***	Y	Y	N	Y	Y	Y	N	N
19 Rangel	Y	Y	Y	Y	Y	Y	Y	N
20 Weiss	Y	Y	Y	Y	?	Y	Y	N
21 Garcia	Y	Y	Y	Y	Y	Y	Y	N
22 Bingham	Y	Y	Y	Y	Y	Y	Y	N
23 Peyser	Y	Y	Y	Y	Y	Y	Y	N
24 Ottinger	P	Y	Y	Y	P	Y	Y	N
25 ***Fish***	Y	Y	Y	Y	Y	Y	Y	N
26 ***Gilman***	Y	Y	Y	Y	?	Y	Y	N
27 McHugh	?	Y	Y	Y	Y	Y	N	N
28 Stratton	Y	Y	N	Y	Y	Y	N	Y
29 ***Solomon***	Y	Y	N	Y	Y	?	N	Y
30 ***Martin***	Y	Y	N	Y	Y	Y	N	Y
31 ***Mitchell***	Y	Y	N	Y	Y	Y	N	N
32 ***Wortley***	Y	Y	Y	Y	Y	Y	N	Y
33 ***Lee***	Y	Y	N	Y	Y	Y	N	Y
34 ***Horton***	Y	Y	Y	Y	Y	Y	Y	N
35 ***Conable***	Y	Y	N	Y	Y	Y	N	Y
36 LaFalce	Y	Y	Y	Y	Y	Y	Y	Y
37 Nowak	Y	Y	Y	Y	Y	Y	N	Y
38 ***Kemp***	Y	Y	N	Y	Y	Y	N	?
39 Lundine	Y	Y	Y	?	?	Y	N	N
NORTH CAROLINA								
1 Jones	?	?	?	?	?	?	X	#
2 Fountain	Y	Y	Y	Y	Y	Y	N	Y
3 Whitley	?	?	?	?	?	Y	N	Y
4 Andrews	?	?	?	?	?	?	N	Y
5 Neal	Y	Y	Y	Y	Y	Y	N	Y
6 ***Johnston***	N	Y	N	?	?	?	?	Y
7 Rose	?	?	?	?	?	Y	N	Y
8 Hefner	Y	Y	Y	Y	Y	Y	N	Y
9 ***Martin***	Y	Y	N	Y	Y	Y	N	Y
10 ***Broyhill***	Y	Y	N	?	?	Y	N	Y
11 ***Hendon***	?	Y	N	Y	Y	Y	N	Y
NORTH DAKOTA								
AL Dorgan	Y	Y	Y	Y	Y	Y	N	Y
OHIO								
1 ***Gradison***	Y	Y	Y	Y	Y	Y	N	N
2 Luken	Y	Y	N	Y	Y	Y	N	N
3 Hall	Y	Y	Y	Y	?	Y	Y	Y
4 Vacancy								
5 ***Latta***	?	?	N	Y	Y	Y	N	Y
6 ***McEwen***	Y	Y	N	Y	Y	Y	N	Y
7 ***Brown***	Y	Y	N	Y	Y	Y	N	Y
8 ***Kindness***	Y	Y	N	Y	Y	Y	N	N
9 ***Weber***	Y	Y	Y	Y	Y	Y	N	Y
10 ***Miller***	Y	Y	N	Y	Y	Y	N	Y
11 ***Stanton***	Y	Y	N	Y	Y	Y	N	Y
12 Shamansky	Y	Y	Y	Y	Y	Y	N	N
13 Pease	Y	Y	Y	Y	Y	Y	Y	N
14 Seiberling	?	Y	Y	Y	Y	Y	Y	N
15 ***Wylie***	Y	Y	N	Y	Y	Y	N	Y
16 ***Regula***	Y	Y	N	Y	Y	Y	N	Y
17 ***Ashbrook***	Y	Y	N	Y	N	Y	N	Y
18 Applegate	?	?	Y	Y	Y	Y	N	?
19 ***Williams***	Y	Y	Y	?	?	Y	N	Y
20 Oakar	Y	Y	?	+	+	Y	Y	N
21 Stokes	?	Y	Y	Y	Y	Y	Y	N
22 Eckart	Y	Y	Y	Y	Y	Y	Y	N
23 Mottl	?	?	?	?	?	Y	Y	Y
OKLAHOMA								
1 Jones	Y	Y	Y	Y	Y	Y	N	Y
2 Synar	Y	Y	Y	Y	Y	Y	Y	N
3 Watkins	Y	Y	N	Y	Y	Y	N	Y
4 McCurdy	Y	Y	N	Y	Y	Y	N	Y
5 ***Edwards***	Y	Y	N	Y	Y	Y	N	Y
6 English	Y	Y	Y	?	Y	Y	Y	Y
OREGON								
1 AuCoin	Y	Y	Y	Y	Y	Y	Y	N
2 ***Smith***	Y	Y	N	Y	Y	Y	N	Y
3 Wyden	?	?	?	?	?	Y	N	N
4 Weaver	N	Y	Y	N	N	Y	Y	N
PENNSYLVANIA								
1 Foglietta	?	Y	Y	?	?	Y	N	N
2 Gray	Y	Y	Y	Y	Y	Y	Y	N
3 Vacancy								
4 ***Dougherty***	?	Y	N	?	?	Y	N	Y
5 ***Schulze***	Y	Y	N	Y	Y	Y	N	Y
6 Yatron	Y	Y	N	Y	Y	Y	N	Y
7 Edgar	Y	Y	Y	Y	Y	Y	Y	N
8 ***Coyne, J.***	?	?	N	Y	Y	Y	N	Y
9 ***Shuster***	Y	Y	N	Y	Y	Y	N	Y
10 ***McDade***	Y	Y	Y	Y	Y	Y	N	Y
11 ***Nelligan***	Y	Y	N	?	?	Y	N	Y
12 Murtha	Y	Y	N	Y	?	Y	N	N
13 ***Coughlin***	Y	Y	N	Y	Y	Y	N	Y
14 Coyne, W.	Y	Y	Y	Y	Y	Y	Y	N
15 ***Ritter***	Y	Y	N	Y	Y	Y	N	Y
16 ***Walker***	N	Y	Y	N	Y	Y	N	N
17 Ertel	Y	Y	Y	N	Y	Y	N	N
18 Walgren	Y	Y	Y	Y	Y	Y	Y	Y
19 ***Goodling***	N	Y	Y	?	?	Y	N	?
20 Gaydos	Y	Y	Y	Y	Y	Y	N	Y
21 Bailey	Y	Y	N	Y	Y	Y	N	N
22 Murphy	?	?	?	?	?	Y	Y	N
23 ***Clinger***	Y	Y	Y	Y	Y	Y	Y	Y
24 ***Marks***	Y	Y	N	Y	Y	Y	N	N
25 Atkinson	?	Y	Y	Y	Y	Y	Y	N
RHODE ISLAND								
1 St Germain	Y	Y	Y	Y	Y	Y	Y	Y
2 ***Schneider***	Y	Y	Y	Y	Y	Y	N	Y
SOUTH CAROLINA								
1 ***Hartnett***	Y	Y	N	Y	?	Y	N	Y
2 ***Spence***	Y	Y	N	Y	Y	Y	N	Y
3 Derrick	?	?	Y	Y	?	Y	?	Y
4 ***Campbell***	Y	Y	N	Y	Y	Y	N	Y
5 Holland	Y	Y	N	Y	Y	Y	N	Y
6 ***Napier***	Y	Y	N	Y	Y	Y	N	Y
SOUTH DAKOTA								
1 Daschle	Y	Y	Y	Y	Y	Y	N	N
2 ***Roberts***	Y	Y	N	Y	Y	Y	N	Y
TENNESSEE								
1 ***Quillen***	?	?	?	?	?	Y	N	Y
2 ***Duncan***	Y	Y	N	Y	Y	Y	N	Y
3 Bouquard	Y	Y	N	Y	Y	Y	N	Y
4 Gore	Y	Y	Y	Y	Y	Y	N	N
5 Boner	?	?	?	?	?	Y	N	Y
6 ***Beard***	Y	Y	N	Y	Y	Y	N	Y
7 Jones	Y	Y	N	Y	Y	Y	N	Y
8 Ford	Y	Y	Y	Y	Y	Y	N	N
TEXAS								
1 Hall, S.	Y	Y	Y	Y	Y	Y	N	N
2 Wilson	Y	Y	N	Y	?	Y	N	Y
3 ***Collins***	Y	Y	Y	Y	Y	Y	N	Y
4 Hall, R.	Y	Y	N	Y	Y	Y	N	N
5 Mattox	Y	Y	Y	Y	Y	Y	Y	N
6 Gramm	?	Y	N	Y	Y	Y	N	Y
7 ***Archer***	Y	Y	N	Y	Y	Y	N	Y
8 ***Fields***	Y	Y	N	Y	Y	Y	N	Y
9 Brooks	Y	Y	Y	Y	?	Y	Y	N
10 Pickle	Y	Y	N	Y	Y	Y	N	N
11 Leath	Y	Y	N	Y	Y	Y	N	Y
12 Wright	Y	Y	?	?	?	Y	N	N
13 Hightower	Y	Y	Y	Y	Y	Y	Y	Y
14 Patman	Y	Y	Y	Y	Y	Y	Y	Y
15 de la Garza	Y	Y	Y	Y	?	Y	N	Y
16 White	Y	Y	N	Y	Y	Y	N	N
17 Stenholm	Y	Y	N	Y	Y	Y	N	Y
18 Leland	Y	Y	Y	Y	Y	Y	Y	N
19 Hance	Y	Y	N	Y	Y	Y	N	Y
20 Gonzalez	Y	Y	N	P	Y	Y	Y	N
21 ***Loeffler***	Y	Y	N	Y	Y	Y	N	Y
22 ***Paul***	Y	Y	Y	N	Y	Y	Y	N
23 Kazen	Y	Y	N	Y	Y	Y	N	Y
24 Frost	Y	Y	N	Y	Y	Y	N	N
UTAH								
1 ***Hansen***	?	Y	N	Y	?	Y	N	Y
2 ***Marriott***	Y	Y	N	Y	Y	Y	N	Y
VERMONT								
AL ***Jeffords***	Y	Y	N	?	?	Y	N	N
VIRGINIA								
1 ***Trible***	?	Y	N	Y	Y	?	N	Y
2 ***Whitehurst***	Y	Y	N	?	?	Y	N	Y
3 ***Bliley***	Y	Y	N	Y	Y	Y	N	Y
4 ***Daniel, R.***	Y	Y	N	Y	Y	Y	N	Y
5 Daniel, D.	Y	Y	N	Y	Y	Y	N	Y
6 ***Butler***	?	?	?	?	?	Y	N	Y
7 ***Robinson***	Y	Y	N	Y	Y	Y	N	Y
8 ***Parris***	Y	Y	N	Y	Y	Y	N	Y
9 ***Wampler***	Y	Y	N	Y	Y	Y	N	Y
10 ***Wolf***	Y	Y	N	Y	Y	Y	N	Y
WASHINGTON								
1 ***Pritchard***	Y	Y	N	Y	Y	Y	N	Y
2 Swift	Y	Y	Y	Y	Y	Y	N	N
3 Bonker	Y	Y	Y	Y	Y	Y	?	N
4 ***Morrison***	Y	Y	N	Y	Y	Y	N	Y
5 Foley	Y	Y	Y	Y	Y	Y	N	N
6 Dicks	Y	Y	N	Y	Y	Y	N	Y
7 Lowry	Y	Y	N	N	Y	Y	Y	N
WEST VIRGINIA								
1 Mollohan	Y	Y	N	Y	Y	Y	N	N
2 ***Benedict***	?	Y	N	Y	Y	Y	N	N
3 ***Staton***	Y	Y	N	Y	Y	Y	N	Y
4 Rahall	Y	Y	Y	Y	Y	Y	N	N
WISCONSIN								
1 Aspin	Y	Y	Y	Y	Y	Y	N	?
2 Kastenmeier	Y	Y	Y	Y	Y	Y	Y	N
3 ***Gunderson***	Y	Y	Y	N	Y	Y	N	N
4 Zablocki	Y	Y	Y	Y	Y	Y	N	Y
5 Reuss	Y	Y	Y	Y	Y	Y	Y	N
6 ***Petri***	Y	Y	N	Y	Y	Y	N	N
7 Obey	Y	Y	Y	?	Y	Y	Y	N
8 ***Roth***	?	?	?	?	?	Y	N	Y
9 ***Sensenbrenner***	Y	Y	N	Y	Y	Y	N	Y
WYOMING								
AL ***Cheney***	Y	Y	N	Y	Y	Y	N	Y

Democrats ***Republicans***

121. HR 3519. Defense Department Authorization. Judiciary Committee amendment, as amended *(see vote 120, p. 46-H)*, to authorize the armed services to cooperate with civilian law enforcement officials in operations against drug smuggling. Adopted 362-49: R 164-22; D 198-27 (ND 138-9, SD 60-18), July 15, 1981. (The original Judiciary Committee amendment specified that the military could assist civilian drug enforcement officials but not make arrests or seize drugs).

122. HR 3519. Defense Department Authorization. Government Operations Committee amendment to place Defense Department procurement under a government-wide procurement system and to authorize multi-year contracting only for purchases meeting certain conditions and specifically approved by Congress. Rejected 133-283: R 8-175; D 125-108 (ND 108-50, SD 17-58), July 15, 1981.

123. HR 3519. Defense Department Authorization. Brooks, D-Texas, amendment to require that all purchases of computers and computer services for the Defense Department be made through the General Services Administration. Rejected 118-299: R 14-171; D 104-128 (ND 91-66, SD 13-62), July 15, 1981.

124. HR 3519. Defense Department Authorization. Hopkins, R-Ky., substitute amendment, to the Hillis, R-Ind., amendment *(see vote 130, p. 50-H)*, to prohibit the armed services from buying automobiles manufactured outside the United States or Canada unless the secretary of defense certified to Congress that suitable automobiles manufactured in the United States or Canada were not available. Rejected 38-371: R 31-150; D 7-221 (ND 3-150, SD 4-71), July 15, 1981.

125. HR 3519. Defense Department Authorization. Weiss, D-N.Y., amendment to delete provisions from the bill requiring Selective Service registrants to provide their Social Security numbers and providing for the departments of Defense, the Treasury and Health and Human Services to share names and addresses of registrants. Rejected 125-290: R 27-158; D 98-132 (ND 90-66, SD 8-66), July 16, 1981.

126. HR 3519. Defense Department Authorization. Schroeder, D-Colo., amendment (to the Courter, R-N.J., substitute amendment *(see vote 127, below)*, to the Schroeder amendment) to direct the president to propose by Jan. 15, 1982, at least $8 billion in rescissions in Defense Department budget authority that was unnecessary or attributable to waste, fraud, abuse or mismanagement. Rejected 142-276: R 17-169; D 125-107 (ND 115-41, SD 10-66), July 16, 1981.

127. HR 3519. Defense Department Authorization. Courter, R-N.J., substitute amendment, to the Schroeder, D-Colo., amendment, to direct the president to submit to Congress by Jan. 15, 1982, his recommendations for improving the efficiency and management in the Defense Department and for eliminating waste, fraud, abuse and mismanagement in the department. The president also would be directed to report on actions taken concerning General Accounting Office reports on waste, fraud, abuse and mismanagement in the Defense Department. Adopted 416-0: R 188-0; D 228-0 (ND 155-0, SD 73-0), July 16, 1981. (The Schroeder amendment, as amended by the Courter substitute, subsequently was adopted by voice vote).

128. HR 3519. Defense Department Authorization. Vento, D-Minn., amendment to prohibit use of funds in the bill for research, development, testing, evaluation or procurement of the F/A-18 fighter/attack aircraft. The amendment directed that the $3.1 billion specified in the bill for the F/A-18 be made available instead for other Navy and Marine Corps aircraft programs. Rejected 101-316: R 13-172; D 88-144 (ND 70-85, SD 18-59), July 16, 1981. A "nay" was a vote supporting the president's position.

	KEY
Y	Voted for (yea).
#	Paired for.
+	Announced for.
N	Voted against (nay).
X	Paired against.
-	Announced against.
P	Voted "present".
C	Voted "present" to avoid possible conflict of interest.
?	Did not vote or otherwise make a position known.

	121	122	123	124	125	126	127	128
ALABAMA								
1 *Edwards*	Y	N	N	N	N	N	Y	N
2 *Dickinson*	Y	N	N	N	N	N	Y	N
3 Nichols	N	N	N	N	N	N	Y	N
4 Bevill	Y	?	?	?	?	?	?	?
5 Flippo	Y	N	N	N	N	N	Y	N
6 *Smith*	Y	N	N	N	N	N	Y	N
7 Shelby	Y	N	N	N	N	N	Y	N
ALASKA								
AL *Young*	Y	N	N	N	N	N	Y	N
ARIZONA								
1 *Rhodes*	Y	N	N	?	?	?	?	?
2 Udall	Y	Y	Y	N	Y	Y	Y	N
3 *Stump*	N	N	N	N	N	N	Y	N
4 *Rudd*	Y	N	N	N	N	N	Y	N
ARKANSAS								
1 Alexander	Y	N	?	N	N	N	Y	N
2 *Bethune*	N	N	N	N	N	N	Y	N
3 *Hammerschmidt*	N	N	N	N	N	N	Y	N
4 Anthony	N	N	N	N	N	N	Y	N
CALIFORNIA								
1 *Chappie*	Y	N	N	N	N	N	Y	N
2 *Clausen*	Y	N	N	?	N	N	Y	N
3 Matsui	Y	?	N	N	Y	N	Y	N
4 Fazio	Y	N	N	N	Y	N	Y	N
5 Burton, J.	Y	Y	Y	N	Y	Y	Y	Y
6 Burton, P.	Y	Y	Y	N	Y	Y	Y	Y
7 Miller	Y	Y	Y	N	Y	Y	Y	Y
8 Dellums	P	Y	Y	N	Y	Y	Y	Y
9 Stark	Y	Y	Y	?	Y	Y	?	Y
10 Edwards	Y	Y	Y	N	Y	Y	Y	?
11 Lantos	+	N	N	N	N	N	Y	N
12 *McCloskey*	Y	N	N	N	?	N	Y	N
13 Mineta	Y	N	N	Y	N	Y	Y	N
14 *Shumway*	Y	N	N	N	N	N	Y	N
15 Coelho	Y	N	N	N	N	N	Y	N
16 Panetta	Y	N	N	Y	N	Y	Y	N
17 *Pashayan*	Y	N	N	Y	N	N	Y	N
18 *Thomas*	Y	N	N	N	N	N	Y	N
19 *Lagomarsino*	Y	N	N	N	N	N	Y	N
20 *Goldwater*	Y	N	N	N	Y	N	Y	?
21 *Fiedler*	Y	N	N	N	N	N	Y	N
22 *Moorhead*	Y	N	N	N	N	N	Y	N
23 Beilenson	Y	Y	Y	N	Y	Y	Y	Y
24 Waxman	Y	Y	Y	N	Y	Y	Y	Y
25 Roybal	Y	Y	Y	N	Y	Y	Y	Y
26 *Rousselot*	Y	?	N	Y	N	N	Y	N
27 *Dornan*	N	?	?	?	?	N	Y	N
28 Dixon	Y	?	N	Y	Y	Y	Y	?
29 Hawkins	P	Y	Y	N	Y	Y	N	Y
30 Danielson	Y	Y	Y	N	N	N	Y	N
31 Dymally	N	Y	?	N	Y	Y	Y	N
32 Anderson	Y	N	N	Y	N	N	Y	N
33 *Grisham*	Y	N	N	Y	N	N	Y	Y
34 *Lungren*	Y	N	N	N	N	N	Y	N
35 *Dreier*	Y	N	N	Y	N	N	Y	N
36 Brown	?	Y	Y	N	Y	Y	?	Y
37 Lewis	Y	N	N	Y	N	N	Y	N
38 Patterson	Y	Y	Y	N	Y	N	Y	Y
39 *Dannemeyer*	Y	N	N	N	N	N	Y	N
40 *Badham*	Y	N	N	N	N	N	Y	?
41 *Lowery*	Y	N	N	N	N	N	Y	N
42 *Hunter*	N	N	N	N	N	N	Y	N
43 *Burgener*	Y	N	N	N	N	N	Y	N
COLORADO								
1 Schroeder	Y	Y	Y	N	Y	Y	Y	Y
2 Wirth	Y	Y	Y	N	Y	Y	Y	Y
3 Kogovsek	Y	N	N	N	Y	N	Y	N
4 *Brown*	Y	Y	Y	N	N	Y	Y	N

	121	122	123	124	125	126	127	128
5 *Kramer*	Y	N	N	N	N	N	Y	N
CONNECTICUT								
1 Cotter	?	?	?	?	?	?	?	?
2 Gejdenson	Y	N	N	N	Y	N	Y	N
3 *DeNardis*	Y	Y	N	N	Y	Y	Y	N
4 *McKinney*	Y	N	N	Y	Y	Y	Y	N
5 Ratchford	Y	Y	Y	N	Y	Y	Y	N
6 Moffett	Y	Y	Y	N	Y	Y	Y	Y
DELAWARE								
AL *Evans*	Y	N	N	N	N	N	Y	N
FLORIDA								
1 Hutto	Y	N	N	N	N	N	Y	N
2 Fuqua	Y	Y	N	N	N	N	Y	N
3 Bennett	N	N	N	N	N	N	Y	N
4 Chappell	N	N	N	N	N	N	Y	Y
5 *McCollum*	Y	N	N	N	N	N	Y	N
6 *Young*	N	N	N	N	N	N	Y	N
7 Gibbons	N	N	N	N	N	N	Y	Y
8 Ireland	Y	N	N	N	Y	Y	Y	N
9 Nelson	Y	N	N	N	N	N	Y	Y
10 *Bafalis*	N	N	N	N	N	N	Y	N
11 Mica	Y	N	N	N	Y	Y	Y	Y
12 *Shaw*	Y	N	Y	N	N	N	Y	N
13 Lehman	Y	N	N	N	Y	Y	Y	N
14 Pepper	Y	N	N	N	N	N	Y	N
15 Fascell	Y	Y	Y	N	Y	Y	Y	Y
GEORGIA								
1 Ginn	N	N	N	N	N	N	Y	N
2 Hatcher	Y	?	N	N	?	?	?	N
3 Brinkley	Y	N	N	N	N	N	Y	N
4 Levitas	Y	Y	N	N	N	N	Y	N
5 Fowler	Y	Y	Y	N	N	N	Y	N
6 *Gingrich*	Y	N	N	N	N	N	Y	Y
7 McDonald	N	N	N	N	N	N	Y	N
8 Evans	Y	N	N	?	N	Y	Y	N
9 Jenkins	Y	N	N	N	N	N	Y	N
10 Barnard	N	N	N	N	N	N	Y	N
HAWAII								
1 Heftel	Y	N	N	N	N	N	Y	N
2 Akaka	Y	Y	N	N	N	N	Y	N
IDAHO								
1 *Craig*	Y	N	N	N	N	N	Y	N
2 *Hansen*	Y	N	N	N	N	N	Y	N
ILLINOIS								
1 Washington	P	Y	Y	N	Y	Y	Y	Y
2 Savage	?	?	?	?	?	?	Y	Y
3 Russo	Y	Y	Y	N	Y	Y	Y	Y
4 *Derwinski*	Y	?	N	N	N	N	Y	N
5 Fary	Y	N	N	N	N	N	Y	N
6 *Hyde*	Y	Y	Y	N	Y	Y	Y	Y
7 Collins	Y	Y	Y	N	Y	Y	Y	Y
8 Rostenkowski	Y	Y	Y	N	N	N	Y	N
9 Yates	Y	Y	Y	N	Y	Y	Y	Y
10 *Porter*	Y	N	-	N	Y	N	Y	N
11 Annunzio	Y	N	N	N	N	N	Y	N
12 *Crane, P.*	Y	?	?	?	?	N	Y	N
13 *McClory*	Y	N	N	N	N	N	Y	N
14 *Erlenborn*	Y	N	N	N	N	N	Y	N
15 *Corcoran*	Y	N	N	N	N	N	Y	N
16 *Martin*	Y	N	N	N	N	N	Y	N
17 *O'Brien*	Y	N	N	N	N	N	?	N
18 *Michel*	Y	N	N	N	N	N	Y	N
19 *Railsback*	Y	N	N	N	N	N	Y	N
20 *Findley*	Y	N	N	N	N	N	Y	N
21 *Madigan*	?	N	N	N	N	N	Y	N
22 *Crane, D.*	Y	N	N	N	Y	N	Y	N
23 Price	Y	N	N	N	N	N	Y	N
24 Simon	Y	Y	N	N	Y	Y	Y	N
INDIANA								
1 Benjamin	Y	Y	N	N	Y	Y	Y	N
2 Fithian	Y	Y	Y	N	?	?	?	?
3 *Hiler*	Y	N	N	N	N	N	Y	N
4 *Coats*	Y	N	N	N	N	N	Y	N
5 *Hillis*	N	N	N	N	N	N	Y	N
6 Evans	Y	Y	Y	N	Y	Y	Y	Y
7 *Myers*	Y	N	N	N	N	N	Y	N
8 *Deckard*	?	N	N	N	Y	?	?	N
9 Hamilton	Y	N	N	N	N	N	Y	N
10 Sharp	Y	N	N	N	N	N	Y	Y
11 Jacobs	N	Y	Y	N	N	Y	Y	Y
IOWA								
1 *Leach*	Y	N	N	N	N	N	Y	N
2 *Tauke*	Y	N	N	Y	N	N	Y	N
3 *Evans*	Y	N	N	N	N	N	Y	N
4 *Smith*	N	Y	Y	N	N	Y	Y	Y
5 Harkin	Y	Y	N	N	Y	Y	Y	N
6 Bedell	Y	Y	Y	N	N	Y	Y	N

Democrats   *Republicans*

	121	122	123	124	125	126	127	128
KANSAS								
1 *Roberts*	Y	N	N	N	N	N	Y	N
2 *Jeffries*	Y	N	N	N	N	N	Y	N
3 *Winn*	Y	N	N	N	N	N	Y	N
4 Glickman	Y	N	N	N	Y	Y	Y	N
5 *Whittaker*	Y	N	N	N	N	N	Y	N
KENTUCKY								
1 Hubbard	Y	N	N	Y	N	N	Y	N
2 Natcher	Y	N	N	Y	N	N	Y	N
3 Mazzoli	Y	Y	N	Y	N	Y	Y	N
4 *Snyder*	Y	N	N	Y	N	Y	Y	N
5 *Rogers*	Y	N	N	Y	N	N	Y	N
6 *Hopkins*	N	N	N	Y	N	N	Y	N
7 Perkins	Y	N	N	N	N	N	Y	N
LOUISIANA								
1 *Livingston*	Y	N	N	N	N	N	Y	N
2 Boggs	Y	N	N	N	Y	N	Y	N
3 Tauzin	Y	N	N	N	N	N	Y	N
4 Roemer	Y	N	N	N	N	N	N	Y
5 Huckaby	Y	N	N	N	N	N	Y	N
6 *Moore*	Y	N	Y	N	N	N	Y	N
7 Breaux	Y	N	N	?	N	N	Y	N
8 Long	Y	N	N	N	N	N	Y	N
MAINE								
1 *Emery*	Y	N	N	N	N	N	Y	N
2 *Snowe*	Y	N	N	N	N	N	Y	N
MARYLAND								
1 Dyson	Y	N	N	N	N	N	Y	N
2 Long	Y	Y	Y	N	N	N	Y	N
3 Mikulski	Y	Y	Y	N	Y	Y	Y	Y
4 *Holt*	N	N	N	?	N	N	Y	?
5 Hoyer	Y	N	Y	N	N	Y	Y	N
6 Byron	Y	N	N	Y	N	N	Y	N
7 Mitchell	?	Y	Y	N	Y	Y	Y	Y
8 Barnes	Y	Y	Y	N	Y	N	Y	N
MASSACHUSETTS								
1 *Conte*	Y	N	N	N	Y	Y	Y	N
2 Boland	Y	Y	N	N	N	Y	Y	N
3 Early	Y	Y	Y	N	Y	?	?	N
4 Frank	Y	Y	N	N	Y	Y	Y	N
5 Shannon	Y	Y	Y	N	Y	Y	Y	Y
6 Mavroules	Y	N	N	N	Y	Y	Y	N
7 Markey	Y	Y	Y	N	Y	Y	Y	N
8 O'Neill								
9 Moakley	Y	Y	N	N	Y	Y	Y	N
10 *Heckler*	Y	N	N	Y	Y	Y	Y	N
11 Donnelly	Y	?	?	?	?	?	?	N
12 Studds	Y	Y	Y	N	Y	Y	Y	Y
MICHIGAN								
1 Conyers	P	Y	Y	N	Y	Y	Y	Y
2 *Pursell*	N	Y	Y	N	Y	Y	Y	N
3 Wolpe	Y	Y	Y	N	Y	Y	Y	N
4 *Siljander*	Y	N	N	N	N	N	Y	N
5 *Sawyer*	Y	N	N	N	N	N	Y	N
6 *Dunn*	Y	N	N	N	Y	N	Y	N
7 Kildee	Y	Y	Y	N	Y	Y	Y	Y
8 Traxler	Y	Y	Y	N	Y	Y	Y	Y
9 *Vander Jagt*	Y	?	Y	N	N	N	Y	N
10 Albosta	Y	N	N	N	N	N	Y	N
11 *Davis*	Y	N	N	N	N	N	Y	N
12 Bonior	Y	Y	?	N	Y	Y	Y	Y
13 Crockett	?	Y	Y	?	Y	Y	?	Y
14 Hertel	Y	N	N	N	N	Y	Y	Y
15 Ford	Y	Y	Y	N	Y	Y	Y	?
16 Dingell	Y	Y	Y	N	N	Y	Y	Y
17 Brodhead	Y	Y	Y	N	Y	Y	Y	Y
18 Blanchard	Y	N	Y	N	N	Y	Y	Y
19 *Broomfield*	Y	N	N	N	N	N	Y	N
MINNESOTA								
1 *Erdahl*	N	N	Y	N	N	N	Y	N
2 *Hagedorn*	N	N	N	N	N	N	Y	N
3 *Frenzel*	Y	N	N	-	N	N	Y	N
4 Vento	Y	Y	Y	N	Y	Y	Y	Y
5 Sabo	Y	Y	Y	N	Y	Y	Y	Y
6 *Weber*	Y	N	N	N	N	N	Y	N
7 *Stangeland*	N	N	N	Y	N	N	Y	N
8 Oberstar	Y	Y	Y	N	Y	Y	Y	Y
MISSISSIPPI								
1 Whitten	Y	Y	Y	N	N	N	Y	N
2 Bowen	Y	N	N	N	N	N	Y	N
3 Montgomery	N	N	N	N	N	N	Y	N
4 Dowdy	N	?	N	N	N	N	Y	N
5 *Lott*	Y	N	N	N	N	N	Y	N
MISSOURI								
1 Clay	Y	Y	Y	N	Y	Y	Y	N
2 Young	Y	N	N	N	N	N	Y	N
3 Gephardt	Y	N	N	N	N	N	Y	N
4 Skelton	N	N	N	N	N	N	Y	N
5 Bolling	Y	Y	Y	?	Y	N	Y	Y
6 *Coleman*	Y	N	N	N	N	N	Y	N
7 *Taylor*	N	N	N	Y	N	N	Y	N
8 *Bailey*	Y	N	N	N	N	N	Y	N
9 Volkmer	Y	N	N	N	Y	N	Y	N
10 *Emerson*	Y	N	N	N	N	N	Y	N
MONTANA								
1 Williams	Y	Y	Y	N	Y	Y	Y	N
2 *Marlenee*	Y	N	N	Y	Y	N	Y	N
NEBRASKA								
1 *Bereuter*	Y	N	N	N	N	N	Y	Y
2 *Daub*	Y	N	Y	N	N	N	Y	N
3 *Smith*	Y	N	N	N	N	N	Y	N
NEVADA								
AL Santini	?	N	N	N	N	N	Y	N
NEW HAMPSHIRE								
1 D'Amours	Y	Y	Y	N	N	Y	Y	?
2 *Gregg*	Y	N	N	N	N	N	Y	N
NEW JERSEY								
1 Florio	Y	Y	Y	?	?	?	?	?
2 Hughes	Y	Y	Y	N	N	N	Y	N
3 Howard	Y	Y	N	N	Y	Y	Y	N
4 *Smith*	Y	N	N	N	N	N	Y	N
5 *Fenwick*	Y	N	N	N	N	N	Y	N
6 *Forsythe*	Y	Y	Y	N	Y	N	Y	Y
7 *Roukema*	Y	N	N	N	N	N	Y	N
8 Roe	Y	Y	Y	?	Y	Y	Y	N
9 *Hollenbeck*	Y	N	Y	N	Y	N	Y	N
10 Rodino	Y	Y	Y	N	Y	Y	Y	Y
11 Minish	Y	Y	N	N	Y	Y	Y	N
12 *Rinaldo*	Y	N	Y	N	N	N	Y	N
13 *Courter*	Y	N	N	N	N	N	Y	N
14 Guarini	Y	Y	N	N	N	Y	Y	N
15 Dwyer	Y	Y	N	N	Y	Y	Y	N
NEW MEXICO								
1 *Lujan*	Y	N	N	Y	N	Y	Y	N
2 *Skeen*	Y	N	N	Y	N	N	Y	N
NEW YORK								
1 *Carney*	Y	N	N	N	N	N	Y	Y
2 Downey	Y	N	N	N	Y	Y	Y	Y
3 *Carman*	Y	N	N	N	N	N	Y	Y
4 *Lent*	Y	N	N	N	N	N	Y	Y
5 *McGrath*	Y	N	N	N	N	N	Y	Y
6 *LeBoutillier*	Y	N	N	N	N	N	Y	N
7 Addabbo	Y	Y	Y	N	Y	Y	Y	N
8 Rosenthal	?	Y	Y	N	Y	Y	Y	Y
9 Ferraro	+	Y	Y	N	Y	Y	Y	N
10 Biaggi	Y	Y	Y	N	Y	Y	Y	N
11 Scheuer	Y	Y	N	?	N	Y	Y	Y
12 Chisholm	P	Y	Y	N	Y	Y	Y	?
13 Solarz	Y	N	N	N	Y	Y	Y	Y
14 Richmond	Y	Y	Y	N	Y	Y	Y	Y
15 Zeferetti	Y	N	N	N	N	N	Y	N
16 Schumer	Y	Y	N	N	Y	Y	Y	Y
17 *Molinari*	Y	N	N	N	N	N	Y	N
18 *Green*	Y	N	N	N	Y	Y	Y	Y
19 Rangel	N	Y	Y	N	Y	Y	Y	N
20 Weiss	P	Y	Y	N	Y	Y	Y	Y
21 Garcia	Y	Y	Y	N	Y	Y	Y	Y
22 Bingham	Y	Y	Y	N	Y	Y	Y	Y
23 Peyser	Y	Y	Y	N	N	N	Y	N
24 Ottinger	Y	Y	Y	N	Y	Y	Y	Y
25 *Fish*	Y	N	N	N	Y	N	Y	N
26 *Gilman*	Y	N	N	Y	N	N	Y	N
27 McHugh	Y	N	N	N	Y	Y	Y	Y
28 Stratton	N	N	N	Y	N	N	Y	N
29 *Solomon*	N	N	N	Y	N	N	Y	N
30 *Martin*	?	N	N	N	N	N	Y	N
31 *Mitchell*	Y	N	N	N	N	N	Y	N
32 *Wortley*	Y	N	N	N	N	N	Y	N
33 *Lee*	Y	N	N	N	N	N	Y	N
34 *Horton*	Y	Y	Y	N	Y	Y	Y	N
35 *Conable*	Y	N	N	N	N	N	Y	N
36 LaFalce	Y	Y	Y	N	N	Y	Y	N
37 Nowak	Y	Y	Y	N	Y	Y	Y	N
38 *Kemp*	Y	N	N	N	?	N	Y	N
39 Lundine	Y	Y	Y	N	N	Y	Y	Y
NORTH CAROLINA								
1 Jones	?	?	?	?	?	?	?	?
2 Fountain	Y	Y	N	N	N	N	Y	N
3 Whitley	N	N	N	N	N	N	Y	N
4 Andrews	Y	N	N	N	N	N	Y	N
5 Neal	Y	N	N	N	N	N	Y	N
6 *Johnston*	Y	N	N	N	N	N	Y	N
7 Rose	Y	N	Y	?	N	N	?	N
8 Hefner	Y	N	N	N	N	N	Y	N
9 *Martin*	Y	N	N	N	N	N	Y	N
10 *Broyhill*	Y	N	N	N	N	N	Y	?
11 *Hendon*	Y	N	N	N	N	N	Y	N
NORTH DAKOTA								
AL Dorgan	Y	N	N	N	-	Y	Y	N
OHIO								
1 *Gradison*	Y	N	N	N	N	N	Y	N
2 Luken	Y	N	N	N	N	N	Y	N
3 Hall	Y	N	N	N	N	Y	Y	N
4 Vacancy								
5 *Latta*	N	N	N	?	?	N	Y	N
6 *McEwen*	Y	N	N	Y	N	N	Y	N
7 *Brown*	Y	N	N	N	N	N	Y	N
8 *Kindness*	Y	N	N	N	Y	N	Y	N
9 *Weber*	Y	N	N	Y	N	N	Y	N
10 *Miller*	Y	N	N	N	N	N	Y	N
11 *Stanton*	Y	N	N	N	N	N	Y	N
12 Shamansky	Y	N	N	N	N	N	Y	N
13 Pease	Y	Y	Y	N	Y	Y	Y	Y
14 Seiberling	Y	Y	Y	N	Y	Y	Y	Y
15 *Wylie*	Y	N	N	N	N	Y	Y	N
16 *Regula*	Y	N	N	N	N	N	Y	N
17 *Ashbrook*	Y	N	N	Y	N	N	Y	N
18 Applegate	Y	N	N	N	N	Y	Y	N
19 *Williams*	Y	N	N	N	N	N	Y	N
20 Oakar	Y	Y	Y	N	Y	Y	Y	N
21 Stokes	Y	Y	Y	N	Y	Y	Y	Y
22 Eckart	Y	Y	N	N	Y	Y	Y	Y
23 Mottl	Y	Y	Y	Y	Y	Y	Y	N
OKLAHOMA								
1 Jones	Y	N	N	N	N	N	Y	N
2 Synar	Y	Y	Y	N	N	Y	Y	N
3 Watkins	Y	N	N	N	N	N	?	N
4 McCurdy	Y	N	N	N	N	N	Y	N
5 *Edwards*	Y	N	N	N	Y	N	Y	N
6 English	Y	Y	N	N	N	N	Y	N
OREGON								
1 AuCoin	Y	Y	Y	N	Y	Y	Y	Y
2 *Smith*	Y	N	N	Y	N	N	Y	N
3 Wyden	Y	Y	Y	N	Y	Y	Y	Y
4 Weaver	Y	Y	Y	N	Y	Y	Y	Y
PENNSYLVANIA								
1 Foglietta	Y	N	?	N	?	Y	Y	N
2 Gray	Y	Y	Y	N	Y	Y	Y	Y
3 Vacancy								
4 *Dougherty*	N	N	N	N	N	N	Y	N
5 *Schulze*	Y	N	N	N	N	N	Y	N
6 Yatron	Y	N	N	N	N	Y	Y	N
7 Edgar	Y	Y	Y	N	Y	Y	Y	Y
8 *Coyne, J.*	Y	N	N	N	N	N	Y	N
9 *Shuster*	Y	N	N	N	N	N	Y	N
10 *McDade*	Y	N	N	N	N	N	Y	N
11 *Nelligan*	Y	N	N	N	N	N	Y	N
12 Murtha	Y	Y	N	N	N	N	Y	N
13 *Coughlin*	Y	N	N	N	N	N	Y	N
14 Coyne, W.	Y	Y	Y	N	N	Y	Y	N
15 *Ritter*	Y	N	N	N	N	N	Y	N
16 *Walker*	Y	Y	N	N	Y	N	Y	N
17 Ertel	Y	N	N	N	N	N	Y	N
18 Walgren	Y	Y	Y	N	Y	Y	Y	N
19 *Goodling*	?	?	?	?	N	Y	Y	N
20 Gaydos	Y	N	N	N	N	Y	Y	N
21 Bailey	Y	N	N	N	N	N	Y	N
22 Murphy	Y	Y	Y	N	N	?	Y	N
23 *Clinger*	Y	N	N	Y	N	N	Y	Y
24 *Marks*	Y	Y	N	N	Y	Y	Y	N
25 Atkinson	Y	Y	Y	N	N	Y	Y	N
RHODE ISLAND								
1 St Germain	Y	N	N	?	Y	Y	Y	Y
2 *Schneider*	Y	N	Y	Y	N	N	Y	Y
SOUTH CAROLINA								
1 *Hartnett*	Y	N	N	N	N	N	Y	N
2 *Spence*	N	N	N	Y	N	N	Y	N
3 Derrick	Y	Y	?	N	Y	N	Y	N
4 *Campbell*	Y	N	N	N	N	N	Y	N
5 Holland	N	N	N	N	N	N	Y	N
6 *Napier*	Y	N	?	?	N	N	Y	N
SOUTH DAKOTA								
1 Daschle	Y	N	N	N	N	Y	Y	N
2 *Roberts*	Y	N	N	N	N	N	Y	N
TENNESSEE								
1 *Quillen*	N	N	N	N	N	N	Y	N
2 *Duncan*	Y	N	N	Y	N	N	Y	N
3 Bouquard	Y	N	N	N	N	N	Y	N
4 Gore	Y	N	N	N	N	N	Y	Y
5 Boner	Y	N	N	N	N	N	Y	N
6 *Beard*	N	N	N	N	N	N	Y	N
7 Jones	Y	N	N	N	N	N	Y	N
8 Ford	Y	Y	Y	N	Y	Y	Y	Y
TEXAS								
1 Hall, S.	Y	N	Y	N	N	N	Y	Y
2 Wilson	N	N	N	N	N	N	Y	Y
3 *Collins*	Y	N	N	N	N	N	Y	N
4 Hall, R.	Y	N	N	N	N	N	Y	N
5 Mattox	Y	Y	Y	N	Y	Y	Y	Y
6 Gramm	N	N	N	N	N	N	Y	N
7 *Archer*	Y	N	N	N	N	N	Y	N
8 *Fields*	Y	N	N	N	N	N	Y	N
9 Brooks	Y	Y	Y	N	Y	Y	Y	N
10 Pickle	Y	N	Y	N	N	Y	Y	N
11 Leath	Y	N	N	N	N	N	Y	N
12 Wright	Y	N	N	N	N	N	Y	N
13 Hightower	Y	Y	Y	N	N	N	Y	Y
14 Patman	N	Y	Y	N	N	N	Y	Y
15 de la Garza	Y	N	N	N	?	N	Y	N
16 White	Y	N	N	N	N	N	+	N
17 Stenholm	N	N	N	N	N	N	Y	Y
18 Leland	Y	Y	Y	N	Y	Y	Y	Y
19 Hance	N	N	N	N	N	N	Y	Y
20 Gonzalez	Y	Y	N	N	Y	N	Y	N
21 *Loeffler*	Y	N	N	N	N	N	Y	N
22 *Paul*	Y	Y	Y	N	Y	Y	Y	Y
23 Kazen	Y	N	N	N	N	N	Y	N
24 Frost	Y	N	N	N	N	N	Y	N
UTAH								
1 *Hansen*	Y	N	N	Y	N	N	Y	N
2 *Marriott*	Y	N	N	N	N	?	Y	N
VERMONT								
AL *Jeffords*	Y	N	N	N	N	N	Y	N
VIRGINIA								
1 *Trible*	N	N	N	N	N	N	Y	N
2 *Whitehurst*	N	N	N	N	N	N	Y	N
3 *Bliley*	Y	N	N	N	N	N	Y	N
4 *Daniel, R.*	Y	N	N	N	N	N	Y	N
5 Daniel, D.	N	N	N	N	N	N	Y	N
6 *Butler*	Y	N	N	N	N	N	Y	N
7 *Robinson*	Y	N	N	N	N	N	Y	N
8 *Parris*	Y	N	N	Y	N	N	Y	N
9 *Wampler*	Y	N	N	N	N	N	Y	N
10 *Wolf*	Y	N	N	N	N	N	Y	N
WASHINGTON								
1 *Pritchard*	Y	N	N	N	Y	N	Y	N
2 Swift	Y	Y	N	N	N	N	Y	N
3 Bonker	Y	Y	N	N	N	Y	Y	Y
4 *Morrison*	Y	N	N	N	N	N	Y	N
5 Foley	Y	Y	Y	N	N	N	Y	N
6 Dicks	Y	N	N	N	N	N	Y	N
7 Lowry	Y	Y	Y	N	Y	Y	Y	Y
WEST VIRGINIA								
1 Mollohan	Y	N	N	N	N	N	Y	N
2 *Benedict*	Y	N	N	N	N	N	Y	N
3 *Staton*	Y	N	N	N	N	N	Y	N
4 Rahall	Y	N	N	N	N	Y	Y	Y
WISCONSIN								
1 Aspin	?	N	N	N	Y	Y	Y	Y
2 Kastenmeier	N	Y	Y	N	Y	Y	Y	Y
3 *Gunderson*	Y	N	N	N	N	N	Y	N
4 Zablocki	Y	N	N	N	N	N	Y	N
5 Reuss	N	Y	N	N	N	Y	Y	Y
6 *Petri*	Y	N	N	N	Y	Y	Y	Y
7 Obey	Y	Y	Y	N	Y	Y	Y	Y
8 *Roth*	Y	?	N	N	N	N	Y	N
9 *Sensenbrenner*	Y	N	N	N	Y	N	Y	N
WYOMING								
AL *Cheney*	Y	N	N	Y	N	N	Y	N

Democrats ***Republicans***

129. HR 3519. Defense Department Authorization. Moffett, D-Conn., amendment to bar procurement of A-7K attack planes and use funds earmarked for that plane to buy instead 13 F-16 fighters. Rejected 148-268: R 60-126; D 88-142 (ND 82-71, SD 6-71), July 16, 1981.

130. HR 3519. Defense Department Authorization. Hillis, R-Ind., amendment to bar the secretary of any armed service from signing a contract worth more than $50,000 to purchase civilian cars or light trucks not made in the United States or Canada, without legislative authorization. Adopted 231-187: R 83-103; D 148-84 (ND 114-41, SD 34-43), July 16, 1981.

131. HR 3519. Defense Department Authorization. Passage of the bill to authorize $136,111,036,000 for Defense Department weapons procurement, military research, operations and maintenance, and civil defense in fiscal 1982. Passed 354-63: R 182-3; D 172-60 (ND 97-59, SD 75-1), July 16, 1981.

132. HR 3519. Defense Department Authorization. Price, D-Ill., motion to allow the House-Senate conference committee on the fiscal 1982 defense authorization bill (S 815) to be closed to the public when classified information was under consideration. Motion agreed to 381-2: R 167-0; D 214-2 (ND 142-2, SD 72-0), July 16, 1981.

133. H Res 177. Nuclear Non-Proliferation Policy. Adoption of the resolution calling on the president to: develop and implement a nuclear non-proliferation policy that would strengthen the barriers to the spread of nuclear weapons and prescribe concrete methods for restraint by all nuclear supplier nations; encourage nations to ratify the Non-Proliferation Treaty; work to develop sanctions against nations that divert nuclear supplies from peaceful purposes into nuclear weapons; and fully implement the Nuclear Non-Proliferation Act of 1978. Adopted 365-0: R 161-0; D 204-0 (ND 133-0, SD 71-0), July 17, 1981.

134. HR 4034. HUD-Independent Agencies Appropriations, Fiscal 1982. Beard, R-Tenn., amendment to reduce the appropriation for the Office of Policy Development and Research in the Department of Housing and Urban Development from $30 million to $20 million. Adopted 202-162: R 123-38; D 79-124 (ND 32-103, SD 47-21), July 17, 1981.

135. HR 4034. HUD-Independent Agencies Appropriations, Fiscal 1982. Dannemeyer, R-Calif., amendments (considered en bloc) to prohibit the Environmental Protection Agency from spending funds to require states to implement or enforce programs for vehicle emission control inspection and maintenance. Rejected 177-184: R 119-43; D 58-141 (ND 23-111, SD 35-30), July 17, 1981.

136. H Res 181. Social Security. Wright, D-Texas, motion to suspend the rules and adopt the resolution stating that the House "strongly urges that the necessary steps be taken to insure that Social Security benefits are not reduced for those currently receiving them." Motion agreed to 405-13: R 176-10; D 229-3 (ND 154-1, SD 75-2), July 21, 1981. A two-thirds majority vote (279 in this case) is required for adoption under suspension of the rules.

KEY

Y Voted for (yea).
Paired for.
+ Announced for.
N Voted against (nay).
X Paired against.
- Announced against.
P Voted "present".
C Voted "present" to avoid possible conflict of interest.
? Did not vote or otherwise make a position known.

	129	130	131	132	133	134	135	136
ALABAMA								
1 *Edwards*	Y	N	Y	Y	Y	N	N	Y
2 *Dickinson*	Y	N	Y	Y	Y	Y	?	Y
3 Nichols	N	Y	Y	Y	Y	Y	Y	Y
4 Bevill	?	?	?	?	?	?	?	Y
5 Flippo	N	Y	Y	Y	Y	N	Y	Y
6 *Smith*	N	N	Y	Y	Y	?	#	#	Y
7 Shelby	N	Y	Y	Y	Y	Y	Y	Y
ALASKA								
AL *Young*	N	N	Y	Y	Y	Y	Y	?
ARIZONA								
1 *Rhodes*	?	?	?	?	?	?	?	Y
2 Udall	N	N	Y	Y	N	N	N	Y
3 *Stump*	N	N	Y	Y	Y	Y	Y	N
4 *Rudd*	N	N	Y	Y	Y	Y	Y	Y
ARKANSAS								
1 Alexander	N	Y	Y	Y	Y	Y	Y	Y
2 *Bethune*	N	Y	Y	Y	Y	Y	Y	Y
3 *Hammerschmidt*	N	Y	Y	Y	Y	Y	Y	Y
4 Anthony	N	Y	Y	Y	?	Y	Y	Y
CALIFORNIA								
1 *Chappie*	N	N	Y	Y	Y	Y	Y	Y
2 *Clausen*	N	N	Y	?	?	Y	Y	Y
3 Matsui	N	N	Y	Y	Y	N	N	Y
4 Fazio	N	N	Y	Y	Y	N	N	Y
5 Burton, J.	Y	Y	N	Y	Y	N	N	Y
6 Burton, P.	Y	N	N	Y	Y	N	N	Y
7 Miller	Y	Y	N	Y	Y	N	N	Y
8 Dellums	Y	N	N	Y	Y	N	N	Y
9 Stark	Y	Y	N	Y	Y	N	N	Y
10 Edwards	Y	Y	N	?	Y	N	N	Y
11 Lantos	N	Y	Y	Y	Y	N	N	Y
12 *McCloskey*	N	N	Y	?	?	X	?
13 Mineta	Y	Y	Y	Y	?	X	?	Y
14 Shumway	N	N	Y	Y	Y	Y	Y	Y
15 Coelho	N	Y	Y	Y	Y	N	N	Y
16 Panetta	N	N	Y	Y	Y	N	N	Y
17 *Pashayan*	N	Y	?	?	Y	N	Y	Y
18 *Thomas*	Y	N	Y	Y	?	?	?	Y
19 *Lagomarsino*	N	N	Y	Y	Y	Y	Y	Y
20 *Goldwater*	Y	N	Y	Y	Y	Y	Y	Y
21 *Fiedler*	Y	Y	Y	Y	Y	Y	Y	Y
22 *Moorhead*	N	N	Y	Y	Y	Y	Y	Y
23 Beilenson	Y	N	N	Y	Y	N	N	Y
24 Waxman	Y	N	Y	Y	Y	N	N	Y
25 Roybal	Y	N	Y	Y	N	Y	N	Y
26 *Rousselot*	N	N	Y	?	?	?	N	Y
27 *Dornan*	N	?	Y	Y	Y	Y	Y	Y
28 Dixon	?	?	?	?	X	?	Y	Y
29 Hawkins	Y	Y	N	Y	Y	N	N	?
30 Danielson	+	+	Y	Y	Y	N	N	Y
31 Dymally	Y	N	N	Y	N	Y	N	Y
32 Anderson	N	N	Y	Y	Y	N	N	Y
33 *Grisham*	N	Y	Y	Y	Y	Y	Y	Y
34 *Lungren*	N	N	Y	Y	Y	Y	Y	N
35 *Dreier*	N	N	Y	Y	Y	Y	Y	Y
36 Brown	?	N	N	Y	N	Y	N	Y
37 Lewis	N	N	Y	Y	Y	N	Y	Y
38 Patterson	Y	Y	Y	Y	Y	N	N	Y
39 *Dannemeyer*	Y	N	Y	Y	Y	Y	Y	Y
40 *Badham*	?	?	?	?	?	?	?	Y
41 *Lowery*	N	N	Y	Y	Y	N	Y	Y
42 *Hunter*	N	Y	Y	Y	Y	Y	Y	Y
43 *Burgener*	Y	N	Y	Y	Y	Y	Y	Y
COLORADO								
1 Schroeder	Y	Y	N	Y	Y	Y	?	Y
2 Wirth	?	?	?	?	?	?	?	Y
3 Kogovsek	Y	Y	Y	Y	Y	Y	N	Y
4 *Brown*	Y	N	Y	Y	Y	Y	N	Y

	129	130	131	132	133	134	135	136
5 *Kramer*	Y	Y	Y	Y	Y	N	Y	Y
CONNECTICUT								
1 Cotter	?	?	?	?	?	?	?	?
2 Gejdenson	Y	Y	Y	Y	Y	N	N	Y
3 *DeNardis*	Y	Y	Y	Y	Y	N	N	Y
4 *McKinney*	Y	Y	Y	Y	Y	N	N	Y
5 Ratchford	Y	Y	Y	Y	Y	N	N	Y
6 Moffett	Y	Y	N	Y	?	?	?	Y
DELAWARE								
AL *Evans*	N	N	Y	?	Y	N	N	Y
FLORIDA								
1 Hutto	N	N	Y	Y	Y	Y	Y	Y
2 Fuqua	N	N	Y	Y	Y	Y	N	Y
3 Bennett	N	N	Y	Y	Y	Y	N	Y
4 Chappell	N	Y	Y	Y	Y	Y	Y	Y
5 *McCollum*	N	Y	Y	Y	?	?	?	Y
6 *Young*	Y	N	Y	Y	?	#	?	Y
7 Gibbons	N	N	Y	Y	Y	N	?	Y
8 Ireland	N	N	Y	Y	Y	Y	Y	Y
9 Nelson	N	N	Y	Y	Y	#	?	Y
10 *Bafalis*	N	N	Y	Y	Y	Y	Y	Y
11 Mica	N	Y	Y	Y	N	?	?	Y
12 *Shaw*	N	N	Y	Y	Y	Y	Y	Y
13 Lehman	N	N	Y	Y	N	N	N	Y
14 Pepper	N	Y	Y	Y	N	N	N	Y
15 Fascell	N	N	Y	Y	N	N	N	Y
GEORGIA								
1 Ginn	N	Y	Y	Y	Y	Y	Y	Y
2 Hatcher	N	N	Y	Y	Y	Y	Y	Y
3 Brinkley	N	N	Y	Y	Y	Y	Y	Y
4 Levitas	N	Y	Y	Y	Y	Y	N	Y
5 Fowler	N	N	Y	Y	Y	N	N	Y
6 *Gingrich*	Y	N	Y	?	Y	Y	Y	Y
7 McDonald	N	N	Y	Y	Y	P	Y	N
8 Evans	N	Y	Y	Y	?	?	?	Y
9 Jenkins	N	N	Y	Y	Y	Y	Y	Y
10 Barnard	N	N	Y	Y	Y	Y	Y	Y
HAWAII								
1 Heftel	N	Y	Y	Y	?	?	N	Y
2 Akaka	Y	Y	Y	Y	Y	N	N	Y
IDAHO								
1 *Craig*	Y	Y	Y	Y	Y	Y	Y	Y
2 *Hansen*	Y	N	Y	Y	Y	Y	Y	Y
ILLINOIS								
1 Washington	Y	Y	N	Y	Y	N	N	Y
2 Savage	?	Y	N	Y	?	N	N	Y
3 Russo	Y	Y	Y	Y	Y	Y	Y	Y
4 *Derwinski*	Y	N	Y	Y	Y	Y	Y	Y
5 Fary	N	N	Y	Y	N	Y	N	Y
6 *Hyde*	N	N	?	?	Y	N	N	Y
7 Collins	Y	Y	N	Y	?	X	?	Y
8 Rostenkowski	Y	Y	N	Y	Y	N	?	Y
9 Yates	Y	N	Y	Y	N	Y	N	Y
10 *Porter*	N	N	Y	Y	N	Y	N	Y
11 Annunzio	N	N	Y	Y	Y	N	N	Y
12 *Crane, P.*	N	N	Y	Y	Y	Y	Y	N
13 *McClory*	N	N	Y	Y	Y	N	N	Y
14 *Erlenborn*	Y	N	Y	Y	Y	N	N	Y
15 *Corcoran*	N	Y	Y	+	#	#	Y
16 *Martin*	Y	Y	Y	Y	Y	Y	Y	Y
17 *O'Brien*	N	N	Y	Y	Y	N	N	Y
18 *Michel*	N	N	Y	Y	Y	N	Y	N
19 *Railsback*	N	Y	Y	Y	?	N	Y	Y
20 *Findley*	Y	Y	Y	Y	Y	N	N	Y
21 *Madigan*	N	Y	Y	Y	Y	N	Y	Y
22 *Crane, D.*	N	N	Y	Y	Y	Y	Y	N
23 Price	N	N	Y	Y	N	Y	N	Y
24 Simon	N	N	Y	?	?	#	?	Y
INDIANA								
1 Benjamin	N	Y	Y	Y	Y	N	N	Y
2 Fithian	?	?	?	?	?	?	?	Y
3 *Hiler*	N	N	Y	Y	Y	Y	Y	Y
4 *Coats*	N	Y	Y	Y	Y	Y	Y	Y
5 *Hillis*	N	Y	Y	Y	Y	Y	Y	Y
6 Evans	N	N	Y	Y	Y	N	N	Y
7 *Myers*	N	Y	Y	Y	Y	Y	Y	Y
8 *Deckard*	Y	Y	Y	Y	?	Y	N	Y
9 Hamilton	N	N	Y	Y	Y	N	Y	Y
10 Sharp	N	Y	Y	Y	N	N	N	Y
11 Jacobs	N	Y	Y	Y	Y	N	Y	Y
IOWA								
1 *Leach*	N	N	Y	Y	Y	N	N	Y
2 *Tauke*	Y	N	N	Y	?	?	?	Y
3 *Evans*	Y	N	Y	Y	Y	Y	Y	Y
4 Smith	N	N	Y	Y	?	?	?	Y
5 Harkin	N	N	Y	Y	Y	N	N	Y
6 Bedell	N	N	N	Y	Y	Y	N	Y

Democrats *Republicans*

Corresponding to Congressional Record Votes 138, 139, 140, 141, 142, 143, 144, 145

	129	130	131	132	133	134	135	136
KANSAS								
1 ***Roberts***	N	N	Y	Y	Y	Y	?	Y
2 ***Jeffries***	N	N	Y	Y	Y	Y	Y	N
3 ***Winn***	N	N	Y	Y	?	?	?	Y
4 Glickman	N	N	Y	Y	Y	Y	?	Y
5 ***Whittaker***	N	N	Y	Y	Y	Y	N	Y
KENTUCKY								
1 Hubbard	N	Y	Y	Y	Y	Y	Y	Y
2 Natcher	N	Y	Y	Y	Y	N	N	Y
3 Mazzoli	N	Y	Y	Y	+	-	-	Y
4 ***Snyder***	N	Y	Y	Y	Y	Y	Y	Y
5 ***Rogers***	N	Y	Y	Y	Y	Y	Y	Y
6 ***Hopkins***	N	Y	Y	Y	Y	Y	Y	Y
7 Perkins	Y	N	Y	?	Y	N	Y	Y
LOUISIANA								
1 ***Livingston***	N	N	Y	Y	Y	N	N	Y
2 Boggs	N	N	Y	Y	Y	N	N	Y
3 Tauzin	N	N	Y	Y	Y	Y	N	Y
4 Roemer	N	Y	Y	Y	Y	Y	N	Y
5 Huckaby	N	N	Y	Y	Y	Y	N	Y
6 ***Moore***	Y	N	Y	Y	Y	Y	N	Y
7 Breaux	N	N	Y	Y	Y	#	N	Y
8 Long	N	N	Y	Y	Y	N	N	Y
MAINE								
1 ***Emery***	N	Y	Y	Y	?	?	X	Y
2 ***Snowe***	Y	Y	Y	Y	Y	Y	N	Y
MARYLAND								
1 Dyson	N	Y	Y	Y	Y	Y	Y	Y
2 Long	N	Y	Y	Y	Y	N	N	Y
3 Mikulski	Y	Y	Y	Y	Y	N	N	Y
4 ***Holt***	?	?	?	?	?	?	?	Y
5 Hoyer	N	Y	Y	Y	Y	N	N	Y
6 Byron	N	Y	Y	Y	Y	Y	Y	Y
7 Mitchell	Y	Y	N	?	?	X	?	Y
8 Barnes	N	Y	Y	Y	Y	N	N	Y
MASSACHUSETTS								
1 ***Conte***	Y	N	Y	Y	Y	N	N	Y
2 Boland	Y	Y	Y	?	Y	N	N	Y
3 Early	Y	Y	N	Y	Y	N	N	Y
4 Frank	N	Y	N	Y	Y	N	N	Y
5 Shannon	Y	Y	Y	Y	Y	N	N	Y
6 Mavroules	N	Y	Y	Y	Y	N	Y	Y
7 Markey	Y	Y	N	Y	Y	N	N	Y
8 O'Neill								
9 Moakley	N	Y	N	Y	Y	N	N	Y
10 ***Heckler***	N	Y	Y	Y	Y	N	N	Y
11 Donnelly	N	Y	N	Y	Y	N	N	Y
12 Studds	Y	N	N	Y	Y	N	N	Y
MICHIGAN								
1 Conyers	Y	Y	N	N	Y	N	N	Y
2 ***Pursell***	Y	Y	Y	Y	Y	N	N	Y
3 Wolpe	Y	Y	N	Y	Y	N	N	Y
4 ***Siljander***	N	Y	Y	Y	?	Y	Y	?
5 ***Sawyer***	N	Y	Y	Y	Y	N	Y	Y
6 ***Dunn***	Y	Y	Y	Y	Y	Y	Y	Y
7 Kildee	Y	Y	N	Y	Y	N	N	Y
8 Traxler	Y	Y	Y	Y	Y	N	N	Y
9 ***Vander Jagt***	N	Y	Y	Y	Y	Y	Y	Y
10 Albosta	N	Y	Y	Y	?	?	?	Y
11 ***Davis***	N	Y	Y	Y	Y	N	Y	Y
12 Bonior	N	Y	N	Y	Y	N	N	Y
13 Crockett	?	Y	N	?	?	N	N	Y
14 Hertel	Y	Y	Y	Y	Y	N	Y	Y
15 Ford	?	Y	Y	Y	?	?	?	+
16 Dingell	Y	Y	Y	Y	Y	?	N	Y
17 Brodhead	Y	Y	Y	Y	Y	N	N	Y
18 Blanchard	N	Y	Y	Y	Y	N	N	Y
19 ***Broomfield***	N	Y	Y	Y	Y	Y	Y	Y
MINNESOTA								
1 ***Erdahl***	Y	N	Y	Y	Y	Y	N	Y
2 ***Hagedorn***	Y	N	Y	?	Y	#	Y	Y
3 ***Frenzel***	N	N	Y	Y	Y	Y	Y	Y
4 Vento	Y	Y	N	Y	Y	N	N	Y
5 Sabo	N	Y	N	Y	Y	N	N	Y
6 ***Weber***	N	N	Y	Y	Y	Y	N	Y
7 ***Stangeland***	Y	N	Y	Y	Y	Y	Y	Y
8 Oberstar	N	Y	N	Y	Y	N	N	Y
MISSISSIPPI								
1 Whitten	N	Y	Y	Y	Y	N	N	Y
2 Bowen	N	N	Y	Y	?	?	?	Y
3 Montgomery	N	N	Y	Y	Y	Y	Y	Y
4 Dowdy	N	Y	Y	Y	Y	Y	Y	Y
5 ***Lott***	N	N	Y	Y	Y	Y	?	Y
MISSOURI								
1 Clay	N	Y	N	?	Y	N	N	Y
2 Young	N	Y	Y	Y	Y	Y	#	Y
3 Gephardt	N	Y	Y	Y	Y	Y	N	Y
4 Skelton	N	Y	Y	Y	Y	Y	Y	Y
5 Bolling	N	N	N	?	?	?	?	Y
6 ***Coleman***	N	Y	Y	?	Y	Y	N	Y
7 ***Taylor***	N	Y	Y	Y	Y	Y	Y	Y
8 ***Bailey***	Y	Y	Y	Y	Y	Y	Y	Y
9 Volkmer	N	Y	Y	Y	Y	Y	Y	Y
10 ***Emerson***	N	Y	Y	Y	Y	Y	Y	Y
MONTANA								
1 Williams	N	Y	Y	Y	Y	N	N	Y
2 ***Marlenee***	N	Y	Y	Y	Y	Y	Y	Y
NEBRASKA								
1 ***Bereuter***	Y	N	Y	Y	Y	P	N	Y
2 ***Daub***	Y	Y	Y	Y	Y	Y	Y	Y
3 ***Smith***	Y	N	Y	Y	Y	N	Y	Y
NEVADA								
AL Santini	N	Y	Y	Y	?	?	?	Y
NEW HAMPSHIRE								
1 D'Amours	Y	Y	Y	Y	Y	N	N	Y
2 ***Gregg***	N	N	Y	Y	Y	Y	?	Y
NEW JERSEY								
1 Florio	?	?	?	?	?	?	?	Y
2 Hughes	N	N	Y	Y	Y	Y	N	Y
3 Howard	Y	Y	Y	Y	Y	Y	N	Y
4 ***Smith***	Y	Y	Y	Y	Y	N	N	Y
5 ***Fenwick***	Y	N	Y	Y	Y	Y	N	Y
6 ***Forsythe***	Y	N	N	?	Y	Y	N	Y
7 ***Roukema***	Y	N	Y	Y	Y	N	N	Y
8 Roe	N	Y	Y	Y	Y	Y	N	Y
9 ***Hollenbeck***	N	Y	Y	?	Y	X	X	Y
10 Rodino	Y	N	N	Y	Y	N	N	Y
11 Minish	N	Y	Y	Y	Y	N	N	Y
12 ***Rinaldo***	N	Y	Y	Y	Y	Y	N	Y
13 ***Courter***	Y	N	Y	Y	?	#	X	Y
14 Guarini	Y	Y	Y	Y	Y	N	N	Y
15 Dwyer	Y	Y	Y	Y	Y	N	N	Y
NEW MEXICO								
1 ***Lujan***	N	Y	Y	Y	Y	Y	N	Y
2 ***Skeen***	N	Y	Y	Y	Y	Y	Y	Y
NEW YORK								
1 ***Carney***	N	N	Y	Y	Y	Y	Y	Y
2 Downey	Y	N	Y	Y	Y	N	N	Y
3 ***Carman***	N	N	Y	Y	Y	Y	Y	Y
4 ***Lent***	N	N	Y	Y	Y	N	Y	Y
5 ***McGrath***	Y	N	Y	Y	Y	N	Y	Y
6 ***LeBoutillier***	N	N	Y	Y	Y	Y	Y	Y
7 Addabbo	Y	Y	Y	?	?	X	X	Y
8 Rosenthal	Y	Y	N	?	Y	N	N	?
9 Ferraro	N	Y	Y	Y	Y	N	N	Y
10 Biaggi	Y	Y	Y	Y	Y	?	?	Y
11 Scheuer	Y	Y	Y	Y	Y	N	N	Y
12 Chisholm	Y	?	N	Y	Y	N	N	Y
13 Solarz	Y	N	Y	Y	Y	N	N	Y
14 Richmond	Y	Y	N	Y	?	X	?	Y
15 Zeferetti	N	Y	Y	?	?	X	X	Y
16 Schumer	Y	?	?	?	Y	N	N	Y
17 ***Molinari***	N	Y	Y	Y	Y	Y	N	Y
18 ***Green***	Y	N	Y	?	Y	N	N	Y
19 Rangel	Y	Y	N	Y	Y	N	N	Y
20 Weiss	Y	Y	N	N	Y	N	N	Y
21 Garcia	Y	Y	N	Y	Y	N	N	Y
22 Bingham	Y	N	N	?	Y	N	N	Y
23 Peyser	Y	Y	Y	Y	Y	N	Y	Y
24 Ottinger	Y	Y	N	Y	Y	N	N	Y
25 ***Fish***	N	Y	Y	Y	Y	N	N	Y
26 ***Gilman***	N	Y	Y	Y	Y	N	Y	Y
27 McHugh	N	N	Y	Y	Y	N	N	Y
28 Stratton	N	Y	Y	Y	Y	Y	N	Y
29 ***Solomon***	N	Y	Y	Y	Y	Y	N	Y
30 ***Martin***	N	Y	Y	Y	Y	Y	N	Y
31 ***Mitchell***	N	N	Y	Y	Y	Y	N	Y
32 ***Wortley***	N	N	Y	Y	Y	Y	Y	Y
33 ***Lee***	N	Y	Y	Y	Y	Y	N	Y
34 ***Horton***	Y	Y	Y	?	?	X	X	Y
35 ***Conable***	Y	N	Y	Y	Y	Y	Y	N
36 LaFalce	Y	N	Y	Y	Y	N	N	Y
37 Nowak	Y	Y	?	Y	Y	?	Y	Y
38 ***Kemp***	N	N	Y	?	?	?	?	Y
39 Lundine	Y	Y	N	Y	?	?	?	Y
NORTH CAROLINA								
1 Jones	?	?	?	?	?	?	?	Y
2 Fountain	N	N	Y	Y	Y	Y	N	Y
3 Whitley	N	N	Y	Y	Y	?	?	Y
4 Andrews	N	Y	Y	?	Y	Y	N	Y
5 Neal	N	N	Y	Y	Y	Y	N	Y
6 ***Johnston***	N	N	Y	Y	Y	Y	Y	Y
7 Rose	Y	N	Y	Y	Y	N	?	Y
8 Hefner	Y	Y	Y	Y	Y	Y	Y	Y
9 ***Martin***	Y	N	Y	Y	Y	Y	Y	N
10 ***Broyhill***	Y	N	Y	?	?	?	?	Y
11 ***Hendon***	N	Y	Y	Y	Y	Y	Y	Y
NORTH DAKOTA								
AL Dorgan	Y	Y	Y	Y	Y	N	N	Y
OHIO								
1 ***Gradison***	N	N	Y	Y	?	?	?	Y
2 Luken	N	Y	Y	Y	Y	Y	Y	Y
3 Hall	N	Y	Y	Y	Y	Y	N	Y
4 ***Oxley****								Y
5 ***Latta***	N	N	Y	Y	?	?	?	Y
6 ***McEwen***	N	Y	Y	Y	Y	Y	Y	Y
7 ***Brown***	N	Y	Y	Y	Y	Y	Y	Y
8 ***Kindness***	N	Y	Y	Y	Y	Y	Y	Y
9 ***Weber***	?	Y	Y	Y	Y	Y	Y	Y
10 ***Miller***	N	Y	Y	Y	Y	Y	Y	Y
11 ***Stanton***	N	N	Y	Y	Y	N	N	Y
12 Shamansky	N	Y	Y	Y	Y	N	N	Y
13 Pease	Y	Y	Y	Y	Y	Y	N	Y
14 Seiberling	N	Y	N	Y	Y	Y	N	Y
15 ***Wylie***	Y	N	Y	Y	Y	Y	N	Y
16 ***Regula***	Y	Y	Y	Y	?	N	Y	Y
17 ***Ashbrook***	N	Y	Y	Y	Y	Y	Y	Y
18 Applegate	N	Y	Y	Y	?	Y	Y	Y
19 ***Williams***	N	Y	Y	Y	Y	N	Y	Y
20 Oakar	N	Y	Y	Y	Y	N	N	Y
21 Stokes	Y	Y	N	Y	Y	N	N	Y
22 Eckart	Y	Y	Y	Y	Y	N	N	Y
23 Mottl	Y	Y	Y	Y	?	?	?	Y
OKLAHOMA								
1 Jones	N	N	Y	Y	Y	Y	N	Y
2 Synar	N	Y	Y	Y	Y	N	N	Y
3 Watkins	N	Y	Y	Y	Y	N	Y	Y
4 McCurdy	N	Y	Y	Y	Y	Y	N	Y
5 ***Edwards***	N	N	Y	?	Y	Y	Y	Y
6 English	N	Y	Y	Y	Y	Y	Y	Y
OREGON								
1 AuCoin	Y	N	N	Y	Y	N	N	Y
2 ***Smith***	N	N	Y	Y	Y	Y	Y	Y
3 Wyden	N	Y	N	Y	Y	Y	N	Y
4 Weaver	Y	Y	N	Y	Y	Y	N	Y
PENNSYLVANIA								
1 Foglietta	N	Y	Y	Y	Y	N	N	?
2 Gray	N	Y	N	Y	Y	N	N	Y
3 Vacancy								
4 ***Dougherty***	N	Y	Y	?	Y	N	Y	Y
5 ***Schulze***	N	N	Y	?	Y	Y	Y	Y
6 Yatron	N	Y	Y	Y	Y	Y	Y	Y
7 Edgar	Y	Y	N	Y	?	N	N	Y
8 ***Coyne, J.***	N	Y	Y	Y	Y	Y	Y	Y
9 ***Shuster***	N	Y	Y	Y	Y	Y	Y	Y
10 ***McDade***	Y	Y	Y	Y	Y	N	N	Y
11 ***Nelligan***	Y	Y	Y	Y	Y	N	Y	Y
12 Murtha	N	N	Y	Y	?	?	Y	Y
13 ***Coughlin***	Y	Y	Y	Y	Y	N	Y	Y
14 Coyne, W.	N	Y	Y	Y	Y	N	N	Y
15 ***Ritter***	Y	Y	Y	Y	Y	Y	Y	Y
16 ***Walker***	N	Y	Y	Y	Y	Y	Y	Y
17 Ertel	N	Y	Y	Y	Y	Y	Y	Y
18 Walgren	Y	Y	Y	Y	Y	N	Y	Y
19 ***Goodling***	Y	Y	Y	Y	?	?	Y	Y
20 Gaydos	Y	Y	Y	Y	?	N	Y	Y
21 Bailey	N	Y	Y	Y	Y	N	Y	Y
22 Murphy	N	Y	Y	Y	Y	Y	Y	Y
23 ***Clinger***	Y	N	Y	Y	Y	N	Y	Y
24 ***Marks***	N	Y	Y	?	Y	Y	Y	Y
25 Atkinson	N	Y	Y	Y	Y	N	Y	Y
RHODE ISLAND								
1 St Germain	Y	Y	Y	Y	?	?	?	Y
2 ***Schneider***	Y	Y	Y	Y	Y	Y	N	Y
SOUTH CAROLINA								
1 ***Hartnett***	N	Y	Y	Y	Y	Y	Y	Y
2 ***Spence***	N	N	Y	Y	Y	Y	Y	Y
3 Derrick	N	Y	?	?	?	?	?	Y
4 ***Campbell***	N	N	Y	?	Y	Y	Y	Y
5 Holland	N	N	Y	Y	?	?	?	Y
6 ***Napier***	N	N	Y	Y	Y	Y	Y	Y
SOUTH DAKOTA								
1 Daschle	Y	Y	Y	Y	Y	N	N	Y
2 ***Roberts***	Y	Y	Y	Y	Y	Y	Y	+
TENNESSEE								
1 ***Quillen***	N	Y	Y	?	?	#	#	Y
2 ***Duncan***	N	Y	Y	Y	Y	Y	Y	Y
3 Bouquard	N	Y	Y	Y	Y	Y	#	Y
4 Gore	N	Y	Y	Y	Y	Y	N	Y
5 Boner	N	Y	Y	Y	Y	Y	N	Y
6 ***Beard***	N	Y	Y	?	Y	Y	Y	Y
7 Jones	N	Y	Y	Y	Y	Y	Y	+
8 Ford	Y	Y	Y	Y	Y	N	N	Y
TEXAS								
1 Hall, S.	N	Y	Y	Y	Y	Y	Y	Y
2 Wilson	N	N	Y	Y	Y	N	Y	Y
3 ***Collins***	N	N	Y	Y	Y	Y	Y	Y
4 Hall, R.	N	Y	Y	Y	Y	N	Y	Y
5 Mattox	N	Y	Y	Y	Y	N	N	?
6 Gramm	N	N	Y	Y	Y	Y	Y	N
7 ***Archer***	N	N	Y	Y	Y	Y	Y	Y
8 ***Fields***	N	N	Y	Y	Y	Y	Y	Y
9 Brooks	N	N	Y	Y	Y	Y	Y	Y
10 Pickle	N	N	Y	?	Y	N	N	Y
11 Leath	N	N	Y	Y	Y	Y	Y	Y
12 Wright	Y	N	Y	Y	Y	Y	Y	Y
13 Hightower	N	Y	Y	Y	Y	N	Y	Y
14 Patman	N	N	Y	Y	Y	Y	Y	Y
15 de la Garza	N	Y	Y	Y	Y	Y	Y	Y
16 White	N	N	Y	Y	Y	Y	Y	Y
17 Stenholm	N	N	Y	Y	Y	?	?	Y
18 Leland	Y	Y	N	Y	Y	N	N	Y
19 Hance	N	N	Y	Y	Y	Y	N	Y
20 Gonzalez	N	N	Y	Y	Y	Y	N	Y
21 ***Loeffler***	N	N	Y	Y	Y	N	Y	Y
22 ***Paul***	Y	Y	N	Y	P	Y	Y	Y
23 Kazen	N	N	Y	Y	Y	Y	Y	Y
24 Frost	N	N	Y	Y	Y	N	N	Y
UTAH								
1 ***Hansen***	Y	N	Y	Y	Y	Y	Y	-
2 ***Marriott***	N	Y	Y	Y	Y	Y	Y	Y
VERMONT								
AL ***Jeffords***	Y	N	Y	Y	Y	Y	N	Y
VIRGINIA								
1 ***Trible***	N	N	Y	Y	Y	Y	Y	Y
2 ***Whitehurst***	N	N	Y	?	Y	Y	Y	Y
3 ***Bliley***	N	N	Y	Y	Y	Y	Y	Y
4 ***Daniel, R.***	N	N	Y	Y	Y	Y	Y	Y
5 Daniel, D.	N	N	Y	Y	Y	Y	Y	Y
6 ***Butler***	N	N	Y	Y	Y	Y	Y	Y
7 ***Robinson***	N	N	Y	Y	?	#	#	Y
8 ***Parris***	N	Y	Y	Y	Y	Y	Y	Y
9 ***Wampler***	N	N	Y	Y	Y	Y	Y	Y
10 ***Wolf***	N	N	Y	Y	Y	Y	Y	Y
WASHINGTON								
1 ***Pritchard***	N	N	Y	Y	Y	N	N	Y
2 Swift	N	Y	Y	Y	Y	N	N	Y
3 Bonker	Y	N	Y	Y	Y	N	N	?
4 ***Morrison***	N	N	Y	Y	Y	Y	Y	Y
5 Foley	Y	N	Y	?	Y	N	?	Y
6 Dicks	Y	N	Y	Y	Y	Y	N	+
7 Lowry	N	N	N	Y	Y	N	N	Y
WEST VIRGINIA								
1 Mollohan	N	N	Y	Y	?	X	?	Y
2 ***Benedict***	N	N	Y	Y	?	#	#	Y
3 ***Staton***	Y	Y	Y	Y	Y	Y	Y	Y
4 Rahall	Y	Y	N	Y	?	X	?	Y
WISCONSIN								
1 Aspin	Y	Y	N	Y	Y	Y	N	Y
2 Kastenmeier	Y	Y	N	Y	Y	N	N	Y
3 ***Gunderson***	Y	Y	Y	Y	Y	Y	N	Y
4 Zablocki	N	N	Y	Y	Y	N	N	Y
5 Reuss	Y	N	N	Y	Y	N	N	Y
6 ***Petri***	N	N	Y	Y	Y	Y	Y	Y
7 Obey	Y	Y	N	Y	Y	N	N	Y
8 ***Roth***	N	N	Y	Y	?	?	?	Y
9 ***Sensenbrenner***	N	Y	Y	Y	Y	Y	Y	Y
WYOMING								
AL ***Cheney***	Y	N	Y	Y	Y	Y	Y	Y

** Rep. Michael G. Oxley, R-Ohio, was sworn in July 21, 1981. The first vote for which he was eligible was CQ vote 136.*

Democrats ***Republicans***

KEY

Y Voted for (yea).
\# Paired for.
\+ Announced for.
N Voted against (nay).
X Paired against.
- Announced against.
P Voted "present".
C Voted "present" to avoid possible conflict of interest.
? Did not vote or otherwise make a position known.

---

137. HR 4034. HUD-Independent Agencies Appropriations, Fiscal 1982. Winn, R-Kan., amendment to cut the appropriation for the National Science Foundation from $1.06 billion to $995 million. Rejected 152-264: R 116-69; D 36-195 (ND 13-141, SD 23-54), July 21, 1981.

138. HR 4034. HUD-Independent Agencies Appropriations, Fiscal 1982. Passage of the bill to appropriate $62,599,958,500 in fiscal 1982 for the Department of Housing and Urban Development and 20 independent agencies. Passed 362-54: R 148-37; D 214-17 (ND 143-12, SD 71-5), July 21, 1981. The president had requested $63,122,794,500.

139. HR 4035. Interior Appropriations, Fiscal 1982. Yates, D-Ill., motion that the House resolve itself into the Committee of the Whole for consideration of the bill. Motion agreed to 378-3: R 173-1; D 205-2 (ND 135-1; SD 70-1), July 21, 1981.

140. HR 4035. Interior Appropriations, Fiscal 1982. Lujan, R-N.M., amendment to provide $100 million for the administrative expenses of the Payments in Lieu of Taxes program. Rejected 96-320: R 55-130; D 41-190 (ND 32-123; SD 9-67), July 21, 1981.

141. HR 4035. Interior Appropriations, Fiscal 1982. Yates, D-Ill., motion that the House resolve itself into the Committee of the Whole for further consideration of the bill. Motion agreed to 383-3: R 179-1; D 204-2 (ND 133-1, SD 71-1), July 22, 1981.

142. HR 4035. Interior Appropriations, Fiscal 1982. Weber, R-Minn., amendment to delete $135 million earmarked for the solvent refined coal demonstration plant at Newman, Ky. Rejected 177-236: R 93-89; D 84-147 (ND 78-76, SD 6-71), July 22, 1981.

143. HR 4035. Interior Appropriations, Fiscal 1982. Glickman, D-Kan., amendment to delete $30,000 earmarked for the Franklin Delano Roosevelt Memorial Commission. Rejected 201-216: R 160-23; D 41-193 (ND 27-131, SD 14-62), July 22, 1981.

144. HR 4035. Interior Appropriations, Fiscal 1982. Passage of the bill to appropriate $11,139,727,000 in fiscal 1982 for the Interior Department and related agencies. Passed 358-46: R 143-33; D 215-13 (ND 150-4, SD 65-9), July 22, 1981. The president had requested $11,216,620,000.

	137	138	139	140	141	142	143	144
ALABAMA								
1 *Edwards*	Y	Y	Y	N	Y	N	Y	Y
2 *Dickinson*	Y	Y	Y	N	Y	N	Y	Y
3 Nichols	N	Y	Y	N	Y	N	N	Y
4 Bevill	N	Y	Y	N	Y	N	N	Y
5 Flippo	N	Y	Y	N	Y	N	N	Y
6 *Smith*	Y	Y	Y	Y	Y	N	Y	Y
7 Shelby	N	Y	Y	N	Y	N	Y	N
ALASKA								
AL *Young*	\#	?	?	?	?	X	?	?
ARIZONA								
1 *Rhodes*	Y	Y	Y	?	Y	Y	Y	Y
2 Udall	N	Y	Y	Y	Y	Y	N	Y
3 *Stump*	Y	N	Y	N	N	N	N	N
4 *Rudd*	Y	Y	Y	Y	Y	N	Y	Y
ARKANSAS								
1 Alexander	N	Y	Y	N	Y	N	N	Y
2 *Bethune*	Y	Y	Y	N	Y	N	Y	N
3 *Hammerschmidt*	Y	Y	Y	Y	Y	N	N	Y
4 Anthony	N	Y	?	?	Y	N	N	Y
CALIFORNIA								
1 *Chappie*	Y	Y	Y	Y	Y	Y	Y	N
2 *Clausen*	N	Y	Y	Y	Y	Y	Y	Y
3 Matsui	N	Y	Y	N	?	N	N	Y
4 Fazio	Y	Y	Y	Y	Y	N	N	Y
5 Burton, J.	N	N	Y	Y	?	Y	N	Y
6 Burton, P.	N	Y	Y	N	Y	Y	N	Y
7 Miller	N	Y	Y	N	Y	Y	N	Y
8 Dellums	N	Y	Y	N	Y	Y	N	Y
9 Stark	N	Y	Y	N	Y	Y	N	Y
10 Edwards	N	Y	Y	N	Y	N	N	Y
11 Lantos	N	Y	Y	N	Y	Y	N	Y
12 *McCloskey*	X	?	?	?	?	\#	?	?
13 Mineta	N	Y	Y	N	Y	N	N	Y
14 *Shumway*	Y	N	Y	Y	Y	N	Y	N
15 Coelho	Y	Y	Y	Y	Y	N	Y	Y
16 Panetta	N	Y	Y	N	Y	N	N	Y
17 *Pashayan*	Y	Y	Y	Y	Y	Y	Y	Y
18 *Thomas*	Y	Y	Y	Y	Y	Y	Y	Y
19 *Lagomarsino*	Y	Y	Y	Y	Y	Y	Y	Y
20 *Goldwater*	\#	Y	Y	Y	Y	Y	Y	Y
21 *Fiedler*	N	Y	Y	Y	Y	N	Y	Y
22 *Moorhead*	Y	N	Y	Y	Y	Y	Y	N
23 Beilenson	N	Y	N	?	Y	N	N	Y
24 Waxman	N	Y	Y	N	Y	Y	N	Y
25 Roybal	N	Y	Y	Y	Y	N	N	Y
26 *Rousselot*	Y	N	Y	N	?	Y	Y	Y
27 *Dornan*	Y	?	?	?	Y	Y	Y	Y
28 Dixon	N	Y	Y	N	N	N	N	Y
29 Hawkins	X	?	?	?	Y	Y	N	Y
30 Danielson	N	Y	Y	N	N	N	N	Y
31 Dymally	?	?	?	?	?	?	?	?
32 Anderson	N	Y	Y	N	?	N	N	Y
33 *Grisham*	Y	Y	Y	Y	Y	Y	Y	N
34 *Lungren*	Y	N	Y	N	Y	Y	Y	N
35 *Dreier*	Y	N	Y	N	Y	Y	Y	Y
36 Brown	N	Y	Y	N	Y	Y	N	Y
37 *Lewis*	N	N	Y	Y	?	?	?	?
38 Patterson	N	Y	Y	N	Y	?	Y	Y
39 *Dannemeyer*	Y	N	Y	N	Y	Y	Y	N
40 *Badham*	Y	N	Y	Y	Y	N	Y	N
41 *Lowery*	N	Y	Y	Y	Y	Y	Y	Y
42 *Hunter*	Y	Y	Y	N	Y	N	Y	N
43 *Burgener*	Y	Y	Y	Y	Y	Y	Y	Y
COLORADO								
1 Schroeder	N	N	Y	Y	Y	Y	Y	Y
2 Wirth	N	Y	Y	Y	Y	Y	N	Y
3 Kogovsek	N	Y	Y	Y	Y	N	N	Y
4 *Brown*	Y	Y	Y	Y	Y	Y	Y	N

	137	138	139	140	141	142	143	144
5 *Kramer*	Y	Y	Y	Y	Y	N	Y	N
CONNECTICUT								
1 Cotter	?	?	?	?	?	?	?	?
2 Gejdenson	N	Y	Y	N	Y	Y	Y	Y
3 *DeNardis*	N	Y	Y	N	?	Y	Y	Y
4 *McKinney*	N	Y	?	N	Y	N	N	Y
5 Ratchford	N	Y	N	N	Y	Y	N	?
6 Moffett	N	Y	Y	N	?	Y	N	Y
DELAWARE								
AL *Evans*	N	Y	Y	N	Y	N	Y	Y
FLORIDA								
1 Hutto	N	Y	Y	N	Y	N	N	Y
2 Fuqua	N	Y	Y	N	Y	N	N	Y
3 Bennett	Y	Y	Y	N	Y	N	N	Y
4 Chappell	Y	Y	Y	N	Y	N	N	Y
5 *McCollum*	Y	Y	Y	N	Y	Y	Y	Y
6 *Young*	N	Y	Y	N	Y	N	Y	?
7 Gibbons	N	Y	Y	N	N	N	N	Y
8 Ireland	N	Y	Y	N	N	N	N	Y
9 Nelson	N	Y	Y	N	Y	N	N	Y
10 *Bafalis*	Y	Y	Y	Y	Y	Y	P	Y
11 Mica	N	Y	Y	N	Y	N	?	?
12 *Shaw*	Y	Y	Y	Y	Y	Y	Y	Y
13 Lehman	N	Y	Y	N	Y	N	N	Y
14 Pepper	N	Y	?	N	?	N	N	Y
15 Fascell	N	Y	Y	Y	X	N	Y	Y
GEORGIA								
1 Ginn	N	Y	Y	N	Y	N	N	Y
2 Hatcher	N	Y	Y	N	Y	N	N	Y
3 Brinkley	Y	Y	Y	N	Y	N	Y	N
4 Levitas	N	Y	Y	N	Y	N	N	Y
5 Fowler	N	Y	Y	N	Y	N	N	Y
6 *Gingrich*	N	Y	Y	N	Y	Y	Y	Y
7 McDonald	Y	N	N	N	Y	Y	Y	N
8 Evans	?	?	?	N	Y	N	N	Y
9 Jenkins	Y	Y	Y	N	Y	N	N	Y
10 Barnard	N	Y	Y	Y	Y	N	N	Y
HAWAII								
1 Heftel	N	N	Y	N	?	Y	N	Y
2 Akaka	N	Y	Y	N	?	N	N	Y
IDAHO								
1 *Craig*	Y	Y	Y	Y	Y	Y	Y	Y
2 *Hansen*	Y	N	Y	Y	?	Y	Y	Y
ILLINOIS								
1 Washington	N	Y	?	N	?	Y	N	Y
2 Savage	N	?	?	?	?	?	N	Y
3 Russo	N	N	Y	N	Y	N	N	Y
4 *Derwinski*	Y	N	Y	N	Y	Y	Y	N
5 Fary	N	Y	?	N	Y	N	N	Y
6 *Hyde*	N	Y	Y	N	Y	Y	Y	Y
7 Collins	N	Y	Y	N	?	Y	N	Y
8 Rostenkowski	N	Y	Y	N	N	N	N	Y
9 Yates	N	Y	Y	N	Y	Y	N	Y
10 *Porter*	N	Y	Y	N	Y	Y	Y	Y
11 Annunzio	N	Y	?	N	Y	N	N	Y
12 *Crane, P.*	Y	N	Y	Y	Y	Y	Y	N
13 *McClory*	N	Y	Y	N	?	Y	N	Y
14 *Erlenborn*	N	Y	Y	N	Y	Y	Y	Y
15 *Corcoran*	Y	Y	Y	Y	Y	Y	Y	Y
16 *Martin*	N	Y	Y	N	Y	N	Y	Y
17 *O'Brien*	N	Y	Y	N	Y	Y	Y	Y
18 *Michel*	Y	N	Y	N	Y	?	?	?
19 *Railsback*	N	Y	Y	N	Y	N	N	Y
20 *Findley*	Y	Y	Y	N	Y	N	Y	Y
21 *Madigan*	N	Y	Y	N	Y	N	Y	?
22 *Crane, D.*	Y	N	Y	Y	Y	Y	Y	Y
23 Price	N	Y	Y	N	N	N	N	Y
24 Simon	N	Y	Y	Y	Y	N	N	Y
INDIANA								
1 Benjamin	N	Y	Y	N	N	N	N	Y
2 Fithian	N	Y	Y	N	Y	N	N	Y
3 *Hiler*	Y	N	Y	N	Y	Y	Y	Y
4 *Coats*	Y	Y	Y	N	Y	Y	Y	Y
5 *Hillis*	Y	Y	Y	N	Y	N	Y	Y
6 Evans	N	Y	?	N	N	N	Y	Y
7 *Myers*	N	Y	Y	N	Y	N	N	Y
8 *Deckard*	N	Y	Y	Y	Y	Y	Y	N
9 Hamilton	N	Y	Y	N	N	N	N	Y
10 Sharp	N	Y	Y	N	Y	N	Y	N
11 Jacobs	N	Y	Y	Y	Y	Y	Y	Y
IOWA								
1 Leach	N	Y	Y	N	Y	Y	Y	Y
2 *Tauke*	N	Y	Y	Y	Y	Y	Y	Y
3 Evans	N	N	N	N	N	N	Y	Y
4 Smith	N	Y	Y	N	?	N	N	Y
5 Harkin	N	Y	Y	N	Y	N	Y	Y
6 Bedell	N	Y	Y	N	Y	N	Y	Y

Democrats   *Republicans*

Corresponding to Congressional Record Votes 146, 147, 148, 149, 150, 151, 152, 153

	137	138	139	140	141	142	143	144
KANSAS								
1 ***Roberts***	Y	Y	Y	Y	Y	Y	Y	Y
2 ***Jeffries***	Y	N	Y	N	Y	Y	Y	N
3 ***Winn***	Y	Y	Y	N	Y	Y	Y	Y
4 Glickman	Y	Y	Y	N	Y	N	Y	Y
5 ***Whittaker***	Y	Y	Y	N	Y	N	Y	Y
KENTUCKY								
1 Hubbard	Y	N	Y	N	Y	N	N	Y
2 Natcher	N	Y	Y	N	Y	N	N	Y
3 Mazzoli	N	Y	Y	N	Y	N	N	Y
4 ***Snyder***	Y	Y	Y	N	Y	N	Y	Y
5 ***Rogers***	Y	Y	Y	Y	Y	N	Y	Y
6 ***Hopkins***	Y	Y	Y	N	Y	N	Y	Y
7 Perkins	N	Y	Y	Y	Y	N	N	Y
LOUISIANA								
1 ***Livingston***	Y	Y	?	N	Y	N	Y	Y
2 Boggs	N	Y	Y	N	?	N	N	Y
3 Tauzin	N	Y	?	N	Y	N	Y	Y
4 Roemer	Y	Y	Y	N	Y	Y	Y	N
5 Huckaby	Y	Y	Y	N	Y	N	Y	Y
6 ***Moore***	Y	Y	Y	N	Y	Y	Y	Y
7 Breaux	N	Y	Y	N	Y	N	Y	Y
8 Long	N	Y	Y	N	Y	N	N	Y
MAINE								
1 ***Emery***	N	Y	Y	N	Y	N	Y	Y
2 ***Snowe***	N	Y	Y	N	Y	N	Y	Y
MARYLAND								
1 Dyson	N	Y	Y	N	Y	N	N	Y
2 Long	N	Y	Y	N	Y	N	Y	Y
3 Mikulski	N	Y	Y	N	Y	Y	N	Y
4 ***Holt***	Y	Y	Y	N	Y	N	Y	N
5 Hoyer	N	Y	Y	N	Y	N	N	Y
6 Byron	N	Y	Y	N	Y	N	Y	Y
7 Mitchell	N	Y	?	N	N	Y	N	?
8 Barnes	N	Y	Y	N	Y	Y	N	Y
MASSACHUSETTS								
1 ***Conte***	N	Y	Y	N	Y	N	N	Y
2 Boland	N	Y	Y	N	Y	Y	N	Y
3 Early	N	Y	Y	N	Y	N	Y	Y
4 Frank	N	Y	Y	N	Y	Y	Y	Y
5 Shannon	N	Y	Y	N	Y	Y	N	Y
6 Mavroules	X	?	?	N	Y	N	N	Y
7 Markey	N	Y	Y	N	Y	Y	N	Y
8 O'Neill								
9 Moakley	N	Y	Y	N	Y	Y	N	Y
10 ***Heckler***	N	Y	Y	N	Y	N	Y	Y
11 Donnelly	N	Y	Y	N	?	N	N	Y
12 Studds	N	Y	Y	Y	Y	Y	Y	Y
MICHIGAN								
1 Conyers	N	Y	Y	Y	Y	Y	N	Y
2 ***Pursell***	N	Y	?	N	Y	N	Y	Y
3 Wolpe	N	Y	Y	Y	Y	Y	N	Y
4 ***Siljander***	Y	Y	Y	Y	Y	Y	Y	Y
5 ***Sawyer***	N	Y	Y	N	Y	N	Y	Y
6 ***Dunn***	N	Y	Y	N	Y	Y	Y	Y
7 Kildee	N	Y	Y	N	Y	Y	Y	Y
8 Traxler	N	Y	Y	Y	Y	Y	N	Y
9 ***Vander Jagt***	Y	Y	Y	Y	Y	Y	N	Y
10 Albosta	N	Y	Y	Y	?	N	N	Y
11 ***Davis***	N	Y	Y	Y	Y	Y	N	N
12 Bonior	N	Y	Y	Y	Y	Y	N	Y
13 Crockett	N	Y	?	?	?	Y	N	Y
14 Hertel	N	Y	Y	N	Y	Y	N	Y
15 Ford	N	Y	Y	N	?	N	N	Y
16 Dingell	N	Y	?	N	Y	N	N	Y
17 Brodhead	N	Y	Y	N	Y	Y	N	Y
18 Blanchard	N	Y	Y	N	Y	?	N	Y
19 ***Broomfield***	Y	Y	Y	N	Y	Y	Y	?
MINNESOTA								
1 ***Erdahl***	N	Y	Y	Y	Y	Y	Y	Y
2 ***Hagedorn***	Y	N	Y	N	Y	Y	Y	Y
3 ***Frenzel***	Y	N	Y	Y	Y	Y	Y	N
4 Vento	N	Y	Y	N	Y	Y	N	Y
5 Sabo	N	Y	Y	N	Y	Y	N	Y
6 ***Weber***	Y	Y	Y	N	Y	Y	Y	N
7 ***Stangeland***	Y	Y	Y	Y	Y	Y	Y	Y
8 Oberstar	N	Y	Y	Y	Y	Y	N	Y
MISSISSIPPI								
1 Whitten	N	Y	Y	Y	Y	N	N	Y
2 Bowen	N	Y	Y	N	Y	N	N	Y
3 Montgomery	Y	Y	Y	N	Y	N	Y	Y
4 Dowdy	Y	Y	Y	N	Y	N	N	Y
5 ***Lott***	Y	Y	Y	N	Y	Y	Y	?
MISSOURI								
1 Clay	N	Y	?	N	Y	Y	N	Y
2 Young	N	Y	Y	N	Y	N	N	Y
3 Gephardt	Y	Y	Y	N	Y	N	Y	Y
4 Skelton	#	Y	Y	Y	Y	N	N	Y
5 Bolling	N	Y	?	N	Y	N	N	Y
6 ***Coleman***	Y	Y	?	N	Y	N	Y	Y
7 ***Taylor***	Y	Y	Y	N	Y	N	Y	Y
8 ***Bailey***	N	N	Y	Y	Y	Y	Y	?
9 Volkmer	N	Y	Y	N	Y	N	Y	Y
10 ***Emerson***	Y	Y	Y	N	Y	N	Y	Y
MONTANA								
1 Williams	N	Y	?	Y	?	Y	N	Y
2 ***Marlenee***	Y	N	Y	Y	Y	N	Y	Y
NEBRASKA								
1 ***Bereuter***	Y	Y	Y	N	Y	Y	Y	Y
2 ***Daub***	Y	Y	Y	Y	Y	Y	Y	Y
3 ***Smith***	Y	Y	Y	Y	Y	Y	Y	Y
NEVADA								
AL Santini	Y	Y	Y	Y	Y	Y	Y	Y
NEW HAMPSHIRE								
1 D'Amours	N	Y	Y	N	?	N	N	Y
2 ***Gregg***	Y	N	Y	N	Y	Y	Y	N
NEW JERSEY								
1 Florio	N	Y	Y	N	Y	Y	N	Y
2 Hughes	Y	Y	Y	N	Y	Y	N	Y
3 Howard	N	Y	Y	N	Y	Y	N	Y
4 ***Smith***	N	Y	Y	N	Y	Y	Y	Y
5 ***Fenwick***	N	Y	Y	N	Y	Y	Y	Y
6 ***Forsythe***	Y	N	Y	N	Y	N	Y	Y
7 ***Roukema***	Y	Y	Y	N	Y	Y	Y	Y
8 Roe	N	Y	Y	N	Y	N	N	Y
9 ***Hollenbeck***	N	Y	Y	N	Y	N	Y	Y
10 Rodino	N	Y	Y	N	?	Y	N	Y
11 Minish	N	Y	Y	N	Y	Y	N	Y
12 ***Rinaldo***	N	Y	Y	N	Y	N	Y	Y
13 ***Courter***	Y	Y	Y	Y	Y	Y	Y	Y
14 Guarini	N	Y	Y	N	Y	Y	N	Y
15 Dwyer	N	Y	Y	N	Y	N	N	Y
NEW MEXICO								
1 ***Lujan***	Y	Y	Y	Y	Y	N	Y	Y
2 ***Skeen***	Y	Y	Y	Y	Y	N	Y	Y
NEW YORK								
1 ***Carney***	N	Y	Y	N	Y	N	Y	N
2 Downey	N	Y	Y	N	Y	Y	N	Y
3 ***Carman***	N	Y	Y	N	Y	Y	Y	Y
4 ***Lent***	N	Y	Y	N	Y	N	N	Y
5 ***McGrath***	N	Y	Y	N	Y	Y	Y	Y
6 ***LeBoutillier***	N	Y	Y	N	Y	N	Y	Y
7 Addabbo	N	Y	Y	N	Y	N	N	Y
8 Rosenthal	?	?	?	?	?	?	?	?
9 Ferraro	N	Y	Y	N	Y	Y	N	Y
10 Biaggi	N	Y	Y	N	Y	N	N	Y
11 Scheuer	N	Y	Y	N	Y	Y	N	Y
12 Chisholm	N	Y	?	N	?	N	N	Y
13 Solarz	N	Y	Y	N	Y	Y	N	Y
14 Richmond	N	Y	?	N	?	Y	N	Y
15 Zeferetti	N	Y	Y	N	Y	N	N	Y
16 Schumer	N	Y	Y	N	Y	N	N	Y
17 ***Molinari***	Y	Y	Y	N	Y	N	Y	Y
18 ***Green***	N	Y	Y	N	Y	Y	N	Y
19 Rangel	N	Y	Y	N	Y	Y	N	?
20 Weiss	N	N	Y	N	Y	Y	N	Y
21 Garcia	N	Y	Y	N	Y	N	N	Y
22 Bingham	N	Y	Y	N	Y	Y	N	Y
23 Peyser	N	Y	Y	N	Y	N	N	?
24 Ottinger	N	Y	P	N	P	Y	Y	Y
25 ***Fish***	N	Y	?	N	Y	Y	N	Y
26 ***Gilman***	N	Y	Y	N	Y	Y	N	Y
27 McHugh	N	Y	Y	N	Y	Y	N	Y
28 Stratton	N	Y	Y	N	Y	N	N	Y
29 ***Solomon***	Y	N	Y	N	Y	Y	Y	N
30 ***Martin***	N	Y	Y	N	Y	N	Y	Y
31 ***Mitchell***	N	Y	Y	N	Y	N	N	Y
32 ***Wortley***	N	Y	Y	N	Y	N	Y	Y
33 ***Lee***	N	Y	Y	N	Y	N	Y	Y
34 ***Horton***	N	Y	Y	N	Y	N	N	Y
35 ***Conable***	Y	N	Y	N	Y	Y	Y	N
36 LaFalce	N	Y	?	N	Y	N	N	Y
37 Nowak	N	Y	Y	N	Y	N	N	Y
38 ***Kemp***	Y	Y	Y	N	Y	Y	N	?
39 Lundine	N	Y	?	Y	Y	N	N	Y
NORTH CAROLINA								
1 Jones	Y	Y	Y	N	?	N	N	Y
2 Fountain	Y	Y	Y	N	Y	N	N	Y
3 Whitley	Y	Y	Y	N	Y	N	N	Y
4 Andrews	N	Y	Y	N	Y	N	N	Y
5 Neal	N	Y	Y	N	Y	N	N	Y
6 ***Johnston***	Y	N	Y	N	Y	Y	Y	?
7 Rose	Y	Y	?	N	Y	N	N	?
8 Hefner	Y	Y	Y	N	Y	N	N	Y
9 ***Martin***	N	Y	Y	N	Y	?	?	?
10 ***Broyhill***	Y	Y	Y	N	Y	Y	Y	Y
11 ***Hendon***	Y	Y	Y	Y	Y	N	Y	Y
NORTH DAKOTA								
AL Dorgan	N	Y	Y	N	Y	Y	N	Y
OHIO								
1 ***Gradison***	N	Y	Y	Y	Y	Y	Y	Y
2 Luken	N	N	Y	N	Y	N	N	Y
3 Hall	Y	Y	Y	N	Y	Y	N	Y
4 ***Oxley***	Y	Y	Y	N	Y	N	Y	Y
5 ***Latta***	Y	N	Y	N	Y	N	N	Y
6 ***McEwen***	Y	Y	Y	N	Y	N	Y	Y
7 ***Brown***	-	Y	Y	N	Y	N	Y	Y
8 ***Kindness***	N	Y	?	N	Y	N	Y	Y
9 ***Weber***	N	Y	Y	N	Y	Y	Y	Y
10 ***Miller***	Y	N	Y	Y	Y	N	Y	Y
11 ***Stanton***	Y	Y	Y	N	Y	N	Y	Y
12 Shamansky	N	Y	Y	N	Y	Y	Y	Y
13 Pease	N	Y	Y	N	Y	N	N	Y
14 Seiberling	N	Y	Y	Y	Y	Y	N	Y
15 ***Wylie***	N	Y	Y	N	Y	N	Y	Y
16 ***Regula***	N	Y	Y	N	Y	N	Y	Y
17 ***Ashbrook***	Y	N	Y	N	Y	N	Y	Y
18 Applegate	Y	N	?	N	?	N	N	N
19 ***Williams***	Y	Y	Y	N	Y	N	N	Y
20 Oakar	N	Y	Y	N	Y	N	N	Y
21 Stokes	N	Y	?	N	Y	N	N	Y
22 Eckart	N	Y	Y	N	Y	N	N	Y
23 Mottl	Y	N	Y	N	Y	N	Y	N
OKLAHOMA								
1 Jones	N	Y	Y	N	Y	N	N	N
2 Synar	N	Y	Y	N	Y	Y	N	Y
3 Watkins	N	Y	Y	N	Y	N	N	Y
4 McCurdy	N	Y	Y	N	Y	N	Y	Y
5 ***Edwards***	Y	Y	?	N	Y	Y	Y	Y
6 English	N	Y	Y	N	Y	N	Y	Y
OREGON								
1 AuCoin	N	Y	Y	N	Y	N	N	Y
2 ***Smith***	Y	N	Y	N	Y	Y	Y	N
3 Wyden	N	Y	Y	N	Y	Y	N	Y
4 Weaver	N	N	Y	Y	Y	Y	N	N
PENNSYLVANIA								
1 Foglietta	?	?	?	?	?	N	Y	Y
2 Gray	N	Y	Y	N	Y	Y	N	Y
3 Vacancy								
4 ***Dougherty***	N	Y	Y	N	Y	X	N	?
5 ***Schulze***	Y	Y	Y	N	Y	N	Y	Y
6 Yatron	Y	Y	Y	N	Y	N	N	Y
7 Edgar	?	Y	Y	N	Y	Y	N	Y
8 ***Coyne, J.***	Y	Y	Y	N	Y	N	Y	Y
9 ***Shuster***	Y	N	Y	N	Y	N	Y	Y
10 ***McDade***	N	Y	Y	N	Y	N	Y	Y
11 ***Nelligan***	N	Y	Y	N	Y	N	Y	Y
12 Murtha	N	Y	Y	N	Y	N	Y	Y
13 ***Coughlin***	N	Y	Y	N	Y	N	Y	Y
14 Coyne, W.	N	Y	Y	N	Y	N	N	Y
15 ***Ritter***	Y	Y	Y	N	Y	N	N	Y
16 ***Walker***	Y	N	Y	N	Y	N	Y	Y
17 Ertel	N	Y	Y	N	?	N	Y	Y
18 Walgren	N	Y	Y	N	Y	N	N	Y
19 ***Goodling***	Y	?	?	Y	Y	N	Y	N
20 Gaydos	N	Y	Y	N	?	?	?	?
21 Bailey	N	Y	Y	Y	Y	N	N	Y
22 Murphy	N	Y	Y	N	Y	N	N	Y
23 ***Clinger***	N	Y	Y	Y	Y	N	Y	Y
24 ***Marks***	N	Y	Y	N	Y	N	N	Y
25 Atkinson	Y	Y	Y	N	Y	N	N	Y
RHODE ISLAND								
1 St Germain	N	Y	?	N	?	Y	N	Y
2 ***Schneider***	N	Y	Y	N	Y	Y	N	Y
SOUTH CAROLINA								
1 ***Hartnett***	Y	N	Y	N	Y	Y	Y	Y
2 ***Spence***	Y	Y	Y	Y	Y	N	Y	Y
3 Derrick	N	Y	Y	Y	Y	Y	N	Y
4 ***Campbell***	N	Y	Y	N	Y	N	Y	Y
5 Holland	N	Y	Y	N	Y	N	N	Y
6 ***Napier***	Y	Y	Y	N	?	N	Y	Y
SOUTH DAKOTA								
1 Daschle	Y	Y	?	N	Y	Y	Y	Y
2 ***Roberts***	+	+	+	+	+	#	+	-
TENNESSEE								
1 ***Quillen***	Y	Y	Y	Y	Y	N	Y	Y
2 ***Duncan***	N	Y	Y	Y	Y	N	Y	Y
3 Bouquard	N	Y	Y	Y	Y	N	N	Y
4 Gore	N	Y	Y	N	Y	N	N	Y
5 Boner	N	Y	Y	N	Y	N	N	Y
6 ***Beard***	Y	Y	Y	N	Y	N	Y	Y
7 Jones	N	Y	Y	N	Y	N	N	Y
8 Ford	N	Y	Y	N	?	N	N	Y
TEXAS								
1 Hall, S.	Y	?	?	N	Y	N	N	Y
2 Wilson	N	Y	Y	N	Y	N	N	?
3 ***Collins***	Y	N	Y	N	Y	Y	Y	N
4 Hall, R.	N	Y	Y	N	Y	N	N	N
5 Mattox	X	?	?	?	?	#	?	?
6 Gramm	Y	N	Y	N	?	N	?	N
7 ***Archer***	Y	N	Y	N	Y	Y	Y	N
8 ***Fields***	Y	N	Y	N	Y	Y	Y	N
9 Brooks	Y	Y	Y	N	Y	N	N	Y
10 Pickle	N	Y	Y	N	Y	N	N	Y
11 Leath	Y	N	Y	N	Y	N	N	?
12 Wright	N	Y	Y	N	Y	N	N	Y
13 Hightower	N	Y	Y	N	Y	N	N	Y
14 Patman	Y	Y	Y	N	Y	N	N	Y
15 de la Garza	N	Y	?	?	Y	N	N	Y
16 White	N	Y	Y	Y	Y	N	Y	Y
17 Stenholm	Y	Y	Y	N	Y	N	Y	Y
18 Leland	N	Y	Y	Y	Y	N	N	Y
19 Hance	Y	N	Y	N	?	N	Y	N
20 Gonzalez	N	Y	Y	N	Y	N	N	Y
21 ***Loeffler***	Y	Y	Y	N	Y	N	Y	Y
22 ***Paul***	Y	N	Y	N	Y	Y	Y	N
23 Kazen	N	Y	Y	N	Y	N	N	Y
24 Frost	N	Y	Y	N	Y	N	N	Y
UTAH								
1 ***Hansen***	#	+	+	+	+	+	?	?
2 ***Marriott***	Y	Y	Y	Y	Y	N	Y	Y
VERMONT								
AL ***Jeffords***	N	Y	?	N	Y	Y	N	Y
VIRGINIA								
1 ***Trible***	Y	Y	Y	N	Y	N	Y	Y
2 ***Whitehurst***	Y	Y	Y	Y	Y	Y	Y	Y
3 ***Bliley***	Y	Y	Y	Y	Y	N	Y	Y
4 ***Daniel, R.***	Y	Y	Y	N	Y	Y	Y	N
5 Daniel, D.	Y	Y	Y	N	Y	N	N	Y
6 ***Butler***	Y	Y	Y	N	Y	N	Y	Y
7 ***Robinson***	Y	Y	Y	N	Y	N	Y	Y
8 ***Parris***	Y	Y	Y	N	Y	Y	Y	Y
9 ***Wampler***	Y	Y	?	Y	Y	N	Y	Y
10 ***Wolf***	N	Y	Y	Y	Y	Y	Y	Y
WASHINGTON								
1 ***Pritchard***	N	Y	?	N	Y	Y	Y	Y
2 Swift	N	Y	Y	Y	Y	N	N	Y
3 Bonker	?	?	?	?	?	?	?	?
4 ***Morrison***	N	Y	Y	Y	Y	Y	Y	Y
5 Foley	N	Y	Y	Y	Y	N	N	Y
6 Dicks	N	N	Y	N	Y	N	N	Y
7 Lowry	N	Y	Y	N	Y	Y	N	Y
WEST VIRGINIA								
1 Mollohan	N	Y	Y	N	Y	N	N	Y
2 ***Benedict***	N	Y	Y	N	Y	N	Y	Y
3 ***Staton***	Y	Y	Y	N	Y	N	Y	Y
4 Rahall	N	Y	Y	Y	Y	N	Y	Y
WISCONSIN								
1 Aspin	N	Y	Y	N	Y	N	N	Y
2 Kastenmeier	N	Y	Y	N	Y	Y	N	Y
3 ***Gunderson***	Y	Y	Y	N	Y	Y	Y	Y
4 Zablocki	N	Y	Y	N	Y	N	N	Y
5 Reuss	N	Y	?	N	Y	Y	N	Y
6 ***Petri***	Y	Y	Y	N	Y	Y	Y	N
7 Obey	N	N	Y	Y	Y	Y	N	Y
8 ***Roth***	Y	Y	Y	N	Y	Y	Y	Y
9 ***Sensenbrenner***	Y	N	Y	N	Y	Y	Y	N
WYOMING								
AL ***Cheney***	Y	N	Y	N	?	Y	Y	Y

Democrats ***Republicans***

145. HR 4144. Energy and Water Development Appropriations, Fiscal 1982. Adoption of the rule (H Res 185) providing for House floor consideration of the fiscal 1982 appropriations bill for energy and water development programs. Adopted 233-178: R 28-153; D 205-25 (ND 135-21, SD 70-4), July 23, 1981.

146. HR 4119. Agriculture Appropriations, Fiscal 1982. Adoption of the rule (H Res 178) providing for House floor consideration of the bill to provide fiscal 1982 funds for the Agriculture Department and related agencies. Adopted 274-131: R 60-118; D 214-13 (ND 141-10, SD 73-3), July 23, 1981.

147. HR 4144. Energy and Water Development Appropriations, Fiscal 1982. Pritchard, R-Wash., amendment, to the Myers, R-Ind., amendment *(see vote 148, below)*, to delete $189 million for the Tennessee-Tombigbee Waterway. Rejected 198-208: R 108-70; D 90-138 (ND 82-70, SD 8-68), July 23, 1981. A "nay" was a vote supporting the president's position.

148. HR 4144. Energy and Water Development Appropriations, Fiscal 1982. Frank, D-Mass., amendment, to the Myers, R-Ind., amendment, to delete $17.8 million for the Stonewall Jackson, W.Va., dam and prohibit further federal spending on the project. Rejected 137-267: R 54-123; D 83-144 (ND 75-77, SD 8-67), July 23, 1981. A "nay" was a vote supporting the president's position. (The Myers amendment to add $9 million for the Big South Fork National River and Recreation Area in Tennessee and Kentucky was adopted subsequently by voice vote.)

149. HR 4144. Energy and Water Development Appropriations, Fiscal 1982. Conte, R-Mass., amendment to delete $4 million for the Garrison Diversion water project in North Dakota. Rejected 188-206: R 111-65; D 77-141 (ND 67-79, SD 10-62), July 23, 1981. A "nay" was a vote supporting the president's position.

150. HR 4144. Energy and Water Development Appropriations, Fiscal 1982. Coughlin, R-Pa., amendment to delete $228 million for the Clinch River (Tenn.) nuclear breeder reactor. Rejected 186-206: R 70-104; D 116-102 (ND 107-38, SD 9-64), July 24, 1981. A "nay" was a vote supporting the president's position.

151. HR 4144. Energy and Water Development Appropriations, Fiscal 1982. Derrick, D-S.C., amendment to transfer $10 million for research at the privately operated Barnwell, S.C., nuclear fuel reprocessing facility to government nuclear waste research. Rejected 157-213: R 28-137; D 129-76 (ND 106-33, SD 23-43), July 24, 1981.

152. HR 4144. Energy and Water Development Appropriations, Fiscal 1982. Passage of the bill to appropriate $13,189,674,000 in fiscal 1982 for energy and water development programs. Passed 244-104: R 112-44; D 132-60 (ND 81-53, SD 51-7), July 24, 1981. The president had requested $13,410,287,000.

KEY		
Y	Voted for (yea).	
#	Paired for.	
+	Announced for.	
N	Voted against (nay).	
X	Paired against.	
-	Announced against.	
P	Voted "present".	
C	Voted "present" to avoid possible conflict of interest.	
?	Did not vote or otherwise make a position known.	

	145	146	147	148	149	150	151	152
ALABAMA								
1 Edwards	Y	Y	N	N	N	N	N	Y
2 *Dickinson*	N	Y	N	N	N	N	N	Y
3 Nichols	Y	Y	N	N	N	N	N	Y
4 Bevill	Y	Y	N	N	N	N	N	Y
5 Flippo	Y	Y	N	N	?	?	?	?
6 *Smith*	N	N	N	N	N	N	N	Y
7 Shelby	Y	Y	N	N	N	N	N	Y
ALASKA								
AL *Young*	N	Y	N	?	N	N	N	Y
ARIZONA								
1 *Rhodes*	N	Y	N	N	N	N	N	Y
2 Udall	Y	?	N	N	Y	Y	Y	Y
3 *Stump*	Y	N	N	N	N	N	N	Y
4 *Rudd*	Y	Y	N	N	N	N	N	Y
ARKANSAS								
1 Alexander	Y	Y	N	?	?	N	Y	Y
2 *Bethune*	N	Y	N	N	N	Y	N	Y
3 *Hammerschmidt*	Y	Y	N	N	N	N	N	Y
4 Anthony	Y	Y	N	N	?	N	X	#
CALIFORNIA								
1 *Chappie*	?	?	?	?	?	?	?	?
2 *Clausen*	Y	N	N	N	N	N	N	Y
3 Matsui	Y	Y	N	N	Y	N	Y	Y
4 Fazio	Y	Y	N	N	Y	N	Y	Y
5 Burton, J.	Y	Y	Y	N	Y	Y	Y	N
6 Burton, P.	Y	Y	#	N	Y	Y	Y	N
7 Miller	Y	Y	Y	Y	Y	Y	Y	N
8 Dellums	Y	Y	Y	Y	Y	Y	Y	N
9 Stark	Y	Y	Y	Y	Y	Y	Y	N
10 Edwards	Y	Y	Y	Y	Y	#	Y	N
11 Lantos	Y	Y	N	N	Y	N	Y	N
12 *McCloskey*	N	N	Y	N	Y	N	Y	N
13 Mineta	Y	Y	N	N	Y	N	Y	N
14 *Shumway*	N	N	N	N	N	N	N	Y
15 Coelho	Y	Y	N	N	N	N	Y	Y
16 Panetta	Y	Y	Y	N	Y	Y	Y	Y
17 *Pashayan*	N	N	N	N	N	N	N	Y
18 *Thomas*	N	N	N	N	N	N	N	Y
19 *Lagomarsino*	N	N	Y	N	Y	N	N	Y
20 *Goldwater*	N	N	N	N	Y	N	N	Y
21 *Fiedler*	N	Y	N	N	Y	N	N	Y
22 *Moorhead*	N	N	N	N	Y	N	N	Y
23 Beilenson	Y	Y	Y	Y	Y	Y	Y	N
24 Waxman	Y	?	Y	Y	Y	Y	Y	N
25 Roybal	Y	Y	N	N	Y	Y	Y	Y
26 *Rousselot*	N	N	Y	N	?	Y	?	Y
27 *Dornan*	?	?	#	?	X	Y	N	?
28 Dixon	Y	Y	N	N	Y	?	?	?
29 Hawkins	Y	Y	N	N	Y	Y	Y	Y
30 Danielson	+	Y	Y	N	N	Y	Y	Y
31 Dymally	?	?	?	?	?	?	?	?
32 Anderson	N	Y	N	N	N	Y	Y	Y
33 *Grisham*	N	N	Y	N	N	Y	N	Y
34 *Lungren*	N	N	Y	N	Y	Y	N	Y
35 *Dreier*	N	N	Y	N	N	N	N	Y
36 Brown	Y	?	N	Y	?	Y	N	Y
37 *Lewis*	?	?	#	?	X	X	?	?
38 Patterson	Y	Y	N	Y	Y	?	?	?
39 *Dannemeyer*	N	N	Y	N	N	N	N	Y
40 *Badham*	N	N	N	N	Y	N	N	Y
41 *Lowery*	N	N	Y	N	N	Y	N	Y
42 *Hunter*	N	N	N	N	Y	Y	N	Y
43 *Burgener*	?	?	X	?	?	X	?	?
COLORADO								
1 Schroeder	N	N	Y	N	Y	N	Y	N
2 Wirth	Y	Y	N	Y	N	Y	Y	Y
3 Kogovsek	Y	Y	N	N	N	Y	N	Y
4 *Brown*	N	N	N	N	Y	N	Y	N

	145	146	147	148	149	150	151	152
5 *Kramer*	N	N	N	N	Y	N	N	Y
CONNECTICUT								
1 Cotter	?	?	?	?	?	?	?	?
2 Gejdenson	Y	Y	Y	Y	N	Y	Y	Y
3 *DeNardis*	N	N	Y	?	Y	Y	Y	N
4 *McKinney*	Y	Y	Y	Y	Y	Y	Y	?
5 Ratchford	Y	Y	Y	Y	N	Y	Y	N
6 Moffett	N	Y	Y	Y	Y	Y	Y	N
DELAWARE								
AL *Evans*	N	N	Y	Y	Y	Y	N	N
FLORIDA								
1 Hutto	Y	Y	N	N	N	N	N	?
2 Fuqua	N	Y	N	N	N	N	N	Y
3 Bennett	Y	Y	N	N	N	N	N	Y
4 Chappell	Y	Y	N	N	N	N	?	?
5 *McCollum*	N	N	N	Y	N	N	N	Y
6 *Young*	N	Y	N	N	N	N	N	Y
7 Gibbons	Y	Y	N	N	N	?	?	?
8 Ireland	Y	Y	N	N	N	N	N	Y
9 Nelson	Y	Y	N	N	N	-	?	#
10 *Bafalis*	N	Y	N	N	N	N	N	Y
11 Mica	Y	Y	N	N	N	N	N	Y
12 *Shaw*	N	N	Y	N	Y	N	N	Y
13 Lehman	Y	Y	N	Y	Y	Y	Y	Y
14 Pepper	Y	Y	N	N	N	?	?	Y
15 Fascell	Y	Y	N	Y	Y	Y	Y	Y
GEORGIA								
1 Ginn	Y	Y	N	N	N	N	Y	Y
2 Hatcher	Y	Y	N	N	N	N	Y	?
3 Brinkley	Y	Y	Y	Y	Y	Y	Y	N
4 Levitas	N	N	N	Y	Y	Y	Y	N
5 Fowler	Y	Y	N	N	Y	Y	Y	?
6 *Gingrich*	N	N	N	N	N	N	N	Y
7 McDonald	N	N	Y	Y	Y	N	N	N
8 Evans	Y	Y	N	N	N	Y	Y	N
9 Jenkins	Y	Y	N	N	?	?	?	?
10 Barnard	Y	Y	N	N	N	N	#	?
HAWAII								
1 Heftel	Y	Y	N	N	N	Y	Y	Y
2 Akaka	Y	Y	N	N	N	N	N	Y
IDAHO								
1 *Craig*	N	N	N	Y	N	N	N	N
2 *Hansen*	N	N	X	N	N	N	N	Y
ILLINOIS								
1 Washington	Y	Y	Y	Y	Y	Y	Y	N
2 Savage	?	?	?	?	?	?	?	?
3 Russo	Y	Y	Y	Y	N	Y	Y	X
4 *Derwinski*	N	N	N	N	N	N	N	Y
5 Fary	Y	Y	N	N	N	N	N	Y
6 *Hyde*	N	N	Y	N	Y	Y	N	Y
7 Collins	Y	Y	Y	N	Y	N	Y	N
8 Rostenkowski	Y	Y	N	N	N	N	N	Y
9 Yates	Y	Y	Y	Y	Y	Y	Y	N
10 *Porter*	N	N	Y	Y	Y	Y	Y	N
11 Annunzio	Y	Y	N	N	N	N	N	Y
12 *Crane, P.*	N	N	Y	N	N	N	N	Y
13 *McClory*	N	Y	N	Y	N	N	N	Y
14 *Erlenborn*	N	N	Y	N	N	N	N	Y
15 *Corcoran*	N	N	Y	N	Y	Y	Y	Y
16 *Martin*	N	?	Y	Y	Y	?	?	?
17 O'Brien	N	Y	N	N	N	N	N	?
18 *Michel*	N	N	Y	N	N	N	N	?
19 *Railsback*	N	N	N	Y	Y	Y	Y	N
20 *Findley*	N	N	N	N	Y	Y	Y	Y
21 *Madigan*	N	N	Y	N	Y	Y	Y	Y
22 *Crane, D.*	N	N	Y	Y	Y	Y	N	N
23 Price	Y	Y	N	N	N	N	N	Y
24 Simon	Y	Y	N	Y	Y	Y	Y	Y
INDIANA								
1 Benjamin	Y	Y	N	N	N	N	N	Y
2 Fithian	N	N	Y	N	Y	N	Y	Y
3 *Hiler*	N	N	Y	N	Y	Y	N	Y
4 *Coats*	N	N	Y	Y	Y	N	N	N
5 *Hillis*	Y	Y	N	N	N	N	N	Y
6 Evans	Y	Y	N	Y	N	Y	N	Y
7 *Myers*	Y	Y	N	N	N	N	N	Y
8 *Deckard*	N	N	Y	Y	Y	Y	N	Y
9 Hamilton	Y	Y	N	N	Y	N	N	Y
10 Sharp	N	N	Y	N	Y	N	Y	N
11 Jacobs	N	N	Y	Y	Y	Y	Y	N
IOWA								
1 *Leach*	N	N	Y	Y	Y	Y	Y	N
2 *Tauke*	N	N	Y	N	Y	Y	?	?
3 *Evans*	N	N	Y	N	N	N	N	Y
4 Smith	Y	Y	N	N	N	N	N	Y
5 Harkin	N	N	Y	Y	Y	Y	Y	N
6 Bedell	N	Y	Y	Y	Y	Y	Y	N

Democrats *Republicans*

Corresponding to Congressional Record Votes 154, 155, 156, 158, 159, 161, 162, 163

	145	146	147	148	149	150	151	152
KANSAS								
1 ***Roberts***	N	Y	Y	N	N	N	N	N
2 ***Jeffries***	N	N	Y	Y	Y	N	N	N
3 ***Winn***	N	N	N	N	N	N	N	Y
4 Glickman	N	Y	Y	N	N	Y	Y	Y
5 ***Whittaker***	N	Y	Y	N	N	N	N	N
KENTUCKY								
1 Hubbard	Y	Y	N	N	N	N	N	Y
2 Natcher	Y	Y	N	N	N	N	N	Y
3 Mazzoli	Y	Y	+	-	+	N	Y	Y
4 ***Snyder***	Y	Y	N	N	Y	Y	N	Y
5 ***Rogers***	Y	Y	N	N	N	N	N	Y
6 ***Hopkins***	N	N	Y	N	N	Y	N	+
7 Perkins	Y	Y	N	N	N	N	N	Y
LOUISIANA								
1 ***Livingston***	N	Y	N	N	Y	N	N	Y
2 Boggs	Y	Y	N	N	N	N	N	Y
3 Tauzin	Y	Y	N	N	N	N	N	Y
4 Roemer	N	N	N	Y	Y	N	Y	N
5 Huckaby	Y	Y	N	N	N	N	N	?
6 ***Moore***	Y	Y	Y	N	Y	Y	Y	Y
7 Breaux	Y	Y	N	N	Y	N	Y	Y
8 Long	Y	Y	N	N	N	N	Y	Y
MAINE								
1 ***Emery***	N	N	Y	Y	Y	Y	N	Y
2 ***Snowe***	N	N	Y	N	Y	Y	N	Y
MARYLAND								
1 Dyson	Y	Y	N	N	N	N	N	N
2 Long	Y	Y	N	N	N	N	N	Y
3 Mikulski	Y	Y	Y	Y	Y	Y	Y	N
4 ***Holt***	N	Y	N	N	N	N	N	N
5 Hoyer	Y	Y	N	Y	?	Y	Y	Y
6 Byron	Y	Y	N	N	Y	N	N	Y
7 Mitchell	Y	Y	?	Y	Y	Y	Y	N
8 Barnes	Y	Y	Y	Y	Y	Y	Y	N
MASSACHUSETTS								
1 ***Conte***	N	Y	Y	Y	Y	Y	N	N
2 Boland	Y	Y	Y	Y	N	Y	?	?
3 Early	Y	Y	Y	Y	Y	Y	?	?
4 Frank	Y	Y	Y	Y	N	Y	Y	N
5 Shannon	Y	Y	Y	Y	Y	Y	Y	N
6 Mavroules	N	Y	Y	Y	N	N	Y	N
7 Markey	N	Y	Y	Y	Y	Y	Y	N
8 O'Neill								
9 Moakley	Y	Y	?	?	N	Y	#	?
10 ***Heckler***	N	Y	Y	Y	Y	Y	N	N
11 Donnelly	Y	Y	N	N	N	Y	Y	Y
12 Studds	Y	Y	Y	Y	Y	Y	Y	N
MICHIGAN								
1 Conyers	Y	Y	N	Y	Y	Y	Y	N
2 ***Pursell***	Y	Y	Y	Y	Y	Y	N	N
3 Wolpe	Y	Y	Y	Y	Y	Y	Y	N
4 ***Siljander***	N	N	Y	Y	?	Y	Y	N
5 ***Sawyer***	Y	Y	Y	N	Y	Y	N	?
6 ***Dunn***	N	N	Y	N	Y	Y	Y	Y
7 Kildee	Y	Y	Y	Y	N	Y	Y	Y
8 Traxler	Y	Y	N	N	N	Y	Y	Y
9 ***Vander Jagt***	N	N	Y	N	#	N	N	Y
10 Albosta	Y	Y	N	N	N	Y	Y	Y
11 ***Davis***	Y	N	Y	N	Y	N	?	?
12 Bonior	Y	Y	Y	Y	?	Y	Y	N
13 Crockett	Y	Y	N	N	X	Y	?	?
14 Hertel	Y	Y	Y	Y	N	Y	Y	N
15 Ford	Y	Y	N	N	N	N	Y	+
16 Dingell	Y	Y	Y	N	Y	Y	Y	Y
17 Brodhead	Y	Y	Y	Y	Y	Y	Y	N
18 Blanchard	Y	Y	Y	N	N	Y	Y	Y
19 ***Broomfield***	N	N	Y	Y	Y	Y	Y	N
MINNESOTA								
1 ***Erdahl***	N	?	Y	Y	N	Y	Y	Y
2 ***Hagedorn***	N	Y	N	Y	Y	N	N	Y
3 ***Frenzel***	N	N	Y	Y	Y	?	?	?
4 Vento	Y	Y	Y	?	#	#	#	X
5 Sabo	Y	Y	N	Y	N	Y	Y	N
6 ***Weber***	N	N	Y	Y	Y	Y	Y	N
7 ***Stangeland***	N	N	N	N	N	N	N	Y
8 Oberstar	Y	Y	N	N	Y	Y	Y	Y
MISSISSIPPI								
1 Whitten	Y	Y	N	N	N	N	N	Y
2 Bowen	Y	Y	N	N	N	N	N	?
3 Montgomery	Y	Y	N	N	N	N	N	Y
4 Dowdy	Y	Y	N	N	N	N	?	?
5 ***Lott***	N	N	N	N	N	N	N	?
MISSOURI								
1 Clay	Y	Y	Y	Y	Y	Y	Y	N
2 Young	Y	Y	N	N	N	N	?	?
3 Gephardt	Y	Y	Y	N	N	Y	Y	Y
4 Skelton	Y	Y	N	N	N	N	Y	Y
5 Bolling	Y	Y	Y	Y	N	?	?	?
6 ***Coleman***	N	Y	N	N	Y	N	?	?
7 ***Taylor***	Y	Y	N	N	N	N	X	?
8 ***Bailey***	?	?	?	?	Y	N	N	Y
9 Volkmer	Y	Y	N	Y	N	N	Y	Y
10 ***Emerson***	Y	Y	N	N	N	N	N	Y
MONTANA								
1 Williams	N	N	N	N	N	Y	Y	Y
2 ***Marlenee***	Y	Y	Y	N	N	Y	N	Y
NEBRASKA								
1 ***Bereuter***	N	N	Y	N	N	N	N	Y
2 ***Daub***	Y	Y	Y	N	N	N	N	Y
3 ***Smith***	Y	Y	N	N	N	N	N	Y
NEVADA								
AL Santini	Y	Y	Y	?	?	?	?	?
NEW HAMPSHIRE								
1 D'Amours	Y	Y	?	Y	Y	Y	Y	Y
2 ***Gregg***	N	N	Y	N	Y	Y	Y	N
NEW JERSEY								
1 Florio	Y	Y	Y	N	?	#	?	?
2 Hughes	N	N	N	Y	Y	Y	Y	N
3 Howard	Y	Y	N	Y	N	Y	N	Y
4 ***Smith***	N	N	Y	N	Y	Y	Y	Y
5 ***Fenwick***	N	N	Y	Y	Y	Y	Y	N
6 ***Forsythe***	N	N	Y	Y	Y	N	N	N
7 ***Roukema***	N	N	Y	Y	Y	N	N	Y
8 Roe	Y	Y	N	N	?	N	N	Y
9 ***Hollenbeck***	N	N	Y	N	Y	N	N	Y
10 Rodino	Y	Y	Y	Y	Y	Y	Y	Y
11 Minish	Y	Y	Y	Y	Y	Y	Y	Y
12 ***Rinaldo***	Y	N	Y	Y	Y	N	N	Y
13 ***Courter***	N	N	Y	Y	Y	N	N	N
14 Guarini	Y	Y	N	N	Y	Y	Y	Y
15 Dwyer	Y	Y	N	N	N	N	N	Y
NEW MEXICO								
1 ***Lujan***	N	N	N	N	N	N	N	Y
2 ***Skeen***	N	N	N	N	N	N	N	Y
NEW YORK								
1 ***Carney***	N	N	N	N	N	N	N	Y
2 Downey	Y	Y	?	?	?	?	?	?
3 ***Carman***	N	N	Y	N	Y	Y	N	N
4 ***Lent***	N	N	Y	N	Y	N	N	Y
5 ***McGrath***	N	N	Y	Y	Y	Y	N	N
6 ***LeBoutillier***	N	Y	Y	N	N	N	?	?
7 Addabbo	Y	Y	N	N	N	N	Y	#
8 Rosenthal	?	?	?	?	?	?	?	?
9 Ferraro	Y	Y	Y	Y	N	Y	Y	Y
10 Biaggi	Y	Y	N	N	?	X	X	#
11 Scheuer	Y	Y	N	Y	Y	Y	Y	Y
12 Chisholm	Y	Y	N	N	N	Y	Y	Y
13 Solarz	Y	Y	Y	Y	N	Y	Y	Y
14 Richmond	Y	Y	Y	Y	Y	#	#	X
15 Zeferetti	Y	Y	N	N	N	N	Y	X
16 Schumer	N	Y	Y	Y	N	Y	Y	N
17 ***Molinari***	N	N	Y	N	Y	Y	N	N
18 ***Green***	N	Y	Y	Y	Y	Y	N	N
19 Rangel	Y	Y	N	Y	N	Y	Y	N
20 Weiss	N	N	Y	Y	N	Y	Y	N
21 Garcia	Y	Y	N	Y	Y	?	#	X
22 Bingham	Y	Y	Y	Y	Y	Y	Y	Y
23 Peyser	Y	Y	Y	N	N	Y	Y	?
24 Ottinger	Y	Y	Y	Y	Y	Y	Y	N
25 ***Fish***	N	N	Y	Y	Y	Y	Y	?
26 ***Gilman***	N	N	-	-	+	Y	Y	Y
27 McHugh	Y	Y	Y	N	N	Y	Y	Y
28 Stratton	Y	Y	N	N	N	N	N	Y
29 ***Solomon***	N	N	Y	Y	Y	N	N	?
30 ***Martin***	N	N	Y	N	Y	?	?	?
31 ***Mitchell***	Y	Y	Y	Y	Y	Y	?	?
32 ***Wortley***	N	N	N	N	Y	Y	N	Y
33 ***Lee***	N	?	N	N	Y	N	N	N
34 ***Horton***	N	N	N	N	Y	?	?	?
35 ***Conable***	N	N	Y	Y	Y	N	N	N
36 LaFalce	Y	Y	N	Y	N	Y	Y	Y
37 Nowak	Y	Y	N	Y	N	Y	Y	Y
38 ***Kemp***	N	N	?	N	Y	?	?	?
39 Lundine	Y	?	Y	N	Y	Y	Y	Y
NORTH CAROLINA								
1 Jones	Y	Y	N	N	N	N	Y	Y
2 Fountain	Y	Y	Y	N	N	N	N	Y
3 Whitley	Y	Y	N	N	N	N	N	Y
4 Andrews	Y	Y	N	N	N	N	N	?
5 Neal	?	Y	Y	Y	?	Y	Y	Y
6 ***Johnston***	N	N	Y	Y	Y	Y	N	N
7 Rose	Y	Y	N	N	?	N	N	Y
8 Hefner	Y	Y	N	N	N	N	N	Y
9 ***Martin***	N	N	Y	Y	Y	?	?	?
10 ***Broyhill***	N	Y	Y	N	Y	N	N	N
11 ***Hendon***	N	Y	N	N	N	?	?	?
NORTH DAKOTA								
AL Dorgan	Y	Y	N	Y	N	Y	Y	Y
OHIO								
1 ***Gradison***	N	N	Y	Y	Y	Y	Y	Y
2 Luken	Y	N	N	N	Y	Y	N	Y
3 Hall	Y	Y	Y	Y	Y	Y	Y	N
4 ***Oxley***	?	?	N	Y	Y	N	N	Y
5 ***Latta***	?	?	X	N	Y	N	N	Y
6 ***McEwen***	N	N	N	N	Y	N	N	Y
7 ***Brown***	N	Y	N	N	Y	?	?	?
8 ***Kindness***	N	Y	N	N	Y	N	N	Y
9 ***Weber***	N	N	Y	N	Y	Y	Y	Y
10 ***Miller***	N	Y	N	N	Y	N	N	Y
11 ***Stanton***	N	N	Y	N	Y	Y	N	Y
12 Shamansky	Y	Y	Y	Y	Y	Y	Y	Y
13 Pease	N	Y	Y	N	Y	Y	Y	N
14 Seiberling	Y	Y	Y	N	Y	Y	Y	N
15 ***Wylie***	N	Y	?	?	?	Y	N	Y
16 ***Regula***	Y	Y	N	N	N	N	N	Y
17 ***Ashbrook***	N	N	N	?	#	N	N	Y
18 Applegate	Y	Y	Y	N	Y	Y	N	N
19 ***Williams***	N	Y	N	N	N	Y	N	Y
20 Oakar	Y	Y	N	N	N	Y	Y	Y
21 Stokes	Y	Y	N	N	N	N	N	Y
22 Eckart	Y	Y	Y	Y	N	Y	Y	N
23 Mottl	N	Y	Y	?	?	?	?	?
OKLAHOMA								
1 Jones	Y	Y	N	N	N	N	Y	Y
2 Synar	Y	Y	Y	Y	Y	Y	Y	Y
3 Watkins	Y	Y	N	N	N	N	N	Y
4 McCurdy	Y	Y	N	N	N	Y	N	Y
5 ***Edwards***	Y	Y	N	N	N	Y	N	Y
6 English	Y	Y	N	N	N	N	N	Y
OREGON								
1 AuCoin	Y	Y	N	Y	Y	Y	Y	Y
2 ***Smith***	N	N	Y	Y	Y	Y	N	N
3 Wyden	Y	Y	Y	Y	Y	Y	Y	N
4 Weaver	N	N	Y	Y	Y	Y	Y	N
PENNSYLVANIA								
1 Foglietta	Y	Y	Y	Y	Y	Y	Y	N
2 Gray	Y	Y	N	N	N	?	?	?
3 Vacancy								
4 ***Dougherty***	?	?	Y	?	Y	N	N	Y
5 ***Schulze***	N	N	Y	N	N	N	N	Y
6 Yatron	Y	Y	Y	N	Y	Y	N	Y
7 Edgar	N	N	Y	Y	Y	Y	Y	N
8 ***Coyne, J.***	N	N	Y	Y	Y	N	Y	Y
9 ***Shuster***	N	N	N	N	N	N	N	Y
10 ***McDade***	Y	Y	N	Y	N	Y	Y	Y
11 ***Nelligan***	N	N	Y	N	Y	N	N	Y
12 Murtha	Y	Y	N	N	N	N	N	Y
13 ***Coughlin***	N	N	Y	N	Y	Y	N	N
14 Coyne, W.	Y	Y	Y	N	N	N	N	Y
15 ***Ritter***	N	N	+	Y	Y	Y	N	N
16 ***Walker***	N	N	Y	Y	Y	N	N	N
17 Ertel	Y	Y	N	N	N	Y	N	Y
18 Walgren	Y	Y	Y	N	Y	Y	Y	Y
19 ***Goodling***	N	N	Y	Y	Y	Y	Y	Y
20 Gaydos	?	?	?	?	?	?	?	?
21 Bailey	Y	Y	N	N	?	N	N	Y
22 Murphy	Y	Y	Y	N	Y	N	N	N
23 ***Clinger***	N	N	Y	N	Y	Y	N	Y
24 ***Marks***	Y	Y	Y	Y	Y	N	N	Y
25 Atkinson	Y	Y	Y	N	N	N	N	Y
RHODE ISLAND								
1 St Germain	Y	?	N	Y	Y	Y	?	?
2 ***Schneider***	N	N	Y	Y	Y	Y	Y	N
SOUTH CAROLINA								
1 ***Hartnett***	N	N	Y	N	Y	N	N	Y
2 ***Spence***	N	Y	N	N	Y	N	N	Y
3 Derrick	Y	Y	Y	Y	Y	N	Y	N
4 ***Campbell***	N	Y	N	N	Y	N	N	Y
5 Holland	Y	Y	N	N	N	N	Y	Y
6 ***Napier***	N	Y	N	N	Y	N	N	Y
SOUTH DAKOTA								
1 Daschle	Y	Y	N	Y	Y	Y	Y	Y
2 ***Roberts***	-	+	+	+	-	-	-	+
TENNESSEE								
1 ***Quillen***	Y	Y	N	N	N	X	X	?
2 ***Duncan***	Y	Y	N	N	N	N	N	Y
3 Bouquard	Y	Y	N	N	N	N	N	Y
4 Gore	Y	Y	N	N	N	N	Y	Y
5 Boner	Y	Y	N	N	N	N	N	Y
6 ***Beard***	Y	Y	N	N	N	N	X	?
7 Jones	Y	Y	N	N	N	N	N	Y
8 Ford	Y	Y	N	N	N	N	Y	Y
TEXAS								
1 Hall, S.	Y	Y	N	N	N	N	N	+
2 Wilson	Y	Y	N	N	N	N	N	Y
3 ***Collins***	N	N	Y	Y	Y	Y	N	N
4 Hall, R.	Y	?	N	N	N	N	N	Y
5 Mattox	?	?	#	?	?	#	#	#
6 Gramm	?	Y	N	N	N	N	N	Y
7 ***Archer***	N	N	Y	Y	Y	N	N	Y
8 ***Fields***	N	N	N	N	N	N	N	Y
9 Brooks	Y	Y	N	N	N	N	N	Y
10 Pickle	Y	Y	N	N	N	N	N	Y
11 Leath	Y	Y	N	N	N	N	?	?
12 Wright	Y	Y	N	N	N	N	N	?
13 Hightower	Y	Y	N	N	N	N	N	?
14 Patman	Y	Y	N	N	N	N	N	Y
15 de la Garza	Y	Y	N	N	N	N	Y	Y
16 White	Y	Y	N	N	N	N	N	Y
17 Stenholm	Y	Y	N	N	N	N	N	Y
18 Leland	Y	Y	Y	Y	N	Y	Y	N
19 Hance	?	Y	N	N	N	N	N	Y
20 Gonzalez	Y	Y	N	N	N	P	P	Y
21 ***Loeffler***	N	Y	N	N	N	N	N	Y
22 ***Paul***	N	N	Y	Y	Y	Y	N	N
23 Kazen	Y	Y	N	N	N	N	N	?
24 Frost	?	?	?	?	?	?	?	?
UTAH								
1 ***Hansen***	?	?	X	?	?	?	?	?
2 ***Marriott***	N	N	N	N	N	N	N	Y
VERMONT								
AL ***Jeffords***	Y	Y	Y	Y	?	Y	Y	N
VIRGINIA								
1 ***Trible***	N	N	N	N	Y	Y	N	Y
2 ***Whitehurst***	N	N	Y	N	Y	N	N	Y
3 ***Bliley***	N	N	N	N	Y	N	N	Y
4 ***Daniel, R.***	N	N	Y	N	Y	Y	N	N
5 Daniel, D.	Y	Y	N	N	Y	N	N	N
6 ***Butler***	N	N	Y	N	Y	N	N	?
7 ***Robinson***	N	Y	N	N	N	N	N	Y
8 ***Parris***	N	N	N	N	Y	N	N	Y
9 ***Wampler***	N	Y	N	N	?	N	N	Y
10 ***Wolf***	N	N	Y	N	N	N	N	Y
WASHINGTON								
1 ***Pritchard***	N	N	Y	?	?	?	?	?
2 Swift	Y	Y	Y	N	N	Y	Y	Y
3 Bonker	?	?	?	?	?	Y	Y	Y
4 ***Morrison***	N	N	N	N	N	N	N	Y
5 Foley	Y	Y	N	N	N	N	Y	Y
6 Dicks	Y	?	N	N	N	N	Y	Y
7 Lowry	N	Y	Y	Y	Y	Y	Y	N
WEST VIRGINIA								
1 Mollohan	Y	Y	N	N	N	N	N	Y
2 ***Benedict***	N	N	N	N	N	Y	?	?
3 ***Staton***	N	N	N	Y	Y	Y	N	Y
4 Rahall	Y	Y	N	N	N	Y	N	Y
WISCONSIN								
1 Aspin	Y	Y	Y	Y	Y	Y	Y	N
2 Kastenmeier	Y	Y	Y	Y	Y	Y	Y	N
3 ***Gunderson***	N	N	Y	N	N	Y	N	Y
4 Zablocki	Y	Y	N	N	N	N	N	Y
5 Reuss	Y	Y	Y	Y	Y	?	?	?
6 ***Petri***	N	N	Y	Y	Y	Y	Y	N
7 Obey	N	Y	Y	Y	Y	Y	Y	N
8 ***Roth***	N	N	Y	Y	Y	N	N	Y
9 ***Sensenbrenner***	N	N	Y	Y	Y	Y	N	N
WYOMING								
AL ***Cheney***	N	Y	N	N	N	X	X	?

Democrats ***Republicans***

153. HR 2819. District of Columbia Federal Payment. Passage of the bill to increase from $300 million to $336.6 million the authorization for fiscal 1982 and each fiscal year thereafter for the annual federal payment to the District of Columbia. Passed 209-179: R 48-123; D 161-56 (ND 122-23, SD 39-33), July 27, 1981.

154. HR 2818. District of Columbia Borrowing Authority. Passage of the bill to extend for two years the authority of the mayor of the District of Columbia to accept certain interim loans from the United States government and to extend the authority of the Treasury secretary to make such loans. Passed 239-149: R 53-118; D 186-31 (ND 134-10, SD 52-21), July 27, 1981.

155. HR 4119. Agriculture Appropriations, Fiscal 1982. Passage of the bill to appropriate $22,730,534,000 for fiscal 1982 for the Agriculture Department and related agencies. Passed 343-33: R 145-22; D 198-11 (ND 128-9; SD 70-2), July 27, 1981. The president had requested $23,792,166,000 in new budget authority.

156. Procedural Motion. Walker, R-Pa., motion to approve the House *Journal* of Monday, July 27. Motion agreed to 379-14: R 172-7; D 207-7 (ND 134-7, SD 73-0), July 28, 1981.

157. HR 1311. National Tourism Policy. Florio, D-N.J., motion to suspend the rules and pass the bill to replace the U.S. Travel Service with a new U.S. Travel and Tourism Administration within the Commerce Department and to authorize $6.5 million in fiscal 1982 for tourism programs. Motion agreed to 321-98: R 123-64; D 198-34 (ND 134-23, SD 64-11), July 28, 1981. A two-thirds majority vote (280 in this case) is required for passage under suspension of the rules. A "yea" was a vote supporting the president's position.

158. H Con Res 160. Monetary Policy and High Interest Rates. Reuss, D-Wis., motion to suspend the rules and adopt the resolution stating it is the "sense of Congress" that since interest rates are "needlessly and destructively" high, Congress and the administration should take actions to reduce future budget deficits; encourage the banking system to provide credit to those who contribute to long-term productivity; and encourage the Federal Reserve to lower interest rates. Motion agreed to 403-17: R 171-15; D 232-2 (ND 158-1, SD 74-1), July 28, 1981. A two-thirds majority vote (280 in this case) is required for adoption under suspension of the rules.

159. HR 4053. Mineral Leasing Act Amendments. Santini, D-Nev., motion to suspend the rules and pass the bill to make it easier for private companies to produce synthetic fuel from oil shale on federal lands. Motion agreed to 408-5: R 180-1; D 228-4 (ND 152-4, SD 76-0), July 28, 1981. A two-thirds majority vote (276 in this case) is required for passage under suspension of the rules. A "yea" was a vote supporting the president's postion.

160. HR 4121. Treasury, Postal Service, General Government Appropriations, Fiscal 1982. Latta, R-Ohio, amendment to delete $5 million earmarked for the Bureau of Alcohol, Tobacco and Firearms in the Treasury Department. Adopted 279-141: R 169-20; D 110-121 (ND 50-106, SD 60-15), July 28, 1981. A "yea" was a vote supporting the president's position.

KEY

- **Y** Voted for (yea).
- **#** Paired for.
- **+** Announced for.
- **N** Voted against (nay).
- **X** Paired against.
- **-** Announced against.
- **P** Voted "present".
- **C** Voted "present" to avoid possible conflict of interest.
- **?** Did not vote or otherwise make a position known.

	153	154	155	156	157	158	159	160
ALABAMA								
1 Edwards	Y	Y	Y	Y	Y	Y	Y	Y
2 Dickinson	N	?	?	Y	N	Y	Y	Y
3 Nichols	N	Y	Y	N	Y	Y	Y	Y
4 Bevill	N	N	Y	Y	Y	Y	Y	N
5 Flippo	N	Y	Y	Y	Y	Y	Y	Y
6 Smith	N	N	Y	Y	Y	Y	Y	Y
7 Shelby	N	N	Y	Y	Y	Y	Y	Y
ALASKA								
AL Young	N	N	Y	N	Y	Y	Y	Y
ARIZONA								
1 Rhodes	?	?	?	?	Y	Y	Y	Y
2 Udall	Y	Y	Y	Y	Y	Y	Y	Y
3 Stump	N	N	N	Y	N	Y	Y	Y
4 Rudd	N	N	N	Y	Y	Y	Y	Y
ARKANSAS								
1 Alexander	Y	Y	Y	Y	Y	Y	?	N
2 Bethune	N	Y	Y	Y	Y	Y	Y	Y
3 Hammerschmidt	N	N	Y	Y	Y	Y	Y	Y
4 Anthony	Y	Y	Y	Y	Y	Y	Y	Y
CALIFORNIA								
1 Chappie	?	X	?	Y	Y	Y	Y	Y
2 Clausen	N	N	Y	Y	Y	Y	Y	Y
3 Matsui	Y	Y	Y	Y	Y	Y	Y	N
4 Fazio	Y	Y	Y	Y	Y	Y	Y	Y
5 Burton, J.	?	?	?	?	Y	Y	Y	?
6 Burton, P.	Y	Y	Y	Y	Y	Y	Y	N
7 Miller	Y	Y	Y	N	Y	Y	N	N
8 Dellums	Y	Y	Y	Y	N	Y	N	N
9 Stark	Y	Y	Y	Y	Y	Y	Y	N
10 Edwards	Y	Y	Y	Y	Y	Y	?	N
11 Lantos	-	+	Y	Y	Y	Y	Y	N
12 McCloskey	N	Y	Y	Y	N	Y	?	N
13 Mineta	Y	Y	Y	Y	Y	Y	Y	N
14 Shumway	N	N	N	N	Y	N	Y	Y
15 Coelho	Y	Y	Y	Y	Y	Y	Y	Y
16 Panetta	Y	Y	Y	Y	Y	Y	Y	N
17 Pashayan	N	Y	Y	Y	Y	Y	Y	Y
18 Thomas	Y	Y	Y	N	Y	N	Y	Y
19 Lagomarsino	N	N	N	Y	Y	Y	Y	Y
20 Goldwater	Y	N	Y	Y	N	N	Y	Y
21 Fiedler	N	Y	Y	Y	N	Y	N	Y
22 Moorhead	N	N	Y	Y	Y	Y	Y	Y
23 Beilenson	Y	Y	Y	?	N	Y	N	Y
24 Waxman	Y	Y	Y	Y	Y	Y	Y	?
25 Roybal	Y	Y	Y	Y	Y	Y	Y	N
26 Rousselot	X	X	?	Y	N	N	Y	Y
27 Dornan	N	N	Y	Y	Y	Y	Y	Y
28 Dixon	Y	Y	Y	?	N	Y	Y	N
29 Hawkins	Y	Y	Y	Y	Y	Y	Y	Y
30 Danielson	Y	Y	Y	Y	Y	Y	Y	N
31 Dymally	Y	Y	Y	Y	Y	Y	Y	N
32 Anderson	?	?	?	Y	Y	Y	Y	N
33 Grisham	?	?	?	Y	Y	Y	Y	Y
34 Lungren	Y	N	Y	N	Y	N	Y	Y
35 Dreier	N	N	N	Y	N	N	N	Y
36 Brown	?	?	?	Y	Y	Y	Y	N
37 Lewis	N	N	Y	N	Y	N	Y	Y
38 Patterson	Y	Y	Y	Y	Y	Y	Y	N
39 Dannemeyer	N	N	N	Y	N	N	Y	Y
40 Badham	N	N	N	?	Y	Y	Y	Y
41 Lowery	N	N	Y	Y	Y	Y	Y	Y
42 Hunter	N	N	Y	Y	Y	Y	?	Y
43 Burgener	N	N	Y	Y	Y	N	Y	N
COLORADO								
1 Schroeder	N	N	N	N	N	Y	N	N
2 Wirth	Y	Y	Y	Y	Y	Y	Y	Y
3 Kogovsek	N	Y	Y	Y	Y	Y	Y	Y
4 Brown	N	N	Y	Y	N	Y	Y	Y

	153	154	155	156	157	158	159	160
5 Kramer	N	Y	Y	Y	Y	Y	Y	Y
CONNECTICUT								
1 Cotter	?	?	?	?	?	?	?	?
2 Gejdenson	Y	Y	Y	Y	Y	Y	N	N
3 DeNardis	#	#	?	?	Y	Y	Y	N
4 McKinney	Y	Y	Y	?	Y	Y	Y	N
5 Ratchford	Y	Y	Y	Y	Y	Y	Y	N
6 Moffett	Y	Y	Y	Y	N	Y	Y	N
DELAWARE								
AL Evans	?	#	?	Y	Y	Y	Y	Y
FLORIDA								
1 Hutto	Y	Y	Y	Y	Y	Y	Y	Y
2 Fuqua	Y	Y	Y	Y	Y	Y	Y	Y
3 Bennett	N	Y	Y	Y	N	Y	Y	N
4 Chappell	N	Y	Y	Y	Y	Y	Y	Y
5 McCollum	N	N	Y	Y	Y	Y	Y	Y
6 Young	Y	N	Y	Y	Y	Y	Y	Y
7 Gibbons	Y	Y	Y	Y	Y	Y	Y	N
8 Ireland	N	N	Y	Y	Y	Y	Y	Y
9 Nelson	Y	Y	Y	Y	Y	Y	Y	Y
10 Bafalis	N	N	Y	Y	Y	?	Y	Y
11 Mica	Y	Y	Y	Y	Y	Y	Y	Y
12 Shaw	N	N	Y	Y	Y	Y	Y	Y
13 Lehman	Y	Y	Y	Y	Y	Y	Y	N
14 Pepper	#	?	?	?	Y	Y	Y	N
15 Fascell	Y	Y	N	?	?	?	?	?
GEORGIA								
1 Ginn	Y	Y	Y	Y	Y	?	Y	Y
2 Hatcher	Y	Y	Y	Y	Y	Y	Y	Y
3 Brinkley	Y	Y	Y	Y	Y	Y	Y	Y
4 Levitas	N	N	Y	Y	Y	Y	Y	N
5 Fowler	Y	Y	Y	Y	Y	Y	Y	N
6 Gingrich	N	Y	Y	Y	Y	Y	Y	Y
7 McDonald	N	N	N	N	N	N	Y	Y
8 Evans	N	N	Y	N	Y	N	Y	Y
9 Jenkins	N	N	Y	Y	Y	Y	Y	Y
10 Barnard	?	?	?	Y	Y	Y	Y	Y
HAWAII								
1 Heftel	N	Y	Y	Y	Y	Y	N	N
2 Akaka	Y	Y	Y	Y	Y	Y	N	N
IDAHO								
1 Craig	N	N	N	Y	Y	Y	Y	Y
2 Hansen	N	N	N	Y	Y	Y	Y	Y
ILLINOIS								
1 Washington	Y	Y	Y	?	Y	Y	N	N
2 Savage	?	?	?	Y	Y	?	N	N
3 Russo	?	?	+	Y	Y	Y	Y	N
4 Derwinski	N	N	Y	N	Y	Y	Y	N
5 Fary	Y	Y	Y	Y	Y	Y	Y	N
6 Hyde	Y	Y	Y	Y	Y	Y	Y	Y
7 Collins	Y	Y	Y	Y	Y	Y	Y	N
8 Rostenkowski	Y	Y	Y	?	Y	Y	Y	N
9 Yates	Y	Y	Y	Y	N	Y	Y	N
10 Porter	Y	Y	N	Y	Y	Y	Y	N
11 Annunzio	Y	Y	Y	Y	Y	Y	Y	N
12 Crane, P.	N	N	N	N	N	Y	N	Y
13 McClory	Y	Y	Y	Y	Y	?	N	Y
14 Erlenborn	N	Y	Y	Y	N	Y	?	N
15 Corcoran	Y	Y	Y	Y	Y	Y	Y	N
16 Martin	?	Y	Y	Y	N	Y	Y	N
17 O'Brien	Y	Y	Y	Y	Y	Y	+	Y
18 Michel	Y	Y	Y	?	N	N	?	Y
19 Railsback	Y	Y	?	Y	Y	Y	Y	N
20 Findley	N	N	Y	N	Y	Y	Y	N
21 Madigan	N	N	Y	Y	Y	Y	Y	N
22 Crane, D.	N	N	N	N	N	Y	N	Y
23 Price	Y	Y	?	Y	Y	Y	Y	Y
24 Simon	?	?	?	Y	Y	Y	Y	N
INDIANA								
1 Benjamin	Y	Y	Y	Y	Y	Y	Y	Y
2 Fithian	Y	Y	Y	Y	Y	Y	Y	Y
3 Hiler	N	N	Y	N	Y	Y	Y	Y
4 Coats	N	N	Y	Y	N	Y	Y	Y
5 Hillis	N	N	Y	N	Y	Y	Y	Y
6 Evans	Y	Y	Y	Y	Y	Y	Y	Y
7 Myers	N	N	Y	N	Y	Y	Y	Y
8 Deckard	Y	X	?	Y	Y	Y	Y	Y
9 Hamilton	N	Y	Y	Y	Y	Y	Y	Y
10 Sharp	Y	Y	Y	Y	Y	Y	Y	Y
11 Jacobs	Y	Y	N	N	N	Y	N	N
IOWA								
1 Leach	N	N	Y	Y	Y	Y	Y	Y
2 Tauke	N	N	Y	Y	Y	Y	Y	Y
3 Evans	?	X	?	N	N	Y	Y	Y
4 Smith	Y	Y	Y	Y	Y	Y	Y	Y
5 Harkin	Y	Y	Y	N	+	Y	Y	Y
6 Bedell	Y	Y	Y	Y	+	Y	Y	Y

Democrats   *Republicans*

Corresponding to Congressional Record Votes 164, 165, 166, 167, 168, 169, 170, 171

	153	154	155	156	157	158	159	160
KANSAS								
1 ***Roberts***	N	N	Y	Y	N	Y	Y	Y
2 ***Jeffries***	N	N	Y	Y	N	N	Y	Y
3 ***Winn***	N	N	Y	Y	Y	Y	Y	Y
4 Glickman	N	Y	Y	Y	Y	Y	Y	Y
5 ***Whittaker***	N	N	Y	Y	Y	Y	Y	Y
KENTUCKY								
1 Hubbard	N	N	Y	Y	Y	Y	Y	Y
2 Natcher	Y	Y	Y	Y	Y	Y	Y	N
3 Mazzoli	Y	Y	Y	Y	N	Y	Y	N
4 ***Snyder***	N	N	Y	Y	Y	Y	Y	Y
5 ***Rogers***	N	N	Y	Y	Y	Y	Y	Y
6 ***Hopkins***	N	N	Y	Y	Y	Y	Y	Y
7 Perkins	Y	Y	Y	Y	Y	Y	Y	N
LOUISIANA								
1 ***Livingston***	N	Y	Y	Y	N	Y	Y	Y
2 Boggs	Y	Y	Y	Y	Y	Y	Y	Y
3 Tauzin	Y	Y	Y	Y	Y	Y	Y	Y
4 Roemer	Y	N	Y	Y	N	Y	Y	Y
5 Huckaby	N	N	Y	Y	N	Y	Y	Y
6 ***Moore***	N	Y	Y	Y	N	Y	Y	Y
7 Breaux	Y	Y	Y	Y	Y	Y	Y	Y
8 Long	Y	Y	Y	Y	Y	Y	Y	Y
MAINE								
1 ***Emery***	Y	N	Y	Y	Y	Y	Y	Y
2 ***Snowe***	Y	N	Y	Y	Y	Y	Y	Y
MARYLAND								
1 Dyson	Y	Y	Y	Y	Y	Y	Y	Y
2 Long	Y	Y	Y	Y	Y	Y	Y	N
3 Mikulski	?	?	?	Y	Y	Y	Y	Y
4 ***Holt***	Y	N	N	?	N	N	Y	Y
5 Hoyer	Y	Y	Y	Y	Y	Y	Y	N
6 Byron	N	Y	Y	Y	Y	Y	Y	N
7 Mitchell	Y	Y	Y	N	Y	Y	Y	N
8 Barnes	Y	Y	Y	Y	Y	Y	Y	N
MASSACHUSETTS								
1 ***Conte***	Y	Y	Y	Y	Y	Y	Y	Y
2 Boland	Y	Y	Y	Y	Y	Y	Y	N
3 Early	N	Y	Y	Y	N	Y	Y	N
4 Frank	Y	Y	?	Y	Y	Y	Y	N
5 Shannon	Y	Y	?	Y	Y	Y	Y	N
6 Mavroules	Y	Y	Y	Y	Y	Y	Y	N
7 Markey	Y	Y	Y	?	Y	Y	Y	N
8 O'Neill								
9 Moakley	Y	Y	Y	?	Y	Y	Y	N
10 ***Heckler***	N	Y	Y	Y	Y	Y	Y	N
11 Donnelly	Y	Y	Y	Y	Y	Y	Y	N
12 Studds	Y	Y	Y	Y	Y	Y	Y	N
MICHIGAN								
1 Conyers	Y	Y	?	?	Y	Y	Y	N
2 ***Pursell***	?	N	Y	Y	Y	?	Y	Y
3 Wolpe	Y	Y	Y	Y	Y	Y	Y	N
4 ***Siljander***	N	N	Y	Y	N	Y	Y	Y
5 ***Sawyer***	N	Y	Y	Y	N	Y	Y	N
6 ***Dunn***	N	Y	Y	Y	N	Y	Y	N
7 Kildee	Y	Y	Y	Y	Y	Y	Y	N
8 Traxler	Y	Y	Y	Y	Y	Y	Y	Y
9 ***Vander Jagt***	N	Y	?	Y	Y	Y	Y	Y
10 Albosta	Y	Y	Y	Y	?	Y	Y	Y
11 ***Davis***	Y	Y	Y	Y	Y	Y	Y	Y
12 Bonior	Y	?	Y	?	Y	Y	Y	N
13 Crockett	Y	Y	Y	Y	Y	Y	?	?
14 Hertel	Y	Y	Y	Y	N	Y	Y	N
15 Ford	Y	Y	Y	Y	N	Y	Y	N
16 Dingell	N	N	Y	Y	Y	Y	Y	Y
17 Brodhead	Y	Y	N	Y	N	Y	Y	N
18 Blanchard	Y	?	?	Y	Y	Y	Y	Y
19 ***Broomfield***	N	N	Y	N	Y	Y	Y	N
MINNESOTA								
1 ***Erdahl***	Y	Y	Y	Y	Y	Y	Y	Y
2 ***Hagedorn***	X	N	Y	Y	Y	Y	Y	Y
3 ***Frenzel***	N	?	?	Y	N	Y	N	Y
4 Vento	Y	Y	Y	Y	Y	Y	N	N
5 Sabo	Y	Y	Y	N	N	Y	Y	N
6 ***Weber***	N	N	Y	Y	N	N	Y	Y
7 ***Stangeland***	?	N	Y	Y	Y	Y	Y	Y
8 Oberstar	Y	Y	Y	Y	Y	Y	Y	Y
MISSISSIPPI								
1 Whitten	N	Y	Y	Y	Y	Y	Y	N
2 Bowen	N	Y	Y	Y	Y	Y	Y	Y
3 Montgomery	N	Y	Y	Y	Y	Y	Y	Y
4 Dowdy	N	Y	Y	Y	Y	Y	Y	Y
5 ***Lott***	N	N	Y	Y	Y	Y	Y	Y
MISSOURI								
1 Clay	Y	Y	Y	?	Y	Y	Y	N
2 Young	N	Y	Y	Y	Y	Y	Y	Y
3 Gephardt	N	?	Y	Y	Y	Y	Y	Y

	153	154	155	156	157	158	159	160
4 Skelton	Y	Y	Y	Y	Y	Y	Y	Y
5 Bolling	Y	Y	Y	?	Y	Y	Y	N
6 ***Coleman***	N	N	Y	Y	Y	Y	Y	Y
7 ***Taylor***	N	N	Y	Y	Y	Y	Y	Y
8 ***Bailey***	N	N	Y	Y	Y	Y	Y	Y
9 Volkmer	N	Y	+	?	-	+	+	+
10 ***Emerson***	N	N	Y	Y	Y	Y	Y	Y
MONTANA								
1 Williams	Y	Y	Y	?	Y	Y	Y	Y
2 ***Marlenee***	N	N	Y	Y	Y	Y	Y	Y
NEBRASKA								
1 ***Bereuter***	Y	Y	Y	Y	N	Y	Y	Y
2 ***Daub***	N	N	Y	Y	Y	Y	Y	Y
3 ***Smith***	N	N	Y	Y	Y	Y	Y	Y
NEVADA								
AL Santini	N	N	?	Y	Y	Y	Y	?
NEW HAMPSHIRE								
1 D'Amours	?	?	?	?	Y	Y	Y	Y
2 ***Gregg***	?	?	?	Y	Y	Y	Y	Y
NEW JERSEY								
1 Florio	Y	Y	Y	Y	Y	Y	Y	N
2 Hughes	N	Y	N	Y	Y	Y	Y	N
3 Howard	Y	Y	Y	Y	Y	Y	Y	N
4 ***Smith***	N	N	Y	Y	Y	Y	Y	Y
5 ***Fenwick***	?	?	N	Y	N	Y	Y	Y
6 ***Forsythe***	Y	Y	Y	N	Y	Y	Y	Y
7 ***Roukema***	N	N	N	Y	N	Y	Y	Y
8 Roe	Y	Y	Y	Y	Y	Y	Y	N
9 ***Hollenbeck***	Y	N	Y	Y	Y	Y	Y	Y
10 Rodino	Y	Y	Y	Y	Y	Y	Y	N
11 Minish	?	?	?	?	?	?	?	?
12 ***Rinaldo***	N	N	Y	Y	Y	Y	Y	Y
13 ***Courter***	N	N	Y	Y	N	Y	Y	Y
14 Guarini	Y	Y	Y	Y	Y	Y	Y	N
15 Dwyer	Y	Y	?	Y	Y	Y	Y	N
NEW MEXICO								
1 ***Lujan***	N	Y	N	Y	Y	Y	Y	Y
2 ***Skeen***	N	N	Y	Y	Y	Y	Y	Y
NEW YORK								
1 ***Carney***	Y	Y	Y	Y	Y	Y	Y	Y
2 Downey	Y	Y	Y	Y	Y	Y	Y	N
3 ***Carman***	N	N	Y	Y	Y	Y	Y	Y
4 ***Lent***	N	N	Y	Y	Y	Y	Y	Y
5 ***McGrath***	Y	N	Y	Y	Y	Y	Y	Y
6 ***LeBoutillier***	N	N	Y	Y	Y	Y	Y	Y
7 Addabbo	Y	Y	Y	Y	Y	Y	Y	N
8 Rosenthal	?	?	?	?	?	?	?	?
9 Ferraro	Y	Y	Y	Y	Y	Y	Y	N
10 Biaggi	N	Y	Y	Y	N	Y	Y	N
11 Scheuer	Y	Y	Y	Y	Y	Y	Y	N
12 Chisholm	Y	Y	Y	?	Y	Y	Y	N
13 Solarz	Y	?	?	Y	Y	Y	Y	N
14 Richmond	Y	Y	Y	Y	Y	Y	Y	N
15 Zeferetti	?	?	?	Y	Y	Y	Y	N
16 Schumer	Y	Y	Y	Y	Y	Y	Y	N
17 ***Molinari***	N	N	Y	Y	Y	Y	Y	Y
18 ***Green***	Y	Y	Y	Y	Y	Y	Y	N
19 Rangel	Y	Y	Y	Y	Y	Y	Y	N
20 Weiss	Y	Y	N	Y	Y	Y	Y	N
21 Garcia	Y	Y	Y	?	Y	Y	Y	N
22 Bingham	Y	Y	Y	Y	N	Y	Y	N
23 Peyser	Y	Y	Y	Y	Y	Y	Y	N
24 Ottinger	Y	Y	Y	P	Y	Y	Y	N
25 ***Fish***	Y	Y	Y	Y	?	Y	Y	N
26 ***Gilman***	N	Y	Y	Y	Y	Y	Y	N
27 McHugh	Y	Y	Y	Y	Y	Y	Y	N
28 Stratton	N	N	Y	Y	Y	N	Y	N
29 ***Solomon***	N	N	Y	Y	Y	Y	Y	Y
30 ***Martin***	N	N	Y	Y	Y	Y	Y	Y
31 ***Mitchell***	Y	N	Y	Y	Y	Y	Y	Y
32 ***Wortley***	Y	Y	Y	Y	Y	Y	Y	Y
33 ***Lee***	N	N	Y	Y	Y	Y	Y	Y
34 ***Horton***	#	?	?	?	?	?	?	?
35 ***Conable***	?	?	?	Y	N	Y	Y	Y
36 LaFalce	N	Y	Y	Y	Y	Y	Y	N
37 Nowak	Y	Y	Y	Y	Y	Y	Y	N
38 ***Kemp***	Y	N	?	Y	Y	N	Y	Y
39 Lundine	Y	Y	Y	Y	Y	Y	Y	Y
NORTH CAROLINA								
1 Jones	Y	Y	Y	?	Y	Y	Y	Y
2 Fountain	N	Y	Y	Y	Y	Y	Y	?
3 Whitley	?	?	?	Y	Y	Y	Y	Y
4 Andrews	Y	Y	Y	?	Y	Y	Y	Y
5 Neal	Y	Y	Y	Y	Y	Y	Y	Y
6 ***Johnston***	N	N	Y	Y	N	Y	Y	Y
7 Rose	Y	Y	Y	Y	Y	Y	Y	Y
8 Hefner	Y	Y	Y	Y	Y	Y	Y	Y

	153	154	155	156	157	158	159	160
9 ***Martin***	N	Y	Y	Y	N	Y	Y	Y
10 ***Broyhill***	N	N	Y	Y	N	Y	?	Y
11 ***Hendon***	N	N	Y	Y	Y	Y	Y	Y
NORTH DAKOTA								
AL Dorgan	N	N	Y	Y	Y	Y	Y	Y
OHIO								
1 ***Gradison***	Y	N	N	Y	N	Y	Y	Y
2 Luken	Y	Y	Y	Y	Y	Y	Y	Y
3 Hall	Y	Y	Y	Y	N	Y	Y	Y
4 ***Oxley***	N	N	Y	Y	?	?	?	Y
5 ***Latta***	N	N	Y	Y	N	Y	Y	Y
6 ***McEwen***	N	N	Y	Y	N	Y	Y	Y
7 ***Brown***	?	?	?	Y	Y	Y	Y	Y
8 ***Kindness***	N	N	Y	Y	N	Y	Y	Y
9 ***Weber***	Y	Y	Y	Y	N	Y	Y	Y
10 ***Miller***	N	N	N	Y	N	Y	Y	Y
11 ***Stanton***	Y	Y	Y	Y	Y	Y	Y	Y
12 Shamansky	Y	Y	Y	Y	N	Y	Y	N
13 Pease	Y	Y	Y	Y	N	Y	Y	N
14 Seiberling	Y	Y	Y	Y	N	Y	Y	N
15 ***Wylie***	N	Y	Y	Y	N	Y	Y	Y
16 ***Regula***	N	N	Y	Y	N	Y	Y	Y
17 ***Ashbrook***	N	N	Y	Y	Y	N	Y	Y
18 Applegate	Y	Y	?	?	Y	Y	?	Y
19 ***Williams***	?	#	?	Y	Y	Y	Y	Y
20 Oakar	Y	Y	Y	Y	Y	Y	Y	N
21 Stokes	Y	Y	Y	Y	Y	Y	Y	N
22 Eckart	Y	Y	Y	Y	Y	Y	Y	N
23 Mottl	N	N	N	Y	Y	Y	Y	N
OKLAHOMA								
1 Jones	Y	Y	Y	Y	N	Y	Y	Y
2 Synar	Y	Y	Y	Y	Y	Y	Y	Y
3 Watkins	N	N	Y	Y	Y	Y	Y	Y
4 McCurdy	Y	Y	Y	Y	Y	Y	Y	Y
5 ***Edwards***	N	N	Y	Y	N	Y	Y	Y
6 English	Y	N	Y	Y	Y	Y	Y	Y
OREGON								
1 AuCoin	N	N	Y	Y	Y	Y	Y	Y
2 ***Smith***	N	N	N	P	N	Y	Y	Y
3 Wyden	Y	Y	Y	Y	Y	Y	Y	Y
4 Weaver	N	N	?	Y	Y	Y	N	Y
PENNSYLVANIA								
1 Foglietta	Y	Y	Y	Y	Y	Y	Y	N
2 Gray	Y	Y	?	Y	Y	Y	Y	N
3 Smith*					Y	Y	Y	Y
4 ***Dougherty***	Y	Y	?	Y	Y	Y	Y	Y
5 ***Schulze***	N	N	Y	Y	Y	Y	Y	Y
6 Yatron	Y	Y	Y	Y	Y	Y	Y	Y
7 Edgar	Y	Y	Y	N	N	Y	Y	N
8 ***Coyne, J.***	N	N	Y	Y	N	N	Y	Y
9 ***Shuster***	N	N	Y	Y	Y	Y	Y	Y
10 ***McDade***	Y	N	Y	?	Y	Y	Y	Y
11 ***Nelligan***	N	N	Y	Y	Y	Y	Y	Y
12 Murtha	Y	Y	Y	Y	Y	Y	Y	Y
13 ***Coughlin***	N	N	Y	Y	Y	Y	Y	N
14 Coyne, W.	Y	Y	Y	Y	Y	Y	Y	N
15 ***Ritter***	N	N	N	Y	Y	Y	Y	Y
16 ***Walker***	N	N	Y	N	Y	Y	Y	Y
17 Ertel	N	Y	Y	Y	Y	Y	Y	Y
18 Walgren	Y	Y	Y	Y	Y	Y	Y	N
19 ***Goodling***	Y	N	Y	N	Y	Y	Y	Y
20 Gaydos	Y	Y	Y	?	Y	Y	Y	Y
21 Bailey	Y	Y	Y	Y	Y	Y	Y	Y
22 Murphy	N	N	N	Y	Y	Y	Y	Y
23 ***Clinger***	Y	N	Y	Y	Y	Y	Y	Y
24 ***Marks***	Y	Y	Y	Y	Y	Y	Y	Y
25 Atkinson	Y	Y	Y	Y	?	Y	Y	Y
RHODE ISLAND								
1 St Germain	P	Y	Y	Y	Y	Y	Y	N
2 ***Schneider***	Y	#	?	Y	Y	Y	Y	N
SOUTH CAROLINA								
1 ***Hartnett***	N	N	Y	Y	N	N	Y	Y
2 ***Spence***	N	N	Y	Y	Y	Y	Y	Y
3 Derrick	Y	Y	Y	?	Y	Y	Y	Y
4 ***Campbell***	N	N	Y	Y	Y	Y	Y	Y
5 Holland	Y	Y	?	Y	?	?	Y	Y
6 ***Napier***	N	Y	Y	Y	Y	Y	Y	Y
SOUTH DAKOTA								
1 Daschle	?	Y	Y	Y	Y	Y	Y	Y
2 ***Roberts***	N	N	Y	Y	Y	Y	Y	Y
TENNESSEE								
1 ***Quillen***	N	N	Y	Y	Y	Y	Y	Y
2 ***Duncan***	N	?	Y	Y	Y	Y	Y	?
3 Bouquard	?	N	Y	Y	Y	Y	Y	Y
4 Gore	N	Y	Y	Y	Y	Y	Y	Y
5 Boner	N	N	Y	Y	Y	Y	Y	Y
6 ***Beard***	N	Y	Y	Y	N	Y	Y	Y

	153	154	155	156	157	158	159	160
7 Jones	N	Y	Y	Y	Y	Y	Y	Y
8 Ford	Y	Y	Y	Y	Y	Y	Y	N
TEXAS								
1 Hall, S.	N	Y	Y	Y	Y	Y	Y	Y
2 Wilson	Y	N	Y	Y	Y	Y	Y	Y
3 ***Collins***	N	N	?	Y	N	N	Y	Y
4 Hall, R.	N	N	Y	Y	Y	Y	Y	Y
5 Mattox	Y	Y	Y	Y	Y	Y	Y	Y
6 Gramm	N	N	Y	Y	?	Y	Y	Y
7 ***Archer***	N	N	N	Y	N	Y	Y	Y
8 ***Fields***	N	N	Y	Y	N	Y	Y	Y
9 Brooks	N	N	Y	Y	N	Y	Y	Y
10 Pickle	?	?	?	Y	Y	Y	Y	Y
11 Leath	N	N	Y	Y	Y	Y	Y	Y
12 Wright	Y	Y	Y	Y	Y	Y	Y	N
13 Hightower	N	Y	Y	Y	Y	Y	Y	Y
14 Patman	N	Y	Y	Y	Y	Y	Y	Y
15 de la Garza	?	?	?	Y	Y	Y	Y	Y
16 White	Y	Y	Y	Y	N	Y	Y	Y
17 Stenholm	N	Y	Y	Y	Y	Y	Y	?
18 Leland	Y	Y	Y	Y	Y	Y	Y	N
19 Hance	N	N	Y	Y	Y	Y	Y	Y
20 Gonzalez	Y	Y	Y	Y	Y	Y	Y	N
21 ***Loeffler***	N	N	Y	Y	Y	Y	Y	Y
22 ***Paul***	X	N	N	Y	N	N	Y	Y
23 Kazen	N	Y	Y	Y	Y	Y	Y	Y
24 Frost	?	?	?	?	?	?	?	?
UTAH								
1 ***Hansen***	?	?	?	?	Y	Y	Y	Y
2 ***Marriott***	Y	Y	Y	Y	Y	Y	Y	Y
VERMONT								
AL ***Jeffords***	Y	Y	Y	Y	Y	Y	Y	Y
VIRGINIA								
1 ***Trible***	Y	Y	Y	Y	Y	Y	Y	Y
2 ***Whitehurst***	N	Y	Y	Y	Y	Y	Y	Y
3 ***Bliley***	Y	Y	Y	Y	N	Y	Y	Y
4 ***Daniel, R.***	N	N	Y	Y	N	Y	Y	Y
5 Daniel, D.	N	N	Y	Y	N	Y	Y	Y
6 ***Butler***	Y	N	Y	Y	N	Y	Y	Y
7 ***Robinson***	N	N	Y	Y	N	Y	Y	Y
8 ***Parris***	Y	Y	Y	Y	Y	Y	Y	Y
9 ***Wampler***	N	Y	Y	?	?	?	?	Y
10 ***Wolf***	Y	Y	Y	Y	Y	Y	Y	Y
WASHINGTON								
1 ***Pritchard***	?	?	?	Y	Y	Y	Y	N
2 Swift	Y	Y	Y	Y	Y	Y	Y	Y
3 Bonker	?	?	?	Y	Y	Y	Y	Y
4 ***Morrison***	N	N	Y	Y	Y	Y	Y	Y
5 Foley	Y	Y	Y	Y	Y	Y	Y	Y
6 Dicks	?	Y	N	Y	Y	Y	Y	Y
7 Lowry	Y	Y	Y	N	Y	Y	Y	Y
WEST VIRGINIA								
1 Mollohan	Y	Y	Y	Y	Y	Y	?	Y
2 ***Benedict***	N	Y	Y	Y	N	Y	Y	Y
3 ***Staton***	Y	Y	?	?	Y	Y	Y	Y
4 Rahall	Y	Y	Y	Y	Y	Y	Y	Y
WISCONSIN								
1 Aspin	Y	Y	?	Y	N	Y	Y	N
2 Kastenmeier	Y	Y	Y	Y	Y	Y	Y	N
3 ***Gunderson***	Y	N	Y	Y	Y	Y	Y	Y
4 Zablocki	Y	Y	Y	Y	Y	Y	Y	N
5 Reuss	Y	Y	Y	Y	Y	Y	Y	N
6 ***Petri***	N	N	Y	Y	Y	Y	Y	Y
7 Obey	?	?	Y	Y	N	Y	Y	Y
8 ***Roth***	N	N	Y	Y	Y	Y	Y	Y
9 ***Sensenbrenner***	N	N	Y	Y	Y	Y	Y	Y
WYOMING								
AL ***Cheney***	N	N	Y	Y	Y	Y	Y	Y

** Rep. Joseph F. Smith, D-Pa., was sworn in July 28, 1981. The first vote for which he was eligible was CQ vote 157.*

Democrats ***Republicans***

161. HR 4121. Treasury, Postal Service, General Government Appropriations, Fiscal 1982. Schroeder, D-Colo., amendment to delete $13.6 million earmarked for the Savings Bond Division of the Treasury Department, which promotes the purchase of government savings bonds. Adopted 223-190: R 43-142; D 180-48 (ND 121-31, SD 59-17), July 28, 1981. (The Schroeder amendment subsequently was rejected on a vote by the full House (see vote 173, p. 60-H).)

162. Procedural Motion. Walker, R-Pa., motion to approve the House *Journal* of Tuesday, July 28. Motion agreed to 350-24: R 161-10; D 189-14 (ND 125-12, SD 64-2), July 29, 1981.

163. HR 4242. Tax Cuts. Bolling, D-Mo., motion to order the previous question (thus ending debate and the possibility of amendments) on the rule (H Res 198) providing for House floor consideration of the bill. Motion agreed to 282-148: R 128-62; D 154-86 (ND 82-80, SD 72-6), July 29, 1981.

164. HR 4242. Tax Cuts. Adoption of the rule (H Res 198) providing for House floor consideration of the bill. Adopted 280-150: R 131-58; D 149-92 (ND 78-85, SD 71-7), July 29, 1981.

165. HR 4242. Tax Cuts. Udall, D-Ariz., substitute amendment, to the bill, to provide a one-year reduction in income tax rates skewed to benefit most those earning less than $50,000 per year and to provide narrowly targeted business and investment tax incentives. Rejected 144-288: R 5-186; D 139-102 (ND 116-46, SD 23-56), July 29, 1981. A "nay" was a vote supporting the president's position.

166. HR 4242. Tax Cuts. Conable, R-N.Y., substitute amendment, to the bill, to reduce individual income tax rates by 25 percent across-the-board over three years, to index tax rates beginning in 1985 and to provide business and investment tax incentives. Adopted 238-195: R 190-1; D 48-194 (ND 12-151, SD 36-43), July 29, 1981. A "yea" was a vote supporting the president's position.

167. HR 4242. Tax Cuts. Passage of the bill to amend the Internal Revenue Service Code of 1954 by reducing individual income tax rates by 25 percent across-the-board over three years, indexing tax rates beginning in 1985 and providing business and investment tax incentives. Passed 323-107: R 190-1; D 133-106 (ND 64-97, SD 69-9), July 29, 1981. A "yea" was a vote supporting the president's position.

KEY

Y	Voted for (yea).
#	Paired for.
+	Announced for.
N	Voted against (nay).
X	Paired against.
-	Announced against.
P	Voted "present".
C	Voted "present" to avoid possible conflict of interest.
?	Did not vote or otherwise make a position known.

	161	162	163	164	165	166	167
ALABAMA							
1 *Edwards*	Y	Y	Y	Y	N	Y	Y
2 *Dickinson*	N	?	Y	Y	N	Y	Y
3 Nichols	Y	Y	Y	Y	Y	Y	Y
4 Bevill	Y	Y	Y	Y	N	Y	Y
5 Flippo	Y	Y	Y	Y	N	Y	Y
6 *Smith*	Y	?	Y	N	Y	N	Y
7 Shelby	Y	?	Y	Y	N	Y	Y
ALASKA							
AL *Young*	N	?	Y	Y	N	Y	Y
ARIZONA							
1 *Rhodes*	N	Y	Y	Y	N	Y	Y
2 Udall	Y	Y	Y	Y	Y	N	N
3 Stump	Y	Y	Y	Y	N	Y	Y
4 *Rudd*	N	Y	Y	Y	N	Y	Y
ARKANSAS							
1 Alexander	Y	Y	Y	Y	Y	N	Y
2 *Bethune*	Y	Y	Y	Y	N	Y	Y
3 *Hammerschmidt*	Y	Y	Y	Y	N	Y	Y
4 Anthony	Y	?	Y	Y	N	N	Y
CALIFORNIA							
1 *Chappie*	Y	Y	Y	Y	N	Y	Y
2 *Clausen*	N	Y	Y	Y	N	Y	Y
3 Matsui	Y	Y	Y	Y	N	N	N
4 Fazio	Y	Y	Y	Y	N	N	Y
5 Burton, J.	?	?	N	N	Y	N	N
6 Burton, P.	Y	Y	N	N	Y	N	N
7 Miller	Y	Y	N	N	Y	N	N
8 Dellums	Y	Y	N	N	Y	N	N
9 Stark	Y	Y	Y	Y	Y	N	Y
10 Edwards	Y	Y	N	N	Y	N	N
11 Lantos	Y	Y	Y	Y	N	N	Y
12 *McCloskey*	Y	Y	Y	Y	N	Y	Y
13 Mineta	Y	Y	Y	N	N	N	Y
14 *Shumway*	N	Y	Y	Y	N	Y	Y
15 Coelho	Y	Y	Y	Y	N	N	Y
16 Panetta	Y	Y	Y	N	Y	N	Y
17 *Pashayan*	N	Y	Y	Y	N	Y	Y
18 *Thomas*	N	Y	Y	Y	N	Y	Y
19 *Lagomarsino*	N	Y	Y	Y	N	Y	Y
20 *Goldwater*	N	Y	Y	Y	N	Y	Y
21 *Fiedler*	N	Y	Y	Y	N	Y	Y
22 *Moorhead*	N	Y	Y	Y	N	Y	Y
23 Beilenson	Y	Y	Y	Y	Y	N	N
24 Waxman	Y	N	Y	N	Y	N	N
25 Roybal	Y	Y	N	N	Y	N	N
26 *Rousselot*	Y	Y	Y	Y	N	Y	Y
27 *Dornan*	N	Y	Y	Y	N	Y	Y
28 Dixon	Y	?	N	N	Y	N	Y
29 Hawkins	N	Y	N	N	Y	N	N
30 Danielson	Y	Y	Y	Y	Y	N	Y
31 Dymally	Y	Y	N	N	Y	N	N
32 Anderson	Y	Y	N	Y	N	Y	Y
33 *Grisham*	Y	Y	Y	Y	N	Y	Y
34 *Lungren*	N	Y	Y	Y	N	Y	Y
35 *Dreier*	N	Y	Y	Y	N	Y	Y
36 Brown	Y	Y	N	Y	N	N	N
37 *Lewis*	N	N	Y	Y	N	Y	Y
38 Patterson	Y	Y	Y	Y	N	Y	Y
39 *Dannemeyer*	N	Y	N	N	N	Y	Y
40 *Badham*	N	Y	Y	Y	N	Y	Y
41 *Lowery*	N	Y	Y	Y	N	Y	Y
42 *Hunter*	N	Y	Y	Y	N	Y	Y
43 *Burgener*	N	Y	Y	Y	N	Y	Y
COLORADO							
1 Schroeder	Y	N	N	N	N	N	N
2 Wirth	Y	?	Y	N	Y	N	N
3 Kogovsek	Y	Y	N	Y	N	N	Y
4 *Brown*	Y	Y	N	Y	N	Y	Y

	161	162	163	164	165	166	167
5 *Kramer*	Y	Y	Y	Y	N	Y	Y
CONNECTICUT							
1 Cotter	?	?	?	?	?	?	?
2 Gejdenson	Y	N	N	N	Y	N	N
3 *DeNardis*	Y	Y	N	N	Y	Y	Y
4 *McKinney*	N	?	N	N	N	Y	Y
5 Ratchford	Y	Y	Y	N	Y	N	N
6 Moffett	Y	?	Y	N	Y	N	N
DELAWARE							
AL *Evans*	N	Y	N	N	N	Y	Y
FLORIDA							
1 Hutto	Y	?	Y	Y	N	Y	Y
2 Fuqua	Y	Y	Y	Y	N	Y	Y
3 Bennett	Y	N	N	N	N	N	N
4 Chappell	N	?	Y	Y	N	Y	Y
5 *McCollum*	Y	Y	Y	Y	N	Y	Y
6 *Young*	N	Y	Y	Y	N	Y	Y
7 Gibbons	Y	Y	Y	Y	N	N	Y
8 Ireland	Y	Y	Y	Y	N	Y	Y
9 Nelson	Y	N	N	N	Y	N	Y
10 *Bafalis*	N	Y	Y	Y	N	Y	Y
11 Mica	Y	Y	Y	Y	Y	Y	Y
12 *Shaw*	N	?	Y	Y	N	Y	Y
13 Lehman	Y	Y	Y	Y	N	Y	N
14 Pepper	N	?	Y	Y	Y	N	Y
15 Fascell	?	?	?	?	Y	N	N
GEORGIA							
1 Ginn	N	Y	Y	Y	N	Y	Y
2 Hatcher	N	?	Y	Y	N	Y	Y
3 Brinkley	Y	Y	Y	Y	N	Y	Y
4 Levitas	Y	Y	N	N	N	Y	Y
5 Fowler	N	Y	Y	Y	N	Y	Y
6 *Gingrich*	N	Y	Y	Y	N	Y	Y
7 McDonald	Y	Y	Y	Y	N	Y	N
8 Evans	N	?	Y	Y	N	Y	?
9 Jenkins	Y	Y	Y	Y	N	Y	Y
10 Barnard	N	Y	Y	Y	N	Y	Y
HAWAII							
1 Heftel	N	?	Y	Y	N	N	Y
2 Akaka	Y	Y	Y	Y	Y	N	Y
IDAHO							
1 *Craig*	N	Y	Y	Y	N	Y	Y
2 *Hansen*	N	Y	Y	Y	N	Y	Y
ILLINOIS							
1 Washington	Y	Y	N	N	Y	N	N
2 Savage	?	?	?	N	P	N	?
3 Russo	N	Y	Y	N	N	N	N
4 *Derwinski*	N	N	N	N	N	Y	Y
5 Fary	Y	Y	Y	N	Y	N	Y
6 *Hyde*	N	Y	Y	Y	N	Y	Y
7 Collins	Y	N	N	N	Y	N	N
8 Rostenkowski	N	Y	Y	N	Y	N	Y
9 Yates	Y	Y	Y	N	Y	N	N
10 *Porter*	Y	Y	N	N	N	Y	Y
11 Annunzio	Y	Y	Y	N	Y	N	Y
12 Crane, P.	Y	Y	Y	N	N	Y	Y
13 *McClory*	N	Y	Y	Y	N	Y	Y
14 *Erlenborn*	Y	Y	Y	Y	N	Y	Y
15 *Corcoran*	N	+	Y	Y	N	Y	Y
16 *Martin*	Y	Y	Y	Y	N	Y	Y
17 *O'Brien*	N	Y	Y	Y	N	Y	Y
18 *Michel*	N	Y	Y	Y	N	Y	Y
19 *Railsback*	N	?	N	N	N	Y	Y
20 *Findley*	Y	N	Y	N	Y	Y	Y
21 *Madigan*	N	?	Y	Y	N	Y	Y
22 Crane, D.	Y	Y	Y	Y	N	Y	Y
23 Price	Y	Y	Y	N	N	N	Y
24 Simon	?	Y	Y	Y	N	N	N
INDIANA							
1 Benjamin	Y	Y	Y	Y	Y	N	Y
2 Fithian	Y	Y	N	N	Y	N	N
3 *Hiler*	N	Y	Y	Y	N	Y	Y
4 *Coats*	N	Y	Y	Y	N	Y	Y
5 *Hillis*	N	Y	Y	Y	N	Y	Y
6 Evans	Y	Y	Y	Y	Y	Y	N
7 *Myers*	N	Y	N	Y	N	Y	Y
8 *Deckard*	N	?	Y	N	N	Y	Y
9 Hamilton	Y	Y	N	Y	N	Y	Y
10 Sharp	Y	Y	N	N	Y	N	Y
11 Jacobs	Y	N	N	N	Y	N	N
IOWA							
1 *Leach*	Y	Y	N	N	N	Y	Y
2 *Tauke*	Y	Y	N	N	N	Y	Y
3 *Evans*	Y	N	N	Y	N	Y	Y
4 Smith	Y	Y	N	N	Y	N	Y
5 Harkin	N	N	N	N	Y	N	N
6 Bedell	Y	?	N	N	Y	N	N

Democrats   **Republicans**

	161	162	163	164	165	166	167
KANSAS							
1 ***Roberts***	N	Y	Y	Y	N	Y	Y
2 ***Jeffries***	Y	Y	Y	Y	N	Y	Y
3 ***Winn***	N	Y	Y	N	N	Y	Y
4 Glickman	Y	Y	N	N	N	Y	Y
5 ***Whittaker***	N	Y	Y	Y	N	Y	Y
KENTUCKY							
1 Hubbard	Y	Y	Y	Y	N	Y	Y
2 Natcher	Y	Y	Y	Y	Y	N	Y
3 Mazzoli	Y	Y	N	Y	N	Y	Y
4 ***Snyder***	N	Y	N	N	N	Y	Y
5 ***Rogers***	N	?	Y	N	N	Y	Y
6 ***Hopkins***	N	Y	N	N	N	Y	Y
7 Perkins	Y	Y	Y	Y	Y	N	Y
LOUISIANA							
1 ***Livingston***	N	?	Y	Y	N	Y	Y
2 Boggs	?	?	Y	Y	N	N	Y
3 Tauzin	N	Y	Y	Y	N	N	Y
4 Roemer	Y	Y	Y	Y	N	Y	Y
5 Huckaby	N	Y	Y	Y	N	Y	Y
6 ***Moore***	Y	Y	N	N	N	Y	Y
7 Breaux	N	Y	Y	Y	N	N	Y
8 Long	Y	Y	Y	Y	N	N	Y
MAINE							
1 ***Emery***	Y	Y	N	N	N	Y	Y
2 ***Snowe***	Y	Y	N	N	N	Y	Y
MARYLAND							
1 Dyson	Y	Y	Y	Y	Y	Y	Y
2 Long	Y	Y	N	Y	Y	N	Y
3 Mikulski	Y	Y	Y	Y	Y	N	N
4 ***Holt***	N	Y	Y	Y	N	Y	Y
5 Hoyer	N	Y	Y	Y	Y	N	N
6 Byron	N	Y	Y	Y	N	Y	Y
7 Mitchell	Y	N	N	N	Y	N	N
8 Barnes	N	Y	N	N	Y	N	N
MASSACHUSETTS							
1 ***Conte***	N	Y	N	N	Y	Y	Y
2 Boland	N	Y	N	N	Y	N	N
3 Early	N	Y	N	N	Y	N	N
4 Frank	Y	Y	N	N	Y	N	N
5 Shannon	N	N	Y	Y	N	N	N
6 Mavroules	N	Y	N	N	Y	N	N
7 Markey	Y	?	Y	N	Y	N	N
8 O'Neill						N	
9 Moakley	Y	Y	Y	Y	Y	N	N
10 ***Heckler***	N	?	N	N	N	Y	Y
11 Donnelly	Y	?	N	N	Y	N	N
12 Studds	Y	Y	N	N	Y	N	N
MICHIGAN							
1 Conyers	Y	?	N	N	Y	N	N
2 ***Pursell***	Y	Y	N	N	N	Y	Y
3 Wolpe	Y	Y	Y	Y	Y	N	Y
4 ***Siljander***	Y	Y	Y	Y	N	Y	Y
5 ***Sawyer***	N	?	Y	Y	N	Y	Y
6 ***Dunn***	Y	Y	N	N	Y	Y	Y
7 Kildee	Y	Y	Y	Y	Y	N	N
8 Traxler	Y	N	Y	Y	N	N	Y
9 ***Vander Jagt***	N	?	Y	Y	N	Y	Y
10 Albosta	N	Y	Y	Y	N	N	Y
11 ***Davis***	N	Y	Y	Y	N	Y	Y
12 Bonior	Y	Y	Y	Y	Y	N	N
13 Crockett	?	?	N	N	Y	N	N
14 Hertel	Y	Y	N	N	Y	N	Y
15 Ford	N	?	Y	Y	Y	N	N
16 Dingell	Y	?	Y	Y	N	N	N
17 Brodhead	Y	?	Y	Y	Y	N	N
18 Blanchard	Y	Y	Y	Y	Y	N	Y
19 ***Broomfield***	N	N	Y	Y	N	Y	Y
MINNESOTA							
1 ***Erdahl***	N	Y	Y	N	N	Y	Y
2 ***Hagedorn***	N	Y	N	N	N	Y	Y
3 ***Frenzel***	N	Y	Y	Y	N	Y	Y
4 Vento	Y	Y	N	N	Y	N	N
5 Sabo	Y	N	Y	N	Y	N	N
6 ***Weber***	Y	Y	Y	Y	N	Y	Y
7 ***Stangeland***	N	Y	N	N	N	Y	Y
8 Oberstar	Y	Y	Y	Y	Y	N	N
MISSISSIPPI							
1 Whitten	Y	Y	Y	Y	Y	N	Y
2 Bowen	Y	Y	Y	Y	N	Y	Y
3 Montgomery	Y	Y	Y	Y	N	Y	Y
4 Dowdy	N	Y	Y	Y	N	N	Y
5 ***Lott***	N	Y	Y	Y	N	Y	Y
MISSOURI							
1 Clay	Y	?	N	N	Y	N	N
2 Young	N	Y	Y	Y	N	N	Y
3 Gephardt	Y	Y	Y	Y	Y	N	Y
4 Skelton	?	Y	Y	Y	N	N	Y
5 Bolling	?	Y	Y	Y	Y	N	N
6 ***Coleman***	N	Y	N	N	N	Y	Y
7 ***Taylor***	N	Y	Y	Y	N	Y	Y
8 ***Bailey***	Y	Y	Y	Y	N	Y	Y
9 Volkmer	Y	Y	Y	N	N	N	Y
10 ***Emerson***	N	Y	Y	Y	N	Y	Y
MONTANA							
1 Williams	Y	Y	Y	Y	Y	N	Y
2 ***Marlenee***	N	Y	Y	Y	N	Y	Y
NEBRASKA							
1 ***Bereuter***	N	Y	N	N	N	Y	Y
2 ***Daub***	N	Y	Y	Y	N	Y	Y
3 ***Smith***	N	Y	Y	Y	N	Y	Y
NEVADA							
AL Santini	?	?	Y	Y	N	Y	Y
NEW HAMPSHIRE							
1 D'Amours	Y	N	N	N	Y	N	N
2 ***Gregg***	Y	Y	N	N	N	Y	Y
NEW JERSEY							
1 Florio	N	Y	N	N	Y	N	N
2 Hughes	Y	Y	N	N	Y	N	N
3 Howard	Y	Y	N	Y	Y	N	N
4 ***Smith***	Y	Y	N	N	N	Y	Y
5 ***Fenwick***	N	Y	N	N	N	Y	Y
6 ***Forsythe***	N	N	Y	Y	N	Y	Y
7 ***Roukema***	N	Y	N	N	N	Y	Y
8 Roe	Y	N	N	N	Y	N	N
9 ***Hollenbeck***	Y	?	N	N	Y	Y	Y
10 Rodino	Y	Y	N	N	Y	N	N
11 Minish	?	Y	N	N	Y	?	?
12 ***Rinaldo***	N	Y	N	N	N	Y	Y
13 ***Courter***	N	Y	Y	Y	N	Y	Y
14 Guarini	Y	Y	N	N	Y	N	N
15 Dwyer	Y	Y	N	N	Y	N	N
NEW MEXICO							
1 ***Lujan***	N	Y	Y	Y	N	Y	Y
2 ***Skeen***	N	Y	Y	Y	N	Y	Y
NEW YORK							
1 ***Carney***	N	Y	Y	Y	N	Y	Y
2 Downey	Y	Y	Y	Y	Y	N	N
3 ***Carman***	N	Y	Y	Y	N	Y	Y
4 ***Lent***	N	Y	N	Y	N	Y	Y
5 ***McGrath***	N	Y	N	N	N	Y	Y
6 ***LeBoutillier***	N	Y	N	Y	N	Y	Y
7 Addabbo	N	Y	Y	Y	N	N	Y
8 Rosenthal	?	Y	N	N	Y	N	N
9 Ferraro	Y	?	Y	Y	Y	N	N
10 Biaggi	N	Y	Y	Y	N	Y	Y
11 Scheuer	Y	Y	N	Y	Y	N	N
12 Chisholm	?	?	N	N	Y	N	N
13 Solarz	Y	?	N	N	Y	N	N
14 Richmond	Y	?	N	N	Y	N	N
15 Zeferetti	N	Y	Y	Y	Y	N	Y
16 Schumer	N	Y	N	N	Y	N	N
17 ***Molinari***	N	Y	Y	Y	N	Y	Y
18 ***Green***	N	Y	N	N	N	Y	Y
19 Rangel	N	?	Y	Y	Y	N	N
20 Weiss	Y	Y	N	N	Y	N	N
21 Garcia	Y	Y	N	N	Y	N	N
22 Bingham	Y	Y	N	N	Y	N	N
23 Peyser	Y	Y	N	N	Y	N	Y
24 Ottinger	Y	P	N	N	Y	N	N
25 ***Fish***	N	Y	N	N	N	Y	Y
26 ***Gilman***	N	Y	N	N	N	Y	Y
27 McHugh	Y	Y	N	N	Y	N	N
28 Stratton	N	Y	Y	Y	N	N	N
29 ***Solomon***	N	N	N	Y	N	Y	Y
30 ***Martin***	N	Y	Y	Y	N	Y	Y
31 ***Mitchell***	N	Y	N	N	N	Y	Y
32 ***Wortley***	N	Y	N	N	N	Y	Y
33 ***Lee***	N	Y	N	N	N	Y	Y
34 ***Horton***	?	Y	N	N	N	Y	Y
35 ***Conable***	?	Y	Y	Y	N	Y	Y
36 LaFalce	?	Y	N	N	Y	N	N
37 Nowak	Y	Y	N	N	N	N	Y
38 ***Kemp***	N	Y	Y	Y	N	Y	Y
39 Lundine	N	Y	N	N	Y	Y	Y
NORTH CAROLINA							
1 Jones	Y	Y	Y	Y	N	N	Y
2 Fountain	Y	?	Y	Y	Y	Y	Y
3 Whitley	Y	Y	Y	Y	Y	N	Y
4 Andrews	Y	Y	Y	Y	Y	N	Y
5 Neal	Y	?	N	N	Y	N	Y
6 ***Johnston***	N	Y	Y	Y	N	Y	Y
7 Rose	Y	Y	Y	Y	Y	N	Y
8 Hefner	Y	Y	Y	Y	Y	N	Y
9 ***Martin***	N	Y	Y	Y	N	Y	Y
10 ***Broyhill***	N	Y	Y	Y	N	Y	Y
11 ***Hendon***	N	Y	Y	Y	N	Y	Y
NORTH DAKOTA							
AL Dorgan	Y	Y	Y	N	N	N	Y
OHIO							
1 ***Gradison***	N	Y	Y	Y	N	Y	Y
2 Luken	N	Y	N	N	N	Y	Y
3 Hall	Y	Y	Y	Y	N	N	Y
4 ***Oxley***	N	?	N	Y	N	Y	Y
5 ***Latta***	N	Y	N	Y	N	Y	Y
6 ***McEwen***	N	Y	Y	Y	N	Y	Y
7 ***Brown***	N	Y	N	Y	N	Y	Y
8 ***Kindness***	Y	Y	N	N	N	Y	Y
9 ***Weber***	N	Y	Y	Y	N	Y	Y
10 ***Miller***	N	Y	Y	Y	N	Y	Y
11 ***Stanton***	N	Y	Y	Y	N	Y	Y
12 Shamansky	Y	Y	Y	Y	Y	N	Y
13 Pease	Y	Y	Y	Y	Y	N	N
14 Seiberling	Y	?	Y	Y	Y	N	N
15 ***Wylie***	N	Y	Y	Y	N	Y	Y
16 ***Regula***	N	Y	N	N	N	Y	Y
17 ***Ashbrook***	N	Y	N	N	N	Y	Y
18 Applegate	N	Y	N	N	N	N	N
19 ***Williams***	?	Y	Y	Y	N	Y	Y
20 Oakar	Y	Y	Y	Y	Y	N	Y
21 Stokes	N	Y	N	N	Y	N	N
22 Eckart	N	Y	N	N	Y	N	Y
23 Mottl	Y	Y	N	N	Y	Y	Y
OKLAHOMA							
1 Jones	Y	N	Y	Y	N	N	Y
2 Synar	Y	N	Y	Y	N	N	Y
3 Watkins	Y	Y	Y	Y	N	N	Y
4 McCurdy	Y	Y	Y	Y	N	Y	Y
5 ***Edwards***	Y	Y	Y	Y	N	Y	Y
6 English	Y	Y	Y	Y	N	Y	Y
OREGON							
1 AuCoin	Y	Y	N	N	N	N	Y
2 ***Smith***	Y	Y	Y	Y	N	Y	Y
3 Wyden	Y	Y	Y	N	Y	N	N
4 Weaver	Y	Y	N	N	Y	N	N
PENNSYLVANIA							
1 Foglietta	Y	?	N	N	Y	N	Y
2 Gray	Y	Y	N	N	Y	N	N
3 Smith	Y	?	Y	Y	Y	N	N
4 ***Dougherty***	N	?	N	N	N	Y	Y
5 ***Schulze***	N	Y	Y	Y	N	Y	Y
6 Yatron	Y	Y	N	N	N	Y	Y
7 Edgar	Y	Y	N	N	Y	N	N
8 ***Coyne, J.***	N	?	N	N	N	Y	Y
9 ***Shuster***	N	Y	Y	Y	N	Y	Y
10 ***McDade***	N	Y	N	Y	N	Y	Y
11 ***Nelligan***	N	Y	N	N	N	Y	Y
12 Murtha	N	Y	Y	Y	Y	N	N
13 ***Coughlin***	N	Y	N	N	N	Y	Y
14 Coyne, W.	N	Y	Y	Y	Y	N	N
15 ***Ritter***	Y	Y	N	N	N	Y	Y
16 ***Walker***	N	N	N	N	N	Y	Y
17 Ertel	Y	Y	N	N	Y	N	Y
18 Walgren	Y	Y	N	N	N	N	N
19 ***Goodling***	N	N	N	N	N	Y	Y
20 Gaydos	Y	Y	Y	Y	N	N	Y
21 Bailey	N	Y	Y	Y	N	N	N
22 Murphy	Y	Y	Y	N	N	N	Y
23 ***Clinger***	N	Y	Y	Y	N	Y	Y
24 ***Marks***	N	Y	Y	Y	N	Y	Y
25 Atkinson	Y	Y	Y	Y	N	Y	Y
RHODE ISLAND							
1 St Germain	Y	Y	N	N	N	N	Y
2 ***Schneider***	N	Y	Y	Y	N	Y	Y
SOUTH CAROLINA							
1 ***Hartnett***	N	Y	Y	Y	N	Y	Y
2 ***Spence***	N	Y	Y	N	N	Y	Y
3 Derrick	Y	Y	Y	Y	N	N	N
4 ***Campbell***	N	Y	?	?	N	Y	Y
5 Holland	Y	Y	Y	Y	N	N	Y
6 ***Napier***	N	Y	Y	Y	N	Y	Y
SOUTH DAKOTA							
1 Daschle	Y	N	Y	N	N	N	Y
2 ***Roberts***	N	Y	Y	Y	N	Y	Y
TENNESSEE							
1 ***Quillen***	N	Y	Y	Y	N	Y	Y
2 ***Duncan***	?	Y	Y	Y	N	Y	Y
3 Bouquard	Y	Y	Y	Y	N	Y	Y
4 Gore	N	Y	Y	Y	Y	N	N
5 Boner	Y	Y	Y	Y	N	Y	Y
6 ***Beard***	N	Y	Y	Y	N	Y	Y
7 Jones	Y	Y	Y	Y	N	Y	Y
8 Ford	Y	Y	Y	N	Y	N	N
TEXAS							
1 Hall, S.	Y	Y	Y	Y	N	Y	Y
2 Wilson	N	Y	Y	Y	N	N	Y
3 ***Collins***	Y	Y	Y	Y	N	Y	Y
4 Hall, R.	Y	?	Y	Y	N	Y	Y
5 Mattox	Y	?	Y	Y	N	N	Y
6 Gramm	Y	Y	Y	Y	N	Y	Y
7 ***Archer***	N	Y	Y	Y	N	Y	Y
8 ***Fields***	Y	Y	Y	Y	N	Y	Y
9 Brooks	Y	Y	Y	Y	N	N	Y
10 Pickle	N	Y	Y	Y	N	N	Y
11 Leath	Y	Y	Y	Y	N	Y	Y
12 Wright	N	Y	Y	Y	N	N	N
13 Hightower	Y	Y	Y	Y	N	Y	Y
14 Patman	Y	Y	Y	Y	N	N	N
15 de la Garza	Y	Y	Y	Y	Y	Y	Y
16 White	Y	Y	Y	Y	N	N	Y
17 Stenholm	Y	Y	Y	Y	N	Y	Y
18 Leland	Y	Y	N	N	Y	N	N
19 Hance	Y	Y	Y	Y	N	Y	Y
20 Gonzalez	N	Y	Y	Y	Y	N	N
21 ***Loeffler***	Y	Y	Y	Y	N	Y	Y
22 ***Paul***	Y	Y	Y	Y	N	Y	Y
23 Kazen	Y	Y	Y	Y	N	N	Y
24 Frost	?	Y	Y	Y	N	N	Y
UTAH							
1 ***Hansen***	N	?	Y	Y	N	Y	Y
2 ***Marriott***	N	Y	Y	Y	N	Y	Y
VERMONT							
AL ***Jeffords***	N	Y	N	N	Y	N	N
VIRGINIA							
1 ***Trible***	N	Y	Y	Y	N	Y	Y
2 ***Whitehurst***	N	Y	Y	Y	N	Y	Y
3 ***Bliley***	N	Y	Y	Y	N	Y	Y
4 ***Daniel, R.***	N	Y	Y	Y	N	Y	Y
5 Daniel, D.	N	Y	Y	Y	N	Y	Y
6 ***Butler***	N	Y	Y	Y	N	Y	Y
7 ***Robinson***	N	Y	Y	Y	N	Y	Y
8 ***Parris***	N	Y	Y	Y	N	Y	Y
9 ***Wampler***	N	Y	Y	Y	N	Y	Y
10 ***Wolf***	N	Y	N	N	N	Y	Y
WASHINGTON							
1 ***Pritchard***	?	Y	N	N	N	Y	Y
2 Swift	Y	Y	N	N	Y	N	Y
3 Bonker	Y	?	Y	Y	Y	N	Y
4 ***Morrison***	N	Y	Y	Y	N	Y	Y
5 Foley	Y	Y	Y	Y	N	N	Y
6 Dicks	Y	Y	Y	Y	N	Y	Y
7 Lowry	Y	N	N	N	Y	N	N
WEST VIRGINIA							
1 Mollohan	Y	Y	Y	Y	N	N	Y
2 ***Benedict***	N	Y	Y	Y	N	Y	Y
3 ***Staton***	N	N	Y	Y	N	Y	Y
4 Rahall	N	Y	Y	N	N	N	Y
WISCONSIN							
1 Aspin	Y	Y	Y	Y	Y	N	N
2 Kastenmeier	Y	Y	N	N	Y	N	N
3 ***Gunderson***	N	Y	N	N	N	Y	Y
4 Zablocki	N	Y	Y	Y	Y	N	Y
5 Reuss	Y	Y	Y	Y	Y	N	N
6 ***Petri***	Y	Y	N	N	N	Y	Y
7 Obey	Y	Y	Y	Y	Y	N	N
8 ***Roth***	?	?	Y	Y	N	Y	Y
9 ***Sensenbrenner***	Y	Y	N	N	N	Y	Y
WYOMING							
AL ***Cheney***	N	Y	Y	Y	N	Y	Y

Democrats ***Republicans***

168. H Res 124. Policy Toward Poland. Adoption of the resolution expressing the sense of the House that the United States could not remain indifferent to any internal repression or external aggression against the people of Poland and that such developments would have serious consequences for East-West relations. Adopted 410-1: R 183-1; D 227-0 (ND 152-0, SD 75-0), July 30, 1981.

169. HR 4121. Treasury, Postal Service, General Government Appropriations, Fiscal 1982. Miller, R-Ohio, amendment to restore $13.6 million to the Treasury Department for the promotion of U.S. Treasury bonds *(see votes 161, p. 58-H and 173, below)*. Rejected 203-210: R 159-25; D 44-185 (ND 30-124; SD 14-61), July 30, 1981.

170. HR 4121. Treasury, Postal Service, General Government Appropriations, Fiscal 1982. Ottinger, D-N.Y., amendment to reduce funding for the Executive Office of the President to the fiscal year 1981 level. Rejected 164-253: R 40-146; D 124-107 (ND 103-55, SD 21-52), July 30, 1981.

171. HR 4121. Treasury, Postal Service, General Government Appropriations, Fiscal 1982. Ashbrook, R-Ohio, amendment to prohibit the use of funds under the Federal Employees Health Benefit Program for abortions, except when the life of the mother is endangered. Adopted 253-167: R 148-40; D 105-127 (ND 58-98, SD 47-29), July 30, 1981.

172. HR 4121. Treasury, Postal Service, General Government Appropriations, Fiscal 1982. Ashbrook, R-Ohio, amendment to prohibit the Internal Revenue Service from implementing or the courts from enforcing IRS regulations to deny tax-exempt status to private schools that discriminate against racial minorities, unless the court order or regulation was in effect prior to Aug. 22, 1978. Adopted 337-83: R 181-5; D 156-78 (ND 83-73, SD 73-5), July 30, 1981.

173. HR 4121. Treasury, Postal Service, General Government Appropriations, Fiscal 1982. Schroeder, D-Colo., amendment to reduce by $13.6 million the appropriations for the Savings Bond Division of the Treasury Department. Rejected 182-233: R 17-170; D 165-63 (ND 110-42, SD 55-21), July 30, 1981. (The Schroeder amendment had been adopted previously *(see vote 161, p. 58-H)* when the House had been sitting as the Committee of the Whole.)

174. HR 4121. Treasury, Postal Service, General Government Appropriations, Fiscal 1982. Passage of the bill to appropriate $9,745,292,000 in fiscal 1982 for the Treasury Department, United States Postal Service, Executive Office of the President and 10 independent agencies. Passed 323-94: R 148-40; D 175-54 (ND 116-37, SD 59-17), July 30, 1981. The president had requested $9,864,638,000.

175. HR 4169. State, Justice, Commerce, Judiciary Appropriations, Fiscal 1982. Adoption of the rule (H Res 188) providing for House floor consideration of the bill to appropriate fiscal 1982 funds for the departments of State, Justice and Commerce, the federal judiciary, and related agencies. Adopted 262-133: R 66-112; D 196-21 (ND 134-8, SD 62-13), July 30, 1981.

KEY

Y	Voted for (yea).
#	Paired for.
+	Announced for.
N	Voted against (nay).
X	Paired against.
-	Announced against.
P	Voted "present".
C	Voted "present" to avoid possible conflict of interest.
?	Did not vote or otherwise make a position known.

	168	169	170	171	172	173	174	175
ALABAMA								
1 *Edwards*	Y	N	N	N	Y	Y	Y	Y
2 *Dickinson*	Y	Y	N	N	Y	N	Y	N
3 Nichols	Y	N	Y	Y	Y	Y	Y	Y
4 Bevill	Y	N	N	Y	Y	Y	Y	Y
5 Flippo	Y	N	N	Y	Y	Y	Y	Y
6 *Smith*	Y	N	N	Y	Y	Y	N	N
7 Shelby	Y	N	N	Y	Y	Y	Y	Y
ALASKA								
AL *Young*	?	Y	N	Y	Y	N	N	Y
ARIZONA								
1 *Rhodes*	Y	Y	N	Y	N	Y	N	Y
2 Udall	Y	N	Y	N	Y	Y	Y	Y
3 *Stump*	Y	N	N	Y	Y	N	Y	N
4 *Rudd*	Y	Y	N	Y	N	Y	N	Y
ARKANSAS								
1 Alexander	Y	N	N	N	Y	Y	Y	Y
2 *Bethune*	Y	Y	N	Y	N	Y	N	N
3 *Hammerschmidt*	Y	Y	N	Y	N	Y	N	N
4 Anthony	Y	N	N	N	Y	Y	Y	N
CALIFORNIA								
1 *Chappie*	Y	Y	N	Y	N	Y	N	Y
2 *Clausen*	Y	Y	N	Y	N	Y	N	?
3 Matsui	Y	N	N	N	N	Y	Y	Y
4 Fazio	Y	N	N	N	Y	Y	Y	Y
5 Burton, J.	?	?	N	N	N	N	N	Y
6 Burton, P.	Y	N	Y	N	N	Y	Y	Y
7 Miller	Y	N	Y	N	?	Y	N	Y
8 Dellums	Y	N	Y	N	N	Y	N	Y
9 Stark	Y	N	Y	N	N	Y	N	Y
10 Edwards	Y	N	Y	N	N	Y	N	Y
11 Lantos	Y	N	Y	N	N	Y	Y	Y
12 *McCloskey*	Y	N	N	N	N	Y	Y	N
13 Mineta	Y	N	Y	N	N	Y	Y	Y
14 *Shumway*	Y	Y	N	Y	N	Y	N	N
15 Coelho	Y	N	N	Y	Y	Y	Y	Y
16 Panetta	Y	N	Y	Y	Y	Y	Y	Y
17 *Pashayan*	Y	Y	N	Y	N	N	Y	?
18 *Thomas*	Y	Y	N	N	Y	Y	Y	N
19 *Lagomarsino*	Y	Y	N	Y	N	N	Y	N
20 *Goldwater*	?	Y	N	Y	N	N	Y	N
21 *Fiedler*	Y	Y	N	Y	N	N	Y	N
22 *Moorhead*	Y	Y	N	Y	N	Y	N	N
23 Beilenson	Y	N	N	N	Y	Y	Y	Y
24 Waxman	Y	N	Y	N	Y	Y	Y	?
25 Roybal	Y	N	N	N	Y	Y	Y	Y
26 *Rousselot*	Y	?	N	Y	N	P	N	N
27 *Dornan*	Y	Y	Y	Y	N	Y	N	N
28 Dixon	Y	N	Y	N	Y	Y	Y	Y
29 Hawkins	Y	N	N	N	Y	Y	Y	Y
30 Danielson	Y	N	N	N	Y	Y	Y	Y
31 Dymally	?	N	N	N	Y	Y	Y	Y
32 Anderson	Y	N	Y	N	Y	Y	Y	Y
33 *Grisham*	Y	Y	N	Y	N	Y	N	N
34 *Lungren*	Y	Y	N	Y	N	Y	N	N
35 *Dreier*	Y	Y	N	Y	N	Y	N	N
36 Brown	Y	N	N	N	Y	Y	Y	Y
37 *Lewis*	Y	Y	N	Y	N	N	Y	N
38 Patterson	Y	N	Y	N	N	Y	Y	Y
39 *Dannemeyer*	Y	Y	N	Y	N	Y	N	N
40 *Badham*	Y	Y	N	Y	N	Y	Y	N
41 *Lowery*	Y	Y	N	Y	N	Y	Y	N
42 *Hunter*	Y	Y	N	Y	N	Y	N	Y
43 *Burgener*	Y	Y	N	N	Y	N	Y	N
COLORADO								
1 Schroeder	Y	N	Y	N	N	Y	N	N
2 Wirth	Y	N	Y	N	N	Y	N	N
3 Kogovsek	Y	N	Y	N	N	Y	Y	Y
4 *Brown*	Y	N	Y	N	Y	Y	N	N

	168	169	170	171	172	173	174	175
5 *Kramer*	Y	N	Y	Y	Y	Y	N	N
CONNECTICUT								
1 Cotter	?	?	?	?	?	?	?	?
2 Gejdenson	Y	N	Y	N	N	Y	N	Y
3 *DeNardis*	Y	N	N	Y	N	Y	N	?
4 *McKinney*	Y	Y	N	N	N	Y	Y	?
5 Ratchford	Y	N	Y	N	N	Y	Y	Y
6 Moffett	Y	N	Y	?	N	Y	N	?
DELAWARE								
AL *Evans*	Y	Y	N	N	Y	N	Y	N
FLORIDA								
1 Hutto	Y	N	N	Y	Y	Y	Y	Y
2 Fuqua	Y	N	?	Y	Y	Y	Y	Y
3 Bennett	Y	N	Y	Y	Y	Y	Y	Y
4 Chappell	Y	N	N	Y	Y	Y	Y	Y
5 *McCollum*	Y	Y	Y	Y	Y	N	Y	N
6 *Young*	Y	N	Y	N	Y	N	Y	N
7 Gibbons	?	N	N	Y	Y	Y	Y	Y
8 Ireland	Y	N	N	Y	Y	Y	Y	Y
9 Nelson	Y	N	N	Y	Y	Y	Y	Y
10 *Bafalis*	Y	N	Y	N	Y	N	Y	Y
11 Mica	Y	N	N	N	Y	Y	Y	Y
12 *Shaw*	Y	N	Y	Y	Y	N	Y	N
13 Lehman	Y	N	Y	N	N	Y	Y	Y
14 Pepper	Y	N	N	Y	Y	Y	Y	Y
15 Fascell	?	?	?	?	?	?	?	?
GEORGIA								
1 Ginn	Y	Y	N	N	Y	Y	Y	Y
2 Hatcher	Y	N	N	N	Y	Y	Y	Y
3 Brinkley	Y	N	N	Y	Y	Y	Y	Y
4 Levitas	Y	N	N	N	Y	Y	N	N
5 Fowler	Y	N	N	Y	N	Y	Y	?
6 *Gingrich*	?	?	?	?	Y	Y	N	Y
7 McDonald	?	N	Y	Y	N	Y	N	Y
8 Evans	?	?	?	?	Y	N	Y	?
9 Jenkins	Y	N	N	Y	Y	Y	N	N
10 Barnard	Y	Y	N	N	Y	N	Y	N
HAWAII								
1 Heftel	?	Y	N	N	Y	N	Y	Y
2 Akaka	Y	N	N	N	Y	Y	Y	Y
IDAHO								
1 *Craig*	Y	Y	N	Y	N	Y	N	N
2 *Hansen*	Y	Y	N	Y	Y	N	N	N
ILLINOIS								
1 Washington	Y	N	Y	N	N	Y	N	Y
2 Savage	?	?	Y	?	?	?	?	?
3 Russo	Y	N	N	Y	Y	Y	Y	Y
4 *Derwinski*	Y	N	Y	N	Y	N	N	N
5 Fary	Y	N	Y	N	Y	Y	Y	Y
6 *Hyde*	Y	Y	N	Y	Y	Y	Y	N
7 Collins	Y	N	N	N	Y	Y	N	Y
8 Rostenkowski	Y	Y	N	Y	Y	Y	Y	?
9 Yates	Y	N	N	N	N	Y	Y	Y
10 *Porter*	Y	N	Y	N	N	Y	N	Y
11 Annunzio	Y	N	Y	N	Y	Y	Y	Y
12 *Crane, P.*	Y	N	Y	Y	Y	N	N	N
13 *McClory*	Y	Y	N	Y	Y	Y	Y	N
14 *Erlenborn*	Y	N	N	Y	N	Y	Y	Y
15 *Corcoran*	Y	Y	N	Y	N	Y	Y	N
16 *Martin*	Y	N	N	?	Y	Y	N	
17 *O'Brien*	Y	Y	N	Y	N	Y	Y	Y
18 *Michel*	Y	Y	N	Y	?	N	Y	N
19 *Railsback*	Y	Y	N	N	Y	Y	N	Y
20 *Findley*	Y	N	Y	N	Y	Y	Y	Y
21 *Madigan*	Y	Y	N	N	N	Y	Y	N
22 *Crane, D.*	Y	N	Y	Y	N	N	N	N
23 Price	Y	N	Y	N	Y	Y	Y	Y
24 Simon	Y	N	N	Y	N	?	?	?
INDIANA								
1 Benjamin	Y	N	Y	N	Y	N	Y	Y
2 Fithian	Y	N	Y	N	Y	N	Y	Y
3 *Hiler*	Y	Y	Y	N	Y	N	Y	N
4 *Coats*	Y	Y	Y	Y	N	Y	N	N
5 *Hillis*	Y	Y	N	N	N	Y	N	Y
6 Evans	Y	N	Y	N	Y	Y	Y	Y
7 *Myers*	Y	N	Y	N	Y	N	Y	Y
8 *Deckard*	Y	?	?	Y	Y	N	Y	N
9 Hamilton	Y	N	N	Y	Y	Y	Y	Y
10 Sharp	Y	N	N	Y	Y	Y	N	?
11 Jacobs	Y	N	N	Y	Y	N	N	N
IOWA								
1 *Leach*	Y	N	N	Y	Y	Y	Y	Y
2 *Tauke*	Y	N	N	Y	Y	Y	N	N
3 *Evans*	Y	N	Y	Y	Y	Y	N	N
4 Smith	Y	N	Y	N	Y	Y	Y	Y
5 Harkin	Y	N	Y	N	N	Y	?	?
6 Bedell	Y	N	Y	N	Y	N	Y	Y

Democrats   *Republicans*

	168	169	170	171	172	173	174	175
KANSAS								
1 ***Roberts***	Y	Y	Y	N	Y	N	Y	N
2 ***Jeffries***	Y	N	Y	Y	Y	Y	N	N
3 ***Winn***	Y	Y	N	N	Y	N	Y	N
4 Glickman	Y	N	Y	N	Y	Y	N	Y
5 ***Whittaker***	Y	Y	Y	N	Y	N	Y	N
KENTUCKY								
1 Hubbard	Y	N	N	Y	Y	Y	N	Y
2 Natcher	Y	N	N	Y	Y	Y	Y	Y
3 Mazzoli	Y	N	N	Y	Y	Y	Y	Y
4 ***Snyder***	Y	Y	Y	Y	Y	N	Y	N
5 ***Rogers***	Y	Y	N	Y	Y	N	Y	N
6 ***Hopkins***	Y	Y	Y	Y	Y	N	Y	N
7 Perkins	Y	N	N	Y	Y	Y	Y	Y
LOUISIANA								
1 ***Livingston***	Y	Y	?	Y	Y	N	Y	N
2 Boggs	Y	Y	N	Y	Y	N	Y	Y
3 Tauzin	Y	Y	N	Y	Y	N	Y	Y
4 Roemer	Y	N	Y	Y	Y	Y	N	N
5 Huckaby	Y	Y	?	N	Y	N	Y	Y
6 ***Moore***	Y	Y	N	Y	Y	N	Y	Y
7 Breaux	Y	Y	N	Y	Y	N	Y	Y
8 Long	Y	N	N	Y	Y	Y	Y	Y
MAINE								
1 ***Emery***	Y	Y	N	Y	Y	N	Y	Y
2 ***Snowe***	Y	N	N	N	Y	Y	Y	N
MARYLAND								
1 Dyson	Y	N	N	Y	Y	Y	Y	Y
2 Long	Y	N	Y	N	N	Y	Y	Y
3 Mikulski	Y	N	Y	N	N	N	Y	Y
4 ***Holt***	Y	Y	N	Y	Y	N	Y	N
5 Hoyer	Y	N	N	N	Y	Y	Y	Y
6 Byron	Y	Y	N	Y	Y	Y	Y	Y
7 Mitchell	Y	N	Y	N	?	?	?	?
8 Barnes	Y	Y	Y	N	N	N	Y	Y
MASSACHUSETTS								
1 ***Conte***	Y	Y	N	Y	Y	N	Y	Y
2 Boland	Y	Y	N	Y	Y	N	Y	Y
3 Early	Y	Y	Y	Y	Y	N	Y	Y
4 Frank	Y	N	N	N	N	Y	Y	Y
5 Shannon	Y	Y	Y	?	N	N	Y	Y
6 Mavroules	Y	N	Y	Y	Y	Y	Y	Y
7 Markey	Y	N	Y	Y	Y	Y	Y	Y
8 O'Neill								
9 Moakley	Y	N	Y	Y	Y	Y	Y	Y
10 ***Heckler***	Y	Y	Y	Y	Y	N	Y	Y
11 Donnelly	Y	N	Y	Y	Y	Y	Y	N
12 Studds	Y	N	Y	N	N	Y	N	Y
MICHIGAN								
1 Conyers	Y	N	Y	N	N	Y	Y	?
2 ***Pursell***	Y	Y	Y	N	Y	N	N	N
3 Wolpe	Y	N	N	N	N	Y	Y	Y
4 ***Siljander***	Y	N	N	Y	Y	N	Y	N
5 ***Sawyer***	Y	Y	N	Y	Y	N	Y	Y
6 ***Dunn***	Y	N	Y	N	Y	N	Y	Y
7 Kildee	Y	N	N	Y	Y	Y	Y	Y
8 Traxler	Y	N	Y	Y	Y	Y	N	Y
9 ***Vander Jagt***	Y	Y	N	Y	Y	N	Y	Y
10 Albosta	Y	Y	N	Y	Y	N	Y	Y
11 ***Davis***	Y	Y	N	Y	Y	N	Y	?
12 Bonior	Y	Y	Y	Y	?	N	Y	Y
13 Crockett	?	?	?	N	N	Y	N	?
14 Hertel	Y	N	N	Y	Y	Y	Y	Y
15 Ford	?	?	Y	N	Y	Y	Y	?
16 Dingell	Y	N	?	N	Y	Y	Y	Y
17 Brodhead	Y	Y	Y	N	N	N	N	Y
18 Blanchard	Y	?	Y	N	Y	N	N	Y
19 ***Broomfield***	Y	Y	N	Y	Y	N	N	?
MINNESOTA								
1 ***Erdahl***	Y	Y	N	Y	Y	N	Y	Y
2 ***Hagedorn***	Y	Y	N	Y	Y	N	Y	N
3 ***Frenzel***	Y	Y	N	N	Y	N	N	Y
4 Vento	Y	Y	Y	N	N	N	Y	Y
5 Sabo	Y	Y	N	N	N	N	Y	Y
6 ***Weber***	Y	Y	N	Y	Y	N	N	N
7 ***Stangeland***	Y	Y	N	Y	Y	N	Y	N
8 Oberstar	Y	N	Y	Y	N	Y	Y	Y
MISSISSIPPI								
1 Whitten	Y	Y	N	Y	Y	Y	Y	Y
2 Bowen	Y	N	Y	Y	Y	Y	Y	Y
3 Montgomery	Y	?	N	Y	Y	Y	Y	N
4 Dowdy	Y	Y	N	Y	Y	Y	Y	Y
5 ***Lott***	Y	Y	N	Y	Y	N	Y	N
MISSOURI								
1 Clay	?	N	Y	N	N	Y	N	?
2 Young	Y	Y	Y	Y	Y	N	Y	Y
3 Gephardt	Y	N	N	Y	Y	Y	Y	Y
4 Skelton	Y	N	N	Y	Y	Y	Y	Y
5 Bolling	Y	?	N	N	N	N	Y	?
6 ***Coleman***	Y	Y	N	Y	Y	N	Y	Y
7 ***Taylor***	Y	Y	N	Y	Y	N	Y	Y
8 ***Bailey***	Y	Y	N	N	Y	N	Y	N
9 Volkmer	Y	N	N	+	+	+	+	?
10 ***Emerson***	Y	Y	N	Y	Y	N	Y	N
MONTANA								
1 Williams	Y	N	Y	N	N	Y	Y	Y
2 ***Marlenee***	Y	Y	Y	N	Y	N	Y	Y
NEBRASKA								
1 ***Bereuter***	Y	Y	N	Y	Y	N	Y	N
2 ***Daub***	Y	Y	Y	Y	Y	N	Y	N
3 ***Smith***	Y	Y	N	Y	Y	N	Y	Y
NEVADA								
AL Santini	Y	N	?	Y	Y	Y	Y	Y
NEW HAMPSHIRE								
1 D'Amours	Y	N	Y	Y	Y	N	Y	Y
2 ***Gregg***	Y	Y	N	Y	Y	N	Y	N
NEW JERSEY								
1 Florio	Y	Y	Y	Y	Y	N	?	?
2 Hughes	Y	N	N	N	N	Y	N	N
3 Howard	Y	N	Y	N	Y	Y	Y	Y
4 ***Smith***	Y	Y	Y	Y	Y	N	Y	Y
5 ***Fenwick***	Y	Y	Y	N	N	N	N	Y
6 ***Forsythe***	Y	Y	N	N	Y	N	Y	Y
7 ***Roukema***	Y	Y	Y	N	Y	N	Y	N
8 Roe	Y	Y	N	Y	Y	N	Y	Y
9 ***Hollenbeck***	Y	Y	N	N	Y	N	Y	Y
10 Rodino	Y	N	Y	N	N	?	Y	Y
11 Minish	?	?	?	?	?	?	?	?
12 ***Rinaldo***	Y	Y	Y	Y	Y	N	Y	Y
13 ***Courter***	Y	Y	N	Y	Y	N	Y	N
14 Guarini	Y	N	Y	N	Y	Y	Y	Y
15 Dwyer	Y	N	Y	Y	Y	Y	Y	Y
NEW MEXICO								
1 ***Lujan***	Y	Y	Y	Y	Y	N	N	Y
2 ***Skeen***	Y	Y	N	Y	Y	N	Y	Y
NEW YORK								
1 ***Carney***	Y	Y	Y	Y	Y	N	Y	N
2 Downey	Y	N	Y	N	N	Y	Y	Y
3 ***Carman***	Y	Y	N	Y	Y	N	Y	Y
4 ***Lent***	Y	Y	N	Y	Y	N	Y	N
5 ***McGrath***	Y	Y	N	Y	Y	N	Y	N
6 ***LeBoutillier***	Y	Y	Y	Y	Y	N	N	N
7 Addabbo	Y	Y	N	N	Y	N	Y	Y
8 Rosenthal	Y	N	N	N	N	Y	Y	Y
9 Ferraro	Y	N	Y	N	Y	Y	Y	Y
10 Biaggi	Y	Y	Y	Y	N	?	?	Y
11 Scheuer	Y	N	Y	N	N	Y	Y	Y
12 Chisholm	?	N	Y	?	N	?	N	?
13 Solarz	Y	N	Y	N	N	Y	Y	Y
14 Richmond	Y	N	Y	N	?	?	X	?
15 Zeferetti	Y	Y	N	Y	Y	N	Y	Y
16 Schumer	?	Y	Y	N	N	N	Y	Y
17 ***Molinari***	Y	Y	N	Y	Y	N	Y	N
18 ***Green***	Y	Y	N	N	N	N	Y	Y
19 Rangel	Y	N	Y	N	N	Y	?	?
20 Weiss	Y	N	Y	N	N	Y	N	Y
21 Garcia	Y	N	Y	N	N	N	Y	Y
22 Bingham	Y	N	N	N	N	Y	Y	Y
23 Peyser	Y	Y	Y	N	Y	N	Y	Y
24 Ottinger	Y	N	Y	N	N	Y	N	Y
25 ***Fish***	Y	Y	N	Y	Y	N	Y	Y
26 ***Gilman***	Y	Y	N	N	Y	N	Y	Y
27 McHugh	Y	N	N	Y	N	Y	Y	Y
28 Stratton	Y	Y	N	Y	Y	N	Y	Y
29 ***Solomon***	Y	Y	N	Y	Y	N	N	N
30 ***Martin***	Y	Y	N	Y	Y	N	Y	N
31 ***Mitchell***	Y	Y	N	Y	Y	N	Y	Y
32 ***Wortley***	Y	Y	N	Y	Y	N	Y	N
33 ***Lee***	Y	Y	N	Y	Y	N	N	N
34 ***Horton***	Y	?	?	?	?	?	?	?
35 ***Conable***	Y	Y	N	N	Y	N	N	Y
36 LaFalce	Y	N	Y	N	N	Y	N	Y
37 Nowak	Y	N	Y	Y	Y	Y	Y	Y
38 ***Kemp***	Y	Y	N	Y	?	?	?	?
39 Lundine	Y	N	Y	N	N	Y	Y	Y
NORTH CAROLINA								
1 Jones	Y	N	Y	N	Y	Y	Y	?
2 Fountain	Y	N	N	?	Y	Y	N	N
3 Whitley	Y	N	N	N	Y	Y	Y	Y
4 Andrews	?	N	N	Y	Y	Y	?	Y
5 Neal	Y	N	Y	N	Y	Y	N	Y
6 ***Johnston***	Y	Y	N	Y	Y	N	N	N
7 Rose	Y	N	N	N	Y	Y	Y	Y
8 Hefner	Y	N	N	N	Y	Y	#	Y
9 ***Martin***	Y	Y	N	N	Y	N	Y	N
10 ***Broyhill***	Y	Y	N	N	Y	N	Y	Y
11 ***Hendon***	Y	Y	Y	Y	Y	N	N	N
NORTH DAKOTA								
AL Dorgan	Y	N	Y	Y	Y	Y	Y	Y
OHIO								
1 ***Gradison***	Y	Y	N	Y	Y	N	N	N
2 Luken	Y	N	Y	Y	Y	N	N	Y
3 Hall	Y	N	Y	N	Y	Y	Y	Y
4 ***Oxley***	Y	Y	Y	Y	Y	N	Y	N
5 ***Latta***	Y	Y	N	Y	Y	N	Y	Y
6 ***McEwen***	Y	Y	Y	Y	Y	N	Y	N
7 ***Brown***	Y	Y	N	Y	Y	N	Y	Y
8 ***Kindness***	Y	N	N	Y	Y	Y	Y	Y
9 ***Weber***	Y	Y	N	Y	Y	N	Y	Y
10 ***Miller***	Y	Y	N	Y	Y	N	Y	Y
11 ***Stanton***	Y	Y	N	Y	Y	N	Y	?
12 Shamansky	Y	N	Y	N	N	Y	Y	Y
13 Pease	Y	N	N	N	Y	Y	Y	Y
14 Seiberling	Y	N	Y	N	N	Y	Y	Y
15 ***Wylie***	Y	Y	N	Y	Y	N	Y	N
16 ***Regula***	Y	Y	N	Y	Y	N	Y	Y
17 ***Ashbrook***	Y	Y	N	Y	Y	N	Y	N
18 Applegate	Y	Y	N	Y	Y	N	N	Y
19 ***Williams***	Y	Y	N	Y	Y	N	Y	Y
20 Oakar	Y	N	Y	Y	Y	?	Y	Y
21 Stokes	Y	?	Y	N	N	Y	N	Y
22 Eckart	Y	N	N	N	Y	N	Y	Y
23 Mottl	Y	N	Y	Y	Y	Y	N	N
OKLAHOMA								
1 Jones	Y	N	Y	Y	Y	Y	N	N
2 Synar	Y	N	Y	N	N	Y	N	Y
3 Watkins	Y	N	N	Y	Y	N	Y	Y
4 McCurdy	Y	N	N	N	Y	Y	Y	?
5 ***Edwards***	Y	N	N	Y	Y	N	Y	N
6 English	Y	N	Y	Y	Y	Y	Y	Y
OREGON								
1 AuCoin	Y	N	Y	N	N	Y	N	Y
2 ***Smith***	Y	Y	N	Y	Y	N	Y	N
3 Wyden	Y	N	Y	N	Y	Y	N	Y
4 Weaver	Y	N	Y	N	Y	Y	N	N
PENNSYLVANIA								
1 Foglietta	Y	N	?	N	Y	Y	Y	Y
2 Gray	?	N	Y	N	N	Y	N	?
3 Smith	Y	N	N	Y	Y	N	Y	Y
4 ***Dougherty***	Y	?	N	Y	Y	N	Y	Y
5 ***Schulze***	Y	Y	N	Y	Y	N	Y	N
6 Yatron	Y	N	Y	Y	Y	Y	Y	Y
7 Edgar	Y	N	Y	N	N	Y	N	N
8 ***Coyne, J.***	Y	Y	Y	N	Y	N	N	Y
9 ***Shuster***	Y	Y	N	Y	Y	N	Y	N
10 ***McDade***	Y	Y	N	Y	Y	N	Y	?
11 ***Nelligan***	Y	N	N	Y	Y	N	Y	N
12 Murtha	Y	Y	N	Y	Y	N	Y	?
13 ***Coughlin***	Y	?	N	N	Y	N	Y	Y
14 Coyne, W.	Y	Y	Y	N	N	N	Y	Y
15 ***Ritter***	Y	Y	Y	Y	Y	N	N	N
16 ***Walker***	Y	Y	N	Y	Y	N	N	N
17 Ertel	Y	N	N	Y	Y	Y	Y	Y
18 Walgren	Y	N	Y	N	Y	Y	Y	Y
19 ***Goodling***	Y	Y	N	Y	Y	N	Y	N
20 Gaydos	Y	N	N	Y	Y	Y	Y	Y
21 Bailey	Y	N	N	Y	Y	Y	Y	Y
22 Murphy	Y	N	Y	Y	Y	Y	Y	Y
23 ***Clinger***	Y	Y	N	Y	Y	N	Y	N
24 ***Marks***	Y	Y	N	N	Y	N	Y	?
25 Atkinson	Y	N	Y	Y	Y	Y	Y	Y
RHODE ISLAND								
1 St Germain	Y	N	N	Y	Y	Y	Y	Y
2 ***Schneider***	?	Y	Y	N	N	N	Y	?
SOUTH CAROLINA								
1 ***Hartnett***	Y	Y	N	Y	Y	N	N	N
2 ***Spence***	Y	Y	N	Y	Y	N	Y	N
3 Derrick	Y	Y	N	N	Y	N	Y	Y
4 ***Campbell***	Y	Y	N	Y	Y	N	Y	Y
5 Holland	Y	N	N	N	Y	N	Y	Y
6 ***Napier***	Y	Y	N	Y	Y	N	Y	N
SOUTH DAKOTA								
1 Daschle	Y	N	Y	N	Y	Y	Y	Y
2 ***Roberts***	Y	Y	Y	Y	Y	N	Y	N
TENNESSEE								
1 ***Quillen***	Y	Y	N	Y	Y	N	Y	?
2 ***Duncan***	Y	Y	N	Y	Y	N	Y	Y
3 Bouquard	Y	N	N	Y	Y	N	Y	Y
4 Gore	Y	Y	N	Y	Y	N	Y	Y
5 Boner	Y	N	Y	Y	Y	N	Y	Y
6 ***Beard***	Y	Y	N	Y	Y	N	Y	N
7 Jones	Y	N	?	Y	Y	N	Y	Y
8 Ford	Y	N	Y	N	N	Y	N	Y
TEXAS								
1 Hall, S.	Y	N	Y	Y	Y	Y	Y	N
2 Wilson	Y	N	N	N	Y	Y	Y	Y
3 ***Collins***	Y	Y	Y	Y	Y	N	N	N
4 Hall, R.	Y	N	Y	Y	Y	Y	Y	Y
5 Mattox	Y	N	Y	N	Y	Y	N	Y
6 Gramm	Y	N	N	Y	Y	Y	N	N
7 ***Archer***	Y	Y	N	Y	Y	N	N	N
8 ***Fields***	Y	Y	N	Y	Y	N	N	N
9 Brooks	Y	N	N	N	Y	Y	Y	Y
10 Pickle	Y	Y	N	N	Y	N	Y	Y
11 Leath	Y	N	N	Y	Y	Y	N	N
12 Wright	Y	N	N	Y	Y	?	Y	Y
13 Hightower	Y	N	Y	Y	Y	Y	Y	Y
14 Patman	Y	N	Y	Y	Y	Y	Y	Y
15 de la Garza	Y	?	N	Y	Y	Y	Y	Y
16 White	Y	N	N	Y	Y	Y	Y	Y
17 Stenholm	Y	N	Y	Y	Y	Y	N	N
18 Leland	Y	N	Y	N	N	Y	Y	Y
19 Hance	Y	N	Y	N	Y	Y	N	Y
20 Gonzalez	Y	N	P	N	N	N	Y	Y
21 ***Loeffler***	Y	Y	N	Y	Y	N	Y	N
22 ***Paul***	N	N	Y	Y	Y	Y	N	N
23 Kazen	Y	N	N	Y	Y	N	Y	Y
24 Frost	Y	N	N	N	Y	N	Y	Y
UTAH								
1 ***Hansen***	Y	Y	Y	Y	Y	N	Y	N
2 ***Marriott***	Y	Y	N	Y	Y	N	Y	N
VERMONT								
AL ***Jeffords***	?	?	?	?	?	?	?	?
VIRGINIA								
1 ***Trible***	?	Y	N	Y	Y	N	Y	N
2 ***Whitehurst***	Y	Y	N	Y	Y	N	Y	Y
3 ***Bliley***	Y	Y	N	Y	Y	N	Y	N
4 ***Daniel, R.***	?	Y	N	Y	Y	N	Y	N
5 Daniel, D.	Y	Y	N	Y	Y	N	Y	Y
6 ***Butler***	Y	Y	N	N	Y	N	Y	Y
7 ***Robinson***	Y	Y	N	Y	Y	N	Y	Y
8 ***Parris***	Y	Y	N	N	Y	N	Y	N
9 ***Wampler***	Y	Y	N	Y	Y	N	Y	Y
10 ***Wolf***	Y	Y	N	Y	Y	N	Y	N
WASHINGTON								
1 ***Pritchard***	Y	N	N	N	Y	N	Y	Y
2 Swift	Y	N	Y	N	N	Y	Y	Y
3 Bonker	Y	N	N	N	Y	N	Y	Y
4 ***Morrison***	Y	Y	N	N	Y	N	Y	Y
5 Foley	Y	N	N	N	Y	Y	Y	Y
6 Dicks	Y	N	N	N	Y	N	Y	Y
7 Lowry	Y	N	Y	N	N	Y	N	Y
WEST VIRGINIA								
1 Mollohan	Y	N	N	N	Y	N	Y	Y
2 ***Benedict***	Y	Y	N	Y	Y	N	Y	Y
3 ***Staton***	Y	Y	N	Y	Y	N	Y	N
4 Rahall	Y	Y	Y	N	Y	N	Y	Y
WISCONSIN								
1 Aspin	Y	N	Y	Y	Y	Y	Y	Y
2 Kastenmeier	Y	Y	Y	N	N	N	Y	Y
3 ***Gunderson***	Y	Y	N	Y	Y	N	Y	N
4 Zablocki	Y	Y	N	Y	Y	N	Y	Y
5 Reuss	Y	N	Y	N	N	Y	N	Y
6 ***Petri***	Y	N	Y	Y	Y	Y	N	Y
7 Obey	Y	N	Y	?	N	Y	Y	Y
8 ***Roth***	Y	Y	Y	Y	Y	N	Y	N
9 ***Sensenbrenner***	Y	N	Y	Y	Y	Y	N	N
WYOMING								
AL ***Cheney***	Y	Y	N	Y	Y	N	Y	N

Democrats ***Republicans***

176. HR 4331/HR 3982. Minimum Social Security Benefits/Budget Reconciliation. Bolling, D-Mo., motion to order the previous question (thus ending debate and the possibility of amendment) on the rule (H Res 203) providing for consideration of 1) the bill (HR 4331) to amend the Omnibus Budget Reconciliation Act of 1981 (HR 3982) to restore minimum Social Security benefits and 2) the reconciliation act conference report. Motion agreed to 271-151: R 166-21; D 105-130 (ND 56-101, SD 49-29), July 31, 1981.

177. HR 4331/HR 3982. Minimum Social Security Benefits/Budget Reconciliation. Adoption of the rule (H Res 203) providing for consideration of 1) the bill (HR 4331) to amend the Omnibus Budget Reconciliation Act of 1981 (HR 3982) to restore minimum Social Security benefits and 2) the reconciliation act conference report. Adopted 370-52: R 180-7; D 190-45 (ND 119-38, SD 71-7), July 31, 1981.

178. HR 4331/HR 3982. Minimum Social Security Benefits/Budget Reconciliation. Passage of the bill (HR 4331) to amend the Omnibus Budget Reconciliation Act of 1981 (HR 3982) to restore minimum Social Security benefits. Passed 404-20: R 172-17; D 232-3 (ND 157-1, SD 75-2), July 31, 1981. (The reconciliation act conference report subsequently was adopted by voice vote.)

179. HR 4242. Tax Cuts. Rostenkowski, D-Ill., motion to suspend the rules and adopt the conference report on the bill to cut individual income tax rates by 25 percent across-the-board over 33 months; require that individual income taxes be adjusted, or indexed, annually to offset the effects of inflation, starting in 1985; allow accelerated depreciation for business investment in new assets; and provide special savings and investment incentives. Motion agreed to (thus clearing the measure for the president) 282-95: R 169-1; D 113-94 (ND 49-91, SD 64-3), Aug. 4, 1981. A two-thirds vote (252 in this case) is required for passage under suspension of the rules. A "yea" was a vote supporting the president's position.

KEY

- Y Voted for (yea).
- \# Paired for.
- \+ Announced for.
- N Voted against (nay).
- X Paired against.
- \- Announced against.
- P Voted "present".
- C Voted "present" to avoid possible conflict of interest.
- ? Did not vote or otherwise make a position known.

	176	177	178	179
ALABAMA				
1 Edwards	Y	Y	Y	Y
2 Dickinson	Y	Y	Y	Y
3 Nichols	N	Y	Y	Y
4 Bevill	Y	Y	Y	Y
5 Flippo	N	Y	Y	Y
6 Smith	Y	Y	Y	Y
7 Shelby	Y	Y	Y	Y
ALASKA				
AL Young	Y	Y	Y	Y
ARIZONA				
1 Rhodes	Y	Y	Y	#
2 Udall	Y	Y	Y	N
3 Stump	Y	Y	N	Y
4 Rudd	Y	Y	Y	Y
ARKANSAS				
1 Alexander	N	Y	Y	Y
2 Bethune	?	?	?	Y
3 Hammerschmidt	Y	Y	Y	Y
4 Anthony	Y	Y	Y	Y
CALIFORNIA				
1 Chappie	Y	Y	Y	Y
2 Clausen	Y	Y	Y	Y
3 Matsui	Y	Y	Y	Y
4 Fazio	Y	Y	Y	Y
5 Burton, J.	N	N	Y	N
6 Burton, P.	N	N	Y	?
7 Miller	N	N	Y	?
8 Dellums	N	N	Y	N
9 Stark	N	Y	Y	N
10 Edwards	N	Y	Y	?
11 Lantos	N	Y	Y	Y
12 McCloskey	Y	Y	N	?
13 Mineta	Y	Y	Y	N
14 Shumway	Y	Y	Y	Y
15 Coelho	Y	Y	?	Y
16 Panetta	Y	Y	Y	Y
17 Pashayan	Y	Y	Y	Y
18 Thomas	Y	Y	Y	Y
19 Lagomarsino	Y	Y	Y	Y
20 Goldwater	?	?	Y	Y
21 Fiedler	Y	Y	Y	Y
22 Moorhead	Y	Y	Y	Y
23 Beilenson	Y	Y	Y	Y
24 Waxman	N	Y	Y	X
25 Roybal	N	N	Y	N
26 Rousselot	Y	Y	N	#
27 Dornan	?	?	?	#
28 Dixon	N	Y	Y	N
29 Hawkins	N	Y	Y	N
30 Danielson	Y	Y	Y	Y
31 Dymally	N	Y	Y	N
32 Anderson	N	Y	Y	?
33 Grisham	Y	Y	Y	Y
34 Lungren	Y	Y	Y	#
35 Dreier	Y	Y	Y	Y
36 Brown	N	Y	Y	N
37 Lewis	Y	Y	Y	Y
38 Patterson	Y	Y	Y	Y
39 Dannemeyer	Y	Y	N	#
40 Badham	Y	Y	N	Y
41 Lowery	Y	Y	Y	Y
42 Hunter	Y	Y	Y	Y
43 Burgener	Y	Y	Y	Y
COLORADO				
1 Schroeder	N	Y	Y	N
2 Wirth	Y	Y	Y	Y
3 Kogovsek	N	Y	Y	N
4 Brown	Y	Y	Y	Y

	176	177	178	179
5 Kramer	Y	Y	Y	Y
CONNECTICUT				
1 Cotter	?	?	?	?
2 Gejdenson	Y	N	Y	N
3 DeNardis	N	N	Y	Y
4 McKinney	Y	Y	Y	Y
5 Ratchford	N	N	Y	N
6 Moffett	N	N	?	X
DELAWARE				
AL Evans	Y	Y	Y	Y
FLORIDA				
1 Hutto	Y	Y	Y	Y
2 Fuqua	Y	Y	Y	Y
3 Bennett	N	Y	Y	N
4 Chappell	Y	Y	Y	Y
5 McCollum	Y	Y	Y	Y
6 Young	Y	Y	Y	Y
7 Gibbons	Y	Y	Y	Y
8 Ireland	Y	Y	Y	Y
9 Nelson	N	Y	Y	Y
10 Bafalis	Y	Y	Y	Y
11 Mica	N	Y	Y	Y
12 Shaw	Y	Y	Y	Y
13 Lehman	N	Y	Y	Y
14 Pepper	Y	Y	Y	Y
15 Fascell	?	?	?	?
GEORGIA				
1 Ginn	Y	Y	Y	Y
2 Hatcher	Y	Y	Y	Y
3 Brinkley	Y	Y	Y	Y
4 Levitas	N	N	Y	Y
5 Fowler	Y	Y	Y	?
6 Gingrich	?	Y	Y	Y
7 McDonald	Y	Y	N	Y
8 Evans	Y	Y	Y	Y
9 Jenkins	Y	Y	Y	?
10 Barnard	Y	Y	Y	Y
HAWAII				
1 Heftel	?	?	Y	Y
2 Akaka	Y	Y	Y	Y
IDAHO				
1 Craig	Y	Y	Y	Y
2 Hansen	Y	Y	N	Y
ILLINOIS				
1 Washington	N	N	Y	N
2 Savage	?	?	Y	N
3 Russo	Y	Y	Y	Y
4 Derwinski	Y	Y	Y	?
5 Fary	Y	Y	Y	Y
6 Hyde	Y	Y	Y	Y
7 Collins	N	N	Y	N
8 Rostenkowski	?	?	Y	Y
9 Yates	N	N	Y	N
10 Porter	Y	Y	Y	Y
11 Annunzio	Y	Y	Y	Y
12 Crane, P.	Y	Y	N	?
13 McClory	Y	Y	Y	Y
14 Erlenborn	Y	Y	N	Y
15 Corcoran	Y	Y	Y	Y
16 Martin	Y	Y	Y	Y
17 O'Brien	Y	Y	Y	Y
18 Michel	Y	Y	N	Y
19 Railsback	Y	?	Y	Y
20 Findley	Y	Y	Y	Y
21 Madigan	Y	Y	Y	Y
22 Crane, D.	Y	Y	N	Y
23 Price	Y	Y	Y	Y
24 Simon	?	?	?	?
INDIANA				
1 Benjamin	Y	Y	Y	Y
2 Fithian	Y	Y	Y	?
3 Hiler	Y	Y	Y	Y
4 Coats	Y	Y	Y	Y
5 Hillis	Y	Y	Y	Y
6 Evans	N	Y	Y	N
7 Myers	N	Y	Y	Y
8 Deckard	Y	Y	Y	Y
9 Hamilton	Y	Y	Y	?
10 Sharp	N	Y	Y	Y
11 Jacobs	N	Y	Y	N
IOWA				
1 Leach	N	Y	Y	Y
2 Tauke	Y	Y	Y	Y
3 Evans	Y	Y	Y	Y
4 Smith	N	Y	Y	Y
5 Harkin	Y	Y	Y	N
6 Bedell	Y	Y	Y	N

Democrats *Republicans*

KANSAS

	176	177	178	179
1 Roberts	Y	Y	Y	Y
2 Jeffries	Y	Y	N	Y
3 Winn	Y	Y	Y	Y
4 Glickman	N	Y	Y	Y
5 Whittaker	Y	Y	Y	Y

KENTUCKY

	176	177	178	179
1 Hubbard	Y	Y	Y	Y
2 Natcher	N	Y	Y	Y
3 Mazzoli	Y	Y	Y	Y
4 Snyder	N	Y	Y	Y
5 Rogers	N	Y	Y	Y
6 Hopkins	N	N	Y	Y
7 Perkins	N	Y	Y	Y

LOUISIANA

	176	177	178	179
1 Livingston	Y	Y	Y	Y
2 Boggs	Y	Y	Y	Y
3 Tauzin	Y	Y	Y	Y
4 Roemer	Y	Y	Y	Y
5 Huckaby	Y	Y	Y	#
6 Moore	Y	Y	Y	Y
7 Breaux	Y	Y	Y	Y
8 Long	Y	Y	Y	Y

MAINE

	176	177	178	179
1 Emery	Y	Y	Y	Y
2 Snowe	Y	Y	Y	Y

MARYLAND

	176	177	178	179
1 Dyson	N	Y	Y	Y
2 Long	N	Y	Y	Y
3 Mikulski	N	N	Y	N
4 Holt	Y	Y	Y	Y
5 Hoyer	Y	Y	Y	Y
6 Byron	Y	Y	Y	Y
7 Mitchell	N	N	Y	N
8 Barnes	N	Y	Y	N

MASSACHUSETTS

	176	177	178	179
1 Conte	Y	Y	Y	Y
2 Boland	Y	Y	Y	N
3 Early	N	N	Y	N
4 Frank	Y	Y	Y	N
5 Shannon	Y	Y	Y	N
6 Mavroules	Y	Y	Y	N
7 Markey	Y	Y	Y	N
8 O'Neill				
9 Moakley	Y	Y	Y	N
10 Heckler	N	N	Y	Y
11 Donnelly	Y	Y	Y	N
12 Studds	N	N	Y	N

MICHIGAN

	176	177	178	179
1 Conyers	N	N	Y	N
2 Pursell	Y	Y	Y	Y
3 Wolpe	N	Y	Y	N
4 Siljander	Y	Y	Y	Y
5 Sawyer	Y	Y	Y	Y
6 Dunn	Y	Y	Y	Y
7 Kildee	N	Y	Y	N
8 Traxler	N	Y	Y	N
9 Vander Jagt	Y	Y	Y	?
10 Albosta	N	Y	Y	Y
11 Davis	N	Y	Y	Y
12 Bonior	N	Y	Y	N
13 Crockett	N	N	Y	N
14 Hertel	N	Y	Y	N
15 Ford	N	Y	Y	X
16 Dingell	Y	Y	Y	Y
17 Brodhead	Y	Y	Y	N
18 Blanchard	N	Y	Y	Y
19 Broomfield	Y	Y	Y	Y

MINNESOTA

	176	177	178	179
1 Erdahl	Y	Y	Y	Y
2 Hagedorn	Y	Y	Y	Y
3 Frenzel	Y	Y	N	Y
4 Vento	N	N	Y	X
5 Sabo	Y	Y	Y	N
6 Weber	Y	Y	Y	Y
7 Stangeland	Y	Y	Y	Y
8 Oberstar	N	Y	Y	N

MISSISSIPPI

	176	177	178	179
1 Whitten	N	Y	Y	Y
2 Bowen	N	Y	Y	Y
3 Montgomery	Y	Y	Y	Y
4 Dowdy	N	Y	Y	Y
5 Lott	Y	Y	Y	Y

MISSOURI

	176	177	178	179
1 Clay	N	N	Y	N
2 Young	?	?	?	#
3 Gephardt	Y	Y	Y	#
4 Skelton	Y	Y	Y	Y
5 Bolling	Y	Y	Y	?
6 Coleman	Y	Y	Y	Y
7 Taylor	Y	Y	Y	#
8 Bailey	Y	Y	Y	Y
9 Volkmer	N	Y	Y	Y
10 Emerson	Y	Y	Y	Y

MONTANA

	176	177	178	179
1 Williams	N	N	Y	N
2 Marlenee	Y	Y	Y	Y

NEBRASKA

	176	177	178	179
1 Bereuter	Y	Y	Y	#
2 Daub	Y	Y	Y	Y
3 Smith	Y	Y	Y	Y

NEVADA

	176	177	178	179
AL Santini	Y	Y	Y	#

NEW HAMPSHIRE

	176	177	178	179
1 D'Amours	N	Y	Y	N
2 Gregg	Y	Y	Y	#

NEW JERSEY

	176	177	178	179
1 Florio	N	Y	Y	N
2 Hughes	N	Y	Y	N
3 Howard	N	Y	Y	N
4 Smith	N	Y	Y	Y
5 Fenwick	Y	Y	Y	Y
6 Forsythe	Y	Y	Y	Y
7 Roukema	Y	Y	Y	Y
8 Roe	N	Y	Y	Y
9 Hollenbeck	N	N	Y	Y
10 Rodino	N	Y	Y	N
11 Minish	N	Y	Y	N
12 Rinaldo	N	Y	Y	Y
13 Courter	Y	Y	Y	Y
14 Guarini	N	Y	Y	N
15 Dwyer	N	N	Y	N

NEW MEXICO

	176	177	178	179
1 Lujan	Y	Y	Y	Y
2 Skeen	Y	Y	Y	Y

NEW YORK

	176	177	178	179
1 Carney	Y	Y	Y	Y
2 Downey	N	N	Y	N
3 Carman	N	Y	Y	Y
4 Lent	N	Y	Y	Y
5 McGrath	N	Y	Y	Y
6 LeBoutillier	Y	Y	Y	Y
7 Addabbo	Y	Y	Y	N
8 Rosenthal	N	Y	Y	N
9 Ferraro	N	Y	Y	N
10 Biaggi	N	Y	Y	#
11 Scheuer	N	Y	Y	N
12 Chisholm	Y	Y	Y	N
13 Solarz	N	N	Y	N
14 Richmond	?	?	?	X
15 Zeferetti	Y	Y	Y	N
16 Schumer	N	N	Y	N
17 Molinari	Y	Y	Y	Y
18 Green	Y	Y	Y	?
19 Rangel	N	N	Y	N
20 Weiss	N	N	Y	N
21 Garcia	N	N	Y	X
22 Bingham	N	N	Y	N
23 Peyser	N	Y	Y	N
24 Ottinger	N	N	Y	N
25 Fish	N	Y	Y	Y
26 Gilman	N	N	Y	#
27 McHugh	Y	Y	Y	N
28 Stratton	N	Y	Y	Y
29 Solomon	Y	Y	Y	#
30 Martin	Y	Y	Y	Y
31 Mitchell	Y	Y	Y	?
32 Wortley	Y	Y	Y	Y
33 Lee	Y	Y	Y	Y
34 Horton	Y	Y	Y	#
35 Conable	Y	Y	N	Y
36 LaFalce	Y	N	Y	N
37 Nowak	N	Y	Y	N
38 Kemp	Y	Y	Y	Y
39 Lundine	N	Y	Y	?

NORTH CAROLINA

	176	177	178	179
1 Jones	Y	Y	Y	?
2 Fountain	Y	Y	Y	Y
3 Whitley	Y	Y	Y	Y
4 Andrews	Y	Y	Y	Y
5 Neal	N	Y	Y	Y
6 Johnston	Y	Y	Y	Y
7 Rose	Y	Y	Y	Y
8 Hefner	Y	Y	Y	Y
9 Martin	N	Y	Y	Y
10 Broyhill	Y	Y	Y	Y
11 Hendon	Y	Y	Y	Y

NORTH DAKOTA

	176	177	178	179
AL Dorgan	Y	Y	Y	Y

OHIO

	176	177	178	179
1 Gradison	Y	Y	Y	Y
2 Luken	N	Y	Y	Y
3 Hall	Y	Y	Y	Y
4 Oxley	Y	Y	Y	Y
5 Latta	Y	Y	Y	Y
6 McEwen	Y	Y	Y	Y
7 Brown	Y	Y	Y	Y
8 Kindness	Y	Y	Y	Y
9 Weber	Y	Y	Y	Y
10 Miller	Y	Y	Y	Y
11 Stanton	Y	Y	Y	Y
12 Shamansky	N	Y	Y	Y
13 Pease	N	N	Y	?
14 Seiberling	N	Y	Y	N
15 Wylie	Y	Y	Y	Y
16 Regula	Y	Y	Y	Y
17 Ashbrook	Y	N	Y	Y
18 Applegate	N	Y	Y	Y
19 Williams	Y	Y	Y	Y
20 Oakar	N	Y	Y	N
21 Stokes	N	N	Y	N
22 Eckart	N	N	Y	N
23 Mottl	N	N	Y	N

OKLAHOMA

	176	177	178	179
1 Jones	Y	Y	Y	Y
2 Synar	N	N	Y	?
3 Watkins	Y	Y	Y	Y
4 McCurdy	Y	Y	Y	Y
5 Edwards	Y	Y	Y	Y
6 English	Y	Y	Y	Y

OREGON

	176	177	178	179
1 AuCoin	N	Y	Y	Y
2 Smith	Y	Y	N	Y
3 Wyden	N	Y	Y	N
4 Weaver	N	Y	Y	?

PENNSYLVANIA

	176	177	178	179
1 Foglietta	N	N	Y	N
2 Gray	N	N	Y	N
3 Smith	Y	Y	Y	N
4 Dougherty	Y	Y	Y	?
5 Schulze	Y	Y	Y	Y
6 Yatron	N	Y	Y	N
7 Edgar	N	Y	Y	N
8 Coyne, J.	Y	Y	Y	Y
9 Shuster	Y	Y	Y	Y
10 McDade	Y	Y	Y	Y
11 Nelligan	Y	Y	Y	Y
12 Murtha	Y	Y	Y	Y
13 Coughlin	Y	Y	Y	Y
14 Coyne, W.	N	N	Y	N
15 Ritter	Y	Y	Y	Y
16 Walker	Y	Y	Y	Y
17 Ertel	N	Y	Y	N
18 Walgren	N	Y	Y	N
19 Goodling	Y	Y	Y	Y
20 Gaydos	Y	Y	Y	Y
21 Bailey	Y	Y	Y	Y
22 Murphy	N	Y	Y	Y
23 Clinger	Y	Y	Y	Y
24 Marks	Y	Y	Y	Y
25 Atkinson	N	Y	Y	?

RHODE ISLAND

	176	177	178	179
1 St Germain	N	Y	Y	Y
2 Schneider	N	N	Y	Y

SOUTH CAROLINA

	176	177	178	179
1 Hartnett	Y	Y	Y	Y
2 Spence	Y	Y	Y	Y
3 Derrick	Y	Y	Y	Y
4 Campbell	Y	Y	Y	Y
5 Holland	Y	Y	?	Y
6 Napier	N	Y	Y	Y

SOUTH DAKOTA

	176	177	178	179
1 Daschle	N	Y	Y	Y
2 Roberts	Y	Y	Y	Y

TENNESSEE

	176	177	178	179
1 Quillen	Y	Y	Y	Y
2 Duncan	Y	Y	Y	Y
3 Bouquard	N	Y	Y	Y
4 Gore	N	N	Y	N
5 Boner	Y	Y	Y	Y
6 Beard	Y	Y	Y	Y
7 Jones	Y	Y	Y	Y
8 Ford	N	N	Y	X

TEXAS

	176	177	178	179
1 Hall, S.	Y	Y	Y	Y
2 Wilson	N	Y	Y	Y
3 Collins	Y	Y	Y	Y
4 Hall, R.	N	Y	Y	Y
5 Mattox	N	N	Y	?
6 Gramm	Y	Y	N	#
7 Archer	Y	Y	N	Y
8 Fields	Y	Y	Y	Y
9 Brooks	N	Y	Y	Y
10 Pickle	Y	Y	Y	Y
11 Leath	Y	Y	Y	?
12 Wright	N	Y	Y	Y
13 Hightower	N	Y	Y	Y
14 Patman	N	N	Y	Y
15 de la Garza	Y	Y	Y	Y
16 White	Y	Y	Y	Y
17 Stenholm	Y	Y	Y	Y
18 Leland	N	N	Y	?
19 Hance	Y	Y	Y	Y
20 Gonzalez	N	Y	Y	N
21 Loeffler	Y	Y	Y	Y
22 Paul	Y	Y	N	Y
23 Kazen	N	Y	Y	Y
24 Frost	Y	Y	Y	?

UTAH

	176	177	178	179
1 Hansen	Y	Y	N	Y
2 Marriott	Y	Y	Y	Y

VERMONT

	176	177	178	179
AL Jeffords	N	Y	Y	N

VIRGINIA

	176	177	178	179
1 Trible	Y	Y	Y	Y
2 Whitehurst	Y	Y	Y	Y
3 Bliley	Y	Y	Y	Y
4 Daniel, R.	Y	Y	Y	Y
5 Daniel, D.	Y	Y	Y	Y
6 Butler	Y	Y	Y	Y
7 Robinson	Y	Y	Y	Y
8 Parris	Y	Y	Y	?
9 Wampler	Y	Y	Y	Y
10 Wolf	N	Y	Y	Y

WASHINGTON

	176	177	178	179
1 Pritchard	Y	Y	Y	?
2 Swift	Y	Y	Y	Y
3 Bonker	Y	Y	Y	Y
4 Morrison	Y	Y	Y	Y
5 Foley	Y	Y	Y	Y
6 Dicks	Y	Y	Y	Y
7 Lowry	Y	Y	Y	N

WEST VIRGINIA

	176	177	178	179
1 Mollohan	Y	Y	N	Y
2 Benedict	Y	Y	Y	Y
3 Staton	Y	Y	Y	Y
4 Rahall	N	Y	Y	N

WISCONSIN

	176	177	178	179
1 Aspin	N	Y	Y	?
2 Kastenmeier	N	N	Y	N
3 Gunderson	Y	Y	Y	Y
4 Zablocki	Y	Y	Y	Y
5 Reuss	N	Y	Y	X
6 Petri	Y	Y	Y	Y
7 Obey	N	Y	Y	N
8 Roth	Y	Y	Y	?
9 Sensenbrenner	Y	Y	Y	Y

WYOMING

	176	177	178	179
AL Cheney	Y	Y	N	Y

Democrats *Republicans*

180. HR 4169. State, Justice, Commerce, Judiciary Appropriations, Fiscal 1982. Mottl, D-Ohio, amendment to prevent the Justice Department from requiring communities to accept subsidized housing as part of the department's enforcement of the 1968 fair housing law. Rejected 188-202: R 120-53; D 68-149 (ND 25-122, SD 43-27), Sept. 9, 1981.

181. HR 4169. State, Justice, Commerce, Judiciary Appropriations, Fiscal 1982. Walker, R-Pa., amendment to bar the Justice Department from using funds contained in the bill to block implementation of voluntary prayer and meditation in public schools. Adopted 333-54: R 166-4; D 167-50 (ND 100-47, SD 67-3), Sept. 9, 1981.

182. HR 4169. State, Justice, Commerce, Judiciary Appropriations, Fiscal 1982. Sensenbrenner, R-Wis., amendment to delete $241 million for the Legal Services Corporation. Rejected 122-272: R 101-74; D 21-198 (ND 1-148, SD 20-50), Sept. 9, 1981.

183. HR 4169. State, Justice, Commerce, Judiciary Appropriations, Fiscal 1982. Passage of the bill to appropriate $8,683,999,000 for the departments of State, Justice and Commerce, the federal judiciary and related agencies. Passed 245-145: R 69-104; D 176-41 (ND 127-22, SD 49-19), Sept. 9, 1981. The president had requested $8,761,102,000.

184. HR 4209. Transportation Appropriations, Fiscal 1982. Benjamin, D-Ind., motion that the House resolve itself into the Committee of the Whole to consider the bill to provide fiscal 1982 funds for the Transportation Department and related agencies. Motion agreed to 367-3: R 171-1; D 196-2 (ND 131-2, SD 65-0), Sept. 10, 1981.

185. HR 4209. Transportation Appropriations, Fiscal 1982. Studds, D-Mass., amendments, considered en bloc, to increase funds for the Coast Guard by $84 million. Rejected 129-260: R 39-136; D 90-124 (ND 66-79, SD 24-45), Sept. 10, 1981.

186. HR 4209. Transportation Appropriations, Fiscal 1982. Dingell, D-Mich., amendment to reduce funds for the Office of the Secretary by $1 million. Adopted 209-172: R 52-124; D 157-48 (ND 98-38, SD 59-10), Sept. 10, 1981.

187. HR 4209. Transportation Appropriations, Fiscal 1982. Studds, D-Mass., amendment to increase funds for the Coast Guard by $6.19 million and to prohibit the use of funds to reduce civilian employment below the fiscal 1981 level. Adopted 283-98: R 91-84; D 192-14 (ND 130-8, SD 62-6), Sept. 10, 1981.

KEY

Y Voted for (yea).
Paired for.
+ Announced for.
N Voted against (nay).
X Paired against.
- Announced against.
P Voted "present".
C Voted "present" to avoid possible conflict of interest.
? Did not vote or otherwise make a position known.

	180	181	182	183	184	185	186	187
ALABAMA								
1 Edwards	N	Y	Y	Y	Y	N	N	Y
2 Dickinson	Y	Y	Y	Y	Y	N	N	Y
3 Nichols	Y	Y	Y	Y	Y	N	Y	Y
4 Bevill	Y	Y	Y	Y	Y	N	N	Y
5 Flippo	?	?	?	?	Y	N	Y	Y
6 Smith	Y	Y	Y	N	Y	N	N	N
7 Shelby	Y	Y	Y	N	Y	N	N	Y
ALASKA								
AL Young	?	?	?	?	?	#	?	#
ARIZONA								
1 Rhodes	?	?	?	?	?	X	?	Y
2 Udall	N	N	N	Y	Y	Y	?	Y
3 Stump	Y	?	Y	N	Y	N	Y	N
4 Rudd	Y	Y	Y	N	Y	N	N	Y
ARKANSAS								
1 Alexander	N	Y	N	Y	Y	Y	N	Y
2 Bethune	N	Y	Y	N	Y	N	N	Y
3 Hammerschmidt	Y	Y	N	Y	Y	N	N	?
4 Anthony	Y	Y	N	?	N	Y	Y	Y
CALIFORNIA								
1 Chappie	Y	Y	Y	N	Y	N	Y	Y
2 Clausen	Y	Y	N	N	Y	Y	N	Y
3 Matsui	N	Y	N	Y	Y	Y	Y	Y
4 Fazio	N	N	N	Y	Y	Y	N	Y
5 Burton, J.	N	N	N	?	Y	Y	?	Y
6 Burton, P.	?	?	?	?	?	?	?	?
7 Miller	N	N	N	Y	Y	Y	Y	Y
8 Dellums	N	N	N	?	Y	Y	Y	Y
9 Stark	N	N	N	Y	Y	Y	Y	Y
10 Edwards	N	N	N	Y	Y	Y	N	Y
11 Lantos	N	Y	N	Y	Y	Y	N	Y
12 McCloskey	N	Y	N	N	?	?	?	Y
13 Mineta	N	N	N	Y	Y	Y	N	Y
14 Shumway	Y	Y	Y	N	Y	N	N	N
15 Coelho	N	?	N	Y	Y	Y	Y	Y
16 Panetta	N	Y	N	Y	Y	Y	Y	Y
17 Pashayan	Y	Y	N	N	Y	N	Y	Y
18 Thomas	Y	Y	Y	N	Y	N	Y	Y
19 Lagomarsino	Y	Y	Y	N	Y	N	N	Y
20 Goldwater	?	?	?	?	?	?	?	?
21 Fiedler	Y	Y	Y	N	Y	N	N	Y
22 Moorhead	Y	Y	Y	N	Y	N	Y	N
23 Beilenson	?	?	?	?	?	?	?	?
24 Waxman	?	?	?	?	?	?	?	?
25 Roybal	N	N	N	Y	Y	Y	Y	Y
26 Rousselot	Y	Y	Y	N	Y	N	Y	N
27 Dornan	Y	Y	Y	N	Y	N	Y	Y
28 Dixon	N	Y	N	Y	?	#	?	?
29 Hawkins	N	N	N	Y	Y	N	N	Y
30 Danielson	N	N	N	Y	+	N	Y	Y
31 Dymally	N	N	N	Y	Y	?	?	Y
32 Anderson	N	Y	N	Y	Y	Y	N	Y
33 Grisham	Y	Y	Y	N	Y	N	N	N
34 Lungren	Y	Y	Y	N	Y	N	N	N
35 Dreier	Y	Y	Y	N	Y	N	Y	N
36 Brown	N	N	N	Y	Y	Y	Y	Y
37 Lewis	Y	Y	Y	N	Y	N	N	N
38 Patterson	N	Y	N	Y	Y	Y	Y	Y
39 Dannemeyer	Y	Y	Y	N	Y	N	N	N
40 Badham	Y	Y	Y	N	Y	N	N	N
41 Lowery	Y	Y	Y	N	?	N	N	N
42 Hunter	Y	Y	Y	Y	Y	?	?	Y
43 Burgener	Y	Y	Y	N	Y	N	N	N
COLORADO								
1 Schroeder	N	Y	N	N	Y	N	?	?
2 Wirth	N	Y	N	N	Y	Y	Y	Y
3 Kogovsek	N	Y	N	Y	Y	N	N	Y
4 Brown	Y	Y	Y	N	Y	N	Y	N

	180	181	182	183	184	185	186	187
5 Kramer	Y	Y	Y	N	Y	N	N	N
CONNECTICUT								
1 Vacancy*								
2 Gejdenson	N	N	N	Y	Y	Y	Y	Y
3 DeNardis	N	Y	N	Y	?	#	?	?
4 McKinney	N	Y	X	?	?	Y	N	Y
5 Ratchford	N	N	N	Y	Y	Y	Y	Y
6 Moffett	N	Y	N	Y	?	Y	Y	Y
DELAWARE								
AL Evans	Y	Y	N	?	Y	N	N	Y
FLORIDA								
1 Hutto	Y	Y	Y	Y	Y	Y	Y	Y
2 Fuqua	Y	Y	N	Y	Y	Y	Y	Y
3 Bennett	Y	Y	Y	Y	Y	Y	Y	Y
4 Chappell	Y	Y	Y	?	?	?	?	?
5 McCollum	Y	Y	N	N	Y	N	N	Y
6 Young	Y	Y	N	N	Y	N	N	Y
7 Gibbons	N	Y	N	Y	Y	Y	Y	Y
8 Ireland	Y	Y	Y	N	?	?	?	?
9 Nelson	N	Y	N	Y	Y	N	N	Y
10 Bafalis	Y	Y	N	Y	Y	N	N	Y
11 Mica	Y	Y	N	Y	Y	N	N	Y
12 Shaw	Y	Y	N	N	Y	N	N	Y
13 Lehman	N	N	N	Y	Y	Y	Y	Y
14 Pepper	N	Y	N	?	?	#	?	?
15 Fascell	N	N	N	Y	?	Y	N	Y
GEORGIA								
1 Ginn	Y	Y	N	Y	Y	Y	Y	Y
2 Hatcher	Y	Y	N	Y	Y	Y	Y	Y
3 Brinkley	Y	Y	Y	Y	Y	N	Y	Y
4 Levitas	Y	Y	N	Y	Y	N	N	Y
5 Fowler	N	Y	N	Y	Y	N	Y	Y
6 Gingrich	Y	Y	Y	N	Y	N	N	N
7 McDonald	Y	Y	Y	N	Y	N	Y	Y
8 Evans	Y	Y	N	Y	Y	Y	Y	Y
9 Jenkins	Y	Y	N	Y	Y	Y	Y	Y
10 Barnard	Y	Y	N	N	Y	N	N	Y
HAWAII								
1 Heftel	?	?	?	?	?	?	?	?
2 Akaka	N	Y	N	Y	Y	Y	Y	Y
IDAHO								
1 Craig	Y	Y	Y	N	Y	N	N	N
2 Hansen	Y	Y	Y	N	Y	N	N	N
ILLINOIS								
1 Washington	N	N	N	Y	?	?	?	N
2 Savage	-	-	-	?	?	?	?	?
3 Russo	Y	Y	N	Y	Y	Y	Y	Y
4 Derwinski	Y	Y	Y	Y	Y	N	N	N
5 Fary	Y	Y	N	Y	Y	Y	Y	Y
6 Hyde	Y	Y	Y	Y	N	N	Y	Y
7 Collins	N	N	N	?	Y	X	?	Y
8 Rostenkowski	N	Y	N	Y	Y	Y	Y	Y
9 Yates	N	N	N	Y	Y	N	Y	N
10 Porter	N	N	Y	N	Y	N	N	N
11 Annunzio	Y	Y	N	Y	Y	N	N	Y
12 Crane, P.	?	?	#	?	?	X	?	X
13 McClory	N	Y	Y	Y	N	N	Y	Y
14 Erlenborn	N	Y	N	N	Y	N	N	N
15 Corcoran	Y	Y	Y	Y	Y	N	N	Y
16 Martin	N	Y	N	N	Y	N	N	N
17 O'Brien	N	Y	Y	Y	Y	N	N	Y
18 Michel	Y	Y	Y	N	Y	N	N	?
19 Railsback	N	Y	N	Y	Y	Y	N	Y
20 Findley	N	Y	N	Y	Y	N	N	N
21 Madigan	?	Y	N	Y	N	N	N	N
22 Crane, D.	Y	Y	Y	N	Y	N	Y	N
23 Price	N	Y	N	Y	Y	N	N	Y
24 Simon	N	N	N	Y	Y	N	N	Y
INDIANA								
1 Benjamin	N	Y	N	Y	Y	N	N	Y
2 Fithian	?	?	?	?	?	?	Y	Y
3 Hiler	Y	Y	Y	N	Y	N	Y	N
4 Coats	Y	Y	Y	N	Y	N	Y	N
5 Hillis	?	?	?	?	Y	N	N	N
6 Evans	?	?	?	?	Y	N	Y	Y
7 Myers	Y	Y	Y	N	Y	N	N	N
8 Deckard	N	Y	Y	N	Y	N	N	N
9 Hamilton	N	Y	N	Y	Y	N	N	Y
10 Sharp	N	Y	N	N	Y	N	Y	?
11 Jacobs	N	Y	N	Y	Y	N	Y	Y
IOWA								
1 Leach	N	Y	N	N	Y	N	N	?
2 Tauke	N	Y	N	N	Y	N	N	Y
3 Evans	N	N	N	N	N	N	N	N
4 Smith	N	Y	N	Y	Y	N	N	Y
5 Harkin	N	Y	N	Y	Y	N	N	Y
6 Bedell	N	Y	N	Y	Y	N	Y	Y

Democrats *Republicans*

	180	181	182	183	184	185	186	187
KANSAS								
1 *Roberts*	Y	Y	Y	N	Y	N	Y	N
2 *Jeffries*	Y	Y	Y	N	Y	N	Y	N
3 *Winn*	Y	Y	Y	Y	Y	N	Y	N
4 Glickman	N	Y	N	N	Y	N	Y	N
5 *Whittaker*	Y	Y	Y	N	Y	N	Y	N
KENTUCKY								
1 Hubbard	Y	Y	N	N	Y	Y	Y	Y
2 Natcher	Y	Y	N	Y	Y	N	Y	Y
3 Mazzoli	N	Y	N	Y	Y	N	Y	N
4 *Snyder*	Y	Y	Y	N	Y	N	N	Y
5 *Rogers*	Y	Y	Y	Y	Y	N	N	N
6 *Hopkins*	Y	Y	N	Y	Y	N	Y	N
7 Perkins	N	Y	N	Y	Y	N	Y	Y
LOUISIANA								
1 *Livingston*	N	Y	N	Y	?	Y	N	Y
2 Boggs	N	Y	N	Y	?	Y	N	Y
3 Tauzin	Y	Y	N	Y	Y	N	Y	Y
4 Roemer	Y	Y	N	Y	Y	N	Y	N
5 Huckaby	Y	Y	N	Y	Y	N	Y	Y
6 *Moore*	Y	Y	N	N	Y	N	Y	N
7 Breaux	Y	Y	N	Y	?	Y	Y	Y
8 Long	Y	Y	N	Y	Y	N	Y	Y
MAINE								
1 *Emery*	N	Y	N	Y	Y	Y	Y	Y
2 *Snowe*	N	Y	N	Y	Y	Y	Y	Y
MARYLAND								
1 Dyson	Y	Y	N	N	Y	Y	Y	Y
2 Long	N	N	N	Y	Y	Y	?	Y
3 Mikulski	N	Y	N	Y	?	Y	Y	Y
4 *Holt*	Y	Y	Y	N	Y	N	Y	Y
5 Hoyer	N	N	N	Y	Y	Y	Y	Y
6 Byron	Y	Y	N	Y	Y	N	Y	Y
7 Mitchell	N	N	N	Y	N	N	?	Y
8 Barnes	N	N	N	Y	Y	Y	N	Y
MASSACHUSETTS								
1 *Conte*	N	Y	N	Y	Y	Y	N	Y
2 Boland	N	Y	N	Y	Y	N	N	Y
3 Early	N	N	N	Y	Y	Y	Y	Y
4 Frank	N	N	N	Y	Y	Y	Y	Y
5 Shannon	N	N	N	Y	Y	Y	Y	Y
6 Mavroules	N	Y	N	Y	Y	Y	Y	Y
7 Markey	N	Y	N	Y	Y	Y	Y	Y
8 O'Neill								
9 Moakley	Y	Y	N	Y	Y	Y	Y	Y
10 *Heckler*	N	Y	N	Y	Y	Y	N	Y
11 Donnelly	N	Y	N	Y	Y	Y	Y	Y
12 Studds	N	N	N	Y	Y	Y	N	Y
MICHIGAN								
1 Conyers	N	N	N	N	?	Y	Y	Y
2 *Pursell*	N	Y	N	Y	Y	N	N	Y
3 Wolpe	N	Y	N	Y	Y	N	Y	Y
4 *Siljander*	Y	Y	Y	N	Y	Y	Y	Y
5 *Sawyer*	Y	Y	N	Y	Y	Y	N	Y
6 *Dunn*	N	Y	N	Y	Y	N	N	Y
7 Kildee	N	Y	N	Y	Y	N	Y	Y
8 Traxler	N	Y	N	Y	Y	N	Y	?
9 *Vander Jagt*	Y	Y	Y	N	Y	Y	N	Y
10 Albosta	Y	Y	N	Y	Y	N	N	Y
11 *Davis*	Y	Y	N	Y	Y	Y	N	Y
12 Bonior	N	Y	N	N	Y	Y	Y	?
13 Crockett	N	N	N	Y	?	N	?	?
14 Hertel	N	Y	N	Y	Y	Y	Y	Y
15 Ford	N	Y	?	?	Y	Y	Y	?
16 Dingell	Y	N	N	Y	?	N	Y	Y
17 Brodhead	N	N	N	N	Y	Y	?	?
18 Blanchard	N	Y	N	N	Y	Y	Y	Y
19 *Broomfield*	Y	Y	N	?	Y	N	N	Y
MINNESOTA								
1 *Erdahl*	?	?	?	?	?	?	?	X
2 *Hagedorn*	Y	Y	N	N	Y	N	N	N
3 *Frenzel*	N	Y	N	N	Y	N	N	N
4 Vento	N	N	N	Y	Y	N	N	Y
5 Sabo	N	N	N	Y	Y	N	N	Y
6 *Weber*	Y	Y	Y	N	Y	N	Y	N
7 *Stangeland*	Y	Y	N	N	Y	N	N	N
8 Oberstar	N	N	N	Y	Y	Y	Y	Y
MISSISSIPPI								
1 Whitten	Y	Y	N	Y	Y	N	N	Y
2 Bowen	Y	Y	N	Y	Y	Y	Y	Y
3 Montgomery	Y	Y	Y	N	Y	N	Y	Y
4 Dowdy	Y	Y	N	Y	Y	N	Y	Y
5 *Lott*	?	?	Y	N	Y	N	N	Y
MISSOURI								
1 Clay	N	N	N	Y	N	Y	Y	Y
2 Young	?	?	N	Y	Y	N	N	Y
3 Gephardt	Y	Y	N	N	Y	N	Y	N
4 Skelton	Y	Y	N	N	Y	?	?	?
5 Bolling	?	?	?	?	Y	Y	Y	?
6 *Coleman*	Y	Y	N	Y	Y	N	N	Y
7 *Taylor*	Y	Y	Y	N	Y	N	Y	N
8 *Bailey*	Y	Y	Y	N	Y	N	N	N
9 Volkmer	Y	Y	N	Y	Y	N	Y	Y
10 *Emerson*	Y	Y	Y	N	Y	X	N	N
MONTANA								
1 Williams	N	Y	N	Y	Y	N	Y	Y
2 *Marlenee*	?	?	?	?	?	X	?	?
NEBRASKA								
1 *Bereuter*	N	Y	N	N	Y	N	N	N
2 *Daub*	Y	Y	Y	N	Y	N	N	Y
3 *Smith*	Y	Y	Y	Y	Y	N	N	Y
NEVADA								
AL Santini	?	?	?	?	?	?	?	?
NEW HAMPSHIRE								
1 D'Amours	N	Y	N	Y	Y	Y	Y	Y
2 *Gregg*	Y	Y	Y	N	Y	N	Y	N
NEW JERSEY								
1 Florio	?	?	X	?	?	#	?	?
2 Hughes	N	Y	N	Y	Y	Y	Y	Y
3 Howard	N	Y	N	Y	Y	Y	Y	Y
4 *Smith*	N	Y	Y	Y	Y	Y	Y	Y
5 *Fenwick*	N	N	N	Y	Y	Y	N	N
6 *Forsythe*	N	Y	N	Y	?	Y	N	N
7 *Roukema*	N	Y	N	N	Y	N	N	N
8 Roe	N	Y	N	Y	Y	Y	Y	Y
9 *Hollenbeck*	N	?	N	?	Y	Y	N	Y
10 Rodino	N	Y	N	Y	Y	Y	Y	Y
11 Minish	N	Y	N	Y	Y	Y	Y	Y
12 *Rinaldo*	N	Y	N	Y	Y	N	N	Y
13 *Courter*	N	Y	N	N	Y	N	?	Y
14 Guarini	N	Y	N	Y	Y	Y	Y	Y
15 Dwyer	N	Y	N	Y	Y	Y	Y	Y
NEW MEXICO								
1 *Lujan*	Y	Y	N	N	Y	N	Y	N
2 *Skeen*	Y	Y	N	Y	Y	N	N	N
NEW YORK								
1 *Carney*	?	?	Y	N	Y	Y	Y	Y
2 Downey	N	Y	N	Y	Y	Y	Y	Y
3 *Carman*	Y	Y	Y	N	Y	N	N	Y
4 *Lent*	?	?	?	?	Y	Y	Y	Y
5 *McGrath*	Y	Y	Y	N	Y	Y	N	Y
6 *LeBoutillier*	Y	Y	Y	N	Y	N	Y	Y
7 Addabbo	N	Y	N	Y	Y	Y	N	Y
8 Rosenthal	N	N	N	Y	Y	Y	Y	Y
9 Ferraro	N	Y	N	Y	Y	Y	N	Y
10 Biaggi	N	Y	N	Y	Y	Y	?	?
11 Scheuer	N	Y	N	Y	Y	Y	Y	Y
12 Chisholm	N	N	N	Y	?	N	?	?
13 Solarz	N	Y	N	Y	Y	N	Y	Y
14 Richmond	N	Y	N	Y	Y	Y	N	Y
15 Zeferetti	N	Y	N	Y	Y	Y	Y	Y
16 Schumer	N	N	N	Y	Y	N	N	Y
17 *Molinari*	N	Y	N	N	Y	N	N	N
18 *Green*	N	N	N	Y	Y	N	N	Y
19 Rangel	N	?	X	?	?	N	N	Y
20 Weiss	N	N	N	Y	Y	Y	Y	Y
21 Garcia	N	Y	N	Y	Y	N	Y	Y
22 Bingham	N	N	N	Y	Y	Y	Y	Y
23 Peyser	N	Y	N	Y	Y	Y	N	Y
24 Ottinger	N	Y	N	Y	P	N	Y	Y
25 *Fish*	N	Y	N	Y	Y	N	N	Y
26 *Gilman*	N	Y	N	Y	+	#	N	Y
27 McHugh	N	Y	N	Y	Y	N	Y	Y
28 Stratton	Y	Y	N	Y	Y	N	N	Y
29 *Solomon*	Y	Y	Y	N	Y	N	Y	N
30 *Martin*	?	?	Y	N	Y	N	N	Y
31 *Mitchell*	Y	Y	N	Y	Y	#	?	#
32 *Wortley*	Y	Y	Y	Y	Y	N	N	N
33 *Lee*	Y	Y	Y	N	Y	Y	Y	Y
34 *Horton*	N	Y	N	Y	Y	Y	?	?
35 *Conable*	N	Y	Y	N	Y	N	N	N
36 LaFalce	?	Y	N	Y	Y	Y	N	Y
37 Nowak	?	Y	N	Y	Y	Y	?	Y
38 *Kemp*	N	Y	Y	N	Y	?	?	?
39 Lundine	N	Y	N	Y	Y	N	Y	Y
NORTH CAROLINA								
1 Jones	?	?	?	?	?	?	?	?
2 Fountain	N	Y	Y	N	N	Y	N	N
3 Whitley	Y	Y	N	Y	Y	Y	Y	Y
4 Andrews	?	?	?	?	?	?	?	?
5 Neal	Y	Y	N	Y	Y	Y	N	Y
6 *Johnston*	?	?	#	?	Y	N	Y	N
7 Rose	Y	Y	Y	Y	?	?	?	?
8 Hefner	Y	Y	N	Y	Y	?	?	?
9 *Martin*	N	Y	N	N	Y	Y	N	Y
10 *Broyhill*	Y	Y	Y	N	Y	N	N	N
11 *Hendon*	Y	Y	Y	N	Y	N	Y	N
NORTH DAKOTA								
AL Dorgan	N	Y	N	Y	Y	N	Y	Y
OHIO								
1 *Gradison*	N	N	N	Y	Y	N	N	N
2 Luken	Y	Y	N	Y	Y	N	Y	Y
3 Hall	N	Y	N	Y	Y	N	Y	?
4 *Oxley*	Y	Y	N	N	Y	N	N	N
5 *Latta*	Y	Y	Y	N	Y	N	Y	N
6 *McEwen*	Y	Y	Y	N	Y	Y	N	Y
7 *Brown*	Y	Y	N	Y	Y	?	?	?
8 *Kindness*	Y	Y	N	N	?	X	N	N
9 *Weber*	N	Y	N	Y	Y	Y	N	N
10 *Miller*	Y	Y	Y	N	Y	N	Y	N
11 *Stanton*	?	?	?	?	Y	N	N	Y
12 Shamansky	N	Y	N	Y	Y	N	Y	Y
13 Pease	N	Y	N	Y	Y	N	Y	Y
14 Seiberling	N	N	N	Y	Y	Y	Y	Y
15 *Wylie*	N	Y	N	N	Y	N	N	N
16 *Regula*	N	Y	N	Y	Y	N	N	N
17 *Ashbrook*	Y	?	?	?	Y	N	Y	?
18 Applegate	Y	Y	N	N	Y	N	N	Y
19 *Williams*	Y	Y	N	Y	Y	N	Y	Y
20 Oakar	N	Y	N	Y	?	Y	N	Y
21 Stokes	N	N	N	Y	Y	N	Y	N
22 Eckart	?	Y	N	Y	Y	Y	Y	Y
23 Mottl	Y	Y	N	N	Y	Y	Y	Y
OKLAHOMA								
1 Jones	N	Y	N	N	Y	N	Y	Y
2 Synar	N	Y	N	Y	Y	N	Y	Y
3 Watkins	N	Y	N	Y	Y	N	Y	?
4 McCurdy	N	Y	N	Y	Y	N	Y	Y
5 *Edwards*	Y	Y	Y	N	Y	N	Y	N
6 English	N	Y	N	N	Y	N	Y	Y
OREGON								
1 AuCoin	N	Y	N	Y	Y	N	Y	Y
2 *Smith*	Y	Y	Y	N	Y	N	Y	N
3 Wyden	N	Y	N	Y	?	?	?	?
4 Weaver	?	?	?	?	?	?	?	?
PENNSYLVANIA								
1 Foglietta	Y	Y	N	Y	Y	Y	N	Y
2 Gray	N	N	N	Y	Y	N	Y	Y
3 Smith	Y	Y	N	Y	Y	Y	Y	Y
4 *Dougherty*	Y	?	N	Y	?	Y	N	Y
5 *Schulze*	Y	Y	Y	N	Y	N	N	N
6 Yatron	Y	Y	N	Y	Y	N	N	Y
7 Edgar	N	N	N	Y	?	?	?	?
8 *Coyne, J.*	N	Y	Y	N	Y	Y	N	Y
9 *Shuster*	Y	Y	Y	N	Y	N	N	N
10 *McDade*	Y	Y	N	Y	Y	N	N	Y
11 *Nelligan*	Y	Y	Y	Y	Y	N	N	Y
12 Murtha	Y	Y	N	Y	Y	N	N	Y
13 *Coughlin*	Y	Y	N	Y	Y	N	N	Y
14 Coyne, W.	N	Y	N	Y	Y	N	N	Y
15 *Ritter*	Y	Y	Y	N	Y	N	N	N
16 *Walker*	Y	Y	Y	N	Y	N	N	N
17 Ertel	Y	Y	N	N	?	?	?	?
18 Walgren	N	Y	N	Y	Y	N	N	Y
19 *Goodling*	?	?	?	?	Y	N	N	N
20 Gaydos	Y	Y	N	Y	Y	N	N	Y
21 Bailey	N	Y	N	Y	Y	N	N	Y
22 Murphy	Y	Y	N	N	Y	N	N	Y
23 *Clinger*	Y	Y	N	Y	Y	N	N	Y
24 *Marks*	N	Y	N	Y	Y	N	N	Y
25 Atkinson	N	Y	N	Y	Y	N	N	Y
RHODE ISLAND								
1 St Germain	N	Y	N	Y	Y	?	Y	Y
2 *Schneider*	N	Y	N	Y	P	Y	N	Y
SOUTH CAROLINA								
1 *Hartnett*	Y	Y	Y	Y	Y	Y	Y	Y
2 *Spence*	Y	Y	Y	N	Y	N	Y	Y
3 Derrick	N	Y	Y	Y	Y	N	Y	Y
4 *Campbell*	Y	Y	Y	Y	Y	N	N	Y
5 Holland	Y	Y	Y	Y	?	?	?	?
6 *Napier*	Y	Y	Y	Y	Y	N	Y	Y
SOUTH DAKOTA								
1 Daschle	N	Y	N	N	?	N	Y	Y
2 *Roberts*	Y	Y	Y	N	Y	N	Y	N
TENNESSEE								
1 *Quillen*	Y	Y	Y	N	Y	N	N	N
2 *Duncan*	Y	Y	N	Y	Y	N	N	Y
3 Bouquard	N	Y	N	Y	Y	N	Y	Y
4 Gore	N	N	N	Y	Y	N	Y	Y
5 Boner	N	Y	N	Y	Y	N	Y	Y
6 *Beard*	Y	Y	Y	Y	?	N	N	Y
7 Jones	+	+	+	+	Y	N	Y	Y
8 Ford	?	?	X	?	Y	N	Y	Y
TEXAS								
1 Hall, S.	Y	Y	Y	N	Y	Y	Y	Y
2 Wilson	?	?	?	?	Y	Y	Y	Y
3 *Collins*	Y	Y	Y	N	Y	N	Y	N
4 Hall, R.	Y	Y	N	Y	?	Y	Y	Y
5 Mattox	N	Y	N	Y	Y	N	Y	Y
6 Gramm	Y	Y	Y	N	Y	N	Y	N
7 *Archer*	Y	Y	Y	N	Y	N	Y	N
8 *Fields*	?	?	#	N	Y	N	Y	N
9 Brooks	?	?	?	?	?	?	?	?
10 Pickle	N	Y	N	Y	Y	N	Y	Y
11 Leath	Y	Y	Y	N	Y	N	Y	Y
12 Wright	?	?	?	?	?	?	?	?
13 Hightower	Y	Y	N	Y	Y	N	Y	Y
14 Patman	Y	Y	Y	N	Y	Y	Y	Y
15 de la Garza	N	Y	N	Y	Y	Y	Y	Y
16 White	Y	Y	N	Y	Y	N	Y	Y
17 Stenholm	Y	Y	Y	N	Y	N	Y	N
18 Leland	N	Y	N	?	Y	N	N	Y
19 Hance	?	?	#	?	Y	N	Y	N
20 Gonzalez	N	Y	N	Y	Y	Y	Y	Y
21 *Loeffler*	Y	Y	Y	N	Y	N	N	N
22 *Paul*	Y	Y	Y	N	Y	N	Y	N
23 Kazen	N	Y	N	Y	Y	N	Y	Y
24 Frost	N	Y	N	Y	Y	N	Y	Y
UTAH								
1 *Hansen*	Y	Y	Y	N	Y	N	Y	Y
2 *Marriott*	Y	Y	Y	Y	Y	N	N	Y
VERMONT								
AL *Jeffords*	?	?	N	Y	Y	?	N	N
VIRGINIA								
1 *Trible*	N	?	?	?	Y	N	N	Y
2 *Whitehurst*	Y	Y	N	N	Y	N	N	Y
3 *Bliley*	Y	Y	Y	N	Y	N	N	N
4 *Daniel, R.*	Y	Y	Y	N	Y	N	N	Y
5 Daniel, D.	Y	Y	Y	N	Y	N	Y	Y
6 *Butler*	Y	Y	N	Y	Y	N	N	N
7 *Robinson*	Y	Y	Y	N	Y	N	N	N
8 *Parris*	Y	Y	Y	Y	Y	Y	N	Y
9 *Wampler*	Y	Y	N	Y	Y	N	N	N
10 *Wolf*	Y	Y	Y	Y	Y	N	N	Y
WASHINGTON								
1 *Pritchard*	N	Y	N	Y	Y	Y	Y	Y
2 Swift	N	N	N	Y	Y	Y	Y	Y
3 Bonker	N	Y	N	Y	Y	Y	Y	Y
4 *Morrison*	Y	Y	Y	Y	Y	N	N	Y
5 Foley	N	Y	N	Y	Y	N	Y	Y
6 Dicks	?	?	?	?	?	N	Y	Y
7 Lowry	N	N	N	Y	Y	Y	Y	Y
WEST VIRGINIA								
1 Mollohan	Y	Y	N	Y	Y	N	Y	Y
2 *Benedict*	?	?	?	?	Y	N	N	N
3 *Staton*	Y	Y	Y	N	Y	N	N	N
4 Rahall	Y	Y	N	Y	Y	N	N	Y
WISCONSIN								
1 Aspin	N	Y	N	Y	Y	N	N	Y
2 Kastenmeier	N	N	N	Y	Y	N	N	N
3 *Gunderson*	N	Y	N	N	Y	N	N	Y
4 Zablocki	N	Y	N	Y	Y	N	Y	Y
5 Reuss	N	N	N	Y	Y	N	Y	Y
6 *Petri*	N	Y	Y	N	Y	N	Y	Y
7 Obey	N	Y	N	Y	Y	N	?	N
8 *Roth*	Y	Y	Y	Y	Y	Y	N	Y
9 *Sensenbrenner*	Y	Y	Y	N	Y	N	Y	N
WYOMING								
AL *Cheney*	N	Y	Y	N	Y	X	?	N

** Rep. William R. Cotter, D-Conn., died Sept. 8, 1981. The last vote for which he was eligible was CQ vote 179.*

Democrats *Republicans*

188. HR 4209. Transportation Appropriations, Fiscal 1982. Wilson, D-Texas, amendment to bar the use of funds to enforce a rule reducing air traffic at Washington, D.C.'s National Airport, below the daily levels of July 31, 1981. Adopted 204-188: R 57-120; D 147-68 (ND 92-52, SD 55-16), Sept. 10, 1981. (The bill to appropriate $11,090,306,439 for the Transportation Department and related agencies in fiscal 1982 was passed by voice vote.)

189. Procedural Motion. Walker, R-Pa., motion to approve the House *Journal* of Monday, Sept. 14. Motion agreed to 366-12: R 165-3; D 201-9 (ND 132-8, SD 69-1), Sept. 15, 1981.

190. H Con Res 153. Martin Luther King Jr. Statue. Hawkins, D-Calif., motion to suspend the rules and adopt the concurrent resolution to authorize $25,000 for a memorial sculpture of Martin Luther King Jr. to be placed in the Capitol building. Motion agreed to 386-16: R 167-14; D 219-2 (ND 150-1, SD 69-1), Sept. 15, 1981. A two-thirds majority vote (268 in this case) is required for adoption under suspension of the rules.

191. HR 4034. HUD-Independent Agencies Appropriations, Fiscal 1982. Adoption of the conference report on the bill to appropriate $60,689,970,200 in fiscal 1982 for the Department of Housing and Urban Development and 20 related agencies. Adopted 209-197: R 27-155; D 182-42 (ND 140-13; SD 42-29), Sept. 15, 1981. President Reagan had requested $63,248,452,500.

192. HR 3380. Military Pay. Addabbo, D-N.Y., amendment to increase the basic pay of senior enlisted personnel by 18-22 percent and the basic pay of junior enlisted personnel by 7-9 percent. Rejected 170-232: R 55-125; D 115-107 (ND 93-56; SD 22-51), Sept. 15, 1981. A "nay" was a vote supporting the president's position.

193. HR 3380. Military Pay. Passage of the bill to increase the basic pay of all military personnel by 14.3 percent. Passed 396-1: R 176-0; D 220-1 (ND 146-1; SD 74-0), Sept. 15, 1981. A "yea" was a vote supporting the president's position.

194. H J Res 325. Fiscal 1982 Continuing Appropriations. Passage of the joint resolution to provide interim spending authority, from Oct. 1 to Nov. 1, 1981, for certain federal agencies whose regular fiscal 1982 appropriations have not become law. Passed 281-107: R 90-77; D 191-30 (ND 129-21, SD 62-9), Sept. 16, 1981.

195. HR 4241. Military Construction Appropriations, Fiscal 1982. Passage of the bill to appropriate $6,887,542,000 for military construction projects in fiscal 1982. Passed 382-24: R 177-5; D 205-19 (ND 132-18, SD 73-1), Sept. 16, 1981. The president had requested $8,016,208,000.

KEY

Y   Voted for (yea).
Paired for.
+   Announced for.
N   Voted against (nay).
X   Paired against.
-   Announced against.
P   Voted "present".
C   Voted "present" to avoid possible conflict of interest.
?   Did not vote or otherwise make a position known.

	188	189	190	191	192	193	194	195
ALABAMA								
1 Edwards	N	Y	Y	N	Y	Y	Y	Y
2 Dickinson	N	Y	Y	N	N	Y	Y	Y
3 Nichols	N	N	Y	Y	N	Y	Y	Y
4 Bevill	N	Y	Y	Y	N	Y	Y	Y
5 Flippo	Y	Y	Y	Y	N	Y	Y	Y
6 Smith	N	Y	Y	N	N	Y	Y	Y
7 Shelby	N	Y	Y	N	N	Y	N	Y
ALASKA								
AL Young	X	?	?	?	?	?	?	?
ARIZONA								
1 Rhodes	?	?	?	X	?	?	?	?
2 Udall	N	Y	Y	Y	N	Y	?	?
3 Stump	Y	Y	N	N	N	Y	N	Y
4 Rudd	Y	?	?	X	?	?	?	?
ARKANSAS								
1 Alexander	Y	Y	Y	Y	Y	Y	Y	Y
2 Bethune	N	Y	Y	N	Y	Y	Y	Y
3 Hammerschmidt	Y	Y	Y	Y	N	Y	Y	Y
4 Anthony	Y	Y	Y	Y	N	Y	Y	Y
CALIFORNIA								
1 Chappie	N	Y	Y	N	N	Y	Y	Y
2 Clausen	N	?	Y	N	Y	Y	Y	Y
3 Matsui	N	Y	Y	Y	Y	Y	Y	Y
4 Fazio	N	Y	Y	Y	Y	Y	Y	Y
5 Burton, J.	?	Y	Y	Y	Y	Y	N	Y
6 Burton, P.	?	?	?	?	?	?	?	?
7 Miller	Y	?	Y	Y	Y	Y	Y	Y
8 Dellums	Y	?	Y	Y	N	Y	Y	N
9 Stark	Y	?	Y	Y	N	Y	N	Y
10 Edwards	X	Y	Y	Y	Y	Y	Y	N
11 Lantos	N	Y	Y	N	Y	Y	Y	Y
12 McCloskey	?	Y	Y	N	Y	Y	?	?
13 Mineta	N	Y	Y	Y	Y	Y	Y	Y
14 Shumway	N	Y	Y	N	N	Y	N	Y
15 Coelho	Y	Y	Y	Y	Y	Y	Y	Y
16 Panetta	N	Y	Y	Y	Y	Y	N	Y
17 Pashayan	N	Y	Y	N	N	Y	Y	Y
18 Thomas	N	?	?	X	N	Y	Y	Y
19 Lagomarsino	N	Y	Y	N	N	Y	Y	Y
20 Goldwater	?	?	?	?	?	?	?	?
21 Fiedler	N	Y	Y	N	N	Y	N	Y
22 Moorhead	N	Y	?	N	N	Y	N	Y
23 Beilenson	?	N	Y	Y	Y	Y	Y	Y
24 Waxman	?	Y	Y	Y	Y	Y	Y	?
25 Roybal	Y	?	Y	Y	Y	Y	Y	N
26 Rousselot	N	Y	N	N	N	Y	?	Y
27 Dornan	N	?	Y	N	N	Y	Y	Y
28 Dixon	#	Y	Y	Y	Y	Y	Y	Y
29 Hawkins	Y	Y	Y	Y	Y	Y	Y	Y
30 Danielson	Y	Y	Y	Y	Y	Y	Y	Y
31 Dymally	Y	Y	Y	Y	N	Y	Y	Y
32 Anderson	N	Y	Y	N	Y	Y	Y	Y
33 Grisham	N	Y	Y	N	N	Y	N	Y
34 Lungren	N	Y	Y	N	N	Y	N	Y
35 Dreier	N	Y	Y	N	N	Y	?	Y
36 Brown	Y	Y	Y	Y	N	Y	?	Y
37 Lewis	X	Y	Y	N	N	Y	Y	Y
38 Patterson	N	Y	Y	Y	Y	Y	N	Y
39 Dannemeyer	N	Y	Y	N	N	Y	N	Y
40 Badham	N	Y	Y	N	N	Y	N	Y
41 Lowery	N	Y	Y	N	Y	Y	?	Y
42 Hunter	N	Y	Y	N	N	Y	?	Y
43 Burgener	N	Y	Y	N	N	?	?	Y
COLORADO								
1 Schroeder	N	N	Y	Y	Y	Y	N	Y
2 Wirth	N	Y	Y	Y	Y	Y	N	Y
3 Kogovsek	N	Y	+	Y	Y	Y	Y	Y
4 Brown	N	Y	Y	N	Y	Y	N	Y
5 Kramer	N	Y	Y	N	N	Y	N	Y
CONNECTICUT								
1 Vacancy								
2 Gejdenson	Y	N	Y	Y	Y	Y	Y	Y
3 DeNardis	N	?	Y	Y	Y	Y	Y	Y
4 McKinney	Y	Y	N	Y	Y	Y	Y	Y
5 Ratchford	Y	Y	Y	Y	Y	Y	Y	Y
6 Moffett	Y	Y	Y	Y	Y	Y	Y	N
DELAWARE								
AL Evans	N	Y	Y	N	N	Y	Y	Y
FLORIDA								
1 Hutto	N	Y	Y	N	Y	Y	Y	Y
2 Fuqua	Y	?	+	+	?	+	?	?
3 Bennett	N	Y	Y	N	N	Y	Y	Y
4 Chappell	#	Y	Y	Y	Y	Y	Y	Y
5 McCollum	N	Y	Y	N	Y	N	Y	Y
6 Young	Y	Y	Y	Y	Y	Y	Y	Y
7 Gibbons	Y	Y	Y	N	Y	Y	Y	Y
8 Ireland	Y	?	?	?	Y	?	Y	Y
9 Nelson	Y	+	+	#	#	+	Y	Y
10 Bafalis	?	Y	Y	N	N	Y	Y	Y
11 Mica	Y	Y	?	Y	N	Y	Y	Y
12 Shaw	N	Y	Y	N	N	Y	N	Y
13 Lehman	N	Y	Y	N	Y	Y	Y	Y
14 Pepper	Y	?	?	#	?	?	#	?
15 Fascell	Y	?	Y	Y	Y	Y	?	?
GEORGIA								
1 Ginn	Y	Y	Y	N	N	Y	Y	Y
2 Hatcher	N	Y	Y	N	N	Y	Y	Y
3 Brinkley	N	Y	Y	N	N	Y	Y	Y
4 Levitas	Y	Y	Y	N	Y	Y	Y	Y
5 Fowler	Y	Y	Y	N	Y	Y	Y	Y
6 Gingrich	N	Y	Y	N	N	Y	N	Y
7 McDonald	Y	N	N	N	N	Y	N	Y
8 Evans	Y	Y	Y	?	N	Y	Y	Y
9 Jenkins	Y	Y	Y	N	N	Y	Y	Y
10 Barnard	Y	Y	Y	N	N	Y	Y	Y
HAWAII								
1 Heftel	Y	Y	Y	N	N	Y	Y	Y
2 Akaka	Y	Y	Y	Y	N	Y	Y	Y
IDAHO								
1 Craig	N	?	N	N	N	Y	N	Y
2 Hansen	Y	Y	N	N	N	Y	N	Y
ILLINOIS								
1 Washington	Y	Y	Y	N	Y	N	Y	Y
2 Savage	?	?	Y	Y	?	?	?	?
3 Russo	Y	Y	Y	Y	N	Y	Y	Y
4 Derwinski	Y	Y	N	Y	N	Y	N	Y
5 Fary	Y	?	Y	N	Y	Y	Y	Y
6 Hyde	N	Y	Y	N	N	Y	N	Y
7 Collins	?	Y	Y	Y	N	Y	Y	Y
8 Rostenkowski	Y	Y	Y	Y	N	Y	Y	Y
9 Yates	Y	Y	Y	Y	N	Y	Y	Y
10 Porter	N	Y	Y	N	N	Y	N	Y
11 Annunzio	Y	Y	Y	Y	Y	Y	Y	Y
12 Crane, P.	X	Y	N	N	Y	?	N	Y
13 McClory	N	Y	Y	N	Y	N	?	Y
14 Erlenborn	N	Y	Y	N	N	Y	N	Y
15 Corcoran	N	Y	Y	N	N	Y	N	Y
16 Martin	N	Y	Y	N	Y	N	Y	Y
17 O'Brien	N	?	Y	N	#	?	#	?
18 Michel	N	Y	Y	N	Y	Y	Y	Y
19 Railsback	N	Y	Y	N	N	Y	Y	Y
20 Findley	N	Y	Y	N	N	Y	Y	Y
21 Madigan	N	?	Y	N	N	Y	?	Y
22 Crane, D.	X	Y	N	N	N	Y	N	Y
23 Price	Y	Y	Y	Y	?	?	Y	Y
24 Simon	Y	Y	Y	Y	Y	Y	Y	Y
INDIANA								
1 Benjamin	N	Y	Y	Y	N	Y	N	Y
2 Fithian	Y	?	?	?	?	?	?	?
3 Hiler	N	Y	Y	N	N	Y	N	Y
4 Coats	N	Y	Y	N	N	Y	N	Y
5 Hillis	N	Y	Y	N	N	Y	Y	Y
6 Evans	Y	Y	Y	Y	Y	Y	?	?
7 Myers	Y	Y	Y	N	Y	Y	Y	Y
8 Deckard	N	Y	Y	N	N	Y	N	Y
9 Hamilton	N	Y	Y	N	N	Y	N	Y
10 Sharp	N	Y	Y	N	N	Y	N	Y
11 Jacobs	Y	N	Y	N	Y	Y	Y	Y
IOWA								
1 Leach	N	Y	Y	N	N	Y	N	Y
2 Tauke	N	Y	Y	N	N	Y	N	Y
3 Evans	N	N	Y	N	Y	Y	N	Y
4 Smith	N	Y	Y	N	Y	Y	N	Y
5 Harkin	N	Y	Y	Y	Y	Y	N	Y
6 Bedell	N	Y	Y	Y	Y	Y	Y	Y

Democrats   *Republicans*

	188	189	190	191	192	193	194	195
KANSAS								
1 ***Roberts***	N	?	Y	N	N	Y	N	Y
2 ***Jeffries***	N	Y	N	N	N	Y	N	Y
3 ***Winn***	N	Y	Y	N	N	Y	N	Y
4 Glickman	N	Y	Y	Y	N	Y	Y	Y
5 ***Whittaker***	N	Y	Y	N	N	Y	N	Y
KENTUCKY								
1 Hubbard	Y	Y	Y	N	N	Y	Y	Y
2 Natcher	Y	Y	Y	Y	N	Y	Y	Y
3 Mazzoli	Y	Y	Y	N	Y	Y	Y	Y
4 ***Snyder***	Y	Y	Y	N	N	Y	Y	Y
5 ***Rogers***	Y	Y	Y	N	N	Y	Y	Y
6 ***Hopkins***	Y	Y	Y	N	N	Y	Y	Y
7 Perkins	Y	Y	Y	Y	Y	Y	Y	Y
LOUISIANA								
1 ***Livingston***	N	Y	Y	N	Y	Y	Y	Y
2 Boggs	N	Y	Y	Y	N	Y	Y	Y
3 Tauzin	N	Y	Y	N	N	Y	Y	Y
4 Roemer	N	?	Y	N	N	Y	N	Y
5 Huckaby	N	Y	Y	N	Y	Y	Y	Y
6 ***Moore***	N	Y	Y	N	N	Y	Y	Y
7 Breaux	N	Y	Y	Y	N	Y	Y	Y
8 Long	N	?	?	?	?	?	Y	Y
MAINE								
1 ***Emery***	N	?	Y	N	N	Y	N	Y
2 ***Snowe***	Y	Y	Y	N	N	Y	N	Y
MARYLAND								
1 Dyson	N	Y	Y	Y	N	Y	Y	Y
2 Long	N	Y	Y	Y	Y	Y	Y	Y
3 Mikulski	N	Y	Y	Y	N	Y	Y	Y
4 ***Holt***	N	Y	Y	N	N	Y	Y	Y
5 Hoyer	N	Y	Y	Y	Y	Y	Y	Y
6 Byron	N	Y	Y	Y	N	Y	Y	Y
7 Mitchell	N	N	Y	Y	Y	Y	Y	N
8 Barnes	N	Y	Y	Y	Y	Y	N	Y
MASSACHUSETTS								
1 ***Conte***	N	Y	Y	Y	Y	Y	Y	Y
2 Boland	Y	Y	Y	Y	Y	?	Y	Y
3 Early	Y	Y	Y	Y	Y	Y	Y	Y
4 Frank	Y	Y	Y	Y	?	?	Y	Y
5 Shannon	Y	Y	Y	Y	Y	Y	Y	Y
6 Mavroules	Y	Y	Y	Y	N	Y	?	Y
7 Markey	Y	Y	Y	Y	Y	Y	Y	Y
8 O'Neill								
9 Moakley	Y	Y	Y	Y	Y	Y	Y	Y
10 ***Heckler***	Y	Y	Y	Y	Y	Y	Y	Y
11 Donnelly	Y	Y	Y	Y	Y	Y	N	Y
12 Studds	Y	Y	Y	Y	Y	Y	Y	N
MICHIGAN								
1 Conyers	Y	N	Y	Y	N	Y	N	N
2 ***Pursell***	N	Y	Y	Y	Y	Y	Y	N
3 Wolpe	N	Y	Y	Y	Y	Y	Y	Y
4 ***Siljander***	N	Y	Y	N	N	Y	N	Y
5 ***Sawyer***	Y	Y	Y	N	Y	Y	Y	Y
6 ***Dunn***	N	Y	Y	Y	N	Y	Y	Y
7 Kildee	N	Y	Y	Y	N	Y	Y	Y
8 Traxler	Y	Y	Y	Y	N	Y	Y	Y
9 ***Vander Jagt***	N	Y	Y	N	?	?	?	Y
10 Albosta	Y	Y	Y	Y	N	Y	Y	Y
11 ***Davis***	N	Y	Y	N	N	Y	Y	Y
12 Bonior	Y	Y	Y	Y	N	Y	Y	N
13 Crockett	?	?	?	#	X	?	?	?
14 Hertel	Y	Y	Y	Y	N	Y	N	Y
15 Ford	Y	Y	Y	Y	Y	Y	Y	?
16 Dingell	Y	Y	Y	Y	Y	Y	Y	Y
17 Brodhead	N	Y	Y	Y	Y	Y	Y	N
18 Blanchard	Y	Y	Y	Y	Y	Y	Y	Y
19 ***Broomfield***	Y	Y	Y	N	N	Y	N	Y
MINNESOTA								
1 ***Erdahl***	#	Y	Y	N	Y	Y	N	Y
2 ***Hagedorn***	N	Y	Y	N	N	Y	?	Y
3 ***Frenzel***	Y	Y	Y	N	N	Y	N	Y
4 Vento	Y	Y	Y	Y	Y	Y	Y	Y
5 Sabo	Y	N	Y	Y	Y	Y	Y	Y
6 ***Weber***	N	Y	Y	N	N	Y	N	Y
7 ***Stangeland***	Y	Y	Y	N	N	Y	N	Y
8 Oberstar	Y	Y	Y	Y	Y	Y	Y	Y
MISSISSIPPI								
1 Whitten	N	Y	Y	Y	Y	Y	Y	Y
2 Bowen	Y	Y	+	Y	N	Y	Y	Y
3 Montgomery	Y	Y	Y	Y	N	Y	?	Y
4 Dowdy	Y	Y	Y	Y	N	Y	Y	?
5 ***Lott***	N	Y	Y	N	N	Y	Y	Y
MISSOURI								
1 Clay	Y	?	?	?	Y	Y	Y	Y
2 Young	Y	Y	Y	Y	N	Y	Y	Y
3 Gephardt	N	Y	Y	Y	N	Y	N	Y

	188	189	190	191	192	193	194	195
4 Skelton	?	Y	Y	Y	N	Y	Y	Y
5 Bolling	N	Y	Y	Y	Y	Y	Y	Y
6 ***Coleman***	N	Y	Y	N	N	Y	N	Y
7 ***Taylor***	Y	?	Y	N	N	Y	N	Y
8 ***Bailey***	N	Y	Y	N	N	Y	N	Y
9 Volkmer	Y	Y	Y	Y	Y	Y	Y	Y
10 ***Emerson***	N	Y	Y	N	N	Y	N	Y
MONTANA								
1 Williams	N	?	Y	Y	Y	Y	Y	Y
2 ***Marlenee***	Y	Y	Y	N	N	Y	Y	Y
NEBRASKA								
1 ***Bereuter***	N	Y	Y	N	N	Y	Y	Y
2 ***Daub***	N	Y	Y	N	N	Y	Y	Y
3 ***Smith***	N	Y	Y	N	Y	Y	Y	Y
NEVADA								
AL Santini	?	Y	Y	N	?	?	Y	Y
NEW HAMPSHIRE								
1 D'Amours	N	Y	Y	Y	Y	Y	Y	?
2 ***Gregg***	N	Y	Y	N	N	Y	N	Y
NEW JERSEY								
1 Florio	#	Y	Y	Y	N	Y	?	?
2 Hughes	N	Y	Y	N	N	Y	N	Y
3 Howard	Y	Y	Y	Y	Y	Y	Y	Y
4 ***Smith***	N	Y	Y	Y	Y	Y	Y	Y
5 ***Fenwick***	Y	Y	Y	N	Y	Y	?	N
6 ***Forsythe***	N	N	Y	N	N	Y	Y	Y
7 ***Roukema***	Y	Y	Y	N	Y	Y	N	Y
8 Roe	Y	Y	Y	Y	N	Y	Y	Y
9 ***Hollenbeck***	Y	Y	?	Y	Y	Y	X	Y
10 Rodino	Y	Y	Y	Y	N	Y	Y	Y
11 Minish	Y	Y	Y	Y	Y	Y	Y	Y
12 ***Rinaldo***	Y	Y	Y	Y	N	Y	Y	Y
13 ***Courter***	Y	Y	Y	N	?	?	Y	Y
14 Guarini	Y	Y	Y	Y	Y	Y	Y	Y
15 Dwyer	Y	Y	Y	Y	Y	Y	Y	Y
NEW MEXICO								
1 ***Lujan***	N	?	?	?	?	?	?	?
2 ***Skeen***	N	?	Y	N	N	Y	Y	Y
NEW YORK								
1 ***Carney***	Y	Y	Y	Y	N	Y	Y	Y
2 Downey	Y	?	?	?	Y	Y	Y	N
3 ***Carman***	N	Y	Y	N	N	Y	N	Y
4 ***Lent***	N	Y	Y	Y	N	Y	Y	Y
5 ***McGrath***	N	Y	Y	Y	N	Y	?	Y
6 ***LeBoutillier***	Y	Y	N	N	Y	Y	Y	Y
7 Addabbo	Y	Y	Y	Y	Y	Y	Y	Y
8 Rosenthal	Y	Y	Y	Y	Y	Y	Y	Y
9 Ferraro	Y	Y	Y	Y	Y	Y	Y	Y
10 Biaggi	Y	?	?	#	?	?	?	?
11 Scheuer	Y	?	Y	Y	Y	Y	Y	Y
12 Chisholm	Y	?	Y	Y	Y	Y	Y	Y
13 Solarz	Y	Y	Y	Y	Y	Y	Y	Y
14 Richmond	#	Y	Y	Y	Y	Y	Y	N
15 Zeferetti	Y	Y	Y	Y	Y	Y	Y	Y
16 Schumer	Y	Y	Y	Y	Y	Y	Y	Y
17 ***Molinari***	Y	Y	Y	Y	Y	Y	N	Y
18 ***Green***	Y	Y	Y	Y	Y	Y	Y	Y
19 Rangel	Y	Y	Y	Y	Y	Y	Y	N
20 Weiss	Y	Y	Y	N	N	Y	Y	Y
21 Garcia	Y	?	Y	Y	Y	Y	?	N
22 Bingham	Y	Y	Y	Y	Y	Y	Y	N
23 Peyser	Y	Y	Y	Y	Y	Y	Y	Y
24 Ottinger	Y	?	+	+	+	+	Y	N
25 ***Fish***	Y	?	Y	N	Y	Y	Y	Y
26 ***Gilman***	Y	+	+	+	-	+	N	Y
27 McHugh	Y	Y	Y	Y	Y	Y	Y	Y
28 Stratton	Y	Y	Y	Y	N	Y	Y	Y
29 ***Solomon***	Y	Y	Y	N	N	Y	N	Y
30 ***Martin***	N	Y	Y	N	N	Y	Y	Y
31 ***Mitchell***	Y	Y	Y	Y	N	Y	Y	Y
32 ***Wortley***	N	Y	Y	N	Y	Y	Y	Y
33 ***Lee***	N	?	?	X	X	?	Y	Y
34 ***Horton***	Y	Y	Y	Y	N	Y	Y	Y
35 ***Conable***	N	Y	Y	N	N	Y	N	Y
36 LaFalce	Y	?	Y	Y	Y	Y	Y	Y
37 Nowak	Y	Y	Y	Y	Y	Y	Y	Y
38 ***Kemp***	Y	Y	Y	X	N	Y	Y	Y
39 Lundine	N	?	Y	Y	N	Y	Y	Y
NORTH CAROLINA								
1 Jones	?	Y	Y	Y	N	Y	Y	Y
2 Fountain	Y	Y	Y	N	N	Y	Y	Y
3 Whitley	Y	Y	Y	N	N	Y	Y	Y
4 Andrews	?	Y	Y	N	N	Y	Y	Y
5 Neal	Y	Y	Y	N	N	Y	Y	Y
6 ***Johnston***	C	Y	Y	N	?	+	N	Y
7 Rose	?	Y	Y	Y	Y	Y	Y	Y
8 Hefner	?	Y	Y	Y	Y	Y	Y	Y

	188	189	190	191	192	193	194	195
9 ***Martin***	Y	Y	Y	N	Y	Y	?	Y
10 ***Broyhill***	N	Y	Y	N	Y	Y	N	Y
11 ***Hendon***	Y	Y	Y	N	Y	Y	N	Y
NORTH DAKOTA								
AL Dorgan	Y	Y	Y	Y	N	Y	Y	Y
OHIO								
1 ***Gradison***	N	Y	Y	N	N	Y	N	Y
2 Luken	N	Y	Y	Y	N	Y	Y	Y
3 Hall	Y	Y	Y	Y	N	Y	Y	Y
4 ***Oxley***	N	?	Y	N	N	Y	N	Y
5 ***Latta***	X	Y	N	N	N	Y	Y	Y
6 ***McEwen***	N	Y	Y	N	N	Y	N	Y
7 ***Brown***	?	Y	Y	N	N	Y	N	Y
8 ***Kindness***	N	Y	Y	N	N	Y	N	Y
9 ***Weber***	Y	Y	Y	N	Y	Y	N	Y
10 ***Miller***	N	Y	Y	N	N	Y	N	N
11 ***Stanton***	Y	Y	Y	N	N	Y	Y	Y
12 Shamansky	#	Y	Y	Y	Y	Y	Y	Y
13 Pease	N	Y	Y	Y	Y	Y	Y	Y
14 Seiberling	N	Y	Y	Y	Y	Y	Y	Y
15 ***Wylie***	N	Y	Y	Y	N	Y	Y	Y
16 ***Regula***	Y	Y	Y	N	N	Y	Y	Y
17 ***Ashbrook***	Y	Y	N	N	N	Y	N	Y
18 Applegate	?	?	Y	N	N	Y	N	Y
19 ***Williams***	Y	Y	Y	Y	N	Y	Y	Y
20 Oakar	Y	Y	Y	Y	N	Y	Y	?
21 Stokes	Y	Y	Y	Y	N	Y	Y	Y
22 Eckart	N	Y	Y	Y	Y	Y	Y	Y
23 Mottl	Y	Y	Y	N	N	Y	N	Y
OKLAHOMA								
1 Jones	Y	Y	Y	Y	N	Y	N	Y
2 Synar	Y	Y	Y	Y	Y	Y	Y	Y
3 Watkins	Y	Y	Y	Y	N	Y	Y	Y
4 McCurdy	Y	Y	Y	Y	N	Y	Y	Y
5 ***Edwards***	Y	Y	Y	N	N	Y	Y	Y
6 English	Y	Y	Y	Y	Y	Y	Y	Y
OREGON								
1 AuCoin	N	?	?	?	?	?	?	?
2 ***Smith***	N	Y	N	N	N	Y	N	Y
3 Wyden	?	Y	Y	Y	Y	Y	N	Y
4 Weaver	?	Y	Y	N	Y	Y	N	N
PENNSYLVANIA								
1 Foglietta	N	?	?	?	?	?	Y	Y
2 Gray	Y	Y	Y	Y	N	Y	Y	Y
3 Smith	Y	Y	Y	Y	Y	Y	Y	Y
4 ***Dougherty***	N	?	Y	Y	N	?	Y	Y
5 ***Schulze***	N	Y	Y	N	N	Y	?	Y
6 Yatron	N	Y	Y	N	?	Y	Y	Y
7 Edgar	?	N	Y	Y	N	Y	Y	N
8 ***Coyne, J.***	N	Y	Y	N	Y	Y	N	Y
9 ***Shuster***	N	Y	Y	N	N	Y	N	Y
10 ***McDade***	N	Y	Y	Y	Y	Y	?	Y
11 ***Nelligan***	N	Y	Y	N	N	?	Y	Y
12 Murtha	Y	Y	Y	Y	?	?	Y	Y
13 ***Coughlin***	N	Y	Y	Y	N	Y	Y	Y
14 Coyne, W.	N	Y	Y	Y	Y	Y	Y	Y
15 ***Ritter***	N	Y	Y	Y	Y	Y	N	Y
16 ***Walker***	N	N	Y	N	N	Y	N	Y
17 Ertel	N	?	?	?	?	?	Y	Y
18 Walgren	N	Y	Y	Y	N	?	Y	Y
19 ***Goodling***	N	?	Y	N	N	Y	N	Y
20 Gaydos	?	?	Y	Y	Y	Y	Y	Y
21 Bailey	Y	Y	Y	Y	N	?	Y	Y
22 Murphy	Y	Y	Y	Y	Y	Y	N	Y
23 ***Clinger***	N	Y	Y	N	Y	Y	Y	Y
24 ***Marks***	N	Y	Y	Y	N	Y	Y	Y
25 Atkinson	N	Y	Y	N	N	Y	Y	Y
RHODE ISLAND								
1 St Germain	Y	Y	Y	Y	N	Y	Y	Y
2 ***Schneider***	N	P	Y	Y	Y	Y	Y	Y
SOUTH CAROLINA								
1 ***Hartnett***	Y	Y	Y	N	N	Y	?	Y
2 ***Spence***	Y	Y	Y	N	N	Y	Y	Y
3 Derrick	Y	Y	Y	Y	N	Y	Y	Y
4 ***Campbell***	?	Y	Y	N	N	Y	Y	?
5 Holland	?	Y	Y	N	N	Y	Y	Y
6 ***Napier***	Y	Y	Y	Y	N	Y	N	Y
SOUTH DAKOTA								
1 Daschle	N	Y	Y	Y	Y	Y	Y	Y
2 ***Roberts***	N	Y	Y	N	N	Y	N	Y
TENNESSEE								
1 ***Quillen***	Y	Y	Y	N	N	Y	Y	Y
2 ***Duncan***	Y	Y	Y	N	N	Y	Y	Y
3 Bouquard	Y	Y	Y	Y	Y	Y	Y	Y
4 Gore	Y	Y	Y	Y	Y	Y	Y	Y
5 Boner	Y	Y	Y	Y	Y	Y	?	Y
6 ***Beard***	N	Y	Y	N	N	Y	Y	Y

	188	189	190	191	192	193	194	195
7 Jones	Y	Y	Y	Y	Y	Y	Y	Y
8 Ford	Y	Y	Y	Y	N	Y	Y	Y
TEXAS								
1 Hall, S.	Y	Y	Y	N	N	Y	Y	Y
2 Wilson	Y	Y	Y	Y	N	Y	Y	Y
3 ***Collins***	Y	Y	N	N	N	Y	N	Y
4 Hall, R.	Y	Y	Y	N	N	Y	Y	Y
5 Mattox	Y	Y	Y	Y	Y	Y	N	Y
6 Gramm	Y	Y	Y	N	N	Y	N	Y
7 ***Archer***	Y	Y	N	N	Y	Y	Y	Y
8 ***Fields***	Y	Y	Y	N	N	Y	N	Y
9 Brooks	?	Y	Y	Y	N	Y	Y	Y
10 Pickle	Y	Y	Y	N	N	Y	X	Y
11 Leath	Y	Y	Y	N	N	Y	Y	Y
12 Wright	?	Y	Y	Y	Y	Y	Y	Y
13 Hightower	Y	Y	Y	Y	N	Y	Y	Y
14 Patman	Y	Y	Y	N	Y	Y	N	Y
15 de la Garza	Y	?	?	?	?	?	?	?
16 White	Y	Y	Y	Y	N	Y	Y	Y
17 Stenholm	Y	Y	Y	N	N	Y	N	Y
18 Leland	Y	?	?	#	N	Y	Y	N
19 Hance	Y	Y	Y	N	N	Y	Y	Y
20 Gonzalez	Y	Y	Y	Y	N	Y	Y	Y
21 ***Loeffler***	Y	Y	Y	N	N	Y	Y	Y
22 ***Paul***	Y	Y	N	N	N	Y	N	N
23 Kazen	Y	Y	Y	Y	N	Y	Y	Y
24 Frost	Y	Y	Y	Y	Y	Y	Y	Y
UTAH								
1 ***Hansen***	N	Y	N	N	Y	Y	N	Y
2 ***Marriott***	N	Y	Y	N	N	Y	+	+
VERMONT								
AL ***Jeffords***	N	Y	Y	Y	Y	Y	Y	Y
VIRGINIA								
1 ***Trible***	N	Y	Y	N	N	Y	Y	Y
2 ***Whitehurst***	Y	Y	Y	N	N	Y	Y	Y
3 ***Bliley***	N	Y	Y	N	N	Y	Y	Y
4 ***Daniel, R.***	Y	Y	Y	N	N	Y	Y	Y
5 Daniel, D.	N	Y	Y	N	N	Y	N	Y
6 ***Butler***	N	Y	Y	N	Y	Y	N	Y
7 ***Robinson***	N	Y	Y	N	N	Y	Y	Y
8 ***Parris***	N	Y	Y	N	N	Y	Y	Y
9 ***Wampler***	Y	Y	Y	N	N	Y	Y	Y
10 ***Wolf***	N	Y	Y	N	N	Y	Y	Y
WASHINGTON								
1 ***Pritchard***	N	Y	Y	N	Y	Y	Y	Y
2 Swift	N	Y	Y	Y	Y	Y	Y	Y
3 Bonker	N	Y	Y	Y	Y	Y	Y	Y
4 ***Morrison***	N	Y	Y	N	Y	Y	Y	Y
5 Foley	Y	Y	Y	Y	Y	Y	Y	Y
6 Dicks	Y	Y	Y	Y	Y	Y	Y	Y
7 Lowry	N	Y	Y	Y	Y	Y	Y	Y
WEST VIRGINIA								
1 Mollohan	N	Y	?	Y	N	Y	Y	Y
2 ***Benedict***	N	Y	Y	N	N	Y	Y	Y
3 ***Staton***	Y	Y	Y	N	N	Y	Y	Y
4 Rahall	N	Y	Y	Y	N	Y	Y	Y
WISCONSIN								
1 Aspin	Y	Y	Y	Y	Y	Y	Y	Y
2 Kastenmeier	Y	Y	Y	Y	Y	Y	Y	N
3 ***Gunderson***	N	Y	Y	N	N	Y	N	Y
4 Zablocki	Y	Y	Y	Y	Y	Y	Y	Y
5 Reuss	N	Y	Y	Y	Y	Y	Y	Y
6 ***Petri***	N	Y	Y	N	N	Y	N	Y
7 Obey	Y	Y	Y	Y	Y	Y	Y	Y
8 ***Roth***	Y	Y	Y	N	N	Y	N	Y
9 ***Sensenbrenner***	Y	Y	Y	N	Y	Y	N	Y
WYOMING								
AL ***Cheney***	N	Y	Y	N	Y	Y	?	Y

Democrats ***Republicans***

196. HR 3518. State Department Authorization. Adoption of the rule (H Res 182) providing for House floor consideration of the bill. Adopted 385-5: R 169-3; D 216-2 (ND 145-1, SD 71-1), Sept. 17, 1981.

197. HR 3518. State Department Authorization. Fascell, D-Fla., motion that the House resolve itself into the Committee of the Whole for consideration of the bill. Motion agreed to 379-3: R 171-1; D 208-2 (ND 137-2, SD 71-0), Sept. 17, 1981.

198. HR 3518. State Department Authorization. Beard, R-Tenn., amendment to prohibit U.S. contributions to the United Nations Educational, Scientific and Cultural Organization (UNESCO) if that organization implements any policy or procedure to license journalists or their publications, censor or otherwise restrict the free flow of information within or among countries, or impose mandatory codes of journalistic practice or ethics. Adopted 372-19: R 171-0; D 201-19 (ND 133-17, SD 68-2), Sept. 17, 1981. A "yea" was a vote supporting the president's position.

199. HR 3518. State Department Authorization. Passage of the bill to authorize fiscal 1982 and 1983 programs of the State Department, the International Communication Agency and the Board for International Broadcasting. Rejected 165-226: R 40-131; D 125-95 (ND 100-49; SD 25-46), Sept. 17, 1981.

200. H J Res 220. Honorary U.S. Citizenship for Raoul Wallenberg. Rodino, D-N.J., motion that the House suspend the rules and pass the joint resolution, as amended, to proclaim as an honorary U.S. citizen the Swedish diplomat Raoul Wallenberg, who helped Hungarian Jews escape Nazi extermination during World War II and was taken prisoner by the Soviet Union after the war. Motion agreed to 396-2: R 178-2; D 218-0 (ND 145-0, SD 73-0), Sept. 22, 1981. A two-thirds majority vote (266 in this case) is required for passage under suspension of the rules.

201. H Con Res 183. National Rugby Team of South Africa. Zablocki, D-Wis., motion that the House suspend the rules and adopt the concurrent resolution stating the sense of Congress that the Springbok National Rugby Team of South Africa, on tour in the United States, should not play rugby in the United States. Motion rejected 201-198: R 31-150: D 170-48 (ND 133-12, SD 37-36), Sept. 22, 1981. A two thirds majority vote (266 in this case) is required for adoption under suspension of the rules.

202. HR 1953. Office of Environmental Quality Reauthorization. Jones, D-N.C., motion that the House suspend the rules and pass the bill, as amended, to authorize $44,000 per year for the Council on Environmental Quality and its staff under the Environmental Quality Improvement Act of 1970 in each of fiscal years 1982, 1983 and 1984. Motion agreed to 360-42: R 151-30; D 209-12 (ND 142-5, SD 67-7), Sept. 22, 1981. A two-thirds majority vote (268 in this case) is required for passage under suspension of the rules.

203. HR 4522. District of Columbia Appropriation, Fiscal 1982. Parris, R-Va., amendment to ban the use of personnel lotteries to hire District of Columbia police officers and fire fighters. Adopted 305-96: R 182-1; D 123-95 (ND 60-84; SD 63-11), Sept. 22, 1981.

KEY

Y	Voted for (yea).
#	Paired for.
+	Announced for.
N	Voted against (nay).
X	Paired against.
-	Announced against.
P	Voted "present".
C	Voted "present" to avoid possible conflict of interest.
?	Did not vote or otherwise make a position known.

	196	197	198	199	200	201	202	203
ALABAMA								
1 *Edwards*	Y	?	Y	Y	?	?	Y	Y
2 *Dickinson*	Y	?	Y	N	Y	N	N	Y
3 Nichols	Y	Y	Y	Y	#	X	?	#
4 Bevill	Y	Y	Y	N	Y	N	Y	Y
5 Flippo	Y	Y	Y	N	Y	N	Y	Y
6 *Smith*	?	Y	Y	N	Y	N	Y	Y
7 Shelby	Y	Y	Y	N	Y	N	N	Y
ALASKA								
AL *Young*	?	?	?	?	Y	N	Y	Y
ARIZONA								
1 *Rhodes*	Y	Y	Y	Y	Y	N	Y	Y
2 Udall	Y	Y	Y	N	Y	Y	Y	?
3 Stump	Y	Y	Y	N	Y	N	N	Y
4 *Rudd*	?	?	?	X	Y	N	N	Y
ARKANSAS								
1 Alexander	Y	Y	Y	N	Y	Y	Y	P
2 *Bethune*	Y	Y	Y	N	Y	N	Y	Y
3 *Hammerschmidt*	Y	Y	Y	N	Y	N	Y	Y
4 Anthony	Y	Y	Y	N	Y	N	Y	?
CALIFORNIA								
1 *Chappie*	Y	Y	Y	N	Y	N	Y	Y
2 *Clausen*	Y	Y	Y	N	?	?	?	Y
3 Matsui	Y	Y	Y	N	Y	Y	Y	N
4 Fazio	Y	Y	Y	N	Y	Y	Y	Y
5 Burton, J.	?	?	Y	Y	+	?	?	?
6 Burton, P.	?	?	?	?	Y	Y	Y	N
7 Miller	Y	Y	Y	X	Y	Y	Y	N
8 Dellums	Y	N	Y	Y	?	?	?	?
9 Stark	Y	Y	Y	N	Y	Y	Y	N
10 Edwards	Y	Y	N	Y	Y	Y	Y	N
11 Lantos	Y	Y	Y	Y	Y	Y	Y	N
12 *McCloskey*	?	?	?	?	Y	Y	Y	Y
13 Mineta	Y	Y	Y	Y	Y	Y	Y	N
14 *Shumway*	Y	Y	Y	N	Y	N	N	Y
15 Coelho	Y	Y	#	N	Y	Y	Y	N
16 Panetta	Y	Y	Y	N	Y	Y	Y	N
17 *Pashayan*	Y	Y	Y	N	?	?	?	?
18 *Thomas*	Y	Y	Y	N	Y	N	Y	Y
19 *Lagomarsino*	Y	Y	Y	N	Y	N	Y	Y
20 *Goldwater*	?	?	?	?	Y	N	Y	Y
21 *Fiedler*	Y	Y	Y	N	Y	N	Y	Y
22 *Moorhead*	Y	Y	Y	N	Y	N	N	Y
23 Beilenson	Y	Y	N	Y	Y	Y	Y	N
24 Waxman	Y	Y	Y	Y	Y	Y	Y	N
25 Roybal	?	?	Y	Y	Y	Y	Y	N
26 *Rousselot*	Y	Y	Y	N	Y	N	N	Y
27 *Dornan*	Y	Y	Y	Y	?	?	?	?
28 Dixon	Y	Y	Y	Y	Y	Y	Y	N
29 Hawkins	Y	Y	N	Y	Y	Y	Y	N
30 Danielson	Y	Y	Y	Y	X	+	+	?
31 Dymally	Y	?	N	Y	Y	Y	Y	N
32 Anderson	Y	Y	Y	N	Y	Y	Y	Y
33 *Grisham*	Y	Y	Y	N	Y	N	N	Y
34 *Lungren*	Y	Y	Y	N	Y	N	N	Y
35 *Dreier*	Y	Y	Y	N	Y	N	Y	Y
36 Brown	Y	N	Y	Y	Y	Y	Y	N
37 *Lewis*	Y	Y	Y	N	Y	Y	Y	Y
38 Patterson	Y	Y	N	Y	Y	Y	Y	N
39 *Dannemeyer*	Y	Y	Y	N	Y	N	N	Y
40 *Badham*	Y	Y	Y	N	Y	N	N	Y
41 *Lowery*	Y	Y	Y	N	Y	N	Y	Y
42 *Hunter*	Y	Y	Y	N	Y	N	Y	Y
43 *Burgener*	?	?	?	?	Y	N	Y	Y
COLORADO								
1 Schroeder	Y	Y	Y	N	Y	Y	Y	N
2 Wirth	Y	Y	Y	N	?	?	?	?
3 Kogovsek	Y	Y	Y	N	Y	Y	Y	N
4 *Brown*	N	Y	N	Y	N	Y	Y	Y

	196	197	198	199	200	201	202	203
5 *Kramer*	Y	Y	?	?	Y	N	Y	Y
CONNECTICUT								
1 Vacancy								
2 Gejdenson	Y	Y	Y	Y	Y	Y	Y	N
3 *DeNardis*	Y	Y	Y	Y	Y	Y	Y	Y
4 *McKinney*	?	Y	Y	Y	Y	N	Y	Y
5 Ratchford	Y	Y	Y	N	Y	Y	Y	Y
6 Moffett	Y	Y	?	N	?	?	?	X
DELAWARE								
AL *Evans*	Y	Y	Y	Y	Y	N	Y	Y
FLORIDA								
1 Hutto	Y	?	Y	N	Y	N	Y	Y
2 Fuqua	Y	Y	Y	Y	Y	Y	Y	Y
3 Bennett	Y	Y	Y	N	Y	N	Y	Y
4 Chappell	Y	Y	Y	?	Y	N	Y	Y
5 *McCollum*	Y	Y	Y	N	Y	N	N	Y
6 *Young*	Y	Y	Y	N	Y	N	N	Y
7 Gibbons	Y	Y	Y	?	?	?	Y	Y
8 Ireland	Y	Y	Y	N	Y	N	Y	Y
9 Nelson	Y	Y	Y	N	Y	Y	Y	Y
10 *Bafalis*	Y	Y	N	Y	N	N	Y	Y
11 Mica	Y	Y	Y	Y	Y	Y	Y	Y
12 *Shaw*	Y	Y	Y	N	Y	N	Y	Y
13 Lehman	Y	Y	?	Y	Y	Y	Y	N
14 Pepper	?	?	?	#	Y	Y	Y	N
15 Fascell	Y	Y	Y	Y	Y	Y	Y	N
GEORGIA								
1 Ginn	?	?	?	?	Y	Y	Y	Y
2 Hatcher	Y	Y	Y	N	Y	N	Y	Y
3 Brinkley	Y	Y	Y	N	Y	N	Y	Y
4 Levitas	Y	Y	Y	N	Y	Y	Y	Y
5 Fowler	Y	Y	Y	N	Y	Y	Y	Y
6 *Gingrich*	Y	Y	Y	N	Y	N	Y	Y
7 McDonald	N	Y	N	N	N	N	Y	Y
8 Evans	Y	Y	N	?	?	?	?	?
9 Jenkins	?	Y	N	Y	N	Y	Y	Y
10 Barnard	?	?	?	?	Y	N	Y	Y
HAWAII								
1 Heftel	Y	Y	Y	Y	Y	Y	Y	Y
2 Akaka	Y	Y	Y	Y	Y	Y	Y	Y
IDAHO								
1 *Craig*	?	?	?	?	Y	N	N	Y
2 *Hansen*	Y	Y	Y	N	Y	N	N	Y
ILLINOIS								
1 Washington	Y	Y	Y	Y	Y	Y	Y	N
2 Savage	?	?	?	?	?	?	?	N
3 Russo	Y	Y	Y	Y	Y	Y	Y	N
4 *Derwinski*	Y	Y	Y	?	?	?	?	Y
5 Fary	Y	Y	Y	Y	Y	Y	Y	#
6 *Hyde*	Y	Y	Y	N	N	N	N	Y
7 Collins	Y	Y	Y	#	#	?	?	X
8 Rostenkowski	?	?	?	?	Y	Y	Y	Y
9 Yates	Y	Y	Y	Y	Y	Y	Y	N
10 *Porter*	Y	Y	Y	Y	Y	Y	Y	Y
11 Annunzio	Y	Y	Y	Y	Y	Y	Y	N
12 *Crane, P.*	Y	Y	N	N	N	N	N	Y
13 *McClory*	Y	Y	Y	Y	Y	N	Y	Y
14 *Erlenborn*	Y	?	Y	N	Y	N	Y	Y
15 *Corcoran*	Y	Y	Y	N	Y	N	Y	Y
16 *Martin*	Y	Y	Y	N	Y	N	Y	Y
17 *O'Brien*	?	?	?	?	Y	N	Y	Y
18 *Michel*	?	Y	Y	N	Y	N	Y	Y
19 *Railsback*	Y	Y	Y	N	Y	N	Y	Y
20 *Findley*	Y	Y	Y	N	Y	N	Y	Y
21 *Madigan*	Y	Y	Y	N	Y	N	Y	Y
22 *Crane, D.*	Y	Y	?	?	N	N	N	Y
23 *Price*	Y	Y	Y	Y	Y	Y	Y	Y
24 Simon	Y	Y	Y	?	?	?	?	Y
INDIANA								
1 Benjamin	Y	Y	Y	Y	Y	Y	Y	N
2 Fithian	?	?	Y	N	Y	N	Y	Y
3 *Hiler*	Y	Y	N	Y	N	N	Y	Y
4 *Coats*	Y	Y	Y	N	Y	N	Y	Y
5 *Hillis*	Y	Y	Y	Y	Y	N	Y	Y
6 Evans	Y	Y	Y	N	Y	N	N	N
7 *Myers*	Y	Y	Y	N	Y	N	N	Y
8 *Deckard*	Y	Y	Y	N	Y	N	N	Y
9 Hamilton	Y	Y	Y	N	Y	N	Y	Y
10 Sharp	Y	Y	Y	N	Y	N	Y	Y
11 Jacobs	Y	Y	N	Y	N	Y	Y	N
IOWA								
1 *Leach*	Y	Y	Y	N	Y	Y	Y	Y
2 *Tauke*	Y	Y	Y	N	Y	Y	Y	Y
3 *Evans*	Y	Y	?	?	Y	Y	Y	Y
4 Smith	Y	Y	Y	N	Y	Y	Y	Y
5 Harkin	Y	Y	N	Y	N	Y	?	N
6 Bedell	Y	Y	Y	Y	Y	Y	Y	Y

Democrats   *Republicans*

Corresponding to Congressional Record Votes 208, 209, 210, 211, 212, 213, 214, 215

	196	197	198	199	200	201	202	203
KANSAS								
1 *Roberts*	Y	Y	Y	N	Y	N	Y	Y
2 *Jeffries*	Y	Y	Y	N	Y	N	Y	Y
3 *Winn*	Y	Y	Y	Y	Y	N	Y	Y
4 Glickman	Y	Y	Y	N	Y	Y	Y	Y
5 *Whittaker*	Y	Y	Y	N	Y	N	Y	Y
KENTUCKY								
1 Hubbard	Y	Y	Y	N	Y	N	Y	Y
2 Natcher	Y	Y	Y	Y	Y	N	Y	Y
3 Mazzoli	Y	Y	Y	N	Y	N	Y	Y
4 *Snyder*	Y	Y	Y	N	Y	N	Y	Y
5 *Rogers*	Y	Y	Y	N	Y	N	Y	Y
6 *Hopkins*	Y	Y	Y	N	Y	N	Y	Y
7 Perkins	Y	Y	Y	N	Y	N	Y	Y
LOUISIANA								
1 *Livingston*	Y	Y	Y	N	Y	N	Y	Y
2 Boggs	Y	Y	Y	Y	Y	Y	?	N
3 Tauzin	Y	Y	Y	N	Y	Y	Y	Y
4 Roemer	Y	Y	Y	N	Y	Y	Y	Y
5 Huckaby	Y	Y	Y	N	Y	N	Y	Y
6 *Moore*	Y	Y	Y	N	Y	N	Y	Y
7 Breaux	Y	Y	Y	N	Y	Y	Y	Y
8 Long	Y	Y	Y	Y	Y	Y	Y	N
MAINE								
1 *Emery*	Y	Y	Y	N	Y	Y	Y	Y
2 *Snowe*	Y	Y	Y	N	Y	Y	Y	Y
MARYLAND								
1 Dyson	Y	Y	Y	N	Y	Y	Y	Y
2 Long	Y	Y	Y	Y	Y	Y	Y	Y
3 Mikulski	Y	Y	Y	Y	Y	Y	Y	N
4 *Holt*	Y	N	Y	N	?	?	?	?
5 Hoyer	Y	Y	Y	Y	Y	Y	Y	Y
6 Byron	?	?	?	N	Y	Y	Y	Y
7 Mitchell	Y	N	N	Y	Y	Y	Y	N
8 Barnes	Y	Y	Y	Y	Y	Y	Y	Y
MASSACHUSETTS								
1 *Conte*	Y	Y	Y	Y	Y	N	Y	Y
2 Boland	Y	Y	Y	#	Y	Y	Y	Y
3 Early	Y	Y	Y	?	Y	Y	Y	Y
4 Frank	Y	Y	Y	Y	Y	Y	Y	N
5 Shannon	Y	Y	Y	Y	Y	Y	Y	Y
6 Mavroules	Y	Y	Y	Y	Y	Y	Y	N
7 Markey	Y	Y	Y	Y	Y	Y	Y	N
8 O'Neill								
9 Moakley	Y	?	Y	N	Y	Y	Y	?
10 *Heckler*	?	Y	Y	Y	Y	Y	Y	Y
11 Donnelly	Y	Y	Y	N	Y	Y	Y	N
12 Studds	Y	Y	Y	Y	Y	Y	Y	N
MICHIGAN								
1 Conyers	N	N	N	N	Y	Y	Y	N
2 *Pursell*	Y	Y	Y	N	Y	Y	?	Y
3 Wolpe	Y	Y	Y	Y	Y	Y	Y	N
4 *Siljander*	Y	Y	Y	N	Y	N	Y	Y
5 *Sawyer*	Y	Y	?	?	Y	N	Y	Y
6 *Dunn*	Y	Y	Y	N	Y	N	N	Y
7 Kildee	Y	Y	Y	Y	Y	Y	Y	N
8 Traxler	Y	Y	Y	Y	Y	Y	Y	N
9 *Vander Jagt*	Y	?	Y	Y	Y	N	Y	Y
10 Albosta	Y	Y	Y	N	Y	Y	Y	Y
11 *Davis*	Y	Y	Y	Y	Y	N	Y	Y
12 Bonior	Y	Y	Y	Y	Y	Y	Y	N
13 Crockett	?	?	X	#	?	Y	Y	N
14 Hertel	Y	Y	Y	Y	Y	Y	Y	N
15 Ford	?	Y	Y	Y	?	?	?	?
16 Dingell	Y	Y	Y	?	Y	?	Y	N
17 Brodhead	Y	Y	N	Y	Y	Y	Y	N
18 Blanchard	Y	Y	Y	Y	?	?	Y	N
19 *Broomfield*	Y	Y	Y	Y	Y	N	N	Y
MINNESOTA								
1 *Erdahl*	Y	Y	Y	Y	Y	Y	Y	Y
2 *Hagedorn*	Y	Y	Y	Y	Y	N	Y	Y
3 *Frenzel*	Y	Y	?	N	Y	N	Y	Y
4 Vento	Y	Y	Y	Y	Y	Y	Y	Y
5 Sabo	Y	Y	Y	Y	Y	Y	Y	N
6 *Weber*	Y	Y	Y	N	Y	N	Y	Y
7 *Stangeland*	Y	Y	Y	N	Y	N	Y	Y
8 Oberstar	Y	Y	Y	Y	Y	Y	Y	N
MISSISSIPPI								
1 Whitten	Y	Y	Y	Y	Y	N	Y	Y
2 Bowen	Y	Y	Y	Y	Y	N	Y	Y
3 Montgomery	Y	Y	Y	N	Y	N	N	Y
4 Dowdy	Y	Y	Y	N	Y	N	Y	Y
5 *Lott*	Y	?	Y	N	Y	N	Y	Y
MISSOURI								
1 Clay	?	?	N	Y	Y	Y	Y	N
2 Young	?	?	Y	Y	Y	Y	Y	Y
3 Gephardt	Y	Y	Y	N	Y	Y	Y	Y
4 Skelton	Y	Y	Y	N	Y	N	Y	?
5 Bolling	?	Y	N	Y	?	?	?	?
6 *Coleman*	Y	Y	Y	Y	Y	N	Y	Y
7 *Taylor*	Y	Y	Y	N	Y	N	Y	Y
8 *Bailey*	Y	Y	Y	N	Y	N	Y	Y
9 Volkmer	Y	Y	Y	N	Y	N	Y	Y
10 *Emerson*	Y	Y	Y	N	Y	N	Y	Y
MONTANA								
1 Williams	Y	?	Y	N	Y	Y	Y	N
2 *Marlenee*	Y	Y	Y	N	Y	N	Y	Y
NEBRASKA								
1 *Bereuter*	Y	Y	Y	N	Y	N	Y	Y
2 *Daub*	?	?	Y	N	Y	N	Y	Y
3 *Smith*	Y	Y	Y	N	Y	N	Y	Y
NEVADA								
AL Santini	?	?	?	#	Y	N	Y	Y
NEW HAMPSHIRE								
1 D'Amours	Y	Y	Y	N	Y	Y	Y	Y
2 *Gregg*	Y	Y	Y	N	Y	N	N	Y
NEW JERSEY								
1 Florio	Y	?	Y	?	Y	Y	Y	Y
2 Hughes	Y	Y	Y	N	Y	Y	Y	Y
3 Howard	Y	Y	Y	Y	Y	Y	Y	Y
4 *Smith*	Y	Y	Y	Y	Y	N	Y	Y
5 *Fenwick*	Y	Y	Y	Y	Y	Y	Y	Y
6 *Forsythe*	Y	Y	Y	Y	Y	N	Y	Y
7 *Roukema*	Y	Y	Y	N	Y	N	Y	Y
8 Roe	Y	Y	Y	N	Y	Y	Y	?
9 *Hollenbeck*	Y	Y	?	?	Y	Y	Y	Y
10 Rodino	Y	Y	Y	Y	Y	Y	Y	N
11 Minish	Y	Y	Y	Y	Y	Y	Y	Y
12 *Rinaldo*	Y	Y	Y	N	Y	Y	Y	Y
13 *Courter*	Y	Y	Y	N	Y	N	Y	Y
14 Guarini	Y	Y	Y	N	Y	Y	Y	N
15 Dwyer	Y	Y	Y	Y	Y	Y	Y	N
NEW MEXICO								
1 *Lujan*	?	?	?	?	Y	N	Y	Y
2 *Skeen*	Y	Y	Y	N	Y	N	Y	Y
NEW YORK								
1 *Carney*	Y	Y	Y	N	Y	N	Y	Y
2 Downey	Y	Y	Y	N	+	+	Y	N
3 *Carman*	Y	Y	Y	N	Y	N	Y	Y
4 *Lent*	Y	Y	Y	Y	Y	Y	Y	Y
5 *McGrath*	Y	Y	Y	N	Y	Y	Y	Y
6 *LeBoutillier*	Y	Y	Y	Y	Y	Y	Y	Y
7 Addabbo	Y	Y	Y	Y	?	?	?	?
8 Rosenthal	?	?	Y	Y	Y	Y	?	?
9 Ferraro	Y	Y	Y	N	Y	Y	Y	Y
10 Biaggi	Y	Y	?	Y	?	?	?	?
11 Scheuer	Y	Y	?	?	Y	Y	Y	Y
12 Chisholm	Y	?	?	Y	Y	Y	Y	N
13 Solarz	Y	Y	Y	Y	Y	Y	Y	N
14 Richmond	Y	Y	N	Y	Y	Y	Y	N
15 Zeferetti	Y	Y	Y	Y	?	?	?	?
16 Schumer	Y	Y	Y	Y	Y	Y	Y	Y
17 *Molinari*	Y	Y	Y	N	Y	N	Y	Y
18 *Green*	Y	Y	Y	Y	Y	Y	Y	N
19 Rangel	?	?	N	N	Y	Y	Y	N
20 Weiss	?	?	Y	Y	Y	Y	Y	N
21 Garcia	Y	Y	Y	Y	+	#	+	N
22 Bingham	Y	Y	Y	Y	Y	Y	Y	N
23 Peyser	Y	Y	Y	Y	Y	Y	Y	N
24 Ottinger	Y	P	Y	Y	Y	Y	Y	N
25 *Fish*	Y	Y	Y	Y	Y	Y	Y	Y
26 *Gilman*	Y	Y	Y	Y	Y	Y	Y	Y
27 McHugh	Y	Y	Y	Y	Y	Y	Y	N
28 Stratton	Y	Y	Y	Y	Y	N	Y	Y
29 *Solomon*	Y	Y	Y	N	Y	N	N	Y
30 *Martin*	Y	Y	Y	?	Y	N	Y	Y
31 *Mitchell*	Y	Y	Y	Y	Y	N	Y	Y
32 *Wortley*	Y	Y	Y	N	Y	N	Y	Y
33 *Lee*	Y	Y	Y	N	Y	N	Y	Y
34 *Horton*	Y	Y	?	?	?	?	?	?
35 *Conable*	Y	Y	Y	N	Y	Y	Y	Y
36 LaFalce	Y	Y	Y	Y	Y	Y	Y	Y
37 Nowak	Y	Y	Y	Y	Y	Y	Y	N
38 *Kemp*	Y	Y	Y	N	Y	N	Y	Y
39 Lundine	Y	?	Y	Y	Y	Y	Y	N
NORTH CAROLINA								
1 Jones	Y	Y	Y	Y	Y	Y	Y	Y
2 Fountain	Y	Y	Y	N	Y	N	Y	Y
3 Whitley	Y	Y	Y	N	Y	Y	Y	Y
4 Andrews	Y	Y	Y	N	Y	Y	Y	Y
5 Neal	Y	Y	Y	N	Y	Y	Y	Y
6 *Johnston*	Y	Y	Y	N	Y	N	N	Y
7 Rose	Y	Y	Y	N	Y	Y	Y	Y
8 Hefner	Y	Y	Y	N	Y	Y	Y	Y
9 *Martin*	Y	Y	Y	N	Y	N	Y	Y
10 *Broyhill*	Y	Y	Y	N	Y	N	Y	Y
11 *Hendon*	Y	Y	Y	N	Y	N	Y	Y
NORTH DAKOTA								
AL Dorgan	Y	Y	Y	Y	Y	Y	Y	N
OHIO								
1 *Gradison*	Y	Y	Y	N	Y	N	Y	Y
2 Luken	Y	Y	Y	N	Y	Y	Y	Y
3 Hall	Y	Y	Y	Y	Y	Y	Y	Y
4 *Oxley*	Y	Y	Y	N	Y	N	Y	Y
5 *Latta*	Y	Y	Y	N	?	?	Y	Y
6 *McEwen*	Y	Y	Y	N	Y	N	Y	Y
7 *Brown*	Y	Y	Y	N	Y	Y	Y	Y
8 *Kindness*	Y	Y	Y	N	Y	N	Y	Y
9 *Weber*	Y	Y	Y	N	Y	N	Y	Y
10 *Miller*	Y	Y	Y	N	Y	N	Y	Y
11 *Stanton*	?	?	?	Y	Y	N	Y	Y
12 Shamansky	Y	Y	Y	Y	Y	Y	Y	Y
13 Pease	Y	Y	Y	Y	Y	Y	Y	N
14 Seiberling	Y	Y	Y	Y	Y	Y	Y	N
15 *Wylie*	Y	Y	Y	N	Y	N	Y	Y
16 *Regula*	Y	Y	Y	Y	Y	N	Y	Y
17 *Ashbrook*	Y	Y	Y	N	N	N	N	Y
18 Applegate	Y	Y	Y	N	Y	N	N	Y
19 *Williams*	Y	Y	Y	N	Y	N	Y	Y
20 Oakar	Y	Y	Y	?	Y	Y	Y	N
21 Stokes	Y	Y	N	Y	Y	Y	Y	N
22 Eckart	Y	Y	Y	N	Y	Y	Y	N
23 Mottl	Y	Y	Y	X	Y	N	N	Y
OKLAHOMA								
1 Jones	Y	Y	Y	N	Y	Y	Y	Y
2 Synar	Y	Y	Y	N	Y	Y	Y	Y
3 Watkins	Y	Y	Y	N	Y	N	N	Y
4 McCurdy	Y	Y	Y	N	Y	?	Y	Y
5 *Edwards*	Y	Y	Y	N	Y	N	N	Y
6 English	Y	Y	Y	N	Y	N	Y	Y
OREGON								
1 AuCoin	Y	Y	Y	N	Y	Y	Y	N
2 *Smith*	Y	Y	Y	N	Y	N	N	Y
3 Wyden	Y	Y	Y	N	Y	Y	Y	N
4 Weaver	Y	Y	Y	N	Y	Y	Y	N
PENNSYLVANIA								
1 Foglietta	Y	Y	Y	Y	Y	Y	Y	N
2 Gray	Y	Y	N	Y	Y	Y	Y	?
3 Smith	Y	Y	Y	Y	Y	Y	Y	Y
4 *Dougherty*	?	?	?	?	?	?	?	?
5 *Schulze*	Y	Y	Y	N	Y	N	Y	Y
6 Yatron	Y	Y	Y	Y	Y	Y	Y	Y
7 Edgar	Y	Y	N	Y	Y	Y	Y	N
8 *Coyne, J.*	Y	Y	Y	N	Y	Y	Y	Y
9 *Shuster*	Y	Y	Y	N	Y	N	Y	Y
10 *McDade*	Y	Y	Y	N	Y	N	Y	Y
11 *Nelligan*	Y	Y	Y	N	Y	N	?	Y
12 Murtha	Y	Y	Y	Y	Y	Y	N	Y
13 *Coughlin*	?	?	?	?	Y	Y	Y	Y
14 Coyne, W.	Y	Y	Y	Y	Y	Y	Y	N
15 *Ritter*	Y	Y	Y	N	Y	N	Y	Y
16 *Walker*	N	Y	Y	N	Y	N	N	Y
17 Ertel	Y	Y	Y	Y	Y	Y	Y	Y
18 Walgren	Y	Y	Y	Y	Y	Y	Y	N
19 *Goodling*	Y	Y	Y	N	Y	Y	N	?
20 Gaydos	Y	Y	Y	N	Y	N	Y	Y
21 Bailey	Y	Y	Y	N	Y	Y	Y	N
22 Murphy	Y	Y	Y	N	Y	N	Y	Y
23 *Clinger*	Y	Y	Y	Y	Y	N	Y	Y
24 *Marks*	Y	Y	Y	Y	Y	Y	Y	Y
25 Atkinson	Y	Y	Y	N	Y	Y	Y	Y
RHODE ISLAND								
1 St Germain	Y	Y	?	?	Y	Y	Y	Y
2 *Schneider*	?	?	Y	N	Y	Y	Y	Y
SOUTH CAROLINA								
1 *Hartnett*	Y	Y	Y	N	Y	N	Y	Y
2 *Spence*	Y	Y	Y	N	Y	N	Y	Y
3 Derrick	Y	Y	Y	Y	Y	Y	Y	Y
4 *Campbell*	Y	Y	Y	N	Y	N	Y	Y
5 Holland	Y	Y	?	?	Y	Y	?	Y
6 *Napier*	Y	Y	Y	N	Y	N	Y	Y
SOUTH DAKOTA								
1 Daschle	Y	?	Y	Y	Y	Y	Y	Y
2 *Roberts*	Y	Y	Y	N	Y	N	N	Y
TENNESSEE								
1 *Quillen*	Y	Y	?	X	Y	N	Y	Y
2 *Duncan*	Y	Y	Y	N	Y	N	Y	Y
3 Bouquard	Y	Y	Y	N	Y	Y	Y	Y
4 Gore	Y	Y	Y	Y	Y	Y	Y	Y
5 Boner	Y	Y	Y	N	Y	Y	Y	Y
6 *Beard*	Y	Y	Y	?	Y	N	Y	Y
7 Jones	Y	Y	Y	N	?	?	?	Y
8 Ford	Y	Y	N	Y	Y	Y	Y	N
TEXAS								
1 Hall, S.	Y	Y	?	N	Y	Y	Y	+
2 Wilson	Y	Y	Y	?	Y	N	Y	Y
3 *Collins*	Y	Y	Y	N	Y	N	N	Y
4 Hall, R.	?	?	?	?	?	?	Y	Y
5 Mattox	Y	Y	Y	N	Y	Y	Y	N
6 Gramm	Y	Y	Y	N	Y	N	N	Y
7 *Archer*	Y	Y	Y	N	Y	N	Y	Y
8 *Fields*	Y	Y	Y	N	Y	N	Y	Y
9 Brooks	Y	Y	Y	Y	Y	N	Y	Y
10 Pickle	Y	Y	Y	N	Y	N	Y	Y
11 Leath	Y	Y	Y	N	Y	N	N	Y
12 Wright	Y	Y	Y	Y	Y	Y	Y	Y
13 Hightower	?	?	?	?	Y	N	Y	Y
14 Patman	Y	Y	Y	N	Y	N	Y	Y
15 de la Garza	?	?	?	?	Y	Y	Y	N
16 White	Y	Y	Y	Y	Y	N	Y	Y
17 Stenholm	Y	?	Y	N	Y	N	N	Y
18 Leland	Y	Y	N	Y	Y	Y	Y	N
19 Hance	Y	Y	Y	N	Y	N	Y	Y
20 Gonzalez	Y	Y	Y	Y	Y	Y	Y	N
21 *Loeffler*	Y	Y	Y	N	Y	N	N	Y
22 *Paul*	N	Y	Y	N	Y	N	N	Y
23 Kazen	Y	Y	Y	Y	Y	N	Y	Y
24 Frost	Y	Y	Y	Y	Y	Y	Y	N
UTAH								
1 *Hansen*	Y	Y	?	N	Y	N	N	Y
2 *Marriott*	Y	Y	Y	N	Y	N	Y	Y
VERMONT								
AL *Jeffords*	Y	Y	Y	Y	Y	N	Y	Y
VIRGINIA								
1 *Trible*	Y	Y	Y	N	Y	N	Y	Y
2 *Whitehurst*	Y	Y	Y	N	Y	N	Y	Y
3 *Bliley*	?	Y	Y	N	Y	N	Y	Y
4 *Daniel, R.*	Y	Y	Y	N	Y	N	Y	Y
5 Daniel, D.	Y	Y	Y	N	Y	N	Y	Y
6 *Butler*	Y	Y	Y	N	Y	N	Y	Y
7 *Robinson*	Y	Y	Y	N	Y	N	Y	Y
8 *Parris*	Y	Y	Y	N	Y	N	Y	Y
9 *Wampler*	?	?	?	?	Y	N	Y	Y
10 *Wolf*	Y	Y	Y	N	Y	N	Y	Y
WASHINGTON								
1 *Pritchard*	Y	Y	Y	Y	Y	Y	Y	Y
2 Swift	Y	Y	Y	Y	Y	Y	Y	N
3 Bonker	Y	Y	Y	Y	Y	Y	Y	Y
4 *Morrison*	Y	Y	Y	N	Y	N	Y	Y
5 Foley	Y	Y	Y	Y	Y	Y	Y	Y
6 Dicks	Y	Y	Y	Y	Y	Y	Y	Y
7 Lowry	Y	Y	Y	Y	Y	Y	Y	N
WEST VIRGINIA								
1 Mollohan	Y	Y	Y	Y	Y	N	Y	Y
2 *Benedict*	Y	Y	Y	N	Y	N	Y	Y
3 *Staton*	Y	Y	Y	N	Y	N	Y	Y
4 Rahall	Y	Y	Y	Y	Y	N	Y	N
WISCONSIN								
1 Aspin	?	?	Y	N	Y	Y	Y	N
2 Kastenmeier	Y	Y	N	Y	Y	Y	Y	Y
3 *Gunderson*	Y	Y	Y	N	Y	Y	Y	Y
4 Zablocki	Y	Y	Y	Y	Y	Y	Y	Y
5 Reuss	Y	?	Y	Y	?	?	?	?
6 *Petri*	Y	Y	Y	Y	?	?	?	Y
7 Obey	Y	Y	?	Y	Y	Y	Y	N
8 *Roth*	Y	Y	Y	Y	Y	N	Y	Y
9 *Sensenbrenner*	Y	Y	Y	N	Y	N	Y	Y
WYOMING								
AL *Cheney*	Y	Y	Y	N	Y	N	N	Y

Democrats *Republicans*

KEY

Y Voted for (yea).
Paired for.
+ Announced for.
N Voted against (nay).
X Paired against.
- Announced against.
P Voted "present".
C Voted "present" to avoid possible conflict of interest.
? Did not vote or otherwise make a position known.

204. HR 4522. District of Columbia Appropriation, Fiscal 1982. Passage of the bill to appropriate $2,389,228,200 for fiscal 1982 for the operations of the District of Columbia government (the appropriation was composed of $520,570,000 in federal funds and $1,868,658,200 in revenues raised by the city). Passed 299-105: R 105-78; D 194-27 (ND 131-14, SD 63-13), Sept. 22, 1981. The president had requested $570,100,000 in federal funds and $1,868,658,200 in D.C. revenues.

205. HR 4. Intelligence Agent Identities Protection Act. Ashbrook, R-Ohio, amendment to provide that anyone exposing the identity of a U.S. covert agent with "reason to believe" the exposure might "impair or impede" U.S. intelligence operations would be guilty of a crime punishable by up to three years in prison and a fine of up to $15,000. The Ashbrook amendment replaced a proposal that such persons would be guilty of a crime only if the exposure was made "with intent to impair or impede" U.S. intelligence. Adopted 226-181: R 151-29; D 75-152 (ND 26-126, SD 49-26), Sept. 23, 1981. A "yea" was a vote supporting the president's position.

206. HR 4. Intelligence Agent Identities Protection Act. Solomon, R-N.Y., amendment to include the identities of retired and other former covert agents among those it would be illegal to expose under the provisions of the bill. Adopted 313-94: R 162-14; D 151-80 (ND 83-70; SD 68-10), Sept. 23, 1981.

207. HR 4. Intelligence Agent Identities Protection Act. Passage of the bill to amend the National Security Act of 1947 to make it a federal crime to disclose the identities of certain U.S. intelligence officers, agents, informants and sources of operational assistance. Passed 354-56: R 178-0; D 176-56 (ND 103-52, SD 73-4), Sept. 23, 1981. A "yea" was a vote supporting the president's position.

208. HR 1520. National Science Foundation Authorization. Fuqua, D-Fla., amendment, to the Weber, R-Minn., amendment (see vote 209, below), to reduce the fiscal 1982 authorization for the agency to $1.08 billion from $1.16 billion. Adopted 245-161: R 38-139; D 207-22 (ND 144-8, SD 63-14), Sept. 23, 1981.

209. HR 1520. National Science Foundation Authorization. Weber, R-Minn., amendment, as amended, to reduce to $1.08 billion from $1.16 billion fiscal 1982 authorizations for the National Science Foundation. Adopted 401-5: R 175-4; D 226-1 (ND 149-1, SD 77-0), Sept. 23, 1981.

210. HR 1520. National Science Foundation Authorization. Passage of the bill to authorize $1.08 billion in fiscal 1982 for the National Science Foundation. Passed 262-149: R 60-122; D 202-27 (ND 147-6, SD 55-21), Sept. 23, 1981.

	204	205	206	207	208	209	210
ALABAMA							
1 Edwards	Y	N	?	Y	N	Y	Y
2 Dickinson	N	Y	Y	Y	N	Y	N
3 Nichols	X	X	Y	?	Y	Y	Y
4 Bevill	Y	Y	Y	Y	Y	Y	Y
5 Flippo	Y	Y	Y	Y	Y	Y	Y
6 Smith	N	Y	Y	N	N	Y	N
7 Shelby	N	Y	Y	Y	Y	Y	N
ALASKA							
AL Young	N	Y	Y	Y	Y	Y	Y
ARIZONA							
1 Rhodes	Y	Y	Y	Y	N	Y	Y
2 Udall	Y	N	Y	Y	Y	Y	Y
3 Stump	N	Y	Y	Y	N	Y	N
4 Rudd	N	Y	Y	Y	N	Y	N
ARKANSAS							
1 Alexander	Y	Y	Y	Y	Y	Y	?
2 Bethune	Y	Y	Y	Y	?	Y	N
3 Hammerschmidt	Y	Y	Y	Y	N	Y	N
4 Anthony	Y	Y	Y	Y	Y	Y	Y
CALIFORNIA							
1 Chappie	N	Y	Y	Y	N	Y	N
2 Clausen	?	Y	Y	Y	N	Y	Y
3 Matsui	Y	N	Y	Y	Y	Y	Y
4 Fazio	Y	N	Y	Y	Y	Y	Y
5 Burton, J.	?	N	N	N	Y	Y	Y
6 Burton, P.	Y	N	N	N	Y	Y	Y
7 Miller	Y	N	Y	N	Y	Y	Y
8 Dellums	?	N	N	N	Y	Y	Y
9 Stark	Y	N	N	N	Y	Y	Y
10 Edwards	Y	N	N	N	Y	?	#
11 Lantos	Y	N	Y	Y	Y	Y	Y
12 McCloskey	Y	?	?	?	?	?	?
13 Mineta	Y	N	N	Y	Y	Y	Y
14 Shumway	N	Y	Y	Y	N	Y	N
15 Coelho	Y	N	Y	Y	Y	Y	?
16 Panetta	Y	N	Y	Y	Y	Y	Y
17 Pashayan	?	?	?	?	?	?	?
18 Thomas	Y	?	Y	Y	N	Y	Y
19 Lagomarsino	N	Y	Y	Y	N	Y	N
20 Goldwater	Y	Y	Y	Y	N	Y	N
21 Fiedler	N	Y	Y	Y	N	Y	N
22 Moorhead	N	Y	Y	Y	N	Y	N
23 Beilenson	Y	N	N	N	Y	Y	Y
24 Waxman	Y	N	N	Y	Y	?	Y
25 Roybal	Y	N	N	Y	Y	Y	Y
26 Rousselot	N	Y	?	Y	N	Y	N
27 Dornan	?	Y	Y	Y	N	Y	Y
28 Dixon	Y	N	N	Y	Y	Y	Y
29 Hawkins	Y	N	N	N	Y	Y	?
30 Danielson	+	-	-	+	+	+	+
31 Dymally	Y	N	N	N	Y	Y	Y
32 Anderson	Y	N	Y	Y	Y	Y	Y
33 Grisham	N	Y	Y	Y	Y	Y	Y
34 Lungren	N	Y	Y	N	Y	N	N
35 Dreier	N	Y	Y	Y	N	Y	N
36 Brown	Y	N	N	Y	Y	Y	Y
37 Lewis	N	Y	Y	Y	N	Y	Y
38 Patterson	Y	N	Y	Y	Y	Y	Y
39 Dannemeyer	N	Y	Y	Y	N	Y	N
40 Badham	N	Y	Y	Y	N	Y	N
41 Lowery	N	Y	?	?	Y	Y	Y
42 Hunter	Y	Y	Y	Y	N	Y	N
43 Burgener	N	Y	Y	Y	N	Y	Y
COLORADO							
1 Schroeder	N	N	Y	Y	Y	Y	Y
2 Wirth	?	N	Y	Y	Y	Y	Y
3 Kogovsek	Y	N	Y	Y	Y	Y	Y
4 Brown	N	Y	Y	Y	N	Y	Y

	204	205	206	207	208	209	210
5 Kramer	N	Y	Y	Y	N	Y	N
CONNECTICUT							
1 Vacancy							
2 Gejdenson	Y	N	N	N	Y	Y	Y
3 DeNardis	Y	N	?	Y	Y	Y	Y
4 McKinney	Y	N	Y	N	Y	Y	Y
5 Ratchford	Y	N	Y	Y	Y	Y	Y
6 Moffett	?	?	N	?	?	?	?
DELAWARE							
AL Evans	Y	Y	Y	Y	N	Y	Y
FLORIDA							
1 Hutto	Y	Y	Y	Y	Y	Y	Y
2 Fuqua	Y	N	Y	Y	Y	Y	Y
3 Bennett	N	Y	Y	Y	Y	Y	Y
4 Chappell	Y	Y	Y	Y	Y	Y	Y
5 McCollum	Y	Y	Y	Y	N	Y	N
6 Young	Y	Y	Y	Y	N	Y	N
7 Gibbons	Y	Y	Y	Y	Y	Y	Y
8 Ireland	N	Y	Y	Y	Y	Y	Y
9 Nelson	Y	#	#	#	#	+	+
10 Bafalis	Y	Y	Y	Y	N	Y	N
11 Mica	Y	Y	Y	Y	Y	Y	Y
12 Shaw	Y	Y	Y	Y	N	Y	N
13 Lehman	Y	N	N	N	Y	Y	Y
14 Pepper	+	Y	Y	Y	+	Y	Y
15 Fascell	Y	N	N	Y	Y	Y	Y
GEORGIA							
1 Ginn	Y	Y	Y	Y	Y	Y	Y
2 Hatcher	Y	N	Y	Y	Y	Y	Y
3 Brinkley	Y	Y	Y	Y	Y	Y	Y
4 Levitas	Y	Y	Y	Y	Y	Y	Y
5 Fowler	Y	N	N	Y	Y	Y	Y
6 Gingrich	Y	Y	Y	Y	N	Y	N
7 McDonald	N	Y	Y	N	N	Y	N
8 Evans	?	?	Y	Y	Y	N	N
9 Jenkins	Y	Y	Y	Y	Y	Y	N
10 Barnard	Y	Y	Y	Y	Y	Y	Y
HAWAII							
1 Heftel	Y	Y	Y	Y	Y	Y	Y
2 Akaka	Y	N	Y	Y	Y	Y	Y
IDAHO							
1 Craig	N	Y	Y	Y	N	Y	N
2 Hansen	N	Y	Y	Y	N	Y	N
ILLINOIS							
1 Washington	Y	N	N	N	Y	Y	Y
2 Savage	Y	?	?	?	?	?	?
3 Russo	N	Y	Y	N	Y	Y	Y
4 Derwinski	?	?	?	?	?	?	?
5 Fary	#	Y	?	?	?	?	?
6 Hyde	Y	Y	Y	Y	?	?	?
7 Collins	?	X	X	X	?	Y	Y
8 Rostenkowski	Y	Y	Y	Y	Y	Y	Y
9 Yates	Y	N	N	N	Y	Y	Y
10 Porter	Y	Y	Y	Y	Y	Y	Y
11 Annunzio	Y	N	Y	Y	Y	Y	Y
12 Crane, P.	N	Y	Y	Y	N	Y	N
13 McClory	Y	N	N	N	Y	N	N
14 Erlenborn	Y	N	Y	N	Y	N	N
15 Corcoran	Y	Y	Y	Y	N	Y	N
16 Martin	Y	Y	Y	Y	N	Y	N
17 O'Brien	Y	Y	Y	Y	N	Y	N
18 Michel	Y	?	Y	Y	?	?	N
19 Railsback	Y	?	N	?	N	Y	Y
20 Findley	Y	N	N	N	Y	N	Y
21 Madigan	Y	Y	Y	Y	N	Y	Y
22 Crane, D.	N	Y	Y	Y	N	Y	N
23 Price	Y	N	Y	Y	Y	Y	Y
24 Simon	Y	N	N	Y	Y	Y	Y
INDIANA							
1 Benjamin	Y	N	Y	Y	Y	Y	Y
2 Fithian	Y	N	Y	Y	Y	Y	Y
3 Hiler	N	Y	Y	Y	N	Y	N
4 Coats	N	Y	Y	N	Y	N	N
5 Hillis	Y	Y	Y	Y	N	Y	Y
6 Evans	N	N	Y	N	Y	N	Y
7 Myers	N	Y	Y	Y	N	Y	Y
8 Deckard	Y	Y	Y	Y	N	Y	N
9 Hamilton	Y	N	N	Y	Y	Y	Y
10 Sharp	Y	N	Y	Y	Y	Y	Y
11 Jacobs	Y	N	N	Y	Y	Y	Y
IOWA							
1 Leach	Y	Y	Y	Y	Y	Y	Y
2 Tauke	N	Y	Y	Y	Y	Y	Y
3 Evans	N	Y	Y	Y	Y	Y	Y
4 Smith	Y	Y	Y	Y	Y	Y	Y
5 Harkin	N	N	N	N	Y	Y	Y
6 Bedell	Y	N	Y	N	Y	Y	Y

Democrats   *Republicans*

Corresponding to Congressional Record Votes 216, 217, 218, 219, 221, 222, 223

	204	205	206	207	208	209	210
KANSAS							
1 ***Roberts***	N	Y	Y	Y	N	Y	N
2 ***Jeffries***	N	Y	Y	Y	N	Y	N
3 ***Winn***	N	Y	Y	Y	N	Y	N
4 Glickman	Y	N	Y	Y	Y	Y	Y
5 ***Whittaker***	N	Y	Y	Y	N	Y	N
KENTUCKY							
1 Hubbard	Y	Y	Y	Y	Y	Y	N
2 Natcher	Y	N	Y	Y	Y	Y	Y
3 Mazzoli	Y	N	N	Y	Y	Y	Y
4 ***Snyder***	Y	N	Y	Y	N	Y	N
5 ***Rogers***	Y	Y	Y	Y	N	Y	N
6 ***Hopkins***	Y	Y	Y	Y	N	Y	N
7 Perkins	Y	N	Y	Y	Y	Y	Y
LOUISIANA							
1 ***Livingston***	Y	N	Y	Y	N	Y	N
2 Boggs	Y	N	Y	Y	Y	Y	Y
3 Tauzin	Y	?	Y	Y	N	Y	N
4 Roemer	Y	Y	Y	Y	N	Y	N
5 Huckaby	Y	Y	Y	Y	N	Y	Y
6 ***Moore***	Y	Y	Y	Y	N	Y	N
7 Breaux	Y	Y	Y	Y	N	Y	N
8 Long	Y	N	Y	Y	Y	Y	Y
MAINE							
1 ***Emery***	Y	Y	Y	Y	N	Y	Y
2 ***Snowe***	Y	Y	Y	Y	N	Y	Y
MARYLAND							
1 Dyson	Y	Y	Y	Y	N	Y	Y
2 Long	Y	N	N	Y	Y	Y	Y
3 Mikulski	Y	N	Y	Y	Y	Y	Y
4 ***Holt***	?	Y	Y	Y	N	Y	N
5 Hoyer	Y	X	?	-	Y	Y	Y
6 Byron	Y	Y	Y	Y	Y	Y	Y
7 Mitchell	Y	N	N	N	Y	Y	Y
8 Barnes	Y	N	Y	N	Y	Y	Y
MASSACHUSETTS							
1 ***Conte***	Y	N	Y	Y	Y	Y	Y
2 Boland	Y	N	N	N	Y	Y	Y
3 Early	Y	N	N	Y	Y	Y	Y
4 Frank	Y	N	N	N	Y	Y	Y
5 Shannon	Y	N	N	N	Y	Y	Y
6 Mavroules	Y	N	N	Y	Y	Y	Y
7 Markey	Y	N	N	N	Y	Y	Y
8 O'Neill							
9 Moakley	?	N	N	Y	Y	Y	Y
10 ***Heckler***	N	N	Y	Y	Y	Y	Y
11 Donnelly	Y	N	N	Y	Y	Y	Y
12 Studds	Y	N	N	N	Y	Y	Y
MICHIGAN							
1 Conyers	Y	N	N	N	Y	Y	Y
2 ***Pursell***	Y	N	N	Y	Y	Y	Y
3 Wolpe	Y	N	N	N	Y	Y	Y
4 ***Siljander***	Y	Y	?	?	N	Y	N
5 ***Sawyer***	Y	N	Y	Y	N	Y	Y
6 ***Dunn***	Y	N	Y	Y	Y	Y	Y
7 Kildee	Y	N	Y	N	Y	Y	Y
8 Traxler	Y	N	Y	Y	Y	Y	Y
9 ***Vander Jagt***	Y	Y	Y	Y	N	N	Y
10 Albosta	Y	Y	Y	Y	Y	Y	Y
11 ***Davis***	Y	Y	Y	Y	Y	Y	Y
12 Bonior	Y	N	N	N	Y	?	Y
13 Crockett	Y	?	?	N	?	?	Y
14 Hertel	N	N	Y	Y	Y	Y	Y
15 Ford	?	N	N	Y	Y	Y	Y
16 Dingell	?	N	Y	Y	Y	Y	Y
17 Brodhead	N	N	Y	N	Y	Y	Y
18 Blanchard	Y	N	Y	Y	Y	Y	Y
19 ***Broomfield***	N	Y	Y	Y	N	N	N
MINNESOTA							
1 ***Erdahl***	Y	Y	Y	Y	Y	Y	Y
2 ***Hagedorn***	Y	Y	Y	Y	?	Y	N
3 ***Frenzel***	Y	Y	N	?	N	Y	N
4 Vento	Y	N	N	Y	Y	Y	Y
5 Sabo	Y	?	N	N	Y	Y	Y
6 ***Weber***	N	Y	Y	Y	N	Y	N
7 ***Stangeland***	N	Y	Y	Y	N	Y	N
8 Oberstar	Y	N	N	Y	Y	Y	Y
MISSISSIPPI							
1 Whitten	Y	Y	Y	Y	N	Y	Y
2 Bowen	Y	Y	Y	Y	Y	Y	Y
3 Montgomery	N	Y	Y	Y	N	?	?
4 Dowdy	Y	Y	Y	Y	N	Y	N
5 ***Lott***	Y	Y	Y	Y	N	Y	N
MISSOURI							
1 Clay	Y	N	N	N	Y	Y	Y
2 Young	Y	N	Y	Y	Y	Y	Y
3 Gephardt	Y	Y	Y	Y	Y	Y	N

	204	205	206	207	208	209	210
4 Skelton	Y	Y	Y	Y	N	N	N
5 Bolling	?	?	?	?	?	?	?
6 ***Coleman***	N	Y	Y	Y	N	Y	N
7 ***Taylor***	N	Y	Y	Y	N	Y	N
8 ***Bailey***	Y	Y	Y	Y	N	Y	N
9 Volkmer	N	N	Y	Y	Y	Y	Y
10 ***Emerson***	N	Y	Y	Y	N	Y	N
MONTANA							
1 Williams	?	N	?	Y	Y	Y	Y
2 ***Marlenee***	N	Y	Y	Y	N	Y	N
NEBRASKA							
1 ***Bereuter***	Y	Y	Y	Y	Y	Y	Y
2 ***Daub***	Y	+	+	?	X	+	X
3 ***Smith***	N	Y	Y	Y	N	Y	N
NEVADA							
AL Santini	N	Y	Y	Y	?	?	?
NEW HAMPSHIRE							
1 D'Amours	Y	N	Y	Y	Y	Y	Y
2 ***Gregg***	Y	Y	Y	Y	N	Y	N
NEW JERSEY							
1 Florio	Y	Y	Y	Y	?	?	Y
2 Hughes	N	N	Y	Y	N	Y	Y
3 Howard	Y	?	Y	Y	Y	Y	Y
4 ***Smith***	N	Y	Y	Y	N	Y	Y
5 ***Fenwick***	Y	Y	Y	Y	Y	Y	Y
6 ***Forsythe***	Y	N	N	Y	N	N	N
7 ***Roukema***	Y	Y	N	Y	N	Y	N
8 Roe	Y	Y	Y	Y	Y	Y	Y
9 ***Hollenbeck***	Y	N	?	?	Y	Y	Y
10 Rodino	Y	N	N	Y	Y	Y	Y
11 Minish	Y	Y	Y	Y	Y	Y	Y
12 ***Rinaldo***	Y	?	?	?	N	Y	N
13 ***Courter***	N	?	?	?	?	?	N
14 Guarini	Y	#	Y	Y	Y	Y	Y
15 Dwyer	Y	N	Y	Y	Y	Y	Y
NEW MEXICO							
1 ***Lujan***	N	Y	Y	Y	Y	Y	N
2 ***Skeen***	Y	Y	Y	Y	N	Y	N
NEW YORK							
1 ***Carney***	Y	Y	?	?	Y	Y	Y
2 Downey	Y	N	N	N	Y	Y	Y
3 ***Carman***	Y	Y	Y	Y	N	Y	N
4 ***Lent***	Y	Y	Y	Y	Y	Y	Y
5 ***McGrath***	Y	Y	Y	Y	Y	Y	Y
6 ***LeBoutillier***	Y	Y	Y	Y	N	Y	N
7 Addabbo	?	N	N	Y	Y	Y	Y
8 Rosenthal	?	N	N	N	Y	Y	Y
9 Ferraro	Y	N	Y	Y	Y	Y	Y
10 Biaggi	Y	Y	Y	Y	Y	Y	Y
11 Scheuer	Y	N	?	?	Y	Y	Y
12 Chisholm	Y	N	Y	Y	Y	Y	Y
13 Solarz	Y	N	N	Y	Y	Y	Y
14 Richmond	Y	N	N	N	Y	Y	Y
15 Zeferetti	?	Y	Y	Y	Y	Y	Y
16 Schumer	Y	N	N	N	Y	Y	Y
17 ***Molinari***	Y	Y	Y	Y	N	Y	N
18 ***Green***	Y	N	N	Y	Y	Y	Y
19 Rangel	Y	N	N	N	Y	Y	Y
20 Weiss	Y	N	N	N	Y	Y	Y
21 Garcia	Y	N	N	N	Y	Y	Y
22 Bingham	Y	N	N	N	N	Y	Y
23 Peyser	Y	N	Y	Y	Y	Y	Y
24 Ottinger	Y	N	Y	N	Y	Y	Y
25 ***Fish***	Y	N	Y	Y	N	Y	Y
26 ***Gilman***	N	Y	Y	Y	Y	Y	Y
27 McHugh	Y	N	Y	Y	Y	Y	Y
28 Stratton	Y	Y	Y	Y	Y	Y	Y
29 ***Solomon***	N	Y	Y	Y	N	Y	N
30 ***Martin***	N	Y	Y	Y	N	Y	N
31 ***Mitchell***	Y	Y	Y	Y	Y	Y	Y
32 ***Wortley***	Y	Y	Y	Y	Y	Y	N
33 ***Lee***	N	Y	Y	Y	N	Y	N
34 ***Horton***	?	?	Y	Y	Y	Y	Y
35 ***Conable***	Y	Y	Y	Y	N	Y	N
36 LaFalce	N	Y	Y	Y	Y	Y	Y
37 Nowak	Y	N	Y	Y	Y	Y	Y
38 ***Kemp***	Y	Y	Y	Y	N	Y	N
39 Lundine	Y	N	N	N	Y	Y	Y
NORTH CAROLINA							
1 Jones	Y	N	Y	Y	Y	Y	Y
2 Fountain	Y	Y	Y	Y	Y	Y	N
3 Whitley	Y	Y	Y	Y	Y	Y	N
4 Andrews	Y	Y	Y	Y	Y	Y	Y
5 Neal	Y	N	Y	Y	Y	Y	Y
6 ***Johnston***	N	Y	Y	Y	N	Y	N
7 Rose	Y	N	N	Y	Y	Y	Y
8 Hefner	Y	Y	Y	Y	Y	Y	N

	204	205	206	207	208	209	210
9 ***Martin***	N	Y	Y	Y	Y	Y	N
10 ***Broyhill***	N	Y	Y	Y	?	?	N
11 ***Hendon***	N	Y	Y	Y	N	Y	N
NORTH DAKOTA							
AL Dorgan	Y	N	Y	Y	Y	Y	Y
OHIO							
1 ***Gradison***	Y	N	Y	Y	N	Y	N
2 Luken	Y	N	Y	Y	Y	Y	Y
3 Hall	Y	Y	Y	Y	Y	?	Y
4 ***Oxley***	Y	Y	Y	Y	N	Y	N
5 ***Latta***	N	Y	Y	Y	N	Y	N
6 ***McEwen***	N	Y	Y	Y	N	Y	N
7 ***Brown***	Y	Y	Y	Y	N	Y	N
8 ***Kindness***	Y	N	Y	Y	N	Y	N
9 ***Weber***	Y	+	+	?	-	+	?
10 ***Miller***	N	Y	Y	Y	N	Y	N
11 ***Stanton***	Y	N	Y	Y	N	Y	N
12 Shamansky	Y	N	Y	Y	Y	Y	Y
13 Pease	Y	N	N	N	Y	Y	Y
14 Seiberling	Y	N	N	N	Y	Y	Y
15 ***Wylie***	Y	Y	Y	Y	?	?	?
16 ***Regula***	Y	Y	Y	Y	N	Y	N
17 ***Ashbrook***	N	Y	Y	Y	N	Y	?
18 Applegate	N	Y	Y	Y	Y	Y	N
19 ***Williams***	Y	Y	Y	Y	N	Y	N
20 Oakar	Y	N	Y	Y	Y	Y	Y
21 Stokes	Y	N	N	N	Y	Y	Y
22 Eckart	Y	N	Y	Y	Y	Y	Y
23 Mottl	N	Y	Y	Y	N	Y	N
OKLAHOMA							
1 Jones	Y	N	Y	Y	Y	Y	N
2 Synar	Y	N	N	Y	Y	Y	Y
3 Watkins	N	Y	Y	Y	Y	Y	N
4 McCurdy	Y	Y	Y	Y	Y	Y	Y
5 ***Edwards***	N	Y	Y	Y	N	Y	N
6 English	N	N	Y	Y	Y	Y	N
OREGON							
1 AuCoin	Y	N	Y	N	Y	Y	Y
2 ***Smith***	N	Y	Y	Y	N	Y	N
3 Wyden	Y	N	Y	N	Y	Y	Y
4 Weaver	N	N	N	N	?	?	?
PENNSYLVANIA							
1 Foglietta	Y	N	Y	Y	Y	Y	Y
2 Gray	Y	N	N	N	Y	Y	Y
3 Smith	Y	N	Y	Y	Y	Y	Y
4 ***Dougherty***	?	Y	Y	Y	Y	Y	Y
5 ***Schulze***	N	Y	Y	Y	N	N	N
6 Yatron	Y	Y	Y	Y	Y	Y	N
7 Edgar	Y	N	N	N	Y	Y	Y
8 ***Coyne, J.***	Y	Y	Y	Y	Y	Y	Y
9 ***Shuster***	N	Y	Y	Y	N	Y	N
10 ***McDade***	Y	Y	N	Y	N	Y	Y
11 ***Nelligan***	Y	Y	Y	Y	?	?	?
12 Murtha	Y	N	Y	Y	Y	Y	Y
13 ***Coughlin***	Y	N	Y	Y	N	Y	Y
14 Coyne, W.	Y	N	N	Y	Y	Y	Y
15 ***Ritter***	N	Y	Y	Y	Y	Y	Y
16 ***Walker***	?	Y	Y	Y	N	Y	N
17 Ertel	Y	N	Y	Y	Y	Y	Y
18 Walgren	Y	N	Y	Y	Y	Y	Y
19 ***Goodling***	Y	Y	Y	Y	N	Y	N
20 Gaydos	Y	Y	Y	Y	Y	Y	Y
21 Bailey	Y	Y	Y	Y	Y	Y	Y
22 Murphy	?	N	Y	Y	?	Y	Y
23 ***Clinger***	Y	N	Y	Y	Y	Y	Y
24 ***Marks***	Y	N	Y	Y	?	Y	Y
25 Atkinson	?	Y	Y	Y	Y	Y	Y
RHODE ISLAND							
1 St Germain	Y	N	N	Y	Y	Y	Y
2 ***Schneider***	Y	Y	Y	Y	Y	?	Y
SOUTH CAROLINA							
1 ***Hartnett***	Y	Y	Y	Y	N	Y	N
2 ***Spence***	N	Y	Y	Y	N	Y	N
3 Derrick	Y	N	Y	Y	N	Y	Y
4 ***Campbell***	N	Y	Y	Y	N	Y	N
5 Holland	Y	N	Y	Y	N	Y	Y
6 ***Napier***	Y	Y	Y	Y	N	Y	N
SOUTH DAKOTA							
1 Daschle	Y	N	Y	Y	Y	Y	Y
2 ***Roberts***	N	Y	Y	Y	N	Y	N
TENNESSEE							
1 ***Quillen***	N	N	N	Y	N	Y	N
2 ***Duncan***	Y	Y	Y	Y	N	Y	Y
3 Bouquard	Y	Y	Y	Y	Y	Y	Y
4 Gore	Y	N	N	Y	Y	Y	Y
5 Boner	Y	Y	Y	Y	Y	Y	Y
6 ***Beard***	Y	Y	Y	Y	Y	Y	N

	204	205	206	207	208	209	210
7 Jones	Y	Y	Y	Y	Y	Y	Y
8 Ford	Y	N	N	N	Y	Y	Y
TEXAS							
1 Hall, S.	-	Y	Y	Y	Y	Y	N
2 Wilson	Y	Y	Y	Y	Y	Y	Y
3 ***Collins***	N	Y	Y	Y	N	Y	N
4 Hall, R.	N	Y	Y	Y	Y	Y	N
5 Mattox	Y	N	Y	Y	Y	Y	Y
6 Gramm	N	Y	Y	Y	N	Y	N
7 ***Archer***	N	Y	Y	Y	N	Y	N
8 ***Fields***	N	Y	Y	Y	N	Y	N
9 Brooks	Y	N	N	Y	Y	Y	Y
10 Pickle	Y	N	Y	Y	Y	Y	Y
11 Leath	N	Y	Y	Y	N	Y	N
12 Wright	Y	Y	Y	Y	Y	Y	Y
13 Hightower	Y	N	Y	Y	Y	Y	Y
14 Patman	Y	Y	Y	Y	Y	Y	Y
15 de la Garza	Y	Y	Y	Y	Y	Y	Y
16 White	Y	Y	Y	Y	Y	Y	Y
17 Stenholm	N	Y	Y	Y	N	Y	N
18 Leland	Y	N	N	N	Y	Y	Y
19 Hance	N	Y	Y	Y	Y	Y	Y
20 Gonzalez	Y	N	Y	N	Y	Y	Y
21 ***Loeffler***	N	Y	Y	Y	N	Y	N
22 ***Paul***	N	N	N	Y	N	Y	N
23 Kazen	Y	Y	Y	Y	Y	Y	Y
24 Frost	Y	Y	Y	Y	Y	Y	Y
UTAH							
1 ***Hansen***	Y	Y	Y	Y	N	Y	N
2 ***Marriott***	Y	Y	Y	Y	N	Y	N
VERMONT							
AL ***Jeffords***	Y	N	Y	Y	Y	Y	Y
VIRGINIA							
1 ***Trible***	Y	Y	Y	Y	N	Y	N
2 ***Whitehurst***	Y	N	N	Y	N	Y	N
3 ***Bliley***	Y	Y	Y	Y	N	Y	N
4 ***Daniel, R.***	N	Y	Y	Y	N	Y	N
5 Daniel, D.	N	Y	Y	Y	N	Y	N
6 ***Butler***	N	Y	Y	Y	N	Y	N
7 ***Robinson***	N	N	N	Y	N	Y	N
8 ***Parris***	Y	Y	Y	Y	N	Y	N
9 ***Wampler***	Y	Y	Y	Y	N	Y	Y
10 ***Wolf***	Y	Y	Y	Y	N	Y	Y
WASHINGTON							
1 ***Pritchard***	Y	Y	?	Y	Y	Y	Y
2 Swift	Y	N	N	Y	Y	Y	Y
3 Bonker	Y	N	Y	Y	Y	Y	Y
4 ***Morrison***	N	Y	Y	Y	N	Y	Y
5 Foley	Y	N	Y	Y	Y	Y	Y
6 Dicks	Y	N	N	Y	Y	Y	Y
7 Lowry	Y	N	N	N	Y	Y	Y
WEST VIRGINIA							
1 Mollohan	Y	Y	Y	Y	Y	Y	Y
2 ***Benedict***	Y	Y	Y	Y	Y	Y	Y
3 ***Staton***	Y	Y	Y	Y	Y	N	N
4 Rahall	Y	N	?	Y	Y	Y	Y
WISCONSIN							
1 Aspin	Y	N	N	N	Y	Y	Y
2 Kastenmeier	Y	N	N	N	Y	Y	Y
3 ***Gunderson***	Y	Y	Y	Y	N	Y	N
4 Zablocki	Y	N	N	Y	Y	Y	Y
5 Reuss	?	N	N	Y	Y	Y	Y
6 ***Petri***	N	Y	Y	Y	N	Y	N
7 Obey	N	N	N	Y	Y	Y	Y
8 ***Roth***	Y	Y	Y	Y	N	Y	N
9 ***Sensenbrenner***	N	Y	Y	Y	N	Y	N
WYOMING							
AL ***Cheney***	N	Y	Y	Y	N	Y	N

Democrats ***Republicans***

211. HR 3210. Federal-Aid Highway Act of 1981. Passage of the bill to authorize $3.1 billion in fiscal 1983 for interstate highway construction and to set a limit of $8.2 billion on obligations from the Highway Trust Fund in fiscal 1982. Passed 377-25: R 156-21; D 221-4 (ND 147-3; SD 74-1), Sept. 24, 1981.

212. Procedural Motion. Walker, R-Pa., motion to approve the House *Journal* of Wednesday, Sept. 30. Motion agreed to 294-71: R 123-40; D 171-31 (ND 114-21, SD 57-10), Oct. 1, 1981.

213. S 304. National Tourism Policy. Florio, D-N.J., motion to suspend the rules and adopt the conference report on the bill to establish the U.S. Travel and Tourism Administration within the Commerce Department and to authorize $8.6 million in fiscal 1982 to carry out national tourism policy. Motion agreed to (thus clearing the measure for the president) 288-112: R 101-75; D 187-37 (ND 130-24, SD 57-13), Oct. 1, 1981. A two-thirds majority vote (267 in this case) is required for adoption under suspension of the rules.

214. H Res 208. District of Columbia Sexual Assault Law. McKinney, R-Conn., motion to table (kill) the P. Crane, R-Ill., motion to discharge the House Committee on the District of Columbia from further consideration of the resolution disapproving the action of the District of Columbia Council (*see vote 218, below*). Motion rejected 117-292: R 22-159; D 95-133 (ND 89-67, SD 6-66), Oct. 1, 1981.

215. H Res 208. District of Columbia Sexual Assault Law. P. Crane, R-Ill., motion to discharge the House Committee on the District of Columbia from further consideration of the resolution disapproving the action of the District of Columbia Council (*see vote 218, below*). Motion agreed to 279-126: R 153-27; D 126-99 (ND 62-90, SD 64-9), Oct. 1, 1981.

216. H Res 208. District of Columbia Sexual Assault Law. P. Crane, R-Ill., motion to proceed to the consideration of the resolution disapproving the action of the District of Columbia Council in revising criminal penalities in certain sex-related offenses. Motion agreed to 287-110: R 150-24; D 137-86 (ND 70-79, SD 67-7), Oct. 1, 1981.

217. H Res 208. District of Columbia Sexual Assault Law. P. Crane, R-Ill., motion to limit debate to two hours on the resolution disapproving the action of the District of Columbia Council in revising criminal penalities in certain sex-related offenses. Motion agreed to 253-141: R 156-22; D 97-119 (ND 48-97, SD 49-22), Oct. 1, 1981.

218. H Res 208. District of Columbia Sexual Assault Law. Adoption of the resolution to disapprove the action of the District of Columbia Council in revising criminal penalties in certain sex-related offenses. Adopted 281-119: R 149-28; D 132-91 (ND 68-82, SD 64-9), Oct. 1, 1981.

KEY

- Y Voted for (yea).
- # Paired for.
- + Announced for.
- N Voted against (nay).
- X Paired against.
- - Announced against.
- P Voted "present".
- C Voted "present" to avoid possible conflict of interest.
- ? Did not vote or otherwise make a position known.

	211	212	213	214	215	216	217	218
ALABAMA								
1 *Edwards*	Y	Y	Y	Y	N	N	Y	N
2 *Dickinson*	Y	?	N	N	Y	Y	Y	Y
3 Nichols	Y	Y	Y	N	Y	Y	Y	Y
4 Bevill	Y	Y	Y	N	Y	Y	N	Y
5 Flippo	Y	Y	Y	N	Y	Y	Y	Y
6 *Smith*	Y	N	N	N	Y	Y	Y	Y
7 Shelby	Y	Y	N	N	Y	Y	Y	Y
ALASKA								
AL *Young*	Y	?	Y	N	Y	Y	Y	Y
ARIZONA								
1 *Rhodes*	Y	Y	Y	Y	N	N	Y	Y
2 Udall	Y	?	Y	Y	N	N	N	N
3 *Stump*	?	N	N	N	Y	Y	Y	Y
4 *Rudd*	Y	Y	Y	N	Y	Y	Y	Y
ARKANSAS								
1 Alexander	Y	Y	Y	N	Y	Y	Y	Y
2 *Bethune*	Y	Y	Y	N	Y	Y	Y	Y
3 *Hammerschmidt*	Y	Y	Y	N	Y	Y	N	Y
4 Anthony	Y	Y	Y	N	Y	Y	N	Y
CALIFORNIA								
1 *Chappie*	Y	Y	N	N	Y	Y	Y	Y
2 *Clausen*	Y	Y	Y	N	Y	Y	Y	Y
3 Matsui	Y	Y	Y	Y	N	N	N	N
4 Fazio	Y	Y	Y	?	N	N	N	N
5 Burton, J.	Y	N	Y	Y	N	N	N	N
6 Burton, P.	Y	Y	Y	N	N	N	N	N
7 Miller	Y	N	N	Y	N	N	N	N
8 Dellums	Y	?	?	Y	N	N	N	N
9 Stark	Y	?	N	Y	N	N	N	N
10 Edwards	Y	Y	Y	Y	N	N	N	N
11 Lantos	Y	Y	Y	N	N	N	Y	N
12 *McCloskey*	?	?	?	?	?	?	?	?
13 Mineta	Y	Y	Y	Y	N	N	N	N
14 *Shumway*	Y	Y	N	N	Y	Y	Y	?
15 Coelho	Y	N	Y	?	N	N	Y	N
16 Panetta	Y	Y	Y	N	Y	N	N	Y
17 *Pashayan*	Y	?	?	?	?	?	?	?
18 *Thomas*	Y	Y	Y	N	Y	Y	Y	Y
19 *Lagomarsino*	Y	Y	Y	N	Y	Y	Y	Y
20 *Goldwater*	Y	?	N	N	?	?	?	?
21 *Fiedler*	Y	Y	N	N	Y	Y	Y	Y
22 *Moorhead*	Y	Y	N	N	Y	Y	Y	Y
23 Beilenson	Y	N	N	Y	N	N	?	N
24 Waxman	Y	Y	Y	N	N	Y	N	N
25 Roybal	Y	Y	Y	Y	N	N	N	N
26 *Rousselot*	Y	N	N	N	Y	Y	Y	Y
27 *Dornan*	Y	?	?	?	?	?	?	?
28 Dixon	?	?	N	N	N	N	N	N
29 Hawkins	Y	Y	Y	Y	N	N	?	N
30 Danielson	+	+	Y	Y	N	N	N	N
31 Dymally	Y	Y	Y	N	N	N	N	N
32 Anderson	Y	Y	Y	N	Y	N	Y	N
33 *Grisham*	Y	Y	Y	N	Y	Y	Y	Y
34 *Lungren*	Y	Y	N	N	Y	Y	Y	N
35 *Dreier*	Y	N	N	N	Y	Y	Y	Y
36 Brown	Y	Y	Y	Y	N	N	N	N
37 *Lewis*	Y	Y	?	N	Y	Y	Y	Y
38 Patterson	Y	Y	Y	Y	Y	Y	Y	Y
39 *Dannemeyer*	Y	N	N	N	Y	Y	Y	Y
40 *Badham*	?	Y	Y	N	Y	Y	Y	Y
41 *Lowery*	Y	?	Y	N	Y	Y	Y	Y
42 *Hunter*	Y	Y	N	N	Y	Y	Y	Y
43 *Burgener*	Y	Y	Y	N	Y	Y	?	Y
COLORADO								
1 Schroeder	Y	N	N	Y	N	N	N	N
2 Wirth	Y	Y	Y	N	N	N	Y	N
3 Kogovsek	Y	Y	Y	N	?	Y	N	Y
4 *Brown*	Y	N	N	N	Y	Y	Y	Y
5 *Kramer*	Y	N	Y	N	Y	Y	Y	Y
CONNECTICUT								
1 Vacancy								
2 Gejdenson	Y	N	Y	Y	N	N	N	N
3 *DeNardis*	Y	Y	Y	Y	N	N	Y	N
4 *McKinney*	Y	Y	Y	Y	N	N	N	N
5 Ratchford	Y	Y	Y	Y	Y	Y	Y	Y
6 Moffett	?	?	N	N	Y	?	N	N
DELAWARE								
AL *Evans*	N	Y	Y	N	Y	Y	Y	Y
FLORIDA								
1 Hutto	Y	Y	Y	N	Y	Y	Y	Y
2 Fuqua	Y	Y	Y	N	Y	Y	Y	Y
3 Bennett	Y	Y	N	N	Y	Y	Y	Y
4 Chappell	Y	Y	Y	N	Y	Y	Y	Y
5 *McCollum*	Y	N	Y	N	Y	Y	Y	Y
6 *Young*	Y	Y	Y	N	Y	Y	N	Y
7 Gibbons	Y	?	Y	N	Y	Y	Y	?
8 Ireland	Y	Y	Y	N	Y	Y	Y	Y
9 Nelson	Y	Y	Y	N	Y	Y	Y	Y
10 *Bafalis*	Y	Y	Y	N	Y	Y	Y	Y
11 Mica	Y	Y	Y	N	Y	Y	Y	Y
12 *Shaw*	Y	Y	N	N	Y	Y	Y	Y
13 Lehman	Y	Y	Y	Y	N	N	N	N
14 Pepper	Y	?	?	?	?	?	?	?
15 Fascell	Y	Y	Y	Y	N	N	N	N
GEORGIA								
1 Ginn	Y	Y	Y	N	Y	Y	Y	Y
2 Hatcher	Y	Y	Y	N	Y	Y	Y	Y
3 Brinkley	Y	Y	Y	N	Y	Y	Y	Y
4 Levitas	Y	Y	Y	N	Y	Y	Y	Y
5 Fowler	Y	Y	Y	N	Y	N	Y	N
6 *Gingrich*	Y	?	?	?	Y	Y	N	Y
7 McDonald	N	Y	N	N	Y	Y	Y	Y
8 Evans	Y	?	?	?	?	Y	N	Y
9 Jenkins	Y	Y	Y	N	Y	Y	Y	Y
10 Barnard	Y	Y	Y	N	Y	Y	Y	Y
HAWAII								
1 Heftel	Y	?	Y	N	N	Y	Y	Y
2 Akaka	Y	Y	Y	N	Y	N	N	N
IDAHO								
1 *Craig*	N	N	N	N	Y	Y	Y	Y
2 *Hansen*	N	?	N	N	Y	Y	Y	Y
ILLINOIS								
1 Washington	Y	?	?	?	?	?	?	X
2 Savage	?	?	?	?	?	?	?	?
3 Russo	N	N	Y	N	Y	Y	Y	Y
4 *Derwinski*	?	N	Y	N	Y	N	Y	Y
5 Fary	?	Y	Y	Y	Y	Y	Y	Y
6 *Hyde*	Y	N	N	Y	Y	Y	Y	Y
7 Collins	Y	Y	Y	Y	N	N	N	N
8 Rostenkowski	Y	N	Y	N	N	N	N	N
9 Yates	Y	N	Y	N	Y	N	N	N
10 *Porter*	Y	Y	Y	N	Y	Y	Y	Y
11 Annunzio	Y	Y	Y	N	Y	Y	Y	Y
12 *Crane, P.*	N	N	N	N	Y	Y	Y	Y
13 *McClory*	?	Y	Y	N	Y	Y	Y	Y
14 *Erlenborn*	Y	N	N	N	Y	Y	Y	Y
15 *Corcoran*	Y	+	-	-	+	+	+	+
16 *Martin*	Y	N	N	N	Y	Y	Y	Y
17 *O'Brien*	Y	?	?	?	?	?	N	Y
18 *Michel*	Y	N	N	N	Y	Y	?	Y
19 *Railsback*	Y	Y	Y	N	Y	Y	Y	Y
20 *Findley*	Y	N	N	N	Y	Y	Y	Y
21 *Madigan*	Y	?	?	N	Y	Y	Y	Y
22 *Crane, D.*	N	N	N	N	Y	Y	Y	Y
23 Price	Y	Y	Y	N	Y	Y	N	Y
24 Simon	Y	Y	Y	N	Y	Y	Y	#
INDIANA								
1 Benjamin	Y	Y	Y	N	Y	N	N	Y
2 Fithian	Y	Y	Y	N	Y	N	N	Y
3 *Hiler*	N	N	N	N	Y	Y	Y	Y
4 *Coats*	N	N	N	N	Y	Y	Y	Y
5 *Hillis*	Y	Y	Y	N	Y	Y	Y	Y
6 Evans	Y	Y	Y	N	Y	Y	N	Y
7 *Myers*	Y	Y	Y	N	Y	Y	Y	Y
8 *Deckard*	Y	?	Y	N	Y	?	Y	N
9 Hamilton	Y	Y	Y	N	Y	Y	Y	Y
10 Sharp	Y	N	N	N	Y	Y	N	Y
11 Jacobs	Y	N	N	Y	N	N	N	N
IOWA								
1 *Leach*	Y	N	N	Y	N	N	N	N
2 *Tauke*	Y	Y	Y	N	Y	Y	Y	Y
3 *Evans*	?	N	N	N	N	Y	N	Y
4 Smith	Y	Y	Y	N	N	N	Y	Y
5 *Harkin*	?	N	Y	Y	Y	Y	N	Y
6 Bedell	Y	Y	Y	N	N	N	N	N

Democrats *Republicans*

Corresponding to Congressional Record Votes 224, 225, 226, 227, 228, 229, 230, 232

	211	212	213	214	215	216	217	218
KANSAS								
1 ***Roberts***	Y	Y	N	N	?	Y	Y	Y
2 ***Jeffries***	N	Y	N	N	Y	Y	Y	Y
3 ***Winn***	Y	Y	Y	N	Y	Y	Y	Y
4 Glickman	Y	Y	N	N	Y	Y	N	Y
5 ***Whittaker***	Y	Y	N	N	Y	Y	Y	Y
KENTUCKY								
1 Hubbard	Y	Y	Y	N	Y	Y	Y	Y
2 Natcher	Y	Y	Y	N	Y	Y	Y	Y
3 Mazzoli	Y	+	-	-	+	+	+	+
4 ***Snyder***	Y	Y	Y	N	Y	Y	Y	Y
5 ***Rogers***	Y	?	Y	N	Y	Y	Y	Y
6 ***Hopkins***	Y	Y	Y	N	Y	Y	Y	Y
7 Perkins	Y	Y	Y	N	Y	Y	Y	Y
LOUISIANA								
1 ***Livingston***	Y	Y	N	N	N	N	Y	N
2 Boggs	Y	Y	Y	N	?	Y	N	N
3 Tauzin	Y	Y	N	N	Y	Y	Y	Y
4 Roemer	Y	N	N	N	Y	Y	N	Y
5 Huckaby	Y	Y	N	N	Y	Y	Y	Y
6 ***Moore***	Y	Y	N	N	Y	Y	N	+
7 Breaux	Y	Y	Y	N	Y	Y	Y	Y
8 Long	Y	Y	Y	N	Y	Y	N	Y
MAINE								
1 ***Emery***	Y	Y	Y	N	Y	Y	Y	Y
2 ***Snowe***	Y	Y	Y	Y	N	Y	Y	N
MARYLAND								
1 Dyson	Y	N	Y	N	Y	Y	Y	Y
2 Long	Y	?	N	Y	N	N	N	N
3 Mikulski	Y	Y	Y	Y	N	N	?	N
4 ***Holt***	Y	N	N	N	Y	Y	Y	Y
5 Hoyer	Y	Y	?	Y	N	N	N	N
6 Byron	Y	?	Y	N	Y	Y	Y	Y
7 Mitchell	Y	?	Y	Y	N	N	N	N
8 Barnes	Y	Y	Y	Y	N	N	N	N
MASSACHUSETTS								
1 ***Conte***	?	Y	Y	N	Y	Y	Y	N
2 Boland	?	Y	Y	N	Y	Y	N	Y
3 Early	?	Y	N	N	Y	Y	N	Y
4 Frank	Y	Y	Y	Y	N	N	N	N
5 Shannon	Y	Y	Y	Y	N	N	N	N
6 Mavroules	Y	Y	Y	N	Y	Y	N	Y
7 Markey	Y	Y	Y	Y	?	N	?	N
8 O'Neill								
9 Moakley	Y	Y	Y	N	Y	Y	N	Y
10 ***Heckler***	Y	N	Y	N	Y	Y	Y	Y
11 Donnelly	Y	Y	Y	N	Y	Y	N	Y
12 Studds	Y	Y	Y	Y	N	N	N	N
MICHIGAN								
1 Conyers	Y	?	Y	Y	N	N	N	N
2 ***Pursell***	?	?	Y	Y	N	N	Y	N
3 Wolpe	Y	Y	Y	Y	N	N	N	N
4 ***Siljander***	Y	Y	N	N	Y	Y	Y	Y
5 ***Sawyer***	Y	Y	Y	N	Y	Y	Y	Y
6 ***Dunn***	Y	Y	Y	N	N	Y	Y	N
7 Kildee	Y	Y	Y	N	Y	Y	Y	Y
8 Traxler	Y	N	Y	N	Y	Y	N	Y
9 ***Vander Jagt***	Y	?	?	N	Y	Y	Y	Y
10 Albosta	Y	Y	Y	N	Y	Y	Y	Y
11 ***Davis***	Y	N	Y	N	Y	Y	Y	Y
12 Bonior	Y	Y	Y	Y	N	N	N	N
13 Crockett	Y	?	Y	Y	N	?	?	N
14 Hertel	Y	Y	N	Y	N	Y	N	Y
15 Ford	?	?	?	Y	N	N	N	Y
16 Dingell	Y	?	?	?	?	?	?	?
17 Brodhead	Y	Y	N	Y	N	Y	Y	Y
18 Blanchard	Y	?	Y	?	?	?	?	?
19 ***Broomfield***	Y	N	N	N	Y	Y	Y	Y
MINNESOTA								
1 ***Erdahl***	Y	Y	Y	Y	Y	Y	Y	N
2 ***Hagedorn***	?	Y	N	N	Y	Y	Y	Y
3 ***Frenzel***	Y	Y	N	Y	N	N	Y	N
4 Vento	Y	Y	Y	Y	N	N	Y	N
5 Sabo	Y	N	Y	Y	N	N	N	N
6 ***Weber***	Y	?	N	N	Y	Y	Y	Y
7 ***Stangeland***	Y	Y	Y	N	Y	Y	Y	Y
8 Oberstar	Y	Y	Y	Y	N	N	N	N
MISSISSIPPI								
1 Whitten	?	Y	Y	N	Y	Y	Y	Y
2 Bowen	Y	Y	Y	N	Y	Y	Y	Y
3 Montgomery	Y	Y	Y	N	Y	Y	Y	Y
4 Dowdy	Y	N	Y	N	Y	Y	Y	Y
5 ***Lott***	Y	Y	Y	N	Y	Y	Y	Y
MISSOURI								
1 Clay	Y	?	Y	Y	N	N	N	N
2 Young	Y	Y	Y	N	Y	Y	Y	#
3 Gephardt	Y	Y	Y	N	N	Y	Y	Y

	211	212	213	214	215	216	217	218
4 Skelton	Y	Y	Y	N	Y	Y	Y	Y
5 Bolling	?	Y	Y	Y	N	N	N	N
6 ***Coleman***	Y	Y	Y	N	Y	Y	Y	Y
7 ***Taylor***	Y	Y	?	N	Y	Y	Y	Y
8 ***Bailey***	Y	N	Y	N	Y	Y	Y	Y
9 Volkmer	Y	N	Y	N	Y	Y	Y	Y
10 ***Emerson***	Y	N	N	N	Y	Y	Y	Y
MONTANA								
1 Williams	N	Y	Y	N	N	Y	Y	N
2 ***Marlenee***	N	Y	Y	N	Y	Y	Y	Y
NEBRASKA								
1 ***Bereuter***	N	?	N	N	Y	Y	Y	Y
2 ***Daub***	N	N	N	N	Y	Y	Y	Y
3 ***Smith***	N	N	N	N	Y	Y	Y	Y
NEVADA								
AL Santini	?	Y	Y	N	Y	Y	N	Y
NEW HAMPSHIRE								
1 D'Amours	Y	Y	Y	N	N	Y	Y	Y
2 ***Gregg***	Y	Y	Y	N	Y	Y	Y	Y
NEW JERSEY								
1 Florio	Y	Y	Y	Y	?	?	?	?
2 Hughes	Y	Y	Y	N	Y	Y	N	Y
3 Howard	Y	Y	Y	Y	N	N	N	N
4 ***Smith***	Y	Y	Y	N	Y	Y	Y	Y
5 ***Fenwick***	Y	Y	N	Y	N	N	Y	N
6 ***Forsythe***	Y	N	Y	N	Y	Y	Y	N
7 ***Roukema***	Y	Y	N	Y	N	N	Y	N
8 Roe	Y	Y	Y	N	?	N	Y	N
9 ***Hollenbeck***	Y	N	Y	Y	N	N	N	N
10 Rodino	?	Y	Y	Y	N	N	N	N
11 Minish	Y	Y	Y	N	Y	Y	N	N
12 ***Rinaldo***	Y	?	Y	N	Y	Y	Y	Y
13 ***Courter***	Y	N	Y	N	Y	Y	Y	Y
14 Guarini	Y	Y	Y	N	Y	Y	N	N
15 Dwyer	Y	Y	Y	Y	N	N	N	N
NEW MEXICO								
1 ***Lujan***	Y	Y	Y	N	Y	Y	Y	Y
2 ***Skeen***	N	Y	Y	N	Y	Y	Y	Y
NEW YORK								
1 ***Carney***	Y	Y	Y	N	Y	Y	Y	Y
2 Downey	Y	Y	Y	Y	N	N	N	N
3 ***Carman***	Y	N	Y	N	Y	Y	Y	Y
4 ***Lent***	Y	Y	Y	N	Y	?	Y	Y
5 ***McGrath***	Y	Y	Y	N	Y	Y	Y	?
6 ***LeBoutillier***	Y	Y	Y	N	Y	Y	Y	Y
7 Addabbo	Y	?	?	?	?	?	?	?
8 Rosenthal	Y	Y	Y	Y	N	N	N	N
9 Ferraro	Y	Y	Y	N	N	Y	N	Y
10 Biaggi	Y	Y	Y	N	Y	?	Y	Y
11 Scheuer	Y	Y	Y	Y	N	N	N	N
12 Chisholm	Y	?	?	?	?	?	?	X
13 Solarz	Y	Y	Y	Y	N	Y	N	N
14 Richmond	Y	?	Y	Y	N	?	?	N
15 Zeferetti	Y	Y	Y	N	Y	Y	Y	Y
16 Schumer	Y	N	Y	Y	Y	Y	N	N
17 ***Molinari***	Y	Y	Y	Y	N	?	Y	N
18 ***Green***	Y	Y	Y	Y	N	N	N	N
19 Rangel	Y	Y	Y	Y	N	N	N	N
20 Weiss	Y	Y	Y	Y	N	N	N	N
21 Garcia	Y	?	?	Y	N	N	N	?
22 Bingham	Y	Y	N	Y	N	N	N	N
23 Peyser	Y	Y	Y	Y	N	N	N	N
24 Ottinger	Y	P	Y	Y	N	?	?	N
25 ***Fish***	?	Y	Y	N	N	N	N	N
26 ***Gilman***	+	Y	Y	N	N	N	N	N
27 McHugh	Y	Y	Y	Y	N	N	N	N
28 Stratton	Y	Y	Y	N	Y	Y	Y	Y
29 ***Solomon***	N	N	Y	N	Y	Y	Y	Y
30 ***Martin***	Y	Y	Y	N	Y	Y	Y	Y
31 ***Mitchell***	Y	Y	Y	N	Y	Y	Y	Y
32 ***Wortley***	Y	N	Y	N	Y	Y	Y	Y
33 ***Lee***	Y	Y	Y	N	Y	Y	Y	Y
34 ***Horton***	Y	Y	Y	Y	N	N	Y	N
35 ***Conable***	Y	N	N	Y	N	N	Y	N
36 LaFalce	Y	Y	Y	Y	Y	Y	Y	Y
37 Nowak	Y	Y	Y	Y	N	N	Y	N
38 ***Kemp***	Y	Y	Y	N	Y	Y	Y	Y
39 Lundine	Y	Y	Y	Y	N	N	Y	N
NORTH CAROLINA								
1 Jones	Y	?	?	?	?	?	?	?
2 Fountain	Y	?	Y	N	Y	Y	Y	Y
3 Whitley	Y	Y	Y	N	Y	Y	Y	Y
4 Andrews	Y	Y	Y	N	Y	Y	Y	Y
5 Neal	Y	?	?	N	Y	Y	N	Y
6 ***Johnston***	N	N	N	N	Y	Y	Y	Y
7 Rose	Y	Y	Y	N	Y	Y	Y	Y
8 Hefner	Y	N	Y	N	Y	Y	N	Y

	211	212	213	214	215	216	217	218
9 ***Martin***	Y	?	N	N	Y	Y	Y	Y
10 ***Broyhill***	N	Y	N	N	Y	Y	Y	Y
11 ***Hendon***	Y	N	Y	N	Y	Y	Y	Y
NORTH DAKOTA								
AL Dorgan	Y	Y	Y	N	Y	Y	Y	Y
OHIO								
1 ***Gradison***	Y	Y	N	Y	N	N	N	N
2 Luken	Y	Y	Y	N	N	N	N	N
3 Hall	Y	?	N	N	Y	Y	Y	Y
4 ***Oxley***	Y	N	N	N	Y	Y	Y	Y
5 ***Latta***	Y	Y	N	N	Y	Y	Y	Y
6 ***McEwen***	Y	Y	N	N	Y	Y	Y	Y
7 ***Brown***	?	Y	N	N	Y	Y	Y	Y
8 ***Kindness***	Y	Y	N	N	Y	Y	Y	Y
9 ***Weber***	Y	Y	N	N	Y	Y	Y	Y
10 ***Miller***	Y	N	N	N	Y	Y	Y	Y
11 ***Stanton***	Y	Y	Y	N	Y	Y	Y	Y
12 Shamansky	Y	Y	Y	Y	N	N	N	Y
13 Pease	Y	Y	N	N	Y	Y	N	Y
14 Seiberling	Y	?	N	Y	N	N	N	N
15 ***Wylie***	Y	Y	N	N	Y	Y	Y	Y
16 ***Regula***	Y	Y	N	N	Y	Y	Y	Y
17 ***Ashbrook***	Y	Y	N	N	Y	Y	Y	?
18 Applegate	Y	?	Y	N	Y	Y	Y	Y
19 ***Williams***	Y	Y	Y	N	Y	Y	Y	?
20 Oakar	Y	Y	Y	N	Y	Y	N	Y
21 Stokes	Y	Y	Y	Y	N	N	N	N
22 Eckart	Y	Y	Y	N	Y	Y	Y	Y
23 Mottl	Y	N	Y	N	Y	Y	Y	Y
OKLAHOMA								
1 Jones	Y	N	Y	N	N	?	N	Y
2 Synar	Y	Y	Y	Y	N	N	N	N
3 Watkins	Y	N	Y	N	Y	Y	Y	Y
4 McCurdy	Y	N	Y	N	Y	Y	Y	Y
5 ***Edwards***	Y	?	N	N	Y	Y	N	Y
6 English	Y	Y	Y	N	Y	Y	Y	Y
OREGON								
1 AuCoin	Y	?	Y	Y	N	N	N	N
2 ***Smith***	N	N	N	N	Y	Y	Y	Y
3 Wyden	Y	Y	Y	Y	N	N	N	N
4 Weaver	N	Y	Y	Y	N	N	N	N
PENNSYLVANIA								
1 Foglietta	Y	Y	Y	Y	N	N	N	N
2 Gray	Y	Y	Y	Y	N	N	N	N
3 Smith	Y	Y	Y	N	Y	Y	N	Y
4 ***Dougherty***	Y	Y	Y	N	Y	Y	Y	Y
5 ***Schulze***	Y	Y	N	N	Y	Y	Y	Y
6 Yatron	Y	Y	Y	N	Y	Y	Y	Y
7 Edgar	Y	Y	N	Y	N	N	N	N
8 ***Coyne, J.***	Y	Y	N	Y	N	N	Y	Y
9 ***Shuster***	Y	Y	N	N	Y	Y	Y	Y
10 ***McDade***	Y	?	?	N	Y	?	Y	Y
11 ***Nelligan***	Y	Y	Y	N	Y	Y	Y	Y
12 Murtha	Y	Y	Y	N	Y	Y	Y	Y
13 ***Coughlin***	?	N	Y	Y	N	N	?	Y
14 Coyne, W.	Y	Y	Y	Y	N	N	N	N
15 ***Ritter***	Y	Y	Y	N	Y	Y	Y	Y
16 ***Walker***	Y	N	N	N	Y	Y	N	Y
17 Ertel	Y	Y	Y	N	Y	Y	N	Y
18 Walgren	Y	Y	Y	Y	N	Y	N	N
19 ***Goodling***	Y	?	N	N	Y	Y	Y	Y
20 Gaydos	Y	Y	Y	N	Y	?	?	Y
21 Bailey	Y	Y	Y	Y	N	Y	N	Y
22 Murphy	Y	Y	Y	N	Y	Y	?	?
23 ***Clinger***	Y	Y	Y	N	Y	Y	Y	Y
24 ***Marks***	Y	Y	Y	N	N	N	N	N
25 Atkinson	Y	Y	Y	N	Y	Y	Y	Y
RHODE ISLAND								
1 St Germain	Y	?	Y	N	Y	Y	Y	Y
2 ***Schneider***	Y	Y	Y	Y	N	N	N	N
SOUTH CAROLINA								
1 ***Hartnett***	Y	Y	N	N	Y	Y	Y	Y
2 ***Spence***	Y	N	N	N	Y	Y	Y	Y
3 Derrick	Y	Y	Y	N	N	Y	N	N
4 ***Campbell***	Y	Y	Y	N	Y	Y	Y	Y
5 Holland	?	?	?	?	?	?	?	?
6 ***Napier***	Y	Y	Y	N	Y	Y	Y	Y
SOUTH DAKOTA								
1 Daschle	Y	Y	Y	Y	N	?	N	N
2 ***Roberts***	N	Y	Y	N	Y	Y	Y	Y
TENNESSEE								
1 ***Quillen***	Y	?	?	?	?	?	?	?
2 ***Duncan***	Y	Y	Y	N	Y	Y	Y	Y
3 Bouquard	Y	Y	Y	N	Y	Y	Y	Y
4 Gore	Y	Y	Y	N	Y	Y	Y	Y
5 Boner	Y	Y	Y	N	Y	Y	Y	Y
6 ***Beard***	Y	?	?	?	?	?	?	?

	211	212	213	214	215	216	217	218
7 Jones	Y	Y	Y	N	Y	Y	Y	Y
8 Ford	Y	?	Y	Y	N	N	N	N
TEXAS								
1 Hall, S.	Y	N	N	N	Y	Y	N	Y
2 Wilson	Y	Y	?	N	Y	Y	?	Y
3 ***Collins***	N	Y	N	N	Y	Y	Y	Y
4 Hall, R.	Y	Y	Y	N	Y	Y	?	Y
5 Mattox	Y	N	N	N	N	N	N	N
6 Gramm	Y	Y	Y	N	Y	Y	Y	Y
7 ***Archer***	Y	N	N	N	Y	Y	Y	Y
8 ***Fields***	Y	Y	N	N	Y	Y	Y	Y
9 Brooks	Y	Y	N	N	Y	Y	?	Y
10 Pickle	Y	+	+	+	Y	Y	N	Y
11 Leath	Y	Y	N	N	Y	Y	Y	Y
12 Wright	Y	Y	Y	N	Y	Y	Y	Y
13 Hightower	Y	Y	N	N	Y	Y	Y	Y
14 Patman	?	N	Y	N	Y	Y	Y	Y
15 de la Garza	Y	Y	Y	N	Y	Y	Y	Y
16 White	Y	?	?	?	Y	Y	Y	Y
17 Stenholm	Y	N	N	N	Y	Y	Y	Y
18 Leland	Y	Y	Y	Y	N	N	?	?
19 Hance	Y	?	Y	N	Y	Y	Y	Y
20 Gonzalez	?	Y	Y	N	N	N	N	N
21 ***Loeffler***	Y	Y	Y	N	Y	Y	Y	Y
22 ***Paul***	N	Y	N	N	Y	Y	Y	Y
23 Kazen	Y	Y	Y	N	Y	Y	N	Y
24 Frost	Y	Y	Y	Y	Y	Y	N	Y
UTAH								
1 ***Hansen***	N	+	+	-	+	+	+	+
2 ***Marriott***	Y	Y	Y	N	Y	Y	Y	Y
VERMONT								
AL ***Jeffords***	N	Y	Y	Y	N	N	N	N
VIRGINIA								
1 ***Trible***	Y	?	?	?	?	?	?	?
2 ***Whitehurst***	Y	Y	Y	N	Y	Y	Y	Y
3 ***Bliley***	Y	Y	N	N	Y	Y	Y	Y
4 ***Daniel, R.***	Y	Y	N	N	Y	Y	Y	Y
5 Daniel, D.	Y	Y	N	N	Y	Y	Y	Y
6 ***Butler***	Y	Y	N	N	Y	Y	Y	Y
7 ***Robinson***	Y	Y	N	N	Y	Y	Y	Y
8 ***Parris***	?	N	Y	N	Y	?	?	Y
9 ***Wampler***	Y	Y	Y	N	Y	Y	N	Y
10 ***Wolf***	Y	Y	Y	N	Y	Y	Y	Y
WASHINGTON								
1 ***Pritchard***	Y	Y	Y	Y	N	N	N	N
2 Swift	Y	N	Y	Y	N	N	Y	N
3 Bonker	Y	Y	Y	N	Y	Y	Y	Y
4 ***Morrison***	Y	Y	Y	N	Y	Y	Y	Y
5 Foley	Y	Y	Y	Y	Y	Y	N	Y
6 Dicks	Y	Y	Y	N	Y	Y	Y	Y
7 Lowry	Y	N	Y	Y	N	N	N	N
WEST VIRGINIA								
1 Mollohan	Y	Y	Y	N	Y	Y	Y	Y
2 ***Benedict***	Y	Y	N	N	Y	Y	Y	Y
3 ***Staton***	Y	Y	Y	N	Y	Y	Y	Y
4 Rahall	Y	Y	Y	N	Y	Y	Y	Y
WISCONSIN								
1 Aspin	Y	N	N	Y	N	Y	?	Y
2 Kastenmeier	Y	Y	N	Y	N	N	N	N
3 ***Gunderson***	Y	Y	Y	N	Y	Y	Y	Y
4 Zablocki	Y	Y	Y	N	Y	Y	Y	Y
5 Reuss	Y	Y	N	Y	N	N	Y	N
6 ***Petri***	Y	?	Y	N	Y	Y	N	Y
7 Obey	Y	N	Y	Y	N	N	N	P
8 ***Roth***	Y	N	Y	N	Y	Y	Y	Y
9 ***Sensenbrenner***	N	Y	Y	N	Y	Y	Y	Y
WYOMING								
AL ***Cheney***	?	Y	Y	N	Y	?	Y	Y

Democrats ***Republicans***

KEY

Y Voted for (yea).
\# Paired for.
+ Announced for.
N Voted against (nay).
X Paired against.
- Announced against.
P Voted "present".
C Voted "present" to avoid possible conflict of interest.
? Did not vote or otherwise make a position known.

219. HR 4612. Dairy Price Supports. Passage of the bill to set dairy price supports at $13.10 per hundredweight until Nov. 15, 1981, and to delay until that date the wheat producer referendum. Passed 328-58: R 157-15; D 171-43 (ND 121-26; SD 50-17), Oct. 1, 1981. A "yea" was a vote supporting the president's position.

220. Procedural Motion. Solomon, R-N.Y., motion to approve the House *Journal* of Thursday, Oct. 1. Motion agreed to 273-28: R 127-13; D 146-15 (ND 96-11; SD 50-4), Oct. 2, 1981.

221. HR 3603. Food and Agriculture Act of 1981. Adoption of the rule (H Res 235) providing for House floor consideration of the bill to authorize appropriations for fiscal years 1982-85 for agricultural price supports and other farm programs and for food stamps. Adopted 343-1: R 155-1; D 188-0 (ND 124-0; SD 64-0), Oct. 2, 1981.

222. HR 3112. Voting Rights Act Extension. Edwards, D-Calif., motion that the House resolve itself into the Committee of the Whole to consider the bill extending enforcement provisions of the 1965 Voting Rights Act. Motion agreed to 350-4: R 152-2; D 198-2 (ND 131-1; SD 67-1), Oct. 5, 1981.

223. HR 3112. Voting Rights Act Extension. Hyde, R-Ill., amendment to eliminate a provision that made the signing of a consent decree in a voting rights lawsuit a bar to bailing out from coverage of the act if the consent decree were signed within 10 years of a jurisdiction's petition to bail out. Rejected 92-285: R 76-88; D 16-197 (ND 3-141; SD 13-56), Oct. 5, 1981.

224. HR 3112. Voting Rights Act Extension. Butler, R-Va., amendment to allow three-judge federal district courts to hear petitions by jurisdictions seeking to bail out from coverage of the Voting Rights Act. Rejected 132-277: R 102-75; D 30-202 (ND 4-153; SD 26-49), Oct. 5, 1981.

225. HR 3112. Voting Rights Act Extension. Campbell, R-S.C., amendment to allow a state covered by the Voting Rights Act to bail out from coverage if two-thirds of its counties are eligible to bail out. Rejected 95-313: R 77-102; D 18-211 (ND 2-153; SD 16-58), Oct. 5, 1981.

226. HR 3112. Voting Rights Act Extension. McClory, R-Ill., amendment to eliminate provisions in the 1965 act requiring certain areas of the country to provide bilingual election materials. Rejected 128-284: R 112-65; D 16-219 (ND 5-153; SD 11-66), Oct. 5, 1981.

	219	220	221	222	223	224	225	226
ALABAMA								
1 *Edwards*	Y	Y	Y	?	#	Y	Y	Y
2 *Dickinson*	Y	N	Y	?	Y	Y	Y	Y
3 Nichols	Y	?	Y	Y	Y	Y	Y	Y
4 Bevill	Y	Y	Y	Y	N	Y	Y	Y
5 Flippo	Y	Y	Y	Y	Y	Y	Y	N
6 *Smith*	Y	?	Y	Y	Y	Y	Y	Y
7 Shelby	Y	N	Y	Y	Y	Y	Y	Y
ALASKA								
AL *Young*	Y	?	?	Y	N	N	N	N
ARIZONA								
1 *Rhodes*	Y	Y	Y	Y	Y	Y	Y	N
2 Udall	Y	Y	Y	?	Y	N	N	N
3 *Stump*	N	?	?	Y	Y	Y	Y	Y
4 *Rudd*	Y	Y	Y	Y	Y	Y	Y	Y
ARKANSAS								
1 Alexander	Y	Y	Y	Y	N	N	N	N
2 *Bethune*	Y	Y	Y	Y	N	N	N	N
3 *Hammerschmidt*	Y	Y	Y	Y	N	N	N	N
4 Anthony	Y	?	Y	Y	N	N	N	N
CALIFORNIA								
1 *Chappie*	Y	Y	Y	Y	Y	Y	Y	N
2 *Clausen*	Y	Y	Y	Y	N	Y	N	N
3 Matsui	Y	Y	Y	N	N	N	N	N
4 Fazio	N	Y	Y	Y	N	N	N	N
5 Burton, J.	Y	?	?	?	?	?	?	?
6 Burton, P.	Y	Y	Y	Y	N	N	N	N
7 Miller	Y	N	Y	N	N	N	N	N
8 Dellums	Y	?	Y	N	N	N	N	N
9 Stark	Y	?	Y	N	N	N	N	N
10 Edwards	Y	Y	Y	N	N	N	N	N
11 Lantos	Y	?	Y	X	N	N	N	N
12 *McCloskey*	?	?	Y	Y	N	N	N	Y
13 Mineta	Y	Y	Y	N	N	N	N	N
14 *Shumway*	?	?	Y	Y	Y	Y	Y	Y
15 Coelho	N	Y	?	Y	N	N	N	N
16 Panetta	Y	Y	Y	N	N	N	N	N
17 *Pashayan*	?	?	?	?	?	?	?	?
18 *Thomas*	Y	Y	Y	?	#	#	#	#
19 *Lagomarsino*	Y	Y	Y	Y	Y	Y	Y	Y
20 *Goldwater*	?	?	Y	Y	Y	N	Y	N
21 *Fiedler*	Y	?	?	?	?	?	?	?
22 *Moorhead*	Y	Y	Y	Y	Y	Y	Y	Y
23 Beilenson	Y	?	Y	Y	N	N	N	N
24 Waxman	Y	Y	Y	N	N	N	N	N
25 Roybal	Y	?	?	Y	N	N	N	N
26 *Rousselot*	?	?	?	Y	Y	Y	Y	Y
27 *Dornan*	?	?	?	Y	N	N	Y	N
28 Dixon	Y	Y	Y	N	N	N	N	N
29 Hawkins	Y	Y	Y	N	N	N	N	N
30 Danielson	Y	Y	Y	N	N	N	N	N
31 Dymally	Y	P	Y	N	N	N	N	N
32 Anderson	Y	?	?	N	N	N	N	N
33 *Grisham*	Y	Y	Y	Y	Y	Y	Y	Y
34 *Lungren*	Y	Y	Y	Y	Y	Y	Y	Y
35 *Dreier*	Y	Y	Y	Y	Y	Y	Y	Y
36 Brown	Y	Y	Y	?	?	N	N	N
37 *Lewis*	Y	?	?	?	?	?	X	N
38 Patterson	Y	N	Y	N	N	N	N	N
39 *Dannemeyer*	Y	Y	Y	?	#	#	#	#
40 *Badham*	Y	?	?	Y	Y	Y	Y	Y
41 *Lowery*	Y	?	Y	Y	Y	Y	Y	Y
42 *Hunter*	Y	Y	Y	Y	N	N	N	Y
43 *Burgener*	Y	Y	Y	Y	Y	Y	Y	Y
COLORADO								
1 Schroeder	Y	N	N	Y	N	N	N	N
2 Wirth	Y	?	?	Y	N	N	N	N
3 Kogovsek	N	Y	Y	N	N	N	N	N
4 *Brown*	Y	Y	Y	Y	N	Y	N	Y

	219	220	221	222	223	224	225	226
5 *Kramer*	Y	Y	Y	Y	Y	Y	N	N
CONNECTICUT								
1 Vacancy								
2 Gejdenson	N	?	?	Y	N	N	N	N
3 *DeNardis*	Y	?	Y	Y	N	N	N	N
4 *McKinney*	Y	?	Y	?	N	N	N	N
5 Ratchford	Y	Y	Y	Y	N	N	N	N
6 Moffett	Y	P	?	?	?	?	X	N
DELAWARE								
AL *Evans*	Y	Y	Y	?	N	Y	N	Y
FLORIDA								
1 Hutto	Y	?	Y	N	N	N	N	N
2 Fuqua	Y	?	?	Y	N	N	N	N
3 Bennett	Y	Y	Y	N	N	N	N	N
4 Chappell	Y	?	?	?	?	Y	Y	Y
5 *McCollum*	Y	Y	Y	Y	N	N	N	N
6 *Young*	Y	Y	Y	Y	Y	Y	Y	Y
7 Gibbons	?	?	?	Y	N	N	N	N
8 Ireland	?	?	?	Y	N	N	N	N
9 Nelson	+	+	+	Y	N	N	N	N
10 *Bafalis*	Y	?	Y	#	?	Y	Y	Y
11 Mica	Y	Y	Y	N	N	N	N	N
12 *Shaw*	Y	Y	Y	Y	N	N	N	N
13 Lehman	Y	Y	Y	Y	N	N	N	?
14 Pepper	?	?	?	?	?	?	?	N
15 Fascell	Y	N	Y	N	N	N	N	N
GEORGIA								
1 Ginn	Y	?	Y	?	?	N	N	N
2 Hatcher	Y	Y	Y	Y	N	N	N	N
3 Brinkley	Y	Y	Y	Y	Y	Y	Y	N
4 Levitas	Y	Y	X	Y	N	Y	N	N
5 Fowler	Y	Y	Y	Y	N	N	N	N
6 *Gingrich*	Y	?	Y	N	Y	N	N	Y
7 McDonald	?	?	Y	N	Y	Y	Y	Y
8 Evans	N	Y	Y	Y	N	Y	Y	Y
9 Jenkins	Y	Y	Y	Y	Y	N	N	N
10 Barnard	Y	Y	Y	Y	Y	Y	Y	N
HAWAII								
1 Heftel	Y	?	Y	N	N	N	N	N
2 Akaka	N	Y	Y	N	N	N	N	N
IDAHO								
1 *Craig*	Y	Y	Y	Y	Y	Y	Y	Y
2 *Hansen*	Y	Y	Y	Y	Y	Y	Y	Y
ILLINOIS								
1 Washington	?	Y	Y	N	N	N	N	N
2 Savage	?	?	?	?	N	N	N	N
3 Russo	Y	Y	Y	N	N	N	N	N
4 *Derwinski*	Y	N	Y	Y	N	Y	N	Y
5 Fary	?	?	?	Y	N	N	N	N
6 *Hyde*	Y	Y	Y	Y	N	N	N	N
7 Collins	Y	?	Y	Y	N	N	N	N
8 Rostenkowski	Y	Y	Y	?	?	N	N	N
9 Yates	Y	Y	Y	N	N	N	N	N
10 *Porter*	Y	Y	Y	N	N	N	N	N
11 Annunzio	Y	Y	Y	N	N	N	N	N
12 *Crane, P.*	?	?	?	?	#	#	#	#
13 *McClory*	?	Y	Y	Y	N	N	N	N
14 *Erlenborn*	Y	Y	Y	N	N	Y	Y	Y
15 *Corcoran*	+	+	+	Y	N	N	N	N
16 *Martin*	Y	Y	Y	N	N	N	N	N
17 *O'Brien*	Y	?	?	?	X	X	Y	N
18 *Michel*	Y	Y	Y	Y	N	N	N	N
19 *Railsback*	Y	?	?	N	N	N	N	N
20 *Findley*	Y	Y	Y	Y	N	N	N	N
21 *Madigan*	Y	Y	Y	N	N	N	N	N
22 *Crane, D.*	Y	Y	Y	N	N	N	N	N
23 Price	Y	Y	Y	N	N	N	N	N
24 Simon	?	?	Y	N	N	N	N	N
INDIANA								
1 Benjamin	Y	Y	Y	Y	N	N	N	N
2 Fithian	Y	?	?	Y	N	N	N	N
3 *Hiler*	Y	Y	Y	Y	N	N	N	N
4 *Coats*	Y	+	+	Y	N	N	N	N
5 *Hillis*	Y	Y	Y	Y	N	N	N	Y
6 Evans	Y	?	?	Y	N	N	N	Y
7 *Myers*	Y	Y	Y	Y	Y	Y	Y	Y
8 *Deckard*	Y	?	Y	Y	N	N	N	N
9 Hamilton	Y	Y	Y	Y	N	N	N	N
10 Sharp	Y	Y	Y	Y	N	N	N	N
11 Jacobs	Y	N	Y	N	N	N	N	N
IOWA								
1 *Leach*	Y	Y	Y	Y	N	N	N	N
2 *Tauke*	Y	?	?	?	?	?	?	?
3 *Evans*	Y	N	Y	Y	N	N	N	N
4 Smith	Y	Y	Y	Y	N	N	N	N
5 Harkin	Y	Y	Y	Y	N	N	N	N
6 Bedell	Y	Y	Y	Y	Y	N	Y	N

Democrats *Republicans*

	219	220	221	222	223	224	225	226
KANSAS								
1 ***Roberts***	Y	Y	Y	Y	Y	Y	N	Y
2 ***Jeffries***	Y	Y	Y	Y	Y	Y	Y	Y
3 ***Winn***	Y	Y	Y	Y	Y	Y	N	Y
4 Glickman	Y	Y	Y	?	N	N	N	N
5 ***Whittaker***	Y	Y	Y	Y	Y	Y	N	Y
KENTUCKY								
1 Hubbard	Y	Y	Y	?	?	?	?	Y
2 Natcher	Y	Y	Y	Y	N	N	N	N
3 Mazzoli	+	+	+	Y	N	N	N	N
4 ***Snyder***	Y	Y	Y	Y	Y	Y	N	Y
5 ***Rogers***	Y	Y	Y	Y	N	Y	Y	Y
6 ***Hopkins***	Y	Y	Y	Y	N	N	N	N
7 Perkins	Y	Y	Y	Y	N	N	N	N
LOUISIANA								
1 ***Livingston***	Y	Y	Y	Y	N	Y	N	N
2 Boggs	?	?	Y	?	?	N	N	N
3 Tauzin	?	Y	Y	?	N	Y	N	N
4 Roemer	Y	Y	Y	Y	N	Y	N	N
5 Huckaby	Y	Y	Y	Y	Y	Y	N	N
6 ***Moore***	N	Y	Y	?	Y	Y	Y	Y
7 Breaux	Y	Y	Y	Y	N	Y	N	N
8 Long	N	Y	Y	Y	N	N	N	N
MAINE								
1 ***Emery***	Y	Y	Y	?	?	N	N	N
2 ***Snowe***	Y	Y	Y	Y	N	N	N	N
MARYLAND								
1 Dyson	Y	?	Y	Y	N	N	N	N
2 Long	Y	?	?	Y	N	N	?	N
3 Mikulski	Y	Y	Y	Y	N	N	N	N
4 ***Holt***	Y	Y	Y	Y	N	N	N	N
5 Hoyer	Y	Y	Y	Y	N	N	N	N
6 Byron	N	N	Y	Y	N	N	N	N
7 Mitchell	Y	N	Y	Y	N	N	N	N
8 Barnes	Y	+	+	Y	N	N	N	N
MASSACHUSETTS								
1 ***Conte***	Y	Y	Y	?	X	N	N	N
2 Boland	Y	?	?	Y	N	N	N	N
3 Early	?	?	?	Y	N	N	N	N
4 Frank	Y	Y	Y	Y	N	N	N	N
5 Shannon	?	?	?	Y	N	N	N	N
6 Mavroules	Y	?	Y	Y	N	N	N	N
7 Markey	Y	Y	Y	?	?	N	N	N
8 O'Neill								
9 Moakley	Y	Y	Y	?	?	N	N	N
10 ***Heckler***	Y	N	Y	Y	X	N	N	N
11 Donnelly	Y	?	?	Y	N	N	N	N
12 Studds	Y	Y	Y	Y	N	N	N	N
MICHIGAN								
1 Conyers	Y	Y	Y	Y	N	N	N	N
2 ***Pursell***	Y	?	Y	Y	N	N	N	N
3 Wolpe	Y	Y	Y	Y	N	N	N	N
4 ***Siljander***	Y	?	?	?	?	Y	Y	?
5 ***Sawyer***	Y	Y	Y	Y	N	Y	N	N
6 ***Dunn***	Y	Y	Y	Y	N	N	N	N
7 Kildee	Y	Y	Y	Y	N	N	N	N
8 Traxler	N	?	?	?	?	N	N	N
9 ***Vander Jagt***	Y	?	Y	Y	N	Y	N	?
10 Albosta	N	?	?	Y	N	N	N	N
11 ***Davis***	Y	Y	Y	Y	N	N	N	N
12 Bonior	N	Y	Y	Y	N	N	N	N
13 Crockett	Y	?	?	Y	N	N	N	N
14 Hertel	Y	Y	Y	Y	N	N	N	N
15 Ford	N	?	?	Y	N	N	N	N
16 Dingell	?	?	?	?	X	X	?	?
17 Brodhead	Y	?	?	Y	N	N	N	N
18 Blanchard	?	?	?	Y	N	N	N	N
19 ***Broomfield***	?	?	?	Y	N	N	N	Y
MINNESOTA								
1 ***Erdahl***	N	Y	Y	Y	N	N	N	Y
2 ***Hagedorn***	Y	?	Y	Y	Y	Y	Y	Y
3 ***Frenzel***	Y	Y	Y	Y	N	Y	N	Y
4 Vento	N	Y	Y	Y	N	N	N	N
5 Sabo	N	N	Y	Y	N	N	N	N
6 ***Weber***	N	Y	Y	Y	N	N	N	N
7 ***Stangeland***	N	?	?	Y	Y	Y	Y	Y
8 Oberstar	N	Y	Y	Y	N	N	N	N
MISSISSIPPI								
1 Whitten	Y	?	Y	Y	N	Y	Y	N
2 Bowen	Y	Y	Y	Y	Y	Y	Y	N
3 Montgomery	Y	Y	Y	Y	Y	Y	Y	Y
4 Dowdy	N	?	?	Y	?	N	N	N
5 ***Lott***	Y	Y	Y	Y	Y	Y	Y	Y
MISSOURI								
1 Clay	Y	?	?	?	N	N	N	N
2 Young	?	?	Y	Y	N	N	N	N
3 Gephardt	Y	Y	Y	Y	N	N	N	N

	219	220	221	222	223	224	225	226
4 Skelton	N	Y	Y	Y	N	N	N	N
5 Bolling	?	Y	Y	Y	?	N	N	N
6 ***Coleman***	Y	Y	Y	Y	N	Y	Y	Y
7 ***Taylor***	N	Y	Y	?	Y	Y	Y	Y
8 ***Bailey***	Y	Y	Y	?	Y	N	N	N
9 Volkmer	N	Y	Y	Y	N	N	N	N
10 ***Emerson***	Y	Y	Y	Y	Y	Y	Y	Y
MONTANA								
1 Williams	N	?	Y	?	N	N	N	N
2 ***Marlenee***	Y	Y	N	Y	Y	Y	Y	Y
NEBRASKA								
1 ***Bereuter***	Y	Y	Y	Y	N	Y	N	N
2 ***Daub***	Y	Y	Y	Y	N	N	N	Y
3 ***Smith***	Y	Y	Y	Y	N	Y	N	Y
NEVADA								
AL Santini	Y	?	Y	Y	N	Y	N	N
NEW HAMPSHIRE								
1 D'Amours	Y	Y	Y	?	?	N	N	N
2 ***Gregg***	Y	Y	Y	Y	N	N	N	Y
NEW JERSEY								
1 Florio	?	?	?	?	N	N	N	N
2 Hughes	Y	Y	Y	Y	N	N	N	N
3 Howard	Y	Y	Y	?	?	N	N	N
4 ***Smith***	Y	Y	Y	Y	N	N	N	N
5 ***Fenwick***	Y	Y	Y	Y	N	N	N	N
6 ***Forsythe***	Y	N	Y	Y	N	N	Y	Y
7 ***Roukema***	Y	Y	Y	Y	N	N	N	Y
8 Roe	Y	Y	Y	?	N	N	N	N
9 ***Hollenbeck***	Y	Y	Y	Y	N	N	N	N
10 Rodino	Y	Y	Y	Y	N	N	N	N
11 Minish	Y	Y	Y	Y	N	N	N	N
12 ***Rinaldo***	Y	Y	Y	Y	N	N	N	N
13 ***Courter***	Y	Y	Y	Y	Y	N	N	N
14 Guarini	Y	Y	Y	?	?	N	N	N
15 Dwyer	Y	Y	Y	Y	N	N	N	N
NEW MEXICO								
1 ***Lujan***	Y	Y	Y	Y	N	N	N	N
2 ***Skeen***	Y	?	?	Y	N	Y	Y	Y
NEW YORK								
1 ***Carney***	Y	Y	Y	Y	N	Y	N	Y
2 Downey	Y	Y	Y	Y	N	N	N	N
3 ***Carman***	Y	Y	Y	Y	Y	Y	N	Y
4 ***Lent***	Y	Y	Y	Y	N	N	N	Y
5 ***McGrath***	Y	?	?	Y	N	N	N	Y
6 ***LeBoutillier***	Y	Y	Y	Y	N	N	N	Y
7 Addabbo	?	?	#	Y	N	N	N	N
8 Rosenthal	Y	?	?	Y	N	N	N	N
9 Ferraro	Y	Y	Y	Y	N	N	N	N
10 Biaggi	Y	Y	Y	Y	N	N	N	N
11 Scheuer	Y	Y	Y	Y	N	N	N	N
12 Chisholm	?	?	?	?	N	N	N	N
13 Solarz	Y	Y	Y	?	?	N	N	N
14 Richmond	Y	Y	Y	Y	N	N	N	N
15 Zeferetti	Y	?	?	Y	N	N	N	N
16 Schumer	Y	Y	Y	Y	N	N	N	N
17 ***Molinari***	Y	Y	Y	Y	N	Y	N	Y
18 ***Green***	Y	Y	Y	Y	N	N	N	N
19 Rangel	Y	Y	Y	Y	N	N	N	N
20 Weiss	Y	?	?	Y	N	N	N	N
21 Garcia	?	?	?	Y	N	N	N	N
22 Bingham	Y	Y	Y	Y	N	N	N	N
23 Peyser	Y	Y	Y	Y	N	?	?	?
24 Ottinger	Y	P	Y	P	N	N	N	N
25 ***Fish***	Y	Y	Y	Y	N	N	N	N
26 ***Gilman***	Y	+	+	?	N	N	N	N
27 McHugh	N	Y	Y	Y	N	N	N	N
28 Stratton	Y	Y	Y	Y	N	N	N	N
29 ***Solomon***	N	N	Y	Y	Y	Y	Y	Y
30 ***Martin***	N	Y	Y	Y	Y	Y	Y	Y
31 ***Mitchell***	N	Y	Y	Y	N	N	N	Y
32 ***Wortley***	N	N	Y	Y	N	N	N	N
33 ***Lee***	N	Y	Y	Y	Y	Y	Y	Y
34 ***Horton***	Y	?	?	?	X	X	X	X
35 ***Conable***	Y	N	Y	Y	?	Y	Y	Y
36 LaFalce	Y	Y	Y	Y	N	N	?	N
37 Nowak	Y	Y	Y	Y	N	N	N	N
38 ***Kemp***	Y	?	Y	Y	N	N	N	N
39 Lundine	N	N	Y	Y	N	N	N	N
NORTH CAROLINA								
1 Jones	?	?	?	?	X	X	?	X
2 Fountain	N	?	Y	Y	Y	N	N	Y
3 Whitley	N	Y	Y	Y	N	N	N	N
4 Andrews	N	Y	Y	?	?	N	N	N
5 Neal	N	Y	Y	Y	N	N	N	N
6 ***Johnston***	Y	N	Y	Y	Y	Y	Y	Y
7 Rose	N	?	Y	Y	N	N	N	N
8 Hefner	N	Y	Y	Y	N	N	N	N

	219	220	221	222	223	224	225	226
9 ***Martin***	Y	Y	Y	?	#	Y	Y	Y
10 ***Broyhill***	Y	Y	Y	Y	Y	Y	Y	N
11 ***Hendon***	Y	Y	Y	Y	N	N	N	Y
NORTH DAKOTA								
AL Dorgan	N	Y	Y	Y	N	N	N	N
OHIO								
1 ***Gradison***	Y	Y	Y	Y	N	N	N	N
2 Luken	N	?	?	?	-	N	N	N
3 Hall	Y	Y	Y	Y	N	N	N	N
4 ***Oxley***	Y	?	Y	?	Y	Y	Y	Y
5 ***Latta***	Y	?	?	Y	N	Y	Y	Y
6 ***McEwen***	Y	Y	Y	Y	N	Y	N	Y
7 ***Brown***	Y	?	?	?	N	N	?	?
8 ***Kindness***	Y	Y	Y	Y	Y	Y	Y	Y
9 ***Weber***	Y	Y	Y	Y	N	N	N	N
10 ***Miller***	Y	Y	Y	Y	Y	Y	Y	Y
11 ***Stanton***	Y	Y	Y	Y	Y	N	N	Y
12 Shamansky	Y	Y	Y	Y	N	N	N	N
13 Pease	Y	Y	Y	Y	N	N	N	N
14 Seiberling	Y	?	Y	Y	N	N	N	N
15 ***Wylie***	Y	Y	Y	Y	N	N	N	Y
16 ***Regula***	Y	Y	Y	Y	N	N	N	Y
17 ***Ashbrook***	?	Y	Y	?	?	?	?	?
18 Applegate	Y	?	Y	?	N	Y	N	Y
19 ***Williams***	?	?	?	?	?	X	X	X
20 Oakar	Y	Y	Y	?	?	?	?	N
21 Stokes	Y	Y	Y	Y	N	N	N	N
22 Eckart	Y	Y	Y	Y	N	N	N	N
23 Mottl	Y	Y	Y	Y	Y	Y	Y	Y
OKLAHOMA								
1 Jones	Y	N	Y	Y	N	N	N	N
2 Synar	Y	Y	Y	Y	N	N	N	N
3 Watkins	N	Y	Y	Y	N	N	N	N
4 McCurdy	N	Y	Y	Y	N	N	N	N
5 ***Edwards***	Y	Y	Y	Y	N	Y	N	Y
6 English	N	Y	Y	Y	N	N	N	N
OREGON								
1 AuCoin	Y	Y	Y	Y	N	N	N	N
2 ***Smith***	Y	N	Y	Y	Y	Y	Y	Y
3 Wyden	Y	Y	Y	Y	N	N	N	N
4 Weaver	Y	Y	Y	Y	N	N	N	N
PENNSYLVANIA								
1 Foglietta	Y	Y	Y	?	N	N	N	N
2 Gray	Y	Y	Y	Y	N	N	N	N
3 Smith	Y	Y	Y	Y	N	N	N	N
4 ***Dougherty***	Y	?	?	?	N	N	N	N
5 ***Schulze***	Y	?	?	Y	N	N	N	Y
6 Yatron	Y	Y	Y	Y	N	N	N	N
7 Edgar	Y	N	Y	Y	N	N	N	N
8 ***Coyne, J.***	Y	?	Y	Y	N	N	N	N
9 ***Shuster***	N	Y	Y	Y	Y	Y	Y	Y
10 ***McDade***	Y	?	Y	Y	N	N	N	N
11 ***Nelligan***	Y	Y	Y	Y	N	N	N	N
12 Murtha	Y	Y	Y	Y	N	N	N	N
13 ***Coughlin***	Y	Y	Y	?	?	N	N	N
14 Coyne, W.	Y	Y	Y	Y	N	N	N	N
15 ***Ritter***	Y	Y	Y	Y	N	N	N	Y
16 ***Walker***	Y	N	Y	Y	N	N	N	N
17 Ertel	Y	Y	Y	Y	N	N	N	N
18 Walgren	Y	Y	Y	Y	N	N	N	N
19 ***Goodling***	?	N	Y	N	Y	Y	N	?
20 Gaydos	Y	Y	Y	Y	N	N	N	N
21 Bailey	Y	Y	Y	Y	N	N	N	N
22 Murphy	?	?	?	Y	N	N	N	N
23 ***Clinger***	Y	Y	Y	Y	N	Y	N	N
24 ***Marks***	Y	Y	Y	Y	N	N	N	N
25 Atkinson	Y	Y	Y	?	?	N	N	N
RHODE ISLAND								
1 St Germain	Y	?	Y	Y	N	N	N	N
2 ***Schneider***	Y	?	Y	Y	N	N	N	N
SOUTH CAROLINA								
1 ***Hartnett***	Y	Y	Y	Y	Y	Y	Y	N
2 ***Spence***	Y	Y	Y	Y	Y	Y	Y	Y
3 Derrick	?	?	?	Y	N	N	N	N
4 ***Campbell***	Y	Y	Y	?	Y	Y	Y	N
5 Holland	?	?	?	?	N	N	N	N
6 ***Napier***	Y	Y	Y	Y	Y	Y	Y	N
SOUTH DAKOTA								
1 Daschle	N	?	?	Y	N	N	?	N
2 ***Roberts***	N	Y	Y	Y	Y	Y	Y	Y
TENNESSEE								
1 ***Quillen***	?	?	?	Y	Y	Y	Y	Y
2 ***Duncan***	Y	Y	Y	Y	N	N	N	Y
3 Bouquard	Y	Y	Y	Y	N	N	N	N
4 Gore	Y	Y	Y	Y	N	N	N	N
5 Boner	Y	Y	Y	Y	N	N	N	N
6 ***Beard***	?	?	?	?	?	?	?	?

	219	220	221	222	223	224	225	226
7 Jones	Y	Y	Y	Y	N	N	N	N
8 Ford	Y	?	Y	?	X	N	N	N
TEXAS								
1 Hall, S.	N	Y	Y	Y	N	Y	Y	N
2 Wilson	Y	?	Y	Y	N	N	N	N
3 ***Collins***	Y	Y	Y	Y	Y	Y	Y	Y
4 Hall, R.	N	Y	Y	Y	N	Y	Y	N
5 Mattox	Y	N	Y	Y	N	N	N	N
6 Gramm	Y	?	?	Y	N	Y	Y	N
7 ***Archer***	Y	Y	Y	Y	Y	Y	Y	Y
8 ***Fields***	Y	Y	Y	Y	Y	Y	Y	Y
9 Brooks	Y	?	?	?	?	?	?	N
10 Pickle	Y	Y	Y	Y	N	N	N	N
11 Leath	?	Y	Y	Y	N	Y	N	N
12 Wright	Y	Y	Y	Y	N	N	N	N
13 Hightower	Y	Y	Y	Y	N	N	N	N
14 Patman	Y	Y	Y	Y	Y	Y	X	Y
15 de la Garza	Y	Y	Y	Y	N	N	N	N
16 White	Y	?	?	Y	N	N	N	N
17 Stenholm	Y	Y	Y	Y	N	Y	N	N
18 Leland	?	Y	Y	Y	N	N	N	N
19 Hance	Y	Y	Y	Y	N	N	N	N
20 Gonzalez	N	Y	Y	Y	N	N	N	N
21 ***Loeffler***	Y	?	?	Y	Y	Y	Y	N
22 ***Paul***	Y	Y	Y	?	#	#	#	?
23 Kazen	N	Y	Y	Y	N	N	N	N
24 Frost	N	Y	Y	Y	N	N	N	N
UTAH								
1 ***Hansen***	+	+	+	Y	Y	Y	Y	Y
2 ***Marriott***	Y	Y	Y	Y	N	N	N	N
VERMONT								
AL ***Jeffords***	Y	Y	Y	N	N	Y	N	Y
VIRGINIA								
1 ***Trible***	?	?	?	Y	#	Y	Y	Y
2 ***Whitehurst***	Y	?	?	Y	Y	Y	Y	Y
3 ***Bliley***	Y	Y	Y	Y	Y	Y	Y	Y
4 ***Daniel, R.***	Y	Y	Y	Y	Y	Y	Y	Y
5 Daniel, D.	Y	Y	Y	Y	Y	Y	Y	Y
6 ***Butler***	Y	Y	Y	Y	Y	Y	Y	Y
7 ***Robinson***	Y	Y	Y	Y	Y	Y	Y	Y
8 ***Parris***	Y	Y	Y	Y	Y	Y	Y	Y
9 ***Wampler***	Y	Y	Y	Y	Y	Y	Y	Y
10 ***Wolf***	Y	Y	Y	Y	N	Y	N	Y
WASHINGTON								
1 ***Pritchard***	?	?	?	?	?	?	N	Y
2 Swift	Y	?	Y	?	N	N	N	N
3 Bonker	Y	Y	Y	Y	N	-	-	-
4 ***Morrison***	Y	Y	Y	Y	N	Y	N	Y
5 Foley	Y	Y	?	Y	N	N	N	N
6 Dicks	Y	?	Y	Y	N	N	N	N
7 Lowry	Y	Y	Y	Y	N	N	N	N
WEST VIRGINIA								
1 Mollohan	Y	?	?	?	N	N	N	Y
2 ***Benedict***	Y	Y	Y	Y	N	#	Y	Y
3 ***Staton***	Y	Y	Y	Y	Y	Y	N	Y
4 Rahall	?	?	?	Y	N	N	N	N
WISCONSIN								
1 Aspin	N	Y	Y	?	?	N	N	N
2 Kastenmeier	N	Y	Y	Y	N	N	N	Y
3 ***Gunderson***	N	Y	Y	Y	N	N	N	N
4 Zablocki	N	Y	Y	Y	N	N	N	N
5 Reuss	Y	Y	Y	Y	N	N	N	N
6 ***Petri***	N	N	Y	?	X	N	N	Y
7 Obey	N	Y	Y	Y	N	N	N	N
8 ***Roth***	?	?	?	?	?	?	N	Y
9 ***Sensenbrenner***	N	Y	Y	Y	N	N	N	N
WYOMING								
AL ***Cheney***	Y	Y	Y	?	#	Y	Y	Y

Democrats ***Republicans***

227. HR 3112. Voting Rights Act Extension. Lungren, R-Calif., amendment to require certain areas of the country to provide bilingual election materials but not bilingual ballots. Rejected 124-285: R 107-68; D 17-217 (ND 9-148; SD 8-69), Oct. 5, 1981.

228. HR 3112. Voting Rights Act Extension. Passage of the bill to extend key enforcement provisions of the 1965 Voting Rights Act. Passed 389-24: R 160-17; D 229-7 (ND 158-1; SD 71-6), Oct. 5, 1981.

229. Procedural Motion. Lott, R-Miss., motion to approve the House *Journal* of Monday, Oct. 5. Motion agreed to 369-18: R 167-11; D 202-7 (ND 134-6; SD 68-1), Oct. 6, 1981.

230. HR 4560. Labor-HHS-Education Appropriations, Fiscal 1982. Natcher, D-Ky., motion that the House resolve itself into the Committee of the Whole for consideration of the bill making fiscal 1982 appropriations for the departments of Labor, Health and Human Services, and Education, and for related agencies. Motion agreed to 360-40: R 147-32; D 213-8 (ND 146-2; SD 67-6), Oct. 6, 1981.

231. HR 4560. Labor-HHS-Education Appropriations, Fiscal 1982. Natcher, D-Ky., amendment to reduce funding for the work incentive (WIN) program by $43.8 million and to require an across-the-board reduction of $30.2 million in spending for salaries and expenses by all the departments and agencies covered by the bill. Adopted 383-30: R 183-0; D 200-30 (ND 127-27; SD 73-3), Oct. 6, 1981.

232. HR 4560. Labor-HHS-Education Appropriations, Fiscal 1982. Bliley, R-Va., amendment to bar enforcement of a provision in the budget reconciliation bill (PL 97-35) that prohibited Medicare and Medicaid reimbursement for drugs for which the Food and Drug Administration had not completed an evaluation of effectiveness. Adopted 271-148: R 178-6; D 93-142 (ND 41-116; SD 52-26), Oct. 6, 1981.

233. HR 4560. Labor-HHS-Education Appropriations, Fiscal 1982. Rousselot, R-Calif., amendment to bar Mine Safety and Health Administration enforcement of regulations relating to the surface mining of stone, clay, colloidal phosphate, sand or gravel. Adopted 254-165: R 166-20; D 88-145 (ND 31-124; SD 57-21), Oct. 6, 1981.

234. HR 4560. Labor-HHS-Education Appropriations, Fiscal 1982. Regula, R-Ohio, motion to recommit the bill to the Appropriations Committee. Motion rejected 168-249: R 140-39; D 28-210 (ND 3-157; SD 25-53), Oct. 6, 1981. (The bill, appropriating $87,181,250,000 for the departments of Labor, Health and Human Services, and Education, and for related agencies, was subsequently passed by voice vote.) A "yea" was a vote supporting the president's position.

KEY

- **Y** Voted for (yea).
- **#** Paired for.
- **+** Announced for.
- **N** Voted against (nay).
- **X** Paired against.
- **-** Announced against.
- **P** Voted "present".
- **C** Voted "present" to avoid possible conflict of interest.
- **?** Did not vote or otherwise make a position known.

	227	228	229	230	231	232	233	234
ALABAMA								
1 *Edwards*	Y	Y	Y	Y	Y	Y	Y	Y
2 *Dickinson*	Y	N	N	Y	Y	Y	Y	Y
3 Nichols	Y	N	Y	Y	Y	Y	Y	N
4 Bevill	Y	Y	Y	Y	Y	Y	N	N
5 Flippo	N	Y	?	?	?	Y	Y	N
6 *Smith*	Y	Y	Y	Y	Y	Y	Y	Y
7 Shelby	Y	N	?	Y	Y	Y	Y	Y
ALASKA								
AL *Young*	N	Y	?	?	Y	Y	Y	N
ARIZONA								
1 *Rhodes*	N	Y	Y	?	Y	Y	Y	Y
2 Udall	N	Y	Y	Y	Y	Y	N	N
3 Stump	Y	N	Y	Y	Y	Y	Y	Y
4 *Rudd*	Y	N	Y	N	Y	Y	Y	Y
ARKANSAS								
1 Alexander	N	Y	Y	Y	Y	N	Y	N
2 *Bethune*	N	Y	Y	Y	?	Y	Y	Y
3 *Hammerschmidt*	Y	Y	Y	Y	Y	Y	Y	Y
4 Anthony	N	Y	Y	Y	Y	Y	Y	N
CALIFORNIA								
1 *Chappie*	Y	Y	Y	Y	Y	Y	Y	Y
2 *Clausen*	Y	Y	Y	Y	Y	Y	Y	Y
3 Matsui	N	Y	Y	Y	Y	N	N	N
4 Fazio	Y	Y	Y	Y	Y	Y	Y	N
5 Burton, J.	?	?	?	?	?	?	?	?
6 Burton, P.	N	Y	Y	Y	N	N	N	N
7 Miller	N	Y	Y	Y	N	N	N	N
8 Dellums	N	Y	?	N	N	N	N	N
9 Stark	N	Y	?	Y	N	N	N	N
10 Edwards	N	Y	Y	Y	N	N	N	N
11 Lantos	N	Y	Y	Y	N	N	N	N
12 *McCloskey*	Y	Y	Y	Y	Y	Y	Y	Y
13 Mineta	N	Y	Y	Y	Y	N	N	N
14 Shumway	Y	Y	Y	N	Y	Y	Y	Y
15 Coelho	Y	Y	Y	Y	Y	Y	N	N
16 Panetta	Y	Y	Y	Y	Y	N	Y	N
17 *Pashayan*	?	?	?	Y	Y	Y	Y	Y
18 *Thomas*	?	?	?	?	?	?	?	?
19 *Lagomarsino*	Y	Y	Y	Y	Y	Y	Y	Y
20 *Goldwater*	N	Y	Y	Y	Y	Y	Y	Y
21 *Fiedler*	?	?	?	?	?	?	?	?
22 *Moorhead*	Y	Y	Y	Y	Y	Y	Y	Y
23 Beilenson	Y	Y	Y	Y	Y	N	N	N
24 Waxman	?	Y	Y	Y	N	N	N	N
25 Roybal	N	Y	Y	Y	Y	N	N	N
26 *Rousselot*	Y	N	Y	N	Y	Y	Y	Y
27 *Dornan*	Y	Y	Y	Y	?	Y	Y	Y
28 Dixon	N	Y	Y	Y	Y	N	N	N
29 Hawkins	N	Y	Y	Y	N	N	N	N
30 Danielson	N	Y	Y	Y	N	N	N	N
31 Dymally	N	Y	Y	Y	N	N	N	N
32 Anderson	N	Y	Y	Y	Y	N	N	N
33 *Grisham*	Y	Y	Y	Y	Y	Y	Y	Y
34 *Lungren*	Y	Y	?	Y	Y	Y	Y	Y
35 *Dreier*	Y	Y	Y	Y	Y	Y	Y	Y
36 Brown	N	Y	?	?	Y	N	N	N
37 *Lewis*	Y	Y	?	N	Y	Y	Y	Y
38 Patterson	N	Y	Y	Y	N	N	N	N
39 *Dannemeyer*	?	?	Y	Y	Y	Y	Y	Y
40 *Badham*	Y	Y	Y	Y	Y	Y	Y	Y
41 *Lowery*	Y	Y	Y	N	Y	Y	Y	Y
42 *Hunter*	Y	Y	Y	Y	Y	Y	Y	Y
43 *Burgener*	Y	Y	Y	Y	Y	Y	Y	Y
COLORADO								
1 Schroeder	N	Y	N	Y	Y	N	N	N
2 Wirth	N	Y	Y	Y	N	Y	N	N
3 Kogovsek	N	Y	Y	Y	N	N	N	N
4 *Brown*	Y	Y	Y	N	Y	Y	Y	Y
5 *Kramer*	Y	Y	Y	Y	Y	Y	Y	Y
CONNECTICUT								
1 Vacancy								
2 Gejdenson	N	Y	N	Y	Y	N	Y	N
3 *DeNardis*	N	Y	Y	Y	Y	Y	N	N
4 *McKinney*	N	Y	Y	Y	?	Y	Y	N
5 Ratchford	N	Y	Y	Y	Y	N	N	N
6 Moffett	N	Y	Y	N	N	N	N	N
DELAWARE								
AL *Evans*	Y	Y	Y	Y	Y	Y	Y	Y
FLORIDA								
1 Hutto	N	Y	?	Y	Y	Y	Y	Y
2 Fuqua	N	Y	Y	Y	Y	N	Y	N
3 Bennett	N	Y	Y	Y	Y	N	Y	N
4 Chappell	Y	Y	Y	Y	Y	N	Y	Y
5 *McCollum*	N	Y	Y	Y	Y	Y	Y	Y
6 *Young*	Y	Y	Y	Y	Y	Y	Y	Y
7 Gibbons	N	Y	Y	Y	Y	Y	N	Y
8 Ireland	N	Y	Y	Y	Y	Y	Y	Y
9 Nelson	N	Y	Y	Y	Y	Y	Y	Y
10 *Bafalis*	Y	Y	Y	Y	Y	Y	C	Y
11 Mica	N	Y	Y	Y	Y	N	Y	N
12 *Shaw*	Y	Y	Y	N	Y	Y	Y	Y
13 Lehman	?	?	?	?	Y	N	N	N
14 Pepper	N	Y	?	Y	Y	N	N	N
15 Fascell	N	Y	Y	Y	Y	N	N	N
GEORGIA								
1 Ginn	N	Y	Y	Y	Y	Y	N	N
2 Hatcher	N	Y	Y	Y	Y	Y	Y	N
3 Brinkley	N	N	Y	Y	Y	Y	Y	N
4 Levitas	N	Y	Y	Y	Y	Y	Y	N
5 Fowler	N	Y	?	?	Y	Y	Y	N
6 *Gingrich*	Y	Y	Y	Y	Y	Y	Y	Y
7 McDonald	Y	N	Y	N	Y	Y	Y	Y
8 Evans	N	Y	Y	Y	Y	Y	Y	N
9 Jenkins	N	Y	Y	Y	Y	Y	Y	N
10 Barnard	N	Y	Y	N	Y	Y	Y	Y
HAWAII								
1 Heftel	N	Y	Y	Y	Y	N	Y	N
2 Akaka	N	Y	Y	Y	N	N	N	N
IDAHO								
1 *Craig*	Y	Y	Y	Y	Y	Y	Y	Y
2 *Hansen*	Y	N	Y	N	Y	Y	Y	Y
ILLINOIS								
1 Washington	N	Y	Y	N	N	N	N	N
2 Savage	N	Y	?	?	N	N	N	N
3 Russo	N	Y	Y	Y	Y	Y	N	N
4 *Derwinski*	Y	Y	N	Y	Y	N	Y	Y
5 Fary	N	Y	Y	Y	Y	N	N	N
6 *Hyde*	N	Y	Y	Y	Y	Y	Y	Y
7 Collins	N	Y	Y	N	N	N	N	N
8 Rostenkowski	N	Y	Y	Y	N	N	N	N
9 Yates	N	Y	Y	N	N	N	N	N
10 *Porter*	N	Y	Y	Y	Y	Y	Y	Y
11 Annunzio	N	Y	Y	Y	N	N	N	N
12 *Crane, P.*	?	?	Y	Y	Y	Y	Y	Y
13 *McClory*	Y	Y	Y	Y	Y	Y	Y	Y
14 *Erlenborn*	Y	Y	Y	Y	Y	Y	Y	Y
15 *Corcoran*	N	Y	Y	Y	Y	Y	Y	Y
16 *Martin*	Y	Y	Y	Y	Y	Y	Y	?
17 O'Brien	N	Y	?	?	Y	Y	Y	Y
18 *Michel*	Y	Y	Y	Y	Y	Y	Y	Y
19 *Railsback*	N	Y	Y	Y	Y	Y	Y	Y
20 *Findley*	Y	Y	Y	Y	Y	Y	Y	Y
21 *Madigan*	Y	Y	Y	Y	Y	Y	Y	Y
22 *Crane, D.*	Y	N	Y	Y	Y	Y	Y	Y
23 Price	N	Y	Y	Y	Y	N	N	N
24 Simon	N	Y	?	Y	Y	N	N	N
INDIANA								
1 Benjamin	N	Y	Y	Y	N	N	N	N
2 Fithian	N	Y	Y	Y	Y	N	Y	N
3 *Hiler*	Y	Y	Y	N	Y	Y	Y	Y
4 *Coats*	N	Y	Y	N	+	Y	N	Y
5 *Hillis*	Y	Y	Y	Y	Y	Y	Y	Y
6 Evans	N	Y	Y	Y	Y	N	N	N
7 *Myers*	Y	Y	Y	N	Y	Y	Y	Y
8 *Deckard*	N	Y	Y	N	Y	Y	Y	Y
9 Hamilton	N	Y	Y	Y	Y	Y	Y	Y
10 Sharp	N	Y	Y	Y	Y	N	Y	N
11 Jacobs	N	Y	N	?	N	Y	N	N
IOWA								
1 *Leach*	N	Y	Y	Y	Y	Y	Y	N
2 *Tauke*	N	Y	Y	Y	Y	Y	Y	Y
3 *Evans*	N	Y	Y	Y	Y	Y	Y	Y
4 Smith	N	Y	Y	Y	Y	N	Y	N
5 Harkin	N	Y	N	Y	Y	N	Y	N
6 Bedell	N	Y	Y	Y	Y	N	Y	N

Corresponding to Congressional Record Votes 241, 242, 243, 244, 245, 246, 247, 248

	227	228	229	230	231	232	233	234
KANSAS								
1 *Roberts*	Y	Y	Y	Y	Y	Y	Y	Y
2 *Jeffries*	Y	Y	Y	Y	Y	Y	Y	Y
3 *Winn*	Y	Y	Y	Y	Y	Y	Y	Y
4 Glickman	N	Y	Y	Y	Y	N	Y	N
5 *Whittaker*	Y	Y	Y	Y	Y	Y	Y	Y
KENTUCKY								
1 Hubbard	Y	Y	Y	Y	Y	Y	N	N
2 Natcher	N	Y	Y	Y	Y	N	N	N
3 Mazzoli	N	Y	Y	Y	Y	Y	N	N
4 *Snyder*	N	Y	Y	Y	Y	N	N	N
5 *Rogers*	N	Y	Y	Y	Y	Y	N	N
6 *Hopkins*	N	Y	Y	Y	Y	Y	N	N
7 Perkins	N	Y	Y	Y	Y	N	N	N
LOUISIANA								
1 *Livingston*	N	Y	Y	Y	Y	Y	Y	N
2 Boggs	N	Y	?	Y	Y	Y	Y	N
3 Tauzin	N	Y	Y	Y	Y	Y	Y	Y
4 Roemer	N	Y	Y	N	Y	N	Y	Y
5 Huckaby	N	Y	Y	Y	Y	Y	Y	Y
6 *Moore*	Y	Y	Y	Y	Y	Y	Y	Y
7 Breaux	N	Y	Y	Y	Y	Y	Y	Y
8 Long	N	Y	Y	Y	Y	Y	N	N
MAINE								
1 *Emery*	N	Y	Y	Y	Y	Y	Y	Y
2 *Snowe*	N	Y	Y	Y	Y	Y	Y	N
MARYLAND								
1 Dyson	N	Y	Y	Y	Y	Y	N	N
2 Long	N	Y	?	Y	Y	N	?	N
3 Mikulski	N	Y	Y	Y	Y	N	N	N
4 *Holt*	N	Y	Y	N	Y	#	Y	N
5 Hoyer	N	Y	Y	?	?	Y	Y	N
6 Byron	N	Y	Y	Y	Y	Y	Y	N
7 Mitchell	N	Y	N	Y	N	N	?	N
8 Barnes	N	Y	Y	Y	Y	N	N	N
MASSACHUSETTS								
1 *Conte*	N	Y	Y	Y	Y	Y	Y	N
2 Boland	N	Y	Y	Y	Y	N	N	N
3 Early	N	Y	Y	Y	Y	N	N	N
4 Frank	N	Y	Y	Y	N	Y	N	N
5 Shannon	N	Y	Y	Y	Y	N	N	N
6 Mavroules	N	Y	Y	Y	Y	N	N	N
7 Markey	N	Y	Y	Y	?	N	N	N
8 O'Neill								
9 Moakley	N	Y	Y	Y	Y	N	N	N
10 *Heckler*	N	Y	N	Y	Y	Y	N	N
11 Donnelly	N	Y	Y	Y	Y	N	N	N
12 Studds	N	Y	Y	Y	Y	N	N	N
MICHIGAN								
1 Conyers	N	Y	Y	Y	N	N	N	N
2 *Pursell*	N	Y	Y	Y	Y	Y	Y	N
3 Wolpe	N	Y	Y	Y	Y	Y	N	N
4 *Siljander*	?	Y	Y	Y	Y	Y	Y	Y
5 *Sawyer*	N	Y	Y	N	Y	Y	Y	Y
6 *Dunn*	N	Y	Y	Y	Y	Y	Y	Y
7 Kildee	N	Y	Y	Y	Y	N	N	N
8 Traxler	N	Y	Y	Y	Y	N	N	N
9 *Vander Jagt*	?	?	Y	Y	Y	Y	Y	Y
10 Albosta	N	Y	Y	Y	Y	Y	N	N
11 *Davis*	N	Y	Y	Y	Y	Y	Y	N
12 Bonior	N	Y	Y	Y	?	?	?	N
13 Crockett	N	Y	?	Y	N	Y	?	N
14 Hertel	N	Y	Y	Y	Y	N	N	N
15 Ford	N	Y	?	Y	Y	N	N	N
16 Dingell	?	?	?	?	?	X	?	N
17 Brodhead	N	Y	Y	N	Y	N	N	N
18 Blanchard	N	Y	?	Y	Y	N	N	N
19 *Broomfield*	N	Y	Y	Y	Y	Y	Y	Y
MINNESOTA								
1 *Erdahl*	Y	Y	Y	Y	Y	Y	Y	N
2 *Hagedorn*	Y	Y	Y	Y	Y	Y	Y	Y
3 *Frenzel*	Y	Y	?	Y	Y	Y	Y	Y
4 Vento	N	Y	Y	Y	Y	N	N	N
5 Sabo	N	Y	N	Y	Y	N	N	N
6 *Weber*	N	Y	Y	Y	Y	Y	Y	Y
7 *Stangeland*	Y	Y	Y	Y	Y	Y	Y	Y
8 Oberstar	N	Y	Y	Y	Y	N	N	N
MISSISSIPPI								
1 Whitten	N	Y	Y	Y	?	N	Y	N
2 Bowen	N	Y	Y	Y	Y	Y	Y	N
3 Montgomery	Y	N	Y	Y	Y	Y	Y	Y
4 Dowdy	N	Y	Y	Y	Y	Y	Y	Y
5 *Lott*	Y	N	Y	N	Y	Y	Y	Y
MISSOURI								
1 Clay	N	Y	?	Y	Y	N	N	N
2 Young	N	Y	Y	Y	Y	N	Y	N
3 Gephardt	N	Y	Y	Y	Y	N	Y	N
4 Skelton	N	Y	?	Y	Y	Y	Y	N
5 Bolling	N	Y	?	?	Y	N	N	N
6 *Coleman*	Y	Y	Y	Y	Y	Y	Y	Y
7 *Taylor*	Y	Y	Y	Y	Y	Y	Y	Y
8 *Bailey*	Y	Y	Y	N	Y	Y	Y	Y
9 Volkmer	N	Y	Y	Y	Y	Y	Y	N
10 *Emerson*	Y	Y	Y	N	Y	Y	Y	Y
MONTANA								
1 Williams	N	Y	Y	Y	Y	N	N	N
2 *Marlenee*	Y	Y	Y	Y	Y	Y	Y	Y
NEBRASKA								
1 *Bereuter*	N	Y	Y	Y	Y	Y	Y	Y
2 *Daub*	Y	Y	Y	N	Y	Y	Y	Y
3 *Smith*	Y	Y	Y	Y	Y	Y	Y	Y
NEVADA								
AL Santini	?	Y	Y	Y	?	Y	Y	N
NEW HAMPSHIRE								
1 D'Amours	N	Y	Y	Y	Y	N	N	N
2 *Gregg*	Y	Y	Y	Y	Y	Y	Y	Y
NEW JERSEY								
1 Florio	N	Y	?	?	?	?	?	?
2 Hughes	N	Y	Y	Y	Y	Y	Y	N
3 Howard	N	Y	Y	Y	Y	Y	N	N
4 *Smith*	N	Y	Y	Y	Y	Y	N	N
5 *Fenwick*	N	Y	Y	Y	Y	N	N	N
6 *Forsythe*	N	Y	N	?	Y	Y	Y	Y
7 *Roukema*	Y	Y	Y	Y	Y	Y	Y	N
8 Roe	N	Y	Y	Y	Y	Y	N	N
9 *Hollenbeck*	N	Y	?	Y	Y	Y	N	N
10 Rodino	N	Y	Y	Y	N	N	N	N
11 Minish	N	Y	Y	Y	Y	Y	N	N
12 *Rinaldo*	N	Y	Y	Y	Y	Y	N	N
13 *Courter*	N	Y	Y	Y	Y	Y	Y	Y
14 Guarini	N	Y	Y	Y	Y	N	N	N
15 Dwyer	N	Y	Y	Y	Y	Y	N	N
NEW MEXICO								
1 *Lujan*	N	Y	Y	Y	Y	Y	Y	Y
2 *Skeen*	N	Y	Y	Y	Y	Y	Y	Y
NEW YORK								
1 *Carney*	Y	Y	Y	Y	Y	Y	Y	N
2 Downey	N	Y	Y	Y	Y	N	N	N
3 *Carman*	Y	Y	Y	Y	Y	Y	Y	Y
4 *Lent*	Y	Y	Y	N	Y	Y	Y	Y
5 *McGrath*	Y	Y	Y	N	Y	Y	Y	Y
6 *LeBoutillier*	Y	Y	Y	Y	Y	Y	Y	Y
7 Addabbo	N	Y	Y	Y	Y	N	N	N
8 Rosenthal	N	Y	Y	Y	Y	N	N	N
9 Ferraro	N	Y	Y	Y	Y	N	N	N
10 Biaggi	N	Y	Y	Y	N	Y	N	N
11 Scheuer	N	Y	Y	Y	Y	N	N	N
12 Chisholm	N	Y	?	Y	N	N	?	?
13 Solarz	N	Y	Y	Y	Y	N	N	N
14 Richmond	N	Y	Y	Y	Y	N	N	N
15 Zeferetti	N	Y	Y	Y	Y	Y	N	N
16 Schumer	N	Y	Y	Y	Y	Y	N	N
17 *Molinari*	Y	Y	Y	Y	Y	Y	Y	Y
18 *Green*	N	Y	Y	Y	Y	Y	Y	N
19 Rangel	N	Y	Y	Y	Y	N	N	N
20 Weiss	N	Y	Y	Y	N	N	N	N
21 Garcia	N	Y	Y	Y	N	N	N	N
22 Bingham	N	Y	Y	Y	N	N	N	N
23 Peyser	?	?	?	?	?	N	N	N
24 Ottinger	N	Y	P	P	N	N	N	N
25 *Fish*	N	Y	Y	Y	Y	Y	Y	N
26 *Gilman*	N	Y	Y	Y	Y	Y	Y	N
27 McHugh	N	Y	Y	Y	Y	N	N	N
28 Stratton	N	Y	Y	Y	Y	Y	Y	N
29 *Solomon*	Y	?	Y	N	Y	Y	Y	Y
30 *Martin*	Y	Y	Y	N	Y	Y	Y	Y
31 *Mitchell*	Y	Y	Y	Y	Y	Y	Y	N
32 *Wortley*	N	Y	N	Y	Y	Y	Y	Y
33 *Lee*	Y	Y	Y	Y	Y	Y	Y	Y
34 *Horton*	?	?	?	?	Y	Y	Y	N
35 *Conable*	?	Y	Y	N	Y	Y	Y	Y
36 LaFalce	N	Y	Y	Y	Y	Y	N	N
37 Nowak	N	Y	Y	Y	Y	N	Y	N
38 *Kemp*	N	Y	Y	Y	Y	Y	Y	Y
39 Lundine	N	Y	Y	Y	Y	N	Y	N
NORTH CAROLINA								
1 Jones	?	?	?	?	?	?	?	?
2 Fountain	N	Y	Y	Y	Y	Y	Y	Y
3 Whitley	N	Y	Y	Y	Y	Y	Y	Y
4 Andrews	N	Y	Y	Y	Y	Y	Y	Y
5 Neal	N	Y	Y	Y	Y	Y	Y	N
6 *Johnston*	Y	N	N	N	Y	Y	Y	?
7 Rose	N	Y	Y	Y	Y	N	N	N
8 Hefner	N	Y	Y	Y	Y	Y	Y	N
9 *Martin*	Y	Y	Y	Y	Y	Y	Y	Y
10 *Broyhill*	Y	Y	Y	Y	Y	Y	Y	Y
11 *Hendon*	Y	Y	+	-	+	#	Y	Y
NORTH DAKOTA								
AL Dorgan	N	Y	Y	N	Y	Y	Y	N
OHIO								
1 *Gradison*	N	Y	Y	Y	Y	N	Y	Y
2 Luken	N	Y	Y	Y	Y	N	N	N
3 Hall	N	Y	Y	Y	Y	N	N	N
4 *Oxley*	Y	Y	?	Y	Y	Y	Y	Y
5 *Latta*	Y	Y	Y	N	Y	Y	N	Y
6 *McEwen*	Y	Y	Y	Y	Y	Y	Y	Y
7 *Brown*	?	?	Y	Y	Y	?	?	?
8 *Kindness*	Y	Y	Y	Y	Y	Y	Y	Y
9 *Weber*	N	Y	Y	Y	Y	Y	N	Y
10 *Miller*	Y	Y	Y	Y	Y	Y	Y	Y
11 *Stanton*	N	Y	Y	Y	Y	Y	Y	Y
12 Shamansky	N	Y	Y	Y	Y	N	N	N
13 Pease	N	Y	Y	Y	Y	N	N	N
14 Seiberling	N	Y	Y	Y	Y	N	N	N
15 *Wylie*	Y	Y	Y	Y	Y	Y	Y	Y
16 *Regula*	Y	Y	Y	Y	Y	Y	Y	Y
17 *Ashbrook*	?	?	Y	Y	Y	Y	Y	Y
18 Applegate	Y	Y	?	?	Y	Y	N	N
19 *Williams*	?	?	Y	Y	Y	Y	Y	N
20 Oakar	N	Y	Y	Y	Y	N	N	N
21 Stokes	N	Y	Y	Y	N	N	N	N
22 Eckart	N	Y	Y	Y	Y	Y	Y	N
23 Mottl	Y	Y	Y	Y	Y	N	N	Y
OKLAHOMA								
1 Jones	N	Y	?	Y	Y	N	Y	N
2 Synar	N	Y	Y	Y	Y	Y	N	N
3 Watkins	N	Y	Y	Y	Y	Y	Y	N
4 McCurdy	N	Y	Y	Y	Y	Y	Y	N
5 *Edwards*	Y	Y	Y	Y	Y	Y	Y	Y
6 English	N	Y	Y	Y	Y	N	Y	N
OREGON								
1 AuCoin	N	Y	Y	Y	Y	N	N	N
2 *Smith*	Y	Y	N	N	Y	Y	Y	Y
3 Wyden	N	Y	Y	Y	Y	N	N	N
4 Weaver	N	Y	Y	Y	Y	N	N	N
PENNSYLVANIA								
1 Foglietta	N	Y	Y	Y	N	N	Y	N
2 Gray	N	Y	Y	Y	N	N	N	N
3 Smith	N	Y	Y	Y	Y	Y	N	N
4 *Dougherty*	?	Y	Y	Y	Y	Y	N	N
5 *Schulze*	Y	Y	Y	N	Y	Y	Y	Y
6 Yatron	N	Y	Y	Y	Y	N	N	N
7 Edgar	N	Y	Y	Y	Y	N	N	N
8 *Coyne, J.*	N	Y	Y	Y	Y	Y	Y	Y
9 *Shuster*	Y	Y	Y	Y	Y	Y	Y	Y
10 *McDade*	N	Y	Y	Y	Y	Y	N	N
11 *Nelligan*	N	Y	Y	Y	Y	Y	Y	N
12 Murtha	N	Y	Y	Y	Y	N	N	N
13 *Coughlin*	N	Y	Y	Y	Y	Y	Y	Y
14 Coyne, W.	N	Y	Y	Y	N	N	N	N
15 *Ritter*	Y	Y	Y	Y	Y	Y	Y	Y
16 *Walker*	N	Y	N	N	Y	Y	N	Y
17 Ertel	N	Y	Y	Y	Y	N	Y	N
18 Walgren	N	Y	Y	Y	Y	Y	N	N
19 *Goodling*	?	?	N	Y	Y	?	Y	N
20 Gaydos	N	Y	Y	Y	Y	N	N	N
21 Bailey	N	Y	Y	Y	Y	N	N	N
22 Murphy	N	Y	Y	Y	Y	Y	N	N
23 *Clinger*	N	Y	Y	Y	Y	N	Y	N
24 *Marks*	N	Y	Y	Y	Y	Y	Y	Y
25 Atkinson	N	Y	Y	Y	Y	N	N	Y
RHODE ISLAND								
1 St Germain	N	Y	Y	Y	Y	Y	N	N
2 *Schneider*	N	Y	Y	Y	Y	Y	N	N
SOUTH CAROLINA								
1 *Hartnett*	N	Y	Y	Y	Y	Y	Y	Y
2 *Spence*	Y	Y	Y	Y	Y	Y	Y	Y
3 Derrick	N	Y	?	?	Y	N	Y	N
4 *Campbell*	N	Y	Y	N	Y	Y	Y	Y
5 Holland	N	Y	Y	Y	Y	Y	N	N
6 *Napier*	N	Y	Y	Y	Y	Y	Y	?
SOUTH DAKOTA								
1 Daschle	N	Y	?	?	Y	Y	Y	N
2 *Roberts*	Y	Y	Y	Y	Y	Y	Y	?
TENNESSEE								
1 *Quillen*	N	Y	Y	Y	Y	Y	Y	Y
2 *Duncan*	N	Y	Y	Y	Y	Y	Y	Y
3 Bouquard	N	Y	Y	Y	Y	N	Y	N
4 Gore	N	Y	Y	Y	Y	N	N	N
5 Boner	N	Y	Y	Y	Y	N	N	N
6 *Beard*	?	?	Y	Y	Y	Y	Y	?
7 Jones	N	Y	Y	Y	Y	N	N	N
8 Ford	N	Y	Y	Y	N	N	N	N
TEXAS								
1 Hall, S.	N	Y	Y	Y	Y	Y	Y	Y
2 Wilson	N	Y	Y	Y	Y	N	N	N
3 *Collins*	Y	N	N	Y	Y	Y	Y	Y
4 Hall, R.	N	Y	Y	N	Y	Y	Y	Y
5 Mattox	N	Y	Y	Y	Y	Y	N	N
6 Gramm	N	Y	Y	N	Y	Y	Y	Y
7 *Archer*	Y	N	Y	?	Y	Y	Y	Y
8 *Fields*	Y	Y	Y	N	Y	Y	Y	Y
9 Brooks	N	Y	Y	?	Y	Y	Y	N
10 Pickle	N	Y	Y	Y	Y	Y	Y	Y
11 Leath	N	Y	Y	N	Y	Y	Y	Y
12 Wright	N	Y	Y	Y	Y	Y	Y	N
13 Hightower	N	Y	Y	Y	Y	Y	Y	N
14 Patman	N	Y	Y	Y	Y	Y	Y	N
15 de la Garza	N	Y	Y	Y	Y	N	Y	N
16 White	N	Y	Y	Y	Y	Y	Y	N
17 Stenholm	N	Y	Y	Y	Y	Y	Y	Y
18 Leland	N	Y	Y	Y	N	Y	N	N
19 Hance	N	Y	Y	Y	Y	N	Y	Y
20 Gonzalez	N	Y	Y	Y	N	Y	N	N
21 *Loeffler*	N	Y	Y	N	?	Y	Y	Y
22 *Paul*	?	?	?	?	Y	Y	Y	Y
23 Kazen	N	Y	Y	Y	Y	Y	Y	N
24 Frost	N	Y	Y	Y	Y	N	N	N
UTAH								
1 *Hansen*	Y	Y	?	Y	Y	Y	Y	Y
2 *Marriott*	N	Y	Y	Y	Y	?	?	?
VERMONT								
AL *Jeffords*	N	Y	Y	Y	Y	N	Y	N
VIRGINIA								
1 *Trible*	Y	N	Y	Y	Y	Y	Y	Y
2 *Whitehurst*	Y	N	Y	Y	Y	Y	Y	Y
3 *Bliley*	Y	N	Y	Y	Y	Y	Y	Y
4 *Daniel, R.*	Y	N	Y	Y	Y	Y	Y	Y
5 Daniel, D.	Y	N	N	Y	Y	Y	Y	Y
6 *Butler*	Y	N	Y	Y	Y	Y	Y	Y
7 *Robinson*	Y	N	Y	Y	Y	Y	Y	Y
8 *Parris*	Y	N	Y	Y	Y	Y	N	?
9 *Wampler*	Y	N	Y	Y	Y	Y	N	N
10 *Wolf*	Y	Y	Y	Y	Y	Y	Y	Y
WASHINGTON								
1 *Pritchard*	N	Y	Y	?	Y	Y	Y	N
2 Swift	N	Y	P	Y	Y	Y	Y	N
3 Bonker	-	+	?	?	Y	?	N	N
4 *Morrison*	N	Y	Y	Y	Y	Y	Y	Y
5 Foley	N	Y	Y	?	Y	Y	Y	N
6 Dicks	N	Y	Y	Y	Y	N	N	N
7 Lowry	N	Y	Y	Y	Y	N	N	N
WEST VIRGINIA								
1 Mollohan	Y	Y	Y	Y	Y	X	N	N
2 *Benedict*	Y	Y	Y	Y	Y	Y	Y	Y
3 *Staton*	Y	Y	Y	Y	Y	Y	N	Y
4 Rahall	N	Y	Y	Y	Y	N	N	N
WISCONSIN								
1 Aspin	N	Y	Y	Y	Y	N	N	N
2 Kastenmeier	Y	Y	Y	Y	Y	N	N	N
3 *Gunderson*	Y	Y	Y	Y	Y	Y	Y	Y
4 Zablocki	N	Y	Y	Y	Y	N	Y	N
5 Reuss	N	Y	?	Y	Y	N	N	N
6 *Petri*	Y	Y	Y	Y	Y	Y	Y	Y
7 Obey	N	Y	Y	Y	Y	N	N	N
8 *Roth*	Y	Y	Y	Y	Y	Y	Y	Y
9 *Sensenbrenner*	N	Y	Y	Y	Y	Y	Y	Y
WYOMING								
AL *Cheney*	Y	Y	Y	?	Y	Y	Y	Y

Democrats *Republicans*

235. H Con Res 200. Anwar Sadat. Adoption of the concurrent resolution expressing the deep regret of the U.S. Congress over the assassination of President Anwar el-Sadat of Egypt. Adopted 411-0: R 180-0; D 231-0 (ND 154-0, SD 77-0), Oct. 6, 1981.

236. Procedural Motion. Lungren, R-Calif., motion to approve the House *Journal* of Tuesday, Oct. 6. Motion agreed to 359-20: R 157-11; D 202-9 (ND 134-8, SD 68-1), Oct. 7, 1981.

237. S 1181. Military Pay Raise. Nichols, D-Ala., motion to order the previous question (thus ending debate and the possibility of an amendment) on the conference report on the bill authorizing $4.5 billion for pay raises for military personnel, effective Oct. 1, 1981. Motion agreed to 416-0: R 183-0; D 233-0 (ND 156-0, SD 77-0), Oct. 7, 1981.

238. S 1181. Military Pay Raise. Adoption of the conference report on the bill authorizing $4.5 billion for pay raises for military personnel, effective Oct. 1, 1981. Adopted 417-1: R 184-0; D 233-1 (ND 156-1, SD 77-0), Oct. 7, 1981.

239. HR 3603. Food and Agriculture Act of 1981. Bedell, D-Iowa, amendments *en bloc* to reduce by $1 billion the committee-approved fiscal 1982 outlays for farm programs, by lowering sugar and dairy price support levels and making certain farm programs discretionary instead of mandatory. Adopted 400-14: R 176-7; D 224-7 (ND 147-7, SD 77-0), Oct. 7, 1981. A "nay" was a vote supporting the president's position.

240. HR 3603. Food and Agriculture Act of 1981. Jeffords, R-Vt., amendment to the Frank, D-Mass., amendment *(see vote 241, below)*, to set the minimum dairy price support level at 70 percent of parity but no less than $13.10 per hundredweight in fiscal 1982. (The effect would be to permit dairy price supports to rise in fiscal 1983 to a minimum of 75 percent of parity, unless Congress blocked the increase.) Rejected 123-277: R 41-138; D 82-139 (ND 40-110, SD 42-29), Oct. 7, 1981. A "nay" was a vote supporting the president's position.

241. HR 3603. Food and Agriculture Act of 1981. Frank, D-Mass., amendment to set dairy price support levels at a minimum of 70 percent of parity for fiscal years 1982-85 with mandatory annual readjustments, except that the secretary of agriculture could forgo the annual adjustment (to bring the actual payment rate back up to 70 percent of parity) in years when anticipated expenditures for surplus dairy purchases exceeded $750 million. In such years, actual payment rates could not go below the previous year's level or $13.10 per hundredweight, whichever was lower. Rejected 153-243: R 75-104; D 78-139 (ND 70-77, SD 8-62), Oct. 7, 1981. A "yea" was a vote supporting the president's position.

KEY

- Y Voted for (yea).
- # Paired for.
- + Announced for.
- N Voted against (nay).
- X Paired against.
- - Announced against.
- P Voted "present".
- C Voted "present" to avoid possible conflict of interest.
- ? Did not vote or otherwise make a position known.

	235	236	237	238	239	240	241
ALABAMA							
1 Edwards	Y	?	Y	Y	Y	N	Y
2 Dickinson	Y	N	Y	Y	Y	Y	N
3 Nichols	Y	Y	Y	Y	Y	?	X
4 Bevill	Y	Y	Y	Y	Y	?	?
5 Flippo	Y	Y	Y	Y	Y	Y	N
6 Smith	Y	?	Y	Y	Y	?	?
7 Shelby	Y	Y	Y	Y	Y	N	N
ALASKA							
AL Young	Y	?	Y	Y	Y	N	N
ARIZONA							
1 Rhodes	?	Y	Y	Y	Y	N	Y
2 Udall	Y	Y	Y	Y	Y	N	Y
3 Stump	Y	Y	Y	Y	Y	N	N
4 Rudd	Y	Y	Y	Y	Y	N	Y
ARKANSAS							
1 Alexander	Y	Y	Y	Y	Y	Y	N
2 Bethune	?	Y	Y	Y	Y	N	N
3 Hammerschmidt	Y	Y	Y	Y	Y	Y	N
4 Anthony	Y	Y	Y	Y	Y	N	N
CALIFORNIA							
1 Chappie	Y	Y	Y	Y	Y	N	Y
2 Clausen	Y	Y	Y	Y	Y	Y	N
3 Matsui	Y	?	Y	Y	Y	N	N
4 Fazio	Y	Y	Y	Y	Y	N	N
5 Burton, J.	?	?	?	?	?	?	?
6 Burton, P.	Y	Y	Y	Y	Y	N	N
7 Miller	Y	Y	Y	Y	Y	N	Y
8 Dellums	Y	Y	Y	Y	Y	N	Y
9 Stark	?	Y	Y	Y	Y	N	Y
10 Edwards	Y	Y	Y	Y	Y	N	Y
11 Lantos	Y	Y	Y	Y	Y	N	N
12 McCloskey	Y	?	Y	Y	?	N	Y
13 Mineta	Y	Y	Y	Y	Y	N	N
14 Shumway	Y	Y	Y	Y	Y	N	N
15 Coelho	Y	Y	Y	Y	Y	Y	N
16 Panetta	Y	Y	Y	Y	Y	N	N
17 Pashayan	?	Y	Y	Y	Y	Y	Y
18 Thomas	?	?	?	?	?	?	?
19 Lagomarsino	Y	Y	Y	Y	Y	N	Y
20 Goldwater	Y	?	?	?	Y	N	N
21 Fiedler	?	?	?	?	?	?	?
22 Moorhead	Y	Y	Y	Y	Y	N	Y
23 Beilenson	Y	Y	Y	Y	Y	N	N
24 Waxman	Y	Y	Y	Y	Y	N	N
25 Roybal	Y	Y	Y	Y	Y	N	Y
26 Rousselot	Y	Y	Y	Y	Y	?	?
27 Dornan	Y	Y	Y	Y	Y	N	Y
28 Dixon	Y	?	?	Y	Y	N	N
29 Hawkins	Y	?	Y	Y	Y	N	N
30 Danielson	Y	Y	Y	Y	Y	N	Y
31 Dymally	Y	Y	Y	Y	Y	N	Y
32 Anderson	Y	Y	Y	Y	Y	N	Y
33 Grisham	Y	Y	Y	Y	Y	N	N
34 Lungren	Y	Y	Y	Y	Y	N	Y
35 Dreier	Y	Y	Y	Y	Y	N	N
36 Brown	Y	Y	Y	Y	Y	Y	N
37 Lewis	Y	Y	Y	Y	N	Y	N
38 Patterson	Y	Y	Y	Y	Y	N	N
39 Dannemeyer	Y	Y	Y	Y	Y	N	Y
40 Badham	Y	Y	Y	Y	?	?	?
41 Lowery	Y	?	Y	Y	Y	N	Y
42 Hunter	Y	Y	Y	Y	Y	N	Y
43 Burgener	Y	Y	Y	Y	Y	N	Y
COLORADO							
1 Schroeder	Y	N	Y	Y	Y	N	Y
2 Wirth	Y	?	?	?	?	?	?
3 Kogovsek	Y	Y	Y	Y	Y	N	N
4 Brown	Y	Y	Y	Y	Y	N	N

	235	236	237	238	239	240	241
5 Kramer	Y	Y	Y	Y	Y	N	N
CONNECTICUT							
1 Vacancy							
2 Gejdenson	Y	N	Y	Y	Y	Y	N
3 DeNardis	Y	Y	Y	Y	Y	N	Y
4 McKinney	Y	?	Y	Y	Y	N	Y
5 Ratchford	Y	Y	Y	Y	Y	N	Y
6 Moffett	Y	?	Y	Y	Y	N	N
DELAWARE							
AL Evans	Y	Y	Y	Y	Y	N	Y
FLORIDA							
1 Hutto	Y	Y	Y	Y	Y	N	N
2 Fuqua	Y	Y	Y	Y	Y	N	N
3 Bennett	Y	Y	Y	Y	Y	N	N
4 Chappell	Y	?	Y	Y	Y	N	N
5 McCollum	Y	Y	Y	Y	Y	N	Y
6 Young	Y	Y	Y	Y	Y	N	N
7 Gibbons	Y	Y	Y	Y	Y	N	Y
8 Ireland	Y	Y	Y	Y	Y	N	N
9 Nelson	Y	Y	Y	Y	Y	N	N
10 Bafalis	Y	Y	Y	Y	Y	N	N
11 Mica	Y	Y	Y	Y	Y	N	N
12 Shaw	Y	Y	Y	Y	Y	N	N
13 Lehman	Y	Y	Y	Y	Y	N	Y
14 Pepper	Y	Y	Y	Y	Y	N	N
15 Fascell	Y	Y	Y	Y	Y	N	Y
GEORGIA							
1 Ginn	Y	Y	Y	Y	Y	Y	N
2 Hatcher	Y	Y	Y	Y	Y	Y	N
3 Brinkley	Y	Y	Y	Y	N	?	?
4 Levitas	Y	?	?	?	?	?	?
5 Fowler	Y	Y	Y	Y	Y	Y	N
6 Gingrich	Y	?	Y	Y	Y	N	N
7 McDonald	Y	?	Y	Y	Y	N	Y
8 Evans	Y	Y	Y	Y	Y	Y	N
9 Jenkins	Y	Y	Y	Y	Y	N	N
10 Barnard	Y	Y	Y	Y	Y	?	?
HAWAII							
1 Heftel	Y	Y	Y	Y	Y	Y	N
2 Akaka	?	Y	Y	Y	Y	Y	N
IDAHO							
1 Craig	Y	?	Y	Y	Y	N	N
2 Hansen	Y	Y	Y	Y	Y	N	N
ILLINOIS							
1 Washington	Y	?	Y	Y	Y	N	Y
2 Savage	?	?	?	?	?	?	?
3 Russo	Y	Y	Y	Y	Y	N	Y
4 Derwinski	Y	Y	Y	Y	Y	N	Y
5 Fary	Y	Y	Y	Y	Y	N	Y
6 Hyde	Y	Y	Y	Y	Y	N	Y
7 Collins	Y	Y	Y	Y	Y	N	Y
8 Rostenkowski	Y	Y	Y	Y	Y	N	Y
9 Yates	?	?	Y	Y	Y	?	?
10 Porter	Y	Y	Y	Y	Y	N	Y
11 Annunzio	Y	Y	Y	Y	Y	N	Y
12 Crane, P.	Y	Y	Y	Y	Y	N	N
13 McClory	Y	Y	Y	Y	Y	N	N
14 Erlenborn	Y	Y	Y	Y	Y	N	Y
15 Corcoran	Y	Y	Y	Y	Y	N	N
16 Martin	Y	Y	Y	Y	Y	N	Y
17 O'Brien	?	?	Y	Y	Y	N	Y
18 Michel	Y	Y	Y	Y	Y	N	N
19 Railsback	Y	Y	Y	Y	Y	N	N
20 Findley	Y	Y	Y	Y	Y	N	N
21 Madigan	Y	Y	Y	Y	Y	N	N
22 Crane, D.	Y	Y	Y	Y	Y	?	#
23 Price	Y	Y	Y	Y	Y	N	N
24 Simon	Y	Y	Y	Y	Y	Y	N
INDIANA							
1 Benjamin	Y	Y	Y	N	Y	N	Y
2 Fithian	Y	Y	Y	Y	Y	Y	N
3 Hiler	Y	Y	Y	Y	Y	N	N
4 Coats	Y	N	Y	Y	Y	N	Y
5 Hillis	Y	Y	Y	Y	Y	N	N
6 Evans	Y	Y	Y	Y	Y	N	N
7 Myers	Y	Y	Y	Y	Y	N	N
8 Deckard	Y	Y	Y	Y	Y	N	N
9 Hamilton	Y	Y	Y	Y	Y	N	N
10 Sharp	Y	Y	Y	Y	Y	N	N
11 Jacobs	Y	N	Y	Y	Y	N	N
IOWA							
1 Leach	Y	Y	Y	Y	Y	N	N
2 Tauke	Y	Y	Y	Y	Y	N	N
3 Evans	Y	N	Y	Y	Y	N	N
4 Smith	Y	Y	Y	Y	Y	N	N
5 Harkin	Y	Y	Y	Y	Y	N	N
6 Bedell	Y	Y	Y	Y	Y	N	N

Democrats *Republicans*

	235	236	237	238	239	240	241
KANSAS							
1 *Roberts*	Y	Y	Y	Y	Y	N	N
2 *Jeffries*	Y	Y	Y	Y	Y	N	N
3 *Winn*	Y	Y	Y	Y	Y	N	N
4 Glickman	Y	Y	Y	Y	Y	N	N
5 *Whittaker*	Y	Y	Y	Y	Y	N	N
KENTUCKY							
1 Hubbard	Y	Y	Y	Y	Y	Y	N
2 Natcher	Y	Y	Y	Y	Y	Y	N
3 Mazzoli	Y	Y	Y	Y	Y	N	Y
4 *Snyder*	Y	Y	Y	Y	Y	Y	N
5 *Rogers*	Y	Y	Y	Y	Y	Y	N
6 *Hopkins*	Y	Y	Y	Y	Y	Y	N
7 Perkins	Y	Y	Y	Y	Y	Y	N
LOUISIANA							
1 *Livingston*	Y	Y	Y	Y	Y	N	N
2 Boggs	Y	?	Y	Y	Y	Y	N
3 Tauzin	Y	Y	Y	Y	Y	Y	N
4 Roemer	Y	Y	Y	Y	Y	N	N
5 Huckaby	Y	Y	Y	Y	Y	Y	N
6 *Moore*	Y	Y	Y	Y	Y	Y	N
7 Breaux	Y	?	Y	Y	Y	Y	N
8 Long	Y	Y	Y	Y	Y	?	?
MAINE							
1 *Emery*	Y	Y	Y	Y	Y	Y	N
2 *Snowe*	Y	Y	Y	Y	Y	N	N
MARYLAND							
1 Dyson	Y	Y	Y	Y	Y	Y	N
2 Long	Y	Y	Y	Y	Y	N	Y
3 Mikulski	Y	Y	Y	Y	Y	N	Y
4 *Holt*	Y	Y	Y	Y	Y	N	N
5 Hoyer	Y	Y	Y	Y	Y	N	Y
6 Byron	Y	Y	Y	Y	Y	Y	N
7 Mitchell	Y	N	Y	Y	Y	N	Y
8 Barnes	Y	Y	Y	Y	Y	N	Y
MASSACHUSETTS							
1 *Conte*	Y	Y	Y	Y	Y	N	Y
2 Boland	Y	Y	Y	Y	Y	N	Y
3 Early	Y	Y	?	?	?	?	?
4 Frank	Y	Y	Y	Y	Y	N	Y
5 Shannon	Y	Y	Y	Y	Y	N	Y
6 Mavroules	Y	Y	Y	Y	Y	N	Y
7 Markey	Y	Y	Y	Y	Y	N	Y
8 O'Neill	Y						
9 Moakley	Y	Y	Y	Y	Y	N	Y
10 *Heckler*	Y	?	Y	?	Y	N	Y
11 Donnelly	Y	Y	Y	Y	Y	N	Y
12 Studds	Y	Y	Y	Y	Y	N	Y
MICHIGAN							
1 Conyers	Y	Y	Y	Y	Y	N	Y
2 *Pursell*	Y	Y	Y	Y	Y	Y	N
3 Wolpe	Y	Y	Y	Y	Y	Y	N
4 *Siljander*	Y	N	Y	Y	Y	N	Y
5 *Sawyer*	Y	Y	Y	Y	Y	N	N
6 *Dunn*	Y	Y	Y	Y	Y	N	N
7 Kildee	Y	Y	Y	Y	Y	Y	N
8 Traxler	Y	?	Y	Y	Y	Y	N
9 *Vander Jagt*	Y	Y	Y	Y	Y	N	N
10 Albosta	Y	Y	Y	Y	Y	Y	N
11 *Davis*	Y	?	?	Y	Y	Y	N
12 Bonior	Y	Y	Y	Y	Y	Y	N
13 Crockett	Y	?	Y	Y	?	?	?
14 Hertel	Y	Y	Y	Y	Y	N	N
15 Ford	Y	Y	Y	Y	Y	N	N
16 Dingell	Y	?	Y	Y	Y	N	N
17 Brodhead	Y	Y	Y	Y	Y	N	Y
18 Blanchard	Y	Y	Y	Y	Y	N	N
19 *Broomfield*	Y	Y	Y	Y	Y	N	Y
MINNESOTA							
1 *Erdahl*	Y	Y	Y	Y	Y	Y	N
2 *Hagedorn*	Y	Y	Y	Y	Y	N	N
3 *Frenzel*	Y	Y	Y	Y	Y	N	Y
4 Vento	Y	Y	Y	Y	Y	N	N
5 Sabo	Y	N	Y	Y	Y	Y	N
6 *Weber*	Y	Y	Y	Y	Y	Y	N
7 *Stangeland*	Y	?	Y	Y	Y	Y	N
8 Oberstar	Y	Y	Y	Y	N	Y	N
MISSISSIPPI							
1 Whitten	Y	Y	Y	Y	Y	Y	N
2 Bowen	Y	Y	Y	Y	Y	Y	N
3 Montgomery	Y	Y	Y	Y	Y	N	N
4 Dowdy	Y	Y	Y	Y	Y	Y	N
5 *Lott*	Y	Y	Y	Y	Y	N	N
MISSOURI							
1 Clay	Y	?	Y	Y	Y	N	N
2 Young	?	Y	Y	Y	Y	Y	N
3 Gephardt	Y	Y	Y	Y	Y	N	?
4 Skelton	Y	Y	Y	Y	Y	Y	N
5 Bolling	Y	Y	Y	Y	?	?	?
6 *Coleman*	Y	Y	Y	Y	Y	N	N
7 *Taylor*	Y	Y	Y	Y	Y	N	N
8 *Bailey*	Y	Y	Y	Y	Y	N	N
9 Volkmer	Y	Y	Y	Y	Y	Y	N
10 *Emerson*	Y	Y	Y	Y	Y	N	N
MONTANA							
1 Williams	Y	Y	Y	Y	N	Y	N
2 *Marlenee*	Y	Y	Y	Y	Y	Y	N
NEBRASKA							
1 *Bereuter*	Y	Y	Y	Y	Y	N	N
2 *Daub*	Y	Y	Y	Y	Y	N	N
3 *Smith*	Y	Y	Y	Y	Y	N	N
NEVADA							
AL Santini	Y	Y	Y	Y	?	?	?
NEW HAMPSHIRE							
1 D'Amours	Y	Y	Y	Y	Y	N	Y
2 *Gregg*	Y	Y	Y	Y	Y	N	Y
NEW JERSEY							
1 Florio	?	?	?	?	?	?	?
2 Hughes	Y	Y	Y	Y	Y	N	Y
3 Howard	Y	Y	Y	Y	Y	N	Y
4 *Smith*	Y	Y	Y	Y	Y	N	Y
5 *Fenwick*	Y	Y	Y	Y	Y	N	Y
6 *Forsythe*	Y	N	Y	Y	Y	N	Y
7 *Roukema*	Y	Y	Y	Y	Y	N	Y
8 Roe	Y	Y	Y	Y	Y	N	Y
9 *Hollenbeck*	Y	Y	Y	Y	Y	N	Y
10 Rodino	Y	Y	Y	Y	Y	N	Y
11 Minish	Y	Y	Y	Y	Y	N	Y
12 *Rinaldo*	Y	Y	Y	Y	Y	N	Y
13 *Courter*	Y	Y	Y	Y	Y	N	Y
14 Guarini	Y	Y	Y	Y	Y	N	Y
15 Dwyer	Y	Y	Y	Y	Y	N	Y
NEW MEXICO							
1 *Lujan*	Y	Y	Y	Y	Y	N	Y
2 *Skeen*	Y	Y	Y	Y	Y	N	N
NEW YORK							
1 *Carney*	Y	Y	Y	Y	Y	N	Y
2 Downey	Y	Y	Y	Y	Y	N	Y
3 *Carman*	Y	Y	Y	Y	Y	N	Y
4 *Lent*	Y	Y	Y	Y	Y	N	Y
5 *McGrath*	Y	Y	Y	Y	Y	N	Y
6 *LeBoutillier*	Y	Y	Y	Y	Y	N	Y
7 Addabbo	Y	?	Y	Y	Y	N	Y
8 Rosenthal	Y	Y	Y	Y	Y	N	Y
9 Ferraro	Y	Y	Y	Y	Y	N	Y
10 Biaggi	Y	Y	Y	Y	Y	N	Y
11 Scheuer	Y	Y	Y	Y	Y	N	Y
12 Chisholm	Y	?	Y	Y	Y	N	Y
13 Solarz	Y	Y	Y	Y	Y	N	Y
14 Richmond	Y	?	Y	Y	Y	?	X
15 Zeferetti	Y	Y	Y	Y	Y	Y	?
16 Schumer	Y	Y	Y	Y	Y	N	Y
17 *Molinari*	Y	Y	Y	Y	Y	N	Y
18 *Green*	Y	Y	Y	Y	Y	N	Y
19 Rangel	Y	Y	Y	Y	Y	N	Y
20 Weiss	Y	Y	Y	Y	Y	N	Y
21 Garcia	Y	Y	Y	Y	Y	N	Y
22 Bingham	Y	Y	Y	Y	Y	N	Y
23 Peyser	Y	Y	Y	Y	Y	N	Y
24 Ottinger	?	P	Y	Y	Y	N	N
25 *Fish*	Y	Y	Y	Y	Y	Y	N
26 *Gilman*	Y	Y	Y	Y	+	-	-
27 McHugh	Y	Y	Y	Y	Y	Y	N
28 Stratton	Y	Y	Y	Y	Y	Y	N
29 *Solomon*	Y	Y	Y	Y	Y	Y	N
30 *Martin*	Y	Y	Y	Y	Y	Y	N
31 *Mitchell*	Y	Y	Y	Y	N	?	?
32 *Wortley*	Y	N	Y	Y	Y	Y	N
33 *Lee*	Y	Y	Y	Y	Y	Y	N
34 *Horton*	Y	Y	Y	Y	Y	Y	N
35 *Conable*	Y	Y	Y	Y	Y	N	N
36 LaFalce	Y	Y	Y	Y	Y	Y	N
37 Nowak	Y	Y	Y	Y	Y	N	Y
38 *Kemp*	Y	Y	Y	Y	Y	N	Y
39 Lundine	Y	Y	Y	Y	Y	Y	N
NORTH CAROLINA							
1 Jones	?	?	?	?	?	?	?
2 Fountain	Y	Y	Y	Y	Y	Y	N
3 Whitley	Y	Y	Y	Y	Y	Y	N
4 Andrews	Y	?	Y	Y	Y	Y	N
5 Neal	Y	?	Y	Y	Y	Y	N
6 *Johnston*	?	N	Y	Y	Y	N	N
7 Rose	Y	Y	Y	Y	Y	Y	N
8 Hefner	Y	Y	Y	Y	Y	Y	N
9 *Martin*	Y	Y	Y	Y	Y	N	Y
10 *Broyhill*	Y	Y	Y	Y	Y	N	Y
11 *Hendon*	Y	Y	Y	Y	Y	N	N
NORTH DAKOTA							
AL Dorgan	Y	N	?	Y	N	Y	N
OHIO							
1 *Gradison*	Y	Y	Y	Y	Y	N	Y
2 Luken	Y	Y	Y	Y	Y	N	N
3 Hall	Y	Y	Y	Y	Y	N	Y
4 *Oxley*	Y	Y	Y	Y	Y	N	N
5 *Latta*	Y	Y	Y	Y	Y	N	N
6 *McEwen*	Y	Y	Y	Y	Y	Y	N
7 *Brown*	?	?	?	?	?	?	?
8 *Kindness*	Y	Y	Y	Y	Y	Y	N
9 *Weber*	Y	Y	Y	Y	Y	N	Y
10 *Miller*	Y	Y	Y	Y	Y	N	N
11 *Stanton*	Y	Y	Y	Y	Y	N	N
12 Shamansky	Y	Y	Y	Y	Y	N	Y
13 Pease	Y	Y	Y	Y	Y	N	N
14 Seiberling	Y	Y	Y	Y	Y	N	Y
15 *Wylie*	Y	Y	Y	Y	Y	N	Y
16 *Regula*	Y	Y	Y	Y	Y	N	N
17 *Ashbrook*	Y	Y	Y	Y	Y	N	N
18 Applegate	Y	Y	Y	Y	Y	N	N
19 *Williams*	Y	Y	Y	Y	Y	Y	N
20 Oakar	Y	Y	Y	Y	Y	N	N
21 Stokes	Y	Y	Y	Y	Y	N	Y
22 Eckart	Y	Y	Y	Y	Y	N	Y
23 Mottl	Y	Y	Y	Y	Y	?	#
OKLAHOMA							
1 Jones	Y	Y	Y	Y	Y	N	N
2 Synar	Y	Y	Y	Y	Y	N	N
3 Watkins	Y	N	Y	Y	Y	Y	N
4 McCurdy	Y	Y	Y	Y	Y	Y	N
5 *Edwards*	Y	Y	Y	Y	Y	N	N
6 English	Y	Y	Y	Y	Y	Y	N
OREGON							
1 AuCoin	Y	Y	Y	Y	Y	N	Y
2 *Smith*	Y	N	?	Y	Y	N	N
3 Wyden	Y	Y	Y	Y	Y	N	Y
4 Weaver	Y	?	Y	Y	Y	N	Y
PENNSYLVANIA							
1 Foglietta	Y	Y	Y	Y	Y	N	Y
2 Gray	Y	Y	Y	Y	Y	N	N
3 Smith	Y	Y	Y	Y	N	N	Y
4 *Dougherty*	Y	?	Y	Y	?	N	Y
5 *Schulze*	Y	Y	Y	Y	Y	?	?
6 Yatron	Y	Y	Y	Y	Y	N	N
7 Edgar	Y	Y	Y	Y	Y	N	N
8 *Coyne, J.*	Y	Y	Y	Y	Y	N	Y
9 *Shuster*	Y	Y	Y	Y	Y	Y	N
10 *McDade*	Y	Y	Y	Y	Y	Y	N
11 *Nelligan*	Y	Y	Y	Y	Y	N	N
12 Murtha	?	Y	Y	Y	Y	N	N
13 *Coughlin*	Y	N	Y	Y	Y	N	Y
14 Coyne, W.	Y	Y	Y	Y	Y	N	Y
15 *Ritter*	Y	?	Y	Y	Y	N	Y
16 *Walker*	Y	N	Y	Y	Y	N	N
17 Ertel	Y	Y	Y	Y	Y	Y	N
18 Walgren	Y	Y	Y	Y	Y	N	N
19 *Goodling*	Y	N	Y	Y	Y	N	N
20 Gaydos	Y	Y	Y	Y	Y	N	N
21 Bailey	Y	Y	Y	Y	Y	N	N
22 Murphy	Y	Y	Y	Y	Y	N	N
23 *Clinger*	Y	Y	Y	Y	Y	Y	N
24 *Marks*	Y	Y	Y	Y	Y	Y	N
25 Atkinson	?	?	Y	Y	Y	N	Y
RHODE ISLAND							
1 St Germain	Y	Y	Y	Y	?	N	Y
2 *Schneider*	Y	Y	Y	Y	Y	N	Y
SOUTH CAROLINA							
1 *Hartnett*	Y	Y	Y	Y	Y	N	N
2 *Spence*	Y	Y	Y	Y	Y	N	N
3 Derrick	Y	Y	Y	Y	Y	Y	N
4 *Campbell*	Y	Y	Y	Y	Y	N	N
5 Holland	?	Y	Y	Y	Y	N	N
6 *Napier*	Y	Y	Y	Y	Y	Y	N
SOUTH DAKOTA							
1 Daschle	Y	Y	Y	Y	N	Y	N
2 *Roberts*	Y	Y	Y	Y	N	Y	N
TENNESSEE							
1 *Quillen*	Y	Y	Y	Y	Y	?	X
2 *Duncan*	Y	Y	Y	Y	Y	Y	N
3 Bouquard	Y	Y	Y	Y	Y	N	N
4 Gore	Y	Y	Y	Y	Y	Y	N
5 Boner	Y	Y	Y	Y	Y	N	N
6 *Beard*	?	?	Y	Y	Y	Y	N
7 Jones	Y	Y	Y	Y	Y	Y	N
8 Ford	Y	?	Y	Y	Y	N	N
TEXAS							
1 Hall, S.	Y	?	Y	Y	Y	Y	N
2 Wilson	Y	Y	Y	Y	Y	Y	N
3 *Collins*	Y	Y	Y	Y	Y	N	N
4 Hall, R.	Y	Y	Y	Y	Y	Y	N
5 Mattox	Y	Y	Y	Y	Y	Y	N
6 Gramm	Y	Y	Y	Y	Y	N	N
7 *Archer*	Y	Y	Y	Y	Y	N	N
8 *Fields*	Y	Y	Y	Y	Y	N	Y
9 Brooks	Y	Y	Y	Y	Y	Y	N
10 Pickle	Y	Y	Y	Y	Y	?	?
11 Leath	Y	Y	Y	Y	Y	Y	N
12 Wright	Y	Y	Y	Y	Y	Y	N
13 Hightower	Y	Y	Y	Y	Y	Y	N
14 Patman	Y	Y	Y	Y	Y	Y	N
15 de la Garza	Y	Y	Y	Y	Y	N	N
16 White	Y	Y	Y	Y	Y	N	N
17 Stenholm	Y	Y	Y	Y	Y	Y	N
18 Leland	Y	Y	Y	Y	Y	N	Y
19 Hance	Y	Y	Y	Y	Y	Y	N
20 Gonzalez	Y	Y	Y	Y	Y	Y	N
21 *Loeffler*	Y	Y	Y	Y	Y	N	N
22 *Paul*	Y	Y	Y	Y	Y	N	Y
23 Kazen	Y	Y	Y	Y	Y	?	?
24 Frost	Y	Y	Y	Y	Y	Y	N
UTAH							
1 *Hansen*	Y	Y	Y	Y	Y	N	Y
2 *Marriott*	?	?	?	?	?	?	#
VERMONT							
AL *Jeffords*	Y	Y	Y	Y	Y	Y	N
VIRGINIA							
1 *Trible*	Y	Y	Y	Y	Y	N	Y
2 *Whitehurst*	Y	Y	Y	Y	Y	N	N
3 *Bliley*	Y	Y	Y	Y	Y	N	N
4 *Daniel, R.*	Y	Y	Y	Y	Y	N	Y
5 Daniel, D.	Y	Y	Y	Y	Y	N	Y
6 *Butler*	Y	?	?	?	Y	N	Y
7 *Robinson*	Y	Y	Y	Y	Y	N	Y
8 *Parris*	?	Y	Y	Y	Y	N	Y
9 *Wampler*	Y	Y	Y	Y	Y	Y	N
10 *Wolf*	Y	Y	Y	Y	Y	N	N
WASHINGTON							
1 *Pritchard*	Y	Y	Y	Y	Y	N	Y
2 Swift	Y	Y	Y	Y	Y	Y	N
3 Bonker	Y	Y	Y	Y	Y	N	N
4 *Morrison*	Y	Y	Y	Y	Y	N	N
5 Foley	Y	Y	Y	Y	Y	Y	N
6 Dicks	Y	Y	Y	Y	Y	?	?
7 Lowry	Y	Y	Y	Y	Y	N	N
WEST VIRGINIA							
1 Mollohan	Y	?	Y	Y	Y	N	N
2 *Benedict*	Y	Y	Y	Y	Y	N	N
3 *Staton*	Y	Y	Y	Y	Y	N	N
4 Rahall	Y	Y	Y	Y	Y	?	?
WISCONSIN							
1 Aspin	Y	N	Y	Y	Y	Y	N
2 Kastenmeier	Y	Y	Y	Y	N	Y	N
3 *Gunderson*	Y	Y	Y	Y	N	Y	N
4 Zablocki	Y	Y	Y	Y	Y	Y	N
5 Reuss	Y	?	Y	Y	Y	Y	N
6 *Petri*	Y	Y	Y	Y	N	Y	N
7 Obey	Y	Y	Y	?	N	Y	N
8 *Roth*	Y	Y	Y	Y	N	Y	N
9 *Sensenbrenner*	Y	Y	Y	Y	N	Y	N
WYOMING							
AL *Cheney*	Y	?	Y	Y	Y	N	Y

Democrats *Republicans*

242. H Con Res 194. Disapproving AWACS Sale. Zablocki, D-Wis., motion that the House resolve itself into the Committee of the Whole for consideration of the resolution disapproving the sale to Saudi Arabia of Airborne Warning and Control System (AWACS) radar planes, conformal fuel tanks for F-15 aircraft, AIM-9L Sidewinder missiles and KC-707 aerial refueling aircraft. Motion agreed to 353-16: R 159-13; D 194-3 (ND 130-1, SD 64-2), Oct. 14, 1981.

243. H Con Res 194. Disapproving AWACS Sale. Adoption of the resolution disapproving the sale to Saudi Arabia of Airborne Warning and Control System (AWACS) radar planes, conformal fuel tanks for F-15 aircraft, AIM-9L Sidewinder missiles and KC-707 aerial refueling aircraft. Adopted 301-111: R 108-78; D 193-33 (ND 149-5, SD 44-28), Oct. 14, 1981. A "nay" was a vote supporting the president's position.

244. HR 3603. Food and Agriculture Act of 1981. Findley, R-Ill., amendment to provide that the dairy price support shall not exceed the support in effect for the previous year, unless the secretary estimates that net government purchases of dairy products in any fiscal year through 1985 will equal or exceed 4.5 billion pounds of milk equivalent. Rejected 153-255: R 91-92; D 62-163 (ND 53-99, SD 9-64), Oct. 14, 1981. A "yea" was a vote supporting the president's position.

245. HR 3603. Food and Agriculture Act of 1981. De la Garza, D-Texas, motion that the House resolve itself into the Committee of the Whole for the consideration of the bill reauthorizing agricultural price supports and other farm programs and for food stamps for fiscal years 1982-1985. Motion agreed to 380-3: R 173-1, D 207-2 (ND 136-2, SD 71-0), Oct. 15, 1981.

246. HR 3603. Food and Agriculture Act of 1981. Lundine, D-N.Y., amendment to repeal the poundage quota and acreage allotment system for peanuts and to eliminate a specified loan rate for peanuts, and instead to authorize the secretary to determine the loan rate. Adopted 250-159: R 120-66, D 130-93 (ND 121-29, SD 9-64), Oct. 15, 1981.

247. HR 3603. Food and Agriculture Act of 1981. Peyser, D-N.Y., amendment to strike the price support program for sugar. Adopted 213-190: R 100-83, D 113-107 (ND 98-50, SD 15-57), Oct. 15, 1981.

KEY

- Y Voted for (yea).
- # Paired for.
- + Announced for.
- N Voted against (nay).
- X Paired against.
- - Announced against.
- P Voted "present".
- C Voted "present" to avoid possible conflict of interest.
- ? Did not vote or otherwise make a position known.

	242	243	244	245	246	247
ALABAMA						
1 Edwards	Y	Y	Y	?	N	Y
2 Dickinson	Y	N	Y	N	N	N
3 Nichols	Y	N	N	Y	N	N
4 Bevill	Y	N	Y	N	N	N
5 Flippo	Y	N	N	Y	N	N
6 Smith	?	Y	Y	N	Y	N
7 Shelby	Y	Y	N	Y	N	N
ALASKA						
AL Young	Y	Y	Y	?	N	N
ARIZONA						
1 Rhodes	?	N	Y	Y	N	N
2 Udall	Y	Y	Y	Y	Y	Y
3 Stump	Y	N	N	Y	N	N
4 Rudd	Y	Y	Y	Y	N	N
ARKANSAS						
1 Alexander	Y	N	N	?	N	N
2 Bethune	Y	Y	?	Y	Y	Y
3 Hammerschmidt	Y	N	N	Y	N	N
4 Anthony	Y	N	N	Y	N	N
CALIFORNIA						
1 Chappie	Y	Y	N	Y	N	N
2 Clausen	Y	Y	N	Y	N	N
3 Matsui	Y	Y	N	Y	N	N
4 Fazio	Y	Y	N	Y	N	N
5 Burton, J.	?	?	?	?	?	X
6 Burton, P.	?	?	?	?	X	X
7 Miller	Y	Y	N	Y	N	N
8 Dellums	Y	Y	Y	Y	Y	Y
9 Stark	Y	Y	N	?	?	?
10 Edwards	Y	Y	Y	Y	Y	Y
11 Lantos	Y	Y	Y	Y	Y	Y
12 McCloskey	?	N	?	Y	Y	Y
13 Mineta	Y	Y	N	Y	N	N
14 Shumway	N	N	Y	N	N	N
15 Coelho	Y	Y	N	Y	N	N
16 Panetta	Y	Y	N	Y	N	N
17 Pashayan	Y	Y	N	Y	N	N
18 Thomas	Y	N	N	Y	N	N
19 Lagomarsino	N	N	Y	N	N	N
20 Goldwater	Y	Y	N	Y	N	N
21 Fiedler	Y	Y	Y	Y	Y	Y
22 Moorhead	Y	N	Y	Y	N	N
23 Beilenson	Y	Y	N	Y	N	N
24 Waxman	Y	Y	N	Y	Y	Y
25 Roybal	Y	Y	N	Y	N	N
26 Rousselot	Y	Y	Y	Y	N	N
27 Dornan	Y	Y	?	Y	N	N
28 Dixon	?	Y	N	N	N	N
29 Hawkins	Y	N	Y	Y	N	Y
30 Danielson	Y	Y	Y	Y	N	N
31 Dymally	Y	Y	N	?	Y	N
32 Anderson	Y	Y	Y	Y	Y	Y
33 Grisham	Y	N	Y	Y	Y	#
34 Lungren	Y	N	Y	Y	Y	Y
35 Dreier	Y	Y	Y	Y	Y	Y
36 Brown	Y	N	Y	N	N	N
37 Lewis	Y	N	Y	Y	Y	X
38 Patterson	Y	N	Y	N	Y	N
39 Dannemeyer	Y	N	Y	Y	N	N
40 Badham	?	?	?	?	#	X
41 Lowery	Y	Y	Y	Y	N	N
42 Hunter	Y	Y	Y	Y	Y	N
43 Burgener	?	?	?	?	?	?
COLORADO						
1 Schroeder	Y	Y	Y	Y	Y	Y
2 Wirth	Y	Y	N	Y	N	N
3 Kogovsek	Y	Y	N	Y	N	N
4 Brown	Y	Y	Y	Y	Y	N

	242	243	244	245	246	247
5 Kramer	Y	Y	N	Y	Y	N
CONNECTICUT						
1 Vacancy						
2 Gejdenson	Y	Y	N	Y	Y	Y
3 DeNardis	Y	Y	Y	?	Y	Y
4 McKinney	?	Y	Y	?	Y	Y
5 Ratchford	Y	Y	Y	Y	Y	Y
6 Moffett	Y	Y	#	?	#	#
DELAWARE						
AL Evans	Y	Y	Y	Y	Y	Y
FLORIDA						
1 Hutto	Y	N	N	Y	N	N
2 Fuqua	Y	N	N	Y	N	N
3 Bennett	Y	Y	Y	Y	N	N
4 Chappell	Y	N	Y	N	N	N
5 McCollum	Y	N	Y	Y	N	N
6 Young	Y	Y	Y	Y	N	N
7 Gibbons	Y	Y	Y	Y	Y	Y
8 Ireland	Y	N	N	N	N	N
9 Nelson	Y	Y	N	Y	N	N
10 Bafalis	?	Y	N	Y	N	N
11 Mica	Y	Y	N	N	N	X
12 Shaw	Y	Y	Y	Y	N	N
13 Lehman	Y	Y	Y	Y	Y	Y
14 Pepper	?	#	?	?	?	X
15 Fascell	Y	Y	Y	Y	Y	Y
GEORGIA						
1 Ginn	?	Y	N	Y	N	Y
2 Hatcher	Y	Y	N	Y	N	N
3 Brinkley	Y	N	N	Y	N	Y
4 Levitas	?	?	?	?	?	Y
5 Fowler	Y	#	?	?	N	Y
6 Gingrich	?	N	N	Y	N	Y
7 McDonald	?	N	Y	Y	Y	Y
8 Evans	Y	N	Y	Y	N	?
9 Jenkins	Y	N	N	Y	N	Y
10 Barnard	Y	X	N	Y	N	Y
HAWAII						
1 Heftel	?	Y	N	Y	N	N
2 Akaka	?	Y	N	Y	N	N
IDAHO						
1 Craig	Y	N	N	Y	Y	X
2 Hansen	Y	N	N	Y	N	N
ILLINOIS						
1 Washington	?	Y	Y	?	Y	Y
2 Savage	?	?	?	?	?	?
3 Russo	Y	Y	N	Y	Y	Y
4 Derwinski	Y	Y	Y	Y	Y	Y
5 Fary	Y	Y	Y	Y	Y	Y
6 Hyde	Y	N	Y	Y	Y	Y
7 Collins	Y	Y	Y	Y	Y	Y
8 Rostenkowski	Y	Y	Y	Y	Y	Y
9 Yates	Y	Y	Y	Y	Y	Y
10 Porter	Y	Y	Y	Y	Y	Y
11 Annunzio	Y	Y	Y	Y	Y	Y
12 Crane, P.	?	?	Y	Y	Y	Y
13 McClory	Y	N	N	Y	Y	Y
14 Erlenborn	Y	N	Y	Y	Y	Y
15 Corcoran	Y	Y	Y	Y	Y	Y
16 Martin	Y	Y	N	?	Y	Y
17 O'Brien	Y	N	Y	Y	Y	#
18 Michel	Y	N	Y	Y	N	N
19 Railsback	Y	Y	N	Y	Y	Y
20 Findley	N	N	Y	Y	Y	Y
21 Madigan	Y	Y	Y	Y	Y	Y
22 Crane, D.	?	Y	Y	Y	Y	Y
23 Price	Y	N	N	Y	Y	Y
24 Simon	Y	Y	N	?	Y	Y
INDIANA						
1 Benjamin	Y	Y	Y	Y	Y	Y
2 Fithian	Y	Y	N	Y	N	N
3 Hiler	N	N	?	Y	Y	Y
4 Coats	Y	Y	Y	Y	Y	Y
5 Hillis	Y	N	N	Y	N	N
6 Evans	Y	N	Y	N	Y	N
7 Myers	N	N	N	Y	N	N
8 Deckard	Y	Y	N	?	Y	Y
9 Hamilton	Y	Y	N	Y	N	N
10 Sharp	Y	Y	Y	Y	Y	Y
11 Jacobs	Y	Y	Y	Y	Y	Y
IOWA						
1 Leach	Y	Y	N	Y	Y	Y
2 Tauke	Y	N	N	Y	Y	N
3 Evans	N	Y	N	N	N	N
4 Smith	Y	Y	Y	Y	N	N
5 Harkin	Y	N	?	N	N	N
6 Bedell	?	Y	N	Y	N	N

Democrats *Republicans*

	242	243	244	245	246	247
KANSAS						
1 ***Roberts***	Y	N	N	Y	N	N
2 ***Jeffries***	Y	N	Y	Y	Y	N
3 ***Winn***	Y	Y	N	Y	N	N
4 Glickman	Y	Y	N	Y	Y	N
5 ***Whittaker***	Y	Y	N	Y	N	N
KENTUCKY						
1 Hubbard	Y	N	N	Y	N	N
2 Natcher	Y	Y	N	Y	N	N
3 Mazzoli	Y	Y	Y	Y	Y	Y
4 ***Snyder***	Y	N	N	Y	N	N
5 ***Rogers***	Y	N	N	Y	N	N
6 ***Hopkins***	Y	N	N	Y	N	N
7 Perkins	Y	Y	N	Y	N	N
LOUISIANA						
1 ***Livingston***	Y	Y	Y	Y	N	N
2 Boggs	?	Y	N	Y	N	N
3 Tauzin	Y	Y	N	Y	N	N
4 Roemer	Y	Y	Y	Y	N	N
5 Huckaby	Y	N	N	Y	N	N
6 ***Moore***	Y	Y	N	Y	N	N
7 Breaux	Y	Y	N	Y	N	N
8 Long	Y	Y	N	Y	N	N
MAINE						
1 ***Emery***	Y	Y	N	?	Y	Y
2 ***Snowe***	Y	Y	N	Y	Y	Y
MARYLAND						
1 Dyson	Y	Y	N	Y	N	N
2 Long	Y	Y	Y	Y	Y	Y
3 Mikulski	Y	Y	Y	Y	Y	Y
4 ***Holt***	Y	N	Y	Y	N	N
5 Hoyer	Y	Y	N	Y	Y	Y
6 Byron	?	Y	N	Y	N	Y
7 Mitchell	N	Y	N	N	Y	Y
8 Barnes	Y	Y	N	Y	Y	Y
MASSACHUSETTS						
1 ***Conte***	Y	Y	Y	Y	Y	Y
2 Boland	?	Y	Y	Y	Y	Y
3 Early	Y	Y	Y	Y	Y	Y
4 Frank	Y	Y	Y	Y	Y	Y
5 Shannon	Y	Y	Y	Y	Y	#
6 Mavroules	Y	Y	Y	Y	Y	Y
7 Markey	Y	Y	Y	Y	Y	Y
8 O'Neill						
9 Moakley	Y	Y	Y	Y	Y	Y
10 ***Heckler***	Y	Y	Y	Y	Y	Y
11 Donnelly	?	Y	Y	Y	Y	Y
12 Studds	Y	Y	Y	Y	Y	Y
MICHIGAN						
1 Conyers	Y	Y	Y	?	Y	Y
2 ***Pursell***	Y	Y	N	Y	Y	Y
3 Wolpe	Y	Y	N	Y	Y	N
4 ***Siljander***	Y	Y	N	Y	Y	N
5 ***Sawyer***	Y	N	Y	Y	N	N
6 ***Dunn***	Y	Y	N	Y	Y	Y
7 Kildee	Y	Y	N	Y	Y	N
8 Traxler	Y	Y	N	Y	N	N
9 ***Vander Jagt***	Y	Y	N	?	Y	N
10 Albosta	?	Y	N	Y	N	N
11 ***Davis***	?	N	N	Y	Y	N
12 Bonior	Y	Y	N	Y	Y	X
13 Crockett	?	Y	?	?	?	#
14 Hertel	Y	Y	N	Y	Y	Y
15 Ford	?	Y	N	Y	N	N
16 Dingell	?	Y	N	Y	N	N
17 Brodhead	Y	Y	N	Y	Y	Y
18 Blanchard	Y	Y	N	Y	Y	N
19 ***Broomfield***	Y	Y	Y	Y	Y	Y
MINNESOTA						
1 ***Erdahl***	Y	Y	N	Y	Y	N
2 ***Hagedorn***	Y	N	N	Y	Y	N
3 ***Frenzel***	Y	Y	Y	Y	Y	N
4 Vento	Y	Y	N	Y	Y	Y
5 Sabo	Y	Y	N	Y	Y	Y
6 ***Weber***	Y	Y	N	Y	N	N
7 ***Stangeland***	Y	N	N	Y	N	N
8 Oberstar	Y	Y	N	Y	N	N
MISSISSIPPI						
1 Whitten	Y	N	N	Y	N	N
2 Bowen	Y	N	N	Y	N	N
3 Montgomery	Y	N	N	Y	N	N
4 Dowdy	Y	Y	N	Y	N	N
5 ***Lott***	Y	N	Y	Y	N	N
MISSOURI						
1 Clay	?	Y	N	Y	Y	Y
2 Young	?	Y	N	Y	Y	N
3 Gephardt	Y	Y	N	Y	Y	N

	242	243	244	245	246	247
4 Skelton	Y	Y	N	Y	N	N
5 Bolling	?	?	?	?	?	N
6 ***Coleman***	Y	N	N	Y	N	N
7 ***Taylor***	?	N	N	Y	N	N
8 ***Bailey***	Y	N	N	Y	Y	Y
9 Volkmer	Y	Y	N	Y	N	N
10 ***Emerson***	N	N	N	Y	N	N
MONTANA						
1 Williams	Y	Y	N	?	N	N
2 ***Marlenee***	Y	N	N	Y	N	N
NEBRASKA						
1 ***Bereuter***	Y	N	N	Y	Y	N
2 ***Daub***	Y	N	N	Y	Y	N
3 ***Smith***	Y	N	N	Y	N	N
NEVADA						
AL Santini	Y	Y	Y	?	?	?
NEW HAMPSHIRE						
1 D'Amours	Y	Y	Y	Y	Y	Y
2 ***Gregg***	Y	Y	Y	Y	Y	Y
NEW JERSEY						
1 Florio	Y	Y	N	?	?	#
2 Hughes	Y	Y	Y	Y	Y	Y
3 Howard	Y	Y	N	Y	Y	Y
4 ***Smith***	Y	Y	N	Y	Y	Y
5 ***Fenwick***	Y	Y	Y	Y	Y	#
6 ***Forsythe***	Y	Y	Y	Y	Y	Y
7 ***Roukema***	Y	Y	Y	Y	Y	Y
8 Roe	?	Y	Y	Y	Y	?
9 ***Hollenbeck***	?	Y	Y	Y	Y	Y
10 Rodino	Y	Y	Y	Y	Y	Y
11 Minish	?	Y	Y	Y	Y	Y
12 ***Rinaldo***	Y	Y	Y	Y	Y	Y
13 ***Courter***	Y	Y	N	Y	Y	Y
14 Guarini	Y	Y	Y	Y	Y	Y
15 Dwyer	Y	Y	Y	Y	Y	Y
NEW MEXICO						
1 ***Lujan***	Y	Y	Y	Y	N	N
2 ***Skeen***	Y	N	N	Y	N	N
NEW YORK						
1 ***Carney***	Y	Y	Y	Y	Y	Y
2 Downey	Y	Y	N	Y	Y	Y
3 ***Carman***	Y	Y	Y	Y	Y	Y
4 ***Lent***	Y	Y	Y	Y	Y	Y
5 ***McGrath***	Y	Y	Y	Y	Y	Y
6 ***LeBoutillier***	Y	Y	Y	Y	Y	Y
7 Addabbo	Y	Y	N	Y	Y	Y
8 Rosenthal	Y	Y	N	Y	Y	Y
9 Ferraro	Y	Y	N	Y	Y	Y
10 Biaggi	Y	Y	N	Y	Y	Y
11 Scheuer	Y	Y	N	Y	Y	Y
12 Chisholm	?	Y	N	Y	Y	Y
13 Solarz	Y	Y	N	Y	Y	Y
14 Richmond	Y	Y	N	Y	N	N
15 Zeferetti	Y	Y	N	Y	Y	Y
16 Schumer	Y	Y	N	Y	Y	Y
17 ***Molinari***	Y	Y	Y	Y	N	Y
18 ***Green***	Y	Y	Y	Y	Y	Y
19 Rangel	Y	Y	X	Y	Y	Y
20 Weiss	Y	Y	Y	?	Y	Y
21 Garcia	?	?	?	?	#	#
22 Bingham	Y	Y	Y	?	Y	Y
23 Peyser	Y	Y	Y	Y	Y	Y
24 Ottinger	?	Y	N	P	Y	Y
25 ***Fish***	Y	Y	Y	Y	N	Y
26 ***Gilman***	Y	Y	N	+	+	Y
27 McHugh	Y	Y	N	Y	Y	Y
28 Stratton	?	X	?	?	?	?
29 ***Solomon***	N	N	N	Y	Y	Y
30 ***Martin***	N	N	N	Y	Y	Y
31 ***Mitchell***	Y	N	N	Y	Y	Y
32 ***Wortley***	Y	Y	N	Y	Y	Y
33 ***Lee***	Y	Y	N	Y	Y	Y
34 ***Horton***	Y	Y	N	Y	Y	Y
35 ***Conable***	N	N	Y	Y	Y	Y
36 LaFalce	Y	Y	N	Y	Y	Y
37 Nowak	?	Y	N	Y	Y	Y
38 ***Kemp***	Y	Y	Y	Y	Y	Y
39 Lundine	Y	Y	N	Y	Y	Y
NORTH CAROLINA						
1 Jones	?	?	?	?	X	?
2 Fountain	Y	N	N	Y	N	N
3 Whitley	Y	N	N	Y	N	N
4 Andrews	?	N	N	Y	N	N
5 Neal	Y	Y	N	?	N	N
6 ***Johnston***	N	N	Y	Y	N	N
7 Rose	?	N	N	Y	N	N
8 Hefner	Y	Y	N	Y	N	N

	242	243	244	245	246	247
9 ***Martin***	Y	Y	Y	Y	N	N
10 ***Broyhill***	Y	N	Y	?	X	Y
11 ***Hendon***	Y	Y	N	Y	N	C
NORTH DAKOTA						
AL Dorgan	Y	Y	N	Y	N	N
OHIO						
1 ***Gradison***	Y	Y	Y	Y	Y	Y
2 Luken	Y	Y	N	Y	Y	Y
3 Hall	Y	Y	Y	Y	Y	Y
4 ***Oxley***	Y	N	N	Y	Y	N
5 ***Latta***	?	N	Y	Y	Y	N
6 ***McEwen***	Y	N	N	Y	Y	Y
7 ***Brown***	Y	Y	?	Y	Y	N
8 ***Kindness***	Y	Y	N	Y	N	N
9 ***Weber***	Y	Y	Y	Y	Y	Y
10 ***Miller***	Y	N	Y	Y	N	Y
11 ***Stanton***	Y	N	Y	Y	Y	Y
12 Shamansky	Y	Y	Y	Y	Y	Y
13 Pease	Y	Y	N	Y	Y	Y
14 Seiberling	Y	Y	Y	Y	Y	Y
15 ***Wylie***	Y	N	N	Y	Y	Y
16 ***Regula***	Y	N	Y	Y	Y	Y
17 ***Ashbrook***	Y	Y	N	Y	Y	Y
18 Applegate	?	Y	N	?	Y	Y
19 ***Williams***	?	Y	N	Y	Y	Y
20 Oakar	Y	Y	N	Y	Y	Y
21 Stokes	?	Y	N	?	Y	Y
22 Eckart	Y	Y	Y	Y	Y	Y
23 Mottl	Y	Y	Y	Y	Y	Y
OKLAHOMA						
1 Jones	Y	Y	N	Y	N	N
2 Synar	Y	Y	N	Y	N	N
3 Watkins	Y	Y	N	Y	N	N
4 McCurdy	Y	Y	N	Y	N	N
5 ***Edwards***	Y	N	N	Y	N	Y
6 English	Y	Y	N	Y	N	N
OREGON						
1 AuCoin	Y	Y	Y	Y	Y	Y
2 ***Smith***	Y	Y	Y	Y	N	N
3 Wyden	Y	Y	Y	Y	Y	Y
4 Weaver	Y	Y	Y	Y	Y	N
PENNSYLVANIA						
1 Foglietta	?	Y	Y	Y	Y	Y
2 Gray	Y	Y	N	Y	N	Y
3 Smith	Y	Y	N	Y	Y	Y
4 ***Dougherty***	?	Y	N	Y	Y	Y
5 ***Schulze***	Y	N	Y	Y	Y	Y
6 Yatron	Y	Y	N	Y	Y	Y
7 Edgar	Y	Y	N	Y	Y	Y
8 ***Coyne, J.***	Y	Y	Y	Y	Y	Y
9 ***Shuster***	Y	Y	N	Y	Y	Y
10 ***McDade***	Y	?	N	Y	Y	Y
11 ***Nelligan***	Y	Y	N	Y	Y	Y
12 Murtha	Y	Y	N	Y	N	N
13 ***Coughlin***	Y	Y	Y	Y	Y	Y
14 Coyne, W.	Y	Y	Y	Y	Y	Y
15 ***Ritter***	Y	Y	Y	Y	Y	Y
16 ***Walker***	N	Y	N	Y	Y	Y
17 Ertel	Y	Y	N	Y	Y	Y
18 Walgren	Y	Y	Y	Y	Y	N
19 ***Goodling***	Y	N	N	Y	Y	Y
20 Gaydos	Y	Y	N	Y	Y	Y
21 Bailey	Y	Y	N	Y	Y	N
22 Murphy	Y	Y	N	N	Y	Y
23 ***Clinger***	Y	N	N	Y	Y	N
24 ***Marks***	?	Y	N	Y	Y	Y
25 ***Atkinson****	?	?	?	?	Y	?
RHODE ISLAND						
1 St Germain	Y	Y	Y	Y	Y	Y
2 ***Schneider***	Y	Y	Y	?	Y	Y
SOUTH CAROLINA						
1 ***Hartnett***	Y	N	Y	Y	N	Y
2 ***Spence***	Y	N	N	Y	N	N
3 Derrick	Y	N	N	Y	N	N
4 ***Campbell***	Y	N	?	?	X	#
5 Holland	?	?	?	?	?	?
6 ***Napier***	?	N	N	Y	N	N
SOUTH DAKOTA						
1 Daschle	Y	Y	N	Y	N	N
2 ***Roberts***	Y	Y	N	Y	N	N
TENNESSEE						
1 ***Quillen***	Y	N	N	Y	N	N
2 ***Duncan***	Y	Y	N	Y	N	Y
3 Bouquard	?	Y	N	Y	Y	N
4 Gore	Y	Y	N	Y	N	N
5 Boner	Y	Y	N	Y	Y	Y
6 ***Beard***	Y	Y	N	Y	Y	N

	242	243	244	245	246	247
7 Jones	Y	Y	N	Y	N	N
8 Ford	Y	Y	N	Y	N	Y
TEXAS						
1 Hall, S.	Y	N	N	Y	N	N
2 Wilson	?	N	N	Y	?	N
3 ***Collins***	Y	Y	Y	Y	Y	Y
4 Hall, R.	?	Y	N	Y	N	N
5 Mattox	N	Y	N	Y	N	Y
6 Gramm	Y	N	Y	Y	N	N
7 ***Archer***	Y	Y	Y	Y	Y	Y
8 ***Fields***	Y	Y	Y	Y	N	Y
9 Brooks	?	?	?	?	?	?
10 Pickle	Y	Y	N	Y	N	N
11 Leath	Y	N	N	Y	N	N
12 Wright	Y	Y	N	Y	N	N
13 Hightower	Y	N	N	Y	N	N
14 Patman	N	N	N	Y	N	N
15 de la Garza	Y	Y	N	Y	N	N
16 White	Y	N	N	Y	N	N
17 Stenholm	Y	N	N	Y	N	N
18 Leland	Y	Y	N	Y	Y	Y
19 Hance	Y	N	N	Y	N	N
20 Gonzalez	Y	Y	N	Y	N	N
21 ***Loeffler***	Y	Y	Y	Y	N	N
22 ***Paul***	Y	Y	Y	Y	Y	Y
23 Kazen	Y	N	N	Y	N	N
24 Frost	Y	Y	N	Y	N	N
UTAH						
1 ***Hansen***	Y	N	Y	Y	Y	Y
2 ***Marriott***	Y	N	N	Y	Y	N
VERMONT						
AL ***Jeffords***	Y	Y	N	Y	N	N
VIRGINIA						
1 ***Trible***	Y	Y	Y	Y	N	Y
2 ***Whitehurst***	?	?	?	Y	N	Y
3 ***Bliley***	Y	Y	Y	Y	N	N
4 ***Daniel, R.***	Y	N	Y	Y	N	Y
5 Daniel, D.	Y	N	Y	Y	N	Y
6 ***Butler***	Y	N	Y	?	N	Y
7 ***Robinson***	Y	N	Y	Y	N	N
8 ***Parris***	N	N	N	Y	N	N
9 ***Wampler***	Y	N	N	Y	N	N
10 ***Wolf***	Y	Y	N	Y	Y	Y
WASHINGTON						
1 ***Pritchard***	Y	N	Y	Y	Y	Y
2 Swift	Y	Y	N	Y	N	N
3 Bonker	Y	?	Y	?	Y	N
4 ***Morrison***	Y	N	N	Y	Y	N
5 Foley	Y	Y	N	Y	N	N
6 Dicks	Y	Y	N	Y	Y	Y
7 Lowry	?	?	?	?	?	?
WEST VIRGINIA						
1 Mollohan	Y	N	N	Y	N	N
2 ***Benedict***	Y	Y	N	Y	N	N
3 ***Staton***	Y	N	N	Y	N	N
4 Rahall	?	N	N	Y	N	Y
WISCONSIN						
1 Aspin	?	Y	N	Y	N	Y
2 Kastenmeier	Y	Y	N	Y	Y	Y
3 ***Gunderson***	Y	N	N	Y	N	N
4 Zablocki	Y	N	N	Y	Y	N
5 Reuss	Y	Y	N	Y	Y	Y
6 ***Petri***	Y	Y	N	Y	Y	Y
7 Obey	Y	Y	N	Y	Y	Y
8 ***Roth***	Y	N	N	Y	Y	Y
9 ***Sensenbrenner***	Y	Y	N	Y	Y	Y
WYOMING						
AL ***Cheney***	Y	N	Y	?	Y	N

**Rep. Eugene V. Atkinson switched his party affiliation from Democrat to Republican effective Oct. 14, 1981.*

Democrats ***Republicans***

248. Procedural Motion. Solomon, R-N.Y., motion to approve the House *Journal* of Monday, Oct. 19. Motion agreed to 363-14: R 166-7; D 197-7 (ND 133-6; SD 64-1), Oct. 20, 1981.

249. H J Res 331. National Mother-in-Law Day. Passage of the joint resolution to designate the fourth Sunday in October as National Mother-in-Law Day. Passed 305-66: R 129-37; D 176-29 (ND 119-22; SD 57-7), Oct. 20, 1981.

250. S J Res 4. National Family Week. Passage of the joint resolution to authorize the president to issue a proclamation designating the week beginning Nov. 22, 1981, as National Family Week. Passed 405-1: R 184-0; D 221-1 (ND 148-1; SD 73-0), Oct. 20, 1981.

251. HR 3403. Hazardous Materials Transportation Act. Anderson, D-Calif., motion that the House resolve itself into the Committee of the Whole for the consideration of the bill. Motion agreed to 392-5: R 177-2; D 215-3 (ND 144-2; SD 71-1). Oct. 20, 1981.

252. HR 3403. Hazardous Materials Transportation Act. Passage of the bill to authorize $8,332,000 annually for fiscal 1982 and 1983 for federal hazardous materials transportation activities and to establish regional training centers for state, local and other personnel to improve enforcement of regulations governing the transportation of hazardous materials and emergency response capability. Passed 410-2: R 183-1; D 227-1 (ND 155-0; SD 72-1). Oct. 20, 1981.

253. HR 3377. Kennedy Center Authorization. Passage of the bill to authorize $4,544,000 for fiscal 1982 to the interior secretary for services necessary to the non-performing arts functions of the John F. Kennedy Center for the Performing Arts. Passed 288-123; R 83-99; D 205-24 (ND 149-5; SD 56-19), Oct. 20, 1981.

254. HR 3603. Food and Agriculture Act of 1981. De la Garza, D-Texas, motion that the House resolve itself into the Committee of the Whole for further consideration of the bill. Motion agreed to 384-3: R 175-0; D 209-3 (ND 138-2; SD 71-1), Oct. 20, 1981.

255. HR 3603. Food and Agriculture Act of 1981. Weaver, D-Ore., amendment to provide discretionary authority to establish a bank to finance U.S. grain exports and to permit the secretary of agriculture to set a minimum price for U.S. grain sold abroad. Rejected 138-270: R 19-164; D 119-106 (ND 90-63; SD 29-43), Oct. 20, 1981. A "nay" was a vote supporting the president's position.

KEY

Y	Voted for (yea).
#	Paired for.
+	Announced for.
N	Voted against (nay).
X	Paired against.
-	Announced against.
P	Voted "present."
C	Voted "present" to avoid possible conflict of interest.
?	Did not vote or otherwise make a position known.

Member	248	249	250	251	252	253	254	255
ALABAMA								
1 *Edwards*	Y	Y	Y	Y	Y	Y	Y	N
2 *Dickinson*	?	Y	Y	Y	Y	N	Y	Y
3 Nichols	?	Y	Y	Y	Y	N	Y	N
4 Bevill	Y	Y	Y	Y	Y	Y	Y	N
5 Flippo	?	?	Y	Y	Y	Y	Y	Y
6 *Smith*	Y	Y	Y	Y	Y	N	Y	N
7 Shelby	Y	Y	Y	Y	Y	Y	Y	N
ALASKA								
AL *Young*	Y	Y	Y	Y	Y	Y	Y	N
ARIZONA								
1 *Rhodes*	?	Y	Y	Y	Y	Y	Y	?
2 Udall	Y	Y	Y	Y	Y	Y	Y	N
3 *Stump*	Y	N	Y	Y	N	Y	N	N
4 *Rudd*	?	?	?	?	?	?	?	?
ARKANSAS								
1 Alexander	Y	Y	Y	Y	Y	Y	Y	N
2 *Bethune*	Y	N	Y	Y	Y	N	Y	N
3 *Hammerschmidt*	Y	N	Y	?	Y	N	Y	N
4 Anthony	Y	Y	Y	Y	Y	Y	Y	Y
CALIFORNIA								
1 *Chappie*	Y	Y	Y	Y	Y	Y	Y	N
2 *Clausen*	Y	Y	Y	Y	Y	Y	Y	N
3 Matsui	Y	Y	Y	Y	Y	Y	Y	N
4 Fazio	Y	Y	Y	Y	Y	Y	Y	N
5 Burton, J.	Y	?	?	?	Y	Y	Y	?
6 Burton, P.	Y	Y	Y	Y	Y	Y	Y	Y
7 Miller	Y	N	Y	Y	Y	Y	Y	Y
8 Dellums	?	Y	Y	Y	Y	Y	?	Y
9 Stark	Y	N	Y	Y	Y	Y	Y	Y
10 Edwards	Y	Y	Y	Y	Y	Y	Y	Y
11 Lantos	Y	Y	Y	Y	Y	Y	Y	N
12 *McCloskey*	?	?	?	?	?	?	?	?
13 Mineta	?	?	?	?	?	?	?	#
14 *Shumway*	Y	N	Y	Y	N	Y	N	N
15 Coelho	?	Y	Y	Y	Y	Y	Y	N
16 Panetta	Y	Y	Y	Y	Y	Y	Y	N
17 *Pashayan*	Y	Y	Y	Y	Y	Y	Y	N
18 *Thomas*	Y	Y	Y	Y	Y	N	Y	N
19 *Lagomarsino*	Y	Y	Y	Y	Y	N	Y	N
20 *Goldwater*	Y	N	Y	Y	Y	N	Y	N
21 *Fiedler*	Y	Y	Y	Y	Y	N	Y	N
22 *Moorhead*	Y	Y	Y	Y	Y	N	Y	N
23 Beilenson	Y	Y	Y	Y	Y	Y	Y	N
24 Waxman	Y	Y	Y	Y	Y	Y	?	Y
25 Roybal	Y	Y	Y	Y	Y	Y	Y	Y
26 *Rousselot*	Y	P	Y	Y	Y	N	Y	N
27 *Dornan*	Y	Y	Y	Y	Y	Y	Y	N
28 Dixon	Y	Y	Y	Y	Y	Y	Y	N
29 Hawkins	Y	Y	Y	Y	Y	Y	Y	Y
30 Danielson	Y	+	Y	Y	Y	Y	+	Y
31 Dymally	Y	Y	Y	Y	Y	Y	Y	Y
32 Anderson	Y	Y	Y	Y	Y	Y	Y	Y
33 *Grisham*	Y	Y	Y	Y	Y	N	Y	N
34 *Lungren*	Y	Y	Y	Y	N	N	Y	N
35 *Dreier*	Y	P	Y	Y	Y	N	Y	N
36 Brown	Y	Y	Y	Y	Y	Y	Y	Y
37 *Lewis*	Y	N	Y	Y	Y	N	Y	N
38 Patterson	Y	Y	Y	Y	Y	Y	Y	N
39 *Dannemeyer*	Y	Y	Y	Y	Y	N	Y	N
40 *Badham*	?	Y	Y	Y	Y	Y	Y	N
41 *Lowery*	Y	Y	Y	Y	Y	Y	Y	N
42 *Hunter*	Y	Y	Y	Y	Y	Y	Y	N
43 *Burgener*	Y	N	Y	Y	Y	Y	Y	N
COLORADO								
1 Schroeder	N	P	Y	Y	Y	Y	Y	Y
2 Wirth	Y	Y	Y	Y	Y	Y	Y	N
3 Kogovsek	Y	N	Y	Y	Y	Y	Y	N
4 *Brown*	Y	P	Y	Y	Y	N	Y	N
5 *Kramer*	Y	Y	Y	Y	Y	N	Y	N
CONNECTICUT								
1 Vacancy								
2 Gejdenson	N	Y	Y	Y	Y	Y	Y	Y
3 *DeNardis*	?	Y	Y	Y	Y	Y	Y	Y
4 *McKinney*	Y	?	Y	Y	Y	Y	Y	N
5 Ratchford	Y	Y	Y	Y	Y	Y	Y	Y
6 Moffett	Y	Y	Y	?	Y	Y	?	Y
DELAWARE								
AL *Evans*	Y	P	Y	Y	Y	Y	Y	N
FLORIDA								
1 Hutto	Y	Y	Y	Y	Y	Y	Y	N
2 Fuqua	Y	Y	Y	Y	Y	Y	Y	N
3 Bennett	Y	Y	Y	Y	Y	Y	Y	Y
4 Chappell	Y	Y	Y	Y	Y	Y	Y	N
5 *McCollum*	Y	N	Y	Y	Y	N	Y	N
6 *Young*	Y	Y	Y	Y	Y	Y	Y	N
7 Gibbons	Y	Y	Y	?	Y	Y	Y	N
8 Ireland	?	P	Y	Y	Y	Y	Y	N
9 Nelson	Y	Y	Y	Y	Y	Y	Y	N
10 *Bafalis*	Y	Y	Y	Y	Y	Y	Y	N
11 Mica	Y	Y	Y	Y	Y	Y	Y	N
12 *Shaw*	Y	Y	Y	Y	Y	N	Y	N
13 Lehman	Y	N	Y	Y	Y	Y	Y	Y
14 Pepper	?	?	?	?	?	?	?	?
15 Fascell	Y	Y	Y	Y	Y	Y	Y	N
GEORGIA								
1 Ginn	?	?	?	?	?	?	?	X
2 Hatcher	Y	Y	Y	Y	Y	Y	Y	Y
3 Brinkley	Y	N	Y	Y	Y	Y	Y	Y
4 Levitas	Y	N	Y	Y	Y	Y	Y	Y
5 Fowler	Y	N	Y	Y	Y	Y	Y	Y
6 *Gingrich*	Y	Y	Y	Y	Y	N	Y	N
7 McDonald	Y	N	Y	N	N	N	Y	N
8 Evans	N	Y	Y	Y	Y	Y	Y	N
9 Jenkins	Y	Y	Y	Y	Y	N	Y	N
10 Barnard	Y	Y	Y	Y	Y	Y	?	N
HAWAII								
1 Heftel	Y	P	Y	Y	Y	Y	Y	N
2 Akaka	Y	Y	+	Y	Y	Y	Y	N
IDAHO								
1 *Craig*	?	?	?	Y	Y	N	Y	N
2 *Hansen*	Y	N	Y	Y	Y	N	Y	N
ILLINOIS								
1 Washington	?	?	?	?	?	?	?	?
2 Savage	?	?	?	?	Y	Y	?	?
3 Russo	Y	Y	Y	Y	Y	Y	Y	N
4 *Derwinski*	Y	Y	Y	Y	Y	N	Y	N
5 Fary	Y	Y	Y	Y	Y	Y	Y	N
6 *Hyde*	Y	N	Y	Y	Y	N	Y	N
7 Collins	Y	Y	Y	Y	+	Y	Y	Y
8 Rostenkowski	Y	Y	Y	Y	Y	Y	Y	N
9 Yates	Y	N	Y	Y	Y	Y	Y	Y
10 *Porter*	Y	P	Y	Y	Y	Y	Y	N
11 Annunzio	?	Y	Y	Y	Y	Y	Y	N
12 *Crane, P.*	Y	Y	Y	N	Y	N	Y	N
13 *McClory*	Y	Y	Y	Y	Y	N	Y	N
14 *Erlenborn*	Y	N	Y	Y	Y	Y	Y	N
15 *Corcoran*	Y	Y	Y	Y	Y	Y	Y	N
16 *Martin*	Y	Y	Y	Y	Y	N	?	N
17 *O'Brien*	Y	Y	Y	Y	Y	N	Y	N
18 *Michel*	Y	N	Y	Y	Y	?	?	N
19 *Railsback*	?	Y	Y	Y	Y	Y	Y	N
20 *Findley*	Y	Y	Y	Y	Y	Y	Y	N
21 *Madigan*	Y	Y	Y	Y	Y	?	Y	N
22 *Crane, D.*	Y	Y	Y	Y	Y	N	Y	N
23 Price	Y	Y	Y	Y	Y	Y	Y	N
24 Simon	Y	Y	Y	Y	Y	Y	Y	N
INDIANA								
1 Benjamin	Y	N	Y	Y	Y	Y	Y	Y
2 Fithian	Y	Y	Y	Y	Y	Y	Y	Y
3 *Hiler*	Y	N	Y	Y	Y	N	Y	N
4 *Coats*	Y	N	Y	Y	Y	N	Y	N
5 *Hillis*	Y	Y	Y	Y	Y	Y	Y	N
6 Evans	Y	Y	Y	Y	Y	Y	Y	N
7 *Myers*	Y	Y	Y	Y	Y	N	Y	N
8 *Deckard*	Y	Y	Y	Y	Y	Y	Y	Y
9 Hamilton	Y	Y	Y	Y	Y	N	Y	N
10 Sharp	Y	Y	Y	Y	Y	Y	Y	N
11 Jacobs	N	Y	Y	Y	Y	Y	Y	Y
IOWA								
1 *Leach*	Y	Y	Y	Y	Y	Y	Y	Y
2 *Tauke*	Y	N	Y	Y	Y	N	Y	N
3 *Evans*	N	N	Y	Y	Y	N	Y	N
4 Smith	Y	N	Y	Y	Y	Y	Y	N
5 Harkin	N	N	Y	Y	Y	Y	Y	Y
6 Bedell	Y	N	Y	Y	Y	Y	Y	N

Democrats   *Republicans*

Corresponding to Congressional Record Votes 262, 263, 264, 265, 266, 267, 268, 269

	248 249 250 251 252 253 254 255
KANSAS	
1 *Roberts*	Y P Y Y Y Y N Y N
2 *Jeffries*	Y N Y Y Y N Y N
3 *Winn*	Y Y Y ? Y N Y N
4 Glickman	Y N Y Y Y Y Y N
5 *Whittaker*	Y Y Y Y Y N Y N
KENTUCKY	
1 Hubbard	Y Y Y Y Y N Y N
2 Natcher	Y Y Y Y Y Y Y N
3 Mazzoli	Y Y Y Y Y Y Y N
4 *Snyder*	Y Y Y Y Y N Y N
5 *Rogers*	Y Y Y Y Y N Y N
6 *Hopkins*	Y Y Y Y Y N Y N
7 Perkins	Y Y Y Y Y Y Y Y
LOUISIANA	
1 *Livingston*	N P Y Y Y Y Y N
2 Boggs	? Y Y Y Y Y ? N
3 Tauzin	Y Y Y Y Y Y Y N
4 Roemer	Y Y Y Y Y N N X
5 Huckaby	Y Y Y Y Y Y Y Y
6 *Moore*	Y Y Y Y Y N Y N
7 Breaux	Y Y Y Y Y Y Y N
8 Long	Y Y Y Y Y Y Y N
MAINE	
1 *Emery*	Y Y Y Y Y Y Y N
2 *Snowe*	Y Y Y Y Y Y Y N
MARYLAND	
1 Dyson	Y Y Y Y Y Y Y N
2 Long	Y Y Y Y Y N Y Y
3 Mikulski	Y Y Y Y Y Y Y Y
4 *Holt*	Y N ? ? ? ? Y N
5 Hoyer	? Y Y Y Y Y ? N
6 Byron	Y P Y Y Y Y Y N
7 Mitchell	? Y Y N Y ? N Y
8 Barnes	Y Y Y Y Y Y Y N
MASSACHUSETTS	
1 Conte	Y Y Y Y Y Y Y N
2 Boland	Y ? Y Y Y Y Y N
3 Early	Y ? Y Y Y Y Y N
4 Frank	Y Y Y Y Y Y Y Y
5 Shannon	Y Y Y Y Y Y Y Y
6 Mavroules	? Y Y Y Y Y Y Y
7 Markey	Y Y Y Y Y Y Y Y
8 O'Neill	
9 Moakley	Y Y Y Y Y Y Y N
10 *Heckler*	Y Y Y Y Y N Y N
11 Donnelly	Y Y Y Y Y Y Y Y
12 Studds	Y N Y Y Y Y Y N
MICHIGAN	
1 Conyers	Y Y Y Y Y Y ? N
2 *Pursell*	? Y Y ? Y N Y N
3 Wolpe	Y Y Y Y Y Y Y Y
4 *Siljander*	Y Y Y Y Y N Y N
5 *Sawyer*	Y Y Y Y Y N Y N
6 *Dunn*	Y Y Y Y Y Y Y N
7 Kildee	Y Y Y Y Y Y Y Y
8 Traxler	Y Y Y Y ? Y Y Y
9 *Vander Jagt*	Y Y Y Y Y Y Y N
10 Albosta	Y P Y Y Y Y Y N
11 *Davis*	Y Y Y Y Y Y Y N
12 Bonior	Y Y Y Y Y Y Y Y
13 Crockett	? ? ? ? Y Y ? ?
14 Hertel	Y Y Y Y Y Y Y N
15 Ford	Y Y ? ? Y Y ? N
16 Dingell	? ? ? ? Y Y Y N
17 Brodhead	Y N Y Y Y Y Y Y
18 Blanchard	Y Y Y Y Y Y Y Y
19 *Broomfield*	Y Y Y Y Y Y Y Y
MINNESOTA	
1 *Erdahl*	Y N Y Y Y Y Y N
2 *Hagedorn*	Y Y Y Y Y Y Y N
3 *Frenzel*	Y Y Y Y Y Y Y N
4 Vento	
5 Sabo	N Y Y Y Y Y Y Y
6 *Weber*	Y N Y Y Y N Y N
7 *Stangeland*	Y Y Y Y Y Y Y N
8 Oberstar	Y Y Y Y Y Y Y Y
MISSISSIPPI	
1 Whitten	Y Y Y Y Y Y Y N
2 Bowen	Y Y Y Y Y Y Y N
3 Montgomery	Y P Y Y Y N Y N
4 Dowdy	Y Y Y Y Y N Y N
5 *Lott*	Y Y Y Y Y N Y N
MISSOURI	
1 Clay	Y Y Y N Y Y Y ? Y
2 Young	Y Y Y Y Y Y Y N
3 Gephardt	Y Y Y Y Y Y Y N

	248 249 250 251 252 253 254 255
4 Skelton	Y ? Y Y ? ? ? N
5 Bolling	Y N Y Y Y Y ? N
6 Coleman	Y Y Y Y Y N Y N
7 Taylor	? Y Y Y Y N Y N
8 Bailey	Y Y Y Y Y N Y N
9 Volkmer	Y Y Y Y Y Y Y N
10 Emerson	Y Y Y Y Y N Y N
MONTANA	
1 Williams	Y Y Y ? Y Y Y ?
2 *Marlenee*	Y N Y Y Y N Y N
NEBRASKA	
1 *Bereuter*	Y Y Y Y Y Y Y N
2 *Daub*	Y Y Y Y Y N Y N
3 *Smith*	Y Y Y Y Y N Y N
NEVADA	
AL Santini	? N Y Y Y Y Y N
NEW HAMPSHIRE	
1 D'Amours	Y Y Y Y Y Y ? Y
2 *Gregg*	Y N Y Y Y Y Y N
NEW JERSEY	
1 Florio	Y Y Y Y Y Y ? ?
2 Hughes	Y Y Y Y Y Y Y Y
3 Howard	Y Y Y Y Y Y Y Y
4 *Smith*	Y Y Y Y Y N Y N
5 *Fenwick*	Y P Y Y Y N Y N
6 *Forsythe*	N Y Y ? Y N ? N
7 *Roukema*	Y Y Y Y N ? -
8 Roe	Y Y Y Y Y Y Y Y
9 *Hollenbeck*	Y N Y Y Y Y Y Y
10 Rodino	Y Y Y Y Y Y Y Y
11 Minish	Y Y Y Y Y Y Y Y
12 *Rinaldo*	Y Y Y Y Y Y Y Y
13 *Courter*	Y Y Y Y Y Y Y N
14 Guarini	Y Y Y Y Y Y Y Y
15 Dwyer	Y Y Y Y Y Y Y Y
NEW MEXICO	
1 Lujan	Y Y Y Y Y N Y N
2 *Skeen*	Y Y Y Y Y Y Y N
NEW YORK	
1 *Carney*	? N Y Y Y N Y Y
2 Downey	Y Y Y Y Y Y Y Y
3 *Carman*	Y Y Y Y Y Y Y Y
4 *Lent*	Y Y Y Y Y N ? Y
5 McGrath	Y P Y Y Y Y Y N
6 *LeBoutillier*	Y Y Y Y Y N Y Y
7 Addabbo	Y Y Y Y Y Y Y Y
8 Rosenthal	Y Y Y Y Y Y Y Y
9 Ferraro	Y Y Y Y Y Y Y Y
10 Biaggi	Y Y Y Y Y Y Y Y
11 Scheuer	Y N Y Y Y Y Y Y
12 Chisholm	? Y Y ? Y Y Y ?
13 Solarz	Y Y Y Y Y Y Y Y
14 Richmond	Y Y Y Y Y Y Y Y
15 Zeferetti	Y Y Y Y Y Y Y N
16 Schumer	Y Y Y Y Y Y Y Y
17 *Molinari*	Y N Y Y Y Y Y N
18 *Green*	Y Y Y Y Y Y Y N
19 Rangel	Y Y Y Y Y ? ? #
20 Weiss	Y Y Y Y Y Y Y Y
21 Garcia	Y Y Y Y Y Y Y Y
22 Bingham	Y Y Y Y Y Y Y Y
23 Peyser	Y Y Y Y Y Y Y Y
24 Ottinger	P N N P Y Y P Y
25 *Fish*	Y Y Y Y Y Y Y N
26 *Gilman*	Y Y Y Y Y Y Y N
27 McHugh	Y Y Y Y Y Y Y Y
28 *Stratton*	? ? ? Y Y Y Y N
29 *Solomon*	N Y Y Y Y N Y N
30 *Martin*	Y Y Y Y Y N Y N
31 *Mitchell*	Y Y Y Y Y Y Y Y
32 *Wortley*	Y Y Y Y Y N Y N
33 Lee	Y Y Y Y Y N Y N
34 Horton	Y ? Y Y Y Y Y N
35 *Conable*	Y N Y Y Y N Y N
36 LaFalce	Y Y Y Y Y Y Y Y
37 Nowak	Y Y Y Y Y Y Y Y
38 *Kemp*	? Y Y Y Y Y Y N
39 Lundine	? ? ? ? ? ? ? ?
NORTH CAROLINA	
1 Jones	Y Y Y Y Y N Y Y
2 Fountain	Y Y Y Y Y Y Y N
3 Whitley	Y Y Y Y Y Y Y N
4 Andrews	Y Y Y Y Y Y Y N
5 Neal	Y Y Y Y Y Y Y Y
6 *Johnston*	N N Y N Y N Y Y
7 Rose	Y Y Y Y Y Y Y Y
8 Hefner	Y Y Y Y Y Y Y Y

	248 249 250 251 252 253 254 255
9 *Martin*	Y Y Y Y Y N Y N
10 *Broyhill*	Y N Y Y Y N Y Y
11 Hendon	Y N Y Y Y N Y Y
NORTH DAKOTA	
AL Dorgan	Y Y Y Y Y Y Y Y
OHIO	
1 *Gradison*	Y Y Y Y Y Y Y N
2 Luken	Y N Y Y Y Y Y N
3 Hall	Y N Y Y Y Y Y Y
4 *Oxley*	Y Y Y Y Y N Y N
5 *Latta*	Y Y Y Y Y N Y N
6 *McEwen*	Y Y Y Y Y Y Y N
7 *Brown*	Y Y Y Y Y Y Y N
8 *Kindness*	Y ? Y Y Y N ? N
9 *Weber*	Y Y Y Y Y Y Y N
10 *Miller*	Y Y Y Y Y N Y N
11 *Stanton*	Y Y Y Y Y Y Y N
12 Shamansky	Y Y Y Y Y Y Y N
13 Pease	Y N Y Y Y Y Y Y
14 Seiberling	Y P P ? Y Y Y Y
15 *Wylie*	Y Y Y Y Y N Y N
16 *Regula*	Y P Y Y Y Y Y N
17 *Ashbrook*	Y Y Y Y Y ? ? ?
18 Applegate	Y Y Y ? Y Y ? N
19 *Williams*	? ? ? ? ? ? ? ?
20 Oakar	? ? ? ? ? ? ? ?
21 Stokes	Y Y Y Y Y Y Y Y
22 Eckart	Y Y Y Y Y Y Y Y
23 Mottl	Y Y Y Y Y Y Y Y
OKLAHOMA	
1 Jones	Y P Y Y Y Y Y N
2 Synar	Y P Y Y Y Y Y N
3 Watkins	? Y Y Y Y N Y N
4 McCurdy	Y P Y Y Y Y Y N
5 *Edwards*	Y Y Y Y Y N Y N
6 English	Y Y Y Y Y N Y N
OREGON	
1 AuCoin	Y Y Y Y Y Y Y N
2 *Smith*	Y N Y Y Y N Y N
3 Wyden	Y Y Y Y Y Y Y N
4 Weaver	Y N Y Y Y Y Y Y
PENNSYLVANIA	
1 Foglietta	? ? ? Y Y Y Y Y
2 Gray	Y Y Y Y Y Y Y Y
3 Smith	Y Y Y Y Y Y Y Y
4 *Dougherty*	Y Y Y Y Y Y Y Y
5 *Schulze*	Y Y Y Y Y N Y N
6 Yatron	Y Y Y Y Y Y Y N
7 Edgar	Y Y Y Y Y Y Y Y
8 Coyne, J.	Y P Y Y ? N Y N
9 *Shuster*	Y N Y Y Y Y Y N
10 *McDade*	Y Y Y ? Y Y Y N
11 *Nelligan*	Y ? Y Y Y Y Y N
12 Murtha	Y Y Y Y Y Y Y N
13 *Coughlin*	Y Y Y Y Y Y Y Y
14 Coyne, W.	Y Y Y Y Y Y Y Y
15 Ritter	Y P Y Y Y N Y N
16 *Walker*	? ? ? ? ? ? ? ?
17 Ertel	Y Y Y Y Y Y Y Y
18 Walgren	Y Y Y Y Y Y Y Y
19 *Goodling*	N N Y Y Y Y ? N
20 Gaydos	Y Y Y Y Y Y Y N
21 Bailey	Y Y Y Y Y Y Y N
22 Murphy	Y ? Y Y Y Y Y Y
23 Clinger	Y Y Y Y Y Y Y N
24 Marks	N Y Y Y Y Y Y Y
25 Atkinson	? ? Y Y Y Y Y N
RHODE ISLAND	
1 St Germain	Y P Y Y Y Y Y Y
2 Schneider	Y Y Y Y Y Y Y Y
SOUTH CAROLINA	
1 *Hartnett*	? N Y Y Y N ? N
2 Spence	Y Y Y Y Y N Y N
3 Derrick	? ? ? ? ? ? ? ?
4 *Campbell*	Y Y Y Y Y Y Y N
5 Holland	? Y Y Y Y Y ? Y
6 *Napier*	Y Y Y Y Y N Y N
SOUTH DAKOTA	
1 Daschle	? Y Y ? Y Y Y Y
2 *Roberts*	? Y Y Y Y N Y Y
TENNESSEE	
1 *Quillen*	Y Y Y Y Y N Y N
2 *Duncan*	Y Y Y Y Y N Y N
3 Bouquard	Y P Y Y Y Y Y Y
4 Gore	Y Y Y Y Y Y Y Y
5 Boner	Y Y Y Y Y N Y N
6 Beard	? ? ? ? ? ? ? ?

	248 249 250 251 252 253 254 255
7 Jones	Y Y Y Y Y Y Y N
8 Ford	? ? ? ? Y Y Y N
TEXAS	
1 Hall, S.	Y Y Y Y Y N Y Y
2 Wilson	Y N Y Y Y Y Y Y
3 Collins	Y Y Y Y Y N Y N
4 Hall, R.	Y Y Y Y Y Y Y Y
5 Mattox	? Y Y Y ? Y Y Y
6 Gramm	Y N Y Y Y N Y N
7 Archer	Y N Y Y Y N Y N
8 Fields	? ? ? ? ? ? ? ?
9 Brooks	Y Y Y Y Y Y Y N
10 Pickle	Y Y Y Y Y Y Y N
11 Leath	Y P Y Y Y N Y Y
12 Wright	Y Y Y Y Y Y Y N
13 Hightower	Y Y Y Y Y Y Y N
14 Patman	? P Y Y Y Y Y Y
15 de la Garza	? ? ? ? Y Y Y N
16 White	Y Y Y Y Y Y Y Y
17 Stenholm	Y Y Y Y Y N Y N
18 Leland	? ? ? ? ? ? ? ?
19 Hance	Y ? ? Y Y Y Y Y
20 Gonzalez	Y Y Y Y ? Y Y Y
21 *Loeffler*	Y Y Y Y Y Y Y N
22 *Paul*	Y N Y Y Y N N Y
23 Kazen	Y Y Y Y Y Y Y N
24 Frost	Y Y Y Y Y ? ? Y
UTAH	
1 *Hansen*	Y Y Y Y Y N Y N
2 *Marriott*	Y Y Y Y Y N Y N
VERMONT	
AL *Jeffords*	Y Y Y Y Y Y Y N
VIRGINIA	
1 *Trible*	Y Y Y Y Y N Y N
2 *Whitehurst*	Y Y Y ? Y N Y N
3 *Bliley*	Y Y Y Y Y N Y N
4 Daniel, R.	Y Y Y Y Y N Y N
5 Daniel, D.	Y Y Y Y Y N Y N
6 *Butler*	Y N Y N Y N Y N
7 *Robinson*	Y Y Y Y Y N Y N
8 *Parris*	Y P Y Y Y Y Y N
9 *Wampler*	Y Y Y Y Y Y Y N
10 *Wolf*	Y Y Y Y Y Y Y N
WASHINGTON	
1 *Pritchard*	Y Y Y Y Y Y Y N
2 Swift	Y N Y Y Y Y Y N
3 Bonker	Y Y Y Y Y Y Y N
4 *Morrison*	Y Y Y Y Y Y Y N
5 Foley	Y Y Y Y Y Y Y N
6 Dicks	Y Y Y Y Y Y Y N
7 Lowry	Y P Y Y Y Y Y N
WEST VIRGINIA	
1 Mollohan	? ? Y Y Y Y Y N
2 *Benedict*	Y Y Y Y Y Y Y N
3 Staton	Y Y Y Y Y Y Y N
4 Rahall	Y Y Y Y Y Y Y Y
WISCONSIN	
1 Aspin	N Y Y Y ? Y Y N
2 Kastenmeier	? Y Y Y Y Y Y Y
3 *Gunderson*	Y N Y Y Y Y Y N
4 Zablocki	? Y Y Y Y Y Y N
5 Reuss	Y Y Y Y Y Y Y N
6 *Petri*	Y Y Y Y Y Y Y N
7 Obey	? N Y Y Y N N Y
8 Roth	Y Y Y Y Y Y Y N
9 *Sensenbrenner*	Y N Y Y Y N Y N
WYOMING	
AL *Cheney*	Y Y Y Y Y N Y N

Democrats   *Republicans*

256. HR 3603. Food and Agriculture Act of 1981. De la Garza, D-Texas, motion that the House resolve itself into the Committee of the Whole for further consideration of the bill. Motion agreed to 386-2: R 176-1; D 210-1 (ND 136-1, SD 74-0), Oct. 21, 1981.

257. HR 3603. Food and Agriculture Act of 1981. Shamansky, D-Ohio, amendment to repeal the tobacco allotment system and tobacco price support loans. Rejected 184-231: R 107-75; D 77-156 (ND 71-85, SD 6-71), Oct. 21, 1981. A "nay" was a vote supporting the president's position.

258. HR 3603. Food and Agriculture Act of 1981. Findley, R-Ill., amendment, as amended by Foley, D-Wash., to direct the secretary of agriculture, acting within existing legal authority, to make the tobacco price support and allotment program self-supporting, without cost to the federal budget except for administrative expenses. (The Foley substitute was adopted by voice vote.) Adopted 412-0: R 180-0; D 232-0 (ND 156-0, SD 76-0), Oct. 21, 1981. A "nay" was a vote supporting the president's position.

259. HR 3603. Food and Agriculture Act of 1981. De la Garza, D-Texas, motion that the House resolve itself into the Committee of the Whole for further consideration of the bill. Motion agreed to 378-1: R 170-0; D 208-1 (ND 142-1, SD 66-0), Oct. 22, 1981.

260. HR 3603. Food and Agriculture Act of 1981. Walker, R-Pa., amendment to require most food stamp recipients to pay for a portion of their stamps. Rejected 147-251: R 134-40; D 13-211 (ND 5-147, SD 8-64), Oct. 22, 1981. A "nay" was a vote supporting the president's position.

261. HR 3603. Food and Agriculture Act of 1981. English, D-Okla., amendment offered as a substitute to the Daschle, D-S.D., amendment *(see vote 262, below)*, to require that meat produced abroad and sold in the United States be produced without drugs or agricultural chemicals that are barred for health reasons in the United States, unless the president determines that such action would harm U.S. farm exports. (The Daschle amendment would have required imported meat to be labeled as to country of origin.) Adopted 223-162: R 84-87; D 139-75 (ND 82-61, SD 57-14), Oct. 22, 1981. A "nay" was a vote supporting the president's position.

262. HR 3603. Food and Agriculture Act of 1981. Daschle, D-S.D., amendment, as amended by English, D-Okla., to require that meat produced abroad and sold in the United States be produced without drugs or agricultural chemicals that are barred for health reasons in the United States, unless the president determines that such action would harm U.S. farm exports. Adopted 211-168: R 80-89; D 131-79 (ND 77-64, SD 54-15), Oct. 22, 1981. A "nay" was a vote supporting the president's position.

263. HR 3603. Food and Agriculture Act of 1981. Coleman, R-Mo., amendment to extend farm and food program authorizations through fiscal 1982-83 only, thereby canceling program reauthorizations for 1984-85. Rejected 180-193: R 159-9; D 21-184 (ND 12-127, SD 9-57), Oct. 22, 1981. A "nay" was a vote supporting the president's position.

KEY

Y Voted for (yea).
\# Paired for.
\+ Announced for.
N Voted against (nay).
X Paired against.
\- Announced against.
P Voted "present".
C Voted "present" to avoid possible conflict of interest.
? Did not vote or otherwise make a position known.

	256	257	258	259	260	261	262	263
ALABAMA								
1 *Edwards*	Y	Y	Y	?	Y	Y	Y	Y
2 *Dickinson*	N	N	Y	Y	N	Y	Y	Y
3 Nichols	Y	N	Y	N	Y	Y	Y	N
4 Bevill	Y	N	Y	N	Y	N	Y	N
5 Flippo	Y	N	Y	N	Y	Y	N	N
6 *Smith*	Y	Y	Y	Y	Y	Y	Y	Y
7 Shelby	Y	N	Y	N	Y	N	Y	N
ALASKA								
AL *Young*	Y	N	Y	?	N	?	?	?
ARIZONA								
1 *Rhodes*	Y	N	Y	Y	?	?	?	?
2 Udall	Y	N	Y	Y	N	?	?	?
3 *Stump*	Y	N	Y	Y	Y	Y	Y	Y
4 *Rudd*	?	X	Y	Y	Y	Y	Y	Y
ARKANSAS								
1 *Alexander*	Y	N	Y	N	N	N	N	?
2 *Bethune*	Y	Y	Y	N	Y	Y	Y	Y
3 *Hammerschmidt*	Y	N	Y	Y	Y	Y	Y	N
4 Anthony	Y	N	Y	N	Y	N	Y	N
CALIFORNIA								
1 *Chappie*	Y	Y	Y	Y	N	N	N	Y
2 *Clausen*	Y	Y	Y	Y	N	N	N	Y
3 Matsui	Y	Y	Y	N	N	N	N	N
4 Fazio	Y	N	Y	N	N	N	N	N
5 Burton, J.	?	N	?	Y	?	?	?	?
6 Burton, P.	Y	N	Y	N	N	N	N	N
7 Miller	Y	Y	Y	N	N	N	N	N
8 Dellums	?	?	?	?	X	X	X	X
9 Stark	Y	N	Y	N	Y	N	Y	N
10 Edwards	Y	N	Y	N	Y	N	Y	N
11 Lantos	Y	Y	Y	N	N	N	N	N
12 *McCloskey*	?	?	?	?	?	?	?	?
13 Mineta	Y	N	Y	N	N	N	N	N
14 *Shumway*	Y	Y	Y	Y	N	Y	N	Y
15 Coelho	Y	N	Y	?	N	N	N	N
16 Panetta	Y	N	Y	N	N	N	N	N
17 Pashayan	Y	N	Y	N	Y	N	N	Y
18 *Thomas*	Y	N	Y	N	Y	N	N	Y
19 *Lagomarsino*	Y	Y	Y	Y	N	N	N	Y
20 *Goldwater*	?	Y	Y	?	?	N	N	Y
21 *Fiedler*	Y	Y	Y	Y	N	N	N	Y
22 *Moorhead*	Y	Y	Y	Y	N	N	N	Y
23 Beilenson	Y	N	Y	N	N	N	N	N
24 Waxman	?	Y	Y	Y	?	?	?	X
25 Roybal	Y	N	Y	N	N	N	N	N
26 *Rousselot*	Y	P	Y	Y	?	?	?	?
27 *Dornan*	Y	Y	Y	Y	N	N	N	Y
28 Dixon	?	N	Y	N	N	N	N	N
29 Hawkins	Y	N	Y	N	N	N	N	N
30 Danielson	Y	N	Y	N	Y	N	N	N
31 Dymally	Y	N	Y	N	Y	?	?	?
32 Anderson	Y	Y	Y	Y	N	N	N	N
33 Grisham	Y	Y	Y	Y	Y	N	Y	Y
34 *Lungren*	Y	Y	Y	?	#	?	?	?
35 *Dreier*	Y	Y	Y	Y	N	N	N	Y
36 Brown	Y	N	Y	N	N	N	N	N
37 *Lewis*	Y	Y	Y	Y	N	N	N	Y
38 Patterson	Y	Y	Y	N	N	N	N	N
39 *Dannemeyer*	Y	Y	Y	Y	N	N	N	Y
40 *Badham*	Y	Y	Y	?	Y	Y	Y	Y
41 *Lowery*	Y	Y	Y	Y	N	N	N	Y
42 *Hunter*	Y	Y	Y	Y	Y	Y	Y	Y
43 *Burgener*	Y	N	Y	Y	N	N	N	Y
COLORADO								
1 Schroeder	Y	Y	Y	N	Y	N	Y	N
2 Wirth	Y	Y	Y	N	Y	N	Y	N
3 Kogovsek	Y	N	Y	N	Y	N	Y	N
4 *Brown*	Y	Y	Y	Y	Y	Y	Y	Y

	256	257	258	259	260	261	262	263
5 *Kramer*	Y	Y	Y	Y	Y	Y	Y	Y
CONNECTICUT								
1 Vacancy								
2 Gejdenson	Y	Y	Y	Y	N	Y	N	N
3 *DeNardis*	Y	Y	Y	Y	N	N	N	Y
4 *McKinney*	Y	Y	Y	Y	N	N	N	?
5 Ratchford	Y	Y	Y	Y	N	Y	N	Y
6 Moffett	?	Y	Y	Y	N	Y	N	Y
DELAWARE								
AL *Evans*	Y	Y	Y	Y	N	N	N	Y
FLORIDA								
1 Hutto	Y	N	Y	?	N	Y	N	Y
2 Fuqua	Y	N	Y	?	N	Y	N	Y
3 Bennett	Y	N	Y	Y	Y	Y	Y	Y
4 Chappell	Y	N	Y	N	Y	N	Y	Y
5 *McCollum*	Y	Y	Y	Y	Y	Y	Y	#
6 *Young*	Y	Y	Y	Y	Y	Y	Y	Y
7 Gibbons	?	Y	Y	Y	N	Y	N	N
8 Ireland	Y	N	Y	N	?	?	?	?
9 Nelson	Y	N	Y	Y	N	Y	Y	Y
10 *Bafalis*	?	N	Y	?	#	#	#	#
11 Mica	Y	N	Y	N	N	N	N	N
12 *Shaw*	Y	Y	Y	Y	N	Y	Y	Y
13 Lehman	?	Y	Y	Y	N	Y	N	N
14 Pepper	?	X	?	?	?	Y	Y	X
15 Fascell	Y	N	Y	N	N	N	N	N
GEORGIA								
1 Ginn	Y	N	Y	N	Y	N	Y	N
2 Hatcher	Y	N	Y	N	Y	N	Y	N
3 Brinkley	Y	Y	Y	N	Y	Y	Y	Y
4 Levitas	Y	N	Y	N	Y	N	Y	N
5 Fowler	Y	N	Y	?	?	?	?	?
6 *Gingrich*	Y	Y	Y	?	?	?	?	#
7 McDonald	Y	+	+	?	Y	N	N	Y
8 Evans	Y	N	Y	?	N	Y	N	N
9 Jenkins	Y	N	Y	N	Y	N	Y	?
10 Barnard	Y	N	Y	?	N	?	?	?
HAWAII								
1 Heftel	?	N	Y	N	Y	N	Y	N
2 Akaka	Y	N	Y	N	Y	N	Y	N
IDAHO								
1 *Craig*	Y	Y	Y	Y	Y	Y	Y	Y
2 *Hansen*	Y	N	Y	Y	Y	Y	Y	Y
ILLINOIS								
1 Washington	Y	Y	Y	N	N	N	N	N
2 Savage	?	Y	Y	?	?	N	?	?
3 Russo	Y	Y	Y	N	N	N	N	N
4 *Derwinski*	Y	Y	?	Y	N	N	Y	N
5 Fary	Y	N	Y	N	N	N	N	N
6 *Hyde*	Y	Y	Y	Y	N	N	N	Y
7 Collins	Y	N	Y	N	Y	N	Y	N
8 Rostenkowski	Y	N	Y	N	N	N	N	N
9 Yates	Y	Y	Y	N	N	N	N	N
10 *Porter*	Y	Y	Y	Y	N	N	N	Y
11 Annunzio	Y	N	Y	N	N	N	N	N
12 *Crane, P.*	Y	Y	Y	Y	N	N	N	Y
13 *McClory*	Y	Y	Y	Y	N	N	N	Y
14 *Erlenborn*	Y	Y	Y	Y	N	N	N	Y
15 *Corcoran*	+	Y	Y	+	#	#	#	#
16 *Martin*	Y	Y	Y	Y	N	N	N	Y
17 *O'Brien*	Y	Y	Y	Y	#	X	X	#
18 *Michel*	Y	N	Y	?	N	Y	N	Y
19 *Railsback*	Y	Y	Y	Y	N	N	N	Y
20 *Findley*	Y	N	Y	N	N	N	N	Y
21 *Madigan*	Y	N	Y	?	N	N	N	Y
22 *Crane, D.*	Y	Y	Y	Y	N	N	N	Y
23 Price	Y	N	Y	N	N	N	N	N
24 Simon	Y	Y	Y	Y	N	N	N	N
INDIANA								
1 Benjamin	Y	N	Y	N	Y	N	Y	N
2 Fithian	Y	N	Y	N	Y	N	Y	N
3 *Hiler*	Y	Y	Y	Y	Y	Y	Y	Y
4 *Coats*	Y	Y	Y	Y	Y	Y	Y	Y
5 *Hillis*	Y	Y	Y	Y	N	N	N	Y
6 Evans	Y	N	Y	N	Y	N	Y	N
7 *Myers*	Y	Y	Y	Y	Y	Y	Y	Y
8 *Deckard*	?	Y	Y	?	?	Y	Y	Y
9 Hamilton	Y	N	Y	N	Y	N	Y	N
10 Sharp	Y	N	Y	Y	Y	Y	Y	N
11 Jacobs	Y	N	Y	N	Y	N	N	N
IOWA								
1 *Leach*	Y	Y	Y	Y	N	N	N	Y
2 *Tauke*	Y	Y	Y	Y	Y	Y	Y	Y
3 Evans	Y	N	Y	N	N	N	N	Y
4 Smith	Y	N	Y	N	N	N	N	Y
5 Harkin	Y	N	Y	N	Y	N	Y	N
6 Bedell	Y	N	Y	N	Y	N	Y	N

Democrats *Republicans*

Corresponding to Congressional Record Votes 270, 271, 272, 273, 274, 275, 276, 277

	256	257	258	259	260	261	262	263
KANSAS								
1 ***Roberts***	Y	N	Y	Y	Y	Y	Y	Y
2 ***Jeffries***	Y	Y	Y	Y	Y	Y	Y	Y
3 ***Winn***	Y	N	Y	Y	Y	Y	Y	Y
4 Glickman	Y	N	Y	Y	N	Y	Y	N
5 ***Whittaker***	Y	Y	Y	Y	Y	Y	Y	Y
KENTUCKY								
1 Hubbard	Y	N	Y	Y	N	Y	Y	N
2 Natcher	Y	N	Y	Y	N	Y	Y	N
3 Mazzoli	Y	N	Y	Y	N	N	N	Y
4 ***Snyder***	Y	N	Y	Y	Y	Y	Y	Y
5 ***Rogers***	Y	N	Y	Y	N	Y	Y	Y
6 ***Hopkins***	Y	N	Y	Y	N	N	N	Y
7 Perkins	Y	N	Y	Y	N	Y	N	N
LOUISIANA								
1 ***Livingston***	Y	N	Y	Y	N	N	N	Y
2 Boggs	Y	N	Y	Y	N	Y	Y	N
3 Tauzin	Y	N	Y	Y	N	Y	Y	N
4 Roemer	Y	N	Y	Y	N	Y	Y	Y
5 Huckaby	Y	N	Y	Y	N	Y	Y	N
6 ***Moore***	Y	N	Y	Y	N	Y	Y	Y
7 Breaux	Y	N	Y	Y	N	Y	Y	N
8 Long	Y	N	Y	Y	N	Y	Y	N
MAINE								
1 ***Emery***	Y	Y	Y	Y	Y	Y	Y	Y
2 ***Snowe***	Y	Y	Y	Y	N	Y	N	Y
MARYLAND								
1 Dyson	Y	N	Y	Y	N	Y	Y	N
2 Long	Y	Y	Y	Y	N	N	N	Y
3 Mikulski	Y	Y	Y	Y	N	Y	Y	N
4 ***Holt***	Y	N	Y	Y	Y	N	N	Y
5 Hoyer	Y	N	Y	Y	N	Y	Y	N
6 Byron	Y	Y	Y	Y	N	N	N	N
7 Mitchell	N	N	Y	N	N	Y	?	N
8 Barnes	Y	Y	Y	Y	N	Y	Y	N
MASSACHUSETTS								
1 ***Conte***	Y	Y	Y	Y	N	N	N	Y
2 Boland	Y	N	Y	Y	N	N	N	N
3 Early	Y	Y	Y	Y	N	?	?	?
4 Frank	Y	Y	Y	Y	N	N	N	Y
5 Shannon	Y	N	Y	Y	N	N	N	N
6 Mavroules	?	N	Y	Y	N	N	N	N
7 Markey	Y	N	Y	Y	N	Y	Y	N
8 O'Neill								
9 Moakley	Y	N	Y	Y	N	N	N	N
10 ***Heckler***	Y	Y	Y	?	N	N	N	Y
11 Donnelly	Y	N	Y	Y	N	Y	Y	N
12 Studds	Y	Y	Y	Y	N	Y	Y	N
MICHIGAN								
1 Conyers	Y	Y	Y	Y	N	Y	Y	N
2 ***Pursell***	Y	Y	?	Y	N	N	N	?
3 Wolpe	Y	Y	Y	Y	N	Y	Y	N
4 ***Siljander***	Y	Y	Y	?	#	Y	Y	Y
5 ***Sawyer***	Y	Y	Y	Y	Y	Y	Y	Y
6 ***Dunn***	Y	Y	Y	Y	Y	N	N	Y
7 Kildee	Y	Y	Y	Y	N	Y	Y	N
8 Traxler	Y	N	Y	Y	N	Y	Y	N
9 ***Vander Jagt***	Y	N	Y	Y	Y	N	?	?
10 Albosta	Y	N	Y	Y	N	Y	Y	N
11 ***Davis***	Y	Y	Y	Y	N	Y	Y	Y
12 Bonior	Y	Y	Y	Y	N	Y	Y	N
13 Crockett	Y	Y	Y	?	N	Y	?	N
14 Hertel	Y	?	?	?	X	#	#	X
15 Ford	?	N	Y	Y	N	Y	Y	N
16 Dingell	Y	N	Y	Y	N	Y	Y	N
17 Brodhead	Y	Y	Y	Y	N	Y	Y	N
18 Blanchard	Y	N	Y	Y	N	Y	Y	N
19 ***Broomfield***	Y	Y	Y	Y	Y	Y	Y	Y
MINNESOTA								
1 ***Erdahl***	Y	Y	Y	Y	Y	Y	Y	Y
2 ***Hagedorn***	Y	Y	Y	Y	Y	Y	Y	Y
3 ***Frenzel***	Y	Y	Y	Y	Y	N	N	Y
4 Vento	Y	Y	Y	Y	N	N	N	N
5 Sabo	Y	N	Y	Y	N	N	N	N
6 ***Weber***	Y	N	Y	Y	Y	Y	Y	N
7 ***Stangeland***	Y	N	Y	Y	Y	Y	Y	Y
8 Oberstar	Y	Y	Y	Y	N	Y	Y	N
MISSISSIPPI								
1 Whitten	Y	N	Y	Y	Y	Y	Y	N
2 Bowen	Y	N	Y	Y	N	Y	Y	N
3 Montgomery	Y	N	?	Y	Y	Y	Y	N
4 Dowdy	Y	N	Y	Y	N	Y	Y	N
5 ***Lott***	Y	N	Y	Y	Y	Y	Y	Y
MISSOURI								
1 Clay	Y	N	Y	Y	N	?	?	?
2 Young	Y	N	Y	Y	N	Y	Y	N
3 Gephardt	Y	N	Y	Y	N	N	N	N
4 Skelton	Y	N	Y	Y	N	Y	Y	N
5 Bolling	Y	N	Y	?	N	?	?	?
6 ***Coleman***	Y	N	Y	Y	Y	Y	Y	Y
7 ***Taylor***	Y	N	Y	Y	Y	Y	Y	Y
8 ***Bailey***	Y	N	Y	Y	Y	Y	Y	Y
9 Volkmer	Y	N	Y	Y	N	Y	Y	N
10 ***Emerson***	Y	N	Y	Y	Y	Y	Y	Y
MONTANA								
1 Williams	?	Y	Y	?	N	Y	Y	N
2 ***Marlenee***	Y	N	Y	Y	Y	Y	Y	Y
NEBRASKA								
1 ***Bereuter***	Y	Y	Y	Y	Y	Y	Y	N
2 ***Daub***	Y	Y	Y	Y	Y	N	N	Y
3 ***Smith***	Y	N	Y	Y	Y	Y	Y	Y
NEVADA								
AL Santini	Y	Y	Y	Y	Y	Y	Y	Y
NEW HAMPSHIRE								
1 D'Amours	Y	Y	Y	Y	N	N	N	N
2 ***Gregg***	Y	Y	Y	Y	Y	N	N	Y
NEW JERSEY								
1 Florio	?	?	?	?	?	?	?	?
2 Hughes	Y	#	Y	Y	N	N	N	Y
3 Howard	Y	N	Y	Y	N	Y	N	N
4 ***Smith***	Y	Y	Y	Y	N	Y	Y	Y
5 ***Fenwick***	Y	Y	Y	Y	Y	N	N	Y
6 ***Forsythe***	Y	Y	Y	Y	Y	N	?	#
7 ***Roukema***	Y	Y	Y	Y	N	N	N	Y
8 Roe	Y	N	Y	Y	N	?	?	?
9 ***Hollenbeck***	Y	Y	?	Y	N	Y	Y	Y
10 Rodino	?	N	Y	Y	N	Y	Y	N
11 Minish	Y	Y	Y	Y	N	Y	Y	N
12 ***Rinaldo***	?	Y	Y	Y	N	Y	Y	Y
13 ***Courter***	?	Y	Y	Y	Y	Y	Y	Y
14 Guarini	Y	Y	Y	Y	N	?	?	X
15 Dwyer	Y	N	Y	Y	N	Y	N	N
NEW MEXICO								
1 ***Lujan***	Y	N	Y	Y	N	Y	Y	Y
2 ***Skeen***	Y	N	Y	Y	Y	Y	Y	Y
NEW YORK								
1 ***Carney***	Y	N	Y	Y	Y	N	N	Y
2 Downey	Y	Y	Y	Y	N	N	N	N
3 ***Carman***	Y	Y	Y	Y	Y	N	N	Y
4 ***Lent***	Y	Y	Y	Y	Y	N	N	Y
5 ***McGrath***	Y	?	Y	Y	Y	N	N	Y
6 ***LeBoutillier***	Y	Y	Y	Y	Y	N	N	Y
7 Addabbo	Y	N	Y	Y	N	Y	Y	N
8 Rosenthal	Y	N	Y	?	?	?	?	?
9 Ferraro	Y	Y	Y	Y	N	Y	Y	N
10 Biaggi	Y	N	Y	?	N	#	#	X
11 Scheuer	Y	Y	Y	Y	N	N	N	N
12 Chisholm	?	N	Y	Y	N	?	N	N
13 Solarz	Y	N	Y	Y	N	N	N	N
14 Richmond	Y	N	Y	Y	N	Y	Y	N
15 Zeferetti	Y	N	Y	Y	N	Y	Y	N
16 Schumer	Y	Y	Y	Y	N	N	N	?
17 ***Molinari***	Y	Y	Y	Y	N	N	N	Y
18 ***Green***	Y	Y	Y	Y	N	N	N	Y
19 Rangel	Y	N	Y	Y	N	N	N	N
20 Weiss	Y	Y	Y	Y	N	N	N	N
21 Garcia	?	Y	Y	Y	N	X	X	X
22 Bingham	Y	N	Y	Y	N	N	N	N
23 Peyser	Y	Y	Y	Y	N	N	N	N
24 Ottinger	?	Y	Y	P	N	N	N	N
25 ***Fish***	?	?	?	Y	N	N	N	Y
26 ***Gilman***	+	+	+	Y	N	+	+	+
27 McHugh	Y	Y	Y	Y	N	N	N	N
28 Stratton	Y	N	Y	Y	N	Y	Y	Y
29 ***Solomon***	Y	?	Y	Y	Y	N	N	Y
30 ***Martin***	Y	N	Y	Y	Y	N	N	Y
31 ***Mitchell***	Y	Y	Y	Y	N	Y	Y	Y
32 ***Wortley***	Y	N	Y	Y	Y	N	N	Y
33 ***Lee***	Y	Y	Y	Y	Y	N	N	Y
34 ***Horton***	Y	Y	?	Y	N	N	N	Y
35 ***Conable***	Y	Y	Y	Y	Y	N	N	Y
36 LaFalce	Y	Y	Y	Y	N	N	N	Y
37 Nowak	Y	Y	Y	Y	N	N	N	N
38 ***Kemp***	Y	Y	Y	?	Y	N	N	Y
39 Lundine	?	?	?	?	?	?	?	?
NORTH CAROLINA								
1 Jones	Y	N	Y	?	X	?	?	X
2 Fountain	Y	N	Y	Y	N	N	Y	N
3 Whitley	Y	N	Y	Y	N	Y	Y	N
4 Andrews	Y	N	Y	Y	N	Y	Y	N
5 Neal	Y	N	Y	Y	N	Y	Y	N
6 ***Johnston***	Y	N	Y	?	#	?	?	?
7 Rose	Y	N	Y	?	N	Y	Y	N
8 Hefner	Y	N	Y	Y	N	?	?	?
9 ***Martin***	Y	N	Y	Y	Y	?	?	?
10 ***Broyhill***	Y	N	Y	Y	Y	?	?	?
11 ***Hendon***	Y	N	Y	Y	Y	Y	Y	N
NORTH DAKOTA								
AL Dorgan	Y	N	Y	Y	N	Y	Y	N
OHIO								
1 ***Gradison***	Y	Y	Y	Y	?	N	N	Y
2 Luken	Y	N	Y	Y	N	N	N	N
3 Hall	Y	Y	Y	Y	N	Y	Y	N
4 ***Oxley***	Y	Y	Y	Y	Y	Y	N	Y
5 ***Latta***	Y	Y	Y	Y	Y	Y	N	Y
6 ***McEwen***	Y	N	Y	Y	Y	N	N	Y
7 ***Brown***	Y	N	Y	?	Y	C	C	Y
8 ***Kindness***	Y	N	Y	Y	#	N	N	Y
9 ***Weber***	Y	N	Y	Y	Y	N	N	Y
10 ***Miller***	Y	N	Y	Y	Y	Y	Y	Y
11 ***Stanton***	Y	N	Y	Y	Y	N	N	Y
12 Shamansky	Y	Y	Y	Y	N	Y	Y	N
13 Pease	Y	Y	Y	Y	N	N	N	N
14 Seiberling	?	N	Y	?	N	Y	Y	N
15 ***Wylie***	Y	Y	Y	Y	Y	Y	Y	Y
16 ***Regula***	Y	Y	Y	Y	Y	Y	Y	Y
17 ***Ashbrook***	Y	N	Y	Y	Y	?	?	?
18 Applegate	?	Y	Y	?	N	Y	Y	Y
19 ***Williams***	?	#	?	?	X	?	?	?
20 Oakar	?	Y	Y	?	N	Y	Y	N
21 Stokes	Y	N	Y	Y	N	Y	Y	N
22 Eckart	Y	Y	Y	Y	N	Y	Y	N
23 Mottl	Y	Y	Y	Y	Y	Y	Y	Y
OKLAHOMA								
1 Jones	Y	N	Y	Y	Y	Y	Y	N
2 Synar	Y	N	Y	Y	N	Y	Y	N
3 Watkins	Y	N	Y	?	N	Y	Y	N
4 McCurdy	Y	N	Y	Y	N	Y	Y	N
5 ***Edwards***	Y	Y	Y	Y	Y	Y	Y	Y
6 English	Y	N	Y	Y	N	Y	Y	N
OREGON								
1 AuCoin	Y	Y	Y	Y	N	Y	Y	N
2 ***Smith***	Y	N	Y	Y	Y	Y	Y	Y
3 Wyden	Y	Y	Y	Y	N	?	?	?
4 Weaver	Y	Y	?	Y	N	Y	Y	Y
PENNSYLVANIA								
1 Foglietta	Y	Y	Y	Y	N	Y	Y	?
2 Gray	Y	N	Y	Y	N	Y	Y	N
3 Smith	Y	N	Y	Y	N	Y	Y	N
4 ***Dougherty***	Y	Y	?	Y	X	N	N	Y
5 ***Schulze***	Y	Y	Y	Y	Y	?	?	?
6 Yatron	Y	Y	Y	Y	N	Y	Y	N
7 Edgar	Y	Y	Y	Y	N	N	N	N
8 ***Coyne, J.***	Y	Y	Y	Y	Y	?	?	Y
9 ***Shuster***	Y	N	Y	Y	Y	Y	Y	N
10 ***McDade***	?	?	?	Y	N	N	N	Y
11 ***Nelligan***	Y	Y	Y	Y	N	Y	N	Y
12 Murtha	Y	N	Y	Y	N	Y	Y	N
13 ***Coughlin***	Y	Y	Y	Y	N	N	N	Y
14 Coyne, W.	Y	Y	Y	?	N	Y	Y	N
15 ***Ritter***	Y	Y	Y	Y	Y	N	N	Y
16 ***Walker***	Y	N	Y	Y	Y	N	N	Y
17 Ertel	Y	Y	Y	?	?	N	N	?
18 Walgren	?	Y	Y	Y	Y	Y	Y	N
19 ***Goodling***	Y	Y	Y	?	Y	Y	Y	Y
20 Gaydos	Y	N	Y	?	N	Y	Y	N
21 Bailey	Y	N	Y	Y	N	Y	Y	N
22 Murphy	?	Y	Y	?	?	?	?	?
23 ***Clinger***	Y	Y	Y	Y	Y	N	N	Y
24 ***Marks***	Y	N	Y	Y	N	?	?	?
25 ***Atkinson***	Y	Y	Y	Y	Y	N	N	N
RHODE ISLAND								
1 St Germain	Y	Y	Y	Y	N	Y	Y	N
2 ***Schneider***	Y	Y	Y	Y	N	Y	Y	Y
SOUTH CAROLINA								
1 ***Hartnett***	Y	N	Y	Y	Y	N	N	Y
2 ***Spence***	Y	N	Y	Y	Y	Y	Y	Y
3 Derrick	Y	N	Y	Y	N	Y	Y	N
4 ***Campbell***	Y	N	Y	?	?	X	X	#
5 Holland	Y	N	Y	Y	N	?	?	?
6 ***Napier***	Y	N	Y	Y	N	N	N	Y
SOUTH DAKOTA								
1 Daschle	?	N	Y	Y	N	N	Y	N
2 ***Roberts***	Y	N	Y	Y	Y	Y	Y	N
TENNESSEE								
1 ***Quillen***	Y	N	Y	Y	Y	Y	Y	Y
2 ***Duncan***	Y	N	Y	Y	Y	Y	Y	Y
3 Bouquard	Y	N	Y	Y	N	N	N	N
4 Gore	Y	N	Y	Y	N	Y	Y	N
5 Boner	Y	N	Y	Y	N	N	N	N
6 ***Beard***	Y	N	Y	Y	?	N	N	Y
7 Jones	Y	N	Y	Y	N	N	N	N
8 Ford	Y	N	Y	?	X	Y	N	N
TEXAS								
1 Hall, S.	Y	N	Y	Y	?	Y	Y	Y
2 Wilson	?	N	Y	Y	?	Y	Y	N
3 ***Collins***	Y	Y	Y	Y	Y	?	?	?
4 Hall, R.	Y	N	Y	Y	N	Y	Y	N
5 Mattox	Y	N	Y	Y	N	Y	Y	N
6 Gramm	Y	Y	Y	Y	Y	Y	Y	Y
7 ***Archer***	Y	Y	Y	Y	Y	N	N	Y
8 ***Fields***	?	?	?	Y	Y	Y	Y	Y
9 Brooks	Y	N	Y	?	?	?	?	?
10 Pickle	Y	N	Y	Y	N	Y	Y	N
11 Leath	Y	N	Y	Y	N	Y	Y	N
12 Wright	Y	N	Y	Y	N	Y	?	?
13 Hightower	Y	N	Y	Y	N	Y	Y	Y
14 Patman	Y	N	Y	Y	N	Y	Y	N
15 de la Garza	Y	N	Y	Y	N	N	N	N
16 White	Y	N	Y	Y	N	Y	?	#
17 Stenholm	Y	N	Y	Y	N	Y	Y	N
18 Leland	Y	N	Y	Y	N	N	N	N
19 Hance	?	N	Y	?	N	Y	Y	N
20 Gonzalez	Y	N	Y	Y	N	Y	Y	N
21 ***Loeffler***	Y	N	Y	Y	Y	Y	Y	Y
22 ***Paul***	Y	Y	Y	Y	Y	N	N	Y
23 Kazen	Y	N	Y	Y	N	Y	Y	N
24 Frost	Y	N	Y	?	?	?	?	?
UTAH								
1 ***Hansen***	Y	Y	Y	Y	Y	N	Y	Y
2 ***Marriott***	Y	Y	Y	Y	Y	Y	Y	Y
VERMONT								
AL ***Jeffords***	Y	N	Y	Y	N	Y	Y	Y
VIRGINIA								
1 ***Trible***	Y	N	Y	Y	Y	N	N	Y
2 ***Whitehurst***	Y	Y	Y	Y	Y	N	N	Y
3 ***Bliley***	Y	N	Y	Y	Y	N	N	Y
4 ***Daniel, R.***	Y	N	Y	Y	Y	N	N	Y
5 Daniel, D.	Y	N	Y	Y	Y	N	N	N
6 ***Butler***	?	N	Y	?	Y	N	N	Y
7 ***Robinson***	Y	N	Y	Y	Y	N	N	Y
8 ***Parris***	Y	N	Y	Y	X	N	N	Y
9 ***Wampler***	Y	N	Y	Y	N	N	N	Y
10 ***Wolf***	Y	N	Y	Y	Y	N	N	Y
WASHINGTON								
1 ***Pritchard***	Y	Y	Y	Y	Y	N	N	Y
2 Swift	Y	Y	Y	Y	N	N	N	N
3 Bonker	Y	Y	Y	Y	N	N	N	N
4 ***Morrison***	Y	Y	Y	Y	Y	Y	Y	Y
5 Foley	Y	N	Y	Y	N	N	N	N
6 Dicks	Y	?	Y	Y	N	N	N	N
7 Lowry	Y	N	Y	Y	N	N	N	N
WEST VIRGINIA								
1 Mollohan	?	N	Y	Y	N	N	N	N
2 ***Benedict***	Y	N	Y	Y	Y	Y	Y	Y
3 ***Staton***	Y	N	Y	Y	Y	N	N	Y
4 Rahall	Y	N	Y	Y	N	Y	Y	N
WISCONSIN								
1 Aspin	Y	N	Y	Y	N	Y	Y	?
2 Kastenmeier	Y	N	Y	Y	N	Y	Y	N
3 ***Gunderson***	Y	N	Y	Y	N	Y	Y	N
4 Zablocki	Y	N	Y	Y	N	N	N	N
5 Reuss	?	Y	Y	Y	N	N	N	N
6 ***Petri***	Y	Y	Y	Y	Y	Y	N	N
7 Obey	?	Y	Y	Y	N	Y	Y	N
8 ***Roth***	Y	Y	Y	Y	Y	Y	Y	Y
9 ***Sensenbrenner***	Y	Y	Y	Y	Y	Y	Y	Y
WYOMING								
AL ***Cheney***	?	Y	Y	?	Y	Y	Y	Y

Democrats ***Republicans***

264. S 884. Agriculture and Food Act of 1981. Passage of the Senate version of the bill, as amended by the provisions of the House-passed bill, reauthorizing for four years price support and other farm programs and food stamps. (HR 3603 previously had passed by voice vote.) Passed 192-160: R 47-114; D 145-46 (ND 95-34, SD 50-12) Oct. 22, 1981. A "nay" was a vote supporting the president's position.

265. HR 4503. Federal Water Pollution Control Act. Roe, D-N.J., motion that the House resolve itself into the Committee of the Whole for consideration of the bill. Motion agreed to 382-4: R 171-1; D 211-3 (ND 138-2, SD 73-1), Oct. 27, 1981.

266. HR 4503. Federal Water Pollution Control Act. Passage of the bill to amend the Federal Water Pollution Control Act to authorize $2.4 billion for fiscal year 1982. Passed 382-18: R 163-17; D 219-1 (ND 144-0, SD 75-1), Oct. 27, 1981. A "nay" was a vote supporting the president's position.

267. H Res 251. House Earned Income Limit. Adoption of the resolution to increase the limitation on House members' outside earned income from 15 percent to 40 percent of their official salary, and to increase the limit on each individual honorarium payment for a speech, article or personal appearance from $1,000 to $2,000, for calendar years 1981 through 1983. Rejected 147-271: R 73-112; D 74-159 (ND 49-107, SD 25-52), Oct. 28, 1981.

268. HR 4603. Depository Institutions Aid. Passage of the bill to authorize federal regulators to provide expanded financial aid to troubled savings institutions and to permit commercial banks or savings and loan associations to acquire failing savings and loans in other states. Passed 371-46: R 173-13; D 198-33 (ND 139-17, SD 59-16), Oct. 28, 1981.

269. HR 4437. Energy Conservation Daylight-Saving Act. Hartnett, R-S.C., amendment to allow states to exempt themselves from the extra two months of daylight-saving time provided in the act. Rejected 170-242: R 109-78; D 61-164 (ND 23-127, SD 38-37). Oct. 28, 1981.

270. HR 4437. Energy Conservation Daylight-Saving Act. Passage of the bill to extend daylight-saving time by two months by starting it on the first Sunday of March. Passed 243-165: R 88-93; D 155-72 (ND 120-32, SD 35-40). Oct. 28, 1981.

KEY	
Y	Voted for (yea).
#	Paired for.
+	Announced for.
N	Voted against (nay).
X	Paired against.
-	Announced against.
P	Voted "present".
C	Voted "present" to avoid possible conflict of interest.
?	Did not vote or otherwise make a position known.

	264	265	266	267	268	269	270
ALABAMA							
1 Edwards	N	Y	Y	Y	Y	N	Y
2 Dickinson	N	Y	Y	Y	Y	Y	N
3 Nichols	Y	Y	Y	N	Y	Y	Y
4 Bevill	Y	Y	N	Y	N	N	Y
5 Flippo	?	Y	Y	N	N	N	Y
6 Smith	N	Y	N	Y	Y	Y	Y
7 Shelby	Y	Y	Y	N	Y	N	Y
ALASKA							
AL Young	X	N	Y	Y	Y	Y	N
ARIZONA							
1 Rhodes	X	?	Y	Y	?	Y	N
2 Udall	?	?	?	Y	Y	Y	Y
3 Stump	N	Y	Y	N	N	Y	N
4 Rudd	N	Y	Y	Y	Y	Y	N
ARKANSAS							
1 Alexander	?	Y	Y	Y	Y	?	?
2 Bethune	N	?	?	N	?	?	?
3 Hammerschmidt	Y	Y	Y	Y	N	Y	N
4 Anthony	Y	Y	N	Y	N	N	N
CALIFORNIA							
1 Chappie	N	Y	Y	N	Y	N	N
2 Clausen	N	Y	N	Y	N	N	N
3 Matsui	Y	Y	Y	Y	Y	N	Y
4 Fazio	Y	Y	Y	Y	N	Y	Y
5 Burton, J.	?	?	?	?	?	?	?
6 Burton, P.	Y	Y	Y	N	Y	N	Y
7 Miller	N	Y	Y	N	Y	N	Y
8 Dellums	#	Y	Y	Y	+	-	+
9 Stark	N	?	?	?	?	?	?
10 Edwards	N	Y	Y	N	Y	Y	Y
11 Lantos	Y	Y	Y	N	Y	N	Y
12 McCloskey	?	Y	Y	Y	Y	Y	Y
13 Mineta	N	Y	Y	N	Y	N	Y
14 Shumway	N	Y	Y	Y	Y	Y	Y
15 Coelho	Y	Y	Y	Y	Y	N	Y
16 Panetta	Y	Y	Y	N	N	N	Y
17 Pashayan	N	?	?	N	Y	N	Y
18 Thomas	N	Y	N	Y	Y	N	Y
19 Lagomarsino	N	Y	Y	N	Y	N	Y
20 Goldwater	N	?	?	Y	Y	Y	Y
21 Fiedler	N	Y	Y	N	Y	Y	Y
22 Moorhead	?	Y	Y	N	Y	Y	Y
23 Beilenson	Y	Y	Y	N	N	?	?
24 Waxman	#	?	Y	Y	Y	Y	Y
25 Roybal	Y	Y	Y	Y	Y	N	Y
26 Rousselot	X	Y	N	Y	Y	Y	Y
27 Dornan	N	Y	Y	Y	Y	Y	N
28 Dixon	Y	Y	N	Y	N	Y	Y
29 Hawkins	Y	Y	N	Y	N	Y	Y
30 Danielson	Y	+	Y	N	Y	N	Y
31 Dymally	#	Y	Y	Y	Y	?	Y
32 Anderson	N	Y	Y	N	Y	N	Y
33 Grisham	N	Y	Y	Y	Y	N	Y
34 Lungren	X	Y	N	Y	Y	Y	Y
35 Dreier	N	N	N	Y	N	Y	Y
36 Brown	Y	Y	N	Y	N	Y	Y
37 Lewis	N	Y	Y	Y	Y	Y	?
38 Patterson	Y	Y	Y	N	Y	N	Y
39 Dannemeyer	N	Y	N	Y	Y	Y	Y
40 Badham	N	Y	Y	Y	Y	Y	N
41 Lowery	N	?	?	?	?	?	?
42 Hunter	N	Y	Y	N	Y	N	Y
43 Burgener	N	Y	Y	Y	Y	Y	Y
COLORADO							
1 Schroeder	?	Y	Y	N	N	N	Y
2 Wirth	Y	Y	Y	N	Y	N	Y
3 Kogovsek	N	Y	Y	N	N	N	Y
4 Brown	N	Y	Y	N	N	N	Y

	264	265	266	267	268	269	270
5 Kramer	N	Y	Y	N	Y	Y	N
CONNECTICUT							
1 Vacancy							
2 Gejdenson	Y	Y	Y	N	Y	N	Y
3 DeNardis	N	?	?	N	?	N	Y
4 McKinney	?	?	Y	Y	Y	N	Y
5 Ratchford	N	Y	Y	N	Y	N	Y
6 Moffett	N	?	?	N	Y	N	Y
DELAWARE							
AL Evans	N	Y	Y	N	Y	N	N
FLORIDA							
1 Hutto	Y	Y	Y	N	Y	N	Y
2 Fuqua	Y	?	?	N	Y	N	Y
3 Bennett	N	Y	Y	N	Y	N	Y
4 Chappell	N	Y	Y	Y	Y	N	N
5 McCollum	?	Y	Y	N	Y	N	N
6 Young	N	Y	Y	N	N	N	N
7 Gibbons	N	Y	Y	Y	N	N	N
8 Ireland	?	Y	Y	N	Y	N	N
9 Nelson	Y	Y	Y	N	Y	N	Y
10 Bafalis	X	Y	Y	N	N	Y	N
11 Mica	Y	Y	Y	N	Y	N	Y
12 Shaw	N	Y	Y	Y	Y	Y	Y
13 Lehman	Y	Y	N	Y	N	N	Y
14 Pepper	#	Y	Y	#	Y	N	Y
15 Fascell	N	Y	Y	N	Y	N	Y
GEORGIA							
1 Ginn	Y	Y	Y	N	Y	N	N
2 Hatcher	Y	Y	Y	N	Y	N	N
3 Brinkley	N	Y	Y	N	Y	N	N
4 Levitas	Y	Y	Y	N	Y	N	N
5 Fowler	?	Y	Y	N	N	N	N
6 Gingrich	?	Y	Y	Y	Y	Y	N
7 McDonald	N	N	N	Y	N	Y	N
8 Evans	Y	Y	Y	N	Y	N	N
9 Jenkins	?	Y	Y	N	Y	N	N
10 Barnard	?	Y	Y	N	Y	N	N
HAWAII							
1 Heftel	Y	Y	Y	N	Y	N	Y
2 Akaka	Y	Y	Y	N	N	N	Y
IDAHO							
1 Craig	N	Y	Y	Y	Y	Y	N
2 Hansen	N	Y	N	Y	Y	Y	N
ILLINOIS							
1 Washington	Y	Y	Y	N	Y	N	Y
2 Savage	?	?	?	Y	Y	?	Y
3 Russo	-	Y	Y	Y	Y	N	Y
4 Derwinski	N	Y	Y	N	Y	N	N
5 Fary	Y	Y	?	?	Y	N	Y
6 Hyde	N	Y	Y	Y	Y	N	Y
7 Collins	Y	Y	Y	Y	N	Y	N
8 Rostenkowski	Y	Y	Y	N	Y	N	Y
9 Yates	N	Y	N	N	N	N	Y
10 Porter	N	Y	Y	Y	N	N	Y
11 Annunzio	Y	Y	Y	N	Y	N	Y
12 Crane, P.	N	Y	N	Y	N	Y	N
13 McClory	N	Y	Y	Y	Y	N	Y
14 Erlenborn	N	Y	Y	Y	Y	N	Y
15 Corcoran	X	Y	Y	X	Y	Y	Y
16 Martin	Y	Y	Y	N	Y	N	N
17 O'Brien	?	Y	Y	N	C	Y	Y
18 Michel	N	Y	Y	Y	Y	N	Y
19 Railsback	Y	Y	Y	Y	N	Y	Y
20 Findley	N	Y	Y	N	Y	N	Y
21 Madigan	N	Y	Y	N	Y	N	Y
22 Crane, D.	N	Y	N	Y	N	Y	N
23 Price	Y	Y	Y	Y	N	Y	Y
24 Simon	Y	Y	Y	N	N	Y	Y
INDIANA							
1 Benjamin	Y	Y	Y	N	Y	N	Y
2 Fithian	Y	?	?	N	Y	N	Y
3 Hiler	N	Y	Y	N	Y	N	N
4 Coats	N	Y	Y	N	Y	N	N
5 Hillis	Y	Y	Y	N	Y	N	Y
6 Evans	Y	Y	Y	N	Y	N	Y
7 Myers	Y	Y	Y	Y	Y	N	Y
8 Deckard	N	Y	Y	N	Y	N	Y
9 Hamilton	?	Y	Y	N	Y	N	Y
10 Sharp	Y	Y	Y	N	Y	N	Y
11 Jacobs	N	Y	Y	N	Y	N	Y
IOWA							
1 Leach	Y	Y	Y	N	Y	N	Y
2 Tauke	Y	Y	Y	N	Y	N	Y
3 Evans	Y	Y	Y	N	N	N	N
4 Smith	Y	Y	Y	N	N	N	N
5 Harkin	Y	Y	Y	N	N	N	N
6 Bedell	Y	Y	Y	N	Y	N	N

	264	265	266	267	268	269	270
KANSAS							
1 *Roberts*	Y	?	Y	N	Y	Y	N
2 *Jeffries*	N	Y	Y	N	N	Y	N
3 *Winn*	Y	Y	Y	N	Y	Y	N
4 Glickman	Y	Y	Y	N	N	N	N
5 *Whittaker*	Y	Y	Y	N	Y	Y	N
KENTUCKY							
1 Hubbard	Y	Y	Y	N	Y	Y	N
2 Natcher	Y	Y	Y	N	Y	Y	N
3 Mazzoli	?	Y	Y	N	Y	Y	N
4 *Snyder*	Y	Y	Y	Y	Y	Y	N
5 *Rogers*	Y	Y	Y	N	Y	Y	N
6 *Hopkins*	Y	Y	Y	N	Y	Y	N
7 Perkins	Y	Y	Y	N	N	Y	N
LOUISIANA							
1 *Livingston*	?	Y	Y	Y	Y	Y	N
2 Boggs	Y	Y	Y	Y	Y	N	Y
3 Tauzin	Y	Y	Y	Y	N	Y	Y
4 Roemer	Y	Y	Y	N	N	Y	N
5 Huckaby	Y	Y	Y	N	Y	N	Y
6 *Moore*	Y	Y	Y	Y	Y	N	Y
7 Breaux	Y	Y	Y	Y	Y	?	?
8 Long	Y	Y	Y	N	Y	N	Y
MAINE							
1 *Emery*	N	Y	Y	N	Y	N	Y
2 *Snowe*	N	Y	Y	N	Y	N	Y
MARYLAND							
1 Dyson	Y	Y	Y	N	Y	Y	N
2 Long	N	Y	Y	N	Y	N	?
3 Mikulski	Y	Y	Y	N	Y	N	Y
4 *Holt*	Y	Y	Y	N	Y	Y	Y
5 Hoyer	Y	Y	Y	Y	Y	N	Y
6 Byron	Y	Y	Y	N	Y	Y	N
7 Mitchell	N	N	Y	Y	N	N	Y
8 Barnes	Y	Y	Y	N	Y	N	Y
MASSACHUSETTS							
1 *Conte*	N	Y	Y	Y	Y	N	Y
2 Boland	Y	Y	Y	N	Y	N	Y
3 Early	?	?	?	Y	Y	N	Y
4 Frank	N	Y	Y	N	Y	N	Y
5 Shannon	Y	Y	Y	N	Y	N	Y
6 Mavroules	Y	Y	Y	N	Y	N	Y
7 Markey	Y	Y	Y	N	Y	N	Y
8 O'Neill							
9 Moakley	Y	Y	Y	Y	Y	N	Y
10 *Heckler*	N	Y	Y	N	Y	Y	Y
11 Donnelly	Y	Y	Y	N	Y	N	Y
12 Studds	N	Y	Y	N	Y	N	Y
MICHIGAN							
1 Conyers	?	Y	Y	#	N	N	Y
2 *Pursell*	#	Y	Y	N	Y	N	Y
3 Wolpe	Y	Y	Y	N	Y	N	Y
4 *Siljander*	N	Y	Y	Y	Y	Y	N
5 *Sawyer*	N	Y	Y	N	Y	Y	Y
6 *Dunn*	Y	Y	Y	N	Y	N	Y
7 Kildee	Y	Y	Y	N	Y	N	Y
8 Traxler	Y	Y	Y	N	Y	Y	N
9 *Vander Jagt*	X	Y	Y	Y	Y	Y	N
10 Albosta	Y	Y	Y	N	Y	N	Y
11 *Davis*	Y	Y	Y	N	Y	Y	N
12 Bonior	Y	Y	Y	N	Y	N	Y
13 Crockett	Y	Y	+	N	Y	?	Y
14 Hertel	X	Y	Y	N	Y	N	Y
15 Ford	Y	Y	Y	Y	Y	N	Y
16 Dingell	Y	Y	?	N	Y	N	Y
17 Brodhead	N	Y	Y	N	Y	N	Y
18 Blanchard	Y	Y	Y	N	Y	N	Y
19 *Broomfield*	N	Y	Y	N	Y	N	Y
MINNESOTA							
1 *Erdahl*	Y	Y	Y	N	Y	N	N
2 *Hagedorn*	Y	Y	Y	Y	Y	Y	N
3 *Frenzel*	N	Y	Y	Y	Y	N	Y
4 Vento	?	Y	Y	N	Y	N	Y
5 Sabo	Y	Y	Y	N	Y	N	Y
6 *Weber*	Y	Y	Y	N	Y	Y	N
7 *Stangeland*	Y	?	Y	N	Y	Y	N
8 Oberstar	Y	Y	Y	N	Y	N	N
MISSISSIPPI							
1 Whitten	?	Y	Y	N	Y	Y	N
2 Bowen	Y	Y	Y	N	Y	N	Y
3 Montgomery	Y	Y	Y	N	Y	N	Y
4 Dowdy	Y	Y	Y	N	Y	N	Y
5 *Lott*	N	Y	Y	Y	Y	Y	Y
MISSOURI							
1 Clay	?	?	?	Y	Y	N	Y
2 Young	Y	Y	Y	N	?	Y	N
3 Gephardt	Y	Y	Y	N	Y	N	Y
4 Skelton	Y	Y	Y	N	Y	Y	N
5 Bolling	?	Y	Y	Y	Y	?	?
6 *Coleman*	N	Y	Y	N	Y	N	Y
7 *Taylor*	Y	Y	Y	Y	Y	Y	N
8 *Bailey*	N	Y	Y	N	Y	Y	N
9 Volkmer	Y	Y	Y	N	N	Y	N
10 *Emerson*	Y	Y	Y	N	Y	Y	N
MONTANA							
1 Williams	N	?	Y	N	Y	N	Y
2 *Marlenee*	Y	?	?	N	Y	N	N
NEBRASKA							
1 *Bereuter*	Y	Y	Y	N	Y	N	N
2 *Daub*	Y	Y	Y	N	Y	Y	N
3 *Smith*	Y	Y	Y	N	Y	Y	N
NEVADA							
AL Santini	N	?	Y	N	N	Y	Y
NEW HAMPSHIRE							
1 D'Amours	Y	Y	Y	N	Y	N	Y
2 *Gregg*	N	Y	Y	N	Y	Y	Y
NEW JERSEY							
1 Florio	X	?	?	?	?	?	?
2 Hughes	N	Y	Y	N	Y	N	Y
3 Howard	N	Y	Y	Y	Y	N	Y
4 *Smith*	Y	Y	Y	N	Y	Y	Y
5 *Fenwick*	N	Y	Y	N	Y	N	Y
6 *Forsythe*	X	Y	Y	N	Y	N	N
7 *Roukema*	N	Y	Y	N	Y	N	Y
8 Roe	?	Y	Y	Y	Y	N	N
9 *Hollenbeck*	N	Y	Y	N	Y	N	Y
10 Rodino	N	Y	Y	Y	Y	N	Y
11 Minish	N	Y	Y	N	Y	N	Y
12 *Rinaldo*	N	Y	Y	N	Y	N	Y
13 *Courter*	N	Y	Y	N	Y	N	Y
14 Guarini	#	Y	Y	Y	Y	N	Y
15 Dwyer	N	Y	Y	N	Y	N	Y
NEW MEXICO							
1 *Lujan*	N	Y	Y	Y	N	Y	N
2 *Skeen*	Y	Y	Y	N	Y	Y	N
NEW YORK							
1 *Carney*	N	Y	Y	N	Y	N	Y
2 Downey	N	Y	Y	N	Y	N	Y
3 *Carman*	N	?	Y	Y	Y	N	Y
4 *Lent*	N	Y	Y	Y	Y	N	Y
5 *McGrath*	N	Y	Y	N	Y	N	Y
6 *LeBoutillier*	N	?	?	N	Y	N	Y
7 Addabbo	Y	Y	Y	Y	Y	N	Y
8 Rosenthal	?	Y	Y	N	Y	N	Y
9 Ferraro	+	Y	Y	Y	Y	N	Y
10 Biaggi	#	?	?	Y	Y	N	Y
11 Scheuer	?	Y	Y	Y	Y	N	Y
12 Chisholm	Y	?	Y	Y	Y	N	Y
13 Solarz	?	Y	Y	N	Y	?	?
14 Richmond	Y	?	?	Y	Y	N	Y
15 Zeferetti	Y	Y	Y	Y	Y	N	Y
16 Schumer	?	Y	Y	N	Y	N	N
17 *Molinari*	N	Y	Y	Y	Y	N	Y
18 *Green*	#	Y	Y	Y	Y	N	Y
19 Rangel	Y	Y	Y	Y	Y	N	Y
20 Weiss	Y	Y	Y	N	Y	N	Y
21 Garcia	#	Y	Y	N	Y	N	Y
22 Bingham	Y	Y	Y	N	Y	N	Y
23 Peyser	Y	Y	Y	Y	Y	N	Y
24 Ottinger	Y	P	Y	Y	Y	N	Y
25 *Fish*	N	Y	Y	Y	Y	N	Y
26 *Gilman*	X	Y	Y	N	Y	N	Y
27 McHugh	Y	Y	Y	N	Y	N	Y
28 Stratton	Y	Y	Y	N	Y	N	Y
29 *Solomon*	?	Y	N	N	Y	Y	N
30 *Martin*	N	Y	Y	Y	Y	N	N
31 *Mitchell*	?	Y	Y	N	Y	N	Y
32 *Wortley*	N	Y	Y	Y	Y	N	?
33 *Lee*	N	Y	N	N	Y	Y	Y
34 *Horton*	N	Y	Y	N	Y	N	Y
35 *Conable*	N	Y	N	Y	Y	Y	?
36 LaFalce	Y	Y	Y	N	Y	N	Y
37 Nowak	Y	Y	Y	N	Y	N	Y
38 *Kemp*	N	?	Y	Y	Y	Y	?
39 Lundine	?	Y	Y	N	Y	N	N
NORTH CAROLINA							
1 Jones	?	?	?	X	?	?	?
2 Fountain	Y	Y	Y	N	Y	N	N
3 Whitley	Y	Y	Y	N	Y	N	Y
4 Andrews	Y	Y	Y	N	Y	N	Y
5 Neal	Y	Y	Y	N	Y	N	N
6 *Johnston*	#	Y	N	#	N	Y	Y
7 Rose	Y	Y	Y	Y	Y	N	Y
8 Hefner	?	Y	Y	N	Y	N	Y
9 *Martin*	?	Y	Y	Y	Y	N	Y
10 *Broyhill*	?	Y	Y	N	Y	N	Y
11 *Hendon*	Y	Y	Y	N	Y	N	Y
NORTH DAKOTA							
AL Dorgan	N	N	Y	N	N	Y	N
OHIO							
1 *Gradison*	N	Y	Y	Y	Y	Y	Y
2 Luken	Y	Y	Y	Y	Y	?	?
3 Hall	N	Y	Y	N	Y	N	Y
4 *Oxley*	Y	Y	Y	N	Y	Y	N
5 *Latta*	N	Y	Y	Y	Y	N	N
6 *McEwen*	Y	Y	Y	N	Y	?	?
7 *Brown*	Y	Y	Y	N	Y	N	N
8 *Kindness*	Y	Y	Y	N	Y	Y	N
9 *Weber*	N	Y	Y	N	Y	N	N
10 *Miller*	Y	Y	Y	N	Y	N	N
11 *Stanton*	N	Y	Y	Y	Y	N	N
12 Shamansky	#	Y	Y	N	Y	Y	N
13 Pease	Y	Y	Y	N	N	N	N
14 Seiberling	N	Y	Y	N	Y	N	Y
15 *Wylie*	N	Y	Y	N	Y	N	N
16 *Regula*	N	Y	Y	N	Y	Y	N
17 *Ashbrook*	?	Y	Y	N	N	Y	N
18 Applegate	Y	?	Y	N	Y	Y	N
19 *Williams*	X	Y	Y	N	Y	N	Y
20 Oakar	Y	Y	Y	N	Y	Y	Y
21 Stokes	Y	Y	Y	Y	Y	N	Y
22 Eckart	N	Y	Y	N	N	N	Y
23 Mottl	N	Y	Y	N	N	Y	N
OKLAHOMA							
1 Jones	?	Y	Y	Y	Y	N	Y
2 Synar	Y	Y	Y	N	Y	N	Y
3 Watkins	Y	Y	Y	N	Y	Y	N
4 McCurdy	Y	Y	Y	N	?	Y	Y
5 *Edwards*	Y	Y	Y	Y	Y	Y	N
6 English	Y	Y	Y	Y	Y	Y	N
OREGON							
1 AuCoin	Y	Y	Y	N	Y	N	Y
2 *Smith*	N	Y	N	Y	N	Y	N
3 Wyden	?	Y	Y	N	Y	N	Y
4 Weaver	N	Y	Y	N	N	N	Y
PENNSYLVANIA							
1 Foglietta	?	Y	Y	Y	Y	N	Y
2 Gray	Y	?	?	Y	Y	N	Y
3 Smith	Y	?	?	Y	Y	N	Y
4 *Dougherty*	N	?	?	?	?	?	?
5 *Schulze*	?	?	Y	Y	Y	Y	Y
6 Yatron	Y	Y	Y	N	Y	Y	N
7 Edgar	Y	Y	Y	N	Y	N	Y
8 *Coyne, J.*	N	Y	Y	N	Y	N	Y
9 *Shuster*	Y	?	?	Y	Y	Y	N
10 *McDade*	N	Y	Y	Y	Y	N	Y
11 *Nelligan*	Y	Y	Y	N	Y	Y	N
12 Murtha	?	Y	Y	Y	Y	Y	Y
13 *Coughlin*	N	Y	Y	?	Y	N	Y
14 Coyne, W.	Y	Y	Y	N	Y	N	Y
15 *Ritter*	N	Y	Y	N	Y	N	Y
16 *Walker*	N	Y	Y	N	N	Y	N
17 Ertel	?	Y	Y	N	Y	N	Y
18 Walgren	N	Y	Y	N	Y	Y	Y
19 *Goodling*	Y	Y	Y	N	Y	Y	N
20 Gaydos	Y	Y	Y	N	Y	N	N
21 Bailey	Y	Y	Y	Y	Y	N	Y
22 Murphy	?	Y	Y	N	Y	N	Y
23 *Clinger*	N	Y	Y	N	Y	N	Y
24 *Marks*	#	Y	Y	N	Y	N	N
25 *Atkinson*	Y	Y	Y	N	Y	Y	N
RHODE ISLAND							
1 St Germain	Y	Y	Y	N	Y	N	Y
2 *Schneider*	N	Y	Y	N	Y	N	Y
SOUTH CAROLINA							
1 *Hartnett*	N	Y	N	Y	N	Y	N
2 *Spence*	Y	Y	Y	N	Y	Y	N
3 Derrick	Y	Y	Y	Y	Y	Y	?
4 *Campbell*	X	?	?	Y	Y	Y	N
5 Holland	?	?	Y	Y	?	Y	N
6 *Napier*	Y	Y	Y	N	Y	Y	Y
SOUTH DAKOTA							
1 Daschle	N	Y	Y	N	Y	Y	N
2 *Roberts*	N	Y	Y	N	Y	Y	N
TENNESSEE							
1 *Quillen*	#	Y	Y	Y	Y	Y	N
2 *Duncan*	Y	Y	Y	N	Y	Y	N
3 Bouquard	Y	?	Y	N	Y	Y	N
4 Gore	Y	Y	Y	N	Y	N	N
5 Boner	Y	Y	Y	N	Y	N	Y
6 *Beard*	?	?	?	X	Y	Y	Y
7 Jones	Y	Y	Y	N	Y	Y	Y
8 Ford	Y	Y	Y	Y	Y	N	Y
TEXAS							
1 Hall, S.	N	Y	Y	N	N	Y	N
2 Wilson	Y	Y	Y	Y	Y	N	Y
3 *Collins*	X	Y	Y	N	Y	N	Y
4 Hall, R.	Y	Y	Y	N	N	Y	N
5 Mattox	Y	Y	Y	Y	N	N	Y
6 Gramm	Y	Y	Y	Y	N	Y	N
7 *Archer*	N	Y	Y	N	Y	Y	N
8 *Fields*	N	Y	Y	Y	N	Y	N
9 Brooks	?	Y	Y	Y	?	N	Y
10 Pickle	Y	Y	Y	N	Y	Y	N
11 Leath	Y	Y	Y	Y	N	N	N
12 Wright	?	Y	Y	Y	N	N	Y
13 Hightower	N	Y	Y	N	Y	N	N
14 Patman	N	Y	Y	N	N	Y	N
15 de la Garza	Y	Y	Y	N	Y	Y	N
16 White	#	Y	Y	Y	Y	Y	N
17 Stenholm	N	Y	Y	N	N	Y	N
18 Leland	Y	?	?	Y	Y	?	Y
19 Hance	N	Y	Y	Y	N	Y	N
20 Gonzalez	Y	Y	Y	Y	Y	Y	N
21 *Loeffler*	N	Y	Y	N	Y	Y	N
22 *Paul*	N	Y	N	Y	N	Y	Y
23 Kazen	Y	Y	Y	N	Y	Y	N
24 Frost	?	Y	Y	N	Y	N	Y
UTAH							
1 *Hansen*	N	+	+	N	Y	Y	N
2 *Marriott*	N	Y	Y	N	Y	N	Y
VERMONT							
AL *Jeffords*	Y	Y	Y	N	Y	Y	Y
VIRGINIA							
1 *Trible*	N	Y	Y	N	Y	Y	N
2 *Whitehurst*	N	Y	Y	N	Y	N	Y
3 *Bliley*	N	Y	Y	?	Y	N	Y
4 *Daniel, R.*	N	Y	Y	Y	Y	Y	N
5 Daniel, D.	N	Y	Y	Y	Y	Y	N
6 *Butler*	N	Y	Y	N	Y	?	?
7 *Robinson*	N	Y	Y	Y	Y	Y	N
8 *Parris*	N	Y	Y	N	Y	N	Y
9 *Wampler*	Y	?	Y	Y	Y	Y	N
10 *Wolf*	N	Y	Y	N	Y	Y	Y
WASHINGTON							
1 *Pritchard*	N	Y	Y	N	Y	N	?
2 Swift	Y	?	Y	N	Y	N	Y
3 Bonker	Y	Y	Y	N	?	?	?
4 *Morrison*	N	Y	Y	N	Y	Y	Y
5 Foley	Y	Y	?	Y	Y	N	Y
6 Dicks	Y	Y	Y	N	Y	N	Y
7 Lowry	Y	Y	Y	N	Y	N	Y
WEST VIRGINIA							
1 Mollohan	Y	Y	Y	?	Y	N	N
2 *Benedict*	Y	Y	Y	Y	Y	Y	N
3 *Staton*	N	Y	Y	Y	Y	Y	N
4 Rahall	Y	?	Y	Y	Y	Y	N
WISCONSIN							
1 Aspin	?	Y	Y	N	Y	N	N
2 Kastenmeier	N	Y	Y	N	Y	N	Y
3 *Gunderson*	N	Y	Y	N	Y	Y	Y
4 Zablocki	Y	Y	Y	Y	Y	N	Y
5 Reuss	Y	Y	Y	Y	Y	N	Y
6 *Petri*	N	Y	Y	N	Y	Y	N
7 Obey	N	Y	Y	N	Y	N	N
8 *Roth*	N	Y	Y	N	Y	Y	Y
9 *Sensenbrenner*	N	Y	Y	N	Y	N	Y
WYOMING							
AL *Cheney*	N	Y	N	Y	Y	N	Y

Democrats *Republicans*

271. Procedural Motion. Solomon, R-N.Y., motion to approve the House *Journal* of Wednesday, Oct. 28. Motion agreed to 346-12: R 164-7; D 182-5 (ND 123-5, SD 59-0), Oct. 29, 1981.

272. S 815. Defense Department Authorization. Dickinson, R-Ala., motion to table (kill) the Schroeder, D-Colo., motion to instruct the House conferees on the bill to concur in a Senate provision requiring the Pentagon to report to Congress certain weapons cost increases. Motion rejected 171-224: R 130-53; D 41-171 (ND 15-130, SD 26-41), Oct. 29, 1981. (The Schroeder motion subsequently was agreed to by voice vote.)

273. S 1193. State Department Authorization. Derwinski, R-Ill., motion to recommit to the Foreign Affairs Committee the bill to authorize fiscal 1982 and 1983 spending by the State Department and related agencies, with instructions to amend it by transferring to the International Communication Agency $36 million in fiscal 1982 and $43 million in fiscal 1983 from the accounts for the administration of foreign affairs and for U.S. participation in international organizations and conferences. Motion rejected 63-318: R 34-142; D 29-176 (ND 25-117, SD 4-59) Oct. 29, 1981.

274. S 1193. State Department Authorization. Passage of the bill to authorize $2.9 billion in fiscal 1982 and $2.8 billion in fiscal 1983 for operations of the State Department and related agencies. Passed 317-58: R 145-30; D 172-28 (ND 126-14, SD 46-14) Oct. 29, 1981.

KEY

Y Voted for (yea).
\# Paired for.
+ Announced for.
N Voted against (nay).
X Paired against.
- Announced against.
P Voted "present".
C Voted "present" to avoid possible conflict of interest.
? Did not vote or otherwise make a position known.

	271	272	273	274
ALABAMA				
1 *Edwards*	Y	Y	N	Y
2 *Dickinson*	Y	Y	N	N
3 Nichols	Y	Y	N	X
4 Bevill	Y	Y	N	Y
5 Flippo	Y	Y	N	Y
6 *Smith*	Y	Y	N	Y
7 Shelby	Y	Y	N	N
ALASKA				
AL *Young*	?	Y	N	Y
ARIZONA				
1 *Rhodes*	Y	Y	N	Y
2 Udall	Y	N	N	Y
3 Stump	Y	Y	N	N
4 *Rudd*	Y	Y	N	N
ARKANSAS				
1 Alexander	?	?	?	?
2 *Bethune*	Y	Y	N	Y
3 *Hammerschmidt*	Y	Y	N	Y
4 Anthony	?	N	N	Y
CALIFORNIA				
1 *Chappie*	Y	Y	N	Y
2 *Clausen*	Y	Y	N	Y
3 Matsui	N	N	N	Y
4 Fazio	?	N	?	?
5 Burton, J.	Y	?	?	?
6 Burton, P.	Y	N	Y	Y
7 Miller	Y	N	N	Y
8 Dellums	?	-	-	+
9 Stark	?	?	?	?
10 Edwards	Y	N	N	Y
11 Lantos	Y	N	Y	Y
12 *McCloskey*	?	?	?	?
13 Mineta	Y	N	N	Y
14 *Shumway*	Y	Y	N	Y
15 Coelho	?	?	?	?
16 Panetta	Y	N	N	Y
17 *Pashayan*	Y	Y	N	Y
18 *Thomas*	Y	Y	N	Y
19 *Lagomarsino*	Y	Y	N	Y
20 *Goldwater*	?	Y	?	?
21 *Fiedler*	Y	Y	N	Y
22 *Moorhead*	Y	Y	N	N
23 Beilenson	?	?	?	?
24 Waxman	?	?	?	?
25 Roybal	Y	N	N	Y
26 *Rousselot*	Y	Y	N	N
27 *Dornan*	Y	Y	N	Y
28 Dixon	Y	N	N	Y
29 Hawkins	Y	N	N	Y
30 Danielson	+	N	N	Y
31 Dymally	Y	N	N	Y
32 Anderson	Y	N	Y	N
33 *Grisham*	Y	Y	N	Y
34 *Lungren*	Y	Y	Y	N
35 *Dreier*	Y	Y	N	N
36 Brown	?	N	N	Y
37 *Lewis*	?	?	?	?
38 Patterson	Y	N	N	Y
39 *Dannemeyer*	Y	Y	Y	Y
40 *Badham*	Y	Y	N	Y
41 *Lowery*	Y	Y	N	Y
42 *Hunter*	Y	Y	N	Y
43 *Burgener*	Y	Y	Y	Y
COLORADO				
1 Schroeder	N	N	N	N
2 Wirth	Y	N	N	Y
3 Kogovsek	Y	N	N	Y
4 *Brown*	Y	N	N	N

	271	272	273	274
5 *Kramer*	Y	Y	N	Y
CONNECTICUT				
1 Vacancy				
2 Gejdenson	N	N	N	Y
3 *DeNardis*	Y	N	Y	Y
4 *McKinney*	?	N	N	Y
5 Ratchford	Y	N	N	Y
6 Moffett	?	N	N	Y
DELAWARE				
AL *Evans*	Y	N	Y	Y
FLORIDA				
1 Hutto	Y	Y	N	Y
2 Fuqua	Y	N	N	Y
3 Bennett	Y	Y	N	Y
4 Chappell	Y	Y	?	?
5 *McCollum*	?	Y	N	Y
6 *Young*	Y	Y	N	Y
7 Gibbons	Y	N	N	Y
8 Ireland	?	?	?	?
9 Nelson	Y	Y	N	Y
10 *Bafalis*	Y	Y	N	Y
11 Mica	Y	Y	N	Y
12 *Shaw*	Y	Y	N	Y
13 Lehman	Y	N	N	Y
14 Pepper	?	?	?	?
15 Fascell	Y	N	N	Y
GEORGIA				
1 Ginn	?	?	?	?
2 Hatcher	Y	N	N	Y
3 Brinkley	Y	N	N	Y
4 Levitas	Y	N	N	Y
5 Fowler	?	?	?	?
6 *Gingrich*	Y	N	N	Y
7 McDonald	?	Y	Y	N
8 Evans	Y	N	N	Y
9 Jenkins	Y	Y	N	Y
10 Barnard	?	?	?	?
HAWAII				
1 Heftel	?	N	N	Y
2 Akaka	Y	Y	N	Y
IDAHO				
1 *Craig*	Y	Y	N	N
2 *Hansen*	Y	Y	N	N
ILLINOIS				
1 Washington	?	N	?	?
2 Savage	?	?	N	Y
3 Russo	Y	N	N	N
4 *Derwinski*	Y	Y	Y	N
5 Fary	Y	N	N	Y
6 *Hyde*	Y	Y	Y	Y
7 Collins	Y	Y	N	Y
8 Rostenkowski	Y	Y	Y	Y
9 Yates	Y	N	Y	Y
10 *Porter*	Y	N	Y	Y
11 Annunzio	?	N	Y	Y
12 *Crane, P.*	?	Y	?	?
13 *McClory*	Y	Y	Y	Y
14 *Erlenborn*	Y	Y	Y	Y
15 Corcoran	+	-	-	+
16 *Martin*	Y	N	?	?
17 *O'Brien*	Y	N	Y	Y
18 *Michel*	Y	Y	N	Y
19 *Railsback*	Y	N	?	?
20 *Findley*	Y	N	N	Y
21 *Madigan*	Y	?	N	Y
22 *Crane, D.*	Y	Y	?	?
23 Price	Y	Y	N	Y
24 Simon	Y	N	Y	Y
INDIANA				
1 Benjamin	Y	N	N	Y
2 Fithian	Y	N	N	Y
3 *Hiler*	Y	N	N	Y
4 *Coats*	Y	N	N	Y
5 *Hillis*	Y	Y	N	Y
6 Evans	Y	N	Y	N
7 *Myers*	Y	Y	N	Y
8 *Deckard*	?	N	N	Y
9 Hamilton	Y	N	N	Y
10 Sharp	Y	N	Y	Y
11 Jacobs	N	N	N	N
IOWA				
1 *Leach*	Y	N	N	Y
2 *Tauke*	Y	?	?	?
3 Evans	N	N	N	Y
4 Smith	Y	N	N	Y
5 Harkin	N	N	N	Y
6 Bedell	Y	N	N	Y

Democrats *Republicans*

	271	272	273	274
KANSAS				
1 *Roberts*	?	Y	N	N
2 *Jeffries*	Y	Y	N	Y
3 *Winn*	Y	Y	N	Y
4 Glickman	Y	N	N	Y
5 *Whittaker*	Y	Y	N	N
KENTUCKY				
1 Hubbard	Y	N	N	Y
2 Natcher	Y	Y	N	Y
3 Mazzoli	Y	N	N	Y
4 *Snyder*	Y	Y	N	Y
5 *Rogers*	Y	Y	N	Y
6 *Hopkins*	Y	Y	N	Y
7 Perkins	Y	Y	N	Y
LOUISIANA				
1 *Livingston*	Y	N	N	Y
2 Boggs	?	N	N	Y
3 Tauzin	Y	N	N	N
4 Roemer	Y	N	Y	N
5 Huckaby	Y	Y	N	Y
6 *Moore*	Y	N	Y	Y
7 Breaux	?	?	?	?
8 Long	Y	N	N	Y
MAINE				
1 *Emery*	Y	Y	N	Y
2 *Snowe*	Y	N	N	Y
MARYLAND				
1 Dyson	Y	Y	N	Y
2 Long	Y	Y	N	Y
3 Mikulski	Y	N	N	Y
4 *Holt*	Y	Y	?	?
5 Hoyer	Y	N	N	Y
6 Byron	?	Y	N	Y
7 Mitchell	?	?	?	#
8 Barnes	Y	N	N	Y
MASSACHUSETTS				
1 *Conte*	Y	N	N	#
2 Boland	Y	N	N	Y
3 Early	Y	N	Y	N
4 Frank	?	N	N	Y
5 Shannon	Y	N	N	Y
6 Mavroules	?	N	N	Y
7 Markey	Y	N	N	Y
8 O'Neill				
9 Moakley	Y	N	N	Y
10 *Heckler*	N	N	N	Y
11 Donnelly	Y	N	Y	Y
12 Studds	Y	N	N	Y
MICHIGAN				
1 Conyers	Y	N	N	Y
2 *Pursell*	Y	N	N	Y
3 Wolpe	Y	N	N	Y
4 *Siljander*	Y	Y	N	Y
5 Sawyer	Y	N	N	Y
6 Dunn	Y	N	N	Y
7 Kildee	Y	N	N	Y
8 Traxler	Y	N	N	Y
9 *Vander Jagt*	Y	Y	N	Y
10 Albosta	Y	Y	N	Y
11 *Davis*	Y	Y	N	Y
12 Bonior	Y	N	N	Y
13 Crockett	Y	N	N	Y
14 Hertel	Y	N	N	N
15 Ford	Y	N	N	Y
16 Dingell	?	N	N	Y
17 Brodhead	Y	N	N	Y
18 Blanchard	Y	N	N	Y
19 *Broomfield*	Y	Y	N	Y
MINNESOTA				
1 *Erdahl*	Y	N	N	Y
2 *Hagedorn*	?	?	N	Y
3 *Frenzel*	Y	N	N	Y
4 Vento	Y	N	Y	N
5 Sabo	N	N	N	Y
6 *Weber*	N	N	N	Y
7 *Stangeland*	?	Y	N	Y
8 Oberstar	Y	N	N	Y
MISSISSIPPI				
1 Whitten	Y	N	N	Y
2 Bowen	Y	N	N	Y
3 Montgomery	Y	N	N	Y
4 Dowdy	?	N	N	N
5 *Lott*	Y	Y	N	Y
MISSOURI				
1 Clay	?	?	?	?
2 Young	Y	N	N	Y
3 Gephardt	Y	N	N	Y

	271	272	273	274
4 Skelton	Y	Y	N	Y
5 Bolling	?	?	?	?
6 *Coleman*	Y	N	N	Y
7 Taylor	Y	Y	N	Y
8 Bailey	Y	Y	N	Y
9 Volkmer	Y	N	N	Y
10 *Emerson*	Y	Y	N	N
MONTANA				
1 Williams	Y	N	N	?
2 *Marlenee*	Y	N	N	Y
NEBRASKA				
1 *Bereuter*	Y	N	N	Y
2 *Daub*	Y	N	?	?
3 *Smith*	Y	Y	N	N
NEVADA				
AL Santini	?	N	N	Y
NEW HAMPSHIRE				
1 D'Amours	Y	N	?	?
2 *Gregg*	Y	Y	N	Y
NEW JERSEY				
1 Florio	?	?	?	?
2 Hughes	Y	N	N	N
3 Howard	Y	N	N	Y
4 *Smith*	Y	N	N	Y
5 *Fenwick*	Y	N	N	Y
6 *Forsythe*	N	N	N	Y
7 *Roukema*	Y	N	N	Y
8 Roe	Y	N	N	Y
9 *Hollenbeck*	Y	N	N	Y
10 Rodino	Y	N	N	Y
11 Minish	Y	N	N	Y
12 *Rinaldo*	Y	N	N	Y
13 *Courter*	Y	Y	Y	Y
14 Guarini	Y	N	N	Y
15 Dwyer	Y	N	N	Y
NEW MEXICO				
1 *Lujan*	Y	N	N	Y
2 *Skeen*	?	Y	N	Y
NEW YORK				
1 *Carney*	?	?	N	N
2 Downey	Y	N	N	Y
3 *Carman*	Y	Y	Y	Y
4 *Lent*	Y	Y	N	Y
5 *McGrath*	Y	Y	Y	Y
6 *LeBoutillier*	?	Y	Y	Y
7 Addabbo	Y	N	N	Y
8 Rosenthal	?	N	N	Y
9 Ferraro	Y	N	N	Y
10 Biaggi	Y	N	Y	Y
11 Scheuer	Y	N	Y	Y
12 Chisholm	?	N	N	Y
13 Solarz	Y	N	Y	Y
14 Richmond	Y	N	N	?
15 Zeferetti	Y	N	N	Y
16 Schumer	Y	N	N	Y
17 *Molinari*	Y	Y	N	Y
18 *Green*	Y	N	N	Y
19 Rangel	Y	N	N	Y
20 Weiss	Y	N	N	Y
21 Garcia	?	?	X	?
22 Bingham	Y	N	N	Y
23 Peyser	Y	N	N	Y
24 Ottinger	?	N	N	Y
25 *Fish*	Y	Y	?	?
26 *Gilman*	+	-	+	+
27 McHugh	Y	Y	N	Y
28 Stratton	Y	Y	N	Y
29 *Solomon*	N	Y	Y	N
30 *Martin*	?	Y	N	Y
31 *Mitchell*	Y	Y	N	Y
32 *Wortley*	Y	Y	N	Y
33 *Lee*	Y	Y	N	Y
34 *Horton*	Y	Y	N	Y
35 *Conable*	Y	Y	Y	Y
36 LaFalce	?	N	N	Y
37 Nowak	Y	N	N	Y
38 *Kemp*	?	Y	Y	Y
39 Lundine	Y	N	N	Y
NORTH CAROLINA				
1 Jones	?	?	?	?
2 Fountain	?	?	?	#
3 Whitley	Y	N	?	?
4 Andrews	?	N	N	Y
5 Neal	?	N	N	Y
6 *Johnston*	Y	Y	N	Y
7 Rose	?	N	N	Y
8 Hefner	Y	N	N	N

	271	272	273	274
9 *Martin*	Y	Y	N	Y
10 *Broyhill*	Y	N	Y	Y
11 *Hendon*	Y	Y	N	Y
NORTH DAKOTA				
AL Dorgan	Y	N	N	Y
OHIO				
1 *Gradison*	Y	Y	N	Y
2 Luken	?	?	?	?
3 Hall	Y	?	N	Y
4 *Oxley*	Y	Y	N	Y
5 *Latta*	Y	Y	N	Y
6 *McEwen*	Y	Y	N	N
7 *Brown*	Y	Y	N	Y
8 *Kindness*	?	Y	N	N
9 *Weber*	Y	Y	N	Y
10 *Miller*	Y	Y	N	Y
11 *Stanton*	Y	Y	N	Y
12 Shamansky	Y	N	Y	Y
13 Pease	Y	N	N	Y
14 Seiberling	Y	N	N	Y
15 *Wylie*	Y	Y	N	Y
16 *Regula*	Y	Y	N	Y
17 *Ashbrook*	Y	Y	Y	N
18 Applegate	?	N	Y	N
19 *Williams*	Y	Y	N	Y
20 Oakar	Y	N	N	Y
21 Stokes	?	?	?	#
22 Eckart	Y	N	Y	Y
23 Mottl	Y	N	#	X
OKLAHOMA				
1 Jones	Y	N	N	N
2 Synar	Y	N	N	Y
3 Watkins	Y	N	Y	N
4 McCurdy	Y	?	?	?
5 *Edwards*	Y	Y	N	Y
6 English	Y	N	Y	N
OREGON				
1 AuCoin	Y	N	N	Y
2 *Smith*	Y	Y	N	N
3 Wyden	Y	N	N	Y
4 Weaver	Y	N	Y	N
PENNSYLVANIA				
1 Foglietta	Y	N	N	Y
2 Gray	Y	N	Y	Y
3 Smith	Y	N	N	Y
4 *Dougherty*	?	Y	Y	Y
5 *Schulze*	Y	Y	Y	N
6 Yatron	Y	N	N	Y
7 Edgar	?	?	?	?
8 *Coyne, J.*	?	?	N	Y
9 *Shuster*	Y	Y	N	Y
10 McDade	Y	N	N	Y
11 *Nelligan*	Y	N	N	Y
12 Murtha	Y	N	N	Y
13 *Coughlin*	Y	N	Y	Y
14 Coyne, W.	?	?	?	?
15 *Ritter*	Y	N	Y	N
16 *Walker*	N	Y	N	N
17 Ertel	Y	N	N	Y
18 Walgren	Y	N	Y	Y
19 *Goodling*	N	Y	N	Y
20 Gaydos	Y	N	N	Y
21 Bailey	Y	N	N	Y
22 Murphy	Y	N	N	Y
23 *Clinger*	Y	N	Y	Y
24 *Marks*	Y	Y	Y	Y
25 Atkinson	Y	Y	N	Y
RHODE ISLAND				
1 St Germain	Y	N	?	?
2 *Schneider*	Y	N	N	Y
SOUTH CAROLINA				
1 *Hartnett*	Y	Y	N	Y
2 *Spence*	Y	Y	Y	N
3 Derrick	Y	?	N	Y
4 *Campbell*	Y	Y	?	?
5 Holland	Y	Y	N	Y
6 *Napier*	Y	Y	?	X
SOUTH DAKOTA				
1 Daschle	Y	N	N	Y
2 *Roberts*	Y	Y	N	N
TENNESSEE				
1 *Quillen*	Y	Y	?	?
2 *Duncan*	Y	Y	N	Y
3 Bouquard	Y	Y	N	Y
4 Gore	Y	N	N	Y
5 Boner	Y	N	N	Y
6 *Beard*	Y	Y	Y	Y

	271	272	273	274
7 Jones	Y	Y	N	N
8 Ford	Y	N	N	Y
TEXAS				
1 Hall, S.	Y	N	N	N
2 Wilson	?	Y	?	?
3 *Collins*	Y	Y	N	N
4 Hall, R.	?	Y	?	?
5 Mattox	Y	N	N	X
6 *Gramm*	Y	Y	N	Y
7 *Archer*	Y	Y	Y	Y
8 *Fields*	Y	Y	N	Y
9 Brooks	Y	N	N	Y
10 Pickle	Y	Y	N	Y
11 Leath	Y	Y	N	N
12 Wright	Y	N	N	?
13 Hightower	Y	N	N	Y
14 Patman	Y	N	N	Y
15 de la Garza	Y	Y	N	Y
16 White	?	Y	N	Y
17 Stenholm	?	?	?	?
18 Leland	Y	N	N	Y
19 Hance	Y	N	N	Y
20 Gonzalez	Y	Y	N	Y
21 *Loeffler*	Y	Y	N	Y
22 *Paul*	Y	N	N	N
23 Kazen	Y	Y	N	Y
24 Frost	Y	N	?	?
UTAH				
1 *Hansen*	Y	Y	N	Y
2 *Marriott*	Y	Y	N	Y
VERMONT				
AL *Jeffords*	Y	N	N	Y
VIRGINIA				
1 *Trible*	Y	Y	N	Y
2 *Whitehurst*	Y	N	N	Y
3 *Bliley*	Y	Y	N	Y
4 *Daniel, R.*	Y	Y	N	N
5 *Daniel, D.*	Y	Y	N	N
6 *Butler*	Y	Y	Y	Y
7 *Robinson*	Y	Y	N	Y
8 *Parris*	Y	Y	N	Y
9 *Wampler*	Y	Y	N	Y
10 *Wolf*	Y	Y	N	Y
WASHINGTON				
1 *Pritchard*	Y	N	N	Y
2 Swift	Y	N	N	Y
3 Bonker	Y	N	N	Y
4 *Morrison*	Y	Y	N	Y
5 Foley	Y	N	N	Y
6 Dicks	Y	N	N	Y
7 Lowry	Y	N	N	Y
WEST VIRGINIA				
1 Mollohan	Y	Y	N	Y
2 *Benedict*	Y	N	N	Y
3 *Staton*	Y	N	N	Y
4 Rahall	?	N	N	Y
WISCONSIN				
1 Aspin	?	N	N	Y
2 Kastenmeier	Y	N	Y	N
3 *Gunderson*	Y	Y	N	Y
4 Zablocki	Y	N	Y	Y
5 Reuss	Y	N	N	Y
6 *Petri*	Y	N	Y	N
7 Obey	Y	N	N	Y
8 *Roth*	Y	Y	Y	Y
9 *Sensenbrenner*	Y	N	N	N
WYOMING				
AL *Cheney*	Y	N	N	Y

Democrats *Republicans*

	KEY		275 276 277 278
Y	Voted for (yea).		
#	Paired for.		
+	Announced for.		
N	Voted against (nay).		
X	Paired against.		
-	Announced against.		
P	Voted "present".		
C	Voted "present" to avoid possible conflict of interest.		
?	Did not vote or otherwise make a position known.		

	275 276 277 278

275. HR 3464. Foreign Construction of U.S. Naval Vessels. Bennett, D-Fla., motion to suspend the rules and pass the bill to prohibit construction of U.S. government naval vessels or their major components in foreign shipyards, except when the president determines, and so notifies Congress, that it is in the national security interest of the United States to do so. Motion agreed to 366-21: R 159-7; D 207-14 (ND 136-13, SD 71-1), Nov. 4, 1981. A two-thirds majority vote (258 in this case) is required for passage under suspension of the rules.

276. HR 3502. Veterans Administration and Defense Department Medical Sharing Act. Montgomery, D-Miss., motion to suspend the rules and pass the bill to mandate the establishment of guidelines providing for increased coordination and sharing of medical facilities by the Veterans Administration and the Defense Department. Motion agreed to 386-0: R 167-0; D 219-0 (ND 148-0, SD 71-0), Nov. 4, 1981. A two-thirds majority vote (258 in this case) is required for passage under suspension of the rules.

277. HR 2330. Nuclear Regulatory Commission Authorization. Markey, D-Mass., amendment to delete the language allowing the Nuclear Regulatory Commission to issue operating licenses to nuclear power plants before the completion of public hearings. Rejected 90-304: R 9-165; D 81-139 (ND 75-72, SD 6-67), Nov. 5, 1981. A "nay" was a vote supporting the president's position.

278. HR 2330. Nuclear Regulatory Commission Authorization. Markey, D-Mass., amendment to prohibit the export of enriched uranium except under certain findings by the Nuclear Regulatory Commission. Rejected 100-293: R 14-161; D 86-132 (ND 82-64, SD 4-68), Nov. 5, 1981. A "nay" was a vote supporting the president's position.

	275	276	277	278
ALABAMA				
1 *Edwards*	Y	Y	N	N
2 *Dickinson*	?	?	?	?
3 Nichols	Y	Y	N	N
4 Bevill	Y	Y	N	N
5 Flippo	Y	Y	N	N
6 *Smith*	Y	Y	N	N
7 Shelby	Y	Y	N	N
ALASKA				
AL *Young*	Y	Y	N	N
ARIZONA				
1 *Rhodes*	?	?	N	N
2 Udall	Y	Y	N	N
3 Stump	Y	Y	N	N
4 *Rudd*	Y	Y	N	N
ARKANSAS				
1 Alexander	Y	Y	N	N
2 *Bethune*	Y	Y	N	N
3 *Hammerschmidt*	Y	Y	N	N
4 Anthony	Y	Y	N	N
CALIFORNIA				
1 *Chappie*	Y	Y	N	N
2 *Clausen*	Y	Y	N	N
3 Matsui	?	?	?	?
4 Fazio	Y	Y	N	Y
5 Burton, J.	Y	Y	Y	Y
6 Burton, P.	Y	Y	Y	Y
7 Miller	Y	Y	Y	Y
8 Dellums	Y	Y	Y	Y
9 Stark	Y	Y	Y	Y
10 Edwards	Y	Y	Y	Y
11 Lantos	Y	Y	N	Y
12 *McCloskey*	?	?	N	Y
13 Mineta	Y	Y	N	N
14 *Shumway*	Y	Y	N	N
15 Coelho	Y	Y	N	N
16 Panetta	Y	Y	Y	Y
17 *Pashayan*	?	?	?	?
18 *Thomas*	Y	Y	N	N
19 *Lagomarsino*	Y	Y	N	N
20 *Goldwater*	?	?	?	?
21 *Fiedler*	Y	Y	N	N
22 *Moorhead*	Y	Y	N	N
23 Beilenson	Y	Y	Y	Y
24 Waxman	Y	Y	Y	Y
25 Roybal	Y	Y	Y	Y
26 *Rousselot*	Y	Y	N	N
27 *Dornan*	?	?	N	N
28 Dixon	Y	Y	N	Y
29 Hawkins	Y	Y	#	#
30 Danielson	Y	Y	?	N
31 Dymally	Y	Y	N	N
32 Anderson	N	Y	Y	?
33 *Grisham*	Y	Y	N	N
34 *Lungren*	Y	Y	N	N
35 *Dreier*	Y	Y	N	N
36 Brown	Y	Y	N	N
37 *Lewis*	Y	Y	N	N
38 Patterson	Y	Y	Y	Y
39 *Dannemeyer*	Y	Y	N	N
40 *Badham*	Y	Y	N	N
41 *Lowery*	Y	Y	N	N
42 *Hunter*	Y	Y	N	N
43 *Burgener*	Y	Y	N	N
COLORADO				
1 Schroeder	Y	Y	Y	Y
2 Wirth	Y	Y	Y	Y
3 Kogovsek	?	Y	N	N
4 *Brown*	N	Y	N	N

	275	276	277	278
5 *Kramer*	Y	Y	N	N
CONNECTICUT				
1 Vacancy				
2 Gejdenson	Y	Y	Y	Y
3 *DeNardis*	Y	Y	N	N
4 *McKinney*	Y	Y	N	N
5 Ratchford	Y	Y	Y	Y
6 Moffett	?	?	Y	Y
DELAWARE				
AL *Evans*	Y	Y	N	N
FLORIDA				
1 Hutto	Y	Y	N	N
2 Fuqua	Y	Y	N	?
3 Bennett	Y	Y	N	Y
4 Chappell	Y	Y	N	N
5 *McCollum*	Y	Y	N	N
6 *Young*	Y	Y	N	N
7 Gibbons	N	Y	N	N
8 Ireland	Y	Y	N	N
9 Nelson	Y	Y	N	N
10 *Bafalis*	Y	Y	N	N
11 Mica	Y	Y	N	N
12 *Shaw*	Y	Y	N	N
13 Lehman	?	?	?	?
14 Pepper	Y	Y	N	N
15 Fascell	Y	?	N	N
GEORGIA				
1 Ginn	Y	Y	N	?
2 Hatcher	Y	Y	N	N
3 Brinkley	Y	Y	N	N
4 Levitas	Y	Y	N	N
5 Fowler	Y	Y	N	N
6 *Gingrich*	?	?	N	N
7 McDonald	Y	Y	N	N
8 Evans	?	?	N	N
9 Jenkins	Y	Y	N	N
10 Barnard	?	?	?	?
HAWAII				
1 Heftel	Y	Y	N	N
2 Akaka	Y	Y	N	Y
IDAHO				
1 *Craig*	Y	Y	N	N
2 *Hansen*	Y	Y	N	N
ILLINOIS				
1 Washington	Y	Y	Y	Y
2 Savage	?	?	#	#
3 Russo	Y	Y	N	N
4 *Derwinski*	Y	Y	N	N
5 Fary	Y	Y	N	N
6 *Hyde*	?	?	?	N
7 Collins	Y	Y	Y	Y
8 Rostenkowski	Y	Y	N	N
9 Yates	Y	Y	Y	Y
10 *Porter*	Y	Y	N	N
11 Annunzio	Y	Y	N	N
12 *Crane, P.*	Y	Y	N	N
13 *McClory*	Y	Y	N	N
14 *Erlenborn*	Y	Y	N	N
15 *Corcoran*	Y	Y	N	N
16 *Martin*	Y	Y	N	N
17 *O'Brien*	Y	Y	N	N
18 *Michel*	Y	Y	N	N
19 *Railsback*	Y	Y	N	N
20 *Findley*	N	Y	N	N
21 *Madigan*	N	Y	?	N
22 *Crane, D.*	Y	Y	N	N
23 Price	Y	Y	N	N
24 Simon	Y	Y	Y	N
INDIANA				
1 Benjamin	N	Y	Y	Y
2 Fithian	Y	Y	Y	N
3 *Hiler*	Y	Y	N	N
4 *Coats*	Y	Y	N	N
5 *Hillis*	Y	Y	N	N
6 Evans	Y	Y	Y	Y
7 *Myers*	Y	Y	N	N
8 *Deckard*	Y	Y	Y	?
9 Hamilton	Y	Y	N	N
10 Sharp	?	?	N	N
11 Jacobs	Y	Y	Y	Y
IOWA				
1 *Leach*	Y	Y	Y	N
2 *Tauke*	Y	Y	N	N
3 *Evans*	Y	Y	N	N
4 *Smith*	?	?	?	?
5 Harkin	Y	Y	N	N
6 Bedell	Y	Y	Y	Y

	275	276	277	278
KANSAS				
1 *Roberts*	Y	Y	N	N
2 *Jeffries*	Y	Y	N	N
3 *Winn*	Y	Y	N	N
4 Glickman	Y	Y	N	Y
5 *Whittaker*	Y	Y	N	N
KENTUCKY				
1 Hubbard	Y	Y	N	N
2 Natcher	Y	Y	N	N
3 Mazzoli	Y	Y	N	N
4 *Snyder*	Y	Y	N	N
5 *Rogers*	Y	Y	N	N
6 *Hopkins*	Y	Y	X	?
7 Perkins	Y	Y	?	?
LOUISIANA				
1 *Livingston*	+	+	N	N
2 Boggs	Y	Y	N	N
3 Tauzin	Y	Y	N	N
4 Roemer	Y	Y	N	N
5 Huckaby	Y	Y	X	X
6 *Moore*	Y	Y	N	N
7 Breaux	Y	Y	N	N
8 Long	Y	Y	N	N
MAINE				
1 *Emery*	Y	Y	N	N
2 *Snowe*	Y	Y	N	Y
MARYLAND				
1 Dyson	Y	Y	N	N
2 Long	Y	Y	Y	Y
3 Mikulski	Y	Y	Y	Y
4 *Holt*	Y	Y	N	N
5 Hoyer	Y	Y	N	N
6 Byron	Y	Y	N	N
7 Mitchell	Y	Y	Y	Y
8 Barnes	Y	Y	Y	N
MASSACHUSETTS				
1 *Conte*	Y	Y	N	Y
2 Boland	Y	Y	N	N
3 Early	N	Y	Y	Y
4 Frank	?	?	Y	Y
5 Shannon	N	Y	Y	Y
6 Mavroules	Y	Y	Y	Y
7 Markey	N	Y	Y	Y
8 O'Neill				
9 Moakley	N	Y	Y	Y
10 *Heckler*	?	?	N	Y
11 Donnelly	N	Y	Y	Y
12 Studds	Y	Y	Y	Y
MICHIGAN				
1 Conyers	Y	Y	Y	Y
2 *Pursell*	Y	Y	N	Y
3 Wolpe	Y	Y	#	Y
4 *Siljander*	?	?	?	?
5 *Sawyer*	Y	Y	N	N
6 *Dunn*	Y	Y	N	N
7 Kildee	Y	Y	Y	Y
8 Traxler	Y	Y	N	N
9 *Vander Jagt*	Y	Y	N	N
10 Albosta	Y	Y	N	N
11 *Davis*	Y	Y	N	N
12 Bonior	N	Y	Y	Y
13 Crockett	?	?	Y	#
14 Hertel	Y	Y	Y	Y
15 Ford	Y	Y	?	Y
16 Dingell	Y	Y	N	N
17 Brodhead	Y	Y	Y	Y
18 Blanchard	Y	Y	N	Y
19 *Broomfield*	Y	Y	N	N
MINNESOTA				
1 *Erdahl*	Y	Y	Y	N
2 *Hagedorn*	Y	Y	N	N
3 *Frenzel*	N	Y	X	X
4 Vento	Y	Y	N	Y
5 Sabo	Y	Y	Y	Y
6 *Weber*	N	Y	Y	Y
7 *Stangeland*	Y	Y	N	N
8 Oberstar	Y	Y	Y	Y
MISSISSIPPI				
1 Whitten	Y	Y	N	N
2 Bowen	Y	Y	N	N
3 Montgomery	Y	Y	N	N
4 Dowdy	Y	Y	N	N
5 *Lott*	Y	Y	N	N
MISSOURI				
1 Clay	Y	Y	Y	?
2 Young	Y	Y	N	N
3 Gephardt	Y	Y	N	N

	275	276	277	278
4 Skelton	Y	Y	N	N
5 Bolling	?	?	?	?
6 *Coleman*	Y	Y	N	N
7 *Taylor*	?	?	X	X
8 Bailey	Y	Y	N	N
9 Volkmer	Y	Y	N	N
10 *Emerson*	+	Y	N	N
MONTANA				
1 Williams	Y	Y	?	?
2 *Marlenee*	Y	Y	N	N
NEBRASKA				
1 *Bereuter*	N	Y	N	N
2 *Daub*	Y	Y	N	N
3 *Smith*	Y	Y	N	N
NEVADA				
AL Santini	Y	Y	N	N
NEW HAMPSHIRE				
1 D'Amours	Y	Y	N	N
2 *Gregg*	Y	Y	N	N
NEW JERSEY				
1 Florio	?	?	?	?
2 Hughes	Y	Y	N	Y
3 Howard	Y	Y	N	N
4 *Smith*	Y	Y	N	Y
5 *Fenwick*	N	Y	N	N
6 *Forsythe*	Y	Y	N	N
7 *Roukema*	Y	Y	N	X
8 Roe	Y	Y	N	N
9 *Hollenbeck*	Y	Y	N	N
10 Rodino	Y	Y	Y	Y
11 Minish	Y	Y	Y	Y
12 *Rinaldo*	Y	Y	N	N
13 *Courter*	Y	Y	N	N
14 Guarini	Y	Y	Y	N
15 Dwyer	Y	Y	N	N
NEW MEXICO				
1 *Lujan*	Y	Y	N	N
2 *Skeen*	Y	Y	N	N
NEW YORK				
1 *Carney*	Y	Y	N	N
2 Downey	Y	Y	Y	Y
3 *Carman*	Y	Y	N	N
4 *Lent*	Y	Y	N	N
5 *McGrath*	Y	Y	N	N
6 *LeBoutillier*	?	?	N	N
7 Addabbo	Y	Y	Y	Y
8 Rosenthal	?	?	Y	Y
9 Ferraro	Y	Y	N	Y
10 Biaggi	Y	Y	N	N
11 Scheuer	Y	Y	N	N
12 Chisholm	Y	Y	#	#
13 Solarz	Y	Y	Y	N
14 Richmond	N	Y	Y	Y
15 Zeferetti	Y	Y	N	N
16 Schumer	Y	Y	Y	Y
17 *Molinari*	Y	Y	Y	N
18 *Green*	Y	Y	N	N
19 Rangel	N	Y	Y	Y
20 Weiss	Y	Y	Y	Y
21 Garcia	Y	Y	#	#
22 Bingham	?	?	Y	N
23 Peyser	Y	Y	N	N
24 Ottinger	Y	Y	N	Y
25 *Fish*	Y	Y	Y	Y
26 *Gilman*	Y	Y	N	Y
27 McHugh	Y	Y	N	Y
28 Stratton	N	Y	N	N
29 *Solomon*	Y	Y	N	N
30 *Martin*	Y	Y	?	?
31 *Mitchell*	Y	Y	N	Y
32 *Wortley*	Y	Y	N	N
33 *Lee*	?	?	?	?
34 *Horton*	Y	Y	?	?
35 *Conable*	Y	Y	N	N
36 LaFalce	Y	Y	N	N
37 Nowak	Y	Y	N	Y
38 *Kemp*	Y	Y	N	N
39 Lundine	Y	Y	N	N
NORTH CAROLINA				
1 Jones	?	?	X	X
2 Fountain	Y	Y	N	N
3 Whitley	Y	Y	N	N
4 Andrews	Y	Y	N	N
5 Neal	Y	Y	N	N
6 *Johnston*	Y	Y	X	X
7 Rose	Y	Y	N	N
8 Hefner	Y	Y	N	N

	275	276	277	278
9 *Martin*	Y	Y	N	N
10 *Broyhill*	Y	Y	N	N
11 *Hendon*	?	?	N	N
NORTH DAKOTA				
AL Dorgan	Y	Y	Y	Y
OHIO				
1 *Gradison*	Y	Y	N	N
2 Luken	Y	Y	N	N
3 Hall	Y	Y	N	Y
4 *Oxley*	Y	Y	N	N
5 *Latta*	?	?	N	N
6 *McEwen*	Y	Y	N	N
7 *Brown*	?	?	?	?
8 *Kindness*	Y	Y	N	N
9 *Weber*	Y	Y	N	N
10 *Miller*	Y	Y	N	N
11 *Stanton*	Y	Y	N	N
12 Shamansky	Y	Y	N	N
13 Pease	Y	Y	N	N
14 Seiberling	Y	Y	Y	Y
15 *Wylie*	Y	Y	N	N
16 *Regula*	Y	Y	N	N
17 *Ashbrook*	Y	Y	N	N
18 Applegate	Y	Y	N	N
19 *Williams*	?	?	?	?
20 Oakar	Y	Y	Y	Y
21 Stokes	?	?	Y	Y
22 Eckart	Y	Y	#	#
23 Mottl	Y	Y	Y	Y
OKLAHOMA				
1 Jones	Y	Y	N	N
2 Synar	?	?	Y	Y
3 Watkins	Y	Y	N	N
4 McCurdy	Y	Y	N	N
5 *Edwards*	Y	Y	N	Y
6 English	Y	Y	N	N
OREGON				
1 AuCoin	N	Y	Y	Y
2 *Smith*	?	?	?	?
3 Wyden	Y	Y	Y	Y
4 Weaver	Y	Y	Y	Y
PENNSYLVANIA				
1 Foglietta	Y	Y	N	N
2 Gray	Y	Y	Y	Y
3 Smith	Y	Y	N	N
4 *Dougherty*	?	?	N	N
5 *Schulze*	?	?	N	N
6 Yatron	Y	Y	N	N
7 Edgar	Y	Y	?	?
8 *Coyne, J.*	Y	Y	N	N
9 *Shuster*	Y	Y	N	N
10 *McDade*	Y	Y	N	Y
11 *Nelligan*	Y	Y	N	N
12 Murtha	Y	Y	N	N
13 *Coughlin*	Y	Y	N	N
14 Coyne, W.	Y	Y	N	Y
15 *Ritter*	Y	Y	N	N
16 *Walker*	Y	Y	N	N
17 Ertel	Y	Y	N	N
18 Walgren	Y	Y	Y	Y
19 *Goodling*	Y	Y	N	N
20 Gaydos	Y	Y	N	N
21 Bailey	Y	Y	N	N
22 Murphy	Y	Y	N	N
23 *Clinger*	Y	Y	N	N
24 *Marks*	Y	Y	N	N
25 Atkinson	Y	Y	N	N
RHODE ISLAND				
1 St Germain	Y	Y	Y	Y
2 *Schneider*	Y	Y	Y	Y
SOUTH CAROLINA				
1 *Hartnett*	Y	Y	N	N
2 *Spence*	Y	Y	N	N
3 Derrick	Y	Y	N	N
4 *Campbell*	Y	Y	N	N
5 Holland	?	?	?	N
6 *Napier*	Y	Y	N	N
SOUTH DAKOTA				
1 Daschle	Y	Y	N	Y
2 *Roberts*	Y	Y	N	N
TENNESSEE				
1 *Quillen*	?	?	?	?
2 *Duncan*	Y	Y	N	N
3 Bouquard	Y	Y	N	N
4 Gore	Y	Y	N	N
5 Boner	Y	Y	N	N
6 Beard	Y	Y	N	N

	275	276	277	278
7 Jones	Y	Y	N	N
8 Ford	Y	Y	Y	N
TEXAS				
1 Hall, S.	Y	Y	N	N
2 Wilson	Y	Y	N	N
3 *Collins*	Y	Y	N	N
4 Hall, R.	Y	Y	N	N
5 Mattox	Y	Y	N	N
6 Gramm	Y	Y	N	N
7 *Archer*	Y	Y	?	N
8 *Fields*	Y	Y	N	N
9 Brooks	Y	Y	N	N
10 Pickle	Y	Y	N	N
11 Leath	Y	Y	N	N
12 Wright	Y	Y	N	N
13 Hightower	Y	Y	N	N
14 Patman	Y	Y	N	N
15 de la Garza	Y	Y	N	N
16 White	Y	Y	N	N
17 Stenholm	Y	Y	N	N
18 Leland	?	?	Y	Y
19 Hance	Y	Y	N	N
20 Gonzalez	Y	Y	Y	Y
21 *Loeffler*	Y	Y	N	N
22 *Paul*	Y	Y	N	N
23 Kazen	Y	Y	N	N
24 Frost	Y	Y	N	N
UTAH				
1 *Hansen*	Y	Y	N	N
2 *Marriott*	?	?	N	N
VERMONT				
AL *Jeffords*	Y	Y	Y	Y
VIRGINIA				
1 *Trible*	Y	Y	N	N
2 *Whitehurst*	Y	Y	N	N
3 *Bliley*	Y	Y	N	N
4 *Daniel, R.*	Y	Y	N	N
5 Daniel, D.	Y	Y	N	N
6 *Butler*	?	?	N	N
7 *Robinson*	Y	Y	N	N
8 *Parris*	Y	Y	N	N
9 *Wampler*	Y	Y	N	N
10 *Wolf*	Y	Y	N	N
WASHINGTON				
1 *Pritchard*	?	?	N	N
2 Swift	Y	?	N	N
3 Bonker	Y	Y	Y	Y
4 *Morrison*	Y	Y	N	N
5 Foley	Y	Y	N	N
6 Dicks	Y	Y	N	?
7 Lowry	Y	Y	Y	Y
WEST VIRGINIA				
1 Mollohan	Y	Y	N	N
2 *Benedict*	Y	Y	N	N
3 *Staton*	Y	Y	N	N
4 Rahall	Y	Y	N	N
WISCONSIN				
1 Aspin	Y	Y	N	N
2 Kastenmeier	Y	Y	Y	Y
3 *Gunderson*	Y	Y	N	N
4 Zablocki	Y	Y	?	?
5 Reuss	N	Y	Y	Y
6 *Petri*	Y	Y	N	N
7 Obey	Y	Y	N	Y
8 *Roth*	Y	Y	N	N
9 *Sensenbrenner*	Y	Y	N	N
WYOMING				
AL *Cheney*	Y	Y	N	N

Democrats   *Republicans*

	KEY		279 280 281
Y	Voted for (yea).		
#	Paired for.		
+	Announced for.		
N	Voted against (nay).		
X	Paired against.		
-	Announced against.		
P	Voted "present".		
C	Voted "present" to avoid possible conflict of interest.		
?	Did not vote or otherwise make a position known.		

279. Procedural Motion. Walker, R-Pa., motion to approve the House *Journal* of Tuesday, Nov. 10. Motion agreed to 337-8: R 158-4; D 179-4 (ND 128-4, SD 51-0), Nov. 12, 1981.

280. HR 3413. Department of Energy National Security Programs Authorization. Price, D-Ill., motion to exclude the public from meetings of the conference committee on HR 3413, the bill making authorizations for national security programs of the Department of Energy, during consideration of classified national security information. Motion agreed to 385-0: R 174-0; D 211-0 (ND 144-0, SD 67-0), Nov. 12, 1981.

281. HR 4035. Interior Appropriations, Fiscal 1982. Loeffler, R-Texas, motion to recommit the conference report of the $7.54 billion bill to the House-Senate conference committee. Motion rejected 19-199: R 170-8; D 29-191 (ND 8-144, SD 21-47), Nov. 12, 1981.

	279	280	281
ALABAMA			
1 *Edwards*	Y	Y	N
2 *Dickinson*	N	Y	Y
3 Nichols	Y	Y	Y
4 Bevill	Y	Y	?
5 Flippo	?	Y	N
6 *Smith*	Y	Y	Y
7 Shelby	Y	Y	Y
ALASKA			
AL *Young*	N	Y	Y
ARIZONA			
1 *Rhodes*	Y	Y	Y
2 Udall	Y	Y	N
3 *Stump*	Y	Y	Y
4 *Rudd*	Y	Y	Y
ARKANSAS			
1 Alexander	Y	Y	N
2 *Bethune*	Y	Y	Y
3 *Hammerschmidt*	Y	Y	Y
4 Anthony	Y	?	N
CALIFORNIA			
1 *Chappie*	Y	Y	Y
2 *Clausen*	Y	Y	Y
3 Matsui	Y	Y	N
4 Fazio	?	?	X
5 Burton, J.	?	Y	N
6 Burton, P.	Y	Y	N
7 Miller	Y	Y	N
8 Dellums	Y	Y	N
9 Stark	?	?	?
10 Edwards	Y	Y	N
11 Lantos	Y	Y	N
12 *McCloskey*	?	?	?
13 Mineta	Y	Y	N
14 *Shumway*	Y	?	?
15 Coelho	Y	Y	N
16 Panetta	?	?	N
17 *Pashayan*	?	Y	Y
18 *Thomas*	Y	Y	Y
19 *Lagomarsino*	Y	Y	Y
20 *Goldwater*	?	?	?
21 *Fiedler*	Y	Y	Y
22 *Moorhead*	Y	Y	Y
23 Beilenson	Y	Y	N
24 Waxman	?	Y	N
25 Roybal	Y	Y	N
26 *Rousselot*	Y	Y	Y
27 *Dornan*	?	?	?
28 Dixon	Y	Y	N
29 Hawkins	Y	Y	N
30 Danielson	Y	Y	N
31 Dymally	Y	Y	N
32 Anderson	Y	Y	N
33 *Grisham*	Y	Y	Y
34 *Lungren*	Y	Y	Y
35 *Dreier*	Y	Y	Y
36 Brown	?	?	N
37 *Lewis*	?	Y	Y
38 Patterson	Y	Y	N
39 *Dannemeyer*	Y	Y	Y
40 *Badham*	?	?	#
41 *Lowery*	?	?	?
42 *Hunter*	Y	Y	Y
43 *Burgener*	Y	Y	Y
COLORADO			
1 Schroeder	N	Y	N
2 Wirth	Y	Y	N
3 Kogovsek	Y	Y	N
4 *Brown*	Y	Y	Y

	279	280	281
5 *Kramer*	Y	Y	Y
CONNECTICUT			
1 Vacancy			
2 Gejdenson	N	Y	N
3 *DeNardis*	?	Y	Y
4 *McKinney*	Y	Y	N
5 Ratchford	Y	Y	N
6 Moffett	Y	?	N
DELAWARE			
AL *Evans*	Y	Y	Y
FLORIDA			
1 Hutto	?	Y	N
2 Fuqua	?	Y	N
3 Bennett	Y	Y	Y
4 Chappell	?	Y	N
5 *McCollum*	Y	Y	Y
6 *Young*	Y	Y	Y
7 Gibbons	?	Y	N
8 Ireland	Y	Y	Y
9 Nelson	+	Y	N
10 *Bafalis*	Y	Y	Y
11 Mica	Y	Y	N
12 *Shaw*	Y	Y	Y
13 Lehman	Y	Y	N
14 Pepper	?	Y	N
15 Fascell	Y	Y	N
GEORGIA			
1 Ginn	?	?	?
2 Hatcher	Y	Y	?
3 Brinkley	Y	Y	N
4 Levitas	Y	Y	N
5 Fowler	Y	Y	N
6 *Gingrich*	Y	Y	Y
7 McDonald	?	?	#
8 Evans	Y	Y	Y
9 Jenkins	?	?	?
10 Barnard	Y	Y	Y
HAWAII			
1 Heftel	Y	Y	N
2 Akaka	Y	Y	N
IDAHO			
1 *Craig*	Y	Y	Y
2 *Hansen*	Y	Y	Y
ILLINOIS			
1 Washington	Y	Y	N
2 Savage	?	?	X
3 Russo	Y	Y	N
4 *Derwinski*	Y	Y	Y
5 Fary	Y	Y	N
6 *Hyde*	Y	Y	Y
7 Collins	Y	Y	N
8 Rostenkowski	Y	Y	N
9 Yates	Y	Y	N
10 *Porter*	Y	Y	Y
11 Annunzio	Y	Y	N
12 *Crane, P.*	Y	Y	Y
13 *McClory*	Y	Y	Y
14 *Erlenborn*	Y	Y	Y
15 *Corcoran*	Y	Y	Y
16 *Martin*	Y	Y	Y
17 *O'Brien*	Y	Y	Y
18 *Michel*	Y	Y	Y
19 *Railsback*	Y	Y	Y
20 *Findley*	Y	Y	Y
21 *Madigan*	?	?	?
22 *Crane, D.*	Y	Y	Y
23 Price	Y	Y	N
24 Simon	?	Y	N
INDIANA			
1 Benjamin	Y	Y	N
2 Fithian	Y	Y	N
3 *Hiler*	Y	Y	Y
4 *Coats*	Y	Y	Y
5 *Hillis*	Y	Y	Y
6 Evans	Y	Y	N
7 *Myers*	Y	Y	Y
8 *Deckard*	Y	Y	Y
9 Hamilton	Y	Y	N
10 Sharp	Y	Y	N
11 Jacobs	Y	Y	N
IOWA			
1 *Leach*	Y	Y	Y
2 *Tauke*	Y	Y	Y
3 *Evans*	N	Y	Y
4 Smith	Y	Y	?
5 Harkin	Y	Y	N
6 Bedell	Y	Y	N

Democrats *Republicans*

	279	280	281
KANSAS			
1 Roberts	Y	Y	Y
2 Jeffries	Y	Y	Y
3 Winn	?	Y	Y
4 Glickman	Y	Y	N
5 Whittaker	Y	Y	Y
KENTUCKY			
1 Hubbard	Y	Y	N
2 Natcher	Y	Y	N
3 Mazzoli	Y	Y	N
4 Snyder	Y	Y	Y
5 Rogers	Y	Y	Y
6 Hopkins	Y	Y	?
7 Perkins	Y	Y	N
LOUISIANA			
1 Livingston	Y	Y	Y
2 Boggs	?	Y	N
3 Tauzin	Y	Y	Y
4 Roemer	?	Y	Y
5 Huckaby	?	?	X
6 Moore	Y	Y	Y
7 Breaux	?	Y	Y
8 Long	?	Y	N
MAINE			
1 Emery	Y	Y	Y
2 Snowe	Y	Y	Y
MARYLAND			
1 Dyson	Y	Y	Y
2 Long	Y	Y	N
3 Mikulski	Y	Y	N
4 Holt	Y	Y	Y
5 Hoyer	Y	Y	N
6 Byron	?	?	?
7 Mitchell	N	Y	N
8 Barnes	Y	Y	N
MASSACHUSETTS			
1 Conte	Y	Y	N
2 Boland	Y	Y	N
3 Early	Y	Y	N
4 Frank	?	Y	N
5 Shannon	Y	Y	N
6 Mavroules	Y	Y	N
7 Markey	Y	Y	N
8 O'Neill			
9 Moakley	?	Y	N
10 Heckler	?	Y	Y
11 Donnelly	Y	Y	N
12 Studds	Y	Y	N
MICHIGAN			
1 Conyers	Y	Y	N
2 Pursell	Y	Y	Y
3 Wolpe	Y	Y	N
4 Siljander	?	Y	Y
5 Sawyer	Y	Y	Y
6 Dunn	?	?	Y
7 Kildee	Y	Y	N
8 Traxler	Y	Y	N
9 Vander Jagt	Y	Y	Y
10 Albosta	?	Y	N
11 Davis	Y	Y	Y
12 Bonior	Y	Y	N
13 Crockett	Y	?	N
14 Hertel	Y	Y	N
15 Ford	Y	Y	N
16 Dingell	Y	Y	N
17 Brodhead	Y	Y	N
18 Blanchard	?	Y	N
19 Broomfield	Y	Y	Y
MINNESOTA			
1 Erdahl	Y	Y	Y
2 Hagedorn	Y	Y	Y
3 Frenzel	Y	Y	Y
4 Vento	Y	?	N
5 Sabo	N	Y	N
6 Weber	Y	Y	Y
7 Stangeland	?	Y	Y
8 Oberstar	Y	Y	N
MISSISSIPPI			
1 Whitten	?	Y	N
2 Bowen	Y	Y	N
3 Montgomery	Y	Y	N
4 Dowdy	?	Y	N
5 Lott	Y	Y	Y
MISSOURI			
1 Clay	?	Y	N
2 Young	Y	Y	N
3 Gephardt	Y	Y	N
4 Skelton	Y	Y	N
5 Bolling	?	?	?
6 Coleman	Y	Y	Y
7 Taylor	Y	Y	Y
8 Bailey	?	Y	Y
9 Volkmer	Y	Y	N
10 Emerson	Y	Y	Y
MONTANA			
1 Williams	?	Y	N
2 Marlenee	Y	Y	Y
NEBRASKA			
1 Bereuter	Y	Y	Y
2 Daub	Y	Y	Y
3 Smith	Y	Y	Y
NEVADA			
AL Santini	Y	Y	N
NEW HAMPSHIRE			
1 D'Amours	Y	Y	N
2 Gregg	Y	Y	Y
NEW JERSEY			
1 Florio	?	?	X
2 Hughes	Y	Y	Y
3 Howard	Y	Y	N
4 Smith	Y	Y	Y
5 Fenwick	Y	Y	Y
6 Forsythe	?	?	#
7 Roukema	Y	Y	Y
8 Roe	Y	Y	N
9 Hollenbeck	Y	Y	Y
10 Rodino	Y	Y	N
11 Minish	Y	Y	N
12 Rinaldo	Y	Y	Y
13 Courter	Y	Y	Y
14 Guarini	Y	Y	N
15 Dwyer	Y	Y	N
NEW MEXICO			
1 Lujan	?	Y	Y
2 Skeen	Y	Y	Y
NEW YORK			
1 Carney	Y	Y	Y
2 Downey	Y	Y	N
3 Carman	Y	Y	Y
4 Lent	Y	Y	Y
5 McGrath	Y	Y	Y
6 LeBoutillier	Y	?	Y
7 Addabbo	Y	Y	N
8 Rosenthal	Y	Y	N
9 Ferraro	Y	Y	N
10 Biaggi	Y	Y	N
11 Scheuer	?	Y	N
12 Chisholm	?	Y	N
13 Solarz	Y	Y	N
14 Richmond	Y	Y	N
15 Zeferetti	?	Y	N
16 Schumer	Y	Y	N
17 Molinari	Y	Y	N
18 Green	Y	Y	N
19 Rangel	?	?	X
20 Weiss	Y	Y	N
21 Garcia	Y	Y	N
22 Bingham	Y	Y	N
23 Peyser	Y	Y	N
24 Ottinger	P	Y	N
25 Fish	Y	Y	Y
26 Gilman	Y	Y	N
27 McHugh	Y	Y	N
28 Stratton	Y	Y	N
29 Solomon	?	?	Y
30 Martin	Y	?	?
31 Mitchell	Y	Y	Y
32 Wortley	Y	Y	Y
33 Lee	Y	Y	Y
34 Horton	?	Y	Y
35 Conable	Y	Y	Y
36 LaFalce	Y	Y	N
37 Nowak	Y	?	N
38 Kemp	Y	Y	Y
39 Lundine	?	Y	N
NORTH CAROLINA			
1 Jones	?	?	N
2 Fountain	Y	Y	N
3 Whitley	Y	Y	N
4 Andrews	?	Y	N
5 Neal	?	Y	?
6 Johnston	Y	Y	Y
7 Rose	Y	Y	N
8 Hefner	?	Y	N
9 Martin	Y	Y	Y
10 Broyhill	Y	Y	Y
11 Hendon	Y	Y	Y
NORTH DAKOTA			
AL Dorgan	Y	Y	N
OHIO			
1 Gradison	Y	Y	Y
2 Luken	Y	Y	N
3 Hall	Y	Y	Y
4 Oxley	Y	Y	Y
5 Latta	Y	Y	Y
6 McEwen	Y	Y	Y
7 Brown	Y	Y	Y
8 Kindness	?	Y	Y
9 Weber	Y	Y	Y
10 Miller	Y	Y	Y
11 Stanton	Y	Y	Y
12 Shamansky	Y	Y	N
13 Pease	Y	Y	N
14 Seiberling	Y	Y	N
15 Wylie	?	Y	Y
16 Regula	Y	Y	N
17 Ashbrook	?	Y	Y
18 Applegate	?	Y	Y
19 Williams	Y	Y	Y
20 Oakar	Y	Y	N
21 Stokes	Y	Y	N
22 Eckart	Y	Y	N
23 Mottl	Y	Y	Y
OKLAHOMA			
1 Jones	Y	Y	?
2 Synar	Y	Y	N
3 Watkins	Y	Y	N
4 McCurdy	Y	Y	Y
5 Edwards	Y	Y	Y
6 English	Y	Y	Y
OREGON			
1 AuCoin	Y	Y	N
2 Smith	?	?	#
3 Wyden	Y	Y	N
4 Weaver	Y	Y	N
PENNSYLVANIA			
1 Foglietta	?	Y	N
2 Gray	Y	?	N
3 Smith	Y	?	N
4 Dougherty	Y	Y	Y
5 Schulze	Y	Y	Y
6 Yatron	Y	Y	Y
7 Edgar	Y	Y	N
8 Coyne, J.	?	Y	Y
9 Shuster	Y	Y	Y
10 McDade	Y	Y	N
11 Nelligan	Y	Y	N
12 Murtha	Y	Y	N
13 Coughlin	Y	Y	Y
14 Coyne, W.	Y	Y	N
15 Ritter	Y	Y	Y
16 Walker	N	Y	N
17 Ertel	Y	Y	N
18 Walgren	Y	Y	N
19 Goodling	?	?	Y
20 Gaydos	Y	Y	N
21 Bailey	Y	Y	N
22 Murphy	Y	Y	Y
23 Clinger	Y	Y	Y
24 Marks	?	Y	Y
25 Atkinson	?	Y	Y
RHODE ISLAND			
1 St Germain	?	Y	N
2 Schneider	Y	Y	Y
SOUTH CAROLINA			
1 Hartnett	Y	Y	Y
2 Spence	Y	Y	Y
3 Derrick	Y	Y	N
4 Campbell	Y	Y	Y
5 Holland	Y	Y	N
6 Napier	Y	Y	Y
SOUTH DAKOTA			
1 Daschle	Y	?	N
2 Roberts	Y	Y	Y
TENNESSEE			
1 Quillen	Y	Y	Y
2 Duncan	Y	Y	Y
3 Bouquard	Y	Y	N
4 Gore	Y	Y	N
5 Boner	?	Y	N
6 Beard	?	?	#
7 Jones	Y	Y	N
8 Ford	Y	Y	N
TEXAS			
1 Hall, S.	Y	Y	Y
2 Wilson	?	?	N
3 Collins	Y	Y	Y
4 Hall, R.	Y	?	Y
5 Mattox	?	?	?
6 Gramm	Y	Y	Y
7 Archer	Y	Y	Y
8 Fields	Y	Y	Y
9 Brooks	Y	Y	N
10 Pickle	Y	Y	Y
11 Leath	Y	Y	Y
12 Wright	Y	Y	N
13 Hightower	Y	Y	N
14 Patman	Y	Y	Y
15 de la Garza	Y	Y	Y
16 White	?	?	?
17 Stenholm	Y	Y	Y
18 Leland	?	?	N
19 Hance	?	?	?
20 Gonzalez	?	Y	N
21 Loeffler	Y	Y	Y
22 Paul	?	?	?
23 Kazen	Y	Y	N
24 Frost	Y	Y	N
UTAH			
1 Hansen	Y	Y	Y
2 Marriott	Y	Y	Y
VERMONT			
AL Jeffords	Y	Y	Y
VIRGINIA			
1 Trible	Y	Y	Y
2 Whitehurst	Y	Y	Y
3 Bliley	Y	Y	Y
4 Daniel, R.	?	?	Y
5 Daniel, D.	Y	Y	Y
6 Butler	Y	Y	Y
7 Robinson	Y	Y	Y
8 Parris	Y	Y	Y
9 Wampler	Y	Y	Y
10 Wolf	Y	Y	Y
WASHINGTON			
1 Pritchard	?	?	?
2 Swift	Y	Y	N
3 Bonker	?	?	?
4 Morrison	Y	Y	Y
5 Foley	Y	Y	N
6 Dicks	Y	Y	N
7 Lowry	Y	Y	N
WEST VIRGINIA			
1 Mollohan	?	Y	N
2 Benedict	Y	Y	Y
3 Staton	Y	Y	Y
4 Rahall	Y	Y	N
WISCONSIN			
1 Aspin	Y	Y	N
2 Kastenmeier	Y	Y	N
3 Gunderson	Y	Y	Y
4 Zablocki	?	?	?
5 Reuss	?	Y	N
6 Petri	Y	Y	Y
7 Obey	Y	Y	N
8 Roth	Y	Y	Y
9 Sensenbrenner	Y	Y	Y
WYOMING			
AL Cheney	Y	Y	Y

Democrats *Republicans*

KEY

Y Voted for (yea).
\# Paired for.
+ Announced for.
N Voted against (nay).
X Paired against.
- Announced against.
P Voted "present".
C Voted "present" to avoid possible conflict of interest.
? Did not vote or otherwise make a position known.

282. Procedural Motion. Walker, R-Pa., motion to approve the House *Journal* of Friday, Nov. 13. Motion agreed to 303-8: R 144-3; D 159-5 (ND 106-5, SD 53-0), Nov. 16, 1981.

283. H J Res 357. Continuing Appropriations, Fiscal 1982. Moakley, D-Mass., motion to order the previous question, thus ending debate and the possibility of amendment, on the resolution (H Res 271) providing for floor consideration of the joint resolution to provide funding authority during the period Nov. 20, 1981, through Sept. 30, 1982, for government agencies whose regular fiscal 1982 appropriations bills had not been enacted. Motion agreed to 185-174: R 26-138; D 159-36 (ND 119-16, SD 40-20), Nov. 16, 1981.

284. H J Res 357. Continuing Appropriations, Fiscal 1982. Adoption of the rule (H Res 271) providing for floor consideration, with no floor amendments allowed, of the joint resolution. Adopted 197-169: R 31-132; D 166-37 (ND 121-21, SD 45-16), Nov. 16, 1981.

285. H J Res 357. Continuing Appropriations, Fiscal 1982. Michel, R-Ill., motion to recommit the joint resolution to the Appropriations Committee with instructions to cut 5 percent from discretionary spending in the joint resolution, except for programs under the defense, military construction and District of Columbia appropriations bills, and Social Security administrative expenses, veterans' medical care and food stamps. Motion rejected 189-201: R 160-18; D 29-183 (ND 2-143, SD 27-40), Nov. 16, 1981. A "yea" was a vote supporting the president's position.

286. H J Res 357. Continuing Appropriations, Fiscal 1982. Passage of the joint resolution to provide funding authority during the period Nov. 20, 1981, through Sept. 30, 1982, for government agencies whose regular fiscal 1982 appropriations bills had not been enacted. Passed 195-187: R 32-144; D 163-43 (ND 122-18, SD 41-25), Nov. 16, 1981.

287. Procedural Motion. Rousselot, R-Calif., motion to approve the House *Journal* of Monday, Nov. 16. Motion agreed to 301-39: R 141-25; D 160-14 (ND 107-9 SD 53-5), Nov. 17, 1981.

288. HR 1797. Authorization of Coastwise Trading Privileges. Adoption of committee amendments which direct the transportation secretary to document the vessel *Capt Tom* for coastwise trade and fishing. Adopted 353-0: R 172-0; D 181-0 (ND 124-0, SD 57-0). Nov. 17, 1981. (The bill, as amended, was subsequently passed by voice vote.)

289. Procedural Motion. Foley, D-Wash., motion that when the House adjourn on Nov. 17, that it adjourn to meet again at 4 p.m. that afternoon. Motion agreed to 191-172: R 3-171; D 188-1 (ND 129-1, SD 59-0), Nov. 17, 1981.

	282	283	284	285	286	287	288	289
ALABAMA								
1 Edwards	Y	Y	Y	Y	N	Y	Y	N
2 Dickinson	N	N	N	Y	N	N	Y	N
3 Nichols	Y	Y	Y	Y	N	?	?	Y
4 Bevill	Y	Y	Y	N	Y	Y	Y	Y
5 Flippo	Y	Y	Y	N	Y	Y	Y	Y
6 Smith	Y	N	N	Y	N	N	Y	N
7 Shelby	Y	N	Y	Y	N	Y	Y	Y
ALASKA								
AL Young	?	X	X	#	X	Y	Y	N
ARIZONA								
1 Rhodes	?	?	?	Y	Y	Y	Y	N
2 Udall	?	#	#	N	Y	Y	?	?
3 Stump	Y	Y	N	N	Y	Y	Y	N
4 Rudd	?	X	X	?	?	Y	Y	N
ARKANSAS								
1 Alexander	Y	Y	Y	N	Y	Y	Y	Y
2 Bethune	Y	N	N	Y	N	Y	Y	N
3 Hammerschmidt	Y	N	Y	N	Y	N	Y	N
4 Anthony	Y	Y	Y	N	Y	?	?	?
CALIFORNIA								
1 Chappie	Y	N	N	N	Y	N	Y	N
2 Clausen	Y	N	?	Y	Y	Y	Y	N
3 Matsui	Y	Y	Y	N	Y	?	?	?
4 Fazio	Y	Y	Y	N	Y	Y	Y	?
5 Burton, J.	?	#	#	?	?	?	Y	Y
6 Burton, P.	Y	Y	Y	N	Y	Y	Y	Y
7 Miller	Y	Y	Y	N	Y	N	Y	Y
8 Dellums	?	Y	Y	N	Y	Y	Y	Y
9 Stark	Y	Y	Y	N	Y	?	?	?
10 Edwards	?	#	#	X	#	Y	?	Y
11 Lantos	Y	Y	Y	N	Y	Y	Y	Y
12 McCloskey	?	N	N	Y	N	?	?	?
13 Mineta	?	Y	Y	N	Y	Y	Y	Y
14 Shumway	Y	N	N	Y	N	Y	Y	N
15 Coelho	?	Y	Y	N	Y	Y	Y	Y
16 Panetta	Y	Y	Y	N	Y	Y	Y	Y
17 Pashayan	Y	N	Y	N	Y	N	Y	Y
18 Thomas	Y	?	?	Y	N	Y	Y	N
19 Lagomarsino	Y	N	N	Y	N	Y	Y	N
20 Goldwater	?	?	?	?	?	?	?	?
21 Fiedler	Y	N	N	Y	N	Y	Y	N
22 Moorhead	Y	N	N	Y	N	Y	Y	N
23 Beilenson	Y	Y	Y	N	Y	Y	Y	Y
24 Waxman	Y	Y	Y	N	Y	Y	Y	Y
25 Roybal	Y	Y	Y	N	Y	Y	Y	Y
26 Rousselot	Y	N	N	Y	N	N	Y	N
27 Dornan	?	X	X	#	X	?	?	?
28 Dixon	Y	Y	Y	N	Y	Y	Y	Y
29 Hawkins	Y	Y	Y	N	Y	Y	Y	Y
30 Danielson	Y	Y	Y	N	Y	Y	Y	Y
31 Dymally	Y	Y	Y	N	Y	Y	?	Y
32 Anderson	Y	N	N	Y	N	Y	Y	Y
33 Grisham	Y	N	N	Y	N	Y	Y	N
34 Lungren	Y	N	N	Y	N	Y	Y	N
35 Dreier	Y	N	N	Y	N	N	Y	N
36 Brown	?	?	?	?	?	?	Y	?
37 Lewis	Y	Y	Y	Y	N	Y	Y	N
38 Patterson	Y	Y	Y	N	Y	Y	Y	Y
39 Dannemeyer	Y	N	N	Y	N	N	Y	N
40 Badham	Y	N	Y	N	Y	N	Y	N
41 Lowery	Y	N	Y	N	Y	N	Y	N
42 Hunter	Y	N	N	Y	N	N	Y	N
43 Burgener	Y	N	N	Y	N	Y	Y	N
COLORADO								
1 Schroeder	N	N	N	N	N	N	Y	N
2 Wirth	Y	Y	Y	N	Y	Y	Y	Y
3 Kogovsek	Y	Y	Y	N	Y	Y	Y	Y
4 Brown	Y	N	N	Y	N	N	Y	N
5 Kramer	Y	N	N	Y	N	N	Y	N
CONNECTICUT								
1 Vacancy								
2 Gejdenson	N	Y	Y	N	Y	N	Y	Y
3 DeNardis	?	N	N	N	Y	?	N	Y
4 McKinney	Y	Y	Y	Y	Y	?	Y	N
5 Ratchford	Y	Y	Y	X	#	Y	Y	Y
6 Moffett	Y	Y	Y	N	Y	?	?	?
DELAWARE								
AL Evans	?	N	N	Y	Y	Y	Y	N
FLORIDA								
1 Hutto	Y	Y	Y	N	Y	Y	Y	Y
2 Fuqua	Y	Y	Y	N	Y	?	?	?
3 Bennett	Y	N	Y	Y	Y	Y	Y	Y
4 Chappell	?	?	N	N	N	Y	Y	?
5 McCollum	?	N	N	N	N	N	Y	N
6 Young	?	N	N	Y	N	N	Y	N
7 Gibbons	?	?	?	Y	Y	Y	Y	Y
8 Ireland	?	N	N	Y	N	?	?	?
9 Nelson	Y	Y	Y	N	Y	Y	Y	Y
10 Bafalis	?	N	N	Y	N	?	?	?
11 Mica	?	?	?	N	Y	Y	Y	Y
12 Shaw	?	N	N	Y	N	N	Y	N
13 Lehman	?	?	?	?	?	?	?	?
14 Pepper	?	Y	Y	N	Y	?	Y	Y
15 Fascell	Y	Y	Y	N	Y	Y	Y	Y
GEORGIA								
1 Ginn	Y	Y	Y	N	Y	?	?	?
2 Hatcher	?	?	?	?	?	Y	Y	Y
3 Brinkley	Y	Y	Y	N	Y	Y	Y	Y
4 Levitas	Y	N	N	Y	N	Y	Y	Y
5 Fowler	Y	N	N	N	Y	?	?	?
6 Gingrich	?	Y	N	Y	N	N	Y	N
7 McDonald	?	X	X	X	N	?	+	?
8 Evans	Y	N	N	Y	N	N	Y	N
9 Jenkins	Y	N	N	Y	N	Y	Y	N
10 Barnard	Y	N	N	Y	N	?	?	?
HAWAII								
1 Heftel	Y	Y	Y	N	N	?	?	?
2 Akaka	?	#	#	N	Y	Y	Y	Y
IDAHO								
1 Craig	Y	N	N	Y	N	N	Y	N
2 Hansen	Y	N	N	Y	N	N	Y	N
ILLINOIS								
1 Washington	Y	Y	Y	N	Y	Y	Y	Y
2 Savage	?	Y	Y	N	Y	?	?	?
3 Russo	Y	N	N	N	N	?	?	?
4 Derwinski	N	N	N	Y	N	N	Y	N
5 Fary	Y	Y	Y	N	Y	Y	Y	Y
6 Hyde	?	?	X	Y	Y	Y	Y	N
7 Collins	Y	Y	Y	N	Y	Y	Y	Y
8 Rostenkowski	Y	Y	Y	N	Y	?	?	?
9 Yates	Y	Y	Y	N	Y	Y	Y	Y
10 Porter	Y	N	N	Y	N	Y	Y	Y
11 Annunzio	Y	Y	Y	N	Y	Y	Y	Y
12 Crane, P.	Y	N	N	Y	N	N	Y	N
13 McClory	Y	N	N	Y	N	Y	Y	Y
14 Erlenborn	?	X	X	Y	Y	Y	Y	N
15 Corcoran	Y	N	N	Y	N	Y	Y	N
16 Martin	Y	N	N	Y	N	Y	?	N
17 O'Brien	Y	Y	Y	Y	N	Y	Y	N
18 Michel	Y	Y	Y	N	Y	Y	Y	N
19 Railsback	Y	N	Y	Y	Y	Y	Y	N
20 Findley	Y	N	N	Y	N	Y	Y	N
21 Madigan	Y	X	N	Y	N	Y	Y	N
22 Crane, D.	?	N	N	Y	N	N	Y	N
23 Price	Y	Y	Y	N	Y	Y	Y	Y
24 Simon	Y	Y	Y	N	?	Y	Y	Y
INDIANA								
1 Benjamin	Y	Y	Y	N	Y	Y	Y	Y
2 Fithian	?	?	?	?	?	?	?	?
3 Hiler	Y	N	N	Y	N	N	Y	N
4 Coats	Y	N	N	Y	N	N	Y	N
5 Hillis	Y	Y	Y	N	Y	Y	Y	Y
6 Evans	Y	Y	Y	N	Y	Y	Y	Y
7 Myers	Y	Y	Y	N	Y	Y	Y	N
8 Deckard	Y	N	N	Y	N	Y	Y	N
9 Hamilton	Y	N	N	Y	N	Y	Y	Y
10 Sharp	Y	N	N	N	N	N	Y	Y
11 Jacobs	N	Y	Y	N	Y	?	?	?
IOWA								
1 Leach	Y	N	N	Y	N	Y	Y	N
2 Tauke	Y	N	N	Y	N	Y	Y	N
3 Evans	Y	N	N	Y	N	Y	Y	N
4 Smith	Y	Y	Y	N	Y	Y	Y	Y
5 Harkin	N	Y	Y	N	Y	Y	Y	Y
6 Bedell	?	?	?	?	?	?	?	?

	282	283	284	285	286	287	288	289
KANSAS								
1 ***Roberts***	Y	N	N	Y	N	Y	Y	N
2 ***Jeffries***	?	?	X	#	X	Y	Y	N
3 ***Winn***	Y	N	Y	Y	N	Y	Y	N
4 Glickman	Y	N	N	N	Y	Y	Y	Y
5 ***Whittaker***	Y	X	X	Y	N	Y	Y	N
KENTUCKY								
1 Hubbard	Y	Y	Y	Y	?	Y	Y	Y
2 Natcher	Y	Y	Y	N	Y	Y	Y	Y
3 Mazzoli	Y	N	N	N	N	Y	Y	Y
4 ***Snyder***	Y	N	N	Y	N	Y	Y	N
5 ***Rogers***	Y	N	N	Y	N	Y	Y	N
6 ***Hopkins***	Y	N	N	Y	N	Y	Y	N
7 Perkins	Y	Y	Y	N	Y	Y	Y	Y
LOUISIANA								
1 ***Livingston***	Y	?	Y	Y	N	Y	Y	N
2 Boggs	?	Y	Y	N	Y	Y	Y	Y
3 Tauzin	Y	N	N	Y	N	Y	Y	Y
4 Roemer	Y	N	N	Y	N	Y	P	Y
5 Huckaby	Y	N	Y	Y	N	Y	Y	Y
6 ***Moore***	Y	N	N	Y	N	Y	Y	N
7 Breaux	Y	Y	Y	Y	N	?	?	?
8 Long	?	?	?	?	?	Y	Y	Y
MAINE								
1 ***Emery***	Y	N	N	Y	N	Y	Y	N
2 ***Snowe***	Y	N	N	Y	N	Y	Y	N
MARYLAND								
1 Dyson	Y	Y	Y	N	Y	Y	Y	Y
2 Long	Y	Y	Y	N	Y	Y	Y	Y
3 Mikulski	?	?	Y	N	Y	?	?	?
4 ***Holt***	?	N	N	Y	N	N	Y	N
5 Hoyer	Y	Y	N	N	Y	Y	Y	Y
6 Byron	?	?	?	?	?	Y	Y	Y
7 Mitchell	?	#	#	X	#	N	Y	Y
8 Barnes	?	Y	N	N	Y	?	?	?
MASSACHUSETTS								
1 ***Conte***	Y	Y	Y	N	Y	Y	Y	N
2 Boland	Y	Y	Y	N	Y	Y	Y	Y
3 Early	Y	Y	Y	N	Y	?	?	?
4 Frank	Y	Y	Y	N	Y	Y	Y	Y
5 Shannon	Y	Y	Y	N	Y	?	?	?
6 Mavroules	?	Y	Y	N	Y	Y	Y	Y
7 Markey	Y	Y	Y	N	Y	Y	Y	Y
8 O'Neill								
9 Moakley	Y	Y	Y	N	Y	Y	Y	Y
10 ***Heckler***	?	Y	N	N	Y	Y	Y	?
11 Donnelly	Y	Y	Y	N	Y	Y	Y	Y
12 Studds	?	Y	Y	N	N	Y	Y	Y
MICHIGAN								
1 Conyers	Y	Y	Y	N	Y	Y	?	Y
2 ***Pursell***	?	N	N	N	Y	Y	Y	N
3 Wolpe	Y	Y	Y	N	Y	Y	Y	Y
4 ***Siljander***	?	X	X	Y	N	Y	Y	N
5 ***Sawyer***	?	?	?	?	?	?	?	?
6 ***Dunn***	Y	Y	Y	Y	N	Y	Y	N
7 Kildee	Y	Y	Y	N	Y	Y	Y	Y
8 Traxler	?	Y	Y	N	Y	Y	Y	Y
9 ***Vander Jagt***	?	N	N	Y	X	?	?	?
10 Albosta	?	Y	Y	N	Y	Y	Y	Y
11 ***Davis***	Y	Y	Y	N	Y	N	Y	N
12 Bonior	?	Y	Y	N	Y	?	?	?
13 Crockett	?	Y	Y	N	Y	Y	?	Y
14 Hertel	?	?	?	?	?	Y	Y	Y
15 Ford	Y	Y	Y	N	Y	?	Y	Y
16 Dingell	Y	Y	Y	N	?	?	?	?
17 Brodhead	Y	Y	Y	N	Y	?	?	?
18 Blanchard	?	?	?	?	?	?	Y	Y
19 ***Broomfield***	Y	N	Y	Y	N	Y	Y	N
MINNESOTA								
1 ***Erdahl***	?	N	N	Y	N	Y	Y	N
2 ***Hagedorn***	?	X	X	#	X	?	?	?
3 ***Frenzel***	Y	N	N	Y	N	N	Y	Y
4 Vento	Y	Y	Y	N	Y	Y	Y	Y
5 Sabo	N	Y	Y	N	Y	N	Y	Y
6 ***Weber***	Y	N	N	Y	N	Y	Y	N
7 ***Stangeland***	?	X	X	Y	N	Y	Y	N
8 Oberstar	Y	Y	N	N	Y	Y	Y	Y
MISSISSIPPI								
1 Whitten	Y	Y	Y	N	Y	Y	Y	Y
2 Bowen	Y	Y	Y	N	Y	Y	Y	Y
3 Montgomery	Y	Y	Y	Y	N	Y	Y	?
4 Dowdy	?	?	?	N	Y	Y	Y	Y
5 ***Lott***	Y	N	N	Y	N	Y	Y	N
MISSOURI								
1 Clay	?	#	Y	N	Y	?	?	?
2 Young	Y	Y	N	N	Y	Y	Y	Y
3 Gephardt	Y	Y	Y	N	Y	Y	Y	Y
4 Skelton	Y	Y	Y	N	Y	Y	Y	Y
5 Bolling	?	?	?	?	?	?	?	?
6 ***Coleman***	?	?	?	?	?	?	?	?
7 ***Taylor***	Y	Y	Y	Y	N	Y	Y	N
8 ***Bailey***	Y	N	N	Y	N	Y	Y	N
9 Volkmer	Y	Y	Y	N	Y	Y	Y	Y
10 ***Emerson***	Y	N	N	Y	N	?	Y	N
MONTANA								
1 Williams	Y	Y	Y	N	Y	Y	?	?
2 ***Marlenee***	Y	N	N	Y	N	Y	Y	N
NEBRASKA								
1 ***Bereuter***	Y	N	N	Y	N	Y	Y	N
2 ***Daub***	Y	N	N	Y	N	N	Y	N
3 ***Smith***	Y	N	N	Y	N	Y	Y	N
NEVADA								
AL Santini	?	?	?	?	?	Y	Y	Y
NEW HAMPSHIRE								
1 D'Amours	Y	Y	Y	N	Y	Y	Y	Y
2 ***Gregg***	Y	N	N	Y	N	Y	Y	N
NEW JERSEY								
1 Florio	?	#	#	X	#	Y	Y	Y
2 Hughes	Y	Y	N	N	N	Y	Y	Y
3 Howard	Y	Y	Y	N	Y	Y	Y	Y
4 ***Smith***	Y	N	N	N	Y	Y	Y	N
5 ***Fenwick***	Y	N	?	Y	N	Y	Y	N
6 ***Forsythe***	?	?	#	#	?	?	?	?
7 ***Roukema***	Y	N	N	Y	N	Y	Y	N
8 Roe	Y	Y	N	N	Y	Y	Y	Y
9 ***Hollenbeck***	?	Y	Y	N	Y	?	?	?
10 Rodino	?	?	Y	N	Y	Y	Y	Y
11 Minish	Y	Y	Y	N	Y	Y	Y	Y
12 ***Rinaldo***	Y	N	N	N	Y	?	?	?
13 ***Courter***	Y	N	N	Y	N	Y	Y	N
14 Guarini	?	#	Y	N	Y	?	?	?
15 Dwyer	Y	Y	Y	N	Y	Y	Y	Y
NEW MEXICO								
1 ***Lujan***	Y	N	N	Y	?	Y	Y	N
2 ***Skeen***	Y	N	Y	Y	N	Y	Y	N
NEW YORK								
1 ***Carney***	Y	N	N	Y	N	Y	Y	N
2 Downey	Y	Y	Y	N	Y	Y	Y	Y
3 ***Carman***	?	N	Y	Y	N	?	?	?
4 ***Lent***	Y	N	N	Y	Y	Y	Y	N
5 ***McGrath***	Y	N	N	Y	Y	Y	Y	N
6 ***LeBoutillier***	Y	N	N	Y	Y	?	Y	N
7 Addabbo	Y	Y	Y	N	Y	Y	Y	Y
8 Rosenthal	?	?	Y	N	Y	Y	Y	Y
9 Ferraro	?	Y	Y	N	Y	Y	Y	Y
10 Biaggi	Y	Y	Y	N	Y	Y	Y	Y
11 Scheuer	?	Y	Y	N	Y	Y	Y	Y
12 Chisholm	?	#	#	X	#	?	?	?
13 Solarz	?	#	#	X	#	Y	Y	Y
14 Richmond	?	#	#	X	#	?	?	?
15 Zeferetti	Y	Y	Y	N	Y	Y	Y	Y
16 Schumer	Y	Y	Y	N	Y	Y	Y	Y
17 ***Molinari***	Y	Y	Y	N	Y	Y	Y	N
18 ***Green***	Y	Y	Y	N	Y	Y	Y	N
19 Rangel	?	Y	Y	N	Y	?	?	?
20 Weiss	?	Y	Y	N	N	?	Y	Y
21 Garcia	?	Y	Y	N	Y	Y	Y	Y
22 Bingham	Y	Y	Y	N	Y	Y	Y	?
23 Peyser	?	#	#	N	Y	Y	Y	Y
24 Ottinger	P	Y	Y	N	Y	P	Y	Y
25 ***Fish***	Y	Y	Y	Y	N	Y	Y	N
26 ***Gilman***	+	-	#	N	Y	+	+	-
27 McHugh	Y	Y	Y	N	Y	?	Y	Y
28 Stratton	Y	Y	Y	N	?	Y	Y	Y
29 ***Solomon***	Y	N	N	Y	N	Y	Y	N
30 ***Martin***	Y	N	N	Y	N	?	?	?
31 ***Mitchell***	Y	N	N	N	Y	Y	Y	N
32 ***Wortley***	?	X	X	Y	N	Y	Y	N
33 ***Lee***	?	-	X	#	?	?	?	?
34 ***Horton***	Y	Y	N	N	Y	?	Y	Y
35 ***Conable***	Y	Y	N	Y	N	Y	Y	N
36 LaFalce	Y	Y	Y	N	Y	?	Y	Y
37 Nowak	Y	Y	Y	N	Y	?	Y	Y
38 ***Kemp***	Y	N	N	Y	N	Y	Y	N
39 Lundine	Y	N	N	N	?	Y	Y	Y
NORTH CAROLINA								
1 Jones	?	Y	Y	N	Y	Y	Y	Y
2 Fountain	?	N	N	N	N	N	Y	Y
3 Whitley	Y	Y	Y	N	Y	Y	Y	Y
4 Andrews	?	?	?	N	Y	?	Y	Y
5 Neal	Y	Y	Y	N	Y	Y	Y	Y
6 ***Johnston***	Y	N	N	Y	N	N	Y	N
7 Rose	?	?	?	?	?	Y	Y	Y
8 Hefner	?	?	?	?	?	?	?	?
9 ***Martin***	Y	N	N	Y	N	?	?	?
10 ***Broyhill***	Y	N	N	Y	N	Y	Y	N
11 ***Hendon***	Y	N	N	Y	N	Y	P	N
NORTH DAKOTA								
AL Dorgan	Y	Y	N	N	N	?	?	Y
OHIO								
1 ***Gradison***	?	X	X	#	X	Y	Y	N
2 Luken	Y	Y	Y	N	Y	Y	Y	Y
3 Hall	Y	Y	Y	N	Y	?	Y	Y
4 ***Oxley***	Y	N	N	Y	N	?	Y	N
5 ***Latta***	Y	N	N	Y	N	N	Y	N
6 ***McEwen***	Y	N	N	Y	N	Y	Y	N
7 ***Brown***	Y	N	N	Y	N	Y	Y	N
8 ***Kindness***	?	N	N	Y	N	Y	Y	N
9 ***Weber***	Y	N	Y	Y	N	Y	Y	N
10 ***Miller***	Y	N	N	Y	N	Y	Y	N
11 ***Stanton***	Y	Y	Y	Y	N	Y	Y	N
12 Shomansky	+	+	Y	N	Y	Y	Y	Y
13 Pease	Y	Y	Y	N	Y	?	?	?
14 Seiberling	Y	Y	Y	N	Y	?	Y	Y
15 ***Wylie***	?	X	?	?	X	Y	Y	N
16 ***Regula***	Y	N	N	Y	N	Y	Y	N
17 ***Ashbrook***	Y	N	N	Y	N	Y	Y	N
18 Applegate	?	N	N	N	N	?	Y	Y
19 ***Williams***	?	#	#	Y	N	Y	Y	N
20 Oakar	?	Y	Y	N	Y	Y	Y	Y
21 Stokes	Y	Y	Y	N	Y	Y	Y	Y
22 Eckart	?	N	N	N	Y	Y	Y	Y
23 Mottl	Y	N	N	Y	N	Y	Y	Y
OKLAHOMA								
1 Jones	Y	Y	N	N	Y	Y	Y	Y
2 Synar	Y	Y	Y	N	Y	Y	Y	Y
3 Watkins	Y	Y	Y	N	Y	Y	Y	Y
4 McCurdy	Y	N	N	N	Y	Y	Y	Y
5 ***Edwards***	Y	N	N	Y	N	Y	Y	N
6 English	Y	N	N	Y	Y	Y	Y	Y
OREGON								
1 AuCoin	Y	Y	Y	N	Y	Y	Y	Y
2 ***Smith***	Y	N	N	Y	N	N	Y	N
3 Wyden	Y	Y	Y	N	Y	Y	Y	Y
4 Weaver	Y	Y	Y	N	N	Y	Y	Y
PENNSYLVANIA								
1 Foglietta	Y	N	Y	N	Y	?	?	?
2 Gray	Y	Y	Y	N	Y	Y	Y	Y
3 Smith	?	Y	Y	N	Y	Y	Y	Y
4 ***Dougherty***	Y	N	N	N	Y	Y	Y	N
5 ***Schulze***	Y	N	N	Y	N	Y	Y	N
6 Yatron	Y	N	N	N	Y	Y	Y	Y
7 Edgar	Y	N	N	N	Y	N	Y	Y
8 ***Coyne, J.***	Y	N	N	Y	N	Y	Y	N
9 ***Shuster***	Y	N	N	Y	N	Y	Y	N
10 ***McDade***	Y	Y	Y	Y	Y	Y	Y	N
11 ***Nelligan***	Y	N	Y	N	Y	Y	Y	N
12 Murtha	Y	Y	Y	N	Y	Y	Y	Y
13 ***Coughlin***	?	?	?	Y	N	N	Y	N
14 Coyne, W.	Y	Y	Y	N	Y	?	?	Y
15 ***Ritter***	Y	N	N	Y	N	Y	Y	N
16 ***Walker***	N	N	N	Y	N	N	Y	N
17 Ertel	?	Y	Y	N	Y	Y	Y	Y
18 Walgren	Y	N	Y	N	Y	Y	?	Y
19 ***Goodling***	?	N	N	Y	N	N	Y	N
20 Gaydos	Y	Y	Y	N	Y	Y	Y	Y
21 Bailey	Y	Y	Y	N	Y	?	?	?
22 Murphy	Y	N	N	N	N	?	?	?
23 ***Clinger***	Y	Y	N	Y	N	Y	Y	N
24 ***Marks***	Y	N	N	Y	Y	Y	Y	N
25 ***Atkinson***	Y	N	N	Y	N	?	Y	N
RHODE ISLAND								
1 St Germain	?	Y	Y	N	Y	Y	Y	Y
2 ***Schneider***	Y	N	N	N	Y	Y	Y	N
SOUTH CAROLINA								
1 ***Hartnett***	Y	N	N	Y	N	Y	Y	N
2 ***Spence***	Y	N	N	Y	N	Y	Y	N
3 Derrick	Y	Y	Y	Y	Y	N	Y	Y
4 ***Campbell***	Y	N	Y	Y	N	Y	Y	N
5 Holland	?	?	?	?	?	?	?	?
6 ***Napier***	?	?	?	Y	Y	Y	Y	N
SOUTH DAKOTA								
1 Daschle	?	?	?	?	?	?	?	Y
2 ***Roberts***	?	N	N	Y	N	N	Y	N
TENNESSEE								
1 ***Quillen***	Y	N	Y	Y	N	Y	Y	N
2 ***Duncan***	Y	N	Y	Y	N	Y	Y	N
3 Bouquard	Y	Y	Y	N	Y	Y	Y	Y
4 Gore	Y	?	?	?	?	Y	Y	Y
5 Boner	Y	Y	Y	N	Y	Y	Y	Y
6 ***Beard***	Y	N	N	Y	N	Y	Y	N
7 Jones	Y	Y	Y	N	Y	Y	Y	Y
8 Ford	Y	Y	Y	N	Y	?	?	?
TEXAS								
1 Hall, S.	Y	N	Y	Y	N	Y	Y	Y
2 Wilson	?	?	?	Y	Y	Y	Y	Y
3 ***Collins***	Y	N	N	Y	N	Y	Y	N
4 Hall, R.	Y	N	Y	Y	N	Y	Y	Y
5 Mattox	?	?	?	?	?	?	?	?
6 Gramm	Y	Y	Y	Y	N	P	P	Y
7 ***Archer***	Y	N	N	Y	N	Y	Y	N
8 ***Fields***	Y	N	N	Y	N	Y	Y	N
9 Brooks	?	?	?	?	?	?	?	?
10 Pickle	?	Y	Y	N	N	?	?	?
11 Leath	?	?	?	?	?	Y	Y	Y
12 Wright	?	Y	Y	N	Y	Y	Y	?
13 Hightower	Y	N	Y	Y	Y	Y	Y	Y
14 Patman	Y	Y	Y	N	N	Y	Y	Y
15 de la Garza	Y	Y	Y	N	Y	Y	Y	Y
16 White	Y	Y	Y	Y	Y	Y	Y	Y
17 Stenholm	Y	N	N	Y	N	N	Y	Y
18 Leland	?	#	#	X	#	?	?	?
19 Hance	?	?	?	?	?	?	?	?
20 Gonzalez	?	Y	Y	N	Y	N	P	Y
21 ***Loeffler***	Y	N	Y	Y	N	Y	Y	N
22 ***Paul***	Y	N	N	Y	N	Y	Y	N
23 Kazen	Y	Y	Y	N	Y	Y	Y	Y
24 Frost	Y	Y	Y	N	Y	Y	?	Y
UTAH								
1 ***Hansen***	Y	N	N	Y	N	Y	Y	N
2 ***Marriott***	Y	N	N	Y	N	Y	Y	N
VERMONT								
AL ***Jeffords***	Y	Y	Y	N	Y	Y	Y	N
VIRGINIA								
1 ***Trible***	Y	N	N	Y	N	Y	Y	N
2 ***Whitehurst***	Y	N	N	Y	N	Y	?	N
3 ***Bliley***	Y	N	N	Y	N	Y	Y	N
4 ***Daniel, R.***	Y	N	N	Y	N	Y	Y	N
5 Daniel, D.	Y	N	N	Y	N	Y	Y	?
6 ***Butler***	?	N	N	Y	N	Y	Y	N
7 ***Robinson***	Y	N	N	Y	N	Y	Y	N
8 ***Parris***	Y	N	N	Y	N	Y	Y	N
9 ***Wampler***	?	X	X	?	X	Y	Y	N
10 ***Wolf***	Y	N	N	Y	N	Y	Y	N
WASHINGTON								
1 ***Pritchard***	Y	Y	#	N	Y	Y	Y	N
2 Swift	Y	Y	Y	N	Y	Y	Y	Y
3 Bonker	?	?	Y	N	Y	Y	Y	Y
4 ***Morrison***	Y	N	N	Y	N	Y	Y	N
5 Foley	?	Y	Y	N	Y	Y	Y	Y
6 Dicks	Y	Y	Y	N	Y	Y	Y	Y
7 Lowry	Y	Y	N	N	Y	N	Y	Y
WEST VIRGINIA								
1 Mollohan	Y	Y	Y	N	?	Y	Y	Y
2 ***Benedict***	Y	N	N	Y	N	Y	Y	N
3 ***Staton***	Y	N	N	Y	N	Y	Y	N
4 Rahall	Y	Y	Y	N	Y	Y	Y	Y
WISCONSIN								
1 Aspin	?	Y	Y	N	Y	?	Y	Y
2 Kastenmeier	Y	Y	Y	N	Y	Y	Y	Y
3 ***Gunderson***	Y	N	N	Y	N	Y	Y	N
4 Zablocki	Y	N	Y	N	Y	Y	Y	Y
5 Reuss	Y	#	#	N	Y	?	?	Y
6 ***Petri***	?	X	X	#	?	?	?	?
7 Obey	Y	Y	Y	N	Y	?	Y	Y
8 ***Roth***	Y	N	N	Y	N	Y	Y	N
9 ***Sensenbrenner***	?	N	N	Y	N	N	Y	N
WYOMING								
AL ***Cheney***	Y	Y	N	Y	N	Y	Y	N

Democrats ***Republicans***

290. Procedural Motion. Foley, D-Wash., motion to adjourn the House. Motion agreed to 188-172: R 0-171; D 188-1 (ND 129-1, SD 59-0), Nov. 17, 1981.

291. Procedural Motion. Walker, R-Pa., motion to approve the House *Journal* of Tuesday, Nov. 17 (first legislative day). Motion agreed to 336-49: R 145-30; D 191-19 (ND 126-15, SD 65-4), Nov. 17, 1981.

292. S 815. Defense Department Authorization. Adoption of the conference report on the bill authorizing $130,696,451,000 for Defense Department programs in fiscal 1982, including weapons procurement, research and development, operations and maintenance, and civil defense. Adopted 335-61: R 168-8; D 167-53 (ND 99-53, SD 68-0), Nov. 17, 1981.

293. HR 4482. Court of Appeals for the Federal Circuit. Kastenmeier, D-Wis., motion to suspend the rules and pass the bill, which creates a new federal court of appeals primarily to handle patent cases. Motion agreed to 321-76: R 120-55; D 201-21 (ND 146-5, SD 55-16), Nov. 18, 1981. A two-thirds majority vote (265 in this case) is required for passage under suspension of the rules.

294. HR 3454. Intelligence Authorization. Adoption of the conference report on the bill authorizing appropriations in secret amounts for U.S. intelligence operations in fiscal 1982. Adopted 379-22: R 176-1; D 203-21 (ND 132-20, SD 71-1), Nov. 18, 1981.

295. HR 4522. District of Columbia Appropriations, Fiscal 1982. Adoption of the conference report on the bill to appropriate $557,170,000 in federal funds and $1,905,258,200 in local funds to the District of Columbia for fiscal 1982. Adopted 228-174: R 58-117; D 170-57 (ND 134-20, SD 36-37), Nov. 18, 1981. (The president had requested $570,170,000 and $1,905,258,200, respectively.)

296. HR 4522. District of Columbia Appropriations, Fiscal 1982. Walker, R-Pa., motion to 1) recede from disagreement with the Senate, and 2) to concur with the Senate position on provisions relating to the salary of the city administrator of the District of Columbia. Motion to recede rejected 186-210: R 59-117; D 127-93 (ND 107-41, SD 20-52), Nov. 18, 1981. (The House later agreed by voice vote to insist on its disagreement with the Senate. The effect of the votes was to deny the administrator a raise.)

297. HR 4995. Defense Department Appropriations, Fiscal 1982. Adoption of H Res 275, waiving certain points of order against the bill to appropriate $196,681,709,000 for Defense Department programs in fiscal 1982. Adopted 398-4: R 174-3; D 224-1 (ND 152-1, SD 72-0), Nov. 18, 1981.

KEY

- **Y** Voted for (yea).
- **#** Paired for.
- **+** Announced for.
- **N** Voted against (nay).
- **X** Paired against.
- **-** Announced against.
- **P** Voted "present".
- **C** Voted "present" to avoid possible conflict of interest.
- **?** Did not vote or otherwise make a position known.

	290	291	292	293	294	295	296	297
ALABAMA								
1 Edwards	N	Y	Y	Y	Y	Y	N	Y
2 Dickinson	N	N	Y	Y	Y	N	Y	Y
3 Nichols	Y	Y	Y	Y	Y	N	N	Y
4 Bevill	Y	Y	Y	N	Y	Y	N	Y
5 Flippo	Y	Y	Y	Y	Y	N	N	Y
6 Smith	N	Y	Y	N	Y	N	N	Y
7 Shelby	Y	N	Y	Y	Y	?	N	Y
ALASKA								
AL Young	N	?	Y	Y	Y	N	N	Y
ARIZONA								
1 Rhodes	N	Y	Y	?	?	?	?	?
2 Udall	?	Y	Y	Y	Y	Y	N	Y
3 Stump	N	Y	Y	N	Y	N	N	Y
4 Rudd	N	Y	Y	Y	Y	N	N	Y
ARKANSAS								
1 Alexander	Y	Y	Y	Y	Y	Y	Y	Y
2 Bethune	N	Y	Y	Y	Y	Y	N	Y
3 Hammerschmidt	N	Y	N	Y	N	N	N	Y
4 Anthony	?	N	Y	Y	Y	Y	N	Y
CALIFORNIA								
1 Chappie	N	Y	Y	Y	Y	N	N	Y
2 Clausen	N	Y	Y	Y	Y	N	N	Y
3 Matsui	?	Y	Y	Y	Y	Y	Y	Y
4 Fazio	Y	Y	Y	Y	Y	Y	Y	Y
5 Burton, J.	?	Y	N	Y	N	Y	Y	Y
6 Burton, P.	Y	Y	N	Y	N	Y	Y	Y
7 Miller	Y	Y	Y	Y	Y	Y	Y	Y
8 Dellums	Y	?	N	?	N	Y	Y	Y
9 Stark	Y	Y	N	Y	N	Y	Y	Y
10 Edwards	Y	Y	N	Y	Y	Y	Y	Y
11 Lantos	Y	Y	Y	Y	Y	Y	N	Y
12 McCloskey	?	?	?	?	?	?	?	?
13 Mineta	Y	Y	Y	Y	Y	Y	Y	Y
14 Shumway	N	Y	Y	Y	Y	N	N	Y
15 Coelho	Y	Y	Y	Y	Y	Y	Y	?
16 Panetta	Y	Y	Y	Y	Y	Y	N	Y
17 Pashayan	N	Y	Y	?	Y	N	Y	Y
18 Thomas	N	Y	N	Y	N	Y	N	Y
19 Lagomarsino	N	Y	Y	Y	Y	N	N	Y
20 Goldwater	?	?	?	?	?	?	?	?
21 Fiedler	N	Y	Y	Y	Y	N	N	Y
22 Moorhead	N	Y	Y	Y	Y	N	N	Y
23 Beilenson	Y	Y	N	Y	Y	Y	Y	Y
24 Waxman	Y	Y	Y	Y	Y	Y	?	Y
25 Roybal	Y	Y	N	Y	Y	Y	Y	Y
26 Rousselot	N	Y	Y	Y	Y	N	N	Y
27 Dornan	?	?	?	?	?	X	?	?
28 Dixon	Y	Y	Y	Y	Y	Y	Y	Y
29 Hawkins	?	N	Y	Y	Y	#	Y	Y
30 Danielson	Y	Y	Y	+	?	Y	?	Y
31 Dymally	Y	Y	Y	Y	Y	Y	Y	Y
32 Anderson	Y	Y	Y	N	Y	Y	Y	Y
33 Grisham	N	Y	Y	Y	Y	Y	N	Y
34 Lungren	N	Y	Y	Y	Y	N	N	Y
35 Dreier	N	N	Y	Y	Y	N	N	Y
36 Brown	Y	Y	N	Y	Y	Y	Y	Y
37 Lewis	N	Y	Y	N	Y	N	Y	Y
38 Patterson	Y	Y	Y	Y	Y	Y	Y	Y
39 Dannemeyer	N	N	Y	Y	Y	N	N	N
40 Badham	N	Y	Y	N	Y	N	N	Y
41 Lowery	N	Y	Y	?	Y	N	Y	Y
42 Hunter	N	Y	Y	Y	Y	N	N	Y
43 Burgener	N	Y	Y	Y	Y	Y	Y	Y
COLORADO								
1 Schroeder	Y	Y	N	Y	Y	N	N	Y
2 Wirth	Y	Y	Y	Y	Y	Y	Y	Y
3 Kogovsek	Y	Y	Y	Y	Y	Y	Y	Y
4 Brown	N	N	N	N	Y	N	N	N
5 Kramer	N	Y	Y	Y	Y	N	N	Y
CONNECTICUT								
1 Vacancy								
2 Gejdenson	Y	N	Y	Y	Y	Y	Y	Y
3 DeNardis	N	Y	Y	Y	Y	Y	Y	Y
4 McKinney	N	?	Y	Y	Y	Y	Y	Y
5 Ratchford	Y	Y	Y	Y	Y	Y	Y	Y
6 Moffett	?	?	N	Y	Y	Y	Y	
DELAWARE								
AL Evans	N	Y	Y	Y	Y	Y	?	?
FLORIDA								
1 Hutto	Y	Y	Y	Y	Y	Y	N	Y
2 Fuqua	?	Y	Y	Y	Y	N	N	Y
3 Bennett	Y	Y	N	Y	N	N	N	Y
4 Chappell	Y	Y	Y	N	Y	N	N	Y
5 McCollum	N	Y	Y	Y	Y	N	N	Y
6 Young	?	Y	Y	Y	Y	N	N	Y
7 Gibbons	Y	Y	Y	Y	Y	N	N	Y
8 Ireland	?	Y	Y	Y	Y	N	N	Y
9 Nelson	Y	Y	Y	Y	Y	N	N	Y
10 Bafalis	?	Y	Y	Y	Y	N	N	Y
11 Mica	Y	Y	Y	N	Y	N	N	Y
12 Shaw	N	Y	Y	Y	Y	N	N	Y
13 Lehman	Y	Y	Y	Y	Y	Y	Y	Y
14 Pepper	Y	?	Y	Y	Y	Y	Y	Y
15 Fascell	Y	Y	Y	Y	Y	Y	Y	Y
GEORGIA								
1 Ginn	?	?	#	Y	Y	N	N	Y
2 Hatcher	Y	Y	Y	Y	Y	N	N	Y
3 Brinkley	Y	Y	Y	Y	Y	Y	Y	Y
4 Levitas	?	Y	Y	Y	Y	Y	N	Y
5 Fowler	?	Y	Y	Y	Y	N	N	Y
6 Gingrich	N	Y	N	Y	Y	Y	Y	Y
7 McDonald	?	?	+	-	+	X	X	+
8 Evans	Y	N	Y	N	Y	Y	N	Y
9 Jenkins	Y	Y	Y	Y	Y	N	N	Y
10 Barnard	?	?	?	Y	Y	N	N	Y
HAWAII								
1 Heftel	?	Y	Y	Y	Y	Y	Y	?
2 Akaka	Y	Y	Y	Y	Y	Y	Y	Y
IDAHO								
1 Craig	N	Y	Y	N	Y	N	N	Y
2 Hansen	N	Y	Y	N	Y	N	N	Y
ILLINOIS								
1 Washington	Y	Y	N	Y	Y	Y	Y	Y
2 Savage	?	?	N	Y	N	Y	Y	?
3 Russo	?	N	N	Y	Y	N	Y	Y
4 Derwinski	N	Y	Y	Y	Y	N	N	Y
5 Fary	Y	Y	Y	Y	Y	Y	Y	Y
6 Hyde	N	Y	Y	Y	Y	Y	Y	Y
7 Collins	Y	N	Y	N	Y	Y	Y	?
8 Rostenkowski	?	?	Y	Y	Y	Y	Y	Y
9 Yates	Y	N	Y	Y	Y	Y	Y	Y
10 Porter	N	Y	Y	Y	Y	Y	Y	Y
11 Annunzio	Y	Y	Y	Y	Y	Y	Y	Y
12 Crane, P.	N	Y	N	Y	N	N	N	N
13 McClory	N	Y	Y	Y	Y	Y	Y	Y
14 Erlenborn	N	Y	Y	Y	Y	Y	Y	Y
15 Corcoran	N	Y	Y	Y	Y	N	N	Y
16 Martin	N	Y	Y	Y	Y	N	N	Y
17 O'Brien	N	Y	Y	Y	Y	Y	Y	Y
18 Michel	N	Y	Y	?	Y	Y	N	Y
19 Railsback	N	Y	Y	Y	Y	N	?	Y
20 Findley	N	Y	Y	Y	N	Y	N	Y
21 Madigan	N	?	?	?	?	?	?	?
22 Crane, D.	N	N	N	Y	N	N	N	Y
23 Price	Y	Y	Y	Y	Y	Y	Y	Y
24 Simon	Y	Y	Y	Y	Y	Y	Y	Y
INDIANA								
1 Benjamin	Y	Y	Y	Y	Y	Y	Y	Y
2 Fithian	?	?	?	?	Y	Y	Y	Y
3 Hiler	N	N	N	Y	N	N	N	Y
4 Coats	N	N	Y	Y	Y	N	N	Y
5 Hillis	N	Y	Y	Y	N	Y	N	Y
6 Evans	Y	Y	Y	Y	Y	Y	Y	Y
7 Myers	N	Y	N	Y	Y	Y	N	Y
8 Deckard	N	Y	Y	Y	Y	?	?	Y
9 Hamilton	Y	Y	Y	Y	Y	N	N	Y
10 Sharp	Y	Y	Y	Y	Y	Y	N	Y
11 Jacobs	?	N	Y	N	Y	Y	N	Y
IOWA								
1 Leach	N	Y	Y	Y	Y	N	Y	Y
2 Tauke	N	Y	N	N	N	Y	N	Y
3 Evans	N	N	Y	Y	N	Y	N	Y
4 Smith	Y	Y	Y	Y	Y	Y	N	Y
5 Harkin	Y	N	Y	N	Y	Y	N	Y
6 Bedell	?	?	?	?	?	?	?	?

Democrats *Republicans*

	290	291	292	293	294	295	296	297
KANSAS								
1 ***Roberts***	N	Y	Y	Y	Y	N	N	Y
2 ***Jeffries***	N	Y	Y	N	Y	N	N	Y
3 ***Winn***	N	Y	Y	Y	Y	N	N	Y
4 Glickman	Y	Y	Y	Y	Y	N	N	Y
5 ***Whittaker***	N	Y	Y	Y	Y	N	Y	Y
KENTUCKY								
1 Hubbard	Y	Y	Y	Y	Y	Y	N	Y
2 Natcher	Y	Y	Y	Y	Y	Y	Y	Y
3 Mazzoli	Y	Y	Y	Y	?	?	?	?
4 ***Snyder***	N	Y	Y	N	Y	N	N	Y
5 ***Rogers***	N	Y	Y	Y	Y	N	N	Y
6 ***Hopkins***	N	Y	Y	N	Y	Y	N	Y
7 Perkins	Y	Y	Y	Y	Y	Y	Y	Y
LOUISIANA								
1 ***Livingston***	N	Y	Y	Y	Y	N	N	Y
2 Boggs	Y	Y	?	Y	Y	Y	Y	Y
3 Tauzin	Y	Y	Y	Y	Y	N	N	Y
4 Roemer	Y	Y	Y	N	Y	N	N	Y
5 Huckaby	?	Y	Y	Y	Y	N	N	Y
6 ***Moore***	N	Y	Y	Y	Y	N	N	Y
7 Breaux	?	?	#	#	?	X	X	?
8 Long	Y	Y	Y	Y	Y	Y	N	Y
MAINE								
1 ***Emery***	N	Y	Y	Y	Y	N	N	Y
2 ***Snowe***	N	Y	Y	Y	Y	Y	N	Y
MARYLAND								
1 Dyson	Y	Y	Y	Y	Y	N	N	Y
2 Long	Y	Y	Y	Y	Y	Y	Y	Y
3 Mikulski	?	Y	N	Y	Y	Y	N	Y
4 ***Holt***	N	Y	Y	N	Y	N	Y	Y
5 Hoyer	Y	Y	Y	Y	Y	Y	Y	Y
6 Byron	Y	Y	Y	Y	Y	N	N	Y
7 Mitchell	Y	N	N	Y	N	Y	Y	Y
8 Barnes	?	N	Y	Y	Y	Y	Y	Y
MASSACHUSETTS								
1 ***Conte***	N	Y	Y	Y	Y	Y	Y	Y
2 Boland	Y	Y	Y	Y	Y	Y	Y	Y
3 Early	?	?	?	Y	Y	N	Y	Y
4 Frank	Y	Y	N	Y	Y	Y	Y	Y
5 Shannon	?	Y	Y	Y	Y	Y	Y	Y
6 Mavroules	Y	Y	Y	Y	Y	Y	Y	Y
7 Markey	Y	Y	N	Y	Y	Y	Y	Y
8 O'Neill								
9 Moakley	Y	Y	Y	Y	Y	Y	Y	Y
10 ***Heckler***	N	Y	Y	Y	Y	N	Y	Y
11 Donnelly	Y	Y	Y	Y	Y	Y	Y	Y
12 Studds	Y	Y	N	Y	Y	Y	Y	Y
MICHIGAN								
1 Conyers	Y	N	N	Y	N	Y	Y	Y
2 ***Pursell***	N	Y	N	Y	Y	Y	Y	Y
3 Wolpe	Y	Y	N	Y	Y	Y	Y	Y
4 ***Siljander***	N	Y	Y	Y	Y	N	N	Y
5 ***Sawyer***	?	Y	Y	Y	Y	N	N	Y
6 ***Dunn***	N	N	Y	Y	Y	Y	Y	Y
7 Kildee	Y	Y	N	Y	Y	Y	Y	Y
8 Traxler	Y	Y	Y	?	Y	Y	?	Y
9 ***Vander Jagt***	?	?	?	?	?	Y	N	Y
10 Albosta	Y	Y	Y	Y	Y	N	N	Y
11 ***Davis***	N	N	N	Y	Y	Y	N	Y
12 Bonior	?	?	N	Y	Y	Y	Y	Y
13 Crockett	?	?	N	Y	N	Y	Y	Y
14 Hertel	Y	Y	N	Y	Y	Y	Y	Y
15 Ford	Y	?	N	?	?	?	?	N
16 Dingell	?	?	#	Y	Y	Y	?	Y
17 Brodhead	?	N	N	Y	Y	Y	Y	Y
18 Blanchard	Y	Y	N	Y	Y	Y	Y	Y
19 ***Broomfield***	N	Y	Y	N	Y	N	N	Y
MINNESOTA								
1 ***Erdahl***	N	Y	Y	Y	Y	Y	N	Y
2 ***Hagedorn***	?	?	?	?	?	?	?	?
3 ***Frenzel***	N	Y	Y	Y	Y	N	Y	Y
4 Vento	Y	N	N	Y	Y	Y	Y	Y
5 Sabo	Y	N	N	Y	Y	Y	Y	Y
6 ***Weber***	N	N	Y	N	Y	N	N	Y
7 ***Stangeland***	N	Y	Y	N	Y	N	N	Y
8 Oberstar	Y	Y	N	Y	Y	Y	N	Y
MISSISSIPPI								
1 Whitten	Y	Y	Y	Y	Y	N	?	Y
2 Bowen	Y	Y	Y	Y	Y	N	N	Y
3 Montgomery	?	Y	Y	N	Y	N	N	Y
4 Dowdy	Y	Y	Y	N	Y	N	N	Y
5 ***Lott***	N	Y	Y	Y	Y	N	N	Y
MISSOURI								
1 Clay	?	?	N	Y	N	Y	Y	Y
2 Young	Y	Y	Y	Y	#	Y	N	Y
3 Gephardt	Y	Y	Y	N	Y	Y	N	Y
4 Skelton	Y	Y	Y	Y	Y	N	N	Y
5 Bolling	?	?	?	?	?	?	?	?
6 ***Coleman***	?	?	?	Y	Y	N	N	Y
7 ***Taylor***	N	Y	Y	Y	Y	N	N	Y
8 ***Bailey***	?	Y	Y	N	Y	N	N	Y
9 Volkmer	Y	?	?	Y	Y	N	N	Y
10 ***Emerson***	N	N	Y	N	Y	N	N	Y
MONTANA								
1 Williams	?	?	N	Y	Y	Y	?	Y
2 ***Marlenee***	N	Y	Y	Y	Y	N	N	Y
NEBRASKA								
1 ***Bereuter***	?	Y	Y	Y	Y	N	Y	Y
2 ***Daub***	N	N	Y	Y	Y	N	N	Y
3 ***Smith***	N	Y	N	Y	Y	N	N	Y
NEVADA								
AL Santini	Y	Y	Y	?	?	N	?	Y
NEW HAMPSHIRE								
1 D'Amours	Y	Y	Y	Y	Y	Y	N	Y
2 ***Gregg***	N	N	Y	N	Y	N	Y	Y
NEW JERSEY								
1 Florio	Y	Y	Y	Y	Y	Y	Y	Y
2 Hughes	Y	Y	Y	Y	Y	N	N	Y
3 Howard	Y	Y	Y	Y	Y	Y	Y	Y
4 ***Smith***	N	Y	Y	Y	Y	N	N	Y
5 ***Fenwick***	N	Y	N	Y	Y	N	N	Y
6 ***Forsythe***	?	?	?	?	?	X	?	?
7 ***Roukema***	N	Y	Y	Y	Y	N	N	Y
8 Roe	Y	Y	Y	Y	Y	Y	?	Y
9 ***Hollenbeck***	?	Y	N	Y	Y	Y	Y	Y
10 Rodino	Y	Y	N	Y	N	Y	Y	Y
11 Minish	Y	Y	Y	Y	Y	Y	N	Y
12 ***Rinaldo***	?	Y	Y	Y	Y	N	N	Y
13 ***Courter***	N	Y	Y	Y	Y	N	N	Y
14 Guarini	?	Y	Y	Y	Y	Y	Y	Y
15 Dwyer	Y	Y	Y	Y	Y	Y	Y	Y
NEW MEXICO								
1 ***Lujan***	N	Y	Y	N	Y	N	N	Y
2 ***Skeen***	N	Y	Y	Y	Y	Y	N	Y
NEW YORK								
1 ***Carney***	N	Y	Y	N	Y	Y	Y	Y
2 Downey	Y	Y	Y	Y	Y	Y	Y	Y
3 ***Carman***	?	Y	Y	Y	Y	Y	N	Y
4 ***Lent***	N	Y	Y	Y	Y	Y	Y	Y
5 ***McGrath***	N	Y	Y	Y	Y	Y	Y	Y
6 ***LeBoutillier***	N	Y	?	Y	Y	Y	N	Y
7 Addabbo	Y	Y	Y	Y	Y	Y	Y	Y
8 Rosenthal	Y	Y	Y	Y	Y	Y	Y	Y
9 Ferraro	Y	Y	Y	Y	Y	Y	Y	Y
10 Biaggi	Y	Y	Y	Y	Y	Y	N	Y
11 Scheuer	Y	Y	Y	Y	N	Y	Y	Y
12 Chisholm	?	?	X	?	X	#	#	?
13 Solarz	Y	Y	Y	Y	Y	Y	Y	Y
14 Richmond	?	?	?	Y	N	#	Y	Y
15 Zeferetti	Y	Y	Y	Y	Y	Y	N	Y
16 Schumer	Y	Y	Y	Y	Y	Y	Y	Y
17 ***Molinari***	N	Y	Y	Y	Y	Y	Y	Y
18 ***Green***	N	Y	Y	N	Y	#	Y	Y
19 Rangel	?	Y	N	?	N	Y	Y	Y
20 Weiss	Y	Y	N	Y	N	Y	Y	Y
21 Garcia	Y	Y	N	Y	N	Y	Y	Y
22 Bingham	Y	Y	N	Y	Y	Y	Y	Y
23 Peyser	Y	Y	Y	Y	Y	Y	Y	Y
24 Ottinger	Y	P	N	Y	Y	Y	Y	Y
25 ***Fish***	N	Y	Y	Y	Y	N	Y	Y
26 ***Gilman***	-	Y	Y	Y	Y	N	Y	Y
27 McHugh	Y	Y	Y	Y	Y	Y	Y	Y
28 Stratton	Y	Y	Y	Y	Y	Y	N	Y
29 ***Solomon***	N	N	Y	N	Y	N	N	Y
30 ***Martin***	?	?	?	?	?	?	?	?
31 ***Mitchell***	N	Y	Y	N	Y	Y	Y	Y
32 ***Wortley***	N	N	Y	Y	Y	Y	Y	Y
33 ***Lee***	?	Y	Y	N	Y	Y	N	Y
34 ***Horton***	N	Y	Y	Y	Y	Y	Y	Y
35 ***Conable***	N	N	Y	N	Y	N	Y	Y
36 LaFalce	Y	Y	Y	Y	Y	Y	Y	Y
37 Nowak	Y	Y	Y	Y	Y	Y	Y	Y
38 ***Kemp***	N	Y	Y	Y	Y	N	Y	Y
39 Lundine	Y	Y	Y	Y	Y	Y	Y	Y
NORTH CAROLINA								
1 Jones	Y	Y	Y	Y	Y	Y	?	?
2 Fountain	Y	Y	Y	N	Y	N	N	Y
3 Whitley	Y	Y	Y	Y	Y	N	N	Y
4 Andrews	Y	?	Y	Y	Y	N	Y	Y
5 Neal	Y	Y	Y	?	?	Y	N	Y
6 ***Johnston***	N	?	?	?	?	?	?	?
7 Rose	Y	?	Y	Y	Y	Y	Y	Y
8 Hefner	?	Y	Y	Y	Y	Y	N	Y
9 ***Martin***	?	?	?	Y	Y	N	Y	Y
10 ***Broyhill***	N	Y	Y	Y	Y	N	N	Y
11 ***Hendon***	N	Y	Y	N	Y	N	N	Y
NORTH DAKOTA								
AL Dorgan	Y	Y	N	Y	Y	Y	Y	Y
OHIO								
1 ***Gradison***	N	Y	Y	Y	Y	Y	Y	Y
2 Luken	Y	Y	Y	Y	Y	N	Y	Y
3 Hall	Y	Y	Y	Y	Y	N	Y	Y
4 ***Oxley***	N	Y	Y	N	Y	N	N	Y
5 ***Latta***	N	N	Y	N	Y	N	N	Y
6 ***McEwen***	N	Y	Y	Y	Y	N	N	Y
7 ***Brown***	N	?	?	Y	Y	N	N	Y
8 ***Kindness***	N	N	Y	Y	Y	Y	N	Y
9 ***Weber***	N	N	Y	Y	Y	Y	Y	Y
10 ***Miller***	N	N	Y	N	Y	N	N	Y
11 ***Stanton***	N	Y	Y	Y	Y	Y	Y	Y
12 Shamansky	Y	Y	Y	Y	Y	Y	N	Y
13 Pease	?	Y	Y	Y	Y	Y	Y	Y
14 Seiberling	Y	Y	N	Y	N	Y	?	?
15 ***Wylie***	N	Y	Y	N	Y	Y	N	Y
16 ***Regula***	N	Y	Y	Y	Y	Y	N	Y
17 ***Ashbrook***	N	Y	Y	Y	Y	N	N	Y
18 Applegate	?	?	Y	Y	Y	N	N	Y
19 ***Williams***	?	Y	Y	Y	Y	Y	N	Y
20 Oakar	Y	Y	Y	Y	Y	Y	Y	Y
21 Stokes	Y	Y	N	Y	N	Y	Y	Y
22 Eckart	Y	Y	Y	Y	Y	Y	N	Y
23 Mottl	Y	Y	Y	N	Y	N	N	Y
OKLAHOMA								
1 Jones	Y	Y	Y	N	Y	Y	N	Y
2 Synar	Y	Y	Y	Y	Y	Y	N	Y
3 Watkins	Y	Y	?	Y	Y	N	N	Y
4 McCurdy	Y	Y	Y	Y	Y	N	N	Y
5 ***Edwards***	N	Y	Y	N	Y	N	N	Y
6 English	Y	Y	Y	N	Y	N	N	Y
OREGON								
1 AuCoin	Y	?	X	Y	?	N	Y	Y
2 ***Smith***	N	Y	Y	N	Y	N	N	Y
3 Wyden	Y	Y	N	Y	Y	Y	Y	Y
4 Weaver	Y	Y	N	Y	N	?	N	Y
PENNSYLVANIA								
1 Foglietta	?	Y	Y	Y	Y	Y	Y	Y
2 Gray	Y	Y	N	?	?	Y	Y	Y
3 Smith	Y	Y	Y	Y	Y	Y	Y	Y
4 ***Dougherty***	N	Y	Y	?	?	?	?	?
5 ***Schulze***	N	Y	Y	Y	Y	N	N	Y
6 Yatron	Y	Y	Y	Y	Y	Y	N	Y
7 Edgar	Y	N	N	Y	Y	Y	Y	Y
8 ***Coyne, J.***	N	N	Y	N	Y	Y	Y	Y
9 ***Shuster***	N	Y	Y	N	Y	N	N	Y
10 ***McDade***	N	Y	Y	Y	Y	Y	Y	Y
11 ***Nelligan***	N	Y	Y	Y	Y	N	N	Y
12 Murtha	Y	Y	Y	Y	Y	Y	Y	Y
13 ***Coughlin***	N	N	Y	Y	Y	Y	Y	Y
14 Coyne, W.	Y	Y	Y	Y	Y	Y	Y	Y
15 ***Ritter***	N	Y	Y	Y	?	?	N	Y
16 ***Walker***	N	N	Y	N	Y	N	N	Y
17 Ertel	Y	Y	Y	Y	Y	N	N	Y
18 Walgren	Y	Y	Y	Y	Y	Y	N	Y
19 ***Goodling***	N	?	Y	N	Y	N	N	?
20 Gaydos	Y	Y	Y	Y	Y	Y	Y	Y
21 Bailey	?	Y	Y	Y	Y	Y	?	Y
22 Murphy	?	?	Y	Y	Y	Y	Y	Y
23 ***Clinger***	N	N	Y	Y	Y	Y	N	Y
24 ***Marks***	N	Y	Y	N	Y	Y	Y	Y
25 ***Atkinson***	N	Y	Y	Y	Y	Y	N	Y
RHODE ISLAND								
1 St Germain	Y	P	Y	Y	Y	Y	N	Y
2 ***Schneider***	N	Y	Y	Y	Y	Y	N	Y
SOUTH CAROLINA								
1 ***Hartnett***	N	N	Y	N	Y	Y	N	Y
2 ***Spence***	N	Y	Y	Y	Y	N	N	Y
3 Derrick	Y	Y	Y	Y	Y	Y	N	Y
4 ***Campbell***	N	N	Y	Y	Y	N	N	Y
5 Holland	?	Y	Y	Y	Y	Y	Y	Y
6 ***Napier***	N	Y	Y	Y	Y	N	N	Y
SOUTH DAKOTA								
1 Daschle	Y	Y	Y	?	Y	Y	Y	Y
2 ***Roberts***	N	N	Y	N	Y	N	N	Y
TENNESSEE								
1 ***Quillen***	N	Y	Y	Y	Y	N	N	Y
2 ***Duncan***	N	?	?	?	?	X	?	?
3 Bouquard	Y	Y	Y	Y	Y	N	N	Y
4 Gore	Y	Y	Y	Y	Y	Y	N	Y
5 Boner	Y	Y	Y	Y	Y	N	N	Y
6 ***Beard***	N	Y	?	?	?	?	N	Y
7 Jones	Y	Y	Y	Y	Y	N	N	Y
8 Ford	?	N	X	?	N	Y	Y	Y
TEXAS								
1 Hall, S.	Y	Y	Y	Y	Y	N	N	Y
2 Wilson	Y	Y	Y	Y	Y	Y	Y	Y
3 ***Collins***	N	Y	Y	N	Y	N	N	Y
4 Hall, R.	Y	Y	Y	Y	Y	N	N	Y
5 Mattox	?	?	?	#	?	?	?	?
6 Gramm	Y	Y	Y	?	Y	N	N	Y
7 ***Archer***	N	Y	Y	N	Y	N	N	Y
8 ***Fields***	N	Y	Y	N	Y	N	N	Y
9 Brooks	?	?	?	N	Y	Y	N	Y
10 Pickle	?	Y	Y	Y	Y	Y	N	Y
11 Leath	Y	Y	Y	Y	Y	N	N	Y
12 Wright	?	Y	?	?	Y	Y	N	Y
13 Hightower	Y	Y	Y	N	Y	N	N	Y
14 Patman	Y	Y	Y	N	Y	N	Y	Y
15 de la Garza	Y	Y	Y	Y	Y	Y	N	?
16 White	Y	Y	Y	Y	Y	Y	Y	Y
17 Stenholm	Y	Y	Y	N	Y	N	N	Y
18 Leland	?	?	X	?	X	#	#	?
19 Hance	?	Y	Y	N	Y	N	Y	Y
20 Gonzalez	Y	Y	Y	Y	Y	Y	Y	Y
21 ***Loeffler***	N	Y	Y	Y	Y	N	N	Y
22 ***Paul***	N	N	N	N	N	N	N	Y
23 Kazen	Y	Y	Y	Y	Y	N	N	Y
24 Frost	Y	Y	Y	Y	Y	Y	N	Y
UTAH								
1 ***Hansen***	N	Y	Y	N	Y	N	N	Y
2 ***Marriott***	N	Y	Y	Y	Y	Y	N	Y
VERMONT								
AL ***Jeffords***	N	Y	Y	Y	Y	Y	Y	Y
VIRGINIA								
1 ***Trible***	N	Y	Y	Y	Y	Y	Y	Y
2 ***Whitehurst***	N	Y	Y	Y	Y	N	Y	Y
3 ***Bliley***	N	Y	Y	Y	Y	Y	Y	Y
4 ***Daniel, R.***	N	Y	Y	Y	Y	N	N	Y
5 Daniel, D.	Y	Y	Y	Y	#	N	N	Y
6 ***Butler***	N	Y	Y	Y	Y	N	Y	Y
7 ***Robinson***	N	Y	Y	Y	Y	N	N	Y
8 ***Parris***	N	N	Y	Y	Y	Y	Y	Y
9 ***Wampler***	N	Y	Y	N	Y	X	?	?
10 ***Wolf***	N	Y	Y	Y	Y	Y	Y	Y
WASHINGTON								
1 ***Pritchard***	N	?	?	?	?	#	?	?
2 Swift	Y	Y	Y	Y	Y	Y	Y	Y
3 Bonker	Y	Y	Y	Y	Y	Y	N	Y
4 ***Morrison***	N	Y	Y	Y	Y	N	N	Y
5 Foley	Y	Y	Y	Y	Y	?	N	Y
6 Dicks	Y	Y	Y	Y	Y	N	N	Y
7 Lowry	Y	N	N	Y	Y	Y	Y	Y
WEST VIRGINIA								
1 Mollohan	Y	Y	Y	Y	Y	Y	N	Y
2 ***Benedict***	N	Y	Y	Y	Y	N	N	Y
3 ***Staton***	N	Y	Y	N	Y	N	N	Y
4 Rahall	Y	Y	#	Y	Y	Y	N	Y
WISCONSIN								
1 Aspin	Y	N	Y	Y	?	Y	Y	Y
2 Kastenmeier	Y	Y	N	Y	N	Y	Y	Y
3 ***Gunderson***	N	Y	Y	Y	Y	Y	Y	Y
4 Zablocki	Y	Y	Y	Y	Y	Y	Y	Y
5 Reuss	Y	Y	N	Y	Y	Y	Y	Y
6 ***Petri***	?	Y	Y	N	Y	N	N	Y
7 Obey	Y	Y	N	Y	Y	N	P	Y
8 ***Roth***	N	Y	Y	N	Y	N	N	Y
9 ***Sensenbrenner***	N	Y	Y	N	Y	N	N	Y
WYOMING								
AL ***Cheney***	N	Y	Y	Y	Y	N	N	Y

Democrats ***Republicans***

298. HR 4995. Defense Department Appropriations, Fiscal 1982. Murtha, D-Pa., substitute for the Addabbo, D-N.Y., amendment, to delete $1.799 billion for Air Force procurement intended for the B-1 bomber. (Although not stated in the amendment, Murtha intended to shift funding to the FB-111 bomber.) Rejected 99-307: R 9-169; D 90-138 (ND 82-72, SD 8-66), Nov. 18, 1981. A "nay" was a vote supporting the president's position. (The Addabbo amendment, to delete $1.801 billion for the B-1 bomber, subsequently was rejected (see vote 299, below).)

299. HR 4995. Defense Department Appropriations, Fiscal 1982. Addabbo, D-N.Y., amendment to delete $1.801 billion from Air Force procurement intended for the B-1 bomber. Rejected 142-263: R 21-157; D 121-106 (ND 111-42, SD 10-64), Nov. 18, 1981. A "nay" was a vote supporting the president's position.

300. HR 4995. Defense Department Appropriations, Fiscal 1982. Addabbo, D-N.Y., amendment to delete $1,913,200,000 in Air Force research, development, test and evaluation funds for the MX missile and basing system. Rejected 139-264: R 27-151; D 112-113 (ND 103-48, SD 9-65), Nov. 18, 1981. A "nay" was a vote supporting the president's position.

301. HR 4995. Defense Department Appropriations, Fiscal 1982. Moffett, D-Conn., amendment to the Schroeder, D-Colo., amendment to cut 2 percent from the funds appropriated in the bill for weapons procurement and for research, development, test and evaluation. Exempted from the cut were funds for procurement of spare parts. Rejected 140-256: R 20-158; D 120-98 (ND 108-39, SD 12-59), Nov. 18, 1981. A "nay" was a vote supporting the president's position. (The Schroeder amendment, to cut 5 percent from the funds appropriated in the bill, subsequently was rejected by voice vote.)

302. HR 4995. Defense Department Appropriations, Fiscal 1982. Roukema, R-N.J., substitute for the Schroeder, D-Colo., amendment to cut 2 percent from the funds appropriated in the bill for weapons procurement and for research, development, test and evaluation. Exempted from the cut were funds for procurement of spare parts, repair parts and ammunition. Rejected 197-202: R 65-114; D 132-88 (ND 117-31, SD 15-57), Nov. 18, 1981. A "nay" was a vote supporting the president's position. (The Schroeder amendment, to cut 5 percent from the funds appropriated in the bill, subsequently was rejected by voice vote.)

303. HR 4995. Defense Department Appropriations, Fiscal 1982. Passage of the bill to appropriate $197,443,289,000 for Department of Defense programs in fiscal 1982. Passed 335-61: R 172-7; D 163-54 (ND 93-52, SD 70-2), Nov. 18, 1981. (The president had requested $200,878,234,000.)

KEY

- Y   Voted for (yea).
- #   Paired for.
- +   Announced for.
- N   Voted against (nay).
- X   Paired against.
- -   Announced against.
- P   Voted "present".
- C   Voted "present" to avoid possible conflict of interest.
- ?   Did not vote or otherwise make a position known.

	298	299	300	301	302	303
ALABAMA						
1 Edwards	N	N	N	N	N	Y
2 Dickinson	N	N	N	N	N	Y
3 Nichols	N	N	N	N	N	Y
4 Bevill	N	N	N	N	N	Y
5 Flippo	N	N	N	N	N	Y
6 Smith	N	N	N	N	N	Y
7 Shelby	N	N	N	N	N	Y
ALASKA						
AL Young	N	N	N	N	N	Y
ARIZONA						
1 Rhodes	?	?	X	X	X	?
2 Udall	Y	Y	N	N	N	Y
3 Stump	N	N	N	N	N	Y
4 Rudd	N	N	N	N	N	Y
ARKANSAS						
1 Alexander	N	N	N	?	?	?
2 Bethune	N	N	N	?	N	Y
3 Hammerschmidt	N	N	N	N	N	Y
4 Anthony	N	N	N	N	N	Y
CALIFORNIA						
1 Chappie	N	N	N	N	N	Y
2 Clausen	N	N	N	N	N	Y
3 Matsui	Y	N	N	N	N	Y
4 Fazio	Y	Y	N	N	N	Y
5 Burton, J.	Y	Y	Y	?	Y	N
6 Burton, P.	N	Y	Y	Y	Y	X
7 Miller	Y	Y	Y	Y	Y	N
8 Dellums	N	Y	Y	Y	Y	N
9 Stark	Y	Y	Y	Y	Y	N
10 Edwards	Y	Y	Y	Y	Y	N
11 Lantos	N	Y	Y	N	Y	Y
12 McCloskey	?	?	?	?	?	?
13 Mineta	Y	Y	Y	N	Y	Y
14 Shumway	N	N	N	N	N	Y
15 Coelho	N	N	Y	Y	Y	Y
16 Panetta	N	Y	Y	N	N	Y
17 Pashayan	N	N	N	N	N	Y
18 Thomas	N	N	N	N	N	Y
19 Lagomarsino	N	N	N	N	N	Y
20 Goldwater	?	?	?	?	?	?
21 Fiedler	N	N	N	N	N	Y
22 Moorhead	N	N	N	N	N	Y
23 Beilenson	N	Y	Y	?	?	X
24 Waxman	Y	Y	Y	Y	Y	Y
25 Roybal	N	Y	Y	N	N	Y
26 Rousselot	N	N	N	N	Y	Y
27 Dornan	?	?	?	X	X	?
28 Dixon	?	X	#	#	#	?
29 Hawkins	N	Y	Y	Y	Y	Y
30 Danielson	N	N	Y	Y	Y	Y
31 Dymally	N	N	?	?	?	?
32 Anderson	N	N	N	Y	Y	Y
33 Grisham	-	-	-	-	-	+
34 Lungren	N	N	N	N	N	Y
35 Dreier	N	N	N	N	N	Y
36 Brown	N	Y	Y	Y	Y	N
37 Lewis	N	N	N	N	N	Y
38 Patterson	Y	N	Y	?	?	?
39 Dannemeyer	N	N	N	N	Y	Y
40 Badham	N	N	N	N	N	Y
41 Lowery	N	N	N	N	N	Y
42 Hunter	N	N	N	N	N	Y
43 Burgener	N	N	N	N	N	Y
COLORADO						
1 Schroeder	Y	Y	Y	Y	Y	N
2 Wirth	N	Y	Y	N	Y	Y
3 Kogovsek	Y	Y	N	Y	Y	Y
4 Brown	Y	Y	N	Y	Y	N
5 Kramer	N	N	N	N	N	Y
CONNECTICUT						
1 Vacancy						
2 Gejdenson	Y	Y	Y	Y	N	Y
3 DeNardis	Y	Y	Y	N	Y	Y
4 McKinney	Y	Y	Y	Y	Y	Y
5 Ratchford	Y	Y	Y	Y	Y	Y
6 Moffett	Y	Y	Y	Y	Y	N
DELAWARE						
AL Evans	N	N	N	N	Y	Y
FLORIDA						
1 Hutto	N	N	N	N	N	Y
2 Fuqua	N	N	N	N	N	Y
3 Bennett	N	N	N	N	N	Y
4 Chappell	N	N	N	N	N	Y
5 McCollum	N	N	N	N	N	Y
6 Young	N	N	N	N	N	Y
7 Gibbons	Y	N	N	N	N	Y
8 Ireland	N	N	N	N	N	Y
9 Nelson	N	N	N	N	N	Y
10 Bafalis	N	N	N	N	N	Y
11 Mica	N	N	N	N	N	Y
12 Shaw	N	N	N	N	N	Y
13 Lehman	Y	Y	Y	Y	N	Y
14 Pepper	?	X	X	X	X	#
15 Fascell	N	Y	Y	Y	Y	Y
GEORGIA						
1 Ginn	N	N	N	N	N	N
2 Hatcher	N	N	N	N	N	Y
3 Brinkley	N	N	N	N	N	Y
4 Levitas	N	N	N	Y	Y	Y
5 Fowler	N	Y	Y	N	Y	Y
6 Gingrich	N	N	N	N	Y	Y
7 McDonald	-	X	X	X	X	#
8 Evans	N	N	N	N	N	Y
9 Jenkins	N	N	N	N	N	Y
10 Barnard	N	N	N	N	N	Y
HAWAII						
1 Heftel	N	N	Y	Y	Y	Y
2 Akaka	N	N	N	N	N	Y
IDAHO						
1 Craig	N	N	N	N	N	Y
2 Hansen	N	N	N	N	N	Y
ILLINOIS						
1 Washington	Y	Y	Y	Y	Y	N
2 Savage	N	Y	Y	Y	Y	N
3 Russo	Y	Y	Y	Y	Y	N
4 Derwinski	N	N	Y	N	N	Y
5 Fary	N	N	N	N	N	Y
6 Hyde	N	N	N	N	N	Y
7 Collins	Y	Y	Y	Y	Y	N
8 Rostenkowski	Y	Y	Y	Y	Y	Y
9 Yates	Y	Y	Y	Y	Y	Y
10 Porter	N	N	Y	N	N	Y
11 Annunzio	N	N	N	N	N	Y
12 Crane, P.	N	N	N	N	N	Y
13 McClory	N	N	N	N	N	Y
14 Erlenborn	N	N	N	N	N	Y
15 Corcoran	N	N	N	N	N	Y
16 Martin	N	N	N	Y	Y	Y
17 O'Brien	N	N	Y	Y	Y	Y
18 Michel	N	N	N	N	N	Y
19 Railsback	N	Y	N	Y	Y	Y
20 Findley	N	Y	Y	N	Y	Y
21 Madigan	?	?	?	X	?	?
22 Crane, D.	N	N	N	N	N	Y
23 Price	N	N	N	N	N	Y
24 Simon	Y	Y	Y	Y	Y	Y
INDIANA						
1 Benjamin	Y	Y	N	Y	Y	Y
2 Fithian	N	Y	N	Y	Y	Y
3 Hiler	N	N	N	N	N	Y
4 Coats	N	N	N	N	N	Y
5 Hillis	N	N	N	N	N	Y
6 Evans	N	Y	Y	Y	Y	Y
7 Myers	N	N	N	N	N	Y
8 Deckard	N	N	N	Y	N	Y
9 Hamilton	N	Y	N	Y	Y	Y
10 Sharp	N	Y	N	Y	Y	Y
11 Jacobs	N	Y	Y	Y	Y	Y
IOWA						
1 Leach	N	Y	Y	Y	Y	Y
2 Tauke	N	N	Y	N	Y	N
3 Evans	N	N	N	Y	N	Y
4 Smith	Y	Y	Y	Y	Y	Y
5 Harkin	Y	Y	Y	Y	Y	N
6 Bedell	?	?	?	?	?	?

Corresponding to Congressional Record Votes 315, 316, 317, 318, 319, 320

	298	299	300	301	302	303
KANSAS						
1 ***Roberts***	N	N	N	N	N	Y
2 ***Jeffries***	N	N	N	N	N	Y
3 ***Winn***	N	N	N	N	N	Y
4 Glickman	Y	Y	Y	N	Y	Y
5 ***Whittaker***	N	N	N	N	Y	Y
KENTUCKY						
1 Hubbard	N	N	N	N	N	Y
2 Natcher	N	N	N	N	N	Y
3 Mazzoli	N	Y	Y	Y	Y	Y
4 ***Snyder***	N	N	N	Y	Y	Y
5 ***Rogers***	N	N	N	N	Y	Y
6 ***Hopkins***	Y	N	N	N	N	Y
7 Perkins	N	N	N	Y	Y	Y
LOUISIANA						
1 ***Livingston***	N	N	N	N	N	Y
2 Boggs	N	N	N	N	N	Y
3 Tauzin	N	N	N	N	N	Y
4 Roemer	N	N	N	N	N	Y
5 Huckaby	N	N	N	N	N	Y
6 ***Moore***	N	N	N	N	N	Y
7 Breaux	?	X	X	X	X	?
8 Long	N	N	N	N	N	Y
MAINE						
1 ***Emery***	N	N	N	N	N	Y
2 ***Snowe***	N	N	N	N	Y	Y
MARYLAND						
1 Dyson	N	N	N	N	N	Y
2 Long	Y	Y	Y	N	N	Y
3 Mikulski	N	Y	Y	Y	Y	N
4 ***Holt***	N	N	N	N	N	Y
5 Hoyer	Y	N	N	Y	Y	Y
6 Byron	N	N	N	N	N	Y
7 Mitchell	N	Y	Y	Y	Y	N
8 Barnes	N	Y	Y	N	N	Y
MASSACHUSETTS						
1 ***Conte***	N	Y	Y	N	N	Y
2 Boland	Y	Y	Y	Y	Y	Y
3 Early	N	Y	Y	Y	Y	N
4 Frank	N	Y	Y	Y	Y	N
5 Shannon	N	Y	Y	Y	Y	Y
6 Mavroules	N	Y	Y	Y	Y	Y
7 Markey	N	Y	Y	Y	Y	N
8 O'Neill						
9 Moakley	?	#	#	?	?	?
10 ***Heckler***	N	Y	N	Y	Y	Y
11 Donnelly	?	#	?	?	?	?
12 Studds	N	Y	Y	Y	Y	N
MICHIGAN						
1 Conyers	N	Y	Y	Y	Y	N
2 ***Pursell***	Y	Y	Y	Y	Y	N
3 Wolpe	Y	Y	Y	Y	Y	N
4 ***Siljander***	N	N	N	N	N	Y
5 ***Sawyer***	N	N	N	N	N	Y
6 ***Dunn***	Y	?	N	N	Y	Y
7 Kildee	Y	Y	Y	Y	Y	N
8 Traxler	Y	Y	Y	Y	Y	Y
9 ***Vander Jagt***	N	N	N	N	Y	Y
10 Albosta	Y	Y	N	Y	Y	Y
11 ***Davis***	?	X	N	N	N	Y
12 Bonior	Y	Y	Y	Y	Y	N
13 Crockett	N	N	Y	Y	Y	N
14 Hertel	Y	Y	Y	N	Y	Y
15 Ford	N	Y	Y	Y	Y	Y
16 Dingell	Y	Y	Y	Y	Y	Y
17 Brodhead	Y	Y	Y	Y	Y	N
18 Blanchard	Y	Y	Y	Y	Y	N
19 ***Broomfield***	N	N	N	N	Y	Y
MINNESOTA						
1 ***Erdahl***	N	Y	Y	N	Y	N
2 ***Hagedorn***	?	?	?	X	?	?
3 ***Frenzel***	N	N	N	N	Y	Y
4 Vento	Y	Y	N	Y	Y	N
5 Sabo	Y	Y	Y	Y	Y	N
6 ***Weber***	N	Y	Y	N	Y	Y
7 ***Stangeland***	N	N	N	N	N	Y
8 Oberstar	N	Y	Y	Y	Y	N
MISSISSIPPI						
1 Whitten	N	N	N	N	N	Y
2 Bowen	N	N	N	N	N	Y
3 Montgomery	N	N	N	N	N	Y
4 Dowdy	N	N	N	N	N	Y
5 ***Lott***	N	N	N	N	N	Y
MISSOURI						
1 Clay	N	Y	Y	Y	Y	N
2 Young	N	N	Y	N	N	Y
3 Gephardt	Y	N	N	N	N	Y

	298	299	300	301	302	303
4 Skelton	N	N	N	N	N	Y
5 Bolling	?	?	?	?	?	?
6 ***Coleman***	N	N	N	N	N	Y
7 ***Taylor***	N	N	N	N	N	Y
8 ***Bailey***	N	N	N	N	N	Y
9 Volkmer	N	N	N	Y	N	Y
10 ***Emerson***	N	N	N	N	N	Y
MONTANA						
1 Williams	Y	Y	Y	Y	Y	N
2 ***Marlenee***	N	N	?	N	N	Y
NEBRASKA						
1 ***Bereuter***	N	N	N	N	Y	Y
2 ***Daub***	N	N	N	N	Y	Y
3 ***Smith***	N	N	Y	Y	Y	N
NEVADA						
AL Santini	N	N	N	Y	Y	Y
NEW HAMPSHIRE						
1 D'Amours	Y	Y	N	Y	Y	Y
2 ***Gregg***	N	N	Y	N	Y	Y
NEW JERSEY						
1 Florio	Y	#	?	?	?	?
2 Hughes	N	Y	N	Y	Y	Y
3 Howard	Y	Y	Y	N	N	Y
4 ***Smith***	N	N	Y	N	Y	Y
5 ***Fenwick***	N	Y	Y	N	Y	N
6 ***Forsythe***	?	?	?	#	#	?
7 ***Roukema***	N	N	N	N	Y	Y
8 Roe	N	N	N	Y	Y	Y
9 ***Hollenbeck***	N	Y	Y	N	Y	Y
10 Rodino	Y	Y	Y	Y	Y	N
11 Minish	Y	Y	Y	Y	Y	Y
12 ***Rinaldo***	N	N	N	N	N	Y
13 ***Courter***	N	N	N	N	N	Y
14 Guarini	N	Y	Y	Y	Y	Y
15 Dwyer	Y	Y	Y	Y	Y	Y
NEW MEXICO						
1 ***Lujan***	N	N	N	Y	Y	Y
2 ***Skeen***	N	N	N	N	N	Y
NEW YORK						
1 ***Carney***	N	N	N	N	N	Y
2 Downey	Y	Y	Y	Y	Y	Y
3 ***Carman***	N	N	N	N	N	Y
4 ***Lent***	N	N	N	N	N	Y
5 ***McGrath***	N	N	N	N	N	Y
6 ***LeBoutillier***	N	N	N	N	N	Y
7 Addabbo	Y	Y	Y	Y	Y	Y
8 Rosenthal	Y	Y	Y	?	?	?
9 Ferraro	Y	Y	Y	Y	Y	Y
10 Biaggi	Y	Y	N	Y	N	?
11 Scheuer	Y	Y	Y	Y	Y	Y
12 Chisholm	?	#	#	#	#	?
13 Solarz	Y	Y	Y	Y	Y	Y
14 Richmond	Y	Y	Y	Y	Y	N
15 Zeferetti	N	N	Y	N	N	Y
16 Schumer	Y	Y	Y	Y	Y	Y
17 ***Molinari***	N	N	Y	N	N	Y
18 ***Green***	N	Y	Y	Y	Y	Y
19 Rangel	Y	Y	Y	Y	Y	N
20 Weiss	N	Y	Y	Y	Y	N
21 Garcia	N	Y	?	#	#	?
22 Bingham	Y	Y	Y	Y	Y	N
23 Peyser	N	Y	N	N	Y	Y
24 Ottinger	Y	Y	Y	Y	Y	N
25 ***Fish***	N	N	N	N	Y	Y
26 ***Gilman***	N	N	N	N	Y	Y
27 McHugh	Y	Y	Y	Y	Y	Y
28 Stratton	N	N	N	N	N	Y
29 ***Solomon***	N	N	N	N	N	Y
30 ***Martin***	?	?	?	?	X	?
31 ***Mitchell***	N	N	N	N	N	Y
32 ***Wortley***	N	N	N	N	N	Y
33 ***Lee***	N	N	N	N	N	Y
34 ***Horton***	N	Y	Y	N	Y	Y
35 ***Conable***	N	N	N	N	N	Y
36 LaFalce	Y	Y	Y	Y	Y	Y
37 Nowak	Y	Y	Y	Y	Y	Y
38 ***Kemp***	N	N	N	N	N	Y
39 Lundine	Y	Y	Y	Y	Y	N
NORTH CAROLINA						
1 Jones	?	?	?	?	?	?
2 Fountain	N	N	N	N	N	Y
3 Whitley	N	N	N	N	N	Y
4 Andrews	N	N	N	?	?	?
5 Neal	N	N	N	?	N	Y
6 ***Johnston***	?	?	?	?	X	?
7 Rose	N	N	N	Y	Y	Y
8 Hefner	N	N	N	N	N	Y

	298	299	300	301	302	303
9 ***Martin***	N	N	N	N	N	Y
10 ***Broyhill***	N	N	N	N	N	Y
11 ***Hendon***	N	N	N	N	N	Y
NORTH DAKOTA						
AL Dorgan	+	+	+	-	-	+
OHIO						
1 ***Gradison***	N	N	N	N	N	Y
2 Luken	N	N	N	N	N	Y
3 Hall	N	N	N	Y	Y	Y
4 ***Oxley***	N	N	N	N	N	Y
5 ***Latta***	N	N	N	N	N	Y
6 ***McEwen***	N	N	N	Y	N	Y
7 ***Brown***	N	N	N	N	N	Y
8 ***Kindness***	N	N	N	N	Y	Y
9 ***Weber***	N	N	N	N	N	Y
10 ***Miller***	N	N	N	Y	Y	Y
11 ***Stanton***	N	N	N	N	Y	Y
12 Shamansky	N	N	N	N	Y	Y
13 Pease	Y	Y	Y	Y	Y	Y
14 Seiberling	Y	Y	Y	Y	Y	N
15 ***Wylie***	N	N	N	N	Y	Y
16 ***Regula***	N	N	N	N	Y	Y
17 ***Ashbrook***	N	N	N	N	N	Y
18 Applegate	N	N	N	Y	Y	Y
19 ***Williams***	N	N	N	N	N	Y
20 Oakar	N	N	N	Y	Y	Y
21 Stokes	N	Y	Y	Y	Y	N
22 Eckart	Y	N	Y	Y	Y	Y
23 Mottl	N	N	N	Y	Y	Y
OKLAHOMA						
1 Jones	N	N	N	N	N	Y
2 Synar	N	N	Y	Y	Y	Y
3 Watkins	N	N	N	N	N	Y
4 McCurdy	N	N	N	N	N	Y
5 ***Edwards***	N	N	N	N	N	Y
6 English	Y	N	N	N	N	Y
OREGON						
1 AuCoin	Y	Y	Y	Y	Y	N
2 ***Smith***	N	N	N	N	N	Y
3 Wyden	Y	Y	Y	Y	Y	N
4 Weaver	Y	Y	Y	Y	Y	?
PENNSYLVANIA						
1 Foglietta	N	Y	Y	Y	Y	Y
2 Gray	N	Y	Y	Y	Y	N
3 Smith	N	N	N	N	N	Y
4 ***Dougherty***	N	N	N	N	N	Y
5 ***Schulze***	N	N	N	N	N	Y
6 Yatron	N	N	N	N	N	Y
7 Edgar	Y	Y	Y	Y	Y	N
8 ***Coyne, J.***	N	N	N	N	Y	Y
9 ***Shuster***	N	N	N	N	N	Y
10 ***McDade***	N	N	N	N	Y	Y
11 ***Nelligan***	N	N	N	N	N	Y
12 Murtha	Y	Y	N	N	N	Y
13 ***Coughlin***	N	N	Y	N	Y	Y
14 Coyne, W.	N	Y	Y	Y	Y	Y
15 ***Ritter***	N	N	N	N	N	Y
16 ***Walker***	N	N	N	N	N	Y
17 Ertel	Y	Y	N	Y	Y	Y
18 Walgren	Y	Y	Y	Y	Y	N
19 ***Goodling***	N	N	Y	Y	Y	N
20 Gaydos	N	N	Y	N	N	Y
21 Bailey	N	N	N	N	N	Y
22 Murphy	N	Y	Y	N	Y	Y
23 ***Clinger***	N	N	N	N	Y	Y
24 ***Marks***	N	N	N	N	Y	Y
25 ***Atkinson***	N	N	N	Y	Y	Y
RHODE ISLAND						
1 St Germain	N	Y	Y	Y	Y	N
2 ***Schneider***	Y	Y	Y	Y	Y	Y
SOUTH CAROLINA						
1 ***Hartnett***	N	N	N	N	N	Y
2 ***Spence***	N	N	N	N	N	Y
3 Derrick	N	Y	N	N	N	Y
4 ***Campbell***	N	N	N	N	N	Y
5 Holland	N	N	N	N	N	Y
6 ***Napier***	N	N	N	N	N	Y
SOUTH DAKOTA						
1 Daschle	Y	N	N	Y	Y	Y
2 ***Roberts***	N	N	N	N	N	Y
TENNESSEE						
1 ***Quillen***	N	N	N	N	N	Y
2 ***Duncan***	?	X	?	?	X	?
3 Bouquard	N	N	N	N	N	Y
4 Gore	Y	Y	N	Y	Y	Y
5 Boner	N	N	N	N	N	Y
6 ***Beard***	N	N	N	N	N	Y

	298	299	300	301	302	303
7 Jones	N	N	N	N	N	Y
8 Ford	N	Y	Y	Y	Y	N
TEXAS						
1 Hall, S.	N	N	N	N	Y	Y
2 Wilson	Y	N	N	N	N	Y
3 ***Collins***	N	N	N	N	N	Y
4 Hall, R.	N	N	N	N	N	Y
5 Mattox	?	#	?	?	?	?
6 Gramm	N	N	N	N	N	Y
7 ***Archer***	N	N	N	N	N	Y
8 ***Fields***	N	N	N	N	N	Y
9 Brooks	Y	Y	Y	N	Y	Y
10 Pickle	N	N	N	N	Y	Y
11 Leath	Y	N	N	N	N	Y
12 Wright	Y	N	N	N	N	Y
13 Hightower	N	N	N	N	N	Y
14 Patman	N	N	N	N	N	Y
15 de la Garza	N	N	N	Y	Y	Y
16 White	N	N	N	N	N	Y
17 Stenholm	N	N	N	N	N	Y
18 Leland	N	Y	Y	Y	Y	N
19 Hance	N	N	N	N	N	Y
20 Gonzalez	N	N	N	N	N	Y
21 ***Loeffler***	N	N	N	N	N	Y
22 ***Paul***	Y	Y	?	#	#	?
23 Kazen	N	N	N	N	N	Y
24 Frost	N	N	N	Y	Y	Y
UTAH						
1 ***Hansen***	N	N	N	N	N	Y
2 ***Marriott***	N	N	N	N	N	Y
VERMONT						
AL ***Jeffords***	Y	Y	Y	Y	Y	Y
VIRGINIA						
1 ***Trible***	N	N	N	N	N	Y
2 ***Whitehurst***	N	N	N	N	N	Y
3 ***Bliley***	N	N	N	N	N	Y
4 ***Daniel, R.***	N	N	N	N	N	Y
5 Daniel, D.	N	N	N	N	N	Y
6 ***Butler***	N	N	N	N	N	Y
7 ***Robinson***	N	N	N	N	N	Y
8 ***Parris***	N	N	N	N	N	Y
9 ***Wampler***	?	N	N	N	N	Y
10 ***Wolf***	N	N	N	N	Y	Y
WASHINGTON						
1 ***Pritchard***	?	?	?	#	#	?
2 Swift	N	Y	N	Y	Y	Y
3 Bonker	Y	Y	Y	Y	Y	Y
4 ***Morrison***	N	N	N	N	N	Y
5 Foley	Y	N	N	N	Y	Y
6 Dicks	Y	N	N	N	Y	Y
7 Lowry	Y	Y	Y	Y	Y	N
WEST VIRGINIA						
1 Mollohan	N	N	N	N	N	Y
2 ***Benedict***	N	N	N	N	Y	Y
3 ***Staton***	N	N	N	N	N	Y
4 Rahall	Y	Y	Y	Y	Y	N
WISCONSIN						
1 Aspin	Y	Y	N	Y	Y	Y
2 Kastenmeier	Y	Y	Y	Y	Y	N
3 ***Gunderson***	N	Y	N	N	Y	Y
4 Zablocki	Y	N	N	N	N	Y
5 Reuss	?	#	#	#	#	?
6 ***Petri***	N	Y	Y	Y	Y	Y
7 Obey	N	Y	Y	N	N	N
8 ***Roth***	N	N	N	N	Y	Y
9 ***Sensenbrenner***	N	N	N	Y	Y	Y
WYOMING						
AL ***Cheney***	N	N	N	N	N	Y

Democrats ***Republicans***

304. H Con Res 224. Strategic Arms Talks. Adoption of the concurrent resolution expressing congressional support for President Reagan's Nov. 18, 1981, proposals for limiting strategic and intermediate range weapons. Adopted 382-3: R 180-0; D 202-3 (ND 132-3, SD 70-0), Nov. 19, 1981.

305. HR 3413. Department of Energy National Security Programs Authorization. Adoption of the conference report on the bill to authorize $5,120,200,000 for national security programs of the Department of Energy in fiscal year 1982. Adopted 335-55: R 166-11; D 169-44 (ND 102-40, SD 67-4), Nov. 19, 1981. (The president had requested $4,996,400,000.)

306. HR 3663. Bus Regulatory Reform. Adoption of the rule (H Res 280) providing for House floor consideration of the bill to reduce regulation of the intercity bus industry. Adopted 306-80: R 111-67; D 195-13 (ND 139-3, SD 56-10), Nov. 19, 1981.

307. HR 3663. Bus Regulatory Reform. Edwards, D-Calif., motion that the House resolve itself into the Committee of the Whole for consideration of the bill to reduce regulation of the intercity bus industry. Motion agreed to 335-33: R 147-20; D 188-13 (ND 131-5, SD 57-8), Nov. 19, 1981.

308. HR 3663. Bus Regulatory Reform. Passage of the bill to reduce government regulation of the intercity bus industry. Passed 305-83: R 146-28; D 159-55 (ND 110-34, SD 49-21), Nov. 19, 1981.

309. H J Res 349. Sinai Peace-keeping Force. Passage of the joint resolution authorizing U.S. participation in the multinational peace-keeping force in the Sinai Peninsula following Israeli withdrawal in April, 1982, and authorizing $125 million in fiscal 1982 as the U.S. contribution to the budget of the peace-keeping force. Passed 368-13: R 161-9; D 207-4 (ND 143-1, SD 64-3), Nov. 19, 1981.

KEY

Y Voted for (yea).
Paired for.
+ Announced for.
N Voted against (nay).
X Paired against.
- Announced against.
P Voted "present".
C Voted "present" to avoid possible conflict of interest.
? Did not vote or otherwise make a position known.

Democrats *Republicans*

	304	305	306	307	308	309
ALABAMA						
1 *Edwards*	Y	Y	Y	Y	?	?
2 *Dickinson*	Y	Y	Y	Y	?	X
3 Nichols	Y	Y	Y	Y	Y	Y
4 Bevill	Y	Y	Y	Y	Y	Y
5 Flippo	Y	Y	Y	Y	Y	Y
6 *Smith*	Y	Y	N	Y	Y	Y
7 Shelby	Y	Y	Y	Y	Y	?
ALASKA						
AL *Young*	Y	Y	N	?	N	Y
ARIZONA						
1 *Rhodes*	?	?	?	?	?	#
2 Udall	Y	Y	Y	Y	Y	Y
3 *Stump*	Y	Y	N	Y	Y	Y
4 *Rudd*	Y	Y	Y	Y	Y	?
ARKANSAS						
1 Alexander	Y	Y	Y	Y	Y	Y
2 *Bethune*	Y	Y	Y	Y	Y	Y
3 *Hammerschmidt*	Y	Y	Y	Y	Y	Y
4 Anthony	Y	Y	Y	Y	Y	Y
CALIFORNIA						
1 *Chappie*	Y	N	Y	Y	Y	Y
2 *Clausen*	Y	Y	Y	Y	Y	Y
3 Matsui	Y	v	Y	?	Y	Y
4 Fazio	Y	Y	Y	Y	Y	Y
5 Burton, J.	P	N	Y	Y	Y	Y
6 Burton, P.	P	N	Y	Y	Y	Y
7 Miller	Y	?	Y	N	Y	Y
8 Dellums	P	N	Y	N	Y	N
9 Stark	Y	N	Y	Y	Y	Y
10 Edwards	Y	N	Y	Y	Y	Y
11 Lantos	Y	Y	Y	Y	Y	Y
12 *McCloskey*	?	?	?	?	?	?
13 Mineta	Y	Y	Y	Y	Y	Y
14 *Shumway*	Y	Y	N	Y	Y	N
15 Coelho	Y	Y	Y	Y	Y	Y
16 Panetta	Y	Y	Y	Y	Y	Y
17 *Pashayan*	Y	Y	N	Y	Y	Y
18 *Thomas*	Y	Y	N	Y	Y	Y
19 *Lagomarsino*	Y	Y	N	Y	Y	Y
20 *Goldwater*	?	?	?	?	?	?
21 *Fiedler*	Y	Y	Y	Y	Y	Y
22 *Moorhead*	+	Y	N	Y	Y	Y
23 Beilenson	P	N	Y	N	Y	Y
24 Waxman	Y	Y	Y	N	Y	Y
25 Roybal	Y	N	Y	Y	Y	Y
26 *Rousselot*	Y	Y	N	N	Y	Y
27 *Dornan*	?	?	?	?	?	?
28 Dixon	?	?	?	?	?	?
29 Hawkins	P	Y	Y	Y	Y	Y
30 Danielson	Y	Y	Y	Y	Y	Y
31 Dymally	?	?	?	?	?	?
32 Anderson	Y	Y	Y	Y	Y	Y
33 *Grisham*	+	+	-	-	+	+
34 *Lungren*	Y	Y	N	Y	Y	Y
35 *Dreier*	Y	Y	N	N	Y	Y
36 Brown	Y	Y	Y	Y	Y	Y
37 *Lewis*	Y	Y	Y	Y	Y	Y
38 Patterson	Y	Y	Y	Y	Y	Y
39 *Dannemeyer*	Y	Y	N	Y	Y	Y
40 *Badham*	Y	Y	N	Y	Y	Y
41 *Lowery*	Y	Y	Y	Y	Y	Y
42 *Hunter*	Y	Y	N	Y	Y	Y
43 *Burgener*	Y	Y	Y	Y	Y	Y
COLORADO						
1 Schroeder	P	N	Y	Y	Y	Y
2 Wirth	Y	Y	Y	Y	Y	Y
3 Kogovsek	Y	Y	Y	Y	Y	Y
4 *Brown*	Y	N	Y	Y	Y	N

	304	305	306	307	308	309
5 *Kramer*	Y	Y	Y	Y	Y	Y
CONNECTICUT						
1 Vacancy						
2 Gejdenson	Y	N	Y	Y	N	Y
3 *DeNardis*	Y	Y	Y	Y	Y	?
4 *McKinney*	Y	Y	Y	?	Y	Y
5 Ratchford	Y	Y	Y	Y	N	Y
6 Moffett	Y	N	?	?	N	Y
DELAWARE						
AL *Evans*	Y	Y	Y	Y	Y	Y
FLORIDA						
1 Hutto	Y	Y	Y	Y	Y	Y
2 Fuqua	Y	Y	Y	Y	Y	Y
3 Bennett	Y	Y	Y	Y	Y	N
4 Chappell	Y	Y	Y	Y	N	Y
5 *McCollum*	Y	Y	Y	Y	Y	Y
6 *Young*	Y	?	?	Y	Y	Y
7 Gibbons	Y	Y	Y	Y	Y	Y
8 Ireland	Y	Y	?	?	Y	Y
9 Nelson	Y	Y	Y	+	Y	Y
10 *Bafalis*	Y	?	?	Y	Y	Y
11 Mica	Y	Y	Y	Y	Y	Y
12 *Shaw*	Y	Y	Y	Y	Y	Y
13 Lehman	P	N	Y	Y	Y	Y
14 Pepper	?	#	?	?	?	?
15 Fascell	Y	N	Y	?	Y	Y
GEORGIA						
1 Ginn	Y	Y	Y	Y	Y	?
2 Hatcher	Y	Y	Y	Y	Y	Y
3 Brinkley	Y	Y	Y	Y	Y	Y
4 Levitas	Y	Y	Y	Y	Y	Y
5 Fowler	Y	Y	Y	Y	Y	Y
6 *Gingrich*	Y	Y	Y	Y	Y	Y
7 McDonald	+	+	X	?	X	X
8 Evans	Y	Y	Y	Y	Y	Y
9 Jenkins	Y	Y	Y	Y	Y	?
10 Barnard	Y	Y	Y	?	?	?
HAWAII						
1 Heftel	Y	Y	Y	Y	Y	Y
2 Akaka	Y	Y	Y	Y	Y	Y
IDAHO						
1 *Craig*	Y	Y	N	?	Y	Y
2 *Hansen*	Y	Y	N	Y	Y	N
ILLINOIS						
1 Washington	P	N	Y	N	N	Y
2 Savage	P	N	Y	?	N	Y
3 Russo	Y	Y	Y	Y	Y	Y
4 *Derwinski*	Y	Y	Y	Y	Y	Y
5 Fary	Y	#	#	Y	Y	Y
6 *Hyde*	Y	Y	Y	Y	Y	Y
7 Collins	P	Y	Y	Y	N	Y
8 Rostenkowski	Y	Y	Y	Y	Y	Y
9 Yates	Y	N	Y	N	Y	Y
10 *Porter*	Y	Y	Y	Y	Y	+
11 Annunzio	Y	Y	Y	Y	Y	Y
12 *Crane, P.*	Y	N	N	Y	Y	Y
13 *McClory*	Y	Y	Y	Y	Y	Y
14 *Erlenborn*	Y	Y	Y	Y	Y	Y
15 *Corcoran*	Y	Y	Y	Y	Y	Y
16 *Martin*	Y	Y	N	Y	Y	Y
17 *O'Brien*	Y	Y	Y	Y	Y	Y
18 *Michel*	Y	Y	Y	Y	Y	Y
19 *Railsback*	Y	Y	Y	Y	?	Y
20 *Findley*	Y	Y	Y	Y	Y	Y
21 *Madigan*	Y	Y	Y	Y	Y	Y
22 *Crane, D.*	Y	N	N	Y	Y	N
23 Price	Y	Y	Y	Y	Y	Y
24 Simon	Y	Y	Y	Y	?	?
INDIANA						
1 Benjamin	Y	Y	Y	Y	Y	Y
2 Fithian	Y	Y	Y	N	Y	Y
3 *Hiler*	Y	Y	N	Y	Y	Y
4 *Coats*	Y	Y	N	N	Y	Y
5 *Hillis*	Y	Y	Y	Y	Y	Y
6 Evans	Y	Y	Y	Y	Y	Y
7 *Myers*	Y	Y	N	Y	?	Y
8 *Deckard*	Y	?	?	?	?	Y
9 Hamilton	Y	Y	Y	Y	Y	Y
10 Sharp	Y	Y	Y	Y	Y	Y
11 Jacobs	Y	N	Y	Y	Y	Y
IOWA						
1 *Leach*	Y	Y	Y	Y	Y	Y
2 *Tauke*	Y	Y	N	N	N	Y
3 *Evans*	Y	Y	Y	N	N	Y
4 Smith	Y	Y	Y	Y	Y	Y
5 Harkin	Y	N	Y	Y	Y	Y
6 Bedell	?	?	?	?	?	?

	304	305	306	307	308	309
KANSAS						
1 ***Roberts***	Y	Y	N	N	N	Y
2 ***Jeffries***	Y	Y	N	Y	Y	N
3 ***Winn***	Y	Y	Y	Y	Y	Y
4 Glickman	Y	Y	Y	?	Y	Y
5 ***Whittaker***	Y	Y	Y	Y	Y	Y
KENTUCKY						
1 Hubbard	Y	Y	Y	Y	Y	Y
2 Natcher	Y	Y	Y	Y	Y	Y
3 Mazzoli	Y	Y	Y	Y	Y	Y
4 ***Snyder***	Y	Y	Y	Y	Y	Y
5 ***Rogers***	Y	Y	Y	Y	N	Y
6 ***Hopkins***	Y	Y	Y	Y	Y	Y
7 Perkins	Y	Y	N	Y	N	Y
LOUISIANA						
1 ***Livingston***	Y	Y	Y	Y	Y	Y
2 Boggs	Y	Y	?	Y	Y	Y
3 Tauzin	Y	Y	Y	Y	Y	Y
4 Roemer	Y	Y	Y	Y	Y	Y
5 Huckaby	Y	Y	Y	Y	Y	Y
6 ***Moore***	Y	Y	Y	Y	Y	Y
7 Breaux	?	?	?	?	?	?
8 Long	?	?	?	?	?	?
MAINE						
1 ***Emery***	Y	Y	N	Y	N	Y
2 ***Snowe***	Y	Y	Y	N	N	Y
MARYLAND						
1 Dyson	Y	Y	Y	Y	N	Y
2 Long	Y	Y	Y	Y	Y	Y
3 Mikulski	Y	Y	Y	Y	Y	Y
4 ***Holt***	Y	Y	Y	Y	Y	Y
5 Hoyer	Y	Y	Y	Y	N	Y
6 Byron	Y	Y	Y	Y	Y	Y
7 Mitchell	Y	?	?	?	Y	Y
8 Barnes	Y	Y	Y	Y	Y	Y
MASSACHUSETTS						
1 ***Conte***	Y	Y	Y	Y	Y	Y
2 Boland	Y	Y	Y	Y	Y	Y
3 Early	Y	Y	Y	Y	Y	Y
4 Frank	Y	N	Y	Y	Y	Y
5 Shannon	Y	Y	Y	Y	?	?
6 Mavroules	Y	Y	?	?	Y	Y
7 Markey	Y	?	Y	Y	Y	Y
8 O'Neill						
9 Moakley	Y	Y	Y	Y	Y	Y
10 ***Heckler***	Y	Y	Y	?	Y	Y
11 Donnelly	Y	N	Y	Y	Y	Y
12 Studds	Y	N	Y	Y	Y	Y
MICHIGAN						
1 Conyers	?	X	?	?	N	Y
2 ***Pursell***	Y	Y	Y	?	Y	Y
3 Wolpe	Y	N	Y	Y	Y	Y
4 ***Siljander***	Y	Y	N	Y	Y	Y
5 ***Sawyer***	Y	Y	N	Y	Y	Y
6 ***Dunn***	Y	Y	Y	Y	Y	Y
7 Kildee	Y	N	Y	Y	N	Y
8 Traxler	Y	Y	Y	Y	N	Y
9 ***Vander Jagt***	Y	Y	N	Y	Y	Y
10 Albosta	Y	Y	Y	Y	Y	Y
11 ***Davis***	Y	Y	Y	Y	N	Y
12 Bonior	Y	N	Y	Y	N	Y
13 Crockett	N	N	N	Y	N	Y
14 Hertel	Y	Y	Y	Y	N	Y
15 Ford	Y	Y	Y	Y	N	Y
16 Dingell	?	?	?	Y	N	Y
17 Brodhead	Y	Y	Y	Y	Y	Y
18 Blanchard	Y	Y	Y	Y	N	Y
19 ***Broomfield***	Y	Y	Y	Y	Y	Y
MINNESOTA						
1 ***Erdahl***	Y	Y	N	?	N	Y
2 ***Hagedorn***	?	?	?	?	?	?
3 ***Frenzel***	Y	Y	N	Y	N	Y
4 Vento	Y	Y	Y	Y	Y	Y
5 Sabo	Y	N	Y	Y	Y	Y
6 ***Weber***	Y	Y	N	Y	N	Y
7 ***Stangeland***	Y	Y	Y	Y	Y	Y
8 Oberstar	Y	N	Y	Y	Y	Y
MISSISSIPPI						
1 Whitten	Y	Y	Y	Y	Y	Y
2 Bowen	?	?	?	?	?	?
3 Montgomery	Y	Y	?	Y	Y	Y
4 Dowdy	?	?	?	?	Y	Y
5 ***Lott***	Y	Y	Y	Y	Y	Y
MISSOURI						
1 Clay	?	?	?	?	?	?
2 Young	Y	Y	Y	Y	#	?
3 Gephardt	Y	Y	Y	Y	Y	Y
4 Skelton	Y	Y	N	N	N	Y
5 Bolling	?	?	?	?	?	?
6 ***Coleman***	Y	Y	N	Y	N	Y
7 ***Taylor***	Y	Y	N	Y	Y	Y
8 ***Bailey***	Y	Y	Y	Y	Y	Y
9 Volkmer	?	?	?	?	?	?
10 ***Emerson***	Y	Y	N	Y	N	?
MONTANA						
1 Williams	Y	N	Y	Y	N	Y
2 ***Marlenee***	Y	Y	Y	Y	N	Y
NEBRASKA						
1 ***Bereuter***	Y	Y	N	N	N	Y
2 ***Daub***	Y	N	N	N	Y	Y
3 ***Smith***	Y	Y	N	N	N	Y
NEVADA						
AL Santini	Y	Y	Y	Y	?	?
NEW HAMPSHIRE						
1 D'Amours	Y	Y	Y	Y	Y	Y
2 ***Gregg***	Y	Y	Y	Y	Y	Y
NEW JERSEY						
1 Florio	?	?	?	?	#	?
2 Hughes	Y	Y	Y	Y	Y	Y
3 Howard	Y	Y	Y	Y	Y	Y
4 ***Smith***	Y	Y	Y	Y	Y	Y
5 ***Fenwick***	Y	N	Y	Y	Y	Y
6 ***Forsythe***	Y	Y	Y	Y	Y	Y
7 ***Roukema***	Y	Y	N	Y	Y	Y
8 Roe	Y	Y	Y	Y	Y	Y
9 ***Hollenbeck***	Y	Y	Y	?	Y	Y
10 Rodino	Y	N	Y	Y	Y	Y
11 Minish	Y	Y	Y	Y	Y	Y
12 ***Rinaldo***	Y	Y	Y	Y	Y	Y
13 ***Courter***	Y	Y	?	?	Y	Y
14 Guarini	Y	Y	Y	Y	Y	Y
15 Dwyer	Y	Y	Y	Y	Y	Y
NEW MEXICO						
1 ***Lujan***	?	Y	Y	Y	Y	Y
2 ***Skeen***	Y	Y	Y	N	Y	Y
NEW YORK						
1 ***Carney***	Y	Y	N	Y	Y	Y
2 Downey	Y	Y	Y	Y	Y	Y
3 ***Carman***	Y	Y	Y	Y	Y	Y
4 ***Lent***	Y	Y	Y	Y	Y	Y
5 ***McGrath***	Y	Y	Y	Y	Y	Y
6 ***LeBoutillier***	Y	Y	Y	Y	Y	Y
7 Addabbo	Y	Y	?	?	Y	Y
8 Rosenthal	Y	Y	Y	Y	?	Y
9 Ferraro	Y	Y	Y	Y	Y	Y
10 Biaggi	?	?	?	?	?	?
11 Scheuer	Y	Y	Y	Y	Y	Y
12 Chisholm	?	X	?	?	X	?
13 Solarz	Y	Y	Y	Y	Y	Y
14 Richmond	?	?	?	?	?	#
15 Zeferetti	Y	Y	Y	Y	Y	Y
16 Schumer	Y	Y	Y	Y	Y	Y
17 ***Molinari***	Y	Y	Y	Y	Y	Y
18 ***Green***	Y	Y	Y	Y	Y	Y
19 Rangel	P	N	Y	Y	N	Y
20 Weiss	N	N	Y	Y	N	Y
21 Garcia	P	N	?	?	N	Y
22 Bingham	Y	N	Y	Y	N	Y
23 Peyser	Y	Y	Y	Y	Y	Y
24 Ottinger	Y	N	Y	P	N	Y
25 ***Fish***	Y	Y	N	Y	N	Y
26 ***Gilman***	Y	Y	Y	Y	Y	Y
27 McHugh	Y	Y	Y	?	N	Y
28 Stratton	Y	Y	Y	Y	Y	Y
29 ***Solomon***	Y	Y	Y	Y	?	Y
30 ***Martin***	?	?	?	?	?	?
31 ***Mitchell***	Y	Y	Y	Y	N	Y
32 ***Wortley***	Y	Y	Y	Y	Y	Y
33 ***Lee***	Y	Y	Y	Y	Y	Y
34 ***Horton***	Y	Y	Y	Y	Y	Y
35 ***Conable***	Y	Y	Y	Y	Y	Y
36 LaFalce	Y	Y	Y	Y	Y	Y
37 Nowak	Y	Y	Y	Y	Y	Y
38 ***Kemp***	Y	Y	Y	Y	Y	Y
39 Lundine	Y	Y	Y	Y	Y	Y
NORTH CAROLINA						
1 Jones	?	?	?	?	?	?
2 Fountain	Y	Y	Y	Y	?	Y
3 Whitley	Y	Y	Y	Y	Y	?
4 Andrews	Y	Y	Y	Y	N	Y
5 Neal	Y	Y	Y	Y	Y	Y
6 ***Johnston***	Y	Y	Y	Y	Y	Y
7 Rose	Y	Y	Y	Y	N	Y
8 Hefner	Y	Y	Y	Y	Y	Y
9 ***Martin***	Y	Y	Y	Y	Y	Y
10 ***Broyhill***	Y	Y	N	Y	Y	Y
11 ***Hendon***	Y	Y	N	Y	N	Y
NORTH DAKOTA						
AL Dorgan	Y	Y	Y	N	N	Y
OHIO						
1 ***Gradison***	Y	Y	Y	Y	Y	Y
2 Luken	Y	Y	Y	Y	Y	Y
3 Hall	Y	Y	Y	Y	Y	Y
4 ***Oxley***	Y	Y	N	Y	Y	Y
5 ***Latta***	Y	N	N	Y	Y	Y
6 ***McEwen***	Y	Y	Y	Y	Y	Y
7 ***Brown***	Y	Y	N	Y	Y	?
8 ***Kindness***	Y	Y	N	N	N	Y
9 ***Weber***	Y	Y	Y	Y	Y	Y
10 ***Miller***	Y	N	Y	Y	Y	N
11 ***Stanton***	Y	Y	Y	Y	N	Y
12 Shamansky	Y	Y	Y	Y	Y	Y
13 Pease	Y	Y	Y	Y	Y	Y
14 Seiberling	Y	N	Y	Y	Y	Y
15 ***Wylie***	Y	Y	N	N	Y	Y
16 ***Regula***	Y	Y	Y	Y	Y	Y
17 ***Ashbrook***	Y	Y	N	Y	Y	?
18 Applegate	Y	Y	Y	?	Y	Y
19 ***Williams***	Y	Y	Y	Y	Y	Y
20 Oakar	Y	Y	Y	Y	Y	Y
21 Stokes	P	N	Y	Y	N	Y
22 Eckart	Y	N	Y	Y	N	Y
23 Mottl	Y	Y	Y	Y	Y	N
OKLAHOMA						
1 Jones	Y	Y	Y	Y	Y	Y
2 Synar	Y	Y	Y	Y	Y	Y
3 Watkins	Y	Y	N	N	N	Y
4 McCurdy	Y	Y	N	N	N	Y
5 ***Edwards***	Y	Y	N	Y	Y	?
6 English	Y	Y	Y	Y	N	Y
OREGON						
1 AuCoin	?	#	?	?	?	?
2 ***Smith***	Y	Y	N	Y	Y	N
3 Wyden	Y	N	Y	Y	Y	Y
4 Weaver	Y	N	Y	Y	Y	Y
PENNSYLVANIA						
1 Foglietta	Y	Y	Y	Y	Y	Y
2 Gray	P	N	Y	Y	Y	Y
3 Smith	Y	Y	Y	?	Y	Y
4 ***Dougherty***	Y	?	Y	?	?	Y
5 ***Schulze***	Y	Y	N	Y	Y	Y
6 Yatron	Y	Y	Y	Y	Y	Y
7 Edgar	Y	N	Y	Y	Y	Y
8 ***Coyne, J.***	Y	Y	Y	Y	Y	Y
9 ***Shuster***	Y	Y	Y	Y	Y	Y
10 ***McDade***	Y	Y	Y	Y	Y	Y
11 ***Nelligan***	Y	Y	Y	Y	Y	Y
12 Murtha	Y	?	Y	Y	Y	Y
13 ***Coughlin***	Y	Y	Y	Y	Y	Y
14 Coyne, W.	Y	Y	Y	Y	Y	Y
15 ***Ritter***	Y	Y	Y	Y	Y	Y
16 ***Walker***	Y	Y	N	N	Y	Y
17 Ertel	Y	Y	Y	Y	Y	Y
18 Walgren	Y	Y	Y	Y	Y	Y
19 ***Goodling***	Y	N	Y	?	?	Y
20 Gaydos	Y	Y	Y	?	Y	Y
21 Bailey	Y	Y	Y	Y	Y	Y
22 Murphy	Y	Y	Y	Y	Y	?
23 ***Clinger***	Y	Y	Y	Y	Y	Y
24 ***Marks***	Y	Y	N	?	Y	Y
25 ***Atkinson***	Y	Y	Y	Y	Y	Y
RHODE ISLAND						
1 St Germain	Y	Y	Y	Y	N	Y
2 ***Schneider***	Y	Y	Y	+	Y	Y
SOUTH CAROLINA						
1 ***Hartnett***	Y	Y	N	Y	Y	Y
2 ***Spence***	Y	Y	N	N	Y	Y
3 Derrick	Y	Y	Y	Y	N	Y
4 ***Campbell***	Y	Y	N	Y	Y	Y
5 Holland	Y	Y	Y	Y	Y	Y
6 ***Napier***	Y	Y	Y	Y	N	Y
SOUTH DAKOTA						
1 Daschle	Y	Y	Y	Y	Y	Y
2 ***Roberts***	Y	Y	N	N	N	Y
TENNESSEE						
1 ***Quillen***	Y	Y	N	?	?	?
2 ***Duncan***	?	?	?	?	?	?
3 Bouquard	Y	Y	Y	Y	Y	Y
4 Gore	Y	Y	Y	Y	N	Y
5 Boner	Y	Y	Y	Y	Y	Y
6 ***Beard***	Y	Y	N	Y	Y	Y
7 Jones	Y	Y	N	Y	N	Y
8 Ford	Y	N	Y	Y	Y	Y
TEXAS						
1 Hall, S.	Y	Y	N	N	N	N
2 Wilson	Y	Y	?	?	N	Y
3 ***Collins***	Y	N	N	Y	Y	N
4 Hall, R.	Y	Y	N	N	N	Y
5 Mattox	?	?	?	?	?	?
6 Gramm	Y	Y	Y	Y	Y	Y
7 ***Archer***	Y	Y	N	N	Y	Y
8 ***Fields***	Y	Y	Y	Y	Y	Y
9 Brooks	Y	Y	Y	Y	Y	Y
10 Pickle	Y	Y	Y	Y	N	Y
11 Leath	Y	Y	N	N	N	Y
12 Wright	Y	Y	Y	Y	Y	Y
13 Hightower	Y	Y	Y	Y	N	Y
14 Patman	Y	Y	N	N	N	N
15 de la Garza	Y	Y	Y	Y	Y	Y
16 White	Y	Y	Y	Y	Y	Y
17 Stenholm	Y	Y	N	Y	Y	Y
18 Leland	Y	N	Y	Y	Y	Y
19 Hance	Y	Y	?	?	N	Y
20 Gonzalez	Y	Y	Y	N	N	Y
21 ***Loeffler***	Y	Y	N	N	Y	Y
22 ***Paul***	?	?	?	?	?	X
23 Kazen	Y	Y	N	N	N	Y
24 Frost	Y	Y	Y	Y	N	Y
UTAH						
1 ***Hansen***	Y	Y	Y	Y	Y	Y
2 ***Marriott***	Y	Y	Y	Y	Y	Y
VERMONT						
AL ***Jeffords***	Y	Y	Y	Y	Y	Y
VIRGINIA						
1 ***Trible***	Y	Y	Y	Y	Y	?
2 ***Whitehurst***	Y	Y	Y	Y	Y	Y
3 ***Bliley***	Y	Y	N	Y	Y	Y
4 ***Daniel, R.***	Y	Y	Y	Y	Y	Y
5 Daniel, D.	Y	Y	Y	Y	Y	Y
6 ***Butler***	Y	Y	N	Y	Y	Y
7 ***Robinson***	Y	Y	N	Y	N	Y
8 ***Parris***	Y	Y	Y	Y	Y	Y
9 ***Wampler***	Y	Y	Y	Y	N	Y
10 ***Wolf***	Y	Y	Y	Y	Y	Y
WASHINGTON						
1 ***Pritchard***	?	?	?	?	?	#
2 Swift	Y	Y	Y	Y	Y	Y
3 Bonker	Y	?	Y	Y	Y	Y
4 ***Morrison***	Y	Y	Y	Y	Y	Y
5 Foley	Y	Y	Y	Y	Y	Y
6 Dicks	Y	Y	Y	Y	?	?
7 Lowry	Y	N	Y	Y	Y	Y
WEST VIRGINIA						
1 Mollohan	Y	Y	Y	Y	Y	Y
2 ***Benedict***	Y	?	N	?	Y	Y
3 ***Staton***	Y	Y	Y	Y	Y	Y
4 Rahall	Y	Y	Y	Y	Y	Y
WISCONSIN						
1 Aspin	Y	Y	Y	Y	Y	Y
2 Kastenmeier	N	N	Y	Y	Y	Y
3 ***Gunderson***	Y	N	N	Y	N	Y
4 Zablocki	Y	Y	Y	Y	Y	Y
5 Reuss	?	X	?	?	?	?
6 ***Petri***	Y	Y	N	N	N	N
7 Obey	Y	Y	Y	N	N	Y
8 ***Roth***	Y	Y	Y	Y	Y	?
9 ***Sensenbrenner***	Y	Y	Y	Y	N	N
WYOMING						
AL ***Cheney***	Y	Y	Y	Y	Y	Y

Democrats ***Republicans***

310. Procedural Motion. Loeffler, R-Texas, motion to approve the House *Journal* of Thursday, Nov. 19. Motion agreed to 323-17: R 144-10; D 179-7 (ND 113-7, SD 66-0), Nov. 20, 1981.

311. HR 4144. Energy and Water Appropriations, Fiscal 1982. Bevill, D-Ala., motion that the House recede from its position and agree to a Senate amendment to allow construction to continue on the Garrison Diversion water project in North Dakota. Work had been halted by a federal court. Motion rejected 67-314: R 23-145; D 44-169 (ND 13-127, SD 31-42), Nov. 20, 1981.

312. HR 3046. Older Americans Act. Passage of the bill to extend Older Americans programs through fiscal 1984 and to grant increased administrative flexibility to state and local providers of services to the elderly. Passed 379-4: R 161-3; D 218-1 (ND 144-0, SD 74-1), Nov. 20, 1981.

313. H Con Res 220. Franklin Delano Roosevelt Commemoration. Adoption of the concurrent resolution to establish a commission to arrange for the convening of a joint session of Congress on Jan. 27, 1982, to commemorate the 100th birthday of President Franklin D. Roosevelt. Adopted 344-18: R 143-17; D 201-1 (ND 130-0, SD 71-1), Nov. 20, 1981.

314. Procedural Motion. Campbell, R-S.C., motion that the House adjourn. Motion rejected 1-370: R 1-162; D 0-208 (ND 0-137, SD 0-71), Nov. 22, 1981.

KEY

Y Voted for (yea).
Paired for.
+ Announced for.
N Voted against (nay).
X Paired against.
- Announced against.
P Voted "present".
C Voted "present" to avoid possible conflict of interest.
? Did not vote or otherwise make a position known.

	310	311	312	313	314
ALABAMA					
1 *Edwards*	?	?	?	?	N
2 *Dickinson*	N	Y	Y	Y	?
3 Nichols	?	Y	Y	Y	N
4 Bevill	Y	Y	Y	Y	N
5 Flippo	Y	Y	Y	Y	N
6 *Smith*	Y	N	Y	N	N
7 Shelby	Y	Y	Y	Y	N
ALASKA					
AL *Young*	?	N	Y	Y	?
ARIZONA					
1 *Rhodes*	Y	Y	Y	Y	N
2 Udall	Y	?	Y	Y	N
3 *Stump*	Y	Y	Y	Y	N
4 *Rudd*	?	?	?	?	N
ARKANSAS					
1 Alexander	Y	Y	Y	Y	N
2 *Bethune*	Y	N	Y	Y	N
3 *Hammerschmidt*	Y	Y	Y	Y	N
4 Anthony	Y	Y	Y	Y	N
CALIFORNIA					
1 *Chappie*	Y	N	Y	Y	N
2 *Clausen*	?	?	Y	Y	N
3 Matsui	Y	Y	Y	Y	N
4 Fazio	Y	N	Y	Y	N
5 Burton, J.	Y	N	Y	Y	?
6 Burton, P.	?	N	Y	?	N
7 Miller	Y	N	Y	Y	N
8 Dellums	?	N	Y	N	N
9 Stark	Y	N	Y	Y	N
10 Edwards	Y	N	Y	Y	?
11 Lantos	Y	N	Y	Y	N
12 *McCloskey*	?	?	?	?	?
13 Mineta	Y	N	Y	Y	N
14 *Shumway*	Y	N	Y	N	N
15 Coelho	Y	Y	Y	Y	N
16 Panetta	Y	N	Y	Y	N
17 *Pashayan*	Y	N	Y	Y	N
18 *Thomas*	Y	N	Y	Y	N
19 *Lagomarsino*	Y	N	Y	Y	N
20 *Goldwater*	?	?	?	?	?
21 *Fiedler*	Y	N	Y	Y	N
22 *Moorhead*	Y	N	Y	Y	N
23 Beilenson	Y	N	Y	Y	N
24 Waxman	?	?	Y	Y	N
25 Roybal	Y	N	Y	Y	N
26 *Rousselot*	Y	N	?	N	?
27 *Dornan*	?	?	?	?	?
28 Dixon	?	?	Y	Y	N
29 Hawkins	Y	N	Y	Y	N
30 Danielson	Y	N	Y	Y	N
31 Dymally	Y	Y	Y	Y	N
32 Anderson	?	N	Y	Y	N
33 *Grisham*	Y	N	Y	Y	?
34 *Lungren*	Y	N	Y	Y	N
35 *Dreier*	Y	N	Y	N	N
36 Brown	?	?	Y	Y	N
37 *Lewis*	Y	Y	Y	Y	N
38 Patterson	Y	N	Y	Y	N
39 *Dannemeyer*	Y	N	N	?	?
40 *Badham*	Y	N	Y	Y	N
41 *Lowery*	Y	N	Y	Y	N
42 *Hunter*	Y	N	Y	Y	N
43 *Burgener*	Y	Y	?	?	N
COLORADO					
1 Schroeder	N	N	Y	Y	N
2 Wirth	Y	N	Y	Y	?
3 Kogovsek	Y	Y	Y	Y	N
4 *Brown*	N	N	Y	Y	N

	310	311	312	313	314
5 *Kramer*	Y	N	Y	Y	N
CONNECTICUT					
1 Vacancy					
2 Gejdenson	N	N	Y	Y	N
3 *DeNardis*	?	N	Y	Y	?
4 *McKinney*	?	?	Y	Y	?
5 Ratchford	Y	N	Y	?	N
6 Moffett	?	?	?	?	N
DELAWARE					
AL *Evans*	Y	?	Y	Y	N
FLORIDA					
1 Hutto	Y	N	Y	Y	N
2 Fuqua	Y	N	Y	Y	?
3 Bennett	Y	N	Y	Y	N
4 Chappell	Y	Y	Y	Y	N
5 *McCollum*	Y	N	Y	Y	N
6 *Young*	Y	N	Y	Y	N
7 Gibbons	Y	Y	Y	Y	N
8 Ireland	Y	N	Y	Y	N
9 Nelson	Y	N	Y	Y	N
10 *Bafalis*	Y	N	Y	Y	N
11 Mica	Y	N	Y	?	N
12 *Shaw*	Y	N	Y	Y	N
13 Lehman	Y	Y	Y	Y	N
14 Pepper	?	N	Y	Y	N
15 Fascell	Y	N	Y	Y	N
GEORGIA					
1 Ginn	?	?	?	Y	N
2 Hatcher	Y	Y	Y	Y	N
3 Brinkley	Y	N	Y	Y	N
4 Levitas	Y	N	Y	?	N
5 Fowler	Y	N	Y	Y	N
6 *Gingrich*	?	N	Y	Y	N
7 McDonald	Y	N	N	N	N
8 Evans	Y	N	Y	Y	?
9 Jenkins	Y	N	Y	Y	N
10 Barnard	?	Y	Y	Y	N
HAWAII					
1 Heftel	?	N	Y	?	N
2 Akaka	Y	N	Y	Y	N
IDAHO					
1 *Craig*	Y	Y	Y	Y	N
2 *Hansen*	Y	Y	?	N	?
ILLINOIS					
1 Washington	?	N	Y	Y	N
2 Savage	?	?	Y	Y	?
3 Russo	Y	N	Y	Y	N
4 *Derwinski*	N	N	Y	Y	N
5 Fary	Y	N	Y	Y	N
6 *Hyde*	Y	N	Y	Y	N
7 Collins	Y	N	Y	Y	N
8 Rostenkowski	Y	N	Y	Y	N
9 Yates	Y	N	Y	Y	N
10 *Porter*	Y	N	Y	Y	N
11 Annunzio	Y	N	Y	Y	N
12 *Crane, P.*	Y	N	N	N	N
13 *McClory*	Y	N	Y	Y	N
14 *Erlenborn*	Y	N	Y	Y	N
15 *Corcoran*	Y	N	Y	Y	N
16 *Martin*	Y	N	Y	Y	N
17 *O'Brien*	Y	Y	Y	Y	N
18 *Michel*	Y	N	Y	Y	N
19 *Railsback*	Y	?	Y	Y	N
20 *Findley*	Y	N	Y	Y	N
21 *Madigan*	Y	?	Y	Y	?
22 *Crane, D.*	Y	N	N	N	?
23 Price	Y	N	Y	Y	N
24 Simon	?	?	?	?	?
INDIANA					
1 Benjamin	Y	Y	Y	Y	N
2 Fithian	Y	N	Y	Y	N
3 *Hiler*	Y	N	Y	Y	N
4 *Coats*	Y	N	Y	Y	N
5 *Hillis*	Y	?	?	?	?
6 Evans	Y	N	Y	Y	N
7 *Myers*	Y	Y	?	?	?
8 *Deckard*	Y	N	Y	Y	N
9 Hamilton	Y	N	Y	Y	N
10 Sharp	Y	N	Y	Y	?
11 Jacobs	Y	N	Y	N	N
IOWA					
1 *Leach*	Y	N	Y	Y	N
2 *Tauke*	Y	N	Y	Y	?
3 Evans	Y	N	Y	Y	N
4 Smith	Y	Y	Y	Y	N
5 Harkin	N	N	Y	Y	?
6 Bedell	?	?	?	?	N

Democrats   *Republicans*

	310	311	312	313	314
KANSAS					
1 *Roberts*	Y	Y	Y	Y	N
2 *Jeffries*	Y	N	Y	N	N
3 *Winn*	Y	Y	Y	Y	?
4 Glickman	Y	N	Y	Y	N
5 *Whittaker*	Y	N	Y	Y	N
KENTUCKY					
1 Hubbard	Y	N	Y	Y	N
2 Natcher	Y	Y	Y	Y	N
3 Mazzoli	Y	Y	Y	Y	N
4 *Snyder*	Y	N	Y	Y	N
5 *Rogers*	Y	N	Y	Y	N
6 *Hopkins*	Y	N	Y	Y	N
7 Perkins	Y	Y	Y	Y	N
LOUISIANA					
1 *Livingston*	Y	N	Y	N	N
2 Boggs	Y	N	Y	Y	N
3 Tauzin	Y	N	Y	Y	N
4 Roemer	Y	N	Y	Y	N
5 Huckaby	Y	N	Y	Y	N
6 *Moore*	Y	N	Y	Y	N
7 Breaux	?	N	Y	Y	N
8 Long	?	N	Y	Y	N
MAINE					
1 *Emery*	Y	N	Y	Y	N
2 *Snowe*	Y	N	Y	Y	N
MARYLAND					
1 Dyson	Y	N	Y	Y	N
2 Long	Y	N	Y	?	N
3 Mikulski	Y	N	Y	Y	N
4 *Holt*	N	N	Y	N	N
5 Hoyer	Y	N	Y	Y	N
6 Byron	?	N	Y	?	N
7 Mitchell	N	N	Y	Y	N
8 Barnes	N	N	Y	Y	N
MASSACHUSETTS					
1 *Conte*	Y	N	Y	Y	N
2 Boland	Y	N	Y	Y	N
3 Early	?	?	?	?	N
4 Frank	Y	N	Y	Y	N
5 Shannon	Y	N	Y	Y	N
6 Mavroules	Y	N	Y	Y	N
7 Markey	Y	N	Y	Y	?
8 O'Neill					
9 Moakley	Y	N	Y	Y	N
10 *Heckler*	N	N	Y	Y	N
11 Donnelly	?	N	Y	Y	N
12 Studds	Y	N	Y	Y	N
MICHIGAN					
1 Conyers	?	N	Y	Y	N
2 *Pursell*	?	N	Y	Y	N
3 Wolpe	Y	N	Y	Y	N
4 *Siljander*	?	?	Y	N	N
5 *Sawyer*	Y	N	Y	Y	N
6 *Dunn*	Y	N	Y	N	N
7 Kildee	Y	N	Y	Y	N
8 Traxler	?	N	Y	Y	N
9 *Vander Jagt*	Y	N	Y	Y	N
10 Albosta	Y	N	Y	Y	N
11 Davis	Y	N	Y	Y	?
12 Bonior	Y	N	?	Y	N
13 Crockett	?	N	Y	Y	?
14 Hertel	Y	N	Y	Y	N
15 Ford	?	N	Y	Y	N
16 Dingell	Y	N	Y	Y	?
17 Brodhead	Y	N	Y	Y	N
18 Blanchard	Y	N	Y	Y	N
19 *Broomfield*	Y	N	Y	Y	N
MINNESOTA					
1 *Erdahl*	Y	N	Y	Y	N
2 *Hagedorn*	?	?	?	?	?
3 *Frenzel*	?	Y	Y	Y	N
4 Vento	?	N	Y	Y	N
5 Sabo	N	N	Y	Y	N
6 *Weber*	Y	N	Y	Y	N
7 *Stangeland*	Y	Y	Y	Y	N
8 Oberstar	Y	N	Y	Y	N
MISSISSIPPI					
1 Whitten	Y	Y	Y	Y	N
2 Bowen	?	?	?	?	?
3 Montgomery	Y	?	Y	Y	N
4 Dowdy	?	Y	Y	Y	N
5 *Lott*	?	?	?	?	N
MISSOURI					
1 Clay	?	?	?	?	N
2 Young	?	N	Y	Y	N
3 Gephardt	?	N	Y	Y	?

	310	311	312	313	314
4 Skelton	Y	N	Y	Y	N
5 Bolling	?	?	?	?	?
6 *Coleman*	?	N	Y	N	N
7 *Taylor*	Y	N	Y	N	N
8 *Bailey*	Y	N	Y	Y	N
9 Volkmer	?	N	Y	?	N
10 *Emerson*	?	N	Y	?	N
MONTANA					
1 Williams	Y	N	Y	Y	N
2 *Marlenee*	Y	Y	Y	N	N
NEBRASKA					
1 *Bereuter*	Y	N	Y	Y	N
2 *Daub*	Y	N	Y	Y	N
3 *Smith*	Y	Y	Y	Y	N
NEVADA					
AL Santini	?	?	?	?	?
NEW HAMPSHIRE					
1 D'Amours	Y	N	Y	Y	N
2 *Gregg*	Y	N	Y	Y	N
NEW JERSEY					
1 Florio	Y	N	Y	?	N
2 Hughes	Y	N	Y	Y	?
3 Howard	Y	?	?	?	N
4 *Smith*	Y	N	Y	Y	N
5 *Fenwick*	?	N	Y	Y	N
6 *Forsythe*	?	N	Y	Y	N
7 *Roukema*	Y	N	Y	Y	N
8 Roe	Y	N	Y	Y	N
9 *Hollenbeck*	Y	N	Y	Y	N
10 Rodino	Y	N	Y	Y	N
11 Minish	Y	N	Y	Y	N
12 *Rinaldo*	Y	N	Y	Y	N
13 *Courter*	Y	N	Y	Y	N
14 Guarini	?	N	Y	Y	N
15 Dwyer	Y	N	Y	Y	N
NEW MEXICO					
1 *Lujan*	Y	Y	Y	Y	?
2 *Skeen*	Y	Y	Y	Y	N
NEW YORK					
1 *Carney*	Y	N	Y	N	N
2 Downey	Y	N	Y	Y	N
3 *Carman*	Y	N	Y	Y	N
4 *Lent*	Y	N	Y	Y	N
5 *McGrath*	Y	N	Y	Y	N
6 *LeBoutillier*	Y	N	Y	Y	N
7 Addabbo	?	N	Y	Y	N
8 Rosenthal	Y	N	Y	Y	N
9 Ferraro	Y	N	Y	?	N
10 Biaggi	?	?	?	?	?
11 Scheuer	Y	N	Y	Y	N
12 Chisholm	?	?	?	?	?
13 Solarz	Y	N	Y	Y	N
14 Richmond	Y	N	Y	Y	N
15 Zeferetti	Y	N	Y	Y	N
16 Schumer	?	?	?	?	N
17 *Molinari*	Y	N	Y	Y	N
18 *Green*	?	N	Y	Y	N
19 Rangel	Y	N	Y	Y	N
20 Weiss	Y	N	Y	Y	N
21 Garcia	?	?	?	?	?
22 Bingham	Y	N	Y	?	?
23 Peyser	Y	N	Y	Y	N
24 Ottinger	P	N	Y	Y	N
25 *Fish*	Y	N	?	?	N
26 *Gilman*	?	?	Y	Y	N
27 McHugh	?	N	Y	Y	N
28 Stratton	Y	N	Y	Y	N
29 *Solomon*	Y	N	Y	N	N
30 *Martin*	Y	N	Y	Y	N
31 *Mitchell*	Y	N	Y	Y	N
32 *Wortley*	Y	N	Y	Y	N
33 *Lee*	?	N	Y	Y	N
34 *Horton*	Y	N	Y	?	N
35 *Conable*	Y	N	Y	Y	N
36 LaFalce	Y	N	Y	Y	N
37 Nowak	Y	N	Y	Y	N
38 *Kemp*	Y	N	Y	Y	N
39 Lundine	Y	N	Y	Y	N
NORTH CAROLINA					
1 Jones	?	?	?	?	?
2 Fountain	?	N	Y	Y	N
3 Whitley	Y	Y	Y	Y	N
4 Andrews	Y	N	Y	Y	N
5 Neal	?	N	Y	Y	N
6 *Johnston*	N	N	Y	Y	N
7 Rose	Y	N	Y	?	?
8 Hefner	Y	Y	Y	Y	N

	310	311	312	313	314
9 *Martin*	Y	N	Y	Y	N
10 *Broyhill*	Y	N	Y	Y	N
11 *Hendon*	Y	N	Y	Y	N
NORTH DAKOTA					
AL Dorgan	Y	Y	Y	Y	N
OHIO					
1 *Gradison*	?	N	Y	Y	N
2 Luken	Y	N	Y	Y	N
3 Hall	Y	N	Y	Y	N
4 *Oxley*	Y	N	?	?	N
5 *Latta*	Y	N	?	?	N
6 *McEwen*	Y	N	Y	?	N
7 *Brown*	?	N	?	?	N
8 *Kindness*	?	?	?	?	N
9 *Weber*	Y	N	?	Y	N
10 *Miller*	N	N	Y	Y	N
11 *Stanton*	Y	N	Y	?	N
12 Shamansky	Y	N	Y	Y	N
13 Pease	Y	N	Y	Y	N
14 Seiberling	Y	N	Y	Y	N
15 *Wylie*	Y	N	?	Y	N
16 *Regula*	Y	Y	Y	?	N
17 *Ashbrook*	Y	N	Y	?	N
18 Applegate	Y	N	Y	Y	N
19 *Williams*	Y	N	?	?	?
20 Oakar	Y	N	Y	Y	N
21 Stokes	Y	Y	Y	Y	N
22 Eckart	Y	N	Y	Y	N
23 Mottl	Y	N	Y	Y	?
OKLAHOMA					
1 Jones	Y	Y	Y	Y	?
2 Synar	Y	N	Y	Y	N
3 Watkins	?	N	Y	Y	N
4 *McCurdy*	Y	N	Y	Y	N
5 *Edwards*	?	Y	Y	Y	?
6 English	Y	Y	Y	Y	N
OREGON					
1 AuCoin	?	?	?	?	?
2 *Smith*	N	N	Y	N	N
3 Wyden	Y	N	Y	Y	N
4 Weaver	Y	N	Y	N	N
PENNSYLVANIA					
1 Foglietta	Y	N	Y	Y	N
2 Gray	Y	N	Y	?	N
3 Smith	?	N	Y	Y	N
4 *Dougherty*	?	N	Y	Y	?
5 *Schulze*	Y	N	?	?	N
6 Yatron	Y	N	Y	Y	N
7 Edgar	Y	N	Y	Y	N
8 *Coyne, J.*	Y	N	Y	Y	N
9 *Shuster*	Y	N	Y	Y	N
10 *McDade*	Y	N	Y	Y	N
11 *Nelligan*	Y	N	Y	Y	N
12 Murtha	Y	Y	Y	Y	N
13 *Coughlin*	N	N	Y	Y	N
14 Coyne, W.	Y	N	Y	Y	N
15 *Ritter*	Y	N	Y	Y	N
16 *Walker*	N	N	Y	Y	N
17 Ertel	Y	Y	Y	?	N
18 Walgren	Y	N	Y	Y	N
19 *Goodling*	?	?	Y	Y	N
20 Gaydos	Y	N	Y	Y	N
21 Bailey	Y	N	Y	Y	N
22 Murphy	?	?	Y	Y	N
23 *Clinger*	Y	N	Y	Y	N
24 *Marks*	?	N	Y	Y	N
25 Atkinson	Y	N	Y	Y	N
RHODE ISLAND					
1 St Germain	?	N	Y	Y	N
2 *Schneider*	Y	N	Y	Y	N
SOUTH CAROLINA					
1 *Hartnett*	Y	N	Y	Y	N
2 *Spence*	Y	N	Y	Y	N
3 Derrick	Y	Y	Y	Y	N
4 *Campbell*	Y	N	Y	Y	N
5 Holland	Y	Y	Y	Y	N
6 *Napier*	Y	N	Y	Y	N
SOUTH DAKOTA					
1 Daschle	?	N	?	Y	N
2 *Roberts*	?	Y	Y	Y	N
TENNESSEE					
1 *Quillen*	?	?	?	?	N
2 *Duncan*	?	?	?	?	?
3 Bouquard	Y	Y	Y	Y	N
4 Gore	Y	Y	Y	Y	N
5 Boner	Y	N	Y	Y	N
6 Beard	?	?	?	?	?

	310	311	312	313	314
7 Jones	Y	Y	Y	Y	N
8 Ford	Y	Y	Y	Y	N
TEXAS					
1 Hall, S.	Y	Y	Y	Y	N
2 Wilson	Y	?	Y	?	N
3 *Collins*	Y	N	Y	Y	N
4 Hall, R.	Y	Y	Y	Y	N
5 Mattox	?	?	?	?	?
6 Gramm	Y	N	Y	Y	N
7 *Archer*	Y	N	Y	N	N
8 *Fields*	Y	N	Y	N	N
9 Brooks	Y	N	Y	Y	N
10 Pickle	Y	N	Y	Y	N
11 Leath	Y	N	Y	Y	N
12 Wright	Y	Y	Y	Y	N
13 Hightower	Y	N	Y	Y	N
14 Patman	Y	N	Y	Y	N
15 de la Garza	Y	Y	Y	Y	N
16 White	Y	N	Y	Y	N
17 Stenholm	Y	Y	Y	Y	N
18 Leland	Y	N	Y	Y	N
19 Hance	Y	N	Y	Y	?
20 Gonzalez	Y	N	Y	Y	N
21 *Loeffler*	Y	N	Y	Y	N
22 *Paul*	?	?	?	?	?
23 Kazen	Y	N	Y	Y	N
24 Frost	Y	N	Y	Y	N
UTAH					
1 *Hansen*	Y	N	Y	Y	N
2 *Marriott*	Y	N	Y	Y	N
VERMONT					
AL *Jeffords*	Y	N	Y	Y	N
VIRGINIA					
1 *Trible*	?	N	Y	?	N
2 *Whitehurst*	Y	N	Y	Y	N
3 *Bliley*	Y	N	Y	Y	N
4 *Daniel, R.*	Y	N	Y	Y	N
5 Daniel, D.	Y	N	Y	Y	N
6 *Butler*	Y	N	Y	Y	N
7 *Robinson*	Y	N	Y	Y	N
8 *Parris*	Y	N	Y	Y	N
9 *Wampler*	Y	Y	?	?	?
10 *Wolf*	Y	N	Y	Y	N
WASHINGTON					
1 *Pritchard*	?	?	?	?	N
2 Swift	Y	N	Y	Y	N
3 Bonker	Y	N	Y	Y	N
4 *Morrison*	Y	Y	Y	Y	N
5 Foley	Y	?	?	?	N
6 Dicks	?	?	?	?	N
7 Lowry	Y	N	Y	Y	N
WEST VIRGINIA					
1 Mollohan	?	Y	?	?	?
2 *Benedict*	?	Y	Y	Y	N
3 Staton	Y	N	Y	Y	N
4 Rahall	Y	Y	Y	?	N
WISCONSIN					
1 Aspin	N	N	Y	Y	?
2 Kastenmeier	Y	N	Y	Y	N
3 *Gunderson*	Y	N	Y	Y	N
4 Zablocki	Y	N	Y	Y	N
5 Reuss	?	?	?	?	?
6 *Petri*	Y	N	Y	Y	N
7 Obey	Y	N	Y	Y	N
8 *Roth*	?	?	?	?	?
9 *Sensenbrenner*	Y	N	Y	Y	N
WYOMING					
AL *Cheney*	Y	?	Y	Y	?

Democrats *Republicans*

315. H J Res 357. Continuing Appropriations, Fiscal 1982. Michel, R-Ill., motion to recommit the conference report on the joint resolution to the conference committee. Motion rejected 184-215: R 175-0; D 9-215 (ND 2-148, SD 7-67), Nov. 22, 1981.

316. H J Res 357. Continuing Appropriations, Fiscal 1982. Adoption of the conference report on the joint resolution to provide funding authority during the period Nov. 20, 1981, through July 15, 1982, for government agencies whose regular fiscal 1982 appropriations bills had not been enacted. Adopted 205-194: R 10-166; D 195-28 (ND 141-8, SD 54-20), Nov. 22, 1981.

317. H J Res 357. Continuing Appropriations, Fiscal 1982. Coughlin, R-Pa., motion that the House recede from its disagreement to a Senate amendment providing additional pay and benefits for air traffic controllers. Motion agreed to 213-183: R 172-2; D 41-181 (ND 11-137, SD 30-44), Nov. 22, 1981.

318. H J Res 368. Continuing Appropriations, Fiscal 1982. Conte, R-Mass., motion to commit the joint resolution to the Appropriations Committee with instructions to advance the expiration date to Dec. 15, 1981, from Feb. 3, 1982, and to add funding for Public Health Service hospitals and clinics. Motion agreed to 221-176: R 178-0; D 43-176 (ND 17-129, SD 26-47), Nov. 23, 1981.

319. H J Res 368. Continuing Appropriations, Fiscal 1982. Passage of the joint resolution to provide funding authority during the period Nov. 20, 1981, through Dec. 15, 1981, for government agencies whose regular fiscal 1982 appropriations bills had not been enacted. Passed 367-26: R 170-6; D 197-20 (ND 130-15, SD 67-5), Nov. 23, 1981.

KEY

Y Voted for (yea).
Paired for.
+ Announced for.
N Voted against (nay).
X Paired against.
- Announced against.
P Voted "present".
C Voted "present" to avoid possible conflict of interest.
? Did not vote or otherwise make a position known.

	315	316	317	318	319
ALABAMA					
1 Edwards	Y	Y	Y	Y	Y
2 Dickinson	Y	N	Y	Y	Y
3 Nichols	N	Y	N	Y	N
4 Bevill	N	Y	N	N	Y
5 Flippo	N	Y	N	N	Y
6 Smith	Y	N	Y	N	Y
7 Shelby	Y	N	Y	Y	Y
ALASKA					
AL Young	Y	N	?	?	?
ARIZONA					
1 Rhodes	Y	N	Y	Y	Y
2 Udall	N	Y	N	N	Y
3 Stump	Y	N	Y	Y	Y
4 Rudd	Y	N	Y	Y	Y
ARKANSAS					
1 Alexander	N	Y	N	N	Y
2 Bethune	Y	N	Y	Y	Y
3 Hammerschmidt	Y	N	Y	Y	Y
4 Anthony	N	Y	N	N	Y
CALIFORNIA					
1 Chappie	Y	N	Y	Y	Y
2 Clausen	Y	N	Y	Y	Y
3 Matsui	N	Y	N	N	Y
4 Fazio	N	Y	N	N	Y
5 Burton, J.	N	Y	N	N	?
6 Burton, P.	?	?	?	?	?
7 Miller	N	Y	N	N	Y
8 Dellums	N	Y	N	N	N
9 Stark	N	Y	N	N	Y
10 Edwards	N	Y	N	N	Y
11 Lantos	?	#	?	X	?
12 McCloskey	?	?	?	?	?
13 Mineta	N	Y	N	N	Y
14 Shumway	Y	N	Y	Y	Y
15 Coelho	N	Y	N	N	Y
16 Panetta	N	Y	N	N	Y
17 Pashayan	Y	N	Y	Y	Y
18 Thomas	Y	N	Y	Y	Y
19 Lagomarsino	Y	N	Y	Y	Y
20 Goldwater	?	?	?	?	?
21 Fiedler	Y	N	Y	Y	Y
22 Moorhead	Y	N	Y	Y	Y
23 Beilenson	N	Y	N	N	N
24 Waxman	N	Y	N	N	Y
25 Roybal	N	Y	N	N	Y
26 Rousselot	Y	N	Y	Y	Y
27 Dornan	?	?	?	?	?
28 Dixon	N	Y	N	N	Y
29 Hawkins	N	P	N	N	N
30 Danielson	N	Y	N	N	Y
31 Dymally	N	Y	N	N	Y
32 Anderson	N	Y	Y	?	?
33 Grisham	Y	N	Y	Y	Y
34 Lungren	Y	N	Y	Y	Y
35 Dreier	Y	N	Y	Y	Y
36 Brown	N	Y	N	N	Y
37 Lewis	Y	N	Y	Y	Y
38 Patterson	N	Y	N	?	?
39 Dannemeyer	Y	N	Y	Y	N
40 Badham	Y	N	Y	Y	Y
41 Lowery	Y	N	Y	Y	Y
42 Hunter	Y	N	Y	Y	Y
43 Burgener	Y	N	Y	Y	Y
COLORADO					
1 Schroeder	N	Y	N	N	N
2 Wirth	N	Y	N	N	Y
3 Kogovsek	N	Y	N	N	Y
4 Brown	Y	N	Y	Y	N

	315	316	317	318	319
5 Kramer	Y	N	?	#	?
CONNECTICUT					
1 Vacancy					
2 Gejdenson	N	Y	N	N	N
3 DeNardis	Y	N	Y	Y	Y
4 McKinney	Y	N	Y	Y	Y
5 Ratchford	N	Y	N	N	Y
6 Moffett	N	Y	N	N	Y
DELAWARE					
AL Evans	Y	N	Y	Y	Y
FLORIDA					
1 Hutto	N	Y	N	Y	Y
2 Fuqua	?	?	?	?	?
3 Bennett	N	N	N	N	Y
4 Chappell	N	N	N	N	Y
5 McCollum	Y	N	Y	Y	Y
6 Young	Y	N	Y	Y	Y
7 Gibbons	N	Y	Y	Y	Y
8 Ireland	Y	N	Y	Y	Y
9 Nelson	N	Y	N	Y	Y
10 Bafalis	Y	N	Y	Y	Y
11 Mica	N	Y	N	Y	N
12 Shaw	Y	N	Y	Y	Y
13 Lehman	N	Y	N	N	N
14 Pepper	N	Y	N	N	N
15 Fascell	N	Y	N	N	N
GEORGIA					
1 Ginn	N	Y	N	N	?
2 Hatcher	N	Y	N	Y	Y
3 Brinkley	N	Y	Y	N	Y
4 Levitas	N	Y	Y	Y	Y
5 Fowler	N	Y	N	N	Y
6 Gingrich	Y	N	Y	Y	Y
7 McDonald	Y	N	Y	Y	N
8 Evans	N	Y	N	N	N
9 Jenkins	N	Y	N	Y	Y
10 Barnard	N	Y	Y	Y	Y
HAWAII					
1 Heftel	N	Y	N	Y	Y
2 Akaka	N	Y	N	N	Y
IDAHO					
1 Craig	Y	N	Y	Y	Y
2 Hansen	?	?	?	Y	Y
ILLINOIS					
1 Washington	N	Y	N	N	Y
2 Savage	N	N	N	N	N
3 Russo	N	N	N	N	N
4 Derwinski	Y	N	Y	Y	Y
5 Fary	N	Y	N	N	Y
6 Hyde	Y	N	Y	Y	Y
7 Collins	N	Y	N	N	Y
8 Rostenkowski	N	Y	N	N	Y
9 Yates	N	Y	N	N	Y
10 Porter	Y	N	Y	Y	Y
11 Annunzio	N	Y	N	N	Y
12 Crane, P.	Y	N	Y	Y	Y
13 McClory	Y	N	Y	Y	Y
14 Erlenborn	Y	N	Y	Y	?
15 Corcoran	Y	N	Y	Y	Y
16 Martin	Y	N	Y	Y	Y
17 O'Brien	Y	N	Y	Y	Y
18 Michel	Y	N	Y	Y	Y
19 Railsback	Y	Y	Y	Y	Y
20 Findley	Y	N	Y	Y	Y
21 Madigan	#	?	?	?	?
22 Crane, D.	?	X	?	#	?
23 Price	N	Y	N	N	Y
24 Simon	?	?	?	N	Y
INDIANA					
1 Benjamin	N	Y	N	N	Y
2 Fithian	N	Y	N	N	Y
3 Hiler	Y	N	Y	Y	Y
4 Coats	Y	N	Y	Y	Y
5 Hillis	?	?	?	?	?
6 Evans	N	Y	N	N	Y
7 Myers	#	X	?	Y	Y
8 Deckard	Y	N	Y	Y	Y
9 Hamilton	N	N	Y	Y	Y
10 Sharp	N	N	?	Y	Y
11 Jacobs	N	Y	N	N	Y
IOWA					
1 Leach	Y	N	Y	Y	Y
2 Tauke	?	?	?	Y	Y
3 Evans	Y	N	Y	Y	Y
4 Smith	N	Y	N	N	Y
5 Harkin	N	Y	N	Y	Y
6 Bedell	N	Y	N	?	?

Democrats *Republicans*

Corresponding to Congressional Record Votes 332, 333, 334, 335, 336

	315	316	317	318	319
KANSAS					
1 *Roberts*	Y	N	Y	Y	Y
2 *Jeffries*	Y	N	Y	Y	Y
3 *Winn*	#	?	?	?	?
4 Glickman	N	Y	Y	Y	Y
5 *Whittaker*	Y	N	Y	Y	Y
KENTUCKY					
1 Hubbard	N	N	N	Y	N
2 Natcher	N	Y	N	N	Y
3 Mazzoli	N	Y	Y	Y	Y
4 *Snyder*	Y	N	Y	Y	Y
5 *Rogers*	Y	N	Y	Y	Y
6 *Hopkins*	Y	N	Y	Y	Y
7 Perkins	N	Y	N	N	Y
LOUISIANA					
1 *Livingston*	Y	N	Y	Y	Y
2 Boggs	N	Y	N	N	Y
3 Tauzin	N	N	Y	Y	Y
4 Roemer	Y	N	Y	Y	Y
5 Huckaby	N	N	N	N	Y
6 *Moore*	Y	N	Y	Y	Y
7 Breaux	N	Y	Y	Y	Y
8 Long	N	Y	N	N	?
MAINE					
1 *Emery*	Y	N	Y	Y	Y
2 *Snowe*	Y	N	Y	Y	Y
MARYLAND					
1 Dyson	N	Y	N	Y	Y
2 Long	N	Y	N	N	Y
3 Mikulski	N	Y	N	N	Y
4 *Holt*	Y	N	Y	Y	Y
5 Hoyer	N	Y	N	N	Y
6 Byron	N	Y	Y	Y	Y
7 Mitchell	N	N	N	N	N
8 Barnes	N	Y	N	N	Y
MASSACHUSETTS					
1 *Conte*	Y	Y	Y	Y	Y
2 Boland	N	Y	N	N	Y
3 Early	N	Y	N	N	Y
4 Frank	N	Y	N	N	Y
5 Shannon	N	Y	N	N	Y
6 Mavroules	N	Y	N	N	Y
7 Markey	N	Y	N	N	Y
8 O'Neill					
9 Moakley	N	Y	N	N	Y
10 *Heckler*	Y	N	Y	Y	Y
11 Donnelly	N	Y	N	N	Y
12 Studds	N	Y	N	N	Y
MICHIGAN					
1 Conyers	N	Y	N	N	N
2 *Pursell*	Y	N	N	Y	Y
3 Wolpe	N	Y	N	N	Y
4 *Siljander*	Y	N	Y	Y	Y
5 *Sawyer*	Y	N	Y	Y	Y
6 *Dunn*	Y	N	Y	Y	Y
7 Kildee	N	Y	N	N	Y
8 Traxler	N	Y	N	N	Y
9 *Vander Jagt*	#	N	Y	Y	Y
10 Albosta	N	Y	N	N	Y
11 *Davis*	Y	N	Y	Y	Y
12 Bonior	N	Y	N	N	Y
13 Crockett	N	Y	N	N	Y
14 Hertel	N	Y	N	N	Y
15 Ford	N	Y	N	N	Y
16 Dingell	N	Y	N	N	Y
17 Brodhead	N	Y	N	N	N
18 Blanchard	N	Y	N	N	Y
19 *Broomfield*	Y	N	Y	Y	Y
MINNESOTA					
1 *Erdahl*	Y	N	Y	Y	Y
2 *Hagedorn*	?	X	?	Y	Y
3 *Frenzel*	Y	N	Y	Y	Y
4 Vento	N	Y	N	Y	Y
5 Sabo	N	Y	N	N	Y
6 *Weber*	Y	N	Y	Y	Y
7 *Stangeland*	Y	N	Y	Y	Y
8 Oberstar	N	Y	N	N	Y
MISSISSIPPI					
1 Whitten	N	Y	N	N	Y
2 Bowen	N	Y	N	Y	N
3 Montgomery	N	N	Y	?	?
4 Dowdy	N	Y	N	N	Y
5 *Lott*	Y	N	Y	Y	Y
MISSOURI					
1 Clay	N	Y	N	N	N
2 Young	N	Y	N	N	Y
3 Gephardt	N	Y	N	N	Y

	315	316	317	318	319
4 Skelton	N	Y	N	Y	Y
5 Bolling	?	?	?	?	?
6 *Coleman*	Y	N	Y	Y	Y
7 *Taylor*	Y	N	Y	Y	Y
8 *Bailey*	Y	N	Y	Y	Y
9 Volkmer	N	Y	N	N	Y
10 *Emerson*	Y	N	Y	Y	Y
MONTANA					
1 Williams	N	Y	N	N	Y
2 *Marlenee*	Y	N	Y	Y	Y
NEBRASKA					
1 *Bereuter*	Y	N	Y	Y	Y
2 *Daub*	Y	N	Y	Y	Y
3 *Smith*	Y	N	Y	Y	Y
NEVADA					
AL Santini	?	?	?	N	Y
NEW HAMPSHIRE					
1 D'Amours	N	Y	N	N	Y
2 *Gregg*	Y	N	Y	Y	Y
NEW JERSEY					
1 Florio	N	Y	N	N	Y
2 Hughes	?	X	?	#	?
3 Howard	N	Y	N	N	Y
4 *Smith*	Y	N	Y	Y	Y
5 *Fenwick*	Y	N	Y	Y	Y
6 *Forsythe*	Y	N	Y	Y	Y
7 *Roukema*	Y	N	Y	Y	Y
8 Roe	N	Y	N	N	Y
9 *Hollenbeck*	Y	N	N	N	Y
10 Rodino	N	Y	N	N	Y
11 Minish	N	Y	N	N	Y
12 *Rinaldo*	Y	N	Y	Y	Y
13 *Courter*	Y	N	Y	Y	Y
14 Guarini	N	Y	N	N	Y
15 Dwyer	N	Y	N	N	Y
NEW MEXICO					
1 *Lujan*	Y	N	Y	Y	Y
2 *Skeen*	Y	N	Y	Y	Y
NEW YORK					
1 *Carney*	Y	N	Y	Y	Y
2 Downey	N	Y	N	N	Y
3 *Carman*	Y	N	Y	?	?
4 *Lent*	Y	N	Y	Y	Y
5 *McGrath*	Y	N	Y	Y	Y
6 *LeBoutillier*	Y	N	Y	Y	Y
7 Addabbo	N	Y	N	N	Y
8 Rosenthal	N	Y	N	N	Y
9 Ferraro	N	Y	N	N	Y
10 Biaggi	X	#	?	?	?
11 Scheuer	N	Y	N	N	Y
12 Chisholm	X	#	?	X	?
13 Solarz	N	Y	N	N	Y
14 Richmond	N	Y	N	N	N
15 Zeferetti	N	Y	N	N	Y
16 Schumer	N	Y	N	X	?
17 *Molinari*	Y	N	Y	Y	Y
18 *Green*	Y	N	Y	Y	Y
19 Rangel	N	Y	N	N	Y
20 Weiss	N	Y	N	N	N
21 Garcia	N	Y	N	N	N
22 Bingham	N	Y	N	N	Y
23 Peyser	N	Y	N	N	Y
24 Ottinger	N	Y	N	N	N
25 *Fish*	Y	N	Y	Y	Y
26 *Gilman*	Y	N	Y	Y	Y
27 McHugh	N	Y	N	N	Y
28 Stratton	N	Y	Y	Y	Y
29 *Solomon*	Y	N	Y	Y	Y
30 *Martin*	Y	N	Y	Y	Y
31 *Mitchell*	Y	N	Y	Y	Y
32 *Wortley*	Y	N	Y	Y	Y
33 *Lee*	Y	N	Y	Y	Y
34 *Horton*	Y	N	Y	Y	Y
35 *Conable*	Y	N	Y	Y	Y
36 LaFalce	N	Y	N	N	Y
37 Nowak	N	Y	N	N	Y
38 *Kemp*	Y	N	Y	Y	Y
39 Lundine	N	Y	N	?	?
NORTH CAROLINA					
1 Jones	?	?	?	?	?
2 Fountain	N	Y	N	Y	N
3 Whitley	N	Y	N	N	Y
4 Andrews	N	Y	Y	N	Y
5 Neal	N	Y	N	N	Y
6 *Johnston*	Y	N	Y	N	Y
7 Rose	?	?	?	?	?
8 Hefner	N	Y	N	N	Y

	315	316	317	318	319
9 *Martin*	Y	N	Y	Y	Y
10 *Broyhill*	Y	N	Y	Y	Y
11 *Hendon*	Y	N	Y	Y	Y
NORTH DAKOTA					
AL Dorgan	N	Y	N	N	Y
OHIO					
1 *Gradison*	Y	N	Y	Y	Y
2 Luken	N	Y	N	N	Y
3 Hall	N	Y	P	Y	Y
4 *Oxley*	Y	N	Y	Y	Y
5 *Latta*	Y	N	Y	Y	Y
6 *McEwen*	Y	N	Y	Y	Y
7 *Brown*	Y	N	Y	#	?
8 *Kindness*	Y	N	Y	Y	Y
9 *Weber*	Y	N	Y	Y	Y
10 *Miller*	Y	N	Y	Y	Y
11 *Stanton*	Y	N	Y	Y	Y
12 Shamansky	N	Y	Y	N	Y
13 Pease	N	Y	N	N	Y
14 Seiberling	N	Y	N	N	Y
15 *Wylie*	Y	N	Y	Y	Y
16 *Regula*	Y	N	Y	Y	Y
17 *Ashbrook*	Y	N	Y	Y	Y
18 Applegate	N	N	Y	N	Y
19 *Williams*	?	?	?	Y	Y
20 Oakar	N	Y	N	N	Y
21 Stokes	N	Y	N	N	Y
22 Eckart	N	Y	N	N	Y
23 Mottl	Y	N	Y	?	?
OKLAHOMA					
1 Jones	?	?	?	?	Y
2 Synar	N	Y	N	N	Y
3 Watkins	N	Y	N	N	Y
4 McCurdy	N	N	Y	Y	Y
5 *Edwards*	Y	N	Y	Y	Y
6 English	N	N	Y	N	Y
OREGON					
1 AuCoin	X	#	?	N	Y
2 *Smith*	Y	N	Y	Y	N
3 Wyden	N	Y	N	Y	Y
4 Weaver	N	Y	N	N	Y
PENNSYLVANIA					
1 Foglietta	N	Y	N	N	Y
2 Gray	N	Y	N	X	?
3 Smith	N	Y	N	N	Y
4 *Dougherty*	Y	Y	Y	Y	Y
5 *Schulze*	Y	N	Y	Y	Y
6 Yatron	N	Y	N	N	Y
7 Edgar	N	Y	N	N	Y
8 *Coyne, J.*	Y	N	Y	Y	Y
9 *Shuster*	Y	N	Y	Y	Y
10 *McDade*	Y	Y	Y	Y	Y
11 *Nelligan*	Y	Y	Y	Y	Y
12 Murtha	N	Y	N	N	Y
13 *Coughlin*	Y	Y	Y	Y	Y
14 Coyne, W.	N	Y	N	N	Y
15 *Ritter*	Y	N	Y	Y	Y
16 *Walker*	Y	N	Y	Y	Y
17 Ertel	N	Y	N	N	Y
18 Walgren	N	Y	N	N	Y
19 *Goodling*	Y	N	Y	Y	Y
20 Gaydos	N	Y	N	N	Y
21 Bailey	N	Y	N	N	Y
22 Murphy	N	Y	N	N	Y
23 *Clinger*	Y	N	Y	Y	Y
24 *Marks*	Y	N	Y	Y	Y
25 *Atkinson*	Y	N	Y	Y	Y
RHODE ISLAND					
1 St Germain	N	Y	N	N	Y
2 *Schneider*	Y	N	Y	Y	Y
SOUTH CAROLINA					
1 *Hartnett*	Y	N	Y	Y	Y
2 *Spence*	Y	N	Y	Y	Y
3 Derrick	N	Y	N	N	Y
4 *Campbell*	Y	N	Y	Y	Y
5 Holland	N	N	Y	N	Y
6 *Napier*	Y	N	Y	Y	Y
SOUTH DAKOTA					
1 Daschle	N	Y	N	N	Y
2 *Roberts*	Y	N	Y	Y	Y
TENNESSEE					
1 *Quillen*	Y	N	Y	Y	Y
2 *Duncan*	?	X	?	#	?
3 Bouquard	N	Y	N	N	Y
4 Gore	N	Y	N	N	Y
5 Boner	N	Y	N	N	Y
6 *Beard*	Y	N	Y	Y	Y

	315	316	317	318	319
7 Jones	N	Y	N	N	Y
8 Ford	N	Y	N	N	Y
TEXAS					
1 Hall, S.	N	N	N	Y	Y
2 Wilson	N	Y	Y	Y	Y
3 *Collins*	Y	N	Y	Y	Y
4 Hall, R.	Y	N	Y	Y	Y
5 Mattox	X	#	?	X	?
6 Gramm	Y	N	Y	Y	Y
7 *Archer*	Y	N	Y	Y	Y
8 *Fields*	Y	N	Y	Y	Y
9 Brooks	N	Y	N	N	Y
10 Pickle	Y	N	N	N	Y
11 Leath	N	N	Y	N	Y
12 Wright	N	Y	N	N	Y
13 Hightower	N	Y	Y	Y	Y
14 Patman	N	Y	Y	Y	Y
15 de la Garza	N	Y	N	N	Y
16 White	N	Y	Y	Y	Y
17 Stenholm	N	N	Y	N	Y
18 Leland	N	Y	N	N	Y
19 Hance	N	N	N	N	Y
20 Gonzalez	N	Y	N	N	Y
21 *Loeffler*	Y	N	Y	Y	Y
22 *Paul*	?	?	?	Y	N
23 Kazen	N	Y	N	N	Y
24 Frost	N	Y	N	N	Y
UTAH					
1 *Hansen*	Y	N	Y	Y	Y
2 *Marriott*	Y	N	Y	Y	Y
VERMONT					
AL *Jeffords*	Y	Y	Y	Y	Y
VIRGINIA					
1 *Trible*	Y	N	Y	Y	Y
2 *Whitehurst*	Y	N	Y	Y	Y
3 *Bliley*	Y	N	Y	Y	Y
4 *Daniel, R.*	N	N	Y	Y	Y
5 Daniel, D.	N	N	Y	N	Y
6 *Butler*	Y	N	Y	Y	Y
7 *Robinson*	Y	Y	Y	Y	Y
8 *Parris*	Y	Y	Y	Y	Y
9 *Wampler*	#	?	?	?	?
10 *Wolf*	Y	N	Y	Y	Y
WASHINGTON					
1 *Pritchard*	Y	N	Y	Y	Y
2 Swift	N	Y	N	Y	Y
3 Bonker	N	Y	N	N	Y
4 *Morrison*	Y	N	Y	Y	Y
5 Foley	N	Y	N	N	Y
6 Dicks	N	Y	N	Y	Y
7 Lowry	N	Y	N	N	Y
WEST VIRGINIA					
1 Mollohan	X	#	?	X	?
2 *Benedict*	Y	N	Y	Y	Y
3 *Staton*	Y	N	Y	Y	Y
4 Rahall	N	Y	N	N	Y
WISCONSIN					
1 Aspin	?	?	?	?	?
2 Kastenmeier	N	Y	N	Y	N
3 *Gunderson*	Y	N	Y	Y	Y
4 Zablocki	N	Y	N	N	Y
5 Reuss	?	?	?	?	?
6 *Petri*	Y	N	Y	Y	N
7 Obey	N	Y	N	N	Y
8 *Roth*	?	X	?	#	?
9 *Sensenbrenner*	Y	N	Y	Y	Y
WYOMING					
AL *Cheney*	Y	N	Y	Y	Y

Democrats *Republicans*

320. H J Res 341. Alaska Natural Gas Transportation System Waivers. Corcoran, R-Ill., motion to postpone until Dec. 10 consideration of the joint resolution approving President Reagan's waivers to the 1977 decision to build the pipeline. The waivers were aimed at securing private financing by putting more financial risk on gas consumers. Motion rejected 50-270: R 21-138; D 29-132 (ND 27-80, SD 2-52), Dec. 8, 1981. (The House subsequently passed H J Res 341, *see vote 322, below.*)

321. Procedural Motion. Corcoran, R-Ill., motion to approve the House *Journal* of Tuesday, Dec. 8. Motion agreed to 348-16: R 157-10; D 191-6 (ND 127-6, SD 64-0), Dec. 9, 1981.

322. H J Res 341. Alaska Natural Gas Transportation System Waivers. Passage of the joint resolution approving the president's waivers of various stipulations in the 1977 decision to build a pipeline to carry natural gas from Alaska to the continental United States. The waivers were aimed at securing private financing for the pipeline. Passed 233-173: R 119-67; D 114-106 (ND 57-88, SD 57-18), Dec. 9, 1981. A "yea" was a vote supporting the president's position. (Because of parliamentary maneuvering, the resolution could not be cleared, and the House subsequently passed an identical Senate joint resolution, S J Res 115 *(see vote 329, p. 108-H),* instead.)

323. HR 3566. Foreign Aid Authorization. Adoption of the resolution (H Res 291) providing for consideration of the bill to authorize appropriations for military, economic and development aid abroad, and to establish the Peace Corps as an independent agency. Adopted 250-151: R 69-114; D 181-37 (ND 137-9, SD 44-28), Dec. 9, 1981.

324. HR 3566. Foreign Aid Authorization. Minish, D-N.J., amendment to prohibit aid to Indonesia. Rejected 55-355: R 13-175; D 42-180 (ND 29-119, SD 13-61), Dec. 9, 1981.

325. HR 3566. Foreign Aid Authorization. Lungren, R-Calif., amendment to delete provisions in the bill removing the Peace Corps from the ACTION agency. Rejected 155-258: R 107-80; D 48-178 (ND 10-140, SD 38-38), Dec. 9, 1981.

326. HR 3566. Foreign Aid Authorization. Markey, D-Mass., amendment, as amended by the Dunn, R-Mich., amendment, stating that Congress condemns the government of Libya for its support of international terrorism, its obstruction of peace in the Middle East and its efforts to destabilize the governments of its neighbors in Africa; and that Congress believes the president should review and report within 180 days of the enactment of HR 3566 on what concrete steps the United States could take, including a ban on importation of Libyan oil, to put economic and political pressure on Libya to force it to abandon its policies. Adopted 356-46: R 143-40; D 213-6 (ND 138-6, SD 75-0), Dec. 9, 1981.

327. HR 3566. Foreign Aid Authorization. Passage of the bill to authorize $5,727,854,000 for fiscal 1982 and $6,415,930,000 for fiscal 1983 (but no more in fiscal 1983 than requested by the president) for military, economic and development aid abroad, and to establish the Peace Corps as an independent agency. Passed 222-184: R 97-86; D 125-98 (ND 102-46, SD 23-52), Dec. 9, 1981. (The president had requested $5,727,854,000.)

KEY

Y Voted for (yea).
\# Paired for.
+ Announced for.
N Voted against (nay).
X Paired against.
- Announced against.
P Voted "present".
C Voted "present" to avoid possible conflict of interest.
? Did not vote or otherwise make a position known.

	320	321	322	323	324	325	326	327
ALABAMA								
1 Edwards	N	?	Y	Y	N	N	Y	N
2 Dickinson	N	N	Y	N	N	Y	N	N
3 Nichols	?	?	?	?	N	Y	Y	N
4 Bevill	N	Y	Y	Y	Y	N	Y	N
5 Flippo	N	Y	Y	Y	Y	N	Y	N
6 Smith	N	Y	Y	N	N	Y	?	X
7 Shelby	?	Y	Y	Y	N	Y	Y	N
ALASKA								
AL Young	N	Y	Y	N	N	Y	N	N
ARIZONA								
1 Rhodes	N	Y	Y	N	N	N	Y	Y
2 Udall	N	Y	Y	Y	N	N	Y	Y
3 Stump	N	Y	Y	N	Y	Y	N	Y
4 Rudd	N	Y	Y	N	N	Y	N	Y
ARKANSAS								
1 Alexander	N	Y	Y	N	N	Y	N	Y
2 Bethune	N	Y	N	N	?	N	Y	X
3 Hammerschmidt	N	Y	Y	N	N	N	Y	N
4 Anthony	?	Y	Y	Y	N	N	?	?
CALIFORNIA								
1 Chappie	N	Y	Y	N	N	N	Y	N
2 Clausen	N	Y	Y	Y	N	Y	N	Y
3 Matsui	?	Y	N	Y	N	N	Y	Y
4 Fazio	N	Y	Y	Y	N	N	Y	Y
5 Burton, J.	Y	Y	N	Y	?	?	?	?
6 Burton, P.	Y	Y	N	N	N	N	Y	Y
7 Miller	Y	?	X	?	?	?	?	?
8 Dellums	?	?	N	Y	N	N	P	N
9 Stark	Y	?	X	Y	Y	N	Y	Y
10 Edwards	Y	Y	N	N	N	Y	Y	Y
11 Lantos	?	Y	Y	N	N	?	?	?
12 McCloskey	?	?	?	?	?	?	?	#
13 Mineta	N	Y	Y	N	N	Y	N	Y
14 Shumway	N	Y	Y	N	Y	Y	N	N
15 Coelho	N	?	Y	Y	N	N	Y	Y
16 Panetta	N	Y	Y	N	N	Y	N	Y
17 Pashayan	N	Y	Y	N	N	Y	N	N
18 Thomas	N	Y	N	N	#	Y	N	Y
19 Lagomarsino	N	Y	Y	Y	N	Y	N	Y
20 Goldwater	?	?	#	?	?	?	?	#
21 Fiedler	?	Y	Y	N	Y	Y	Y	Y
22 Moorhead	N	Y	Y	N	N	Y	N	N
23 Beilenson	N	Y	N	N	N	Y	Y	Y
24 Waxman	?	Y	N	Y	N	Y	N	Y
25 Roybal	?	Y	N	Y	N	N	Y	N
26 Rousselot	N	N	Y	N	N	N	?	X
27 Dornan	N	Y	Y	N	N	Y	Y	Y
28 Dixon	?	Y	Y	Y	N	N	Y	Y
29 Hawkins	?	Y	Y	Y	N	N	Y	N
30 Danielson	N	Y	N	N	N	Y	N	Y
31 Dymally	?	?	#	?	?	X	?	?
32 Anderson	N	Y	Y	Y	N	Y	Y	N
33 Grisham	N	Y	Y	N	N	Y	N	N
34 Lungren	N	Y	Y	N	Y	Y	Y	Y
35 Dreier	?	N	Y	N	Y	Y	Y	N
36 Brown	N	Y	Y	Y	N	N	N	N
37 Lewis	N	Y	Y	N	N	N	N	Y
38 Patterson	N	Y	Y	Y	N	N	Y	Y
39 Dannemeyer	N	Y	Y	N	N	Y	N	Y
40 Badham	N	Y	N	N	N	Y	N	Y
41 Lowery	N	Y	Y	N	N	Y	Y	?
42 Hunter	N	Y	Y	N	N	Y	N	Y
43 Burgener	N	?	Y	Y	N	Y	N	Y
COLORADO								
1 Schroeder	N	N	N	N	Y	Y	Y	N
2 Wirth	?	Y	N	Y	N	N	Y	Y
3 Kogovsek	?	Y	Y	Y	N	N	Y	N
4 Brown	Y	Y	N	N	Y	Y	Y	N

	320	321	322	323	324	325	326	327
5 Kramer	N	Y	Y	N	N	Y	Y	N
CONNECTICUT								
1 Vacancy								
2 Gejdenson	N	N	N	Y	N	N	Y	Y
3 DeNardis	N	Y	N	N	N	N	Y	Y
4 McKinney	?	Y	Y	N	N	N	Y	Y
5 Ratchford	N	Y	N	N	N	N	Y	Y
6 Moffett	?	Y	N	?	N	N	Y	Y
DELAWARE								
AL Evans	N	?	Y	N	N	Y	Y	Y
FLORIDA								
1 Hutto	N	?	Y	Y	N	Y	Y	N
2 Fuqua	N	Y	Y	Y	N	N	Y	Y
3 Bennett	N	Y	Y	Y	Y	Y	Y	N
4 Chappell	N	?	Y	Y	N	Y	Y	N
5 McCollum	N	Y	Y	N	N	Y	Y	N
6 Young	N	Y	Y	N	N	Y	Y	N
7 Gibbons	?	Y	Y	N	Y	Y	Y	Y
8 Ireland	N	Y	Y	?	N	Y	Y	Y
9 Nelson	N	Y	Y	N	N	Y	Y	N
10 Bafalis	N	Y	Y	N	N	Y	Y	N
11 Mica	N	Y	N	Y	N	N	Y	Y
12 Shaw	N	Y	Y	N	N	Y	Y	Y
13 Lehman	?	Y	Y	Y	N	N	Y	Y
14 Pepper	N	?	#	?	N	N	Y	Y
15 Fascell	N	?	N	Y	N	N	Y	Y
GEORGIA								
1 Ginn	?	?	?	?	?	?	?	?
2 Hatcher	N	Y	N	Y	N	N	N	Y
3 Brinkley	N	Y	Y	N	N	N	Y	N
4 Levitas	?	Y	N	Y	N	N	Y	N
5 Fowler	?	?	N	N	N	N	Y	N
6 Gingrich	?	Y	Y	N	N	Y	N	Y
7 McDonald	?	Y	Y	N	Y	N	Y	N
8 Evans	?	Y	N	?	N	Y	N	Y
9 Jenkins	?	Y	Y	N	Y	Y	Y	N
10 Barnard	N	Y	Y	N	Y	Y	Y	N
HAWAII								
1 Heftel	?	Y	Y	Y	Y	N	Y	Y
2 Akaka	N	Y	Y	Y	Y	N	Y	N
IDAHO								
1 Craig	N	Y	?	N	N	Y	N	N
2 Hansen	N	Y	Y	N	N	N	Y	N
ILLINOIS								
1 Washington	?	Y	N	Y	N	N	Y	Y
2 Savage	?	Y	N	Y	N	N	P	N
3 Russo	?	Y	N	Y	N	Y	N	Y
4 Derwinski	N	Y	N	N	N	Y	Y	Y
5 Fary	?	?	X	Y	N	N	Y	Y
6 Hyde	Y	Y	N	Y	N	Y	N	Y
7 Collins	N	Y	N	Y	N	Y	Y	Y
8 Rostenkowski	?	Y	Y	N	N	N	Y	Y
9 Yates	Y	Y	Y	Y	N	N	Y	Y
10 Porter	N	Y	N	N	Y	N	Y	Y
11 Annunzio	N	Y	N	Y	N	N	Y	Y
12 Crane, P.	N	?	N	N	N	N	Y	N
13 McClory	?	Y	Y	N	N	Y	Y	Y
14 Erlenborn	N	Y	N	N	N	Y	Y	N
15 Corcoran	Y	Y	N	N	N	Y	Y	N
16 Martin	N	Y	N	N	N	N	N	Y
17 O'Brien	N	Y	Y	N	N	Y	N	N
18 Michel	Y	?	N	?	N	Y	N	Y
19 Railsback	Y	Y	N	N	N	N	Y	N
20 Findley	N	Y	N	N	N	Y	N	Y
21 Madigan	N	?	Y	N	Y	N	N	Y
22 Crane, D.	N	Y	N	N	N	Y	Y	N
23 Price	N	Y	N	N	N	Y	Y	Y
24 Simon	?	Y	N	Y	N	N	Y	Y
INDIANA								
1 Benjamin	N	Y	Y	N	N	Y	N	Y
2 Fithian	?	?	?	?	?	?	?	?
3 Hiler	N	Y	N	Y	N	N	Y	N
4 Coats	N	Y	N	N	N	Y	Y	N
5 Hillis	?	Y	Y	Y	N	N	N	Y
6 Evans	?	Y	Y	N	N	N	N	N
7 Myers	N	Y	N	N	N	N	N	N
8 Deckard	N	N	?	N	N	Y	N	N
9 Hamilton	N	Y	Y	N	N	Y	Y	N
10 Sharp	N	Y	Y	Y	N	N	Y	Y
11 Jacobs	?	N	N	N	Y	Y	N	Y
IOWA								
1 Leach	Y	Y	N	Y	N	N	N	Y
2 Tauke	Y	Y	N	N	N	N	Y	Y
3 Evans	Y	N	N	Y	N	N	N	Y
4 Smith	N	Y	N	Y	N	N	N	Y
5 Harkin	N	N	N	Y	N	N	Y	Y
6 Bedell	Y	Y	N	Y	?	?	?	?

Democrats *Republicans*

	320	321	322	323	324	325	326	327
KANSAS								
1 ***Roberts***	N	Y	Y	N	N	N	Y	N
2 ***Jeffries***	?	Y	Y	N	N	Y	N	N
3 ***Winn***	N	Y	Y	Y	N	N	Y	Y
4 Glickman	N	Y	Y	Y	N	N	Y	Y
5 ***Whittaker***	N	Y	Y	N	N	Y	Y	N
KENTUCKY								
1 Hubbard	N	Y	Y	N	Y	Y	Y	N
2 Natcher	N	Y	N	Y	N	N	Y	N
3 Mazzoli	N	Y	N	Y	N	N	Y	N
4 ***Snyder***	?	Y	N	N	N	Y	Y	N
5 ***Rogers***	Y	Y	N	Y	N	Y	Y	Y
6 ***Hopkins***	N	Y	N	N	N	N	N	N
7 Perkins	?	Y	N	Y	N	N	Y	N
LOUISIANA								
1 ***Livingston***	N	Y	Y	Y	N	Y	N	Y
2 Boggs	N	?	#	?	?	N	Y	Y
3 Tauzin	?	Y	Y	Y	N	Y	Y	N
4 Roemer	N	Y	Y	N	N	Y	Y	N
5 Huckaby	?	Y	Y	N	N	N	Y	N
6 ***Moore***	N	Y	Y	Y	N	Y	N	Y
7 Breaux	?	Y	Y	Y	N	Y	Y	Y
8 Long	N	Y	Y	Y	N	N	Y	Y
MAINE								
1 ***Emery***	?	Y	N	N	N	N	Y	N
2 ***Snowe***	Y	Y	N	Y	N	N	Y	Y
MARYLAND								
1 Dyson	N	Y	N	N	N	N	Y	N
2 Long	N	Y	N	Y	N	N	Y	Y
3 Mikulski	N	Y	Y	Y	N	N	Y	Y
4 ***Holt***	N	Y	Y	Y	N	Y	Y	Y
5 Hoyer	N	Y	Y	Y	N	N	Y	Y
6 Byron	N	?	Y	Y	N	N	Y	N
7 Mitchell	Y	?	N	?	Y	N	?	Y
8 Barnes	N	N	N	Y	N	N	Y	Y
MASSACHUSETTS								
1 ***Conte***	N	?	N	Y	N	N	Y	Y
2 Boland	N	Y	N	Y	N	N	Y	Y
3 Early	N	Y	N	Y	Y	N	Y	N
4 Frank	?	Y	N	Y	N	N	Y	Y
5 Shannon	N	Y	N	Y	N	N	Y	Y
6 Mavroules	N	?	N	Y	N	N	Y	Y
7 Markey	Y	Y	N	Y	N	N	Y	Y
8 O'Neill								
9 Moakley	N	Y	?	Y	N	N	Y	Y
10 ***Heckler***	?	Y	N	Y	N	N	Y	Y
11 Donnelly	Y	?	N	N	N	N	Y	N
12 Studds	N	Y	N	Y	N	N	Y	Y
MICHIGAN								
1 Conyers	Y	Y	N	Y	Y	N	N	N
2 ***Pursell***	Y	Y	N	Y	N	N	?	Y
3 Wolpe	?	Y	N	Y	N	N	Y	Y
4 ***Siljander***	?	Y	Y	N	N	Y	Y	N
5 ***Sawyer***	N	Y	N	Y	N	N	Y	Y
6 ***Dunn***	N	Y	N	N	N	N	Y	N
7 Kildee	Y	Y	N	Y	N	N	Y	Y
8 Traxler	?	Y	N	Y	N	N	Y	N
9 ***Vander Jagt***	N	?	Y	Y	N	N	?	#
10 Albosta	?	Y	Y	Y	N	N	Y	N
11 ***Davis***	?	Y	N	N	N	N	Y	N
12 Bonior	Y	Y	N	?	N	N	Y	Y
13 Crockett	?	Y	N	?	?	N	?	Y
14 Hertel	?	Y	N	Y	N	N	Y	N
15 Ford	?	?	Y	?	N	N	Y	N
16 Dingell	N	Y	?	Y	N	N	Y	Y
17 Brodhead	?	?	N	Y	N	N	Y	Y
18 Blanchard	?	Y	N	Y	N	N	Y	Y
19 ***Broomfield***	N	?	N	Y	N	N	N	Y
MINNESOTA								
1 ***Erdahl***	N	Y	N	Y	N	N	Y	Y
2 ***Hagedorn***	N	Y	N	N	N	Y	Y	Y
3 ***Frenzel***	N	Y	Y	Y	N	N	Y	Y
4 Vento	N	Y	Y	N	N	N	Y	Y
5 Sabo	N	N	Y	Y	N	N	Y	Y
6 ***Weber***	N	Y	N	N	N	Y	Y	N
7 ***Stangeland***	N	Y	Y	Y	N	Y	Y	Y
8 Oberstar	N	Y	Y	Y	N	N	Y	Y
MISSISSIPPI								
1 Whitten	N	?	N	N	N	Y	Y	N
2 Bowen	N	Y	Y	Y	N	N	Y	Y
3 Montgomery	?	Y	Y	N	?	Y	Y	N
4 Dowdy	?	Y	Y	N	Y	Y	Y	N
5 ***Lott***	N	?	Y	?	N	Y	N	N
MISSOURI								
1 Clay	?	?	N	Y	N	N	Y	Y
2 Young	N	Y	Y	Y	N	N	Y	Y
3 Gephardt	?	?	Y	Y	N	N	Y	Y
4 Skelton	Y	Y	Y	Y	N	Y	Y	N
5 Bolling	?	?	?	?	?	?	?	?
6 ***Coleman***	N	Y	N	N	N	N	Y	N
7 ***Taylor***	N	Y	N	N	N	Y	Y	N
8 ***Bailey***	N	Y	Y	N	N	Y	N	N
9 Volkmer	Y	Y	N	Y	N	Y	Y	N
10 ***Emerson***	N	N	Y	N	N	Y	Y	N
MONTANA								
1 Williams	N	?	Y	Y	N	N	Y	N
2 ***Marlenee***	N	Y	Y	Y	N	Y	Y	N
NEBRASKA								
1 ***Bereuter***	N	Y	Y	N	N	N	Y	Y
2 ***Daub***	N	Y	Y	N	N	N	Y	Y
3 ***Smith***	N	Y	Y	N	N	N	Y	N
NEVADA								
AL Santini	?	?	#	Y	N	Y	Y	N
NEW HAMPSHIRE								
1 D'Amours	N	Y	N	N	N	N	Y	N
2 ***Gregg***	N	Y	N	N	N	N	Y	Y
NEW JERSEY								
1 Florio	Y	?	N	Y	Y	N	Y	N
2 Hughes	N	Y	N	Y	N	N	Y	N
3 Howard	?	?	?	?	?	?	?	?
4 ***Smith***	N	Y	Y	Y	N	N	Y	Y
5 ***Fenwick***	N	N	Y	N	Y	N	N	Y
6 ***Forsythe***	N	N	Y	?	N	N	N	Y
7 ***Roukema***	N	Y	N	Y	N	N	Y	N
8 Roe	N	Y	N	Y	Y	N	Y	Y
9 ***Hollenbeck***	?	Y	N	Y	N	N	Y	Y
10 Rodino	Y	Y	N	Y	Y	N	Y	N
11 Minish	N	Y	N	Y	Y	N	Y	Y
12 ***Rinaldo***	?	?	Y	Y	Y	N	Y	Y
13 ***Courter***	Y	Y	Y	Y	N	N	Y	N
14 Guarini	?	Y	N	Y	Y	N	Y	N
15 Dwyer	N	Y	N	Y	Y	N	Y	Y
NEW MEXICO								
1 ***Lujan***	N	Y	Y	Y	Y	Y	Y	N
2 ***Skeen***	?	Y	Y	N	N	Y	Y	N
NEW YORK								
1 ***Carney***	N	Y	N	N	Y	Y	Y	Y
2 Downey	Y	Y	N	Y	N	N	Y	Y
3 ***Carman***	?	Y	Y	Y	N	Y	Y	Y
4 ***Lent***	N	Y	Y	Y	N	N	Y	Y
5 ***McGrath***	N	Y	N	N	N	Y	Y	Y
6 ***LeBoutillier***	N	Y	Y	N	N	Y	Y	Y
7 Addabbo	N	Y	N	Y	Y	N	Y	#
8 Rosenthal	Y	Y	N	?	N	N	Y	Y
9 Ferraro	?	Y	Y	Y	N	Y	Y	Y
10 Biaggi	N	Y	N	Y	Y	N	Y	Y
11 Scheuer	N	Y	Y	Y	N	N	Y	Y
12 Chisholm	?	?	N	Y	N	N	Y	N
13 Solarz	N	Y	Y	Y	N	N	Y	Y
14 Richmond	N	Y	N	Y	N	N	Y	Y
15 Zeferetti	N	Y	Y	Y	Y	N	Y	Y
16 Schumer	?	Y	Y	Y	Y	N	Y	Y
17 ***Molinari***	N	Y	Y	N	N	Y	Y	Y
18 ***Green***	?	?	Y	Y	N	N	Y	Y
19 Rangel	?	Y	N	Y	N	N	N	Y
20 Weiss	Y	Y	N	N	N	N	Y	Y
21 Garcia	?	?	X	?	?	X	?	?
22 Bingham	N	Y	Y	Y	N	N	Y	Y
23 Peyser	N	Y	N	Y	N	N	Y	Y
24 Ottinger	Y	P	N	Y	N	N	Y	Y
25 ***Fish***	N	Y	N	N	?	N	Y	Y
26 ***Gilman***	?	Y	N	Y	N	N	Y	Y
27 McHugh	?	Y	Y	Y	N	N	Y	Y
28 Stratton	N	Y	Y	Y	N	N	Y	Y
29 ***Solomon***	N	Y	Y	N	Y	Y	Y	N
30 ***Martin***	N	Y	Y	N	N	Y	Y	Y
31 ***Mitchell***	?	Y	N	Y	N	Y	Y	Y
32 ***Wortley***	N	Y	Y	Y	N	Y	Y	Y
33 ***Lee***	N	?	N	N	N	N	Y	N
34 ***Horton***	?	Y	N	Y	N	Y	Y	Y
35 ***Conable***	?	Y	Y	Y	N	N	N	Y
36 LaFalce	N	Y	N	Y	N	N	Y	Y
37 Nowak	N	Y	?	Y	N	N	Y	Y
38 ***Kemp***	N	?	N	Y	N	Y	Y	Y
39 Lundine	N	Y	?	Y	?	N	Y	Y
NORTH CAROLINA								
1 Jones	N	?	Y	N	Y	Y	Y	N
2 Fountain	N	?	N	Y	N	N	Y	N
3 Whitley	N	Y	Y	N	Y	N	Y	N
4 Andrews	?	Y	N	N	N	N	Y	N
5 Neal	N	?	N	N	N	N	Y	N
6 ***Johnston***	N	N	Y	N	N	Y	Y	Y
7 Rose	N	Y	Y	Y	?	N	Y	Y
8 Hefner	N	Y	N	N	N	N	Y	N
9 ***Martin***	N	?	Y	N	N	Y	?	Y
10 ***Broyhill***	?	Y	N	N	N	Y	Y	N
11 ***Hendon***	N	Y	Y	N	N	Y	Y	N
NORTH DAKOTA								
AL Dorgan	N	Y	N	Y	N	N	Y	Y
OHIO								
1 ***Gradison***	Y	Y	N	N	N	N	Y	Y
2 Luken	?	Y	Y	Y	N	N	Y	N
3 Hall	?	?	?	?	?	?	?	?
4 ***Oxley***	N	Y	N	Y	N	Y	Y	Y
5 ***Latta***	?	Y	N	Y	N	Y	Y	N
6 ***McEwen***	N	Y	Y	Y	N	Y	Y	N
7 ***Brown***	?	Y	N	N	N	Y	Y	N
8 ***Kindness***	N	Y	Y	?	N	Y	N	N
9 ***Weber***	N	Y	N	Y	N	Y	Y	Y
10 ***Miller***	N	N	Y	N	Y	Y	Y	N
11 ***Stanton***	N	Y	N	Y	N	N	Y	Y
12 Shamansky	N	Y	N	Y	N	N	Y	Y
13 Pease	N	Y	N	Y	N	N	Y	Y
14 Seiberling	Y	Y	N	Y	N	N	Y	Y
15 ***Wylie***	N	Y	N	N	N	N	Y	Y
16 ***Regula***	N	Y	N	N	N	N	Y	N
17 ***Ashbrook***	?	Y	N	N	Y	Y	Y	N
18 Applegate	?	?	?	?	?	?	?	?
19 ***Williams***	N	Y	N	Y	N	N	Y	N
20 Oakar	N	Y	N	Y	?	?	?	?
21 Stokes	N	?	?	?	N	N	Y	Y
22 Eckart	N	Y	N	Y	N	N	Y	Y
23 Mottl	Y	Y	N	Y	Y	Y	Y	N
OKLAHOMA								
1 Jones	?	Y	Y	N	N	Y	Y	N
2 Synar	N	Y	Y	Y	N	N	Y	Y
3 Watkins	N	Y	Y	N	N	Y	Y	N
4 McCurdy	N	Y	Y	Y	N	Y	Y	N
5 ***Edwards***	N	Y	Y	N	N	Y	Y	N
6 English	N	Y	Y	N	N	Y	Y	N
OREGON								
1 AuCoin	?	?	X	?	?	?	?	?
2 ***Smith***	N	Y	Y	N	N	Y	Y	N
3 Wyden	N	Y	N	Y	Y	N	Y	Y
4 Weaver	Y	Y	N	Y	N	N	Y	N
PENNSYLVANIA								
1 Foglietta	?	Y	N	Y	N	N	Y	Y
2 Gray	?	Y	N	Y	N	N	P	Y
3 Smith	?	Y	Y	Y	N	N	Y	Y
4 ***Dougherty***	?	?	N	Y	N	?	Y	Y
5 ***Schulze***	?	Y	Y	Y	N	Y	N	N
6 Yatron	N	Y	Y	Y	N	N	Y	Y
7 Edgar	N	?	N	Y	N	N	Y	Y
8 ***Coyne, J.***	?	Y	Y	N	N	N	Y	Y
9 ***Shuster***	N	Y	Y	N	N	Y	Y	N
10 ***McDade***	Y	?	Y	N	N	N	Y	Y
11 ***Nelligan***	N	Y	Y	N	N	Y	Y	N
12 Murtha	?	Y	Y	Y	Y	N	Y	Y
13 ***Coughlin***	Y	N	Y	N	N	N	Y	Y
14 Coyne, W.	?	Y	Y	Y	N	N	Y	Y
15 ***Ritter***	N	Y	Y	N	N	Y	Y	N
16 ***Walker***	N	N	Y	N	N	Y	N	N
17 Ertel	Y	Y	N	Y	N	N	Y	N
18 Walgren	N	Y	Y	Y	N	N	Y	Y
19 ***Goodling***	N	Y	Y	N	N	N	Y	N
20 Gaydos	N	Y	Y	Y	Y	N	Y	N
21 Bailey	?	Y	Y	Y	N	Y	Y	N
22 Murphy	N	Y	Y	Y	Y	N	Y	N
23 ***Clinger***	N	Y	Y	N	N	N	Y	Y
24 ***Marks***	N	Y	Y	Y	N	N	N	Y
25 ***Atkinson***	?	?	Y	Y	N	N	Y	N
RHODE ISLAND								
1 St Germain	?	?	N	Y	N	Y	Y	Y
2 ***Schneider***	N	Y	N	Y	N	Y	Y	Y
SOUTH CAROLINA								
1 ***Hartnett***	N	Y	Y	?	N	N	Y	Y
2 ***Spence***	N	Y	N	N	N	Y	Y	N
3 Derrick	N	?	N	Y	N	N	Y	N
4 ***Campbell***	N	Y	Y	N	N	Y	?	#
5 Holland	Y	Y	Y	N	N	?	?	?
6 ***Napier***	N	Y	Y	N	N	Y	Y	Y
SOUTH DAKOTA								
1 Daschle	N	Y	Y	Y	N	N	Y	N
2 ***Roberts***	N	Y	Y	N	N	Y	Y	N
TENNESSEE								
1 ***Quillen***	N	?	Y	Y	N	N	Y	Y
2 ***Duncan***	N	Y	Y	N	N	Y	Y	N
3 Bouquard	N	Y	Y	N	N	Y	Y	N
4 Gore	N	Y	Y	Y	N	N	Y	Y
5 Boner	N	Y	Y	Y	N	N	Y	N
6 ***Beard***	?	?	?	N	N	Y	Y	N
7 Jones	?	Y	Y	N	N	Y	Y	N
8 Ford	N	Y	N	Y	N	N	Y	Y
TEXAS								
1 Hall, S.	N	?	Y	Y	N	Y	Y	N
2 Wilson	?	Y	Y	Y	N	Y	Y	Y
3 ***Collins***	N	Y	Y	N	Y	Y	Y	N
4 Hall, R.	?	Y	N	Y	Y	Y	Y	N
5 Mattox	?	Y	Y	Y	N	N	Y	Y
6 Gramm	N	Y	Y	N	N	Y	Y	N
7 ***Archer***	N	Y	Y	N	Y	Y	N	N
8 ***Fields***	?	Y	Y	Y	N	Y	Y	N
9 Brooks	N	Y	Y	Y	?	?	?	X
10 Pickle	N	Y	Y	Y	N	N	Y	Y
11 Leath	N	Y	Y	Y	N	Y	Y	N
12 Wright	N	?	Y	Y	N	N	Y	Y
13 Hightower	N	Y	Y	N	N	Y	Y	N
14 Patman	N	Y	Y	N	Y	Y	Y	N
15 de la Garza	?	Y	Y	Y	N	N	Y	N
16 White	N	Y	Y	?	N	Y	Y	N
17 Stenholm	N	Y	Y	N	N	Y	Y	N
18 Leland	N	Y	Y	Y	N	N	Y	Y
19 Hance	?	Y	Y	Y	N	Y	Y	N
20 Gonzalez	Y	Y	N	Y	N	N	Y	N
21 ***Loeffler***	N	Y	Y	N	N	Y	Y	Y
22 ***Paul***	N	Y	Y	N	Y	Y	N	N
23 Kazen	N	Y	Y	N	N	Y	Y	N
24 Frost	N	Y	Y	Y	N	N	Y	Y
UTAH								
1 ***Hansen***	N	Y	Y	N	N	Y	Y	N
2 ***Marriott***	N	Y	Y	N	N	Y	Y	N
VERMONT								
AL ***Jeffords***	Y	Y	N	Y	N	Y	N	Y
VIRGINIA								
1 ***Trible***	N	Y	Y	N	N	Y	Y	N
2 ***Whitehurst***	N	Y	Y	N	N	N	Y	N
3 ***Bliley***	N	Y	Y	N	N	Y	Y	Y
4 ***Daniel, R.***	N	Y	Y	N	N	Y	Y	N
5 Daniel, D.	N	Y	N	Y	N	Y	Y	N
6 ***Butler***	N	?	?	?	N	N	N	Y
7 ***Robinson***	N	Y	Y	N	Y	Y	Y	N
8 ***Parris***	N	Y	N	N	N	#	?	X
9 ***Wampler***	N	?	N	Y	N	N	Y	N
10 ***Wolf***	N	Y	C	N	N	Y	Y	Y
WASHINGTON								
1 ***Pritchard***	N	Y	Y	Y	N	N	N	Y
2 Swift	N	Y	Y	Y	N	N	Y	Y
3 Bonker	?	Y	N	Y	Y	N	Y	Y
4 ***Morrison***	N	Y	Y	Y	N	N	Y	Y
5 Foley	N	Y	Y	Y	N	N	Y	Y
6 Dicks	N	Y	Y	Y	N	N	Y	Y
7 Lowry	Y	Y	Y	Y	N	N	Y	Y
WEST VIRGINIA								
1 Mollohan	N	Y	N	Y	N	N	Y	Y
2 ***Benedict***	N	Y	Y	N	N	Y	Y	N
3 ***Staton***	N	Y	Y	N	N	Y	Y	N
4 Rahall	N	Y	Y	N	Y	N	N	N
WISCONSIN								
1 Aspin	N	Y	N	Y	N	N	Y	Y
2 Kastenmeier	Y	Y	N	Y	Y	N	N	N
3 ***Gunderson***	Y	Y	N	N	N	N	N	N
4 Zablocki	N	Y	Y	Y	N	N	N	Y
5 Reuss	?	Y	Y	Y	N	N	Y	Y
6 ***Petri***	Y	Y	N	N	Y	N	Y	N
7 Obey	N	Y	Y	N	N	N	Y	N
8 ***Roth***	N	Y	N	Y	N	N	N	N
9 ***Sensenbrenner***	Y	Y	N	N	N	N	Y	N
WYOMING								
AL ***Cheney***	N	?	Y	Y	N	Y	Y	Y

Democrats ***Republicans***

328. Procedural Motion. Corcoran, R-Ill., motion to approve the House *Journal* of Wednesday, Dec. 9. Motion agreed to 346-29: R 163-16; D 183-13 (ND 112-12, SD 71-1), Dec. 10, 1981.

329. S J Res 115. Alaska Natural Gas Transportation System Waivers. Passage of the joint resolution approving the president's waivers of various stipulations in the 1977 decision to build a pipeline to carry natural gas from Alaska to the continental United States. The waivers were aimed at securing private financing for the pipeline. Passed 230-188: R 112-76; D 118-112 (ND 61-93, SD 57-19), Dec. 10, 1981. A "yea" was a vote supporting the president's position. (Because of parliamentary maneuvering, a joint resolution passed by the House the day before *(see vote 322, p. 106-H)* could not be cleared, so the House adopted the identical Senate joint resolution instead.)

330. H J Res 370. Continuing Appropriations, Fiscal 1982. Conte, R-Mass., motion to recommit the joint resolution to the Appropriations Committee with instructions to report it back immediately with a substitute amendment making a 4 percent cut in spending contained in seven domestic spending programs, with exemptions for entitlements, law enforcement and certain other programs. Motion agreed to 222-194: R 186-3; D 36-191 (ND 4-148, SD 32-43), Dec. 10, 1981. A "yea" was a vote supporting the president's position.

331. H J Res 370. Continuing Appropriations, Fiscal 1982. Passage of the joint resolution providing funding authority during the period Dec. 15, 1981, through March 31, 1982, for government agencies whose regular fiscal 1982 appropriations bills had not been enacted. Passed 218-197: R 164-25; D 54-172 (ND 15-135, SD 39-37), Dec. 10, 1981. A "yea" was a vote supporting the president's position.

332. H Con Res 230. Second Budget Resolution, Fiscal 1982. Adoption of the rule (H Res 295) providing for House floor consideration of the second concurrent budget resolution for fiscal 1982. Adopted 248-154: R 79-107; D 169-47 (ND 110-33, SD 59-14), Dec. 10, 1981.

333. S Con Res 50. Second Budget Resolution, Fiscal 1982. Adoption of the concurrent resolution to reaffirm the first fiscal 1982 budget resolution and to express the sense of the Senate that: 1) the Budget Committee by March 31, 1982, report a budget resolution containing a balanced budget for fiscal 1984; 2) a balanced budget should be achieved through spending reductions in all parts of the budget, including entitlement programs, and revenue increases, excluding changes in the Accelerated Cost Recovery System and individual rate reductions provided by the Economic Recovery Tax Act of 1981 (PL 97-34); and 3) under the committee plan, federal outlays should not exceed 20.5 percent of the gross national product in fiscal 1984. Adopted 206-200: R 136-50; D 70-150 (ND 25-123, SD 45-27), Dec. 10, 1981.

KEY

Y	Voted for (yea).
#	Paired for.
+	Announced for.
N	Voted against (nay).
X	Paired against.
-	Announced against.
P	Voted "present".
C	Voted "present" to avoid possible conflict of interest.
?	Did not vote or otherwise make a position known.

Member	328	329	330	331	332	333
ALABAMA						
1 Edwards	Y	Y	Y	Y	Y	Y
2 Dickinson	N	Y	Y	Y	Y	Y
3 Nichols	?	Y	Y	Y	Y	Y
4 Bevill	Y	Y	N	N	Y	Y
5 Flippo	Y	Y	N	Y	Y	Y
6 Smith	Y	Y	Y	Y	Y	Y
7 Shelby	Y	Y	Y	Y	Y	Y
ALASKA						
AL Young	N	Y	Y	Y	Y	Y
ARIZONA						
1 Rhodes	?	Y	Y	Y	Y	Y
2 Udall	Y	Y	N	N	Y	N
3 Stump	Y	Y	Y	Y	Y	Y
4 Rudd	Y	Y	Y	Y	Y	Y
ARKANSAS						
1 Alexander	Y	Y	N	N	Y	N
2 Bethune	Y	N	Y	Y	Y	Y
3 Hammerschmidt	Y	Y	Y	Y	N	Y
4 Anthony	Y	Y	N	N	Y	Y
CALIFORNIA						
1 Chappie	Y	Y	Y	Y	N	Y
2 Clausen	Y	Y	Y	Y	Y	Y
3 Matsui	Y	N	N	N	Y	N
4 Fazio	Y	Y	N	N	Y	N
5 Burton, J.	?	N	N	N	N	N
6 Burton, P.	Y	N	N	N	Y	N
7 Miller	?	N	N	N	N	N
8 Dellums	?	N	N	N	N	N
9 Stark	?	N	N	N	Y	N
10 Edwards	Y	N	N	N	Y	N
11 Lantos	Y	Y	N	N	?	?
12 McCloskey	?	#	#	#	?	#
13 Mineta	Y	Y	N	N	Y	N
14 Shumway	Y	Y	Y	Y	N	N
15 Coelho	Y	Y	N	N	Y	N
16 Panetta	Y	Y	N	N	Y	N
17 Pashayan	Y	Y	Y	Y	Y	Y
18 Thomas	Y	Y	Y	Y	Y	Y
19 Lagomarsino	Y	Y	Y	Y	N	N
20 Goldwater	?	#	#	#	?	#
21 Fiedler	Y	Y	Y	N	N	Y
22 Moorhead	Y	Y	Y	Y	N	N
23 Beilenson	Y	N	N	N	Y	N
24 Waxman	?	N	N	N	Y	N
25 Roybal	Y	N	N	N	Y	N
26 Rousselot	Y	Y	Y	N	?	N
27 Dornan	Y	Y	Y	?	?	?
28 Dixon	Y	Y	N	N	Y	N
29 Hawkins	N	Y	N	N	N	N
30 Danielson	?	N	X	N	Y	N
31 Dymally	?	#	?	?	?	N
32 Anderson	Y	Y	N	N	Y	N
33 Grisham	Y	Y	Y	Y	N	Y
34 Lungren	Y	Y	Y	Y	N	Y
35 Dreier	N	Y	Y	N	N	N
36 Brown	?	Y	N	N	?	?
37 Lewis	Y	Y	Y	Y	N	N
38 Patterson	Y	Y	N	N	Y	N
39 Dannemeyer	N	Y	Y	N	N	N
40 Badham	Y	Y	Y	Y	N	N
41 Lowery	?	Y	Y	Y	N	N
42 Hunter	Y	Y	Y	Y	N	Y
43 Burgener	Y	Y	Y	Y	N	N
COLORADO						
1 Schroeder	N	N	N	N	N	N
2 Wirth	Y	N	N	N	Y	N
3 Kogovsek	Y	Y	N	N	?	N
4 Brown	N	N	Y	N	N	N
5 Kramer	N	N	Y	N	N	Y
CONNECTICUT						
1 Vacancy						
2 Gejdenson	N	N	N	N	N	N
3 DeNardis	Y	N	Y	Y	N	Y
4 McKinney	Y	Y	Y	Y	Y	Y
5 Ratchford	Y	N	N	N	N	N
6 Moffett	Y	N	N	N	N	N
DELAWARE						
AL Evans	Y	Y	Y	Y	Y	Y
FLORIDA						
1 Hutto	Y	Y	Y	Y	Y	Y
2 Fuqua	Y	Y	Y	Y	Y	Y
3 Bennett	Y	Y	Y	Y	Y	Y
4 Chappell	Y	Y	Y	Y	Y	Y
5 McCollum	Y	N	Y	Y	Y	N
6 Young	Y	Y	Y	Y	N	Y
7 Gibbons	Y	Y	N	Y	Y	Y
8 Ireland	Y	Y	Y	Y	Y	Y
9 Nelson	Y	Y	Y	Y	Y	Y
10 Bafalis	Y	Y	Y	Y	Y	N
11 Mica	Y	N	Y	Y	Y	Y
12 Shaw	Y	Y	Y	Y	Y	Y
13 Lehman	Y	Y	N	N	Y	N
14 Pepper	?	N	N	N	Y	N
15 Fascell	Y	N	N	N	Y	N
GEORGIA						
1 Ginn	Y	N	N	Y	Y	Y
2 Hatcher	Y	N	N	Y	Y	Y
3 Brinkley	Y	Y	N	Y	Y	Y
4 Levitas	Y	N	N	N	Y	N
5 Fowler	Y	N	N	Y	Y	Y
6 Gingrich	Y	N	Y	N	Y	Y
7 McDonald	Y	Y	N	Y	X	-
8 Evans	Y	?	?	N	N	?
9 Jenkins	Y	Y	Y	Y	N	Y
10 Barnard	Y	Y	Y	Y	N	Y
HAWAII						
1 Heftel	?	Y	N	Y	Y	Y
2 Akaka	?	Y	N	N	Y	Y
IDAHO						
1 Craig	Y	Y	Y	N	N	Y
2 Hansen	Y	Y	Y	N	N	N
ILLINOIS						
1 Washington	Y	N	N	N	N	N
2 Savage	?	N	N	N	N	N
3 Russo	Y	N	N	N	N	N
4 Derwinski	Y	N	Y	N	Y	N
5 Fary	Y	N	N	N	N	N
6 Hyde	Y	N	Y	Y	Y	Y
7 Collins	Y	N	N	N	N	N
8 Rostenkowski	Y	N	N	N	Y	N
9 Yates	Y	N	N	N	N	N
10 Porter	Y	Y	Y	Y	Y	Y
11 Annunzio	Y	N	N	N	Y	N
12 Crane, P.	?	N	Y	N	N	N
13 McClory	Y	Y	Y	N	N	Y
14 Erlenborn	Y	Y	Y	Y	Y	Y
15 Corcoran	Y	N	Y	Y	Y	Y
16 Martin	Y	N	Y	N	Y	Y
17 O'Brien	Y	N	Y	N	Y	Y
18 Michel	Y	N	Y	Y	N	Y
19 Railsback	Y	N	Y	Y	Y	Y
20 Findley	Y	N	Y	Y	Y	Y
21 Madigan	?	N	Y	Y	N	Y
22 Crane, D.	Y	N	N	N	N	N
23 Price	Y	N	N	N	Y	N
24 Simon	Y	N	N	Y	N	N
INDIANA						
1 Benjamin	Y	N	N	Y	N	N
2 Fithian	?	?	?	?	?	?
3 Hiler	Y	Y	Y	Y	N	N
4 Coats	Y	Y	Y	Y	N	N
5 Hillis	Y	Y	Y	Y	Y	Y
6 Evans	Y	N	N	Y	N	N
7 Myers	Y	Y	Y	Y	N	N
8 Deckard	Y	N	Y	Y	?	Y
9 Hamilton	Y	Y	N	N	N	N
10 Sharp	Y	N	N	N	N	N
11 Jacobs	N	N	N	N	N	N
IOWA						
1 Leach	Y	N	Y	Y	N	Y
2 Tauke	Y	N	Y	Y	N	Y
3 Evans	N	N	Y	Y	Y	Y
4 Smith	Y	N	N	N	N	N
5 Harkin	N	N	N	N	N	N
6 Bedell	Y	N	Y	Y	Y	?

Democrats **Republicans**

	328	329	330	331	332	333
KANSAS						
1 ***Roberts***	Y	Y	Y	Y	N	Y
2 ***Jeffries***	Y	Y	Y	Y	N	Y
3 ***Winn***	Y	Y	Y	Y	N	Y
4 Glickman	Y	Y	N	N	N	Y
5 ***Whittaker***	Y	Y	Y	Y	N	Y
KENTUCKY						
1 Hubbard	Y	Y	N	N	N	N
2 Natcher	Y	N	N	N	Y	Y
3 Mazzoli	Y	N	N	N	Y	Y
4 ***Snyder***	Y	N	Y	N	N	N
5 ***Rogers***	Y	N	Y	Y	Y	Y
6 ***Hopkins***	Y	N	Y	Y	N	N
7 Perkins	Y	N	N	N	Y	N
LOUISIANA						
1 ***Livingston***	Y	Y	Y	Y	Y	Y
2 Boggs	?	Y	N	N	Y	Y
3 Tauzin	Y	Y	Y	Y	N	N
4 Roemer	Y	Y	Y	Y	N	N
5 Huckaby	Y	Y	Y	Y	Y	N
6 ***Moore***	Y	Y	Y	Y	N	N
7 Breaux	Y	Y	Y	Y	Y	N
8 Long	Y	Y	N	N	Y	Y
MAINE						
1 ***Emery***	Y	N	Y	Y	N	Y
2 ***Snowe***	Y	N	Y	Y	Y	N
MARYLAND						
1 Dyson	Y	N	N	Y	Y	Y
2 Long	Y	N	N	N	Y	Y
3 Mikulski	Y	Y	N	N	Y	N
4 ***Holt***	N	Y	Y	Y	Y	Y
5 Hoyer	Y	Y	N	N	N	N
6 Byron	?	Y	N	Y	Y	Y
7 Mitchell	N	N	N	N	N	N
8 Barnes	N	N	N	N	N	N
MASSACHUSETTS						
1 ***Conte***	Y	N	Y	Y	Y	Y
2 Boland	Y	N	N	N	Y	Y
3 Early	?	N	N	N	?	N
4 Frank	Y	N	N	N	N	N
5 Shannon	Y	N	N	N	Y	N
6 Mavroules	?	N	N	N	Y	N
7 Markey	Y	N	N	N	Y	N
8 O'Neill						
9 Moakley	Y	X	X	X	#	X
10 ***Heckler***	Y	N	Y	Y	Y	N
11 Donnelly	Y	N	N	N	Y	Y
12 Studds	Y	N	N	N	Y	N
MICHIGAN						
1 Conyers	Y	N	N	N	N	N
2 ***Pursell***	Y	N	Y	Y	Y	N
3 Wolpe	Y	N	N	N	Y	N
4 ***Siljander***	Y	Y	Y	N	N	N
5 ***Sawyer***	Y	N	Y	Y	Y	Y
6 ***Dunn***	Y	N	Y	Y	N	Y
7 Kildee	Y	N	N	N	Y	N
8 Traxler	Y	N	N	N	Y	N
9 ***Vander Jagt***	Y	N	Y	Y	Y	Y
10 Albosta	Y	Y	N	N	Y	N
11 ***Davis***	?	N	Y	Y	N	Y
12 Bonior	?	N	N	N	Y	N
13 Crockett	?	X	?	?	?	?
14 Hertel	Y	N	N	N	Y	N
15 Ford	Y	Y	N	N	Y	N
16 Dingell	Y	Y	N	N	Y	N
17 Brodhead	Y	N	N	N	Y	N
18 Blanchard	Y	N	N	N	Y	N
19 ***Broomfield***	Y	N	Y	Y	N	Y
MINNESOTA						
1 ***Erdahl***	Y	N	Y	Y	N	Y
2 ***Hagedorn***	Y	N	Y	Y	N	Y
3 ***Frenzel***	Y	Y	Y	Y	N	Y
4 Vento	Y	Y	N	N	N	N
5 Sabo	N	Y	N	N	N	N
6 ***Weber***	Y	N	Y	Y	N	N
7 ***Stangeland***	Y	Y	Y	Y	N	Y
8 Oberstar	Y	Y	N	N	Y	N
MISSISSIPPI						
1 Whitten	Y	N	N	N	N	N
2 Bowen	Y	Y	N	Y	Y	Y
3 Montgomery	Y	Y	Y	Y	?	Y
4 Dowdy	N	Y	N	N	Y	Y
5 ***Lott***	Y	Y	Y	Y	Y	Y
MISSOURI						
1 Clay	N	N	N	N	Y	N
2 Young	Y	Y	N	Y	Y	Y
3 Gephardt	?	Y	N	N	Y	Y
4 Skelton	Y	Y	N	N	Y	Y
5 Bolling	?	Y	N	?	?	?
6 ***Coleman***	Y	N	Y	Y	N	Y
7 ***Taylor***	Y	N	Y	Y	N	Y
8 ***Bailey***	Y	Y	Y	Y	Y	Y
9 Volkmer	?	N	N	N	Y	N
10 ***Emerson***	N	Y	Y	Y	N	Y
MONTANA						
1 Williams	Y	Y	N	N	N	N
2 ***Marlenee***	Y	Y	Y	Y	N	Y
NEBRASKA						
1 ***Bereuter***	Y	Y	Y	Y	N	Y
2 ***Daub***	Y	Y	Y	Y	N	Y
3 ***Smith***	Y	Y	Y	Y	N	Y
NEVADA						
AL Santini	?	Y	N	N	?	Y
NEW HAMPSHIRE						
1 D'Amours	Y	N	N	N	Y	N
2 ***Gregg***	Y	N	Y	N	N	N
NEW JERSEY						
1 Florio	Y	N	N	N	N	N
2 Hughes	Y	N	N	N	N	N
3 Howard	?	?	?	?	?	?
4 ***Smith***	Y	Y	Y	Y	N	Y
5 ***Fenwick***	Y	N	Y	Y	N	Y
6 ***Forsythe***	?	Y	Y	Y	N	Y
7 ***Roukema***	Y	N	Y	Y	Y	Y
8 Roe	Y	N	N	N	Y	N
9 ***Hollenbeck***	Y	N	N	N	N	N
10 Rodino	Y	N	N	N	Y	N
11 Minish	Y	N	N	N	Y	N
12 ***Rinaldo***	Y	Y	Y	Y	Y	N
13 ***Courter***	Y	Y	Y	Y	N	N
14 Guarini	Y	N	N	?	Y	N
15 Dwyer	Y	N	N	N	Y	N
NEW MEXICO						
1 ***Lujan***	Y	Y	Y	Y	Y	Y
2 ***Skeen***	Y	Y	Y	Y	N	Y
NEW YORK						
1 ***Carney***	Y	N	Y	Y	N	Y
2 Downey	Y	N	N	N	Y	Y
3 ***Carman***	Y	Y	Y	Y	N	Y
4 ***Lent***	Y	Y	Y	Y	N	Y
5 ***McGrath***	Y	N	Y	Y	N	Y
6 ***LeBoutillier***	Y	Y	Y	Y	Y	Y
7 Addabbo	?	N	N	N	Y	N
8 Rosenthal	Y	N	N	N	Y	N
9 Ferraro	Y	Y	N	N	Y	N
10 Biaggi	Y	N	N	N	Y	?
11 Scheuer	?	Y	N	N	Y	N
12 Chisholm	?	N	N	N	?	N
13 Solarz	Y	Y	N	?	Y	N
14 Richmond	?	N	N	N	Y	N
15 Zeferetti	Y	Y	N	N	Y	N
16 Schumer	Y	Y	N	N	Y	N
17 ***Molinari***	Y	Y	Y	Y	N	?
18 ***Green***	Y	Y	N	N	Y	Y
19 Rangel	Y	N	N	N	N	N
20 Weiss	Y	N	N	N	N	N
21 Garcia	?	X	?	?	X	?
22 Bingham	?	Y	N	N	Y	N
23 Peyser	Y	N	N	N	Y	N
24 Ottinger	P	N	N	N	N	Y
25 ***Fish***	Y	N	Y	Y	N	N
26 ***Gilman***	Y	N	Y	Y	N	N
27 McHugh	Y	Y	N	N	Y	N
28 Stratton	Y	Y	N	N	Y	Y
29 ***Solomon***	N	Y	Y	Y	N	Y
30 ***Martin***	Y	Y	Y	Y	Y	Y
31 ***Mitchell***	Y	N	Y	Y	N	Y
32 ***Wortley***	Y	Y	Y	Y	N	Y
33 ***Lee***	Y	N	Y	Y	N	Y
34 ***Horton***	Y	N	Y	Y	Y	Y
35 ***Conable***	Y	Y	Y	Y	Y	Y
36 LaFalce	?	N	N	N	N	N
37 Nowak	Y	N	N	N	Y	N
38 ***Kemp***	?	N	Y	Y	Y	N
39 Lundine	?	Y	N	Y	Y	N
NORTH CAROLINA						
1 Jones	Y	Y	N	N	#	Y
2 Fountain	?	N	Y	Y	Y	Y
3 Whitley	Y	Y	Y	Y	Y	Y
4 Andrews	Y	N	Y	Y	Y	Y
5 Neal	?	N	N	Y	N	?
6 ***Johnston***	N	Y	Y	N	N	N
7 Rose	?	Y	N	Y	Y	Y
8 Hefner	Y	N	Y	Y	Y	Y
9 ***Martin***	Y	Y	Y	Y	Y	Y
10 ***Broyhill***	Y	N	Y	Y	Y	Y
11 ***Hendon***	Y	Y	Y	Y	Y	N
NORTH DAKOTA						
AL Dorgan	N	N	N	N	Y	N
OHIO						
1 ***Gradison***	Y	N	Y	Y	Y	Y
2 Luken	Y	Y	N	Y	?	N
3 Hall	?	?	?	?	?	?
4 ***Oxley***	Y	N	Y	Y	Y	Y
5 ***Latta***	Y	N	Y	Y	Y	Y
6 ***McEwen***	Y	N	Y	Y	N	Y
7 ***Brown***	Y	N	Y	Y	N	#
8 ***Kindness***	Y	Y	Y	Y	N	Y
9 ***Weber***	Y	N	Y	Y	Y	Y
10 ***Miller***	N	Y	Y	Y	N	Y
11 ***Stanton***	Y	N	Y	Y	Y	Y
12 Shamansky	Y	N	N	N	Y	N
13 Pease	Y	N	N	N	Y	N
14 Seiberling	?	N	N	N	Y	N
15 ***Wylie***	Y	N	Y	Y	Y	Y
16 ***Regula***	Y	N	Y	Y	Y	Y
17 ***Ashbrook***	Y	N	Y	N	N	Y
18 Applegate	?	N	N	N	N	N
19 ***Williams***	?	N	Y	Y	N	Y
20 Oakar	Y	N	X	?	?	?
21 Stokes	Y	N	N	N	Y	N
22 Eckart	Y	N	N	N	N	N
23 Mottl	Y	N	Y	N	Y	N
OKLAHOMA						
1 Jones	Y	Y	N	N	Y	Y
2 Synar	Y	Y	N	N	Y	N
3 Watkins	Y	Y	Y	N	Y	Y
4 McCurdy	Y	Y	Y	Y	Y	Y
5 ***Edwards***	Y	Y	Y	N	Y	N
6 English	Y	Y	Y	N	Y	Y
OREGON						
1 AuCoin	?	X	X	?	?	X
2 ***Smith***	Y	Y	Y	N	N	N
3 Wyden	Y	N	N	N	Y	N
4 Weaver	Y	N	N	N	N	N
PENNSYLVANIA						
1 Foglietta	Y	N	N	N	Y	N
2 Gray	?	N	N	N	Y	N
3 Smith	Y	Y	N	N	Y	Y
4 ***Dougherty***	?	N	N	N	N	Y
5 ***Schulze***	Y	Y	Y	Y	N	Y
6 Yatron	Y	Y	N	N	Y	N
7 Edgar	Y	N	N	N	?	N
8 ***Coyne, J.***	Y	Y	Y	Y	N	Y
9 ***Shuster***	Y	Y	Y	Y	Y	Y
10 ***McDade***	Y	N	Y	Y	N	Y
11 ***Nelligan***	?	Y	Y	Y	N	Y
12 Murtha	Y	Y	N	N	Y	Y
13 ***Coughlin***	N	Y	Y	Y	N	Y
14 Coyne, W.	Y	Y	N	N	Y	N
15 ***Ritter***	Y	?	Y	Y	N	Y
16 ***Walker***	N	Y	Y	Y	N	N
17 Ertel	Y	N	N	Y	Y	N
18 Walgren	Y	Y	Y	Y	Y	Y
19 ***Goodling***	N	N	Y	Y	N	Y
20 Gaydos	Y	Y	N	N	Y	N
21 Bailey	Y	Y	N	N	Y	N
22 Murphy	Y	Y	N	N	Y	N
23 ***Clinger***	Y	Y	Y	Y	Y	Y
24 ***Marks***	Y	Y	Y	Y	Y	Y
25 ***Atkinson***	Y	Y	Y	Y	Y	Y
RHODE ISLAND						
1 St Germain	Y	N	N	N	Y	N
2 ***Schneider***	Y	N	Y	Y	Y	N
SOUTH CAROLINA						
1 ***Hartnett***	Y	Y	Y	Y	N	Y
2 ***Spence***	Y	N	Y	Y	N	Y
3 Derrick	Y	N	N	Y	Y	Y
4 ***Campbell***	Y	Y	Y	Y	Y	Y
5 Holland	Y	Y	Y	Y	Y	Y
6 ***Napier***	Y	Y	Y	Y	Y	Y
SOUTH DAKOTA						
1 Daschle	N	Y	N	N	Y	-
2 ***Roberts***	Y	Y	Y	Y	N	Y
TENNESSEE						
1 ***Quillen***	Y	Y	Y	Y	Y	Y
2 ***Duncan***	Y	Y	Y	Y	Y	Y
3 Bouquard	Y	Y	N	N	Y	Y
4 Gore	Y	Y	N	N	Y	N
5 Boner	Y	#	?	?	?	?
6 ***Beard***	Y	N	#	#	?	#
7 Jones	Y	Y	N	N	Y	X
8 Ford	Y	N	N	N	N	N
TEXAS						
1 Hall, S.	Y	Y	N	N	Y	Y
2 Wilson	Y	Y	N	N	Y	Y
3 ***Collins***	Y	Y	Y	N	N	N
4 Hall, R.	Y	Y	Y	N	Y	N
5 Mattox	Y	Y	N	N	N	N
6 Gramm	Y	Y	Y	Y	N	Y
7 ***Archer***	Y	Y	Y	N	N	N
8 ***Fields***	Y	Y	Y	Y	N	N
9 Brooks	?	?	?	X	?	?
10 Pickle	Y	Y	Y	Y	Y	Y
11 Leath	Y	Y	Y	Y	Y	N
12 Wright	Y	Y	N	N	Y	N
13 Hightower	Y	Y	Y	Y	Y	Y
14 Patman	Y	Y	N	N	N	N
15 de la Garza	Y	Y	N	N	Y	Y
16 White	Y	Y	Y	Y	Y	Y
17 Stenholm	Y	Y	Y	Y	Y	N
18 Leland	Y	Y	N	N	Y	N
19 Hance	Y	Y	Y	N	Y	Y
20 Gonzalez	Y	N	N	N	N	N
21 ***Loeffler***	Y	Y	Y	Y	N	N
22 ***Paul***	N	Y	Y	N	N	N
23 Kazen	Y	Y	N	N	Y	N
24 Frost	Y	Y	N	N	Y	N
UTAH						
1 ***Hansen***	Y	Y	Y	Y	N	Y
2 ***Marriott***	Y	Y	Y	Y	Y	Y
VERMONT						
AL ***Jeffords***	Y	N	Y	Y	N	N
VIRGINIA						
1 ***Trible***	Y	Y	Y	Y	N	Y
2 ***Whitehurst***	Y	Y	Y	Y	Y	Y
3 ***Bliley***	?	Y	Y	Y	Y	Y
4 ***Daniel, R.***	Y	Y	Y	Y	Y	Y
5 Daniel, D.	Y	N	#	X	?	X
6 ***Butler***	Y	Y	Y	Y	Y	Y
7 ***Robinson***	Y	Y	Y	Y	Y	Y
8 ***Parris***	Y	N	Y	Y	Y	Y
9 ***Wampler***	Y	N	Y	Y	Y	Y
10 ***Wolf***	Y	C	Y	Y	Y	Y
WASHINGTON						
1 ***Pritchard***	Y	Y	Y	Y	Y	Y
2 Swift	P	Y	N	N	Y	N
3 Bonker	Y	N	N	Y	?	N
4 ***Morrison***	Y	Y	Y	Y	Y	Y
5 Foley	Y	Y	N	Y	Y	Y
6 Dicks	Y	Y	N	Y	Y	N
7 Lowry	N	Y	N	N	Y	N
WEST VIRGINIA						
1 Mollohan	Y	N	N	N	Y	Y
2 ***Benedict***	Y	Y	Y	Y	Y	Y
3 ***Staton***	Y	Y	Y	Y	Y	Y
4 Rahall	?	Y	N	N	Y	N
WISCONSIN						
1 Aspin	Y	N	N	Y	Y	Y
2 Kastenmeier	Y	N	N	N	Y	N
3 ***Gunderson***	Y	N	Y	Y	N	Y
4 Zablocki	Y	Y	N	N	Y	Y
5 Reuss	Y	Y	N	N	Y	N
6 ***Petri***	Y	N	Y	N	N	N
7 Obey	Y	N	N	N	Y	N
8 ***Roth***	Y	N	Y	Y	N	N
9 ***Sensenbrenner***	Y	N	Y	N	N	N
WYOMING						
AL ***Cheney***	Y	Y	Y	Y	Y	Y

Democrats ***Republicans***

334. Procedural Motion. Livingston, R-La., motion to approve the House *Journal* of Thursday, Dec. 10. Motion agreed to 328-23: R 148-12; D 180-11 (ND 117-10, SD 63-1), Dec. 11, 1981.

335. HR 4559. Foreign Aid Appropriations, Fiscal 1982. Long, D-Md., motion that the House resolve itself into the Committee of the Whole for the purpose of considering the bill making appropriations for foreign aid and related programs in fiscal 1982. Motion agreed to 363-16: R 165-8; D 198-8 (ND 134-4, SD 64-4), Dec. 11, 1981.

336. HR 4559. Foreign Aid Appropriations, Fiscal 1982. Kemp, R-N.Y., amendment to the Edwards, R-Okla., amendment, to reduce the contribution to the sixth replenishment of the International Development Association from $850 million to $725 million. The Edwards amendment would have reduced the contribution to $520 million. Adopted 281-114: R 113-68; D 168-46 (ND 130-14, SD 38-32), Dec. 11, 1981. (The Edwards amendment, as amended by the Kemp amendment, subsequently was adopted, *see vote 337, below*.)

337. HR 4559. Foreign Aid Appropriations, Fiscal 1982. Edwards, R-Okla., amendment as amended by the Kemp, R-N.Y., amendment, to reduce the contribution to the sixth replenishment of the International Development Association from $850 million to $725 million. Adopted 372-17: R 175-3; D 197-14 (ND 129-12, SD 68-2), Dec. 11, 1981.

338. HR 4559. Foreign Aid Appropriations, Fiscal 1982. Passage of the bill to appropriate $7,440,280,064 for foreign aid and related programs in fiscal 1982. Passed 199-166: R 84-87; D 115-79 (ND 95-36, SD 20-43), Dec. 11, 1981. (The president had requested $7,775,098,683.)

339. HR 4995. Defense Department Appropriations, Fiscal 1982. Addabbo, D-N.Y., motion to close to the public conference committee meetings on HR 4995 when information relating to the national security was under discussion. Motion agreed to 359-1: R 162-0; D 197-1 (ND 132-1, SD 65-0), Dec. 14, 1981.

340. HR 4910. District of Columbia Bond Authority. Passage of the bill to allow the District of Columbia to issue general obligation bonds and notes and revenue bonds and other obligations. Passed 375-6: R 170-5; D 205-1 (ND 136-1, SD 69-0), Dec. 14, 1981.

341. HR 2559. Coast Guard Authorization. Studds, D-Mass., amendment to the Snyder, R-Ky., amendment to bar the use of funds for specified Coast Guard facilities. Rejected 0-389: R 0-182; D 0-207 (ND 0-138, SD 0-69), Dec. 14, 1981. (The Snyder amendment, which would have reduced Coast Guard authorizations, subsequently was rejected by voice vote.)

KEY

Y Voted for (yea).
Paired for.
+ Announced for.
N Voted against (nay).
X Paired against.
- Announced against.
P Voted "present".
C Voted "present" to avoid possible conflict of interest.
? Did not vote or otherwise make a position known.

	334	335	336	337	338	339	340	341
ALABAMA								
1 *Edwards*	?	Y	Y	Y	Y	Y	Y	N
2 *Dickinson*	N	?	Y	Y	?	Y	Y	N
3 Nichols	?	?	Y	Y	N	Y	Y	N
4 Bevill	Y	Y	Y	Y	N	Y	Y	N
5 Flippo	Y	Y	Y	Y	?	?	Y	N
6 *Smith*	?	Y	N	?	Y	Y	Y	N
7 Shelby	Y	Y	N	Y	N	Y	?	?
ALASKA								
AL *Young*	?	Y	Y	Y	N	Y	Y	N
ARIZONA								
1 *Rhodes*	Y	Y	Y	Y	Y	Y	Y	N
2 Udall	Y	Y	Y	Y	Y	Y	Y	N
3 *Stump*	Y	Y	N	Y	N	Y	Y	N
4 *Rudd*	Y	Y	N	Y	N	Y	Y	N
ARKANSAS								
1 Alexander	Y	Y	Y	Y	?	Y	Y	N
2 *Bethune*	Y	Y	N	Y	N	Y	Y	N
3 *Hammerschmidt*	Y	Y	N	Y	N	Y	Y	N
4 Anthony	?	?	?	?	?	Y	Y	N
CALIFORNIA								
1 *Chappie*	?	?	X	?	?	Y	Y	N
2 *Clausen*	Y	Y	Y	Y	Y	Y	Y	N
3 Matsui	Y	Y	Y	Y	Y	Y	Y	N
4 Fazio	Y	Y	Y	Y	?	Y	Y	N
5 Burton, J.	?	?	?	?	?	?	?	?
6 Burton, P.	Y	Y	Y	N	Y	Y	Y	N
7 Miller	N	Y	Y	Y	Y	Y	Y	N
8 Dellums	?	Y	Y	N	N	?	?	?
9 Stark	?	Y	Y	Y	Y	Y	Y	N
10 Edwards	Y	Y	Y	Y	Y	Y	Y	N
11 Lantos	Y	Y	Y	Y	Y	Y	Y	N
12 *McCloskey*	?	?	?	?	?	?	?	?
13 Mineta	Y	Y	Y	Y	Y	Y	Y	N
14 *Shumway*	Y	Y	N	Y	N	Y	Y	N
15 Coelho	Y	Y	Y	Y	Y	Y	Y	N
16 Panetta	Y	Y	Y	N	Y	Y	Y	N
17 *Pashayan*	Y	Y	Y	N	Y	Y	Y	N
18 *Thomas*	Y	Y	Y	Y	Y	Y	Y	N
19 *Lagomarsino*	Y	Y	N	Y	Y	Y	Y	N
20 *Goldwater*	Y	P	?	?	X	?	Y	N
21 *Fiedler*	Y	Y	Y	Y	?	Y	Y	N
22 *Moorhead*	Y	Y	N	Y	N	?	Y	N
23 Beilenson	Y	Y	Y	Y	Y	Y	Y	N
24 Waxman	Y	Y	Y	Y	Y	Y	Y	N
25 Roybal	Y	Y	Y	Y	N	Y	Y	N
26 *Rousselot*	?	N	N	Y	N	?	Y	N
27 *Dornan*	?	?	?	?	?	?	Y	N
28 Dixon	Y	Y	Y	Y	Y	Y	Y	N
29 Hawkins	N	N	Y	Y	Y	Y	Y	N
30 Danielson	Y	Y	Y	Y	Y	Y	Y	N
31 Dymally	Y	Y	Y	Y	Y	Y	Y	N
32 Anderson	Y	Y	N	Y	N	Y	Y	N
33 *Grisham*	Y	Y	N	Y	N	Y	Y	N
34 *Lungren*	?	Y	N	Y	N	Y	Y	N
35 *Dreier*	N	N	N	Y	N	?	Y	N
36 Brown	?	?	?	?	?	?	?	?
37 Lewis	?	Y	Y	Y	Y	Y	Y	N
38 Patterson	Y	Y	Y	Y	Y	?	?	?
39 *Dannemeyer*	Y	?	X	?	?	Y	Y	N
40 *Badham*	Y	Y	Y	Y	Y	Y	Y	N
41 *Lowery*	?	Y	Y	Y	Y	Y	Y	N
42 *Hunter*	Y	Y	Y	Y	N	?	Y	N
43 *Burgener*	Y	Y	Y	Y	Y	Y	Y	N
COLORADO								
1 Schroeder	N	Y	Y	Y	N	Y	Y	N
2 Wirth	Y	Y	Y	Y	Y	Y	Y	N
3 Kogovsek	Y	Y	Y	Y	N	Y	Y	N
4 *Brown*	N	Y	N	Y	N	Y	N	N

	334	335	336	337	338	339	340	341
5 *Kramer*	?	?	?	?	?	Y	Y	N
CONNECTICUT								
1 Vacancy								
2 Gejdenson	N	Y	Y	Y	Y	Y	Y	P
3 *DeNardis*	?	Y	Y	Y	Y	Y	Y	N
4 *McKinney*	Y	Y	Y	Y	Y	?	?	?
5 Ratchford	N	Y	Y	Y	Y	Y	Y	N
6 Moffett	?	Y	Y	Y	Y	Y	Y	N
DELAWARE								
AL *Evans*	Y	Y	Y	Y	Y	Y	Y	N
FLORIDA								
1 Hutto	Y	Y	Y	Y	?	Y	Y	N
2 Fuqua	Y	Y	Y	Y	Y	Y	Y	N
3 Bennett	Y	Y	N	Y	N	Y	Y	N
4 Chappell	Y	Y	Y	Y	N	Y	Y	N
5 *McCollum*	Y	Y	N	Y	N	Y	Y	N
6 *Young*	Y	?	Y	Y	N	Y	Y	N
7 Gibbons	?	Y	Y	Y	N	?	Y	N
8 Ireland	Y	Y	Y	Y	Y	Y	Y	N
9 Nelson	Y	Y	Y	Y	Y	Y	Y	N
10 *Bafalis*	Y	Y	Y	Y	N	Y	Y	N
11 Mica	Y	Y	Y	Y	?	Y	Y	N
12 *Shaw*	Y	Y	N	Y	N	Y	Y	N
13 Lehman	?	Y	Y	Y	Y	Y	Y	N
14 Pepper	?	?	Y	Y	Y	Y	Y	N
15 Fascell	Y	Y	Y	Y	Y	Y	Y	N
GEORGIA								
1 Ginn	?	Y	N	Y	N	Y	Y	N
2 Hatcher	?	?	?	?	?	?	?	?
3 Brinkley	Y	Y	N	Y	N	Y	Y	N
4 Levitas	Y	Y	N	Y	Y	Y	Y	N
5 Fowler	Y	Y	N	Y	N	Y	Y	N
6 *Gingrich*	?	Y	Y	Y	Y	Y	?	N
7 McDonald	Y	N	N	Y	-	+	+	-
8 Evans	N	Y	Y	N	Y	Y	Y	N
9 Jenkins	Y	Y	N	Y	?	Y	Y	N
10 Barnard	Y	Y	N	Y	?	Y	Y	N
HAWAII								
1 Heftel	?	Y	Y	Y	Y	Y	Y	N
2 Akaka	Y	Y	Y	Y	N	Y	Y	N
IDAHO								
1 *Craig*	Y	Y	N	N	N	Y	Y	N
2 *Hansen*	Y	Y	N	Y	N	Y	Y	N
ILLINOIS								
1 Washington	Y	?	Y	Y	Y	Y	Y	N
2 Savage	?	?	Y	N	N	Y	Y	N
3 Russo	Y	Y	Y	Y	X	?	?	?
4 *Derwinski*	Y	Y	Y	Y	?	Y	Y	N
5 Fary	Y	Y	Y	Y	Y	Y	Y	N
6 *Hyde*	Y	Y	Y	Y	Y	Y	Y	N
7 Collins	?	?	?	?	#	Y	Y	N
8 Rostenkowski	Y	Y	Y	Y	Y	Y	Y	N
9 Yates	Y	Y	Y	Y	Y	Y	Y	N
10 *Porter*	Y	Y	Y	Y	+	+	Y	N
11 Annunzio	Y	Y	Y	Y	Y	Y	Y	N
12 *Crane, P.*	Y	Y	N	Y	N	Y	Y	N
13 *McClory*	Y	Y	Y	Y	Y	Y	Y	N
14 *Erlenborn*	?	?	Y	Y	Y	Y	Y	N
15 *Corcoran*	Y	Y	N	Y	N	Y	Y	N
16 *Martin*	Y	Y	N	Y	N	+	+	N
17 *O'Brien*	?	?	?	?	Y	Y	Y	N
18 *Michel*	?	Y	Y	Y	Y	Y	Y	N
19 *Railsback*	Y	Y	Y	?	?	Y	Y	N
20 *Findley*	Y	Y	Y	Y	Y	Y	Y	N
21 *Madigan*	?	Y	Y	Y	Y	Y	Y	N
22 *Crane, D.*	Y	Y	N	Y	N	Y	Y	N
23 Price	Y	Y	Y	Y	Y	Y	Y	N
24 Simon	?	?	?	?	?	Y	Y	N
INDIANA								
1 Benjamin	Y	Y	N	Y	N	Y	Y	N
2 Fithian	Y	Y	Y	Y	N	?	?	?
3 *Hiler*	?	Y	Y	Y	Y	Y	Y	N
4 *Coats*	N	Y	Y	Y	Y	Y	Y	N
5 *Hillis*	Y	Y	Y	Y	Y	Y	?	N
6 Evans	Y	Y	?	?	?	Y	Y	N
7 *Myers*	Y	Y	N	Y	N	Y	Y	N
8 *Deckard*	Y	Y	N	N	N	Y	Y	N
9 Hamilton	Y	Y	Y	Y	Y	Y	Y	N
10 Sharp	Y	Y	Y	Y	Y	Y	Y	N
11 Jacobs	?	N	Y	N	Y	Y	Y	N
IOWA								
1 *Leach*	Y	Y	Y	Y	Y	Y	N	N
2 *Tauke*	Y	Y	Y	Y	Y	Y	?	N
3 *Evans*	N	Y	N	Y	N	Y	Y	N
4 Smith	Y	Y	Y	Y	Y	Y	Y	N
5 Harkin	N	Y	Y	Y	Y	Y	Y	N
6 Bedell	?	?	?	?	?	Y	Y	N

Member	334	335	336	337	338	339	340	341
KANSAS								
1 ***Roberts***	Y	Y	N	Y	N	Y	Y	N
2 ***Jeffries***	Y	Y	N	Y	N	Y	Y	N
3 ***Winn***	Y	Y	Y	Y	Y	Y	Y	N
4 Glickman	Y	Y	Y	Y	Y	Y	Y	N
5 ***Whittaker***	Y	Y	Y	Y	N	Y	Y	N
KENTUCKY								
1 Hubbard	Y	Y	N	Y	N	?	?	?
2 Natcher	Y	Y	Y	Y	N	Y	Y	N
3 Mazzoli	Y	Y	Y	Y	Y	?	Y	N
4 ***Snyder***	Y	N	N	Y	N	Y	Y	N
5 ***Rogers***	Y	Y	N	Y	N	Y	Y	N
6 ***Hopkins***	Y	Y	N	Y	N	Y	Y	N
7 Perkins	Y	Y	N	Y	N	Y	Y	N
LOUISIANA								
1 ***Livingston***	Y	Y	Y	Y	Y	Y	?	N
2 Boggs	?	Y	Y	Y	Y	Y	Y	N
3 Tauzin	Y	Y	N	Y	N	Y	Y	N
4 Roemer	Y	N	N	Y	N	Y	Y	N
5 Huckaby	Y	Y	N	Y	N	Y	Y	?
6 ***Moore***	Y	Y	N	Y	N	Y	Y	N
7 Breaux	Y	Y	Y	Y	Y	?	?	N
8 Long	Y	Y	Y	Y	Y	Y	Y	N
MAINE								
1 ***Emery***	Y	Y	N	Y	N	Y	Y	N
2 ***Snowe***	Y	Y	Y	Y	Y	Y	Y	N
MARYLAND								
1 Dyson	Y	N	Y	Y	N	Y	Y	N
2 Long	Y	Y	Y	Y	Y	Y	Y	N
3 Mikulski	Y	Y	Y	Y	Y	?	Y	N
4 ***Holt***	N	N	Y	Y	N	Y	Y	N
5 Hoyer	Y	Y	Y	Y	Y	Y	Y	N
6 Byron	?	Y	Y	Y	N	Y	Y	N
7 Mitchell	N	N	Y	?	Y	N	Y	N
8 Barnes	N	Y	Y	Y	Y	Y	Y	N
MASSACHUSETTS								
1 ***Conte***	Y	Y	Y	Y	Y	Y	Y	N
2 Boland	Y	Y	?	?	#	Y	Y	N
3 Early	Y	Y	N	Y	?	Y	Y	N
4 Frank	Y	Y	Y	Y	Y	?	?	?
5 Shannon	Y	Y	Y	?	?	Y	Y	N
6 Mavroules	?	Y	Y	Y	Y	Y	?	N
7 Markey	?	Y	Y	Y	Y	Y	Y	N
8 O'Neill								
9 Moakley	?	?	?	Y	Y	Y	?	?
10 ***Heckler***	Y	Y	Y	Y	Y	?	Y	N
11 Donnelly	?	Y	Y	Y	N	?	?	?
12 Studds	Y	Y	Y	Y	Y	Y	Y	P
MICHIGAN								
1 Conyers	P	Y	Y	Y	N	Y	Y	N
2 ***Pursell***	?	Y	Y	Y	#	Y	Y	N
3 Wolpe	Y	Y	Y	Y	Y	Y	Y	N
4 ***Siljander***	Y	Y	Y	Y	Y	Y	Y	N
5 ***Sawyer***	Y	Y	Y	Y	Y	Y	Y	N
6 ***Dunn***	N	Y	Y	Y	N	Y	Y	N
7 Kildee	Y	Y	Y	Y	Y	Y	Y	N
8 Traxler	Y	Y	Y	Y	?	Y	Y	N
9 ***Vander Jagt***	?	Y	Y	?	Y	Y	Y	N
10 Albosta	Y	Y	N	Y	?	Y	Y	N
11 ***Davis***	Y	Y	N	Y	N	Y	Y	N
12 Bonior	?	Y	Y	Y	Y	Y	Y	N
13 Crockett	?	?	?	?	?	?	?	?
14 Hertel	Y	Y	Y	Y	Y	Y	Y	N
15 Ford	?	?	Y	?	N	?	?	N
16 Dingell	Y	Y	Y	Y	Y	Y	N	N
17 Brodhead	Y	Y	Y	Y	N	Y	Y	N
18 Blanchard	Y	Y	Y	Y	Y	?	Y	N
19 ***Broomfield***	Y	Y	Y	Y	Y	Y	Y	N
MINNESOTA								
1 ***Erdahl***	Y	Y	Y	Y	Y	Y	Y	N
2 ***Hagedorn***	Y	Y	N	Y	Y	Y	Y	N
3 ***Frenzel***	?	Y	Y	Y	Y	Y	Y	N
4 Vento	Y	Y	Y	Y	Y	?	Y	N
5 Sabo	N	Y	Y	Y	Y	Y	Y	N
6 ***Weber***	?	?	N	Y	N	?	Y	N
7 ***Stangeland***	Y	Y	N	Y	Y	?	?	N
8 Oberstar	Y	Y	Y	Y	Y	?	Y	N
MISSISSIPPI								
1 Whitten	Y	Y	Y	Y	N	Y	Y	N
2 Bowen	Y	Y	Y	Y	Y	Y	Y	N
3 Montgomery	Y	?	N	Y	N	Y	Y	N
4 Dowdy	Y	N	N	Y	N	Y	Y	N
5 ***Lott***	?	Y	Y	Y	N	Y	Y	N
MISSOURI								
1 Clay	?	?	?	?	?	Y	Y	N
2 Young	Y	Y	Y	Y	N	Y	Y	N
3 Gephardt	Y	Y	Y	Y	N	Y	Y	N
4 Skelton	Y	Y	N	Y	N	Y	Y	N
5 Bolling	?	?	?	?	?	?	?	?
6 ***Coleman***	Y	Y	N	Y	N	Y	Y	N
7 ***Taylor***	Y	Y	N	Y	N	Y	Y	N
8 ***Bailey***	Y	Y	N	Y	N	Y	Y	N
9 Volkmer	Y	Y	N	Y	N	Y	Y	N
10 ***Emerson***	N	Y	N	Y	N	Y	Y	N
MONTANA								
1 Williams	Y	?	Y	Y	N	Y	Y	?
2 ***Marlenee***	Y	Y	N	Y	N	Y	Y	N
NEBRASKA								
1 ***Bereuter***	Y	Y	Y	Y	Y	Y	Y	N
2 ***Daub***	Y	Y	N	Y	N	Y	Y	N
3 ***Smith***	Y	Y	Y	Y	N	Y	Y	N
NEVADA								
AL Santini	?	Y	N	N	N	Y	Y	N
NEW HAMPSHIRE								
1 D'Amours	Y	Y	Y	Y	N	Y	Y	N
2 ***Gregg***	Y	Y	Y	Y	Y	Y	Y	N
NEW JERSEY								
1 Florio	Y	Y	Y	Y	Y	Y	Y	N
2 Hughes	Y	Y	N	Y	N	Y	Y	N
3 Howard	Y	Y	Y	Y	Y	Y	Y	N
4 ***Smith***	Y	Y	Y	Y	Y	Y	Y	N
5 ***Fenwick***	Y	Y	Y	Y	Y	Y	N	N
6 ***Forsythe***	N	Y	Y	Y	Y	Y	Y	N
7 ***Roukema***	Y	Y	Y	Y	Y	?	Y	N
8 Roe	Y	Y	Y	Y	Y	?	?	?
9 ***Hollenbeck***	Y	Y	Y	Y	Y	?	Y	N
10 Rodino	Y	Y	Y	Y	N	?	Y	N
11 Minish	Y	?	Y	Y	Y	Y	Y	N
12 ***Rinaldo***	Y	Y	Y	Y	Y	?	Y	N
13 ***Courter***	?	?	N	Y	Y	Y	Y	N
14 Guarini	Y	Y	Y	Y	N	Y	Y	N
15 Dwyer	Y	Y	Y	Y	Y	Y	Y	N
NEW MEXICO								
1 ***Lujan***	Y	Y	Y	Y	N	Y	Y	N
2 ***Skeen***	Y	Y	N	Y	N	Y	Y	N
NEW YORK								
1 ***Carney***	Y	Y	Y	Y	Y	Y	Y	N
2 Downey	Y	Y	Y	Y	Y	Y	Y	N
3 ***Carman***	Y	Y	Y	Y	Y	Y	Y	N
4 ***Lent***	Y	Y	Y	Y	Y	Y	Y	?
5 ***McGrath***	Y	Y	Y	Y	Y	Y	Y	N
6 ***LeBoutillier***	Y	Y	Y	Y	Y	Y	Y	N
7 Addabbo	?	Y	Y	Y	Y	Y	Y	N
8 Rosenthal	Y	Y	Y	Y	?	Y	Y	N
9 Ferraro	Y	Y	Y	Y	Y	?	?	N
10 Biaggi	?	?	?	?	?	Y	Y	N
11 Scheuer	Y	Y	Y	N	Y	?	Y	N
12 Chisholm	?	?	?	?	?	Y	Y	N
13 Solarz	Y	Y	Y	N	Y	Y	Y	N
14 Richmond	?	?	?	?	#	Y	Y	N
15 Zeferetti	Y	Y	Y	Y	Y	Y	Y	N
16 Schumer	Y	Y	Y	Y	Y	Y	Y	N
17 ***Molinari***	Y	Y	Y	Y	Y	?	Y	N
18 ***Green***	Y	Y	Y	N	Y	Y	Y	N
19 Rangel	Y	Y	Y	Y	Y	Y	Y	N
20 Weiss	Y	Y	Y	N	Y	Y	Y	N
21 Garcia	?	?	?	?	?	?	?	?
22 Bingham	?	Y	Y	N	Y	Y	Y	N
23 Peyser	Y	Y	Y	Y	Y	Y	Y	N
24 Ottinger	P	P	Y	Y	Y	Y	Y	N
25 ***Fish***	?	Y	Y	Y	#	?	Y	N
26 ***Gilman***	Y	Y	Y	Y	Y	Y	Y	N
27 McHugh	Y	Y	Y	Y	Y	Y	Y	N
28 Stratton	Y	Y	Y	Y	Y	Y	Y	N
29 ***Solomon***	Y	N	N	Y	N	Y	Y	N
30 ***Martin***	Y	Y	Y	Y	N	Y	Y	N
31 ***Mitchell***	Y	Y	Y	Y	Y	Y	Y	N
32 ***Wortley***	Y	Y	Y	Y	Y	Y	Y	N
33 ***Lee***	Y	Y	Y	Y	N	Y	Y	N
34 ***Horton***	?	Y	Y	Y	Y	Y	?	N
35 ***Conable***	Y	Y	Y	Y	Y	Y	Y	N
36 LaFalce	?	?	Y	N	Y	Y	Y	N
37 Nowak	Y	Y	Y	Y	?	Y	Y	N
38 ***Kemp***	?	Y	Y	Y	Y	Y	Y	?
39 Lundine	Y	Y	Y	Y	Y	Y	Y	N
NORTH CAROLINA								
1 Jones	Y	Y	N	Y	N	Y	Y	N
2 Fountain	?	Y	N	Y	N	Y	Y	N
3 Whitley	Y	Y	?	?	?	Y	Y	N
4 Andrews	Y	Y	Y	Y	N	Y	Y	N
5 Neal	Y	Y	Y	Y	N	Y	Y	N
6 ***Johnston***	Y	N	Y	Y	Y	Y	Y	N
7 Rose	Y	?	?	?	?	Y	Y	N
8 Hefner	?	?	?	?	X	Y	Y	N
9 ***Martin***	Y	Y	N	Y	N	Y	Y	N
10 ***Broyhill***	Y	Y	N	Y	N	Y	Y	N
11 ***Hendon***	Y	N	N	Y	N	Y	Y	N
NORTH DAKOTA								
AL Dorgan	Y	Y	Y	Y	Y	Y	Y	N
OHIO								
1 ***Gradison***	Y	Y	Y	Y	Y	Y	Y	N
2 Luken	Y	Y	Y	Y	Y	Y	Y	N
3 Hall	Y	Y	Y	Y	Y	Y	Y	N
4 ***Oxley***	Y	Y	Y	Y	Y	Y	Y	N
5 ***Latta***	Y	Y	Y	Y	N	Y	Y	N
6 ***McEwen***	Y	Y	Y	Y	N	Y	Y	N
7 ***Brown***	?	?	?	?	?	?	?	?
8 ***Kindness***	Y	N	Y	Y	N	?	?	?
9 ***Weber***	Y	Y	Y	Y	Y	Y	Y	N
10 ***Miller***	N	Y	N	Y	N	Y	Y	N
11 ***Stanton***	Y	Y	Y	Y	Y	Y	Y	N
12 Shamansky	Y	Y	Y	Y	Y	?	?	?
13 Pease	?	Y	Y	Y	?	Y	Y	N
14 Seiberling	Y	Y	Y	Y	Y	Y	Y	N
15 ***Wylie***	Y	Y	Y	Y	Y	?	?	N
16 ***Regula***	?	Y	Y	Y	Y	Y	Y	N
17 ***Ashbrook***	Y	?	N	Y	N	Y	Y	N
18 Applegate	?	?	N	Y	N	Y	Y	N
19 ***Williams***	Y	Y	Y	Y	?	?	?	N
20 Oakar	?	?	?	?	?	Y	Y	N
21 Stokes	N	Y	Y	Y	Y	Y	Y	N
22 Eckart	Y	Y	Y	Y	Y	Y	Y	N
23 Mottl	Y	Y	N	Y	?	Y	Y	N
OKLAHOMA								
1 Jones	Y	Y	N	Y	N	Y	Y	N
2 Synar	Y	Y	Y	Y	Y	Y	Y	N
3 Watkins	Y	?	N	Y	N	?	Y	N
4 McCurdy	Y	Y	N	Y	N	Y	Y	N
5 ***Edwards***	Y	Y	N	Y	N	Y	Y	N
6 English	Y	Y	N	Y	N	Y	Y	N
OREGON								
1 AuCoin	?	?	?	?	?	?	?	?
2 ***Smith***	Y	Y	N	Y	N	Y	Y	N
3 Wyden	Y	Y	Y	Y	Y	Y	Y	N
4 Weaver	Y	Y	Y	Y	N	Y	Y	N
PENNSYLVANIA								
1 Foglietta	Y	Y	Y	Y	Y	Y	Y	?
2 Gray	Y	Y	Y	Y	Y	?	?	?
3 Smith	Y	Y	Y	Y	Y	Y	Y	N
4 ***Dougherty***	Y	?	Y	Y	Y	?	?	?
5 ***Schulze***	Y	Y	N	Y	N	Y	Y	N
6 Yatron	Y	Y	Y	Y	?	Y	Y	N
7 Edgar	Y	Y	Y	Y	Y	?	Y	N
8 ***Coyne, J.***	Y	Y	Y	Y	Y	Y	Y	N
9 ***Shuster***	Y	Y	N	Y	N	Y	Y	N
10 ***McDade***	Y	Y	Y	Y	N	Y	Y	N
11 ***Nelligan***	Y	Y	N	Y	N	Y	Y	N
12 Murtha	Y	Y	Y	Y	Y	Y	Y	N
13 ***Coughlin***	N	Y	Y	Y	Y	Y	Y	N
14 Coyne, W.	Y	Y	Y	Y	Y	Y	Y	N
15 ***Ritter***	Y	Y	N	Y	N	Y	Y	N
16 ***Walker***	?	Y	N	Y	N	Y	Y	N
17 Ertel	Y	Y	Y	Y	?	?	?	?
18 Walgren	Y	Y	Y	Y	?	?	?	?
19 ***Goodling***	N	Y	Y	Y	N	?	?	?
20 Gaydos	Y	Y	Y	Y	N	Y	Y	N
21 Bailey	Y	Y	Y	Y	N	Y	Y	N
22 Murphy	Y	Y	Y	Y	?	?	?	?
23 ***Clinger***	Y	Y	Y	Y	Y	Y	Y	N
24 ***Marks***	?	Y	Y	Y	Y	?	Y	N
25 ***Atkinson***	Y	Y	Y	Y	N	Y	Y	N
RHODE ISLAND								
1 St Germain	Y	Y	?	?	?	Y	?	N
2 ***Schneider***	Y	Y	Y	Y	Y	Y	Y	N
SOUTH CAROLINA								
1 ***Hartnett***	Y	Y	Y	Y	#	Y	Y	?
2 ***Spence***	Y	Y	Y	Y	N	?	Y	N
3 Derrick	Y	Y	Y	Y	N	Y	Y	N
4 ***Campbell***	Y	Y	Y	Y	Y	Y	Y	N
5 Holland	?	Y	Y	Y	?	?	?	?
6 ***Napier***	Y	Y	Y	Y	N	Y	Y	N
SOUTH DAKOTA								
1 Daschle	Y	Y	Y	Y	N	Y	Y	N
2 ***Roberts***	Y	Y	N	Y	N	Y	Y	N
TENNESSEE								
1 ***Quillen***	Y	Y	#	?	X	Y	Y	N
2 ***Duncan***	Y	Y	Y	Y	?	Y	Y	N
3 Bouquard	Y	Y	N	Y	N	Y	Y	N
4 Gore	Y	Y	Y	Y	Y	Y	Y	N
5 Boner	Y	Y	Y	Y	N	Y	Y	N
6 ***Beard***	?	?	?	?	?	?	?	?
7 Jones	?	?	?	?	X	Y	Y	N
8 Ford	Y	Y	Y	Y	Y	Y	Y	N
TEXAS								
1 Hall, S.	Y	Y	N	Y	N	Y	Y	N
2 Wilson	Y	Y	Y	Y	Y	Y	Y	N
3 ***Collins***	Y	Y	N	Y	N	Y	N	N
4 Hall, R.	Y	N	N	Y	N	Y	Y	N
5 Mattox	Y	Y	Y	Y	Y	?	?	?
6 Gramm	Y	Y	N	Y	N	Y	Y	N
7 ***Archer***	Y	Y	N	Y	N	Y	Y	N
8 ***Fields***	Y	Y	N	Y	N	Y	Y	N
9 Brooks	?	?	?	?	?	?	?	?
10 Pickle	Y	Y	N	Y	Y	Y	Y	N
11 Leath	Y	Y	N	Y	N	Y	Y	N
12 Wright	Y	Y	?	?	?	?	?	?
13 Hightower	Y	Y	Y	Y	N	Y	Y	N
14 Patman	Y	Y	N	Y	N	Y	Y	N
15 de la Garza	Y	Y	Y	Y	N	Y	Y	N
16 White	Y	Y	N	Y	N	Y	Y	N
17 Stenholm	Y	Y	N	Y	N	Y	Y	N
18 Leland	Y	Y	Y	N	Y	Y	Y	N
19 Hance	?	?	?	?	?	Y	Y	N
20 Gonzalez	Y	Y	Y	N	N	Y	Y	N
21 ***Loeffler***	Y	Y	N	Y	Y	Y	Y	N
22 ***Paul***	Y	Y	N	Y	N	Y	N	N
23 Kazen	Y	Y	N	Y	N	Y	Y	N
24 Frost	Y	Y	Y	Y	Y	?	?	?
UTAH								
1 ***Hansen***	Y	Y	N	Y	N	Y	Y	N
2 ***Marriott***	Y	Y	N	Y	N	Y	Y	N
VERMONT								
AL ***Jeffords***	Y	Y	Y	Y	Y	Y	Y	N
VIRGINIA								
1 ***Trible***	Y	Y	Y	Y	N	?	Y	N
2 ***Whitehurst***	Y	Y	#	?	?	Y	Y	N
3 ***Bliley***	Y	Y	Y	Y	Y	Y	Y	N
4 ***Daniel, R.***	Y	Y	N	Y	N	Y	Y	N
5 Daniel, D.	?	Y	Y	Y	N	Y	Y	N
6 ***Butler***	Y	Y	Y	Y	Y	Y	Y	N
7 ***Robinson***	Y	Y	Y	Y	N	Y	Y	N
8 ***Parris***	Y	?	N	Y	N	Y	Y	N
9 ***Wampler***	Y	?	Y	Y	N	Y	Y	N
10 ***Wolf***	Y	Y	Y	Y	Y	Y	Y	N
WASHINGTON								
1 ***Pritchard***	Y	Y	Y	Y	Y	Y	Y	N
2 Swift	Y	Y	Y	Y	Y	Y	?	N
3 Bonker	Y	Y	Y	Y	Y	Y	Y	N
4 ***Morrison***	Y	Y	Y	Y	Y	Y	Y	N
5 Foley	Y	Y	Y	?	Y	Y	Y	N
6 Dicks	Y	Y	Y	Y	Y	Y	Y	N
7 Lowry	Y	Y	Y	N	Y	Y	Y	N
WEST VIRGINIA								
1 Mollohan	Y	Y	N	N	Y	Y	Y	N
2 ***Benedict***	Y	Y	N	Y	N	Y	Y	N
3 ***Staton***	?	?	?	?	X	Y	Y	N
4 Rahall	Y	Y	N	Y	N	Y	Y	?
WISCONSIN								
1 Aspin	Y	Y	Y	Y	?	Y	Y	N
2 Kastenmeier	Y	Y	Y	Y	N	Y	Y	N
3 ***Gunderson***	Y	Y	Y	Y	N	Y	Y	N
4 Zablocki	Y	Y	Y	Y	Y	Y	Y	N
5 Reuss	Y	Y	Y	N	Y	Y	Y	N
6 ***Petri***	Y	Y	N	Y	N	Y	Y	N
7 Obey	Y	?	Y	Y	N	Y	Y	N
8 ***Roth***	Y	Y	N	Y	N	Y	Y	N
9 ***Sensenbrenner***	Y	Y	N	Y	N	Y	Y	N
WYOMING								
AL ***Cheney***	Y	Y	Y	Y	Y	Y	Y	N

Democrats ***Republicans***

342. HR 2559. Coast Guard Authorization. Passage of the bill to authorize $1.9 billion in fiscal 1982 for Coast Guard activities. Passed 391-2: R 179-2; D 212-0 (ND 142-0, SD 70-0), Dec. 14, 1981.

343. HR 4700. Standby Petroleum Emergency Authority Act. Adoption of the rule (H Res 288) providing for House floor consideration of the bill to provide the president with standby authority to allocate supplies and control prices of oil during a severe petroleum supply interruption. Adopted 272-113: R 72-106; D 200-7 (ND 136-2, SD 64-5), Dec. 14, 1981.

344. HR 4700. Standby Petroleum Emergency Authority Act. Passage of the bill to give the president standby authority to control oil supplies and prices in the event of a severe petroleum supply interruption. Passed 244-136: R 65-116; D 179-20 (ND 126-6, SD 53-14), Dec. 14, 1981. A "nay" was a vote supporting the president's position.

345. HR 4995. Defense Department Appropriations, Fiscal 1982. Adoption of the conference report on the bill to appropriate $199,899,264,000 for the Department of Defense in fiscal year 1982. Adopted 334-84: R 170-16; D 164-68 (ND 91-65, SD 73-3), Dec. 15, 1981. (The president had requested $200,878,234,000.)

346. Procedural Motion. Walker, R-Pa., motion to approve the House *Journal* of Tuesday, Dec. 15. Motion agreed to 200-171: R 72-98; D 128-73 (ND 79-55, SD 49-18), Dec. 16, 1981.

347. HR 4331. Minimum Social Security Benefits. Rostenkowski, D-Ill., motion to suspend the rules and adopt the conference report on the bill to restore the minimum Social Security benefit; to extend the payroll tax to the first six months of sick pay; and to permit the borrowing of assets among the three Social Security trust funds through Dec. 31, 1982. Motion agreed to (thus cleared for the president) 412-10: R 181-7; D 231-3 (ND 154-3, SD 77-0), Dec. 16, 1981. A two-thirds majority vote (282 in this case) is required for adoption under suspension of the rules. A "yea" was a vote supporting the president's position.

348. HR 4559. Foreign Aid Appropriations, Fiscal 1982. Adoption of the conference report on the bill to appropriate $7,495,221,970 for foreign assistance and related programs in fiscal 1982. Adopted 217-201: R 91-93; D 126-108 (ND 105-52, SD 21-56), Dec. 16, 1981. (The president had requested $7,775,098,683.)

KEY

Y	Voted for (yea).
#	Paired for.
+	Announced for.
N	Voted against (nay).
X	Paired against.
-	Announced against.
P	Voted "present".
C	Voted "present" to avoid possible conflict of interest.
?	Did not vote or otherwise make a position known.

	342	343	344	345	346	347	348
ALABAMA							
1 Edwards	Y	Y	N	Y	Y	Y	Y
2 Dickinson	Y	Y	N	Y	Y	Y	N
3 Nichols	Y	Y	X	Y	?	Y	N
4 Bevill	Y	Y	Y	?	Y	Y	N
5 Flippo	Y	Y	Y	Y	Y	Y	N
6 Smith	Y	N	N	Y	N	Y	N
7 Shelby	?	?	?	Y	?	Y	N
ALASKA							
AL Young	Y	N	N	Y	?	Y	N
ARIZONA							
1 Rhodes	Y	N	N	Y	Y	Y	Y
2 Udall	Y	Y	?	Y	N	Y	Y
3 Stump	Y	N	N	Y	N	Y	N
4 Rudd	Y	N	N	Y	N	Y	N
ARKANSAS							
1 Alexander	Y	Y	Y	Y	Y	Y	Y
2 Bethune	Y	N	N	Y	N	Y	N
3 Hammerschmidt	Y	N	N	Y	N	Y	N
4 Anthony	Y	Y	Y	Y	Y	Y	N
CALIFORNIA							
1 Chappie	Y	N	N	Y	N	Y	N
2 Clausen	Y	N	N	Y	N	Y	Y
3 Matsui	Y	Y	Y	Y	?	Y	Y
4 Fazio	Y	Y	Y	Y	Y	Y	Y
5 Burton, J.	?	?	?	?	?	?	?
6 Burton, P.	Y	Y	Y	N	Y	Y	Y
7 Miller	Y	Y	Y	N	N	Y	Y
8 Dellums	?	?	?	N	Y	Y	N
9 Stark	Y	Y	Y	N	N	Y	N
10 Edwards	Y	Y	Y	N	Y	Y	Y
11 Lantos	Y	?	#	Y	Y	Y	Y
12 McCloskey	?	?	X	Y	?	Y	N
13 Mineta	Y	Y	Y	Y	Y	Y	Y
14 Shumway	Y	N	N	Y	Y	Y	N
15 Coelho	Y	Y	Y	Y	Y	Y	Y
16 Panetta	Y	Y	Y	N	Y	Y	N
17 Pashayan	Y	N	N	Y	Y	Y	N
18 Thomas	Y	N	N	Y	Y	Y	Y
19 Lagomarsino	Y	N	N	Y	Y	Y	Y
20 Goldwater	?	N	N	?	?	Y	#
21 Fiedler	Y	Y	N	N	Y	Y	Y
22 Moorhead	Y	N	N	Y	?	?	X
23 Beilenson	Y	Y	Y	N	Y	Y	Y
24 Waxman	Y	?	?	Y	?	Y	Y
25 Roybal	Y	Y	Y	N	Y	Y	N
26 Rousselot	Y	N	N	Y	?	N	N
27 Dornan	Y	N	N	Y	?	Y	Y
28 Dixon	Y	Y	Y	Y	Y	Y	Y
29 Hawkins	Y	Y	Y	Y	Y	Y	Y
30 Danielson	Y	Y	Y	Y	Y	Y	Y
31 Dymally	Y	Y	Y	Y	?	Y	Y
32 Anderson	Y	Y	N	Y	N	Y	N
33 Grisham	Y	Y	N	Y	Y	Y	N
34 Lungren	Y	N	N	Y	Y	Y	N
35 Dreier	Y	N	N	Y	N	Y	N
36 Brown	Y	Y	?	N	N	Y	N
37 Lewis	Y	Y	N	Y	Y	Y	Y
38 Patterson	?	?	?	Y	Y	Y	Y
39 Dannemeyer	Y	N	N	Y	N	Y	N
40 Badham	Y	?	X	Y	Y	Y	Y
41 Lowery	Y	N	N	Y	N	Y	N
42 Hunter	Y	N	N	Y	N	Y	N
43 Burgener	Y	N	N	Y	?	?	#
COLORADO							
1 Schroeder	Y	Y	N	N	N	Y	N
2 Wirth	Y	Y	Y	Y	Y	Y	Y
3 Kogovsek	Y	Y	Y	N	Y	N	N
4 Brown	Y	N	N	Y	N	Y	N
5 Kramer	Y	N	N	Y	N	Y	N
CONNECTICUT							
1 Vacancy							
2 Gejdenson	Y	Y	Y	Y	Y	Y	Y
3 DeNardis	Y	?	Y	Y	?	Y	Y
4 McKinney	?	?	#	?	N	Y	Y
5 Ratchford	Y	Y	Y	Y	Y	Y	Y
6 Moffett	Y	?	Y	N	Y	Y	Y
DELAWARE							
AL Evans	Y	Y	Y	Y	Y	Y	Y
FLORIDA							
1 Hutto	Y	Y	N	Y	Y	Y	N
2 Fuqua	Y	Y	Y	Y	Y	Y	N
3 Bennett	Y	Y	Y	N	Y	N	N
4 Chappell	Y	Y	?	Y	?	Y	N
5 McCollum	Y	N	N	Y	N	Y	N
6 Young	Y	N	N	Y	N	Y	X
7 Gibbons	Y	N	Y	Y	N	Y	Y
8 Ireland	Y	N	N	Y	Y	Y	N
9 Nelson	Y	Y	Y	Y	Y	Y	Y
10 Bafalis	Y	N	N	Y	N	Y	N
11 Mica	Y	Y	Y	Y	Y	Y	Y
12 Shaw	Y	N	N	Y	Y	Y	N
13 Lehman	Y	Y	Y	N	Y	Y	Y
14 Pepper	Y	Y	Y	Y	?	Y	Y
15 Fascell	Y	Y	Y	Y	Y	Y	Y
GEORGIA							
1 Ginn	Y	Y	Y	Y	Y	Y	N
2 Hatcher	?	?	?	Y	Y	Y	N
3 Brinkley	Y	Y	Y	Y	Y	Y	N
4 Levitas	Y	Y	Y	Y	Y	Y	N
5 Fowler	Y	Y	Y	Y	N	Y	N
6 Gingrich	Y	N	N	Y	Y	Y	Y
7 McDonald	+	-	X	#	?	-	X
8 Evans	Y	N	N	Y	?	Y	N
9 Jenkins	Y	Y	Y	Y	Y	Y	N
10 Barnard	Y	Y	N	Y	Y	Y	N
HAWAII							
1 Heftel	Y	Y	Y	Y	Y	Y	Y
2 Akaka	Y	Y	Y	Y	Y	Y	Y
IDAHO							
1 Craig	Y	N	Y	Y	N	Y	N
2 Hansen	Y	N	N	Y	N	Y	N
ILLINOIS							
1 Washington	Y	Y	Y	N	Y	Y	Y
2 Savage	Y	Y	Y	N	?	Y	N
3 Russo	?	?	?	N	?	?	X
4 Derwinski	Y	N	N	Y	N	Y	Y
5 Fary	Y	Y	Y	Y	Y	Y	Y
6 Hyde	Y	N	N	Y	Y	Y	Y
7 Collins	Y	Y	Y	N	Y	Y	Y
8 Rostenkowski	Y	Y	Y	N	Y	Y	Y
9 Yates	Y	Y	Y	N	N	Y	Y
10 Porter	Y	N	N	Y	?	Y	Y
11 Annunzio	Y	Y	Y	Y	Y	Y	Y
12 Crane, P.	Y	Y	Y	N	N	Y	N
13 McClory	Y	N	N	Y	Y	Y	Y
14 Erlenborn	Y	N	N	Y	N	Y	N
15 Corcoran	Y	N	N	Y	N	Y	Y
16 Martin	Y	Y	Y	Y	Y	Y	Y
17 O'Brien	Y	N	N	Y	?	Y	Y
18 Michel	Y	N	N	Y	Y	Y	Y
19 Railsback	Y	Y	Y	Y	Y	Y	Y
20 Findley	Y	N	N	Y	Y	Y	Y
21 Madigan	Y	N	X	Y	?	Y	Y
22 Crane, D.	Y	?	N	Y	N	Y	N
23 Price	Y	Y	Y	Y	Y	Y	Y
24 Simon	Y	Y	Y	Y	Y	Y	Y
INDIANA							
1 Benjamin	Y	Y	Y	N	Y	N	Y
2 Fithian	?	?	?	?	N	Y	N
3 Hiler	Y	N	N	Y	N	Y	N
4 Coats	Y	Y	Y	N	Y	N	N
5 Hillis	Y	N	N	Y	Y	Y	N
6 Evans	Y	Y	Y	N	Y	N	N
7 Myers	Y	N	N	Y	N	Y	N
8 Deckard	Y	Y	Y	N	Y	Y	N
9 Hamilton	Y	Y	Y	Y	Y	Y	N
10 Sharp	Y	Y	Y	Y	Y	Y	N
11 Jacobs	Y	Y	Y	N	Y	N	N
IOWA							
1 Leach	Y	Y	Y	Y	N	Y	Y
2 Tauke	Y	Y	Y	N	Y	Y	Y
3 Evans	Y	Y	Y	N	N	Y	Y
4 Smith	Y	Y	Y	N	N	Y	N
5 Harkin	Y	Y	Y	N	N	Y	N
6 Bedell	Y	Y	Y	N	N	Y	Y

Democrats   *Republicans*

Corresponding to Congressional Record Votes 360, 361, 362, 363, 364, 365, 366

	342	343	344	345	346	347	348
KANSAS							
1 ***Roberts***	Y	Y	Y	Y	N	Y	N
2 ***Jeffries***	Y	N	N	Y	N	Y	N
3 ***Winn***	Y	N	N	Y	Y	Y	Y
4 Glickman	Y	Y	Y	Y	N	Y	Y
5 ***Whittaker***	Y	Y	Y	Y	N	Y	N
KENTUCKY							
1 Hubbard	?	?	?	Y	Y	Y	N
2 Natcher	Y	Y	Y	Y	Y	Y	N
3 Mazzoli	Y	Y	Y	Y	Y	Y	Y
4 ***Snyder***	Y	Y	Y	Y	Y	Y	N
5 ***Rogers***	Y	Y	Y	Y	N	Y	N
6 ***Hopkins***	Y	N	Y	Y	N	Y	N
7 Perkins	Y	Y	Y	Y	Y	Y	N
LOUISIANA							
1 ***Livingston***	Y	N	N	Y	Y	Y	Y
2 Boggs	Y	Y	Y	Y	Y	Y	Y
3 Tauzin	Y	Y	Y	Y	Y	Y	N
4 Roemer	Y	Y	N	Y	N	Y	N
5 Huckaby	Y	Y	N	Y	N	Y	N
6 ***Moore***	Y	Y	N	Y	?	Y	N
7 Breaux	Y	Y	N	Y	Y	Y	Y
8 Long	Y	Y	Y	Y	Y	Y	Y
MAINE							
1 ***Emery***	Y	Y	Y	Y	N	Y	N
2 ***Snowe***	Y	Y	Y	Y	N	Y	Y
MARYLAND							
1 Dyson	Y	Y	N	Y	N	Y	N
2 Long	Y	Y	Y	Y	Y	Y	Y
3 Mikulski	Y	Y	Y	N	N	Y	Y
4 ***Holt***	Y	N	N	Y	N	Y	N
5 Hoyer	Y	Y	Y	Y	Y	Y	Y
6 Byron	Y	Y	N	Y	N	Y	N
7 Mitchell	Y	Y	Y	N	Y	Y	Y
8 Barnes	Y	Y	Y	Y	Y	Y	Y
MASSACHUSETTS							
1 ***Conte***	Y	Y	Y	Y	Y	Y	Y
2 Boland	Y	Y	Y	Y	N	Y	Y
3 Early	Y	Y	Y	N	N	Y	N
4 Frank	?	?	?	?	N	Y	N
5 Shannon	Y	Y	Y	N	Y	Y	N
6 Mavroules	Y	Y	Y	Y	?	Y	Y
7 Markey	Y	Y	Y	N	N	Y	Y
8 O'Neill							
9 Moakley	?	?	?	Y	Y	Y	Y
10 ***Heckler***	Y	Y	Y	Y	N	Y	Y
11 Donnelly	?	?	?	N	Y	Y	N
12 Studds	Y	Y	Y	N	Y	Y	N
MICHIGAN							
1 Conyers	Y	Y	Y	N	?	Y	N
2 ***Pursell***	Y	N	Y	N	N	Y	Y
3 Wolpe	Y	Y	Y	N	N	Y	Y
4 ***Siljander***	Y	N	N	Y	N	Y	Y
5 ***Sawyer***	Y	N	Y	Y	N	Y	Y
6 ***Dunn***	Y	N	Y	Y	N	Y	N
7 Kildee	Y	Y	Y	N	N	Y	Y
8 Traxler	Y	Y	?	Y	?	Y	N
9 ***Vander Jagt***	Y	Y	X	Y	Y	Y	Y
10 Albosta	Y	Y	Y	Y	Y	Y	N
11 ***Davis***	Y	?	N	Y	N	Y	N
12 Bonior	?	Y	Y	N	Y	Y	Y
13 Crockett	?	?	?	N	?	Y	Y
14 Hertel	Y	Y	Y	N	N	Y	Y
15 Ford	Y	Y	Y	N	?	Y	Y
16 Dingell	Y	Y	Y	Y	?	Y	Y
17 Brodhead	Y	Y	Y	N	Y	Y	Y
18 Blanchard	Y	Y	Y	N	N	Y	Y
19 ***Broomfield***	Y	N	N	Y	N	Y	Y
MINNESOTA							
1 ***Erdahl***	Y	Y	Y	N	N	Y	Y
2 ***Hagedorn***	Y	N	Y	Y	Y	Y	Y
3 ***Frenzel***	Y	Y	N	Y	Y	Y	Y
4 Vento	Y	Y	Y	N	Y	X	#
5 Sabo	Y	?	Y	N	N	Y	Y
6 ***Weber***	Y	Y	Y	Y	N	Y	N
7 ***Stangeland***	Y	Y	Y	Y	Y	Y	Y
8 Oberstar	Y	Y	Y	N	Y	Y	Y
MISSISSIPPI							
1 Whitten	Y	Y	Y	Y	Y	Y	N
2 Bowen	Y	Y	Y	Y	Y	Y	Y
3 Montgomery	Y	Y	Y	Y	Y	Y	N
4 Dowdy	Y	Y	Y	Y	N	Y	N
5 ***Lott***	Y	N	N	Y	Y	Y	N
MISSOURI							
1 Clay	Y	Y	Y	N	Y	Y	Y
2 Young	Y	Y	Y	Y	Y	Y	N
3 Gephardt	Y	Y	Y	Y	Y	Y	N

	342	343	344	345	346	347	348
4 Skelton	Y	Y	Y	Y	N	Y	N
5 Bolling	?	?	?	?	?	?	?
6 ***Coleman***	Y	Y	Y	Y	N	Y	N
7 ***Taylor***	Y	N	N	Y	Y	Y	N
8 ***Bailey***	Y	Y	Y	Y	N	Y	N
9 Volkmer	Y	Y	Y	Y	N	Y	N
10 ***Emerson***	Y	Y	Y	Y	N	Y	N
MONTANA							
1 Williams	Y	?	Y	N	?	N	N
2 ***Marlenee***	Y	Y	Y	Y	Y	Y	N
NEBRASKA							
1 ***Bereuter***	Y	Y	Y	Y	N	Y	Y
2 ***Daub***	Y	Y	Y	Y	N	Y	N
3 ***Smith***	Y	N	Y	N	N	Y	N
NEVADA							
AL Santini	Y	Y	Y	Y	N	Y	N
NEW HAMPSHIRE							
1 D'Amours	Y	Y	Y	Y	?	Y	N
2 ***Gregg***	Y	N	N	Y	N	Y	Y
NEW JERSEY							
1 Florio	Y	Y	Y	Y	Y	Y	N
2 Hughes	Y	Y	Y	N	N	Y	N
3 Howard	Y	Y	Y	Y	Y	Y	Y
4 ***Smith***	Y	Y	Y	Y	Y	Y	Y
5 ***Fenwick***	Y	N	N	Y	N	Y	Y
6 ***Forsythe***	Y	N	N	N	?	Y	#
7 ***Roukema***	Y	Y	Y	N	N	Y	Y
8 Roe	?	?	?	Y	Y	Y	Y
9 ***Hollenbeck***	Y	Y	Y	N	?	Y	Y
10 Rodino	Y	Y	Y	N	Y	Y	N
11 Minish	Y	Y	Y	Y	Y	Y	Y
12 ***Rinaldo***	Y	Y	N	Y	N	Y	Y
13 ***Courter***	Y	N	Y	?	N	Y	Y
14 Guarini	Y	Y	Y	Y	Y	Y	N
15 Dwyer	Y	Y	Y	Y	Y	Y	Y
NEW MEXICO							
1 ***Lujan***	Y	Y	N	Y	N	Y	N
2 ***Skeen***	Y	N	N	Y	Y	Y	N
NEW YORK							
1 ***Carney***	Y	Y	Y	Y	N	Y	Y
2 Downey	Y	?	Y	N	Y	Y	Y
3 ***Carman***	Y	Y	Y	Y	N	Y	Y
4 ***Lent***	Y	Y	Y	Y	N	Y	Y
5 ***McGrath***	Y	Y	Y	Y	N	Y	Y
6 ***LeBoutillier***	Y	Y	Y	Y	N	Y	Y
7 Addabbo	Y	Y	Y	Y	Y	Y	Y
8 Rosenthal	Y	Y	Y	?	Y	Y	Y
9 Ferraro	Y	Y	Y	Y	Y	Y	Y
10 Biaggi	?	?	?	Y	Y	Y	Y
11 Scheuer	Y	Y	Y	Y	Y	Y	Y
12 Chisholm	Y	Y	Y	N	?	Y	N
13 Solarz	Y	Y	?	Y	Y	Y	Y
14 Richmond	Y	Y	Y	N	?	Y	Y
15 Zeferetti	Y	Y	?	Y	Y	Y	Y
16 Schumer	Y	Y	Y	N	N	Y	Y
17 ***Molinari***	Y	Y	Y	Y	N	Y	Y
18 ***Green***	Y	Y	N	Y	Y	Y	Y
19 Rangel	Y	Y	Y	N	Y	Y	Y
20 Weiss	Y	Y	Y	N	Y	Y	Y
21 Garcia	?	?	?	N	Y	Y	N
22 Bingham	Y	Y	Y	N	Y	Y	Y
23 Peyser	Y	Y	?	Y	Y	Y	Y
24 Ottinger	Y	Y	Y	N	?	Y	Y
25 ***Fish***	Y	Y	Y	Y	Y	Y	Y
26 ***Gilman***	Y	Y	Y	Y	N	N	Y
27 McHugh	Y	Y	Y	Y	N	Y	Y
28 Stratton	Y	Y	Y	Y	Y	Y	Y
29 ***Solomon***	Y	Y	Y	Y	N	Y	N
30 ***Martin***	Y	Y	Y	Y	N	Y	?
31 ***Mitchell***	Y	Y	Y	Y	N	Y	Y
32 ***Wortley***	Y	Y	Y	Y	Y	Y	Y
33 ***Lee***	Y	Y	Y	Y	N	Y	X
34 ***Horton***	Y	Y	#	Y	Y	Y	Y
35 ***Conable***	?	?	?	Y	Y	Y	Y
36 LaFalce	Y	Y	?	N	N	Y	Y
37 Nowak	Y	Y	Y	N	Y	Y	Y
38 ***Kemp***	?	?	?	Y	Y	Y	Y
39 Lundine	Y	Y	Y	Y	N	N	Y
NORTH CAROLINA							
1 Jones	Y	Y	Y	Y	Y	Y	N
2 Fountain	Y	Y	Y	Y	N	Y	N
3 Whitley	Y	Y	Y	Y	Y	Y	N
4 Andrews	Y	Y	Y	Y	Y	Y	N
5 Neal	Y	Y	Y	Y	Y	Y	N
6 ***Johnston***	N	N	N	Y	Y	N	Y
7 Rose	Y	?	?	Y	?	Y	N
8 Hefner	Y	Y	Y	Y	Y	Y	N

	342	343	344	345	346	347	348
9 ***Martin***	Y	N	N	Y	Y	Y	N
10 ***Broyhill***	Y	N	N	Y	N	Y	N
11 ***Hendon***	Y	N	N	?	N	Y	N
NORTH DAKOTA							
AL Dorgan	Y	Y	Y	N	Y	Y	N
OHIO							
1 ***Gradison***	Y	N	N	Y	Y	Y	Y
2 Luken	Y	Y	Y	Y	Y	Y	Y
3 Hall	Y	Y	Y	Y	?	Y	Y
4 ***Oxley***	Y	N	N	Y	N	Y	Y
5 ***Latta***	Y	N	N	Y	Y	Y	N
6 ***McEwen***	Y	N	N	Y	N	Y	N
7 ***Brown***	Y	N	N	Y	?	Y	Y
8 ***Kindness***	?	?	N	Y	N	Y	N
9 ***Weber***	Y	N	N	Y	N	Y	Y
10 ***Miller***	Y	Y	N	Y	N	Y	N
11 ***Stanton***	Y	N	N	Y	Y	Y	Y
12 Shamansky	Y	Y	Y	Y	N	Y	Y
13 Pease	Y	Y	?	Y	?	Y	Y
14 Seiberling	Y	Y	Y	N	?	Y	Y
15 ***Wylie***	Y	N	N	Y	Y	Y	Y
16 ***Regula***	Y	Y	N	Y	N	Y	Y
17 ***Ashbrook***	Y	N	N	Y	N	Y	N
18 Applegate	Y	N	N	Y	?	Y	N
19 ***Williams***	Y	N	N	Y	N	Y	N
20 Oakar	Y	Y	Y	Y	N	Y	N
21 Stokes	Y	Y	Y	N	Y	Y	Y
22 Eckart	Y	Y	Y	Y	N	Y	N
23 Mottl	Y	Y	Y	Y	N	N	N
OKLAHOMA							
1 Jones	Y	Y	Y	Y	Y	Y	N
2 Synar	Y	Y	Y	Y	N	Y	Y
3 Watkins	Y	Y	Y	Y	Y	Y	N
4 McCurdy	Y	Y	N	Y	N	Y	N
5 ***Edwards***	Y	Y	N	Y	N	Y	N
6 English	Y	Y	Y	Y	N	Y	N
OREGON							
1 AuCoin	?	?	#	X	?	#	?
2 ***Smith***	Y	N	N	Y	Y	Y	N
3 Wyden	Y	Y	Y	N	N	Y	Y
4 Weaver	Y	Y	Y	N	Y	Y	N
PENNSYLVANIA							
1 Foglietta	Y	Y	Y	Y	?	Y	Y
2 Gray	?	?	?	N	?	Y	Y
3 Smith	Y	Y	?	Y	Y	Y	Y
4 ***Dougherty***	?	?	?	Y	?	+	Y
5 ***Schulze***	Y	N	N	Y	Y	Y	N
6 Yatron	Y	Y	Y	Y	N	Y	Y
7 Edgar	Y	Y	?	N	N	Y	Y
8 ***Coyne, J.***	Y	N	Y	N	N	Y	Y
9 ***Shuster***	Y	?	N	Y	Y	Y	N
10 ***McDade***	Y	Y	Y	Y	?	Y	N
11 ***Nelligan***	Y	Y	Y	Y	N	Y	N
12 Murtha	Y	Y	Y	Y	Y	Y	Y
13 ***Coughlin***	Y	Y	N	N	N	Y	Y
14 Coyne, W.	Y	Y	Y	Y	Y	Y	Y
15 ***Ritter***	Y	N	N	N	Y	Y	N
16 ***Walker***	Y	N	N	Y	N	Y	N
17 Ertel	Y	Y	Y	Y	Y	Y	N
18 Walgren	?	?	?	N	N	Y	N
19 ***Goodling***	Y	N	N	?	N	Y	N
20 Gaydos	Y	Y	Y	Y	?	Y	N
21 Bailey	Y	Y	Y	Y	Y	Y	N
22 Murphy	?	?	?	Y	N	Y	N
23 ***Clinger***	Y	N	Y	Y	Y	Y	Y
24 ***Marks***	?	Y	Y	Y	Y	Y	Y
25 ***Atkinson***	Y	Y	N	Y	N	Y	N
RHODE ISLAND							
1 St Germain	Y	Y	Y	Y	Y	Y	N
2 ***Schneider***	Y	Y	Y	Y	?	Y	Y
SOUTH CAROLINA							
1 ***Hartnett***	?	?	?	Y	N	Y	Y
2 ***Spence***	Y	N	N	Y	Y	Y	N
3 Derrick	Y	Y	Y	Y	?	Y	N
4 ***Campbell***	Y	N	N	Y	Y	Y	Y
5 Holland	?	?	?	Y	Y	Y	N
6 ***Napier***	Y	Y	Y	Y	Y	Y	N
SOUTH DAKOTA							
1 Daschle	Y	Y	Y	Y	N	Y	N
2 ***Roberts***	Y	Y	Y	Y	N	Y	N
TENNESSEE							
1 ***Quillen***	Y	N	N	Y	Y	Y	N
2 ***Duncan***	Y	Y	Y	Y	Y	Y	N
3 Bouquard	Y	Y	Y	Y	N	Y	N
4 Gore	Y	Y	Y	Y	N	Y	Y
5 Boner	Y	Y	Y	Y	N	Y	N
6 ***Beard***	?	?	?	Y	?	Y	N

	342	343	344	345	346	347	348
7 Jones	Y	Y	Y	Y	Y	Y	N
8 Ford	Y	Y	Y	N	Y	Y	Y
TEXAS							
1 Hall, S.	Y	Y	Y	Y	N	Y	N
2 Wilson	Y	Y	Y	Y	?	Y	Y
3 ***Collins***	Y	N	N	Y	Y	Y	Y
4 Hall, R.	Y	Y	Y	Y	N	Y	N
5 Mattox	?	?	#	?	?	Y	Y
6 Gramm	Y	N	N	Y	?	Y	N
7 ***Archer***	Y	N	N	Y	N	N	N
8 ***Fields***	Y	N	N	Y	?	Y	N
9 Brooks	?	?	?	Y	Y	Y	N
10 Pickle	Y	Y	Y	Y	Y	Y	Y
11 Leath	Y	N	N	Y	Y	Y	N
12 Wright	?	?	?	Y	Y	Y	Y
13 Hightower	Y	Y	Y	Y	Y	Y	N
14 Patman	Y	Y	N	Y	N	Y	N
15 de la Garza	Y	Y	N	Y	Y	Y	N
16 White	Y	Y	Y	Y	Y	Y	N
17 Stenholm	Y	Y	Y	Y	N	Y	N
18 Leland	Y	Y	Y	N	?	#	#
19 Hance	Y	Y	Y	Y	Y	Y	N
20 Gonzalez	Y	Y	Y	Y	Y	Y	N
21 ***Loeffler***	Y	N	N	Y	N	Y	Y
22 ***Paul***	N	N	N	N	Y	N	N
23 Kazen	Y	Y	Y	Y	N	Y	N
24 Frost	?	?	?	Y	Y	Y	Y
UTAH							
1 ***Hansen***	Y	N	N	Y	Y	Y	N
2 ***Marriott***	Y	?	N	Y	Y	Y	N
VERMONT							
AL ***Jeffords***	?	Y	Y	N	N	Y	Y
VIRGINIA							
1 ***Trible***	Y	N	N	Y	?	?	?
2 ***Whitehurst***	Y	N	N	?	?	Y	N
3 ***Bliley***	Y	N	N	Y	N	Y	Y
4 ***Daniel, R.***	Y	N	N	Y	Y	Y	N
5 Daniel, D.	Y	N	N	Y	Y	Y	N
6 ***Butler***	Y	N	N	Y	N	Y	Y
7 ***Robinson***	Y	N	N	Y	Y	Y	N
8 ***Parris***	Y	Y	N	Y	N	Y	N
9 ***Wampler***	Y	Y	Y	Y	Y	Y	N
10 ***Wolf***	Y	N	Y	Y	Y	Y	Y
WASHINGTON							
1 ***Pritchard***	Y	N	Y	Y	N	Y	Y
2 Swift	Y	Y	Y	Y	N	Y	Y
3 Bonker	Y	Y	Y	Y	Y	Y	Y
4 ***Morrison***	Y	N	N	Y	N	Y	Y
5 Foley	Y	Y	Y	Y	Y	Y	Y
6 Dicks	Y	Y	Y	Y	Y	Y	Y
7 Lowry	Y	Y	Y	N	Y	Y	Y
WEST VIRGINIA							
1 Mollohan	?	Y	Y	Y	?	Y	Y
2 ***Benedict***	Y	Y	Y	Y	Y	Y	N
3 ***Staton***	Y	N	N	Y	Y	Y	N
4 Rahall	?	?	#	Y	Y	Y	N
WISCONSIN							
1 Aspin	Y	Y	Y	N	N	Y	Y
2 Kastenmeier	Y	Y	Y	N	N	Y	N
3 ***Gunderson***	Y	Y	Y	N	N	Y	N
4 Zablocki	Y	Y	Y	Y	Y	Y	Y
5 Reuss	Y	Y	Y	N	Y	Y	Y
6 ***Petri***	Y	N	N	N	N	Y	N
7 Obey	Y	Y	Y	N	N	Y	Y
8 ***Roth***	Y	Y	N	Y	N	Y	N
9 ***Sensenbrenner***	Y	N	N	Y	N	Y	N
WYOMING							
AL ***Cheney***	Y	N	N	Y	Y	Y	Y

Democrats ***Republicans***

KEY			
Y Voted for (yea).			
# Paired for.			
+ Announced for.			
N Voted against (nay).			
X Paired against.			
- Announced against.			
P Voted "present".			
C Voted "present" to avoid possible conflict of interest.			
? Did not vote or otherwise make a position known.			

349. HR 5159. Black Lung Benefits. Rostenkowski, D-Ill., motion to suspend the rules and concur with the Senate amendment to the bill to double temporarily the excise tax on coal; to tighten rules used in determining eligibility for black lung disability benefits; to liberalize rules governing business tax deductions for the cost of maintaining a second home; to allow business deductions for costs related to the rental of a dwelling to a relative for use as a primary residence; to require businesses involved in the leasing of equipment for tax benefits to report such activities to the Internal Revenue Service within 30 days of the transaction; and to delay for two years the effective date of new limits on how long corporations can carry over net operating losses. Motion agreed to (thus cleared for the president) 363-47: R 155-28; D 208-19 (ND 140-11, SD 68-8), Dec. 16, 1981. A two-thirds majority vote (274 in this case) is required for adoption under suspension of the rules.

350. S 884. Agriculture and Food Act of 1981. Adoption of the rule (H Res 303) providing for House floor consideration of the conference report on the bill to reauthorize for four years price support and other farm programs and, for one year, food stamps. Adopted 284-116: R 131-47; D 153-69 (ND 91-54, SD 62-15), Dec. 16, 1981. A "yea" was a vote supporting the president's position.

351. S 884. Agriculture and Food Act of 1981. Adoption of the conference report on the bill to reauthorize for four years price support and other farm programs and, for one year, food stamps. Adopted 205-203: R 125-59; D 80-144 (ND 27-121, SD 53-23), Dec. 16, 1981. A "yea" was a vote supporting the president's position.

	349	350	351
ALABAMA			
1 *Edwards*	Y	Y	Y
2 *Dickinson*	Y	Y	Y
3 Nichols	Y	Y	Y
4 Bevill	Y	Y	Y
5 Flippo	Y	Y	Y
6 *Smith*	N	Y	Y
7 Shelby	Y	Y	Y
ALASKA			
AL *Young*	Y	Y	Y
ARIZONA			
1 *Rhodes*	Y	Y	Y
2 Udall	Y	Y	Y
3 Stump	N	Y	Y
4 *Rudd*	Y	Y	Y
ARKANSAS			
1 Alexander	Y	Y	Y
2 *Bethune*	N	Y	Y
3 *Hammerschmidt*	Y	Y	Y
4 Anthony	Y	Y	Y
CALIFORNIA			
1 *Chappie*	Y	Y	Y
2 *Clausen*	Y	Y	Y
3 Matsui	Y	Y	Y
4 Fazio	Y	Y	Y
5 Burton, J.	?	?	#
6 Burton, P.			Y
7 Miller	Y	N	N
8 Dellums	Y	N	N
9 Stark	Y	N	N
10 Edwards	Y	N	N
11 Lantos	Y	N	N
12 *McCloskey*	Y	Y	Y
13 Mineta	Y	Y	Y
14 Shumway	N	Y	Y
15 Coelho	Y	Y	Y
16 Panetta	Y	Y	Y
17 *Pashayan*	Y	Y	Y
18 *Thomas*	Y	Y	Y
19 *Lagomarsino*	Y	Y	Y
20 *Goldwater*	Y	Y	Y
21 *Fiedler*	Y	N	Y
22 *Moorhead*	?	?	?
23 Beilenson	Y	?	Y
24 Waxman	Y	Y	N
25 Roybal	Y	Y	Y
26 *Rousselot*	Y	N	Y
27 *Dornan*	Y	N	Y
28 Dixon	Y	Y	Y
29 Hawkins	Y	?	N
30 Danielson	Y	Y	Y
31 Dymally	Y	Y	Y
32 Anderson	Y	N	N
33 *Grisham*	Y	Y	Y
34 *Lungren*	Y	N	Y
35 *Dreier*	Y	N	Y
36 Brown	Y	Y	Y
37 *Lewis*	Y	Y	Y
38 Patterson	Y	Y	N
39 *Dannemeyer*	Y	N	Y
40 *Badham*	N	?	Y
41 *Lowery*	Y	Y	Y
42 *Hunter*	Y	Y	Y
43 *Burgener*	?	?	#
COLORADO			
1 Schroeder	Y	Y	N
2 Wirth	Y	N	N
3 Kogovsek	Y	N	N
4 *Brown*	Y	Y	Y

	349	350	351
5 *Kramer*	Y	N	N
CONNECTICUT			
1 Vacancy			
2 Gejdenson	Y	N	N
3 *DeNardis*	Y	Y	N
4 *McKinney*	Y	N	N
5 Ratchford	Y	Y	N
6 Moffett	?	?	?
DELAWARE			
AL *Evans*	Y	Y	N
FLORIDA			
1 Hutto	Y	Y	Y
2 Fuqua	Y	Y	Y
3 Bennett	N	Y	Y
4 Chappell	Y	Y	Y
5 *McCollum*	Y	N	Y
6 *Young*	?	?	#
7 Gibbons	Y	Y	Y
8 Ireland	Y	Y	Y
9 Nelson	Y	Y	Y
10 *Bafalis*	P	Y	Y
11 Mica	Y	Y	Y
12 *Shaw*	Y	N	Y
13 Lehman	Y	Y	Y
14 Pepper	Y	Y	Y
15 Fascell	Y	Y	N
GEORGIA			
1 Ginn	Y	Y	Y
2 Hatcher	Y	Y	Y
3 Brinkley	Y	Y	Y
4 Levitas	Y	Y	Y
5 Fowler	Y	Y	Y
6 *Gingrich*	Y	N	Y
7 McDonald	-	-	-
8 Evans	Y	Y	Y
9 Jenkins	Y	N	Y
10 Barnard	Y	Y	Y
HAWAII			
1 Heftel	Y	Y	Y
2 Akaka	Y	Y	Y
IDAHO			
1 *Craig*	N	?	Y
2 *Hansen*	N	Y	Y
ILLINOIS			
1 Washington	Y	N	N
2 Savage	Y	Y	N
3 Russo	?	?	X
4 *Derwinski*	Y	N	Y
5 Fary	Y	Y	N
6 *Hyde*	Y	Y	Y
7 Collins	Y	N	N
8 Rostenkowski	Y	Y	N
9 Yates	Y	N	N
10 *Porter*	Y	N	N
11 Annunzio	Y	Y	N
12 *Crane, P.*	N	N	Y
13 *McClory*	Y	N	N
14 *Erlenborn*	N	?	Y
15 *Corcoran*	Y	Y	Y
16 *Martin*	N	Y	Y
17 O'Brien	Y	Y	Y
18 *Michel*	Y	Y	Y
19 *Railsback*	Y	Y	Y
20 *Findley*	Y	Y	Y
21 *Madigan*	Y	Y	Y
22 *Crane, D.*	N	N	Y
23 Price	Y	Y	Y
24 Simon	Y	Y	Y
INDIANA			
1 Benjamin	Y	Y	N
2 Fithian	Y	N	N
3 *Hiler*	Y	Y	Y
4 *Coats*	Y	Y	Y
5 *Hillis*	Y	Y	Y
6 Evans	Y	N	N
7 *Myers*	Y	Y	Y
8 *Deckard*	Y	N	N
9 Hamilton	Y	Y	Y
10 Sharp	Y	N	N
11 Jacobs	P	?	N
IOWA			
1 *Leach*	Y	Y	Y
2 *Tauke*	Y	Y	Y
3 *Evans*	Y	Y	Y
4 Smith	Y	N	N
5 Harkin	Y	N	N
6 Bedell	Y	N	N

Democrats *Republicans*

	349	350	351
KANSAS			
1 *Roberts*	Y	N	N
2 *Jeffries*	Y	Y	Y
3 *Winn*	Y	Y	Y
4 Glickman	N	Y	N
5 *Whittaker*	Y	Y	Y
KENTUCKY			
1 Hubbard	Y	N	N
2 Natcher	Y	Y	Y
3 Mazzoli	Y	Y	Y
4 *Snyder*	Y	Y	Y
5 *Rogers*	Y	Y	Y
6 *Hopkins*	Y	Y	Y
7 Perkins	Y	Y	Y
LOUISIANA			
1 *Livingston*	Y	Y	Y
2 Boggs	Y	Y	Y
3 Tauzin	Y	Y	Y
4 Roemer	N	Y	Y
5 Huckaby	Y	Y	Y
6 *Moore*	Y	Y	Y
7 Breaux	Y	Y	Y
8 Long	Y	Y	Y
MAINE			
1 *Emery*	Y	N	Y
2 *Snowe*	Y	N	Y
MARYLAND			
1 Dyson	Y	Y	Y
2 Long	Y	Y	Y
3 Mikulski	Y	N	N
4 *Holt*	Y	Y	Y
5 Hoyer	Y	Y	N
6 Byron	Y	N	N
7 Mitchell	Y	Y	N
8 Barnes	Y	N	N
MASSACHUSETTS			
1 *Conte*	?	?	?
2 Boland	Y	N	N
3 Early	Y	N	N
4 Frank	N	N	N
5 Shannon	Y	N	N
6 Mavroules	Y	N	N
7 Markey	Y	Y	N
8 O'Neill			
9 Moakley	Y	Y	N
10 *Heckler*	Y	N	N
11 Donnelly	Y	N	N
12 Studds	Y	Y	N
MICHIGAN			
1 Conyers	Y	N	N
2 *Pursell*	Y	Y	N
3 Wolpe	N	N	N
4 *Siljander*	Y	Y	N
5 *Sawyer*	Y	Y	Y
6 *Dunn*	Y	Y	Y
7 Kildee	N	N	N
8 Traxler	Y	Y	N
9 *Vander Jagt*	Y	Y	Y
10 Albosta	Y	Y	N
11 *Davis*	Y	N	N
12 Bonior	?	Y	N
13 Crockett	Y	N	N
14 Hertel	N	Y	N
15 Ford	?	?	?
16 Dingell	Y	Y	Y
17 Brodhead	Y	Y	N
18 Blanchard	Y	?	?
19 *Broomfield*	?	?	X
MINNESOTA			
1 *Erdahl*	Y	Y	Y
2 *Hagedorn*	Y	?	Y
3 *Frenzel*	Y	Y	Y
4 Vento	?	?	?
5 Sabo	Y	N	N
6 *Weber*	Y	N	N
7 *Stangeland*	Y	Y	Y
8 Oberstar	Y	Y	N
MISSISSIPPI			
1 Whitten	Y	Y	Y
2 Bowen	Y	Y	Y
3 Montgomery	N	Y	Y
4 Dowdy	Y	Y	N
5 *Lott*	Y	Y	Y
MISSOURI			
1 Clay	Y	N	N
2 Young	Y	Y	?
3 Gephardt	Y	Y	N

	349	350	351
4 Skelton	Y	Y	N
5 Bolling	?	?	?
6 *Coleman*	Y	Y	Y
7 *Taylor*	Y	Y	Y
8 *Bailey*	Y	Y	Y
9 Volkmer	N	N	N
10 *Emerson*	Y	Y	Y
MONTANA			
1 Williams	N	N	N
2 *Marlenee*	Y	N	N
NEBRASKA			
1 *Bereuter*	Y	N	N
2 *Daub*	Y	N	N
3 *Smith*	Y	N	N
NEVADA			
AL Santini	?	X	X
NEW HAMPSHIRE			
1 D'Amours	Y	N	N
2 *Gregg*	Y	N	N
NEW JERSEY			
1 Florio	Y	Y	N
2 Hughes	Y	Y	N
3 Howard	Y	Y	N
4 *Smith*	Y	Y	Y
5 *Fenwick*	Y	Y	N
6 *Forsythe*	N	Y	Y
7 *Roukema*	Y	Y	N
8 Roe	Y	?	N
9 *Hollenbeck*	Y	N	Y
10 Rodino	Y	Y	N
11 Minish	Y	Y	N
12 *Rinaldo*	Y	Y	N
13 *Courter*	Y	Y	N
14 Guarini	Y	Y	N
15 Dwyer	Y	?	X
NEW MEXICO			
1 *Lujan*	Y	Y	N
2 *Skeen*	Y	Y	Y
NEW YORK			
1 *Carney*	Y	Y	N
2 Downey	Y	Y	N
3 *Carman*	N	?	N
4 *Lent*	Y	Y	N
5 *McGrath*	Y	Y	N
6 *LeBoutillier*	Y	Y	N
7 Addabbo	Y	#	N
8 Rosenthal	Y	N	N
9 Ferraro	Y	Y	N
10 Biaggi	Y	Y	N
11 Scheuer	Y	Y	N
12 Chisholm	Y	N	N
13 Solarz	Y	Y	N
14 Richmond	Y	Y	Y
15 Zeferetti	Y	Y	N
16 Schumer	Y	Y	N
17 *Molinari*	Y	Y	N
18 *Green*	Y	Y	Y
19 Rangel	Y	Y	N
20 Weiss	Y	Y	N
21 Garcia	Y	Y	N
22 Bingham	Y	Y	N
23 Peyser	Y	Y	N
24 Ottinger	Y	N	N
25 *Fish*	Y	Y	N
26 *Gilman*	Y	Y	N
27 McHugh	Y	N	N
28 Stratton	N	Y	N
29 *Solomon*	N	Y	N
30 *Martin*	Y	Y	N
31 *Mitchell*	N	N	N
32 *Wortley*	Y	Y	N
33 *Lee*	Y	N	N
34 *Horton*	Y	Y	N
35 *Conable*	Y	Y	Y
36 LaFalce	N	N	?
37 Nowak	Y	N	N
38 *Kemp*	Y	Y	Y
39 Lundine	Y	N	N
NORTH CAROLINA			
1 Jones	Y	Y	Y
2 Fountain	Y	Y	Y
3 Whitley	Y	Y	Y
4 Andrews	Y	Y	Y
5 Neal	Y	Y	Y
6 *Johnston*	N	Y	Y
7 Rose	Y	Y	Y
8 Hefner	Y	Y	Y

	349	350	351
9 *Martin*	Y	Y	Y
10 *Broyhill*	N	Y	Y
11 *Hendon*	Y	Y	Y
NORTH DAKOTA			
AL Dorgan	Y	N	N
OHIO			
1 *Gradison*	Y	Y	N
2 Luken	Y	N	N
3 Hall	Y	Y	N
4 *Oxley*	Y	Y	Y
5 *Latta*	Y	Y	Y
6 *McEwen*	Y	Y	Y
7 *Brown*	Y	N	Y
8 *Kindness*	N	Y	N
9 Weber	Y	Y	Y
10 *Miller*	Y	Y	N
11 *Stanton*	Y	Y	Y
12 Shamansky	Y	N	N
13 Pease	Y	Y	N
14 Seiberling	Y	Y	N
15 *Wylie*	Y	Y	Y
16 *Regula*	Y	Y	N
17 *Ashbrook*	N	Y	Y
18 Applegate	Y	Y	N
19 *Williams*	Y	?	N
20 Oakar	Y	N	N
21 Stokes	Y	N	N
22 Eckart	Y	Y	N
23 Mottl	Y	N	N
OKLAHOMA			
1 Jones	Y	Y	Y
2 Synar	P	N	N
3 Watkins	Y	N	N
4 McCurdy	Y	N	N
5 *Edwards*	Y	Y	Y
6 English	Y	N	N
OREGON			
1 AuCoin	?	?	?
2 *Smith*	N	Y	Y
3 Wyden	Y	Y	N
4 Weaver	Y	N	N
PENNSYLVANIA			
1 Foglietta	Y	Y	N
2 Gray	Y	Y	N
3 Smith	Y	Y	N
4 *Dougherty*	Y	Y	N
5 *Schulze*	Y	N	Y
6 Yatron	Y	N	N
7 Edgar	Y	N	N
8 *Coyne, J.*	Y	N	N
9 *Shuster*	Y	N	Y
10 *McDade*	Y	Y	?
11 *Nelligan*	Y	Y	Y
12 Murtha	Y	?	N
13 *Coughlin*	Y	N	N
14 Coyne, W.	Y	Y	N
15 *Ritter*	Y	N	N
16 *Walker*	N	N	N
17 Ertel	Y	N	N
18 Walgren	Y	Y	N
19 *Goodling*	N	Y	N
20 Gaydos	Y	?	?
21 Bailey	Y	Y	Y
22 Murphy	Y	N	N
23 *Clinger*	Y	N	Y
24 *Marks*	Y	Y	Y
25 *Atkinson*	Y	Y	Y
RHODE ISLAND			
1 St Germain	Y	N	N
2 *Schneider*	Y	N	N
SOUTH CAROLINA			
1 *Hartnett*	Y	Y	Y
2 *Spence*	Y	Y	Y
3 Derrick	Y	Y	Y
4 *Campbell*	Y	Y	Y
5 Holland	Y	?	?
6 *Napier*	Y	Y	Y
SOUTH DAKOTA			
1 Daschle	P	N	N
2 *Roberts*	N	N	N
TENNESSEE			
1 *Quillen*	?	?	#
2 *Duncan*	Y	Y	Y
3 Bouquard	Y	N	N
4 Gore	Y	N	N
5 Boner	Y	N	N
6 *Beard*	Y	Y	Y

	349	350	351
7 Jones	Y	N	N
8 Ford	Y	Y	P
TEXAS			
1 Hall, S.	N	Y	N
2 Wilson	Y	N	N
3 *Collins*	N	Y	Y
4 Hall, R.	N	N	N
5 Mattox	Y	N	N
6 Gramm	N	Y	Y
7 *Archer*	Y	N	N
8 *Fields*	Y	Y	Y
9 Brooks	Y	Y	Y
10 Pickle	Y	Y	Y
11 Leath	Y	Y	N
12 Wright	Y	Y	Y
13 Hightower	Y	N	N
14 Patman	N	Y	N
15 de la Garza	Y	Y	Y
16 White	Y	Y	Y
17 Stenholm	N	Y	N
18 Leland	?	Y	N
19 Hance	Y	Y	N
20 Gonzalez	Y	N	N
21 *Loeffler*	Y	Y	Y
22 *Paul*	N	N	N
23 Kazen	Y	Y	Y
24 Frost	Y	Y	N
UTAH			
1 *Hansen*	Y	Y	Y
2 *Marriott*	Y	Y	Y
VERMONT			
AL *Jeffords*	Y	Y	N
VIRGINIA			
1 *Trible*	?	?	?
2 *Whitehurst*	?	?	?
3 *Bliley*	Y	Y	Y
4 *Daniel, R.*	Y	Y	Y
5 *Daniel, D.*	Y	Y	Y
6 *Butler*	N	Y	Y
7 *Robinson*	Y	Y	Y
8 *Parris*	Y	Y	Y
9 *Wampler*	Y	Y	Y
10 *Wolf*	Y	Y	Y
WASHINGTON			
1 *Pritchard*	Y	Y	N
2 Swift	Y	Y	N
3 Bonker	Y	Y	Y
4 *Morrison*	Y	Y	N
5 Foley	Y	Y	Y
6 Dicks	Y	Y	Y
7 Lowry	Y	Y	N
WEST VIRGINIA			
1 Mollohan	Y	Y	N
2 *Benedict*	Y	Y	Y
3 *Staton*	Y	Y	Y
4 Rahall	Y	Y	N
WISCONSIN			
1 Aspin	N	N	N
2 Kastenmeier	Y	N	N
3 *Gunderson*	N	N	N
4 Zablocki	Y	Y	N
5 Reuss	Y	Y	N
6 *Petri*	N	N	N
7 Obey	Y	N	N
8 *Roth*	Y	N	N
9 *Sensenbrenner*	N	N	N
WYOMING			
AL *Cheney*	Y	Y	Y

Democrats   *Republicans*

352. HR 5274. Oil Company Merger Moratorium. Livingston, R-La., motion that the House adjourn. The purpose of the motion was to block consideration of the bill to place a moratorium on the acquisition of U.S. oil companies by larger oil companies. Motion rejected 73-249: R 53-98; D 20-151 (ND 2-106, SD 18-45), Dec. 16, 1981.

353. HR 5274. Oil Company Merger Moratorium. Dingell, D-Mich., motion to suspend the rules and pass the bill to prohibit the nine largest U.S. oil companies or major foreign oil-producing governments or companies from acquiring any of the top 40 U.S. oil-producing companies between Dec. 1, 1981, and June 30, 1982. Motion agreed to 223-107: R 75-74; D 148-33 (ND 111-6, SD 37-27), Dec. 16, 1981. A two-thirds majority (220 in this case) is required for passage under suspension of the rules.

KEY

Y   Voted for (yea).
Paired for.
+   Announced for.
N   Voted against (nay).
X   Paired against.
-   Announced against.
P   Voted "present".
C   Voted "present" to avoid possible conflict of interest.
?   Did not vote or otherwise make a position known.

	352	353
ALABAMA		
1 *Edwards*	N	N
2 *Dickinson*	N	N
3 Nichols	?	?
4 Bevill	N	Y
5 Flippo	N	Y
6 *Smith*	Y	N
7 Shelby	?	Y
ALASKA		
AL *Young*	N	N
ARIZONA		
1 *Rhodes*	N	Y
2 Udall	N	Y
3 Stump	Y	N
4 *Rudd*	N	N
ARKANSAS		
1 Alexander	N	Y
2 *Bethune*	?	?
3 *Hammerschmidt*	N	N
4 Anthony	Y	N
CALIFORNIA		
1 *Chappie*	N	N
2 *Clausen*	N	Y
3 Matsui	N	Y
4 Fazio	N	Y
5 Burton, J.	?	?
6 Burton, P.	?	?
7 Miller	N	Y
8 Dellums	N	Y
9 Stark	N	Y
10 Edwards	N	Y
11 Lantos	?	?
12 *McCloskey*	?	?
13 Mineta	N	Y
14 *Shumway*	Y	N
15 Coelho	N	Y
16 Panetta	N	Y
17 *Pashayan*	Y	N
18 *Thomas*	Y	N
19 *Lagomarsino*	Y	N
20 *Goldwater*	Y	N
21 *Fiedler*	Y	N
22 *Moorhead*	?	?
23 Beilenson	?	Y
24 Waxman	?	?
25 Roybal	N	Y
26 *Rousselot*	N	N
27 *Dornan*	N	N
28 Dixon	?	?
29 Hawkins	?	?
30 Danielson	N	Y
31 Dymally	N	Y
32 Anderson	N	N
33 *Grisham*	Y	N
34 *Lungren*	Y	N
35 *Dreier*	Y	N
36 Brown	N	Y
37 *Lewis*	Y	N
38 Patterson	N	Y
39 *Dannemeyer*	N	Y
40 *Badham*	Y	N
41 *Lowery*	N	N
42 *Hunter*	Y	N
43 *Burgener*	?	?
COLORADO		
1 Schroeder	N	Y
2 Wirth	N	Y
3 Kogovsek	N	Y
4 *Brown*	N	Y

	352	353
5 *Kramer*	N	Y
CONNECTICUT		
1 Vacancy		
2 Gejdenson	?	?
3 *DeNardis*	N	Y
4 *McKinney*	?	?
5 Ratchford	N	Y
6 Moffett	?	?
DELAWARE		
AL *Evans*	N	N
FLORIDA		
1 Hutto	N	Y
2 Fuqua	N	Y
3 Bennett	N	Y
4 Chappell	Y	N
5 *McCollum*	N	C
6 *Young*	?	?
7 Gibbons	?	?
8 Ireland	?	?
9 Nelson	N	Y
10 *Bafalis*	Y	N
11 Mica	?	Y
12 *Shaw*	N	N
13 Lehman	N	Y
14 Pepper	N	Y
15 Fascell	?	?
GEORGIA		
1 Ginn	N	Y
2 Hatcher	N	Y
3 Brinkley	N	N
4 Levitas	N	Y
5 Fowler	N	Y
6 *Gingrich*	?	?
7 McDonald	?	-
8 Evans	N	?
9 Jenkins	N	Y
10 Barnard	Y	N
HAWAII		
1 Heftel	N	Y
2 Akaka	?	Y
IDAHO		
1 *Craig*	N	N
2 *Hansen*	N	N
ILLINOIS		
1 Washington	N	Y
2 Savage	N	Y
3 Russo	?	?
4 *Derwinski*	?	Y
5 Fary	N	N
6 *Hyde*	Y	N
7 Collins	N	Y
8 Rostenkowski	N	N
9 Yates	N	Y
10 *Porter*	Y	N
11 Annunzio	N	N
12 *Crane, P.*	Y	N
13 *McClory*	?	Y
14 *Erlenborn*	Y	N
15 Corcoran	N	Y
16 Martin	N	Y
17 O'Brien	Y	N
18 Michel	N	N
19 *Railsback*	Y	?
20 *Findley*	N	Y
21 *Madigan*	?	?
22 *Crane, D.*	N	Y
23 Price	N	Y
24 Simon	N	Y
INDIANA		
1 Benjamin	N	Y
2 Fithian	N	Y
3 *Hiler*	Y	N
4 *Coats*	N	Y
5 *Hillis*	?	?
6 *Evans*	?	Y
7 *Myers*	Y	N
8 *Deckard*	?	Y
9 Hamilton	N	Y
10 Sharp	N	Y
11 Jacobs	N	Y
IOWA		
1 *Leach*	N	Y
2 *Tauke*	N	Y
3 *Evans*	N	Y
4 Smith	N	Y
5 Harkin	?	?
6 Bedell	N	Y

	352 353		352 353		352 353		352 353
KANSAS		4 Skelton	Y Y	9 *Martin*	N Y	7 Jones	N Y
1 *Roberts*	N N	5 Bolling	? ?	10 *Broyhill*	N Y	8 Ford	? ?
2 *Jeffries*	Y N	6 *Coleman*	N P	11 *Hendon*	Y N	**TEXAS**	
3 *Winn*	N N	7 *Taylor*	? ?	**NORTH DAKOTA**		1 Hall, S.	Y N
4 Glickman	N Y	8 *Bailey*	Y N	AL Dorgan	N Y	2 Wilson	? ?
5 *Whittaker*	N Y	9 Volkmer	? Y	**OHIO**		3 *Collins*	? ?
KENTUCKY		10 *Emerson*	N Y	1 *Gradison*	? ?	4 Hall, R.	Y N
1 Hubbard	N N	**MONTANA**		2 Luken	N Y	5 Mattox	Y N
2 Natcher	N Y	1 Williams	? ?	3 Hall	? ?	6 *Gramm*	Y N
3 Mazzoli	? Y	2 *Marlenee*	Y ?	4 *Oxley*	N Y	7 *Archer*	Y N
4 *Snyder*	? ?	**NEBRASKA**		5 *Latta*	N Y	8 *Fields*	Y N
5 *Rogers*	N Y	1 *Bereuter*	N Y	6 *McEwen*	N Y	9 Brooks	N N
6 *Hopkins*	N Y	2 *Daub*	N Y	7 *Brown*	N Y	10 Pickle	N N
7 Perkins	N Y	3 *Smith*	N Y	8 *Kindness*	N N	11 Leath	Y N
LOUISIANA		**NEVADA**		9 *Weber*	N Y	12 Wright	N Y
1 *Livingston*	Y N	AL Santini	? ?	10 *Miller*	N Y	13 Hightower	? ?
2 Boggs	N ?	**NEW HAMPSHIRE**		11 *Stanton*	? Y	14 Patman	N Y
3 Tauzin	Y N	1 D'Amours	N Y	12 Shamansky	N Y	15 de la Garza	Y Y
4 Roemer	N N	2 *Gregg*	Y Y	13 Pease	N Y	16 White	N N
5 Huckaby	Y N	**NEW JERSEY**		14 Seiberling	? Y	17 Stenholm	Y N
6 *Moore*	Y N	1 Florio	? ?	15 *Wylie*	N Y	18 Leland	N Y
7 Breaux	Y N	2 Hughes	N Y	16 *Regula*	N Y	19 Hance	Y N
8 Long	? ?	3 Howard	N Y	17 *Ashbrook*	? ?	20 Gonzalez	N Y
MAINE		4 *Smith*	N Y	18 Applegate	N Y	21 *Loeffler*	Y N
1 *Emery*	N Y	5 *Fenwick*	N Y	19 *Williams*	? ?	22 *Paul*	Y N
2 *Snowe*	N Y	6 *Forsythe*	Y N	20 Oakar	N Y	23 Kazen	N Y
MARYLAND		7 *Roukema*	N Y	21 Stokes	N Y	24 Frost	N N
1 Dyson	N Y	8 Roe	N Y	22 Eckart	N Y	**UTAH**	
2 Long	N Y	9 *Hollenbeck*	? ?	23 Mottl	? ?	1 *Hansen*	Y N
3 Mikulski	N Y	10 Rodino	N Y	**OKLAHOMA**		2 *Marriott*	N Y
4 *Holt*	? ?	11 Minish	N Y	1 Jones	Y N	**VERMONT**	
5 Hoyer	N Y	12 *Rinaldo*	N Y	2 Synar	Y N	AL *Jeffords*	N Y
6 Byron	? ?	13 *Courter*	N Y	3 Watkins	Y N	**VIRGINIA**	
7 Mitchell	? ?	14 Guarini	N Y	4 McCurdy	Y N	1 *Trible*	? ?
8 Barnes	N Y	15 Dwyer	? ?	5 *Edwards*	Y ?	2 *Whitehurst*	? ?
MASSACHUSETTS		**NEW MEXICO**		6 English	Y N	3 *Bliley*	Y N
1 *Conte*	? ?	1 *Lujan*	N Y	**OREGON**		4 *Daniel, R.*	N Y
2 Boland	N Y	2 *Skeen*	Y N	1 AuCoin	? ?	5 Daniel, D.	N N
3 Early	N Y	**NEW YORK**		2 *Smith*	Y N	6 *Butler*	? ?
4 Frank	N Y	1 *Carney*	N Y	3 Wyden	N Y	7 *Robinson*	N N
5 Shannon	N Y	2 Downey	N Y	4 Weaver	? ?	8 *Parris*	N Y
6 Mavroules	? ?	3 *Carman*	? ?	**PENNSYLVANIA**		9 *Wampler*	N Y
7 Markey	? ?	4 *Lent*	? ?	1 Foglietta	? ?	10 *Wolf*	N N
8 O'Neill		5 *McGrath*	N Y	2 Gray	N Y	**WASHINGTON**	
9 Moakley	N ?	6 *LeBoutillier*	Y N	3 Smith	? ?	1 *Pritchard*	N N
10 *Heckler*	N Y	7 Addabbo	? Y	4 *Dougherty*	N Y	2 Swift	N Y
11 Donnelly	N Y	8 Rosenthal	? ?	5 *Schulze*	? Y	3 Bonker	? ?
12 Studds	N Y	9 Ferraro	N Y	6 Yatron	N Y	4 *Morrison*	Y N
MICHIGAN		10 Biaggi	N Y	7 Edgar	N Y	5 Foley	N Y
1 Conyers	? ?	11 Scheuer	N Y	8 *Coyne, J.*	N Y	6 Dicks	? Y
2 *Pursell*	N Y	12 Chisholm	N Y	9 *Shuster*	? ?	7 Lowry	N Y
3 Wolpe	N Y	13 Solarz	N Y	10 *McDade*	? ?	**WEST VIRGINIA**	
4 *Siljander*	N Y	14 Richmond	N Y	11 Nelligan	Y Y	1 *Mollohan*	N Y
5 *Sawyer*	N Y	15 Zeferetti	? Y	12 Murtha	N Y	2 *Benedict*	N N
6 *Dunn*	Y N	16 Schumer	? ?	13 *Coughlin*	? ?	3 Staton	Y N
7 Kildee	N Y	17 *Molinari*	Y N	14 Coyne, W.	N Y	4 Rahall	N Y
8 Traxler	N Y	18 *Green*	? ?	15 *Ritter*	N Y	**WISCONSIN**	
9 *Vander Jagt*	? ?	19 Rangel	? ?	16 *Walker*	N N	1 Aspin	? ?
10 Albosta	N Y	20 Weiss	N N	17 Ertel	N Y	2 Kastenmeier	N Y
11 *Davis*	N Y	21 Garcia	N Y	18 Walgren	? Y	3 *Gunderson*	N N
12 Bonior	? ?	22 Bingham	? ?	19 *Goodling*	N Y	4 Zablocki	N Y
13 Crockett	? ?	23 Peyser	? ?	20 Gaydos	? ?	5 Reuss	? ?
14 Hertel	? Y	24 Ottinger	N Y	21 Bailey	N Y	6 *Petri*	N Y
15 Ford	? ?	25 *Fish*	N Y	22 Murphy	N Y	7 Obey	N Y
16 Dingell	N Y	26 *Gilman*	N Y	23 *Clinger*	N C	8 *Roth*	N Y
17 Brodhead	N Y	27 McHugh	N Y	24 *Marks*	? ?	9 *Sensenbrenner*	Y C
18 Blanchard	N Y	28 Stratton	N Y	25 *Atkinson*	? ?	**WYOMING**	
19 *Broomfield*	? ?	29 *Solomon*	N Y	**RHODE ISLAND**		AL *Cheney*	N N
MINNESOTA		30 *Martin*	N Y	1 St Germain	N Y		
1 *Erdahl*	Y N	31 *Mitchell*	N Y	2 *Schneider*	N Y		
2 *Hagedorn*	? ?	32 *Wortley*	N Y	**SOUTH CAROLINA**			
3 *Frenzel*	Y N	33 *Lee*	? ?	1 *Hartnett*	Y N		
4 Vento	? ?	34 *Horton*	N N	2 *Spence*	N Y		
5 Sabo	N Y	35 *Conable*	Y N	3 Derrick	N Y		
6 *Weber*	N Y	36 LaFalce	? ?	4 *Campbell*	? N		
7 *Stangeland*	Y Y	37 Nowak	N Y	5 Holland	? ?		
8 Oberstar	N Y	38 *Kemp*	? ?	6 *Napier*	Y N		
MISSISSIPPI		39 Lundine	? ?	**SOUTH DAKOTA**			
1 Whitten	N Y	**NORTH CAROLINA**		1 Daschle	N Y		
2 Bowen	N Y	1 Jones	? ?	2 *Roberts*	N N		
3 Montgomery	? ?	2 Fountain	N Y	**TENNESSEE**			
4 Dowdy	N N	3 Whitley	N Y	1 *Quillen*	? ?		
5 *Lott*	N N	4 Andrews	N Y	2 *Duncan*	N Y		
MISSOURI		5 Neal	N Y	3 Bouquard	N Y		
1 Clay	? ?	6 *Johnston*	Y N	4 Gore	N Y		
2 Young	? ?	7 Rose	N N	5 Boner	N Y		
3 Gephardt	N Y	8 Hefner	? ?	6 *Beard*	N Y		

Democrats   *Republicans*

HOUSE ROLL-CALL VOTES

SENATE ROLL-CALL VOTES

INDEX

INDEX